POPULAR SONGS OF THE TWENTIETH CENTURY

A CHARTED HISTORY

Volume 1 – Chart Detail & Encyclopedia, 1900–1949

POPULAR SONGS OF THE TWENTIETH CENTURY

A CHARTED HISTORY

Volume 1 – Chart Detail & Encyclopedia, 1900–1949

Compiled by

Edward Foote Gardner

Mathematician, Musicologist

PARAGON HOUSE

St. Paul, Minnesota

First Edition, 2000

Published in the United States by
Paragon House
2700 University Avenue West
St. Paul, MN 55114

Manufactured in the United States of America.

Library of Congress Cataloging-in-Publication Data

Gardner, Edward F., 1937-
Popular songs of the twentieth century : a charted history / compiled by Edward F. Gardner.
p. cm.
Includes bibliographical references.
Contents: v. 1. Chart detail & encyclopedia, 1900-1949
ISBN 1-55778-789-1 (pbk. : alk. paper)
1. Popular music--United States--Indexes. 2. Popular music--United States--Statistics.
I. Title.

ML128.S3 G3 2000
782.421164'0973--dc2l

00-020315
CIP

10 9 8 7 6 5 4 3 2 1

For current information about all releases from Paragon House,
visit the web site at http://www.paragonhouse.com

CONTENTS

PREFACE TO VOLUME I

PREFACE TO VOLUME I

This compendium is the result of a lifelong research project aimed at producing the most accurate rankings possible for all songs popularized across the USA during the twentieth century. Many different surveys developed at various times during that period. Many diverse styles of pop music have come and gone as well. Based on scores of references, this book was developed to establish and summarize the historical rankings of all mainstream pop songs. We proceed from the ballads and marches of 1900 to the Big Band Era of the 1940s to early rock music all the way up to the pop, rock and hip-hop music of the 1990s. Whatever topped the music charts, indeed whatever made the Top 20, you'll find them all listed here. Volume I presents the charts and an encyclopedia of the songs in the INDEX OF CHARTED SONGS, some 4000 of them, and Volume II features summaries of chart data of all 10,000 songs that charted during this unique and amazing century—1900–1999.

In the early 1900s simple ballads, marches, and comic songs were dominant while ragtime musicians and Negro bands exerted increasing influence. These popular subcultural movements, mostly from the South and from Chicago, eventually paved the way for the Jazz and Dance Band craze that swept the nation during World War I and the 1920s. Romantic singing stylists emerged toward the end of the 20s and they, the Crooners, along with the so-called Sweet Bands, held sway in the early 1930s. But again, an underground movement, this time called Swing, would gradually transport us from the Sweet Band sounds into the Big Band Era of the late 30s and the 1940s. Band vocalists were gradually introduced in the mid-20s, but mostly in a musically subordinate role. By the end of the 1930s, they began taking a larger part in the presentation of a song, and eventually more and more of them left their bands to go out on their own. Little by little, these singers became predominant as the era of the Song Stylists carried us from the late 40s to the advent of Rock and Roll in the mid-50s.

Rock, indeed, was the primary music form that dominated the second half of the century. The story of rock, and all of the genres within it, has been chronicled extensively. *Billboard* and other trade papers have done the job of charting and ranking these latter songs much more thoroughly than was done for the pre-rock songs of the first fifty years. This book attempts to correct that imbalance by providing greater detail for the first half of the century, including the many years when there was little or no chart information. Not until *Billboard*'s "Honor Roll of Hits" appeared in 1945 were there any really reliable song rankings in the trade papers despite the steady growth of the music business.

Thus, the driving force behind this 100-year summary was the desire to create "the charts that would have been" for songs of the period 1900-1945. This awesome task was achieved by extracting information from two principal source types. Thousands of pages were examined in pop-music history books and reference books, such as those of Spaeth, Kinkle, and others. Likewise, thousands of issues of weekly trade papers such as *The Music Trades, Variety,* and *Billboard* were consulted. See the Bibliography for a complete list of books and periodicals involved.

The data extracted from these sources were taken through a number of stages, as outlined below, to produce the charts displayed in this first volume. For the period 1900–1945 most chart rankings given here are approximate, at best. This is because my challenge was to produce numerical rankings from sources that largely contained only prose or qualitative information about the songs of the day. However, no effort has been spared in utilizing all sources to make these charts as accurate and realistic as possible.

It is worth noting that to compile monthly charts of best-selling songs would have been impossible much before 1900. To produce national hits, the needed ingredients are song promotion and a communications network that brings the nation together. The first song to be nationally promoted through an ad campaign was "Grandfather's Clock" in 1876. This, coincidentally, was the year the telephone was invented. It wasn't until 1893 that a single song swept the country and could be considered a national hit. This phenomenon began at the Chicago World's Fair in 1893, when "After the Ball" by Charles K. Harris was featured endlessly. The fairgoers took the song back to all parts of the country, and the first #1 hit was established.

TRADE PAPER INFORMATION AVAILABLE, 1900-1949

At the turn of the century, about the only source of information on popularity of contemporary songs was *The Music Trades,* a trade paper serving the entire music industry. Every week *The Music Trades* printed a rich "chatter" column about the songs being sung most frequently by the vaudeville stars of the day. Also included were articles about sheet-music sales of the most popular songs. This column continued weekly until the early 1920s. By 1921, weekly papers such as *Variety* and *Metronome* had become quite active in listing the top sheet music sellers and best-selling records along with commentary about regional sales around the country. The *Variety* listings expanded little by little so that, by 1930, there were separate sheet-music and record-sales rankings reported monthly for three major sections of the country.

On April 20, 1935, a major step in song ranking took place as "Your Hit Parade" went on the air, playing the Top 15 songs each week. The show continued until 1958. Over the years their survey sometimes received criticism that, while it reflected sheet music sales and radio play fairly well, it did not take sufficient account of record sales and juke-box play. Thus, some immensely popular Big Band hits such as "In the Mood" did not get a fair ranking. That imbalance has been corrected in the compilations presented here.

Finally, on March 17, 1945, *Billboard* magazine introduced the "Honor Roll of Hits," an evenhanded weekly ranking of songs. For the summaries presented in Volume II, this author began by following the "Honor Roll" closely through the end of its run in 1963. Thereafter, I have roughly followed the *Billboard* "Hot 100" to establish song ranking. See the Preface of Volume II for more details on the "Hot 100."

THE RESEARCH

For the period 1900–1929, I started by forming a file containing every song mentioned at least once in several well-known history books, those by Mattfeld, Spaeth, and Kinkle (see bibliography). I then turned to the weekly trade papers of the time (*Music Trades, Variety, Metro-*

nome, and others). I found weekly accounts of most of the songs in my file plus additional important songs overlooked by the history books along with the names of vaudeville singers promoting the songs. I then took notes on every mention of these songs and recorded these notes week by week on spreadsheets, from the week ending January 6, 1900 to the week ending January 4, 1930. Also noted on these sheets were the artists who recorded the song and the dates of recording. This information came from *Talking Machine World,* a trade paper for the young phonograph industry. *Talking Machine World* was invaluable for determining record release dates and for supporting the data extracted from *The Music Trades.* Songs that were being touted as popular in the latter ought to show up on records in the former at about the same time.

The completed spreadsheets indicated the period of peak popularity of each song. Generally, the mentions would begin in a flurry of excitement about the success of a new song, say in early March, then the commentary and recording activity would dwindle a few months later, perhaps in September or October, indicating the song had run its course. For each song, the sheer number of mentions, with factoring for the enthusiasm of the mentions, helped form the basis for assigning three key numbers to each song: A start-month number, a stop-month number, and a strength-of-popularity number. These three numbers, when fed to a computer program I wrote, led to a set of chart rankings for each given song, for the relevant months of popularity, that might look like this:

Mar	Apr	May	June	July	Aug	Sept	Oct	Nov
19	11	5	3	3	2	10	17	OFF

This computer result clearly shows the song's rise and fall on the would-be charts. The final chart rankings were worked out largely by hand, using the computer results as a starting point, according to what seemed best to this author based on the complete data and knowledge on hand for each song. This led to the Month-By-Month charts found in Section 2. These were subsequently broken down to the semi-monthly finished spreadsheets seen in Section 3.

Overall, for the period 1900–1929, this author accumulated and processed over a million bits of information regarding about 5000 song candidates. Thus, the rankings are hardly based on thin or spotty data. My rankings represent the only known song charts that completely cover this period with any measure of reliability. They take into account three major areas of popularity: frequency of performance in vaudeville, sheet-music sales, and record and piano-roll sales. In later years, as vaudeville gave way to radio, airplay became a major factor.

For the Depression years of the 1930s, I relied heavily on the record and sheet-music rankings in *Variety* and *Metronome,* rankings on "Your Hit Parade," and sheet-music and jukebox charts in *Billboard.* This led to a different kind of point system whereby my charts, month by month, were essentially an average of the available weekly chart information. The working idea was that if one averages the information found in several somewhat-reliable sources, one hopes the average will be more reliable than any single source.

On July 20, 1940, *Billboard* began featuring weekly charts of the best-selling records along with their ongoing charts on sheet-music sales and radio performances. There was thus a plethora of information to be averaged together to produce my rankings for the early 1940s. When the "Honor Roll of Hits" began in 1945, the averaging process was no longer needed, and I have roughly followed *Billboard* ever since. However, the "Honor Roll" often ranked only the Top Ten or Top Fifteen songs and didn't expand to a Top Twenty until October 1952. So, in the meantime *Billboard's* other charts, on jukebox plays, jockey plays and record sales, helped to fill out the lower-ranked positions on my charts. As mentioned above, when the "Honor Roll" was discontinued in 1963, the "Hot 100" served as a basis for the rest of the century.

THE FOUR SECTIONS OF VOLUME 1

Please note, the key to abbreviations and symbols in each section is found in the Introduction to that section.

SECTION 1: AN INDEX OF CHARTED SONGS, 1900-1949

The index occupies Section 1 because it is central to the use of Volume I. To find information on a particular song, look it up alphabetically in this index and note the year. Then look up the song in any subsequent section. Sections 2 through 4 each display their charts year by year. For those songs whose dates lie between 1900 and 1949, information regarding these songs will be found in Sections 2 through 4.

Generally, songs for the years 1950–1999 are indexed and summarized in Volume II. However, there were many instances throughout the century when two different charted songs had the same title but different writers. Also, many songs initially popularized in or before 1949 were successfully revived and charted again post-1949. Both of these types of song pairings are a perennial source of confusion in musicology, so all such songs are listed in this index alongside their pre-1950 namesakes in order to eliminate such confusion.

When two different songs have the same title, a writer is listed for each song to distinguish them. For example, see "Beautiful Eyes" (Snyder): 1909 and "Beautiful Eyes" (Adams): 1949. When a song is listed multiple times with the same writer, it means this one song enjoyed separate waves of popularity on two or more occasions during the century. See "Ain't She Sweet" (Ager), for example, which is listed as having been popular in 1927, 1949, and 1964.

Shown opposite each song is the highest chart rank it attained along with the month and year when it first reached this high. For example, the designation #13 – Apr. 1929 means the song reached #13 in April 1929 and never went higher during this wave of popularity. The month and year are particularly useful for locating songs in the chronological listings of Sections 2, 3, and 4. For more detail on the use of the Index, see the Introduction at the beginning of Section 1.

SECTION 2: THE MONTHLY TOP-20 SONG CHARTS, 1900-1949

This Section contains the Top-20 Song Charts, month by month, from January 1900 to December 1949. Such listings have never been published before. These include the years for which no charts existed prior to this research. Each chart shows the rankings for the given month (T.M.) as well as those of the previous month (L.M.) so that the song's progress up or down the chart can be seen. The number in parentheses indicates how many months the song has been on the charts so far during its current wave of popularity. For more detail, see the Introduction at the beginning of Section 2.

SECTION 3: SEMI-MONTHLY TOP-20 SONG SPREADSHEETS, 1900-1949

Section 3 breaks the monthly charts into semi-monthly intervals and shows the chart activity of songs from a different, and more detailed, viewpoint. The chart success of any given song can be seen at a glance as a series of numerical rankings shows the song climbing toward the top and eventually descending in favor of the next songs to come along. Two chart rankings appear for each month. For example, Jy Jy in the heading refer to the first and second halves of July respectively, and there are rankings listed underneath for each half-month for each song. For more detail on these spreadsheets, see the Introduction at the beginning of Section 3.

SECTION 4: THE ENCYCLOPEDIA OF CHARTED SONGS, 1900-1949

Section 4 contains complete details of every song mentioned in Volume I for the period in the INDEX OF CHARTED SONGS. Each song's description includes the following: the title followed by its rank for the year, its publisher at the time of popularity, publication date, and the month, year, and rank when peak popularity was attained. Following those entries are the writers of the song and any contemporary show or movie in which the song was featured. The third level of information details the artists connected with the song and how they were connected.

For complete details on using the Encyclopedia, see the Introduction at the beginning of Section 4.

BIBLIOGRAPHY

Volume I contains a complete bibliography of sources for this project. The listing is broken into several categories, including expository books and articles, periodicals, discographies, record catalogs, and libraries.

SUPPORT

My thanks go out to:

(1) The Free Library of Philadelphia, where my requests have numbered in the thousands, and especially the expert and patient staff members in the departments of Music, Newspapers/Microfilm, Theater, and Government Publications;

(2) The Library of Congress, Music Division and Recorded Sound Reference Center, where I filled many chronological gaps and uncovered obscure information of all types;

(3) The New York Public Library, Music Division and the Rodgers and Hammerstein Recorded Sound Archives, where I used the Rigler and Deutsch Index to research long-forgotten band vocalists and the library's vast collection of Uncataloged Pop Song microfilms to get songwriter information;

(4) The Boston Public Library, which furnished some turn-of-the-century materials apparently not available elsewhere on the planet;

(5) The Van Pelt Library of the University of Pennsylvania, rich with discographies;

(6) The Ludington Library of Bryn Mawr, PA, my local library, which contains excellent music and film references;

(7) The Agnes Irwin School in Rosemont, PA, my place of work, which provided the necessary computer facilities and, frequently, some welcome encouragement and advice; and

(8) My wife, Ildiko, and children, Vanessa and Justin, who have been sympathetic, loving, and patient in allowing me to search endlessly for truth and order.

ERRATA

Clearly, a work of this magnitude cannot be totally free of errors. Any readers who discover inconsistencies or typos are encouraged to contact the author at Box 407, Rosemont, PA 19010. After a suitable period of time, a list of errata will be mailed to everyone who contributed.

THE CENTURY IN REVIEW

Now you are ready to browse through the music of this astounding century and review more than 10,000 top songs that millions of us have listened to and sung, lots of them well-remembered by many, some of them long-forgotten by most.

SECTION 1

AN INDEX OF CHARTED SONGS, 1900-1949

INTRODUCTION TO SECTION 1:

AN INDEX OF CHARTED SONGS, 1900-1949

The index occupies Section 1 because it is central to the use of Volume I. To find information on a particular song, look it up alphabetically in this index and note the year. Then look up the song in any subsequent section. Sections 2 through 4 each display their charts year by year. For those songs whose dates lie between 1900 and 1949, information regarding these songs will be found in Sections 2 through 4.

Generally, songs for the years 1950-1999 are indexed and summarized in Volume II. However, there were many instances throughout the century when two different charted songs had the same title but different writers. Also, many songs initially popularized in or before 1949 were successfully revived and charted again post-1949 with, of course, the same writers. Both of these types of song pairings are a perennial source of confusion in musicology, so all such later songs are listed in this index alongside their pre-1950 namesakes in order to eliminate this kind of confusion.

When two different songs have the same title, a writer is listed for each song to distinguish them. For example, see "Beautiful Eyes" (Snyder): 1909 and "Beautiful Eyes" (Adams): 1949. When a song is listed multiple times with the same writer, it means this one song enjoyed separate waves of popularity on two or more occasions during the century. See "Ain't She Sweet" (Ager), for example, which is listed as having been popular in 1927, 1949, and 1964. For more complete songwriter information, see the Encyclopedia of Section 4.

Shown opposite each song is the highest chart rank it attained along with the month and year when it first reached this high. For example, the designation #13 – Apr. 1929 means the song reached #13 in April 1929 and never went higher during this wave of popularity. The month and year are particularly useful for locating songs in the chronologically arranged listings of Sections 2, 3, and 4.

An apparent disagreement can appear between the year assigned to the song (: 1912, for example) and the year it reached its chart high. As an illustration, perhaps a 1912 song was strong in the late fall of 1912 and early winter, but happened to reach its high in January 1913, before quickly tumbling downward. Or perhaps a 1937 song soared quickly to Number One in December 1936 but stayed strong all winter and into early spring of 1937, thus accumulating most of its chart credits in 1937.

For this index, the charts used to determine the listed "high" are largely those of the Section 3 Spreadsheets with two exceptions: (1) On rare occasions a song failed to make the Semi-monthly charts in Section 3 but did make a minimal showing on the Monthly charts of Section 2. In such a case, the "chart high" is that monthly high. (2) Occasionally, a steady-selling song would fail to make the Top 20 on either chart yet make the Annual Top 50 in Section 7 of Volume II. The designation T30 – Apr. 1911 means, for example, that such a song first made the Top 30 in April 1911 but never made the Top 20 during that wave of popularity. For 1950 onward, the charts used to determine the highs were from my unpublished work based closely, but not exactly, on the *Billboard* charts.

99 OUT OF 100 (WANNA BE LOVED): 1931	#17 – Apr. 1931

A

"A"-YOU'RE ADORABLE: 1949	# 3 – May 1949
A-TISKET, A-TASKET: 1938	# 1 – Aug. 1938
ABA DABA HONEYMOON (Fields): 1914	# 1 – Oct. 1914
ABA DABA HONEYMOON (Fields): 1951	# 3 – Apr. 1951
ABOUT A QUARTER TO NINE: 1935	# 1 – June 1935
ABSENCE MAKES THE HEART GROW FONDER (Dillea): 1901	# 5 – Apr. 1901
ABSENCE MAKES THE HEART GROW FONDER (FOR SOMEBODY ELSE) (Warren): 1930	#11 – Aug. 1930
ABSINTHE FRAPPE: 1905	#12 – Apr. 1905
AC-CENT-TCHU-ATE THE POSITIVE: 1945	# 1 – Feb. 1945
ACCENT ON YOUTH: 1935	# 3 – Sept. 1935
ACROSS THE ALLEY FROM THE ALAMO: 1947	# 5 – July 1947
ADDRESS UNKNOWN: 1939	#13 – Nov. 1939
ADORABLE: 1933	# 8 – June 1933
AFGHANISTAN: 1920	#15 – Apr. 1920
AFRAID TO DREAM: 1937	# 8 – Sept. 1937
AFTER ALL, YOU'RE ALL I'M AFTER: 1933	#18 – Dec. 1933
AFTER ALL THAT I'VE BEEN TO YOU: 1912	#20 – Jan. 1913
AFTER EVERY PARTY: 1923	#19 – May 1923
(What can I say) AFTER I SAY I'M SORRY: 1926	# 2 – May 1926
AFTER THE ROSES HAVE FADED AWAY: 1915	#12 – Mar. 1915
AFTER THEY GATHER THE HAY: 1906	#19 – July 1906
AFTER YOU GET WHAT YOU WANT, YOU DON'T WANT IT: 1920	# 7 – Oct. 1920
AFTER YOU'VE GONE (Creamer): 1918	# 7 – Nov. 1918
AFTER YOU'VE GONE (Creamer): 1927	#16 – Aug. 1927
AGAIN (Newman): 1949	# 2 – June 1949
AGAIN (Jackson): 1993	# 1 – Dec. 1993
AGGRAVATIN' PAPA: 1923	# 1 – Apr. 1923
AH, BUT IS IT LOVE? 1933	#13 – Oct. 1933
AH! SWEET MYSTERY OF LIFE (V. Herbert): 1911	T30 – May 1911
AH! SWEET MYSTERY OF LIFE (V. Herbert): 1928	# 9 – Apr. 1928
Reached second peak at	#11 – Sept. 1928
AH! SWEET MYSTERY OF LIFE (V. Herbert): 1935	#19 – July 1935
AIN'T DAT A SHAME? (Wilson): 1901	# 2 – Nov. 1901
AIN'T IT FUNNY WHAT A DIFFERENCE JUST A FEW HOURS MAKE? 1904	#16 – June 1904
AIN'T MISBEHAVIN': 1929	#11 – Oct. 1929
AIN'T NOBODY HERE BUT US CHICKENS: 1947	#17 – Feb. 1947
AIN'T SHE SWEET (Ager): 1927	# 2 – June 1927
AIN'T SHE SWEET (Ager): 1949	#19 – Aug. 1949
AIN'T SHE SWEET (Ager): 1964	#19 – Aug. 1964
AIN'T THAT A SHAME (Domino): 1955	# 2 – Sept. 1955
AIN'T WE GOT FUN? 1921	# 1 – July 1921
AL FRESCO: 1905	#16 – Jan. 1905
ALABAMA JUBILEE (Cobb): 1915	# 3 – Aug. 1915
ALABAMA JUBILEE (Cobb): 1955	#15 – July 1955
ALABAMA MOON: 1920	#13 – July 1920
ALABAMY BOUND: 1925	# 1 – May 1925
ALCOHOLIC BLUES: 1919	#13 – July 1919
ALEXANDER (DON'T YOU LOVE YOUR BABY NO MORE?): 1904	# 4 – Oct. 1904
ALEXANDER THE SWOOSE: 1941	#14 – May 1941
ALEXANDER'S BAND IS BACK IN DIXIE LAND: 1919	#10 – Nov. 1919
ALEXANDER'S RAGTIME BAND (Berlin): 1911	# 1 – Oct. 1911
ALEXANDER'S RAGTIME BAND (Berlin): 1938	# 3 – Sept. 1938
ALICE, WHERE ART THOU GOING? 1906	#12 – Sept. 1906
ALICE BLUE GOWN (Tierney): 1920	#10 – June 1920
Reached second peak at	#20 – Jan. 1921
ALICE BLUE GOWN (Tierney): 1940	#12 – May 1940
ALL ABOARD FOR BLANKET BAY: 1911	# 4 – June 1911
ALL ABOARD FOR DIXIE LAND: 1914	# 3 – July 1914
ALL ALONE (H. Von Tilzer): 1911	# 2 – Aug. 1911
ALL ALONE (Berlin): 1925	# 1 – Jan. 1925
ALL ALONE MONDAY: 1927	# 8 – Jan. 1927
ALL ASHORE: 1938	# 2 – Dec. 1938
ALL BY MYSELF (Berlin): 1921	# 1 – Aug. 1921
ALL BY MYSELF (Carmen): 1976	# 2 – Mar. 1976
ALL BY MYSELF (Carmen): 1997	# 4 – Apr. 1997
ALL DRESSED UP WITH A BROKEN HEART: 1948	#20 – Apr. 1948
ALL I DO IS DREAM OF YOU: 1934	# 1 – Aug. 1934
ALL I WANT FOR CHRISTMAS (IS MY TWO FRONT TEETH): 1948	# 5 – Dec. 1948
ALL IN, DOWN AND OUT: 1907	#13 – Mar. 1907
ALL MY LIFE (Stept): 1936	# 4 – June 1936
ALL MY LOVE (Akst): 1947	#15 – Oct. 1947
ALL MY LOVE (Durand): 1950	# 2 – Nov. 1950
(You were made for) ALL MY LOVE (J. Wilson): 1960	#18 – Sept. 1960
ALL NIGHT LONG (S. Brooks): 1912	#13 – Dec. 1912
ALL NIGHT LONG (Walsh): 1980	#19 – July 1980
ALL NIGHT LONG (Combs): 1999	# 9 – Apr. 1999
ALL NIGHT LONG (ALL NIGHT) (Richie): 1983	# 1 – Nov. 1983
ALL OF A SUDDEN MY HEART SINGS; *SEE: (All of a sudden) MY HEART SINGS: 1945, 1959*	
ALL OF ME (Simons): 1932	# 1 – Feb. 1932
ALL OF ME (Simons): 1952	#18 – Aug. 1952
ALL OF MY LIFE: 1945	# 9 – May 1945
ALL OR NOTHING AT ALL: 1943	# 3 – Sept. 1943
ALL OVER NOTHING AT ALL: 1922	# 7 – Aug. 1922
ALL SHE'D SAY WAS "UMH-HUM": 1921	# 7 – Feb. 1921
ALL THAT I ASK OF YOU IS LOVE: 1910	# 5 – Nov. 1910
ALL THAT I'M ASKING IS SYMPATHY: 1929	#20 – Jan. 1930
ALL THE QUAKERS ARE SHOULDER SHAKERS (DOWN IN QUAKER TOWN): 1920	# 9 – Feb. 1920
ALL THE THINGS YOU ARE: 1940	# 1 – Jan. 1940
ALL THE WORLD WILL BE JEALOUS OF ME: 1917	# 1 – Aug. 1917
ALL THIS AND HEAVEN TOO: 1940	# 9 – Aug. 1940
ALL THROUGH THE DAY: 1946	# 4 – May 1946
ALL-AMERICAN GIRL: 1932	# 3 – Nov. 1932
ALLA EN EL RANCHO GRANDE; *SEE: (Alla en) EL RANCHO GRANDE: 1939*	
ALLAH'S HOLIDAY: 1917	# 7 – June 1917
ALMA (WHERE DO YOU LIVE?): 1911	#17 – Sept. 1911
ALMOST LIKE BEING IN LOVE: 1947	#14 – July 1947
ALONE (N.H.Brown): 1936	# 1 – Feb. 1936
ALONE (Steinberg): 1987	# 1 – July 1987
ALONE AT A TABLE FOR TWO: 1936	#10 – Mar. 1936
ALONE TOGETHER: 1932	#17 – Oct. 1932
ALONG THE NAVAJO TRAIL: 1945	# 4 – Oct. 1945
ALONG THE ROCKY ROAD TO DUBLIN: 1916	# 2 – Feb. 1916
ALONG THE SANTA FE TRAIL: 1941	# 9 – Jan. 1941
ALONG WITH ME: 1946	#18 – Aug. 1946
ALWAYS (Bowers): 1900	# 3 – Feb. 1900
ALWAYS (Berlin): 1926	# 1 – Apr. 1926
ALWAYS (Berlin): 1944	# 6 – Nov. 1944
ALWAYS (Bon Jovi): 1994	# 4 – Dec. 1994
ALWAYS (Bell): 1994	#20 – Aug. 1994
ALWAYS (Lewis): 1987	# 1 – June 1987
ALWAYS AND ALWAYS: 1938	#18 – May 1938
ALWAYS IN MY HEART (Lecuona): 1942	# 9 – July 1942
ALWAYS IN MY HEART (Babyface): 1994	#20 – Aug. 1994
ALWAYS IN THE WAY: 1903	# 1 – Oct. 1903
ALWAYS LEAVE THEM LAUGHING: 1904	#15 – Mar. 1904
AM I BLUE: 1929	# 1 – Sept. 1929

AM I WASTING MY TIME ON YOU? 1926 .... #12 – Aug. 1926
AMAPOLA: 1941 .... # 1 – Apr. 1941
AMEN (Schoen): 1942 .... #12 – Oct. 1942
AMEN (Mayfield): 1965 .... # 7 – Jan. 1965
AMERICA, I LOVE YOU (Gottler): 1916 .... # 2 – Jan. 1916
AMERICA, I LOVE YOU (Gottler): 1941 .... #16 – Mar. 1941
AMINA: 1909 .... # 6 – Oct. 1909
AMONG MY SOUVENIRS (Nicholls): 1928 .... # 1 – Mar. 1928
AMONG MY SOUVENIRS (Nicholls): 1960 .... # 6 – Jan. 1960
AMOR (Ruiz): 1944 .... # 4 – July 1944
AMOR (Ruiz): 1961 .... #19 – Sept. 1961
AND A LITTLE BIT MORE: 1907 .... # 4 – June 1907
AND A LITTLE CHILD SHALL LEAD THEM: 1907 .... #13 – Mar. 1907
AND HE'D SAY OOH-LA-LA! WEE WEE: 1919 .... # 9 – Nov. 1919
AND HER TEARS FLOWED LIKE WINE: 1944 .... #13 – Nov. 1944
–AND MIMI: 1947 .... # 8 – Dec. 1947
AND THE ANGELS SING: 1939 .... # 1 – May 1939
AND THE BAND PLAYED ON; *SEE: BAND PLAYED ON, THE: 1941*
AND THE GREEN GRASS GREW ALL AROUND: 1913 .... # 4 – Apr. 1913
AND THEN IT'S HEAVEN: 1946 .... #10 – Nov. 1946
AND THEN SOME: 1935 .... # 4 – Aug. 1935
AND THEN YOU KISSED ME: 1944 .... #19 – Aug. 1944
AND THERE YOU ARE: 1945 .... #14 – Oct. 1945
ANGEL CHILD: 1922 .... # 1 – May 1922
ANGEL IN DISGUISE, AN: 1940 .... #20 – June 1940
ANGELA MIA (MY ANGEL): 1928 .... # 1 – Aug. 1928
ANGELS WITH DIRTY FACES: 1939 .... #15 – Jan. 1939
ANGELUS, THE: 1913 .... T30 – Aug. 1913
ANGRY: 1925 .... # 7 – Nov. 1925
ANIMAL CRACKERS; *SEE: I'M JUST WILD ABOUT ANIMAL CRACKERS: 1926*
ANIMAL CRACKERS IN MY SOUP: 1935 .... #13 – Sept. 1935
ANNABELLE: 1923 .... # 6 – Oct. 1923
ANNIE DOESN'T LIVE HERE ANYMORE: 1933 .... # 2 – Dec. 1933
ANNIVERSARY SONG: 1947 .... # 1 – Mar. 1947
ANONA: 1903 .... # 2 – Oct. 1903
ANOTHER RAG: 1912 .... #12 – Mar. 1912
ANVIL CHORUS: 1941 .... #11 – Mar. 1941
ANY LITTLE GIRL THAT'S A NICE LITTLE GIRL: 1910 .... # 1 – Sept. 1910
ANY OLD PLACE I CAN HANG MY HAT IS HOME SWEET HOME TO ME: 1901 .... # 5 – June 1901
ANY OLD PORT IN A STORM: 1908 .... # 9 – Nov. 1908
ANY OLD TIME AT ALL: 1907 .... #20 – May 1907
ANY RAGS? 1904 .... #10 – Jan. 1904
ANYTHING GOES: 1935 .... #13 – Feb. 1935
APPLE BLOSSOM WEDDING, AN: 1947 .... # 6 – Nov. 1947
APPLE FOR THE TEACHER, AN: 1939 .... # 4 – Oct. 1939
APRIL IN PARIS: 1933 .... #11 – Dec. 1933
APRIL SHOWERS (Silvers): 1922 .... # 1 – Feb. 1922
APRIL SHOWERS (Silvers): 1947 .... # 6 – May 1947
ARABY: 1916 .... #13 – Jan. 1916
ARE YOU FROM DIXIE? 1916 .... # 6 – May 1916
ARE YOU FROM HEAVEN? 1918 .... # 2 – Apr. 1918
ARE YOU HAVIN' ANY FUN? 1939 .... #11 – Nov. 1939
ARE YOU LONESOME? 1910 .... #15 – Mar. 1910
ARE YOU LONESOME TONIGHT? (Handman): 1927 .... # 6 – Oct. 1927
ARE YOU LONESOME TONIGHT? (Handman): 1950 .... #18 – May 1950
ARE YOU LONESOME TONIGHT? (Handman): 1960 .... # 1 – Dec. 1960
ARE YOU LONESOME TONIGHT? (Handman): 1974 .... #15 – Jan. 1974
ARE YOU MAKIN' ANY MONEY? 1933 .... #16 – Oct. 1933
ARE YOU SINCERE? (Gumble): 1908 .... #10 – Aug. 1908
ARE YOU SINCERE? (Walker): 1958 .... # 5 – Mar. 1958
(I'm a dreamer) AREN'T WE ALL? 1930 .... # 1 – Feb. 1930
AREN'T YOU GLAD YOU'RE YOU? 1946 .... # 6 – Feb. 1946
ARGENTINES, THE PORTUGUESE, AND THE GREEKS, THE: 1920 .... #13 – Aug. 1920
ARMY AIR CORPS SONG, THE: 1942 .... #11 – Sept. 1942
AROUND THE CORNER: 1930 .... #15 – Aug. 1930
ARRAH, GO ON, I'M GONNA GO BACK TO OREGON: 1916 .... # 5 – July 1916
ARRAH WANNA: 1907 .... # 1 – Jan. 1907
AS LONG AS THE WORLD ROLLS ON: 1908 .... # 2 – Feb. 1908
AS TIME GOES BY (Hupfeld): 1943 .... # 1 – May 1943
AS TIME GOES BY (Hupfeld): 1952 .... #20 – June 1952
AS YOU DESIRE ME: 1932 .... # 4 – Sept. 1932
ASK ANYONE WHO KNOWS: 1947 .... # 7 – Aug. 1947
ASK HER WHILE THE BAND IS PLAYING: 1909 .... # 8 – Feb. 1909
AT A MISSISSIPPI CABARET: 1914 .... # 6 – Jan. 1915
AT A PERFUME COUNTER: 1938 .... #14 – May 1938
AT LAST (Warren): 1942 .... #11 – Oct. 1942
AT LAST (Warren): 1952 .... #14 – Mar. 1952
AT LONG LAST LOVE: 1938 .... # 9 – Nov. 1938
AT PEACE WITH THE WORLD: 1926 .... # 7 – July 1926
AT SUNDOWN: 1927 .... # 2 – July 1927
AT THE BALALAIKA: 1940 .... # 4 – Feb. 1940
AT THE DEVIL'S BALL: 1913 .... # 6 – Apr. 1913
AT THE END OF A BEAUTIFUL DAY: 1916 .... #19 – Sept. 1916
AT THE RAGTIME BALL: 1912 .... #18 – May 1912
AT YOUR COMMAND: 1931 .... # 6 – Aug. 1931
ATLANTA, G.A.: 1946 .... #10 – Apr. 1946
AUF WIEDERSEH'N (Romberg): 1915 .... # 3 – Jan. 1916
AUF WIEDERSEH'N, MY DEAR (Ager): 1932 .... # 1 – Mar. 1932
AUF WIEDERSEH'N, SWEETHEART (Storch): 1952 .... # 1 – July 1952
AUNT HAGAR'S BLUES; *SEE: AUNT HAGAR'S CHILDREN (BLUES): 1923*
AUNT HAGAR'S CHILDREN (BLUES): 1923 .... #19 – May 1923
AURORA: 1941 .... #18 – July 1941
AVALON: 1921 .... # 1 – Jan. 1921
AVALON TOWN: 1929 .... # 8 – Mar. 1929
AWAY DOWN SOUTH IN HEAVEN: 1928 .... # 4 – Mar. 1928

B

BABES IN THE WOOD: 1916 .... # 8 – July 1916
BABY, IT'S COLD OUTSIDE: 1949 .... # 4 – July 1949
BABY, WON'T YOU PLEASE COME HOME: 1920 .... #17 – Feb. 1920
BABY FACE (Akst): 1926 .... # 1 – Oct. 1926
BABY FACE (Akst): 1948 .... # 4 – May 1948
BABY FACE (Akst): 1976 .... #14 – Feb. 1976
BABY MINE: 1901 .... #10 – Nov. 1901
BABY ROSE: 1911 .... # 3 – Aug. 1911
BABY SHOES: 1916 .... # 1 – Aug. 1916
BABY'S BIRTHDAY PARTY: 1930 .... #18 – Dec. 1930
BACK, BACK, BACK TO BALTIMORE: 1904 .... # 1 – Jan. 1905
BACK HOME AGAIN IN INDIANA; *SEE: INDIANA: 1917*
BACK HOME IN TENNESSEE: 1915 .... # 1 – Dec. 1915
BACK IN YOUR OWN BACK YARD: 1928 .... # 2 – May 1928
BACK TO THE CAROLINA YOU LOVE: 1915 .... # 7 – Jan. 1915
BAGDAD (V. Herbert): 1913 .... #16 – Feb. 1913
BAGDAD (Ager): 1924 .... #11 – Nov. 1924
BAIA: 1945 .... #16 – June 1945
BALI HA'I: 1949 .... # 5 – July 1949
BALLERINA: 1948 .... # 1 – Jan. 1948
BALLIN' THE JACK: 1914 .... # 1 – Nov. 1914
BAM, BAM, BAMY SHORE: 1926 .... # 9 – Jan. 1926
BAMBALINA: 1923 .... # 1 – May 1923
BAMBINA: 1938 .... #17 – Sept. 1938
BAND PLAYED ON, THE (C. Ward): 1941 .... #11 – June 1941

BANDANA DAYS: 1922	#12 – Apr. 1922
BARCELONA: 1926	#15 – Oct. 1926
BARNEY GOOGLE: 1923	# 2 – July 1923
BE CAREFUL, IT'S MY HEART: 1942	# 5 – Sept. 1942
BE MY LITTLE BABY BUMBLE BEE: 1913	# 3 – Jan. 1913
BE STILL, MY HEART: 1934	#11 – Dec. 1934
BEALE STREET BLUES: 1918	T30 – Jan. 1918
BEAT ME, DADDY, EIGHT TO THE BAR: 1940	#11 – Nov. 1940
BEAT OF MY HEART, THE: 1934	#12 – June 1934
BEAUTIFUL ANNABELLE LEE: 1921	#12 – Feb. 1921
BEAUTIFUL EYES (Snyder): 1909	# 5 – June 1909
BEAUTIFUL EYES (Adams): 1949	#20 – Mar. 1949
BEAUTIFUL LADY IN BLUE, A: 1936	# 3 – Mar. 1936
BEAUTIFUL OHIO: 1919	# 2 – Mar. 1919
BEBE: 1923	#11 – Sept. 1923
BECAUSE (D'Hardelot): 1948	#11 – Apr. 1948
BECAUSE (D'Hardelot): 1951	#20 – Sept. 1951
BECAUSE (Clark): 1964	# 3 – Sept. 1964
BECAUSE I LOVE YOU (Berlin): 1926	# 1 – Dec. 1926
BECAUSE I LOVE YOU (THE POSTMAN SONG) (Brooks): 1990	# 1 – Dec. 1990
BECAUSE I'M MARRIED NOW: 1907	# 2 – July 1907
BECAUSE MY BABY DON'T MEAN MAYBE NOW: 1928	#20 – Aug. 1928
BECAUSE YOU WERE AN OLD SWEETHEART OF MINE: 1904	#13 – July 1904
BECAUSE YOU'RE YOU: 1907	# 8 – Feb. 1907
BEDELIA: 1903	# 1 – Dec. 1903
BEER BARREL POLKA: 1939	# 2 – June 1939
BEG YOUR PARDON: 1948	# 3 – Mar. 1948
BEGIN THE BEGUINE: 1938	#12 – Oct. 1938
BEI MIR BIST DU SCHOEN: 1938	# 1 – Jan. 1938
BELGIAN ROSE; *SEE: MY BELGIAN ROSE: 1918*	
BELIEVE IT, BELOVED: 1935	# 5 – Feb. 1935
BELL-BOTTOM TROUSERS: 1945	# 2 – June 1945
BELLS OF SAN RAQUEL, THE: 1942	# 8 – Jan. 1942
BELLS OF ST. MARY'S, THE (Adams): 1919	#15 – Sept. 1919
BELLS OF ST. MARY'S, THE (Adams): 1946	#15 – Feb. 1946
BELOVED: 1928	# 5 – July 1928
BESAME MUCHO: 1944	# 1 – Mar. 1944
BESIDE A BABBLING BROOK: 1923	# 4 – July 1923
BESIDE AN OPEN FIREPLACE: 1930	#18 – Apr. 1930
BEST I GET IS MUCH OBLIGED TO YOU, THE: 1908	# 1 – Feb. 1908
BEST THING IN LIFE, THE: 1907	#14 – Apr. 1907
BEST THINGS IN LIFE ARE FREE, THE (Henderson): 1927	# 7 – Dec. 1927
BEST THINGS IN LIFE ARE FREE, THE (Henderson): 1948	# 9 – Mar. 1948
BEST THINGS IN LIFE ARE FREE, THE (Tresvant): 1992	#10 – June 1992
BETTY CO-ED: 1930	# 4 – Oct. 1930
BETWEEN THE DEVIL AND THE DEEP BLUE SEA: 1932	#18 – Mar. 1932
BEWILDERED: 1938	#17 – May 1938
BEYOND THE BLUE HORIZON: 1930	# 6 – Dec. 1930
BIFF, BANG; *SEE: HEIDELBERG (STEIN SONG): 1903*	
BIG APPLE, THE: 1937	#11 – Oct. 1937
BIG BASS VIOL: 1910	T30 – July 1910
BIG BOY: 1943	#20 – June 1943
BIG CITY BLUES: 1929	#17 – July 1929
BILL BAILEY, WON'T YOU PLEASE COME HOME? 1902	# 1 – Sept. 1902
BILL SIMMONS: 1906	# 4 – July 1906
BILLY (Kendis): 1911	# 4 – Dec. 1911
BILLY (Kendis): 1958	#15 – Apr. 1958
BIMINI BAY: 1921	#11 – Jan. 1922
BIRD IN A GILDED CAGE, A: 1900	# 1 – Mar. 1900
BIRD ON NELLIE'S HAT, THE: 1907	# 1 – Mar. 1907
BIRTH OF THE BLUES, THE: 1926	# 6 – Dec. 1926
BIT O' BLARNEY, A: 1904	# 2 – Sept. 1904
"BL-ND" AND "P-G" SPELLS "BLIND PIG": 1909	#18 – Mar. 1909
BLACK BOTTOM: 1926	# 1 – Dec. 1926
BLACK COFFEE: 1949	#20 – June 1949
BLACK PEARL (Brill): 1900; *SEE: MA BLACK PEARL: 1900*	
BLACK PEARL (Spector): 1969	#13 – July 1969
BLAZE AWAY! 1902	# 5 – July 1902
BLESS YOU (FOR BEING AN ANGEL) (D. Baker): 1947	#12 – Apr. 1947
BLESS YOU (Mann): 1961	#16 – Oct. 1961
BLESS YOUR HEART: 1933	#19 – Nov. 1933
BLOND SAILOR, THE: 1945	#18 – Oct. 1945
BLOSSOMS ON BROADWAY: 1937	# 5 – Nov. 1937
BLUE (AND BROKEN-HEARTED): 1922	# 4 – Nov. 1922
BLUE AGAIN: 1931	# 7 – Feb. 1931
BLUE AND THE GRAY, THE: 1900	# 1 – May 1900
BLUE BELL: 1904	# 1 – May 1904
BLUE BIRD (BRING BACK MY HAPPINESS): 1918	#15 – May 1918
BLUE CHAMPAGNE: 1941	# 7 – Aug. 1941
BLUE CHRISTMAS: 1949	#12 – Dec. 1949
BLUE DANUBE BLUES: 1922	#20 – Apr. 1922
BLUE DANUBE WALTZ: 1935	#17 – Dec. 1934
BLUE EVENING: 1939	#18 – June 1939
BLUE FLAME: 1941	#16 – Apr. 1941
BLUE HAWAII: 1937	# 7 – July 1937
BLUE LOVEBIRD: 1940	#10 – July 1940
BLUE MOON (Rodgers): 1935	# 2 – Feb. 1935
BLUE MOON (Rodgers): 1961	# 1 – Apr. 1961
BLUE ORCHIDS: 1939	# 3 – Nov. 1939
BLUE PRELUDE: 1933	# 7 – Aug. 1933
BLUE RAIN: 1943	#15 – Oct. 1943
BLUE ROOM, THE: 1926	# 8 – Sept. 1926
BLUE SKIES (Berlin): 1927	# 1 – Mar. 1927
BLUE SKIES (Berlin): 1946	#12 – Nov. 1946
BLUE SKIRT WALTZ, THE: 1949	#11 – June 1949
BLUE SKY AVENUE: 1934	#20 – Nov. 1934
BLUEBERRY HILL (Rose): 1940	# 1 – Oct. 1940
BLUEBERRY HILL (Rose): 1956	# 4 – Jan. 1957
BLUEBIRD OF HAPPINESS: 1948	#10 – Oct. 1948
BLUEBIRDS IN THE MOONLIGHT: 1940	#18 – Jan. 1940
BLUES (MY NAUGHTY SWEETIE GIVES TO ME): 1919	# 4 – Sept. 1919
BLUES IN THE NIGHT: 1942	# 1 – Feb. 1942
BOB WHITE (WHATCHA GONNA SWING TONIGHT?): 1937	# 6 – Jan. 1938
BOBBIN' UP AND DOWN: 1913	#13 – Aug. 1913
BODY AND SOUL (J. Green): 1930	# 5 – Dec. 1930
BON BON BUDDY: 1908	# 4 – Oct. 1908
BOO-HOO: 1937	# 1 – Apr. 1937
BOOG-IT: 1940	#19 – June 1940
BOOGIE WOOGIE (P. Smith): 1938	#18 – Nov. 1938
BOOGIE WOOGIE (P. Smith): 1943	#12 – Jan. 1944
BOOGIE WOOGIE (P. Smith): 1945	#16 – Sept. 1945
BOOGIE WOOGIE BUGLE BOY, THE (H. Prince): 1941	#15 – Mar. 1941
BOOGIE WOOGIE BUGLE BOY, THE (H. Prince): 1973	# 8 – July 1973
BOOGLIE-WOOGLIE PIGGY, THE: 1941	#15 – Aug. 1941
BOOLA, BOOLA (YALE BOOLA): 1901	# 5 – Sept. 1901
BOULEVARD OF BROKEN DREAMS: 1934	# 7 – Apr. 1934
BOUQUET OF ROSES: 1948	#17 – Aug. 1948
BOY AND A GIRL WERE DANCING, A: 1932	#18 – Jan. 1933
BOYS ARE COMING HOME TODAY, THE: 1903	# 9 – July 1903
BOYS IN THE GALL'RY FOR MINE, THE: 1903	# 5 – Sept. 1903
BRAZIL (Barroso): 1943	# 3 – Mar. 1943
BRAZIL (Barroso): 1975	#11 – Oct. 1975
BREAK THE NEWS TO MOTHER: 1917	#10 – Nov. 1917
BREAKAWAY, THE: 1929	#14 – July 1929
BREATHLESS (J. Press): 1942	#17 – June 1942
BREEZE AND I, THE (Lecuona): 1940	# 3 – July 1940

BREEZE AND I, THE (Lecuona): 1955 ..... #13 – May 1955
BREEZIN' ALONG WITH THE BREEZE: 1926 ..... # 2 – Nov. 1926
BRIDGE OF SIGHS, THE: 1900 ..... # 5 – Dec. 1900
BRIGHT EYES: 1921 ..... # 1 – Apr. 1921
BRIGHT EYES, GOODBYE: 1905 ..... #17 – July 1905
BRING BACK MY DADDY TO ME: 1918 ..... # 5 – June 1918
BROADWAY MELODY: 1929 ..... # 7 – May 1929
BROADWAY ROSE: 1921 ..... # 4 – Feb. 1921
(Here am I) BROKEN HEARTED (Henderson): 1927 ..... # 2 – Oct. 1927
(Here am I) BROKEN HEARTED (Henderson): 1952 ..... #13 – Mar. 1952
BROKEN RECORD, THE: 1936 ..... # 7 – Jan. 1936
BROTHER, CAN YOU SPARE A DIME? 1932 ..... # 8 – Dec. 1932
BROWN EYES, WHY ARE YOU BLUE? 1925 ..... # 2 – Dec. 1925
BRUSH THOSE TEARS FROM YOUR EYES: 1949 ..... #15 – Jan. 1949
BUDWEISER'S A FRIEND OF MINE: 1907 ..... # 8 – Oct. 1907
BUGLE CALL RAG (Schoebel): 1932 ..... #17 – Sept. 1932
BUGLE CALL RAG (Schoebel): 1934 ..... #16 – Nov. 1934
BUMBLE BOOGIE (Fina): 1946 ..... #20 – May 1946
BUMBLE BOOGIE (Fina): 1961 ..... #15 – June 1961
BURNING OF ROME, THE: 1904 ..... # 7 – Mar. 1904
BUT BEAUTIFUL: 1948 ..... # 5 – Apr. 1948
BUT I DID: 1945 ..... #20 – Dec. 1945
BUTTON UP YOUR OVERCOAT: 1929 ..... # 4 – Apr. 1929
BUTTONS AND BOWS: 1948 ..... # 1 – Nov. 1948
BUZZ ME: 1946 ..... #18 – Feb. 1946
BY A RIPPLING STREAM: 1932 ..... #10 – June 1932
BY A WATERFALL: 1933 ..... # 4 – Dec. 1933
BY HECK: 1915 ..... # 5 – May 1915
BY THE BEAUTIFUL SEA: 1914 ..... # 1 – Aug. 1914
BY THE FIRESIDE: 1932 ..... # 4 – Apr. 1932
BY THE LIGHT OF THE SILVERY MOON: 1909 ..... # 1 – Dec. 1909
BY THE LIGHT OF THE STARS: 1925 ..... #20 – Aug. 1925
BY THE RIVER OF THE ROSES: 1944 ..... #12 – Apr. 1944
BY THE RIVER STE. MARIE: 1931 ..... # 6 – Apr. 1931
BY THE SASKATCHEWAN: 1911 ..... #17 – July 1911
BY THE SYCAMORE TREE: 1932 ..... # 8 – Feb. 1932
BY THE WATERMELON VINE, LINDY LOU: 1904 ..... # 6 – Jan. 1905
BY-U, BY-O: 1941 ..... # 9 – Jan. 1942
BYE BYE BABY (Handman): 1936 ..... # 5 – Sept. 1936
BYE, BYE, BLACKBIRD: 1926 ..... # 1 – Sept. 1926
BYE BYE BLUES (Lown): 1930 ..... # 7 – Sept. 1930
BYE BYE BLUES (Lown): 1953 ..... #14 – Feb. 1953

C

C'EST VOUS (IT'S YOU): 1927 ..... # 7 – Oct. 1927
C-H-I-C-K-E-N; *SEE: DAT'S DE WAY TO SPELL CHICKEN: 1903*
C-O-N-S-T-A-N-T-I-N-O-P-L-E: 1928 ..... # 8 – Aug. 1928
CABIN IN THE COTTON: 1932 ..... #12 – July 1932
CALDONIA: 1945 ..... # 7 – June 1945
CALDONIA BOOGIE; *SEE: CALDONIA: 1945*
CALIFORNIA: 1922 ..... # 4 – June 1922
CALIFORNIA, HERE I COME: 1924 ..... # 1 – Apr. 1924
CALIFORNIA AND YOU: 1914 ..... # 5 – Oct. 1914
CALL ME DARLING: 1931 ..... # 6 – Dec. 1931
CALL ME UP SOME RAINY AFTERNOON: 1910 ..... # 5 – July 1910
CALL OF THE CANYON, THE: 1940 ..... #11 – Oct. 1940
CALLING TO HER BOY JUST ONCE AGAIN: 1900 ..... # 7 – Nov. 1900
CAMP MEETIN' TIME: 1906 ..... #17 – Sept. 1906
CAMP MEETING BAND: 1914 ..... #18 – June 1914
CAN I FORGET YOU? 1937 ..... #17 – Oct. 1937
CAN'T GET INDIANA OFF MY MIND: 1940 ..... #14 – Sept. 1940
CAN'T GET OUT OF THIS MOOD: 1943 ..... # 9 – Jan. 1943
CAN'T HELP LOVIN' DAT MAN: 1928 ..... #11 – Apr. 1928
CAN'T WE BE FRIENDS? 1929 ..... #14 – Oct. 1929
CAN'T WE TALK IT OVER? 1932 ..... # 9 – Mar. 1932
CAN'T YOU HEAR ME CALLING, CAROLINE? 1914 ..... # 4 – Oct. 1914
CAN'T YOU SEE I'M LONELY? 1906 ..... #10 – Mar. 1906
CAN'T YOU TAKE IT BACK AND CHANGE IT FOR A BOY? 1911 ..... #19 – Aug. 1911
CANADIAN CAPERS (Chandler): 1921 ..... #10 – Dec. 1921
CANADIAN CAPERS (Chandler, Warren): 1949 ..... #19 – Nov. 1949
CANDY: 1945 ..... # 2 – Apr. 1945
CANDY KISSES: 1949 ..... #16 – May 1949
CARAMBA! IT'S THE SAMBA! 1948 ..... #20 – June 1948
CARAVAN (Ellington): 1937 ..... #11 – Aug. 1937
CARELESS: 1940 ..... # 1 – Feb. 1940
CARELESS HANDS: 1949 ..... # 4 – Apr. 1949
CARELESSLY: 1937 ..... # 2 – May 1937
CARIOCA (Youmans): 1934 ..... # 4 – Feb. 1934
CARIOCA (Youmans): 1952 ..... #15 – May 1952
CARISSIMA: 1905 ..... # 5 – June 1905
CAROLINA IN THE MORNING: 1923 ..... # 1 – Jan. 1923
CAROLINA MOON: 1929 ..... # 1 – Mar. 1929
CAROLINA SUNSHINE: 1919 ..... # 9 – Dec. 1919
CARRIE (MARRY HARRY): 1909 ..... # 4 – Dec. 1909
CARRY ME BACK TO OLD VIRGINNY: 1915 ..... #11 – May 1915
CASEY JONES: 1910 ..... # 3 – Jan. 1911
CATHEDRAL IN THE PINES: 1938 ..... # 4 – June 1938
'CAUSE MY BABY SAYS IT'S SO: 1937 ..... #16 – July 1937
CECILIA (Dreyer): 1925 ..... # 2 – Nov. 1925
CECILIA (Simon): 1970 ..... # 4 – May 1970
CEMENT MIXER (PUT-TI, PUT-TI): 1946 ..... #10 – May 1946
CENTRAL, GIVE ME BACK MY DIME: 1905 ..... #17 – Sept. 1905
CHAMPAGNE WALTZ, THE: 1934 ..... #10 – June 1934
CHANGE PARTNERS: 1938 ..... # 2 – Oct. 1938
CHANSON DU COEUR BRISE; *SEE: SONG OF SONGS, THE: 1915*
CHANSONETTE: 1924 ..... #13 – Dec. 1923
CHANT OF THE JUNGLE: 1930 ..... # 1 – Jan. 1930
CHANTICLEER RAG, THE: 1910 ..... #18 – Aug. 1910
CHARLESTON, THE (J.P.Johnson): 1924 ..... #20 – Jan. 1924
CHARLESTON, THE (J.P.Johnson): 1925 ..... #10 – Dec. 1925
CHARLEY, MY BOY (FioRito): 1924 ..... # 1 – Oct. 1924
CHARLEY, MY BOY (FioRito): 1950 ..... #13 – Jan. 1950
CHARMAINE (Rapee): 1927 ..... # 1 – Sept. 1927
CHARMAINE (Rapee): 1952 ..... # 8 – Feb. 1952
CHASING SHADOWS: 1935 ..... # 2 – July 1935
CHATTANOOGA CHOO CHOO: 1941 ..... # 1 – Dec. 1941
CHATTERBOX: 1940 ..... #13 – Jan. 1940
CHEATIN' ON ME: 1925 ..... # 7 – June 1925
CHEEK TO CHEEK: 1935 ..... # 1 – Sept. 1935
CHEER UP, MARY: 1906 ..... # 4 – Dec. 1906
CHEERFUL LITTLE EARFUL: 1931 ..... # 9 – Jan. 1931
CHERIE: 1921 ..... # 5 – Aug. 1921
CHERIE, I LOVE YOU: 1926 ..... # 5 – Sept. 1926
CHERRY (Redman): 1928 ..... #16 – Dec. 1928
CHERRY (Redman): 1944 ..... #12 – Feb. 1944
CHEYENNE: 1906 ..... # 3 – June 1906
CHI-BABA, CHI-BABA: 1947 ..... # 3 – July 1947
CHICAGO (THAT TODDLIN' TOWN): 1922 ..... # 2 – Dec. 1922
CHICKEN RAG: 1911 ..... #18 – Jan. 1912
CHICKEN REEL: 1911 ..... #10 – Oct. 1911
CHICKERY CHICK: 1945 ..... # 4 – Dec. 1945
CHILD LOVE: 1911 ..... #20 – Oct. 1911
CHILI BEAN: 1920 ..... # 5 – Dec. 1920

CHIMES OF SPRING; *SEE: SPRING, BEAUTIFUL SPRING: 1907*	
CHINATOWN, MY CHINATOWN (J. Schwartz): 1910	T30 – Oct. 1910
CHINATOWN, MY CHINATOWN (J. Schwartz): 1915	# 5 – Feb. 1915
CHINESE LULLABY: 1919	# 9 – Oct. 1919
CHIQUITA: 1928	# 3 – Oct. 1928
CHLOE (Moret): 1928	# 3 – Apr. 1928
CHLOE (Moret): 1945	#12 – May 1945
CHONG, HE COME FROM HONG KONG: 1919	# 4 – May 1919
CHOO CHOO CH'BOOGIE: 1946	#14 – Sept. 1946
CHOPIN'S POLONAISE: 1945	# 8 – Aug. 1945
CHRISTMAS ISLAND: 1947	#13 – Jan. 1947
CHRISTMAS SONG, THE: 1946	#11 – Dec. 1946
CHRISTOPHER COLUMBUS: 1936	#11 – May 1936
CINDERELLA, STAY IN MY ARMS: 1939	# 8 – Aug. 1939
CIRIBIRIBIN (Pestalozza): 1910	#11 – Mar. 1910
CIRIBIRIBIN (Pestalozza): 1940	#20 – Jan. 1940
CITY CALLED HEAVEN, A: 1941	#16 – Nov. 1941
CIVILIZATION: 1947	# 5 – Dec. 1947
CLAP YO' HANDS: 1927	#10 – Mar. 1927
CLIMBING UP THE LADDER OF LOVE: 1926	#12 – Dec. 1926
CLING TO ME: 1936	#11 – Mar. 1936
CLOSE TO ME: 1936	#14 – Nov. 1936
CLOSE TO MY HEART: 1915	# 7 – Dec. 1915
CLOSE TO YOU (Livingston): 1943	#14 – Oct. 1943
(They long to be) CLOSE TO YOU (Bacharach): 1970	# 1 – July 1970
CLOSE YOUR EYES (Petkere): 1933	#17 – Nov. 1933
CLOUDS: 1935	# 6 – Mar. 1935
COAL-BLACK MAMMY: 1922	# 6 – Nov. 1922
COAX ME: 1905	#17 – Mar. 1905
COAX ME A LITTLE BIT: 1946	#18 – June 1946
COCKTAILS FOR TWO (Coslow): 1934	# 3 – July 1934
COCKTAILS FOR TWO (Coslow): 1945	# 9 – Feb. 1945
COFFEE SONG, THE: 1946	#12 – Nov. 1946
COHEN ON THE TELEPHONE: 1914	#11 – Sept. 1914
COLLEGE LIFE: 1905	#10 – Oct. 1905
COLLEGIATE: 1925	# 1 – Aug. 1925
COLORADO: 1924	# 8 – June 1924
COME, JOSEPHINE, IN MY FLYING MACHINE: 1911	# 1 – Mar. 1911
COME AFTER BREAKFAST, BRING 'LONG YOUR LUNCH, AND LEAVE 'FORE SUPPER TIME: 1910	# 3 – Feb. 1910
COME ALONG, MY MANDY! 1910	# 7 – May 1910
COME BACK, MA HONEY BOY, TO ME: 1901	#17 – Jan. 1901
COME DOWN, MA EVENIN' STAR: 1903	# 4 – Aug. 1903
COME ON, PAPA: 1919	# 7 – Apr. 1919
COME OUT OF THE KITCHEN, MARY ANN: 1917	# 7 – May 1917
COME OVER ON MY VERANDA: 1905	#20 – July 1905
COME RAIN OR COME SHINE: 1946	#13 – July 1946
COME TAKE A TRIP IN MY AIRSHIP: 1904	# 1 – Sept. 1904
COME TO BABY DO! 1946	#14 – Feb. 1946
COME TO ME (Henderson): 1931	# 9 – Aug. 1931
COME TO ME (T. Green): 1979	#15 – Nov. 1979
COMES LOVE: 1939	# 7 – Sept. 1939
COMIN' IN ON A WING AND A PRAYER: 1943	# 1 – June 1943
CONCERT IN THE PARK: 1939	#12 – July 1939
CONCERTO FOR TWO: 1941	#13 – Dec. 1941
CONEY ISLAND COON: 1903	#18 – Jan. 1903
CONFESS: 1948	#12 – Aug. 1948
CONFESSIN' (THAT I LOVE YOU); *SEE: I'M CONFESSIN' (THAT I LOVE YOU): 1930, 1945, 1952*	
CONFUCIUS SAY: 1940	#13 – Mar. 1940
CONGO LOVE SONG: 1903	# 1 – Aug. 1903
CONGRATULATIONS (Stept): 1930	#16 – Jan. 1930
CONGRATULATIONS (P. Weston): 1949	#20 – Feb. 1949
CONSOLATION: 1908	#13 – July 1908
CONTINENTAL, THE: 1934	# 1 – Nov. 1934
COOL WATER: 1948	#12 – Sept. 1948
COON! COON! COON! 1901	# 1 – Feb. 1901
COON BAND CONCERT, A; *SEE: COON BAND CONTEST, A: 1900*	
COON BAND CONTEST, A: 1900	# 9 – Aug. 1900
COON UP A TREE: 1901	#10 – June 1901
COPENHAGEN: 1925	# 2 – Feb. 1925
COQUETTE (C. Lombardo): 1928	# 5 – June 1928
COQUETTE (Berlin): 1929	#20 – May 1929
COSSACK LOVE SONG (DON'T FORGET ME): 1926	#14 – May 1926
COTTAGE FOR SALE, A (L. Conley): 1930	# 3 – May 1930
COTTAGE FOR SALE, A (L. Conley): 1945	#15 – Oct. 1945
COULD BE: 1939	# 4 – Mar. 1939
COULD YOU BE TRUE TO EYES OF BLUE? 1902	# 4 – Dec. 1902
COVERED WAGON DAYS: 1924	#10 – Feb. 1924
COW-COW BOOGIE (D. Raye): 1942	#18 – Aug. 1942
COW-COW BOOGIE (D. Raye): 1944	#18 – Apr. 1944
COZY CORNER; *SEE: IN A COZY CORNER: 1902*	
CRAZY BLUES: 1921	#10 – Apr. 1921
CRAZY RHYTHM: 1928	# 8 – Aug. 1928
CRAZY WORDS, CRAZY TUNE: 1927	# 9 – May 1927
CREOLE BELLES: 1902	# 1 – Jan. 1902
CRINOLINE DAYS: 1923	# 4 – Feb. 1923
CROCODILE ISLE: 1906	#13 – Sept. 1906
CROONING: 1921	# 8 – Sept. 1921
CROONY MELODY; *SEE: MY CROONY MELODY: 1914*	
CROSS PATCH: 1936	#12 – July 1936
CROSS YOUR HEART: 1926	#11 – Dec. 1926
CROSSTOWN: 1940	#17 – Oct. 1940
CRUISING DOWN THE RIVER: 1949	# 1 – Mar. 1949
CRY, BABY, CRY: 1938	# 1 – June 1938
CRYIN' FOR THE CAROLINES: 1930	# 3 – Mar. 1930
CRYING FOR YOU: 1923	#15 – May 1923
CUANTO LE GUSTA: 1948	#10 – Jan. 1949
CUBAN LOVE SONG: 1932	# 7 – Jan. 1932
CUBAN MOON: 1920	#19 – Nov. 1920
CUBANOLA GLIDE, THE: 1910	# 2 – Jan. 1910
CUCKOO WALTZ: 1948	#19 – July 1948
CUDDLE UP A LITTLE CLOSER: 1908	# 2 – Oct. 1908
CUP OF COFFEE, A SANDWICH, AND YOU, A: 1926	# 7 – Feb. 1926
CUPID'S GARDEN: 1902	#11 – July 1902
CURSE OF AN ACHING HEART, THE: 1913	# 2 – Aug. 1913
CUT YOURSELF A PIECE OF CAKE: 1923	#18 – Oct. 1923

D

DADDY: 1941	# 2 – Aug. 1941
DADDY, YOU'VE BEEN A MOTHER TO ME: 1920	# 3 – May 1920
DADDY HAS A SWEETHEART, AND MOTHER IS HER NAME: 1913	# 5 – May 1913
DADDY LONG LEGS: 1919	#11 – Sept. 1919
DADDY'S LITTLE GIRL (Morse): 1906	# 8 – Feb. 1906
DADDY'S LITTLE GIRL (Gerlach): 1950	# 7 – Apr. 1950
DAISIES WON'T TELL: 1909	#10 – Nov. 1909
DAMES: 1934	#14 – Aug. 1934
DANCE OF THE GRIZZLY BEAR: 1910	T30 – Sept. 1910
DANCE OF THE HONEYBEES: 1902	#13 – Dec. 1902
DANCE OF THE HOURS: 1949	#20 – Sept. 1949
DANCE WITH A DOLLY: 1944	# 2 – Dec. 1944
DANCING AROUND; *SEE: WHILE THEY WERE DANCING AROUND: 1914*	
DANCING FOOL: 1922	# 3 – Sept. 1922
DANCING IN THE DARK (A. Schwartz): 1931	# 5 – Aug. 1931

DANCING IN THE DARK (Springsteen): 1984	# 2 – June 1984
DANCING ON THE CEILING (Rodgers): 1932	# 8 – Mar. 1932
DANCING ON THE CEILING (Richie): 1986	# 2 – Sept. 1986
DANCING TAMBOURINE: 1927	# 7 – Dec. 1927
DANCING WITH MY SHADOW: 1935	# 8 – Feb. 1935
DANCING WITH TEARS IN MY EYES: 1930	# 1 – July 1930
DAPPER DAN: 1922	# 4 – Jan. 1922
DARDANELLA: 1920	# 1 – Feb. 1920
DARKNESS ON THE DELTA: 1933	#17 – Mar. 1933
DARKTOWN STRUTTERS' BALL, THE (S. Brooks): 1917	# 1 – Feb. 1918
DARKTOWN STRUTTERS' BALL, THE (S. Brooks): 1954	#13 – Mar. 1954
DARN THAT DREAM: 1940	# 4 – Mar. 1940
DAT'S DE WAY TO SPELL CHICKEN: 1903	# 8 – Feb. 1903
(She's) THE DAUGHTER OF ROSIE O'GRADY: 1918	# 4 – June 1918
DAWN OF THE CENTURY MARCH: 1900	#12 – Aug. 1900
DAY AFTER DAY (R. Himber): 1938	#19 – Dec. 1938
DAY AFTER DAY (W.P.Ham): 1972	# 4 – Feb. 1972
DAY AFTER FOREVER, THE: 1944	#19 – Sept. 1944
DAY BY DAY (P. Weston): 1946	# 6 – Mar. 1946
DAY BY DAY (S. Schwartz): 1972	#13 – July 1972
DAY BY DAY (R. Hyman): 1986	#18 – Feb. 1986
DAY DREAMING (Kern): 1942	#17 – Feb. 1942
DAY DREAMING (A. Franklin): 1972	# 5 – May 1972
DAY DREAMING (ALL NIGHT LONG) (Warren): 1938	#17 – July 1938
DAY DREAMS (VISIONS OF BLISS): 1911	# 6 – May 1911
DAY IN – DAY OUT: 1939	# 3 – Oct. 1939
DAY THAT YOU GREW COLDER, THE: 1905	#18 – Apr. 1905
DAY YOU CAME ALONG, THE: 1933	# 4 – Oct. 1933
DAYBREAK: 1942	#12 – Dec. 1942
DAYDREAMIN' (Jerkins):1998	# 6 – Sept. 1998
DEAR LITTLE BOY OF MINE: 1919	# 7 – Feb. 1919
DEAR MOM: 1942	#18 – Mar. 1942
DEAR OLD GIRL (Morse): 1903	# 2 – Nov. 1903
DEAR OLD GIRL (Morse): 1913	T30 – June 1913
DEAR OLD MOONLIGHT: 1910	T30 – Apr. 1910
DEAR OLD PAL OF MINE: 1919	#10 – Feb. 1919
DEAR OLD ROSE: 1912	#20 – July 1912
DEAR OLD SOUTHLAND: 1922	# 2 – Apr. 1922
DEAREST, YOU'RE THE NEAREST TO MY HEART: 1923	# 4 – June 1923
DEARIE (Kummer): 1905	# 1 – Mar. 1906
DEARIE (Hilliard): 1950	# 5 – Apr. 1950
DEARLY BELOVED: 1942	# 5 – Nov. 1942
DEEP IN A DREAM: 1939	# 3 – Feb. 1939
DEEP IN MY HEART, DEAR: 1925	# 9 – Mar. 1925
DEEP IN THE HEART OF TEXAS: 1942	# 1 – Mar. 1942
DEEP NIGHT: 1929	# 6 – May 1929
DEEP PURPLE (DeRose): 1939	# 1 – Mar. 1939
DEEP PURPLE (DeRose): 1963	# 1 – Nov. 1963
DEEP PURPLE (DeRose): 1976	#14 – Mar. 1976
DELISHIOUS: 1932	#15 – Feb. 1932
DER FUEHRER'S FACE: 1942	# 8 – Dec. 1942
DESERT SONG, THE: 1929	#12 – July 1929
DEVIL MAY CARE: 1940	#12 – July 1940
DEW, DEW, DEWY DAY; *SEE: WHAT DO WE DO ON A DEW, DEW, DEWY DAY: 1927*	
DIANE (Rapee): 1928	# 3 – Dec. 1927
DIANE (Rapee): 1964	#10 – June 1964
DICKEY-BIRD SONG, THE: 1948	# 7 – May 1948
DID I REMEMBER: 1936	# 1 – Aug. 1936
DID YOU EVER GET THAT FEELING IN THE MOONLIGHT *SEE: (Did you ever get) THAT FEELING IN THE MOONLIGHT: 1945*	
DID YOU EVER SEE A DREAM WALKING? 1933	# 1 – Dec. 1933
DID YOU MEAN IT? (Lyman)): 1928	# 8 – Jan. 1928
DID YOU MEAN IT? (J. Greer): 1936	#10 – Dec. 1936
DIG YOU LATER (A HUBBA-HUBBA-HUBBA): 1946	# 9 – Jan. 1946
DIGA-DIGA-DOO: 1928	# 6 – Oct. 1928
DINAH (Akst): 1926	# 1 – Mar. 1926
DINAH (Akst): 1932	#11 – Feb. 1932
DINNER AT EIGHT: 1933	# 8 – Nov. 1933
DINNER FOR ONE, PLEASE, JAMES: 1936	#11 – Feb. 1936
DIPSY DOODLE, THE: 1938	# 2 – Feb. 1938
DIRTY HANDS! DIRTY FACE! 1923	#15 – Sept. 1923
DIXIE MADE US JAZZ BAND MAD: 1920	#16 – Dec. 1920
DIXIELAND BAND, THE: 1935	#20 – May 1935
DIZZY FINGERS: 1924	#16 – June 1924
DO, DO, DO: 1927	# 9 – Feb. 1927
DO I LOVE YOU? 1940	# 8 – Mar. 1940
DO I WORRY? 1941	# 3 – May 1941
DO IT AGAIN (Gershwin): 1922	# 5 – Aug. 1922
DO IT AGAIN (Wilson): 1968	#20 – Sept. 1968
DO IT AGAIN (Becker): 1973	# 6 – Feb. 1973
DO NOTHIN' TILL YOU HEAR FROM ME: 1944	#15 – Mar. 1944
DO YOU CARE? 1941	# 8 – Oct. 1941
DO YOU EVER THINK OF ME? 1921	# 8 – May 1921
DO YOU LOVE ME? (Ruby): 1946	# 9 – June 1946
DO YOU LOVE ME? (Gordy): 1962	# 3 – Oct. 1962
DO YOU LOVE ME? (Gordy): 1964	#11 – June 1964
DO YOU LOVE ME? (Gordy): 1988	#11 – Aug. 1988
DO YOU TAKE THIS WOMAN: 1914	# 4 – Apr. 1914
DOAN YE CRY, MA HONEY: 1900	# 2 – Mar. 1900
DOCTOR, LAWYER, INDIAN CHIEF: 1946	# 3 – Mar. 1946
DOCTOR TINKLE TINKER: 1911	#20 – Sept. 1911
DOIN' THE NEW LOW DOWN: 1928	#14 – Oct. 1928
DOIN' THE RACCOON: 1928	# 5 – Dec. 1928
DOIN' THE UPTOWN LOWDOWN: 1933	#20 – Dec. 1933
DOIN' WHAT COMES NATUR'LLY: 1946	# 2 – Aug. 1946
DOLL DANCE, THE: 1927	# 5 – July 1927
DOLORES: 1941	# 6 – May 1941
DON'T BE LIKE THAT: 1929	#18 – Feb. 1929
DON'T BE THAT WAY: 1938	# 4 – May 1938
DON'T BITE THE HAND THAT'S FEEDING YOU: 1916	#10 – Mar. 1916
DON'T BLAME IT ALL ON BROADWAY: 1914	#11 – Feb. 1914
DON'T BLAME ME: 1933	# 5 – Sept. 1933
DON'T BRING LULU: 1925	# 2 – July 1925
DON'T CRY, BABY: 1943	#19 – Oct. 1942
DON'T CRY, FRENCHY, DON'T CRY: 1919	#19 – May 1919
DON'T CRY, JOE: 1949	# 5 – Nov. 1949
DON'T EVER LEAVE ME: 1930	#20 – Feb. 1930
DON'T FENCE ME IN: 1945	# 1 – Jan. 1945
DON'T FORGET ME (Gershwin); *SEE: COSSACK LOVE SONG: 1926*	
DON'T FORGET TONIGHT, TOMORROW: 1945	#19 – Nov. 1945
DON'T GET AROUND MUCH ANYMORE: 1943	# 2 – May 1943
DON'T GET MARRIED ANY MORE, MA: 1907	#18 – Dec. 1907
DON'T GIVE UP THE SHIP: 1935	# 8 – Dec. 1935
DON'T HOLD EVERYTHING: 1929	#15 – Jan. 1929
DON'T LET IT BOTHER YOU: 1934	#17 – Nov. 1934
DON'T PUT ME OFF AT BUFFALO ANY MORE: 1901	#19 – Jan. 1902
DON'T SIT UNDER THE APPLE TREE (WITH ANYONE ELSE BUT ME): 1942	# 1 – June 1942
DON'T SWEETHEART ME: 1944	# 7 – May 1944
DON'T TAKE ME HOME: 1908	#10 – Dec. 1908
DON'T TELL HER (HIM) WHAT HAPPENED TO ME: 1930	#14 – Oct. 1930
DON'T WAIT TILL THE NIGHT BEFORE CHRISTMAS; *SEE: (Don't wait till) THE NIGHT BEFORE CHRISTMAS: 1938*	
DON'T WAKE ME UP, I'M DREAMING: 1911	# 9 – June 1911
DON'T WAKE ME UP (LET ME DREAM): 1926	#20 – Feb. 1926

DON'T WORRY 'BOUT ME (Bloom): 1939	# 6 – June 1939
DON'T WORRY 'BOUT ME (Bloom): 1954	#20 – June 1954
DON'T WORRY, BILL; *SEE: SYMPATHY: 1906*	
DON'T YOU LOVE ME ANYMORE? 1947	#12 – Jan. 1948
DONKEY SERENADE, THE: 1938	#20 – May 1938
DOO DAH BLUES: 1922	#19 – May 1922
DOO WACKA DOO: 1924	# 7 – Dec. 1924
DOODLE DOO DOO: 1924	#10 – Sept. 1924
DOWN AMONG THE SHELTERING PALMS: 1915	# 4 – May 1915
DOWN AMONG THE SUGAR CANE: 1909	# 2 – Oct. 1909
DOWN ARGENTINA WAY: 1940	# 3 – Jan. 1941
DOWN AT THE HUSKING BEE: 1909	#11 – Apr. 1909
DOWN BY THE O-HI-O: 1921	# 5 – Mar. 1921
DOWN BY THE OLD MILL STREAM: 1911	# 1 – July 1911
DOWN BY THE RIVER: 1935	#16 – Apr. 1935
DOWN BY THE RIVERSIDE (P. Barnes): 1901	#18 – Mar. 1901
DOWN BY THE STATION (S. Gaillard): 1949	#15 – Feb. 1949
DOWN BY THE STATION (Belland): 1960	#14 – Feb. 1960
DOWN BY THE WINEGAR WOIKS: 1926	#10 – Mar. 1926
DOWN HOME IN TENNESSEE; *SEE: BACK HOME IN TENNESSEE: 1915*	
DOWN IN BOM-BOMBAY: 1915	# 2 – Oct. 1915
DOWN IN DEAR OLD NEW ORLEANS: 1913	#18 – Apr. 1913
DOWN IN JUNGLE TOWN: 1908	# 1 – Sept. 1908
DOWN IN TENNESSEE; *SEE: TEN LITTLE FINGERS AND TEN LITTLE TOES: 1922*	
DOWN IN THE DEEP, LET ME SLEEP WHEN I DIE: 1903	#12 – Aug. 1903
DOWN IN THE DEPTHS: 1901	#18 – July 1901
DOWN IN THE VALE OF SHENANDOAH: 1904	#18 – Nov. 1904
DOWN ON THE BRANDYWINE: 1904	#18 – Sept. 1904
DOWN ON THE FARM (H. Von Tilzer): 1903	# 5 – Jan. 1904
DOWN ON THE FARM (Berlin); *SEE: I WANT TO GO BACK TO MICHIGAN: 1914*	
DOWN SOUTH (Myddleton): 1901	T30 – July 1901
DOWN SOUTH (Myddleton, Spaeth): 1927	#16 – Oct. 1927
DOWN THE OLD CHURCH AISLE: 1922	#20 – May 1922
DOWN THE OLD OX ROAD: 1933	#10 – Aug. 1933
DOWN THE RIVER OF GOLDEN DREAMS: 1930	# 9 – Aug. 1930
DOWN WHERE THE COTTON BLOSSOMS GROW: 1902	# 2 – Feb. 1902
DOWN WHERE THE SILV'RY MOHAWK FLOWS: 1905	#14 – Sept. 1905
DOWN WHERE THE SWANEE RIVER FLOWS: 1916	#19 – Oct. 1916
DOWN WHERE THE WURTZBURGER FLOWS: 1903	# 1 – Jan. 1903
DOWN YONDER (Gilbert): 1921	# 5 – Aug. 1921
DOWN YONDER (Gilbert): 1951	# 3 – Dec. 1951
DOWNHEARTED BLUES: 1923	#18 – Sept. 1923
DREAM: 1945	# 3 – June 1945
DREAM A LITTLE DREAM OF ME (Schwandt): 1931	# 3 – June 1931
DREAM A LITTLE DREAM OF ME (Schwandt): 1950	#18 – Nov. 1950
DREAM A LITTLE DREAM OF ME (Schwandt): 1968	#12 – Aug. 1968
DREAM DADDY: 1924	# 8 – Apr. 1924
DREAM HOUSE: 1928	# 9 – Oct. 1928
DREAM IN MY HEART, THE: 1937	#17 – July 1937
DREAM TRAIN: 1929	#20 – Apr. 1929
DREAM VALLEY: 1940	# 8 – Dec. 1940
DREAMER, THE (A. Schwartz): 1943	#15 – Jan. 1944
DREAMER (Davies): 1980	#15 – Nov. 1980
DREAMER'S HOLIDAY, A: 1949	# 4 – Dec. 1949
DREAMIN' (Ellis): 1960	#14 – Aug. 1960
DREAMIN' (Paschal): 1989	# 8 – Apr. 1989
DREAMING (Dailey): 1907	# 2 – Sept. 1907
DREAMING (Sayer): 1980	#10 – Nov. 1980
DREAMING (J. McCluskey): 1988	#16 – May 1988
DREAMING, LOVE, OF YOU: 1906	T30 – Apr. 1906
DREAMS OF LONG AGO: 1912	# 8 – Oct. 1912
DREAMY ALABAMA: 1919	#15 – Nov. 1919
DREAMY BLUES; *SEE: MOOD INDIGO: 1931*	
DREAMY MELODY: 1923	# 4 – Nov. 1923
DRIFTING AND DREAMING: 1926	# 6 – Aug. 1926
DRUNKARD SONG, THE (THERE IS A TAVERN IN THE TOWN): 1934	# 8 – Nov. 1934
DUSKY STEVEDORE: 1928	# 6 – Nov. 1928
DUST ON THE MOON: 1934	#11 – Aug. 1934
DUTY TO HOME AND FLAG: 1903	#17 – Jan. 1903

E

EADIE WAS A LADY: 1933	# 7 – Feb. 1933
EAST OF THE SUN: 1935	# 1 – Sept. 1935
EAST SIDE OF HEAVEN, THE: 1939	#11 – May 1939
EASTER PARADE (Berlin): 1934	# 5 – Jan. 1934
EASTER PARADE (Berlin): 1946	#16 – Apr. 1946
EASY COME, EASY GO (J. Green): 1934	# 7 – June 1934
EASY COME, EASY GO (J. Keller): 1970	# 9 – Apr. 1970
EASY TO LOVE: 1936	#12 – Jan. 1937
EBB TIDE (Rainger): 1937	#12 – Dec. 1937
EBB TIDE (Maxwell): 1953	# 2 – Dec. 1953
EBB TIDE (Maxwell): 1966	# 5 – Jan. 1966
EENY MEENY MINEY MO: 1936	# 7 – Jan. 1936
EGYPT: 1904	# 5 – July 1904
EL MANISERO; *SEE: PEANUT VENDOR, THE: 1931*	
(Alla en) EL RANCHO GRANDE: 1939	# 7 – Nov. 1939
ELMER'S TUNE: 1941	# 2 – Dec. 1941
EMALINE (McHugh): 1921	#17 – Oct. 1921
EMALINE (Perkins): 1934	#20 – July 1934
EMBRACEABLE YOU: 1931	#18 – Jan. 1931
EMPTY SADDLES: 1936	#11 – Sept. 1936
ENVY: 1949	#20 – Nov. 1949
ESPECIALLY FOR YOU: 1939	#17 – Aug. 1939
EUGENIA WALTZES: 1901	#17 – Mar. 1901
EV'RY DAY (Barron): 1910	#20 – Mar. 1910
EV'RY DAY (Fain): 1935	# 4 – Mar. 1935
EV'RY DAY I LOVE YOU (JUST A LITTLE BIT MORE): 1948	#13 – Oct. 1948
EV'RY LITTLE BIT HELPS: 1905	#17 – June 1905
EV'RYTHING I LOVE: 1942	#10 – Feb. 1942
EVELINA: 1945	#17 – Feb. 1945
EVENIN': 1933	#16 – Dec. 1933
EVENING IN CAROLINE, AN: 1931	# 5 – Dec. 1931
EVERY DAY IS LADIES' DAY WITH ME: 1907	# 9 – Jan. 1907
EVERY DAY WILL BE SUNDAY WHEN THE TOWN GOES DRY: 1919	#20 – Apr. 1919
EVERY LITTLE BIT ADDED TO WHAT YOU'VE GOT MAKES JUST A LITTLE BIT MORE: 1907	#15 – Aug. 1907
EVERY LITTLE MOMENT: 1935	#13 – Aug. 1935
EVERY LITTLE MOVEMENT: 1910	# 1 – Jan. 1911
EVERY MAN IS A VOLUNTEER: 1903	#15 – June 1903
EVERY MINUTE OF THE HOUR: 1936	#11 – Apr. 1936
EVERY MORN I BRING THEE VIOLETS; *SEE: VIOLETS: 1902*	
EVERY NOW AND THEN: 1935	#16 – Oct. 1935
EVERY RACE HAS A FLAG BUT THE COON: 1900	# 6 – Aug. 1900
EVERYBODY LOVES ME BUT THE ONE I LOVE: 1909	# 8 – Mar. 1909
EVERYBODY LOVES MY BABY: 1925	# 2 – Mar. 1925
EVERYBODY OUGHT TO KNOW HOW TO DO THE TICKLE TOE: 1918	# 7 – June 1918
EVERYBODY RAG WITH ME: 1915	#11 – May 1915
EVERYBODY SHIMMIES NOW: 1919	#15 – Mar. 1919
EVERYBODY STEP: 1922	# 4 – Mar. 1922
EVERYBODY TWO-STEP: 1912	# 5 – Dec. 1912
EVERYBODY WANTS A KEY TO MY CELLAR: 1919	#20 – Sept. 1919
EVERYBODY WORKS BUT FATHER: 1905	# 3 – Oct. 1905

EVERYBODY'S (GONE) CRAZY 'BOUT THE DOGGONE
BLUES: 1918 .... #17 – Aug. 1918
EVERYBODY'S DOIN' IT NOW: 1912 .... # 1 – May 1912
EVERYTHING HAPPENS TO ME: 1941 .... #19 – June 1941
EVERYTHING I HAVE IS YOURS: 1934 .... # 4 – Feb. 1934
EVERYTHING IS HOTSY-TOTSY NOW: 1925 .... #16 – Aug. 1925
EVERYTHING IS PEACHES DOWN IN GEORGIA: 1918 .... # 2 – Nov. 1918
EVERYTHING'S BEEN DONE BEFORE: 1935 .... #10 – May 1935
EVERYWHERE YOU GO: 1949 .... #16 – June 1949
EXACTLY LIKE YOU (McHugh): 1930 .... # 8 – June 1930
EXACTLY LIKE YOU (McHugh): 1936 .... #19 – Dec. 1936

F

F.D.R. JONES: 1939 .... #10 – Feb. 1939
FADED SUMMER LOVE, A: 1931 .... # 2 – Dec. 1931
FAITHFUL FOREVER: 1940 .... # 5 – Feb. 1940
FAR AWAY PLACES: 1949 .... # 1 – Feb. 1949
FARE THEE WELL, ANNABELLE: 1935 .... # 4 – Mar. 1935
FARE THEE WELL, MOLLIE DARLING: 1902 .... # 6 – Nov. 1902
FAREWELL, MY LOVE: 1937 .... #12 – Dec. 1937
FAREWELL BLUES: 1923 .... # 6 – June 1923
FAREWELL TO ARMS: 1933 .... # 3 – Apr. 1933
FASCINATING RHYTHM: 1925 .... # 6 – Mar. 1925
FAT MEAT IS GOOD MEAT: 1943 .... #19 – Feb. 1943
FATAL ROSE OF RED, THE: 1900 .... # 1 – Sept. 1900
FEATHER YOUR NEST: 1921 .... # 3 – Jan. 1921
FELLOW ON A FURLOUGH, A: 1944 .... #13 – Sept. 1944
FERDINAND THE BULL: 1939 .... #17 – Jan. 1939
FERRY-BOAT SERENADE: 1940 .... # 1 – Nov. 1940
FEUDIN' AND FIGHTIN': 1947 .... # 4 – Oct. 1947
FIDDLE DEE DEE: 1949 .... #18 – Oct. 1949
FIDO IS A HOT DOG NOW: 1914 .... #19 – Oct. 1914
FIFTY MILLION FRENCHMEN (CAN'T BE WRONG): 1927 .... #13 – July 1927
FILIPINO SHUFFLE: 1900 .... #10 – May 1900
FINE AND DANDY: 1930 .... #13 – Dec. 1930
FINE ROMANCE, A: 1936 .... # 3 – Oct. 1936
FIRST TIME I SAW YOU, THE: 1937 .... # 6 – Sept. 1937
FIT AS A FIDDLE: 1932 .... # 3 – Jan. 1933
FIVE FOOT TWO, EYES OF BLUE (Henderson): 1926 .... # 3 – Feb. 1926
FIVE FOOT TWO, EYES OF BLUE (Henderson): 1949 .... #15 – June 1949
FIVE MINUTES MORE: 1946 .... # 2 – Sept. 1946
FIVE O'CLOCK WHISTLE: 1940 .... #15 – Dec. 1940
FLAT FOOT FLUGEY: 1938 .... # 7 – July 1938
FLIRTATION WALK: 1935 .... # 9 – Jan. 1935
FLOATING ALONG: 1907 .... #18 – Apr. 1907
FLOATING DOWN THE SLEEPY LAGOON; *SEE: WATERS OF VENICE: 1918*
FLORADORA SEXTET; *SEE: TELL ME, PRETTY MAIDEN: 1901*
FLOWERS FOR MADAME: 1935 .... #12 – June 1935
FLYING ARROW: 1906 .... #18 – Oct. 1906
FLYING DOWN TO RIO: 1934 .... #14 – Mar. 1934
FOGGY DAY, A: 1937 .... #14 – Dec. 1937
FOLLOW THE SWALLOW: 1924 .... # 2 – Nov. 1924
FOLLOWING THE SUN AROUND: 1927 .... #15 – May 1927
FOOL IN LOVE, A: 1933 .... #18 – July 1933
FOOLS RUSH IN (Blume): 1940 .... # 3 – Aug. 1940
FOOLS RUSH IN (Blume): 1963 .... #11 – Nov. 1963
FOOTLOOSE AND FANCY FREE: 1935 .... #13 – July 1935
FOR ALL WE KNOW (Coots): 1934 .... # 3 – Sept. 1934
FOR ALL WE KNOW (Karlin): 1971 .... # 3 – Mar. 1971
FOR ME AND MY GAL (G.W.Meyer): 1917 .... # 1 – May 1917
FOR ME AND MY GAL (G.W.Meyer): 1943 .... # 6 – Mar. 1943
FOR MY SWEETHEART: 1926 .... #13 – Dec. 1926
FOR OLD TIMES' SAKE: 1900 .... # 1 – Dec. 1900
FOR SALE, A BABY: 1904 .... # 8 – May 1904
(I Love you) FOR SENTIMENTAL REASONS: 1947 .... # 1 – Feb. 1947
FOR THE FIRST TIME: 1943 .... #11 – Jan. 1944
FOR YOU (Burke): 1931 .... #15 – May 1931
FOR YOU (Burke): 1949 .... #20 – Jan. 1949
FOR YOU (Burke): 1964 .... # 6 – Feb. 1964
FOR YOU, FOR ME, FOREVERMORE: 1947 .... #12 – Jan. 1947
FOR YOU A ROSE: 1917 .... # 7 – July 1917
FOREVER AND EVER: 1949 .... # 1 – May 1949
FOREVER IS A LONG, LONG TIME: 1918 .... # 8 – June 1918
FORGIVE ME (Ager): 1927 .... # 5 – June 1927
FORGIVE ME (Ager): 1952 .... #10 – May 1952
FORTY-FIVE MINUTES FROM BROADWAY: 1906 .... # 5 – Apr. 1906
FORTY-SECOND STREET: 1933 .... # 2 – Apr. 1933
FOUR KINGS MARCH, THE: 1901 .... #17 – May 1901
FOUR WINDS AND THE SEVEN SEAS, THE: 1949 .... # 7 – Aug. 1949
FRASQUITA SERENADE; *SEE: MY LITTLE NEST OF HEAVENLY BLUE: 1926*
FRECKLE FACE, YOU'RE BEAUTIFUL: 1934 .... #19 – July 1934
FRECKLES: 1920 .... # 7 – Feb. 1920
FREE EATS: 1947 .... #16 – May 1947
FRENESI: 1941 .... # 1 – Jan. 1941
FRIEND OF YOURS, A: 1945 .... #12 – Aug. 1945
FRIENDLY TAVERN POLKA: 1941 .... #17 – June 1941
FROLIC OF THE TEDDY BEARS, THE;
SEE: TEDDY BEARS' PICNIC, THE: 1907, 1908
FROM THE LAND OF THE SKY-BLUE WATER: 1909 .... T40 – Aug. 1909
FUDDY DUDDY WATCHMAKER, THE: 1943 .... #18 – June 1943
FULL MOON: 1942 .... #18 – May 1942
FULL MOON AND EMPTY ARMS: 1946 .... # 8 – June 1946
FUNNY, DEAR, WHAT LOVE CAN DO: 1930 .... #20 – Feb. 1930
FUNNY OLD HILLS, THE: 1939 .... #15 – Feb. 1939
FUZZY WUZZY: 1945 .... #20 – Aug. 1945

G

G'BYE NOW: 1941 .... # 9 – May 1941
G.I. JIVE: 1944 .... # 8 – July 1944
GABY GLIDE, THE: 1912 .... # 2 – May 1912
GAL IN CALICO, A: 1947 .... # 3 – Feb. 1947
GALWAY BAY: 1949 .... # 4 – Mar. 1949
GAMBLING MAN, THE: 1903 .... # 3 – Apr. 1903
GAMES OF CHILDHOOD DAYS: 1909 .... #14 – May 1909
GARDEN IN THE RAIN, A (Gibbons): 1929 .... #13 – June 1929
GARDEN IN THE RAIN, A (Gibbons): 1952 .... #16 – Jan. 1952
GARDEN OF ROSES, THE: 1910 .... #11 – Jan. 1910
GARDEN OF THE MOON: 1938 .... #17 – Sept. 1938
GARLAND OF OLD FASHIONED ROSES, A: 1912 .... #15 – Oct. 1912
GAUCHO SERENADE, THE: 1940 .... # 6 – Apr. 1940
GEE, BUT I HATE TO GO HOME ALONE: 1922 .... #11 – Aug. 1922
GEE, BUT IT'S GREAT TO MEET A FRIEND FROM YOUR OWN
HOME TOWN: 1911 .... # 3 – June 1911
GEE, BUT THERE'S CLASS TO A GIRL LIKE YOU: 1909 .... # 9 – Oct. 1909
GEORGETTE: 1922 .... # 4 – Oct. 1922
GEORGIA: 1922 .... # 2 – June 1922
GEORGIA ON MY MIND (Carmichael): 1941 .... #11 – Apr. 1941
GEORGIA ON MY MIND (Carmichael): 1960 .... # 3 – Nov. 1960
GET HAPPY: 1930 .... #13 – July 1930

GET OUT AND GET UNDER (Abrahams); *SEE: HE'D HAVE TO GET UNDER, GET OUT AND GET UNDER, TO FIX UP HIS AUTOMOBILE: 1914*	
GET OUT AND GET UNDER THE MOON: 1928	# 2 – Aug. 1928
GET OUT OF TOWN: 1939	#13 – Feb. 1939
GETTING SOME FUN OUT OF LIFE: 1937	#20 – Nov. 1937
GHOST OF A COON, A: 1901	#19 – June 1901
GHOST OF THE VIOLIN, THE: 1912	# 9 – Jan. 1913
GIANNINA MIA: 1913	T30 – Sept. 1913
GIMME A LITTLE KISS, WILL YA, HUH? 1926	# 2 – June 1926
GIRL FRIEND, THE (Rodgers): 1926	#14 – Sept. 1926
GIRL IN THE BONNET OF BLUE, THE: 1938	#15 – June 1938
GIRL IN THE LITTLE GREEN HAT, THE: 1933	#10 – Feb. 1933
GIRL OF MY DREAMS (Emerson): 1911	T30 – Jan. 1911
GIRL OF MY DREAMS (Clapp): 1928	# 2 – June 1928
GIRL THAT I MARRY, THE: 1946	#16 – Jan. 1947
GIRLS OF AMERICA MARCH, THE: 1900	#11 – Jan. 1900
GIVE ME A NIGHT IN JUNE: 1927	# 4 – Nov. 1927
GIVE ME THE MOONLIGHT, GIVE ME THE GIRL: 1918	#18 – Feb. 1918
GIVE MY REGARDS TO BROADWAY: 1905	# 3 – June 1905
GLORIA (L. Rene): 1949	#16 – Dec. 1948
GLORIA (V. Morrison): 1966	# 9 – May 1966
GLORIA (Tozzi): 1982	# 2 – Nov. 1982
GLORY OF LOVE, THE (B. Hill): 1936	# 2 – July 1936
GLORY OF LOVE (THEME FROM KARATE KID II) (P. Cetera): 1986	# 1 – Aug. 1986
GLOW-WORM, THE (Lincke, Robinson): 1908	# 1 – May 1908
GLOW-WORM, THE (Lincke, Robinson): 1910	#16 – Apr. 1910
GLOW-WORM, THE (Lincke, Mercer): 1952	# 2 – Dec. 1952
GO 'WAY BACK AND SIT DOWN: 1901	# 2 – Aug. 1901
GO FLY A KITE: 1939	#19 – Sept. 1939
GO HOME AND TELL YOUR MOTHER: 1930	# 3 – Oct. 1930
GO ON, GOOD-A-BYE: 1910	#19 – June 1910
GOBS OF LOVE: 1942	#20 – Nov. 1942
GOD BLESS AMERICA (Berlin): 1939	#11 – Apr. 1939
GOD BLESS AMERICA (Berlin): 1940	# 8 – Aug. 1940
GOIN' TO HEAVEN ON A MULE: 1934	# 9 – Mar. 1934
GOING MY WAY: 1944	#15 – Aug. 1944
GOLD DIGGERS' LULLABY; *SEE: WITH PLENTY OF MONEY AND YOU: 1937*	
GOLD DIGGERS' SONG, THE; *SEE: WE'RE IN THE MONEY: 1933*	
GOLDEN EARRINGS: 1948	# 4 – Jan. 1948
GOLDEN ROD: 1907	#12 – June 1907
GONDOLIER, THE: 1904	# 6 – June 1904
GONE WITH THE WIND: 1937	# 8 – Aug. 1937
GOOD, GOOD, GOOD: 1945	#14 – June 1945
GOOD EVENING, CAROLINE: 1909	# 5 – Jan. 1909
GOOD FOR NOTHIN' BUT LOVE: 1939	#16 – Mar. 1939
GOOD MAN IS HARD TO FIND, A: 1919	#11 – May 1919
GOOD MORNING: 1939	#12 – Nov. 1939
GOOD MORNING, CARRIE: 1901	# 1 – Oct. 1901
GOOD MORNING, GLORY: 1933	#11 – Jan. 1934
GOOD MORNING, MR. ZIP-ZIP-ZIP! 1918	# 4 – July 1918
GOOD NEWS (Henderson): 1927	# 8 – Dec. 1927
GOOD NEWS (S. Cooke): 1964	#11 – Mar. 1964
GOOD NIGHT, DEAR: 1909	#10 – Jan. 1910
GOOD NIGHT, LITTLE GIRL OF MY DREAMS: 1933	# 1 – Dec. 1933
GOOD NIGHT, NURSE: 1913	# 4 – May 1913
GOOD OLD U.S.A., THE: 1906	# 2 – Sept. 1906
GOODBYE, BOYS: 1913	# 4 – July 1913
GOODBYE, DOLLY GRAY: 1901	# 1 – Mar. 1901
GOODBYE, ELIZA JANE: 1904	# 3 – Feb. 1904
GOODBYE, FLO: 1905	T30 – Mar. 1905
GOODBYE, GIRLS, I'M THROUGH: 1915	# 4 – Mar. 1915
GOODBYE, GOOD LUCK, AND GOD BLESS YOU: 1916	# 1 – May 1916
GOODBYE, LITTLE GIRL, GOODBYE: 1904	# 1 – Oct. 1904
GOOD-BYE, MA! GOOD-BYE, PA! GOOD-BYE MULE; *SEE: LONG BOY: 1917*	
GOODBYE, MY LADY LOVE: 1904	# 2 – May 1904
GOODBYE, ROSE: 1912	#10 – June 1912
GOODBYE, SIS: 1905	#19 – May 1905
GOODBYE BROADWAY, HELLO FRANCE! 1917	# 2 – Sept. 1917
GOODNIGHT, ANGEL: 1938	# 4 – Mar. 1938
GOODNIGHT, BELOVED, GOODNIGHT: 1903	#10 – Aug. 1903
GOODNIGHT, LOVELY LITTLE LADY: 1934	# 3 – May 1934
GOODNIGHT, MY LOVE: 1937	# 1 – Feb. 1937
GOODNIGHT, MY STARLIGHT; *SEE: STARLIGHT: 1906*	
GOODNIGHT, SWEETHEART: 1931	# 1 – Nov. 1931
GOODNIGHT, WHEREVER YOU ARE: 1944	# 6 – July 1944
GOODY GOODBYE: 1939	#11 – Dec. 1939
GOODY-GOODY: 1936	# 1 – Mar. 1936
GOOFUS: 1932	# 5 – July 1932
GOT A DATE WITH AN ANGEL: 1932	#19 – June 1932
GOT THE BENCH, GOT THE PARK: 1931	#16 – Apr. 1931
GOTTA BE THIS OR THAT: 1945	# 4 – Aug. 1945
GOTTA GET SOME SHUTEYE: 1939	#10 – Apr. 1939
GRANNY, YOU'RE MY MAMMY'S MAMMY: 1922	#16 – Feb. 1922
GREAT DAY: 1930	# 9 – Jan. 1930
GREEN EYES: 1941	# 3 – Sept. 1941
GRIEVING FOR YOU: 1949	#19 – Feb. 1949
GUILTY (R. Whiting): 1931	# 2 – Nov. 1931
GUILTY (R. Whiting): 1947	# 5 – Mar. 1947
GUILTY (Gibb): 1980	# 3 – Jan. 1981
GULF COAST BLUES: 1923	#15 – Aug. 1923
GYPSY, THE (B. Reid): 1946	# 1 – June 1946
GYPSY (S. Nicks): 1982	#12 – Oct. 1982
GYPSY FIDDLES: 1933	#15 – June 1933
GYPSY TOLD ME, A: 1938	#12 – Mar. 1938

H

HA-CHA-CHA: 1934	#20 – Nov. 1934
HAB EIN BLAUES HIMMELBETT; *SEE: MY LITTLE NEST OF HEAVENLY BLUE: 1926*	
HAIL, HAIL, THE GANG'S ALL HERE: 1918	#11 – Jan. 1918
HAIR OF GOLD, EYES OF BLUE: 1948	# 7 – Oct. 1948
HALFWAY TO HEAVEN: 1928	# 7 – Dec. 1928
HALLELUJAH! 1927	# 8 – Oct. 1927
HAMLET WAS A MELANCHOLY DANE: 1903	# 9 – Mar. 1903
HANDS ACROSS THE TABLE: 1934	# 8 – Jan. 1935
HANNAH, WON'T YOU OPEN THAT DOOR? 1904	# 9 – June 1904
HAPPY DAYS AND LONELY NIGHTS: 1929	#19 – Mar. 1929
HAPPY DAYS ARE HERE AGAIN: 1930	# 1 – Feb. 1930
HAPPY IN LOVE: 1942	#19 – Apr. 1942
HAPPY-GO-LUCKY LANE: 1928	# 7 – July 1928
HARBOR LIGHTS (Grosz): 1937	# 5 – Oct. 1937
HARBOR LIGHTS (Grosz): 1950	# 1 – Nov. 1950
HARBOR LIGHTS (Grosz): 1960	# 8 – Apr. 1960
HARBOR OF LOVE, THE: 1911	# 5 – Nov. 1911
HARD-HEARTED HANNAH: 1924	# 8 – Sept. 1924
HARRIGAN: 1907	# 1 – Oct. 1907
HAS ANYBODY HERE SEEN KELLY? 1910	# 1 – June 1910
HAUNTED HEART: 1948	#15 – July 1948
HAVE YOU EVER BEEN LONELY? 1933	# 4 – May 1933
HAVE YOU FORGOTTEN SO SOON? 1938	# 9 – Dec. 1938
HAVE YOU GOT ANY CASTLES, BABY? 1937	# 4 – Oct. 1937
HAWAIIAN BUTTERFLY: 1917	# 9 – July 1917

HAWAIIAN SUNSHINE; *SEE: MY HAWAIIAN SUNSHINE: 1917*
HE GOES TO CHURCH ON SUNDAY: 1907 .... # 6 – July 1907
HE LAID AWAY A SUIT OF GRAY: 1901 .... # 9 – Oct. 1901
HE WALKED RIGHT IN, TURNED AROUND, AND WALKED
RIGHT OUT AGAIN: 1906 .... # 3 – Oct. 1906
HE WEARS A PAIR OF SILVER WINGS: 1942 .... # 1 – Sept. 1942
HE'D HAVE TO GET UNDER, GET OUT AND GET UNDER,
TO FIX UP HIS AUTOMOBILE: 1914 .... # 1 – Feb. 1914
HE'S A COUSIN OF MINE: 1907 .... # 2 – Mar. 1907
HE'S A DEVIL IN HIS OWN HOME TOWN: 1914 .... # 2 – June 1914
HE'S A RAG PICKER: 1914 .... #10 – Jan. 1915
HE'S ME PAL: 1905 .... # 2 – May 1905
HE'S MY GUY: 1942 .... #11 – Oct. 1942
HEAR MY SONG, VIOLETTA: 1940 .... #17 – Aug. 1940
HEART AND SOUL (Carmichael): 1938 .... # 2 – Nov. 1938
HEART AND SOUL (Carmichael): 1952 .... #17 – Jan. 1953
HEART AND SOUL (Carmichael): 1961 .... #18 – July 1961
HEART AND SOUL (Chinn): 1983 .... # 8 – Nov. 1983
HEART AND SOUL (Decker): 1987 .... # 4 – Aug. 1987
HEARTACHES (Hoffman): 1931 .... #13 – Apr. 1931
HEARTACHES (Hoffman): 1947 .... # 1 – Apr. 1947
HEARTACHES (Hoffman): 1961 .... # 9 – Nov. 1961
HEARTBREAKER (Freedman): 1948 .... #19 – June 1948
HEARTBREAKER (Foxx); *SEE: SHE'S A HEARTBREAKER: 1968*
HEARTBREAKER (Gibb): 1982 .... #10 – Jan. 1983
HEARTBREAKER (Carey): 1999 .... # 1 – Oct. 1999
HEARTS ARE TRUMPS: 1900 .... #18 – Apr. 1900
HEAT WAVE (Berlin): 1933 .... #10 – Dec. 1933
HEAT WAVE (Holland): 1963 .... # 4 – Sept. 1963
HEAT WAVE (Holland): 1975 .... # 5 – Nov. 1975
HEAVEN CAN WAIT: 1939 .... # 2 – Apr. 1939
HEAVEN WILL PROTECT THE WORKING GIRL: 1910 .... #13 – Oct. 1910
HEIDELBERG (STEIN SONG): 1903 .... #20 – Feb. 1903
HEIGH-HO: 1938 .... # 3 – Apr. 1938
HELL'S BELLS: 1932 .... #13 – Nov. 1932
HELLO, ALOHA! HOW ARE YOU? 1926 .... #12 – Sept. 1926
HELLO, BEAUTIFUL: 1931 .... #10 – Apr. 1931
HELLO, BLUEBIRD: 1927 .... #10 – Jan. 1927
HELLO, CENTRAL, GIVE ME 603; *SEE: ALL ALONE (Von Tilzer): 1911*
HELLO, CENTRAL, GIVE ME HEAVEN: 1901 .... # 1 – July 1901
HELLO, CENTRAL, GIVE ME NO-MAN'S-LAND: 1918 .... # 2 – Aug. 1918
HELLO, FRISCO! 1915 .... # 1 – Oct. 1915
HELLO, HAWAII, HOW ARE YOU? 1916 .... # 2 – Mar. 1916
HER NAME IS ROSE: 1900 .... #20 – Apr. 1900
HERE AM I, BROKEN HEARTED;
SEE: (Here am I) BROKEN HEARTED (Henderson): 1927, 1952
(Lookie lookie lookie) HERE COMES COOKIE: 1935 .... # 8 – Apr. 1935
HERE COMES HEAVEN AGAIN: 1946 .... #16 – Mar. 1946
HERE COMES MY DADDY NOW: 1913 .... #12 – May 1913
HERE COMES SANTA CLAUS (Haldeman): 1947 .... #18 – Dec. 1947
HERE COMES SANTA CLAUS (Haldeman): 1948 .... #13 – Dec. 1948
HERE COMES SANTA CLAUS (Haldeman): 1949 .... #16 – Dec. 1949
HERE COMES THE SHOW BOAT: 1927 .... # 9 – Jan. 1928
HERE COMES THE SUN (H. Woods): 1930 .... #20 – Oct. 1930
HERE COMES THE SUN (Harrison): 1971 .... #16 – May 1971
HERE LIES LOVE: 1932 .... #12 – Dec. 1932
HERE YOU ARE: 1942 .... #19 – July 1942
HERE'S LOVE IN YOUR EYES: 1936 .... #12 – Dec. 1936
HERE'S YOUR HAT, WHAT'S YOUR HURRY? 1904 .... #17 – Mar. 1904
HEY! BA-BA-RE-BOP: 1946 .... #13 – June 1946
HEY! YOUNG FELLA: 1933 .... #15 – Apr. 1933
HI, NEIGHBOR! 1941 .... #17 – Oct. 1941
HIAWATHA: 1903 .... # 1 – May 1903
HIAWATHA'S MELODY OF LOVE: 1920 .... # 3 – Sept. 1920
HIGH AND LOW: 1931 .... #16 – Aug. 1931
HIGH ON A WINDY HILL: 1941 .... # 1 – Mar. 1941
HINDUSTAN: 1918 .... # 3 – Dec. 1918
HINKY DINKY PARLAY VOO (McHugh);
SEE: WHAT HAS BECOME OF HINKY DINKY PARLAY VOO: 1924
HIS ROCKING HORSE RAN AWAY: 1944 .... #14 – Sept. 1944
HITCHY KOO: 1912 .... # 4 – Dec. 1912
HO-HUM: 1931 .... # 5 – June 1931
HOLD ME (Hickman): 1920 .... # 1 – July 1920
HOLD ME (Little): 1933 .... # 3 – June 1933
HOLD ME (McVie): 1982 .... # 4 – July 1982
HOLD MY HAND (N. Gay): 1932 .... # 6 – Aug. 1932
HOLD MY HAND (Lawrence): 1954 .... # 5 – Nov. 1954
HOLD MY HAND (Bryan): 1995 .... #10 – Feb. 1995
HOLD TIGHT, HOLD TIGHT: 1939 .... # 8 – Apr. 1939
HOLD YOUR MAN: 1933 .... # 7 – Aug. 1933
HOLIDAY FOR STRINGS: 1944 .... #10 – Mar. 1944
HOME (WHEN SHADOWS FALL): 1932 .... # 1 – Feb. 1932
HOME AGAIN BLUES: 1921 .... #12 – July 1921
HOMESICK: 1922 .... #10 – Dec. 1922
HONEY (R. Whiting): 1929 .... # 1 – May 1929
HONEY, I'M WAITING: 1905 .... # 9 – May 1905
HONEY BOY: 1907 .... # 2 – Nov. 1907
HONEY MAN; *SEE: MY LOVIN' HONEY MAN: 1911*
HONEYMOON HOTEL: 1933 .... # 8 – Dec. 1933
HONEYSUCKLE AND THE BEE, THE: 1901 .... # 4 – Aug. 1901
HONG KONG BLUES: 1945 .... #15 – Aug. 1945
HONKY TONKY MONKEY RAG; *SEE: (Honky tonky) MONKEY RAG: 1911*
HOO-OO (AIN'T YOU COMIN' OUT TONIGHT?): 1908 .... # 7 – July 1908
HOP-SCOTCH POLKA: 1949 .... #11 – Oct. 1949
HORSES: 1926 .... # 1 – June 1926
HOT CANARY, THE (Nero): 1949 .... #20 – Mar. 1949
HOT CANARY, THE (Nero): 1951 .... #18 – Apr. 1951
HOT LIPS: 1922 .... # 2 – Oct. 1922
HOTTENTOT LOVE SONG, A: 1906 .... #20 – Nov. 1906
HOUR NEVER PASSES, AN: 1944 .... #14 – Oct. 1944
HOUSE OF BLUE LIGHTS, THE (D. Raye): 1946 .... #18 – July 1946
HOUSE OF BLUE LIGHTS, THE (D. Raye): 1955 .... #19 – Aug. 1955
HOW ABOUT ME? 1929 .... # 8 – Feb. 1929
HOW ABOUT YOU? 1942 .... # 8 – Mar. 1942
HOW AM I TO KNOW? 1929 .... # 5 – Nov. 1929
HOW ARE THINGS IN GLOCCA MORRA? 1947 .... # 4 – Mar. 1947
HOW BLUE THE NIGHT: 1944 .... #18 – July 1944
HOW COME YOU DO MY LIKE YOU DO? 1924 .... # 9 – Sept. 1924
HOW COULD YOU? 1937 .... #17 – May 1937
HOW DEEP IS THE OCEAN? (Berlin): 1932 .... # 3 – Nov. 1932
HOW DEEP IS THE OCEAN? (Berlin): 1945 .... # 9 – Nov. 1945
HOW DO I KNOW IT'S REAL? 1942 .... #15 – Apr. 1942
HOW HIGH THE MOON (Hamilton): 1940 .... #10 – Apr. 1940
HOW HIGH THE MOON (Hamilton): 1951 .... # 1 – May 1951
HOW LUCKY YOU ARE: 1948 .... #16 – Feb. 1948
HOW MANY HEARTS HAVE YOU BROKEN: 1944 .... # 4 – Oct. 1944
HOW MANY TIMES: 1926 .... # 9 – Oct. 1926
HOW SOON (WILL I BE SEEING YOU): 1947 .... # 2 – Jan. 1948
HOW SWEET YOU ARE: 1943 .... #11 – Dec. 1943
HOW YA GONNA KEEP 'EM DOWN ON THE FARM? 1919 .... # 1 – May 1919
HOW'D YOU LIKE TO BE MY DADDY? 1918 .... #20 – July 1918
HOW'D YOU LIKE TO SPOON WITH ME? 1905 .... # 4 – Dec. 1905
HOW'S EVERY LITTLE THING IN DIXIE? 1917 .... #10 – Feb. 1917
HOWDJA LIKE TO LOVE ME: 1938 .... #10 – Apr. 1938
HUCKLEBUCK, THE (Gibson): 1949 .... # 7 – Sept. 1949
HUCKLEBERRY FINN: 1917 .... # 9 – Aug. 1917

HUGGIN' AND CHALKIN': 1947 .... # 5 – Feb. 1947
HUMMIN' TO MYSELF: 1932 .... # 7 – July 1932
HUMMING: 1921 .... # 9 – June 1921
HURRAH FOR BAFFIN'S BAY: 1903 .... # 8 – May 1903
HURRY HOME: 1939 .... # 9 – Feb. 1939
HUSH-A-BYE MA BABY; *SEE: MISSOURI WALTZ: 1916, 1918*
HUT-SUT SONG: 1941 .... # 2 – June 1941
HYMNS OF THE OLD CHURCH CHOIR: 1907 .... #13 – July 1907

I

I AIN'T GOT NOBODY (S. Williams): 1917 .... # 3 – Mar. 1917
I AIN'T GOT NOBODY (S. Williams): 1928 .... # 8 – Feb. 1928
I AIN'T GOT NOBODY (S. Williams): 1985;
SEE: JUST A GIGOLO/I AIN'T GOT NOBODY: 1985
I AIN'T LAZY, I'M JUST DREAMIN': 1934 .... #11 – June 1934
I AIN'T MAD (AT YOU): 1947 .... #20 – Aug. 1947
I AIN'T NOBODY'S DARLING: 1921 .... # 7 – Nov. 1921
I AM AN AMERICAN: 1940 .... #13 – Nov. 1940
I AM THE WORDS, YOU ARE THE MELODY;
SEE: (I am the words) YOU ARE THE MELODY: 1931
I APOLOGIZE (Hoffman): 1931 .... # 6 – Nov. 1931
I APOLOGIZE (Hoffman): 1951 .... # 6 – May 1951
I BELIEVE (J. Styne): 1947 .... # 8 – May 1947
I BELIEVE (E. Drake): 1953 .... # 2 – Apr. 1953
I BELIEVE (LOVE IS THE ANSWER): 1995 .... # 8 – May 1995
I BELIEVE IN MIRACLES: 1935 .... # 3 – Feb. 1935
I CAME HERE TO TALK FOR JOE: 1942 .... #11 – Nov. 1942
I CAN DANCE WITH EVERYBODY BUT MY WIFE: 1916 .... # 2 – July 1916
I CAN DREAM, CAN'T I? (Fain): 1938 .... # 9 – Mar. 1938
I CAN DREAM, CAN'T I? (Fain): 1949 .... # 1 – Jan. 1950
I CAN'T BEGIN TO TELL YOU: 1945 .... # 2 – Dec. 1945
I CAN'T BELIEVE IT'S TRUE: 1932 .... # 7 – Sept. 1932
I CAN'T BELIEVE THAT YOU'RE IN LOVE WITH ME: 1927 .... #15 – Sept. 1927
I CAN'T DO THE SUM: 1904 .... # 4 – Mar. 1904
I CAN'T DO WITHOUT YOU: 1928 .... # 4 – June 1928
I CAN'T ESCAPE FROM YOU: 1936 .... # 9 – Sept. 1936
I CAN'T GIVE YOU ANYTHING BUT LOVE: 1928 .... # 2 – Oct. 1928
I CAN'T LOVE YOU ANY MORE (THAN I DO): 1940 .... # 7 – July 1940
I CAN'T TELL WHY I LOVE YOU BUT I DO: 1900 .... # 1 – Oct. 1900
I COULDN'T BELIEVE MY EYES: 1935 .... #14 – Sept. 1935
I COULDN'T SLEEP A WINK LAST NIGHT: 1944 .... # 3 – Apr. 1944
I COULDN'T STAND TO SEE MY BABY LOSE: 1900 .... # 7 – Mar. 1900
I COVER THE WATERFRONT: 1933 .... #11 – July 1933
I CRIED FOR YOU (A. Lyman): 1923 .... # 5 – Aug. 1923
I CRIED FOR YOU (A. Lyman): 1939 .... # 5 – Mar. 1939
I DIDN'T KNOW WHAT TIME IT WAS: 1939 .... # 6 – Dec. 1939
I DIDN'T RAISE MY BOY TO BE A SOLDIER: 1915 .... # 1 – Mar. 1915
I DON'T BELIEVE IT, BUT SAY IT AGAIN;
SEE: (I don't believe it but) SAY IT AGAIN: 1926
I DON'T CARE WHO KNOWS IT: 1945 .... #16 – Apr. 1945
Reached second peak at .... # 9 – Sept. 1945
I DON'T KNOW ENOUGH ABOUT YOU: 1946 .... # 6 – July 1946
I DON'T KNOW WHERE I'M GOING, BUT I'M ON MY WAY: 1917 .... # 9 – Dec. 1917
I DON'T KNOW WHY (I JUST DO) (Ahlert): 1931 .... # 2 – Nov. 1931
I DON'T KNOW WHY (I JUST DO) (Ahlert): 1946 .... #10 – Sept. 1946
I DON'T KNOW WHY (I JUST DO) (Ahlert): 1961 .... #11 – Dec. 1961
I DON'T KNOW WHY I LOVE YOU LIKE I DO;
SEE: I DON'T KNOW WHY (I JUST DO): 1931, 1946, 1961
I DON'T SEE ME IN YOUR EYES ANYMORE: 1949 .... # 7 – July 1949
I DON'T WANT TO GET WELL: 1917 .... # 3 – Jan. 1918
I DON'T WANT TO LOVE YOU (LIKE I DO): 1945 .... #11 – Jan. 1945
I DON'T WANT TO SET THE WORLD ON FIRE: 1941 .... # 1 – Oct. 1941
I DON'T WANT TO WALK WITHOUT YOU: 1942 .... # 3 – Mar. 1942
I DOUBLE DARE YOU: 1938 .... # 2 – Feb. 1938
I DREAM OF YOU: 1945 .... # 3 – Jan. 1945
I DREAMT I DWELT IN HARLEM: 1941 .... #12 – Mar. 1941
I FALL IN LOVE WITH YOU EVERY DAY: 1938 .... #11 – Apr. 1938
I FAW DOWN AN' GO BOOM! 1929 .... #12 – Mar. 1929
I FEEL LIKE A FEATHER IN THE BREEZE: 1936 .... # 6 – Feb. 1936
I FOUND A DREAM: 1935 .... #15 – Dec. 1935
I FOUND A MILLION-DOLLAR BABY: 1931 .... # 2 – Aug. 1931
I FOUND A ROSE IN THE DEVIL'S GARDEN: 1921 .... # 4 – May 1921
I GAVE YOU UP JUST BEFORE YOU THREW ME DOWN: 1923 .... #14 – Mar. 1923
I GET A KICK OUT OF YOU: 1935 .... #17 – Jan. 1935
I GET ALONG WITHOUT YOU VERY WELL: 1939 .... # 3 – Apr. 1939
I GET THE BLUES WHEN IT RAINS: 1929 .... # 9 – Aug. 1929
I GIVE YOU MY WORD: 1941 .... # 3 – Feb. 1941
I GOT IT BAD (AND THAT AIN'T GOOD): 1942 .... #20 – Feb. 1942
I GOT RHYTHM (Gershwin): 1931 .... #16 – Jan. 1931
I GOT RHYTHM (Gershwin): 1967 .... # 3 – May 1967
I GOT THE SUN IN THE MORNING: 1946 .... # 8 – July 1946
I GOTTA RIGHT TO SING THE BLUES: 1933 .... #18 – Mar. 1933
I GUESS I'LL GET THE PAPERS AND GO HOME: 1946 .... #14 – Oct. 1946
I GUESS I'LL HAVE TO CHANGE MY PLAN: 1932 .... #14 – Oct. 1932
I GUESS I'LL HAVE TO DREAM THE REST: 1941 .... # 5 – Oct. 1941
I HAD A DREAM, DEAR;
SEE: YOU TELL ME YOUR DREAM (AND I WILL TELL YOU MINE): 1900
I HAD THE CRAZIEST DREAM: 1943 .... # 3 – Jan. 1943
I HADN'T ANYONE TILL YOU: 1938 .... # 4 – July 1938
I HATE TO LOSE YOU: 1918 .... # 6 – June 1918
I HAVE BUT ONE HEART: 1947 .... #11 – Oct. 1947
I HAVE EYES: 1939 .... # 3 – Feb. 1939
I HEAR A RHAPSODY (Fragos): 1941 .... # 1 – Feb. 1941
I HEAR A RHAPSODY (Fragos): 1952 .... #20 – May 1952
I HEAR A THRUSH AT EVE: 1913 .... T30 – Dec. 1913
I HEAR YOU CALLING ME: 1913 .... #17 – Mar. 1914
I HEARD: 1932 .... #15 – Apr. 1932
I HEARD YOU CRIED LAST NIGHT: 1943 .... # 4 – Oct. 1943
I JUST CAN'T MAKE MY EYES BEHAVE: 1907 .... # 4 – Mar. 1907
I JUST KISSED YOUR PICTURE GOODNIGHT: 1943 .... #13 – Apr. 1943
I JUST ROLL ALONG (HAVIN' MY UPS AND DOWNS): 1928 .... # 9 – May 1928
I KISS YOUR HAND, MADAME: 1929 .... # 7 – June 1929
I KNOW I GOT MORE THAN MY SHARE: 1916 .... #17 – Jan. 1917
I KNOW NOW: 1937 .... # 4 – Aug. 1937
I KNOW THAT YOU KNOW: 1927 .... # 4 – Mar. 1927
I LEFT MY HEART AT THE STAGE DOOR CANTEEN: 1942 .... # 4 – Sept. 1942
I LET A SONG GO OUT OF MY HEART: 1938 .... # 2 – June 1938
I LIKE THE HAT, I LIKE THE DRESS, AND I LIKE
THE GIRL THAT'S IN IT: 1911 .... # 6 – Sept. 1911
I LOVE, I LOVE, I LOVE MY WIFE, BUT OH, YOU KID
(H. Von Tilzer): 1909 .... # 5 – July 1909
I LOVE A LASSIE: 1908 .... #13 – Dec. 1907
I LOVE A PIANO: 1916 .... #15 – July 1916
I LOVE LOUISA: 1931 .... # 6 – Sept. 1931
I LOVE LOVE: 1912 .... #20 – Feb. 1912
I LOVE MY BABY: 1926 .... # 5 – Mar. 1926
I LOVE MY WIFE, BUT OH, YOU KID! (Armstrong): 1909 .... # 7 – July 1909
I LOVE THE LADIES: 1914 .... # 1 – July 1914
I LOVE THE LAND OF OLD BLACK JOE: 1920 .... #10 – Nov. 1920
I LOVE THE NAME OF MARY: 1911 .... T30 – Apr. 1911
I LOVE TO WHISTLE: 1938 .... # 7 – May 1938
I LOVE YOU (Archer): 1923 .... # 1 – Dec. 1923
I LOVE YOU (Porter): 1944 .... # 1 – May 1944

I LOVE YOU (White): 1968 .... #14 – June 1968
I LOVE YOU (Holt): 1981 .... #12 – June 1981
I LOVE YOU, SWEETHEART OF ALL MY DREAMS;
SEE: (I love you) SWEETHEART OF ALL MY DREAMS: 1929, 1945
I LOVE YOU, THAT'S ONE THING I KNOW: 1916 .... #11 – May 1916
I LOVE YOU, YES I DO: 1948 .... #19 – Apr. 1948
I LOVE YOU FOR SENTIMENTAL REASONS;
SEE: (I love you) FOR SENTIMENTAL REASONS: 1947
I LOVE YOU SO (MERRY WIDOW WALTZ): 1908 .... # 1 – Feb. 1908
I LOVE YOU SO MUCH: 1930 .... #14 – Aug. 1930
I LOVE YOU SO MUCH IT HURTS: 1949 .... #11 – Feb. 1949
I LOVE YOU SUNDAY: 1920 .... #20 – Nov. 1920
I LOVE YOU TRULY (Jacobs-Bond): 1907 .... T40 – May 1907
I LOVE YOU TRULY (Jacobs-Bond): 1912 .... # 9 – Oct. 1912
I MARRIED AN ANGEL: 1938 .... # 6 – July 1938
I MAY BE CRAZY, BUT I AIN'T NO FOOL: 1904 .... # 1 – Dec. 1904
I MAY BE GONE FOR A LONG, LONG TIME: 1917 .... # 2 – Dec. 1917
I MAY BE WRONG (BUT I THINK YOU'RE WONDERFUL): 1929 .. #20 – Dec. 1929
I MET HER ON MONDAY: 1942 .... #17 – Oct. 1942
I MIGHT BE YOUR ONCE-IN-A-WHILE: 1920 .... # 9 – Feb. 1920
I MISS MY SWISS: 1925 .... # 5 – Oct. 1925
I MISS YOU MOST OF ALL: 1914 .... # 3 – Mar. 1914
I MUST A-BEEN A-DREAMIN': 1900 .... # 9 – Sept. 1900
I MUST HAVE THAT MAN: 1928 .... #14 – Oct. 1928
I MUST SEE ANNIE TONIGHT: 1939 .... # 9 – Jan. 1939
I NEVER DREAMT: 1930 .... #19 – June 1930
I NEVER HAD A CHANCE: 1934 .... # 2 – Aug. 1934
I NEVER KNEW (I COULD LOVE ANYBODY): 1921 .... # 2 – Apr. 1921
I NEVER KNEW (THAT ROSES GREW) (FioRito): 1926 .... #11 – Feb. 1926
I NEVER KNEW (THAT ROSES GREW) (FioRito): 1947 .... #14 – Aug. 1947
I NEVER KNEW HEAVEN COULD SPEAK: 1939 .... #13 – June 1939
I NEVER MENTION YOUR NAME: 1943 .... #12 – Sept. 1943
I NEVER SEE MAGGIE ALONE: 1949 .... #11 – Nov. 1949
I ONLY HAVE EYES FOR YOU (Warren): 1934 .... # 2 – Sept. 1934
I ONLY HAVE EYES FOR YOU (Warren): 1959 .... #13 – July 1959
I ONLY HAVE EYES FOR YOU (Warren): 1975 .... #18 – Nov. 1975
I POURED MY HEART INTO A SONG: 1939 .... # 4 – Aug. 1939
I PROMISE YOU: 1939 .... #13 – Mar. 1939
I REMEMBER YOU (Schertzinger): 1942 .... #10 – May 1942
I REMEMBER YOU (Schertzinger): 1962 .... # 6 – Oct. 1962
I REMEMBER YOU (Bolan): 1990 .... # 6 – Feb. 1990
I SAID NO! 1942 .... #10 – Feb. 1942
I SAW STARS: 1934 .... # 3 – Oct. 1934
I SCREAM, YOU SCREAM, WE ALL SCREAM FOR ICE CREAM: 1928 # 7 – Feb. 1928
I SEE A MILLION PEOPLE: 1941 .... #14 – Nov. 1941
I SHOULD CARE (P. Weston): 1945 .... #10 – June 1945
I SHOULD CARE (P. Weston): 1952 .... #19 – Oct. 1952
I STILL GET A THRILL: 1930 .... # 6 – Oct. 1930
I STILL LOVE TO KISS YOU GOODNIGHT: 1937 .... # 7 – Dec. 1937
I STILL LOVE YOU (Ager): 1928 .... #11 – June 1928
I STILL LOVE YOU (Huggar): 1998 .... #17 – Oct. 1998
I STILL REMEMBER: 1930 .... #19 – June 1930
I SURRENDER, DEAR: 1931 .... # 3 – Mar. 1931
I TAKE THINGS EASY: 1903 .... #17 – Apr. 1903
I THREW A KISS IN THE OCEAN: 1942 .... #11 – June 1942
I UPS TO HER (AND SHE UPS TO ME): 1939 .... #19 – Jan. 1939
I USED TO LOVE YOU, BUT IT'S ALL OVER NOW: 1921 .... # 3 – May 1921
I WAKE UP SMILING: 1933 .... #15 – May 1933
I WANNA BE LOVED BY YOU (Stothart): 1929 .... # 4 – Jan. 1929
I WANNA GET MARRIED: 1945 .... #16 – Mar. 1945
I WANNA GO WHERE YOU GO, DO WHAT YOU DO;
SEE: THEN I'LL BE HAPPY: 1926
I WANNA SING ABOUT YOU: 1931 .... # 3 – July 1931
I WANT A GIRL (JUST LIKE THE GIRL WHO MARRIED
DEAR OLD DAD): 1911 .... # 2 – Nov. 1911
I WANT TO BE A MILITARY MAN: 1901 .... #13 – Mar. 1901
I WANT TO BE HAPPY (Youmans): 1924 .... # 6 – Dec. 1924
I WANT TO BE HAPPY (Youmans): 1926 .... #20 – Jan. 1926
I WANT TO GO BACK TO MICHIGAN (DOWN ON THE FARM): 1914 # 1 – Dec. 1914
I WANT WHAT I WANT WHEN I WANT IT: 1906 .... #11 – Apr. 1906
I WANT YOU (G.M.Cohan): 1908 .... #13 – Apr. 1908
I WANT YOU (Dylan): 1966 .... #20 – July 1966
I WANT YOU (Ware): 1976 .... #15 – June 1976
I WANT YOU (Ware): 1991;
SEE: MERCY MERCY ME (THE ECOLOGY)/I WANT YOU: 1991
I WANT YOU (D. Jones): 1997 .... # 4 – May 1997
I WANTS A PING PONG MAN: 1902 .... #19 – Nov. 1902
I WAS LUCKY: 1935 .... # 8 – Apr. 1935
I WENT OUT OF MY WAY: 1941 .... #13 – Sept. 1941
I WISH (D. Fisher): 1945 .... #15 – June 1945
I WISH (S. Wonder): 1977 .... # 1 – Jan. 1977
I WISH (Skee-Lo): 1995 .... #13 – Sept. 1995
I WISH I COULD SHIMMY LIKE MY SISTER KATE: 1922 .... # 7 – Dec. 1922
I WISH I DIDN'T LOVE YOU SO: 1947 .... # 2 – Oct. 1947
I WISH I HAD A GIRL (LeBoy, Kahn): 1908 .... # 2 – Dec. 1908
I WISH I HAD A GIRL (Summer): 1988 .... #20 – Apr. 1988
I WISH I HAD MY OLD GIRL BACK AGAIN: 1909 .... # 5 – Nov. 1909
I WISH I KNEW: 1945 .... # 6 – Sept. 1945
I WISH I KNEW (YOU REALLY LOVED ME): 1922 .... #20 – Dec. 1922
I WISH I WERE ALADDIN: 1935 .... #14 – Oct. 1935
I WISH I WERE TWINS: 1934 .... #14 – July 1934
I WISH THAT I COULD HIDE INSIDE THIS LETTER: 1944 .... #17 – Apr. 1944
I WISH WE'D NEVER MET: 1901 .... #18 – Jan. 1901
I WISHED ON THE MOON: 1935 .... # 9 – Oct. 1935
I WON'T DANCE: 1935 .... # 7 – Apr. 1935
I WON'T TELL A SOUL: 1938 .... # 6 – Dec. 1938
I WONDER, I WONDER, I WONDER: 1947 .... # 2 – July 1947
I WONDER WHAT'S BECOME OF SALLY: 1924 .... # 1 – Nov. 1924
I WONDER WHO'S KISSING HER NOW (J. Howard): 1909 .... # 1 – Sept. 1909
I WONDER WHO'S KISSING HER NOW (J. Howard): 1947 .... # 2 – Oct. 1947
I YUST GO NUTS AT CHRISTMAS: 1949 .... #14 – Dec. 1949
I'D BE LOST WITHOUT YOU: 1946 .... # 9 – Oct. 1946
I'D CLIMB THE HIGHEST MOUNTAIN: 1926 .... # 2 – July 1926
I'D LOVE TO LIVE IN LOVELAND WITH A GIRL LIKE YOU: 1912 .. #13 – Mar. 1912
I'D RATHER LISTEN TO YOUR EYES: 1935 .... #18 – Nov. 1935
I'D RATHER SAY HELLO THAN SAY GOODBYE: 1910 .... T30 – Dec. 1910
I'D STILL BELIEVE YOU TRUE: 1901 .... #10 – Jan. 1901
I'LL ALWAYS BE IN LOVE WITH YOU: 1929 .... # 4 – Aug. 1929
I'LL BE BLUE JUST THINKING OF YOU: 1930 .... #15 – Nov. 1930
I'LL BE FAITHFUL: 1933 .... # 6 – Dec. 1933
I'LL BE GLAD WHEN YOU'RE DEAD, YOU RASCAL YOU;
SEE: (I'll be glad when you're dead) YOU RASCAL YOU: 1932
I'LL BE HAPPY WHEN THE PREACHER MAKE YOU MINE: 1919 .. # 7 – Dec. 1919
I'LL BE HOME FOR CHRISTMAS (W. Kent): 1943 .... # 7 – Dec. 1943
I'LL BE HOME FOR CHRISTMAS (W. Kent): 1944 .... #17 – Dec. 1944
I'LL BE IN VIRGINIA IN THE MORNING; *SEE: LET IT RAIN! LET IT POUR! 1925*
I'LL BE SEEING YOU: 1944 .... # 1 – June 1944
I'LL BE THERE, MARY DEAR: 1902 .... T30 – July 1902
I'LL BE WALKIN' WITH MY HONEY; *SEE: (I'll be) WALKIN' WITH MY HONEY: 1945*
I'LL BE WITH YOU IN APPLE BLOSSOM TIME (A. Von Tilzer): 1920 # 4 – Nov. 1920
I'LL BE WITH YOU IN APPLE BLOSSOM TIME (A. Von Tilzer): 1941 # 7 – June 1941
I'LL BE WITH YOU WHEN THE ROSES BLOOM AGAIN: 1901 .... # 1 – Dec. 1901
I'LL BE YOUR RAINBEAU: 1902 .... # 7 – Oct. 1902
I'LL BUILD A STAIRWAY TO PARADISE: 1922 .... # 8 – Nov. 1922
I'LL BUY THAT DREAM: 1945 .... # 2 – Oct. 1945
I'LL CHANGE THE THORNS TO ROSES: 1911 .... #18 – Jan. 1911

I'LL CLOSE MY EYES: 1947	# 8 – Apr. 1947
I'LL DANCE AT YOUR WEDDING: 1948	# 5 – Jan. 1948
I'LL DO IT ALL OVER AGAIN: 1914	#20 – June 1914
I'LL FOLLOW MY SECRET HEART: 1934	#18 – Dec. 1934
I'LL GET BY (AS LONG AS I HAVE YOU) (Ahlert): 1929	# 1 – Mar. 1929
I'LL GET BY (AS LONG AS I HAVE YOU) (Ahlert): 1944	# 2 – July 1944
I'LL KEEP A WARM SPOT IN MY HEART FOR YOU: 1906	#11 – July 1906
I'LL KEEP THE LOVELIGHT BURNING: 1942	#15 – July 1942
I'LL MAKE A RING AROUND ROSIE: 1910	# 8 – June 1910
I'LL NEVER BE THE SAME: 1932	# 5 – Sept. 1932
I'LL NEVER SAY "NEVER AGAIN" AGAIN: 1935	# 3 – Aug. 1935
I'LL NEVER SLIP AROUND AGAIN: 1949	#13 – Nov. 1949
I'LL NEVER SMILE AGAIN: 1940	# 1 – Aug. 1940
I'LL PRAY FOR YOU: 1942	#13 – Apr. 1942
I'LL SAY SHE DOES: 1919	# 5 – June 1919
I'LL SEE YOU AGAIN: 1930	#20 – Mar. 1930
I'LL SEE YOU IN C-U-B-A: 1920	# 4 – May 1920
I'LL SEE YOU IN MY DREAMS (I. Jones): 1925	# 1 – Apr. 1925
I'LL SEE YOU IN MY DREAMS (A. Pasqua): 1990	#20 – June 1990
I'LL SING YOU A THOUSAND LOVE SONGS: 1936	# 3 – Nov. 1936
I'LL STRING ALONG WITH YOU: 1934	# 1 – June 1934
I'LL TAKE AN OPTION ON YOU: 1933	# 7 – Apr. 1933
I'LL WALK ALONE (J. Styne): 1944	# 1 – Sept. 1944
I'LL WALK ALONE (J. Styne): 1952	# 6 – May 1952
I'M A BIG GIRL NOW: 1946	# 9 – May 1946
I'M A DREAMER, AREN'T WE ALL; *SEE: (I'm a dreamer) AREN'T WE ALL: 1930*	
I'M A JAZZ VAMPIRE: 1920	# 7 – Sept. 1920
I'M A JONAH MAN: 1903	# 4 – May 1903
I'M A POPULAR MAN: 1907	#11 – Oct. 1907
I'M A-COMIN' A-COURTIN', CORABELLE: 1948	#18 – Mar. 1948
I'M AFRAID TO COME HOME IN THE DARK: 1908	# 1 – Apr. 1908
I'M ALL BOUND 'ROUND WITH THE MASON-DIXON LINE: 1918	# 6 – Jan. 1918
I'M ALONE BECAUSE I LOVE YOU: 1931	# 2 – Feb. 1931
I'M ALWAYS CHASING RAINBOWS (H. Carroll): 1918	# 1 – Jan. 1919
I'M ALWAYS CHASING RAINBOWS (H. Carroll): 1946	# 4 – Feb. 1946
I'M AN OLD COWHAND: 1936	# 7 – Sept. 1936
I'M AWFULLY GLAD I MET YOU: 1909	#17 – July 1909
I'M BEGINNING TO SEE THE LIGHT: 1945	# 2 – Apr. 1945
I'M BRINGING A RED, RED ROSE: 1929	#14 – Mar. 1929
I'M BUILDING A SAILBOAT OF DREAMS: 1939	#10 – May 1939
I'M BUILDING UP TO AN AWFUL LETDOWN: 1936	#10 – Feb. 1936
I'M CERTAINLY LIVING A RAGTIME LIFE: 1900	# 4 – June 1900
I'M COMING, VIRGINIA: 1927	# 8 – Oct. 1927
I'M CONFESSIN' (THAT I LOVE YOU) (Reynolds): 1930	# 7 – Oct. 1930
I'M CONFESSIN' (THAT I LOVE YOU) (Reynolds): 1945	#12 – Feb. 1945
I'M CONFESSIN' (THAT I LOVE YOU) (Reynolds): 1952	#14 – May 1952
I'M FALLING IN LOVE WITH SOMEONE (V. Herbert): 1911	# 7 – Apr. 1911
I'M FALLING IN LOVE WITH SOMEONE (V. Herbert): 1935	#15 – July 1935
I'M FOLLOWING YOU: 1930	# 4 – Feb. 1930
I'M FOREVER BLOWING BUBBLES (Kellette): 1919	# 1 – June 1919
I'M FOREVER BLOWING BUBBLES (Kellette): 1950	#11 – Oct. 1950
I'M GETTING TIRED SO I CAN SLEEP: 1943	#16 – Feb. 1943
I'M GLAD I CAN MAKE YOU CRY: 1918	#16 – Jan. 1919
I'M GLAD I MET YOU, MARY: 1900	#16 – Jan. 1900
I'M GLAD I WAITED FOR YOU: 1946	#17 – Mar. 1946
I'M GOIN' SOUTH: 1924	# 3 – Apr. 1924
I'M GOING TO FOLLOW THE BOYS: 1918	#10 – Apr. 1918
I'M GONNA CHARLESTON BACK TO CHARLESTON: 1925	#20 – Nov. 1925
I'M GONNA LOCK MY HEART: 1938	# 4 – Sept. 1938
I'M GONNA LOVE THAT GAL (GUY): 1945	# 4 – Oct. 1945
I'M GONNA PIN MY MEDAL ON THE GIRL I LEFT BEHIND: 1918	#14 – Sept. 1918
I'M GONNA SEE MY BABY: 1945	#19 – Mar. 1945
I'M GONNA SIT RIGHT DOWN AND WRITE MYSELF A LETTER (Ahlert): 1936	# 4 – Mar. 1936
I'M GONNA SIT RIGHT DOWN AND WRITE MYSELF A LETTER (Ahlert): 1957	# 4 – Aug. 1957
I'M IN A DANCING MOOD: 1936	# 5 – Jan. 1937
I'M IN LOVE AGAIN (C. Porter): 1927	# 8 – July 1927
I'M IN LOVE AGAIN (C. Porter): 1951	#11 – June 1951
I'M IN LOVE AGAIN (Domino): 1956	# 7 – June 1956
I'M IN THE MARKET FOR YOU: 1930	# 5 – June 1930
I'M IN THE MOOD FOR LOVE: 1935	# 2 – Sept. 1935
I'M JUST A VAGABOND LOVER: 1929	# 2 – July 1929
I'M JUST WILD ABOUT ANIMAL CRACKERS: 1926	#20 – Sept. 1926
I'M JUST WILD ABOUT HARRY: 1922	# 4 – Sept. 1922
I'M LIVING IN A GREAT BIG WAY: 1935	#18 – July 1935
I'M LOOKING FOR A NICE YOUNG FELLOW: 1911	# 3 – Mar. 1911
I'M LOOKING OVER A FOUR LEAF CLOVER (H. Woods): 1927	# 1 – June 1927
I'M LOOKING OVER A FOUR LEAF CLOVER (H. Woods): 1948	# 1 – Feb. 1948
I'M MAKING BELIEVE: 1944	# 3 – Dec. 1944
I'M MISSIN' MAMMY'S KISSIN': 1921	#10 – May 1921
I'M MY OWN GRANDPAW (GRANDMAW): 1948	#11 – Feb. 1948
I'M NOBODY'S BABY (Ager): 1921	# 3 – Sept. 1921
I'M NOBODY'S BABY (Ager): 1940	# 4 – Sept. 1940
I'M NOT THAT KIND OF GIRL: 1910	#20 – June 1910
I'M ON A SEE SAW: 1935	# 3 – Oct. 1935
I'M ON MY WAY TO DUBLIN BAY: 1915	# 1 – July 1915
I'M ON MY WAY TO MANDALAY: 1914	# 2 – Mar. 1914
I'M ON THE WATER WAGON NOW: 1904	#10 – Feb. 1904
I'M PUTTING ALL MY EGGS IN ONE BASKET: 1936	# 2 – Apr. 1936
I'M SHOOTING HIGH: 1936	# 6 – Feb. 1936
I'M SITTIN' HIGH ON A HILLTOP: 1935	# 8 – Dec. 1935
I'M SITTING ON TOP OF THE WORLD (Henderson): 1926	# 2 – Feb. 1926
I'M SITTING ON TOP OF THE WORLD (Henderson): 1953	#14 – Apr. 1953
I'M SITTING PRETTY IN A PRETTY LITTLE CITY: 1924	# 5 – Jan. 1924
I'M SORRY, SALLY: 1929	# 8 – Jan. 1929
I'M SORRY I MADE YOU CRY: 1918	# 1 – June 1918
I'M STARVING FOR ONE SIGHT OF YOU: 1908	#12 – Apr. 1908
I'M STEPPING OUT WITH A MEMORY TONIGHT: 1940	#11 – Aug. 1940
I'M STILL WITHOUT A SWEETHEART WITH SUMMER COMIN' ON; *SEE: (I'm still without a sweetheart) WITH SUMMER COMIN' ON: 1932*	
I'M SURE OF EVERYTHING BUT YOU: 1932	# 9 – Jan. 1933
I'M TALKING THROUGH MY HEART: 1936	#15 – Dec. 1936
I'M THE LONESOMEST GAL IN TOWN (A. Von Tilzer): 1912	#20 – Oct. 1912
I'M THROUGH WITH LOVE: 1931	# 4 – Aug. 1931
I'M TIRED: 1901	# 8 – Dec. 1901
I'M TOO ROMANTIC; *SEE: (I'm) TOO ROMANTIC: 1940*	
I'M TRYING SO HARD TO FORGET YOU: 1905	# 3 – Apr. 1905
I'M WASTIN' MY TEARS ON YOU: 1945	#16 – Jan. 1945
I'M WEARING MY HEART AWAY FOR YOU, LOUISE: 1902	# 5 – Dec. 1902
I'M YOUNG AND HEALTHY: 1933	#12 – Mar. 1933
I'M YOURS (J. Green): 1930	# 2 – Nov. 1930
I'M YOURS (Mellin): 1952	# 3 – June 1952
I'M YOURS (Robertson): 1965	#11 – Oct. 1965
I'VE A LONGING IN MY HEART FOR YOU, LOUISE: 1901	# 2 – Apr. 1901
I'VE BEEN FLOATING DOWN THE OLD GREEN RIVER: 1916	#10 – Jan. 1916
I'VE GOT A DATE WITH A DREAM: 1938	# 7 – Oct. 1938
I'VE GOT A FEELIN' FOR YOU: 1904	# 3 – Apr. 1904
I'VE GOT A FEELIN' YOU'RE FOOLIN': 1935	# 5 – Nov. 1935
I'VE GOT A FEELING I'M FALLING: 1929	#12 – Aug. 1929
I'VE GOT A GAL IN KALAMAZOO; *SEE: (I've got a gal in) KALAMAZOO: 1942*	
I'VE GOT A LOVELY BUNCH OF COCONUTS: 1949	#10 – Nov. 1949
I'VE GOT A PAIN IN MY SAWDUST: 1909	T30 – July 1909
I'VE GOT A POCKETFUL OF DREAMS: 1938	# 1 – Sept. 1938

I'VE GOT A WHITE MAN WORKING FOR ME: 1900 .... #18 – Oct. 1900
I'VE GOT AN INVITATION TO A DANCE: 1935 .... #11 – Jan. 1935
I'VE GOT FIVE DOLLARS: 1931 .... #19 – Apr. 1931
I'VE GOT MY CAPTAIN WORKING FOR ME NOW: 1919.......... # 6 – Nov. 1919
I'VE GOT MY EYES ON YOU (T. Morse): 1902................. #11 – Oct. 1902
I'VE GOT MY EYES ON YOU (C. Porter): 1940 .... # 8 – Mar. 1940
I'VE GOT MY LOVE TO KEEP ME WARM (Berlin): 1937......... # 4 – Apr. 1937
I'VE GOT MY LOVE TO KEEP ME WARM (Berlin): 1949......... # 5 – Feb. 1949
I'VE GOT RINGS ON MY FINGERS: 1909..................... # 1 – Nov. 1909
I'VE GOT THE GIRL: 1927 .... #20 – Feb. 1927
I'VE GOT THE TIME, I'VE GOT THE PLACE, BUT IT'S
HARD TO FIND THE GIRL: 1910.................... # 2 – Aug. 1910
I'VE GOT THE WORDS, I'VE GOT THE TUNE; *SEE: HUMMIN' TO MYSELF: 1932*
I'VE GOT THE WORLD ON A STRING: 1933 .... #19 – Mar. 1933
I'VE GOT TO GO NOW 'CAUSE I THINK IT'S GOING TO RAIN: 1903 #11 – Aug. 1903
I'VE GOT TO SING A TORCH SONG: 1933.................... #18 – July 1933
I'VE GOT YOU UNDER MY SKIN (C. Porter): 1936 .... # 4 – Dec. 1936
I'VE GOT YOU UNDER MY SKIN (C. Porter): 1966 .... # 9 – Oct. 1966
I'VE GROWN SO LONESOME THINKING OF YOU;
SEE: (I've grown so lonesome) THINKING OF YOU: 1927
I'VE GROWN SO USED TO YOU: 1901 .... #16 – Aug. 1901
I'VE HAD MY MOMENTS: 1934............................ #17 – July 1934
I'VE HEARD THAT SONG BEFORE: 1943 .... # 1 – Mar. 1943
I'VE MADE MY PLANS FOR THE SUMMER: 1907 .... #20 – Aug. 1907
I'VE TAKEN QUITE A FANCY TO YOU: 1908.................. # 5 – Sept. 1908
I'VE TOLD EVERY LITTLE STAR (J. Kern): 1933 .... #17 – Jan. 1933
I'VE TOLD EVERY LITTLE STAR (J. Kern): 1961 .... # 4 – May 1961
ICE CREAM;
SEE: I SCREAM, YOU SCREAM, WE ALL SCREAM FOR ICE CREAM: 1928
IDA (SWEET AS APPLE CIDER) (E. Leonard): 1904 .... #14 – July 1904
IDA (SWEET AS APPLE CIDER) (E. Leonard): 1928 .... #11 – Jan. 1928
IDAHO: 1942.. # 3 – Aug. 1942
IF A GIRL LIKE YOU LOVED A BOY LIKE ME: 1906 .... # 4 – Apr. 1906
IF HE CAN FIGHT LIKE HE CAN LOVE, GOOD NIGHT GERMANY!
1918... # 9 – Sept. 1918
IF HE COMES IN, I'M GOING OUT: 1910 .... # 8 – Nov. 1910
IF I BUT DARE: 1902 .... #16 – Aug. 1902
IF I COULD BE WITH YOU (ONE HOUR TONIGHT): 1930 .... # 2 – Sept. 1930
IF I DIDN'T CARE: 1939 .... # 6 – July 1939
IF I HAD A GIRL LIKE YOU: 1930 .... # 4 – June 1930
IF I HAD A TALKING PICTURE OF YOU: 1929................. # 3 – Dec. 1929
IF I HAD A THOUSAND LIVES TO LIVE: 1909................. # 2 – Apr. 1909
IF I HAD MY LIFE TO LIVE OVER: 1947 .... #12 – July 1947
IF I HAD MY WAY (J. Kendis): 1914 .... #13 – June 1914
IF I HAD MY WAY (J. Kendis): 1939 .... #19 – July 1939
IF I HAD YOU: 1929 .... # 5 – Mar. 1929
IF I KNOCK THE "L" OUT OF KELLY: 1916 .... # 3 – Sept. 1916
IF I LOVED YOU: 1945 .... # 2 – Aug. 1945
IF I ONLY HAD A DOLLAH OF MY OWN: 1901 .... # 8 – Apr. 1901
IF I SHOULD LOSE YOU: 1936 .... #20 – Jan. 1936
IF I WERE ON THE STAGE; *SEE: KISS ME AGAIN: 1906, 1916*
IF IT AIN'T LOVE: 1932................................. #18 – July 1932
IF IT'S THE LAST THING I DO: 1937 .... # 6 – Dec. 1937
IF MONEY TALKS, IT AIN'T ON SPEAKIN' TERMS WITH ME: 1902. # 4 – June 1902
IF THE MAN IN THE MOON WERE A COON: 1906 .... # 8 – Oct. 1906
IF THE MOON TURNS GREEN: 1935 .... # 9 – Apr. 1935
IF TIME WAS MONEY, I'D BE A MILLIONAIRE: 1902 .... # 6 – July 1902
IF WE CAN'T BE THE SAME OLD SWEETHEARTS: 1915 .... # 5 – Sept. 1915
IF YOU CAN'T BE A BELL COW, FALL IN BEHIND: 1903......... #16 – Jan. 1903
IF YOU HAD ALL THE WORLD AND ITS GOLD: 1917 .... #12 – Mar. 1917
IF YOU KNEW SUSIE: 1925 .... # 1 – July 1925
IF YOU LOOK IN HER EYES: 1918 .... #20 – May 1918
IF YOU PLEASE: 1943 .... # 8 – Oct. 1943
IF YOU SEE SALLY: 1927 .... #19 – May 1927
IF YOU TALK IN YOUR SLEEP, DON'T MENTION MY NAME
(Ayer): 1912 .... # 5 – Feb. 1912
IF YOU TALK IN YOUR SLEEP (West): 1974 .... #17 – Aug. 1974
IF YOU WERE THE ONLY GIRL: 1946 .... # 6 – Sept. 1946
ILL WIND: 1934 .... #15 – May 1934
IMAGINATION: 1940 .... # 1 – June 1940
IMPECUNIOUS DAVIS: 1900 .... # 9 – Jan. 1900
IN A COZY CORNER: 1902 .... T30 – June 1902
IN A LITTLE GYPSY TEAROOM: 1935 .... # 1 – July 1935
IN A LITTLE SPANISH TOWN: 1927 .... # 1 – Jan. 1927
IN A SHANTY IN OLD SHANTY TOWN: 1932 .... # 1 – July 1932
IN ALL MY DREAMS I DREAM OF YOU: 1911 .... T30 – Aug. 1911
IN AN EIGHTEENTH CENTURY DRAWING ROOM: 1939 .... # 9 – Oct. 1939
IN AN OLD DUTCH GARDEN: 1940......................... # 2 – Apr. 1940
IN APPLE BLOSSOM TIME;
SEE: I'LL BE WITH YOU IN APPLE BLOSSOM TIME: 1920, 1941
IN DEAR OLD GEORGIA: 1905 .... # 5 – Jan. 1906
IN DEAR OLD ILLINOIS: 1903 .... # 4 – Feb. 1903
IN GOOD OLD NEW YORK TOWN: 1900 .... # 6 – Feb. 1900
IN LOVE IN VAIN: 1946 .... # 8 – Aug. 1946
IN MONKEYLAND: 1907 .... # 5 – Nov. 1907
IN MY ARMS: 1943 .... # 5 – Aug. 1943
IN MY HAREM: 1913.................................... # 2 – Aug. 1913
IN MY HIDEAWAY: 1932 .... #17 – July 1932
IN MY MERRY OLDSMOBILE: 1906 .... # 2 – Jan. 1906
IN NAPLES FAIR: 1900 .... # 9 – Apr. 1900
IN OLD ALABAMA: 1903................................. # 3 – July 1903
IN OLD NEW YORK: 1907 .... # 6 – Jan. 1907
IN SHADOWLAND: 1925 .... #13 – June 1925
IN THE BLUE OF THE EVENING: 1943...................... # 2 – Aug. 1943
IN THE CANDLELIGHT: 1914 .... #17 – June 1914
IN THE CATHEDRAL: 1901 .... #16 – May 1901
IN THE CHAPEL IN THE MOONLIGHT (B. Hill): 1936.......... # 1 – Dec. 1936
IN THE CHAPEL IN THE MOONLIGHT (B. Hill): 1954.......... # 6 – Aug. 1954
IN THE CITY OF SIGHS AND TEARS: 1902 .... # 8 – Jan. 1903
IN THE EVENING BY THE MOONLIGHT, DEAR LOUISE: 1907 .... #20 – Jan. 1907
IN THE GARDEN OF MY HEART: 1910 .... # 8 – Apr. 1910
"IN THE GLOAMING" WAS THE SONG SHE SANG TO ME: 1912 .. #16 – June 1912
IN THE GOOD OLD SUMMERTIME (Evans): 1902............. # 1 – Sept. 1902
IN THE GOOD OLD SUMMERTIME (Evans): 1952............. #17 – July 1952
IN THE GREAT SOMEWHERE: 1901 .... #17 – Dec. 1901
IN THE HOUSE OF TOO MUCH TROUBLE: 1901 .... # 6 – May 1901
IN THE LAND OF HARMONY: 1911........................ #10 – Aug. 1911
IN THE LITTLE RED SCHOOL HOUSE: 1922 .... # 5 – July 1922
IN THE MIDDLE OF A DREAM: 1939 .... #11 – July 1939
IN THE MIDDLE OF A KISS: 1935.......................... # 3 – July 1935
IN THE MIDDLE OF MAY: 1946 .... #15 – Jan. 1946
IN THE MIDDLE OF THE NIGHT: 1926 .... #14 – June 1926
IN THE MOOD (Garland): 1940 .... # 5 – Feb. 1940
IN THE MOOD (Garland): 1959 .... # 5 – Dec. 1959
IN THE MOOD (Garland): 1990; *SEE: SWING THE MOOD: 1990*
IN THE MOON MIST: 1946 .... #18 – June 1946
IN THE PARK IN PAREE: 1933 .... #18 – June 1933
IN THE SHADE OF THE OLD APPLE TREE: 1905.............. # 1 – Apr. 1905
IN THE SHADE OF THE SHELTERING PALM; *SEE: SHADE OF THE PALM: 1901*
IN THE SHADOWS: 1912 .... # 4 – Mar. 1912
IN THE STILL OF THE NIGHT (C. Porter): 1938 .... #12 – Jan. 1938
IN THE STILL OF THE NIGHT (F. Parris): 1993 .... # 3 – Jan. 1993
IN THE SWEET BYE AND BYE: 1903....................... # 4 – June 1903
IN THE TOWN WHERE I WAS BORN: 1914................... #20 – Sept. 1914
IN THE VALLEY OF THE MOON: 1933 .... # 1 – July 1933
IN THE WILDWOOD WHERE THE BLUE BELLS GREW: 1907 .... # 6 – May 1907

IN ZANZIBAR: 1904	# 4 – Apr. 1904
INDIAN LOVE CALL (Friml): 1925	# 7 – Mar. 1925
INDIAN LOVE CALL (Friml): 1937	#20 – Jan. 1937
INDIAN LOVE CALL (Friml): 1952	#13 – Sept. 1952
INDIAN SUMMER: 1940	# 2 – Jan. 1940
INDIANA: 1917	# 3 – June 1917
INDIANA MOON: 1923	# 2 – Oct. 1923
INDIANOLA: 1918	# 3 – Apr. 1918
INTERMEZZO (A LOVE STORY): 1941	# 1 – June 1941
INTERNATIONAL RAG; *SEE: THAT INTERNATIONAL RAG: 1913*	
INTO EACH LIFE SOME RAIN MUST FALL: 1944	# 7 – Jan. 1945
INVITATION TO A DANCE; *SEE: I'VE GOT AN INVITATION TO A DANCE: 1935*	
IOLA: 1906	# 4 – Nov. 1906
IRELAND MUST BE HEAVEN FOR MY MOTHER CAME FROM THERE: 1916	# 2 – Nov. 1916
IRENE: 1920	# 7 – July 1920
IS EVERYBODY HAPPY? 1906	#18 – May 1906
IS I IN LOVE? I IS: 1932	#14 – July 1932
IS IT TRUE WHAT THEY SAY ABOUT DIXIE? 1936	# 1 – June 1936
IS YOU IS OR IS YOU AIN'T (MA' BABY): 1944	# 3 – Sept. 1944
ISLE D'AMOUR: 1914	# 5 – Feb. 1914
ISLE O'DREAMS: 1913	T30 – June 1913
ISLE OF CAPRI (Grosz): 1935	# 1 – Feb. 1935
ISLE OF CAPRI (Grosz): 1954	#12 – June 1954
ISLE OF OUR DREAMS, THE: 1907	#16 – Dec. 1906
ISN'T IT HEAVENLY? 1933	# 7 – July 1933
ISN'T THIS A LOVELY DAY (TO BE CAUGHT IN THE RAIN)? 1935	# 4 – Oct. 1935
IT AIN'T GONNA RAIN NO MO': 1924	# 1 – May 1924
IT ALL COMES BACK TO ME NOW: 1941	# 4 – Mar. 1941
IT ALL DEPENDS ON YOU: 1927	# 1 – May 1927
IT CAN'T BE WRONG: 1943	# 3 – May 1943
IT COULD HAPPEN TO YOU: 1944	# 8 – Sept. 1944
IT DON'T MEAN A THING (IF IT AIN'T GOT THAT SWING): 1932	#18 – May 1932
Reached second peak at	#20 – Nov. 1932
IT HAD TO BE YOU (I. Jones): 1924	# 2 – Aug. 1924
IT HAD TO BE YOU (I. Jones): 1944	# 5 – Sept. 1944
IT HAPPENED IN MONTEREY: 1930	# 3 – May 1930
IT LOOKS LIKE A BIG NIGHT TONIGHT: 1908	# 4 – Dec. 1908
IT LOOKS LIKE RAIN IN CHERRY BLOSSOM LANE: 1937	# 1 – July 1937
IT MADE YOU HAPPY WHEN YOU MADE ME CRY: 1927	# 5 – Feb. 1927
IT MIGHT AS WELL BE SPRING: 1945	# 3 – Dec. 1945
IT MUST BE TRUE: 1930	# 6 – Dec. 1930
IT ONLY HAPPENS WHEN I DANCE WITH YOU: 1948	#10 – Aug. 1948
IT STARTED ALL OVER AGAIN: 1943	#10 – Apr. 1943
IT TAKES A LITTLE RAIN WITH THE SUNSHINE TO MAKE THE WORLD GO 'ROUND: 1913	# 8 – Oct. 1913
IT TAKES A LONG, TALL, BROWN-SKIN GAL: 1917	# 8 – July 1917
IT WAS ONLY A SUN SHOWER: 1927	# 9 – Dec. 1927
IT WAS SO BEAUTIFUL: 1932	# 5 – Sept. 1932
IT'S A BIG, WIDE, WONDERFUL WORLD: 1949	#19 – May 1949
IT'S A BLUE WORLD: 1940	# 2 – Mar. 1940
IT'S A GOOD DAY: 1947	# 9 – Apr. 1947
IT'S A HUNDRED TO ONE (I'M IN LOVE): 1939	#13 – Oct. 1939
IT'S A LONG, LONG WAY TO TIPPERARY: 1915	# 1 – Jan. 1915
IT'S A SIN TO TELL A LIE (Mayhew): 1936	# 2 – July 1936
IT'S A SIN TO TELL A LIE (Mayhew): 1955	# 9 – July 1955
IT'S A WONDERFUL WORLD: 1940	#19 – June 1940
IT'S ALL FORGOTTEN NOW: 1934	#13 – Oct. 1934
IT'S ALL OVER NOW: 1946	#17 – Dec. 1946
IT'S ALL RIGHT, MAYME: 1901	#20 – Nov. 1901
IT'S ALWAYS YOU: 1943	# 5 – July 1943
IT'S AN OLD SOUTHERN CUSTOM: 1935	# 9 – May 1935
IT'S BEEN A LONG, LONG TIME: 1945	# 1 – Nov. 1945
IT'S BEEN SO LONG: 1936	# 4 – Mar. 1936
IT'S DARK ON OBSERVATORY HILL: 1935	#16 – Jan. 1935
IT'S DE-LOVELY: 1936	# 3 – Dec. 1936
IT'S DELIGHTFUL TO BE MARRIED: 1907	# 5 – July 1907
IT'S EASY TO REMEMBER: 1935	#10 – Apr. 1935
IT'S FOR HER, HER, HER: 1902	T30 – Sept. 1902
IT'S GREAT TO BE A SOLDIER MAN: 1907	# 9 – July 1907
IT'S LOVE, LOVE, LOVE: 1944	# 1 – Apr. 1944
IT'S MAGIC: 1948	# 3 – Aug. 1948
IT'S MIGHTY STRANGE; *SEE: BEST I GET IS MUCH OBLIGED TO YOU, THE: 1908*	
IT'S NOBODY'S BUSINESS BUT MY OWN: 1919	# 8 – Aug. 1919
IT'S ONLY A PAPER MOON (Arlen): 1933	#11 – Nov. 1933
IT'S ONLY A PAPER MOON (Arlen): 1945	# 8 – Nov. 1945
IT'S THE GIRL: 1931	#14 – Sept. 1931
IT'S THE MAN BEHIND THE GUN (J.P. Sousa); *SEE: (It's the) MAN BEHIND THE GUN: 1900*	
IT'S THE MAN BEHIND THE GUN THAT DOES THE WORK (T. Morse): 1900	#19 – Dec. 1900
IT'S THE NATURAL THING TO DO: 1937	#12 – Sept. 1937
IT'S THE TALK OF THE TOWN: 1933	# 6 – Nov. 1933
IT'S TULIP TIME IN HOLLAND: 1915	# 1 – Nov. 1915
IT'S WONDERFUL (S. Smith): 1938	#13 – Mar. 1938
IT'S YOU (Silver); *SEE: C'EST VOUS: 1927*	
ITALIAN STREET SONG: 1911	#11 – Mar. 1911
IVY: 1947	#13 – Aug. 1947

J

JA-DA: 1919	# 2 – Mar. 1919
JAPANESE SANDMAN, THE: 1920	# 2 – Nov. 1920
JAZZ BABIES' BALL: 1920	#18 – July 1920
JAZZ ME BLUES, THE: 1921	# 8 – Aug. 1921
JEALOUS: 1924	# 2 – Sept. 1924
JEALOUS HEART: 1949	# 5 – Oct. 1949
JEANNINE, I DREAM OF LILAC TIME: 1928	# 1 – Oct. 1928
JEEPERS CREEPERS: 1939	# 1 – Feb. 1939
JENNIE LEE (H. Von Tilzer): 1902	# 4 – Apr. 1902
JENNIE LEE (J. Berry): 1958	#12 – June 1958
JERICHO: 1929	#10 – May 1929
JERSEY BOUNCE: 1942	# 3 – June 1942
JIM: 1941	# 2 – Oct. 1941
JIM JUDSON (FROM THE TOWN OF HACKENSACK): 1905	#18 – May 1905
JIMMY, THE PRIDE OF NEWSPAPER ROW: 1901	#10 – Aug. 1901
JIMMY VALENTINE: 1911	#14 – June 1911
JINGLE, JANGLE, JINGLE: 1942	# 1 – July 1942
JINGLE BELLS (Pierpont): 1941	#15 – Dec. 1941
JINGLE BELLS (Pierpont): 1951	#16 – Dec. 1951
JINGLE BELLS (Pierpont, Stewart); *SEE: YINGLE BELLS: 1949*	
JOAN OF ARC, THEY ARE CALLING YOU: 1917	# 4 – Nov. 1917
JOHNNY DOUGHBOY FOUND A ROSE IN IRELAND: 1942	# 2 – June 1942
JOHNNY ZERO: 1943	# 4 – July 1943
JOLLY ME ALONG: 1905	#10 – Feb. 1905
JOSEPHINE (W. King): 1937	#16 – Apr. 1937
Reached second peak at	#12 – Oct. 1937
JOSEPHINE (W. King): 1951	#16 – July 1951
JOSEPHINE, MY JO: 1902	# 5 – May 1902
JUKE BOX SATURDAY NIGHT: 1942	#15 – Jan. 1943
JUMPIN' JIVE, THE: 1939	#10 – Sept. 1939
JUNE BROUGHT THE ROSES: 1925	# 7 – Apr. 1925
JUNE IN JANUARY: 1935	# 1 – Jan. 1935
JUNE IS BUSTIN' OUT ALL OVER: 1945	#16 – Aug. 1945

JUNE NIGHT: 1924	# 2 – Oct. 1924
JUST A BABY'S PRAYER AT TWILIGHT: 1918	# 1 – Apr. 1918
JUST A BIRD'S-EYE VIEW OF MY OLD KENTUCKY HOME: 1927	#15 – Jan. 1927
JUST A COTTAGE SMALL (BY A WATERFALL): 1926	# 4 – May 1926
JUST A GIGOLO (Casucci): 1931	# 1 – Feb. 1931
JUST A GIGOLO (Casucci): 1985; *SEE: JUST A GIGOLO/I AIN'T GOT NOBODY: 1985*	
JUST A GIGOLO/I AIN'T GOT NOBODY: 1985	#12 – June 1985
JUST A GIRL THAT MEN FORGET: 1923	# 1 – Sept. 1923
JUST A GLEAM OF HEAVEN IN HER EYES: 1904	#14 – Aug. 1904
JUST A LITTLE BIT SOUTH OF NORTH CAROLINA: 1941	# 7 – July 1941
JUST A LITTLE CLOSER: 1930	#16 – Sept. 1930
JUST A LITTLE DRINK: 1925	#19 – Aug. 1925
JUST A LITTLE FOND AFFECTION: 1946	# 9 – Feb. 1946
JUST A LITTLE HOME FOR THE OLD FOLKS: 1932	#12 – Dec. 1932
JUST A LITTLE LOVE SONG: 1922	#10 – Apr. 1922
JUST A LITTLE ROCKING CHAIR AND YOU: 1906	# 5 – May 1906
JUST A MEMORY: 1927	# 1 – Dec. 1927
JUST A PRAYER AWAY: 1945	# 5 – Apr. 1945
JUST A-WEARYIN' FOR YOU: 1902	T40 – May 1902
JUST AN ECHO IN THE VALLEY: 1933	# 1 – Mar. 1933
JUST ANOTHER DAY WASTED AWAY (WAITING FOR YOU): 1927	# 7 – Sept. 1927
JUST AROUND THE CORNER: 1926	#10 – Jan. 1926
JUST AS THOUGH YOU WERE HERE: 1942	#11 – Aug. 1942
JUST BECAUSE (Shelton): 1948	#13 – June 1948
JUST BECAUSE (O'Hara): 1989	#14 – Apr. 1989
JUST BECAUSE I LOVED YOU SO: 1907	#19 – July 1907
JUST BECAUSE SHE MADE DEM GOO-GOO EYES: 1900	# 4 – Dec. 1900
JUST FOR A GIRL: 1910	# 9 – July 1910
JUST FOR TONIGHT: 1923	#15 – Nov. 1923
JUST FRIENDS: 1932	# 3 – Mar. 1932
JUST KISS YOURSELF GOODBYE: 1903	# 4 – Mar. 1903
JUST LIKE A BUTTERFLY (THAT'S CAUGHT IN THE RAIN): 1927	# 4 – Sept. 1927
JUST LIKE A GYPSY: 1920	# 7 – May 1920
JUST LIKE A MELODY OUT OF THE SKY: 1928	# 2 – Sept. 1928
JUST LIKE A RAINBOW: 1921	#17 – Nov. 1921
JUST LIKE WASHINGTON CROSSED THE DELAWARE: 1918	# 6 – July 1918
JUST NEXT DOOR: 1902	# 9 – Aug. 1902
JUST ONCE AGAIN: 1927	#14 – Nov. 1927
JUST ONE KISS: 1900	#12 – Aug. 1900
JUST ONE MORE CHANCE (Johnston): 1931	# 1 – July 1931
JUST ONE MORE CHANCE (Johnston): 1951	#11 – Nov. 1951
JUST ONE WAY TO SAY I LOVE YOU: 1949	#15 – Sept. 1949
JUST ONE WORD OF CONSOLATION: 1906	T30 – June 1906
JUST SOMEONE: 1908	# 3 – June 1908
JUST THE OTHER DAY: 1946	#20 – Sept. 1946
JUST TRY TO PICTURE ME DOWN HOME IN TENNESSEE; *SEE: BACK HOME IN TENNESSEE: 1915*	
JUST WHEN I NEEDED YOU MOST (W.B.Gray): 1900	#20 – Oct. 1900
JUST WHEN I NEEDED YOU MOST (Vanwarmer): 1979	# 4 – Mar. 1979

K

K-K-K-KATY: 1918	# 1 – July 1918
KA-LU-A: 1922	# 2 – Mar. 1922
(I've got a gal in) KALAMAZOO: 1942	# 1 – Oct. 1942
KARAMA: 1904	#12 – Nov. 1904
KATE (HAVE I COME TOO EARLY, TOO LATE): 1947	#14 – Oct. 1947
KATE KEARNEY: 1904	#12 – Jan. 1905
KATEY DEAR: 1906	#13 – Jan. 1906
KATINKA: 1926	#16 – Aug. 1926
KEEP A LITTLE COZY CORNER IN YOUR HEART FOR ME: 1905	# 1 – Aug. 1905
KEEP ON THE SUNNY SIDE: 1906	# 2 – May 1906
KEEP SMILING AT TROUBLE: 1925	# 8 – Apr. 1925
KEEP SWEEPING THE COBWEBS OFF THE MOON: 1928	# 7 – Mar. 1928
KEEP THE HOME FIRES BURNING (Novello): 1916	#14 – Mar. 1916
KEEP THE HOME FIRES BURNING (Novello): 1917	# 7 – Oct. 1917
KEEP YOUNG AND BEAUTIFUL: 1934	#13 – Feb. 1934
KEEP YOUR HEAD DOWN, FRITZIE BOY: 1918	#11 – Aug. 1918
KEEPIN' OUT OF MISCHIEF NOW: 1932	# 9 – May 1932
KENTUCKY DAYS: 1912	#11 – Sept. 1912
KENTUCKY DREAM WALTZ: 1919	#10 – May 1919
KENTUCKY DREAMS; *SEE: KENTUCKY DREAM WALTZ: 1919*	
KERRY MILLS BARN DANCE: 1909	#13 – June 1909
KICKIN' THE GONG AROUND: 1931	#15 – Dec. 1931
KING FOR A DAY (FioRito): 1928	#14 – Nov. 1928
KING FOR A DAY (Currie): 1986	# 8 – Mar. 1986
KING'S HORSES, THE: 1931	#13 – Mar. 1931
KINKAJOU, THE: 1927	#12 – May 1927
KISS GOODNIGHT, A: 1945	#19 – Aug. 1945
KISS IN THE DARK, A: 1923	# 5 – May 1923
KISS ME, MY HONEY, KISS ME: 1911	# 4 – Apr. 1911
KISS ME AGAIN (V. Herbert): 1906	T30 – May 1906
KISS ME AGAIN (V. Herbert): 1916	#17 – Oct. 1916
KISS ME GOODNIGHT: 1932	# 8 – Apr. 1932
KISS ME SWEET: 1949	#14 – June 1949
KISS THE BOYS GOODBYE: 1941	#11 – Sept. 1941
KISS WALTZ, THE: 1930	# 3 – Oct. 1930
KISSES, THE SWEETEST KISSES OF ALL: 1919	#10 – Mar. 1919
KITTEN ON THE KEYS: 1922	# 3 – Aug. 1922
KITTY FROM KANSAS CITY: 1930	#14 – July 1930
KNOCK, KNOCK, WHO'S THERE? 1936	#14 – Sept. 1936
KNOCK WOOD: 1911	#16 – Dec. 1911
KOKOMO, INDIANA: 1947	#16 – Oct. 1947
KOONVILLE KOONLETS: 1900	#11 – June 1900

L

LA ROSITA: 1924	#14 – Feb. 1924
LA VEEDA: 1920	# 2 – July 1920
LADDER OF ROSES, THE: 1916	#12 – Apr. 1916
LADDIE BOY: 1917	#11 – Nov. 1917
LADY, PLAY YOUR MANDOLIN: 1931	# 9 – Feb. 1931
LADY ANGELINE: 1912	#15 – June 1912
LADY BE GOOD; *SEE: OH, LADY BE GOOD: 1925*	
LADY FROM 29 PALMS, THE: 1947	# 8 – Oct. 1947
LADY IN RED, THE (Wrubel): 1935	# 6 – July 1935
LADY IN RED, THE (DeBurgh): 1987	# 3 – May 1987
LADY OF SPAIN (T. Evans): 1931	# 9 – Nov. 1931
LADY OF SPAIN (T. Evans): 1949	#19 – Mar. 1949
LADY OF SPAIN (T. Evans): 1952	# 5 – Dec. 1952
LADY OF THE EVENING: 1923	# 5 – Mar. 1923
LADY'S IN LOVE WITH YOU, THE: 1939	# 3 – July 1939
LAM' LAM' LAM': 1900	# 6 – Dec. 1900
LAMBETH WALK, THE: 1938	# 5 – Oct. 1938
LAMP IS LOW, THE: 1939	# 6 – Aug. 1939
LANKY YANKEE BOYS IN BLUE, THE: 1908	# 7 – May 1908
LAROO, LAROO, LILLI BOLERO: 1948	#15 – May 1948
LAST MILE HOME, THE: 1949	#20 – Oct. 1949
(Why couldn't it last) LAST NIGHT: 1939	# 8 – Nov. 1939
LAST NIGHT I DREAMED YOU KISSED ME: 1928	#19 – Sept. 1928
LAST NIGHT ON THE BACK PORCH: 1923	# 2 – Dec. 1923

LAST NIGHT WAS THE END OF THE WORLD: 1913	# 6 – Nov. 1913
LAST ROUNDUP, THE: 1933	# 1 – Oct. 1933
LAST TIME I SAW PARIS, THE: 1941	#12 – Feb. 1941
LAUGH! CLOWN, LAUGH! 1928	# 3 – June 1928
LAUGHING ON THE OUTSIDE: 1946	# 1 – May 1946
LAUGHING WATER: 1903	# 3 – Jan. 1904
LAURA: 1945	# 2 – June 1945
LAVENDER BLUE (L. Morey): 1949	# 4 – Feb. 1949
LAVENDER BLUE (L. Morey): 1959	# 4 – Aug. 1959
LAWD, YOU MADE THE NIGHT TOO LONG: 1932	# 5 – June 1932
LAZY: 1924	# 5 – June 1924
LAZY BONES: 1933	# 1 – Aug. 1933
LAZY DAY (Posford): 1932	# 5 – July 1932
LAZY DAY (Fischoff): 1967	#14 – Dec. 1967
LAZY LOU'SIANA MOON: 1930	# 8 – Apr. 1930
LAZY MOON: 1904	# 6 – Oct. 1904
LEADER OF THE GERMAN BAND, THE: 1905	# 7 – Nov. 1905
LEANIN' ON THE OLE TOP RAIL: 1940	#10 – Apr. 1940
LEARN TO CROON: 1933	# 4 – Aug. 1933
LEARN TO SMILE: 1921	# 5 – Sept. 1921
LEAVE ME WITH A SMILE: 1922	# 9 – Feb. 1922
LEFT ALL ALONE AGAIN BLUES: 1920	# 8 – July 1920
LEMON IN THE GARDEN OF LOVE, A: 1907	# 4 – Feb. 1907
LENA FROM PALESTEENA; *SEE: (Lena from) PALESTEENA: 1921*	
LET A SMILE BE YOUR UMBRELLA: 1928	# 3 – Apr. 1928
LET IT ALONE: 1907	# 3 – Apr. 1907
LET IT RAIN! LET IT POUR! (I'LL BE IN VIRGINIA IN THE MORNING): 1925	#17 – June 1925
LET IT SNOW! LET IT SNOW! LET IT SNOW! 1946	# 2 – Feb. 1946
LET ME CALL YOU SWEETHEART (L. Friedman): 1911	# 1 – Feb. 1911
LET ME CALL YOU SWEETHEART (L. Friedman): 1925	# 9 – Oct. 1925
LET ME LINGER (LONGER) IN YOUR ARMS: 1925	#14 – Aug. 1925
LET ME LOVE YOU TONIGHT (Touzet): 1944	#15 – Dec. 1944
LET ME LOVE YOU TONIGHT (Woodard): 1980	#10 – July 1980
LET ME OFF UPTOWN: 1941	#20 – Aug. 1941
LET ME WHISPER (I LOVE YOU): 1938	#16 – June 1938
LET THE REST OF THE WORLD GO BY: 1920	# 1 – Jan. 1920
LET THERE BE LOVE: 1940	# 6 – May 1940
LET YOURSELF GO: 1936	# 5 – Apr. 1936
LET'S CALL IT A DAY: 1933	#17 – May 1933
LET'S CALL THE WHOLE THING OFF: 1937	#14 – May 1937
LET'S DO IT (LET'S FALL IN LOVE): 1929	# 5 – Jan. 1929
LET'S DREAM THIS ONE OUT: 1941	#20 – Feb. 1941
LET'S FACE THE MUSIC AND DANCE: 1936	# 8 – Mar. 1936
LET'S FALL IN LOVE: 1934	# 6 – Mar. 1934
LET'S GET AWAY FROM IT ALL: 1941	#17 – May 1941
LET'S GET LOST: 1943	# 3 – June 1943
LET'S GO BACK TO BABY DAYS: 1909	#13 – May 1909
LET'S HAVE ANOTHER CUP OF COFFEE: 1932	#14 – Apr. 1932
LET'S PUT OUT THE LIGHTS (AND GO TO SLEEP): 1932	# 1 – Nov. 1932
LET'S SAIL TO DREAMLAND: 1938	#10 – Apr. 1938
LET'S SING AGAIN: 1936	#14 – July 1936
LET'S SWING IT: 1935	#12 – July 1935
LET'S TAKE AN OLD-FASHIONED WALK: 1949	# 8 – Sept. 1949
LET'S TAKE THE LONG WAY HOME: 1945	#20 – Feb. 1945
LET'S TALK ABOUT MY SWEETIE: 1926	# 7 – June 1926
LI'L LIZA JANE: 1918	#13 – Mar. 1918
LIBERTY BELL, IT'S TIME TO RING AGAIN: 1918	#20 – Mar. 1918
LIES (H. Barris): 1932	#14 – Jan. 1932
LIES (Randell): 1966	#20 – Jan. 1966
LIFE GITS TEE-JUS, DON'T IT? 1948	#19 – Nov. 1948
LIFE IS A SONG: 1935	# 3 – June 1935
LIFE IS JUST A BOWL OF CHERRIES: 1931	# 9 – Nov. 1931
LIFE'S A FUNNY PROPOSITION AFTER ALL: 1905	# 9 – Mar. 1905
LIGHTS OUT (B. Hill): 1936	# 2 – Mar. 1936
LIGHTS OUT (Wolf): 1984	#12 – Sept. 1984
LILACS IN THE RAIN: 1939	# 4 – Dec. 1939
LILY BELLE: 1945	#16 – Dec. 1945
LILY OF THE VALLEY: 1917	# 3 – July 1917
LIMEHOUSE BLUES: 1924	# 2 – May 1924
LINCOLN, GRANT, OR LEE: 1903	#19 – Dec. 1903
LINDA: 1947	# 2 – Apr. 1947
LINDBERGH, THE EAGLE OF THE U.S.A.: 1927	#10 – Aug. 1927
LINDY LOO: 1900	#13 – June 1900
LINGER AWHILE: 1924	# 1 – Feb. 1924
LINGER IN MY ARMS A LITTLE LONGER, BABY: 1946	#11 – Oct. 1946
LINGER LONGER GIRL, THE: 1906	#12 – Nov. 1906
LISTENING: 1925	#20 – May 1925
LITTLE BIRD TOLD ME, A: 1949	# 1 – Jan. 1949
LITTLE BIT INDEPENDENT, A: 1935	# 1 – Jan. 1936
LITTLE BIT OF HEAVEN, A (E. Ball): 1915	# 1 – May 1915
LITTLE BIT OF HEAVEN, A (Resnick): 1965	#16 – July 1965
LITTLE BOY CALLED TAPS, A: 1904	# 8 – Dec. 1904
LITTLE BUNCH OF SHAMROCKS, A: 1913	#10 – July 1913
LITTLE BUTTERFLY: 1924	#19 – Feb. 1924
LITTLE CHURCH WHERE YOU AND I WERE WED, THE: 1904	#19 – Nov. 1904
LITTLE COQUETTE; *SEE: COQUETTE (C. Lombardo): 1928*	
LITTLE CURLY HAIR IN A HIGH CHAIR: 1940	# 9 – June 1940
LITTLE DID I KNOW: 1944	#19 – Jan. 1944
LITTLE DUTCH MILL, A: 1934	# 1 – May 1934
LITTLE GIRL (F. Henry): 1931	#11 – Aug. 1931
LITTLE GIRL (Gonzalez): 1966	# 8 – July 1966
LITTLE GREY HOME IN THE WEST: 1914	#10 – May 1914
LITTLE GREY MOTHER, THE: 1915	#11 – Dec. 1915
LITTLE HOUSE UPON THE HILL, THE: 1915	# 7 – May 1915
LITTLE KISS EACH MORNING, A: 1930	# 3 – Jan. 1930
LITTLE LADY MAKE BELIEVE: 1938	#11 – July 1938
LITTLE LOVE, A LITTLE KISS, A: 1914	#18 – Mar. 1914
LITTLE MAN, YOU'VE HAD A BUSY DAY: 1934	# 2 – July 1934
LITTLE MAN WHO WASN'T THERE, THE: 1939	#16 – Oct. 1939
LITTLE OLD LADY: 1937	# 2 – Apr. 1937
LITTLE ON THE LONELY SIDE, A: 1945	# 4 – Feb. 1945
LITTLE PAL: 1929	# 7 – Sept. 1929
LITTLE RED FOX, THE: 1940	# 9 – Feb. 1940
LITTLE RED SCHOOLHOUSE; *SEE: IN THE LITTLE RED SCHOOLHOUSE: 1922*	
LITTLE RENDEZVOUS IN HONOLULU, A: 1936	#16 – Mar. 1936
LITTLE SIR ECHO: 1939	# 2 – May 1939
LITTLE SKIPPER: 1939	# 5 – May 1939
LITTLE STREET WHERE OLD FRIENDS MEET, A: 1932	# 1 – Jan. 1933
LITTLE THINGS IN LIFE, THE: 1931	# 4 – Jan. 1931
LITTLE WHITE GARDENIA, A: 1935	# 6 – Mar. 1935
LITTLE WHITE HOUSE (AT THE END OF HONEYMOON LANE), THE: 1927	# 2 – Jan. 1927
LITTLE WHITE LIES (Donaldson): 1930	# 1 – Sept. 1930
LITTLE WHITE LIES (Donaldson): 1948	# 3 – June 1948
LIVERY STABLE BLUES: 1917	#20 – Oct. 1917
LIVIN' IN THE SUNLIGHT, LOVIN' IN THE MOONLIGHT: 1930	#10 – July 1930
LONELY TROUBADOUR: 1929	# 5 – Nov. 1929
LONESOME: 1909	#13 – Aug. 1909
LONESOME AND SORRY: 1926	# 2 – July 1926
LONESOME LOVER: 1931	# 6 – Feb. 1931
LONESOMEST GAL IN TOWN, THE (A. Von Tilzer); *SEE: I'M THE LONESOMEST GAL IN TOWN: 1912*	
LONESOMEST GIRL IN TOWN, THE (McHugh): 1926	#16 – Jan. 1926
LONG AGO AND FAR AWAY: 1944	# 1 – June 1944
LONG BOY (GOODBYE, MA! GOODBYE, PA! GOODBYE, MULE): 1917	#16 – Jan. 1918

LONGING FOR YOU (T. Morse): 1905 .... # 9 – May 1905
LONGING FOR YOU (Dana): 1951 .... #11 – Aug. 1951
LOOK FOR THE SILVER LINING: 1921 .... # 6 – Apr. 1921
LOOK OUT FOR JIMMY VALENTINE; *SEE: JIMMY VALENTINE: 1911*
LOOKIE LOOKIE LOOKIE, HERE COMES COOKIE;
SEE: (Lookie, lookie, lookie) HERE COMES COOKIE: 1935
LOOKING AT THE WORLD THROUGH ROSE-COLORED
GLASSES: 1926 .... # 8 – Oct. 1926
LORRAINE (MY BEAUTIFUL ALSACE LORRAINE): 1918 .... # 6 – May 1918
LOST (Ohman): 1936 .... # 1 – May 1936
LOST (A WONDERFUL GIRL) (Hanley): 1923 .... #20 – Feb. 1923
LOST IN A FOG: 1934 .... # 4 – Nov. 1934
LOUISE: 1929 .... # 3 – June 1929
LOUISIANA: 1928 .... #16 – Nov. 1928
LOUISIANA HAYRIDE: 1932 .... #15 – Dec. 1932
LOUISVILLE LOU, THE VAMPIN' LADY: 1923 .... # 3 – Sept. 1923
LOVABLE: 1932 .... #10 – May 1932
LOVE, HERE IS MY HEART: 1915 .... #14 – Dec. 1915
LOVE, YOU FUNNY THING: 1932 .... # 8 – May 1932
LOVE (YOUR SPELL IS EVERYWHERE): 1929 .... # 4 – Dec. 1929
LOVE AND A DIME: 1935 .... #14 – June 1935
LOVE AND LEARN: 1937 .... #15 – Feb. 1937
LOVE BIRD: 1921 .... #11 – Apr. 1921
LOVE BUG WILL BITE YOU, THE: 1937 .... # 4 – May 1937
LOVE DAYS: 1908 .... #19 – Sept. 1908
LOVE FOR SALE: 1931 .... #20 – Mar. 1931
LOVE IN BLOOM: 1934 .... # 1 – Sept. 1934
LOVE IN THE MOONLIGHT: 1933 .... #10 – Mar. 1933
LOVE IS A DREAM: 1933 .... #11 – Mar. 1933
LOVE IS JUST AROUND THE CORNER: 1935 .... #12 – Feb. 1935
LOVE IS LIKE A CIGARETTE (V. Herbert): 1909 .... #11 – Feb. 1909
LOVE IS LIKE A CIGARETTE (W. Kent): 1936 .... #12 – May 1936
LOVE IS MINE: 1912 .... #13 – June 1912
LOVE IS THE SWEETEST THING: 1933 .... # 3 – Oct. 1933
LOVE LETTERS (V. Young): 1945 .... #12 – Nov. 1945
LOVE LETTERS (V. Young): 1962 .... # 7 – Apr. 1962
LOVE LETTERS (V. Young): 1966 .... #19 – July 1966
LOVE LETTERS IN THE SAND (Coots): 1931 .... # 4 – Oct. 1931
LOVE LETTERS IN THE SAND (Coots): 1957 .... # 1 – June 1957
LOVE LOCKED OUT: 1934 .... #15 – Feb. 1934
LOVE ME (E. Golden): 1929 .... # 4 – Nov. 1929
LOVE ME (Lieber): 1957 .... # 7 – Jan. 1957
LOVE ME (Gibb): 1976 .... #14 – Dec. 1976
LOVE ME (Brathwaite, Vandross): 1998 .... #19 – Dec. 1998
LOVE ME AND THE WORLD IS MINE: 1906 .... # 1 – Dec. 1906
LOVE ME FOREVER: 1935 .... # 4 – Aug. 1935
LOVE ME OR LEAVE ME (Donaldson): 1929 .... #15 – May 1929
LOVE ME OR LEAVE ME (Donaldson): 1955 .... #17 – June 1955
LOVE ME TONIGHT (Rodgers): 1932 .... # 4 – Oct. 1932
LOVE ME TONIGHT (Panzeri): 1969 .... #13 – July 1969
LOVE NEST, THE: 1920 .... # 1 – Sept. 1920
LOVE SENDS A LITTLE GIFT OF ROSES (Openshaw): 1921 .... #12 – Sept. 1921
LOVE SENDS A LITTLE GIFT OF ROSES (Openshaw): 1923 .... #12 – Apr. 1923
LOVE SOMEBODY (Kramer): 1948 .... # 6 – Sept. 1948
LOVE SOMEBODY (Springfield): 1984 .... # 5 – May 1984
LOVE SONGS OF THE NILE: 1933 .... # 4 – June 1933
LOVE TALES: 1923 .... #11 – Nov. 1923
LOVE THY NEIGHBOR: 1934 .... # 1 – June 1934
LOVE WALKED IN (Gershwin): 1938 .... # 1 – May 1938
LOVE WALKED IN (Gershwin): 1953 .... #13 – Nov. 1953
LOVE WILL FIND A WAY (E. Blake): 1921 .... #15 – Oct. 1921
LOVE WILL FIND A WAY (Lerios): 1978 .... # 7 – Aug. 1978
LOVE'S OWN SWEET SONG: 1914 .... #19 – Aug. 1914
LOVE'S ROUNDELAY: 1908 .... #10 – June 1908
LOVELIGHT IN THE STARLIGHT: 1938 .... # 5 – June 1938
LOVELY LADY: 1936 .... #20 – Apr. 1936
LOVELY TO LOOK AT: 1935 .... # 3 – Apr. 1935
LOVELY WAY TO SPEND AN EVENING, A: 1944 .... # 9 – Mar. 1944
LOVER (Rodgers): 1933 .... # 4 – May 1933
LOVER (Rodgers): 1952 .... #12 – July 1952
LOVER, COME BACK TO ME: 1929 .... # 3 – Apr. 1929
LOVER'S LULLABY, A: 1940 .... #13 – May 1940
LOVEY CAME BACK: 1924 .... # 5 – Feb. 1924
LOVIN' SAM, THE SHEIK OF ALABAM': 1923 .... # 2 – Feb. 1923
LUCKY DAY: 1926 .... # 3 – Nov. 1926
LUCKY IN LOVE: 1927 .... # 7 – Nov. 1927
LUCKY LINDY: 1927 .... #13 – Aug. 1927
LULLABY OF BROADWAY: 1935 .... # 1 – Apr. 1935
LULLABY OF THE LEAVES: 1932 .... # 1 – June 1932
LULU'S BACK IN TOWN: 1935 .... #10 – Aug. 1935
LYING IN THE HAY: 1933 .... #10 – June 1933

M

M-I-S-S-I-S-S-I-P-P-I: 1917 .... # 3 – May 1917
M-O-T-H-E-R (Morse): 1916 .... # 1 – Feb. 1916
MA! (HE'S MAKIN' EYES AT ME): 1921 .... # 1 – Nov. 1921
MA BLACK PEARL: 1900 .... # 6 – Nov. 1900
MA BLUSHIN' ROSIE: 1901 .... # 3 – Feb. 1901
MA SCOTCH BLUE BELL; *SEE: I LOVE A LASSIE: 1908*
MA TIGER LILY: 1900 .... # 2 – July 1900
MacNAMARA'S BAND: 1946 .... #16 – Mar. 1946
MACUSHLA: 1912 .... T30 – Jan. 1912
MAD BOOGIE, THE: 1946 .... #20 – June 1946
MADELAINE: 1942 .... #11 – Jan. 1942
MADELON: 1919 .... # 5 – Apr. 1919
MAGIC MELODY, THE: 1915 .... #19 – July 1915
MAGIC OF YOUR EYES, THE: 1917 .... #15 – July 1917
MAGNOLIA: 1927 .... #12 – Aug. 1927
MAH JONG; *SEE: SINCE MA IS PLAYING MAH JONG: 1924*
MAHARAJAH OF MAGADOR, THE: 1948 .... #19 – Aug. 1948
MAIDEN WITH THE DREAMY EYES: 1902 .... # 5 – Mar. 1902
MAINE STEIN SONG; *SEE: STEIN SONG: 1930*
MAIRZY DOATS: 1944 .... # 1 – Apr. 1944
MAKE BELIEVE (T. Morse): 1908 .... # 4 – Mar. 1908
MAKE BELIEVE (J. Shilkret): 1921 .... # 2 – June 1921
MAKE BELIEVE (Kern): 1928 .... #15 – Apr. 1928
MAKE BELIEVE (Kern): 1951 .... #18 – Sept. 1951
MAKE BELIEVE ISLAND: 1940 .... # 1 – July 1940
MAKIN' WHOOPIE: 1929 .... # 6 – Mar. 1929
MAM'SELLE: 1947 .... # 1 – May 1947
MAMA, THAT MOON IS HERE AGAIN: 1938 .... #15 – Feb. 1938
MAMA INEZ: 1931 .... #19 – May 1931
MAMIE: 1901 .... # 4 – July 1901
MAMMA GOES WHERE PAPA GOES: 1924 .... # 5 – Jan. 1924
MAMMA LOVES PAPA (PAPA LOVES MAMMA): 1924 .... # 7 – Feb. 1924
MAMMA'S BOY: 1905 .... # 3 – Feb. 1905
MAMMY JINNY'S JUBILEE: 1913 .... # 9 – Dec. 1913
MAMMY O' MINE: 1919 .... # 2 – July 1919
MAMMY'S CHOCOLATE SOLDIER: 1918 .... #13 – Nov. 1918
MAMMY'S LITTLE COAL BLACK ROSE: 1916 .... # 1 – Jan. 1917
MAN AND HIS DREAM, A: 1939 .... # 8 – Oct. 1939
(It's the) MAN BEHIND THE GUN (J.P. Sousa): 1900 .... # 7 – Aug. 1900
MAN FROM THE SOUTH, THE: 1930 .... # 9 – Feb. 1930

MAN I LOVE, THE: 1928	# 4 – May 1928
MAN ON THE FLYING TRAPEZE, THE: 1934	# 8 – July 1934
MAN WITH THE LADDER AND THE HOSE, THE: 1904	# 9 – Aug. 1904
MAN WITH THE MANDOLIN, THE: 1939	# 2 – Sept. 1939
MANAGUA, NICARAGUA: 1947	# 2 – Mar. 1947
MANANA: 1948	# 2 – Apr. 1948
MANDALAY: 1924	# 3 – Sept. 1924
MANDY (Berlin): 1919	# 1 – Oct. 1919
MANDY (English): 1975	# 1 – Jan. 1975
MANDY, MAKE UP YOUR MIND: 1925	#12 – Jan. 1925
MANDY 'N' ME: 1921	#16 – Dec. 1921
MANHATTAN: 1925	# 5 – Oct. 1925
MANHATTAN SERENADE (Alter): 1928	#19 – June 1928
MANHATTAN SERENADE (Alter): 1942	# 6 – Nov. 1942
MANSION OF ACHING HEARTS, THE: 1902	# 2 – May 1902
MANY HAPPY RETURNS OF THE DAY: 1931	# 2 – Sept. 1931
MARCH OF THE TOYS: 1904	#15 – Feb. 1904
MARCH OF THE VAGABONDS, THE; *SEE: SONG OF THE VAGABONDS, THE: 1926*	
MARCHETA: 1923	# 5 – Oct. 1923
MARGIE: 1921	# 1 – Feb. 1921
MARIA ELENA (Barcelata): 1941	# 1 – July 1941
MARIA ELENA (Barcelata): 1963	# 6 – Nov. 1963
MARIE (Berlin): 1929	# 2 – Feb. 1929
MARIE (Berlin): 1937	#11 – Apr. 1937
MARIE (Berlin): 1954	#17 – Jan. 1954
MARIE (Berlin): 1965	#15 – July 1965
MARINES' HYMN, THE: 1942	#17 – July 1942
MARTHA: 1938	#13 – June 1938
MARY, YOU'RE A LITTLE BIT OLD FASHIONED: 1914	# 7 – Aug. 1914
MARY ANN: 1928	# 5 – May 1928
MARY LOU: 1927	# 4 – Jan. 1927
MARY'S A GRAND OLD NAME: 1906	#14 – Apr. 1906
MASQUERADE: 1932	# 3 – Aug. 1932
MASQUERADE IS OVER, THE: 1939	# 5 – Apr. 1939
MAY I? 1934	#10 – May 1934
MAY I HAVE THE NEXT ROMANCE WITH YOU? 1937	#13 – Mar. 1937
MAY I NEVER LOVE AGAIN: 1941	#13 – Feb. 1941
MAYBE (Flynn): 1940	# 2 – Oct. 1940
MAYBE (Flynn): 1952	# 8 – Aug. 1952
MAYBE (IT'S BECAUSE) I LOVE YOU TOO MUCH: 1933	#12 – June 1933
MAYBE IT'S BECAUSE: 1949	# 5 – Sept. 1949
MAYBE YOU'LL BE THERE: 1948	# 5 – Nov. 1948
MAYTIME: 1924	#17 – Oct. 1924
MAZIE: 1921	#15 – Apr. 1921
ME! 1931	# 6 – Oct. 1931
ME, MYSELF AND I (ARE ALL IN LOVE WITH YOU): 1937	#20 – Aug. 1937
ME AND MY MELINDA: 1942	#16 – Apr. 1942
ME AND MY SHADOW: 1927	# 1 – Aug. 1927
ME AND THE MAN IN THE MOON: 1929	#18 – Mar. 1929
ME AND THE MOON: 1936	# 6 – Oct. 1936
ME TOO: 1926	# 5 – Nov. 1926
ME-OW: 1919	#19 – July 1919
MEAN TO ME (Ahlert): 1929	# 3 – May 1929
MEAN TO ME (Ahlert): 1937	#19 – July 1937
MEET ME IN ST. LOUIS, LOUIS (K. Mills): 1904	# 1 – July 1904
MEET ME IN ST. LOUIS, LOUIS (K. Mills): 1945	#19 – Jan. 1945
MEET ME TONIGHT IN DREAMLAND: 1910	# 1 – July 1910
MELINDA'S WEDDING DAY: 1913	# 5 – June 1913
MELODY FROM THE SKY, A: 1936	# 1 – May 1936
MEMORIES: 1916	# 1 – Apr. 1916
MEMORIES OF FRANCE: 1928	# 4 – Oct. 1928
MEMORY LANE: 1924	# 4 – Oct. 1924
MEMPHIS BLUES, THE: 1914	#17 – Nov. 1914
MERRY WIDOW WALTZ, THE; *SEE: I LOVE YOU SO: 1908*	
MERRY-GO-ROUND BROKE DOWN, THE: 1937	# 1 – July 1937
MERRY-GO-ROUND WALTZ: 1949	#17 – June 1949
MESSAGE OF THE VIOLET, THE: 1903	# 3 – Feb. 1903
MEXICALI ROSE (Tenney): 1924	#15 – June 1924
MEXICALI ROSE (Tenney): 1938	#16 – Nov. 1938
MICK WHO THREW THE BRICK, THE: 1900	#14 – June 1900
MICKEY (Moret): 1919	# 2 – Feb. 1919
MICKEY (Moret): 1947	#11 – Nov. 1947
MICKEY (Chinn): 1982	# 1 – Dec. 1982
MIDNIGHT BLUE (Burke): 1936	#14 – Dec. 1936
MIDNIGHT BLUE (Manchester): 1975	# 6 – Aug. 1975
MIDNIGHT BLUE (Gramm): 1987	# 5 – Apr. 1987
MIDNIGHT FIRE ALARM: 1900	# 4 – Sept. 1900
MIDNIGHT MASQUERADE: 1947	#10 – July 1947
MIDNIGHT ROSE: 1923	#13 – Nov. 1923
MIDNIGHT WALTZ: 1925	# 8 – July 1925
MIGHTY LAK' A ROSE: 1902	#16 – June 1902
MILENBERG JOYS: 1925	#11 – Sept. 1925
MILKMAN, KEEP THOSE BOTTLES QUIET: 1944	# 9 – July 1944
MILLION DREAMS AGO, A: 1940	#18 – Nov. 1940
MILO: 1906	# 9 – Aug. 1906
MIMI: 1932	#17 – Sept. 1932
MINDIN' MY BUS'NESS: 1924	#11 – May 1924
MINE: 1933	#19 – Dec. 1933
MINNIE THE MOOCHER: 1931	#18 – May 1931
MISS ANNABELLE LEE: 1927	# 1 – Nov. 1927
MISS YOU (Tobias): 1929	#12 – Sept. 1929
MISS YOU (Tobias): 1942	# 5 – Apr. 1942
MISS YOU (K. Richards): 1978	# 1 – Aug. 1978
MISSISSIPPI MUD: 1928	#15 – June 1928
MISSOURI WALTZ (HUSH-A-BYE MA BABY) (Eppell): 1916	#19 – Aug. 1916
Reached second peak at	#19 – Apr. 1917
MISSOURI WALTZ (HUSH-A-BYE MA BABY) (Eppell): 1918	# 4 – May 1918
MOANIN' LOW: 1929	# 5 – Sept. 1929
MOLLIE (A DAINTY BIT OF JOLLY): 1903	# 7 – Apr. 1903
MOLLY DEAR, IT'S YOU I'M AFTER: 1916	# 8 – Feb. 1916
MOMENT I MET YOU, THE: 1946	#19 – Feb. 1946
MON COEUR EST POUR TOI; *SEE: LOVE, HERE IS MY HEART: 1915*	
MON HOMME; *SEE: MY MAN: 1921*	
MONEY IS THE ROOT OF ALL EVIL (TAKE IT AWAY): 1946	#18 – Feb. 1946
(Honky Tonky) MONKEY RAG: 1911	#12 – Jan. 1912
MONTMARTRE ROSE: 1925	# 9 – Oct. 1925
MOOD INDIGO: 1931	#16 – Mar. 1931
MOON GOT IN MY EYES, THE: 1937	# 3 – Oct. 1937
MOON IS A SILVER DOLLAR, THE: 1939	#10 – Apr. 1939
MOON IS LOW, THE: 1930	# 5 – May 1930
MOON LOVE: 1939	# 1 – Sept. 1939
MOON OF MANAKOORA, THE: 1938	#13 – Mar. 1938
MOON OVER MIAMI: 1936	# 2 – Feb. 1936
MOON RIVER (David): 1922	#15 – June 1922
MOON RIVER (Mancini): 1961	# 2 – Dec. 1961
MOON SHINES ON THE MOONSHINE, THE: 1920	#20 – May 1920
MOON SONG: 1933	# 2 – Feb. 1933
MOON-FACED, STARRY-EYED: 1947	#20 – May 1947
MOONBEAM! KISS HER FOR ME: 1927	#16 – May 1927
MOONBEAMS: 1907	#14 – Mar. 1907
MOONGLOW (DeLange): 1934	# 6 – Aug. 1934
MOONGLOW (DeLange): 1956; *SEE: MOONGLOW AND THEME FROM PICNIC: 1956*	
MOONGLOW & THEME FROM PICNIC: 1956	# 1 – June 1956
MOONLIGHT (SERENADE) (N. Moret): 1905	# 6 – June 1905
MOONLIGHT (Conrad): 1921	#12 – Oct. 1921

MOONLIGHT AND ROSES: 1925 ... # 2 – Oct. 1925
MOONLIGHT AND SHADOWS: 1937 ... # 1 – Mar. 1937
MOONLIGHT BAY (Wenrich): 1912 ... # 1 – July 1912
MOONLIGHT BAY (Wenrich): 1951 ... #19 – May 1951
MOONLIGHT BECOMES YOU: 1943 ... # 1 – Feb. 1943
MOONLIGHT COCKTAIL: 1942 ... # 1 – Apr. 1942
MOONLIGHT IN VERMONT: 1945 ... #20 – Feb. 1945
MOONLIGHT MOOD: 1943 ... # 8 – Feb. 1943
MOONLIGHT ON THE COLORADO: 1930 ... # 3 – Dec. 1930
MOONLIGHT ON THE GANGES: 1927 ... # 3 – Jan. 1927
MOONLIGHT SAVING TIME: 1931 ... # 1 – June 1931
MOONLIGHT SERENADE (G. Miller): 1939 ... # 9 – Sept. 1939
MORE AND MORE (Kern): 1945 ... #10 – Mar. 1945
MORE AND MORE (Schein): 1993 ... #17 – June 1993
MORE I SEE YOU, THE (Warren): 1945 ... # 7 – July 1945
MORE I SEE YOU, THE (Warren): 1966 ... #16 – June 1966
MORE THAN EVER (I. Jones): 1938 ... #11 – Mar. 1938
MORE THAN EVER (Nelson): 1991 ... #14 – May 1991
MORE THAN YOU KNOW (Youmans): 1930 ... #17 – Jan. 1930
MORE THAN YOU KNOW (Martika): 1989 ... #18 – Apr. 1989
MORNING AFTER THE NIGHT BEFORE, THE: 1910 ... #20 – Aug. 1910
MORNING CY: 1908 ... # 9 – Feb. 1909
MOSQUITO'S PARADE, THE: 1900 ... #11 – Dec. 1900
MOTHER (Romberg): 1917 ... #19 – Apr. 1917
MOTHER (Morse): *SEE; M-O-T-H-E-R*
MOTHER MACHREE (E. Ball): 1912 ... # 9 – Feb. 1912
MOTHER MACHREE (E. Ball): 1914 ... #17 – Oct. 1914
MOTHER'S GIFT TO HER COUNTRY, A; *SEE: BLUE AND THE GRAY, THE: 1900*
MOUNTAIN GREENERY: 1926 ... #20 – Sept. 1926
MOVE IT OVER: 1943 ... #20 – Feb. 1943
MR. AND MRS. IS THE NAME: 1934 ... #15 – Dec. 1934
MR. DOOLEY: 1902 ... # 1 – Dec. 1902
MR. FIVE BY FIVE: 1942 ... # 3 – Dec. 1942
MR. GALLAGHER AND MR. SHEAN: 1922 ... # 1 – Nov. 1922
MR. VOLUNTEER: 1901 ... # 6 – Dec. 1901
MUCH OBLIGED TO YOU;
SEE: BEST I GET IS MUCH OBLIGED TO YOU, THE: 1908
MUDDY WATER: 1927 ... # 3 – June 1927
MULE TRAIN: 1949 ... # 1 – Dec. 1949
"MURDER" HE SAYS: 1943 ... #14 – May 1943
MUSETTE: 1908 ... #20 – Feb. 1908
MUSIC, MAESTRO, PLEASE (Wrubel): 1938 ... # 1 – July 1938
MUSIC, MAESTRO, PLEASE (Wrubel): 1950 ... #19 – Sept. 1950
MUSIC GOES 'ROUND AND AROUND: 1936 ... # 1 – Jan. 1936
MUSIC MAKERS: 1941 ... #20 – May 1941
MUSIC MAKES ME: 1934 ... #17 – Mar. 1934
MY ADOBE HACIENDA: 1947 ... # 4 – May 1947
MY ANGEL; *SEE: ANGELA MIA: 1928*
MY BABY JUST CARES FOR ME: 1930 ... #10 – Oct. 1930
MY BABY'S ARMS: 1919 ... #19 – Jan. 1920
MY BARNEY LIES OVER THE OCEAN (JUST THE WAY HE LIED TO ME): 1919 ... #18 – July 1919
MY BEAUTIFUL LADY: 1911 ... # 7 – Dec. 1911
MY BELGIAN ROSE: 1918 ... # 4 – Sept. 1918
MY BESSIE'S WEDDING DAY: 1903 ... # 8 – Aug. 1903
MY BEST GIRL: 1925 ... # 2 – Feb. 1925
MY BIRD OF PARADISE: 1915 ... # 3 – July 1915
MY BLACKBIRDS ARE BLUEBIRDS NOW: 1929 ... #14 – Jan. 1929
MY BLUE HEAVEN: 1928 ... # 1 – Jan. 1928
MY BLUE MOUNTAIN HOME; *SEE: MY BLUE RIDGE MOUNTAIN HOME: 1928*
MY BLUE RIDGE MOUNTAIN HOME: 1928 ... #17 – Jan. 1928
MY BOLERO: 1949 ... #19 – Sept. 1949
MY BRUDDAH SYLVEST': 1908 ... # 7 – Dec. 1908
MY BUDDY: 1923 ... # 1 – Dec. 1922
MY CABIN OF DREAMS: 1937 ... # 3 – Sept. 1937
MY CAROLINA CAROLINE: 1902 ... # 4 – Mar. 1902
MY CASTLE ON THE NILE: 1901 ... # 5 – Dec. 1901
MY COUSIN CARUS': 1909 ... # 2 – Aug. 1909
MY COZY CORNER GIRL; *SEE: IN A COZY CORNER: 1902*
MY CROONY MELODY: 1914 ... #11 – Oct. 1914
MY DARLING: 1933 ... # 4 – Feb. 1933
MY DARLING, MY DARLING: 1948 ... # 3 – Dec. 1948
MY DEVOTION: 1942 ... # 1 – Sept. 1942
MY DREAM GIRL: 1924 ... # 8 – Nov. 1924
MY DREAM OF THE BIG PARADE: 1926 ... #14 – Aug. 1926
MY DREAMS ARE GETTING BETTER ALL THE TIME: 1945 ... # 1 – Apr. 1945
MY DREAMY CHINA LADY: 1916 ... #20 – June 1916
MY ELINORE: 1901 ... #11 – May 1901
MY EXTRAORDINARY GAL: 1932 ... # 7 – June 1932
MY FATE IS IN YOUR HANDS: 1930 ... #14 – Jan. 1930
MY FUTURE JUST PASSED: 1930 ... # 6 – Aug. 1930
MY GAL SAL: 1906 ... # 3 – Oct. 1906
MY GIRL FROM DIXIE: 1901 ... #14 – Mar. 1901
MY HAPPINESS (Bergantine): 1948 ... # 1 – Aug. 1948
MY HAPPINESS (Bergantine): 1959 ... # 3 – Jan. 1959
MY HAT'S ON THE SIDE OF MY HEAD: 1934 ... #18 – Aug. 1934
MY HAWAIIAN SUNSHINE: 1917 ... # 4 – Feb. 1917
MY HEART BELONGS TO DADDY: 1939 ... #15 – Mar. 1939
MY HEART HAS LEARNED TO LOVE YOU, NOW DO NOT SAY GOODBYE: 1910 ... # 5 – Oct. 1910
(All of a sudden) MY HEART SINGS (Herpin): 1945 ... #15 – Mar. 1945
(All of a sudden) MY HEART SINGS (Herpin): 1959 ... #14 – Feb. 1959
MY HEART STOOD STILL: 1928 ... # 4 – Feb. 1928
MY HEART TELLS ME: 1944 ... # 1 – Jan. 1944
MY HEART'S TONIGHT IN TEXAS: 1900 ... # 7 – Nov. 1900
MY HERO: 1911 ... #11 – Aug. 1911
MY HOME TOWN IS A ONE-HORSE TOWN: 1920 ... # 7 – Jan. 1921
MY HONEY'S LOVIN' ARMS: 1922 ... #13 – July 1922
MY IDEAL (R. Whiting): 1931 ... #16 – Jan. 1931
MY IDEAL (R. Whiting): 1944 ... # 5 – Jan. 1944
MY INDIANA HOME; *SEE: INDIANA: 1917*
MY IRISH MOLLY-O: 1905 ... # 1 – Sept. 1905
MY IRISH ROSIE: 1907 ... # 7 – Feb. 1907
MY ISLE OF GOLDEN DREAMS: 1920 ... # 3 – Feb. 1920
MY JERSEY LILY: 1900 ... # 3 – June 1900
MY LADY HOTTENTOT: 1901 ... # 6 – Oct. 1901
(This is) MY LAST AFFAIR: 1937 ... #17 – Apr. 1937
MY LAST GOODBYE: 1939 ... #19 – July 1939
MY LIFE, I LOVE THEE; *SEE: ROSE OF THE WORLD: 1909*
MY LITTLE BIMBO (FROM THE BAMBOO ISLE): 1920 ... # 9 – Nov. 1920
MY LITTLE BUCKAROO: 1937 ... #19 – Apr. 1937
MY LITTLE CHIMPANZEE; *SEE: IN ZANZIBAR: 1904*
MY LITTLE DREAM GIRL: 1915 ... # 1 – Sept. 1915
MY LITTLE GIRL: 1915 ... # 6 – Sept. 1915
MY LITTLE GRASS SHACK IN KEALEKUA, HAWAII: 1934 ... # 1 – Apr. 1934
MY LITTLE NEST OF HEAVENLY BLUE: 1926 ... # 5 – Aug. 1926
MY LITTLE ZULU BABE: 1901 ... #10 – Jan. 1901
MY LOVIN' HONEY MAN: 1911 ... # 7 – Dec. 1911
MY LUCKY STAR: 1929 ... #19 – Apr. 1929
MY MAMMY (Donaldson): 1921 ... # 1 – May 1921
MY MAMMY (Donaldson): 1967 ... #13 – Aug. 1967
MY MAN: 1921 ... # 2 – Sept. 1921
MY MARGARITA: 1938 ... #19 – July 1938
MY MARIUCCIA TAKE A STEAMBOAT: 1907 ... # 3 – Jan. 1907
MY MELANCHOLY BABY (E. Burnett): 1928 ... #15 – Mar. 1928
MY MELANCHOLY BABY (E. Burnett): 1947 ... #10 – May 1947

MY MISSISSIPPI SUE: 1902	# 7 – Feb. 1902
MY MOM: 1932	# 4 – May 1932
MY MOONLIGHT MADONNA: 1933	#10 – Sept. 1933
MY MOTHER WAS A NORTHERN GIRL: 1902	#17 – July 1902
MY MOTHER'S EYES: 1929	#10 – Apr. 1929
MY MOTHER'S ROSARY: 1916	# 3 – May 1916
MY ONE AND ONLY HIGHLAND FLING: 1949	#18 – July 1949
MY OWN: 1938	# 6 – Dec. 1938
MY OWN IONA: 1916	# 2 – Sept. 1916
MY OWN UNITED STATES (J. Edwards): 1903	# 3 – Mar. 1903
MY OWN UNITED STATES (J. Edwards): 1909	# 7 – Jan. 1909
MY PONY BOY: 1909	# 1 – Aug. 1909
MY PRAYER (Boulanger): 1939	# 3 – Nov. 1939
MY PRAYER (Boulanger): 1956	# 1 – Aug. 1956
MY REVERIE: 1938	# 1 – Nov. 1938
MY SHINING HOUR: 1944	# 8 – Jan. 1944
MY SILENT LOVE: 1932	# 2 – July 1932
MY SIN: 1929	# 4 – July 1929
MY SISTER AND I: 1941	# 2 – June 1941
MY SONG: 1931	#15 – Nov. 1931
MY SONG OF THE NILE: 1929	# 2 – Oct. 1929
MY SUNBEAM FROM THE SOUTH: 1900	#19 – June 1900
MY SUNNY TENNESSEE: 1921	# 5 – Dec. 1921
MY SUNSHINE JANE: 1917	T30 – Dec. 1917
MY SWEET ADAIR: 1915	# 1 – Dec. 1915
MY SWEET KIMONA: 1901	#15 – Aug. 1901
MY SWEETER THAN SWEET: 1930	#11 – Jan. 1930
MY SWEETIE TURNED ME DOWN: 1925	# 6 – Oct. 1925
MY SWEETIE WENT AWAY: 1923	# 3 – Oct. 1923
MY WIFE'S GONE TO THE COUNTRY (HURAH! HURAH!): 1909	# 3 – Sept. 1909

N

N'EVERYTHING: 1918	#11 – July 1918
NAGASAKI: 1928	#13 – Nov. 1928
NANCY (WITH THE LAUGHING FACE): 1945	#20 – Dec. 1945
NANCY BROWN: 1902	# 4 – Aug. 1902
NASTY MAN: 1934	#12 – May 1934
NAT'AN, FOR WHAT ARE YOU WAITIN', NAT'AN? 1916	#16 – June 1916
NATIONAL EMBLEM MARCH: 1912	#20 – Aug. 1912
NATURE BOY: 1948	# 1 – May 1948
NAUGHTY! NAUGHTY! NAUGHTY! 1917	#12 – Feb. 1917
NAVAJO: 1904	# 1 – Mar. 1904
NEAPOLITAN NIGHTS (Zamecnik): 1926	#17 – July 1926
NEAPOLITAN NIGHTS (Zamecnik): 1928	# 9 – Nov. 1928
NEAR YOU (F. Craig): 1947	# 1 – Oct. 1947
NEAR YOU (F. Craig): 1958	# 8 – Oct. 1958
NEARNESS OF YOU, THE: 1940	# 6 – Sept. 1940
'NEATH THE SOUTH SEA MOON: 1922	# 2 – Sept. 1922
NEED YOU: 1949	#11 – May 1949
NEEDLE IN A HAYSTACK, A: 1934	#13 – Nov. 1934
NEIGHBORS: 1934	#15 – Apr. 1934
NELLIE KELLY, I LOVE YOU: 1922	# 5 – Nov. 1922
NEVER A DAY GOES BY: 1943	#20 – July 1943
NEVER IN A MILLION YEARS: 1937	# 4 – June 1937
NEVER NO LAMENT; *SEE: DO NOTHIN' TILL YOU HEAR FROM ME: 1944*	
NEVERTHELESS (H. Ruby): 1931	# 8 – July 1931
NEVERTHELESS (H. Ruby): 1950	# 2 – Dec. 1950
NEW MOON AND AN OLD SERENADE, A: 1939	# 9 – June 1939
NEW MOON IS OVER MY SHOULDER, A: 1934	#19 – Sept. 1934
NEW SAN ANTONIO ROSE; *SEE: SAN ANTONIO ROSE: 1941, 1961*	
NEW SUN IN THE SKY: 1931	#19 – Aug. 1931
NEXT TO YOUR MOTHER, WHO DO YOU LOVE? 1909	# 9 – Dec. 1909
NICE WORK IF YOU CAN GET IT: 1937	# 3 – Dec. 1937
NIGHT AND DAY: 1933	# 1 – Jan. 1933
(Don't wait till) THE NIGHT BEFORE CHRISTMAS: 1938	#10 – Dec. 1938
NIGHT IS YOUNG AND YOU'RE SO BEAUTIFUL, THE: 1937	# 5 – Feb. 1937
NIGHT MUST FALL (OVER ALL): 1939	#20 – May 1939
NIGHT WHEN LOVE WAS BORN, THE: 1932	#18 – Aug. 1932
NIGHTINGALE (X. Cugat): 1942	#16 – June 1942
NIGHTINGALE (C. King): 1975	# 9 – Mar. 1975
NIGHTINGALE SANG IN BERKELEY SQUARE, A: 1940	# 2 – Dec. 1940
NIGHTS OF GLADNESS: 1914	# 7 – Mar. 1914
NO, NO, NORA: 1923	# 2 – Nov. 1923
NO CAN DO: 1945	#15 – Nov. 1945
NO LETTER TODAY: 1943	#17 – Sept. 1943
NO LOVE, NO NOTHIN': 1944	# 4 – Mar. 1944
NO OTHER ONE: 1935	# 7 – Dec. 1935
NO REGRETS: 1936	# 7 – Aug. 1936
NO STRINGS (I'M FANCY FREE): 1935	#18 – Oct. 1935
NO WEDDING BELLS FOR ME: 1907	# 5 – Sept. 1907
NOBODY (B. Williams): 1905	# 7 – Sept. 1905
NOBODY (B. Williams): 1906	#19 – Sept. 1906
NOBODY (Fleming): 1982	#15 – Nov. 1982
NOBODY (Sweat): 1996	# 3 – Dec. 1996
NOBODY KNOWS, AND NOBODY SEEMS TO CARE (Berlin): 1919	# 2 – Dec. 1919
NOBODY KNOWS, NOBODY CARES (Harris): 1909	# 4 – May 1909
NOBODY KNOWS WHAT A RED-HEADED MAMA CAN DO: 1925	#16 – Mar. 1925
NOBODY LIED: 1922	# 8 – Sept. 1922
NOBODY'S LITTLE GIRL: 1907	# 6 – June 1907
NOBODY'S LOOKING BUT THE OWL AND THE MOON: 1903	# 3 – June 1903
NOBODY'S SWEETHEART: 1924	# 3 – June 1924
NOLA (Arndt): 1922	# 8 – July 1922
NOLA (Arndt): 1924	#14 – July 1924
NOLA (Arndt): 1950	#11 – Aug. 1950
NORWAY: 1915	#17 – Oct. 1915
NOT BECAUSE YOUR HAIR IS CURLY: 1906	# 7 – July 1906
NOW I LAY ME DOWN TO DREAM: 1940	# 9 – Nov. 1940
NOW IS THE HOUR: 1948	# 1 – Mar. 1948
NOW IT CAN BE TOLD: 1938	# 2 – Sept. 1938
NOW THAT I NEED YOU: 1949	#13 – Oct. 1949
NOW THAT YOU'RE GONE: 1931	# 7 – Nov. 1931
NOW YOU'RE IN MY ARMS: 1931	# 6 – July 1931
NOW'S THE TIME TO FALL IN LOVE: 1932	#11 – Feb. 1932
NUMBER TEN LULLABY LANE: 1941	#12 – May 1941

O

O DEATH, WHERE IS THY STING? 1919	#20 – Feb. 1919
O KATHARINA; *SEE: OH, KATHARINA: 1925*	
O-HI-O (OH MY-O); *SEE: DOWN BY THE OHIO: 1921*	
O-OO, ERNEST (ARE YOU EARNEST WITH ME?): 1922	# 7 – June 1922
OBJECT OF MY AFFECTION, THE: 1934	# 1 – Jan. 1935
OCEANA ROLL: 1911	# 2 – Sept. 1911
OF THEE I SING: 1932	#20 – Mar. 1932
OH! (B. Gay): 1920	#12 – Apr. 1920
OH! (B. Gay): 1953	# 3 – Oct. 1953
OH, BUT I DO! 1947	# 7 – Jan. 1947
OH, DIDN'T HE RAMBLE: 1902	# 4 – Sept. 1902
OH! FRENCHY: 1918	# 9 – Oct. 1918
OH! GEE, OH! GOSH, OH! GOLLY, I'M IN LOVE: 1923	# 2 – Sept. 1923
OH! HOW I HATE TO GET UP IN THE MORNING: 1918	# 3 – Nov. 1918

OH! HOW I LAUGH WHEN I THINK HOW I CRIED OVER YOU: 1920 # 7 – May 1920
OH, HOW I MISS YOU TONIGHT: 1925 .... # 3 – July 1925
OH! HOW I WISH I COULD SLEEP UNTIL MY DADDY COMES HOME: 1918 .... # 3 – Nov. 1918
OH! HOW SHE COULD YACKI, HACKI, WICKI, WACKI, WOO: 1916 . # 6 – Nov. 1916
OH, KATHARINA! 1925 .... # 2 – May 1925
OH, LADY BE GOOD: 1925 .... # 8 – Mar. 1925
OH, LOOK AT ME NOW: 1941 .... # 4 – Apr. 1941
OH! MA-MA: 1938...................................... # 8 – July 1938
OH, MABEL: 1925...................................... #12 – Apr. 1925
OH, MISS MALINDA: 1909 .... # 4 – Apr. 1909
OH, MR. DREAM MAN: 1912 .... # 6 – June 1912
OH! OH! DELPHINE: 1913 .... #19 – Jan. 1913
OH, SHINING LIGHT: 1900 .... #10 – Nov. 1900
OH, WHAT A BEAUTIFUL MORNIN': 1943 .... # 4 – Dec. 1943
OH! WHAT A PAL WAS MARY: 1919......................... # 1 – Dec. 1919
OH! WHAT IT SEEMED TO BE: 1946 .... # 1 – Mar. 1946
OH, WOULDN'T IT JAR YOU?
SEE: WOULDN'T IT MAKE YOU MAD, WOULDN'T IT JAR YOU? 1900
OH, YOU BEAR CAT RAG: 1911 .... T30 – Feb. 1911
OH, YOU BEAUTIFUL DOLL: 1912 .... # 1 – Feb. 1912
OH! YOU CIRCUS DAY: 1912.............................. # 2 – Aug. 1912
OH, YOU CRAZY MOON: 1939.............................. # 3 – Sept. 1939
OH, YOU KID! 1908 .... #14 – Oct. 1908
OH, YOU MILLION DOLLAR DOLL: 1913 .... #12 – Dec. 1913
OH BY JINGO, OH BY GEE! (YOU'RE THE ONLY GIRL FOR ME): 1920 .... # 4 – June 1920
OH JOHNNY, OH JOHNNY, OH! (Olman): 1917 .... # 2 – June 1917
OH JOHNNY, OH JOHNNY, OH! (Olman): 1939 .... # 3 – Jan. 1940
OH ME! OH MY! (OH YOU!): 1921 .... #13 – Sept. 1921
OH POP-OH POP-OH POP; *SEE: HERE COMES MY DADDY NOW: 1913*
OL' MAN MOSE: 1938 .... #12 – Sept. 1938
OL' MAN RIVER: 1928................................... # 8 – May 1928
OLD APPLE TREE, THE: 1938 .... #14 – Apr. 1938
OLD DEVIL MOON: 1947 .... #15 – June 1947
OLD FAITHFUL (Holzmann): 1907 .... # 7 – Nov. 1907
OLD FASHION LOVE (M. Williams): 1980 .... #20 – Aug. 1980
OLD FASHIONED LOVE (J.P. Johnson): 1924 .... #18 – Feb. 1924
OLD GREY MARE, THE: 1918.............................. #15 – Feb. 1918
OLD LAMP-LIGHTER, THE (N. Simon): 1946 .... # 1 – Dec. 1946
OLD LAMP-LIGHTER, THE (N. Simon): 1960 .... # 6 – May 1960
OLD MAN JAZZ: 1920 .... #19 – June 1920
OLD MAN SUNSHINE: 1928 .... # 5 – Nov. 1928
OLD NEW ENGLAND MOON: 1930 .... #14 – Aug. 1930
OLD PAL, WHY DON'T YOU ANSWER ME? 1921 .... # 3 – Feb. 1921
OLD SPINNING WHEEL: 1934 .... # 1 – Jan. 1934
OLE BUTTERMILK SKY: 1946.............................. # 1 – Dec. 1946
OLE EPH'S VISION: 1900 .... # 9 – Mar. 1900
OLE FAITHFUL (Kennedy): 1935 .... #11 – Mar. 1935
ON A BUS; *SEE: US ON A BUS: 1936*
ON A LITTLE BAMBOO BRIDGE: 1937........................ #10 – Mar. 1937
ON A LITTLE DREAM RANCH: 1937 .... #20 – June 1937
ON A SATURDAY NIGHT: 1902 .... # 6 – June 1902
ON A SLOW BOAT TO CHINA: 1948 .... # 2 – Nov. 1948
ON A SUNDAY AFTERNOON: 1902 .... # 1 – Apr. 1902
ON MIAMI SHORE: 1920 .... # 5 – Feb. 1920
ON MOBILE BAY: 1911 .... #10 – June 1911
ON THE 5:15: 1915 .... # 2 – Mar. 1915
ON THE ALAMO: 1922 .... # 8 – Aug. 1922
ON THE ATCHISON, TOPEKA, AND THE SANTA FE: 1945........ # 1 – Aug. 1945
ON THE BEACH AT BALI BALI: 1936 .... # 3 – Aug. 1936
ON THE BEACH AT WAIKIKI: 1916 .... #19 – July 1916
ON THE BEACH WITH YOU: 1931............................ #16 – July 1931
ON THE FIRING LINE: 1900 .... #14 – July 1900
ON THE GIN-GIN-GINNY SHORE: 1922 .... # 1 – Apr. 1922
ON THE GOOD SHIP LOLLIPOP: 1935 .... # 3 – Feb. 1935
ON THE GOOD SHIP MARY ANN: 1914........................ # 7 – Apr. 1914
ON THE ISLE OF MAY: 1940 .... # 3 – Apr. 1940
ON THE MISSISSIPPI: 1913 .... # 1 – Feb. 1913
ON THE OLD FALL RIVER LINE: 1913 .... # 6 – Nov. 1913
ON THE ROAD TO HOME SWEET HOME: 1918 .... #18 – Apr. 1918
ON THE SENTIMENTAL SIDE: 1938 .... # 5 – May 1938
ON THE SHORES OF TRIPOLI; *SEE: TRIPOLI: 1920*
ON THE SOUTH SEA ISLE: 1916............................ #13 – Oct. 1916
ON THE SUNNY SIDE OF THE STREET: 1930.................. #12 – May 1930
ON TREASURE ISLAND: 1935............................... # 2 – Nov. 1935
ONCE IN AWHILE (M. Edwards): 1937...................... # 1 – Dec. 1937
ONCE IN AWHILE (M. Edwards): 1952...................... #16 – July 1952
ONCE IN AWHILE (M. Edwards): 1961...................... #15 – Jan. 1961
ONCE IN LOVE WITH AMY: 1949 .... #20 – May 1949
ONE, TWO, BUTTON YOUR SHOE: 1937....................... #11 – Jan. 1937
ONE ALONE: 1927 .... #11 – Mar. 1927
ONE DOZEN ROSES: 1942 .... # 5 – June 1942
ONE HAS MY NAME (THE OTHER HAS MY HEART) (Dean): 1948 #20 – Nov. 1948
ONE HAS MY NAME (THE OTHER HAS MY HEART) (Dean): 1966 #13 – Jan. 1966
ONE HOUR WITH YOU: 1932 .... # 2 – May 1932
ONE I LOVE BELONGS TO SOMEBODY ELSE, THE: 1924 .... # 2 – Apr. 1924
ONE MINUTE TO ONE: 1934 .... #16 – Jan. 1934
ONE MORE TIME: 1931 .... #12 – June 1931
ONE MORE TOMORROW: 1946 .... #14 – Aug. 1946
ONE NIGHT IN MONTE CARLO: 1936......................... #14 – Jan. 1936
ONE NIGHT OF LOVE: 1934 .... # 7 – Nov. 1934
ONE ROSE, THE: 1937 .... # 6 – Nov. 1937
ONE STRIKE, TWO STRIKES, THREE STRIKES OUT: 1902 ...... # 9 – Apr. 1902
ONE-ZY, TWO-ZY (I LOVE YOU-ZY): 1946 .... # 2 – Apr. 1946
ONLY A ROSE: 1926 .... #18 – Feb. 1926
ONLY A SOLDIER BOY: 1903.............................. #12 – June 1903
ONLY FOREVER: 1940..................................... # 1 – Oct. 1940
ONLY MAKE BELIEVE; *SEE: MAKE BELIEVE (Kern): 1928, 1951*
OOGIE OOGIE WA WA: 1922............................... #19 – June 1922
OOH! THAT KISS: 1932................................... #10 – Jan. 1932
OPEN THE DOOR, RICHARD! 1947 .... # 1 – Mar. 1947
OPUS NO. 1: 1945....................................... #16 – Mar. 1945
ORANGE BLOSSOM LANE: 1941.............................. #16 – Dec. 1941
ORANGE GROVE IN CALIFORNIA, AN: 1924 .... # 6 – Feb. 1924
ORCHID TO YOU, AN: 1933 .... #12 – July 1933
ORCHIDS FOR REMEMBRANCE: 1940.......................... #17 – Aug. 1940
ORCHIDS IN THE MOONLIGHT: 1934 .... # 6 – Feb. 1934
ORGAN GRINDER'S SWING: 1936............................ # 5 – Nov. 1936
OS-KA-LOO-SA-LOO: 1906 .... #11 – Nov. 1906
OUI, OUI, MARIE: 1918 .... #10 – Dec. 1918
OUR DIRECTOR (MARCH): 1902 .... # 5 – May 1902
OUR LOVE (L. Clinton): 1939............................ # 1 – May 1939
OUR LOVE (M. Yancy): 1978 .... #10 – Apr. 1978
OUR LOVE, DON'T THROW IT ALL AWAY (Gibb): 1978 .... # 9 – Dec. 1978
OUR LOVE AFFAIR: 1940 .... # 6 – Nov. 1940
OUR PENTHOUSE ON THIRD AVENUE: 1937.................... #15 – Aug. 1937
OUT IN THE COLD AGAIN (Bloom): 1934 .... # 8 – Nov. 1934
OUT IN THE COLD AGAIN (Bloom): 1951 .... #20 – Dec. 1951
(You came along) OUT OF NOWHERE (Green): 1931 .... # 3 – May 1931
(You came along) OUT OF NOWHERE (Green): 1945 .... # 8 – Oct. 1945
OUT OF THE CRADLE, INTO MY HEART: 1916................. #11 – Jan. 1917
OUT OF THE DAWN: 1928 .... #20 – Nov. 1928
OVER SOMEBODY ELSE'S SHOULDER: 1934.................... #17 – Apr. 1934
OVER THE HILLS AND FAR AWAY: 1908 .... #20 – June 1908
OVER THE RAINBOW (Arlen): 1939 .... # 1 – Sept. 1939

OVER THE RAINBOW (Arlen): 1960 .... #17 – Sept. 1960
OVER THERE: 1917 .... # 1 – Aug. 1917
OVERNIGHT: 1931 .... #20 – Feb. 1931
OWL AND THE MOON, THE;
SEE: NOBODY'S LOOKING BUT THE OWL AND THE MOON: 1903

P

P. S. I LOVE YOU (Jenkins): 1934 .... #20 – Dec. 1934
P. S. I LOVE YOU (Jenkins): 1953 .... # 6 – Aug. 1953
P. S. I LOVE YOU (McCartney): 1964 .... #10 – June 1964
PACK UP YOUR SINS (AND GO TO THE DEVIL): 1923 .... #14 – Feb. 1923
PACK UP YOUR TROUBLES IN YOUR OLD KIT BAG: 1917 .... # 2 – June 1917
PADDLIN' MADELIN' HOME: 1926 .... #12 – Jan. 1926
PAGAN LOVE SONG: 1929 .... # 1 – July 1929
PAGE MISS GLORY: 1935 .... #12 – Sept. 1935
PAINTING THE CLOUDS WITH SUNSHINE: 1929 .... # 2 – Nov. 1929
PAL OF MINE: 1905 .... #10 – May 1905
PAL OF MY CRADLE DAYS: 1925 .... # 4 – Oct. 1925
PAL THAT I LOVED STOLE THE GAL THAT LOVED, THE: 1925 ... # 4 – Jan. 1925
PALE MOON: 1921 .... #14 – July 1921
(Lena from) PALESTEENA: 1921 .... # 2 – Jan. 1921
PANAMERICANA: 1902 .... #16 – June 1902
PANSIES MEAN THOUGHTS, AND THOUGHTS MEAN YOU: 1909 .. #19 – Aug. 1909
PAPER DOLL: 1943 .... # 1 – Oct. 1943
PARA VIGO ME VOY; *SEE: SAY SI SI: 1940*
PARADE OF THE WOODEN SOLDIERS: 1922 .... # 3 – Mar. 1923
PARADISE (N.H.Brown): 1932 .... # 1 – Apr. 1932
PARADISE (Adu): 1988 .... #16 – July 1988
PARDON MY SOUTHERN ACCENT: 1934 .... # 6 – Oct. 1934
PARIS IN THE SPRING: 1935 .... # 6 – Aug. 1935
PARLEZ MOI D'AMOUR; *SEE: SPEAK TO ME OF LOVE: 1933*
PASS THAT PEACE PIPE: 1948 .... #16 – Jan. 1948
PASSE: 1946 .... #20 – Nov. 1946
PATTY-CAKE MAN, THE: 1944 .... #18 – Oct. 1944
PEANUT VENDOR, THE: 1931 .... # 2 – Jan. 1931
PEG O' MY HEART (F. Fisher): 1913 .... # 1 – Dec. 1913
PEG O' MY HEART (F. Fisher): 1947 .... # 1 – July 1947
PEGGY: 1920 .... # 3 – Mar. 1920
PEGGY O'NEILL: 1921 .... # 2 – July 1921
PENNIES FROM HEAVEN: 1937 .... # 1 – Jan. 1937
PENNSYLVANIA 6-5000: 1940 .... #14 – Aug. 1940
PENNY SERENADE: 1939 .... # 2 – Mar. 1939
PENTHOUSE SERENADE; *SEE: WHEN WE'RE ALONE: 1932*
PEOPLE WILL SAY WE'RE IN LOVE: 1943 .... # 3 – Nov. 1943
PERFECT DAY, A (C. Jacobs-Bond): 1911 .... T30 – May 1911
PERFECT DAY, A (C. Jacobs-Bond): 1916 .... #13 – Aug. 1916
PERFIDIA (TONIGHT) (Dominguez): 1941 .... # 4 – Feb. 1941
PERFIDIA (TONIGHT) (Dominguez): 1952 .... #13 – May 1952
PERFIDIA (TONIGHT) (Dominguez): 1960 .... #16 – Dec. 1960
PERSIAN RUG: 1928 .... #10 – June 1928
PERSONALITY (Van Heusen): 1946 .... # 2 – Mar. 1946
PERSONALITY (Price): 1959 .... # 2 – June 1959
PIANISSIMO: 1948 .... #18 – Apr. 1948
PIANO CONCERTO: 1941 .... # 2 – Nov. 1941
PICCOLINO, THE: 1935 .... #19 – Oct. 1935
PICCOLO PETE: 1929 .... # 6 – Nov. 1929
PINEY RIDGE: 1915 .... #20 – Jan. 1916
PINK ELEPHANTS: 1932 .... # 3 – Dec. 1932
PISTOL PACKIN' MAMA: 1943 .... # 1 – Nov. 1943
PLACE A LIGHT TO GUIDE ME HOME: 1902 .... #13 – Nov. 1902
PLAY, FIDDLE, PLAY: 1933 .... # 4 – Jan. 1933
PLAY A SIMPLE MELODY (Berlin): 1915 .... #17 – July 1915
PLAY A SIMPLE MELODY (Berlin): 1950 .... # 3 – Aug. 1950
PLAY GYPSIES – DANCE GYPSIES: 1926 .... #11 – Nov. 1926
PLAY THAT BARBERSHOP CHORD: 1910 .... # 1 – Nov. 1910
PLAY TO ME, GYPSY: 1934 .... #18 – May 1934
PLAYMATES: 1940 .... # 5 – June 1940
PLEASE: 1932 .... # 1 – Dec. 1932
PLEASE BE KIND: 1938 .... # 2 – Apr. 1938
PLEASE BELIEVE ME: 1936 .... # 8 – Mar. 1936
PLEASE COME AND PLAY IN MY YARD: 1904 .... # 3 – Jan. 1905
PLEASE COME OUT OF YOUR DREAM: 1939 .... #20 – Jan. 1939
PLEASE DON'T TALK ABOUT ME (WHEN I'M GONE): 1931 ..... # 2 – May 1931
PLEASE GO 'WAY AND LET ME SLEEP: 1902 .... # 1 – Aug. 1902
PLEASE LET ME SLEEP; *SEE: PLEASE GO 'WAY AND LET ME SLEEP: 1902*
PLEASE THINK OF ME: 1943 .... #16 – Mar. 1943
POINCIANA: 1944 .... # 4 – Apr. 1944
POLONAISE IN A FLAT; *SEE: CHOPIN'S POLONAISE: 1945*
POMPTON TURNPIKE: 1940 .... #15 – Jan. 1941
POOR BUTTERFLY (Hubbell): 1917 .... # 1 – Feb. 1917
POOR BUTTERFLY (Hubbell): 1954 .... #19 – May 1954
POOR JOHN! 1907 .... # 1 – Apr. 1907
POOR LITTLE RHODE ISLAND: 1945 .... #19 – May 1945
POOR PAPA, HE GOT NUTHIN' AT ALL: 1926 .... # 5 – May 1926
POOR PAULINE: 1914 .... # 7 – Dec. 1914
POP GOES YOUR HEART: 1934 .... #12 – Dec. 1934
POWDER YOUR FACE WITH SUNSHINE: 1949 .... # 3 – Feb. 1949
PRACTICE MAKES PERFECT: 1940 .... # 5 – Oct. 1940
PRAISE THE LORD AND PASS THE AMMUNITION: 1942 .... # 2 – Nov. 1942
PRAY FOR THE LIGHTS TO GO OUT: 1916 .... #12 – Oct. 1916
PREACHER AND THE BEAR, THE: 1905 .... # 5 – Sept. 1905
PRECIOUS LITTLE THING CALLED LOVE: 1929 .... # 1 – Apr. 1929
PRETENDING: 1946 .... #19 – Sept. 1946
PRETTY BABY: 1916 .... # 1 – Sept. 1916
PRETTY GIRL IS LIKE A MELODY, A: 1919 .... # 1 – Sept. 1919
PRETTY KITTY BLUE EYES: 1944 .... #10 – Sept. 1944
PRETTY KITTY KELLY: 1920 .... # 3 – Aug. 1920
PRETTY MOLLIE SHANNON: 1902 .... # 8 – July 1902
PRINCE CHARMING: 1943 .... #19 – June 1943
PRINCESS POCAHONTAS: 1903 .... #20 – Sept. 1903
PRISONER OF LOVE (R. Columbo): 1946 .... # 3 – June 1946
PRISONER OF LOVE (R. Columbo): 1963 .... #18 – June 1963
PRISONER'S SONG, THE: 1926 .... # 1 – Jan. 1926
PRIZE WALTZ, THE: 1934 .... #16 – Aug. 1934
PU-LEEZE, MR. HEMINGWAY! 1932 .... #14 – Nov. 1932
PUDDIN' HEAD JONES: 1933 .... #20 – Jan. 1934
PULLMAN PORTERS ON PARADE, THE: 1913 .... #12 – Dec. 1913
PUSSY CAT SONG, THE: 1949 .... #13 – Feb. 1949
PUT 'EM IN A BOX, TIE 'EM WITH A RIBBON: 1948 .... #11 – Aug. 1948
PUT AWAY A LITTLE RAY OF GOLDEN SUNSHINE FOR A RAINY
DAY: 1924 .... # 5 – Dec. 1924
PUT ME TO SLEEP WITH AN OLD FASHIONED MELODY: 1915 ... #19 – Nov. 1915
PUT ON YOUR OLD GRAY BONNET: 1910 .... # 1 – Mar. 1910
PUT YOUR ARMS AROUND ME, HONEY (A. Von Tilzer): 1911 .... # 1 – May 1911
PUT YOUR ARMS AROUND ME, HONEY (A. Von Tilzer): 1943 .... # 5 – Oct. 1943
PUTTIN' ON THE RITZ (Berlin): 1930 .... # 6 – May 1930
PUTTIN' ON THE RITZ (Berlin): 1983 .... # 4 – Sept. 1983

Q

QUAND MADELON; *SEE: MADELON: 1919*
QUIEREME MUCHO; *SEE: YOURS: 1941*

R

RACKETY COO! 1916 .... #12 – May 1916
RAGGEDY ANN: 1924 .... # 5 – Mar. 1924
RAGGING THE BABY TO SLEEP: 1912 .... # 5 – Sept. 1912
RAGGING THE SCALE: 1915 .... # 7 – Oct. 1915
RAGTIME COWBOY JOE (Muir): 1912 .... #12 – Oct. 1912
RAGTIME COWBOY JOE (Muir): 1949 .... #19 – Oct. 1949
RAGTIME COWBOY JOE (Muir): 1959 .... #15 – Aug. 1959
RAGTIME VIOLIN: 1912 .... # 3 – June 1912
RAILROAD JIM : 1915 .... #18 – July 1915
RAIN (DeRose): 1934 .... # 5 – Dec. 1934
RAIN (Ford): 1928 .... # 3 – Mar. 1928
RAIN (Ford): 1950 .... #15 – May 1950
RAIN (Madonna): 1993 .... #14 – Sept. 1993
RAIN, THE (V. Bell): 1986 .... # 9 – Nov. 1986
RAIN ON THE ROOF (Ronell): 1932 .... #13 – Mar. 1932
RAIN ON THE ROOF (Ronell): 1966 .... #10 – Nov. 1966
RAINBOW (Wenrich): 1908 .... # 9 – Aug. 1908
RAINBOW ON THE RIVER: 1937 .... #10 – Feb. 1937
RAINBOW 'ROUND MY SHOULDER;
SEE: THERE'S A RAINBOW 'ROUND MY SHOULDER: 1928
RAINY NIGHT IN RIO, A: 1947 .... #13 – Apr. 1947
RAMBLIN' ROSE (Sherman): 1962 .... # 2 – Sept. 1962
RAMBLING ROSE (J. Burke): 1948 .... #12 – Oct. 1948
RAMONA: 1928 .... # 1 – May 1928
RANGER'S SONG, THE: 1927 .... #11 – May 1927
REACHING FOR THE MOON (Greer): 1926 .... #15 – July 1926
REACHING FOR THE MOON (Berlin): 1931 .... # 5 – Mar. 1931
READY FOR THE RIVER: 1928 .... #10 – July 1928
REBECCA OF SUNNYBROOK FARM: 1914 .... # 1 – Apr. 1914
RED, RED ROSE: 1909 .... #15 – July 1909
RED HEAD: 1909 .... # 9 – Sept. 1909
RED HOT MAMMA: 1924 .... #11 – Aug. 1924
RED LIPS, KISS MY BLUES AWAY: 1927 .... # 9 – July 1927
RED ROSES FOR A BLUE LADY (Tepper): 1949 .... # 3 – Apr. 1949
RED ROSES FOR A BLUE LADY (Tepper): 1965 .... # 5 – Mar. 1965
RED SAILS IN THE SUNSET: 1935 .... # 1 – Nov. 1935
RED SILK STOCKINGS AND GREEN PERFUME: 1947 .... #13 – June 1947
RED WING: 1908 .... # 3 – Jan. 1908
REMEMB'RING: 1924 .... # 2 – Mar. 1924
REMEMBER (Berlin): 1925 .... # 1 – Nov. 1925
REMEMBER (WALKIN' IN THE SAND) (Morton): 1964 .... # 5 – Sept. 1964
REMEMBER ME (O'Brien): 1933 .... #13 – May 1933
REMEMBER ME (Ashford): 1971 .... #16 – Feb. 1971
REMEMBER ME? (Warren): 1937 .... # 2 – Oct. 1937
REMEMBER PEARL HARBOR: 1942 .... # 5 – Feb. 1942
RENDEZVOUS WITH A DREAM: 1936 .... # 5 – Aug. 1936
REVENGE (H. Akst): 1928 .... # 8 – Nov. 1928
REVENGE (B. Benton): 1962 .... #15 – Jan. 1962
RHAPSODY IN BLUE (Gershwin): 1924 .... #14 – Oct. 1924
RHAPSODY IN BLUE (Gershwin): 1943 .... #18 – Nov. 1943
RHYTHM AND ROMANCE: 1935 .... #13 – Oct. 1935
RHYTHM IN MY NURSERY RHYMES: 1936 .... # 8 – Feb. 1936
RHYTHM IS OUR BUSINESS: 1935 .... #14 – July 1935
RIDE, RED, RIDE: 1936 .... #20 – Mar. 1936
RIDERS IN THE SKY: 1949 .... # 1 – June 1949
RIDIN' AROUND IN THE RAIN: 1934 .... # 8 – June 1934
(You're in) THE RIGHT CHURCH BUT THE WRONG PEW: 1909 .... # 1 – Feb. 1909
RIGHT CHURCH, WRONG PEW;
SEE: (You're in) THE RIGHT CHURCH BUT THE WRONG PEW: 1909
RIO RITA: 1927 .... # 4 – May 1927
RIP VAN WINKLE WAS A LUCKY MAN: 1902 .... # 1 – July 1902
RIPTIDE: 1934 .... # 6 – June 1934
RISE 'N SHINE: 1933 .... #16 – Feb. 1933
RIVER, STAY 'WAY FROM MY DOOR: 1931 .... #13 – Dec. 1931
RIVERBOAT SHUFFLE: 1925 .... #11 – Aug. 1925
ROAMIN' IN THE GLOAMIN': 1911 .... #19 – Dec. 1911
ROBINS AND ROSES: 1936 .... # 2 – June 1936
ROCK-A-BYE MY BABY BLUES: 1924 .... #15 – Nov. 1924
ROCK-A-BYE YOUR BABY WITH A DIXIE MELODY
(J. Schwartz): 1918 .... # 3 – Sept. 1918
ROCK-A-BYE YOUR BABY WITH A DIXIE MELODY
(J. Schwartz): 1957 .... #12 – Jan. 1957
ROCKABYE MOON: 1933 .... # 6 – Feb. 1933
ROCKIN' CHAIR (Carmichael): 1932 .... #18 – June 1932
ROCKIN' CHAIR (Reid): 1975 .... # 9 – Aug. 1975
ROLL ALONG, PRAIRIE MOON: 1935 .... # 6 – Nov. 1935
ROLL DEM ROLY BOLY EYES: 1912 .... #20 – June 1912
ROLL ON, MISSISSIPPI, ROLL ON: 1931 .... #16 – June 1931
ROLL THEM COTTON BALES: 1914 .... # 8 – Sept. 1914
ROLLING STONES (ALL COME ROLLING HOME AGAIN): 1917 .... # 8 – Apr. 1917
ROMANCE: 1930 .... #19 – Apr. 1930
ROOM FULL OF ROSES: 1949 .... # 1 – Sept. 1949
ROSALIE: 1938 .... # 1 – Jan. 1938
ROSE ANN OF CHARING CROSS: 1943 .... #11 – Feb. 1943
ROSE IN HER HAIR, THE: 1935 .... # 6 – Sept. 1935
ROSE O'DAY: 1942 .... # 3 – Feb. 1942
ROSE OF NO MAN'S LAND: 1919 .... # 1 – Jan. 1919
ROSE OF THE RIO GRANDE: 1923 .... # 4 – Apr. 1923
ROSE OF THE WORLD: 1909 .... # 5 – Feb. 1909
ROSE OF WASHINGTON SQUARE: 1920 .... # 1 – June 1920
ROSE-MARIE: 1925 .... # 3 – Feb. 1925
ROSES BRING DREAMS OF YOU: 1908 .... # 3 – July 1908
ROSES IN DECEMBER: 1937 .... # 5 – Nov. 1937
ROSES IN THE RAIN: 1947 .... #14 – May 1947
ROSES OF PICARDY (H. Wood): 1918 .... #19 – Oct. 1918
ROSES OF PICARDY (H. Wood): 1923 .... # 7 – Dec. 1923
ROSES OF YESTERDAY: 1928 .... # 7 – Nov. 1928
ROW, ROW, ROW: 1913 .... # 1 – Mar. 1913
RUDOLPH, THE RED-NOSED REINDEER: 1949 .... # 6 – Dec. 1949
RUDOLPH, THE RED-NOSED REINDEER: 1950 .... # 4 – Dec. 1950
RUDOLPH, THE RED-NOSED REINDEER: 1951 .... #11 – Dec. 1951
RUDOLPH, THE RED-NOSED REINDEER: 1952 .... #10 – Dec. 1952
RUDOLPH, THE RED-NOSED REINDEER: 1953 .... #16 – Dec. 1953
RUDOLPH, THE RED-NOSED REINDEER: 1954 .... #17 – Dec. 1954
RUDOLPH, THE RED-NOSED REINDEER: 1960 .... #16 – Dec. 1960
RUFUS RASTUS JOHNSON BROWN;
SEE: WHAT YOU GOIN' TO DO WHEN THE RENT COMES 'ROUND? 1905
RUM AND COCA COLA: 1945 .... # 2 – Mar. 1945
RUM TUM TIDDLE: 1912 .... # 3 – Apr. 1912
RUMORS ARE FLYING: 1946 .... # 1 – Nov. 1946
RUNNIN' WILD: 1923 .... # 2 – Apr. 1923
RUSSIAN LULLABY: 1927 .... # 1 – July 1927

S

'S WONDERFUL: 1928 .... #20 – May 1928
S'POSIN': 1929 .... #14 – Aug. 1929
S. R. HENRY'S BARN DANCE; *SEE: DOWN AT THE HUSKING BEE: 1909*
SABRE DANCE: 1948 .... # 6 – Apr. 1948

SABRE DANCE BOOGIE; *SEE: SABRE DANCE: 1948*	
SADIE GREEN: 1903	#14 – Aug. 1903
SADIE SALOME, GO HOME: 1909	#18 – Sept. 1909
SADIE SAY YOU WON'T SAY NAY: 1902	#15 – Aug. 1902
SAFTEST O' THE FAMILY: 1908	#19 – Jan. 1908
SAIL ALONG, SILV'RY MOON (Wenrich): 1938	#14 – Jan. 1938
SAIL ALONG, SILV'RY MOON (Wenrich): 1958	# 3 – Feb. 1958
SAILBOAT IN THE MOONLIGHT, A: 1937	# 1 – Aug. 1937
SAILIN' AWAY ON THE HENRY CLAY: 1917	# 6 – Oct. 1917
SAILING DOWN THE CHESAPEAKE BAY: 1913	# 5 – Jan. 1914
SALLY OF MY DREAMS: 1928	# 8 – Dec. 1928
SALVATION LASSIE OF MINE: 1919	#18 – Apr. 1919
SAM, THE OLD ACCORDION MAN: 1927	# 2 – Apr. 1927
SAME OLD STORY, THE: 1940	#15 – Oct. 1940
SAMMY: 1903	#18 – Apr. 1903
SAN: 1924	#11 – Sept. 1924
SAN ANTONIO: 1907	# 1 – May 1907
SAN ANTONIO ROSE (Wills): 1941	# 5 – Apr. 1941
SAN ANTONIO ROSE (Wills): 1961	# 7 – July 1961
SAN FERNANDO VALLEY: 1944	# 2 – May 1944
SANTA CLAUS IS COMIN' TO TOWN: 1934	# 3 – Dec. 1934
SANTA CLAUS IS COMIN' TO TOWN: 1935	#11 – Dec. 1935
SANTA CLAUS IS COMIN' TO TOWN: 1936	#11 – Dec. 1936
SANTA CLAUS IS COMIN' TO TOWN: 1947	#16 – Dec. 1947
SANTA CLAUS IS COMIN' TO TOWN: 1948	#18 – Dec. 1948
SARI WALTZ: 1914	#17 – Apr. 1914
SATAN TAKES A HOLIDAY: 1937	#12 – Aug. 1937
SATISFIED (C. Friend): 1929	#11 – Dec. 1929
SATURDAY NIGHT (IS THE LONELIEST NIGHT OF THE WEEK) (J. Styne): 1945	# 5 – Mar. 1945
SAVE YOUR SORROW (FOR TOMORROW): 1925	# 6 – Nov. 1925
SAW MILL RIVER ROAD: 1923	#10 – July 1923
SAY A PRAYER FOR THE BOYS OVER THERE: 1943	#10 – Oct. 1943
SAY IT (McHugh): 1940	# 4 – June 1940
SAY IT (McKetney): 1998	#12 – July 1998
(I don't believe it but) SAY IT AGAIN: 1926	# 7 – June 1926
SAY IT ISN'T SO (Berlin): 1932	# 1 – Oct. 1932
SAY IT ISN'T SO (D. Hall): 1983	# 2 – Dec. 1983
SAY IT WHILE DANCING: 1922	# 3 – Oct. 1922
SAY IT WITH MUSIC: 1921	# 1 – Dec. 1921
SAY SI SI (PARA VIGO ME VOY) (Lecuona): 1940	#11 – Apr. 1940
SAY SI SI (PARA VIGO ME VOY) (Lecuona): 1953	#19 – June 1953
SAY SOMETHING SWEET TO YOUR SWEETHEART: 1948	#17 – Nov. 1948
SAYS MY HEART: 1938	# 1 – June 1938
SCATTERBRAIN: 1939	# 1 – Dec. 1939
SCHOOL DAY (C. Berry): 1957	# 7 – May 1957
SCHOOL DAYS (G. Edwards): 1907	# 1 – June 1907
SCHOOL MATES: 1909	# 6 – June 1909
SCRUB ME, MAMA, WITH A BOOGIE BEAT: 1940	#12 – Dec. 1940
SECOND HAND ROSE: 1921	# 7 – Dec. 1921
SEEMS LIKE OLD TIMES: 1946	#11 – May 1946
SEMINOLE: 1904	# 6 – Sept. 1904
SEND ME AWAY WITH A SMILE: 1917	#15 – Nov. 1917
SENORA: 1909	#12 – Dec. 1909
SENTIMENTAL JOURNEY: 1945	# 1 – June 1945
SENTIMENTAL ME (Morehead): 1950	# 4 – May 1950
SENTIMENTAL ME (AND ROMANTIC YOU) (Rodgers): 1925	# 8 – Nov. 1925
SEPTEMBER IN THE RAIN: 1937	# 1 – May 1937
SEPTEMBER SONG: 1946	#12 – Dec. 1946
SERENADE (Romberg): 1925	#14 – Mar. 1925
SERENADE IN BLUE: 1942	# 3 – Nov. 1942
SERENADE IN THE NIGHT: 1937	# 9 – Mar. 1937
SERENADE OF THE BELLS: 1948	# 3 – Jan. 1948
SEVEN OR ELEVEN (MY DIXIE PAIR O'DICE): 1923	#11 – June 1923
SEVENTEEN (Rosoff): 1925; *SEE: WHEN YOU AND I WERE SEVENTEEN: 1925*	
SEVENTEEN (B. Bennett): 1955	# 3 – Sept. 1955
SHABBY OLD CABBY, THE: 1939	#16 – Aug. 1939
SHADE OF THE PALM, THE: 1901	# 5 – Mar. 1901
SHADES OF NIGHT: 1916	# 5 – Aug. 1916
SHADOW WALTZ: 1933	# 1 – July 1933
SHADOWLAND: 1915	#10 – July 1915
SHAKE DOWN THE STARS: 1940	#11 – June 1940
SHAKING THE BLUES AWAY: 1927	# 6 – Nov. 1927
SHAKY EYES: 1910	# 4 – Apr. 1910
SHAME ON YOU: 1905	#13 – Jan. 1905
SHANGHAI LIL: 1933	#17 – Dec. 1933
SHANTY IN OLD SHANTY TOWN; *SEE: IN A SHANTY IN OLD SHANTY TOWN: 1932*	
SHANTY TOWN; *SEE: IN A SHANTY IN OLD SHANTY TOWN: 1932*	
SHE DIDN'T SAY "YES": 1932	#19 – Feb. 1932
SHE IS MA DAISY: 1908	#17 – Jan. 1908
SHE IS THE SUNSHINE OF VIRGINIA: 1916	# 3 – Dec. 1916
SHE REMINDS ME OF YOU: 1934	#11 – May 1934
SHE SHALL HAVE MUSIC: 1936	# 7 – June 1936
SHE WAITS BY THE DEEP BLUE SEA: 1905	# 7 – July 1905
SHE WAS A GRAND OLD LADY: 1907	#20 – Oct. 1907
SHE WOULDN'T DO (WHAT I ASKED HER TO): 1924	#10 – Apr. 1924
SHE'LL ALWAYS REMEMBER: 1942	#19 – Apr. 1942
SHE'S A LATIN FROM MANHATTAN: 1935	# 6 – June 1935
SHE'S DIXIE ALL THE TIME: 1917	#17 – Apr. 1917
SHE'S FUNNY THAT WAY: 1929	# 7 – Feb. 1929
SHE'S THE DAUGHTER OF MOTHER MACHREE: 1916	# 7 – Mar. 1916
SHE'S THE DAUGHTER OF ROSIE O'GRADY; *SEE: (She's the) DAUGHTER OF ROSIE O'GRADY: 1918*	
SHEIK (OF ARABY), THE: 1922	# 1 – Feb. 1922
SHEPHERD SERENADE: 1941	# 3 – Dec. 1941
SHIM-ME-SHA-WABBLE: 1917	#19 – Aug. 1917
SHINE (F. Dabney): 1924	# 5 – July 1924
SHINE (F. Dabney): 1948	#14 – Apr. 1948
SHINE (Roland): 1994	#11 – Aug. 1994
SHINE ON, HARVEST MOON (N. Bayes): 1909	# 1 – Mar. 1909
SHINE ON, HARVEST MOON (N. Bayes): 1931	#16 – Oct. 1931
SHINE ON YOUR SHOES, A: 1932	#17 – Dec. 1932
SHOE SHINE BOY (Chaplin): 1936	#17 – July 1936
SHOO-FLY PIE AND APPLE PAN DOWDY: 1946	# 3 – May 1946
SHOO-SHOO BABY: 1944	# 1 – Feb. 1944
SHOULD I? (N.H.Brown): 1930	# 2 – Mar. 1930
SHOULD I? (N.H.Brown): 1952	#16 – Aug. 1952
SHOW ME THE WAY (T. Lewis): 1925	#13 – Feb. 1925
SHOW ME THE WAY (Frampton): 1976	# 6 – May 1976
SHOW ME THE WAY (DeYoung): 1991	# 3 – Mar. 1991
SHOW ME THE WAY TO GO HOME (R. Connelly): 1926	# 4 – Jan. 1926
SHOW ME THE WHITE OF YO' EYE: 1903	# 2 – Sept. 1903
SHRINE OF ST. CECILIA, THE: 1942	# 4 – Feb. 1942
SHUFFLE OFF TO BUFFALO: 1933	# 1 – Apr. 1933
SIAM: 1916	#10 – May 1916
SIBONEY: 1931	#20 – June 1931
SIDE BY SIDE (Woods): 1927	# 3 – Aug. 1927
SIDE BY SIDE (Woods): 1953	# 6 – Apr. 1953
SIDEWALKS OF NEW YORK, THE: 1928	# 9 – Sept. 1928
SIERRA SUE: 1940	# 2 – July 1940
SIGNAL FROM MARS, A: 1902	#13 – Apr. 1902
SILENT NIGHT: 1935	#19 – Dec. 1935
SILVER BELL (Wenrich): 1910	# 5 – Jan. 1911
SILVER BELLS (Livingston): 1952	#20 – Jan. 1953
SILVER MOON: 1927	#20 – Aug. 1927
SILVER THREADS AMONG THE GOLD: 1911	T30 – Mar. 1911

SILVERHEELS: 1906 .... # 6 – Feb. 1906
SIMPLE MELODY; *SEE: PLAY A SIMPLE MELODY: 1915, 1950*
SINCE FATHER WENT TO WORK: 1906 .... #19 – Mar. 1906
SINCE I FIRST MET YOU: 1903 .... # 8 – July 1903
SINCE MA IS PLAYING MAH JONG: 1924 .... #15 – June 1924
SINCE NELLIE WENT AWAY: 1906 .... #15 – June 1906
SINCE SALLY LEFT OUR ALLEY: 1903 .... # 6 – May 1903
SING, BABY, SING: 1936 .... # 6 – Nov. 1936
SING, SING, SING: 1936 .... #12 – Oct. 1936
SING, YOU SINNERS: 1930 .... # 8 – May 1930
SING AN OLD FASHIONED SONG: 1936 .... #14 – Apr. 1936
SING ME A SONG OF THE ISLANDS: 1942 .... #19 – June 1942
SING ME A SONG OF THE SOUTH: 1900 .... # 6 – Jan. 1900
SING ME A SWING SONG (AND LET ME DANCE): 1936 .... #15 – July 1936
SING ME LOVE'S LULLABY: 1917 .... T30 – Oct. 1917
SING SOMETHING SIMPLE: 1930 .... #12 – Nov. 1930
SINGIN' IN THE BATHTUB: 1930 .... # 7 – Jan. 1930
SINGIN' IN THE RAIN: 1929 .... # 3 – Nov. 1929
SINGING A SONG TO THE STARS: 1930 .... # 7 – Aug. 1930
SINGING A VAGABOND SONG: 1930 .... #20 – Apr. 1930
SINGING HILLS, THE: 1940 .... # 3 – May 1940
SINNER KISSED AN ANGEL, A: 1941 .... #19 – Dec. 1941
SIOUX CITY SUE: 1946 .... # 6 – May 1946
SIPPING CIDER THROUGH A STRAW: 1919 .... # 8 – Oct. 1919
SISTER KATE; *SEE: I WISH I COULD SHIMMY LIKE MY SISTER KATE: 1922*
SISTER SUSIE'S SEWING SHIRTS FOR SOLDIERS: 1915 .... # 9 – Feb. 1915
SIT DOWN, YOU'RE ROCKING THE BOAT: 1914 .... #16 – Mar. 1914
SITTIN' IN A CORNER: 1924 .... # 2 – Jan. 1924
SIX LESSONS FROM MADAME LA ZONGA: 1940 .... # 9 – Sept. 1940
SIXTY SECONDS GOT TOGETHER: 1938 .... #14 – Nov. 1938
SKYLARK: 1942 .... # 5 – May 1942
SLAP 'ER DOWN AGIN, PAW: 1948 .... #10 – Mar. 1948
SLEEP (Lebieg): 1924 .... # 2 – Feb. 1924
SLEEP (Lebieg): 1960 .... #14 – Nov. 1960
SLEEPY HEAD (Greer): 1926 .... # 4 – Aug. 1926
SLEEPY HEAD (Donaldson): 1934 .... # 6 – Aug. 1934
SLEEPY LAGOON: 1942 .... # 1 – June 1942
SLEEPY TIME GAL: 1926 .... # 2 – Feb. 1926
SLEEPY VALLEY: 1929 .... # 4 – Sept. 1929
SLEIGH RIDE IN JULY: 1945 .... #15 – Feb. 1945
SLIPPING AROUND: 1949 .... # 3 – Nov. 1949
SLOW RIVER: 1927 .... #19 – Sept. 1927
SLUMMING ON PARK AVENUE: 1937 .... #16 – Mar. 1937
SMALL FRY: 1938 .... # 6 – Oct. 1938
SMARTY (A. Von Tilzer): 1908 .... # 2 – June 1908
(You know it all) SMARTY (B. Lane): 1937 .... #20 – Aug. 1937
SMILE WILL GO A LONG, LONG WAY, A: 1924 .... # 2 – Apr. 1924
SMILES: 1918 .... # 1 – Sept. 1918
SMILIN' THROUGH (A. Penn): 1919 .... # 2 – Sept. 1919
SMILIN' THROUGH (A. Penn): 1922 .... #14 – Aug. 1922
SMOKE! SMOKE! SMOKE! (THAT CIGARETTE): 1947 .... # 4 – Sept. 1947
SMOKE DREAMS: 1937 .... #17 – Mar. 1937
SMOKE GETS IN YOUR EYES (Kern): 1934 .... # 2 – Feb. 1934
SMOKE GETS IN YOUR EYES (Kern): 1959 .... # 1 – Jan. 1959
SMOKE ON THE WATER (Z. Clements): 1944 .... #17 – Oct. 1944
SMOKE ON THE WATER (Blackmore): 1973 .... # 4 – July 1973
SMOKE RINGS (Clifford): 1933 .... #13 – Aug. 1933
SMOKE RINGS (Clifford): 1952 .... #19 – July 1952
SNEAK, THE: 1922 .... #18 – Sept. 1922
SNOOKEY OOKUMS: 1913 .... # 6 – July 1913
SNUGGLED ON YOUR SHOULDER: 1932 .... # 6 – Apr. 1932
SO ASHAMED: 1932 .... #17 – Aug. 1932
SO BEATS MY HEART FOR YOU: 1930 .... # 4 – Aug. 1930
SO BLUE: 1927 .... #10 – June 1927
SO FAR: 1947 .... #12 – Dec. 1947
SO FAR, SO GOOD: 1940 .... #17 – Apr. 1940
SO HELP ME (IF I DON'T LOVE YOU): 1938 .... # 3 – Oct. 1938
SO IN LOVE: 1949 .... #11 – Apr. 1949
SO LITTLE TIME: 1938 .... #19 – June 1938
SO LONG, LETTY: 1916 .... #15 – Apr. 1916
SO LONG, MARY: 1906 .... # 3 – May 1906
SO LONG! OO-LONG: 1920 .... # 4 – July 1920
SO MANY MEMORIES: 1937 .... #11 – Oct. 1937
SO RARE (Herst): 1937 .... # 1 – Sept. 1937
SO RARE (Herst): 1957 .... # 2 – July 1957
SO TIRED: 1949 .... # 8 – Mar. 1949
SO YOU'RE THE ONE: 1941 .... # 8 – Feb. 1941
SOFT LIGHTS AND SWEET MUSIC: 1932 .... #11 – May 1932
SOLITUDE: 1935 .... # 8 – Mar. 1935
SOME BOY: 1913 .... # 7 – May 1913
SOME DAY WHEN DREAMS COME TRUE: 1907 .... # 8 – Jan. 1908
SOME ENCHANTED EVENING (Rodgers): 1949 .... # 1 – July 1949
SOME ENCHANTED EVENING (Rodgers): 1965 .... #13 – Oct. 1965
SOME LITTLE BIRD: 1921 .... #19 – May 1921
SOME OF THESE DAYS: 1910 .... # 1 – Oct. 1910
SOME SUNDAY MORNING (R. Whiting): 1917 .... # 2 – Dec. 1917
SOME SUNDAY MORNING (M.K.Jerome): 1946 .... # 8 – Jan. 1946
SOME SUNNY DAY: 1922 .... # 3 – July 1922
SOME SWEET DAY: 1929 .... #20 – May 1929
SOMEBODY ELSE, IT'S ALWAYS SOMEBODY ELSE: 1910 .... # 9 – Oct. 1910
SOMEBODY ELSE IS TAKING MY PLACE: 1942 .... # 1 – May 1942
SOMEBODY LIED: 1908 .... #16 – Oct. 1908
SOMEBODY LOVES ME: 1924 .... # 4 – Nov. 1924
SOMEBODY LOVES YOU: 1932 .... # 3 – Apr. 1932
SOMEBODY STOLE MY GAL (L. Wood): 1924 .... # 4 – Mar. 1924
SOMEBODY'S COMING TO MY HOUSE: 1913 .... # 4 – Nov. 1913
SOMEBODY'S SWEETHEART I LONG TO BE: 1906 .... T30 – Feb. 1906
SOMEBODY'S WAITING 'NEATH SOUTHERN SKIES: 1903 .... #14 – Jan. 1903
SOMEBODY'S WAITING FOR YOU: 1907 .... #12 – Apr. 1907
SOMEDAY (YOU'LL WANT ME TO WANT YOU) (Hodges): 1949 ... # 2 – Oct. 1949
SOMEDAY I'LL MEET YOU AGAIN: 1944 .... #12 – July 1944
SOMEONE LIKE YOU: 1949 .... #13 – May 1949
SOMEONE TO WATCH OVER ME: 1927 .... # 5 – Mar. 1927
SOMETHING TELLS ME: 1938 .... #19 – May 1938
SOMETHING TO REMEMBER YOU BY: 1930 .... #20 – Dec. 1930
SOMETIME (FioRito): 1925 .... # 3 – Dec. 1925
SOMETIME (FioRito): 1950 .... #16 – Sept. 1950
SOMETIMES: 1942 .... #10 – Apr. 1942
SOMETIMES I'M HAPPY: 1927 .... # 8 – Aug. 1927
SOMEWHERE (Harris): 1906 .... # 9 – Nov. 1906
SOMEWHERE (Wisner): 1964 .... #19 – Feb. 1964
SOMEWHERE A VOICE IS CALLING: 1914 .... #20 – Apr. 1914
SOMEWHERE IN FRANCE IS THE LILY: 1918 .... #11 – Feb. 1918
SOMEWHERE IN OLD WYOMING: 1930 .... #17 – Sept. 1930
SONATA: 1947 .... #12 – Feb. 1947
SONG IS ENDED (BUT THE MELODY LINGERS ON), THE: 1928 .. # 3 – Feb. 1928
SONG IS YOU, THE: 1933 .... #19 – Feb. 1933
SONG OF LOVE: 1922 .... #12 – Feb. 1922
SONG OF SONGS, THE: 1915 .... #15 – Apr. 1915
SONG OF THE FLAME: 1926 .... #13 – Apr. 1926
SONG OF THE ISLANDS (Gordon);
SEE: SING ME A SONG OF THE ISLANDS: 1942
SONG OF THE VAGABONDS: 1926 .... #13 – Feb. 1926
SONG OF THE VOLGA BOATMEN: 1941 .... #10 – Mar. 1941
SONG OF THE WANDERER: 1927 .... #10 – Apr. 1927
SONG THAT REACHES IRISH HEARTS, THE: 1912 .... T30 – May 1912

Song	Chart
SONNY BOY: 1928	# 1 – Nov. 1928
SOON: 1935	# 5 – Apr. 1935
SOONER OR LATER (Wolcott): 1947	#11 – Jan. 1947
SOONER OR LATER (Paris): 1971	# 9 – July 1971
SOPHISTICATED LADY: 1933	#12 – Aug. 1933
SOUTH AMERICA, TAKE IT AWAY: 1946	# 3 – Sept. 1946
SOUTH AMERICAN WAY: 1939	#18 – Aug. 1939
SOUTH OF THE BORDER: 1939	# 1 – Nov. 1939
SOUTH SEA ISLAND MAGIC: 1936	# 7 – Nov. 1936
SOUTH SEA ROSE: 1930	#17 – Mar. 1930
SOUVENIR DE VIENNE; *SEE: INTERMEZZO (A LOVE STORY): 1941*	
SPAIN: 1924	# 4 – July 1924
SPANGLES: 1907	#16 – July 1907
SPANIARD THAT BLIGHTED MY LIFE, THE: 1913	# 7 – July 1913
SPEAK LOW: 1944	#11 – Feb. 1944
SPEAK TO ME OF LOVE: 1933	#13 – Feb. 1933
SPEAKING OF HEAVEN: 1939	#15 – Jan. 1940
SPELLBOUND: 1934	#15 – Aug. 1934
SPIDER AND THE FLY, THE: 1901	#16 – Jan. 1901
SPIRIT OF '76, THE: 1903	#18 – Feb. 1903
SPIRIT OF INDEPENDENCE: 1912	#18 – Oct. 1912
SPLASH ME; *SEE: YOU SPLASH ME AND I'LL SPLASH YOU: 1907*	
SPREAD YO' STUFF: 1921	#16 – June 1921
SPREADIN' RHYTHM AROUND: 1936	#20 – Mar. 1936
SPRING, BEAUTIFUL SPRING: 1907	#14 – Nov. 1907
SPRING WILL BE A LITTLE LATE THIS YEAR: 1944	#20 – May 1944
ST. JAMES INFIRMARY (Mills): 1930	# 8 – Mar. 1930
ST. JAMES INFIRMARY (Mills): 1931	#19 – June 1931
ST. LOUIS BLUES (W.C.Handy): 1920	#16 – Sept. 1920
ST. LOUIS BLUES (W.C.Handy): 1948; *SEE: ST. LOUIS BLUES (MARCH): 1948*	
ST. LOUIS BLUES (MARCH) (W.C.Handy): 1948	#11 – May 1948
STAIRWAY TO THE STARS: 1939	# 1 – July 1939
STAR DUST (Carmichael): 1931	#12 – July 1931
STAR DUST (Carmichael): 1941	# 8 – Feb. 1941
STAR DUST (Carmichael): 1957	#16 – Aug. 1957
STAR EYES: 1944	# 8 – Feb. 1944
STAR FELL OUT OF HEAVEN, A: 1936	# 2 – Sept. 1936
STAR GAZING: 1935	#20 – July 1935
STARDUST ON THE MOON: 1937	#14 – Sept. 1937
STARLIGHT (Morse): 1906	# 5 – Feb. 1906
STARLIGHT (Petkere): 1932	#19 – Mar. 1932
STARLIT HOUR, THE: 1940	# 5 – Apr. 1940
STARS FELL ON ALABAMA: 1934	# 2 – Nov. 1934
STARS WILL REMEMBER (SO WILL I), THE: 1948	#13 – Mar. 1948
STAY AS SWEET AS YOU ARE: 1934	# 1 – Dec. 1934
STAY IN YOUR OWN BACK YARD: 1902	#17 – Oct. 1902
STEALING: 1922	#15 – Apr. 1922
STEAMBOAT BILL: 1911	# 3 – July 1911
STEIN SONG (Fenstad): 1930	# 1 – Apr. 1930
STEIN SONG, A (Luders); *SEE: HEIDELBERG (STEIN SONG): 1903*	
STELLA: 1923	# 9 – Aug. 1923
STOLEN KISSES: 1921	T30 – Nov. 1921
STOMPIN' AT THE SAVOY: 1936	#17 – July 1936
STONE COLD DEAD IN DE MARKET: 1946	#18 – July 1946
STOP! IT'S WONDERFUL: 1939	# 7 – Dec. 1939
STOP! YOU'RE BREAKING MY HEART: 1937	#18 – Aug. 1937
STOP BEATIN' 'ROUND THE MULBERRY BUSH: 1938	# 6 – Sept. 1938
STOP YER TICKLIN', JOCK! 1908	#20 – Dec. 1907
STORMY WEATHER: 1933	# 1 – May 1933
STRAIGHTEN UP AND FLY RIGHT: 1944	#15 – July 1944
STRANGE ENCHANTMENT: 1939	# 7 – July 1939
STRANGE INTERLUDE: 1932	# 6 – Sept. 1932
STRANGE MUSIC: 1944	#19 – Nov. 1944
STREET OF DREAMS (V. Young): 1933	# 9 – Feb. 1933
STREET OF DREAMS (Sturken): 1991	#17 – Nov. 1991
STREETS OF NEW YORK, THE; *SEE: IN OLD NEW YORK: 1907*	
STRICTLY INSTRUMENTAL: 1942	#12 – Sept. 1942
STRIKE UP THE BAND: 1930	#13 – Apr. 1930
STRIKE UP THE BAND, HERE COMES A SAILOR: 1900	# 1 – Aug. 1900
STRING OF PEARLS, A: 1942	# 6 – Mar. 1942
STRIP POLKA: 1942	# 4 – Oct. 1942
STRUT, MISS LIZZIE: 1921	# 5 – July 1921
STUFF LIKE THAT THERE: 1945	#13 – May 1945
STUMBLING: 1922	# 1 – July 1922
SUDDENLY IT'S SPRING: 1944	#14 – June 1944
SUEZ: 1922	#17 – Sept. 1922
SUGAR BLUES (C. Williams): 1931	#20 – Apr. 1931
SUGAR BLUES (C. Williams): 1935	#16 – Aug. 1935
SUGAR BLUES (C. Williams): 1947	#15 – Nov. 1947
SUGAR MOON (Wenrich): 1910	#14 – Dec. 1910
SUGAR MOON (Wolfe): 1958	# 7 – June 1958
SUMMER SOUVENIRS: 1938	# 9 – Nov. 1938
SUN DANCE, THE: 1903	# 6 – Oct. 1903
SUNBONNET SUE: 1908	# 1 – Oct. 1908
SUNDAY: 1927	# 7 – Feb. 1927
SUNDAY, MONDAY, OR ALWAYS: 1943	# 1 – Oct. 1943
SUNDAY IN THE PARK: 1938	#18 – Apr. 1938
SUNDAY KIND OF LOVE, A: 1947	#14 – June 1947
SUNFLOWER: 1949	# 4 – Apr. 1949
SUNNY SIDE UP: 1929	# 9 – Dec. 1929
SUNRISE SERENADE: 1939	# 4 – June 1939
SUNSHINE (Berlin): 1928	# 8 – May 1928
SUNSHINE (Kim): 1972	# 4 – Jan. 1972
SUNSHINE AND ROSES: 1913	#15 – Dec. 1913
SUNSHINE OF YOUR SMILE, THE: 1916	# 4 – Sept. 1916
SURRENDER (G. Weiss): 1946	# 3 – Aug. 1946
SURRENDER (DeCurtis): 1961	# 1 – Mar. 1961
SWANEE: 1920	# 1 – May 1920
SWANEE BUTTERFLY: 1925	#16 – June 1925
SWANEE RIVER MOON: 1922	# 4 – May 1922
SWEET ADELINE: 1904	# 2 – Feb. 1905
SWEET AND LOVELY (G. Arnheim): 1931	# 1 – Oct. 1931
SWEET AND LOVELY (G. Arnheim): 1944	#15 – Oct. 1944
SWEET AND LOW-DOWN: 1926	#12 – Apr. 1926
SWEET AND SLOW: 1935	#15 – Aug. 1935
SWEET ANNIE MOORE: 1901	# 1 – Aug. 1901
SWEET AS A SONG: 1938	# 4 – Mar. 1938
SWEET DREAMS, SWEETHEART: 1945	# 7 – Feb. 1945
SWEET ELOISE: 1942	#13 – July 1942
SWEET EMALINA, MY GAL: 1917	#16 – Oct. 1917
SWEET GEORGIA BROWN (M. Pinkard): 1925	# 2 – Aug. 1925
SWEET GEORGIA BROWN (M. Pinkard): 1949	#15 – Feb. 1949
SWEET HAWAIIAN MOONLIGHT: 1919	# 3 – July 1919
SWEET INDIANA HOME: 1922	#14 – Sept. 1922
SWEET IS THE WORD FOR YOU: 1937	#15 – May 1937
SWEET JENNIE LEE: 1930	# 9 – Dec. 1930
SWEET KENTUCKY LADY: 1915	#12 – May 1915
SWEET LADY (Crumit): 1921	# 3 – Nov. 1921
SWEET LADY (C. Farrar): 1999	#12 – May 1999
SWEET LEILANI: 1937	# 3 – May 1937
SWEET LITTLE BUTTERCUP: 1918	# 9 – Apr. 1918
SWEET LITTLE YOU: 1924	#20 – Nov. 1924
SWEET LORRAINE (Burwell): 1928	#15 – Aug. 1928
SWEET LORRAINE (Burwell): 1944	#18 – July 1944
SWEET MAMA (PAPA'S GETTIN' MAD): 1921	#17 – Feb. 1921
SWEET MUSIC: 1935	#16 – Mar. 1935

SWEET SOMEONE: 1938 .... #10 – Feb. 1938
SWEET SUE (JUST YOU): 1928 .... #11 – Sept. 1928
SWEETEST FLOWER THAT GROWS IN TENNESSEE, THE: 1904 .. #19 – Feb. 1904
SWEETEST GIRL IN DIXIE, THE: 1904 .... #17 – Aug. 1904
SWEETEST MAID OF ALL, THE: 1908 .... # 7 – June 1908
SWEETHEART, DARLIN': 1933 .... # 3 – July 1933
SWEETHEART, SWEETHEART, SWEETHEART;
SEE: WILL YOU REMEMBER (SWEETHEART) (Romberg): 1918, 1937
SWEETHEART DAYS: 1908 .... # 9 – June 1908
(I love you) SWEETHEART OF ALL MY DREAMS (Fitch): 1929 ... # 9 – Mar. 1929
(I love you) SWEETHEART OF ALL MY DREAMS (Fitch): 1945 ... #17 – May 1945
SWEETHEART OF MY STUDENT DAYS: 1930 .... # 8 – Dec. 1930
SWEETHEART OF SIGMA CHI: 1928 .... # 6 – Jan. 1928
SWEETHEARTS (Herbert, Smith): 1913 .... #14 – Aug. 1913
SWEETHEARTS (Herbert, Forrest): 1939 .... #18 – Feb. 1939
SWEETHEARTS FOREVER: 1932 .... # 7 – Oct. 1932
SWEETHEARTS ON PARADE: 1929 .... # 1 – Feb. 1929
SWEETIE PIE: 1934 .... #14 – Nov. 1934
SWING HIGH, SWING LOW: 1937 .... #19 – Apr. 1937
SWINGIN' DOWN THE LANE: 1923 .... # 2 – Aug. 1923
SWINGIN' IN A HAMMOCK: 1930 .... # 6 – Sept. 1930
SWINGING ON A STAR: 1944 .... # 1 – Aug. 1944
SWINGTIME IN THE ROCKIES: 1936 .... #18 – Aug. 1936
SYMPATHY (Paley): 1906 .... # 9 – Feb. 1906
SYMPATHY (Friml): 1913 .... #18 – Aug. 1913
SYMPATHY (Burke): 1929; *SEE: ALL THAT I'M ASKING IS SYMPATHY: 1929*
SYMPHONY: 1946 .... # 1 – Jan. 1946
SYNCOPATED WALK: 1915 .... #18 – Apr. 1915

T

'TAIN'T NO SIN (TO DANCE AROUND IN YOUR BONES): 1930 ... #15 – Mar. 1930
TAKE A LITTLE TIP FROM FATHER: 1912 .... # 6 – Aug. 1912
TAKE IT EASY (V. Mizzy): 1944 .... #20 – Mar. 1944
TAKE IT EASY (G. Frey): 1972 .... #12 – July 1972
TAKE IT FROM THERE: 1943 .... #16 – July 1943
TAKE ME: 1942 .... # 6 – Sept. 1942
TAKE ME BACK TO BABYLAND: 1910 .... #17 – Dec. 1910
TAKE ME BACK TO MY BOOTS AND SADDLE: 1935 .... # 4 – Dec. 1935
TAKE ME BACK TO NEW YORK TOWN: 1907 .... # 3 – Nov. 1907
TAKE ME BACK TO THE GARDEN OF LOVE: 1912 .... #10 – May 1912
TAKE ME BACK TO YOUR HEART AGAIN: 1906 .... #10 – June 1906
TAKE ME IN YOUR ARMS AGAIN: 1912 .... #20 – May 1912
TAKE ME OUT TO THE BALL GAME (A. Von Tilzer): 1908 .... # 1 – Aug. 1908
TAKE ME OUT TO THE BALL GAME (A. Von Tilzer): 1909 .... #20 – June 1909
TAKE ME TO THE LAND OF JAZZ: 1919 .... #14 – Nov. 1919
TAKE ME TO THE MIDNIGHT CAKE WALK BALL: 1915 .... T30 – Dec. 1915
TAKE ME UP WITH YOU, DEARIE: 1909 .... #10 – Aug. 1909
TAKE MY HEART (Ahlert): 1936 .... # 4 – July 1936
TAKE MY HEART (Smith): 1981 .... #17 – Dec. 1981
TAKE MY HEART (IT'S YOURS FOREVER) (Borrelli): 1952 ...... #17 – July 1952
TAKE OH TAKE THOSE LIPS AWAY: 1924 .... #11 – Feb. 1924
TAKE YOUR TOMORROW (AND GIVE ME TODAY): 1928 .... # 9 – Jan. 1929
TAKING A CHANCE ON LOVE: 1943 .... # 6 – June 1943
TALE OF A BUMBLE BEE, THE: 1901 .... #13 – Dec. 1901
TALE OF THE KANGAROO, THE: 1901 .... # 5 – Apr. 1901
TALE OF THE SEASHELL, THE: 1903 .... #15 – Feb. 1903
TALE OF THE TURTLE DOVE, THE: 1905 .... # 5 – Mar. 1905
TALE THE CHURCH BELLS TOLLED, THE: 1907 .... # 4 – May 1907
TALK OF THE TOWN, THE; *SEE: IT'S THE TALK OF THE TOWN: 1933*
TALKIN' TO MYSELF: 1934 .... #12 – Oct. 1934
TALKING THROUGH MY HEART; *SEE: I'M TALKING THROUGH MY HEART: 1936*
TALLAHASSEE: 1947 .... #11 – Aug. 1947
TAMIAMI TRAIL: 1926 .... # 9 – May 1926
TAMMANY: 1905 .... # 2 – June 1905
TAMPICO: 1945 .... #12 – Aug. 1945
TANGERINE (Schertzinger): 1942 .... # 3 – May 1942
TANGERINE (Schertzinger): 1976 .... #18 – Apr. 1976
TARA TALARA TALA: 1949 .... #19 – Feb. 1949
TEA FOR TWO (Youmans): 1924 .... # 3 – Dec. 1924
TEA FOR TWO (Youmans): 1926 .... #19 – Jan. 1926
TEA FOR TWO CHA-CHA (Youmans): 1958 .... # 6 – Oct. 1958
TEA LEAVES: 1948 .... #20 – Aug. 1948
TEARS: 1931 .... #13 – Feb. 1931
TEARS FROM MY INKWELL: 1939 .... #18 – May 1939
TEASING: 1904 .... # 1 – Dec. 1904
TEDDY BEARS' PICNIC, THE (Bratton): 1907 .... #19 – Aug. 1907
TEDDY BEARS' PICNIC, THE (Bratton): 1908 .... #11 – June 1908
TELL HER IN THE SPRINGTIME: 1925 .... #18 – Mar. 1925
TELL ME, LITTLE GYPSY: 1920 .... # 4 – Oct. 1920
TELL ME, PRETTY MAIDEN: 1901 .... # 3 – Mar. 1901
TELL ME (Wilson): 1995 .... # 5 – Nov. 1995
TELL ME (Cantrell): 1996 .... #19 – Nov. 1996
TELL ME (WHY NIGHTS ARE LONELY): 1919 .... # 2 – Nov. 1919
TELL ME A STORY (L. Stock): 1948 .... #10 – June 1948
TELL ME A STORY (Gilkyson): 1953 .... # 6 – Apr. 1953
TELL ME THAT YOU LOVE ME: 1935 .... # 7 – June 1935
TELL ME TONIGHT: 1933 .... #20 – July 1933
TELL ME WITH YOUR EYES: 1905 .... #17 – Mar. 1905
TELLING IT TO THE DAISIES: 1930 .... #18 – June 1930
TEMPTATION (N.H.Brown): 1934 .... # 8 – Feb. 1934
TEMPTATION (TIM-TAY-SHUN) (N.H.Brown, R. Ingle): 1947 .... # 7 – July 1947
TEMPTATION (Corina): 1991 .... # 6 – Aug. 1991
TEMPTATION RAG: 1910 .... # 7 – Aug. 1910
TEN BABY FINGERS AND TEN BABY TOES;
SEE: MY MOTHER'S ROSARY: 1916
TEN CENTS A DANCE: 1930 .... # 9 – July 1930
TEN LITTLE FINGERS AND TEN LITTLE TOES: 1922 .... # 5 – Jan. 1922
TEN LITTLE MILES FROM TOWN: 1928 .... #15 – Oct. 1928
TEN PRETTY GIRLS: 1938 .... #13 – Feb. 1938
TEN THOUSAND YEARS FROM NOW: 1923 .... # 8 – Nov. 1923
TENNESSEE FISH FRY: 1940 .... #19 – July 1940
TESS'S TORCH SONG: 1944 .... #19 – June 1944
TESSIE, YOU ARE THE ONLY, ONLY, ONLY: 1903 .... # 4 – Mar. 1903
THANK YOU FOR A LOVELY EVENING: 1934 .... #17 – Aug. 1934
THANKS: 1933 .... # 3 – Nov. 1933
THANKS A MILLION: 1935 .... # 6 – Dec. 1935
THANKS FOR EVERYTHING: 1939 .... # 7 – Feb. 1939
THANKS FOR THE BUGGY RIDE: 1926 .... # 6 – May 1926
THANKS FOR THE MEMORY: 1938 .... # 1 – Mar. 1938
THAT BABOON BABY DANCE: 1912 .... #18 – June 1912
THAT BEAUTIFUL RAG: 1911 .... #20 – Jan. 1911
THAT CERTAIN FEELING: 1926 .... #12 – Apr. 1926
THAT CERTAIN PARTY (Donaldson): 1926 .... # 4 – Feb. 1926
THAT CERTAIN PARTY (Donaldson): 1948 .... #14 – Nov. 1948
THAT CROONY MELODY; *SEE: MY CROONY MELODY: 1914*
THAT DAFFYDIL RAG: 1912 .... #20 – Mar. 1912
THAT DREAMY ITALIAN WALTZ: 1911 .... #17 – Mar. 1911
(Did you ever get) THAT FEELING IN THE MOONLIGHT: 1945 ... # 9 – Dec. 1945
THAT HAUNTING MELODY: 1912 .... # 6 – Apr. 1912
THAT INTERNATIONAL RAG: 1913 .... # 3 – Nov. 1913
THAT ITALIAN RAG: 1910 .... # 8 – May 1910
THAT LOVIN' RAG: 1909 .... T30 – June 1909
THAT LUCKY OLD SUN (B. Smith): 1949 .... # 1 – Nov. 1949

THAT LUCKY OLD SUN (B. Smith): 1964	#20 – Jan. 1964
THAT MELLOW MELODY: 1912	# 7 – Nov. 1912
THAT MESMERIZING MENDELSSOHN TUNE: 1910	# 2 – Mar. 1910
THAT MINOR STRAIN: 1911	#19 – Jan. 1911
THAT MYSTERIOUS RAG: 1912	# 2 – Mar. 1912
THAT NAUGHTY WALTZ: 1920	# 6 – May 1920
THAT OLD BLACK MAGIC (Arlen): 1943	# 2 – Mar. 1943
THAT OLD BLACK MAGIC (Arlen): 1955	#20 – July 1955
THAT OLD FEELING: 1937	# 1 – Oct. 1937
THAT OLD GANG OF MINE: 1923	# 1 – Oct. 1923
THAT OLD GIRL OF MINE: 1913	# 2 – Mar. 1913
THAT OLD IRISH MOTHER OF MINE: 1920	#12 – Nov. 1920
THAT RAILROAD RAG: 1911	#18 – July 1911
THAT RED-HEAD GAL: 1923	#17 – June 1923
THAT TUMBLEDOWN SHACK IN ATHLONE (Sanders): 1919	#18 – May 1919
THAT TUMBLEDOWN SHACK IN ATHLONE (Sanders): 1920	#17 – Apr. 1920
THAT WAS BEFORE I MET YOU: 1911	#15 – May 1911
THAT WONDERFUL MOTHER OF MINE: 1919	# 5 – Apr. 1919
THAT WONDERFUL SOMETHING: 1930	#19 – Feb. 1930
THAT'S A-PLENTY: 1909	# 4 – Nov. 1909
THAT'S AN IRISH LULLABY; *SEE: TOO-RA LOO-RA LOO-RAL: 1914, 1944*	
THAT'S FOR ME (Monaco): 1940	#10 – Oct. 1940
THAT'S FOR ME (Rodgers): 1945	# 4 – Nov. 1945
THAT'S GRATITUDE: 1908	#12 – Feb. 1908
THAT'S HOW I NEED YOU: 1912	# 1 – Jan. 1913
THAT'S HOW MUCH I LOVE YOU: 1947	#20 – Apr. 1947
THAT'S MY DESIRE: 1947	# 2 – Aug. 1947
THAT'S MY WEAKNESS NOW: 1928	# 2 – Sept. 1928
THAT'S THE SONG OF SONGS FOR ME: 1915	#12 – Nov. 1915
THAT'S WHAT THE ROSE SAID TO ME: 1907	# 5 – Dec. 1907
THAT'S WHERE I CAME IN: 1947	#18 – May 1947
THAT'S YIDDISHA LOVE: 1910	# 8 – Nov. 1910
THEN I'D BE SATISFIED WITH LIFE: 1903	#10 – Feb. 1903
THEN I'LL BE HAPPY: 1926	# 5 – Apr. 1926
THEN I'LL BE TIRED OF YOU: 1934	#15 – Oct. 1934
THEN I'LL STOP LOVING YOU: 1913	#13 – Apr. 1913
THERE! I'VE SAID IT AGAIN (Evans): 1945	# 3 – July 1945
THERE! I'VE SAID IT AGAIN (Evans): 1964	# 1 – Jan. 1964
THERE ARE SUCH THINGS: 1943	# 1 – Jan. 1943
THERE GOES MY HEART: 1934	#19 – Mar. 1934
THERE GOES THAT SONG AGAIN: 1945	# 2 – Jan. 1945
THERE I GO: 1940	# 3 – Nov. 1940
THERE IS NO GREATER LOVE: 1936	#15 – May 1936
THERE MUST BE A WAY: 1945	# 8 – Sept. 1945
THERE NEVER WAS A GIRL LIKE YOU: 1908	# 4 – Aug. 1908
THERE WILL NEVER BE ANOTHER YOU: 1942	#16 – Dec. 1942
THERE'LL BE A HOT TIME IN THE TOWN OF BERLIN: 1944	#10 – Nov. 1944
THERE'LL BE SOME CHANGES MADE (Overstreet): 1924	#17 – Dec. 1924
THERE'LL BE SOME CHANGES MADE (Overstreet): 1941	# 1 – Apr. 1941
THERE'LL COME A TIME: 1911	#13 – May 1911
THERE'S A BROKEN HEART FOR EVERY LIGHT ON BROADWAY: 1916	# 8 – Apr. 1916
THERE'S A DARK MAN COMING WITH A BUNDLE: 1905	# 2 – Jan. 1905
THERE'S A FARAWAY LOOK IN YOUR EYE: 1938	#15 – Sept. 1938
THERE'S A GIRL IN HAVANA: 1912	#14 – Feb. 1912
THERE'S A GIRL IN THE HEART OF MARYLAND: 1913	# 1 – Jan. 1914
THERE'S A GOLD MINE IN THE SKY: 1938	# 4 – Jan. 1938
THERE'S A HARBOR OF DREAMBOATS: 1943	#12 – May 1943
THERE'S A LITTLE BIT OF BAD IN EVERY GOOD LITTLE GIRL: 1916	# 1 – Dec. 1916
THERE'S A LITTLE LANE WITHOUT A TURNING ON THE WAY TO HOME SWEET HOME: 1915	# 5 – Nov. 1915
THERE'S A LITTLE SPARK OF LOVE STILL BURNING: 1915	# 2 – May 1915
THERE'S A LONG, LONG TRAIL (Elliott): 1916	# 6 – Oct. 1916
THERE'S A LONG, LONG TRAIL (Elliott): 1918	# 3 – Mar. 1918
THERE'S A LULL IN MY LIFE: 1937	# 5 – June 1937
THERE'S A NEW STAR IN HEAVEN TONIGHT (RUDOLPH VALENTINO): 1926	#18 – Nov. 1926
THERE'S A QUAKER DOWN IN QUAKER TOWN: 1916	# 3 – Aug. 1916
THERE'S A RAINBOW 'ROUND MY SHOULDER: 1928	# 2 – Dec. 1928
THERE'S A SHANTY IN OLD SHANTY TOWN; *SEE: IN A SHANTY IN OLD SHANTY TOWN: 1932*	
THERE'S A SMALL HOTEL: 1936	# 5 – July 1936
THERE'S A STAR-SPANGLED BANNER WAVING SOMEWHERE: 1943	# 8 – Dec. 1942
THERE'S DANGER IN YOUR EYES, CHERIE: 1930	# 4 – Apr. 1930
THERE'S EGYPT IN YOUR DREAMY EYES: 1917	# 8 – Apr. 1917
THERE'S EVERYTHING NICE ABOUT YOU: 1927	#12 – June 1927
THERE'S FROST ON THE MOON: 1937	#16 – Jan. 1937
THERE'S HONEY ON THE MOON TONIGHT: 1938	#13 – July 1938
THERE'S NO NORTH OR SOUTH TODAY: 1901	#12 – June 1901
THERE'S NO ONE BUT YOU: 1946	#17 – Aug. 1946
THERE'S NO YOU: 1945	#16 – Sept. 1945
THERE'S SOMEONE MORE LONESOME THAN YOU: 1917	#13 – Apr. 1917
THERE'S SOMETHING IN THE AIR: 1937	# 7 – Feb. 1937
THERE'S SOMETHING NICE ABOUT EVERYONE; *SEE: THERE'S EVERYTHING NICE ABOUT YOU: 1927*	
THERE'S YES! YES! IN YOUR EYES (Santly): 1924	# 2 – July 1924
THERE'S YES! YES! IN YOUR EYES (Santly): 1949	#15 – Sept. 1949
THESE FOOLISH THINGS: 1936	# 1 – July 1936
THEY ALL HAD A FINGER IN THE PIE: 1914	#17 – Dec. 1914
THEY ALL LAUGHED: 1937	#16 – May 1937
THEY ALWAYS PICK ON ME: 1911	#12 – Oct. 1911
THEY CAN'T TAKE THAT AWAY FROM ME: 1937	# 6 – June 1937
THEY DIDN'T BELIEVE ME: 1916	# 2 – Feb. 1916
THEY GO WILD, SIMPLY WILD, OVER ME: 1917	# 3 – Oct. 1917
THEY GOTTA QUIT KICKIN' MY DAWG AROUND: 1912	#11 – May 1912
THEY SAY: 1939	#7 – Feb. 1939
THEY SAY IT'S WONDERFUL: 1946	# 2 – July 1946
THEY WERE ALL OUT OF STEP BUT JIM: 1918	# 5 – Aug. 1918
THEY'RE ALL SWEETIES: 1919	#19 – Dec. 1919
THEY'RE EITHER TOO YOUNG OR TOO OLD: 1943	# 6 – Dec. 1943
THEY'RE ON THEIR WAY TO MEXICO: 1914	T30 – July 1914
THEY'RE WEARIN' 'EM HIGHER IN HAWAII: 1917	# 2 – Feb. 1917
THINGS I LOVE, THE: 1941	# 5 – July 1941
THINGS WE DID LAST SUMMER, THE: 1946	# 9 – Nov. 1946
THINKING OF YOU (Ruby): 1950	# 4 – Nov. 1950
THINKING OF YOU (Messina): 1973	#18 – May 1973
THINKING OF YOU (DeSalvo): 1989	#12 – May 1989
(I've grown so lonesome) THINKING OF YOU (Donaldson): 1927	# 6 – Mar. 1927
THIS CAN'T BE LOVE: 1939	# 4 – Jan. 1939
THIS CHANGING WORLD: 1940	#13 – Feb. 1940
THIS IS ALWAYS: 1946	# 8 – Nov. 1946
THIS IS IT (A. Schwartz): 1939	#12 – Apr. 1939
THIS IS IT (K. Loggins): 1980	#11 – Feb. 1980
THIS IS MY LAST AFFAIR; *SEE: (This is) MY LAST AFFAIR: 1937*	
THIS IS NO DREAM: 1939	#13 – Aug. 1939
THIS IS NO LAUGHING MATTER: 1942	#10 – Jan. 1942
THIS IS THE LIFE: 1914	# 1 – June 1914
THIS IS THE MISSUS: 1931	#14 – Oct. 1931
THIS IS WORTH FIGHTING FOR: 1942	#12 – Aug. 1942
THIS LITTLE PIGGIE WENT TO MARKET: 1934	# 2 – Mar. 1934
THIS LOVE OF MINE: 1941	# 4 – Dec. 1941
THIS NIGHT (WILL BE MY SOUVENIR): 1939	#19 – Apr. 1939
THIS ROSE BRINGS MY HEART TO YOU: 1909	#15 – May 1909

THIS TIME IT'S LOVE: 1933 .... # 9 – Oct. 1933
THIS TIME IT'S REAL: 1938 .... #12 – July 1938
THIS TIME THE DREAM'S ON ME: 1941 .... #14 – Dec. 1941
THIS YEAR'S KISSES: 1937 .... # 2 – Mar. 1937
THOU SWELL: 1928 .... # 6 – Mar. 1928
THOUSAND GOODNIGHTS, A: 1934 .... # 2 – May 1934
THREE CABALLEROS: 1945 .... #12 – Mar. 1945
THREE LITTLE FISHIES (ITTY BITTY POO): 1939............ # 1 – June 1939
THREE LITTLE SISTERS: 1942............................ # 7 – July 1942
THREE LITTLE WORDS: 1930 .... # 1 – Nov. 1930
THREE O'CLOCK IN THE MORNING: 1922.................. # 1 – June 1922
THREE ON A MATCH: 1932............................... # 9 – Sept. 1932
THREE STRIKES OUT;
SEE: ONE STRIKE, TWO STRIKES, THREE STRIKES OUT: 1902
THREE WONDERFUL LETTERS FROM HOME: 1918 .... #13 – June 1918
THREE'S A CROWD: 1932............................... # 5 – Oct. 1932
THRILL IS GONE, THE (Henderson): 1931 .... #14 – Oct. 1931
THRILL IS GONE, THE (Hawkins): 1970 .... #16 – Feb. 1970
THRILLED: 1935 .... #12 – July 1935
THROUGH: 1929...................................... #12 – Dec. 1929
THROUGH A LONG AND SLEEPLESS NIGHT: 1949 .... #18 – Nov. 1949
THROUGH THE COURTESY OF LOVE: 1936................. #20 – Oct. 1936
THROW ANOTHER LOG ON THE FIRE: 1934 .... # 6 – Mar. 1934
THROW ME A ROSE: 1917 .... # 9 – Jan. 1917
TI-PI-TIN: 1938....................................... # 1 – Apr. 1938
TICKLE TOE, THE;
SEE: EVERYBODY OUGHT TO KNOW HOW TO DO THE TICKLE TOE: 1918
TIE THAT BINDS, THE: 1901 .... #12 – Oct. 1901
TIE YOUR LITTLE BULL OUTSIDE: 1910.................... #11 – Apr. 1910
TIGER RAG (LaRocca): 1918 .... #15 – Oct. 1918
TIGER RAG (LaRocca): 1931 .... #17 – Dec. 1931
TIGER RAG (LaRocca): 1952 .... # 8 – Feb. 1952
'TIL REVEILLE: 1941 .... # 2 – Sept. 1941
TILL THE CLOUDS ROLL BY: 1917........................ # 9 – Aug. 1917
TILL THE END OF TIME: 1945........................... # 1 – Sept. 1945
TILL THE SANDS OF THE DESERT GROW COLD: 1912......... # 4 – Sept. 1912
TILL THEN (Seiler): 1944............................... #17 – Sept. 1944
TILL THEN (Seiler): 1954............................... #11 – Mar. 1954
TILL WE MEET AGAIN: 1919............................. # 1 – Feb. 1919
TIM-TAY-SHUN; *SEE: TEMPTATION (TIM-TAY-SHUN): 1947*
TIMBUCTOO: 1921 .... #12 – May 1921
TIME AFTER TIME (J. Styne): 1947....................... #17 – July 1947
TIME AFTER TIME (C. Lauper): 1984 .... # 1 – June 1984
TIME AFTER TIME (C. Lauper): 1998 .... # 6 – Sept. 1998
TIME ALONE WILL TELL: 1944 .... #17 – June 1944
TIME ON MY HANDS: 1931.............................. # 4 – Dec. 1931
TIME WAITS FOR NO ONE: 1944 .... # 3 – Sept. 1944
TIME WAS: 1941 .... #12 – Oct. 1941
TING-A-LING (THE WALTZ OF THE BELLS): 1926............ #13 – Oct. 1926
TINY LITTLE FINGERPRINTS: 1935 .... # 7 – Mar. 1935
TIP TOE THROUGH THE TULIPS WITH ME (Burke): 1929 ...... # 1 – Oct. 1929
TIP TOE THROUGH THE TULIPS WITH ME (Burke): 1968 ...... #17 – June 1968
TIP TOP TIPPERARY MARY: 1915 .... #11 – Feb. 1915
TIPPERARY: 1908 .... #20 – May 1908
TIPPIN' IN: 1945...................................... #19 – May 1945
'TIS AUTUMN: 1942 .... #13 – Feb. 1942
TISHOMINGO BLUES: 1918 .... #14 – July 1918
TO EACH HIS OWN: 1946 .... # 1 – Aug. 1946
TO HAVE, TO HOLD, TO LOVE: 1913 .... # 8 – Aug. 1913
TO THE END OF THE WORLD WITH YOU: 1909 .... # 5 – Sept. 1909
TO WHOM IT MAY CONCERN: 1931 .... #13 – Feb. 1931
TO YOU: 1939 .... #11 – Aug. 1939
TO YOU, SWEETHEART, ALOHA: 1940 .... #13 – Feb. 1940
TOGETHER (Henderson): 1928 .... # 1 – Apr. 1928
TOGETHER (Henderson): 1944 .... # 2 – Nov. 1944
TOGETHER (Henderson): 1961 .... # 6 – Aug. 1961
TOGETHER (Gamble): 1981............................. #18 – Feb. 1981
TOGETHER, WE TWO: 1928 .... #15 – Feb. 1928
TONIGHT (Dominguez); *SEE: PERFIDIA: 1941, 1952, 1960*
TONIGHT (Bernstein): 1961 .... # 9 – Dec. 1961
TONIGHT (Taylor): 1984................................ #13 – May 1984
TONIGHT (Starr): 1990 .... # 7 – Sept. 1990
TONIGHT WE LOVE: 1941 .... # 5 – Nov. 1941
TONIGHT YOU BELONG TO ME (L. David): 1927 .... # 2 – Feb. 1927
TONIGHT YOU BELONG TO ME (L. David): 1956 .... # 3 – Sept. 1956
TOO FAT POLKA: 1947 .... # 4 – Dec. 1947
TOO MANY TEARS: 1932................................ # 6 – May 1932
TOO MARVELOUS FOR WORDS: 1937 .... # 3 – May 1937
TOO MUCH MUSTARD: 1913 .... T30 – June 1913
(I'm) TOO ROMANTIC: 1940............................. # 5 – May 1940
TOO-RA LOO-RA LOO-RAL (Shannon): 1914 .... #10 – Mar. 1914
TOO-RA LOO-RA LOO-RAL (Shannon): 1944 .... #13 – Dec. 1944
TOODLE-OO: 1937 .... #14 – July 1937
TOOLIE OOLIE DOOLIE (THE YODEL POLKA): 1948 .... # 4 – May 1948
TOOT, TOOT, TOOTSIE! (GOODBYE): 1923 .... # 2 – Jan. 1923
TOP HAT, WHITE TIE, AND TAILS: 1935.................... # 6 – Sept. 1935
TORMENTED: 1936 .... # 7 – May 1936
TOUCH OF YOUR LIPS, THE: 1936........................ # 6 – May 1936
TOWN WHERE I WAS BORN, THE: 1905 .... #13 – Jan. 1906
TOYLAND: 1904 .... # 6 – Mar. 1904
TRADE WINDS: 1940................................... # 2 – Oct. 1940
TRAIL OF THE LONESOME PINE, THE: 1913................. # 1 – July 1913
TREE IN THE MEADOW, A: 1948 .... # 1 – Oct. 1948
TRES MOUTARD; *SEE: TOO MUCH MUSTARD: 1913*
TRIPOLI: 1920 .... # 7 – Nov. 1920
TROLLEY SONG, THE: 1944 .... # 1 – Dec. 1944
TROUBADOUR, THE: 1904.............................. #16 – Nov. 1904
TROUBLE IN PARADISE: 1933 .... #16 – Aug. 1933
TRUCKIN': 1935 .... # 8 – Nov. 1935
TRUE (Samuels): 1934................................. #11 – Apr. 1934
TRUE (Jolley): 1983 .... # 4 – Oct. 1983
TRUE BLUE LOU: 1929................................. #12 – Oct. 1929
TRUE CONFESSION: 1938 .... # 3 – Jan. 1938
TRUE HEART: 1908.................................... # 8 – June 1908
TRUST IN ME: 1937 .... # 5 – Mar. 1937
TRY A LITTLE TENDERNESS: 1933 .... # 5 – Apr. 1933
TRY TO FORGET: 1932 .... #19 – Jan. 1932
TSCHAIKOVSKY'S PIANO CONCERTO IN B FLAT; *SEE: PIANO CONCERTO: 1941*
TUCK ME TO SLEEP IN MY OLD 'TUCKY HOME: 1921.......... # 2 – Jan. 1922
TULIE TULIP TIME: 1938................................ #19 – Sept. 1938
TULIP TIME: 1919 .... # 6 – Oct. 1919
TUMBLING TUMBLEWEEDS: 1934......................... #18 – Sept. 1934
TURN BACK THE UNIVERSE AND GIVE ME YESTERDAY: 1916 ... # 3 – Nov. 1916
TURN ON THE HEAT: 1929 .... #13 – Dec. 1929
TUXEDO JUNCTION: 1940 .... # 7 – Apr. 1940
TWELFTH STREET RAG (Bowman): 1920 .... #15 – Nov. 1920
TWELFTH STREET RAG (Bowman): 1948 .... # 2 – Oct. 1948
TWENTY-FOUR HOURS A DAY: 1935....................... # 5 – Dec. 1935
TWENTY-FOUR HOURS OF SUNSHINE: 1949................. #11 – Sept. 1949
TWILIGHT ON THE TRAIL: 1936.......................... #18 – July 1936
TWILIGHT TIME (Nevins): 1945.......................... #14 – Feb. 1945
TWILIGHT TIME (Nevins): 1958.......................... # 2 – Apr. 1958
TWO BLACK CROWS, PARTS 1 AND 2: 1927................. #15 – Aug. 1927
TWO BLUE EYES: 1908................................. # 1 – Jan. 1908
TWO CIGARETTES IN THE DARK: 1934 .... # 2 – Oct. 1934
TWO DIRTY LITTLE HANDS: 1906 .... #17 – June 1906

TWO DREAMS GOT TOGETHER: 1938	#18 – Feb. 1938
TWO DREAMS MET: 1940	#13 – Nov. 1940
TWO HEARTS IN THREE-QUARTER TIME: 1931	# 8 – May 1931
TWO HEARTS THAT PASS IN THE NIGHT: 1941	#17 – July 1941
TWO IN LOVE: 1941	#10 – Dec. 1941
TWO IS COMPANY, THREE IS A CROWD: 1903	# 7 – Mar. 1903
TWO LITTLE BABY SHOES: 1908	#14 – Apr. 1908
TWO LITTLE LOVE BEES: 1911	#11 – July 1911
TWO SLEEPY PEOPLE: 1938	# 2 – Dec. 1938
TWO TICKETS TO GEORGIA: 1933	#12 – May 1933

U

UKULELE LADY: 1925	# 2 – Aug. 1925
UMBRELLA MAN, THE: 1939	# 2 – Feb. 1939
UN PEU D'AMOUR; *SEE: LITTLE LOVE, A LITTLE KISS, A: 1914*	
UNDECIDED (Shavers): 1939	#20 – Apr. 1939
UNDECIDED (Shavers): 1951	# 5 – Dec. 1951
UNDER A BLANKET OF BLUE: 1933	# 6 – Aug. 1933
UNDER A TEXAS MOON: 1930	# 4 – May 1930
UNDER ANY OLD FLAG AT ALL: 1908	#15 – Apr. 1908
UNDER THE AMERICAN FLAG: 1915	#19 – Sept. 1915
UNDER THE ANHEUSER BUSH: 1904	# 4 – June 1904
UNDER THE BAMBOO TREE: 1903	# 1 – Feb. 1903
UNDER THE MOON: 1927	#15 – Oct. 1927
UNDER THE TROPICAL MOON: 1907	#19 – Oct. 1907
UNDER THE YUM YUM TREE: 1911	# 4 – Feb. 1911
UNDERNEATH THE ARCHES: 1948	# 6 – Oct. 1948
UNDERNEATH THE HARLEM MOON: 1932	# 9 – Dec. 1932
UNDERNEATH THE MELLOW MOON: 1923	#14 – July 1923
UNDERNEATH THE STARS: 1916	# 4 – Mar. 1916
UNTER DEN LINDEN: 1904	# 8 – July 1904
UNTIL: 1948	# 7 – Dec. 1948
UNTIL THE REAL THING COMES ALONG: 1936	# 3 – Sept. 1936
UNTIL TODAY: 1936	#20 – Sept. 1936
UNTIL TOMORROW: 1941	#14 – July 1941
UP, UP, UP IN MY AEROPLANE: 1909	#12 – Nov. 1909
UP IN A COCONUT TREE: 1903	# 5 – Dec. 1903
UP IN THE CLOUDS: 1928	#12 – Jan. 1928
US ON A BUS: 1936	#16 – May 1936

V

VALENCIA (Padilla): 1926	# 1 – July 1926
VALENCIA (Padilla): 1950	#18 – May 1950
VAMP, THE: 1919	# 5 – Oct. 1919
VARSITY DRAG, THE: 1927	# 4 – Dec. 1927
VELVET MOON: 1943	#11 – May 1943
VENETIAN MOON: 1920	# 4 – Aug. 1920
VERY THOUGHT OF YOU, THE (R. Noble): 1934	# 9 – Oct. 1934
VERY THOUGHT OF YOU, THE (R. Noble): 1944	#18 – Dec. 1944
VESPER BELLS WERE RINGING, THE: 1901	#20 – Apr. 1901
VESTI LA GIUBBA: 1907	# 9 – Oct. 1907
VICT'RY POLKA: 1943	# 9 – Dec. 1943
VIENI, VIENI: 1937	# 1 – Nov. 1937
VILIA: 1908	# 7 – Feb. 1908
VIOLETS: 1902	# 6 – Oct. 1902
VIOLETTE: 1905	#16 – Sept. 1905
VOICE IN THE OLD VILLAGE CHOIR, THE: 1932	#14 – July 1932
VOICE OF THE HUDSON: 1903	# 7 – June 1903

W

WABASH BLUES: 1922	# 1 – Jan. 1922
WABASH MOON: 1931	# 9 – May 1931
WAGON WHEELS: 1934	# 3 – Apr. 1934
WAH-HOO! 1936	# 6 – Apr. 1936
WAIT (Bowers): 1900	# 3 – Sept. 1900
WAIT (Bowers): 1902	# 9 – Nov. 1902
WAIT AND SEE: 1946	#18 – Mar. 1946
WAIT FOR ME, MARY: 1943	#16 – Oct. 1943
WAIT TILL THE COWS COME HOME: 1918	# 2 – Mar. 1918
WAIT TILL THE SUN SHINES, NELLIE: 1906	# 1 – Dec. 1905
WAIT TILL YOU GET THEM UP IN THE AIR, BOYS: 1919	# 8 – Dec. 1919
WAITIN' FOR THE TRAIN TO COME IN: 1945	# 5 – Dec. 1945
WAITING AT THE CHURCH (MY WIFE WON'T LET ME): 1906	# 1 – July 1906
WAITING AT THE END OF THE ROAD: 1929	#14 – Nov. 1929
WAITING FOR THE ROBERT E. LEE: 1912	# 1 – Sept. 1912
WALKIN' MY BABY BACK HOME (Ahlert): 1931	# 2 – Apr. 1931
WALKIN' MY BABY BACK HOME (Ahlert): 1952	# 3 – Aug. 1952
(I'll be) WALKIN' WITH MY HONEY: 1945	#17 – Dec. 1945
WALKING BY THE RIVER: 1941	# 4 – May 1941
WALKING WITH SUSIE: 1929	#16 – July 1929
WALTZ ME AROUND AGAIN, WILLIE: 1906	# 1 – Sept. 1906
WALTZ OF LONG AGO, THE: 1924	# 7 – Mar. 1924
WALTZ OF THE BELLS, THE; *SEE: TING-A-LING: 1926*	
WALTZ YOU SAVED FOR ME, THE: 1931	# 1 – May 1931
WANG WANG BLUES, THE: 1921	# 5 – Apr. 1921
WAR IS OVER MANY YEARS, THE; *SEE: LINCOLN, GRANT, OR LEE: 1903*	
WARSAW CONCERTO: 1943	#17 – Aug. 1943
WAS IT A DREAM? 1928	# 5 – July 1928
WAS IT RAIN? 1937	#11 – June 1937
WAS THAT THE HUMAN THING TO DO? 1932	# 1 – Mar. 1932
WAS THERE EVER A PAL LIKE YOU: 1920	#12 – Mar. 1920
WATERS OF VENICE: 1918	#16 – Nov. 1918
WAY BACK HOME: 1935	#12 – June 1935
WAY DOWN IN COTTON TOWN: 1910	#13 – Mar. 1910
WAY DOWN IN MY HEART; *SEE: I'VE GOT A FEELIN' FOR YOU: 1904*	
WAY DOWN IN OLD INDIANA: 1901	#11 – Dec. 1901
WAY DOWN SOUTH (Fairman): 1912	#11 – Oct. 1912
WAY DOWN SOUTH (Myddleton); *SEE: DOWN SOUTH: 1901, 1927*	
WAY DOWN YONDER IN NEW ORLEANS (Layton): 1923	# 5 – Feb. 1923
WAY DOWN YONDER IN NEW ORLEANS (Layton): 1960	# 4 – Jan. 1960
WAY DOWN YONDER IN THE CORNFIELD: 1902	# 1 – Apr. 1902
WAY YOU LOOK TONIGHT, THE (Kern): 1936	# 1 – Nov. 1936
WAY YOU LOOK TONIGHT, THE (Kern): 1961	#13 – Oct. 1961
WE DID IT BEFORE (AND WE CAN DO IT AGAIN): 1942	# 9 – Feb. 1942
WE HAVE MUCH TO BE THANKFUL FOR: 1913	#18 – Nov. 1913
WE JUST COULDN'T SAY GOODBYE: 1932	# 1 – Sept. 1932
WE THREE: 1940	# 1 – Dec. 1940
WE'LL GATHER LILACS: 1946	#12 – June 1946
WE'LL MAKE HAY WHILE THE SUN SHINES: 1934	# 8 – Feb. 1934
WE'LL MEET AGAIN: 1942	#15 – June 1942
WE'RE ALL PALS TOGETHER; *SEE: RANGER'S SONG, THE: 1927*	
WE'RE GOING OVER: 1917	#20 – Dec. 1917
WE'RE IN THE MONEY (THE GOLD DIGGERS' SONG): 1933	#14 – July 1933
WE'RE THE COUPLE IN THE CASTLE: 1942	#15 – Mar. 1942
WE'VE COME A LONG WAY TOGETHER: 1939	#18 – Apr. 1939
WEARY RIVER: 1929	# 1 – Apr. 1929
WEDDING BELLS (ARE BREAKING UP THAT OLD GANG OF MINE) (Fain): 1929	# 5 – Apr. 1929

WEDDING BELLS (ARE BREAKING UP THAT OLD GANG OF MINE) (Fain): 1955 ... #17 – Mar. 1955
WEDDING OF THE PAINTED DOLL, THE: 1929 ... # 1 – June 1929
WEDDING OF THE WINDS: 1914 ... T30 – Mar. 1914
WEE LITTLE DROP O' THE CRUISKEEN LAWN, A: 1912 ... #13 – Mar. 1912
WELL, ALL RIGHT! 1939 ... #13 – Aug. 1939
WERE YOU SINCERE? 1931 ... #16 – May 1931
WEST, A NEST, AND YOU, THE: 1923 ... #11 – Dec. 1923
WEST OF THE GREAT DIVIDE: 1925 ... #11 – May 1925
WEST WIND: 1936 ... #13 – Apr. 1936
WHAT A DIFF'RENCE A DAY MADE (Grever): 1944 ... #18 – Nov. 1944
WHAT A DIFF'RENCE A DAY MADE (Grever): 1959 ... # 9 – Aug. 1959
WHAT A DIFF'RENCE A DAY MADE (Grever): 1975 ... #20 – Nov. 1975
WHAT A DIFF'RENCE A DAY MAKES;
SEE: WHAT A DIFF'RENCE A DAY MADE: 1944, 1959, 1975
WHAT A LITTLE MOONLIGHT CAN DO: 1935 ... #15 – Aug. 1935
WHAT A NASTY DISPOSITION FOR A LADY LIKE YOU: 1903 ... # 7 – July 1903
WHAT A WONDERFUL MOTHER YOU'D BE: 1916 ... # 9 – Apr. 1916
WHAT CAN I SAY, AFTER I SAY I'M SORRY;
SEE: (What can I say) AFTER I SAY I'M SORRY: 1926
WHAT DO WE DO ON A DEW-DEW-DEWY DAY? 1927 ... # 2 – Sept. 1927
WHAT DO YOU WANT TO MAKE THOSE EYES AT ME FOR? 1917 ... # 2 – Mar. 1917
WHAT DOES IT MATTER? 1927 ... # 7 – June 1927
WHAT GOES ON HERE IN MY HEART: 1938 ... # 9 – Sept. 1938
WHAT HAS BECOME OF HINKY DINKY PARLAY VOO: 1924 ... # 9 – Aug. 1924
WHAT HAVE YOU GOT THAT GETS ME? 1938 ... #12 – Dec. 1938
WHAT IS A HOME WITHOUT LOVE? 1900 ... # 9 – May 1900
WHAT IS THIS THING CALLED LOVE? 1930 ... # 4 – Mar. 1930
WHAT THE BRASS BAND PLAYED: 1905 ... # 4 – Mar. 1905
WHAT WILL I TELL MY HEART: 1937 ... # 4 – Apr. 1937
WHAT YOU GOIN' TO DO WHEN THE RENT COMES 'ROUND? (RUFUS RASTUS JOHNSON BROWN): 1905 ... # 4 – Nov. 1905
WHAT'LL I DO? 1924 ... # 1 – June 1924
WHAT'S NEW? 1939 ... # 7 – Oct. 1939
WHAT'S THE GOOD WORD, MR. BLUEBIRD? 1943 ... #14 – May 1943
WHAT'S THE MATTER WITH FATHER? 1910 ... # 3 – Aug. 1910
WHAT'S THE NAME OF THAT SONG? 1936 ... # 9 – Apr. 1936
WHAT'S THE REASON? 1935 ... # 2 – June 1935
WHEN A FELLOW'S ON THE LEVEL WITH A GIRL WHO'S ON THE SQUARE: 1908 ... # 8 – Apr. 1908
WHEN A LADY MEETS A GENTLEMAN DOWN SOUTH: 1936 ... #13 – Oct. 1936
WHEN BOB WHITE IS WHISTLING IN THE MEADOW: 1907 ... #11 – Mar. 1907
WHEN BUDDHA SMILES: 1922 ... # 7 – Mar. 1922
WHEN CHLOE SINGS A SONG: 1900 ... # 4 – May 1900
WHEN DAY IS DONE: 1927 ... # 2 – Sept. 1927
WHEN DID YOU LEAVE HEAVEN? 1936 ... # 1 – Oct. 1936
WHEN FRANCES DANCES WITH ME: 1921 ... # 8 – Dec. 1921
WHEN HEARTS ARE YOUNG: 1923 ... # 1 – Mar. 1923
WHEN I DREAM IN THE GLOAMING OF YOU: 1909 ... # 2 – July 1909
WHEN I GET YOU ALONE TONIGHT: 1912 ... # 2 – Nov. 1912
WHEN I GROW TOO OLD TO DREAM: 1935 ... # 1 – May 1935
WHEN I LEAVE THE WORLD BEHIND: 1915 ... # 1 – Sept. 1915
WHEN I LOST YOU: 1913 ... # 1 – June 1913
WHEN I TAKE MY SUGAR TO TEA: 1931 ... #13 – May 1931
WHEN I WAS A DREAMER (AND YOU WERE MY DREAM): 1915 ... # 6 – Aug. 1915
WHEN I WAS TWENTY-ONE AND YOU WERE SWEET SIXTEEN: 1912 ... # 3 – May 1912
WHEN I'M AWAY FROM YOU, DEAR: 1904 ... #17 – May 1904
WHEN I'M GONE I WON'T FORGET;
SEE: WHEN YOU'RE GONE I WON'T FORGET: 1920
WHEN I'M LOOKING AT YOU: 1930 ... #17 – Apr. 1930
WHEN I'M WITH YOU (Revel): 1936 ... # 2 – Aug. 1936
WHEN I'M WITH YOU (Lanni): 1989 ... # 1 – Feb. 1989
WHEN IRISH EYES ARE SMILING: 1913 ... #15 – July 1913
WHEN IT'S ALL GOIN' OUT AND NOTHIN' COMIN' IN: 1903 ... # 3 – Feb. 1903
WHEN IT'S APPLE BLOSSOM TIME IN NORMANDY: 1913 ... # 3 – Sept. 1913
WHEN IT'S NIGHT TIME DOWN IN BURGUNDY: 1914 ... # 7 – Oct. 1914
WHEN IT'S NIGHT TIME IN DIXIE LAND: 1915 ... #20 – Apr. 1915
WHEN IT'S NIGHT TIME IN ITALY, IT'S WEDNESDAY OVER HERE: 1923 ... #20 – Nov. 1923
WHEN IT'S SLEEPY TIME DOWN SOUTH: 1931 ... # 2 – Jan. 1932
WHEN IT'S SPRINGTIME IN THE ROCKIES: 1930 ... # 1 – June 1930
WHEN KATE AND I WERE COMIN' THRO' THE RYE: 1902 ... # 5 – Oct. 1902
WHEN LIGHTS ARE LOW: 1924 ... # 7 – Apr. 1924
WHEN MOTHER NATURE SINGS HER LULLABY: 1938 ... # 4 – Aug. 1938
WHEN MR. SHAKESPEARE COMES TO TOWN: 1901 ... #11 – Jan. 1902
WHEN MY BABY SMILES AT ME: 1920 ... # 1 – May 1920
WHEN MY DREAMBOAT COMES HOME: 1937 ... # 2 – Feb. 1937
WHEN MY DREAMS COME TRUE: 1929 ... # 8 – Oct. 1929
WHEN MY SHIP COMES IN: 1915 ... #17 – Apr. 1915
WHEN MY SUGAR WALKS DOWN THE STREET: 1925 ... # 6 – June 1925
WHEN OLD BILL BAILEY PLAYS THE UKULELE: 1915 ... #15 – Jan. 1916
WHEN SHADOWS FALL; *SEE: HOME (WHEN SHADOWS FALL): 1932*
WHEN SHALL WE MEET AGAIN? 1922 ... # 8 – Mar. 1922
WHEN SWEET MARIE WAS SWEET SIXTEEN: 1908 ... # 4 – June 1908
WHEN THE (MIGHTY) ORGAN PLAYED "OH PROMISE ME": 1938 ... #11 – Jan. 1938
WHEN THE ANGELUS IS RINGING: 1914 ... # 8 – June 1914
WHEN THE BEES ARE IN THE HIVE: 1905 ... #13 – Feb. 1905
WHEN THE BELL IN THE LIGHTHOUSE RINGS, DING DONG: 1905 ... # 6 – Oct. 1905
WHEN THE BLACK SHEEP RETURNS TO THE FOLD: 1916 ... #19 – Dec. 1916
WHEN THE BLOOM IS ON THE SAGE: 1930 ... #10 – June 1930
WHEN THE EVENING BREEZE IS SIGHING HOME SWEET HOME: 1906 ... #14 – Mar. 1906
WHEN THE GROWN UP LADIES ACT LIKE BABIES: 1915 ... #16 – Feb. 1915
WHEN THE HARVEST DAYS ARE OVER, JESSIE, DEAR: 1900 ... # 2 – Jan. 1901
WHEN THE HARVEST MOON IS SHINING ON THE RIVER: 1905 ... # 9 – June 1905
WHEN THE LEAVES BID THE TREES GOODBYE: 1935 ... #17 – Nov. 1935
WHEN THE LEAVES COME TUMBLING DOWN: 1923 ... # 7 – Jan. 1923
WHEN THE LIGHTS GO ON AGAIN: 1942 ... # 1 – Jan. 1943
WHEN THE LITTLE RED ROSES GET THE BLUES: 1930 ... #17 – May 1930
WHEN THE MIDNIGHT CHOO CHOO LEAVES FOR ALABAM': 1913 ... # 1 – May 1913
WHEN THE MOCKING BIRDS ARE SINGING IN THE WILDWOOD: 1906 ... # 6 – May 1906
WHEN THE MOON COMES OVER THE MOUNTAIN: 1931 ... # 1 – Aug. 1931
WHEN THE MOON PLAYS PEEK-A-BOO WITH YOU: 1908 ... #20 – July 1908
WHEN THE MOON SHINES ON THE MOONSHINE;
SEE: MOON SHINES ON THE MOONSHINE, THE: 1920
WHEN THE ORGAN PLAYED AT TWILIGHT: 1930 ... # 4 – Dec. 1930
WHEN THE POPPIES BLOOM AGAIN: 1937 ... # 6 – Apr. 1937
WHEN THE RED, RED, ROBIN COMES BOB, BOB, BOBBIN' ALONG: 1926 ... # 2 – Oct. 1926
WHEN THE ROSES BLOOM AGAIN (Edwards);
SEE: I'LL BE WITH YOU WHEN THE ROSES BLOOM AGAIN: 1901
WHEN THE SUNSET TURNS THE OCEAN'S BLUE TO GOLD: 1904 ... # 5 – Jan. 1904
WHEN THE SWALLOWS COME BACK TO CAPISTRANO: 1940 ... # 2 – Sept. 1940
WHEN THEY ASK ABOUT YOU: 1944 ... # 4 – Mar. 1944
WHEN THEY PLAYED THE POLKA: 1938 ... #10 – Aug. 1938
WHEN TOMORROW COMES: 1934 ... #15 – Mar. 1934
WHEN UNCLE JOE PLAYS A RAG ON HIS OLD BANJO: 1912 ... # 9 – Dec. 1912
WHEN WE ARE M-A-DOUBLE-R-I-E-D: 1908 ... # 5 – May 1908
WHEN WE'RE ALONE (PENTHOUSE SERENADE): 1932 ... # 4 – Feb. 1932
WHEN YANKEE DOODLE LEARNS TO PARLEZ-VOUS FRANCAIS: 1917 ... #11 – Nov. 1917
WHEN YOU AND I WERE SEVENTEEN: 1925 ... # 5 – Apr. 1925
WHEN YOU AND I WERE YOUNG MAGGIE BLUES (Butterfield, McHugh): 1922 ... #19 – Dec. 1922

WHEN YOU AND I WERE YOUNG MAGGIE BLUES (Butterfield, McHugh): 1951	#13 – May 1951
WHEN YOU COME BACK (AND YOU WILL COME BACK): 1918	# 5 – Oct. 1918
WHEN YOU KNOW YOU'RE NOT FORGOTTEN BY THE GIRL YOU CAN'T FORGET: 1907	# 5 – Aug. 1907
WHEN YOU LOOK IN THE HEART OF A ROSE: 1919	# 3 – Aug. 1919
WHEN YOU PLAY IN THE GAME OF LOVE: 1914	# 2 – Aug. 1914
WHEN YOU WALKED OUT, SOMEONE ELSE WALKED RIGHT IN: 1923	# 6 – Aug. 1923
WHEN YOU WERE SWEET SIXTEEN (Thornton): 1900	# 2 – Apr. 1900
WHEN YOU WERE SWEET SIXTEEN (Thornton): 1947	# 7 – Sept. 1947
WHEN YOU WISH UPON A STAR: 1940	# 1 – Mar. 1940
WHEN YOU WORE A PINAFORE: 1908	#20 – June 1908
WHEN YOU WORE A TULIP: 1915	# 2 – Jan. 1915
WHEN YOU'RE A LONG, LONG WAY FROM HOME: 1914	# 1 – Dec. 1914
WHEN YOU'RE ALL DRESSED UP AND NO PLACE TO GO: 1914	# 5 – Aug. 1914
WHEN YOU'RE AWAY (Grant): 1912	# 9 – Nov. 1912
WHEN YOU'RE AWAY (V. Herbert): 1915	# 9 – June 1915
WHEN YOU'RE GONE I WON'T FORGET: 1920	#18 – Nov. 1920
WHEN YOU'RE SMILING: 1929	T30 – Nov. 1928
WHEN YOUR HAIR HAS TURNED TO SILVER: 1931	# 1 – Apr. 1931
WHEN YOUR LOVER HAS GONE: 1931	#14 – May 1931
WHEN YUBA PLAYS RUMBA ON THE TUBA: 1931	# 9 – Aug. 1931
WHERE AM I? 1935	#13 – Jan. 1936
WHERE ARE THE FRIENDS OF OTHER DAYS? 1903	# 8 – Dec. 1903
WHERE ARE YOU? 1937	# 9 – June 1937
WHERE DID ROBINSON CRUSOE GO WITH FRIDAY ON SATURDAY NIGHT? 1916	# 7 – June 1916
WHERE DID YOU GET THAT GIRL? 1914	# 2 – Mar. 1914
WHERE DO WE GO FROM HERE? 1917	# 3 – Sept. 1917
WHERE DO YOU WORK-A JOHN? 1927	# 2 – Mar. 1927
WHERE IN THE WORLD: 1938	#16 – Aug. 1938
WHERE IS THE SONG OF SONGS FOR ME? 1929	#16 – Apr. 1929
WHERE OR WHEN (Rodgers): 1937	# 4 – July 1937
WHERE OR WHEN (Rodgers): 1960	# 5 – Feb. 1960
WHERE THE BLACK-EYED SUSANS GROW: 1917	# 4 – May 1917
WHERE THE BLUE OF THE NIGHT MEETS THE GOLD OF THE DAY: 1932	# 3 – Jan. 1932
WHERE THE LAZY DAISIES GROW: 1924	# 2 – May 1924
WHERE THE MORNING GLORIES GROW: 1917	#16 – Dec. 1917
WHERE THE MORNING GLORIES TWINE AROUND THE DOOR: 1905	# 6 – Jan. 1906
WHERE THE RIVER SHANNON FLOWS: 1910	#11 – Nov. 1910
WHERE THE SHY LITTLE VIOLETS GROW: 1929	# 9 – Mar. 1929
WHERE THE SILV'RY COLORADO WENDS ITS WAY (Avril): 1902	#15 – July 1902
WHERE THE SILV'RY COLORADO WENDS ITS WAY (Avril): 1904	#11 – May 1904
WHERE THE SOUTHERN ROSES GROW: 1905	# 7 – Apr. 1905
WHERE THE SUNSET TURNS THE OCEAN'S BLUE TO GOLD; *SEE: WHEN THE SUNSET TURNS THE OCEAN'S BLUE TO GOLD: 1904*	
WHERE WAS I? 1940	# 4 – June 1940
WHERE'D YOU GET THOSE EYES? 1926	# 4 – Sept. 1926
WHIFFENPOOF SONG, THE: 1947	# 6 – Nov. 1947
WHILE A CIGARETTE WAS BURNING: 1938	# 3 – Nov. 1938
WHILE THEY WERE DANCING AROUND: 1914	# 5 – Apr. 1914
WHIP-POOR-WILL: 1921	#11 – May 1921
WHISPERING (Schonberger): 1920	# 1 – Oct. 1920
WHISPERING (Schonberger): 1944	#18 – Nov. 1944
WHISPERING (Schonberger): 1951	#11 – Sept. 1951
WHISPERING (Schonberger): 1964	#11 – Jan. 1964
WHISPERING HOPE: 1949	#10 – Oct. 1949
WHISPERS IN THE DARK: 1937	# 1 – Sept. 1937
WHISTLE WHILE YOU WORK: 1938	# 2 – Mar. 1938
WHISTLER, THE: 1947	#19 – Jan. 1948
WHISTLER AND HIS DOG, THE: 1905	#12 – Nov. 1905
WHISTLING IN THE DARK: 1931	# 4 – June 1931
WHITE CHRISTMAS: 1942	# 1 – Nov. 1942
WHITE CHRISTMAS: 1943	# 8 – Dec. 1943
WHITE CHRISTMAS: 1944	# 7 – Dec. 1944
WHITE CHRISTMAS: 1945	# 7 – Dec. 1945
WHITE CHRISTMAS: 1946	# 3 – Dec. 1946
WHITE CHRISTMAS: 1947	#10 – Dec. 1947
WHITE CHRISTMAS: 1948	# 9 – Dec. 1948
WHITE CHRISTMAS: 1949	#10 – Dec. 1949
WHITE CHRISTMAS: 1950	#12 – Jan. 1951
WHITE CHRISTMAS: 1951	#16 – Dec. 1951
WHITE CHRISTMAS: 1952	#10 – Jan. 1953
WHITE CHRISTMAS: 1953	#14 – Dec. 1953
WHITE CHRISTMAS: 1954	#12 – Dec. 1954
WHITE CHRISTMAS: 1955	#16 – Jan. 1956
WHITE CHRISTMAS: 1960	#20 – Dec. 1960
WHITE CHRISTMAS: 1961	#13 – Dec. 1961
WHITE CLIFFS OF DOVER, THE: 1942	# 1 – Jan. 1942
WHITE SAILS: 1939	# 3 – July 1939
WHO? 1926	# 5 – Feb. 1926
WHO BLEW OUT THE FLAME? 1938	#11 – Dec. 1938
WHO CARES? 1923	# 9 – Feb. 1923
WHO DO YOU LOVE, I HOPE? 1946	#19 – July 1946
WHO LOVES YOU? (Coots): 1936	#10 – Nov. 1936
WHO PAID THE RENT FOR MRS. RIP VAN WINKLE? 1914	# 6 – June 1914
WHO TAKES CARE OF THE CARETAKER'S DAUGHTER (WHILE THE CARETAKER'S BUSY TAKING CARE): 1925	# 8 – June 1925
WHO THREW THE WHISKEY IN THE WELL? 1945	#17 – Aug. 1945
WHO TOLD YOU THAT LIE? 1946	#14 – Aug. 1946
WHO WOULDN'T LOVE YOU: 1942	# 4 – July 1942
WHO'LL BE THE NEXT ONE TO CRY OVER YOU? 1921	# 8 – Oct. 1921
WHO'S AFRAID OF LOVE: 1937	#20 – Feb. 1937
WHO'S AFRAID OF THE BIG BAD WOLF? 1933	# 2 – Oct. 1933
WHO'S SORRY NOW? (Snyder): 1923	# 1 – June 1923
WHO'S SORRY NOW? (Snyder): 1958	# 5 – Apr. 1958
WHO'S WONDERFUL, WHO'S MARVELOUS? *SEE: MISS ANNABELLE LEE: 1927*	
WHOLE WORLD IS SINGING MY SONG, THE: 1946	# 4 – Dec. 1946
WHOSE BABY ARE YOU? 1920	# 7 – June 1920
WHOSE HONEY ARE YOU? 1935	#18 – Apr. 1935
WHY (Cohn): 1900	# 5 – May 1900
WHY? (Coots): 1930	#14 – Mar. 1930
WHY (Marcucci): 1960	# 1 – Dec. 1959
WHY (Marcucci): 1972	#13 – Oct. 1972
WHY COULDN'T IT LAST, LAST NIGHT; *SEE: (Why couldn't it last) LAST NIGHT: 1939*	
WHY DANCE? 1931	#20 – Oct. 1931
WHY DID I KISS THAT GIRL? 1924	# 5 – June 1924
WHY DID THEY SELL KILLARNEY? 1902	T30 – June 1902
WHY DO I DREAM THOSE DREAMS? 1934	# 6 – May 1934
WHY DO I LOVE YOU? 1928	#18 – Apr. 1928
WHY DO I LOVE YOU SO? 1925	#20 – Aug. 1925
WHY DON'T WE DO THIS MORE OFTEN? 1941	#13 – Nov. 1941
WHY DON'T YOU DO RIGHT? 1943	#11 – Mar. 1943
WHY DON'T YOU FALL IN LOVE WITH ME? 1943	# 4 – Feb. 1943
WHY DON'T YOU GO, GO, GO: 1903	# 9 – Apr. 1903
WHY DON'T YOU TRY? 1906	#16 – July 1906
WHY SHOULD I CRY OVER YOU? 1922	# 4 – Sept. 1922
WHY SHOULDN'T I? 1935	#19 – Dec. 1935
WHY WAS I BORN? 1930	#16 – Feb. 1930
WILD CHERRIES RAG: 1909	# 7 – Dec. 1909
WILDFLOWER (Youmans): 1923	# 5 – July 1923
WILDFLOWER (Richardson): 1973	# 9 – May 1973

WILL YOU LOVE ME IN DECEMBER AS YOU DO IN MAY? 1906 . . . # 1 – Apr. 1906
WILL YOU REMEMBER (SWEETHEART) (Romberg): 1918 . . . . . . #14 – Jan. 1918
WILL YOU REMEMBER (SWEETHEART) (Romberg): 1937 . . . . . . # 8 – May 1937
WILL YOU REMEMBER TONIGHT TOMORROW? 1938 . . . . #20 – Aug. 1938
WILLIAM TELL OVERTURE (IT'S A BEAUTIFUL DAY FOR THE RACES): 1948 . . . . . . #12 – June 1948
WILLOW, WEEP FOR ME (Ronell): 1933 . . . . . . # 5 – Jan. 1933
WILLOW, WEEP FOR ME (Ronell): 1965 . . . . . . #16 – Jan. 1965
WINTER WONDERLAND: 1935 . . . . . . # 4 – Jan. 1935
WINTER WONDERLAND: 1946 . . . . . . #14 – Jan. 1947
WINTER WONDERLAND: 1950 . . . . . . #16 – Dec. 1950
WINTER WONDERLAND: 1952 . . . . . . #17 – Dec. 1952
WISE OLD OWL, A: 1941 . . . . . . # 2 – Apr. 1941
WISHING: 1939 . . . . . . # 1 – June 1939
WITH A SONG IN MY HEART: 1929 . . . . . . # 8 – July 1929
WITH ALL MY HEART: 1936 . . . . . . # 8 – Feb. 1936
WITH EVERY BREATH I TAKE: 1935 . . . . . . # 7 – Feb. 1935
WITH MY EYES WIDE OPEN, I'M DREAMING (Revel): 1934 . . . . . # 3 – Aug. 1934
WITH MY EYES WIDE OPEN, I'M DREAMING (Revel): 1950 . . . . . #15 – Feb. 1950
WITH PLENTY OF MONEY AND YOU: 1937 . . . . . . # 2 – Feb. 1937
(I'm still without a sweetheart) WITH SUMMER COMIN' ON: 1932 #10 – July 1932
WITH THE WIND AND THE RAIN IN YOUR HAIR (Lawrence): 1940 # 2 – May 1940
WITH THE WIND AND THE RAIN IN YOUR HAIR (Lawrence): 1959 #19 – Feb. 1959
WITH YOU IN ETERNITY: 1907 . . . . . . # 8 – Sept. 1907
WITHOUT A SONG: 1930 . . . . . . #20 – Jan. 1930
WITHOUT A WORD OF WARNING: 1935 . . . . . . # 7 – Oct. 1935
WITHOUT THAT CERTAIN THING: 1934 . . . . . . #15 – Mar. 1934
WITHOUT THAT GAL: 1931 . . . . . . # 7 – Aug. 1931
WITHOUT YOU (Farres): 1946 . . . . . . #18 – Sept. 1946
WITHOUT YOU (Tillotson): 1961 . . . . . . # 7 – Sept. 1961
WITHOUT YOU (Evans): 1972 . . . . . . # 1 – Feb. 1972
WITHOUT YOU (Sixx): 1990 . . . . . . # 8 – May 1990
WITHOUT YOU (Ham): 1994 . . . . . . # 3 – Mar. 1994
WITHOUT YOU THE WORLD DON'T SEEM THE SAME: 1910 . . . . #17 – Nov. 1910
WOMAN IS ONLY A WOMAN, BUT A GOOD CIGAR IS A SMOKE, A: 1905 . . . . . . #18 – Dec. 1905
WON'T YOU BE MY HONEY? 1907 . . . . . . # 3 – Sept. 1907
WON'T YOU COME OVER TO MY HOUSE? 1906 . . . . . . # 1 – Dec. 1906
WON'T YOU FONDLE ME? 1905 . . . . . . #12 – Mar. 1905
WON'T YOU WALTZ HOME SWEET HOME WITH ME? 1908 . . . . . . # 7 – Apr. 1908
WONDER WHEN MY BABY'S COMING HOME: 1942 . . . . . . #14 – Nov. 1942
WONDERFUL GUY, A: 1949 . . . . . . # 9 – July 1949
WONDERFUL ONE (Neilan): 1923 . . . . . . # 2 – June 1923
WONDERFUL ONE (Holland); *SEE: YOU'RE A WONDERFUL ONE: 1964*
WOODCHOPPERS' BALL: 1939 . . . . . . #19 – June 1939
WOODEN SOLDIER AND THE CHINA DOLL, THE: 1932 . . . . #10 – Mar. 1932
WOODMAN, WOODMAN, SPARE THAT TREE! 1911 . . . . . . T30 – Sept. 1911
WOODPECKER SONG, THE: 1940 . . . . . . # 1 – May 1940
WOODY WOODPECKER: 1948 . . . . . . # 1 – July 1948
WORLD IS WAITING FOR THE SUNRISE, THE (Seitz): 1922 . . . . . #15 – May 1922
Reached second peak at . . . . . . #14 – Jan. 1923
WORLD IS WAITING FOR THE SUNRISE, THE (Seitz): 1951 . . . . . # 6 – Sept. 1951
WOULD YOU? 1936 . . . . . . # 6 – June 1936
WOULD YOU CARE? 1905 . . . . . . # 1 – Oct. 1905
WOULD YOU LIKE TO TAKE A WALK? 1931 . . . . . . # 5 – Mar. 1931
WOULD YOU RATHER BE A COLONEL WITH AN EAGLE ON YOUR SHOULDER OR A PRIVATE WITH A CHICKEN ON YOUR KNEE? 1919 . . . . . . #16 – Jan. 1919
WOULDN'T IT MAKE YOU MAD, WOULDN'T IT JAR YOU? 1900 . . . # 5 – July 1900
WRAP YOUR TROUBLES IN DREAMS: 1931 . . . . . . # 8 – June 1931
WYOMING: 1921 . . . . . . #20 – July 1921

X

Y

Y.M.C.A. MARCH: 1904 . . . . . . #18 – May 1904
YAAKA HULA, HICKEY DULA: 1916 . . . . . . # 1 – June 1916
YAH-TA-TA, YAH-TA-TA (TALK, TALK, TALK): 1945 . . . . . . #12 – May 1945
YALE BOOLA; *SEE: BOOLA, BOOLA: 1901*
YAMA-YAMA MAN, THE: 1908 . . . . . . # 5 – Aug. 1908
Reached second peak at . . . . . . # 8 – Aug. 1909
YANKEE DOODLE BLUES: 1922 . . . . . . # 7 – Oct. 1922
YANKEE DOODLE BOY: 1905 . . . . . . # 1 – Mar. 1905
YANKEE GRIT: 1905 . . . . . . # 7 – Aug. 1905
YANKEE ROSE (Frankel): 1927 . . . . . . # 5 – Apr. 1927
YANKEE ROSE (Roth): 1986 . . . . . . #16 – Aug. 1986
YEARNING (JUST FOR YOU): 1925 . . . . . . # 1 – June 1925
YELLOW DOG BLUES: 1920 . . . . . . #16 – Mar. 1920
YES, INDEED! 1941 . . . . . . #13 – Oct. 1941
YES, MY DARLING DAUGHTER: 1941 . . . . . . #16 – Feb. 1941
YES SIR! THAT'S MY BABY: 1925 . . . . . . # 1 – Sept. 1925
YES! WE HAVE NO BANANAS: 1923 . . . . . . # 1 – July 1923
YESTERDAY (Harris): 1907 . . . . . . #13 – Nov. 1907
YESTERDAY (McCartney): 1965 . . . . . . # 1 – Oct. 1965
YESTERDAYS (Kern): 1934 . . . . . . #20 – Jan. 1934
YIDDLE ON YOUR FIDDLE: 1910 . . . . . . # 7 – Feb. 1910
YINGLE BELLS (JINGLE BELLS): 1949 . . . . . . #17 – Dec. 1949
YIP-I-ADDY-I-AY! 1909 . . . . . . # 1 – June 1909
YODELIN' JIVE: 1939 . . . . . . #17 – Jan. 1940
YOO-HOO: 1922 . . . . . . # 2 – Feb. 1922
YOU (Donaldson): 1936 . . . . . . # 4 – May 1936
YOU (Vanata): 1958 . . . . . . #20 – May 1958
YOU (Powell): 1999 . . . . . . #10 – Mar. 1999
YOU, YOU, DARLIN': 1940 . . . . . . #17 – May 1940
YOU AIN'T HEARD NOTHIN' YET: 1920 . . . . . . #14 – Apr. 1920
YOU AIN'T TALKIN' TO ME: 1909 . . . . . . #15 – Sept. 1909
YOU ALWAYS HURT THE ONE YOU LOVE (Roberts): 1944 . . . . # 7 – Sept. 1944
YOU ALWAYS HURT THE ONE YOU LOVE (Roberts): 1961 . . . . #12 – June 1961
YOU AND I (Willson): 1941 . . . . . . # 1 – Sept. 1941
YOU AND I (R. James): 1978 . . . . . . #13 – Sept. 1978
YOU AND I (Myers): 1983 . . . . . . # 7 – Feb. 1983
YOU AND I KNOW: 1937 . . . . . . #19 – Nov. 1937
YOU AND ME THAT USED TO BE, THE: 1937 . . . . . . # 6 – July 1937
YOU ARE MY LUCKY STAR: 1935 . . . . . . # 2 – Nov. 1935
YOU ARE MY SUNSHINE (Davis): 1941 . . . . . . #10 – July 1941
YOU ARE MY SUNSHINE (Davis): 1962 . . . . . . # 7 – Dec. 1962
YOU ARE THE IDEAL OF MY DREAMS: 1910 . . . . . . # 4 – June 1910
(I am the words) YOU ARE THE MELODY: 1931 . . . . . . #18 – Jan. 1931
YOU BELONG TO MY HEART: 1945 . . . . . . # 5 – July 1945
YOU BROUGHT A NEW KIND OF LOVE TO ME: 1930 . . . . . . # 3 – Aug. 1930
YOU CALL EVERYBODY DARLIN': 1948 . . . . . . # 1 – Sept. 1948
YOU CALL IT MADNESS (BUT I CALL IT LOVE): 1931 . . . . . . #10 – Nov. 1931
YOU CAME A LONG WAY FROM ST. LOUIS: 1948 . . . . . . #16 – Sept. 1948
YOU CAME ALONG (OUT OF NOWHERE); *SEE: (You came along) OUT OF NOWHERE: 1931, 1945*
YOU CAN DEPEND ON ME (E. Hines): 1932 . . . . . . #16 – Mar. 1932
YOU CAN DEPEND ON ME (E. Hines): 1961 . . . . . . # 6 – May 1961
YOU CAN HAVE EVERY LIGHT ON BROADWAY: 1922 . . . . . . #11 – May 1922
YOU CAN'T BE TRUE, DEAR: 1948 . . . . . . # 1 – June 1948
YOU CAN'T FOOL ALL THE PEOPLE ALL OF THE TIME: 1903 . . . . #18 – Sept. 1903
YOU CAN'T KEEP A GOOD MAN DOWN (M. F. Carey): 1901 . . . . . . #20 – Feb. 1901
YOU CAN'T KEEP A GOOD MAN DOWN (P. Bradford): 1920 . . . . . . #19 – Aug. 1920
YOU CAN'T PULL THE WOOL OVER MY EYES: 1936 . . . . . . # 7 – Aug. 1936

YOU CAN'T SEE THE SUN WHEN YOU'RE CRYIN': 1947	#10 – Apr. 1947
YOU CAN'T STOP ME FROM DREAMING: 1937	# 1 – Nov. 1937
YOU CAN'T STOP ME FROM LOVING YOU: 1913	#18 – Dec. 1913
YOU COULDN'T BE CUTER: 1938	# 6 – May 1938
YOU DIDN'T WANT ME WHEN YOU HAD ME: 1919	#16 – Dec. 1919
YOU DO: 1947	# 2 – Dec. 1947
YOU DO THE DARNDEST THINGS, BABY: 1936	#16 – Nov. 1936
YOU DON'T BELONG TO THE REGULARS; *SEE: MR. VOLUNTEER: 1901*	
YOU DON'T LIKE IT, NOT MUCH: 1927	#18 – Sept. 1927
YOU FORGOT TO REMEMBER; *SEE: REMEMBER (Berlin): 1925*	
YOU FORGOT YOUR GLOVES: 1931	#17 – Nov. 1931
YOU GAVE ME YOUR HEART: 1923	#12 – Jan. 1923
YOU GO TO MY HEAD: 1938	# 4 – Sept. 1938
YOU GOTTA QUIT KICKIN' MY DAWG AROUND; *SEE: THEY GOTTA QUIT KICKIN' MY DAWG AROUND: 1912*	
YOU KEEP COMING BACK LIKE A SONG: 1946	# 5 – Nov. 1946
YOU KNOW AND I KNOW (AND WE BOTH UNDERSTAND): 1915	#15 – Aug. 1915
YOU KNOW IT ALL, SMARTY; *SEE: (You know it all) SMARTY: 1937*	
YOU KNOW YOU BELONG TO SOMEBODY ELSE: 1923	# 7 – Apr. 1923
YOU LEAVE ME BREATHLESS: 1938	# 4 – July 1938
YOU MADE ME LOVE YOU (Monaco): 1913	# 1 – Sept. 1913
YOU MADE ME LOVE YOU (Monaco): 1942	#12 – Dec. 1941
YOU MADE ME WHAT I AM TODAY; *SEE: CURSE OF AN ACHING HEART, THE: 1913*	
YOU MUST HAVE BEEN A BEAUTIFUL BABY (Warren): 1938	# 1 – Jan. 1939
YOU MUST HAVE BEEN A BEAUTIFUL BABY (Warren): 1961	# 4 – Oct. 1961
YOU NEEDN'T SAY THE KISSES CAME FROM ME: 1900	#15 – Sept. 1900
YOU NEVER SPOKE TO ME LIKE THAT BEFORE: 1904	#19 – May 1904
YOU OUGHTA BE IN PICTURES: 1934	# 4 – May 1934
YOU PLANTED A ROSE IN THE GARDEN OF LOVE: 1914	# 8 – Aug. 1914
(I'll be glad when you're dead) YOU RASCAL YOU: 1932	#19 – Jan. 1932
YOU REMIND ME OF MY MOTHER: 1922	# 4 – Nov. 1922
YOU SAID SOMETHING: 1917	#14 – May 1917
YOU SPLASH ME AND I'LL SPLASH YOU: 1907	# 2 – Aug. 1907
YOU STARTED ME DREAMING: 1936	# 4 – May 1936
YOU TAUGHT ME HOW TO LOVE YOU, NOW TEACH ME TO FORGET: 1910	#11 – June 1910
YOU TELL HER, I S-T-U-T-T-E-R: 1923	# 5 – Apr. 1923
YOU TELL ME YOUR DREAM (AND I WILL TELL YOU MINE): 1900	# 4 – Nov. 1900
YOU TOOK ADVANTAGE OF ME: 1928	# 8 – Sept. 1928
YOU TOOK THE WORDS RIGHT OUT OF MY HEART: 1938	#11 – Feb. 1938
YOU TRY SOMEBODY ELSE: 1931	# 9 – Jan. 1932
YOU TURNED THE TABLES ON ME: 1936	# 5 – Nov. 1936
YOU WALK BY: 1941	# 3 – Feb. 1941
YOU WERE MEANT FOR ME (N.H.Brown): 1929	# 4 – May 1929
YOU WERE MEANT FOR ME (N.H.Brown): 1948	#11 – Apr. 1948
YOU WERE MEANT FOR ME (J. Kilcher): 1997	# 2 – May 1997
YOU WERE ONLY FOOLING: 1948	# 4 – Dec. 1948
YOU WON'T BE SATISFIED (UNTIL YOU BREAK MY HEART): 1946	# 3 – Apr. 1946
YOU'D BE SO NICE TO COME HOME TO: 1943	# 5 – Apr. 1943
YOU'D BE SURPRISED (Berlin): 1920	# 2 – Jan. 1920
YOU'D BE SURPRISED (Berlin): 1940	#14 – Feb. 1940
YOU'LL ALWAYS BE THE ONE I LOVE: 1947	#17 – Mar. 1947
YOU'LL ALWAYS BE THE SAME SWEET GIRL: 1915	# 8 – Dec. 1915
YOU'LL NEVER KNOW: 1943	# 1 – Aug. 1943
YOU'RE A BUILDER UPPER: 1934	#13 – Nov. 1934
YOU'RE A DANGEROUS GIRL: 1916	#10 – Sept. 1916
YOU'RE A GRAND OLD FLAG: 1906	# 1 – June 1906
YOU'RE A GREAT BIG BLUE-EYED BABY: 1913	# 3 – June 1913
YOU'RE A HEAVENLY THING: 1935	#13 – June 1935
YOU'RE A MILLION MILES FROM NOWHERE: 1920	# 5 – Mar. 1920
YOU'RE A REAL SWEETHEART: 1928	#15 – Sept. 1928
YOU'RE A SWEET LITTLE HEADACHE: 1939	# 5 – Mar. 1939
YOU'RE A SWEETHEART: 1938	# 3 – Feb. 1938
YOU'RE ALL I NEED: 1935	# 3 – Sept. 1935
YOU'RE ALL I WANT FOR CHRISTMAS: 1948	#19 – Dec. 1948
YOU'RE AN EDUCATION: 1938	# 6 – May 1938
YOU'RE AN OLD SMOOTHIE: 1933	#15 – Feb. 1933
YOU'RE AS WELCOME AS THE FLOWERS IN MAY: 1903	#13 – Dec. 1903
YOU'RE BLASÉ: 1932	# 7 – Aug. 1932
YOU'RE BREAKING MY HEART: 1949	# 1 – Sept. 1949
YOU'RE DEVASTATING: 1934	#19 – Jan. 1934
YOU'RE DRIVING ME CRAZY: 1931	# 1 – Jan. 1931
YOU'RE GETTING TO BE A HABIT WITH ME: 1933	# 9 – Apr. 1933
YOU'RE GONNA LOSE YOUR GAL: 1933	# 7 – Dec. 1933
YOU'RE HERE AND I'M HERE: 1914	# 3 – Sept. 1914
YOU'RE IN THE RIGHT CHURCH BUT THE WRONG PEW; *SEE: (you're in) THE RIGHT CHURCH BUT THE WRONG PEW: 1909*	
YOU'RE JUST A FLOWER FROM AN OLD BOUQUET: 1925	# 7 – Feb. 1925
YOU'RE LAUGHING AT ME: 1937	#14 – Mar. 1937
YOU'RE LONELY AND I'M LONELY: 1940	#13 – July 1940
YOU'RE MORE THAN THE WORLD TO ME: 1915	# 5 – Jan. 1915
YOU'RE MY BABY: 1912	# 4 – Nov. 1912
YOU'RE MY EVERYTHING (Warren): 1932	#10 – Feb. 1932
YOU'RE MY EVERYTHING (Whitfield): 1967	# 6 – Sept. 1967
YOU'RE NOT THE KIND: 1936	#16 – Aug. 1936
YOU'RE SO UNDERSTANDING: 1949	#18 – Aug. 1949
YOU'RE THE CREAM IN MY COFFEE: 1929	# 1 – Jan. 1929
YOU'RE THE FLOWER OF MY HEART, SWEET ADELINE; *SEE: SWEET ADELINE: 1904*	
YOU'RE THE ONE (YOU BEAUTIFUL SON-OF-A-GUN): 1932	#17 – May 1932
YOU'RE THE ONE I CARE FOR: 1931	#11 – Feb. 1931
YOU'RE THE ONLY STAR (IN MY BLUE HEAVEN): 1939	#17 – Jan. 1939
YOU'RE THE TOP: 1935	# 6 – Jan. 1935
YOU'VE GOT EVERYTHING: 1933	#19 – Nov. 1933
YOU'VE GOT ME CRYING AGAIN: 1933	#14 – Apr. 1933
YOU'VE GOT ME IN THE PALM OF YOUR HAND: 1932	#11 – Sept. 1932
YOU'VE GOT ME THIS WAY: 1941	#19 – Jan. 1941
YOU'VE GOT THAT THING: 1930	#11 – Feb. 1930
YOU'VE GOT TO SEE MAMMA EV'RY NIGHT: 1923	# 1 – May 1923
YOU'VE GOT YOUR MOTHER'S BIG BLUE EYES: 1913	#10 – Jan. 1914
YOUNG AND HEALTHY; *SEE: I'M YOUNG AND HEALTHY: 1933*	
YOUNG MAN'S FANCY, A: 1920	# 3 – Sept. 1920
YOUR EYES HAVE TOLD ME SO: 1920	# 8 – Apr. 1920
YOUR MOTHER AND MINE: 1929	#19 – Sept. 1929
YOUR MOTHER WANTS YOU HOME, BOY: 1904	#11 – Mar. 1904
YOURS (QUIEREME MUCHO) (Roig): 1941	# 3 – Sept. 1941
YOURS (QUIEREME MUCHO) (Roig): 1952	#12 – Nov. 1952
YOURS AND MINE (J. Burke): 1931	#14 – Jan. 1931
YOURS AND MINE (N. H. Brown): 1937	#15 – Sept. 1937
YOURS IS MY HEART ALONE: 1940	#18 – June 1940
YOURS TRULY IS TRULY YOURS: 1936	#17 – May 1936

Z

ZIP-A-DEE-DOO-DAH (Wrubel): 1947	# 5 – Jan. 1947
ZIP-A-DEE-DOO-DAH (Wrubel): 1963	# 8 – Jan. 1963
ZOOT SUIT, A: 1942	#13 – Apr. 1942
ZULU WEDDING DANCE: 1900	#15 – Mar. 1900

SECTION 2

THE MONTHLY TOP-20 SONG CHARTS, 1900-1949

INTRODUCTION TO SECTION 2:

THE MONTHLY TOP-20 SONG CHARTS, 1900-1949

This section contains the Top-20 Song Charts, month by month, from January 1900 to December 1949. Such listings have never been published before. These include the years for which no charts existed prior to this research. Each chart shows the rankings for the given month (T.M.) as well as those of the previous month (L.M.) so that every song's progress up or down the chart can be seen. The number in parentheses indicates how many months the song was on the charts during its wave of popularity.

To get the best sense of the chart run of any given song, look for its year in the Index (Section 1) then consult that year here in Section 2. Since the charts in this section are listed chronologically, note the month of its chart "high" in Section 1 to help track it down on the Section 2 Monthly Charts.

Information about the author, original publisher, and performers associated with each song can be found in the Encyclopedia of Section 4.

One will notice readily that in the early part of the century (1900–1924) songs would often stay on the charts for many months, and there were fewer hit songs altogether. With the coming of electrical recordings and radio in the mid-twenties, a greater number of songs received exposure and had chart runs. With the increased competition, most songs stayed on the charts for only two or three months during the period 1925–1939. During World War II, the American Society of Composers, Authors, and Publishers' (ASCAP) publishing ban and the Petrillo recording ban all conspired to decrease the number of songs popularized and long chart runs became frequent once again. Gradually, the proliferation of songs increased after the war and reached its peak in the 1960s following the Rock explosion. From then on, short chart runs were the rule until the 1990s when the industry seemed to suffer, oddly, from a scarcity of good new songs. So once again the very best songs would stay on the charts for many months, just as they did in the earliest days of the century.

JANUARY 1900

LM	TM	
1	1.	I'D LEAVE MY HAPPY HOME FOR YOU (4)
2	2.	A PICTURE NO ARTIST CAN PAINT (6)
4	3.	MA LADY LU (4)
6	4.	THE STORY OF THE ROSE (4)
9	5.	ALWAYS (3)
12	6.	SING ME A SONG OF THE SOUTH (3)
3	7.	MY CREOLE SUE (5)
7	8.	MY WILD IRISH ROSE (8)
5	9.	BEN HUR CHARIOT RACE (4)
10	10.	CAKEWALK IN THE SKY (3)
–	11.	IMPECUNIOUS DAVIS (1)
14	12.	THE GIRLS OF AMERICA MARCH (3)
19	13.	WHEN YOU WERE SWEET SIXTEEN (2)
8	14.	SMOKEY MOKES (7)
–	15.	IN GOOD OLD NEW YORK TOWN (1)
11	16.	ONE NIGHT IN JUNE (6)
–	17.	DOAN YE CRY, MA HONEY (1)
17	18.	I'M GLAD I MET YOU, MARY (2)
13	19.	MANDY LEE (7)
15	20.	HEARTS AND FLOWERS (6)

FEBRUARY 1900

LM	TM	
1	1.	I'D LEAVE MY HAPPY HOME FOR YOU (5)
2	2.	A PICTURE NO ARTIST CAN PAINT (7)
5	3.	ALWAYS (4)
17	4.	DOAN YE CRY, MA HONEY (2)
–	5.	A BIRD IN A GILDED CAGE (1)
4	6.	THE STORY OF THE ROSE (5)
15	7.	IN GOOD OLD NEW YORK TOWN (2)
3	8.	MA LADY LU (5)
6	9.	SING ME A SONG OF THE SOUTH (4)
13	10.	WHEN YOU WERE SWEET SIXTEEN (3)
–	11.	I COULDN'T STAND TO SEE MY BABY LOSE (1)
8	12.	MY WILD IRISH ROSE (9)
11	13.	IMPECUNIOUS DAVIS (2)
–	14.	OLE EPH'S VISION (1)
10	15.	CAKEWALK IN THE SKY (4)
12	16.	THE GIRLS OF AMERICA MARCH (4)
9	17.	BEN HUR CHARIOT RACE (5)
7	18.	MY CREOLE SUE (6)
–	19.	ZULU WEDDING DANCE (1)
–	20.	THE ROSARY (9)

MARCH 1900

LM	TM	
5	1.	A BIRD IN A GILDED CAGE (2)
4	2.	DOAN YE CRY, MA HONEY (3)
1	3.	I'D LEAVE MY HAPPY HOME FOR YOU (6)
2	4.	A PICTURE NO ARTIST CAN PAINT (8)
10	5.	WHEN YOU WERE SWEET SIXTEEN (4)
3	6.	ALWAYS (5)
11	7.	I COULDN'T STAND TO SEE MY BABY LOSE (2)
14	8.	OLE EPH'S VISION (2)
8	9.	MA LADY LU (6)
–	10.	THE BLUE AND THE GRAY (1)
7	11.	IN GOOD OLD NEW YORK TOWN (3)
9	12.	SING ME A SONG OF THE SOUTH (5)
19	13.	ZULU WEDDING DANCE (2)
12	14.	MY WILD IRISH ROSE (10)
6	15.	THE STORY OF THE ROSE (6)
–	16.	FILIPINO SHUFFLE (1)
–	17.	IN NAPLES FAIR (1)
16	18.	THE GIRLS OF AMERICA MARCH (4)
–	19.	WHEN CHLOE SINGS A SONG (1)
–	20.	HEARTS ARE TRUMPS (1)

APRIL 1900

LM	TM	
1	1.	A BIRD IN A GILDED CAGE (3)
5	2.	WHEN YOU WERE SWEET SIXTEEN (5)
10	3.	THE BLUE AND THE GRAY (2)
4	4.	A PICTURE NO ARTIST CAN PAINT (9)
2	5.	DOAN YE CRY, MA HONEY (4)
6	6.	ALWAYS (6)
3	7.	I'D LEAVE MY HAPPY HOME FOR YOU (7)
7	8.	I COULDN'T STAND TO SEE MY BABY LOSE (3)
17	9.	IN NAPLES FAIR (2)
19	10.	WHEN CHLOE SINGS A SONG (2)
–	11.	WHY (1)
12	12.	SING ME A SONG OF THE SOUTH (6)
8	13.	OLE EPH'S VISION (3)
9	14.	MA LADY LU (7)
16	15.	FILIPINO SHUFFLE (2)
14	16.	MY WILD IRISH ROSE (11)
20	17.	HEARTS ARE TRUMPS (2)
–	18.	I'M CERTAINLY LIVING A RAGTIME LIFE (1)
–	19.	WHAT IS A HOME WITHOUT LOVE? (1)
13	20.	ZULU WEDDING DANCE (3)

MAY 1900

LM	TM	
3	1.	THE BLUE AND THE GRAY (3)
1	2.	A BIRD IN A GILDED CAGE (4)
2	3.	WHEN YOU WERE SWEET SIXTEEN (6)
10	4.	WHEN CHLOE SINGS A SONG (3)
11	5.	WHY (2)
18	6.	I'M CERTAINLY LIVING A RAGTIME LIFE (2)
6	7.	ALWAYS (7)
4	8.	A PICTURE NO ARTIST CAN PAINT (10)
19	9.	WHAT IS A HOME WITHOUT LOVE? (2)
15	10.	FILIPINO SHUFFLE (3)
7	11.	I'D LEAVE MY HAPPY HOME FOR YOU (8)
5	12.	DOAN YE CRY, MA HONEY (5)
9	13.	IN NAPLES FAIR (3)
16	14.	MY WILD IRISH ROSE (12)
–	15.	KOONVILLE KOONLETS (1)
8	16.	I COULDN'T STAND TO SEE MY BABY LOSE (4)
–	17.	MY JERSEY LILY (1)
12	18.	SING ME A SONG OF THE SOUTH (7)
–	19.	MA TIGER LILY (1)
–	20.	LINDY LOO (1)

JUNE 1900

LM	TM	
1	1.	THE BLUE AND THE GRAY (4)
3	2.	WHEN YOU WERE SWEET SIXTEEN (7)
2	3.	A BIRD IN A GILDED CAGE (5)
6	4.	I'M CERTAINLY LIVING A RAGTIME LIFE (3)
17	5.	MY JERSEY LILY (2)
19	6.	MA TIGER LILY (2)
4	7.	WHEN CHLOE SINGS A SONG (4)
–	8.	WOULDN'T IT MAKE YOU MAD, WOULDN'T IT JAR YOU? (1)
5	9.	WHY (3)
8	12.	A PICTURE NO ARTIST CAN PAINT (11)
7	10.	ALWAYS (8)
15	11.	KOONVILLE KOONLETS (2)
20	13.	LINDY LOO (2)
–	14.	THE FATAL ROSE OF RED (1)
–	15.	THE MICK WHO THREW THE BRICK (1)
–	16.	STRIKE UP THE BAND, HERE COMES A SAILOR (1)
9	17.	WHAT IS A HOME WITHOUT LOVE? (3)
10	18.	FILIPINO SHUFFLE (4)
–	19.	MY SUNBEAM FROM THE SOUTH (1)
–	20.	A COON BAND CONTEST (1)

JULY 1900

LM	TM	
1	1.	THE BLUE AND THE GRAY (5)
2	2.	WHEN YOU WERE SWEET SIXTEEN (8)
6	3.	MA TIGER LILY (3)
16	4.	STRIKE UP THE BAND, HERE COMES A SAILOR (2)
5	5.	MY JERSEY LILY (3)
8	6.	WOULDN'T IT MAKE YOU MAD, WOULDN'T IT JAR YOU? (2)
4	7.	I'M CERTAINLY LIVING A RAGTIME LIFE (4)
–	8.	EVERY RACE HAS A FLAG BUT THE COON (1)
–	9.	(IT'S THE) MAN BEHIND THE GUN (1)
14	10.	THE FATAL ROSE OF RED (2)
11	11.	KOONVILLE KOONLETS (3)
20	12.	A COON BAND CONTEST (2)
7	13.	WHEN CHLOE SINGS A SONG (5)
–	14.	JUST ONE KISS (1)
3	15.	A BIRD IN A GILDED CAGE (6)
–	16.	ON THE FIRING LINE (1)
9	17.	WHY (4)
15	18.	THE MICK WHO THREW THE BRICK (2)
10	19.	ALWAYS (9)
–	20.	WAIT (1)

AUGUST 1900

LM	TM	
1	1.	THE BLUE AND THE GRAY (6)
4	2.	STRIKE UP THE BAND, HERE COMES A SAILOR (3)
3	3.	MA TIGER LILY (4)
2	4.	WHEN YOU WERE SWEET SIXTEEN (9)
10	5.	THE FATAL ROSE OF RED (3)
8	6.	EVERY RACE HAS A FLAG BUT THE COON (2)
9	7.	(IT'S THE) MAN BEHIND THE GUN (2)
12	8.	A COON BAND CONTEST (3)
20	9.	WAIT (2)
11	10.	KOONVILLE KOONLETS (4)
14	11.	JUST ONE KISS (2)
–	12.	MIDNIGHT FIRE ALARM (1)
5	13.	MY JERSEY LILY (4)
7	14.	I'M CERTAINLY LIVING A RAGTIME LIFE (5)
–	15.	DAWN OF THE CENTURY MARCH (1)
16	16.	ON THE FIRING LINE (2)
6	17.	WOULDN'T IT MAKE YOU MAD, WOULDN'T IT JAR YOU? (3)
–	18.	YOU TELL ME YOUR DREAM (AND I WILL TELL YOU MINE) (1)
13	19.	WHEN CHLOE SINGS A SONG (6)
–	20.	MY HEART'S TONIGHT IN TEXAS (1)

SEPTEMBER 1900

LM	TM	
2	1.	STRIKE UP THE BAND, HERE COMES A SAILOR (4)
5	2.	THE FATAL ROSE OF RED (4)
1	3.	THE BLUE AND THE GRAY (7)
12	4.	MIDNIGHT FIRE ALARM (2)
9	5.	WAIT (3)
3	6.	MA TIGER LILY (5)
4	7.	WHEN YOU WERE SWEET SIXTEEN (10)
–	8.	I CAN'T TELL WHY I LOVE YOU BUT I DO (1)
18	9.	YOU TELL ME YOUR DREAM (AND I WILL TELL YOU MINE) (2)
–	10	I MUST A-BEEN A-DREAMIN' (1)
–	11.	FOR OLD TIMES' SAKE (1)
–	12.	WHEN THE HARVEST DAYS ARE OVER, JESSIE DEAR (1)
20	13.	MY HEART'S TONIGHT IN TEXAS (2)
7	14.	(IT'S THE) MAN BEHIND THE GUN (3)
15	15.	DAWN OF THE CENTURY MARCH (2)
–	16.	YOU NEEDN'T SAY THE KISSES CAME FROM ME (1)
–	17.	MA BLACK PEARL (1)
10	18.	KOONVILLE KOONLETS (5)
6	19.	EVERY RACE HAS A FLAG BUT THE COON (3)
8	20.	A COON BAND CONTEST (4)

OCTOBER 1900

LM	TM	
2	1.	THE FATAL ROSE OF RED (5)
8	2.	I CAN'T TELL WHY I LOVE YOU BUT I DO (2)
11	3.	FOR OLD TIMES' SAKE (2)
12	4.	WHEN THE HARVEST DAYS ARE OVER, JESSIE DEAR (2)
5	5.	WAIT (4)
1	6.	STRIKE UP THE BAND, HERE COMES A SAILOR (5)
9	7.	YOU TELL ME YOUR DREAM (AND I WILL TELL YOU MINE) (3)
17	8.	MA BLACK PEARL (2)
10	9	I MUST A-BEEN A-DREAMIN' (2)
4	10.	MIDNIGHT FIRE ALARM (3)
13	11.	MY HEART'S TONIGHT IN TEXAS (3)
6	12.	MA TIGER LILY (6)
7	13.	WHEN YOU WERE SWEET SIXTEEN (11)
3	14.	THE BLUE AND THE GRAY (8)
–	15.	OH, SHINING LIGHT (1)
–	16.	JUST BECAUSE SHE MADE DEM GOO-GOO EYES (1)
16	17.	YOU NEEDN'T SAY THE KISSES CAME FROM ME (2)
–	18.	I'VE GOT A WHITE MAN WORKING FOR ME (1)
–	19.	THE MOSQUITO'S PARADE (1)
–	20.	JUST WHEN I NEEDED YOU MOST (1)

NOVEMBER 1900

LM	TM	
2	1.	I CAN'T TELL WHY I LOVE YOU BUT I DO (3)
3	2.	FOR OLD TIMES' SAKE (3)
4	3.	WHEN THE HARVEST DAYS ARE OVER, JESSIE DEAR (3)
1	4.	THE FATAL ROSE OF RED (6)
7	5.	YOU TELL ME YOUR DREAM (AND I WILL TELL YOU MINE) (4)
8	6.	MA BLACK PEARL (3)
16	7.	JUST BECAUSE SHE MADE DEM GOO-GOO EYES (2)
11	8.	MY HEART'S TONIGHT IN TEXAS (4)
–	9.	CALLING TO HER BOY JUST ONCE AGAIN (1)
5	10.	WAIT (5)
–	11.	THE BRIDGE OF SIGHS (1)
–	12.	LAM' LAM' LAM (1)
19	13.	THE MOSQUITO'S PARADE (2)
15	14.	OH, SHINING LIGHT (2)
–	15.	MA BLUSHIN' ROSIE (1)
9	16	I MUST A-BEEN A-DREAMIN' (3)
12	17.	MA TIGER LILY (7)
6	18.	STRIKE UP THE BAND, HERE COMES A SAILOR (6)
13	19.	WHEN YOU WERE SWEET SIXTEEN (12)
–	20.	MY LITTLE ZULU BABE (1)

DECEMBER 1900

LM	TM	
2	1.	FOR OLD TIMES' SAKE (4)
1	2.	I CAN'T TELL WHY I LOVE YOU BUT I DO (4)
3	3.	WHEN THE HARVEST DAYS ARE OVER, JESSIE DEAR (4)
7	4.	JUST BECAUSE SHE MADE DEM GOO-GOO EYES (3)
11	5.	THE BRIDGE OF SIGHS (2)
12	6.	LAM' LAM' LAM (2)
15	7.	MA BLUSHIN' ROSIE (2)
9	8.	CALLING TO HER BOY JUST ONCE AGAIN (2)
5	9.	YOU TELL ME YOUR DREAM (AND I WILL TELL YOU MINE) (5)
13	10.	THE MOSQUITO'S PARADE (3)
4	11.	THE FATAL ROSE OF RED (7)
–	12.	COON! COON! COON! (1)
20	13.	MY LITTLE ZULU BABE (2)
–	14.	I'D STILL BELIEVE YOU TRUE (1)
6	15.	MA BLACK PEARL (2)
8	16.	MY HEART'S TONIGHT IN TEXAS (5)
–	17.	GOODBYE, DOLLY GRAY (1)
10	18.	WAIT (6)
14	19.	OH, SHINING LIGHT (3)
–	20.	IT'S THE MAN BEHIND THE GUN (THAT DOES THE WORK) (1)

JANUARY 1901

LM	TM	
2	1.	I CAN'T TELL WHY I LOVE YOU BUT I DO (5)
3	2.	WHEN THE HARVEST DAYS ARE OVER, JESSIE DEAR (5)
1	3.	FOR OLD TIMES' SAKE (5)
4	4.	JUST BECAUSE SHE MADE DEM GOO-GOO EYES (4)
12	5.	COON! COON! COON! (2)
7	6.	MA BLUSHIN' ROSIE (3)
17	7.	GOODBYE, DOLLY GRAY (2)
5	8.	THE BRIDGE OF SIGHS (3)
6	9.	LAM' LAM' LAM (3)
14	10.	I'D STILL BELIEVE YOU TRUE (2)
13	11.	MY LITTLE ZULU BABE (3)
11	12.	THE FATAL ROSE OF RED (8)
9	13.	YOU TELL ME YOUR DREAM (AND I WILL TELL YOU MINE) (6)
10	14.	THE MOSQUITO'S PARADE (4)
8	15.	CALLING TO HER BOY JUST ONCE AGAIN (3)
–	16.	THE SPIDER AND THE FLY (1)
–	17.	COME BACK, MA HONEY BOY, TO ME (1)
–	18.	COON UP A TREE (1)
–	19.	I WISH WE'D NEVER MET (1)
16	20.	MY HEART'S TONIGHT IN TEXAS (5)

FEBRUARY 1901

LM	TM	
5	1.	COON! COON! COON! (3)
7	2.	GOODBYE, DOLLY GRAY (3)
6	3.	MA BLUSHIN' ROSIE (4)
2	4.	WHEN THE HARVEST DAYS ARE OVER, JESSIE DEAR (6)
1	5.	I CAN'T TELL WHY I LOVE YOU BUT I DO (6)
3	6.	FOR OLD TIMES' SAKE (6)
4	7.	JUST BECAUSE SHE MADE DEM GOO-GOO EYES (5)
8	8.	THE BRIDGE OF SIGHS (4)
9	9.	LAM' LAM' LAM (4)
–	10.	TELL ME, PRETTY MAIDEN (1)
–	11.	I'VE A LONGING IN MY HEART FOR YOU, LOUISE (1)
–	12.	THE SHADE OF THE PALM (1)
11	13.	MY LITTLE ZULU BABE (4)
–	14.	ABSENCE MAKES THE HEART GROW FONDER (1)
–	15.	I WANT TO BE A MILITARY MAN (1)
–	16.	MY GIRL FROM DIXIE (1)
10	17.	I'D STILL BELIEVE YOU TRUE (3)
14	18.	THE MOSQUITO'S PARADE (5)
12	19.	THE FATAL ROSE OF RED (9)
20	20.	I WISH WE'D NEVER MET (2)

MARCH 1901

LM	TM	
1	1.	COON! COON! COON! (4)
2	2.	GOODBYE, DOLLY GRAY (4)
10	3.	TELL ME, PRETTY MAIDEN (2)
11	4.	I'VE A LONGING IN MY HEART FOR YOU, LOUISE (2)
3	5.	MA BLUSHIN' ROSIE (5)
12	6.	THE SHADE OF THE PALM (2)
14	7.	ABSENCE MAKES THE HEART GROW FONDER (2)
4	8.	WHEN THE HARVEST DAYS ARE OVER, JESSIE DEAR (7)
6	9.	FOR OLD TIMES' SAKE (7)
–	10.	THE TALE OF THE KANGAROO (1)
7	11.	JUST BECAUSE SHE MADE DEM GOO-GOO EYES (6)
5	12.	I CAN'T TELL WHY I LOVE YOU BUT I DO (7)
–	13.	IF I ONLY HAD A DOLLAH OF MY OWN (1)
15	14.	I WANT TO BE A MILITARY MAN (2)
16	15.	MY GIRL FROM DIXIE (2)
8	16.	THE BRIDGE OF SIGHS (5)
9	17.	LAM' LAM' LAM (5)
–	18.	EUGENIA WALTZES (1)
–	19.	DOWN BY THE RIVERSIDE (1)
13	20.	MY LITTLE ZULU BABE (5)

APRIL 1901

LM	TM	
2	1.	GOODBYE, DOLLY GRAY (5)
4	2.	I'VE A LONGING IN MY HEART FOR YOU, LOUISE (3)
3	3.	TELL ME, PRETTY MAIDEN (3)
1	4.	COON! COON! COON! (5)
10	5.	THE TALE OF THE KANGAROO (2)
7	6.	ABSENCE MAKES THE HEART GROW FONDER (3)
13	7.	IF I ONLY HAD A DOLLAH OF MY OWN (2)
5	8.	MA BLUSHIN' ROSIE (6)
6	9.	THE SHADE OF THE PALM (3)
–	10.	IN THE HOUSE OF TOO MUCH TROUBLE (1)
8	11.	WHEN THE HARVEST DAYS ARE OVER, JESSIE DEAR (8)
11	12.	JUST BECAUSE SHE MADE DEM GOO-GOO EYES (7)
–	13.	MY ELINORE (1)
9	14.	FOR OLD TIMES' SAKE (8)
15	15.	MY GIRL FROM DIXIE (3)
–	16.	COON UP A TREE (2)
–	17.	HELLO, CENTRAL, GIVE ME HEAVEN (1)
–	18.	DOWN BY THE RIVERSIDE (1)
12	19.	I CAN'T TELL WHY I LOVE YOU BUT I DO (8)
–	20.	THE VESPER BELLS WERE RINGING (1)

MAY 1901

LM	TM	
1	1.	GOODBYE, DOLLY GRAY (6)
2	2.	I'VE A LONGING IN MY HEART FOR YOU, LOUISE (4)
3	3.	TELL ME, PRETTY MAIDEN (4)
4	4.	COON! COON! COON! (6)
6	5.	ABSENCE MAKES THE HEART GROW FONDER (4)
10	6.	IN THE HOUSE OF TOO MUCH TROUBLE (2)
17	7.	HELLO, CENTRAL, GIVE ME HEAVEN (2)
8	8.	MA BLUSHIN' ROSIE (7)
5	9.	THE TALE OF THE KANGAROO (3)
7	10.	IF I ONLY HAD A DOLLAH OF MY OWN (3)
–	11.	SWEET ANNIE MOORE (1)
–	12.	ANY OLD PLACE I CAN HANG MY HAT IS HOME SWEET HOME TO ME (1)
13	13.	MY ELINORE (2)
16	14.	COON UP A TREE (3)
–	15.	THERE'S NO NORTH OR SOUTH TODAY (1)
11	16.	WHEN THE HARVEST DAYS ARE OVER, JESSIE DEAR (9)
–	17.	IN THE CATHEDRAL (1)
–	18.	THE FOUR KINGS MARCH (1)
9	19.	THE SHADE OF THE PALM (4)
20	20.	THE VESPER BELLS WERE RINGING (2)

JUNE 1901

LM	TM	
1	1.	GOODBYE, DOLLY GRAY (7)
7	2.	HELLO, CENTRAL, GIVE ME HEAVEN (3)
2	3.	I'VE A LONGING IN MY HEART FOR YOU, LOUISE (5)
11	4.	SWEET ANNIE MOORE (2)
12	5.	ANY OLD PLACE I CAN HANG MY HAT IS HOME SWEET HOME TO ME (2)
4	6.	COON! COON! COON! (7)
3	7.	TELL ME, PRETTY MAIDEN (5)
5	8.	ABSENCE MAKES THE HEART GROW FONDER (5)
–	9.	MAMIE (1)
6	10.	IN THE HOUSE OF TOO MUCH TROUBLE (3)
14	11.	COON UP A TREE (4)
15	12.	THERE'S NO NORTH OR SOUTH TODAY (2)
8	13.	MA BLUSHIN' ROSIE (8)
–	14.	BOOLA, BOOLA (YALE BOOLA) (1)
13	15.	MY ELINORE (3)
10	16.	IF I ONLY HAD A DOLLAH OF MY OWN (4)
–	17.	THE HONEYSUCKLE AND THE BEE (1)
–	18.	JIMMY, THE PRIDE OF NEWSPAPER ROW (1)
18	19.	THE FOUR KINGS MARCH (2)
–	20.	A GHOST OF A COON (1)

JULY 1901

LM	TM	
2	1.	HELLO, CENTRAL, GIVE ME HEAVEN (4)
4	2.	SWEET ANNIE MOORE (3)
1	3.	GOODBYE, DOLLY GRAY (8)
9	4.	MAMIE (2)
5	5.	ANY OLD PLACE I CAN HANG MY HAT IS HOME SWEET HOME TO ME (3)
3	6.	I'VE A LONGING IN MY HEART FOR YOU, LOUISE (6)
8	7.	ABSENCE MAKES THE HEART GROW FONDER (6)
6	8.	COON! COON! COON! (8)
14	9.	BOOLA, BOOLA (YALE BOOLA) (2)
17	10.	THE HONEYSUCKLE AND THE BEE (2)
7	11.	TELL ME, PRETTY MAIDEN (6)
11	12.	COON UP A TREE (5)
18	13.	JIMMY, THE PRIDE OF NEWSPAPER ROW (2)
–	14.	GOOD MORNING, CARRIE (1)
–	15.	GO 'WAY BACK AND SIT DOWN (1)
10	16.	IN THE HOUSE OF TOO MUCH TROUBLE (4)
12	17.	THERE'S NO NORTH OR SOUTH TODAY (3)
–	18.	DOWN IN THE DEPTHS (1)
–	19.	MY SWEET KIMONA (1)
13	20.	MA BLUSHIN' ROSIE (9)

AUGUST 1901

LM	TM	
1	1.	HELLO, CENTRAL, GIVE ME HEAVEN (5)
2	2.	SWEET ANNIE MOORE (4)
15	3.	GO 'WAY BACK AND SIT DOWN (2)
10	4.	THE HONEYSUCKLE AND THE BEE (3)
3	5.	GOODBYE, DOLLY GRAY (9)
14	6.	GOOD MORNING, CARRIE (2)
9	7.	BOOLA, BOOLA (YALE BOOLA) (3)
4	8.	MAMIE (3)
7	9.	ABSENCE MAKES THE HEART GROW FONDER (7)
8	10.	COON! COON! COON! (9)
13	11.	JIMMY, THE PRIDE OF NEWSPAPER ROW (3)
5	12.	ANY OLD PLACE I CAN HANG MY HAT IS HOME SWEET HOME TO ME (4)
6	13.	I'VE A LONGING IN MY HEART FOR YOU, LOUISE (7)
12	14.	COON UP A TREE (6)
–	15.	AIN'T DAT A SHAME? (1)
–	16.	I'VE GROWN SO USED TO YOU (1)
19	17.	MY SWEET KIMONA (2)
–	18.	HE LAID AWAY A SUIT OF GRAY (1)
18	19.	DOWN IN THE DEPTHS (2)
–	20.	A GHOST OF A COON (2)

SEPTEMBER 1901

LM	TM	
1	1.	HELLO, CENTRAL, GIVE ME HEAVEN (6)
3	2.	GO 'WAY BACK AND SIT DOWN (3)
6	3.	GOOD MORNING, CARRIE (3)
4	4.	THE HONEYSUCKLE AND THE BEE (4)
15	5.	AIN'T DAT A SHAME? (2)
7	6.	BOOLA, BOOLA (YALE BOOLA) (4)
5	7.	GOODBYE, DOLLY GRAY (10)
9	8.	ABSENCE MAKES THE HEART GROW FONDER (8)
2	9.	SWEET ANNIE MOORE (5)
8	10.	MAMIE (4)
11	11.	JIMMY, THE PRIDE OF NEWSPAPER ROW (4)
–	12.	MR. VOLUNTEER (1)
–	13.	MY LADY HOTTENTOT (1)
18	14.	HE LAID AWAY A SUIT OF GRAY (2)
14	15.	COON UP A TREE (7)
10	16.	COON! COON! COON! (10)
–	17.	DOWN WHERE THE COTTON BLOSSOMS GROW (1)
16	18.	I'VE GROWN SO USED TO YOU (2)
20	19.	A GHOST OF A COON (2)
–	20.	THE TALE OF A BUMBLE BEE (1)

OCTOBER 1901

LM	TM	
3	1.	GOOD MORNING, CARRIE (4)
1	2.	HELLO, CENTRAL, GIVE ME HEAVEN (7)
2	3.	GO 'WAY BACK AND SIT DOWN (4)
4	4.	THE HONEYSUCKLE AND THE BEE (5)
5	5.	AIN'T DAT A SHAME? (3)
12	6.	MR. VOLUNTEER (2)
13	7.	MY LADY HOTTENTOT (2)
–	8.	I'LL BE WITH YOU WHEN THE ROSES BLOOM AGAIN (1)
17	9.	DOWN WHERE THE COTTON BLOSSOMS GROW (2)
6	10.	BOOLA, BOOLA (YALE BOOLA) (5)
14	11.	HE LAID AWAY A SUIT OF GRAY (3)
–	12.	I'M TIRED (1)
–	13.	MY CASTLE ON THE NILE (1)
–	14.	THE TIE THAT BINDS (1)
20	15.	THE TALE OF A BUMBLE BEE (2)
–	16.	BABY MINE (1)
–	17.	CREOLE BELLES (1)
15	18.	COON UP A TREE (8)
7	19.	GOODBYE, DOLLY GRAY (11)
8	20.	ABSENCE MAKES THE HEART GROW FONDER (9)

NOVEMBER 1901

LM	TM	
1	1.	GOOD MORNING, CARRIE (5)
8	2.	I'LL BE WITH YOU WHEN THE ROSES BLOOM AGAIN (2)
5	3.	AIN'T DAT A SHAME? (4)
2	4.	HELLO, CENTRAL, GIVE ME HEAVEN (8)
9	5.	DOWN WHERE THE COTTON BLOSSOMS GROW (3)
4	6.	THE HONEYSUCKLE AND THE BEE (6)
13	7.	MY CASTLE ON THE NILE (2)
17	8.	CREOLE BELLES (2)
6	9.	MR. VOLUNTEER (3)
16	10.	BABY MINE (2)
12	11.	I'M TIRED (2)
3	12.	GO 'WAY BACK AND SIT DOWN (5)
14	13.	THE TIE THAT BINDS (2)
7	14.	MY LADY HOTTENTOT (3)
15	15.	THE TALE OF A BUMBLE BEE (3)
11	16.	HE LAID AWAY A SUIT OF GRAY (4)
–	17.	WHEN MR. SHAKESPEARE COMES TO TOWN (1)
–	18.	IN THE GREAT SOMEWHERE (1)
10	19.	BOOLA, BOOLA (YALE BOOLA) (6)
–	20.	A GHOST OF A COON (3)

DECEMBER 1901

LM	TM	
2	1.	I'LL BE WITH YOU WHEN THE ROSES BLOOM AGAIN (3)
1	2.	GOOD MORNING, CARRIE (6)
8	3.	CREOLE BELLES (3)
5	4.	DOWN WHERE THE COTTON BLOSSOMS GROW (4)
7	5.	MY CASTLE ON THE NILE (3)
9	6.	MR. VOLUNTEER (4)
4	7.	HELLO, CENTRAL, GIVE ME HEAVEN (9)
3	8.	AIN'T DAT A SHAME? (5)
11	9.	I'M TIRED (3)
6	10.	THE HONEYSUCKLE AND THE BEE (7)
10	11.	BABY MINE (3)
13	12.	THE TIE THAT BINDS (3)
–	13.	WAY DOWN IN OLD INDIANA (1)
17	14.	WHEN MR. SHAKESPEARE COMES TO TOWN (2)
15	15.	THE TALE OF A BUMBLE BEE (4)
14	16.	MY LADY HOTTENTOT (4)
–	17.	MY MISSISSIPPI SUE (1)
18	18.	IN THE GREAT SOMEWHERE (2)
16	19.	HE LAID AWAY A SUIT OF GRAY (5)
–	20.	IT'S ALL RIGHT, MAYME (1)

JANUARY 1902

LM	TM	
3	1.	CREOLE BELLES (4)
1	2.	I'LL BE WITH YOU WHEN THE ROSES BLOOM AGAIN (4)
4	3.	DOWN WHERE THE COTTON BLOSSOMS GROW (5)
2	4.	GOOD MORNING, CARRIE (7)
6	5.	MR. VOLUNTEER (5)
5	6.	MY CASTLE ON THE NILE (4)
7	7.	HELLO, CENTRAL, GIVE ME HEAVEN (10)
8	8.	AIN'T DAT A SHAME? (6)
14	9.	WHEN MR. SHAKESPEARE COMES TO TOWN (3)
17	10.	MY MISSISSIPPI SUE (2)
10	11.	HONEYSUCKLE AND THE BEE (8)
13	12.	WAY DOWN IN OLD INDIANA (2)
9	13.	I'M TIRED (4)
–	14.	MY CAROLINA CAROLINE (1)
12	15.	THE TIE THAT BINDS (4)
15	16.	TALE OF A BUMBLE BEE (5)
–	17.	ONE STRIKE, TWO STRIKES, THREE STRIKES OUT (1)
19	18.	HE LAID AWAY A SUIT OF GRAY (6)
–	19.	DON'T PUT ME OFF AT BUFFALO ANYMORE (1)
–	20.	BOOLA, BOOLA (YALE BOOLA) (7)

FEBRUARY 1902

LM	TM	
1	1.	CREOLE BELLES (5)
2	2.	I'LL BE WITH YOU WHEN THE ROSES BLOOM AGAIN (5)
3	3.	DOWN WHERE THE COTTON BLOSSOMS GROW (6)
4	4.	GOOD MORNING, CARRIE (8)
5	5.	MR. VOLUNTEER (6)
7	6.	HELLO, CENTRAL, GIVE ME HEAVEN (11)
10	7.	MY MISSISSIPPI SUE (3)
8	8.	AIN'T DAT A SHAME? (7)
14	9.	MY CAROLINA CAROLINE (2)
11	10.	HONEYSUCKLE AND THE BEE (9)
6	11.	MY CASTLE ON THE NILE (5)
–	12.	WAY DOWN YONDER IN THE CORNFIELD (1)
9	13.	WHEN MR. SHAKESPEARE COMES TO TOWN (4)
17	14.	ONE STRIKE, TWO STRIKES, THREE STRIKES OUT (2)
16	15.	TALE OF A BUMBLE BEE (6)
–	16.	MAIDEN WITH THE DREAMY EYES (1)
12	17.	WAY DOWN IN OLD INDIANA (3)
18	18.	HE LAID AWAY A SUIT OF GRAY (7)
13	19.	I'M TIRED (5)
–	20.	SADIE, SAY YOU WON'T SAY NAY (1)

MARCH 1902

LM	TM	
1	1.	CREOLE BELLES (6)
3	2.	DOWN WHERE THE COTTON BLOSSOMS GROW (7)
12	3.	WAY DOWN YONDER IN THE CORNFIELD (2)
4	4.	GOOD MORNING, CARRIE (9)
9	5.	MY CAROLINA CAROLINE (3)
16	6.	MAIDEN WITH THE DREAMY EYES (2)
2	7.	I'LL BE WITH YOU WHEN THE ROSES BLOOM AGAIN (6)
–	8.	ON A SUNDAY AFTERNOON (1)
7	9.	MY MISSISSIPPI SUE (4)
5	10.	MR. VOLUNTEER (7)
–	11.	MANSION OF ACHING HEARTS (1)
6	12.	HELLO, CENTRAL, GIVE ME HEAVEN (12)
14	13.	ONE STRIKE, TWO STRIKES, THREE STRIKES OUT (3)
–	14.	OUR DIRECTOR (MARCH) (1)
8	15.	AIN'T DAT A SHAME? (8)
–	16.	BLAZE AWAY! (1)
–	17.	JENNIE LEE (1)
–	18.	A SIGNAL FROM MARS (1)
10	19.	THE HONEYSUCKLE AND THE BEE (10)
13	20.	WHEN MR. SHAKESPEARE COMES TO TOWN (5)

APRIL 1902

LM	TM	
3	1.	WAY DOWN YONDER IN THE CORNFIELD (3)
8	2.	ON A SUNDAY AFTERNOON (2)
11	3.	MANSION OF ACHING HEARTS (2)
1	4.	CREOLE BELLES (7)
17	5.	JENNIE LEE (2)
2	6.	DOWN WHERE THE COTTON BLOSSOMS GROW (8)
5	7.	MY CAROLINA CAROLINE (4)
14	8.	OUR DIRECTOR (MARCH) (2)
–	9.	JOSEPHINE, MY JO (1)
16	10.	BLAZE AWAY! (2)
13	11.	ONE STRIKE, TWO STRIKES, THREE STRIKES OUT (4)
6	12.	MAIDEN WITH THE DREAMY EYES (3)
18	13.	A SIGNAL FROM MARS (2)
4	14.	GOOD MORNING, CARRIE (10)
9	15.	MY MISSISSIPPI SUE (5)
10	16.	MR. VOLUNTEER (8)
12	17.	HELLO, CENTRAL, GIVE ME HEAVEN (13)
–	18.	TALE OF A BUMBLE BEE (6)
–	19.	RIP VAN WINKLE WAS A LUCKY MAN (1)
–	20.	CUPID'S GARDEN (1)

MAY 1902

LM	TM	
2	1.	ON A SUNDAY AFTERNOON (3)
3	2.	MANSION OF ACHING HEARTS (3)
1	3.	WAY DOWN YONDER IN THE CORNFIELD (4)
5	4.	JENNIE LEE (3)
9	5.	JOSEPHINE, MY JO (2)
8	6.	OUR DIRECTOR (MARCH) (3)
19	7.	RIP VAN WINKLE WAS A LUCKY MAN (2)
10	8.	BLAZE AWAY! (3)
–	9.	ON A SATURDAY NIGHT (1)
–	10.	IF MONEY TALKS, IT AIN'T ON SPEAKIN' TERMS WITH ME (1)
7	11.	MY CAROLINA CAROLINE (5)
6	12.	DOWN WHERE THE COTTON BLOSSOMS GROW (9)
4	13.	CREOLE BELLES (8)
11	14.	ONE STRIKE, TWO STRIKES, THREE STRIKES OUT (5)
13	15.	A SIGNAL FROM MARS (3)
12	16.	MAIDEN WITH THE DREAMY EYES (4)
–	17.	IF TIME WAS MONEY, I'D BE A MILLIONAIRE (1)
20	18.	CUPID'S GARDEN (2)
–	19.	MIGHTY LAK' A ROSE (1)
–	20.	STAY IN YOUR OWN BACK YARD (1)

JUNE 1902

LM	TM	
1	1.	ON A SUNDAY AFTERNOON (4)
2	2.	MANSION OF ACHING HEARTS (4)
7	3.	RIP VAN WINKLE WAS A LUCKY MAN (3)
10	4.	IF MONEY TALKS, IT AIN'T ON SPEAKIN' TERMS WITH ME (2)
6	5.	OUR DIRECTOR (MARCH) (4)
3	6.	WAY DOWN YONDER IN THE CORNFIELD (5)
9	7.	ON A SATURDAY NIGHT (2)
8	8.	BLAZE AWAY! (4)
4	9.	JENNIE LEE (4)
17	10.	IF TIME WAS MONEY, I'D BE A MILLIONAIRE (2)
11	11.	MY CAROLINA CAROLINE (6)
12	12.	DOWN WHERE THE COTTON BLOSSOMS GROW (10)
5	13.	JOSEPHINE, MY JO (3)
14	14.	ONE STRIKE, TWO STRIKES, THREE STRIKES OUT (6)
18	15.	CUPID'S GARDEN (3)
19	16.	MIGHTY LAK' A ROSE (2)
–	17.	PANAMERICANA (1)
20	18.	STAY IN YOUR OWN BACK YARD (2)
–	19.	PRETTY MOLLIE SHANNON (1)
15	20.	A SIGNAL FROM MARS (4)

JULY 1902

LM	TM	
1	1.	ON A SUNDAY AFTERNOON (5)
3	2.	RIP VAN WINKLE WAS A LUCKY MAN (4)
2	3.	MANSION OF ACHING HEARTS (5)
4	4.	IF MONEY TALKS, IT AIN'T ON SPEAKIN' TERMS WITH ME (3)
8	5.	BLAZE AWAY! (5)
10	6.	IF TIME WAS MONEY, I'D BE A MILLION-AIRE (3)
5	7.	OUR DIRECTOR (MARCH) (5)
7	8.	ON A SATURDAY NIGHT (3)
6	9.	WAY DOWN YONDER IN THE CORNFIELD (6)
–	10.	PLEASE GO 'WAY AND LET ME SLEEP (1)
19	11.	PRETTY MOLLIE SHANNON (2)
11	12.	MY CAROLINA CAROLINE (7)
15	13.	CUPID'S GARDEN (4)
–	14.	WHERE THE SILV'RY COLORADO WENDS ITS WAY (1)
9	15.	JENNIE LEE (5)
–	16.	MY MOTHER WAS A NORTHERN GIRL (1)
–	17.	VIOLETS (1)
–	18.	BILL BAILEY, WON'T YOU PLEASE COME HOME? (1)
–	19.	NANCY BROWN (1)
16	20.	MIGHTY LAK' A ROSE (3)

AUGUST 1902

LM	TM	
10	1.	PLEASE GO 'WAY AND LET ME SLEEP (2)
1	2.	ON A SUNDAY AFTERNOON (6)
2	3.	RIP VAN WINKLE WAS A LUCKY MAN (5)
3	4.	MANSION OF ACHING HEARTS (6)
18	5.	BILL BAILEY, WON'T YOU PLEASE COME HOME? (2)
4	6.	IF MONEY TALKS, IT AIN'T ON SPEAKIN' TERMS WITH ME (4)
19	7.	NANCY BROWN (2)
–	8.	OH, DIDN'T HE RAMBLE (1)
11	9.	PRETTY MOLLIE SHANNON (3)
6	10.	IF TIME WAS MONEY, I'D BE A MILLION-AIRE (4)
–	11.	JUST NEXT DOOR (1)
17	12.	VIOLETS (2)
9	13.	WAY DOWN YONDER IN THE CORNFIELD (7)
–	14.	IN THE GOOD OLD SUMMERTIME (1)
5	15.	BLAZE AWAY! (6)
13	16.	CUPID'S GARDEN (5)
14	17.	WHERE THE SILV'RY COLORADO WENDS ITS WAY (2)
20	18.	MIGHTY LAK' A ROSE (4)
–	19.	SADIE, SAY YOU WON'T SAY NAY (2)
–	20.	IF I BUT DARE (1)

SEPTEMBER 1902

LM	TM	
5	1.	BILL BAILEY, WON'T YOU PLEASE COME HOME? (3)
14	2.	IN THE GOOD OLD SUMMERTIME (2)
1	3.	PLEASE GO 'WAY AND LET ME SLEEP (3)
8	4.	OH, DIDN'T HE RAMBLE (2)
7	5.	NANCY BROWN (3)
2	6.	ON A SUNDAY AFTERNOON (7)
12	7.	VIOLETS (3)
–	8.	WHEN KATE AND I WERE COMIN' THRO' THE RYE (1)
11	9.	JUST NEXT DOOR (2)
4	10.	MANSION OF ACHING HEARTS (7)
9	11.	PRETTY MOLLIE SHANNON (4)
–	12.	I'LL BE YOUR RAINBEAU (1)
–	13.	I'VE GOT MY EYES ON YOU (1)
3	14.	RIP VAN WINKLE WAS A LUCKY MAN (6)
17	15.	WHERE THE SILV'RY COLORADO WENDS ITS WAY (3)
–	16.	FARE THEE WELL, MOLLIE DARLING (1)
19	17.	SADIE, SAY YOU WON'T SAY NAY (3)
18	18.	MIGHTY LAK' A ROSE (5)
20	19.	IF I BUT DARE (2)
–	20.	MR. DOOLEY (1)

OCTOBER 1902

LM	TM	
2	1.	IN THE GOOD OLD SUMMERTIME (3)
1	2.	BILL BAILEY, WON'T YOU PLEASE COME HOME? (4)
3	3.	PLEASE GO 'WAY AND LET ME SLEEP (4)
4	4.	OH, DIDN'T HE RAMBLE (3)
8	5.	WHEN KATE AND I WERE COMIN' THRO' THE RYE (2)
7	6.	VIOLETS (4)
20	7.	MR. DOOLEY (2)
16	8.	FARE THEE WELL, MOLLIE DARLING (2)
12	9.	I'LL BE YOUR RAINBEAU (2)
13	10.	I'VE GOT MY EYES ON YOU (2)
11	11.	PRETTY MOLLIE SHANNON (5)
5	12.	NANCY BROWN (4)
–	13.	WAIT (1)
9	14.	JUST NEXT DOOR (3)
–	15.	PLACE A LIGHT TO GUIDE ME HOME (1)
6	16.	ON A SUNDAY AFTERNOON (8)
15	17.	WHERE THE SILV'RY COLORADO WENDS ITS WAY (4)
–	18.	STAY IN YOUR OWN BACK YARD (3)
18	19.	SADIE, SAY YOU WON'T SAY NAY (4)
–	20.	COULD YOU BE TRUE TO EYES OF BLUE? (1)

NOVEMBER 1902

LM	TM	
1	1.	IN THE GOOD OLD SUMMERTIME (4)
2	2.	BILL BAILEY, WON'T YOU PLEASE COME HOME? (5)
7	3.	MR. DOOLEY (3)
3	4.	PLEASE GO 'WAY AND LET ME SLEEP (5)
4	5.	OH, DIDN'T HE RAMBLE (4)
8	6.	FARE THEE WELL, MOLLIE DARLING (3)
5	7.	WHEN KATE AND I WERE COMIN' THRO' THE RYE (3)
6	8.	VIOLETS (5)
20	9.	COULD YOU BE TRUE TO EYES OF BLUE? (2)
–	10.	DOWN WHERE THE WURTZBURGER FLOWS (1)
–	11.	I'M WEARING MY HEART AWAY FOR YOU, LOUISE (1)
13	12.	WAIT (2)
15	13.	PLACE A LIGHT TO GUIDE ME HOME (2)
11	14.	PRETTY MOLLIE SHANNON (6)
9	15.	I'LL BE YOUR RAINBEAU (3)
–	16.	DANCE OF THE HONEYBEES (1)
10	17.	I'VE GOT MY EYES ON YOU (3)
–	18.	CUPID'S GARDEN (6)
–	19.	I WANTS A PING PONG MAN (1)
17	20.	WHERE THE SILV'RY COLORADO WENDS ITS WAY (5)

DECEMBER 1902

LM	TM	
3	1.	MR. DOOLEY (4)
1	2.	IN THE GOOD OLD SUMMERTIME (5)
10	3.	DOWN WHERE THE WURTZBURGER FLOWS (2)
2	4.	BILL BAILEY, WON'T YOU PLEASE COME HOME? (6)
9	5.	COULD YOU BE TRUE TO EYES OF BLUE? (3)
11	6.	I'M WEARING MY HEART AWAY FOR YOU, LOUISE (2)
4	7.	PLEASE GO 'WAY AND LET ME SLEEP (6)
–	8.	UNDER THE BAMBOO TREE (1)
5	9.	OH, DIDN'T HE RAMBLE (5)
6	10.	FARE THEE WELL, MOLLIE DARLING (4)
–	11.	IN THE CITY OF SIGHS AND TEARS (1)
–	12.	WHEN IT'S ALL GOIN' OUT AND NOTHIN' COMIN' IN (1)
16	13.	DANCE OF THE HONEYBEES (2)
–	14.	DAT'S DE WAY TO SPELL CHICKEN (1)
–	15.	IN DEAR OLD ILLINOIS (1)
8	16.	VIOLETS (6)
12	17.	WAIT (3)
13	18.	PLACE A LIGHT TO GUIDE ME HOME (3)
7	19.	WHEN KATE AND I WERE COMIN' THRO' THE RYE (4)
–	20.	STAY IN YOUR OWN BACK YARD (4)

JANUARY 1903

LM	TM	
3	1.	DOWN WHERE THE WURTZBURGER FLOWS (3)
8	2.	UNDER THE BAMBOO TREE (2)
1	3.	MR. DOOLEY (5)
12	4.	WHEN IT'S ALL GOIN' OUT AND NOTHIN' COMIN' IN (2)
2	5.	IN THE GOOD OLD SUMMERTIME (7)
5	6.	COULD YOU BE TRUE TO EYES OF BLUE? (4)
6	7.	I'M WEARING MY HEART AWAY FOR YOU, LOUISE (3)
15	8.	IN DEAR OLD ILLINOIS (2)
14	9.	DAT'S DE WAY TO SPELL CHICKEN (2)
–	10.	THE MESSAGE OF THE VIOLET (1)
11	11.	IN THE CITY OF SIGHS AND TEARS (2)
–	12.	THEN I'D BE SATISFIED WITH LIFE (1)
4	13.	BILL BAILEY, WON'T YOU PLEASE COME HOME? (7)
–	14.	JUST KISS YOURSELF GOODBYE (1)
–	15.	SOMEBODY'S WAITING 'NEATH SOUTHERN SKIES (1)
–	16.	DUTY TO HOME AND FLAG (1)
–	17.	IF YOU CAN'T BE A BELL COW, FALL IN BEHIND (1)
–	18.	CONEY ISLAND COON (1)
13	19.	DANCE OF THE HONEYBEES (3)
7	20.	PLEASE GO 'WAY AND LET ME SLEEP (7)

FEBRUARY 1903

LM	TM	
2	1.	UNDER THE BAMBOO TREE (3)
1	2.	DOWN WHERE THE WURTZBURGER FLOWS (4)
4	3.	WHEN IT'S ALL GOIN' OUT AND NOTHIN' COMIN' IN (3)
8	4.	IN DEAR OLD ILLINOIS (3)
10	5.	THE MESSAGE OF THE VIOLET (2)
14	6.	JUST KISS YOURSELF GOODBYE (2)
3	7.	MR. DOOLEY (6)
9	8.	DAT'S DE WAY TO SPELL CHICKEN (3)
6	9.	COULD YOU BE TRUE TO EYES OF BLUE? (5)
12	10.	THEN I'D BE SATISFIED WITH LIFE (2)
–	11.	TWO IS COMPANY, THREE IS A CROWD (1)
–	12.	HAMLET WAS A MELANCHOLY DANE (1)
7	13.	I'M WEARING MY HEART AWAY FOR YOU, LOUISE (4)
–	14.	THE TALE OF THE SEASHELL (1)
–	15.	MY OWN UNITED STATES (1)
15	16.	SOMEBODY'S WAITING 'NEATH SOUTHERN SKIES (2)
5	17.	IN THE GOOD OLD SUMMERTIME (8)
–	18.	THE SPIRIT OF '76 (1)
–	19.	TESSIE, YOU ARE THE ONLY, ONLY, ONLY (1)
–	20.	HEIDELBERG (STEIN SONG) (1)

MARCH 1903

LM	TM	
1	1.	UNDER THE BAMBOO TREE (4)
2	2.	DOWN WHERE THE WURTZBURGER FLOWS (5)
5	3.	THE MESSAGE OF THE VIOLET (3)
15	4.	MY OWN UNITED STATES (2)
6	5.	JUST KISS YOURSELF GOODBYE (3)
19	6.	TESSIE, YOU ARE THE ONLY, ONLY, ONLY (2)
11	7.	TWO IS COMPANY, THREE IS A CROWD (2)
3	8.	WHEN IT'S ALL GOIN' OUT AND NOTHIN' COMIN' IN (4)
–	9.	MOLLIE (A DAINTY BIT OF JOLLY) (1)
–	10.	HIAWATHA (1)
12	11.	HAMLET WAS A MELANCHOLY DANE (2)
4	12.	IN DEAR OLD ILLINOIS (4)
7	13.	MR. DOOLEY (7)
–	14.	THE GAMBLING MAN (1)
8	15.	DAT'S DE WAY TO SPELL CHICKEN (4)
–	16.	IN THE SWEET BYE AND BYE (1)
18	17.	THE SPIRIT OF '76 (2)
14	18.	THE TALE OF THE SEASHELL (2)
–	19.	WHY DON'T YOU GO, GO, GO (1)
–	20.	NOBODY'S LOOKING BUT THE OWL AND THE MOON (1)

APRIL 1903

LM	TM	
1	1.	UNDER THE BAMBOO TREE (5)
10	2.	HIAWATHA (2)
4	3.	MY OWN UNITED STATES (3)
14	4.	THE GAMBLING MAN (2)
6	5.	TESSIE, YOU ARE THE ONLY, ONLY, ONLY (3)
2	6.	DOWN WHERE THE WURTZBURGER FLOWS (6)
16	7.	IN THE SWEET BYE AND BYE (2)
9	8.	MOLLIE (A DAINTY BIT OF JOLLY) (2)
19	9.	WHY DON'T YOU GO, GO, GO (2)
–	10.	I'M A JONAH MAN (1)
–	11.	SINCE SALLY LEFT OUR ALLEY (1)
3	12.	THE MESSAGE OF THE VIOLET (4)
–	13.	HURRAH FOR BAFFIN'S BAY (1)
20	14.	NOBODY'S LOOKING BUT THE OWL AND THE MOON (2)
5	15.	JUST KISS YOURSELF GOODBYE (4)
7	16.	TWO IS COMPANY, THREE IS A CROWD (3)
–	17.	I TAKE THINGS EASY (1)
–	18.	SAMMY (1)
–	19.	DOWN IN THE DEEP, LET ME SLEEP WHEN I DIE (1)
8	20.	WHEN IT'S ALL GOIN' OUT AND NOTHIN' COMIN' IN (5)

MAY 1903

LM	TM	
2	1.	HIAWATHA (3)
1	2.	UNDER THE BAMBOO TREE (6)
4	3.	THE GAMBLING MAN (3)
10	4.	I'M A JONAH MAN (2)
7	5.	IN THE SWEET BYE AND BYE (3)
11	6.	SINCE SALLY LEFT OUR ALLEY (2)
14	7.	NOBODY'S LOOKING BUT THE OWL AND THE MOON (3)
13	8.	HURRAH FOR BAFFIN'S BAY (2)
5	9.	TESSIE, YOU ARE THE ONLY, ONLY, ONLY (4)
–	10.	THE VOICE OF THE HUDSON (1)
–	11.	CONGO LOVE SONG (1)
3	12.	MY OWN UNITED STATES (4)
–	13.	ONLY A SOLDIER BOY (1)
8	14.	MOLLIE (A DAINTY BIT OF JOLLY) (3)
–	15.	EVERY MAN IS A VOLUNTEER (1)
–	16.	WHAT A NASTY DISPOSITION FOR A GIRL LIKE YOU (1)
–	17.	COME DOWN, MA EVENIN' STAR (1)
–	18.	IN OLD ALABAMA (1)
12	19.	THE MESSAGE OF THE VIOLET (5)
9	20.	WHY DON'T YOU GO, GO, GO (3)

JUNE 1903

LM	TM	
1	1.	HIAWATHA (4)
11	2.	CONGO LOVE SONG (2)
2	3.	UNDER THE BAMBOO TREE (7)
7	4.	NOBODY'S LOOKING BUT THE OWL AND THE MOON (4)
3	5.	THE GAMBLING MAN (4)
5	6.	IN THE SWEET BYE AND BYE (4)
18	7.	IN OLD ALABAMA (2)
10	8.	THE VOICE OF THE HUDSON (2)
17	9.	COME DOWN, MA EVENIN' STAR (2)
16	10.	WHAT A NASTY DISPOSITION FOR A GIRL LIKE YOU (2)
4	11.	I'M A JONAH MAN (3)
8	12.	HURRAH FOR BAFFIN'S BAY (3)
13	13.	ONLY A SOLDIER BOY (2)
6	14.	SINCE SALLY LEFT OUR ALLEY (3)
–	15.	THE BOYS ARE COMING HOME TODAY (1)
15	16.	EVERY MAN IS A VOLUNTEER (2)
9	17.	TESSIE, YOU ARE THE ONLY, ONLY, ONLY (5)
–	18.	SINCE I FIRST MET YOU (1)
–	19.	MY BESSIE'S WEDDING DAY (1)
–	20.	GOODNIGHT, BELOVED, GOODNIGHT (1)

JULY 1903

LM	TM	
1	1.	HIAWATHA (5)
2	2.	CONGO LOVE SONG (3)
7	3.	IN OLD ALABAMA (3)
4	4.	NOBODY'S LOOKING BUT THE OWL AND THE MOON (5)
9	5.	COME DOWN, MA EVENIN' STAR (3)
6	6.	IN THE SWEET BYE AND BYE (5)
18	7.	SINCE I FIRST MET YOU (2)
15	8.	THE BOYS ARE COMING HOME TODAY (2)
19	9.	MY BESSIE'S WEDDING DAY (2)
10	10.	WHAT A NASTY DISPOSITION FOR A GIRL LIKE YOU (3)
3	11.	UNDER THE BAMBOO TREE (8)
–	12.	SHOW ME THE WHITE OF YO' EYE (1)
5	13.	THE GAMBLING MAN (5)
8	14.	THE VOICE OF THE HUDSON (3)
13	15.	ONLY A SOLDIER BOY (3)
14	16.	SINCE SALLY LEFT OUR ALLEY (4)
20	17.	GOODNIGHT, BELOVED, GOODNIGHT (2)
16	18.	EVERY MAN IS A VOLUNTEER (3)
–	19.	DOWN IN THE DEEP, LET ME SLEEP WHEN I DIE (2)
12	20.	HURRAH FOR BAFFIN'S BAY (4)

AUGUST 1903

LM	TM	
2	1.	CONGO LOVE SONG (4)
1	2.	HIAWATHA (6)
3	3.	IN OLD ALABAMA (4)
12	4.	SHOW ME THE WHITE OF YO' EYE (2)
5	5.	COME DOWN, MA EVENIN' STAR (4)
4	6.	NOBODY'S LOOKING BUT THE OWL AND THE MOON (6)
6	7.	IN THE SWEET BYE AND BYE (6)
9	8.	MY BESSIE'S WEDDING DAY (3)
–	9.	THE BOYS IN THE GALL'RY FOR MINE (1)
17	10.	GOODNIGHT, BELOVED, GOODNIGHT (3)
7	11.	SINCE I FIRST MET YOU (3)
19	12.	DOWN IN THE DEEP, LET ME SLEEP WHEN I DIE (3)
–	13.	I'VE GOT TO GO NOW 'CAUSE I THINK IT'S GOING TO RAIN (1)
8	14.	THE BOYS ARE COMING HOME TODAY (3)
–	15.	SADIE GREEN (1)
10	16.	WHAT A NASTY DISPOSITION FOR A GIRL LIKE YOU (4)
15	17.	ONLY A SOLDIER BOY (4)
18	18.	EVERY MAN IS A VOLUNTEER (4)
–	19.	YOU CAN'T FOOL ALL THE PEOPLE ALL THE TIME (1)
16	20.	SINCE SALLY LEFT OUR ALLEY (5)

SEPTEMBER 1903

LM	TM	
1	1.	CONGO LOVE SONG (5)
4	2.	SHOW ME THE WHITE OF YO' EYE (3)
3	3.	IN OLD ALABAMA (5)
2	4.	HIAWATHA (7)
9	5.	THE BOYS IN THE GALL'RY FOR MINE (2)
5	6.	COME DOWN, MA EVENIN' STAR (5)
6	7.	NOBODY'S LOOKING BUT THE OWL AND THE MOON (7)
–	8.	ALWAYS IN THE WAY (1)
8	9.	MY BESSIE'S WEDDING DAY (4)
–	10	ANONA (1)
–	11.	THE SUN DANCE (1)
13	12.	I'VE GOT TO GO NOW 'CAUSE I THINK IT'S GOING TO RAIN (2)
10	13.	GOODNIGHT, BELOVED, GOODNIGHT (4)
12	14.	DOWN IN THE DEEP, LET ME SLEEP WHEN I DIE (4)
7	15.	IN THE SWEET BYE AND BYE (7)
15	16.	SADIE GREEN (2)
11	17.	SINCE I FIRST MET YOU (4)
16	18.	WHAT A NASTY DISPOSITION FOR A GIRL LIKE YOU (5)
–	19.	DEAR OLD GIRL (1)
–	20.	YOU CAN'T FOOL ALL THE PEOPLE ALL THE TIME (1)

OCTOBER 1903

LM	TM	
8	1.	ALWAYS IN THE WAY (2)
10	2.	ANONA (2)
1	3.	CONGO LOVE SONG (6)
2	4.	SHOW ME THE WHITE OF YO' EYE (4)
11	5.	THE SUN DANCE (2)
19	6.	DEAR OLD GIRL (2)
5	7.	THE BOYS IN THE GALL'RY FOR MINE (3)
6	8.	COME DOWN, MA EVENIN' STAR (6)
3	9.	IN OLD ALABAMA (6)
–	10.	LAUGHING WATER (1)
4	11.	HIAWATHA (8)
–	12.	UP IN A COCONUT TREE (1)
7	13.	NOBODY'S LOOKING BUT THE OWL AND THE MOON (8)
9	14.	MY BESSIE'S WEDDING DAY (5)
12	15.	I'VE GOT TO GO NOW 'CAUSE I THINK IT'S GOING TO RAIN (3)
13	16.	GOODNIGHT, BELOVED, GOODNIGHT (5)
14	17.	DOWN IN THE DEEP, LET ME SLEEP WHEN I DIE (5)
–	18.	DOWN ON THE FARM (1)
15	19.	IN THE SWEET BYE AND BYE (8)
–	20.	PRINCESS POCAHONTAS (1)

NOVEMBER 1903

LM	TM	
1	1.	ALWAYS IN THE WAY (3)
6	2.	DEAR OLD GIRL (3)
2	3.	ANONA (3)
10	4.	LAUGHING WATER (2)
–	5.	BEDELIA (1)
12	6.	UP IN A COCONUT TREE (2)
3	7.	CONGO LOVE SONG (7)
8	8.	COME DOWN, MA EVENIN' STAR (7)
4	9.	SHOW ME THE WHITE OF YO' EYE (5)
18	10.	DOWN ON THE FARM (2)
–	11.	WHERE ARE THE FRIENDS OF OTHER DAYS? (1)
5	12.	THE SUN DANCE (3)
13	13.	NOBODY'S LOOKING BUT THE OWL AND THE MOON (9)
16	14.	GOODNIGHT, BELOVED, GOODNIGHT (6)
7	15.	THE BOYS IN THE GALL'RY FOR MINE (4)
14	16.	MY BESSIE'S WEDDING DAY (6)
–	17.	YOU'RE AS WELCOME AS THE FLOWERS IN MAY (1)
9	18.	IN OLD ALABAMA (7)
15	19.	I'VE GOT TO GO NOW 'CAUSE I THINK IT'S GOING TO RAIN (4)
–	20.	WHEN THE SUNSET TURNS THE OCEAN'S BLUE TO GOLD (1)

DECEMBER 1903

LM	TM	
5	1.	BEDELIA (2)
2	2.	DEAR OLD GIRL (4)
1	3.	ALWAYS IN THE WAY (4)
4	4.	LAUGHING WATER (3)
6	5.	UP IN A COCONUT TREE (3)
3	6.	ANONA (4)
10	7.	DOWN ON THE FARM (3)
11	8.	WHERE ARE THE FRIENDS OF OTHER DAYS? (2)
7	9.	CONGO LOVE SONG (8)
8	10.	COME DOWN, MA EVENIN' STAR (8)
20	11.	WHEN THE SUNSET TURNS THE OCEAN'S BLUE TO GOLD (2)
14	12.	GOODNIGHT, BELOVED, GOODNIGHT (7)
17	13.	YOU'RE AS WELCOME AS THE FLOWERS IN MAY (2)
–	14.	GOODBYE, ELIZA JANE (1)
13	15.	NOBODY'S LOOKING BUT THE OWL AND THE MOON (10)
9	16.	SHOW ME THE WHITE OF YO' EYE (6)
12	17.	THE SUN DANCE (4)
–	18.	ANY RAGS? (1)
–	19.	I CAN'T DO THE SUM (1)
16	20.	MY BESSIE'S WEDDING DAY (7)

JANUARY 1904

LM	TM	
1	1.	BEDELIA (3)
3	2.	ALWAYS IN THE WAY (5)
4	3.	LAUGHING WATER (4)
2	4.	DEAR OLD GIRL (5)
7	5.	DOWN ON THE FARM (4)
5	6.	UP IN A COCONUT TREE (4)
11	7.	WHEN THE SUNSET TURNS THE OCEAN'S BLUE TO GOLD (3)
14	8.	GOODBYE, ELIZA JANE (2)
6	9.	ANONA (5)
19	10.	I CAN'T DO THE SUM (2)
9	11.	CONGO LOVE SONG (9)
18	12.	ANY RAGS? (2)
10	13.	COME DOWN, MA EVENIN' STAR (9)
–	14.	THE BURNING OF ROME (1)
–	15.	TOYLAND (1)
12	16.	GOODNIGHT, BELOVED, GOODNIGHT (8)
13	17.	YOU'RE AS WELCOME AS THE FLOWERS IN MAY (3)
8	18.	WHERE ARE THE FRIENDS OF OTHER DAYS? (3)
–	19.	BECAUSE YOU WERE AN OLD SWEETHEART OF MINE (1)
–	20.	NAVAJO (1)

FEBRUARY 1904

LM	TM	
1	1.	BEDELIA (4)
2	2.	ALWAYS IN THE WAY (6)
3	3.	LAUGHING WATER (5)
8	4.	GOODBYE, ELIZA JANE (3)
10	5.	I CAN'T DO THE SUM (3)
7	6.	WHEN THE SUNSET TURNS THE OCEAN'S BLUE TO GOLD (4)
20	7.	NAVAJO (2)
14	8.	THE BURNING OF ROME (2)
5	9.	DOWN ON THE FARM (5)
4	10.	DEAR OLD GIRL (6)
–	11.	I'M ON THE WATER WAGON NOW (1)
12	12.	ANY RAGS? (3)
15	13.	TOYLAND (2)
–	14.	YOUR MOTHER WANTS YOU HOME, BOY (1)
–	15.	MARCH OF THE TOYS (1)
6	16.	UP IN A COCONUT TREE (5)
11	17.	CONGO LOVE SONG (10)
–	18.	HERE'S YOUR HAT, WHAT'S YOUR HURRY? (1)
19	19.	BECAUSE YOU WERE AN OLD SWEETHEART OF MINE (2)
–	20.	THE SWEETEST FLOWER THAT GROWS IN TENNESSEE (1)

MARCH 1904

LM	TM	
7	1.	NAVAJO (3)
2	2.	ALWAYS IN THE WAY (7)
1	3.	BEDELIA (5)
4	4.	GOODBYE, ELIZA JANE (4)
5	5.	I CAN'T DO THE SUM (4)
6	6.	WHEN THE SUNSET TURNS THE OCEAN'S BLUE TO GOLD (5)
8	7.	THE BURNING OF ROME (3)
13	8.	TOYLAND (3)
–	9.	BLUE BELL (1)
3	10.	LAUGHING WATER (6)
14	11.	YOUR MOTHER WANTS YOU HOME, BOY (2)
12	12.	ANY RAGS? (4)
–	13.	I'VE GOT A FEELIN' FOR YOU (1)
11	14.	I'M ON THE WATER WAGON NOW (2)
–	15.	ALWAYS LEAVE THEM LAUGHING (1)
–	16.	IN ZANZIBAR (1)
15	17.	MARCH OF THE TOYS (2)
9	18.	DOWN ON THE FARM (6)
18	19.	HERE'S YOUR HAT, WHAT'S YOUR HURRY? (2)
19	20.	BECAUSE YOU WERE AN OLD SWEETHEART OF MINE (3)

APRIL 1904

LM	TM	
1	1.	NAVAJO (4)
9	2.	BLUE BELL (2)
13	3.	I'VE GOT A FEELIN' FOR YOU (2)
2	4.	ALWAYS IN THE WAY (8)
16	5.	IN ZANZIBAR (2)
4	6.	GOODBYE, ELIZA JANE (5)
8	7.	TOYLAND (4)
5	8.	I CAN'T DO THE SUM (5)
–	9.	GOODBYE, MY LADY LOVE (1)
–	10.	FOR SALE, A BABY (1)
6	11.	WHEN THE SUNSET TURNS THE OCEAN'S BLUE TO GOLD (6)
15	12.	ALWAYS LEAVE THEM LAUGHING (2)
12	13.	ANY RAGS? (5)
7	14.	THE BURNING OF ROME (4)
–	15.	WHERE THE SILV'RY COLORADO WENDS ITS WAY (1)
3	16.	BEDELIA (6)
–	17.	UNDER THE ANHEUSER BUSH (1)
–	18.	THE GONDOLIER (1)
20	19.	BECAUSE YOU WERE AN OLD SWEETHEART OF MINE (4)
11	20.	YOUR MOTHER WANTS YOU HOME, BOY (3)

MAY 1904

LM	TM	
2	1.	BLUE BELL (3)
9	2.	GOODBYE, MY LADY LOVE (2)
3	3.	I'VE GOT A FEELIN' FOR YOU (3)
1	4.	NAVAJO (5)
5	5.	IN ZANZIBAR (3)
17	6.	UNDER THE ANHEUSER BUSCH (2)
4	7.	ALWAYS IN THE WAY (9)
18	8.	THE GONDOLIER (2)
10	9.	FOR SALE, A BABY (2)
7	10.	TOYLAND (5)
15	11.	WHERE THE SILV'RY COLORADO WENDS ITS WAY (2)
6	12.	GOODBYE, ELIZA JANE (6)
–	13.	HANNAH, WON'T YOU OPEN THAT DOOR? (1)
8	14.	I CAN'T DO THE SUM (6)
11	15.	WHEN THE SUNSET TURNS THE OCEAN'S BLUE TO GOLD (7)
19	16.	BECAUSE YOU WERE AN OLD SWEETHEART OF MINE (5)
–	17.	Y.M.C.A. MARCH (1)
–	18.	WHEN I'M AWAY FROM YOU, DEAR (1)
–	19.	YOU NEVER SPOKE TO ME LIKE THAT BEFORE (1)
13	20.	ANY RAGS? (6)

JUNE 1904

LM	TM	
1	1.	BLUE BELL (4)
2	2.	GOODBYE, MY LADY LOVE (3)
3	3.	I'VE GOT A FEELIN' FOR YOU (4)
6	4.	UNDER THE ANHEUSER BUSCH (3)
4	5.	NAVAJO (6)
8	6.	THE GONDOLIER (3)
5	7.	IN ZANZIBAR (4)
13	8.	HANNAH, WON'T YOU OPEN THAT DOOR? (2)
9	9.	FOR SALE, A BABY (3)
–	10.	MEET ME IN ST. LOUIS, LOUIS (1)
–	11.	UNTER DEN LINDEN (1)
7	12.	ALWAYS IN THE WAY (10)
11	13.	WHERE THE SILV'RY COLORADO WENDS ITS WAY (3)
10	14.	TOYLAND (6)
–	15.	AIN'T IT FUNNY WHAT A DIFFERENCE JUST A FEW HOURS MAKE? (1)
12	16.	GOODBYE, ELIZA JANE (7)
16	17.	BECAUSE YOU WERE AN OLD SWEETHEART OF MINE (6)
–	18.	EGYPT (1)
–	19.	SWEET ADELINE (1)
15	20.	WHEN THE SUNSET TURNS THE OCEAN'S BLUE TO GOLD (8)

JULY 1904

LM	TM	
1	1.	BLUE BELL (5)
10	2.	MEET ME IN ST. LOUIS, LOUIS (2)
2	3.	GOODBYE, MY LADY LOVE (4)
3	4.	I'VE GOT A FEELIN' FOR YOU (5)
5	5.	NAVAJO (7)
18	6.	EGYPT (2)
4	7.	UNDER THE ANHEUSER BUSCH (4)
11	8.	UNTER DEN LINDEN (2)
6	9.	THE GONDOLIER (4)
–	10.	A BIT O' BLARNEY (1)
7	11.	IN ZANZIBAR (5)
14	12.	TOYLAND (7)
19	13.	SWEET ADELINE (2)
8	14.	HANNAH, WON'T YOU OPEN THAT DOOR? (3)
17	15.	BECAUSE YOU WERE AN OLD SWEETHEART OF MINE (7)
–	16.	IDA (SWEET AS APPLE CIDER) (1)
13	17.	WHERE THE SILV'RY COLORADO WENDS ITS WAY (4)
9	18.	FOR SALE, A BABY (4)
–	19.	Y.M.C.A. MARCH (2)
16	20.	GOODBYE, ELIZA JANE (8)

AUGUST 1904

LM	TM	
2	1.	MEET ME IN ST. LOUIS, LOUIS (3)
1	2.	BLUE BELL (6)
10	3.	A BIT O' BLARNEY (2)
3	4.	GOODBYE, MY LADY LOVE (5)
4	5.	I'VE GOT A FEELIN' FOR YOU (6)
6	6.	EGYPT (3)
13	7.	SWEET ADELINE (3)
–	8.	THE MAN WITH THE LADDER AND THE HOSE (1)
–	9.	COME TAKE A TRIP IN MY AIRSHIP (1)
5	10.	NAVAJO (8)
–	11.	SEMINOLE (1)
7	12.	UNDER THE ANHEUSER BUSCH (5)
8	13.	UNTER DEN LINDEN (3)
–	14.	LAZY MOON (1)
9	15.	THE GONDOLIER (5)
–	16.	GOODBYE, LITTLE GIRL, GOODBYE (1)
–	17.	JUST A GLEAM OF HEAVEN IN HER EYES (1)
–	18.	THE SWEETEST GIRL IN DIXIE (1)
16	19.	IDA (SWEET AS APPLE CIDER) (2)
–	20.	BY THE WATERMELON VINE, LINDY LOU (1)

SEPTEMBER 1904

LM	TM	
1	1.	MEET ME IN ST. LOUIS, LOUIS (4)
3	2.	A BIT O' BLARNEY (3)
9	3.	COME TAKE A TRIP IN MY AIRSHIP (2)
16	5.	GOODBYE, LITTLE GIRL, GOODBYE (2)
7	4.	SWEET ADELINE (4)
2	6.	BLUE BELL (7)
11	7.	SEMINOLE (2)
–	8.	TEASING (1)
–	9.	ALEXANDER (DON'T YOU LOVE YOUR BABY NO MORE?) (1)
8	10.	THE MAN WITH THE LADDER AND THE HOSE (2)
14	11.	LAZY MOON (2)
4	12.	GOODBYE, MY LADY LOVE (6)
5	13.	I'VE GOT A FEELIN' FOR YOU (7)
6	14.	EGYPT (4)
17	15.	JUST A GLEAM OF HEAVEN IN HER EYES (2)
20	16.	BY THE WATERMELON VINE, LINDY LOU (2)
–	17.	PLEASE COME AND PLAY IN MY YARD (1)
–	18.	DOWN ON THE BRANDYWINE (1)
18	19.	THE SWEETEST GIRL IN DIXIE (2)
19	20.	IDA (SWEET AS APPLE CIDER) (3)

OCTOBER 1904

LM	TM	
3	1.	COME TAKE A TRIP IN MY AIRSHIP (3)
5	2.	GOODBYE, LITTLE GIRL, GOODBYE (3)
8	3.	TEASING (2)
9	4.	ALEXANDER (DON'T YOU LOVE YOUR BABY NO MORE?) (2)
4	5.	SWEET ADELINE (5)
7	6.	SEMINOLE (3)
2	7.	A BIT O' BLARNEY (4)
1	8.	MEET ME IN ST. LOUIS, LOUIS (5)
17	9.	PLEASE COME AND PLAY IN MY YARD (2)
11	10.	LAZY MOON (3)
16	11.	BY THE WATERMELON VINE, LINDY LOU (3)
6	12.	BLUE BELL (8)
10	13.	THE MAN WITH THE LADDER AND THE HOSE (3)
–	14.	BACK, BACK, BACK TO BALTIMORE (1)
–	15.	KARAMA (1)
–	16.	KATE KEARNEY (1)
15	17.	JUST A GLEAM OF HEAVEN IN HER EYES (3)
–	18.	I MAY BE CRAZY, BUT I AIN'T NO FOOL (1)
19	19.	THE SWEETEST GIRL IN DIXIE (3)
–	20.	THE LITTLE CHURCH WHERE YOU AND I WERE WED (1)

NOVEMBER 1904

LM	TM	
2	1.	GOODBYE, LITTLE GIRL, GOODBYE (4)
3	2.	TEASING (3)
1	3.	COME TAKE A TRIP IN MY AIRSHIP (4)
4	4.	ALEXANDER (DON'T YOU LOVE YOUR BABY NO MORE?) (3)
5	5.	SWEET ADELINE (6)
18	6.	I MAY BE CRAZY, BUT I AIN'T NO FOOL (2)
9	7.	PLEASE COME AND PLAY IN MY YARD (3)
–	8.	A LITTLE BOY CALLED TAPS (1)
14	9.	BACK, BACK, BACK TO BALTIMORE (2)
10	10.	LAZY MOON (4)
11	11.	BY THE WATERMELON VINE, LINDY LOU (4)
7	12.	A BIT O' BLARNEY (5)
15	13.	KARAMA (2)
6	14.	SEMINOLE (4)
16	15.	KATE KEARNEY (2)
–	16.	THE TROUBADOUR (1)
–	17.	SHAME ON YOU (1)
–	18.	DOWN IN THE VALE OF SHENANDOAH (1)
20	19.	THE LITTLE CHURCH WHERE YOU AND I WERE WED (2)
–	20.	IDA (SWEET AS APPLE CIDER) (4)

DECEMBER 1904

LM	TM	
6	1.	I MAY BE CRAZY, BUT I AIN'T NO FOOL (3)
1	2.	GOODBYE, LITTLE GIRL, GOODBYE (5)
2	3.	TEASING (4)
9	4.	BACK, BACK, BACK TO BALTIMORE (3)
7	5.	PLEASE COME AND PLAY IN MY YARD (4)
3	6.	COME TAKE A TRIP IN MY AIRSHIP (5)
5	7.	SWEET ADELINE (7)
8	8.	A LITTLE BOY CALLED TAPS (2)
10	9.	LAZY MOON (5)
11	10.	BY THE WATERMELON VINE, LINDY LOU (5)
–	11.	THERE'S A DARK MAN COMING WITH A BUNDLE (1)
4	12.	ALEXANDER (DON'T YOU LOVE YOUR BABY NO MORE?) (4)
13	13.	KARAMA (3)
15	14.	KATE KEARNEY (3)
12	15.	A BIT O' BLARNEY (6)
17	16.	SHAME ON YOU (2)
16	17.	THE TROUBADOUR (2)
18	18.	DOWN IN THE VALE OF SHENANDOAH (2)
14	19.	SEMINOLE (5)
–	20.	THE SWEETEST GIRL IN DIXIE (4)

JANUARY 1905

LM	TM	
4	1.	BACK, BACK, BACK TO BALTIMORE (4)
1	2.	I MAY BE CRAZY, BUT I AIN'T NO FOOL (4)
5	3.	PLEASE COME AND PLAY IN MY YARD (5)
11	4.	THERE'S A DARK MAN COMING WITH A BUNDLE (2)
7	5.	SWEET ADELINE (8)
2	6.	GOODBYE, LITTLE GIRL, GOODBYE (6)
6	7.	COME TAKE A TRIP IN MY AIRSHIP (6)
9	8.	LAZY MOON (6)
10	9.	BY THE WATERMELON VINE, LINDY LOU (6)
3	10.	TEASING (5)
8	11.	A LITTLE BOY CALLED TAPS (3)
14	12.	KATE KEARNEY (4)
16	13.	SHAME ON YOU (3)
–	14.	JOLLY ME ALONG (1)
12	15.	ALEXANDER (DON'T YOU LOVE YOUR BABY NO MORE?) (5)
–	16.	MAMMA'S BOY (1)
–	17.	AL FRESCO (1)
–	18.	WHEN THE BEES ARE IN THE HIVE (1)
13	19.	KARAMA (4)
–	20.	THE TALE OF THE TURTLE DOVE (1)

FEBRUARY 1905

LM	TM	
1	1.	BACK, BACK, BACK TO BALTIMORE (5)
5	2.	SWEET ADELINE (9)
4	3.	THERE'S A DARK MAN COMING WITH A BUNDLE (3)
16	4.	MAMMA'S BOY (2)
3	5.	PLEASE COME AND PLAY IN MY YARD (6)
20	6.	THE TALE OF THE TURTLE DOVE (2)
–	7.	YANKEE DOODLE BOY (1)
8	8.	LAZY MOON (7)
9	9.	BY THE WATERMELON VINE, LINDY LOU (7)
14	10.	JOLLY ME ALONG (2)
6	11.	GOODBYE, LITTLE GIRL, GOODBYE (7)
2	12.	I MAY BE CRAZY, BUT I AIN'T NO FOOL (5)
18	13.	WHEN THE BEES ARE IN THE HIVE (2)
7	14.	COME TAKE A TRIP IN MY AIRSHIP (7)
–	15.	WHAT THE BRASS BAND PLAYED (1)
13	16.	SHAME ON YOU (4)
–	17.	LIFE'S A FUNNY PROPOSITION AFTER ALL (1)
10	18.	TEASING (6)
–	19.	WON'T YOU FONDLE ME? (1)
17	20.	AL FRESCO (2)

MARCH 1905

LM	TM	
7	1.	YANKEE DOODLE BOY (2)
2	2.	SWEET ADELINE (10)
1	3.	BACK, BACK, BACK TO BALTIMORE (6)
4	4.	MAMMA'S BOY (3)
15	5.	WHAT THE BRASS BAND PLAYED (2)
6	6.	THE TALE OF THE TURTLE DOVE (3)
–	7.	IN THE SHADE OF THE OLD APPLE TREE (1)
8	8.	LAZY MOON (8)
17	9.	LIFE'S A FUNNY PROPOSITION AFTER ALL (2)
9	10.	BY THE WATERMELON VINE, LINDY LOU (8)
19	11.	WON'T YOU FONDLE ME? (2)
–	12.	GIVE MY REGARDS TO BROADWAY (1)
–	13.	I'M TRYING SO HARD TO FORGET YOU (1)
5	14.	PLEASE COME AND PLAY IN MY YARD (7)
3	15.	THERE'S A DARK MAN COMING WITH A BUNDLE (4)
–	16.	COAX ME (1)
10	17.	JOLLY ME ALONG (3)
–	18.	TELL ME WITH YOUR EYES (1)
11	19.	GOODBYE, LITTLE GIRL, GOODBYE (8)
13	20.	WHEN THE BEES ARE IN THE HIVE (3)

APRIL 1905

LM	TM	
1	1.	YANKEE DOODLE BOY (3)
7	2.	IN THE SHADE OF THE OLD APPLE TREE (2)
13	3.	I'M TRYING SO HARD TO FORGET YOU (2)
2	4.	SWEET ADELINE (11)
12	5.	GIVE MY REGARDS TO BROADWAY (2)
–	6.	CARISSIMA (1)
–	7.	HE'S ME PAL (1)
5	8.	WHAT THE BRASS BAND PLAYED (3)
–	9.	WHERE THE SOUTHERN ROSES GROW (1)
9	10.	LIFE'S A FUNNY PROPOSITION AFTER ALL (3)
–	11.	HONEY, I'M WAITING (1)
3	12.	BACK, BACK, BACK TO BALTIMORE (7)
–	13.	MOONLIGHT (SERENADE) (1)
10	14.	BY THE WATERMELON VINE, LINDY LOU (9)
–	15.	ABSINTHE FRAPPE (1)
8	16.	LAZY MOON (9)
4	17.	MAMMA'S BOY (4)
–	18.	WHEN THE HARVEST MOON IS SHINING ON THE RIVER (1)
11	19.	WON'T YOU FONDLE ME? (2)
–	20.	THE DAY THAT YOU GREW COLDER (1)

MAY 1905

LM	TM	
2	1.	IN THE SHADE OF THE OLD APPLE TREE (3)
7	2.	HE'S ME PAL (2)
1	3.	YANKEE DOODLE BOY (4)
5	4.	GIVE MY REGARDS TO BROADWAY (3)
6	5.	CARISSIMA (2)
3	6.	I'M TRYING SO HARD TO FORGET YOU (3)
13	7.	MOONLIGHT (SERENADE) (2)
–	8.	TAMMANY (1)
9	9.	WHERE THE SOUTHERN ROSES GROW (2)
11	10.	HONEY, I'M WAITING (2)
–	11.	LONGING FOR YOU (1)
18	12.	WHEN THE HARVEST MOON IS SHINING ON THE RIVER (2)
–	13.	PAL OF MINE (1)
4	14.	SWEET ADELINE (12)
8	15.	WHAT THE BRASS BAND PLAYED (4)
15	16.	ABSINTHE FRAPPE (2)
10	17.	LIFE'S A FUNNY PROPOSITION AFTER ALL (4)
–	18.	JIM JUDSON (FROM THE TOWN OF HACKENSACK) (1)
–	19.	GOODBYE, SIS (1)
–	20.	EV'RY LITTLE BIT HELPS (1)

JUNE 1905

LM	TM	
1	1.	IN THE SHADE OF THE OLD APPLE TREE (4)
8	2.	TAMMANY (2)
4	3.	GIVE MY REGARDS TO BROADWAY (4)
3	4.	YANKEE DOODLE BOY (5)
2	5.	HE'S ME PAL (3)
5	6.	CARISSIMA (3)
7	7.	MOONLIGHT (SERENADE) (3)
6	8.	I'M TRYING SO HARD TO FORGET YOU (4)
12	9.	WHEN THE HARVEST MOON IS SHINING ON THE RIVER (3)
–	10.	SHE WAITS BY THE DEEP BLUE SEA (1)
11	11.	LONGING FOR YOU (2)
13	12.	PAL OF MINE (2)
–	13.	KEEP A LITTLE COZY CORNER IN YOUR HEART FOR ME (1)
9	14.	WHERE THE SOUTHERN ROSES GROW (3)
10	15.	HONEY, I'M WAITING (3)
–	16.	YANKEE GRIT (1)
15	17.	WHAT THE BRASS BAND PLAYED (5)
–	18.	MY IRISH MOLLY-O (1)
20	19.	EV'RY LITTLE BIT HELPS (2)
14	20.	SWEET ADELINE (13)

JULY 1905

LM	TM	
1	1.	IN THE SHADE OF THE OLD APPLE TREE (5)
2	2.	TAMMANY (3)
13	3.	KEEP A LITTLE COZY CORNER IN YOUR HEART FOR ME (2)
3	4.	GIVE MY REGARDS TO BROADWAY (5)
4	5.	YANKEE DOODLE BOY (6)
6	6.	CARISSIMA (4)
10	7.	SHE WAITS BY THE DEEP BLUE SEA (2)
18	8.	MY IRISH MOLLY-O (2)
7	9.	MOONLIGHT (SERENADE) (4)
5	10.	HE'S ME PAL (4)
–	11.	THE PREACHER AND THE BEAR (1)
16	12.	YANKEE GRIT (2)
9	13.	WHEN THE HARVEST MOON IS SHINING ON THE RIVER (4)
11	14.	LONGING FOR YOU (3)
12	15.	PAL OF MINE (3)
–	16.	BRIGHT EYES, GOODBYE (1)
8	17.	I'M TRYING SO HARD TO FORGET YOU (5)
19	18.	EV'RY LITTLE BIT HELPS (3)
–	19.	COLLEGE LIFE (1)
–	20.	COME OVER ON MY VERANDA (1)

AUGUST 1905

LM	TM	
1	1.	IN THE SHADE OF THE OLD APPLE TREE (6)
3	2.	KEEP A LITTLE COZY CORNER IN YOUR HEART FOR ME (3)
2	3.	TAMMANY (4)
8	4.	MY IRISH MOLLY-O (3)
11	5.	THE PREACHER AND THE BEAR (2)
6	6.	CARISSIMA (5)
–	7.	EVERYBODY WORKS BUT FATHER (1)
4	8.	GIVE MY REGARDS TO BROADWAY (6)
12	9.	YANKEE GRIT (3)
5	10.	YANKEE DOODLE BOY (7)
–	11.	NOBODY (1)
–	12.	WOULD YOU CARE? (1)
9	13.	MOONLIGHT (SERENADE) (5)
19	14.	COLLEGE LIFE (2)
13	15.	WHEN THE HARVEST MOON IS SHINING ON THE RIVER (5)
7	16.	SHE WAITS BY THE DEEP BLUE SEA (3)
–	17.	DEARIE (1)
–	18.	VIOLETTE (1)
16	19.	BRIGHT EYES, GOODBYE (2)
–	20.	WHEN THE BELL IN THE LIGHTHOUSE RINGS, DING DONG (1)

SEPTEMBER 1905

LM	TM	
4	1.	MY IRISH MOLLY-O (4)
2	2.	KEEP A LITTLE COZY CORNER IN YOUR HEART FOR ME (4)
7	3.	EVERYBODY WORKS BUT FATHER (2)
1	4.	IN THE SHADE OF THE OLD APPLE TREE (7)
12	5.	WOULD YOU CARE? (2)
5	6.	THE PREACHER AND THE BEAR (3)
11	7.	NOBODY (2)
3	8.	TAMMANY (5)
9	9.	YANKEE GRIT (4)
20	10.	WHEN THE BELL IN THE LIGHTHOUSE RINGS, DING DONG (2)
17	11.	DEARIE (2)
6	12.	CARISSIMA (6)
14	13.	COLLEGE LIFE (3)
8	14.	GIVE MY REGARDS TO BROADWAY (7)
–	15.	DOWN WHERE THE SILV'RY MOHAWK FLOWS (1)
18	16.	VIOLETTE (2)
15	17.	WHEN THE HARVEST MOON IS SHINING ON THE RIVER (6)
10	18.	YANKEE DOODLE BOY (8)
–	19.	CENTRAL, GIVE ME BACK MY DIME (1)
13	20.	MOONLIGHT (SERENADE) (6)

OCTOBER 1905

LM	TM	
5	1.	WOULD YOU CARE? (3)
1	2.	MY IRISH MOLLY-O (5)
3	3.	EVERYBODY WORKS BUT FATHER (3)
2	4.	KEEP A LITTLE COZY CORNER IN YOUR HEART FOR ME (5)
11	5.	DEARIE (3)
10	6.	WHEN THE BELL IN THE LIGHTHOUSE RINGS, DING DONG (3)
6	7.	THE PREACHER AND THE BEAR (4)
7	8.	NOBODY (3)
13	9.	COLLEGE LIFE (4)
–	10.	WHAT YOU GOIN' TO DO WHEN THE RENT COMES 'ROUND? (RUFUS RASTUS JOHNSON BROWN) (1)
4	11.	IN THE SHADE OF THE OLD APPLE TREE (8)
–	12.	THE LEADER OF THE GERMAN BAND (1)
–	13.	WAIT TILL THE SUN SHINES, NELLIE (1)
15	14.	DOWN WHERE THE SILV'RY MOHAWK FLOWS (2)
9	15.	YANKEE GRIT (5)
–	16.	IN DEAR OLD GEORGIA (1)
–	17.	IN MY MERRY OLDSMOBILE (1)
8	18.	TAMMANY (6)
12	19.	CARISSIMA (7)
19	20.	CENTRAL, GIVE ME BACK MY DIME (2)

NOVEMBER 1905

LM	TM	
1	1.	WOULD YOU CARE? (4)
5	2.	DEARIE (4)
2	3.	MY IRISH MOLLY-O (6)
10	4.	WHAT YOU GOIN' TO DO WHEN THE RENT COMES ROUND? (RUFUS RASTUS JOHNSON BROWN) (2)
13	5.	WAIT TILL THE SUN SHINES, NELLIE (2)
3	6.	EVERYBODY WORKS BUT FATHER (4)
12	7.	THE LEADER OF THE GERMAN BAND (2)
4	8.	KEEP A LITTLE COZY CORNER IN YOUR HEART FOR ME (6)
17	9.	IN MY MERRY OLDSMOBILE (2)
–	10.	HOW'D YOU LIKE TO SPOON WITH ME? (1)
–	11.	THE WHISTLER AND HIS DOG (1)
16	12.	IN DEAR OLD GEORGIA (2)
14	13.	DOWN WHERE THE SILV'RY MOHAWK FLOWS (3)
6	14.	WHEN THE BELL IN THE LIGHTHOUSE RINGS, DING DONG (4)
9	15.	COLLEGE LIFE (5)
–	16.	WHERE THE MORNING GLORIES TWINE AROUND THE DOOR (1)
7	17.	THE PREACHER AND THE BEAR (5)
8	18.	NOBODY (4)
–	19.	STARLIGHT (1)
15	20.	YANKEE GRIT (6)

DECEMBER 1905

LM	TM	
5	1.	WAIT TILL THE SUN SHINES, NELLIE (3)
2	2.	DEARIE (5)
1	3.	WOULD YOU CARE? (5)
10	4.	HOW'D YOU LIKE TO SPOON WITH ME? (2)
4	5.	WHAT YOU GOIN' TO DO WHEN THE RENT COMES ROUND? (RUFUS RASTUS JOHNSON BROWN) (3)
9	6.	IN MY MERRY OLDSMOBILE (3)
7	7.	THE LEADER OF THE GERMAN BAND (3)
12	8.	IN DEAR OLD GEORGIA (3)
16	9.	WHERE THE MORNING GLORIES TWINE AROUND THE DOOR (2)
3	10.	MY IRISH MOLLY-O (7)
6	11.	EVERYBODY WORKS BUT FATHER (5)
11	12.	THE WHISTLER AND HIS DOG (2)
19	13.	STARLIGHT (2)
–	14.	THE TOWN WHERE I WAS BORN (1)
8	15.	KEEP A LITTLE COZY CORNER IN YOUR HEART FOR ME (7)
13	16.	DOWN WHERE THE SILV'RY MOHAWK FLOWS (4)
–	17.	SILVERHEELS (1)
15	18.	COLLEGE LIFE (6)
–	19.	A WOMAN IS ONLY A WOMAN, BUT A GOOD CIGAR IS A SMOKE (1)
–	20.	KATEY DEAR (1)

JANUARY 1906

LM	TM	
1	1.	WAIT TILL THE SUN SHINES, NELLIE (4)
3	2.	WOULD YOU CARE? (6)
2	3.	DEARIE (6)
6	4.	IN MY MERRY OLDSMOBILE (4)
9	5.	WHERE THE MORNING GLORIES TWINE AROUND THE DOOR (3)
8	6.	IN DEAR OLD GEORGIA (4)
4	7.	HOW'D YOU LIKE TO SPOON WITH ME? (3)
5	8.	WHAT YOU GOIN' TO DO WHEN THE RENT COMES 'ROUND? (RUFUS RASTUS JOHNSON BROWN) (4)
13	9.	STARLIGHT (3)
17	10.	SILVERHEELS (2)
7	11.	THE LEADER OF THE GERMAN BAND (4)
14	12.	THE TOWN WHERE I WAS BORN (2)
10	13.	MY IRISH MOLLY-O (8)
–	14.	SYMPATHY (1)
11	15.	EVERYBODY WORKS BUT FATHER (6)
20	16.	KATEY DEAR (2)
16	17.	DOWN WHERE THE SILV'RY MOHAWK FLOWS (5)
12	18.	THE WHISTLER AND HIS DOG (3)
19	19.	A WOMAN IS ONLY A WOMAN, BUT A GOOD CIGAR IS A SMOKE (2)
–	20.	CAN'T YOU SEE I'M LONELY? (1)

FEBRUARY 1906

LM	TM	
1	1.	WAIT TILL THE SUN SHINES, NELLIE (5)
4	2.	IN MY MERRY OLDSMOBILE (5)
3	3.	DEARIE (7)
2	4.	WOULD YOU CARE? (7)
9	5.	STARLIGHT (4)
10	6.	SILVERHEELS (3)
6	7.	IN DEAR OLD GEORGIA (5)
5	8.	WHERE THE MORNING GLORIES TWINE AROUND THE DOOR (4)
–	9.	IF A GIRL LIKE YOU LOVED A BOY LIKE ME (1)
–	10.	DADDY'S LITTLE GIRL (1)
14	11.	SYMPATHY (2)
8	12.	WHAT YOU GOIN' TO DO WHEN THE RENT COMES 'ROUND? (RUFUS RASTUS JOHNSON BROWN) (5)
7	13.	HOW'D YOU LIKE TO SPOON WITH ME? (4)
–	14.	WILL YOU LOVE ME IN DECEMBER AS YOU DO IN MAY? (1)
20	15.	CAN'T YOU SEE I'M LONELY? (2)
11	16.	THE LEADER OF THE GERMAN BAND (5)
–	17.	JUST A LITTLE ROCKING CHAIR AND YOU (1)
16	18.	KATEY DEAR (3)
17	19.	DOWN WHERE THE SILV'RY MOHAWK FLOWS (6)
12	20.	THE TOWN WHERE I WAS BORN (3)

MARCH 1906

LM	TM	
3	1.	DEARIE (8)
1	2.	WAIT TILL THE SUN SHINES, NELLIE (6)
4	3.	WOULD YOU CARE? (8)
2	4.	IN MY MERRY OLDSMOBILE (6)
9	5.	IF A GIRL LIKE YOU LOVED A BOY LIKE ME (2)
14	6.	WILL YOU LOVE ME IN DECEMBER AS YOU DO IN MAY? (2)
5	7.	STARLIGHT (5)
10	8.	DADDY'S LITTLE GIRL (2)
6	9.	SILVERHEELS (4)
15	10.	CAN'T YOU SEE I'M LONELY? (3)
–	11.	SO LONG, MARY (1)
17	12.	JUST A LITTLE ROCKING CHAIR AND YOU (2)
–	13.	FORTY-FIVE MINUTES FROM BROADWAY (1)
7	14.	IN DEAR OLD GEORGIA (6)
–	15.	WHEN THE EVENING BREEZE IS SIGHING HOME SWEET HOME (1)
8	16.	WHERE THE MORNING GLORIES TWINE AROUND THE DOOR (5)
–	17.	I WANT WHAT I WANT WHEN I WANT IT (1)
–	18.	SINCE FATHER WENT TO WORK (1)
11	19.	SYMPATHY (3)
–	20.	MARY'S A GRAND OLD NAME (1)

APRIL 1906

LM	TM	
6	1.	WILL YOU LOVE ME IN DECEMBER AS YOU DO IN MAY? (3)
1	2.	DEARIE (9)
2	3.	WAIT TILL THE SUN SHINES, NELLIE (7)
5	4.	IF A GIRL LIKE YOU LOVED A BOY LIKE ME (3)
11	5.	SO LONG, MARY (2)
13	6.	FORTY-FIVE MINUTES FROM BROADWAY (2)
3	7.	WOULD YOU CARE? (9)
4	8.	IN MY MERRY OLDSMOBILE (7)
12	9.	JUST A LITTLE ROCKING CHAIR AND YOU (3)
–	10.	YOU'RE A GRAND OLD FLAG (1)
–	11.	WHEN THE MOCKING BIRDS ARE SINGING IN THE WILDWOOD (1)
–	12.	KEEP ON THE SUNNY SIDE (1)
17	13.	I WANT WHAT I WANT WHEN I WANT IT (2)
20	14.	MARY'S A GRAND OLD NAME (2)
7	15.	STARLIGHT (6)
–	16.	CHEYENNE (1)
10	17.	CAN'T YOU SEE I'M LONELY? (4)
15	18.	WHEN THE EVENING BREEZE IS SIGHING HOME SWEET HOME (2)
9	19.	SILVERHEELS (5)
18	20.	SINCE FATHER WENT TO WORK (2)

MAY 1906

LM	TM	
1	1.	WILL YOU LOVE ME IN DECEMBER AS YOU DO IN MAY? (4)
12	2.	KEEP ON THE SUNNY SIDE (2)
5	3.	SO LONG, MARY (3)
10	4.	YOU'RE A GRAND OLD FLAG (2)
9	5.	JUST A LITTLE ROCKING CHAIR AND YOU (4)
2	6.	DEARIE (10)
11	7.	WHEN THE MOCKING BIRDS ARE SINGING IN THE WILDWOOD (2)
6	8.	FORTY-FIVE MINUTES FROM BROADWAY (3)
16	9.	CHEYENNE (2)
3	10.	WAIT TILL THE SUN SHINES, NELLIE (8)
13	11.	I WANT WHAT I WANT WHEN I WANT IT (3)
4	12.	IF A GIRL LIKE YOU LOVED A BOY LIKE ME (4)
14	13.	MARY'S A GRAND OLD NAME (3)
8	14.	IN MY MERRY OLDSMOBILE (8)
–	15.	WAITING AT THE CHURCH (MY WIFE WON'T LET ME) (1)
–	16.	TAKE ME BACK TO YOUR HEART (1)
7	17.	WOULD YOU CARE? (10)
–	18.	SINCE NELLIE WENT AWAY (1)
–	19.	TWO DIRTY LITTLE HANDS (1)
–	20.	MY GAL SAL (1)

JUNE 1906

LM	TM	
4	1.	YOU'RE A GRAND OLD FLAG (3)
2	2.	KEEP ON THE SUNNY SIDE (3)
9	3.	CHEYENNE (3)
1	4.	WILL YOU LOVE ME IN DECEMBER AS YOU DO IN MAY? (5)
15	5.	WAITING AT THE CHURCH (MY WIFE WON'T LET ME) (2)
7	6.	WHEN THE MOCKING BIRDS ARE SINGING IN THE WILDWOOD (3)
5	7.	JUST A LITTLE ROCKING CHAIR AND YOU (5)
6	8.	DEARIE (11)
3	9.	SO LONG, MARY (4)
–	10.	BILL SIMMONS (1)
16	11.	TAKE ME BACK TO YOUR HEART (2)
10	12.	WAIT TILL THE SUN SHINES, NELLIE (9)
18	13.	SINCE NELLIE WENT AWAY (2)
8	14.	FORTY-FIVE MINUTES FROM BROADWAY (4)
20	15.	MY GAL SAL (2)
11	16.	I WANT WHAT I WANT WHEN I WANT IT (4)
–	17.	NOT BECAUSE YOUR HAIR IS CURLY (1)
–	18.	I'LL KEEP A WARM SPOT IN MY HEART FOR YOU (1)
19	19.	TWO DIRTY LITTLE HANDS (2)
–	20.	WHY DON'T YOU TRY? (1)

JULY 1906

LM	TM	
1	1.	YOU'RE A GRAND OLD FLAG (4)
5	2.	WAITING AT THE CHURCH (MY WIFE WON'T LET ME) (3)
3	3.	CHEYENNE (4)
10	4.	BILL SIMMONS (2)
2	5.	KEEP ON THE SUNNY SIDE (4)
4	6.	WILL YOU LOVE ME IN DECEMBER AS YOU DO IN MAY? (6)
15	7.	MY GAL SAL (3)
17	8.	NOT BECAUSE YOUR HAIR IS CURLY (2)
–	9.	THE GOOD OLD U.S.A. (1)
–	10.	MILO (1)
18	11.	I'LL KEEP A WARM SPOT IN MY HEART FOR YOU (2)
6	12.	WHEN THE MOCKING BIRDS ARE SINGING IN THE WILDWOOD (4)
8	13.	DEARIE (12)
7	14.	JUST A LITTLE ROCKING CHAIR AND YOU (6)
11	15.	TAKE ME BACK TO YOUR HEART (3)
–	16.	IF THE MAN IN THE MOON WERE A COON (1)
20	17.	WHY DON'T YOU TRY? (2)
–	18.	CROCODILE ISLE (1)
13	19.	SINCE NELLIE WENT AWAY (3)
–	20.	AFTER THEY GATHER THE HAY (1)

AUGUST 1906

LM	TM	
2	1.	WAITING AT THE CHURCH (MY WIFE WON'T LET ME) (4)
1	2.	YOU'RE A GRAND OLD FLAG (5)
3	3.	CHEYENNE (5)
4	4.	BILL SIMMONS (3)
9	5.	THE GOOD OLD U.S.A. (2)
7	6.	MY GAL SAL (4)
8	7.	NOT BECAUSE YOUR HAIR IS CURLY (3)
–	8.	WALTZ ME AROUND AGAIN, WILLIE (1)
10	9.	MILO (2)
5	10.	KEEP ON THE SUNNY SIDE (5)
6	11.	WILL YOU LOVE ME IN DECEMBER AS YOU DO IN MAY? (7)
16	12.	IF THE MAN IN THE MOON WERE A COON (2)
–	13.	LOVE ME AND THE WORLD IS MINE (1)
18	14.	CROCODILE ISLE (2)
–	15.	ALICE, WHERE ART THOU GOING? (1)
13	16.	DEARIE (13)
–	17.	HE WALKED RIGHT IN, TURNED AROUND AND WALKED RIGHT OUT AGAIN (1)
11	18.	I'LL KEEP A WARM SPOT IN MY HEART FOR YOU (3)
14	19.	JUST A LITTLE ROCKING CHAIR AND YOU (7)
20	20.	AFTER THEY GATHER THE HAY (2)

SEPTEMBER 1906

LM	TM	
1	1.	WAITING AT THE CHURCH (MY WIFE WON'T LET ME) (5)
5	2.	THE GOOD OLD U.S.A. (3)
8	3.	WALTZ ME AROUND AGAIN, WILLIE (2)
6	4.	MY GAL SAL (5)
2	5.	YOU'RE A GRAND OLD FLAG (6)
3	6.	CHEYENNE (6)
4	7.	BILL SIMMONS (4)
17	8.	HE WALKED RIGHT IN, TURNED AROUND AND WALKED RIGHT OUT AGAIN (2)
13	9.	LOVE ME AND THE WORLD IS MINE (2)
12	10.	IF THE MAN IN THE MOON WERE A COON (3)
15	11.	ALICE, WHERE ART THOU GOING? (2)
7	12.	NOT BECAUSE YOUR HAIR IS CURLY (4)
–	13.	SOMEWHERE (1)
14	14.	CROCODILE ISLE (3)
9	15.	MILO (3)
–	16.	THE LINGER LONGER GIRL (1)
–	17.	CAMP MEETIN' TIME (1)
–	18.	OS-KA-LOO-SA-LOO (1)
10.	19.	KEEP ON THE SUNNY SIDE (6)
–	20.	FLYING ARROW (1)

OCTOBER 1906

LM	TM	
3	1.	WALTZ ME AROUND AGAIN, WILLIE (3)
2	2.	THE GOOD OLD U.S.A. (4)
8	3.	HE WALKED RIGHT IN, TURNED AROUND AND WALKED RIGHT OUT AGAIN (3)
9	4.	LOVE ME AND THE WORLD IS MINE (3)
4	5.	MY GAL SAL (6)
1	6.	WAITING AT THE CHURCH (MY WIFE WON'T LET ME) (6)
–	7.	WON'T YOU COME OVER TO MY HOUSE (1)
5	8.	YOU'RE A GRAND OLD FLAG (7)
6	9.	CHEYENNE (7)
10	10.	IF THE MAN IN THE MOON WERE A COON (4)
13	11.	SOMEWHERE (2)
–	12.	IOLA (1)
7	13.	BILL SIMMONS (5)
18	14.	OS-KA-LOO-SA-LOO (2)
16	15.	THE LINGER LONGER GIRL (2)
12	16.	NOT BECAUSE YOUR HAIR IS CURLY (5)
14	17.	CROCODILE ISLE (4)
11	18.	ALICE, WHERE ART THOU GOING? (3)
20	19.	FLYING ARROW (2)
15	20.	MILO (4)

NOVEMBER 1906

LM	TM	
1	1.	WALTZ ME AROUND AGAIN, WILLIE (4)
8	2.	WON'T YOU COME OVER TO MY HOUSE (2)
4	3.	LOVE ME AND THE WORLD IS MINE (4)
12	4.	IOLA (2)
5	5.	MY GAL SAL (7)
2	6.	THE GOOD OLD U.S.A. (5)
3	7.	HE WALKED RIGHT IN, TURNED AROUND AND WALKED RIGHT OUT AGAIN (4)
10	8.	IF THE MAN IN THE MOON WERE A COON (5)
–	9.	CHEER UP, MARY (1)
–	10.	ARRAH WANNA (1)
14	11.	OS-KA-LOO-SA-LOO (3)
11	12.	SOMEWHERE (3)
15	13.	THE LINGER LONGER GIRL (3)
6	14.	WAITING AT THE CHURCH (MY WIFE WON'T LET ME) (7)
8	15.	YOU'RE A GRAND OLD FLAG (8)
9	16.	CHEYENNE (8)
17	17.	CROCODILE ISLE (5)
–	18.	MY MARIUCCIA TAKE A STEAMBOAT (1)
19	20.	FLYING ARROW (3)
13	19.	BILL SIMMONS (6)

DECEMBER 1906

LM	TM	
2	1.	WON'T YOU COME OVER TO MY HOUSE (3)
3	2.	LOVE ME AND THE WORLD IS MINE (5)
10	3.	ARRAH WANNA (2)
9	4.	CHEER UP, MARY (2)
4	5.	IOLA (3)
1	6.	WALTZ ME AROUND AGAIN, WILLIE (5)
18	7.	MY MARIUCCIA TAKE A STEAMBOAT (2)
5	8.	MY GAL SAL (8)
–	9.	IN OLD NEW YORK (1)
11	10.	OS-KA-LOO-SA-LOO (4)
12	11.	SOMEWHERE (4)
–	12.	EVERY DAY IS LADIES' DAY WITH ME (1)
7	13.	HE WALKED RIGHT IN, TURNED AROUND AND WALKED RIGHT OUT AGAIN (5)
–	14.	THE BIRD ON NELLIE'S HAT (1)
–	15.	I JUST CAN'T MAKE MY EYES BEHAVE (1)
–	16.	THE ISLE OF OUR DREAMS (2)
8	17.	IF THE MAN IN THE MOON WERE A COON (6)
6	18.	THE GOOD OLD U.S.A. (6)
–	19.	HE'S A COUSIN OF MINE (1)
–	20.	BECAUSE YOU'RE YOU (1)

JANUARY 1907

LM	TM	
3	1.	ARRAH WANNA (3)
2	2.	LOVE ME AND THE WORLD IS MINE (6)
7	3.	MY MARIUCCIA TAKE A STEAMBOAT (3)
1	4.	WON'T YOU COME OVER TO MY HOUSE (4)
14	5.	THE BIRD ON NELLIE'S HAT (2)
4	6.	CHEER UP, MARY (3)
15	7.	I JUST CAN'T MAKE MY EYES BEHAVE (2)
9	8.	IN OLD NEW YORK (2)
20	9.	BECAUSE YOU'RE YOU (2)
12	10.	EVERY DAY IS LADIES' DAY WITH ME (3)
19	11.	HE'S A COUSIN OF MINE (2)
–	12.	A LEMON IN THE GARDEN OF LOVE (1)
5	13.	IOLA (4)
11	14.	SOMEWHERE (5)
10	15.	OS-KA-LOO-SA-LOO (5)
8	16.	MY GAL SAL (9)
16	17.	THE ISLE OF OUR DREAMS (2)
–	18.	MY IRISH ROSIE (1)
6	19.	WALTZ ME AROUND AGAIN, WILLIE (6)
–	20.	LET IT ALONE (1)

FEBRUARY 1907

LM	TM	
1	1.	ARRAH WANNA (4)
5	2.	THE BIRD ON NELLIE'S HAT (3)
2	3.	LOVE ME AND THE WORLD IS MINE (7)
12	4.	A LEMON IN THE GARDEN OF LOVE (2)
7	5.	I JUST CAN'T MAKE MY EYES BEHAVE (3)
11	6.	HE'S A COUSIN OF MINE (3)
3	7.	MY MARIUCCIA TAKE A STEAMBOAT (4)
9	8.	BECAUSE YOU'RE YOU (3)
18	9.	MY IRISH ROSIE (2)
4	10.	WON'T YOU COME OVER TO MY HOUSE (5)
20	11.	LET IT ALONE (2)
8	12.	IN OLD NEW YORK (3)
10	13.	EVERY DAY IS LADIES' DAY WITH ME (4)
14	14.	SOMEWHERE (6)
–	15.	MOONBEAMS (1)
–	16.	AND A LITTLE CHILD SHALL LEAD THEM (1)
13	17.	IOLA (5)
15	18.	OS-KA-LOO-SA-LOO (6)
17	19.	THE ISLE OF OUR DREAMS (3)
6	20.	CHEER UP, MARY (4)

MARCH 1907

LM	TM	
2	1.	THE BIRD ON NELLIE'S HAT (4)
6	2.	HE'S A COUSIN OF MINE (4)
1	3.	ARRAH WANNA (5)
5	4.	I JUST CAN'T MAKE MY EYES BEHAVE (4)
3	5.	LOVE ME AND THE WORLD IS MINE (8)
11	6.	LET IT ALONE (3)
–	7.	POOR JOHN! (1)
8	8.	BECAUSE YOU'RE YOU (4)
9	9.	MY IRISH ROSIE (3)
–	10.	SAN ANTONIO (1)
4	11.	A LEMON IN THE GARDEN OF LOVE (3)
7	12.	MY MARIUCCIA TAKE A STEAMBOAT (5)
–	13.	WHEN BOB WHITE IS WHISTLING IN THE MEADOW (1)
–	14.	ALL IN, DOWN AND OUT (1)
16	15.	AND A LITTLE CHILD SHALL LEAD THEM (2)
15	16.	MOONBEAMS (2)
14	17.	SOMEWHERE (7)
13	18.	EVERY DAY IS LADIES' DAY WITH ME (5)
–	19.	SOMEBODY'S WAITING FOR YOU (1)
12	20.	IN OLD NEW YORK (4)

APRIL 1907

LM	TM	
7	1.	POOR JOHN! (2)
10	2.	SAN ANTONIO (2)
1	3.	THE BIRD ON NELLIE'S HAT (5)
6	4.	LET IT ALONE (4)
3	5.	ARRAH WANNA (6)
5	6.	LOVE ME AND THE WORLD IS MINE (9)
2	7.	HE'S A COUSIN OF MINE (5)
4	8.	I JUST CAN'T MAKE MY EYES BEHAVE (5)
9	9.	MY IRISH ROSIE (4)
–	10.	IN THE WILDWOOD WHERE THE BLUE BELLS GREW (1)
–	11.	THE TALE THE CHURCH BELLS TOLLED (1)
19	12.	SOMEBODY'S WAITING FOR YOU (2)
8	13.	BECAUSE YOU'RE YOU (5)
–	14.	GOLDEN ROD (1)
13	15.	WHEN BOB WHITE IS WHISTLING IN THE MEADOW (2)
–	16.	THE BEST THING IN LIFE (1)
–	17.	FLOATING ALONG (1)
14	18.	ALL IN, DOWN AND OUT (2)
11	19.	A LEMON IN THE GARDEN OF LOVE (4)
–	20.	SPANGLES (1)

MAY 1907

LM	TM	
2	1.	SAN ANTONIO (3)
1	2.	POOR JOHN! (3)
–	3.	SCHOOL DAYS (1)
6	4.	LOVE ME AND THE WORLD IS MINE (10)
11	5.	THE TALE THE CHURCH BELLS TOLLED (2)
10	6.	IN THE WILDWOOD WHERE THE BLUE BELLS GREW (2)
4	7.	LET IT ALONE (5)
7	8.	HE'S A COUSIN OF MINE (6)
–	9.	NOBODY'S LITTLE GIRL (1)
5	10.	ARRAH WANNA (7)
–	11.	BECAUSE I'M MARRIED NOW (1)
3	12.	THE BIRD ON NELLIE'S HAT (6)
12	13.	SOMEBODY'S WAITING FOR YOU (3)
–	14.	AND A LITTLE BIT MORE (1)
9	15.	MY IRISH ROSIE (5)
14	16.	GOLDEN ROD (2)
16	17.	THE BEST THING IN LIFE (2)
17	18.	FLOATING ALONG (2)
8	19.	I JUST CAN'T MAKE MY EYES BEHAVE (6)
–	20.	ANY OLD TIME AT ALL (1)

JUNE 1907

LM	TM	
3	1.	SCHOOL DAYS (2)
1	2.	SAN ANTONIO (4)
11	3.	BECAUSE I'M MARRIED NOW (2)
2	4.	POOR JOHN! (4)
14	5.	AND A LITTLE BIT MORE (2)
9	6.	NOBODY'S LITTLE GIRL (2)
4	7.	LOVE ME AND THE WORLD IS MINE (11)
5	8.	THE TALE THE CHURCH BELLS TOLLED (3)
–	9.	HE GOES TO CHURCH ON SUNDAY (1)
–	10.	IT'S DELIGHTFUL TO BE MARRIED (1)
8	11.	HE'S A COUSIN OF MINE (7)
10	12.	ARRAH WANNA (8)
6	13.	IN THE WILDWOOD WHERE THE BLUE BELLS GREW (3)
16	14.	GOLDEN ROD (3)
7	15.	LET IT ALONE (6)
–	16.	HYMNS OF THE OLD CHURCH CHOIR (1)
–	17.	YOU SPLASH ME AND I'LL SPLASH YOU (1)
–	18.	IT'S GREAT TO BE A SOLDIER MAN (1)
13	19.	SOMEBODY'S WAITING FOR YOU (4)
–	20.	SPANGLES (2)

JULY 1907

LM	TM	
1	1.	SCHOOL DAYS (3)
3	2.	BECAUSE I'M MARRIED NOW (3)
2	3.	SAN ANTONIO (5)
17	4.	YOU SPLASH ME AND I'LL SPLASH YOU (2)
10	5.	IT'S DELIGHTFUL TO BE MARRIED (2)
9	6.	HE GOES TO CHURCH ON SUNDAY (2)
5	7.	AND A LITTLE BIT MORE (3)
–	8.	WHEN YOU KNOW YOU'RE NOT FORGOTTEN BY THE GIRL YOU CAN'T FORGET (1)
18	9.	IT'S GREAT TO BE A SOLDIER MAN (2)
6	10.	NOBODY'S LITTLE GIRL (3)
7	11.	LOVE ME AND THE WORLD IS MINE (12)
4	12.	POOR JOHN! (5)
16	13.	HYMNS OF THE OLD CHURCH CHOIR (2)
–	14.	NO WEDDING BELLS FOR ME (1)
–	15.	WON'T YOU BE MY HONEY? (1)
20	16.	SPANGLES (3)
12	17.	ARRAH WANNA (9)
11	18.	HE'S A COUSIN OF MINE (8)
–	19.	JUST BECAUSE I LOVED YOU SO (1)
8	20.	THE TALE THE CHURCH BELLS TOLLED (4)

AUGUST 1907

LM	TM	
1	1.	SCHOOL DAYS (4)
4	2.	YOU SPLASH ME AND I'LL SPLASH YOU (3)
2	3.	BECAUSE I'M MARRIED NOW (4)
3	4.	SAN ANTONIO (6)
15	5.	WON'T YOU BE MY HONEY? (2)
5	6.	IT'S DELIGHTFUL TO BE MARRIED (3)
14	7.	NO WEDDING BELLS FOR ME (2)
8	8.	WHEN YOU KNOW YOU'RE NOT FORGOTTEN BY THE GIRL YOU CAN'T FORGET (2)
9	9.	IT'S GREAT TO BE A SOLDIER MAN (3)
–	10.	DREAMING (1)
–	11.	HARRIGAN (1)
–	12.	EVERY LITTLE BIT ADDED (TO WHAT YOU'VE GOT) (1)
–	13.	WITH YOU IN ETERNITY (1)
–	14.	HONEY BOY (1)
7	15.	AND A LITTLE BIT MORE (4)
6	16.	HE GOES TO CHURCH ON SUNDAY (3)
11	17.	LOVE ME AND THE WORLD IS MINE (13)
–	18.	TAKE ME BACK TO NEW YORK TOWN (1)
–	19.	I'VE MADE MY PLANS FOR THE SUMMER (1)
–	20.	THE TEDDY BEARS' PICNIC (1)

SEPTEMBER 1907

LM	TM	
1	1.	SCHOOL DAYS (5)
10	2.	DREAMING (2)
5	3.	WON'T YOU BE MY HONEY? (3)
11	4.	HARRIGAN (2)
14	5.	HONEY BOY (2)
18	6.	TAKE ME BACK TO NEW YORK TOWN (2)
7	7.	NO WEDDING BELLS FOR ME (3)
13	8.	WITH YOU IN ETERNITY (2)
2	9.	YOU SPLASH ME AND I'LL SPLASH YOU (4)
9	10.	IT'S GREAT TO BE A SOLDIER MAN (4)
4	11.	SAN ANTONIO (7)
–	12.	VESTI LA GIUBBA (1)
3	13.	BECAUSE I'M MARRIED NOW (5)
–	14.	I'M A POPULAR MAN (1)
–	15.	BUDWEISER'S A FRIEND OF MINE (1)
–	16.	THAT'S WHAT THE ROSE SAID TO ME (1)
6	17.	IT'S DELIGHTFUL TO BE MARRIED (4)
8	18.	WHEN YOU KNOW YOU'RE NOT FORGOTTEN BY THE GIRL YOU CAN'T FORGET (3)
–	19.	SOME DAY WHEN DREAMS COME TRUE (1)
12	20.	EVERY LITTLE BIT ADDED (TO WHAT YOU'VE GOT) (2)

OCTOBER 1907

LM	TM	
1	1.	SCHOOL DAYS (6)
4	2.	HARRIGAN (3)
2	3.	DREAMING (3)
5	4.	HONEY BOY (3)
3	5.	WON'T YOU BE MY HONEY? (4)
6	6.	TAKE ME BACK TO NEW YORK TOWN (3)
7	7.	NO WEDDING BELLS FOR ME (4)
15	8.	BUDWEISER'S A FRIEND OF MINE (2)
12	9.	VESTI LA GIUBBA (2)
–	10.	IN MONKEYLAND (1)
14	11.	I'M A POPULAR MAN (2)
16	12.	THAT'S WHAT THE ROSE SAID TO ME (2)
19	13.	SOME DAY WHEN DREAMS COME TRUE (2)
8	14.	WITH YOU IN ETERNITY (3)
10	15.	IT'S GREAT TO BE A SOLDIER MAN (5)
–	16.	YESTERDAY (1)
–	17.	OLD FAITHFUL (1)
–	18.	UNDER THE TROPICAL MOON (1)
–	19.	SHE WAS A GRAND OLD LADY (1)
9	20.	YOU SPLASH ME, AND I'LL SPLASH YOU (5)

NOVEMBER 1907

LM	TM	
2	1.	HARRIGAN (4)
4	2.	HONEY BOY (4)
6	3.	TAKE ME BACK TO NEW YORK TOWN (4)
5	4.	WON'T YOU BE MY HONEY? (5)
1	5.	SCHOOL DAYS (7)
10	6.	IN MONKEYLAND (2)
3	7.	DREAMING (4)
17	8.	OLD FAITHFUL (2)
–	9.	RED WING (1)
12	10.	THAT'S WHAT THE ROSE SAID TO ME (3)
13	11.	SOME DAY WHEN DREAMS COME TRUE (3)
16	12.	YESTERDAY (2)
7	13.	NO WEDDING BELLS FOR ME (5)
14	14.	WITH YOU IN ETERNITY (4)
–	15.	SPRING, BEAUTIFUL SPRING (1)
9	16.	VESTI LA GIUBBA (3)
–	17.	TWO BLUE EYES (1)
8	18.	BUDWEISER'S A FRIEND OF MINE (3)
11	19.	I'M A POPULAR MAN (3)
15	20.	IT'S GREAT TO BE A SOLDIER MAN (6)

DECEMBER 1907

LM	TM	
1	1.	HARRIGAN (5)
2	2.	HONEY BOY (5)
17	3.	TWO BLUE EYES (2)
9	4.	RED WING (2)
3	5.	TAKE ME BACK TO NEW YORK TOWN (5)
6	6.	IN MONKEYLAND (3)
10	7.	THAT'S WHAT THE ROSE SAID TO ME (4)
8	8.	OLD FAITHFUL (3)
–	9.	THE BEST I GET IS MUCH OBLIGED TO YOU (1)
4	10.	WON'T YOU BE MY HONEY? (6)
11	11.	SOME DAY WHEN DREAMS COME TRUE (4)
–	12.	AS LONG AS THE WORLD ROLLS ON (1)
7	13.	DREAMING (5)
–	14.	I LOVE A LASSIE (1)
–	15.	THAT'S GRATITUDE (1)
–	16.	SHE IS MA DAISY (1)
15	17.	SPRING, BEAUTIFUL SPRING (2)
–	18.	DON'T GET MARRIED ANY MORE, MA (1)
5	19.	SCHOOL DAYS (8)
13	20.	NO WEDDING BELLS FOR ME (6)

JANUARY 1908

LM	TM	
3	1.	TWO BLUE EYES (3)
1	2.	HARRIGAN (6)
9	3.	THE BEST I GET IS MUCH OBLIGED TO YOU (2)
4	4.	RED WING (3)
2	5.	HONEY BOY (6)
12	6.	AS LONG AS THE WORLD ROLLS ON (2)
–	7.	I LOVE YOU SO (MERRY WIDOW WALTZ) (1)
11	8.	SOME DAY WHEN DREAMS COME TRUE (5)
6	9.	IN MONKEYLAND (4)
7	10.	THAT'S WHAT THE ROSE SAID TO ME (5)
5	11.	TAKE ME BACK TO NEW YORK TOWN (6)
8	12.	OLD FAITHFUL (4)
–	13.	MAKE BELIEVE (1)
10	14.	WON'T YOU BE MY HONEY? (7)
15	15.	THAT'S GRATITUDE (2)
–	16.	VILIA (1)
14	17.	I LOVE A LASSIE (2)
16	18.	SHE IS MA DAISY (2)
17	19.	SPRING, BEAUTIFUL SPRING (3)
18	20.	DON'T GET MARRIED ANY MORE, MA (2)

FEBRUARY 1908

LM	TM	
7	1.	I LOVE YOU SO (MERRY WIDOW WALTZ) (2)
3	2.	THE BEST I GET IS MUCH OBLIGED TO YOU (3)
1	3.	TWO BLUE EYES (4)
6	4.	AS LONG AS THE WORLD ROLLS ON (3)
4	5.	RED WING (4)
16	6.	VILIA (2)
13	7.	MAKE BELIEVE (2)
2	8.	HARRIGAN (7)
5	9.	HONEY BOY (7)
15	10.	THAT'S GRATITUDE (3)
10	11.	THAT'S WHAT THE ROSE SAID TO ME (6)
8	12.	SOME DAY WHEN DREAMS COME TRUE (6)
–	13.	THE GLOW-WORM (1)
12	14.	OLD FAITHFUL (5)
9	15.	IN MONKEYLAND (5)
14	16.	WON'T YOU BE MY HONEY? (8)
–	17.	WON'T YOU WALTZ HOME SWEET HOME WITH ME? (1)
–	18.	MUSETTE (1)
11	19.	TAKE ME BACK TO NEW YORK TOWN (7)
17	20	I LOVE A LASSIE (3)

MARCH 1908

LM	TM	
1	1.	I LOVE YOU SO (MERRY WIDOW WALTZ) (3)
4	2.	AS LONG AS THE WORLD ROLLS ON (4)
5	3.	RED WING (5)
7	4.	MAKE BELIEVE (3)
3	5.	TWO BLUE EYES (5)
13	6.	THE GLOW-WORM (2)
–	7.	I'M AFRAID TO COME HOME IN THE DARK (1)
2	8.	THE BEST I GET IS MUCH OBLIGED TO YOU (4)
12	9.	SOME DAY WHEN DREAMS COME TRUE (7)
11	10.	THAT'S WHAT THE ROSE SAID TO ME (7)
17	11.	WON'T YOU WALTZ HOME SWEET HOME WITH ME? (2)
–	12.	WHEN A FELLOW'S ON THE LEVEL WITH A GIRL WHO'S ON THE SQUARE (1)
6	13.	VILIA (3)
9	14.	HONEY BOY (8)
10	15.	THAT'S GRATITUDE (4)
–	16.	I'M STARVING FOR ONE SIGHT OF YOU (1)
–	17.	UNDER ANY OLD FLAG AT ALL (1)
–	18.	TWO LITTLE BABY SHOES (1)
–	19.	WHEN WE ARE M-A-DOUBLE-R-I-E-D (1)
8	20.	HARRIGAN (8)

APRIL 1908

LM	TM	
7	1.	I'M AFRAID TO COME HOME IN THE DARK (2)
2	2.	AS LONG AS THE WORLD ROLLS ON (5)
1	3.	I LOVE YOU SO (MERRY WIDOW WALTZ) (4)
6	4.	THE GLOW-WORM (3)
3	5.	RED WING (6)
4	6.	MAKE BELIEVE (4)
19	7.	WHEN WE ARE M-A-DOUBLE-R-I-E-D (2)
12	8.	WHEN A FELLOW'S ON THE LEVEL WITH A GIRL WHO'S ON THE SQUARE (2)
11	9.	WON'T YOU WALTZ HOME SWEET HOME WITH ME? (3)
–	10.	THE LANKY YANKEE BOYS IN BLUE (1)
9	11.	SOME DAY WHEN DREAMS COME TRUE (8)
–	12.	SMARTY (1)
16	13.	I'M STARVING FOR ONE SIGHT OF YOU (2)
10	14.	THAT'S WHAT THE ROSE SAID TO ME (8)
–	15.	I WANT YOU (1)
18	16.	TWO LITTLE BABY SHOES (2)
17	17.	UNDER ANY OLD FLAG AT ALL (2)
5	18.	TWO BLUE EYES (6)
15	19.	THAT'S GRATITUDE (5)
–	20.	WHEN SWEET MARIE WAS SWEET SIXTEEN (1)

MAY 1908

LM	TM	
1	1.	I'M AFRAID TO COME HOME IN THE DARK (3)
4	2.	THE GLOW-WORM (4)
2	3.	AS LONG AS THE WORLD ROLLS ON (6)
12	4.	SMARTY (2)
7	5.	WHEN WE ARE M-A-DOUBLE-R-I-E-D (3)
3	6.	I LOVE YOU SO (MERRY WIDOW WALTZ) (5)
20	7.	WHEN SWEET MARIE WAS SWEET SIXTEEN (2)
–	8.	JUST SOMEONE (1)
–	9.	THE SWEETEST MAID OF ALL (1)
10	10.	THE LANKY YANKEE BOYS IN BLUE (2)
–	11.	TRUE HEART (1)
5	12.	RED WING (7)
6	13.	MAKE BELIEVE (5)
8	14.	WHEN A FELLOW'S ON THE LEVEL WITH A GIRL WHO'S ON THE SQUARE (3)
15	15.	I WANT YOU (2)
–	16.	LOVE'S ROUNDELAY (1)
9	17.	WON'T YOU WALTZ HOME SWEET HOME WITH ME? (4)
11	18.	SOME DAY WHEN DREAMS COME TRUE (9)
–	19.	I LOVE A LASSIE (4)
–	20.	SWEETHEART DAYS (1)

JUNE 1908

LM	TM	
2	1.	THE GLOW-WORM (5)
4	2.	SMARTY (3)
8	3.	JUST SOMEONE (2)
7	4.	WHEN SWEET MARIE WAS SWEET SIXTEEN (3)
3	5.	AS LONG AS THE WORLD ROLLS ON (7)
1	6.	I'M AFRAID TO COME HOME IN THE DARK (4)
9	7.	THE SWEETEST MAID OF ALL (2)
11	8.	TRUE HEART (2)
5	9.	WHEN WE ARE M-A-DOUBLE-R-I-E-D (4)
16	10.	LOVE'S ROUNDELAY (2)
–	11.	ROSES BRING DREAMS OF YOU (1)
–	12.	THE TEDDY BEARS' PICNIC (2)
20	13.	SWEETHEART DAYS (2)
–	14.	HOO-OO (AIN'T YOU COMIN' OUT TONIGHT?) (1)
18	15.	SOME DAY WHEN DREAMS COME TRUE (10)
6	16.	I LOVE YOU SO (MERRY WIDOW WALTZ) (6)
10	17.	THE LANKY YANKEE BOYS IN BLUE (3)
14	18.	WHEN A FELLOW'S ON THE LEVEL WITH A GIRL WHO'S ON THE SQUARE (4)
–	19.	THERE NEVER WAS A GIRL LIKE YOU (1)
–	20.	OVER THE HILLS AND FAR AWAY (1)

JULY 1908

LM	TM	
1	1.	THE GLOW-WORM (6)
2	2.	SMARTY (4)
3	3.	JUST SOMEONE (3)
11	4.	ROSES BRING DREAMS OF YOU (2)
–	5.	TAKE ME OUT TO THE BALL GAME (1)
19	6.	THERE NEVER WAS A GIRL LIKE YOU (2)
4	7.	WHEN SWEET MARIE WAS SWEET SIXTEEN (4)
14	8.	HOO-OO (AIN'T YOU COMIN' OUT TONIGHT?) (2)
5	9.	AS LONG AS THE WORLD ROLLS ON (8)
–	10.	THE YAMA-YAMA MAN (1)
13	11.	SWEETHEART DAYS (3)
–	12.	ARE YOU SINCERE? (1)
–	13.	CONSOLATION (1)
12	14.	THE TEDDY BEARS' PICNIC (3)
–	15.	BON BON BUDDY (1)
–	16.	RAINBOW (1)
8	17.	TRUE HEART (3)
6	18.	I'M AFRAID TO COME HOME IN THE DARK (5)
7	19.	THE SWEETEST MAID OF ALL (3)
–	20.	SHE IS MA DAISY (3)

AUGUST 1908

LM	TM	
5	1.	TAKE ME OUT TO THE BALL GAME (2)
1	2.	THE GLOW-WORM (7)
4	3.	ROSES BRING DREAMS OF YOU (3)
6	4.	THERE NEVER WAS A GIRL LIKE YOU (3)
10	5.	THE YAMA-YAMA MAN (2)
3	6.	JUST SOMEONE (4)
2	7.	SMARTY (5)
–	8.	I'VE TAKEN QUITE A FANCY TO YOU (1)
16	9.	RAINBOW (2)
–	10.	DOWN IN JUNGLE TOWN (1)
–	11.	SUNBONNET SUE (1)
15	12.	BON BON BUDDY (2)
8	13.	HOO-OO (AIN'T YOU COMIN' OUT TONIGHT?) (3)
12	14.	ARE YOU SINCERE? (2)
–	15.	CUDDLE UP A LITTLE CLOSER (1)
–	16.	I LOVE A LASSIE (5)
13	17.	CONSOLATION (2)
9	18.	AS LONG AS THE WORLD ROLLS ON (9)
7	19.	WHEN SWEET MARIE WAS SWEET SIXTEEN (5)
11	20.	SWEETHEART DAYS (4)

SEPTEMBER 1908

LM	TM	
1	1.	TAKE ME OUT TO THE BALL GAME (3)
10	2.	DOWN IN JUNGLE TOWN (2)
11	3.	SUNBONNET SUE (2)
8	4.	I'VE TAKEN QUITE A FANCY TO YOU (2)
15	5.	CUDDLE UP A LITTLE CLOSER (2)
5	6.	THE YAMA-YAMA MAN (3)
2	7.	THE GLOW-WORM (8)
12	8.	BON BON BUDDY (3)
3	9.	ROSES BRING DREAMS OF YOU (4)
4	10.	THERE NEVER WAS A GIRL LIKE YOU (4)
9	11.	RAINBOW (3)
13	12.	HOO-OO (AIN'T YOU COMIN' OUT TONIGHT?) (4)
16	13.	I LOVE A LASSIE (6)
–	14.	IT LOOKS LIKE A BIG NIGHT TONIGHT (1)
7	15.	SMARTY (6)
6	16.	JUST SOMEONE (5)
–	17.	I WISH I HAD A GIRL (1)
–	18.	SOMEBODY LIED (1)
–	19.	LOVE DAYS (1)
14	20.	ARE YOU SINCERE? (3)

OCTOBER 1908

LM	TM	
3	1.	SUNBONNET SUE (3)
5	2.	CUDDLE UP A LITTLE CLOSER (3)
2	3.	DOWN IN JUNGLE TOWN (3)
8	4.	BON BON BUDDY (4)
4	5.	I'VE TAKEN QUITE A FANCY TO YOU (3)
1	6.	TAKE ME OUT TO THE BALL GAME (4)
7	7.	THE GLOW-WORM (9)
14	8.	IT LOOKS LIKE A BIG NIGHT TONIGHT (2)
17	9.	I WISH I HAD A GIRL (2)
6	10.	THE YAMA-YAMA MAN (4)
9	11.	ROSES BRING DREAMS OF YOU (5)
10	12.	THERE NEVER WAS A GIRL LIKE YOU (5)
11	13.	RAINBOW (4)
12	14.	HOO-OO (AIN'T YOU COMIN' OUT TONIGHT?) (5)
–	15.	ANY OLD PORT IN A STORM (1)
18	16.	SOMEBODY LIED (2)
13	17.	I LOVE A LASSIE (7)
–	18.	OH, YOU KID! (1)
19	19.	LOVE DAYS (2)
–	20.	WHEN THE MOON PLAYS PEEK-A-BOO (1)

NOVEMBER 1908

LM	TM	
1	1.	SUNBONNET SUE (4)
2	2.	CUDDLE UP A LITTLE CLOSER (4)
9	3.	I WISH I HAD A GIRL (3)
3	4.	DOWN IN JUNGLE TOWN (4)
8	5.	IT LOOKS LIKE A BIG NIGHT TONIGHT (3)
4	6.	BON BON BUDDY (5)
7	7.	THE GLOW-WORM (10)
15	8.	ANY OLD PORT IN A STORM (2)
11	9.	ROSES BRING DREAMS OF YOU (6)
–	10.	MY BRUDDAH SYLVEST' (1)
10	11.	THE YAMA-YAMA MAN (5)
5	12.	I'VE TAKEN QUITE A FANCY TO YOU (4)
–	13.	MORNING CY (1)
–	14.	DON'T TAKE ME HOME (1)
14	15.	HOO-OO (AIN'T YOU COMIN' OUT TONIGHT?) (6)
6	16.	TAKE ME OUT TO THE BALL GAME (5)
18	17.	OH, YOU KID! (2)
–	18.	YOU'RE IN THE RIGHT CHURCH BUT THE WRONG PEW (1)
12	19.	THERE NEVER WAS A GIRL LIKE YOU (6)
13	20.	RAINBOW (5)

DECEMBER 1908

LM	TM	
1	1.	SUNBONNET SUE (5)
3	2.	I WISH I HAD A GIRL (4)
2	3.	CUDDLE UP A LITTLE CLOSER (5)
5	4.	IT LOOKS LIKE A BIG NIGHT TONIGHT (4)
4	5.	DOWN IN JUNGLE TOWN (5)
6	6.	BON BON BUDDY (6)
10	7.	MY BRUDDAH SYLVEST' (2)
18	8.	YOU'RE IN THE RIGHT CHURCH BUT THE WRONG PEW (2)
–	9.	IF I HAD A THOUSAND LIVES TO LIVE (1)
14	10.	DON'T TAKE ME HOME (2)
7	11.	THE GLOW-WORM (11)
–	12.	GOOD EVENING, CAROLINE (1)
13	13.	MORNING CY (2)
9	14.	ROSES BRING DREAMS OF YOU (7)
–	15.	MY OWN UNITED STATES (1)
8	16.	ANY OLD PORT IN A STORM (3)
–	17.	ROSE OF THE WORLD (1)
–	18.	ASK HER WHILE THE BAND IS PLAYING (1)
15	19.	HOO-OO (AIN'T YOU COMIN' OUT TONIGHT?) (7)
11	20.	THE YAMA-YAMA MAN (6)

JANUARY 1909

LM	TM	
1	1.	SUNBONNET SUE (6)
8	2.	YOU'RE IN THE RIGHT CHURCH BUT THE WRONG PEW (3)
2	3.	I WISH I HAD A GIRL (5)
12	4.	GOOD EVENING, CAROLINE (2)
6	5.	BON BON BUDDY (7)
9	6.	IF I HAD A THOUSAND LIVES TO LIVE (2)
4	7.	IT LOOKS LIKE A BIG NIGHT TONIGHT (5)
17	8.	ROSE OF THE WORLD (2)
3	9.	CUDDLE UP A LITTLE CLOSER (6)
15	10.	MY OWN UNITED STATES (2)
18	11.	ASK HER WHILE THE BAND IS PLAYING (2)
10	12.	DON'T TAKE ME HOME (3)
13	13.	MORNING CY (3)
–	14.	LOVE IS LIKE A CIGARETTE (1)
11	15.	THE GLOW-WORM (12)
7	16.	MY BRUDDAH SYLVEST' (3)
5	17.	DOWN IN JUNGLE TOWN (6)
14	18.	ROSES BRING DREAMS OF YOU (8)
–	19.	I LOVE A LASSIE (8)
–	20.	SHE IS MA DAISY (4)

FEBRUARY 1909

LM	TM	
2	1.	YOU'RE IN THE RIGHT CHURCH BUT THE WRONG PEW (4)
1	2.	SUNBONNET SUE (7)
6	3.	IF I HAD A THOUSAND LIVES TO LIVE (3)
3	4.	I WISH I HAD A GIRL (6)
8	5.	ROSE OF THE WORLD (3)
4	6.	GOOD EVENING, CAROLINE (3)
10	7.	MY OWN UNITED STATES (3)
–	8.	SHINE ON, HARVEST MOON (1)
13	9.	MORNING CY (4)
11	10.	ASK HER WHILE THE BAND IS PLAYING (3)
14	11.	LOVE IS LIKE A CIGARETTE (2)
5	12.	BON BON BUDDY (8)
–	13.	OH, MISS MALINDA (1)
12	14.	DON'T TAKE ME HOME (4)
15	15.	THE GLOW-WORM (13)
16	16.	MY BRUDDAH SYLVEST' (4)
18	17.	ROSES BRING DREAMS OF YOU (9)
7	18.	IT LOOKS LIKE A BIG NIGHT TONIGHT (6)
9	19.	CUDDLE UP A LITTLE CLOSER (7)
19	20.	I LOVE A LASSIE (9)

MARCH 1909

LM	TM	
8	1.	SHINE ON, HARVEST MOON (2)
1	2.	YOU'RE IN THE RIGHT CHURCH BUT THE WRONG PEW (5)
3	3.	IF I HAD A THOUSAND LIVES TO LIVE (4)
4	4.	I WISH I HAD A GIRL (7)
2	5.	SUNBONNET SUE (8)
5	6.	ROSE OF THE WORLD (4)
13	7.	OH, MISS MALINDA (2)
–	8.	WHEN I DREAM IN THE GLOAMING OF YOU (1)
–	9.	EVERYBODY LOVES ME BUT THE ONE I LOVE (1)
7	10.	MY OWN UNITED STATES (4)
11	11.	LOVE IS LIKE A CIGARETTE (3)
9	12.	MORNING CY (5)
6	13.	GOOD EVENING, CAROLINE (4)
12	14.	BON BON BUDDY (9)
16	15.	MY BRUDDAH SYLVEST' (5)
10	16.	ASK HER WHILE THE BAND IS PLAYING (4)
–	17.	NOBODY KNOWS, NOBODY CARES (1)
14	18.	DON'T TAKE ME HOME (5)
–	19.	"BL-ND" AND "P-G" SPELLS "BLIND PIG" (1)
20	20.	I LOVE A LASSIE (10)

APRIL 1909

LM	TM	
1	1.	SHINE ON, HARVEST MOON (3)
3	2.	IF I HAD A THOUSAND LIVES TO LIVE (5)
8	3.	WHEN I DREAM IN THE GLOAMING OF YOU (2)
2	4.	YOU'RE IN THE RIGHT CHURCH BUT THE WRONG PEW (6)
7	5.	OH, MISS MALINDA (3)
4	6.	I WISH I HAD A GIRL (8)
–	7.	YIP-I-ADDY-I-AY! (1)
17	8.	NOBODY KNOWS, NOBODY CARES (2)
5	9.	SUNBONNET SUE (9)
9	10.	EVERYBODY LOVES ME BUT THE ONE I LOVE (2)
6	11.	ROSE OF THE WORLD (5)
12	12.	MORNING CY (6)
–	13.	DOWN AT HUSKING BEE (1)
10	14.	MY OWN UNITED STATES (5)
11	15.	LOVE IS LIKE A CIGARETTE (4)
–	16.	GAMES OF CHILDHOOD DAYS (1)
–	17.	TO THE END OF THE WORLD WITH YOU (1)
20	18.	I LOVE A LASSIE (12)
13	19.	GOOD EVENING, CAROLINE (5)
–	20.	KERRY MILLS BARN DANCE (1)

MAY 1909

LM	TM	
1	1.	SHINE ON, HARVEST MOON (4)
7	2.	YIP-I-ADDY-I-AY! (2)
3	3.	WHEN I DREAM IN THE GLOAMING OF YOU (3)
8	4.	NOBODY KNOWS, NOBODY CARES (3)
2	5.	IF I HAD A THOUSAND LIVES TO LIVE (6)
5	6.	OH, MISS MALINDA (4)
–	7.	MY COUSIN CARUS' (1)
6	8.	I WISH I HAD A GIRL (9)
4	9.	YOU'RE IN THE RIGHT CHURCH BUT THE WRONG PEW (7)
13	10.	DOWN AT HUSKING BEE (2)
17	11.	TO THE END OF THE WORLD WITH YOU (2)
9	12.	SUNBONNET SUE (10)
–	13.	LET'S GO BACK TO BABY DAYS (1)
–	14.	DOWN AMONG THE SUGAR CANE (1)
–	15.	THIS ROSE BRINGS MY HEART TO YOU (1)
20	16.	KERRY MILLS BARN DANCE (2)
16	17.	GAMES OF CHILDHOOD DAYS (2)
–	18.	SCHOOL MATES (1)
10	19.	EVERYBODY LOVES ME BUT THE ONE I LOVE (3)
12	20.	MORNING CY (7)

JUNE 1909

LM	TM	
2	1.	YIP-I-ADDY-I-AY! (3)
1	2.	SHINE ON, HARVEST MOON (5)
3	3.	WHEN I DREAM IN THE GLOAMING OF YOU (4)
7	4.	MY COUSIN CARUS' (2)
18	5.	SCHOOL MATES (2)
4	6.	NOBODY KNOWS, NOBODY CARES (4)
–	7.	BEAUTIFUL EYES (1)
–	8.	I LOVE MY WIFE, BUT OH, YOU KID! (1)
–	9.	I LOVE, I LOVE, I LOVE MY WIFE, BUT OH, YOU KID (1)
14	10.	DOWN AMONG THE SUGAR CANE (2)
–	11.	I WONDER WHO'S KISSING HER NOW (1)
11	12.	TO THE END OF THE WORLD WITH YOU (3)
8	13.	I WISH I HAD A GIRL (10)
16	14.	KERRY MILLS BARN DANCE (3)
6	15.	OH, MISS MALINDA (5)
–	16.	MY PONY BOY (1)
–	17.	THE YAMA-YAMA MAN (7)
–	18.	RED, RED ROSE (1)
13	19.	LET'S GO BACK TO BABY DAYS (2)
15	20.	THIS ROSE BRINGS MY HEART TO YOU (2)

JULY 1909

LM	TM	
1	1.	YIP-I-ADDY-I-AY! (4)
3	2.	WHEN I DREAM IN THE GLOAMING OF YOU (5)
4	3.	MY COUSIN CARUS' (3)
16	4.	MY PONY BOY (2)
2	5.	SHINE ON, HARVEST MOON (6)
11	6.	I WONDER WHO'S KISSING HER NOW (2)
9	7.	I LOVE, I LOVE, I LOVE MY WIFE, BUT OH, YOU KID (2)
8	8.	I LOVE MY WIFE, BUT OH, YOU KID! (2)
7	9.	BEAUTIFUL EYES (2)
10	10.	DOWN AMONG THE SUGAR CANE (3)
5	11.	SCHOOL MATES (3)
17	12.	THE YAMA-YAMA MAN (8)
12	13.	TO THE END OF THE WORLD WITH YOU (4)
6	14.	NOBODY KNOWS, NOBODY CARES (5)
–	15.	TAKE ME UP WITH YOU, DEARIE (1)
–	16.	LONESOME (1)
–	17.	YOU AIN'T TALKIN' TO ME (1)
–	18.	I'M AWFULLY GLAD I MET YOU (1)
–	19.	RED HEAD (1)
18	20.	RED, RED ROSE (2)

AUGUST 1909

LM	TM	
4	1.	MY PONY BOY (3)
6	2.	I WONDER WHO'S KISSING HER NOW (3)
3	3.	MY COUSIN CARUS' (4)
1	4.	YIP-I-ADDY-I-AY! (5)
10	5.	DOWN AMONG THE SUGAR CANE (4)
2	6.	WHEN I DREAM IN THE GLOAMING OF YOU (6)
13	7.	TO THE END OF THE WORLD WITH YOU (5)
12	8.	THE YAMA-YAMA MAN (9)
–	9.	MY WIFE'S GONE TO THE COUNTRY (HURAH! HURAH!) (1)
5	10.	SHINE ON, HARVEST MOON (7)
15	11.	TAKE ME UP WITH YOU, DEARIE (2)
19	12.	RED HEAD (2)
8	13.	I LOVE MY WIFE, BUT OH, YOU KID! (3)
7	14.	I LOVE, I LOVE, I LOVE MY WIFE, BUT OH, YOU KID (3)
16	15.	LONESOME (2)
–	16.	I WISH I HAD MY OLD GIRL BACK AGAIN (1)
9	17.	BEAUTIFUL EYES (3)
–	18.	I'VE GOT RINGS ON MY FINGERS (1)
17	19.	YOU AIN'T TALKIN' TO ME (2)
–	20.	PANSIES MEAN THOUGHTS, AND THOUGHTS MEAN YOU (1)

SEPTEMBER 1909

LM	TM	
2	1.	I WONDER WHO'S KISSING HER NOW (4)
1	2.	MY PONY BOY (4)
9	3.	MY WIFE'S GONE TO THE COUNTRY (HURAH! HURAH!) (2)
5	4.	DOWN AMONG THE SUGAR CANE (5)
4	5.	YIP-I-ADDY-I-AY! (6)
7	6.	TO THE END OF THE WORLD WITH YOU (6)
3	7.	MY COUSIN CARUS' (5)
18	8.	I'VE GOT RINGS ON MY FINGERS (2)
16	9.	I WISH I HAD MY OLD GIRL BACK AGAIN (2)
12	10.	RED HEAD (3)
6	11.	WHEN I DREAM IN THE GLOAMING OF YOU (7)
8	12.	THE YAMA-YAMA MAN (10)
–	13.	AMINA (1)
11	14.	TAKE ME UP WITH YOU, DEARIE (3)
15	15.	LONESOME (3)
–	16.	GEE, BUT THERE'S CLASS TO A GIRL LIKE YOU (1)
19	17.	YOU AIN'T TALKIN' TO ME (3)
–	18.	SADIE SALOME, GO HOME (1)
10	19.	SHINE ON, HARVEST MOON (8)
–	20.	KERRY MILLS BARN DANCE (4)

OCTOBER 1909

LM	TM	
1	1.	I WONDER WHO'S KISSING HER NOW (5)
8	2.	I'VE GOT RINGS ON MY FINGERS (3)
4	3.	DOWN AMONG THE SUGAR CANE (6)
6	4.	TO THE END OF THE WORLD WITH YOU (7)
2	5.	MY PONY BOY (5)
–	6.	BY THE LIGHT OF THE SILVERY MOON (1)
9	7.	I WISH I HAD MY OLD GIRL BACK AGAIN (3)
3	8.	MY WIFE'S GONE TO THE COUNTRY (HURAH! HURAH!) (3)
13	9.	AMINA (2)
7	10.	MY COUSIN CARUS' (6)
16	11.	GEE, BUT THERE'S CLASS TO A GIRL LIKE YOU (2)
5	12.	YIP-I-ADDY-I-AY! (7)
–	13.	DAISIES WON'T TELL (1)
10	14.	RED HEAD (4)
–	15.	UP, UP, UP IN MY AEROPLANE (1)
11	16.	WHEN I DREAM IN THE GLOAMING OF YOU (8)
–	17.	THAT'S A-PLENTY (1)
12	18.	THE YAMA-YAMA MAN (11)
–	19.	WILD CHERRIES RAG (1)
–	20.	GOOD NIGHT, DEAR (1)

NOVEMBER 1909

LM	TM	
2	1.	I'VE GOT RINGS ON MY FINGERS (4)
6	2.	BY THE LIGHT OF THE SILVERY MOON (2)
1	3.	I WONDER WHO'S KISSING HER NOW (6)
3	4.	DOWN AMONG THE SUGAR CANE (7)
17	5.	THAT'S A-PLENTY (2)
7	6.	I WISH I HAD MY OLD GIRL BACK AGAIN (4)
4	7.	TO THE END OF THE WORLD WITH YOU (8)
–	8.	CARRIE (MARRY HARRY) (1)
19	9.	WILD CHERRIES RAG (2)
9	10.	AMINA (3)
13	11.	DAISIES WON'T TELL (2)
–	12.	THE CUBANOLA GLIDE (1)
15	13.	UP, UP, UP IN MY AEROPLANE (2)
11	14.	GEE, BUT THERE'S CLASS TO A GIRL LIKE YOU (3)
–	15.	MEET ME TONIGHT IN DREAMLAND (1)
–	16.	SENORA (1)
10	17.	MY COUSIN CARUS' (7)
5	18.	MY PONY BOY (6)
20	19.	GOOD NIGHT, DEAR (2)
12	20.	YIP-I-ADDY-I-AY! (8)

DECEMBER 1909

LM	TM	
2	1.	BY THE LIGHT OF THE SILVERY MOON (3)
1	2.	I'VE GOT RINGS ON MY FINGERS (5)
3	3.	I WONDER WHO'S KISSING HER NOW (7)
8	4.	CARRIE (MARRY HARRY) (2)
6	5.	I WISH I HAD MY OLD GIRL BACK AGAIN (5)
12	6.	THE CUBANOLA GLIDE (2)
5	7.	THAT'S A-PLENTY (3)
9	8.	WILD CHERRIES RAG (3)
7	9.	TO THE END OF THE WORLD WITH YOU (9)
–	10.	NEXT TO YOUR MOTHER, WHO DO YOU LOVE? (1)
4	11.	DOWN AMONG THE SUGAR CANE (8)
19	12.	GOOD NIGHT, DEAR (3)
–	13.	THE GARDEN OF ROSES (1)
15	14.	MEET ME TONIGHT IN DREAMLAND (2)
–	15.	COME AFTER BREAKFAST, BRING 'LONG YOUR LUNCH, AND LEAVE 'FORE SUPPER TIME (1)
16	16.	SENORA (2)
10	17.	AMINA (4)
11	18.	DAISIES WON'T TELL (3)
–	19.	CIRIBIRIBIN (1)
–	20.	IN THE GARDEN OF MY HEART (1)

JANUARY 1910

LM	TM	
1	1.	BY THE LIGHT OF THE SILVERY MOON (4)
6	2.	THE CUBANOLA GLIDE (3)
2	3.	I'VE GOT RINGS ON MY FINGERS (6)
3	4.	I WONDER WHO'S KISSING HER NOW (8)
15	5.	COME AFTER BREAKFAST, BRING 'LONG YOUR LUNCH, AND LEAVE 'FORE SUPPER TIME (2)
4	6.	CARRIE (MARRY HARRY) (3)
5	7.	I WISH I HAD MY OLD GIRL BACK AGAIN (6)
9	8.	TO THE END OF THE WORLD WITH YOU (10)
–	9.	PUT ON YOUR OLD GRAY BONNET (1)
13	10.	THE GARDEN OF ROSES (2)
14	11.	MEET ME TONIGHT IN DREAMLAND (3)
10	12.	NEXT TO YOUR MOTHER, WHO DO YOU LOVE? (2)
7	13.	THAT'S A-PLENTY (4)
12	14.	GOOD NIGHT, DEAR (4)
8	15.	WILD CHERRIES RAG (4)
11	16.	DOWN AMONG THE SUGAR CANE (9)
–	17.	YIDDLE ON YOUR FIDDLE (1)
17	18.	AMINA (5)
18	19.	DAISIES WON'T TELL (4)
20	20.	IN THE GARDEN OF MY HEART (2)

FEBRUARY 1910

LM	TM	
1	1.	BY THE LIGHT OF THE SILVERY MOON (5)
2	2.	THE CUBANOLA GLIDE (4)
9	3.	PUT ON YOUR OLD GRAY BONNET (2)
5	4.	COME AFTER BREAKFAST, BRING 'LONG YOUR LUNCH, AND LEAVE 'FORE SUPPER TIME (3)
3	5.	I'VE GOT RINGS ON MY FINGERS (7)
8	6.	TO THE END OF THE WORLD WITH YOU (11)
17	7.	YIDDLE ON YOUR FIDDLE (2)
–	8.	THAT MESMERIZING MENDELSSOHN TUNE (1)
11	9.	MEET ME TONIGHT IN DREAMLAND (4)
4	10.	I WONDER WHO'S KISSING HER NOW (9)
7	11.	I WISH I HAD MY OLD GIRL BACK AGAIN (7)
–	12.	SHAKY EYES (1)
13	13.	THAT'S A-PLENTY (5)
10	14.	THE GARDEN OF ROSES (3)
18	15.	AMINA (6)
20	16.	IN THE GARDEN OF MY HEART (3)
–	17.	CIRIBIRIBIN (2)
6	18.	CARRIE (MARRY HARRY) (4)
14	19.	GOOD NIGHT, DEAR (5)
15	20.	WILD CHERRIES RAG (5)

MARCH 1910

LM	TM	
3	1.	PUT ON YOUR OLD GRAY BONNET (3)
8	2.	THAT MESMERIZING MENDELSSOHN TUNE (2)
1	3.	BY THE LIGHT OF THE SILVERY MOON (6)
2	4.	THE CUBANOLA GLIDE (5)
9	5.	MEET ME TONIGHT IN DREAMLAND (5)
4	6.	COME AFTER BREAKFAST, BRING 'LONG YOUR LUNCH, AND LEAVE 'FORE SUPPER TIME (4)
12	7.	SHAKY EYES (2)
5	8.	I'VE GOT RINGS ON MY FINGERS (8)
6	9.	TO THE END OF THE WORLD WITH YOU (12)
7	10.	YIDDLE ON YOUR FIDDLE (3)
17	11.	CIRIBIRIBIN (3)
16	12.	IN THE GARDEN OF MY HEART (4)
–	13.	WAY DOWN IN COTTON TOWN (1)
15	14.	AMINA (7)
–	15.	ARE YOU LONESOME? (1)
14	16.	THE GARDEN OF ROSES (4)
10	17.	I WONDER WHO'S KISSING HER NOW (10)
11	18.	I WISH I HAD MY OLD GIRL BACK AGAIN (8)
–	19.	TIE YOUR LITTLE BULL OUTSIDE (1)
–	20.	EV'RY DAY (1)

APRIL 1910

LM	TM	
1	1.	PUT ON YOUR OLD GRAY BONNET (4)
2	2.	THAT MESMERIZING MENDELSSOHN TUNE (3)
5	3.	MEET ME TONIGHT IN DREAMLAND (6)
7	4.	SHAKY EYES (3)
4	5.	THE CUBANOLA GLIDE (6)
–	6.	HAS ANYBODY HERE SEEN KELLY? (1)
3	7.	BY THE LIGHT OF THE SILVERY MOON (7)
8	8.	I'VE GOT RINGS ON MY FINGERS (9)
12	9.	IN THE GARDEN OF MY HEART (5)
6	10.	COME AFTER BREAKFAST, BRING 'LONG YOUR LUNCH, AND LEAVE 'FORE SUPPER TIME (5)
19	11.	TIE YOUR LITTLE BULL OUTSIDE (2)
–	12.	COME ALONG, MY MANDY! (1)
9	13.	TO THE END OF THE WORLD WITH YOU (13)
–	14.	THAT ITALIAN RAG (1)
–	15.	YOU ARE THE IDEAL OF MY DREAMS (1)
–	16.	I'LL MAKE A RING AROUND ROSIE (1)
11	17.	CIRIBIRIBIN (4)
10	18.	YIDDLE ON YOUR FIDDLE (4)
16	19.	THE GARDEN OF ROSES (5)
–	20.	THE GLOW-WORM (1)

MAY 1910

LM	TM	
1	1.	PUT ON YOUR OLD GRAY BONNET (5)
6	2.	HAS ANYBODY HERE SEEN KELLY? (2)
3	3.	MEET ME TONIGHT IN DREAMLAND (7)
2	4.	THAT MESMERIZING MENDELSSOHN TUNE (4)
15	5.	YOU ARE THE IDEAL OF MY DREAMS (2)
4	6.	SHAKY EYES (4)
12	7.	COME ALONG, MY MANDY! (2)
14	8.	THAT ITALIAN RAG (2)
16	9.	I'LL MAKE A RING AROUND ROSIE (2)
9	10.	IN THE GARDEN OF MY HEART (6)
5	11.	THE CUBANOLA GLIDE (7)
–	12.	WHAT'S THE MATTER WITH FATHER? (1)
–	13.	I'VE GOT THE TIME, I'VE GOT THE PLACE, BUT IT'S HARD TO FIND THE GIRL (1)
–	14.	YOU TAUGHT ME HOW TO LOVE YOU, NOW TEACH ME TO FORGET (1)
7	15.	BY THE LIGHT OF THE SILVERY MOON (8)
11	16.	TIE YOUR LITTLE BULL OUTSIDE (3)
20	17.	THE GLOW-WORM (2)
–	18.	JUST FOR A GIRL (1)
–	19.	TEMPTATION RAG (1)
–	20.	WHERE THE RIVER SHANNON FLOWS (1)

JUNE 1910

LM	TM	
2	1.	HAS ANYBODY HERE SEEN KELLY? (3)
3	2.	MEET ME TONIGHT IN DREAMLAND (8)
1	3.	PUT ON YOUR OLD GRAY BONNET (6)
5	4.	YOU ARE THE IDEAL OF MY DREAMS (3)
13	5.	I'VE GOT THE TIME, I'VE GOT THE PLACE, BUT IT'S HARD TO FIND THE GIRL (2)
4	6.	THAT MESMERIZING MENDELSSOHN TUNE (5)
6	7.	SHAKY EYES (5)
12	8.	WHAT'S THE MATTER WITH FATHER? (2)
10	9.	IN THE GARDEN OF MY HEART (7)
–	10.	CALL ME UP SOME RAINY AFTERNOON (1)
14	11.	YOU TAUGHT ME HOW TO LOVE YOU, NOW TEACH ME TO FORGET (2)
8	12.	THAT ITALIAN RAG (3)
9	13.	I'LL MAKE A RING AROUND ROSIE (3)
18	14.	JUST FOR A GIRL (2)
7	15.	COME ALONG, MY MANDY! (3)
19	16.	TEMPTATION RAG (2)
17	17.	THE GLOW-WORM (3)
20	18.	WHERE THE RIVER SHANNON FLOWS (2)
–	19.	GO ON, GOOD-A-BYE (1)
–	20.	I'M NOT THAT KIND OF GIRL (1)

JULY 1910

LM	TM	
2	1.	MEET ME TONIGHT IN DREAMLAND (9)
1	2.	HAS ANYBODY HERE SEEN KELLY? (4)
5	3.	I'VE GOT THE TIME, I'VE GOT THE PLACE, BUT IT'S HARD TO FIND THE GIRL (3)
10	4.	CALL ME UP SOME RAINY AFTERNOON (2)
4	5.	PUT ON YOUR OLD GRAY BONNET (7)
3	6.	YOU ARE THE IDEAL OF MY DREAMS (4)
8	7.	WHAT'S THE MATTER WITH FATHER? (3)
16	8.	TEMPTATION RAG (3)
7	9.	SHAKY EYES (6)
14	10.	JUST FOR A GIRL (3)
9	11.	IN THE GARDEN OF MY HEART (8)
14	12.	COME ALONG, MY MANDY! (4)
18	13.	WHERE THE RIVER SHANNON FLOWS (3)
11	14.	YOU TAUGHT ME HOW TO LOVE YOU, NOW TEACH ME TO FORGET (3)
–	15.	MY HEART HAS LEARNED TO LOVE YOU, NOW DO NOT SAY GOOD-BYE (1)
12	16.	THAT ITALIAN RAG (4)
13	17.	I'LL MAKE A RING AROUND ROSIE (4)
6	18.	THAT MESMERIZING MENDELSSOHN TUNE (6)
17	19.	THE GLOW-WORM (4)
19	20.	GO ON, GOOD-A-BYE (2)

AUGUST 1910

LM	TM	
1	1.	MEET ME TONIGHT IN DREAMLAND (10)
3	2.	I'VE GOT THE TIME, I'VE GOT THE PLACE, BUT IT'S HARD TO FIND THE GIRL (4)
2	3.	HAS ANYBODY HERE SEEN KELLY? (5)
7	4.	WHAT'S THE MATTER WITH FATHER? (4)
4	5.	CALL ME UP SOME RAINY AFTERNOON (3)
6	6.	YOU ARE THE IDEAL OF MY DREAMS (5)
8	7.	TEMPTATION RAG (4)
–	8.	ANY LITTLE GIRL THAT'S A NICE LITTLE GIRL (1)
15	9.	MY HEART HAS LEARNED TO LOVE YOU, NOW DO NOT SAY GOOD-BYE (2)
11	10.	IN THE GARDEN OF MY HEART (9)
–	11.	EVERY LITTLE MOVEMENT (1)
5	12.	PUT ON YOUR OLD GRAY BONNET (8)
–	13.	SOMEBODY ELSE, IT'S ALWAYS SOMEBODY ELSE (1)
–	14.	HEAVEN WILL PROTECT THE WORKING GIRL (1)
13	15.	WHERE THE RIVER SHANNON FLOWS (4)
10	16.	JUST FOR A GIRL (4)
9	17.	SHAKY EYES (7)
16	18.	THAT ITALIAN RAG (5)
–	19.	THE CHANTICLEER RAG (1)
–	20.	CASEY JONES (1)

SEPTEMBER 1910

LM	TM	
1	1.	MEET ME TONIGHT IN DREAMLAND (11)
8	2.	ANY LITTLE GIRL THAT'S A NICE LITTLE GIRL (2)
2	3.	I'VE GOT THE TIME, I'VE GOT THE PLACE, BUT IT'S HARD TO FIND THE GIRL (5)
4	4.	WHAT'S THE MATTER WITH FATHER? (5)
–	5.	SOME OF THESE DAYS (1)
–	6.	PLAY THAT BARBERSHOP CHORD (1)
11	7.	EVERY LITTLE MOVEMENT (2)
9	8.	MY HEART HAS LEARNED TO LOVE YOU, NOW DO NOT SAY GOOD-BYE (3)
3	9.	HAS ANYBODY HERE SEEN KELLY? (6)
5	10.	CALL ME UP SOME RAINY AFTERNOON (4)
13	11.	SOMEBODY ELSE, IT'S ALWAYS SOMEBODY ELSE (2)
10	12.	IN THE GARDEN OF MY HEART (10)
20	13.	CASEY JONES (2)
6	14.	YOU ARE THE IDEAL OF MY DREAMS (6)
7	15.	TEMPTATION RAG (5)
14	16.	HEAVEN WILL PROTECT THE WORKING GIRL (2)
–	17.	THAT'S YIDDISHA LOVE (1)
–	18.	ALL THAT I ASK OF YOU IS LOVE (1)
15	19.	WHERE THE RIVER SHANNON FLOWS (5)
–	20.	WITHOUT YOU THE WORLD DON'T SEEM THE SAME (1)

OCTOBER 1910

LM	TM	
5	1.	SOME OF THESE DAYS (2)
6	2.	PLAY THAT BARBERSHOP CHORD (2)
2	3.	ANY LITTLE GIRL THAT'S A NICE LITTLE GIRL (3)
7	4.	EVERY LITTLE MOVEMENT (3)
1	5.	MEET ME TONIGHT IN DREAMLAND (12)
8	6.	MY HEART HAS LEARNED TO LOVE YOU, NOW DO NOT SAY GOOD-BYE (4)
13	7.	CASEY JONES (3)
18	8.	ALL THAT I ASK OF YOU IS LOVE (2)
4	9.	WHAT'S THE MATTER WITH FATHER? (6)
11	10.	SOMEBODY ELSE, IT'S ALWAYS SOMEBODY ELSE (3)
3	11.	I'VE GOT THE TIME, I'VE GOT THE PLACE, BUT IT'S HARD TO FIND THE GIRL (6)
17	12.	THAT'S YIDDISHA LOVE (2)
16	13.	HEAVEN WILL PROTECT THE WORKING GIRL (3)
12	14.	IN THE GARDEN OF MY HEART (11)
19	15.	WHERE THE RIVER SHANNON FLOWS (6)
–	16.	IF HE COMES IN, I'M GOING OUT (1)
15	17.	TEMPTATION RAG (6)
10	18.	CALL ME UP SOME RAINY AFTERNOON (5)
–	19.	SILVER BELL (1)
20	20.	WITHOUT YOU THE WORLD DON'T SEEM THE SAME (2)

NOVEMBER 1910

LM	TM	
1	1.	SOME OF THESE DAYS (3)
2	2.	PLAY THAT BARBERSHOP CHORD (3)
4	3.	EVERY LITTLE MOVEMENT (4)
3	4.	ANY LITTLE GIRL THAT'S A NICE LITTLE GIRL (4)
8	5.	ALL THAT I ASK OF YOU IS LOVE (3)
6	6.	MY HEART HAS LEARNED TO LOVE YOU, NOW DO NOT SAY GOOD-BYE (5)
7	7.	CASEY JONES (4)
12	8.	THAT'S YIDDISHA LOVE (3)
16	9.	IF HE COMES IN, I'M GOING OUT (2)
19	10.	SILVER BELL (2)
15	11.	WHERE THE RIVER SHANNON FLOWS (7)
5	12.	MEET ME TONIGHT IN DREAMLAND (13)
11	13.	I'VE GOT THE TIME, I'VE GOT THE PLACE, BUT IT'S HARD TO FIND THE GIRL (7)
14	14.	IN THE GARDEN OF MY HEART (12)
10	15.	SOMEBODY ELSE, IT'S ALWAYS SOMEBODY ELSE (4)
9	16.	WHAT'S THE MATTER WITH FATHER? (7)
–	17.	UNDER THE YUM YUM TREE (1)
20	18.	WITHOUT YOU THE WORLD DON'T SEEM THE SAME (3)
–	19.	LET ME CALL YOU SWEETHEART (1)
13	20.	HEAVEN WILL PROTECT THE WORKING GIRL (4)

DECEMBER 1910

LM	TM	
1	1.	SOME OF THESE DAYS (4)
3	2.	EVERY LITTLE MOVEMENT (5)
2	3.	PLAY THAT BARBERSHOP CHORD (4)
4	4.	ANY LITTLE GIRL THAT'S A NICE LITTLE GIRL (5)
7	5.	CASEY JONES (5)
5	6.	ALL THAT I ASK OF YOU IS LOVE (4)
10	7	SILVER BELL (3)
6	8.	MY HEART HAS LEARNED TO LOVE YOU, NOW DO NOT SAY GOOD-BYE (6)
9	9.	IF HE COMES IN, I'M GOING OUT (3)
17	10.	UNDER THE YUM YUM TREE (2)
19	11.	LET ME CALL YOU SWEETHEART (2)
8	12.	THAT'S YIDDISHA LOVE (4)
11	13.	WHERE THE RIVER SHANNON FLOWS (8)
14	14.	IN THE GARDEN OF MY HEART (13)
–	15.	SUGAR MOON (1)
16	16.	WHAT'S THE MATTER WITH FATHER? (8)
12	17.	MEET ME TONIGHT IN DREAMLAND (14)
15	18.	SOMEBODY ELSE, IT'S ALWAYS SOMEBODY ELSE (5)
–	19.	TEMPTATION RAG (7)
–	20.	TAKE ME BACK TO BABYLAND (1)

JANUARY 1911

LM	TM	
2	1.	EVERY LITTLE MOVEMENT (6)
1	2.	SOME OF THESE DAYS (5)
5	3.	CASEY JONES (6)
11	4.	LET ME CALL YOU SWEETHEART (3)
3	5.	PLAY THAT BARBERSHOP CHORD (5)
7	6	SILVER BELL (4)
10	7.	UNDER THE YUM YUM TREE (3)
6	8.	ALL THAT I ASK OF YOU IS LOVE (5)
4	9.	ANY LITTLE GIRL THAT'S A NICE LITTLE GIRL (6)
8	10.	MY HEART HAS LEARNED TO LOVE YOU, NOW DO NOT SAY GOOD-BYE (7)
9	11.	IF HE COMES IN, I'M GOING OUT (4)
13	12.	WHERE THE RIVER SHANNON FLOWS (9)
14	13.	IN THE GARDEN OF MY HEART (14)
15	14.	SUGAR MOON (2)
12	15.	THAT'S YIDDISHA LOVE (5)
16	16.	WHAT'S THE MATTER WITH FATHER? (9)
20	17.	TAKE ME BACK TO BABYLAND (2)
–	18.	I'LL CHANGE THE THORNS TO ROSES (1)
–	19.	THAT MINOR STRAIN (1)
–	20.	THAT BEAUTIFUL RAG (1)

FEBRUARY 1911

LM	TM	
4	1.	LET ME CALL YOU SWEETHEART (4)
1	2.	EVERY LITTLE MOVEMENT (7)
2	3.	SOME OF THESE DAYS (6)
7	4.	UNDER THE YUM YUM TREE (4)
3	5.	CASEY JONES (7)
6	6	SILVER BELL (5)
8	7.	ALL THAT I ASK OF YOU IS LOVE (6)
–	8.	COME, JOSEPHINE, IN MY FLYING MACHINE (1)
–	9.	I'M LOOKING FOR A NICE YOUNG FELLOW (1)
5	10.	PLAY THAT BARBERSHOP CHORD (6)
10	11.	MY HEART HAS LEARNED TO LOVE YOU, NOW DO NOT SAY GOOD-BYE (8)
9	12.	ANY LITTLE GIRL THAT'S A NICE LITTLE GIRL (7)
–	13.	I'M FALLING IN LOVE WITH SOMEONE (1)
11	14.	IF HE COMES IN, I'M GOING OUT (5)
12	15.	WHERE THE RIVER SHANNON FLOWS (10)
13	16.	IN THE GARDEN OF MY HEART (15)
–	17.	ITALIAN STREET SONG (1)
18	18.	I'LL CHANGE THE THORNS TO ROSES (2)
14	19.	SUGAR MOON (3)
–	20.	MY HERO (1)

MARCH 1911

LM	TM	
1	1.	LET ME CALL YOU SWEETHEART (5)
8	2.	COME, JOSEPHINE, IN MY FLYING MACHINE (2)
9	3.	I'M LOOKING FOR A NICE YOUNG FELLOW (2)
5	4.	CASEY JONES (8)
2	5.	EVERY LITTLE MOVEMENT (8)
–	6.	PUT YOUR ARMS AROUND ME, HONEY (1)
–	7.	KISS ME, MY HONEY, KISS ME (1)
3	8.	SOME OF THESE DAYS (7)
4	9.	UNDER THE YUM YUM TREE (5)
13	10.	I'M FALLING IN LOVE WITH SOMEONE (2)
–	11.	GEE, BUT IT'S GREAT TO MEET A FRIEND FROM YOUR HOME TOWN (1)
6	12	SILVER BELL (6)
17	13.	ITALIAN STREET SONG (2)
–	14.	ALL ABOARD FOR BLANKET BAY (1)
7	15.	ALL THAT I ASK OF YOU IS LOVE (7)
20	16.	MY HERO (2)
–	17.	THAT DREAMY ITALIAN WALTZ (1)
–	18.	DAY DREAMS (VISIONS OF BLISS) (1)
11	19.	MY HEART HAS LEARNED TO LOVE YOU, NOW DO NOT SAY GOOD-BYE (9)
–	20.	ALMA (WHERE DO YOU LIVE?) (1)

APRIL 1911

LM	TM	
2	1.	COME, JOSEPHINE, IN MY FLYING MACHINE (3)
1	2.	LET ME CALL YOU SWEETHEART (6)
6	3.	PUT YOUR ARMS AROUND ME, HONEY (2)
7	4.	KISS ME, MY HONEY, KISS ME (2)
11	5.	GEE, BUT IT'S GREAT TO MEET A FRIEND FROM YOUR HOME TOWN (2)
14	6.	ALL ABOARD FOR BLANKET BAY (2)
3	7.	I'M LOOKING FOR A NICE YOUNG FELLOW (3)
10	8.	I'M FALLING IN LOVE WITH SOMEONE (3)
18	9.	DAY DREAMS (VISIONS OF BLISS) (2)
4	10.	CASEY JONES (9)
–	11.	STEAMBOAT BILL (1)
–	12.	ON MOBILE BAY (1)
–	13.	DOWN BY THE OLD MILL STREAM (1)
5	14.	EVERY LITTLE MOVEMENT (9)
13	15.	ITALIAN STREET SONG (3)
12	16.	SILVER BELL (7)
–	17.	THERE'LL COME A TIME (1)
–	18.	DON'T WAKE ME UP, I'M DREAMING (1)
–	19.	THAT WAS BEFORE I MET YOU (1)
16	20.	MY HERO (3)

MAY 1911

LM	TM	
3	1.	PUT YOUR ARMS AROUND ME, HONEY (3)
2	2.	LET ME CALL YOU SWEETHEART (7)
1	3.	COME, JOSEPHINE, IN MY FLYING MACHINE (4)
5	4.	GEE, BUT IT'S GREAT TO MEET A FRIEND FROM YOUR HOME TOWN (3)
6	5.	ALL ABOARD FOR BLANKET BAY (3)
9	6.	DAY DREAMS (VISIONS OF BLISS) (3)
4	7.	KISS ME, MY HONEY, KISS ME (3)
11	8.	STEAMBOAT BILL (2)
8	9.	I'M FALLING IN LOVE WITH SOMEONE (4)
13	10.	DOWN BY THE OLD MILL STREAM (2)
18	11.	DON'T WAKE ME UP, I'M DREAMING (2)
12	12.	ON MOBILE BAY (2)
17	13.	THERE'LL COME A TIME (2)
7	14.	I'M LOOKING FOR A NICE YOUNG FELLOW (4)
19	15.	THAT WAS BEFORE I MET YOU (2)
–	16.	TWO LITTLE LOVE BEES (1)
20	17.	MY HERO (4)
–	18.	JIMMY VALENTINE (1)
15	19.	ITALIAN STREET SONG (4)
–	20.	ALMA (WHERE DO YOU LIVE?) (2)

JUNE 1911

LM	TM	
1	1.	PUT YOUR ARMS AROUND ME, HONEY (4)
4	2.	GEE, BUT IT'S GREAT TO MEET A FRIEND FROM YOUR HOME TOWN (4)
2	3.	LET ME CALL YOU SWEETHEART (8)
10	4.	DOWN BY THE OLD MILL STREAM (3)
5	5.	ALL ABOARD FOR BLANKET BAY (4)
6	6.	DAY DREAMS (VISIONS OF BLISS) (4)
8	7.	STEAMBOAT BILL (3)
3	8.	COME, JOSEPHINE, IN MY FLYING MACHINE (5)
11	9.	DON'T WAKE ME UP, I'M DREAMING (3)
12	10.	ON MOBILE BAY (3)
7	11.	KISS ME, MY HONEY, KISS ME (4)
16	12.	TWO LITTLE LOVE BEES (2)
–	13.	ALL ALONE (1)
18	14.	JIMMY VALENTINE (2)
17	15.	MY HERO (5)
9	16.	I'M FALLING IN LOVE WITH SOMEONE (5)
15	17.	THAT WAS BEFORE I MET YOU (3)
13	18.	THERE'LL COME A TIME (3)
–	19.	BABY ROSE (1)
20	20.	ALMA (WHERE DO YOU LIVE?) (3)

JULY 1911

LM	TM	
4	1.	DOWN BY THE OLD MILL STREAM (4)
1	2.	PUT YOUR ARMS AROUND ME, HONEY (5)
7	3.	STEAMBOAT BILL (4)
13	4.	ALL ALONE (2)
5	5.	ALL ABOARD FOR BLANKET BAY (5)
3	6.	LET ME CALL YOU SWEETHEART (9)
2	7.	GEE, BUT IT'S GREAT TO MEET A FRIEND FROM YOUR HOME TOWN (5)
19	8.	BABY ROSE (2)
6	9.	DAY DREAMS (VISIONS OF BLISS) (5)
12	10.	TWO LITTLE LOVE BEES (3)
9	11.	DON'T WAKE ME UP, I'M DREAMING (4)
15	12.	MY HERO (6)
8	13.	COME, JOSEPHINE, IN MY FLYING MACHINE (6)
14	14.	JIMMY VALENTINE (3)
10	15.	ON MOBILE BAY (4)
–	16.	I LIKE THE HAT, I LIKE THE DRESS, AND I LIKE THE GIRL THAT'S IN IT (1)
–	17.	BY THE SASKATCHEWAN (1)
11	18.	KISS ME, MY HONEY, KISS ME (5)
–	19.	THAT RAILROAD RAG (1)
–	20.	OCEANA ROLL (1)

AUGUST 1911

LM	TM	
1	1.	DOWN BY THE OLD MILL STREAM (5)
4	2.	ALL ALONE (3)
8	3.	BABY ROSE (3)
3	4.	STEAMBOAT BILL (5)
5	5.	ALL ABOARD FOR BLANKET BAY (6)
2	6.	PUT YOUR ARMS AROUND ME, HONEY (6)
6	7.	LET ME CALL YOU SWEETHEART (10)
20	8.	OCEANA ROLL (2)
16	9.	I LIKE THE HAT, I LIKE THE DRESS, AND I LIKE THE GIRL THAT'S IN IT (2)
7	10.	GEE, BUT IT'S GREAT TO MEET A FRIEND FROM YOUR HOME TOWN (6)
12	11.	MY HERO (7)
–	12.	IN THE LAND OF HARMONY (1)
10	13.	TWO LITTLE LOVE BEES (4)
11	14.	DON'T WAKE ME UP, I'M DREAMING (5)
14	15.	JIMMY VALENTINE (4)
–	16.	CHICKEN REEL (1)
9	17.	DAY DREAMS (VISIONS OF BLISS) (6)
19	18.	THAT RAILROAD RAG (2)
–	19.	CAN'T YOU TAKE IT BACK AND CHANGE IT FOR A BOY? (1)
–	20.	IN THE GARDEN OF MY HEART (16)

SEPTEMBER 1911

LM	TM	
1	1.	DOWN BY THE OLD MILL STREAM (6)
8	2.	OCEANA ROLL (3)
2	3.	ALL ALONE (4)
3	4.	BABY ROSE (4)
–	5.	ALEXANDER'S RAGTIME BAND (1)
4	6.	STEAMBOAT BILL (6)
9	7.	I LIKE THE HAT, I LIKE THE DRESS, AND I LIKE THE GIRL THAT'S IN IT (3)
7	8.	LET ME CALL YOU SWEETHEART (11)
5	9.	ALL ABOARD FOR BLANKET BAY (7)
12	10.	IN THE LAND OF HARMONY (2)
–	11.	I WANT A GIRL (JUST LIKE THE GIRL WHO MARRIED DEAR OLD DAD) (1)
16	12.	CHICKEN REEL (2)
–	13.	MY BEAUTIFUL LADY (1)
11	14.	MY HERO (8)
10	15.	GEE, BUT IT'S GREAT TO MEET A FRIEND FROM YOUR HOME TOWN (7)
6	16.	PUT YOUR ARMS AROUND ME, HONEY (7)
–	17.	BILLY (1)
–	18.	ALMA (WHERE DO YOU LIVE?) (4)
–	19.	THE HARBOR OF LOVE (1)
20	20.	IN THE GARDEN OF MY HEART (17)

OCTOBER 1911

LM	TM	
5	1.	ALEXANDER'S RAGTIME BAND (2)
2	2.	OCEANA ROLL (4)
1	3.	DOWN BY THE OLD MILL STREAM (7)
11	4.	I WANT A GIRL (JUST LIKE THE GIRL WHO MARRIED DEAR OLD DAD) (2)
4	5.	BABY ROSE (5)
7	6.	I LIKE THE HAT, I LIKE THE DRESS, AND I LIKE THE GIRL THAT'S IN IT (4)
19	7.	THE HARBOR OF LOVE (2)
13	8.	MY BEAUTIFUL LADY (2)
17	9.	BILLY (2)
3	10.	ALL ALONE (5)
8	11.	LET ME CALL YOU SWEETHEART (12)
12	12.	CHICKEN REEL (3)
10	13.	IN THE LAND OF HARMONY (3)
–	14.	THEY ALWAYS PICK ON ME (1)
–	15.	MY LOVIN' HONEY MAN (1)
14	16.	MY HERO (9)
9	17.	ALL ABOARD FOR BLANKET BAY (8)
6	18.	STEAMBOAT BILL (7)
–	19.	MOTHER MACHREE (1)
–	20.	CHILD LOVE (1)

NOVEMBER 1911

LM	TM	
1	1.	ALEXANDER'S RAGTIME BAND (3)
4	2.	I WANT A GIRL (JUST LIKE THE GIRL WHO MARRIED DEAR OLD DAD) (3)
2	3.	OCEANA ROLL (5)
3	4.	DOWN BY THE OLD MILL STREAM (8)
7	5.	THE HARBOR OF LOVE (3)
9	6.	BILLY (3)
5	7.	BABY ROSE (6)
6	8.	I LIKE THE HAT, I LIKE THE DRESS, AND I LIKE THE GIRL THAT'S IN IT (5)
8	9.	MY BEAUTIFUL LADY (3)
15	10.	MY LOVIN' HONEY MAN (2)
14	11.	THEY ALWAYS PICK ON ME (2)
12	12.	CHICKEN REEL (4)
–	13.	THAT MYSTERIOUS RAG (1)
11	14.	LET ME CALL YOU SWEETHEART (13)
–	15.	IN THE SHADOWS (1)
13	16.	IN THE LAND OF HARMONY (4)
–	17.	(HONKY TONKY) MONKEY RAG (1)
–	18.	OH, YOU BEAUTIFUL DOLL (1)
10	19.	ALL ALONE (6)
19	20.	MOTHER MACHREE (2)

DECEMBER 1911

LM	TM	
1	1.	ALEXANDER'S RAGTIME BAND (4)
2	2.	I WANT A GIRL (JUST LIKE THE GIRL WHO MARRIED DEAR OLD DAD) (4)
3	3.	OCEANA ROLL (6)
6	4.	BILLY (4)
18	5.	OH, YOU BEAUTIFUL DOLL (2)
4	6.	DOWN BY THE OLD MILL STREAM (9)
10	7.	MY LOVIN' HONEY MAN (3)
9	8.	MY BEAUTIFUL LADY (4)
13	9.	THAT MYSTERIOUS RAG (2)
5	10.	THE HARBOR OF LOVE (4)
8	11.	I LIKE THE HAT, I LIKE THE DRESS, AND I LIKE THE GIRL THAT'S IN IT (6)
7	12.	BABY ROSE (7)
17	13.	(HONKY TONKY) MONKEY RAG (2)
15	14.	IN THE SHADOWS (2)
20	15.	MOTHER MACHREE (3)
–	16.	KNOCK WOOD (1)
11	17.	THEY ALWAYS PICK ON ME (3)
14	18.	LET ME CALL YOU SWEETHEART (14)
–	19.	ROAMIN' IN THE GLOAMIN' (1)
–	20.	CHICKEN RAG (1)

JANUARY 1912

LM	TM	
1	1.	ALEXANDER'S RAGTIME BAND (5)
2	2.	I WANT A GIRL (JUST LIKE THE GIRL WHO MARRIED DEAR OLD DAD) (5)
5	3.	OH, YOU BEAUTIFUL DOLL (3)
3	4.	OCEANA ROLL (7)
9	5.	THAT MYSTERIOUS RAG (3)
4	6.	BILLY (5)
6	7.	DOWN BY THE OLD MILL STREAM (10)
8	8.	MY BEAUTIFUL LADY (5)
11	9.	I LIKE THE HAT, I LIKE THE DRESS, AND I LIKE THE GIRL THAT'S IN IT (7)
14	10.	IN THE SHADOWS (3)
–	11.	IF YOU TALK IN YOUR SLEEP, DON'T MENTION MY NAME (1)
7	12.	MY LOVIN' HONEY MAN (4)
13	13.	(HONKY TONKY) MONKEY RAG (3)
10	14.	THE HARBOR OF LOVE (5)
12	15.	BABY ROSE (8)
15	16.	MOTHER MACHREE (4)
–	17.	THERE'S A GIRL IN HAVANA (1)
20	18.	CHICKEN RAG (2)
–	19.	I'D LOVE TO LIVE IN LOVELAND WITH A GIRL LIKE YOU (1)
–	20.	MY HERO (10)

FEBRUARY 1912

LM	TM	
3	1.	OH, YOU BEAUTIFUL DOLL (4)
2	2.	I WANT A GIRL (JUST LIKE THE GIRL WHO MARRIED DEAR OLD DAD) (6)
1	3.	ALEXANDER'S RAGTIME BAND (6)
5	4.	THAT MYSTERIOUS RAG (4)
11	5.	IF YOU TALK IN YOUR SLEEP, DON'T MENTION MY NAME (2)
10	6.	IN THE SHADOWS (4)
4	7.	OCEANA ROLL (8)
8	8.	MY BEAUTIFUL LADY (6)
6	9.	BILLY (6)
16	10.	MOTHER MACHREE (5)
7	11.	DOWN BY THE OLD MILL STREAM (11)
9	12.	I LIKE THE HAT, I LIKE THE DRESS, AND I LIKE THE GIRL THAT'S IN IT (8)
–	13.	RUM TUM TIDDLE (1)
13	14.	(HONKY TONKY) MONKEY RAG (4)
17	15.	THERE'S A GIRL IN HAVANA (2)
19	16.	I'D LOVE TO LIVE IN LOVELAND WITH A GIRL LIKE YOU (2)
12	17.	MY LOVIN' HONEY MAN (5)
14	18.	THE HARBOR OF LOVE (6)
15	19.	BABY ROSE (9)
–	20.	I LOVE LOVE (1)

MARCH 1912

LM	TM	
1	1.	OH, YOU BEAUTIFUL DOLL (5)
4	2.	THAT MYSTERIOUS RAG (5)
3	3.	ALEXANDER'S RAGTIME BAND (7)
2	4.	I WANT A GIRL (JUST LIKE THE GIRL WHO MARRIED DEAR OLD DAD) (7)
5	5.	IF YOU TALK IN YOUR SLEEP, DON'T MENTION MY NAME (3)
6	6.	IN THE SHADOWS (5)
13	7.	RUM TUM TIDDLE (2)
–	8.	EVERYBODY'S DOIN' IT NOW (1)
8	9.	MY BEAUTIFUL LADY (7)
10	10.	MOTHER MACHREE (6)
–	11.	THAT HAUNTING MELODY (1)
7	12.	OCEANA ROLL (9)
–	13.	ANOTHER RAG (1)
–	14.	A WEE LITTLE DROP O' THE CRUISKEEN LAWN (1)
16	15.	I'D LOVE TO LIVE IN LOVELAND WITH A GIRL LIKE YOU (3)
9	16.	BILLY (7)
12	17.	I LIKE THE HAT, I LIKE THE DRESS, AND I LIKE THE GIRL THAT'S IN IT (9)
–	18.	OH, MR. DREAM MAN (1)
14	19.	(HONKY TONKY) MONKEY RAG (5)
11	20.	DOWN BY THE OLD MILL STREAM (12)

APRIL 1912

LM	TM	
1	1.	OH, YOU BEAUTIFUL DOLL (6)
8	2.	EVERYBODY'S DOIN' IT NOW (2)
7	3.	RUM TUM TIDDLE (3)
3	4.	ALEXANDER'S RAGTIME BAND (8)
11	5.	THAT HAUNTING MELODY (2)
6	6.	IN THE SHADOWS (6)
–	7.	THE GABY GLIDE (1)
2	8.	THAT MYSTERIOUS RAG (6)
5	9.	IF YOU TALK IN YOUR SLEEP, DON'T MENTION MY NAME (4)
10	10.	MOTHER MACHREE (7)
4	11.	I WANT A GIRL (JUST LIKE THE GIRL WHO MARRIED DEAR OLD DAD) (8)
–	12.	WHEN I WAS TWENTY-ONE AND YOU WERE SWEET SIXTEEN (1)
–	13.	RAGTIME VIOLIN (1)
–	14.	TAKE ME BACK TO THE GARDEN OF LOVE (1)
18	15.	OH, MR. DREAM MAN (2)
–	16.	MOONLIGHT BAY (1)
9	17.	MY BEAUTIFUL LADY (8)
14	18.	A WEE LITTLE DROP O' THE CRUISKEEN LAWN (2)
13	19.	ANOTHER RAG (2)
–	20.	JIMMY VALENTINE (5)

MAY 1912

LM	TM	
2	1.	EVERYBODY'S DOIN' IT NOW (3)
7	2.	THE GABY GLIDE (2)
1	3.	OH, YOU BEAUTIFUL DOLL (7)
12	4.	WHEN I WAS TWENTY-ONE AND YOU WERE SWEET SIXTEEN (2)
3	5.	RUM TUM TIDDLE (4)
13	6.	RAGTIME VIOLIN (2)
5	7.	THAT HAUNTING MELODY (3)
15	8.	OH, MR. DREAM MAN (3)
6	9.	IN THE SHADOWS (7)
16	10.	MOONLIGHT BAY (2)
14	11.	TAKE ME BACK TO THE GARDEN OF LOVE (2)
–	12.	THEY GOTTA QUIT KICKIN' MY DAWG AROUND (1)
4	13.	ALEXANDER'S RAGTIME BAND (9)
–	14.	GOODBYE, ROSE (1)
8	15.	THAT MYSTERIOUS RAG (7)
10	16.	MOTHER MACHREE (8)
–	17.	AT THE RAGTIME BALL (1)
–	18.	"IN THE GLOAMING" WAS THE SONG SHE SANG TO ME (1)
–	19.	LADY ANGELINE (1)
9	20.	IF YOU TALK IN YOUR SLEEP, DON'T MENTION MY NAME (5)

JUNE 1912

LM	TM	
1	1.	EVERYBODY'S DOIN' IT NOW (4)
2	2.	THE GABY GLIDE (3)
6	3.	RAGTIME VIOLIN (3)
4	4.	WHEN I WAS TWENTY-ONE AND YOU WERE SWEET SIXTEEN (3)
10	5.	MOONLIGHT BAY (3)
8	6.	OH, MR. DREAM MAN (4)
3	7.	OH, YOU BEAUTIFUL DOLL (8)
5	8.	RUM TUM TIDDLE (5)
9	9.	IN THE SHADOWS (8)
14	10.	GOODBYE, ROSE (2)
12	11.	THEY GOTTA QUIT KICKIN' MY DAWG AROUND (2)
16	12.	MOTHER MACHREE (9)
–	13.	LOVE IS MINE (1)
19	14.	LADY ANGELINE (2)
7	15.	THAT HAUNTING MELODY (4)
18	16.	"IN THE GLOAMING" WAS THE SONG SHE SANG TO ME (2)
–	17.	RAGGING THE BABY TO SLEEP (1)
–	18.	OH! YOU CIRCUS DAY (1)
15	19.	THAT MYSTERIOUS RAG (8)
11	20.	TAKE ME BACK TO THE GARDEN OF LOVE (3)

JULY 1912

LM	TM	
5	1.	MOONLIGHT BAY (4)
1	2.	EVERYBODY'S DOIN' IT NOW (5)
2	3.	THE GABY GLIDE (4)
3	4.	RAGTIME VIOLIN (4)
4	5.	WHEN I WAS TWENTY-ONE AND YOU WERE SWEET SIXTEEN (4)
6	6.	OH, MR. DREAM MAN (5)
18	7.	OH! YOU CIRCUS DAY (2)
9	8.	IN THE SHADOWS (9)
17	9.	RAGGING THE BABY TO SLEEP (2)
8	10.	RUM TUM TIDDLE (6)
–	11.	TAKE A LITTLE TIP FROM FATHER (1)
10	12.	GOODBYE, ROSE (3)
13	13.	LOVE IS MINE (2)
12	14.	MOTHER MACHREE (10)
–	15.	TILL THE SANDS OF THE DESERT GROW COLD (1)
11	16.	THEY GOTTA QUIT KICKIN' MY DAWG AROUND (3)
16	17.	"IN THE GLOAMING" WAS THE SONG SHE SANG TO ME (3)
–	18.	A GARLAND OF OLD FASHIONED ROSES (1)
14	19.	LADY ANGELINE (3)
7	20.	OH, YOU BEAUTIFUL DOLL (9)

AUGUST 1912

LM	TM	
1	1.	MOONLIGHT BAY (5)
7	2.	OH! YOU CIRCUS DAY (3)
4	3.	RAGTIME VIOLIN (5)
3	4.	THE GABY GLIDE (5)
2	5.	EVERYBODY'S DOIN' IT NOW (6)
11	6.	TAKE A LITTLE TIP FROM FATHER (2)
9	7.	RAGGING THE BABY TO SLEEP (3)
–	8.	WAITING FOR THE ROBERT E. LEE (1)
15	9.	TILL THE SANDS OF THE DESERT GROW COLD (2)
6	10.	OH, MR. DREAM MAN (6)
8	11.	IN THE SHADOWS (10)
14	12.	MOTHER MACHREE (11)
10	13.	RUM TUM TIDDLE (7)
12	14.	GOODBYE, ROSE (4)
18	15.	A GARLAND OF OLD FASHIONED ROSES (2)
–	16.	WAY DOWN SOUTH (1)
13	17.	LOVE IS MINE (3)
–	18.	KENTUCKY DAYS (1)
5	19.	WHEN I WAS TWENTY-ONE AND YOU WERE SWEET SIXTEEN (5)
17	20.	"IN THE GLOAMING" WAS THE SONG SHE SANG TO ME (4)

SEPTEMBER 1912

LM	TM	
1	1.	MOONLIGHT BAY (6)
8	2.	WAITING FOR THE ROBERT E. LEE (2)
2	3.	OH! YOU CIRCUS DAY (4)
9	4.	TILL THE SANDS OF THE DESERT GROW COLD (3)
3	5.	RAGTIME VIOLIN (6)
7	6.	RAGGING THE BABY TO SLEEP (4)
6	7.	TAKE A LITTLE TIP FROM FATHER (3)
11	8.	IN THE SHADOWS (11)
–	9.	WHEN I GET YOU ALONE TONIGHT (1)
18	10.	KENTUCKY DAYS (2)
–	11.	DREAMS OF LONG AGO (1)
4	12.	THE GABY GLIDE (6)
–	13.	I LOVE YOU TRULY ' (1)
5	14.	EVERYBODY'S DOIN' IT NOW (7)
16	15.	WAY DOWN SOUTH (2)
15	16.	A GARLAND OF OLD FASHIONED ROSES (3)
10	17.	OH, MR. DREAM MAN (7)
–	18.	RAGTIME COWBOY JOE (1)
–	19.	THAT'S HOW I NEED YOU (1)
–	20.	YOU'RE MY BABY (1)

OCTOBER 1912

LM	TM	
2	1.	WAITING FOR THE ROBERT E. LEE (3)
1	2.	MOONLIGHT BAY (7)
3	3.	OH! YOU CIRCUS DAY (5)
9	4.	WHEN I GET YOU ALONE TONIGHT (2)
4	5.	TILL THE SANDS OF THE DESERT GROW COLD (4)
19	6.	THAT'S HOW I NEED YOU (2)
20	7.	YOU'RE MY BABY (2)
11	8.	DREAMS OF LONG AGO (2)
13	9.	I LOVE YOU TRULY (2)
–	10.	THAT MELLOW MELODY (1)
18	11.	RAGTIME COWBOY JOE (2)
15	12.	WAY DOWN SOUTH (3)
7	13.	TAKE A LITTLE TIP FROM FATHER (4)
10	14.	KENTUCKY DAYS (3)
–	15.	WHEN YOU'RE AWAY (1)
16	16.	A GARLAND OF OLD FASHIONED ROSES (4)
8	17.	IN THE SHADOWS (12)
6	18.	RAGGING THE BABY TO SLEEP (5)
–	19.	THE SPIRIT OF INDEPENDENCE (1)
–	20.	ALL NIGHT LONG (1)

NOVEMBER 1912

LM	TM	
1	1.	WAITING FOR THE ROBERT E. LEE (4)
4	2.	WHEN I GET YOU ALONE TONIGHT (3)
6	3.	THAT'S HOW I NEED YOU (3)
7	4.	YOU'RE MY BABY (3)
5	5.	TILL THE SANDS OF THE DESERT GROW COLD (5)
10	6.	THAT MELLOW MELODY (2)
2	7.	MOONLIGHT BAY (8)
–	8.	HITCHY KOO (1)
3	9.	OH! YOU CIRCUS DAY (6)
–	10.	EVERYBODY TWO-STEP (1)
15	11.	WHEN YOU'RE AWAY (2)
11	12.	RAGTIME COWBOY JOE (3)
8	13.	DREAMS OF LONG AGO (3)
–	14.	WHEN UNCLE JOE PLAYS A RAG ON HIS OLD BANJO (1)
20	15.	ALL NIGHT LONG (2)
14	16.	KENTUCKY DAYS (4)
9	17.	I LOVE YOU TRULY (3)
16	18.	A GARLAND OF OLD FASHIONED ROSES (5)
–	19.	BE MY LITTLE BABY BUMBLE BEE (1)
12	20.	WAY DOWN SOUTH (4)

DECEMBER 1912

LM	TM	
1	1.	WAITING FOR THE ROBERT E. LEE (5)
3	2.	THAT'S HOW I NEED YOU (4)
2	3.	WHEN I GET YOU ALONE TONIGHT (4)
8	4.	HITCHY KOO (2)
10	5.	EVERYBODY TWO-STEP (2)
5	6.	TILL THE SANDS OF THE DESERT GROW COLD (6)
4	7.	YOU'RE MY BABY (4)
–	8.	ON THE MISSISSIPPI (1)
19	9.	BE MY LITTLE BABY BUMBLE BEE (2)
6	10.	THAT MELLOW MELODY (3)
14	11.	WHEN UNCLE JOE PLAYS A RAG ON HIS OLD BANJO (2)
–	12.	THE GHOST OF THE VIOLIN (1)
12	13.	RAGTIME COWBOY JOE (4)
15	14.	ALL NIGHT LONG (3)
9	15.	OH! YOU CIRCUS DAY (7)
7	16.	MOONLIGHT BAY (9)
–	17.	MOTHER MACHREE (12)
16	18.	KENTUCKY DAYS (5)
11	19.	WHEN YOU'RE AWAY (3)
20	20.	WAY DOWN SOUTH (5)

JANUARY 1913

LM	TM	
2	1.	THAT'S HOW I NEED YOU (5)
8	2.	ON THE MISSISSIPPI (2)
1	3.	WAITING FOR THE ROBERT E. LEE (6)
9	4.	BE MY LITTLE BABY BUMBLE BEE (3)
4	5.	HITCHY KOO (3)
3	6.	WHEN I GET YOU ALONE TONIGHT (5)
5	7.	EVERYBODY TWO-STEP (3)
6	8.	TILL THE SANDS OF THE DESERT GROW COLD (7)
–	9.	ROW, ROW, ROW (1)
12	10.	THE GHOST OF THE VIOLIN (2)
11	11.	WHEN UNCLE JOE PLAYS A RAG ON HIS OLD BANJO (3)
7	12.	YOU'RE MY BABY (5)
10	13.	THAT MELLOW MELODY (4)
14	14.	ALL NIGHT LONG (4)
13	15.	RAGTIME COWBOY JOE (5)
–	16.	THAT OLD GIRL OF MINE (1)
–	17.	BAGDAD (1)
15	18.	OH! YOU CIRCUS DAY (8)
16	19.	MOONLIGHT BAY (10)
–	20.	AFTER ALL THAT I'VE BEEN TO YOU (1)

FEBRUARY 1913

LM	TM	
2	1.	ON THE MISSISSIPPI (3)
1	2.	THAT'S HOW I NEED YOU (6)
4	3.	BE MY LITTLE BABY BUMBLE BEE (4)
9	4.	ROW, ROW, ROW (2)
16	7.	THAT OLD GIRL OF MINE (2)
3	5.	WAITING FOR THE ROBERT E. LEE (7)
8	6.	TILL THE SANDS OF THE DESERT GROW COLD (8)
5	8.	HITCHY KOO (4)
6	9.	WHEN I GET YOU ALONE TONIGHT (6)
7	10.	EVERYBODY TWO-STEP (4)
11	11.	WHEN UNCLE JOE PLAYS A RAG ON HIS OLD BANJO (4)
12	12.	YOU'RE MY BABY (6)
13	13.	THAT MELLOW MELODY (5)
15	14.	RAGTIME COWBOY JOE (6)
14	15.	ALL NIGHT LONG (5)
17	16.	BAGDAD (2)
18	17.	OH! YOU CIRCUS DAY (9)
–	18.	AT THE DEVIL'S BALL (1)
10	19.	THE GHOST OF THE VIOLIN (3)
–	20.	WAY DOWN SOUTH (6)

MARCH 1913

LM	TM	
4	1.	ROW, ROW, ROW (3)
7	2.	THAT OLD GIRL OF MINE (3)
1	3.	ON THE MISSISSIPPI (4)
2	4.	THAT'S HOW I NEED YOU (7)
3	5.	BE MY LITTLE BABY BUMBLE BEE (5)
5	6.	WAITING FOR THE ROBERT E. LEE (8)
6	7.	TILL THE SANDS OF THE DESERT GROW COLD (9)
18	8.	AT THE DEVIL'S BALL (2)
–	9.	WHEN THE MIDNIGHT CHOO-CHOO LEAVES FOR ALABAM' (1)
10	10.	EVERYBODY TWO-STEP (5)
11	11.	WHEN UNCLE JOE PLAYS A RAG ON HIS OLD BANJO (5)
9	12.	WHEN I GET YOU ALONE TONIGHT (7)
–	13.	AND THE GREEN GRASS GREW ALL AROUND (1)
8	14.	HITCHY KOO (5)
–	15.	WHEN I LOST YOU (1)
–	16.	THEN I'LL STOP LOVING YOU (1)
20	17.	WAY DOWN SOUTH (7)
13	18.	THAT MELLOW MELODY (6)
–	19.	DOWN IN DEAR OLD NEW ORLEANS (1)
12	20.	YOU'RE MY BABY (7)

APRIL 1913

LM	TM	
1	1.	ROW, ROW, ROW (4)
9	2.	WHEN THE MIDNIGHT CHOO-CHOO LEAVES FOR ALABAM' (2)
2	3.	THAT OLD GIRL OF MINE (4)
15	4.	WHEN I LOST YOU (2)
13	5.	AND THE GREEN GRASS GREW ALL AROUND (2)
8	6.	AT THE DEVIL'S BALL (3)
3	7.	ON THE MISSISSIPPI (5)
4	8.	THAT'S HOW I NEED YOU (8)
6	9.	WAITING FOR THE ROBERT E. LEE (9)
5	10.	BE MY LITTLE BABY BUMBLE BEE (6)
–	11.	DADDY HAS A SWEETHEART, AND MOTHER IS HER NAME (1)
–	12.	SOME BOY (1)
7	13.	TILL THE SANDS OF THE DESERT GROW COLD (10)
16	14.	THEN I'LL STOP LOVING YOU (2)
–	15.	GOOD NIGHT, NURSE (1)
10	16.	EVERYBODY TWO-STEP (6)
–	17.	MELINDA'S WEDDING DAY (1)
–	18.	ALL NIGHT LONG (6)
–	19.	YOU'RE A GREAT BIG BLUE-EYED BABY (1)
19	20.	DOWN IN DEAR OLD NEW ORLEANS (2)

MAY 1913

LM	TM	
2	1.	WHEN THE MIDNIGHT CHOO-CHOO LEAVES FOR ALABAM' (3)
4	2.	WHEN I LOST YOU (3)
1	3.	ROW, ROW, ROW (5)
11	4.	DADDY HAS A SWEETHEART, AND MOTHER IS HER NAME (2)
15	5.	GOOD NIGHT, NURSE (2)
5	6.	AND THE GREEN GRASS GREW ALL AROUND (3)
12	7.	SOME BOY (2)
6	8.	AT THE DEVIL'S BALL (4)
19	9.	YOU'RE A GREAT BIG BLUE-EYED BABY (2)
–	10.	THE TRAIL OF THE LONESOME PINE (1)
17	11.	MELINDA'S WEDDING DAY (2)
–	12.	HERE COMES MY DADDY NOW (1)
–	13.	GOODBYE, BOYS (1)
3	14.	THAT OLD GIRL OF MINE (5)
–	15.	WHEN IT'S APPLE BLOSSOM TIME IN NORMANDY (1)
9	16.	WAITING FOR THE ROBERT E. LEE (10)
–	17.	IN MY HAREM (1)
–	18.	WHEN IRISH EYES ARE SMILING (1)
–	19.	LAST NIGHT WAS THE END OF THE WORLD (1)
7	20.	ON THE MISSISSIPPI (6)

JUNE 1913

LM	TM	
2	1.	WHEN I LOST YOU (4)
10	2.	THE TRAIL OF THE LONESOME PINE (2)
9	3.	YOU'RE A GREAT BIG BLUE-EYED BABY (3)
1	4.	WHEN THE MIDNIGHT CHOO-CHOO LEAVES FOR ALABAM' (4)
11	5.	MELINDA'S WEDDING DAY (3)
3	6.	ROW, ROW, ROW (6)
17	7.	IN MY HAREM (2)
5	8.	GOOD NIGHT, NURSE (3)
7	9.	SOME BOY (3)
13	10.	GOODBYE, BOYS (2)
15	11.	WHEN IT'S APPLE BLOSSOM TIME IN NORMANDY (2)
4	12.	DADDY HAS A SWEETHEART, AND MOTHER IS HER NAME (3)
–	13.	SNOOKEY OOKUMS (1)
–	14.	THE CURSE OF AN ACHING HEART (1)
–	16.	A LITTLE BUNCH OF SHAMROCKS (1)
6	15.	AND THE GREEN GRASS GREW ALL AROUND (4)
18	17.	WHEN IRISH EYES ARE SMILING (2)
–	18.	THE SPANIARD THAT BLIGHTED MY LIFE (1)
12	19.	HERE COMES MY DADDY NOW (2)
8	20.	AT THE DEVIL'S BALL (5)

JULY 1913

LM	TM	
1	1.	WHEN I LOST YOU (5)
2	2.	THE TRAIL OF THE LONESOME PINE (3)
7	3.	IN MY HAREM (3)
3	4.	YOU'RE A GREAT BIG BLUE-EYED BABY (4)
10	5.	GOODBYE, BOYS (3)
13	6.	SNOOKEY OOKUMS (2)
11	7.	WHEN IT'S APPLE BLOSSOM TIME IN NORMANDY (3)
18	8.	THE SPANIARD THAT BLIGHTED MY LIFE (2)
14	9.	THE CURSE OF AN ACHING HEART (2)
4	10.	WHEN THE MIDNIGHT CHOO-CHOO LEAVES FOR ALABAM' (5)
5	11.	MELINDA'S WEDDING DAY (4)
16	12.	A LITTLE BUNCH OF SHAMROCKS (2)
6	13.	ROW, ROW, ROW (7)
–	14.	TO HAVE, TO HOLD, TO LOVE (1)
17	15.	WHEN IRISH EYES ARE SMILING (3)
9	16.	SOME BOY (4)
–	17.	LAST NIGHT WAS THE END OF THE WORLD (2)
–	18.	I HEAR YOU CALLING ME (1)
8	19.	GOOD NIGHT, NURSE (4)
–	20.	YOU MADE ME LOVE YOU (1)

AUGUST 1913

LM	TM	
2	1.	THE TRAIL OF THE LONESOME PINE (4)
9	2.	THE CURSE OF AN ACHING HEART (3)
3	3.	IN MY HAREM (4)
7	4.	WHEN IT'S APPLE BLOSSOM TIME IN NORMANDY (4)
1	5.	WHEN I LOST YOU (6)
5	6.	GOODBYE, BOYS (4)
20	7.	YOU MADE ME LOVE YOU (2)
14	8.	TO HAVE, TO HOLD, TO LOVE (2)
6	9.	SNOOKEY OOKUMS (3)
8	10.	THE SPANIARD THAT BLIGHTED MY LIFE (3)
4	11.	YOU'RE A GREAT BIG BLUE-EYED BABY (5)
12	12.	A LITTLE BUNCH OF SHAMROCKS (3)
11	13.	MELINDA'S WEDDING DAY (5)
–	14.	SWEETHEARTS (1)
–	15.	BOBBIN' UP AND DOWN (1)
17	16.	LAST NIGHT WAS THE END OF THE WORLD (3)
9	17.	WHEN THE MIDNIGHT CHOO-CHOO LEAVES FOR ALABAM' (6)
15	18.	WHEN IRISH EYES ARE SMILING (4)
–	19.	SYMPATHY (1)
13	20.	ROW, ROW, ROW (8)

SEPTEMBER 1913

LM	TM	
7	1.	YOU MADE ME LOVE YOU (3)
1	2.	THE TRAIL OF THE LONESOME PINE (5)
2	3.	THE CURSE OF AN ACHING HEART (4)
4	4.	WHEN IT'S APPLE BLOSSOM TIME IN NORMANDY (5)
3	5.	IN MY HAREM (5)
6	6.	GOODBYE, BOYS (5)
–	7.	PEG O' MY HEART (1)
5	8.	WHEN I LOST YOU (7)
8	9.	TO HAVE, TO HOLD, TO LOVE (3)
10	10.	THE SPANIARD THAT BLIGHTED MY LIFE (4)
9	11.	SNOOKEY OOKUMS (4)
–	12.	IT TAKES A LITTLE RAIN WITH THE SUNSHINE TO MAKE THE WORLD GO ROUND (1)
16	13.	LAST NIGHT WAS THE END OF THE WORLD (4)
15	14.	BOBBIN' UP AND DOWN (2)
11	15.	YOU'RE A GREAT BIG BLUE-EYED BABY (6)
14	16.	SWEETHEARTS (3)
12	17.	A LITTLE BUNCH OF SHAMROCKS (4)
19	18.	SYMPATHY (2)
–	19.	SOMEBODY'S COMING TO MY HOUSE (1)
18	20.	WHEN IRISH EYES ARE SMILING (5)

OCTOBER 1913

LM	TM	
1	1.	YOU MADE ME LOVE YOU (4)
7	2.	PEG O' MY HEART (2)
4	3.	WHEN IT'S APPLE BLOSSOM TIME IN NORMANDY (6)
2	4.	THE TRAIL OF THE LONESOME PINE (6)
–	5.	THAT INTERNATIONAL RAG (1)
3	6.	THE CURSE OF AN ACHING HEART (5)
19	7.	SOMEBODY'S COMING TO MY HOUSE (2)
12	8.	IT TAKES A LITTLE RAIN WITH THE SUNSHINE TO MAKE THE WORLD GO ROUND (2)
6	9.	GOODBYE, BOYS (6)
13	10.	LAST NIGHT WAS THE END OF THE WORLD (5)
9	11.	TO HAVE, TO HOLD, TO LOVE (4)
–	12.	THERE'S A GIRL IN THE HEART OF MARYLAND (1)
5	13.	IN MY HAREM (6)
–	14.	ON THE OLD FALL RIVER LINE (1)
8	15.	WHEN I LOST YOU (8)
–	16.	SAILING DOWN THE CHESAPEAKE BAY (1)
10	17.	THE SPANIARD THAT BLIGHTED MY LIFE (5)
–	18.	MAMMY JINNY'S JUBILEE (1)
18	19.	SYMPATHY (3)
11	20.	SNOOKEY OOKUMS (5)

NOVEMBER 1913

LM	TM	
1	1.	YOU MADE ME LOVE YOU (5)
2	2.	PEG O' MY HEART (3)
5	3.	THAT INTERNATIONAL RAG (2)
7	4.	SOMEBODY'S COMING TO MY HOUSE (3)
12	5.	THERE'S A GIRL IN THE HEART OF MARYLAND (2)
14	6.	ON THE OLD FALL RIVER LINE (2)
3	7.	WHEN IT'S APPLE BLOSSOM TIME IN NORMANDY (7)
10	8.	LAST NIGHT WAS THE END OF THE WORLD (6)
16	9.	SAILING DOWN THE CHESAPEAKE BAY (2)
4	10.	THE TRAIL OF THE LONESOME PINE (7)
18	11.	MAMMY JINNY'S JUBILEE (2)
9	12.	GOODBYE, BOYS (7)
6	13.	THE CURSE OF AN ACHING HEART (6)
–	14.	THE PULLMAN PORTERS ON PARADE (1)
–	15.	OH, YOU MILLION DOLLAR DOLL (1)
–	16.	WHERE DID YOU GET THAT GIRL? (1)
8	17.	IT TAKES A LITTLE RAIN WITH THE SUNSHINE TO MAKE THE WORLD GO ROUND (3)
11	18.	TO HAVE, TO HOLD, TO LOVE (5)
–	19.	YOU'VE GOT YOUR MOTHER'S BIG BLUE EYES (1)
–	20.	WHEN IRISH EYES ARE SMILING (6)

DECEMBER 1913

LM	TM	
2	1.	PEG O' MY HEART (4)
1	2.	YOU MADE ME LOVE YOU (6)
3	3.	THAT INTERNATIONAL RAG (3)
5	4.	THERE'S A GIRL IN THE HEART OF MARYLAND (3)
4	5.	SOMEBODY'S COMING TO MY HOUSE (4)
9	6.	SAILING DOWN THE CHESAPEAKE BAY (3)
6	7.	ON THE OLD FALL RIVER LINE (3)
16	8.	WHERE DID YOU GET THAT GIRL? (2)
8	9.	LAST NIGHT WAS THE END OF THE WORLD (7)
11	10.	MAMMY JINNY'S JUBILEE (3)
19	11.	YOU'VE GOT YOUR MOTHER'S BIG BLUE EYES (2)
15	12.	OH, YOU MILLION DOLLAR DOLL (2)
–	13.	ISLE D'AMOUR (1)
14	14.	THE PULLMAN PORTERS ON PARADE (2)
7	15.	WHEN IT'S APPLE BLOSSOM TIME IN NORMANDY (8)
–	16.	YOU CAN'T STOP ME FROM LOVING YOU (1)
–	17.	SUNSHINE AND ROSES (1)
20	18.	WHEN IRISH EYES ARE SMILING (7)
12	19.	GOODBYE, BOYS (8)
10	20.	THE TRAIL OF THE LONESOME PINE (8)

JANUARY 1914

LM	TM	
1	1.	PEG O' MY HEART (5)
4	2.	THERE'S A GIRL IN THE HEART OF MARYLAND (4)
3	3.	THAT INTERNATIONAL RAG (4)
2	4.	YOU MADE ME LOVE YOU (7)
8	5.	WHERE DID YOU GET THAT GIRL? (3)
6	6.	SAILING DOWN THE CHESAPEAKE BAY (4)
5	7.	SOMEBODY'S COMING TO MY HOUSE (5)
–	8.	HE'D HAVE TO GET UNDER, GET OUT AND GET UNDER, TO FIX UP HIS AUTOMOBILE (1)
13	9.	ISLE D'AMOUR (2)
11	10.	YOU'VE GOT YOUR MOTHER'S BIG BLUE EYES (3)
7	11.	ON THE OLD FALL RIVER LINE (4)
9	12.	LAST NIGHT WAS THE END OF THE WORLD (8)
12	13.	OH, YOU MILLION DOLLAR DOLL (3)
–	14.	DON'T BLAME IT ALL ON BROADWAY (1)
10	15.	MAMMY JINNY'S JUBILEE (4)
14	16.	THE PULLMAN PORTERS ON PARADE (3)
–	17.	NIGHTS OF GLADNESS (1)
17	18.	SUNSHINE AND ROSES (2)
18	19.	WHEN IRISH EYES ARE SMILING (8)
–	20.	I MISS YOU MOST OF ALL (1)

FEBRUARY 1914

LM	TM	
2	1.	THERE'S A GIRL IN THE HEART OF MARYLAND (5)
8	2.	HE'D HAVE TO GET UNDER, GET OUT AND GET UNDER, TO FIX UP HIS AUTOMOBILE (2)
5	3.	WHERE DID YOU GET THAT GIRL? (4)
1	4.	PEG O' MY HEART (6)
9	5.	ISLE D'AMOUR (3)
20	6.	I MISS YOU MOST OF ALL (2)
3	7.	THAT INTERNATIONAL RAG (5)
6	8.	SAILING DOWN THE CHESAPEAKE BAY (5)
4	9.	YOU MADE ME LOVE YOU (8)
17	10.	NIGHTS OF GLADNESS (2)
–	11.	I'M ON MY WAY TO MANDALAY (1)
12	13.	LAST NIGHT WAS THE END OF THE WORLD (9)
10	14.	YOU'VE GOT YOUR MOTHER'S BIG BLUE EYES (4)
14	12.	DON'T BLAME IT ALL ON BROADWAY (2)
13	15.	OH, YOU MILLION DOLLAR DOLL (4)
15	17.	MAMMY JINNY'S JUBILEE (5)
–	16.	DO YOU TAKE THIS WOMAN (1)
7	18.	SOMEBODY'S COMING TO MY HOUSE (6)
18	19.	SUNSHINE AND ROSES (3)
–	20.	TOO-RA LOO-RA LOO-RAL (1)

MARCH 1914

LM	TM	
2	1.	HE'D HAVE TO GET UNDER, GET OUT AND GET UNDER, TO FIX UP HIS AUTOMOBILE (3)
11	2.	I'M ON MY WAY TO MANDALAY (2)
6	3.	I MISS YOU MOST OF ALL (3)
3	4.	WHERE DID YOU GET THAT GIRL? (5)
16	5.	DO YOU TAKE THIS WOMAN (2)
5	6.	ISLE D'AMOUR (4)
10	7.	NIGHTS OF GLADNESS (3)
1	8.	THERE'S A GIRL IN THE HEART OF MARYLAND (6)
4	9.	PEG O' MY HEART (7)
–	10.	REBECCA OF SUNNYBROOK FARM (1)
8	11.	SAILING DOWN THE CHESAPEAKE BAY (6)
20	12.	TOO-RA LOO-RA LOO-RAL (2)
–	13.	WHILE THEY WERE DANCING AROUND (1)
7	14.	THAT INTERNATIONAL RAG (6)
–	15.	SIT DOWN, YOU'RE ROCKING THE BOAT (1)
–	16.	A LITTLE LOVE, A LITTLE KISS (1)
–	17.	ON THE GOOD SHIP MARY ANN (1)
13	18.	LAST NIGHT WAS THE END OF THE WORLD (10)
–	19.	I HEAR YOU CALLING ME (2)
–	20.	THIS IS THE LIFE (1)

APRIL 1914

LM	TM	
1	1.	HE'D HAVE TO GET UNDER, GET OUT AND GET UNDER, TO FIX UP HIS AUTOMOBILE (4)
10	2.	REBECCA OF SUNNYBROOK FARM (2)
20	3.	THIS IS THE LIFE (2)
2	4.	I'M ON MY WAY TO MANDALAY (3)
5	5.	DO YOU TAKE THIS WOMAN (3)
13	6.	WHILE THEY WERE DANCING AROUND (2)
3	7.	I MISS YOU MOST OF ALL (4)
17	8.	ON THE GOOD SHIP MARY ANN (2)
7	9.	NIGHTS OF GLADNESS (4)
–	10.	ALL ABOARD FOR DIXIE LAND (1)
–	11.	HE'S A DEVIL IN HIS OWN HOME TOWN (1)
12	12.	TOO-RA LOO-RA LOO-RAL (3)
4	13.	WHERE DID YOU GET THAT GIRL? (6)
6	14.	ISLE D'AMOUR (5)
–	15.	LITTLE GREY HOME IN THE WEST (1)
15	16.	SIT DOWN, YOU'RE ROCKING THE BOAT (2)
8	17.	THERE'S A GIRL IN THE HEART OF MARYLAND (7)
–	18.	SARI WALTZ (1)
16	19.	A LITTLE LOVE, A LITTLE KISS (2)
–	20.	DON'T BLAME IT ALL ON BROADWAY (3)

MAY 1914

LM	TM	
2	1.	REBECCA OF SUNNYBROOK FARM (3)
3	2.	THIS IS THE LIFE (3)
4	3.	I'M ON MY WAY TO MANDALAY (4)
1	4.	HE'D HAVE TO GET UNDER, GET OUT AND GET UNDER, TO FIX UP HIS AUTOMOBILE (5)
11	5.	HE'S A DEVIL IN HIS OWN HOME TOWN (2)
10	6.	ALL ABOARD FOR DIXIE LAND (2)
6	7.	WHILE THEY WERE DANCING AROUND (3)
8	8.	ON THE GOOD SHIP MARY ANN (3)
15	9.	LITTLE GREY HOME IN THE WEST (2)
–	10.	WHO PAID THE RENT FOR MRS. RIP VAN WINKLE? (1)
5	11.	DO YOU TAKE THIS WOMAN (4)
12	12.	TOO-RA LOO-RA LOO-RAL (4)
–	13.	MARY, YOU'RE A LITTLE BIT OLD FASHIONED (1)
9	14.	NIGHTS OF GLADNESS (5)
–	15.	WHEN THE ANGELUS IS RINGING (1)
–	16.	I LOVE THE LADIES (1)
16	17.	SIT DOWN, YOU'RE ROCKING THE BOAT (3)
–	18.	I MISS YOU MOST OF ALL (5)
–	19.	IF I HAD MY WAY (1)
18	20.	SARI WALTZ (2)

JUNE 1914

LM	TM	
2	1.	THIS IS THE LIFE (4)
5	2.	HE'S A DEVIL IN HIS OWN HOME TOWN (3)
1	3.	REBECCA OF SUNNYBROOK FARM (4)
3	4.	I'M ON MY WAY TO MANDALAY (5)
6	5.	ALL ABOARD FOR DIXIE LAND (3)
10	6.	WHO PAID THE RENT FOR MRS. RIP VAN WINKLE? (2)
4	7.	HE'D HAVE TO GET UNDER, GET OUT AND GET UNDER, TO FIX UP HIS AUTOMOBILE (6)
15	8.	WHEN THE ANGELUS IS RINGING (2)
16	9.	I LOVE THE LADIES (2)
13	10.	MARY, YOU'RE A LITTLE BIT OLD FASHIONED (2)
8	11.	ON THE GOOD SHIP MARY ANN (4)
9	12.	LITTLE GREY HOME IN THE WEST (3)
19	13.	IF I HAD MY WAY (2)
–	14.	WHEN YOU'RE ALL DRESSED UP AND NO PLACE TO GO (1)
–	15.	YOU PLANTED A ROSE IN THE GARDEN OF LOVE (1)
12	16.	TOO-RA LOO-RA LOO-RAL (5)
–	17.	IN THE CANDLELIGHT (1)
–	18.	CAMP MEETING BAND (1)
–	19.	BY THE BEAUTIFUL SEA (1)
7	20.	WHILE THEY WERE DANCING AROUND (4)

JULY 1914

LM	TM	
1	1.	THIS IS THE LIFE (5)
9	2.	I LOVE THE LADIES (3)
5	3.	ALL ABOARD FOR DIXIE LAND (4)
3	4.	REBECCA OF SUNNYBROOK FARM (5)
19	5.	BY THE BEAUTIFUL SEA (2)
2	6.	HE'S A DEVIL IN HIS OWN HOME TOWN (4)
6	7.	WHO PAID THE RENT FOR MRS. RIP VAN WINKLE? (3)
10	8.	MARY, YOU'RE A LITTLE BIT OLD FASHIONED (3)
8	9.	WHEN THE ANGELUS IS RINGING (3)
4	10.	I'M ON MY WAY TO MANDALAY (6)
14	11.	WHEN YOU'RE ALL DRESSED UP AND NO PLACE TO GO (2)
15	12.	YOU PLANTED A ROSE IN THE GARDEN OF LOVE (2)
–	13.	YOU'RE HERE AND I'M HERE (1)
–	14.	WHEN YOU PLAY IN THE GAME OF LOVE (1)
13	15.	IF I HAD MY WAY (3)
12	16.	LITTLE GREY HOME IN THE WEST (4)
11	17.	ON THE GOOD SHIP MARY ANN (5)
7	18.	HE'D HAVE TO GET UNDER, GET OUT AND GET UNDER, TO FIX UP HIS AUTOMOBILE (7)
17	19.	IN THE CANDLELIGHT (2)
–	20.	ROLL THEM COTTON BALES (1)

AUGUST 1914

LM	TM	
5	1.	BY THE BEAUTIFUL SEA (3)
2	2.	I LOVE THE LADIES (4)
14	3.	WHEN YOU PLAY IN THE GAME OF LOVE (2)
13	4.	YOU'RE HERE AND I'M HERE (2)
1	5.	THIS IS THE LIFE (6)
11	6.	WHEN YOU'RE ALL DRESSED UP AND NO PLACE TO GO (3)
8	7.	MARY, YOU'RE A LITTLE BIT OLD FASHIONED (4)
3	8.	ALL ABOARD FOR DIXIE LAND (5)
4	9.	REBECCA OF SUNNYBROOK FARM (6)
12	10.	YOU PLANTED A ROSE IN THE GARDEN OF LOVE (3)
20	11.	ROLL THEM COTTON BALES (2)
7	12.	WHO PAID THE RENT FOR MRS. RIP VAN WINKLE? (4)
9	13.	WHEN THE ANGELUS IS RINGING (4)
–	14.	BALLIN' THE JACK (1)
–	15.	CALIFORNIA AND YOU (1)
10	16.	I'M ON MY WAY TO MANDALAY (7)
6	17.	HE'S A DEVIL IN HIS OWN HOME TOWN (5)
–	18.	MOTHER MACHREE (1)
–	19.	LOVE'S OWN SWEET SONG (1)
–	20.	CAN'T YOU HEAR ME CALLING, CAROLINE? (1)

SEPTEMBER 1914

LM	TM	
1	1.	BY THE BEAUTIFUL SEA (4)
3	2.	WHEN YOU PLAY IN THE GAME OF LOVE (3)
4	3.	YOU'RE HERE AND I'M HERE (3)
14	4.	BALLIN' THE JACK (2)
2	5.	I LOVE THE LADIES (5)
15	6.	CALIFORNIA AND YOU (2)
–	7.	ABA DABA HONEYMOON (1)
11	8.	ROLL THEM COTTON BALES (3)
–	9.	WHEN IT'S NIGHT TIME DOWN IN BURGUNDY (1)
6	10.	WHEN YOU'RE ALL DRESSED UP AND NO PLACE TO GO (4)
10	11.	YOU PLANTED A ROSE IN THE GARDEN OF LOVE (4)
–	12.	COHEN ON THE TELEPHONE (1)
20	13.	CAN'T YOU HEAR ME CALLING, CAROLINE? (2)
7	14.	MARY, YOU'RE A LITTLE BIT OLD FASHIONED (5)
5	15.	THIS IS THE LIFE (7)
8	16.	ALL ABOARD FOR DIXIE LAND (6)
13	17.	WHEN THE ANGELUS IS RINGING (5)
19	18.	LOVE'S OWN SWEET SONG (2)
9	19.	REBECCA OF SUNNYBROOK FARM (7)
–	20.	IN THE TOWN WHERE I WAS BORN (1)

OCTOBER 1914

LM	TM	
1	1.	BY THE BEAUTIFUL SEA (5)
4	2.	BALLIN' THE JACK (3)
7	3.	ABA DABA HONEYMOON (2)
2	4.	WHEN YOU PLAY IN THE GAME OF LOVE (4)
6	5.	CALIFORNIA AND YOU (3)
13	6.	CAN'T YOU HEAR ME CALLING, CAROLINE? (3)
9	7.	WHEN IT'S NIGHT TIME DOWN IN BURGUNDY (2)
3	8.	YOU'RE HERE AND I'M HERE (4)
–	9.	WHEN YOU'RE A LONG, LONG WAY FROM HOME (1)
8	10.	ROLL THEM COTTON BALES (4)
5	11.	I LOVE THE LADIES (6)
10	12.	WHEN YOU'RE ALL DRESSED UP AND NO PLACE TO GO (5)
–	13.	MY CROONY MELODY (1)
11	14.	YOU PLANTED A ROSE IN THE GARDEN OF LOVE (5)
–	15.	POOR PAULINE (1)
12	16.	COHEN ON THE TELEPHONE (2)
–	17.	MOTHER MACHREE (2)
14	18.	MARY, YOU'RE A LITTLE BIT OLD FASHIONED (6)
–	19.	THE MEMPHIS BLUES (1)
–	20.	FIDO IS A HOT DOG NOW (1)

NOVEMBER 1914

LM	TM	
2	1.	BALLIN' THE JACK (4)
3	2.	ABA DABA HONEYMOON (3)
9	3.	WHEN YOU'RE A LONG, LONG WAY FROM HOME (2)
6	4.	CAN'T YOU HEAR ME CALLING, CAROLINE? (4)
5	5.	CALIFORNIA AND YOU (4)
1	6.	BY THE BEAUTIFUL SEA (6)
8	7.	YOU'RE HERE AND I'M HERE (5)
15	8.	POOR PAULINE (2)
–	9.	I WANT TO GO BACK TO MICHIGAN (1)
–	10.	WHEN YOU WORE A TULIP (1)
–	11.	IT'S A LONG, LONG WAY TO TIPPERARY (1)
7	12.	WHEN IT'S NIGHT TIME DOWN IN BURGUNDY (3)
–	13.	AT A MISSISSIPPI CABARET (1)
10	14.	ROLL THEM COTTON BALES (5)
4	15.	WHEN YOU PLAY IN THE GAME OF LOVE (5)
13	16.	MY CROONY MELODY (2)
19	17.	THE MEMPHIS BLUES (2)
–	18.	HE'S A RAG PICKER (1)
16	19.	COHEN ON THE TELEPHONE (3)
–	20.	YOU'RE MORE THAN THE WORLD TO ME (1)

DECEMBER 1914

LM	TM	
3	1.	WHEN YOU'RE A LONG, LONG WAY FROM HOME (3)
9	2.	I WANT TO GO BACK TO MICHIGAN (2)
11	3.	IT'S A LONG, LONG WAY TO TIPPERARY (2)
1	4.	BALLIN' THE JACK (5)
10	5.	WHEN YOU WORE A TULIP (2)
4	6.	CAN'T YOU HEAR ME CALLING, CAROLINE? (5)
8	7.	POOR PAULINE (3)
2	8.	ABA DABA HONEYMOON (4)
13	9.	AT A MISSISSIPPI CABARET (2)
20	10.	YOU'RE MORE THAN THE WORLD TO ME (2)
–	11.	BACK TO THE CAROLINA YOU LOVE (1)
5	12.	CALIFORNIA AND YOU (5)
18	13.	HE'S A RAG PICKER (2)
7	14.	YOU'RE HERE AND I'M HERE (6)
–	15.	TIP TOP TIPPERARY MARY (1)
12	16.	WHEN IT'S NIGHT TIME DOWN IN BURGUNDY (4)
–	17.	THEY ALL HAD A FINGER IN THE PIE (1)
6	18.	BY THE BEAUTIFUL SEA (7)
–	19.	WHEN THE GROWN UP LADIES ACT LIKE BABIES (1)
16	20.	MY CROONY MELODY (3)

JANUARY 1915

LM	TM	
3	1.	IT'S A LONG, LONG WAY TO TIPPERARY (3)
2	2.	I WANT TO GO BACK TO MICHIGAN (3)
5	3.	WHEN YOU WORE A TULIP (3)
1	4.	WHEN YOU'RE A LONG, LONG WAY FROM HOME (4)
10	5.	YOU'RE MORE THAN THE WORLD TO ME (3)
9	6.	AT A MISSISSIPPI CABARET (3)
11	7.	BACK TO THE CAROLINA YOU LOVE (2)
7	8.	POOR PAULINE (4)
6	9.	CAN'T YOU HEAR ME CALLING, CAROLINE? (6)
–	10.	CHINATOWN, MY CHINATOWN (1)
13	11.	HE'S A RAG PICKER (3)
–	12.	SISTER SUSIE'S SEWING SHIRTS FOR SOLDIERS (1)
4	13.	BALLIN' THE JACK (6)
15	14.	TIP TOP TIPPERARY MARY (2)
8	15.	ABA DABA HONEYMOON (5)
19	16.	WHEN THE GROWN UP LADIES ACT LIKE BABIES (2)
12	17.	CALIFORNIA AND YOU (6)
14	18.	YOU'RE HERE AND I'M HERE (7)
–	19.	THE MEMPHIS BLUES (3)
–	20.	I DIDN'T RAISE MY BOY TO BE A SOLDIER (1)

FEBRUARY 1915

LM	TM	
1	1.	IT'S A LONG, LONG WAY TO TIPPERARY (4)
3	2.	WHEN YOU WORE A TULIP (4)
20	3.	I DIDN'T RAISE MY BOY TO BE A SOLDIER (2)
4	4.	WHEN YOU'RE A LONG, LONG WAY FROM HOME (5)
2	5.	I WANT TO GO BACK TO MICHIGAN (4)
10	6.	CHINATOWN, MY CHINATOWN (2)
5	7.	YOU'RE MORE THAN THE WORLD TO ME (4)
–	8.	ON THE 5:15 (1)
–	9.	GOODBYE, GIRLS, I'M THROUGH (1)
12	10.	SISTER SUSIE'S SEWING SHIRTS FOR SOLDIERS (2)
7	11.	BACK TO THE CAROLINA YOU LOVE (3)
14	12.	TIP TOP TIPPERARY MARY (3)
6	13.	AT A MISSISSIPPI CABARET (4)
–	14.	DOWN AMONG THE SHELTERING PALMS (1)
9	15.	CAN'T YOU HEAR ME CALLING, CAROLINE? (7)
–	16.	A LITTLE BIT OF HEAVEN (1)
16	17.	WHEN THE GROWN UP LADIES ACT LIKE BABIES (3)
–	18.	AFTER THE ROSES HAVE FADED AWAY (1)
8	19.	POOR PAULINE (5)
19	20.	THE MEMPHIS BLUES (4)

MARCH 1915

LM	TM	
3	1.	I DIDN'T RAISE MY BOY TO BE A SOLDIER (3)
1	2.	IT'S A LONG, LONG WAY TO TIPPERARY (5)
8	3.	ON THE 5:15 (2)
9	4.	GOODBYE, GIRLS, I'M THROUGH (2)
2	5.	WHEN YOU WORE A TULIP (5)
16	6.	A LITTLE BIT OF HEAVEN (2)
6	7.	CHINATOWN, MY CHINATOWN (3)
14	8.	DOWN AMONG THE SHELTERING PALMS (2)
4	9.	WHEN YOU'RE A LONG, LONG WAY FROM HOME (6)
10	10.	SISTER SUSIE'S SEWING SHIRTS FOR SOLDIERS (3)
–	11.	THERE'S A LITTLE SPARK OF LOVE STILL BURNING (1)
18	12.	AFTER THE ROSES HAVE FADED AWAY (2)
7	13.	YOU'RE MORE THAN THE WORLD TO ME (5)
–	14.	BY HECK (1)
12	15.	TIP TOP TIPPERARY MARY (4)
–	16.	THE LITTLE HOUSE UPON THE HILL (1)
–	17.	EVERYBODY RAG WITH ME (1)
5	18.	I WANT TO GO BACK TO MICHIGAN (5)
11	19.	BACK TO THE CAROLINA YOU LOVE (4)
–	20.	SWEET KENTUCKY LADY (1)

APRIL 1915

LM	TM	
1	1.	I DIDN'T RAISE MY BOY TO BE A SOLDIER (4)
6	2.	A LITTLE BIT OF HEAVEN (3)
11	3.	THERE'S A LITTLE SPARK OF LOVE STILL BURNING (2)
3	4.	ON THE 5:15 (3)
4	5.	GOODBYE, GIRLS, I'M THROUGH (3)
8	6.	DOWN AMONG THE SHELTERING PALMS (3)
2	7.	IT'S A LONG, LONG WAY TO TIPPERARY (6)
14	8.	BY HECK (2)
16	9.	THE LITTLE HOUSE UPON THE HILL (2)
5	10.	WHEN YOU WORE A TULIP (6)
7	11.	CHINATOWN, MY CHINATOWN (4)
10	12.	SISTER SUSIE'S SEWING SHIRTS FOR SOLDIERS (4)
17	13.	EVERYBODY RAG WITH ME (2)
20	14.	SWEET KENTUCKY LADY (2)
–	15.	THE SONG OF SONGS (1)
12	16.	AFTER THE ROSES HAVE FADED AWAY (3)
–	17.	CARRY ME BACK TO OLD VIRGINNY (1)
–	18.	SYNCOPATED WALK (1)
–	19.	WHEN MY SHIP COMES IN (1)
–	20.	THEY ALL HAD A FINGER IN THE PIE (2)

MAY 1915

LM	TM	
2	1.	A LITTLE BIT OF HEAVEN (4)
3	2.	THERE'S A LITTLE SPARK OF LOVE STILL BURNING (3)
1	3.	I DIDN'T RAISE MY BOY TO BE A SOLDIER (5)
6	4.	DOWN AMONG THE SHELTERING PALMS (4)
8	5.	BY HECK (3)
5	6.	GOODBYE, GIRLS, I'M THROUGH (4)
4	7.	ON THE 5:15 (4)
9	8.	THE LITTLE HOUSE UPON THE HILL (3)
7	9.	IT'S A LONG, LONG WAY TO TIPPERARY (7)
–	10.	I'M ON MY WAY TO DUBLIN BAY (1)
11	11.	CHINATOWN, MY CHINATOWN (5)
17	12.	CARRY ME BACK TO OLD VIRGINNY (2)
14	13.	SWEET KENTUCKY LADY (3)
13	14.	EVERYBODY RAG WITH ME (3)
12	15.	SISTER SUSIE'S SEWING SHIRTS FOR SOLDIERS (5)
–	16.	WHEN YOU'RE AWAY (1)
19	17.	WHEN MY SHIP COMES IN (2)
10	18.	WHEN YOU WORE A TULIP (7)
15	19.	THE SONG OF SONGS (2)
–	20.	PLAY A SIMPLE MELODY (1)

JUNE 1915

LM	TM	
1	1.	A LITTLE BIT OF HEAVEN (5)
2	2.	THERE'S A LITTLE SPARK OF LOVE STILL BURNING (4)
10	3.	I'M ON MY WAY TO DUBLIN BAY (2)
4	4.	DOWN AMONG THE SHELTERING PALMS (5)
3	5.	I DIDN'T RAISE MY BOY TO BE A SOLDIER (6)
5	6.	BY HECK (4)
8	7.	THE LITTLE HOUSE UPON THE HILL (4)
6	8.	GOODBYE, GIRLS, I'M THROUGH (5)
–	9.	MY BIRD OF PARADISE (1)
16	10.	WHEN YOU'RE AWAY (2)
–	11.	MY LITTLE DREAM GIRL (1)
–	12.	ALABAMA JUBILEE (1)
12	13.	CARRY ME BACK TO OLD VIRGINNY (3)
9	14.	IT'S A LONG, LONG WAY TO TIPPERARY (8)
–	15.	WHEN I WAS A DREAMER (AND YOU WERE MY DREAM) (1)
14	16.	EVERYBODY RAG WITH ME (4)
13	17.	SWEET KENTUCKY LADY (4)
–	18.	SHADOWLAND (1)
7	19.	ON THE 5:15 (5)
20	20.	PLAY A SIMPLE MELODY (2)

JULY 1915

LM	TM	
3	1.	I'M ON MY WAY TO DUBLIN BAY (3)
1	2.	A LITTLE BIT OF HEAVEN (6)
9	3.	MY BIRD OF PARADISE (2)
11	4.	MY LITTLE DREAM GIRL (2)
12	5.	ALABAMA JUBILEE (2)
4	6.	DOWN AMONG THE SHELTERING PALMS (6)
2	7.	THERE'S A LITTLE SPARK OF LOVE STILL BURNING (5)
15	8.	WHEN I WAS A DREAMER (AND YOU WERE MY DREAM) (2)
10	9.	WHEN YOU'RE AWAY (3)
5	10.	I DIDN'T RAISE MY BOY TO BE A SOLDIER (7)
6	11.	BY HECK (5)
13	12.	CARRY ME BACK TO OLD VIRGINNY (4)
18	13.	SHADOWLAND (2)
7	14.	THE LITTLE HOUSE UPON THE HILL (5)
8	15.	GOODBYE, GIRLS, I'M THROUGH (6)
–	16.	WHEN I LEAVE THE WORLD BEHIND (1)
–	17.	YOU KNOW AND I KNOW (AND WE BOTH UNDERSTAND (1)
17	18.	SWEET KENTUCKY LADY (5)
20	19.	PLAY A SIMPLE MELODY (3)
–	20.	RAILROAD JIM (1)

AUGUST 1915

LM	TM	
2	1.	A LITTLE BIT OF HEAVEN (7)
4	2.	MY LITTLE DREAM GIRL (3)
3	3.	MY BIRD OF PARADISE (3)
1	4.	I'M ON MY WAY TO DUBLIN BAY (4)
5	5.	ALABAMA JUBILEE (3)
16	6.	WHEN I LEAVE THE WORLD BEHIND (2)
8	7.	WHEN I WAS A DREAMER (AND YOU WERE MY DREAM) (3)
–	8.	IF WE CAN'T BE THE SAME OLD SWEETHEARTS (1)
6	9.	DOWN AMONG THE SHELTERING PALMS (7)
9	10.	WHEN YOU'RE AWAY (4)
–	11.	MY LITTLE GIRL (1)
13	12.	SHADOWLAND (3)
12	13.	CARRY ME BACK TO OLD VIRGINNY (5)
7	14.	THERE'S A LITTLE SPARK OF LOVE STILL BURNING (6)
17	15.	YOU KNOW AND I KNOW (AND WE BOTH UNDERSTAND (2)
11	16.	BY HECK (6)
20	17.	RAILROAD JIM (2)
–	18.	THE MEMPHIS BLUES (5)
–	19.	THE MAGIC MELODY (1)
–	20.	HELLO, FRISCO! (1)

SEPTEMBER 1915

LM	TM	
2	1.	MY LITTLE DREAM GIRL (4)
1	2.	A LITTLE BIT OF HEAVEN (8)
6	3.	WHEN I LEAVE THE WORLD BEHIND (3)
20	4.	HELLO, FRISCO! (2)
5	5.	ALABAMA JUBILEE (4)
–	6.	DOWN IN BOM-BOMBAY (1)
8	7.	IF WE CAN'T BE THE SAME OLD SWEETHEARTS (2)
11	8.	MY LITTLE GIRL (2)
–	9.	IT'S TULIP TIME IN HOLLAND (1)
3	10.	MY BIRD OF PARADISE (4)
4	11.	I'M ON MY WAY TO DUBLIN BAY (5)
7	12.	WHEN I WAS A DREAMER (AND YOU WERE MY DREAM) (4)
10	13.	WHEN YOU'RE AWAY (5)
–	14.	RAGGING THE SCALE (1)
9	15.	DOWN AMONG THE SHELTERING PALMS (8)
–	16.	YOU'LL ALWAYS BE THE SAME SWEET GIRL (1)
13	17.	CARRY ME BACK TO OLD VIRGINNY (6)
–	18.	MY SWEET ADAIR (1)
–	19.	UNDER THE AMERICAN FLAG (1)
14	20.	SHADOWLAND (4)

OCTOBER 1915

LM	TM	
4	1.	HELLO, FRISCO! (3)
3	2.	WHEN I LEAVE THE WORLD BEHIND (4)
6	3.	DOWN IN BOM-BOMBAY (2)
2	4.	A LITTLE BIT OF HEAVEN (9)
9	5.	IT'S TULIP TIME IN HOLLAND (2)
18	6.	MY SWEET ADAIR (2)
1	7.	MY LITTLE DREAM GIRL (5)
14	8.	RAGGING THE SCALE (2)
8	9.	MY LITTLE GIRL (3)
–	10.	CLOSE TO MY HEART (1)
16	11.	YOU'LL ALWAYS BE THE SAME SWEET GIRL (2)
7	12.	IF WE CAN'T BE THE SAME OLD SWEETHEARTS (3)
5	13.	ALABAMA JUBILEE (5)
12	14.	WHEN I WAS A DREAMER (AND YOU WERE MY DREAM) (5)
13	15.	WHEN YOU'RE AWAY (6)
–	16.	NORWAY (1)
10	17.	MY BIRD OF PARADISE (5)
–	18.	THERE'S A LITTLE LANE WITHOUT A TURNING ON THE WAY TO HOME SWEET HOME (1)
11	19.	I'M ON MY WAY TO DUBLIN BAY (6)
17	20.	CARRY ME BACK TO OLD VIRGINNY (7)

NOVEMBER 1915

LM	TM	
5	1.	IT'S TULIP TIME IN HOLLAND (3)
1	2.	HELLO, FRISCO! (4)
6	3.	MY SWEET ADAIR (3)
2	4.	WHEN I LEAVE THE WORLD BEHIND (5)
3	5.	DOWN IN BOM-BOMBAY (3)
4	6.	A LITTLE BIT OF HEAVEN (10)
18	7.	THERE'S A LITTLE LANE WITHOUT A TURNING ON THE WAY TO HOME SWEET HOME (2)
–	8.	BACK HOME IN TENNESSEE (1)
10	9.	CLOSE TO MY HEART (2)
8	10.	RAGGING THE SCALE (3)
–	11.	AMERICA, I LOVE YOU (1)
11	12.	YOU'LL ALWAYS BE THE SAME SWEET GIRL (3)
–	13.	AUF WIEDERSEH'N (1)
7	14.	MY LITTLE DREAM GIRL (6)
–	15.	THAT'S THE SONG OF SONGS FOR ME (1)
9	16.	MY LITTLE GIRL (4)
16	17.	NORWAY (2)
–	18.	THE LITTLE GREY MOTHER (1)
–	19.	PUT ME TO SLEEP WITH AN OLD FASHIONED MELODY (1)
–	20.	LOVE, HERE IS MY HEART (1)

DECEMBER 1915

LM	TM	
3	1.	MY SWEET ADAIR (4)
8	2.	BACK HOME IN TENNESSEE (2)
1	3.	IT'S TULIP TIME IN HOLLAND (4)
11	4.	AMERICA, I LOVE YOU (2)
13	5.	AUF WIEDERSEH'N (2)
7	6.	THERE'S A LITTLE LANE WITHOUT A TURNING ON THE WAY TO HOME SWEET HOME (3)
9	7.	CLOSE TO MY HEART (3)
4	8.	WHEN I LEAVE THE WORLD BEHIND (6)
12	9.	YOU'LL ALWAYS BE THE SAME SWEET GIRL (4)
6	10.	A LITTLE BIT OF HEAVEN (11)
2	11.	HELLO, FRISCO! (5)
18	12.	THE LITTLE GREY MOTHER (2)
5	13.	DOWN IN BOM-BOMBAY (4)
20	14.	LOVE, HERE IS MY HEART (2)
–	15.	I'VE BEEN FLOATING DOWN THE OLD GREEN RIVER (1)
–	16.	WHEN OLD BILL BAILEY PLAYS THE UKULELE (1)
–	17.	ALONG THE ROCKY ROAD TO DUBLIN (1)
–	18.	M-O-T-H-E-R (1)
17	19.	NORWAY (3)
10	20.	RAGGING THE SCALE (4)

JANUARY 1916

LM	TM	
2	1.	BACK HOME IN TENNESSEE (3)
4	2.	AMERICA, I LOVE YOU (3)
18	3.	M-O-T-H-E-R (2)
5	4.	AUF WIEDERSEH'N (3)
1	5.	MY SWEET ADAIR (5)
17	6.	ALONG THE ROCKY ROAD TO DUBLIN (2)
3	7.	IT'S TULIP TIME IN HOLLAND (5)
–	8.	THEY DIDN'T BELIEVE ME (1)
9	9.	YOU'LL ALWAYS BE THE SAME SWEET GIRL (5)
15	10.	I'VE BEEN FLOATING DOWN THE OLD GREEN RIVER (2)
–	11.	MOLLY, DEAR, IT'S YOU I'M AFTER (1)
6	12.	THERE'S A LITTLE LANE WITHOUT A TURNING ON THE WAY TO HOME SWEET HOME (4)
10	13.	A LITTLE BIT OF HEAVEN (12)
–	14.	ARABY (1)
12	15.	THE LITTLE GREY MOTHER (3)
16	16.	WHEN OLD BILL BAILEY PLAYS THE UKULELE (2)
7	17.	CLOSE TO MY HEART (4)
8	18.	WHEN I LEAVE THE WORLD BEHIND (7)
–	19.	SHE'S THE DAUGHTER OF MOTHER MACHREE (1)
–	20.	PINEY RIDGE (1)

FEBRUARY 1916

LM	TM	
3	1.	M-O-T-H-E-R (3)
6	2.	ALONG THE ROCKY ROAD TO DUBLIN (3)
8	3.	THEY DIDN'T BELIEVE ME (2)
2	4.	AMERICA, I LOVE YOU (4)
1	5.	BACK HOME IN TENNESSEE (4)
–	6.	HELLO, HAWAII, HOW ARE YOU? (1)
–	7.	UNDERNEATH THE STARS (1)
4	8.	AUF WIEDERSEH'N (4)
9	9.	YOU'LL ALWAYS BE THE SAME SWEET GIRL (6)
19	10.	SHE'S THE DAUGHTER OF MOTHER MACHREE (2)
11	11.	MOLLY, DEAR, IT'S YOU I'M AFTER (2)
–	12.	MEMORIES (1)
10	13.	I'VE BEEN FLOATING DOWN THE OLD GREEN RIVER (3)
–	14.	DON'T BITE THE HAND THAT'S FEEDING YOU (1)
5	15.	MY SWEET ADAIR (6)
14	16.	ARABY (2)
7	17.	IT'S TULIP TIME IN HOLLAND (6)
–	18.	KEEP THE HOME FIRES BURNING (1)
–	19.	WHAT A WONDERFUL MOTHER YOU'D BE (1)
13	20.	A LITTLE BIT OF HEAVEN (13)

MARCH 1916

LM	TM	
1	1.	M-O-T-H-E-R (4)
3	2.	THEY DIDN'T BELIEVE ME (3)
6	3.	HELLO, HAWAII, HOW ARE YOU? (2)
7	4.	UNDERNEATH THE STARS (2)
12	5.	MEMORIES (2)
2	6.	ALONG THE ROCKY ROAD TO DUBLIN (4)
10	7.	SHE'S THE DAUGHTER OF MOTHER MACHREE (3)
–	8.	GOODBYE, GOOD LUCK, AND GOD BLESS YOU (1)
5	9.	BACK HOME IN TENNESSEE (5)
14	10.	DON'T BITE THE HAND THAT'S FEEDING YOU (2)
–	11.	MY MOTHER'S ROSARY (1)
4	12.	AMERICA, I LOVE YOU (5)
18	13.	KEEP THE HOME FIRES BURNING (2)
9	14.	YOU'LL ALWAYS BE THE SAME SWEET GIRL (7)
19	15.	WHAT A WONDERFUL MOTHER YOU'D BE (2)
–	16.	THE LADDER OF ROSES (1)
8	17.	AUF WIEDERSEH'N (5)
11	18.	MOLLY, DEAR, IT'S YOU I'M AFTER (3)
–	19.	ARE YOU FROM DIXIE? (1)
16	20.	ARABY (3)

APRIL 1916

LM	TM	
5	1.	MEMORIES (3)
8	2.	GOODBYE, GOOD LUCK, AND GOD BLESS YOU (2)
3	3.	HELLO, HAWAII, HOW ARE YOU? (3)
1	4.	M-O-T-H-E-R (5)
4	5.	UNDERNEATH THE STARS (3)
11	6.	MY MOTHER'S ROSARY (2)
2	7.	THEY DIDN'T BELIEVE ME (4)
–	8.	THERE'S A BROKEN HEART FOR EVERY LIGHT ON BROADWAY (1)
19	9.	ARE YOU FROM DIXIE? (2)
15	10.	WHAT A WONDERFUL MOTHER YOU'D BE (3)
7	11.	SHE'S THE DAUGHTER OF MOTHER MACHREE (4)
16	12.	THE LADDER OF ROSES (2)
–	13.	I LOVE YOU, THAT'S ONE THING I KNOW (1)
–	14.	RACKETY COO! (1)
12	15.	AMERICA, I LOVE YOU (6)
–	16.	SO LONG, LETTY (1)
9	17.	BACK HOME IN TENNESSEE (6)
–	18.	THERE'S A LONG, LONG TRAIL (1)
6	19.	ALONG THE ROCKY ROAD TO DUBLIN (5)
13	20.	KEEP THE HOME FIRES BURNING (3)

MAY 1916

LM	TM	
2	1.	GOODBYE, GOOD LUCK, AND GOD BLESS YOU (3)
1	2.	MEMORIES (4)
6	3.	MY MOTHER'S ROSARY (3)
5	4.	UNDERNEATH THE STARS (4)
3	5.	HELLO, HAWAII, HOW ARE YOU? (4)
–	6.	YAAKA HULA, HICKEY DULA (1)
4	7.	M-O-T-H-E-R (6)
9	8.	ARE YOU FROM DIXIE? (3)
8	9.	THERE'S A BROKEN HEART FOR EVERY LIGHT ON BROADWAY (2)
–	10.	I CAN DANCE WITH EVERYBODY BUT MY WIFE (1)
7	11.	THEY DIDN'T BELIEVE ME (5)
13	12.	I LOVE YOU, THAT'S ONE THING I KNOW (2)
–	13.	SIAM (1)
14	14.	RACKETY COO! (2)
16	15.	SO LONG, LETTY (2)
–	16.	WHERE DID ROBINSON CRUSOE GO WITH FRIDAY ON A SATURDAY NIGHT? (1)
18	17.	THERE'S A LONG, LONG TRAIL (2)
–	18.	BABES IN THE WOOD (1)
–	19.	NAT'AN, FOR WHAT ARE YOU WAITIN', NAT'AN? (1)
10	20.	WHAT A WONDERFUL MOTHER YOU'D BE (4)

JUNE 1916

LM	TM	
6	1.	YAAKA HULA, HICKEY DULA (2)
2	2.	MEMORIES (5)
1	3.	GOODBYE, GOOD LUCK, AND GOD BLESS YOU (4)
3	4.	MY MOTHER'S ROSARY (4)
10	5.	I CAN DANCE WITH EVERYBODY BUT MY WIFE (2)
8	6.	ARE YOU FROM DIXIE? (4)
17	7.	WHERE DID ROBINSON CRUSOE GO WITH FRIDAY ON A SATURDAY NIGHT? (2)
5	8.	HELLO, HAWAII, HOW ARE YOU? (5)
18	9.	BABES IN THE WOOD (2)
4	10.	UNDERNEATH THE STARS (5)
–	11.	BABY SHOES (1)
–	12.	THERE'S A QUAKER DOWN IN QUAKER TOWN (1)
–	13.	ARRAH, GO ON, I'M GONNA GO BACK TO OREGON (1)
17	14.	THERE'S A LONG, LONG TRAIL (3)
13	15.	SIAM (2)
–	16.	SHADES OF NIGHT (1)
–	17.	I LOVE A PIANO (1)
19	18.	NAT'AN, FOR WHAT ARE YOU WAITIN', NAT'AN? (2)
–	19.	A PERFECT DAY (1)
9	20.	THERE'S A BROKEN HEART FOR EVERY LIGHT ON BROADWAY (3)

JULY 1916

LM	TM	
1	1.	YAAKA HULA, HICKEY DULA (3)
5	2.	I CAN DANCE WITH EVERYBODY BUT MY WIFE (3)
11	3.	BABY SHOES (2)
3	4.	GOODBYE, GOOD LUCK, AND GOD BLESS YOU (5)
12	5.	THERE'S A QUAKER DOWN IN QUAKER TOWN (2)
13	6.	ARRAH, GO ON, I'M GONNA GO BACK TO OREGON (2)
4	7.	MY MOTHER'S ROSARY (5)
9	8.	BABES IN THE WOOD (3)
14	9.	THERE'S A LONG, LONG TRAIL (4)
2	10.	MEMORIES (6)
7	11.	WHERE DID ROBINSON CRUSOE GO WITH FRIDAY ON A SATURDAY NIGHT? (3)
–	12.	MY OWN IONA (1)
16	13.	SHADES OF NIGHT (2)
–	14.	THE SUNSHINE OF YOUR SMILE (1)
6	15.	ARE YOU FROM DIXIE? (5)
17	16.	I LOVE A PIANO (2)
19	17.	A PERFECT DAY (2)
–	18.	ON THE BEACH AT WAIKIKI (1)
–	19.	MY DREAMY CHINA LADY (1)
–	20.	PRETTY BABY (1)

AUGUST 1916

LM	TM	
3	1.	BABY SHOES (3)
1	2.	YAAKA HULA, HICKEY DULA (4)
12	3.	MY OWN IONA (2)
20	4.	PRETTY BABY (2)
5	5.	THERE'S A QUAKER DOWN IN QUAKER TOWN (3)
6	6.	ARRAH, GO ON, I'M GONNA GO BACK TO OREGON (3)
14	7.	THE SUNSHINE OF YOUR SMILE (2)
13	8.	SHADES OF NIGHT (3)
9	9.	THERE'S A LONG, LONG TRAIL (5)
2	11.	I CAN DANCE WITH EVERYBODY BUT MY WIFE (4)
8	10.	BABES IN THE WOOD (4)
17	12.	A PERFECT DAY (3)
–	13.	YOU'RE A DANGEROUS GIRL (1)
11	14.	WHERE DID ROBINSON CRUSOE GO WITH FRIDAY ON A SATURDAY NIGHT? (4)
7	15.	MY MOTHER'S ROSARY (6)
–	16.	IF I KNOCK THE "L" OUT OF KELLY (1)
4	17.	GOODBYE, GOOD LUCK, AND GOD BLESS YOU (6)
–	18.	PRAY FOR THE LIGHTS TO GO OUT (1)
–	19.	MISSOURI WALTZ (1)
10	20.	MEMORIES (7)

SEPTEMBER 1916

LM	TM	
4	1.	PRETTY BABY (3)
3	2.	MY OWN IONA (3)
16	3.	IF I KNOCK THE "L" OUT OF KELLY (2)
1	4.	BABY SHOES (4)
7	5.	THE SUNSHINE OF YOUR SMILE (3)
8	6.	SHADES OF NIGHT (4)
–	7.	IRELAND MUST BE HEAVEN FOR MY MOTHER CAME FROM THERE (1)
9	8.	THERE'S A LONG, LONG TRAIL (6)
6	9.	ARRAH, GO ON, I'M GONNA GO BACK TO OREGON (4)
5	10.	THERE'S A QUAKER DOWN IN QUAKER TOWN (4)
–	11.	TURN BACK THE UNIVERSE AND GIVE ME YESTERDAY (1)
13	12.	YOU'RE A DANGEROUS GIRL (2)
2	13.	YAAKA HULA, HICKEY DULA (5)
12	14.	A PERFECT DAY (4)
18	15.	PRAY FOR THE LIGHTS TO GO OUT (2)
–	16.	ON THE SOUTH SEA ISLE (1)
10	17.	BABES IN THE WOOD (5)
–	18.	OH! HOW SHE COULD YACKI, HACKI, WICKI, WACKI, WOO (1)
–	19.	AT THE END OF A BEAUTIFUL DAY (1)
–	20.	DOWN WHERE THE SWANEE RIVER FLOWS (1)

OCTOBER 1916

LM	TM	
1	1.	PRETTY BABY (4)
2	2.	MY OWN IONA (4)
7	3.	IRELAND MUST BE HEAVEN FOR MY MOTHER CAME FROM THERE (2)
3	4.	IF I KNOCK THE "L" OUT OF KELLY (3)
11	5.	TURN BACK THE UNIVERSE AND GIVE ME YESTERDAY (2)
18	6.	OH! HOW SHE COULD YACKI, HACKI, WICKI, WACKI, WOO (2)
8	7.	THERE'S A LONG, LONG TRAIL (7)
–	8.	THERE'S A LITTLE BIT OF BAD IN EVERY GOOD LITTLE GIRL (1)
5	9.	THE SUNSHINE OF YOUR SMILE (4)
6	10.	SHADES OF NIGHT (5)
4	11.	BABY SHOES (5)
15	12.	PRAY FOR THE LIGHTS TO GO OUT (3)
16	13.	ON THE SOUTH SEA ISLE (2)
10	14.	THERE'S A QUAKER DOWN IN QUAKER TOWN (5)
14	15.	A PERFECT DAY (5)
9	16.	ARRAH, GO ON, I'M GONNA GO BACK TO OREGON (5)
–	17.	KISS ME AGAIN (1)
12	18.	YOU'RE A DANGEROUS GIRL (3)
20	19.	DOWN WHERE THE SWANEE RIVER FLOWS (1)
–	20.	MISSOURI WALTZ (2)

NOVEMBER 1916

LM	TM	
1	1.	PRETTY BABY (5)
3	2.	IRELAND MUST BE HEAVEN FOR MY MOTHER CAME FROM THERE (3)
8	3.	THERE'S A LITTLE BIT OF BAD IN EVERY GOOD LITTLE GIRL (2)
5	4.	TURN BACK THE UNIVERSE AND GIVE ME YESTERDAY (3)
2	5.	MY OWN IONA (5)
6	6.	OH! HOW SHE COULD YACKI, HACKI, WICKI, WACKI, WOO (3)
4	7.	IF I KNOCK THE "L" OUT OF KELLY (4)
–	8.	MAMMY'S LITTLE COAL BLACK ROSE (1)
7	9.	THERE'S A LONG, LONG TRAIL (8)
10	10.	SHADES OF NIGHT (6)
–	11.	SHE IS THE SUNSHINE OF VIRGINIA (1)
9	12.	THE SUNSHINE OF YOUR SMILE (5)
12	13.	PRAY FOR THE LIGHTS TO GO OUT (4)
13	14.	ON THE SOUTH SEA ISLE (3)
15	15.	A PERFECT DAY (6)
11	16.	BABY SHOES (6)
–	17.	OUT OF THE CRADLE, INTO MY HEART (1)
–	18.	I KNOW I GOT MORE THAN MY SHARE (1)
–	19.	SO LONG, LETTY (3)
17	20.	KISS ME AGAIN (2)

DECEMBER 1916

LM	TM	
3	1.	THERE'S A LITTLE BIT OF BAD IN EVERY GOOD LITTLE GIRL (3)
8	2.	MAMMY'S LITTLE COAL BLACK ROSE (2)
1	3.	PRETTY BABY (6)
2	4.	IRELAND MUST BE HEAVEN FOR MY MOTHER CAME FROM THERE (4)
11	5.	SHE IS THE SUNSHINE OF VIRGINIA (2)
4	6.	TURN BACK THE UNIVERSE AND GIVE ME YESTERDAY (4)
5	7.	MY OWN IONA (6)
9	8.	THERE'S A LONG, LONG TRAIL (9)
12	9.	THE SUNSHINE OF YOUR SMILE (6)
10	10.	SHADES OF NIGHT (7)
–	11.	MY HAWAIIAN SUNSHINE (1)
6	12.	OH! HOW SHE COULD YACKI HACKI WICKI WACKI WOO (4)
7	13.	IF I KNOCK THE "L" OUT OF KELLY (5)
17	14.	OUT OF THE CRADLE, INTO MY HEART (2)
13	15.	PRAY FOR THE LIGHTS TO GO OUT (5)
15	16.	A PERFECT DAY (7)
19	17.	SO LONG, LETTY (4)
18	18.	I KNOW I GOT MORE THAN MY SHARE (2)
–	19.	WHEN THE BLACK SHEEP RETURNS TO THE FOLD (1)
–	20.	POOR BUTTERFLY (1)

JANUARY 1917

LM	TM	
2	1.	MAMMY'S LITTLE COAL BLACK ROSE (3)
1	2.	THERE'S A LITTLE BIT OF BAD IN EVERY GOOD LITTLE GIRL (4)
5	3.	SHE IS THE SUNSHINE OF VIRGINIA (3)
4	4.	IRELAND MUST BE HEAVEN FOR MY MOTHER CAME FROM THERE (5)
20	5.	POOR BUTTERFLY (2)
–	6.	THEY'RE WEARIN' 'EM HIGHER IN HAWAII (1)
11	7.	MY HAWAIIAN SUNSHINE (2)
3	8.	PRETTY BABY (7)
–	9.	I AIN'T GOT NOBODY (1)
8	10.	THERE'S A LONG, LONG TRAIL (10)
–	11.	THROW ME A ROSE (1)
14	12.	OUT OF THE CRADLE, INTO MY HEART (3)
9	13.	THE SUNSHINE OF YOUR SMILE (7)
7	14.	MY OWN IONA (7)
–	15.	HOW'S EVERY LITTLE THING IN DIXIE? (1)
10	16.	SHADES OF NIGHT (8)
–	17.	NAUGHTY! NAUGHTY! NAUGHTY! (1)
18	18.	I KNOW I GOT MORE THAN MY SHARE (3)
6	19.	TURN BACK THE UNIVERSE AND GIVE ME YESTERDAY (5)
16	20.	A PERFECT DAY (8)

FEBRUARY 1917

LM	TM	
5	1.	POOR BUTTERFLY (3)
6	2.	THEY'RE WEARIN' 'EM HIGHER IN HAWAII (2)
1	3.	MAMMY'S LITTLE COAL BLACK ROSE (4)
–	4.	WHAT DO YOU WANT TO MAKE THOSE EYES AT ME FOR? (1)
7	5.	MY HAWAIIAN SUNSHINE (3)
3	6.	SHE IS THE SUNSHINE OF VIRGINIA (4)
2	7.	THERE'S A LITTLE BIT OF BAD IN EVERY GOOD LITTLE GIRL (5)
9	8.	I AIN'T GOT NOBODY (2)
15	9.	HOW'S EVERY LITTLE THING IN DIXIE? (2)
11	10.	THROW ME A ROSE (2)
17	11.	NAUGHTY! NAUGHTY! NAUGHTY! (2)
4	12.	IRELAND MUST BE HEAVEN FOR MY MOTHER CAME FROM THERE (6)
–	13.	M-I-S-S-I-S-S-I-P-P-I (1)
–	14.	ROLLING STONES (ALL COME ROLLING HOME AGAIN) (1)
10	15.	THERE'S A LONG, LONG TRAIL (11)
–	16.	IF YOU HAD ALL THE WORLD AND ITS GOLD (1)
–	17.	PRAY FOR THE LIGHTS TO GO OUT (6)
20	18.	A PERFECT DAY (9)
12	19.	OUT OF THE CRADLE, INTO MY HEART (4)
8	20.	PRETTY BABY (8)

MARCH 1917

LM	TM	
1	1.	POOR BUTTERFLY (4)
4	2.	WHAT DO YOU WANT TO MAKE THOSE EYES AT ME FOR? (2)
8	3.	I AIN'T GOT NOBODY (3)
13	4.	M-I-S-S-I-S-S-I-P-P-I (2)
2	5.	THEY'RE WEARIN' 'EM HIGHER IN HAWAII (3)
–	6.	WHERE THE BLACK-EYED SUSANS GROW (1)
3	7.	MAMMY'S LITTLE COAL BLACK ROSE (5)
5	8.	MY HAWAIIAN SUNSHINE (4)
14	9.	ROLLING STONES (ALL COME ROLLING HOME AGAIN) (2)
–	10.	FOR ME AND MY GAL (1)
–	11.	PACK UP YOUR TROUBLES IN YOUR OLD KIT BAG (1)
16	12.	IF YOU HAD ALL THE WORLD AND ITS GOLD(2)
6	13.	SHE IS THE SUNSHINE OF VIRGINIA (5)
9	14.	HOW'S EVERY LITTLE THING IN DIXIE? (3)
7	15.	THERE'S A LITTLE BIT OF BAD IN EVERY GOOD LITTLE GIRL (6)
11	16.	NAUGHTY! NAUGHTY! NAUGHTY! (3)
–	17.	THERE'S SOMEONE MORE LONESOME THAN YOU (1)
17	18.	PRAY FOR THE LIGHTS TO GO OUT (7)
10	19.	THROW ME A ROSE (3)
–	20.	SHE'S DIXIE ALL THE TIME (1)

APRIL 1917

LM	TM	
1	1.	POOR BUTTERFLY (5)
2	2.	WHAT DO YOU WANT TO MAKE THOSE EYES AT ME FOR? (3)
10	3.	FOR ME AND MY GAL (2)
4	4.	M-I-S-S-I-S-S-I-P-P-I (3)
6	5.	WHERE THE BLACK-EYED SUSANS GROW (2)
3	6.	I AIN'T GOT NOBODY (4)
5	7.	THEY'RE WEARIN' 'EM HIGHER IN HAWAII (4)
11	8.	PACK UP YOUR TROUBLES IN YOUR OLD KIT BAG(2)
–	10.	THERE'S EGYPT IN YOUR DREAMY EYES (1)
9	10.	ROLLING STONES (ALL COME ROLLING HOME AGAIN) (3)
–	11.	INDIANA (1)
17	12.	THERE'S SOMEONE MORE LONESOME THAN YOU (2)
12	13.	IF YOU HAD ALL THE WORLD AND ITS GOLD (3)
–	14.	COME OUT OF THE KITCHEN, MARY ANN (1)
7	15.	MAMMY'S LITTLE COAL BLACK ROSE (6)
–	16.	ALLAH'S HOLIDAY (1)
–	17.	OH JOHNNY, OH JOHNNY, OH! (1)
20	18.	SHE'S DIXIE ALL THE TIME (2)
–	19.	MOTHER (1)
–	20.	MISSOURI WALTZ (HUSH-A-BYE MA BABY) (3)

MAY 1917

LM	TM	
3	1.	FOR ME AND MY GAL (3)
1	2.	POOR BUTTERFLY (6)
8	3.	PACK UP YOUR TROUBLES IN YOUR OLD KIT BAG (3)
5	4.	WHERE THE BLACK-EYED SUSANS GROW (3)
4	5.	M-I-S-S-I-S-S-I-P-P-I (4)
2	6.	WHAT DO YOU WANT TO MAKE THOSE EYES AT ME FOR? (4)
17	7.	OH JOHNNY, OH JOHNNY, OH! (2)
11	8.	INDIANA (2)
6	9.	I AIN'T GOT NOBODY (5)
14	10.	COME OUT OF THE KITCHEN, MARY ANN (2)
9	11.	THERE'S EGYPT IN YOUR DREAMY EYES (2)
16	12.	ALLAH'S HOLIDAY (2)
12	13.	THERE'S SOMEONE MORE LONESOME THAN YOU (3)
13	14.	IF YOU HAD ALL THE WORLD AND ITS GOLD (4)
–	15.	HAWAIIAN BUTTERFLY (1)
–	16.	YOU SAID SOMETHING (1)
7	17.	THEY'RE WEARIN' 'EM HIGHER IN HAWAII (5)
10	18.	ROLLING STONES (ALL COME ROLLING HOME AGAIN) (4)
18	19.	SHE'S DIXIE ALL THE TIME (3)
–	20.	ALL THE WORLD WILL BE JEALOUS OF ME (1)

JUNE 1917

LM	TM	
1	1.	FOR ME AND MY GAL (4)
7	2.	OH JOHNNY, OH JOHNNY, OH! (3)
3	3.	PACK UP YOUR TROUBLES IN YOUR OLD KIT BAG (4)
8	4.	INDIANA (3)
2	5.	POOR BUTTERFLY (7)
4	6.	WHERE THE BLACK-EYED SUSANS GROW (4)
–	7.	LILY OF THE VALLEY (1)
5	8.	M-I-S-S-I-S-S-I-P-P-I (5)
12	9.	ALLAH'S HOLIDAY (3)
10	10.	COME OUT OF THE KITCHEN, MARY ANN (3)
20	11.	ALL THE WORLD WILL BE JEALOUS OF ME (2)
9	12.	I AIN'T GOT NOBODY (6)
15	13.	HAWAIIAN BUTTERFLY (2)
–	14.	TILL THE CLOUDS ROLL BY (1)
6	15.	WHAT DO YOU WANT TO MAKE THOSE EYES AT ME FOR? (5)
14	16.	IF YOU HAD ALL THE WORLD AND IT'S GOLD (5)
–	17.	THE DARKTOWN STRUTTERS' BALL (1)
–	18.	FOR YOU, A ROSE (1)
–	19.	HUCKLEBERRY FINN (1)
–	20.	IT TAKES A LONG, TALL, BROWN-SKIN GAL (1)

JULY 1917

LM	TM	Title
1	1.	FOR ME AND MY GAL (5)
2	2.	OH JOHNNY, OH JOHNNY, OH! (4)
7	3.	LILY OF THE VALLEY (2)
4	4.	INDIANA (4)
11	5.	ALL THE WORLD WILL BE JEALOUS OF ME (3)
18	6.	FOR YOU, A ROSE (2)
3	7.	PACK UP YOUR TROUBLES IN YOUR OLD KIT BAG (5)
–	8.	OVER THERE (1)
20	9.	IT TAKES A LONG, TALL, BROWN-SKIN GAL (2)
14	10.	TILL THE CLOUDS ROLL BY (2)
13	11.	HAWAIIAN BUTTERFLY (3)
9	12.	ALLAH'S HOLIDAY (4)
8	13.	M-I-S-S-I-S-S-I-P-P-I (6)
19	14.	HUCKLEBERRY FINN (2)
–	15.	THE MAGIC OF YOUR EYES (1)
17	16.	THE DARKTOWN STRUTTERS' BALL (2)
6	17.	WHERE THE BLACK-EYED SUSANS GROW (5)
5	18.	POOR BUTTERFLY (8)
–	19.	KEEP THE HOME FIRES BURNING (4)
16	20.	IF YOU HAD ALL THE WORLD AND IT'S GOLD (6)

AUGUST 1917

LM	TM	Title
5	1.	ALL THE WORLD WILL BE JEALOUS OF ME (4)
8	2.	OVER THERE (2)
3	3.	LILY OF THE VALLEY (3)
–	4.	GOODBYE BROADWAY, HELLO FRANCE! (1)
2	5.	OH JOHNNY, OH JOHNNY, OH! (5)
1	6.	FOR ME AND MY GAL (6)
4	7.	INDIANA (5)
–	8.	WHERE DO WE GO FROM HERE? (1)
6	9.	FOR YOU, A ROSE (3)
7	10.	PACK UP YOUR TROUBLES IN YOUR OLD KIT BAG (6)
19	11.	KEEP THE HOME FIRES BURNING (5)
14	12.	HUCKLEBERRY FINN (3)
10	13.	TILL THE CLOUDS ROLL BY (3)
9	14.	IT TAKES A LONG, TALL, BROWN-SKIN GAL (3)
–	15.	JOAN OF ARC, THEY ARE CALLING YOU (1)
16	16.	THE DARKTOWN STRUTTERS' BALL (3)
15	17.	THE MAGIC OF YOUR EYES (2)
–	18.	I MAY BE GONE FOR A LONG, LONG TIME (1)
11	19.	HAWAIIAN BUTTERFLY (4)
–	20.	SHIM-ME-SHA-WABBLE (1)

SEPTEMBER 1917

LM	TM	Title
2	1.	OVER THERE (3)
4	2.	GOODBYE BROADWAY, HELLO FRANCE! (2)
8	3.	WHERE DO WE GO FROM HERE? (2)
1	4.	ALL THE WORLD WILL BE JEALOUS OF ME (5)
3	5.	LILY OF THE VALLEY (4)
18	6.	I MAY BE GONE FOR A LONG, LONG TIME (2)
–	7.	THEY GO WILD, SIMPLY WILD, OVER ME (1)
–	8.	SAILIN' AWAY ON THE HENRY CLAY (1)
15	9.	JOAN OF ARC, THEY ARE CALLING YOU (2)
7	10.	INDIANA (6)
11	11.	KEEP THE HOME FIRES BURNING (6)
6	12.	FOR ME AND MY GAL (7)
5	13.	OH JOHNNY, OH JOHNNY, OH! (6)
16	14.	THE DARKTOWN STRUTTERS' BALL (4)
12	15.	HUCKLEBERRY FINN (4)
–	16.	SEND ME AWAY WITH A SMILE (1)
10	17.	PACK UP YOUR TROUBLES IN YOUR OLD KIT BAG (7)
–	18.	I DON'T KNOW WHERE I'M GOING, BUT I'M ON MY WAY (1)
–	19.	BREAK THE NEWS TO MOTHER (1)
9	20.	FOR YOU, A ROSE (4)

OCTOBER 1917

LM	TM	Title
1	1.	OVER THERE (4)
2	2.	GOODBYE BROADWAY, HELLO FRANCE! (3)
3	3.	WHERE DO WE GO FROM HERE? (3)
7	4.	THEY GO WILD, SIMPLY WILD, OVER ME (2)
6	5.	I MAY BE GONE FOR A LONG, LONG TIME (3)
9	6.	JOAN OF ARC, THEY ARE CALLING YOU (3)
8	7.	SAILIN' AWAY ON THE HENRY CLAY (2)
11	8.	KEEP THE HOME FIRES BURNING (7)
4	9.	ALL THE WORLD WILL BE JEALOUS OF ME (6)
14	10.	THE DARKTOWN STRUTTERS' BALL (5)
5	11.	LILY OF THE VALLEY (5)
18	12.	I DON'T KNOW WHERE I'M GOING, BUT I'M ON MY WAY (2)
19	13.	BREAK THE NEWS TO MOTHER (2)
–	14.	LADDIE BOY (1)
10	15.	INDIANA (7)
16	16.	SEND ME AWAY WITH A SMILE (2)
–	17.	WHEN YANKEE DOODLE LEARNS TO PARLEZ-VOUS FRANCAIS (1)
20	18.	FOR YOU, A ROSE (5)
–	19.	SWEET EMALINA, MY GAL (1)
12	20.	FOR ME AND MY GAL (8)

NOVEMBER 1917

LM	TM	Title
1	1.	OVER THERE (5)
2	2.	GOODBYE BROADWAY, HELLO FRANCE! (4)
5	3.	I MAY BE GONE FOR A LONG, LONG TIME (4)
4	4.	THEY GO WILD, SIMPLY WILD, OVER ME (3)
3	5.	WHERE DO WE GO FROM HERE? (4)
6	6.	JOAN OF ARC, THEY ARE CALLING YOU (4)
10	7.	THE DARKTOWN STRUTTERS' BALL (6)
8	8.	KEEP THE HOME FIRES BURNING (8)
13	9.	BREAK THE NEWS TO MOTHER (3)
7	10.	SAILIN' AWAY ON THE HENRY CLAY (3)
–	11.	SOME SUNDAY MORNING (1)
17	12.	WHEN YANKEE DOODLE LEARNS TO PARLEZ-VOUS FRANCAIS (2)
12	13.	I DON'T KNOW WHERE I'M GOING, BUT I'M ON MY WAY (3)
14	14.	LADDIE BOY (2)
–	15.	THERE'S A LONG, LONG TRAIL (12)
–	16.	I'M ALL BOUND 'ROUND WITH THE MASON-DIXON LINE (1)
16	17.	SEND ME AWAY WITH A SMILE (3)
11	18.	LILY OF THE VALLEY (6)
9	19.	ALL THE WORLD WILL BE JEALOUS OF ME (7)
–	20.	I DON'T WANT TO GET WELL (1)

DECEMBER 1917

LM	TM	Title
1	1.	OVER THERE (6)
11	2.	SOME SUNDAY MORNING (2)
7	3.	THE DARKTOWN STRUTTERS' BALL (7)
3	4.	I MAY BE GONE FOR A LONG, LONG TIME (5)
2	5.	GOODBYE BROADWAY, HELLO FRANCE! (5)
6	6.	JOAN OF ARC, THEY ARE CALLING YOU (5)
20	7.	I DON'T WANT TO GET WELL (2)
15	8.	THERE'S A LONG, LONG TRAIL (13)
13	9.	I DON'T KNOW WHERE I'M GOING, BUT I'M ON MY WAY (4)
16	10.	I'M ALL BOUND 'ROUND WITH THE MASON-DIXON LINE (2)
4	11.	THEY GO WILD, SIMPLY WILD, OVER ME (4)
8	12.	KEEP THE HOME FIRES BURNING (9)
12	13.	WHEN YANKEE DOODLE LEARNS TO PARLEZ-VOUS FRANCAIS (3)
9	14.	BREAK THE NEWS TO MOTHER (4)
–	15.	HAIL, HAIL, THE GANG'S ALL HERE (1)
–	16.	WHERE THE MORNING GLORIES GROW (1)
5	17.	WHERE DO WE GO FROM HERE? (5)
–	18.	LONG BOY (GOODBYE MA! GOODBYE PA! GOODBYE MULE) (1)
–	19.	WILL YOU REMEMBER (SWEETHEART) (1)
–	20.	SOMEWHERE IN FRANCE IS THE LILY (1)

JANUARY 1918

LM	TM	
1	1.	OVER THERE (7)
3	2.	THE DARKTOWN STRUTTERS' BALL (8)
2	3.	SOME SUNDAY MORNING (3)
7	4.	I DON'T WANT TO GET WELL (3)
8	5.	THERE'S A LONG, LONG TRAIL (14)
10	6.	I'M ALL BOUND 'ROUND WITH THE MASON-DIXON LINE (3)
–	7.	WAIT TILL THE COWS COME HOME (1)
6	8.	JOAN OF ARC, THEY ARE CALLING YOU (6)
12	9.	KEEP THE HOME FIRES BURNING (10)
14	10.	BREAK THE NEWS TO MOTHER (5)
13	11.	WHEN YANKEE DOODLE LEARNS TO PARLEZ-VOUS FRANCAIS (4)
15	12.	HAIL, HAIL, THE GANG'S ALL HERE (2)
4	13.	I MAY BE GONE FOR A LONG, LONG TIME (6)
19	14.	WILL YOU REMEMBER (SWEETHEART) (2)
20	15.	SOMEWHERE IN FRANCE IS THE LILY (2)
9	16.	I DON'T KNOW WHERE I'M GOING, BUT I'M ON MY WAY (5)
18	17.	LONG BOY (GOODBYE MA! GOODBYE PA! GOODBYE MULE) (2)
–	18.	LI'L LIZA JANE (1)
5	19.	GOODBYE BROADWAY, HELLO FRANCE! (6)
–	20.	MY SUNSHINE JANE (1)

FEBRUARY 1918

LM	TM	
2	1.	THE DARKTOWN STRUTTERS' BALL (9)
1	2.	OVER THERE (8)
7	3.	WAIT TILL THE COWS COME HOME (2)
4	4.	I DON'T WANT TO GET WELL (4)
5	5.	THERE'S A LONG, LONG TRAIL (15)
6	6.	I'M ALL BOUND 'ROUND WITH THE MASON-DIXON LINE (4)
3	7.	SOME SUNDAY MORNING (4)
8	8.	JOAN OF ARC, THEY ARE CALLING YOU (7)
9	9.	KEEP THE HOME FIRES BURNING (11)
10	10.	BREAK THE NEWS TO MOTHER (6)
15	11.	SOMEWHERE IN FRANCE IS THE LILY (3)
11	12.	WHEN YANKEE DOODLE LEARNS TO PARLEZ-VOUS FRANCAIS (5)
–	13.	INDIANOLA (1)
–	14.	ARE YOU FROM HEAVEN? (1)
18	15.	LI'L LIZA JANE (2)
–	16.	THE OLD GREY MARE (1)
12	17.	HAIL, HAIL, THE GANG'S ALL HERE (3)
17	18.	LONG BOY (GOODBYE MA! GOODBYE PA! GOODBYE MULE) (3)
14	19.	WILL YOU REMEMBER (SWEETHEART) (3)
–	20.	GIVE ME THE MOONLIGHT, GIVE ME THE GIRL (1)

MARCH 1918

LM	TM	
1	1.	THE DARKTOWN STRUTTERS' BALL (10)
3	2.	WAIT TILL THE COWS COME HOME (3)
5	3.	THERE'S A LONG, LONG TRAIL (16)
–	4.	JUST A BABY'S PRAYER AT TWILIGHT (1)
14	5.	ARE YOU FROM HEAVEN? (2)
2	6.	OVER THERE (9)
13	7.	INDIANOLA (2)
6	8.	I'M ALL BOUND 'ROUND WITH THE MASON-DIXON LINE (5)
4	9.	I DON'T WANT TO GET WELL (5)
9	10.	KEEP THE HOME FIRES BURNING (12)
8	11.	JOAN OF ARC, THEY ARE CALLING YOU (8)
–	12.	MISSOURI WALTZ (HUSH-A-BYE MA BABY) (4)
10	13.	BREAK THE NEWS TO MOTHER (7)
11	14.	SOMEWHERE IN FRANCE IS THE LILY (4)
15	15.	LI'L LIZA JANE (3)
12	16.	WHEN YANKEE DOODLE LEARNS TO PARLEZ-VOUS FRANCAIS (6)
–	17.	I'M GOING TO FOLLOW THE BOYS (1)
–	18.	SWEET LITTLE BUTTERCUP (1)
7	19.	SOME SUNDAY MORNING (5)
16	20.	THE OLD GREY MARE (2)

APRIL 1918

LM	TM	
4	1.	JUST A BABY'S PRAYER AT TWILIGHT (2)
5	2.	ARE YOU FROM HEAVEN? (3)
1	3.	THE DARKTOWN STRUTTERS' BALL (11)
7	4.	INDIANOLA (3)
–	5.	I'M SORRY I MADE YOU CRY (1)
12	6.	MISSOURI WALTZ (HUSH-A-BYE MA BABY) (5)
3	7.	THERE'S A LONG, LONG TRAIL (17)
–	8.	LORRAINE (MY BEAUTIFUL ALSACE LORRAINE) (1)
18	9.	SWEET LITTLE BUTTERCUP (2)
17	10.	I'M GOING TO FOLLOW THE BOYS (2)
–	11.	(SHE'S) THE DAUGHTER OF ROSIE O'GRADY (1)
6	12.	OVER THERE (10)
8	13.	I'M ALL BOUND 'ROUND WITH THE MASON-DIXON LINE (6)
2	14.	WAIT TILL THE COWS COME HOME (4)
–	15.	FOREVER IS A LONG, LONG TIME (1)
–	16.	EVERYBODY OUGHT TO KNOW HOW TO DO THE TICKLE TOE (1)
13	17.	BREAK THE NEWS TO MOTHER (8)
–	18.	BRING BACK MY DADDY TO ME (1)
–	19.	BLUE BIRD (BRING BACK MY HAPPINESS) (1)
–	20.	ON THE ROAD TO HOME SWEET HOME (1)

MAY 1918

LM	TM	
1	1.	JUST A BABY'S PRAYER AT TWILIGHT (3)
5	2.	I'M SORRY I MADE YOU CRY (2)
4	3.	INDIANOLA (4)
6	4.	MISSOURI WALTZ (HUSH-A-BYE MA BABY) (6)
2	5.	ARE YOU FROM HEAVEN? (4)
11	6.	(SHE'S) THE DAUGHTER OF ROSIE O'GRADY (2)
18	7.	BRING BACK MY DADDY TO ME (2)
8	8.	LORRAINE (MY BEAUTIFUL ALSACE LORRAINE) (2)
–	9.	I HATE TO LOSE YOU (1)
16	10.	EVERYBODY OUGHT TO KNOW HOW TO DO THE TICKLE TOE (2)
3	11.	THE DARKTOWN STRUTTERS' BALL (12)
15	12.	FOREVER IS A LONG, LONG TIME (2)
9	13.	SWEET LITTLE BUTTERCUP (3)
7	14.	THERE'S A LONG, LONG TRAIL (18)
–	15.	THREE WONDERFUL LETTERS FROM HOME (1)
19	16.	BLUE BIRD (BRING BACK MY HAPPINESS) (2)
20	17.	ON THE ROAD TO HOME SWEET HOME (2)
–	18.	K-K-K-KATY (1)
12	19.	OVER THERE (11)
–	20.	IF YOU LOOK IN HER EYES (1)

JUNE 1918

LM	TM	
2	1.	I'M SORRY I MADE YOU CRY (3)
1	2.	JUST A BABY'S PRAYER AT TWILIGHT (4)
6	3.	(SHE'S) THE DAUGHTER OF ROSIE O'GRADY (3)
3	4.	INDIANOLA (5)
18	5.	K-K-K-KATY (2)
9	6.	I HATE TO LOSE YOU (2)
–	7.	HELLO, CENTRAL, GIVE ME NO-MAN'S-LAND (1)
7	8.	BRING BACK MY DADDY TO ME (3)
12	9.	FOREVER IS A LONG, LONG TIME (3)
10	10.	EVERYBODY OUGHT TO KNOW HOW TO DO THE TICKLE TOE (3)
4	11.	MISSOURI WALTZ (HUSH-A-BYE MA BABY) (7)
–	12.	JUST LIKE WASHINGTON CROSSED THE DELAWARE (1)
–	13.	GOOD MORNING, MR. ZIP-ZIP-ZIP! (1)
15	14.	THREE WONDERFUL LETTERS FROM HOME (2)
8	15.	LORRAINE (MY BEAUTIFUL ALSACE LORRAINE) (3)
5	16.	ARE YOU FROM HEAVEN? (5)
–	17.	N'EVERYTHING (1)
13	18.	SWEET LITTLE BUTTERCUP (4)
–	19.	TISHOMINGO BLUES (1)
16	20.	BLUE BIRD (BRING BACK MY HAPPINESS) (3)

JULY 1918

LM	TM	Title
1	1.	I'M SORRY I MADE YOU CRY (4)
7	2.	HELLO, CENTRAL, GIVE ME NO-MAN'S- LAND (2)
5	3.	K-K-K-KATY (3)
2	4.	JUST A BABY'S PRAYER AT TWILIGHT (5)
13	5.	GOOD MORNING, MR. ZIP-ZIP-ZIP! (2)
3	6.	(SHE'S) THE DAUGHTER OF ROSIE O'GRADY (4)
9	7.	FOREVER IS A LONG, LONG TIME (4)
12	8.	JUST LIKE WASHINGTON CROSSED THE DELAWARE (2)
4	9.	INDIANOLA (6)
–	10.	THEY WERE ALL OUT OF STEP BUT JIM (1)
6	11.	I HATE TO LOSE YOU (3)
17	12.	N'EVERYTHING (2)
–	13.	IF HE CAN FIGHT LIKE HE CAN LOVE, GOOD NIGHT, GERMANY! (1)
19	14.	TISHOMINGO BLUES (2)
–	15.	MY BELGIAN ROSE (1)
8	16.	BRING BACK MY DADDY TO ME (4)
10	17.	EVERYBODY OUGHT TO KNOW HOW TO DO THE TICKLE TOE (4)
11	18.	MISSOURI WALTZ (HUSH-A-BYE MA BABY) (8)
–	19.	EVERYBODY'S (GONE) CRAZY 'BOUT THE DOGGONE BLUES (1)
–	20.	ROCK-A-BYE YOUR BABY WITH A DIXIE MELODY (1)

AUGUST 1918

LM	TM	Title
3	1.	K-K-K-KATY (4)
2	2.	HELLO, CENTRAL, GIVE ME NO-MAN'S- LAND(3)
1	3.	I'M SORRY I MADE YOU CRY (5)
10	4.	THEY WERE ALL OUT OF STEP BUT JIM (2)
–	5.	SMILES (1)
5	6.	GOOD MORNING, MR. ZIP-ZIP-ZIP! (3)
4	7.	JUST A BABY'S PRAYER AT TWILIGHT (6)
15	8.	MY BELGIAN ROSE (2)
13	9.	IF HE CAN FIGHT LIKE HE CAN LOVE, GOOD NIGHT, GERMANY! (2)
20	10.	ROCK-A-BYE YOUR BABY WITH A DIXIE MELODY (2)
7	11.	FOREVER IS A LONG, LONG TIME (5)
6	12.	(SHE'S) THE DAUGHTER OF ROSIE O'GRADY (5)
–	13.	KEEP YOUR HEAD DOWN, FRITZIE BOY (1)
9	14.	INDIANOLA (7)
–	15.	I'M GONNA PIN MY MEDAL ON THE GIRL I LEFT BEHIND (1)
19	16.	EVERYBODY'S (GONE) CRAZY 'BOUT THE DOGGONE BLUES (2)
14	17.	TISHOMINGO BLUES (3)
–	18.	I'M ALWAYS CHASING RAINBOWS (1)
8	19.	JUST LIKE WASHINGTON CROSSED THE DELAWARE (3)
–	20.	HOW'D YOU LIKE TO BE MY DADDY? (1)

SEPTEMBER 1918

LM	TM	Title
1	1.	K-K-K-KATY (5)
5	2.	SMILES (2)
10	3.	ROCK-A-BYE YOUR BABY WITH A DIXIE MELODY (3)
2	4.	HELLO, CENTRAL, GIVE ME NO-MAN'S- LAND (4)
8	5.	MY BELGIAN ROSE (3)
3	6.	I'M SORRY I MADE YOU CRY (6)
–	7.	WHEN YOU COME BACK (AND YOU WILL COME BACK) (1)
–	8.	OH! HOW I HATE TO GET UP IN THE MORNING (1)
4	9.	THEY WERE ALL OUT OF STEP BUT JIM (3)
6	10.	GOOD MORNING, MR. ZIP-ZIP-ZIP! (4)
9	11.	IF HE CAN FIGHT LIKE HE CAN LOVE, GOOD NIGHT, GERMANY! (3)
18	12.	I'M ALWAYS CHASING RAINBOWS (2)
13	13.	KEEP YOUR HEAD DOWN, FRITZIE BOY (2)
7	14.	JUST A BABY'S PRAYER AT TWILIGHT (7)
–	15.	OH! FRENCHY (1)
15	16.	I'M GONNA PIN MY MEDAL ON THE GIRL I LEFT BEHIND (2)
–	17.	OUI, OUI, MARIE (1)
11	18.	FOREVER IS A LONG, LONG TIME (6)
14	19.	INDIANOLA (8)
–	20.	TIGER RAG (1)

OCTOBER 1918

LM	TM	Title
2	1.	SMILES (3)
1	2.	K-K-K-KATY (6)
3	3.	ROCK-A-BYE YOUR BABY WITH A DIXIE MELODY (4)
8	4.	OH! HOW I HATE TO GET UP IN THE MORNING (2)
7	5.	WHEN YOU COME BACK (AND YOU WILL COME BACK) (2)
–	6.	EVERYTHING IS PEACHES DOWN IN GEORGIA (1)
5	7.	MY BELGIAN ROSE (4)
12	8.	I'M ALWAYS CHASING RAINBOWS (3)
15	9.	OH! FRENCHY (2)
–	10.	AFTER YOU'VE GONE (1)
17	11.	OUI, OUI, MARIE (2)
4	12.	HELLO, CENTRAL, GIVE ME NO-MAN'S- LAND (5)
–	13.	HINDUSTAN (1)
–	14.	MAMMY'S CHOCOLATE SOLDIER (1)
20	15.	TIGER RAG (2)
–	16.	OH! HOW I WISH I COULD SLEEP UNTIL MY DADDY COMES HOME (1)
10	17.	GOOD MORNING, MR. ZIP-ZIP-ZIP! (5)
11	18.	IF HE CAN FIGHT LIKE HE CAN LOVE, GOOD NIGHT, GERMANY! (4)
–	19.	ROSES OF PICARDY (1)
–	20.	WATERS OF VENICE (1)

NOVEMBER 1918

LM	TM	Title
1	1.	SMILES (4)
6	2.	EVERYTHING IS PEACHES DOWN IN GEORGIA (2)
4	3.	OH! HOW I HATE TO GET UP IN THE MORNING (3)
16	4.	OH! HOW I WISH I COULD SLEEP UNTIL MY DADDY COMES HOME (2)
3	5.	ROCK-A-BYE YOUR BABY WITH A DIXIE MELODY (5)
8	6.	I'M ALWAYS CHASING RAINBOWS (4)
2	7.	K-K-K-KATY (7)
5	8.	WHEN YOU COME BACK (AND YOU WILL COME BACK) (3)
10	9.	AFTER YOU'VE GONE (2)
9	10.	OH! FRENCHY (3)
11	11.	OUI, OUI, MARIE (3)
13	12.	HINDUSTAN (2)
7	13.	MY BELGIAN ROSE (5)
14	14.	MAMMY'S CHOCOLATE SOLDIER (2)
15	15.	TIGER RAG (3)
–	16.	DEAR LITTLE BOY OF MINE (1)
20	17.	WATERS OF VENICE (2)
19	18.	ROSES OF PICARDY (2)
–	19.	BEAUTIFUL OHIO (1)
17	20.	GOOD MORNING, MR. ZIP-ZIP-ZIP! (6)

DECEMBER 1918

LM	TM	Title
1	1.	SMILES (5)
6	2.	I'M ALWAYS CHASING RAINBOWS (5)
4	3.	OH! HOW I WISH I COULD SLEEP UNTIL MY DADDY COMES HOME (3)
2	4.	EVERYTHING IS PEACHES DOWN IN GEORGIA (3)
12	5.	HINDUSTAN (3)
3	6.	OH! HOW I HATE TO GET UP IN THE MORNING (4)
5	7.	ROCK-A-BYE YOUR BABY WITH A DIXIE MELODY (6)
9	8.	AFTER YOU'VE GONE (3)
10	9.	OH! FRENCHY (4)
19	10.	BEAUTIFUL OHIO (2)
–	11.	ROSE OF NO MAN'S LAND (1)
11	12.	OUI, OUI, MARIE (4)
–	13.	TILL WE MEET AGAIN (1)
7	14.	K-K-K-KATY (8)
8	15.	WHEN YOU COME BACK (AND YOU WILL COME BACK) (4)
16	16.	DEAR LITTLE BOY OF MINE (2)
–	17.	MICKEY (1)
–	18.	I'M GLAD I CAN MAKE YOU CRY (1)
–	19.	WOULD YOU RATHER BE A COLONEL WITH AN EAGLE ON YOUR SHOULDER OR A PRIVATE WITH A CHICKEN ON YOUR KNEE? (1)
–	20.	A GOOD MAN IS HARD TO FIND (1)

JANUARY 1919

LM	TM	
11	1.	ROSE OF NO MAN'S LAND (2)
2	2.	I'M ALWAYS CHASING RAINBOWS (6)
5	3.	HINDUSTAN (4)
1	4.	SMILES (6)
13	5.	TILL WE MEET AGAIN (2)
10	6.	BEAUTIFUL OHIO (3)
4	7.	EVERYTHING IS PEACHES DOWN IN GEORGIA (4)
17	8.	MICKEY (2)
3	9.	OH! HOW I WISH I COULD SLEEP UNTIL MY DADDY COMES HOME (4)
16	10.	DEAR LITTLE BOY OF MINE (3)
9	11.	OH! FRENCHY (5)
7	12.	ROCK-A-BYE YOUR BABY WITH A DIXIE MELODY (7)
6	13.	OH! HOW I HATE TO GET UP IN THE MORNING (5)
12	14.	OUI, OUI, MARIE (5)
8	15.	AFTER YOU'VE GONE (4)
19	16.	WOULD YOU RATHER BE A COLONEL WITH AN EAGLE ON YOUR SHOULDER OR A PRIVATE WITH A CHICKEN ON YOUR KNEE? (2)
18	17.	I'M GLAD I CAN MAKE YOU CRY (2)
20	18.	A GOOD MAN IS HARD TO FIND (2)
–	19.	DEAR OLD PAL OF MINE (1)
14	20.	K-K-K-KATY (9)

FEBRUARY 1919

LM	TM	
5	1.	TILL WE MEET AGAIN (3)
1	2.	ROSE OF NO MAN'S LAND (3)
8	3.	MICKEY (3)
6	4.	BEAUTIFUL OHIO (4)
2	5.	I'M ALWAYS CHASING RAINBOWS (7)
10	6.	DEAR LITTLE BOY OF MINE (4)
3	7.	HINDUSTAN (5)
–	8.	JA-DA (1)
4	9.	SMILES (7)
–	10.	MADELON (1)
11	11.	OH! FRENCHY (6)
–	12.	KISSES, THE SWEETEST KISSES OF ALL (1)
19	13.	DEAR OLD PAL OF MINE (2)
14	14.	OUI, OUI, MARIE (6)
18	15.	A GOOD MAN IS HARD TO FIND (3)
7	16.	EVERYTHING IS PEACHES DOWN IN GEORGIA (5)
16	17.	WOULD YOU RATHER BE A COLONEL WITH AN EAGLE ON YOUR SHOULDER OR A PRIVATE WITH A CHICKEN ON YOUR KNEE? (3)
12	18.	ROCK-A-BYE YOUR BABY WITH A DIXIE MELODY (8)
–	19.	THAT WONDERFUL MOTHER OF MINE (1)
–	20.	EVERYBODY SHIMMIES NOW (1)

MARCH 1919

LM	TM	
1	1.	TILL WE MEET AGAIN (4)
4	2.	BEAUTIFUL OHIO (5)
8	3.	JA-DA (2)
3	4.	MICKEY (4)
–	5.	HOW YA GONNA KEEP 'EM DOWN ON THE FARM? (1)
10	6.	MADELON (2)
2	7.	ROSE OF NO MAN'S LAND (4)
6	8.	DEAR LITTLE BOY OF MINE (5)
5	9.	I'M ALWAYS CHASING RAINBOWS (8)
12	10.	KISSES, THE SWEETEST KISSES OF ALL (2)
19	11.	THAT WONDERFUL MOTHER OF MINE (2)
7	12.	HINDUSTAN (6)
–	13.	KENTUCKY DREAM WALTZ (1)
15	14.	A GOOD MAN IS HARD TO FIND (4)
20	15.	EVERYBODY SHIMMIES NOW (2)
–	16.	COME ON, PAPA (1)
13	17.	DEAR OLD PAL OF MINE (3)
–	18.	SALVATION LASSIE OF MINE (1)
9	19.	SMILES (8)
11	20.	OH! FRENCHY (7)

APRIL 1919

LM	TM	
1	1.	TILL WE MEET AGAIN (5)
5	2.	HOW YA GONNA KEEP 'EM DOWN ON THE FARM? (2)
3	3.	JA-DA (3)
2	4.	BEAUTIFUL OHIO (6)
6	5.	MADELON (3)
11	6.	THAT WONDERFUL MOTHER OF MINE (3)
4	7.	MICKEY (5)
8	8.	DEAR LITTLE BOY OF MINE (6)
16	9.	COME ON, PAPA (2)
–	10.	CHONG, HE COME FROM HONG KONG (1)
13	11.	KENTUCKY DREAM WALTZ (2)
7	12.	ROSE OF NO MAN'S LAND (5)
14	13.	A GOOD MAN IS HARD TO FIND (5)
–	14.	I'LL SAY SHE DOES (1)
10	15.	KISSES, THE SWEETEST KISSES OF ALL (3)
15	16.	EVERYBODY SHIMMIES NOW (3)
–	17.	WHEN YOU LOOK IN THE HEART OF A ROSE (1)
9	18.	I'M ALWAYS CHASING RAINBOWS (9)
18	19.	SALVATION LASSIE OF MINE (2)
–	20.	EVERY DAY WILL BE SUNDAY WHEN THE TOWN GOES DRY (1)

MAY 1919

LM	TM	
2	1.	HOW YA GONNA KEEP 'EM DOWN ON THE FARM? (3)
1	2.	TILL WE MEET AGAIN (6)
3	3.	JA-DA (4)
–	4.	I'M FOREVER BLOWING BUBBLES (1)
4	5.	BEAUTIFUL OHIO (7)
10	6.	CHONG, HE COME FROM HONG KONG (2)
6	7.	THAT WONDERFUL MOTHER OF MINE (4)
14	8.	I'LL SAY SHE DOES (2)
9	9.	COME ON, PAPA (3)
11	10.	KENTUCKY DREAM WALTZ (3)
13	11.	A GOOD MAN IS HARD TO FIND (6)
17	12.	WHEN YOU LOOK IN THE HEART OF A ROSE (2)
5	13.	MADELON (4)
8	14.	DEAR LITTLE BOY OF MINE (7)
–	15.	SWEET HAWAIIAN MOONLIGHT (1)
–	16.	MAMMY O' MINE (1)
–	17.	THAT TUMBLEDOWN SHACK IN ATHLONE (1)
–	18.	DON'T CRY, FRENCHY, DON'T CRY (1)
7	19.	MICKEY (6)
–	20.	SMILIN' THROUGH (1)

JUNE 1919

LM	TM	
4	1.	I'M FOREVER BLOWING BUBBLES (2)
1	2.	HOW YA GONNA KEEP 'EM DOWN ON THE FARM? (4)
2	3.	TILL WE MEET AGAIN (7)
6	4.	CHONG, HE COME FROM HONG KONG (3)
8	5.	I'LL SAY SHE DOES (3)
16	6.	MAMMY O' MINE (2)
15	7.	SWEET HAWAIIAN MOONLIGHT (2)
12	8.	WHEN YOU LOOK IN THE HEART OF A ROSE (3)
5	9.	BEAUTIFUL OHIO (8)
20	10.	SMILIN' THROUGH (2)
3	11.	JA-DA (5)
11	12.	A GOOD MAN IS HARD TO FIND (7)
–	13.	IT'S NOBODY'S BUSINESS BUT MY OWN (1)
7	14.	THAT WONDERFUL MOTHER OF MINE (5)
10	15.	KENTUCKY DREAM WALTZ (4)
–	16.	ALCOHOLIC BLUES (1)
9	17.	COME ON, PAPA (4)
14	18.	DEAR LITTLE BOY OF MINE (8)
17	19.	THAT TUMBLEDOWN SHACK IN ATHLONE (2)
18	20.	DON'T CRY, FRENCHY, DON'T CRY (2)

JULY 1919

LM	TM	
1	1.	I'M FOREVER BLOWING BUBBLES (3)
6	2.	MAMMY O' MINE (3)
7	3.	SWEET HAWAIIAN MOONLIGHT (3)
10	4.	SMILIN' THROUGH (3)
2	5.	HOW YA GONNA KEEP 'EM DOWN ON THE FARM? (5)
8	6.	WHEN YOU LOOK IN THE HEART OF A ROSE (4)
3	7.	TILL WE MEET AGAIN (8)
4	8.	CHONG, HE COME FROM HONG KONG (4)
5	9.	I'LL SAY SHE DOES (4)
9	10.	BEAUTIFUL OHIO (9)
13	11.	IT'S NOBODY'S BUSINESS BUT MY OWN (2)
16	12.	ALCOHOLIC BLUES (2)
12	13.	A GOOD MAN IS HARD TO FIND (8)
15	14.	KENTUCKY DREAM WALTZ (5)
14	15.	THAT WONDERFUL MOTHER OF MINE (6)
18	16.	DEAR LITTLE BOY OF MINE (9)
–	17.	BLUES (MY NAUGHTY SWEETIE GIVES TO ME) (1)
–	18.	THE BELLS OF ST. MARY'S (1)
–	19.	MY BARNEY LIES OVER THE OCEAN (1)
–	20.	ME-OW (1)

AUGUST 1919

LM	TM	
1	1.	I'M FOREVER BLOWING BUBBLES (4)
2	2.	MAMMY O' MINE (4)
6	3.	WHEN YOU LOOK IN THE HEART OF A ROSE (5)
4	4.	SMILIN' THROUGH (4)
3	5.	SWEET HAWAIIAN MOONLIGHT (4)
17	6.	BLUES (MY NAUGHTY SWEETIE GIVES TO ME) (2)
7	7.	TILL WE MEET AGAIN (9)
8	8.	CHONG, HE COME FROM HONG KONG (5)
9	9.	I'LL SAY SHE DOES (5)
11	10.	IT'S NOBODY'S BUSINESS BUT MY OWN (3)
10	11.	BEAUTIFUL OHIO (10)
–	12.	DADDY LONG LEGS (1)
14	13.	KENTUCKY DREAM WALTZ (6)
13	14.	A GOOD MAN IS HARD TO FIND (9)
–	15.	A PRETTY GIRL IS LIKE A MELODY (1)
5	16.	HOW YA GONNA KEEP 'EM DOWN ON THE FARM? (6)
18	17.	THE BELLS OF ST. MARY'S (2)
15	18.	THAT WONDERFUL MOTHER OF MINE (7)
–	19.	EVERYBODY WANTS A KEY TO MY CELLAR (1)
12	20.	ALCOHOLIC BLUES (3)

SEPTEMBER 1919

LM	TM	
1	1.	I'M FOREVER BLOWING BUBBLES (5)
15	2.	A PRETTY GIRL IS LIKE A MELODY (2)
4	3.	SMILIN' THROUGH (5)
6	4.	BLUES (MY NAUGHTY SWEETIE GIVES TO ME) (3)
–	5.	MANDY (1)
–	6.	TELL ME (WHY NIGHTS ARE LONELY) (1)
3	7.	WHEN YOU LOOK IN THE HEART OF A ROSE (6)
10	8.	IT'S NOBODY'S BUSINESS BUT MY OWN (4)
–	9.	THE VAMP (1)
–	10.	SIPPING CIDER THROUGH A STRAW (1)
12	11.	DADDY LONG LEGS (2)
2	12.	MAMMY O' MINE (5)
–	13.	TULIP TIME (1)
9	14.	I'LL SAY SHE DOES (6)
17	15.	THE BELLS OF ST. MARY'S (3)
–	16.	I'LL BE HAPPY WHEN THE PREACHER MAKES YOU MINE (1)
7	17.	TILL WE MEET AGAIN (10)
5	18.	SWEET HAWAIIAN MOONLIGHT (5)
–	19.	CHINESE LULLABY (1)
14	20.	A GOOD MAN IS HARD TO FIND (10)

OCTOBER 1919

LM	TM	
2	1.	A PRETTY GIRL IS LIKE A MELODY (3)
5	2.	MANDY (2)
6	3.	TELL ME (WHY NIGHTS ARE LONELY) (2)
–	4.	OH! WHAT A PAL WAS MARY (1)
13	5.	TULIP TIME (2)
9	6.	THE VAMP (2)
4	7.	BLUES (MY NAUGHTY SWEETIE GIVES TO ME) (4)
10	8.	SIPPING CIDER THROUGH A STRAW (2)
–	9.	NOBODY KNOWS, AND NOBODY SEEMS TO CARE (1)
19	10.	CHINESE LULLABY (2)
16	11.	I'LL BE HAPPY WHEN THE PREACHER MAKES YOU MINE (2)
3	12.	SMILIN' THROUGH (6)
7	13.	WHEN YOU LOOK IN THE HEART OF A ROSE (7)
1	14.	I'M FOREVER BLOWING BUBBLES (6)
–	15.	I'VE GOT MY CAPTAIN WORKING FOR ME NOW (1)
–	16.	AND HE'D SAY OOH-LA-LA! WEE WEE (1)
–	17.	ALEXANDER'S BAND IS BACK IN DIXIE LAND(1)
13	18.	THE BELLS OF ST. MARY'S (4)
–	19.	TAKE ME TO THE LAND OF JAZZ (1)
–	20.	EVERYBODY WANTS A KEY TO MY CELLAR (1)

NOVEMBER 1919

LM	TM	
2	1.	MANDY (3)
3	2.	TELL ME (WHY NIGHTS ARE LONELY) (3)
4	3.	OH! WHAT A PAL WAS MARY (2)
1	4.	A PRETTY GIRL IS LIKE A MELODY (4)
9	5.	NOBODY KNOWS, AND NOBODY SEEMS TO CARE (2)
6	6.	THE VAMP (3)
15	7.	I'VE GOT MY CAPTAIN WORKING FOR ME NOW (2)
5	8.	TULIP TIME (3)
11	9.	I'LL BE HAPPY WHEN THE PREACHER MAKES YOU MINE (3)
10	10.	CHINESE LULLABY (3)
17	11.	ALEXANDER'S BAND IS BACK IN DIXIE LAND(2)
16	12.	AND HE'D SAY OOH-LA-LA! WEE WEE (2)
7	13.	BLUES (MY NAUGHTY SWEETIE GIVES TO ME) (5)
–	14.	WAIT TILL YOU GET THEM UP IN THE AIR, BOYS (1)
19	15.	TAKE ME TO THE LAND OF JAZZ (2)
–	16.	CAROLINA SUNSHINE (1)
–	17.	DREAMY ALABAMA (1)
–	18.	YOU DIDN'T WANT ME WHEN YOU HAD ME (1)
8	19.	SIPPING CIDER THROUGH A STRAW (3)
18	20.	THE BELLS OF ST. MARY'S (5)

DECEMBER 1919

LM	TM	
3	1.	OH! WHAT A PAL WAS MARY (3)
1	2.	MANDY (4)
5	3.	NOBODY KNOWS, AND NOBODY SEEMS TO CARE (3)
2	4.	TELL ME (WHY NIGHTS ARE LONELY) (4)
4	5.	A PRETTY GIRL IS LIKE A MELODY (5)
7	6.	I'VE GOT MY CAPTAIN WORKING FOR ME NOW (3)
–	7.	LET THE REST OF THE WORLD GO BY (1)
14	8.	WAIT TILL YOU GET THEM UP IN THE AIR, BOYS (2)
9	9.	I'LL BE HAPPY WHEN THE PREACHER MAKES YOU MINE (4)
16	10.	CAROLINA SUNSHINE (2)
–	11.	YOU'D BE SURPRISED (1)
–	12.	MY ISLE OF GOLDEN DREAMS (1)
12	13.	AND HE'D SAY OOH-LA-LA! WEE WEE (3)
6	14.	THE VAMP (4)
11	15.	ALEXANDER'S BAND IS BACK IN DIXIE LAND (3)
18	16.	YOU DIDN'T WANT ME WHEN YOU HAD ME (2)
–	17.	THAT NAUGHTY WALTZ (1)
13	18.	BLUES (MY NAUGHTY SWEETIE GIVES TO ME) (6)
8	19.	TULIP TIME (4)
–	20.	THEY'RE ALL SWEETIES (1)

JANUARY 1920

LM	TM	
7	1.	LET THE REST OF THE WORLD GO BY (2)
1	2.	OH! WHAT A PAL WAS MARY (4)
11	3.	YOU'D BE SURPRISED (2)
12	4.	MY ISLE OF GOLDEN DREAMS (2)
3	5.	NOBODY KNOWS, AND NOBODY SEEMS TO CARE (4)
4	6.	TELL ME (WHY NIGHTS ARE LONELY) (5)
–	7.	PEGGY (1)
–	8.	DARDANELLA (1)
8	9.	WAIT TILL YOU GET THEM UP IN THE AIR, BOYS (3)
2	10.	MANDY (5)
–	11.	ON MIAMI SHORE (1)
17	12.	THAT NAUGHTY WALTZ (2)
10	13.	CAROLINA SUNSHINE (3)
5	14.	A PRETTY GIRL IS LIKE A MELODY (6)
–	15.	FRECKLES (1)
9	16.	I'LL BE HAPPY WHEN THE PREACHER MAKES YOU MINE (5)
–	17.	I MIGHT BE YOUR ONCE-IN-A-WHILE (1)
6	18.	I'VE GOT MY CAPTAIN WORKING FOR ME NOW (4)
–	19.	YOU AIN'T HEARD NOTHIN' YET (1)
18	20.	BLUES (MY NAUGHTY SWEETIE GIVES TO ME) (7)

FEBRUARY 1920

LM	TM	
1	1.	LET THE REST OF THE WORLD GO BY (3)
8	2.	DARDANELLA (2)
4	3.	MY ISLE OF GOLDEN DREAMS (3)
7	4.	PEGGY (2)
3	5.	YOU'D BE SURPRISED (3)
11	6.	ON MIAMI SHORE (2)
15	7.	FRECKLES (2)
2	8.	OH! WHAT A PAL WAS MARY (5)
–	9.	YOU'RE A MILLION MILES FROM NOWHERE (1)
17	10.	I MIGHT BE YOUR ONCE-IN-A-WHILE (2)
12	11.	THAT NAUGHTY WALTZ (3)
–	12.	ALL THE QUAKERS ARE SHOULDER SHAKERS (DOWN IN QUAKER TOWN) (1)
13	13.	CAROLINA SUNSHINE (4)
5	14.	NOBODY KNOWS, AND NOBODY SEEMS TO CARE (5)
19	15.	YOU AIN'T HEARD NOTHIN' YET (2)
–	16.	YOUR EYES HAVE TOLD ME SO (1)
6	17.	TELL ME (WHY NIGHTS ARE LONELY) (6)
–	18.	BABY, WON'T YOU PLEASE COME HOME (1)
9	19.	WAIT TILL YOU GET THEM UP IN THE AIR, BOYS (4)
–	20.	YELLOW DOG BLUES (1)

MARCH 1920

LM	TM	
2	1.	DARDANELLA (3)
1	2.	LET THE REST OF THE WORLD GO BY (4)
4	3.	PEGGY (3)
3	4.	MY ISLE OF GOLDEN DREAMS (4)
9	5.	YOU'RE A MILLION MILES FROM NOWHERE (2)
–	6.	SWANEE (1)
6	7.	ON MIAMI SHORE (3)
11	8.	THAT NAUGHTY WALTZ (4)
12	9.	ALL THE QUAKERS ARE SHOULDER SHAKERS (DOWN IN QUAKER TOWN) (2)
–	10.	WHEN MY BABY SMILES AT ME (1)
16	11.	YOUR EYES HAVE TOLD ME SO (2)
–	12.	WAS THERE EVER A PAL LIKE YOU? (1)
10	13.	I MIGHT BE YOUR ONCE-IN-A-WHILE (3)
5	14.	YOU'D BE SURPRISED (4)
7	15.	FRECKLES (3)
15	16.	YOU AIN'T HEARD NOTHIN' YET (3)
18	17.	BABY, WON'T YOU PLEASE COME HOME (2)
20	18.	YELLOW DOG BLUES (2)
–	19.	DADDY, YOU'VE BEEN A MOTHER TO ME (1)
–	20.	JUST LIKE A GYPSY (1)

APRIL 1920

LM	TM	
2	1.	LET THE REST OF THE WORLD GO BY (5)
10	2.	WHEN MY BABY SMILES AT ME (2)
6	3.	SWANEE (2)
1	4.	DARDANELLA (4)
19	5.	DADDY, YOU'VE BEEN A MOTHER TO ME (2)
3	6.	PEGGY (4)
8	7.	THAT NAUGHTY WALTZ (5)
–	8.	I'LL SEE YOU IN C-U-B-A (1)
4	9.	MY ISLE OF GOLDEN DREAMS (5)
11	10.	YOUR EYES HAVE TOLD ME SO (3)
–	11.	OH! HOW I LAUGH WHEN I THINK HOW I CRIED OVER YOU (1)
5	12.	YOU'RE A MILLION MILES FROM NOWHERE (3)
–	13.	OH! (1)
7	14.	ON MIAMI SHORE (4)
20	15.	JUST LIKE A GYPSY (2)
–	16.	AFGHANISTAN (1)
16	17.	YOU AIN'T HEARD NOTHIN' YET (4)
–	18.	THAT TUMBLEDOWN SHACK IN ATHLONE (3)
12	19.	WAS THERE EVER A PAL LIKE YOU? (2)
–	20.	OH BY JINGO! OH BY GEE! (YOU'RE THE ONLY GIRL FOR ME) (1)

MAY 1920

LM	TM	
3	1.	SWANEE (3)
2	2.	WHEN MY BABY SMILES AT ME (3)
5	3.	DADDY, YOU'VE BEEN A MOTHER TO ME (3)
8	4.	I'LL SEE YOU IN C-U-B-A (2)
–	5.	ROSE OF WASHINGTON SQUARE (1)
7	6.	THAT NAUGHTY WALTZ (6)
11	7.	OH! HOW I LAUGH WHEN I THINK HOW I CRIED OVER YOU (2)
10	8.	YOUR EYES HAVE TOLD ME SO (4)
1	9.	LET THE REST OF THE WORLD GO BY (6)
15	10.	JUST LIKE A GYPSY (3)
20	11.	OH BY JINGO! OH BY GEE! (YOU'RE THE ONLY GIRL FOR ME) (2)
–	12.	WHOSE BABY ARE YOU? (1)
–	13.	IRENE (1)
9	14.	MY ISLE OF GOLDEN DREAMS (6)
–	15.	ALICE BLUE GOWN (1)
16	16.	AFGHANISTAN (2)
4	17.	DARDANELLA (5)
13	18.	OH! (2)
–	19.	LA VEEDA (1)
–	20.	VENETIAN MOON (1)

JUNE 1920

LM	TM	
5	1.	ROSE OF WASHINGTON SQUARE (2)
1	2.	SWANEE (4)
2	3.	WHEN MY BABY SMILES AT ME (4)
11	4.	OH BY JINGO! OH BY GEE! (YOU'RE THE ONLY GIRL FOR ME) (3)
4	5.	I'LL SEE YOU IN C-U-B-A (3)
–	6.	HOLD ME (1)
19	7.	LA VEEDA (2)
–	8.	SO LONG! 00-LONG (1)
13	9.	IRENE (2)
10	10.	JUST LIKE A GYPSY (4)
15	11.	ALICE BLUE GOWN (2)
12	12.	WHOSE BABY ARE YOU? (2)
6	13.	THAT NAUGHTY WALTZ (7)
3	14.	DADDY, YOU'VE BEEN A MOTHER TO ME (4)
20	15.	VENETIAN MOON (2)
8	16.	YOUR EYES HAVE TOLD ME SO (5)
–	17.	LEFT ALL ALONE AGAIN BLUES (1)
–	18.	ALABAMA MOON (1)
–	19.	OLD MAN JAZZ (1)
7	20.	OH! HOW I LAUGH WHEN I THINK HOW I CRIED OVER YOU (3)

JULY 1920

LM	TM	
6	1.	HOLD ME (2)
1	2.	ROSE OF WASHINGTON SQUARE (3)
7	3.	LA VEEDA (3)
2	4.	SWANEE (5)
4	5.	OH BY JINGO! OH BY GEE! (YOU'RE THE ONLY GIRL FOR ME) (4)
8	6.	SO LONG! 00-LONG (2)
15	7.	VENETIAN MOON (3)
9	8.	IRENE (3)
17	9.	LEFT ALL ALONE AGAIN BLUES (2)
–	10.	PRETTY KITTY KELLY (1)
10	11.	JUST LIKE A GYPSY (5)
11	12.	ALICE BLUE GOWN (3)
5	13.	I'LL SEE YOU IN C-U-B-A (4)
18	14.	ALABAMA MOON (2)
16	15.	YOUR EYES HAVE TOLD ME SO (6)
–	16.	HIAWATHA'S MELODY OF LOVE (1)
–	17.	THE ARGENTINES, THE PORTUGUESE, AND THE GREEKS (1)
13	18.	THAT NAUGHTY WALTZ (8)
3	19.	WHEN MY BABY SMILES AT ME (5)
19	20.	OLD MAN JAZZ (2)

AUGUST 1920

LM	TM	
1	1.	HOLD ME (3)
3	2.	LA VEEDA (4)
10	3.	PRETTY KITTY KELLY (2)
16	4.	HIAWATHA'S MELODY OF LOVE (2)
7	5.	VENETIAN MOON (4)
5	6.	OH BY JINGO! OH BY GEE! (YOU'RE THE ONLY GIRL FOR ME) (5)
–	7.	THE LOVE NEST (1)
11	8.	JUST LIKE A GYPSY (6)
8	9.	IRENE (4)
9	10.	LEFT ALL ALONE AGAIN BLUES (3)
2	11.	ROSE OF WASHINGTON SQUARE (4)
–	12.	AFTER YOU GET WHAT YOU WANT, YOU DON'T WANT IT (1)
4	13.	SWANEE (6)
17	14.	THE ARGENTINES, THE PORTUGUESE, AND THE GREEKS (2)
6	15.	SO LONG! 00-LONG (3)
–	16.	I'M A JAZZ VAMPIRE (1)
–	17.	A YOUNG MAN'S FANCY (1)
14	18.	ALABAMA MOON (3)
12	19.	ALICE BLUE GOWN (4)
20	20.	OLD MAN JAZZ (3)

SEPTEMBER 1920

LM	TM	
7	1.	THE LOVE NEST (2)
1	2.	HOLD ME (4)
4	3.	HIAWATHA'S MELODY OF LOVE (3)
17	4.	A YOUNG MAN'S FANCY (2)
–	5.	TELL ME, LITTLE GYPSY (1)
2	6.	LA VEEDA (5)
3	7.	PRETTY KITTY KELLY (3)
–	8.	WHISPERING (1)
16	9.	I'M A JAZZ VAMPIRE (2)
12	10.	AFTER YOU GET WHAT YOU WANT, YOU DON'T WANT IT (2)
5	11.	VENETIAN MOON (5)
8	12.	JUST LIKE A GYPSY (7)
6	13.	OH BY JINGO! OH BY GEE! (YOU'RE THE ONLY GIRL FOR ME) (6)
9	14.	IRENE (5)
14	15.	THE ARGENTINES, THE PORTUGUESE, AND THE GREEKS (3)
–	16.	TWELFTH STREET RAG (1)
–	17.	MY LITTLE BIMBO (FROM THE BAMBOO ISLE) (1)
–	18.	TRIPOLI (1)
–	19.	JAZZ BABIES' BALL (1)
–	20.	ST. LOUIS BLUES (1)

OCTOBER 1920

LM	TM	
1	1.	THE LOVE NEST (3)
8	2.	WHISPERING (2)
4	3.	A YOUNG MAN'S FANCY (3)
5	4.	TELL ME, LITTLE GYPSY (2)
–	5.	THE JAPANESE SANDMAN (1)
3	6.	HIAWATHA'S MELODY OF LOVE (4)
10	7.	AFTER YOU GET WHAT YOU WANT, YOU DON'T WANT IT (3)
2	8.	HOLD ME (5)
17	10.	MY LITTLE BIMBO (FROM THE BAMBOO ISLE) (2)
–	9.	I'LL BE WITH YOU IN APPLE BLOSSOM TIME (1)
18	11.	TRIPOLI (2)
11	12.	VENETIAN MOON (6)
–	13.	CHILI BEAN (1)
9	14.	I'M A JAZZ VAMPIRE (3)
7	15.	PRETTY KITTY KELLY (4)
16	16.	TWELFTH STREET RAG (2)
–	17.	THAT OLD IRISH MOTHER OF MINE (1)
–	18.	I LOVE THE LAND OF OLD BLACK JOE (1)
6	19.	LA VEEDA (6)
–	20.	MY HOME TOWN IS A ONE-HORSE TOWN (1)

NOVEMBER 1920

LM	TM	
2	1.	WHISPERING (3)
1	2.	THE LOVE NEST (4)
5	3.	THE JAPANESE SANDMAN (2)
9	4.	I'LL BE WITH YOU IN APPLE BLOSSOM TIME (2)
4	5.	TELL ME, LITTLE GYPSY (3)
3	6.	A YOUNG MAN'S FANCY (4)
13	7.	CHILI BEAN (2)
11	8.	TRIPOLI (3)
10	9.	MY LITTLE BIMBO (FROM THE BAMBOO ISLE) (3)
20	10.	MY HOME TOWN IS A ONE-HORSE TOWN (2)
7	11.	AFTER YOU GET WHAT YOU WANT, YOU DON'T WANT IT (4)
18	12.	I LOVE THE LAND OF OLD BLACK JOE (2)
8	13.	HOLD ME (6)
17	14.	THAT OLD IRISH MOTHER OF MINE (2)
–	15.	AVALON (1)
16	16.	TWELFTH STREET RAG (3)
6	17.	HIAWATHA'S MELODY OF LOVE (5)
–	18.	WHEN YOU'RE GONE, I WON'T FORGET (1)
12	19.	VENETIAN MOON (7)
–	20.	I LOVE YOU SUNDAY (1)

DECEMBER 1920

LM	TM	
1	1.	WHISPERING (4)
3	2.	THE JAPANESE SANDMAN (3)
4	3.	I'LL BE WITH YOU IN APPLE BLOSSOM TIME (3)
15	4.	AVALON (2)
2	5.	THE LOVE NEST (5)
7	6.	CHILI BEAN (3)
–	7.	FEATHER YOUR NEST (1)
10	8.	MY HOME TOWN IS A ONE-HORSE TOWN (3)
5	9.	TELL ME, LITTLE GYPSY (4)
12	10.	I LOVE THE LAND OF OLD BLACK JOE (3)
–	11.	(LENA FROM) PALESTEENA (1)
14	12.	THAT OLD IRISH MOTHER OF MINE (3)
–	13.	BROADWAY ROSE (1)
8	14.	TRIPOLI (4)
6	15.	A YOUNG MAN'S FANCY (5)
–	16.	BEAUTIFUL ANNABELLE LEE (1)
–	17.	DIXIE MADE US JAZZ BAND MAD (1)
16	18.	TWELFTH STREET RAG (4)
11	19.	AFTER YOU GET WHAT YOU WANT, YOU DON'T WANT IT (5)
9	20.	MY LITTLE BIMBO (FROM THE BAMBOO ISLE) (4)

JANUARY 1921

LM	TM	
4	1.	AVALON (3)
11	2.	(LENA FROM) PALESTEENA (2)
7	3.	FEATHER YOUR NEST (2)
2	4.	THE JAPANESE SANDMAN (4)
1	5.	WHISPERING (5)
–	6.	MARGIE (1)
13	7.	BROADWAY ROSE (2)
3	8.	I'LL BE WITH YOU IN APPLE BLOSSOM TIME (4)
8	9.	MY HOME TOWN IS A ONE-HORSE TOWN (4)
6	10.	CHILI BEAN (4)
–	11.	OLD PAL, WHY DON'T YOU ANSWER ME? (1)
5	12.	THE LOVE NEST (6)
10	13.	I LOVE THE LAND OF OLD BLACK JOE (4)
9	14.	TELL ME, LITTLE GYPSY (5)
16	15.	BEAUTIFUL ANNABELLE LEE (2)
12	16.	THAT OLD IRISH MOTHER OF MINE (4)
14	17.	TRIPOLI (5)
–	18.	SWEET MAMA (PAPA'S GETTIN' MAD) (1)
17	19.	DIXIE MADE US JAZZ BAND MAD (2)
–	20.	ALL SHE'D SAY WAS "UMH-HUM" (1)

FEBRUARY 1921

LM	TM	
6	1.	MARGIE (2)
2	2.	(LENA FROM) PALESTEENA (3)
1	3.	AVALON (4)
11	4.	OLD PAL, WHY DON'T YOU ANSWER ME? (2)
3	5.	FEATHER YOUR NEST (3)
7	6.	BROADWAY ROSE (3)
5	7.	WHISPERING (6)
8	8.	I'LL BE WITH YOU IN APPLE BLOSSOM TIME (5)
20	9.	ALL SHE'D SAY WAS "UMH-HUM" (2)
4	10.	THE JAPANESE SANDMAN (5)
10	11.	CHILI BEAN (5)
13	12.	I LOVE THE LAND OF OLD BLACK JOE (5)
15	13.	BEAUTIFUL ANNABELLE LEE (3)
9	14.	MY HOME TOWN IS A ONE-HORSE TOWN (5)
–	15.	I NEVER KNEW (1)
–	16.	THE WANG WANG BLUES (1)
–	17.	DOWN BY THE O-HI-O (1)
16	18.	THAT OLD IRISH MOTHER OF MINE (5)
18	19.	SWEET MAMA (PAPA'S GETTIN' MAD) (2)
–	20.	CRAZY BLUES (1)

MARCH 1921

LM	TM	
1	1.	MARGIE (3)
15	2.	I NEVER KNEW (2)
2	3.	(LENA FROM) PALESTEENA (4)
–	4.	BRIGHT EYES (1)
17	5.	DOWN BY THE O-HI-O (2)
–	6.	MY MAMMY (1)
4	7.	OLD PAL, WHY DON'T YOU ANSWER ME? (3)
6	8.	BROADWAY ROSE (4)
16	9.	THE WANG WANG BLUES (2)
–	10.	I USED TO LOVE YOU, BUT IT'S ALL OVER NOW (1)
–	11.	DO YOU EVER THINK OF ME (1)
9	12.	ALL SHE'D SAY WAS "UMH-HUM" (3)
20	13.	CRAZY BLUES (2)
–	14.	LOOK FOR THE SILVER LINING (1)
3	15.	AVALON (5)
5	16.	FEATHER YOUR NEST (4)
–	17.	LOVE BIRD (1)
–	18.	MAZIE (1)
8	19.	I'LL BE WITH YOU IN APPLE BLOSSOM TIME (6)
13	20.	BEAUTIFUL ANNABELLE LEE (4)

APRIL 1921

LM	TM	
4	1.	BRIGHT EYES (2)
6	2.	MY MAMMY (2)
2	3.	I NEVER KNEW (3)
10	4.	I USED TO LOVE YOU, BUT IT'S ALL OVER NOW (2)
9	5.	THE WANG WANG BLUES (3)
1	6.	MARGIE (4)
14	7.	LOOK FOR THE SILVER LINING (2)
5	8.	DOWN BY THE O-HI-O (3)
11	9.	DO YOU EVER THINK OF ME (2)
13	10.	CRAZY BLUES (3)
–	11.	I'M MISSIN' MAMMY'S KISSIN' (1)
17	12.	LOVE BIRD (2)
–	13.	I FOUND A ROSE IN THE DEVIL'S GARDEN (1)
–	14.	MAKE BELIEVE (1)
–	15.	TIMBUCTOO (1)
18	16.	MAZIE (2)
7	17.	OLD PAL, WHY DON'T YOU ANSWER ME? (4)
–	18.	WHIP-POOR-WILL (1)
3	19.	(LENA FROM) PALESTEENA (5)
–	20.	STRUT, MISS LIZZIE (1)

MAY 1921

LM	TM	
2	1.	MY MAMMY (3)
1	2.	BRIGHT EYES (3)
4	3.	I USED TO LOVE YOU, BUT IT'S ALL OVER NOW (3)
13	4.	I FOUND A ROSE IN THE DEVIL'S GARDEN (2)
3	5.	I NEVER KNEW (4)
14	6.	MAKE BELIEVE (2)
5	7.	THE WANG WANG BLUES (4)
7	8.	LOOK FOR THE SILVER LINING (3)
11	9.	I'M MISSIN' MAMMY'S KISSIN' (2)
–	10.	AIN'T WE GOT FUN? (1)
9	11.	DO YOU EVER THINK OF ME (3)
18	12.	WHIP-POOR-WILL (2)
15	13.	TIMBUCTOO (2)
20	14.	STRUT, MISS LIZZIE (2)
10	15.	CRAZY BLUES (4)
6	16.	MARGIE (5)
12	17.	LOVE BIRD (3)
8	18.	DOWN BY THE O-HI-O (4)
–	19.	HOME AGAIN BLUES (1)
–	20.	HUMMING (1)

JUNE 1921

LM	TM	
1	1.	MY MAMMY (4)
6	2.	MAKE BELIEVE (3)
10	3.	AIN'T WE GOT FUN? (2)
4	4.	I FOUND A ROSE IN THE DEVIL'S GARDEN (3)
7	5.	THE WANG WANG BLUES (5)
2	6.	BRIGHT EYES (4)
14	7.	STRUT, MISS LIZZIE (3)
3	8.	I USED TO LOVE YOU, BUT IT'S ALL OVER NOW (4)
20	9.	HUMMING (2)
–	10.	PEGGY O'NEILL (1)
5	11.	I NEVER KNEW (5)
–	12.	MY MAN (1)
19	13.	HOME AGAIN BLUES (2)
–	14.	DOWN YONDER (1)
8	15.	LOOK FOR THE SILVER LINING (4)
9	16.	I'M MISSIN' MAMMY'S KISSIN' (3)
–	17.	CHERIE (1)
–	18.	SPREAD YO' STUFF (1)
–	19.	PALE MOON (1)
11	20.	DO YOU EVER THINK OF ME (4)

JULY 1921

LM	TM	
3	1.	AIN'T WE GOT FUN? (3)
10	2.	PEGGY O'NEILL (2)
2	3.	MAKE BELIEVE (4)
12	4.	MY MAN (2)
7	5.	STRUT, MISS LIZZIE (4)
1	6.	MY MAMMY (5)
14	7.	DOWN YONDER (2)
17	8.	CHERIE (2)
5	9.	THE WANG WANG BLUES (6)
–	10.	ALL BY MYSELF (1)
4	11.	I FOUND A ROSE IN THE DEVIL'S GARDEN (4)
–	12.	I'M NOBODY'S BABY (1)
13	13.	HOME AGAIN BLUES (3)
9	14.	HUMMING (3)
–	15.	WHO'LL BE THE NEXT ONE TO CRY OVER YOU? (1)
19	16.	PALE MOON (2)
–	17.	THE JAZZ ME BLUES (1)
18	18.	SPREAD YO' STUFF (2)
–	19.	CROONING (1)
8	20.	I USED TO LOVE YOU, BUT IT'S ALL OVER NOW (5)

AUGUST 1921

LM	TM	
2	1.	PEGGY O'NEILL (3)
10	2.	ALL BY MYSELF (2)
1	3.	AIN'T WE GOT FUN? (4)
4	4.	MY MAN (3)
8	5.	CHERIE (3)
7	6.	DOWN YONDER (3)
12	7.	I'M NOBODY'S BABY (2)
5	8.	STRUT, MISS LIZZIE (5)
17	9.	THE JAZZ ME BLUES (2)
15	10.	WHO'LL BE THE NEXT ONE TO CRY OVER YOU? (2)
3	11.	MAKE BELIEVE (5)
19	12.	CROONING (2)
13	13.	HOME AGAIN BLUES (4)
9	14.	THE WANG WANG BLUES (7)
6	15.	MY MAMMY (6)
16	16.	PALE MOON (3)
–	17.	LOVE SENDS A LITTLE GIFT OF ROSES (1)
14	18.	HUMMING (4)
–	19.	MOONLIGHT (1)
18	20.	SPREAD YO' STUFF (3)

SEPTEMBER 1921

LM	TM	
2	1.	ALL BY MYSELF (3)
4	2.	MY MAN (4)
7	3.	I'M NOBODY'S BABY (3)
1	4.	PEGGY O'NEILL (4)
6	5.	DOWN YONDER (4)
5	6.	CHERIE (4)
12	7.	CROONING (3)
–	8.	LEARN TO SMILE (1)
10	9.	WHO'LL BE THE NEXT ONE TO CRY OVER YOU? (3)
3	10.	AIN'T WE GOT FUN? (5)
9	11.	THE JAZZ ME BLUES (3)
8	12.	STRUT, MISS LIZZIE (6)
17	13.	LOVE SENDS A LITTLE GIFT OF ROSES (2)
19	14.	MOONLIGHT (2)
13	15.	HOME AGAIN BLUES (5)
–	16.	OH ME! OH MY! (OH YOU!) (1)
–	17.	LOVE WILL FIND A WAY (1)
–	18.	MA! (HE'S MAKIN' EYES AT ME) (1)
16	19.	PALE MOON (4)
14	20.	THE WANG WANG BLUES (8)

OCTOBER 1921

LM	TM	
1	1.	ALL BY MYSELF (4)
2	2.	MY MAN (5)
3	3.	I'M NOBODY'S BABY (4)
18	4.	MA! (HE'S MAKIN' EYES AT ME) (2)
4	5.	PEGGY O'NEILL (5)
8	6.	LEARN TO SMILE (2)
–	7.	TUCK ME TO SLEEP IN MY OLD 'TUCKY HOME (1)
9	8.	WHO'LL BE THE NEXT ONE TO CRY OVER YOU? (4)
–	9.	SWEET LADY (1)
5	10.	DOWN YONDER (5)
–	11.	MY SUNNY TENNESSEE (1)
7	12.	CROONING (4)
14	13.	MOONLIGHT (3)
6	14.	CHERIE (5)
12	15.	STRUT, MISS LIZZIE (7)
17	16.	LOVE WILL FIND A WAY (2)
11	17.	THE JAZZ ME BLUES (4)
–	18.	SAY IT WITH MUSIC (1)
–	19.	EMALINE (1)
–	20.	SECOND HAND ROSE (1)

NOVEMBER 1921

LM	TM	
4	1.	MA! (HE'S MAKIN' EYES AT ME) (3)
9	2.	SWEET LADY (2)
18	3.	SAY IT WITH MUSIC (2)
1	4.	ALL BY MYSELF (5)
7	5.	TUCK ME TO SLEEP IN MY OLD 'TUCKY HOME (2)
11	6.	MY SUNNY TENNESSEE (2)
–	7.	I AIN'T NOBODY'S DARLING (1)
2	8.	MY MAN (6)
20	9.	SECOND HAND ROSE (2)
3	10.	I'M NOBODY'S BABY (5)
8	11.	WHO'LL BE THE NEXT ONE TO CRY OVER YOU (5)
–	12.	WHEN FRANCES DANCES WITH ME (1)
–	13.	TEN LITTLE FINGERS AND TEN LITTLE TOES (1)
5	14.	PEGGY O'NEILL (6)
13	15.	MOONLIGHT (4)
6	16.	LEARN TO SMILE (3)
16	17.	LOVE WILL FIND A WAY (3)
–	18.	CANADIAN CAPERS (1)
–	19.	WABASH BLUES (1)
19	20.	EMALINE (2)

DECEMBER 1921

LM	TM	
3	1.	SAY IT WITH MUSIC (3)
1	2.	MA! (HE'S MAKIN' EYES AT ME) (4)
5	3.	TUCK ME TO SLEEP IN MY OLD 'TUCKY HOME (3)
19	4.	WABASH BLUES (2)
6	5.	MY SUNNY TENNESSEE (3)
2	6.	SWEET LADY (3)
–	7.	DAPPER DAN (1)
12	8.	WHEN FRANCES DANCES WITH ME (2)
9	9.	SECOND HAND ROSE (3)
13	10.	TEN LITTLE FINGERS AND TEN LITTLE TOES (2)
–	11.	APRIL SHOWERS (1)
18	12.	CANADIAN CAPERS (2)
4	13.	ALL BY MYSELF (6)
–	14.	BIMINI BAY (1)
–	15.	YOO HOO (1)
7	16.	I AIN'T NOBODY'S DARLING (2)
11	17.	WHO'LL BE THE NEXT ONE TO CRY OVER YOU (6)
10	18.	I'M NOBODY'S BABY (6)
–	19.	MANDY 'N' ME (1)
–	20.	JUST LIKE A RAINBOW (1)

JANUARY 1922

LM	TM	
1	1.	SAY IT WITH MUSIC (4)
4	2.	WABASH BLUES (3)
11	3.	APRIL SHOWERS (2)
3	4.	TUCK ME TO SLEEP IN MY OLD 'TUCKY HOME (4)
10	5.	TEN LITTLE FINGERS AND TEN LITTLE TOES (3)
7	6.	DAPPER DAN (2)
15	7.	YOO-HOO (2)
5	8.	MY SUNNY TENNESSEE (4)
2	9.	MA! (HE'S MAKIN' EYES AT ME) (5)
–	10.	LEAVE ME WITH A SMILE (1)
14	11.	BIMINI BAY (2)
9	12.	SECOND HAND ROSE (4)
8	13.	WHEN FRANCES DANCES WITH ME (3)
–	14.	KA-LU-A (1)
–	15.	SONG OF LOVE (1)
–	16.	THE SHEIK (OF ARABY) (1)
–	17.	WHEN SHALL WE MEET AGAIN? (1)
12	18.	CANADIAN CAPERS (3)
19	19.	MANDY 'N' ME (2)
6	20.	SWEET LADY (4)

FEBRUARY 1922

LM	TM	
7	1.	YOO-HOO (3)
16	2.	THE SHEIK (OF ARABY) (2)
3	3.	APRIL SHOWERS (3)
2	4.	WABASH BLUES (4)
14	5.	KA-LU-A (2)
5	6.	TEN LITTLE FINGERS AND TEN LITTLE TOES (4)
1	7.	SAY IT WITH MUSIC (5)
4	8.	TUCK ME TO SLEEP IN MY OLD 'TUCKY HOME (5)
10	9.	LEAVE ME WITH A SMILE (2)
6	10.	DAPPER DAN (3)
17	11.	WHEN SHALL WE MEET AGAIN? (2)
15	12.	SONG OF LOVE (2)
8	13.	MY SUNNY TENNESSEE (5)
–	14.	EVERYBODY STEP (1)
12	15.	SECOND HAND ROSE (5)
19	16.	MANDY 'N' ME (3)
–	17.	GRANNY, YOU'RE MY MAMMY'S MAMMY (1)
10	18.	MA! (HE'S MAKIN' EYES AT ME) (6)
–	19.	MY MAN (7)
–	20.	BANDANA DAYS (1)

MARCH 1922

LM	TM	
2	1.	THE SHEIK (OF ARABY) (3)
5	2.	KA-LU-A (3)
1	3.	YOO-HOO (4)
14	4.	EVERYBODY STEP (2)
3	5.	APRIL SHOWERS (4)
6	6.	TEN LITTLE FINGERS AND TEN LITTLE TOES (5)
–	7.	WHEN BUDDHA SMILES (1)
–	8.	DEAR OLD SOUTHLAND (1)
11	9.	WHEN SHALL WE MEET AGAIN? (3)
–	10.	ON THE GIN-GIN-GINNY SHORE (1)
4	11.	WABASH BLUES (5)
9	12.	LEAVE ME WITH A SMILE (3)
8	13.	TUCK ME TO SLEEP IN MY OLD 'TUCKY HOME (6)
–	14.	SWANEE RIVER MOON (1)
12	15.	SONG OF LOVE (3)
20	16.	BANDANA DAYS (2)
7	17.	SAY IT WITH MUSIC (6)
17	18.	GRANNY, YOU'RE MY MAMMY'S MAMMY (2)
–	19.	JUST A LITTLE LOVE SONG (1)
10	20.	DAPPER DAN (4)

APRIL 1922

LM	TM	
10	1.	ON THE GIN-GIN-GINNY SHORE (2)
1	2.	THE SHEIK (OF ARABY) (4)
8	3.	DEAR OLD SOUTHLAND (2)
3	4.	YOO-HOO (5)
14	5.	SWANEE RIVER MOON (2)
–	6.	ANGEL CHILD (1)
2	7.	KA-LU-A (4)
5	8.	APRIL SHOWERS (5)
7	9.	WHEN BUDDHA SMILES (2)
9	10.	WHEN SHALL WE MEET AGAIN? (4)
4	11.	EVERYBODY STEP (3)
16	12.	BANDANA DAYS (3)
19	13.	JUST A LITTLE LOVE SONG (2)
6	14.	TEN LITTLE FINGERS AND TEN LITTLE TOES (6)
–	15.	THREE O'CLOCK IN THE MORNING (1)
15	16.	SONG OF LOVE (4)
–	17.	THE WORLD IS WAITING FOR THE SUNRISE (1)
–	18.	STEALING (1)
12	19.	LEAVE ME WITH A SMILE (4)
18	20.	GRANNY, YOU'RE MY MAMMY'S MAMMY (3)

MAY 1922

LM	TM	
6	1.	ANGEL CHILD (2)
3	2.	DEAR OLD SOUTHLAND (3)
15	3.	THREE O'CLOCK IN THE MORNING (2)
5	4.	SWANEE RIVER MOON (3)
1	5.	ON THE GIN-GIN-GINNY SHORE (3)
–	6.	GEORGIA (1)
2	7.	THE SHEIK (OF ARABY) (5)
–	8.	CALIFORNIA (1)
–	9.	O-OO, ERNEST (ARE YOU EARNEST WITH ME?) (1)
4	10.	YOO-HOO (6)
7	11.	KA-LU-A (5)
–	12.	YOU CAN HAVE EVERY LIGHT ON BROADWAY (1)
12	13.	BANDANA DAYS (4)
–	14.	SOME SUNNY DAY (1)
18	15.	STEALING (2)
17	16.	THE WORLD IS WAITING FOR THE SUNRISE (2)
10	17.	WHEN SHALL WE MEET AGAIN? (5)
–	18.	DOO DAH BLUES (1)
–	19.	DOWN THE OLD CHURCH AISLE (1)
–	20.	IN THE LITTLE RED SCHOOL HOUSE (1)

JUNE 1922

LM	TM	
3	1.	THREE O'CLOCK IN THE MORNING (3)
6	2.	GEORGIA (2)
1	3.	ANGEL CHILD (3)
14	4.	SOME SUNNY DAY (2)
8	5.	CALIFORNIA (2)
2	6.	DEAR OLD SOUTHLAND (4)
20	7.	IN THE LITTLE RED SCHOOL HOUSE (2)
9	8.	O-OO, ERNEST (ARE YOU EARNEST WITH ME?) (2)
–	9.	STUMBLING (1)
4	10.	SWANEE RIVER MOON (4)
–	11.	NOLA (1)
–	12.	KITTEN ON THE KEYS (1)
5	13.	ON THE GIN-GIN-GINNY SHORE (4)
–	14.	MOON RIVER (1)
–	15.	SMILIN' THROUGH (1)
7	16.	THE SHEIK (OF ARABY) (6)
–	17.	ON THE ALAMO (1)
–	18.	MY HONEY'S LOVIN' ARMS (1)
12	19.	YOU CAN HAVE EVERY LIGHT ON BROADWAY (2)
13	20.	BANDANA DAYS (5)

JULY 1922

LM	TM	
9	1.	STUMBLING (2)
1	2.	THREE O'CLOCK IN THE MORNING (4)
4	3.	SOME SUNNY DAY (3)
2	4.	GEORGIA (3)
12	5.	KITTEN ON THE KEYS (2)
7	6.	IN THE LITTLE RED SCHOOL HOUSE (3)
3	7.	ANGEL CHILD (4)
–	8.	DO IT AGAIN (1)
17	9.	ON THE ALAMO (2)
11	10.	NOLA (2)
–	11.	I'M JUST WILD ABOUT HARRY (1)
18	12.	MY HONEY'S LOVIN' ARMS (2)
6	13.	DEAR OLD SOUTHLAND (5)
–	14.	ALL OVER NOTHING AT ALL (1)
10	15.	SWANEE RIVER MOON (5)
–	16.	GEE, BUT I HATE TO GO HOME ALONE (1)
5	17.	CALIFORNIA (3)
15	18.	SMILIN' THROUGH (2)
–	19.	DANCING FOOL (1)
8	20.	O-OO, ERNEST, ARE YOU EARNEST WITH ME? (3)

AUGUST 1922

LM	TM	
1	1.	STUMBLING (3)
2	2.	THREE O'CLOCK IN THE MORNING (5)
5	3.	KITTEN ON THE KEYS (3)
19	4.	DANCING FOOL (2)
11	5.	I'M JUST WILD ABOUT HARRY (2)
8	6.	DO IT AGAIN (2)
3	7.	SOME SUNNY DAY (4)
14	8.	ALL OVER NOTHING AT ALL (2)
–	9.	NOBODY LIED (1)
–	10.	'NEATH THE SOUTH SEA MOON (1)
9	11.	ON THE ALAMO (3)
–	12.	WHY SHOULD I CRY OVER YOU? (1)
16	13.	GEE, BUT I HATE TO GO HOME ALONE (2)
4	14.	GEORGIA (4)
12	15.	MY HONEY'S LOVIN' ARMS (3)
–	16.	MR. GALLAGHER AND MR. SHEAN (1)
18	17.	SMILIN' THROUGH (3)
10	18.	NOLA (3)
7	19.	ANGEL CHILD (5)
6	20.	IN THE LITTLE RED SCHOOL HOUSE (4)

SEPTEMBER 1922

LM	TM	
2	1.	THREE O'CLOCK IN THE MORNING (6)
10	2.	'NEATH THE SOUTH SEA MOON (2)
4	3.	DANCING FOOL (3)
12	4.	WHY SHOULD I CRY OVER YOU? (2)
5	5.	I'M JUST WILD ABOUT HARRY (3)
–	6.	SAY IT WHILE DANCING (1)
8	7.	ALL OVER NOTHING AT ALL (3)
1	8.	STUMBLING (4)
–	9.	GEORGETTE (1)
3	10.	KITTEN ON THE KEYS (4)
–	11.	HOT LIPS (1)
16	12.	MR. GALLAGHER AND MR. SHEAN (2)
9	13.	NOBODY LIED (2)
–	14.	SWEET INDIANA HOME (1)
17	15.	SMILIN' THROUGH (4)
–	16.	PARADE OF THE WOODEN SOLDIERS (1)
6	17.	DO IT AGAIN (3)
11	18.	ON THE ALAMO (4)
–	19.	SUEZ (1)
–	20.	THE SNEAK (1)

OCTOBER 1922

LM	TM	
1	1.	THREE O'CLOCK IN THE MORNING (7)
11	2.	HOT LIPS (2)
12	3.	MR. GALLAGHER AND MR. SHEAN (3)
6	4.	SAY IT WHILE DANCING (2)
9	5.	GEORGETTE (2)
5	6.	I'M JUST WILD ABOUT HARRY (4)
3	7.	DANCING FOOL (4)
–	8.	BLUE (AND BROKEN HEARTED) (1)
10	9.	KITTEN ON THE KEYS (5)
2	10.	'NEATH THE SOUTH SEA MOON (3)
–	11.	YANKEE DOODLE BLUES (1)
4	12.	WHY SHOULD I CRY OVER YOU? (3)
–	13.	COAL-BLACK MAMMY (1)
16	14.	PARADE OF THE WOODEN SOLDIERS (2)
13	15.	NOBODY LIED (3)
7	16.	ALL OVER NOTHING AT ALL (4)
–	17.	YOU REMIND ME OF MY MOTHER (1)
14	18.	SWEET INDIANA HOME (2)
20	19.	THE SNEAK (2)
19	20.	SUEZ (2)

NOVEMBER 1922

LM	TM	
3	1.	MR. GALLAGHER AND MR. SHEAN (4)
1	2.	THREE O'CLOCK IN THE MORNING (8)
2	3.	HOT LIPS (3)
17	4.	YOU REMIND ME OF MY MOTHER (2)
–	5.	NELLIE KELLY, I LOVE YOU (1)
8	6.	BLUE (AND BROKEN HEARTED) (2)
–	7.	CHICAGO (THAT TODDLIN' TOWN) (1)
13	8.	COAL-BLACK MAMMY (2)
–	9.	I WISH I COULD SHIMMY LIKE MY SISTER KATE (1)
11	10.	YANKEE DOODLE BLUES (2)
14	11.	PARADE OF THE WOODEN SOLDIERS (3)
–	12.	HOMESICK (1)
–	13.	MY BUDDY (1)
–	14.	I'LL BUILD A STAIRWAY TO PARADISE (1)
5	15.	GEORGETTE (3)
4	16.	SAY IT WHILE DANCING (3)
6	17.	I'M JUST WILD ABOUT HARRY (5)
9	18.	KITTEN ON THE KEYS (6)
12	19.	WHY SHOULD I CRY OVER YOU? (4)
–	20.	THE WORLD IS WAITING FOR THE SUNRISE (3)

DECEMBER 1922

LM	TM	
1	1.	MR. GALLAGHER AND MR. SHEAN (5)
13	2.	MY BUDDY (2)
7	3.	CHICAGO (THAT TODDLIN' TOWN) (2)
–	4.	CAROLINA IN THE MORNING (1)
5	5.	NELLIE KELLY, I LOVE YOU (2)
2	6.	THREE O'CLOCK IN THE MORNING (9)
9	7.	I WISH I COULD SHIMMY LIKE MY SISTER KATE (2)
4	8.	YOU REMIND ME OF MY MOTHER (3)
11	9.	PARADE OF THE WOODEN SOLDIERS (4)
–	10.	TOOT, TOOT, TOOTSIE! (GOODBYE) (1)
12	11.	HOMESICK (2)
14	12.	I'LL BUILD A STAIRWAY TO PARADISE (2)
–	13.	WAY DOWN YONDER IN NEW ORLEANS (1)
3	14.	HOT LIPS (4)
20	15.	THE WORLD IS WAITING FOR THE SUNRISE (4)
6	16.	BLUE (AND BROKEN HEARTED) (3)
10	17.	YANKEE DOODLE BLUES (3)
–	18.	WHEN YOU AND I WERE YOUNG MAGGIE BLUES (1)
–	19.	LOVIN' SAM, THE SHEIK OF ALABAM' (1)
8	20.	COAL-BLACK MAMMY (3)

JANUARY 1923

LM	TM	
4	1.	CAROLINA IN THE MORNING (2)
2	2.	MY BUDDY (3)
10	3.	TOOT, TOOT, TOOTSIE! (GOODBYE) (2)
19	4.	LOVIN' SAM, THE SHEIK OF ALABAM' (2)
–	5.	CRINOLINE DAYS (1)
3	6.	CHICAGO (THAT TODDLIN' TOWN) (3)
9	7.	PARADE OF THE WOODEN SOLDIERS (5)
13	8.	WAY DOWN YONDER IN NEW ORLEANS (2)
–	9.	WHEN THE LEAVES COME TUMBLING DOWN (1)
1	10.	MR. GALLAGHER AND MR. SHEAN (6)
7	11.	I WISH I COULD SHIMMY LIKE MY SISTER KATE (3)
–	12.	YOU GAVE ME YOUR HEART (1)
–	13.	LADY OF THE EVENING (1)
6	14.	THREE O'CLOCK IN THE MORNING (10)
15	15.	THE WORLD IS WAITING FOR THE SUNRISE (5)
5	16.	NELLIE KELLY, I LOVE YOU (3)
11	17.	HOMESICK (3)
–	18.	I GAVE YOU UP JUST BEFORE YOU PUT ME DOWN (2)
–	19.	PACK UP YOUR SINS (AND GO TO THE DEVIL) (1)
–	20.	WHO CARES? (1)

FEBRUARY 1923

LM	TM	
1	1.	CAROLINA IN THE MORNING (3)
4	2.	LOVIN' SAM, THE SHEIK OF ALABAM' (3)
2	3.	MY BUDDY (4)
5	4.	CRINOLINE DAYS (2)
3	5.	TOOT, TOOT, TOOTSIE! (GOODBYE) (3)
8	6.	WAY DOWN YONDER IN NEW ORLEANS (3)
–	7.	WHEN HEARTS ARE YOUNG (1)
13	8.	LADY OF THE EVENING (2)
7	9.	PARADE OF THE WOODEN SOLDIERS (6)
9	10.	WHEN THE LEAVES COME TUMBLING DOWN (2)
20	11.	WHO CARES? (2)
10	12.	MR. GALLAGHER AND MR. SHEAN (7)
6	13.	CHICAGO (THAT TODDLIN' TOWN) (4)
19	14.	PACK UP YOUR SINS (AND GO TO THE DEVIL) (2)
–	15.	LOVE SENDS A LITTLE GIFT OF ROSES (1)
18	16.	I GAVE YOU UP JUST BEFORE YOU PUT ME DOWN (2)
15	17.	THE WORLD IS WAITING FOR THE SUNRISE (6)
–	18.	YOU TELL HER, I S-T-U-T-T-E-R (1)
12	19.	YOU GAVE ME YOUR HEART (2)
–	20.	A KISS IN THE DARK (1)

MARCH 1923

LM	TM	
7	1.	WHEN HEARTS ARE YOUNG (2)
1	2.	CAROLINA IN THE MORNING (4)
2	3.	LOVIN' SAM, THE SHEIK OF ALABAM' (4)
9	4.	PARADE OF THE WOODEN SOLDIERS (7)
3	5.	MY BUDDY (5)
18	6.	YOU TELL HER, I S-T-U-T-T-E-R (2)
4	7.	CRINOLINE DAYS (3)
8	8.	LADY OF THE EVENING (3)
–	9.	AGGRAVATIN' PAPA (1)
–	10.	ROSE OF THE RIO GRANDE (1)
11	11.	WHO CARES? (3)
6	12.	WAY DOWN YONDER IN NEW ORLEANS (4)
–	13.	YOU KNOW YOU BELONG TO SOMEBODY ELSE (1)
5	14.	TOOT, TOOT, TOOTSIE! (GOODBYE) (4)
10	15.	WHEN THE LEAVES COME TUMBLING DOWN (3)
16	16.	I GAVE YOU UP JUST BEFORE YOU THREW ME DOWN (3)
15	17.	LOVE SENDS A LITTLE GIFT OF ROSES (2)
20	18.	A KISS IN THE DARK (2)
12	19.	MR. GALLAGHER AND MR. SHEAN (8)
–	20.	DEAREST, YOU'RE THE NEAREST TO MY HEART (1)

APRIL 1923

LM	TM	
9	1.	AGGRAVATIN' PAPA (2)
4	2.	PARADE OF THE WOODEN SOLDIERS (8)
1	3.	WHEN HEARTS ARE YOUNG (3)
–	4.	RUNNIN' WILD (1)
10	5.	ROSE OF THE RIO GRANDE (2)
–	6.	YOU'VE GOT TO SEE MAMMA EV'RY NIGHT (1)
20	7.	DEAREST, YOU'RE THE NEAREST TO MY HEART (2)
13	8.	YOU KNOW YOU BELONG TO SOMEBODY ELSE (2)
6	9.	YOU TELL HER, I S-T-U-T-T-E-R (3)
2	10.	CAROLINA IN THE MORNING (5)
18	11.	A KISS IN THE DARK (3)
–	12.	BAMBALINA (1)
8	13.	LADY OF THE EVENING (4)
16	14.	I GAVE YOU UP JUST BEFORE YOU THREW ME DOWN (4)
11	15.	WHO CARES? (4)
17	16.	LOVE SENDS A LITTLE GIFT OF ROSES (3)
5	17.	MY BUDDY (6)
12	18.	WAY DOWN YONDER IN NEW ORLEANS (5)
–	19.	WHO'S SORRY NOW? (1)
7	20.	CRINOLINE DAYS (4)

MAY 1923

LM	TM	
6	1.	YOU'VE GOT TO SEE MAMMA EV'RY NIGHT (2)
12	2.	BAMBALINA (2)
4	3.	RUNNIN' WILD (2)
19	4.	WHO'S SORRY NOW? (2)
1	5.	AGGRAVATIN' PAPA (3)
7	6.	DEAREST, YOU'RE THE NEAREST TO MY HEART (3)
11	7.	A KISS IN THE DARK (4)
2	8.	PARADE OF THE WOODEN SOLDIERS (9)
8	9.	YOU KNOW YOU BELONG TO SOMEBODY ELSE (3)
–	10.	WONDERFUL ONE (1)
9	11.	YOU TELL HER, I S-T-U-T-T-E-R (4)
3	12.	WHEN HEARTS ARE YOUNG (4)
16	13.	LOVE SENDS A LITTLE GIFT OF ROSES (4)
–	14.	FAREWELL BLUES (1)
–	15.	CRYING FOR YOU (1)
5	16.	ROSE OF THE RIO GRANDE (3)
–	17.	WILDFLOWER (1)
–	18.	UNDERNEATH THE MELLOW MOON (1)
–	19.	AUNT HAGAR'S CHILDREN (BLUES) (1)
–	20.	SEVEN OR ELEVEN (MY DIXIE PAIR O' DICE) (1)

JUNE 1923

LM	TM	
4	1.	WHO'S SORRY NOW? (3)
2	2.	BAMBALINA (3)
10	3.	WONDERFUL ONE (2)
1	4.	YOU'VE GOT TO SEE MAMMA EV'RY NIGHT (3)
6	5.	DEAREST, YOU'RE THE NEAREST TO MY HEART (4)
14	6.	FAREWELL BLUES (2)
7	7.	A KISS IN THE DARK (5)
–	8.	YES! WE HAVE NO BANANAS (1)
17	9.	WILDFLOWER (2)
–	10.	BARNEY GOOGLE (1)
3	11.	RUNNIN' WILD (3)
20	12.	SEVEN OR ELEVEN (MY DIXIE PAIR O' DICE) (2)
–	13.	SAW MILL RIVER ROAD (1)
5	14.	AGGRAVATIN' PAPA (4)
–	15.	BESIDE A BABBLING BROOK (1)
9	16.	YOU KNOW YOU BELONG TO SOMEBODY ELSE (4)
18	17.	UNDERNEATH THE MELLOW MOON (2)
13	18.	LOVE SENDS A LITTLE GIFT OF ROSES (5)
–	19.	THAT RED-HEAD GAL (1)
8	20.	PARADE OF THE WOODEN SOLDIERS (10)

JULY 1923

LM	TM	
8	1.	YES! WE HAVE NO BANANAS (2)
10	2.	BARNEY GOOGLE (2)
1	3.	WHO'S SORRY NOW? (4)
3	4.	WONDERFUL ONE (3)
15	5.	BESIDE A BABBLING BROOK (2)
9	6.	WILDFLOWER (3)
–	7.	SWINGIN' DOWN THE LANE (1)
7	8.	A KISS IN THE DARK (6)
6	9.	FAREWELL BLUES (3)
13	10.	SAW MILL RIVER ROAD (2)
–	11.	LOUISVILLE LOU, THE VAMPIN' LADY (1)
2	12.	BAMBALINA (4)
5	13.	DEAREST, YOU'RE THE NEAREST TO MY HEART (5)
–	14.	JUST A GIRL THAT MEN FORGET (1)
–	15.	MARCHETA (1)
–	16.	STELLA (1)
4	17.	YOU'VE GOT TO SEE MAMMA EV'RY NIGHT (4)
17	18.	UNDERNEATH THE MELLOW MOON (3)
12	19.	SEVEN OR ELEVEN (MY DIXIE PAIR O' DICE) (3)
–	20.	I CRIED FOR YOU (1)

AUGUST 1923

LM	TM	
1	1.	YES! WE HAVE NO BANANAS (3)
7	2.	SWINGIN' DOWN THE LANE (2)
2	3.	BARNEY GOOGLE (3)
5	4.	BESIDE A BABBLING BROOK (3)
20	5.	I CRIED FOR YOU (2)
4	6.	WONDERFUL ONE (4)
11	7.	LOUISVILLE LOU, THE VAMPIN' LADY (2)
–	8.	WHEN YOU WALKED OUT, SOMEONE ELSE WALKED RIGHT IN (1)
16	9.	STELLA (2)
14	10.	JUST A GIRL THAT MEN FORGET (2)
6	11.	WILDFLOWER (4)
3	12.	WHO'S SORRY NOW? (5)
15	13.	MARCHETA (2)
–	14.	OH! GEE, OH! GOSH, OH! GOLLY, I'M IN LOVE (1)
8	15.	A KISS IN THE DARK (7)
–	16.	DIRTY HANDS! DIRTY FACE! (1)
–	17.	GULF COAST BLUES (1)
–	18.	BEBE (1)
10	19.	SAW MILL RIVER ROAD (3)
–	20.	DOWNHEARTED BLUES (1)

SEPTEMBER 1923

LM	TM	
10	1.	JUST A GIRL THAT MEN FORGET (3)
2	2.	SWINGIN' DOWN THE LANE (3)
14	3.	OH! GEE, OH! GOSH, OH! GOLLY, I'M IN LOVE (2)
1	4.	YES! WE HAVE NO BANANAS (4)
–	5.	MY SWEETIE WENT AWAY (1)
7	6.	LOUISVILLE LOU, THE VAMPIN' LADY (3)
5	7.	I CRIED FOR YOU (3)
13	8.	MARCHETA (3)
–	9.	THAT OLD GANG OF MINE (1)
8	10.	WHEN YOU WALKED OUT, SOMEONE ELSE WALKED RIGHT IN (2)
18	11.	BEBE (2)
6	12.	WONDERFUL ONE (5)
4	13.	BESIDE A BABBLING BROOK (4)
3	14.	BARNEY GOOGLE (4)
15	15.	A KISS IN THE DARK (8)
16	16.	DIRTY HANDS! DIRTY FACE! (2)
–	17.	INDIANA MOON (1)
–	18.	DREAMY MELODY (1)
9	19.	STELLA (3)
–	20.	ANNABELLE (1)

OCTOBER 1923

LM	TM	
9	1.	THAT OLD GANG OF MINE (2)
1	2.	JUST A GIRL THAT MEN FORGET (4)
17	3.	INDIANA MOON (2)
5	4.	MY SWEETIE WENT AWAY (2)
8	5.	MARCHETA (4)
20	6.	ANNABELLE (2)
3	7.	OH! GEE, OH! GOSH, OH! GOLLY, I'M IN LOVE (3)
6	8.	LOUISVILLE LOU, THE VAMPIN' LADY (4)
18	9.	DREAMY MELODY (2)
–	10.	NO, NO, NORA (1)
11	11.	BEBE (3)
2	12.	SWINGIN' DOWN THE LANE (4)
15	13.	A KISS IN THE DARK (9)
–	14.	TEN THOUSAND YEARS FROM NOW (1)
–	15.	ROSES OF PICARDY (1)
12	16.	WONDERFUL ONE (6)
7	17.	I CRIED FOR YOU (4)
–	18.	CUT YOURSELF A PIECE OF CAKE (1)
–	19.	LOVE TALES (1)
16	20.	DIRTY HANDS! DIRTY FACE! (3)

NOVEMBER 1923

LM	TM	
1	1.	THAT OLD GANG OF MINE (3)
10	2.	NO, NO, NORA (2)
3	3.	INDIANA MOON (3)
9	4.	DREAMY MELODY (3)
–	5.	LAST NIGHT ON THE BACK PORCH (1)
5	6.	MARCHETA (5)
–	7.	I LOVE YOU (1)
4	8.	MY SWEETIE WENT AWAY (3)
14	9.	TEN THOUSAND YEARS FROM NOW (2)
2	10.	JUST A GIRL THAT MEN FORGET (5)
15	11.	ROSES OF PICARDY (2)
19	12.	LOVE TALES (2)
6	13.	ANNABELLE (3)
–	14.	MIDNIGHT ROSE (1)
13	15.	A KISS IN THE DARK (10)
–	16.	JUST FOR TONIGHT (1)
8	17.	LOUISVILLE LOU, THE VAMPIN' LADY (5)
11	18.	BEBE (4)
–	19.	WHEN IT'S NIGHT TIME IN ITALY, IT'S WEDNESDAY OVER HERE (1)
–	20.	SITTIN' IN A CORNER (1)

DECEMBER 1923

LM	TM	
7	1.	I LOVE YOU (2)
5	2.	LAST NIGHT ON THE BACK PORCH (2)
1	3.	THAT OLD GANG OF MINE (4)
2	4.	NO, NO, NORA (3)
4	5.	DREAMY MELODY (4)
20	6.	SITTIN' IN A CORNER (2)
6	7.	MARCHETA (6)
11	8.	ROSES OF PICARDY (3)
3	9.	INDIANA MOON (4)
9	10.	TEN THOUSAND YEARS FROM NOW (3)
–	11.	THE WEST, A NEST, AND YOU (1)
–	12.	I'M SITTING PRETTY IN A PRETTY LITTLE CITY (1)
–	13.	MAMMA GOES WHERE PAPA GOES (1)
12	14.	LOVE TALES (3)
–	15.	SLEEP (1)
–	16.	CHANSONETTE (1)
14	17.	MIDNIGHT ROSE (2)
10	18.	JUST A GIRL THAT MEN FORGET (6)
16	19.	JUST FOR TONIGHT (2)
8	20.	MY SWEETIE WENT AWAY (4)

JANUARY 1924

LM	TM	
1	1.	I LOVE YOU (3)
6	2.	SITTIN' IN A CORNER (3
2	3.	LAST NIGHT ON THE BACK PORCH (3)
15	4.	SLEEP (2)
12	5.	I'M SITTING PRETTY IN A PRETTY LITTLE CITY (2)
3	6.	THAT OLD GANG OF MINE (5)
13	7.	MAMMA GOES WHERE PAPA GOES (2)
7	8.	MARCHETA (7)
–	9.	LINGER AWHILE (1)
–	10.	MAMMA LOVES PAPA (PAPA LOVES MAMMA) (1)
5	11.	DREAMY MELODY (5)
–	12.	LOVEY CAME BACK (1)
–	13.	COVERED WAGON DAYS (1)
–	14.	REMEMB'RING (1)
8	15.	ROSES OF PICARDY (4)
11	16.	THE WEST, A NEST, AND YOU (2)
4	17.	NO, NO, NORA (4)
–	18.	TAKE OH TAKE THOSE LIPS AWAY (1)
–	19.	LA ROSITA (1)
–	20.	OLD FASHIONED LOVE (1)

FEBRUARY 1924

LM	TM	
9	1.	LINGER AWHILE (2)
1	2.	I LOVE YOU (4)
4	3.	SLEEP (3)
14	4.	REMEMB'RING (2)
12	5.	LOVEY CAME BACK (2)
5	6.	I'M SITTING PRETTY IN A PRETTY LITTLE CITY (3)
10	7.	MAMMA LOVES PAPA (PAPA LOVES MAMMA) (2)
2	8.	SITTIN' IN A CORNER (4)
13	9.	COVERED WAGON DAYS (2)
–	10.	AN ORANGE GROVE IN CALIFORNIA (1)
18	11.	TAKE OH TAKE THOSE LIPS AWAY (2)
15	12.	ROSES OF PICARDY (5)
–	13.	RAGGEDY ANN (1)
3	14.	LAST NIGHT ON THE BACK PORCH (4)
19	15.	LA ROSITA (2)
7	16.	MAMMA GOES WHERE PAPA GOES (3)
–	17.	THE WALTZ OF LONG AGO (1)
6	18.	THAT OLD GANG OF MINE (6)
20	19.	OLD FASHIONED LOVE (2)
–	20.	LITTLE BUTTERFLY (1)

MARCH 1924

LM	TM	
1	1.	LINGER AWHILE (3)
4	2.	REMEMB'RING (3)
–	3.	CALIFORNIA, HERE I COME (1)
3	4.	SLEEP (4)
2	5.	I LOVE YOU (5)
–	6.	SOMEBODY STOLE MY GAL (1)
–	7.	A SMILE WILL GO A LONG, LONG WAY (1)
13	8.	RAGGEDY ANN (2)
–	9.	I'M GOIN' SOUTH (1)
–	10.	WHEN LIGHTS ARE LOW (1)
10	11.	AN ORANGE GROVE IN CALIFORNIA (2)
–	12.	DREAM DADDY (1)
17	13.	THE WALTZ OF LONG AGO (2)
–	14.	SHE WOULDN'T DO (WHAT I ASKED HER TO) (1)
5	15.	LOVEY CAME BACK (3)
–	16.	THE ONE I LOVE BELONGS TO SOMEBODY ELSE (1)
12	17.	ROSES OF PICARDY (6)
9	18.	COVERED WAGON DAYS (3)
6	19.	I'M SITTING PRETTY IN A PRETTY LITTLE CITY (4)
20	20.	LITTLE BUTTERFLY (2)

APRIL 1924

LM	TM	
3	1.	CALIFORNIA, HERE I COME (2)
7	2.	A SMILE WILL GO A LONG, LONG WAY (2)
16	3.	THE ONE I LOVE BELONGS TO SOMEBODY ELSE (2)
9	4.	I'M GOIN' SOUTH (2)
6	5.	SOMEBODY STOLE MY GAL (2)
–	6.	WHERE THE LAZY DAISIES GROW (1)
1	7.	LINGER AWHILE (4)
10	8.	WHEN LIGHTS ARE LOW (2)
–	9.	IT AIN'T GONNA RAIN NO MO' (1)
12	10.	DREAM DADDY (2)
2	11.	REMEMB'RING (4)
–	12.	LIMEHOUSE BLUES (1)
14	13.	SHE WOULDN'T DO (WHAT I ASKED HER TO) (2)
–	14.	NOBODY'S SWEETHEART (1)
4	15.	SLEEP (5)
5	16.	I LOVE YOU (6)
11	17.	AN ORANGE GROVE IN CALIFORNIA (3)
13	18.	THE WALTZ OF LONG AGO (3)
17	19.	ROSES OF PICARDY (7)
8	20.	RAGGEDY ANN (3)

MAY 1924

LM	TM	
9	1.	IT AIN'T GONNA RAIN NO MO' (2)
6	2.	WHERE THE LAZY DAISIES GROW (2)
1	3.	CALIFORNIA, HERE I COME (3)
12	4.	LIMEHOUSE BLUES (2)
3	5.	THE ONE I LOVE BELONGS TO SOMEBODY ELSE (3)
14	6.	NOBODY'S SWEETHEART (2)
–	7.	WHY DID I KISS THAT GIRL? (1)
2	8.	A SMILE WILL GO A LONG, LONG WAY (3)
–	9.	COLORADO (1)
–	10.	MINDIN' MY BUS'NESS (1)
5	11.	SOMEBODY STOLE MY GAL (3)
–	12.	WHAT'LL I DO? (1)
4	13.	I'M GOIN' SOUTH (3)
8	14.	WHEN LIGHTS ARE LOW (3)
–	15.	LAZY (1)
11	16.	REMEMB'RING (5)
7	17.	LINGER AWHILE (5)
13	18.	SHE WOULDN'T DO (WHAT I ASKED HER TO) (3)
–	19.	DON'T MIND THE RAIN (1)
–	20.	MEXICALI ROSE (1)

JUNE 1924

LM	TM	
1	1.	IT AIN'T GONNA RAIN NO MO' (3)
12	2.	WHAT'LL I DO? (2)
4	3.	LIMEHOUSE BLUES (3)
6	4.	NOBODY'S SWEETHEART (3)
15	5.	LAZY (2)
7	6.	WHY DID I KISS THAT GIRL? (2)
19	7.	DON'T MIND THE RAIN (2)
9	8.	COLORADO (2)
2	9.	WHERE THE LAZY DAISIES GROW (3)
10	10.	MINDIN' MY BUS'NESS (2)
–	11.	IT HAD TO BE YOU (1)
5	12.	THE ONE I LOVE BELONGS TO SOMEBODY ELSE (4)
3	13.	CALIFORNIA, HERE I COME (4)
–	14.	THERE'S YES! YES! IN YOUR EYES (1)
20	15.	MEXICALI ROSE (2)
–	16.	DIZZY FINGERS (1)
–	17.	NOLA (4)
14	18.	WHEN LIGHTS ARE LOW (4)
8	19.	A SMILE WILL GO A LONG, LONG WAY (4)
–	20.	SINCE MA IS PLAYING MAH JONG (1)

JULY 1924

LM	TM	
2	1.	WHAT'LL I DO? (3)
14	2.	THERE'S YES! YES! IN YOUR EYES (2)
11	3.	IT HAD TO BE YOU (2)
1	4.	IT AIN'T GONNA RAIN NO MO' (4)
–	5.	SPAIN (1)
–	6.	SHINE (1)
4	7.	NOBODY'S SWEETHEART (4)
6	8.	WHY DID I KISS THAT GIRL? (3)
5	9.	LAZY (3)
3	10.	LIMEHOUSE BLUES (4)
–	11.	JEALOUS (1)
–	12.	MANDALAY (1)
7	13.	DON'T MIND THE RAIN (3)
–	14.	WHAT HAS BECOME OF HINKY DINKY PARLAY VOO (1)
8	15.	COLORADO (3)
17	16.	NOLA (5)
9	17.	WHERE THE LAZY DAISIES GROW (4)
15	18.	MEXICALI ROSE (3)
–	19.	MEMORY LANE (1)
–	20.	RHAPSODY IN BLUE (1)

AUGUST 1924

LM	TM	
1	1.	WHAT'LL I DO? (4)
3	2.	IT HAD TO BE YOU (3)
2	3.	THERE'S YES! YES! IN YOUR EYES (3)
11	4.	JEALOUS (2)
12	5.	MANDALAY (2)
5	6.	SPAIN (2)
6	7.	SHINE (2)
19	8.	MEMORY LANE (2)
4	9.	IT AIN'T GONNA RAIN NO MO' (5)
14	10.	WHAT HAS BECOME OF HINKY DINKY PARLAY VOO (2)
7	11.	NOBODY'S SWEETHEART (5)
–	12.	RED HOT MAMMA (1)
–	13.	SAN (1)
8	14.	WHY DID I KISS THAT GIRL? (4)
16	15.	NOLA (6)
20	16.	RHAPSODY IN BLUE (2)
10	17.	LIMEHOUSE BLUES (5)
9	18.	LAZY (4)
–	19.	HOW COME YOU DO ME LIKE YOU DO? (1)
–	20.	HARD-HEARTED HANNAH (1)

SEPTEMBER 1924

LM	TM	
1	1.	WHAT'LL I DO? (5)
4	2.	JEALOUS (3)
5	3.	MANDALAY (3)
2	4.	IT HAD TO BE YOU (4)
8	5.	MEMORY LANE (3)
–	6.	JUNE NIGHT (1)
20	7.	HARD-HEARTED HANNAH (2)
19	8.	HOW COME YOU DO ME LIKE YOU DO? (2)
3	9.	THERE'S YES! YES! IN YOUR EYES (4)
–	10.	DOODLE DOO DOO (1)
–	11.	CHARLEY, MY BOY (1)
13	12.	SAN (2)
12	13.	RED HOT MAMMA (2)
–	14.	I WONDER WHAT'S BECOME OF SALLY (1)
6	15.	SPAIN (3)
10	16.	WHAT HAS BECOME OF HINKY DINKY PARLAY VOO (3)
–	17.	SOMEBODY LOVES ME (1)
9	18.	IT AIN'T GONNA RAIN NO MO' (6)
16	19.	RHAPSODY IN BLUE (3)
–	20.	I WANT TO BE HAPPY (1)

OCTOBER 1924

LM	TM	
11	1.	CHARLEY, MY BOY (2)
1	2.	WHAT'LL I DO? (6)
6	3.	JUNE NIGHT (2)
5	4.	MEMORY LANE (4)
14	5.	I WONDER WHAT'S BECOME OF SALLY (2)
2	6.	JEALOUS (4)
17	7.	SOMEBODY LOVES ME (2)
3	8.	MANDALAY (4)
7	9.	HARD-HEARTED HANNAH (3)
20	10.	I WANT TO BE HAPPY (2)
–	11.	MY DREAM GIRL (1)
4	12.	IT HAD TO BE YOU (5)
8	13.	HOW COME YOU DO ME LIKE YOU DO? (3)
19	14.	RHAPSODY IN BLUE (4)
10	15.	DOODLE DOO DOO (2)
–	16.	BAGDAD (1)
–	17.	MAYTIME (1)
–	18.	FOLLOW THE SWALLOW (1)
–	19.	ROCK-A-BYE MY BABY BLUES (1)
16	20.	WHAT HAS BECOME OF HINKY DINKY PARLAY VOO (4)

NOVEMBER 1924

LM	TM	
5	1.	I WONDER WHAT'S BECOME OF SALLY (3)
1	2.	CHARLEY, MY BOY (3)
3	3.	JUNE NIGHT (3)
18	4.	FOLLOW THE SWALLOW (2)
7	5.	SOMEBODY LOVES ME (3)
–	6.	PUT AWAY A LITTLE RAY OF SUNSHINE FOR A RAINY DAY (1)
2	7.	WHAT'LL I DO? (7)
10	8.	I WANT TO BE HAPPY (3)
11	9.	MY DREAM GIRL (2)
4	10.	MEMORY LANE (5)
16	11.	BAGDAD (2)
9	12.	HARD-HEARTED HANNAH (4)
–	13.	TEA FOR TWO (1)
13	14.	HOW COME YOU DO ME LIKE YOU DO? (4)
14	15.	RHAPSODY IN BLUE (5)
6	16.	JEALOUS (5)
15	17.	DOODLE DOO DOO (3)
19	18.	ROCK-A-BYE MY BABY BLUES (2)
8	19.	MANDALAY (5)
–	20.	THERE'LL BE SOME CHANGES MADE (1)

DECEMBER 1924

LM	TM	
1	1.	I WONDER WHAT'S BECOME OF SALLY (4)
4	2.	FOLLOW THE SWALLOW (3)
5	3.	SOMEBODY LOVES ME (4)
13	4.	TEA FOR TWO (2)
2	5.	CHARLEY, MY BOY (4)
8	6.	I WANT TO BE HAPPY (4)
6	7.	PUT AWAY A LITTLE RAY OF SUNSHINE FOR A RAINY DAY (2)
–	8.	DOO WACKA DOO (1)
–	9.	THE PAL THAT I LOVED STOLE THE GAL THAT I LOVED (1)
3	10.	JUNE NIGHT (4)
10	11.	MEMORY LANE (6)
9	12.	MY DREAM GIRL (3)
–	13.	COPENHAGEN (1)
7	14.	WHAT'LL I DO? (8)
18	15.	ROCK-A-BYE MY BABY BLUES (3)
11	16.	BAGDAD (3)
–	17.	ALL ALONE (1)
20	18.	THERE'LL BE SOME CHANGES MADE (2)
12	19.	HARD-HEARTED HANNAH (5)
–	20.	ROSE MARIE (1)

JANUARY 1925

LM	TM	
1	1.	I WONDER WHAT'S BECOME OF SALLY (5)
17	2.	ALL ALONE (2)
2	3.	FOLLOW THE SWALLOW (4)
13	4.	COPENHAGEN (2)
9	5.	THE PAL THAT I LOVED STOLE THE GAL THAT I LOVED (2)
4	6.	TEA FOR TWO (3)
20	7.	ROSE-MARIE (2)
8	8.	DOO WACKA DOO (2)
–	9.	YOU'RE JUST A FLOWER FROM AN OLD BOUQUET (1)
3	10.	SOMEBODY LOVES ME (5)
–	11.	MY BEST GIRL (1)
11	12.	MEMORY LANE (7)
6	13.	I WANT TO BE HAPPY (5)
12	14.	MY DREAM GIRL (4)
–	15.	MANDY, MAKE UP YOUR MIND (1)
15	16.	ROCK-A-BYE MY BABY BLUES (4)
5	17.	CHARLEY, MY BOY (5)
–	18.	INDIAN LOVE CALL (1)
18	19.	THERE'LL BE SOME CHANGES MADE (3)
–	20.	SHOW ME THE WAY (1)

FEBRUARY 1925

LM	TM	
2	1.	ALL ALONE (3)
11	2.	MY BEST GIRL (2)
4	3.	COPENHAGEN (3)
7	4.	ROSE-MARIE (3)
1	5.	I WONDER WHAT'S BECOME OF SALLY (6)
5	6.	THE PAL THAT I LOVED STOLE THE GAL THAT I LOVED (3)
–	7.	EVERYBODY LOVES MY BABY (1)
18	8.	INDIAN LOVE CALL (2)
9	9.	YOU'RE JUST A FLOWER FROM AN OLD BOUQUET (2)
6	10.	TEA FOR TWO (4)
–	11.	I'LL SEE YOU IN MY DREAMS (1)
8	12.	DOO WACKA DOO (3)
–	13.	DEEP IN MY HEART, DEAR (1)
–	14.	FASCINATING RHYTHM (1)
20	15.	SHOW ME THE WAY (2)
–	16.	SERENADE (1)
3	17.	FOLLOW THE SWALLOW (5)
15	18.	MANDY, MAKE UP YOUR MIND (2)
–	19.	WEST OF THE GREAT DIVIDE (1)
–	20.	OH, LADY BE GOOD (1)

MARCH 1925

LM	TM	
1	1.	ALL ALONE (4)
7	2.	EVERYBODY LOVES MY BABY (2)
2	3.	MY BEST GIRL (3)
11	4.	I'LL SEE YOU IN MY DREAMS (2)
4	5.	ROSE-MARIE (4)
14	6.	FASCINATING RHYTHM (2)
–	7.	OH, KATHARINA! (1)
20	8.	OH, LADY BE GOOD (2)
8	9.	INDIAN LOVE CALL (3)
13	10.	DEEP IN MY HEART, DEAR (2)
–	11.	WHEN YOU AND I WERE SEVENTEEN (1)
16	12.	SERENADE (2)
–	13.	KEEP SMILING AT TROUBLE (1)
3	14.	COPENHAGEN (4)
19	15.	WEST OF THE GREAT DIVIDE (2)
–	16.	NOBODY KNOWS WHAT A RED-HEADED MAMA CAN DO (1)
6	17.	THE PAL THAT I LOVED STOLE THE GAL THAT I LOVED (4)
–	18.	JUNE BROUGHT THE ROSES (1)
–	19.	TELL HER IN THE SPRINGTIME (1)
–	20.	OH, MABEL (1)

APRIL 1925

LM	TM	
4	1.	I'LL SEE YOU IN MY DREAMS (3)
1	2.	ALL ALONE (5)
7	3.	OH, KATHARINA! (2)
2	4.	EVERYBODY LOVES MY BABY (3)
11	5.	WHEN YOU AND I WERE SEVENTEEN (2)
–	6.	ALABAMY BOUND (1)
18	7.	JUNE BROUGHT THE ROSES (2)
5	8.	ROSE-MARIE (5)
13	9.	KEEP SMILING AT TROUBLE (2)
9	10.	INDIAN LOVE CALL (4)
6	11.	FASCINATING RHYTHM (3)
3	12.	MY BEST GIRL (4)
20	13.	OH, MABEL (2)
–	14.	YEARNING (JUST FOR YOU) (1)
15	15.	WEST OF THE GREAT DIVIDE (3)
–	16.	THE CHARLESTON (1)
8	17.	OH, LADY BE GOOD (3)
10	18.	DEEP IN MY HEART, DEAR (3)
16	19.	NOBODY KNOWS WHAT A RED-HEADED MAMA CAN DO (2)
19	20.	TELL HER IN THE SPRINGTIME (2)

MAY 1925

LM	TM	
6	1.	ALABAMY BOUND (2)
1	2.	I'LL SEE YOU IN MY DREAMS (4)
3	3.	OH, KATHARINA! (3)
2	4.	ALL ALONE (6)
14	5.	YEARNING (JUST FOR YOU) (2)
5	6.	WHEN YOU AND I WERE SEVENTEEN (3)
–	7.	OH, HOW I MISS YOU TONIGHT (1)
–	8.	CHEATIN' ON ME (1)
–	9.	WHO TAKES CARE OF THE CARETAKER'S DAUGHTER (WHILE THE CARETAKER'S BUSY TAKING CARE) (1)
7	10.	JUNE BROUGHT THE ROSES (3)
10	11.	INDIAN LOVE CALL (5)
4	12.	EVERYBODY LOVES MY BABY (4)
15	13.	WEST OF THE GREAT DIVIDE (4)
–	14.	WHEN MY SUGAR WALKS DOWN THE STREET (1)
–	15.	UKULELE LADY (1)
9	16.	KEEP SMILING AT TROUBLE (3)
–	17.	IN SHADOWLAND (1)
8	18.	ROSE-MARIE (6)
16	19.	THE CHARLESTON (2)
–	20.	LET IT RAIN! LET IT POUR! (I'LL BE IN VIRGINIA IN THE MORNING) (1)

JUNE 1925

LM	TM	
5	1.	YEARNING (JUST FOR YOU) (3)
1	2.	ALABAMY BOUND (3)
3	3.	OH, KATHARINA! (4)
15	7.	UKULELE LADY (2)
7	4.	OH, HOW I MISS YOU TONIGHT (2)
2	5.	I'LL SEE YOU IN MY DREAMS (5)
14	6.	WHEN MY SUGAR WALKS DOWN THE STREET (2)
–	8.	MIDNIGHT WALTZ (1)
8	9.	CHEATIN' ON ME (2)
9	10.	WHO TAKES CARE OF THE CARETAKER'S DAUGHTER (WHILE THE CARETAKER'S BUSY TAKING CARE) (2)
6	11.	WHEN YOU AND I WERE SEVENTEEN (4)
11	12.	INDIAN LOVE CALL (6)
–	13.	IF YOU KNEW SUSIE (1)
4	14.	ALL ALONE (7)
17	15.	IN SHADOWLAND (2)
13	16.	WEST OF THE GREAT DIVIDE (5)
–	17.	SWANEE BUTTERFLY (1)
20	18.	LET IT RAIN! LET IT POUR! (I'LL BE IN VIRGINIA IN THE MORNING) (2)
–	19.	MOONLIGHT AND ROSES (1)
–	20.	SWEET GEORGIA BROWN (1)

JULY 1925

LM	TM	
13	1.	IF YOU KNEW SUSIE (2)
1	2.	YEARNING (JUST FOR YOU) (4)
–	3.	DON'T BRING LULU (1)
4	4.	OH, HOW I MISS YOU TONIGHT (3)
7	5.	UKULELE LADY (3)
20	6.	SWEET GEORGIA BROWN (2)
3	7.	OH, KATHARINA! (5)
2	8.	ALABAMY BOUND (4)
12	9.	INDIAN LOVE CALL (7)
19	10.	MOONLIGHT AND ROSES (2)
8	11.	MIDNIGHT WALTZ (2)
5	12.	I'LL SEE YOU IN MY DREAMS (6)
–	13.	PAL OF MY CRADLE DAYS (1)
6	14.	WHEN MY SUGAR WALKS DOWN THE STREET (3)
–	15.	THE CHARLESTON (3)
16	16.	WEST OF THE GREAT DIVIDE (6)
10	17.	WHO TAKES CARE OF THE CARETAKER'S DAUGHTER (WHILE THE CARETAKER'S BUSY TAKING CARE) (3)
11	18.	WHEN YOU AND I WERE SEVENTEEN (5)
–	19.	COLLEGIATE (1)
–	20.	EVERYTHING IS HOTSY-TOTSY NOW (1)

AUGUST 1925

LM	TM	
1	1.	IF YOU KNEW SUSIE (3)
6	2.	SWEET GEORGIA BROWN (3)
5	3.	UKULELE LADY (4)
19	4.	COLLEGIATE (2)
3	5.	DON'T BRING LULU (2)
–	6.	YES SIR! THAT'S MY BABY (1)
10	7.	MOONLIGHT AND ROSES (3)
4	8.	OH, HOW I MISS YOU TONIGHT (4)
2	9.	YEARNING (JUST FOR YOU) (5)
13	10.	PAL OF MY CRADLE DAYS (2)
9	11.	INDIAN LOVE CALL (8)
–	12.	RIVERBOAT SHUFFLE (1)
11	13.	MIDNIGHT WALTZ (3)
15	14.	THE CHARLESTON (4)
–	15.	MILENBERG JOYS (1)
7	16.	OH, KATHARINA! (6)
–	17.	LET ME CALL YOU SWEETHEART (1)
–	18.	LET ME LINGER (LONGER) IN YOUR ARMS (1)
–	19.	EVERYTHING IS HOTSY-TOTSY NOW (1)
8	20.	ALABAMY BOUND (5)

SEPTEMBER 1925

LM	TM	
4	1.	COLLEGIATE (3)
6	2.	YES SIR! THAT'S MY BABY (2)
3	3.	UKULELE LADY (5)
7	4.	MOONLIGHT AND ROSES (4)
1	5.	IF YOU KNEW SUSIE (4)
10	6.	PAL OF MY CRADLE DAYS (3)
–	7.	I MISS MY SWISS (1)
2	8.	SWEET GEORGIA BROWN (4)
5	9.	DON'T BRING LULU (3)
–	10.	MANHATTAN (1)
8	11.	OH, HOW I MISS YOU TONIGHT (5)
15	12.	MILENBERG JOYS (2)
12	13.	RIVERBOAT SHUFFLE (2)
–	14.	MONTMARTRE ROSE (1)
11	15.	INDIAN LOVE CALL (9)
14	16.	THE CHARLESTON (5)
9	17.	YEARNING (JUST FOR YOU) (6)
17	18.	LET ME CALL YOU SWEETHEART (2)
18	19.	LET ME LINGER (LONGER) IN YOUR ARMS (2)
–	20.	BY THE LIGHT OF THE STARS (1)

OCTOBER 1925

LM	TM	
2	1.	YES SIR! THAT'S MY BABY (3)
4	2.	MOONLIGHT AND ROSES (5)
1	3.	COLLEGIATE (4)
6	4.	PAL OF MY CRADLE DAYS (4)
10	5.	MANHATTAN (2)
7	6.	I MISS MY SWISS (2)
–	7.	MY SWEETIE TURNED ME DOWN (1)
–	8.	CECILIA (1)
18	9.	LET ME CALL YOU SWEETHEART (3)
14	10.	MONTMARTRE ROSE (2)
3	11.	UKULELE LADY (6)
15	12.	INDIAN LOVE CALL (10)
–	13.	SENTIMENTAL ME (AND ROMANTIC YOU) (1)
12	14.	MILENBERG JOYS (3)
5	15.	IF YOU KNEW SUSIE (5)
11	16.	OH, HOW I MISS YOU TONIGHT (6)
16	17.	THE CHARLESTON (6)
–	18.	REMEMBER (1)
–	19.	THE PRISONER'S SONG (1)
8	20.	SWEET GEORGIA BROWN (5)

NOVEMBER 1925

LM	TM	
2	1.	MOONLIGHT AND ROSES (6)
18	2.	REMEMBER (2)
8	3.	CECILIA (2)
1	4.	YES SIR! THAT'S MY BABY (4)
–	5.	BROWN EYES, WHY ARE YOU BLUE? (1)
3	6.	COLLEGIATE (5)
5	7.	MANHATTAN (3)
13	8.	SENTIMENTAL ME (AND ROMANTIC YOU) (2)
–	9.	SAVE YOUR SORROW (FOR TOMORROW) (1)
4	10.	PAL OF MY CRADLE DAYS (5)
9	11.	LET ME CALL YOU SWEETHEART (4)
7	12.	MY SWEETIE TURNED ME DOWN (2)
–	13.	SOMETIME (1)
–	14.	ANGRY (1)
17	15.	THE CHARLESTON (7)
19	16.	THE PRISONER'S SONG (2)
12	17.	INDIAN LOVE CALL (11)
6	18.	I MISS MY SWISS (3)
–	19.	I'M GONNA CHARLESTON BACK TO CHARLESTON (1)
–	20.	CLOSE YOUR EYES (1)

DECEMBER 1925

LM	TM	
2	1.	REMEMBER (3)
5	2.	BROWN EYES, WHY ARE YOU BLUE? (2)
13	3.	SOMETIME (2)
3	4.	CECILIA (3)
16	5.	THE PRISONER'S SONG (3)
1	6.	MOONLIGHT AND ROSES (7)
9	7.	SAVE YOUR SORROW (FOR TOMORROW) (2)
–	8.	SLEEPY TIME GAL (1)
14	9.	ANGRY (2)
15	10.	THE CHARLESTON (8)
–	11.	I'M SITTING ON TOP OF THE WORLD (1)
11	12.	LET ME CALL YOU SWEETHEART (5)
–	13.	JUST AROUND THE CORNER (1)
4	14.	YES SIR! THAT'S MY BABY (5)
8	15.	SENTIMENTAL ME (AND ROMANTIC YOU) (3)
10	16.	PAL OF MY CRADLE DAYS (6)
–	17.	SHOW ME THE WAY TO GO HOME (1)
–	18.	SONG OF THE VAGABONDS (1)
17	19.	INDIAN LOVE CALL (12)
–	20.	PADDLIN' MADELIN' HOME (1)

JANUARY 1926

LM	TM	
1	1.	REMEMBER (4)
5	2.	THE PRISONER'S SONG (4)
8	3.	SLEEPY TIME GAL (2)
2	4.	BROWN EYES, WHY ARE YOU BLUE? (3)
17	5.	SHOW ME THE WAY TO GO HOME (2)
11	6.	I'M SITTING ON TOP OF THE WORLD (2)
–	7.	WHO? (1)
3	8.	SOMETIME (3)
–	9.	FIVE FOOT TWO, EYES OF BLUE (1)
–	10.	BAM, BAM, BAMY SHORE (1)
13	11.	JUST AROUND THE CORNER (2)
10	12.	THE CHARLESTON (9)
18	13.	SONG OF THE VAGABONDS (2)
4	14.	CECILIA (4)
20	15.	PADDLIN' MADELIN' HOME (2)
–	16.	THEN I'LL BE HAPPY (1)
–	17.	THAT CERTAIN PARTY (1)
–	18.	THE LONESOMEST GIRL IN TOWN (1)
–	19.	TEA FOR TWO (5)
–	20.	I WANT TO BE HAPPY (6)

FEBRUARY 1926

LM	TM	
2	1.	THE PRISONER'S SONG (5)
6	2.	I'M SITTING ON TOP OF THE WORLD (3)
9	3.	FIVE FOOT TWO, EYES OF BLUE (2)
3	4.	SLEEPY TIME GAL (3)
17	5.	THAT CERTAIN PARTY (2)
5	6.	SHOW ME THE WAY TO GO HOME (3)
7	7.	WHO? (2)
1	8.	REMEMBER (5)
–	9.	A CUP OF COFFEE, A SANDWICH, AND YOU (1)
16	10.	THEN I'LL BE HAPPY (2)
–	11.	I NEVER KNEW (THAT ROSES GREW) (1)
4	12.	BROWN EYES, WHY ARE YOU BLUE? (4)
10	13.	BAM, BAM, BAMY SHORE (2)
11	14.	JUST AROUND THE CORNER (3)
–	15.	DINAH (1)
13	16.	SONG OF THE VAGABONDS (3)
12	17.	THE CHARLESTON (10)
–	18.	ONLY A ROSE (1)
–	19.	I LOVE MY BABY (1)
–	20.	DON'T WAKE ME UP, LET ME DREAM (1)

MARCH 1926

LM	TM	
1	1.	THE PRISONER'S SONG (6)
2	2.	I'M SITTING ON TOP OF THE WORLD (4)
15	3.	DINAH (2)
3	4.	FIVE FOOT TWO, EYES OF BLUE (3)
10	5.	THEN I'LL BE HAPPY (3)
–	6.	ALWAYS (1)
5	7.	THAT CERTAIN PARTY (3)
4	8.	SLEEPY TIME GAL (4)
7	9.	WHO? (3)
19	10.	I LOVE MY BABY (2)
6	11.	SHOW ME THE WAY TO GO HOME (4)
8	12.	REMEMBER (6)
9	13.	A CUP OF COFFEE, A SANDWICH, AND YOU (2)
–	14.	DOWN BY THE WINEGAR WOIKS (1)
16	15.	SONG OF THE VAGABONDS (4)
17	16.	THE CHARLESTON (11)
13	17.	BAM, BAM, BAMY SHORE (3)
11	18.	I NEVER KNEW (THAT ROSES GREW) (2)
14	19.	JUST AROUND THE CORNER (4)
–	20.	(WHAT CAN I SAY) AFTER I SAY I'M SORRY (1)

APRIL 1926

LM	TM	
6	1.	ALWAYS (2)
3	2.	DINAH (3)
1	3.	THE PRISONER'S SONG (7)
2	4.	I'M SITTING ON TOP OF THE WORLD (5)
5	5.	THEN I'LL BE HAPPY (4)
20	6.	(WHAT CAN I SAY) AFTER I SAY I'M SORRY (2)
10	7.	I LOVE MY BABY (3)
8	8.	SLEEPY TIME GAL (5)
9	9.	WHO? (4)
–	10.	THANKS FOR THE BUGGY RIDE (1)
4	11.	FIVE FOOT TWO, EYES OF BLUE (4)
–	12.	SONG OF THE FLAME (1)
14	13.	DOWN BY THE WINEGAR WOIKS (2)
–	14.	SWEET AND LOW-DOWN (1)
–	15.	THAT CERTAIN FEELING (1)
–	16.	JUST A COTTAGE SMALL (BY A WATER-FALL) (1)
–	17.	POOR PAPA, HE GOT NUTHIN' AT ALL (1)
13	18.	A CUP OF COFFEE, A SANDWICH, AND YOU (3)
15	19.	SONG OF THE VAGABONDS (5)
–	20.	GIMME A LITTLE KISS, WILL YA, HUH? (1)

MAY 1926

LM	TM	
1	1.	ALWAYS (3)
6	2.	(WHAT CAN I SAY) AFTER I SAY I'M SORRY (3)
2	3.	DINAH (4)
16	4.	JUST A COTTAGE SMALL (BY A WATER-FALL) (2)
20	5.	GIMME A LITTLE KISS, WILL YA, HUH? (2)
17	6.	POOR PAPA, HE GOT NUTHIN' AT ALL (2)
3	7.	THE PRISONER'S SONG (8)
10	8.	THANKS FOR THE BUGGY RIDE (2)
–	9.	LET'S TALK ABOUT MY SWEETIE (1)
5	10.	THEN I'LL BE HAPPY (5)
–	11.	TAMIAMI TRAIL (1)
7	12.	I LOVE MY BABY (4)
–	13.	HORSES (1)
4	14.	I'M SITTING ON TOP OF THE WORLD (6)
12	15.	SONG OF THE FLAME (2)
–	16.	COSSACK LOVE SONG (DON'T FORGET ME) (1)
14	17.	SWEET AND LOW-DOWN (2)
–	18.	IN THE MIDDLE OF THE NIGHT (1)
8	19.	SLEEPY TIME GAL (6)
9	20.	WHO? (5)

JUNE 1926

LM	TM	
1	1.	ALWAYS (4)
13	2.	HORSES (2)
5	3.	GIMME A LITTLE KISS, WILL YA, HUH? (3)
2	4.	(WHAT CAN I SAY) AFTER I SAY I'M SORRY (4)
4	5.	JUST A COTTAGE SMALL (BY A WATER-FALL) (3)
9	6.	LET'S TALK ABOUT MY SWEETIE (2)
–	7.	I'D CLIMB THE HIGHEST MOUNTAIN (1)
–	8.	(I DON'T BELIEVE IT BUT) SAY IT AGAIN (1)
6	9.	POOR PAPA, HE GOT NUTHIN' AT ALL (3)
11	10.	TAMIAMI TRAIL (2)
3	11.	DINAH (5)
7	12.	THE PRISONER'S SONG (9)
–	13.	AT PEACE WITH THE WORLD (1)
–	14.	DRIFTING AND DREAMING (1)
–	15.	REACHING FOR THE MOON (1)
8	16.	THANKS FOR THE BUGGY RIDE (3)
18	17.	IN THE MIDDLE OF THE NIGHT (2)
–	18.	LONESOME AND SORRY (1)
–	19.	MY LITTLE NEST OF HEAVENLY BLUE (1)
16	20.	COSSACK LOVE SONG (DON'T FORGET ME) (2)

JULY 1926

LM	TM	
7	1.	I'D CLIMB THE HIGHEST MOUNTAIN (2)
2	2.	HORSES (3)
1	3.	ALWAYS (5)
18	4.	LONESOME AND SORRY (2)
–	5.	VALENCIA (1)
3	6.	GIMME A LITTLE KISS, WILL YA, HUH? (4)
13	7.	AT PEACE WITH THE WORLD (2)
19	8.	MY LITTLE NEST OF HEAVENLY BLUE (2)
14	9.	DRIFTING AND DREAMING (2)
4	10.	(WHAT CAN I SAY) AFTER I SAY I'M SORRY (5)
5	11.	JUST A COTTAGE SMALL (BY A WATERFALL) (4)
8	12.	(I DON'T BELIEVE IT BUT) SAY IT AGAIN (2)
–	13.	BYE, BYE, BLACKBIRD (1)
15	14.	REACHING FOR THE MOON (2)
6	15.	LET'S TALK ABOUT MY SWEETIE (3)
–	16.	NEAPOLITAN NIGHTS (1)
–	17.	THE BLUE ROOM (1)
9	18.	POOR PAPA, HE GOT NUTHIN' AT ALL (4)
–	19.	SLEEPY HEAD (1)
11	20.	DINAH (6)

AUGUST 1926

LM	TM	
5	1.	VALENCIA (2)
13	2.	BYE, BYE, BLACKBIRD (2)
4	3.	LONESOME AND SORRY (3)
1	4.	I'D CLIMB THE HIGHEST MOUNTAIN (3)
9	5.	DRIFTING AND DREAMING (3)
19	6.	SLEEPY HEAD (2)
8	7.	MY LITTLE NEST OF HEAVENLY BLUE (3)
3	8.	ALWAYS (6)
–	9.	WHEN THE RED, RED ROBIN COMES BOB, BOB, BOBBIN' ALONG (1)
7	10.	AT PEACE WITH THE WORLD (3)
–	11.	CHERIE, I LOVE YOU (1)
17	12.	THE BLUE ROOM (2)
–	13.	AM I WASTING MY TIME ON YOU? (1)
2	14.	HORSES (4)
–	15.	MY DREAM OF THE BIG PARADE (1)
14	16.	REACHING FOR THE MOON (3)
–	17.	HELLO, ALOHA! HOW ARE YOU? (1)
–	18.	THE GIRL FRIEND (1)
–	19.	WHERE'D YOU GET THOSE EYES? (1)
11	20.	JUST A COTTAGE SMALL (BY A WATERFALL) (5)

SEPTEMBER 1926

LM	TM	
1	1.	VALENCIA (3)
2	2.	BYE, BYE, BLACKBIRD (3)
9	3.	WHEN THE RED, RED ROBIN COMES BOB, BOB, BOBBIN' ALONG (2)
6	4.	SLEEPY HEAD (3)
11	5.	CHERIE, I LOVE YOU (2)
19	6.	WHERE'D YOU GET THOSE EYES? (2)
5	7.	DRIFTING AND DREAMING (4)
3	8.	LONESOME AND SORRY (4)
12	9.	THE BLUE ROOM (3)
17	10.	HELLO, ALOHA, HOW ARE YOU? (2)
–	11.	LOOKING AT THE WORLD THROUGH ROSE-COLORED GLASSES (1)
18	12.	THE GIRL FRIEND (2)
13	13.	AM I WASTING MY TIME ON YOU? (2)
–	14.	BABY FACE (1)
–	15.	BREEZIN' ALONG WITH THE BREEZE (1)
8	16.	ALWAYS (7)
4	17.	I'D CLIMB THE HIGHEST MOUNTAIN (4)
–	18.	HOW MANY TIMES (1)
15	19.	MY DREAM OF THE BIG PARADE (2)
–	20.	KATINKA (1)

OCTOBER 1926

LM	TM	
2	1.	BYE, BYE, BLACKBIRD (4)
3	2.	WHEN THE RED, RED ROBIN COMES BOB, BOB, BOBBIN' ALONG (3)
14	3.	BABY FACE (2)
15	4.	BREEZIN' ALONG WITH THE BREEZE (2)
6	5.	WHERE'D YOU GET THOSE EYES? (3)
1	6.	VALENCIA (4)
5	7.	CHERIE, I LOVE YOU (3)
–	8.	ME TOO (1)
18	9.	HOW MANY TIMES (2)
–	10.	BLACK BOTTOM (1)
11	11.	LOOKING AT THE WORLD THROUGH ROSE-COLORED GLASSES (2)
–	12.	LUCKY DAY (1)
9	13.	THE BLUE ROOM (4)
–	14.	TING-A-LING (THE WALTZ OF THE BELLS) (1)
7	15.	DRIFTING AND DREAMING (5)
11	16.	HELLO, ALOHA, HOW ARE YOU? (3)
12	17.	THE GIRL FRIEND (3)
–	18.	BARCELONA (1)
4	19.	SLEEPY HEAD (4)
–	20.	THE BIRTH OF THE BLUES (1)

NOVEMBER 1926

LM	TM	
3	1.	BABY FACE (3)
10	2.	BLACK BOTTOM (2)
4	3.	BREEZIN' ALONG WITH THE BREEZE (3)
12	4.	LUCKY DAY (2)
1	5.	BYE, BYE, BLACKBIRD (5)
8	6.	ME TOO (2)
5	7.	WHERE'D YOU GET THOSE EYES? (4)
–	8.	BECAUSE I LOVE YOU (1)
9	9.	HOW MANY TIMES (3)
7	10.	CHERIE, I LOVE YOU (4)
2	11.	WHEN THE RED, RED ROBIN COMES BOB, BOB, BOBBIN' ALONG (4)
20	12.	THE BIRTH OF THE BLUES (2)
–	13.	PLAY GYPSIES - DANCE GYPSIES (1)
6	14.	VALENCIA (5)
–	15.	IN A LITTLE SPANISH TOWN (1)
14	16.	TING-A-LING (THE WALTZ OF THE BELLS) (2)
13	17.	THE BLUE ROOM (5)
11	18.	LOOKING AT THE WORLD THROUGH ROSE-COLORED GLASSES (3)
–	19.	MOONLIGHT ON THE GANGES (1)
–	20.	THERE'S A NEW STAR IN HEAVEN TONIGHT (RUDOLPH VALENTINO) (1)

DECEMBER 1926

LM	TM	
8	1.	BECAUSE I LOVE YOU (2)
2	2.	BLACK BOTTOM (3)
15	3.	IN A LITTLE SPANISH TOWN (2)
19	4.	MOONLIGHT ON THE GANGES (2)
1	5.	BABY FACE (4)
–	6.	MARY LOU (1)
4	7.	LUCKY DAY (3)
–	8.	TONIGHT YOU BELONG TO ME (1)
12	9.	THE BIRTH OF THE BLUES (3)
3	10.	BREEZIN' ALONG WITH THE BREEZE (4)
–	11.	THE LITTLE WHITE HOUSE (AT THE END OF HONEYMOON LANE) (1)
–	12.	CROSS YOUR HEART (1)
13	13.	PLAY GYPSIES - DANCE, GYPSIES (2)
–	14.	FOR MY SWEETHEART (1)
–	15.	CLIMBING UP THE LADDER OF LOVE (1)
10	16.	CHERIE, I LOVE YOU (5)
6	17.	ME TOO (3)
5	18.	BYE, BYE, BLACKBIRD (6)
–	19.	ALL ALONE MONDAY (1)
9	20.	HOW MANY TIMES (4)

JANUARY 1927

LM	TM	Title
3	1.	IN A LITTLE SPANISH TOWN (3)
4	2.	MOONLIGHT ON THE GANGES (3)
11	3.	THE LITTLE WHITE HOUSE (AT THE END OF HONEYMOON LANE) (2)
1	4.	BECAUSE I LOVE YOU (3)
8	5.	TONIGHT YOU BELONG TO ME (2)
6	6.	MARY LOU (2)
19	7.	ALL ALONE MONDAY (2)
2	8.	BLACK BOTTOM (4)
–	9.	IT MADE YOU HAPPY WHEN YOU MADE ME CRY (1)
7	10.	LUCKY DAY (4)
9	11.	THE BIRTH OF THE BLUES (4)
–	12.	SUNDAY (1)
–	13.	HELLO, BLUEBIRD (1)
12	14.	CROSS YOUR HEART (2)
–	15.	DO, DO, DO (1)
5	16.	BABY FACE (5)
–	17.	JUST A BIRD'S-EYE VIEW OF MY OLD KENTUCKY HOME (1)
15	18.	CLIMBING UP THE LADDER OF LOVE (2)
13	19.	PLAY GYPSIES - DANCE GYPSIES (3)
–	20.	SOMEONE TO WATCH OVER ME (1)

FEBRUARY 1927

LM	TM	Title
1	1.	IN A LITTLE SPANISH TOWN (4)
5	2.	TONIGHT YOU BELONG TO ME (3)
3	3.	THE LITTLE WHITE HOUSE (AT THE END OF HONEYMOON LANE) (3)
9	4.	IT MADE YOU HAPPY WHEN YOU MADE ME CRY (2)
6	5.	MARY LOU (3)
–	6.	WHERE DO YOU WORK-A JOHN? (1)
12	7.	SUNDAY (2)
2	8.	MOONLIGHT ON THE GANGES (4)
15	9.	DO, DO, DO (2)
4	10.	BECAUSE I LOVE YOU (4)
20	11.	SOMEONE TO WATCH OVER ME (2)
–	12.	BLUE SKIES (1)
13	13.	HELLO, BLUEBIRD (2)
–	14.	(I'VE GROWN SO LONESOME) THINKING OF YOU (1)
–	15.	ONE ALONE (1)
7	16.	ALL ALONE MONDAY (3)
–	17.	CLAP YO' HANDS (1)
11	18.	THE BIRTH OF THE BLUES (5)
8	19.	BLACK BOTTOM (5)
–	20.	I'VE GOT THE GIRL (1)

MARCH 1927

LM	TM	Title
12	1.	BLUE SKIES (2)
6	2.	WHERE DO YOU WORK-A JOHN? (2)
1	3.	IN A LITTLE SPANISH TOWN (5)
11	4.	SOMEONE TO WATCH OVER ME (3)
14	5.	(I'VE GROWN SO LONESOME) THINKING OF YOU (2)
–	6.	I KNOW THAT YOU KNOW (1)
2	7.	TONIGHT YOU BELONG TO ME (4)
7	8.	SUNDAY (3)
–	9.	IT ALL DEPENDS ON YOU (1)
17	10.	CLAP YO' HANDS (2)
15	11.	ONE ALONE (2)
–	12.	SAM, THE OLD ACCORDION MAN (1)
–	13.	YANKEE ROSE (1)
5	14.	MARY LOU (4)
13	15.	HELLO, BLUEBIRD (3)
10	16.	BECAUSE I LOVE YOU (5)
–	17.	MUDDY WATER (1)
4	18.	IT MADE YOU HAPPY WHEN YOU MADE ME CRY (3)
9	19.	DO, DO, DO (3)
–	20.	SONG OF THE WANDERER (1)

APRIL 1927

LM	TM	Title
1	1.	BLUE SKIES (3)
12	2.	SAM, THE OLD ACCORDION MAN (2)
9	3.	IT ALL DEPENDS ON YOU (2)
2	4.	WHERE DO YOU WORK-A JOHN? (3)
13	5.	YANKEE ROSE (2)
17	6.	MUDDY WATER (2)
3	7.	IN A LITTLE SPANISH TOWN (6)
6	8.	I KNOW THAT YOU KNOW (2)
–	9.	RIO RITA (1)
20	10.	SONG OF THE WANDERER (2)
–	11.	WHAT DOES IT MATTER? (1)
7	12.	TONIGHT YOU BELONG TO ME (5)
4	13.	SOMEONE TO WATCH OVER ME (4)
–	14.	I'M LOOKING OVER A FOUR LEAF CLOVER (1)
11	15.	ONE ALONE (3)
–	16.	AIN'T SHE SWEET? (1)
–	17.	THE RANGER'S SONG (1)
–	18.	THE KINKAJOU (1)
5	19.	(I'VE GROWN SO LONESOME) THINKING OF YOU (3)
15	20.	HELLO, BLUEBIRD (4)

MAY 1927

LM	TM	Title
3	1.	IT ALL DEPENDS ON YOU (3)
2	2.	SAM, THE OLD ACCORDION MAN (3)
14	3.	I'M LOOKING OVER A FOUR LEAF CLOVER (2)
9	4.	RIO RITA (2)
1	5.	BLUE SKIES (4)
6	6.	MUDDY WATER (3)
16	7.	AIN'T SHE SWEET? (2)
11	8.	WHAT DOES IT MATTER? (2)
–	9.	FORGIVE ME (1)
10	10.	SONG OF THE WANDERER (3)
5	11.	YANKEE ROSE (3)
–	12.	CRAZY WORDS, CRAZY TUNE (1)
17	13.	THE RANGER'S SONG (2)
18	14.	THE KINKAJOU (2)
–	15.	FOLLOWING THE SUN AROUND (1)
–	16.	SO BLUE (1)
–	17.	MOONBEAM! KISS HER FOR ME (1)
–	18.	IF YOU SEE SALLY (1)
7	19.	IN A LITTLE SPANISH TOWN (7)
–	20.	AFTER YOU'VE GONE (1)

JUNE 1927

LM	TM	Title
3	1.	I'M LOOKING OVER A FOUR LEAF CLOVER (3)
7	2.	AIN'T SHE SWEET? (3)
6	3.	MUDDY WATER (4)
4	4.	RIO RITA (3)
9	5.	FORGIVE ME (2)
–	6.	RUSSIAN LULLABY (1)
8	7.	WHAT DOES IT MATTER? (3)
–	8.	THE DOLL DANCE (1)
1	9.	IT ALL DEPENDS ON YOU (4)
–	10.	AT SUNDOWN (1)
16	11.	SO BLUE (2)
2	12.	SAM, THE OLD ACCORDION MAN (4)
12	13.	CRAZY WORDS, CRAZY TUNE (2)
–	14.	THERE'S EVERYTHING NICE ABOUT YOU (1)
5	15.	BLUE SKIES (5)
10	16.	SONG OF THE WANDERER (4)
–	17.	I'M IN LOVE AGAIN (1)
14	18.	THE KINKAJOU (3)
–	19.	ME AND MY SHADOW (1)
17	20.	MOONBEAM! KISS HER FOR ME (2)

JULY 1927

LM	TM	
6	1.	RUSSIAN LULLABY (2)
10	2.	AT SUNDOWN (2)
19	3.	ME AND MY SHADOW (2)
8	4.	THE DOLL DANCE (2)
1	5.	I'M LOOKING OVER A FOUR LEAF CLOVER (4)
–	6.	SIDE BY SIDE (1)
2	7.	AIN'T SHE SWEET? (4)
3	8.	MUDDY WATER (5)
–	9.	WHEN DAY IS DONE (1)
17	10.	I'M IN LOVE AGAIN (2)
–	11.	RED LIPS, KISS MY BLUES AWAY (1)
7	12.	WHAT DOES IT MATTER? (4)
4	13.	RIO RITA (4)
–	14.	FIFTY MILLION FRENCHMEN (CAN'T BE WRONG) (1)
–	15.	LINDBERGH, THE EAGLE OF THE U.S.A. (1)
14	16.	THERE'S EVERYTHING NICE ABOUT YOU (2)
–	17.	AFTER YOU'VE GONE (2)
11	18.	SO BLUE (3)
–	19.	LUCKY LINDY (1)
9	20.	IT ALL DEPENDS ON YOU (5)

AUGUST 1927

LM	TM	
3	1.	ME AND MY SHADOW (3)
1	2.	RUSSIAN LULLABY (3)
6	3.	SIDE BY SIDE (2)
–	4.	CHARMAINE (1)
2	5.	AT SUNDOWN (3)
9	6.	WHEN DAY IS DONE (2)
4	7.	THE DOLL DANCE (3)
–	8.	SOMETIMES I'M HAPPY (1)
–	9.	JUST LIKE A BUTTERFLY (THAT'S CAUGHT IN THE RAIN) (1)
11	10.	RED LIPS, KISS MY BLUES AWAY (2)
–	11.	HALLELUJAH! (1)
15	12.	LINDBERGH, THE EAGLE OF THE U.S.A. (2)
–	13.	JUST ANOTHER DAY WASTED AWAY (WAITING FOR YOU) (1)
–	14.	MAGNOLIA (1)
19	15.	LUCKY LINDY (2)
17	16.	AFTER YOU'VE GONE (3)
–	17.	TWO BLACK CROWS, PARTS 1 AND 2 (1)
–	18.	WHAT DO WE DO ON A DEW-DEW-DEWY DAY? (1)
–	19.	I CAN'T BELIEVE THAT YOU'RE IN LOVE WITH ME (1)
–	20.	SLOW RIVER (1)

SEPTEMBER 1927

LM	TM	
4	1.	CHARMAINE (2)
6	2.	WHEN DAY IS DONE (3)
1	3.	ME AND MY SHADOW (4)
18	4.	WHAT DO WE DO ON A DEW-DEW-DEWY DAY? (2)
9	5.	JUST LIKE A BUTTERFLY (THAT'S CAUGHT IN THE RAIN) (2)
3	6.	SIDE BY SIDE (3)
13	7.	JUST ANOTHER DAY WASTED AWAY (WAITING FOR YOU) (2)
2	8.	RUSSIAN LULLABY (4)
5	9.	AT SUNDOWN (4)
–	10.	(HERE AM I) BROKEN HEARTED (1)
8	11.	SOMETIMES I'M HAPPY (2)
11	12.	HALLELUJAH! (2)
7	13.	THE DOLL DANCE (4)
–	14.	ARE YOU LONESOME TONIGHT? (1)
19	15.	I CAN'T BELIEVE THAT YOU'RE IN LOVE WITH ME (2)
–	16.	DOWN SOUTH (1)
17	17.	TWO BLACK CROWS, PARTS 1 AND 2 (2)
14	18.	MAGNOLIA (2)
20	19.	SLOW RIVER (2)
–	20.	YOU DON'T LIKE IT, NOT MUCH (1)

OCTOBER 1927

LM	TM	
1	1.	CHARMAINE (3)
10	2.	(HERE AM I) BROKEN HEARTED (2)
4	3.	WHAT DO WE DO ON A DEW-DEW-DEWY DAY? (3)
2	4.	WHEN DAY IS DONE (4)
14	5.	ARE YOU LONESOME TONIGHT? (2)
3	6.	ME AND MY SHADOW (5)
–	7.	C'EST VOUS (IT'S YOU) (1)
–	8.	MISS ANNABELLE LEE (1)
12	9.	HALLELUJAH! (3)
–	10.	I'M COMING, VIRGINIA (1)
7	11.	JUST ANOTHER DAY WASTED AWAY (WAITING FOR YOU) (3)
–	12.	GIVE ME A NIGHT IN JUNE (1)
13	13.	THE DOLL DANCE (5)
–	14.	SHAKING THE BLUES AWAY (1)
5	15.	JUST LIKE A BUTTERFLY (THAT'S CAUGHT IN THE RAIN) (3)
16	16.	DOWN SOUTH (2)
9	17.	AT SUNDOWN (5)
6	18.	SIDE BY SIDE (4)
–	19.	UNDER THE MOON (1)
–	20.	JUST ONCE AGAIN (1)

NOVEMBER 1927

LM	TM	
8	1.	MISS ANNABELLE LEE (2)
1	2.	CHARMAINE (4)
12	3.	GIVE ME A NIGHT IN JUNE (2)
3	4.	WHAT DO WE DO ON A DEW-DEW-DEWY DAY? (4)
2	5.	(HERE AM I) BROKEN HEARTED (3)
–	6.	JUST A MEMORY (1)
–	7.	LUCKY IN LOVE (1)
14	8.	SHAKING THE BLUES AWAY (2)
–	9.	DANCING TAMBOURINE (1)
4	10.	WHEN DAY IS DONE (5)
7	11.	C'EST VOUS (IT'S YOU) (2)
–	12.	THE VARSITY DRAG (1)
5	13.	ARE YOU LONESOME TONIGHT? (3)
10	14.	I'M COMING, VIRGINIA (2)
16	15.	DOWN SOUTH (3)
–	16.	DIANE (1)
9	17.	HALLELUJAH! (4)
20	18.	JUST ONCE AGAIN (2)
19	19.	UNDER THE MOON (2)
–	20.	HERE COMES THE SHOW BOAT (1)

DECEMBER 1927

LM	TM	
6	1.	JUST A MEMORY (2)
16	2.	DIANE (2)
2	3.	CHARMAINE (5)
1	4.	MISS ANNABELLE LEE (3)
12	5.	THE VARSITY DRAG (2)
–	6.	MY BLUE HEAVEN (1)
9	7.	DANCING TAMBOURINE (2)
3	8.	GIVE ME A NIGHT IN JUNE (3)
–	9.	THE BEST THINGS IN LIFE ARE FREE (1)
20	10.	HERE COMES THE SHOW BOAT (2)
–	11.	GOOD NEWS (1)
–	12.	THE SWEETHEART OF SIGMA CHI (1)
–	13.	IT WAS ONLY A SUN SHOWER (1)
–	14.	I AIN'T GOT NOBODY (1)
7	15.	LUCKY IN LOVE (2)
5	16.	(HERE AM I) BROKEN HEARTED (4)
–	17.	IDA (SWEET AS APPLE CIDER) (1)
4	18.	WHAT DO WE DO ON A DEW-DEW-DEWY DAY? (5)
–	19.	AMONG MY SOUVENIRS (1)
–	20.	DID YOU MEAN IT? (1)

JANUARY 1928

LM	TM	
6	1.	MY BLUE HEAVEN (2)
1	2.	JUST A MEMORY (3)
2	3.	DIANE (3)
19	4.	AMONG MY SOUVENIRS (2)
5	5.	THE VARSITY DRAG (3)
12	6.	THE SWEETHEART OF SIGMA CHI (2)
–	7.	THE SONG IS ENDED (1)
20	8.	DID YOU MEAN IT? (2)
9	9.	THE BEST THINGS IN LIFE ARE FREE (2)
14	10.	I AIN'T GOT NOBODY (2)
10	11.	HERE COMES THE SHOW BOAT (3)
17	12.	IDA (SWEET AS APPLE CIDER) (2)
–	13.	UP IN THE CLOUDS (1)
11	14.	GOOD NEWS (2)
–	15.	MY BLUE RIDGE MOUNTAIN HOME (1)
3	16.	CHARMAINE (6)
4	17.	MISS ANNABELLE LEE (4)
–	18.	MY HEART STOOD STILL (1)
–	19.	TOGETHER, WE TWO (1)
–	20.	I SCREAM, YOU SCREAM, WE ALL SCREAM FOR ICE CREAM (1)

FEBRUARY 1928

LM	TM	
1	1.	MY BLUE HEAVEN (3)
4	2.	AMONG MY SOUVENIRS (3)
7	3.	THE SONG IS ENDED (2)
3	4.	DIANE (4)
18	5.	MY HEART STOOD STILL (2)
–	6.	AWAY DOWN SOUTH IN HEAVEN (1)
6	7.	THE SWEETHEART OF SIGMA CHI (3)
20	8.	I SCREAM, YOU SCREAM, WE ALL SCREAM FOR ICE CREAM (2)
5	9.	THE VARSITY DRAG (4)
–	10.	THOU SWELL (1)
10	11.	I AIN'T GOT NOBODY (3)
2	12.	JUST A MEMORY (4)
–	13.	RAIN (1)
8	14.	DID YOU MEAN IT? (3)
9	15.	THE BEST THINGS IN LIFE ARE FREE (3)
11	16.	HERE COMES THE SHOW BOAT (4)
–	17.	CHLOE (1)
19	18.	TOGETHER, WE TWO (2)
–	19.	MY MELANCHOLY BABY (1)
–	20.	LET A SMILE BE YOUR UMBRELLA (1)

MARCH 1928

LM	TM	
2	1.	AMONG MY SOUVENIRS (4)
1	2.	MY BLUE HEAVEN (4)
13	3.	RAIN (2)
3	4.	THE SONG IS ENDED (3)
20	5.	LET A SMILE BE YOUR UMBRELLA (2)
17	6.	CHLOE (2)
6	7.	AWAY DOWN SOUTH IN HEAVEN (2)
10	8.	THOU SWELL (2)
–	9.	KEEP SWEEPING THE COBWEBS OFF THE MOON (1)
4	10.	DIANE (5)
5	11.	MY HEART STOOD STILL (3)
–	12.	THE MAN I LOVE (1)
11	13.	I AIN'T GOT NOBODY (4)
–	14.	TOGETHER (1)
–	15.	AH! SWEET MYSTERY OF LIFE (1)
–	16.	CAN'T HELP LOVIN' DAT MAN (1)
8	17.	I SCREAM, YOU SCREAM, WE ALL SCREAM FOR ICE CREAM (3)
7	18.	THE SWEETHEART OF SIGMA CHI (4)
19	19.	MY MELANCHOLY BABY (2)
–	20.	OL' MAN RIVER (1)

APRIL 1928

LM	TM	
14	1.	TOGETHER (2)
5	2.	LET A SMILE BE YOUR UMBRELLA (3)
6	3.	CHLOE (3)
–	4.	RAMONA (1)
1	5.	AMONG MY SOUVENIRS (5)
2	6.	MY BLUE HEAVEN (5)
–	7.	BACK IN YOUR OWN BACK YARD (1)
12	8.	THE MAN I LOVE (2)
3	9.	RAIN (3)
15	10.	AH! SWEET MYSTERY OF LIFE (2)
16	11.	CAN'T HELP LOVIN' DAT MAN (2)
20	12.	OL' MAN RIVER (2)
4	13.	THE SONG IS ENDED (4)
–	14.	MAKE BELIEVE (1)
9	15.	KEEP SWEEPING THE COBWEBS OFF THE MOON (2)
–	16.	MARY ANN (1)
–	17.	GIRL OF MY DREAMS (1)
–	18.	WHY DO I LOVE YOU? (1)
13	19.	I AIN'T GOT NOBODY (5)
–	20.	COQUETTE (1)

MAY 1928

LM	TM	
4	1.	RAMONA (2)
7	2.	BACK IN YOUR OWN BACK YARD (2)
3	3.	CHLOE (4)
8	4.	THE MAN I LOVE (3)
1	5.	TOGETHER (3)
2	6.	LET A SMILE BE YOUR UMBRELLA (4)
16	7.	MARY ANN (2)
20	8.	COQUETTE (2)
17	9.	GIRL OF MY DREAMS (2)
–	10.	I JUST ROLL ALONG (HAVIN' MY UPS AND DOWNS) (1)
–	11.	SUNSHINE (1)
12	12.	OL' MAN RIVER (3)
11	13.	CAN'T HELP LOVIN' DAT MAN (3)
10	14.	AH! SWEET MYSTERY OF LIFE (3)
6	15.	MY BLUE HEAVEN (6)
–	16.	PERSIAN RUG (1)
14	17.	MAKE BELIEVE (2)
19	18.	I AIN'T GOT NOBODY (6)
–	19.	I STILL LOVE YOU (1)
–	20.	LAUGH, CLOWN, LAUGH (1)

JUNE 1928

LM	TM	
1	1.	RAMONA (3)
9	2.	GIRL OF MY DREAMS (3)
20	3.	LAUGH, CLOWN, LAUGH (2)
2	4.	BACK IN YOUR OWN BACK YARD (3)
8	5.	COQUETTE (3)
–	6.	I CAN'T DO WITHOUT YOU (1)
3	7.	CHLOE (5)
12	8.	OL' MAN RIVER (4)
4	9.	THE MAN I LOVE (4)
–	10.	WAS IT A DREAM? (1)
19	11.	I STILL LOVE YOU (2)
16	12.	PERSIAN RUG (2)
10	13.	I JUST ROLL ALONG (HAVIN' MY UPS AND DOWNS) (2)
13	14.	CAN'T HELP LOVIN' DAT MAN (4)
–	15.	MISSISSIPPI MUD (1)
–	16.	ANGELA MIA (MY ANGEL) (1)
18	17.	I AIN'T GOT NOBODY (7)
14	18.	AH! SWEET MYSTERY OF LIFE (4)
–	19.	MANHATTAN SERENADE (1)
11	20.	SUNSHINE (2)

JULY 1928

LM	TM	
1	1.	RAMONA (4)
2	2.	GIRL OF MY DREAMS (4)
3	3.	LAUGH, CLOWN, LAUGH (3)
16	4.	ANGELA MIA (MY ANGEL) (2)
–	5.	BELOVED (1)
–	6.	GET OUT AND GET UNDER THE MOON (1)
10	7.	WAS IT A DREAM? (2)
–	8.	HAPPY-GO-LUCKY LANE (1)
–	9.	READY FOR THE RIVER (1)
6	10.	I CAN'T DO WITHOUT YOU (2)
–	11.	C-O-N-S-T-A-N-T-I-N-O-P-L-E (1)
8	12.	OL' MAN RIVER (5)
7	13.	CHLOE (6)
–	14.	CRAZY RHYTHM (1)
5	15.	COQUETTE (4)
9	16.	THE MAN I LOVE (5)
4	17.	BACK IN YOUR OWN BACK YARD (4)
18	18.	AH! SWEET MYSTERY OF LIFE (5)
–	19.	JUST LIKE A MELODY OUT OF THE SKY (1)
–	20.	THAT'S MY WEAKNESS NOW (1)

AUGUST 1928

LM	TM	
4	1.	ANGELA MIA (MY ANGEL) (3)
1	2.	RAMONA (5)
6	3.	GET OUT AND GET UNDER THE MOON (2)
2	4.	GIRL OF MY DREAMS (5)
5	5.	BELOVED (2)
19	6.	JUST LIKE A MELODY OUT OF THE SKY (2)
3	7.	LAUGH, CLOWN, LAUGH (4)
20	8.	THAT'S MY WEAKNESS NOW (2)
14	9.	CRAZY RHYTHM (2)
11	10.	C-O-N-S-T-A-N-T-I-N-O-P-L-E (2)
–	11.	THE SIDEWALKS OF NEW YORK (1)
–	12.	YOU TOOK ADVANTAGE OF ME (1)
18	13.	AH! SWEET MYSTERY OF LIFE (6)
9	14.	READY FOR THE RIVER (2)
–	15.	SWEET SUE (JUST YOU) (1)
–	16.	SWEET LORRAINE (1)
–	17.	YOU'RE A REAL SWEETHEART (1)
7	18.	WAS IT A DREAM? (3)
12	19.	OL' MAN RIVER (6)
–	20.	BECAUSE MY BABY DON'T MEAN MAYBE NOW (1)

SEPTEMBER 1928

LM	TM	
1	1.	ANGELA MIA (MY ANGEL) (4)
8	2.	THAT'S MY WEAKNESS NOW (3)
6	3.	JUST LIKE A MELODY OUT OF THE SKY (3)
3	4.	GET OUT AND GET UNDER THE MOON (3)
–	5.	CHIQUITA (1)
4	6.	GIRL OF MY DREAMS (6)
19	7.	I CAN'T GIVE YOU ANYTHING BUT LOVE (1)
2	8.	RAMONA (6)
12	9.	YOU TOOK ADVANTAGE OF ME (2)
11	10.	THE SIDEWALKS OF NEW YORK (2)
–	11.	DIGA-DIGA-DOO (1)
15	12.	SWEET SUE (JUST YOU) (2)
13	13.	AH! SWEET MYSTERY OF LIFE (7)
5	14.	BELOVED (3)
–	15.	MEMORIES OF FRANCE (1)
–	16.	JEANNINE, I DREAM OF LILAC TIME (1)
9	17.	CRAZY RHYTHM (3)
17	18.	YOU'RE A REAL SWEETHEART (2)
–	19.	DREAM HOUSE (1)
16	20.	SWEET LORRAINE (2)

OCTOBER 1928

LM	TM	
16	1.	JEANNINE, I DREAM OF LILAC TIME (2)
7	2.	I CAN'T GIVE YOU ANYTHING BUT LOVE (2)
1	3.	ANGELA MIA (MY ANGEL) (5)
5	4.	CHIQUITA (2)
15	5.	MEMORIES OF FRANCE (2)
11	6.	DIGA-DIGA-DOO (2)
2	7.	THAT'S MY WEAKNESS NOW (4)
19	8.	DREAM HOUSE (2)
3	9.	JUST LIKE A MELODY OUT OF THE SKY (4)
–	10.	DUSKY STEVEDORE (1)
–	11.	SONNY BOY (1)
–	12.	OLD MAN SUNSHINE (1)
–	13.	TEN LITTLE MILES FROM TOWN (1)
–	14.	THERE'S A RAINBOW 'ROUND MY SHOULDER (1)
–	15.	DOIN' THE NEW LOW-DOWN (1)
4	16.	GET OUT AND GET UNDER THE MOON (4)
–	17.	REVENGE (1)
–	18.	I MUST HAVE THAT MAN (1)
10	19.	THE SIDEWALKS OF NEW YORK (3)
12	20.	SWEET SUE (JUST YOU) (3)

NOVEMBER 1928

LM	TM	
1	1.	JEANNINE, I DREAM OF LILAC TIME (3)
11	2.	SONNY BOY (2)
2	3.	I CAN'T GIVE YOU ANYTHING BUT LOVE (3)
14	4.	THERE'S A RAINBOW 'ROUND MY SHOULDER (2)
12	5.	OLD MAN SUNSHINE (2)
10	6.	DUSKY STEVEDORE (2)
17	7.	REVENGE (2)
–	8.	NEAPOLITAN NIGHTS (2)
–	9.	ROSES OF YESTERDAY (1)
4	10.	CHIQUITA (3)
8	11.	DREAM HOUSE (3)
–	12.	HALFWAY TO HEAVEN (1)
3	13.	ANGELA MIA (MY ANGEL) (6)
5	14.	MEMORIES OF FRANCE (3)
–	15.	NAGASAKI (1)
6	16.	DIGA-DIGA-DOO (3)
–	17.	KING FOR A DAY (1)
–	18.	DOIN' THE RACCOON (1)
–	19.	TAKE YOUR TOMORROW (AND GIVE ME TODAY) (1)
–	20.	LOUISIANA (1)

DECEMBER 1928

LM	TM	
2	1.	SONNY BOY (3)
4	2.	THERE'S A RAINBOW 'ROUND MY SHOULDER (3)
1	3.	JEANNINE, I DREAM OF LILAC TIME (4)
3	4.	I CAN'T GIVE YOU ANYTHING BUT LOVE (4)
18	5.	DOIN' THE RACCOON (2)
–	6.	YOU'RE THE CREAM IN MY COFFEE (1)
5	7.	OLD MAN SUNSHINE (3)
–	8.	SALLY OF MY DREAMS (1)
6	9.	DUSKY STEVEDORE (3)
19	10.	TAKE YOUR TOMORROW (AND GIVE ME TODAY) (2)
–	11.	I WANNA BE LOVED BY YOU (1)
12	12.	HALFWAY TO HEAVEN (2)
9	13.	ROSES OF YESTERDAY (2)
–	14.	I'M SORRY, SALLY (1)
8	15.	NEAPOLITAN NIGHTS (3)
–	16.	CHERRY (1)
11	17.	DREAM HOUSE (4)
20	18.	LOUISIANA (2)
–	19.	LET'S DO IT (LET'S FALL IN LOVE) (1)
–	20.	DON'T HOLD EVERYTHING (1)

JANUARY 1929

LM	TM	
1	1.	SONNY BOY (4)
6	2.	YOU'RE THE CREAM IN MY COFFEE (2)
2	3.	THERE'S A RAINBOW 'ROUND MY SHOULDER (4)
11	4.	I WANNA BE LOVED BY YOU (2)
–	5.	MARIE (1)
19	6.	LET'S DO IT (LET'S FALL IN LOVE) (2)
–	7.	SWEETHEARTS ON PARADE (1)
14	8.	I'M SORRY, SALLY (2)
4	9.	I CAN'T GIVE YOU ANYTHING BUT LOVE (5)
–	10.	SHE'S FUNNY THAT WAY (1)
10	11.	TAKE YOUR TOMORROW (AND GIVE ME TODAY) (3)
3	12.	JEANNINE, I DREAM OF LILAC TIME (5)
–	13.	CAROLINA MOON (1)
–	14.	AVALON TOWN (1)
–	15.	I'LL GET BY (AS LONG AS I HAVE YOU) (1)
5	16.	DOIN' THE RACCOON (3)
20	17.	DON'T HOLD EVERYTHING (2)
–	18.	MY BLACKBIRDS ARE BLUEBIRDS NOW (1)
–	19.	MAKIN' WHOOPIE (1)
–	20.	SALLY OF MY DREAMS (2)

FEBRUARY 1929

LM	TM	
7	1.	SWEETHEARTS ON PARADE (2)
5	2.	MARIE (2)
15	3.	I'LL GET BY (AS LONG AS I HAVE YOU) (2)
2	4.	YOU'RE THE CREAM IN MY COFFEE (3)
13	5.	CAROLINA MOON (2)
1	6.	SONNY BOY (5)
–	7.	IF I HAD YOU (1)
–	8.	HOW ABOUT ME? (1)
19	9.	MAKIN' WHOOPIE (2)
–	10.	WHERE THE SHY LITTLE VIOLETS GROW (1)
14	11.	AVALON TOWN (2)
3	12.	THERE'S A RAINBOW 'ROUND MY SHOULDER (5)
10	13.	SHE'S FUNNY THAT WAY (2)
–	14.	(I LOVE YOU) SWEETHEART OF ALL MY DREAMS (1)
4	15.	I WANNA BE LOVED BY YOU (3)
6	16.	LET'S DO IT (LET'S FALL IN LOVE) (3)
–	17.	A PRECIOUS LITTLE THING CALLED LOVE (1)
–	18.	I FAW DOWN AN' GO BOOM! (1)
8	19.	I'M SORRY, SALLY (3)
–	20.	DON'T BE LIKE THAT (1)

MARCH 1929

LM	TM	
5	1.	CAROLINA MOON (3)
3	2.	I'LL GET BY (AS LONG AS I HAVE YOU) (3)
1	3.	SWEETHEARTS ON PARADE (3)
17	4.	A PRECIOUS LITTLE THING CALLED LOVE (2)
7	5.	IF I HAD YOU (2)
2	6.	MARIE (3)
9	7.	MAKIN' WHOOPIE (3)
–	8.	WEDDING BELLS (ARE BREAKING UP THAT OLD GANG OF MINE) (1)
14	9.	(I LOVE YOU) SWEETHEART OF ALL MY DREAMS (2)
11	10.	AVALON TOWN (3)
10	11.	WHERE THE SHY LITTLE VIOLETS GROW (2)
4	12.	YOU'RE THE CREAM IN MY COFFEE (4)
–	13.	WEARY RIVER (1)
18	14.	I FAW DOWN AN' GO BOOM! (2)
–	15.	MY MOTHER'S EYES (1)
–	16.	I'M BRINGING A RED, RED ROSE (1)
–	17.	WHERE IS THE SONG OF SONGS FOR ME? (1)
–	18.	ME AND THE MAN IN THE MOON (1)
–	19.	HAPPY DAYS AND LONELY NIGHTS (1)
–	20.	BUTTON UP YOUR OVERCOAT (1)

APRIL 1929

LM	TM	
13	1.	WEARY RIVER (2)
1	2.	CAROLINA MOON (4)
4	3.	A PRECIOUS LITTLE THING CALLED LOVE (3)
20	4.	BUTTON UP YOUR OVERCOAT (2)
–	5.	LOVER, COME BACK TO ME! (1)
8	6.	WEDDING BELLS (ARE BREAKING UP THAT OLD GANG OF MINE) (2)
–	7.	THE WEDDING OF THE PAINTED DOLL (1)
5	8.	IF I HAD YOU (3)
–	9.	BROADWAY MELODY (1)
15	10.	MY MOTHER'S EYES (2)
–	11.	YOU WERE MEANT FOR ME (1)
–	12.	DEEP NIGHT (1)
2	13.	I'LL GET BY (AS LONG AS I HAVE YOU) (4)
3	14.	SWEETHEARTS ON PARADE (4)
9	15.	(I LOVE YOU) SWEETHEART OF ALL MY DREAMS (3)
17	16.	WHERE IS THE SONG OF SONGS FOR ME? (2)
–	17.	HONEY (1)
6	18.	MARIE (4)
–	19.	MY LUCKY STAR (1)
14	20.	I FAW DOWN AN' GO BOOM! (3)

MAY 1929

LM	TM	
7	1.	THE WEDDING OF THE PAINTED DOLL (2)
17	2.	HONEY (2)
2	3.	CAROLINA MOON (5)
5	4.	LOVER, COME BACK TO ME! (2)
–	5.	MEAN TO ME (1)
11	6.	YOU WERE MEANT FOR ME (2)
12	7.	DEEP NIGHT (2)
9	8.	BROADWAY MELODY (2)
1	9.	WEARY RIVER (3)
–	10.	JERICHO (1)
–	11.	I'LL ALWAYS BE IN LOVE WITH YOU (1)
4	12.	BUTTON UP YOUR OVERCOAT (3)
3	13.	A PRECIOUS LITTLE THING CALLED LOVE (4)
–	14.	A GARDEN IN THE RAIN (1)
10	15.	MY MOTHER'S EYES (3)
–	16.	LOVE ME OR LEAVE ME (1)
6	17.	WEDDING BELLS (ARE BREAKING UP THAT OLD GANG OF MINE) (3)
–	18.	LOUISE (1)
–	19.	PAGAN LOVE SONG (1)
–	20.	I KISS YOUR HAND, MADAME (1)

JUNE 1929

LM	TM	
1	1.	THE WEDDING OF THE PAINTED DOLL (3)
2	2.	HONEY (3)
19	3.	PAGAN LOVE SONG (2)
18	4.	LOUISE (2)
5	5.	MEAN TO ME (2)
11	6.	I'LL ALWAYS BE IN LOVE WITH YOU (2)
6	7.	YOU WERE MEANT FOR ME (3)
20	8.	I KISS YOUR HAND, MADAME (2)
–	9.	MY SIN (1)
8	10.	BROADWAY MELODY (3)
3	11.	CAROLINA MOON (6)
–	12.	WITH A SONG IN MY HEART (1)
10	13.	JERICHO (2)
14	14.	A GARDEN IN THE RAIN (2)
4	15.	LOVER, COME BACK TO ME! (3)
–	16.	I'M JUST A VAGABOND LOVER (1)
7	17.	DEEP NIGHT (3)
9	18.	WEARY RIVER (4)
–	19.	I'VE GOT A FEELING I'M FALLING (1)
–	20.	THE BREAKAWAY (1)

JULY 1929

LM	TM	
3	1.	PAGAN LOVE SONG (3)
1	2.	THE WEDDING OF THE PAINTED DOLL (4)
4	3.	LOUISE (3)
16	4.	I'M JUST A VAGABOND LOVER (2)
9	5.	MY SIN (2)
6	6.	I'LL ALWAYS BE IN LOVE WITH YOU (3)
8	7.	I KISS YOUR HAND, MADAME (3)
12	8.	WITH A SONG IN MY HEART (2)
2	9.	HONEY (4)
–	10.	I GET THE BLUES WHEN IT RAINS (1)
5	11.	MEAN TO ME (3)
–	12.	THE DESERT SONG (1)
19	13.	I'VE GOT A FEELING I'M FALLING (2)
20	14.	THE BREAKAWAY (2)
–	15.	SLEEPY VALLEY (1)
–	16.	BIG CITY BLUES (1)
13	17.	JERICHO (3)
–	18.	WALKING WITH SUSIE (1)
–	19.	SINGIN' IN THE RAIN (1)
14	20.	A GARDEN IN THE RAIN (3)

AUGUST 1929

LM	TM	
1	1.	PAGAN LOVE SONG (4)
4	2.	I'M JUST A VAGABOND LOVER (3)
–	3.	AM I BLUE (1)
2	4.	THE WEDDING OF THE PAINTED DOLL (5)
6	5.	I'LL ALWAYS BE IN LOVE WITH YOU (4)
15	6.	SLEEPY VALLEY (2)
–	7.	MY SONG OF THE NILE (1)
19	8.	SINGIN' IN THE RAIN (2)
10	9.	I GET THE BLUES WHEN IT RAINS (2)
3	10.	LOUISE (4)
–	11.	WHEN MY DREAMS COME TRUE (1)
13	12.	I'VE GOT A FEELING I'M FALLING (3)
–	13.	LITTLE PAL (1)
–	14.	S'POSIN' (1)
5	15.	MY SIN (3)
–	16.	MOANIN' LOW (1)
18	17.	WALKING WITH SUSIE (2)
12	18.	THE DESERT SONG (2)
7	19.	I KISS YOUR HAND, MADAME (4)
–	20.	MISS YOU (1)

SEPTEMBER 1929

LM	TM	
3	1.	AM I BLUE (2)
1	2.	PAGAN LOVE SONG (5)
7	3.	MY SONG OF THE NILE (2)
6	4.	SLEEPY VALLEY (3)
16	5.	MOANIN' LOW (2)
2	6.	I'M JUST A VAGABOND LOVER (4)
8	7.	SINGIN' IN THE RAIN (3)
13	8.	LITTLE PAL (2)
11	9.	WHEN MY DREAMS COME TRUE (2)
4	10.	THE WEDDING OF THE PAINTED DOLL (6)
–	11.	TIP TOE THROUGH THE TULIPS WITH ME (1)
20	12.	MISS YOU (2)
9	13.	I GET THE BLUES WHEN IT RAINS (3)
12	14.	I'VE GOT A FEELING I'M FALLING (4)
5	15.	I'LL ALWAYS BE IN LOVE WITH YOU (5)
–	16.	PAINTING THE CLOUDS WITH SUNSHINE (1)
–	17.	HOW AM I TO KNOW? (1)
–	18.	TRUE BLUE LOU (1)
14	19.	S'POSIN' (2)
–	20.	YOUR MOTHER AND MINE (1)

OCTOBER 1929

LM	TM	
1	1.	AM I BLUE (3)
11	2.	TIP TOE THROUGH THE TULIPS WITH ME (2)
3	3.	MY SONG OF THE NILE (3)
7	4.	SINGIN' IN THE RAIN (4)
5	5.	MOANIN' LOW (3)
16	6.	PAINTING THE CLOUDS WITH SUNSHINE (2)
2	7.	PAGAN LOVE SONG (6)
9	8.	WHEN MY DREAMS COME TRUE (3)
17	9.	HOW AM I TO KNOW? (2)
4	10.	SLEEPY VALLEY (4)
8	11.	LITTLE PAL (3)
–	12.	PICCOLO PETE (1)
18	13.	TRUE BLUE LOU (2)
–	14.	AIN'T MISBEHAVIN' (1)
12	15.	MISS YOU (3)
10	16.	THE WEDDING OF THE PAINTED DOLL (7)
–	17.	CAN'T WE BE FRIENDS? (1)
–	18.	WAITING AT THE END OF THE ROAD (1)
6	19.	I'M JUST A VAGABOND LOVER (5)
20	20.	YOUR MOTHER AND MINE (2)

NOVEMBER 1929

LM	TM	
2	1.	TIP TOE THROUGH THE TULIPS WITH ME (3)
6	2.	PAINTING THE CLOUDS WITH SUNSHINE (3)
4	3.	SINGIN' IN THE RAIN (5)
1	4.	AM I BLUE (4)
12	5.	PICCOLO PETE (2)
–	6.	LONELY TROUBADOUR (1)
–	7.	LOVE ME (1)
3	8.	MY SONG OF THE NILE (4)
9	9.	HOW AM I TO KNOW? (3)
5	10.	MOANIN' LOW (4)
–	11.	IF I HAD A TALKING PICTURE OF YOU (1)
–	12.	SUNNY SIDE UP (1)
–	13.	LOVE (YOUR SPELL IS EVERYWHERE) (1)
14	14.	AIN'T MISBEHAVIN' (2)
–	15.	(I'M A DREAMER) AREN'T WE ALL? (1)
8	16.	WHEN MY DREAMS COME TRUE (4)
–	17.	THROUGH (1)
18	18.	WAITING AT THE END OF THE ROAD (2)
–	19.	SATISFIED (1)
11	20.	LITTLE PAL (4)

DECEMBER 1929

LM	TM	
1	1.	TIP TOE THROUGH THE TULIPS WITH ME (4)
2	2.	PAINTING THE CLOUDS WITH SUNSHINE (4)
11	3.	IF I HAD A TALKING PICTURE OF YOU (2)
13	4.	LOVE (YOUR SPELL IS EVERYWHERE) (2)
3	5.	SINGIN' IN THE RAIN (6)
7	6.	LOVE ME (2)
15	7.	(I'M A DREAMER) AREN'T WE ALL? (2)
6	8.	LONELY TROUBADOUR (2)
12	9.	SUNNY SIDE UP (2)
–	10.	CHANT OF THE JUNGLE (1)
5	11.	PICCOLO PETE (3)
19	12.	SATISFIED (2)
–	13.	MY SWEETER THAN SWEET (1)
–	14.	TURN ON THE HEAT (1)
–	15.	SINGIN' IN THE BATHTUB (1)
–	16.	GREAT DAY (1)
17	17.	THROUGH (2)
–	18.	CONGRATULATIONS (1)
4	19.	AM I BLUE (5)
–	20.	I MAY BE WRONG (BUT I THINK YOU'RE WONDERFUL) (1)

JANUARY 1930

LM	TM	
10	1.	CHANT OF THE JUNGLE (2)
7	2.	(I'M A DREAMER) AREN'T WE ALL? (3)
1	3.	TIP TOE THROUGH THE TULIPS WITH ME (5)
3	4.	IF I HAD A TALKING PICTURE OF YOU (3)
–	5.	A LITTLE KISS EACH MORNING (1)
2	6.	PAINTING THE CLOUDS WITH SUNSHINE (5)
15	7.	SINGIN' IN THE BATHTUB (2)
–	8.	I'M FOLLOWING YOU (1)
16	9.	GREAT DAY (2)
4	10.	LOVE (YOUR SPELL IS EVERYWHERE) (3)
9	11.	SUNNY SIDE UP (3)
6	12.	LOVE ME (3)
13	13.	MY SWEETER THAN SWEET (2)
–	14.	MY FATE IS IN YOUR HANDS (1)
5	15.	SINGIN' IN THE RAIN (7)
18	16.	CONGRATULATIONS (2)
14	17.	TURN ON THE HEAT (2)
–	18.	MORE THAN YOU KNOW (1)
–	19.	HAPPY DAYS ARE HERE AGAIN (1)
–	20.	WITHOUT A SONG (1)

FEBRUARY 1930

LM	TM	
2	1.	(I'M A DREAMER) AREN'T WE ALL? (4)
19	2.	HAPPY DAYS ARE HERE AGAIN (2)
1	3.	CHANT OF THE JUNGLE (3)
8	4.	I'M FOLLOWING YOU (2)
5	5.	A LITTLE KISS EACH MORNING (2)
4	6.	IF I HAD A TALKING PICTURE OF YOU (4)
–	7.	SHOULD I? (1)
–	8.	CRYIN' FOR THE CAROLINES (1)
–	9.	THE MAN FROM THE SOUTH (1)
7	10.	SINGIN' IN THE BATHTUB (3)
3	11.	TIP TOE THROUGH THE TULIPS WITH ME (6)
–	12.	YOU'VE GOT THAT THING (1)
–	13.	WHAT IS THIS THING CALLED LOVE? (1)
6	14.	PAINTING THE CLOUDS WITH SUNSHINE (6)
9	15.	GREAT DAY (3)
–	16.	ST. JAMES INFIRMARY (1)
–	17.	WHY WAS I BORN? (1)
13	18.	MY SWEETER THAN SWEET (3)
–	19.	THAT WONDERFUL SOMETHING (1)
–	20.	FUNNY, DEAR, WHAT LOVE CAN DO (1)

MARCH 1930

LM	TM	
2	1.	HAPPY DAYS ARE HERE AGAIN (3)
7	2.	SHOULD I? (2)
8	3.	CRYIN' FOR THE CAROLINES (2)
4	4.	I'M FOLLOWING YOU (3)
13	5.	WHAT IS THIS THING CALLED LOVE? (2)
5	6.	A LITTLE KISS EACH MORNING (3)
–	7.	THERE'S DANGER IN YOUR EYES, CHERIE (1)
16	8.	ST. JAMES INFIRMARY (2)
1	9.	(I'M A DREAMER) AREN'T WE ALL? (5)
–	10.	STEIN SONG (1)
6	11.	IF I HAD A TALKING PICTURE OF YOU (5)
12	12.	YOU'VE GOT THAT THING (2)
9	13.	THE MAN FROM THE SOUTH (2)
–	14.	WHY? (1)
–	15.	WHEN IT'S SPRINGTIME IN THE ROCKIES (1)
–	16.	'TAIN'T NO SIN (TO DANCE AROUND IN YOUR BONES) (1)
–	17.	SOUTH SEA ROSE (1)
–	18.	A COTTAGE FOR SALE (1)
–	19.	LAZY LOU'SIANA MOON (1)
3	20.	CHANT OF THE JUNGLE (4)

APRIL 1930

LM	TM	
10	1.	STEIN SONG (2)
2	2.	SHOULD I? (3)
15	3.	WHEN IT'S SPRINGTIME IN THE ROCKIES (2)
1	4.	HAPPY DAYS ARE HERE AGAIN (4)
7	5.	THERE'S DANGER IN YOUR EYES, CHERIE (2)
18	6.	A COTTAGE FOR SALE (2)
–	7.	UNDER A TEXAS MOON (1)
3	8.	CRYIN' FOR THE CAROLINES (3)
19	9.	LAZY LOU'SIANA MOON (2)
–	10.	PUTTIN' ON THE RITZ (1)
–	11.	SING, YOU SINNERS (1)
4	12.	I'M FOLLOWING YOU (4)
5	13.	WHAT IS THIS THING CALLED LOVE? (3)
–	14.	ON THE SUNNY SIDE OF THE STREET (1)
–	15.	STRIKE UP THE BAND (1)
9	16.	(I'M A DREAMER) AREN'T WE ALL? (6)
–	17.	BESIDE AN OPEN FIREPLACE (1)
–	18.	ROMANCE (1)
–	19.	WHEN I'M LOOKING AT YOU (1)
–	20.	SINGING A VAGABOND SONG (1)

MAY 1930

LM	TM	
1	1.	STEIN SONG (3)
3	2.	WHEN IT'S SPRINGTIME IN THE ROCKIES (3)
6	3.	A COTTAGE FOR SALE (3)
7	4.	UNDER A TEXAS MOON (2)
–	5.	IT HAPPENED IN MONTEREY (1)
–	6.	THE MOON IS LOW (1)
10	7.	PUTTIN' ON THE RITZ (2)
2	8.	SHOULD I? (4)
11	9.	SING, YOU SINNERS (2)
–	10.	I'M IN THE MARKET FOR YOU (1)
9	11.	LAZY LOU'SIANA MOON (3)
4	12.	HAPPY DAYS ARE HERE AGAIN (5)
8	13.	CRYIN' FOR THE CAROLINES (4)
14	14.	ON THE SUNNY SIDE OF THE STREET (2)
–	15.	DANCING WITH TEARS IN MY EYES (1)
5	16.	THERE'S DANGER IN YOUR EYES, CHERIE (3)
–	17.	IF I HAD A GIRL LIKE YOU (1)
15	18.	STRIKE UP THE BAND (2)
–	19.	TELLING IT TO THE DAISIES (1)
–	20.	EXACTLY LIKE YOU (1)

JUNE 1930

LM	TM	
2	1.	WHEN IT'S SPRINGTIME IN THE ROCKIES (4)
1	2.	STEIN SONG (4)
15	3.	DANCING WITH TEARS IN MY EYES (2)
5	4.	IT HAPPENED IN MONTEREY (2)
17	5.	IF I HAD A GIRL LIKE YOU (2)
10	6.	I'M IN THE MARKET FOR YOU (2)
20	7.	EXACTLY LIKE YOU (2)
–	8.	YOU BROUGHT A NEW KIND OF LOVE TO ME (1)
6	9.	THE MOON IS LOW (2)
3	10.	A COTTAGE FOR SALE (4)
–	11.	LIVIN' IN THE SUNLIGHT, LOVIN' IN THE MOONLIGHT (1)
–	12.	WHEN THE BLOOM IS ON THE SAGE (1)
9	13.	SING, YOU SINNERS (3)
14	14.	ON THE SUNNY SIDE OF THE STREET (3)
4	15.	UNDER A TEXAS MOON (3)
–	16.	GET HAPPY (1)
–	17.	TEN CENTS A DANCE (1)
19	18.	TELLING IT TO THE DAISIES (2)
–	19.	I STILL REMEMBER (1)
–	20.	I NEVER DREAMT (1)

JULY 1930

LM	TM	
3	1.	DANCING WITH TEARS IN MY EYES (3)
1	2.	WHEN IT'S SPRINGTIME IN THE ROCKIES (5)
2	3.	STEIN SONG (5)
8	4.	YOU BROUGHT A NEW KIND OF LOVE TO ME (2)
5	5.	IF I HAD A GIRL LIKE YOU (3)
6	6.	I'M IN THE MARKET FOR YOU (3)
4	7.	IT HAPPENED IN MONTEREY (3)
–	8.	SO BEATS MY HEART FOR YOU (1)
–	9.	SINGING A SONG TO THE STARS (1)
–	10.	MY FUTURE JUST PASSED (1)
17	11.	TEN CENTS A DANCE (2)
–	12.	DOWN THE RIVER OF GOLDEN DREAMS (1)
7	13.	EXACTLY LIKE YOU (3)
11	14.	LIVIN' IN THE SUNLIGHT, LOVIN' IN THE MOONLIGHT (2)
12	15.	WHEN THE BLOOM IS ON THE SAGE (2)
–	16.	ABSENCE MAKES THE HEART GROW FONDER (FOR SOMEBODY ELSE) (1)
–	17.	KITTY FROM KANSAS CITY (1)
16	18.	GET HAPPY (2)
–	19.	OLD NEW ENGLAND MOON (1)
–	20.	AROUND THE CORNER (1)

AUGUST 1930

LM	TM	
1	1.	DANCING WITH TEARS IN MY EYES (4)
2	2.	WHEN IT'S SPRINGTIME IN THE ROCKIES (6)
4	3.	YOU BROUGHT A NEW KIND OF LOVE TO ME (3)
–	4.	LITTLE WHITE LIES (1)
3	5.	STEIN SONG (6)
8	6.	SO BEATS MY HEART FOR YOU (2)
10	7.	MY FUTURE JUST PASSED (2)
9	8.	SINGING A SONG TO THE STARS (2)
12	9.	DOWN THE RIVER OF GOLDEN DREAMS (2)
–	10.	BYE BYE BLUES (1)
–	11.	SWINGIN' IN A HAMMOCK (1)
–	12.	IF I COULD BE WITH YOU (ONE HOUR TONIGHT) (1)
5	13.	IF I HAD A GIRL LIKE YOU (4)
–	14.	I LOVE YOU SO MUCH (1)
19	15.	OLD NEW ENGLAND MOON (2)
20	16.	AROUND THE CORNER (2)
–	17.	BETTY CO-ED (1)
16	18.	ABSENCE MAKES THE HEART GROW FONDER (FOR SOMEBODY ELSE) (2)
7	19.	IT HAPPENED IN MONTEREY (4)
–	20.	SOMEWHERE IN OLD WYOMING (1)

SEPTEMBER 1930

LM	TM	
4	1.	LITTLE WHITE LIES (2)
1	2.	DANCING WITH TEARS IN MY EYES (5)
12	3.	IF I COULD BE WITH YOU (ONE HOUR TONIGHT) (2)
2	4.	WHEN IT'S SPRINGTIME IN THE ROCKIES (7)
11	5.	SWINGIN' IN A HAMMOCK (2)
6	6.	SO BEATS MY HEART FOR YOU (3)
17	7.	BETTY CO-ED (2)
10	8.	BYE BYE BLUES (2)
–	9.	THE KISS WALTZ (1)
–	10.	I'M CONFESSIN' (THAT I LOVE YOU) (1)
3	11.	YOU BROUGHT A NEW KIND OF LOVE TO ME (4)
9	12.	DOWN THE RIVER OF GOLDEN DREAMS (3)
–	13.	GO HOME AND TELL YOUR MOTHER (1)
–	14	MY BABY JUST CARES FOR ME (1)
7	15.	MY FUTURE JUST PASSED (3)
20	16.	SOMEWHERE IN OLD WYOMING (2)
14	17.	I LOVE YOU SO MUCH (2)
–	18.	JUST A LITTLE CLOSER (1)
–	19.	I STILL GET A THRILL (1)
5	20.	STEIN SONG (7)

OCTOBER 1930

LM	TM	
1	1.	LITTLE WHITE LIES (3)
3	2.	IF I COULD BE WITH YOU (ONE HOUR TONIGHT) (3)
13	3.	GO HOME AND TELL YOUR MOTHER (2)
9	4.	THE KISS WALTZ (2)
7	5.	BETTY CO-ED (3)
4	6.	WHEN IT'S SPRINGTIME IN THE ROCKIES (8)
10	7.	I'M CONFESSIN' (THAT I LOVE YOU) (2)
19	8.	I STILL GET A THRILL (2)
–	9.	MOONLIGHT ON THE COLORADO (1)
14	10	MY BABY JUST CARES FOR ME (2)
–	11.	WHEN THE ORGAN PLAYED AT TWILIGHT (1)
2	12.	DANCING WITH TEARS IN MY EYES (6)
–	13.	DON'T TELL HER (HIM) WHAT HAPPENED TO ME (1)
–	14.	BODY AND SOUL (1)
–	15.	I'M YOURS (1)
–	16.	SING SOMETHING SIMPLE (1)
18	17.	JUST A LITTLE CLOSER (2)
5	18.	SWINGIN' IN A HAMMOCK (3)
6	19.	SO BEATS MY HEART FOR YOU (4)
–	20.	HERE COMES THE SUN (1)

NOVEMBER 1930

LM	TM	
1	1.	LITTLE WHITE LIES (4)
2	2.	IF I COULD BE WITH YOU (ONE HOUR TONIGHT) (4)
3	3.	GO HOME AND TELL YOUR MOTHER (3)
–	4.	THREE LITTLE WORDS (1)
9	5.	MOONLIGHT ON THE COLORADO (2)
15	6.	I'M YOURS (2)
5	7.	BETTY CO-ED (4)
11	8.	WHEN THE ORGAN PLAYED AT TWILIGHT (2)
14	9.	BODY AND SOUL (2)
–	10.	BEYOND THE BLUE HORIZON (1)
4	11.	THE KISS WALTZ (3)
–	12.	IT MUST BE TRUE (1)
6	13.	WHEN IT'S SPRINGTIME IN THE ROCKIES (9)
16	14.	SING SOMETHING SIMPLE (2)
10	15	MY BABY JUST CARES FOR ME (3)
8	16.	I STILL GET A THRILL (3)
–	17.	I'LL BE BLUE JUST THINKING OF YOU (1)
–	18.	SOMEWHERE IN OLD WYOMING (3)
–	19.	SWEETHEART OF MY STUDENT DAYS (1)
7	20.	I'M CONFESSIN' (THAT I LOVE YOU) (3)

DECEMBER 1930

LM	TM	
4	1.	THREE LITTLE WORDS (2)
6	2.	I'M YOURS (3)
5	3.	MOONLIGHT ON THE COLORADO (3)
8	4.	WHEN THE ORGAN PLAYED AT TWILIGHT (3)
–	5.	YOU'RE DRIVING ME CRAZY (1)
9	6.	BODY AND SOUL (3)
12	7.	IT MUST BE TRUE (2)
–	8.	THE PEANUT VENDOR (1)
19	9.	SWEETHEART OF MY STUDENT DAYS (2)
10	10.	BEYOND THE BLUE HORIZON (2)
–	11.	SWEET JENNIE LEE (1)
–	12.	THE LITTLE THINGS IN LIFE (1)
2	13.	IF I COULD BE WITH YOU (ONE HOUR TONIGHT) (5)
7	14.	BETTY CO-ED (5)
14	15.	SING SOMETHING SIMPLE (3)
–	16.	FINE AND DANDY (1)
1	17.	LITTLE WHITE LIES (5)
–	18.	CHEERFUL LITTLE EARFUL (1)
3	19.	GO HOME AND TELL YOUR MOTHER (4)
–	20.	BABY'S BIRTHDAY PARTY (1)

JANUARY 1931

LM	TM	
5	1.	YOU'RE DRIVING ME CRAZY (2)
1	2.	THREE LITTLE WORDS (3)
8	3.	THE PEANUT VENDOR (2)
3	4.	MOONLIGHT ON THE COLORADO (4)
4	5.	WHEN THE ORGAN PLAYED AT TWILIGHT (4)
7	6.	IT MUST BE TRUE (3)
6	7.	BODY AND SOUL (4)
12	8.	THE LITTLE THINGS IN LIFE (2)
2	9.	I'M YOURS (4)
18	10.	CHEERFUL LITTLE EARFUL (2)
–	11.	I'M ALONE BECAUSE I LOVE YOU (1)
–	12.	BLUE AGAIN (1)
–	13.	YOURS AND MINE (1)
–	14.	TO WHOM IT MAY CONCERN (1)
11	15.	SWEET JENNIE LEE (2)
–	16.	JUST A GIGOLO (1)
9	17.	SWEETHEART OF MY STUDENT DAYS (3)
–	18.	MY IDEAL (1)
–	19.	I GOT RHYTHM (1)
–	20	EMBRACEABLE YOU (1)

FEBRUARY 1931

LM	TM	
16	1.	JUST A GIGOLO (2)
11	2.	I'M ALONE BECAUSE I LOVE YOU (2)
1	3.	YOU'RE DRIVING ME CRAZY (3)
3	4.	THE PEANUT VENDOR (3)
8	5.	THE LITTLE THINGS IN LIFE (3)
–	6.	WHEN YOUR HAIR HAS TURNED TO SILVER (1)
12	7.	BLUE AGAIN (2)
–	8.	LONESOME LOVER (1)
–	9.	LADY, PLAY YOUR MANDOLIN (1)
2	10.	THREE LITTLE WORDS (4)
5	11.	WHEN THE ORGAN PLAYED AT TWILIGHT (5)
–	12.	REACHING FOR THE MOON (1)
–	13.	YOU'RE THE ONE I CARE FOR (1)
7	14.	BODY AND SOUL (5)
–	15.	TEARS (1)
–	16.	I SURRENDER, DEAR (1)
14	17.	TO WHOM IT MAY CONCERN (2)
6	18.	IT MUST BE TRUE (4)
–	19.	WOULD YOU LIKE TO TAKE A WALK? (1)
19	20.	I GOT RHYTHM (2)

MARCH 1931

LM	TM	
1	1.	JUST A GIGOLO (3)
6	2.	WHEN YOUR HAIR HAS TURNED TO SILVER (2)
16	3.	I SURRENDER, DEAR (2)
2	4.	I'M ALONE BECAUSE I LOVE YOU (3)
12	5.	REACHING FOR THE MOON (2)
–	6.	WALKIN' MY BABY BACK HOME (1)
19	7.	WOULD YOU LIKE TO TAKE A WALK? (2)
4	8.	THE PEANUT VENDOR (4)
7	9.	BLUE AGAIN (3)
8	10.	LONESOME LOVER (2)
13	11.	YOU'RE THE ONE I CARE FOR (2)
–	12.	THE WALTZ YOU SAVED FOR ME (1)
15	13.	TEARS (2)
–	14.	HELLO, BEAUTIFUL (1)
9	15.	LADY, PLAY YOUR MANDOLIN (2)
–	16.	THE KING'S HORSES (1)
3	17.	YOU'RE DRIVING ME CRAZY (4)
–	18.	MOOD INDIGO (1)
–	19.	DREAM A LITTLE DREAM OF ME (1)
–	20.	STAR DUST (1)

APRIL 1931

LM	TM	
2	1.	WHEN YOUR HAIR HAS TURNED TO SILVER (3)
6	2.	WALKIN' MY BABY BACK HOME (2)
1	3.	JUST A GIGOLO (4)
3	4.	I SURRENDER, DEAR (3)
12	5.	THE WALTZ YOU SAVED FOR ME (2)
7	6.	WOULD YOU LIKE TO TAKE A WALK? (3)
19	7.	DREAM A LITTLE DREAM OF ME (2)
–	8.	BY THE RIVER STE. MARIE (1)
–	9.	PLEASE DON'T TALK ABOUT ME (WHEN I'M GONE) (1)
–	10.	TWO HEARTS IN THREE-QUARTER TIME (1)
–	11.	WABASH MOON (1)
8	12.	THE PEANUT VENDOR (5)
5	13.	REACHING FOR THE MOON (3)
14	14.	HELLO, BEAUTIFUL (2)
–	15.	HEARTACHES (1)
–	16.	99 OUT OF 100 (WANNA BE LOVED) (1)
16	17.	THE KING'S HORSES (2)
–	18.	GOT THE BENCH, GOT THE PARK (1)
–	19.	I'VE GOT FIVE DOLLARS (1)
20	20.	STAR DUST (2)

MAY 1931

LM	TM	
5	1.	THE WALTZ YOU SAVED FOR ME (3)
9	2.	PLEASE DON'T TALK ABOUT ME (WHEN I'M GONE) (2)
1	3.	WHEN YOUR HAIR HAS TURNED TO SILVER (4)
–	4.	(YOU CAME ALONG) OUT OF NOWHERE (1)
7	5.	DREAM A LITTLE DREAM OF ME (3)
8	6.	BY THE RIVER STE. MARIE (2)
2	7.	WALKIN' MY BABY BACK HOME (3)
10	8.	TWO HEARTS IN THREE-QUARTER TIME (2)
–	9.	MOONLIGHT SAVING TIME (1)
11	10.	WABASH MOON (2)
–	11.	WHISTLING IN THE DARK (1)
–	12.	WHEN I TAKE MY SUGAR TO TEA (1)
–	13.	WRAP YOUR TROUBLES IN DREAMS (1)
–	14.	WHEN YOUR LOVER HAS GONE (1)
4	15.	I SURRENDER, DEAR (4)
–	16.	FOR YOU (1)
–	17.	WERE YOU SINCERE? (1)
–	18.	HO-HUM (1)
3	19.	JUST A GIGOLO (5)
–	20.	MINNIE THE MOOCHER (1)

JUNE 1931

LM	TM	
9	1.	MOONLIGHT SAVING TIME (2)
1	2.	THE WALTZ YOU SAVED FOR ME (4)
5	3.	DREAM A LITTLE DREAM OF ME (4)
4	4.	(YOU CAME ALONG) OUT OF NOWHERE (2)
11	5.	WHISTLING IN THE DARK (2)
18	6.	HO-HUM (2)
2	7.	PLEASE DON'T TALK ABOUT ME WHEN I'M GONE (3)
13	8.	WRAP YOUR TROUBLES IN DREAMS (2)
8	9.	TWO HEARTS IN THREE-QUARTER TIME (3)
–	10.	JUST ONE MORE CHANCE (1)
–	11.	NEVERTHELESS (1)
–	12.	I WANNA SING ABOUT YOU (1)
–	13.	NOW YOU'RE IN MY ARMS (1)
10	14.	WABASH MOON (3)
6	15.	BY THE RIVER STE. MARIE (3)
–	16.	ONE MORE TIME (1)
–	17.	STAR DUST (3)
3	18.	WHEN YOUR HAIR HAS TURNED TO SILVER (5)
16	19.	FOR YOU (2)
–	20.	ROLL ON, MISSISSIPPI, ROLL ON (1)

JULY 1931

LM	TM	
1	1.	MOONLIGHT SAVING TIME (3)
10	2.	JUST ONE MORE CHANCE (2)
12	3.	I WANNA SING ABOUT YOU (2)
3	4.	DREAM A LITTLE DREAM OF ME (5)
2	5.	THE WALTZ YOU SAVED FOR ME (5)
–	6.	WHEN THE MOON COMES OVER THE MOUNTAIN (1)
13	7.	NOW YOU'RE IN MY ARMS (2)
6	8.	HO-HUM (3)
11	9.	NEVERTHELESS (2)
–	10.	I FOUND A MILLION DOLLAR BABY (1)
–	11.	I'M THROUGH WITH LOVE (1)
17	12.	STAR DUST (4)
–	13.	WITHOUT THAT GAL (1)
–	14.	DANCING IN THE DARK (1)
–	15.	LITTLE GIRL (1)
5	16.	WHISTLING IN THE DARK (3)
8	17.	WRAP YOUR TROUBLES IN DREAMS (3)
4	18.	(YOU CAME ALONG) OUT OF NOWHERE (3)
–	19.	ON THE BEACH WITH YOU (1)
9	20.	TWO HEARTS IN THREE-QUARTER TIME (4)

AUGUST 1931

LM	TM	
6	1.	WHEN THE MOON COMES OVER THE MOUNTAIN (2)
10	2.	I FOUND A MILLION DOLLAR BABY (2)
2	3.	JUST ONE MORE CHANCE (3)
11	4.	I'M THROUGH WITH LOVE (2)
1	5.	MOONLIGHT SAVING TIME (4)
14	6.	DANCING IN THE DARK (2)
13	7.	WITHOUT THAT GAL (2)
–	8.	AT YOUR COMMAND (1)
–	9.	COME TO ME (1)
–	10.	WHEN YUBA PLAYS RUMBA ON THE TUBA (1)
–	11.	MANY HAPPY RETURNS OF THE DAY (1)
3	12.	I WANNA SING ABOUT YOU (3)
15	13.	LITTLE GIRL (2)
–	14.	I LOVE LOUISA (1)
–	15.	SWEET AND LOVELY (1)
5	16.	THE WALTZ YOU SAVED FOR ME (6)
12	17.	STAR DUST (5)
4	18.	DREAM A LITTLE DREAM OF ME (6)
7	19.	NOW YOU'RE IN MY ARMS (3)
–	20.	HIGH AND LOW (1)

SEPTEMBER 1931

LM	TM	
1	1.	WHEN THE MOON COMES OVER THE MOUNTAIN (3)
11	2.	MANY HAPPY RETURNS OF THE DAY (2)
15	3.	SWEET AND LOVELY (2)
2	4.	I FOUND A MILLION DOLLAR BABY (3)
3	5.	JUST ONE MORE CHANCE (4)
14	6.	I LOVE LOUISA (2)
8	7.	AT YOUR COMMAND (2)
4	8.	I'M THROUGH WITH LOVE (3)
6	9.	DANCING IN THE DARK (3)
–	10.	ME! (1)
–	11.	I APOLOGIZE (1)
10	12.	WHEN YUBA PLAYS RUMBA ON THE TUBA (2)
–	13.	LOVE LETTERS IN THE SAND (1)
9	14.	COME TO ME (2)
–	15.	I DON'T KNOW WHY (I JUST DO) (1)
–	16.	IT'S THE GIRL (1)
–	17.	LIFE IS JUST A BOWL OF CHERRIES (1)
20	18.	HIGH AND LOW (2)
5	19.	MOONLIGHT SAVING TIME (5)
17	20.	STAR DUST (6)

OCTOBER 1931

LM	TM	
3	1.	SWEET AND LOVELY (3)
1	2.	WHEN THE MOON COMES OVER THE MOUNTAIN (4)
2	3.	MANY HAPPY RETURNS OF THE DAY (3)
15	4.	I DON'T KNOW WHY (I JUST DO) (2)
13	5.	LOVE LETTERS IN THE SAND (2)
–	6.	GUILTY (1)
–	7.	GOODNIGHT, SWEETHEART (1)
11	8.	I APOLOGIZE (2)
10	9.	ME! (2)
–	10.	NOW THAT YOU'RE GONE (1)
9	11.	DANCING IN THE DARK (4)
17	12.	LIFE IS JUST A BOWL OF CHERRIES (2)
–	13.	THIS IS THE MISSUS (1)
5	14.	JUST ONE MORE CHANCE (5)
–	15.	YOU CALL IT MADNESS (BUT I CALL IT LOVE) (1)
–	16.	MY SONG (1)
–	17.	THE THRILL IS GONE (1)
4	18.	I FOUND A MILLION DOLLAR BABY (4)
–	19.	SHINE ON, HARVEST MOON (1)
16	20.	IT'S THE GIRL (2)

NOVEMBER 1931

LM	TM	
7	1.	GOODNIGHT, SWEETHEART (2)
6	2.	GUILTY (2)
4	3.	I DON'T KNOW WHY (I JUST DO) (3)
5	4.	LOVE LETTERS IN THE SAND (3)
2	5.	WHEN THE MOON COMES OVER THE MOUNTAIN (5)
1	6.	SWEET AND LOVELY (4)
8	7.	I APOLOGIZE (3)
–	8.	A FADED SUMMER LOVE (1)
10	9.	NOW THAT YOU'RE GONE (2)
–	10.	WHEN IT'S SLEEPY TIME DOWN SOUTH (1)
–	11.	LADY OF SPAIN (1)
12	12.	LIFE IS JUST A BOWL OF CHERRIES (3)
15	13.	YOU CALL IT MADNESS (BUT I CALL IT LOVE) (2)
–	14.	TIME ON MY HANDS (1)
3	15.	MANY HAPPY RETURNS OF THE DAY (4)
16	16.	MY SONG (2)
17	17.	THE THRILL IS GONE (2)
–	18.	YOU FORGOT YOUR GLOVES (1)
–	19.	AN EVENING IN CAROLINE (1)
13	20.	THIS IS THE MISSUS (2)

DECEMBER 1931

LM	TM	
1	1.	GOODNIGHT, SWEETHEART (3)
8	2.	A FADED SUMMER LOVE (2)
14	3.	TIME ON MY HANDS (2)
10	4.	WHEN IT'S SLEEPY TIME DOWN SOUTH (2)
4	5.	LOVE LETTERS IN THE SAND (4)
3	6.	I DON'T KNOW WHY (I JUST DO) (4)
5	7.	WHEN THE MOON COMES OVER THE MOUNTAIN (6)
2	8.	GUILTY (3)
19	9.	AN EVENING IN CAROLINE (2)
–	10.	CALL ME DARLING (1)
–	11.	YOU TRY SOMEBODY ELSE (1)
11	12.	LADY OF SPAIN (2)
–	13.	RIVER, STAY 'WAY FROM MY DOOR (1)
–	14.	WHERE THE BLUE OF THE NIGHT MEETS THE GOLD OF THE DAY (1)
–	15.	HOME (WHEN SHADOWS FALL) (1)
–	16.	CUBAN LOVE SONG (1)
–	17.	TIGER RAG (1)
6	18.	SWEET AND LOVELY (5)
–	19.	KICKIN' THE GONG AROUND (1)
–	20.	OOH! THAT KISS (1)

JANUARY 1932

LM	TM	
1	1.	GOODNIGHT, SWEETHEART (4)
14	2.	WHERE THE BLUE OF THE NIGHT MEETS THE GOLD OF THE DAY (2)
4	3.	WHEN IT'S SLEEPY TIME DOWN SOUTH (3)
15	4.	HOME (WHEN SHADOWS FALL) (2)
9	5.	AN EVENING IN CAROLINE (3)
2	6.	A FADED SUMMER LOVE (3)
10	7.	CALL ME DARLING (2)
–	8.	ALL OF ME (1)
16	9.	CUBAN LOVE SONG (2)
3	10.	TIME ON MY HANDS (3)
20	11.	OOH! THAT KISS (2)
–	12.	BY THE SYCAMORE TREE (1)
11	13.	YOU TRY SOMEBODY ELSE (2)
–	14.	LIES (1)
–	15.	NOW'S THE TIME TO FALL IN LOVE (1)
13	16.	RIVER, STAY 'WAY FROM MY DOOR (2)
7	17.	WHEN THE MOON COMES OVER THE MOUNTAIN (7)
–	18.	WAS THAT THE HUMAN THING TO DO? (1)
–	19.	DELISHIOUS (1)
17	20.	TIGER RAG (2)

FEBRUARY 1932

LM	TM	
8	1.	ALL OF ME (2)
4	2.	HOME (WHEN SHADOWS FALL) (3)
18	3.	WAS THAT THE HUMAN THING TO DO? (2)
1	4.	GOODNIGHT, SWEETHEART (5)
2	5.	WHERE THE BLUE OF THE NIGHT MEETS THE GOLD OF THE DAY (3)
–	6.	WHEN WE'RE ALONE (PENTHOUSE SERENADE (1)
3	7.	WHEN IT'S SLEEPY TIME DOWN SOUTH (4)
–	8.	JUST FRIENDS (1)
12	9.	BY THE SYCAMORE TREE (2)
–	10.	YOU'RE MY EVERYTHING (1)
5	11.	AN EVENING IN CAROLINE (4)
–	12.	AUF WIEDERSEH'N, MY DEAR (1)
–	13.	DINAH (1)
–	14.	SNUGGLED ON YOUR SHOULDER (1)
15	15.	NOW'S THE TIME TO FALL IN LOVE (2)
9	16.	CUBAN LOVE SONG (3)
–	17.	DANCING ON THE CEILING (1)
7	18.	CALL ME DARLING (3)
–	19.	YOU CAN DEPEND ON ME (1)
–	20.	THE WOODEN SOLDIER AND THE CHINA DOLL (1)

MARCH 1932

LM	TM	
3	1.	WAS THAT THE HUMAN THING TO DO? (3)
12	2.	AUF WIEDERSEH'N, MY DEAR (2)
1	3.	ALL OF ME (3)
2	4.	HOME (WHEN SHADOWS FALL) (4)
8	5.	JUST FRIENDS (2)
14	6.	SNUGGLED ON YOUR SHOULDER (2)
6	7.	WHEN WE'RE ALONE (PENTHOUSE SERENADE (2)
–	8.	SOMEBODY LOVES YOU (1)
–	9.	PARADISE (1)
17	10.	DANCING ON THE CEILING (2)
–	11.	CAN'T WE TALK IT OVER? (1)
20	12.	THE WOODEN SOLDIER AND THE CHINA DOLL (2)
5	13.	WHERE THE BLUE OF THE NIGHT MEETS THE GOLD OF THE DAY (4)
–	14.	RAIN ON THE ROOF (1)
–	15.	BY THE FIRESIDE (1)
–	16.	KISS ME GOODNIGHT (1)
10	17.	YOU'RE MY EVERYTHING (2)
–	18.	BETWEEN THE DEVIL AND THE DEEP BLUE SEA (1)
19	19.	YOU CAN DEPEND ON ME (2)
–	20.	OF THEE I SING (BABY) (1)

APRIL 1932

LM	TM	
9	1.	PARADISE (2)
2	2.	AUF WIEDERSEH'N, MY DEAR (3)
8	3.	SOMEBODY LOVES YOU (2)
15	4.	BY THE FIRESIDE (2)
6	5.	SNUGGLED ON YOUR SHOULDER (3)
1	6.	WAS THAT THE HUMAN THING TO DO? (4)
–	7.	ONE HOUR WITH YOU (1)
–	8.	TOO MANY TEARS (1)
5	9.	JUST FRIENDS (3)
16	10.	KISS ME GOODNIGHT (2)
3	11.	ALL OF ME (4)
–	12.	LOVE, YOU FUNNY THING (1)
–	13.	KEEPIN' OUT OF MISCHIEF NOW (1)
–	14.	MY MOM (1)
–	15.	LET'S HAVE ANOTHER CUP OF COFFEE (1)
–	16.	I HEARD (1)
4	17.	HOME (WHEN SHADOWS FALL) (5)
11	18.	CAN'T WE TALK IT OVER? (2)
–	19.	IT DON'T MEAN A THING (IF IT AIN'T GOT THAT SWING) (1)
–	20.	BY A RIPPLING STREAM (1)

MAY 1932

LM	TM	
1	1.	PARADISE (3)
7	2.	ONE HOUR WITH YOU (2)
3	3.	SOMEBODY LOVES YOU (3)
2	4.	AUF WIEDERSEH'N, MY DEAR (4)
4	5.	BY THE FIRESIDE (3)
14	6.	MY MOM (2)
8	7.	TOO MANY TEARS (2)
–	8.	LULLABY OF THE LEAVES (1)
–	9.	LAWD, YOU MADE THE NIGHT TOO LONG (1)
13	10.	KEEPIN' OUT OF MISCHIEF NOW (2)
20	11.	BY A RIPPLING STREAM (2)
–	12.	GOOFUS (1)
10	13.	KISS ME GOODNIGHT (3)
12	14.	LOVE, YOU FUNNY THING (2)
–	15.	LOVABLE (1)
–	16.	SOFT LIGHTS AND SWEET MUSIC (1)
5	17.	SNUGGLED ON YOUR SHOULDER (4)
–	18.	YOU'RE THE ONE (YOU BEAUTIFUL SON OF A GUN) (1)
–	19.	YOU CAN DEPEND ON ME (3)
–	20.	BETWEEN THE DEVIL AND THE DEEP BLUE SEA (2)

JUNE 1932

LM	TM	
1	1.	PARADISE (4)
8	2.	LULLABY OF THE LEAVES (2)
2	3.	ONE HOUR WITH YOU (3)
–	4.	MY SILENT LOVE (1)
3	5.	SOMEBODY LOVES YOU (4)
12	6.	GOOFUS (2)
4	7.	AUF WIEDERSEH'N, MY DEAR (5)
6	8.	MY MOM (3)
–	9.	MY EXTRAORDINARY GAL (1)
–	10.	IN A SHANTY IN OLD SHANTY TOWN (1)
9	11.	LAWD, YOU MADE THE NIGHT TOO LONG (2)
–	12.	HUMMIN' TO MYSELF (1)
–	13.	LAZY DAY (1)
11	14.	BY A RIPPLING STREAM (3)
5	15.	BY THE FIRESIDE (4)
15	16.	LOVABLE (2)
–	17.	THE VOICE IN THE OLD VILLAGE CHOIR (1)
–	18.	CABIN IN THE COTTON (1)
–	19.	GOT A DATE WITH AN ANGEL (1)
13	20.	KISS ME GOODNIGHT (4)

JULY 1932

LM	TM	
10	1.	IN A SHANTY IN OLD SHANTY TOWN (2)
2	2.	LULLABY OF THE LEAVES (3)
4	3.	MY SILENT LOVE (2)
1	4.	PARADISE (5)
6	5.	GOOFUS (3)
13	6.	LAZY DAY (2)
12	7.	HUMMIN' TO MYSELF (2)
3	8.	ONE HOUR WITH YOU (4)
7	9.	AUF WIEDERSEH'N, MY DEAR (6)
–	10.	YOU'RE BLASE (1)
–	11.	(I'M STILL WITHOUT A SWEETHEART) WITH SUMMER COMIN' ON (1)
–	12.	HOLD MY HAND (1)
18	13.	CABIN IN THE COTTON (2)
9	14.	MY EXTRAORDINARY GAL (2)
5	15.	SOMEBODY LOVES YOU (5)
17	16.	THE VOICE IN THE OLD VILLAGE CHOIR (2)
–	17.	IS I IN LOVE? I IS (1)
–	18.	IN MY HIDEAWAY (1)
–	19.	ROCKIN' CHAIR (1)
8	20.	MY MOM (4)

AUGUST 1932

LM	TM	
1	1.	IN A SHANTY IN OLD SHANTY TOWN (3)
3	2.	MY SILENT LOVE (3)
2	3.	LULLABY OF THE LEAVES (4)
–	4.	WE JUST COULDN'T SAY GOODBYE (1)
–	5.	MASQUERADE (1)
5	6.	GOOFUS (4)
–	7.	IT WAS SO BEAUTIFUL (1)
10	8.	YOU'RE BLASE (2)
12	9.	HOLD MY HAND (2)
4	10.	PARADISE (6)
–	11.	I CAN'T BELIEVE IT'S TRUE (1)
–	12.	AS YOU DESIRE ME (1)
6	13.	LAZY DAY (3)
–	14.	STRANGE INTERLUDE (1)
7	15.	HUMMIN' TO MYSELF (3)
–	16.	YOU'VE GOT ME IN THE PALM OF YOUR HAND (1)
17	17.	IS I IN LOVE? I IS (2)
–	18.	THREE ON A MATCH (1)
–	19.	SO ASHAMED (1)
–	20.	THE NIGHT WHEN LOVE WAS BORN (1)

SEPTEMBER 1932

LM	TM	
4	1.	WE JUST COULDN'T SAY GOODBYE (2)
1	2.	IN A SHANTY IN OLD SHANTY TOWN (4)
5	3.	MASQUERADE (2)
14	4.	STRANGE INTERLUDE (2)
12	5.	AS YOU DESIRE ME (2)
7	6.	IT WAS SO BEAUTIFUL (2)
–	7.	THREE'S A CROWD (1)
–	8.	I'LL NEVER BE THE SAME (1)
–	9.	SAY IT ISN'T SO (1)
11	10.	I CAN'T BELIEVE IT'S TRUE (2)
–	11.	LOVE ME TONIGHT (1)
18	12.	THREE ON A MATCH (2)
6	13.	GOOFUS (5)
16	14.	YOU'VE GOT ME IN THE PALM OF YOUR HAND (2)
–	15.	SWEETHEARTS FOREVER (1)
–	16.	MIMI (1)
3	17.	LULLABY OF THE LEAVES (5)
2	18.	MY SILENT LOVE (4)
–	19.	I GUESS I'LL HAVE TO CHANGE MY PLAN (1)
19	20.	SO ASHAMED (2)

OCTOBER 1932

LM	TM	
9	1.	SAY IT ISN'T SO (2)
2	2.	IN A SHANTY IN OLD SHANTY TOWN (5)
1	3.	WE JUST COULDN'T SAY GOODBYE (3)
11	4.	LOVE ME TONIGHT (2)
–	5.	LET'S PUT OUT THE LIGHTS (AND GO TO SLEEP) (1)
7	6.	THREE'S A CROWD (2)
–	7.	ALL-AMERICAN GIRL (1)
3	8.	MASQUERADE (3)
8	9.	I'LL NEVER BE THE SAME (2)
15	10.	SWEETHEARTS FOREVER (2)
–	11.	PLEASE (1)
12	12.	THREE ON A MATCH (3)
4	13.	STRANGE INTERLUDE (3)
–	14.	HOW DEEP IS THE OCEAN? (1)
19	15.	I GUESS I'LL HAVE TO CHANGE MY PLAN (2)
5	16.	AS YOU DESIRE ME (3)
–	17.	ALONE TOGETHER (1)
–	18.	PINK ELEPHANTS (1)
13	19.	GOOFUS (6)
–	20.	PU-LEEZE, MR. HEMINGWAY! (1)

NOVEMBER 1932

LM	TM	
5	1.	LET'S PUT OUT THE LIGHTS (AND GO TO SLEEP) (2)
11	2.	PLEASE (2)
7	3.	ALL-AMERICAN GIRL (2)
1	4.	SAY IT ISN'T SO (3)
14	5.	HOW DEEP IS THE OCEAN? (2)
2	6.	IN A SHANTY IN OLD SHANTY TOWN (6)
–	7.	A LITTLE STREET WHERE OLD FRIENDS MEET (1)
18	8.	PINK ELEPHANTS (2)
10	9.	SWEETHEARTS FOREVER (3)
3	10.	WE JUST COULDN'T SAY GOODBYE (4)
–	11.	FIT AS A FIDDLE (1)
–	12.	PLAY, FIDDLE, PLAY (1)
–	13.	HERE LIES LOVE (1)
–	14.	ROCKABYE MOON (1)
–	15.	BROTHER, CAN YOU SPARE A DIME? (1)
–	16.	HELL'S BELLS (1)
6	17.	THREE'S A CROWD (3)
4	18.	LOVE ME TONIGHT (3)
9	19.	I'LL NEVER BE THE SAME (3)
20	20.	PU-LEEZE, MR. HEMINGWAY! (2)

DECEMBER 1932

LM	TM	
2	1.	PLEASE (3)
7	2.	A LITTLE STREET WHERE OLD FRIENDS MEET (2)
3	3.	ALL-AMERICAN GIRL (3)
8	4.	PINK ELEPHANTS (3)
1	5.	LET'S PUT OUT THE LIGHTS (AND GO TO SLEEP) (3)
11	6.	FIT AS A FIDDLE (2)
5	7.	HOW DEEP IS THE OCEAN? (3)
12	8.	PLAY, FIDDLE, PLAY (2)
15	9.	BROTHER, CAN YOU SPARE A DIME? (2)
–	10.	UNDERNEATH THE HARLEM MOON (1)
14	11.	ROCKABYE MOON (2)
–	12.	JUST A LITTLE HOME FOR THE OLD FOLKS (1)
4	13.	SAY IT ISN'T SO (4)
–	14.	I'M SURE OF EVERYTHING BUT YOU (1)
13	15.	HERE LIES LOVE (2)
–	16.	WILLOW, WEEP FOR ME (1)
16	17.	HELL'S BELLS (2)
–	18.	LOUISIANA HAYRIDE (1)
6	19.	IN A SHANTY IN OLD SHANTY TOWN (7)
–	20.	A SHINE ON YOUR SHOES (1)

JANUARY 1933

LM	TM	
2	1.	A LITTLE STREET WHERE OLD FRIENDS MEET (3)
6	2.	FIT AS A FIDDLE (3)
8	3.	PLAY, FIDDLE, PLAY (3)
–	4.	NIGHT AND DAY (1)
1	5.	PLEASE (4)
16	6.	WILLOW, WEEP FOR ME (2)
4	7.	PINK ELEPHANTS (4)
–	8.	MY DARLING (1)
14	9.	I'M SURE OF EVERYTHING BUT YOU (2)
3	10.	ALL-AMERICAN GIRL (4)
11	11.	ROCKABYE MOON (3)
–	12.	MOON SONG (1)
10	13.	UNDERNEATH THE HARLEM MOON (2)
12	14.	JUST A LITTLE HOME FOR THE OLD FOLKS (2)
–	15.	JUST AN ECHO IN THE VALLEY (1)
–	16.	EADIE WAS A LADY (1)
9	17.	BROTHER, CAN YOU SPARE A DIME? (3)
17	18.	HELL'S BELLS (3)
–	19.	I'VE TOLD EVERY LITTLE STAR (1)
–	20.	A BOY AND A GIRL WERE DANCING (1)

FEBRUARY 1933

LM	TM	
4	1.	NIGHT AND DAY (2)
12	2.	MOON SONG (2)
15	3.	JUST AN ECHO IN THE VALLEY (2)
1	4.	A LITTLE STREET WHERE OLD FRIENDS MEET (4)
8	5.	MY DARLING (2)
11	6.	ROCKABYE MOON (4)
3	7.	PLAY, FIDDLE, PLAY (4)
16	8.	EADIE WAS A LADY (2)
6	9.	WILLOW, WEEP FOR ME (3)
–	10.	STREET OF DREAMS (1)
–	11.	THE GIRL IN THE LITTLE GREEN HAT (1)
–	12.	LOVE IN THE MOONLIGHT (1)
2	13.	FIT AS A FIDDLE (4)
–	14.	SPEAK TO ME OF LOVE (1)
–	15.	YOU'RE AN OLD SMOOTHIE (1)
–	16.	RISE 'N SHINE (1)
–	17.	LOVE IS A DREAM (1)
19	18.	I'VE TOLD EVERY LITTLE STAR (2)
–	19.	THE SONG IS YOU (1)
9	20.	I'M SURE OF EVERYTHING BUT YOU (3)

MARCH 1933

LM	TM	
3	1.	JUST AN ECHO IN THE VALLEY (3)
2	2.	MOON SONG (3)
1	3.	NIGHT AND DAY (3)
–	4.	FAREWELL TO ARMS (1)
5	5.	MY DARLING (3)
–	6.	SHUFFLE OFF TO BUFFALO (1)
4	7.	A LITTLE STREET WHERE OLD FRIENDS MEET (5)
–	8.	TRY A LITTLE TENDERNESS (1)
–	9.	FORTY-SECOND STREET (1)
12	10.	LOVE IN THE MOONLIGHT (2)
17	11.	LOVE IS A DREAM (2)
–	12.	YOU'RE GETTING TO A HABIT WITH ME (1)
6	13.	ROCKABYE MOON (5)
7	14.	PLAY, FIDDLE, PLAY (5)
11	15.	THE GIRL IN THE LITTLE GREEN HAT (2)
–	16.	I'M YOUNG AND HEALTHY (1)
–	17.	I GOTTA RIGHT TO SING THE BLUES (1)
–	18.	DARKNESS ON THE DELTA (1)
–	19.	I'VE GOT THE WORLD ON A STRING (1)
10	20.	STREET OF DREAMS (2)

APRIL 1933

LM	TM	
6	1.	SHUFFLE OFF TO BUFFALO (2)
1	2.	JUST AN ECHO IN THE VALLEY (4)
4	3.	FAREWELL TO ARMS (2)
9	4.	FORTY-SECOND STREET (2)
8	5.	TRY A LITTLE TENDERNESS (2)
2	6.	MOON SONG (4)
–	7.	HAVE YOU EVER BEEN LONELY? (1)
3	8.	NIGHT AND DAY (4)
–	9.	IN THE VALLEY OF THE MOON (1)
–	10.	I'LL TAKE AN OPTION ON YOU (1)
5	11.	MY DARLING (4)
–	12.	LOVER (1)
12	13.	YOU'RE GETTING TO A HABIT WITH ME (2)
–	14.	YOU'VE GOT ME CRYING AGAIN (1)
16	15.	I'M YOUNG AND HEALTHY (2)
–	16.	HEY! YOUNG FELLA (1)
18	17.	DARKNESS ON THE DELTA (2)
10	18.	LOVE IN THE MOONLIGHT (3)
–	19.	STORMY WEATHER (1)
–	20.	I WAKE UP SMILING (1)

MAY 1933

LM	TM	
1	1.	SHUFFLE OFF TO BUFFALO (3)
19	2.	STORMY WEATHER (2)
4	3.	FORTY-SECOND STREET (3)
12	4.	LOVER (2)
7	5.	HAVE YOU EVER BEEN LONELY? (2)
9	6.	IN THE VALLEY OF THE MOON (2)
–	7.	HOLD ME (1)
2	8.	JUST AN ECHO IN THE VALLEY (5)
3	9.	FAREWELL TO ARMS (3)
–	10.	TWO TICKETS TO GEORGIA (1)
10	11.	I'LL TAKE AN OPTION ON YOU (2)
–	12.	ADORABLE (1)
–	13.	REMEMBER ME (1)
–	14.	LOVE SONGS OF THE NILE (1)
5	15.	TRY A LITTLE TENDERNESS (3)
–	16.	MAYBE (IT'S BECAUSE) I LOVE YOU TOO MUCH (1)
20	17.	I WAKE UP SMILING (2)
–	18.	LET'S CALL IT A DAY (1)
–	19.	LYING IN THE HAY (1)
8	20.	NIGHT AND DAY (5)

JUNE 1933

LM	TM	
2	1.	STORMY WEATHER (3)
6	2.	IN THE VALLEY OF THE MOON (3)
7	3.	HOLD ME (2)
5	4.	HAVE YOU EVER BEEN LONELY? (3)
1	5.	SHUFFLE OFF TO BUFFALO (4)
14	6.	LOVE SONGS OF THE NILE (2)
–	7.	SWEETHEART, DARLIN' (1)
12	8.	ADORABLE (2)
4	9.	LOVER (3)
19	10.	LYING IN THE HAY (2)
–	11.	ISN'T IT HEAVENLY? (1)
3	12.	FORTY-SECOND STREET (4)
–	13.	SHADOW WALTZ (1)
–	14.	I COVER THE WATERFRONT (1)
–	15.	GYPSY FIDDLES (1)
–	16.	AN ORCHID TO YOU (1)
16	17.	MAYBE (IT'S BECAUSE) I LOVE YOU TOO MUCH (2)
–	18.	IN THE PARK IN PAREE (1)
10	19.	TWO TICKETS TO GEORGIA (2)
–	20.	WE'RE IN THE MONEY (THE GOLD DIGGERS' SONG) (1)

JULY 1933

LM	TM	
2	1.	IN THE VALLEY OF THE MOON (4)
13	2.	SHADOW WALTZ (2)
7	3.	SWEETHEART, DARLIN' (2)
1	4.	STORMY WEATHER (4)
6	5.	LOVE SONGS OF THE NILE (3)
3	6.	HOLD ME (3)
–	7.	LEARN TO CROON (1)
11	8.	ISN'T IT HEAVENLY? (2)
–	9.	LAZY BONES (1)
14	10.	I COVER THE WATERFRONT (2)
4	11.	HAVE YOU EVER BEEN LONELY? (4)
8	12.	ADORABLE (3)
–	13.	HOLD YOUR MAN (1)
16	14.	AN ORCHID TO YOU (2)
20	15.	WE'RE IN THE MONEY (THE GOLD DIGGERS' SONG) (2)
–	16.	SOPHISTICATED LADY (1)
15	17.	GYPSY FIDDLES (2)
–	18.	I'VE GOT TO SING A TORCH SONG (1)
–	19.	BLUE PRELUDE (1)
10	20.	LYING IN THE HAY (3)

AUGUST 1933

LM	TM	
2	1.	SHADOW WALTZ (3)
9	2.	LAZY BONES (2)
1	3.	IN THE VALLEY OF THE MOON (5)
3	4.	SWEETHEART, DARLIN' (3)
7	5.	LEARN TO CROON (2)
13	6.	HOLD YOUR MAN (2)
19	7.	BLUE PRELUDE (2)
–	8.	UNDER A BLANKET OF BLUE (1)
5	9.	LOVE SONGS OF THE NILE (4)
–	10.	LOVE IS THE SWEETEST THING (1)
–	11.	DOWN THE OLD OX ROAD (1)
4	12.	STORMY WEATHER (5)
16	13.	SOPHISTICATED LADY (2)
6	14.	HOLD ME (4)
–	15.	SMOKE RINGS (1)
–	16.	MY MOONLIGHT MADONNA (1)
12	17.	ADORABLE (4)
–	18.	TROUBLE IN PARADISE (1)
17	19.	GYPSY FIDDLES (3)
8	20.	ISN'T IT HEAVENLY (3)

SEPTEMBER 1933

LM	TM	
2	1.	LAZY BONES (3)
1	2.	SHADOW WALTZ (4)
–	3.	THE LAST ROUNDUP (1)
10	4.	LOVE IS THE SWEETEST THING (2)
3	5.	IN THE VALLEY OF THE MOON (6)
8	6.	UNDER A BLANKET OF BLUE (2)
5	7.	LEARN TO CROON (3)
–	8.	DON'T BLAME ME (1)
7	9.	BLUE PRELUDE (3)
16	10.	MY MOONLIGHT MADONNA (2)
4	11.	SWEETHEART, DARLIN' (4)
6	12.	HOLD YOUR MAN (3)
11	13.	DOWN THE OLD OX ROAD (2)
13	14.	SOPHISTICATED LADY (3)
–	15.	THIS TIME IT'S LOVE (1)
15	16.	SMOKE RINGS (2)
–	17.	WHO'S AFRAID OF THE BIG BAD WOLF? (1)
–	18.	AH, BUT IS IT LOVE? (1)
18	19.	TROUBLE IN PARADISE (2)
19	20.	GYPSY FIDDLES (4)

OCTOBER 1933

LM	TM	
3	1.	THE LAST ROUNDUP (2)
1	2.	LAZY BONES (4)
17	3.	WHO'S AFRAID OF THE BIG BAD WOLF? (2)
4	4.	LOVE IS THE SWEETEST THING (3)
–	5.	THE DAY YOU CAME ALONG (1)
8	6.	DON'T BLAME ME (2)
2	7.	SHADOW WALTZ (5)
–	8.	THANKS (1)
5	9.	IN THE VALLEY OF THE MOON (7)
15	10.	THIS TIME IT'S LOVE (2)
–	11.	GOOD NIGHT, LITTLE GIRL OF MY DREAMS (1)
–	12.	IT'S ONLY A PAPER MOON (1)
–	13.	DINNER AT EIGHT (1)
–	14.	IT'S THE TALK OF THE TOWN (1)
7	15.	LEARN TO CROON (4)
6	16.	UNDER A BLANKET OF BLUE (3)
–	17.	ARE YOU MAKIN' ANY MONEY? (1)
18	18.	AH, BUT IS IT LOVE? (2)
14	19.	SOPHISTICATED LADY (4)
9	20.	BLUE PRELUDE (4)

NOVEMBER 1933

LM	TM	
1	1.	THE LAST ROUNDUP (3)
3	2.	WHO'S AFRAID OF THE BIG BAD WOLF? (3)
8	3.	THANKS (2)
11	4.	GOOD NIGHT, LITTLE GIRL OF MY DREAMS (2)
5	5.	THE DAY YOU CAME ALONG (2)
14	6.	IT'S THE TALK OF THE TOWN (2)
–	7.	BY A WATERFALL (1)
4	8.	LOVE IS THE SWEETEST THING (4)
13	9.	DINNER AT EIGHT (2)
–	10.	ANNIE DOESN'T LIVE HERE ANYMORE (1)
–	11.	I'LL BE FAITHFUL (1)
2	12.	LAZY BONES (5)
12	13.	IT'S ONLY A PAPER MOON (2)
6	14.	DON'T BLAME ME (3)
–	15.	THE OLD SPINNING WHEEL (1)
7	16.	SHADOW WALTZ (6)
–	17.	HEAT WAVE (1)
–	18.	DID YOU EVER SEE A DREAM WALKING? (1)
–	19.	YOU'VE GOT EVERYTHING (1)
–	20.	CLOSE YOUR EYES (1)

DECEMBER 1933

LM	TM	
4	1.	GOOD NIGHT, LITTLE GIRL OF MY DREAMS (3)
18	2.	DID YOU EVER SEE A DREAM WALKING? (2)
10	3.	ANNIE DOESN'T LIVE HERE ANYMORE (2)
7	4.	BY A WATERFALL (2)
11	5.	I'LL BE FAITHFUL (2)
1	6.	THE LAST ROUNDUP (4)
2	7.	WHO'S AFRAID OF THE BIG BAD WOLF? (4)
–	8.	YOU'RE GONNA LOSE YOUR GAL (1)
–	9.	HONEYMOON HOTEL (1)
15	10.	THE OLD SPINNING WHEEL (2)
17	11.	HEAT WAVE (2)
3	12.	THANKS (3)
5	13.	THE DAY YOU CAME ALONG (3)
–	14.	APRIL IN PARIS (1)
–	15.	EASTER PARADE (1)
–	16.	GOOD MORNING GLORY (1)
6	17.	IT'S THE TALK OF THE TOWN (3)
–	18.	SHANGHAI LIL (1)
–	19.	EVENIN' (1)
–	20.	DOIN' THE UPTOWN LOWDOWN (1)

JANUARY 1934

LM	TM	
10	1.	THE OLD SPINNING WHEEL (3)
2	2.	DID YOU EVER SEE A DREAM WALKING? (3)
1	3.	GOOD NIGHT, LITTLE GIRL OF MY DREAMS (4)
–	4.	SMOKE GETS IN YOUR EYES (1)
3	5.	ANNIE DOESN'T LIVE HERE ANYMORE (3)
15	6.	EASTER PARADE (2)
6	7.	THE LAST ROUNDUP (5)
9	8.	HONEYMOON HOTEL (2)
–	9.	EVERYTHING I HAVE IS YOURS (1)
4	10.	BY A WATERFALL (3)
–	11.	TEMPTATION (1)
8	12.	YOU'RE GONNA LOSE YOUR GAL (2)
16	13.	GOOD MORNING GLORY (2)
–	14.	ONE MINUTE TO ONE (1)
–	15.	MY LITTLE GRASS SHACK IN KEALEKUA, HAWAII (1)
–	16.	ORCHIDS IN THE MOONLIGHT (1)
14	17.	APRIL IN PARIS (2)
5	18.	I'LL BE FAITHFUL (3)
–	19.	YOU'RE DEVASTATING (1)
–	20.	CARIOCA (1)

FEBRUARY 1934

LM	TM	
1	1.	THE OLD SPINNING WHEEL (4)
4	2.	SMOKE GETS IN YOUR EYES (2)
3	3.	GOOD NIGHT, LITTLE GIRL OF MY DREAMS (5)
15	4.	MY LITTLE GRASS SHACK IN KEALEKUA, HAWAII (2)
20	5.	CARIOCA (2)
9	6.	EVERYTHING I HAVE IS YOURS (2)
16	7.	ORCHIDS IN THE MOONLIGHT (2)
–	8.	THROW ANOTHER LOG ON THE FIRE (1)
–	9.	WE'LL MAKE HAY WHILE THE SUN SHINES (1)
11	10.	TEMPTATION (2)
2	11.	DID YOU EVER SEE A DREAM WALKING? (4)
–	12.	THIS LITTLE PIGGIE WENT TO MARKET (1)
–	13.	KEEP YOUNG AND BEAUTIFUL (1)
6	14.	EASTER PARADE (3)
–	15.	LET'S FALL IN LOVE (1)
–	16.	LOVE LOCKED OUT (1)
–	17.	WHEN TOMORROW COMES (1)
–	18.	GOIN' TO HEAVEN ON A MULE (1)
–	19.	FLYING DOWN TO RIO (1)
–	20.	WAGON WHEELS (1)

MARCH 1934

LM	TM	
1	1.	THE OLD SPINNING WHEEL (5)
12	2.	THIS LITTLE PIGGIE WENT TO MARKET (2)
4	3.	MY LITTLE GRASS SHACK IN KEALEKUA, HAWAII (3)
5	4.	CARIOCA (3)
2	5.	SMOKE GETS IN YOUR EYES (3)
15	6.	LET'S FALL IN LOVE (2)
20	7.	WAGON WHEELS (2)
8	8.	THROW ANOTHER LOG ON THE FIRE (2)
18	9.	GOIN' TO HEAVEN ON A MULE (2)
9	10.	WE'LL MAKE HAY WHILE THE SUN SHINES (2)
3	11.	GOOD NIGHT, LITTLE GIRL OF MY DREAMS (6)
7	12.	ORCHIDS IN THE MOONLIGHT (3)
–	13.	BOULEVARD OF BROKEN DREAMS (1)
10	14.	TEMPTATION (3)
19	15.	FLYING DOWN TO RIO (2)
–	16.	YOU OUGHTA BE IN PICTURES (1)
–	17.	WITHOUT THAT CERTAIN THING (1)
6	18.	EVERYTHING I HAVE IS YOURS (3)
–	19.	THERE GOES MY HEART (1)
–	20.	MUSIC MAKES ME (1)

APRIL 1934

LM	TM	
1	1.	THE OLD SPINNING WHEEL (6)
3	2.	MY LITTLE GRASS SHACK IN KEALEKUA, HAWAII (4)
7	3.	WAGON WHEELS (3)
4	4.	CARIOCA (4)
–	5.	A LITTLE DUTCH MILL (1)
16	6.	YOU OUGHTA BE IN PICTURES (2)
13	7.	BOULEVARD OF BROKEN DREAMS (2)
2	8.	THIS LITTLE PIGGIE WENT TO MARKET (3)
5	9.	SMOKE GETS IN YOUR EYES (4)
–	10.	WHY DO I DREAM THOSE DREAMS? (1)
6	11.	LET'S FALL IN LOVE (3)
–	12.	GOODNIGHT, LOVELY LITTLE LADY (1)
9	13.	GOIN' TO HEAVEN ON A MULE (3)
–	14.	TRUE (1)
14	15.	TEMPTATION (4)
8	16.	THROW ANOTHER LOG ON THE FIRE (3)
–	17.	A THOUSAND GOODNIGHTS (1)
10	18.	WE'LL MAKE HAY WHILE THE SUN SHINES (3)
–	19.	NEIGHBORS (1)
–	20.	OVER SOMEBODY ELSE'S SHOULDER (1)

MAY 1934

LM	TM	
5	1.	A LITTLE DUTCH MILL (2)
2	2.	MY LITTLE GRASS SHACK IN KEALEKUA, HAWAII (5)
1	3.	THE OLD SPINNING WHEEL (7)
12	4.	GOODNIGHT, LOVELY LITTLE LADY (2)
6	5.	YOU OUGHTA BE IN PICTURES (3)
17	6.	A THOUSAND GOODNIGHTS (2)
10	7.	WHY DO I DREAM THOSE DREAMS? (2)
–	8.	LOVE THY NEIGHBOR (1)
3	9.	WAGON WHEELS (4)
–	10.	SHE REMINDS ME OF YOU (1)
4	11.	CARIOCA (5)
–	12.	COCKTAILS FOR TWO (1)
–	13.	I'LL STRING ALONG WITH YOU (1)
–	14.	MAY I? (1)
–	15.	NASTY MAN (1)
–	16.	THE BEAT OF MY HEART (1)
14	17.	TRUE (2)
–	18.	LITTLE MAN, YOU'VE HAD A BUSY DAY (1)
–	19.	ILL WIND (1)
–	20.	PLAY TO ME, GYPSY (1)

JUNE 1934

LM	TM	
13	1.	I'LL STRING ALONG WITH YOU (2)
8	2.	LOVE THY NEIGHBOR (2)
18	3.	LITTLE MAN, YOU'VE HAD A BUSY DAY (2)
12	4.	COCKTAILS FOR TWO (2)
1	5.	A LITTLE DUTCH MILL (3)
6	6.	A THOUSAND GOODNIGHTS (3)
–	7.	ALL I DO IS DREAM OF YOU (1)
–	8.	RIPTIDE (1)
–	9.	EASY COME, EASY GO (1)
–	10.	RIDIN' AROUND IN THE RAIN (1)
4	11.	GOODNIGHT, LOVELY LITTLE LADY (3)
16	12.	THE BEAT OF MY HEART (2)
14	13.	MAY I? (2)
–	14.	THE MAN ON THE FLYING TRAPEZE (1)
–	15.	I AIN'T LAZY, I'M JUST DREAMIN' (1)
–	16.	THE CHAMPAGNE WALTZ (1)
–	17.	WITH MY EYES WIDE OPEN, I'M DREAMING (1)
3	18.	THE OLD SPINNING WHEEL (8)
10	19.	SHE REMINDS ME OF YOU (2)
–	20.	SLEEPY HEAD (1)

JULY 1934

LM	TM	
1	1.	I'LL STRING ALONG WITH YOU (3)
7	2.	ALL I DO IS DREAM OF YOU (2)
3	3.	LITTLE MAN, YOU'VE HAD A BUSY DAY (3)
4	4.	COCKTAILS FOR TWO (3)
17	5.	WITH MY EYES WIDE OPEN, I'M DREAMING (2)
2	6.	LOVE THY NEIGHBOR (3)
20	7.	SLEEPY HEAD (2)
14	8.	THE MAN ON THE FLYING TRAPEZE (2)
–	9.	MOONGLOW (1)
16	10.	THE CHAMPAGNE WALTZ (2)
9	11.	EASY COME, EASY GO (2)
15	12.	I AIN'T LAZY, I'M JUST DREAMIN' (2)
–	13.	I NEVER HAD A CHANCE (1)
8	14.	RIPTIDE (2)
10	15.	RIDIN' AROUND IN THE RAIN (2)
–	16.	I WISH I WERE TWINS (1)
5	17.	A LITTLE DUTCH MILL (4)
6	18.	A THOUSAND GOODNIGHTS (4)
–	19.	SPELLBOUND (1)
–	20.	FRECKLE FACE, YOU'RE BEAUTIFUL (1)

AUGUST 1934

LM	TM	
2	1.	ALL I DO IS DREAM OF YOU (3)
1	2.	I'LL STRING ALONG WITH YOU (4)
13	3.	I NEVER HAD A CHANCE (2)
5	4.	WITH MY EYES WIDE OPEN, I'M DREAMING (3)
4	5.	COCKTAILS FOR TWO (4)
–	6.	LOVE IN BLOOM (1)
9	7.	MOONGLOW (2)
7	8.	SLEEPY HEAD (3)
–	9.	FOR ALL WE KNOW (1)
3	10.	LITTLE MAN, YOU'VE HAD A BUSY DAY (4)
–	11.	THE VERY THOUGHT OF YOU (1)
–	12.	DUST ON THE MOON (1)
8	13.	THE MAN ON THE FLYING TRAPEZE (3)
–	14.	I ONLY HAVE EYES FOR YOU (1)
–	15.	DAMES (1)
–	16.	THE PRIZE WALTZ (1)
19	17.	SPELLBOUND (2)
–	18.	MY HAT'S ON THE SIDE OF MY HEAD (1)
–	19.	PARDON MY SOUTHERN ACCENT (1)
–	20.	THANK YOU FOR A LOVELY EVENING (1)

SEPTEMBER 1934

LM	TM	
6	1.	LOVE IN BLOOM (2)
14	2.	I ONLY HAVE EYES FOR YOU (2)
9	3.	FOR ALL WE KNOW (2)
3	4.	I NEVER HAD A CHANCE (3)
–	5.	I SAW STARS (1)
–	6.	TWO CIGARETTES IN THE DARK (1)
1	7.	ALL I DO IS DREAM OF YOU (4)
7	8.	MOONGLOW (3)
2	9.	I'LL STRING ALONG WITH YOU (5)
19	10.	PARDON MY SOUTHERN ACCENT (2)
11	12.	THE VERY THOUGHT OF YOU (2)
4	11.	WITH MY EYES WIDE OPEN, I'M DREAMING (4)
5	13.	COCKTAILS FOR TWO (5)
12	14.	DUST ON THE MOON (2)
8	15.	SLEEPY HEAD (4)
13	16.	THE MAN ON THE FLYING TRAPEZE (4)
–	17.	TUMBLING TUMBLEWEEDS (1)
–	18.	THEN I'LL BE TIRED OF YOU (1)
–	19.	A NEW MOON IS OVER MY SHOULDER (1)
16	20.	THE PRIZE WALTZ (2)

OCTOBER 1934

LM	TM	
1	1.	LOVE IN BLOOM (3)
6	2.	TWO CIGARETTES IN THE DARK (2)
5	3.	I SAW STARS (2)
2	4.	I ONLY HAVE EYES FOR YOU (3)
–	5.	THE CONTINENTAL (1)
–	6.	STARS FELL ON ALABAMA (1)
4	7.	I NEVER HAD A CHANCE (4)
–	8.	LOST IN A FOG (1)
10	9.	PARDON MY SOUTHERN ACCENT (3)
12	10.	THE VERY THOUGHT OF YOU (3)
8	11.	MOONGLOW (4)
3	12.	FOR ALL WE KNOW (3)
–	13.	ONE NIGHT OF LOVE (1)
–	14.	IT'S ALL FORGOTTEN NOW (1)
–	15.	TALKIN' TO MYSELF (1)
–	16.	THE DRUNKARD SONG (THERE IS A TAVERN IN THE TOWN) (1)
7	17.	ALL I DO IS DREAM OF YOU (5)
18	18.	THEN I'LL BE TIRED OF YOU (2)
9	19.	I'LL STRING ALONG WITH YOU (6)
–	20.	RAIN (1)

NOVEMBER 1934

LM	TM	
5	1.	THE CONTINENTAL (2)
6	2.	STARS FELL ON ALABAMA (2)
1	3.	LOVE IN BLOOM (4)
2	4.	TWO CIGARETTES IN THE DARK (3)
8	5.	LOST IN A FOG (2)
3	6.	I SAW STARS (3)
20	7.	RAIN (2)
13	8.	ONE NIGHT OF LOVE (2)
16	9.	THE DRUNKARD SONG (THERE IS A TAVERN IN THE TOWN) (2)
–	10.	OUT IN THE COLD AGAIN (1)
4	11.	I ONLY HAVE EYES FOR YOU (4)
–	12.	STAY AS SWEET AS YOU ARE (1)
10	13.	THE VERY THOUGHT OF YOU (4)
–	14.	BE STILL, MY HEART (1)
–	15.	SWEETIE PIE (1)
–	16.	THE OBJECT OF MY AFFECTION (1)
–	17.	YOU'RE A BUILDER UPPER (1)
–	18.	DON'T LET IT BOTHER YOU (1)
–	19.	BUGLE CALL RAG (1)
–	20.	A NEEDLE IN A HAYSTACK (1)

DECEMBER 1934

LM	TM	
12	1.	STAY AS SWEET AS YOU ARE (2)
16	2.	THE OBJECT OF MY AFFECTION (2)
1	3.	THE CONTINENTAL (3)
2	4.	STARS FELL ON ALABAMA (3)
–	5.	SANTA CLAUS IS COMIN' TO TOWN (1)
7	6.	RAIN (3)
3	7.	LOVE IN BLOOM (5)
5	8.	LOST IN A FOG (3)
–	9.	JUNE IN JANUARY (1)
10	10.	OUT IN THE COLD AGAIN (2)
–	11.	WINTER WONDERLAND (1)
–	12.	HANDS ACROSS THE TABLE (1)
14	13.	BE STILL, MY HEART (2)
4	14.	TWO CIGARETTES IN THE DARK (4)
–	15.	POP GOES YOUR HEART (1)
–	16.	YOU'RE THE TOP (1)
–	17.	FLIRTATION WALK (1)
17	18.	YOU'RE A BUILDER UPPER (2)
15	19.	SWEETIE PIE (2)
–	20.	MR. AND MRS. IS THE NAME (1)

JANUARY 1935

LM	TM	
2	1.	THE OBJECT OF MY AFFECTION (3)
9	2.	JUNE IN JANUARY (2)
1	3.	STAY AS SWEET AS YOU ARE (3)
11	4.	WINTER WONDERLAND (2)
16	5.	YOU'RE THE TOP (2)
–	6.	BLUE MOON (1)
4	7.	STARS FELL ON ALABAMA (4)
–	8.	ON THE GOOD SHIP LOLLIPOP (1)
17	9.	FLIRTATION WALK (2)
12	10.	HANDS ACROSS THE TABLE (2)
–	11.	WITH EVERY BREATH I TAKE (1)
5	12.	SANTA CLAUS IS COMIN' TO TOWN (2)
–	13.	I'VE GOT AN INVITATION TO A DANCE (1)
–	14.	BELIEVE IT, BELOVED (1)
3	15.	THE CONTINENTAL (4)
6	16.	RAIN (4)
–	17.	DANCING WITH MY SHADOW (1)
–	18.	ON OBSERVATORY HILL (1)
–	19.	LOVE IS JUST AROUND THE CORNER (1)
–	20.	ANYTHING GOES (1)

FEBRUARY 1935

LM	TM	
6	1.	BLUE MOON (2)
–	2.	ISLE OF CAPRI (1)
2	3.	JUNE IN JANUARY (3)
8	4.	ON THE GOOD SHIP LOLLIPOP (2)
–	5.	I BELIEVE IN MIRACLES (1)
14	6.	BELIEVE IT, BELOVED (2)
17	7.	DANCING WITH MY SHADOW (2)
1	8.	THE OBJECT OF MY AFFECTION (4)
11	9.	WITH EVERY BREATH I TAKE (2)
–	10.	TINY LITTLE FINGERPRINTS (1)
5	11.	YOU'RE THE TOP (3)
19	12.	LOVE IS JUST AROUND THE CORNER (2)
3	13.	STAY AS SWEET AS YOU ARE (4)
–	14.	SOLITUDE (1)
–	15.	FARE THEE WELL, ANNABELLE (1)
–	16.	OLE FAITHFUL (1)
–	17.	CLOUDS (1)
20	18.	ANYTHING GOES (2)
18	19.	ON OBSERVATORY HILL (2)
–	20.	BLUE DANUBE WALTZ (1)

MARCH 1935

LM	TM	
2	1.	ISLE OF CAPRI (2)
1	2.	BLUE MOON (3)
–	3.	LULLABY OF BROADWAY (1)
–	4.	WHEN I GROW TOO OLD TO DREAM (1)
4	5.	ON THE GOOD SHIP LOLLIPOP (3)
15	6.	FARE THEE WELL, ANNABELLE (2)
5	7.	I BELIEVE IN MIRACLES (2)
17	8.	CLOUDS (2)
–	9.	EV'RY DAY (1)
–	10.	A LITTLE WHITE GARDENIA (1)
14	11.	SOLITUDE (2)
–	12.	IF THE MOON TURNS GREEN (1)
16	13.	OLE FAITHFUL (2)
–	14.	(LOOKIE LOOKIE LOOKIE) HERE COMES COOKIE (1)
10	15.	TINY LITTLE FINGERPRINTS (2)
–	16.	SOON (1)
20	17.	BLUE DANUBE WALTZ (2)
6	18.	BELIEVE IT, BELOVED (3)
–	19.	SWEET MUSIC (1)
–	20.	IT'S EASY TO REMEMBER (1)

APRIL 1935

LM	TM	
3	1.	LULLABY OF BROADWAY (2)
4	2.	WHEN I GROW TOO OLD TO DREAM (2)
1	3.	ISLE OF CAPRI (3)
9	4.	EV'RY DAY (2)
16	5.	SOON (2)
–	6.	LOVELY TO LOOK AT (1)
8	7.	CLOUDS (3)
14	8.	(LOOKIE LOOKIE LOOKIE) HERE COMES COOKIE (2)
–	9.	I WAS LUCKY (1)
–	10.	I WON'T DANCE (1)
20	11.	IT'S EASY TO REMEMBER (2)
11	12.	SOLITUDE (3)
12	13.	IF THE MOON TURNS GREEN (2)
10	14.	A LITTLE WHITE GARDENIA (2)
–	15.	WHAT'S THE REASON? (1)
5	16.	ON THE GOOD SHIP LOLLIPOP (4)
–	17.	IT'S AN OLD SOUTHERN CUSTOM (1)
–	18.	EVERYTHING'S BEEN DONE BEFORE (1)
–	19.	DOWN BY THE RIVER (1)
–	20.	WHOSE HONEY ARE YOU? (1)

MAY 1935

LM	TM	
2	1.	WHEN I GROW TOO OLD TO DREAM (3)
1	2.	LULLABY OF BROADWAY (3)
6	3.	LOVELY TO LOOK AT (2)
3	4.	ISLE OF CAPRI (4)
15	5.	WHAT'S THE REASON? (2)
–	6.	ABOUT A QUARTER TO NINE (1)
5	7.	SOON (3)
10	8.	I WON'T DANCE (2)
17	9.	IT'S AN OLD SOUTHERN CUSTOM (2)
18	10.	EVERYTHING'S BEEN DONE BEFORE (2)
–	11.	TELL ME THAT YOU LOVE ME (1)
–	12.	SHE'S A LATIN FROM MANHATTAN (1)
9	13.	I WAS LUCKY (2)
4	14.	EV'RY DAY (3)
11	15.	IT'S EASY TO REMEMBER (3)
–	16.	FLOWERS FOR MADAME (1)
–	17.	LOVE AND A DIME (1)
7	18.	CLOUDS (4)
–	19.	IN A LITTLE GYPSY TEAROOM (1)
–	20.	YOU'RE A HEAVENLY THING (1)

JUNE 1935

LM	TM	
6	1.	ABOUT A QUARTER TO NINE (2)
5	2.	WHAT'S THE REASON? (3)
19	3.	IN A LITTLE GYPSY TEAROOM (2)
–	4.	LIFE IS A SONG (1)
1	5.	WHEN I GROW TOO OLD TO DREAM (4)
12	6.	SHE'S A LATIN FROM MANHATTAN (2)
11	7.	TELL ME THAT YOU LOVE ME (2)
–	8.	CHASING SHADOWS (1)
–	9.	IN THE MIDDLE OF A KISS (1)
–	10.	THE LADY IN RED (1)
8	11.	I WON'T DANCE (3)
10	12.	EVERYTHING'S BEEN DONE BEFORE (3)
–	13.	I'LL NEVER SAY "NEVER AGAIN" AGAIN (1)
–	14.	WAY BACK HOME (1)
2	15.	LULLABY OF BROADWAY (4)
16	16.	FLOWERS FOR MADAME (2)
17	17.	LOVE AND A DIME (2)
4	18.	ISLE OF CAPRI (5)
20	19.	YOU'RE A HEAVENLY THING (2)
3	20.	LOVELY TO LOOK AT (3)

JULY 1935

LM	TM	
3	1.	IN A LITTLE GYPSY TEAROOM (3)
8	2.	CHASING SHADOWS (2)
9	3.	IN THE MIDDLE OF A KISS (2)
1	4.	ABOUT A QUARTER TO NINE (3)
13	5.	I'LL NEVER SAY "NEVER AGAIN" AGAIN (2)
4	6.	LIFE IS A SONG (2)
10	7.	THE LADY IN RED (2)
2	8.	WHAT'S THE REASON? (4)
7	9.	TELL ME THAT YOU LOVE ME (3)
5	10.	WHEN I GROW TOO OLD TO DREAM (5)
–	11.	LET'S SWING IT (1)
–	12.	RHYTHM IS OUR BUSINESS (1)
–	13.	PARIS IN THE SPRING (1)
6	14.	SHE'S A LATIN FROM MANHATTAN (3)
–	15.	AND THEN SOME (1)
–	16.	THRILLED (1)
–	17.	FOOTLOOSE AND FANCY FREE (1)
–	18.	I'M FALLING IN LOVE WITH SOMEONE (1)
–	19.	EAST OF THE SUN (1)
–	20.	LOVE ME FOREVER (1)

AUGUST 1935

LM	TM	
1	1.	IN A LITTLE GYPSY TEAROOM (4)
5	2.	I'LL NEVER SAY "NEVER AGAIN" AGAIN (3)
19	3.	EAST OF THE SUN (2)
2	4.	CHASING SHADOWS (3)
15	5.	AND THEN SOME (2)
3	6.	IN THE MIDDLE OF A KISS (3)
13	7.	PARIS IN THE SPRING (2)
20	8.	LOVE ME FOREVER (2)
–	9.	YOU'RE ALL I NEED (1)
7	10.	THE LADY IN RED (3)
–	11.	LULU'S BACK IN TOWN (1)
4	12.	ABOUT A QUARTER TO NINE (4)
–	13.	SWEET AND SLOW (1)
12	14.	RHYTHM IS OUR BUSINESS (2)
–	15.	EVERY LITTLE MOMENT (1)
–	16.	I'M IN THE MOOD FOR LOVE (1)
6	17.	LIFE IS A SONG (3)
–	18.	WHAT A LITTLE MOONLIGHT CAN DO (1)
–	19.	THE ROSE IN HER HAIR (1)
10	20.	WHEN I GROW TOO OLD TO DREAM (6)

SEPTEMBER 1935

LM	TM	
3	1.	EAST OF THE SUN (3)
16	2.	I'M IN THE MOOD FOR LOVE (2)
–	3.	CHEEK TO CHEEK (1)
9	4.	YOU'RE ALL I NEED (2)
–	5.	ACCENT ON YOUTH (1)
1	6.	IN A LITTLE GYPSY TEAROOM (5)
19	7.	THE ROSE IN HER HAIR (2)
–	8.	TOP HAT, WHITE TIE, AND TAILS (1)
8	9.	LOVE ME FOREVER (3)
5	10.	AND THEN SOME (3)
–	11.	I'M ON A SEE SAW (1)
–	12.	PAGE MISS GLORY (1)
–	13.	ANIMAL CRACKERS IN MY SOUP (1)
–	14.	ISN'T THIS A LOVELY DAY (TO BE CAUGHT IN THE RAIN)? (1)
2	15.	I'LL NEVER SAY "NEVER AGAIN" AGAIN (4)
–	16.	I WISHED ON THE MOON (1)
–	17.	I COULDN'T BELIEVE MY EYES (1)
6	18.	IN THE MIDDLE OF A KISS (4)
–	19.	WITHOUT A WORD OF WARNING (1)
7	20.	PARIS IN THE SPRING (3)

OCTOBER 1935

LM	TM	
3	1.	CHEEK TO CHEEK (2)
2	2.	I'M IN THE MOOD FOR LOVE (3)
11	3.	I'M ON A SEE SAW (2)
14	4.	ISN'T THIS A LOVELY DAY (TO BE CAUGHT IN THE RAIN)? (2)
8	5.	TOP HAT, WHITE TIE, AND TAILS (2)
5	6.	ACCENT ON YOUTH (2)
19	7.	WITHOUT A WORD OF WARNING (2)
–	8.	I'VE GOT A FEELIN' YOU'RE FOOLIN' (1)
–	9.	YOU ARE MY LUCKY STAR (1)
16	10.	I WISHED ON THE MOON (2)
7	11.	THE ROSE IN HER HAIR (3)
–	12.	TRUCKIN' (1)
–	13.	ROLL ALONG, PRAIRIE MOON (1)
–	14.	RHYTHM AND ROMANCE (1)
1	15.	EAST OF THE SUN (4)
4	16.	YOU'RE ALL I NEED (3)
–	17.	I WISH I WERE TWINS (1)
–	18.	EVERY NOW AND THEN (1)
–	19.	ON TREASURE ISLAND (1)
–	20.	NO STRINGS (I'M FANCY FREE) (1)

NOVEMBER 1935

LM	TM	
19	1.	ON TREASURE ISLAND (2)
–	2.	RED SAILS IN THE SUNSET (1)
1	3.	CHEEK TO CHEEK (3)
9	4.	YOU ARE MY LUCKY STAR (2)
8	5.	I'VE GOT A FEELIN' YOU'RE FOOLIN' (2)
13	6.	ROLL ALONG, PRAIRIE MOON (2)
2	7.	I'M IN THE MOOD FOR LOVE (4)
12	8.	TRUCKIN' (2)
3	9.	I'M ON A SEE SAW (3)
–	10.	TWENTY-FOUR HOURS A DAY (1)
4	11.	ISN'T THIS A LOVELY DAY (TO BE CAUGHT IN THE RAIN)? (3)
5	12.	TOP HAT, WHITE TIE, AND TAILS (3)
–	13.	A LITTLE BIT INDEPENDENT (1)
–	14.	TAKE ME BACK TO MY BOOTS AND SADDLE (1)
–	15.	DON'T GIVE UP THE SHIP (1)
–	16.	I'M SITTIN' HIGH ON A HILLTOP (1)
–	17.	THANKS A MILLION (1)
10	18.	I WISHED ON THE MOON (3)
–	19.	I FOUND A DREAM (1)
17	20.	I WISH I WERE TWINS (2)

DECEMBER 1935

LM	TM	
2	1.	RED SAILS IN THE SUNSET (2)
1	2.	ON TREASURE ISLAND (3)
13	3.	A LITTLE BIT INDEPENDENT (2)
14	4.	TAKE ME BACK TO MY BOOTS AND SADDLE (2)
10	5.	TWENTY-FOUR HOURS A DAY (2)
17	6.	THANKS A MILLION (2)
15	7.	DON'T GIVE UP THE SHIP (2)
16	8.	I'M SITTIN' HIGH ON A HILLTOP (2)
–	9.	NO OTHER ONE (1)
4	10.	YOU ARE MY LUCKY STAR (3)
6	11.	ROLL ALONG, PRAIRIE MOON (3)
–	12.	SANTA CLAUS IS COMIN' TO TOWN (1)
5	13.	I'VE GOT A FEELIN' YOU'RE FOOLIN' (3)
–	14.	WHERE AM I? (1)
19	15.	I FOUND A DREAM (2)
8	16.	TRUCKIN' (3)
–	17.	EENY MEENY MINEY MO (1)
3	18.	CHEEK TO CHEEK (4)
–	19.	WHY SHOULDN'T I? (1)
7	20	I'M IN THE MOOD FOR LOVE (5)

JANUARY 1936

LM	TM	
–	1.	THE MUSIC GOES 'ROUND AND AROUND (1)
3	2.	A LITTLE BIT INDEPENDENT (3)
2	3.	ON TREASURE ISLAND (4)
1	4.	RED SAILS IN THE SUNSET (3)
–	5.	ALONE (1)
–	6.	MOON OVER MIAMI (1)
4	7.	TAKE ME BACK TO MY BOOTS AND SADDLE (3)
17	8.	EENY MEENY MINEY MO (2)
6	9.	THANKS A MILLION (3)
–	10.	THE BROKEN RECORD (1)
–	11.	WITH ALL MY HEART (1)
–	12.	A BEAUTIFUL LADY IN BLUE (1)
9	13.	NO OTHER ONE (2)
8	14.	I'M SITTIN' HIGH ON A HILLTOP (3)
–	15.	ONE NIGHT IN MONTE CARLO (1)
7	16.	DON'T GIVE UP THE SHIP (3)
–	17.	DINNER FOR ONE, PLEASE, JAMES (1)
–	18.	LIGHTS OUT (1)
5	19.	TWENTY-FOUR HOURS A DAY (3)
–	20.	I FEEL LIKE A FEATHER IN THE BREEZE (1)

FEBRUARY 1936

LM	TM	
5	1.	ALONE (2)
6	2.	MOON OVER MIAMI (2)
18	3.	LIGHTS OUT (2)
12	4.	A BEAUTIFUL LADY IN BLUE (2)
1	5.	THE MUSIC GOES 'ROUND AND AROUND (2)
20	6.	I FEEL LIKE A FEATHER IN THE BREEZE (2)
–	7.	I'M GONNA SIT RIGHT DOWN AND WRITE MYSELF A LETTER (1)
–	8.	I'M SHOOTING HIGH (1)
–	9.	RHYTHM IN MY NURSERY RHYMES (1)
10	10.	THE BROKEN RECORD (2)
17	11.	DINNER FOR ONE, PLEASE, JAMES (2)
11	12.	WITH ALL MY HEART (2)
4	13.	RED SAILS IN THE SUNSET (4)
–	14.	I'M BUILDING UP TO AN AWFUL LET-DOWN (1)
–	15.	PLEASE BELIEVE ME (1)
3	16.	ON TREASURE ISLAND (5)
–	17.	IT'S BEEN SO LONG (1)
2	18.	A LITTLE BIT INDEPENDENT (4)
–	19.	CLING TO ME (1)
7	20.	TAKE ME BACK TO MY BOOTS AND SADDLE (4)

MARCH 1936

LM	TM	
3	1.	LIGHTS OUT (3)
1	2.	ALONE (3)
–	3.	GOODY-GOODY (1)
17	4.	IT'S BEEN SO LONG (2)
4	5.	A BEAUTIFUL LADY IN BLUE (3)
7	6.	I'M GONNA SIT RIGHT DOWN AND WRITE MYSELF A LETTER (2)
–	7.	I'M PUTTING ALL MY EGGS IN ONE BASKET (1)
15	8.	PLEASE BELIEVE ME (2)
–	9.	WA-HOO (1)
2	10.	MOON OVER MIAMI (3)
–	11.	LET'S FACE THE MUSIC AND DANCE (1)
–	12.	ALONE AT A TABLE FOR TWO (1)
8	13.	I'M SHOOTING HIGH (2)
19	14.	CLING TO ME (2)
–	15.	WHAT'S THE NAME OF THAT SONG? (1)
–	16.	LET YOURSELF GO (1)
9	17.	RHYTHM IN MY NURSERY RHYMES (2)
–	18.	A LITTLE RENDEZVOUS IN HONOLULU (1)
–	19.	WEST WIND (1)
–	20.	LOST (1)

APRIL 1936

LM	TM	
3	1.	GOODY-GOODY (2)
20	2.	LOST (2)
7	3.	I'M PUTTING ALL MY EGGS IN ONE BASKET (2)
4	4.	IT'S BEEN SO LONG (3)
16	5.	LET YOURSELF GO (2)
5	6.	A BEAUTIFUL LADY IN BLUE (4)
1	7.	LIGHTS OUT (4)
–	8.	A MELODY FROM THE SKY (1)
9	9.	WA-HOO (2)
15	10.	WHAT'S THE NAME OF THAT SONG? (2)
–	11.	YOU STARTED ME DREAMING (1)
–	12.	EVERY MINUTE OF THE HOUR (1)
–	13.	CHRISTOPHER COLUMBUS (1)
11	14.	LET'S FACE THE MUSIC AND DANCE (2)
–	15.	THE TOUCH OF YOUR LIPS (1)
–	16.	THERE IS NO GREATER LOVE (1)
2	17.	ALONE (4)
–	18.	I'M GONNA SIT RIGHT DOWN AND WRITE MYSELF A LETTER (3)
–	19.	SING AN OLD FASHIONED SONG (1)
19	20.	WEST WIND (2)

MAY 1936

LM	TM	
2	1.	LOST (3)
8	2.	A MELODY FROM THE SKY (2)
–	3.	YOU (1)
–	4.	IS IT TRUE WHAT THEY SAY ABOUT DIXIE? (1)
11	5.	YOU STARTED ME DREAMING (2)
1	6.	GOODY-GOODY (3)
–	7.	TORMENTED (1)
15	8.	THE TOUCH OF YOUR LIPS (2)
–	9.	ALL MY LIFE (1)
–	10.	ROBINS AND ROSES (1)
4	11.	IT'S BEEN SO LONG (4)
–	12.	LOVE IS LIKE A CIGARETTE (1)
13	13.	CHRISTOPHER COLUMBUS (2)
3	14.	I'M PUTTING ALL MY EGGS IN ONE BASKET (3)
–	15.	SHE SHALL HAVE MUSIC (1)
16	16.	THERE IS NO GREATER LOVE (2)
–	17.	WOULD YOU? (1)
–	18.	IT'S A SIN TO TELL A LIE (1)
–	19.	YOURS TRULY IS TRULY YOURS (1)
5	20.	LET YOURSELF GO (3)

JUNE 1936

LM	TM	
4	1.	IS IT TRUE WHAT THEY SAY ABOUT DIXIE? (2)
10	2.	ROBINS AND ROSES (2)
9	3.	ALL MY LIFE (2)
2	4.	A MELODY FROM THE SKY (3)
–	5.	THE GLORY OF LOVE (1)
18	6.	IT'S A SIN TO TELL A LIE (2)
15	7.	SHE SHALL HAVE MUSIC (2)
3	8.	YOU (2)
17	9.	WOULD YOU? (2)
1	10.	LOST (4)
–	11.	THERE'S A SMALL HOTEL (1)
7	12.	TORMENTED (2)
5	13.	YOU STARTED ME DREAMING (3)
–	14.	YOU CAN'T PULL THE WOOL OVER MY EYES (1)
8	15.	THE TOUCH OF YOUR LIPS (3)
13	16.	CHRISTOPHER COLUMBUS (3)
–	17.	THESE FOOLISH THINGS (1)
–	18.	TAKE MY HEART (1)
12	19.	LOVE IS LIKE A CIGARETTE (2)
–	20.	TWILIGHT ON THE TRAIL (1)

JULY 1936

LM	TM	Song
6	1.	IT'S A SIN TO TELL A LIE (3)
5	2.	THE GLORY OF LOVE (2)
1	3.	IS IT TRUE WHAT THEY SAY ABOUT DIXIE? (3)
17	4.	THESE FOOLISH THINGS (2)
18	5.	TAKE MY HEART (2)
11	6.	THERE'S A SMALL HOTEL (2)
9	7.	WOULD YOU? (3)
2	8.	ROBINS AND ROSES (3)
–	9.	ON THE BEACH AT BALI BALI (1)
14	10.	YOU CAN'T PULL THE WOOL OVER MY EYES (2)
7	11.	SHE SHALL HAVE MUSIC (3)
4	12.	A MELODY FROM THE SKY (4)
–	13.	LET'S SING AGAIN (1)
–	14.	NO REGRETS (1)
–	15.	CROSS PATCH (1)
–	16.	RENDEZVOUS WITH A DREAM (1)
–	17.	SHOE SHINE BOY (1)
3	18.	ALL MY LIFE (3)
–	19.	SING ME A SWING SONG (AND LET ME DANCE) (1)
8	20.	YOU (3)

AUGUST 1936

LM	TM	Song
4	1.	THESE FOOLISH THINGS (3)
9	2.	ON THE BEACH AT BALI BALI (2)
1	3.	IT'S A SIN TO TELL A LIE (4)
–	4.	WHEN I'M WITH YOU (1)
–	5.	DID I REMEMBER (1)
5	6.	TAKE MY HEART (3)
16	7.	RENDEZVOUS WITH A DREAM (2)
2	8.	THE GLORY OF LOVE (3)
14	9.	NO REGRETS (2)
7	10.	WOULD YOU? (4)
–	11.	UNTIL THE REAL THING COMES ALONG (1)
10	12.	YOU CAN'T PULL THE WOOL OVER MY EYES (3)
–	13.	A STAR FELL OUT OF HEAVEN (1)
3	14.	IS IT TRUE WHAT THEY SAY ABOUT DIXIE? (4)
15	15.	CROSS PATCH (2)
6	16.	THERE'S A SMALL HOTEL (3)
–	17.	EMPTY SADDLES (1)
–	18.	KNOCK, KNOCK, WHO'S THERE? (1)
13	19.	LET'S SING AGAIN (2)
–	20.	SWINGTIME IN THE ROCKIES (1)

SEPTEMBER 1936

LM	TM	Song
5	1.	DID I REMEMBER (2)
13	2.	A STAR FELL OUT OF HEAVEN (2)
11	3.	UNTIL THE REAL THING COMES ALONG (2)
4	4.	WHEN I'M WITH YOU (2)
–	5.	WHEN DID YOU LEAVE HEAVEN? (1)
–	6.	BYE BYE BABY (1)
7	7.	RENDEZVOUS WITH A DREAM (3)
–	8.	ME AND THE MOON (1)
–	9.	I CAN'T ESCAPE FROM YOU (1)
–	10.	I'M AN OLD COWHAND (1)
9	11.	NO REGRETS (3)
17	12.	EMPTY SADDLES (2)
2	13.	ON THE BEACH AT BALI BALI (3)
–	14.	SING, BABY, SING (1)
1	15.	THESE FOOLISH THINGS (4)
–	16.	THE WAY YOU LOOK TONIGHT (1)
18	17.	KNOCK, KNOCK, WHO'S THERE? (2)
–	18.	ORGAN GRINDER'S SWING (1)
–	19.	SING, SING, SING (1)
–	20.	SOUTH SEA ISLAND MAGIC (1)

OCTOBER 1936

LM	TM	Song
5	1.	WHEN DID YOU LEAVE HEAVEN? (2)
1	2.	DID I REMEMBER (3)
2	3.	A STAR FELL OUT OF HEAVEN (3)
16	4.	THE WAY YOU LOOK TONIGHT (2)
–	5.	A FINE ROMANCE (1)
3	6.	UNTIL THE REAL THING COMES ALONG (3)
8	7.	ME AND THE MOON (2)
14	8.	SING, BABY, SING (2)
9	9.	I CAN'T ESCAPE FROM YOU (2)
18	10.	ORGAN GRINDER'S SWING (2)
6	11.	BYE BYE BABY (2)
10	12.	I'M AN OLD COWHAND (2)
–	13.	I'LL SING YOU A THOUSAND LOVE SONGS (1)
–	14.	YOU TURNED THE TABLES ON ME (1)
–	15.	WHEN A LADY MEETS A GENTLEMAN DOWN SOUTH (1)
20	16.	SOUTH SEA ISLAND MAGIC (2)
19	17.	SING, SING, SING (2)
12	18.	EMPTY SADDLES (3)
7	19.	RENDEZVOUS WITH A DREAM (4)
–	20.	WHO LOVES YOU? (1)

NOVEMBER 1936

LM	TM	Song
4	1.	THE WAY YOU LOOK TONIGHT (3)
1	2.	WHEN DID YOU LEAVE HEAVEN? (3)
13	3.	I'LL SING YOU A THOUSAND LOVE SONGS (2)
5	4.	A FINE ROMANCE (2)
10	5.	ORGAN GRINDER'S SWING (3)
14	6.	YOU TURNED THE TABLES ON ME (2)
–	7.	IN THE CHAPEL IN THE MOONLIGHT (1)
16	8.	SOUTH SEA ISLAND MAGIC (3)
7	9.	ME AND THE MOON (3)
8	10.	SING, BABY, SING (3)
20	11.	WHO LOVES YOU? (2)
–	12.	PENNIES FROM HEAVEN (1)
–	13.	CLOSE TO ME (1)
–	14.	DID YOU MEAN IT? (1)
2	15.	DID I REMEMBER (4)
3	16.	A STAR FELL OUT OF HEAVEN (4)
–	17.	IT'S DE-LOVELY (1)
9	18.	I CAN'T ESCAPE FROM YOU (3)
–	19.	MIDNIGHT BLUE (1)
–	20.	YOU DO THE DARNDEST THINGS, BABY (1)

DECEMBER 1936

LM	TM	Song
7	1.	IN THE CHAPEL IN THE MOONLIGHT (2)
12	2.	PENNIES FROM HEAVEN (2)
1	3.	THE WAY YOU LOOK TONIGHT (4)
3	4.	I'LL SING YOU A THOUSAND LOVE SONGS (3)
17	5.	IT'S DE-LOVELY (2)
6	6.	YOU TURNED THE TABLES ON ME (3)
8	7.	SOUTH SEA ISLAND MAGIC (4)
–	8.	I'VE GOT YOU UNDER MY SKIN (1)
5	9.	ORGAN GRINDER'S SWING (4)
–	10.	I'M IN A DANCING MOOD (1)
2	11.	WHEN DID YOU LEAVE HEAVEN? (4)
14	12.	DID YOU MEAN IT? (2)
–	13.	HERE'S LOVE IN YOUR EYES (1)
4	14.	A FINE ROMANCE (3)
19	15.	MIDNIGHT BLUE (2)
–	16.	WITH PLENTY OF MONEY AND YOU (1)
–	17.	SANTA CLAUS IS COMIN' TO TOWN (1)
11	18.	WHO LOVES YOU? (3)
–	19.	I'M TALKING THROUGH MY HEART (1)
20	20.	YOU DO THE DARNDEST THINGS, BABY (2)

JANUARY 1937

LM	TM	
2	1.	PENNIES FROM HEAVEN (3)
1	2.	IN THE CHAPEL IN THE MOONLIGHT (3)
5	3.	IT'S DE-LOVELY (3)
–	4.	WHEN MY DREAM BOAT COMES HOME (1)
8	5.	I'VE GOT YOU UNDER MY SKIN (2)
10	6.	I'M IN A DANCING MOOD (2)
–	7.	THERE'S SOMETHING IN THE AIR (1)
–	8.	THE NIGHT IS YOUNG AND YOU'RE SO BEAUTIFUL (1)
–	9.	GOODNIGHT, MY LOVE (1)
–	10.	ONE, TWO, BUTTON YOUR SHOE (1)
16	11.	WITH PLENTY OF MONEY AND YOU (2)
–	12.	EASY TO LOVE (1)
4	13.	I'LL SING YOU A THOUSAND LOVE SONGS (4)
7	14.	SOUTH SEA ISLAND MAGIC (5)
3	15.	THE WAY YOU LOOK TONIGHT (5)
9	16.	ORGAN GRINDER'S SWING (5)
–	17.	SERENADE IN THE NIGHT (1)
–	18.	THERE'S FROST ON THE MOON (1)
–	19.	RAINBOW (1)
11	20.	WHEN DID YOU LEAVE HEAVEN? (5)

FEBRUARY 1937

LM	TM	
9	1.	GOODNIGHT, MY LOVE (2)
4	2.	WHEN MY DREAM BOAT COMES HOME (2)
11	3.	WITH PLENTY OF MONEY AND YOU (3)
1	4.	PENNIES FROM HEAVEN (4)
8	5.	THE NIGHT IS YOUNG AND YOU'RE SO BEAUTIFUL (2)
–	6.	THIS YEAR'S KISSES (1)
2	7.	IN THE CHAPEL IN THE MOONLIGHT (4)
–	8.	TRUST IN ME (1)
7	9.	THERE'S SOMETHING IN THE AIR (2)
19	10.	RAINBOW (2)
5	11.	I'VE GOT YOU UNDER MY SKIN (3)
17	12.	SERENADE IN THE NIGHT (2)
–	13.	MOONLIGHT AND SHADOWS (1)
–	14.	WHAT WILL I TELL MY HEART (1)
–	15.	LOVE AND LEARN (1)
3	16.	IT'S DE-LOVELY (4)
12	17.	EASY TO LOVE (2)
–	18.	I'VE GOT MY LOVE TO KEEP ME WARM (1)
10	19.	ONE, TWO, BUTTON YOUR SHOE (2)
–	20.	MAY I HAVE THE NEXT ROMANCE WITH YOU? (1)

MARCH 1937

LM	TM	
1	1.	GOODNIGHT, MY LOVE (3)
2	2.	WHEN MY DREAM BOAT COMES HOME (3)
6	3.	THIS YEAR'S KISSES (2)
13	4.	MOONLIGHT AND SHADOWS (2)
8	5.	TRUST IN ME (2)
3	6.	WITH PLENTY OF MONEY AND YOU (4)
18	7.	I'VE GOT MY LOVE TO KEEP ME WARM (2)
–	8.	LITTLE OLD LADY (1)
14	9.	WHAT WILL I TELL MY HEART (2)
12	10.	SERENADE IN THE NIGHT (3)
–	11.	BOO-HOO (1)
–	12.	ON A LITTLE BAMBOO BRIDGE (1)
20	13.	MAY I HAVE THE NEXT ROMANCE WITH YOU? (2)
–	14.	YOU'RE LAUGHING AT ME (1)
–	15.	SLUMMING ON PARK AVENUE (1)
–	16.	SMOKE DREAMS (1)
–	17.	WHEN THE POPPIES BLOOM AGAIN (1)
5	18.	THE NIGHT IS YOUNG AND YOU'RE SO BEAUTIFUL (3)
4	19.	PENNIES FROM HEAVEN (5)
–	20.	MARIE (1)

APRIL 1937

LM	TM	
11	1.	BOO-HOO (2)
8	2.	LITTLE OLD LADY (2)
4	3.	MOONLIGHT AND SHADOWS (3)
9	4.	WHAT WILL I TELL MY HEART (3)
7	5.	I'VE GOT MY LOVE TO KEEP ME WARM (3)
5	6.	TRUST IN ME (3)
17	7.	WHEN THE POPPIES BLOOM AGAIN (2)
2	8.	WHEN MY DREAM BOAT COMES HOME (4)
–	9.	TOO MARVELOUS FOR WORDS (1)
1	10.	GOODNIGHT, MY LOVE (4)
20	11.	MARIE (2)
–	12.	SEPTEMBER IN THE RAIN (1)
–	13.	WILL YOU REMEMBER (SWEETHEART) (1)
12	14.	ON A LITTLE BAMBOO BRIDGE (2)
3	15.	THIS YEAR'S KISSES (3)
–	16.	SWEET IS THE WORD FOR YOU (1)
–	17.	WHERE ARE YOU? (1)
–	18.	JOSEPHINE (1)
–	19.	SWEET LEILANI (1)
10	20.	SERENADE IN THE NIGHT (4)

MAY 1937

LM	TM	
12	1.	SEPTEMBER IN THE RAIN (2)
2	2.	LITTLE OLD LADY (3)
1	3.	BOO-HOO (3)
–	4.	CARELESSLY (1)
9	5.	TOO MARVELOUS FOR WORDS (2)
–	6.	THE LOVE BUG WILL BITE YOU (1)
19	7.	SWEET LEILANI (2)
–	8.	NEVER IN A MILLION YEARS (1)
3	9.	MOONLIGHT AND SHADOWS (4)
13	10.	WILL YOU REMEMBER (SWEETHEART) (2)
17	11.	WHERE ARE YOU? (2)
–	12.	THEY CAN'T TAKE THAT AWAY FROM ME (1)
–	13.	BLUE HAWAII (1)
4	14.	WHAT WILL I TELL MY HEART (4)
–	15.	LET'S CALL THE WHOLE THING OFF (1)
–	16.	THERE'S A LULL IN MY LIFE (1)
16	17.	SWEET IS THE WORD FOR YOU (2)
–	18.	HOW COULD YOU? (1)
–	19.	THEY ALL LAUGHED (1)
–	20.	WAS IT RAIN? (1)

JUNE 1937

LM	TM	
1	1.	SEPTEMBER IN THE RAIN (3)
7	2.	SWEET LEILANI (3)
4	3.	CARELESSLY (2)
8	4.	NEVER IN A MILLION YEARS (2)
–	5.	IT LOOKS LIKE RAIN IN CHERRY BLOSSOM LANE (1)
12	6.	THEY CAN'T TAKE THAT AWAY FROM ME (2)
16	7.	THERE'S A LULL IN MY LIFE (2)
13	8.	BLUE HAWAII (2)
6	9.	THE LOVE BUG WILL BITE YOU (2)
11	10.	WHERE ARE YOU? (3)
–	11.	THE MERRY GO ROUND BROKE DOWN (1)
20	12.	WAS IT RAIN? (2)
2	13.	LITTLE OLD LADY (4)
–	14.	WHERE OR WHEN (1)
10	15.	WILL YOU REMEMBER (SWEETHEART) (3)
19	16.	THEY ALL LAUGHED (2)
–	17.	A SAILBOAT IN THE MOONLIGHT (1)
5	18.	TOO MARVELOUS FOR WORDS (3)
15	19.	LET'S CALL THE WHOLE THING OFF (2)
–	20.	THE YOU AND ME THAT USED TO BE (1)

JULY 1937

LM	TM	
5	1.	IT LOOKS LIKE RAIN IN CHERRY BLOSSOM LANE (2)
11	2.	THE MERRY GO ROUND BROKE DOWN (2)
17	3.	A SAILBOAT IN THE MOONLIGHT (2)
2	4.	SWEET LEILANI (4)
14	5.	WHERE OR WHEN (2)
1	6.	SEPTEMBER IN THE RAIN (4)
20	7.	THE YOU AND ME THAT USED TO BE (2)
8	8.	BLUE HAWAII (3)
4	9.	NEVER IN A MILLION YEARS (3)
–	10.	I KNOW NOW (1)
7	11.	THERE'S A LULL IN MY LIFE (3)
6	12.	THEY CAN'T TAKE THAT AWAY FROM ME (3)
12	13.	WAS IT RAIN? (3)
3	14.	CARELESSLY (3)
–	15.	GONE WITH THE WIND (1)
–	16.	OUR PENTHOUSE ON THIRD AVENUE (1)
–	17.	TOODLE-OO (1)
–	18.	SO RARE (1)
–	19.	THE DREAM IN MY HEART (1)
–	20.	'CAUSE MY BABY SAYS IT'S SO (1)

AUGUST 1937

LM	TM	
3	1.	A SAILBOAT IN THE MOONLIGHT (3)
1	2.	IT LOOKS LIKE RAIN IN CHERRY BLOSSOM LANE (3)
18	3.	SO RARE (2)
10	4.	I KNOW NOW (2)
2	5.	THE MERRY GO ROUND BROKE DOWN (3)
5	6.	WHERE OR WHEN (3)
4	7.	SWEET LEILANI (5)
15	8.	GONE WITH THE WIND (2)
–	9.	WHISPERS IN THE DARK (1)
–	10.	THE FIRST TIME I SAW YOU (1)
–	11.	MY CABIN OF DREAMS (1)
–	12.	SATAN TAKES A HOLIDAY (1)
8	13.	BLUE HAWAII (4)
–	14.	CARAVAN (1)
7	15.	THE YOU AND ME THAT USED TO BE (3)
–	16.	HARBOR LIGHTS (1)
–	17.	STARDUST ON THE MOON (1)
16	18.	OUR PENTHOUSE ON THIRD AVENUE (2)
–	19.	STOP! YOU'RE BREAKING MY HEART (1)
–	20.	ME, MYSELF AND I (ARE ALL IN LOVE WITH YOU) (1)

SEPTEMBER 1937

LM	TM	
3	1.	SO RARE (3)
9	2.	WHISPERS IN THE DARK (2)
11	3.	MY CABIN OF DREAMS (2)
–	4.	THAT OLD FEELING (1)
16	5.	HARBOR LIGHTS (2)
4	6.	I KNOW NOW (3)
10	7.	THE FIRST TIME I SAW YOU (2)
1	8.	A SAILBOAT IN THE MOONLIGHT (4)
–	9.	HAVE YOU GOT ANY CASTLES, BABY? (1)
–	10.	AFRAID TO DREAM (1)
–	11.	THE MOON GOT IN MY EYES (1)
2	12.	IT LOOKS LIKE RAIN IN CHERRY BLOSSOM LANE (4)
12	13.	SATAN TAKES A HOLIDAY (2)
–	14.	IT'S THE NATURAL THING TO DO (1)
17	15.	STARDUST ON THE MOON (2)
8	16.	GONE WITH THE WIND (3)
14	17.	CARAVAN (2)
–	18.	REMEMBER ME? (1)
–	19.	THE BIG APPLE (1)
–	20.	YOURS AND MINE (1)

OCTOBER 1937

LM	TM	
4	1.	THAT OLD FEELING (2)
11	2.	THE MOON GOT IN MY EYES (2)
18	3.	REMEMBER ME? (2)
2	4.	WHISPERS IN THE DARK (3)
9	5.	HAVE YOU GOT ANY CASTLES, BABY? (2)
3	6.	MY CABIN OF DREAMS (3)
5	7.	HARBOR LIGHTS (3)
–	8.	ROSES IN DECEMBER (1)
–	9.	YOU CAN'T STOP ME FROM DREAMING (1)
10	10.	AFRAID TO DREAM (2)
1	11.	SO RARE (4)
–	12.	JOSEPHINE (2)
19	13.	THE BIG APPLE (2)
–	14.	SO MANY MEMORIES (1)
–	15.	THE ONE ROSE (1)
7	16.	THE FIRST TIME I SAW YOU (3)
14	17.	IT'S THE NATURAL THING TO DO (2)
–	18.	CAN I FORGET YOU? (1)
–	19.	VIENI, VIENI (1)
–	20.	BLOSSOMS ON BROADWAY (1)

NOVEMBER 1937

LM	TM	
9	1.	YOU CAN'T STOP ME FROM DREAMING (2)
19	2.	VIENI, VIENI (2)
3	3.	REMEMBER ME? (3)
20	4.	BLOSSOMS ON BROADWAY (2)
–	5.	ONCE IN AWHILE (1)
8	6.	ROSES IN DECEMBER (2)
7	7.	HARBOR LIGHTS (4)
15	8.	THE ONE ROSE (2)
1	9.	THAT OLD FEELING (3)
2	10.	THE MOON GOT IN MY EYES (3)
–	11.	IF IT'S THE LAST THING I DO (1)
6	12.	MY CABIN OF DREAMS (4)
–	13.	I STILL LOVE TO KISS YOU GOODNIGHT (1)
14	14.	SO MANY MEMORIES (2)
–	15.	NICE WORK IF YOU CAN GET IT (1)
12	16.	JOSEPHINE (3)
5	17.	HAVE YOU GOT ANY CASTLES, BABY? (3)
–	18.	FAREWELL, MY LOVE (1)
–	19.	EBB TIDE (1)
–	20.	YOU AND I KNOW (1)

DECEMBER 1937

LM	TM	
5	1.	ONCE IN AWHILE (2)
2	2.	VIENI, VIENI (3)
15	3.	NICE WORK IF YOU CAN GET IT (2)
1	4.	YOU CAN'T STOP ME FROM DREAMING (3)
–	5.	ROSALIE (1)
4	6.	BLOSSOMS ON BROADWAY (3)
13	7.	I STILL LOVE TO KISS YOU GOODNIGHT (2)
11	8.	IF IT'S THE LAST THING I DO (2)
8	9.	THE ONE ROSE (3)
–	10.	BOB WHITE (WHATCHA GONNA SWING TONIGHT?) (1)
7	11.	HARBOR LIGHTS (5)
18	12.	FAREWELL, MY LOVE (2)
19	13.	EBB TIDE (2)
–	14.	THERE'S A GOLD MINE IN THE SKY (1)
–	15.	A FOGGY DAY (1)
6	16.	ROSES IN DECEMBER (3)
–	17.	IN THE STILL OF THE NIGHT (1)
–	18.	THE DIPSY DOODLE (1)
–	19.	WHEN THE (MIGHTY) ORGAN PLAYED OH PROMISE ME (1)
3	20.	REMEMBER ME? (4)

JANUARY 1938

LM	TM	
5	1.	ROSALIE (2)
–	2.	TRUE CONFESSION (1)
1	3.	ONCE IN AWHILE (3)
14	4.	THERE'S A GOLD MINE IN THE SKY (2)
–	5.	BEI MIR BIST DU SCHOEN (1)
18	6.	THE DIPSY DOODLE (2)
3	7.	NICE WORK IF YOU CAN GET IT (3)
–	8.	YOU'RE A SWEETHEART (1)
10	9.	BOB WHITE (WHATCHA GONNA SWING TONIGHT?) (2)
19	10.	WHEN THE (MIGHTY) ORGAN PLAYED OH PROMISE ME (2)
9	11.	THE ONE ROSE (4)
–	12.	I DOUBLE DARE YOU (1)
2	14.	VIENI, VIENI (4)
–	13.	SWEET SOMEONE (1)
4	15.	YOU CAN'T STOP ME FROM DREAMING (4)
–	16.	JOSEPHINE (4)
17	17.	IN THE STILL OF THE NIGHT (2)
–	18.	SAIL ALONG, SILV'RY MOON (1)
–	19.	THANKS FOR THE MEMORY (1)
–	20.	YOU TOOK THE WORDS RIGHT OUT OF MY HEART (1)

FEBRUARY 1938

LM	TM	
5	1.	BEI MIR BIST DU SCHOEN (2)
12	2.	I DOUBLE DARE YOU (2)
8	3.	YOU'RE A SWEETHEART (2)
6	4.	THE DIPSY DOODLE (3)
19	5.	THANKS FOR THE MEMORY (2)
1	6.	ROSALIE (3)
3	7.	THERE'S A GOLD MINE IN THE SKY (3)
–	8.	WHISTLE WHILE YOU WORK (1)
2	9.	TRUE CONFESSION (2)
20	10.	YOU TOOK THE WORDS RIGHT OUT OF MY HEART (2)
–	11.	SWEET AS A SONG (1)
–	12.	TEN PRETTY GIRLS (1)
13	13.	SWEET SOMEONE (2)
7	14.	NICE WORK IF YOU CAN GET IT (4)
–	15.	MAMA, THAT MOON IS HERE AGAIN (1)
10	16.	WHEN THE (MIGHTY) ORGAN PLAYED OH PROMISE ME (3)
–	17.	I CAN DREAM, CAN'T I? (1)
–	18.	THE MOON OF MANAKOORA (1)
18	19.	SAIL ALONG, SILV'RY MOON (2)
–	20.	A GYPSY TOLD ME (1)

MARCH 1938

LM	TM	
5	1.	THANKS FOR THE MEMORY (3)
8	2.	WHISTLE WHILE YOU WORK (2)
2	3.	I DOUBLE DARE YOU (3)
11	4.	SWEET AS A SONG (2)
–	5.	GOODNIGHT, ANGEL (1)
7	6.	THERE'S A GOLD MINE IN THE SKY (4)
–	7.	HEIGH-HO (1)
–	8.	TI-PI-TIN (1)
17	9.	I CAN DREAM, CAN'T I? (2)
4	10.	THE DIPSY DOODLE (4)
1	11.	BEI MIR BIST DU SCHOEN (3)
20	12.	A GYPSY TOLD ME (2)
–	13.	MORE THAN EVER (1)
18	14.	THE MOON OF MANAKOORA (2)
3	15.	YOU'RE A SWEETHEART (3)
–	16.	IT'S WONDERFUL (1)
12	17.	TEN PRETTY GIRLS (2)
–	18.	PLEASE BE KIND (1)
–	19.	LOVE WALKED IN (1)
–	20.	YOU'RE AN EDUCATION (1)

APRIL 1938

LM	TM	
8	1.	TI-PI-TIN (2)
7	2.	HEIGH-HO (2)
18	3.	PLEASE BE KIND (2)
2	4.	WHISTLE WHILE YOU WORK (3)
5	5.	GOODNIGHT, ANGEL (2)
19	6.	LOVE WALKED IN (2)
1	7.	THANKS FOR THE MEMORY (4)
20	8.	YOU'RE AN EDUCATION (2)
6	9.	THERE'S A GOLD MINE IN THE SKY (5)
–	10.	HOWDJA LIKE TO LOVE ME (1)
–	11.	DON'T BE THAT WAY (1)
–	12.	ON THE SENTIMENTAL SIDE (1)
16	13.	IT'S WONDERFUL (2)
–	14.	LET'S SAIL TO DREAMLAND (1)
3	15.	I DOUBLE DARE YOU (4)
–	16.	I LOVE TO WHISTLE (1)
–	17.	I FALL IN LOVE WITH YOU EVERY DAY (1)
–	18.	THE OLD APPLE TREE (1)
12	19.	A GYPSY TOLD ME (3)
–	20.	ALWAYS AND ALWAYS (1)

MAY 1938

LM	TM	
6	1.	LOVE WALKED IN (3)
1	2.	TI-PI-TIN (3)
3	3.	PLEASE BE KIND (3)
11	4.	DON'T BE THAT WAY (2)
–	5.	CRY, BABY, CRY (1)
12	6.	ON THE SENTIMENTAL SIDE (2)
16	7.	I LOVE TO WHISTLE (2)
–	8.	YOU COULDN'T BE CUTER (1)
2	9.	HEIGH-HO (3)
5	10.	GOODNIGHT, ANGEL (3)
8	11.	YOU'RE AN EDUCATION (3)
10	12.	HOWDJA LIKE TO LOVE ME (2)
17	13.	I FALL IN LOVE WITH YOU EVERY DAY (2)
–	14.	AT A PERFUME COUNTER (1)
–	15.	MARTHA (1)
–	16.	I LET A SONG GO OUT OF MY HEART (1)
4	17.	WHISTLE WHILE YOU WORK (4)
–	18.	BEWILDERED (1)
–	19.	SOMETHING TELLS ME (1)
20	20.	ALWAYS AND ALWAYS (2)

JUNE 1938

LM	TM	
5	1.	CRY, BABY, CRY (2)
–	2.	SAYS MY HEART (1)
3	3.	PLEASE BE KIND (4)
–	4.	CATHEDRAL IN THE PINES (1)
16	5.	I LET A SONG GO OUT OF MY HEART (2)
1	6.	LOVE WALKED IN (4)
–	7.	LOVELIGHT IN THE STARLIGHT (1)
4	8.	DON'T BE THAT WAY (3)
–	9.	YOU LEAVE ME BREATHLESS (1)
–	10.	OH! MA-MA (1)
8	11.	YOU COULDN'T BE CUTER (2)
–	12.	THIS TIME IT'S REAL (1)
15	13.	MARTHA (2)
–	14.	MUSIC, MAESTRO, PLEASE (1)
2	15.	TI-PI-TIN (4)
–	16.	FLAT FOOT FLUGEY (1)
7	17.	I LOVE TO WHISTLE (3)
–	18.	LITTLE LADY MAKE BELIEVE (1)
–	19.	THE GIRL IN THE BONNET OF BLUE (1)
14	20.	AT A PERFUME COUNTER (2)

JULY 1938

LM	TM	
5	1.	I LET A SONG GO OUT OF MY HEART (3)
2	2.	SAYS MY HEART (2)
14	3.	MUSIC, MAESTRO, PLEASE (2)
4	4.	CATHEDRAL IN THE PINES (2)
9	5.	YOU LEAVE ME BREATHLESS (2)
–	6.	I HADN'T ANYONE TILL YOU (1)
7	7.	LOVELIGHT IN THE STARLIGHT (2)
16	8.	FLAT FOOT FLUGEY (2)
–	9.	I MARRIED AN ANGEL (1)
10	10.	OH! MA-MA (2)
1	11.	CRY, BABY, CRY (3)
18	12.	LITTLE LADY MAKE BELIEVE (2)
12	13.	THIS TIME IT'S REAL (2)
–	14.	A-TISKET, A-TASKET (1)
3	15.	PLEASE BE KIND (5)
–	16.	THERE'S HONEY ON THE MOON TONIGHT (1)
–	17.	LET ME WHISPER (I LOVE YOU) (1)
6	18.	LOVE WALKED IN (5)
–	19.	WHEN THEY PLAYED THE POLKA (1)
–	20.	DAY DREAMING (ALL NIGHT LONG) (1)

AUGUST 1938

LM	TM	
3	1.	MUSIC, MAESTRO, PLEASE (3)
14	2.	A-TISKET, A-TASKET (2)
1	3.	I LET A SONG GO OUT OF MY HEART (4)
–	4.	WHEN MOTHER NATURE SINGS HER LULLABY (1)
–	5.	NOW IT CAN BE TOLD (1)
2	6.	SAYS MY HEART (3)
–	7.	I'M GONNA LOCK MY HEART (1)
4	8.	CATHEDRAL IN THE PINES (3)
6	9.	I HADN'T ANYONE TILL YOU (2)
–	10.	YOU GO TO MY HEAD (1)
8	11.	FLAT FOOT FLUGEY (3)
19	12.	WHEN THEY PLAYED THE POLKA (2)
12	13.	LITTLE LADY MAKE BELIEVE (3)
–	14.	OL' MAN MOSE (1)
9	15.	I MARRIED AN ANGEL (2)
–	16.	I'VE GOT A POCKETFUL OF DREAMS (1)
–	17.	WHERE IN THE WORLD (1)
–	18.	WHAT GOES ON HERE IN MY HEART (1)
16	19.	THERE'S HONEY ON THE MOON TONIGHT (2)
7	20.	LOVELIGHT IN THE STARLIGHT (3)

SEPTEMBER 1938

LM	TM	
2	1.	A-TISKET, A-TASKET (3)
16	2.	I'VE GOT A POCKETFUL OF DREAMS (2)
5	3.	NOW IT CAN BE TOLD (2)
–	4.	ALEXANDER'S RAGTIME BAND (1)
10	5.	YOU GO TO MY HEAD (2)
7	6.	I'M GONNA LOCK MY HEART (2)
1	7.	MUSIC, MAESTRO, PLEASE (4)
–	8.	STOP BEATIN' 'ROUND THE MULBERRY BUSH (1)
4	9.	WHEN MOTHER NATURE SINGS HER LULLABY (2)
–	10.	SO HELP ME (IF I DON'T LOVE YOU) (1)
18	11.	WHAT GOES ON HERE IN MY HEART (2)
–	12.	SMALL FRY (1)
14	13.	OL' MAN MOSE (2)
–	14.	CHANGE PARTNERS (1)
3	15.	I LET A SONG GO OUT OF MY HEART (5)
–	16.	GARDEN OF THE MOON (1)
–	17.	I'VE GOT A DATE WITH A DREAM (1)
–	18.	BAMBINA (1)
–	19.	THERE'S A FARAWAY LOOK IN YOUR EYE (1)
9	20.	I HADN'T ANYONE TILL YOU (3)

OCTOBER 1938

LM	TM	
2	1.	I'VE GOT A POCKETFUL OF DREAMS (3)
14	2.	CHANGE PARTNERS (2)
4	3.	ALEXANDER'S RAGTIME BAND (2)
10	4.	SO HELP ME (IF I DON'T LOVE YOU) (2)
17	5.	I'VE GOT A DATE WITH A DREAM (2)
–	6.	THE LAMBETH WALK (1)
8	7.	STOP BEATIN' 'ROUND THE MULBERRY BUSH (2)
12	8.	SMALL FRY (2)
1	9.	A-TISKET, A-TASKET (4)
–	10.	MY REVERIE (1)
11	11.	WHAT GOES ON HERE IN MY HEART (3)
–	12.	BEGIN THE BEGUINE (1)
–	13.	AT LONG LAST LOVE (1)
3	14.	NOW IT CAN BE TOLD (3)
–	15.	HEART AND SOUL (1)
9	16.	WHEN MOTHER NATURE SINGS HER LULLABY (3)
6	17.	I'M GONNA LOCK MY HEART (3)
16	18.	GARDEN OF THE MOON (2)
5	19.	YOU GO TO MY HEAD (3)
–	20.	WHILE A CIGARETTE WAS BURNING (1)

NOVEMBER 1938

LM	TM	
10	1.	MY REVERIE (2)
1	2.	I'VE GOT A POCKETFUL OF DREAMS (4)
15	3.	HEART AND SOUL (2)
20	4.	WHILE A CIGARETTE WAS BURNING (2)
2	5.	CHANGE PARTNERS (3)
–	6.	ALL ASHORE (1)
–	7.	MY OWN (1)
6	8.	THE LAMBETH WALK (2)
3	9.	ALEXANDER'S RAGTIME BAND (3)
–	10.	SUMMER SOUVENIRS (1)
–	11.	TWO SLEEPY PEOPLE (1)
12	12.	BEGIN THE BEGUINE (2)
–	13.	I WON'T TELL A SOUL (1)
13	14.	AT LONG LAST LOVE (2)
–	15.	WHO BLEW OUT THE FLAME? (1)
–	16.	MEXICALI ROSE (1)
4	17.	SO HELP ME (IF I DON'T LOVE YOU) (3)
8	18.	SMALL FRY (3)
–	19.	BOOGIE WOOGIE (1)
–	20.	SIXTY SECONDS GOT TOGETHER (1)

DECEMBER 1938

LM	TM	
1	1.	MY REVERIE (3)
11	2.	TWO SLEEPY PEOPLE (2)
6	3.	ALL ASHORE (2)
–	4.	YOU MUST HAVE BEEN A BEAUTIFUL BABY (1)
3	5.	HEART AND SOUL (3)
13	6.	I WON'T TELL A SOUL (2)
4	7.	WHILE A CIGARETTE WAS BURNING (3)
–	8.	HAVE YOU FORGOTTEN SO SOON? (1)
7	9.	MY OWN (2)
–	10.	DEEP IN A DREAM (1)
8	11.	THE LAMBETH WALK (3)
–	12.	THE UMBRELLA MAN (1)
12	13.	BEGIN THE BEGUINE (3)
–	14.	(DON'T WAIT TIL) THE NIGHT BEFORE CHRISTMAS (1)
15	15.	WHO BLEW OUT THE FLAME? (2)
–	16.	WHAT HAVE YOU GOT THAT GETS ME? (1)
2	17.	I'VE GOT A POCKETFUL OF DREAMS (5)
10	18.	SUMMER SOUVENIRS (2)
–	19.	DAY AFTER DAY (1)
–	20.	THEY SAY (1)

JANUARY 1939

LM	TM	
4	1.	YOU MUST HAVE BEEN A BEAUTIFUL BABY (2)
1	2.	MY REVERIE (4)
10	3.	DEEP IN A DREAM (2)
12	4.	THE UMBRELLA MAN (2)
–	5.	JEEPERS, CREEPERS (1)
–	6.	THIS CAN'T BE LOVE (1)
2	7.	TWO SLEEPY PEOPLE (3)
–	8.	THANKS FOR EVERYTHING (1)
–	9.	I MUST SEE ANNIE TONIGHT (1)
20	10.	THEY SAY (2)
3	11.	ALL ASHORE (3)
–	12.	I HAVE EYES (1)
–	13.	F.D.R. JONES (1)
–	14.	HURRY HOME (1)
–	15.	ANGELS WITH DIRTY FACES (1)
6	16.	I WON'T TELL A SOUL (3)
–	17.	YOU'RE A SWEET LITTLE HEADACHE (1)
–	18.	YOU'RE THE ONLY STAR (IN MY BLUE HEAVEN) (1)
–	19.	GET OUT OF TOWN (1)
–	20.	FERDINAND THE BULL (1)

FEBRUARY 1939

LM	TM	
5	1.	JEEPERS, CREEPERS (2)
4	2.	THE UMBRELLA MAN (3)
3	3.	DEEP IN A DREAM (3)
12	4.	I HAVE EYES (2)
6	5.	THIS CAN'T BE LOVE (2)
10	6.	THEY SAY (3)
14	7.	HURRY HOME (2)
8	8.	THANKS FOR EVERYTHING (2)
17	9.	YOU'RE A SWEET LITTLE HEADACHE (2)
1	10.	YOU MUST HAVE BEEN A BEAUTIFUL BABY (3)
13	11.	F.D.R. JONES (2)
–	12.	DEEP PURPLE (1)
–	13.	COULD BE (1)
19	14.	GET OUT OF TOWN (2)
–	15.	THE FUNNY OLD HILLS (1)
–	16.	PENNY SERENADE (1)
9	17.	I MUST SEE ANNIE TONIGHT (2)
7	18.	TWO SLEEPY PEOPLE (4)
–	19.	HOLD TIGHT, HOLD TIGHT (1)
2	20.	MY REVERIE (5)

MARCH 1939

LM	TM	
12	1.	DEEP PURPLE (2)
16	2.	PENNY SERENADE (2)
2	3.	THE UMBRELLA MAN (4)
13	4.	COULD BE (2)
4	5.	I HAVE EYES (3)
9	6.	YOU'RE A SWEET LITTLE HEADACHE (3)
–	7.	I CRIED FOR YOU (1)
–	8.	THE MASQUERADE IS OVER (1)
–	9.	LITTLE SIR ECHO (1)
–	10.	I GET ALONG WITHOUT YOU VERY WELL (1)
5	11.	THIS CAN'T BE LOVE (3)
3	12.	DEEP IN A DREAM (4)
19	13.	HOLD TIGHT, HOLD TIGHT (2)
6	14.	THEY SAY (4)
–	15.	I PROMISE YOU (1)
1	16.	JEEPERS, CREEPERS (3)
–	17.	GOD BLESS AMERICA (1)
–	18.	GOTTA GET SOME SHUTEYE (1)
–	19.	GOOD FOR NOTHIN' BUT LOVE (1)
–	20.	MY HEART BELONGS TO DADDY (1)

APRIL 1939

LM	TM	
1	1.	DEEP PURPLE (3)
2	2.	PENNY SERENADE (3)
9	3.	LITTLE SIR ECHO (2)
10	4.	I GET ALONG WITHOUT YOU VERY WELL (2)
–	5.	HEAVEN CAN WAIT (1)
8	6.	THE MASQUERADE IS OVER (2)
13	7.	HOLD TIGHT, HOLD TIGHT (3)
4	8.	COULD BE (3)
17	9.	GOD BLESS AMERICA (2)
3	10.	THE UMBRELLA MAN (5)
–	11.	THE MOON IS A SILVER DOLLAR (1)
–	12.	OUR LOVE (1)
7	13.	I CRIED FOR YOU (2)
–	14.	THIS IS IT (1)
18	15.	GOTTA GET SOME SHUTEYE (2)
–	16.	LITTLE SKIPPER (1)
–	17.	AND THE ANGELS SING (1)
6	18.	YOU'RE A SWEET LITTLE HEADACHE (4)
15	19.	I PROMISE YOU (2)
–	20.	WE'VE COME A LONG WAY TOGETHER (1)

MAY 1939

LM	TM	
17	1.	AND THE ANGELS SING (2)
12	2.	OUR LOVE (2)
3	3.	LITTLE SIR ECHO (3)
–	4.	THREE LITTLE FISHIES (ITTY BITTY POO) (1)
5	5.	HEAVEN CAN WAIT (2)
16	6.	LITTLE SKIPPER (2)
–	7.	BEER BARREL POLKA (1)
–	8.	DON'T WORRY 'BOUT ME (1)
–	9.	WISHING (1)
2	10.	PENNY SERENADE (4)
–	11.	I'M BUILDING A SAILBOAT OF DREAMS (1)
1	12.	DEEP PURPLE (4)
–	13.	THE EAST SIDE OF HEAVEN (1)
–	14.	SUNRISE SERENADE (1)
4	15.	I GET ALONG WITHOUT YOU VERY WELL (3)
6	16.	THE MASQUERADE IS OVER (3)
–	17.	IF I DIDN'T CARE (1)
9	18.	GOD BLESS AMERICA (3)
–	19.	TEARS FROM MY INKWELL (1)
–	20.	THE LADY'S IN LOVE WITH YOU (1)

JUNE 1939

LM	TM	
9	1.	WISHING (2)
4	2.	THREE LITTLE FISHIES (ITTY BITTY POO) (2)
7	3.	BEER BARREL POLKA (2)
1	4.	AND THE ANGELS SING (3)
8	5.	DON'T WORRY 'BOUT ME (2)
14	6.	SUNRISE SERENADE (2)
2	7.	OUR LOVE (3)
20	8.	THE LADY'S IN LOVE WITH YOU (2)
3	9.	LITTLE SIR ECHO (4)
17	10.	IF I DIDN'T CARE (2)
6	11.	LITTLE SKIPPER (3)
–	12.	A NEW MOON AND AN OLD SERENADE (1)
–	13.	I NEVER KNEW HEAVEN COULD SPEAK (1)
–	14.	IN THE MIDDLE OF A DREAM (1)
5	15.	HEAVEN CAN WAIT (3)
–	16.	STRANGE ENCHANTMENT (1)
–	17.	WOODCHOPPERS' BALL (1)
–	18.	MY LAST GOODBYE (1)
18	19.	GOD BLESS AMERICA (4)
13	20.	THE EAST SIDE OF HEAVEN (2)

JULY 1939

LM	TM	
1	1.	WISHING (3)
–	2.	STAIRWAY TO THE STARS (1)
3	3.	BEER BARREL POLKA (3)
6	4.	SUNRISE SERENADE (3)
–	5.	WHITE SAILS (1)
8	6.	THE LADY'S IN LOVE WITH YOU (3)
16	7.	STRANGE ENCHANTMENT (2)
10	8.	IF I DIDN'T CARE (3)
–	9.	MOON LOVE (1)
14	10.	IN THE MIDDLE OF A DREAM (2)
5	11.	DON'T WORRY 'BOUT ME (3)
2	12.	THREE LITTLE FISHIES (ITTY BITTY POO) (3)
–	13.	COMES LOVE (1)
–	14.	WELL, ALL RIGHT! (1)
–	15.	I POURED MY HEART INTO A SONG (1)
–	16.	CONCERT IN THE PARK (1)
12	17.	A NEW MOON AND AN OLD SERENADE (2)
–	18.	THIS IS NO DREAM (1)
9	19.	LITTLE SIR ECHO (5)
–	20.	CINDERELLA, STAY IN MY ARMS (1)

AUGUST 1939

LM	TM	
2	1.	STAIRWAY TO THE STARS (2)
9	2.	MOON LOVE (2)
3	3.	BEER BARREL POLKA (4)
5	4.	WHITE SAILS (2)
15	5.	I POURED MY HEART INTO A SONG (2)
4	6.	SUNRISE SERENADE (4)
–	7.	THE LAMP IS LOW (1)
1	8.	WISHING (4)
20	9.	CINDERELLA, STAY IN MY ARMS (2)
13	10.	COMES LOVE (2)
–	11.	TO YOU (1)
14	12.	WELL, ALL RIGHT! (2)
–	13.	OVER THE RAINBOW (1)
8	14.	IF I DIDN'T CARE (4)
–	15.	OH, YOU CRAZY MOON (1)
–	16.	MOONLIGHT SERENADE (1)
18	17.	THIS IS NO DREAM (2)
–	18.	THE MAN WITH THE MANDOLIN (1)
–	19.	THE JUMPIN' JIVE (1)
–	20.	ESPECIALLY FOR YOU (1)

SEPTEMBER 1939

LM	TM	
13	1.	OVER THE RAINBOW (2)
2	2.	MOON LOVE (3)
3	3.	BEER BARREL POLKA (5)
18	4.	THE MAN WITH THE MANDOLIN (2)
15	5.	OH, YOU CRAZY MOON (2)
10	6.	COMES LOVE (3)
1	7.	STAIRWAY TO THE STARS (3)
5	8.	I POURED MY HEART INTO A SONG (3)
7	9.	THE LAMP IS LOW (2)
6	10.	SUNRISE SERENADE (5)
19	11.	THE JUMPIN' JIVE (2)
16	12.	MOONLIGHT SERENADE (2)
9	13.	CINDERELLA, STAY IN MY ARMS (3)
–	14.	AN APPLE FOR THE TEACHER (1)
11	15.	TO YOU (2)
–	16.	A MAN AND HIS DREAM (1)
–	17.	DAY IN - DAY OUT (1)
4	18.	WHITE SAILS (3)
–	19.	GO FLY A KITE (1)
–	20.	IN AN EIGHTEENTH CENTURY DRAWING ROOM (1)

OCTOBER 1939

LM	TM	
1	1.	OVER THE RAINBOW (3)
4	2.	THE MAN WITH THE MANDOLIN (3)
17	3.	DAY IN - DAY OUT (2)
14	4.	AN APPLE FOR THE TEACHER (2)
–	5.	BLUE ORCHIDS (1)
5	6.	OH, YOU CRAZY MOON (3)
–	7.	WHAT'S NEW? (1)
–	8.	SOUTH OF THE BORDER (1)
3	9.	BEER BARREL POLKA (6)
20	10.	IN AN EIGHTEENTH CENTURY DRAWING ROOM (2)
16	11.	A MAN AND HIS DREAM (2)
12	12.	MOONLIGHT SERENADE (3)
2	13.	MOON LOVE (4)
–	14.	MY PRAYER (1)
10	15.	SUNRISE SERENADE (6)
–	16.	ARE YOU HAVIN' ANY FUN? (1)
–	17.	(ALLA EN) EL RANCHO GRANDE (1)
–	18.	THE LITTLE MAN WHO WASN'T THERE (1)
11	19.	THE JUMPIN' JIVE (3)
–	20.	ADDRESS UNKNOWN (1)

NOVEMBER 1939

LM	TM	
8	1.	SOUTH OF THE BORDER (2)
–	2.	SCATTERBRAIN (1)
5	3.	BLUE ORCHIDS (2)
1	4.	OVER THE RAINBOW (4)
14	5.	MY PRAYER (2)
–	6.	LILACS IN THE RAIN (1)
2	7.	THE MAN WITH THE MANDOLIN (4)
17	8.	(ALLA EN) EL RANCHO GRANDE (2)
7	9.	WHAT'S NEW? (2)
3	10.	DAY IN - DAY OUT (3)
–	11.	(WHY COULDN'T IT LAST) LAST NIGHT? (1)
16	12.	ARE YOU HAVIN' ANY FUN? (2)
20	13.	ADDRESS UNKNOWN (2)
4	14.	AN APPLE FOR THE TEACHER (3)
–	15.	GOOD MORNING (1)
–	16.	IN THE MOOD (1)
10	17.	IN AN EIGHTEENTH CENTURY DRAWING ROOM (3)
9	18.	BEER BARREL POLKA (7)
–	19.	I DIDN'T KNOW WHAT TIME IT WAS (1)
–	20.	IT'S A HUNDRED TO ONE (1)

DECEMBER 1939

LM	TM	
2	1.	SCATTERBRAIN (2)
1	2.	SOUTH OF THE BORDER (3)
5	3.	MY PRAYER (3)
6	4.	LILACS IN THE RAIN (2)
–	5.	OH JOHNNY, OH JOHNNY, OH! (1)
19	6.	I DIDN'T KNOW WHAT TIME IT WAS (2)
8	7.	(ALLA EN) EL RANCHO GRANDE (3)
3	8.	BLUE ORCHIDS (3)
16	9.	IN THE MOOD (2)
11	10.	(WHY COULDN'T IT LAST) LAST NIGHT? (2)
–	11.	STOP! IT'S WONDERFUL (1)
4	12.	OVER THE RAINBOW (5)
–	13.	GOODY GOODBYE (1)
–	14.	ALL THE THINGS YOU ARE (1)
9	15.	WHAT'S NEW? (3)
–	16.	SPEAKING OF HEAVEN (1)
7	17.	THE MAN WITH THE MANDOLIN (5)
–	18.	CHATTERBOX (1)
–	19.	YODELIN' JIVE (1)
–	20.	THE LITTLE RED FOX (1)

JANUARY 1940

LM	TM	
1	1.	SCATTERBRAIN (3)
14	2.	ALL THE THINGS YOU ARE (2)
–	3.	INDIAN SUMMER (1)
5	4.	OH JOHNNY, OH JOHNNY, OH! (2)
2	5.	SOUTH OF THE BORDER (4)
–	6.	CARELESS (1)
9	7.	IN THE MOOD (3)
–	8.	FAITHFUL FOREVER (1)
11	9.	STOP! IT'S WONDERFUL (2)
3	10.	MY PRAYER (4)
20	11.	THE LITTLE RED FOX (2)
4	12.	LILACS IN THE RAIN (3)
18	13.	CHATTERBOX (2)
–	14.	IN AN OLD DUTCH GARDEN (1)
–	15.	AT THE BALALAIKA (1)
19	16.	YODELIN' JIVE (2)
7	17.	(ALLA EN) EL RANCHO GRANDE (4)
16	18.	SPEAKING OF HEAVEN (2)
–	19.	BLUEBIRDS IN THE MOONLIGHT (1)
13	20.	GOODY GOODBYE (2)

FEBRUARY 1940

LM	TM	
6	1.	CARELESS (2)
3	2.	INDIAN SUMMER (2)
2	3.	ALL THE THINGS YOU ARE (3)
8	4.	FAITHFUL FOREVER (2)
7	5.	IN THE MOOD (4)
15	6.	AT THE BALALAIKA (2)
–	7.	DARN THAT DREAM (1)
4	8.	OH JOHNNY, OH JOHNNY, OH! (3)
11	9.	THE LITTLE RED FOX (3)
14	10.	IN AN OLD DUTCH GARDEN (2)
1	11.	SCATTERBRAIN (4)
5	12.	SOUTH OF THE BORDER (5)
–	13.	TO YOU, SWEETHEART, ALOHA (1)
–	14.	IT'S A BLUE WORLD (1)
–	15.	THIS CHANGING WORLD (1)
–	16.	YOU'D BE SURPRISED (1)
–	17.	DO I LOVE YOU? (1)
–	18.	THE GAUCHO SERENADE (1)
–	19.	CONFUCIUS SAY (1)
10	20.	MY PRAYER (5)

MARCH 1940

LM	TM	
10	1.	IN AN OLD DUTCH GARDEN (3)
1	2.	CARELESS (3)
2	3.	INDIAN SUMMER (3)
14	4.	IT'S A BLUE WORLD (2)
–	5.	WHEN YOU WISH UPON A STAR (1)
6	6.	AT THE BALALAIKA (3)
7	7.	DARN THAT DREAM (2)
5	8.	IN THE MOOD (5)
–	9.	ON THE ISLE OF MAY (1)
18	10.	THE GAUCHO SERENADE (2)
–	11.	I'VE GOT MY EYES ON YOU (1)
17	12.	DO I LOVE YOU? (2)
–	13.	THE STARLIT HOUR (1)
3	14.	ALL THE THINGS YOU ARE (4)
–	15.	TUXEDO JUNCTION (1)
19	16.	CONFUCIUS SAY (2)
4	17.	FAITHFUL FOREVER (3)
–	18.	LEANIN' ON THE OLE TOP RAIL (1)
–	19.	THE SINGING HILLS (1)
16	20.	YOU'D BE SURPRISED (2)

APRIL 1940

LM	TM	
5	1.	WHEN YOU WISH UPON A STAR (2)
1	2.	IN AN OLD DUTCH GARDEN (4)
9	3.	ON THE ISLE OF MAY (2)
–	4.	THE WOODPECKER SONG (1)
–	5.	WITH THE WIND AND THE RAIN IN YOUR HAIR (1)
13	6.	THE STARLIT HOUR (2)
15	7.	TUXEDO JUNCTION (2)
4	8.	IT'S A BLUE WORLD (3)
19	9.	THE SINGING HILLS (2)
–	10.	(I'M) TOO ROMANTIC (1)
10	11.	THE GAUCHO SERENADE (3)
18	12.	LEANIN' ON THE OLE TOP RAIL (2)
–	13.	SAY SI SI (1)
–	14.	HOW HIGH THE MOON (1)
11	15.	I'VE GOT MY EYES ON YOU (2)
3	16.	INDIAN SUMMER (4)
8	17.	IN THE MOOD (6)
–	18.	LET THERE BE LOVE (1)
–	19.	ALICE BLUE GOWN (1)
–	20.	SO FAR, SO GOOD (1)

MAY 1940

LM	TM	
4	1.	THE WOODPECKER SONG (2)
5	2.	WITH THE WIND AND THE RAIN IN YOUR HAIR (2)
1	3.	WHEN YOU WISH UPON A STAR (3)
9	4.	THE SINGING HILLS (3)
10	5.	(I'M) TOO ROMANTIC (2)
18	6.	LET THERE BE LOVE (2)
2	7.	IN AN OLD DUTCH GARDEN (5)
7	8.	TUXEDO JUNCTION (3)
–	9.	PLAYMATES (1)
–	10.	SAY IT (1)
–	11.	IMAGINATION (1)
19	12.	ALICE BLUE GOWN (2)
12	13.	LEANIN' ON THE OLE TOP RAIL (3)
–	14.	LITTLE CURLY HAIR IN A HIGH CHAIR (1)
–	15.	SHAKE DOWN THE STARS (1)
3	16.	ON THE ISLE OF MAY (3)
14	17.	HOW HIGH THE MOON (2)
–	18.	A LOVER'S LULLABY (1)
–	19.	YOU, YOU, DARLIN' (1)
13	20.	SAY SI SI (2)

JUNE 1940

LM	TM	
1	1.	THE WOODPECKER SONG (3)
11	2.	IMAGINATION (2)
2	3.	WITH THE WIND AND THE RAIN IN YOUR HAIR (3)
10	4.	SAY IT (2)
–	5.	MAKE BELIEVE ISLAND (1)
9	6.	PLAYMATES (2)
–	7.	WHERE WAS I? (1)
4	8.	THE SINGING HILLS (4)
14	9.	LITTLE CURLY HAIR IN A HIGH CHAIR (2)
15	10.	SHAKE DOWN THE STARS (2)
–	11.	THE BREEZE AND I (1)
8	12.	TUXEDO JUNCTION (4)
12	13.	ALICE BLUE GOWN (3)
–	14.	I CAN'T LOVE YOU ANY MORE (THAN I DO) (1)
3	15.	WHEN YOU WISH UPON A STAR (4)
5	16.	(I'M) TOO ROMANTIC (3)
–	17.	BLUE LOVEBIRD (1)
–	18.	BOOG-IT (1)
7	19.	IN AN OLD DUTCH GARDEN (6)
–	20.	SIERRA SUE (1)

JULY 1940

LM	TM	
5	1.	MAKE BELIEVE ISLAND (2)
2	2.	IMAGINATION (3)
11	3.	THE BREEZE AND I (2)
20	4.	SIERRA SUE (2)
7	5.	WHERE WAS I? (2)
1	6.	THE WOODPECKER SONG (4)
6	7.	PLAYMATES (3)
–	8.	FOOLS RUSH IN (1)
14	9.	I CAN'T LOVE YOU ANY MORE (THAN I DO) (2)
–	10.	I'LL NEVER SMILE AGAIN (1)
17	11.	BLUE LOVEBIRD (2)
–	12.	GOD BLESS AMERICA (5)
–	13.	DEVIL MAY CARE (1)
4	14.	SAY IT (3)
8	15.	THE SINGING HILLS (5)
–	16.	YOU'RE LONELY AND I'M LONELY (1)
–	17.	I'M STEPPING OUT WITH A MEMORY TONIGHT (1)
–	18.	THE NEARNESS OF YOU (1)
3	19.	WITH THE WIND AND THE RAIN IN YOUR HAIR (4)
–	20.	SIX LESSONS FROM MADAME LA ZONGA (1)

AUGUST 1940

LM	TM	
10	1.	I'LL NEVER SMILE AGAIN (2)
4	2.	SIERRA SUE (3)
8	3.	FOOLS RUSH IN (2)
3	4.	THE BREEZE AND I (3)
–	5.	WHEN THE SWALLOWS COME BACK TO CAPISTRANO (1)
–	6.	I'M NOBODY'S BABY (1)
1	7.	MAKE BELIEVE ISLAND (3)
12	8.	GOD BLESS AMERICA (6)
18	9.	THE NEARNESS OF YOU (2)
–	10.	ALL THIS AND HEAVEN TOO (1)
7	11.	PLAYMATES (4)
17	12.	I'M STEPPING OUT WITH A MEMORY TONIGHT (2)
20	13.	SIX LESSONS FROM MADAME LA ZONGA (2)
–	14.	BLUEBERRY HILL (1)
2	15.	IMAGINATION (4)
5	16.	WHERE WAS I? (3)
–	17.	PENNSYLVANIA 6-5000 (1)
–	18.	HEAR MY SONG, VIOLETTA (1)
13	19.	DEVIL MAY CARE (2)
9	20.	I CAN'T LOVE YOU ANY MORE (THAN I DO) (3)

SEPTEMBER 1940

LM	TM	
1	1.	I'LL NEVER SMILE AGAIN (3)
5	2.	WHEN THE SWALLOWS COME BACK TO CAPISTRANO (2)
14	3.	BLUEBERRY HILL (2)
6	4.	I'M NOBODY'S BABY (2)
2	5.	SIERRA SUE (4)
–	6.	MAYBE (1)
8	7.	GOD BLESS AMERICA (7)
9	8.	THE NEARNESS OF YOU (3)
–	9.	TRADE WINDS (1)
–	10.	PRACTICE MAKE PERFECT (1)
13	11.	SIX LESSONS FROM MADAME LA ZONGA (3)
10	12.	ALL THIS AND HEAVEN TOO (2)
3	13.	FOOLS RUSH IN (3)
–	14.	ONLY FOREVER (1)
4	15.	THE BREEZE AND I (4)
–	16.	CAN'T GET INDIANA OFF MY MIND (1)
–	17.	BEAT ME, DADDY, EIGHT TO THE BAR (1)
–	18.	THAT'S FOR ME (1)
17	19.	PENNSYLVANIA 6-5000 (2)
12	20.	I'M STEPPING OUT WITH A MEMORY TONIGHT (3)

OCTOBER 1940

LM	TM	
3	1.	BLUEBERRY HILL (3)
9	2.	TRADE WINDS (2)
6	3.	MAYBE (2)
14	4.	ONLY FOREVER (2)
10	5.	PRACTICE MAKE PERFECT (2)
2	6.	WHEN THE SWALLOWS COME BACK TO CAPISTRANO (3)
1	7.	I'LL NEVER SMILE AGAIN (4)
–	8.	FERRY-BOAT SERENADE (1)
4	9.	I'M NOBODY'S BABY (3)
7	10.	GOD BLESS AMERICA (8)
–	11.	THE CALL OF THE CANYON (1)
17	12.	BEAT ME, DADDY, EIGHT TO THE BAR (2)
–	13.	NOW I LAY ME DOWN TO DREAM (1)
–	14.	OUR LOVE AFFAIR (1)
18	15.	THAT'S FOR ME (2)
5	16.	SIERRA SUE (5)
–	17.	WE THREE (1)
–	18.	THE SAME OLD STORY (1)
–	19.	CROSSTOWN (1)
–	20.	THERE I GO (1)

NOVEMBER 1940

LM	TM	
4	1.	ONLY FOREVER (3)
8	2.	FERRY-BOAT SERENADE (2)
2	3.	TRADE WINDS (3)
20	4.	THERE I GO (2)
3	5.	MAYBE (3)
14	6.	OUR LOVE AFFAIR (2)
17	7.	WE THREE (2)
5	8.	PRACTICE MAKE PERFECT (3)
1	9.	BLUEBERRY HILL (4)
13	10.	NOW I LAY ME DOWN TO DREAM (2)
12	11.	BEAT ME, DADDY, EIGHT TO THE BAR (3)
–	12.	I AM AN AMERICAN (1)
10	13.	GOD BLESS AMERICA (9)
–	14.	POMPTON TURNPIKE (1)
7	15.	I'LL NEVER SMILE AGAIN (5)
–	16.	DOWN ARGENTINA WAY (1)
–	17.	FIVE O'CLOCK WHISTLE (1)
–	18.	TWO DREAMS MET (1)
6	19.	WHEN THE SWALLOWS COME BACK TO CAPISTRANO (4)
–	20.	DREAM VALLEY (1)

DECEMBER 1940

LM	TM	
7	1.	WE THREE (3)
2	2.	FERRY-BOAT SERENADE (3)
1	3.	ONLY FOREVER (4)
–	4.	A NIGHTINGALE SANG IN BERKELEY SQUARE (1)
4	5.	THERE I GO (3)
–	6.	FRENESI (1)
16	7.	DOWN ARGENTINA WAY (2)
3	8.	TRADE WINDS (4)
20	9.	DREAM VALLEY (2)
11	10.	BEAT ME, DADDY, EIGHT TO THE BAR (4)
9	11.	BLUEBERRY HILL (5)
–	12.	SO YOU'RE THE ONE (1)
–	13.	I GIVE YOU MY WORD (1)
17	14.	FIVE O'CLOCK WHISTLE (2)
–	15.	SCRUB ME, MAMA, WITH A BOOGIE BEAT (1)
5	16.	MAYBE (4)
8	17.	PRACTICE MAKE PERFECT (4)
14	18.	POMPTON TURNPIKE (2)
6	19.	OUR LOVE AFFAIR (3)
18	20.	TWO DREAMS MET (2)

JANUARY 1941

LM	TM	
6	1.	FRENESI (2)
7	2.	DOWN ARGENTINA WAY (3)
4	3.	A NIGHTINGALE SANG IN BERKELEY SQUARE (2)
5	4.	THERE I GO (4)
2	5.	FERRY-BOAT SERENADE (4)
–	6.	I HEAR A RHAPSODY (1)
13	7.	I GIVE YOU MY WORD (2)
1	8.	WE THREE (4)
9	9.	DREAM VALLEY (3)
3	10.	ONLY FOREVER (5)
–	11.	ALONG THE SANTA FE TRAIL (1)
12	12.	SO YOU'RE THE ONE (2)
–	13.	PERFIDIA (TONIGHT) (1)
15	14.	SCRUB ME, MAMA, WITH A BOOGIE BEAT (2)
–	15.	YOU WALK BY (1)
8	16.	TRADE WINDS (5)
18	17.	POMPTON TURNPIKE (3)
–	18.	STAR DUST (1)
–	19.	YOU'VE GOT ME THIS WAY (1)
10	20.	BEAT ME, DADDY, EIGHT TO THE BAR (5)

FEBRUARY 1941

LM	TM	
1	1.	FRENESI (3)
6	2.	I HEAR A RHAPSODY (2)
15	3.	YOU WALK BY (2)
7	4.	I GIVE YOU MY WORD (3)
13	5.	PERFIDIA (TONIGHT) (2)
4	6.	THERE I GO (5)
–	7.	IT ALL COMES BACK TO ME NOW (1)
3	8.	A NIGHTINGALE SANG IN BERKELEY SQUARE (3)
12	9.	SO YOU'RE THE ONE (3)
18	10.	STAR DUST (2)
–	11.	HIGH ON A WINDY HILL (1)
–	12.	ANVIL CHORUS (1)
–	13.	MAY I NEVER LOVE AGAIN (1)
11	14.	ALONG THE SANTA FE TRAIL (2)
–	15.	THE LAST TIME I SAW PARIS (1)
2	16.	DOWN ARGENTINA WAY (4)
–	17.	YES, MY DARLING DAUGHTER (1)
–	18.	SAN ANTONIO ROSE (1)
–	19.	THERE'LL BE SOME CHANGES MADE (1)
9	20.	DREAM VALLEY (4)

MARCH 1941

LM	TM	
2	1.	I HEAR A RHAPSODY (3)
11	2.	HIGH ON A WINDY HILL (2)
1	3.	FRENESI (4)
7	4.	IT ALL COMES BACK TO ME NOW (2)
5	5.	PERFIDIA (TONIGHT) (3)
19	6.	THERE'LL BE SOME CHANGES MADE (2)
3	7.	YOU WALK BY (3)
18	8.	SAN ANTONIO ROSE (2)
–	9.	SONG OF THE VOLGA BOATMEN (1)
12	10.	ANVIL CHORUS (2)
–	11.	I DREAMT I DWELT IN HARLEM (1)
–	12.	AMAPOLA (1)
4	13.	I GIVE YOU MY WORD (4)
8	14.	A NIGHTINGALE SANG IN BERKELEY SQUARE (4)
–	15.	A WISE OLD OWL (1)
10	16.	STAR DUST (3)
13	17.	MAY I NEVER LOVE AGAIN (2)
15	18.	THE LAST TIME I SAW PARIS (2)
–	19.	OH, LOOK AT ME NOW (1)
–	20.	THE BOOGIE WOOGIE BUGLE BOY (1)

APRIL 1941

LM	TM	
12	1.	AMAPOLA (2)
6	2.	THERE'LL BE SOME CHANGES MADE (3)
15	3.	A WISE OLD OWL (2)
2	4.	HIGH ON A WINDY HILL (3)
19	5.	OH, LOOK AT ME NOW (2)
8	6.	SAN ANTONIO ROSE (3)
4	7.	IT ALL COMES BACK TO ME NOW (3)
3	8.	FRENESI (5)
1	9.	I HEAR A RHAPSODY (4)
–	10.	WALKING BY THE RIVER (1)
9	11.	SONG OF THE VOLGA BOATMEN (2)
5	12.	PERFIDIA (TONIGHT) (4)
–	13.	GEORGIA ON MY MIND (1)
7	14.	YOU WALK BY (4)
–	15.	G'BYE NOW (1)
–	16.	DOLORES (1)
–	17.	BLUE FLAME (1)
–	18.	DO I WORRY? (1)
10	19.	ANVIL CHORUS (3)
–	20.	NUMBER TEN LULLABY LANE (1)

MAY 1941

LM	TM	
1	1.	AMAPOLA (3)
18	2.	DO I WORRY? (2)
–	3.	MY SISTER AND I (1)
3	4.	A WISE OLD OWL (3)
10	5.	WALKING BY THE RIVER (2)
–	6.	INTERMEZZO (A LOVE STORY) (1)
16	7.	DOLORES (2)
5	8.	OH, LOOK AT ME NOW (3)
–	9.	MARIA ELENA (1)
2	10.	THERE'LL BE SOME CHANGES MADE (4)
15	11.	G'BYE NOW (2)
20	12.	NUMBER TEN LULLABY LANE (2)
6	13.	SAN ANTONIO ROSE (4)
–	14.	I'LL BE WITH YOU IN APPLE BLOSSOM TIME (1)
–	15.	ALEXANDER THE SWOOSE (1)
–	16.	THE HUT-SUT SONG (1)
–	17.	THE BAND PLAYED ON (1)
13	18.	GEORGIA ON MY MIND (2)
–	19.	LET'S GET AWAY FROM IT ALL (1)
–	20.	FRIENDLY TAVERN POLKA (1)

JUNE 1941

LM	TM	
6	1.	INTERMEZZO (A LOVE STORY) (2)
3	2.	MY SISTER AND I (2)
16	3.	THE HUT-SUT SONG (2)
9	4.	MARIA ELENA (2)
1	5.	AMAPOLA (4)
–	6.	THE THINGS I LOVE (1)
2	7.	DO I WORRY? (3)
14	8.	I'LL BE WITH YOU IN APPLE BLOSSOM TIME (2)
7	9.	DOLORES (3)
11	10.	G'BYE NOW (3)
–	11.	DADDY (1)
–	12.	JUST A LITTLE BIT SOUTH OF NORTH CAROLINA (1)
17	13.	THE BAND PLAYED ON (2)
–	14.	YOU ARE MY SUNSHINE (1)
5	15.	WALKING BY THE RIVER (3)
–	16.	GREEN EYES (1)
20	17.	FRIENDLY TAVERN POLKA (2)
–	18.	EVERYTHING HAPPENS TO ME (1)
12	19.	NUMBER TEN LULLABY LANE (3)
–	20.	TWO HEARTS THAT PASS IN THE NIGHT (1)

JULY 1941

LM	TM	
4	1.	MARIA ELENA (3)
3	2.	THE HUT-SUT SONG (3)
1	3.	INTERMEZZO (A LOVE STORY) (3)
11	4.	DADDY (2)
2	5.	MY SISTER AND I (3)
6	6.	THE THINGS I LOVE (2)
12	7.	JUST A LITTLE BIT SOUTH OF NORTH CAROLINA (2)
16	8.	GREEN EYES (2)
8	9.	I'LL BE WITH YOU IN APPLE BLOSSOM TIME (3)
5	10.	AMAPOLA (5)
14	11.	YOU ARE MY SUNSHINE (2)
–	12.	YOURS (QUIEREME MUCHO) (1)
7	13.	DO I WORRY? (4)
13	14.	THE BAND PLAYED ON (3)
–	15.	UNTIL TOMORROW (1)
9	16.	DOLORES (4)
–	17.	AURORA (1)
20	18.	TWO HEARTS THAT PASS IN THE NIGHT (2)
10	19.	G'BYE NOW (4)
–	20.	'TIL REVEILLE (1)

AUGUST 1941

LM	TM	
1	1.	MARIA ELENA (4)
4	2.	DADDY (3)
8	3.	GREEN EYES (3)
12	4.	YOURS (QUIEREME MUCHO) (2)
20	5.	'TIL REVEILLE (2)
2	6.	THE HUT-SUT SONG (4)
3	7.	INTERMEZZO (A LOVE STORY) (4)
6	8.	THE THINGS I LOVE (3)
–	9.	BLUE CHAMPAGNE (1)
–	10.	YOU AND I (1)
7	11.	JUST A LITTLE BIT SOUTH OF NORTH CAROLINA (3)
11	12.	YOU ARE MY SUNSHINE (3)
–	13.	YES, INDEED! (1)
–	14.	KISS THE BOYS GOODBYE (1)
–	15.	THE BOOGLIE-WOOGLIE PIGGIE (1)
9	16.	I'LL BE WITH YOU IN APPLE BLOSSOM TIME (4)
5	17.	MY SISTER AND I (4)
–	18.	PIANO CONCERTO (1)
–	19.	I WENT OUT OF MY WAY (1)
17	20.	AURORA (2)

SEPTEMBER 1941

LM	TM	
10	1.	YOU AND I (2)
5	2.	'TIL REVEILLE (3)
4	3.	YOURS (QUIEREME MUCHO) (3)
3	4.	GREEN EYES (4)
1	5.	MARIA ELENA (5)
2	6.	DADDY (4)
9	7.	BLUE CHAMPAGNE (2)
7	8.	INTERMEZZO (A LOVE STORY) (5)
18	9.	PIANO CONCERTO (2)
–	10.	DO YOU CARE? (1)
–	11.	I GUESS I'LL HAVE TO DREAM THE REST (1)
–	12.	I DON'T WANT TO SET THE WORLD ON FIRE (1)
14	13.	KISS THE BOYS GOODBYE (2)
13	14.	YES, INDEED! (2)
8	15.	THE THINGS I LOVE (4)
–	16.	ELMER'S TUNE (1)
–	17.	JIM (1)
19	18.	I WENT OUT OF MY WAY (2)
15	19.	THE BOOGLIE-WOOGLIE PIGGY (2)
12	20.	YOU ARE MY SUNSHINE (4)

OCTOBER 1941

LM	TM	
12	1.	I DON'T WANT TO SET THE WORLD ON FIRE (2)
1	2.	YOU AND I (3)
17	3.	JIM (2)
9	4.	PIANO CONCERTO (3)
2	5.	'TIL REVEILLE (4)
11	6.	I GUESS I'LL HAVE TO DREAM THE REST (2)
3	7.	YOURS (QUIEREME MUCHO) (4)
10	8.	DO YOU CARE? (2)
7	9.	BLUE CHAMPAGNE (3)
16	10.	ELMER'S TUNE (2)
–	11.	CHATTANOOGA CHOO CHOO (1)
5	12.	MARIA ELENA (6)
–	13.	TIME WAS (1)
14	14.	YES, INDEED! (3)
–	15.	TONIGHT WE LOVE (1)
–	16.	THIS LOVE OF MINE (1)
8	17.	INTERMEZZO (A LOVE STORY) (6)
4	18.	GREEN EYES (5)
–	19.	WHY DON'T WE DO THIS MORE OFTEN? (1)
–	20.	HI, NEIGHBOR! (1)

NOVEMBER 1941

LM	TM	
1	1.	I DON'T WANT TO SET THE WORLD ON FIRE (3)
4	2.	PIANO CONCERTO (4)
3	3.	JIM (3)
10	4.	ELMER'S TUNE (3)
11	5.	CHATTANOOGA CHOO CHOO (2)
2	6.	YOU AND I (4)
15	7.	TONIGHT WE LOVE (2)
6	8.	I GUESS I'LL HAVE TO DREAM THE REST (3)
16	9.	THIS LOVE OF MINE (2)
7	10.	YOURS (QUIEREME MUCHO) (5)
8	11.	DO YOU CARE? (3)
13	12.	TIME WAS (2)
–	13.	SHEPHERD SERENADE (1)
5	14.	'TIL REVEILLE (5)
19	15.	WHY DON'T WE DO THIS MORE OFTEN? (2)
–	16.	I SEE A MILLION PEOPLE (1)
14	17.	YES, INDEED! (4)
9	18.	BLUE CHAMPAGNE (4)
–	19.	A CITY CALLED HEAVEN (1)
–	20.	CONCERTO FOR TWO (1)

DECEMBER 1941

LM	TM	
5	1.	CHATTANOOGA CHOO CHOO (3)
4	2.	ELMER'S TUNE (4)
13	3.	SHEPHERD SERENADE (2)
2	4.	PIANO CONCERTO (5)
9	5.	THIS LOVE OF MINE (3)
7	6.	TONIGHT WE LOVE (3)
1	7.	I DON'T WANT TO SET THE WORLD ON FIRE (4)
6	8.	YOU AND I (5)
–	9.	THE BELLS OF SAN RAQUEL (1)
–	10.	BY-U, BY-O (1)
–	11.	TWO IN LOVE (1)
3	12.	JIM (4)
–	13.	THE WHITE CLIFFS OF DOVER (1)
–	14.	YOU MADE ME LOVE YOU (1)
–	15.	THIS TIME THE DREAM'S ON ME (1)
15	16.	WHY DON'T WE DO THIS MORE OFTEN? (3)
20	17.	CONCERTO FOR TWO (2)
–	18.	ROSE O'DAY (1)
–	19.	JINGLE BELLS (1)
–	20.	ORANGE BLOSSOM LANE (1)

JANUARY 1942

LM	TM	
1	1.	CHATTANOOGA CHOO CHOO (4)
13	2.	THE WHITE CLIFFS OF DOVER (2)
2	3.	ELMER'S TUNE (5)
5	4.	THIS LOVE OF MINE (4)
3	5.	SHEPHERD SERENADE (3)
18	6.	ROSE O'DAY (2)
9	7.	THE BELLS OF SAN RAQUEL (2)
–	8.	THE SHRINE OF ST. CECILIA (1)
4	9.	PIANO CONCERTO (6)
–	10.	BLUES IN THE NIGHT (1)
6	11.	TONIGHT WE LOVE (4)
–	12.	MADELAINE (1)
–	13.	THIS IS NO LAUGHING MATTER (1)
14	14.	YOU MADE ME LOVE YOU (2)
10	15.	BY-U, BY-O (2)
19	16.	JINGLE BELLS (2)
11	17.	TWO IN LOVE (2)
–	18.	'TIS AUTUMN (1)
–	19.	REMEMBER PEARL HARBOR (1)
–	20.	EV'RYTHING I LOVE (1)

FEBRUARY 1942

LM	TM	
2	1.	THE WHITE CLIFFS OF DOVER (3)
10	2.	BLUES IN THE NIGHT (2)
6	3.	ROSE O'DAY (3)
8	4.	THE SHRINE OF ST. CECILIA (2)
19	5.	REMEMBER PEARL HARBOR (2)
1	6.	CHATTANOOGA CHOO CHOO (5)
3	7.	ELMER'S TUNE (6)
20	8.	EV'RYTHING I LOVE (2)
–	9.	WE DID IT BEFORE (AND WE CAN DO IT AGAIN) (1)
4	10.	THIS LOVE OF MINE (5)
–	11.	I SAID NO! (1)
–	12.	A STRING OF PEARLS (1)
–	13.	DEEP IN THE HEART OF TEXAS (1)
–	14.	MOONLIGHT COCKTAIL (1)
18	15.	'TIS AUTUMN (2)
14	16.	YOU MADE ME LOVE YOU (3)
13	17.	THIS IS NO LAUGHING MATTER (2)
7	18.	THE BELLS OF SAN RAQUEL (3)
–	19.	I DON'T WANT TO WALK WITHOUT YOU (1)
–	20.	WE'RE THE COUPLE IN THE CASTLE (1)

MARCH 1942

LM	TM	
13	1.	DEEP IN THE HEART OF TEXAS (2)
2	2.	BLUES IN THE NIGHT (3)
1	3.	THE WHITE CLIFFS OF DOVER (4)
14	4.	MOONLIGHT COCKTAIL (2)
19	5.	I DON'T WANT TO WALK WITHOUT YOU (2)
3	6.	ROSE O'DAY (4)
12	7.	A STRING OF PEARLS (2)
4	8.	THE SHRINE OF ST. CECILIA (3)
5	9.	REMEMBER PEARL HARBOR (3)
–	10.	HOW ABOUT YOU? (1)
11	11.	I SAID NO! (2)
–	12.	SOMEBODY ELSE IS TAKING MY PLACE (1)
8	13.	EV'RYTHING I LOVE (3)
7	14.	ELMER'S TUNE (7)
–	15.	MISS YOU (1)
20	16.	WE'RE THE COUPLE IN THE CASTLE (2)
6	17.	CHATTANOOGA CHOO CHOO (6)
–	18.	SOMETIMES (1)
–	19.	A ZOOT SUIT (1)
–	20.	DEAR MOM (1)

APRIL 1942

LM	TM	
4	1.	MOONLIGHT COCKTAIL (3)
1	2.	DEEP IN THE HEART OF TEXAS (3)
12	3.	SOMEBODY ELSE IS TAKING MY PLACE (2)
5	4.	I DON'T WANT TO WALK WITHOUT YOU (3)
15	5.	MISS YOU (2)
2	6.	BLUES IN THE NIGHT (4)
7	7.	A STRING OF PEARLS (3)
3	8.	THE WHITE CLIFFS OF DOVER (5)
–	9	TANGERINE (1)
10	10.	HOW ABOUT YOU? (2)
19	11.	A ZOOT SUIT (2)
18	12.	SOMETIMES (2)
–	13.	DON'T SIT UNDER THE APPLE TREE (WITH ANYONE ELSE BUT ME) (1)
8	14.	THE SHRINE OF ST. CECILIA (4)
–	15.	I REMEMBER YOU (1)
6	16.	ROSE O'DAY (5)
–	17.	SKYLARK (1)
–	18.	I'LL PRAY FOR YOU (1)
–	19.	JERSEY BOUNCE (1)
–	20.	ALWAYS IN MY HEART (1)

MAY 1942

LM	TM	
3	1.	SOMEBODY ELSE IS TAKING MY PLACE (3)
1	2.	MOONLIGHT COCKTAIL (4)
13	3.	DON'T SIT UNDER THE APPLE TREE (WITH ANYONE ELSE BUT ME) (2)
9	4	TANGERINE (2)
4	5.	I DON'T WANT TO WALK WITHOUT YOU (4)
17	6.	SKYLARK (2)
19	7.	JERSEY BOUNCE (2)
–	8.	JOHNNY DOUGHBOY FOUND A ROSE IN IRELAND (1)
5	9.	MISS YOU (3)
–	10.	SLEEPY LAGOON (1)
2	11.	DEEP IN THE HEART OF TEXAS (4)
15	12.	I REMEMBER YOU (2)
7	13.	A STRING OF PEARLS (4)
–	14.	WHO WOULDN'T LOVE YOU (1)
–	15.	ONE DOZEN ROSES (1)
20	16.	ALWAYS IN MY HEART (2)
18	17.	I'LL PRAY FOR YOU (2)
–	18.	I THREW A KISS IN THE OCEAN (1)
6	19.	BLUES IN THE NIGHT (5)
–	20.	THREE LITTLE SISTERS (1)

JUNE 1942

LM	TM	
10	1.	SLEEPY LAGOON (2)
8	2.	JOHNNY DOUGHBOY FOUND A ROSE IN IRELAND (2)
3	3.	DON'T SIT UNDER THE APPLE TREE (WITH ANYONE ELSE BUT ME) (3)
7	4.	JERSEY BOUNCE (3)
15	5.	ONE DOZEN ROSES (2)
4	6	TANGERINE (3)
14	7.	WHO WOULDN'T LOVE YOU (2)
6	8.	SKYLARK (3)
1	9.	SOMEBODY ELSE IS TAKING MY PLACE (4)
20	10.	THREE LITTLE SISTERS (2)
18	11.	I THREW A KISS IN THE OCEAN (2)
2	12.	MOONLIGHT COCKTAIL (5)
16	13.	ALWAYS IN MY HEART (3)
–	14.	JINGLE, JANGLE, JINGLE (1)
9	15.	MISS YOU (4)
–	16.	WE'LL MEET AGAIN (1)
5	17.	I DON'T WANT TO WALK WITHOUT YOU (5)
12	18.	I REMEMBER YOU (3)
–	19.	BREATHLESS (1)
–	20.	NIGHTINGALE (1)

JULY 1942

LM	TM	
1	1.	SLEEPY LAGOON (3)
2	2.	JOHNNY DOUGHBOY FOUND A ROSE IN IRELAND (3)
14	3.	JINGLE, JANGLE, JINGLE (2)
4	4.	JERSEY BOUNCE (4)
5	5.	ONE DOZEN ROSES (3)
7	6.	WHO WOULDN'T LOVE YOU (3)
3	7.	DON'T SIT UNDER THE APPLE TREE (WITH ANYONE ELSE BUT ME) (4)
10	8.	THREE LITTLE SISTERS (3)
13	9.	ALWAYS IN MY HEART (4)
6	10	TANGERINE (4)
11	11.	I THREW A KISS IN THE OCEAN (3)
8	12.	SKYLARK (4)
–	13.	SWEET ELOISE (1)
–	14.	HE WEARS A PAIR OF SILVER WINGS (1)
–	15.	THE ARMY AIR CORPS SONG (1)
12	16.	MOONLIGHT COCKTAIL (6)
–	17.	I'LL KEEP THE LOVELIGHT BURNING (1)
–	18.	IDAHO (1)
–	19.	THIS IS WORTH FIGHTING FOR (1)
–	20.	THE MARINES' HYMN (1)

AUGUST 1942

LM	TM	
3	1.	JINGLE, JANGLE, JINGLE (3)
14	2.	HE WEARS A PAIR OF SILVER WINGS (2)
6	3.	WHO WOULDN'T LOVE YOU (4)
1	4.	SLEEPY LAGOON (4)
2	5.	JOHNNY DOUGHBOY FOUND A ROSE IN IRELAND (4)
18	6.	IDAHO (2)
–	7.	I LEFT MY HEART AT THE STAGE DOOR CANTEEN (1)
4	8.	JERSEY BOUNCE (5)
9	9.	ALWAYS IN MY HEART (5)
–	10.	TAKE ME (1)
8	11.	THREE LITTLE SISTERS (4)
–	12.	AMEN (1)
–	13.	JUST AS THOUGH YOU WERE HERE (1)
–	14.	MY DEVOTION (1)
13	15.	SWEET ELOISE (2)
19	16.	THIS IS WORTH FIGHTING FOR (2)
5	17.	ONE DOZEN ROSES (4)
–	18.	STRICTLY INSTRUMENTAL (1)
–	19.	(I'VE GOT A GAL IN) KALAMAZOO (1)
–	20.	BE CAREFUL, IT'S MY HEART (1)

SEPTEMBER 1942

LM	TM	
2	1.	HE WEARS A PAIR OF SILVER WINGS (3)
14	2.	MY DEVOTION (2)
7	3.	I LEFT MY HEART AT THE STAGE DOOR CANTEEN (2)
1	4.	JINGLE, JANGLE, JINGLE (4)
19	5.	(I'VE GOT A GAL IN) KALAMAZOO (2)
10	6.	TAKE ME (2)
20	7.	BE CAREFUL, IT'S MY HEART (2)
6	8.	IDAHO (3)
4	9.	SLEEPY LAGOON (5)
–	10.	STRIP POLKA (1)
18	11.	STRICTLY INSTRUMENTAL (2)
13	12.	JUST AS THOUGH YOU WERE HERE (2)
3	13.	WHO WOULDN'T LOVE YOU (5)
–	14.	THE ARMY AIR CORPS SONG (2)
9	15.	ALWAYS IN MY HEART (6)
12	16.	AMEN (2)
–	17.	THERE'S A STAR-SPANGLED BANNER WAVING SOMEWHERE (1)
5	18.	JOHNNY DOUGHBOY FOUND A ROSE IN IRELAND (5)
–	19.	SERENADE IN BLUE (1)
–	20.	COW-COW BOOGIE (1)

OCTOBER 1942

LM	TM	
5	1.	(I'VE GOT A GAL IN) KALAMAZOO (3)
2	2.	MY DEVOTION (3)
10	3.	STRIP POLKA (2)
–	4.	WHITE CHRISTMAS (1)
1	5.	HE WEARS A PAIR OF SILVER WINGS (4)
3	6.	I LEFT MY HEART AT THE STAGE DOOR CANTEEN (3)
19	7.	SERENADE IN BLUE (2)
7	8.	BE CAREFUL, IT'S MY HEART (3)
–	9.	AT LAST (1)
–	10.	HE'S MY GUY (1)
16	11.	AMEN (3)
–	12.	PRAISE THE LORD AND PASS THE AMMUNITION (1)
–	13.	WHEN THE LIGHTS GO ON AGAIN (1)
6	14.	TAKE ME (3)
17	15.	THERE'S A STAR-SPANGLED BANNER WAVING SOMEWHERE (2)
8	16.	IDAHO (4)
–	17.	WONDER WHEN MY BABY'S COMING HOME (1)
4	18.	JINGLE, JANGLE, JINGLE (5)
–	19.	I CAME HERE TO TALK FOR JOE (1)
–	20.	DEARLY BELOVED (1)

NOVEMBER 1942

LM	TM	
4	1.	WHITE CHRISTMAS (2)
12	2.	PRAISE THE LORD AND PASS THE AMMUNITION (2)
7	3.	SERENADE IN BLUE (3)
13	4.	WHEN THE LIGHTS GO ON AGAIN (2)
2	5.	MY DEVOTION (4)
3	6.	STRIP POLKA (3)
20	7.	DEARLY BELOVED (2)
1	8.	(I'VE GOT A GAL IN) KALAMAZOO (4)
–	9.	MANHATTAN SERENADE (1)
–	10.	MR. FIVE BY FIVE (1)
15	11.	THERE'S A STAR-SPANGLED BANNER WAVING SOMEWHERE (3)
8	12.	BE CAREFUL, IT'S MY HEART (4)
–	13.	DER FUEHRER'S FACE (1)
9	14.	AT LAST (2)
17	15.	WONDER WHEN MY BABY'S COMING HOME (2)
19	16.	I CAME HERE TO TALK FOR JOE (2)
6	17.	I LEFT MY HEART AT THE STAGE DOOR CANTEEN (4)
–	18.	THE ARMY AIR CORPS SONG (3)
5	19.	HE WEARS A PAIR OF SILVER WINGS (5)
10	20.	HE'S MY GUY (2)

DECEMBER 1942

LM	TM	
1	1.	WHITE CHRISTMAS (3)
4	2.	WHEN THE LIGHTS GO ON AGAIN (3)
2	3.	PRAISE THE LORD AND PASS THE AMMUNITION (3)
10	4.	MR. FIVE BY FIVE (2)
7	5.	DEARLY BELOVED (3)
9	6.	MANHATTAN SERENADE (2)
–	7.	THERE ARE SUCH THINGS (1)
13	8.	DER FUEHRER'S FACE (2)
11	9.	THERE'S A STAR-SPANGLED BANNER WAVING SOMEWHERE (4)
3	10.	SERENADE IN BLUE (4)
–	11.	I HAD THE CRAZIEST DREAM (1)
–	12.	DAYBREAK (1)
6	13.	STRIP POLKA (4)
5	14.	MY DEVOTION (5)
–	15.	WHY DON'T YOU FALL IN LOVE WITH ME? (1)
–	16.	THERE WILL NEVER BE ANOTHER YOU (1)
18	17.	THE ARMY AIR CORPS SONG (4)
–	18.	MOONLIGHT BECOMES YOU (1)
8	19.	(I'VE GOT A GAL IN) KALAMAZOO (5)
–	20.	JUKE BOX SATURDAY NIGHT (1)

JANUARY 1943

LM	TM	
7	1.	THERE ARE SUCH THINGS (2)
2	2.	WHEN THE LIGHTS GO ON AGAIN (4)
18	3.	MOONLIGHT BECOMES YOU (2)
11	4.	I HAD THE CRAZIEST DREAM (2)
4	5.	MR. FIVE BY FIVE (3)
15	6.	WHY DON'T YOU FALL IN LOVE WITH ME? (2)
3	7.	PRAISE THE LORD AND PASS THE AMMUNITION (4)
5	8.	DEARLY BELOVED (4)
1	9.	WHITE CHRISTMAS (4)
9	10.	THERE'S A STAR-SPANGLED BANNER WAVING SOMEWHERE (5)
–	11.	CAN'T GET OUT OF THIS MOOD (1)
–	12.	FOR ME AND MY GAL (1)
6	13.	MANHATTAN SERENADE (3)
20	14.	JUKE BOX SATURDAY NIGHT (2)
–	15.	MOONLIGHT MOOD (1)
–	16.	ROSE ANN OF CHARING CROSS (1)
8	17.	DER FUEHRER'S FACE (3)
12	18.	DAYBREAK (2)
–	19.	A TOUCH OF TEXAS (1)
17	20.	THE ARMY AIR CORPS SONG (5)

FEBRUARY 1943

LM	TM	
3	1.	MOONLIGHT BECOMES YOU (3)
1	2.	THERE ARE SUCH THINGS (3)
4	3.	I HAD THE CRAZIEST DREAM (3)
6	4.	WHY DON'T YOU FALL IN LOVE WITH ME? (3)
–	5.	YOU'D BE SO NICE TO COME HOME TO (1)
–	6.	BRAZIL (1)
–	7.	I'VE HEARD THAT SONG BEFORE (1)
2	8.	WHEN THE LIGHTS GO ON AGAIN (5)
12	9.	FOR ME AND MY GAL (2)
15	10.	MOONLIGHT MOOD (2)
10	11.	THERE'S A STAR-SPANGLED BANNER WAVING SOMEWHERE (6)
16	12.	ROSE ANN OF CHARING CROSS (2)
–	13.	WHY DON'T YOU DO RIGHT? (1)
8	14.	DEARLY BELOVED (5)
11	15.	CAN'T GET OUT OF THIS MOOD (2)
–	16.	DON'T GET AROUND MUCH ANYMORE (1)
–	17.	THAT OLD BLACK MAGIC (1)
20	18.	THE ARMY AIR CORPS SONG (6)
–	19.	I'M GETTING TIRED SO I CAN SLEEP (1)
–	20.	FAT MEAT IS GOOD MEAT (1)

MARCH 1943

LM	TM	
7	1.	I'VE HEARD THAT SONG BEFORE (2)
2	2.	THERE ARE SUCH THINGS (4)
6	3.	BRAZIL (2)
17	4.	THAT OLD BLACK MAGIC (2)
1	5.	MOONLIGHT BECOMES YOU (4)
5	6.	YOU'D BE SO NICE TO COME HOME TO (2)
9	7.	FOR ME AND MY GAL (3)
3	8.	I HAD THE CRAZIEST DREAM (4)
–	9.	AS TIME GOES BY (1)
4	10.	WHY DON'T YOU FALL IN LOVE WITH ME? (4)
11	11.	THERE'S A STAR-SPANGLED BANNER WAVING SOMEWHERE (7)
13	12.	WHY DON'T YOU DO RIGHT? (2)
16	13.	DON'T GET AROUND MUCH ANYMORE (2)
10	14.	MOONLIGHT MOOD (3)
–	15.	IT STARTED ALL OVER AGAIN (1)
–	16.	PLEASE THINK OF ME (1)
8	17.	WHEN THE LIGHTS GO ON AGAIN (6)
18	18.	THE ARMY AIR CORPS SONG (7)
12	19.	ROSE ANN OF CHARING CROSS (3)
20	20.	FAT MEAT IS GOOD MEAT (2)

APRIL 1943

LM	TM	
1	1.	I'VE HEARD THAT SONG BEFORE (3)
9	2.	AS TIME GOES BY (2)
4	3.	THAT OLD BLACK MAGIC (3)
3	4.	BRAZIL (3)
6	5.	YOU'D BE SO NICE TO COME HOME TO (3)
13	6.	DON'T GET AROUND MUCH ANYMORE (3)
7	7.	FOR ME AND MY GAL (4)
2	8.	THERE ARE SUCH THINGS (5)
15	9.	IT STARTED ALL OVER AGAIN (2)
–	10.	IT CAN'T BE WRONG (1)
5	11.	MOONLIGHT BECOMES YOU (5)
–	12.	TAKING A CHANCE ON LOVE (1)
11	13.	THERE'S A STAR-SPANGLED BANNER WAVING SOMEWHERE (8)
8	14.	I HAD THE CRAZIEST DREAM (5)
–	15.	I JUST KISSED YOUR PICTURE GOODNIGHT (1)
12	16.	WHY DON'T YOU DO RIGHT? (3)
–	17.	"MURDER" HE SAYS (1)
14	18.	MOONLIGHT MOOD (4)
–	19.	VELVET MOON (1)
18	20.	THE ARMY AIR CORPS SONG (8)

MAY 1943

LM	TM	
2	1.	AS TIME GOES BY (3)
6	2.	DON'T GET AROUND MUCH ANYMORE (4)
1	3.	I'VE HEARD THAT SONG BEFORE (4)
3	4.	THAT OLD BLACK MAGIC (4)
10	5.	IT CAN'T BE WRONG (2)
–	6.	COMIN' IN ON A WING AND A PRAYER (1)
12	7.	TAKING A CHANCE ON LOVE (2)
4	8.	BRAZIL (4)
7	9.	FOR ME AND MY GAL (5)
–	10.	LET'S GET LOST (1)
19	11.	VELVET MOON (2)
–	12.	THERE'S A HARBOR OF DREAMBOATS (1)
–	13.	YOU'LL NEVER KNOW (1)
5	14.	YOU'D BE SO NICE TO COME HOME TO (4)
13	15.	THERE'S A STAR-SPANGLED BANNER WAVING SOMEWHERE (9)
17	16.	"MURDER" HE SAYS (2)
–	17.	WHAT'S THE GOOD WORD, MR. BLUEBIRD? (1)
9	18.	IT STARTED ALL OVER AGAIN (3)
–	19.	JOHNNY ZERO (1)
16	20.	WHY DON'T YOU DO RIGHT? (4)

JUNE 1943

LM	TM	
1	1.	AS TIME GOES BY (4)
6	2.	COMIN' IN ON A WING AND A PRAYER (2)
10	3.	LET'S GET LOST (2)
2	4.	DON'T GET AROUND MUCH ANYMORE (5)
13	5.	YOU'LL NEVER KNOW (2)
5	6.	IT CAN'T BE WRONG (3)
7	7.	TAKING A CHANCE ON LOVE (3)
4	8.	THAT OLD BLACK MAGIC (5)
19	9.	JOHNNY ZERO (2)
3	10.	I'VE HEARD THAT SONG BEFORE (5)
11	11.	VELVET MOON (3)
–	12.	IN THE BLUE OF THE EVENING (1)
15	13.	THERE'S A STAR-SPANGLED BANNER WAVING SOMEWHERE (10)
–	14.	IT'S ALWAYS YOU (1)
16	15.	"MURDER" HE SAYS (3)
8	16.	BRAZIL (5)
–	17.	IN MY ARMS (1)
17	18.	WHAT'S THE GOOD WORD, MR. BLUEBIRD? (2)
–	19.	BIG BOY (1)
–	20.	THE FUDDY DUDDY WATCHMAKER (1)

JULY 1943

LM	TM	
2	1.	COMIN' IN ON A WING AND A PRAYER (3)
5	2.	YOU'LL NEVER KNOW (3)
3	3.	LET'S GET LOST (3)
12	4.	IN THE BLUE OF THE EVENING (2)
9	5.	JOHNNY ZERO (3)
6	6.	IT CAN'T BE WRONG (4)
4	7.	DON'T GET AROUND MUCH ANYMORE (6)
1	8.	AS TIME GOES BY (5)
14	9.	IT'S ALWAYS YOU (2)
–	10.	ALL OR NOTHING AT ALL (1)
17	11.	IN MY ARMS (2)
7	12.	TAKING A CHANCE ON LOVE (4)
–	13.	PISTOL PACKIN' MAMA (1)
11	14.	VELVET MOON (4)
13	15.	THERE'S A STAR-SPANGLED BANNER WAVING SOMEWHERE (11)
–	16.	PEOPLE WILL SAY WE'RE IN LOVE (1)
–	17.	BOOGIE WOOGIE (1)
18	18.	WHAT'S THE GOOD WORD, MR. BLUEBIRD? (3)
–	19.	WAIT FOR ME, MARY (1)
8	20.	THAT OLD BLACK MAGIC (6)

AUGUST 1943

LM	TM	
2	1.	YOU'LL NEVER KNOW (4)
1	2.	COMIN' IN ON A WING AND A PRAYER (4)
4	3.	IN THE BLUE OF THE EVENING (3)
10	4.	ALL OR NOTHING AT ALL (2)
11	5.	IN MY ARMS (3)
6	6.	IT CAN'T BE WRONG (5)
16	7.	PEOPLE WILL SAY WE'RE IN LOVE (2)
9	8.	IT'S ALWAYS YOU (3)
5	9.	JOHNNY ZERO (4)
–	10.	SUNDAY, MONDAY, OR ALWAYS (1)
13	11.	PISTOL PACKIN' MAMA (2)
3	12.	LET'S GET LOST (4)
–	13.	PAPER DOLL (1)
8	14.	AS TIME GOES BY (6)
–	15.	I HEARD YOU CRIED LAST NIGHT (1)
–	16.	PUT YOUR ARMS AROUND ME, HONEY (1)
–	17.	WARSAW CONCERTO (1)
7	18.	DON'T GET AROUND MUCH ANYMORE (7)
19	19.	WAIT FOR ME, MARY (2)
17	20.	BOOGIE WOOGIE (2)

SEPTEMBER 1943

LM	TM	
1	1.	YOU'LL NEVER KNOW (5)
10	2.	SUNDAY, MONDAY, OR ALWAYS (2)
4	3.	ALL OR NOTHING AT ALL (3)
3	4.	IN THE BLUE OF THE EVENING (4)
13	5.	PAPER DOLL (2)
7	6.	PEOPLE WILL SAY WE'RE IN LOVE (3)
5	7.	IN MY ARMS (4)
11	8.	PISTOL PACKIN' MAMA (3)
15	9.	I HEARD YOU CRIED LAST NIGHT (2)
2	10.	COMIN' IN ON A WING AND A PRAYER (5)
16	11.	PUT YOUR ARMS AROUND ME, HONEY (2)
6	12.	IT CAN'T BE WRONG (6)
8	13.	IT'S ALWAYS YOU (4)
–	14.	I NEVER MENTION YOUR NAME (1)
–	15.	SAY A PRAYER FOR THE BOYS OVER THERE (1)
–	16.	IF YOU PLEASE (1)
–	17.	NO LETTER TODAY (1)
9	18.	JOHNNY ZERO (5)
19	19.	WAIT FOR ME, MARY (3)
17	20.	WARSAW CONCERTO (2)

OCTOBER 1943

LM	TM	
5	1.	PAPER DOLL (3)
2	2.	SUNDAY, MONDAY, OR ALWAYS (3)
8	3.	PISTOL PACKIN' MAMA (4)
1	4.	YOU'LL NEVER KNOW (6)
6	5.	PEOPLE WILL SAY WE'RE IN LOVE (4)
9	6.	I HEARD YOU CRIED LAST NIGHT (3)
11	7.	PUT YOUR ARMS AROUND ME, HONEY (3)
3	8.	ALL OR NOTHING AT ALL (4)
7	9.	IN MY ARMS (5)
16	10.	IF YOU PLEASE (2)
15	11.	SAY A PRAYER FOR THE BOYS OVER THERE (2)
4	12.	IN THE BLUE OF THE EVENING (5)
14	13.	I NEVER MENTION YOUR NAME (2)
–	14.	BLUE RAIN (1)
–	15.	CLOSE TO YOU (1)
17	16.	NO LETTER TODAY (2)
–	17.	VICT'RY POLKA (1)
–	18.	THEY'RE EITHER TOO YOUNG OR TOO OLD (1)
19	19.	WAIT FOR ME, MARY (4)
–	20.	DON'T CRY, BABY (1)

NOVEMBER 1943

LM	TM	
3	1.	PISTOL PACKIN' MAMA (5)
1	2.	PAPER DOLL (4)
5	3.	PEOPLE WILL SAY WE'RE IN LOVE (5)
2	4.	SUNDAY, MONDAY, OR ALWAYS (4)
7	5.	PUT YOUR ARMS AROUND ME, HONEY (4)
6	6.	I HEARD YOU CRIED LAST NIGHT (4)
18	7.	THEY'RE EITHER TOO YOUNG OR TOO OLD (2)
–	8.	OH, WHAT A BEAUTIFUL MORNIN' (1)
10	9.	IF YOU PLEASE (3)
17	10.	VICT'RY POLKA (2)
11	11.	SAY A PRAYER FOR THE BOYS OVER THERE (3)
–	12.	HOW SWEET YOU ARE (1)
–	13.	MY HEART TELLS ME (1)
14	14.	BLUE RAIN (2)
9	15.	IN MY ARMS (6)
4	16.	YOU'LL NEVER KNOW (7)
–	17.	BOOGIE WOOGIE (3)
20	18.	DON'T CRY, BABY (2)
–	19.	FOR THE FIRST TIME (1)
–	20.	THE DREAMER (1)

DECEMBER 1943

LM	TM	
2	1.	PAPER DOLL (5)
1	2.	PISTOL PACKIN' MAMA (6)
3	3.	PEOPLE WILL SAY WE'RE IN LOVE (6)
13	4.	MY HEART TELLS ME (2)
8	5.	OH, WHAT A BEAUTIFUL MORNIN' (2)
7	6.	THEY'RE EITHER TOO YOUNG OR TOO OLD (3)
4	7.	SUNDAY, MONDAY, OR ALWAYS (5)
10	8.	VICT'RY POLKA (3)
–	9.	I'LL BE HOME FOR CHRISTMAS (1)
–	10.	WHITE CHRISTMAS (1)
12	11.	HOW SWEET YOU ARE (2)
11	12.	SAY A PRAYER FOR THE BOYS OVER THERE (4)
6	13.	PUT YOUR ARMS AROUND ME, HONEY (5)
19	14.	FOR THE FIRST TIME (2)
17	15.	BOOGIE WOOGIE (4)
–	16.	SHOO-SHOO BABY (1)
20	17.	THE DREAMER (2)
9	18.	IF YOU PLEASE (4)
–	19.	MY IDEAL (1)
6	20.	I HEARD YOU CRIED LAST NIGHT (5)

JANUARY 1944

LM	TM	
1	1.	PAPER DOLL (6)
4	2.	MY HEART TELLS ME (3)
3	3.	PEOPLE WILL SAY WE'RE IN LOVE (7)
5	4.	OH, WHAT A BEAUTIFUL MORNIN' (3)
16	5.	SHOO-SHOO BABY (2)
2	6.	PISTOL PACKIN' MAMA (7)
19	7.	MY IDEAL (2)
6	8.	THEY'RE EITHER TOO YOUNG OR TOO OLD (4)
–	9.	MY SHINING HOUR (1)
8	10.	VICT'RY POLKA (4)
14	11.	FOR THE FIRST TIME (3)
9	12.	I'LL BE HOME FOR CHRISTMAS (2)
–	13.	NO LOVE, NO NOTHIN' (1)
15	14.	BOOGIE WOOGIE (5)
–	15.	MAIRZY DOATS (1)
–	16.	SPEAK LOW (1)
–	17.	STAR EYES (1)
–	18.	BESAME MUCHO (1)
10	19.	WHITE CHRISTMAS (2)
–	20.	LITTLE DID I KNOW (1)

FEBRUARY 1944

LM	TM	
5	1.	SHOO-SHOO BABY (3)
2	2.	MY HEART TELLS ME (4)
15	3.	MAIRZY DOATS (2)
13	4.	NO LOVE, NO NOTHIN' (2)
18	5.	BESAME MUCHO (2)
1	6.	PAPER DOLL (7)
7	7.	MY IDEAL (3)
17	8.	STAR EYES (2)
4	9.	OH, WHAT A BEAUTIFUL MORNIN' (4)
9	10.	MY SHINING HOUR (2)
–	11.	I COULDN'T SLEEP A WINK LAST NIGHT (1)
16	12.	SPEAK LOW (2)
–	13.	CHERRY (1)
11	14.	FOR THE FIRST TIME (4)
3	15.	PEOPLE WILL SAY WE'RE IN LOVE (8)
–	16.	HOLIDAY FOR STRINGS (1)
–	17.	WHEN THEY ASK ABOUT YOU (1)
14	18.	BOOGIE WOOGIE (6)
–	19.	A LOVELY WAY TO SPEND AN EVENING (1)
6	20.	PISTOL PACKIN' MAMA (8)

MARCH 1944

LM	TM	
5	1.	BESAME MUCHO (3)
1	2.	SHOO-SHOO BABY (4)
3	3.	MAIRZY DOATS (3)
4	4.	NO LOVE, NO NOTHIN' (3)
17	5.	WHEN THEY ASK ABOUT YOU (2)
11	6.	I COULDN'T SLEEP A WINK LAST NIGHT (2)
2	7.	MY HEART TELLS ME (5)
–	8.	POINCIANA (1)
7	9.	MY IDEAL (4)
19	10.	A LOVELY WAY TO SPEND AN EVENING (2)
8	11.	STAR EYES (3)
16	12.	HOLIDAY FOR STRINGS (2)
13	13.	CHERRY (2)
6	14.	PAPER DOLL (8)
–	15.	DO NOTHIN' TILL YOU HEAR FROM ME (1)
–	16.	DON'T SWEETHEART ME (1)
9	17.	OH, WHAT A BEAUTIFUL MORNIN' (5)
–	18.	I LOVE YOU (1)
–	19.	TAKE IT EASY (1)
12	20.	SPEAK LOW (3)

APRIL 1944

LM	TM	
1	1.	BESAME MUCHO (4)
–	2.	IT'S LOVE, LOVE, LOVE (1)
3	3.	MAIRZY DOATS (4)
8	4.	POINCIANA (2)
18	5.	I LOVE YOU (2)
6	6.	I COULDN'T SLEEP A WINK LAST NIGHT (3)
5	7.	WHEN THEY ASK ABOUT YOU (3)
16	8.	DON'T SWEETHEART ME (2)
–	9.	SAN FERNANDO VALLEY (1)
2	10.	SHOO-SHOO BABY (5)
12	11.	HOLIDAY FOR STRINGS (3)
10	12.	A LOVELY WAY TO SPEND AN EVENING (3)
–	13.	BY THE RIVER OF THE ROSES (1)
4	14.	NO LOVE, NO NOTHIN' (4)
15	15.	DO NOTHIN' TILL YOU HEAR FROM ME (2)
–	16.	I WISH I COULD HIDE INSIDE THIS LETTER (1)
–	17.	I'LL GET BY (AS LONG AS I HAVE YOU) (1)
–	18.	COW-COW BOOGIE (1)
–	19.	LONG AGO AND FAR AWAY (1)
19	20.	TAKE IT EASY (2)

MAY 1944

LM	TM	
5	1.	I LOVE YOU (3)
2	2.	IT'S LOVE, LOVE, LOVE (2)
9	3.	SAN FERNANDO VALLEY (2)
19	4.	LONG AGO AND FAR AWAY (2)
17	5.	I'LL GET BY (AS LONG AS I HAVE YOU) (2)
1	6.	BESAME MUCHO (5)
4	7.	POINCIANA (3)
8	8.	DON'T SWEETHEART ME (3)
–	9.	I'LL BE SEEING YOU (1)
7	10.	WHEN THEY ASK ABOUT YOU (4)
11	11.	HOLIDAY FOR STRINGS (4)
3	12.	MAIRZY DOATS (5)
–	13.	GOODNIGHT, WHEREVER YOU ARE (1)
6	14.	I COULDN'T SLEEP A WINK LAST NIGHT (4)
13	15.	BY THE RIVER OF THE ROSES (2)
–	16.	G.I. JIVE (1)
–	17.	AMOR (1)
10	18.	SHOO-SHOO BABY (6)
15	19.	DO NOTHIN' TILL YOU HEAR FROM ME (3)
–	20.	SUDDENLY IT'S SPRING (1)

JUNE 1944

LM	TM	
4	1.	LONG AGO AND FAR AWAY (3)
9	2.	I'LL BE SEEING YOU (2)
5	3.	I'LL GET BY (AS LONG AS I HAVE YOU) (3)
2	4.	IT'S LOVE, LOVE, LOVE (3)
1	5.	I LOVE YOU (4)
3	6.	SAN FERNANDO VALLEY (3)
13	7.	GOODNIGHT, WHEREVER YOU ARE (2)
17	8.	AMOR (2)
8	9.	DON'T SWEETHEART ME (4)
16	10.	G.I. JIVE (2)
–	11.	SWINGING ON A STAR (1)
–	12.	MILKMAN, KEEP THOSE BOTTLES QUIET (1)
11	13.	HOLIDAY FOR STRINGS (5)
–	14.	SOMEDAY I'LL MEET YOU AGAIN (1)
20	15.	SUDDENLY IT'S SPRING (2)
7	16.	POINCIANA (4)
–	17.	IT HAD TO BE YOU (1)
6	18.	BESAME MUCHO (6)
–	19.	TIME WAITS FOR NO ONE (1)
–	20.	TIME ALONE WILL TELL (1)

JULY 1944

LM	TM	
2	1.	I'LL BE SEEING YOU (3)
3	2.	I'LL GET BY (AS LONG AS I HAVE YOU) (4)
1	3.	LONG AGO AND FAR AWAY (4)
11	4.	SWINGING ON A STAR (2)
8	5.	AMOR (3)
7	6.	GOODNIGHT, WHEREVER YOU ARE (3)
10	7.	G.I. JIVE (3)
6	8.	SAN FERNANDO VALLEY (4)
19	9.	TIME WAITS FOR NO ONE (2)
12	10.	MILKMAN, KEEP THOSE BOTTLES QUIET (2)
5	11.	I LOVE YOU (5)
–	12.	YOU ALWAYS HURT THE ONE YOU LOVE (1)
4	13.	IT'S LOVE, LOVE, LOVE (4)
14	14.	SOMEDAY I'LL MEET YOU AGAIN (2)
–	15.	I'LL WALK ALONE (1)
17	16.	IT HAD TO BE YOU (2)
–	17.	STRAIGHTEN UP AND FLY RIGHT (1)
–	18.	HOW BLUE THE NIGHT (1)
9	19.	DON'T SWEETHEART ME (5)
–	20.	SWEET LORRAINE (1)

AUGUST 1944

LM	TM	
1	1.	I'LL BE SEEING YOU (4)
4	2.	SWINGING ON A STAR (3)
2	3.	I'LL GET BY (AS LONG AS I HAVE YOU) (5)
15	4.	I'LL WALK ALONE (2)
5	5.	AMOR (4)
9	6.	TIME WAITS FOR NO ONE (3)
3	7.	LONG AGO AND FAR AWAY (5)
16	8.	IT HAD TO BE YOU (3)
12	9.	YOU ALWAYS HURT THE ONE YOU LOVE (2)
7	10.	G.I. JIVE (4)
6	11.	GOODNIGHT, WHEREVER YOU ARE (4)
–	12.	IS YOU IS OR IS YOU AIN'T (MA' BABY) (1)
10	13.	MILKMAN, KEEP THOSE BOTTLES QUIET (3)
–	14.	IT COULD HAPPEN TO YOU (1)
17	15.	STRAIGHTEN UP AND FLY RIGHT (2)
–	16.	HIS ROCKING HORSE RAN AWAY (1)
–	17.	GOING MY WAY (1)
8	18.	SAN FERNANDO VALLEY (5)
–	19.	A FELLOW ON A FURLOUGH (1)
–	20.	TILL THEN (1)

SEPTEMBER 1944

LM	TM	
4	1.	I'LL WALK ALONE (3)
2	2.	SWINGING ON A STAR (4)
6	3.	TIME WAITS FOR NO ONE (4)
12	4.	IS YOU IS OR IS YOU AIN'T (MA' BABY) (2)
1	5.	I'LL BE SEEING YOU (5)
8	6.	IT HAD TO BE YOU (4)
5	7.	AMOR (5)
9	8.	YOU ALWAYS HURT THE ONE YOU LOVE (3)
14	9.	IT COULD HAPPEN TO YOU (2)
3	10.	I'LL GET BY (AS LONG AS I HAVE YOU) (6)
–	11.	PRETTY KITTY BLUE EYES (1)
10	12.	G.I. JIVE (5)
19	13.	A FELLOW ON A FURLOUGH (2)
–	14.	HOW MANY HEARTS HAVE YOU BROKEN (1)
16	15.	HIS ROCKING HORSE RAN AWAY (2)
–	16.	DANCE WITH A DOLLY (1)
20	17.	TILL THEN (2)
11	18.	GOODNIGHT, WHEREVER YOU ARE (5)
7	19.	LONG AGO AND FAR AWAY (6)
–	20.	THE DAY AFTER FOREVER (1)

OCTOBER 1944

LM	TM	
1	1.	I'LL WALK ALONE (4)
2	2.	SWINGING ON A STAR (5)
4	3.	IS YOU IS OR IS YOU AIN'T (MA' BABY) (3)
14	4.	HOW MANY HEARTS HAVE YOU BROKEN (2)
3	5.	TIME WAITS FOR NO ONE (5)
6	6.	IT HAD TO BE YOU (5)
16	7.	DANCE WITH A DOLLY (2)
8	8.	YOU ALWAYS HURT THE ONE YOU LOVE (4)
–	9.	TOGETHER (1)
5	10.	I'LL BE SEEING YOU (6)
–	11.	THERE'LL BE A HOT TIME IN THE TOWN OF BERLIN (1)
9	12.	IT COULD HAPPEN TO YOU (3)
11	13.	PRETTY KITTY BLUE EYES (2)
–	14.	THE TROLLEY SONG (1)
–	15.	AND HER TEARS FLOWED LIKE WINE (1)
–	16.	AN HOUR NEVER PASSES (1)
–	17.	SWEET AND LOVELY (1)
–	18.	ALWAYS (1)
–	19.	SMOKE ON THE WATER (1)
–	20.	THE PATTY-CAKE MAN (1)

NOVEMBER 1944

LM	TM	
1	1.	I'LL WALK ALONE (5)
14	2.	THE TROLLEY SONG (2)
7	3.	DANCE WITH A DOLLY (3)
9	4.	TOGETHER (2)
4	5.	HOW MANY HEARTS HAVE YOU BROKEN (3)
2	6.	SWINGING ON A STAR (6)
18	7.	ALWAYS (2)
8	8.	YOU ALWAYS HURT THE ONE YOU LOVE (5)
–	9.	I'M MAKING BELIEVE (1)
11	10.	THERE'LL BE A HOT TIME IN THE TOWN OF BERLIN (2)
3	11.	IS YOU IS OR IS YOU AIN'T (MA' BABY) (4)
15	12.	AND HER TEARS FLOWED LIKE WINE (2)
–	13.	TOO-RA LOO-RA LOO-RAL (1)
6	14.	IT HAD TO BE YOU (6)
–	15.	I DREAM OF YOU (1)
10	16.	I'LL BE SEEING YOU (7)
–	17.	THERE GOES THAT SONG AGAIN (1)
–	18.	INTO EACH LIFE SOME RAIN MUST FALL (1)
–	19.	WHAT A DIFF'RENCE A DAY MAKES (1)
5	20.	TIME WAITS FOR NO ONE (6)

DECEMBER 1944

LM	TM	
2	1.	THE TROLLEY SONG (3)
3	2.	DANCE WITH A DOLLY (4)
9	3.	I'M MAKING BELIEVE (2)
4	4.	TOGETHER (3)
–	5.	DON'T FENCE ME IN (1)
1	6.	I'LL WALK ALONE (6)
–	7.	WHITE CHRISTMAS (1)
7	8.	ALWAYS (3)
17	9.	THERE GOES THAT SONG AGAIN (2)
15	10.	I DREAM OF YOU (2)
18	11.	INTO EACH LIFE SOME RAIN MUST FALL (2)
8	12.	YOU ALWAYS HURT THE ONE YOU LOVE (6)
13	13.	TOO-RA LOO-RA LOO-RAL (2)
5	14.	HOW MANY HEARTS HAVE YOU BROKEN (4)
12	15.	AND HER TEARS FLOWED LIKE WINE (3)
–	16.	I'LL BE HOME FOR CHRISTMAS (1)
10	17.	THERE'LL BE A HOT TIME IN THE TOWN OF BERLIN (3)
–	18.	LET ME LOVE YOU TONIGHT (1)
–	19.	I DON'T WANT TO LOVE YOU (LIKE I DO) (1)
–	20.	THE VERY THOUGHT OF YOU (1)

JANUARY 1945

LM	TM	
5	1.	DON'T FENCE ME IN (2)
9	2.	THERE GOES THAT SONG AGAIN (3)
1	3.	THE TROLLEY SONG (4)
10	4.	I DREAM OF YOU (3)
3	5.	I'M MAKING BELIEVE (3)
2	6.	DANCE WITH A DOLLY (5)
–	7.	AC-CENT-TCHU-ATE THE POSITIVE (1)
8	8.	ALWAYS (4)
11	9.	INTO EACH LIFE SOME RAIN MUST FALL (3)
–	10.	RUM AND COCA COLA (1)
19	11.	I DON'T WANT TO LOVE YOU (LIKE I DO) (2)
4	12.	TOGETHER (4)
15	13.	AND HER TEARS FLOWED LIKE WINE (4)
12	14.	YOU ALWAYS HURT THE ONE YOU LOVE (7)
6	15.	I'LL WALK ALONE (7)
–	16.	SWEET DREAMS, SWEETHEART (1)
–	17.	I'M CONFESSIN' (THAT I LOVE YOU) (1)
–	18.	I'M WASTIN' MY TEARS ON YOU (1)
–	19.	COCKTAILS FOR TWO (1)
–	20.	MEET ME IN ST. LOUIS, LOUIS (1)

FEBRUARY 1945

LM	TM	
7	1.	AC-CENT-TCHU-ATE THE POSITIVE (2)
1	2.	DON'T FENCE ME IN (3)
10	3.	RUM AND COCA COLA (2)
4	4.	I DREAM OF YOU (4)
2	5.	THERE GOES THAT SONG AGAIN (4)
–	6.	A LITTLE ON THE LONELY SIDE (1)
–	7.	SATURDAY NIGHT (IS THE LONELIEST NIGHT OF THE WEEK) (1)
16	8.	SWEET DREAMS, SWEETHEART (2)
19	9.	COCKTAILS FOR TWO (2)
–	10.	I'M BEGINNING TO SEE THE LIGHT (1)
5	11.	I'M MAKING BELIEVE (4)
–	12.	MY DREAMS ARE GETTING BETTER ALL THE TIME (1)
17	13.	I'M CONFESSIN' (THAT I LOVE YOU) (2)
9	14.	INTO EACH LIFE SOME RAIN MUST FALL (4)
8	15.	ALWAYS (5)
–	16.	TWILIGHT TIME (1)
3	17.	THE TROLLEY SONG (5)
–	18.	SLEIGH RIDE IN JULY (1)
–	19.	EVELINA (1)
–	20.	LET'S TAKE THE LONG WAY HOME (1)

MARCH 1945

LM	TM	
1	1.	AC-CENT-TCHU-ATE THE POSITIVE (3)
3	2.	RUM AND COCA COLA (3)
6	3.	A LITTLE ON THE LONELY SIDE (2)
12	4.	MY DREAMS ARE GETTING BETTER ALL THE TIME (2)
2	5.	DON'T FENCE ME IN (4)
7	6.	SATURDAY NIGHT (IS THE LONELIEST NIGHT OF THE WEEK) (2)
10	7.	I'M BEGINNING TO SEE THE LIGHT (2)
–	8.	CANDY (1)
8	9.	SWEET DREAMS, SWEETHEART (3)
4	10.	I DREAM OF YOU (5)
–	11.	MORE AND MORE (1)
9	12.	COCKTAILS FOR TWO (3)
–	13.	DREAM (1)
–	14.	THE THREE CABALLEROS (1)
–	15.	SENTIMENTAL JOURNEY (1)
13	16.	I'M CONFESSIN' (THAT I LOVE YOU) (3)
–	17.	THERE! I'VE SAID IT AGAIN (1)
–	18.	(ALL OF A SUDDEN) MY HEART SINGS (1)
–	19.	I WANNA GET MARRIED (1)
–	20.	OPUS NO. 1 (1)

APRIL 1945

LM	TM	
4	1.	MY DREAMS ARE GETTING BETTER ALL THE TIME (3)
8	2.	CANDY (2)
7	3.	I'M BEGINNING TO SEE THE LIGHT (3)
3	4.	A LITTLE ON THE LONELY SIDE (3)
–	5.	JUST A PRAYER AWAY (1)
2	6.	RUM AND COCA COLA (4)
1	7.	AC-CENT-TCHU-ATE THE POSITIVE (4)
13	8.	DREAM (2)
6	9.	SATURDAY NIGHT (IS THE LONELIEST NIGHT OF THE WEEK) (3)
–	10.	LAURA (1)
15	11.	SENTIMENTAL JOURNEY (2)
17	12.	THERE! I'VE SAID IT AGAIN (2)
9	13.	SWEET DREAMS, SWEETHEART (4)
–	14.	ALL OF MY LIFE (1)
11	15.	MORE AND MORE (2)
–	16.	STUFF LIKE THAT THERE (1)
–	17.	I SHOULD CARE (1)
–	18.	I DON'T CARE WHO KNOWS IT (1)
18	19.	(ALL OF A SUDDEN) MY HEART SINGS (2)
20	20.	OPUS NO. 1 (2)

MAY 1945

LM	TM	
1	1.	MY DREAMS ARE GETTING BETTER ALL THE TIME (4)
2	2.	CANDY (3)
10	3.	LAURA (2)
11	4.	SENTIMENTAL JOURNEY (3)
3	5.	I'M BEGINNING TO SEE THE LIGHT (4)
8	6.	DREAM (3)
12	7.	THERE! I'VE SAID IT AGAIN (3)
5	8.	JUST A PRAYER AWAY (2)
14	9.	ALL OF MY LIFE (2)
–	10.	CALDONIA (1)
–	11.	BELL-BOTTOM TROUSERS (1)
–	12.	CHLOE (1)
16	13.	STUFF LIKE THAT THERE (2)
4	14.	A LITTLE ON THE LONELY SIDE (4)
17	15.	I SHOULD CARE (2)
–	16.	YAH-TA-TA, YAH-TA-TA (TALK, TALK, TALK) (1)
–	17.	TIPPIN' IN (1)
–	18.	POOR LITTLE RHODE ISLAND (1)
–	19.	I WISH (1)
9	20.	SATURDAY NIGHT (IS THE LONELIEST NIGHT OF THE WEEK) (4)

JUNE 1945

LM	TM	
4	1.	SENTIMENTAL JOURNEY (4)
11	2.	BELL-BOTTOM TROUSERS (2)
3	3.	LAURA (3)
6	4.	DREAM (4)
2	5.	CANDY (4)
7	6.	THERE! I'VE SAID IT AGAIN (4)
1	7.	MY DREAMS ARE GETTING BETTER ALL THE TIME (5)
10	8.	CALDONIA (2)
–	9.	YOU BELONG TO MY HEART (1)
8	10.	JUST A PRAYER AWAY (3)
15	11.	I SHOULD CARE (3)
9	12.	ALL OF MY LIFE (3)
–	13.	THE MORE I SEE YOU (1)
19	14.	I WISH (2)
13	15.	STUFF LIKE THAT THERE (3)
–	16.	GOOD, GOOD, GOOD (1)
5	17.	I'M BEGINNING TO SEE THE LIGHT (5)
–	18.	BAIA (1)
–	19.	(I LOVE YOU) SWEETHEART OF ALL MY DREAMS (1)
16	20.	YAH-TA-TA, YAH-TA-TA (TALK, TALK, TALK) (2)

JULY 1945

LM	TM	
1	1.	SENTIMENTAL JOURNEY (5)
2	2.	BELL-BOTTOM TROUSERS (3)
6	3.	THERE! I'VE SAID IT AGAIN (5)
4	4.	DREAM (5)
–	5.	GOTTA BE THIS OR THAT (1)
13	6.	THE MORE I SEE YOU (2)
9	7.	YOU BELONG TO MY HEART (2)
–	8.	IF I LOVED YOU (1)
3	9.	LAURA (4)
–	10.	ON THE ATCHESON, TOPEKA, AND THE SANTA FE (1)
–	11.	I WISH I KNEW (1)
12	12.	ALL OF MY LIFE (4)
–	13.	CHOPIN'S POLONAISE (1)
8	14.	CALDONIA (3)
11	15.	I SHOULD CARE (4)
10	16.	JUST A PRAYER AWAY (4)
16	17.	GOOD, GOOD, GOOD (2)
–	18.	THERE MUST BE A WAY (1)
–	19.	A FRIEND OF YOURS (1)
5	20.	CANDY (5)

AUGUST 1945

LM	TM	
10	1.	ON THE ATCHESON, TOPEKA, AND THE SANTA FE (2)
1	2.	SENTIMENTAL JOURNEY (6)
8	3.	IF I LOVED YOU (2)
2	4.	BELL-BOTTOM TROUSERS (4)
5	5.	GOTTA BE THIS OR THAT (2)
4	6.	DREAM (6)
11	7.	I WISH I KNEW (2)
13	8.	CHOPIN'S POLONAISE (2)
3	9.	THERE! I'VE SAID IT AGAIN (6)
–	10.	TILL THE END OF TIME (1)
6	11.	THE MORE I SEE YOU (3)
7	12.	YOU BELONG TO MY HEART (3)
–	13.	TAMPICO (1)
19	14.	A FRIEND OF YOURS (2)
18	15.	THERE MUST BE A WAY (2)
–	16.	I'M GONNA LOVE THAT GAL (GUY) (1)
9	17.	LAURA (5)
–	18.	WHO THREW THE WHISKEY IN THE WELL? (1)
–	19.	HONG KONG BLUES (1)
–	20.	JUNE IS BUSTIN' OUT ALL OVER (1)

SEPTEMBER 1945

LM	TM	
1	1.	ON THE ATCHESON, TOPEKA, AND THE SANTA FE (3)
10	2.	TILL THE END OF TIME (2)
3	3.	IF I LOVED YOU (3)
5	4.	GOTTA BE THIS OR THAT (3)
16	5.	I'M GONNA LOVE THAT GAL (GUY) (2)
7	6.	I WISH I KNEW (3)
–	7.	ALONG THE NAVAJO TRAIL (1)
2	8.	SENTIMENTAL JOURNEY (7)
15	9.	THERE MUST BE A WAY (3)
4	10.	BELL-BOTTOM TROUSERS (5)
–	11.	I DON'T CARE WHO KNOWS IT (2)
8	12.	CHOPIN'S POLONAISE (3)
11	13.	THE MORE I SEE YOU (4)
13	14.	TAMPICO (2)
6	15.	DREAM (7)
–	16.	(YOU CAME ALONG) OUT OF NOWHERE (1)
–	17.	I'LL BUY THAT DREAM (1)
–	18.	THERE'S NO YOU (1)
9	19.	THERE! I'VE SAID IT AGAIN (7)
–	20.	BOOGIE WOOGIE (1)

OCTOBER 1945

LM	TM	
2	1.	TILL THE END OF TIME (3)
1	2.	ON THE ATCHESON, TOPEKA, AND THE SANTA FE (4)
17	3.	I'LL BUY THAT DREAM (2)
7	4.	ALONG THE NAVAJO TRAIL (2)
5	5.	I'M GONNA LOVE THAT GAL (GUY) (3)
3	6.	IF I LOVED YOU (4)
4	7.	GOTTA BE THIS OR THAT (4)
–	8.	THAT'S FOR ME (1)
–	9.	IT'S ONLY A PAPER MOON (1)
–	10.	IT'S BEEN A LONG, LONG TIME (1)
16	11.	(YOU CAME ALONG) OUT OF NOWHERE (2)
–	12.	HOW DEEP IS THE OCEAN? (1)
6	13.	I WISH I KNEW (4)
–	14.	LOVE LETTERS (1)
–	15.	AND THERE YOU ARE (1)
14	16.	TAMPICO (3)
–	17.	A COTTAGE FOR SALE (1)
11	18.	I DON'T CARE WHO KNOWS IT (3)
–	19.	HONG KONG BLUES (2)
–	20.	THE BLOND SAILOR (1)

NOVEMBER 1945

LM	TM	
1	1.	TILL THE END OF TIME (4)
10	2.	IT'S BEEN A LONG, LONG TIME (2)
3	3.	I'LL BUY THAT DREAM (3)
8	4.	THAT'S FOR ME (2)
4	5.	ALONG THE NAVAJO TRAIL (3)
2	6.	ON THE ATCHESON, TOPEKA, AND THE SANTA FE (5)
–	7.	CHICKERY CHICK (1)
9	8.	IT'S ONLY A PAPER MOON (2)
–	9.	IT MIGHT AS WELL BE SPRING (1)
5	10.	I'M GONNA LOVE THAT GAL (GUY) (4)
12	11.	HOW DEEP IS THE OCEAN? (2)
6	12.	IF I LOVED YOU (5)
–	13.	(DID YOU EVER GET) THAT FEELING IN THE MOONLIGHT (1)
14	14.	LOVE LETTERS (2)
–	15.	I CAN'T BEGIN TO TELL YOU (1)
–	16.	WAITIN' FOR THE TRAIN TO COME IN (1)
7	17.	GOTTA BE THIS OR THAT (5)
–	18.	NO CAN DO (1)
16	19.	TAMPICO (4)
20	20.	THE BLOND SAILOR (2)

DECEMBER 1945

LM	TM	
2	1.	IT'S BEEN A LONG, LONG TIME (3)
9	2.	IT MIGHT AS WELL BE SPRING (2)
7	3.	CHICKERY CHICK (2)
15	4.	I CAN'T BEGIN TO TELL YOU (2)
3	5.	I'LL BUY THAT DREAM (4)
16	6.	WAITIN' FOR THE TRAIN TO COME IN (2)
4	7.	THAT'S FOR ME (3)
1	8.	TILL THE END OF TIME (5)
–	9.	SYMPHONY (1)
–	10.	WHITE CHRISTMAS (1)
13	11.	(DID YOU EVER GET) THAT FEELING IN THE MOONLIGHT (2)
8	12.	IT'S ONLY A PAPER MOON (3)
5	13.	ALONG THE NAVAJO TRAIL (4)
14	14.	LOVE LETTERS (3)
–	15.	JUST A LITTLE FOND AFFECTION (1)
12	16.	IF I LOVED YOU (6)
–	17.	LET IT SNOW! LET IT SNOW! LET IT SNOW! (1)
–	18.	LILY BELLE (1)
–	19.	IN THE MIDDLE OF MAY (1)
–	20.	SOME SUNDAY MORNING (1)

JANUARY 1946

LM	TM	
9	1.	SYMPHONY (2)
4	2.	I CAN'T BEGIN TO TELL YOU (3)
2	3.	IT MIGHT AS WELL BE SPRING (3)
1	4.	IT'S BEEN A LONG, LONG TIME (4)
17	5.	LET IT SNOW! LET IT SNOW! LET IT SNOW! (2)
6	6.	WAITIN' FOR THE TRAIN TO COME IN (3)
3	7.	CHICKERY CHICK (3)
–	8.	AREN'T YOU GLAD YOU'RE YOU? (1)
20	9.	SOME SUNDAY MORNING (2)
–	10.	DIG YOU LATER (A HUBBA-HUBBA-HUBBA) (1)
–	11.	DOCTOR, LAWYER, INDIAN CHIEF (1)
7	12.	THAT'S FOR ME (4)
–	13.	I'M ALWAYS CHASING RAINBOWS (1)
15	14.	JUST A LITTLE FOND AFFECTION (2)
–	15.	COME TO BABY, DO! (1)
19	16.	IN THE MIDDLE OF MAY (2)
11	17.	(DID YOU EVER GET) THAT FEELING IN THE MOONLIGHT (3)
10	18.	WHITE CHRISTMAS (2)
–	19.	THE BELLS OF ST. MARY'S (1)
–	20.	BUZZ ME (1)

FEBRUARY 1946

LM	TM	
1	1.	SYMPHONY (3)
5	2.	LET IT SNOW! LET IT SNOW! LET IT SNOW! (3)
2	3.	I CAN'T BEGIN TO TELL YOU (4)
13	4.	I'M ALWAYS CHASING RAINBOWS (2)
3	5.	IT MIGHT AS WELL BE SPRING (4)
8	6.	AREN'T YOU GLAD YOU'RE YOU? (2)
11	7.	DOCTOR, LAWYER, INDIAN CHIEF (2)
–	8.	PERSONALITY (1)
14	9.	JUST A LITTLE FOND AFFECTION (3)
9	10.	SOME SUNDAY MORNING (3)
7	11.	CHICKERY CHICK (4)
10	12.	DIG YOU LATER (A HUBBA-HUBBA-HUBBA) (2)
–	13.	DAY BY DAY (1)
–	14.	OH! WHAT IT SEEMED TO BE (1)
6	15.	WAITIN' FOR THE TRAIN TO COME IN (4)
19	16.	THE BELLS OF ST. MARY'S (2)
15	17.	COME TO BABY, DO! (2)
12	18.	THAT'S FOR ME (5)
20	19.	BUZZ ME (2)
4	20.	IT'S BEEN A LONG, LONG TIME (5)

MARCH 1946

LM	TM	
14	1.	OH! WHAT IT SEEMED TO BE (2)
1	2.	SYMPHONY (4)
8	3.	PERSONALITY (2)
7	4.	DOCTOR, LAWYER, INDIAN CHIEF (3)
2	5.	LET IT SNOW! LET IT SNOW! LET IT SNOW! (4)
–	6.	YOU WON'T BE SATISFIED (UNTIL YOU BREAK MY HEART) (1)
13	7.	DAY BY DAY (2)
3	8.	I CAN'T BEGIN TO TELL YOU (5)
4	9.	I'M ALWAYS CHASING RAINBOWS (3)
10	10.	SOME SUNDAY MORNING (4)
–	11.	ONE-ZY, TWO-ZY (I LOVE YOU-ZY) (1)
6	12.	AREN'T YOU GLAD YOU'RE YOU? (3)
–	13.	ATLANTA, GA. (1)
12	14.	DIG YOU LATER (A HUBBA-HUBBA-HUBBA) (3)
5	15.	IT MIGHT AS WELL BE SPRING (5)
–	16.	HERE COMES HEAVEN AGAIN (1)
–	17.	SHOO-FLY PIE AND APPLE PAN DOWDY (1)
9	18.	JUST A LITTLE FOND AFFECTION (4)
–	19.	SEEMS LIKE OLD TIMES (1)
–	20.	MacNAMARA'S BAND (1)

APRIL 1946

LM	TM	
1	1.	OH! WHAT IT SEEMED TO BE (3)
11	2.	ONE-ZY, TWO-ZY (I LOVE YOU-ZY) (2)
6	3.	YOU WON'T BE SATISFIED (UNTIL YOU BREAK MY HEART) (2)
3	4.	PERSONALITY (3)
17	5.	SHOO-FLY PIE AND APPLE PAN DOWDY (2)
7	6.	DAY BY DAY (3)
–	7.	LAUGHING ON THE OUTSIDE (1)
4	8.	DOCTOR, LAWYER, INDIAN CHIEF (4)
–	9.	SIOUX CITY SUE (1)
–	10.	ALL THROUGH THE DAY (1)
13	11.	ATLANTA, GA. (2)
19	12.	SEEMS LIKE OLD TIMES (2)
9	13.	I'M ALWAYS CHASING RAINBOWS (4)
2	14.	SYMPHONY (5)
–	15.	PRISONER OF LOVE (1)
–	16.	I'M A BIG GIRL NOW (1)
–	17.	I'M GLAD I WAITED FOR YOU (1)
10	18.	SOME SUNDAY MORNING (5)
–	19.	EASTER PARADE (1)
–	20.	HEY! BA BA RE-BOP (1)

MAY 1946

LM	TM	
7	1.	LAUGHING ON THE OUTSIDE (2)
1	2.	OH! WHAT IT SEEMED TO BE (4)
–	3.	THE GYPSY (1)
5	4.	SHOO-FLY PIE AND APPLE PAN DOWDY (3)
10	5.	ALL THROUGH THE DAY (2)
9	6.	SIOUX CITY SUE (2)
15	7.	PRISONER OF LOVE (2)
2	8.	ONE-ZY, TWO-ZY (I LOVE YOU-ZY) (3)
3	9.	YOU WON'T BE SATISFIED (UNTIL YOU BREAK MY HEART) (3)
16	10.	I'M A BIG GIRL NOW (2)
–	11.	CEMENT MIXER (PUT-TI, PUT-TI) (1)
12	12.	SEEMS LIKE OLD TIMES (3)
–	13.	THEY SAY IT'S WONDERFUL (1)
6	14.	DAY BY DAY (4)
–	15.	IN LOVE IN VAIN (1)
4	16.	PERSONALITY (4)
–	17.	FULL MOON AND EMPTY ARMS (1)
–	18.	WE'LL GATHER LILACS (1)
13	19.	I'M ALWAYS CHASING RAINBOWS (5)
–	20.	I DON'T KNOW ENOUGH ABOUT YOU (1)

JUNE 1946

LM	TM	
3	1.	THE GYPSY (2)
1	2.	LAUGHING ON THE OUTSIDE (3)
13	3.	THEY SAY IT'S WONDERFUL (2)
7	4.	PRISONER OF LOVE (3)
5	5.	ALL THROUGH THE DAY (3)
6	6.	SIOUX CITY SUE (3)
20	7.	I DON'T KNOW ENOUGH ABOUT YOU (2)
17	8.	FULL MOON AND EMPTY ARMS (2)
4	9.	SHOO-FLY PIE AND APPLE PAN DOWDY (4)
11	10.	CEMENT MIXER (PUT-TI, PUT-TI) (2)
15	11.	IN LOVE IN VAIN (2)
–	12.	DOIN' WHAT COMES NATUR'LY (1)
2	13.	OH! WHAT IT SEEMED TO BE (5)
–	14.	DO YOU LOVE ME? (1)
–	15.	HEY! BA BA RE-BOP (2)
10	16.	I'M A BIG GIRL NOW (3)
18	17.	WE'LL GATHER LILACS (2)
–	18.	COME RAIN OR COME SHINE (1)
12	19.	SEEMS LIKE OLD TIMES (4)
–	20.	COAX ME A LITTLE BIT (1)

JULY 1946

LM	TM	
1	1.	THE GYPSY (3)
3	2.	THEY SAY IT'S WONDERFUL (3)
12	3.	DOIN' WHAT COMES NATUR'LY (2)
4	4.	PRISONER OF LOVE (4)
7	5.	I DON'T KNOW ENOUGH ABOUT YOU (3)
2	6.	LAUGHING ON THE OUTSIDE (4)
–	7.	SURRENDER (1)
6	8.	SIOUX CITY SUE (4)
–	9.	I GOT THE SUN IN THE MORNING (1)
5	10.	ALL THROUGH THE DAY (4)
8	11.	FULL MOON AND EMPTY ARMS (3)
11	12.	IN LOVE IN VAIN (3)
–	13.	TO EACH HIS OWN (1)
–	14.	I DON'T KNOW WHY (I JUST DO) (1)
18	15.	COME RAIN OR COME SHINE (2)
14	16.	DO YOU LOVE ME? (2)
–	17.	ONE MORE TOMORROW (1)
10	18.	CEMENT MIXER (PUT-TI, PUT-TI) (3)
–	19.	THE HOUSE OF BLUE LIGHTS (1)
15	20.	HEY! BA BA RE-BOP (3)

AUGUST 1946

LM	TM	
1	1.	THE GYPSY (4)
13	2.	TO EACH HIS OWN (2)
3	3.	DOIN' WHAT COMES NATUR'LY (3)
7	4.	SURRENDER (2)
2	5.	THEY SAY IT'S WONDERFUL (4)
5	6.	I DON'T KNOW ENOUGH ABOUT YOU (4)
4	7.	PRISONER OF LOVE (5)
9	8.	I GOT THE SUN IN THE MORNING (2)
–	9.	FIVE MINUTES MORE (1)
12	10.	IN LOVE IN VAIN (4)
14	11.	I DON'T KNOW WHY (I JUST DO) (2)
10	12.	ALL THROUGH THE DAY (5)
–	13.	WHO TOLD YOU THAT LIE? (1)
17	14.	ONE MORE TOMORROW (2)
–	15.	SOUTH AMERICA, TAKE IT AWAY (1)
11	16.	FULL MOON AND EMPTY ARMS (4)
–	17.	IF YOU WERE THE ONLY GIRL (1)
8	18.	SIOUX CITY SUE (5)
–	19.	THERE'S NO ONE BUT YOU (1)
–	20.	I'D BE LOST WITHOUT YOU (1)

SEPTEMBER 1946

LM	TM	
2	1.	TO EACH HIS OWN (3)
9	2.	FIVE MINUTES MORE (2)
4	3.	SURRENDER (3)
15	4.	SOUTH AMERICA, TAKE IT AWAY (2)
5	5.	THEY SAY IT'S WONDERFUL (5)
1	6.	THE GYPSY (5)
17	7.	IF YOU WERE THE ONLY GIRL (2)
3	8.	DOIN' WHAT COMES NATUR'LY (4)
8	9.	I GOT THE SUN IN THE MORNING (3)
11	10.	I DON'T KNOW WHY (I JUST DO) (3)
6	11.	I DON'T KNOW ENOUGH ABOUT YOU (5)
20	12.	I'D BE LOST WITHOUT YOU (2)
–	13.	RUMORS ARE FLYING (1)
–	14.	BLUE SKIES (1)
14	15.	ONE MORE TOMORROW (3)
–	16.	CHOO CHOO CH'BOOGIE (1)
7	17.	PRISONER OF LOVE (6)
10	18.	IN LOVE IN VAIN (5)
–	19.	WITHOUT YOU (1)
–	20.	THIS IS ALWAYS (1)

OCTOBER 1946

LM	TM	
1	1.	TO EACH HIS OWN (4)
2	2.	FIVE MINUTES MORE (3)
13	3.	RUMORS ARE FLYING (2)
4	4.	SOUTH AMERICA, TAKE IT AWAY (3)
3	5.	SURRENDER (4)
7	6.	IF YOU WERE THE ONLY GIRL (3)
8	7.	DOIN' WHAT COMES NATUR'LY (5)
–	8.	OLE BUTTERMILK SKY (1)
5	9.	THEY SAY IT'S WONDERFUL (6)
–	10.	YOU KEEP COMING BACK LIKE A SONG (1)
12	11.	I'D BE LOST WITHOUT YOU (3)
–	12.	LINGER IN MY ARMS A LITTLE LONGER, BABY (1)
–	13.	SEPTEMBER SONG (1)
10	14.	I DON'T KNOW WHY (I JUST DO) (4)
20	15.	THIS IS ALWAYS (2)
16	16.	CHOO CHOO CH'BOOGIE (2)
14	17.	BLUE SKIES (2)
–	18.	I GUESS I'LL GET THE PAPERS AND GO HOME (1)
–	19.	AND THEN IT'S HEAVEN (1)
9	20.	I GOT THE SUN IN THE MORNING (4)

NOVEMBER 1946

LM	TM	
3	1.	RUMORS ARE FLYING (3)
2	2.	FIVE MINUTES MORE (4)
8	3.	OLE BUTTERMILK SKY (2)
1	4.	TO EACH HIS OWN (5)
10	5.	YOU KEEP COMING BACK LIKE A SONG (2)
4	6.	SOUTH AMERICA, TAKE IT AWAY (4)
–	7.	THE WHOLE WORLD IS SINGING MY SONG (1)
–	8.	THE OLD LAMP-LIGHTER (1)
15	9.	THIS IS ALWAYS (3)
6	10.	IF YOU WERE THE ONLY GIRL (4)
–	11.	THE THINGS WE DID LAST SUMMER (1)
17	12.	BLUE SKIES (3)
19	13.	AND THEN IT'S HEAVEN (2)
13	14.	SEPTEMBER SONG (2)
–	15.	(I LOVE YOU) FOR SENTIMENTAL REASONS) (1)
–	16.	THE COFFEE SONG (1)
12	17.	LINGER IN MY ARMS A LITTLE LONGER, BABY (2)
18	18.	I GUESS I'LL GET THE PAPERS AND GO HOME (2)
5	19.	SURRENDER (5)
–	20.	THE GIRL THAT I MARRY (1)

DECEMBER 1946

LM	TM	
3	1.	OLE BUTTERMILK SKY (3)
8	2.	THE OLD LAMP-LIGHTER (2)
1	3.	RUMORS ARE FLYING (4)
7	4.	THE WHOLE WORLD IS SINGING MY SONG (2)
15	5.	(I LOVE YOU) FOR SENTIMENTAL REASONS) (2)
–	6.	WHITE CHRISTMAS (1)
–	7.	ZIP-A-DEE-DOO-DAH (1)
11	8.	THE THINGS WE DID LAST SUMMER (2)
2	9.	FIVE MINUTES MORE (5)
5	10.	YOU KEEP COMING BACK LIKE A SONG (3)
–	11.	A GAL IN CALICO (1)
–	12.	HUGGIN' AND CHALKIN' (1)
14	13.	SEPTEMBER SONG (3)
4	14.	TO EACH HIS OWN (6)
–	15.	THE CHRISTMAS SONG (1)
16	16.	THE COFFEE SONG (2)
–	17.	IT'S ALL OVER NOW (1)
–	18.	SOONER OR LATER (1)
–	19.	WINTER WONDERLAND (1)
20	20.	THE GIRL THAT I MARRY (2)

JANUARY 1947

LM	TM	
2	1.	THE OLD LAMP-LIGHTER (3)
5	2.	(I LOVE YOU) FOR SENTIMENTAL REASONS) (3)
1	3.	OLE BUTTERMILK SKY (4)
11	4.	A GAL IN CALICO (2)
7	5.	ZIP-A-DEE-DOO-DAH (2)
12	6.	HUGGIN' AND CHALKIN' (2)
4	7.	THE WHOLE WORLD IS SINGING MY SONG (3)
3	8.	RUMORS ARE FLYING (5)
8	9.	THE THINGS WE DID LAST SUMMER (3)
–	10.	OH, BUT I DO! (1)
18	11.	SOONER OR LATER (2)
10	12.	YOU KEEP COMING BACK LIKE A SONG (4)
–	13.	FOR YOU, FOR ME, FOREVERMORE (1)
–	14.	MANAGUA, NICARAGUA (1)
20	15.	THE GIRL THAT I MARRY (3)
13	16.	SEPTEMBER SONG (4)
6	17.	WHITE CHRISTMAS (2)
–	18.	I'LL CLOSE MY EYES (1)
–	19.	CHRISTMAS ISLAND (1)
19	20.	WINTER WONDERLAND (2)

FEBRUARY 1947

LM	TM	
2	1.	(I LOVE YOU) FOR SENTIMENTAL REASONS) (4)
1	2.	THE OLD LAMP-LIGHTER (4)
4	3.	A GAL IN CALICO (3)
14	4.	MANAGUA, NICARAGUA (2)
–	5.	OPEN THE DOOR, RICHARD! (1)
6	6.	HUGGIN' AND CHALKIN' (3)
3	7.	OLE BUTTERMILK SKY (5)
5	8.	ZIP-A-DEE-DOO-DAH (3)
–	9.	ANNIVERSARY SONG (1)
10	10.	OH, BUT I DO! (2)
18	11.	I'LL CLOSE MY EYES (2)
–	12.	SONATA (1)
11	13.	SOONER OR LATER (3)
–	14.	GUILTY (1)
7	15.	THE WHOLE WORLD IS SINGING MY SONG (4)
9	16.	THE THINGS WE DID LAST SUMMER (4)
15	17.	THE GIRL THAT I MARRY (4)
–	18.	AIN'T NOBODY HERE BUT US CHICKENS (1)
–	19.	A RAINY NIGHT IN RIO (1)
–	20.	HOW ARE THINGS IN GLOCCA MORRA? (1)

MARCH 1947

LM	TM	
9	1.	ANNIVERSARY SONG (2)
4	2.	MANAGUA, NICARAGUA (3)
5	3.	OPEN THE DOOR, RICHARD! (2)
–	4.	HEARTACHES (1)
1	5.	(I LOVE YOU) FOR SENTIMENTAL REASONS) (5)
14	6.	GUILTY (2)
20	7.	HOW ARE THINGS IN GLOCCA MORRA? (2)
2	8.	THE OLD LAMP-LIGHTER (5)
–	9.	LINDA (1)
11	10.	I'LL CLOSE MY EYES (3)
8	11.	ZIP-A-DEE-DOO-DAH (4)
3	12.	A GAL IN CALICO (4)
10	13.	OH, BUT I DO! (3)
12	14.	SONATA (2)
–	15.	IT'S A GOOD DAY (1)
19	16.	A RAINY NIGHT IN RIO (2)
–	17.	YOU'LL ALWAYS BE THE ONE I LOVE (1)
–	18.	BLESS YOU (FOR BEING AN ANGEL) (1)
6	19.	HUGGIN' AND CHALKIN' (4)
–	20.	YOU CAN'T SEE THE SUN WHEN YOU'RE CRYIN' (1)

APRIL 1947

LM	TM	
4	1.	HEARTACHES (2)
1	2.	ANNIVERSARY SONG (3)
9	3.	LINDA (2)
2	4.	MANAGUA, NICARAGUA (4)
7	5.	HOW ARE THINGS IN GLOCCA MORRA? (3)
6	6.	GUILTY (3)
15	7.	IT'S A GOOD DAY (2)
10	8.	I'LL CLOSE MY EYES (4)
–	9.	MY ADOBE HACIENDA (1)
–	10.	MAM'SELLE (1)
20	11.	YOU CAN'T SEE THE SUN WHEN YOU'RE CRYIN' (2)
5	12.	(I LOVE YOU) FOR SENTIMENTAL REASONS) (6)
–	13.	APRIL SHOWERS (1)
18	14.	BLESS YOU (FOR BEING AN ANGEL) (2)
16	15.	A RAINY NIGHT IN RIO (3)
14	16.	SONATA (3)
–	17.	THAT'S MY DESIRE (1)
–	18.	ROSES IN THE RAIN (1)
–	19.	IF I HAD MY LIFE TO LIVE OVER (1)
3	20.	OPEN THE DOOR, RICHARD! (3)

MAY 1947

LM	TM	
10	1.	MAM'SELLE (2)
1	2.	HEARTACHES (3)
3	3.	LINDA (3)
9	4.	MY ADOBE HACIENDA (2)
2	5.	ANNIVERSARY SONG (4)
13	6.	APRIL SHOWERS (2)
4	7.	MANAGUA, NICARAGUA (5)
17	8.	THAT'S MY DESIRE (2)
5	9.	HOW ARE THINGS IN GLOCCA MORRA? (4)
–	10.	I BELIEVE (1)
–	11.	MY MELANCHOLY BABY (1)
–	12.	PEG O' MY HEART (1)
6	13.	GUILTY (4)
18	14.	ROSES IN THE RAIN (2)
–	15.	I WONDER, I WONDER, I WONDER (1)
7	16.	IT'S A GOOD DAY (3)
–	17.	ACROSS THE ALLEY FROM THE ALAMO (1)
11	18.	YOU CAN'T SEE THE SUN WHEN YOU'RE CRYIN' (3)
19	19.	IF I HAD MY LIFE TO LIVE OVER (2)
–	20.	FREE EATS (1)

JUNE 1947

LM	TM	
1	1.	MAM'SELLE (3)
12	2.	PEG O' MY HEART (2)
3	3.	LINDA (4)
15	4.	I WONDER, I WONDER, I WONDER (2)
4	5.	MY ADOBE HACIENDA (3)
8	6.	THAT'S MY DESIRE (3)
2	7.	HEARTACHES (4)
–	8.	CHI-BABA, CHI-BABA (1)
17	9.	ACROSS THE ALLEY FROM THE ALAMO (2)
5	10.	ANNIVERSARY SONG (5)
10	11.	I BELIEVE (2)
19	12.	IF I HAD MY LIFE TO LIVE OVER (3)
–	13.	RED SILK STOCKINGS AND GREEN PERFUME (1)
–	14.	MIDNIGHT MASQUERADE (1)
6	15.	APRIL SHOWERS (3)
–	16.	A SUNDAY KIND OF LOVE (1)
–	17.	OLD DEVIL MOON (1)
–	18.	I NEVER KNEW (THAT ROSES GREW) (1)
–	19.	TEMPTATION (TIM-TAY-SHUN) (1)
–	20.	TIME AFTER TIME (1)

JULY 1947

LM	TM	
2	1.	PEG O' MY HEART (3)
4	2.	I WONDER, I WONDER, I WONDER (3)
8	3.	CHI-BABA, CHI-BABA (2)
6	4.	THAT'S MY DESIRE (4)
1	5.	MAM'SELLE (4)
9	6.	ACROSS THE ALLEY FROM THE ALAMO (3)
3	7.	LINDA (5)
19	8.	TEMPTATION (TIM-TAY-SHUN) (2)
5	9.	MY ADOBE HACIENDA (4)
14	10.	MIDNIGHT MASQUERADE (2)
–	11.	ASK ANYONE WHO KNOWS (1)
12	12.	IF I HAD MY LIFE TO LIVE OVER (4)
–	13.	WHEN YOU WERE SWEET SIXTEEN (1)
–	14.	ALMOST LIKE BEING IN LOVE (1)
7	15.	HEARTACHES (5)
10	16.	ANNIVERSARY SONG (6)
–	17.	SMOKE! SMOKE! SMOKE! (THAT CIGARETTE) (1)
–	18.	I WONDER WHO'S KISSING HER NOW (1)
13	19.	RED SILK STOCKINGS AND GREEN PERFUME (2)
18	20.	I NEVER KNEW (THAT ROSES GREW) (2)

AUGUST 1947

LM	TM	
1	1.	PEG O' MY HEART (4)
4	2.	THAT'S MY DESIRE (5)
2	3.	I WONDER, I WONDER, I WONDER (4)
18	4.	I WONDER WHO'S KISSING HER NOW (2)
3	5	CHI-BABA, CHI-BABA (3)
17	6.	SMOKE! SMOKE! SMOKE! (THAT CIGARETTE) (2)
8	7.	TEMPTATION (TIM-TAY-SHUN) (3)
11	8.	ASK ANYONE WHO KNOWS (2)
6	9.	ACROSS THE ALLEY FROM THE ALAMO (4)
13	10.	WHEN YOU WERE SWEET SIXTEEN (2)
–	11.	TALLAHASSEE (1)
–	12.	FEUDIN' AND FIGHTIN' (1)
–	13.	IVY (1)
5	14.	MAM'SELLE (5)
20	15.	I NEVER KNEW (THAT ROSES GREW) (3)
14	16.	ALMOST LIKE BEING IN LOVE (2)
–	17.	I WISH I DIDN'T LOVE YOU SO (1)
7	18.	LINDA (6)
–	19.	NEAR YOU (1)
12	20.	IF I HAD MY LIFE TO LIVE OVER (5)

SEPTEMBER 1947

LM	TM	
1	1.	PEG O' MY HEART (5)
4	2.	I WONDER WHO'S KISSING HER NOW (3)
2	3.	THAT'S MY DESIRE (6)
19	4.	NEAR YOU (2)
6	5.	SMOKE! SMOKE! SMOKE! (THAT CIGARETTE) (3)
12	6.	FEUDIN' AND FIGHTIN' (2)
10	7.	WHEN YOU WERE SWEET SIXTEEN (3)
17	8.	I WISH I DIDN'T LOVE YOU SO (2)
–	9.	THE LADY FROM 29 PALMS (1)
3	10.	I WONDER, I WONDER, I WONDER (5)
7	11.	TEMPTATION (TIM-TAY-SHUN) (4)
–	12.	AN APPLE BLOSSOM WEDDING (1)
8	13.	ASK ANYONE WHO KNOWS (3)
11	14.	TALLAHASSEE (2)
–	15.	I HAVE BUT ONE HEART (1)
16	16.	ALMOST LIKE BEING IN LOVE (3)
–	17.	KATE (HAVE I COME TOO EARLY, TOO LATE) (1)
13	18.	IVY (2)
–	19.	YOU DO (1)
5	20	CHI-BABA, CHI-BABA (4)

OCTOBER 1947

LM	TM	
4	1.	NEAR YOU (3)
2	2.	I WONDER WHO'S KISSING HER NOW (4)
8	3.	I WISH I DIDN'T LOVE YOU SO (3)
1	4.	PEG O' MY HEART (6)
6	5.	FEUDIN' AND FIGHTIN' (3)
12	6.	AN APPLE BLOSSOM WEDDING (2)
3	7.	THAT'S MY DESIRE (7)
7	8.	WHEN YOU WERE SWEET SIXTEEN (4)
19	9.	YOU DO (2)
9	10.	THE LADY FROM 29 PALMS (2)
5	11.	SMOKE! SMOKE! SMOKE! (THAT CIGARETTE) (4)
15	12.	I HAVE BUT ONE HEART (2)
13	13.	ASK ANYONE WHO KNOWS (4)
17	14.	KATE (HAVE I COME TOO EARLY, TOO LATE) (2)
–	15.	HOW SOON (WILL I BE SEEING YOU) (1)
–	16.	THE WHIFFENPOOF SONG (1)
–	17.	ALL MY LOVE (1)
–	18.	KOKOMO, INDIANA (1)
–	19.	CIVILIZATION (1)
–	20.	SUGAR BLUES (1)

NOVEMBER 1947

LM	TM	
1	1.	NEAR YOU (4)
3	2.	I WISH I DIDN'T LOVE YOU SO (4)
9	3.	YOU DO (3)
15	4.	HOW SOON (WILL I BE SEEING YOU) (2)
6	5.	AN APPLE BLOSSOM WEDDING (3)
16	6.	THE WHIFFENPOOF SONG (2)
2	7.	I WONDER WHO'S KISSING HER NOW (5)
5	8.	FEUDIN' AND FIGHTIN' (4)
8	9.	WHEN YOU WERE SWEET SIXTEEN (5)
–	10.	BALLERINA (1)
–	11.	TOO FAT POLKA (1)
19	12.	CIVILIZATION (2)
–	13.	MICKEY (1)
10	14.	THE LADY FROM 29 PALMS (3)
–	15.	—AND MIMI (1)
12	16.	I HAVE BUT ONE HEART (3)
4	17.	PEG O' MY HEART (7)
14	18.	KATE (HAVE I COME TOO EARLY TOO LATE?) (3)
20	19.	SUGAR BLUES (2)
–	20.	SO FAR (1)

DECEMBER 1947

LM	TM	
1	1.	NEAR YOU (5)
4	2.	HOW SOON (WILL I BE SEEING YOU) (3)
10	3.	BALLERINA (2)
3	4.	YOU DO (4)
11	5.	TOO FAT POLKA (2)
12	6.	CIVILIZATION (3)
2	7.	I WISH I DIDN'T LOVE YOU SO (5)
–	8.	SERENADE OF THE BELLS (1)
15	9.	—AND MIMI (2)
–	10.	GOLDEN EARRINGS (1)
6	11.	THE WHIFFENPOOF SONG (3)
–	12.	WHITE CHRISTMAS (1)
–	13.	I'LL DANCE AT YOUR WEDDING (1)
20	14.	SO FAR (2)
13	15.	MICKEY (2)
5	16.	AN APPLE BLOSSOM WEDDING (4)
–	17.	DON'T YOU LOVE ME ANYMORE? (1)
–	18.	SANTA CLAUS IS COMIN' TO TOWN (1)
8	19.	FEUDIN' AND FIGHTIN' (5)
–	20.	HERE COMES SANTA CLAUS (1)

JANUARY 1948

LM	TM	
3	1.	BALLERINA (3)
2	2.	HOW SOON (WILL I BE SEEING YOU) (4)
8	3.	SERENADE OF THE BELLS (2)
5	4.	TOO FAT POLKA (3)
1	5.	NEAR YOU (6)
10	6.	GOLDEN EARRINGS (2)
13	7.	I'LL DANCE AT YOUR WEDDING (2)
6	8.	CIVILIZATION (4)
9	9.	—AND MIMI (3)
4	10.	YOU DO (5)
–	11.	BEG YOUR PARDON (1)
–	12.	I'M LOOKING OVER A FOUR LEAF CLOVER (1)
–	13.	NOW IS THE HOUR (1)
15	14.	MICKEY (3)
–	15.	THE BEST THINGS IN LIFE ARE FREE (1)
14	16.	SO FAR (3)
17	17.	DON'T YOU LOVE ME ANYMORE? (2)
–	18.	THE STARS WILL REMEMBER (SO WILL I) (1)
–	19.	PASS THAT PEACE PIPE (1)
7	20.	I WISH I DIDN'T LOVE YOU SO (6)

FEBRUARY 1948

LM	TM	
12	1.	I'M LOOKING OVER A FOUR LEAF CLOVER (2)
1	2.	BALLERINA (4)
13	3.	NOW IS THE HOUR (2)
3	4.	SERENADE OF THE BELLS (3)
6	5.	GOLDEN EARRINGS (3)
2	6.	HOW SOON (WILL I BE SEEING YOU) (5)
11	7.	BEG YOUR PARDON (2)
–	8.	MANANA (1)
7	9.	I'LL DANCE AT YOUR WEDDING (3)
4	10.	TOO FAT POLKA (4)
15	11.	THE BEST THINGS IN LIFE ARE FREE (2)
–	12.	I'M MY OWN GRANDPAW (GRANDMAW) (1)
18	13.	THE STARS WILL REMEMBER (SO WILL I) (2)
5	14.	NEAR YOU (7)
–	15.	HOW LUCKY YOU ARE (1)
–	16.	BUT BEAUTIFUL (1)
–	17.	SLAP 'ER DOWN AGIN, PAW (1)
14	18.	MICKEY (4)
–	19.	I'M A-COMIN' A-COURTIN' CORABELLE (1)
–	20.	SHINE (1)

MARCH 1948

LM	TM	
3	1.	NOW IS THE HOUR (3)
1	2.	I'M LOOKING OVER A FOUR LEAF CLOVER (3)
8	3.	MANANA (2)
7	4.	BEG YOUR PARDON (3)
2	5.	BALLERINA (5)
4	6.	SERENADE OF THE BELLS (4)
16	7.	BUT BEAUTIFUL (2)
5	8.	GOLDEN EARRINGS (4)
9	9.	I'LL DANCE AT YOUR WEDDING (4)
17	10.	SLAP 'ER DOWN AGIN, PAW (2)
11	11.	THE BEST THINGS IN LIFE ARE FREE (3)
13	12.	THE STARS WILL REMEMBER (SO WILL I) (3)
12	13.	I'M MY OWN GRANDPAW (GRANDMAW) (2)
–	14.	THE DICKEY-BIRD SONG (1)
6	15.	HOW SOON (WILL I BE SEEING YOU) (6)
20	16.	SHINE (2)
–	17.	BECAUSE (1)
–	18.	YOU WERE MEANT FOR ME (1)
19	19.	I'M A-COMIN' A-COURTIN' CORABELLE (2)
10	20.	TOO FAT POLKA (5)

APRIL 1948

LM	TM	
1	1.	NOW IS THE HOUR (4)
3	2.	MANANA (3)
2	3.	I'M LOOKING OVER A FOUR LEAF CLOVER (4)
4	4.	BEG YOUR PARDON (4)
–	5.	BABY FACE (1)
7	6.	BUT BEAUTIFUL (3)
–	7.	SABRE DANCE (1)
14	8.	THE DICKEY-BIRD SONG (2)
6	9.	SERENADE OF THE BELLS (5)
18	10.	YOU WERE MEANT FOR ME (2)
17	11.	BECAUSE (2)
–	12.	TOOLIE OOLIE DOOLIE (THE YODEL POLKA) (1)
10	13.	SLAP 'ER DOWN AGIN, PAW (3)
5	14.	BALLERINA (6)
16	15.	SHINE (3)
–	16.	YOU CAN'T BE TRUE, DEAR (1)
11	17.	THE BEST THINGS IN LIFE ARE FREE (4)
–	18.	ST. LOUIS BLUES (MARCH) (1)
–	19.	NATURE BOY (1)
–	20.	PIANISSIMO (1)

MAY 1948

LM	TM	
1	1.	NOW IS THE HOUR (5)
16	2.	YOU CAN'T BE TRUE, DEAR (2)
19	3.	NATURE BOY (2)
2	4.	MANANA (4)
5	5.	BABY FACE (2)
12	6.	TOOLIE OOLIE DOOLIE (THE YODEL POLKA) (2)
7	7.	SABRE DANCE (2)
8	8.	THE DICKEY-BIRD SONG (3)
–	9.	LITTLE WHITE LIES (1)
3	10.	I'M LOOKING OVER A FOUR LEAF CLOVER (5)
18	11.	ST. LOUIS BLUES (MARCH) (2)
4	12.	BEG YOUR PARDON (5)
–	13.	MY HAPPINESS (1)
–	14.	TELL ME A STORY (1)
11	15.	BECAUSE (3)
15	16.	SHINE (4)
–	17.	HAUNTED HEART (1)
–	18.	LAROO, LAROO LILI BOLERO (1)
–	19.	JUST BECAUSE (1)
6	20.	BUT BEAUTIFUL (4)

JUNE 1948

LM	TM	
3	1.	NATURE BOY (3)
2	2.	YOU CAN'T BE TRUE, DEAR (3)
9	3.	LITTLE WHITE LIES (2)
13	4.	MY HAPPINESS (2)
1	5.	NOW IS THE HOUR (6)
6	6.	TOOLIE OOLIE DOOLIE (THE YODEL POLKA) (3)
5	7.	BABY FACE (3)
8	8.	THE DICKEY-BIRD SONG (4)
–	9.	WOODY WOODPECKER (1)
–	10.	LOVE SOMEBODY (1)
14	11.	TELL ME A STORY (2)
7	12.	SABRE DANCE (3)
19	13.	JUST BECAUSE (2)
4	14.	MANANA (5)
11	15.	ST. LOUIS BLUES (MARCH) (3)
–	16.	WILLIAM TELL OVERTURE (IT'S A BEAUTIFUL DAY FOR THE RACES) (1)
17	17.	HAUNTED HEART (2)
18	18.	LAROO, LAROO LILI BOLERO (2)
–	19.	HEARTBREAKER (1)
15	20.	BECAUSE (4)

JULY 1948

LM	TM	
9	1.	WOODY WOODPECKER (2)
2	2.	YOU CAN'T BE TRUE, DEAR (4)
4	3.	MY HAPPINESS (3)
3	4.	LITTLE WHITE LIES (3)
1	5.	NATURE BOY (4)
6	6.	TOOLIE OOLIE DOOLIE (THE YODEL POLKA) (4)
–	7.	YOU CALL EVERYBODY DARLIN' (1)
10	8.	LOVE SOMEBODY (2)
5	9.	NOW IS THE HOUR (7)
8	10.	THE DICKEY-BIRD SONG (5)
–	11.	IT'S MAGIC (1)
7	12.	BABY FACE (4)
–	13.	A TREE IN THE MEADOW (1)
16	14.	WILLIAM TELL OVERTURE (IT'S A BEAUTIFUL DAY FOR THE RACES) (2)
–	15.	TWELFTH STREET RAG (1)
11	16.	TELL ME A STORY (3)
–	17.	MAYBE YOU'LL BE THERE (1)
17	18.	HAUNTED HEART (3)
–	19.	PUT 'EM IN A BOX, TIE 'EM WITH A RIBBON (1)
13	20.	JUST BECAUSE (3)

AUGUST 1948

LM	TM	
3	1.	MY HAPPINESS (4)
7	2.	YOU CALL EVERYBODY DARLIN' (2)
1	3.	WOODY WOODPECKER (3)
11	4.	IT'S MAGIC (2)
2	5.	YOU CAN'T BE TRUE, DEAR (5)
13	6.	A TREE IN THE MEADOW (2)
8	7.	LOVE SOMEBODY (3)
15	8.	TWELFTH STREET RAG (2)
4	9.	LITTLE WHITE LIES (4)
19	10.	PUT 'EM IN A BOX, TIE 'EM WITH A RIBBON (2)
17	11.	MAYBE YOU'LL BE THERE (2)
–	12.	IT ONLY HAPPENS WHEN I DANCE WITH YOU (1)
–	13.	BLUEBIRD OF HAPPINESS (1)
–	14.	CONFESS (1)
–	15.	COOL WATER (1)
5	16.	NATURE BOY (5)
6	17.	TOOLIE OOLIE DOOLIE (THE YODEL POLKA) (5)
–	18.	BOUQUET OF ROSES (1)
–	19.	UNDERNEATH THE ARCHES (1)
–	20.	TEA LEAVES (1)

SEPTEMBER 1948

LM	TM	
2	1.	YOU CALL EVERYBODY DARLIN' (3)
6	2.	A TREE IN THE MEADOW (3)
1	3.	MY HAPPINESS (5)
4	4.	IT'S MAGIC (3)
8	5.	TWELFTH STREET RAG (3)
7	6.	LOVE SOMEBODY (4)
11	7.	MAYBE YOU'LL BE THERE (3)
5	8.	YOU CAN'T BE TRUE, DEAR (6)
19	9.	UNDERNEATH THE ARCHES (2)
3	10.	WOODY WOODPECKER (4)
13	11.	BLUEBIRD OF HAPPINESS (2)
–	12.	HAIR OF GOLD, EYES OF BLUE (1)
14	13.	CONFESS (2)
15	14.	COOL WATER (2)
–	15.	RAMBLING ROSE (1)
–	16.	YOU CAME A LONG WAY FROM ST. LOUIS (1)
12	17.	IT ONLY HAPPENS WHEN I DANCE WITH YOU (2)
9	18.	LITTLE WHITE LIES (5)
18	19.	BOUQUET OF ROSES (2)
–	20.	UNTIL (1)

OCTOBER 1948

LM	TM	
2	1.	A TREE IN THE MEADOW (4)
1	2.	YOU CALL EVERYBODY DARLIN' (4)
5	3.	TWELFTH STREET RAG (4)
4	4.	IT'S MAGIC (4)
3	5.	MY HAPPINESS (6)
9	6.	UNDERNEATH THE ARCHES (3)
12	7.	HAIR OF GOLD, EYES OF BLUE (2)
7	8.	MAYBE YOU'LL BE THERE (4)
11	9.	BLUEBIRD OF HAPPINESS (3)
–	10.	BUTTONS AND BOWS (1)
20	11.	UNTIL (2)
6	12.	LOVE SOMEBODY (5)
14	13.	COOL WATER (3)
–	14.	EV'RY DAY I LOVE YOU (1)
15	15.	RAMBLING ROSE (2)
8	16.	YOU CAN'T BE TRUE, DEAR (7)
16	17.	YOU CAME A LONG WAY FROM ST. LOUIS (2)
19	18.	BOUQUET OF ROSES (3)
13	19.	CONFESS (3)
–	20.	ON A SLOW BOAT TO CHINA (1)

NOVEMBER 1948

LM	TM	
10	1.	BUTTONS AND BOWS (2)
1	2.	A TREE IN THE MEADOW (5)
20	3.	ON A SLOW BOAT TO CHINA (2)
3	4.	TWELFTH STREET RAG (5)
8	5.	MAYBE YOU'LL BE THERE (5)
2	6.	YOU CALL EVERYBODY DARLIN' (5)
7	7.	HAIR OF GOLD, EYES OF BLUE (3)
5	8.	MY HAPPINESS (7)
4	9.	IT'S MAGIC (5)
–	10.	YOU WERE ONLY FOOLING (1)
–	11.	MY DARLING, MY DARLING (1)
11	12.	UNTIL (3)
6	13.	UNDERNEATH THE ARCHES (4)
–	14.	THAT CERTAIN PARTY (1)
9	15.	BLUEBIRD OF HAPPINESS (4)
14	16.	EV'RY DAY I LOVE YOU (2)
–	17.	CUANTO LE GUSTA (1)
15	18.	RAMBLING ROSE (3)
–	19.	SAY SOMETHING SWEET TO YOUR SWEETHEART (1)
18	20.	BOUQUET OF ROSES (4)

DECEMBER 1948

LM	TM	
1	1.	BUTTONS AND BOWS (3)
3	2.	ON A SLOW BOAT TO CHINA (3)
11	3.	MY DARLING, MY DARLING (2)
–	4.	A LITTLE BIRD TOLD ME (1)
10	5.	YOU WERE ONLY FOOLING (2)
–	6.	ALL I WANT FOR CHRISTMAS (IS MY TWO FRONT TEETH) (1)
12	7.	UNTIL (4)
5	8.	MAYBE YOU'LL BE THERE (6)
2	9.	A TREE IN THE MEADOW (6)
4	10.	TWELFTH STREET RAG (6)
–	11.	WHITE CHRISTMAS (1)
–	12.	LAVENDER BLUE (1)
17	13.	CUANTO LE GUSTA (2)
8	14.	MY HAPPINESS (8)
7	15.	HAIR OF GOLD, EYES OF BLUE (4)
–	16.	HERE COMES SANTA CLAUS (1)
–	17.	SANTA CLAUS IS COMIN' TO TOWN (1)
–	18.	GLORIA (1)
6	19.	YOU CALL EVERYBODY DARLIN' (6)
14	20.	THAT CERTAIN PARTY (2)

JANUARY 1949

LM	TM	
1	1.	BUTTONS AND BOWS (4)
4	2.	A LITTLE BIRD TOLD ME (2)
2	3.	ON A SLOW BOAT TO CHINA (4)
3	4.	MY DARLING, MY DARLING (3)
–	5.	FAR AWAY PLACES (1)
12	6.	LAVENDER BLUE (2)
5	7.	YOU WERE ONLY FOOLING (3)
7	8.	UNTIL (5)
13	9.	CUANTO LE GUSTA (3)
–	10.	POWDER YOUR FACE WITH SUNSHINE (1)
6	11.	ALL I WANT FOR CHRISTMAS (IS MY TWO FRONT TEETH) (2)
–	12.	SO TIRED (1)
–	13.	GALWAY BAY (1)
–	14.	BRUSH THOSE TEARS FROM YOUR EYES (1)
–	15.	I'VE GOT MY LOVE TO KEEP ME WARM (1)
–	16.	THE PUSSY CAT SONG (1)
10	17.	TWELFTH STREET RAG (7)
–	18.	SWEET GEORGIA BROWN (1)
–	19.	I LOVE YOU SO MUCH IT HURTS (1)
11	20.	WHITE CHRISTMAS (2)

FEBRUARY 1949

LM	TM	
2	1.	A LITTLE BIRD TOLD ME (3)
5	2.	FAR AWAY PLACES (2)
10	3.	POWDER YOUR FACE WITH SUNSHINE (2)
6	4.	LAVENDER BLUE (3)
1	5.	BUTTONS AND BOWS (5)
15	6.	I'VE GOT MY LOVE TO KEEP ME WARM (2)
13	7.	GALWAY BAY (2)
4	8.	MY DARLING, MY DARLING (4)
3	9.	ON A SLOW BOAT TO CHINA (5)
12	10.	SO TIRED (2)
–	11.	CRUISING DOWN THE RIVER (1)
–	12.	RED ROSES FOR A BLUE LADY (1)
19	13.	I LOVE YOU SO MUCH IT HURTS (2)
16	14.	THE PUSSY CAT SONG (2)
18	15.	SWEET GEORGIA BROWN (2)
–	16.	DOWN BY THE STATION (1)
–	17.	SO IN LOVE (1)
–	18.	TARA TALARA TALA (1)
7	19.	YOU WERE ONLY FOOLING (4)
–	20.	GLORIA (2)

MARCH 1949

LM	TM	
11	1.	CRUISING DOWN THE RIVER (2)
2	2.	FAR AWAY PLACES (3)
3	3.	POWDER YOUR FACE WITH SUNSHINE (3)
7	4.	GALWAY BAY (3)
6	5.	I'VE GOT MY LOVE TO KEEP ME WARM (3)
1	6.	A LITTLE BIRD TOLD ME (4)
12	7.	RED ROSES FOR A BLUE LADY (2)
4	8.	LAVENDER BLUE (4)
10	9.	SO TIRED (3)
–	10.	SUNFLOWER (1)
–	11.	CARELESS HANDS (1)
13	12.	I LOVE YOU SO MUCH IT HURTS (3)
17	13.	SO IN LOVE (2)
5	14.	BUTTONS AND BOWS (6)
16	15.	DOWN BY THE STATION (2)
15	16.	SWEET GEORGIA BROWN (3)
–	17.	FOREVER AND EVER (1)
8	18.	MY DARLING, MY DARLING (5)
–	19.	THE BLUE SKIRT WALTZ (1)
–	20.	LADY OF SPAIN (1)

APRIL 1949

LM	TM	
1	1.	CRUISING DOWN THE RIVER (3)
7	2.	RED ROSES FOR A BLUE LADY (3)
2	3.	FAR AWAY PLACES (4)
17	4.	FOREVER AND EVER (2)
10	5.	SUNFLOWER (2)
11	6.	CARELESS HANDS (2)
3	7.	POWDER YOUR FACE WITH SUNSHINE (4)
4	8.	GALWAY BAY (4)
9	9.	SO TIRED (4)
–	10.	"A" - YOU'RE ADORABLE (1)
5	11.	I'VE GOT MY LOVE TO KEEP ME WARM (4)
–	12.	AGAIN (1)
19	13.	THE BLUE SKIRT WALTZ (2)
13	14.	SO IN LOVE (3)
–	15.	NEED YOU (1)
8	16.	LAVENDER BLUE (5)
12	17.	I LOVE YOU SO MUCH IT HURTS (4)
6	18.	A LITTLE BIRD TOLD ME (5)
–	19.	SOMEONE LIKE YOU (1)
15	20.	DOWN BY THE STATION (3)

MAY 1949

LM	TM	
4	1.	FOREVER AND EVER (3)
1	2.	CRUISING DOWN THE RIVER (4)
–	3.	RIDERS IN THE SKY (1)
10	4.	"A" - YOU'RE ADORABLE (2)
6	5.	CARELESS HANDS (3)
12	6.	AGAIN (2)
2	7.	RED ROSES FOR A BLUE LADY (4)
–	8.	SOME ENCHANTED EVENING (1)
5	9.	SUNFLOWER (3)
–	10.	I DON'T SEE ME IN YOUR EYES ANYMORE (1)
15	11.	NEED YOU (2)
–	12.	BALI HA'I (1)
13	13.	THE BLUE SKIRT WALTZ (3)
3	14.	FAR AWAY PLACES (5)
9	15.	SO TIRED (5)
–	16.	SOMEONE LIKE YOU (1)
7	17.	POWDER YOUR FACE WITH SUNSHINE (5)
–	18.	CANDY KISSES (1)
–	19.	BABY, IT'S COLD OUTSIDE (1)
–	20.	IT'S A BIG, WIDE, WONDERFUL WORLD (1)

JUNE 1949

LM	TM	
3	1.	RIDERS IN THE SKY (2)
6	2.	AGAIN (3)
1	3.	FOREVER AND EVER (4)
8	4.	SOME ENCHANTED EVENING (2)
4	5.	"A" - YOU'RE ADORABLE (3)
2	6.	CRUISING DOWN THE RIVER (5)
5	7.	CARELESS HANDS (4)
12	8.	BALI HA'I (2)
19	9.	BABY, IT'S COLD OUTSIDE (2)
10	10.	I DON'T SEE ME IN YOUR EYES ANYMORE (2)
–	11.	A WONDERFUL GUY (1)
13	12.	THE BLUE SKIRT WALTZ (4)
–	13.	KISS ME SWEET (1)
–	14.	THE HUCKLEBUCK (1)
18	15.	CANDY KISSES (2)
7	16.	RED ROSES FOR A BLUE LADY (5)
9	17.	SUNFLOWER (4)
–	18.	FIVE FOOT TWO, EYES OF BLUE (1)
–	19.	EVERYWHERE YOU GO (1)
–	20.	MERRY-GO-ROUND WALTZ (1)

JULY 1949

LM	TM	
1	1.	RIDERS IN THE SKY (3)
4	2.	SOME ENCHANTED EVENING (3)
2	3.	AGAIN (4)
3	4.	FOREVER AND EVER (5)
9	5.	BABY, IT'S COLD OUTSIDE (3)
8	6.	BALI HA'I (3)
10	7.	I DON'T SEE ME IN YOUR EYES ANYMORE (3)
11	8.	A WONDERFUL GUY (2)
5	9.	"A" - YOU'RE ADORABLE (4)
–	10.	THE FOUR WINDS AND THE SEVEN SEAS (1)
–	11.	ROOM FULL OF ROSES (1)
6	12.	CRUISING DOWN THE RIVER (6)
14	13.	THE HUCKLEBUCK (2)
–	14.	YOU'RE BREAKING MY HEART (1)
7	15.	CARELESS HANDS (5)
12	16.	THE BLUE SKIRT WALTZ (5)
18	17.	FIVE FOOT TWO, EYES OF BLUE (2)
–	18.	MY ONE AND ONLY HIGHLAND FLING (1)
–	19.	LET'S TAKE AN OLD-FASHIONED WALK (1)
13	20.	KISS ME SWEET (2)

AUGUST 1949

LM	TM	
2	1.	SOME ENCHANTED EVENING (4)
11	2.	ROOM FULL OF ROSES (2)
3	3.	AGAIN (5)
5	4.	BABY, IT'S COLD OUTSIDE (4)
1	5.	RIDERS IN THE SKY (4)
14	6.	YOU'RE BREAKING MY HEART (2)
4	7.	FOREVER AND EVER (6)
10	8.	THE FOUR WINDS AND THE SEVEN SEAS (2)
6	9.	BALI HA'I (4)
–	10.	MAYBE IT'S BECAUSE (1)
7	11.	I DON'T SEE ME IN YOUR EYES ANYMORE (4)
8	12.	A WONDERFUL GUY (3)
–	13.	SOMEDAY (YOU'LL WANT ME TO WANT YOU) (1)
13	14.	THE HUCKLEBUCK (3)
19	15.	LET'S TAKE AN OLD-FASHIONED WALK (2)
–	16.	JEALOUS HEART (1)
–	17.	THERE'S YES! YES! IN YOUR EYES (1)
–	18.	YOU'RE SO UNDERSTANDING (1)
16	19.	THE BLUE SKIRT WALTZ (6)
–	20.	AIN'T SHE SWEET (1)

SEPTEMBER 1949

LM	TM	
6	1.	YOU'RE BREAKING MY HEART (3)
2	2.	ROOM FULL OF ROSES (3)
1	3.	SOME ENCHANTED EVENING (5)
13	4.	SOMEDAY (YOU'LL WANT ME TO WANT YOU) (2)
10	5.	MAYBE IT'S BECAUSE (2)
–	6.	THAT LUCKY OLD SUN (1)
14	7.	THE HUCKLEBUCK (4)
16	8.	JEALOUS HEART (2)
3	9.	AGAIN (6)
15	10.	LET'S TAKE AN OLD-FASHIONED WALK (3)
4	11.	BABY, IT'S COLD OUTSIDE (5)
9	12.	BALI HA'I (5)
–	13.	TWENTY-FOUR HOURS OF SUNSHINE (1)
17	14.	THERE'S YES! YES! IN YOUR EYES (2)
5	15.	RIDERS IN THE SKY (5)
–	16.	WHISPERING HOPE (1)
–	17.	JUST ONE WAY TO SAY I LOVE YOU (1)
18	18.	YOU'RE SO UNDERSTANDING (2)
8	19.	THE FOUR WINDS AND THE SEVEN SEAS (3)
–	20.	DANCE OF THE HOURS (1)

OCTOBER 1949

LM	TM	
1	1.	YOU'RE BREAKING MY HEART (4)
6	2.	THAT LUCKY OLD SUN (2)
4	3.	SOMEDAY (YOU'LL WANT ME TO WANT YOU) (3)
2	4.	ROOM FULL OF ROSES (4)
8	5.	JEALOUS HEART (3)
5	6.	MAYBE IT'S BECAUSE (3)
–	7.	SLIPPING AROUND (1)
3	8.	SOME ENCHANTED EVENING (6)
–	9.	DON'T CRY, JOE (1)
16	10.	WHISPERING HOPE (2)
–	11.	HOP-SCOTCH POLKA (1)
10	12.	LET'S TAKE AN OLD-FASHIONED WALK (4)
–	13.	NOW THAT I NEED YOU (1)
–	14.	I CAN DREAM, CAN'T I? (1)
7	15.	THE HUCKLEBUCK (5)
–	16.	I NEVER SEE MAGGIE ALONE (1)
–	17.	KISS ME SWEET (1)
–	18.	A DREAMER'S HOLIDAY (1)
–	19.	RAGTIME COWBOY JOE (1)
9	20.	AGAIN (7)

NOVEMBER 1949

LM	TM	
2	1.	THAT LUCKY OLD SUN (3)
7	2.	SLIPPING AROUND (2)
1	3.	YOU'RE BREAKING MY HEART (5)
14	4.	I CAN DREAM, CAN'T I? (2)
9	5.	DON'T CRY, JOE (2)
–	6.	MULE TRAIN (1)
5	7.	JEALOUS HEART (4)
3	8.	SOMEDAY (YOU'LL WANT ME TO WANT YOU) (4)
18	9.	A DREAMER'S HOLIDAY (2)
4	10.	ROOM FULL OF ROSES (5)
–	11.	I'VE GOT A LOVELY BUNCH OF COCOANUTS (1)
16	12.	I NEVER SEE MAGGIE ALONE (2)
6	13.	MAYBE IT'S BECAUSE (4)
11	14.	HOP-SCOTCH POLKA (2)
–	15.	I'LL NEVER SLIP AROUND AGAIN (1)
10	16.	WHISPERING HOPE (3)
–	17.	JOHNSON RAG (1)
–	18.	CANADIAN CAPERS (1)
–	19.	DEAR HEARTS AND GENTLE PEOPLE (1)
13	20.	NOW THAT I NEED YOU (2)

DECEMBER 1949

LM	TM	
6	1.	MULE TRAIN (2)
4	2.	I CAN DREAM, CAN'T I? (3)
2	3.	SLIPPING AROUND (3)
9	4.	A DREAMER'S HOLIDAY (3)
1	5.	THAT LUCKY OLD SUN (4)
5	6.	DON'T CRY, JOE (3)
19	7.	DEAR HEARTS AND GENTLE PEOPLE (2)
–	8.	RUDOLPH, THE RED-NOSED REINDEER (1)
–	9.	THE OLD MASTER PAINTER (1)
7	10.	JEALOUS HEART (5)
3	11.	YOU'RE BREAKING MY HEART (6)
–	12.	WHITE CHRISTMAS (1)
15	13.	I'LL NEVER SLIP AROUND AGAIN (2)
11	14.	I'VE GOT A LOVELY BUNCH OF COCOANUTS (2)
8	15.	SOMEDAY (YOU'LL WANT ME TO WANT YOU) (5)
17	16.	JOHNSON RAG (2)
–	17.	BLUE CHRISTMAS (1)
–	18.	THERE'S NO TOMORROW (1)
–	19.	I YUST GO NUTS AT CHRISTMAS (1)
–	20.	HERE COMES SANTA CLAUS (1)

SECTION 3

SEMI-MONTHLY TOP-20 SONG SPREADSHEETS, 1900-1949

INTRODUCTION TO SECTION 3:

SEMI-MONTHLY TOP-20 SONG SPREADSHEETS, 1900-1949

Section 3 breaks the monthly charts into semi-monthly intervals and thus shows the chart actions of songs from a different, and more detailed, viewpoint. If the reader scans horizontally, the chart success of any given song can be seen at a glance. A series of numerical rankings shows the song climbing toward the top and eventually descending in favor of the next songs to come along. The == marks indicate months when the song was probably in the Top 40 but not in the Top 20. Two chart rankings appear for each month. For example, Jy Jy in the heading refer to the first and second halves of July respectively, and there are rankings listed underneath for each half-month for each song. The larger, underlined portion of the heading contains the months of the given year (12 months, 24 intervals). But since many songs straddle two years, a few months are shown for the preceding year or the following year as needed. Songs not officially belonging to the given year are marked as belonging to the previous year or following year as appropriate.

To get the best sense of the chart run of any given song, look for its year in the Index (Section 1) then consult that year here in Section 3. Since the songs in this section are listed chronologically, note the month of its chart "high" in Section 1 to help track it down on these Section 3 Spreadsheets.

Information about the author, original publisher, and performers associated with each song listed here can be found in the Encyclopedia of Section 4.

As with the Monthly Charts of Section 2, one will notice readily here that in the early part of the century (1900-1924) songs would often stay on the charts for many months, and there were fewer hit songs all told. With the coming of electrical recordings and radio in the mid-twenties, a greater number of songs received exposure and had chart runs. With the increased competition, most songs stayed on the charts for only two or three months during the period 1925-1939. During World War II the ASCAP publishing ban and the Petrillo recording ban all conspired to decrease the number of songs popularized, and long chart runs became frequent once again. Gradually, the proliferation of songs increased after the war and reached its peak in the 1960s following the Rock explosion. From then on, short chart runs were the rule until the 1990s when the industry seemed to suffer, oddly, from a scarcity of good new songs. So once again the very best songs would stay on the charts for many months, just as they did in the earliest days of the century.

1899						1900																								
Oc	Oc	Nv	Nv	Dc	Dc	Ja	Ja	Fb	Fb	Ma	Ma	Ap	Ap	My	My	Jn	Jn	Jy	Jy	Ag	Ag	Sp	Sp	Oc	Oc	Nv	Nv	Dc	Dc	
14	12	13	13	14	18	20	==	20	20	==	==	==	==	==	==	==	==	==	==	==	==	==	==	==	==	==	==	==	==	THE ROSARY (1899)
17	17	15	16	17	15	18	==	==	==	==	==	==	==	==	==	==	==	==	==	==	==	==	==	==	==	==	==	–	–	HEARTS AND FLOWERS (1899)
5	5	8	9	7	7	9	7	10	13	14	13	16	16	14	17	==	==	==	==	==	==	–	–	–	–	–	–	–	–	MY WILD IRISH ROSE (1899)
4	4	7	10	12	14	17	20	==	==	==	==	–	–	–	–	–	–	–	–	–	–	–	–	–	–	–	–	–	–	MANDY LEE (1899)
2	2	2	3	8	10	12	16	19	==	==	==	–	–	–	–	–	–	–	–	–	–	–	–	–	–	–	–	–	–	SMOKEY MOKES (1899)
3	3	4	6	9	12	15	17	==	==	–	–	–	–	–	–	–	–	–	–	–	–	–	–	–	–	–	–	–	–	ONE NIGHT IN JUNE (1899)
1	1	1	1	2	4	5	8	15	==	==	==	–	–	–	–	–	–	–	–	–	–	–	–	–	–	–	–	–	–	MY CREOLE SUE (1899)
15	10	5	5	4	6	8	12	17	18	==	==	==	==	–	–	–	–	–	–	–	–	–	–	–	–	–	–	–	–	BEN HUR CHARIOT RACE (1899)
==	==	16	14	11	11	10	10	14	16	20	==	==	==	==	==	–	–	–	–	–	–	–	–	–	–	–	–	–	–	CAKEWALK IN THE SKY (1899)
13	7	3	2	1	1	1	1	1	1	2	4	6	7	9	13	==	==	–	–	–	–	–	–	–	–	–	–	–	–	I'D LEAVE MY HAPPY HOME FOR YOU (1899)
18	13	11	7	5	3	3	3	5	7	8	10	14	18	==	==	==	==	–	–	–	–	–	–	–	–	–	–	–	–	MA LADY LU (1899)
16	11	10	7	6	5	4	4	4	8	13	18	==	==	–	–	–	–	–	–	–	–	–	–	–	–	–	–	–	–	THE STORY OF THE ROSE (1899)
8	8	6	4	3	2	2	2	2	3	4	5	4	5	7	8	11	16	20	==	==	==	–	–	–	–	–	–	–	–	A PICTURE NO ARTIST CAN PAINT (1899)
==	==	==	==	18	17	16	18	==	==	==	==	==	==	==	==	–	–	–	–	–	–	–	–	–	–	–	–	–	–	I'M GLAD I MET YOU, MARY
==	==	==	18	15	13	11	15	16	15	18	==	==	==	==	==	==	==	==	==	–	–	–	–	–	–	–	–	–	–	THE GIRLS OF AMERICA MARCH
==	==	==	17	13	9	7	6	9	10	11	11	11	12	16	==	==	==	==	==	–	–	–	–	–	–	–	–	–	–	SING ME A SONG OF THE SOUTH
==	==	==	15	10	8	6	5	3	5	5	6	7	4	6	7	9	13	17	==	==	==	==	==	–	–	–	–	–	–	ALWAYS
–	–	==	==	==	16	14	11	11	9	6	3	2	2	3	3	2	2	2	3	4	5	7	12	14	15	19	==	==	==	WHEN YOU WERE SWEET SIXTEEN
–	–	–	–	==	20	13	9	12	14	17	==	==	–	–	–	–	–	–	–	–	–	–	–	–	–	–	–	–	–	IMPECUNIOUS DAVIS
–	–	–	–	==	==	19	13	8	6	10	12	17	==	==	–	–	–	–	–	–	–	–	–	–	–	–	–	–	–	IN GOOD OLD NEW YORK TOWN
–	–	–	–	==	==	==	==	18	12	9	9	12	14	18	==	==	==	–	–	–	–	–	–	–	–	–	–	–	–	OLE EPH'S VISION
–	–	–	–	–	==	==	==	==	==	16	15	16	13	10	10	16	==	==	==	==	==	–	–	–	–	–	–	–	–	FILIPINO SHUFFLE
–	–	–	–	–	–	==	==	==	17	15	15	19	==	==	==	–	–	–	–	–	–	–	–	–	–	–	–	–	–	ZULU WEDDING DANCE
–	–	–	–	–	==	==	14	6	4	3	2	3	6	12	14	20	==	==	–	–	–	–	–	–	–	–	–	–	–	DOAN YE CRY, MA HONEY
–	–	–	–	–	–	==	==	13	11	7	7	8	11	15	==	==	==	–	–	–	–	–	–	–	–	–	–	–	–	I COULDN'T STAND TO SEE MY BABY LOSE
–	–	–	–	–	–	==	19	7	2	1	1	1	1	1	2	3	6	8	17	==	==	–	–	–	–	–	–	–	–	A BIRD IN A GILDED CAGE
–	–	–	–	–	–	==	==	==	==	==	17	10	8	4	4	5	8	13	15	18	==	==	==	==	==	–	–	–	–	WHEN CHLOE SINGS A SONG
–	–	–	–	–	–	–	==	==	19	12	8	5	3	2	1	1	1	1	1	1	2	3	5	12	17	==	==	–	–	THE BLUE AND THE GRAY
–	–	–	–	–	–	–	–	==	==	==	==	==	==	17	15	12	11	12	12	11	11	18	18	==	==	==	==	==	==	KOONVILLE KOONLETS
–	–	–	–	–	–	–	–	==	==	19	14	9	10	13	16	18	==	==	–	–	–	–	–	–	–	–	–	–	–	IN NAPLES FAIR
–	–	–	–	–	–	–	–	==	==	==	19	18	19	==	==	==	==	==	==	–	–	–	–	–	–	–	–	–	–	HEARTS ARE TRUMPS
–	–	–	–	–	–	–	–	==	==	==	20	13	9	5	6	6	9	15	18	==	==	==	==	–	–	–	–	–	–	WHY
–	–	–	–	–	–	–	–	==	==	==	==	20	20	==	==	==	==	==	==	==	==	–	–	–	–	–	–	–	–	HER NAME IS ROSE
–	–	–	–	–	–	–	–	–	–	==	==	==	==	==	==	17	14	18	20	==	==	==	==	==	–	–	–	–	–	THE MICK WHO THREW THE BRICK
–	–	–	–	–	–	–	–	–	–	==	==	==	17	11	9	15	==	==	==	==	==	–	–	–	–	–	–	–	–	WHAT IS A HOME WITHOUT LOVE?
–	–	–	–	–	–	–	–	–	–	==	==	==	15	8	5	4	5	7	10	13	16	==	==	==	==	–	–	–	–	I'M CERTAINLY LIVING A RAGTIME LIFE
–	–	–	–	–	–	–	–	–	–	–	–	==	==	==	18	13	15	==	==	==	==	–	–	–	–	–	–	–	–	LINDY LOO
–	–	–	–	–	–	–	–	–	–	–	–	==	==	19	11	7	3	4	6	8	15	==	==	==	==	–	–	–	–	MY JERSEY LILY
–	–	–	–	–	–	–	–	–	–	–	–	==	==	20	12	8	4	3	2	2	3	4	8	13	11	16	18	==	==	MA TIGER LILY
Oc	Oc	Nv	Nv	Dc	Dc	Ja	Ja	Fb	Fb	Ma	Ma	Ap	Ap	My	My	Jn	Jn	Jy	Jy	Ag	Ag	Sp	Sp	Oc	Oc	Nv	Nv	Dc	Dc	

1 9 0 0 (Ap–Dc) — 1 9 0 1 (Ja–Jn)

Ap	Ap	My	My	Jn	Jn	Jy	Jy	Ag	Ag	Sp	Sp	Oc	Oc	Nv	Nv	Dc	Dc	Ja	Ja	Fb	Fb	Ma	Ma	Ap	Ap	My	My	Jn	Jn	
==	==	==	20	14	10	9	5	5	4	2	**1**	**1**	2	3	6	10	12	13	13	19	==	==	==	==	==	–	–	–	–	THE FATAL ROSE OF RED
–	==	==	19	10	7	5	9	14	==	==	==	–	–	–	–	–	–	–	–	–	–	–	–	–	–	–	–	–	–	WOULDN'T IT MAKE YOU MAD, WOULDN'T IT JAR YOU
–	–	==	==	==	==	19	14	15	20	==	==	==	==	==	==	–	–	–	–	–	–	–	–	–	–	–	–	–	–	ON THE FIRING LINE
–	–	==	==	==	17	14	11	9	10	17	==	==	==	==	==	–	–	–	–	–	–	–	–	–	–	–	–	–	–	A COON BAND CONTEST
–	–	==	==	19	20	==	19	19	==	==	–	–	–	–	–	–	–	–	–	–	–	–	–	–	–	–	–	–	–	MY SUNBEAM FROM THE SOUTH
–	–	–	==	==	18	10	7	6	7	14	==	==	==	–	–	–	–	–	–	–	–	–	–	–	–	–	–	–	–	EVERY RACE HAS A FLAG BUT THE COON
–	–	–	==	==	19	11	8	7	8	10	16	==	==	==	==	–	–	–	–	–	–	–	–	–	–	–	–	–	–	(IT'S THE) MAN BEHIND THE GUN
–	–	–	==	==	12	6	4	3	**1**	**1**	2	4	8	15	==	==	–	–	–	–	–	–	–	–	–	–	–	–	–	STRIKE UP THE BAND, HERE COMES A SAILOR
–	–	–	–	==	==	16	13	12	14	20	==	==	–	–	–	–	–	–	–	–	–	–	–	–	–	–	–	–	–	JUST ONE KISS
–	–	–	–	==	==	==	16	10	6	5	3	3	5	9	14	17	18	==	==	==	==	==	==	–	–	–	–	–	–	WAIT
–	–	–	–	–	–	==	==	17	12	12	17	17	==	==	==	==	==	–	–	–	–	–	–	–	–	–	–	–	–	DAWN OF THE CENTURY MARCH
–	–	–	–	–	–	==	==	16	9	6	4	8	12	18	==	==	==	–	–	–	–	–	–	–	–	–	–	–	–	MIDNIGHT FIRE ALARM
–	–	–	–	–	–	==	==	20	13	8	10	7	6	5	4	7	9	12	15	20	==	==	==	==	==	–	–	–	–	YOU TELL ME YOUR DREAM (AND I WILL TELL YOU MINE)
–	–	–	–	–	–	==	==	==	==	19	15	16	==	==	==	==	==	==	==	–	–	–	–	–	–	–	–	–	–	YOU NEEDN'T SAY THE KISSES CAME FROM ME
–	–	–	–	–	–	==	==	==	==	==	20	20	==	==	==	20	19	==	==	==	==	==	==	–	–	–	–	–	–	IT'S THE MAN BEHIND THE GUN THAT DOES THE WORK
–	–	–	–	–	–	==	==	==	17	13	13	11	10	7	11	13	17	19	==	==	==	==	==	–	–	–	–	–	–	MY HEART'S TONIGHT IN TEXAS
–	–	–	–	–	–	–	–	==	==	==	19	15	13	10	15	18	==	==	==	==	==	==	==	==	==	–	–	–	–	OH, SHINING LIGHT
–	–	–	–	–	–	–	==	==	18	11	9	9	9	12	16	19	==	==	==	–	–	–	–	–	–	–	–	–	–	I MUST A-BEEN A-DREAMIN'
–	–	–	–	–	–	–	–	==	==	==	14	10	7	6	8	12	16	18	==	==	==	–	–	–	–	–	–	–	–	MA BLACK PEARL
–	–	–	–	–	–	–	–	==	19	9	6	2	**1**	**1**	**1**	2	2	**1**	**1**	4	5	12	13	17	==	==	==	–	–	I CAN'T TELL WHY I LOVE YOU BUT I DO
–	–	–	–	–	–	–	–	==	==	15	7	5	3	2	2	**1**	**1**	2	4	6	6	9	10	12	16	==	==	==	==	FOR OLD TIMES' SAKE
–	–	–	–	–	–	–	–	==	==	16	11	6	4	4	3	3	3	3	2	2	4	7	9	10	11	13	19	==	==	WHEN THE HARVEST DAYS ARE OVER, JESSIE DEAR
–	–	–	–	–	–	–	–	==	==	==	==	19	18	14	12	11	11	14	12	13	==	==	==	==	==	–	–	–	–	THE MOSQUITO'S PARADE
–	–	–	–	–	–	–	–	==	==	==	==	18	==	==	==	==	==	==	==	–	–	–	–	–	–	–	–	–	–	I'VE GOT A WHITE MAN WORKING FOR ME
–	–	–	–	–	–	–	–	==	==	==	==	==	20	==	==	==	==	==	==	–	–	–	–	–	–	–	–	–	–	JUST WHEN I NEEDED YOU MOST
–	–	–	–	–	–	–	–	–	–	==	==	==	16	11	7	8	8	15	14	==	==	==	==	–	–	–	–	–	–	CALLING TO HER BOY JUST ONCE AGAIN
–	–	–	–	–	–	–	–	–	–	==	==	==	==	17	10	6	7	8	9	9	12	16	19	==	==	==	==	–	–	LAM' LAM' LAM'
–	–	–	–	–	–	–	–	–	–	==	==	==	19	13	9	5	5	7	8	8	11	15	==	==	==	==	==	–	–	THE BRIDGE OF SIGHS
–	–	–	–	–	–	–	–	–	–	==	==	==	14	8	5	4	4	4	6	7	7	8	11	13	15	19	==	==	==	JUST BECAUSE SHE MADE DEM GOO-GOO EYES
–	–	–	–	–	–	–	–	–	–	–	–	==	==	==	17	15	13	11	10	10	16	18	==	==	==	==	==	==	==	MY LITTLE ZULU BABE (1901)
–	–	–	–	–	–	–	–	–	–	–	–	==	==	20	13	9	6	5	5	5	3	3	7	7	7	7	10	13	14	MA BLUSHIN' ROSIE (1901)
–	–	–	–	–	–	–	–	–	–	–	–	–	==	==	20	16	14	10	11	11	17	==	==	==	==	–	–	–	–	I'D STILL BELIEVE YOU TRUE (1901)
–	–	–	–	–	–	–	–	–	–	–	–	–	–	==	19	14	10	6	3	**1**	**1**	**1**	2	4	4	4	4	5	6	COON! COON! COON! (1901)
–	–	–	–	–	–	–	–	–	–	–	–	–	–	==	==	==	15	9	7	3	2	2	**1**	**1**	**1**	**1**	**1**	**1**	1	GOODBYE, DOLLY GRAY (1901)
–	–	–	–	–	–	–	–	–	–	–	–	–	–	==	==	==	20	16	16	==	==	==	20	==	==	==	==	==	==	THE SPIDER AND THE FLY (1901)
Ap	Ap	My	My	Jn	Jn	Jy	Jy	Ag	Ag	Sp	Sp	Oc	Oc	Nv	Nv	Dc	Dc	Ja	Ja	Fb	Fb	Ma	Ma	Ap	Ap	My	My	Jn	Jn	

1900						1901																								
Oc	Oc	Nv	Nv	Dc	Dc	Ja	Ja	Fb	Fb	Ma	Ma	Ap	Ap	My	My	Jn	Jn	Jy	Jy	Ag	Ag	Sp	Sp	Oc	Oc	Nv	Nv	Dc	Dc	
1	2	3	6	10	12	13	13	19	==	==	==	==	==	–	–	–	–	–	–	–	–	–	–	–	–	–	–	–	–	THE FATAL ROSE OF RED (1900)
11	10	7	11	13	17	19	==	==	==	==	==	–	–	–	–	–	–	–	–	–	–	–	–	–	–	–	–	–	–	MY HEART'S TONIGHT IN TEXAS (1900)
7	6	5	4	7	9	12	15	20	==	==	==	==	==	–	–	–	–	–	–	–	–	–	–	–	–	–	–	–	–	YOU TELL ME YOUR DREAM (AND I WILL TELL YOU MINE)(1900)
19	18	14	12	11	11	14	12	13	==	==	==	==	==	–	–	–	–	–	–	–	–	–	–	–	–	–	–	–	–	THE MOSQUITO'S PARADE (1900)
10	7	6	8	12	16	18	==	==	==	–	–	–	–	–	–	–	–	–	–	–	–	–	–	–	–	–	–	–	–	MA BLACK PEARL (1900)
2	**1**	**1**	**1**	2	2	**1**	**1**	4	5	10	13	17	==	==	==	–	–	–	–	–	–	–	–	–	–	–	–	–	–	I CAN'T TELL WHY I LOVE YOU BUT I DO (1900)
5	3	2	2	**1**	**1**	2	4	6	6	9	10	12	16	==	==	==	==	–	–	–	–	–	–	–	–	–	–	–	–	FOR OLD TIMES' SAKE (1900)
6	4	4	3	3	3	3	2	2	4	7	9	10	11	13	19	==	==	==	==	–	–	–	–	–	–	–	–	–	–	WHEN THE HARVEST DAYS ARE OVER, JESSIE DEAR (1900)
==	16	11	7	8	8	15	14	==	==	==	==	–	–	–	–	–	–	–	–	–	–	–	–	–	–	–	–	–	–	CALLING TO HER BOY JUST ONCE AGAIN (1900)
==	==	17	10	6	7	8	9	9	12	16	19	==	==	==	==	–	–	–	–	–	–	–	–	–	–	–	–	–	–	LAM' LAM' LAM' (1900)
==	19	13	9	5	5	7	8	8	11	15	18	==	==	==	==	–	–	–	–	–	–	–	–	–	–	–	–	–	–	THE BRIDGE OF SIGHS (1900)
==	14	8	5	4	4	4	6	7	7	8	11	13	13	19	==	==	==	–	–	–	–	–	–	–	–	–	–	–	–	JUST BECAUSE SHE MADE DEM GOO-GOO EYES (1900)
==	==	==	17	15	13	11	10	10	16	18	==	==	==	==	==	==	==	–	–	–	–	–	–	–	–	–	–	–	–	MY LITTLE ZULU BABE
==	==	20	13	9	6	5	5	5	3	3	7	7	7	7	10	13	14	17	==	==	==	–	–	–	–	–	–	–	–	MA BLUSHIN' ROSIE
–	==	==	20	16	14	10	11	11	17	==	==	==	==	–	–	–	–	–	–	–	–	–	–	–	–	–	–	–	–	I'D STILL BELIEVE YOU TRUE
–	–	==	19	14	10	6	3	**1**	**1**	**1**	2	4	4	4	4	5	6	8	10	12	11	12	17	==	==	–	–	–	–	COON! COON! COON!
–	–	==	==	==	15	9	7	3	2	2	**1**	**1**	**1**	**1**	**1**	**1**	**1**	3	3	3	6	6	9	13	20	==	==	–	–	GOODBYE, DOLLY GRAY
–	–	==	==	==	==	20	19	==	==	==	==	18	14	12	12	10	10	11	14	14	13	13	15	19	18	==	==	==	==	== == == 20 == == == == COON UP A TREE
–	–	==	==	==	==	17	17	==	==	==	==	==	==	–	–	–	–	–	–	–	–	–	–	–	–	–	–	–	–	COME BACK, MA HONEY BOY, TO ME
–	–	==	==	==	20	16	16	==	==	==	20	==	==	==	==	==	==	–	–	–	–	–	–	–	–	–	–	–	–	THE SPIDER AND THE FLY
–	–	–	–	==	==	==	18	==	18	==	==	==	==	–	–	–	–	–	–	–	–	–	–	–	–	–	–	–	–	I WISH WE'D NEVER MET
–	–	–	–	==	==	==	==	==	20	==	==	==	==	==	==	–	–	–	–	–	–	–	–	–	–	–	–	–	–	YOU CAN'T KEEP A GOOD MAN DOWN
–	–	–	–	==	==	==	==	17	15	14	14	14	17	==	==	==	==	–	–	–	–	–	–	–	–	–	–	–	–	MY GIRL FROM DIXIE
–	–	–	–	==	==	==	20	16	13	11	6	6	5	5	6	8	8	7	7	9	9	10	10	14	==	==	==	==	==	ABSENCE MAKES THE HEART GROW FONDER
–	–	–	–	–	–	==	==	18	14	13	15	16	==	==	==	–	–	–	–	–	–	–	–	–	–	–	–	–	–	I WANT TO BE A MILITARY MAN
–	–	–	–	–	–	==	==	15	10	6	5	8	10	16	==	==	–	–	–	–	–	–	–	–	–	–	–	–	–	THE SHADE OF THE PALM
–	–	–	–	–	–	==	==	12	8	5	3	3	3	3	3	4	9	10	15	16	==	==	–	–	–	–	–	–	–	TELL ME, PRETTY MAIDEN
–	–	–	–	–	–	==	==	14	9	4	4	2	2	2	2	2	4	4	6	11	15	==	==	–	–	–	–	–	–	I'VE A LONGING IN MY HEART FOR YOU, LOUISE
–	–	–	–	–	–	==	==	==	==	19	18	==	==	==	==	==	==	–	–	–	–	–	–	–	–	–	–	–	–	DOWN BY THE RIVERSIDE
–	–	–	–	–	–	==	==	==	==	20	17	19	==	==	==	==	==	–	–	–	–	–	–	–	–	–	–	–	–	EUGENIA WALTZES
–	–	–	–	–	–	–	–	==	19	12	8	5	6	8	14	17	==	==	–	–	–	–	–	–	–	–	–	–	–	THE TALE OF THE KANGAROO
–	–	–	–	–	–	–	–	==	==	==	==	20	==	==	20	==	==	==	==	–	–	–	–	–	–	–	–	–	–	THE VESPER BELLS WERE RINGING
–	–	–	–	–	–	–	–	==	==	17	12	9	8	9	11	15	18	==	==	–	–	–	–	–	–	–	–	–	–	IF I ONLY HAD A DOLLAH OF MY OWN
–	–	–	–	–	–	–	–	==	==	==	==	==	==	17	18	20	==	==	==	==	–	–	–	–	–	–	–	–	–	THE FOUR KINGS MARCH
–	–	–	–	–	–	–	–	==	==	==	==	15	12	11	13	14	17	==	20	==	==	–	–	–	–	–	–	–	–	MY ELINORE
–	–	–	–	–	–	–	–	–	==	==	16	11	9	6	7	9	11	14	18	==	==	–	–	–	–	–	–	–	–	IN THE HOUSE OF TOO MUCH TROUBLE
–	–	–	–	–	–	–	–	–	–	==	==	==	18	18	16	20	==	==	==	–	–	–	–	–	–	–	–	–	–	IN THE CATHEDRAL
–	–	–	–	–	–	–	–	–	–	==	==	==	==	20	==	19	==	==	==	20	19	19	20	==	==	==	==	==	==	A GHOST OF A COON
Oc	Oc	Nv	Nv	Dc	Dc	Ja	Ja	Fb	Fb	Ma	Ma	Ap	Ap	My	My	Jn	Jn	Jy	Jy	Ag	Ag	Sp	Sp	Oc	Oc	Nv	Nv	Dc	Dc	

1901																		1902												
Ap	Ap	My	My	Jn	Jn	Jy	Jy	Ag	Ag	Sp	Sp	Oc	Oc	Nv	Nv	Dc	Dc	Ja	Ja	Fb	Fb	Ma	Ma	Ap	Ap	My	My	Jn	Jn	
==	15	10	5	3	2	**1**	**1**	2	**1**	**1**	**1**	2	2	4	5	8	7	7	7	6	6	10	15	17	19	==	==	==	==	HELLO, CENTRAL, GIVE ME HEAVEN
==	==	17	15	12	12	15	17	==	==	==	==	–	–	–	–	–	–	–	–	–	–	–	–	–	–	–	–	–	–	THERE'S NO NORTH OR SOUTH TODAY
==	19	15	8	7	5	6	5	10	14	20	==	==	–	–	–	–	–	–	–	–	–	–	–	–	–	–	–	–	–	ANY OLD PLACE I CAN HANG MY HAT IS HOME SWEET HOME TO ME
==	20	14	9	6	3	2	2	**1**	3	8	11	18	==	==	–	–	–	–	–	–	–	–	–	–	–	–	–	–	–	SWEET ANNIE MOORE
==	==	==	==	==	19	18	19	19	20	==	==	==	==	==	==	–	–	–	–	–	–	–	–	–	–	–	–	–	–	DOWN IN THE DEPTHS
–	–	==	==	16	13	9	8	7	7	5	6	8	16	17	==	==	==	==	20	==	==	==	==	–	–	–	–	–	–	BOOLA, BOOLA (YALE BOOLA)
–	–	==	==	==	==	20	16	15	18	==	==	==	==	–	–	–	–	–	–	–	–	–	–	–	–	–	–	–	–	MY SWEET KIMONA
–	–	==	18	11	7	5	4	6	8	9	13	==	==	–	–	–	–	–	–	–	–	–	–	–	–	–	–	–	–	MAMIE
–	–	==	==	==	16	13	13	13	10	11	14	==	==	==	==	–	–	–	–	–	–	–	–	–	–	–	–	–	–	JIMMY, THE PRIDE OF NEWSPAPER ROW
–	–	==	==	==	15	12	9	4	4	4	4	4	4	5	9	9	10	9	10	11	9	14	20	20	==	==	==	–	–	THE HONEYSUCKLE AND THE BEE
–	–	–	–	==	==	==	==	==	17	14	12	9	14	15	17	18	18	16	18	18	19	==	==	==	==	–	–	–	–	HE LAID AWAY A SUIT OF GRAY
–	–	–	–	==	==	16	11	8	5	3	3	**1**	**1**	**1**	**1**	2	3	4	4	4	4	3	7	14	14	==	==	==	==	GOOD MORNING, CARRIE
–	–	–	–	–	–	==	==	18	16	18	==	==	==	==	==	–	–	–	–	–	–	–	–	–	–	–	–	–	–	I'VE GROWN SO USED TO YOU
–	–	–	–	–	==	19	12	5	2	2	2	3	5	12	15	==	==	==	–	–	–	–	–	–	–	–	–	–	–	GO 'WAY BACK AND SIT DOWN
–	–	–	–	–	–	==	==	17	12	7	5	5	3	2	3	7	9	8	8	8	13	12	18	==	==	–	–	–	–	AIN'T DAT A SHAME?
–	–	–	–	–	–	–	–	==	==	15	7	6	9	14	13	16	17	==	==	==	–	–	–	–	–	–	–	–	–	MY LADY HOTTENTOT
–	–	–	–	–	–	–	–	==	==	16	8	7	7	7	8	6	6	6	5	5	5	9	11	16	18	==	==	==	==	MR. VOLUNTEER
–	–	–	–	–	–	–	–	==	==	==	18	12	17	16	14	13	16	15	17	14	15	19	==	18	20	==	==	==	==	THE TALE OF A BUMBLE BEE
–	–	–	–	–	–	–	–	–	–	==	==	20	15	11	10	11	15	20	==	==	–	–	–	–	–	–	–	–	–	BABY MINE
–	–	–	–	–	–	–	–	–	–	==	==	17	12	13	12	12	12	14	16	20	==	==	==	–	–	–	–	–	–	THE TIE THAT BINDS
–	–	–	–	–	–	–	–	–	–	==	==	15	11	10	11	10	8	11	15	16	==	==	==	–	–	–	–	–	–	I'M TIRED
–	–	–	–	–	–	–	–	–	–	==	19	10	6	3	2	**1**	**1**	2	2	2	3	5	13	==	==	–	–	–	–	I'LL BE WITH YOU WHEN THE ROSES BLOOM AGAIN
–	–	–	–	–	–	–	–	–	–	==	==	16	10	8	7	5	5	5	6	9	12	17	==	==	==	–	–	–	–	MY CASTLE ON THE NILE
–	–	–	–	–	–	–	–	–	–	–	–	==	==	18	16	15	13	10	11	13	16	18	==	==	==	==	==	–	–	WHEN MR. SHAKESPEARE COMES TO TOWN
–	–	–	–	–	–	–	–	–	–	–	–	==	==	==	20	20	==	==	==	–	–	–	–	–	–	–	–	–	–	IT'S ALL RIGHT, MAYME
–	–	–	–	–	–	–	–	–	–	–	–	==	==	19	18	17	19	==	==	==	==	–	–	–	–	–	–	–	–	IN THE GREAT SOMEWHERE
–	–	–	–	–	–	–	–	–	–	–	–	==	==	==	==	==	20	19	19	==	==	–	–	–	–	–	–	–	–	DON'T PUT ME OFF AT BUFFALO ANY MORE
–	–	–	–	–	–	–	–	–	–	–	–	–	–	==	19	14	11	12	14	15	17	==	==	–	–	–	–	–	–	WAY DOWN IN OLD INDIANA
–	–	–	–	–	–	==	==	==	==	==	==	==	19	20	==	==	==	==	==	==	18	==	==	==	==	==	==	==	==	SADIE SAY YOU WON'T SAY NAY (1902)
–	–	–	–	–	–	–	–	–	–	==	==	==	13	9	6	3	2	**1**	**1**	**1**	**1**	**1**	**1**	2	5	11	15	17	==	CREOLE BELLES (1902)
–	–	–	–	–	–	–	–	==	==	17	16	11	8	6	4	4	4	3	3	3	2	2	3	5	8	10	12	13	13	DOWN WHERE THE COTTON BLOSSOMS GROW (1902)
–	–	–	–	–	–	–	–	–	–	–	–	–	–	==	==	19	14	13	9	7	7	8	10	13	16	==	==	–	–	MY MISSISSIPPI SUE (1902)
Ap	Ap	My	My	Jn	Jn	Jy	Jy	Ag	Ag	Sp	Sp	Oc	Oc	Nv	Nv	Dc	Dc	Ja	Ja	Fb	Fb	Ma	Ma	Ap	Ap	My	My	Jn	Jn	

1901						1902																								
Oc	Oc	Nv	Nv	Dc	Dc	Ja	Ja	Fb	Fb	Ma	Ma	Ap	Ap	My	My	Jn	Jn	Jy	Jy	Ag	Ag	Sp	Sp	Oc	Oc	Nv	Nv	Dc	Dc	
19	18	==	==	==	==	==	==	==	20	==	==	==	==	–	–	–	–	–	–	–	–	–	–	–	–	–	–	–	–	COON UP A TREE (1901)
2	2	4	5	8	7	7	7	6	6	10	15	17	19	==	==	==	==	–	–	–	–	–	–	–	–	–	–	–	–	HELLO, CENTRAL, GIVE ME HEAVEN (1901)
8	16	17	==	==	==	==	20	==	==	==	==	–	–	–	–	–	–	–	–	–	–	–	–	–	–	–	–	–	–	BOOLA, BOOLA (YALE BOOLA) (1901)
4	4	5	9	9	10	9	10	11	9	14	20	20	==	==	==	–	–	–	–	–	–	–	–	–	–	–	–	–	–	THE HONEYSUCKLE AND THE BEE (1901)
9	14	15	17	18	18	16	18	18	19	==	==	==	==	–	–	–	–	–	–	–	–	–	–	–	–	–	–	–	–	HE LAID AWAY A SUIT OF GRAY (1901)
1	1	1	1	2	3	4	4	4	4	3	7	14	14	==	==	==	==	–	–	–	–	–	–	–	–	–	–	–	–	GOOD MORNING, CARRIE (1901)
5	3	2	3	7	9	8	8	8	13	12	18	==	==	–	–	–	–	–	–	–	–	–	–	–	–	–	–	–	–	AIN'T DAT A SHAME? (1901)
7	7	7	8	6	6	6	5	5	5	9	11	16	18	==	==	==	==	–	–	–	–	–	–	–	–	–	–	–	–	MR. VOLUNTEER (1901)
12	17	16	14	13	16	15	17	14	15	19	==	18	20	==	==	==	==	–	–	–	–	–	–	–	–	–	–	–	–	THE TALE OF A BUMBLE BEE (1901)
20	15	11	10	11	15	20	==	==	–	–	–	–	–	–	–	–	–	–	–	–	–	–	–	–	–	–	–	–	–	BABY MINE (1901)
17	12	13	12	12	12	14	16	20	==	==	==	–	–	–	–	–	–	–	–	–	–	–	–	–	–	–	–	–	–	THE TIE THAT BINDS (1901)
15	11	10	11	10	8	11	15	16	==	==	==	–	–	–	–	–	–	–	–	–	–	–	–	–	–	–	–	–	–	I'M TIRED (1901)
16	10	8	7	5	5	5	6	9	12	17	==	==	==	–	–	–	–	–	–	–	–	–	–	–	–	–	–	–	–	MY CASTLE ON THE NILE (1901)
10	6	3	2	1	1	2	2	2	3	5	13	==	==	–	–	–	–	–	–	–	–	–	–	–	–	–	–	–	–	I'LL BE WITH YOU WHEN THE ROSES BLOOM AGAIN (1901)
11	8	6	4	4	4	3	3	3	2	2	3	5	8	10	12	13	13	16	==	==	==	==	==	==	==	–	–	–	–	DOWN WHERE THE COTTON BLOSSOMS GROW
==	19	==	==	==	==	==	==	==	18	==	==	==	==	==	==	==	==	==	==	==	15	18	15	==	19	==	==	==	==	SADIE SAY YOU WON'T SAY NAY
==	13	9	6	3	2	1	1	1	1	1	1	2	5	11	15	17	==	==	==	–	–	–	–	–	–	–	–	–	–	CREOLE BELLES
==	==	18	16	15	13	10	11	13	16	18	==	==	==	==	==	–	–	–	–	–	–	–	–	–	–	–	–	–	–	WHEN MR. SHAKESPEARE COMES TO TOWN (1901)
–	–	==	==	==	20	19	19	==	==	–	–	–	–	–	–	–	–	–	–	–	–	–	–	–	–	–	–	–	–	DON'T PUT ME OFF AT BUFFALO ANY MORE (1901)
–	–	==	19	14	11	12	14	15	17	==	==	–	–	–	–	–	–	–	–	–	–	–	–	–	–	–	–	–	–	WAY DOWN IN OLD INDIANA (1901)
–	–	==	==	19	14	13	9	7	7	8	10	13	16	==	==	–	–	–	–	–	–	–	–	–	–	–	–	–	–	MY MISSISSIPPI SUE
==	==	==	==	==	==	17	12	10	8	7	4	6	9	9	11	12	11	10	15	==	==	==	==	==	==	==	==	==	==	MY CAROLINA CAROLINE
–	–	==	==	==	==	18	13	12	14	11	9	9	11	14	13	14	15	==	==	==	==	==	==	==	==	==	==	==	==	ONE STRIKE, TWO STRIKES, THREE STRIKES OUT
–	–	–	–	==	==	==	==	==	==	==	==	==	17	17	17	15	12	11	12	15	20	17	==	==	==	18	==	==	==	CUPID'S GARDEN
–	–	–	–	==	==	==	==	==	==	==	==	==	==	18	18	16	17	20	18	16	18	==	17	19	==	==	==	==	==	MIGHTY LAK' A ROSE
–	–	–	–	==	==	==	==	==	==	==	==	19	==	19	==	20	20	19	==	==	==	==	20	17	20	==	19	==	==	STAY IN YOUR OWN BACK YARD
–	–	–	–	–	–	==	==	17	10	4	2	1	2	3	3	3	7	9	9	11	14	==	==	==	==	–	–	–	–	WAY DOWN YONDER IN THE CORNFIELD
–	–	–	–	–	–	==	==	19	11	6	5	10	12	16	19	==	==	==	==	–	–	–	–	–	–	–	–	–	–	MAIDEN WITH THE DREAMY EYES
–	–	–	–	–	–	==	==	==	==	==	==	==	==	==	==	==	18	15	16	19	17	16	16	18	17	==	18	20	==	WHERE THE SILV'RY COLORADO WENDS ITS WAY
–	–	–	–	–	–	–	–	==	==	==	17	15	13	15	16	19	==	==	==	==	==	–	–	–	–	–	–	–	–	A SIGNAL FROM MARS
–	–	–	–	–	–	–	–	–	==	==	14	7	4	4	4	7	10	13	20	==	==	–	–	–	–	–	–	–	–	JENNIE LEE
–	–	–	–	–	–	–	–	==	==	16	12	8	6	6	5	5	5	7	10	17	==	==	==	==	==	–	–	–	–	OUR DIRECTOR (MARCH)
–	–	–	–	–	–	–	–	==	==	13	8	4	3	2	2	2	2	3	3	4	5	8	14	20	==	==	–	–	–	THE MANSION OF ACHING HEARTS
–	–	–	–	–	–	–	–	==	==	15	6	3	1	1	1	1	1	1	2	2	2	6	8	14	==	==	==	==	==	ON A SUNDAY AFTERNOON
–	–	–	–	–	–	–	–	==	==	20	16	11	10	7	8	9	8	5	6	10	19	==	==	==	==	==	==	–	–	BLAZE AWAY!
–	–	–	–	–	–	–	–	–	–	==	19	12	7	5	7	11	14	==	==	–	–	–	–	–	–	–	–	–	–	JOSEPHINE, MY JO
–	–	–	–	–	–	–	–	–	–	–	==	==	15	8	6	4	3	2	1	3	6	11	19	==	==	–	–	–	–	RIP VAN WINKLE WAS A LUCKY MAN
–	–	–	–	–	–	–	–	–	–	–	–	==	==	==	20	18	16	==	==	==	==	–	–	–	–	–	–	–	–	PANAMERICANA
Oc	Oc	Nv	Nv	Dc	Dc	Ja	Ja	Fb	Fb	Ma	Ma	Ap	Ap	My	My	Jn	Jn	Jy	Jy	Ag	Ag	Sp	Sp	Oc	Oc	Nv	Nv	Dc	Dc	

1902 | 1903

Ap	Ap	My	My	Jn	Jn	Jy	Jy	Ag	Ag	Sp	Sp	Oc	Oc	Nv	Nv	Dc	Dc	Ja	Ja	Fb	Fb	Ma	Ma	Ap	Ap	My	My	Jn	Jn	
==	==	12	9	8	6	8	11	20	==	==	==	–	–	–	–	–	–	–	–	–	–	–	–	–	–	–	–	–	–	ON A SATURDAY NIGHT
==	==	20	14	10	9	6	7	6	13	20	==	==	==	–	–	–	–	–	–	–	–	–	–	–	–	–	–	–	–	IF TIME WAS MONEY, I'D BE A MILLIONAIRE
==	==	13	10	6	4	4	4	5	11	13	==	==	==	–	–	–	–	–	–	–	–	–	–	–	–	–	–	–	–	IF MONEY TALKS, IT AIN'T ON SPEAKIN' TERMS WITH ME
==	==	==	==	==	==	17	19	==	==	==	==	==	==	==	==	==	==	–	–	–	–	–	–	–	–	–	–	–	–	MY MOTHER WAS A NORTHERN GIRL
==	==	==	==	==	19	12	8	8	12	10	9	12	12	14	14	==	==	==	==	==	==	==	==	–	–	–	–	–	–	PRETTY MOLLIE SHANNON
–	–	==	==	==	==	18	17	14	10	7	7	6	7	8	11	10	16	20	==	==	==	–	–	–	–	–	–	–	–	VIOLETS
–	–	–	–	–	==	==	14	9	4	5	5	9	13	==	==	–	–	–	–	–	–	–	–	–	–	–	–	–	–	NANCY BROWN
–	–	–	–	–	–	==	==	==	16	19	==	==	==	==	==	–	–	–	–	–	–	–	–	–	–	–	–	–	–	IF I BUT DARE
–	–	–	–	==	==	==	==	13	9	9	10	13	16	17	==	==	==	–	–	–	–	–	–	–	–	–	–	–	–	JUST NEXT DOOR
–	–	–	–	–	–	==	==	==	==	==	==	==	==	19	20	==	==	==	==	==	–	–	–	–	–	–	–	–	–	I WANTS A PING PONG MAN
–	–	–	–	==	==	14	5	**1**	**1**	2	3	3	3	3	4	6	8	15	==	==	==	–	–	–	–	–	–	–	–	PLEASE GO 'WAY AND LET ME SLEEP
–	–	–	–	–	==	==	13	7	3	**1**	2	2	2	2	3	3	7	11	15	==	==	–	–	–	–	–	–	–	–	BILL BAILEY, WON'T YOU PLEASE COME HOME?
–	–	–	–	–	–	==	==	==	==	14	11	7	9	15	17	==	==	==	==	–	–	–	–	–	–	–	–	–	–	I'LL BE YOUR RAINBEAU
–	–	–	–	–	–	==	==	12	7	4	4	4	4	5	5	8	11	13	==	==	==	–	–	–	–	–	–	–	–	OH, DIDN'T HE RAMBLE
–	–	–	–	–	–	–	==	18	8	3	**1**	**1**	**1**	**1**	**1**	2	3	4	6	12	==	==	==	–	–	–	–	–	–	IN THE GOOD OLD SUMMERTIME
–	–	–	–	–	–	–	–	==	==	==	==	15	10	9	12	16	17	==	==	==	==	==	==	==	==	–	–	–	–	WAIT
–	–	–	–	–	–	–	–	==	==	==	13	8	8	7	6	9	15	==	==	==	==	==	==	–	–	–	–	–	–	FARE THEE WELL, MOLLIE DARLING
–	–	–	–	–	–	–	–	==	==	==	==	16	14	13	13	18	19	==	==	==	==	==	==	==	==	–	–	–	–	PLACE A LIGHT TO GUIDE ME HOME
–	–	–	–	–	–	–	–	==	==	==	==	==	==	20	16	13	14	19	==	==	==	==	==	==	==	==	==	==	==	DANCE OF THE HONEYBEES
–	–	–	–	–	–	–	–	==	==	15	12	11	11	16	==	==	==	==	==	–	–	–	–	–	–	–	–	–	–	I'VE GOT MY EYES ON YOU
–	–	–	–	–	–	–	–	==	==	12	6	5	5	6	10	17	==	==	==	–	–	–	–	–	–	–	–	–	–	WHEN KATE AND I WERE COMIN' THRO' THE RYE
–	–	–	–	–	–	–	–	==	==	==	18	10	6	4	2	**1**	**1**	2	3	6	7	11	15	==	==	==	==	–	–	MR. DOOLEY
–	–	–	–	–	–	–	–	–	–	==	==	==	15	10	7	5	4	6	5	8	13	16	==	==	==	==	==	–	–	COULD YOU BE TRUE TO EYES OF BLUE?
–	–	–	–	–	–	–	–	–	–	==	==	==	18	11	9	7	5	7	10	11	16	==	==	==	==	–	–	–	–	I'M WEARING MY HEART AWAY FOR YOU, LOUISE
–	–	–	–	–	–	–	–	–	–	–	–	–	–	==	==	14	10	8	13	17	==	==	–	–	–	–	–	–	–	IN THE CITY OF SIGHS AND TEARS
–	–	–	–	–	–	–	–	–	–	–	–	==	==	==	==	==	20	18	17	==	==	==	==	==	==	==	==	–	–	DUTY TO HOME AND FLAG (1903)
–	–	–	–	–	–	–	–	–	–	–	–	==	==	12	8	4	2	**1**	**1**	2	2	2	2	6	9	14	==	==	==	DOWN WHERE THE WURTZBURGER FLOWS (1903)
–	–	–	–	–	–	–	–	–	–	–	–	==	==	==	15	12	12	9	9	9	8	13	17	==	==	==	==	==	==	DAT'S DE WAY TO SPELL CHICKEN (1903)
–	–	–	–	–	–	–	–	–	–	–	–	–	–	==	==	19	13	10	7	4	6	10	14	19	==	==	–	–	–	IN DEAR OLD ILLINOIS (1903)
–	–	–	–	–	–	–	–	–	–	–	–	–	–	==	==	15	9	5	4	3	4	5	10	17	==	==	==	–	–	WHEN IT'S ALL GOIN' OUT AND NOTHIN' COMIN' IN (1903)
–	–	–	–	–	–	–	–	–	–	–	–	–	–	==	==	==	18	12	8	5	3	3	5	10	14	16	19	==	==	THE MESSAGE OF THE VIOLET (1903)
–	–	–	–	–	–	–	–	–	–	–	–	–	–	==	==	11	6	3	2	**1**	**1**	**1**	**1**	**1**	**1**	2	2	3	6	UNDER THE BAMBOO TREE (1903)
Ap	Ap	My	My	Jn	Jn	Jy	Jy	Ag	Ag	Sp	Sp	Oc	Oc	Nv	Nv	Dc	Dc	Ja	Ja	Fb	Fb	Ma	Ma	Ap	Ap	My	My	Jn	Jn	

1902						1903																								
Oc	Oc	Nv	Nv	Dc	Dc	Ja	Ja	Fb	Fb	Ma	Ma	Ap	Ap	My	My	Jn	Jn	Jy	Jy	Ag	Ag	Sp	Sp	Oc	Oc	Nv	Nv	Dc	Dc	
6	7	8	11	10	16	20	==	==	==	–	–	–	–	–	–	–	–	–	–	–	–	–	–	–	–	–	–	–	–	VIOLETS (1902)
3	3	3	4	6	8	15	==	==	==	–	–	–	–	–	–	–	–	–	–	–	–	–	–	–	–	–	–	–	–	PLEASE GO 'WAY AND LET ME SLEEP (1902)
4	4	5	5	8	11	13	==	==	==	–	–	–	–	–	–	–	–	–	–	–	–	–	–	–	–	–	–	–	–	OH, DIDN'T HE RAMBLE (1902)
2	2	2	3	3	7	11	15	==	==	–	–	–	–	–	–	–	–	–	–	–	–	–	–	–	–	–	–	–	–	BILL BAILEY WON'T YOU PLEASE COME HOME? (1902)
1	**1**	**1**	**1**	2	3	4	6	12	==	==	==	–	–	–	–	–	–	–	–	–	–	–	–	–	–	–	–	–	–	IN THE GOOD OLD SUMMERTIME (1902)
==	==	20	16	13	14	19	==	==	==	==	==	==	==	==	==	==	==	==	==	–	–	–	–	–	–	–	–	–	–	DANCE OF THE HONEYBEES (1902)
10	6	4	2	**1**	**1**	2	3	6	7	11	15	==	==	==	==	–	–	–	–	–	–	–	–	–	–	–	–	–	–	MR. DOOLEY (1902)
==	15	10	7	5	4	6	5	8	13	16	==	==	==	==	==	–	–	–	–	–	–	–	–	–	–	–	–	–	–	COULD YOU BE TRUE TO EYES OF BLUE? (1902)
==	18	11	9	7	5	7	10	11	16	==	==	==	==	–	–	–	–	–	–	–	–	–	–	–	–	–	–	–	–	I'M WEARING MY HEART AWAY FOR YOU, LOUISE (1902)
–	–	==	==	14	10	8	13	17	==	==	–	–	–	–	–	–	–	–	–	–	–	–	–	–	–	–	–	–	–	IN THE CITY OF SIGHS AND TEARS (1902)
==	==	==	==	==	20	18	17	==	==	==	==	==	==	==	==	–	–	–	–	–	–	–	–	–	–	–	–	–	–	DUTY TO HOME AND FLAG
==	==	12	8	4	2	**1**	**1**	2	2	2	2	6	9	14	==	==	==	–	–	–	–	–	–	–	–	–	–	–	–	DOWN WHERE THE WURTZBURGER FLOWS
==	==	==	==	==	==	==	18	==	==	==	==	==	==	==	==	==	==	–	–	–	–	–	–	–	–	–	–	–	–	CONEY ISLAND COON
==	==	==	15	12	12	9	9	9	8	13	17	==	==	==	==	==	==	–	–	–	–	–	–	–	–	–	–	–	–	DAT'S DE WAY TO SPELL CHICKEN
–	–	==	==	11	6	3	2	**1**	**1**	**1**	**1**	**1**	**1**	2	2	3	6	10	12	==	==	–	–	–	–	–	–	–	–	UNDER THE BAMBOO TREE
–	–	==	==	19	13	10	7	4	6	10	14	19	==	==	–	–	–	–	–	–	–	–	–	–	–	–	–	–	–	IN DEAR OLD ILLINOIS
–	–	==	==	15	9	5	4	3	4	5	10	17	==	==	==	–	–	–	–	–	–	–	–	–	–	–	–	–	–	WHEN IT'S ALL GOIN' OUT AND NOTHIN' COMIN' IN
–	–	==	==	==	==	==	16	18	==	==	==	==	==	==	==	–	–	–	–	–	–	–	–	–	–	–	–	–	–	IF YOU CAN'T BE A BELL COW, FALL IN BEHIND
–	–	==	==	==	==	17	14	15	19	==	==	==	==	==	==	–	–	–	–	–	–	–	–	–	–	–	–	–	–	SOMEBODY'S WAITING 'NEATH SOUTHERN SKIES
–	–	==	==	==	==	16	12	7	5	4	6	11	15	==	==	==	==	–	–	–	–	–	–	–	–	–	–	–	–	JUST KISS YOURSELF GOODBYE
–	–	==	==	==	18	12	8	5	3	3	5	10	14	16	19	==	==	==	==	–	–	–	–	–	–	–	–	–	–	THE MESSAGE OF THE VIOLET
–	–	–	–	==	==	==	==	16	15	18	==	==	==	==	==	==	==	–	–	–	–	–	–	–	–	–	–	–	–	THE TALE OF THE SEASHELL
–	–	–	–	==	==	==	==	19	18	19	19	==	==	==	==	==	==	–	–	–	–	–	–	–	–	–	–	–	–	THE SPIRIT OF '76
–	–	–	–	==	==	14	11	10	12	15	==	==	==	==	==	–	–	–	–	–	–	–	–	–	–	–	–	–	–	THEN I'D BE SATISFIED WITH LIFE
–	–	–	–	==	==	==	==	==	20	==	==	==	==	==	==	–	–	–	–	–	–	–	–	–	–	–	–	–	–	HEIDELBERG (STEIN SONG)
–	–	–	–	==	==	==	20	14	10	9	13	18	==	==	==	==	==	–	–	–	–	–	–	–	–	–	–	–	–	HAMLET WAS A MELANCHOLY DANE
–	–	–	–	==	==	==	19	13	9	7	9	12	16	==	==	==	==	–	–	–	–	–	–	–	–	–	–	–	–	TWO IS COMPANY, THREE IS A CROWD
–	–	–	–	–	–	==	==	==	==	==	18	16	13	10	5	4	3	4	4	6	6	7	10	11	12	13	14	15	15	19 == NOBODY'S LOOKING BUT THE OWL AND THE MOON
–	–	–	–	–	–	==	==	==	17	12	8	7	8	11	18	==	==	==	==	–	–	–	–	–	–	–	–	–	–	MOLLIE (A DAINTY BIT OF JOLLY)
–	–	–	–	–	–	==	==	20	11	6	3	3	4	7	16	19	==	==	==	–	–	–	–	–	–	–	–	–	–	MY OWN UNITED STATES
–	–	–	–	–	–	==	==	==	14	8	4	4	5	9	11	16	19	==	==	==	==	–	–	–	–	–	–	–	–	TESSIE, YOU ARE THE ONLY, ONLY, ONLY
–	–	–	–	–	–	==	==	==	==	20	12	8	7	5	6	6	4	5	6	7	9	15	16	18	==	==	==	–	–	IN THE SWEET BYE AND BYE
–	–	–	–	–	–	–	–	==	==	==	==	20	17	==	==	==	==	–	–	–	–	–	–	–	–	–	–	–	–	I TAKE THINGS EASY
–	–	–	–	–	–	–	–	==	==	==	16	9	12	19	20	==	==	==	==	–	–	–	–	–	–	–	–	–	–	WHY DON'T YOU GO, GO, GO
–	–	–	–	–	–	–	–	==	==	17	11	5	3	3	3	5	7	11	16	==	==	–	–	–	–	–	–	–	–	THE GAMBLING MAN
–	–	–	–	–	–	–	–	==	==	==	20	13	10	6	9	14	16	15	18	20	==	==	==	–	–	–	–	–	–	SINCE SALLY LEFT OUR ALLEY
–	–	–	–	–	–	–	–	==	==	14	7	2	2	**1**	**1**	**1**	**1**	**1**	**1**	2	2	4	5	10	13	20	==	==	–	HIAWATHA
–	–	–	–	–	–	–	–	–	–	==	==	==	18	==	==	==	==	–	–	–	–	–	–	–	–	–	–	–	–	SAMMY
Oc	Oc	Nv	Nv	Dc	Dc	Ja	Ja	Fb	Fb	Ma	Ma	Ap	Ap	My	My	Jn	Jn	Jy	Jy	Ag	Ag	Sp	Sp	Oc	Oc	Nv	Nv	Dc	Dc	

1903																				1904										
Ma	Ma	Ap	Ap	My	My	Jn	Jn	Jy	Jy	Ag	Ag	Sp	Sp	Oc	Oc	Nv	Nv	Dc	Dc	Ja	Ja	Fb	Fb	Ma	Ma	Ap	Ap	My	My	
==	==	14	6	4	4	8	13	19	==	==	–	–	–	–	–	–	–	–	–	–	–	–	–	–	–	–	–	–	–	I'M A JONAH MAN
==	==	15	11	8	8	9	14	18	==	==	==	–	–	–	–	–	–	–	–	–	–	–	–	–	–	–	–	–	–	HURRAH FOR BAFFIN'S BAY
==	==	==	==	20	13	11	8	6	5	4	5	6	8	9	7	8	8	10	11	12	15	==	==	==	==	==	==	==	==	COME DOWN, MA EVENIN' STAR
==	==	==	==	17	17	15	18	17	19	18	==	==	==	–	–	–	–	–	–	–	–	–	–	–	–	–	–	–	–	EVERY MAN IS A VOLUNTEER
==	==	==	==	13	14	13	12	14	14	17	17	==	==	–	–	–	–	–	–	–	–	–	–	–	–	–	–	–	–	ONLY A SOLDIER BOY
==	==	==	19	==	==	==	==	20	15	13	12	12	14	17	19	==	==	==	==	==	==	==	==	==	==	==	==	–	–	DOWN IN THE DEEP, LET ME SLEEP WHEN I DIE
==	==	==	==	==	==	20	20	==	13	10	10	10	13	16	18	15	13	11	13	15	17	==	==	==	==	==	==	==	==	GOODNIGHT, BELOVED, GOODNIGHT
==	==	==	==	18	12	12	9	7	11	14	16	18	==	==	–	–	–	–	–	–	–	–	–	–	–	–	–	–	–	WHAT A NASTY DISPOSITION FOR A LADY LIKE YOU
–	==	==	20	12	10	7	10	13	17	==	==	–	–	–	–	–	–	–	–	–	–	–	–	–	–	–	–	–	–	VOICE OF THE HUDSON
–	–	==	==	==	==	18	15	8	8	9	13	17	==	==	==	–	–	–	–	–	–	–	–	–	–	–	–	–	–	SINCE I FIRST MET YOU
–	–	==	==	==	15	10	5	3	3	3	3	3	3	7	11	17	==	==	==	–	–	–	–	–	–	–	–	–	–	IN OLD ALABAMA
–	–	==	==	==	==	==	17	12	9	8	8	8	11	12	14	16	18	20	==	==	==	–	–	–	–	–	–	–	–	MY BESSIE'S WEDDING DAY
–	–	==	==	==	==	==	==	==	==	16	14	16	17	==	==	==	19	==	==	==	==	==	==	==	==	–	–	–	–	SADIE GREEN
–	–	==	==	15	7	2	2	2	2	**1**	**1**	**1**	**1**	**1**	4	5	7	9	8	10	13	17	17	==	==	==	==	–	–	CONGO LOVE SONG
–	–	–	–	==	==	17	11	9	10	12	15	19	==	==	–	–	–	–	–	–	–	–	–	–	–	–	–	–	–	THE BOYS ARE COMING HOME TODAY
–	–	–	–	–	–	==	==	16	7	5	4	2	2	4	5	9	11	14	18	==	==	–	–	–	–	–	–	–	–	SHOW ME THE WHITE OF YO' EYE
–	–	–	–	–	–	–	–	==	==	==	==	20	==	==	20	==	==	==	==	–	–	–	–	–	–	–	–	–	–	PRINCESS POCAHONTAS
–	–	–	–	–	–	–	–	==	==	19	20	==	18	19	==	==	==	==	==	–	–	–	–	–	–	–	–	–	–	YOU CAN'T FOOL ALL THE PEOPLE ALL THE TIME
–	–	–	–	–	–	–	–	==	==	15	11	11	12	15	16	18	==	==	==	–	–	–	–	–	–	–	–	–	–	I'VE GOT TO GO NOW 'CAUSE I THINK IT'S GOING TO RAIN
–	–	–	–	–	–	–	–	==	20	11	7	5	7	5	9	12	16	18	==	==	–	–	–	–	–	–	–	–	–	THE BOYS IN THE GALL'RY FOR MINE
–	–	–	–	–	–	–	–	–	–	==	19	14	9	6	6	10	12	16	19	==	==	–	–	–	–	–	–	–	–	THE SUN DANCE
–	–	–	–	–	–	–	–	–	–	==	==	13	6	3	2	3	5	6	7	8	11	15	==	==	–	–	–	–	–	ANONA
–	–	–	–	–	–	–	–	–	–	==	18	9	4	2	**1**	**1**	**1**	3	3	2	2	2	2	3	2	2	5	6	9	10 13 20 == ALWAYS IN THE WAY
–	–	–	–	–	–	–	–	–	–	–	==	==	15	8	3	2	3	2	2	4	4	8	13	17	==	==	–	–	–	DEAR OLD GIRL
–	–	–	–	–	–	–	–	–	–	–	–	==	20	14	10	6	6	5	5	6	8	12	16	==	==	–	–	–	–	UP IN A COCONUT TREE
–	–	–	–	–	–	–	–	–	–	–	–	==	19	13	8	4	4	4	4	3	3	3	6	8	12	17	==	==	==	LAUGHING WATER
–	–	–	–	–	–	–	–	–	–	–	–	==	==	20	15	11	10	7	6	5	6	7	9	13	20	==	==	==	==	DOWN ON THE FARM
–	–	–	–	–	–	–	–	–	–	–	–	==	==	==	==	19	15	13	14	17	19	==	20	==	==	==	==	==	==	YOU'RE AS WELCOME AS THE FLOWERS IN MAY
–	–	–	–	–	–	–	–	–	–	–	–	–	–	==	==	14	9	8	9	14	==	==	–	–	–	–	–	–	–	WHERE ARE THE FRIENDS OF OTHER DAYS?
–	–	–	–	–	–	–	–	–	–	–	–	–	–	==	17	7	2	**1**	**1**	**1**	**1**	**1**	**1**	**1**	5	12	==	==	–	BEDELIA
–	–	–	–	–	–	–	–	–	–	–	–	–	–	–	–	==	==	19	==	==	==	==	==	–	–	–	–	–	–	LINCOLN, GRANT, OR LEE
–	–	–	–	–	–	–	–	–	–	–	–	==	==	==	==	==	20	==	20	20	20	20	==	==	==	==	18	16	15	BECAUSE YOU WERE AN OLD SWEETHEART OF MINE (1904)
–	–	–	–	–	–	–	–	–	–	–	–	–	–	==	==	==	17	12	10	7	5	5	7	6	8	9	11	14	16	WHEN THE SUNSET TURNS THE OCEAN'S BLUE TO GOLD (1904)
–	–	–	–	–	–	–	–	–	–	–	–	–	–	–	–	==	==	==	16	13	10	11	12	10	13	11	15	17	==	ANY RAGS? (1904)
–	–	–	–	–	–	–	–	–	–	–	–	–	–	–	–	==	==	17	12	9	7	4	3	4	3	5	8	12	13	GOODBYE, ELIZA JANE (1904)
–	–	–	–	–	–	–	–	–	–	–	–	–	–	–	–	–	==	==	17	11	9	6	5	5	4	7	9	13	14	I CAN'T DO THE SUM (1904)
Ma	Ma	Ap	Ap	My	My	Jn	Jn	Jy	Jy	Ag	Ag	Sp	Sp	Oc	Oc	Nv	Nv	Dc	Dc	Ja	Ja	Fb	Fb	Ma	Ma	Ap	Ap	My	My	

1903						1904																								
Oc	Oc	Nv	Nv	Dc	Dc	Ja	Ja	Fb	Fb	Ma	Ma	Ap	Ap	My	My	Jn	Jn	Jy	Jy	Ag	Ag	Sp	Sp	Oc	Oc	Nv	Nv	Dc	Dc	
16	18	15	13	11	13	15	17	==	–	–	–	–	–	–	–	–	–	–	–	–	–	–	–	–	–	–	–	–	–	GOODNIGHT, BELOVED, GOODNIGHT (1903)
11	12	13	14	15	15	19	==	–	–	–	–	–	–	–	–	–	–	–	–	–	–	–	–	–	–	–	–	–	–	NOBODY'S LOOKING BUT THE OWL AND THE MOON (1903)
9	7	8	8	10	11	12	15	==	–	–	–	–	–	–	–	–	–	–	–	–	–	–	–	–	–	–	–	–	–	COME DOWN, MA EVENIN' STAR (1903)
1	4	5	7	9	8	10	13	17	17	==	==	==	==	–	–	–	–	–	–	–	–	–	–	–	–	–	–	–	–	CONGO LOVE SONG (1903)
3	2	3	5	6	7	8	11	15	==	==	–	–	–	–	–	–	–	–	–	–	–	–	–	–	–	–	–	–	–	ANONA (1903)
==	==	19	15	13	14	17	19	==	20	==	==	==	==	==	==	–	–	–	–	–	–	–	–	–	–	–	–	–	–	YOU'RE AS WELCOME AS THE FLOWERS IN MAY (1903)
2	**1**	**1**	**1**	3	3	2	2	2	2	3	2	2	5	6	9	10	13	20	==	==	==	–	–	–	–	–	–	–	–	ALWAYS IN THE WAY (1903)
14	10	6	6	5	5	6	8	12	16	==	==	–	–	–	–	–	–	–	–	–	–	–	–	–	–	–	–	–	–	UP IN A COCONUT TREE (1903)
8	3	2	3	2	2	4	4	8	13	17	==	==	–	–	–	–	–	–	–	–	–	–	–	–	–	–	–	–	–	DEAR OLD GIRL (1903)
13	8	4	4	4	4	3	3	3	6	8	12	17	==	==	==	–	–	–	–	–	–	–	–	–	–	–	–	–	–	LAUGHING WATER (1903)
==	==	14	9	8	9	14	==	==	–	–	–	–	–	–	–	–	–	–	–	–	–	–	–	–	–	–	–	–	–	WHERE ARE THE FRIENDS OF OTHER DAYS? (1903)
==	17	7	2	**1**	**1**	**1**	**1**	**1**	**1**	**1**	5	12	==	==	–	–	–	–	–	–	–	–	–	–	–	–	–	–	–	BEDELIA (1903)
20	15	11	10	7	6	5	6	7	9	13	20	==	==	==	==	==	==	–	–	–	–	–	–	–	–	–	–	–	–	DOWN ON THE FARM (1903)
==	==	==	20	==	20	20	20	20	==	==	==	==	18	16	15	17	16	15	16	==	==	==	==	==	==	==	==	==	==	BECAUSE YOU WERE AN OLD SWEETHEART OF MINE
==	==	==	17	12	10	7	5	5	7	6	8	9	11	14	16	20	==	==	==	==	==	==	==	==	==	–	–	–	–	WHEN THE SUNSET TURNS THE OCEAN'S BLUE TO GOLD
–	–	==	==	==	16	13	10	11	12	10	13	11	15	17	==	==	==	==	==	==	==	==	==	==	==	–	–	–	–	ANY RAGS?
–	–	==	==	17	12	9	7	4	3	4	3	5	8	12	13	14	19	19	==	==	==	==	==	==	==	–	–	–	–	GOODBYE, ELIZA JANE
–	–	–	==	==	17	11	9	6	5	5	4	7	9	13	14	18	==	==	==	–	–	–	–	–	–	–	–	–	–	I CAN'T DO THE SUM
–	–	–	–	==	==	16	12	10	8	7	9	13	16	==	==	–	–	–	–	–	–	–	–	–	–	–	–	–	–	THE BURNING OF ROME
–	–	–	–	==	==	==	18	16	15	16	18	==	==	==	==	==	==	–	–	–	–	–	–	–	–	–	–	–	–	MARCH OF THE TOYS
–	–	–	–	==	==	18	14	13	11	9	6	8	7	9	10	11	12	12	13	15	==	==	==	==	==	–	–	–	–	TOYLAND
–	–	–	–	==	==	==	==	==	19	==	==	==	==	==	==	==	==	==	==	==	==	==	==	–	–	–	–	–	–	THE SWEETEST FLOWER THAT GROWS IN TENNESSEE
–	–	–	–	–	==	==	16	9	4	2	**1**	**1**	**1**	2	4	4	5	6	6	8	11	==	==	==	==	–	–	–	–	NAVAJO
–	–	–	–	–	–	==	==	14	10	12	16	==	==	–	–	–	–	–	–	–	–	–	–	–	–	–	–	–	–	I'M ON THE WATER WAGON NOW
–	–	–	–	–	–	==	==	19	18	20	17	==	==	==	==	==	==	–	–	–	–	–	–	–	–	–	–	–	–	HERE'S YOUR HAT, WHAT'S YOUR HURRY?
–	–	–	–	–	–	==	==	18	14	11	14	18	==	==	==	–	–	–	–	–	–	–	–	–	–	–	–	–	–	YOUR MOTHER WANTS YOU HOME, BOY
–	–	–	–	–	–	==	==	==	==	==	==	==	19	18	18	==	==	==	18	==	==	==	==	–	–	–	–	–	–	Y.M.C.A. MARCH
–	–	–	–	–	–	–	–	==	==	==	==	==	20	19	19	==	==	==	==	–	–	–	–	–	–	–	–	–	–	YOU NEVER SPOKE TO ME LIKE THAT BEFORE
–	–	–	–	–	–	–	–	==	==	==	==	14	10	8	8	8	11	17	==	==	==	–	–	–	–	–	–	–	–	FOR SALE, A BABY
–	–	–	–	–	–	–	–	==	==	==	==	15	14	11	11	13	14	16	19	==	==	==	==	–	–	–	–	–	–	WHERE THE SILV'RY COLORADO WENDS ITS WAY
–	–	–	–	–	–	–	–	==	==	19	11	6	4	5	5	7	8	10	12	17	==	==	==	–	–	–	–	–	–	IN ZANZIBAR
–	–	–	–	–	–	–	–	==	==	18	15	16	13	20	==	==	–	–	–	–	–	–	–	–	–	–	–	–	–	ALWAYS LEAVE THEM LAUGHING
–	–	–	–	–	–	–	–	==	==	==	==	19	12	7	6	5	4	5	8	12	15	17	==	==	==	–	–	–	–	UNDER THE ANHEUSER BUSH
–	–	–	–	–	–	–	–	==	==	==	==	20	17	10	7	6	6	7	10	10	18	18	==	==	==	–	–	–	–	THE GONDOLIER
–	–	–	–	–	–	–	–	==	==	15	10	4	3	3	3	3	3	4	4	5	6	10	13	15	==	==	–	–	–	I'VE GOT A FEELIN' FOR YOU
–	–	–	–	–	–	–	–	==	==	14	7	3	2	**1**	**1**	**1**	**1**	**1**	2	2	2	5	9	11	17	==	==	–	–	BLUE BELL
Oc	Oc	Nv	Nv	Dc	Dc	Ja	Ja	Fb	Fb	Ma	Ma	Ap	Ap	My	My	Jn	Jn	Jy	Jy	Ag	Ag	Sp	Sp	Oc	Oc	Nv	Nv	Dc	Dc	

1904																				1905										
Ma	Ma	Ap	Ap	My	My	Jn	Jn	Jy	Jy	Ag	Ag	Sp	Sp	Oc	Oc	Nv	Nv	Dc	Dc	Ja	Ja	Fb	Fb	Ma	Ma	Ap	Ap	My	My	
==	19	10	6	4	2	2	2	2	3	3	5	9	12	14	==	==	–	–	–	–	–	–	–	–	–	–	–	–	–	GOODBYE, MY LADY LOVE
==	==	==	==	==	==	==	==	18	14	16	==	==	20	==	==	==	20	==	==	==	==	==	==	==	–	–	–	–	–	IDA (SWEET AS APPLE CIDER)
==	==	==	==	==	==	==	==	==	==	==	==	==	==	==	20	20	19	==	==	==	==	==	==	==	==	==	==	==	==	THE LITTLE CHURCH WHERE YOU AND I WERE WED
–	–	==	==	==	17	19	==	==	==	–	–	–	–	–	–	–	–	–	–	–	–	–	–	–	–	–	–	–	–	WHEN I'M AWAY FROM YOU, DEAR
–	–	==	==	==	20	16	17	==	==	==	==	–	–	–	–	–	–	–	–	–	–	–	–	–	–	–	–	–	–	AIN'T IT FUNNY WHAT A DIFFERENCE JUST A FEW HOURS MAKE?
–	–	==	==	15	12	9	10	13	17	==	==	–	–	–	–	–	–	–	–	–	–	–	–	–	–	–	–	–	–	HANNAH, WON'T YOU OPEN THAT DOOR?
–	–	==	==	==	==	15	9	8	9	11	16	==	==	==	==	–	–	–	–	–	–	–	–	–	–	–	–	–	–	UNTER DEN LINDEN
–	–	==	==	==	==	==	18	14	11	7	4	4	5	4	5	5	5	7	7	6	5	3	2	3	2	3	8	11	14	19 20 ==SWEET ADELINE
–	–	–	–	==	==	==	15	9	5	6	8	13	17	==	==	==	==	–	–	–	–	–	–	–	–	–	–	–	–	EGYPT
–	–	–	–	==	==	12	7	3	**1**	**1**	**1**	**1**	2	8	11	16	==	==	–	–	–	–	–	–	–	–	–	–	–	MEET ME IN ST. LOUIS, LOUIS
–	–	–	–	==	==	==	==	==	20	20	17	19	19	20	==	==	==	20	20	==	==	–	–	–	–	–	–	–	–	THE SWEETEST GIRL IN DIXIE
–	–	–	–	==	==	==	20	11	7	4	3	2	4	6	9	11	13	13	16	18	==	==	==	==	==	==	==	–	–	A BIT O' BLARNEY
–	–	–	–	–	–	==	==	==	==	==	20	16	15	12	10	10	11	11	11	11	6	7	9	8	13	13	16	20	==	BY THE WATERMELON VINE, LINDY LOU
–	–	–	–	–	–	==	==	==	15	9	9	14	11	13	16	19	==	==	==	–	–	–	–	–	–	–	–	–	–	THE MAN WITH THE LADDER AND THE HOSE
–	–	–	–	–	–	–	–	==	==	==	==	20	18	==	==	==	==	–	–	–	–	–	–	–	–	–	–	–	–	DOWN ON THE BRANDYWINE
–	–	–	–	–	–	–	–	==	==	19	14	15	16	18	18	==	==	==	==	–	–	–	–	–	–	–	–	–	–	JUST A GLEAM OF HEAVEN IN HER EYES
–	–	–	–	–	–	–	–	==	==	14	10	6	7	7	7	12	15	19	==	==	==	–	–	–	–	–	–	–	–	SEMINOLE
–	–	–	–	–	–	–	–	==	==	13	7	3	**1**	**1**	2	2	3	6	6	7	8	13	16	==	==	–	–	–	–	COME TAKE A TRIP IN MY AIRSHIP
–	–	–	–	–	–	–	–	==	==	18	13	12	10	9	6	6	10	9	8	8	9	6	8	7	11	15	20	==	==	LAZY MOON
–	–	–	–	–	–	–	–	–	==	==	12	7	3	2	**1**	**1**	**1**	2	3	5	7	9	12	14	==	==	==	–	–	GOODBYE, LITTLE GIRL, GOODBYE
–	–	–	–	–	–	–	–	–	–	==	==	11	8	5	4	4	8	10	12	14	20	==	==	–	–	–	–	–	–	ALEXANDER (DON'T YOU LOVE YOUR BABY NO MORE?)
–	–	–	–	–	–	–	–	–	–	==	19	8	6	3	3	3	2	**1**	5	9	11	16	==	==	==	–	–	–	–	TEASING
–	–	–	–	–	–	–	–	–	–	==	==	==	==	==	==	==	18	18	18	19	==	==	==	==	==	–	–	–	–	DOWN IN THE VALE OF SHENANDOAH
–	–	–	–	–	–	–	–	–	–	==	==	==	14	10	8	7	6	5	4	3	3	4	7	10	15	==	==	==	==	PLEASE COME AND PLAY IN MY YARD
–	–	–	–	–	–	–	–	–	–	==	==	==	==	19	15	15	14	14	13	12	15	20	==	==	==	==	==	–	–	KATE KEARNEY
–	–	–	–	–	–	–	–	–	–	–	–	==	==	==	==	17	16	17	17	20	==	==	==	==	==	–	–	–	–	THE TROUBADOUR
–	–	–	–	–	–	–	–	–	–	–	–	==	==	17	14	14	12	12	14	15	==	==	==	==	==	–	–	–	–	KARAMA
–	–	–	–	–	–	–	–	–	–	–	–	==	==	16	12	9	7	4	2	**1**	**1**	**1**	**1**	2	3	7	15	==	==	BACK, BACK, BACK TO BALTIMORE
–	–	–	–	–	–	–	–	–	–	–	–	–	–	==	19	13	9	8	10	10	13	17	==	==	–	–	–	–	–	A LITTLE BOY CALLED TAPS
–	–	–	–	–	–	–	–	–	–	–	–	–	==	==	13	8	4	3	**1**	2	4	12	14	==	==	–	–	–	–	I MAY BE CRAZY, BUT I AIN'T NO FOOL
–	–	–	–	–	–	–	–	–	–	–	–	–	==	==	==	18	17	16	15	13	14	15	19	==	==	==	==	==	==	SHAME ON YOU (1905)
–	–	–	–	–	–	–	–	–	–	–	–	–	–	–	–	==	==	15	9	4	2	2	5	9	14	==	==	–	–	THERE'S A DARK MAN COMING WITH A BUNDLE (1905)
–	–	–	–	–	–	–	–	–	–	–	–	–	–	–	–	–	==	==	19	16	19	19	==	==	==	==	==	==	==	AL FRESCO (1905)
Ma	Ma	Ap	Ap	My	My	Jn	Jn	Jy	Jy	Ag	Ag	Sp	Sp	Oc	Oc	Nv	Nv	Dc	Dc	Ja	Ja	Fb	Fb	Ma	Ma	Ap	Ap	My	My	

		1904															1905													
Oc	Oc	Nv	Nv	Dc	Dc	Ja	Ja	Fb	Fb	Ma	Ma	Ap	Ap	My	My	Jn	Jn	Jy	Jy	Ag	Ag	Sp	Sp	Oc	Oc	Nv	Nv	Dc	Dc	
4	5	5	5	7	7	6	5	3	2	3	2	3	8	11	14	19	20	==	==	==	==	–	–	–	–	–	–	–	–	SWEET ADELINE (1904)
6	9	11	13	13	16	18	==	==	==	==	==	==	==	–	–	–	–	–	–	–	–	–	–	–	–	–	–	–	–	A BIT O' BLARNEY (1904)
12	10	10	11	11	11	11	6	7	9	8	13	13	16	20	==	==	==	–	–	–	–	–	–	–	–	–	–	–	–	BY THE WATERMELON VINE, LINDY LOU (1904)
2	1	1	1	2	3	5	7	9	12	14	20	==	==	–	–	–	–	–	–	–	–	–	–	–	–	–	–	–	–	GOODBYE, LITTLE GIRL, GOODBYE (1904)
1	2	2	3	6	6	7	8	13	16	==	==	–	–	–	–	–	–	–	–	–	–	–	–	–	–	–	–	–	–	COME TAKE A TRIP IN MY AIRSHIP (1904)
9	6	6	10	9	8	8	9	6	8	7	11	15	20	==	==	–	–	–	–	–	–	–	–	–	–	–	–	–	–	LAZY MOON (1904)
5	4	4	8	10	12	14	20	==	==	–	–	–	–	–	–	–	–	–	–	–	–	–	–	–	–	–	–	–	–	ALEXANDER (DON'T YOU LOVE YOUR BABY NO MORE? (1904)
3	3	3	2	1	5	9	11	16	==	==	==	–	–	–	–	–	–	–	–	–	–	–	–	–	–	–	–	–	–	TEASING (1904)
==	==	==	18	18	18	19	==	==	==	==	==	–	–	–	–	–	–	–	–	–	–	–	–	–	–	–	–	–	–	DOWN IN THE VALE OF SHENANDOAH (1904)
10	8	7	6	5	4	3	3	4	7	10	15	==	==	==	==	–	–	–	–	–	–	–	–	–	–	–	–	–	–	PLEASE COME AND PLAY IN MY YARD (1904)
19	15	15	14	14	13	12	15	20	==	==	==	==	==	–	–	–	–	–	–	–	–	–	–	–	–	–	–	–	–	KATE KEARNEY (1904)
==	==	17	16	17	17	20	==	==	==	==	==	–	–	–	–	–	–	–	–	–	–	–	–	–	–	–	–	–	–	THE TROUBADOUR (1904)
17	14	14	12	12	14	15	==	==	==	==	==	–	–	–	–	–	–	–	–	–	–	–	–	–	–	–	–	–	–	KARAMA (1904)
16	12	9	7	4	2	1	1	1	1	2	3	7	15	==	==	–	–	–	–	–	–	–	–	–	–	–	–	–	–	BACK, BACK, BACK TO BALTIMORE (1904)
==	19	13	9	8	10	10	13	17	==	==	–	–	–	–	–	–	–	–	–	–	–	–	–	–	–	–	–	–	–	A LITTLE BOY CALLED TAPS (1904)
==	13	8	4	3	1	2	4	12	14	==	==	–	–	–	–	–	–	–	–	–	–	–	–	–	–	–	–	–	–	I MAY BE CRAZY, BUT I AIN'T NO FOOL (1904)
==	==	18	17	16	15	13	14	15	19	==	==	==	==	==	==	==	==	==	==	–	–	–	–	–	–	–	–	–	–	SHAME ON YOU
–	–	==	==	15	9	4	2	2	5	9	14	==	==	–	–	–	–	–	–	–	–	–	–	–	–	–	–	–	–	THERE'S A DARK MAN COMING WITH A BUNDLE
–	–	–	==	==	19	16	19	19	==	==	==	==	==	==	–	–	–	–	–	–	–	–	–	–	–	–	–	–	–	AL FRESCO
–	–	–	–	==	==	17	12	11	10	18	18	==	==	==	==	–	–	–	–	–	–	–	–	–	–	–	–	–	–	JOLLY ME ALONG
–	–	–	–	==	==	==	==	18	11	6	4	6	9	14	15	16	19	==	==	==	==	–	–	–	–	–	–	–	–	WHAT THE BRASS BAND PLAYED
–	–	–	–	–	==	==	17	14	13	15	==	==	==	–	–	–	–	–	–	–	–	–	–	–	–	–	–	–	–	WHEN THE BEES ARE IN THE HIVE
–	–	–	–	–	==	==	16	8	6	5	7	16	==	==	–	–	–	–	–	–	–	–	–	–	–	–	–	–	–	THE TALE OF THE TURTLE DOVE
–	–	–	–	–	==	==	10	5	3	4	6	10	==	==	–	–	–	–	–	–	–	–	–	–	–	–	–	–	–	MAMMA'S BOY
–	–	–	–	–	==	==	==	==	20	17	19	==	==	==	==	==	–	–	–	–	–	–	–	–	–	–	–	–	–	COAX ME
–	–	–	–	–	–	==	==	==	18	13	12	17	==	==	==	==	==	–	–	–	–	–	–	–	–	–	–	–	–	WON'T YOU FONDLE ME?
–	–	–	–	–	–	==	==	==	15	11	9	9	13	15	19	==	==	–	–	–	–	–	–	–	–	–	–	–	–	LIFE'S A FUNNY PROPOSITION AFTER ALL
–	–	–	–	–	–	==	18	10	4	1	1	1	2	2	3	3	4	4	5	8	12	15	==	==	==	–	–	–	–	YANKEE DOODLE BOY
–	–	–	–	–	–	==	==	==	==	==	==	==	14	13	11	9	11	11	13	14	16	16	19	==	==	==	==	==	==	WHEN THE HARVEST MOON IS SHINING ON THE RIVER
–	–	–	–	–	–	–	==	==	==	20	17	19	==	==	==	==	==	–	–	–	–	–	–	–	–	–	–	–	–	TELL ME WITH YOUR EYES
–	–	–	–	–	–	–	–	==	==	==	==	==	18	==	==	–	–	–	–	–	–	–	–	–	–	–	–	–	–	THE DAY THAT YOU GREW COLDER
–	–	–	–	–	–	–	–	==	==	==	==	20	12	17	16	17	==	==	==	–	–	–	–	–	–	–	–	–	–	ABSINTHE FRAPPE
–	–	–	–	–	–	–	–	==	==	19	8	4	3	5	8	8	10	16	20	==	==	–	–	–	–	–	–	–	–	I'M TRYING SO HARD TO FORGET YOU
–	–	–	–	–	–	–	–	==	==	16	10	5	4	4	4	4	3	3	4	7	11	13	15	==	==	==	==	–	–	GIVE MY REGARDS TO BROADWAY
–	–	–	–	–	–	–	–	==	17	12	5	2	1	1	1	1	1	1	1	1	2	3	5	9	16	20	==	–	–	IN THE SHADE OF THE OLD APPLE TREE
–	–	–	–	–	–	–	–	==	==	==	16	8	6	7	6	7	5	6	6	5	8	10	13	17	20	==	==	==	==	CARISSIMA
–	–	–	–	–	–	–	–	–	–	==	==	12	7	6	12	13	16	19	==	==	–	–	–	–	–	–	–	–	–	WHERE THE SOUTHERN ROSES GROW
–	–	–	–	–	–	–	–	–	–	==	==	14	10	9	13	14	18	20	==	==	–	–	–	–	–	–	–	–	–	HONEY, I'M WAITING
Oc	Oc	Nv	Nv	Dc	Dc	Ja	Ja	Fb	Fb	Ma	Ma	Ap	Ap	My	My	Jn	Jn	Jy	Jy	Ag	Ag	Sp	Sp	Oc	Oc	Nv	Nv	Dc	Dc	

1905																				1906										
Ma	Ma	Ap	Ap	My	My	Jn	Jn	Jy	Jy	Ag	Ag	Sp	Sp	Oc	Oc	Nv	Nv	Dc	Dc	Ja	Ja	Fb	Fb	Ma	Ma	Ap	Ap	My	My	
==	20	11	5	3	2	5	7	9	12	17	==	==	–	–	–	–	–	–	–	–	–	–	–	–	–	–	–	–	–	HE'S ME PAL
==	==	18	11	8	7	6	6	8	10	11	15	19	==	==	==	–	–	–	–	–	–	–	–	–	–	–	–	–	–	MOONLIGHT (SERENADE)
–	==	==	17	12	9	10	12	12	14	==	==	–	–	–	–	–	–	–	–	–	–	–	–	–	–	–	–	–	–	LONGING FOR YOU
–	–	==	==	18	18	==	==	==	–	–	–	–	–	–	–	–	–	–	–	–	–	–	–	–	–	–	–	–	–	JIM JUDSON (FROM THE TOWN OF HACKENSACK)
–	–	==	==	19	20	==	==	–	–	–	–	–	–	–	–	–	–	–	–	–	–	–	–	–	–	–	–	–	–	GOODBYE, SIS
–	–	==	==	16	10	11	13	15	15	==	==	==	==	–	–	–	–	–	–	–	–	–	–	–	–	–	–	–	–	PAL OF MINE
–	–	==	19	10	5	2	2	2	2	3	4	6	10	12	==	==	==	–	–	–	–	–	–	–	–	–	–	–	–	TAMMANY
–	–	==	==	==	==	20	17	17	19	==	==	–	–	–	–	–	–	–	–	–	–	–	–	–	–	–	–	–	–	EV'RY LITTLE BIT HELPS
–	–	–	–	==	17	12	8	7	8	12	19	==	==	–	–	–	–	–	–	–	–	–	–	–	–	–	–	–	–	SHE WAITS BY THE DEEP BLUE SEA
–	–	–	–	==	==	18	15	14	11	9	7	9	11	11	17	18	==	==	==	==	==	–	–	–	–	–	–	–	–	YANKEE GRIT
–	–	–	–	==	==	15	9	5	3	2	1	2	3	4	5	7	11	13	17	20	==	==	==	–	–	–	–	–	–	KEEP A LITTLE COZY CORNER IN YOUR HEART FOR ME
–	–	–	–	–	–	==	==	18	17	19	==	==	==	==	==	–	–	–	–	–	–	–	–	–	–	–	–	–	–	BRIGHT EYES, GOODBYE
–	–	–	–	–	–	==	==	13	9	6	6	5	6	6	7	15	18	==	==	–	–	–	–	–	–	–	–	–	–	THE PREACHER AND THE BEAR
–	–	–	–	–	==	==	14	10	7	4	3	1	1	2	2	3	5	7	10	12	15	20	==	==	–	–	–	–	–	MY IRISH MOLLY–O
–	–	–	–	–	–	==	==	==	16	16	13	14	12	10	11	14	15	17	20	==	==	==	==	==	==	==	==	–	–	COLLEGE LIFE
–	–	–	–	–	–	==	==	==	==	20	14	12	9	5	4	2	2	3	2	3	4	4	3	1	1	1	2	2	8	10 12 13 18 == DEARIE
–	–	–	–	–	–	–	–	==	==	18	18	17	16	20	==	==	==	–	–	–	–	–	–	–	–	–	–	–	–	VIOLETTE
–	–	–	–	–	–	–	–	==	==	13	9	8	7	8	12	16	20	==	==	–	–	–	–	–	–	–	–	–	–	NOBODY
–	–	–	–	–	–	–	–	==	18	10	5	4	4	3	3	4	6	11	12	14	16	==	==	–	–	–	–	–	–	EVERYBODY WORKS BUT FATHER
–	–	–	–	–	–	–	–	==	==	==	==	18	14	15	15	17	14	15	16	17	17	19	19	==	==	==	==	–	–	DOWN WHERE THE SILV'RY MOHAWK FLOWS
–	–	–	–	–	–	–	–	==	==	15	10	7	2	1	1	1	1	2	3	2	3	3	4	3	3	5	11	15	==	WOULD YOU CARE?
–	–	–	–	–	–	–	–	–	–	==	==	20	17	==	==	==	==	==	==	–	–	–	–	–	–	–	–	–	–	CENTRAL, GIVE ME BACK MY DIME
–	–	–	–	–	–	–	–	–	–	==	17	11	8	7	6	10	16	18	==	==	–	–	–	–	–	–	–	–	–	WHEN THE BELL IN THE LIGHTHOUSE RINGS, DING DONG
–	–	–	–	–	–	–	–	–	–	–	–	==	18	14	10	8	7	8	8	10	11	12	17	==	==	–	–	–	–	THE LEADER OF THE GERMAN BAND
–	–	–	–	–	–	–	–	–	–	–	–	==	20	13	8	5	4	4	5	8	10	10	13	18	==	==	==	–	–	WHAT YOU GOIN' TO DO WHEN THE RENT COMES 'ROUND?
																														(RUFUS RASTUS JOHNSON BROWN)
–	–	–	–	–	–	–	–	–	–	–	–	==	==	18	13	13	10	9	7	5	5	6	9	11	17	==	==	==	==	IN DEAR OLD GEORGIA
–	–	–	–	–	–	–	–	–	–	–	–	–	–	==	19	12	12	12	13	15	==	==	==	–	–	–	–	–	–	THE WHISTLER AND HIS DOG
–	–	–	–	–	–	–	–	–	–	–	–	–	–	==	18	11	9	5	4	7	9	11	15	==	==	–	–	–	–	HOW'D YOU LIKE TO SPOON WITH ME?
–	–	–	–	–	–	–	–	–	–	–	–	–	–	==	==	19	13	10	9	6	6	8	10	13	20	==	==	–	–	WHERE THE MORNING GLORIES TWINE AROUND THE DOOR
–	–	–	–	–	–	–	–	–	–	–	–	–	–	–	==	==	==	20	18	19	==	==	==	–	–	–	–	–	–	A WOMAN IS ONLY A WOMAN, BUT A GOOD CIGAR IS A SMOKE
–	–	–	–	–	–	–	–	–	–	–	–	–	–	–	==	==	19	16	14	13	14	18	==	==	–	–	–	–	–	THE TOWN WHERE I WAS BORN
–	–	–	–	–	–	–	–	–	–	–	–	==	==	19	14	9	8	6	6	4	2	2	2	4	6	8	12	13	16	IN MY MERRY OLDSMOBILE (1906)
–	–	–	–	–	–	–	–	–	–	–	–	==	==	16	9	6	3	1	1	1	1	1	1	2	2	3	3	9	10	WAIT TILL THE SUN SHINES, NELLIE (1906)
–	–	–	–	–	–	–	–	–	–	–	–	–	–	==	==	==	17	14	11	9	7	5	5	5	7	10	16	==	==	STARLIGHT (1906)
–	–	–	–	–	–	–	–	–	–	–	–	–	–	–	–	==	==	==	19	16	13	17	20	==	==	==	==	–	–	KATEY DEAR (1906)
–	–	–	–	–	–	–	–	–	–	–	–	–	–	–	–	==	==	19	15	11	8	7	6	7	12	18	19	==	==	SILVERHEELS (1906)
Ma	Ma	Ap	Ap	My	My	Jn	Jn	Jy	Jy	Ag	Ag	Sp	Sp	Oc	Oc	Nv	Nv	Dc	Dc	Ja	Ja	Fb	Fb	Ma	Ma	Ap	Ap	My	My	

1905						1906																								
Oc	Oc	Nv	Nv	Dc	Dc	Ja	Ja	Fb	Fb	Ma	Ma	Ap	Ap	My	My	Jn	Jn	Jy	Jy	Ag	Ag	Sp	Sp	Oc	Oc	Nv	Nv	Dc	Dc	
4	5	7	11	13	17	20	==	==	==	–	–	–	–	–	–	–	–	–	–	–	–	–	–	–	–	–	–	–	–	KEEP A LITTLE COZY CORNER IN YOUR HEART FOR ME (1905)
2	2	3	5	7	10	12	15	20	==	==	–	–	–	–	–	–	–	–	–	–	–	–	–	–	–	–	–	–	–	MY IRISH MOLLY–O (1905)
5	4	2	2	3	2	3	4	4	3	**1**	**1**	**1**	2	2	8	8	9	10	12	13	18	==	==	==	==	==	==	–	–	DEARIE (1905)
3	3	4	6	11	12	14	16	==	==	–	–	–	–	–	–	–	–	–	–	–	–	–	–	–	–	–	–	–	–	EVERYBODY WORKS BUT FATHER (1905)
15	15	17	14	15	16	17	17	19	19	==	==	==	==	–	–	–	–	–	–	–	–	–	–	–	–	–	–	–	–	DOWN WHERE THE SILV'RY MOHAWK FLOWS (1905)
1	**1**	**1**	**1**	2	3	2	3	3	4	3	3	5	11	15	==	==	==	==	==	–	–	–	–	–	–	–	–	–	–	WOULD YOU CARE? (1905)
14	10	8	7	8	8	10	11	12	17	==	==	–	–	–	–	–	–	–	–	–	–	–	–	–	–	–	–	–	–	THE LEADER OF THE GERMAN BAND (1905)
13	8	5	4	4	5	8	10	10	13	18	==	==	==	–	–	–	–	–	–	–	–	–	–	–	–	–	–	–	–	WHAT YOU GOIN' TO DO WHEN THE RENT COMES 'ROUND? (RUFUS RASTUS JOHNSON BROWN) (1905)
18	13	13	10	9	7	5	5	6	9	11	17	==	==	==	==	–	–	–	–	–	–	–	–	–	–	–	–	–	–	IN DEAR OLD GEORGIA (1905)
==	19	12	12	12	13	15	==	==	==	–	–	–	–	–	–	–	–	–	–	–	–	–	–	–	–	–	–	–	–	THE WHISTLER AND HIS DOG (1905)
==	18	11	9	5	4	7	9	11	15	==	==	–	–	–	–	–	–	–	–	–	–	–	–	–	–	–	–	–	–	HOW'D YOU LIKE TO SPOON WITH ME? (1905)
==	==	19	13	10	9	6	6	8	10	13	20	==	==	–	–	–	–	–	–	–	–	–	–	–	–	–	–	–	–	WHERE THE MORNING GLORIES TWINE AROUND THE DOOR (1905)
–	==	==	==	20	18	19	==	==	==	–	–	–	–	–	–	–	–	–	–	–	–	–	–	–	–	–	–	–	–	A WOMAN IS ONLY A WOMAN, BUT A GOOD CIGAR IS A SMOKE
–	==	==	19	16	14	13	14	18	==	==	–	–	–	–	–	–	–	–	–	–	–	–	–	–	–	–	–	–	–	THE TOWN WHERE I WAS BORN (1905)
19	14	9	8	6	6	4	2	2	2	4	6	8	12	13	16	20	==	–	–	–	–	–	–	–	–	–	–	–	–	IN MY MERRY OLDSMOBILE
16	9	6	3	**1**	**1**	**1**	**1**	**1**	**1**	2	2	3	3	9	10	10	17	20	==	==	==	–	–	–	–	–	–	–	–	WAIT TILL THE SUN SHINES, NELLIE
==	==	==	17	14	11	9	7	5	5	5	7	10	16	==	==	==	==	–	–	–	–	–	–	–	–	–	–	–	–	STARLIGHT
–	–	==	==	==	19	16	13	17	20	==	==	==	==	–	–	–	–	–	–	–	–	–	–	–	–	–	–	–	–	KATEY DEAR
–	–	==	==	19	15	11	8	7	6	7	12	18	19	==	==	==	==	–	–	–	–	–	–	–	–	–	–	–	–	SILVERHEELS
–	–	==	==	==	==	==	18	16	14	10	11	16	17	19	==	==	==	==	==	==	==	–	–	–	–	–	–	–	–	CAN'T YOU SEE I'M LONELY?
–	–	==	==	==	==	==	==	==	18	16	14	17	18	==	==	==	==	==	==	==	==	–	–	–	–	–	–	–	–	WHEN THE EVENING BREEZE IS SIGHING HOME SWEET HOME
–	–	–	–	==	==	18	12	9	12	17	==	==	==	–	–	–	–	–	–	–	–	–	–	–	–	–	–	–	–	SYMPATHY
–	–	–	–	–	–	==	20	14	8	9	13	19	==	–	–	–	–	–	–	–	–	–	–	–	–	–	–	–	–	DADDY'S LITTLE GIRL
–	–	–	–	–	–	==	19	13	7	6	5	4	6	11	14	==	==	–	–	–	–	–	–	–	–	–	–	–	–	IF A GIRL LIKE YOU LOVED A BOY LIKE ME
–	–	–	–	–	–	==	==	==	16	12	9	9	9	7	5	5	8	12	13	17	==	==	==	==	==	–	–	–	–	JUST A LITTLE ROCKING CHAIR AND YOU
–	–	–	–	–	–	==	==	15	11	8	4	2	**1**	**1**	**1**	3	5	6	9	11	17	20	==	==	==	==	==	–	–	WILL YOU LOVE ME IN DECEMBER AS YOU DO IN MAY?
–	–	–	–	–	–	–	–	==	==	19	19	20	==	==	==	–	–	–	–	–	–	–	–	–	–	–	–	–	–	SINCE FATHER WENT TO WORK
–	–	–	–	–	–	–	–	==	==	15	10	7	5	5	9	12	18	==	==	–	–	–	–	–	–	–	–	–	–	FORTY–FIVE MINUTES FROM BROADWAY
–	–	–	–	–	–	–	–	==	==	==	18	14	15	14	15	18	==	==	==	==	==	–	–	–	–	–	–	–	–	MARY'S A GRAND OLD NAME
–	–	–	–	–	–	–	–	==	==	20	16	11	13	12	11	13	19	==	==	==	==	–	–	–	–	–	–	–	–	I WANT WHAT I WANT WHEN I WANT IT
–	–	–	–	–	–	–	–	==	==	==	==	==	20	18	==	==	==	==	==	–	–	–	–	–	–	–	–	–	–	IS EVERYBODY HAPPY?
–	–	–	–	–	–	–	–	==	==	14	8	6	4	3	4	9	11	18	==	==	==	–	–	–	–	–	–	–	–	SO LONG, MARY
–	–	–	–	–	–	–	–	==	==	==	15	13	10	8	6	6	6	9	14	20	==	==	==	–	–	–	–	–	–	WHEN THE MOCKING BIRDS ARE SINGING IN THE WILDWOOD
–	–	–	–	–	–	–	–	–	–	==	==	==	==	20	17	15	16	17	==	==	==	==	==	==	==	==	==	–	–	SINCE NELLIE WENT AWAY
–	–	–	–	–	–	–	–	–	–	==	==	==	==	17	13	11	10	13	18	==	==	==	==	–	–	–	–	–	–	TAKE ME BACK TO YOUR HEART
Oc	Oc	Nv	Nv	Dc	Dc	Ja	Ja	Fb	Fb	Ma	Ma	Ap	Ap	My	My	Jn	Jn	Jy	Jy	Ag	Ag	Sp	Sp	Oc	Oc	Nv	Nv	Dc	Dc	

1906																				1907										
Ma	Ma	Ap	Ap	My	My	Jn	Jn	Jy	Jy	Ag	Ag	Sp	Sp	Oc	Oc	Nv	Nv	Dc	Dc	Ja	Ja	Fb	Fb	Ma	Ma	Ap	Ap	My	My	
==	==	==	==	==	==	==	==	19	15	12	11	11	10	10	8	8	10	13	20	==	==	==	==	==	==	==	==	–	–	IF THE MAN IN THE MOON WERE A COON
==	==	15	7	4	2	2	2	4	5	8	10	16	==	==	==	–	–	–	–	–	–	–	–	–	–	–	–	–	–	KEEP ON THE SUNNY SIDE
==	==	==	14	10	7	4	3	3	3	3	3	6	7	8	13	15	17	==	==	–	–	–	–	–	–	–	–	–	–	CHEYENNE
==	==	12	8	6	3	1	1	1	2	2	2	5	5	7	11	14	16	==	==	–	–	–	–	–	–	–	–	–	–	YOU'RE A GRAND OLD FLAG
==	==	==	==	==	18	16	12	7	6	5	5	4	4	3	4	4	6	7	9	16	18	==	==	==	==	==	==	==	==	MY GAL SAL
–	–	==	==	==	==	==	20	16	20	==	==	==	==	==	==	==	==	–	–	–	–	–	–	–	–	–	–	–	–	WHY DON'T YOU TRY?
–	–	==	==	==	19	17	==	==	==	–	–	–	–	–	–	–	–	–	–	–	–	–	–	–	–	–	–	–	–	TWO DIRTY LITTLE HANDS
–	–	==	==	==	20	14	7	5	4	4	6	7	9	9	15	18	==	==	==	–	–	–	–	–	–	–	–	–	–	BILL SIMMONS
–	–	==	==	16	12	7	4	2	1	1	1	1	3	6	7	10	14	20	==	==	–	–	–	–	–	–	–	–	–	WAITING AT THE CHURCH (MY WIFE WON'T LET ME)
–	–	==	==	==	==	19	13	8	7	7	8	10	14	16	16	20	==	==	==	==	==	–	–	–	–	–	–	–	–	NOT BECAUSE YOUR HAIR IS CURLY
–	–	–	–	==	==	==	==	==	19	19	==	==	==	==	==	==	==	==	==	===	==	==	==	–	–	–	–	–	–	AFTER THEY GATHER THE HAY
–	–	–	–	==	==	==	14	14	11	15	==	==	==	–	–	–	–	–	–	–	–	–	–	–	–	–	–	–	–	I'LL KEEP A WARM SPOT IN MY HEART FOR YOU
–	–	–	–	==	==	==	==	15	10	9	9	13	18	19	==	==	==	==	==	–	–	–	–	–	–	–	–	–	–	MILO
–	–	–	–	==	==	==	==	==	16	14	14	14	13	17	17	17	18	==	==	==	==	–	–	–	–	–	–	–	–	CROCODILE ISLE
–	–	–	–	==	==	==	==	==	==	==	==	19	20	18	19	==	==	==	==	==	==	==	–	–	–	–	–	–	–	FLYING ARROW
–	–	–	–	==	==	==	15	11	8	6	4	2	2	2	5	6	9	16	19	==	==	==	==	==	==	–	–	–	–	THE GOOD OLD U.S.A.
–	–	–	–	–	–	==	==	==	==	==	==	18	15	14	14	12	13	19	==	==	==	==	==	==	==	==	==	==	==	THE LINGER LONGER GIRL
–	–	–	–	–	–	==	==	==	==	18	13	12	12	18	19	==	==	==	==	–	–	–	–	–	–	–	–	–	–	ALICE, WHERE ART THOU GOING?
–	–	–	–	–	==	==	==	==	16	12	9	8	5	2	2	3	2	1	2	2	3	3	5	5	7	4	4	5	5	9 9 12 14 17 == == == == LOVE ME AND THE WORLD IS MINE
–	–	–	–	–	–	–	–	==	==	==	19	17	17	==	==	==	==	==	==	==	==	==	==	==	==	==	–	–	–	CAMP MEETIN' TIME
–	–	–	–	–	–	–	–	==	==	17	10	7	3	1	1	1	1	1	3	7	17	==	==	–	–	–	–	–	–	WALTZ ME AROUND AGAIN, WILLIE
–	–	–	–	–	–	–	–	==	==	==	16	8	6	4	3	7	8	10	17	20	==	==	==	–	–	–	–	–	–	HE WALKED RIGHT IN, TURNED AROUND, AND WALKED RIGHT OUT AGAIN
–	–	–	–	–	–	–	–	==	==	==	==	==	16	13	12	11	11	11	11	14	16	16	19	==	==	==	==	==	==	OS–KA–LOO–SA–LOO
–	–	–	–	–	–	–	–	==	==	==	15	15	11	11	10	9	12	9	14	15	13	14	12	15	17	==	==	==	==	SOMEWHERE
–	–	–	–	–	–	–	–	–	==	==	20	19	==	==	–	–	–	–	–	–	–	–	–	–	–	–	–	–	–	NOBODY
–	–	–	–	–	–	–	–	–	–	==	==	==	20	15	9	5	4	4	6	10	14	15	18	==	==	==	==	–	–	IOLA
–	–	–	–	–	–	–	–	–	–	–	–	==	==	12	6	3	2	1	3	3	5	9	11	20	==	==	–	–	–	WON'T YOU COME OVER TO MY HOUSE?
–	–	–	–	–	–	–	–	–	–	–	–	–	–	==	20	13	5	5	4	5	8	18	==	==	==	–	–	–	–	CHEER UP, MARY
–	–	–	–	–	–	–	–	–	–	–	–	–	–	==	==	==	20	==	==	==	==	==	==	==	==	==	==	==	==	A HOTTENTOT LOVE SONG
–	–	–	–	–	–	–	–	–	–	–	–	–	–	==	==	16	7	6	2	1	1	1	1	2	3	4	6	9	12	ARRAH WANNA (1907)
–	–	–	–	–	–	–	–	–	–	–	–	–	–	–	–	==	==	18	16	18	17	17	==	==	==	==	==	–	–	THE ISLE OF OUR DREAMS (1907)
–	–	–	–	–	–	–	–	–	–	–	–	–	–	–	–	==	19	12	8	6	11	11	13	19	==	==	==	–	–	IN OLD NEW YORK (1907)
–	–	–	–	–	–	–	–	–	–	–	–	–	–	–	–	==	==	14	10	9	12	12	14	17	==	==	==	–	–	EVERY DAY IS LADIES' DAY WITH ME (1907)
–	–	–	–	–	–	–	–	–	–	–	–	–	–	–	==	==	15	8	5	4	3	6	9	11	14	20	==	==	–	MY MARIUCCIA TAKE A STEAMBOAT (1907)
–	–	–	–	–	–	–	–	–	–	–	–	–	–	–	–	==	==	17	13	8	6	5	5	4	7	8	10	18	==	I JUST CAN'T MAKE MY EYES BEHAVE (1907)
–	–	–	–	–	–	–	–	–	–	–	–	–	–	–	–	==	==	15	12	7	4	2	2	1	1	2	5	10	15	THE BIRD ON NELLIE'S HAT (1907)
–	–	–	–	–	–	–	–	–	–	–	–	–	–	–	–	==	==	==	15	12	10	7	4	3	2	6	7	8	10	HE'S A COUSIN OF MINE (1907)
–	–	–	–	–	–	–	–	–	–	–	–	–	–	–	–	–	==	==	18	11	9	8	8	8	10	10	16	20	==	BECAUSE YOU'RE YOU (1907)
Ma	Ma	Ap	Ap	My	My	Jn	Jn	Jy	Jy	Ag	Ag	Sp	Sp	Oc	Oc	Nv	Nv	Dc	Dc	Ja	Ja	Fb	Fb	Ma	Ma	Ap	Ap	My	My	

1906 1907

Oc	Oc	Nv	Nv	Dc	Dc	Ja	Ja	Fb	Fb	Ma	Ma	Ap	Ap	My	My	Jn	Jn	Jy	Jy	Ag	Ag	Sp	Sp	Oc	Oc	Nv	Nv	Dc	Dc	
3	4	4	6	7	9	16	18	==	==	==	==	==	==	==	==	==	==	–	–	–	–	–	–	–	–	–	–	–	–	MY GAL SAL (1906)
5	2	2	3	2	**1**	2	2	3	3	5	5	7	4	4	5	5	9	9	12	14	17	==	==	==	==	==	==	–	–	LOVE ME AND THE WORLD IS MINE (1906)
1	**1**	**1**	**1**	3	7	17	==	==	–	–	–	–	–	–	–	–	–	–	–	–	–	–	–	–	–	–	–	–	–	WALTZ ME AROUND AGAIN, WILLIE (1906)
4	3	7	8	10	17	20	==	==	==	–	–	–	–	–	–	–	–	–	–	–	–	–	–	–	–	–	–	–	–	HE WALKED RIGHT IN, TURNED AROUND, AND WALKED RIGHT OUT AGAIN (1906)
13	12	11	11	11	11	14	16	16	19	==	==	==	==	==	==	==	==	==	==	–	–	–	–	–	–	–	–	–	–	OS–KA–LOO–SA–LOO (1906)
11	10	9	12	9	14	15	13	14	12	15	17	==	==	==	==	==	==	–	–	–	–	–	–	–	–	–	–	–	–	SOMEWHERE (1906)
15	9	5	4	4	6	10	14	15	18	==	==	==	==	–	–	–	–	–	–	–	–	–	–	–	–	–	–	–	–	IOLA (1906)
12	6	3	2	**1**	3	3	5	9	11	20	==	==	–	–	–	–	–	–	–	–	–	–	–	–	–	–	–	–	–	WON'T YOU COME OVER TO MY HOUSE (1906)
==	20	13	5	5	4	5	8	18	==	==	==	–	–	–	–	–	–	–	–	–	–	–	–	–	–	–	–	–	–	CHEER UP, MARY (1906)
==	==	16	7	6	2	**1**	**1**	**1**	**1**	2	3	4	6	9	12	11	13	14	17	==	==	==	==	–	–	–	–	–	–	ARRAH WANNA
–	–	==	==	18	16	18	17	17	==	==	==	==	==	–	–	–	–	–	–	–	–	–	–	–	–	–	–	–	–	THE ISLE OF OUR DREAMS
–	–	==	19	12	8	6	11	11	13	19	==	==	==	–	–	–	–	–	–	–	–	–	–	–	–	–	–	–	–	IN OLD NEW YORK
–	–	==	==	14	10	9	12	12	14	17	==	==	==	–	–	–	–	–	–	–	–	–	–	–	–	–	–	–	–	EVERY DAY IS LADIES' DAY WITH ME
–	==	==	15	8	5	4	3	6	9	11	14	20	==	==	–	–	–	–	–	–	–	–	–	–	–	–	–	–	–	MY MARIUCCIA TAKE A STEAMBOAT
–	–	==	==	17	13	8	6	5	5	4	7	8	10	18	==	==	==	–	–	–	–	–	–	–	–	–	–	–	–	I JUST CAN'T MAKE MY EYES BEHAVE
–	–	==	==	15	12	7	4	2	2	**1**	**1**	2	5	10	15	17	==	==	==	–	–	–	–	–	–	–	–	–	–	THE BIRD ON NELLIE'S HAT
–	–	==	==	==	15	12	10	7	4	3	2	6	7	8	10	9	11	15	18	==	==	==	==	–	–	–	–	–	–	HE'S A COUSIN OF MINE
–	–	==	==	==	==	==	20	==	20	==	==	==	==	–	–	–	–	–	–	–	–	–	–	–	–	–	–	–	–	IN THE EVENING BY THE MOONLIGHT, DEAR LOUISE
–	–	–	==	==	18	11	9	8	8	8	10	10	15	20	==	==	–	–	–	–	–	–	–	–	–	–	–	–	–	BECAUSE YOU'RE YOU
–	–	–	–	==	==	==	==	19	15	14	16	==	==	==	==	–	–	–	–	–	–	–	–	–	–	–	–	–	–	MOONBEAMS
–	–	–	–	==	==	==	==	20	16	13	15	==	==	==	==	–	–	–	–	–	–	–	–	–	–	–	–	–	–	AND A LITTLE CHILD SHALL LEAD THEM
–	–	–	–	==	==	19	15	10	7	9	9	9	11	12	16	==	==	==	==	–	–	–	–	–	–	–	–	–	–	MY IRISH ROSIE
–	–	–	–	==	==	13	7	4	6	7	12	19	==	==	–	–	–	–	–	–	–	–	–	–	–	–	–	–	–	A LEMON IN THE GARDEN OF LOVE
–	–	–	–	==	==	==	19	13	10	6	6	5	3	3	7	14	17	==	==	==	==	–	–	–	–	–	–	–	–	LET IT ALONE
–	–	–	–	–	–	==	==	==	==	18	13	17	==	==	==	==	==	–	–	–	–	–	–	–	–	–	–	–	–	ALL IN, DOWN AND OUT
–	–	–	–	–	–	–	==	==	==	16	11	11	17	==	==	==	==	–	–	–	–	–	–	–	–	–	–	–	–	WHEN BOB WHITE IS WHISTLING IN THE MEADOW
–	–	–	–	–	–	–	–	==	==	==	18	12	12	13	14	18	==	==	==	==	==	–	–	–	–	–	–	–	–	SOMEBODY'S WAITING FOR YOU
–	–	–	–	–	–	–	==	==	17	10	4	**1**	**1**	2	3	3	5	11	14	18	==	==	–	–	–	–	–	–	–	POOR JOHN!
–	–	–	–	–	–	–	–	==	==	==	==	18	19	19	18	==	==	==	==	==	==	–	–	–	–	–	–	–	–	FLOATING ALONG
–	–	–	–	–	–	–	–	==	==	==	20	15	13	15	13	15	12	19	==	==	==	==	==	–	–	–	–	–	–	GOLDEN ROD
–	–	–	–	–	–	–	–	==	==	12	8	3	2	**1**	**1**	2	2	3	4	4	5	11	15	==	==	–	–	–	–	SAN ANTONIO
–	–	–	–	–	–	–	–	–	–	==	==	16	14	17	19	==	==	–	–	–	–	–	–	–	–	–	–	–	–	THE BEST THING IN LIFE
–	–	–	–	–	–	–	–	–	–	==	19	13	8	6	6	10	16	==	==	–	–	–	–	–	–	–	–	–	–	IN THE WILDWOOD WHERE THE BLUE BELLS GREW
–	–	–	–	–	–	–	–	–	–	==	==	14	9	5	4	8	10	16	==	==	==	–	–	–	–	–	–	–	–	THE TALE THE CHURCH BELLS TOLLED
–	–	–	–	–	–	–	–	–	–	==	==	==	20	==	==	==	20	==	16	==	==	==	==	==	==	==	==	–	–	SPANGLES
–	–	–	–	–	–	–	–	–	–	–	–	==	18	11	8	7	6	8	13	==	==	–	–	–	–	–	–	–	–	NOBODY'S LITTLE GIRL
–	–	–	–	–	–	–	–	–	–	–	–	==	==	16	11	6	4	4	8	11	18	==	==	–	–	–	–	–	–	AND A LITTLE BIT MORE
–	–	–	–	–	–	–	–	–	–	–	–	==	==	14	9	4	3	2	2	2	3	12	16	==	==	–	–	–	–	BECAUSE I'M MARRIED NOW
–	–	–	–	–	–	–	–	–	–	–	–	–	16	7	2	**1**	**1**	**1**	**1**	**1**	**1**	**1**	**1**	**1**	2	4	9	14	==	SCHOOL DAYS
Oc	Oc	Nv	Nv	Dc	Dc	Ja	Ja	Fb	Fb	Ma	Ma	Ap	Ap	My	My	Jn	Jn	Jy	Jy	Ag	Ag	Sp	Sp	Oc	Oc	Nv	Nv	Dc	Dc	

								1907																1908						
Ap	Ap	My	My	Jn	Jn	Jy	Jy	Ag	Ag	Sp	Sp	Oc	Oc	Nv	Nv	Dc	Dc	Ja	Ja	Fb	Fb	Ma	Ma	Ap	Ap	My	My	Jn	Jn	
==	==	==	==	20	==	==	==	19	==	==	==	==	==	==	==	–	–	–	–	–	–	–	–	–	–	–	–	–	–	THE TEDDY BEARS' PICNIC
==	==	==	==	19	15	12	9	9	11	10	9	13	18	18	==	==	==	–	–	–	–	–	–	–	–	–	–	–	–	IT'S GREAT TO BE A SOLDIER MAN
–	==	==	20	13	7	5	5	6	7	13	19	==	==	–	–	–	–	–	–	–	–	–	–	–	–	–	–	–	–	IT'S DELIGHTFUL TO BE MARRIED
–	–	==	==	16	18	13	15	==	==	–	–	–	–	–	–	–	–	–	–	–	–	–	–	–	–	–	–	–	–	HYMNS OF THE OLD CHURCH CHOIR
–	–	==	==	==	==	20	19	==	==	==	==	–	–	–	–	–	–	–	–	–	–	–	–	–	–	–	–	–	–	JUST BECAUSE I LOVED YOU SO
–	–	==	17	12	8	6	7	10	16	20	==	–	–	–	–	–	–	–	–	–	–	–	–	–	–	–	–	–	–	HE GOES TO CHURCH ON SUNDAY
–	–	==	==	==	==	==	==	==	==	==	17	14	10	9	11	10	12	8	8	11	10	10	8	8	12	18	16	13	16	==SOME DAY WHEN DREAMS COME TRUE
–	–	==	==	==	19	10	6	5	9	15	18	==	==	==	==	–	–	–	–	–	–	–	–	–	–	–	–	–	–	WHEN YOU KNOW YOU'RE NOT FORGOTTEN BY THE GIRL YOU CAN'T FORGET
–	–	==	==	==	==	17	10	7	6	5	7	7	7	11	15	18	==	==	==	==	==	–	–	–	–	–	–	–	–	NO WEDDING BELLS FOR ME
–	–	==	==	==	==	==	==	16	13	9	8	9	16	15	17	==	==	==	==	==	==	==	==	–	–	–	–	–	–	WITH YOU IN ETERNITY
–	–	–	–	==	==	==	==	==	==	==	==	20	20	==	==	==	==	==	==	==	==	==	==	–	–	–	–	–	–	SHE WAS A GRAND OLD LADY
–	–	–	==	==	==	18	11	8	4	3	4	5	6	5	4	9	11	13	16	14	19	==	==	==	==	–	–	–	–	WON'T YOU BE MY HONEY?
–	–	–	–	==	==	==	==	==	19	18	14	11	12	10	8	5	8	9	11	9	11	9	12	13	15	==	==	==	==	THAT'S WHAT THE ROSE SAID TO ME
–	–	–	–	==	==	==	==	==	20	==	==	–	–	–	–	–	–	–	–	–	–	–	–	–	–	–	–	–	–	I'VE MADE MY PLANS FOR THE SUMMER
–	–	–	==	==	14	7	3	3	2	7	10	16	==	==	–	–	–	–	–	–	–	–	–	–	–	–	–	–	–	YOU SPLASH ME AND I'LL SPLASH YOU
–	–	–	–	–	–	==	==	==	==	==	==	19	19	20	==	==	==	==	==	==	==	==	==	–	–	–	–	–	–	UNDER THE TROPICAL MOON
–	–	–	–	–	–	==	==	15	15	19	==	==	==	–	–	–	–	–	–	–	–	–	–	–	–	–	–	–	–	EVERY LITTLE BIT ADDED TO WHAT YOU'VE GOT
–	–	–	–	–	–	==	20	12	8	2	2	3	4	6	10	11	14	20	==	==	–	–	–	–	–	–	–	–	–	DREAMING
–	–	–	–	–	–	==	==	20	14	8	6	6	5	3	3	3	5	7	13	17	==	==	==	–	–	–	–	–	–	TAKE ME BACK TO NEW YORK TOWN
–	–	–	–	–	–	==	==	13	10	4	3	2	**1**	**1**	**1**	**1**	**1**	**1**	4	6	9	16	==	==	==	–	–	–	–	HARRIGAN
–	–	–	–	–	–	==	==	17	12	6	5	4	3	2	2	2	2	5	6	8	8	12	19	==	==	==	==	–	–	HONEY BOY
–	–	–	–	–	–	–	–	==	==	17	12	8	13	17	20	==	==	–	–	–	–	–	–	–	–	–	–	–	–	BUDWEISER'S A FRIEND OF MINE
–	–	–	–	–	–	–	–	==	==	16	13	12	11	16	==	==	==	–	–	–	–	–	–	–	–	–	–	–	–	I'M A POPULAR MAN
–	–	–	–	–	–	–	–	==	==	14	11	10	9	14	19	==	==	==	==	==	==	–	–	–	–	–	–	–	–	VESTI LA GIUBBA
–	–	–	–	–	–	–	–	–	==	==	20	15	8	7	5	6	7	10	12	15	15	==	==	==	==	–	–	–	–	IN MONKEYLAND
–	–	–	–	–	–	–	–	–	–	==	==	17	15	13	13	17	==	==	–	–	–	–	–	–	–	–	–	–	–	YESTERDAY
–	–	–	–	–	–	–	–	–	–	==	==	18	14	8	7	8	9	11	10	13	17	==	==	==	==	–	–	–	–	OLD FAITHFUL
–	–	–	–	–	–	–	–	–	–	–	==	==	==	19	14	16	17	18	20	==	==	==	==	–	–	–	–	–	–	SPRING, BEAUTIFUL SPRING
–	–	–	–	–	–	–	–	–	–	–	–	–	–	==	==	==	18	19	==	==	==	==	==	–	–	–	–	–	–	DON'T GET MARRIED ANY MORE, MA
–	–	–	–	–	–	–	–	–	–	==	==	==	17	12	6	4	4	3	3	5	5	3	3	5	5	9	14	19	==	RED WING (1908)
–	–	–	–	–	–	–	–	–	–	–	–	==	==	==	==	19	15	14	15	12	13	15	17	19	20	==	==	==	==	THAT'S GRATITUDE (1908)
–	–	–	–	–	–	–	–	–	–	–	–	==	==	==	16	13	10	6	5	4	2	2	2	2	2	3	3	5	5	AS LONG AS THE WORLD ROLLS ON (1908)
–	–	–	–	–	–	–	–	–	–	–	–	–	–	==	18	12	6	4	2	**1**	3	6	11	18	==	==	–	–	–	THE BEST I GET IS MUCH OBLIGED TO YOU (1908)
–	–	–	–	–	–	–	–	–	–	–	–	–	==	==	12	7	3	2	**1**	2	4	5	7	16	==	==	–	–	–	TWO BLUE EYES (1908)
–	–	–	–	–	–	–	–	–	–	–	–	–	–	==	==	20	16	17	18	==	==	==	==	==	==	==	==	==	==	SHE IS MA DAISY (1908)
–	–	–	–	–	–	–	–	–	–	–	–	–	–	==	==	15	13	15	17	19	16	20	==	==	==	20	==	==	==	I LOVE A LASSIE (1908)
–	–	–	–	–	–	–	–	–	–	–	–	–	–	==	==	==	20	==	==	==	==	==	==	==	==	==	==	==	==	STOP YER TICKLIN' JOCK! (1908)
–	–	–	–	–	–	–	–	–	–	–	–	–	–	–	–	==	19	12	7	3	**1**	**1**	**1**	3	4	4	9	11	18	I LOVE YOU SO (MERRY WIDOW WALTZ) (1908)
Ap	Ap	My	My	Jn	Jn	Jy	Jy	Ag	Ag	Sp	Sp	Oc	Oc	Nv	Nv	Dc	Dc	Ja	Ja	Fb	Fb	Ma	Ma	Ap	Ap	My	My	Jn	Jn	

1907						1908																									
Oc	Oc	Nv	Nv	Dc	Dc	Ja	Ja	Fb	Fb	Ma	Ma	Ap	Ap	My	My	Jn	Jn	Jy	Jy	Ag	Ag	Sp	Sp	Oc	Oc	Nv	Nv	Dc	Dc		
14	10	9	11	10	12	8	8	11	10	10	8	8	12	18	16	13	16	==	==	==	==	==	==	==	==	==	==	==	==		SOME DAY WHEN DREAMS COME TRUE (1907)
5	6	5	4	9	11	13	16	14	19	==	==	==	==	–	–	–	–	–	–	–	–	–	–	–	–	–	–	–	–		WON'T YOU BE MY HONEY? (1907)
11	12	10	8	5	8	9	11	9	11	9	12	13	15	==	==	==	==	==	==	==	==	–	–	–	–	–	–	–	–		THAT'S WHAT THE ROSE SAID TO ME (1907)
3	4	6	10	11	14	20	==	==	–	–	–	–	–	–	–	–	–	–	–	–	–	–	–	–	–	–	–	–	–		DREAMING (1907)
6	5	3	3	3	5	7	13	17	==	==	==	–	–	–	–	–	–	–	–	–	–	–	–	–	–	–	–	–	–		TAKE ME BACK TO NEW YORK TOWN (1907)
2	**1**	**1**	**1**	**1**	**1**	**1**	4	6	9	16	==	==	==	–	–	–	–	–	–	–	–	–	–	–	–	–	–	–	–		HARRIGAN (1907)
4	3	2	2	2	2	5	6	8	8	12	19	==	==	==	–	–	–	–	–	–	–	–	–	–	–	–	–	–	–		HONEY BOY (1907)
14	8	7	5	6	7	10	12	15	15	==	==	==	==	–	–	–	–	–	–	–	–	–	–	–	–	–	–	–	–		IN MONKEYLAND (1907)
18	14	8	7	8	9	11	10	13	17	==	==	==	==	–	–	–	–	–	–	–	–	–	–	–	–	–	–	–	–		OLD FAITHFUL (1907)
==	==	19	14	16	17	18	20	==	==	==	==	–	–	–	–	–	–	–	–	–	–	–	–	–	–	–	–	–	–		SPRING, BEAUTIFUL SPRING (1907)
–	–	==	==	==	18	19	==	==	==	==	–	–	–	–	–	–	–	–	–	–	–	–	–	–	–	–	–	–	–		DON'T GET MARRIED ANY MORE, MA (1907)
==	17	12	6	4	4	3	3	5	5	3	3	5	5	9	14	19	==	==	==	==	==	–	–	–	–	–	–	–	–		RED WING
==	==	==	==	19	15	14	15	12	13	15	17	19	20	==	==	==	==	–	–	–	–	–	–	–	–	–	–	–	–		THAT'S GRATITUDE
==	==	==	16	13	10	6	5	4	2	2	2	2	2	3	3	5	5	6	10	15	18	==	==	==	==	–	–	–	–		AS LONG AS THE WORLD ROLLS ON
–	–	==	18	12	6	4	2	**1**	3	6	11	18	==	==	–	–	–	–	–	–	–	–	–	–	–	–	–	–	–		THE BEST I GET IS MUCH OBLIGED TO YOU
–	==	==	12	7	3	2	**1**	2	4	5	7	16	==	==	–	–	–	–	–	–	–	–	–	–	–	–	–	–	–		TWO BLUE EYES
–	–	==	==	20	16	17	18	==	==	==	==	==	==	==	==	==	==	==	==	==	19	20	==	==	==	==	==	==	==	20 ==	SHE IS MA DAISY
–	–	==	==	15	13	15	17	19	16	20	==	==	==	20	==	==	==	==	18	20	16	15	14	15	19	==	==	==	19	19 19 == == == 16 18 20 ==	I LOVE A LASSIE
–	–	==	==	==	20	==	==	==	==	==	==	==	==	==	==	==	==	==	==	==	20	==	==	==	==	==	==	==	==		STOP YER TICKLIN' JOCK!
–	–	==	==	==	==	16	9	10	6	4	5	6	6	12	15	==	==	==	==	==	==	–	–	–	–	–	–	–	–		MAKE BELIEVE
–	–	==	==	==	==	==	19	==	==	==	==	==	==	==	==	==	==	==	==	==	==	==	==	==	==	==	==	==	==		SAFTEST O' THE FAMILY
–	–	–	–	==	19	12	7	3	**1**	**1**	**1**	3	4	4	9	11	18	==	==	–	–	–	–	–	–	–	–	–	–		I LOVE YOU SO (MERRY WIDOW WALTZ)
–	–	–	–	==	==	==	==	20	20	==	==	==	==	==	==	–	–	–	–	–	–	–	–	–	–	–	–	–	–		MUSETTE
–	–	–	–	==	==	==	14	7	7	8	15	20	==	==	==	–	–	–	–	–	–	–	–	–	–	–	–	–	–		VILIA
–	–	–	–	==	==	==	==	18	14	14	9	7	10	16	19	==	==	==	==	==	==	–	–	–	–	–	–	–	–		WON'T YOU WALTZ HOME SWEET HOME WITH ME?
–	–	–	–	==	==	==	==	16	12	7	6	4	3	2	**1**	**1**	**1**	**1**	**1**	**1**	2	4	8	7	8	7	7	9	12	17 15 14 17 19 ==	THE GLOW–WORM
–	–	–	–	–	–	–	–	==	==	18	18	14	19	==	==	–	–	–	–	–	–	–	–	–	–	–	–	–	–		TWO LITTLE BABY SHOES
–	–	–	–	–	–	–	–	==	==	13	10	9	8	13	13	16	19	==	==	==	–	–	–	–	–	–	–	–	–		WHEN A FELLOW'S ON THE LEVEL WITH A GIRL WHO'S ON THE SQUARE
–	–	–	–	–	–	–	–	==	==	19	16	15	18	==	==	–	–	–	–	–	–	–	–	–	–	–	–	–	–		UNDER ANY OLD FLAG AT ALL
–	–	–	–	–	–	–	–	==	==	17	14	12	16	19	==	==	==	==	==	–	–	–	–	–	–	–	–	–	–		I'M STARVING FOR ONE SIGHT OF YOU
–	–	–	–	–	–	–	–	==	18	11	4	**1**	**1**	**1**	2	6	6	13	==	==	–	–	–	–	–	–	–	–	–		I'M AFRAID TO COME HOME IN THE DARK
–	–	–	–	–	–	–	–	–	==	==	==	==	13	14	17	==	==	==	==	–	–	–	–	–	–	–	–	–	–		I WANT YOU
–	–	–	–	–	–	–	–	–	==	==	13	10	7	5	5	8	13	18	==	==	==	==	–	–	–	–	–	–	–		WHEN WE ARE M–A–DOUBLE–R–I–E–D
–	–	–	–	–	–	–	–	–	–	==	20	11	9	7	11	14	==	==	==	==	==	–	–	–	–	–	–	–	–		THE LANKY YANKEE BOYS IN BLUE
–	–	–	–	–	–	–	–	–	–	==	==	17	11	6	4	2	2	2	2	7	10	14	17	20	==	==	==	–	–		SMARTY
–	–	–	–	–	–	–	–	–	–	–	==	==	14	8	6	4	4	5	9	16	==	==	==	–	–	–	–	–	–		WHEN SWEET MARIE WAS SWEET SIXTEEN
–	–	–	–	–	–	–	–	–	–	–	==	==	17	10	7	3	3	3	4	5	8	13	16	==	==	==	==	–	–		JUST SOMEONE
–	–	–	–	–	–	–	–	–	–	–	–	==	==	11	8	7	7	16	==	==	==	–	–	–	–	–	–	–	–		THE SWEETEST MAID OF ALL
Oc	Oc	Nv	Nv	Dc	Dc	Ja	Ja	Fb	Fb	Ma	Ma	Ap	Ap	My	My	Jn	Jn	Jy	Jy	Ag	Ag	Sp	Sp	Oc	Oc	Nv	Nv	Dc	Dc		

1908																		1909												
Ap	Ap	My	My	Jn	Jn	Jy	Jy	Ag	Ag	Sp	Sp	Oc	Oc	Nv	Nv	Dc	Dc	Ja	Ja	Fb	Fb	Ma	Ma	Ap	Ap	My	My	Jn	Jn	
==	==	15	10	9	8	14	17	==	==	==	==	–	–	–	–	–	–	–	–	–	–	–	–	–	–	–	–	–	–	TRUE HEART
==	==	17	12	10	14	19	==	==	==	–	–	–	–	–	–	–	–	–	–	–	–	–	–	–	–	–	–	–	–	LOVE'S ROUNDELAY
==	==	==	20	==	==	==	==	==	==	==	==	–	–	–	–	–	–	–	–	–	–	–	–	–	–	–	–	–	–	TIPPERARY
==	==	==	18	12	9	10	12	18	==	==	==	==	==	–	–	–	–	–	–	–	–	–	–	–	–	–	–	–	–	SWEETHEART DAYS
–	==	==	==	17	10	4	3	3	3	7	9	11	11	8	8	12	16	18	17	19	19	==	==	==	==	==	==	–	–	ROSES BRING DREAMS OF YOU
–	–	==	==	==	20	==	==	==	==	==	==	–	–	–	–	–	–	–	–	–	–	–	–	–	–	–	–	–	–	WHEN YOU WORE A PINAFORE
–	–	==	==	20	==	==	==	==	==	==	==	–	–	–	–	–	–	–	–	–	–	–	–	–	–	–	–	–	–	OVER THE HILLS AND FAR AWAY
–	–	==	==	15	11	12	16	==	==	==	==	==	==	–	–	–	–	–	–	–	–	–	–	–	–	–	–	–	–	THE TEDDY BEARS' PICNIC
–	–	==	==	==	15	8	6	4	4	9	10	12	13	17	==	==	==	==	==	–	–	–	–	–	–	–	–	–	–	THERE NEVER WAS A GIRL LIKE YOU
–	–	==	==	18	12	7	7	8	14	12	12	14	15	15	17	16	==	==	==	==	==	–	–	–	–	–	–	–	–	HOO–OO (AIN'T YOU COMIN' OUT TONIGHT?)
–	–	–	==	==	==	11	8	6	5	6	6	9	10	11	12	18	==	==	==	==	==	==	==	==	==	==	==	==	14	13 11 8 9 10 11 15 == THE YAMA–YAMA MAN
–	–	–	–	==	==	17	13	17	17	==	==	–	–	–	–	–	–	–	–	–	–	–	–	–	–	–	–	–	–	CONSOLATION
–	–	–	–	==	==	15	11	10	15	17	==	==	==	–	–	–	–	–	–	–	–	–	–	–	–	–	–	–	–	ARE YOU SINCERE?
–	–	–	–	==	17	9	5	2	1	1	2	4	9	13	19	==	==	–	–	–	–	–	–	–	–	–	–	–	–	TAKE ME OUT TO THE BALL GAME
–	–	–	–	==	==	==	14	9	11	11	11	13	14	19	==	==	==	==	==	–	–	–	–	–	–	–	–	–	–	RAINBOW
–	–	–	–	==	==	==	20	==	==	==	20	==	==	==	==	==	==	==	==	==	==	–	–	–	–	–	–	–	–	WHEN THE MOON PLAYS PEEK–A–BOO WITH YOU
–	–	–	–	==	==	20	15	12	12	10	7	5	4	6	6	6	6	4	8	10	13	13	15	==	==	–	–	–	–	BON BON BUDDY
–	–	–	–	–	–	==	==	==	==	18	18	16	17	20	==	==	==	==	==	–	–	–	–	–	–	–	–	–	–	SOMEBODY LIED
–	–	–	–	–	–	==	==	==	==	19	19	19	==	==	==	==	==	==	==	==	==	–	–	–	–	–	–	–	–	LOVE DAYS
–	–	–	–	–	–	==	==	13	6	5	5	6	7	10	15	19	==	==	–	–	–	–	–	–	–	–	–	–	–	I'VE TAKEN QUITE A FANCY TO YOU
–	–	–	–	–	–	==	19	11	7	2	1	2	3	3	4	5	7	15	20	==	==	–	–	–	–	–	–	–	–	DOWN IN JUNGLE TOWN
–	–	–	–	–	–	==	==	19	13	8	4	3	2	2	2	3	3	7	11	18	==	==	==	–	–	–	–	–	–	CUDDLE UP A LITTLE CLOSER
–	–	–	–	–	–	==	==	14	9	3	3	1	1	1	1	1	1	1	1	2	2	5	6	7	9	9	20	==	==	SUNBONNET SUE
–	–	–	–	–	–	–	–	==	==	==	==	18	16	14	18	==	==	==	==	==	==	–	–	–	–	–	–	–	–	OH, YOU KID!
–	–	–	–	–	–	–	–	==	==	16	13	8	5	5	5	4	4	5	9	17	20	==	==	–	–	–	–	–	–	IT LOOKS LIKE A BIG NIGHT TONIGHT
–	–	–	–	–	–	–	–	==	==	==	==	==	==	18	13	10	11	10	13	13	14	17	==	==	==	–	–	–	–	DON'T TAKE ME HOME
–	–	–	–	–	–	–	–	==	==	==	==	==	20	16	11	14	13	14	12	9	9	14	11	12	12	18	==	==	==	MORNING CY
–	–	–	–	–	–	–	–	==	==	==	15	10	6	4	3	2	2	2	3	4	4	4	4	6	8	7	8	11	16	==I WISH I HAD A GIRL
–	–	–	–	–	–	–	–	–	–	==	==	17	12	9	10	13	18	==	==	==	==	–	–	–	–	–	–	–	–	ANY OLD PORT IN A STORM
–	–	–	–	–	–	–	–	–	–	==	==	==	18	12	9	7	9	13	16	15	15	16	17	==	==	–	–	–	–	MY BRUDDAH SYLVEST'
–	–	–	–	–	–	–	–	–	–	–	–	==	==	==	20	17	15	11	7	7	8	7	10	13	15	==	==	==	==	MY OWN UNITED STATES (1909)
–	–	–	–	–	–	–	–	–	–	–	–	==	==	==	14	8	5	3	2	1	1	1	2	2	5	8	9	17	==	(YOU'RE IN) THE RIGHT CHURCH BUT THE WRONG PEW (1909)
–	–	–	–	–	–	–	–	–	–	–	–	==	==	==	16	11	8	8	4	3	3	3	3	4	2	4	7	12	==	IF I HAD A THOUSAND LIVES TO LIVE (1909)
–	–	–	–	–	–	–	–	–	–	–	–	–	–	==	==	==	20	16	14	11	12	11	13	14	18	==	==	–	–	LOVE IS LIKE A CIGARETTE (1909)
–	–	–	–	–	–	–	–	–	–	–	–	–	–	==	==	20	14	9	6	5	5	6	8	11	14	==	==	==	–	ROSE OF THE WORLD (1909)
–	–	–	–	–	–	–	–	–	–	–	–	–	–	==	==	==	17	12	10	8	11	15	19	==	==	–	–	–	–	ASK HER WHILE THE BAND IS PLAYING (1909)
–	–	–	–	–	–	–	–	–	–	–	–	–	–	==	==	15	10	6	5	6	6	9	14	16	==	==	–	–	–	GOOD EVENING, CAROLINE (1909)
Ap	Ap	My	My	Jn	Jn	Jy	Jy	Ag	Ag	Sp	Sp	Oc	Oc	Nv	Nv	Dc	Dc	Ja	Ja	Fb	Fb	Ma	Ma	Ap	Ap	My	My	Jn	Jn	

1908						1909																								
Oc	Oc	Nv	Nv	Dc	Dc	Ja	Ja	Fb	Fb	Ma	Ma	Ap	Ap	My	My	Jn	Jn	Jy	Jy	Ag	Ag	Sp	Sp	Oc	Oc	Nv	Nv	Dc	Dc	
==	==	==	==	==	==	20	==	==	==	==	==	==	==	==	==	==	==	==	==	==	==	–	–	–	–	–	–	–	–	SHE IS MA DAISY (1908)
15	19	==	==	==	19	19	19	==	==	==	16	18	20	==	==	==	==	==	==	==	==	==	==	==	==	==	==	==	==	I LOVE A LASSIE (1908)
7	8	7	7	9	12	17	15	14	17	19	==	==	==	–	–	–	–	–	–	–	–	–	–	–	–	–	–	–	–	THE GLOW-WORM (1908)
11	11	8	8	12	16	18	17	19	19	==	==	==	==	==	==	–	–	–	–	–	–	–	–	–	–	–	–	–	–	ROSES BRING DREAMS OF YOU (1908)
9	10	11	12	18	==	==	==	==	==	==	==	==	==	==	==	==	14	13	11	8	9	10	11	15	==	==	==	–	–	THE YAMA-YAMA MAN (1908)
5	4	6	6	6	6	4	8	10	13	13	15	==	==	–	–	–	–	–	–	–	–	–	–	–	–	–	–	–	–	BON BON BUDDY (1908)
2	3	3	4	5	7	15	20	==	==	–	–	–	–	–	–	–	–	–	–	–	–	–	–	–	–	–	–	–	–	DOWN IN JUNGLE TOWN (1908)
3	2	2	2	3	3	7	11	18	==	==	==	–	–	–	–	–	–	–	–	–	–	–	–	–	–	–	–	–	–	CUDDLE UP A LITTLE CLOSER (1908)
1	**1**	**1**	**1**	**1**	**1**	**1**	**1**	2	2	5	6	7	9	9	20	==	==	–	–	–	–	–	–	–	–	–	–	–	–	SUNBONNET SUE (1908)
8	5	5	5	4	4	5	9	17	20	==	==	–	–	–	–	–	–	–	–	–	–	–	–	–	–	–	–	–	–	IT LOOKS LIKE A BIG NIGHT TONIGHT (1908)
==	==	18	13	10	11	10	13	13	14	17	==	==	==	–	–	–	–	–	–	–	–	–	–	–	–	–	–	–	–	DON'T TAKE ME HOME (1908)
==	20	16	11	14	13	14	12	9	9	14	11	12	12	18	==	==	==	==	==	–	–	–	–	–	–	–	–	–	–	MORNING CY (1908)
10	6	4	3	2	2	2	3	4	4	4	4	6	8	7	8	11	16	==	==	–	–	–	–	–	–	–	–	–	–	I WISH I HAD A GIRL (1908)
==	18	12	9	7	9	13	16	15	15	16	17	==	==	–	–	–	–	–	–	–	–	–	–	–	–	–	–	–	–	MY BRUDDAH SYLVEST' (1908)
==	==	==	20	17	15	11	7	7	8	7	10	13	15	==	==	==	==	==	==	–	–	–	–	–	–	–	–	–	–	MY OWN UNITED STATES
==	==	==	14	8	5	3	2	**1**	**1**	**1**	2	2	5	8	9	17	==	==	–	–	–	–	–	–	–	–	–	–	–	(YOU'RE IN) THE RIGHT CHURCH BUT THE WRONG PEW
==	==	==	16	11	8	8	4	3	3	3	3	4	2	4	7	12	==	==	==	–	–	–	–	–	–	–	–	–	–	IF I HAD A THOUSAND LIVES TO LIVE
–	–	==	==	==	20	16	14	11	12	11	13	14	18	==	==	–	–	–	–	–	–	–	–	–	–	–	–	–	–	LOVE IS LIKE A CIGARETTE
–	–	==	==	20	14	9	6	5	5	6	8	11	14	==	==	==	–	–	–	–	–	–	–	–	–	–	–	–	–	ROSE OF THE WORLD
–	–	==	==	==	17	12	10	8	11	15	19	==	==	–	–	–	–	–	–	–	–	–	–	–	–	–	–	–	–	ASK HER WHILE THE BAND IS PLAYING
–	–	==	==	15	10	6	5	6	6	9	14	16	==	==	–	–	–	–	–	–	–	–	–	–	–	–	–	–	–	GOOD EVENING, CAROLINE
–	–	==	==	==	==	==	==	20	==	18	20	==	==	==	==	–	–	–	–	–	–	–	–	–	–	–	–	–	–	"BL-ND" AND "P-G" SPELLS "BLIND PIG"
–	–	==	==	==	==	==	==	==	==	20	==	20	19	19	16	13	15	19	==	==	==	==	20	==	==	==	==	==	==	KERRY MILLS BARN DANCE
–	–	–	–	==	==	==	==	16	10	8	7	5	4	6	6	7	19	==	==	==	==	==	==	–	–	–	–	–	–	OH, MISS MALINDA
–	–	–	–	–	–	==	==	==	16	12	9	8	10	13	19	==	==	==	==	–	–	–	–	–	–	–	–	–	–	EVERYBODY LOVES ME BUT THE ONE I LOVE
–	–	–	–	–	–	==	18	12	7	2	**1**	**1**	**1**	**1**	**1**	2	2	4	6	9	12	17	==	==	==	–	–	–	–	SHINE ON, HARVEST MOON
–	–	–	–	–	–	==	==	==	==	==	==	15	11	12	11	18	==	==	==	==	==	==	==	==	==	==	==	==	==	DOWN AT THE HUSKING BEE
–	–	–	–	–	–	–	–	==	==	==	==	17	16	14	18	==	==	==	==	==	==	–	–	–	–	–	–	–	–	GAMES OF CHILDHOOD DAYS
–	–	–	–	–	–	–	–	==	18	10	5	3	3	3	3	3	4	2	3	5	7	8	13	14	19	==	==	==	==	WHEN I DREAM IN THE GLOAMING OF YOU
–	–	–	–	–	–	–	–	==	==	==	12	9	7	5	4	5	9	12	15	==	==	==	–	–	–	–	–	–	–	NOBODY KNOWS, NOBODY CARES
–	–	–	–	–	–	–	==	==	==	==	19	13	11	14	10	13	14	10	7	6	7	5	5	4	5	8	10	10	8	8 6 9 9 9 11 17 == TO THE END OF THE WORLD WITH YOU
–	–	–	–	–	–	–	–	–	–	==	18	10	6	2	2	**1**	**1**	**1**	**1**	4	3	3	7	12	14	17	==	==	–	YIP-I-ADDY-I-AY!
–	–	–	–	–	–	–	–	–	–	==	==	==	==	==	==	==	18	18	19	20	16	15	19	18	==	==	==	==	==	YOU AIN'T TALKIN' TO ME
–	–	–	–	–	–	–	–	–	–	–	–	==	==	15	13	19	==	==	==	==	==	–	–	–	–	–	–	–	–	LET'S GO BACK TO BABY DAYS
–	–	–	–	–	–	–	–	–	–	–	–	==	==	16	15	20	==	==	==	==	==	==	–	–	–	–	–	–	–	THIS ROSE BRINGS MY HEART TO YOU
–	–	–	–	–	–	–	–	–	–	–	–	==	17	14	5	4	3	3	4	2	4	6	9	8	11	15	==	==	==	MY COUSIN CARUS'
–	–	–	–	–	–	–	–	–	–	–	–	==	==	20	14	6	6	8	14	==	==	==	==	==	==	–	–	–	–	SCHOOL MATES
Oc	Oc	Nv	Nv	Dc	Dc	Ja	Ja	Fb	Fb	Ma	Ma	Ap	Ap	My	My	Jn	Jn	Jy	Jy	Ag	Ag	Sp	Sp	Oc	Oc	Nv	Nv	Dc	Dc	

1909																		1910												
Ap	Ap	My	My	Jn	Jn	Jy	Jy	Ag	Ag	Sp	Sp	Oc	Oc	Nv	Nv	Dc	Dc	Ja	Ja	Fb	Fb	Ma	Ma	Ap	Ap	My	My	Jn	Jn	
==	==	==	==	==	==	==	==	==	==	16	12	10	6	8	12	16	16	17	18	15	16	14	14	==	==	==	==	==	==	AMINA
==	==	==	==	==	17	15	==	==	==	==	==	==	==	–	–	–	–	–	–	–	–	–	–	–	–	–	–	–	–	RED, RED ROSE
==	==	17	12	8	11	11	8	6	5	5	4	2	3	4	6	9	15	16	17	==	20	==	==	==	==	–	–	–	–	DOWN AMONG THE SUGAR CANE
–	–	==	==	==	20	==	20	==	==	==	==	–	–	–	–	–	–	–	–	–	–	–	–	–	–	–	–	–	–	TAKE ME OUT TO THE BALL GAME
–	–	==	==	16	8	7	9	11	19	==	==	–	–	–	–	–	–	–	–	–	–	–	–	–	–	–	–	–	–	I LOVE MY WIFE, BUT OH, YOU KID!
–	–	==	==	14	7	5	7	10	17	==	==	–	–	–	–	–	–	–	–	–	–	–	–	–	–	–	–	–	–	I LOVE, I LOVE, I LOVE MY WIFE, BUT OH, YOU KID
–	==	==	17	9	5	10	12	15	18	==	==	==	==	–	–	–	–	–	–	–	–	–	–	–	–	–	–	–	–	BEAUTIFUL EYES
–	–	==	==	==	==	==	18	14	11	9	10	13	17	==	==	==	==	==	==	–	–	–	–	–	–	–	–	–	–	RED HEAD
–	–	==	==	15	10	9	5	3	2	**1**	**1**	**1**	**1**	2	3	3	3	4	4	8	11	17	19	==	==	==	–	–	–	I WONDER WHO'S KISSING HER NOW
–	–	–	==	==	12	6	2	**1**	**1**	2	2	3	8	16	==	==	–	–	–	–	–	–	–	–	–	–	–	–	–	MY PONY BOY
–	–	–	–	==	==	20	17	18	==	==	==	==	==	–	–	–	–	–	–	–	–	–	–	–	–	–	–	–	–	I'M AWFULLY GLAD I MET YOU
–	–	–	–	==	==	==	==	19	20	20	==	==	==	==	–	–	–	–	–	–	–	–	–	–	–	–	–	–	–	PANSIES MEAN THOUGHTS, AND THOUGHTS MEAN YOU
–	–	–	–	==	==	17	16	16	13	14	17	==	==	==	==	–	–	–	–	–	–	–	–	–	–	–	–	–	–	LONESOME
–	–	–	–	==	==	16	13	13	10	13	15	19	==	==	==	–	–	–	–	–	–	–	–	–	–	–	–	–	–	TAKE ME UP WITH YOU, DEARIE
–	–	–	–	==	==	==	==	==	==	18	18	==	==	==	==	==	–	–	–	–	–	–	–	–	–	–	–	–	–	SADIE SALOME, GO HOME
–	–	–	–	==	==	==	==	17	14	12	8	7	7	6	5	5	6	7	9	9	12	18	==	==	–	–	–	–	–	I WISH I HAD MY OLD GIRL BACK AGAIN
–	–	–	–	–	–	==	==	12	8	4	3	6	10	19	==	==	–	–	–	–	–	–	–	–	–	–	–	–	–	MY WIFE'S GONE TO THE COUNTRY (HURAH! HURAH!)
–	–	–	–	–	–	==	==	==	==	==	==	16	13	11	10	15	17	18	==	==	==	==	==	==	==	==	==	–	–	DAISIES WON'T TELL
–	–	–	–	–	–	==	==	==	15	11	6	4	2	**1**	**1**	2	2	2	3	5	5	7	8	8	9	18	==	==	==	I'VE GOT RINGS ON MY FINGERS
–	–	–	–	–	–	–	–	==	==	19	14	11	9	13	16	==	==	==	==	–	–	–	–	–	–	–	–	–	–	GEE, BUT THERE'S CLASS TO A GIRL LIKE YOU
–	–	–	–	–	–	–	–	==	==	==	==	==	16	10	9	7	8	15	15	19	==	==	==	==	==	–	–	–	–	WILD CHERRIES RAG
–	–	–	–	–	–	–	–	==	==	==	==	20	12	7	4	6	7	13	13	12	17	19	==	==	==	–	–	–	–	THAT'S A–PLENTY
–	–	–	–	–	–	–	–	==	==	==	==	==	20	20	17	14	11	10	16	18	==	==	==	==	==	==	==	==	==	GOOD NIGHT, DEAR
–	–	–	–	–	–	–	–	–	==	==	16	9	5	3	2	**1**	**1**	**1**	**1**	**1**	**1**	2	3	6	7	13	19	==	==	BY THE LIGHT OF THE SILVERY MOON
–	–	–	–	–	–	–	–	–	–	==	==	17	15	12	14	19	==	==	–	–	–	–	–	–	–	–	–	–	–	UP, UP, UP IN MY AEROPLANE
–	–	–	–	–	–	–	–	–	–	–	–	==	==	==	13	12	18	==	==	==	==	–	–	–	–	–	–	–	–	SENORA
–	–	–	–	–	–	–	–	–	–	–	–	==	18	9	7	4	5	5	7	13	==	==	==	–	–	–	–	–	–	CARRIE (MARRY HARRY)
–	–	–	–	–	–	–	–	–	–	–	–	–	–	==	20	13	9	9	14	==	==	–	–	–	–	–	–	–	–	NEXT TO YOUR MOTHER, WHO DO YOU LOVE?
–	–	–	–	–	–	–	–	==	==	==	==	==	==	18	15	11	14	14	10	10	7	6	4	3	3	3	3	2	2	MEET ME TONIGHT IN DREAMLAND (1910)
–	–	–	–	–	–	–	–	–	–	==	==	==	==	==	18	20	20	==	==	20	14	11	11	12	20	==	==	==	==	CIRIBIRIBIN (1910)
–	–	–	–	–	–	–	–	==	==	==	==	==	==	==	19	==	==	19	20	17	15	12	12	9	8	10	11	10	11	IN THE GARDEN OF MY HEART (1910)
–	–	–	–	–	–	–	–	–	–	–	–	==	==	14	11	8	4	3	2	2	3	3	5	5	6	9	13	==	==	THE CUBANOLA GLIDE (1910)
–	–	–	–	–	–	–	–	–	–	–	–	–	–	==	==	17	12	11	11	14	13	16	16	16	==	==	==	–	–	THE GARDEN OF ROSES (1910)
–	–	–	–	–	–	–	–	–	–	–	–	–	–	==	==	18	13	6	5	3	4	5	7	7	14	19	==	==	==	COME AFTER BREAKFAST, BRING 'LONG YOUR LUNCH, AND LEAVE 'FORE SUPPER TIME (1910)
–	–	–	–	–	–	–	–	–	–	–	–	–	–	–	–	==	19	12	6	4	2	**1**	**1**	**1**	**1**	**1**	**1**	3	3	PUT ON YOUR OLD GRAY BONNET (1910)
Ap	Ap	My	My	Jn	Jn	Jy	Jy	Ag	Ag	Sp	Sp	Oc	Oc	Nv	Nv	Dc	Dc	Ja	Ja	Fb	Fb	Ma	Ma	Ap	Ap	My	My	Jn	Jn	

1909						1910																								
Oc	Oc	Nv	Nv	Dc	Dc	Ja	Ja	Fb	Fb	Ma	Ma	Ap	Ap	My	My	Jn	Jn	Jy	Jy	Ag	Ag	Sp	Sp	Oc	Oc	Nv	Nv	Dc	Dc	
5	4	5	8	10	10	8	8	6	9	9	9	11	17	==	==	==	==	==	==	–	–	–	–	–	–	–	–	–	–	TO THE END OF THE WORLD WITH YOU (1909)
10	6	8	12	16	16	17	18	15	16	14	14	==	==	==	==	==	==	==	==	==	==	–	–	–	–	–	–	–	–	AMINA (1909)
2	3	4	6	9	15	16	17	==	20	==	==	==	==	–	–	–	–	–	–	–	–	–	–	–	–	–	–	–	–	DOWN AMONG THE SUGAR CANE (1909)
1	**1**	2	3	3	3	4	4	8	11	17	19	==	==	–	–	–	–	–	–	–	–	–	–	–	–	–	–	–	–	I WONDER WHO'S KISSING HER NOW (1909)
7	7	6	5	5	6	7	9	9	12	18	==	==	==	–	–	–	–	–	–	–	–	–	–	–	–	–	–	–	–	I WISH I HAD MY OLD GIRL BACK AGAIN (1909)
16	13	11	10	15	17	18	==	==	==	==	==	==	==	==	==	–	–	–	–	–	–	–	–	–	–	–	–	–	–	DAISIES WON'T TELL (1909)
4	2	**1**	**1**	2	2	2	3	5	5	7	8	8	9	18	==	==	==	–	–	–	–	–	–	–	–	–	–	–	–	I'VE GOT RINGS ON MY FINGERS (1909)
==	16	10	9	7	8	15	15	19	==	==	==	==	==	–	–	–	–	–	–	–	–	–	–	–	–	–	–	–	–	WILD CHERRIES RAG (1909)
20	12	7	4	6	7	13	13	12	17	19	==	==	==	–	–	–	–	–	–	–	–	–	–	–	–	–	–	–	–	THAT'S A-PLENTY (1909)
==	20	20	17	14	11	10	16	18	==	==	==	==	==	==	==	==	==	–	–	–	–	–	–	–	–	–	–	–	–	GOOD NIGHT, DEAR (1909)
9	5	3	2	**1**	**1**	**1**	**1**	**1**	**1**	2	3	6	7	13	19	==	==	–	–	–	–	–	–	–	–	–	–	–	–	BY THE LIGHT OF THE SILVERY MOON (1909)
==	18	9	7	4	5	5	7	13	==	==	==	–	–	–	–	–	–	–	–	–	–	–	–	–	–	–	–	–	–	CARRIE (MARRY HARRY) (1909)
–	–	==	20	13	9	9	14	==	==	–	–	–	–	–	–	–	–	–	–	–	–	–	–	–	–	–	–	–	–	NEXT TO YOUR MOTHER, WHO DO YOU LOVE? (1909)
==	==	18	15	11	14	14	10	10	7	6	4	3	3	3	3	2	2	**1**	**1**	**1**	**1**	**1**	2	4	7	11	12	14	18	==MEET ME TONIGHT IN DREAMLAND
==	==	==	18	20	20	==	==	20	14	11	11	12	20	==	==	==	==	==	==	==	==	==	==	==	==	–	–	–	–	CIRIBIRIBIN
==	==	==	19	==	==	19	20	17	15	12	12	9	8	10	11	10	11	11	10	10	11	15	13	16	15	15	13	15	15	15 13 15 17 == IN THE GARDEN OF MY HEART
==	==	14	11	8	4	3	2	2	3	3	5	5	6	9	13	==	==	==	–	–	–	–	–	–	–	–	–	–	–	THE CUBANOLA GLIDE
==	==	==	==	==	==	==	==	==	==	20	20	==	==	==	==	–	–	–	–	–	–	–	–	–	–	–	–	–	–	EV'RY DAY
–	–	==	==	17	12	11	11	14	13	16	16	16	==	==	==	–	–	–	–	–	–	–	–	–	–	–	–	–	–	THE GARDEN OF ROSES
–	–	==	==	18	13	6	5	3	4	5	7	7	14	19	==	==	==	–	–	–	–	–	–	–	–	–	–	–	–	COME AFTER BREAKFAST, BRING 'LONG YOUR LUNCH, AND LEAVE 'FORE SUPPER TIME
–	–	–	–	==	==	20	12	7	8	10	10	13	==	==	–	–	–	–	–	–	–	–	–	–	–	–	–	–	–	YIDDLE ON YOUR FIDDLE
–	–	–	–	==	19	12	6	4	2	**1**	**1**	**1**	**1**	**1**	**1**	3	3	3	7	8	13	==	==	==	==	–	–	–	–	PUT ON YOUR OLD GRAY BONNET
–	–	–	–	==	==	==	==	16	10	8	6	4	4	5	6	6	6	8	11	15	==	==	==	==	==	==	==	–	–	SHAKY EYES
–	–	–	–	–	–	==	==	==	18	15	15	==	==	–	–	–	–	–	–	–	–	–	–	–	–	–	–	–	–	ARE YOU LONESOME?
–	–	–	–	–	–	==	==	==	19	13	13	18	==	==	==	–	–	–	–	–	–	–	–	–	–	–	–	–	–	WAY DOWN IN COTTON TOWN
–	–	–	–	–	–	==	19	11	6	4	2	2	2	4	4	5	7	14	19	==	==	–	–	–	–	–	–	–	–	THAT MESMERIZING MENDELSSOHN TUNE
–	–	–	–	–	–	–	–	==	==	==	17	14	11	12	18	==	==	==	==	–	–	–	–	–	–	–	–	–	–	TIE YOUR LITTLE BULL OUTSIDE
–	–	–	–	–	–	–	–	==	==	==	==	==	==	==	20	18	18	15	13	12	16	17	19	17	14	14	11	13	13	13 12 14 17 == WHERE THE RIVER SHANNON FLOWS
–	–	–	–	–	–	–	–	–	–	==	==	17	15	11	9	8	15	16	18	==	==	–	–	–	–	–	–	–	–	I'LL MAKE A RING AROUND ROSIE
–	–	–	–	–	–	–	–	–	–	==	==	20	12	10	8	10	14	17	16	16	==	==	==	==	==	–	–	–	–	THAT ITALIAN RAG
–	–	–	–	–	–	–	–	–	–	==	==	==	16	17	16	17	17	19	17	==	==	==	==	–	–	–	–	–	–	THE GLOW-WORM
–	–	–	–	–	–	–	–	–	–	==	==	15	10	7	7	13	13	13	14	17	==	==	==	–	–	–	–	–	–	COME ALONG, MY MANDY!
–	–	–	–	–	–	–	–	–	–	==	==	19	13	6	5	4	4	6	6	6	7	12	17	==	==	–	–	–	–	YOU ARE THE IDEAL OF MY DREAMS
–	–	–	–	–	–	–	–	–	–	==	18	10	5	2	2	**1**	**1**	2	2	3	4	5	9	18	==	==	==	–	–	HAS ANYBODY HERE SEEN KELLY?
–	–	–	–	–	–	–	–	–	–	==	==	==	==	==	==	==	==	==	==	==	==	20	==	19	19	17	19	==	==	WITHOUT YOU THE WORLD DON'T SEEM THE SAME
–	–	–	–	–	–	–	–	–	–	==	==	==	==	20	17	16	16	9	8	7	8	13	18	15	18	==	==	19	20	==TEMPTATION RAG
–	–	–	–	–	–	–	–	–	–	==	==	==	18	14	12	12	10	7	4	4	3	4	7	7	11	16	18	16	16	16 == WHAT'S THE MATTER WITH FATHER?
–	–	–	–	–	–	–	–	–	–	==	==	==	==	==	==	19	19	20	==	==	==	==	==	==	==	==	==	==	==	GO ON, GOOD-A-BYE
Oc	Oc	Nv	Nv	Dc	Dc	Ja	Ja	Fb	Fb	Ma	Ma	Ap	Ap	My	My	Jn	Jn	Jy	Jy	Ag	Ag	Sp	Sp	Oc	Oc	Nv	Nv	Dc	Dc	

1910																		1911												
Ap	Ap	My	My	Jn	Jn	Jy	Jy	Ag	Ag	Sp	Sp	Oc	Oc	Nv	Nv	Dc	Dc	Ja	Ja	Fb	Fb	Ma	Ma	Ap	Ap	My	My	Jn	Jn	
==	19	15	14	11	12	12	15	==	==	–	–	–	–	–	–	–	–	–	–	–	–	–	–	–	–	–	–	–	–	YOU TAUGHT ME HOW TO LOVE YOU, NOW TEACH ME TO FORGET
==	==	==	15	14	10	10	9	14	17	==	==	==	==	–	–	–	–	–	–	–	–	–	–	–	–	–	–	–	–	JUST FOR A GIRL
==	==	==	==	20	20	==	==	==	==	==	==	==	==	==	==	–	–	–	–	–	–	–	–	–	–	–	–	–	–	I'M NOT THAT KIND OF GIRL
==	==	16	10	7	5	4	3	2	2	3	5	8	12	12	14	20	==	==	==	–	–	–	–	–	–	–	–	–	–	I'VE GOT THE TIME, I'VE GOT THE PLACE, BUT IT'S HARD TO FIND THE GIRL
–	–	==	==	15	8	5	5	5	6	6	11	14	==	==	–	–	–	–	–	–	–	–	–	–	–	–	–	–	–	CALL ME UP SOME RAINY AFTERNOON
–	–	–	–	==	==	==	20	18	==	==	20	==	==	–	–	–	–	–	–	–	–	–	–	–	–	–	–	–	–	THE CHANTICLEER RAG
–	–	–	–	==	==	18	12	9	10	8	8	6	5	5	6	8	8	10	10	11	10	15	==	==	==	==	==	==	==	MY HEART HAS LEARNED TO LOVE YOU, NOW DO NOT SAY GOODBYE
–	–	–	==	==	==	==	==	==	18	16	12	9	6	7	7	5	4	3	4	5	3	4	4	9	13	18	==	==	==	CASEY JONES
–	–	–	–	–	–	==	==	20	14	14	16	13	16	19	==	==	==	–	–	–	–	–	–	–	–	–	–	–	–	HEAVEN WILL PROTECT THE WORKING GIRL
–	–	–	–	–	–	==	==	19	12	11	10	11	9	13	16	18	19	==	20	19	==	==	==	–	–	–	–	–	–	SOMEBODY ELSE, IT'S ALWAYS SOMEBODY ELSE
–	–	–	–	–	–	==	==	11	5	2	**1**	3	4	4	4	4	5	9	9	12	13	18	==	–	–	–	–	–	–	ANY LITTLE GIRL THAT'S A NICE LITTLE GIRL
–	–	–	–	–	–	==	==	13	9	7	6	5	3	3	3	2	2	**1**	**1**	2	2	5	6	11	==	==	==	–	–	EVERY LITTLE MOVEMENT
–	–	–	–	–	–	==	==	==	20	==	==	==	==	==	==	–	–	–	–	–	–	–	–	–	–	–	–	–	–	THE MORNING AFTER THE NIGHT BEFORE
–	–	–	–	–	–	–	==	==	15	9	4	2	2	**1**	**1**	3	3	4	7	8	11	19	==	–	–	–	–	–	–	PLAY THAT BARBERSHOP CHORD
–	–	–	–	–	–	–	–	==	==	18	14	12	10	8	9	10	12	12	15	==	==	==	–	–	–	–	–	–	–	THAT'S YIDDISHA LOVE
–	–	–	–	–	–	–	–	==	==	==	==	20	13	9	8	9	11	11	11	13	16	==	==	==	==	–	–	–	–	IF HE COMES IN, I'M GOING OUT
–	–	–	–	–	–	–	–	==	19	10	3	**1**	**1**	2	2	**1**	**1**	2	2	3	5	6	9	15	==	==	==	==	==	SOME OF THESE DAYS
–	–	–	–	–	–	–	–	==	==	19	15	10	8	6	5	6	6	7	8	7	9	13	17	==	==	==	==	==	==	ALL THAT I ASK OF YOU IS LOVE
–	–	–	–	–	–	–	–	==	==	==	==	==	==	==	==	==	17	17	19	==	==	==	==	==	==	==	==	==	==	TAKE ME BACK TO BABYLAND
–	–	–	–	–	–	–	–	==	==	==	==	==	17	10	10	7	7	6	5	6	8	8	13	14	20	==	==	==	==	SILVER BELL
–	–	–	–	–	–	–	–	–	–	==	==	==	20	18	20	17	14	14	16	16	==	==	==	==	==	==	==	–	–	SUGAR MOON
–	–	–	–	–	–	–	–	–	–	–	–	==	==	==	17	12	9	5	3	**1**	**1**	**1**	2	2	**1**	2	2	2	4	LET ME CALL YOU SWEETHEART (1911)
–	–	–	–	–	–	–	–	–	–	–	–	==	==	20	15	11	10	8	6	4	4	7	11	17	==	==	==	==	==	UNDER THE YUM YUM TREE (1911)
Ap	Ap	My	My	Jn	Jn	Jy	Jy	Ag	Ag	Sp	Sp	Oc	Oc	Nv	Nv	Dc	Dc	Ja	Ja	Fb	Fb	Ma	Ma	Ap	Ap	My	My	Jn	Jn	

1910 | 1911

Oc	Oc	Nv	Nv	Dc	Dc	Ja	Ja	Fb	Fb	Ma	Ma	Ap	Ap	My	My	Jn	Jn	Jy	Jy	Ag	Ag	Sp	Sp	Oc	Oc	Nv	Nv	Dc	Dc	
16	15	15	13	15	15	15	13	15	17	==	==	==	==	==	==	==	==	==	==	20	17	19	==	==	==	==	==	–	–	IN THE GARDEN OF MY HEART (1910)
17	14	14	11	13	13	13	12	14	17	==	==	==	==	==	==	==	==	==	==	==	==	==	==	==	==	==	==	==	==	WHERE THE RIVER SHANNON FLOWS (1910)
7	11	16	18	16	16	16	==	==	==	==	==	==	==	–	–	–	–	–	–	–	–	–	–	–	–	–	–	–	–	WHAT'S THE MATTER WITH FATHER? (1910)
6	5	5	6	8	8	10	10	11	10	15	==	==	==	==	==	==	==	–	–	–	–	–	–	–	–	–	–	–	–	MY HEART HAS LEARNED TO LOVE YOU, NOW DO NOT SAY GOODBYE (1910)
11	9	13	16	18	19	==	20	19	==	==	==	–	–	–	–	–	–	–	–	–	–	–	–	–	–	–	–	–	–	SOMEBODY ELSE, IT'S ALWAYS SOMEBODY ELSE (1910)
3	4	4	4	4	5	9	9	12	13	18	==	–	–	–	–	–	–	–	–	–	–	–	–	–	–	–	–	–	–	ANY LITTLE GIRL THAT'S A NICE LITTLE GIRL (1910)
5	3	3	3	2	2	**1**	**1**	2	2	5	6	11	==	==	==	–	–	–	–	–	–	–	–	–	–	–	–	–	–	EVERY LITTLE MOVEMENT (1910)
9	6	7	7	5	4	3	4	5	3	4	4	9	13	18	==	==	==	==	==	–	–	–	–	–	–	–	–	–	–	CASEY JONES (1910)
12	10	8	9	10	12	12	15	==	==	==	–	–	–	–	–	–	–	–	–	–	–	–	–	–	–	–	–	–	–	THAT'S YIDDISHA LOVE (1910)
2	2	**1**	**1**	3	3	4	7	8	11	19	==	–	–	–	–	–	–	–	–	–	–	–	–	–	–	–	–	–	–	PLAY THAT BARBERSHOP CHORD (1910)
20	13	9	8	9	11	11	11	13	16	==	==	==	==	–	–	–	–	–	–	–	–	–	–	–	–	–	–	–	–	IF HE COMES IN, I'M GOING OUT (1910)
1	**1**	2	2	**1**	**1**	2	2	3	5	6	9	15	==	==	==	==	==	–	–	–	–	–	–	–	–	–	–	–	–	SOME OF THESE DAYS (1910)
10	8	6	5	6	6	7	8	7	9	13	17	==	==	==	==	==	==	–	–	–	–	–	–	–	–	–	–	–	–	ALL THAT I ASK OF YOU IS LOVE (1910)
==	==	==	==	==	17	17	19	==	==	==	==	==	==	==	==	==	==	==	==	–	–	–	–	–	–	–	–	–	–	TAKE ME BACK TO BABYLAND (1910)
==	17	10	10	7	7	6	5	6	8	8	13	14	20	==	==	==	==	==	==	–	–	–	–	–	–	–	–	–	–	SILVER BELL (1910)
==	20	18	20	17	14	14	16	16	==	==	==	==	==	==	==	–	–	–	–	–	–	–	–	–	–	–	–	–	–	SUGAR MOON (1910)
==	==	==	==	==	==	18	18	18	==	==	==	==	==	–	–	–	–	–	–	–	–	–	–	–	–	–	–	–	–	I'LL CHANGE THE THORNS TO ROSES
==	==	==	==	==	==	19	==	20	==	==	==	==	==	–	–	–	–	–	–	–	–	–	–	–	–	–	–	–	–	THAT MINOR STRAIN
==	==	==	==	==	==	20	==	==	==	==	==	==	==	==	==	–	–	–	–	–	–	–	–	–	–	–	–	–	–	THAT BEAUTIFUL RAG
==	==	==	17	12	9	5	3	**1**	**1**	**1**	2	2	**1**	2	2	2	4	6	6	7	7	7	9	8	13	13	15	16	==	LET ME CALL YOU SWEETHEART
==	==	20	15	11	10	8	6	4	4	7	11	17	==	==	==	==	==	–	–	–	–	–	–	–	–	–	–	–	–	UNDER THE YUM YUM TREE
==	==	==	==	==	==	==	==	==	19	20	16	==	18	17	15	17	15	15	12	11	11	12	15	16	16	19	==	==	==	== 20 20 == MY HERO
–	–	–	–	==	==	==	==	==	20	==	20	20	19	==	20	19	20	20	==	==	==	17	18	==	==	==	==	==	==	ALMA (WHERE DO YOU LIVE?)
–	–	–	–	==	==	==	==	==	==	17	18	==	==	==	==	==	==	==	==	==	==	–	–	–	–	–	–	–	–	THAT DREAMY ITALIAN WALTZ
–	–	–	–	–	–	==	==	==	14	11	14	18	14	16	19	==	==	–	–	–	–	–	–	–	–	–	–	–	–	ITALIAN STREET SONG
–	–	–	–	–	==	==	17	10	7	3	3	5	9	13	18	20	==	==	==	–	–	–	–	–	–	–	–	–	–	I'M LOOKING FOR A NICE YOUNG FELLOW
–	–	–	–	–	==	==	14	9	6	2	**1**	**1**	2	3	3	7	8	12	14	==	==	–	–	–	–	–	–	–	–	COME, JOSEPHINE, IN MY FLYING MACHINE
–	–	–	–	–	–	==	==	17	12	9	10	7	7	8	10	12	18	19	==	==	==	==	==	==	==	–	–	–	–	I'M FALLING IN LOVE WITH SOMEONE
–	–	–	–	–	–	–	==	==	15	10	5	4	4	4	8	11	13	16	==	==	==	==	==	–	–	–	–	–	–	KISS ME, MY HONEY, KISS ME
–	–	–	–	–	–	–	–	==	==	12	8	6	6	6	4	3	3	5	8	8	13	14	17	==	==	==	–	–	–	GEE, BUT IT'S GREAT TO MEET A FRIEND FROM YOUR OWN HOME TOWN
–	–	–	–	–	–	–	–	==	==	14	7	3	3	**1**	**1**	**1**	**1**	**1**	2	5	8	13	19	==	==	–	–	–	–	PUT YOUR ARMS AROUND ME, HONEY
–	–	–	–	–	–	–	–	==	==	16	12	8	5	5	5	4	5	4	5	6	6	6	10	14	19	==	==	==	==	ALL ABOARD FOR BLANKET BAY
–	–	–	–	–	–	–	–	–	==	==	15	10	8	7	6	6	7	8	9	15	==	==	==	–	–	–	–	–	–	DAY DREAMS (VISIONS OF BLISS)
–	–	–	–	–	–	–	–	–	–	==	19	13	11	11	12	10	10	13	16	==	==	==	==	–	–	–	–	–	–	ON MOBILE BAY
Oc	Oc	Nv	Nv	Dc	Dc	Ja	Ja	Fb	Fb	Ma	Ma	Ap	Ap	My	My	Jn	Jn	Jy	Jy	Ag	Ag	Sp	Sp	Oc	Oc	Nv	Nv	Dc	Dc	

1911																				1912										
Ma	Ma	Ap	Ap	My	My	Jn	Jn	Jy	Jy	Ag	Ag	Sp	Sp	Oc	Oc	Nv	Nv	Dc	Dc	Ja	Ja	Fb	Fb	Ma	Ma	Ap	Ap	My	My	
==	==	==	17	15	16	16	17	==	==	==	–	–	–	–	–	–	–	–	–	–	–	–	–	–	–	–	–	–	–	THAT WAS BEFORE I MET YOU
==	==	19	16	12	11	9	9	9	10	12	14	==	==	==	–	–	–	–	–	–	–	–	–	–	–	–	–	–	–	DON'T WAKE ME UP, I'M DREAMING
==	==	==	15	14	13	14	19	==	==	==	==	==	==	–	–	–	–	–	–	–	–	–	–	–	–	–	–	–	–	THERE'LL COME A TIME
==	==	==	==	20	14	13	12	11	11	13	18	==	==	==	==	==	==	–	–	–	–	–	–	–	–	–	–	–	–	TWO LITTLE LOVE BEES
==	==	==	==	19	17	15	14	14	15	14	15	18	==	==	==	==	20	==	==	==	==	==	==	==	==	20	19	==	==	JIMMY VALENTINE
==	==	12	10	9	7	8	6	3	3	4	4	5	7	15	==	==	==	–	–	–	–	–	–	–	–	–	–	–	–	STEAMBOAT BILL
==	==	16	12	10	9	5	2	2	1	1	1	1	1	3	4	4	4	5	6	7	7	10	12	18	==	==	==	==	==	DOWN BY THE OLD MILL STREAM
–	–	==	==	==	==	==	==	18	20	18	19	==	20	==	==	==	==	–	–	–	–	–	–	–	–	–	–	–	–	THAT RAILROAD RAG
–	–	–	–	==	==	==	==	==	18	16	12	11	14	12	10	10	13	20	==	==	==	==	==	==	==	–	–	–	–	CHICKEN REEL
–	–	–	–	==	==	==	==	==	==	19	==	==	==	–	–	–	–	–	–	–	–	–	–	–	–	–	–	–	–	CAN'T YOU TAKE IT BACK AND CHANGE IT FOR A BOY?
–	–	–	–	==	==	==	==	==	==	==	==	16	12	9	9	9	9	8	7	8	8	9	7	7	11	12	==	==	==	MY BEAUTIFUL LADY
–	–	–	–	==	==	==	==	17	19	==	==	==	==	–	–	–	–	–	–	–	–	–	–	–	–	–	–	–	–	BY THE SASKATCHEWAN
–	–	–	–	==	==	18	11	7	4	2	2	2	5	7	11	15	==	==	–	–	–	–	–	–	–	–	–	–	–	ALL ALONE
–	–	–	–	==	==	==	==	==	==	17	10	10	11	13	14	14	18	==	==	==	==	–	–	–	–	–	–	–	–	IN THE LAND OF HARMONY
–	–	–	–	==	==	==	16	10	7	3	3	3	4	4	5	6	7	12	12	14	16	==	==	==	==	==	==	–	–	BABY ROSE
–	–	–	–	==	==	==	==	==	13	10	9	9	6	6	7	8	8	11	11	9	11	12	13	17	18	==	==	==	==	I LIKE THE HAT, I LIKE THE DRESS, AND I LIKE THE GIRL THAT'S IN IT
–	–	–	–	–	–	==	==	==	17	9	5	4	2	2	2	3	3	3	3	4	4	6	8	10	14	==	==	==	==	OCEANA ROLL
–	–	–	–	–	–	–	–	–	==	==	==	==	20	==	==	==	==	==	==	==	–	–	–	–	–	–	–	–	–	DOCTOR TINKLE TINKER
–	–	–	–	–	–	–	–	–	==	==	==	==	==	==	==	==	==	==	19	20	==	==	19	==	==	==	==	==	==	ROAMIN' IN THE GLOAMIN'
–	–	–	–	–	–	–	–	–	–	==	16	8	3	1	1	1	1	1	1	1	1	3	3	3	3	4	5	11	16	ALEXANDER'S RAGTIME BAND
–	–	–	–	–	–	–	–	–	–	==	==	15	8	5	3	2	2	2	2	2	2	2	2	4	5	9	16	==	==	I WANT A GIRL (JUST LIKE THE GIRL THAT MARRIED DEAR OLD DAD)
–	–	–	–	–	–	–	–	–	–	==	==	==	16	10	6	5	6	10	10	13	13	17	==	==	==	==	==	–	–	THE HARBOR OF LOVE
–	–	–	–	–	–	–	–	–	–	==	==	==	==	18	15	11	10	7	9	10	14	18	17	==	==	==	==	–	–	MY LOVIN' HONEY MAN
–	–	–	–	–	–	–	–	–	–	==	==	==	13	11	8	7	5	4	5	5	6	8	10	14	17	==	==	==	==	BILLY
–	–	–	–	–	–	–	–	–	–	==	==	==	==	20	20	==	==	==	==	–	–	–	–	–	–	–	–	–	–	CHILD LOVE
–	–	–	–	–	–	–	–	–	–	==	==	==	==	17	12	12	12	15	17	==	==	–	–	–	–	–	–	–	–	THEY ALWAYS PICK ON ME
–	–	–	–	–	–	–	–	–	–	–	–	–	–	==	==	==	==	==	19	18	19	==	==	==	==	–	–	–	–	CHICKEN RAG
–	–	–	–	–	–	–	–	–	–	–	–	–	–	==	==	18	17	13	13	12	12	13	15	19	==	==	==	–	–	(HONKY TONKY) MONKEY RAG
–	–	–	–	–	–	–	–	–	–	–	–	–	–	==	==	==	==	18	16	20	==	==	–	–	–	–	–	–	–	KNOCK WOOD
–	–	–	–	–	–	–	–	==	==	==	20	==	==	19	17	20	19	17	15	16	15	11	9	9	10	10	12	16	15	MOTHER MACHREE (1912)
–	–	–	–	–	–	–	–	–	==	==	==	==	==	==	18	17	14	14	14	11	10	7	6	6	4	6	7	8	10	IN THE SHADOWS (1912)
–	–	–	–	–	–	–	–	–	–	–	–	–	–	==	==	16	11	9	8	6	5	4	4	2	2	5	10	14	15	THAT MYSTERIOUS RAG (1912)
–	–	–	–	–	–	–	–	–	–	–	–	–	–	–	==	==	16	6	4	3	3	1	1	1	1	1	1	3	4	OH, YOU BEAUTIFUL DOLL (1912)
–	–	–	–	–	–	–	–	–	–	–	–	–	–	–	–	==	==	==	18	17	17	14	16	20	==	==	==	==	==	THERE'S A GIRL IN HAVANA (1912)
Ma	Ma	Ap	Ap	My	My	Jn	Jn	Jy	Jy	Ag	Ag	Sp	Sp	Oc	Oc	Nv	Nv	Dc	Dc	Ja	Ja	Fb	Fb	Ma	Ma	Ap	Ap	My	My	

1911						1912																								
Oc	Oc	Nv	Nv	Dc	Dc	Ja	Ja	Fb	Fb	Ma	Ma	Ap	Ap	My	My	Jn	Jn	Jy	Jy	Ag	Ag	Sp	Sp	Oc	Oc	Nv	Nv	Dc	Dc	
16	16	19	==	==	==	==	20	20	==	==	==	==	==	==	==	==	==	–	–	–	–	–	–	–	–	–	–	–	–	MY HERO (1911)
==	==	==	20	==	==	==	==	==	==	==	==	20	19	==	==	==	==	–	–	–	–	–	–	–	–	–	–	–	–	JIMMY VALENTINE (1911)
3	4	4	4	5	6	7	7	10	12	18	==	==	==	==	==	–	–	–	–	–	–	–	–	–	–	–	–	–	–	DOWN BY THE OLD MILL STREAM (1911)
9	9	9	9	8	7	8	8	9	7	7	11	12	==	==	==	==	==	==	==	==	==	–	–	–	–	–	–	–	–	MY BEAUTIFUL LADY (1911)
4	5	6	7	12	12	14	16	==	==	==	==	==	==	–	–	–	–	–	–	–	–	–	–	–	–	–	–	–	–	BABY ROSE (1911)
6	7	8	8	11	11	9	11	12	13	17	18	==	==	==	==	==	==	–	–	–	–	–	–	–	–	–	–	–	–	I LIKE THE HAT, I LIKE THE DRESS, AND I LIKE THE GIRL THAT'S IN IT (1911)
2	2	3	3	3	3	4	4	6	8	10	14	==	==	==	==	–	–	–	–	–	–	–	–	–	–	–	–	–	–	OCEANA ROLL (1911)
==	==	==	==	19	20	==	==	19	==	==	==	==	==	==	==	–	–	–	–	–	–	–	–	–	–	–	–	–	–	ROAMIN' IN THE GLOAMIN' (1911)
10	6	5	6	10	10	13	13	17	==	==	==	==	==	==	–	–	–	–	–	–	–	–	–	–	–	–	–	–	–	HARBOR OF LOVE (1911)
1	1	1	1	1	1	1	1	3	3	3	3	4	5	11	16	==	==	==	==	–	–	–	–	–	–	–	–	–	–	ALEXANDER'S RAGTIME BAND (1911)
5	3	2	2	2	2	2	2	2	2	4	5	9	16	==	==	==	==	–	–	–	–	–	–	–	–	–	–	–	–	I WANT A GIRL (JUST LIKE THE GIRL THAT MARRIED DEAR OLD DAD) (1911)
18	15	11	10	7	9	10	14	18	17	==	==	==	==	–	–	–	–	–	–	–	–	–	–	–	–	–	–	–	–	MY LOVIN' HONEY MAN (1911)
11	8	7	5	4	5	5	6	8	10	14	17	==	==	==	==	–	–	–	–	–	–	–	–	–	–	–	–	–	–	BILLY (1911)
==	==	==	==	==	19	18	19	==	==	==	==	–	–	–	–	–	–	–	–	–	–	–	–	–	–	–	–	–	–	CHICKEN RAG (1911)
==	==	18	16	13	13	12	12	13	15	19	==	==	==	–	–	–	–	–	–	–	–	–	–	–	–	–	–	–	–	(HONKY TONKY) MONKEY RAG (1911)
==	==	==	==	18	16	20	==	==	–	–	–	–	–	–	–	–	–	–	–	–	–	–	–	–	–	–	–	–	–	KNOCK WOOD (1911)
19	17	20	19	17	15	16	15	11	9	9	10	10	12	16	15	14	11	15	13	12	11	19	==	==	==	==	==	18	17	==MOTHER MACHREE
==	18	17	14	14	14	11	10	7	6	6	4	6	7	8	10	9	7	7	9	11	10	10	9	18	19	==	==	==	==	IN THE SHADOWS
==	==	==	==	==	==	19	18	16	14	13	15	==	==	==	==	==	==	==	==	==	==	==	==	–	–	–	–	–	–	I'D LOVE TO LIVE IN LOVELAND WITH A GIRL LIKE YOU
==	==	16	11	9	8	6	5	4	4	2	2	5	10	14	14	17	==	==	==	==	==	==	==	–	–	–	–	–	–	THAT MYSTERIOUS RAG
–	==	==	16	6	4	3	3	1	1	1	1	1	1	2	4	6	9	16	==	==	==	–	–	–	–	–	–	–	–	OH, YOU BEAUTIFUL DOLL
–	–	==	==	==	18	17	17	14	16	20	==	==	==	==	==	==	==	–	–	–	–	–	–	–	–	–	–	–	–	THERE'S A GIRL IN HAVANA
–	–	–	–	==	==	15	9	5	5	5	8	8	11	17	==	==	==	==	==	–	–	–	–	–	–	–	–	–	–	IF YOU TALK IN YOUR SLEEP (DON'T MENTION MY NAME)
–	–	–	–	–	–	==	==	15	11	8	6	3	3	4	6	8	8	8	10	13	13	==	==	==	==	==	–	–	–	RUM TUM TIDDLE
–	–	–	–	–	–	–	==	==	18	15	12	14	==	==	–	–	–	–	–	–	–	–	–	–	–	–	–	–	–	ANOTHER RAG
–	–	–	–	–	–	–	–	==	==	==	20	==	==	==	==	–	–	–	–	–	–	–	–	–	–	–	–	–	–	THAT DAFFYDIL RAG
–	–	–	–	–	–	–	–	==	==	16	13	13	20	==	==	==	==	–	–	–	–	–	–	–	–	–	–	–	–	A WEE LITTLE DROP O' THE CRUISKEEN LAWN
–	–	–	–	–	–	–	–	==	20	11	9	7	6	6	8	12	20	==	==	–	–	–	–	–	–	–	–	–	–	THAT HAUNTING MELODY
–	–	–	–	–	–	–	–	==	==	==	19	==	==	19	==	==	19	==	==	==	==	==	==	–	–	–	–	–	–	THAT BABOON BABY DANCE
–	–	–	–	–	–	–	–	==	19	12	7	2	2	1	1	1	1	1	2	5	8	9	19	==	==	–	–	–	–	EVERYBODY'S DOIN' IT NOW
–	–	–	–	–	–	–	–	==	==	==	16	15	14	9	7	7	6	6	6	8	12	11	==	==	==	==	==	==	==	OH, MR. DREAM MAN
–	–	–	–	–	–	–	–	–	–	==	==	18	13	10	13	18	==	==	==	–	–	–	–	–	–	–	–	–	–	TAKE ME BACK TO THE GARDEN OF LOVE
–	–	–	–	–	–	–	–	–	–	==	==	16	8	5	3	4	5	5	11	15	==	==	–	–	–	–	–	–	–	WHEN I WAS TWENTY-ONE AND YOU WERE SWEET SIXTEEN
Oc	Oc	Nv	Nv	Dc	Dc	Ja	Ja	Fb	Fb	Ma	Ma	Ap	Ap	My	My	Jn	Jn	Jy	Jy	Ag	Ag	Sp	Sp	Oc	Oc	Nv	Nv	Dc	Dc	

								1 9 1 2																1 9 1 3						
Ma	Ma	Ap	Ap	My	My	Jn	Jn	Jy	Jy	Ag	Ag	Sp	Sp	Oc	Oc	Nv	Nv	Dc	Dc	Ja	Ja	Fb	Fb	Ma	Ma	Ap	Ap	My	My	
==	==	==	18	13	11	11	12	14	17	19	==	==	–	–	–	–	–	–	–	–	–	–	–	–	–	–	–	–	–	THEY GOTTA QUIT KICKIN' MY DAWG AROUND
==	==	==	==	==	17	16	17	17	18	18	==	==	==	–	–	–	–	–	–	–	–	–	–	–	–	–	–	–	–	"IN THE GLOAMING" WAS THE SONG SHE SANG TO ME
==	==	==	==	==	18	15	16	19	19	20	==	==	==	–	–	–	–	–	–	–	–	–	–	–	–	–	–	–	–	LADY ANGELINE
==	==	==	==	18	20	==	==	==	==	–	–	–	–	–	–	–	–	–	–	–	–	–	–	–	–	–	–	–	–	AT THE RAGTIME BALL
==	==	==	==	20	==	==	==	==	==	==	==	==	==	–	–	–	–	–	–	–	–	–	–	–	–	–	–	–	–	TAKE ME IN YOUR ARMS AGAIN
==	==	==	17	15	12	10	10	10	15	14	14	==	==	–	–	–	–	–	–	–	–	–	–	–	–	–	–	–	–	GOODBYE, ROSE
==	==	11	4	3	2	2	2	3	3	3	5	8	18	==	==	–	–	–	–	–	–	–	–	–	–	–	–	–	–	THE GABY GLIDE
==	==	17	9	7	5	3	3	4	4	4	3	4	6	16	==	==	==	–	–	–	–	–	–	–	–	–	–	–	–	RAGTIME VIOLIN
==	==	19	15	12	9	5	4	2	1	1	1	1	2	2	2	6	9	16	15	17	==	–	–	–	–	–	–	–	–	MOONLIGHT BAY
==	==	==	==	==	==	==	==	20	16	17	18	16	17	17	15	19	20	==	==	==	–	–	–	–	–	–	–	–	–	A GARLAND OF OLD FASHIONED ROSES
–	–	==	==	==	==	==	==	18	12	9	9	6	4	4	4	5	4	5	8	8	8	7	7	7	9	11	18	==	19	==TILL THE SANDS OF THE DESERT GROW COLD
–	–	==	==	==	==	20	==	==	==	==	==	20	==	==	==	–	–	–	–	–	–	–	–	–	–	–	–	–	–	ROLL DEM ROLY BOLY EYES
–	–	–	==	==	19	13	13	13	14	16	==	==	==	–	–	–	–	–	–	–	–	–	–	–	–	–	–	–	–	LOVE IS MINE
–	–	–	==	==	==	19	15	11	7	7	6	5	5	13	==	==	==	–	–	–	–	–	–	–	–	–	–	–	–	RAGGING THE BABY TO SLEEP
–	–	–	–	==	==	==	==	==	20	==	==	–	–	–	–	–	–	–	–	–	–	–	–	–	–	–	–	–	–	DEAR OLD ROSE
–	–	–	–	==	==	==	18	12	8	6	7	7	7	10	17	==	==	==	–	–	–	–	–	–	–	–	–	–	–	TAKE A LITTLE TIP FROM FATHER
–	–	–	–	==	==	==	14	9	5	2	2	3	3	3	5	8	10	15	16	16	18	18	==	==	==	–	–	–	–	OH! YOU CIRCUS DAY
–	–	–	–	–	–	==	==	==	==	==	20	==	==	==	==	–	–	–	–	–	–	–	–	–	–	–	–	–	–	NATIONAL EMBLEM MARCH
–	–	–	–	–	–	==	==	==	==	==	16	17	13	11	13	18	==	==	20	==	==	19	18	17	17	==	==	==	==	WAY DOWN SOUTH
–	–	–	–	–	–	–	–	==	==	==	15	12	11	14	14	13	17	17	18	==	==	==	==	–	–	–	–	–	–	KENTUCKY DAYS
–	–	–	–	–	–	–	–	==	==	10	4	2	1	1	1	1	1	1	1	2	4	5	5	6	7	9	11	15	==	WAITING FOR THE ROBERT E. LEE
–	–	–	–	–	–	–	–	–	==	==	17	18	16	12	12	15	12	12	13	15	15	14	16	==	==	–	–	–	–	RAGTIME COWBOY JOE
–	–	–	–	–	–	–	–	–	==	==	19	14	10	8	9	12	15	==	==	==	–	–	–	–	–	–	–	–	–	DREAMS OF LONG AGO
–	–	–	–	–	–	–	–	–	–	==	==	==	20	20	18	20	==	==	==	==	==	–	–	–	–	–	–	–	–	SPIRIT OF INDEPENDENCE
–	–	–	–	–	–	–	–	–	–	==	==	15	12	9	10	14	19	==	==	==	–	–	–	–	–	–	–	–	–	I LOVE YOU TRULY
–	–	–	–	–	–	–	–	–	–	==	==	13	8	5	3	2	2	3	3	4	6	8	11	11	14	==	==	==	–	WHEN I GET YOU ALONE TONIGHT
–	–	–	–	–	–	–	–	–	–	–	–	==	==	19	11	9	13	19	19	==	==	–	–	–	–	–	–	–	–	WHEN YOU'RE AWAY
–	–	–	–	–	–	–	–	–	–	–	–	==	==	==	20	==	==	20	==	==	==	==	==	–	–	–	–	–	–	I'M THE LONESOMEST GAL IN TOWN
–	–	–	–	–	–	–	–	–	–	–	–	==	==	15	8	7	7	8	11	13	14	13	12	15	==	==	–	–	–	THAT MELLOW MELODY
–	–	–	–	–	–	–	–	–	–	–	==	==	15	7	7	4	5	7	9	11	12	12	13	18	20	==	==	–	–	YOU'RE MY BABY
–	–	–	–	–	–	–	–	–	–	–	–	==	==	==	16	16	14	13	14	14	16	15	15	20	==	19	19	==	==	ALL NIGHT LONG
–	–	–	–	–	–	–	–	–	–	–	==	==	14	6	6	3	3	2	2	1	1	2	2	4	4	6	10	18	==	THAT'S HOW I NEED YOU
–	–	–	–	–	–	–	–	–	–	–	–	–	–	==	==	10	6	4	4	6	5	6	10	12	15	==	==	–	–	HITCHY KOO
–	–	–	–	–	–	–	–	–	–	–	–	–	==	==	==	17	11	9	12	10	10	11	9	9	13	17	==	==	–	WHEN UNCLE JOE PLAYS A RAG ON HIS OLD BANJO
–	–	–	–	–	–	–	–	–	–	–	–	–	–	==	==	11	8	6	5	7	9	10	8	8	12	15	17	==	==	EVERYBODY TWO–STEP
–	–	–	–	–	–	–	–	–	–	–	–	–	–	–	–	==	==	14	10	9	11	17	==	==	–	–	–	–	–	THE GHOST OF THE VIOLIN
–	–	–	–	–	–	–	–	–	–	–	–	–	–	–	==	==	16	10	7	5	3	3	4	5	5	10	13	==	==	BE MY LITTLE BABY BUMBLE BEE (1913)
–	–	–	–	–	–	–	–	–	–	–	–	–	–	–	–	==	18	11	6	3	2	1	1	2	3	5	9	16	==	ON THE MISSISSIPPI (1913)
Ma	Ma	Ap	Ap	My	My	Jn	Jn	Jy	Jy	Ag	Ag	Sp	Sp	Oc	Oc	Nv	Nv	Dc	Dc	Ja	Ja	Fb	Fb	Ma	Ma	Ap	Ap	My	My	

1912						1913																								
Oc	Oc	Nv	Nv	Dc	Dc	Ja	Ja	Fb	Fb	Ma	Ma	Ap	Ap	My	My	Jn	Jn	Jy	Jy	Ag	Ag	Sp	Sp	Oc	Oc	Nv	Nv	Dc	Dc	
2	2	6	9	16	15	17	==	==	==	–	–	–	–	–	–	–	–	–	–	–	–	–	–	–	–	–	–	–	–	MOONLIGHT BAY (1912)
4	4	5	4	5	8	8	8	7	7	7	9	11	18	==	19	==	==	==	==	==	==	==	==	==	==	==	==	==	==	TILL THE SANDS OF THE DESERT GROW COLD (1912)
3	5	8	10	15	16	16	18	18	==	==	==	–	–	–	–	–	–	–	–	–	–	–	–	–	–	–	–	–	–	OH! YOU CIRCUS DAY (1912)
11	13	18	==	==	20	==	==	19	18	17	17	==	==	==	==	–	–	–	–	–	–	–	–	–	–	–	–	–	–	WAY DOWN SOUTH (1912)
1	**1**	**1**	**1**	**1**	**1**	2	4	5	5	6	7	9	11	15	==	==	==	–	–	–	–	–	–	–	–	–	–	–	–	WAITING FOR THE ROBERT E. LEE (1912)
5	3	2	2	3	3	4	6	8	11	11	14	==	==	==	–	–	–	–	–	–	–	–	–	–	–	–	–	–	–	WHEN I GET YOU ALONE TONIGHT (1912)
15	8	7	7	8	11	13	14	13	12	15	==	==	–	–	–	–	–	–	–	–	–	–	–	–	–	–	–	–	–	THAT MELLOW MELODY (1912)
7	7	4	5	7	9	11	12	12	13	18	20	==	==	–	–	–	–	–	–	–	–	–	–	–	–	–	–	–	–	YOU'RE MY BABY (1912)
==	16	16	14	13	14	14	16	15	15	20	==	19	19	==	==	==	–	–	–	–	–	–	–	–	–	–	–	–	–	ALL NIGHT LONG (1912)
6	6	3	3	2	2	**1**	**1**	2	2	4	4	6	10	18	==	==	==	–	–	–	–	–	–	–	–	–	–	–	–	THAT'S HOW I NEED YOU (1912)
11	11	16	12	12	13	15	15	14	16	==	==	–	–	–	–	–	–	–	–	–	–	–	–	–	–	–	–	–	–	RAGTIME COWBOY JOE (1912)
==	==	10	6	4	4	6	5	6	10	12	15	==	==	–	–	–	–	–	–	–	–	–	–	–	–	–	–	–	–	HITCHY KOO (1912)
==	==	17	11	9	12	10	10	11	9	9	13	17	==	==	–	–	–	–	–	–	–	–	–	–	–	–	–	–	–	WHEN UNCLE JOE PLAYS A RAG ON HIS OLD BANJO (1912)
==	==	11	8	6	5	7	9	10	8	8	12	15	17	==	==	–	–	–	–	–	–	–	–	–	–	–	–	–	–	EVERYBODY TWO–STEP (1912)
–	–	==	==	==	==	20	20	==	==	–	–	–	–	–	–	–	–	–	–	–	–	–	–	–	–	–	–	–	–	AFTER ALL THAT I'VE BEEN TO YOU (1912)
–	–	==	==	14	10	9	11	17	==	==	–	–	–	–	–	–	–	–	–	–	–	–	–	–	–	–	–	–	–	THE GHOST OF THE VIOLIN (1912)
==	==	==	==	==	==	==	==	==	==	==	==	20	==	==	==	==	==	20	19	==	==	==	==	==	==	==	==	==	==	== == == == 20 17 18 == == I HEAR YOU CALLING ME
–	==	==	16	10	7	5	3	3	4	5	5	10	13	==	==	–	–	–	–	–	–	–	–	–	–	–	–	–	–	BE MY LITTLE BABY BUMBLE BEE
–	–	==	18	11	6	3	2	**1**	**1**	2	3	5	9	16	==	==	==	–	–	–	–	–	–	–	–	–	–	–	–	ON THE MISSISSIPPI
–	–	–	–	==	==	==	19	20	==	==	==	–	–	–	–	–	–	–	–	–	–	–	–	–	–	–	–	–	–	OH! OH! DELPHINE
–	–	–	–	==	==	19	17	16	17	==	==	–	–	–	–	–	–	–	–	–	–	–	–	–	–	–	–	–	–	BAGDAD
–	–	–	–	==	==	18	13	9	6	3	2	3	5	10	16	==	==	–	–	–	–	–	–	–	–	–	–	–	–	THAT OLD GIRL OF MINE
–	–	–	–	==	==	12	7	4	3	**1**	**1**	**1**	**1**	3	3	5	6	12	14	19	==	==	==	==	==	==	==	–	–	ROW, ROW, ROW
–	–	–	–	–	–	–	==	==	14	10	8	8	6	6	9	15	==	==	==	–	–	–	–	–	–	–	–	–	–	AT THE DEVIL'S BALL
–	–	–	–	–	–	–	–	==	==	16	16	13	14	17	==	==	–	–	–	–	–	–	–	–	–	–	–	–	–	THEN I'LL STOP LOVING YOU
–	–	–	–	–	–	–	–	==	19	14	11	7	4	4	10	13	17	17	==	==	–	–	–	–	–	–	–	–	–	AND THE GREEN GRASS GREW ALL AROUND
–	–	–	–	–	–	–	–	==	==	==	19	18	==	==	==	–	–	–	–	–	–	–	–	–	–	–	–	–	–	DOWN IN DEAR OLD NEW ORLEANS
–	–	–	–	–	–	–	–	==	20	13	6	2	2	**1**	**1**	2	4	8	12	14	20	==	==	–	–	–	–	–	–	WHEN THE MIDNIGHT CHOO–CHOO LEAVES FOR ALABAM'
–	–	–	–	–	–	–	–	==	==	19	10	4	3	2	2	**1**	**1**	**1**	2	5	7	7	9	13	17	==	==	==	==	WHEN I LOST YOU
–	–	–	–	–	–	–	–	–	–	==	18	12	7	5	5	9	14	==	==	==	==	–	–	–	–	–	–	–	–	DADDY HAS A SWEETHEART, AND MOTHER IS HER NAME
–	–	–	–	–	–	–	–	–	–	==	==	14	8	7	8	8	12	14	17	20	==	==	==	–	–	–	–	–	–	SOME BOY
–	–	–	–	–	–	–	–	–	–	==	==	16	12	8	4	7	11	16	==	==	==	==	==	–	–	–	–	–	–	GOOD NIGHT, NURSE
–	–	–	–	–	–	–	–	–	–	==	==	==	==	19	17	17	18	15	15	17	19	19	==	==	18	20	18	18	16	19 == WHEN IRISH EYES ARE SMILING
Oc	Oc	Nv	Nv	Dc	Dc	Ja	Ja	Fb	Fb	Ma	Ma	Ap	Ap	My	My	Jn	Jn	Jy	Jy	Ag	Ag	Sp	Sp	Oc	Oc	Nv	Nv	Dc	Dc	

1913																		1914												
Ap	Ap	My	My	Jn	Jn	Jy	Jy	Ag	Ag	Sp	Sp	Oc	Oc	Nv	Nv	Dc	Dc	Ja	Ja	Fb	Fb	Ma	Ma	Ap	Ap	My	My	Jn	Jn	
==	==	20	18	==	20	18	18	16	16	12	12	10	8	6	7	8	9	11	11	12	14	17	19	==	==	==	==	==	==	LAST NIGHT WAS THE END OF THE WORLD
==	16	9	7	4	3	3	5	11	11	13	19	==	==	–	–	–	–	–	–	–	–	–	–	–	–	–	–	–	–	YOU'RE A GREAT BIG BLUE-EYED BABY
==	15	11	11	6	5	10	11	13	15	20	==	==	==	–	–	–	–	–	–	–	–	–	–	–	–	–	–	–	–	MELINDA'S WEDDING DAY
==	20	13	12	19	19	==	==	==	==	–	–	–	–	–	–	–	–	–	–	–	–	–	–	–	–	–	–	–	–	HERE COMES MY DADDY NOW
==	==	==	==	16	16	13	10	12	12	15	17	==	==	==	19	==	==	–	–	–	–	–	–	–	–	–	–	–	–	A LITTLE BUNCH OF SHAMROCKS
==	==	14	13	12	8	5	4	6	6	6	7	7	11	13	12	17	19	==	==	==	==	–	–	–	–	–	–	–	–	GOODBYE, BOYS
==	==	12	6	3	2	2	**1**	**1**	1	2	2	4	5	9	11	16	==	==	==	==	==	–	–	–	–	–	–	–	–	THE TRAIL OF THE THE LONESOME PINE
==	==	==	14	11	9	7	6	4	4	4	3	3	3	5	9	14	17	20	==	==	==	==	==	–	–	–	–	–	–	WHEN IT'S APPLE BLOSSOM TIME IN NORMANDY
–	==	==	15	10	7	4	3	2	3	5	6	11	16	==	==	==	–	–	–	–	–	–	–	–	–	–	–	–	–	IN MY HAREM
–	–	==	20	14	10	6	9	7	9	11	13	20	==	==	==	–	–	–	–	–	–	–	–	–	–	–	–	–	–	SNOOKEY OOKUMS
–	–	==	==	18	13	11	8	3	2	3	4	5	7	11	16	==	==	==	==	–	–	–	–	–	–	–	–	–	–	THE CURSE OF AN ACHING HEART
–	–	==	==	20	15	9	7	8	10	10	11	14	19	==	==	==	==	–	–	–	–	–	–	–	–	–	–	–	–	THE SPANIARD THE BLIGHTED MY LIFE
–	–	==	==	==	==	19	13	9	8	9	8	12	14	16	==	==	==	==	==	==	==	–	–	–	–	–	–	–	–	TO HAVE, TO HOLD, TO LOVE
–	–	==	==	==	==	==	20	15	14	16	20	==	==	==	==	==	==	==	==	==	==	==	==	–	–	–	–	–	–	SWEETHEARTS
–	–	==	==	==	==	==	==	==	18	18	18	19	==	==	==	==	==	==	==	==	==	==	==	==	–	–	–	–	–	SYMPATHY
–	–	–	–	==	==	==	==	18	13	14	15	17	==	==	==	==	==	–	–	–	–	–	–	–	–	–	–	–	–	BOBBIN' UP AND DOWN
–	–	–	–	–	==	==	16	10	5	**1**	**1**	**1**	**1**	**1**	**1**	2	2	4	6	9	12	13	==	==	==	–	–	–	–	YOU MADE ME LOVE YOU
–	–	–	–	–	–	==	==	==	==	==	==	==	==	==	==	20	15	18	19	19	19	==	==	==	==	==	==	==	==	SUNSHINE AND ROSES
–	–	–	–	–	–	–	–	==	==	17	10	8	10	14	==	==	==	–	–	–	–	–	–	–	–	–	–	–	–	IT TAKES A LITTLE RAIN WITH THE SUNSHINE TO MAKE THE WORLD GO 'ROUND
–	–	–	–	–	–	–	–	==	==	==	==	==	20	15	14	12	14	15	17	20	==	==	==	==	==	–	–	–	–	THE PULLMAN PORTERS ON PARADE
–	–	–	–	–	–	–	–	==	17	8	5	2	2	2	2	**1**	**1**	**1**	2	4	5	9	12	19	==	==	==	–	–	PEG O' MY HEART
–	–	–	–	–	–	–	–	==	==	==	==	==	15	12	10	9	10	13	15	17	18	==	==	==	==	==	==	==	==	MAMMY JINNY'S JUBILEE
–	–	–	–	–	–	–	–	–	==	==	14	9	6	4	4	5	5	7	9	16	==	==	–	–	–	–	–	–	–	SOMEBODY'S COMING TO MY HOUSE
–	–	–	–	–	–	–	–	–	–	==	==	16	12	8	6	7	8	8	12	18	==	==	–	–	–	–	–	–	–	ON THE OLD FALL RIVER LINE
–	–	–	–	–	–	–	–	–	–	==	==	==	==	17	13	13	12	12	13	14	17	==	==	==	==	–	–	–	–	OH, YOU MILLION DOLLAR DOLL
–	–	–	–	–	–	–	–	–	–	==	==	==	==	18	==	==	==	==	==	==	==	==	==	==	==	–	–	–	–	WE HAVE MUCH TO BE THANKFUL FOR
–	–	–	–	–	–	–	–	–	–	==	16	6	4	3	3	3	3	3	4	6	10	12	==	==	==	–	–	–	–	THAT INTERNATIONAL RAG
–	–	–	–	–	–	–	–	–	–	==	==	15	9	7	5	4	4	2	**1**	**1**	2	6	9	15	==	==	==	–	–	THERE'S A GIRL IN THE HEART OF MARYLAND
–	–	–	–	–	–	–	–	–	–	==	==	18	13	10	8	6	6	5	7	7	8	10	13	20	==	==	==	==	==	SAILING DOWN THE CHESAPEAKE BAY
–	–	–	–	–	–	–	–	–	–	–	–	==	==	==	==	19	18	==	==	–	–	–	–	–	–	–	–	–	–	YOU CAN'T STOP ME FROM LOVING YOU
–	–	–	–	–	–	–	–	–	–	–	–	==	==	==	17	11	11	10	10	10	15	==	==	==	==	–	–	–	–	YOU'VE GOT YOUR MOTHER'S BIG BLUE EYES
–	–	–	–	–	–	–	–	–	–	==	==	==	==	==	20	15	13	9	8	5	6	5	8	14	14	20	==	==	==	ISLE D'AMOUR (1914)
–	–	–	–	–	–	–	–	–	–	==	==	==	==	==	==	==	20	17	16	11	9	8	7	8	10	12	16	==	==	NIGHTS OF GLADNESS (1914)
–	–	–	–	–	–	–	–	–	–	–	–	==	==	19	15	10	7	6	3	3	3	2	4	9	15	==	==	==	==	WHERE DID YOU GET THAT GIRL? (1914)
Ap	Ap	My	My	Jn	Jn	Jy	Jy	Ag	Ag	Sp	Sp	Oc	Oc	Nv	Nv	Dc	Dc	Ja	Ja	Fb	Fb	Ma	Ma	Ap	Ap	My	My	Jn	Jn	

1913						1914																								
Oc	Oc	Nv	Nv	Dc	Dc	Ja	Ja	Fb	Fb	Ma	Ma	Ap	Ap	My	My	Jn	Jn	Jy	Jy	Ag	Ag	Sp	Sp	Oc	Oc	Nv	Nv	Dc	Dc	
==	==	==	==	==	==	==	==	==	==	20	17	18	==	==	==	==	==	==	==	==	==	==	==	==	==	==	==	==	==	I HEAR YOU CALLING ME (1913)
10	8	6	7	8	9	11	11	12	14	17	19	==	==	==	==	==	==	==	==	==	==	==	==	==	==	–	–	–	–	LAST NIGHT WAS THE END OF THE WORLD (1913)
==	18	20	18	18	16	19	==	==	==	==	==	==	==	==	==	==	==	==	==	==	==	==	==	==	==	==	==	==	==	WHEN IRISH EYES ARE SMILING (1913)
3	3	5	9	14	17	20	==	==	==	==	==	–	–	–	–	–	–	–	–	–	–	–	–	–	–	–	–	–	–	WHEN IT'S APPLE BLOSSOM TIME IN NORMANDY (1913)
1	**1**	**1**	**1**	2	2	4	6	9	12	13	==	==	==	–	–	–	–	–	–	–	–	–	–	–	–	–	–	–	–	YOU MADE ME LOVE YOU (1913)
==	==	==	==	20	15	18	19	19	19	==	==	==	==	==	==	==	==	==	==	==	==	–	–	–	–	–	–	–	–	SUNSHINE AND ROSES (1913)
==	20	15	14	12	14	15	17	20	==	==	==	==	==	–	–	–	–	–	–	–	–	–	–	–	–	–	–	–	–	THE PULLMAN PORTERS ON PARADE (1913)
2	2	2	2	**1**	**1**	**1**	2	4	5	9	12	19	==	==	==	–	–	–	–	–	–	–	–	–	–	–	–	–	–	PEG O' MY HEART (1913)
==	15	12	10	9	10	13	15	17	18	==	==	==	==	==	==	==	==	–	–	–	–	–	–	–	–	–	–	–	–	MAMMY JINNY'S JUBILEE (1913)
16	12	8	6	7	8	8	12	18	==	==	–	–	–	–	–	–	–	–	–	–	–	–	–	–	–	–	–	–	–	ON THE OLD FALL RIVER LINE (1913)
9	6	4	4	5	5	7	9	16	==	==	–	–	–	–	–	–	–	–	–	–	–	–	–	–	–	–	–	–	–	SOMEBODY'S COMING TO MY HOUSE (1913)
==	==	17	13	13	12	12	13	14	17	==	==	==	==	–	–	–	–	–	–	–	–	–	–	–	–	–	–	–	–	OH, YOU MILLION DOLLAR DOLL (1913)
6	4	3	3	3	3	3	4	6	10	12	==	==	==	–	–	–	–	–	–	–	–	–	–	–	–	–	–	–	–	THAT INTERNATIONAL RAG (1913)
15	9	7	5	4	4	2	**1**	**1**	2	6	9	15	==	==	==	–	–	–	–	–	–	–	–	–	–	–	–	–	–	THERE'S A GIRL IN THE HEART OF MARYLAND (1913)
18	13	10	8	6	6	5	7	7	8	10	13	20	==	==	==	==	==	–	–	–	–	–	–	–	–	–	–	–	–	SAILING DOWN THE CHESAPEAKE BAY (1913)
==	==	==	17	11	11	10	10	10	15	==	==	==	==	–	–	–	–	–	–	–	–	–	–	–	–	–	–	–	–	YOU'VE GOT YOUR MOTHER'S BIG BLUE EYES (1913)
==	==	==	==	==	==	==	==	==	20	18	18	==	18	==	==	==	==	==	==	==	==	==	==	==	==	==	==	==	==	A LITTLE LOVE, A LITTLE KISS
==	==	==	==	==	==	==	==	==	==	==	==	==	==	==	==	==	==	==	==	==	==	==	==	20	18	17	20	==	==	18 == == 20 == == THE MEMPHIS BLUES
==	==	==	20	15	13	9	8	5	6	5	8	14	14	20	==	==	==	–	–	–	–	–	–	–	–	–	–	–	–	ISLE D'AMOUR
==	==	==	==	==	20	17	16	11	9	8	7	8	10	12	16	==	==	–	–	–	–	–	–	–	–	–	–	–	–	NIGHTS OF GLADNESS
==	==	==	==	==	==	==	20	==	16	14	10	11	12	11	14	16	19	==	==	==	==	==	==	==	==	==	==	==	==	TOO-RA LOO-RA LOO-RAL
==	==	19	15	10	7	6	3	3	3	2	4	9	15	==	==	==	==	–	–	–	–	–	–	–	–	–	–	–	–	WHERE DID YOU GET THAT GIRL?
–	–	==	==	==	==	16	14	13	11	15	20	==	19	==	==	–	–	–	–	–	–	–	–	–	–	–	–	–	–	DON'T BLAME IT ALL ON BROADWAY
–	–	–	–	==	==	14	5	2	**1**	**1**	**1**	**1**	2	3	6	6	9	13	==	==	==	–	–	–	–	–	–	–	–	HE'D HAVE TO GET UNDER, GET OUT AND GET UNDER, TO FIX UP HIS AUTOMOBILE
–	–	–	–	==	==	==	==	==	==	16	16	17	16	17	18	==	==	==	==	==	==	==	==	–	–	–	–	–	–	SIT DOWN, YOU'RE ROCKING THE BOAT
–	–	–	–	==	==	==	==	==	==	==	==	16	13	10	10	12	12	15	16	==	==	==	==	==	==	==	==	==	==	LITTLE GREY HOME IN THE WEST
–	–	–	–	–	==	==	18	8	4	4	3	6	11	14	==	==	–	–	–	–	–	–	–	–	–	–	–	–	–	I MISS YOU MOST OF ALL
–	–	–	–	–	–	==	==	15	7	3	2	2	4	4	3	4	5	9	13	15	==	==	==	==	–	–	–	–	–	I'M ON MY WAY TO MANDALAY
–	–	–	–	–	–	==	==	==	13	7	5	4	6	9	13	19	==	==	–	–	–	–	–	–	–	–	–	–	–	DO YOU TAKE THIS WOMAN
–	–	–	–	–	–	==	==	==	==	==	==	==	20	==	==	==	==	==	==	==	==	==	==	==	==	==	==	==	==	SOMEWHERE A VOICE IS CALLING
–	–	–	–	–	–	–	–	==	==	19	11	7	5	7	9	17	==	==	==	–	–	–	–	–	–	–	–	–	–	WHILE THEY WERE DANCING AROUND
–	–	–	–	–	–	–	–	==	==	11	6	3	**1**	**1**	**1**	2	3	4	5	8	13	18	==	==	==	–	–	–	–	REBECCA OF SUNNYBROOK FARM
–	–	–	–	–	–	–	–	==	==	==	15	10	7	8	7	8	11	16	17	==	==	–	–	–	–	–	–	–	–	ON THE GOOD SHIP MARY ANN
–	–	–	–	–	–	–	–	–	–	==	==	==	17	19	==	==	==	==	==	–	–	–	–	–	–	–	–	–	–	SARI WALTZ
–	–	–	–	–	–	–	–	–	–	==	==	13	9	5	4	3	2	5	7	12	==	==	–	–	–	–	–	–	–	HE'S A DEVIL IN HIS OWN HOME TOWN
–	–	–	–	–	–	–	–	–	–	==	14	5	3	2	2	**1**	**1**	**1**	3	3	6	12	15	==	==	–	–	–	–	THIS IS THE LIFE
–	–	–	–	–	–	–	–	–	–	==	==	==	==	==	17	13	16	14	15	20	==	==	==	==	==	–	–	–	–	IF I HAD MY WAY
–	–	–	–	–	–	–	–	–	–	==	==	12	8	6	5	5	4	3	4	7	11	16	16	==	==	–	–	–	–	ALL ABOARD FOR DIXIE LAND
Oc	Oc	Nv	Nv	Dc	Dc	Ja	Ja	Fb	Fb	Ma	Ma	Ap	Ap	My	My	Jn	Jn	Jy	Jy	Ag	Ag	Sp	Sp	Oc	Oc	Nv	Nv	Dc	Dc	

							1914																1915							
Ap	Ap	My	My	Jn	Jn	Jy	Jy	Ag	Ag	Sp	Sp	Oc	Oc	Nv	Nv	Dc	Dc	Ja	Ja	Fb	Fb	Ma	Ma	Ap	Ap	My	My	Jn	Jn	
==	==	==	19	18	18	20	==	==	==	==	==	==	==	–	–	–	–	–	–	–	–	–	–	–	–	–	–	–	–	CAMP MEETING BAND
==	==	==	20	20	17	19	20	==	==	==	==	==	==	==	==	–	–	–	–	–	–	–	–	–	–	–	–	–	–	IN THE CANDELELIGHT
==	==	==	==	==	20	==	==	==	==	==	==	==	==	–	–	–	–	–	–	–	–	–	–	–	–	–	–	–	–	I'LL DO IT ALL OVER AGAIN
==	==	13	8	7	6	6	6	9	15	==	==	–	–	–	–	–	–	–	–	–	–	–	–	–	–	–	–	–	–	WHO PAID THE RENT FOR MRS. RIP VAN WINKLE?
==	==	15	11	9	8	10	8	11	14	17	17	==	==	–	–	–	–	–	–	–	–	–	–	–	–	–	–	–	–	WHEN THE ANGELUS IS RINGING
==	==	16	12	10	10	8	9	10	7	13	14	15	==	==	==	==	==	–	–	–	–	–	–	–	–	–	–	–	–	MARY, YOU'RE A LITTLE BIT OLD FASHIONED
==	==	18	15	11	7	2	**1**	2	3	4	7	10	12	19	==	==	==	–	–	–	–	–	–	–	–	–	–	–	–	I LOVE THE LADIES
==	==	==	==	15	15	12	14	14	8	9	12	13	16	==	==	==	==	–	–	–	–	–	–	–	–	–	–	–	–	YOU PLANTED A ROSE IN THE GARDEN OF LOVE
==	==	==	==	==	==	==	19	19	19	19	==	==	==	==	==	==	==	==	==	–	–	–	–	–	–	–	–	–	–	LOVE'S OWN SWEET SONG
==	==	==	==	==	==	==	18	18	20	20	==	17	17	==	==	==	==	20	==	==	==	–	–	–	–	–	–	–	–	MOTHER MACHREE
–	–	==	==	14	14	11	10	6	5	6	10	12	14	==	==	==	==	–	–	–	–	–	–	–	–	–	–	–	–	WHEN YOU'RE ALL DRESSED UP AND NO PLACE TO GO
–	–	–	==	==	13	7	2	**1**	**1**	**1**	**1**	**1**	3	5	10	15	==	==	–	–	–	–	–	–	–	–	–	–	–	BY THE BEAUTIFUL SEA
–	–	–	–	==	==	17	12	5	4	3	4	6	9	7	11	12	14	17	==	==	==	–	–	–	–	–	–	–	–	YOU'RE HERE AND I'M HERE
–	–	–	–	==	==	==	19	13	9	8	9	8	10	14	14	20	==	==	–	–	–	–	–	–	–	–	–	–	–	ROLL THEM COTTON BALES
–	–	–	–	–	–	==	==	==	==	==	==	19	20	==	==	==	–	–	–	–	–	–	–	–	–	–	–	–	–	FIDO IS A HOT DOG NOW
–	–	–	–	==	==	18	11	4	2	2	2	2	5	10	15	==	==	==	==	–	–	–	–	–	–	–	–	–	–	WHEN YOU PLAY IN THE GAME OF LOVE
–	–	–	–	–	==	==	==	17	12	7	6	5	7	6	6	11	13	16	20	==	==	–	–	–	–	–	–	–	–	CALIFORNIA AND YOU
–	–	–	–	–	–	==	==	==	17	11	8	7	8	8	13	16	16	==	==	–	–	–	–	–	–	–	–	–	–	WHEN IT'S NIGHT TIME DOWN IN BURGUNDY
–	–	–	–	–	–	==	==	==	18	15	11	14	15	18	==	==	==	==	==	==	==	–	–	–	–	–	–	–	–	COHEN ON THE TELEPHONE
–	–	–	–	–	–	==	==	16	10	5	3	3	2	**1**	**1**	3	5	11	15	==	==	==	==	–	–	–	–	–	–	BALLIN' THE JACK
–	–	–	–	–	–	==	==	==	16	14	13	9	4	4	4	6	6	8	10	14	16	20	==	==	==	==	==	–	–	CAN'T YOU HEAR ME CALLING, CAROLINE?
–	–	–	–	–	–	–	–	==	==	10	5	4	**1**	2	3	7	10	13	16	==	==	==	==	–	–	–	–	–	–	ABA DABA HONEYMOON
–	–	–	–	–	–	–	–	–	–	==	==	16	11	11	18	19	==	==	==	–	–	–	–	–	–	–	–	–	–	MY CROONY MELODY
–	–	–	–	–	–	–	–	–	–	==	==	18	13	9	8	8	7	7	9	15	==	==	–	–	–	–	–	–	–	POOR PAULINE
–	–	–	–	–	–	–	–	–	–	==	18	11	6	3	2	**1**	3	3	4	4	4	6	11	17	==	==	==	–	–	WHEN YOU'RE A LONG, LONG WAY FROM HOME
–	–	–	–	–	–	–	–	–	–	–	–	==	==	==	19	17	20	==	==	==	==	==	20	19	==	==	==	–	–	THEY ALL HAD A FINGER IN THE PIE
–	–	–	–	–	–	–	–	–	–	–	–	==	==	20	16	13	12	10	12	19	==	==	–	–	–	–	–	–	–	HE'S A RAG PICKER
–	–	–	–	–	–	–	–	–	–	–	–	==	19	12	5	2	**1**	**1**	3	3	6	14	==	==	–	–	–	–	–	I WANT TO GO BACK TO MICHIGAN (DOWN ON THE FARM)
–	–	–	–	–	–	–	–	–	–	–	–	==	==	16	12	9	8	6	8	13	18	==	==	==	==	–	–	–	–	AT A MISSISSIPPI CABARET
–	–	–	–	–	–	–	–	–	–	–	–	==	==	13	7	4	4	4	2	2	3	3	7	9	11	16	==	==	==	WHEN YOU WORE A TULIP (1915)
–	–	–	–	–	–	–	–	–	–	–	–	==	==	15	9	5	2	2	**1**	**1**	**1**	2	3	5	8	9	10	11	17	IT'S A LONG, LONG WAY TO TIPPERARY (1915)
–	–	–	–	–	–	–	–	–	–	–	–	–	–	==	==	==	19	19	17	16	17	18	==	==	==	–	–	–	–	WHEN THE GROWN UP LADIES ACT LIKE BABIES (1915)
–	–	–	–	–	–	–	–	–	–	–	–	–	–	==	==	14	11	9	7	8	13	17	==	==	==	–	–	–	–	BACK TO THE CAROLINA YOU LOVE (1915)
–	–	–	–	–	–	–	–	–	–	–	–	–	==	==	17	10	9	5	5	7	9	10	16	16	==	==	–	–	–	YOU'RE MORE THAN THE WORLD TO ME (1915)
–	–	–	–	–	–	–	–	–	–	–	–	–	–	==	==	18	15	15	13	12	11	15	15	==	==	==	==	–	–	TIP TOP TIPPERARY MARY (1915)
–	–	–	–	–	–	–	–	–	–	–	–	–	–	–	–	==	18	14	11	9	10	9	10	12	14	15	16	==	==	SISTER SUSIE'S SEWING SHIRTS FOR SOLDIERS (1915)
–	–	–	–	–	–	–	–	–	–	–	–	–	–	–	–	==	17	12	6	6	5	7	6	10	10	10	14	19	==	CHINATOWN, MY CHINATOWN (1915)
Ap	Ap	My	My	Jn	Jn	Jy	Jy	Ag	Ag	Sp	Sp	Oc	Oc	Nv	Nv	Dc	Dc	Ja	Ja	Fb	Fb	Ma	Ma	Ap	Ap	My	My	Jn	Jn	

1 9 1 4																	1 9 1 5													
Oc	Oc	Nv	Nv	Dc	Dc	Ja	Ja	Fb	Fb	Ma	Ma	Ap	Ap	My	My	Jn	Jn	Jy	Jy	Ag	Ag	Sp	Sp	Oc	Oc	Nv	Nv	Dc	Dc	
20	18	17	20	==	==	18	==	==	20	==	==	==	==	==	==	==	==	==	==	19	==	==	==	==	==	==	==	==	==	THE MEMPHIS BLUES (1914)
17	17	==	==	==	==	20	==	==	==	–	–	–	–	–	–	–	–	–	–	–	–	–	–	–	–	–	–	–	–	MOTHER MACHREE (1914)
6	9	7	11	12	14	17	==	==	==	–	–	–	–	–	–	–	–	–	–	–	–	–	–	–	–	–	–	–	–	YOU'RE HERE AND I'M HERE (1914)
5	7	6	6	11	13	16	20	==	==	–	–	–	–	–	–	–	–	–	–	–	–	–	–	–	–	–	–	–	–	CALIFORNIA AND YOU (1914)
3	2	**1**	**1**	3	5	11	15	==	==	==	==	–	–	–	–	–	–	–	–	–	–	–	–	–	–	–	–	–	–	BALLIN' THE JACK (1914)
9	4	4	4	6	6	8	10	14	16	20	==	==	==	==	==	–	–	–	–	–	–	–	–	–	–	–	–	–	–	CAN'T YOU HEAR ME CALLING, CAROLINE? (1914)
4	**1**	2	3	7	10	13	16	==	==	==	==	–	–	–	–	–	–	–	–	–	–	–	–	–	–	–	–	–	–	ABA DABA HONEYMOON (1914)
18	13	9	8	8	7	7	9	15	==	==	–	–	–	–	–	–	–	–	–	–	–	–	–	–	–	–	–	–	–	POOR PAULINE (1914)
11	6	3	2	**1**	3	3	4	4	4	6	11	17	==	==	==	–	–	–	–	–	–	–	–	–	–	–	–	–	–	WHEN YOU'RE A LONG, LONG WAY FROM HOME (1914)
==	==	==	19	17	20	==	==	==	==	==	20	19	==	==	==	–	–	–	–	–	–	–	–	–	–	–	–	–	–	THEY ALL HAD A FINGER IN THE PIE (1914)
==	==	20	16	13	12	10	12	19	==	–	–	–	–	–	–	–	–	–	–	–	–	–	–	–	–	–	–	–	–	HE'S A RAG PICKER (1914)
==	19	12	5	2	**1**	**1**	3	3	6	14	==	==	–	–	–	–	–	–	–	–	–	–	–	–	–	–	–	–	–	I WANT TO GO BACK TO MICHIGAN (1914)
==	==	16	12	9	8	6	8	13	18	==	==	==	==	–	–	–	–	–	–	–	–	–	–	–	–	–	–	–	–	AT A MISSISSIPPI CABARET (1914)
==	==	13	7	4	4	4	2	2	3	3	7	9	11	16	==	==	==	–	–	–	–	–	–	–	–	–	–	–	–	WHEN YOU WORE A TULIP
==	==	15	9	5	2	2	**1**	**1**	**1**	2	3	5	8	9	10	11	17	19	==	==	–	–	–	–	–	–	–	–	–	IT'S A LONG, LONG WAY TO TIPPERARY
–	==	==	17	10	9	5	5	7	9	10	16	16	==	==	–	–	–	–	–	–	–	–	–	–	–	–	–	–	–	YOU'RE MORE THAN THE WORLD TO ME
–	–	==	==	==	19	19	17	16	17	18	==	==	==	–	–	–	–	–	–	–	–	–	–	–	–	–	–	–	–	WHEN THE GROWN UP LADIES ACT LIKE BABIES
–	–	==	==	14	11	9	7	8	13	17	==	==	==	–	–	–	–	–	–	–	–	–	–	–	–	–	–	–	–	BACK TO THE CAROLINA YOU LOVE
–	–	==	==	18	15	15	13	12	11	15	15	==	==	==	==	–	–	–	–	–	–	–	–	–	–	–	–	–	–	TIP TOP TIPPERARY MARY
–	–	–	–	==	18	14	11	9	10	9	10	12	14	15	16	==	==	–	–	–	–	–	–	–	–	–	–	–	–	SISTER SUSIE'S SEWING SHIRTS FOR SOLDIERS
–	–	–	–	==	17	12	6	6	5	7	6	10	10	10	14	19	==	–	–	–	–	–	–	–	–	–	–	–	–	CHINATOWN, MY CHINATOWN
–	–	–	–	==	==	==	==	20	15	12	14	15	19	20	==	==	==	–	–	–	–	–	–	–	–	–	–	–	–	AFTER THE ROSES HAVE FADED AWAY
–	–	–	–	==	==	==	==	==	==	19	17	13	12	11	13	15	16	20	==	==	==	–	–	–	–	–	–	–	–	EVERYBODY RAG WITH ME
–	–	–	–	–	–	==	==	18	14	11	8	7	5	4	4	4	4	4	5	8	9	13	18	==	==	==	–	–	–	DOWN AMONG THE SHELTERING PALMS
–	–	–	–	–	–	==	18	10	7	5	2	3	4	7	8	14	==	==	–	–	–	–	–	–	–	–	–	–	–	ON THE 5:15
–	–	–	–	–	–	==	14	5	2	**1**	**1**	**1**	**1**	2	3	3	5	8	15	==	==	–	–	–	–	–	–	–	–	I DIDN'T RAISE MY BOY TO BE A SOLDIER
–	–	–	–	–	–	==	==	==	==	==	==	20	15	19	==	==	==	==	==	–	–	–	–	–	–	–	–	–	–	THE SONG OF SONGS
–	–	–	–	–	–	==	19	11	8	4	4	4	6	6	6	7	10	15	20	==	==	–	–	–	–	–	–	–	–	GOODBYE, GIRLS, I'M THROUGH
–	–	–	–	–	–	==	==	==	==	==	19	14	13	12	12	13	18	16	==	==	==	==	==	–	–	–	–	–	–	SWEET KENTUCKY LADY
–	–	–	–	–	–	==	==	==	==	==	==	==	==	17	15	9	12	10	9	9	11	14	13	15	18	20	==	==	==	WHEN YOU'RE AWAY
–	–	–	–	–	–	==	==	17	12	8	5	2	2	**1**	**1**	**1**	**1**	2	2	**1**	**1**	2	3	4	5	6	9	10	10	13 12 18 == A LITTLE BIT OF HEAVEN
–	–	–	–	–	–	–	–	==	==	==	==	==	20	==	==	==	==	–	–	–	–	–	–	–	–	–	–	–	–	WHEN IT'S NIGHT TIME IN DIXIE LAND
–	–	–	–	–	–	–	–	==	==	==	==	==	17	18	17	==	20	==	==	–	–	–	–	–	–	–	–	–	–	WHEN MY SHIP COMES IN
–	–	–	–	–	–	–	–	==	19	13	9	6	3	3	2	2	3	6	8	12	20	==	==	–	–	–	–	–	–	THERE'S A LITTLE SPARK OF LOVE STILL BURNING
–	–	–	–	–	–	–	–	==	==	==	13	11	9	8	7	8	8	13	16	17	==	==	–	–	–	–	–	–	–	THE LITTLE HOUSE UPON THE HILL
–	–	–	–	–	–	–	–	==	==	16	12	8	7	5	5	6	7	11	11	16	==	==	–	–	–	–	–	–	–	BY HECK
–	–	–	–	–	–	–	–	==	==	==	18	18	16	13	11	12	14	12	12	14	12	16	19	18	20	==	==	==	==	CARRY ME BACK TO OLD VIRGINNY
–	–	–	–	–	–	–	–	–	–	==	==	==	18	==	19	==	==	==	==	==	–	–	–	–	–	–	–	–	–	SYNCOPATED WALK
Oc	Oc	Nv	Nv	Dc	Dc	Ja	Ja	Fb	Fb	Ma	Ma	Ap	Ap	My	My	Jn	Jn	Jy	Jy	Ag	Ag	Sp	Sp	Oc	Oc	Nv	Nv	Dc	Dc	

								1 9 1 5														1 9 1 6								
Ap	Ap	My	My	Jn	Jn	Jy	Jy	Ag	Ag	Sp	Sp	Oc	Oc	Nv	Nv	Dc	Dc	Ja	Ja	Fb	Fb	Ma	Ma	Ap	Ap	My	My	Jn	Jn	
==	==	==	20	20	19	17	==	==	==	–	–	–	–	–	–	–	–	–	–	–	–	–	–	–	–	–	–	–	–	PLAY A SIMPLE MELODY
==	==	==	==	==	15	14	10	11	13	18	==	==	==	–	–	–	–	–	–	–	–	–	–	–	–	–	–	–	–	SHADOWLAND
==	==	14	9	5	2	**1**	**1**	4	6	10	12	17	==	==	–	–	–	–	–	–	–	–	–	–	–	–	–	–	–	I'M ON MY WAY TO DUBLIN BAY
–	–	==	18	10	6	3	3	3	5	9	11	14	==	==	–	–	–	–	–	–	–	–	–	–	–	–	–	–	–	MY BIRD OF PARADISE
–	–	==	==	18	13	9	7	6	8	12	16	16	13	19	==	==	==	–	–	–	–	–	–	–	–	–	–	–	–	WHEN I WAS A DREAMER (AND YOU WERE MY DREAM)
–	–	==	==	17	11	7	6	5	3	4	7	11	15	==	==	==	==	–	–	–	–	–	–	–	–	–	–	–	–	ALABAMA JUBILEE
–	–	==	==	16	9	5	4	2	2	**1**	2	5	8	12	15	20	==	==	==	–	–	–	–	–	–	–	–	–	–	MY LITTLE DREAM GIRL
–	–	–	–	==	==	==	19	20	19	==	==	–	–	–	–	–	–	–	–	–	–	–	–	–	–	–	–	–	–	THE MAGIC MELODY
–	–	–	–	==	==	18	17	15	17	==	==	–	–	–	–	–	–	–	–	–	–	–	–	–	–	–	–	–	–	YOU KNOW AND I KNOW (AND WE BOTH UNDERSTAND)
–	–	–	–	==	==	==	18	18	18	20	==	==	==	–	–	–	–	–	–	–	–	–	–	–	–	–	–	–	–	RAILROAD JIM
–	–	–	–	–	==	==	14	10	7	5	9	10	12	18	==	==	–	–	–	–	–	–	–	–	–	–	–	–	–	IF WE CAN'T BE THE SAME OLD SWEETHEARTS
–	–	–	–	–	==	==	13	7	4	3	**1**	**1**	3	5	4	7	9	17	20	==	==	==	==	–	–	–	–	–	–	WHEN I LEAVE THE WORLD BEHIND
–	–	–	–	–	–	==	==	13	10	6	6	9	9	15	==	==	==	–	–	–	–	–	–	–	–	–	–	–	–	MY LITTLE GIRL
–	–	–	–	–	–	–	==	==	16	11	8	6	4	**1**	**1**	3	3	6	8	15	==	==	==	==	==	–	–	–	–	IT'S TULIP TIME IN HOLLAND
–	–	–	–	–	–	–	–	==	15	8	5	3	2	3	7	12	18	==	==	–	–	–	–	–	–	–	–	–	–	DOWN IN BOM-BOMBAY
–	–	–	–	–	–	–	–	==	14	7	4	2	**1**	2	3	9	13	19	==	==	–	–	–	–	–	–	–	–	–	HELLO, FRISCO!
–	–	–	–	–	–	–	–	==	==	17	15	13	11	11	13	11	8	8	9	7	10	13	17	==	==	==	==	==	==	YOU'LL ALWAYS BE THE SAME SWEET GIRL
–	–	–	–	–	–	–	–	==	==	19	20	20	==	==	==	==	==	–	–	–	–	–	–	–	–	–	–	–	–	UNDER THE AMERICAN FLAG
–	–	–	–	–	–	–	–	–	==	15	10	8	7	7	14	16	==	==	–	–	–	–	–	–	–	–	–	–	–	RAGGING THE SCALE
–	–	–	–	–	–	–	–	–	==	==	14	7	6	4	2	**1**	2	4	6	13	18	==	==	–	–	–	–	–	–	MY SWEET ADAIR
–	–	–	–	–	–	–	–	–	==	==	17	12	10	9	10	8	7	14	18	==	==	==	==	==	–	–	–	–	–	CLOSE TO MY HEART
–	–	–	–	–	–	–	–	–	–	==	==	19	17	17	18	18	20	==	==	==	==	–	–	–	–	–	–	–	–	NORWAY
–	–	–	–	–	–	–	–	–	–	==	==	==	19	13	12	17	==	==	==	–	–	–	–	–	–	–	–	–	–	THAT'S THE SONG OF SONGS FOR ME
–	–	–	–	–	–	–	–	–	–	–	==	==	==	19	==	==	==	==	–	–	–	–	–	–	–	–	–	–	–	PUT ME TO SLEEP WITH AN OLD FASHIONED MELODY
–	–	–	–	–	–	–	–	–	–	–	==	==	14	8	5	5	6	9	16	==	==	–	–	–	–	–	–	–	–	THERE'S A LITTLE LANE WITHOUT A TURNING ON THE WAY TO HOME SWEET HOME
–	–	–	–	–	–	–	–	–	–	–	–	==	==	==	20	19	16	16	15	19	==	==	==	–	–	–	–	–	–	WHEN OLD BILL BAILEY PLAYS THE UKULELE
–	–	–	–	–	–	–	–	–	–	–	–	==	==	==	17	14	17	==	==	==	==	–	–	–	–	–	–	–	–	LOVE, HERE IS MY HEART
–	–	–	–	–	–	–	–	–	–	–	–	==	==	==	16	13	11	15	17	20	==	==	==	==	==	–	–	–	–	THE LITTLE GREY MOTHER
–	–	–	–	–	–	–	–	–	–	–	–	==	16	10	6	2	**1**	**1**	**1**	5	7	7	11	15	19	==	==	–	–	BACK HOME IN TENNESSEE
–	–	–	–	–	–	–	–	–	–	–	–	==	==	16	11	6	5	3	5	6	11	15	19	==	==	==	==	–	–	AUF WIEDERSEH'N
–	–	–	–	–	–	–	–	–	–	–	–	–	==	==	==	==	20	==	==	==	–	–	–	–	–	–	–	–	–	PINEY RIDGE
–	–	–	–	–	–	–	–	–	–	–	–	==	==	14	8	4	4	2	3	3	4	9	12	13	18	==	==	–	–	AMERICA, I LOVE YOU (1916)
–	–	–	–	–	–	–	–	–	–	–	–	–	==	==	15	15	11	10	12	14	20	==	==	==	–	–	–	–	–	I'VE BEEN FLOATING DOWN THE OLD GREEN RIVER (1916)
–	–	–	–	–	–	–	–	–	–	–	–	–	==	==	==	19	12	11	8	12	16	18	==	==	==	==	–	–	–	MOLLY DEAR, IT'S YOU I'M AFTER (1916)
–	–	–	–	–	–	–	–	–	–	–	–	–	–	==	==	14	7	4	2	3	5	9	14	==	==	–	–	–	–	ALONG THE ROCKY ROAD TO DUBLIN (1916)
–	–	–	–	–	–	–	–	–	–	–	–	–	–	–	–	==	12	5	2	**1**	**1**	**1**	**1**	3	5	7	9	16	==	M-O-T-H-E-R (1916)
Ap	Ap	My	My	Jn	Jn	Jy	Jy	Ag	Ag	Sp	Sp	Oc	Oc	Nv	Nv	Dc	Dc	Ja	Ja	Fb	Fb	Ma	Ma	Ap	Ap	My	My	Jn	Jn	

1915						1916																								
Oc	Oc	Nv	Nv	Dc	Dc	Ja	Ja	Fb	Fb	Ma	Ma	Ap	Ap	My	My	Jn	Jn	Jy	Jy	Ag	Ag	Sp	Sp	Oc	Oc	Nv	Nv	Dc	Dc	
4	5	6	9	10	10	13	12	18	==	==	==	==	==	==	==	==	==	–	–	–	–	–	–	–	–	–	–	–	–	A LITTLE BIT OF HEAVEN (1915)
1	3	5	4	7	9	17	20	==	==	==	==	–	–	–	–	–	–	–	–	–	–	–	–	–	–	–	–	–	–	WHEN I LEAVE THE WORLD BEHIND (1915)
2	**1**	2	3	9	13	19	==	==	–	–	–	–	–	–	–	–	–	–	–	–	–	–	–	–	–	–	–	–	–	HELLO, FRISCO! (1915)
6	4	**1**	**1**	3	3	6	8	15	==	==	==	==	==	–	–	–	–	–	–	–	–	–	–	–	–	–	–	–	–	IT'S TULIP TIME IN HOLLAND (1915)
13	11	11	13	11	8	8	9	7	10	13	17	==	==	==	==	==	==	–	–	–	–	–	–	–	–	–	–	–	–	YOU'LL ALWAYS BE THE SAME SWEET GIRL (1915)
7	6	4	2	**1**	2	4	6	13	18	==	==	–	–	–	–	–	–	–	–	–	–	–	–	–	–	–	–	–	–	MY SWEET ADAIR (1915)
12	10	9	10	8	7	14	18	==	==	==	==	==	–	–	–	–	–	–	–	–	–	–	–	–	–	–	–	–	–	CLOSE TO MY HEART (1915)
==	14	8	5	5	6	9	16	==	==	–	–	–	–	–	–	–	–	–	–	–	–	–	–	–	–	–	–	–	–	THERE'S A LITTLE LANE WITHOUT A TURNING ON THE WAY TO HOME SWEET HOME (1915)
==	==	==	20	19	16	16	15	19	==	==	==	–	–	–	–	–	–	–	–	–	–	–	–	–	–	–	–	–	–	WHEN OLD BILL BAILEY PLAYS THE UKULELE (1915)
==	==	==	16	13	11	15	17	20	==	==	==	==	==	–	–	–	–	–	–	–	–	–	–	–	–	–	–	–	–	THE LITTLE GREY MOTHER (1915)
==	16	10	6	2	**1**	**1**	**1**	5	7	7	11	15	19	==	==	–	–	–	–	–	–	–	–	–	–	–	–	–	–	BACK HOME IN TENNESSEE (1915)
==	==	16	11	6	5	3	5	6	11	15	19	==	==	==	==	–	–	–	–	–	–	–	–	–	–	–	–	–	–	AUF WIEDERSEH'N (1915)
–	–	==	==	==	==	20	==	==	==	–	–	–	–	–	–	–	–	–	–	–	–	–	–	–	–	–	–	–	–	PINEY RIDGE (1915)
==	==	14	8	4	4	2	3	3	4	9	12	13	18	==	==	–	–	–	–	–	–	–	–	–	–	–	–	–	–	AMERICA, I LOVE YOU
–	–	==	==	==	==	18	13	16	15	19	==	==	==	–	–	–	–	–	–	–	–	–	–	–	–	–	–	–	–	ARABY
–	–	==	==	15	15	11	10	12	14	20	==	==	==	–	–	–	–	–	–	–	–	–	–	–	–	–	–	–	–	I'VE BEEN FLOATING DOWN THE OLD GREEN RIVER
–	–	==	==	==	19	12	11	8	12	16	18	==	==	==	==	–	–	–	–	–	–	–	–	–	–	–	–	–	–	MOLLY DEAR, IT'S YOU I'M AFTER
–	–	–	==	==	14	7	4	2	3	5	9	14	==	==	–	–	–	–	–	–	–	–	–	–	–	–	–	–	–	ALONG THE ROCKY ROAD TO DUBLIN
–	–	–	–	==	12	5	2	**1**	**1**	**1**	**1**	3	5	7	9	16	==	–	–	–	–	–	–	–	–	–	–	–	–	M-O-T-H-E-R
–	–	–	–	==	==	==	14	11	8	8	7	8	11	17	==	==	==	–	–	–	–	–	–	–	–	–	–	–	–	SHE'S THE DAUGHTER OF MOTHER MACHREE
–	–	–	–	==	==	10	7	4	2	2	4	7	7	10	13	==	==	==	==	–	–	–	–	–	–	–	–	–	–	THEY DIDN'T BELIEVE ME
–	–	–	–	==	==	==	==	==	==	==	==	==	==	==	==	==	==	==	==	==	==	==	==	18	17	20	==	==	==	KISS ME AGAIN
–	–	–	–	–	–	==	==	17	13	10	10	17	==	==	–	–	–	–	–	–	–	–	–	–	–	–	–	–	–	DON'T BITE THE HAND THAT'S FEEDING YOU
–	–	–	–	–	–	==	==	==	16	14	16	20	20	==	==	–	–	–	–	–	–	–	–	–	–	–	–	–	–	KEEP THE HOME FIRES BURNING
–	–	–	–	–	–	==	==	==	17	17	13	9	10	14	==	==	==	–	–	–	–	–	–	–	–	–	–	–	–	WHAT A WONDERFUL MOTHER YOU'D BE
–	–	–	–	–	–	==	19	9	5	3	2	2	3	5	5	7	13	17	==	==	–	–	–	–	–	–	–	–	–	HELLO, HAWAII, HOW ARE YOU?
–	–	–	–	–	–	==	==	10	6	4	5	5	4	4	6	8	14	==	==	–	–	–	–	–	–	–	–	–	–	UNDERNEATH THE STARS
–	–	–	–	–	–	==	==	==	==	==	==	16	12	11	15	==	==	==	==	==	==	==	==	–	–	–	–	–	–	I LOVE YOU, THAT'S ONE THING I KNOW
–	–	–	–	–	–	==	==	==	==	==	==	==	==	==	20	20	19	18	16	15	13	14	13	15	14	16	14	17	19	== 19 16 19 == A PERFECT DAY
–	–	–	–	–	–	==	==	==	==	==	==	==	17	19	16	15	12	10	7	7	9	8	8	6	8	8	10	8	8	12 10 13 18 20 == THERE'S A LONG, LONG TRAIL
–	–	–	–	–	–	==	==	14	9	6	3	**1**	**1**	2	2	2	4	9	14	17	==	==	==	–	–	–	–	–	–	MEMORIES
–	–	–	–	–	–	–	–	==	==	18	14	12	14	18	==	==	==	–	–	–	–	–	–	–	–	–	–	–	–	THE LADDER OF ROSES
–	–	–	–	–	–	–	–	==	19	11	6	4	2	**1**	**1**	3	2	3	6	13	==	==	–	–	–	–	–	–	–	GOODBYE, GOOD LUCK, AND GOD BLESS YOU
–	–	–	–	–	–	–	–	==	20	12	8	6	6	3	4	4	5	6	9	14	17	==	==	–	–	–	–	–	–	MY MOTHER'S ROSARY
–	–	–	–	–	–	–	–	==	==	==	15	10	9	6	7	6	6	12	17	18	==	==	==	==	==	–	–	–	–	ARE YOU FROM DIXIE?
–	–	–	–	–	–	–	–	==	==	==	==	19	15	15	18	==	==	==	==	==	==	==	==	==	==	19	17	16	==	SO LONG, LETTY
–	–	–	–	–	–	–	–	–	–	==	==	18	13	12	19	==	==	==	==	–	–	–	–	–	–	–	–	–	–	RACKETY COO!
Oc	Oc	Nv	Nv	Dc	Dc	Ja	Ja	Fb	Fb	Ma	Ma	Ap	Ap	My	My	Jn	Jn	Jy	Jy	Ag	Ag	Sp	Sp	Oc	Oc	Nv	Nv	Dc	Dc	

1916																				1917										
Ma	Ma	Ap	Ap	My	My	Jn	Jn	Jy	Jy	Ag	Ag	Sp	Sp	Oc	Oc	Nv	Nv	Dc	Dc	Ja	Ja	Fb	Fb	Ma	Ma	Ap	Ap	My	My	
==	==	==	==	==	==	==	==	==	==	19	==	==	==	==	20	==	==	==	==	==	==	==	==	==	==	19	20	==	==	MISSOURI WALTZ (HUSH-A-BYE, MA BABY)
==	20	11	8	9	11	17	==	==	–	–	–	–	–	–	–	–	–	–	–	–	–	–	–	–	–	–	–	–	–	THERE'S A BROKEN HEART FOR EVERY LIGHT ON BROADWAY
==	==	==	==	20	17	18	16	19	==	==	==	–	–	–	–	–	–	–	–	–	–	–	–	–	–	–	–	–	–	NAT'AN, FOR WHAT ARE YOU WAITIN', NAT'AN?
==	==	==	==	16	10	10	18	==	==	==	==	==	==	–	–	–	–	–	–	–	–	–	–	–	–	–	–	–	–	SIAM
–	–	==	==	13	8	5	3	2	3	8	14	18	==	==	–	–	–	–	–	–	–	–	–	–	–	–	–	–	–	I CAN DANCE WITH EVERYBODY BUT MY WIFE
–	–	==	==	==	12	9	7	11	11	12	15	==	==	–	–	–	–	–	–	–	–	–	–	–	–	–	–	–	–	WHERE DID ROBINSON CRUSOE GO WITH FRIDAY ON A SATURDAY NIGHT?
–	–	==	==	==	==	==	20	==	20	==	==	==	==	–	–	–	–	–	–	–	–	–	–	–	–	–	–	–	–	MY DREAMY CHINA LADY
–	–	==	==	==	==	==	17	15	18	==	==	==	==	–	–	–	–	–	–	–	–	–	–	–	–	–	–	–	–	I LOVE A PIANO
–	–	==	16	8	3	1	1	1	1	2	4	9	18	==	==	–	–	–	–	–	–	–	–	–	–	–	–	–	–	YAAKA HULA, HICKEY DULA
–	–	==	==	==	14	11	9	8	8	10	10	15	==	==	==	==	==	==	==	==	–	–	–	–	–	–	–	–	–	BABES IN THE WOOD
–	–	==	==	==	==	==	20	19	20	==	==	==	==	==	–	–	–	–	–	–	–	–	–	–	–	–	–	–	–	ON THE BEACH AT WAIKIKI
–	–	==	==	==	==	19	15	13	12	11	5	6	7	10	9	9	11	10	11	13	20	==	==	==	==	–	–	–	–	SHADES OF NIGHT
–	–	–	–	==	==	13	10	5	4	3	7	10	12	14	15	==	==	==	==	–	–	–	–	–	–	–	–	–	–	THERE'S A QUAKER DOWN IN QUAKER TOWN
–	–	–	–	==	==	14	11	7	5	5	8	7	11	16	16	==	==	==	==	–	–	–	–	–	–	–	–	–	–	ARRAH, GO ON, I'M GONNA GO BACK TO OREGON
–	–	–	–	==	==	12	8	4	2	1	1	3	4	9	11	15	19	==	==	–	–	–	–	–	–	–	–	–	–	BABY SHOES
–	–	–	–	==	==	==	==	16	13	9	6	4	6	8	10	10	12	11	10	10	14	==	==	==	==	==	==	–	–	THE SUNSHINE OF YOUR SMILE
–	–	–	–	–	–	==	==	==	==	==	16	17	14	12	12	13	13	14	17	==	==	20	15	16	==	==	==	==	==	PRAY FOR THE LIGHTS TO GO OUT
–	–	–	–	–	–	==	==	==	==	==	==	19	19	20	==	==	==	==	==	–	–	–	–	–	–	–	–	–	–	AT THE END OF A BEAUTIFUL DAY
–	–	–	–	–	–	==	==	14	10	4	3	2	2	2	2	5	5	6	6	9	16	==	==	–	–	–	–	–	–	MY OWN IONA
–	–	–	–	–	–	==	==	==	==	==	==	20	20	19	==	==	==	==	==	==	==	==	==	==	==	–	–	–	–	DOWN WHERE THE SWANEE RIVER FLOWS
–	–	–	–	–	–	–	–	==	==	16	12	11	10	17	19	==	==	–	–	–	–	–	–	–	–	–	–	–	–	YOU'RE A DANGEROUS GIRL
–	–	–	–	–	–	–	–	==	==	==	20	16	16	13	13	14	16	18	==	==	–	–	–	–	–	–	–	–	–	ON THE SOUTH SEA ISLE
–	–	–	–	–	–	–	–	–	==	15	6	2	1	1	1	1	1	1	2	5	5	11	14	==	==	–	–	–	–	PRETTY BABY
–	–	–	–	–	–	–	–	–	–	==	==	11	5	3	4	4	7	8	12	14	==	==	–	–	–	–	–	–	–	IF I KNOCK THE "L" OUT OF KELLY
–	–	–	–	–	–	–	–	–	–	–	==	19	13	9	5	5	3	4	5	7	15	==	==	–	–	–	–	–	–	TURN BACK THE UNIVERSE AND GIVE ME YESTERDAY
–	–	–	–	–	–	–	–	–	–	–	==	18	12	5	3	3	2	2	3	4	4	7	9	14	==	==	–	–	–	IRELAND MUST BE HEAVEN FOR MY MOTHER CAME FROM THERE
–	–	–	–	–	–	–	–	–	–	–	==	==	15	7	7	6	7	9	12	18	==	–	–	–	–	–	–	–	–	OH! HOW SHE COULD YACKI HACKI WICKI WACKI WOO
–	–	–	–	–	–	–	–	–	–	–	–	==	17	11	6	4	3	1	1	2	2	5	7	11	18	==	==	–	–	THERE'S A LITTLE BIT OF BAD IN EVERY GOOD LITTLE GIRL
–	–	–	–	–	–	–	–	–	–	–	–	–	–	==	==	17	15	15	13	11	12	15	==	==	==	–	–	–	–	OUT OF THE CRADLE, INTO MY HEART
–	–	–	–	–	–	–	–	–	–	–	–	–	–	==	==	18	18	20	18	17	18	==	==	==	==	–	–	–	–	I KNOW I GOT MORE THAN MY SHARE
–	–	–	–	–	–	–	–	–	–	–	–	–	–	==	18	11	6	4	2	1	1	3	5	6	8	10	==	==	–	MAMMY'S LITTLE COAL BLACK ROSE
–	–	–	–	–	–	–	–	–	–	–	–	–	–	==	==	==	==	19	==	==	==	–	–	–	–	–	–	–	–	WHEN THE BLACK SHEEP RETURNS TO THE FOLD
–	–	–	–	–	–	–	–	–	–	–	–	–	–	==	==	12	9	7	3	3	3	4	8	8	15	==	==	==	–	SHE IS THE SUNSHINE OF VIRGINIA
–	–	–	–	–	–	–	–	–	–	–	–	–	–	–	–	==	20	13	9	7	6	6	4	7	10	15	==	==	–	MY HAWAIIAN SUNSHINE (1917)
–	–	–	–	–	–	–	–	–	–	–	–	–	–	–	–	–	–	==	16	8	5	2	2	3	6	7	9	14	19	THEY'RE WEARIN' 'EM HIGHER IN HAWAII (1917)
–	–	–	–	–	–	–	–	–	–	–	–	–	–	–	–	–	–	==	15	6	4	1	1	1	1	1	1	2	2	POOR BUTTERFLY (1917)
–	–	–	–	–	–	–	–	–	–	–	–	–	–	–	–	==	==	==	20	14	8	8	6	4	3	3	6	7	10	I AIN'T GOT NOBODY (1917)
Ma	Ma	Ap	Ap	My	My	Jn	Jn	Jy	Jy	Ag	Ag	Sp	Sp	Oc	Oc	Nv	Nv	Dc	Dc	Ja	Ja	Fb	Fb	Ma	Ma	Ap	Ap	My	My	

1916						1917																								
Oc	Oc	Nv	Nv	Dc	Dc	Ja	Ja	Fb	Fb	Ma	Ma	Ap	Ap	My	My	Jn	Jn	Jy	Jy	Ag	Ag	Sp	Sp	Oc	Oc	Nv	Nv	Dc	Dc	
15	14	16	14	17	19	==	19	16	19	==	==	==	==	==	==	==	==	==	==	–	–	–	–	–	–	–	–	–	–	A PERFECT DAY (1916)
6	8	8	10	8	8	12	10	13	18	20	==	==	==	==	==	==	==	==	==											THERE'S A LONG, LONG TRAIL (1916)*
10	9	9	11	10	11	13	20	==	==	==	==	–	–	–	–	–	–	–	–	–	–	–	–	–	–	–	–	–	–	SHADES OF NIGHT (1916)
8	10	10	12	11	10	10	14	==	==	==	==	==	==	–	–	–	–	–	–	–	–	–	–	–	–	–	–	–	–	THE SUNSHINE OF YOUR SMILE (1916)
12	12	13	13	14	17	==	==	20	15	16	==	==	==	==	==	–	–	–	–	–	–	–	–	–	–	–	–	–	–	PRAY FOR THE LIGHTS TO GO OUT (1916)
2	2	5	5	6	6	9	16	==	==	–	–	–	–	–	–	–	–	–	–	–	–	–	–	–	–	–	–	–	–	MY OWN IONA (1916)
1	1	1	1	2	5	5	11	14	==	==	–	–	–	–	–	–	–	–	–	–	–	–	–	–	–	–	–	–	–	PRETTY BABY (1916)
5	5	3	4	5	7	15	==	==	–	–	–	–	–	–	–	–	–	–	–	–	–	–	–	–	–	–	–	–	–	TURN BACK THE UNIVERSE AND GIVE ME YESTERDAY (1916)
3	3	2	2	3	4	4	7	9	14	==	==	–	–	–	–	–	–	–	–	–	–	–	–	–	–	–	–	–	–	IRELAND MUST BE HEAVEN FOR MY MOTHER CAME FROM THERE (1916)
7	7	6	7	9	12	18	==	–	–	–	–	–	–	–	–	–	–	–	–	–	–	–	–	–	–	–	–	–	–	OH! HOW SHE COULD YACKI HACKI WICKI WACKI WOO(1916)
11	6	4	3	1	1	2	2	5	7	11	18	==	==	–	–	–	–	–	–	–	–	–	–	–	–	–	–	–	–	THERE'S A LITTLE BIT OF BAD IN EVERY GOOD LITTLE GIRL (1916)
==	==	17	15	15	13	11	12	15	==	==	==	–	–	–	–	–	–	–	–	–	–	–	–	–	–	–	–	–	–	OUT OF THE CRADLE, INTO MY HEART (1916)
==	==	18	18	20	18	17	18	==	==	==	==	–	–	–	–	–	–	–	–	–	–	–	–	–	–	–	–	–	–	I KNOW I GOT MORE THAN MY SHARE (1916)
==	18	11	6	4	2	1	1	3	5	6	8	10	==	==	–	–	–	–	–	–	–	–	–	–	–	–	–	–	–	MAMMY'S LITTLE COAL BLACK ROSE (1916)
==	==	12	9	7	3	3	3	4	8	8	15	==	==	==	–	–	–	–	–	–	–	–	–	–	–	–	–	–	–	SHE IS THE SUNSHINE OF VIRGINIA (1916)
==	20	==	==	==	==	==	==	==	==	==	==	19	20	==	==	==	==	==	==	–	–	–	–	–	–	–	–	–	–	MISSOURI WALTZ (HUSH-A-BYE, MA BABY) (1916)
–	–	==	==	==	20	14	8	8	6	4	3	3	6	7	10	11	14	==	==	==	==	==	==	==	==	–	–	–	–	I AIN'T GOT NOBODY
–	–	==	20	13	9	7	6	6	4	7	10	15	==	==	–	–	–	–	–	–	–	–	–	–	–	–	–	–	–	MY HAWAIIAN SUNSHINE
–	–	–	–	==	==	20	15	12	12	15	17	==	==	==	–	–	–	–	–	–	–	–	–	–	–	–	–	–	–	NAUGHTY! NAUGHTY! NAUGHTY!
–	–	–	–	==	16	8	5	2	2	3	6	7	9	14	19	==	==	–	–	–	–	–	–	–	–	–	–	–	–	THEY'RE WEARIN' 'EM HIGHER IN HAWAII
–	–	–	–	==	15	6	4	1	1	1	1	1	1	2	2	4	6	14	==	==	==	–	–	–	–	–	–	–	–	POOR BUTTERFLY
–	–	–	–	==	==	16	9	10	13	19	20	==	==	–	–	–	–	–	–	–	–	–	–	–	–	–	–	–	–	THROW ME A ROSE
–	–	–	–	==	==	19	13	11	10	12	14	20	==	==	–	–	–	–	–	–	–	–	–	–	–	–	–	–	–	HOW'S EVERY LITTLE THING IN DIXIE?
–	–	–	–	–	–	==	17	7	3	2	2	2	5	6	9	12	==	==	==	–	–	–	–	–	–	–	–	–	–	WHAT DO YOU WANT TO MAKE THOSE EYES AT ME FOR?
–	–	–	–	–	–	==	==	19	11	10	9	8	16	17	==	==	==	–	–	–	–	–	–	–	–	–	–	–	–	ROLLING STONES (ALL COME ROLLING HOME AGAIN)
–	–	–	–	–	–	==	==	17	9	5	4	4	4	3	5	7	9	12	12	==	==	–	–	–	–	–	–	–	–	M-I-S-S-I-S-S-I-P-P-I
–	–	–	–	–	–	==	==	18	16	13	12	12	15	13	16	16	15	19	==	==	==	==	==	==	–	–	–	–	–	IF YOU HAD ALL THE WORLD AND ITS GOLD
–	–	–	–	–	==	==	==	==	==	==	19	17	18	18	17	==	==	==	–	–	–	–	–	–	–	–	–	–	–	SHE'S DIXIE ALL THE TIME
–	–	–	–	–	–	==	==	==	20	14	11	11	7	4	3	2	4	6	9	10	10	16	19	==	==	==	==	–	–	PACK UP YOUR TROUBLES IN YOUR OLD KIT BAG
–	–	–	–	–	–	==	==	==	==	18	16	13	13	16	18	20	==	==	==	–	–	–	–	–	–	–	–	–	–	THERE'S SOMEONE MORE LONESOME THAN YOU
–	–	–	–	–	–	–	–	==	17	9	5	6	5	5	4	6	8	13	==	==	–	–	–	–	–	–	–	–	–	WHERE THE BLACK-EYED SUSANS GROW
–	–	–	–	–	–	–	–	==	==	==	==	==	19	20	==	==	–	–	–	–	–	–	–	–	–	–	–	–	–	MOTHER
–	–	–	–	–	–	–	–	–	==	==	13	9	8	10	12	15	==	==	==	–	–	–	–	–	–	–	–	–	–	THERE'S EGYPT IN YOUR DREAMY EYES
–	–	–	–	–	–	–	–	–	==	17	7	5	2	1	1	1	1	1	1	4	7	7	13	17	==	==	==	–	–	FOR ME AND MY GAL
–	–	–	–	–	–	–	–	–	–	==	==	16	11	12	7	8	16	20	==	==	==	–	–	–	–	–	–	–	–	COME OUT OF THE KITCHEN, MARY ANN
–	–	–	–	–	–	–	–	–	–	==	==	18	12	11	11	10	7	7	14	20	==	==	==	–	–	–	–	–	–	ALLAH'S HOLIDAY
–	–	–	–	–	–	–	–	–	–	==	==	14	10	8	8	5	3	4	6	6	8	10	10	12	18	==	==	–	–	INDIANA
Oc	Oc	Nv	Nv	Dc	Dc	Ja	Ja	Fb	Fb	Ma	Ma	Ap	Ap	My	My	Jn	Jn	Jy	Jy	Ag	Ag	Sp	Sp	Oc	Oc	Nv	Nv	Dc	Dc	

* 1916 SONG LEAVES TOP TWENTY IN MARCH AND REAPPEARS IN OCTOBER (BELOW) TO BECOME A 1918 SONG.

1917																		1918												
Ap	Ap	My	My	Jn	Jn	Jy	Jy	Ag	Ag	Sp	Sp	Oc	Oc	Nv	Nv	Dc	Dc	Ja	Ja	Fb	Fb	Ma	Ma	Ap	Ap	My	My	Jn	Jn	
==	17	15	14	19	==	==	==	–	–	–	–	–	–	–	–	–	–	–	–	–	–	–	–	–	–	–	–	–	–	YOU SAID SOMETHING
==	14	9	6	3	2	2	2	5	6	6	14	==	==	==	–	–	–	–	–	–	–	–	–	–	–	–	–	–	–	OH JOHNNY, OH JOHNNY, OH!
==	==	==	==	==	==	==	==	19	==	==	==	–	–	–	–	–	–	–	–	–	–	–	–	–	–	–	–	–	–	SHIM-ME-SHA-WABBLE
==	==	19	13	14	12	9	13	18	==	==	==	–	–	–	–	–	–	–	–	–	–	–	–	–	–	–	–	–	–	HAWAIIAN BUTTERFLY
==	==	==	==	20	17	15	15	20	==	==	==	==	==	==	==	==	==	–	–	–	–	–	–	–	–	–	–	–	–	THE MAGIC OF YOUR EYES
==	==	==	20	18	17	18	16	16	17	15	12	10	9	8	5	3	3	2	2	**1**	**1**	**1**	**1**	2	5	9	12	18	==	THE DARKTOWN STUTTERS' BALL
==	==	==	==	==	==	==	18	14	12	9	11	8	7	7	8	12	11	8	9	9	8	10	10	18	==	==	==	–	–	KEEP THE HOME FIRES BURNING
–	==	==	15	13	10	5	4	**1**	2	4	6	9	11	15	20	==	==	==	==	–	–	–	–	–	–	–	–	–	–	ALL THE WORLD WILL BE JEALOUS OF ME
–	–	==	==	17	11	10	11	9	13	==	==	==	–	–	–	–	–	–	–	–	–	–	–	–	–	–	–	–	–	TILL THE CLOUDS ROLL BY
–	–	==	==	==	18	11	8	12	16	19	==	==	==	==	==	–	–	–	–	–	–	–	–	–	–	–	–	–	–	IT TAKES A LONG, TALL, BROWN-SKIN GAL
–	–	==	==	==	13	8	7	8	11	18	==	19	17	==	==	==	==	–	–	–	–	–	–	–	–	–	–	–	–	FOR YOU A ROSE
–	–	==	==	9	5	3	3	3	4	5	8	11	10	12	19	==	==	==	–	–	–	–	–	–	–	–	–	–	–	LILY OF THE VALLEY
–	–	==	==	==	19	15	10	13	9	14	18	18	==	==	==	==	==	–	–	–	–	–	–	–	–	–	–	–	–	HUCKLEBERRY FINN
–	–	–	–	==	==	==	20	17	14	11	9	7	6	6	4	6	4	5	8	8	7	11	12	19	==	==	==	–	–	JOAN OF ARC, THEY ARE CALLING YOU
–	–	–	–	–	==	16	5	2	**1**	**1**	**1**	**1**	**1**	**1**	**1**	**1**	**1**	**1**	**1**	2	2	4	7	8	16	17	==	–	–	OVER THERE
–	–	–	–	–	–	==	19	11	5	3	3	3	4	5	7	15	==	==	–	–	–	–	–	–	–	–	–	–	–	WHERE DO WE GO FROM HERE?
–	–	–	–	–	–	==	17	7	3	2	2	2	2	2	2	5	7	16	==	==	==	–	–	–	–	–	–	–	–	GOODBYE BROADWAY, HELLO FRANCE!
–	–	–	–	–	–	==	==	==	==	==	==	20	==	==	==	==	==	==	==	==	==	–	–	–	–	–	–	–	–	LIVERY STABLE BLUES
–	–	–	–	–	–	==	==	==	==	20	17	14	14	10	10	14	12	11	10	10	14	15	13	14	19	==	==	–	–	BREAK THE NEWS TO MOTHER
–	–	–	–	–	–	–	==	==	15	8	4	5	5	4	3	2	5	10	15	20	==	==	–	–	–	–	–	–	–	I MAY BE GONE FOR A LONG, LONG TIME
–	–	–	–	–	–	–	–	==	==	17	16	16	19	17	15	18	==	–	–	–	–	–	–	–	–	–	–	–	–	SEND ME AWAY WITH A SMILE
–	–	–	–	–	–	–	–	==	18	12	7	6	8	9	17	==	==	–	–	–	–	–	–	–	–	–	–	–	–	SAILIN' AWAY ON THE HENRY CLAY
–	–	–	–	–	–	–	–	==	19	13	5	4	3	3	6	7	14	19	==	==	–	–	–	–	–	–	–	–	–	THEY GO WILD, SIMPLY WILD, OVER ME
–	–	–	–	–	–	–	–	==	==	==	15	13	12	14	12	9	10	13	18	==	==	–	–	–	–	–	–	–	–	I DON'T KNOW WHERE I'M GOING, BUT I'M ON MY WAY
–	–	–	–	–	–	–	–	==	==	==	20	15	13	11	18	==	==	==	==	==	==	–	–	–	–	–	–	–	–	LADDIE BOY
–	–	–	–	–	–	–	–	–	–	==	==	==	16	20	==	==	==	–	–	–	–	–	–	–	–	–	–	–	–	SWEET EMALINA, MY GAL
–	–	–	–	–	–	–	–	–	–	==	==	==	15	13	11	13	13	14	13	12	12	12	19	==	==	–	–	–	–	WHEN YANKEE DOODLE LEARNS TO PARLEZ-VOUS FRANCAIS
–	–	–	–	–	–	–	–	–	–	–	–	==	==	==	==	19	18	18	16	18	==	==	==	–	–	–	–	–	–	LONG BOY (GOODBYE, MA! GOODBYE, PA! GOODBYE, MULE)
–	–	–	–	–	–	–	–	–	–	–	–	==	==	16	9	4	2	3	4	6	9	16	==	==	–	–	–	–	–	SOME SUNDAY MORNING
–	–	–	–	–	–	–	–	–	–	–	–	==	==	==	16	8	6	4	3	3	5	7	11	15	==	==	–	–	–	I DON'T WANT TO GET WELL
–	–	–	–	–	–	–	–	–	–	–	–	–	==	==	==	20	==	==	==	==	–	–	–	–	–	–	–	–	–	WE'RE GOING OVER
–	–	–	–	–	–	–	–	–	–	–	–	–	–	==	==	16	16	20	==	==	–	–	–	–	–	–	–	–	–	WHERE THE MORNING GLORIES GROW
–	–	–	–	–	–	–	–	–	–	–	–	–	–	==	==	17	15	12	11	17	19	==	==	–	–	–	–	–	–	HAIL, HAIL, THE GANG'S ALL HERE (1918)
								==	==	==	==	==	20	19	13	10	9	6	5	5	4	3	5	5	7	12	17	–	–	THERE'S A LONG, LONG TRAIL (1918)*
–	–	–	–	–	–	–	–	–	–	–	–	==	==	18	14	11	8	7	6	7	6	8	8	11	15	==	==	–	–	I'M ALL BOUND 'ROUND WITH THE MASON-DIXON LINE (1918)
–	–	–	–	–	–	–	–	–	–	–	–	==	==	==	==	==	17	15	14	19	==	==	==	==	==	==	==	–	–	WILL YOU REMEMBER (SWEETHEART) (1918)
–	–	–	–	–	–	–	–	–	–	–	–	–	–	==	==	==	20	17	12	11	13	14	17	==	==	–	–	–	–	SOMEWHERE IN FRANCE IS THE LILY (1918)
–	–	–	–	–	–	–	–	–	–	–	–	–	–	–	==	==	19	9	7	4	3	2	3	9	20	==	–	–	–	WAIT TILL THE COWS COME HOME (1918)
Ap	Ap	My	My	Jn	Jn	Jy	Jy	Ag	Ag	Sp	Sp	Oc	Oc	Nv	Nv	Dc	Dc	Ja	Ja	Fb	Fb	Ma	Ma	Ap	Ap	My	My	Jn	Jn	

1917						1918																								
Oc	Oc	Nv	Nv	Dc	Dc	Ja	Ja	Fb	Fb	Ma	Ma	Ap	Ap	My	My	Jn	Jn	Jy	Jy	Ag	Ag	Sp	Sp	Oc	Oc	Nv	Nv	Dc	DC	
10	9	8	5	3	3	2	2	1	1	1	1	2	5	9	12	18	==	==	==	–	–	–	–	–	–	–	–	–	–	THE DARKTOWN STUTTERS' BALL (1917)
8	7	7	8	12	11	8	9	9	8	10	10	18	==	==	==	==	==	–	–	–	–	–	–	–	–	–	–	–	–	KEEP THE HOME FIRES BURNING (1917)
7	6	6	4	6	4	5	8	8	7	11	12	19	==	==	==	==	==	–	–	–	–	–	–	–	–	–	–	–	–	JOAN OF ARC, THEY ARE CALLING YOU (1917)
2	2	2	2	5	7	16	==	==	==	–	–	–	–	–	–	–	–	–	–	–	–	–	–	–	–	–	–	–	–	GOODBYE BROADWAY, HELLO FRANCE! (1917)
1	1	1	1	1	1	1	1	2	2	4	7	8	16	17	==	==	==	==	==	==	–	–	–	–	–	–	–	–	–	OVER THERE (1917)
13	12	14	12	9	10	13	18	==	==	–	–	–	–	–	–	–	–	–	–	–	–	–	–	–	–	–	–	–	–	I DON'T KNOW WHERE I'M GOING, BUT I'M ON MY WAY
14	14	10	10	14	12	11	10	10	14	15	13	14	19	==	==	==	==	==	==	–	–	–	–	–	–	–	–	–	–	BREAK THE NEWS TO MOTHER (1917)
5	5	4	3	2	5	10	15	20	==	==	–	–	–	–	–	–	–	–	–	–	–	–	–	–	–	–	–	–	–	I MAY BE GONE FOR A LONG, LONG TIME (1917)
4	3	3	6	7	14	19	==	==	–	–	–	–	–	–	–	–	–	–	–	–	–	–	–	–	–	–	–	–	–	THEY GO WILD, SIMPLY WILD, OVER ME (1917)
==	15	13	11	13	13	14	13	12	12	12	19	==	==	–	–	–	–	–	–	–	–	–	–	–	–	–	–	–	–	WHEN YANKEE DOODLE LEARNS TO PARLEZ-VOUS FRANCAIS
==	==	==	==	19	18	18	16	18	==	==	==	–	–	–	–	–	–	–	–	–	–	–	–	–	–	–	–	–	–	LONG BOY (GOODBYE, MA! GOODBYE, PA! GOODBYE, MULE)
==	==	16	9	4	2	3	4	6	9	16	==	==	–	–	–	–	–	–	–	–	–	–	–	–	–	–	–	–	–	SOME SUNDAY MORNING (1917)
==	==	==	16	8	6	4	3	3	5	7	11	15	==	==	–	–	–	–	–	–	–	–	–	–	–	–	–	–	–	I DON'T WANT TO GET WELL (1917)
–	–	==	==	16	16	20	==	==	–	–	–	–	–	–	–	–	–	–	–	–	–	–	–	–	–	–	–	–	–	WHERE THE MORNING GLORIES GROW (1917)
–	–	==	==	17	15	12	11	17	19	==	==	–	–	–	–	–	–	–	–	–	–	–	–	–	–	–	–	–	–	HAIL, HAIL, THE GANG'S ALL HERE
==	20	19	13	10	9	6	5	5	4	3	5	5	7	12	17	==	==	==	==	==	==	–	–	–	–	–	–	–	–	THERE'S A LONG, LONG TRAIL
==	==	18	14	11	8	7	6	7	6	8	8	11	15	==	==	–	–	–	–	–	–	–	–	–	–	–	–	–	–	I'M ALL BOUND 'ROUND WITH THE MASON-DIXON LINE
==	==	==	==	==	17	15	14	19	==	==	==	==	==	==	==	–	–	–	–	–	–	–	–	–	–	–	–	–	–	WILL YOU REMEMBER (SWEETHEART)
–	–	==	==	==	20	17	12	11	13	14	17	==	==	–	–	–	–	–	–	–	–	–	–	–	–	–	–	–	–	SOMEWHERE IN FRANCE IS THE LILY
–	–	–	==	==	19	9	7	4	3	2	3	9	20	==	–	–	–	–	–	–	–	–	–	–	–	–	–	–	–	WAIT TILL THE COWS COME HOME
–	–	==	==	==	==	==	17	14	15	13	16	==	==	==	==	–	–	–	–	–	–	–	–	–	–	–	–	–	–	LI'L LIZA JANE
–	–	==	==	==	==	==	20	13	11	9	6	4	3	3	3	3	7	9	10	14	13	17	==	==	==	==	==	–	–	INDIANOLA
–	–	–	–	==	==	==	19	15	17	18	==	==	–	–	–	–	–	–	–	–	–	–	–	–	–	–	–	–	–	THE OLD GREY MARE
–	–	–	–	==	==	==	==	==	18	20	==	==	==	–	–	–	–	–	–	–	–	–	–	–	–	–	–	–	–	GIVE ME THE MOONLIGHT, GIVE ME THE GIRL
–	–	–	–	–	–	==	==	==	==	==	20	==	==	–	–	–	–	–	–	–	–	–	–	–	–	–	–	–	–	LIBERTY BELL, IT'S TIME TO RING AGAIN
–	–	–	–	–	–	==	==	16	10	5	4	3	2	4	5	11	15	==	==	==	==	–	–	–	–	–	–	–	–	ARE YOU FROM HEAVEN?
–	–	–	–	–	–	==	==	==	==	==	==	20	17	15	16	==	20	==	==	==	==	==	==	–	–	–	–	–	–	BLUE BIRD (BRING BACK MY HAPPINESS)
–	–	–	–	–	–	==	==	==	20	17	9	6	6	5	4	8	13	17	==	==	==	==	==	==	==	–	–	–	–	MISSOURI WALTZ (HUSH-A-BYE, MA BABY)
–	–	–	–	–	–	–	–	==	16	6	2	1	1	1	1	2	2	4	5	6	9	15	17	==	==	==	==	–	–	JUST A BABY'S PRAYER AT TWILIGHT
–	–	–	–	–	–	–	–	==	==	19	14	10	14	18	==	==	–	–	–	–	–	–	–	–	–	–	–	–	–	I'M GOING TO FOLLOW THE BOYS
–	–	–	–	–	–	–	–	==	==	==	15	12	9	13	13	17	==	==	==	–	–	–	–	–	–	–	–	–	–	SWEET LITTLE BUTTERCUP
–	–	–	–	–	–	–	–	==	==	==	==	==	18	19	20	==	==	==	==	–	–	–	–	–	–	–	–	–	–	ON THE ROAD TO HOME SWEET HOME
–	–	–	–	–	–	–	–	==	==	==	==	17	12	14	11	12	8	8	9	9	12	16	==	==	==	==	==	–	–	FOREVER IS A LONG, LONG TIME
–	–	–	–	–	–	–	–	==	==	==	==	==	==	==	==	==	==	==	==	==	==	==	==	==	19	19	19	==	==	ROSES OF PICARDY
–	–	–	–	–	–	–	–	==	==	==	==	==	==	20	==	==	==	–	–	–	–	–	–	–	–	–	–	–	–	IF YOU LOOK IN HER EYES
–	–	–	–	–	–	–	–	–	–	==	18	7	4	2	2	1	1	1	2	3	3	6	8	18	==	==	==	–	–	I'M SORRY I MADE YOU CRY
–	–	–	–	–	–	–	–	–	–	==	==	13	8	6	10	15	18	==	==	–	–	–	–	–	–	–	–	–	–	LORRAINE (MY BEAUTIFUL ALSACE LORRAINE)
–	–	–	–	–	–	–	–	–	–	==	==	==	11	10	9	7	12	14	==	==	==	–	–	–	–	–	–	–	–	EVERYBODY OUGHT TO KNOW HOW TO DO THE TICKLE TOE
–	–	–	–	–	–	–	–	–	–	==	==	16	10	7	6	4	5	5	6	8	14	==	==	–	–	–	–	–	–	(SHE'S) THE DAUGHTER OF ROSIE O'GRADY
Oc	Oc	Nv	Nv	Dc	Dc	Ja	Ja	Fb	Fb	Ma	Ma	Ap	Ap	My	My	Jn	Jn	Jy	Jy	Ag	Ag	Sp	Sp	Oc	Oc	Nv	Nv	Dc	Dc	

1918																		1919												
Ap	Ap	My	My	Jn	Jn	Jy	Jy	Ag	Ag	Sp	Sp	Oc	Oc	Nv	Nv	Dc	Dc	Ja	Ja	Fb	Fb	Ma	Ma	Ap	Ap	My	My	Jn	Jn	
==	13	8	7	5	10	13	==	==	–	–	–	–	–	–	–	–	–	–	–	–	–	–	–	–	–	–	–	–	–	BRING BACK MY DADDY TO ME
==	==	16	14	13	14	18	==	==	==	–	–	–	–	–	–	–	–	–	–	–	–	–	–	–	–	–	–	–	–	THREE WONDERFUL LETTERS FROM HOME
==	==	11	8	6	6	10	12	18	==	==	–	–	–	–	–	–	–	–	–	–	–	–	–	–	–	–	–	–	–	I HATE TO LOSE YOU
==	==	==	==	20	17	16	14	16	18	==	==	==	==	==	==	==	==	–	–	–	–	–	–	–	–	–	–	–	–	TISHOMINGO BLUES
–	==	==	15	9	4	2	1	1	1	1	2	2	2	5	8	13	16	19	==	==	==	==	==	==	==	–	–	–	–	K-K-K-KATY
–	–	==	==	19	16	11	15	==	==	==	–	–	–	–	–	–	–	–	–	–	–	–	–	–	–	–	–	–	–	N'EVERYTHING
–	–	==	19	14	9	6	8	15	==	==	–	–	–	–	–	–	–	–	–	–	–	–	–	–	–	–	–	–	–	JUST LIKE WASHINGTON CROSSED THE DELAWARE
–	–	==	18	10	3	3	3	2	2	3	5	10	16	20	==	–	–	–	–	–	–	–	–	–	–	–	–	–	–	HELLO, CENTRAL, GIVE ME NO-MAN'S-LAND
–	–	==	==	16	11	7	4	4	7	8	10	13	17	18	==	==	==	–	–	–	–	–	–	–	–	–	–	–	–	GOOD MORNING, MR. ZIP-ZIP-ZIP!
–	–	==	==	==	==	20	19	17	17	==	==	==	–	–	–	–	–	–	–	–	–	–	–	–	–	–	–	–	–	EVERYBODY'S (GONE) CRAZY 'BOUT THE DOGGONE BLUES
–	–	–	–	==	19	12	7	5	5	7	11	19	==	==	–	–	–	–	–	–	–	–	–	–	–	–	–	–	–	THEY WERE ALL OUT OF STEP BUT JIM
–	–	–	–	==	==	==	20	==	20	==	==	==	==	–	–	–	–	–	–	–	–	–	–	–	–	–	–	–	–	HOW'D YOU LIKE TO BE MY DADDY?
–	–	–	–	==	==	15	11	10	10	9	12	16	18	==	==	–	–	–	–	–	–	–	–	–	–	–	–	–	–	IF HE CAN FIGHT LIKE HE CAN LOVE, GOOD NIGHT GERMANY!
–	–	–	–	==	==	19	13	11	6	4	4	5	8	12	14	17	==	==	==	==	==	–	–	–	–	–	–	–	–	MY BELGIAN ROSE
–	–	–	–	–	==	==	17	12	8	5	3	3	3	4	6	6	9	9	12	14	19	==	==	==	==	–	–	–	–	ROCK-A-BYE YOUR BABY WITH A DIXIE MELODY
–	–	–	–	–	==	==	16	13	11	12	14	20	==	==	==	–	–	–	–	–	–	–	–	–	–	–	–	–	–	KEEP YOUR HEAD DOWN, FRITZIE BOY
–	–	–	–	–	–	==	==	19	15	14	18	==	==	–	–	–	–	–	–	–	–	–	–	–	–	–	–	–	–	I'M GONNA PIN MY MEDAL ON THE GIRL I LEFT BEHIND
–	–	–	–	–	–	==	18	7	4	2	1	1	1	1	1	1	1	3	7	8	11	17	==	==	==	–	–	–	–	SMILES
–	–	–	–	–	–	==	==	20	16	13	9	8	7	6	4	2	2	1	2	3	5	9	11	15	==	==	==	–	–	I'M ALWAYS CHASING RAINBOWS
–	–	–	–	–	–	–	–	==	19	10	6	6	5	7	9	15	18	==	==	–	–	–	–	–	–	–	–	–	–	WHEN YOU COME BACK (AND YOU WILL COME BACK)
–	–	–	–	–	–	–	–	==	==	11	7	4	4	3	5	5	8	12	14	==	==	–	–	–	–	–	–	–	–	OH! HOW I HATE TO GET UP IN THE MORNING
–	–	–	–	–	–	–	–	==	==	==	==	15	14	14	13	18	==	==	==	==	==	–	–	–	–	–	–	–	–	MAMMY'S CHOCOLATE SOLDIER
–	–	–	–	–	–	–	–	==	==	==	==	==	20	16	18	==	==	==	==	==	==	==	==	==	==	–	–	–	–	WATERS OF VENICE
–	–	–	–	–	–	–	–	==	==	20	19	17	15	15	17	==	==	==	==	–	–	–	–	–	–	–	–	–	–	TIGER RAG
–	–	–	–	–	–	–	–	==	==	19	15	11	11	11	12	10	13	14	13	11	18	==	==	==	==	–	–	–	–	OUI, OUI, MARIE
–	–	–	–	–	–	–	–	==	==	18	13	9	9	10	10	9	11	10	10	9	13	18	==	==	==	==	==	–	–	OH! FRENCHY
–	–	–	–	–	–	–	–	–	–	==	16	7	6	2	2	4	4	6	9	12	==	==	–	–	–	–	–	–	–	EVERYTHING IS PEACHES DOWN IN GEORGIA
–	–	–	–	–	–	–	–	–	–	==	20	12	10	9	7	8	12	15	15	==	==	–	–	–	–	–	–	–	–	AFTER YOU'VE GONE
–	–	–	–	–	–	–	–	–	–	==	==	14	13	13	11	7	3	4	4	6	8	11	12	18	==	==	==	–	–	HINDUSTAN
–	–	–	–	–	–	–	–	–	–	–	==	==	12	8	3	3	5	8	11	19	==	==	–	–	–	–	–	–	–	OH! HOW I WISH I COULD SLEEP UNTIL MY DADDY COMES HOME)
–	–	–	–	–	–	–	–	–	–	–	–	==	==	==	==	==	17	16	20	==	==	==	==	==	==	–	–	–	–	I'M GLAD I CAN MAKE YOU CRY
–	–	–	–	–	–	–	–	–	–	–	–	–	==	==	==	19	19	17	16	17	16	20	==	==	–	–	–	–	–	WOULD YOU RATHER BE A COLONEL WITH AN EAGLE ON YOUR SHOULDER OR A PRIVATE WITH A CHICKEN ON YOUR KNEE?(1919)
–	–	–	–	–	–	–	–	–	–	==	==	==	==	17	16	16	14	13	8	7	7	7	7	7	9	13	16	20	17	DEAR LITTLE BOY OF MINE (1919)
–	–	–	–	–	–	–	–	–	–	==	==	==	==	==	==	20	20	18	19	18	14	16	15	13	12	11	12	11	13	A GOOD MAN IS HARD TO FIND (1919)
–	–	–	–	–	–	–	–	–	–	–	–	–	–	==	==	12	6	2	1	2	4	5	8	10	16	==	==	–	–	ROSE OF NO MAN'S LAND (1919)
–	–	–	–	–	–	–	–	–	–	–	–	–	–	==	==	==	15	11	6	4	2	3	5	6	8	15	==	==	–	MICKEY (1919)
–	–	–	–	–	–	–	–	–	–	–	–	–	==	==	15	11	7	7	5	5	3	2	3	4	4	4	6	6	10	BEAUTIFUL OHIO (1919)
–	–	–	–	–	–	–	–	–	–	–	–	–	–	==	20	14	10	5	3	1	1	1	1	1	1	2	2	3	3	TILL WE MEET AGAIN (1919)
Ap	Ap	My	My	Jn	Jn	Jy	Jy	Ag	Ag	Sp	Sp	Oc	Oc	Nv	Nv	Dc	Dc	Ja	Ja	Fb	Fb	Ma	Ma	Ap	Ap	My	My	Jn	Jn	

1918						1919																								
Oc	Oc	Nv	Nv	Dc	Dc	Ja	Ja	Fb	Fb	Ma	Ma	Ap	Ap	My	My	Jn	Jn	Jy	Jy	Ag	Ag	Sp	Sp	Oc	Oc	Nv	Nv	Dc	Dc	
2	2	5	8	13	16	19	==	==	==	==	==	==	==	–	–	–	–	–	–	–	–	–	–	–	–	–	–	–	–	K-K-K-KATY (1918)
3	3	4	6	6	9	9	12	14	19	==	==	==	==	–	–	–	–	–	–	–	–	–	–	–	–	–	–	–	–	ROCK-A-BYE YOUR BABY WITH A DIXIE MELODY (1918)
1	1	1	1	1	1	3	7	8	11	17	==	==	==	–	–	–	–	–	–	–	–	–	–	–	–	–	–	–	–	SMILES (1918)
8	7	6	4	2	2	1	2	3	5	9	11	15	==	==	==	==	==	–	–	–	–	–	–	–	–	–	–	–	–	I'M ALWAYS CHASING RAINBOWS (1918)
4	4	3	5	5	8	12	14	==	==	–	–	–	–	–	–	–	–	–	–	–	–	–	–	–	–	–	–	–	–	OH! HOW I HATE TO GET UP IN THE MORNING (1918)
11	11	11	12	10	13	14	13	11	18	==	==	==	==	–	–	–	–	–	–	–	–	–	–	–	–	–	–	–	–	OUI, OUI, MARIE (1918)
9	9	10	10	9	11	10	10	9	13	18	==	==	==	==	==	–	–	–	–	–	–	–	–	–	–	–	–	–	–	OH! FRENCHY (1918)
7	6	2	2	4	4	6	9	12	==	==	–	–	–	–	–	–	–	–	–	–	–	–	–	–	–	–	–	–	–	EVERYTHING IS PEACHES DOWN IN GEORGIA (1918)
12	10	9	7	8	12	15	15	==	==	==	–	–	–	–	–	–	–	–	–	–	–	–	–	–	–	–	–	–	–	AFTER YOU'VE GONE (1918)
14	13	13	11	7	3	4	4	6	8	11	12	18	==	==	==	==	==	–	–	–	–	–	–	–	–	–	–	–	–	HINDUSTAN (1918)
==	12	8	3	3	5	8	11	19	==	==	–	–	–	–	–	–	–	–	–	–	–	–	–	–	–	–	–	–	–	OH! HOW I WISH I COULD SLEEP UNTIL MY DADDY COMES HOME
==	==	==	==	==	17	16	20	==	==	==	==	==	==	–	–	–	–	–	–	–	–	–	–	–	–	–	–	–	–	I'M GLAD I CAN MAKE YOU CRY (1918)
–	–	==	==	19	19	17	16	17	16	20	==	==	–	–	–	–	–	–	–	–	–	–	–	–	–	–	–	–	–	WOULD YOU RATHER BE A COLONEL WITH AN EAGLE ON YOUR SHOULDER OR A PRIVATE WITH A CHICKEN ON YOUR KNEE?
==	==	==	==	20	20	18	19	18	14	16	15	13	12	11	12	11	13	12	13	15	14	18	==	==	==	==	==	==	==	A GOOD MAN IS HARD TO FIND
==	==	17	16	16	14	13	8	7	7	7	7	7	9	13	16	20	17	16	17	20	==	==	==	==	==	==	==	–	–	DEAR LITTLE BOY OF MINE
==	==	==	==	==	==	==	==	20	==	==	20	==	==	==	–	–	–	–	–	–	–	–	–	–	–	–	–	–	–	O DEATH, WHERE IS THY STING?
–	–	==	==	12	6	2	1	2	4	5	8	10	16	==	==	–	–	–	–	–	–	–	–	–	–	–	–	–	–	ROSE OF NO MAN'S LAND
–	–	==	==	==	15	11	6	4	2	3	5	6	8	15	==	==	==	==	==	–	–	–	–	–	–	–	–	–	–	MICKEY
–	–	==	==	==	==	20	17	13	10	13	17	==	==	==	==	==	==	==	==	==	==	–	–	–	–	–	–	–	–	DEAR OLD PAL OF MINE
–	==	==	15	11	7	7	5	5	3	2	3	4	4	4	6	6	10	10	10	10	13	19	==	==	==	==	==	==	==	BEAUTIFUL OHIO
–	–	==	20	14	10	5	3	1	1	1	1	1	1	2	2	3	3	6	6	6	7	13	==	==	==	–	–	–	–	TILL WE MEET AGAIN
–	–	==	==	==	==	==	==	==	20	14	14	12	11	12	10	14	16	15	12	13	18	==	==	==	==	==	==	==	==	KENTUCKY DREAM WALTZ
–	–	–	–	==	==	==	==	16	12	10	10	14	17	==	==	==	==	–	–	–	–	–	–	–	–	–	–	–	–	KISSES, THE SWEETEST KISSES OF ALL
–	–	–	–	–	–	==	==	15	9	6	6	5	6	10	14	==	==	–	–	–	–	–	–	–	–	–	–	–	–	MADELON
–	–	–	–	–	–	==	==	==	==	19	19	20	18	==	==	==	==	–	–	–	–	–	–	–	–	–	–	–	–	SALVATION LASSIE OF MINE
–	–	–	–	–	–	==	==	==	17	15	16	16	19	20	==	==	==	==	==	–	–	–	–	–	–	–	–	–	–	EVERYBODY SHIMMIES NOW
–	–	–	–	–	–	==	18	10	6	4	2	2	3	3	5	10	12	17	==	==	–	–	–	–	–	–	–	–	–	JA-DA
–	–	–	–	–	–	==	==	==	15	12	9	8	5	5	8	12	14	14	15	16	20	==	==	==	==	==	==	–	–	THAT WONDERFUL MOTHER OF MINE
–	–	–	–	–	–	==	==	==	==	==	==	19	15	14	9	9	8	7	5	4	3	3	7	9	16	==	==	==	==	WHEN YOU LOOK IN THE HEART OF A ROSE
–	–	–	–	–	–	–	==	==	==	==	==	==	20	==	==	==	==	–	–	–	–	–	–	–	–	–	–	–	–	EVERY DAY WILL BE SUNDAY WHEN THE TOWN GOES DRY
–	–	–	–	–	–	–	–	==	==	==	13	9	7	8	11	16	18	==	==	==	–	–	–	–	–	–	–	–	–	COME ON, PAPA
–	–	–	–	–	–	–	–	==	==	8	4	3	2	1	1	2	2	3	7	12	==	==	–	–	–	–	–	–	–	HOW YA GONNA KEEP 'EM DOWN ON THE FARM?
–	–	–	–	–	–	–	–	–	–	==	==	17	13	9	7	5	6	8	9	9	9	10	17	==	==	–	–	–	–	I'LL SAY SHE DOES
–	–	–	–	–	–	–	–	–	–	==	==	==	==	==	==	==	20	19	20	==	==	==	==	–	–	–	–	–	–	ME-OW
–	–	–	–	–	–	–	–	–	–	==	==	==	==	==	==	==	19	18	==	==	==	–	–	–	–	–	–	–	–	MY BARNEY LIES OVER THE OCEAN (JUST THE WAY HE LIED TO ME)
Oc	Oc	Nv	Nv	Dc	Dc	Ja	Ja	Fb	Fb	Ma	Ma	Ap	Ap	My	My	Jn	Jn	Jy	Jy	Ag	Ag	Sp	Sp	Oc	Oc	Nv	Nv	Dc	Dc	

1919																				1920										
Ma	Ma	Ap	Ap	My	My	Jn	Jn	Jy	Jy	Ag	Ag	Sp	Sp	Oc	Oc	Nv	Nv	Dc	Dc	Ja	Ja	Fb	Fb	Ma	Ma	Ap	Ap	My	My	
==	==	==	==	19	19	19	==	==	==	==	==	–	–	–	–	–	–	–	–	–	–	–	–	–	–	–	–	–	–	DON'T CRY, FRENCHY, DON'T CRY
==	==	==	==	17	18	18	==	==	==	==	–	–	–	–	–	–	–	==	==	==	==	==	==	==	20	17	==	==	==	THAT TUMBLEDOWN SHACK IN ATHLONE
==	18	11	10	7	4	4	5	9	8	7	10	20	==	–	–	–	–	–	–	–	–	–	–	–	–	–	–	–	–	CHONG, HE COME FROM HONG KONG
==	==	==	==	16	13	8	7	4	3	5	6	16	==	==	==	==	==	–	–	–	–	–	–	–	–	–	–	–	–	SWEET HAWAIIAN MOONLIGHT
–	–	==	==	18	15	7	4	2	2	2	2	8	14	==	==	==	==	–	–	–	–	–	–	–	–	–	–	–	–	MAMMY O' MINE
–	–	==	14	6	3	**1**	**1**	**1**	**1**	**1**	**1**	**1**	3	11	19	==	==	–	–	–	–	–	–	–	–	–	–	–	–	I'M FOREVER BLOWING BUBBLES
–	–	==	==	==	17	13	9	5	4	3	4	2	6	10	14	19	==	==	==	==	==	–	–	–	–	–	–	–	–	SMILIN' THROUGH
–	–	–	–	==	==	17	15	13	14	17	==	==	–	–	–	–	–	–	–	–	–	–	–	–	–	–	–	–	–	ALCOHOLIC BLUES
–	–	–	–	==	20	15	11	11	11	11	8	9	10	15	==	==	–	–	–	–	–	–	–	–	–	–	–	–	–	IT'S NOBODY'S BUSINESS BUT MY OWN
–	–	–	–	–	–	==	==	==	18	18	17	15	16	16	20	20	==	==	==	==	==	==	==	==	–	–	–	–	–	THE BELLS OF ST. MARY'S
–	–	–	–	–	–	==	==	20	16	8	5	4	5	4	8	13	15	18	17	17	==	==	==	==	–	–	–	–	–	BLUES (MY NAUGHTY SWEETIE GIVES TO ME)
–	–	–	–	–	–	–	–	==	19	14	12	11	12	==	==	–	–	–	–	–	–	–	–	–	–	–	–	–	–	DADDY LONG LEGS
–	–	–	–	–	–	–	–	==	==	==	==	==	20	20	==	==	==	==	–	–	–	–	–	–	–	–	–	–	–	EVERYBODY WANTS A KEY TO MY CELLAR
–	–	–	–	–	–	–	–	==	==	==	==	==	==	==	17	14	18	==	==	==	==	==	==	==	==	==	==	–	–	TAKE ME TO THE LAND OF JAZZ
–	–	–	–	–	–	–	–	–	==	19	11	5	**1**	**1**	2	3	4	5	6	8	16	==	==	–	–	–	–	–	–	A PRETTY GIRL IS LIKE A MELODY
–	–	–	–	–	–	–	–	–	–	==	15	6	4	3	3	2	3	3	4	7	7	14	==	==	–	–	–	–	–	TELL ME (WHY NIGHTS ARE LONELY)
–	–	–	–	–	–	–	–	–	–	==	16	7	2	2	**1**	**1**	**1**	2	3	6	15	==	==	==	–	–	–	–	–	MANDY
–	–	–	–	–	–	–	–	–	–	==	19	12	8	6	5	5	7	11	14	==	==	==	==	–	–	–	–	–	–	THE VAMP
–	–	–	–	–	–	–	–	–	–	==	==	14	9	8	11	16	==	==	–	–	–	–	–	–	–	–	–	–	–	SIPPING CIDER THROUGH A STRAW
–	–	–	–	–	–	–	–	–	–	==	==	17	11	5	6	6	11	17	==	==	==	–	–	–	–	–	–	–	–	TULIP TIME
–	–	–	–	–	–	–	–	–	–	==	==	==	15	13	9	10	13	==	==	==	==	==	==	–	–	–	–	–	–	CHINESE LULLABY
–	–	–	–	–	–	–	–	–	–	==	==	==	13	14	10	9	8	7	10	15	19	20	==	==	==	==	==	–	–	I'LL BE HAPPY WHEN THE PREACHER MAKES YOU MINE
–	–	–	–	–	–	–	–	–	–	==	==	==	==	17	13	11	9	12	13	18	==	==	==	==	==	==	==	–	–	AND HE'D SAY OOH-LA-LA! WEE WEE
–	–	–	–	–	–	–	–	–	–	–	==	==	==	==	18	15	19	==	==	==	==	–	–	–	–	–	–	–	–	DREAMY ALABAMA
–	–	–	–	–	–	–	–	–	–	–	==	==	==	19	15	12	10	13	15	20	==	==	==	==	==	==	==	–	–	ALEXANDER'S BAND IS BACK IN DIXIE LAND
–	–	–	–	–	–	–	–	–	–	–	–	==	==	18	12	8	6	6	9	16	==	==	==	–	–	–	–	–	–	I'VE GOT MY CAPTAIN WORKING FOR ME NOW
–	–	–	–	–	–	–	–	–	–	–	–	==	19	12	7	7	5	4	2	3	8	10	19	==	==	–	–	–	–	NOBODY KNOWS, AND NOBODY SEEMS TO CARE
–	–	–	–	–	–	–	–	–	–	–	–	==	18	7	4	4	2	**1**	**1**	**1**	3	6	12	18	==	==	==	–	–	OH! WHAT A PAL WAS MARY
–	–	–	–	–	–	–	–	–	–	–	–	==	==	==	==	==	==	20	==	19	==	==	==	==	==	==	==	–	–	MY BABY'S ARMS
–	–	–	–	–	–	–	–	–	–	–	–	–	–	==	==	==	17	16	18	==	20	==	==	==	==	–	–	–	–	YOU DIDN'T WANT ME WHEN YOU HAD ME
–	–	–	–	–	–	–	–	–	–	–	–	–	–	==	==	==	==	19	20	==	==	==	==	==	==	–	–	–	–	THEY'RE ALL SWEETIES
–	–	–	–	–	–	–	–	–	–	–	–	–	–	==	==	17	12	8	8	9	10	15	==	==	==	–	–	–	–	WAIT TILL YOU GET THEM UP IN THE AIR, BOYS
–	–	–	–	–	–	–	–	–	–	–	–	–	–	==	==	18	14	9	12	10	11	12	16	==	==	==	==	–	–	CAROLINA SUNSHINE
–	–	–	–	–	–	–	–	–	–	–	–	–	–	==	==	==	==	==	16	12	13	11	10	8	10	9	7	6	6	THAT NAUGHTY WALTZ (1920)
–	–	–	–	–	–	–	–	–	–	–	–	–	–	–	–	==	==	15	11	5	4	3	3	4	3	6	10	10	17	MY ISLE OF GOLDEN DREAMS (1920)
–	–	–	–	–	–	–	–	–	–	–	–	–	–	–	–	==	16	10	5	2	**1**	**1**	2	2	2	**1**	**1**	5	14	LET THE REST OF THE WORLD GO BY (1920)
–	–	–	–	–	–	–	–	–	–	–	–	–	–	–	–	==	20	14	7	4	2	5	6	10	17	==	==	–	–	YOU'D BE SURPRISED (1920)
–	–	–	–	–	–	–	–	–	–	–	–	–	–	–	–	–	–	==	19	11	6	2	**1**	**1**	**1**	2	6	11	==	DARDANELLA (1920)
Ma	Ma	Ap	Ap	My	My	Jn	Jn	Jy	Jy	Ag	Ag	Sp	Sp	Oc	Oc	Nv	Nv	Dc	Dc	Ja	Ja	Fb	Fb	Ma	Ma	Ap	Ap	My	My	

1919												1920														
Oc	Oc	Nv	Nv	Dc	Dc	Ja	Ja	Fb	Fb	Ma	Ma	Ap	Ap	My	My	Jn	Jn	Jy	Jy	Ag	Ag	Sp	Sp	Oc	Oc	
4	8	13	15	18	17	17	==	==	==	==	==	==	==	==	==	–	–	–	–	–	–	–	–	–	–	BLUES (MY NAUGHTY SWEETIE GIVES TO ME) (1919)
1	2	3	4	5	6	8	16	==	==	==	–	–	–	–	–	–	–	–	–	–	–	–	–	–	–	A PRETTY GIRL IS LIKE A MELODY (1919)
3	3	2	3	3	4	7	7	14	==	==	–	–	–	–	–	–	–	–	–	–	–	–	–	–	–	TELL ME (WHY NIGHTS ARE LONELY) (1919)
2	1	1	1	2	3	6	15	==	==	==	–	–	–	–	–	–	–	–	–	–	–	–	–	–	–	MANDY (1919)
14	10	9	8	7	10	15	19	20	==	==	==	==	==	–	–	–	–	–	–	–	–	–	–	–	–	I'LL BE HAPPY WHEN THE PREACHER MAKES YOU MINE (1919)
17	13	11	9	12	13	18	==	==	==	==	==	==	==	–	–	–	–	–	–	–	–	–	–	–	–	AND HE'D SAY OOH-LA-LA! WEE WEE (1919)
19	15	12	10	13	15	20	==	==	==	==	==	==	==	–	–	–	–	–	–	–	–	–	–	–	–	ALEXANDER'S BAND IS BACK IN DIXIE LAND (1919)
18	12	8	6	6	9	16	==	==	==	–	–	–	–	–	–	–	–	–	–	–	–	–	–	–	–	I'VE GOT MY CAPTAIN WORKING FOR ME NOW (1919)
12	7	7	5	4	2	3	8	10	19	==	==	–	–	–	–	–	–	–	–	–	–	–	–	–	–	NOBODY KNOWS, AND NOBODY SEEMS TO CARE (1919)
7	4	4	2	1	1	1	3	6	12	18	==	==	==	–	–	–	–	–	–	–	–	–	–	–	–	OH! WHAT A PAL WAS MARY (1919)
==	==	==	17	16	18	==	20	==	==	==	==	–	–	–	–	–	–	–	–	–	–	–	–	–	–	YOU DIDN'T WANT ME WHEN YOU HAD ME (1919)
==	==	17	12	8	8	9	10	15	==	==	==	–	–	–	–	–	–	–	–	–	–	–	–	–	–	WAIT TILL YOU GET THEM UP IN THE AIR, BOYS (1919)
==	==	18	14	9	12	10	11	12	16	==	==	==	==	–	–	–	–	–	–	–	–	–	–	–	–	CAROLINA SUNSHINE (1919)
==	==	==	==	20	==	19	==	==	==	==	==	==	==	==	==	==	==	–	–	–	–	–	–	–	–	MY BABY'S ARMS (1919)
==	==	==	==	==	==	14	9	8	5	6	8	12	19	==	==	==	==	==	–	–	–	–	–	–	–	ON MIAMI SHORE
==	==	==	==	==	==	==	==	==	20	==	==	==	==	==	==	==	==	==	==	==	20	16	==	==	==	ST. LOUIS BLUES
==	==	==	==	==	==	==	18	18	17	17	19	==	==	==	==	==	==	==	–	–	–	–	–	–	–	BABY, WON'T YOU PLEASE COME HOME
==	==	==	==	==	==	==	==	19	13	11	11	10	8	8	8	14	16	16	17	17	==	==	==	==	==	YOUR EYES HAVE TOLD ME SO
–	–	==	==	==	16	12	13	11	10	8	10	9	7	6	6	9	14	17	19	==	==	==	==	==	==	THAT NAUGHTY WALTZ
–	–	==	==	15	11	5	4	3	3	4	3	6	10	10	17	==	==	==	–	–	–	–	–	–	–	MY ISLE OF GOLDEN DREAMS
–	–	==	16	10	5	2	1	1	2	2	2	1	1	5	14	20	==	==	==	–	–	–	–	–	–	LET THE REST OF THE WORLD GO BY
–	–	==	20	14	7	4	2	5	6	10	17	==	==	–	–	–	–	–	–	–	–	–	–	–	–	YOU'D BE SURPRISED
–	–	–	==	==	==	13	5	4	4	3	4	5	11	19	==	==	==	==	–	–	–	–	–	–	–	PEGGY
–	–	–	–	==	19	11	6	2	1	1	1	2	6	11	==	==	–	–	–	–	–	–	–	–	–	DARDANELLA
–	–	==	==	==	==	==	14	9	11	13	13	20	==	==	==	==	–	–	–	–	–	–	–	–	–	I MIGHT BE YOUR ONCE-IN-A-WHILE
–	–	–	==	==	==	==	17	18	17	19	14	15	18	==	==	==	==	–	–	–	–	–	–	–	–	YOU AIN'T HEARD NOTHIN' YET
–	–	–	==	==	==	==	12	7	8	12	18	==	==	==	–	–	–	–	–	–	–	–	–	–	–	FRECKLES
–	–	–	–	==	==	==	==	==	==	==	20	17	==	==	==	–	–	–	–	–	–	–	–	–	–	THAT TUMBLEDOWN SHACK IN ATHLONE
–	–	–	–	–	–	==	==	17	9	9	9	==	==	==	–	–	–	–	–	–	–	–	–	–	–	ALL THE QUAKERS ARE SHOULDER SHAKERS (DOWN IN QUAKER TOWN)
–	–	–	–	–	–	==	==	13	7	5	5	8	14	==	==	–	–	–	–	–	–	–	–	–	–	YOU'RE A MILLION MILES FROM NOWHERE
–	–	–	–	–	–	==	==	==	18	16	==	==	==	==	==	==	–	–	–	–	–	–	–	–	–	YELLOW DOG BLUES
–	–	–	–	–	–	==	==	==	==	20	==	19	13	13	7	8	12	11	11	10	8	14	12	20	==	JUST LIKE A GYPSY
–	–	–	–	–	–	–	–	==	==	15	12	16	==	==	–	–	–	–	–	–	–	–	–	–	–	WAS THERE EVER A PAL LIKE YOU
–	–	–	–	–	–	–	–	==	14	7	6	3	3	2	1	1	2	3	5	12	14	==	==	–	–	SWANEE
–	–	–	–	–	–	–	–	==	==	==	==	==	==	17	13	12	10	10	15	19	==	==	==	==	==	== == == == == 20 20 == == == ALICE BLUE GOWN
–	–	–	–	–	–	–	–	–	==	==	==	18	15	15	16	==	==	–	–	–	–	–	–	–	–	AFGHANISTAN
–	–	–	–	–	–	–	–	–	==	14	7	4	2	1	2	2	3	15	==	==	–	–	–	–	–	WHEN MY BABY SMILES AT ME
–	–	–	–	–	–	–	–	–	==	==	==	==	==	==	19	16	13	9	8	4	6	8	11	9	13	17 == VENETIAN MOON
–	–	–	–	–	–	–	–	–	–	==	==	14	12	14	20	==	==	==	–	–	–	–	–	–	–	OH!
–	–	–	–	–	–	–	–	–	–	==	15	7	4	3	3	6	18	==	==	–	–	–	–	–	–	DADDY, YOU'VE BEEN A MOTHER TO ME
–	–	–	–	–	–	–	–	–	–	==	16	11	5	4	5	4	9	12	13	==	==	–	–	–	–	I'LL SEE YOU IN C-U-B-A
Oc	Oc	Nv	Nv	Dc	Dc	Ja	Ja	Fb	Fb	Ma	Ma	Ap	Ap	My	My	Jn	Jn	Jy	Jy	Ag	Ag	Sp	Sp	Oc	Oc	

1920																				1921						
Ma	Ma	Ap	Ap	My	My	Jn	Jn	Jy	Jy	Ag	Ag	Sp	Sp	Oc	Oc	Nv	Nv	Dc	Dc	Ja	Ja	Fb	Fb	Ma	Ma	
==	==	13	9	7	10	18	==	==	–	–	–	–	–	–	–	–	–	–	–	–	–	–	–	–	–	OH! HOW I LAUGH WHEN I THINK I CRIED OVER YOU
–	==	==	20	16	12	10	8	7	10	9	11	13	19	==	==	–	–	–	–	–	–	–	–	–	–	IRENE
–	==	==	17	12	11	5	4	5	6	5	7	9	==	==	–	–	–	–	–	–	–	–	–	–	–	OH BY JINGO! OH BY GEE! (YOU'RE THE ONLY GIRL FOR ME)
–	==	==	==	20	==	==	==	==	==	–	–	–	–	–	–	–	–	–	–	–	–	–	–	–	–	THE MOON SHINES ON THE MOONSHINE
–	–	==	==	18	9	7	15	18	==	==	–	–	–	–	–	–	–	–	–	–	–	–	–	–	–	WHOSE BABY ARE YOU?
–	–	==	16	9	4	3	**1**	**1**	3	7	18	==	–	–	–	–	–	–	–	–	–	–	–	–	–	ROSE OF WASHINGTON SQUARE
–	–	==	==	==	==	==	20	==	==	==	19	==	==	==	==	–	–	–	–	–	–	–	–	–	–	YOU CAN'T KEEP A GOOD MAN DOWN
–	–	==	==	==	==	==	19	19	20	==	==	==	==	==	–	–	–	–	–	–	–	–	–	–	–	OLD MAN JAZZ
–	–	==	==	==	==	17	17	13	14	15	==	==	==	==	–	–	–	–	–	–	–	–	–	–	–	ALABAMA MOON
–	–	==	==	==	==	==	==	==	18	20	==	18	==	==	==	==	==	==	–	–	–	–	–	–	–	JAZZ BABIES' BALL
–	–	==	==	==	15	11	6	4	2	2	2	4	8	15	==	==	==	==	–	–	–	–	–	–	–	LA VEEDA
–	–	==	==	==	18	13	5	2	**1**	**1**	**1**	**1**	2	5	9	11	14	20	==	==	==	==	–	–	–	HOLD ME
–	–	–	–	==	==	19	11	8	9	8	15	20	==	==	–	–	–	–	–	–	–	–	–	–	–	LEFT ALL ALONE AGAIN BLUES
–	–	–	–	==	==	==	==	20	16	14	13	15	17	==	==	==	==	==	–	–	–	–	–	–	–	THE ARGENTINES, THE PORTUGUESE, AND THE GREEKS
–	–	–	–	==	==	15	7	6	4	11	17	==	==	–	–	–	–	–	–	–	–	–	–	–	–	SO LONG! OO-LONG
–	–	–	–	–	–	==	==	14	7	3	3	5	7	13	20	==	==	==	–	–	–	–	–	–	–	PRETTY KITTY KELLY
–	–	–	–	–	–	==	==	==	==	18	10	7	10	14	18	19	==	==	==	==	==	==	–	–	–	I'M A JAZZ VAMPIRE
–	–	–	–	–	–	==	==	==	12	6	4	3	4	6	8	15	18	==	==	==	==	==	–	–	–	HIAWATHA'S MELODY OF LOVE
–	–	–	–	–	–	–	–	==	==	16	12	11	9	7	7	10	16	14	==	==	==	==	–	–	–	AFTER YOU GET WHAT YOU WANT YOU DON'T WANT IT
–	–	–	–	–	–	–	–	==	==	13	5	2	**1**	**1**	2	2	3	3	7	11	15	==	==	–	–	THE LOVE NEST
–	–	–	–	–	–	–	–	–	==	==	9	6	3	3	3	5	8	13	18	==	–	–	–	–	–	A YOUNG MAN'S FANCY
–	–	–	–	–	–	–	–	–	–	==	16	10	6	4	4	4	5	7	11	12	16	==	==	–	–	TELL ME, LITTLE GYPSY
–	–	–	–	–	–	–	–	–	–	==	==	17	16	16	17	16	15	17	20	18	==	==	==	==	–	TWELFTH STREET RAG
–	–	–	–	–	–	–	–	–	–	–	==	19	15	11	10	9	11	16	==	==	–	–	–	–	–	MY LITTLE BIMBO (FROM THE BAMBOO ISLE)
–	–	–	–	–	–	–	–	–	–	–	==	==	13	12	11	8	7	11	15	17	19	==	==	==	==	TRIPOLI
–	–	–	–	–	–	–	–	–	–	–	==	12	5	2	**1**	**1**	**1**	**1**	**1**	3	6	7	8	17	==	WHISPERING
–	–	–	–	–	–	–	–	–	–	–	==	==	18	18	15	14	10	10	12	14	12	13	17	==	==	I LOVE THE LAND OF OLD BLACK JOE
–	–	–	–	–	–	–	–	–	–	–	–	==	==	==	19	18	20	==	==	==	–	–	–	–	–	WHEN YOU'RE GONE I WON'T FORGET
–	–	–	–	–	–	–	–	–	–	–	–	==	14	8	5	3	2	2	2	2	5	9	13	==	==	THE JAPANESE SANDMAN
–	–	–	–	–	–	–	–	–	–	–	–	==	==	19	14	12	13	12	13	16	13	15	==	==	==	THAT OLD IRISH MOTHER OF MINE
–	–	–	–	–	–	–	–	–	–	–	–	==	==	==	==	==	==	==	16	20	==	18	==	==	==	DIXIE MADE US JAZZ BAND MAD
–	–	–	–	–	–	–	–	–	–	–	–	==	20	10	6	6	4	4	4	6	8	8	9	18	==	I'LL BE WITH YOU IN APPLE BLOSSOM TIME
–	–	–	–	–	–	–	–	–	–	–	–	==	==	17	12	7	6	5	6	9	11	10	15	==	==	CHILI BEAN
–	–	–	–	–	–	–	–	–	–	–	–	–	==	==	16	13	9	9	8	7	9	11	16	==	==	MY HOME TOWN IS A ONE-HORSE TOWN
–	–	–	–	–	–	–	–	–	–	–	–	–	==	==	==	==	19	==	19	==	==	==	==	==	==	CUBAN MOON
–	–	–	–	–	–	–	–	–	–	–	–	–	–	–	==	20	12	6	3	**1**	**1**	3	5	11	18	AVALON (1921)
–	–	–	–	–	–	–	–	–	–	–	–	–	–	–	==	==	==	19	14	15	14	14	12	19	==	BEAUTIFUL ANNABELLE LEE (1921)
–	–	–	–	–	–	–	–	–	–	–	–	–	–	–	–	==	17	8	5	4	3	4	6	14	19	FEATHER YOUR NEST (1921)
–	–	–	–	–	–	–	–	–	–	–	–	–	–	–	–	–	==	18	10	8	7	5	4	5	10	BROADWAY ROSE (1921)
–	–	–	–	–	–	–	–	–	–	–	–	–	–	–	–	–	==	15	9	5	2	2	2	2	6	(LENA FROM) PALESTEENA (1921)
–	–	–	–	–	–	–	–	–	–	–	–	–	–	–	–	–	–	==	17	10	4	**1**	**1**	**1**	1	MARGIE (1921)
Ma	Ma	Ap	Ap	My	My	Jn	Jn	Jy	Jy	Ag	Ag	Sp	Sp	Oc	Oc	Nv	Nv	Dc	Dc	Ja	Ja	Fb	Fb	Ma	Ma	

1920														1921												
Oc	Oc	Nv	Nv	Dc	Dc	Ja	Ja	Fb	Fb	Ma	Ma	Ap	Ap	My	My	Jn	Jn	Jy	Jy	Ag	Ag	Sp	Sp	Oc	Oc	
1	2	2	3	3	7	11	15	==	==	–	–	–	–	–	–	–	–	–	–	–	–	–	–	–	–	THE LOVE NEST (1920)
4	4	4	5	7	11	12	16	==	==	–	–	–	–	–	–	–	–	–	–	–	–	–	–	–	–	TELL ME, LITTLE GYPSY (1920)
16	17	16	15	17	20	18	==	==	==	==	–	–	–	–	–	–	–	–	–	–	–	–	–	–	–	TWELFTH STREET RAG (1920)
12	11	8	7	11	15	17	19	==	==	==	==	–	–	–	–	–	–	–	–	–	–	–	–	–	–	TRIPOLI (1920)
2	1	1	1	1	1	3	6	7	8	17	==	–	–	–	–	–	–	–	–	–	–	–	–	–	–	WHISPERING (1920)
18	15	14	10	10	12	14	12	13	17	==	==	==	==	–	–	–	–	–	–	–	–	–	–	–	–	I LOVE THE LAND OF OLD BLACK JOE (1920)
8	5	3	2	2	2	2	5	9	13	==	==	–	–	–	–	–	–	–	–	–	–	–	–	–	–	THE JAPANESE SANDMAN (1920)
19	14	12	13	12	13	16	13	15	==	==	==	==	–	–	–	–	–	–	–	–	–	–	–	–	–	THAT OLD IRISH MOTHER OF MINE (1920)
==	==	==	==	==	16	20	==	18	==	==	==	==	==	==	==	==	–	–	–	–	–	–	–	–	–	DIXIE MADE US JAZZ BAND MAD (1920)
10	6	6	4	4	4	6	8	8	9	18	==	==	–	–	–	–	–	–	–	–	–	–	–	–	–	I'LL BE WITH YOU IN APPLE BLOSSOM TIME (1920)
17	12	7	6	5	6	9	11	10	15	==	==	==	==	==	–	–	–	–	–	–	–	–	–	–	–	CHILI BEAN (1920)
==	16	13	9	9	8	7	9	11	16	==	==	–	–	–	–	–	–	–	–	–	–	–	–	–	–	MY HOME TOWN IS A ONE-HORSE TOWN (1920)
==	==	==	==	==	==	==	20	20	==	==	==	==	==	==	–	–	–	–	–	–	–	–	–	–	–	ALICE BLUE GOWN (1920)
–	==	20	12	6	3	1	1	3	5	11	18	==	–	–	–	–	–	–	–	–	–	–	–	–	–	AVALON
–	==	==	==	19	14	15	14	14	12	19	==	==	==	–	–	–	–	–	–	–	–	–	–	–	–	BEAUTIFUL ANNABELLE LEE
–	–	==	17	8	5	4	3	4	6	14	19	==	–	–	–	–	–	–	–	–	–	–	–	–	–	FEATHER YOUR NEST
–	–	–	==	18	10	8	7	5	4	5	10	==	==	–	–	–	–	–	–	–	–	–	–	–	–	BROADWAY ROSE
–	–	–	==	15	9	5	2	2	2	2	6	13	==	==	–	–	–	–	–	–	–	–	–	–	–	(LENA FROM) PALESTEENA
–	–	–	–	==	17	10	4	1	1	1	1	4	7	13	20	==	–	–	–	–	–	–	–	–	–	MARGIE
–	–	==	==	==	==	19	18	17	==	==	==	==	==	–	–	–	–	–	–	–	–	–	–	–	–	SWEET MAMA (PAPA'S GETTIN' MAD)
–	–	–	–	–	==	13	10	6	3	3	11	14	19	==	==	–	–	–	–	–	–	–	–	–	–	OLD PAL, WHY DON'T YOU ANSWER ME?
–	–	–	–	–	–	–	==	19	10	4	3	2	3	4	6	10	14	18	==	–	–	–	–	–	–	I NEVER KNEW (I COULD LOVE ANYBODY)
–	–	–	–	–	–	–	==	==	11	6	5	6	8	14	==	==	–	–	–	–	–	–	–	–	–	DOWN BY THE O-HI-O
–	–	–	–	–	==	==	17	12	7	7	13	16	==	==	==	=	=	–	–	–	–	–	–	–	–	ALL SHE'D SAY WAS "UMH-HUM"
–	–	–	–	–	–	==	==	16	14	10	8	7	5	6	8	6	5	7	11	15	15	18	==	==	==	THE WANG WANG BLUES
–	–	–	–	–	–	==	==	==	==	==	20	==	17	17	11	8	7	5	5	8	9	11	12	14	18	==STRUT, MISS LIZZIE
–	–	–	–	–	–	–	==	==	19	15	12	10	13	16	14	19	==	==	–	–	–	–	–	–	–	CRAZY BLUES
–	–	–	–	–	–	–	–	==	20	13	9	9	9	8	12	17	==	==	–	–	–	–	–	–	–	DO YOU EVER THINK OF ME?
–	–	–	–	–	–	–	–	==	==	20	16	15	18	==	==	==	==	==	–	–	–	–	–	–	–	MAZIE
–	–	–	–	–	–	–	–	==	==	12	7	5	4	3	5	7	8	15	==	==	–	–	–	–	–	I USED TO LOVE YOU, BUT IT'S ALL OVER NOW
–	–	–	–	–	–	–	–	==	==	9	4	3	2	2	1	1	1	4	9	12	17	==	==	–	–	MY MAMMY
–	–	–	–	–	–	–	–	==	==	==	==	==	==	20	17	14	13	12	15	13	13	15	18	==	==	HOME AGAIN BLUES
–	–	–	–	–	–	–	–	==	18	8	2	1	1	1	2	4	10	20	==	–	–	–	–	–	–	BRIGHT EYES
–	–	–	–	–	–	–	–	==	==	16	14	8	6	7	9	11	18	==	==	==	–	–	–	–	–	LOOK FOR THE SILVER LINING
–	–	–	–	–	–	–	–	–	==	==	15	11	16	18	18	==	==	==	–	–	–	–	–	–	–	LOVE BIRD
–	–	–	–	–	–	–	–	–	–	==	17	12	12	10	10	15	19	==	–	–	–	–	–	–	–	I'M MISSIN' MAMMY'S KISSIN'
–	–	–	–	–	–	–	–	–	–	==	==	17	14	12	15	==	==	==	–	–	–	–	–	–	–	TIMBUCTOO
–	–	–	–	–	–	–	–	–	–	==	==	==	20	19	==	==	–	–	–	–	–	–	–	–	–	SOME LITTLE BIRD
–	–	–	–	–	–	–	–	–	–	–	==	20	15	11	13	18	==	==	–	–	–	–	–	–	–	WHIP-POOR-WILL
–	–	–	–	–	–	–	–	–	–	–	==	18	10	5	4	5	4	9	13	19	–	–	–	–	–	I FOUND A ROSE IN THE DEVIL'S GARDEN
–	–	–	–	–	–	–	–	–	–	–	==	19	11	9	3	2	2	2	4	9	12	17	==	–	–	MAKE BELIEVE
Oc	Oc	Nv	Nv	Dc	Dc	Ja	Ja	Fb	Fb	Ma	Ma	Ap	Ap	My	My	Jn	Jn	Jy	Jy	Ag	Ag	Sp	Sp	Oc	Oc	

						1 9 2 1															1 9 2 2					
Ap	**Ap**	**My**	**My**	**Jn**	**Jn**	**Jy**	**Jy**	**Ag**	**Ag**	**Sp**	**Sp**	**Oc**	**Oc**	**Nv**	**Nv**	**Dc**	**Dc**	**Ja**	**Ja**	**Fb**	**Fb**	**Ma**	**Ma**	**Ap**	**Ap**	
–	==	15	7	3	3	**1**	**1**	**1**	3	7	11	==	==	–	–	–	–	–	–	–	–	–	–	–	–	AIN'T WE GOT FUN?
–	==	==	16	9	9	11	18	17	18	==	–	–	–	–	–	–	–	–	–	–	–	–	–	–	–	HUMMING
–	–	==	==	==	16	19	19	20	20	==	==	–	–	–	–	–	–	–	–	–	–	–	–	–	–	SPREAD YO' STUFF
–	==	==	19	16	12	8	6	6	5	6	6	7	13	19	==	==	==	==	==	==	–	–	–	–	–	DOWN YONDER
–	–	==	==	==	17	14	17	16	16	19	19	18	==	==	–	–	–	–	–	–	–	–	–	–	–	PALE MOON
–	–	==	==	12	6	3	2	2	2	3	4	4	9	12	==	==	==	==	–	–	–	–	–	–	–	PEGGY O'NEILL
–	–	–	==	20	15	10	8	5	6	5	7	8	20	==	==	==	–	–	–	–	–	–	–	–	–	CHERIE
–	–	==	==	13	11	6	3	4	4	2	2	2	3	7	10	20	==	==	==	20	19	==	==	==	–	MY MAN
–	–	–	–	==	==	==	20	==	==	==	==	–	–	–	–	–	–	–	–	–	–	–	–	–	–	WYOMING
–	–	–	–	==	==	17	12	10	11	10	9	9	8	9	13	17	17	==	==	–	–	–	–	–	–	WHO'LL BE THE NEXT ONE TO CRY OVER YOU?
–	–	–	–	==	==	==	16	14	10	8	8	10	14	20	==	==	==	==	==	==	–	–	–	–	–	CROONING
–	–	–	–	–	==	==	14	11	8	9	10	15	==	==	==	==	–	–	–	–	–	–	–	–	–	THE JAZZ ME BLUES
–	–	–	–	==	20	13	7	3	**1**	**1**	**1**	**1**	**1**	2	5	11	19	==	==	==	–	–	–	–	–	ALL BY MYSELF
–	–	–	–	==	==	16	10	7	7	4	3	3	4	8	12	16	20	==	==	==	–	–	–	–	–	I'M NOBODY'S BABY
–	–	–	–	–	–	==	==	18	14	12	15	20	==	==	==	–	–	–	–	–	–	–	–	–	–	LOVE SENDS A LITTLE GIFT OF ROSES
–	–	–	–	–	–	–	==	==	19	16	14	12	12	15	19	==	==	==	==	==	==	==	==	–	–	MOONLIGHT
–	–	–	–	–	–	–	==	==	==	13	17	19	==	==	–	–	–	–	–	–	–	–	–	–	–	OH ME! OH MY! (OH YOU!)
–	–	–	–	–	–	–	–	==	==	20	16	17	15	17	==	==	==	–	–	–	–	–	–	–	–	LOVE WILL FIND A WAY
–	–	–	–	–	–	–	–	==	==	14	5	5	10	13	18	==	==	–	–	–	–	–	–	–	–	LEARN TO SMILE
–	–	–	–	–	–	–	–	–	–	==	==	==	17	18	==	==	==	==	==	==	–	–	–	–	–	EMALINE
–	–	–	–	–	–	–	–	–	–	==	13	6	2	**1**	**1**	2	2	7	9	14	==	==	–	–	–	MA! (HE'S MAKIN' EYES AT ME)
–	–	–	–	–	–	–	–	–	–	–	==	16	7	6	6	5	5	8	8	11	15	==	==	==	–	MY SUNNY TENNESSEE
–	–	–	–	–	–	–	–	–	–	==	20	11	5	5	4	4	4	2	6	8	9	9	12	18	==	TUCK ME TO SLEEP IN MY OLD 'TUCKY HOME
–	–	–	–	–	–	–	–	–	–	–	==	13	6	3	3	3	7	15	==	==	–	–	–	–	–	SWEET LADY
–	–	–	–	–	–	–	–	–	–	–	–	==	16	11	8	7	11	13	13	15	14	19	==	–	–	SECOND HAND ROSE
–	–	–	–	–	–	–	–	–	–	–	–	==	11	4	2	**1**	**1**	**1**	2	7	7	10	==	–	–	SAY IT WITH MUSIC
–	–	–	–	–	–	–	–	–	–	–	–	==	19	10	7	14	==	==	==	–	–	–	–	–	–	I AIN'T NOBODY'S DARLING
–	–	–	–	–	–	–	–	–	–	–	–	==	==	==	17	==	18	20	==	==	==	==	–	–	–	JUST LIKE A RAINBOW
–	–	–	–	–	–	–	–	–	–	–	–	–	==	16	9	8	10	10	15	==	==	==	–	–	–	WHEN FRANCES DANCES WITH ME
–	–	–	–	–	–	–	–	–	–	–	–	–	==	==	==	19	16	17	18	16	18	==	==	==	==	MANDY 'N' ME
–	–	–	–	–	–	–	–	–	–	–	–	–	==	==	14	10	13	14	19	==	–	–	–	–	–	CANADIAN CAPERS
–	–	–	–	–	–	–	–	–	–	–	–	–	–	==	20	13	12	11	16	17	==	==	–	–	–	BIMINI BAY
–	–	–	–	–	–	–	–	–	–	–	–	==	==	14	11	12	9	6	5	5	6	6	9	13	17	TEN LITTLE FINGERS AND TEN LITTLE TOES (1922)
–	–	–	–	–	–	–	–	–	–	–	–	–	–	==	16	9	6	4	7	10	11	16	==	==	–	DAPPER DAN (1922)
–	–	–	–	–	–	–	–	–	–	–	–	–	–	==	==	==	15	12	10	9	10	12	13	14	==	LEAVE ME WITH A SMILE (1922)
–	–	–	–	–	–	–	–	–	–	–	–	–	–	–	==	18	8	5	3	**1**	4	5	8	8	8	APRIL SHOWERS (1922)
–	–	–	–	–	–	–	–	–	–	–	–	–	–	==	==	15	14	9	4	2	2	3	3	4	6	YOO-HOO (1922)
–	–	–	–	–	–	–	–	–	–	–	–	–	–	==	15	6	3	3	**1**	3	5	7	17	==	–	WABASH BLUES (1922)
Ap	**Ap**	**My**	**My**	**Jn**	**Jn**	**Jy**	**Jy**	**Ag**	**Ag**	**Sp**	**Sp**	**Oc**	**Oc**	**Nv**	**Nv**	**Dc**	**Dc**	**Ja**	**Ja**	**Fb**	**Fb**	**Ma**	**Ma**	**Ap**	**Ap**	

1921						1922																				
Oc	Oc	Nv	Nv	Dc	Dc	Ja	Ja	Fb	Fb	Ma	Ma	Ap	Ap	My	My	Jn	Jn	Jy	Jy	Ag	Ag	Sp	Sp	Oc	Oc	
2	3	7	10	20	==	==	==	20	19	==	==	==	–	–	–	–	–	–	–	–	–	–	–	–	–	MY MAN (1921)
6	2	**1**	**1**	2	2	7	9	14	==	==	–	–	–	–	–	–	–	–	–	–	–	–	–	–	–	MA! (HE'S MAKIN' EYES AT ME) (1921)
16	7	6	6	5	5	8	8	11	15	==	==	==	–	–	–	–	–	–	–	–	–	–	–	–	–	MY SUNNY TENNESSEE (1921)
11	5	5	4	4	4	2	6	8	9	9	12	18	==	–	–	–	–	–	–	–	–	–	–	–	–	TUCK ME TO SLEEP IN MY OLD 'TUCKY HOME (1921)
13	6	3	3	3	7	15	==	==	–	–	–	–	–	–	–	–	–	–	–	–	–	–	–	–	–	SWEET LADY (1921)
==	16	11	8	7	11	13	13	15	14	19	==	==	–	–	–	–	–	–	–	–	–	–	–	–	–	SECOND HAND ROSE (1921)
==	11	4	2	**1**	**1**	**1**	2	7	7	10	==	–	–	–	–	–	–	–	–	–	–	–	–	–	–	SAY IT WITH MUSIC (1921)
==	==	==	==	==	18	20	==	==	==	==	–	–	–	–	–	–	–	–	–	–	–	–	–	–	–	JUST LIKE A RAINBOW (1921)
–	==	16	9	8	10	10	15	==	==	==	–	–	–	–	–	–	–	–	–	–	–	–	–	–	–	WHEN FRANCES DANCES WITH ME (1921)
–	==	==	==	19	16	17	18	16	18	==	==	==	==	–	–	–	–	–	–	–	–	–	–	–	–	MANDY 'N' ME (1921)
–	==	==	14	10	13	14	19	==	–	–	–	–	–	–	–	–	–	–	–	–	–	–	–	–	–	CANADIAN CAPERS (1921)
–	–	==	20	13	12	11	16	17	==	==	–	–	–	–	–	–	–	–	–	–	–	–	–	–	–	BIMINI BAY (1921)
==	==	14	11	12	9	6	5	5	6	6	9	13	17	==	–	–	–	–	–	–	–	–	–	–	–	TEN LITTLE FINGERS AND TEN LITTLE TOES
–	–	==	16	9	6	4	7	10	11	16	==	==	–	–	–	–	–	–	–	–	–	–	–	–	–	DAPPER DAN
–	–	==	==	==	15	12	10	9	10	12	13	14	==	==	–	–	–	–	–	–	–	–	–	–	–	LEAVE ME WITH A SMILE
–	–	–	==	18	8	5	3	**1**	4	5	8	8	8	20	==	–	–	–	–	–	–	–	–	–	–	APRIL SHOWERS
–	–	==	==	15	14	9	4	2	2	3	3	4	6	6	12	==	==	–	–	–	–	–	–	–	–	YOO-HOO
–	–	==	15	6	3	3	**1**	3	5	7	17	==	–	–	–	–	–	–	–	–	–	–	–	–	–	WABASH BLUES
==	==	==	==	==	==	==	==	==	==	==	20	17	19	15	17	20	==	==	==	==	==	==	==	==	==	THE WORLD IS WAITING FOR THE SUNRISE *
–	–	–	–	==	==	19	14	12	13	13	14	16	16	==	==	–	–	–	–	–	–	–	–	–	–	SONG OF LOVE
–	–	–	–	==	==	16	11	6	3	2	2	5	7	8	13	==	==	–	–	–	–	–	–	–	–	KA-LU-A
–	–	–	–	==	==	18	17	13	12	8	11	11	9	14	==	==	==	–	–	–	–	–	–	–	–	WHEN SHALL WE MEET AGAIN?
–	–	–	–	==	==	==	==	==	17	18	16	12	13	13	14	17	==	==	==	==	==	–	–	–	–	BANDANA DAYS
–	–	–	–	–	==	==	20	18	16	17	18	19	==	==	==	–	–	–	–	–	–	–	–	–	–	GRANNY, YOU'RE MY MAMMY'S MAMMY
–	–	–	–	–	==	==	12	4	**1**	**1**	**1**	**1**	3	5	8	12	18	==	–	–	–	–	–	–	–	THE SHEIK (OF ARABY)
–	–	–	–	–	–	==	==	==	==	20	10	6	5	4	4	8	10	12	18	==	==	==	==	==	–	SWANEE RIVER MOON
–	–	–	–	–	–	–	==	19	8	4	4	10	14	==	==	–	–	–	–	–	–	–	–	–	–	EVERYBODY STEP
–	–	–	–	–	–	–	–	==	20	11	7	9	12	19	==	–	–	–	–	–	–	–	–	–	–	WHEN BUDDHA SMILES
–	–	–	–	–	–	–	–	==	==	==	19	15	10	17	==	–	–	–	–	–	–	–	–	–	–	JUST A LITTLE LOVE SONG
–	–	–	–	–	–	–	–	==	==	==	==	==	20	==	==	–	–	–	–	–	–	–	–	–	–	BLUE DANUBE BLUES
–	–	–	–	–	–	–	–	–	==	15	6	2	**1**	3	7	10	20	==	–	–	–	–	–	–	–	ON THE GIN-GIN-GINNY SHORE
–	–	–	–	–	–	–	–	–	==	14	5	3	2	2	2	6	7	11	19	==	–	–	–	–	–	DEAR OLD SOUTHLAND
–	–	–	–	–	–	–	–	–	–	==	==	20	15	16	15	==	==	–	–	–	–	–	–	–	–	STEALING
–	–	–	–	–	–	–	–	–	–	==	15	7	4	**1**	**1**	3	3	6	8	19	==	==	–	–	–	ANGEL CHILD
–	–	–	–	–	–	–	–	–	–	–	==	==	==	==	20	==	==	–	–	–	–	–	–	–	–	DOWN THE OLD CHURCH AISLE
–	–	–	–	–	–	–	–	–	–	–	–	==	==	==	19	19	==	==	–	–	–	–	–	–	–	DOO DAH BLUES
–	–	–	–	–	–	–	–	–	–	–	–	==	18	11	11	14	==	==	–	–	–	–	–	–	–	YOU CAN HAVE EVERY LIGHT ON BROADWAY
–	–	–	–	–	–	–	–	–	–	–	–	==	==	9	6	2	2	4	5	10	==	==	–	–	–	GEORGIA
–	–	–	–	–	–	–	–	–	–	–	–	–	==	12	9	7	8	15	==	==	–	–	–	–	–	O-OO, ERNEST (ARE YOU EARNEST WITH ME?)
–	–	–	–	–	–	–	–	–	–	–	–	–	==	10	5	4	9	13	20	==	–	–	–	–	–	CALIFORNIA
–	–	–	–	–	–	–	–	–	–	–	–	–	==	==	==	16	15	18	==	==	==	==	==	–	–	MOON RIVER
–	–	–	–	–	–	–	–	–	–	–	–	–	==	18	10	5	4	3	3	3	10	19	==	–	–	SOME SUNNY DAY
–	–	–	–	–	–	–	–	–	–	–	–	–	–	==	18	11	11	8	11	16	==	==	==	==	–	NOLA
Oc	Oc	Nv	Nv	Dc	Dc	Ja	Ja	Fb	Fb	Ma	Ma	Ap	Ap	My	My	Jn	Jn	Jy	Jy	Ag	Ag	Sp	Sp	Oc	Oc	

* SONG LEAVES TOP TWENTY IN JUNE AND RETURNS IN DECEMBER 1922

							1 9 2 2															1 9 2 3				
Ma	**Ma**	**Ap**	**Ap**	**My**	**My**	**Jn**	**Jn**	**Jy**	**Jy**	**Ag**	**Ag**	**Sp**	**Sp**	**Oc**	**Oc**	**Nv**	**Nv**	**Dc**	**Dc**	**Ja**	**Ja**	**Fb**	**Fb**	**Ma**	**Ma**	
–	==	==	11	7	3	**1**	**1**	2	2	2	2	**1**	**1**	**1**	**1**	**1**	2	3	9	13	17	==	–	–	–	THREE O'CLOCK IN THE MORNING
–	–	==	==	==	==	15	12	7	4	4	3	9	11	9	10	16	18	==	–	–	–	–	–	–	–	KITTEN ON THE KEYS
–	–	–	–	==	16	9	6	5	7	14	==	==	–	–	–	–	–	–	–	–	–	–	–	–	–	IN THE LITTLE RED SCHOOL HOUSE
–	–	–	–	==	==	18	16	20	16	18	14	16	16	==	==	–	–	–	–	–	–	–	–	–	–	SMILIN' THROUGH
–	–	–	–	–	==	==	19	==	==	==	==	–	–	–	–	–	–	–	–	–	–	–	–	–	–	OOGIE OOGIE WA WA
–	–	–	–	–	==	13	5	**1**	**1**	**1**	**1**	5	12	19	==	–	–	–	–	–	–	–	–	–	–	STUMBLING
–	–	–	–	–	==	==	14	14	13	13	16	20	==	==	–	–	–	–	–	–	–	–	–	–	–	MY HONEY'S LOVIN' ARMS
–	–	–	–	–	–	==	==	17	14	11	19	==	==	==	–	–	–	–	–	–	–	–	–	–	–	GEE, BUT I HATE TO GO HOME ALONE
–	–	–	–	–	==	==	13	9	9	8	12	17	==	==	–	–	–	–	–	–	–	–	–	–	–	ON THE ALAMO
–	–	–	–	–	–	==	==	16	10	6	5	4	6	6	8	14	20	==	==	==	==	–	–	–	–	I'M JUST WILD ABOUT HARRY
–	–	–	–	–	–	==	17	10	6	5	6	14	19	==	–	–	–	–	–	–	–	–	–	–	–	DO IT AGAIN
–	–	–	–	–	–	–	==	19	12	9	7	7	10	13	16	==	==	==	–	–	–	–	–	–	–	ALL OVER NOTHING AT ALL
–	–	–	–	–	–	–	–	==	17	12	9	8	13	11	17	==	==	–	–	–	–	–	–	–	–	NOBODY LIED
–	–	–	–	–	–	–	==	==	15	7	4	3	3	7	11	20	==	–	–	–	–	–	–	–	–	DANCING FOOL
–	–	–	–	–	–	–	–	==	==	20	13	12	9	5	2	2	**1**	**1**	3	5	10	12	13	19	19	20 == MR. GALLAGHER AND MR. SHEAN
–	–	–	–	–	–	–	–	–	==	15	8	2	2	8	12	==	==	–	–	–	–	–	–	–	–	'NEATH THE SOUTH SEA MOON
–	–	–	–	–	–	–	–	–	==	17	11	6	4	10	15	18	==	==	–	–	–	–	–	–	–	WHY SHOULD I CRY OVER YOU?
–	–	–	–	–	–	–	–	–	==	==	20	15	14	16	20	==	==	==	==	==	–	–	–	–	–	SWEET INDIANA HOME
–	–	–	–	–	–	–	–	–	–	==	==	==	18	18	==	==	–	–	–	–	–	–	–	–	–	THE SNEAK
–	–	–	–	–	–	–	–	–	–	==	==	==	17	20	==	==	==	==	–	–	–	–	–	–	–	SUEZ
–	–	–	–	–	–	–	–	–	–	==	15	10	5	3	4	8	19	==	–	–	–	–	–	–	–	SAY IT WHILE DANCING
–	–	–	–	–	–	–	–	–	–	==	17	11	7	4	5	13	16	–	–	–	–	–	–	–	–	GEORGETTE
–	–	–	–	–	–	–	–	–	–	==	18	13	8	2	3	3	3	10	20	==	==	==	–	–	–	HOT LIPS
–	–	–	–	–	–	–	–	–	–	==	==	18	15	14	14	12	10	9	8	6	8	8	10	7	3	3 4 7 10 16 == PARADE OF THE WOODEN SOLDIERS
–	–	–	–	–	–	–	–	–	–	–	–	==	20	15	7	7	14	16	==	==	==	==	–	–	–	YANKEE DOODLE BLUES
–	–	–	–	–	–	–	–	–	–	–	–	–	==	17	9	6	13	17	==	==	–	–	–	–	–	COAL-BLACK MAMMY
–	–	–	–	–	–	–	–	–	–	–	–	==	==	12	6	4	12	15	==	==	–	–	–	–	–	BLUE (AND BROKEN HEARTED)
–	–	–	–	–	–	–	–	–	–	–	–	–	==	==	18	10	6	2	4	4	9	13	14	==	==	CHICAGO (THAT TODDLIN' TOWN)
–	–	–	–	–	–	–	–	–	–	–	–	–	–	==	==	==	==	20	==	==	–	–	–	–	–	I WISH I KNEW (YOU REALLY LOVED ME)
–	–	–	–	–	–	–	–	–	–	–	–	–	==	==	13	5	4	6	11	18	==	–	–	–	–	YOU REMIND ME OF MY MOTHER
–	–	–	–	–	–	–	–	–	–	–	–	–	–	==	==	11	9	7	7	11	13	19	==	==	–	I WISH I COULD SHIMMY LIKE MY SISTER KATE
–	–	–	–	–	–	–	–	–	–	–	–	–	–	==	19	15	11	11	10	17	20	==	==	==	–	HOMESICK
–	–	–	–	–	–	–	–	–	–	–	–	–	–	–	==	17	8	12	13	20	==	–	–	–	–	I'LL BUILD A STAIRWAY TO PARADISE
–	–	–	–	–	–	–	–	–	–	–	–	–	–	==	==	9	5	5	6	12	==	==	–	–	–	NELLIE KELLY, I LOVE YOU
–	–	–	–	–	–	–	–	–	–	–	–	–	–	–	==	==	==	19	==	==	==	20	==	==	==	WHEN YOU AND I WERE YOUNG MAGGIE BLUES
																==	==	18	15	15	14	18	18	18	==	THE WORLD IS WAITING FOR THE SUNRISE *
–	–	–	–	–	–	–	–	–	–	–	–	–	–	–	==	19	7	4	**1**	2	3	4	3	4	8	MY BUDDY (1923)
–	–	–	–	–	–	–	–	–	–	–	–	–	–	–	–	==	==	==	19	19	18	16	19	17	14	I GAVE YOU UP JUST BEFORE YOU THREW ME DOWN (1923)
–	–	–	–	–	–	–	–	–	–	–	–	–	–	–	–	==	17	14	12	9	6	6	5	10	13	WAY DOWN YONDER IN NEW ORLEANS (1923)
–	–	–	–	–	–	–	–	–	–	–	–	–	–	–	–	–	==	==	18	14	12	15	==	==	==	YOU GAVE ME YOUR HEART (1923)
–	–	–	–	–	–	–	–	–	–	–	–	–	–	–	–	–	==	13	5	3	2	3	8	11	20	TOOT, TOOT, TOOTSIE! (GOODBYE) (1923)
–	–	–	–	–	–	–	–	–	–	–	–	–	–	–	–	==	==	==	17	10	7	7	11	12	18	WHEN THE LEAVES COME TUMBLING DOWN (1923)
–	–	–	–	–	–	–	–	–	–	–	–	–	–	–	–	==	15	8	2	**1**	**1**	**1**	**1**	2	2	CAROLINA IN THE MORNING (1923)
–	–	–	–	–	–	–	–	–	–	–	–	–	–	–	–	–	–	==	14	8	4	2	2	**1**	7	LOVIN' SAM, THE SHEIK OF ALABAM' (1923)
–	–	–	–	–	–	–	–	–	–	–	–	–	–	–	–	–	–	==	16	7	5	5	4	6	9	CRINOLINE DAYS (1923)
Ma	**Ma**	**Ap**	**Ap**	**My**	**My**	**Jn**	**Jn**	**Jy**	**Jy**	**Ag**	**Ag**	**Sp**	**Sp**	**Oc**	**Oc**	**Nv**	**Nv**	**Dc**	**Dc**	**Ja**	**Ja**	**Fb**	**Fb**	**Ma**	**Ma**	

Oc	Oc	Nv	Nv	Dc	Dc	Ja	Ja	Fb	Fb	Ma	Ma	Ap	Ap	My	My	Jn	Jn	Jy	Jy	Ag	Ag	Sp	Sp	Oc	Oc	
1922						1923																				
1	**1**	**1**	2	3	9	13	17	==	–	–	–	–	–	–	–	–	–	–	–	–	–	–	–	–	–	THREE O'CLOCK IN THE MORNING (1922)
5	2	2	**1**	**1**	3	5	10	12	13	19	19	20	==	==	–	–	–	–	–	–	–	–	–	–	–	MR. GALLAGHER AND MR. SHEAN (1922)
14	14	12	10	9	8	6	8	8	10	7	3	3	4	7	10	16	==	==	–	–	–	–	–	–	–	PARADE OF THE WOODEN SOLDIERS (1922)
==	18	10	6	2	4	4	9	13	14	==	==	==	–	–	–	–	–	–	–	–	–	–	–	–	–	CHICAGO (THAT TODDLIN' TOWN) (1922)
==	13	5	4	6	11	18	==	–	–	–	–	–	–	–	–	–	–	–	–	–	–	–	–	–	–	YOU REMIND ME OF MY MOTHER (1922)
==	==	11	9	7	7	11	13	19	==	==	–	–	–	–	–	–	–	–	–	–	–	–	–	–	–	I WISH I COULD SHIMMY LIKE MY SISTER KATE (1922)
==	19	15	11	11	10	17	20	==	==	==	–	–	–	–	–	–	–	–	–	–	–	–	–	–	–	HOMESICK (1922)
–	==	17	8	12	13	20	==	–	–	–	–	–	–	–	–	–	–	–	–	–	–	–	–	–	–	I'LL BUILD A STAIRWAY TO PARADISE (1922)
==	==	9	5	5	6	12	==	==	–	–	–	–	–	–	–	–	–	–	–	–	–	–	–	–	–	NELLIE KELLY, I LOVE YOU (1922)
–	==	==	==	19	==	==	==	20	==	==	==	==	–	–	–	–	–	–	–	–	–	–	–	–	–	WHEN YOU AND I WERE YOUNG MAGGIE BLUES (1922)
==	==	==	==	18	15	15	14	18	18	18	==	==	==	==	==	==	==	==	–	–	–	–	–	–	–	THE WORLD IS WAITING FOR THE SUNRISE (1922)
–	==	19	7	4	**1**	2	3	4	3	4	8	12	18	17	==	==	–	–	–	–	–	–	–	–	–	MY BUDDY
–	–	==	==	==	19	19	18	16	19	17	14	14	16	==	==	–	–	–	–	–	–	–	–	–	–	I GAVE YOU UP JUST BEFORE YOU THREW ME DOWN
–	–	==	17	14	12	9	6	6	5	10	13	17	19	==	20	==	–	–	–	–	–	–	–	–	–	WAY DOWN YONDER IN NEW ORLEANS
–	–	==	15	8	2	**1**	**1**	**1**	**1**	2	2	6	13	==	==	–	–	–	–	–	–	–	–	–	–	CAROLINA IN THE MORNING
–	–	–	==	==	18	14	12	15	==	==	==	–	–	–	–	–	–	–	–	–	–	–	–	–	–	YOU GAVE ME YOUR HEART
–	–	–	==	13	5	3	2	3	8	11	20	==	–	–	–	–	–	–	–	–	–	–	–	–	–	TOOT, TOOT, TOOTSIE! (GOODBYE)
–	–	==	==	==	17	10	7	7	11	12	18	==	==	==	–	–	–	–	–	–	–	–	–	–	–	WHEN THE LEAVES COME TUMBLING DOWN
–	–	–	–	==	14	8	4	2	2	**1**	7	18	==	–	–	–	–	–	–	–	–	–	–	–	–	LOVIN' SAM, THE SHEIK OF ALABAM'
–	–	–	–	==	16	7	5	5	4	6	9	19	==	==	–	–	–	–	–	–	–	–	–	–	–	CRINOLINE DAYS
==	==	==	==	==	==	==	==	17	15	14	17	16	12	13	14	18	16	19	==	==	==	==	==	==	==	LOVE SENDS A LITTLE GIFT OF ROSES
–	–	–	–	==	==	==	==	==	17	16	16	11	11	8	5	6	9	7	8	13	15	16	15	12	11	14 17 == A KISS IN THE DARK
–	–	–	–	–	==	==	15	14	16	==	==	–	–	–	–	–	–	–	–	–	–	–	–	–	–	PACK UP YOUR SINS (AND GO TO THE DEVIL)
–	–	–	–	–	==	16	11	10	7	5	10	13	15	18	==	==	–	–	–	–	–	–	–	–	–	LADY OF THE EVENING
–	–	–	–	–	–	==	==	==	20	==	==	==	==	==	–	–	–	–	–	–	–	–	–	–	–	LOST (A WONDERFUL GIRL)
–	–	–	–	–	–	==	16	11	9	9	12	15	17	==	==	–	–	–	–	–	–	–	–	–	–	WHO CARES?
–	–	–	–	–	–	==	19	9	6	3	**1**	2	5	10	16	==	–	–	–	–	–	–	–	–	–	WHEN HEARTS ARE YOUNG
–	–	–	–	–	–	–	–	==	12	8	6	5	10	11	12	==	==	–	–	–	–	–	–	–	–	YOU TELL HER, I S-T-U-T-T-E-R
–	–	–	–	–	–	–	–	==	==	13	4	**1**	**1**	4	7	10	18	==	–	–	–	–	–	–	–	AGGRAVATIN' PAPA
–	–	–	–	–	–	–	–	–	==	15	5	4	6	12	==	==	–	–	–	–	–	–	–	–	–	ROSE OF THE RIO GRANDE
–	–	–	–	–	–	–	–	–	==	20	11	7	8	9	9	14	19	==	–	–	–	–	–	–	–	YOU KNOW YOU BELONG TO SOMEBODY ELSE
–	–	–	–	–	–	–	–	–	–	==	==	==	==	19	==	==	==	==	–	–	–	–	–	–	–	AUNT HAGAR'S CHILDREN (BLUES)
–	–	–	–	–	–	–	–	–	–	==	15	10	7	6	6	4	7	11	16	==	==	–	–	–	–	DEAREST, YOU'RE THE NEAREST TO MY HEART
–	–	–	–	–	–	–	–	–	–	==	==	8	2	2	4	7	14	==	==	–	–	–	–	–	–	RUNNIN' WILD
–	–	–	–	–	–	–	–	–	–	==	==	9	3	**1**	2	3	10	13	==	==	–	–	–	–	–	YOU'VE GOT TO SEE MAMMA EV'RY NIGHT
–	–	–	–	–	–	–	–	–	–	–	==	==	==	20	19	==	==	==	==	==	–	–	–	–	–	AFTER EVERY PARTY
–	–	–	–	–	–	–	–	–	–	–	==	==	9	3	**1**	2	5	10	18	==	–	–	–	–	–	BAMBALINA
–	–	–	–	–	–	–	–	–	–	–	==	==	==	==	17	19	15	14	==	==	==	==	==	–	–	UNDERNEATH THE MELLOW MOON
–	–	–	–	–	–	–	–	–	–	–	==	==	20	14	8	5	2	4	5	5	9	12	13	16	20	== WONDERFUL ONE
–	–	–	–	–	–	–	–	–	–	–	–	==	==	16	15	17	==	==	–	–	–	–	–	–	–	CRYING FOR YOU
–	–	–	–	–	–	–	–	–	–	–	–	==	14	5	3	**1**	**1**	3	6	6	10	==	==	–	–	WHO'S SORRY NOW?
–	–	–	–	–	–	–	–	–	–	–	–	==	==	15	11	8	6	8	13	20	==	–	–	–	–	FAREWELL BLUES
–	–	–	–	–	–	–	–	–	–	–	–	–	==	==	18	12	11	15	==	==	–	–	–	–	–	SEVEN OR ELEVEN (MY DIXIE PAIR O'DICE)
–	–	–	–	–	–	–	–	–	–	–	–	–	==	==	==	==	17	20	==	==	==	==	==	–	–	THAT RED-HEAD GAL
Oc	Oc	Nv	Nv	Dc	Dc	Ja	Ja	Fb	Fb	Ma	Ma	Ap	Ap	My	My	Jn	Jn	Jy	Jy	Ag	Ag	Sp	Sp	Oc	Oc	

1923																		1924								
Ap	Ap	My	My	Jn	Jn	Jy	Jy	Ag	Ag	Sp	Sp	Oc	Oc	Nv	Nv	Dc	Dc	Ja	Ja	Fb	Fb	Ma	Ma	Ap	Ap	
–	==	==	13	9	8	5	7	7	14	==	==	–	–	–	–	–	–	–	–	–	–	–	–	–	–	WILDFLOWER
–	==	==	==	15	13	12	10	18	20	==	==	==	==	–	–	–	–	–	–	–	–	–	–	–	–	SAW MILL RIVER ROAD
–	–	–	==	13	4	2	2	2	3	11	20	==	–	–	–	–	–	–	–	–	–	–	–	–	–	BARNEY GOOGLE
–	–	–	==	11	3	**1**	**1**	**1**	**1**	**1**	8	14	==	–	–	–	–	–	–	–	–	–	–	–	–	YES! WE HAVE NO BANANAS
–	–	–	==	20	12	6	4	4	7	13	16	==	==	–	–	–	–	–	–	–	–	–	–	–	–	BESIDE A BABBLING BROOK
–	–	–	==	==	==	==	==	==	==	==	==	==	19	15	15	19	20	==	==	==	==	==	==	==	==	JUST FOR TONIGHT
–	–	–	–	==	==	16	12	12	8	4	**1**	2	3	7	12	15	==	==	–	–	–	–	–	–	–	JUST A GIRL THAT MEN FORGET
–	–	–	–	==	==	17	15	14	13	8	6	7	5	5	7	6	8	8	13	20	==	==	==	==	–	MARCHETA
–	–	–	–	–	20	9	3	3	2	2	3	9	12	==	==	–	–	–	–	–	–	–	–	–	–	SWINGIN' DOWN THE LANE
–	–	–	–	–	==	==	20	19	==	18	==	==	–	–	–	–	–	–	–	–	–	–	–	–	–	DOWNHEARTED BLUES
–	–	–	–	–	==	==	11	9	11	14	==	==	–	–	–	–	–	–	–	–	–	–	–	–	–	STELLA
–	–	–	–	–	==	==	==	15	18	20	==	==	==	–	–	–	–	–	–	–	–	–	–	–	–	GULF COAST BLUES
–	–	–	–	–	==	==	19	16	16	15	18	18	==	==	==	–	–	–	–	–	–	–	–	–	–	DIRTY HANDS! DIRTY FACE!
–	–	–	–	–	==	18	9	10	4	3	9	8	9	16	19	==	–	–	–	–	–	–	–	–	–	LOUISVILLE LOU, THE VAMPIN' LADY
–	–	–	–	–	–	==	14	8	5	7	7	13	==	==	–	–	–	–	–	–	–	–	–	–	–	I CRIED FOR YOU
–	–	–	–	–	–	==	17	11	6	6	10	17	==	==	–	–	–	–	–	–	–	–	–	–	–	WHEN YOU WALKED OUT, SOMEONE ELSE WALKED RIGHT IN
–	–	–	–	–	–	==	==	==	==	==	==	20	15	13	10	8	7	11	15	11	13	18	18	20	20	== ROSES OF PICARDY
–	–	–	–	–	–	–	==	17	12	5	2	4	10	19	–	–	–	–	–	–	–	–	–	–	–	OH! GEE, OH! GOSH, OH! GOLLY, I'M IN LOVE
–	–	–	–	–	–	–	==	==	17	17	11	11	13	18	==	==	==	–	–	–	–	–	–	–	–	BEBE
–	–	–	–	–	–	–	–	==	==	19	17	10	8	4	5	5	6	9	16	==	==	==	–	–	–	DREAMY MELODY
–	–	–	–	–	–	–	–	–	==	==	19	19	18	==	==	==	–	–	–	–	–	–	–	–	–	CUT YOURSELF A PIECE OF CAKE
–	–	–	–	–	–	–	–	–	19	9	4	3	4	6	9	16	==	–	–	–	–	–	–	–	–	MY SWEETIE WENT AWAY
–	–	–	–	–	–	–	–	–	==	10	5	**1**	**1**	**1**	**1**	3	3	4	8	14	==	==	–	–	–	THAT OLD GANG OF MINE
–	–	–	–	–	–	–	–	–	–	==	14	6	7	9	14	==	–	–	–	–	–	–	–	–	–	ANNABELLE
–	–	–	–	–	–	–	–	–	–	==	12	5	2	2	6	7	16	==	–	–	–	–	–	–	–	INDIANA MOON
–	–	–	–	–	–	–	–	–	–	==	==	==	==	20	20	==	==	==	==	==	==	==	–	–	–	WHEN IT'S NIGHT TIME IN ITALY, IT'S WEDNESDAY OVER HERE
–	–	–	–	–	–	–	–	–	–	==	==	==	14	10	8	10	14	==	==	==	==	==	–	–	–	TEN THOUSAND YEARS FROM NOW
–	–	–	–	–	–	–	–	–	–	–	==	==	16	12	11	11	15	==	==	==	–	–	–	–	–	LOVE TALES
–	–	–	–	–	–	–	–	–	–	–	==	15	6	3	2	4	5	10	19	==	–	–	–	–	–	NO, NO, NORA
–	–	–	–	–	–	–	–	–	–	–	–	==	==	17	13	13	19	==	–	–	–	–	–	–	–	MIDNIGHT ROSE
–	–	–	–	–	–	–	–	–	–	–	–	==	17	8	3	2	2	3	3	8	16	==	–	–	–	LAST NIGHT ON THE BACK PORCH
–	–	–	–	–	–	–	–	–	–	–	–	–	==	11	4	**1**	**1**	**1**	**1**	**1**	4	4	8	12	==	I LOVE YOU
–	–	–	–	–	–	–	–	–	–	–	–	–	–	==	18	12	11	13	17	==	==	==	–	–	–	THE WEST, A NEST, AND YOU
–	–	–	–	–	–	–	–	–	–	–	–	–	–	==	==	14	9	6	5	6	9	16	==	==	–	I'M SITTING PRETTY IN A PRETTY LITTLE CITY (1924)
–	–	–	–	–	–	–	–	–	–	–	–	–	–	–	==	17	10	5	7	13	==	==	–	–	–	MAMA GOES WHERE PAPA GOES (1924)
–	–	–	–	–	–	–	–	–	–	–	–	–	–	==	16	9	4	2	2	5	12	==	==	–	–	SITTIN' IN A CORNER (1924)
–	–	–	–	–	–	–	–	–	–	–	–	–	–	==	==	20	13	18	==	==	==	==	==	==	–	CHANSONETTE (1924)
–	–	–	–	–	–	–	–	–	–	–	–	–	–	–	==	==	18	19	18	16	14	==	==	==	==	LA ROSITA (1924)
–	–	–	–	–	–	–	–	–	–	–	–	–	–	–	==	18	12	7	4	3	2	3	7	11	15	SLEEP (1924)
–	–	–	–	–	–	–	–	–	–	–	–	–	–	–	–	==	17	12	12	10	10	13	==	==	–	COVERED WAGON DAYS (1924)
Ap	Ap	My	My	Jn	Jn	Jy	Jy	Ag	Ag	Sp	Sp	Oc	Oc	Nv	Nv	Dc	Dc	Ja	Ja	Fb	Fb	Ma	Ma	Ap	Ap	

1923														1924												
Oc	Oc	Nv	Nv	Dc	Dc	Ja	Ja	Fb	Fb	Ma	Ma	Ap	Ap	My	My	Jn	Jn	Jy	Jy	Ag	Ag	Sp	Sp	Oc	Oc	
7	5	5	7	6	8	8	13	20	==	==	==	==	==	==	==	==	==	==	==	==	==	–	–	–	–	MARCHETA (1923)
20	15	13	10	8	7	11	15	11	13	18	18	20	20	==	==	==	==	==	==	==	–	–	–	–	–	ROSES OF PICARDY (1923)
10	8	4	5	5	6	9	16	==	==	==	–	–	–	–	–	–	–	–	–	–	–	–	–	–	–	DREAMY MELODY (1923)
1	1	1	1	3	3	4	8	14	==	==	–	–	–	–	–	–	–	–	–	–	–	–	–	–	–	THAT OLD GANG OF MINE (1923)
15	6	3	2	4	5	10	19	==	–	–	–	–	–	–	–	–	–	–	–	–	–	–	–	–	–	NO, NO, NORA (1923)
==	17	8	3	2	2	3	3	8	16	==	–	–	–	–	–	–	–	–	–	–	–	–	–	–	–	LAST NIGHT ON THE BACK PORCH (1923)
–	==	11	4	1	1	1	1	1	4	4	8	12	==	==	–	–	–	–	–	–	–	–	–	–	–	I LOVE YOU (1923)
–	–	==	18	12	11	13	17	==	==	==	–	–	–	–	–	–	–	–	–	–	–	–	–	–	–	THE WEST, A NEST, AND YOU (1923)
–	–	==	==	14	9	6	5	6	9	16	==	==	–	–	–	–	–	–	–	–	–	–	–	–	–	I'M SITTING PRETTY IN A PRETTY LITTLE CITY
–	–	==	16	9	4	2	2	5	12	==	==	–	–	–	–	–	–	–	–	–	–	–	–	–	–	SITTIN' IN A CORNER
–	–	==	==	20	13	18	==	==	==	==	==	==	–	–	–	–	–	–	–	–	–	–	–	–	–	CHANSONETTE
–	–	–	==	17	10	5	7	13	==	==	–	–	–	–	–	–	–	–	–	–	–	–	–	–	–	MAMMA GOES WHERE PAPA GOES
–	–	–	==	==	18	19	18	16	14	==	==	==	==	==	–	–	–	–	–	–	–	–	–	–	–	LA ROSITA
–	–	–	==	18	12	7	4	3	2	3	7	11	15	16	==	==	==	==	–	–	–	–	–	–	–	SLEEP
–	–	–	–	==	==	==	20	==	==	==	–	–	–	–	–	–	–	–	–	–	–	–	–	–	–	THE CHARLESTON
–	–	–	–	==	17	12	12	10	10	13	==	==	–	–	–	–	–	–	–	–	–	–	–	–	–	COVERED WAGON DAYS
–	–	–	–	==	==	20	==	18	19	==	==	==	–	–	–	–	–	–	–	–	–	–	–	–	–	OLD FASHIONED LOVE
–	–	–	–	==	==	==	==	19	20	==	20	==	==	==	–	–	–	–	–	–	–	–	–	–	–	LITTLE BUTTERFLY
–	–	–	–	==	==	14	10	9	5	15	17	==	==	==	–	–	–	–	–	–	–	–	–	–	–	LOVEY CAME BACK
–	–	–	–	==	==	16	11	4	3	2	5	9	13	17	17	==	==	==	==	–	–	–	–	–	–	REMEMB'RING
–	–	–	–	–	==	15	9	7	7	17	==	==	–	–	–	–	–	–	–	–	–	–	–	–	–	MAMMA LOVES PAPA (PAPA LOVES MAMMA)
–	–	–	–	–	==	17	6	2	1	1	1	4	8	14	==	==	–	–	–	–	–	–	–	–	–	LINGER AWHILE
–	–	–	–	–	–	==	14	12	11	19	==	–	–	–	–	–	–	–	–	–	–	–	–	–	–	TAKE OH TAKE THOSE LIPS AWAY
–	–	–	–	–	–	==	==	15	6	6	14	17	==	==	–	–	–	–	–	–	–	–	–	–	–	AN ORANGE GROVE IN CALIFORNIA
–	–	–	–	–	–	==	==	==	15	7	15	19	19	==	==	==	–	–	–	–	–	–	–	–	–	THE WALTZ OF LONG AGO
–	–	–	–	–	–	–	==	17	8	5	12	18	==	==	–	–	–	–	–	–	–	–	–	–	–	RAGGEDY ANN
–	–	–	–	–	–	–	–	==	18	9	4	6	4	7	14	==	–	–	–	–	–	–	–	–	–	SOMEBODY STOLE MY GAL
–	–	–	–	–	–	–	–	==	17	10	9	7	10	13	15	14	20	==	–	–	–	–	–	–	–	WHEN LIGHTS ARE LOW
–	–	–	–	–	–	–	–	==	==	12	10	8	12	==	==	–	–	–	–	–	–	–	–	–	–	DREAM DADDY
–	–	–	–	–	–	–	–	==	==	11	3	2	3	6	10	13	==	==	–	–	–	–	–	–	–	A SMILE WILL GO A LONG, LONG WAY
–	–	–	–	–	–	–	–	–	==	20	13	10	14	15	==	==	–	–	–	–	–	–	–	–	–	SHE WOULDN'T DO (WHAT I ASKED HER TO)
–	–	–	–	–	–	–	–	–	==	14	6	3	6	9	16	==	–	–	–	–	–	–	–	–	–	I'M GOIN' SOUTH
–	–	–	–	–	–	–	–	–	==	8	2	1	1	1	5	10	19	==	–	–	–	–	–	–	–	CALIFORNIA, HERE I COME
–	–	–	–	–	–	–	–	–	–	==	11	5	2	5	7	12	12	==	==	–	–	–	–	–	–	THE ONE I LOVE BELONGS TO SOMEBODY ELSE
–	–	–	–	–	–	–	–	–	–	==	19	16	11	8	4	4	3	3	9	10	13	17	==	==	–	NOBODY'S SWEETHEART
–	–	–	–	–	–	–	–	–	–	==	16	13	7	3	1	1	2	2	6	8	10	16	==	==	–	IT AIN'T GONNA RAIN NO MO'
–	–	–	–	–	–	–	–	–	–	–	==	14	5	2	3	6	11	13	==	–	–	–	–	–	–	WHERE THE LAZY DAISIES GROW
–	–	–	–	–	–	–	–	–	–	–	==	15	9	4	2	2	4	10	11	15	==	–	–	–	–	LIMEHOUSE BLUES
–	–	–	–	–	–	–	–	–	–	==	==	==	==	==	19	18	16	18	20	20	==	==	==	==	–	DIZZY FINGERS
–	–	–	–	–	–	–	–	–	–	–	–	==	==	==	20	15	==	==	–	–	–	–	–	–	–	SINCE MA IS PLAYING MAH JONG
–	–	–	–	–	–	–	–	–	–	–	–	==	18	12	11	11	14	==	==	–	–	–	–	–	–	MINDIN' MY BUS'NESS
–	–	–	–	–	–	–	–	–	–	–	–	==	==	20	18	16	15	17	==	==	–	–	–	–	–	MEXICALI ROSE
–	–	–	–	–	–	–	–	–	–	–	–	==	17	11	9	9	8	12	16	19	==	==	–	–	–	COLORADO
–	–	–	–	–	–	–	–	–	–	–	–	==	16	10	6	5	6	9	10	13	19	==	–	–	–	WHY DID I KISS THAT GIRL?
Oc	Oc	Nv	Nv	Dc	Dc	Ja	Ja	Fb	Fb	Ma	Ma	Ap	Ap	My	My	Jn	Jn	Jy	Jy	Ag	Ag	Sp	Sp	Oc	Oc	

							1924													1925						
Ap	Ap	My	My	Jn	Jn	Jy	Jy	Ag	Ag	Sp	Sp	Oc	Oc	Nv	Nv	Dc	Dc	Ja	Ja	Fb	Fb	Ma	Ma	Ap	Ap	
==	==	==	==	17	17	14	17	17	17	==	==	==	==	–	–	–	–	–	–	–	–	–	–	–	–	NOLA
–	–	==	13	7	7	11	15	==	–	–	–	–	–	–	–	–	–	–	–	–	–	–	–	–	–	DON'T MIND THE RAIN
–	–	19	12	8	5	8	12	16	==	==	–	–	–	–	–	–	–	–	–	–	–	–	–	–	–	LAZY
–	–	18	8	3	**1**	**1**	**1**	**1**	**1**	**1**	**1**	**1**	3	5	7	11	17	==	–	–	–	–	–	–	–	WHAT'LL I DO?
–	–	==	==	20	==	20	==	18	18	==	19	16	14	14	17	19	==	==	==	==	==	==	–	–	–	RHAPSODY IN BLUE
–	–	–	==	==	10	4	2	3	5	6	15	==	==	–	–	–	–	–	–	–	–	–	–	–	–	THERE'S YES! YES! IN YOUR EYES
–	–	–	==	19	9	5	3	2	2	4	4	6	15	==	==	==	–	–	–	–	–	–	–	–	–	IT HAD TO BE YOU
–	–	–	–	==	13	6	5	7	8	18	==	–	–	–	–	–	–	–	–	–	–	–	–	–	–	SHINE
–	–	–	–	==	18	7	4	4	6	7	20	==	–	–	–	–	–	–	–	–	–	–	–	–	–	SPAIN
–	–	–	–	==	==	16	13	11	9	14	18	19	==	==	==	==	–	–	–	–	–	–	–	–	–	WHAT HAS BECOME OF HINKY DINKY PARLAY VOO
–	–	–	–	–	==	15	7	5	3	2	2	5	8	13	19	==	–	–	–	–	–	–	–	–	–	JEALOUS
–	–	–	–	–	==	==	19	14	12	11	14	==	==	–	–	–	–	–	–	–	–	–	–	–	–	SAN
–	–	–	–	–	–	==	18	12	11	13	12	18	==	==	–	–	–	–	–	–	–	–	–	–	–	RED HOT MAMMA
–	–	–	–	–	–	19	8	6	4	3	3	7	11	16	==	==	–	–	–	–	–	–	–	–	–	MANDALAY
–	–	–	–	–	–	==	14	9	7	5	6	4	6	10	10	10	12	11	14	20	==	–	–	–	–	MEMORY LANE
–	–	–	–	–	–	–	–	==	16	12	10	14	18	18	16	==	==	==	–	–	–	–	–	–	–	DOODLE DOO DOO
–	–	–	–	–	–	–	–	==	14	9	9	11	12	15	14	18	==	==	–	–	–	–	–	–	–	HOW COME YOU DO ME LIKE YOU DO?
–	–	–	–	–	–	–	–	==	15	8	8	8	10	12	13	15	20	==	–	–	–	–	–	–	–	HARD-HEARTED HANNAH
–	–	–	–	–	–	–	–	==	==	20	==	20	20	19	15	16	16	15	18	==	==	–	–	–	–	ROCK-A-BYE MY BABY BLUES
–	–	–	–	–	–	–	–	–	20	10	5	2	2	3	4	7	14	19	==	–	–	–	–	–	–	JUNE NIGHT
–	–	–	–	–	–	–	–	–	==	15	11	9	4	2	**1**	**1**	**1**	**1**	2	4	7	14	==	==	–	I WONDER WHAT'S BECOME OF SALLY
–	–	–	–	–	–	–	–	–	–	==	==	17	19	==	==	==	–	–	–	–	–	–	–	–	–	MAYTIME
–	–	–	–	–	–	–	–	–	–	==	==	15	16	11	12	14	19	==	–	–	–	–	–	–	–	BAGDAD
–	–	–	–	–	–	–	–	–	–	19	7	3	**1**	**1**	3	3	5	14	20	==	–	–	–	–	–	CHARLEY, MY BOY
–	–	–	–	–	–	–	–	–	–	==	17	13	9	8	9	9	13	13	17	==	–	–	–	–	–	MY DREAM GIRL
–	–	–	–	–	–	–	–	–	–	==	16	12	7	7	8	8	6	10	15	==	==	–	–	–	–	I WANT TO BE HAPPY
–	–	–	–	–	–	–	–	–	–	==	13	10	5	4	5	4	4	8	11	15	==	–	–	–	–	SOMEBODY LOVES ME
–	–	–	–	–	–	–	–	–	–	==	==	==	==	==	18	17	18	18	19	==	==	==	–	–	–	THERE'LL BE SOME CHANGES MADE
–	–	–	–	–	–	–	–	–	–	–	==	==	==	20	==	==	==	==	–	–	–	–	–	–	–	SWEET LITTLE YOU
–	–	–	–	–	–	–	–	–	–	–	==	==	13	6	2	2	2	2	5	10	==	==	–	–	–	FOLLOW THE SWALLOW
–	–	–	–	–	–	–	–	–	–	–	–	==	==	17	11	6	3	4	8	8	14	==	==	–	–	TEA FOR TWO
–	–	–	–	–	–	–	–	–	–	–	–	==	17	9	6	5	11	17	==	–	–	–	–	–	–	PUT AWAY A LITTLE RAY OF GOLDEN SUNSHINE FOR A RAINY DAY
–	–	–	–	–	–	–	–	–	–	–	–	–	–	==	20	12	7	7	10	11	16	==	==	–	–	DOO WACKA DOO
–	–	–	–	–	–	–	–	–	–	–	–	–	–	==	==	13	8	6	4	5	6	13	==	==	==	THE PAL THAT I LOVED STOLE THE GAL THAT I LOVED (1925)
–	–	–	–	–	–	–	–	–	–	–	–	–	–	–	==	20	9	5	3	2	4	11	==	==	–	COPENHAGEN (1925)
–	–	–	–	–	–	–	–	–	–	–	–	–	–	–	==	==	15	9	6	6	3	4	6	6	9	ROSE MARIE (1925)
–	–	–	–	–	–	–	–	–	–	–	–	–	–	–	–	==	10	3	**1**	**1**	**1**	**1**	**1**	**1**	2	ALL ALONE (1925)
Ap	Ap	My	My	Jn	Jn	Jy	Jy	Ag	Ag	Sp	Sp	Oc	Oc	Nv	Nv	Dc	Dc	Ja	Ja	Fb	Fb	Ma	Ma	Ap	Ap	

1924															1925											
Oc	Oc	Nv	Nv	Dc	Dc	Ja	Ja	Fb	Fb	Ma	Ma	Ap	Ap	My	My	Jn	Jn	Jy	Jy	Ag	Ag	Sp	Sp	Oc	Oc	
4	6	10	10	10	12	11	14	20	==	–	–	–	–	–	–	–	–	–	–	–	–	–	–	–	–	MEMORY LANE (1924)
20	20	19	15	16	16	15	18	==	–	–	–	–	–	–	–	–	–	–	–	–	–	–	–	–	–	ROCK-A-BYE MY BABY BLUES (1924)
2	2	3	4	7	14	19	==	–	–	–	–	–	–	–	–	–	–	–	–	–	–	–	–	–	–	JUNE NIGHT (1924)
9	4	2	1	1	1	1	2	4	7	14	==	==	–	–	–	–	–	–	–	–	–	–	–	–	–	I WONDER WHAT'S BECOME OF SALLY (1924)
3	1	1	3	3	5	14	20	==	–	–	–	–	–	–	–	–	–	–	–	–	–	–	–	–	–	CHARLEY, MY BOY (1924)
13	9	8	9	9	13	13	17	==	–	–	–	–	–	–	–	–	–	–	–	–	–	–	–	–	–	MY DREAM GIRL (1924)
12	7	7	8	8	6	10	15	==	–	–	–	–	–	–	–	–	–	–	–	–	–	–	–	–	–	I WANT TO BE HAPPY (1924)
10	5	4	5	4	4	8	11	15	==	–	–	–	–	–	–	–	–	–	–	–	–	–	–	–	–	SOMEBODY LOVES ME (1924)
==	==	==	18	17	18	18	19	==	==	==	–	–	–	–	–	–	–	–	–	–	–	–	–	–	–	THERE'LL BE SOME CHANGES MADE (1924)
==	13	6	2	2	2	2	5	10	==	==	–	–	–	–	–	–	–	–	–	–	–	–	–	–	–	FOLLOW THE SWALLOW (1924)
==	==	17	11	6	3	4	8	8	14	==	==	–	–	–	–	–	–	–	–	–	–	–	–	–	–	TEA FOR TWO (1924)
==	17	9	6	5	11	17	==	–	–	–	–	–	–	–	–	–	–	–	–	–	–	–	–	–	–	PUT AWAY A LITTLE RAY OF GOLDEN SUNSHINE FOR A RAINY DAY (1924)
–	–	==	20	12	7	7	10	11	16	==	==	–	–	–	–	–	–	–	–	–	–	–	–	–	–	DOO WACKA DOO (1924)
–	–	==	==	13	8	6	4	5	6	13	==	==	==	–	–	–	–	–	–	–	–	–	–	–	–	THE PAL THAT I LOVED STOLE THE GAL THAT ILOVED
–	–	–	==	20	9	5	3	2	4	11	==	==	–	–	–	–	–	–	–	–	–	–	–	–	–	COPENHAGEN
–	–	–	==	==	15	9	6	6	3	4	6	6	9	15	19	==	==	==	–	–	–	–	–	–	–	ROSE-MARIE
–	–	–	–	==	10	3	1	1	1	1	1	1	2	4	5	10	==	==	–	–	–	–	–	–	–	ALL ALONE
–	–	–	–	==	==	12	9	7	11	19	==	==	==	–	–	–	–	–	–	–	–	–	–	–	–	YOU'RE JUST A FLOWER FROM AN OLD BOUQUET
–	–	–	–	–	==	20	12	14	20	==	==	–	–	–	–	–	–	–	–	–	–	–	–	–	–	MANDY, MAKE UP YOUR MIND
–	–	–	–	–	==	==	13	9	8	7	9	12	11	9	12	14	10	10	11	11	13	13	16	12	12	17 17 15 == INDIAN LOVE CALL
–	–	–	–	–	–	==	==	16	17	15	14	19	==	==	–	–	–	–	–	–	–	–	–	–	–	SERENADE
–	–	–	–	–	–	==	16	13	15	20	==	==	==	==	–	–	–	–	–	–	–	–	–	–	–	SHOW ME THE WAY
–	–	–	–	–	==	16	7	3	2	2	4	7	16	==	–	–	–	–	–	–	–	–	–	–	–	MY BEST GIRL
–	–	–	–	–	–	==	==	==	19	16	15	14	15	13	11	15	17	16	18	==	==	==	–	–	–	WEST OF THE GREAT DIVIDE
–	–	–	–	–	–	==	==	==	==	==	20	20	14	16	==	==	==	19	17	14	16	16	15	19	15	13 15 13 10 10 13 15 16 17 16 20 == == == THE CHARLESTON
–	–	–	–	–	–	–	==	18	10	9	11	15	==	==	==	–	–	–	–	–	–	–	–	–	–	DEEP IN MY HEART, DEAR
–	–	–	–	–	–	–	==	19	12	6	7	11	13	==	==	–	–	–	–	–	–	–	–	–	–	FASCINATING RHYTHM
–	–	–	–	–	–	==	==	12	5	3	2	3	6	7	16	==	==	–	–	–	–	–	–	–	–	EVERYBODY LOVES MY BABY
–	–	–	–	–	–	–	–	==	==	17	16	17	==	==	–	–	–	–	–	–	–	–	–	–	–	NOBODY KNOWS WHAT A RED-HEADED MAMA CAN DO
–	–	–	–	–	–	–	==	==	13	8	8	16	20	==	==	–	–	–	–	–	–	–	–	–	–	OH, LADY BE GOOD
–	–	–	–	–	–	–	–	==	==	==	18	18	==	==	==	==	–	–	–	–	–	–	–	–	–	TELL HER IN THE SPRINGTIME
–	–	–	–	–	–	–	==	17	9	5	3	2	1	1	3	4	5	11	16	==	==	–	–	–	–	I'LL SEE YOU IN MY DREAMS
–	–	–	–	–	–	–	–	==	18	12	10	5	5	6	6	11	12	15	==	==	==	==	–	–	–	WHEN YOU AND I WERE SEVENTEEN
–	–	–	–	–	–	–	–	–	==	18	13	10	8	11	20	==	–	–	–	–	–	–	–	–	–	KEEP SMILING AT TROUBLE
–	–	–	–	–	–	–	–	–	==	==	17	13	12	19	==	==	==	–	–	–	–	–	–	–	–	OH, MABEL
–	–	–	–	–	–	–	–	–	==	==	12	9	7	8	15	18	==	==	==	–	–	–	–	–	–	JUNE BROUGHT THE ROSES
–	–	–	–	–	–	–	–	–	==	10	5	4	3	3	2	3	2	4	9	13	==	==	–	–	–	OH, KATHARINA!
–	–	–	–	–	–	–	–	–	–	==	==	==	==	20	==	==	==	==	–	–	–	–	–	–	–	LISTENING
–	–	–	–	–	–	–	–	–	–	==	19	8	4	2	1	1	3	6	8	17	==	==	–	–	–	ALABAMY BOUND
–	–	–	–	–	–	–	–	–	–	–	==	==	10	5	4	2	1	1	4	8	10	14	20	==	==	YEARNING (JUST FOR YOU)
–	–	–	–	–	–	–	–	–	–	–	–	==	17	14	8	7	11	18	==	==	–	–	–	–	–	CHEATIN' ON ME
–	–	–	–	–	–	–	–	–	–	–	–	==	18	10	10	8	13	17	20	==	==	–	–	–	–	WHO TAKES CARE OF THE CARETAKER'S DAUGHTER
–	–	–	–	–	–	–	–	–	–	–	–	==	19	12	7	5	4	3	6	7	9	10	13	15	18	== OH, HOW I MISS YOU TONIGHT
–	–	–	–	–	–	–	–	–	–	–	–	–	==	==	14	13	19	==	==	–	–	–	–	–	–	IN SHADOWLAND
–	–	–	–	–	–	–	–	–	–	–	–	–	==	17	9	6	6	13	15	==	==	–	–	–	–	WHEN MY SUGAR WALKS DOWN THE STREET
–	–	–	–	–	–	–	–	–	–	–	–	–	==	==	18	17	20	20	==	==	==	==	–	–	–	LET IT RAIN! LET IT POUR! (I'LL BE IN VIRGINIA IN THE MORNING)
Oc	Oc	Nv	Nv	Dc	Dc	Ja	Ja	Fb	Fb	Ma	Ma	Ap	Ap	My	My	Jn	Jn	Jy	Jy	Ag	Ag	Sp	Sp	Oc	Oc	

1925																		1926								
Ap	Ap	My	My	Jn	Jn	Jy	Jy	Ag	Ag	Sp	Sp	Oc	Oc	Nv	Nv	Dc	Dc	Ja	Ja	Fb	Fb	Ma	Ma	Ap	Ap	
–	==	18	13	9	7	5	5	3	2	2	3	7	16	==	==	–	–	–	–	–	–	–	–	–	–	UKULELE LADY
–	–	==	==	16	16	==	==	==	–	–	–	–	–	–	–	–	–	–	–	–	–	–	–	–	–	SWANEE BUTTERFLY
–	–	==	17	12	9	8	10	12	12	==	==	==	–	–	–	–	–	–	–	–	–	–	–	–	–	MIDNIGHT WALTZ
–	–	==	==	20	15	12	7	5	7	4	4	2	2	2	3	5	8	19	==	==	==	==	–	–	–	MOONLIGHT AND ROSES
–	–	–	==	==	==	==	19	16	==	==	==	–	–	–	–	–	–	–	–	–	–	–	–	–	–	EVERYTHING IS HOTSY-TOTSY NOW
–	–	–	==	==	==	14	12	10	8	7	5	4	4	9	12	14	==	==	==	==	–	–	–	–	–	PAL OF MY CRADLE DAYS
–	–	–	==	19	8	2	**1**	**1**	4	5	7	10	==	==	–	–	–	–	–	–	–	–	–	–	–	IF YOU KNEW SUSIE
–	–	–	–	==	18	7	2	4	6	8	10	18	==	==	–	–	–	–	–	–	–	–	–	–	–	DON'T BRING LULU
–	–	–	–	==	14	9	3	2	3	6	9	16	==	==	–	–	–	–	–	–	–	–	–	–	–	SWEET GEORGIA BROWN
–	–	–	–	==	==	==	==	18	18	19	19	13	9	10	13	9	12	==	==	==	==	==	–	–	–	LET ME CALL YOU SWEETHEART
–	–	–	–	–	–	==	==	20	==	==	==	==	–	–	–	–	–	–	–	–	–	–	–	–	–	WHY DO I LOVE YOU SO?
–	–	–	–	–	–	==	==	==	19	20	==	==	==	==	–	–	–	–	–	–	–	–	–	–	–	JUST A LITTLE DRINK
–	–	–	–	–	–	==	==	==	20	==	==	==	==	==	–	–	–	–	–	–	–	–	–	–	–	BY THE LIGHT OF THE STARS
–	–	–	–	–	–	==	==	15	11	12	14	==	==	==	==	==	–	–	–	–	–	–	–	–	–	RIVERBOAT SHUFFLE
–	–	–	–	–	–	==	==	19	15	11	12	14	14	20	==	==	–	–	–	–	–	–	–	–	–	MILENBERG JOYS
–	–	–	–	–	–	==	13	6	**1**	**1**	2	3	3	4	11	==	==	–	–	–	–	–	–	–	–	COLLEGIATE
–	–	–	–	–	–	==	14	9	5	3	**1**	**1**	**1**	**1**	5	10	==	==	–	–	–	–	–	–	–	YES SIR! THAT'S MY BABY
–	–	–	–	–	==	==	==	==	14	18	==	==	–	–	–	–	–	–	–	–	–	–	–	–	–	LET ME LINGER (LONGER) IN YOUR ARMS
–	–	–	–	–	–	–	–	==	17	9	6	5	8	14	18	==	–	–	–	–	–	–	–	–	–	I MISS MY SWISS
–	–	–	–	–	–	–	–	==	==	17	11	9	13	19	==	==	–	–	–	–	–	–	–	–	–	MONTMARTRE ROSE
–	–	–	–	–	–	–	–	–	==	15	8	6	5	6	10	16	==	–	–	–	–	–	–	–	–	MANHATTAN
–	–	–	–	–	–	–	–	–	–	==	17	8	6	7	16	==	–	–	–	–	–	–	–	–	–	MY SWEETIE TURNED ME DOWN
–	–	–	–	–	–	–	–	–	–	==	18	11	7	3	2	4	4	8	==	==	–	–	–	–	–	CECILIA
–	–	–	–	–	–	–	–	–	–	==	==	17	10	8	9	11	18	==	–	–	–	–	–	–	–	SENTIMENTAL ME (AND ROMANTIC YOU)
–	–	–	–	–	–	–	–	–	–	–	–	==	17	12	6	6	11	18	==	==	–	–	–	–	–	SAVE YOUR SORROW (FOR TOMORROW)
–	–	–	–	–	–	–	–	–	–	–	–	==	==	18	7	7	9	20	==	==	==	–	–	–	–	ANGRY
–	–	–	–	–	–	–	–	–	–	–	–	==	20	15	8	3	3	5	11	20	==	==	–	–	–	SOMETIME
–	–	–	–	–	–	–	–	–	–	–	–	==	==	11	4	2	2	3	5	9	18	20	==	==	–	BROWN EYES, WHY ARE YOU BLUE?
–	–	–	–	–	–	–	–	–	–	–	–	==	11	5	**1**	**1**	**1**	**1**	2	7	10	12	12	19	==	REMEMBER
–	–	–	–	–	–	–	–	–	–	–	–	==	==	==	20	==	==	==	–	–	–	–	–	–	–	I'M GONNA CHARLESTON BACK TO CHARLESTON
–	–	–	–	–	–	–	–	–	–	–	–	–	==	==	19	17	==	==	–	–	–	–	–	–	–	CLOSE YOUR EYES
==	==	==	==	==	==	==	==	==	==	==	==	20	19	16	14	8	5	2	**1**	**1**	**1**	**1**	2	3	3	THE PRISONER'S SONG (1926)
–	–	–	–	–	–	–	–	–	–	–	–	–	–	==	==	==	20	16	==	==	==	==	==	==	–	THE LONESOMEST GIRL IN TOWN (1926)
–	–	–	–	–	–	–	–	–	–	–	–	–	–	–	==	19	14	13	10	13	15	19	==	==	==	JUST AROUND THE CORNER (1926)
–	–	–	–	–	–	–	–	–	–	–	–	–	–	–	==	12	6	4	3	2	6	8	8	8	11	SLEEPY TIME GAL (1926)
–	–	–	–	–	–	–	–	–	–	–	–	–	–	–	==	20	17	12	16	19	==	==	–	–	–	PADDLIN' MADELIN' HOME (1926)
–	–	–	–	–	–	–	–	–	–	–	–	–	–	–	–	==	16	11	9	12	14	15	19	==	==	BAM, BAM, BAMY SHORE (1926)
–	–	–	–	–	–	–	–	–	–	–	–	–	–	–	–	==	13	7	4	5	8	9	13	==	==	SHOW ME THE WAY TO GO HOME (1926)
–	–	–	–	–	–	–	–	–	–	–	–	–	–	–	–	==	19	14	14	16	13	14	17	15	==	SONG OF THE VAGABONDS (1926)
–	–	–	–	–	–	–	–	–	–	–	–	–	–	–	–	==	15	9	8	8	5	6	9	10	9	WHO? (1926)
–	–	–	–	–	–	–	–	–	–	–	–	–	–	–	–	18	7	6	6	4	2	2	3	4	6	I'M SITTING ON TOP OF THE WORLD (1926)
Ap	Ap	My	My	Jn	Jn	Jy	Jy	Ag	Ag	Sp	Sp	Oc	Oc	Nv	Nv	Dc	Dc	Ja	Ja	Fb	Fb	Ma	Ma	Ap	Ap	

1925						1926																				
Oc	Oc	Nv	Nv	Dc	Dc	Ja	Ja	Fb	Fb	Ma	Ma	Ap	Ap	My	My	Jn	Jn	Jy	Jy	Ag	Ag	Sp	Sp	Oc	Oc	
19	15	13	15	13	10	10	13	15	16	17	16	20	==	==	==	==	==	==	–	–	–	–	–	–	–	THE CHARLESTON (1925)
2	2	2	3	5	8	19	==	==	==	==	–	–	–	–	–	–	–	–	–	–	–	–	–	–	–	MOONLIGHT AND ROSES (1925)
11	7	3	2	4	4	8	==	==	–	–	–	–	–	–	–	–	–	–	–	–	–	–	–	–	–	CECILIA (1925)
==	17	12	6	6	11	18	==	==	–	–	–	–	–	–	–	–	–	–	–	–	–	–	–	–	–	SAVE YOUR SORROW (FOR TOMORROW) (1925)
==	==	18	7	7	9	20	==	==	==	–	–	–	–	–	–	–	–	–	–	–	–	–	–	–	–	ANGRY (1925)
==	20	15	8	3	3	5	11	20	==	==	–	–	–	–	–	–	–	–	–	–	–	–	–	–	–	SOMETIME (1925)
==	==	11	4	2	2	3	5	9	18	20	==	==	–	–	–	–	–	–	–	–	–	–	–	–	–	BROWN EYES, WHY ARE YOU BLUE? (1925)
==	11	5	**1**	**1**	**1**	**1**	2	7	10	12	12	19	==	==	–	–	–	–	–	–	–	–	–	–	–	REMEMBER (1925)
20	19	16	14	8	5	2	**1**	**1**	**1**	**1**	2	3	3	5	10	11	17	==	==	==	–	–	–	–	–	THE PRISONER'S SONG
–	–	==	==	==	20	16	==	==	==	==	==	==	–	–	–	–	–	–	–	–	–	–	–	–	–	THE LONESOMEST GIRL IN TOWN
–	–	–	==	19	14	13	10	13	15	19	==	==	==	==	–	–	–	–	–	–	–	–	–	–	–	JUST AROUND THE CORNER
–	–	–	==	12	6	4	3	2	6	8	8	8	11	17	==	–	–	–	–	–	–	–	–	–	–	SLEEPY TIME GAL
–	–	–	==	20	17	12	16	19	==	==	–	–	–	–	–	–	–	–	–	–	–	–	–	–	–	PADDLIN' MADELIN' HOME
–	–	–	–	==	==	==	20	==	==	==	==	==	–	–	–	–	–	–	–	–	–	–	–	–	–	I WANT TO BE HAPPY
–	–	–	–	==	==	==	19	==	==	==	==	==	–	–	–	–	–	–	–	–	–	–	–	–	–	TEA FOR TWO
–	–	–	–	==	16	11	9	12	14	15	19	==	==	–	–	–	–	–	–	–	–	–	–	–	–	BAM, BAM, BAMY SHORE
–	–	–	–	==	13	7	4	5	8	9	13	==	==	–	–	–	–	–	–	–	–	–	–	–	–	SHOW ME THE WAY TO GO HOME
–	–	–	–	==	19	14	14	16	13	14	17	15	==	==	–	–	–	–	–	–	–	–	–	–	–	SONG OF THE VAGABONDS
–	–	–	–	==	==	==	==	18	19	==	==	==	==	==	==	==	–	–	–	–	–	–	–	–	–	ONLY A ROSE
–	–	–	–	==	15	9	8	8	5	6	9	10	9	18	==	==	–	–	–	–	–	–	–	–	–	WHO?
–	–	–	–	18	7	6	6	4	2	2	3	4	6	11	18	==	–	–	–	–	–	–	–	–	–	I'M SITTING ON TOP OF THE WORLD
–	–	–	–	–	==	15	7	3	3	3	7	7	14	20	==	–	–	–	–	–	–	–	–	–	–	FIVE FOOT TWO, EYES OF BLUE
–	–	–	–	–	==	17	15	10	9	7	6	5	5	7	13	19	==	==	–	–	–	–	–	–	–	THEN I'LL BE HAPPY
–	–	–	–	–	–	==	==	==	20	==	==	==	–	–	–	–	–	–	–	–	–	–	–	–	–	DON'T WAKE ME UP (LET ME DREAM)
–	–	–	–	–	–	==	18	14	11	16	18	==	==	–	–	–	–	–	–	–	–	–	–	–	–	I NEVER KNEW (THAT ROSES GREW)
–	–	–	–	–	–	==	17	11	7	11	14	14	==	==	–	–	–	–	–	–	–	–	–	–	–	A CUP OF COFFEE, A SANDWICH, AND YOU
–	–	–	–	–	–	==	12	6	4	4	11	18	==	–	–	–	–	–	–	–	–	–	–	–	–	THAT CERTAIN PARTY
–	–	–	–	–	–	==	==	17	12	5	**1**	2	2	3	4	8	12	16	==	==	–	–	–	–	–	DINAH
–	–	–	–	–	–	–	==	==	17	13	5	6	7	12	12	20	==	–	–	–	–	–	–	–	–	I LOVE MY BABY
–	–	–	–	–	–	–	–	==	==	18	10	11	17	==	==	–	–	–	–	–	–	–	–	–	–	DOWN BY THE WINEGAR WOIKS
–	–	–	–	–	–	–	–	–	==	==	20	12	18	==	==	==	–	–	–	–	–	–	–	–	–	THAT CERTAIN FEELING
–	–	–	–	–	–	–	–	–	==	==	==	13	8	6	11	13	19	==	==	==	–	–	–	–	–	THANKS FOR THE BUGGY RIDE
–	–	–	–	–	–	–	–	–	==	10	4	**1**	**1**	**1**	**1**	**1**	2	3	4	6	8	11	19	==	==	ALWAYS
–	–	–	–	–	–	–	–	–	–	==	==	16	13	14	17	==	–	–	–	–	–	–	–	–	–	SONG OF THE FLAME
–	–	–	–	–	–	–	–	–	–	==	==	17	12	15	20	==	–	–	–	–	–	–	–	–	–	SWEET AND LOW-DOWN
–	–	–	–	–	–	–	–	–	–	==	==	==	20	16	14	17	==	==	–	–	–	–	–	–	–	COSSACK LOVE SONG (DON'T FORGET ME)
–	–	–	–	–	–	–	–	–	–	==	15	9	4	2	2	4	4	9	12	==	==	–	–	–	–	(WHAT CAN I SAY) AFTER I SAY I'M SORRY
–	–	–	–	–	–	–	–	–	–	==	==	==	10	4	6	6	6	11	11	15	==	==	==	==	–	JUST A COTTAGE SMALL (BY A WATERFALL)
–	–	–	–	–	–	–	–	–	–	–	–	==	==	==	16	14	20	==	==	==	–	–	–	–	–	IN THE MIDDLE OF THE NIGHT
–	–	–	–	–	–	–	–	–	–	–	–	==	19	10	8	7	8	14	18	==	==	–	–	–	–	LET'S TALK ABOUT MY SWEETIE
–	–	–	–	–	–	–	–	–	–	–	–	==	16	8	3	2	3	4	10	16	==	–	–	–	–	GIMME A LITTLE KISS, WILL YA, HUH?
–	–	–	–	–	–	–	–	–	–	–	–	==	15	9	5	5	13	13	==	–	–	–	–	–	–	POOR PAPA, HE GOT NUTHIN' AT ALL
–	–	–	–	–	–	–	–	–	–	–	–	–	==	13	9	9	9	17	==	–	–	–	–	–	–	TAMIAMI TRAIL
–	–	–	–	–	–	–	–	–	–	–	–	–	–	==	15	10	7	12	14	==	–	–	–	–	–	(I DON'T BELIEVE IT BUT) SAY IT AGAIN
–	–	–	–	–	–	–	–	–	–	–	–	–	–	19	7	3	**1**	**1**	5	10	20	==	–	–	–	HORSES
–	–	–	–	–	–	–	–	–	–	–	–	–	–	==	==	16	16	15	15	18	18	==	==	==	–	REACHING FOR THE MOON
Oc	Oc	Nv	Nv	Dc	Dc	Ja	Ja	Fb	Fb	Ma	Ma	Ap	Ap	My	My	Jn	Jn	Jy	Jy	Ag	Ag	Sp	Sp	Oc	Oc	

						1926												1927								
Ap	Ap	My	My	Jn	Jn	Jy	Jy	Ag	Ag	Sp	Sp	Oc	Oc	Nv	Nv	Dc	Dc	Ja	Ja	Fb	Fb	Ma	Ma	Ap	Ap	
–	–	==	==	==	==	19	17	==	==	==	==	==	==	==	–	–	–	–	–	–	–	–	–	–	–	NEAPOLITAN NIGHTS
–	–	==	19	12	5	2	3	4	7	10	==	==	–	–	–	–	–	–	–	–	–	–	–	–	–	I'D CLIMB THE HIGHEST MOUNTAIN
–	–	–	==	15	14	10	8	7	6	6	7	14	16	20	==	==	–	–	–	–	–	–	–	–	–	DRIFTING AND DREAMING
–	–	–	==	18	10	7	7	8	10	19	==	–	–	–	–	–	–	–	–	–	–	–	–	–	–	AT PEACE WITH THE WORLD
–	–	–	–	==	15	8	6	5	9	17	==	==	–	–	–	–	–	–	–	–	–	–	–	–	–	MY LITTLE NEST OF HEAVENLY BLUE
–	–	–	–	==	11	5	2	2	3	5	11	19	==	–	–	–	–	–	–	–	–	–	–	–	–	LONESOME AND SORRY
–	–	–	–	==	==	==	19	19	19	14	15	17	18	==	==	==	==	==	==	==	–	–	–	–	–	THE GIRL FRIEND
–	–	–	–	==	==	20	16	11	13	8	13	12	14	16	==	==	==	==	==	==	–	–	–	–	–	THE BLUE ROOM
–	–	–	–	==	18	6	1	1	1	1	2	3	6	9	==	==	–	–	–	–	–	–	–	–	–	VALENCIA
–	–	–	–	–	–	==	==	17	14	15	==	==	–	–	–	–	–	–	–	–	–	–	–	–	–	MY DREAM OF THE BIG PARADE
–	–	–	–	–	–	==	13	9	4	4	6	18	==	==	–	–	–	–	–	–	–	–	–	–	–	SLEEPY HEAD
–	–	–	–	–	–	==	==	==	==	==	20	==	==	==	==	==	–	–	–	–	–	–	–	–	–	MOUNTAIN GREENERY
–	–	–	–	–	–	==	==	14	12	12	18	20	==	==	==	==	–	–	–	–	–	–	–	–	–	AM I WASTING MY TIME ON YOU?
–	–	–	–	–	–	18	9	3	2	2	1	1	2	4	6	14	==	==	–	–	–	–	–	–	–	BYE, BYE, BLACKBIRD
–	–	–	–	–	–	==	20	13	11	7	5	7	9	10	10	17	17	==	==	==	–	–	–	–	–	CHERIE, I LOVE YOU
–	–	–	–	–	–	–	==	==	16	16	==	==	==	–	–	–	–	–	–	–	–	–	–	–	–	KATINKA
–	–	–	–	–	–	–	==	20	17	13	12	15	17	==	==	==	–	–	–	–	–	–	–	–	–	HELLO, ALOHA! HOW ARE YOU?
–	–	–	–	–	–	–	==	12	5	3	3	2	4	8	13	20	==	–	–	–	–	–	–	–	–	WHEN THE RED, RED ROBIN COMES BOB, BOB, BOBBIN' ALONG
–	–	–	–	–	–	–	–	==	==	20	==	==	==	==	–	–	–	–	–	–	–	–	–	–	–	I'M JUST WILD ABOUT ANIMAL CRACKERS
–	–	–	–	–	–	–	–	==	15	9	4	4	5	7	8	19	==	==	–	–	–	–	–	–	–	WHERE'D YOU GET THOSE EYES?
–	–	–	–	–	–	–	–	==	==	==	==	16	13	13	20	==	==	==	==	–	–	–	–	–	–	TING-A-LING (THE WALTZ OF THE BELLS)
–	–	–	–	–	–	–	–	==	==	==	==	==	15	17	==	==	==	==	==	==	–	–	–	–	–	BARCELONA
–	–	–	–	–	–	–	–	==	==	==	14	9	10	11	9	18	18	==	==	==	–	–	–	–	–	HOW MANY TIMES
–	–	–	–	–	–	–	–	–	==	18	9	8	12	14	==	==	–	–	–	–	–	–	–	–	–	LOOKING AT THE WORLD THROUGH ROSE-COLORED GLASSES
–	–	–	–	–	–	–	–	–	==	==	17	11	8	3	2	1	3	7	13	18	==	==	==	–	–	BLACK BOTTOM
–	–	–	–	–	–	–	–	–	==	==	==	13	11	6	3	4	8	8	14	20	==	==	==	==	–	LUCKY DAY
–	–	–	–	–	–	–	–	–	==	==	10	6	3	2	4	8	13	19	==	–	–	–	–	–	–	BREEZIN' ALONG WITH THE BREEZE
–	–	–	–	–	–	–	–	–	–	==	16	10	7	5	5	15	20	==	–	–	–	–	–	–	–	ME TOO
–	–	–	–	–	–	–	–	–	–	==	8	5	1	1	1	3	9	11	==	==	–	–	–	–	–	BABY FACE
–	–	–	–	–	–	–	–	–	–	==	==	==	19	15	12	6	10	10	11	16	19	==	==	==	==	THE BIRTH OF THE BLUES
–	–	–	–	–	–	–	–	–	–	–	–	==	20	18	==	==	==	–	–	–	–	–	–	–	–	THERE'S A NEW STAR IN HEAVEN TONIGHT (RUDOLPH VALENTINO)
–	–	–	–	–	–	–	–	–	–	–	–	–	==	==	17	13	16	==	==	==	–	–	–	–	–	FOR MY SWEETHEART
–	–	–	–	–	–	–	–	–	–	–	–	–	==	19	11	11	15	18	==	==	–	–	–	–	–	PLAY GYPSIES – DANCE GYPSIES
–	–	–	–	–	–	–	–	–	–	–	–	–	==	==	19	12	11	13	17	==	==	–	–	–	–	CROSS YOUR HEART
–	–	–	–	–	–	–	–	–	–	–	–	–	==	12	7	2	1	2	5	6	13	14	19	==	–	BECAUSE I LOVE YOU
–	–	–	–	–	–	–	–	–	–	–	–	–	–	==	==	==	12	12	20	==	–	–	–	–	–	CLIMBING UP THE LADDER OF LOVE
–	–	–	–	–	–	–	–	–	–	–	–	–	==	==	18	10	6	6	4	2	2	4	10	10	15	TONIGHT YOU BELONG TO ME (1927)
–	–	–	–	–	–	–	–	–	–	–	–	–	–	==	16	9	5	4	6	7	8	8	18	==	–	MARY LOU (1927)
–	–	–	–	–	–	–	–	–	–	–	–	–	–	==	15	7	4	3	3	4	14	20	==	==	–	MOONLIGHT ON THE GANGES (1927)
–	–	–	–	–	–	–	–	–	–	–	–	–	–	==	14	5	2	1	1	1	1	1	3	6	8	IN A LITTLE SPANISH TOWN (1927)
–	–	–	–	–	–	–	–	–	–	–	–	–	–	–	==	16	7	5	2	3	3	15	==	–	–	THE LITTLE WHITE HOUSE (AT THE END OF HONEYMOON LANE) (1927)
–	–	–	–	–	–	–	–	–	–	–	–	–	–	–	==	==	14	9	8	13	17	==	==	–	–	ALL ALONE MONDAY (1927)
–	–	–	–	–	–	–	–	–	–	–	–	–	–	–	–	==	19	14	9	8	7	7	14	17	==	SUNDAY (1927)
Ap	Ap	My	My	Jn	Jn	Jy	Jy	Ag	Ag	Sp	Sp	Oc	Oc	Nv	Nv	Dc	Dc	Ja	Ja	Fb	Fb	Ma	Ma	Ap	Ap	

1926						1927																				
Oc	Oc	Nv	Nv	Dc	Dc	Ja	Ja	Fb	Fb	Ma	Ma	Ap	Ap	My	My	Jn	Jn	Jy	Jy	Ag	Ag	Sp	Sp	Oc	Oc	
11	8	3	2	**1**	3	7	13	18	==	==	==	–	–	–	–	–	–	–	–	–	–	–	–	–	–	BLACK BOTTOM (1926)
13	11	6	3	4	8	8	14	20	==	==	==	==	–	–	–	–	–	–	–	–	–	–	–	–	–	LUCKY DAY (1926)
6	3	2	4	8	13	19	==	–	–	–	–	–	–	–	–	–	–	–	–	–	–	–	–	–	–	BREEZIN' ALONG WITH THE BREEZE (1926)
5	**1**	**1**	**1**	3	9	11	==	==	–	–	–	–	–	–	–	–	–	–	–	–	–	–	–	–	–	BABY FACE (1926)
==	19	15	12	6	10	10	11	16	19	==	==	==	==	==	–	–	–	–	–	–	–	–	–	–	–	THE BIRTH OF THE BLUES (1926)
–	==	==	17	13	16	==	==	==	–	–	–	–	–	–	–	–	–	–	–	–	–	–	–	–	–	FOR MY SWEETHEART (1926)
–	==	19	11	11	15	18	==	==	–	–	–	–	–	–	–	–	–	–	–	–	–	–	–	–	–	PLAY GYPSIES – DANCE GYPSIES (1926)
–	==	==	19	12	11	13	17	==	==	–	–	–	–	–	–	–	–	–	–	–	–	–	–	–	–	CROSS YOUR HEART (1926)
–	==	13	7	2	**1**	2	5	6	13	14	19	==	–	–	–	–	–	–	–	–	–	–	–	–	–	BECAUSE I LOVE YOU (1926)
–	–	==	==	==	12	12	20	==	–	–	–	–	–	–	–	–	–	–	–	–	–	–	–	–	–	CLIMBING UP THE LADDER OF LOVE (1926)
–	==	==	18	10	6	6	4	2	2	4	10	10	15	==	==	–	–	–	–	–	–	–	–	–	–	TONIGHT YOU BELONG TO ME
–	–	==	16	9	5	4	6	7	8	8	18	==	–	–	–	–	–	–	–	–	–	–	–	–	–	MARY LOU
–	–	==	15	7	4	3	3	4	14	20	==	==	–	–	–	–	–	–	–	–	–	–	–	–	–	MOONLIGHT ON THE GANGES
–	–	==	14	5	2	**1**	**1**	**1**	**1**	**1**	3	6	8	16	==	==	–	–	–	–	–	–	–	–	–	IN A LITTLE SPANISH TOWN
–	–	–	==	16	7	5	2	3	3	15	==	–	–	–	–	–	–	–	–	–	–	–	–	–	–	THE LITTLE WHITE HOUSE (AT THE END OF HONEYMOON LANE)
–	–	–	==	==	14	9	8	13	17	==	==	–	–	–	–	–	–	–	–	–	–	–	–	–	–	ALL ALONE MONDAY
–	–	–	==	==	==	17	15	==	==	==	==	–	–	–	–	–	–	–	–	–	–	–	–	–	–	JUST A BIRD'S-EYE VIEW OF MY OLD KENTUCKY HOME
–	–	–	–	==	19	14	9	8	7	7	14	17	==	==	–	–	–	–	–	–	–	–	–	–	–	SUNDAY
–	–	–	–	==	==	16	10	10	15	12	16	16	==	–	–	–	–	–	–	–	–	–	–	–	–	HELLO, BLUEBIRD
–	–	–	–	–	==	20	12	9	9	13	20	==	==	–	–	–	–	–	–	–	–	–	–	–	–	DO, DO, DO
–	–	–	–	–	==	15	7	5	6	17	17	==	–	–	–	–	–	–	–	–	–	–	–	–	–	IT MADE YOU HAPPY WHEN YOU MADE ME CRY
–	–	–	–	–	–	==	18	15	12	11	11	12	20	==	==	–	–	–	–	–	–	–	–	–	–	ONE ALONE
–	–	–	–	–	–	==	16	12	10	5	5	9	16	==	==	–	–	–	–	–	–	–	–	–	–	SOMEONE TO WATCH OVER ME
–	–	–	–	–	–	–	19	11	4	2	2	2	6	17	–	–	–	–	–	–	–	–	–	–	–	WHERE DO YOU WORK-A JOHN?
–	–	–	–	–	–	–	==	19	16	10	12	18	–	–	–	–	–	–	–	–	–	–	–	–	–	CLAP YO' HANDS
–	–	–	–	–	–	–	==	14	11	6	6	15	==	–	–	–	–	–	–	–	–	–	–	–	–	(I'VE GROWN SO LONESOME) THINKING OF YOU
–	–	–	–	–	–	–	==	==	20	==	==	==	–	–	–	–	–	–	–	–	–	–	–	–	–	I'VE GOT THE GIRL
–	–	–	–	–	–	–	–	==	18	9	4	7	12	20	==	==	–	–	–	–	–	–	–	–	–	I KNOW THAT YOU KNOW
–	–	–	–	–	–	–	–	17	5	3	**1**	**1**	**1**	3	7	11	19	==	–	–	–	–	–	–	–	BLUE SKIES
–	–	–	–	–	–	–	–	==	==	==	13	8	4	5	6	3	3	7	10	18	==	==	==	==	==	MUDDY WATER
–	–	–	–	–	–	–	–	==	==	==	15	11	10	10	11	14	17	==	==	==	==	–	–	–	–	SONG OF THE WANDERER
–	–	–	–	–	–	–	–	–	==	18	9	5	5	6	15	==	–	–	–	–	–	–	–	–	–	YANKEE ROSE
–	–	–	–	–	–	–	–	–	==	16	8	4	3	**1**	**1**	6	14	15	==	==	–	–	–	–	–	IT ALL DEPENDS ON YOU
–	–	–	–	–	–	–	–	–	–	19	7	3	2	2	5	8	16	==	–	–	–	–	–	–	–	SAM, THE OLD ACCORDION MAN
–	–	–	–	–	–	–	–	–	–	–	==	==	==	19	19	==	==	==	==	==	–	–	–	–	–	IF YOU SEE SALLY
–	–	–	–	–	–	–	–	–	–	–	==	14	7	4	4	4	6	11	20	==	–	–	–	–	–	RIO RITA
–	–	–	–	–	–	–	–	–	–	–	==	20	14	11	14	19	==	==	==	==	–	–	–	–	–	THE RANGER'S SONG
–	–	–	–	–	–	–	–	–	–	–	==	==	19	15	17	20	==	==	==	==	==	–	–	–	–	FOLLOWING THE SUN AROUND
–	–	–	–	–	–	–	–	–	–	–	==	19	17	14	12	17	18	==	==	==	==	==	–	–	–	THE KINKAJOU
–	–	–	–	–	–	–	–	–	–	–	==	13	9	8	10	7	9	10	17	==	==	==	–	–	–	WHAT DOES IT MATTER?
–	–	–	–	–	–	–	–	–	–	–	–	==	18	13	9	9	15	==	==	–	–	–	–	–	–	CRAZY WORDS, CRAZY TUNE
–	–	–	–	–	–	–	–	–	–	–	–	==	==	18	16	18	==	==	==	==	==	–	–	–	–	MOONBEAM! KISS HER FOR ME
–	–	–	–	–	–	–	–	–	–	–	–	==	13	9	3	2	2	3	8	17	==	–	–	–	–	AIN'T SHE SWEET
–	–	–	–	–	–	–	–	–	–	–	–	==	11	7	2	**1**	**1**	5	7	11	==	==	–	–	–	I'M LOOKING OVER A FOUR LEAF CLOVER
–	–	–	–	–	–	–	–	–	–	–	–	==	==	==	20	==	==	18	18	16	18	==	==	==	==	AFTER YOU'VE GONE
–	–	–	–	–	–	–	–	–	–	–	–	–	==	12	8	5	7	17	==	==	–	–	–	–	–	FORGIVE ME
–	–	–	–	–	–	–	–	–	–	–	–	–	==	==	13	13	10	14	==	==	==	==	–	–	–	SO BLUE
–	–	–	–	–	–	–	–	–	–	–	–	–	==	18	15	12	16	16	==	==	–	–	–	–	–	THERE'S EVERYTHING NICE ABOUT YOU

1927																		1928								
Ap	Ap	My	My	Jn	Jn	Jy	Jy	Ag	Ag	Sp	Sp	Oc	Oc	Nv	Nv	Dc	Dc	Ja	Ja	Fb	Fb	Ma	Ma	Ap	Ap	
–	–	==	==	==	==	==	==	==	20	20	==	==	==	==	==	==	==	==	–	–	–	–	–	–	–	SILVER MOON
–	–	==	==	10	8	6	5	5	9	11	13	10	14	20	==	==	==	==	–	–	–	–	–	–	–	THE DOLL DANCE
–	–	–	==	12	4	**1**	**1**	2	4	6	10	18	==	–	–	–	–	–	–	–	–	–	–	–	–	RUSSIAN LULLABY
–	–	–	==	16	5	2	2	3	6	8	9	12	==	==	–	–	–	–	–	–	–	–	–	–	–	AT SUNDOWN
–	–	–	==	==	11	8	11	==	==	–	–	–	–	–	–	–	–	–	–	–	–	–	–	–	–	I'M IN LOVE AGAIN
–	–	–	–	==	20	13	19	==	–	–	–	–	–	–	–	–	–	–	–	–	–	–	–	–	–	FIFTY MILLION FRENCHMEN (CAN'T BE WRONG)
–	–	–	–	==	13	4	3	**1**	**1**	3	4	5	11	==	==	–	–	–	–	–	–	–	–	–	–	ME AND MY SHADOW
–	–	–	–	==	==	==	==	20	15	17	20	==	==	==	==	==	–	–	–	–	–	–	–	–	–	TWO BLACK CROWS, PARTS 1 AND 2
–	–	–	–	==	==	12	6	7	5	2	3	4	4	7	11	18	==	==	–	–	–	–	–	–	–	WHEN DAY IS DONE
–	–	–	–	–	==	==	14	13	19	==	==	–	–	–	–	–	–	–	–	–	–	–	–	–	–	LUCKY LINDY
–	–	–	–	–	==	20	13	10	17	==	==	–	–	–	–	–	–	–	–	–	–	–	–	–	–	LINDBERGH, THE EAGLE OF THE U.S.A.
–	–	–	–	–	==	19	9	9	13	==	==	–	–	–	–	–	–	–	–	–	–	–	–	–	–	RED LIPS, KISS MY BLUES AWAY
–	–	–	–	–	==	9	4	4	3	5	8	15	==	==	–	–	–	–	–	–	–	–	–	–	–	SIDE BY SIDE
–	–	–	–	–	==	==	==	==	==	19	19	==	==	==	==	–	–	–	–	–	–	–	–	–	–	SLOW RIVER
–	–	–	–	–	–	==	==	14	12	16	==	==	–	–	–	–	–	–	–	–	–	–	–	–	–	MAGNOLIA
–	–	–	–	–	–	==	15	8	8	9	12	19	==	==	–	–	–	–	–	–	–	–	–	–	–	SOMETIMES I'M HAPPY
–	–	–	–	–	–	==	==	==	16	15	15	20	==	==	==	==	==	==	–	–	–	–	–	–	–	I CAN'T BELIEVE THAT YOU'RE IN LOVE WITH ME
–	–	–	–	–	–	==	==	15	11	12	11	8	12	16	19	==	==	==	–	–	–	–	–	–	–	HALLELUJAH!
–	–	–	–	–	–	==	12	6	2	**1**	**1**	**1**	**1**	**1**	2	3	5	13	==	==	–	–	–	–	–	CHARMAINE
–	–	–	–	–	–	–	==	12	7	4	5	11	==	–	–	–	–	–	–	–	–	–	–	–	–	JUST LIKE A BUTTERFLY (THAT'S CAUGHT IN THE RAIN)
–	–	–	–	–	–	–	==	19	10	10	7	7	13	19	==	==	–	–	–	–	–	–	–	–	–	JUST ANOTHER DAY WASTED AWAY (WAITING FOR YOU)
–	–	–	–	–	–	–	==	==	==	18	17	17	16	17	17	==	==	==	==	==	==	–	–	–	–	DOWN SOUTH
–	–	–	–	–	–	–	–	==	==	14	14	6	9	12	18	==	==	==	–	–	–	–	–	–	–	ARE YOU LONESOME TONIGHT?
–	–	–	–	–	–	–	–	==	14	7	2	2	3	3	6	16	==	==	–	–	–	–	–	–	–	WHAT DO WE DO ON A DEW-DEW-DEWY DAY?
–	–	–	–	–	–	–	–	–	==	==	18	==	==	==	==	==	–	–	–	–	–	–	–	–	–	YOU DON'T LIKE IT, NOT MUCH
–	–	–	–	–	–	–	–	–	==	13	6	3	2	4	5	10	20	==	–	–	–	–	–	–	–	(HERE AM I) BROKEN HEARTED
–	–	–	–	–	–	–	–	–	–	==	==	13	8	13	==	==	–	–	–	–	–	–	–	–	–	I'M COMING, VIRGINIA
–	–	–	–	–	–	–	–	–	–	==	16	9	7	11	13	20	==	–	–	–	–	–	–	–	–	C'EST VOUS (IT'S YOU)
–	–	–	–	–	–	–	–	–	–	==	==	==	18	14	==	==	==	==	–	–	–	–	–	–	–	JUST ONCE AGAIN
–	–	–	–	–	–	–	–	–	–	==	==	==	15	15	==	==	==	==	–	–	–	–	–	–	–	UNDER THE MOON
–	–	–	–	–	–	–	–	–	–	–	==	==	10	6	10	19	==	–	–	–	–	–	–	–	–	SHAKING THE BLUES AWAY
–	–	–	–	–	–	–	–	–	–	–	==	16	6	5	4	6	14	19	==	–	–	–	–	–	–	GIVE ME A NIGHT IN JUNE
–	–	–	–	–	–	–	–	–	–	–	==	14	5	2	**1**	2	6	14	==	==	–	–	–	–	–	MISS ANNABELLE LEE
–	–	–	–	–	–	–	–	–	–	–	–	==	19	10	7	12	18	==	–	–	–	–	–	–	–	LUCKY IN LOVE
–	–	–	–	–	–	–	–	–	–	–	–	==	17	9	8	7	11	18	==	==	–	–	–	–	–	DANCING TAMBOURINE
–	–	–	–	–	–	–	–	–	–	–	–	==	==	==	16	13	8	15	16	20	==	==	==	==	–	GOOD NEWS
–	–	–	–	–	–	–	–	–	–	–	–	==	==	==	20	14	7	7	10	14	17	==	==	==	==	THE BEST THINGS IN LIFE ARE FREE
–	–	–	–	–	–	–	–	–	–	–	–	==	==	18	9	5	4	5	5	5	11	17	==	==	==	THE VARSITY DRAG
–	–	–	–	–	–	–	–	–	–	–	–	–	20	8	3	**1**	**1**	2	4	7	18	==	–	–	–	JUST A MEMORY
–	–	–	–	–	–	–	–	–	–	–	–	–	==	==	15	11	10	9	11	16	20	==	==	–	–	HERE COMES THE SHOW BOAT
–	–	–	–	–	–	–	–	–	–	–	–	–	–	==	14	9	16	20	==	–	–	–	–	–	–	IT WAS ONLY A SUN SHOWER
–	–	–	–	–	–	–	–	==	==	==	==	==	==	==	==	17	13	12	9	8	12	12	16	17	20	I AIN'T GOT NOBODY (1928)
–	–	–	–	–	–	–	–	–	–	–	==	==	==	==	==	15	9	6	6	6	10	14	==	==	==	THE SWEETHEART OF SIGMA CHI (1928)
–	–	–	–	–	–	–	–	–	–	–	–	–	–	==	==	==	19	17	18	==	==	==	==	==	==	MY BLUE RIDGE MOUNTAIN HOME (1928)
–	–	–	–	–	–	–	–	–	–	–	–	–	–	==	12	4	3	3	3	3	6	8	12	20	==	DIANE (1928)
–	–	–	–	–	–	–	–	–	–	–	–	–	–	–	==	==	12	11	13	18	==	==	–	–	–	IDA (SWEET AS APPLE CIDER) (1928)
–	–	–	–	–	–	–	–	–	–	–	–	–	–	–	==	==	17	8	8	13	13	==	==	==	–	DID YOU MEAN IT? (1928)
–	–	–	–	–	–	–	–	–	–	–	–	–	–	–	–	==	8	2	**1**	**1**	**1**	**1**	2	2	5	6	MY BLUE HEAVEN (1928)
–	–	–	–	–	–	–	–	–	–	–	–	–	–	–	–	–	==	15	4	2	2	2	**1**	**1**	**1**	7	AMONG MY SOUVENIRS (1928)
Ap	Ap	My	My	Jn	Jn	Jy	Jy	Ag	Ag	Sp	Sp	Oc	Oc	Nv	Nv	Dc	Dc	Ja	Ja	Fb	Fb	Ma	Ma	Ap	Ap	

1927														1928												
Oc	Oc	Nv	Nv	Dc	Dc	Ja	Ja	Fb	Fb	Ma	Ma	Ap	Ap	My	My	Jn	Jn	Jy	Jy	Ag	Ag	Sp	Sp	Oc	Oc	
1	1	1	2	3	5	13	==	==	–	–	–	–	–	–	–	–	–	–	–	–	–	–	–	–	–	CHARMAINE (1927)
16	6	5	4	6	14	19	==	–	–	–	–	–	–	–	–	–	–	–	–	–	–	–	–	–	–	GIVE ME A NIGHT IN JUNE (1927)
14	5	2	1	2	6	14	==	==	–	–	–	–	–	–	–	–	–	–	–	–	–	–	–	–	–	MISS ANNABELLE LEE (1927)
==	17	9	8	7	11	18	==	==	–	–	–	–	–	–	–	–	–	–	–	–	–	–	–	–	–	DANCING TAMBOURINE (1927)
==	==	==	16	13	8	15	16	20	==	==	==	==	–	–	–	–	–	–	–	–	–	–	–	–	–	GOOD NEWS (1927)
==	==	==	20	14	7	7	10	14	17	==	==	==	==	–	–	–	–	–	–	–	–	–	–	–	–	THE BEST THINGS IN LIFE ARE FREE (1927)
–	–	==	14	9	16	20	==	–	–	–	–	–	–	–	–	–	–	–	–	–	–	–	–	–	–	IT WAS ONLY A SUN SHOWER (1927)
==	==	18	9	5	4	5	5	5	11	17	==	==	==	==	–	–	–	–	–	–	–	–	–	–	–	VARSITY DRAG (1927)
–	20	8	3	1	1	2	4	7	18	==	–	–	–	–	–	–	–	–	–	–	–	–	–	–	–	JUST A MEMORY (1927)
–	==	==	15	11	10	9	11	16	20	==	==	–	–	–	–	–	–	–	–	–	–	–	–	–	–	HERE COMES THE SHOW BOAT (1927)
==	==	==	==	17	13	12	9	8	12	12	16	17	20	19	==	19	17	20	==	==	==	==	==	==	==	I AIN'T GOT NOBODY
==	==	==	==	15	9	6	6	6	10	14	==	==	==	==	==	==	==	==	–	–	–	–	–	–	–	THE SWEETHEART OF SIGMA CHI
–	–	==	==	==	19	17	18	==	==	==	==	==	==	–	–	–	–	–	–	–	–	–	–	–	–	MY BLUE RIDGE MOUNTAIN HOME
–	–	==	12	4	3	3	3	3	6	8	12	20	==	–	–	–	–	–	–	–	–	–	–	–	–	DIANE
–	–	–	==	==	12	11	13	18	==	==	–	–	–	–	–	–	–	–	–	–	–	–	–	–	–	IDA (SWEET AS APPLE CIDER)
–	–	–	==	==	17	8	8	13	13	==	==	==	–	–	–	–	–	–	–	–	–	–	–	–	–	DID YOU MEAN IT?
–	–	–	==	8	2	1	1	1	1	2	2	5	6	13	20	==	–	–	–	–	–	–	–	–	–	MY BLUE HEAVEN
–	–	–	–	==	==	16	12	19	==	–	–	–	–	–	–	–	–	–	–	–	–	–	–	–	–	UP IN THE CLOUDS
–	–	–	–	==	15	4	2	2	2	1	1	1	7	16	==	–	–	–	–	–	–	–	–	–	–	AMONG MY SOUVENIRS
–	–	–	–	==	==	10	7	4	3	3	6	9	==	==	–	–	–	–	–	–	–	–	–	–	–	THE SONG IS ENDED (BUT THE MELODY LINGERS ON)
–	–	–	–	–	==	==	17	15	==	==	–	–	–	–	–	–	–	–	–	–	–	–	–	–	–	TOGETHER, WE TWO
–	–	–	–	–	–	==	15	9	7	13	==	==	–	–	–	–	–	–	–	–	–	–	–	–	–	I SCREAM, YOU SCREAM, WE ALL SCREAM FOR ICE CREAM
–	–	–	–	–	–	==	20	10	5	4	10	16	==	–	–	–	–	–	–	–	–	–	–	–	–	AWAY DOWN SOUTH IN HEAVEN
–	–	–	–	–	–	==	14	11	4	7	14	==	==	==	–	–	–	–	–	–	–	–	–	–	–	MY HEART STOOD STILL
–	–	–	–	–	–	==	==	==	16	15	==	==	==	==	==	==	–	–	–	–	–	–	–	–	–	MY MELANCHOLY BABY
–	–	–	–	–	–	==	19	12	9	6	11	19	==	==	–	–	–	–	–	–	–	–	–	–	–	THOU SWELL
–	–	–	–	–	–	–	==	==	==	==	==	==	==	20	==	==	==	==	==	–	–	–	–	–	–	'S WONDERFUL
–	–	–	–	–	–	–	==	==	==	16	13	10	9	14	15	17	==	==	16	14	13	11	15	20	==	AH! SWEET MYSTERY OF LIFE
–	–	–	–	–	–	–	==	17	8	5	3	7	12	==	–	–	–	–	–	–	–	–	–	–	–	RAIN
–	–	–	–	–	–	–	–	==	19	11	7	13	==	==	–	–	–	–	–	–	–	–	–	–	–	KEEP SWEEPING THE COBWEBS OFF THE MOON
–	–	–	–	–	–	–	–	==	15	9	4	3	4	4	12	==	==	–	–	–	–	–	–	–	–	LET A SMILE BE YOUR UMBRELLA
–	–	–	–	–	–	–	–	==	14	10	5	4	3	3	3	3	7	10	==	==	–	–	–	–	–	CHLOE
–	–	–	–	–	–	–	–	==	==	==	18	11	10	8	11	9	9	14	12	19	==	==	–	–	–	OL' MAN RIVER
–	–	–	–	–	–	–	–	==	==	==	==	==	==	==	19	18	15	18	==	==	==	==	==	==	–	MISSISSIPPI MUD
–	–	–	–	–	–	–	–	–	==	==	20	18	19	18	==	==	==	==	–	–	–	–	–	–	–	WHY DO I LOVE YOU?
–	–	–	–	–	–	–	–	–	==	==	19	15	18	17	==	==	==	==	–	–	–	–	–	–	–	MAKE BELIEVE
–	–	–	–	–	–	–	–	–	==	19	15	12	11	15	13	14	==	==	–	–	–	–	–	–	–	CAN'T HELP LOVIN' DAT MAN
–	–	–	–	–	–	–	–	–	==	18	9	8	8	6	4	8	10	15	==	==	==	–	–	–	–	THE MAN I LOVE
–	–	–	–	–	–	–	–	–	==	20	8	2	1	5	10	20	==	–	–	–	–	–	–	–	–	TOGETHER
–	–	–	–	–	–	–	–	–	–	==	17	6	2	1	1	1	1	1	1	2	3	5	16	==	==	RAMONA
–	–	–	–	–	–	–	–	–	–	–	==	==	13	7	5	16	==	–	–	–	–	–	–	–	–	MARY ANN
–	–	–	–	–	–	–	–	–	–	–	==	==	17	12	8	15	==	==	–	–	–	–	–	–	–	SUNSHINE
–	–	–	–	–	–	–	–	–	–	–	==	==	14	9	9	12	20	==	–	–	–	–	–	–	–	I JUST ROLL ALONG (HAVIN' MY UPS AND DOWNS)
–	–	–	–	–	–	–	–	–	–	–	==	14	5	2	2	2	6	13	==	–	–	–	–	–	–	BACK IN YOUR OWN BACK YARD
–	–	–	–	–	–	–	–	–	–	–	==	==	15	11	7	4	2	2	2	4	4	6	9	11	==	GIRL OF MY DREAMS
–	–	–	–	–	–	–	–	–	–	–	–	==	16	10	6	6	5	11	==	==	–	–	–	–	–	COQUETTE
–	–	–	–	–	–	–	–	–	–	–	–	==	==	==	17	11	11	19	==	==	==	==	–	–	–	I STILL LOVE YOU
–	–	–	–	–	–	–	–	–	–	–	–	–	==	==	16	10	13	17	==	==	–	–	–	–	–	PERSIAN RUG
–	–	–	–	–	–	–	–	–	–	–	–	–	–	==	==	==	19	==	==	–	–	–	–	–	–	MANHATTAN SERENADE
Oc	Oc	Nv	Nv	Dc	Dc	Ja	Ja	Fb	Fb	Ma	Ma	Ap	Ap	My	My	Jn	Jn	Jy	Jy	Ag	Ag	Sp	Sp	Oc	Oc	

						1928												1929								
Ap	Ap	My	My	Jn	Jn	Jy	Jy	Ag	Ag	Sp	Sp	Oc	Oc	Nv	Nv	Dc	Dc	Ja	Ja	Fb	Fb	Ma	Ma	Ap	Ap	
–	–	==	18	7	4	6	18	==	–	–	–	–	–	–	–	–	–	–	–	–	–	–	–	–	–	I CAN'T DO WITHOUT YOU
–	–	==	14	5	3	3	4	6	9	20	==	==	–	–	–	–	–	–	–	–	–	–	–	–	–	LAUGH! CLOWN, LAUGH!
–	–	–	==	==	18	12	10	12	16	==	==	–	–	–	–	–	–	–	–	–	–	–	–	–	–	READY FOR THE RIVER
–	–	–	==	13	8	5	8	13	==	==	–	–	–	–	–	–	–	–	–	–	–	–	–	–	–	WAS IT A DREAM?
–	–	–	–	==	14	7	7	18	==	–	–	–	–	–	–	–	–	–	–	–	–	–	–	–	–	HAPPY-GO-LUCKY LANE
–	–	–	–	==	12	4	3	**1**	**1**	**1**	**1**	2	5	11	19	==	–	–	–	–	–	–	–	–	–	ANGELA MIA (MY ANGEL)
–	–	–	–	==	16	8	5	5	7	7	18	==	==	–	–	–	–	–	–	–	–	–	–	–	–	BELOVED
–	–	–	–	–	==	9	6	3	2	4	6	10	==	==	–	–	–	–	–	–	–	–	–	–	–	GET OUT AND GET UNDER THE MOON
–	–	–	–	–	==	16	9	8	10	17	==	–	–	–	–	–	–	–	–	–	–	–	–	–	–	C-O-N-S-T-A-N-T-I-N-O-P-L-E
–	–	–	–	–	–	==	20	17	15	18	19	==	–	–	–	–	–	–	–	–	–	–	–	–	–	SWEET LORRAINE
–	–	–	–	–	==	==	11	10	8	10	==	==	–	–	–	–	–	–	–	–	–	–	–	–	–	CRAZY RHYTHM
–	–	–	–	–	–	==	15	11	11	9	13	13	==	==	–	–	–	–	–	–	–	–	–	–	–	THE SIDEWALKS OF NEW YORK
–	–	–	–	–	–	==	17	15	12	8	14	==	==	==	–	–	–	–	–	–	–	–	–	–	–	YOU TOOK ADVANTAGE OF ME
–	–	–	–	–	–	==	19	16	14	14	11	17	==	==	==	–	–	–	–	–	–	–	–	–	–	SWEET SUE (JUST YOU)
–	–	–	–	–	–	==	13	7	5	2	3	8	16	==	==	–	–	–	–	–	–	–	–	–	–	JUST LIKE A MELODY OUT OF THE SKY
–	–	–	–	–	–	==	14	9	6	3	2	5	10	==	==	–	–	–	–	–	–	–	–	–	–	THAT'S MY WEAKNESS NOW
–	–	–	–	–	–	==	==	==	20	19	==	==	–	–	–	–	–	–	–	–	–	–	–	–	–	LAST NIGHT I DREAMED YOU KISSED ME
–	–	–	–	–	–	–	==	20	17	15	17	==	==	==	–	–	–	–	–	–	–	–	–	–	–	YOU'RE A REAL SWEETHEART
–	–	–	–	–	–	–	==	==	==	==	12	9	12	12	12	14	20	==	–	–	–	–	–	–	–	DREAM HOUSE
–	–	–	–	–	–	–	–	==	==	16	8	7	6	13	18	==	–	–	–	–	–	–	–	–	–	DIGA-DIGA-DOO
–	–	–	–	–	–	–	–	==	19	12	4	4	3	7	17	==	–	–	–	–	–	–	–	–	–	CHIQUITA
–	–	–	–	–	–	–	–	==	==	==	20	12	11	6	6	9	9	18	==	==	–	–	–	–	–	DUSKY STEVEDORE
–	–	–	–	–	–	–	–	==	18	13	5	3	2	2	4	4	4	6	15	19	==	==	–	–	–	I CAN'T GIVE YOU ANYTHING BUT LOVE
–	–	–	–	–	–	–	–	–	==	==	==	16	14	16	==	==	–	–	–	–	–	–	–	–	–	DOIN' THE NEW LOW DOWN
–	–	–	–	–	–	–	–	–	==	==	==	14	20	==	==	–	–	–	–	–	–	–	–	–	–	I MUST HAVE THAT MAN
–	–	–	–	–	–	–	–	–	==	==	10	6	4	10	20	==	–	–	–	–	–	–	–	–	–	MEMORIES OF FRANCE
–	–	–	–	–	–	–	–	–	–	==	==	==	==	20	==	==	–	–	–	–	–	–	–	–	–	OUT OF THE DAWN
–	–	–	–	–	–	–	–	–	–	==	==	15	15	18	==	==	–	–	–	–	–	–	–	–	–	TEN LITTLE MILES FROM TOWN
–	–	–	–	–	–	–	–	–	–	==	==	==	18	9	10	13	18	==	==	==	–	–	–	–	–	NEAPOLITAN NIGHTS
–	–	–	–	–	–	–	–	–	–	==	7	**1**	**1**	**1**	2	3	3	7	19	==	–	–	–	–	–	JEANNINE, I DREAM OF LILAC TIME
–	–	–	–	–	–	–	–	–	–	==	==	==	==	==	16	15	==	==	==	==	==	–	–	–	–	LOUISIANA
–	–	–	–	–	–	–	–	–	–	–	==	==	19	15	13	==	==	–	–	–	–	–	–	–	–	NAGASAKI
–	–	–	–	–	–	–	–	–	–	–	==	==	13	8	8	20	==	–	–	–	–	–	–	–	–	REVENGE
–	–	–	–	–	–	–	–	–	–	–	==	==	17	17	14	16	==	==	–	–	–	–	–	–	–	KING FOR A DAY
–	–	–	–	–	–	–	–	–	–	–	==	19	8	5	5	6	13	==	–	–	–	–	–	–	–	OLD MAN SUNSHINE
–	–	–	–	–	–	–	–	–	–	–	–	18	7	3	**1**	**1**	**1**	**1**	2	4	10	19	==	–	–	SONNY BOY
–	–	–	–	–	–	–	–	–	–	–	–	==	9	4	3	2	2	3	3	8	17	==	–	–	–	THERE'S A RAINBOW 'ROUND MY SHOULDER
–	–	–	–	–	–	–	–	–	–	–	–	==	==	14	7	8	15	==	–	–	–	–	–	–	–	ROSES OF YESTERDAY
–	–	–	–	–	–	–	–	–	–	–	–	==	==	==	15	11	10	9	12	20	==	–	–	–	–	TAKE YOUR TOMORROW (AND GIVE ME TODAY)
–	–	–	–	–	–	–	–	–	–	–	–	–	==	19	9	7	14	==	–	–	–	–	–	–	–	HALFWAY TO HEAVEN
–	–	–	–	–	–	–	–	–	–	–	–	–	–	==	==	10	8	16	==	–	–	–	–	–	–	SALLY OF MY DREAMS
–	–	–	–	–	–	–	–	–	–	–	–	–	–	==	11	5	6	11	20	==	–	–	–	–	–	DOIN' THE RACCOON
–	–	–	–	–	–	–	–	–	–	–	–	–	–	–	==	18	16	==	==	–	–	–	–	–	–	CHERRY
–	–	–	–	–	–	–	–	–	–	–	–	–	–	–	==	12	5	2	**1**	3	5	11	13	==	==	YOU'RE THE CREAM IN MY COFFEE (1929)
–	–	–	–	–	–	–	–	–	–	–	–	–	–	–	==	19	11	8	9	17	==	–	–	–	–	I'M SORRY, SALLY (1929)
–	–	–	–	–	–	–	–	–	–	–	–	–	–	–	==	17	7	4	6	13	18	==	–	–	–	I WANNA BE LOVED BY YOU (1929)
–	–	–	–	–	–	–	–	–	–	–	–	–	–	–	==	==	17	15	17	==	==	==	==	–	–	DON'T HOLD EVERYTHING (1929)
–	–	–	–	–	–	–	–	–	–	–	–	–	–	–	–	==	12	5	8	16	16	==	==	–	–	LET'S DO IT (LET'S FALL IN LOVE) (1929)
–	–	–	–	–	–	–	–	–	–	–	–	–	–	–	–	==	19	14	18	==	==	–	–	–	–	MY BLACKBIRDS ARE BLUEBIRDS NOW (1929)
Ap	Ap	My	My	Jn	Jn	Jy	Jy	Ag	Ag	Sp	Sp	Oc	Oc	Nv	Nv	Dc	Dc	Ja	Ja	Fb	Fb	Ma	Ma	Ap	Ap	

	1928														1929											
Oc	Oc	Nv	Nv	Dc	Dc	Ja	Ja	Fb	Fb	Ma	Ma	Ap	Ap	My	My	Jn	Jn	Jy	Jy	Ag	Ag	Sp	Sp	Oc	Oc	
12	11	6	6	9	9	18	==	==	–	–	–	–	–	–	–	–	–	–	–	–	–	–	–	–	–	DUSKY STEVEDORE (1928)
3	2	2	4	4	4	6	15	19	==	==	–	–	–	–	–	–	–	–	–	–	–	–	–	–	–	I CAN'T GIVE YOU ANYTHING BUT VE (1928)
1	**1**	**1**	2	3	3	7	19	==	–	–	–	–	–	–	–	–	–	–	–	–	–	–	–	–	–	JEANNINE, I DREAM OF LILAC TIME (1928)
18	7	3	**1**	**1**	**1**	**1**	2	4	10	19	==	–	–	–	–	–	–	–	–	–	–	–	–	–	–	SONNY BOY (1928)
==	9	4	3	2	2	3	3	8	17	==	–	–	–	–	–	–	–	–	–	–	–	–	–	–	–	THERE'S A RAINBOW 'ROUND MY SHOULDER (1928)
–	–	==	==	10	8	16	==	–	–	–	–	–	–	–	–	–	–	–	–	–	–	–	–	–	–	SALLY OF MY DREAMS (1928)
==	==	==	15	11	10	9	12	20	==	–	–	–	–	–	–	–	–	–	–	–	–	–	–	–	–	TAKE YOUR TOMORROW (AND GIVE ME TODAY) (1928)
–	–	==	11	5	6	11	20	==	–	–	–	–	–	–	–	–	–	–	–	–	–	–	–	–	–	DOIN' THE RACCOON (1928)
–	–	–	==	12	5	2	**1**	3	5	11	13	==	==	–	–	–	–	–	–	–	–	–	–	–	–	YOU'RE THE CREAM IN MY COFFEE
–	–	–	==	19	11	8	9	17	==	–	–	–	–	–	–	–	–	–	–	–	–	–	–	–	–	I'M SORRY, SALLY
–	–	–	==	17	7	4	6	13	18	==	–	–	–	–	–	–	–	–	–	–	–	–	–	–	–	I WANNA BE LOVED BY YOU
–	–	–	==	==	17	15	17	==	==	==	==	–	–	–	–	–	–	–	–	–	–	–	–	–	–	DON'T HOLD EVERYTHING
–	–	–	–	==	12	5	7	16	16	==	==	–	–	–	–	–	–	–	–	–	–	–	–	–	–	LET'S DO IT (LET'S FALL IN LOVE)
–	–	–	–	==	==	17	13	11	9	8	12	==	==	–	–	–	–	–	–	–	–	–	–	–	–	AVALON TOWN
–	–	–	–	==	19	14	18	==	==	–	–	–	–	–	–	–	–	–	–	–	–	–	–	–	–	MY BLACKBIRDS ARE BLUEBIRDS NOW
–	–	–	–	–	==	==	==	18	==	==	==	–	–	–	–	–	–	–	–	–	–	–	–	–	–	DON'T BE LIKE THAT
–	–	–	–	–	==	13	8	7	14	20	==	–	–	–	–	–	–	–	–	–	–	–	–	–	–	SHE'S FUNNY THAT WAY
–	–	–	–	–	==	10	4	2	3	4	7	15	==	==	–	–	–	–	–	–	–	–	–	–	–	MARIE
–	–	–	–	–	==	12	5	**1**	**1**	3	3	9	==	==	–	–	–	–	–	–	–	–	–	–	–	SWEETHEARTS ON PARADE
–	–	–	–	–	==	19	10	6	4	2	**1**	2	2	**1**	6	9	16	19	==	==	–	–	–	–	–	CAROLINA MOON
–	–	–	–	–	–	20	11	5	2	**1**	4	8	14	18	==	–	–	–	–	–	–	–	–	–	–	I'LL GET BY (AS LONG AS I HAVE YOU)
–	–	–	–	–	–	==	16	9	8	17	==	–	–	–	–	–	–	–	–	–	–	–	–	–	–	HOW ABOUT ME?
–	–	–	–	–	–	==	14	10	7	6	10	13	==	==	–	–	–	–	–	–	–	–	–	–	–	MAKIN' WHOOPIE
–	–	–	–	–	–	–	==	14	11	9	11	20	==	==	–	–	–	–	–	–	–	–	–	–	–	WHERE THE SHY LITTLE VIOLETS GROW
–	–	–	–	–	–	–	==	15	12	10	9	16	17	==	==	–	–	–	–	–	–	–	–	–	–	(I LOVE YOU) SWEETHEART OF ALL MY DREAMS
–	–	–	–	–	–	–	==	12	6	5	5	6	13	17	==	–	–	–	–	–	–	–	–	–	–	IF I HAD YOU
–	–	–	–	–	–	–	–	==	20	14	==	==	==	–	–	–	–	–	–	–	–	–	–	–	–	I'M BRINGING A RED, RED ROSE
–	–	–	–	–	–	–	–	==	15	12	17	18	==	==	–	–	–	–	–	–	–	–	–	–	–	I FAW DOWN AN' GO BOOM!
–	–	–	–	–	–	–	–	==	19	16	15	10	10	12	==	==	–	–	–	–	–	–	–	–	–	MY MOTHER'S EYES
–	–	–	–	–	–	–	–	==	13	7	2	**1**	6	11	19	==	==	–	–	–	–	–	–	–	–	A PRECIOUS LITTLE THING CALLED LOVE
–	–	–	–	–	–	–	–	–	==	18	18	17	16	==	==	–	–	–	–	–	–	–	–	–	–	WHERE IS THE SONG OF SONGS FOR ME?
–	–	–	–	–	–	–	–	–	==	13	6	5	11	13	==	==	–	–	–	–	–	–	–	–	–	WEDDING BELLS (ARE BREAKING UP THAT OLD GANG OF MINE)
–	–	–	–	–	–	–	–	–	==	15	8	3	**1**	5	11	18	==	==	–	–	–	–	–	–	–	WEARY RIVER
–	–	–	–	–	–	–	–	–	–	==	==	==	20	==	==	–	–	–	–	–	–	–	–	–	–	DREAM TRAIN
–	–	–	–	–	–	–	–	–	–	==	==	==	19	==	==	–	–	–	–	–	–	–	–	–	–	MY LUCKY STAR
–	–	–	–	–	–	–	–	–	–	==	14	4	4	10	14	19	==	–	–	–	–	–	–	–	–	BUTTON UP YOUR OVERCOAT
–	–	–	–	–	–	–	–	–	–	==	==	14	7	6	8	15	==	==	–	–	–	–	–	–	–	DEEP NIGHT
–	–	–	–	–	–	–	–	–	–	==	16	7	3	3	5	12	15	==	==	–	–	–	–	–	–	LOVER, COME BACK TO ME!
–	–	–	–	–	–	–	–	–	–	==	19	11	8	9	7	8	12	20	==	==	–	–	–	–	–	BROADWAY MELODY
–	–	–	–	–	–	–	–	–	–	==	==	==	18	15	17	20	==	==	==	==	==	==	–	–	–	LOVE ME OR LEAVE ME
–	–	–	–	–	–	–	–	–	–	==	20	12	5	2	2	**1**	**1**	2	3	3	6	9	11	13	20	== THE WEDDING OF THE PAINTED DOLL
–	–	–	–	–	–	–	–	–	–	–	==	19	9	7	4	4	10	18	==	==	–	–	–	–	–	YOU WERE MEANT FOR ME
–	–	–	–	–	–	–	–	–	–	–	==	==	20	==	==	==	–	–	–	–	–	–	–	–	–	SOME SWEET DAY
–	–	–	–	–	–	–	–	–	–	–	==	==	==	20	==	==	==	–	–	–	–	–	–	–	–	COQUETTE
–	–	–	–	–	–	–	–	–	–	–	==	15	8	3	3	8	10	15	==	==	–	–	–	–	–	MEAN TO ME
–	–	–	–	–	–	–	–	–	–	–	==	12	4	**1**	2	4	8	9	20	==	==	–	–	–	–	HONEY
–	–	–	–	–	–	–	–	–	–	–	–	==	14	10	11	14	15	==	==	==	==	–	–	–	–	JERICHO
–	–	–	–	–	–	–	–	–	–	–	–	==	19	16	14	13	16	==	==	==	–	–	–	–	–	A GARDEN IN THE RAIN
Oc	Oc	Nv	Nv	Dc	Dc	Ja	Ja	Fb	Fb	Ma	Ma	Ap	Ap	My	My	Jn	Jn	Jy	Jy	Ag	Ag	Sp	Sp	Oc	Oc	

						1929														1930						
Ap	Ap	My	My	Jn	Jn	Jy	Jy	Ag	Ag	Sp	Sp	Oc	Oc	Nv	Nv	Dc	Dc	Ja	Ja	Fb	Fb	Ma	Ma	Ap	Ap	
–	==	16	9	7	5	5	6	4	7	11	18	==	–	–	–	–	–	–	–	–	–	–	–	–	–	I'LL ALWAYS BE IN LOVE WITH YOU
–	–	==	15	10	7	7	7	13	==	==	–	–	–	–	–	–	–	–	–	–	–	–	–	–	–	I KISS YOUR HAND, MADAME
–	–	==	12	6	3	3	4	6	16	==	–	–	–	–	–	–	–	–	–	–	–	–	–	–	–	LOUISE
–	–	==	18	13	6	4	5	11	19	==	==	–	–	–	–	–	–	–	–	–	–	–	–	–	–	MY SIN
–	–	==	==	==	==	17	20	==	==	==	==	==	–	–	–	–	–	–	–	–	–	–	–	–	–	BIG CITY BLUES
–	–	==	==	==	18	14	17	==	==	==	==	==	–	–	–	–	–	–	–	–	–	–	–	–	–	THE BREAKAWAY
–	–	==	13	5	2	**1**	**1**	**1**	**1**	2	2	4	10	19	==	–	–	–	–	–	–	–	–	–	–	PAGAN LOVE SONG
–	–	–	==	16	9	9	8	17	==	==	–	–	–	–	–	–	–	–	–	–	–	–	–	–	–	WITH A SONG IN MY HEART
–	–	–	==	==	17	13	13	12	15	13	14	19	==	==	–	–	–	–	–	–	–	–	–	–	–	I'VE GOT A FEELING I'M FALLING
–	–	–	==	17	11	6	2	2	3	5	9	15	==	==	==	–	–	–	–	–	–	–	–	–	–	I'M JUST A VAGABOND LOVER
–	–	–	–	==	20	12	12	16	18	18	==	==	–	–	–	–	–	–	–	–	–	–	–	–	–	THE DESERT SONG
–	–	–	–	==	19	11	10	9	10	14	16	==	==	–	–	–	–	–	–	–	–	–	–	–	–	I GET THE BLUES WHEN IT RAINS
–	–	–	–	–	==	==	16	18	17	==	==	–	–	–	–	–	–	–	–	–	–	–	–	–	–	WALKING WITH SUSIE
–	–	–	–	–	==	==	11	5	5	4	4	7	12	==	–	–	–	–	–	–	–	–	–	–	–	SLEEPY VALLEY
–	–	–	–	–	–	==	==	15	12	10	10	9	8	12	20	–	–	–	–	–	–	–	–	–	–	WHEN MY DREAMS COME TRUE
–	–	–	–	–	–	==	==	19	11	8	7	10	13	15	–	–	–	–	–	–	–	–	–	–	–	LITTLE PAL
–	–	–	–	–	–	==	==	14	14	16	==	==	==	–	–	–	–	–	–	–	–	–	–	–	–	S'POSIN'
–	–	–	–	–	–	==	18	7	2	**1**	**1**	**1**	2	4	7	14	==	–	–	–	–	–	–	–	–	AM I BLUE
–	–	–	–	–	–	==	14	10	8	6	8	5	4	3	3	3	7	13	==	–	–	–	–	–	–	SINGIN' IN THE RAIN
–	–	–	–	–	–	==	19	8	4	3	3	2	5	7	14	==	–	–	–	–	–	–	–	–	–	MY SONG OF THE NILE
–	–	–	–	–	–	–	–	==	==	19	==	20	==	–	–	–	–	–	–	–	–	–	–	–	–	YOUR MOTHER AND MINE
–	–	–	–	–	–	–	–	==	13	12	15	14	16	==	–	–	–	–	–	–	–	–	–	–	–	MISS YOU
–	–	–	–	–	–	–	–	==	20	17	17	12	15	==	–	–	–	–	–	–	–	–	–	–	–	TRUE BLUE LOU
–	–	–	–	–	–	–	–	==	9	7	5	6	7	9	12	15	==	–	–	–	–	–	–	–	–	MOANIN' LOW
–	–	–	–	–	–	–	–	–	==	==	13	11	6	5	13	==	==	–	–	–	–	–	–	–	–	HOW AM I TO KNOW?
–	–	–	–	–	–	–	–	–	==	20	12	8	3	2	2	2	2	5	8	10	18	==	–	–	–	PAINTING THE CLOUDS WITH SUNSHINE
–	–	–	–	–	–	–	–	–	==	15	6	3	**1**	**1**	**1**	**1**	**1**	**1**	5	7	14	==	–	–	–	TIP TOE THROUGH THE TULIPS WITH ME
–	–	–	–	–	–	–	–	–	–	==	20	18	14	18	==	==	–	–	–	–	–	–	–	–	–	CAN'T WE BE FRIENDS?
–	–	–	–	–	–	–	–	–	–	==	19	16	11	11	16	==	==	–	–	–	–	–	–	–	–	AIN'T MISBEHAVIN'
–	–	–	–	–	–	–	–	–	–	–	==	==	17	14	==	==	–	–	–	–	–	–	–	–	–	WAITING AT THE END OF THE ROAD
–	–	–	–	–	–	–	–	–	–	–	==	17	9	6	6	9	15	==	==	–	–	–	–	–	–	PICCOLO PETE
–	–	–	–	–	–	–	–	–	–	–	–	==	19	10	4	5	8	10	15	==	–	–	–	–	–	LOVE ME
–	–	–	–	–	–	–	–	–	–	–	–	==	18	8	5	7	10	19	==	–	–	–	–	–	–	LONELY TROUBADOUR
–	–	–	–	–	–	–	–	–	–	–	–	–	==	16	9	6	4	6	10	18	==	–	–	–	–	LOVE (YOUR MAGIC SPELL IS EVERYWHERE)
–	–	–	–	–	–	–	–	–	–	–	–	–	==	13	8	4	3	4	4	5	8	9	13	==	==	IF I HAD A TALKING PICTURE OF YOU
–	–	–	–	–	–	–	–	–	–	–	–	–	==	==	17	11	16	==	==	–	–	–	–	–	–	SATISFIED
–	–	–	–	–	–	–	–	–	–	–	–	–	==	==	15	12	==	==	–	–	–	–	–	–	–	THROUGH
–	–	–	–	–	–	–	–	–	–	–	–	–	==	17	10	10	9	9	12	==	==	–	–	–	–	SUNNY SIDE UP
–	–	–	–	–	–	–	–	–	–	–	–	–	–	==	==	20	20	==	==	–	–	–	–	–	–	I MAY BE WRONG (BUT I THINK YOU'RE WONDERFUL)
–	–	–	–	–	–	–	–	–	–	–	–	–	–	==	18	16	13	15	18	==	==	–	–	–	–	TURN ON THE HEAT
–	–	–	–	–	–	–	–	–	–	–	–	–	–	–	==	==	==	20	==	==	–	–	–	–	–	ALL THAT I'M ASKING IS SYMPATHY
–	–	–	–	–	–	–	–	–	–	–	–	–	==	20	11	8	5	3	2	**1**	2	7	11	13	==	(I'M A DREAMER) AREN'T WE ALL (1930)
–	–	–	–	–	–	–	–	–	–	–	–	–	–	==	==	19	18	16	16	==	==	==	==	==	==	CONGRATULATIONS (1930)
–	–	–	–	–	–	–	–	–	–	–	–	–	–	–	==	==	14	11	9	12	15	==	==	–	–	GREAT DAY (1930)
–	–	–	–	–	–	–	–	–	–	–	–	–	–	–	==	==	19	18	17	==	==	==	–	–	–	MORE THAN YOU KNOW (1930)
–	–	–	–	–	–	–	–	–	–	–	–	–	–	–	==	17	12	14	11	15	==	==	–	–	–	MY SWEETER THAN SWEET (1930)
–	–	–	–	–	–	–	–	–	–	–	–	–	–	–	19	13	6	2	**1**	2	6	14	==	–	–	CHANT OF THE JUNGLE (1930)
–	–	–	–	–	–	–	–	–	–	–	–	–	–	–	==	18	11	8	7	8	13	18	==	–	–	SINGIN' IN THE BATHTUB (1930)
–	–	–	–	–	–	–	–	–	–	–	–	–	–	–	–	==	17	7	3	3	5	5	8	15	==	A LITTLE KISS EACH MORNING (1930)
Ap	Ap	My	My	Jn	Jn	Jy	Jy	Ag	Ag	Sp	Sp	Oc	Oc	Nv	Nv	Dc	Dc	Ja	Ja	Fb	Fb	Ma	Ma	Ap	Ap	

1929															1930											
Oc	Oc	Nv	Nv	Dc	Dc	Ja	Ja	Fb	Fb	Ma	Ma	Ap	Ap	My	My	Jn	Jn	Jy	Jy	Ag	Ag	Sp	Sp	Oc	Oc	
5	4	3	3	3	7	13	==	–	–	–	–	–	–	–	–	–	–	–	–	–	–	–	–	–	–	SINGIN' IN THE RAIN (1929)
8	3	2	2	2	2	5	8	10	18	==	–	–	–	–	–	–	–	–	–	–	–	–	–	–	–	PAINTING THE CLOUDS WITH SUNSHINE (1929)
3	**1**	**1**	**1**	**1**	**1**	**1**	5	7	14	==	–	–	–	–	–	–	–	–	–	–	–	–	–	–	–	TIP TOE THROUGH THE TULIPS WITH ME (1929)
==	19	10	4	5	8	10	15	==	–	–	–	–	–	–	–	–	–	–	–	–	–	–	–	–	–	LOVE ME (1929)
–	==	16	9	6	4	6	10	18	==	–	–	–	–	–	–	–	–	–	–	–	–	–	–	–	–	LOVE (YOUR MAGIC SPELL IS EVERYWHERE) (1929)
–	==	13	8	4	3	4	4	5	8	9	13	==	==	–	–	–	–	–	–	–	–	–	–	–	–	IF I HAD A TALKING PICTURE OF YOU (1929)
==	18	8	5	7	10	19	==	–	–	–	–	–	–	–	–	–	–	–	–	–	–	–	–	–	–	LONELY TROUBADOUR (1929)
–	==	17	10	10	9	9	12	==	==	–	–	–	–	–	–	–	–	–	–	–	–	–	–	–	–	SUNNY SIDE UP (1929)
–	–	==	18	16	13	15	18	==	==	–	–	–	–	–	–	–	–	–	–	–	–	–	–	–	–	TURN ON THE HEAT (1929)
–	–	–	==	==	==	20	==	==	–	–	–	–	–	–	–	–	–	–	–	–	–	–	–	–	–	ALL THAT I'M ASKING IS SYMPATHY (1929)
–	==	20	11	8	5	3	2	**1**	2	7	11	13	==	–	–	–	–	–	–	–	–	–	–	–	–	(I'M A DREAMER) AREN'T WE ALL?
–	–	==	==	19	18	16	16	==	==	==	==	==	==	–	–	–	–	–	–	–	–	–	–	–	–	CONGRATULATIONS
–	–	–	==	==	14	11	9	12	15	==	==	–	–	–	–	–	–	–	–	–	–	–	–	–	–	GREAT DAY
–	–	–	==	==	19	18	17	==	==	==	–	–	–	–	–	–	–	–	–	–	–	–	–	–	–	MORE THAN YOU KNOW
–	–	–	==	17	12	14	11	15	==	==	–	–	–	–	–	–	–	–	–	–	–	–	–	–	–	MY SWEETER THAN SWEET
–	–	–	19	13	6	2	**1**	2	6	14	==	–	–	–	–	–	–	–	–	–	–	–	–	–	–	CHANT OF THE JUNGLE
–	–	–	==	18	11	8	7	8	13	18	==	–	–	–	–	–	–	–	–	–	–	–	–	–	–	SINGIN' IN THE BATHTUB
–	–	–	–	==	17	7	3	3	5	5	8	15	==	–	–	–	–	–	–	–	–	–	–	–	–	A LITTLE KISS EACH MORNING
–	–	–	–	==	==	17	14	==	==	–	–	–	–	–	–	–	–	–	–	–	–	–	–	–	–	MY FATE IS IN YOUR HANDS
–	–	–	–	–	==	==	==	20	==	==	–	–	–	–	–	–	–	–	–	–	–	–	–	–	–	DON'T EVER LEAVE ME
–	–	–	–	–	==	==	==	19	17	==	==	–	–	–	–	–	–	–	–	–	–	–	–	–	–	THAT WONDERFUL SOMETHING
–	–	–	–	–	==	==	19	16	19	==	==	–	–	–	–	–	–	–	–	–	–	–	–	–	–	WHY WAS I BORN?
–	–	–	–	–	==	12	6	4	4	4	6	9	12	18	==	–	–	–	–	–	–	–	–	–	–	I'M FOLLOWING YOU
–	–	–	–	–	–	==	20	13	11	12	12	==	==	–	–	–	–	–	–	–	–	–	–	–	–	YOU'VE GOT THAT THING
–	–	–	–	–	–	==	13	6	**1**	**1**	**1**	**1**	6	10	15	==	–	–	–	–	–	–	–	–	–	HAPPY DAYS ARE HERE AGAIN
–	–	–	–	–	–	–	==	14	9	11	18	==	–	–	–	–	–	–	–	–	–	–	–	–	–	THE MAN FROM THE SOUTH
–	–	–	–	–	–	–	==	9	7	3	3	6	10	12	17	==	–	–	–	–	–	–	–	–	–	CRYIN' FOR THE CAROLINES
–	–	–	–	–	–	–	==	17	10	6	4	11	16	==	==	–	–	–	–	–	–	–	–	–	–	WHAT IS THIS THING CALLED LOVE?
–	–	–	–	–	–	–	==	11	3	2	2	2	3	5	11	20	–	–	–	–	–	–	–	–	–	SHOULD I?
–	–	–	–	–	–	–	==	==	12	8	9	16	==	==	–	–	–	–	–	–	–	–	–	–	–	ST. JAMES INFIRMARY
–	–	–	–	–	–	–	==	==	16	16	14	==	==	==	–	–	–	–	–	–	–	–	–	–	–	WHY?
–	–	–	–	–	–	–	==	==	==	15	19	==	==	–	–	–	–	–	–	–	–	–	–	–	–	'TAIN'T NO SIN (TO DANCE AROUND IN YOUR BONES)
–	–	–	–	–	–	–	==	==	==	17	20	==	==	–	–	–	–	–	–	–	–	–	–	–	–	SOUTH SEA ROSE
–	–	–	–	–	–	–	==	==	==	20	==	==	==	–	–	–	–	–	–	–	–	–	–	–	–	I'LL SEE YOU AGAIN
–	–	–	–	–	–	–	–	==	20	10	5	4	7	14	20	–	–	–	–	–	–	–	–	–	–	THERE'S DANGER IN YOUR EYES, CHERIE
–	–	–	–	–	–	–	–	==	==	19	10	5	2	2	2	**1**	**1**	2	2	2	3	3	3	6	8	11 == WHEN IT'S SPRINGTIME IN THE ROCKIES
–	–	–	–	–	–	–	–	–	==	13	7	3	**1**	**1**	**1**	2	3	3	3	4	6	14	==	–	–	STEIN SONG
–	–	–	–	–	–	–	–	–	==	==	17	10	8	9	13	==	–	–	–	–	–	–	–	–	–	LAZY LOU'SIANA MOON
–	–	–	–	–	–	–	–	–	–	==	==	20	18	19	==	==	–	–	–	–	–	–	–	–	–	BESIDE AN OPEN FIREPLACE
–	–	–	–	–	–	–	–	–	–	==	==	17	==	==	–	–	–	–	–	–	–	–	–	–	–	WHEN I'M LOOKING AT YOU
–	–	–	–	–	–	–	–	–	–	==	==	==	19	==	==	–	–	–	–	–	–	–	–	–	–	ROMANCE
–	–	–	–	–	–	–	–	–	–	==	==	12	9	6	9	16	==	–	–	–	–	–	–	–	–	PUTTIN' ON THE RITZ
–	–	–	–	–	–	–	–	–	–	==	16	8	5	4	6	11	==	==	–	–	–	–	–	–	–	UNDER A TEXAS MOON
–	–	–	–	–	–	–	–	–	–	==	15	7	4	3	4	8	12	==	==	–	–	–	–	–	–	A COTTAGE FOR SALE
–	–	–	–	–	–	–	–	–	–	==	==	19	13	16	==	==	–	–	–	–	–	–	–	–	–	STRIKE UP THE BAND
–	–	–	–	–	–	–	–	–	–	==	==	14	11	8	8	10	14	20	–	–	–	–	–	–	–	SING, YOU SINNERS
–	–	–	–	–	–	–	–	–	–	–	==	18	14	15	12	14	15	==	–	–	–	–	–	–	–	ON THE SUNNY SIDE OF THE STREET
–	–	–	–	–	–	–	–	–	–	–	==	==	17	13	7	5	6	6	9	17	==	–	–	–	–	I'M IN THE MARKET FOR YOU
–	–	–	–	–	–	–	–	–	–	–	–	==	15	7	3	3	5	7	10	18	20	==	–	–	–	IT HAPPENED IN MONTEREY
–	–	–	–	–	–	–	–	–	–	–	–	==	==	17	==	==	–	–	–	–	–	–	–	–	–	WHEN THE LITTLE RED ROSES GET THE BLUES
–	–	–	–	–	–	–	–	–	–	–	–	==	==	==	19	18	18	==	==	–	–	–	–	–	–	TELLING IT TO THE DAISIES
Oc	Oc	Nv	Nv	Dc	Dc	Ja	Ja	Fb	Fb	Ma	Ma	Ap	Ap	My	My	Jn	Jn	Jy	Jy	Ag	Ag	Sp	Sp	Oc	Oc	

1930																		1931								
Ap	Ap	My	My	Jn	Jn	Jy	Jy	Ag	Ag	Sp	Sp	Oc	Oc	Nv	Nv	Dc	Dc	Ja	Ja	Fb	Fb	Ma	Ma	Ap	Ap	
–	20	11	5	6	9	16	==	–	–	–	–	–	–	–	–	–	–	–	–	–	–	–	–	–	–	THE MOON IS LOW
–	–	==	==	17	16	13	20	==	–	–	–	–	–	–	–	–	–	–	–	–	–	–	–	–	–	GET HAPPY
–	–	==	16	9	8	8	13	–	–	–	–	–	–	–	–	–	–	–	–	–	–	–	–	–	–	EXACTLY LIKE YOU
–	–	==	==	19	20	==	==	–	–	–	–	–	–	–	–	–	–	–	–	–	–	–	–	–	–	I NEVER DREAMT
–	–	==	18	13	11	10	19	==	–	–	–	–	–	–	–	–	–	–	–	–	–	–	–	–	–	LIVIN' IN THE SUNLIGHT, LOVIN' IN THE MOONLIGHT
–	–	==	==	==	19	==	==	–	–	–	–	–	–	–	–	–	–	–	–	–	–	–	–	–	–	I STILL REMEMBER
–	–	–	==	==	13	9	16	==	==	–	–	–	–	–	–	–	–	–	–	–	–	–	–	–	–	TEN CENTS A DANCE
–	–	==	14	7	4	4	5	10	16	==	–	–	–	–	–	–	–	–	–	–	–	–	–	–	–	IF I HAD A GIRL LIKE YOU
–	–	==	==	12	7	5	4	3	5	8	13	==	–	–	–	–	–	–	–	–	–	–	–	–	–	YOU BROUGHT A NEW KIND OF LOVE TO ME
–	–	20	10	4	2	**1**	**1**	**1**	**1**	2	4	9	18	==	–	–	–	–	–	–	–	–	–	–	–	DANCING WITH TEARS IN MY EYES
–	–	–	==	15	10	14	18	==	==	–	–	–	–	–	–	–	–	–	–	–	–	–	–	–	–	WHEN THE BLOOM IS ON THE SAGE
–	–	–	–	==	17	11	8	7	12	==	==	–	–	–	–	–	–	–	–	–	–	–	–	–	–	SINGING A SONG TO THE STARS
–	–	–	–	==	==	18	12	11	19	==	==	–	–	–	–	–	–	–	–	–	–	–	–	–	–	ABSENCE MAKES THE HEART GROW FONDER (FOR SOMEBODYELSE)
–	–	–	–	–	==	19	14	20	==	–	–	–	–	–	–	–	–	–	–	–	–	–	–	–	–	KITTY FROM KANSAS CITY
–	–	–	–	–	==	15	7	6	8	11	18	==	–	–	–	–	–	–	–	–	–	–	–	–	–	MY FUTURE JUST PASSED
–	–	–	–	–	==	17	11	9	11	10	14	==	==	–	–	–	–	–	–	–	–	–	–	–	–	DOWN THE RIVER OF GOLDEN DREAMS
–	–	–	–	–	==	12	6	5	4	5	7	14	==	==	–	–	–	–	–	–	–	–	–	–	–	SO BEATS MY HEART FOR YOU
–	–	–	–	–	==	==	17	15	17	==	==	–	–	–	–	–	–	–	–	–	–	–	–	–	–	AROUND THE CORNER
–	–	–	–	–	–	==	==	13	9	6	9	13	==	==	–	–	–	–	–	–	–	–	–	–	–	SWINGIN' IN A HAMMOCK
–	–	–	–	–	–	==	15	14	15	20	==	–	–	–	–	–	–	–	–	–	–	–	–	–	–	OLD NEW ENGLAND MOON
–	–	–	–	–	–	==	==	16	14	15	==	==	–	–	–	–	–	–	–	–	–	–	–	–	–	I LOVE YOU SO MUCH
–	–	–	–	–	–	–	==	8	2	**1**	**1**	**1**	**1**	**1**	3	14	==	==	–	–	–	–	–	–	–	LITTLE WHITE LIES
–	–	–	–	–	–	–	==	12	10	7	11	18	==	–	–	–	–	–	–	–	–	–	–	–	–	BYE BYE BLUES
–	–	–	–	–	–	–	–	19	7	4	2	2	2	2	4	10	17	==	==	–	–	–	–	–	–	IF I COULD BE WITH YOU (ONE HOUR TONIGHT)
–	–	–	–	–	–	–	==	==	18	17	17	19	==	19	20	==	==	–	–	–	–	–	–	–	–	SOMEWHERE IN OLD WYOMING
–	–	–	–	–	–	–	–	==	13	9	5	4	4	4	9	12	15	==	–	–	–	–	–	–	–	BETTY CO–ED
–	–	–	–	–	–	–	–	==	==	13	8	7	10	17	==	==	–	–	–	–	–	–	–	–	–	I'M CONFESSIN' (THAT I LOVE YOU)
–	–	–	–	–	–	–	–	–	==	19	16	17	19	==	–	–	–	–	–	–	–	–	–	–	–	JUST A LITTLE CLOSER
–	–	–	–	–	–	–	–	–	==	12	6	3	5	9	13	==	==	–	–	–	–	–	–	–	–	THE KISS WALTZ
–	–	–	–	–	–	–	–	–	==	18	12	10	13	15	18	==	–	–	–	–	–	–	–	–	–	MY BABY JUST CARES FOR ME
–	–	–	–	–	–	–	–	–	==	16	10	5	3	3	6	15	==	–	–	–	–	–	–	–	–	GO HOME AND TELL YOUR MOTHER
–	–	–	–	–	–	–	–	–	==	==	19	11	7	5	5	3	5	4	7	15	==	==	–	–	–	MOONLIGHT ON THE COLORADO
–	–	–	–	–	–	–	–	–	==	==	15	8	6	12	19	==	–	–	–	–	–	–	–	–	–	I STILL GET A THRILL
–	–	–	–	–	–	–	–	–	==	==	20	12	9	8	7	4	4	5	5	9	16	==	==	–	–	WHEN THE ORGAN PLAYED AT TWILIGHT
–	–	–	–	–	–	–	–	–	–	==	==	==	20	==	==	–	–	–	–	–	–	–	–	–	–	HERE COMES THE SUN
–	–	–	–	–	–	–	–	–	–	==	==	15	14	20	==	==	–	–	–	–	–	–	–	–	–	DON'T TELL HER (HIM) WHAT HAPPENED TO ME
–	–	–	–	–	–	–	–	–	–	–	==	==	11	7	2	2	2	8	12	==	==	–	–	–	–	I'M YOURS
–	–	–	–	–	–	–	–	–	–	–	==	16	12	10	8	5	8	7	9	12	17	==	–	–	–	BODY AND SOUL
–	–	–	–	–	–	–	–	–	–	–	==	20	15	14	12	13	16	==	==	==	–	–	–	–	–	SING SOMETHING SIMPLE
–	–	–	–	–	–	–	–	–	–	–	==	==	17	13	10	6	12	20	==	==	–	–	–	–	–	BEYOND THE BLUE HORIZON
–	–	–	–	–	–	–	–	–	–	–	–	==	==	16	11	7	6	6	8	14	==	==	–	–	–	IT MUST BE TRUE
–	–	–	–	–	–	–	–	–	–	–	–	==	==	18	15	19	==	==	–	–	–	–	–	–	–	I'LL BE BLUE JUST THINKING OF YOU
–	–	–	–	–	–	–	–	–	–	–	–	==	16	6	**1**	**1**	**1**	**1**	3	6	15	==	–	–	–	THREE LITTLE WORDS
–	–	–	–	–	–	–	–	–	–	–	–	–	==	==	14	8	11	12	==	==	–	–	–	–	–	SWEETHEART OF MY STUDENT DAYS
–	–	–	–	–	–	–	–	–	–	–	–	–	–	==	==	20	18	==	==	–	–	–	–	–	–	BABY'S BIRTHDAY PARTY
–	–	–	–	–	–	–	–	–	–	–	–	–	–	==	==	18	13	==	==	–	–	–	–	–	–	FINE AND DANDY
–	–	–	–	–	–	–	–	–	–	–	–	–	–	==	==	16	9	11	==	==	–	–	–	–	–	SWEET JENNIE LEE
–	–	–	–	–	–	–	–	–	–	–	–	–	–	–	==	==	20	==	==	==	–	–	–	–	–	SOMETHING TO REMEMBER YOU BY
–	–	–	–	–	–	–	–	–	–	–	–	–	–	==	==	17	10	10	4	5	7	18	==	–	–	THE LITTLE THINGS IN LIFE (1931)
–	–	–	–	–	–	–	–	–	–	–	–	–	–	==	17	9	3	2	**1**	**1**	5	12	==	==	–	YOU'RE DRIVING ME CRAZY (1931)
–	–	–	–	–	–	–	–	–	–	–	–	–	–	==	16	11	7	3	2	3	3	6	9	12	15	THE PEANUT VENDOR (1931)
–	–	–	–	–	–	–	–	–	–	–	–	–	–	–	==	==	19	19	16	18	==	==	–	–	–	I GOT RHYTHM (1931)
–	–	–	–	–	–	–	–	–	–	–	–	–	–	–	–	==	14	9	13	==	==	–	–	–	–	CHEERFUL LITTLE EARFUL (1931)
Ap	Ap	My	My	Jn	Jn	Jy	Jy	Ag	Ag	Sp	Sp	Oc	Oc	Nv	Nv	Dc	Dc	Ja	Ja	Fb	Fb	Ma	Ma	Ap	Ap	

1930 Oc	Oc	Nv	Nv	Dc	Dc	1931 Ja	Ja	Fb	Fb	Ma	Ma	Ap	Ap	My	My	Jn	Jn	Jy	Jy	Ag	Ag	Sp	Sp	Oc	Oc	
11	7	5	5	3	5	4	7	15	==	==	–	–	–	–	–	–	–	–	–	–	–	–	–	–	–	MOONLIGHT ON THE COLORADO (1930)
12	9	8	7	4	4	5	5	9	16	==	==	–	–	–	–	–	–	–	–	–	–	–	–	–	–	WHEN THE ORGAN PLAYED AT TWILIGHT (1930)
==	11	7	2	2	2	8	12	==	==	–	–	–	–	–	–	–	–	–	–	–	–	–	–	–	–	I'M YOURS (1930)
==	==	16	11	7	6	6	8	14	==	==	–	–	–	–	–	–	–	–	–	–	–	–	–	–	–	IT MUST BE TRUE (1930)
16	12	10	8	5	8	7	9	12	17	==	–	–	–	–	–	–	–	–	–	–	–	–	–	–	–	BODY AND SOUL (1930)
==	17	13	10	6	12	20	==	==	–	–	–	–	–	–	–	–	–	–	–	–	–	–	–	–	–	BEYOND THE BLUE HORIZON (1930)
==	16	6	1	1	1	1	3	6	15	==	–	–	–	–	–	–	–	–	–	–	–	–	–	–	–	THREE LITTLE WORDS (1930)
–	==	==	14	8	11	12	==	==	–	–	–	–	–	–	–	–	–	–	–	–	–	–	–	–	–	SWEETHEART OF MY STUDENT DAYS (1930)
–	–	==	==	16	9	11	==	==	–	–	–	–	–	–	–	–	–	–	–	–	–	–	–	–	–	SWEET JENNIE LEE (1930)
–	–	==	==	17	10	10	4	5	7	18	==	–	–	–	–	–	–	–	–	–	–	–	–	–	–	THE LITTLE THINGS IN LIFE
–	–	==	17	9	3	2	1	1	5	12	==	==	–	–	–	–	–	–	–	–	–	–	–	–	–	YOU'RE DRIVING ME CRAZY
–	–	==	16	11	7	3	2	3	3	6	9	12	15	–	–	–	–	–	–	–	–	–	–	–	–	THE PEANUT VENDOR
–	–	–	==	==	19	19	16	18	==	==	–	–	–	–	–	–	–	–	–	–	–	–	–	–	–	I GOT RHYTHM
–	–	–	–	==	14	9	13	==	==	–	–	–	–	–	–	–	–	–	–	–	–	–	–	–	–	CHEERFUL LITTLE EARFUL
–	–	–	–	==	==	17	15	13	19	==	–	–	–	–	–	–	–	–	–	–	–	–	–	–	–	TO WHOM IT MAY CONCERN
–	–	–	–	==	==	==	18	==	==	==	–	–	–	–	–	–	–	–	–	–	–	–	–	–	–	EMBRACEABLE YOU
–	–	–	–	==	==	18	==	==	–	–	–	–	–	–	–	–	–	–	–	–	–	–	–	–	–	(I AM THE WORDS) YOU ARE THE MELODY
–	–	–	–	==	==	15	14	==	==	–	–	–	–	–	–	–	–	–	–	–	–	–	–	–	–	YOURS AND MINE
–	–	–	–	==	==	16	20	==	==	–	–	–	–	–	–	–	–	–	–	–	–	–	–	–	–	MY IDEAL
–	–	–	–	–	==	13	6	2	2	3	6	11	==	–	–	–	–	–	–	–	–	–	–	–	–	I'M ALONE BECAUSE I LOVE YOU
–	–	–	–	–	==	14	10	7	8	7	10	18	==	–	–	–	–	–	–	–	–	–	–	–	–	BLUE AGAIN
–	–	–	–	–	–	==	==	20	==	==	–	–	–	–	–	–	–	–	–	–	–	–	–	–	–	OVERNIGHT
–	–	–	–	–	–	==	17	8	6	8	11	==	==	–	–	–	–	–	–	–	–	–	–	–	–	LONESOME LOVER
–	–	–	–	–	–	==	==	11	9	14	17	==	–	–	–	–	–	–	–	–	–	–	–	–	–	LADY, PLAY YOUR MANDOLIN
–	–	–	–	–	–	==	==	16	11	11	12	==	==	–	–	–	–	–	–	–	–	–	–	–	–	YOU'RE THE ONE I CARE FOR
–	–	–	–	–	–	==	11	4	1	1	1	2	4	11	==	–	–	–	–	–	–	–	–	–	–	JUST A GIGOLO
–	–	–	–	–	–	==	19	10	4	2	2	1	1	2	6	13	==	==	–	–	–	–	–	–	–	WHEN YOUR HAIR HAS TURNED TO SILVER
–	–	–	–	–	–	==	==	==	==	==	20	19	==	==	==	18	15	12	15	18	17	19	==	==	==	STAR DUST
–	–	–	–	–	–	–	==	19	13	13	16	==	–	–	–	–	–	–	–	–	–	–	–	–	–	TEARS
–	–	–	–	–	–	–	==	17	10	5	7	9	==	==	–	–	–	–	–	–	–	–	–	–	–	REACHING FOR THE MOON
–	–	–	–	–	–	–	==	==	14	9	5	5	9	16	==	==	–	–	–	–	–	–	–	–	–	WOULD YOU LIKE TO TAKE A WALK?
–	–	–	–	–	–	–	==	==	20	15	8	6	3	1	1	2	2	5	6	12	20	==	==	–	–	THE WALTZ YOU SAVED FOR ME
–	–	–	–	–	–	–	–	==	12	4	3	4	5	10	==	==	–	–	–	–	–	–	–	–	–	I SURRENDER, DEAR
–	–	–	–	–	–	–	–	==	18	10	4	3	2	4	10	==	==	–	–	–	–	–	–	–	–	WALKIN' MY BABY BACK HOME
–	–	–	–	–	–	–	–	==	==	20	==	==	==	–	–	–	–	–	–	–	–	–	–	–	–	LOVE FOR SALE
–	–	–	–	–	–	–	–	==	==	16	19	==	==	19	==	==	==	–	–	–	–	–	–	–	–	MOOD INDIGO
–	–	–	–	–	–	–	–	–	==	19	13	16	==	==	–	–	–	–	–	–	–	–	–	–	–	THE KING'S HORSES
–	–	–	–	–	–	–	–	–	==	17	14	10	14	==	==	–	–	–	–	–	–	–	–	–	–	HELLO, BEAUTIFUL
–	–	–	–	–	–	–	–	–	–	==	==	17	17	==	==	–	–	–	–	–	–	–	–	–	–	99 OUT OF 100 (WANNA BE LOVED)
–	–	–	–	–	–	–	–	–	–	==	==	==	19	==	==	–	–	–	–	–	–	–	–	–	–	I'VE GOT FIVE DOLLARS
–	–	–	–	–	–	–	–	–	–	==	==	20	13	18	==	–	–	–	–	–	–	–	–	–	–	HEARTACHES
–	–	–	–	–	–	–	–	–	–	==	18	8	6	6	7	10	17	==	–	–	–	–	–	–	–	BY THE RIVER STE. MARIE
–	–	–	–	–	–	–	–	–	–	==	15	7	7	7	4	3	3	4	5	13	==	–	–	–	–	DREAM A LITTLE DREAM OF ME
–	–	–	–	–	–	–	–	–	–	–	==	13	8	3	2	5	12	20	–	–	–	–	–	–	–	PLEASE DON'T TALK ABOUT ME (WHEN I'M GONE)
–	–	–	–	–	–	–	–	–	–	–	==	==	16	20	==	–	–	–	–	–	–	–	–	–	–	GOT THE BENCH, GOT THE PARK
–	–	–	–	–	–	–	–	–	–	–	==	==	==	14	17	==	==	–	–	–	–	–	–	–	–	WHEN YOUR LOVER HAS GONE
–	–	–	–	–	–	–	–	–	–	–	==	15	11	9	9	11	14	==	–	–	–	–	–	–	–	WABASH MOON
–	–	–	–	–	–	–	–	–	–	–	==	14	10	8	8	9	13	17	==	–	–	–	–	–	–	TWO HEARTS IN THREE-QUARTER TIME
–	–	–	–	–	–	–	–	–	–	–	==	==	20	==	==	==	==	–	–	–	–	–	–	–	–	SUGAR BLUES
–	–	–	–	–	–	–	–	–	–	–	–	==	==	==	19	==	==	==	–	–	–	–	–	–	–	MAMA INEZ
–	–	–	–	–	–	–	–	–	–	–	–	==	18	13	13	==	==	–	–	–	–	–	–	–	–	WHEN I TAKE MY SUGAR TO TEA
–	–	–	–	–	–	–	–	–	–	–	–	==	12	5	3	4	6	11	==	–	–	–	–	–	–	(YOU CAME ALONG) OUT OF NOWHERE
–	–	–	–	–	–	–	–	–	–	–	–	==	==	==	15	17	19	==	==	–	–	–	–	–	–	FOR YOU
–	–	–	–	–	–	–	–	–	==	==	==	==	==	==	==	20	==	==	==	–	–	–	–	–	–	SIBONEY
–	–	–	–	–	–	–	–	–	–	–	–	–	==	==	16	==	==	–	–	–	–	–	–	–	–	WERE YOU SINCERE?
–	–	–	–	–	–	–	–	–	–	–	–	–	==	==	18	==	==	==	==	==	–	–	–	–	–	MINNIE THE MOOCHER
Oc	Oc	Nv	Nv	Dc	Dc	Ja	Ja	Fb	Fb	Ma	Ma	Ap	Ap	My	My	Jn	Jn	Jy	Jy	Ag	Ag	Sp	Sp	Oc	Oc	

						1931														1932						
Ap	Ap	My	My	Jn	Jn	Jy	Jy	Ag	Ag	Sp	Sp	Oc	Oc	Nv	Nv	Dc	Dc	Ja	Ja	Fb	Fb	Ma	Ma	Ap	Ap	
–	==	==	20	12	18	==	==	–	–	–	–	–	–	–	–	–	–	–	–	–	–	–	–	–	–	ONE MORE TIME
–	==	15	11	6	4	10	19	==	–	–	–	–	–	–	–	–	–	–	–	–	–	–	–	–	–	WHISTLING IN THE DARK
–	==	17	12	8	11	13	==	==	–	–	–	–	–	–	–	–	–	–	–	–	–	–	–	–	–	WRAP YOUR TROUBLES IN DREAMS
–	==	12	5	**1**	**1**	**1**	2	4	8	13	==	–	–	–	–	–	–	–	–	–	–	–	–	–	–	MOONLIGHT SAVING TIME
–	–	==	14	7	5	7	10	19	==	–	–	–	–	–	–	–	–	–	–	–	–	–	–	–	–	HO–HUM
–	–	==	==	19	20	==	==	==	–	–	–	–	–	–	–	–	–	–	–	–	–	–	–	–	–	ST. JAMES INFIRMARY
–	–	–	==	==	16	==	==	–	–	–	–	–	–	–	–	–	–	–	–	–	–	–	–	–	–	ROLL ON, MISSISSIPPI, ROLL ON
–	–	–	==	16	8	3	4	8	15	==	–	–	–	–	–	–	–	–	–	–	–	–	–	–	–	I WANNA SING ABOUT YOU
–	–	–	==	==	10	6	9	17	==	–	–	–	–	–	–	–	–	–	–	–	–	–	–	–	–	NOW YOU'RE IN MY ARMS
–	–	–	==	14	9	8	13	==	==	–	–	–	–	–	–	–	–	–	–	–	–	–	–	–	–	NEVERTHELESS
–	–	–	==	15	7	2	**1**	2	3	4	5	10	==	==	–	–	–	–	–	–	–	–	–	–	–	JUST ONE MORE CHANCE
–	–	–	–	==	==	14	7	3	2	3	4	15	==	–	–	–	–	–	–	–	–	–	–	–	–	I FOUND A MILLION–DOLLAR BABY
–	–	–	–	–	==	16	11	7	10	17	==	–	–	–	–	–	–	–	–	–	–	–	–	–	–	WITHOUT THAT GAL
–	–	–	–	–	==	15	8	5	4	7	12	==	–	–	–	–	–	–	–	–	–	–	–	–	–	I'M THROUGH WITH LOVE
–	–	–	–	–	==	19	14	11	14	==	==	–	–	–	–	–	–	–	–	–	–	–	–	–	–	LITTLE GIRL
–	–	–	–	–	==	18	12	6	5	9	10	7	13	==	==	–	–	–	–	–	–	–	–	–	–	DANCING IN THE DARK
–	–	–	–	–	==	9	3	**1**	**1**	**1**	**1**	2	2	6	6	7	9	12	==	==	–	–	–	–	–	WHEN THE MOON COMES OVER THE MOUNTAIN
–	–	–	–	–	==	==	16	==	==	–	–	–	–	–	–	–	–	–	–	–	–	–	–	–	–	ON THE BEACH WITH YOU
–	–	–	–	–	–	==	17	9	13	11	15	==	–	–	–	–	–	–	–	–	–	–	–	–	–	WHEN YUBA PLAYS RUMBA ON THE TUBA
–	–	–	–	–	–	==	20	15	7	2	3	3	7	12	18	==	–	–	–	–	–	–	–	–	–	MANY HAPPY RETURNS OF THE DAY
–	–	–	–	–	–	–	18	10	6	6	7	19	==	–	–	–	–	–	–	–	–	–	–	–	–	AT YOUR COMMAND
–	–	–	–	–	–	–	==	14	9	10	18	==	–	–	–	–	–	–	–	–	–	–	–	–	–	COME TO ME
–	–	–	–	–	–	–	==	16	11	8	6	18	==	–	–	–	–	–	–	–	–	–	–	–	–	I LOVE LOUISA
–	–	–	–	–	–	–	==	20	12	5	2	**1**	**1**	5	8	11	==	==	–	–	–	–	–	–	–	SWEET AND LOVELY
–	–	–	–	–	–	–	==	==	16	18	==	==	–	–	–	–	–	–	–	–	–	–	–	–	–	HIGH AND LOW
–	–	–	–	–	–	–	==	==	19	==	==	==	–	–	–	–	–	–	–	–	–	–	–	–	–	NEW SUN IN THE SKY
–	–	–	–	–	–	–	–	==	18	14	16	17	==	–	–	–	–	–	–	–	–	–	–	–	–	IT'S THE GIRL
–	–	–	–	–	–	–	–	–	==	12	8	6	10	20	==	–	–	–	–	–	–	–	–	–	–	ME!
–	–	–	–	–	–	–	–	–	==	15	13	8	8	7	10	16	==	–	–	–	–	–	–	–	–	I APOLOGIZE
–	–	–	–	–	–	–	–	–	==	16	9	5	4	4	4	4	7	16	==	==	–	–	–	–	–	LOVE LETTERS IN THE SAND
–	–	–	–	–	–	–	–	–	–	==	17	16	19	==	==	–	–	–	–	–	–	–	–	–	–	SHINE ON, HARVEST MOON
–	–	–	–	–	–	–	–	–	–	==	20	14	15	18	==	–	–	–	–	–	–	–	–	–	–	THIS IS THE MISSUS
–	–	–	–	–	–	–	–	–	–	==	14	13	11	9	14	==	–	–	–	–	–	–	–	–	–	LIFE IS JUST A BOWL OF CHERRIES
–	–	–	–	–	–	–	–	–	–	==	==	12	9	8	11	12	==	–	–	–	–	–	–	–	–	NOW THAT YOU'RE GONE
–	–	–	–	–	–	–	–	–	–	20	11	4	3	2	3	3	8	==	–	–	–	–	–	–	–	I DON'T KNOW WHY (I JUST DO)
–	–	–	–	–	–	–	–	–	–	==	19	9	6	3	2	8	16	==	–	–	–	–	–	–	–	GUILTY
–	–	–	–	–	–	–	–	–	–	–	==	11	5	**1**	**1**	**1**	**1**	**1**	**1**	2	6	12	==	–	–	GOODNIGHT, SWEETHEART
–	–	–	–	–	–	–	–	–	–	–	==	20	12	10	13	13	==	==	–	–	–	–	–	–	–	YOU CALL IT MADNESS (BUT I CALL IT LOVE)
–	–	–	–	–	–	–	–	–	–	–	==	==	20	==	==	==	–	–	–	–	–	–	–	–	–	WHY DANCE?
–	–	–	–	–	–	–	–	–	–	–	==	==	14	16	17	==	–	–	–	–	–	–	–	–	–	THE THRILL IS GONE
–	–	–	–	–	–	–	–	–	–	–	==	==	16	15	16	==	–	–	–	–	–	–	–	–	–	MY SONG
–	–	–	–	–	–	–	–	–	–	–	==	==	==	17	==	==	–	–	–	–	–	–	–	–	–	YOU FORGOT YOUR GLOVES
–	–	–	–	–	–	–	–	–	–	–	–	==	17	13	9	10	18	20	==	==	==	==	–	–	–	LADY OF SPAIN
–	–	–	–	–	–	–	–	–	–	–	–	==	18	11	5	2	2	4	10	==	==	–	–	–	–	A FADED SUMMER LOVE
–	–	–	–	–	–	–	–	–	–	–	–	–	==	19	12	5	4	8	13	==	==	–	–	–	–	TIME ON MY HANDS
–	–	–	–	–	–	–	–	–	–	–	–	–	==	14	7	6	3	2	4	6	15	==	==	–	–	WHEN IT'S SLEEPY TIME DOWN SOUTH
–	–	–	–	–	–	–	–	–	–	–	–	–	–	==	15	9	5	7	5	10	12	==	–	–	–	AN EVENING IN CAROLINE
–	–	–	–	–	–	–	–	–	–	–	–	–	–	==	20	14	13	13	20	==	–	–	–	–	–	RIVER, STAY 'WAY FROM MY DOOR
–	–	–	–	–	–	–	–	–	–	–	–	–	–	==	19	15	20	==	–	–	–	–	–	–	–	KICKIN' THE GONG AROUND
–	–	–	–	–	–	–	–	–	–	–	–	–	–	–	==	17	6	6	8	12	==	–	–	–	–	CALL ME DARLING
–	–	–	–	–	–	–	–	–	–	–	–	–	–	–	==	18	10	9	17	==	==	–	–	–	–	YOU TRY SOMEBODY ELSE
–	–	–	–	–	–	–	–	–	–	–	–	–	–	–	==	20	17	18	==	==	==	–	–	–	–	TIGER RAG
–	–	–	–	–	–	–	–	–	–	–	–	–	–	==	==	19	12	5	2	**1**	3	3	8	12	==	HOME (WHEN SHADOWS FALL) (1932)
–	–	–	–	–	–	–	–	–	–	–	–	–	–	–	==	==	11	3	3	4	5	9	15	==	–	WHERE THE BLUE OF THE NIGHT MEETS THE GOLD OF THE DAY (1932)
–	–	–	–	–	–	–	–	–	–	–	–	–	–	–	–	==	19	14	15	==	==	–	–	–	–	LIES (1932)
–	–	–	–	–	–	–	–	–	–	–	–	–	–	–	–	==	14	10	11	17	==	–	–	–	–	OOH! THAT KISS (1932)
–	–	–	–	–	–	–	–	–	–	–	–	–	–	–	–	==	15	11	7	9	20	==	–	–	–	CUBAN LOVE SONG (1932)
Ap	Ap	My	My	Jn	Jn	Jy	Jy	Ag	Ag	Sp	Sp	Oc	Oc	Nv	Nv	Dc	Dc	Ja	Ja	Fb	Fb	Ma	Ma	Ap	Ap	

	1931						1932																			
Oc	Oc	Nv	Nv	Dc	Dc	Ja	Ja	Fb	Fb	Ma	Ma	Ap	Ap	My	My	Jn	Jn	Jy	Jy	Ag	Ag	Sp	Sp	Oc	Oc	
2	2	6	6	7	9	12	==	==	–	–	–	–	–	–	–	–	–	–	–	–	–	–	–	–	–	WHEN THE MOON COMES OVER THE MOUNTAIN (1931)
5	4	4	4	7	7	16	==	==	–	–	–	–	–	–	–	–	–	–	–	–	–	–	–	–	–	LOVE LETTERS IN THE SAND (1931)
11	5	**1**	**1**	**1**	**1**	**1**	**1**	2	6	12	==	–	–	–	–	–	–	–	–	–	–	–	–	–	–	GOODNIGHT, SWEETHEART (1931)
==	17	13	9	10	18	20	==	==	==	==	–	–	–	–	–	–	–	–	–	–	–	–	–	–	–	LADY OF SPAIN (1931)
==	18	11	5	2	2	4	10	==	==	–	–	–	–	–	–	–	–	–	–	–	–	–	–	–	–	A FADED SUMMER LOVE (1931)
–	==	19	12	5	4	8	13	==	==	–	–	–	–	–	–	–	–	–	–	–	–	–	–	–	–	TIME ON MY HANDS (1931)
–	==	14	7	6	3	2	4	6	15	==	==	–	–	–	–	–	–	–	–	–	–	–	–	–	–	WHEN IT'S SLEEPY TIME DOWN SOUTH (1931)
–	–	==	15	9	5	7	5	10	12	==	–	–	–	–	–	–	–	–	–	–	–	–	–	–	–	AN EVENING IN CAROLINE (1931)
–	–	==	20	14	13	13	20	==	–	–	–	–	–	–	–	–	–	–	–	–	–	–	–	–	–	RIVER, STAY 'WAY FROM MY DOOR (1931)
–	–	–	==	17	6	6	8	12	==	–	–	–	–	–	–	–	–	–	–	–	–	–	–	–	–	CALL ME DARLING (1931)
–	–	–	==	18	10	9	17	==	==	–	–	–	–	–	–	–	–	–	–	–	–	–	–	–	–	YOU TRY SOMEBODY ELSE (1931)
–	–	–	==	20	17	18	==	==	==	–	–	–	–	–	–	–	–	–	–	–	–	–	–	–	–	TIGER RAG (1931)
–	–	==	==	19	12	5	2	**1**	3	3	8	12	==	–	–	–	–	–	–	–	–	–	–	–	–	HOME (WHEN SHADOWS FALL)
–	–	–	==	==	11	3	3	4	5	9	15	==	–	–	–	–	–	–	–	–	–	–	–	–	–	WHERE THE BLUE OF THE NIGHT MEETS THE GOLD OF THE DAY
–	–	–	–	==	19	14	15	==	==	–	–	–	–	–	–	–	–	–	–	–	–	–	–	–	–	LIES
–	–	–	–	==	14	10	11	17	==	–	–	–	–	–	–	–	–	–	–	–	–	–	–	–	–	OOH! THAT KISS
–	–	–	–	==	15	11	7	9	20	==	–	–	–	–	–	–	–	–	–	–	–	–	–	–	–	CUBAN LOVE SONG
–	–	–	–	==	==	19	==	==	–	–	–	–	–	–	–	–	–	–	–	–	–	–	–	–	–	TRY TO FORGET
–	–	–	–	==	==	==	19	==	==	–	–	–	–	–	–	–	–	–	–	–	–	–	–	–	–	(I'LL BE GLAD WHEN YOU'RE DEAD) YOU RASCAL YOU
–	–	–	–	–	==	==	12	11	==	20	==	–	–	–	–	–	–	–	–	–	–	–	–	–	–	NOW'S THE TIME TO FALL IN LOVE
–	–	–	–	–	==	==	==	19	==	==	–	–	–	–	–	–	–	–	–	–	–	–	–	–	–	SHE DIDN'T SAY "YES"
–	–	–	–	–	==	17	9	8	16	==	–	–	–	–	–	–	–	–	–	–	–	–	–	–	–	BY THE SYCAMORE TREE
–	–	–	–	–	==	15	6	3	**1**	2	4	8	13	==	==	–	–	–	–	–	–	–	–	–	–	ALL OF ME
–	–	–	–	–	–	==	==	13	10	15	==	==	–	–	–	–	–	–	–	–	–	–	–	–	–	YOU'RE MY EVERYTHING
–	–	–	–	–	–	==	==	16	11	19	==	–	–	–	–	–	–	–	–	–	–	–	–	–	–	DINAH
–	–	–	–	–	–	==	16	15	==	==	–	–	–	–	–	–	–	–	–	–	–	–	–	–	–	DELISHIOUS
–	–	–	–	–	–	==	18	7	4	6	10	==	==	–	–	–	–	–	–	–	–	–	–	–	–	WHEN WE'RE ALONE (PENTHOUSE SERENADE)
–	–	–	–	–	–	==	14	5	2	**1**	2	4	10	20	–	–	–	–	–	–	–	–	–	–	–	WAS THAT THE HUMAN THING TO DO?
–	–	–	–	–	–	–	==	18	9	7	7	6	6	14	==	–	–	–	–	–	–	–	–	–	–	SNUGGLED ON YOUR SHOULDER
–	–	–	–	–	–	–	==	14	7	5	3	7	17	==	–	–	–	–	–	–	–	–	–	–	–	JUST FRIENDS
–	–	–	–	–	–	–	==	==	17	16	==	==	==	==	18	==	==	–	–	–	–	–	–	–	–	YOU CAN DEPEND ON ME
–	–	–	–	–	–	–	==	==	==	18	18	==	==	==	20	==	==	–	–	–	–	–	–	–	–	BETWEEN THE DEVIL AND THE DEEP BLUE SEA
–	–	–	–	–	–	–	–	20	8	4	**1**	**1**	2	3	5	7	8	9	11	16	==	–	–	–	–	AUF WIEDERSEH'N, MY DEAR
–	–	–	–	–	–	–	–	==	18	17	13	==	–	–	–	–	–	–	–	–	–	–	–	–	–	RAIN ON THE ROOF
–	–	–	–	–	–	–	–	==	14	10	17	==	==	–	–	–	–	–	–	–	–	–	–	–	–	THE WOODEN SOLDIER AND THE CHINA DOLL
–	–	–	–	–	–	–	–	==	19	14	9	14	==	==	–	–	–	–	–	–	–	–	–	–	–	CAN'T WE TALK IT OVER?
–	–	–	–	–	–	–	–	==	13	8	11	17	==	==	–	–	–	–	–	–	–	–	–	–	–	DANCING ON THE CEILING
–	–	–	–	–	–	–	–	–	==	11	5	3	3	4	3	4	9	13	==	==	–	–	–	–	–	SOMEBODY LOVES YOU
–	–	–	–	–	–	–	–	–	==	13	6	2	**1**	**1**	**1**	**1**	2	4	4	4	13	==	–	–	–	PARADISE
–	–	–	–	–	–	–	–	–	==	==	20	15	20	==	==	–	–	–	–	–	–	–	–	–	–	I HEARD
–	–	–	–	–	–	–	–	–	==	==	14	9	8	10	13	18	==	==	–	–	–	–	–	–	–	KISS ME GOODNIGHT
–	–	–	–	–	–	–	–	–	==	==	19	==	==	==	–	–	–	–	–	–	–	–	–	–	–	STARLIGHT
–	–	–	–	–	–	–	–	–	–	==	==	16	14	19	==	==	–	–	–	–	–	–	–	–	–	LET'S HAVE ANOTHER CUP OF COFFEE
–	–	–	–	–	–	–	–	–	–	==	==	13	9	8	15	==	==	–	–	–	–	–	–	–	–	LOVE, YOU FUNNY THING
–	–	–	–	–	–	–	–	–	–	==	16	10	7	6	9	17	==	–	–	–	–	–	–	–	–	TOO MANY TEARS
–	–	–	–	–	–	–	–	–	–	==	12	5	4	5	7	11	16	==	–	–	–	–	–	–	–	BY THE FIRESIDE
–	–	–	–	–	–	–	–	–	–	==	==	20	19	18	==	==	==	–	–	–	–	–	–	==	==	20 == IT DON'T MEAN A THING (IF IT AIN'T GOT THAT SWING)
–	–	–	–	–	–	–	–	–	–	–	==	18	11	9	14	20	==	–	–	–	–	–	–	–	–	KEEPIN' OUT OF MISCHIEF NOW
–	–	–	–	–	–	–	–	–	–	–	==	11	5	2	2	2	4	7	12	==	–	–	–	–	–	ONE HOUR WITH YOU
–	–	–	–	–	–	–	–	–	–	–	==	==	18	17	==	==	–	–	–	–	–	–	–	–	–	YOU'RE THE ONE (YOU BEAUTIFUL SON–OF–A–GUN)
–	–	–	–	–	–	–	–	–	–	–	–	19	12	7	4	6	12	15	==	–	–	–	–	–	–	MY MOM
–	–	–	–	–	–	–	–	–	–	–	–	==	15	11	16	==	==	–	–	–	–	–	–	–	–	SOFT LIGHTS AND SWEET MUSIC
–	–	–	–	–	–	–	–	–	–	–	–	==	16	12	11	10	14	==	==	–	–	–	–	–	–	BY A RIPPLING STREAM
–	–	–	–	–	–	–	–	–	–	–	–	==	==	16	10	13	==	==	–	–	–	–	–	–	–	LOVABLE
Oc	Oc	Nv	Nv	Dc	Dc	Ja	Ja	Fb	Fb	Ma	Ma	Ap	Ap	My	My	Jn	Jn	Jy	Jy	Ag	Ag	Sp	Sp	Oc	Oc	

							1932												1933							
Ap	Ap	My	My	Jn	Jn	Jy	Jy	Ag	Ag	Sp	Sp	Oc	Oc	Nv	Nv	Dc	Dc	Ja	Ja	Fb	Fb	Ma	Ma	Ap	Ap	
–	==	13	8	5	13	==	==	–	–	–	–	–	–	–	–	–	–	–	–	–	–	–	–	–	–	LAWD, YOU MADE THE NIGHT TOO LONG
–	==	15	6	3	**1**	**1**	3	3	5	13	18	==	–	–	–	–	–	–	–	–	–	–	–	–	–	LULLABY OF THE LEAVES
–	==	==	12	9	6	5	6	5	7	8	13	18	==	==	–	–	–	–	–	–	–	–	–	–	–	GOOFUS
–	–	==	17	12	7	10	16	==	–	–	–	–	–	–	–	–	–	–	–	–	–	–	–	–	–	MY EXTRAORDINARY GAL
–	–	==	19	8	3	2	2	2	4	16	==	–	–	–	–	–	–	–	–	–	–	–	–	–	–	MY SILENT LOVE
–	–	–	==	14	11	8	7	13	==	==	–	–	–	–	–	–	–	–	–	–	–	–	–	–	–	HUMMIN' TO MYSELF
–	–	–	==	19	15	14	==	==	–	–	–	–	–	–	–	–	–	–	–	–	–	–	–	–	–	THE VOICE IN THE OLD VILLAGE CHOIR
–	–	–	==	16	10	6	5	8	15	==	–	–	–	–	–	–	–	–	–	–	–	–	–	–	–	LAZY DAY
–	–	–	==	15	5	3	**1**	**1**	**1**	**1**	2	3	2	4	8	13	==	==	–	–	–	–	–	–	–	IN A SHANTY IN OLD SHANTY TOWN
–	–	–	==	==	17	12	13	==	==	–	–	–	–	–	–	–	–	–	–	–	–	–	–	–	–	CABIN IN THE COTTON
–	–	–	==	==	18	19	18	==	==	==	20	==	==	==	==	==	==	–	–	–	–	–	–	–	–	ROCKIN' CHAIR
–	–	–	–	==	19	11	10	15	==	–	–	–	–	–	–	–	–	–	–	–	–	–	–	–	–	(I'M STILL WITHOUT A SWEETHEART) WITH SUMMER COMIN' ON
–	–	–	–	==	20	18	==	==	–	–	–	–	–	–	–	–	–	–	–	–	–	–	–	–	–	IF IT AIN'T LOVE
–	–	–	–	–	==	20	17	20	==	–	–	–	–	–	–	–	–	–	–	–	–	–	–	–	–	IN MY HIDEAWAY
–	–	–	–	–	==	17	9	6	11	18	==	–	–	–	–	–	–	–	–	–	–	–	–	–	–	HOLD MY HAND
–	–	–	–	–	==	16	8	7	14	==	==	–	–	–	–	–	–	–	–	–	–	–	–	–	–	YOU'RE BLASE
–	–	–	–	–	==	==	14	14	==	==	–	–	–	–	–	–	–	–	–	–	–	–	–	–	–	IS I IN LOVE? I IS
–	–	–	–	–	–	==	==	19	18	==	==	–	–	–	–	–	–	–	–	–	–	–	–	–	–	THE NIGHT WHEN LOVE WAS BORN
–	–	–	–	–	–	==	15	9	3	3	4	6	12	==	–	–	–	–	–	–	–	–	–	–	–	MASQUERADE
–	–	–	–	–	–	==	19	==	17	20	19	==	==	==	–	–	–	–	–	–	–	–	–	–	–	SO ASHAMED
–	–	–	–	–	–	–	20	10	2	2	**1**	2	4	9	16	==	–	–	–	–	–	–	–	–	–	WE JUST COULDN'T SAY GOODBYE
–	–	–	–	–	–	–	==	12	9	7	12	16	==	–	–	–	–	–	–	–	–	–	–	–	–	I CAN'T BELIEVE IT'S TRUE
–	–	–	–	–	–	–	==	17	19	14	9	9	15	==	–	–	–	–	–	–	–	–	–	–	–	THREE ON A MATCH
–	–	–	–	–	–	–	==	18	8	4	10	12	==	==	–	–	–	–	–	–	–	–	–	–	–	AS YOU DESIRE ME
–	–	–	–	–	–	–	==	11	6	5	11	15	==	–	–	–	–	–	–	–	–	–	–	–	–	IT WAS SO BEAUTIFUL
–	–	–	–	–	–	–	==	==	12	11	14	==	==	–	–	–	–	–	–	–	–	–	–	–	–	YOU'VE GOT ME IN THE PALM OF YOUR HAND
–	–	–	–	–	–	–	==	==	10	6	7	8	17	==	–	–	–	–	–	–	–	–	–	–	–	STRANGE INTERLUDE
–	–	–	–	–	–	–	–	==	20	17	==	==	–	–	–	–	–	–	–	–	–	–	–	–	–	BUGLE CALL RAG
–	–	–	–	–	–	–	–	==	16	9	5	7	11	15	==	==	–	–	–	–	–	–	–	–	–	I'LL NEVER BE THE SAME
–	–	–	–	–	–	–	–	–	==	19	17	==	==	–	–	–	–	–	–	–	–	–	–	–	–	MIMI
–	–	–	–	–	–	–	–	–	==	10	6	5	9	12	18	==	–	–	–	–	–	–	–	–	–	THREE'S A CROWD
–	–	–	–	–	–	–	–	–	==	15	8	4	6	11	20	==	–	–	–	–	–	–	–	–	–	LOVE ME TONIGHT
–	–	–	–	–	–	–	–	–	==	12	3	**1**	**1**	2	5	10	19	==	–	–	–	–	–	–	–	SAY IT ISN'T SO
–	–	–	–	–	–	–	–	–	==	==	15	13	7	10	12	==	==	–	–	–	–	–	–	–	–	SWEETHEARTS FOREVER
–	–	–	–	–	–	–	–	–	–	==	16	14	16	==	==	–	–	–	–	–	–	–	–	–	–	I GUESS I'LL HAVE TO CHANGE MY PLAN
–	–	–	–	–	–	–	–	–	–	==	==	11	5	3	4	3	5	8	15	==	–	–	–	–	–	ALL-AMERICAN GIRL
–	–	–	–	–	–	–	–	–	–	==	==	17	19	==	==	–	–	–	–	–	–	–	–	–	–	ALONE TOGETHER
–	–	–	–	–	–	–	–	–	–	–	==	==	18	14	==	==	–	–	–	–	–	–	–	–	–	PU-LEEZE, MR. HEMINGWAY!
–	–	–	–	–	–	–	–	–	–	–	==	10	3	**1**	**1**	2	7	15	==	–	–	–	–	–	–	LET'S PUT OUT THE LIGHTS (AND GO TO SLEEP)
–	–	–	–	–	–	–	–	–	–	–	==	20	10	5	3	4	10	19	==	–	–	–	–	–	–	HOW DEEP IS THE OCEAN?
–	–	–	–	–	–	–	–	–	–	–	==	19	8	6	2	**1**	**1**	2	7	13	==	–	–	–	–	PLEASE
–	–	–	–	–	–	–	–	–	–	–	–	==	13	8	7	6	3	4	10	18	==	–	–	–	–	PINK ELEPHANTS
–	–	–	–	–	–	–	–	–	–	–	–	==	20	13	15	16	17	17	==	==	–	–	–	–	–	HELL'S BELLS
–	–	–	–	–	–	–	–	–	–	–	–	==	14	7	6	5	2	**1**	2	4	5	5	9	19	==	A LITTLE STREET WHERE OLD FRIENDS MEET
–	–	–	–	–	–	–	–	–	–	–	–	–	==	17	13	12	18	==	–	–	–	–	–	–	–	HERE LIES LOVE
–	–	–	–	–	–	–	–	–	–	–	–	–	==	19	11	8	8	14	==	==	–	–	–	–	–	BROTHER, CAN YOU SPARE A DIME?
–	–	–	–	–	–	–	–	–	–	–	–	–	==	16	9	7	4	3	3	8	18	==	–	–	–	FIT AS A FIDDLE
–	–	–	–	–	–	–	–	–	–	–	–	–	==	==	19	17	==	==	–	–	–	–	–	–	–	A SHINE ON YOUR SHOES
–	–	–	–	–	–	–	–	–	–	–	–	–	–	==	17	14	12	13	19	==	–	–	–	–	–	JUST A LITTLE HOME FOR THE OLD FOLKS
–	–	–	–	–	–	–	–	–	–	–	–	–	–	==	==	15	9	10	13	==	==	–	–	–	–	UNDERNEATH THE HARLEM MOON
–	–	–	–	–	–	–	–	–	–	–	–	–	–	==	==	18	11	9	12	15	==	–	–	–	–	I'M SURE OF EVERYTHING BUT YOU
–	–	–	–	–	–	–	–	–	–	–	–	–	–	–	==	20	15	20	==	==	–	–	–	–	–	LOUISIANA HAYRIDE
–	–	–	–	–	–	–	–	–	–	–	–	–	–	–	==	==	20	18	==	==	–	–	–	–	–	A BOY AND A GIRL WERE DANCING
–	–	–	–	–	–	–	–	–	–	–	–	–	==	18	14	11	13	11	11	7	6	8	15	==	–	ROCKABYE MOON (1933)
–	–	–	–	–	–	–	–	–	–	–	–	–	–	20	10	9	6	5	4	6	8	12	20	==	–	PLAY, FIDDLE, PLAY (1933)
–	–	–	–	–	–	–	–	–	–	–	–	–	–	–	==	19	14	6	5	9	14	==	–	–	–	WILLOW, WEEP FOR ME (1933)
–	–	–	–	–	–	–	–	–	–	–	–	–	–	–	–	==	16	7	**1**	**1**	**1**	2	3	7	11	NIGHT AND DAY (1933)
Ap	Ap	My	My	Jn	Jn	Jy	Jy	Ag	Ag	Sp	Sp	Oc	Oc	Nv	Nv	Dc	Dc	Ja	Ja	Fb	Fb	Ma	Ma	Ap	Ap	

1932														1933												
Oc	Oc	Nv	Nv	Dc	Dc	Ja	Ja	Fb	Fb	Ma	Ma	Ap	Ap	My	My	Jn	Jn	Jy	Jy	Ag	Ag	Sp	Sp	Oc	Oc	
10	3	**1**	**1**	2	7	15	==	–	–	–	–	–	–	–	–	–	–	–	–	–	–	–	–	–	–	LET'S PUT OUT THE LIGHTS (AND GO TO SLEEP) (1932)
20	10	5	3	4	10	19	==	–	–	–	–	–	–	–	–	–	–	–	–	–	–	–	–	–	–	HOW DEEP IS THE OCEAN? (1932)
19	8	6	2	**1**	**1**	2	7	13	==	–	–	–	–	–	–	–	–	–	–	–	–	–	–	–	–	PLEASE (1932)
==	13	8	7	6	3	4	10	18	==	–	–	–	–	–	–	–	–	–	–	–	–	–	–	–	–	PINK ELEPHANTS (1932)
11	5	3	4	3	5	8	15	==	–	–	–	–	–	–	–	–	–	–	–	–	–	–	–	–	–	ALL-AMERICAN GIRL (1932)
==	20	13	15	16	17	17	==	==	–	–	–	–	–	–	–	–	–	–	–	–	–	–	–	–	–	HELL'S BELLS (1932)
==	14	7	6	5	2	**1**	2	4	5	5	9	19	==	–	–	–	–	–	–	–	–	–	–	–	–	A LITTLE STREET WHERE OLD FRIENDS MEET (1932)
–	==	19	11	8	8	14	==	==	–	–	–	–	–	–	–	–	–	–	–	–	–	–	–	–	–	BROTHER, CAN YOU SPARE A DIME? (1932)
–	==	16	9	7	4	3	3	8	18	==	–	–	–	–	–	–	–	–	–	–	–	–	–	–	–	FIT AS A FIDDLE (1932)
–	–	==	17	14	12	13	19	==	–	–	–	–	–	–	–	–	–	–	–	–	–	–	–	–	–	JUST A LITTLE HOME FOR THE OLD FOLKS (1932)
–	–	==	==	15	9	10	13	==	==	–	–	–	–	–	–	–	–	–	–	–	–	–	–	–	–	UNDERNEATH THE HARLEM MOON (1932)
–	–	==	==	18	11	9	12	15	==	–	–	–	–	–	–	–	–	–	–	–	–	–	–	–	–	I'M SURE OF EVERYTHING BUT YOU (1932)
–	–	–	==	20	15	20	==	==	–	–	–	–	–	–	–	–	–	–	–	–	–	–	–	–	–	LOUISIANA HAYRIDE (1932)
–	==	18	14	11	13	11	11	7	6	8	15	==	–	–	–	–	–	–	–	–	–	–	–	–	–	ROCKABYE MOON
–	–	20	10	9	6	5	4	6	8	12	20	==	–	–	–	–	–	–	–	–	–	–	–	–	–	PLAY, FIDDLE, PLAY
–	–	–	==	19	14	6	5	9	14	==	–	–	–	–	–	–	–	–	–	–	–	–	–	–	–	WILLOW, WEEP FOR ME
–	–	–	==	==	20	18	==	==	–	–	–	–	–	–	–	–	–	–	–	–	–	–	–	–	–	A BOY AND A GIRL WERE DANCING (1932)
–	–	–	–	==	16	7	**1**	**1**	**1**	2	3	7	11	14	==	==	–	–	–	–	–	–	–	–	–	NIGHT AND DAY
–	–	–	–	==	==	12	6	5	4	4	7	8	14	==	–	–	–	–	–	–	–	–	–	–	–	MY DARLING
–	–	–	–	–	==	==	17	17	20	==	==	–	–	–	–	–	–	–	–	–	–	–	–	–	–	I'VE TOLD EVERY LITTLE STAR
–	–	–	–	–	==	16	8	2	2	3	2	4	12	18	==	–	–	–	–	–	–	–	–	–	–	MOON SONG
–	–	–	–	–	==	==	14	10	7	16	==	–	–	–	–	–	–	–	–	–	–	–	–	–	–	EADIE WAS A LADY
–	–	–	–	–	==	==	9	3	3	**1**	**1**	**1**	3	7	8	13	==	–	–	–	–	–	–	–	–	JUST AN ECHO IN THE VALLEY
–	–	–	–	–	–	==	16	12	9	17	==	==	–	–	–	–	–	–	–	–	–	–	–	–	–	STREET OF DREAMS
–	–	–	–	–	–	==	20	11	10	13	==	==	–	–	–	–	–	–	–	–	–	–	–	–	–	THE GIRL IN THE LITTLE GREEN HAT
–	–	–	–	–	–	==	18	14	11	10	11	16	==	==	–	–	–	–	–	–	–	–	–	–	–	LOVE IN THE MOONLIGHT
–	–	–	–	–	–	==	==	16	13	==	==	–	–	–	–	–	–	–	–	–	–	–	–	–	–	SPEAK TO ME OF LOVE
–	–	–	–	–	–	==	==	20	16	==	==	–	–	–	–	–	–	–	–	–	–	–	–	–	–	RISE 'N SHINE
–	–	–	–	–	–	==	==	19	15	==	==	–	–	–	–	–	–	–	–	–	–	–	–	–	–	YOU'RE AN OLD SMOOTHIE
–	–	–	–	–	–	–	==	==	12	11	13	20	==	–	–	–	–	–	–	–	–	–	–	–	–	LOVE IS A DREAM
–	–	–	–	–	–	–	==	==	==	20	19	==	==	–	–	–	–	–	–	–	–	–	–	–	–	I'VE GOT THE WORLD ON A STRING
–	–	–	–	–	–	–	–	==	17	7	8	6	5	11	20	==	–	–	–	–	–	–	–	–	–	TRY A LITTLE TENDERNESS
–	–	–	–	–	–	–	–	==	19	6	4	3	4	8	11	17	==	–	–	–	–	–	–	–	–	FAREWELL TO ARMS
–	–	–	–	–	–	–	–	==	==	19	18	==	==	–	–	–	–	–	–	–	–	–	–	–	–	I GOTTA RIGHT TO SING THE BLUES
–	–	–	–	–	–	–	–	==	==	9	5	2	**1**	**1**	2	5	7	16	==	–	–	–	–	–	–	SHUFFLE OFF TO BUFFALO
–	–	–	–	–	–	–	–	–	==	15	10	9	13	==	==	–	–	–	–	–	–	–	–	–	–	YOU'RE GETTING TO BE A HABIT WITH ME
–	–	–	–	–	–	–	–	–	==	14	6	5	2	2	6	8	17	==	–	–	–	–	–	–	–	FORTY-SECOND STREET
–	–	–	–	–	–	–	–	–	==	18	12	12	20	==	–	–	–	–	–	–	–	–	–	–	–	I'M YOUNG AND HEALTHY
–	–	–	–	–	–	–	–	–	==	==	17	18	18	==	==	–	–	–	–	–	–	–	–	–	–	DARKNESS ON THE DELTA
–	–	–	–	–	–	–	–	–	–	==	16	14	15	20	==	–	–	–	–	–	–	–	–	–	–	YOU'VE GOT ME CRYING AGAIN
–	–	–	–	–	–	–	–	–	–	==	14	10	6	5	4	4	6	9	14	==	–	–	–	–	–	HAVE YOU EVER BEEN LONELY?
–	–	–	–	–	–	–	–	–	–	==	==	15	17	==	==	–	–	–	–	–	–	–	–	–	–	HEY! YOUNG FELLA
–	–	–	–	–	–	–	–	–	–	==	==	13	7	10	16	==	–	–	–	–	–	–	–	–	–	I'LL TAKE AN OPTION ON YOU
–	–	–	–	–	–	–	–	–	–	==	==	11	8	6	3	2	2	**1**	2	2	3	3	6	8	13	== IN THE VALLEY OF THE MOON
–	–	–	–	–	–	–	–	–	–	–	==	17	10	4	7	7	12	==	==	–	–	–	–	–	–	LOVER
–	–	–	–	–	–	–	–	–	–	–	==	==	19	15	18	==	==	–	–	–	–	–	–	–	–	I WAKE UP SMILING
–	–	–	–	–	–	–	–	–	–	–	–	==	16	9	5	3	3	6	8	11	19	==	–	–	–	HOLD ME
–	–	–	–	–	–	–	–	–	–	–	–	==	9	3	**1**	**1**	**1**	2	6	9	15	==	–	–	–	STORMY WEATHER
–	–	–	–	–	–	–	–	–	–	–	–	==	==	16	15	12	20	==	–	–	–	–	–	–	–	MAYBE (IT'S BECAUSE) I LOVE YOU TOO MUCH
–	–	–	–	–	–	–	–	–	–	–	–	==	==	13	14	20	==	–	–	–	–	–	–	–	–	REMEMBER ME
–	–	–	–	–	–	–	–	–	–	–	–	==	==	12	12	14	==	==	–	–	–	–	–	–	–	TWO TICKETS TO GEORGIA
–	–	–	–	–	–	–	–	–	–	–	–	–	==	==	17	==	==	–	–	–	–	–	–	–	–	LET'S CALL IT A DAY
Oc	Oc	Nv	Nv	Dc	Dc	Ja	Ja	Fb	Fb	Ma	Ma	Ap	Ap	My	My	Jn	Jn	Jy	Jy	Ag	Ag	Sp	Sp	Oc	Oc	

1933																		1934								
Ap	**Ap**	**My**	**My**	**Jn**	**Jn**	**Jy**	**Jy**	**Ag**	**Ag**	**Sp**	**Sp**	**Oc**	**Oc**	**Nv**	**Nv**	**Dc**	**Dc**	**Ja**	**Ja**	**Fb**	**Fb**	**Ma**	**Ma**	**Ap**	**Ap**	
–	==	17	9	9	8	10	12	15	==	==	–	–	–	–	–	–	–	–	–	–	–	–	–	–	–	ADORABLE
–	–	==	13	10	11	15	==	–	–	–	–	–	–	–	–	–	–	–	–	–	–	–	–	–	–	LYING IN THE HAY
–	–	==	18	19	==	==	–	–	–	–	–	–	–	–	–	–	–	–	–	–	–	–	–	–	–	IN THE PARK IN PAREE
–	–	19	10	6	4	5	4	6	18	==	–	–	–	–	–	–	–	–	–	–	–	–	–	–	–	LOVE SONGS OF THE NILE
–	–	–	19	11	5	3	3	4	5	9	15	==	–	–	–	–	–	–	–	–	–	–	–	–	–	SWEETHEART, DARLIN'
–	–	–	==	==	14	12	16	==	==	–	–	–	–	–	–	–	–	–	–	–	–	–	–	–	–	AN ORCHID TO YOU
–	–	–	==	15	10	7	9	16	==	–	–	–	–	–	–	–	–	–	–	–	–	–	–	–	–	ISN'T IT HEAVENLY?
–	–	–	==	19	13	11	11	17	==	–	–	–	–	–	–	–	–	–	–	–	–	–	–	–	–	I COVER THE WATERFRONT
–	–	–	==	16	15	17	==	18	20	17	==	==	–	–	–	–	–	–	–	–	–	–	–	–	–	GYPSY FIDDLES
–	–	–	==	==	16	14	17	==	==	–	–	–	–	–	–	–	–	–	–	–	–	–	–	–	–	WE'RE IN THE MONEY (THE GOLD DIGGERS' SONG)
–	–	–	–	==	==	==	18	==	==	–	–	–	–	–	–	–	–	–	–	–	–	–	–	–	–	I'VE GOT TO SING A TORCH SONG
–	–	–	–	==	==	19	15	13	12	14	16	18	==	==	–	–	–	–	–	–	–	–	–	–	–	SOPHISTICATED LADY
–	–	–	–	==	==	18	==	==	–	–	–	–	–	–	–	–	–	–	–	–	–	–	–	–	–	A FOOL IN LOVE
–	–	–	–	==	==	==	20	==	==	20	==	==	–	–	–	–	–	–	–	–	–	–	–	–	–	TELL ME TONIGHT
–	–	–	–	==	9	4	**1**	**1**	2	2	3	6	11	15	17	==	–	–	–	–	–	–	–	–	–	SHADOW WALTZ
–	–	–	–	–	18	8	7	5	4	6	7	11	17	==	–	–	–	–	–	–	–	–	–	–	–	LEARN TO CROON
–	–	–	–	–	==	20	10	7	8	11	18	==	–	–	–	–	–	–	–	–	–	–	–	–	–	HOLD YOUR MAN
–	–	–	–	–	==	13	5	3	**1**	**1**	**1**	2	3	9	16	==	–	–	–	–	–	–	–	–	–	LAZY BONES
–	–	–	–	–	–	==	==	14	10	13	19	==	–	–	–	–	–	–	–	–	–	–	–	–	–	DOWN THE OLD OX ROAD
–	–	–	–	–	–	==	19	10	6	7	8	12	18	==	–	–	–	–	–	–	–	–	–	–	–	UNDER A BLANKET OF BLUE
–	–	–	–	–	–	==	13	8	7	8	9	16	==	–	–	–	–	–	–	–	–	–	–	–	–	BLUE PRELUDE
–	–	–	–	–	–	–	==	20	16	16	==	==	–	–	–	–	–	–	–	–	–	–	–	–	–	TROUBLE IN PARADISE
–	–	–	–	–	–	–	==	==	14	12	10	==	==	–	–	–	–	–	–	–	–	–	–	–	–	MY MOONLIGHT MADONNA
–	–	–	–	–	–	–	==	19	13	15	17	==	–	–	–	–	–	–	–	–	–	–	–	–	–	SMOKE RINGS
–	–	–	–	–	–	–	==	12	9	5	4	3	5	7	11	15	==	–	–	–	–	–	–	–	–	LOVE IS THE SWEETEST THING
–	–	–	–	–	–	–	–	==	==	18	12	9	14	18	==	==	–	–	–	–	–	–	–	–	–	THIS TIME IT'S LOVE
–	–	–	–	–	–	–	–	==	17	10	5	5	7	12	19	==	–	–	–	–	–	–	–	–	–	DON'T BLAME ME
–	–	–	–	–	–	–	–	==	11	4	2	**1**	**1**	**1**	**1**	2	6	5	8	17	==	–	–	–	–	THE LAST ROUNDUP
–	–	–	–	–	–	–	–	–	==	19	14	13	==	==	–	–	–	–	–	–	–	–	–	–	–	AH, BUT IS IT LOVE?
–	–	–	–	–	–	–	–	–	–	==	13	7	4	4	6	9	17	==	–	–	–	–	–	–	–	THE DAY YOU CAME ALONG
–	–	–	–	–	–	–	–	–	–	==	20	10	6	3	4	8	14	==	–	–	–	–	–	–	–	THANKS
–	–	–	–	–	–	–	–	–	–	==	11	4	2	2	2	7	10	16	==	–	–	–	–	–	–	WHO'S AFRAID OF THE BIG BAD WOLF?
–	–	–	–	–	–	–	–	–	–	==	==	17	16	20	==	–	–	–	–	–	–	–	–	–	–	ARE YOU MAKIN' ANY MONEY?
–	–	–	–	–	–	–	–	–	–	–	==	15	12	11	14	==	==	–	–	–	–	–	–	–	–	IT'S ONLY A PAPER MOON
–	–	–	–	–	–	–	–	–	–	–	==	19	10	8	10	18	==	–	–	–	–	–	–	–	–	DINNER AT EIGHT
–	–	–	–	–	–	–	–	–	–	–	==	20	9	6	9	14	==	–	–	–	–	–	–	–	–	IT'S THE TALK OF THE TOWN
–	–	–	–	–	–	–	–	–	–	–	==	14	8	5	3	**1**	3	3	2	3	5	12	16	==	==	GOOD NIGHT, LITTLE GIRL OF MY DREAMS
–	–	–	–	–	–	–	–	–	–	–	==	==	19	17	==	==	–	–	–	–	–	–	–	–	–	CLOSE YOUR EYES
–	–	–	–	–	–	–	–	–	–	–	==	==	==	19	==	==	–	–	–	–	–	–	–	–	–	BLESS YOUR HEART
–	–	–	–	–	–	–	–	–	–	–	–	==	20	13	7	3	2	4	7	14	==	–	–	–	–	ANNIE DOESN'T LIVE HERE ANYMORE
–	–	–	–	–	–	–	–	–	–	–	–	==	15	10	5	5	4	9	14	==	–	–	–	–	–	BY A WATERFALL
–	–	–	–	–	–	–	–	–	–	–	–	==	==	14	8	6	9	13	==	–	–	–	–	–	–	I'LL BE FAITHFUL
–	–	–	–	–	–	–	–	–	–	–	–	–	==	==	13	10	13	17	==	==	–	–	–	–	–	HEAT WAVE
–	–	–	–	–	–	–	–	–	–	–	–	–	==	==	18	17	==	==	–	–	–	–	–	–	–	SHANGHAI LIL
–	–	–	–	–	–	–	–	–	–	–	–	–	==	==	==	16	==	==	–	–	–	–	–	–	–	EVENIN'
–	–	–	–	–	–	–	–	–	–	–	–	–	–	==	20	11	7	10	17	==	–	–	–	–	–	YOU'RE GONNA LOSE YOUR GAL
–	–	–	–	–	–	–	–	–	–	–	–	–	–	==	==	13	8	8	12	20	==	–	–	–	–	HONEYMOON HOTEL
–	–	–	–	–	–	–	–	–	–	–	–	–	–	==	12	4	**1**	**1**	4	6	18	==	–	–	–	DID YOU EVER SEE A DREAM WALKING?
–	–	–	–	–	–	–	–	–	–	–	–	–	–	==	==	19	11	12	==	==	–	–	–	–	–	APRIL IN PARIS
–	–	–	–	–	–	–	–	–	–	–	–	–	–	–	==	==	==	20	==	–	–	–	–	–	–	PUDDIN' HEAD JONES
–	–	–	–	–	–	–	–	–	–	–	–	–	–	–	==	==	19	==	==	==	–	–	–	–	–	MINE
–	–	–	–	–	–	–	–	–	–	–	–	–	–	–	==	==	18	==	==	–	–	–	–	–	–	AFTER ALL, YOU'RE ALL I'M AFTER
–	–	–	–	–	–	–	–	–	–	–	–	–	–	–	==	==	16	11	13	==	==	–	–	–	–	GOOD MORNING, GLORY
–	–	–	–	–	–	–	–	–	–	–	–	–	–	–	–	20	20	==	==	–	–	–	–	–	–	DOIN' THE UPTOWN LOWDOWN
–	–	–	–	–	–	–	–	–	–	–	–	==	==	16	15	12	5	2	**1**	**1**	**1**	**1**	**1**	**1**	2	THE OLD SPINNING WHEEL (1934)
–	–	–	–	–	–	–	–	–	–	–	–	–	–	–	==	==	12	7	5	10	==	==	–	–	–	EASTER PARADE (1934)
–	–	–	–	–	–	–	–	–	–	–	–	–	–	–	–	==	15	6	3	2	2	5	7	8	12	SMOKE GETS IN YOUR EYES (1934)
Ap	**Ap**	**My**	**My**	**Jn**	**Jn**	**Jy**	**Jy**	**Ag**	**Ag**	**Sp**	**Sp**	**Oc**	**Oc**	**Nv**	**Nv**	**Dc**	**Dc**	**Ja**	**Ja**	**Fb**	**Fb**	**Ma**	**Ma**	**Ap**	**Ap**	

1933														1934												
Oc	Oc	Nv	Nv	Dc	Dc	Ja	Ja	Fb	Fb	Ma	Ma	Ap	Ap	My	My	Jn	Jn	Jy	Jy	Ag	Ag	Sp	Sp	Oc	Oc	
1	**1**	**1**	**1**	2	6	5	8	17	==	–	–	–	–	–	–	–	–	–	–	–	–	–	–	–	–	THE LAST ROUNDUP (1933)
4	2	2	2	7	10	16	==	–	–	–	–	–	–	–	–	–	–	–	–	–	–	–	–	–	–	WHO'S AFRAID OF THE BIG BAD WOLF? (1933)
==	==	14	8	6	9	13	==	–	–	–	–	–	–	–	–	–	–	–	–	–	–	–	–	–	–	I'LL BE FAITHFUL (1933)
==	20	13	7	3	2	4	7	14	==	–	–	–	–	–	–	–	–	–	–	–	–	–	–	–	–	ANNIE DOESN'T LIVE HERE ANYMORE (1933)
==	15	10	5	5	4	9	14	==	–	–	–	–	–	–	–	–	–	–	–	–	–	–	–	–	–	BY A WATERFALL (1933)
14	8	5	3	**1**	3	3	2	3	5	12	16	==	==	–	–	–	–	–	–	–	–	–	–	–	–	GOOD NIGHT, LITTLE GIRL OF MY DREAMS (1933)
–	==	==	13	10	13	17	==	==	–	–	–	–	–	–	–	–	–	–	–	–	–	–	–	–	–	HEAT WAVE (1933)
–	–	==	20	11	7	10	17	==	–	–	–	–	–	–	–	–	–	–	–	–	–	–	–	–	–	YOU'RE GONNA LOSE YOUR GAL (1933)
–	–	==	==	13	8	8	12	20	==	–	–	–	–	–	–	–	–	–	–	–	–	–	–	–	–	HONEYMOON HOTEL (1933)
–	–	==	12	4	**1**	**1**	4	6	18	==	–	–	–	–	–	–	–	–	–	–	–	–	–	–	–	DID YOU EVER SEE A DREAM WALKING? (1933)
–	–	==	==	19	11	12	==	==	–	–	–	–	–	–	–	–	–	–	–	–	–	–	–	–	–	APRIL IN PARIS (1933)
–	–	–	==	==	16	11	13	==	==	–	–	–	–	–	–	–	–	–	–	–	–	–	–	–	–	GOOD MORNING, GLORY (1933)
–	–	–	==	==	==	20	==	–	–	–	–	–	–	–	–	–	–	–	–	–	–	–	–	–	–	PUDDIN' HEAD JONES (1933)
==	==	16	15	12	5	2	**1**	**1**	**1**	**1**	**1**	**1**	2	3	4	14	==	==	–	–	–	–	–	–	–	THE OLD SPINNING WHEEL
–	–	–	==	==	12	7	5	10	==	==	–	–	–	–	–	–	–	–	–	–	–	–	–	–	–	EASTER PARADE
–	–	–	–	==	15	6	3	2	2	5	7	8	12	==	–	–	–	–	–	–	–	–	–	–	–	SMOKE GETS IN YOUR EYES
–	–	–	–	–	==	18	16	==	==	–	–	–	–	–	–	–	–	–	–	–	–	–	–	–	–	ONE MINUTE TO ONE
–	–	–	–	–	==	14	6	4	10	16	==	–	–	–	–	–	–	–	–	–	–	–	–	–	–	EVERYTHING I HAVE IS YOURS
–	–	–	–	–	==	15	9	8	11	13	13	12	19	==	–	–	–	–	–	–	–	–	–	–	–	TEMPTATION
–	–	–	–	–	==	==	19	==	==	–	–	–	–	–	–	–	–	–	–	–	–	–	–	–	–	YOU'RE DEVASTATING
–	–	–	–	–	==	==	20	==	==	–	–	–	–	–	–	–	–	–	–	–	–	–	–	–	–	YESTERDAYS
–	–	–	–	–	–	19	10	5	3	3	3	2	**1**	2	6	17	==	–	–	–	–	–	–	–	–	MY LITTLE GRASS SHACK IN KEALEKUA, HAWAII
–	–	–	–	–	–	==	11	9	6	8	14	15	==	–	–	–	–	–	–	–	–	–	–	–	–	ORCHIDS IN THE MOONLIGHT
–	–	–	–	–	–	==	15	7	4	4	4	4	5	9	18	==	–	–	–	–	–	–	–	–	–	CARIOCA
–	–	–	–	–	–	==	18	11	8	11	12	16	==	==	–	–	–	–	–	–	–	–	–	–	–	WE'LL MAKE HAY WHILE THE SUN SHINES
–	–	–	–	–	–	==	==	15	19	==	==	–	–	–	–	–	–	–	–	–	–	–	–	–	–	LOVE LOCKED OUT
–	–	–	–	–	–	==	==	13	15	20	==	–	–	–	–	–	–	–	–	–	–	–	–	–	–	KEEP YOUNG AND BEAUTIFUL
–	–	–	–	–	–	==	==	12	7	6	9	13	20	==	–	–	–	–	–	–	–	–	–	–	–	THROW ANOTHER LOG ON THE FIRE
–	–	–	–	–	–	–	==	16	9	2	2	5	10	==	==	–	–	–	–	–	–	–	–	–	–	THIS LITTLE PIGGIE WENT TO MARKET
–	–	–	–	–	–	–	==	18	12	7	6	7	14	==	–	–	–	–	–	–	–	–	–	–	–	LET'S FALL IN LOVE
–	–	–	–	–	–	–	==	19	16	15	==	==	–	–	–	–	–	–	–	–	–	–	–	–	–	WHEN TOMORROW COMES
–	–	–	–	–	–	–	==	==	20	17	==	==	–	–	–	–	–	–	–	–	–	–	–	–	–	MUSIC MAKES ME
–	–	–	–	–	–	–	==	==	17	14	18	==	–	–	–	–	–	–	–	–	–	–	–	–	–	FLYING DOWN TO RIO
–	–	–	–	–	–	–	–	==	14	10	5	3	4	7	15	==	==	–	–	–	–	–	–	–	–	WAGON WHEELS
–	–	–	–	–	–	–	–	==	13	9	10	11	18	==	–	–	–	–	–	–	–	–	–	–	–	GOIN' TO HEAVEN ON A MULE
–	–	–	–	–	–	–	–	==	==	19	15	19	==	–	–	–	–	–	–	–	–	–	–	–	–	WITHOUT THAT CERTAIN THING
–	–	–	–	–	–	–	–	==	==	18	8	10	7	13	==	==	–	–	–	–	–	–	–	–	–	BOULEVARD OF BROKEN DREAMS
–	–	–	–	–	–	–	–	–	==	==	20	17	==	==	–	–	–	–	–	–	–	–	–	–	–	OVER SOMEBODY ELSE'S SHOULDER
–	–	–	–	–	–	–	–	–	==	==	19	==	==	–	–	–	–	–	–	–	–	–	–	–	–	THERE GOES MY HEART
–	–	–	–	–	–	–	–	–	==	==	11	6	6	4	9	==	==	–	–	–	–	–	–	–	–	YOU OUGHTA BE IN PICTURES
–	–	–	–	–	–	–	–	–	–	==	17	9	3	**1**	**1**	3	8	14	==	–	–	–	–	–	–	A LITTLE DUTCH MILL
–	–	–	–	–	–	–	–	–	–	==	==	14	9	6	11	20	==	–	–	–	–	–	–	–	–	WHY DO I DREAM THOSE DREAMS?
–	–	–	–	–	–	–	–	–	–	–	==	18	8	5	3	7	17	==	–	–	–	–	–	–	–	GOODNIGHT, LOVELY LITTLE LADY
–	–	–	–	–	–	–	–	–	–	–	==	20	11	14	==	==	–	–	–	–	–	–	–	–	–	TRUE
–	–	–	–	–	–	–	–	–	–	–	==	==	15	17	==	==	–	–	–	–	–	–	–	–	–	NEIGHBORS
–	–	–	–	–	–	–	–	–	–	–	–	==	16	12	16	16	==	==	–	–	–	–	–	–	–	NASTY MAN
–	–	–	–	–	–	–	–	–	–	–	–	==	17	11	13	15	==	==	–	–	–	–	–	–	–	SHE REMINDS ME OF YOU
–	–	–	–	–	–	–	–	–	–	–	–	==	13	8	2	4	9	15	==	–	–	–	–	–	–	A THOUSAND GOODNIGHTS
–	–	–	–	–	–	–	–	–	–	–	–	==	==	18	==	==	–	–	–	–	–	–	–	–	–	PLAY TO ME, GYPSY
–	–	–	–	–	–	–	–	–	–	–	–	==	==	15	==	==	–	–	–	–	–	–	–	–	–	ILL WIND
–	–	–	–	–	–	–	–	–	–	–	–	==	==	16	10	11	20	==	–	–	–	–	–	–	–	MAY I?
–	–	–	–	–	–	–	–	–	–	–	–	–	==	10	5	**1**	2	5	6	19	==	–	–	–	–	LOVE THY NEIGHBOR
–	–	–	–	–	–	–	–	–	–	–	–	–	==	==	19	9	6	13	==	==	–	–	–	–	–	RIPTIDE
–	–	–	–	–	–	–	–	–	–	–	–	–	–	20	14	12	16	==	–	–	–	–	–	–	–	THE BEAT OF MY HEART
–	–	–	–	–	–	–	–	–	–	–	–	–	–	19	8	5	4	4	3	5	7	12	13	==	–	COCKTAILS FOR TWO
–	–	–	–	–	–	–	–	–	–	–	–	–	–	==	17	8	14	16	19	==	–	–	–	–	–	RIDIN' AROUND IN THE RAIN
–	–	–	–	–	–	–	–	–	–	–	–	–	–	==	12	6	3	2	4	8	13	19	==	–	–	LITTLE MAN, YOU'VE HAD A BUSY DAY
–	–	–	–	–	–	–	–	–	–	–	–	–	–	==	7	2	**1**	**1**	**1**	2	4	6	10	14	==	I'LL STRING ALONG WITH YOU
–	–	–	–	–	–	–	–	–	–	–	–	–	–	==	==	13	7	7	12	==	–	–	–	–	–	EASY COME, EASY GO
Oc	Oc	Nv	Nv	Dc	Dc	Ja	Ja	Fb	Fb	Ma	Ma	Ap	Ap	My	My	Jn	Jn	Jy	Jy	Ag	Ag	Sp	Sp	Oc	Oc	

							1 9 3 4												1 9 3 5							
Ap	Ap	My	My	Jn	Jn	Jy	Jy	Ag	Ag	Sp	Sp	Oc	Oc	Nv	Nv	Dc	Dc	Ja	Ja	Fb	Fb	Ma	Ma	Ap	Ap	
–	–	==	==	18	12	8	9	10	14	16	17	==	==	–	–	–	–	–	–	–	–	–	–	–	–	THE MAN ON THE FLYING TRAPEZE
–	–	–	20	10	5	3	2	**1**	**1**	5	9	13	==	==	–	–	–	–	–	–	–	–	–	–	–	ALL I DO IS DREAM OF YOU
–	–	–	==	==	19	17	==	–	–	–	–	–	–	–	–	–	–	–	–	–	–	–	–	–	–	I'VE HAD MY MOMENTS
–	–	–	==	==	==	20	==	–	–	–	–	–	–	–	–	–	–	–	–	–	–	–	–	–	–	EMALINE
–	–	–	==	19	11	12	13	==	==	–	–	–	–	–	–	–	–	–	–	–	–	–	–	–	–	I AIN'T LAZY, I'M JUST DREAMIN'
–	–	–	==	==	10	10	11	==	==	–	–	–	–	–	–	–	–	–	–	–	–	–	–	–	–	THE CHAMPAGNE WALTZ
–	–	–	–	==	13	6	5	3	5	11	12	20	==	–	–	–	–	–	–	–	–	–	–	–	–	WITH MY EYES WIDE OPEN, I'M DREAMING
–	–	–	–	==	==	19	==	==	–	–	–	–	–	–	–	–	–	–	–	–	–	–	–	–	–	FRECKLE FACE, YOU'RE BEAUTIFUL
–	–	–	–	==	15	9	7	6	9	10	15	==	–	–	–	–	–	–	–	–	–	–	–	–	–	SLEEPY HEAD
–	–	–	–	==	18	11	8	7	6	7	8	8	19	==	–	–	–	–	–	–	–	–	–	–	–	MOONGLOW
–	–	–	–	–	==	18	10	4	2	2	6	5	10	==	–	–	–	–	–	–	–	–	–	–	–	I NEVER HAD A CHANCE
–	–	–	–	–	==	==	14	18	==	==	–	–	–	–	–	–	–	–	–	–	–	–	–	–	–	I WISH I WERE TWINS
–	–	–	–	–	==	==	20	17	==	==	–	–	–	–	–	–	–	–	–	–	–	–	–	–	–	THANK YOU FOR A LOVELY EVENING
–	–	–	–	–	==	==	16	15	20	==	–	–	–	–	–	–	–	–	–	–	–	–	–	–	–	SPELLBOUND
–	–	–	–	–	==	==	==	14	17	17	==	–	–	–	–	–	–	–	–	–	–	–	–	–	–	DAMES
–	–	–	–	–	–	==	15	11	12	15	14	==	–	–	–	–	–	–	–	–	–	–	–	–	–	DUST ON THE MOON
–	–	–	–	–	–	==	18	13	8	3	3	7	20	==	–	–	–	–	–	–	–	–	–	–	–	FOR ALL WE KNOW
–	–	–	–	–	–	==	17	12	10	14	11	12	9	10	18	==	–	–	–	–	–	–	–	–	–	THE VERY THOUGHT OF YOU
–	–	–	–	–	–	==	==	16	16	20	==	==	–	–	–	–	–	–	–	–	–	–	–	–	–	THE PRIZE WALTZ
–	–	–	–	–	–	==	==	==	18	==	–	–	–	–	–	–	–	–	–	–	–	–	–	–	–	MY HAT'S ON THE SIDE OF MY HEAD
–	–	–	–	–	–	–	==	20	11	4	2	4	6	9	16	==	–	–	–	–	–	–	–	–	–	I ONLY HAVE EYES FOR YOU
–	–	–	–	–	–	–	==	9	3	**1**	**1**	**1**	**1**	3	3	6	11	==	–	–	–	–	–	–	–	LOVE IN BLOOM
–	–	–	–	–	–	–	–	==	15	13	7	6	14	==	–	–	–	–	–	–	–	–	–	–	–	PARDON MY SOUTHERN ACCENT
–	–	–	–	–	–	–	–	==	19	18	18	==	==	==	==	–	–	–	–	–	–	–	–	–	–	TUMBLING TUMBLEWEEDS
–	–	–	–	–	–	–	–	–	==	8	4	3	3	5	9	==	==	–	–	–	–	–	–	–	–	I SAW STARS
–	–	–	–	–	–	–	–	–	==	9	5	2	2	4	5	10	==	==	–	–	–	–	–	–	–	TWO CIGARETTES IN THE DARK
–	–	–	–	–	–	–	–	–	==	==	16	15	==	==	–	–	–	–	–	–	–	–	–	–	–	THEN I'LL BE TIRED OF YOU
–	–	–	–	–	–	–	–	–	==	==	19	19	==	–	–	–	–	–	–	–	–	–	–	–	–	A NEW MOON IS OVER MY SHOULDER
–	–	–	–	–	–	–	–	–	–	==	==	11	7	6	4	7	12	==	–	–	–	–	–	–	–	LOST IN A FOG
–	–	–	–	–	–	–	–	–	–	–	20	9	4	**1**	**1**	**1**	4	10	==	==	–	–	–	–	–	THE CONTINENTAL
–	–	–	–	–	–	–	–	–	–	–	==	18	13	18	==	–	–	–	–	–	–	–	–	–	–	IT'S ALL FORGOTTEN NOW
–	–	–	–	–	–	–	–	–	–	–	==	10	5	2	2	4	5	5	12	==	–	–	–	–	–	STARS FELL ON ALABAMA
–	–	–	–	–	–	–	–	–	–	–	==	17	12	14	==	==	–	–	–	–	–	–	–	–	–	TALKIN' TO MYSELF
–	–	–	–	–	–	–	–	–	–	–	==	16	8	7	12	18	==	–	–	–	–	–	–	–	–	ONE NIGHT OF LOVE
–	–	–	–	–	–	–	–	–	–	–	–	==	16	13	==	==	–	–	–	–	–	–	–	–	–	A NEEDLE IN A HAYSTACK
–	–	–	–	–	–	–	–	–	–	–	–	==	17	16	==	==	–	–	–	–	–	–	–	–	–	BUGLE CALL RAG
–	–	–	–	–	–	–	–	–	–	–	–	==	11	8	11	17	==	–	–	–	–	–	–	–	–	THE DRUNKARD SONG (THERE IS A TAVERN IN THE TOWN)
–	–	–	–	–	–	–	–	–	–	–	–	==	18	12	8	9	13	==	==	–	–	–	–	–	–	OUT IN THE COLD AGAIN
–	–	–	–	–	–	–	–	–	–	–	–	==	15	11	7	5	8	12	==	==	–	–	–	–	–	RAIN
–	–	–	–	–	–	–	–	–	–	–	–	==	==	20	==	==	–	–	–	–	–	–	–	–	–	BLUE SKY AVENUE
–	–	–	–	–	–	–	–	–	–	–	–	==	==	15	15	11	16	==	–	–	–	–	–	–	–	BE STILL, MY HEART
–	–	–	–	–	–	–	–	–	–	–	–	==	==	17	14	16	==	–	–	–	–	–	–	–	–	SWEETIE PIE
–	–	–	–	–	–	–	–	–	–	–	–	–	==	19	6	2	**1**	3	5	10	19	==	–	–	–	STAY AS SWEET AS YOU ARE
–	–	–	–	–	–	–	–	–	–	–	–	–	==	==	17	==	==	–	–	–	–	–	–	–	–	DON'T LET IT BOTHER YOU
–	–	–	–	–	–	–	–	–	–	–	–	–	==	==	13	15	==	==	–	–	–	–	–	–	–	YOU'RE A BUILDER UPPER
–	–	–	–	–	–	–	–	–	–	–	–	–	==	==	20	==	==	–	–	–	–	–	–	–	–	HA–CHA–CHA
–	–	–	–	–	–	–	–	–	–	–	–	–	–	==	10	3	2	**1**	2	4	16	==	–	–	–	THE OBJECT OF MY AFFECTION
–	–	–	–	–	–	–	–	–	–	–	–	–	–	==	19	12	19	==	–	–	–	–	–	–	–	POP GOES YOUR HEART
–	–	–	–	–	–	–	–	–	–	–	–	–	–	==	==	20	==	==	–	–	–	–	–	–	–	P. S. I LOVE YOU
–	–	–	–	–	–	–	–	–	–	–	–	–	–	==	==	14	9	8	13	==	==	–	–	–	–	HANDS ACROSS THE TABLE
–	–	–	–	–	–	–	–	–	–	–	–	–	–	–	==	8	3	7	==	–	–	–	–	–	–	SANTA CLAUS IS COMIN' TO TOWN
–	–	–	–	–	–	–	–	–	–	–	–	–	–	–	==	==	18	==	==	==	–	–	–	–	–	I'LL FOLLOW MY SECRET HEART
–	–	–	–	–	–	–	–	–	–	–	–	–	–	–	–	==	15	17	==	==	–	–	–	–	–	MR. AND MRS. IS THE NAME
–	–	–	–	–	–	–	–	–	–	–	–	–	–	–	==	19	7	4	4	15	==	–	–	–	–	WINTER WONDERLAND (1935)
–	–	–	–	–	–	–	–	–	–	–	–	–	–	–	–	==	10	6	7	11	13	==	–	–	–	YOU'RE THE TOP (1935)
–	–	–	–	–	–	–	–	–	–	–	–	–	–	–	==	==	14	9	9	18	==	–	–	–	–	FLIRTATION WALK (1935)
–	–	–	–	–	–	–	–	–	–	–	–	–	–	–	==	13	6	2	**1**	**1**	5	15	==	–	–	JUNE IN JANUARY (1935)
–	–	–	–	–	–	–	–	–	–	–	–	–	–	–	–	==	17	18	==	==	20	18	18	==	==	BLUE DANUBE WALTZ (1935)
–	–	–	–	–	–	–	–	–	–	–	–	–	–	–	–	==	20	11	15	==	–	–	–	–	–	I'VE GOT AN INVITATION TO A DANCE (1935)
Ap	Ap	My	My	Jn	Jn	Jy	Jy	Ag	Ag	Sp	Sp	Oc	Oc	Nv	Nv	Dc	Dc	Ja	Ja	Fb	Fb	Ma	Ma	Ap	Ap	

1934 Oc	Oc	Nv	Nv	Dc	Dc	1935 Ja	Ja	Fb	Fb	Ma	Ma	Ap	Ap	My	My	Jn	Jn	Jy	Jy	Ag	Ag	Sp	Sp	Oc	Oc	
10	5	2	2	4	5	5	12	==	–	–	–	–	–	–	–	–	–	–	–	–	–	–	–	–	–	STARS FELL ON ALABAMA (1934)
9	4	**1**	**1**	**1**	4	10	==	==	–	–	–	–	–	–	–	–	–	–	–	–	–	–	–	–	–	THE CONTINENTAL (1934)
==	15	11	7	5	8	12	==	==	–	–	–	–	–	–	–	–	–	–	–	–	–	–	–	–	–	RAIN (1934)
–	==	19	6	2	**1**	3	5	10	19	==	–	–	–	–	–	–	–	–	–	–	–	–	–	–	–	STAY AS SWEET AS YOU ARE (1934)
–	–	==	10	3	2	**1**	2	4	16	==	–	–	–	–	–	–	–	–	–	–	–	–	–	–	–	THE OBJECT OF MY AFFECTION (1934)
–	–	==	==	14	9	8	13	==	==	–	–	–	–	–	–	–	–	–	–	–	–	–	–	–	–	HANDS ACROSS THE TABLE (1934)
–	–	–	==	8	3	7	==	–	–	–	–	–	–	–	–	–	–	–	–	–	–	–	–	–	–	SANTA CLAUS IS COMIN' TO TOWN (1934)
–	–	–	–	==	15	17	==	==	–	–	–	–	–	–	–	–	–	–	–	–	–	–	–	–	–	MR. AND MRS. IS THE NAME (1934)
–	–	–	==	19	7	4	4	15	==	–	–	–	–	–	–	–	–	–	–	–	–	–	–	–	–	WINTER WONDERLAND
–	–	–	==	13	6	2	**1**	**1**	5	15	==	–	–	–	–	–	–	–	–	–	–	–	–	–	–	JUNE IN JANUARY
–	–	–	==	==	14	9	9	18	==	–	–	–	–	–	–	–	–	–	–	–	–	–	–	–	–	FLIRTATION WALK
–	–	–	–	==	10	6	7	11	13	==	–	–	–	–	–	–	–	–	–	–	–	–	–	–	–	YOU'RE THE TOP
–	–	–	–	==	17	18	==	==	20	18	18	==	==	–	–	–	–	–	–	–	–	–	–	–	–	BLUE DANUBE WALTZ
–	–	–	–	==	20	11	15	==	–	–	–	–	–	–	–	–	–	–	–	–	–	–	–	–	–	I'VE GOT AN INVITATION TO A DANCE
–	–	–	–	==	==	==	17	==	==	–	–	–	–	–	–	–	–	–	–	–	–	–	–	–	–	I GET A KICK OUT OF YOU
–	–	–	–	==	==	==	==	19	9	8	15	12	13	16	==	==	–	–	–	–	–	–	–	–	–	SOLITUDE
–	–	–	–	–	==	16	19	16	==	==	–	–	–	–	–	–	–	–	–	–	–	–	–	–	–	IT'S DARK ON OBSERVATORY HILL
–	–	–	–	–	==	14	3	2	2	2	5	16	==	–	–	–	–	–	–	–	–	–	–	–	–	BLUE MOON
–	–	–	–	–	==	19	18	12	12	==	==	–	–	–	–	–	–	–	–	–	–	–	–	–	–	LOVE IS JUST AROUND THE CORNER
–	–	–	–	–	==	20	10	5	6	12	==	==	–	–	–	–	–	–	–	–	–	–	–	–	–	BELIEVE IT, BELOVED
–	–	–	–	–	==	15	8	7	14	==	==	–	–	–	–	–	–	–	–	–	–	–	–	–	–	WITH EVERY BREATH I TAKE
–	–	–	–	–	==	13	6	3	4	5	8	11	==	==	–	–	–	–	–	–	–	–	–	–	–	ON THE GOOD SHIP LOLLIPOP
–	–	–	–	–	==	==	14	13	==	==	–	–	–	–	–	–	–	–	–	–	–	–	–	–	–	ANYTHING GOES
–	–	–	–	–	==	==	11	8	10	20	==	–	–	–	–	–	–	–	–	–	–	–	–	–	–	DANCING WITH MY SHADOW
–	–	–	–	–	–	==	20	9	3	3	12	19	==	–	–	–	–	–	–	–	–	–	–	–	–	I BELIEVE IN MIRACLES
–	–	–	–	–	–	==	16	6	**1**	**1**	**1**	**1**	4	4	6	11	==	==	–	–	–	–	–	–	–	ISLE OF CAPRI
–	–	–	–	–	–	==	==	14	8	7	20	==	–	–	–	–	–	–	–	–	–	–	–	–	–	TINY LITTLE FINGERPRINTS
–	–	–	–	–	–	–	==	17	15	11	14	==	==	–	–	–	–	–	–	–	–	–	–	–	–	OLE FAITHFUL
–	–	–	–	–	–	–	==	==	17	9	3	3	2	2	**1**	3	6	9	8	14	==	==	–	–	–	WHEN I GROW TOO OLD TO DREAM
–	–	–	–	–	–	–	–	20	7	4	9	20	==	–	–	–	–	–	–	–	–	–	–	–	–	FARE THEE WELL, ANNABELLE
–	–	–	–	–	–	–	–	==	11	6	7	6	11	14	==	–	–	–	–	–	–	–	–	–	–	CLOUDS
–	–	–	–	–	–	–	–	==	18	14	6	7	19	==	–	–	–	–	–	–	–	–	–	–	–	A LITTLE WHITE GARDENIA
–	–	–	–	–	–	–	–	==	==	16	==	==	–	–	–	–	–	–	–	–	–	–	–	–	–	SWEET MUSIC
–	–	–	–	–	–	–	–	–	==	17	10	9	17	==	–	–	–	–	–	–	–	–	–	–	–	IF THE MOON TURNS GREEN
–	–	–	–	–	–	–	–	–	==	13	4	4	6	13	16	==	–	–	–	–	–	–	–	–	–	EV'RY DAY
–	–	–	–	–	–	–	–	–	==	10	2	2	**1**	**1**	2	8	==	==	–	–	–	–	–	–	–	LULLABY OF BROADWAY
–	–	–	–	–	–	–	–	–	–	19	11	8	9	==	==	–	–	–	–	–	–	–	–	–	–	(LOOKIE LOOKIE LOOKIE) HERE COMES COOKIE
–	–	–	–	–	–	–	–	–	–	==	19	13	8	8	==	==	–	–	–	–	–	–	–	–	–	I WAS LUCKY
–	–	–	–	–	–	–	–	–	–	==	13	5	5	6	7	==	==	–	–	–	–	–	–	–	–	SOON
–	–	–	–	–	–	–	–	–	–	==	16	10	3	3	5	14	==	–	–	–	–	–	–	–	–	LOVELY TO LOOK AT
–	–	–	–	–	–	–	–	–	–	==	17	14	10	11	18	==	==	–	–	–	–	–	–	–	–	IT'S EASY TO REMEMBER
–	–	–	–	–	–	–	–	–	–	==	==	18	15	9	13	==	==	–	–	–	–	–	–	–	–	IT'S AN OLD SOUTHERN CUSTOM
–	–	–	–	–	–	–	–	–	–	–	==	==	18	==	==	–	–	–	–	–	–	–	–	–	–	WHOSE HONEY ARE YOU?
–	–	–	–	–	–	–	–	–	–	–	==	17	12	5	4	2	4	8	10	19	==	==	–	–	–	WHAT'S THE REASON?
–	–	–	–	–	–	–	–	–	–	–	==	15	7	7	8	9	16	==	–	–	–	–	–	–	–	I WON'T DANCE
–	–	–	–	–	–	–	–	–	–	–	==	==	16	18	==	==	==	–	–	–	–	–	–	–	–	DOWN BY THE RIVER
–	–	–	–	–	–	–	–	–	–	–	–	==	14	10	12	10	13	==	–	–	–	–	–	–	–	EVERYTHING'S BEEN DONE BEFORE
–	–	–	–	–	–	–	–	–	–	–	–	==	20	17	19	20	12	17	==	–	–	–	–	–	–	FLOWERS FOR MADAME
–	–	–	–	–	–	–	–	–	–	–	–	==	==	12	3	**1**	**1**	4	5	9	19	==	–	–	–	ABOUT A QUARTER TO NINE
–	–	–	–	–	–	–	–	–	–	–	–	==	==	==	17	13	==	==	–	–	–	–	–	–	–	YOU'RE A HEAVENLY THING
–	–	–	–	–	–	–	–	–	–	–	–	–	==	20	15	19	14	==	==	–	–	–	–	–	–	LOVE AND A DIME
–	–	–	–	–	–	–	–	–	–	–	–	–	==	19	10	6	9	11	==	==	–	–	–	–	–	SHE'S A LATIN FROM MANHATTAN
–	–	–	–	–	–	–	–	–	–	–	–	–	==	15	9	7	11	10	9	17	==	–	–	–	–	TELL ME THAT YOU LOVE ME
–	–	–	–	–	–	–	–	–	–	–	–	–	==	==	20	==	==	–	–	–	–	–	–	–	–	THE DIXIELAND BAND
–	–	–	–	–	–	–	–	–	–	–	–	–	==	==	14	5	3	3	7	13	==	–	–	–	–	LIFE IS A SONG
–	–	–	–	–	–	–	–	–	–	–	–	–	==	==	==	==	18	14	18	20	17	==	==	–	–	RHYTHM IS OUR BUSINESS
–	–	–	–	–	–	–	–	–	–	–	–	–	==	==	==	==	–	–	==	==	16	20	==	–	–	SUGAR BLUES
–	–	–	–	–	–	–	–	–	–	–	–	–	–	==	11	4	2	**1**	**1**	**1**	**1**	2	9	17	==	IN A LITTLE GYPSY TEAROOM
–	–	–	–	–	–	–	–	–	–	–	–	–	–	==	==	12	15	==	==	–	–	–	–	–	–	WAY BACK HOME
Oc	Oc	Nv	Nv	Dc	Dc	Ja	Ja	Fb	Fb	Ma	Ma	Ap	Ap	My	My	Jn	Jn	Jy	Jy	Ag	Ag	Sp	Sp	Oc	Oc	

							1935													1936						
Ap	Ap	My	My	Jn	Jn	Jy	Jy	Ag	Ag	Sp	Sp	Oc	Oc	Nv	Nv	Dc	Dc	Ja	Ja	Fb	Fb	Ma	Ma	Ap	Ap	
–	–	–	==	16	7	5	3	5	8	11	==	==	–	–	–	–	–	–	–	–	–	–	–	–	–	IN THE MIDDLE OF A KISS
–	–	–	==	17	8	7	6	8	10	14	==	–	–	–	–	–	–	–	–	–	–	–	–	–	–	THE LADY IN RED
–	–	–	==	15	10	6	4	3	3	10	==	–	–	–	–	–	–	–	–	–	–	–	–	–	–	I'LL NEVER SAY "NEVER AGAIN" AGAIN
–	–	–	==	18	5	2	2	2	9	18	==	–	–	–	–	–	–	–	–	–	–	–	–	–	–	CHASING SHADOWS
–	–	–	==	==	==	15	==	==	–	–	–	–	–	–	–	–	–	–	–	–	–	–	–	–	–	I'M FALLING IN LOVE WITH SOMEONE
–	–	–	==	==	==	19	==	==	–	–	–	–	–	–	–	–	–	–	–	–	–	–	–	–	–	AH! SWEET MYSTERY OF LIFE
–	–	–	–	==	20	18	==	==	–	–	–	–	–	–	–	–	–	–	–	–	–	–	–	–	–	I'M LIVING IN A GREAT BIG WAY
–	–	–	–	==	17	12	==	==	–	–	–	–	–	–	–	–	–	–	–	–	–	–	–	–	–	THRILLED
–	–	–	–	==	19	13	==	==	–	–	–	–	–	–	–	–	–	–	–	–	–	–	–	–	–	FOOTLOOSE AND FANCY FREE
–	–	–	–	==	==	16	12	16	==	==	–	–	–	–	–	–	–	–	–	–	–	–	–	–	–	LET'S SWING IT
–	–	–	–	–	==	20	15	7	6	12	==	==	–	–	–	–	–	–	–	–	–	–	–	–	–	PARIS IN THE SPRING
–	–	–	–	–	==	==	19	==	13	==	==	–	–	–	–	–	–	–	–	–	–	–	–	–	–	EVERY LITTLE MOMENT
–	–	–	–	–	==	==	20	==	==	–	–	–	–	–	–	–	–	–	–	–	–	–	–	–	–	STAR GAZING
–	–	–	–	–	==	==	11	4	7	8	19	==	–	–	–	–	–	–	–	–	–	–	–	–	–	AND THEN SOME
–	–	–	–	–	==	==	13	6	2	**1**	4	9	==	==	–	–	–	–	–	–	–	–	–	–	–	EAST OF THE SUN
–	–	–	–	–	==	==	16	10	11	17	==	==	==	–	–	–	–	–	–	–	–	–	–	–	–	LULU'S BACK IN TOWN
–	–	–	–	–	–	==	17	15	==	==	==	==	–	–	–	–	–	–	–	–	–	–	–	–	–	WHAT A LITTLE MOONLIGHT CAN DO
–	–	–	–	–	–	==	14	11	4	9	17	==	–	–	–	–	–	–	–	–	–	–	–	–	–	LOVE ME FOREVER
–	–	–	–	–	–	–	==	12	5	3	5	10	==	==	–	–	–	–	–	–	–	–	–	–	–	YOU'RE ALL I NEED
–	–	–	–	–	–	–	==	18	15	==	==	–	–	–	–	–	–	–	–	–	–	–	–	–	–	SWEET AND SLOW
–	–	–	–	–	–	–	==	==	==	19	14	==	==	–	–	–	–	–	–	–	–	–	–	–	–	I COULDN'T BELIEVE MY EYES
–	–	–	–	–	–	–	–	==	12	4	2	2	2	5	15	15	==	–	–	–	–	–	–	–	–	I'M IN THE MOOD FOR LOVE
–	–	–	–	–	–	–	–	==	14	6	8	8	15	15	==	–	–	–	–	–	–	–	–	–	–	THE ROSE IN HER HAIR
–	–	–	–	–	–	–	–	==	20	7	3	4	10	20	==	–	–	–	–	–	–	–	–	–	–	ACCENT ON YOUTH
–	–	–	–	–	–	–	–	==	18	5	**1**	**1**	**1**	**1**	4	13	==	==	–	–	–	–	–	–	–	CHEEK TO CHEEK
–	–	–	–	–	–	–	–	==	==	13	15	==	==	–	–	–	–	–	–	–	–	–	–	–	–	ANIMAL CRACKERS IN MY SOUP
–	–	–	–	–	–	–	–	–	==	15	12	20	==	==	–	–	–	–	–	–	–	–	–	–	–	PAGE MISS GLORY
–	–	–	–	–	–	–	–	–	==	==	16	19	13	16	==	–	–	–	–	–	–	–	–	–	–	RHYTHM AND ROMANCE
–	–	–	–	–	–	–	–	–	==	16	6	6	6	11	19	==	==	–	–	–	–	–	–	–	–	TOP HAT, WHITE TIE, AND TAILS
–	–	–	–	–	–	–	–	–	==	==	10	5	4	6	17	==	–	–	–	–	–	–	–	–	–	ISN'T THIS A LOVELY DAY (TO BE CAUGHT IN THE RAIN)?
–	–	–	–	–	–	–	–	–	==	==	11	11	9	13	==	–	–	–	–	–	–	–	–	–	–	I WISHED ON THE MOON
–	–	–	–	–	–	–	–	–	==	==	7	3	3	8	11	==	–	–	–	–	–	–	–	–	–	I'M ON A SEE SAW
–	–	–	–	–	–	–	–	–	==	==	==	==	19	==	–	–	–	–	–	–	–	–	–	–	–	THE PICCOLINO
–	–	–	–	–	–	–	–	–	–	==	13	7	8	12	==	==	–	–	–	–	–	–	–	–	–	WITHOUT A WORD OF WARNING
–	–	–	–	–	–	–	–	–	–	==	18	14	20	18	20	==	–	–	–	–	–	–	–	–	–	I WISH I WERE ALADDIN
–	–	–	–	–	–	–	–	–	–	==	20	13	12	9	8	14	17	==	==	–	–	–	–	–	–	TRUCKIN'
–	–	–	–	–	–	–	–	–	–	==	==	18	16	==	–	–	–	–	–	–	–	–	–	–	–	EVERY NOW AND THEN
–	–	–	–	–	–	–	–	–	–	–	==	16	5	2	3	5	16	==	–	–	–	–	–	–	–	YOU ARE MY LUCKY STAR
–	–	–	–	–	–	–	–	–	–	–	==	15	14	10	6	9	13	15	==	==	–	–	–	–	–	ROLL ALONG, PRAIRIE MOON
–	–	–	–	–	–	–	–	–	–	–	==	12	7	7	5	11	==	==	–	–	–	–	–	–	–	I'VE GOT A FEELIN' YOU'RE FOOLIN'
–	–	–	–	–	–	–	–	–	–	–	==	==	18	==	==	–	–	–	–	–	–	–	–	–	–	NO STRINGS (I'M FANCY FREE)
–	–	–	–	–	–	–	–	–	–	–	==	==	11	3	2	2	3	2	6	12	==	==	–	–	–	ON TREASURE ISLAND
–	–	–	–	–	–	–	–	–	–	–	–	==	17	4	**1**	**1**	**1**	4	3	9	17	==	–	–	–	RED SAILS IN THE SUNSET
–	–	–	–	–	–	–	–	–	–	–	–	==	==	17	==	==	–	–	–	–	–	–	–	–	–	WHEN THE LEAVES BID THE TREES GOODBYE
–	–	–	–	–	–	–	–	–	–	–	–	==	==	==	18	==	==	–	–	–	–	–	–	–	–	I'D RATHER LISTEN TO YOUR EYES
–	–	–	–	–	–	–	–	–	–	–	–	–	==	14	7	6	5	14	==	==	–	–	–	–	–	TWENTY–FOUR HOURS A DAY
–	–	–	–	–	–	–	–	–	–	–	–	–	==	19	14	8	9	12	==	==	–	–	–	–	–	DON'T GIVE UP THE SHIP
–	–	–	–	–	–	–	–	–	–	–	–	–	==	==	16	16	15	==	==	–	–	–	–	–	–	I FOUND A DREAM
–	–	–	–	–	–	–	–	–	–	–	–	–	–	==	12	7	6	6	16	==	–	–	–	–	–	THANKS A MILLION
–	–	–	–	–	–	–	–	–	–	–	–	–	–	==	9	3	2	**1**	2	10	==	–	–	–	–	A LITTLE BIT INDEPENDENT
–	–	–	–	–	–	–	–	–	–	–	–	–	–	==	13	10	8	11	==	==	–	–	–	–	–	I'M SITTIN' HIGH ON A HILLTOP
–	–	–	–	–	–	–	–	–	–	–	–	–	–	==	10	4	4	5	8	15	==	–	–	–	–	TAKE ME BACK TO MY BOOTS AND SADDLE
–	–	–	–	–	–	–	–	–	–	–	–	–	–	==	==	19	20	==	==	–	–	–	–	–	–	WHY SHOULDN'T I?
–	–	–	–	–	–	–	–	–	–	–	–	–	–	==	==	12	7	10	19	==	–	–	–	–	–	NO OTHER ONE
–	–	–	–	–	–	–	–	–	–	–	–	–	–	–	==	17	14	13	==	==	–	–	–	–	–	WHERE AM I?
–	–	–	–	–	–	–	–	–	–	–	–	–	–	–	==	18	11	==	–	–	–	–	–	–	–	SANTA CLAUS IS COMIN' TO TOWN
–	–	–	–	–	–	–	–	–	–	–	–	–	–	–	–	==	19	==	–	–	–	–	–	–	–	SILENT NIGHT
–	–	–	–	–	–	–	–	–	–	–	–	–	–	–	==	20	10	7	13	19	==	–	–	–	–	EENY MEENY MINEY MO (1936)
–	–	–	–	–	–	–	–	–	–	–	–	–	–	–	–	==	18	16	9	8	15	==	==	–	–	WITH ALL MY HEART (1936)
–	–	–	–	–	–	–	–	–	–	–	–	–	–	–	–	==	12	3	**1**	**1**	9	16	==	–	–	THE MUSIC GOES 'ROUND AND AROUND (1936)
Ap	Ap	My	My	Jn	Jn	Jy	Jy	Ag	Ag	Sp	Sp	Oc	Oc	Nv	Nv	Dc	Dc	Ja	Ja	Fb	Fb	Ma	Ma	Ap	Ap	

	1935														1936											
Oc	Oc	Nv	Nv	Dc	Dc	Ja	Ja	Fb	Fb	Ma	Ma	Ap	Ap	My	My	Jn	Jn	Jy	Jy	Ag	Ag	Sp	Sp	Oc	Oc	
==	11	3	2	2	3	2	6	12	==	==	–	–	–	–	–	–	–	–	–	–	–	–	–	–	–	ON TREASURE ISLAND (1935)
15	14	10	6	9	13	15	==	==	–	–	–	–	–	–	–	–	–	–	–	–	–	–	–	–	–	ROLL ALONG, PRAIRIE MOON (1935)
–	==	14	7	6	5	14	==	==	–	–	–	–	–	–	–	–	–	–	–	–	–	–	–	–	–	TWENTY-FOUR HOURS A DAY (1935)
==	17	4	1	1	1	4	3	9	17	==	–	–	–	–	–	–	–	–	–	–	–	–	–	–	–	RED SAILS IN THE SUNSET (1935)
–	==	19	14	8	9	12	==	==	–	–	–	–	–	–	–	–	–	–	–	–	–	–	–	–	–	DON'T GIVE UP THE SHIP (1935)
–	–	==	==	12	7	10	19	==	–	–	–	–	–	–	–	–	–	–	–	–	–	–	–	–	–	NO OTHER ONE (1935)
–	–	==	12	7	6	6	16	==	–	–	–	–	–	–	–	–	–	–	–	–	–	–	–	–	–	THANKS A MILLION (1935)
–	–	==	9	3	2	1	2	10	==	–	–	–	–	–	–	–	–	–	–	–	–	–	–	–	–	A LITTLE BIT INDEPENDENT (1935)
–	–	==	13	10	8	11	==	==	–	–	–	–	–	–	–	–	–	–	–	–	–	–	–	–	–	I'M SITTIN' HIGH ON A HILLTOP (1935)
–	–	==	10	4	4	5	8	15	==	–	–	–	–	–	–	–	–	–	–	–	–	–	–	–	–	TAKE ME BACK TO MY BOOTS AND SADDLE (1935)
–	–	–	==	17	14	13	==	==	–	–	–	–	–	–	–	–	–	–	–	–	–	–	–	–	–	WHERE AM I? (1935)
–	–	–	==	20	10	7	13	19	==	–	–	–	–	–	–	–	–	–	–	–	–	–	–	–	–	EENY MEENY MINEY MO
–	–	–	–	==	18	16	9	8	15	==	==	–	–	–	–	–	–	–	–	–	–	–	–	–	–	WITH ALL MY HEART
–	–	–	–	==	12	3	1	1	9	16	==	–	–	–	–	–	–	–	–	–	–	–	–	–	–	THE MUSIC GOES 'ROUND AND AROUND
–	–	–	–	==	==	19	14	20	==	==	–	–	–	–	–	–	–	–	–	–	–	–	–	–	–	ONE NIGHT IN MONTE CARLO
–	–	–	–	–	==	9	5	2	2	6	17	==	–	–	–	–	–	–	–	–	–	–	–	–	–	MOON OVER MIAMI
–	–	–	–	–	==	17	7	7	18	==	–	–	–	–	–	–	–	–	–	–	–	–	–	–	–	THE BROKEN RECORD
–	–	–	–	–	==	8	4	3	1	1	5	11	==	==	–	–	–	–	–	–	–	–	–	–	–	ALONE
–	–	–	–	–	==	18	10	4	4	3	6	7	7	14	==	–	–	–	–	–	–	–	–	–	–	A BEAUTIFUL LADY IN BLUE
–	–	–	–	–	==	20	15	11	13	19	==	–	–	–	–	–	–	–	–	–	–	–	–	–	–	DINNER FOR ONE, PLEASE, JAMES
–	–	–	–	–	–	==	20	==	==	–	–	–	–	–	–	–	–	–	–	–	–	–	–	–	–	IF I SHOULD LOSE YOU
–	–	–	–	–	–	==	12	6	7	17	==	–	–	–	–	–	–	–	–	–	–	–	–	–	–	I FEEL LIKE A FEATHER IN THE BREEZE
–	–	–	–	–	–	==	17	13	8	13	==	==	–	–	–	–	–	–	–	–	–	–	–	–	–	RHYTHM IN MY NURSERY RHYMES
–	–	–	–	–	–	==	11	5	3	2	2	8	10	==	==	–	–	–	–	–	–	–	–	–	–	LIGHTS OUT
–	–	–	–	–	–	==	18	14	6	9	18	==	–	–	–	–	–	–	–	–	–	–	–	–	–	I'M SHOOTING HIGH
–	–	–	–	–	–	–	==	18	11	8	11	==	==	–	–	–	–	–	–	–	–	–	–	–	–	PLEASE BELIEVE ME
–	–	–	–	–	–	–	==	16	5	4	9	12	==	==	–	–	–	–	–	–	–	–	–	–	–	I'M GONNA SIT RIGHT DOWN AND WRITE MYSELF A LETTER
–	–	–	–	–	–	–	==	==	14	11	19	==	–	–	–	–	–	–	–	–	–	–	–	–	–	CLING TO ME
–	–	–	–	–	–	–	==	17	10	18	==	–	–	–	–	–	–	–	–	–	–	–	–	–	–	I'M BUILDING UP TO AN AWFUL LETDOWN
–	–	–	–	–	–	–	==	==	20	10	13	==	–	–	–	–	–	–	–	–	–	–	–	–	–	ALONE AT A TABLE FOR TWO
–	–	–	–	–	–	–	==	==	12	5	4	4	4	9	17	==	==	–	–	–	–	–	–	–	–	IT'S BEEN SO LONG
–	–	–	–	–	–	–	==	==	==	20	==	==	==	–	–	–	–	–	–	–	–	–	–	–	–	RIDE, RED, RIDE
–	–	–	–	–	–	–	–	==	16	7	1	1	1	3	9	15	==	–	–	–	–	–	–	–	–	GOODY-GOODY
–	–	–	–	–	–	–	–	==	19	15	8	10	19	==	==	–	–	–	–	–	–	–	–	–	–	LET'S FACE THE MUSIC AND DANCE
–	–	–	–	–	–	–	–	==	==	14	7	6	18	==	–	–	–	–	–	–	–	–	–	–	–	WAH-HOO!
–	–	–	–	–	–	–	–	–	==	20	==	==	–	–	–	–	–	–	–	–	–	–	–	–	–	SPREADIN' RHYTHM AROUND
–	–	–	–	–	–	–	–	–	==	12	3	2	3	10	19	==	–	–	–	–	–	–	–	–	–	I'M PUTTING ALL MY EGGS IN ONE BASKET
–	–	–	–	–	–	–	–	–	==	==	16	==	==	–	–	–	–	–	–	–	–	–	–	–	–	A LITTLE RENDEZVOUS IN HONOLULU
–	–	–	–	–	–	–	–	–	==	==	15	13	==	==	–	–	–	–	–	–	–	–	–	–	–	WEST WIND
–	–	–	–	–	–	–	–	–	==	==	12	9	16	==	==	–	–	–	–	–	–	–	–	–	–	WHAT'S THE NAME OF THAT SONG?
–	–	–	–	–	–	–	–	–	–	==	10	5	6	16	==	–	–	–	–	–	–	–	–	–	–	LET YOURSELF GO
–	–	–	–	–	–	–	–	–	–	==	14	3	2	1	2	6	14	==	–	–	–	–	–	–	–	LOST
–	–	–	–	–	–	–	–	–	–	==	==	14	==	==	–	–	–	–	–	–	–	–	–	–	–	SING AN OLD FASHIONED SONG
–	–	–	–	–	–	–	–	–	–	==	==	==	20	20	==	==	–	–	–	–	–	–	–	–	–	LOVELY LADY
–	–	–	–	–	–	–	–	–	–	–	==	19	8	4	7	13	18	==	–	–	–	–	–	–	–	YOU STARTED ME DREAMING
–	–	–	–	–	–	–	–	–	–	–	==	17	5	2	1	2	8	12	19	==	–	–	–	–	–	A MELODY FROM THE SKY
–	–	–	–	–	–	–	–	–	–	–	==	16	17	15	20	==	–	–	–	–	–	–	–	–	–	THERE IS NO GREATER LOVE
–	–	–	–	–	–	–	–	–	–	–	==	18	12	11	15	14	20	16	==	–	–	–	–	–	–	CHRISTOPHER COLUMBUS
–	–	–	–	–	–	–	–	–	–	–	==	15	11	19	==	–	–	–	–	–	–	–	–	–	–	EVERY MINUTE OF THE HOUR
–	–	–	–	–	–	–	–	–	–	–	==	20	9	6	11	11	==	==	–	–	–	–	–	–	–	THE TOUCH OF YOUR LIPS
–	–	–	–	–	–	–	–	–	–	–	–	==	13	12	14	16	==	==	–	–	–	–	–	–	–	LOVE IS LIKE A CIGARETTE
–	–	–	–	–	–	–	–	–	–	–	–	==	14	5	4	5	9	14	==	–	–	–	–	–	–	YOU
–	–	–	–	–	–	–	–	–	–	–	–	==	15	7	8	12	15	==	–	–	–	–	–	–	–	TORMENTED
–	–	–	–	–	–	–	–	–	–	–	–	==	==	17	==	==	–	–	–	–	–	–	–	–	–	YOURS TRULY IS TRULY YOURS
–	–	–	–	–	–	–	–	–	–	–	–	==	==	13	6	4	5	13	==	==	–	–	–	–	–	ALL MY LIFE
–	–	–	–	–	–	–	–	–	–	–	–	–	==	8	3	1	1	1	6	12	==	==	–	–	–	IS IT TRUE WHAT THEY SAY ABOUT DIXIE?
–	–	–	–	–	–	–	–	–	–	–	–	–	==	==	13	9	4	3	2	2	6	11	==	==	–	IT'S A SIN TO TELL A LIE
–	–	–	–	–	–	–	–	–	–	–	–	–	==	==	12	8	6	6	7	6	14	==	–	–	–	WOULD YOU?
–	–	–	–	–	–	–	–	–	–	–	–	–	==	==	10	7	7	8	15	==	–	–	–	–	–	SHE SHALL HAVE MUSIC
–	–	–	–	–	–	–	–	–	–	–	–	–	==	==	==	19	==	18	==	==	–	–	–	–	–	TWILIGHT ON THE TRAIL
Oc	Oc	Nv	Nv	Dc	Dc	Ja	Ja	Fb	Fb	Ma	Ma	Ap	Ap	My	My	Jn	Jn	Jy	Jy	Ag	Ag	Sp	Sp	Oc	Oc	

							1936														1937					
Ap	Ap	My	My	Jn	Jn	Jy	Jy	Ag	Ag	Sp	Sp	Oc	Oc	Nv	Nv	Dc	Dc	Ja	Ja	Fb	Fb	Ma	Ma	Ap	Ap	
–	==	18	5	3	2	4	10	15	==	–	–	–	–	–	–	–	–	–	–	–	–	–	–	–	–	ROBINS AND ROSES
–	–	==	16	18	==	–	–	–	–	–	–	–	–	–	–	–	–	–	–	–	–	–	–	–	–	US ON A BUS
–	–	==	18	10	3	2	3	5	11	==	==	–	–	–	–	–	–	–	–	–	–	–	–	–	–	THE GLORY OF LOVE
–	–	–	==	17	10	5	8	13	==	==	–	–	–	–	–	–	–	–	–	–	–	–	–	–	–	THERE'S A SMALL HOTEL
–	–	–	==	20	12	11	9	7	19	==	–	–	–	–	–	–	–	–	–	–	–	–	–	–	–	YOU CAN'T PULL THE WOOL OVER MY EYES
–	–	–	–	==	16	10	5	3	4	9	20	==	–	–	–	–	–	–	–	–	–	–	–	–	–	ON THE BEACH AT BALI BALI
–	–	–	–	==	17	20	14	16	==	==	–	–	–	–	–	–	–	–	–	–	–	–	–	–	–	LET'S SING AGAIN
–	–	–	–	==	11	7	1	1	3	13	==	–	–	–	–	–	–	–	–	–	–	–	–	–	–	THESE FOOLISH THINGS
–	–	–	–	==	13	9	4	4	8	17	==	–	–	–	–	–	–	–	–	–	–	–	–	–	–	TAKE MY HEART
–	–	–	–	==	19	15	==	==	–	–	–	–	–	–	–	–	–	–	–	–	–	–	–	–	–	SING ME A SWING SONG (AND LET ME DANCE)
–	–	–	–	==	==	17	18	19	==	==	–	–	–	–	–	–	–	–	–	–	–	–	–	–	–	SHOE SHINE BOY
–	–	–	–	–	==	19	17	18	==	–	–	–	–	–	–	–	–	–	–	–	–	–	–	–	–	STOMPIN' AT THE SAVOY
–	–	–	–	–	==	==	11	10	7	8	17	==	–	–	–	–	–	–	–	–	–	–	–	–	–	NO REGRETS
–	–	–	–	–	==	==	13	9	5	5	12	16	==	==	–	–	–	–	–	–	–	–	–	–	–	RENDEZVOUS WITH A DREAM
–	–	–	–	–	==	==	12	14	20	==	–	–	–	–	–	–	–	–	–	–	–	–	–	–	–	CROSS PATCH
–	–	–	–	–	–	==	16	8	2	2	6	18	==	–	–	–	–	–	–	–	–	–	–	–	–	WHEN I'M WITH YOU
–	–	–	–	–	–	==	20	11	1	1	1	1	5	10	==	==	–	–	–	–	–	–	–	–	–	DID I REMEMBER
–	–	–	–	–	–	–	==	17	9	3	3	3	8	19	==	–	–	–	–	–	–	–	–	–	–	UNTIL THE REAL THING COMES ALONG
–	–	–	–	–	–	–	==	20	15	14	18	==	–	–	–	–	–	–	–	–	–	–	–	–	–	KNOCK, KNOCK, WHO'S THERE?
–	–	–	–	–	–	–	==	==	18	==	==	–	–	–	–	–	–	–	–	–	–	–	–	–	–	SWINGTIME IN THE ROCKIES
–	–	–	–	–	–	–	==	==	16	18	==	==	–	–	–	–	–	–	–	–	–	–	–	–	–	YOU'RE NOT THE KIND
–	–	–	–	–	–	–	–	==	12	15	11	14	==	==	–	–	–	–	–	–	–	–	–	–	–	EMPTY SADDLES
–	–	–	–	–	–	–	–	==	10	4	2	2	4	11	==	==	–	–	–	–	–	–	–	–	–	A STAR FELL OUT OF HEAVEN
–	–	–	–	–	–	–	–	==	13	6	5	9	15	==	–	–	–	–	–	–	–	–	–	–	–	BYE BYE BABY
–	–	–	–	–	–	–	–	==	==	10	9	10	11	13	==	==	–	–	–	–	–	–	–	–	–	I CAN'T ESCAPE FROM YOU
–	–	–	–	–	–	–	–	==	==	16	7	11	12	20	==	–	–	–	–	–	–	–	–	–	–	I'M AN OLD COWHAND
–	–	–	–	–	–	–	–	==	17	7	4	4	1	1	4	9	16	16	==	–	–	–	–	–	–	WHEN DID YOU LEAVE HEAVEN?
–	–	–	–	–	–	–	–	==	==	12	8	6	6	7	13	18	==	–	–	–	–	–	–	–	–	ME AND THE MOON
–	–	–	–	–	–	–	–	–	==	20	==	==	==	–	–	–	–	–	–	–	–	–	–	–	–	UNTIL TODAY
–	–	–	–	–	–	–	–	–	==	19	10	7	7	6	18	==	–	–	–	–	–	–	–	–	–	SING, BABY, SING
–	–	–	–	–	–	–	–	–	==	==	15	12	==	==	–	–	–	–	–	–	–	–	–	–	–	SING, SING, SING
–	–	–	–	–	–	–	–	–	==	==	13	5	2	2	1	2	6	10	==	–	–	–	–	–	–	THE WAY YOU LOOK TONIGHT
–	–	–	–	–	–	–	–	–	==	==	19	8	3	3	8	11	==	==	–	–	–	–	–	–	–	A FINE ROMANCE
–	–	–	–	–	–	–	–	–	–	==	16	15	17	9	7	7	8	9	19	==	–	–	–	–	–	SOUTH SEA ISLAND MAGIC
–	–	–	–	–	–	–	–	–	–	==	14	13	9	5	6	8	9	11	==	==	–	–	–	–	–	ORGAN GRINDER'S SWING
–	–	–	–	–	–	–	–	–	–	==	==	19	13	16	==	–	–	–	–	–	–	–	–	–	–	WHEN A LADY MEETS A GENTLEMAN DOWN SOUTH
–	–	–	–	–	–	–	–	–	–	==	==	17	14	8	5	5	10	17	==	–	–	–	–	–	–	YOU TURNED THE TABLES ON ME
–	–	–	–	–	–	–	–	–	–	–	==	20	10	4	3	3	5	7	18	==	–	–	–	–	–	I'LL SING YOU A THOUSAND LOVE SONGS
–	–	–	–	–	–	–	–	–	–	–	==	==	==	15	14	20	==	–	–	–	–	–	–	–	–	CLOSE TO ME
–	–	–	–	–	–	–	–	–	–	–	–	==	20	==	==	–	–	–	–	–	–	–	–	–	–	THROUGH THE COURTESY OF LOVE
–	–	–	–	–	–	–	–	–	–	–	–	==	16	14	10	13	==	==	–	–	–	–	–	–	–	WHO LOVES YOU?
–	–	–	–	–	–	–	–	–	–	–	–	==	18	18	==	==	==	15	12	13	==	==	–	–	–	EASY TO LOVE
–	–	–	–	–	–	–	–	–	–	–	–	==	19	==	16	17	==	19	==	–	–	–	–	–	–	YOU DO THE DARNDEST THINGS, BABY
–	–	–	–	–	–	–	–	–	–	–	–	–	==	12	2	1	1	2	2	6	8	20	==	–	–	IN THE CHAPEL IN THE MOONLIGHT
–	–	–	–	–	–	–	–	–	–	–	–	–	==	==	20	19	==	==	–	–	–	–	–	–	–	EXACTLY LIKE YOU
–	–	–	–	–	–	–	–	–	–	–	–	–	–	==	15	14	20	==	–	–	–	–	–	–	–	MIDNIGHT BLUE
–	–	–	–	–	–	–	–	–	–	–	–	–	==	==	11	10	17	20	==	–	–	–	–	–	–	DID YOU MEAN IT?
–	–	–	–	–	–	–	–	–	–	–	–	–	==	==	12	6	3	3	4	10	18	==	–	–	–	IT'S DE–LOVELY
–	–	–	–	–	–	–	–	–	–	–	–	–	==	==	==	16	12	==	==	–	–	–	–	–	–	HERE'S LOVE IN YOUR EYES
–	–	–	–	–	–	–	–	–	–	–	–	–	==	==	==	==	15	==	==	–	–	–	–	–	–	I'M TALKING THROUGH MY HEART
–	–	–	–	–	–	–	–	–	–	–	–	–	–	==	19	12	4	4	8	9	17	==	–	–	–	I'VE GOT YOU UNDER MY SKIN
–	–	–	–	–	–	–	–	–	–	–	–	–	–	==	17	15	7	5	9	17	==	–	–	–	–	I'M IN A DANCING MOOD
–	–	–	–	–	–	–	–	–	–	–	–	–	–	–	–	==	11	==	–	–	–	–	–	–	–	SANTA CLAUS IS COMIN' TO TOWN
–	–	–	–	–	–	–	–	–	–	–	–	–	==	17	9	4	2	1	1	1	5	12	==	–	–	PENNIES FROM HEAVEN (1937)
–	–	–	–	–	–	–	–	–	–	–	–	–	==	==	==	==	19	12	11	15	==	==	–	–	–	ONE, TWO, BUTTON YOUR SHOE (1937)
–	–	–	–	–	–	–	–	–	–	–	–	–	–	–	–	==	13	14	7	4	2	4	11	==	==	WITH PLENTY OF MONEY AND YOU (1937)
–	–	–	–	–	–	–	–	–	–	–	–	–	–	–	–	==	18	13	6	5	6	11	==	==	–	THE NIGHT IS YOUNG AND YOU'RE SO BEAUTIFUL (1937)
–	–	–	–	–	–	–	–	–	–	–	–	–	–	–	–	==	14	6	3	2	3	3	2	8	9	WHEN MY DREAM BOAT COMES HOME (1937)
Ap	Ap	My	My	Jn	Jn	Jy	Jy	Ag	Ag	Sp	Sp	Oc	Oc	Nv	Nv	Dc	Dc	Ja	Ja	Fb	Fb	Ma	Ma	Ap	Ap	

1936														1937												
Oc	Oc	Nv	Nv	Dc	Dc	Ja	Ja	Fb	Fb	Ma	Ma	Ap	Ap	My	My	Jn	Jn	Jy	Jy	Ag	Ag	Sp	Sp	Oc	Oc	
4	1	1	4	9	16	16	==	–	–	–	–	–	–	–	–	–	–	–	–	–	–	–	–	–	–	WHEN DID YOU LEAVE HEAVEN? (1936)
5	2	2	1	2	6	10	==	–	–	–	–	–	–	–	–	–	–	–	–	–	–	–	–	–	–	THE WAY YOU LOOK TONIGHT (1936)
15	17	9	7	7	8	9	19	==	–	–	–	–	–	–	–	–	–	–	–	–	–	–	–	–	–	SOUTH SEA ISLAND MAGIC (1936)
13	9	5	6	8	9	11	==	==	–	–	–	–	–	–	–	–	–	–	–	–	–	–	–	–	–	ORGAN GRINDER'S SWING (1936)
17	14	8	5	5	10	17	==	–	–	–	–	–	–	–	–	–	–	–	–	–	–	–	–	–	–	YOU TURNED THE TABLES ON ME (1936)
20	10	4	3	3	5	7	18	==	–	–	–	–	–	–	–	–	–	–	–	–	–	–	–	–	–	I'LL SING YOU A THOUSAND LOVE SONGS (1936)
==	18	18	==	==	==	15	12	13	==	==	–	–	–	–	–	–	–	–	–	–	–	–	–	–	–	EASY TO LOVE (1936)
==	19	==	16	17	==	19	==	–	–	–	–	–	–	–	–	–	–	–	–	–	–	–	–	–	–	YOU DO THE DARNDEST THINGS, BABY
–	==	12	2	1	1	2	2	6	8	20	==	–	–	–	–	–	–	–	–	–	–	–	–	–	–	IN THE CHAPEL IN THE MOONLIGHT (1936)
–	–	==	19	12	4	4	8	9	17	==	–	–	–	–	–	–	–	–	–	–	–	–	–	–	–	I'VE GOT YOU UNDER MY SKIN (1936)
–	–	==	17	15	7	5	9	17	==	–	–	–	–	–	–	–	–	–	–	–	–	–	–	–	–	I'M IN A DANCING MOOD (1936)
–	==	==	11	10	17	20	==	–	–	–	–	–	–	–	–	–	–	–	–	–	–	–	–	–	–	DID YOU MEAN IT? (1936)
–	==	==	12	6	3	3	4	10	18	==	–	–	–	–	–	–	–	–	–	–	–	–	–	–	–	IT'S DE–LOVELY (1936)
–	==	17	9	4	2	1	1	1	5	12	==	–	–	–	–	–	–	–	–	–	–	–	–	–	–	PENNIES FROM HEAVEN
–	==	==	==	==	19	12	11	15	==	==	–	–	–	–	–	–	–	–	–	–	–	–	–	–	–	ONE, TWO, BUTTON YOUR SHOE
–	–	–	–	==	13	14	7	4	2	4	11	==	==	–	–	–	–	–	–	–	–	–	–	–	–	WITH PLENTY OF MONEY AND YOU
–	–	–	–	==	18	13	6	5	6	11	==	==	–	–	–	–	–	–	–	–	–	–	–	–	–	THE NIGHT IS YOUNG AND YOU'RE SO BEAUTIFUL
–	–	–	–	==	14	6	3	2	3	3	2	8	9	20	==	–	–	–	–	–	–	–	–	–	–	WHEN MY DREAM BOAT COMES HOME
–	–	–	–	==	==	==	16	==	==	–	–	–	–	–	–	–	–	–	–	–	–	–	–	–	–	THERE'S FROST ON THE MOON
–	–	–	–	–	==	8	10	7	9	==	==	–	–	–	–	–	–	–	–	–	–	–	–	–	–	THERE'S SOMETHING IN THE AIR
–	–	–	–	–	==	==	20	20	==	==	==	==	==	–	–	–	–	–	–	–	–	–	–	–	–	INDIAN LOVE CALL
–	–	–	–	–	==	==	13	12	14	9	10	14	==	==	–	–	–	–	–	–	–	–	–	–	–	SERENADE IN THE NIGHT
–	–	–	–	–	–	18	5	3	1	1	3	7	18	==	–	–	–	–	–	–	–	–	–	–	–	GOODNIGHT, MY LOVE
–	–	–	–	–	–	==	17	16	15	==	==	–	–	–	–	–	–	–	–	–	–	–	–	–	–	LOVE AND LEARN
–	–	–	–	–	–	==	15	8	7	5	7	5	7	19	==	–	–	–	–	–	–	–	–	–	–	TRUST IN ME
–	–	–	–	–	–	==	14	11	10	19	==	–	–	–	–	–	–	–	–	–	–	–	–	–	–	RAINBOW ON THE RIVER
–	–	–	–	–	–	–	==	14	4	2	6	12	==	==	–	–	–	–	–	–	–	–	–	–	–	THIS YEAR'S KISSES
–	–	–	–	–	–	–	==	19	11	6	1	3	3	5	15	==	–	–	–	–	–	–	–	–	–	MOONLIGHT AND SHADOWS
–	–	–	–	–	–	–	==	18	13	8	9	6	4	10	19	==	–	–	–	–	–	–	–	–	–	WHAT WILL I TELL MY HEART
–	–	–	–	–	–	–	==	==	20	==	==	–	–	–	–	–	–	–	–	–	–	–	–	–	–	WHO'S AFRAID OF LOVE
–	–	–	–	–	–	–	==	==	16	15	13	==	–	–	–	–	–	–	–	–	–	–	–	–	–	MAY I HAVE THE NEXT ROMANCE WITH YOU?
–	–	–	–	–	–	–	–	==	12	7	8	4	8	==	==	–	–	–	–	–	–	–	–	–	–	I'VE GOT MY LOVE TO KEEP ME WARM
–	–	–	–	–	–	–	–	==	19	10	14	13	==	==	–	–	–	–	–	–	–	–	–	–	–	ON A LITTLE BAMBOO BRIDGE
–	–	–	–	–	–	–	–	==	==	14	15	15	==	==	–	–	–	–	–	–	–	–	–	–	–	YOU'RE LAUGHING AT ME
–	–	–	–	–	–	–	–	–	==	18	4	1	1	1	9	16	==	–	–	–	–	–	–	–	–	BOO–HOO
–	–	–	–	–	–	–	–	–	==	16	16	==	==	–	–	–	–	–	–	–	–	–	–	–	–	SLUMMING ON PARK AVENUE
–	–	–	–	–	–	–	–	–	==	13	5	2	2	2	6	11	15	==	==	–	–	–	–	–	–	LITTLE OLD LADY
–	–	–	–	–	–	–	–	–	==	17	17	==	==	–	–	–	–	–	–	–	–	–	–	–	–	SMOKE DREAMS
–	–	–	–	–	–	–	–	–	==	==	19	17	==	==	–	–	–	–	–	–	–	–	–	–	–	(THIS IS) MY LAST AFFAIR
–	–	–	–	–	–	–	–	–	==	==	12	9	6	18	==	–	–	–	–	–	–	–	–	–	–	WHEN THE POPPIES BLOOM AGAIN
–	–	–	–	–	–	–	–	–	–	==	18	11	12	==	==	==	–	–	–	–	–	–	–	–	–	MARIE
–	–	–	–	–	–	–	–	–	–	==	==	10	5	3	7	14	19	==	–	–	–	–	–	–	–	TOO MARVELOUS FOR WORDS
–	–	–	–	–	–	–	–	–	–	==	==	==	19	==	==	–	–	–	–	–	–	–	–	–	–	SWING HIGH, SWING LOW
–	–	–	–	–	–	–	–	–	–	–	==	19	==	==	==	–	–	–	–	–	–	–	–	–	–	MY LITTLE BUCKAROO
–	–	–	–	–	–	–	–	–	–	–	==	18	16	15	==	–	–	–	–	–	–	–	–	–	–	SWEET IS THE WORD FOR YOU
–	–	–	–	–	–	–	–	–	–	–	==	==	==	17	==	==	–	–	–	–	–	–	–	–	–	HOW COULD YOU?
–	–	–	–	–	–	–	–	–	–	–	–	20	10	4	1	1	1	4	9	==	==	–	–	–	–	SEPTEMBER IN THE RAIN
–	–	–	–	–	–	–	–	–	–	–	–	==	13	11	10	9	13	==	–	–	–	–	–	–	–	WHERE ARE YOU?
–	–	–	–	–	–	–	–	–	–	–	–	==	17	12	13	8	8	11	7	10	16	16	==	–	–	BLUE HAWAII
–	–	–	–	–	–	–	–	–	–	–	–	==	15	6	4	7	14	==	–	–	–	–	–	–	–	THE LOVE BUG WILL BITE YOU
–	–	–	–	–	–	–	–	–	–	–	–	==	14	7	3	3	3	3	5	6	10	19	==	–	–	SWEET LEILANI
–	–	–	–	–	–	–	–	–	–	–	–	==	11	8	12	12	17	15	==	==	–	–	–	–	–	WILL YOU REMEMBER (SWEETHEART)
–	–	–	–	–	–	–	–	–	–	–	–	–	==	9	2	2	5	10	==	==	–	–	–	–	–	CARELESSLY
–	–	–	–	–	–	–	–	–	–	–	–	–	==	16	14	15	20	==	–	–	–	–	–	–	–	LET'S CALL THE WHOLE THING OFF
–	–	–	–	–	–	–	–	–	–	–	–	–	==	13	5	4	4	7	13	==	–	–	–	–	–	NEVER IN A MILLION YEARS
–	–	–	–	–	–	–	–	–	–	–	–	–	==	14	8	6	7	8	15	==	–	–	–	–	–	THEY CAN'T TAKE THAT AWAY FROM ME
–	–	–	–	–	–	–	–	–	–	–	–	–	==	==	18	13	11	13	12	==	==	–	–	–	–	WAS IT RAIN?
Oc	Oc	Nv	Nv	Dc	Dc	Ja	Ja	Fb	Fb	Ma	Ma	Ap	Ap	My	My	Jn	Jn	Jy	Jy	Ag	Ag	Sp	Sp	Oc	Oc	

								1937												1938						
Ma	Ma	Ap	Ap	My	My	Jn	Jn	Jy	Jy	Ag	Ag	Sp	Sp	Oc	Oc	Nv	Nv	Dc	Dc	Ja	Ja	Fb	Fb	Ma	Ma	
==	20	16	20	==	==	–	–	–	–	–	==	==	==	14	12	14	18	17	==	15	16	==	==	–	–	JOSEPHINE
–	–	–	==	==	16	17	16	20	==	–	–	–	–	–	–	–	–	–	–	–	–	–	–	–	–	THEY ALL LAUGHED
–	–	–	–	==	11	5	10	12	11	==	–	–	–	–	–	–	–	–	–	–	–	–	–	–	–	THERE'S A LULL IN MY LIFE
–	–	–	–	==	17	10	2	**1**	2	**1**	3	9	18	==	–	–	–	–	–	–	–	–	–	–	–	IT LOOKS LIKE RAIN IN CHERRY BLOSSOM LANE
–	–	–	–	==	20	19	9	6	4	4	7	15	==	–	–	–	–	–	–	–	–	–	–	–	–	WHERE OR WHEN
–	–	–	–	==	==	20	==	==	==	–	–	–	–	–	–	–	–	–	–	–	–	–	–	–	–	ON A LITTLE DREAM RANCH
–	–	–	–	–	==	==	18	9	6	9	19	==	–	–	–	–	–	–	–	–	–	–	–	–	–	THE YOU AND ME THAT USED TO BE
–	–	–	–	–	–	18	6	2	**1**	3	6	==	–	–	–	–	–	–	–	–	–	–	–	–	–	THE MERRY–GO–ROUND BROKE DOWN
–	–	–	–	–	–	==	12	5	3	2	**1**	5	11	==	–	–	–	–	–	–	–	–	–	–	–	A SAILBOAT IN THE MOONLIGHT
–	–	–	–	–	–	==	==	14	==	==	–	–	–	–	–	–	–	–	–	–	–	–	–	–	–	TOODLE–OO
–	–	–	–	–	–	–	==	16	8	5	4	4	10	17	==	–	–	–	–	–	–	–	–	–	–	I KNOW NOW
–	–	–	–	–	–	–	==	19	==	==	–	–	–	–	–	–	–	–	–	–	–	–	–	–	–	MEAN TO ME
–	–	–	–	–	–	–	==	17	==	==	–	–	–	–	–	–	–	–	–	–	–	–	–	–	–	THE DREAM IN MY HEART
–	–	–	–	–	–	–	==	18	17	15	==	==	–	–	–	–	–	–	–	–	–	–	–	–	–	OUR PENTHOUSE ON THIRD AVENUE
–	–	–	–	–	–	–	–	==	16	19	==	–	–	–	–	–	–	–	–	–	–	–	–	–	–	'CAUSE MY BABY SAYS IT'S SO
–	–	–	–	–	–	–	–	==	10	8	8	12	==	–	–	–	–	–	–	–	–	–	–	–	–	GONE WITH THE WIND
–	–	–	–	–	–	–	–	==	20	14	12	13	17	==	==	–	–	–	–	–	–	–	–	–	–	SATAN TAKES A HOLIDAY
–	–	–	–	–	–	–	–	==	14	7	2	**1**	2	7	19	==	–	–	–	–	–	–	–	–	–	SO RARE
–	–	–	–	–	–	–	–	==	19	11	14	17	19	19	==	–	–	–	–	–	–	–	–	–	–	CARAVAN
–	–	–	–	–	–	–	–	==	18	12	5	2	**1**	2	7	16	==	–	–	–	–	–	–	–	–	WHISPERS IN THE DARK
–	–	–	–	–	–	–	–	–	==	20	==	==	==	==	==	–	–	–	–	–	–	–	–	–	–	(YOU KNOW IT ALL) SMARTY
–	–	–	–	–	–	–	–	–	==	17	15	14	16	==	==	–	–	–	–	–	–	–	–	–	–	STARDUST ON THE MOON
–	–	–	–	–	–	–	–	–	==	13	11	6	9	12	==	–	–	–	–	–	–	–	–	–	–	THE FIRST TIME I SAW YOU
–	–	–	–	–	–	–	–	–	==	16	9	3	3	4	9	11	15	==	–	–	–	–	–	–	–	MY CABIN OF DREAMS
–	–	–	–	–	–	–	–	–	==	18	13	7	6	8	5	6	7	10	11	==	–	–	–	–	–	HARBOR LIGHTS
–	–	–	–	–	–	–	–	–	==	==	18	==	==	–	–	–	–	–	–	–	–	–	–	–	–	STOP! YOU'RE BREAKING MY HEART
–	–	–	–	–	–	–	–	–	–	==	17	8	4	**1**	**1**	4	12	==	==	–	–	–	–	–	–	THAT OLD FEELING
–	–	–	–	–	–	–	–	–	–	==	==	10	8	10	15	==	–	–	–	–	–	–	–	–	–	AFRAID TO DREAM
–	–	–	–	–	–	–	–	–	–	==	==	==	15	16	==	–	–	–	–	–	–	–	–	–	–	YOURS AND MINE
–	–	–	–	–	–	–	–	–	–	–	20	11	5	5	4	12	==	==	–	–	–	–	–	–	–	HAVE YOU GOT ANY CASTLES, BABY?
–	–	–	–	–	–	–	–	–	–	–	==	18	12	13	==	==	–	–	–	–	–	–	–	–	–	IT'S THE NATURAL THING TO DO
–	–	–	–	–	–	–	–	–	–	–	==	20	7	3	3	7	13	==	–	–	–	–	–	–	–	THE MOON GOT IN MY EYES
–	–	–	–	–	–	–	–	–	–	–	==	==	==	20	17	==	==	–	–	–	–	–	–	–	–	CAN I FORGET YOU?
–	–	–	–	–	–	–	–	–	–	–	–	==	13	6	2	2	4	15	==	–	–	–	–	–	–	REMEMBER ME?
–	–	–	–	–	–	–	–	–	–	–	–	==	14	11	16	==	==	–	–	–	–	–	–	–	–	THE BIG APPLE
–	–	–	–	–	–	–	–	–	–	–	–	==	20	9	6	5	8	11	==	==	–	–	–	–	–	ROSES IN DECEMBER
–	–	–	–	–	–	–	–	–	–	–	–	–	==	18	11	13	16	==	–	–	–	–	–	–	–	SO MANY MEMORIES
–	–	–	–	–	–	–	–	–	–	–	–	–	==	15	8	**1**	2	3	5	9	20	==	–	–	–	YOU CAN'T STOP ME FROM DREAMING
–	–	–	–	–	–	–	–	–	–	–	–	–	–	==	10	9	6	9	10	12	15	==	–	–	–	THE ONE ROSE
–	–	–	–	–	–	–	–	–	–	–	–	–	–	==	14	8	5	5	6	16	==	–	–	–	–	BLOSSOMS ON BROADWAY
–	–	–	–	–	–	–	–	–	–	–	–	–	–	==	13	3	**1**	2	4	8	==	==	–	–	–	VIENI, VIENI
–	–	–	–	–	–	–	–	–	–	–	–	–	–	==	18	18	20	16	12	20	==	–	–	–	–	EBB TIDE
–	–	–	–	–	–	–	–	–	–	–	–	–	–	==	20	10	3	**1**	**1**	2	8	17	==	–	–	ONCE IN AWHILE
–	–	–	–	–	–	–	–	–	–	–	–	–	–	==	==	19	==	==	–	–	–	–	–	–	–	YOU AND I KNOW
–	–	–	–	–	–	–	–	–	–	–	–	–	–	==	==	20	==	==	–	–	–	–	–	–	–	GETTING SOME FUN OUT OF LIFE
–	–	–	–	–	–	–	–	–	–	–	–	–	–	–	==	==	14	12	15	==	–	–	–	–	–	FAREWELL, MY LOVE
–	–	–	–	–	–	–	–	–	–	–	–	–	–	–	==	15	9	6	13	==	–	–	–	–	–	IF IT'S THE LAST THING I DO
–	–	–	–	–	–	–	–	–	–	–	–	–	–	–	==	17	11	7	9	19	==	–	–	–	–	I STILL LOVE TO KISS YOU GOODNIGHT
–	–	–	–	–	–	–	–	–	–	–	–	–	–	–	==	==	10	4	3	3	9	11	==	–	–	NICE WORK IF YOU CAN GET IT
–	–	–	–	–	–	–	–	–	–	–	–	–	–	–	–	==	19	14	17	18	==	–	–	–	–	A FOGGY DAY
–	–	–	–	–	–	–	–	–	–	–	–	–	–	–	–	==	==	13	7	6	10	15	==	–	–	BOB WHITE (WHATCHA GONNA SWING TONIGHT?)
–	–	–	–	–	–	–	–	–	–	–	–	–	–	–	–	==	17	8	2	**1**	2	4	8	16	==	ROSALIE (1938)
–	–	–	–	–	–	–	–	–	–	–	–	–	–	–	–	==	==	19	20	13	11	12	==	–	–	WHEN THE(MIGHTY ORGAN PLAYED "OH PROMISE ME" (1938)
–	–	–	–	–	–	–	–	–	–	–	–	–	–	–	–	–	–	==	8	4	6	7	7	6	8	THERE'S A GOLD MINE IN THE SKY (1938)
–	–	–	–	–	–	–	–	–	–	–	–	–	–	–	–	–	–	==	16	5	3	6	9	18	==	TRUE CONFESSION (1938)
–	–	–	–	–	–	–	–	–	–	–	–	–	–	–	–	==	==	18	18	==	12	18	==	–	–	IN THE STILL OF THE NIGHT (1938)
–	–	–	–	–	–	–	–	–	–	–	–	–	–	–	–	–	==	20	14	7	4	2	6	7	10	THE DIPSY DOODLE (1938)
–	–	–	–	–	–	–	–	–	–	–	–	–	–	–	–	–	–	==	19	14	18	20	19	20	==	SAIL ALONG, SILV'RY MOON (1938)
Ma	Ma	Ap	Ap	My	My	Jn	Jn	Jy	Jy	Ag	Ag	Sp	Sp	Oc	Oc	Nv	Nv	Dc	Dc	Ja	Ja	Fb	Fb	Ma	Ma	

1937						1938																				
Oc	Oc	Nv	Nv	Dc	Dc	Ja	Ja	Fb	Fb	Ma	Ma	Ap	Ap	My	My	Jn	Jn	Jy	Jy	Ag	Ag	Sp	Sp	Oc	Oc	
14	12	14	18	17	==	15	16	==	==	–	–	–	–	–	–	–	–	–	–	–	–	–	–	–	–	JOSEPHINE (1937)
==	10	9	6	9	10	12	15	==	–	–	–	–	–	–	–	–	–	–	–	–	–	–	–	–	–	THE ONE ROSE (1937)
==	14	8	5	5	6	16	==	–	–	–	–	–	–	–	–	–	–	–	–	–	–	–	–	–	–	BLOSSOMS ON BROADWAY (1937)
15	8	**1**	2	3	5	9	20	==	–	–	–	–	–	–	–	–	–	–	–	–	–	–	–	–	–	YOU CAN'T STOP ME FROM DREAMING
==	13	3	**1**	2	4	8	==	==	–	–	–	–	–	–	–	–	–	–	–	–	–	–	–	–	–	VIENI, VIENI (1937)
==	18	18	20	16	12	20	==	–	–	–	–	–	–	–	–	–	–	–	–	–	–	–	–	–	–	EBB TIDE (1937)
==	20	10	3	**1**	**1**	2	8	17	==	–	–	–	–	–	–	–	–	–	–	–	–	–	–	–	–	ONCE IN AWHILE (1937)
–	==	17	11	7	9	19	==	–	–	–	–	–	–	–	–	–	–	–	–	–	–	–	–	–	–	I STILL LOVE TO KISS YOU GOODNIGHT (1937)
–	–	==	19	14	17	18	==	–	–	–	–	–	–	–	–	–	–	–	–	–	–	–	–	–	–	A FOGGY DAY (1937)
–	==	==	10	4	3	3	9	11	==	–	–	–	–	–	–	–	–	–	–	–	–	–	–	–	–	NICE WORK IF YOU CAN GET IT (1937)
–	–	==	==	13	7	6	10	15	==	–	–	–	–	–	–	–	–	–	–	–	–	–	–	–	–	BOB WHITE (WHATCHA GONNA SWING TONIGHT?) (1937)
–	–	==	17	8	2	**1**	2	4	8	16	==	–	–	–	–	–	–	–	–	–	–	–	–	–	–	ROSALIE
–	–	==	==	19	20	13	11	12	==	–	–	–	–	–	–	–	–	–	–	–	–	–	–	–	–	WHEN THE (MIGHTY) ORGAN PLAYED "OH PROMISE ME"
–	–	==	==	18	18	==	12	18	==	–	–	–	–	–	–	–	–	–	–	–	–	–	–	–	–	IN THE STILL OF THE NIGHT
–	–	–	==	20	14	7	4	2	6	7	10	==	–	–	–	–	–	–	–	–	–	–	–	–	–	THE DIPSY DOODLE
–	–	–	–	==	8	4	6	7	7	6	8	7	13	==	–	–	–	–	–	–	–	–	–	–	–	THERE'S A GOLD MINE IN THE SKY
–	–	–	–	==	16	5	3	6	9	18	==	–	–	–	–	–	–	–	–	–	–	–	–	–	–	TRUE CONFESSION
–	–	–	–	==	19	14	18	20	19	20	==	–	–	–	–	–	–	–	–	–	–	–	–	–	–	SAIL ALONG, SILV'RY MOON
–	–	–	–	–	==	10	5	3	4	8	==	==	–	–	–	–	–	–	–	–	–	–	–	–	–	YOU'RE A SWEETHEART
–	–	–	–	–	==	17	13	10	20	==	–	–	–	–	–	–	–	–	–	–	–	–	–	–	–	SWEET SOMEONE
–	–	–	–	–	==	11	**1**	**1**	**1**	5	19	–	–	–	–	–	–	–	–	–	–	–	–	–	–	BEI MIR BIST DU SCHOEN
–	–	–	–	–	–	==	7	5	2	3	7	11	==	–	–	–	–	–	–	–	–	–	–	–	–	I DOUBLE DARE YOU
–	–	–	–	–	–	==	17	14	11	19	==	–	–	–	–	–	–	–	–	–	–	–	–	–	–	YOU TOOK THE WORDS RIGHT OUT OF MY HEART
–	–	–	–	–	–	==	19	13	13	17	==	==	–	–	–	–	–	–	–	–	–	–	–	–	–	TEN PRETTY GIRLS
–	–	–	–	–	–	==	14	8	3	**1**	**1**	2	16	==	–	–	–	–	–	–	–	–	–	–	–	THANKS FOR THE MEMORY
–	–	–	–	–	–	==	==	19	15	==	–	–	–	–	–	–	–	–	–	–	–	–	–	–	–	MAMA, THAT MOON IS HERE AGAIN
–	–	–	–	–	–	–	==	16	10	4	6	20	==	–	–	–	–	–	–	–	–	–	–	–	–	SWEET AS A SONG
–	–	–	–	–	–	–	==	9	5	2	2	4	5	13	==	==	–	–	–	–	–	–	–	–	–	WHISTLE WHILE YOU WORK
–	–	–	–	–	–	–	==	==	14	13	17	16	==	==	==	–	–	–	–	–	–	–	–	–	–	THE MOON OF MANAKOORA
–	–	–	–	–	–	–	–	==	18	==	==	–	–	–	–	–	–	–	–	–	–	–	–	–	–	TWO DREAMS GOT TOGETHER
–	–	–	–	–	–	–	–	==	12	9	9	17	==	–	–	–	–	–	–	–	–	–	–	–	–	I CAN DREAM, CAN'T I?
–	–	–	–	–	–	–	–	==	16	12	12	13	==	==	–	–	–	–	–	–	–	–	–	–	–	A GYPSY TOLD ME
–	–	–	–	–	–	–	–	==	17	10	4	6	4	7	11	==	==	–	–	–	–	–	–	–	–	GOODNIGHT, ANGEL
–	–	–	–	–	–	–	–	–	==	14	11	==	==	–	–	–	–	–	–	–	–	–	–	–	–	MORE THAN EVER
–	–	–	–	–	–	–	–	–	==	11	5	3	3	9	9	16	==	–	–	–	–	–	–	–	–	HEIGH–HO
–	–	–	–	–	–	–	–	–	==	15	3	**1**	**1**	**1**	5	10	==	–	–	–	–	–	–	–	–	TI–PI–TIN
–	–	–	–	–	–	–	–	–	==	==	18	12	10	12	10	==	–	–	–	–	–	–	–	–	–	HOWDJA LIKE TO LOVE ME
–	–	–	–	–	–	–	–	–	–	==	13	14	15	==	–	–	–	–	–	–	–	–	–	–	–	IT'S WONDERFUL
–	–	–	–	–	–	–	–	–	–	==	20	10	==	==	–	–	–	–	–	–	–	–	–	–	–	LET'S SAIL TO DREAMLAND
–	–	–	–	–	–	–	–	–	–	==	16	9	8	6	13	==	==	–	–	–	–	–	–	–	–	YOU'RE AN EDUCATION
–	–	–	–	–	–	–	–	–	–	==	14	5	2	3	3	2	6	9	20	==	–	–	–	–	–	PLEASE BE KIND
–	–	–	–	–	–	–	–	–	–	==	15	8	6	2	**1**	3	8	15	==	–	–	–	–	–	–	LOVE WALKED IN
–	–	–	–	–	–	–	–	–	–	==	==	19	19	18	==	==	–	–	–	–	–	–	–	–	–	ALWAYS AND ALWAYS
–	–	–	–	–	–	–	–	–	–	–	==	18	7	5	8	20	==	–	–	–	–	–	–	–	–	ON THE SENTIMENTAL SIDE
–	–	–	–	–	–	–	–	–	–	–	==	15	9	4	4	4	11	==	–	–	–	–	–	–	–	DON'T BE THAT WAY
–	–	–	–	–	–	–	–	–	–	–	==	==	14	==	==	–	–	–	–	–	–	–	–	–	–	THE OLD APPLE TREE
–	–	–	–	–	–	–	–	–	–	–	==	==	17	15	15	13	18	==	==	–	–	–	–	–	–	MARTHA
–	–	–	–	–	–	–	–	–	–	–	–	==	18	==	==	–	–	–	–	–	–	–	–	–	–	SUNDAY IN THE PARK
–	–	–	–	–	–	–	–	–	–	–	–	==	11	14	16	==	–	–	–	–	–	–	–	–	–	I FALL IN LOVE WITH YOU EVERY DAY
–	–	–	–	–	–	–	–	–	–	–	–	==	==	16	14	15	==	–	–	–	–	–	–	–	–	AT A PERFUME COUNTER
–	–	–	–	–	–	–	–	–	–	–	–	==	20	11	6	9	19	==	–	–	–	–	–	–	–	YOU COULDN'T BE CUTER
–	–	–	–	–	–	–	–	–	–	–	–	==	12	10	7	11	==	==	–	–	–	–	–	–	–	I LOVE TO WHISTLE
–	–	–	–	–	–	–	–	–	–	–	–	==	==	17	==	==	–	–	–	–	–	–	–	–	–	BEWILDERED
–	–	–	–	–	–	–	–	–	–	–	–	–	==	20	==	==	–	–	–	–	–	–	–	–	–	THE DONKEY SERENADE
–	–	–	–	–	–	–	–	–	–	–	–	–	==	8	2	**1**	3	6	16	==	–	–	–	–	–	CRY, BABY, CRY
–	–	–	–	–	–	–	–	–	–	–	–	–	==	19	12	7	2	2	2	3	6	11	==	–	–	I LET A SONG GO OUT OF MY HEART
–	–	–	–	–	–	–	–	–	–	–	–	–	==	==	19	==	==	–	–	–	–	–	–	–	–	SOMETHING TELLS ME
–	–	–	–	–	–	–	–	–	–	–	–	–	–	==	20	8	5	7	9	15	==	==	–	–	–	LOVELIGHT IN THE STARLIGHT
–	–	–	–	–	–	–	–	–	–	–	–	–	–	==	17	6	4	5	5	8	9	16	==	–	–	CATHEDRAL IN THE PINES
–	–	–	–	–	–	–	–	–	–	–	–	–	–	==	==	19	==	==	–	–	–	–	–	–	–	SO LITTLE TIME
Oc	Oc	Nv	Nv	Dc	Dc	Ja	Ja	Fb	Fb	Ma	Ma	Ap	Ap	My	My	Jn	Jn	Jy	Jy	Ag	Ag	Sp	Sp	Oc	Oc	

1938																		1939								
Ap	Ap	My	My	Jn	Jn	Jy	Jy	Ag	Ag	Sp	Sp	Oc	Oc	Nv	Nv	Dc	Dc	Ja	Ja	Fb	Fb	Ma	Ma	Ap	Ap	
–	–	==	==	18	14	11	7	9	15	==	==	–	–	–	–	–	–	–	–	–	–	–	–	–	–	FLAT FOOT FLUGEY
–	–	==	==	17	10	4	6	12	15	==	–	–	–	–	–	–	–	–	–	–	–	–	–	–	–	I HADN'T ANYONE TILL YOU
–	–	–	18	5	**1**	**1**	3	4	11	==	–	–	–	–	–	–	–	–	–	–	–	–	–	–	–	SAYS MY HEART
–	–	–	==	12	7	4	8	17	==	==	–	–	–	–	–	–	–	–	–	–	–	–	–	–	–	YOU LEAVE ME BREATHLESS
–	–	–	==	17	13	12	15	==	–	–	–	–	–	–	–	–	–	–	–	–	–	–	–	–	–	THIS TIME IT'S REAL
–	–	–	==	14	9	8	12	==	==	–	–	–	–	–	–	–	–	–	–	–	–	–	–	–	–	OH! MA–MA
–	–	–	==	==	15	==	==	–	–	–	–	–	–	–	–	–	–	–	–	–	–	–	–	–	–	THE GIRL IN THE BONNET OF BLUE
–	–	–	==	==	12	14	11	11	17	==	==	–	–	–	–	–	–	–	–	–	–	–	–	–	–	LITTLE LADY MAKE BELIEVE
–	–	–	–	==	16	16	19	==	–	–	–	–	–	–	–	–	–	–	–	–	–	–	–	–	–	LET ME WHISPER (I LOVE YOU)
–	–	–	–	==	10	3	**1**	**1**	2	5	9	17	==	==	–	–	–	–	–	–	–	–	–	–	–	MUSIC, MAESTRO, PLEASE
–	–	–	–	==	20	13	6	10	19	==	–	–	–	–	–	–	–	–	–	–	–	–	–	–	–	I MARRIED AN ANGEL
–	–	–	–	==	==	17	==	–	–	–	–	–	–	–	–	–	–	–	–	–	–	–	–	–	–	DAY DREAMING (ALL NIGHT LONG)
–	–	–	–	–	==	19	==	–	–	–	–	–	–	–	–	–	–	–	–	–	–	–	–	–	–	MY MARGARITA
–	–	–	–	–	==	20	13	18	20	==	–	–	–	–	–	–	–	–	–	–	–	–	–	–	–	THERE'S HONEY ON THE MOON TONIGHT
–	–	–	–	–	==	18	10	2	**1**	**1**	2	4	15	==	==	–	–	–	–	–	–	–	–	–	–	A–TISKET, A–TASKET
–	–	–	–	–	==	==	18	16	13	12	16	==	==	–	–	–	–	–	–	–	–	–	–	–	–	OL' MAN MOSE
–	–	–	–	–	==	==	17	5	4	6	13	13	17	==	==	–	–	–	–	–	–	–	–	–	–	WHEN MOTHER NATURE SINGS HER LULLABY
–	–	–	–	–	–	==	14	14	10	==	–	–	–	–	–	–	–	–	–	–	–	–	–	–	–	WHEN THEY PLAYED THE POLKA
–	–	–	–	–	–	==	==	19	16	==	==	–	–	–	–	–	–	–	–	–	–	–	–	–	–	WHERE IN THE WORLD
–	–	–	–	–	–	==	==	7	3	2	5	9	==	==	–	–	–	–	–	–	–	–	–	–	–	NOW IT CAN BE TOLD
–	–	–	–	–	–	–	==	20	==	==	==	–	–	–	–	–	–	–	–	–	–	–	–	–	–	WILL YOU REMEMBER TONIGHT TOMORROW?
–	–	–	–	–	–	–	==	12	5	4	8	11	==	–	–	–	–	–	–	–	–	–	–	–	–	I'M GONNA LOCK MY HEART
–	–	–	–	–	–	–	==	13	7	7	4	14	==	–	–	–	–	–	–	–	–	–	–	–	–	YOU GO TO MY HEAD
–	–	–	–	–	–	–	–	==	8	3	**1**	**1**	**1**	**1**	5	12	==	==	–	–	–	–	–	–	–	I'VE GOT A POCKETFUL OF DREAMS
–	–	–	–	–	–	–	–	==	18	8	3	3	4	7	15	15	==	==	–	–	–	–	–	–	–	ALEXANDER'S RAGTIME BAND
–	–	–	–	–	–	–	–	==	14	9	14	12	14	==	–	–	–	–	–	–	–	–	–	–	–	WHAT GOES ON HERE IN MY HEART
–	–	–	–	–	–	–	–	==	==	17	18	==	==	–	–	–	–	–	–	–	–	–	–	–	–	BAMBINA
–	–	–	–	–	–	–	–	==	==	20	15	19	==	==	–	–	–	–	–	–	–	–	–	–	–	THERE'S A FARAWAY LOOK IN YOUR EYE
–	–	–	–	–	–	–	–	–	==	10	6	6	8	==	==	–	–	–	–	–	–	–	–	–	–	STOP BEATIN' 'ROUND THE MULBERRY BUSH
–	–	–	–	–	–	–	–	–	==	19	==	==	–	–	–	–	–	–	–	–	–	–	–	–	–	TULIE TULIP TIME
–	–	–	–	–	–	–	–	–	==	14	10	8	6	13	==	==	–	–	–	–	–	–	–	–	–	SMALL FRY
–	–	–	–	–	–	–	–	–	==	13	7	5	3	10	==	==	–	–	–	–	–	–	–	–	–	SO HELP ME (IF I DON'T LOVE YOU)
–	–	–	–	–	–	–	–	–	==	18	17	20	18	==	–	–	–	–	–	–	–	–	–	–	–	GARDEN OF THE MOON
–	–	–	–	–	–	–	–	–	–	==	12	7	7	20	==	–	–	–	–	–	–	–	–	–	–	I'VE GOT A DATE WITH A DREAM
–	–	–	–	–	–	–	–	–	–	==	11	2	2	2	7	16	==	–	–	–	–	–	–	–	–	CHANGE PARTNERS
–	–	–	–	–	–	–	–	–	–	==	20	16	12	12	13	14	20	==	==	–	–	–	–	–	–	BEGIN THE BEGUINE
–	–	–	–	–	–	–	–	–	–	==	19	15	9	3	**1**	**1**	**1**	**1**	6	16	==	–	–	–	–	MY REVERIE
–	–	–	–	–	–	–	–	–	–	–	==	18	11	9	17	==	–	–	–	–	–	–	–	–	–	AT LONG LAST LOVE
–	–	–	–	–	–	–	–	–	–	–	==	10	5	6	11	9	14	==	==	–	–	–	–	–	–	THE LAMBETH WALK
–	–	–	–	–	–	–	–	–	–	–	–	==	10	4	2	4	8	19	==	–	–	–	–	–	–	HEART AND SOUL
–	–	–	–	–	–	–	–	–	–	–	–	==	16	8	8	6	15	==	–	–	–	–	–	–	–	MY OWN
–	–	–	–	–	–	–	–	–	–	–	–	==	13	5	3	5	13	==	–	–	–	–	–	–	–	WHILE A CIGARETTE WAS BURNING
–	–	–	–	–	–	–	–	–	–	–	–	==	19	14	9	13	==	–	–	–	–	–	–	–	–	SUMMER SOUVENIRS
–	–	–	–	–	–	–	–	–	–	–	–	==	20	16	10	8	6	14	==	==	–	–	–	–	–	I WON'T TELL A SOUL
–	–	–	–	–	–	–	–	–	–	–	–	==	==	17	16	==	==	–	–	–	–	–	–	–	–	MEXICALI ROSE
–	–	–	–	–	–	–	–	–	–	–	–	==	==	11	4	2	4	8	15	==	–	–	–	–	–	ALL ASHORE
–	–	–	–	–	–	–	–	–	–	–	–	–	==	19	18	==	–	–	–	–	–	–	–	–	–	BOOGIE WOOGIE
–	–	–	–	–	–	–	–	–	–	–	–	–	==	15	12	11	==	==	–	–	–	–	–	–	–	WHO BLEW OUT THE FLAME?
–	–	–	–	–	–	–	–	–	–	–	–	–	==	18	6	3	2	2	7	14	==	–	–	–	–	TWO SLEEPY PEOPLE
–	–	–	–	–	–	–	–	–	–	–	–	–	–	==	14	20	==	–	–	–	–	–	–	–	–	SIXTY SECONDS GOT TOGETHER
–	–	–	–	–	–	–	–	–	–	–	–	–	–	==	20	10	9	20	==	–	–	–	–	–	–	HAVE YOU FORGOTTEN SO SOON?
–	–	–	–	–	–	–	–	–	–	–	–	–	–	==	19	7	3	3	**1**	6	14	==	–	–	–	YOU MUST HAVE BEEN A BEAUTIFUL BABY
–	–	–	–	–	–	–	–	–	–	–	–	–	–	==	==	19	19	==	==	–	–	–	–	–	–	DAY AFTER DAY
–	–	–	–	–	–	–	–	–	–	–	–	–	–	–	==	==	12	16	==	–	–	–	–	–	–	WHAT HAVE YOU GOT THAT GETS ME?
–	–	–	–	–	–	–	–	–	–	–	–	–	–	–	==	==	10	==	–	–	–	–	–	–	–	(DON'T WAIT TILL) THE NIGHT BEFORE CHRISTMAS
–	–	–	–	–	–	–	–	–	–	–	–	–	–	–	==	18	5	4	5	4	3	6	==	==	–	DEEP IN A DREAM (1939)
–	–	–	–	–	–	–	–	–	–	–	–	–	–	–	==	==	18	10	10	8	6	8	==	–	–	THEY SAY (1939)
–	–	–	–	–	–	–	–	–	–	–	–	–	–	–	==	==	16	18	12	9	9	17	==	–	–	HURRY HOME (1939)
–	–	–	–	–	–	–	–	–	–	–	–	–	–	–	==	17	7	6	3	2	2	2	3	9	16	THE UMBRELLA MAN (1939)
–	–	–	–	–	–	–	–	–	–	–	–	–	–	–	–	==	11	5	4	5	7	10	14	==	–	THIS CAN'T BE LOVE (1939)
–	–	–	–	–	–	–	–	–	–	–	–	–	–	–	–	==	17	11	9	12	==	==	–	–	–	I MUST SEE ANNIE TONIGHT (1939)
Ap	Ap	My	My	Jn	Jn	Jy	Jy	Ag	Ag	Sp	Sp	Oc	Oc	Nv	Nv	Dc	Dc	Ja	Ja	Fb	Fb	Ma	Ma	Ap	Ap	

1938															1939											
Oc	Oc	Nv	Nv	Dc	Dc	Ja	Ja	Fb	Fb	Ma	Ma	Ap	Ap	My	My	Jn	Jn	Jy	Jy	Ag	Ag	Sp	Sp	Oc	Oc	
==	10	4	2	4	8	19	==	–	–	–	–	–	–	–	–	–	–	–	–	–	–	–	–	–	–	HEART AND SOUL (1938)
15	9	3	**1**	**1**	**1**	**1**	6	16	==	–	–	–	–	–	–	–	–	–	–	–	–	–	–	–	–	MY REVERIE (1938)
==	==	11	4	2	4	8	15	==	–	–	–	–	–	–	–	–	–	–	–	–	–	–	–	–	–	ALL ASHORE (1938)
==	20	16	10	8	6	14	==	==	–	–	–	–	–	–	–	–	–	–	–	–	–	–	–	–	–	I WON'T TELL A SOUL (1938)
–	==	18	6	3	2	2	7	14	==	–	–	–	–	–	–	–	–	–	–	–	–	–	–	–	–	TWO SLEEPY PEOPLE (1938)
–	–	==	20	10	9	20	==	–	–	–	–	–	–	–	–	–	–	–	–	–	–	–	–	–	–	HAVE YOU FORGOTTEN? (1938)
–	–	==	19	7	3	3	**1**	6	14	==	–	–	–	–	–	–	–	–	–	–	–	–	–	–	–	YOU MUST HAVE BEEN A BEAUTIFUL BABY (1938)
–	–	–	==	==	12	16	==	–	–	–	–	–	–	–	–	–	–	–	–	–	–	–	–	–	–	WHAT HAVE YOU GOT THAT GETS ME? (1938)
–	–	–	==	18	5	4	5	4	3	6	==	==	–	–	–	–	–	–	–	–	–	–	–	–	–	DEEP IN A DREAM
–	–	–	==	17	7	6	3	2	2	2	3	9	16	==	–	–	–	–	–	–	–	–	–	–	–	THE UMBRELLA MAN
–	–	–	==	==	18	10	10	8	6	8	==	–	–	–	–	–	–	–	–	–	–	–	–	–	–	THEY SAY
–	–	–	==	==	16	18	12	9	9	17	==	–	–	–	–	–	–	–	–	–	–	–	–	–	–	HURRY HOME
–	–	–	–	==	11	5	4	5	7	10	14	==	–	–	–	–	–	–	–	–	–	–	–	–	–	THIS CAN'T BE LOVE
–	–	–	–	==	17	11	9	12	==	==	–	–	–	–	–	–	–	–	–	–	–	–	–	–	–	I MUST SEE ANNIE TONIGHT
–	–	–	–	==	==	17	==	==	==	–	–	–	–	–	–	–	–	–	–	–	–	–	–	–	–	YOU'RE THE ONLY STAR (IN MY BLUE HEAVEN)
–	–	–	–	==	==	15	18	==	–	–	–	–	–	–	–	–	–	–	–	–	–	–	–	–	–	ANGELS WITH DIRTY FACES
–	–	–	–	==	==	12	13	10	13	==	–	–	–	–	–	–	–	–	–	–	–	–	–	–	–	F.D.R. JONES
–	–	–	–	==	==	7	2	**1**	**1**	9	==	==	–	–	–	–	–	–	–	–	–	–	–	–	–	JEEPERS CREEPERS
–	–	–	–	–	==	9	8	7	12	==	==	–	–	–	–	–	–	–	–	–	–	–	–	–	–	THANKS FOR EVERYTHING
–	–	–	–	–	==	13	11	3	4	4	9	17	==	–	–	–	–	–	–	–	–	–	–	–	–	I HAVE EYES
–	–	–	–	–	==	==	17	==	–	–	–	–	–	–	–	–	–	–	–	–	–	–	–	–	–	FERDINAND THE BULL
–	–	–	–	–	==	==	20	==	–	–	–	–	–	–	–	–	–	–	–	–	–	–	–	–	–	PLEASE COME OUT OF YOUR DREAM
–	–	–	–	–	==	==	16	13	18	==	–	–	–	–	–	–	–	–	–	–	–	–	–	–	–	GET OUT OF TOWN
–	–	–	–	–	==	==	14	11	8	5	10	13	==	–	–	–	–	–	–	–	–	–	–	–	–	YOU'RE A SWEET LITTLE HEADACHE
–	–	–	–	–	==	==	==	18	==	–	–	–	–	–	–	–	–	–	–	–	–	–	–	–	–	SWEETHEARTS
–	–	–	–	–	–	==	==	15	19	==	==	==	–	–	–	–	–	–	–	–	–	–	–	–	–	THE FUNNY OLD HILLS
–	–	–	–	–	–	==	19	20	==	–	–	–	–	–	–	–	–	–	–	–	–	–	–	–	–	I UPS TO HER (AND SHE UPS TO ME)
–	–	–	–	–	–	–	==	17	10	7	4	7	14	==	–	–	–	–	–	–	–	–	–	–	–	COULD BE
–	–	–	–	–	–	–	==	19	5	**1**	**1**	**1**	**1**	6	17	18	==	–	–	–	–	–	–	–	–	DEEP PURPLE
–	–	–	–	–	–	–	==	==	15	14	11	8	12	==	==	–	–	–	–	–	–	–	–	–	–	HOLD TIGHT, HOLD TIGHT
–	–	–	–	–	–	–	==	==	16	15	==	==	–	–	–	–	–	–	–	–	–	–	–	–	–	MY HEART BELONGS TO DADDY
–	–	–	–	–	–	–	–	==	20	12	7	5	6	10	==	–	–	–	–	–	–	–	–	–	–	THE MASQUERADE IS OVER
–	–	–	–	–	–	–	–	==	17	11	5	14	13	==	–	–	–	–	–	–	–	–	–	–	–	I CRIED FOR YOU
–	–	–	–	–	–	–	–	==	11	3	2	2	4	8	14	17	==	–	–	–	–	–	–	–	–	PENNY SERENADE
–	–	–	–	–	–	–	–	==	==	19	15	11	11	17	19	==	17	==	20	==	==	==	==	==	==	GOD BLESS AMERICA
–	–	–	–	–	–	–	–	–	==	20	16	==	–	–	–	–	–	–	–	–	–	–	–	–	–	GOOD FOR NOTHIN' BUT LOVE
–	–	–	–	–	–	–	–	–	==	16	13	16	==	–	–	–	–	–	–	–	–	–	–	–	–	I PROMISE YOU
–	–	–	–	–	–	–	–	–	==	13	8	4	3	2	4	6	10	14	==	–	–	–	–	–	–	LITTLE SIR ECHO
–	–	–	–	–	–	–	–	–	==	18	6	3	5	9	==	–	–	–	–	–	–	–	–	–	–	I GET ALONG WITHOUT YOU VERY WELL
–	–	–	–	–	–	–	–	–	==	==	12	10	18	==	–	–	–	–	–	–	–	–	–	–	–	GOTTA GET SOME SHUTEYE
–	–	–	–	–	–	–	–	–	–	==	20	19	==	–	–	–	–	–	–	–	–	–	–	–	–	THIS NIGHT (WILL BE MY SOUVENIR)
–	–	–	–	–	–	–	–	–	–	==	19	18	==	==	–	–	–	–	–	–	–	–	–	–	–	WE'VE COME A LONG WAY TOGETHER
–	–	–	–	–	–	–	–	–	–	==	17	12	15	==	–	–	–	–	–	–	–	–	–	–	–	THIS IS IT
–	–	–	–	–	–	–	–	–	–	==	18	6	2	4	6	14	==	–	–	–	–	–	–	–	–	HEAVEN CAN WAIT
–	–	–	–	–	–	–	–	–	–	–	==	20	==	==	–	–	–	–	–	–	–	–	–	–	–	UNDECIDED
–	–	–	–	–	–	–	–	–	–	–	==	15	10	16	==	–	–	–	–	–	–	–	–	–	–	THE MOON IS A SILVER DOLLAR
–	–	–	–	–	–	–	–	–	–	–	–	==	7	**1**	3	4	11	15	==	–	–	–	–	–	–	OUR LOVE
–	–	–	–	–	–	–	–	–	–	–	–	==	8	5	5	8	12	16	==	–	–	–	–	–	–	LITTLE SKIPPER
–	–	–	–	–	–	–	–	–	–	–	–	==	9	3	**1**	3	8	==	==	–	–	–	–	–	–	AND THE ANGELS SING
–	–	–	–	–	–	–	–	–	–	–	–	==	20	12	9	7	6	9	==	–	–	–	–	–	–	DON'T WORRY 'BOUT ME
–	–	–	–	–	–	–	–	–	–	–	–	==	17	14	11	15	==	–	–	–	–	–	–	–	–	THE EAST SIDE OF HEAVEN
–	–	–	–	–	–	–	–	–	–	–	–	==	==	==	20	==	–	–	–	–	–	–	–	–	–	NIGHT MUST FALL (OVER ALL)
–	–	–	–	–	–	–	–	–	–	–	–	–	19	7	2	**1**	3	10	==	==	–	–	–	–	–	THREE LITTLE FISHIES (ITTY BITTY POO)
–	–	–	–	–	–	–	–	–	–	–	–	–	==	20	18	==	–	–	–	–	–	–	–	–	–	TEARS FROM MY INKWELL
–	–	–	–	–	–	–	–	–	–	–	–	–	==	13	10	16	==	–	–	–	–	–	–	–	–	I'M BUILDING A SAILBOAT OF DREAMS
–	–	–	–	–	–	–	–	–	–	–	–	–	==	15	7	2	**1**	**1**	2	7	11	17	==	–	–	WISHING
–	–	–	–	–	–	–	–	–	–	–	–	–	==	19	15	9	7	6	9	12	20	==	–	–	–	IF I DIDN'T CARE
–	–	–	–	–	–	–	–	–	–	–	–	–	–	==	16	12	9	12	==	–	–	–	–	–	–	A NEW MOON AND AN OLD SERENADE
–	–	–	–	–	–	–	–	–	–	–	–	–	–	==	13	11	5	3	7	==	==	–	–	–	–	THE LADY'S IN LOVE WITH YOU
Oc	Oc	Nv	Nv	Dc	Dc	Ja	Ja	Fb	Fb	Ma	Ma	Ap	Ap	My	My	Jn	Jn	Jy	Jy	Ag	Ag	Sp	Sp	Oc	Oc	

1939																		1940								
Ap	Ap	My	My	Jn	Jn	Jy	Jy	Ag	Ag	Sp	Sp	Oc	Oc	Nv	Nv	Dc	Dc	Ja	Ja	Fb	Fb	Ma	Ma	Ap	Ap	
–	==	11	8	5	2	2	4	4	3	3	5	9	11	14	==	==	–	–	–	–	–	–	–	–	–	BEER BARREL POLKA
–	==	18	12	10	4	5	5	5	7	11	10	12	==	==	–	–	–	–	–	–	–	–	–	–	–	SUNRISE SERENADE
–	–	==	==	13	16	==	–	–	–	–	–	–	–	–	–	–	–	–	–	–	–	–	–	–	–	I NEVER KNEW HEAVEN COULD SPEAK
–	–	–	==	19	19	==	==	–	–	–	–	–	–	–	–	–	–	–	–	–	–	–	–	–	–	WOODCHOPPERS' BALL
–	–	–	==	20	20	19	==	==	==	–	–	–	–	–	–	–	–	–	–	–	–	–	–	–	–	MY LAST GOODBYE
–	–	–	–	==	14	7	8	20	==	–	–	–	–	–	–	–	–	–	–	–	–	–	–	–	–	STRANGE ENCHANTMENT
–	–	–	–	==	18	20	==	==	19	==	–	–	–	–	–	–	–	–	–	–	–	–	–	–	–	BLUE EVENING
–	–	–	–	==	13	11	11	15	==	–	–	–	–	–	–	–	–	–	–	–	–	–	–	–	–	IN THE MIDDLE OF A DREAM
–	–	–	–	==	15	4	**1**	**1**	**1**	4	17	==	–	–	–	–	–	–	–	–	–	–	–	–	–	STAIRWAY TO THE STARS
–	–	–	–	–	==	17	15	14	13	20	==	–	–	–	–	–	–	–	–	–	–	–	–	–	–	WELL, ALL RIGHT!
–	–	–	–	–	==	8	3	3	5	13	==	–	–	–	–	–	–	–	–	–	–	–	–	–	–	WHITE SAILS
–	–	–	–	–	==	13	6	2	2	**1**	4	7	==	==	–	–	–	–	–	–	–	–	–	–	–	MOON LOVE
–	–	–	–	–	==	18	13	10	8	7	8	20	==	==	–	–	–	–	–	–	–	–	–	–	–	COMES LOVE
–	–	–	–	–	==	==	12	==	==	–	–	–	–	–	–	–	–	–	–	–	–	–	–	–	–	CONCERT IN THE PARK
–	–	–	–	–	–	==	19	==	==	–	–	–	–	–	–	–	–	–	–	–	–	–	–	–	–	IF I HAD MY WAY
–	–	–	–	–	–	==	14	13	==	==	–	–	–	–	–	–	–	–	–	–	–	–	–	–	–	THIS IS NO DREAM
–	–	–	–	–	–	==	18	11	12	15	12	==	–	–	–	–	–	–	–	–	–	–	–	–	–	TO YOU
–	–	–	–	–	–	==	10	6	4	5	16	==	–	–	–	–	–	–	–	–	–	–	–	–	–	I POURED MY HEART INTO A SONG
–	–	–	–	–	–	==	17	9	6	6	15	==	==	–	–	–	–	–	–	–	–	–	–	–	–	THE LAMP IS LOW
–	–	–	–	–	–	==	16	8	9	12	14	14	==	==	–	–	–	–	–	–	–	–	–	–	–	CINDERELLA, STAY IN MY ARMS
–	–	–	–	–	–	==	==	16	==	==	–	–	–	–	–	–	–	–	–	–	–	–	–	–	–	THE SHABBY OLD CABBY
–	–	–	–	–	–	==	==	18	==	==	–	–	–	–	–	–	–	–	–	–	–	–	–	–	–	SOUTH AMERICAN WAY
–	–	–	–	–	–	==	==	19	16	14	9	11	15	==	==	–	–	–	–	–	–	–	–	–	–	MOONLIGHT SERENADE
–	–	–	–	–	–	–	==	17	15	8	3	6	10	==	–	–	–	–	–	–	–	–	–	–	–	OH, YOU CRAZY MOON
–	–	–	–	–	–	–	–	==	18	10	13	17	19	==	==	–	–	–	–	–	–	–	–	–	–	THE JUMPIN' JIVE
–	–	–	–	–	–	–	–	==	17	==	==	–	–	–	–	–	–	–	–	–	–	–	–	–	–	ESPECIALLY FOR YOU
–	–	–	–	–	–	–	–	==	14	9	2	2	2	7	10	13	==	–	–	–	–	–	–	–	–	THE MAN WITH THE MANDOLIN
–	–	–	–	–	–	–	–	==	10	2	**1**	**1**	**1**	2	6	10	14	==	–	–	–	–	–	–	–	OVER THE RAINBOW
–	–	–	–	–	–	–	–	==	==	16	11	8	18	==	–	–	–	–	–	–	–	–	–	–	–	A MAN AND HIS DREAM
–	–	–	–	–	–	–	–	–	==	18	6	4	6	9	19	==	–	–	–	–	–	–	–	–	–	AN APPLE FOR THE TEACHER
–	–	–	–	–	–	–	–	–	==	19	7	3	4	6	11	==	==	–	–	–	–	–	–	–	–	DAY IN – DAY OUT
–	–	–	–	–	–	–	–	–	==	==	18	13	9	16	16	16	==	–	–	–	–	–	–	–	–	IN AN EIGHTEENTH CENTURY DRAWING ROOM
–	–	–	–	–	–	–	–	–	–	==	20	10	7	8	9	12	==	==	–	–	–	–	–	–	–	WHAT'S NEW?
–	–	–	–	–	–	–	–	–	–	==	19	5	5	3	4	5	13	==	==	–	–	–	–	–	–	BLUE ORCHIDS
–	–	–	–	–	–	–	–	–	–	==	==	16	20	==	==	–	–	–	–	–	–	–	–	–	–	THE LITTLE MAN WHO WASN'T THERE
–	–	–	–	–	–	–	–	–	–	==	==	19	16	10	7	7	10	12	==	==	–	–	–	–	–	(ALLA EN) EL RANCHO GRANDE
–	–	–	–	–	–	–	–	–	–	–	==	18	12	11	14	15	==	–	–	–	–	–	–	–	–	ARE YOU HAVIN' ANY FUN?
–	–	–	–	–	–	–	–	–	–	–	==	15	3	**1**	**1**	2	2	2	8	12	16	==	–	–	–	SOUTH OF THE BORDER
–	–	–	–	–	–	–	–	–	–	–	==	==	14	13	13	20	==	–	–	–	–	–	–	–	–	ADDRESS UNKNOWN
–	–	–	–	–	–	–	–	–	–	–	==	==	8	5	3	3	3	6	11	15	==	–	–	–	–	MY PRAYER
–	–	–	–	–	–	–	–	–	–	–	–	==	13	17	==	==	–	–	–	–	–	–	–	–	–	IT'S A HUNDRED TO ONE (I'M IN LOVE)
–	–	–	–	–	–	–	–	–	–	–	–	==	17	4	2	**1**	**1**	**1**	3	10	18	==	–	–	–	SCATTERBRAIN
–	–	–	–	–	–	–	–	–	–	–	–	==	==	19	12	==	==	–	–	–	–	–	–	–	–	GOOD MORNING
–	–	–	–	–	–	–	–	–	–	–	–	==	==	12	5	4	5	11	14	20	==	–	–	–	–	LILACS IN THE RAIN
–	–	–	–	–	–	–	–	–	–	–	–	–	==	15	8	8	12	==	==	–	–	–	–	–	–	(WHY COULDN'T IT LAST) LAST NIGHT
–	–	–	–	–	–	–	–	–	–	–	–	–	==	20	17	9	6	19	==	–	–	–	–	–	–	I DIDN'T KNOW WHAT TIME IT WAS
–	–	–	–	–	–	–	–	–	–	–	–	–	–	==	20	14	11	16	==	–	–	–	–	–	–	GOODY GOODBYE
–	–	–	–	–	–	–	–	–	–	–	–	–	–	==	18	6	4	3	4	4	11	17	==	–	–	OH JOHNNY, OH JOHNNY, OH!
–	–	–	–	–	–	–	–	–	–	–	–	–	–	–	==	17	7	9	9	18	==	–	–	–	–	STOP! IT'S WONDERFUL
–	–	–	–	–	–	–	–	–	–	–	–	–	–	–	==	18	17	15	==	==	–	–	–	–	–	SPEAKING OF HEAVEN
–	–	–	–	–	–	–	–	–	–	–	–	–	–	–	==	19	20	17	17	==	–	–	–	–	–	YODELIN' JIVE
–	–	–	–	–	–	–	–	–	–	–	–	==	==	18	15	11	8	7	7	6	5	7	10	14	19	IN THE MOOD (1940)
–	–	–	–	–	–	–	–	–	–	–	–	–	–	–	–	==	9	4	**1**	2	3	9	==	==	–	ALL THE THINGS YOU ARE (1940)
–	–	–	–	–	–	–	–	–	–	–	–	–	–	–	–	==	18	5	2	3	2	2	5	12	==	INDIAN SUMMER (1940)
–	–	–	–	–	–	–	–	–	–	–	–	–	–	–	–	==	15	13	15	==	==	–	–	–	–	CHATTERBOX (1940)
–	–	–	–	–	–	–	–	–	–	–	–	–	–	–	–	==	19	8	5	**1**	**1**	**1**	6	17	==	CARELESS (1940)
–	–	–	–	–	–	–	–	–	–	–	–	–	–	–	–	==	16	14	10	9	10	20	==	–	–	THE LITTLE RED FOX (1940)
Ap	Ap	My	My	Jn	Jn	Jy	Jy	Ag	Ag	Sp	Sp	Oc	Oc	Nv	Nv	Dc	Dc	Ja	Ja	Fb	Fb	Ma	Ma	Ap	Ap	

		1939													1940											
Oc	Oc	Nv	Nv	Dc	Dc	Ja	Ja	Fb	Fb	Ma	Ma	Ap	Ap	My	My	Jn	Jn	Jy	Jy	Ag	Ag	Sp	Sp	Oc	Oc	
==	8	5	3	3	3	6	11	15	==	–	–	–	–	–	–	–	–	–	–	–	–	–	–	–	–	MY PRAYER (1939)
15	3	**1**	**1**	2	2	2	8	12	16	==	–	–	–	–	–	–	–	–	–	–	–	–	–	–	–	SOUTH OF THE BORDER (1939)
==	==	12	5	4	5	11	14	20	==	–	–	–	–	–	–	–	–	–	–	–	–	–	–	–	–	LILACS IN THE RAIN (1939)
==	17	4	2	**1**	**1**	**1**	3	10	18	==	–	–	–	–	–	–	–	–	–	–	–	–	–	–	–	SCATTERBRAIN (1939)
–	==	20	17	9	6	19	==	–	–	–	–	–	–	–	–	–	–	–	–	–	–	–	–	–	–	I DIDN'T KNOW WHAT TIME IT WAS (1939)
19	16	10	7	7	10	12	==	==	–	–	–	–	–	–	–	–	–	–	–	–	–	–	–	–	–	(ALLA EN) EL RANCHO GRANDE (1939)
–	–	==	20	14	11	16	==	–	–	–	–	–	–	–	–	–	–	–	–	–	–	–	–	–	–	GOODY GOODBYE (1939)
–	–	==	18	6	4	3	4	4	11	17	==	–	–	–	–	–	–	–	–	–	–	–	–	–	–	OH JOHNNY, OH JOHNNY, OH! (1939)
–	–	–	==	17	7	9	9	18	==	–	–	–	–	–	–	–	–	–	–	–	–	–	–	–	–	STOP! IT'S WONDERFUL (1939)
–	–	–	==	18	17	15	==	==	–	–	–	–	–	–	–	–	–	–	–	–	–	–	–	–	–	SPEAKING OF HEAVEN (1939)
–	–	–	==	19	20	17	17	==	–	–	–	–	–	–	–	–	–	–	–	–	–	–	–	–	–	YODELIN' JIVE (1939)
==	==	18	15	11	8	7	7	6	5	7	10	14	19	==	–	–	–	–	–	–	–	–	–	–	–	IN THE MOOD
–	–	–	–	==	9	4	**1**	2	3	9	==	==	–	–	–	–	–	–	–	–	–	–	–	–	–	ALL THE THINGS YOU ARE
–	–	–	–	==	18	5	2	3	2	2	5	12	==	==	–	–	–	–	–	–	–	–	–	–	–	INDIAN SUMMER
–	–	–	–	==	15	13	15	==	==	–	–	–	–	–	–	–	–	–	–	–	–	–	–	–	–	CHATTERBOX
–	–	–	–	==	19	8	5	**1**	**1**	**1**	6	17	==	–	–	–	–	–	–	–	–	–	–	–	–	CARELESS
–	–	–	–	==	16	14	10	9	10	20	==	–	–	–	–	–	–	–	–	–	–	–	–	–	–	THE LITTLE RED FOX
–	–	–	–	==	==	10	6	5	7	12	==	–	–	–	–	–	–	–	–	–	–	–	–	–	–	FAITHFUL FOREVER
–	–	–	–	–	==	20	12	8	4	5	9	19	==	–	–	–	–	–	–	–	–	–	–	–	–	AT THE BALALAIKA
–	–	–	–	–	==	18	13	11	9	3	3	2	4	7	11	15	==	==	–	–	–	–	–	–	–	IN AN OLD DUTCH GARDEN
–	–	–	–	–	==	==	18	19	==	==	–	–	–	–	–	–	–	–	–	–	–	–	–	–	–	BLUEBIRDS IN THE MOONLIGHT
–	–	–	–	–	–	==	20	==	==	–	–	–	–	–	–	–	–	–	–	–	–	–	–	–	–	CIRIBIRIBIN
–	–	–	–	–	–	==	19	13	20	==	–	–	–	–	–	–	–	–	–	–	–	–	–	–	–	THIS CHANGING WORLD
–	–	–	–	–	–	==	16	7	6	4	12	20	==	–	–	–	–	–	–	–	–	–	–	–	–	DARN THAT DREAM
–	–	–	–	–	–	–	==	17	13	==	==	–	–	–	–	–	–	–	–	–	–	–	–	–	–	TO YOU, SWEETHEART, ALOHA
–	–	–	–	–	–	–	==	16	17	8	15	==	–	–	–	–	–	–	–	–	–	–	–	–	–	DO I LOVE YOU?
–	–	–	–	–	–	–	==	14	19	18	==	–	–	–	–	–	–	–	–	–	–	–	–	–	–	YOU'D BE SURPRISED
–	–	–	–	–	–	–	==	==	8	6	2	4	12	==	==	–	–	–	–	–	–	–	–	–	–	IT'S A BLUE WORLD
–	–	–	–	–	–	–	==	==	==	15	13	7	8	8	10	12	17	==	==	–	–	–	–	–	–	TUXEDO JUNCTION
–	–	–	–	–	–	–	–	==	12	11	11	6	16	==	–	–	–	–	–	–	–	–	–	–	–	THE GAUCHO SERENADE
–	–	–	–	–	–	–	–	==	14	14	8	16	20	==	–	–	–	–	–	–	–	–	–	–	–	I'VE GOT MY EYES ON YOU
–	–	–	–	–	–	–	–	==	15	13	==	==	–	–	–	–	–	–	–	–	–	–	–	–	–	CONFUCIUS SAY
–	–	–	–	–	–	–	–	==	==	10	**1**	**1**	**1**	2	4	10	==	==	–	–	–	–	–	–	–	WHEN YOU WISH UPON A STAR
–	–	–	–	–	–	–	–	–	==	16	4	3	5	9	==	==	–	–	–	–	–	–	–	–	–	ON THE ISLE OF MAY
–	–	–	–	–	–	–	–	–	==	19	7	5	9	==	==	–	–	–	–	–	–	–	–	–	–	THE STARLIT HOUR
–	–	–	–	–	–	–	–	–	==	==	14	10	13	10	18	==	–	–	–	–	–	–	–	–	–	LEANIN' ON THE OLE TOP RAIL
–	–	–	–	–	–	–	–	–	==	==	16	11	6	4	3	6	8	12	16	==	–	–	–	–	–	THE SINGING HILLS
–	–	–	–	–	–	–	–	–	==	==	==	8	2	**1**	**1**	**1**	2	3	10	18	==	–	–	–	–	THE WOODPECKER SONG
–	–	–	–	–	–	–	–	–	–	==	19	18	10	11	19	==	–	–	–	–	–	–	–	–	–	HOW HIGH THE MOON
–	–	–	–	–	–	–	–	–	–	==	18	15	7	5	9	14	==	==	–	–	–	–	–	–	–	(I'M) TOO ROMANTIC
–	–	–	–	–	–	–	–	–	–	==	17	13	11	14	20	==	–	–	–	–	–	–	–	–	–	SAY SI SI (PARA VIGO ME VOY)
–	–	–	–	–	–	–	–	–	–	==	20	9	3	3	2	2	7	16	==	==	–	–	–	–	–	WITH THE WIND AND THE RAIN IN YOUR HAIR
–	–	–	–	–	–	–	–	–	–	–	==	==	14	6	8	18	==	==	–	–	–	–	–	–	–	LET THERE BE LOVE
–	–	–	–	–	–	–	–	–	–	–	==	==	15	12	15	13	20	==	–	–	–	–	–	–	–	ALICE BLUE GOWN
–	–	–	–	–	–	–	–	–	–	–	==	==	17	==	==	–	–	–	–	–	–	–	–	–	–	SO FAR, SO GOOD
–	–	–	–	–	–	–	–	–	–	–	==	==	==	19	13	16	==	–	–	–	–	–	–	–	–	A LOVER'S LULLABY
–	–	–	–	–	–	–	–	–	–	–	–	==	18	15	14	11	12	19	==	–	–	–	–	–	–	SHAKE DOWN THE STARS
–	–	–	–	–	–	–	–	–	–	–	–	–	==	17	17	==	–	–	–	–	–	–	–	–	–	YOU, YOU, DARLIN'
–	–	–	–	–	–	–	–	–	–	–	–	–	==	13	6	5	6	6	7	9	15	==	–	–	–	PLAYMATES
–	–	–	–	–	–	–	–	–	–	–	–	–	==	16	12	9	13	==	==	–	–	–	–	–	–	LITTLE CURLY HAIR IN A HIGH CHAIR
–	–	–	–	–	–	–	–	–	–	–	–	–	==	18	5	4	5	8	20	==	–	–	–	–	–	SAY IT
–	–	–	–	–	–	–	–	–	–	–	–	–	–	20	7	3	**1**	2	6	12	19	==	–	–	–	IMAGINATION
–	–	–	–	–	–	–	–	–	–	–	–	–	–	==	16	7	3	**1**	**1**	5	12	18	==	–	–	MAKE BELIEVE ISLAND
Oc	Oc	Nv	Nv	Dc	Dc	Ja	Ja	Fb	Fb	Ma	Ma	Ap	Ap	My	My	Jn	Jn	Jy	Jy	Ag	Ag	Sp	Sp	Oc	Oc	

1940																		1941								
Ap	Ap	My	My	Jn	Jn	Jy	Jy	Ag	Ag	Sp	Sp	Oc	Oc	Nv	Nv	Dc	Dc	Ja	Ja	Fb	Fb	Ma	Ma	Ap	Ap	
–	==	==	==	==	==	14	11	8	10	8	9	9	14	14	18	==	==	18	==	==	==	==	==	–	–	GOD BLESS AMERICA
–	–	==	==	20	==	–	–	–	–	–	–	–	–	–	–	–	–	–	–	–	–	–	–	–	–	AN ANGEL IN DISGUISE
–	–	==	==	8	4	4	8	11	==	==	–	–	–	–	–	–	–	–	–	–	–	–	–	–	–	WHERE WAS I?
–	–	–	==	19	==	==	–	–	–	–	–	–	–	–	–	–	–	–	–	–	–	–	–	–	–	IT'S A WONDERFUL WORLD
–	–	–	==	17	10	5	3	4	6	10	==	==	–	–	–	–	–	–	–	–	–	–	–	–	–	THE BREEZE AND I
–	–	–	==	==	19	20	==	==	–	–	–	–	–	–	–	–	–	–	–	–	–	–	–	–	–	BOOG-IT
–	–	–	==	==	11	10	13	==	==	–	–	–	–	–	–	–	–	–	–	–	–	–	–	–	–	BLUE LOVEBIRD
–	–	–	==	==	9	7	9	16	==	–	–	–	–	–	–	–	–	–	–	–	–	–	–	–	–	I CAN'T LOVE YOU ANY MORE (THAN I DO)
–	–	–	–	==	18	18	==	–	–	–	–	–	–	–	–	–	–	–	–	–	–	–	–	–	–	YOURS IS MY HEART ALONE
–	–	–	–	==	14	13	==	==	==	–	–	–	–	–	–	–	–	–	–	–	–	–	–	–	–	YOU'RE LONELY AND I'M LONELY
–	–	–	–	==	15	9	2	2	2	3	8	11	==	–	–	–	–	–	–	–	–	–	–	–	–	SIERRA SUE
–	–	–	–	==	16	11	5	3	3	7	18	==	–	–	–	–	–	–	–	–	–	–	–	–	–	FOOLS RUSH IN
–	–	–	–	–	==	15	12	20	20	==	–	–	–	–	–	–	–	–	–	–	–	–	–	–	–	DEVIL MAY CARE
–	–	–	–	–	==	17	4	**1**	**1**	**1**	**1**	6	6	11	==	==	–	–	–	–	–	–	–	–	–	I'LL NEVER SMILE AGAIN
–	–	–	–	–	==	==	19	==	==	–	–	–	–	–	–	–	–	–	–	–	–	–	–	–	–	TENNESSEE FISH FRY
–	–	–	–	–	==	==	==	17	18	==	–	–	–	–	–	–	–	–	–	–	–	–	–	–	–	HEAR MY SONG, VIOLETTA
–	–	–	–	–	–	==	15	10	8	6	13	==	–	–	–	–	–	–	–	–	–	–	–	–	–	THE NEARNESS OF YOU
–	–	–	–	–	–	==	17	15	13	9	11	16	==	–	–	–	–	–	–	–	–	–	–	–	–	SIX LESSONS FROM MADAME LA ZONGA
–	–	–	–	–	–	==	14	13	11	15	==	–	–	–	–	–	–	–	–	–	–	–	–	–	–	I'M STEPPING OUT WITH A MEMORY TONIGHT
–	–	–	–	–	–	==	18	6	4	2	3	4	9	16	==	==	–	–	–	–	–	–	–	–	–	WHEN THE SWALLOWS COME BACK TO CAPISTRANO
–	–	–	–	–	–	==	==	7	5	4	5	8	15	==	–	–	–	–	–	–	–	–	–	–	–	I'M NOBODY'S BABY
–	–	–	–	–	–	–	==	14	9	11	12	==	–	–	–	–	–	–	–	–	–	–	–	–	–	ALL THIS AND HEAVEN TOO
–	–	–	–	–	–	–	==	19	14	19	19	==	–	–	–	–	–	–	–	–	–	–	–	–	–	PENNSYLVANIA 6-5000
–	–	–	–	–	–	–	==	==	7	5	2	**1**	3	5	9	10	14	==	==	–	–	–	–	–	–	BLUEBERRY HILL
–	–	–	–	–	–	–	–	==	17	==	==	–	–	–	–	–	–	–	–	–	–	–	–	–	–	ORCHIDS FOR REMEMBRANCE
–	–	–	–	–	–	–	–	==	16	16	16	14	12	12	11	13	13	17	==	==	–	–	–	–	–	BEAT ME, DADDY, EIGHT TO THE BAR
–	–	–	–	–	–	–	–	–	==	17	14	==	==	–	–	–	–	–	–	–	–	–	–	–	–	CAN'T GET INDIANA OFF MY MIND
–	–	–	–	–	–	–	–	–	==	14	6	5	5	6	8	11	==	==	–	–	–	–	–	–	–	PRACTICE MAKES PERFECT
–	–	–	–	–	–	–	–	–	==	13	4	2	4	4	7	12	20	==	–	–	–	–	–	–	–	MAYBE
–	–	–	–	–	–	–	–	–	==	12	7	3	2	3	5	5	11	14	==	–	–	–	–	–	–	TRADE WINDS
–	–	–	–	–	–	–	–	–	==	20	15	10	==	==	–	–	–	–	–	–	–	–	–	–	–	THAT'S FOR ME
–	–	–	–	–	–	–	–	–	==	==	20	==	18	13	15	==	==	–	–	–	–	–	–	–	–	I AM AN AMERICAN
–	–	–	–	–	–	–	–	–	==	==	10	7	**1**	**1**	2	**1**	7	7	10	==	==	–	–	–	–	ONLY FOREVER
–	–	–	–	–	–	–	–	–	==	==	==	15	20	==	==	==	==	–	–	–	–	–	–	–	–	THE SAME OLD STORY
–	–	–	–	–	–	–	–	–	–	==	17	13	11	15	==	–	–	–	–	–	–	–	–	–	–	THE CALL OF THE CANYON
–	–	–	–	–	–	–	–	–	–	–	==	19	17	20	==	–	–	–	–	–	–	–	–	–	–	CROSSTOWN
–	–	–	–	–	–	–	–	–	–	–	==	20	8	7	6	14	19	==	–	–	–	–	–	–	–	OUR LOVE AFFAIR
–	–	–	–	–	–	–	–	–	–	–	==	18	16	10	4	2	**1**	5	11	17	==	–	–	–	–	WE THREE
–	–	–	–	–	–	–	–	–	–	–	==	12	7	2	**1**	3	3	4	7	18	==	–	–	–	–	FERRY-BOAT SERENADE
–	–	–	–	–	–	–	–	–	–	–	==	17	10	9	12	==	==	–	–	–	–	–	–	–	–	NOW I LAY ME DOWN TO DREAM
–	–	–	–	–	–	–	–	–	–	–	==	==	19	18	==	==	–	–	–	–	–	–	–	–	–	A MILLION DREAMS AGO
–	–	–	–	–	–	–	–	–	–	–	==	==	13	8	3	4	6	6	4	4	10	20	==	–	–	THERE I GO
–	–	–	–	–	–	–	–	–	–	–	–	==	==	17	17	18	16	15	==	==	–	–	–	–	–	POMPTON TURNPIKE
–	–	–	–	–	–	–	–	–	–	–	–	–	==	19	16	15	17	==	==	–	–	–	–	–	–	FIVE O'CLOCK WHISTLE
–	–	–	–	–	–	–	–	–	–	–	–	–	==	==	20	8	2	2	5	6	11	10	==	==	–	A NIGHTINGALE SANG IN BERKELEY SQUARE
–	–	–	–	–	–	–	–	–	–	–	–	–	–	==	13	16	==	==	–	–	–	–	–	–	–	TWO DREAMS MET
–	–	–	–	–	–	–	–	–	–	–	–	–	–	==	14	9	8	9	8	15	==	==	–	–	–	DREAM VALLEY
–	–	–	–	–	–	–	–	–	–	–	–	–	–	==	10	6	5	3	3	9	==	==	–	–	–	DOWN ARGENTINA WAY
–	–	–	–	–	–	–	–	–	–	–	–	–	–	–	==	20	12	13	16	==	==	–	–	–	–	SCRUB ME, MAMA, WITH A BOOGIE BEAT
–	–	–	–	–	–	–	–	–	–	–	–	–	–	==	==	19	9	8	6	3	7	9	==	==	–	I GIVE YOU MY WORD (1941)
–	–	–	–	–	–	–	–	–	–	–	–	–	–	–	==	17	10	11	14	8	9	19	==	–	–	SO YOU'RE THE ONE (1941)
–	–	–	–	–	–	–	–	–	–	–	–	–	–	–	==	19	7	4	**1**	**1**	1	2	**1**	3	5	9	FRENESI (1941)
–	–	–	–	–	–	–	–	–	–	–	–	–	–	–	–	==	15	10	9	14	19	==	–	–	–	ALONG THE SANTA FE TRAIL (1941)
–	–	–	–	–	–	–	–	–	–	–	–	–	–	–	–	==	18	12	2	2	**1**	2	2	4	15	I HEAR A RHAPSODY (1941)
Ap	Ap	My	My	Jn	Jn	Jy	Jy	Ag	Ag	Sp	Sp	Oc	Oc	Nv	Nv	Dc	Dc	Ja	Ja	Fb	Fb	Ma	Ma	Ap	Ap	

1940						1941																				
Oc	Oc	Nv	Nv	Dc	Dc	Ja	Ja	Fb	Fb	Ma	Ma	Ap	Ap	My	My	Jn	Jn	Jy	Jy	Ag	Ag	Sp	Sp	Oc	Oc	
9	14	14	18	==	==	18	==	==	==	==	==	–	–	–	–	–	–	–	–	–	–	–	–	–	–	GOD BLESS AMERICA (1940)
14	12	12	11	13	13	17	==	==	–	–	–	–	–	–	–	–	–	–	–	–	–	–	–	–	–	BEAT ME, DADDY, EIGHT TO THE BAR (1940)
7	1	1	2	1	7	7	10	==	==	–	–	–	–	–	–	–	–	–	–	–	–	–	–	–	–	ONLY FOREVER (1940)
3	2	3	5	5	11	14	==	–	–	–	–	–	–	–	–	–	–	–	–	–	–	–	–	–	–	TRADE WINDS (1940)
==	13	8	3	4	6	6	4	4	10	20	==	–	–	–	–	–	–	–	–	–	–	–	–	–	–	THERE I GO (1940)
18	16	10	4	2	1	5	11	17	==	–	–	–	–	–	–	–	–	–	–	–	–	–	–	–	–	WE THREE (1940)
==	==	17	17	18	16	15	==	==	–	–	–	–	–	–	–	–	–	–	–	–	–	–	–	–	–	POMPTON TURNPIKE (1940)
12	7	2	1	3	3	4	7	18	==	–	–	–	–	–	–	–	–	–	–	–	–	–	–	–	–	FERRY-BOAT SERENADE (1940)
–	==	==	20	8	2	2	5	6	11	10	==	==	–	–	–	–	–	–	–	–	–	–	–	–	–	A NIGHTINGALE SANG IN BERKELEY SQUARE (1940)
–	–	==	14	9	8	9	8	15	==	==	–	–	–	–	–	–	–	–	–	–	–	–	–	–	–	DREAM VALLEY (1940)
–	–	==	10	6	5	3	3	9	==	==	–	–	–	–	–	–	–	–	–	–	–	–	–	–	–	DOWN ARGENTINA WAY (1940)
–	–	==	19	7	4	1	1	1	2	1	3	5	9	18	==	–	–	–	–	–	–	–	–	–	–	FRENESI
–	–	==	==	19	9	8	6	3	7	9	==	==	–	–	–	–	–	–	–	–	–	–	–	–	–	I GIVE YOU MY WORD
–	–	–	==	20	12	13	16	==	==	–	–	–	–	–	–	–	–	–	–	–	–	–	–	–	–	SCRUB ME, MAMA, WITH A BOOGIE BEAT (1940)
–	–	–	==	17	10	11	14	8	9	19	==	–	–	–	–	–	–	–	–	–	–	–	–	–	–	SO YOU'RE THE ONE
–	–	–	==	==	==	19	20	==	–	–	–	–	–	–	–	–	–	–	–	–	–	–	–	–	–	YOU'VE GOT ME THIS WAY
–	–	–	–	==	15	10	9	14	19	==	–	–	–	–	–	–	–	–	–	–	–	–	–	–	–	ALONG THE SANTA FE TRAIL
–	–	–	–	==	18	12	2	2	1	2	2	4	15	==	–	–	–	–	–	–	–	–	–	–	–	I HEAR A RHAPSODY
–	–	–	–	==	==	16	12	7	4	5	6	11	16	==	–	–	–	–	–	–	–	–	–	–	–	PERFIDIA (TONIGHT)
–	–	–	–	==	==	20	13	5	3	6	7	8	==	==	–	–	–	–	–	–	–	–	–	–	–	YOU WALK BY
–	–	–	–	–	==	==	15	11	8	18	17	==	==	–	–	–	–	–	–	–	–	–	–	–	–	STAR DUST
–	–	–	–	–	==	==	==	==	14	7	9	9	5	10	12	==	==	==	==	–	–	–	–	–	–	SAN ANTONIO ROSE
–	–	–	–	–	–	==	17	12	17	14	==	–	–	–	–	–	–	–	–	–	–	–	–	–	–	THE LAST TIME I SAW PARIS
–	–	–	–	–	–	==	19	19	16	17	==	==	–	–	–	–	–	–	–	–	–	–	–	–	–	YES, MY DARLING DAUGHTER
–	–	–	–	–	–	==	18	16	12	11	13	14	20	==	–	–	–	–	–	–	–	–	–	–	–	ANVIL CHORUS
–	–	–	–	–	–	–	==	13	15	13	==	–	–	–	–	–	–	–	–	–	–	–	–	–	–	MAY I NEVER LOVE AGAIN
–	–	–	–	–	–	–	==	10	5	4	5	7	8	==	==	–	–	–	–	–	–	–	–	–	–	IT ALL COMES BACK TO ME NOW
–	–	–	–	–	–	–	==	20	6	3	1	2	7	19	==	–	–	–	–	–	–	–	–	–	–	HIGH ON A WINDY HILL
–	–	–	–	–	–	–	==	==	20	==	20	==	==	–	–	–	–	–	–	–	–	–	–	–	–	LET'S DREAM THIS ONE OUT
–	–	–	–	–	–	–	–	==	18	12	10	12	12	==	==	–	–	–	–	–	–	–	–	–	–	SONG OF THE VOLGA BOATMEN
–	–	–	–	–	–	–	–	==	13	8	4	1	3	7	16	==	–	–	–	–	–	–	–	–	–	THERE'LL BE SOME CHANGES MADE
–	–	–	–	–	–	–	–	==	==	16	==	==	–	–	–	–	–	–	–	–	–	–	–	–	–	AMERICA, I LOVE YOU
–	–	–	–	–	–	–	–	–	==	15	12	18	==	–	–	–	–	–	–	–	–	–	–	–	–	I DREAMT I DWELT IN HARLEM
–	–	–	–	–	–	–	–	–	==	==	15	17	==	==	–	–	–	–	–	–	–	–	–	–	–	THE BOOGIE WOOGIE BUGLE BOY
–	–	–	–	–	–	–	–	–	–	==	18	16	17	17	==	–	–	–	–	–	–	–	–	–	–	BLUE FLAME
–	–	–	–	–	–	–	–	–	–	==	11	6	2	2	8	==	==	–	–	–	–	–	–	–	–	A WISE OLD OWL
–	–	–	–	–	–	–	–	–	–	==	14	10	4	5	15	==	–	–	–	–	–	–	–	–	–	OH, LOOK AT ME NOW
–	–	–	–	–	–	–	–	–	–	==	16	19	18	12	14	16	==	==	–	–	–	–	–	–	–	NUMBER TEN LULLABY LANE
–	–	–	–	–	–	–	–	–	–	==	8	3	1	1	1	3	5	9	11	==	==	–	–	–	–	AMAPOLA
–	–	–	–	–	–	–	–	–	–	==	19	13	6	4	7	12	16	==	==	–	–	–	–	–	–	WALKING BY THE RIVER
–	–	–	–	–	–	–	–	–	–	–	==	15	11	11	19	==	==	–	–	–	–	–	–	–	–	GEORGIA ON MY MIND
–	–	–	–	–	–	–	–	–	–	–	==	20	14	8	6	7	11	14	==	==	==	–	–	–	–	DOLORES
–	–	–	–	–	–	–	–	–	–	–	==	==	13	3	4	6	10	12	12	==	==	–	–	–	–	DO I WORRY?
–	–	–	–	–	–	–	–	–	–	–	–	==	19	14	==	==	–	–	–	–	–	–	–	–	–	ALEXANDER THE SWOOSE
–	–	–	–	–	–	–	–	–	–	–	–	==	10	13	9	10	12	16	==	–	–	–	–	–	–	G'BYE NOW
–	–	–	–	–	–	–	–	–	–	–	–	–	==	16	10	9	7	8	13	13	17	==	==	–	–	I'LL BE WITH YOU IN APPLE BLOSSOM TIME
–	–	–	–	–	–	–	–	–	–	–	–	–	==	6	3	2	4	4	8	10	==	==	–	–	–	MY SISTER AND I
–	–	–	–	–	–	–	–	–	–	–	–	–	==	==	==	==	18	17	==	==	–	–	–	–	–	TWO HEARTS THAT PASS IN THE NIGHT
–	–	–	–	–	–	–	–	–	–	–	–	–	==	==	==	==	19	20	14	18	==	–	–	–	–	UNTIL TOMORROW
Oc	Oc	Nv	Nv	Dc	Dc	Ja	Ja	Fb	Fb	Ma	Ma	Ap	Ap	My	My	Jn	Jn	Jy	Jy	Ag	Ag	Sp	Sp	Oc	Oc	

1941																		1942								
Ap	Ap	My	My	Jn	Jn	Jy	Jy	Ag	Ag	Sp	Sp	Oc	Oc	Nv	Nv	Dc	Dc	Ja	Ja	Fb	Fb	Ma	Ma	Ap	Ap	
==	==	==	==	14	13	11	10	12	13	15	==	==	==	20	==	==	–	–	–	–	–	–	–	–	–	YOU ARE MY SUNSHINE
==	==	15	5	4	3	**1**	**1**	**1**	**1**	5	4	10	16	==	==	–	–	–	–	–	–	–	–	–	–	MARIA ELENA
==	==	9	2	**1**	**1**	3	3	5	8	8	10	17	18	==	==	–	–	–	–	–	–	–	–	–	–	INTERMEZZO (A LOVE STORY)
–	==	20	==	==	–	–	–	–	–	–	–	–	–	–	–	–	–	–	–	–	–	–	–	–	–	MUSIC MAKERS
–	==	==	20	19	20	==	==	–	–	–	–	–	–	–	–	–	–	–	–	–	–	–	–	–	–	EVERYTHING HAPPENS TO ME
–	==	==	18	17	17	19	==	–	–	–	–	–	–	–	–	–	–	–	–	–	–	–	–	–	–	FRIENDLY TAVERN POLKA
–	==	==	13	11	15	13	15	20	==	–	–	–	–	–	–	–	–	–	–	–	–	–	–	–	–	THE BAND PLAYED ON
–	–	==	17	20	==	–	–	–	–	–	–	–	–	–	–	–	–	–	–	–	–	–	–	–	–	LET'S GET AWAY FROM IT ALL
–	–	==	11	5	2	2	2	3	10	20	==	–	–	–	–	–	–	–	–	–	–	–	–	–	–	THE HUT-SUT SONG
–	–	==	==	8	6	5	6	7	9	12	18	==	–	–	–	–	–	–	–	–	–	–	–	–	–	THE THINGS I LOVE
–	–	–	==	18	8	7	7	8	18	==	–	–	–	–	–	–	–	–	–	–	–	–	–	–	–	JUST A LITTLE BIT SOUTH OF NORTH CAROLINA
–	–	–	==	13	9	6	4	2	2	6	5	15	==	–	–	–	–	–	–	–	–	–	–	–	–	DADDY
–	–	–	==	15	14	10	5	4	6	3	6	16	20	==	–	–	–	–	–	–	–	–	–	–	–	GREEN EYES
–	–	–	–	==	==	18	20	19	==	==	–	–	–	–	–	–	–	–	–	–	–	–	–	–	–	AURORA
–	–	–	–	–	==	15	9	6	4	4	3	6	7	10	11	==	–	–	–	–	–	–	–	–	–	YOURS (QUIEREME MUCHO)
–	–	–	–	–	==	==	17	11	7	7	9	8	11	14	==	==	–	–	–	–	–	–	–	–	–	BLUE CHAMPAGNE
–	–	–	–	–	==	==	==	16	5	**1**	**1**	**1**	3	4	7	8	11	17	==	–	–	–	–	–	–	YOU AND I
–	–	–	–	–	–	==	19	17	12	11	15	==	–	–	–	–	–	–	–	–	–	–	–	–	–	KISS THE BOYS GOODBYE
–	–	–	–	–	–	==	18	15	15	17	19	==	–	–	–	–	–	–	–	–	–	–	–	–	–	THE BOOGLIE-WOOGLIE PIGGIE
–	–	–	–	–	–	==	16	9	3	2	2	3	6	8	==	==	–	–	–	–	–	–	–	–	–	'TIL REVEILLE
–	–	–	–	–	–	–	==	14	14	14	14	13	15	15	20	==	–	–	–	–	–	–	–	–	–	YES, INDEED!
–	–	–	–	–	–	–	==	==	20	==	==	==	==	–	–	–	–	–	–	–	–	–	–	–	–	LET ME OFF UPTOWN
–	–	–	–	–	–	–	–	==	16	13	==	==	==	–	–	–	–	–	–	–	–	–	–	–	–	I WENT OUT OF MY WAY
–	–	–	–	–	–	–	–	==	19	16	8	7	5	6	10	18	==	–	–	–	–	–	–	–	–	I GUESS I'LL HAVE TO DREAM THE REST
–	–	–	–	–	–	–	–	==	11	10	11	4	4	3	2	4	6	6	14	==	==	–	–	–	–	PIANO CONCERTO
–	–	–	–	–	–	–	–	==	==	9	13	9	8	11	12	==	–	–	–	–	–	–	–	–	–	DO YOU CARE?
–	–	–	–	–	–	–	–	==	==	19	16	12	9	5	3	2	2	2	3	6	7	13	16	==	–	ELMER'S TUNE
–	–	–	–	–	–	–	–	–	==	18	7	2	**1**	**1**	**1**	5	8	==	==	–	–	–	–	–	–	I DON'T WANT TO SET THE WORLD ON FIRE
–	–	–	–	–	–	–	–	–	–	==	12	5	2	2	6	9	17	==	–	–	–	–	–	–	–	JIM
–	–	–	–	–	–	–	–	–	–	==	20	14	12	13	15	19	==	–	–	–	–	–	–	–	–	TIME WAS
–	–	–	–	–	–	–	–	–	–	==	17	11	10	7	4	**1**	**1**	**1**	2	5	8	14	==	==	–	CHATTANOOGA CHOO CHOO
–	–	–	–	–	–	–	–	–	–	–	==	20	19	17	13	17	18	==	–	–	–	–	–	–	–	WHY DON'T WE DO THIS MORE OFTEN?
–	–	–	–	–	–	–	–	–	–	–	==	18	14	12	9	6	4	5	5	8	14	==	==	–	–	THIS LOVE OF MINE
–	–	–	–	–	–	–	–	–	–	–	==	19	13	9	5	7	5	7	16	==	–	–	–	–	–	TONIGHT WE LOVE
–	–	–	–	–	–	–	–	–	–	–	–	==	17	==	==	–	–	–	–	–	–	–	–	–	–	HI, NEIGHBOR!
–	–	–	–	–	–	–	–	–	–	–	–	==	==	16	==	==	–	–	–	–	–	–	–	–	–	A CITY CALLED HEAVEN
–	–	–	–	–	–	–	–	–	–	–	–	–	==	18	14	==	==	–	–	–	–	–	–	–	–	I SEE A MILLION PEOPLE
–	–	–	–	–	–	–	–	–	–	–	–	–	==	19	8	3	3	3	8	==	==	–	–	–	–	SHEPHERD SERENADE
–	–	–	–	–	–	–	–	–	–	–	–	–	–	==	17	13	==	==	–	–	–	–	–	–	–	CONCERTO FOR TWO
–	–	–	–	–	–	–	–	–	–	–	–	–	–	==	16	11	10	9	==	==	–	–	–	–	–	BY-U, BY-O
–	–	–	–	–	–	–	–	–	–	–	–	–	–	==	18	14	16	20	==	==	–	–	–	–	–	THIS TIME THE DREAM'S ON ME
–	–	–	–	–	–	–	–	–	–	–	–	–	–	==	==	10	13	11	==	==	–	–	–	–	–	TWO IN LOVE
–	–	–	–	–	–	–	–	–	–	–	–	–	–	–	==	16	==	==	–	–	–	–	–	–	–	ORANGE BLOSSOM LANE
–	–	–	–	–	–	–	–	–	–	–	–	–	–	–	–	==	19	==	==	–	–	–	–	–	–	A SINNER KISSED AN ANGEL
–	–	–	–	–	–	–	–	–	–	–	–	–	–	–	–	==	15	15	20	==	–	–	–	–	–	JINGLE BELLS
–	–	–	–	–	–	–	–	–	–	–	–	–	–	==	19	15	12	14	15	16	19	==	20	18	==	YOU MADE ME LOVE YOU (1942)
–	–	–	–	–	–	–	–	–	–	–	–	–	–	–	==	12	9	8	9	12	==	==	–	–	–	THE BELLS OF SAN RAQUEL (1942)
–	–	–	–	–	–	–	–	–	–	–	–	–	–	–	==	20	7	4	**1**	**1**	2	3	5	8	9	THE WHITE CLIFFS OF DOVER (1942)
–	–	–	–	–	–	–	–	–	–	–	–	–	–	–	–	==	14	10	4	3	3	5	7	12	==	ROSE O'DAY (1942)
–	–	–	–	–	–	–	–	–	–	–	–	–	–	–	–	==	20	13	7	2	**1**	**1**	2	5	6	BLUES IN THE NIGHT (1942)
Ap	Ap	My	My	Jn	Jn	Jy	Jy	Ag	Ag	Sp	Sp	Oc	Oc	Nv	Nv	Dc	Dc	Ja	Ja	Fb	Fb	Ma	Ma	Ap	Ap	

1941						1942																				
Oc	**Oc**	**Nv**	**Nv**	**Dc**	**Dc**	**Ja**	**Ja**	**Fb**	**Fb**	**Ma**	**Ma**	**Ap**	**Ap**	**My**	**My**	**Jn**	**Jn**	**Jy**	**Jy**	**Ag**	**Ag**	**Sp**	**Sp**	**Oc**	**Oc**	
1	3	4	7	8	11	17	==	–	–	–	–	–	–	–	–	–	–	–	–	–	–	–	–	–	–	YOU AND I (1941)
4	4	3	2	4	6	6	14	==	==	–	–	–	–	–	–	–	–	–	–	–	–	–	–	–	–	PIANO CONCERTO (1941)
12	9	5	3	2	2	2	3	6	7	13	16	==	–	–	–	–	–	–	–	–	–	–	–	–	–	ELMER'S TUNE (1941)
18	14	12	9	6	4	5	5	8	14	==	==	–	–	–	–	–	–	–	–	–	–	–	–	–	–	THIS LOVE OF MINE (1941)
19	13	9	5	7	5	7	16	==	–	–	–	–	–	–	–	–	–	–	–	–	–	–	–	–	–	TONIGHT WE LOVE (1941)
–	==	19	8	3	3	3	8	==	==	–	–	–	–	–	–	–	–	–	–	–	–	–	–	–	–	SHEPHERD SERENADE (1941)
11	10	7	4	**1**	**1**	**1**	2	5	8	14	==	==	–	–	–	–	–	–	–	–	–	–	–	–	–	CHATTANOOGA CHOO CHOO (1941)
–	–	==	16	11	10	9	==	==	–	–	–	–	–	–	–	–	–	–	–	–	–	–	–	–	–	BY-U, BY-O (1941)
–	–	==	18	14	16	20	==	==	–	–	–	–	–	–	–	–	–	–	–	–	–	–	–	–	–	THIS TIME THE DREAM'S ON ME (1941)
–	–	==	==	10	13	11	==	==	–	–	–	–	–	–	–	–	–	–	–	–	–	–	–	–	–	TWO IN LOVE (1941)
–	–	–	–	==	15	15	20	==	–	–	–	–	–	–	–	–	–	–	–	–	–	–	–	–	–	JINGLE BELLS (1941)
–	–	==	19	15	12	14	15	16	19	==	20	18	==	–	–	–	–	–	–	–	–	–	–	–	–	YOU MADE ME LOVE YOU
–	–	–	==	12	9	8	9	12	==	==	–	–	–	–	–	–	–	–	–	–	–	–	–	–	–	THE BELLS OF SAN RAQUEL
–	–	–	==	20	7	4	**1**	**1**	2	3	5	8	9	16	==	–	–	–	–	–	–	–	–	–	–	THE WHITE CLIFFS OF DOVER
–	–	–	–	==	14	10	4	3	3	5	7	12	==	==	–	–	–	–	–	–	–	–	–	–	–	ROSE O'DAY
–	–	–	–	==	20	13	7	2	**1**	**1**	2	5	6	14	==	–	–	–	–	–	–	–	–	–	–	BLUES IN THE NIGHT
–	–	–	–	==	==	16	11	18	==	–	–	–	–	–	–	–	–	–	–	–	–	–	–	–	–	MADELAINE
–	–	–	–	==	==	19	17	13	18	20	==	–	–	–	–	–	–	–	–	–	–	–	–	–	–	'TIS AUTUMN
–	–	–	–	–	==	18	10	15	20	==	–	–	–	–	–	–	–	–	–	–	–	–	–	–	–	THIS IS NO LAUGHING MATTER
–	–	–	–	–	==	12	6	4	4	7	9	11	==	==	–	–	–	–	–	–	–	–	–	–	–	THE SHRINE OF ST. CECILIA
–	–	–	–	–	==	==	13	11	10	10	19	==	–	–	–	–	–	–	–	–	–	–	–	–	–	EV'RYTHING I LOVE
–	–	–	–	–	==	==	18	14	11	9	6	7	8	11	15	20	==	==	–	–	–	–	–	–	–	A STRING OF PEARLS
–	–	–	–	–	–	==	12	7	5	8	12	20	==	–	–	–	–	–	–	–	–	–	–	–	–	REMEMBER PEARL HARBOR
–	–	–	–	–	–	==	19	10	12	11	13	16	==	–	–	–	–	–	–	–	–	–	–	–	–	I SAID NO!
–	–	–	–	–	–	==	==	20	==	==	–	–	–	–	–	–	–	–	–	–	–	–	–	–	–	I GOT IT BAD (AND THAT AIN'T GOOD)
–	–	–	–	–	–	==	==	9	13	17	==	–	–	–	–	–	–	–	–	–	–	–	–	–	–	WE DID IT BEFORE (AND WE CAN DO IT AGAIN)
–	–	–	–	–	–	–	==	17	==	15	17	==	–	–	–	–	–	–	–	–	–	–	–	–	–	WE'RE THE COUPLE IN THE CASTLE
–	–	–	–	–	–	–	==	19	9	4	4	2	**1**	2	4	9	14	14	==	–	–	–	–	–	–	MOONLIGHT COCKTAIL
–	–	–	–	–	–	–	==	==	16	12	8	9	17	==	–	–	–	–	–	–	–	–	–	–	–	HOW ABOUT YOU?
–	–	–	–	–	–	–	–	==	17	==	18	==	–	–	–	–	–	–	–	–	–	–	–	–	–	DAY DREAMING
–	–	–	–	–	–	–	–	==	6	2	**1**	**1**	3	6	18	==	–	–	–	–	–	–	–	–	–	DEEP IN THE HEART OF TEXAS
–	–	–	–	–	–	–	–	==	15	6	3	3	4	3	9	15	==	–	–	–	–	–	–	–	–	I DON'T WANT TO WALK WITHOUT YOU
–	–	–	–	–	–	–	–	==	==	==	14	10	==	==	==	–	–	–	–	–	–	–	–	–	–	SOMETIMES
–	–	–	–	–	–	–	–	–	==	18	==	==	–	–	–	–	–	–	–	–	–	–	–	–	–	DEAR MOM
–	–	–	–	–	–	–	–	–	==	16	11	4	2	**1**	**1**	7	13	18	==	–	–	–	–	–	–	SOMEBODY ELSE IS TAKING MY PLACE
–	–	–	–	–	–	–	–	–	==	19	10	6	5	7	11	13	20	==	–	–	–	–	–	–	–	MISS YOU
–	–	–	–	–	–	–	–	–	–	==	15	13	15	==	–	–	–	–	–	–	–	–	–	–	–	A ZOOT SUIT
–	–	–	–	–	–	–	–	–	–	==	==	15	==	==	–	–	–	–	–	–	–	–	–	–	–	HOW DO I KNOW IT'S REAL?
–	–	–	–	–	–	–	–	–	–	==	==	17	20	19	13	14	10	10	9	11	12	12	20	20	==	ALWAYS IN MY HEART
–	–	–	–	–	–	–	–	–	–	–	==	19	==	==	–	–	–	–	–	–	–	–	–	–	–	SHE'LL ALWAYS REMEMBER
–	–	–	–	–	–	–	–	–	–	–	==	14	7	4	3	5	6	8	11	==	==	–	–	–	–	TANGERINE
–	–	–	–	–	–	–	–	–	–	–	==	==	16	==	==	–	–	–	–	–	–	–	–	–	–	ME AND MY MELINDA
–	–	–	–	–	–	–	–	–	–	–	==	==	19	==	==	–	–	–	–	–	–	–	–	–	–	HAPPY IN LOVE
–	–	–	–	–	–	–	–	–	–	–	==	==	13	13	==	==	–	–	–	–	–	–	–	–	–	I'LL PRAY FOR YOU
–	–	–	–	–	–	–	–	–	–	–	==	==	14	9	7	4	3	3	5	6	16	==	–	–	–	JERSEY BOUNCE
–	–	–	–	–	–	–	–	–	–	–	–	==	11	10	16	16	==	–	–	–	–	–	–	–	–	I REMEMBER YOU
–	–	–	–	–	–	–	–	–	–	–	–	==	12	8	5	8	9	11	14	==	==	–	–	–	–	SKYLARK
–	–	–	–	–	–	–	–	–	–	–	–	==	18	==	14	11	11	12	12	20	==	–	–	–	–	I THREW A KISS IN THE OCEAN
–	–	–	–	–	–	–	–	–	–	–	–	==	10	5	2	**1**	4	4	8	15	==	–	–	–	–	DON'T SIT UNDER THE APPLE TREE WITH ANYONE ELSE BUT ME
–	–	–	–	–	–	–	–	–	–	–	–	==	==	15	8	3	**1**	**1**	2	2	7	9	10	==	==	SLEEPY LAGOON
–	–	–	–	–	–	–	–	–	–	–	–	–	==	12	6	2	2	2	3	3	6	14	==	–	–	JOHNNY DOUGHBOY FOUND A ROSE IN IRELAND
Oc	**Oc**	**Nv**	**Nv**	**Dc**	**Dc**	**Ja**	**Ja**	**Fb**	**Fb**	**Ma**	**Ma**	**Ap**	**Ap**	**My**	**My**	**Jn**	**Jn**	**Jy**	**Jy**	**Ag**	**Ag**	**Sp**	**Sp**	**Oc**	**Oc**	

1942																		1943								
Ap	Ap	My	My	Jn	Jn	Jy	Jy	Ag	Ag	Sp	Sp	Oc	Oc	Nv	Nv	Dc	Dc	Ja	Ja	Fb	Fb	Ma	Ma	Ap	Ap	
==	==	==	20	19	15	==	==	–	–	–	–	–	–	–	–	–	–	–	–	–	–	–	–	–	–	WE'LL MEET AGAIN
==	==	==	==	==	19	==	==	–	–	–	–	–	–	–	–	–	–	–	–	–	–	–	–	–	–	SING ME A SONG OF THE ISLANDS
–	==	18	==	==	–	–	–	–	–	–	–	–	–	–	–	–	–	–	–	–	–	–	–	–	–	FULL MOON
–	==	17	12	10	7	7	4	4	4	10	18	==	–	–	–	–	–	–	–	–	–	–	–	–	–	WHO WOULDN'T LOVE YOU
–	==	==	==	17	==	==	–	–	–	–	–	–	–	–	–	–	–	–	–	–	–	–	–	–	–	BREATHLESS
–	==	==	==	==	==	17	==	==	==	==	==	==	==	==	==	==	==	==	==	==	==	==	==	==	==	THE MARINES' HYMN
–	–	20	10	6	5	5	6	10	==	==	–	–	–	–	–	–	–	–	–	–	–	–	–	–	–	ONE DOZEN ROSES
–	–	==	17	12	8	9	7	7	19	==	–	–	–	–	–	–	–	–	–	–	–	–	–	–	–	THREE LITTLE SISTERS
–	–	==	19	==	18	15	==	==	–	–	–	–	–	–	–	–	–	–	–	–	–	–	–	–	–	I'LL KEEP THE LOVELIGHT BURNING
–	–	–	==	==	16	19	==	–	–	–	–	–	–	–	–	–	–	–	–	–	–	–	–	–	–	NIGHTINGALE
–	–	–	==	==	==	13	==	19	==	17	11	17	==	==	14	17	17	16	==	16	==	20	18	20	==	THE ARMY AIR CORPS SONG
–	–	–	–	18	12	6	**1**	**1**	**1**	2	7	12	==	==	–	–	–	–	–	–	–	–	–	–	–	JINGLE, JANGLE, JINGLE
–	–	–	–	==	17	16	13	14	17	20	==	–	–	–	–	–	–	–	–	–	–	–	–	–	–	SWEET ELOISE
–	–	–	–	–	==	20	10	5	2	**1**	2	3	9	16	==	–	–	–	–	–	–	–	–	–	–	HE WEARS A PAIR OF SILVER WINGS
–	–	–	–	–	==	==	16	12	20	==	==	–	–	–	–	–	–	–	–	–	–	–	–	–	–	THIS IS WORTH FIGHTING FOR
–	–	–	–	–	==	==	15	9	3	5	8	10	==	==	–	–	–	–	–	–	–	–	–	–	–	IDAHO
–	–	–	–	–	–	==	19	==	==	–	–	–	–	–	–	–	–	–	–	–	–	–	–	–	–	HERE YOU ARE
–	–	–	–	–	–	==	18	17	11	11	15	==	–	–	–	–	–	–	–	–	–	–	–	–	–	JUST AS THOUGH YOU WERE HERE
–	–	–	–	–	–	==	17	13	14	15	16	13	12	18	==	–	–	–	–	–	–	–	–	–	–	AMEN
–	–	–	–	–	–	==	==	16	8	6	6	8	20	==	–	–	–	–	–	–	–	–	–	–	–	TAKE ME
–	–	–	–	–	–	–	20	8	5	4	4	4	8	15	17	==	–	–	–	–	–	–	–	–	–	I LEFT MY HEART AT THE STAGE DOOR CANTEEN
–	–	–	–	–	–	–	==	18	15	13	12	==	==	–	–	–	–	–	–	–	–	–	–	–	–	STRICTLY INSTRUMENTAL
–	–	–	–	–	–	–	==	==	13	7	5	6	6	8	15	==	==	–	–	–	–	–	–	–	–	BE CAREFUL, IT'S MY HEART
–	–	–	–	–	–	–	==	==	9	3	**1**	**1**	3	4	7	12	20	==	–	–	–	–	–	–	–	MY DEVOTION
–	–	–	–	–	–	–	–	==	10	8	3	2	**1**	7	10	13	==	==	–	–	–	–	–	–	–	(I'VE GOT A GAL IN) KALAMAZOO
–	–	–	–	–	–	–	–	==	18	19	==	==	–	–	–	–	–	–	–	–	–	–	–	–	–	COW-COW BOOGIE
–	–	–	–	–	–	–	–	==	==	18	==	19	15	14	16	==	==	–	–	–	–	–	–	–	–	WONDER WHEN MY BABY'S COMING HOME
–	–	–	–	–	–	–	–	–	==	16	9	5	4	5	9	9	19	==	==	–	–	–	–	–	–	STRIP POLKA
–	–	–	–	–	–	–	–	–	==	==	17	11	13	12	18	==	–	–	–	–	–	–	–	–	–	AT LAST
–	–	–	–	–	–	–	–	–	–	==	14	7	5	3	4	7	14	17	==	–	–	–	–	–	–	SERENADE IN BLUE
–	–	–	–	–	–	–	–	–	–	==	19	14	11	20	==	==	–	–	–	–	–	–	–	–	–	HE'S MY GUY
–	–	–	–	–	–	–	–	–	–	==	==	16	10	6	3	3	2	**1**	4	5	9	17	17	==	–	WHEN THE LIGHTS GO ON AGAIN
–	–	–	–	–	–	–	–	–	–	–	==	9	2	**1**	**1**	**1**	**1**	2	16	–	–	–	–	–	–	WHITE CHRISTMAS
–	–	–	–	–	–	–	–	–	–	–	==	18	==	10	5	5	5	9	6	12	15	==	==	–	–	DEARLY BELOVED
–	–	–	–	–	–	–	–	–	–	–	==	==	17	==	==	==	–	–	–	–	–	–	–	–	–	I MET HER ON MONDAY
–	–	–	–	–	–	–	–	–	–	–	==	==	14	19	11	14	==	==	–	–	–	–	–	–	–	I CAME HERE TO TALK FOR JOE
–	–	–	–	–	–	–	–	–	–	–	==	==	7	2	2	2	4	4	10	==	==	–	–	–	–	PRAISE THE LORD AND PASS THE AMMUNITION
–	–	–	–	–	–	–	–	–	–	–	==	==	==	13	6	6	7	11	==	==	–	–	–	–	–	MANHATTAN SERENADE
–	–	–	–	–	–	–	–	–	–	–	–	==	18	17	12	8	10	13	==	==	–	–	–	–	–	DER FUEHRER'S FACE
–	–	–	–	–	–	–	–	–	–	–	–	==	19	11	8	4	3	6	7	17	==	–	–	–	–	MR. FIVE BY FIVE
–	–	–	–	–	–	–	–	–	–	–	–	==	==	==	==	16	18	19	==	–	–	–	–	–	–	THERE WILL NEVER BE ANOTHER YOU
–	–	–	–	–	–	–	–	–	–	–	–	–	==	==	20	==	==	–	–	–	–	–	–	–	–	GOBS OF LOVE
–	–	–	–	–	–	–	–	–	–	–	–	–	==	==	==	15	12	14	==	==	–	–	–	–	–	DAYBREAK
–	–	–	–	–	–	–	–	–	–	–	–	–	–	–	==	20	16	15	19	==	==	–	–	–	–	JUKE BOX SATURDAY NIGHT
–	–	–	–	–	–	–	–	–	–	==	13	15	16	9	13	10	8	10	11	13	11	12	11	13	12	THERE'S A STAR SPANGLED BANNER WAVING SOMEWHERE (1943)
–	–	–	–	–	–	–	–	–	–	–	–	–	–	==	19	11	6	3	**1**	2	2	2	4	6	8	THERE ARE SUCH THINGS (1943)
–	–	–	–	–	–	–	–	–	–	–	–	–	–	==	==	19	13	8	5	4	4	9	14	==	==	WHY DON'T YOU FALL IN LOVE WITH ME? (1943)
–	–	–	–	–	–	–	–	–	–	–	–	–	–	–	==	18	9	5	3	3	3	5	9	11	20	I HAD THE CRAZIEST DREAM (1943)
–	–	–	–	–	–	–	–	–	–	–	–	–	–	–	==	==	11	7	2	**1**	**1**	3	8	9	14	MOONLIGHT BECOMES YOU (1943)
–	–	–	–	–	–	–	–	–	–	–	–	–	==	==	==	==	15	12	9	14	19	==	–	–	–	CAN'T GET OUT OF THIS MOOD (1943)
Ap	Ap	My	My	Jn	Jn	Jy	Jy	Ag	Ag	Sp	Sp	Oc	Oc	Nv	Nv	Dc	Dc	Ja	Ja	Fb	Fb	Ma	Ma	Ap	Ap	

1942															1943											
Oc	Oc	Nv	Nv	Dc	Dc	Ja	Ja	Fb	Fb	Ma	Ma	Ap	Ap	My	My	Jn	Jn	Jy	Jy	Ag	Ag	Sp	Sp	Oc	Oc	
17	==	==	14	17	17	16	==	16	==	20	18	20	==	==	==	==	—	—	—	—	—	—	—	—	—	THE ARMY AIR CORPS SONG (1942)
7	5	3	4	7	14	17	==	—	—	—	—	—	—	—	—	—	—	—	—	—	—	—	—	—	—	SERENADE IN BLUE (1942)
16	10	6	3	3	2	**1**	4	5	9	17	17	==	—	—	—	—	—	—	—	—	—	—	—	—	—	WHEN THE LIGHTS GO ON AGAIN (1942)
9	2	**1**	**1**	**1**	**1**	2	16	—	—	—	—	—	—	—	—	—	—	—	—	—	—	—	—	—	—	WHITE CHRISTMAS (1942)
18	==	10	5	5	5	9	6	12	15	==	==	—	—	—	—	—	—	—	—	—	—	—	—	—	—	DEARLY BELOVED (1942)
==	7	2	2	2	4	4	10	==	==	—	—	—	—	—	—	—	—	—	—	—	—	—	—	—	—	PRAISE THE LORD AND PASS THE AMMUNITION (1942)
==	==	13	6	6	7	11	==	==	—	—	—	—	—	—	—	—	—	—	—	—	—	—	—	—	—	MANHATTAN SERENADE (1942)
—	==	==	==	16	18	19	==	—	—	—	—	—	—	—	—	—	—	—	—	—	—	—	—	—	—	THERE WILL NEVER BE ANOTHER YOU (1942)
—	==	==	==	15	12	14	==	==	—	—	—	—	—	—	—	—	—	—	—	—	—	—	—	—	—	DAYBREAK (1942)
==	19	11	8	4	3	6	7	17	==	—	—	—	—	—	—	—	—	—	—	—	—	—	—	—	—	MR. FIVE BY FIVE (1942)
==	18	17	12	8	10	13	==	==	—	—	—	—	—	—	—	—	—	—	—	—	—	—	—	—	—	DER FUEHRER'S FACE (1942)
—	—	—	==	20	16	15	19	==	==	—	—	—	—	—	—	—	—	—	—	—	—	—	—	—	—	JUKE BOX SATURDAY NIGHT (1942)
15	16	9	13	10	8	10	11	13	11	12	11	13	12	11	17	13	15	14	20	==	==	==	==	—	—	THERE'S A STAR SPANGLED BANNER WAVING SOMEWHERE
—	==	==	==	==	15	12	9	14	19	==	—	—	—	—	—	—	—	—	—	—	—	—	—	—	—	CAN'T GET OUT OF THIS MOOD
—	—	==	19	11	6	3	**1**	2	2	2	4	6	8	==	==	—	—	—	—	—	—	—	—	—	—	THERE ARE SUCH THINGS
—	—	==	==	19	13	8	5	4	4	9	14	==	==	—	—	—	—	—	—	—	—	—	—	—	—	WHY DON'T YOU FALL IN LOVE WITH ME?
—	—	—	==	18	9	5	3	3	3	5	9	11	20	—	—	—	—	—	—	—	—	—	—	—	—	I HAD THE CRAZIEST DREAM
—	—	—	==	==	11	7	2	**1**	1	3	8	9	14	==	==	—	—	—	—	—	—	—	—	—	—	MOONLIGHT BECOMES YOU
—	—	—	—	==	==	==	==	==	16	==	==	—	—	—	—	—	—	—	—	—	—	—	—	—	—	I'M GETTING TIRED SO I CAN SLEEP
—	—	—	—	—	==	20	17	18	==	==	—	—	—	—	—	—	—	—	—	—	—	—	—	—	—	A TOUCH OF TEXAS
—	—	—	—	—	==	18	8	8	10	6	7	7	7	9	12	17	==	==	—	—	—	—	—	—	—	FOR ME AND MY GAL
—	—	—	—	—	==	==	13	11	14	13	==	==	—	—	—	—	—	—	—	—	—	—	—	—	—	ROSE ANN OF CHARING CROSS
—	—	—	—	—	==	==	18	15	12	11	12	15	15	19	==	==	—	—	—	—	—	—	—	—	—	WHY DON'T YOU DO RIGHT?
—	—	—	—	—	==	==	12	10	8	10	15	16	18	==	==	—	—	—	—	—	—	—	—	—	—	MOONLIGHT MOOD
—	—	—	—	—	==	==	14	7	6	4	3	4	4	6	10	12	==	==	—	—	—	—	—	—	—	BRAZIL
—	—	—	—	—	—	==	15	6	7	7	6	5	6	10	18	==	==	—	—	—	—	—	—	—	—	YOU'D BE SO NICE TO COME HOME TO
—	—	—	—	—	—	==	20	9	5	**1**	**1**	**1**	**1**	2	5	9	12	18	==	==	—	—	—	—	—	I'VE HEARD THAT SONG BEFORE
—	—	—	—	—	—	==	==	19	==	19	20	==	==	—	—	—	—	—	—	—	—	—	—	—	—	FAT MEAT IS GOOD MEAT
—	—	—	—	—	—	==	==	20	18	14	10	8	5	4	2	2	5	4	10	14	==	==	—	—	—	DON'T GET AROUND MUCH ANYMORE
—	—	—	—	—	—	—	—	==	20	==	==	—	—	—	—	—	—	—	—	—	—	—	—	—	—	MOVE IT OVER
—	—	—	—	—	—	—	—	==	17	15	13	10	11	15	19	==	—	—	—	—	—	—	—	—	—	IT STARTED ALL OVER AGAIN
—	—	—	—	—	—	—	—	==	13	8	2	3	3	3	4	8	8	17	==	==	—	—	—	—	—	THAT OLD BLACK MAGIC
—	—	—	—	—	—	—	—	==	==	16	5	2	2	**1**	**1**	**1**	2	5	9	13	16	==	==	—	—	AS TIME GOES BY
—	—	—	—	—	—	—	—	==	==	==	19	14	9	7	7	6	7	9	13	==	==	—	—	—	—	TAKING A CHANCE ON LOVE
—	—	—	—	—	—	—	—	—	==	18	16	19	==	==	—	—	—	—	—	—	—	—	—	—	—	PLEASE THINK OF ME
—	—	—	—	—	—	—	—	—	==	==	==	12	10	5	3	5	6	6	7	6	7	12	13	19	==	IT CAN'T BE WRONG
—	—	—	—	—	—	—	—	—	—	==	==	==	==	12	13	19	==	==	—	—	—	—	—	—	—	THERE'S A HARBOR OF DREAMBOATS
—	—	—	—	—	—	—	—	—	—	—	==	17	13	==	==	—	—	—	—	—	—	—	—	—	—	I JUST KISSED YOUR PICTURE GOODNIGHT
—	—	—	—	—	—	—	—	—	—	—	==	18	16	14	16	15	17	==	==	—	—	—	—	—	—	"MURDER" HE SAYS
—	—	—	—	—	—	—	—	—	—	—	—	==	17	13	11	11	11	12	15	==	==	—	—	—	—	VELVET MOON
—	—	—	—	—	—	—	—	—	—	—	—	==	19	8	6	4	**1**	**1**	**1**	2	3	9	11	18	==	COMIN' IN ON A WING AND A PRAYER
—	—	—	—	—	—	—	—	—	—	—	—	==	==	16	8	3	3	3	6	9	13	==	==	—	—	LET'S GET LOST
—	—	—	—	—	—	—	—	—	—	—	—	—	==	20	15	10	9	7	4	8	11	16	20	==	—	JOHNNY ZERO
Oc	Oc	Nv	Nv	Dc	Dc	Ja	Ja	Fb	Fb	Ma	Ma	Ap	Ap	My	My	Jn	Jn	Jy	Jy	Ag	Ag	Sp	Sp	Oc	Oc	

1943																		1944								
Ap	Ap	My	My	Jn	Jn	Jy	Jy	Ag	Ag	Sp	Sp	Oc	Oc	Nv	Nv	Dc	Dc	Ja	Ja	Fb	Fb	Ma	Ma	Ap	Ap	
==	==	18	14	14	==	16	==	==	–	–	–	–	–	–	–	–	–	–	–	–	–	–	–	–	–	WHAT'S THE GOOD WORD, MR. BLUEBIRD?
–	==	17	9	7	4	2	2	**1**	**1**	**1**	**1**	2	7	14	==	==	–	–	–	–	–	–	–	–	–	YOU'LL NEVER KNOW
–	==	==	20	==	==	19	19	19	19	20	==	==	==	==	17	17	15	12	17	16	==	==	–	–	–	BOOGIE WOOGIE
–	–	==	==	18	10	8	3	3	2	4	6	9	14	==	==	–	–	–	–	–	–	–	–	–	–	IN THE BLUE OF THE EVENING
–	–	==	==	==	==	==	18	17	20	==	19	16	==	==	==	==	–	–	–	–	–	–	–	–	–	WAIT FOR ME, MARY
–	–	–	==	20	20	==	==	–	–	–	–	–	–	–	–	–	–	–	–	–	–	–	–	–	–	BIG BOY
–	–	–	==	16	14	10	5	7	10	11	16	==	==	–	–	–	–	–	–	–	–	–	–	–	–	IT'S ALWAYS YOU
–	–	–	==	==	19	==	==	–	–	–	–	–	–	–	–	–	–	–	–	–	–	–	–	–	–	PRINCE CHARMING
–	–	–	==	==	18	==	==	–	–	–	–	–	–	–	–	–	–	–	–	–	–	–	–	–	–	THE FUDDY DUDDY WATCHMAKER
–	–	–	==	==	13	11	11	5	5	5	9	10	9	13	20	==	==	–	–	–	–	–	–	–	–	IN MY ARMS
–	–	–	–	==	16	13	8	4	4	3	4	7	11	18	==	–	–	–	–	–	–	–	–	–	–	ALL OR NOTHING AT ALL
–	–	–	–	==	==	20	==	==	==	–	–	==	==	==	==	–	–	–	–	–	–	–	–	–	–	NEVER A DAY GOES BY
–	–	–	–	==	==	15	12	11	9	7	7	6	2	**1**	2	2	2	4	10	17	==	–	–	–	–	PISTOL PACKIN' MAMA
–	–	–	–	–	==	==	16	==	==	==	==	–	–	–	–	–	–	–	–	–	–	–	–	–	–	TAKE IT FROM THERE
–	–	–	–	–	==	==	14	10	6	6	5	5	4	4	3	3	3	3	6	12	==	==	–	–	–	PEOPLE WILL SAY WE'RE IN LOVE
–	–	–	–	–	==	==	==	18	15	13	10	8	5	5	5	8	18	==	==	–	–	–	–	–	–	PUT YOUR ARMS AROUND ME, HONEY
–	–	–	–	–	–	==	17	12	8	2	2	1	3	3	4	6	11	==	==	–	–	–	–	–	–	SUNDAY, MONDAY, OR ALWAYS
–	–	–	–	–	–	==	==	15	12	8	3	3	**1**	2	**1**	**1**	**1**	**1**	2	5	7	11	20	==	==	PAPER DOLL
–	–	–	–	–	–	==	==	16	14	10	8	4	6	6	8	16	==	==	–	–	–	–	–	–	–	I HEARD YOU CRIED LAST NIGHT
–	–	–	–	–	–	==	==	20	17	19	==	==	==	–	–	–	–	–	–	–	–	–	–	–	–	WARSAW CONCERTO
–	–	–	–	–	–	==	==	==	==	15	12	13	17	17	==	==	–	–	–	–	–	–	–	–	–	I NEVER MENTION YOUR NAME
–	–	–	–	–	–	–	==	==	18	17	17	17	18	20	==	==	–	–	–	–	–	–	–	–	–	NO LETTER TODAY
–	–	–	–	–	–	–	–	==	==	14	14	11	10	11	12	10	14	18	==	==	–	–	–	–	–	SAY A PRAYER FOR THE BOYS OVER THERE
–	–	–	–	–	–	–	–	==	==	18	15	12	8	8	9	13	==	==	–	–	–	–	–	–	–	IF YOU PLEASE
–	–	–	–	–	–	–	–	–	–	==	18	14	20	==	==	–	–	–	–	–	–	–	–	–	–	CLOSE TO YOU
–	–	–	–	–	–	–	–	–	–	==	==	15	15	15	15	19	==	–	–	–	–	–	–	–	–	BLUE RAIN
–	–	–	–	–	–	–	–	–	–	==	==	20	19	19	19	==	==	–	–	–	–	–	–	–	–	DON'T CRY, BABY
–	–	–	–	–	–	–	–	–	–	==	==	==	12	10	11	9	9	9	13	18	==	–	–	–	–	VICT'RY POLKA
–	–	–	–	–	–	–	–	–	–	–	==	==	16	9	6	4	5	5	4	8	10	12	==	==	==	OH, WHAT A BEAUTIFUL MORNIN'
–	–	–	–	–	–	–	–	–	–	–	==	==	13	7	7	7	6	6	15	19	==	==	–	–	–	THEY'RE EITHER TOO YOUNG OR TOO OLD
–	–	–	–	–	–	–	–	–	–	–	==	==	==	12	13	11	12	16	==	==	–	–	–	–	–	HOW SWEET YOU ARE
–	–	–	–	–	–	–	–	–	–	–	–	–	==	==	16	18	16	15	==	–	–	–	–	–	–	THE DREAMER
–	–	–	–	–	–	–	–	–	–	–	–	–	==	==	14	14	13	11	11	13	15	19	==	–	–	FOR THE FIRST TIME
–	–	–	–	–	–	–	–	–	–	–	–	–	–	==	18	==	==	–	–	–	–	–	–	–	–	RHAPSODY IN BLUE
–	–	–	–	–	–	–	–	–	–	–	–	–	–	==	==	15	8	14	==	–	–	–	–	–	–	WHITE CHRISTMAS
–	–	–	–	–	–	–	–	–	–	–	–	–	–	–	==	12	7	8	18	–	–	–	–	–	–	I'LL BE HOME FOR CHRISTMAS
–	–	–	–	–	–	–	–	–	–	–	–	–	==	==	16	10	5	4	2	**1**	2	2	5	8	15	==	MY HEART TELLS ME (1944)
–	–	–	–	–	–	–	–	–	–	–	–	–	–	–	==	==	10	7	3	**1**	**1**	**1**	3	6	13	SHOO-SHOO BABY (1944)
–	–	–	–	–	–	–	–	–	–	–	–	–	–	==	==	20	17	10	5	6	6	8	14	==	==	MY IDEAL (1944)
–	–	–	–	–	–	–	–	–	–	–	–	–	–	–	==	==	20	17	16	10	8	10	13	18	==	STAR EYES (1944)
–	–	–	–	–	–	–	–	–	–	–	–	–	–	==	==	==	19	13	8	9	11	18	==	==	–	MY SHINING HOUR (1944)
Ap	Ap	My	My	Jn	Jn	Jy	Jy	Ag	Ag	Sp	Sp	Oc	Oc	Nv	Nv	Dc	Dc	Ja	Ja	Fb	Fb	Ma	Ma	Ap	Ap	

1943						1944																				
Oc	Oc	Nv	Nv	Dc	Dc	Ja	Ja	Fb	Fb	Ma	Ma	Ap	Ap	My	My	Jn	Jn	Jy	Jy	Ag	Ag	Sp	Sp	Oc	Oc	
==	==	==	17	17	15	12	17	16	==	==	–	–	–	–	–	–	–	–	–	–	–	–	–	–	–	BOOGIE WOOGIE (1943)
6	2	1	2	2	2	4	10	17	==	–	–	–	–	–	–	–	–	–	–	–	–	–	–	–	–	PISTOL PACKIN' MAMA (1943)
5	4	4	3	3	3	3	6	12	==	==	–	–	–	–	–	–	–	–	–	–	–	–	–	–	–	PEOPLE WILL SAY WE'RE IN LOVE (1943)
3	1	2	1	1	1	1	2	5	7	11	20	==	==	–	–	–	–	–	–	–	–	–	–	–	–	PAPER DOLL (1943)
11	10	11	12	10	14	18	==	==	–	–	–	–	–	–	–	–	–	–	–	–	–	–	–	–	–	SAY A PRAYER FOR THE BOYS OVER THERE (1943)
==	16	9	6	4	5	5	4	8	10	12	==	==	==	–	–	–	–	–	–	–	–	–	–	–	–	OH, WHAT A BEAUTIFUL MORNIN' (1943)
==	12	10	11	9	9	9	13	18	==	–	–	–	–	–	–	–	–	–	–	–	–	–	–	–	–	VICT'RY POLKA (1943)
==	13	7	7	7	6	6	15	19	==	==	–	–	–	–	–	–	–	–	–	–	–	–	–	–	–	THEY'RE EITHER TOO YOUNG OR TOO OLD (1943)
==	==	12	13	11	12	16	==	==	–	–	–	–	–	–	–	–	–	–	–	–	–	–	–	–	–	HOW SWEET YOU ARE (1943)
–	==	==	16	18	16	15	==	–	–	–	–	–	–	–	–	–	–	–	–	–	–	–	–	–	–	THE DREAMER (1943)
–	–	==	==	15	8	14	==	–	–	–	–	–	–	–	–	–	–	–	–	–	–	–	–	–	–	WHITE CHRISTMAS (1943)
–	==	==	14	14	13	11	11	13	15	19	==	–	–	–	–	–	–	–	–	–	–	–	–	–	–	FOR THE FIRST TIME (1943)
==	==	16	10	5	4	2	1	2	2	5	8	15	==	==	–	–	–	–	–	–	–	–	–	–	–	MY HEART TELLS ME
–	–	==	==	20	17	10	5	6	6	8	14	==	==	–	–	–	–	–	–	–	–	–	–	–	–	MY IDEAL
–	–	==	==	==	19	13	8	9	11	18	==	==	–	–	–	–	–	–	–	–	–	–	–	–	–	MY SHINING HOUR
–	–	–	==	12	7	8	18	–	–	–	–	–	–	–	–	–	–	–	–	–	–	–	–	–	–	I'LL BE HOME FOR CHRISTMAS (1943)
–	–	–	==	==	20	17	16	10	8	10	13	18	==	==	–	–	–	–	–	–	–	–	–	–	–	STAR EYES
–	–	–	==	==	10	7	3	1	1	1	3	6	13	15	==	==	–	–	–	–	–	–	–	–	–	SHOO-SHOO BABY
–	–	–	==	==	==	==	7	4	5	4	6	12	19	==	==	–	–	–	–	–	–	–	–	–	–	NO LOVE, NO NOTHIN'
–	–	–	–	–	==	20	19	==	==	–	–	–	–	–	–	–	–	–	–	–	–	–	–	–	–	LITTLE DID I KNOW
–	–	–	–	–	==	19	14	11	14	17	==	==	–	–	–	–	–	–	–	–	–	–	–	–	–	SPEAK LOW
–	–	–	–	–	==	==	9	3	4	3	2	1	6	10	13	20	==	–	–	–	–	–	–	–	–	MAIRZY DOATS
–	–	–	–	–	–	==	12	7	3	2	1	2	2	5	9	16	==	–	–	–	–	–	–	–	–	BESAME MUCHO
–	–	–	–	–	–	==	20	14	9	7	5	3	9	12	16	==	–	–	–	–	–	–	–	–	–	I COULDN'T SLEEP A WINK LAST NIGHT
–	–	–	–	–	–	–	==	15	12	13	16	==	–	–	–	–	–	–	–	–	–	–	–	–	–	CHERRY
–	–	–	–	–	–	–	==	20	16	14	10	11	10	11	11	15	15	20	==	–	–	–	–	–	–	HOLIDAY FOR STRINGS
–	–	–	–	–	–	–	==	==	13	6	4	5	7	9	12	==	==	–	–	–	–	–	–	–	–	WHEN THEY ASK ABOUT YOU
–	–	–	–	–	–	–	==	==	20	==	==	14	12	13	19	17	==	–	–	–	–	–	–	–	–	BY THE RIVER OF THE ROSES
–	–	–	–	–	–	–	–	==	17	15	9	9	15	==	==	–	–	–	–	–	–	–	–	–	–	A LOVELY WAY TO SPEND AN EVENING
–	–	–	–	–	–	–	–	==	19	16	15	16	16	17	==	==	–	–	–	–	–	–	–	–	–	DO NOTHIN' TILL YOU HEAR FROM ME
–	–	–	–	–	–	–	–	==	18	9	7	7	4	6	8	12	==	==	–	–	–	–	–	–	–	POINCIANA
–	–	–	–	–	–	–	–	==	==	==	12	10	8	7	7	7	12	16	==	–	–	–	–	–	–	DON'T SWEETHEART ME
–	–	–	–	–	–	–	–	–	==	20	==	20	==	==	–	–	–	–	–	–	–	–	–	–	–	TAKE IT EASY
–	–	–	–	–	–	–	–	–	==	==	11	8	3	2	1	5	5	9	13	==	==	–	–	–	–	I LOVE YOU
–	–	–	–	–	–	–	–	–	==	==	18	13	5	3	2	6	4	7	12	13	==	==	–	–	–	SAN FERNANDO VALLEY
–	–	–	–	–	–	–	–	–	–	==	19	17	17	==	20	==	==	–	–	–	–	–	–	–	–	I WISH I COULD HIDE INSIDE THIS LETTER
–	–	–	–	–	–	–	–	–	–	==	17	4	1	1	4	3	6	10	17	==	==	–	–	–	–	IT'S LOVE, LOVE, LOVE
–	–	–	–	–	–	–	–	–	–	==	==	19	18	==	==	–	–	–	–	–	–	–	–	–	–	COW-COW BOOGIE
–	–	–	–	–	–	–	–	–	–	–	==	==	11	8	5	4	3	3	2	3	6	7	12	17	==	I'LL GET BY (AS LONG AS I HAVE YOU)
–	–	–	–	–	–	–	–	–	–	–	==	==	14	4	3	1	2	2	5	7	10	16	==	==	–	LONG AGO AND FAR AWAY
–	–	–	–	–	–	–	–	–	–	–	==	==	==	16	10	8	7	6	6	8	12	12	==	==	–	GOODNIGHT, WHEREVER YOU ARE
–	–	–	–	–	–	–	–	–	–	–	==	==	==	==	18	14	20	==	–	–	–	–	–	–	–	SUDDENLY IT'S SPRING
–	–	–	–	–	–	–	–	–	–	–	–	==	==	20	==	==	–	–	–	–	–	–	–	–	–	SPRING WILL BE A LITTLE LATE THIS YEAR
–	–	–	–	–	–	–	–	–	–	–	–	==	==	19	15	10	10	8	8	9	9	11	15	16	==	G.I. JIVE
–	–	–	–	–	–	–	–	–	–	–	–	–	==	18	==	18	13	12	15	==	==	–	–	–	–	SOMEDAY I'LL MEET YOU AGAIN
–	–	–	–	–	–	–	–	–	–	–	–	–	==	==	17	11	11	11	9	12	14	==	==	–	–	MILKMAN, KEEP THOSE BOTTLES QUIET
Oc	Oc	Nv	Nv	Dc	Dc	Ja	Ja	Fb	Fb	Ma	Ma	Ap	Ap	My	My	Jn	Jn	Jy	Jy	Ag	Ag	Sp	Sp	Oc	Oc	

						1944													1945							
Ap	Ap	My	My	Jn	Jn	Jy	Jy	Ag	Ag	Sp	Sp	Oc	Oc	Nv	Nv	Dc	Dc	Ja	Ja	Fb	Fb	Ma	Ma	Ap	Ap	
==	20	14	6	2	1	1	1	1	2	4	6	6	13	15	==	==	–	–	–	–	–	–	–	–	–	I'LL BE SEEING YOU
–	–	==	14	9	8	5	4	4	5	5	9	19	==	–	–	–	–	–	–	–	–	–	–	–	–	AMOR
–	–	==	==	19	==	==	–	–	–	–	–	–	–	–	–	–	–	–	–	–	–	–	–	–	–	TESS'S TORCH SONG
–	–	–	==	13	9	4	3	2	1	1	2	2	2	6	8	19	==	–	–	–	–	–	–	–	–	SWINGING ON A STAR
–	–	–	==	==	17	==	==	–	–	–	–	–	–	–	–	–	–	–	–	–	–	–	–	–	–	TIME ALONE WILL TELL
–	–	–	==	==	18	15	16	15	17	==	==	==	–	–	–	–	–	–	–	–	–	–	–	–	–	STRAIGHTEN UP AND FLY RIGHT
–	–	–	==	==	14	17	14	11	7	9	5	5	8	11	20	==	–	–	–	–	–	–	–	–	–	IT HAD TO BE YOU
–	–	–	==	==	16	13	7	5	4	3	4	4	9	16	==	==	–	–	–	–	–	–	–	–	–	TIME WAITS FOR NO ONE
–	–	–	==	==	==	18	19	18	==	==	–	–	–	–	–	–	–	–	–	–	–	–	–	–	–	HOW BLUE THE NIGHT
–	–	–	–	==	19	14	10	10	8	8	7	8	7	7	9	8	12	14	14	==	==	–	–	–	–	YOU ALWAYS HURT THE ONE YOU LOVE
–	–	–	–	–	==	19	11	6	3	2	1	1	1	1	1	3	9	10	==	==	–	–	–	–	–	I'LL WALK ALONE
–	–	–	–	–	==	==	18	==	==	–	–	–	–	–	–	–	–	–	–	–	–	–	–	–	–	SWEET LORRAINE
–	–	–	–	–	==	==	==	20	15	18	==	==	–	–	–	–	–	–	–	–	–	–	–	–	–	GOING MY WAY
–	–	–	–	–	==	==	==	16	13	10	8	11	14	==	==	–	–	–	–	–	–	–	–	–	–	IT COULD HAPPEN TO YOU
–	–	–	–	–	–	==	20	14	11	6	3	3	3	8	12	==	==	–	–	–	–	–	–	–	–	IS YOU IS OR IS YOU AIN'T (MA' BABY)
–	–	–	–	–	–	==	==	==	18	15	13	==	==	–	–	–	–	–	–	–	–	–	–	–	–	A FELLOW ON A FURLOUGH
–	–	–	–	–	–	==	==	==	20	13	10	10	16	==	==	–	–	–	–	–	–	–	–	–	–	PRETTY KITTY BLUE EYES
–	–	–	–	–	–	–	==	19	==	==	==	==	–	–	–	–	–	–	–	–	–	–	–	–	–	AND THEN YOU KISSED ME
–	–	–	–	–	–	–	==	17	16	14	16	==	==	–	–	–	–	–	–	–	–	–	–	–	–	HIS ROCKING HORSE RAN AWAY
–	–	–	–	–	–	–	==	==	19	17	17	==	20	==	–	–	–	–	–	–	–	–	–	–	–	TILL THEN
–	–	–	–	–	–	–	==	==	==	19	11	7	4	5	5	11	19	==	==	–	–	–	–	–	–	HOW MANY HEARTS HAVE YOU BROKEN
–	–	–	–	–	–	–	–	–	==	20	14	9	6	3	3	2	4	6	9	18	==	–	–	–	–	DANCE WITH A DOLLY
–	–	–	–	–	–	–	–	–	==	==	19	==	==	==	==	==	–	–	–	–	–	–	–	–	–	THE DAY AFTER FOREVER
–	–	–	–	–	–	–	–	–	==	==	18	12	5	2	4	4	6	8	17	==	–	–	–	–	–	TOGETHER
–	–	–	–	–	–	–	–	–	==	==	==	15	==	20	==	==	–	–	–	–	–	–	–	–	–	SWEET AND LOVELY
–	–	–	–	–	–	–	–	–	–	==	20	13	11	10	10	15	20	==	–	–	–	–	–	–	–	THERE'LL BE A HOT TIME IN THE TOWN OF BERLIN
–	–	–	–	–	–	–	–	–	–	==	==	14	==	==	–	–	–	–	–	–	–	–	–	–	–	AN HOUR NEVER PASSES
–	–	–	–	–	–	–	–	–	–	==	==	18	==	==	–	–	–	–	–	–	–	–	–	–	–	THE PATTY-CAKE MAN
–	–	–	–	–	–	–	–	–	–	–	==	20	10	4	2	1	1	2	6	15	==	–	–	–	–	THE TROLLEY SONG
–	–	–	–	–	–	–	–	–	–	–	==	==	17	17	==	==	–	–	–	–	–	–	–	–	–	SMOKE ON THE WATER
–	–	–	–	–	–	–	–	–	–	–	==	==	15	13	13	16	14	15	13	==	==	–	–	–	–	AND HER TEARS FLOWED LIKE WINE
–	–	–	–	–	–	–	–	–	–	–	==	==	19	12	7	5	3	4	5	6	13	==	==	–	–	I'M MAKING BELIEVE
–	–	–	–	–	–	–	–	–	–	–	–	==	12	9	6	6	11	9	8	14	18	==	–	–	–	ALWAYS
–	–	–	–	–	–	–	–	–	–	–	–	==	==	18	==	==	–	–	–	–	–	–	–	–	–	WHISPERING
–	–	–	–	–	–	–	–	–	–	–	–	==	18	14	14	14	13	20	==	–	–	–	–	–	–	TOO-RA LOO-RA LOO-RAL
–	–	–	–	–	–	–	–	–	–	–	–	–	==	19	==	==	–	–	–	–	–	–	–	–	–	STRANGE MUSIC
–	–	–	–	–	–	–	–	–	–	–	–	–	==	==	18	==	==	–	–	–	–	–	–	–	–	WHAT A DIFF'RENCE A DAY MAKES
–	–	–	–	–	–	–	–	–	–	–	–	–	==	==	16	10	10	7	10	12	16	==	==	–	–	INTO EACH LIFE SOME RAIN MUST FALL
–	–	–	–	–	–	–	–	–	–	–	–	–	–	==	==	20	15	==	==	–	–	–	–	–	–	LET ME LOVE YOU TONIGHT
–	–	–	–	–	–	–	–	–	–	–	–	–	–	–	17	7	8	18	–	–	–	–	–	–	–	WHITE CHRISTMAS
–	–	–	–	–	–	–	–	–	–	–	–	–	–	–	==	18	==	==	–	–	–	–	–	–	–	THE VERY THOUGHT OF YOU
–	–	–	–	–	–	–	–	–	–	–	–	–	–	–	==	17	17	==	–	–	–	–	–	–	–	I'LL BE HOME FOR CHRISTMAS
–	–	–	–	–	–	–	–	–	–	–	–	–	–	==	19	9	2	1	1	2	2	3	8	18	==	DON'T FENCE ME IN (1945)
–	–	–	–	–	–	–	–	–	–	–	–	–	–	==	15	13	5	3	2	5	7	15	==	==	–	THERE GOES THAT SONG AGAIN (1945)
–	–	–	–	–	–	–	–	–	–	–	–	–	–	==	11	12	7	5	3	4	5	9	13	==	==	I DREAM OF YOU (1945)
–	–	–	–	–	–	–	–	–	–	–	–	–	–	–	==	==	16	11	12	19	==	–	–	–	–	I DON'T WANT TO LOVE YOU (LIKE I DO) (1945)
–	–	–	–	–	–	–	–	–	–	–	–	–	–	–	==	==	18	17	15	13	12	14	==	==	–	I'M CONFESSIN' (THAT I LOVE YOU) (1945)
Ap	Ap	My	My	Jn	Jn	Jy	Jy	Ag	Ag	Sp	Sp	Oc	Oc	Nv	Nv	Dc	Dc	Ja	Ja	Fb	Fb	Ma	Ma	Ap	Ap	

1944						1945																				
Oc	Oc	Nv	Nv	Dc	Dc	Ja	Ja	Fb	Fb	Ma	Ma	Ap	Ap	My	My	Jn	Jn	Jy	Jy	Ag	Ag	Sp	Sp	Oc	Oc	
8	7	7	9	8	12	14	14	==	==	–	–	–	–	–	–	–	–	–	–	–	–	–	–	–	–	YOU ALWAYS HURT THE ONE YOU LOVE (1944)
1	1	1	1	3	9	10	==	==	–	–	–	–	–	–	–	–	–	–	–	–	–	–	–	–	–	I'LL WALK ALONE (1944)
9	6	3	3	2	4	6	9	18	==	–	–	–	–	–	–	–	–	–	–	–	–	–	–	–	–	DANCE WITH A DOLLY (1944)
12	5	2	4	4	6	8	17	==	–	–	–	–	–	–	–	–	–	–	–	–	–	–	–	–	–	TOGETHER (1944)
==	15	13	13	16	14	15	13	==	==	–	–	–	–	–	–	–	–	–	–	–	–	–	–	–	–	AND HER TEARS FLOWED LIKE WINE (1944)
20	10	4	2	1	1	2	6	15	==	–	–	–	–	–	–	–	–	–	–	–	–	–	–	–	–	THE TROLLEY SONG (1944)
==	12	9	6	6	11	9	8	14	18	==	–	–	–	–	–	–	–	–	–	–	–	–	–	–	–	ALWAYS (1944)
==	19	12	7	5	3	4	5	6	13	==	==	–	–	–	–	–	–	–	–	–	–	–	–	–	–	I'M MAKING BELIEVE (1944)
==	18	14	14	14	13	20	==	–	–	–	–	–	–	–	–	–	–	–	–	–	–	–	–	–	–	TOO-RA LOO-RA LOO-RAL (1944)
–	==	==	16	10	10	7	10	12	16	==	==	–	–	–	–	–	–	–	–	–	–	–	–	–	–	INTO EACH LIFE SOME RAIN MUST FALL (1944)
–	–	–	17	7	8	18	–	–	–	–	–	–	–	–	–	–	–	–	–	–	–	–	–	–	–	WHITE CHRISTMAS (1944)
–	–	==	19	9	2	1	1	2	2	3	8	18	==	–	–	–	–	–	–	–	–	–	–	–	–	DON'T FENCE ME IN
–	–	==	15	13	5	3	2	5	7	15	==	==	–	–	–	–	–	–	–	–	–	–	–	–	–	THERE GOES THAT SONG AGAIN
–	–	==	11	12	7	5	3	4	5	9	13	==	==	–	–	–	–	–	–	–	–	–	–	–	–	I DREAM OF YOU
–	–	==	==	==	==	==	==	==	14	19	==	==	–	–	–	–	–	–	–	–	–	–	–	–	–	TWILIGHT TIME
–	–	–	==	==	16	11	12	19	==	–	–	–	–	–	–	–	–	–	–	–	–	–	–	–	–	I DON'T WANT TO LOVE YOU (LIKE I DO)
–	–	–	==	==	18	17	15	13	12	14	==	==	–	–	–	–	–	–	–	–	–	–	–	–	–	I'M CONFESSIN' (THAT I LOVE YOU)
–	–	–	–	==	==	19	==	==	==	–	–	–	–	–	–	–	–	–	–	–	–	–	–	–	–	MEET ME IN ST. LOUIS, LOUIS
–	–	–	–	==	==	16	==	==	–	–	–	–	–	–	–	–	–	–	–	–	–	–	–	–	–	I'M WASTIN' MY TEARS ON YOU
–	–	–	–	–	==	13	4	1	1	1	1	5	11	18	==	==	–	–	–	–	–	–	–	–	–	AC-CENT-TCHU-ATE THE POSITIVE
–	–	–	–	–	==	12	7	3	3	2	3	6	8	17	==	–	–	–	–	–	–	–	–	–	–	RUM AND COCA COLA
–	–	–	–	–	==	==	11	7	11	10	9	9	16	==	–	–	–	–	–	–	–	–	–	–	–	SWEET DREAMS, SWEETHEART
–	–	–	–	–	==	==	==	17	==	==	–	–	–	–	–	–	–	–	–	–	–	–	–	–	–	EVELINA
–	–	–	–	–	–	==	16	9	9	11	17	==	–	–	–	–	–	–	–	–	–	–	–	–	–	COCKTAILS FOR TWO
–	–	–	–	–	–	==	18	8	4	4	4	4	10	18	==	–	–	–	–	–	–	–	–	–	–	A LITTLE ON THE LONELY SIDE
–	–	–	–	–	–	==	19	10	8	6	5	2	3	3	6	13	==	==	–	–	–	–	–	–	–	I'M BEGINNING TO SEE THE LIGHT
–	–	–	–	–	–	==	==	20	==	==	==	–	–	–	–	–	–	–	–	–	–	–	–	–	–	MOONLIGHT IN VERMONT
–	–	–	–	–	–	==	==	==	15	17	==	==	–	–	–	–	–	–	–	–	–	–	–	–	–	SLEIGH RIDE IN JULY
–	–	–	–	–	–	==	==	==	==	==	15	19	==	==	–	–	–	–	–	–	–	–	–	–	–	(ALL OF A SUDDEN) MY HEART SINGS
–	–	–	–	–	–	–	20	11	6	5	6	7	12	16	==	==	–	–	–	–	–	–	–	–	–	SATURDAY NIGHT (IS THE LONELIEST NIGHT OF THE WEEK)
–	–	–	–	–	–	–	==	16	10	7	2	1	1	1	1	4	13	==	==	–	–	–	–	–	–	MY DREAMS ARE GETTING BETTER ALL THE TIME
–	–	–	–	–	–	–	==	==	20	==	==	==	–	–	–	–	–	–	–	–	–	–	–	–	–	LET'S TAKE THE LONG WAY HOME
–	–	–	–	–	–	–	–	==	17	8	7	3	2	2	2	3	7	16	==	–	–	–	–	–	–	CANDY
–	–	–	–	–	–	–	–	==	19	12	20	==	==	–	–	–	–	–	–	–	–	–	–	–	–	THE THREE CABALLEROS
–	–	–	–	–	–	–	–	==	==	16	==	==	–	–	–	–	–	–	–	–	–	–	–	–	–	I WANNA GET MARRIED
–	–	–	–	–	–	–	–	==	==	13	10	12	17	==	==	–	–	–	–	–	–	–	–	–	–	MORE AND MORE
–	–	–	–	–	–	–	–	–	==	20	12	11	10	5	4	1	1	1	1	1	3	5	15	==	–	SENTIMENTAL JOURNEY
–	–	–	–	–	–	–	–	–	==	18	11	10	6	6	5	6	3	4	4	6	7	10	==	==	–	DREAM
–	–	–	–	–	–	–	–	–	==	==	19	==	==	–	–	–	–	–	–	–	–	–	–	–	–	I'M GONNA SEE MY BABY
–	–	–	–	–	–	–	–	–	==	==	16	20	==	==	==	–	–	–	–	–	–	–	–	–	–	OPUS NO. 1
–	–	–	–	–	–	–	–	–	==	==	18	8	5	8	8	9	10	15	15	==	==	–	–	–	–	JUST A PRAYER AWAY
–	–	–	–	–	–	–	–	–	–	==	14	14	9	7	7	8	4	3	3	9	10	15	==	==	–	THERE! I'VE SAID IT AGAIN
–	–	–	–	–	–	–	–	–	–	==	==	==	15	15	15	10	11	12	19	==	==	–	–	–	–	I SHOULD CARE
–	–	–	–	–	–	–	–	–	–	–	==	16	20	==	==	–	–	–	–	==	==	14	9	17	==	I DON'T CARE WHO KNOWS IT
–	–	–	–	–	–	–	–	–	–	–	==	13	13	9	11	12	12	14	14	19	==	–	–	–	–	ALL OF MY LIFE
–	–	–	–	–	–	–	–	–	–	–	==	15	7	4	3	2	5	6	12	14	==	==	–	–	–	LAURA
–	–	–	–	–	–	–	–	–	–	–	==	17	14	14	13	14	19	==	–	–	–	–	–	–	–	STUFF LIKE THAT THERE
–	–	–	–	–	–	–	–	–	–	–	–	==	19	11	9	7	9	11	17	==	==	–	–	–	–	CALDONIA
–	–	–	–	–	–	–	–	–	–	–	–	==	18	12	14	==	==	–	–	–	–	–	–	–	–	CHLOE
–	–	–	–	–	–	–	–	–	–	–	–	==	==	19	20	==	==	–	–	–	–	–	–	–	–	POOR LITTLE RHODE ISLAND
–	–	–	–	–	–	–	–	–	–	–	–	==	==	20	19	19	==	==	==	–	–	–	–	–	–	TIPPIN' IN
–	–	–	–	–	–	–	–	–	–	–	–	–	==	==	12	16	==	==	–	–	–	–	–	–	–	YAH-TA-TA, YAH-TA-TA (TALK, TALK, TALK)
–	–	–	–	–	–	–	–	–	–	–	–	–	==	==	17	17	==	==	–	–	–	–	–	–	–	(I LOVE YOU) SWEETHEART OF ALL MY DREAMS
Oc	Oc	Nv	Nv	Dc	Dc	Ja	Ja	Fb	Fb	Ma	Ma	Ap	Ap	My	My	Jn	Jn	Jy	Jy	Ag	Ag	Sp	Sp	Oc	Oc	

						1945														1946						
Ap	Ap	My	My	Jn	Jn	Jy	Jy	Ag	Ag	Sp	Sp	Oc	Oc	Nv	Nv	Dc	Dc	Ja	Ja	Fb	Fb	Ma	Ma	Ap	Ap	
–	==	13	10	5	2	2	2	3	4	8	14	==	==	–	–	–	–	–	–	–	–	–	–	–	–	BELL-BOTTOM TROUSERS
–	==	==	==	20	16	20	==	–	–	–	–	–	–	–	–	–	–	–	–	–	–	–	–	–	–	BAIA
–	==	==	==	11	6	5	10	8	14	18	==	==	–	–	–	–	–	–	–	–	–	–	–	–	–	YOU BELONG TO MY HEART
–	==	==	==	18	8	7	7	10	11	9	18	==	==	–	–	–	–	–	–	–	–	–	–	–	–	THE MORE I SEE YOU
–	–	==	16	15	15	19	==	–	–	–	–	–	–	–	–	–	–	–	–	–	–	–	–	–	–	I WISH
–	–	==	==	==	14	18	16	18	==	==	–	–	–	–	–	–	–	–	–	–	–	–	–	–	–	GOOD, GOOD, GOOD
–	–	–	–	==	17	8	5	4	5	4	4	7	10	13	==	==	–	–	–	–	–	–	–	–	–	GOTTA BE THIS OR THAT
–	–	–	–	==	18	9	8	5	2	3	3	5	8	11	14	15	==	==	–	–	–	–	–	–	–	IF I LOVED YOU
–	–	–	–	==	20	10	9	7	9	6	7	11	17	==	==	–	–	–	–	–	–	–	–	–	–	I WISH I KNEW
–	–	–	–	==	==	==	20	17	18	==	==	–	–	–	–	–	–	–	–	–	–	–	–	–	–	WHO THREW THE WHISKEY IN THE WELL?
–	–	–	–	==	==	==	18	12	20	==	==	–	–	–	–	–	–	–	–	–	–	–	–	–	–	A FRIEND OF YOURS
–	–	–	–	==	==	==	13	16	17	13	8	18	==	==	–	–	–	–	–	–	–	–	–	–	–	THERE MUST BE A WAY
–	–	–	–	–	==	17	11	11	8	12	13	20	==	==	–	–	–	–	–	–	–	–	–	–	–	CHOPIN'S POLONAISE
–	–	–	–	–	==	13	6	2	**1**	**1**	2	2	3	5	10	16	==	–	–	–	–	–	–	–	–	ON THE ATCHESON, TOPEKA AND THE SANTA FE
–	–	–	–	–	==	==	==	==	16	19	==	==	–	–	–	–	–	–	–	–	–	–	–	–	–	JUNE IS BUSTIN' OUT ALL OVER
–	–	–	–	–	==	==	==	==	==	17	17	==	==	–	–	–	–	–	–	–	–	–	–	–	–	THERE'S NO YOU
–	–	–	–	–	–	==	==	13	12	16	12	13	16	15	==	==	–	–	–	–	–	–	–	–	–	TAMPICO
–	–	–	–	–	–	–	==	20	==	==	–	–	–	–	–	–	–	–	–	–	–	–	–	–	–	FUZZY WUZZY
–	–	–	–	–	–	–	==	15	6	2	**1**	**1**	**1**	**1**	2	5	10	==	==	–	–	–	–	–	–	TILL THE END OF TIME
–	–	–	–	–	–	–	==	==	19	==	==	–	–	–	–	–	–	–	–	–	–	–	–	–	–	A KISS GOODNIGHT
–	–	–	–	–	–	–	==	==	15	20	==	19	==	==	==	–	–	–	–	–	–	–	–	–	–	HONG KONG BLUES
–	–	–	–	–	–	–	==	==	==	==	10	8	12	17	==	–	–	–	–	–	–	–	–	–	–	(YOU CAME ALONG) OUT OF NOWHERE
–	–	–	–	–	–	–	–	==	13	7	5	4	6	7	17	==	==	–	–	–	–	–	–	–	–	I'M GONNA LOVE THAT GAL (GUY)
–	–	–	–	–	–	–	–	==	==	11	6	6	4	6	7	13	==	==	–	–	–	–	–	–	–	ALONG THE NAVAJO TRAIL
–	–	–	–	–	–	–	–	–	==	==	11	3	2	3	3	2	9	20	==	–	–	–	–	–	–	I'LL BUY THAT DREAM
–	–	–	–	–	–	–	–	–	–	==	16	==	==	–	–	–	–	–	–	–	–	–	–	–	–	BOOGIE WOOGIE
–	–	–	–	–	–	–	–	–	–	==	19	10	7	4	4	6	8	8	14	16	==	–	–	–	–	THAT'S FOR ME
–	–	–	–	–	–	–	–	–	–	==	20	9	9	8	11	10	11	19	==	–	–	–	–	–	–	IT'S ONLY A PAPER MOON
–	–	–	–	–	–	–	–	–	–	==	==	14	14	18	==	==	–	–	–	–	–	–	–	–	–	AND THERE YOU ARE
–	–	–	–	–	–	–	–	–	–	==	==	12	11	9	16	==	==	–	–	–	–	–	–	–	–	HOW DEEP IS THE OCEAN?
–	–	–	–	–	–	–	–	–	–	==	==	15	13	12	13	14	==	==	–	–	–	–	–	–	–	LOVE LETTERS
–	–	–	–	–	–	–	–	–	–	–	==	16	5	2	**1**	**1**	**1**	3	6	15	==	–	–	–	–	IT'S BEEN A LONG, LONG TIME
–	–	–	–	–	–	–	–	–	–	–	==	==	15	19	==	==	–	–	–	–	–	–	–	–	–	A COTTAGE FOR SALE
–	–	–	–	–	–	–	–	–	–	–	==	==	18	20	20	==	==	–	–	–	–	–	–	–	–	THE BLOND SAILOR
–	–	–	–	–	–	–	–	–	–	–	–	==	19	10	5	4	4	5	7	8	14	==	–	–	–	CHICKERY CHICK
–	–	–	–	–	–	–	–	–	–	–	–	==	20	14	6	3	3	4	4	4	8	13	==	==	–	IT MIGHT AS WELL BE SPRING
–	–	–	–	–	–	–	–	–	–	–	–	==	==	16	12	9	12	14	==	==	–	–	–	–	–	(DID YOU EVER GET) THAT FEELING IN THE MOONLIGHT
–	–	–	–	–	–	–	–	–	–	–	–	==	==	==	15	19	==	–	–	–	–	–	–	–	–	NO CAN DO
–	–	–	–	–	–	–	–	–	–	–	–	==	==	==	18	17	==	==	–	–	–	–	–	–	–	(I'LL BE) WALKIN' WITH MY HONEY
–	–	–	–	–	–	–	–	–	–	–	–	==	==	==	==	==	16	==	==	–	–	–	–	–	–	LILY BELLE
–	–	–	–	–	–	–	–	–	–	–	–	–	==	==	19	==	==	–	–	–	–	–	–	–	–	DON'T FORGET TONIGHT, TOMORROW
–	–	–	–	–	–	–	–	–	–	–	–	–	==	==	8	7	2	2	2	3	3	6	10	16	==	I CAN'T BEGIN TO TELL YOU
–	–	–	–	–	–	–	–	–	–	–	–	–	==	==	9	8	5	6	5	13	17	==	–	–	–	WAITIN' FOR THE TRAIN TO COME IN
–	–	–	–	–	–	–	–	–	–	–	–	–	–	==	==	20	==	==	–	–	–	–	–	–	–	BUT I DID
–	–	–	–	–	–	–	–	–	–	–	–	–	–	–	==	11	7	13	–	–	–	–	–	–	–	WHITE CHRISTMAS
–	–	–	–	–	–	–	–	–	–	–	–	–	–	–	==	==	20	==	==	–	–	–	–	–	–	NANCY (WITH THE LAUGHING FACE)
–	–	–	–	–	–	–	–	–	–	–	–	–	–	–	==	18	==	12	8	11	10	11	12	15	==	SOME SUNDAY MORNING (1946)
–	–	–	–	–	–	–	–	–	–	–	–	–	–	–	==	12	6	**1**	**1**	**1**	**1**	**1**	5	9	18	SYMPHONY (1946)
–	–	–	–	–	–	–	–	–	–	–	–	–	–	–	==	==	14	17	13	9	12	15	20	==	–	JUST A LITTLE FOND AFFECTION (1946)
–	–	–	–	–	–	–	–	–	–	–	–	–	–	–	==	==	18	18	15	20	==	–	–	–	–	IN THE MIDDLE OF MAY (1946)
–	–	–	–	–	–	–	–	–	–	–	–	–	–	–	–	==	13	7	3	2	2	3	8	==	==	LET IT SNOW! LET IT SNOW! LET IT SNOW! (1946)
–	–	–	–	–	–	–	–	–	–	–	–	–	–	–	–	==	15	10	9	6	7	10	14	==	==	AREN'T YOU GLAD YOU'RE YOU? (1946)
–	–	–	–	–	–	–	–	–	–	–	–	–	–	–	–	==	17	15	16	14	19	==	–	–	–	COME TO BABY, DO! (1946)
–	–	–	–	–	–	–	–	–	–	–	–	–	–	–	–	==	19	9	12	12	13	12	19	==	–	DIG YOU LATER (A HUBBA-HUBBA-HUBBA) (1946)
Ap	Ap	My	My	Jn	Jn	Jy	Jy	Ag	Ag	Sp	Sp	Oc	Oc	Nv	Nv	Dc	Dc	Ja	Ja	Fb	Fb	Ma	Ma	Ap	Ap	

1945															1946											
Oc	Oc	Nv	Nv	Dc	Dc	Ja	Ja	Fb	Fb	Ma	Ma	Ap	Ap	My	My	Jn	Jn	Jy	Jy	Ag	Ag	Sp	Sp	Oc	Oc	
3	2	3	3	2	9	20	==	–	–	–	–	–	–	–	–	–	–	–	–	–	–	–	–	–	–	I'LL BUY THAT DREAM (1945)
10	7	4	4	6	8	8	14	16	==	–	–	–	–	–	–	–	–	–	–	–	–	–	–	–	–	THAT'S FOR ME (1945)
9	9	8	11	10	11	19	==	–	–	–	–	–	–	–	–	–	–	–	–	–	–	–	–	–	–	IT'S ONLY A PAPER MOON (1945)
16	5	2	**1**	**1**	**1**	3	6	15	==	–	–	–	–	–	–	–	–	–	–	–	–	–	–	–	–	IT'S BEEN A LONG, LONG TIME (1945)
==	19	10	5	4	4	5	7	8	14	==	–	–	–	–	–	–	–	–	–	–	–	–	–	–	–	CHICKERY CHICK (1945)
==	20	14	6	3	3	4	4	4	8	13	==	==	–	–	–	–	–	–	–	–	–	–	–	–	–	IT MIGHT AS WELL BE SPRING (1945)
==	==	16	12	9	12	14	==	==	–	–	–	–	–	–	–	–	–	–	–	–	–	–	–	–	–	THAT FEELING IN THE MOONLIGHT (1945)
–	==	==	8	7	2	2	2	3	3	6	10	16	==	–	–	–	–	–	–	–	–	–	–	–	–	I CAN'T BEGIN TO TELL YOU (1945)
–	==	==	9	8	5	6	5	13	17	==	–	–	–	–	–	–	–	–	–	–	–	–	–	–	–	WAITIN' FOR THE TRAIN TO COME IN (1945)
–	–	–	==	11	7	13	–	–	–	–	–	–	–	–	–	–	–	–	–	–	–	–	–	–	–	WHITE CHRISTMAS (1945)
–	–	–	==	18	==	12	8	11	10	11	12	15	==	–	–	–	–	–	–	–	–	–	–	–	–	SOME SUNDAY MORNING
–	–	–	==	12	6	**1**	**1**	**1**	**1**	**1**	5	9	18	–	–	–	–	–	–	–	–	–	–	–	–	SYMPHONY
–	–	–	==	==	14	17	13	9	12	15	20	==	–	–	–	–	–	–	–	–	–	–	–	–	–	JUST A LITTLE FOND AFFECTION
–	–	–	==	==	18	18	15	20	==	–	–	–	–	–	–	–	–	–	–	–	–	–	–	–	–	IN THE MIDDLE OF MAY
–	–	–	–	==	13	7	3	2	2	3	8	==	==	–	–	–	–	–	–	–	–	–	–	–	–	LET IT SNOW! LET IT SNOW! LET IT SNOW!
–	–	–	–	==	15	10	9	6	7	10	14	==	==	–	–	–	–	–	–	–	–	–	–	–	–	AREN'T YOU GLAD YOU'RE YOU?
–	–	–	–	==	17	15	16	14	19	==	–	–	–	–	–	–	–	–	–	–	–	–	–	–	–	COME TO BABY, DO!
–	–	–	–	==	19	9	12	12	13	12	19	==	–	–	–	–	–	–	–	–	–	–	–	–	–	DIG YOU LATER (A HUBBA-HUBBA-HUBBA)
–	–	–	–	==	==	11	10	7	6	4	3	6	11	16	==	–	–	–	–	–	–	–	–	–	–	DOCTOR, LAWYER, INDIAN CHIEF
–	–	–	–	–	==	16	11	5	4	7	9	11	15	15	==	–	–	–	–	–	–	–	–	–	–	I'M ALWAYS CHASING RAINBOWS
–	–	–	–	–	==	==	20	19	==	–	–	–	–	–	–	–	–	–	–	–	–	–	–	–	–	THE MOMENT I MET YOU
–	–	–	–	–	–	==	19	18	20	==	–	–	–	–	–	–	–	–	–	–	–	–	–	–	–	BUZZ ME
–	–	–	–	–	–	==	17	17	15	19	==	==	–	–	–	–	–	–	–	–	–	–	–	–	–	THE BELLS OF ST. MARY'S
–	–	–	–	–	–	–	18	10	5	5	2	3	5	12	==	==	–	–	–	–	–	–	–	–	–	PERSONALITY
–	–	–	–	–	–	–	==	==	9	2	**1**	**1**	**1**	**1**	3	7	==	==	–	–	–	–	–	–	–	OH! WHAT IT SEEMED TO BE
–	–	–	–	–	–	–	==	==	16	8	4	4	3	8	11	14	==	–	–	–	–	–	–	–	–	YOU WON'T BE SATISFIED (UNTIL YOU BREAK MY HEART)
–	–	–	–	–	–	–	==	==	==	16	18	==	==	–	–	–	–	–	–	–	–	–	–	–	–	HERE COMES HEAVEN AGAIN
–	–	–	–	–	–	–	–	==	18	20	==	–	–	–	–	–	–	–	–	–	–	–	–	–	–	MONEY IS THE ROOT OF ALL EVIL (TAKE IT AWAY!)
–	–	–	–	–	–	–	–	==	11	9	6	7	6	13	14	==	==	–	–	–	–	–	–	–	–	DAY BY DAY
–	–	–	–	–	–	–	–	==	==	18	==	==	–	–	–	–	–	–	–	–	–	–	–	–	–	WAIT AND SEE
–	–	–	–	–	–	–	–	==	==	14	11	10	13	20	==	–	–	–	–	–	–	–	–	–	–	ATLANTA, GA
–	–	–	–	–	–	–	–	–	==	17	7	2	2	4	13	==	–	–	–	–	–	–	–	–	–	ONE-ZY, TWO-ZY (I LOVE YOU-ZY)
–	–	–	–	–	–	–	–	–	–	==	16	19	==	–	–	–	–	–	–	–	–	–	–	–	–	MacNAMARA'S BAND
–	–	–	–	–	–	–	–	–	–	==	15	13	12	11	15	13	==	–	–	–	–	–	–	–	–	SEEMS LIKE OLD TIMES
–	–	–	–	–	–	–	–	–	–	==	13	5	4	3	5	10	14	==	==	–	–	–	–	–	–	SHOO-FLY PIE AND APPLE PAN DOWDY
–	–	–	–	–	–	–	–	–	–	==	17	18	20	==	–	–	–	–	–	–	–	–	–	–	–	I'M GLAD I WAITED FOR YOU
–	–	–	–	–	–	–	–	–	–	==	==	20	19	==	==	17	13	16	==	==	–	–	–	–	–	HEY! BA-BA-RE-BOP
–	–	–	–	–	–	–	–	–	–	–	==	12	8	7	6	6	6	7	10	13	==	==	–	–	–	SIOUX CITY SUE
–	–	–	–	–	–	–	–	–	–	–	==	8	7	2	**1**	2	2	5	9	20	==	–	–	–	–	LAUGHING ON THE OUTSIDE
–	–	–	–	–	–	–	–	–	–	–	==	14	9	6	4	5	5	9	11	10	15	17	==	==	–	ALL THROUGH THE DAY
–	–	–	–	–	–	–	–	–	–	–	–	17	10	9	7	3	4	3	5	6	9	13	==	==	–	PRISONER OF LOVE
–	–	–	–	–	–	–	–	–	–	–	–	==	16	==	–	–	–	–	–	–	–	–	–	–	–	EASTER PARADE
–	–	–	–	–	–	–	–	–	–	–	–	==	14	10	9	16	16	==	==	–	–	–	–	–	–	I'M A BIG GIRL NOW
–	–	–	–	–	–	–	–	–	–	–	–	==	17	5	2	**1**	**1**	**1**	**1**	**1**	2	5	7	17	==	THE GYPSY
–	–	–	–	–	–	–	–	–	–	–	–	==	==	19	17	12	20	==	–	–	–	–	–	–	–	WE'LL GATHER LILACS
–	–	–	–	–	–	–	–	–	–	–	–	==	==	17	16	15	11	10	12	8	12	15	==	–	–	IN LOVE IN VAIN
–	–	–	–	–	–	–	–	–	–	–	–	==	==	==	==	20	==	==	–	–	–	–	–	–	–	THE MAD BOOGIE
–	–	–	–	–	–	–	–	–	–	–	–	–	==	14	10	11	12	17	==	==	–	–	–	–	–	CEMENT MIXER (PUT-TI, PUT-TI)
–	–	–	–	–	–	–	–	–	–	–	–	–	==	==	12	8	9	8	15	12	19	==	–	–	–	FULL MOON AND EMPTY ARMS
–	–	–	–	–	–	–	–	–	–	–	–	–	==	==	18	9	8	6	6	7	7	10	13	==	==	I DON'T KNOW ENOUGH ABOUT YOU
Oc	Oc	Nv	Nv	Dc	Dc	Ja	Ja	Fb	Fb	Ma	Ma	Ap	Ap	My	My	Jn	Jn	Jy	Jy	Ag	Ag	Sp	Sp	Oc	Oc	

1946																		1947								
Ap	Ap	My	My	Jn	Jn	Jy	Jy	Ag	Ag	Sp	Sp	Oc	Oc	Nv	Nv	Dc	Dc	Ja	Ja	Fb	Fb	Ma	Ma	Ap	Ap	
–	==	18	8	4	3	2	2	5	6	6	5	8	11	==	==	–	–	–	–	–	–	–	–	–	–	THEY SAY IT'S WONDERFUL
–	–	==	20	==	==	–	–	–	–	–	–	–	–	–	–	–	–	–	–	–	–	–	–	–	–	BUMBLE BOOGIE
–	–	==	19	==	15	13	14	19	==	==	–	–	–	–	–	–	–	–	–	–	–	–	–	–	–	COME RAIN OR COME SHINE
–	–	==	==	18	==	==	–	–	–	–	–	–	–	–	–	–	–	–	–	–	–	–	–	–	–	COAX ME A LITTLE BIT
–	–	==	==	==	18	==	==	–	–	–	–	–	–	–	–	–	–	–	–	–	–	–	–	–	–	IN THE MOON MIST
–	–	==	==	==	17	18	17	14	16	16	15	==	==	–	–	–	–	–	–	–	–	–	–	–	–	ONE MORE TOMORROW
–	–	–	==	19	10	15	16	==	==	–	–	–	–	–	–	–	–	–	–	–	–	–	–	–	–	DO YOU LOVE ME?
–	–	–	==	==	==	19	==	==	–	–	–	–	–	–	–	–	–	–	–	–	–	–	–	–	–	THE HOUSE OF BLUE LIGHTS
–	–	–	–	==	7	4	3	2	4	7	8	7	9	16	==	–	–	–	–	–	–	–	–	–	–	DOIN' WHAT COMES NATUR'LY
–	–	–	–	==	19	12	8	9	8	8	11	16	==	==	–	–	–	–	–	–	–	–	–	–	–	I GOT THE SUN IN THE MORNING
–	–	–	–	==	==	14	13	11	11	11	10	10	18	==	==	–	–	–	–	–	–	–	–	–	–	I DON'T KNOW WHY (I JUST DO)
–	–	–	–	–	==	11	4	4	3	3	4	5	8	11	==	–	–	–	–	–	–	–	–	–	–	SURRENDER
–	–	–	–	–	–	20	7	3	1	1	1	1	1	3	6	11	20	==	–	–	–	–	–	–	–	TO EACH HIS OWN
–	–	–	–	–	–	==	19	==	==	–	–	–	–	–	–	–	–	–	–	–	–	–	–	–	–	WHO DO YOU LOVE, I HOPE?
–	–	–	–	–	–	==	18	18	==	–	–	–	–	–	–	–	–	–	–	–	–	–	–	–	–	STONE COLD DEAD IN DE MARKET
–	–	–	–	–	–	==	20	15	14	==	==	–	–	–	–	–	–	–	–	–	–	–	–	–	–	WHO TOLD YOU THAT LIE?
–	–	–	–	–	–	==	==	17	20	==	–	–	–	–	–	–	–	–	–	–	–	–	–	–	–	THERE'S NO ONE BUT YOU
–	–	–	–	–	–	==	==	==	17	12	12	9	12	==	==	–	–	–	–	–	–	–	–	–	–	I'D BE LOST WITHOUT YOU
–	–	–	–	–	–	–	==	16	5	2	2	2	3	2	3	5	14	==	–	–	–	–	–	–	–	FIVE MINUTES MORE
–	–	–	–	–	–	–	==	==	18	==	==	–	–	–	–	–	–	–	–	–	–	–	–	–	–	ALONG WITH ME
–	–	–	–	–	–	–	==	==	13	9	6	6	7	9	13	19	==	–	–	–	–	–	–	–	–	IF YOU WERE THE ONLY GIRL
–	–	–	–	–	–	–	–	==	10	4	3	3	4	5	8	17	==	–	–	–	–	–	–	–	–	SOUTH AMERICA, TAKE IT AWAY
–	–	–	–	–	–	–	–	==	==	18	==	==	–	–	–	–	–	–	–	–	–	–	–	–	–	WITHOUT YOU
–	–	–	–	–	–	–	–	==	==	==	20	==	–	–	–	–	–	–	–	–	–	–	–	–	–	JUST THE OTHER DAY
–	–	–	–	–	–	–	–	–	==	20	14	14	19	==	==	–	–	–	–	–	–	–	–	–	–	CHOO CHOO CH'BOOGIE
–	–	–	–	–	–	–	–	–	==	14	16	18	16	12	15	==	==	–	–	–	–	–	–	–	–	BLUE SKIES
–	–	–	–	–	–	–	–	–	==	==	19	20	==	==	==	–	–	–	–	–	–	–	–	–	–	PRETENDING
–	–	–	–	–	–	–	–	–	==	==	18	11	15	14	20	==	==	–	–	–	–	–	–	–	–	LINGER IN MY ARMS A LITTLE LONGER, BABY
–	–	–	–	–	–	–	–	–	–	19	9	4	2	**1**	**1**	2	5	5	13	19	==	–	–	–	–	RUMORS ARE FLYING
–	–	–	–	–	–	–	–	–	–	==	17	19	10	8	11	16	==	==	–	–	–	–	–	–	–	THIS IS ALWAYS
–	–	–	–	–	–	–	–	–	–	==	==	==	17	10	19	==	==	–	–	–	–	–	–	–	–	AND THEN IT'S HEAVEN
–	–	–	–	–	–	–	–	–	–	–	==	12	5	4	2	**1**	2	2	3	4	9	16	==	–	–	OLE BUTTERMILK SKY
–	–	–	–	–	–	–	–	–	–	–	==	13	13	18	14	12	13	18	17	==	==	–	–	–	–	SEPTEMBER SONG
–	–	–	–	–	–	–	–	–	–	–	==	15	6	6	5	8	12	11	14	20	==	–	–	–	–	YOU KEEP COMING BACK LIKE A SONG
–	–	–	–	–	–	–	–	–	–	–	==	==	14	17	16	==	==	–	–	–	–	–	–	–	–	I GUESS I'LL GET THE PAPERS AND GO HOME
–	–	–	–	–	–	–	–	–	–	–	==	==	==	20	==	==	–	–	–	–	–	–	–	–	–	PASSE
–	–	–	–	–	–	–	–	–	–	–	–	==	20	7	7	4	6	8	8	14	19	==	–	–	–	THE WHOLE WORLD IS SINGING MY SONG
–	–	–	–	–	–	–	–	–	–	–	–	==	==	19	18	==	18	19	16	18	17	==	==	==	–	THE GIRL THAT I MARRY
–	–	–	–	–	–	–	–	–	–	–	–	==	==	==	12	14	19	==	==	–	–	–	–	–	–	THE COFFEE SONG
–	–	–	–	–	–	–	–	–	–	–	–	–	==	13	4	3	**1**	**1**	**1**	2	4	6	11	==	==	THE OLD LAMP-LIGHTER
–	–	–	–	–	–	–	–	–	–	–	–	–	==	15	9	9	9	10	10	15	20	==	==	–	–	THE THINGS WE DID LAST SUMMER
–	–	–	–	–	–	–	–	–	–	–	–	–	–	–	==	18	17	==	==	–	–	–	–	–	–	IT'S ALL OVER NOW
–	–	–	–	–	–	–	–	–	–	–	–	–	–	–	==	10	3	9	==	–	–	–	–	–	–	WHITE CHRISTMAS
–	–	–	–	–	–	–	–	–	–	–	–	–	–	–	–	20	11	15	==	–	–	–	–	–	–	THE CHRISTMAS SONG
–	–	–	–	–	–	–	–	–	–	–	–	–	–	–	–	==	16	14	==	–	–	–	–	–	–	WINTER WONDERLAND
–	–	–	–	–	–	–	–	–	–	–	–	–	–	==	10	6	4	3	2	**1**	**1**	4	6	7	13	(I LOVE YOU) FOR SENTIMENTAL REASONS (1947)
–	–	–	–	–	–	–	–	–	–	–	–	–	–	==	17	7	8	7	5	7	8	11	10	17	==	ZIP-A-DEE-DO-DAH (1947)
–	–	–	–	–	–	–	–	–	–	–	–	–	–	==	==	13	10	6	6	5	7	14	20	==	–	HUGGIN' AND CHALKIN' (1947)
–	–	–	–	–	–	–	–	–	–	–	–	–	–	–	==	15	7	4	4	3	5	9	16	==	–	A GAL IN CALICO (1947)
–	–	–	–	–	–	–	–	–	–	–	–	–	–	–	==	==	15	12	11	12	13	19	==	–	–	SOONER OR LATER (1947)
Ap	Ap	My	My	Jn	Jn	Jy	Jy	Ag	Ag	Sp	Sp	Oc	Oc	Nv	Nv	Dc	Dc	Ja	Ja	Fb	Fb	Ma	Ma	Ap	Ap	

1946													1947													
Oc	**Oc**	**Nv**	**Nv**	**Dc**	**Dc**	**Ja**	**Ja**	**Fb**	**Fb**	**Ma**	**Ma**	**Ap**	**Ap**	**My**	**My**	**Jn**	**Jn**	**Jy**	**Jy**	**Ag**	**Ag**	**Sp**	**Sp**	**Oc**	**Oc**	
4	2	**1**	**1**	2	5	5	13	19	==	–	–	–	–	–	–	–	–	–	–	–	–	–	–	–	–	RUMORS ARE FLYING (1946)
12	5	4	2	**1**	2	2	3	4	9	16	==	–	–	–	–	–	–	–	–	–	–	–	–	–	–	OLE BUTTERMILK SKY (1946)
13	13	18	14	12	13	18	17	==	==	–	–	–	–	–	–	–	–	–	–	–	–	–	–	–	–	SEPTEMBER SONG (1946)
15	6	6	5	8	12	11	14	20	==	–	–	–	–	–	–	–	–	–	–	–	–	–	–	–	–	YOU KEEP COMING BACK LIKE A SONG (1946)
==	20	7	7	4	6	8	8	14	19	==	–	–	–	–	–	–	–	–	–	–	–	–	–	–	–	THE WHOLE WORLD IS SINGING MY SONG (1946)
==	==	19	18	==	18	19	16	18	17	==	==	==	–	–	–	–	–	–	–	–	–	–	–	–	–	THE GIRL THAT I MARRY (1946)
–	==	13	4	3	**1**	**1**	**1**	2	4	6	11	==	==	–	–	–	–	–	–	–	–	–	–	–	–	THE OLD LAMP-LIGHTER (1946)
–	==	15	9	9	9	10	10	15	20	==	==	–	–	–	–	–	–	–	–	–	–	–	–	–	–	THE THINGS WE DID LAST SUMMER (1946)
–	–	–	==	10	3	9	==	–	–	–	–	–	–	–	–	–	–	–	–	–	–	–	–	–	–	WHITE CHRISTMAS (1946)
–	–	–	–	20	11	15	==	–	–	–	–	–	–	–	–	–	–	–	–	–	–	–	–	–	–	THE CHRISTMAS SONG (1946)
–	–	–	–	==	16	14	==	–	–	–	–	–	–	–	–	–	–	–	–	–	–	–	–	–	–	WINTER WONDERLAND (1946)
–	–	–	–	–	==	13	==	–	–	–	–	–	–	–	–	–	–	–	–	–	–	–	–	–	–	CHRISTMAS ISLAND
–	–	==	10	6	4	3	2	**1**	**1**	4	6	7	13	==	==	–	–	–	–	–	–	–	–	–	–	(I LOVE YOU) FOR SENTIMENTAL REASONS
–	–	==	17	7	8	7	5	7	8	11	10	17	==	–	–	–	–	–	–	–	–	–	–	–	–	ZIP-A-DEE-DOO-DAH
–	–	==	==	13	10	6	6	5	7	14	20	==	–	–	–	–	–	–	–	–	–	–	–	–	–	HUGGIN' AND CHALKIN'
–	–	–	==	15	7	4	4	3	5	9	16	==	–	–	–	–	–	–	–	–	–	–	–	–	–	A GAL IN CALICO
–	–	–	==	==	15	12	11	12	13	19	==	–	–	–	–	–	–	–	–	–	–	–	–	–	–	SOONER OR LATER
–	–	–	–	==	==	16	7	8	10	12	15	==	==	–	–	–	–	–	–	–	–	–	–	–	–	OH, BUT I DO!
–	–	–	–	==	==	17	12	==	==	–	–	–	–	–	–	–	–	–	–	–	–	–	–	–	–	FOR YOU, FOR ME, FOREVERMORE
–	–	–	–	==	==	20	18	9	11	10	9	8	12	==	==	–	–	–	–	–	–	–	–	–	–	I'LL CLOSE MY EYES
–	–	–	–	==	==	==	==	==	18	20	14	13	19	==	==	–	–	–	–	–	–	–	–	–	–	A RAINY NIGHT IN RIO
–	–	–	–	–	–	==	19	17	==	==	–	–	–	–	–	–	–	–	–	–	–	–	–	–	–	AIN'T NOBODY HERE BUT US CHICKENS
–	–	–	–	–	–	==	15	13	12	15	12	14	==	==	–	–	–	–	–	–	–	–	–	–	–	SONATA
–	–	–	–	–	–	==	9	6	3	3	2	5	4	8	12	==	==	–	–	–	–	–	–	–	–	MANAGUA, NICARAGUA
–	–	–	–	–	–	==	==	16	14	5	5	6	7	9	19	==	–	–	–	–	–	–	–	–	–	GUILTY
–	–	–	–	–	–	==	==	==	==	17	13	9	9	11	20	==	–	–	–	–	–	–	–	–	–	IT'S A GOOD DAY
–	–	–	–	–	–	–	20	11	6	2	**1**	**1**	3	4	5	9	11	16	17	==	==	–	–	–	–	ANNIVERSARY SONG
–	–	–	–	–	–	–	==	10	2	**1**	7	15	==	–	–	–	–	–	–	–	–	–	–	–	–	OPEN THE DOOR, RICHARD!
–	–	–	–	–	–	–	–	==	15	13	8	3	2	3	3	2	5	7	8	14	==	–	–	–	–	LINDA
–	–	–	–	–	–	–	–	==	16	8	4	4	6	7	13	18	==	–	–	–	–	–	–	–	–	HOW ARE THINGS IN GLOCCA MORRA?
–	–	–	–	–	–	–	–	==	==	18	17	==	==	–	–	–	–	–	–	–	–	–	–	–	–	YOU'LL ALWAYS BE THE ONE I LOVE
–	–	–	–	–	–	–	–	==	==	==	18	12	16	==	==	–	–	–	–	–	–	–	–	–	–	BLESS YOU (FOR BEING AN ANGEL)
–	–	–	–	–	–	–	–	–	==	7	3	2	**1**	**1**	2	5	9	11	20	==	–	–	–	–	–	HEARTACHES
–	–	–	–	–	–	–	–	–	==	==	19	10	11	12	==	==	–	–	–	–	–	–	–	–	–	YOU CAN'T SEE THE SUN WHEN YOU'RE CRYIN'
–	–	–	–	–	–	–	–	–	–	==	==	11	8	5	4	4	7	9	11	20	==	–	–	–	–	MY ADOBE HACIENDA
–	–	–	–	–	–	–	–	–	–	==	==	==	20	==	–	–	–	–	–	–	–	–	–	–	–	THAT'S HOW MUCH I LOVE YOU
–	–	–	–	–	–	–	–	–	–	–	==	18	10	6	6	12	18	==	–	–	–	–	–	–	–	APRIL SHOWERS
–	–	–	–	–	–	–	–	–	–	–	==	19	17	13	7	7	6	5	4	3	2	2	5	6	10	== == THAT'S MY DESIRE
–	–	–	–	–	–	–	–	–	–	–	–	20	18	14	14	20	==	–	–	–	–	–	–	–	–	ROSES IN THE RAIN
–	–	–	–	–	–	–	–	–	–	–	–	16	5	2	**1**	**1**	**1**	4	6	10	18	==	–	–	–	MAM'SELLE
–	–	–	–	–	–	–	–	–	–	–	–	==	14	10	15	==	==	–	–	–	–	–	–	–	–	MY MELANCHOLY BABY
–	–	–	–	–	–	–	–	–	–	–	–	==	15	19	18	16	13	12	15	16	==	==	–	–	–	IF I HAD MY LIFE TO LIVE OVER
–	–	–	–	–	–	–	–	–	–	–	–	==	==	16	==	==	–	–	–	–	–	–	–	–	–	FREE EATS
–	–	–	–	–	–	–	–	–	–	–	–	==	==	18	==	==	–	–	–	–	–	–	–	–	–	THAT'S WERE I CAME IN
–	–	–	–	–	–	–	–	–	–	–	–	–	==	20	==	==	–	–	–	–	–	–	–	–	–	MOON-FACED, STARRY-EYED
–	–	–	–	–	–	–	–	–	–	–	–	–	==	==	16	13	15	13	==	==	–	–	–	–	–	RED SILK STOCKINGS AND GREEN PERFUME
–	–	–	–	–	–	–	–	–	–	–	–	–	==	==	17	14	16	15	==	==	==	–	–	–	–	A SUNDAY KIND OF LOVE
–	–	–	–	–	–	–	–	–	–	–	–	–	==	==	11	8	8	6	5	5	12	19	==	–	–	ACROSS THE ALLEY FROM THE ALAMO
–	–	–	–	–	–	–	–	–	–	–	–	–	==	==	==	19	12	10	13	19	==	–	–	–	–	MIDNIGHT MASQUERADE
Oc	**Oc**	**Nv**	**Nv**	**Dc**	**Dc**	**Ja**	**Ja**	**Fb**	**Fb**	**Ma**	**Ma**	**Ap**	**Ap**	**My**	**My**	**Jn**	**Jn**	**Jy**	**Jy**	**Ag**	**Ag**	**Sp**	**Sp**	**Oc**	**Oc**	

1947																		1948								
Ap	Ap	My	My	Jn	Jn	Jy	Jy	Ag	Ag	Sp	Sp	Oc	Oc	Nv	Nv	Dc	Dc	Ja	Ja	Fb	Fb	Ma	Ma	Ap	Ap	
–	==	15	8	10	14	==	==	–	–	–	–	–	–	–	–	–	–	–	–	–	–	–	–	–	–	I BELIEVE
–	==	17	10	3	2	1	1	1	1	1	1	3	5	12	==	==	–	–	–	–	–	–	–	–	–	PEG O' MY HEART
–	==	==	==	==	==	17	==	==	–	–	–	–	–	–	–	–	–	–	–	–	–	–	–	–	–	TIME AFTER TIME
–	–	==	9	6	3	2	2	2	4	8	13	17	==	–	–	–	–	–	–	–	–	–	–	–	–	I WONDER, I WONDER, I WONDER
–	–	==	==	15	17	==	==	–	–	–	–	–	–	–	–	–	–	–	–	–	–	–	–	–	–	OLD DEVIL MOON
–	–	–	==	11	4	3	3	4	6	15	==	–	–	–	–	–	–	–	–	–	–	–	–	–	–	CHI-BABA, CHI-BABA
–	–	–	==	17	19	==	18	17	14	20	==	==	==	==	–	–	–	–	–	–	–	–	–	–	–	I NEVER KNEW (THAT ROSES GREW)
–	–	–	==	==	20	14	16	15	17	16	19	20	==	==	–	–	–	–	–	–	–	–	–	–	–	ALMOST LIKE BEING IN LOVE
–	–	–	–	==	10	8	7	8	7	9	14	==	–	–	–	–	–	–	–	–	–	–	–	–	–	TEMPTATION (TIM-TAY-SHUN)
–	–	–	–	==	==	18	9	7	9	13	11	13	17	==	–	–	–	–	–	–	–	–	–	–	–	ASK ANYONE WHO KNOWS
–	–	–	–	–	==	19	10	12	8	7	7	7	9	7	13	19	==	–	–	–	–	–	–	–	–	WHEN YOU WERE SWEET SIXTEEN
–	–	–	–	–	==	==	==	13	16	17	==	==	–	–	–	–	–	–	–	–	–	–	–	–	–	IVY
–	–	–	–	–	–	20	14	9	5	4	4	9	11	==	==	–	–	–	–	–	–	–	–	–	–	SMOKE! SMOKE! SMOKE! (THAT CIGARETTE)
–	–	–	–	–	–	==	19	11	11	12	17	==	–	–	–	–	–	–	–	–	–	–	–	–	–	TALLAHASSEE
–	–	–	–	–	–	==	12	6	3	3	3	2	3	4	12	18	==	–	–	–	–	–	–	–	–	I WONDER WHO'S KISSING HER NOW
–	–	–	–	–	–	==	==	18	10	5	6	5	4	5	11	16	==	–	–	–	–	–	–	–	–	FEUDIN' AND FIGHTIN'
–	–	–	–	–	–	–	==	==	20	==	==	–	–	–	–	–	–	–	–	–	–	–	–	–	–	I AIN'T MAD (AT YOU)
–	–	–	–	–	–	–	==	==	13	10	8	4	2	2	2	4	12	13	==	==	–	–	–	–	–	I WISH I DIDN'T LOVE YOU SO
–	–	–	–	–	–	–	–	==	19	11	9	10	8	8	19	==	–	–	–	–	–	–	–	–	–	THE LADY FROM 29 PALMS
–	–	–	–	–	–	–	–	==	15	6	2	1	1	1	1	1	1	3	7	13	17	==	==	–	–	NEAR YOU
–	–	–	–	–	–	–	–	==	==	14	10	8	7	6	8	14	20	==	–	–	–	–	–	–	–	AN APPLE BLOSSOM WEDDING
–	–	–	–	–	–	–	–	–	==	18	12	11	12	13	20	==	–	–	–	–	–	–	–	–	–	I HAVE BUT ONE HEART
–	–	–	–	–	–	–	–	–	==	==	15	14	20	19	18	==	–	–	–	–	–	–	–	–	–	KATE (HAVE I COME TOO EARLY, TOO LATE)
–	–	–	–	–	–	–	–	–	==	==	20	16	15	9	6	11	13	18	==	–	–	–	–	–	–	THE WHIFFENPOOF SONG
–	–	–	–	–	–	–	–	–	–	==	16	12	6	3	3	2	6	9	18	==	–	–	–	–	–	YOU DO
–	–	–	–	–	–	–	–	–	–	==	18	15	18	==	==	–	–	–	–	–	–	–	–	–	–	ALL MY LOVE
–	–	–	–	–	–	–	–	–	–	==	==	18	16	==	==	==	–	–	–	–	–	–	–	–	–	KOKOMO, INDIANA
–	–	–	–	–	–	–	–	–	–	–	==	19	13	10	4	3	3	2	2	3	9	11	20	==	–	HOW SOON (WILL I BE SEEING YOU)
–	–	–	–	–	–	–	–	–	–	–	==	==	19	15	==	–	–	–	–	–	–	–	–	–	–	SUGAR BLUES
–	–	–	–	–	–	–	–	–	–	–	–	==	14	14	9	7	5	5	8	15	==	–	–	–	–	CIVILIZATION
–	–	–	–	–	–	–	–	–	–	–	–	–	==	11	15	17	17	15	16	19	20	==	==	–	–	MICKEY
–	–	–	–	–	–	–	–	–	–	–	–	–	==	16	7	6	4	4	6	8	12	15	==	–	–	TOO FAT POLKA
–	–	–	–	–	–	–	–	–	–	–	–	–	==	18	10	8	9	10	12	17	==	–	–	–	–	–AND MIMI
–	–	–	–	–	–	–	–	–	–	–	–	–	–	20	==	==	==	19	==	==	–	–	–	–	–	THE WHISTLER
–	–	–	–	–	–	–	–	–	–	–	–	–	–	==	14	12	15	14	20	==	–	–	–	–	–	SO FAR
–	–	–	–	–	–	–	–	–	–	–	–	–	–	==	==	13	10	11	==	–	–	–	–	–	–	WHITE CHRISTMAS
–	–	–	–	–	–	–	–	–	–	–	–	–	–	==	==	20	14	12	==	==	–	–	–	–	–	DON'T YOU LOVE ME ANYMORE?
–	–	–	–	–	–	–	–	–	–	–	–	–	–	–	–	==	16	==	–	–	–	–	–	–	–	SANTA CLAUS IS COMIN' TO TOWN
–	–	–	–	–	–	–	–	–	–	–	–	–	–	–	–	==	18	==	–	–	–	–	–	–	–	HERE COMES SANTA CLAUS
–	–	–	–	–	–	–	–	–	–	–	–	–	–	17	5	5	2	1	1	1	3	5	5	10	20	BALLERINA (1948)
–	–	–	–	–	–	–	–	–	–	–	–	–	–	==	16	9	7	6	3	4	7	6	6	9	12	SERENADE OF THE BELLS (1948)
–	–	–	–	–	–	–	–	–	–	–	–	–	–	==	17	10	8	7	4	5	6	7	8	16	==	GOLDEN EARRINGS (1948)
–	–	–	–	–	–	–	–	–	–	–	–	–	–	–	==	15	11	8	5	7	8	9	11	==	==	I'LL DANCE AT YOUR WEDDING (1948)
–	–	–	–	–	–	–	–	–	–	–	–	–	–	–	–	==	19	16	19	==	–	–	–	–	–	PASS THAT PEACE PIPE (1948)
Ap	Ap	My	My	Jn	Jn	Jy	Jy	Ag	Ag	Sp	Sp	Oc	Oc	Nv	Nv	Dc	Dc	Ja	Ja	Fb	Fb	Ma	Ma	Ap	Ap	

		1947													1948											
Oc	Oc	Nv	Nv	Dc	Dc	Ja	Ja	Fb	Fb	Ma	Ma	Ap	Ap	My	My	Jn	Jn	Jy	Jy	Ag	Ag	Sp	Sp	Oc	Oc	
4	2	2	2	4	12	13	==	–	–	–	–	–	–	–	–	–	–	–	–	–	–	–	–	–	–	I WISH I DIDN'T LOVE YOU SO (1947)
1	1	1	1	1	1	3	7	13	17	==	==	–	–	–	–	–	–	–	–	–	–	–	–	–	–	NEAR YOU (1947)
12	6	3	3	2	6	9	18	==	–	–	–	–	–	–	–	–	–	–	–	–	–	–	–	–	–	YOU DO (1947)
16	15	9	6	11	13	18	==	–	–	–	–	–	–	–	–	–	–	–	–	–	–	–	–	–	–	THE WHIFFENPOOF SONG (1947)
==	14	14	9	7	5	5	8	15	==	–	–	–	–	–	–	–	–	–	–	–	–	–	–	–	–	CIVILIZATION (1947)
19	13	10	4	3	3	2	2	3	9	11	20	==	–	–	–	–	–	–	–	–	–	–	–	–	–	HOW SOON (WILL I BE SEEING YOU) (1947)
–	==	11	15	17	17	15	16	19	20	==	==	–	–	–	–	–	–	–	–	–	–	–	–	–	–	MICKEY (1947)
–	==	16	7	6	4	4	6	8	12	15	==	–	–	–	–	–	–	–	–	–	–	–	–	–	–	TOO FAT POLKA (1947)
–	–	==	14	12	15	14	20	==	–	–	–	–	–	–	–	–	–	–	–	–	–	–	–	–	–	SO FAR (1947)
–	==	18	10	8	9	10	12	17	==	–	–	–	–	–	–	–	–	–	–	–	–	–	–	–	–	–AND MIMI (1947)
–	–	==	==	13	10	11	==	–	–	–	–	–	–	–	–	–	–	–	–	–	–	–	–	–	–	WHITE CHRISTMAS (1947)
–	–	20	==	==	==	19	==	==	–	–	–	–	–	–	–	–	–	–	–	–	–	–	–	–	–	THE WHISTLER (1947)
–	–	==	==	20	14	12	==	==	–	–	–	–	–	–	–	–	–	–	–	–	–	–	–	–	–	DON'T YOU LOVE ME ANYMORE? (1947)
–	–	17	5	5	2	1	1	1	3	5	5	10	20	–	–	–	–	–	–	–	–	–	–	–	–	BALLERINA
–	–	==	16	9	7	6	3	4	7	6	6	9	12	==	–	–	–	–	–	–	–	–	–	–	–	SERENADE OF THE BELLS
–	–	==	17	10	8	7	4	5	6	7	8	16	==	–	–	–	–	–	–	–	–	–	–	–	–	GOLDEN EARRINGS
–	–	–	==	15	11	8	5	7	8	9	11	==	==	–	–	–	–	–	–	–	–	–	–	–	–	I'LL DANCE AT YOUR WEDDING
–	–	–	–	==	19	16	19	==	–	–	–	–	–	–	–	–	–	–	–	–	–	–	–	–	–	PASS THAT PEACE PIPE
–	–	–	–	==	==	==	17	16	16	19	==	==	==	–	–	–	–	–	–	–	–	–	–	–	–	HOW LUCKY YOU ARE
–	–	–	–	==	==	==	14	14	14	14	13	==	==	–	–	–	–	–	–	–	–	–	–	–	–	THE STARS WILL REMEMBER (SO WILL I)
–	–	–	–	==	==	==	13	11	10	12	9	15	==	==	–	–	–	–	–	–	–	–	–	–	–	THE BEST THINGS IN LIFE ARE FREE
–	–	–	–	–	–	17	10	9	4	3	4	4	4	9	16	==	–	–	–	–	–	–	–	–	–	BEG YOUR PARDON
–	–	–	–	–	–	20	11	6	2	2	1	1	1	1	2	4	7	7	11	==	–	–	–	–	–	NOW IS THE HOUR
–	–	–	–	–	–	==	9	2	1	1	2	3	3	8	13	==	–	–	–	–	–	–	–	–	–	I'M LOOKING OVER A FOUR LEAF CLOVER
–	–	–	–	–	–	==	15	10	5	4	3	2	2	2	6	11	18	==	–	–	–	–	–	–	–	MANANA
–	–	–	–	–	–	–	==	12	11	13	14	18	==	==	–	–	–	–	–	–	–	–	–	–	–	I'M MY OWN GRANDPAW (GRANDMAW)
–	–	–	–	–	–	–	==	18	15	8	7	5	7	15	==	–	–	–	–	–	–	–	–	–	–	BUT BEAUTIFUL
–	–	–	–	–	–	–	==	20	19	18	==	==	–	–	–	–	–	–	–	–	–	–	–	–	–	I'M A-COMIN' A-COURTIN', CORABELLE
–	–	–	–	–	–	–	==	==	18	17	16	14	16	14	20	==	==	–	–	–	–	–	–	–	–	SHINE
–	–	–	–	–	–	–	–	==	13	10	10	12	17	==	==	–	–	–	–	–	–	–	–	–	–	SLAP 'ER DOWN AGIN' PAW
–	–	–	–	–	–	–	–	==	==	16	12	8	9	10	7	8	8	8	13	==	==	–	–	–	–	THE DICKEY-BIRD SONG
–	–	–	–	–	–	–	–	==	==	==	==	20	==	==	–	–	–	–	–	–	–	–	–	–	–	ALL DRESSED UP WITH A BROKEN HEART
–	–	–	–	–	–	–	–	–	==	20	19	11	13	19	==	–	–	–	–	–	–	–	–	–	–	YOU WERE MEANT FOR ME
–	–	–	–	–	–	–	–	–	–	==	17	7	6	6	8	12	13	19	==	==	–	–	–	–	–	SABRE DANCE
–	–	–	–	–	–	–	–	–	–	==	15	13	11	13	17	17	==	==	==	–	–	–	–	–	–	BECAUSE
–	–	–	–	–	–	–	–	–	–	==	==	==	18	==	==	–	–	–	–	–	–	–	–	–	–	PIANISSIMO
–	–	–	–	–	–	–	–	–	–	==	==	==	==	18	12	10	10	13	20	==	==	–	–	–	–	TELL ME A STORY
–	–	–	–	–	–	–	–	–	–	–	18	6	5	4	5	6	9	9	16	==	–	–	–	–	–	BABY FACE
–	–	–	–	–	–	–	–	–	–	–	==	19	==	==	–	–	–	–	–	–	–	–	–	–	–	I LOVE YOU, YES I DO
–	–	–	–	–	–	–	–	–	–	–	==	17	8	5	4	5	6	6	8	14	==	–	–	–	–	TOOLIE OOLIE DOOLIE (THE YODEL POLKA)
–	–	–	–	–	–	–	–	–	–	–	–	==	15	12	11	15	15	20	==	–	–	–	–	–	–	ST. LOUIS BLUES (MARCH)
–	–	–	–	–	–	–	–	–	–	–	–	==	14	7	1	1	2	4	6	15	20	==	–	–	–	NATURE BOY
–	–	–	–	–	–	–	–	–	–	–	–	==	10	3	3	2	1	1	2	3	6	7	9	12	==	YOU CAN'T BE TRUE, DEAR
–	–	–	–	–	–	–	–	–	–	–	–	==	19	11	9	3	4	5	4	8	9	14	==	–	–	LITTLE WHITE LIES
–	–	–	–	–	–	–	–	–	–	–	–	==	==	16	19	18	16	15	==	==	–	–	–	–	–	HAUNTED HEART
–	–	–	–	–	–	–	–	–	–	–	–	==	==	20	15	16	==	==	–	–	–	–	–	–	–	LAROO, LAROO, LILI BOLERO
Oc	Oc	Nv	Nv	Dc	Dc	Ja	Ja	Fb	Fb	Ma	Ma	Ap	Ap	My	My	Jn	Jn	Jy	Jy	Ag	Ag	Sp	Sp	Oc	Oc	

							1 9 4 8												1 9 4 9							
Ap	Ap	My	My	Jn	Jn	Jy	Jy	Ag	Ag	Sp	Sp	Oc	Oc	Nv	Nv	Dc	Dc	Ja	Ja	Fb	Fb	Ma	Ma	Ap	Ap	
–	==	17	10	7	3	3	3	**1**	**1**	2	4	4	5	9	7	11	17	==	–	–	–	–	–	–	–	MY HAPPINESS
–	–	==	14	13	14	17	==	==	–	–	–	–	–	–	–	–	–	–	–	–	–	–	–	–	–	JUST BECAUSE
–	–	==	18	9	11	10	7	7	7	6	6	9	16	==	–	–	–	–	–	–	–	–	–	–	–	LOVE SOMEBODY
–	–	==	==	19	==	==	–	–	–	–	–	–	–	–	–	–	–	–	–	–	–	–	–	–	–	HEARTBREAKER
–	–	–	==	14	5	2	**1**	2	4	9	13	19	==	–	–	–	–	–	–	–	–	–	–	–	–	WOODY WOODPECKER
–	–	–	–	20	12	12	15	18	==	==	–	–	–	–	–	–	–	–	–	–	–	–	–	–	–	WILLIAM TELL OVERTURE (IT'S A BEAUTIFUL DAY FOR THE RACES)
–	–	–	–	==	20	==	==	–	–	–	–	–	–	–	–	–	–	–	–	–	–	–	–	–	–	CARAMBA! IT'S THE SAMBA
–	–	–	–	==	17	14	10	5	3	4	3	3	4	8	12	18	==	–	–	–	–	–	–	–	–	IT'S MAGIC
–	–	–	–	==	==	==	19	==	==	==	–	–	–	–	–	–	–	–	–	–	–	–	–	–	–	CUCKOO WALTZ
–	–	–	–	==	==	==	17	11	11	17	==	==	–	–	–	–	–	–	–	–	–	–	–	–	–	PUT 'EM IN A BOX, TIE 'EM WITH A RIBBON
–	–	–	–	==	==	==	==	17	12	12	14	18	==	==	–	–	–	–	–	–	–	–	–	–	–	CONFESS
–	–	–	–	–	19	11	5	4	2	**1**	**1**	**1**	3	4	11	15	==	–	–	–	–	–	–	–	–	YOU CALL EVERYBODY DARLIN'
–	–	–	–	–	==	16	9	6	5	3	2	2	**1**	2	3	7	10	19	==	–	–	–	–	–	–	A TREE IN THE MEADOW
–	–	–	–	–	==	18	12	9	8	5	5	5	2	3	4	8	14	14	==	==	–	–	–	–	–	TWELFTH STREET RAG
–	–	–	–	–	==	==	14	13	10	8	7	8	8	6	5	6	11	18	==	–	–	–	–	–	–	MAYBE YOU'LL BE THERE
–	–	–	–	–	==	==	==	20	==	==	==	–	–	–	–	–	–	–	–	–	–	–	–	–	–	TEA LEAVES
–	–	–	–	–	–	==	==	19	==	–	–	–	–	–	–	–	–	–	–	–	–	–	–	–	–	THE MAHARAJAH OF MAGADOR
–	–	–	–	–	–	==	==	12	13	11	11	10	10	13	16	==	–	–	–	–	–	–	–	–	–	BLUEBIRD OF HAPPINESS
–	–	–	–	–	–	==	==	==	17	19	20	20	19	==	18	20	==	==	==	==	==	–	–	–	–	BOUQUET OF ROSES
–	–	–	–	–	–	–	18	10	14	16	18	==	–	–	–	–	–	–	–	–	–	–	–	–	–	IT ONLY HAPPENS WHEN I DANCE WITH YOU
–	–	–	–	–	–	–	==	16	16	18	12	14	13	20	==	–	–	–	–	–	–	–	–	–	–	COOL WATER
–	–	–	–	–	–	–	–	==	15	10	8	6	6	10	13	==	==	–	–	–	–	–	–	–	–	UNDERNEATH THE ARCHES
–	–	–	–	–	–	–	–	==	19	15	17	16	12	16	==	==	–	–	–	–	–	–	–	–	–	RAMBLING ROSE
–	–	–	–	–	–	–	–	==	==	20	16	17	==	==	–	–	–	–	–	–	–	–	–	–	–	YOU CAME A LONG WAY FROM ST. LOUIS
–	–	–	–	–	–	–	–	==	==	==	19	13	14	15	19	==	==	–	–	–	–	–	–	–	–	EV'RY DAY I LOVE YOU (JUST A LITTLE BIT MORE)
–	–	–	–	–	–	–	–	–	18	13	10	7	9	7	8	12	20	==	–	–	–	–	–	–	–	HAIR OF GOLD, EYES OF BLUE
–	–	–	–	–	–	–	–	–	–	==	15	11	11	12	10	9	7	8	12	==	==	–	–	–	–	UNTIL
–	–	–	–	–	–	–	–	–	–	–	==	15	7	**1**	**1**	**1**	**1**	**1**	2	3	8	10	18	==	–	BUTTONS AND BOWS
–	–	–	–	–	–	–	–	–	–	–	==	==	17	14	14	16	==	==	–	–	–	–	–	–	–	THAT CERTAIN PARTY
–	–	–	–	–	–	–	–	–	–	–	==	==	20	11	9	4	6	9	9	16	==	–	–	–	–	YOU WERE ONLY FOOLING
–	–	–	–	–	–	–	–	–	–	–	==	==	==	19	==	==	–	–	–	–	–	–	–	–	–	LIFE GITS TEE-JUS, DON'T IT?
–	–	–	–	–	–	–	–	–	–	–	–	==	15	5	2	2	2	2	3	6	12	18	==	–	–	ON A SLOW BOAT TO CHINA
–	–	–	–	–	–	–	–	–	–	–	–	==	18	17	==	==	==	–	–	–	–	–	–	–	–	SAY SOMETHING SWEET TO YOUR SWEETHEART
–	–	–	–	–	–	–	–	–	–	–	–	==	==	==	17	13	12	10	10	17	==	–	–	–	–	CUANTO LE GUSTA
–	–	–	–	–	–	–	–	–	–	–	–	–	==	18	6	3	3	4	4	7	10	14	==	–	–	MY DARLING, MY DARLING
–	–	–	–	–	–	–	–	–	–	–	–	–	==	==	20	==	==	–	–	–	–	–	–	–	–	ONE HAS MY NAME (THE OTHER HAS MY HEART)
–	–	–	–	–	–	–	–	–	–	–	–	–	–	–	==	19	18	==	–	–	–	–	–	–	–	SANTA CLAUS IS COMIN' TO TOWN
–	–	–	–	–	–	–	–	–	–	–	–	–	–	–	==	14	9	11	–	–	–	–	–	–	–	WHITE CHRISTMAS
–	–	–	–	–	–	–	–	–	–	–	–	–	–	–	==	10	5	5	19	–	–	–	–	–	–	ALL I WANT FOR CHRISTMAS (IS MY TWO FRONT TEETH)
–	–	–	–	–	–	–	–	–	–	–	–	–	–	–	==	==	13	13	–	–	–	–	–	–	–	HERE COMES SANTA CLAUS
–	–	–	–	–	–	–	–	–	–	–	–	–	–	–	–	==	19	==	–	–	–	–	–	–	–	YOU'RE ALL I WANT FOR CHRISTMAS
–	–	–	–	–	–	–	–	–	–	–	–	–	–	==	15	5	4	3	**1**	**1**	2	4	10	15	==	A LITTLE BIRD TOLD ME (1949)
–	–	–	–	–	–	–	–	–	–	–	–	–	–	–	==	17	8	6	6	4	4	6	9	13	==	LAVENDER BLUE (DILLY DILLY) (1949)
–	–	–	–	–	–	–	–	–	–	–	–	–	–	–	==	==	16	20	==	20	==	==	–	–	–	GLORIA (1949)
–	–	–	–	–	–	–	–	–	–	–	–	–	–	–	–	==	15	7	5	2	**1**	2	2	2	5	FAR AWAY PLACES (1949)
Ap	Ap	My	My	Jn	Jn	Jy	Jy	Ag	Ag	Sp	Sp	Oc	Oc	Nv	Nv	Dc	Dc	Ja	Ja	Fb	Fb	Ma	Ma	Ap	Ap	

1948						1949																				
Oc	Oc	Nv	Nv	Dc	Dc	Ja	Ja	Fb	Fb	Ma	Ma	Ap	Ap	My	My	Jn	Jn	Jy	Jy	Ag	Ag	Sp	Sp	Oc	Oc	
2	**1**	2	3	7	10	19	==	–	–	–	–	–	–	–	–	–	–	–	–	–	–	–	–	–	–	A TREE IN THE MEADOW (1948)
5	2	3	4	8	14	14	==	==	–	–	–	–	–	–	–	–	–	–	–	–	–	–	–	–	–	TWELFTH STREET RAG (1948)
8	8	6	5	6	11	18	==	–	–	–	–	–	–	–	–	–	–	–	–	–	–	–	–	–	–	MAYBE YOU'LL BE THERE (1948)
11	11	12	10	9	7	8	12	==	==	–	–	–	–	–	–	–	–	–	–	–	–	–	–	–	–	UNTIL (1948)
15	7	**1**	**1**	**1**	**1**	**1**	2	3	8	10	18	==	–	–	–	–	–	–	–	–	–	–	–	–	–	BUTTONS AND BOWS (1948)
==	15	5	2	2	2	2	3	6	12	18	==	–	–	–	–	–	–	–	–	–	–	–	–	–	–	ON A SLOW BOAT TO CHINA (1948)
==	20	11	9	4	6	9	9	16	==	–	–	–	–	–	–	–	–	–	–	–	–	–	–	–	–	YOU WERE ONLY FOOLING (1948)
–	==	18	6	3	3	4	4	7	10	14	==	–	–	–	–	–	–	–	–	–	–	–	–	–	–	MY DARLING, MY DARLING (1948)
==	==	==	17	13	12	10	10	17	==	–	–	–	–	–	–	–	–	–	–	–	–	–	–	–	–	CUANTO LE GUSTA (1948)
–	–	–	==	10	5	5	19	–	–	–	–	–	–	–	–	–	–	–	–	–	–	–	–	–	–	ALL I WANT FOR CHRISTMAS (IS MY TWO FRONT TEETH (1948)
–	–	–	==	14	9	11	–	–	–	–	–	–	–	–	–	–	–	–	–	–	–	–	–	–	–	WHITE CHRISTMAS (1948)
–	–	–	==	==	13	13	–	–	–	–	–	–	–	–	–	–	–	–	–	–	–	–	–	–	–	HERE COMES SANTA CLAUS (1948)
–	–	==	15	5	4	3	**1**	**1**	2	4	10	15	==	–	–	–	–	–	–	–	–	–	–	–	–	A LITTLE BIRD TOLD ME
–	–	–	==	17	8	6	6	4	4	6	9	13	==	==	–	–	–	–	–	–	–	–	–	–	–	LAVENDER BLUE (DILLY DILLY)
–	–	–	==	==	16	20	==	20	==	==	–	–	–	–	–	–	–	–	–	–	–	–	–	–	–	GLORIA
–	–	–	–	==	15	7	5	2	**1**	2	2	2	5	11	17	==	–	–	–	–	–	–	–	–	–	FAR AWAY PLACES
–	–	–	–	==	==	17	15	==	==	==	–	–	–	–	–	–	–	–	–	–	–	–	–	–	–	BRUSH THOSE TEARS FROM YOUR EYES
–	–	–	–	==	==	12	11	10	9	8	8	9	8	10	19	==	==	–	–	–	–	–	–	–	–	SO TIRED
–	–	–	–	==	==	16	8	8	7	7	4	7	9	16	==	–	–	–	–	–	–	–	–	–	–	GALWAY BAY
–	–	–	–	–	==	15	7	5	3	3	3	5	11	15	==	==	–	–	–	–	–	–	–	–	–	POWDER YOUR FACE WITH SUNSHINE
–	–	–	–	–	==	==	16	15	16	17	17	==	==	–	–	–	–	–	–	–	–	–	–	–	–	SWEET GEORGIA BROWN
–	–	–	–	–	==	==	17	11	13	11	14	14	==	==	–	–	–	–	–	–	–	–	–	–	–	I LOVE YOU SO MUCH IT HURTS
–	–	–	–	–	–	==	20	==	==	–	–	–	–	–	–	–	–	–	–	–	–	–	–	–	–	FOR YOU
–	–	–	–	–	–	==	14	13	17	19	==	==	–	–	–	–	–	–	–	–	–	–	–	–	–	THE PUSSY CAT SONG
–	–	–	–	–	–	==	13	9	5	5	6	10	14	==	==	–	–	–	–	–	–	–	–	–	–	I'VE GOT MY LOVE TO KEEP ME WARM
–	–	–	–	–	–	==	18	12	11	9	5	3	3	5	8	13	==	==	–	–	–	–	–	–	–	RED ROSES FOR A BLUE LADY
–	–	–	–	–	–	==	==	19	==	==	==	–	–	–	–	–	–	–	–	–	–	–	–	–	–	TARA TALARA TALA
–	–	–	–	–	–	–	==	18	15	16	15	17	==	==	–	–	–	–	–	–	–	–	–	–	–	DOWN BY THE STATION
–	–	–	–	–	–	–	==	14	6	**1**	**1**	**1**	**1**	2	3	6	6	9	15	==	–	–	–	–	–	CRUISING DOWN THE RIVER
–	–	–	–	–	–	–	==	==	20	==	==	==	–	–	–	–	–	–	–	–	–	–	–	–	–	CONGRATULATIONS
–	–	–	–	–	–	–	==	==	14	12	13	11	18	==	==	–	–	–	–	–	–	–	–	–	–	SO IN LOVE
–	–	–	–	–	–	–	–	==	19	==	==	–	–	–	–	–	–	–	–	–	–	–	–	–	–	GRIEVING FOR YOU
–	–	–	–	–	–	–	–	==	18	13	11	8	4	4	6	7	10	11	17	==	–	–	–	–	–	CARELESS HANDS
–	–	–	–	–	–	–	–	–	==	20	==	==	==	–	–	–	–	–	–	–	–	–	–	–	–	BEAUTIFUL EYES
–	–	–	–	–	–	–	–	–	==	15	7	4	6	8	12	14	==	==	–	–	–	–	–	–	–	SUNFLOWER
–	–	–	–	–	–	–	–	–	–	==	19	==	==	–	–	–	–	–	–	–	–	–	–	–	–	LADY OF SPAIN
–	–	–	–	–	–	–	–	–	–	==	20	20	==	==	==	==	==	–	–	–	–	–	–	–	–	THE HOT CANARY
–	–	–	–	–	–	–	–	–	–	==	12	6	2	**1**	**1**	3	4	4	5	7	9	16	==	==	–	FOREVER AND EVER
–	–	–	–	–	–	–	–	–	–	==	16	16	12	14	15	11	12	15	13	17	==	==	–	–	–	THE BLUE SKIRT WALTZ
–	–	–	–	–	–	–	–	–	–	==	==	12	7	3	5	5	5	7	14	==	==	–	–	–	–	"A" – YOU'RE ADORABLE
–	–	–	–	–	–	–	–	–	–	==	==	==	20	19	==	20	==	==	–	–	–	–	–	–	–	IT'S A BIG, WIDE, WONDERFUL WORLD
–	–	–	–	–	–	–	–	–	–	–	==	==	16	17	13	18	==	==	–	–	–	–	–	–	–	SOMEONE LIKE YOU
–	–	–	–	–	–	–	–	–	–	–	==	==	==	==	16	16	19	==	==	==	–	–	–	–	–	CANDY KISSES
–	–	–	–	–	–	–	–	–	–	–	–	19	13	12	11	19	==	–	–	–	–	–	–	–	–	NEED YOU
–	–	–	–	–	–	–	–	–	–	–	–	18	10	7	4	2	2	2	3	2	3	6	10	15	==	AGAIN
–	–	–	–	–	–	–	–	–	–	–	–	==	19	13	9	8	9	8	7	11	12	==	==	–	–	I DON'T SEE ME IN YOUR EYES ANYMORE
–	–	–	–	–	–	–	–	–	–	–	–	–	17	6	2	**1**	**1**	**1**	2	4	6	13	==	==	–	RIDERS IN THE SKY
–	–	–	–	–	–	–	–	–	–	–	–	–	==	20	==	==	–	–	–	–	–	–	–	–	–	ONCE IN LOVE WITH AMY
–	–	–	–	–	–	–	–	–	–	–	–	–	==	18	10	10	7	5	6	8	10	12	14	==	==	BALI HA'I
–	–	–	–	–	–	–	–	–	–	–	–	–	==	==	18	12	11	10	9	10	15	==	==	–	–	A WONDERFUL GUY
–	–	–	–	–	–	–	–	–	–	–	–	–	==	==	==	==	16	19	==	==	–	–	–	–	–	EVERYWHERE YOU GO
Oc	Oc	Nv	Nv	Dc	Dc	Ja	Ja	Fb	Fb	Ma	Ma	Ap	Ap	My	My	Jn	Jn	Jy	Jy	Ag	Ag	Sp	Sp	Oc	Oc	

1949																		1950								
Ap	Ap	My	My	Jn	Jn	Jy	Jy	Ag	Ag	Sp	Sp	Oc	Oc	Nv	Nv	Dc	Dc	Ja	Ja	Fb	Fb	Ma	Ma	Ap	Ap	
==	15	9	7	4	3	3	**1**	**1**	**1**	2	4	6	10	20	==	–	–	–	–	–	–	–	–	–	–	SOME ENCHANTED EVENING
–	==	==	20	15	14	17	==	==	–	–	–	–	–	–	–	–	–	–	–	–	–	–	–	–	–	KISS ME SWEET
–	–	==	14	9	8	6	4	5	5	8	12	17	==	–	–	–	–	–	–	–	–	–	–	–	–	BABY, IT'S COLD OUTSIDE
–	–	–	==	17	13	12	12	13	13	7	9	11	17	==	==	–	–	–	–	–	–	–	–	–	–	THE HUCKLE BUCK
–	–	–	==	==	17	20	==	==	–	–	–	–	–	–	–	–	–	–	–	–	–	–	–	–	–	MERRY-GO-ROUND WALTZ
–	–	–	==	==	15	18	20	==	–	–	–	–	–	–	–	–	–	–	–	–	–	–	–	–	–	FIVE FOOT TWO, EYES OF BLUE
–	–	–	–	==	20	==	==	–	–	–	–	–	–	–	–	–	–	–	–	–	–	–	–	–	–	BLACK COFFEE
–	–	–	–	==	==	16	8	3	2	**1**	2	4	4	9	11	16	==	–	–	–	–	–	–	–	–	ROOM FULL OF ROSES
–	–	–	–	==	==	==	18	==	==	–	–	–	–	–	–	–	–	–	–	–	–	–	–	–	–	MY ONE AND ONLY HIGHLAND FLING
–	–	–	–	–	18	13	10	9	7	14	==	==	==	–	–	–	–	–	–	–	–	–	–	–	–	THE FOUR WINDS AND THE SEVEN SEAS
–	–	–	–	–	–	==	14	11	6	4	3	**1**	**1**	**1**	2	6	8	==	==	–	–	–	–	–	–	YOU'RE BREAKING MY HEART
–	–	–	–	–	–	–	==	16	14	14	10	8	9	16	==	–	–	–	–	–	–	–	–	–	–	LET'S TAKE AN OLD-FASHIONED WALK
–	–	–	–	–	–	–	==	19	12	11	5	6	5	7	10	16	==	==	–	–	–	–	–	–	–	MAYBE IT'S BECAUSE
–	–	–	–	–	–	==	==	20	18	==	18	==	–	–	–	–	–	–	–	–	–	–	–	–	–	YOU'RE SO UNDERSTANDING
–	–	–	–	–	–	==	==	18	8	4	3	2	3	6	9	12	==	==	–	–	–	–	–	–	–	SOMEDAY (YOU'LL WANT ME TO WANT YOU)
–	–	–	–	–	–	–	==	19	==	==	–	–	–	–	–	–	–	–	–	–	–	–	–	–	–	AIN'T SHE SWEET
–	–	–	–	–	–	–	==	16	17	17	15	==	==	–	–	–	–	–	–	–	–	–	–	–	–	THERE'S YES! YES! IN YOUR EYES
–	–	–	–	–	–	–	==	15	16	9	7	7	5	7	8	9	11	17	==	–	–	–	–	–	–	JEALOUS HEART
–	–	–	–	–	–	–	==	==	19	15	19	==	==	==	–	–	–	–	–	–	–	–	–	–	–	JUST ONE WAY TO SAY I LOVE YOU
–	–	–	–	–	–	–	==	==	20	18	11	20	==	==	–	–	–	–	–	–	–	–	–	–	–	TWENTY-FOUR HOURS OF SUNSHINE
–	–	–	–	–	–	–	–	==	19	==	==	–	–	–	–	–	–	–	–	–	–	–	–	–	–	MY BOLERO
–	–	–	–	–	–	–	–	–	==	11	5	3	2	**1**	**1**	3	8	9	15	==	–	–	–	–	–	THAT LUCKY OLD SUN
–	–	–	–	–	–	–	–	–	==	20	20	==	==	==	–	–	–	–	–	–	–	–	–	–	–	DANCE OF THE HOURS
–	–	–	–	–	–	–	–	–	==	==	13	10	12	14	18	19	20	==	–	–	–	–	–	–	–	WHISPERING HOPE
–	–	–	–	–	–	–	–	–	==	==	==	18	18	==	==	–	–	–	–	–	–	–	–	–	–	FIDDLE DEE DEE
–	–	–	–	–	–	–	–	–	==	==	==	13	14	16	==	==	–	–	–	–	–	–	–	–	–	NOW THAT I NEED YOU
–	–	–	–	–	–	–	–	–	–	==	16	16	15	11	14	17	==	==	–	–	–	–	–	–	–	I NEVER SEE MAGGIE ALONE
–	–	–	–	–	–	–	–	–	–	==	==	==	==	18	==	–	–	–	–	–	–	–	–	–	–	THROUGH A LONG AND SLEEPLESS NIGHT
–	–	–	–	–	–	–	–	–	–	–	==	12	11	12	17	20	==	–	–	–	–	–	–	–	–	HOP-SCOTCH POLKA
–	–	–	–	–	–	–	–	–	–	–	17	8	6	3	3	4	3	6	6	10	==	–	–	–	–	SLIPPING AROUND
–	–	–	–	–	–	–	–	–	–	–	==	19	19	==	==	–	–	–	–	–	–	–	–	–	–	RAGTIME COWBOY JOE
–	–	–	–	–	–	–	–	–	–	–	==	14	8	5	5	5	7	7	11	==	==	–	–	–	–	DON'T CRY, JOE
–	–	–	–	–	–	–	–	–	–	–	==	==	9	4	4	2	2	2	**1**	3	7	14	==	==	–	I CAN DREAM, CAN'T I?
–	–	–	–	–	–	–	–	–	–	–	–	==	20	==	–	–	–	–	–	–	–	–	–	–	–	THE LAST MILE HOME
–	–	–	–	–	–	–	–	–	–	–	–	==	13	8	7	6	4	5	5	9	13	==	==	–	–	A DREAMER'S HOLIDAY
–	–	–	–	–	–	–	–	–	–	–	–	–	==	19	19	==	–	–	–	–	–	–	–	–	–	CANADIAN CAPERS
–	–	–	–	–	–	–	–	–	–	–	–	–	==	13	10	11	18	13	10	12	15	==	–	–	–	I'VE GOT A LOVELY BUNCH OF COCOANUTS
–	–	–	–	–	–	–	–	–	–	–	–	–	==	==	20	==	==	–	–	–	–	–	–	–	–	ENVY
–	–	–	–	–	–	–	–	–	–	–	–	–	–	17	13	13	15	==	==	–	–	–	–	–	–	I'LL NEVER SLIP AROUND AGAIN
–	–	–	–	–	–	–	–	–	–	–	–	–	–	15	2	**1**	**1**	**1**	4	14	==	–	–	–	–	MULE TRAIN
–	–	–	–	–	–	–	–	–	–	–	–	–	–	–	==	14	6	8	==	–	–	–	–	–	–	RUDOLPH, THE RED-NOSED REINDEER
–	–	–	–	–	–	–	–	–	–	–	–	–	–	–	–	18	10	15	–	–	–	–	–	–	–	WHITE CHRISTMAS
–	–	–	–	–	–	–	–	–	–	–	–	–	–	–	–	==	16	==	–	–	–	–	–	–	–	HERE COMES SANTA CLAUS
–	–	–	–	–	–	–	–	–	–	–	–	–	–	–	–	==	14	16	–	–	–	–	–	–	–	I YUST GO NUTS AT CHRISTMAS
–	–	–	–	–	–	–	–	–	–	–	–	–	–	–	–	==	17	20	–	–	–	–	–	–	–	YINGLE BELLS (JINGLE BELLS)
–	–	–	–	–	–	–	–	–	–	–	–	–	–	–	–	==	12	14	==	–	–	–	–	–	–	BLUE CHRISTMAS
–	–	–	–	–	–	–	–	–	–	–	–	–	==	==	15	15	19	11	9	7	10	11	17	==	==	JOHNSON RAG (1950)
–	–	–	–	–	–	–	–	–	–	–	–	–	–	==	12	7	5	3	2	**1**	3	5	9	==	==	DEAR HEARTS AND GENTLE PEOPLE (1950)
–	–	–	–	–	–	–	–	–	–	–	–	–	–	–	==	10	9	4	3	4	6	10	19	==	–	THE OLD MASTER PAINTER (1950)
–	–	–	–	–	–	–	–	–	–	–	–	–	–	–	==	13	10	7	6	4	4	6	6	11	THERE'S NO TOMORROW (1950)
Ap	Ap	My	My	Jn	Jn	Jy	Jy	Ag	Ag	Sp	Sp	Oc	Oc	Nv	Nv	Dc	Dc	Ja	Ja	Fb	Fb	Ma	Ma	Ap	Ap	

SECTION 4

THE ENCYCLOPEDIA OF CHARTED SONGS, 1900-1949

INTRODUCTION TO SECTION 4:

THE ENCYCLOPEDIA OF CHARTED SONGS, 1900-1949

Section 4 contains complete details of every song mentioned in this book for the period 1900-1949. Each song's description includes the following: the title followed by its rank for the year, its publisher at the time of popularity, publication date, and the month, year, and rank when peak popularity was attained. It should be carefully noted that, generally, the latter rankings are taken from the spreadsheets of Section 3 rather than the monthly listings of Section 2. (Exceptions are noted in footnotes.) Following those entries are the writers of the song, and any contemporary show or movie in which the song was featured. The opening show date or movie release date is also given (month and year). This often provides evidence that the song's popularity resulted from its inclusion in the show or movie and from sales of a show's score in sheet music form.

The third level of information details the artists connected with the song and how they were connected. These include vaudeville singers, show singers, movie singers, radio singers, bandleaders, and recording artists. (Key: vv = vaudeville, db = dance band, ri = reissue of an earlier record.) The artists are listed in order of strongest proponents of the song at the time of popularity. An artist who became associated with the song at some later time is not listed, unless that artist was able to bring the song back into the Top 20. In that case, the song gets an additional encyclopedic listing under that subsequent year and a second mention in the Index of Section 1. For any song revived in 1950 or beyond, the artist who revived it can be found in Volume II.

For recording artists, the details include record label, approximate record release date (month and year), and record issue number. Actually, the record date is roughly the month when the record began selling significantly. This was usually one month after the release date and two or three months after the recording date. Again, these dates help to pinpoint the period when a given song was most popular. Another fact to be noted is that between 1900 and 1955 it was almost universal that several different artists would record and release the same song at about the same time. Thus the spoils might be divided among two or three top artists. In contrast, from 1955 onward, it was generally one artist per song at any one time, although a successful song would often experience a "remake," a revival by a different artist in a subsequent year.

It should be noted that, prior to 1920, artists generally did not record a song until it was clear that the song was gaining considerable popularity through vaudeville performances and sheet-music sales. Thus, a song would often reach its peak of popularity just as the record was coming out, and the record sales would then help in sustaining the song's popularity. Record sales were not a strong factor in the early days, but they became a steadily increasing factor over the first quarter of the century. A typical best seller in 1905 might sell about 5000 records in all, compared with 500,000 copies of sheet music. But by 1925, the same caliber of top seller would sell 500,000 records and about the same for sheet music. Reflecting this trend, the charts attach increasing importance to record sales as the years go by.

No attempt is made here to chronicle the most popular recordings of all time. This is a book about the popularity of songs. Nevertheless, the Φ symbol next to the recording artist's name is included to indicate approximately the sales strength of the record. No Φ denotes mediocre to moderate sales. One Φ indicates strong sales, ΦΦ means very strong sales (probably making the Top Four or so), and ΦΦΦ indicates a million-seller. However, if a record is known to have sold a million copies over many years as a catalog item, and not mainly during the song's wave of popularity, it does not get the ΦΦΦ accolade. Likewise, a ΦΦΦ next to a publisher's name indicates the sale of a million copies of sheet music, not a rare feat in the early days.

In summary, a typical entry in Section 4 has this form:

SONG TITLE (rank for the year)
Publisher, copyright year, highest chart position with month & year
Songwriters: lyricists (w) & composers (m)
Show or movie that featured the song, if any, with premier date (month & year)
Artist, with details of his/her association with song
Artist may be the one who sang the song in a show or movie
Artist may be one who popularized the song in vaudeville (vv stage)
Artist may be a recording singer, a group, or an orchestra.

For orchestra recordings, the abbreviation "Orch" indicates that this was an instrumental recording with no vocalist. Example: Paul Whiteman Orch. When there is a vocal, the credit shows the names of bandleader/vocalist in that order, and "Orch" is omitted. Example: Tommy Dorsey/Frank Sinatra. If the vocalist gets top billing on the record label but the orchestra is still a major factor, the listing is reversed. Example: Boswell Sisters/Dorsey Bros Orch. When the band vocal is a duet or group effort, the names are often omitted unless the names are highly significant, as with Bob Eberly and Helen O'Connell. The designation: w.vocal indicates that the vocalist's identity is uncertain or unknown. The designation: <vocal indicates that the bandleader served as vocalist. Example: Rudy Vallee/<vocal.

Throughout the Encyclopedia, the publishers' names and the record label names are usually abbreviated. The keys to these abbreviations can be found in the Appendix. The abbreviation "cyl" stands for a cylinder recording. Cylinders, the standard configuration for the 1890s, were still very popular at the turn of the century. However, the disk format made swift and steady gains during the first decade, and the cylinder gradually approached extinction during the period 1910–1919.

Here are two examples of an artist entry under a particular song:

1) J Aldrich Libbey Φ vv stage, 06/02 Ed 8018 cyl

This says J. Aldrich Libbey sang this song on the vaudeville stage (vv stage) and also recorded it on Edison cylinder (cyl) records, issue number 8018, and the cylinder enjoyed strong sales (Φ) beginning around June 1902 (06/02).

2) George Olsen/Fran Frey ΦΦ performed in show, 09/27 Vic 19870, 11/27 Col 2211-D

This says the George Olsen orchestra, with Fran Frey on vocal, performed this song in the Broadway show cited in the line just above the artists, and Olsen also recorded it on two record labels with very strong sales (ΦΦ) overall. The Victor record (issue #19870) began selling in September 1927 (09/27) and the Columbia record (issue #2211-D) began selling in November 1927 (11/27). (This is probably because the Columbia recording was made and issued about two months after the Victor.)

Just for the record, the first example is real, the second one fictitious.

As stated above, the number in parentheses following each song title is the song's rank for the year, provided it ranked in the Top Fifty for its year. Complete listings of the Top Fifty Songs of Each Year, 1900–1999, can be found in Volume II.

1900

ALWAYS (8)
Witmark, pub. 1899, reached #3 in February 1900
Charles Horwitz w, Fred Bowers m
Harry Macdonough Φ 12/99 Ed 7302 cyl
Currier & Reidy, vv stage
May Kelso 10/99 Ed 7239 cyl

A BIRD IN A GILDED CAGE (5)
Shapiro, B & Von T, ΦΦΦ pub. 1900, reached #1 in March 1900
Arthur Lamb w, Harry Von Tilzer m
Imogene Comer, vv stage
Dick Jose, vv stage
Steve Porter Φ 05/00 Col 4608 cyl
Jere Mahoney Φ 05/00 Ed 7440 cyl
Joe Natus, vv stage

THE BLUE AND THE GRAY (2)
Howley, Haviland ΦΦΦ, pub. 1900, reached #1 in May 1900
Paul Dresser w & m
Dick Jose, vv stage
Joe Natus, vv stage, 10/00 Ed 7570 cyl, 1900 Berliner 01205 disk
Byron G Harlan Φ 04/00 Ed 7433 cyl
Harry Macdonough 09/00 $Gram^2$ 83 disk
Myrtle Tressider, vv stage

THE BRIDGE OF SIGHS (13)
Witmark, pub. 1900, reached #5 in December 1900
James Thornton w & m
James Thornton, vv stage
Lydia Barry, vv stage
Harry J Howard, vv stage

CALLING TO HER BOY JUST ONCE AGAIN (28)
Howley, Haviland, pub. 1900, reached #7 in November 1900
Paul Dresser w & m
Dick Jose, vv stage
Joe Natus, vv stage, 05/01 Vic 680 disk

A COON BAND CONTEST (39)
Bell Mus Co, pub. 1900, reached #9 in August 1900
Arthur Pryor m
Arthur Pryor, band concerts (Later: 1904 Vic 4069 disk)
Vess Ossman 10/00 Ed 7561 cyl, 10/00 Col 31412 cyl, 01/01 Gram 154 disk
Sousa's Band 1900 Col 538 cyl, 1900 Berliner 01170 disk

DAWN OF THE CENTURY MARCH (47)
E T Paull, pub. 1900, reached #12 in August 1900
Edward T Paull m
Concert bands

DOAN YE CRY, MA HONEY (14)
Oliver Ditson Co, pub. 1899, reached #2 in March 1900
Albert W Noll w & m
Concert singers
Sam Dudley Φ 06/00 Ed 7459 cyl, 02/01 Gram 22 disk
Haydn Quartet 1900 Berliner 01304 disk

EVERY RACE HAS A FLAG BUT THE COON (35)
J W Stern, pub. 1900, reached #6 in August 1900
Will Heelan & J Fred Helf w & m
Lew Dockstader, vv stage
Marie Dressler, vv stage
Arthur Collins 08/00 Col 31342 cyl, 10/00 Ed 7580 cyl
Lottie Gilson, vv stage

THE FATAL ROSE OF RED (7)
F A Mills, pub. 1900, reached #1 in September 1900
J Fred Helf & Ed Gardenier w & m
Joe Natus Φ 11/00 Ed 7601 cyl, 05/01 Vic 683 disk
Emma Carus, vv stage
Nora Bayes, vv stage
Dan Quinn 1900 Col 5851 cyl

FILIPINO SHUFFLE (29)
H F Odell, pub. 1899, reached #10 in May 1900
H F Odell, m
Concert bands

FOR OLD TIMES' SAKE (4)
C K Harris, pub. 1900, reached #1 in December 1900
Charles K Harris w & m
J Aldrich Libbey, vv stage
Jere Mahoney Φ 01/01 Ed 7680 cyl
Imogene Comer, vv stage
Will F Denny 1900 Berliner 01164 disk
Aurie Dagwell, vv stage

THE GIRLS OF AMERICA MARCH (21)
Keystone Mus Co, pub. 1899, reached #11 in January 1900
J Mahlon Duganne m
Metropolitan Orch 12/00 Gram 254 disk, 1900 Berliner 0837 disk
Other concert bands

HEARTS ARE TRUMPS
Whitney-Warner, pub. 1899, reached #18 in April 1900
L W Young m
Concert bands

HER NAME IS ROSE (50)
Shapiro, B & Von T, pub. 1899, reached #20 in April 1900
Irene Franklin w, Harry Von Tilzer m
Irene Franklin, vv stage
Jere Mahoney 09/00 Ed 7537 cyl
Steve Porter 1900 Col 4646 cyl

I CAN'T TELL WHY I LOVE YOU BUT I DO (3)
Howley, Haviland, pub. 1900, reached #1 in October 1900
Will D Cobb w, Gus Edwards m
Emma Carus, vv stage
Harry Macdonough Φ 11/00 Ed 7595 cyl, 02/01 Gram 533 disk
Myrtle Tressider, vv stage
Albert Campbell 12/00 Gram 222 disk
Steve Porter 1900 Col 4644 cyl

I COULDN'T STAND TO SEE MY BABY LOSE (31)
Howley, Haviland, pub. 1899, reached #7 in March 1900
Will D Cobb w, Gus Edwards m
May Irwin, vv stage
Emma Carus, vv stage
Len Spencer 1900 Col 7497 cyl

I MUST A-BEEN A-DREAMIN' (36)
Howley, Haviland, pub. 1900, reached #9 in September 1900
Bob Cole w & m
Cole & Johnson, vv stage
Harcourt & May, vv stage
Arthur Collins 07/01 Ed 7850 cyl

I'M CERTAINLY LIVING A RAGTIME LIFE (24)
Sol Bloom, pub. 1900, reached #4 in June 1900
Gene Jefferson w, Robert S Roberts m
Artie Hall, vv stage
Anna Held, vv stage
Arthur Collins 1900 Col 31323 cyl

I'M GLAD I MET YOU, MARY (33)
Windsor Mus Co, pub. 1899, reached #16 in January 1900
Monroe Rosenfeld w & m
J Aldrich Libbey, vv stage
Emma Carus, vv stage
Harry Talley, vv stage

I'VE GOT A WHITE MAN WORKING FOR ME (49)
F A Mills, pub. 1900, reached #18 in October 1900
Andrew Sterling w & m
Blanche Ring, vv stage
Jack Norworth, vv stage
Arthur Collins 1900 Col 31321 cyl, 04/01 Gram 650 disk

IMPECUNIOUS DAVIS (43)
F A Mills, pub. 1899, reached #9 in January 1900
Kerry Mills m
Vess Ossman 12/00 Ed 7646 cyl
Concert bands

IN GOOD OLD NEW YORK TOWN (27)
Howley, Haviland, pub. 1899, reached #6 in February 1900
Paul Dresser w & m
Lottie Gilson, vv stage
Samuel Dudley & Harry Macdonough 1900 Col 31345 cyl
Steve Porter 1900 Col 4613 cyl

IN NAPLES FAIR (44)
Hill, H & B, pub. 1900, reached #9 in April 1900
Charles Horwitz w, Fred Bowers m
Camille D'Arville, vv stage
Other vv singers

IT'S THE MAN BEHIND THE GUN THAT DOES THE WORK (42)
Sol Bloom, pub. 1900, reached #19 in December 1900
Robert Browne w, Theodore F Morse m
Frank C. Stanley 05/01 Ed 7802 cyl
Belle Stewart, vv stage
Hamilton Hill, vv stage

JUST BECAUSE SHE MADE DEM GOO-GOO EYES (9)
Howley, Haviland, pub. 1900, reached #4 in December 1900
John Queen & Hughie Cannon w & m
Arthur Collins Φ 11/00 Col 31441 cyl, 01/01 Ed 7693 cyl
Johnny Queen, vv stage
Dan Quinn 01/01 Gram 475 disk

JUST ONE KISS
C K Harris, pub. 1900, reached #12 in August 1900
Charles K Harris w & m
Marie Rose, vv stage
George J Gaskin 1900 Col 4355 cyl

JUST WHEN I NEEDED YOU MOST
W B Gray, pub. 1900, reached #20 in October 1900
William B Gray w & m
Harry Ellis, vv stage
Reese Prosser, vv stage
George J Gaskin 1900 Col 4272 cyl

KOONVILLE KOONLETS (19)
W Jacobs, pub. 1899, reached #11 in June 1900
A J Weidt, m
Metropolitan Orch 04/01 Gram 259 disk
Concert bands

LAM' LAM' LAM' (16)
Howley, Haviland, pub. 1900, reached #6 in December 1900
Frank Abbott w, Ben Jerome m
Ernest Hogan, vv stage
Arthur Collins 10/00 Ed 7572 cyl, 02/01 Gram 502 disk
Myrtle Tressider, vv stage

LINDY LOO
John T Hall, pub. 1899, reached #13 in June 1900
C Kennedy w, L Newcombe m
Grace Belmont, vv stage
Violet Hulls, vv stage

MA BLACK PEARL (25)
Doty & Brill, pub. 1900, reached #6 in November 1900
Charles W Doty w, Edwin S Brill m
Bessie Taylor, vv stage
Sisson & Wallace, vv stage
John W Myers 02/01 Col 31473 cyl

MA TIGER LILY (11)
Witmark, pub. 1900, reached #2 in July 1900
Clay F Greene w, A Baldwin Sloane m
Featured in AUNT HANNAH, show (opened 02/00)
Fay Templeton, sung in show
Len Spencer Φ 06/00 Col 7502 cyl
Arthur Collins Φ 08/00 Ed 7517 cyl,
07/00 Berliner 01291 disk, 10/00 Gram 156 disk
Steve Porter 1900 Col 4647 cyl

(IT'S THE) MAN BEHIND THE GUN (38)
John Church, pub. 1900, reached #7 in August 1900
John Philip Sousa m
Sousa's Band 1900 Berliner 01169 disk, 1900 Col 537 cyl, 01/01 Gram 307 disk
Vess Ossman 1900 Berliner 01101 disk, 04/ 01 Gram 152 disk
Metropolitan Orch 1900 Berliner 0909 disk, 02/01 Gram 86 disk

THE MICK WHO THREW THE BRICK (41)
Hugo V Schlam, pub. 1899, reached #14 in June 1900
William C Davies w, Charles B Lawlor m
Arthur Collins 06/00 Ed 7489 cyl
W C Davies, vv stage
Dan Quinn 1900 Col 31482 cyl

MIDNIGHT FIRE ALARM (26)
E T Paull, pub. 1900, reached #4 in September 1900
Harry J Lincoln m
Peerless Orch 12/00 Ed 7642 cyl
Edison Military Band, band concerts

THE MOSQUITO'S PARADE (18)
Witmark, pub. 1899, reached #11 in December 1900
Howard Whitney m
Sousa's Band 1900 Berliner 01199 disk, 01/01 Gram 337 disk
Vess Ossman 11/00 Ed 7635 cyl, 02/01 Gram 485 disk
Whitney Brothers Band, band concerts

MY HEART'S TONIGHT IN TEXAS (20)
J W Stern, pub. 1900, reached #7 in November 1900
Robert F Roden w, Max S Witt m
Irene Franklin, vv stage
Lottie Gilson, vv stage
Gilmore's band/Bert Morphy 1900 Col 27507 cyl

MY JERSEY LILY (34)
Shapiro, B & Von T, pub. 1900, reached #3 in June 1900
Arthur Trevelyan w, Harry Von Tilzer m
J Aldrich Libbey, vv stage
Elinore Falk, vv stage
Dan Quinn 03/01 Ed 7729 cyl

MY SUNBEAM FROM THE SOUTH
Witmark, pub. 1900, reached #19 in June 1900
Walter H Ford w, John W Bratton m
George J Gaskin 1900 Col 4263 cyl
vv singers

OH, SHINING LIGHT (23)
Vandersloot, pub. 1900, reached #10 in November 1900
Spencer Adams w & m
Frank Stanley 08/01 Ed 7874 cyl
Concert singers

OLE EPH'S VISION (32)
Vandersloot, pub. 1899, reached #9 in March 1900
Lee Orean Smith w & m
Edison Grand Concert Band 12/99 Ed 7349 cyl
other concert bands

ON THE FIRING LINE (48)
A W Tams, pub. 1900, reached #14 in July 1900
L F Mabie, m
Concert bands

SING ME A SONG OF THE SOUTH (17)
Witmark, pub. 1899, reached #6 in January 1900
George A Norton w, James W Casey m
Harry Macdonough 11/99 Ed 7242 cyl
Esther Wallace, vv stage
Will Thompson, vv stage

STRIKE UP THE BAND, HERE COMES A SAILOR (10)
Shapiro, B & Von T, pub. 1900, reached #1 in August 1900
Andrew Sterling w, Charles B Ward m
Annie Hart, vv stage
Dan Quinn Φ 09/00 Ed 7552 cyl, 09/00 Gram 9 disk
Charles B Ward, vv stage
George J Gaskin 1900 Col 4270 cyl

WAIT (15)
Hill, H & B, pub. 1900, reached #3 in September 1900 (Also reached #9 in November 1902)
Charles Horwitz w, Fred Bowers m
Emma Carus, vv stage
Camille D'Arville, vv stage
Frank Stanley 01/01 Ed 7689 cyl
Aurie Dagwell, vv stage

WHAT IS A HOME WITHOUT LOVE? (46)
C K Harris, pub. 1900, reached #9 in May 1900
Charles K Harris w & m
Marie Rose, vv stage
George J Gaskin 1900 Col 4256 cyl
John W Myers 1900 Col 31382 cyl

WHEN CHLOE SINGS A SONG (22)
Witmark, pub. 1899, reached #4 in May 1900
Harry B Smith w, John Stromberg m
Featured in WHIRLIGIG, show (opened 09/99)
Lillian Russell, sung in show
George J Gaskin Φ 02/00 Col 4248 cyl
Steve Porter 1900 Col 4652 cyl

WHEN THE HARVEST DAYS ARE OVER, JESSIE, DEAR (6)
Shapiro,B & Von T ΦΦΦ, pub. 1900, reached #2 in January 1901
Howard Graham w, Harry Von Tilzer m
Emma Carus, vv stage
Byron G Harlan Φ 01/01 Ed 7670 cyl, 01/01 Col 31521 cyl
Harry Ellis, vv stage
Maude Nugent, vv stage
Dan J. Sullivan, vv stage

WHEN YOU WERE SWEET SIXTEEN (1)
Witmark ΦΦΦ, pub. 1898, reached #2 in April 1900
(Also reached #7 in September 1947)
James Thornton w & m
Jere Mahoney Φ 01/00 Ed 7410 cyl
George J Gaskin Φ 07/00 Col 4281 cyl
Master Joe Santly, vv stage
Victoria Ladies' Quartet, vv stage

WHY (30)
Windsor Mus Co, pub. 1899, reached #5 in May 1900
Fred J Hamill w, Paul Cohn m
J Aldrich Libbey, vv stage
Frank Stanley 08/00 Ed 7520 cyl
Cheridah Simpson, vv stage

WOULDN'T IT MAKE YOU MAD, WOULDN'T IT JAR YOU? (37)
Willis Woodward, pub. 1900, reached #5 in July 1900
Will J Hardman
George J Gaskin 1900 Col 4274 cyl
Samuel H Dudley 01/01 Gram 512 disk
vv singers

YOU NEEDN'T SAY THE KISSES CAME FROM ME (40)
Loomis P C, pub. 1900, reached #15 in September 1900
Stanley Carter w & m
Imogene Comer, vv stage
Bennett & Young, vv stage

YOU TELL ME YOUR DREAM (AND I WILL TELL YOU MINE) (12)
Western M P C, pub. 1900, reached #4 in November 1900
Seymour A Rice & Al H Brown w, Neil Moret[1] m
Empire Quartet, vv stage
Etta Butler, vv stage

ZULU WEDDING DANCE (45)
Berge Mus Co, pub. 1899, reached #15 in March 1900
D A Epler w & m
Clarice Vance, vv stage
Kelly & Violette, vv stage
Vess Ossman 07/00 Ed 7485 cyl, 1900 Berliner 01099 disk

[1]Neil Moret was a pen name for Charles N Daniels.
[2]Gram-o-phone became Victor in 1901

1901

ABSENCE MAKES THE HEART GROW FONDER (7)
Witmark, pub. 1900, reached #5 in April 1901
Arthur Gillespie w, Herbert Dillea m
Featured in THE FLOOR WALKERS, show (opened 01/00)
Blanche Ring, vv stage
Harry Macdonough Φ 07/01 Ed 7870 cyl, 10/01 Vic 907 disk
John W Early, sung in show
George J Gaskin 04/01 Col 31549 cyl, 01/02 Col 221 disk
Currier & Reidy, vv stage

AIN'T DAT A SHAME? (13)
Howley, H & D, pub. 1901, reached #2 in November 1901
John Queen w, Walter Wilson m
Tascott, vv stage
Dan Quinn Φ 10/01 Vic 923 disk
Johnnie Queen, vv stage
Carmen Sisters, vv stage
Will F Denny 08/01 Ed 7875 cyl

ANY OLD PLACE I CAN HANG MY HAT IS HOME SWEET HOME TO ME (20)
Shapiro, B & Von T, pub. 1901, reached #5 in June 1901
William Jerome w, Jean Schwartz m
Emma Carus, vv stage
Lew Dockstader, vv stage
Will F Denny Φ 09/01 Ed 7901 cyl, 12/01 Vic 956 disk
Nat Wills, vv stage

BABY MINE (27)
Sol Bloom, pub. 1901, reached #10 in November 1901
Raymond A Browne w, Leo Friedman m
Featured in THE STROLLERS, show (opened 06/01)
Marie George, sung in show
Emma Carus, vv stage
Blanche Ring, vv stage
Sam Dudley 02/02 Vic 1089 disk
Harry Macdonough 02/02 Vic 1098 disk

BOOLA, BOOLA (YALE BOOLA) (17)
Loomis P C, pub. 1901, reached #5 in September 1901
Billy Johnson, Bob Cole & Allen M Hirsch w & m
Haydn Quartet 01/02 Vic 1068 disk
Sousa's Band, band concerts
Peerless Orch 07/01 Ed 7859 cyl

COME BACK, MA HONEY BOY, TO ME (45)
Witmark, pub. 1900, reached #17 in January 1901
Edgar Smith w, John Stromberg m
Featured in FIDDLE DEE DEE, show (opened 07/00)
Lillian Russell, sung in show
vv singers

COON! COON! COON! (4)
Sol Bloom, pub. 1900, reached #1 in February 1901
Leo Friedman & Gene Jefferson w & m
Lew Dockstader, vv stage
Arthur Collins & Joe Natus Φ 04/01 Ed 7750 cyl
Len Spencer/Vess Ossman Φ 08/01 Vic 817 disk
Josephine Sabel, vv stage
Violet Dale, vv stage

COON UP A TREE (15)
A Scull, pub. 1900, reached #10 in June 1901
Gustav Schmull m
Concert bands

DON'T PUT ME OFF AT BUFFALO ANY MORE
Shapiro, B & Von T, pub. 1901, reached #19 in January 1902
William Jerome w, Jean Schwartz m
Maude Nugent, vv stage
other vv singers

DOWN BY THE RIVERSIDE (48)
Howley, H & D. pub. 1900, reached #18 in March 1901
Paul Barnes w & m
John W Myers 12/00 Col 31440 cyl
Joe Natus 03/01 Ed 7736 cyl
vv singers

DOWN IN THE DEPTHS (47)
J W Stern, pub. 1901, reached #18 in July 1901
Henry W Petrie w & m
John W Myers, concert stage
John W Early, concert stage
Frank Stanley 10/02 Ed 8178 cyl

DOWN SOUTH (50)
J W Stern, pub. 1900, reached Top 30 in July 1901
(Also reached #16 in October 1927)
William H Myddleton m
Sousa's Band, band concerts, 03/02 Vic 1173 disk

EUGENIA WALTZES (42)
Ellis Mus Co, pub. 1900, reached #17 in March 1901
Florence McPherran m
Concert bands and orchestras

THE FOUR KINGS MARCH (46)
J W York, pub. 1901, reached #17 in May 1901
C W Dalbey, Ellis Brooks, A F Weldon, W H Scouton m
Concert bands

A GHOST OF A COON (39)
J W Stern, pub. 1900, reached #19 in June 1901
George Walker w, Bert Williams m
Bert Williams, vv stage, 01/02 Vic 998 disk
Arthur Collins 02/01 Col 31460 cyl
George H Primrose, vv stage
Fred Warren, vv stage

GO 'WAY BACK AND SIT DOWN (14)
F A Mills, pub. 1901, reached #2 in August 1901
Elmer Bowman w, Al Johns m
Lottie Gilson, vv stage
Ernest Hogan, vv stage
Dan Quinn 10/01 Vic 919 disk

GOOD MORNING, CARRIE (3)
Windsor Mus Co, pub. 1901, reached #1 in October 1901
Cecil Mack & Chris Smith w, James T Brymn m
Bert Williams & George Walker Φ vv stage, 01/02 Vic 997 disk
Emma Carus, vv stage
Dan Quinn Φ 08/01 Ed 7893 cyl, 10/01 Vic 920 disk
Arthur Collins 08/01 Col 31645 cyl

GOODBYE, DOLLY GRAY (1)
Howley, Haviland ΦΦΦ, pub. 1900, reached #1 in March 1901
Will D Cobb w, Paul Barnes m
Dick Jose, vv stage
Harry Ellis, vv stage
Big Four Quartet Φ 03/01 Ed 7728 cyl
Harry Macdonough 05/01 Gram 655 disk
John W Myers 1900 Col 7502 cyl, 1900 Col 31311 cyl

HE LAID AWAY A SUIT OF GRAY (24)
L Feist, pub. 1900, reached #9 in October 1901
Edward W Wicks w, Ben Janson m
J Aldrich Libbey, vv stage
Lydia Barry, vv stage
Byron G Harlan 08/01 Ed 7892 cyl, 02/02 Col 326 disk
Lillian Mack, vv stage

HELLO, CENTRAL, GIVE ME HEAVEN (2)
C K Harris ΦΦΦ, pub. 1901, reached #1 in July 1901
Charles K Harris w & m
J Aldrich Libbey, vv stage
Byron G Harlan Φ 07/01 Ed 7852 cyl, 12/01 Col 230 disk
Steve Porter 09/01 Vic 861 disk, 12/01 Vic 1069 disk
Harry Ellis, vv stage
Will C Cook, vv stage

THE HONEYSUCKLE AND THE BEE (8)
Sol Bloom, pub. 1901, reached #4 in August 1901
Albert H Fitz w, William H Penn m
Featured in THE PRIMA DONNA, show (opened 04/01)
J Aldrich Libbey, vv stage
Lulu Glaser, sung in show
Arthur Collins 08/01 Col 31646 cyl
Harry Macdonough 10/01 Ed 7954 cyl, 12/01 Vic 948 disk
Della Fox, vv stage

I WANT TO BE A MILITARY MAN (37)
Francis D & H, pub. 1900, reached #13 in March 1901
Owen Hall w, Leslie Stuart m
Featured in FLORADORA, show (opened 11/00)
Cyril Scott, sung in show
Dan Quinn 04/01 Ed 7756 cyl

I WISH WE'D NEVER MET
George P Jennings, pub. 1900, reached #18 in January 1901
Monroe Rosenfeld w & m
Art Chapman, vv stage

I'D STILL BELIEVE YOU TRUE (33)
Howley, H & D, pub. 1900, reached #10 in January 1901
Paul Dresser w & m
Charles Kent, vv stage
Joe Natus 05/01 Vic 678 disk

I'LL BE WITH YOU WHEN THE ROSES BLOOM AGAIN (6)
F A Mills, pub. 1901, reached #1 in December 1901
Will D Cobb w, Gus Edwards m
Harry Macdonough 10/01 Ed 7942 cyl, 02/02 Vic 1097 disk
Dorothy Morton, vv stage
Joe Natus, vv stage, 02/02 Vic 1116 disk
May Hoey, vv stage

I'M TIRED (22)
Shapiro, B & Von T, pub. 1901, reached #8 in December 1901
William Jerome w, Jean Schwartz m
Featured in THE STROLLERS, show (opened 06/01)
Eddie Foy, sung in show
Sam Dudley 09/01 Ed 7919 cyl, 02/02 Vic 1091 disk
vv singers

I'VE A LONGING IN MY HEART FOR YOU, LOUISE (5)
C K Harris, pub. 1900, reached #2 in April 1901
Charles K Harris w & m
Charles Falk, vv stage
Lydia Barry, vv stage
Joe Natus 07/01 Ed 7871 cyl
Harry Macdonough 10/01 Vic 909 disk

I'VE GROWN SO USED TO YOU (44)
Howley, H & D, pub. 1901, reached #16 in August 1901
Thurland Chattaway w & m
Dick Jose, vv stage
Hazel Burt, vv stage
Columbia Orch 09/02 Col 31868 cyl

IF I ONLY HAD A DOLLAH OF MY OWN (31)
Whitney-Warner, pub. 1900, reached #8 in April 1901
Bogert & O'Brien w & m
Belle Williams, vv stage
Beatrice Golden, vv stage
Laura Comstock, vv stage
Arthur Collins 11/01 Ed 7956 cyl

IN THE CATHEDRAL (43)
W H Anstead, pub. 1900, reached #16 in May 1901
Louis Voight w, G S DeChaneet m
J Aldrich Libbey, concert stage
Mrs. Charles Babcock, concert stage

IN THE GREAT SOMEWHERE (41)
Howley, H & D, pub. 1901, reached #17 in December 1901
Paul Dresser w & m
Dick Jose, vv stage

IN THE HOUSE OF TOO MUCH TROUBLE (29)
J W Stern, pub. 1900, reached #6 in May 1901
Will Heelan & J Fred Helf w & m
Lottie Gilson, vv stage
George H Diamond, vv stage
Byron G Harlan 03/01 Ed 7731 cyl, 10/01 Col 55 disk
Harry Macdonough 08/01 Vic 768 disk

IT'S ALL RIGHT, MAYME
Shapiro, B & Von T, pub. 1901, reached #20 in November 1901
William Jerome w, Jean Schwartz m
Maude Nugent, vv stage

JIMMY, THE PRIDE OF NEWSPAPER ROW (34)
Witmark, pub. 1900, reached #10 in August 1901
A Baldwin Sloane w & m
Nellie O'Neill, vv stage
Nellie Parker, vv stage
Polly Allison, vv stage

MA BLUSHIN' ROSIE (9)
Witmark, pub. 1900, reached #3 in February 1901
Edgar Smith w, John Stromberg m
Featured in FIDDLE DEE DEE, show (opened 07/00)
Fay Templeton, sung in show
Arthur Collins 04/01 Col 31510 cyl
Albert Campbell Φ 12/00 Gram 219 disk
Sam Dudley 02/01 Gram 517 disk, 08/01 Ed 7883 cyl
Carol Ladies' Quartette, vv stage

MAMIE (25)
Howley, H & D, pub. 1901, reached #4 in July 1901
Will D Cobb w, Gus Edwards m
Orpheus Quartet, vv stage
Elizabeth Murray, vv stage
John W Myers 06/01 Ed 7821 cyl, 08/01 Vic 828 disk

MR. VOLUNTEER (12)
Howley, H & D, pub. 1901, reached #6 in December 1901
Paul Dresser w & m
J Aldrich Libbey, vv stage
Dorothy Morton, vv stage
Joe Natus 08/01 Ed 7895 cyl, 02/02 Vic 1115 disk
Carmen Sisters, vv stage

MY CASTLE ON THE NILE (16)
J W Stern, pub. 1901, reached #5 in December 1901
James Weldon Johnson & Bob Cole w, J Rosamond Johnson m
Bert Williams & George Walker, vv stage, 01/02 Vic 991 disk
Cole & Johnson, vv stage
Arthur Collins 04/02 Col 31729 cyl, 08/02 Ed 8094 cyl

MY ELINORE (36)
Witmark, pub. 1900, reached #11 in May 1901
Joseph W Standish w, J A Silberburg m
Eleanor Barry, vv stage
Harry Macdonough 05/02 Col 31742 cyl,
08/02 Vic 1410 disk

MY GIRL FROM DIXIE (32)
Sol Bloom, pub. 1900, reached #14 in March 1901
Raymond A Browne & Robert J Adams w & m
Josie Sabel, vv stage
Belle Stewart, vv stage
Lawrence Sisters, vv stage

MY LADY HOTTENTOT (30)
Shapiro, B & Von T, pub. 1901, reached #6 in October 1901
William Jerome w, Harry Von Tilzer m
Maude Nugent, vv stage
Bonita, vv stage
Silas Leachman 03/02 Vic 1123 disk

MY LITTLE ZULU BABE (19)
Windsor Mus Co, pub. 1900, reached #10 in January 1901
William S Estren w, James T Brymn m
Williams & Walker, vv stage
Eddie Foy & Eva Tanguay, vv stage
Arthur Collins 11/00 Col 31322 cyl

MY SWEET KIMONA
Shapiro, B & Von T, pub. 1901, reached #15 in August 1901
Maude Nugent
Maude Nugent, vv stage

THE SHADE OF THE PALM (23)
Francis, D & H, pub. 1900, reached #5 in March 1901
Owen Hall w, Leslie Stuart m
Featured in FLORADORA, show (opened 11/00)
Bertram Godfrey, sung in show
Frank Stanley 03/01 Ed 7721 cyl
Herbert Goddard[1] 08/01 Vic 780 disk
John W Myers 07/01 Col 31620 cyl

THE SPIDER AND THE FLY (38)
Shapiro, B & Von T, pub. 1900, reached #16 in January 1901
Arthur Lamb w, Harry Von Tilzer m
Dan J. Sullivan, vv stage
Steve Porter 04/01 Col 31546 cyl, 09/01 Vic 869 disk
Byron G Harlan 10/01 Ed 7944 cyl
George H Diamond, vv stage

SWEET ANNIE MOORE (11)
Howley, H & D, pub. 1901, reached #1 in August 1901
John H Flynn & Alex Rogers w & m
Harry Macdonough & Sam Dudley Φ 08/01 Vic 775 disk
Joe Natus 05/01 Ed 7791 cyl, 06/01 Col 31584 cyl
Agnes Miles, vv stage

THE TALE OF A BUMBLE BEE (21)
Witmark, pub. 1901, reached #13 in December 1901
Frank Pixley w, Gustav Luders m
Featured in KING DODO, show (opened 05/02)
Louise Montrose & Raymond Hitchcock, sung in show
Harry Macdonough Φ 10/01 Vic 908 disk
Mina Hickman & Harry Macdonough 11/01 Ed 7976 cyl

THE TALE OF THE KANGAROO (18)
Witmark, pub. 1900, reached #5 in April 1901
Frank Pixley w, Gustav Luders m
Featured in THE BURGOMASTER, show (opened 12/00)
Della Stacey, sung in show
Sam Dudley 01/01 Ed 7685 cyl, 03/01 Gram 64 disk
Sousa's Band 07/01 Vic 728 disk

TELL ME, PRETTY MAIDEN (10)
Francis, D & H, pub. 1900, reached #3 in March 1901
Owen Hall w, Leslie Stuart m
Featured in FLORADORA, show (opened 11/00)
First show tune to be recorded by members of original cast
Floradora Girls, sung in show
Floradora Girls/w.male quartet Φ 07/01 Col 31604 cyl
Grace Spencer & Harry Macdonough Φ 04/01 Ed 7758 cyl

THERE'S NO NORTH OR SOUTH TODAY (40)
Howley, H & D, pub. 1901, reached #12 in June 1901
Paul Dresser w & m
Dick Jose, vv stage
Bernard Dyllyn, vv stage
Joe Natus 05/01 Gram 677 disk, 06/01 Col 31586 cyl

THE TIE THAT BINDS (28)
C K Harris, pub. 1901, reached #12 in October 1901
Charles K Harris w & m
Henry & Gallot, vv stage
Jere Mahoney 09/01 Ed 7921 cyl

THE VESPER BELLS WERE RINGING (49)
Windsor Mus Co, pub. 1900, reached #20 in April 1901
Henry V Neal w, C H Bennett m
Harry Leighton, vv stage
other vv singers

WAY DOWN IN OLD INDIANA (35)
Howley, H & D, pub. 1901, reached #11 in December 1901
Paul Dresser w & m
Dick Jose, vv stage
John W Myers 05/02 Vic 1228 disk, 05/02 Col 31749 cyl

WHEN MR. SHAKESPEARE COMES TO TOWN (26)
Howley, H & D, pub. 1901, reached #11 in January 1902
William Jerome w, Jean Schwartz m
Featured in KING'S CARNIVAL, show (opened 05/01)
Emma Carus & Harry Bulger, sung in show
Dan Quinn Φ 09/01 Ed 7906 cyl, 10/01 Vic 922 disk
Carmen Sisters, vv stage

YOU CAN'T KEEP A GOOD MAN DOWN
J W Stern, pub. 1900, reached #20 in February 1901
M F Carey w & m
Dan Quinn 01/01 Ed 7687 cyl, 07/01 Vic 746 disk
vv singers

[1]Herbert Goddard was a pseudonym for Emilio deGogorza.

1902

BILL BAILEY, WON'T YOU PLEASE COME HOME? (6)
Howley, H & D, pub. 1902, reached #1 in September 1902
Hughie Cannon & Johnnie Queen w & m
Tascott, vv stage
Dan Quinn Φ 08/02 Vic 1411 disk
Artie Hall, vv stage
Arthur Collins Φ 09/02 Ed 8112 cyl, 11/02 Col 872 disk
Silas Leachman 10/02 Vic 1458 disk

BLAZE AWAY! (18)
L Feist, pub. 1901, reached #5 in July 1902
Abe Holzmann m
Sousa's Band, band concerts
Fred Van Eps 06/02 Ed 8025 cyl
Columbia Orch 10/01 Col 48 disk

COULD YOU BE TRUE TO EYES OF BLUE? (16)
F A Mills, pub. 1902, reached #4 in December 1902
Will D Cobb w, G Edwards m
Featured in A CHINESE HONEYMOON, show (opened 06/02)
Van Rensselar Wheeler, sung in show
Emma Carus, vv stage
Katherine Trayer, vv stage
Harry Macdonough 12/02 Vic 1658 disk

CREOLE BELLES (4)
J H Remick, pub. 1900, reached #1 in January 1902
George Sidney w, J Bodewald Lampe m
Sousa's Band Φ band concerts, 04/02 Vic 1182 disk
Kelly & Violette, vv stage
Columbia Orch Φ 12/01 Col 31688 cyl, 03/02 Col 330 disk
Edison Grand Concert Band 10/01 Ed 7926 cyl
Hawthorne Sisters, vv stage

CUPID'S GARDEN (13)
T B Harms, pub. 1901, reached #11 in July 1902
Max C. Eugene m
Peerless Orch 08/02 Ed 8095 cyl
Concert bands & orchestras

DANCE OF THE HONEYBEES (29)
Willis Woodward, pub. 1902, reached #13 in December 1902
Benjamin Richmond m
Concert bands and orchestras

DOWN WHERE THE COTTON BLOSSOMS GROW (5)
Shapiro, B & Von T ΦΦΦ, pub. 1901, reached #2 in Feb. 1902
Andrew Sterling w, Harry Von Tilzer m
Harry Ellis, vv stage
George H Diamond, vv stage
Frank Stanley 09/01 Ed 7917 cyl
Helene Mora, vv stage
Harry Macdonough 12/02 Vic 1621 disk

FARE THEE WELL, MOLLIE DARLING (21)
F A Mills, pub. 1902, reached #6 in November 1902
Will D Cobb m, Kerry Mills m
Charles Falk, vv stage
Daisy Dumont, vv stage
Harry Macdonough 11/02 Vic 1656 disk
John W Myers 09/02 Col 31851 cyl

I WANTS A PING PONG MAN (39)
Witmark, pub. 1902, reached #19 in November 1902
Howard Whitney w & m
The Hamlins, vv stage
Carrie Scott, vv stage

I'LL BE THERE, MARY DEAR (50)
H Von Tilzer, pub. 1902, reached Top 30 in July 1902
Andrew Sterling w, Harry Von Tilzer m
Byron G Harlan 10/02 Ed 8164 cyl
Jenny Eddy, vv stage

I'LL BE YOUR RAINBEAU (38)
Sol Bloom, pub. 1902, reached #7 in October 1902
Ed Gardenier w, J Fred Helf m
Featured in THE DEFENDER, show (opened 07/02)
Emma Carus, sung in show
Josie Sabel, vv stage
Dan Quinn 10/02 Vic 1467 disk, 10/02 Ed 8174 cyl
Anna Held, vv stage

I'M WEARING MY HEART AWAY FOR YOU, LOUISE (17)
C K Harris, pub. 1902, reached #5 in December 1902
Charles K Harris w & m
Frank Morrell, vv stage
Harry Macdonough & John H Bieling 02/03 Vic 1854 disk
Jere Sanford, vv stage

I'VE GOT MY EYES ON YOU (41)
American Advance, pub. 1902, reached #11 in October 1902
F W Hager & Justus Ringleben w, Theodore F Morse m
William H Thompson 08/02 Ed 8092 cyl
John J Nestor, vv stage

IF I BUT DARE (42)
G W Fager, pub. 1901, reached #16 in August 1902
F Dupree w, Arthur Trevelyan m
Jessie Stevens, vv stage
other vv singers

IF MONEY TALKS, IT AIN'T ON SPEAKIN' TERMS WITH ME (20)
Sol Bloom, pub. 1902, reached #4 in June 1902
J Fred Helf w & m
Tascott, vv stage
Lottie Gilson, vv stage
Clarice Vance, vv stage, 09/02 Col 731 disk
Arthur Collins 12/02 Vic 1631 disk
Jack Norworth, vv stage

IF TIME WAS MONEY, I'D BE A MILLIONAIRE (33)
L Feist, pub. 1902, reached #6 in July 1902
Felix Feist w, Ted S Barron m
Clarice Vance, vv stage
Arthur Collins 04/02 Col 31706 cyl

IN A COZY CORNER (48)
Witmark, pub. 1901, reached Top 30 in June 1902
Grace E Kimball & John W Bratton m
Gilmore's Band 06/02 Col 31775 cyl
Concert bands and orchestras

IN THE CITY OF SIGHS AND TEARS (49)
F A Mills, pub. 1902, reached #8 in January 1903
Andrew Sterling w, Kerry Mills m
Charles Falke, vv stage
Josie Flynn, vv stage
John W Myers 01/03 Vic 1696 disk, 02/03 Col 1014 disk

IN THE GOOD OLD SUMMERTIME (2)
Howley, H & D ΦΦΦ, pub. 1902, reached #1 in September 1902
(Also reached #17 in July 1952)
Ren Shields w, George Evans m
Featured in THE DEFENDER, show (opened 07/02)
All-time pop standard
Blanche Ring, sung in show
J Aldrich Libbey, vv stage
Harry Macdonough Φ 01/03 Vic 1655 disk
John W Myers Φ 11/02 Col 31879 cyl, 11/02 Col 940 disk
William H Redmond Φ 10/02 Ed 8118 cyl

IT'S FOR HER, HER, HER (47)
Witmark, pub. 1902, reached Top 30 in September 1902
Ren Shields w, Billee Taylor m
Josie Sabel, vv stage
Phyllis Allen, vv stage

JENNIE LEE (30)
Shapiro, B & Von T, pub. 1902, reached #4 in April 1902
Arthur Lamb w, Harry Von Tilzer m
Helene Mora, vv stage
John P Curran, vv stage
Harry Macdonough 08/02 Vic 1395 disk
Byron G Harlan 08/02 Ed 8082 cyl

JOSEPHINE, MY JO (36)
Shapiro, B & Von T, pub. 1901, reached #5 in May 1902
Cecil Mack w, James T Brymn m
Flossie Allen & the Blondells, vv stage
Arthur Collins 07/02 Col 31787 cyl
Harry Macdonough 08/02 Vic 1393 disk

JUST A-WEARYIN' FOR YOU (45)
C Jacobs-Bond, pub. 1901; reached Top 40 in May 1902
Frank Stanton w, Carrie Jacobs-Bond m
Steady seller, beginning 1902
Jessie Bartlett Davis, concert stage

JUST NEXT DOOR (34)
C K Harris, pub. 1902, reached #9 in August 1902
Charles K Harris w & m
J Aldrich Libbey, vv stage
Aurie Dagwell, vv stage
Harry Macdonough 11/02 Vic 1618 disk

MAIDEN WITH THE DREAMY EYES (44)
J W Stern, pub. 1901, reached #5 in March 1902
James W Johnson w, Bob Cole m
Featured in THE LITTLE DUCHESS, show (opened 10/01)
Featured in THE SUPPER CLUB, show (opened 12/01)
Anna Held, sung in show (LD)
Tom Seabrooke, sung in show (SC)
Lucille Jocelyn & Harry Macdonough 03/02 Col 31705 cyl
Harry Macdonough 07/02 Vic 1353 disk

THE MANSION OF ACHING HEARTS (3)
Shapiro, B & Von T ΦΦΦ, pub. 1902, reached #2 in May 1902
Arthur Lamb w, Harry Von Tilzer m
Emma Carus, vv stage
Kathryn Miley, vv stage
John W Myers Φ 06/02 Col 31776 cyl, 09/02 Col 861 disk
Byron G Harlan Φ 08/02 Ed 8093 cyl
Harry Macdonough 11/02 Vic 1415 disk

MIGHTY LAK' A ROSE (23)
John Church Co ΦΦΦ, Pub. 1901, reached #16 in June 1902
Frank Stanton w, Ethelbert Nevin m
Steady seller 1902-1910
Concert singers
Arthur Clifford 07/03 Ed 8430 cyl
George Alexander 12/03 Col 1585 disk, 12/03 Col 32295 cyl

MR. DOOLEY (7)
Shapiro, B & Von T, pub. 1902, reached #1 in December 1902
William Jerome w, Jean Schwartz m
Featured in THE CHINESE HONEYMOON, show (opened 06/02)
Tom Seabrooke, sung in show
Dan Quinn Φ 09/02 Col 31779 cyl, 10/02 Vic 1466 disk
Elizabeth Murray, vv stage
Edward Φ Favor 09/02 Ed 8125 cyl

MY CAROLINA CAROLINE (12)
Windsor Mus Co, pub. 1901, reached #4 in March 1902
Billy Johnson w & m
Sawtell Sisters, vv stage
Murphy & Slater, vv stage
Arthur Collins 04/02 Col 31730 cyl

MY MISSISSIPPI SUE (40)
G M Krey, pub. 1901, reached #7 in February 1902
Will Toland w, Fred Meloy m
Will Hagen, vv stage
Marjorie King, vv stage

MY MOTHER WAS A NORTHERN GIRL (35)
Sol Bloom, pub. 1902, reached #17 in July 1902
J Fred Helf w & m
Louise Dresser, vv stage
Lottie Gilson, vv stage
Ada Jones, vv stage, 09/02 Col 730 disk

NANCY BROWN (26)
Howley, H & D, pub. 1901, reached #4 in August 1902
Clifton Crawford w & m
Featured in THE WILD ROSE, show (opened 05/02)
Marie Cahill, sung in show
Harry Macdonough 08/02 Vic 1409 disk
Estelle Wells, vv stage

OH, DIDN'T HE RAMBLE (11)
J W Stern, pub. 1902, reached #4 in September 1902
Bob Cole w, J Rosamond Johnson m
George Primrose, vv stage
Dan Quinn 06/02 Vic 1327 disk
Arthur Collins 08/02 Ed 8081 cyl

ON A SATURDAY NIGHT (37)
Vandersloot, pub. 1902, reached #6 in June 1902
Ida Emerson w, Joe Howard m
Joe Howard, vv stage
Edward Daly, vv stage
Joe Natus 06/02 Vic 1300 disk

ON A SUNDAY AFTERNOON (1)
H Von Tilzer ΦΦΦ, pub. 1902, reached #1 in April 1902
Andrew Sterling w, Harry Von Tilzer m
J Aldrich Libbey Φ vv stage, 06/02 Ed 8018 cyl
Emma Carus, vv stage
John W Myers Φ 04/02 Col 106 disk, 05/02 Col 31755 cyl
Alice Dorothy, vv stage
Harry Macdonough Φ 08/02 Vic 1391 disk

ONE STRIKE, TWO STRIKES, THREE STRIKES OUT (22)
Windsor Mus Co, pub. 1901, reached #9 in April 1902
Ed Gardenier w, Ed Rogers m
Henry & Gallot, vv stage
Sawtell Sisters, vv stage
Dudley & Orme, vv stage

OUR DIRECTOR (MARCH) (24)
W Jacobs, pub. 1901, reached #5 in May 1902
Frederick E. Bigelow m
Sousa's Band, band concerts
Gilmore's Band 08/02 Col 31848 cyl

PANAMERICANA
Witmark, pub. 1901, reached #16 in June 1902
Victor Herbert m
Clarke's Band of Providence, band concerts
other concert bands, band concerts

PLACE A LIGHT TO GUIDE ME HOME (28)
Witmark, pub. 1898, reached #13 in November 1902
J Everett Fay w, James B Oliver m
Henry & Gallot, vv stage
Edgar Manley, vv stage

PLEASE GO 'WAY AND LET ME SLEEP (8)
H Von Tilzer, pub. 1902, reached #1 in August 1902
Cecil Mack w, James T Brymn m
Arthur Deming, vv stage
Arthur Collins Φ 07/02 Col 31788 cyl, 11/02 Vic 1630 disk
Raymond Teal, vv stage

PRETTY MOLLIE SHANNON (15)
Witmark, pub. 1901, reached #8 in July 1902
George H Ryan w, Walter Wolff m
Featured in THE LITTLE DUCHESS, show (opened 10/01)
Anna Held, sung in show
John W Myers 05/02 Vic 1240 disk, 05/02 Col 31751 cyl
Harry Macdonough 05/02 Vic 1268 disk, 05/02 Col 31735 cyl
Sousa's Band 09/02 Vic 1425 disk

RIP VAN WINKLE WAS A LUCKY MAN (14)
Shapiro, B & Von T, pub. 1901, reached #1 in July 1902
William Jerome w, Jean Schwartz m
Featured in SLEEPING BEAUTY AND THE BEAST, show (opened 11/01)
Harry Bulger, sung in show
Maude Nugent, vv stage
Dan Quinn Φ 05/02 Col 890 disk, 06/02 Vic 1326 disk
Will F Denny 05/02 Col 31726 cyl

SADIE SAY YOU WON'T SAY NAY (25)
Witmark, pub. 1901, reached #15 in August 1902
Will R Anderson w & m
Master Willie Howard, vv stage
Ethel Robinson, vv stage
William H Thompson 03/02 Ed 8037 cyl

A SIGNAL FROM MARS (46)
E T Paull, pub. 1901, reached #13 in April 1902
Edward T Paull m
Concert bands, band concerts

STAY IN YOUR OWN BACK YARD (10)
Witmark, pub. 1899, reached #17 in October 1902
Karl Kennett w, Lyn Udall m
Steady seller, 1901-1903
Harry Macdonough Φ 09/02 Vic 1419 disk
Arthur Collins 10/02 Ed 8165 cyl
Sousa's Band 11/02 Vic 1551 disk

VIOLETS (19)
G Ricordi, pub. 1900, reached #6 in October 1902
Heinrich Heine & Julian Fane w, Ellen Wright m
Featured in THE LITTLE DUCHESS, show (opened 10/01)
Sydney Barraclough, sung in show
Herbert Goddard[1] 06/02 Vic 1332 disk
John W Myers 03/02 Vic 1141 disk, 06/02 Col 557 disk
Mlle. St. Andre, stage

WAIT (31)
Hill, H & B, pub. 1900, reached #9 in November 1902
(Also reached #3 in September 1900)
Charles Horwitz w, Fred Bowers m
Herbert Goddard[1] 05/02 Vic 1247 disk
stage singers

WAY DOWN YONDER IN THE CORNFIELD (9)
F A Mills, pub. 1901, reached #1 in April 1902
Will D Cobb w, Gus Edwards m
Lottie Gilson, vv stage
George Diamond, vv stage
John W Myers 11/01 Ed 7978 cyl, 03/02 Vic 1136 disk
Hazel Burt, vv stage

WHEN KATE AND I WERE COMIN' THRO' THE RYE (27)
H Von Tilzer, pub. 1902, reached #5 in October 1902
Andrew Sterling w, Harry Von Tilzer m
Lillian Washburn, vv stage
Byron G Harlan 10/02 Ed 8201 cyl, 05/03 Col 1191 disk

WHERE THE SILV'RY COLORADO WENDS ITS WAY (32)
T R Ingram, pub. 1901, reached #15 in July 1902
(Also reached #11 in May 1904)
C H Scoggins w, Charles Avril m
Steady seller, 1901-1905
J Aldrich Libbey, vv stage, 06/02 Ed 8020 cyl
Reese Prosser, vv stage

WHY DID THEY SELL KILLARNEY? (43)
Witmark, pub. 1900, reached Top 30 in June 1902
Harry Dillon w, John Dillon m
Phyllis Allen, vv stage
Joe Natus 07/00 Ed 7497 cyl

[1]Herbert Goddard was a pseudonym for Emilio deGogorza.

1903

ALWAYS IN THE WAY (1)
C K Harris ΦΦΦ, pub. 1903, reached #1 in October 1903
Charles K Harris w & m
Jere Sanford, vv stage
Byron G Harlan ΦΦ 10/03 Ed 8501 cyl, 01/04 Col 1662 disk
Bennett & Young, vv stage
John W Myers 02/04 Col 1674 disk

ANONA (17)
L Feist, pub. 1903, reached #2 in October 1903
Mabel McKinley w, Robert A King m
Mabel McKinley, vv stage
Charles Falke, vv stage
Harry Macdonough 12/03 Col 1602 disk,
02/04 Vic 2551 disk
Pryor's Band 02/04 Vic 2521 disk

BEDELIA (3)
Shapiro, B, pub. 1903, reached #1 in December 1903
William Jerome w, Jean Schwartz m
Featured in THE JERSEY LILY, show (opened 09/03)
Blanche Ring, vv stage
Billy Murray Φ 12/03 Ed 8550 cyl
Elizabeth Murray, vv stage
Emma Carus, vv stage
Haydn Quartet Φ 02/04 Vic 2559 disk

THE BOYS ARE COMING HOME TODAY (43)
Howley, H & D, pub. 1903, reached #9 in July 1903
Paul Dresser w & m
Flossie Allen, vv stage
Joe Natus 08/03 Vic 2334 disk
Boston Comedy Four, vv stage

THE BOYS IN THE GALL'RY FOR MINE (35)
Sol Bloom, pub. 1903, reached #5 in September 1903
Will Heelan & J Fred Helf w & m
Anna Driver, vv stage
Marie Culp, vv stage
Johnnie Carroll, vv stage

COME DOWN, MA EVENIN' STAR (9)
Witmark, pub. 1902, reached #4 in August 1903
Robert B Smith w, John Stromberg w
Featured in TWIRLY WHIRLY, show (opened 09/02)
Lillian Russell, sung in show
Mina Hickman Φ 01/03 Col 955 disk, 05/03 Vic 1980 disk
Henry Burr 07/03 Col 1405 disk, 07/03 Col 32174 cyl
Everett Quartet, vv stage

CONEY ISLAND COON (34)
Windsor Mus Co, pub. 1902, reached #18 in January 1903
William C Welp w & m
Edith Arnold, vv stage
Edna Murrell, vv stage

CONGO LOVE SONG (5)
J W Stern, pub. 1903, reached #1 in August 1903
Bob Cole w, J Rosamond Johnson m
Featured in NANCY BROWN, show (opened 02/03)
Marie Cahill, sung in show
Mina Hickman 08/03 Vic 2374 disk
Sousa's Band 11/03 Vic 2436 disk
Harry Macdonough 08/03 Ed 8456 cyl

DAT'S DE WAY TO SPELL CHICKEN (20)
Witmark, pub. 1902, reached #8 in February 1903
Bob Slater & Sidney Perrin w & m
Josie Sabel, vv stage
Dumont's Minstrels, vv stage
Arthur Collins 01/03 Ed 8301 cyl, 04/03 Col 1152 disk
Len Spencer 04/03 Vic 1900 disk

DEAR OLD GIRL (10)
Howley, H & D, pub. 1903, reached #2 in November 1903
Richard H Buck w, Theodore F Morse m
Dick Jose, vv stage
John W Myers Φ 11/03 Col 32282 cyl, 12/03 Col 1573 disk
Harry Macdonough 02/04 Ed 8613 cyl, 04/04 Vic 2643 disk
Tally-Ho Duo, vv stage

DOWN IN THE DEEP, LET ME SLEEP WHEN I DIE (11)
Albright, pub. 1900, reached #12 in August 1903
W L Titus w, Henry W Petrie m
Steady seller for several years, peaking in 1903
Fred Barnes, concert stage
Lillian Edwards, concert stage
Arthur Hahn, stage

DOWN ON THE FARM (16)
H Von Tilzer, pub. 1902, reached #5 in January 1904
Raymond A Browne w, Harry Von Tilzer m
George H Diamond, vv stage
Haydn Quartet 02/04 Vic 2580 disk
Francklyn Wallace 10/03 Ed 8517 cyl
John W Myers 01/04 Col 1612 disk

DOWN WHERE THE WURTZBURGER FLOWS (6)
H Von Tilzer ΦΦΦ, pub. 1902, reached #1 in January 1903
Vincent Bryan w, Harry Von Tilzer m
Lew Dockstader, vv stage
Collins & Harlan Φ 11/02 Ed 8238 cyl, 01/03 Zono 5441 disk
Empire City Quartet, vv stage
Arthur Collins 12/02 Vic 1635 disk
Madge Ellis, vv stage

DUTY TO HOME AND FLAG (37)
Windsor Mus Co, pub. 1903, reached #17 in January 1903
Ed Rogers w & m
Hazel Burt, vv stage
Florence Emmett, vv stage

EVERY MAN IS A VOLUNTEER (45)
Sol Bloom, pub. 1903, reached #15 in June 1903
Will Heelan w, J Fred Helf m
Florine, vv stage
The Klinerts, vv stage

THE GAMBLING MAN (21)
Shapiro, B, pub. 1902, reached #3 in April 1903
William Jerome w, Jean Schwartz m
Emma Carus, vv stage
Tascott, vv stage
Maude Nugent, vv stage
Silas Leachman 04/03 Vic 1898 disk
Anna Driver, vv stage

GOODNIGHT, BELOVED, GOODNIGHT (15)
Witmark, pub. 1900, reached #10 in August 1903
J Everett Fay w, James B Oliver m
Phyllis Allen, vv stage
Mina Hickman 05/03 Vic 1979 disk
Paloma Ladies' Quartette, vv stage
William H Thompson 12/02 Ed 8262 cyl
Josie Turner, vv stage

HAMLET WAS A MELANCHOLY DANE (36)
Shapiro, B, pub. 1902, reached #9 in March 1903
William Jerome w, Jean Schwartz m
Featured in MR. BLUEBEARD, show (opened 01/03)
Eddie Foy, sung in show
Edward M Favor 05/03 Ed 8400 cyl
Dan Quinn 10/03 Vic 2421 disk

HEIDELBERG (STEIN SONG)
Witmark, pub. 1902, reached #20 in February 1903
Frank Pixley w, Gustav Luders m
Featured by ensemble in THE PRINCE OF PILSEN, show (opened 03/03)
John W Myers 02/03 Col 1054 disk, 02/03 Col 31994 cyl
Harry Macdonough 04/03 Vic 1920 disk, 04/03 Ed 8385 cyl

HIAWATHA (4)
Whitney-Warner, pub. 1903, reached #1 in May 1903
James O'Dea w, Neil Moret m
Initially published as instrumental in 1901
Clara Morton, vv stage
Grace LaRue, vv stage
Harry Macdonough Φ 07/03 Ed 8425 cyl, 07/03 Col 32175 cyl, 09/03 Vic 2351 disk
Metropolitan Orch 03/03 Vic 1923 disk
Columbia Orch 04/03 Col 1155 disk, 04/03 Col 32092 cyl

HURRAH FOR BAFFIN'S BAY (38)
Howley, H & D, pub. 1903, reached #8 in May 1903
Vincent Bryan w, Theodore F Morse m
Featured in THE WIZARD OF OZ, show (opened 01/03)
Dave Montgomery & Fred Stone, sung in show
Bob Roberts 07/03 Col 1404 disk
Collins & Harlan 07/03 Ed 8447 cyl, 09/03 Col 1491 disk

I TAKE THINGS EASY (50)
Shapiro, B, pub. 1903, reached #17 in April 1903
Cecil Mack w, James T Brymn m
Bert Williams & George Walker, vv stage
Tascott, vv stage
Len Spencer 03/03 Vic 1903 disk
Maude Raymond, vv stage

I'M A JONAH MAN (28)
Witmark, pub. 1903, reached #4 in May 1903
Alex Rogers w & m
Featured in IN DAHOMEY, show (opened 02/03)
Bert Williams, sung in show
Arthur Collins 06/03 Vic 2052 disk, 07/03 Ed 8440 cyl
Dan Quinn 04/03 Vic 1989 disk

I'VE GOT TO GO NOW 'CAUSE I THINK IT'S GOING TO RAIN
Witmark, pub. 1903, reached #11 in August 1903
Ed Rose w, Nat Osborne m
Bob Roberts 07/03 Col 1389 disk
Harry Wardell, vv stage
Arthur Collins 08/03 Col 32163 cyl

IF YOU CAN'T BE A BELL COW, FALL IN BEHIND (46)
Sol Bloom, pub. 1902, reached #16 in January 1903
A L Robb & J Fred Helf w & m
Tascott, vv stage
Clarice Vance, vv stage
The Leightons, vv stage

IN DEAR OLD ILLINOIS (19)
Howley, H & D, pub. 1902, reached #4 in February 1903
Paul Dresser w & m
Dick Jose, vv stage
William H Thompson 12/02 Ed 8273 cyl
Harry Macdonough & John H Bieling 04/03 Vic 1856 disk

IN OLD ALABAMA (14)
Manhattan Mus Co, pub. 1903, reached #3 in July 1903
Dox Cruger w & m
Leeds & Catlin, vv stage
Peerless Orch 05/03 Ed 8392 cyl
Columbia Orch 09/03 Col 1549 disk

IN THE SWEET BYE AND BYE (13)
H Von Tilzer, pub. 1902, reached #4 in June 1903
Vincent Bryan w, Harry Von Tilzer m
J Aldrich Libbey, vv stage, 01/03 Ed 8300 cyl
Harry Macdonough & John H Bieling 06/03 Vic 1855 disk
other vv singers

JUST KISS YOURSELF GOODBYE (23)
Shapiro, B, pub. 1902, reached #4 in March 1903
William Jerome w, Jean Schwartz m
Artie Hall, vv stage
Arthur Collins 12/02 Ed 8275 cyl, 04/03 Col 32081 cyl
Belle Williams, vv stage
DeGraff Sisters, vv stage

LAUGHING WATER (8)
Sol Bloom, pub. 1903, reached #3 in January 1904
George Totten Smith w, Frederick W Hager m
Featured in MOTHER GOOSE, show (opened 12/03)
Harry Bulger, sung in show
Columbia Orch 11/03 Col 1571 disk, 11/03 Col 32283 cyl
Edison Grand Concert Band 11/03 Ed 8532 cyl

LINCOLN, GRANT, OR LEE
Howley, H & D, pub. 1903, reached #19 in December 1903
Paul Dresser w & m
Haverly's Minstrels, vv stage
Tom McKenna, vv stage

THE MESSAGE OF THE VIOLET (12)
Witmark, pub. 1902, reached #3 in February 1903
Frank Pixley w, Gustav Luders m
Featured in THE PRINCE OF PILSEN, show (opened 03/03)
Albert Paar & Anna Lichter, sung in show
John W Myers Φ 02/03 Col 1055 disk,
02/03 Col 31995 cyl, 03/03 Vic 1796 disk

MOLLIE (A DAINTY BIT OF JOLLY) (32)
Windsor Mus Co, pub. 1902, reached #7 in April 1903
Harry S Melville w, Ellis Ephraim m
Charles Hart, vv stage
Flo Irwin, vv stage
Daisy Linden, vv stage

MY BESSIE'S WEDDING DAY (30)
Peerless Pub Co, pub. 1902, reached #8 in August 1903
Sidney J Mullen w & m
J Aldrich Libbey, vv stage
J Aldrich Libbey & Katherine Trayer, vv stage
Florence Emery, vv stage

MY OWN UNITED STATES (24)
Witmark, pub. 1902, reached #3 in March 1903
(Also reached #7 in January 1909)
Stanislaus Stange w, Julian Edwards m
Featured in WHEN JOHNNY COMES MARCHING HOME, show
(opened 12/02)
William G Stewart, sung in show
John W Myers 02/03 Vic 1795 disk, 03/03 Col 1119 disk
Harry Joelson, vv stage

NOBODY'S LOOKING BUT THE OWL AND THE MOON (7)
J W Stern, pub. 1901, reached #3 in June 1903
Bob Cole w, J Rosamond Johnson m
Featured in SLEEPING BEAUTY AND THE BEAST, show
(opened 11/01)
Cole & Johnson, sung in show and on vv stage
Florence Bindley, vv stage
Sam Dudley Φ 09/02 Vic 1388 disk

ONLY A SOLDIER BOY (39)
Doty & Brill, pub. 1902, reached #12 in June 1903
Charles W Doty w, Edwin S Brill m
Harry Wise, vv stage

PRINCESS POCAHONTAS
Windsor Mus Co, pub. 1903, reached #20 in September 1903
Al Trahern w, Richmond F Hoyt m
vv singers
Concert bands

SADIE GREEN
Peerless Pub Co, pub. 1903. reached #14 in August 1903
Sidney J Mullen w & m
J Aldrich Libbey, vv stage
The Colby Family, vv stage

SAMMY
Sol Bloom, pub. 1902, reached #18 in April 1903
James O'Dea w, Edward Hutchinson m
Featured in THE WIZARD OF OZ, show (opened 01/03)
Mabel Barrison & Lotta Faust, sung in show
Harry Macdonough 01/03 Vic 1657 disk

SHOW ME THE WHITE OF YO' EYE (18)
Shapiro, B, pub. 1903, reached #2 in September 1903
Stanley Crawford w & m
Lottie Gilson, vv stage
The Leightons, vv stage
Tom Moore, vv stage

SINCE I FIRST MET YOU
Witmark, pub. 1902, reached #8 in July 1903
George Ade w, Alfred J Wathall m
Featured by ensemble in THE SULTAN OF SULU, show (opened 12/02)
Harry Macdonough 04/03 Vic 1922 disk
William H Thompson 03/03 Ed 8350 cyl

SINCE SALLY LEFT OUR ALLEY (26)
Sol Bloom, pub. 1903, reached #6 in May 1903
Will Heelan w, J Fred Helf m
Nellie Beaumont, vv stage
Concert bands

SOMEBODY'S WAITING 'NEATH SOUTHERN SKIES (40)
Witmark, pub. 1902, reached #14 in January 1903
Arthur Lamb w, John T Bratton m
Violet Staley, vv stage
Harry Macdonough & John H Bieling 01/04 Vic 2504 disk
Jones & Ryan, vv stage

THE SPIRIT OF '76 (33)
Sol Bloom, pub. 1902, reached #18 in February 1903
J Fred Helf w & m
Henry & Gallot, vv stage
Ada Jones, vv stage

THE SUN DANCE (47)
Sol Bloom, pub. 1901, reached #6 in October 1903
Leo Friedman m
Edison Symphony Orch 11/03 Ed 8548 cyl
Concert bands & orchestras

THE TALE OF THE SEASHELL (31)
Witmark, pub. 1902, reached #15 in February 1903
Frank Pixley w, Gustav Luders m
Featured in THE PRINCE OF PILSEN, show (opened 03/03)
Arthur Donaldson & Lillian Cole, sung in show
John W Myers 02/03 Col 31992 cyl
William H Thompson 11/02 Ed 8212 cyl, 02/03 Col 1052 disk

TESSIE, YOU ARE THE ONLY, ONLY, ONLY (25)
Witmark, pub. 1902, reached #4 in March 1903
Will R Anderson w & m
Featured in THE SILVER SLIPPER, show (opened 10/02)
Harry Macdonough 05/03 Col 32099 cyl, 06/03 Vic 2056 disk
Billy Murray 04/03 Col 1163 disk
Stanley Hawkins, sung in show

THEN I'D BE SATISFIED WITH LIFE (44)
F A Mills, pub. 1902, reached #10 in February 1903
George M Cohan w & m
Featured in THE SILVER SLIPPER, show (opened 10/02)
George M Cohan, vv stage
Sam Bernard, sung in show
Edward M Favor 03/03 Ed 8365 cyl

TWO IS COMPANY, THREE IS A CROWD (29)
Windsor Mus Co, pub. 1902, reached #7 in March 1903
Chris Smith & Elmer Bowman w & m
Bessie Taylor, vv stage
Charles Downing, vv stage
Bessie Howard, vv stage

UNDER THE BAMBOO TREE (2)
J W Stern, pub. 1902, reached #1 in February 1903
Bob Cole w, J Rosamond Johnson m
Featured in SALLY IN OUR ALLEY, show (opened 08/02)
Marie Cahill, sung in show (Later: 1917 Vic 45125)
Arthur Collins Φ 11/02 Ed 8215 cyl, 12/02 Vic 1633 disk
Cole & Johnson, vv stage
Irene Franklin, vv stage

UP IN A COCONUT TREE (27)
Howley, H & D, pub. 1903, reached #5 in December 1903
Edward Madden w, Theodore F Morse m
Billy Murray 11/03 Vic 2453 disk, 12/03 Ed 8564 cyl
Carmen Sisters, vv stage
Tallyho Duo, vv stage

VOICE OF THE HUDSON (42)
Howley, H & D, pub. 1903, reached #7 in June 1903
Paul Dresser w & m
Dick Jose, vv stage
Joe Natus 08/03 Vic 2336 disk

WHAT A NASTY DISPOSITION FOR A LADY LIKE YOU (41)
Sol Bloom, pub. 1903, reached #7 in July 1903
Will Heelan w, J Fred Helf m
Tascott, vv stage
Josephine Gassman, vv stage
Lydia Hall, vv stage

WHEN IT'S ALL GOIN' OUT AND NOTHIN' COMIN' IN (22)
J W Stern, pub. 1902, reached #3 in February 1903
George Walker w, Bert Williams m
Bert Williams & George Walker, vv stage, 01/02 Vic 994 disk
Lottie Gilson, vv stage
Elizabeth Murray, vv stage

WHERE ARE THE FRIENDS OF OTHER DAYS?
Howley, H & D, pub. 1903, reached #8 in December 1903
Paul Dresser w & m
Dick Jose, vv stage
Kitty Mitchell, vv stage

WHY DON'T YOU GO, GO, GO (48)
Shapiro, B, pub. 1903, reached #9 in April 1903
William Jerome w, Jean Schwartz m
Wood & Ray, vv stage
other vv singers

YOU CAN'T FOOL ALL THE PEOPLE ALL OF THE TIME
J W Stern, pub. 1903, reached #18 in September 1903
Shepard N Edmonds w & m
Featured in NANCY BROWN, show (opened 02/03)
Marie Cahill, sung in show
Arthur Collins 08/03 Ed 8460 cyl, 09/03 Vic 2407 disk

YOU'RE AS WELCOME AS THE FLOWERS IN MAY (49)
J W Stern, pub. 1902, reached #13 in December 1903
Dan J Sullivan w & m
John W Myers 12/03 Col 1600 disk, 12/03 Col 32314 cyl
vv singers

1904

AIN'T IT FUNNY WHAT A DIFFERENCE JUST A FEW HOURS MAKE? (49)
Witmark, pub. 1903, reached #16 in June 1904
Henry M Blossom w, Alfred G Robyn m
Featured in THE YANKEE CONSUL, show (opened 02/04)
Raymond Hitchcock, sung in show
Billy Murray 05/04 Col 1790 disk, 06/04 Vic 2731 disk

ALEXANDER (DON'T YOU LOVE YOUR BABY NO MORE?) (17)
H Von Tilzer, pub. 1904, reached #4 in October 1904
Andrew Sterling w, Harry Von Tilzer m
Billy Murray Φ 08/04 Ed 8765 cyl
McIntyre & Heath, vv stage
May Ward, vv stage
Bob Roberts 09/04 Vic 2988 disk, 10/04 Col 32563 cyl

ALWAYS LEAVE THEM LAUGHING (47)
F A Mills, pub. 1903, reached #15 in March 1904
George M Cohan w & m
Featured in MOTHER GOOSE, show (opened 12/03)
Harry Bulger, sung in show
vv singers

ANY RAGS? (27)
W Jacobs, pub. 1902, reached #10 in January 1904
Thomas S Allen w & m
Dan Coleman, vv stage
Arthur Collins Φ 12/03 Ed 8525 cyl, 01/04 Vic 2519 disk, 02/04 Col 1669 disk
Tascott, vv stage

BACK, BACK, BACK TO BALTIMORE (9)
Shapiro, Remick, pub. 1904, reached #1 in January 1905
Harry H Williams w, Egbert Van Alstyne m
Clarice Vance, vv stage
Bob Roberts Φ 11/04 Col 32564 cyl, 12/04 Vic 4134 disk
Elizabeth Murray, vv stage
Tascott, vv stage
Collins & Harlan Φ 01/05 Ed 8860 cyl

BECAUSE YOU WERE AN OLD SWEETHEART OF MINE (19)
Witmark, pub. 1901, reached #13 in July 1904
Harry I Robinson w, Maurice L Jacobs m
Lottie Gilson, vv stage
May Bryant, vv stage
John W Myers 12/03 Col 1577 disk, 12/03 Col 32287 cyl

A BIT O' BLARNEY (14)
Sol Bloom, pub. 1904, reached #2 in September 1904
Will Heelan w, J Fred Helf m
Blanche Ring, vv stage
Josie Sabel, vv stage
Pryor's Orch Φ 08/04 Vic 2824 disk
Billy Murray 10/04 Vic 2939 disk

BLUE BELL (1)
F B Haviland ΦΦΦ, pub. 1904, reached #1 in May 1904
Edward Madden w, Theodore F Morse m
Harry Macdonough/Haydn Quartet Φ 06/04 Vic 2750 disk
Byron Harlan & Frank Stanley Φ 04/04 Ed 8655 cyl
Helen Trix, vv stage
Anna Driver, vv stage
Albert Campbell 03/04 Zono 5808 disk

THE BURNING OF ROME (33)
E T Paull, pub. 1903, reached #7 in March 1904
Edward T Paull m
Pryor's Orch 06/04 Vic 2742 disk
other concert bands, band concerts

BY THE WATERMELON VINE, LINDY LOU (11)
W Jacobs, pub. 1904, reached #6 in January 1905
Thomas S Allen w & m
Ernest Hogan, vv stage
Bob Roberts 11/04 Col 1882 disk
Harry Macdonough 01/05 Vic 4137 disk
Gladys Fisher, vv stage
Alabama Comedy Four, vv stage

COME TAKE A TRIP IN MY AIRSHIP (6)
C K Harris, pub. 1904, reached #1 in September 1904
Ren Shields w, George Evans m
George Evans, vv stage
Edna Wallace Hopper, vv stage
Ethel Robinson, vv stage
Billy Murray Φ 10/04 Vic 2986 disk, 01/05 Ed 8874 cyl
John W Myers 11/04 Col 1878 disk

DOWN IN THE VALE OF SHENANDOAH (44)
C K Harris, pub. 1904, reached #18 in November 1904
Charles K Harris w & m
Harry Macdonough 09/04 Ed 8788 cyl, 11/04 Vic 4051 disk
West's Minstrels, vv stage
Marie Welsh, vv stage

DOWN ON THE BRANDYWINE
Shapiro, Remick, pub. 1904, reached #18 in Sept 1904
Vincent Bryan w, James B Mullen m
Collins & Harlan 06/04 Ed 8712 cyl, 07/04 Vic 2754 disk, 08/04 Col 32551 cyl, 12/04 Col 3027 disk
Artie Hall, vv stage
Mamie Lincoln Pixley, vv stage

EGYPT (32)
J W Stern, pub. 1903, reached #5 in July 1904
Clare Kummer w & m
Featured in THE GIRL FROM KAY'S, show (opened 11/03)
Sallie Fisher, sung in show
Harry Tally 09/04 Col 1853 disk, 12/04 Vic 4148 disk

FOR SALE, A BABY (31)
C K Harris, pub. 1903, reached #8 in May 1904
Charles K Harris w & m
Byron G Harlan 03/04 Ed 8626 cyl, 05/04 Vic 2683 disk, 08/04 Col 1827 disk
Bennett & Young, vv stage
West's Minstrels, vv stage

THE GONDOLIER (23)
Shapiro, Remick, pub. 1903, reached #6 in June 1904
Harry Williams w, W C Powell m
Pryor's Orch 05/04 Vic 2652 disk
Harry Macdonough 06/04 Vic 2753 disk
Harry Tally 06/04 Col 1784 disk, 06/04 Zono 5896 disk

GOODBYE, ELIZA JANE (16)
H Von Tilzer, pub. 1903, reached #3 in February 1904
Andrew Sterling w, Harry Von Tilzer m
McIntyre & Heath, vv stage
Arthur Collins Φ 10/03 Ed 8515 cyl
Bob Roberts 08/04 Vic 2832 disk, 08/04 Col 32539 cyl

GOODBYE, LITTLE GIRL, GOODBYE (5)
Witmark, pub. 1904, reached #1 in October 1904
Will D Cobb w, Gus Edwards m
Emma Carus, vv stage
Mina Hickman 09/04 Vic 2908 disk
Byron G Harlan 08/04 Col 1840 disk, 08/04 Col 32546 cyl
Raymond & Clark, vv stage

GOODBYE, MY LADY LOVE (7)
C K Harris, pub. 1904, reached #2 in May 1904
Joe Howard w & m
Joe Howard, vv stage (Later: 1936 Voc 3357)
Blanche Ring, vv stage
Ida Emerson, vv stage
Harry Macdonough Φ 05/04 Ed 8684 cyl, 08/04 Vic 2851 disk
Pryor's Band 06/04 Vic 2744 disk

HANNAH, WON'T YOU OPEN THAT DOOR? (42)
H Von Tilzer, pub. 1904, reached #9 in June 1904
Andrew Sterling w, Harry Von Tilzer m
Tascott, vv stage
Elizabeth Murray, vv stage
Arthur Collins 03/04 Ed 8637 cyl, 05/04 Col 1800 disk
Bob Roberts 04/04 Vic 2627 disk

HERE'S YOUR HAT, WHAT'S YOUR HURRY?
Witmark, pub. 1903, reached #17 in March 1904
Bartley Costello w, Nat Osborne m
Byron Sisters, vv stage
Delmore & Darrell, vv stage
Bob Roberts 07/04 Ed 8743 cyl

I CAN'T DO THE SUM (25)
Witmark, pub. 1903, reached #4 in March 1904
Glen MacDonough w, Victor Herbert m
Featured in BABES IN TOYLAND, show (opened 10/03)
Mabel Barrison, sung in show
Billy Murray 02/04 Col 1687 disk
Sam Dudley/Haydn Quartet 05/04 Vic 2722 disk

I MAY BE CRAZY, BUT I AIN'T NO FOOL (15)
Attucks, pub. 1904, reached #1 in December 1904
Alex Rogers w & m
Bert Williams, vv stage
Lew Dockstader, vv stage
Bob Roberts Φ 11/04 Col 1889 disk, 11/04 Ed 8847 cyl, 12/04 Vic 4108 disk
Tascott, vv stage

I'M ON THE WATER WAGON NOW (45)
Witmark, pub. 1903, reached #10 in February 1904
Paul West w, John W Bratton m
Featured in THE OFFICE BOY, show (opened 11/03)
Frank Daniels, sung in show
Bob Roberts 01/04 Col 1644 disk
Billy Murray 04/04 Vic 2662 disk

I'VE GOT A FEELIN' FOR YOU (4)
F B Haviland, pub. 1904, reached #3 in April 1904
Edward Madden w, Theodore F Morse m
Tascott, vv stage
Hazel Burt, vv stage
Arthur Collins Φ 04/04 Ed 8661 cyl, 05/04 Zono 5889 disk
Austin Sisters, vv stage

IDA (SWEET AS APPLE CIDER) (28)
J W Stern, pub. 1903, reached #14 in July 1904
(Also reached #11 in January 1928)
Eddie Leonard & Eddie Munson w & m
Eddie Leonard, vv stage
Elizabeth Murray, vv stage
Nellie Howe, vv stage

IN ZANZIBAR (22)
Shapiro, Remick, pub. 1904, reached #4 in April 1904
Will D Cobb w, Gus Edwards m
Featured in THE MEDAL AND THE MAID, show (opened 01/04)
Emma Carus, sung in show, 04/04 Col 1763 disk
Harry Macdonough 04/04 Ed 8651 cyl, 05/04 Vic 2690 disk
Billy Murray 04/04 Col 1722 disk

JUST A GLEAM OF HEAVEN IN HER EYES (48)
C K Harris, pub. 1904, reached #14 in August 1904
Charles K Harris w & m
Byron G Harlan 07/04 Ed 8733 cyl
Helen Bertram, vv stage
Pauline Hall, vv stage

KARAMA (36)
L Feist, pub. 1904, reached #12 in November 1904
Mabel McKinley w & m
Mabel McKinley, vv stage
Vess Ossman 09/04 Ed 8780 cyl
Pryor's Orch 01/05 Vic 4133 disk

KATE KEARNEY (29)
Witmark, pub. 1904, reached #12 in January 1905
J Everett Fay w, James B Oliver m
Blanche Ring, vv stage
Phyllis Allen, vv stage
Harry Macdonough 02/05 Vic 4178 disk

LAZY MOON (12)
J W Stern, pub. 1903, reached #6 in October 1904
Bob Cole w, J Rosamond Johnson m
George Primrose, vv stage
Edna Wallace Hopper, vv stage
Billy Murray 10/05 Vic 4471 disk

A LITTLE BOY CALLED TAPS (26)
F B Haviland, pub. 1904, reached #8 in December 1904
Edward Madden w, Theodore F Morse m
Kathryn Miley, vv stage
Byron G Harlan 11/04 Ed 8846 cyl, 01/05 Vic 4135 disk, 03/05 Zono 99 disk
Madeline Clark, vv stage

THE LITTLE CHURCH WHERE YOU AND I WERE WED (24)
W Rolfe, pub. 1903, reached #19 in November 1904
Walter Rolfe w & m
Reese Prosser, vv stage
George Hammond, vv stage

THE MAN WITH THE LADDER AND THE HOSE (40)
American Advance, pub. 1904, reached #9 in August 1904
T Mayo Geary, Harry J Breen & Bartley Costello w & m
Maxwell & Simpson, vv stage
Billy Murray 08/04 Vic 2848 disk
William H Thompson 07/04 Ed 8728 cyl

MARCH OF THE TOYS (41)
Witmark, pub. 1903, reached #15 in February 1904
Glen MacDonough w, Victor Herbert m
Featured in BABES IN TOYLAND, show (opened 10/03)
William Norris & Mabel Barrison, sung in show
vv singers

MEET ME IN ST. LOUIS, LOUIS (8)
F A Mills, pub. 1904, reached #1 in July 1904
Andrew Sterling w, Kerry Mills m
(Also reached #19 in January 1945)
All-time pop standard
Ethel Levy, vv stage
Lottie Gilson, vv stage
Billy Murray Φ 06/04 Col 1792 disk, 07/04 Ed 8722 cyl, 08/04 Vic 2850 disk
Sam Dudley 08/04 Vic 2807 disk
John W Myers 09/04 Col 1848 disk

NAVAJO (3)
Shapiro, B, pub. 1903, reached #1 in March 1904
Harry H Williams w, Egbert Van Alstyne m
Featured in NANCY BROWN, show (opened 02/03)
Marie Cahill, sung in show
Emma Carus, vv stage, 04/04 Col 1765 disk
Billy Murray Φ 02/04 Col 1655 disk
Harry Macdonough 03/04 Ed 8640 cyl, 04/04 Vic 2656 disk
John W Myers 02/04 Col 1721 disk

PLEASE COME AND PLAY IN MY YARD (13)
F B Haviland, pub. 1904, reached #3 in January 1905
Edward Madden w, Theodore F Morse m
Madge O'Brien, vv stage
Billy Murray 10/04 Vic 2987 disk
Byron G Harlan 09/04 Ed 8778 cyl
Morse Trio, vv stage

SEMINOLE (30)
Shapiro, Remick, pub. 1904, reached #6 in September 1904
Harry H Williams w, Egbert Van Alstyne m
Emma Carus, vv stage
Blanche Ring, vv stage
Harry Tally 09/04 Col 1852 disk, 10/04 Vic 2937 disk, 01/04 Ed 8808 cyl

SWEET ADELINE (2)
Witmark, pub. 1903, reached #2 in February 1905
Richard Gerard Husch w, Harry Armstrong m
Quaker City Quartet, vv stage
Columbia Male Quartet[1] Φ 10/04 Col 32584 cyl
Haydn Quartet Φ 10/04 Vic 2934 disk
Albert Campbell & James F Harrison 05/04 Ed 8677 cyl
Messenger Boys Trio, vv stage

THE SWEETEST FLOWER THAT GROWS IN TENNESSEE (38)
C K Harris, pub. 1903, reached #19 in February 1904
Ren Shields w, George Evans m
Featured in IN THE GOOD OLD SUMMERTIME, revue (1903)
George Evans, sung in revue
Charlotte Ravenscroft, vv stage
Joe Natus 08/03 Zono 5884 disk, 04/04 Vic 2666 disk

THE SWEETEST GIRL IN DIXIE (37)
Shapiro, Remick, pub. 1903, reached #17 in August 1904
James O'Dea w, Robert J Adams m
Harry Macdonough 04/04 Vic 2657 disk, 04/04 Ed 8646 cyl, 12/04 Col 31513 cyl
Marie Laurent, vv stage

TEASING (10)
New York Mus Co, pub. 1904, reached #1 in December 1904
Cecil Mack w, Albert Von Tilzer m
Featured in THE SOUTHERNERS, show (opened 05/04)
Davis & Bentley, sung in show
Billy Murray Φ 09/04 Col 1857 disk, 11/04 Vic 4054 disk
Harry & Eva Puck, vv stage
Bob Roberts 10/04 Ed 8804 cyl
Harry Macdonough/Haydn Quartet 12/04 Vic 4065 disk

TOYLAND (21)
Witmark, pub. 1903, reached #6 in March 1904
Glen MacDonough w, Victor Herbert m
Featured in BABES IN TOYLAND, show (opened 10/03)
Bessie Wynn, sung in show
Corinne Morgan & Billy Murray 06/04 Vic 2721 disk
Rogers' Orch[2] 06/04 Vic 2737 disk

THE TROUBADOUR (46)
Shapiro, Remick, pub. 1904, reached #16 in November 1904
Harry H Williams w, W C Powell m
Viola Gillette, vv stage
Hager's Orch 01/05 Zono 6079 disk

UNDER THE ANHEUSER BUSCH (20)
H Von Tilzer, pub. 1903, reached #4 in June 1904
Andrew Sterling w, Harry Von Tilzer m
Josie Sabel, vv stage
Billy Murray Φ 01/04 Ed 8575 cyl, 02/04 Col 1676 disk, 04/04 Vic 2639 disk
May Booth, vv stage
Elizabeth Murray, vv stage
Collins & Harlan 05/04 Vic 2668 disk, 04/04 Col 1742 disk, 04/04 Col 32409 cyl

UNTER DEN LINDEN (39)
Sol Bloom, pub. 1904, reached #8 in July 1904
Arthur Penn m
Pryor's Orch 07/04 Vic 2780 disk
Concert bands and orchestras

WHEN I'M AWAY FROM YOU, DEAR
Howley & Dresser, pub. 1904, reached #17 in May 1904
Paul Dresser w & m
Dick Jose, vv stage, 02/04 Vic 31154 disk
Jessie Bartlett Davis, stage

WHEN THE SUNSET TURNS THE OCEAN'S BLUE TO GOLD (18)
J W Stern, pub. 1902, reached #5 in January 1904
Eva Fern Buckner w, Henry W Petrie m
Manuel Romain, vv stage
Byron G Harlan 03/04 Ed 8645 cyl, 03/05 Col 3100 disk

WHERE THE SILV'RY COLORADO WENDS ITS WAY (35)
T R Ingram, pub. 1901, reached #11 in May 1904
(Also reached #15 in July 1902)
C H Scoggins w, Charles Avril m
Reese Prosser, vv stage
Marion Cook, vv stage

Y.M.C.A. MARCH (34)
W H Anstead, pub. 1903, reached #18 in May 1904
W H Anstead m
Concert bands

YOU NEVER SPOKE TO ME LIKE THAT BEFORE (50)
C K Harris, pub. 1903, reached #19 in May 1904
Charles K Harris w & m
Kelly & Gallot, vv stage
Nellie Hanley, vv stage

YOUR MOTHER WANTS YOU HOME, BOY (43)
Howley & Dresser, pub. 1903, reached #11 in March 1904
Paul Dresser w & m
Dick Jose, vv stage, 04/04 Vic 2632 disk
Haverly's Minstrels, vv stage
Byron G Harlan 02/04 Ed 8600 cyl

[1]The Columbia Male Quartet eventually became known as the Peerless Quartet.
[2]Rogers' Orch was actually Pryor's Band.

1905

ABSINTHE FRAPPE (41)
Witmark, pub. 1904, reached #12 in April 1905
Glen MacDonough w, Victor Herbert m
Featured in IT HAPPENED IN NORDLAND, show (opened 12/04)
Harry Davenport, sung in show
Billy Murray 11/05 Vic 2048[1]

AL FRESCO (43)
Witmark, pub. 1904, reached #16 in January 1905
Victor Herbert m
Featured in IT HAPPENED IN NORDLAND, show (opened 12/04)
Pryor's Orch 03/05 Vic 4247
Prince's Band 03/05 Col 32648 cyl, 07/05 Col 3194

BRIGHT EYES, GOODBYE (49)
J H Remick, pub. 1905, reached #17 in July 1905
Harry H Williams w, Egbert Van Alstyne m
Louise Dresser, vv stage
Empire City Quartet, vv stage
Byron G Harlan 10/05 Vic 4464

CARISSIMA (12)
Sol Bloom, pub. 1904, reached #5 in June 1905
Arthur Penn w & m
Featured in THE RED FEATHER, show (opened 11/03)
Emma Carus, vv stage
Cherida Simpson, sung in show
Maude Williams, vv stage

CENTRAL, GIVE ME BACK MY DIME (50)
C K Harris, pub. 1905, reached #17 in September 1905
Joe Howard w & m
Joe Howard, vv stage
Kathryn Trayer, vv stage
Collins & Harlan 10/05 Vic 4484, 01/06 Zon 340

COAX ME (45)
H Von Tilzer, pub. 1904, reached #17 in March 1905
Andrew Sterling w, Harry Von Tilzer m
Lottie Gilson, vv stage
Collins & Harlan 02/05 Vic 4174, 02/05 Col 3052, 02/05 Ed 8907 cyl, 04/05 Zono 114

COLLEGE LIFE (18)
F B Haviland, pub. 1905, reached #10 in October 1905
Porter Emerson Browne w, Henry Frantzen m
Pryor's Orch 06/05 Vic 4318
Kelly & Reno, vv stage
Billy Murray, vv stage (Later: 1906 Vic 4721)

COME OVER ON MY VERANDA
W Jacobs, pub. 1905, reached #20 in July 1905[5]
John Kemble w, Lester Keith m
Harry Macdonough 09/05 Vic 2047[1]
Julian Eltinge, vv stage

THE DAY THAT YOU GREW COLDER
Paul Dresser P C, pub. 1905, reached #18 in April 1905
Paul Dresser w & m
Dick Jose, vv stage, 03/05 Vic 31348

DEARIE (2)
J W Stern, pub. 1905, reached #1 in March 1906
Clare Kummer w & m
Featured in SARGENT BRUE, show (opened 04/05)
Sallie Fisher, sung in show
Corinne Morgan/Haydn Quartet Φ 08/05 Vic 4396, 08/05 Vic 31408
Harry Macdonough 08/05 Ed 9054 cyl
Billy Murray 10/05 Zono 6186
The Three Troubadours, vv stage

DOWN WHERE THE SILV'RY MOHAWK FLOWS (19)
J W Stern, pub. 1905, reached #14 in September 1905
Monroe Rosenfeld w, John Heinzman & Otto Heinzman m
Kelly & Violette, vv stage
Harry Macdonough/Haydn Quartet 08/05 Vic 4378
Quaker City Quartet, vv stage

EV'RY LITTLE BIT HELPS (48)
H Von Tilzer, pub. 1904, reached #17 in June 1905
George Whiting w, Fred Fisher m
Arthur Collins 04/05 Zono 6129, 06/05 Col 32725 cyl, 07/05 Col 3196
Ada Jones & Len Spencer 06/05 Col 32730 cyl, 06/05 Ed 9016 cyl, 07/05 Col 3190

EVERYBODY WORKS BUT FATHER (9)
Helf & Hager, pub. 1905, reached #3 in October 1905
Jean Havez w & m
Lew Dockstader, vv stage, 11/05 Col 3251
Billy Murray Φ 12/05 Vic 4519
Bob Roberts 10/05 Ed 9100 cyl, 10/05 Zono 258, 12/05 Col 32830 cyl
Sousa's Band, band concerts

GIVE MY REGARDS TO BROADWAY (8)
F A Mills, pub. 1904, reached #3 in June 1905
George M Cohan w & m
Featured in LITTLE JOHNNY JONES, show (opened 11/04)
All time pop standard
George M Cohan, sung in show
Billy Murray Φ 05/05 Zono 140, 06/05 Col 3165, 09/05 Ed 9095 cyl
Sam Dudley 08/05 Vic 4385
vv singers

GOODBYE, FLO (47)
F A Mills, pub. 1904, reached Top 30 in February 1905
George M Cohan w & m
Featured in LITTLE JOHNNY JONES, show (opened 11/04)
Ethel Levey, sung in show
Billy Murray 01/06 Vic 4545

GOODBYE, SIS
F B Haviland, pub. 1904, reached #19 in May 1905
Will D Cobb w, Theodore F Morse m
Madge O'Brien, vv stage
Morse Trio, vv stage
Billy Murray 03/05 Col 3064, 04/05 Col 32686 cyl

HE'S ME PAL (14)
Witmark, pub. 1905, reached #2 in May 1905
Vincent Bryan w, Gus Edwards m
Eleanor Falk, vv stage
Ada Jones 03/05 Ed 8957 cyl, 08/05 Vic 4386
May Ward, vv stage
Violet Staley, vv stage

HONEY, I'M WAITING (42)
L Feist, pub. 1905, reached #9 in May 1905
Ted S Barron w & m
Louise Taylor, vv stage
Delmore & Darrell, vv stage
The Three Kuhns, vv stage

HOW'D YOU LIKE TO SPOON WITH ME? (15)
T B Harms, pub. 1905, reached #4 in December 1905
Edward Laska w, Jerome Kern m
Featured in THE EARL AND THE GIRL, show (opened 11/05)
Victor Morley & Georgia Caine, sung in show
Corinne Morgan/Haydn Quartet Φ 01/06 Vic 4532
Billy Murray 01/06 Zono 344

I'M TRYING SO HARD TO FORGET YOU (23)
C K Harris, pub. 1904, reached #3 in April 1905
Charles K Harris w & m
Harlan & Stanley 01/05 Ed 8870 cyl, 04/05 Col 3091
Cheridah Simpson, vv stage
Lydia Barry, vv stage

IN DEAR OLD GEORGIA (10)
J H Remick, pub. 1905, reached #5 in January 1906
Harry H Williams w, Egbert Van Alstyne m
Empire City Quartet, vv stage
Quaker City Quartet, vv stage
Kelly & Violette, vv stage
Haydn Quartet Φ 12/05 Vic 4522
Frank Stanley Φ 11/05 Col 3256, 12/05 Vic 4503

IN THE SHADE OF THE OLD APPLE TREE (1)
Shapiro, Remick ΦΦΦ, pub. 1905, reached #1 in April 1905
Harry H Williams w, Egbert Van Alstyne m
Kelly & Violette, vv stage
Louise Dresser, vv stage
Henry Burr Φ 04/05 Ed 8958 cyl[2], 06/05 Vic 4338
Harry Macdonough/Haydn Quartet Φ 06/05 Vic 4337
Albert Campbell Φ 04/05 Col 32664 cyl, 06/05 Col 3153

JIM JUDSON (FROM THE TOWN OF HACKENSACK)
Paul Dresser P C, pub. 1905, reached #18 in May 1905
Paul Dresser w & m
Arthur Collins 09/05 Col 3213, 09/05 Imper 44479
vv singers

JOLLY ME ALONG (36)
W C Polla, pub. 1904, reached #10 in February 1905
C P McDonald w, Albert Gumble m
Flo Adler, vv stage
Rocca Vocca, vv stage

KEEP A LITTLE COZY CORNER IN YOUR HEART FOR ME (6)
F B Haviland, pub. 1905, reached #1 in August 1905
Jack Drislane w, Theodore F Morse m
Flo Allen, vv stage
Hazel Burt, vv stage
Ada Jones 08/05 Ed 9060 cyl
Harry Macdonough/Haydn Quartet 08/05 Vic 4390
Lillian Held, vv stage

THE LEADER OF THE GERMAN BAND (17)
F B Haviland, pub. 1905, reached #7 in November 1905
Edward Madden w, Theodore F Morse m
Mamie Remington, vv stage
Sheppard & Ward, vv stage
Collins & Harlan 10/05 Ed 9115 cyl, 01/06 Vic 4555

LIFE'S A FUNNY PROPOSITION AFTER ALL (33)
F A Mills, pub. 1904, reached #9 in March 1905
George M Cohan w & m
Featured in LITTLE JOHNNY JONES, show (opened 11/04)
George M Cohan, sung in show (Later: 1911 Vic 60042)
vv singers

LONGING FOR YOU (30)
F B Haviland, pub. 1905, reached #9 in May 1905
Jack Drislane w, Theodore F Morse m
Madge O'Brien, vv stage
Byron G Harlan 04/05 Ed 8961 cyl, 07/05 Col 3187
Morse Trio, vv stage

MAMMA'S BOY (29)
Helf & Hager, pub. 1904, reached #3 in February 1905
Harry Sinclair w, J Fred Helf m
Lew Dockstader, vv stage
Byron G Harlan 02/05 Col 3045, 02/05 Ed 8914 cyl, 03/05 Vic 4207

MOONLIGHT (SERENADE) (20)
J H Remick, pub. 1905, reached #6 in June 1905
James O'Dea w, Neil Moret m
Kelly & Violette, vv stage
Marie Laurent, vv stage
Pryor's Orch 06/05 Vic 4319
Sousa's Band, band concerts, 12/05 Vic 4528

MY IRISH MOLLY-O (5)
J H Remick, pub. 1905, reached #1 in September 1905
William Jerome w, Jean Schwartz m
Featured in SARGENT BRUE, show (opened 04/05)
Blanche Ring, sung in show
Nellie Beaumont, vv stage
Arthur Collins Φ 06/05 Vic 4371
Billy Murray Φ 08/05 Ed 9063 cyl, 08/05 Zono 219
Harry Tally Φ 09/05 Col 3238, 02/06 Vic 4580

NOBODY (27)
Attucks, pub. 1905, reached #7 in September 1905
(Also reached #19 in September 1906)
Alex Rogers w, Bert Williams m
Bert Williams, vv stage (Later: 1906 Col 3423)
Arthur Collins 08/05 Vic 4391, 09/05 Ed 9084 cyl, 11/05 Col 3264
Lew Dockstader, vv stage

PAL OF MINE (37)
L Feist, pub. 1905, reached #10 in May 1905
Bartley Costello w, Joseph S Nathan m
George Gaskin, vv stage
Frances Gerard, vv stage
Frank Stanley 06/05 Vic 4530

THE PREACHER AND THE BEAR (24)
A Longbrake, pub. 1904, reached #5 in September 1905
Joe Arzonia w & m
Arthur Collins ΦΦ 04/05 Zono 120, 05/05 Ed 9000 cyl, 06/05 Col 3146, 06/05 Col 32720 cyl, 09/05 Vic 4431

SHAME ON YOU (28)
J W Stern, pub. 1904, reached #13 in January 1905
Chris Smith w, John Larkins m
Tascott, vv stage, 07/05 Ed 9033 cyl
Lew Dockstader, vv stage
Josephine Gassman, vv stage
Chris Smith, vv stage
Len Spencer & Billy Murray 01/05 Vic 4153

SHE WAITS BY THE DEEP BLUE SEA (32)
F B Haviland, pub. 1905, reached #7 in July 1905
Edward Madden w, Gus Edwards m
Leola Pearl, vv stage
John W Myers 07/05 Vic 4341
Irving Gillette[3] 05/05 Ed 9032 cyl

THE TALE OF THE TURTLE DOVE (34)
Witmark, pub. 1904, reached #5 in March 1905
Frank Pixley w, Gustav Luders m
Featured in WOODLAND, show (opened 11/04)
Margaret Sayre, sung in show
Billy Murray 01/05 Zono 6076
Harry Macdonough 04/05 Col 32687 cyl

TAMMANY (7)
Witmark, pub. 1905, reached #2 in June 1905
Vincent Bryan w, Gus Edwards m
Featured in FANTANA, show (opened 01/05)
Jeff DeAngelis, sung in show
Collins & Harlan Φ 05/05 Ed 8979 cyl, 07/05 Vic 4373, 08/05 Zono 223
Eddie Foy, vv stage
Pryor's Orch Φ 07/05 Vic 31397, 12/05 Vic 4526

TELL ME WITH YOUR EYES (46)
H Von Tilzer, pub. 1904, reached #17 in March 1905
Arthur Lamb w, Harry Von Tilzer m
Harry Macdonough/Haydn Quartet 02/05 Vic 4170
Columbia Male Quartet[4] 05/05 Col 32703 cyl

THERE'S A DARK MAN COMING WITH A BUNDLE (22)
Helf & Hager, pub. 1904, reached #2 in January 1905
Bert Leighton & Frank Leighton w & m
Lew Dockstader, vv stage
Arthur Collins 02/05 Col 32622 cyl, 04/05 Col 3077
Bob Roberts 01/05 Zono 6078, 01/05 Ed 8857 cyl
Viola Gillette, vv stage

THE TOWN WHERE I WAS BORN (39)
J H Remick, pub. 1905, reached #13 in January 1906
Paul Dresser w & m
John P Curran, vv stage
John W Myers 03/06 Imperial 44706

VIOLETTE (44)
P J Howley, pub. 1905, reached #16 in September 1905
Dorothy Jardon w, James B Mullen m
Della Fox, vv stage
Joe Natus, vv stage
Byron Harlan & Frank Stanley 08/05 Ed 9061 cyl

WHAT THE BRASS BAND PLAYED (25)
F B Haviland, pub. 1904, reached #4 in March 1905
Jack Drislane w, Theodore F Morse m
Helen Trix, vv stage
Bob Roberts, vv stage
Billy Murray 02/05 Vic 4151, 03/05 Zono 6104
John W Myers 02/05 Col 32614 cyl, 03/05 Col 3030

WHAT YOU GOIN' TO DO WHEN THE RENT COMES 'ROUND? (RUFUS RASTUS JOHNSON BROWN) (11)
H Von Tilzer, pub. 1905, reached #4 in November 1905
Andrew Sterling w, Harry Von Tilzer m
Arthur Collins ΦΦ 09/05 Vic 4432, 10/05 Col 3250, 10/05 Ed 9111 cyl, 11/05 Zono 298
Emma Carus, vv stage

WHEN THE BEES ARE IN THE HIVE (40)
F A Mills, pub. 1904, reached #13 in February 1905
Alfred Bryan w, Kerry Mills m
Macdonough & Bieling/Haydn Quartet 03/05 Vic 4230
Dietrich & Sheridan, vv stage
Byron G Harlan 05/05 Zono 148

WHEN THE BELL IN THE LIGHTHOUSE RINGS, DING DONG (26)
J W Stern, pub. 1905, reached #6 in October 1905
Arthur Lamb w, Alfred Solman m
Wilford Glenn, stage (Later: 1923 Vic 19116)
Gus Reed, stage
Frank Stanley 10/05 Vic 31426, 01/06 Col 3305

WHEN THE HARVEST MOON IS SHINING ON THE RIVER (13)
J W Stern, pub. 1904, reached #9 in June 1905
Arthur Lamb w, S R Henry m
Manuel Romain, vv stage, 12/04 Col 3045
Byron G Harlan 04/05 Vic 4254
Knickerbocker Four, vv stage

WHERE THE MORNING GLORIES TWINE AROUND THE DOOR (16)
H Von Tilzer, pub. 1905, reached #6 in January 1906
Andrew Sterling w, Harry Von Tilzer m
Byron G Harlan Φ 11/05 Col 32814 cyl, 12/05 Col 3282, 04/06 Vic 4616
Harry & Eva Puck, vv stage
Daphne Pollard, vv stage

WHERE THE SOUTHERN ROSES GROW (35)
F B Haviland, pub. 1904, reached #7 in April 1905
Richard H Buck w, Theodore F Morse m
Harry Macdonough/Haydn Quartet 04/05 Vic 4277
May Alpine & Picks, vv stage
Edison Male Quartet 04/05 Ed 8976 cyl

THE WHISTLER AND HIS DOG (31)
Carl Fischer, pub. 1905, reached #12 in November 1905
Arthur Pryor m
Pryor's Band 09/05 Vic 4418, 10/05 Ed 9107 cyl
Prince's Band 12/05 Col 3290
Zon-o-phone Concert Band 01/06 Zono 332

A WOMAN IS ONLY A WOMAN, BUT A GOOD CIGAR IS A SMOKE
Witmark, pub. 1905, reached #18 in December 1905
Harry B Smith w, Victor Herbert m
Featured in MISS DOLLY DOLLARS, show (opened 09/05)
Melville Stewart, sung in show
vv singers

WON'T YOU FONDLE ME? (38)
Shapiro, Remick, pub. 1904, reached #12 in March 1905
Jack Kendis & Herman Paley w & m
Grace LaRue, vv stage
Arthur Collins 03/05 Ed 8944 cyl
Bob Roberts & Billy Murray 05/05 Vic 4301, 05/05 Zono 149
Josephine Aimsley, vv stage

WOULD YOU CARE? (3)
C K Harris ΦΦΦ, pub. 1905, reached #1 in October 1905
Charles K Harris w & m
J Aldrich Libbey, vv stage
Byron G Harlan Φ 09/05 Vic 4425
Kathryn Trayer, vv stage
Kelly & Violette, vv stage
Irving Gillette[3] 08/05 Ed 9070

YANKEE DOODLE BOY (4)
F A Mills, pub. 1904, reached #1 in March 1905
George M Cohan w & m
Featured in LITTLE JOHNNY JONES, show (opened 11/04)
All-time patriotic standard
George M Cohan, sung in show
Billy Murray ΦΦ 01/05 Zono 75, 02/05 Col 3051, 02/05 Ed 8910, 03/05 Vic 4229
vv singers

YANKEE GRIT (21)
L Feist, pub. 1905, reached #7 in August 1905
Abe Holzmann m
Pryor's Band 08/05 Vic 4379
Columbia Orch 09/05 Col 32769 cyl
Edison Concert Band 10/05 Ed 9116

[1]Victor 2000's from 1905 were 7-inch records.
[2]Burr's Edison recording was listed as Irving Gillette.
[3]Irving Gillette was a pseudonym for Henry Burr.
[4]The Columbia Male Quartet eventually became known (in 1906) as the Peerless Quartet.
[5]Reached #20 on monthly chart only.

1906

AFTER THEY GATHER THE HAY (31)
J W Stern, pub. 1906, reached #19 in July 1906
James J Walker w, S R Henry m
Lottie Gilson, vv stage
Harry Macdonough & John H Bieling 07/06 Vic 4710
Jane Allen, vv stage

ALICE, WHERE ART THOU GOING? (40)
J H Remick, pub. 1906, reached #12 in September 1906
Will Heelan w, Albert Gumble m
Della Fox, vv stage
Harry Tally 09/06 Vic 4775
Billy Murray 01/07 Col 3533, 02/07 Ed 9474 cyl

BILL SIMMONS (14)
Witmark, pub. 1906, reached #4 in July 1906
George A Spink w & m
Maude Raymond, vv stage
Artie Hall, vv stage
Arthur Collins Φ 07/06 Vic 4724, 08/06 Col 3438, 08/06 Ed 9320 cyl
Mabel Barrison, vv stage

CAMP MEETIN' TIME (49)
J H Remick, pub. 1906, reached #17 in September 1906
Harry H Williams w, Egbert Van Alstyne m
Ernest Hogan, vv stage
Villiers & Lee, vv stage
Collins & Harlan Φ 12/06 Col 3513, 03/07 Vic 4995

CAN'T YOU SEE I'M LONELY? (28)
L Feist, pub. 1905, reached #10 in March 1906
Felix Feist w, Harry Armstrong m
Emma Carus, vv stage
Billy Murray 11/05 Zono 286
Harry Tally 04/06 Vic 4619, 06/06 Col 3400

CHEER UP, MARY (39)
Cooper, K & P, pub. 1906, reached #4 in December 1906
Jack Kendis & Herman Paley w & m
Empire City Quartet, vv stage
Byron G Harlan 09/06 Zono 536, 11/06 Ed 9403 cyl, 01/07 Vic 4938
Harry Tally 11/06 Col 3501, 11/06 Col 33023 cyl

CHEYENNE (7)
J H Remick, pub. 1906, reached #3 in June 1906
Harry H Williams w, Egbert Van Alstyne m
Irene Franklin, vv stage
Billy Murray 05/06 Internat 2099, 06/06 Col 3389, 08/06 Vic 4719, 10/06 Zono 565
Empire City Quartet, vv stage

CROCODILE ISLE (34)
F B Haviland, pub. 1906, reached #13 in September 1906
Jack Drislane w, Theodore F Morse m
Billy Murray 08/06 Zono 537, 10/06 Vic 4817
York Comedy Four, vv stage
Mills & Morris, vv stage

DADDY'S LITTLE GIRL (43)
F B Haviland, pub. 1905, reached #8 in February 1906
Edward Madden w, Theodore F Morse m
Baby Ethel Shute, vv stage
Byron G Harlan 02/06 Ed 9202 cyl, 03/06 Vic 4604
Kathryn Miley, vv stage

DREAMING, LOVE, OF YOU (38)
C K Harris, pub. 1905, reached Top 30 in April 1906
Charles K Harris w & m
J Aldrich Libbey, vv stage
Byron G Harlan 02/06 Zono 365
Marie Laurent, vv stage

FLYING ARROW (41)
L Feist, pub. 1906, reached #18 in October 1906
Abe Holzmann m
Sousa's Band 07/06 Vic 4718
Edison Military Band 07/06 Ed 9313 cyl

FORTY-FIVE MINUTES FROM BROADWAY (26)
F A Mills, pub. 1905, reached #5 in April 1906
George M Cohan w & m
Featured in FORTY-FIVE MINUTES FROM BROADWAY, show (opened 01/06)
Victor Moore, sung in show
Billy Murray 02/06 American 170, 02/06 Col 32877 cyl, 03/06 Ed 9231 cyl
vv singers

THE GOOD OLD U.S.A. (11)
F B Haviland, pub. 1906, reached #2 in September 1906
Jack Drislane w, Theodore F Morse m
Byron G Harlan Φ 08/06 Col 3463, 09/06 Ed 9350 cyl, 09/06 Zono 539, 09/06 Col 32997 cyl
John W Myers Φ 08/06 Vic 4761
The Kaufman Brothers, vv stage

HE WALKED RIGHT IN, TURNED AROUND, AND WALKED RIGHT OUT AGAIN (21)
F A Mills, pub. 1906, reached #3 in October 1906
Ed Rose w, Maxwell Silver m
Bob Roberts 08/06 Zono 518, 10/06 Vic 4816, 11/06 Col 33020 cyl, 12/06 Col 3519
vv singers

A HOTTENTOT LOVE SONG (45)
J W Stern, pub. 1906, reached #20 in November 1906
Silvio Hein w & m
Featured in MARRYING MARY, show (opened 08/06)
Marie Cahill, sung in show
Bob Cole & J R Johnson, vv stage
Ada Jones 12/06 Vic 4892, 12/06 Col 3523, 12/06 Ed 9418 cyl

I WANT WHAT I WANT WHEN I WANT IT (33)
Witmark, pub. 1905, reached #11 in April 1906
Henry Blossom w, Victor Herbert m
Featured in MLLE. MODISTE, show (opened 12/05)
William Pruette, sung in show
Frank Stanley 04/06 Vic 31509, 07/06 Ed 9307 cyl
George Alexander 07/06 Col 3412

I'LL KEEP A WARM SPOT IN MY HEART FOR YOU (47)
Attucks, pub. 1906, reached #11 in July 1906
George Walker w, Bert Williams m
Featured in ABYSSINIA, show (opened 02/06)
Williams & Walker, vv stage
Aida Overton Walker, sung in show
Cole & Johnson, vv stage

IF A GIRL LIKE YOU LOVED A BOY LIKE ME (23)
Gus Edwards M P C, pub. 1905, reached #4 in April 1906
Will D Cobb w, Gus Edwards m
Harry Macdonough 02/06 Ed 9175 cyl, 03/06 Vic 4601
Lillian Russell, vv stage
other vv singers

IF THE MAN IN THE MOON WERE A COON (12)
Will Rossiter ΦΦΦ, pub. 1905, reached #8 in October 1906
Fred Fisher w & m
Steady seller for several years, peaking in late 1906
Ada Jones Φ 09/06 Imperial 45215, 10/06 Ed 9372 cyl, 02/07 Col 3565, 02/07 Col 33083 cyl, 10/07 Vic 5226
Bob Roberts 02/07 Col 85100 cyl
Chris Bruno, vv stage

IN MY MERRY OLDSMOBILE (4)
Witmark ΦΦΦ, pub. 1905, reached #2 in January 1906
Vincent Bryan w, Gus Edwards m
Billy Murray ΦΦ 10/05 Vic 4467, 02/07 Col 3564
Nellie Beaumont, vv stage
Kathryn Trayer, vv stage
Charlotte Ravenscroft, vv stage
Anna Fitzhugh, vv stage

IOLA (22)
J H Remick, pub. 1906, reached #4 in November 1906
James O'Dea w, Charles L Johnson m
Sousa's Band 11/06 Vic 4862
Bessie Wynn, vv stage
Kelly & Violette, vv stage
Harry Ellis, vv stage

IS EVERYBODY HAPPY?
C K Harris, pub. 1905, reached #18 in May 1906
Frank Williams w, Tom Lemonier & Ernest Hogan m
Featured in RUFUS RASTUS, vv revue (opened 01/06)
Ernest Hogan, sung in revue
Arthur Collins 03/06 Col 3332
Abbie Mitchell, vv stage

JUST A LITTLE ROCKING CHAIR AND YOU (15)
F B Haviland, pub. 1905, reached #5 in May 1906
Bert Fitzgibbon & Jack Drislane w, Theodore F Morse m
Billy Murray/Haydn Quartet 04/06 Vic 31501
Nellie Beaumont, vv stage
The Kaufman Brothers, vv stage
Ada Jones 03/06 Ed 9222 cyl
Flo Allen, vv stage

JUST ONE WORD OF CONSOLATION (44)
C K Harris, pub. 1906, reached Top 30 in June 1906
Frank Williams w, Tom Lemonier m
Featured in RUFUS RASTUS, show (opened 01/06)
Ernest Hogan, sung in show
Frank Coombs, vv stage
Harry Tally 08/06 Vic 31549

KATEY DEAR (50)
New York M P H, pub. 1905, reached #13 in January 1906
Sara Posey w & m
Dick Jose, vv stage, 03/06 Vic 31484
Adele Richie, vv stage

KEEP ON THE SUNNY SIDE (13)
F B Haviland, pub. 1906, reached #2 in May 1906
Jack Drislane w, Theodore F Morse m
Billy Murray Φ 04/06 Vic 31507
Kathryn Miley, vv stage
Byron G Harlan 05/06 Ed 9271 cyl, 06/06 Col 3398
Madge O'Brien, vv stage
Mamie Remington, vv stage

KISS ME AGAIN (48)
Witmark ΦΦΦ, pub. 1905, reached Top 30 in May 1906
(Also reached #17 in October 1916)
Henry Blossom w, Victor Herbert m
Featured in MLLE. MODISTE, show (opened 12/05)
Steady seller 1906-1920
Fritzie Scheff, sung in show

THE LINGER LONGER GIRL (24)
J W Stern, pub. 1906, reached #12 in November 1906
Arthur Lamb w, Alfred Solman m
Maude Lambert, vv stage
Elise Stevenson & Frank Stanley Φ 12/06 Vic 4876, 02/07 Col 33074 cyl, 03/07 Col 3573
The Three Troubadours, vv stage

LOVE ME AND THE WORLD IS MINE (1)
Witmark ΦΦΦ, pub. 1906, reached #1 in December 1906
Dave Reed w, Ernest Ball m
Maude Lambert, vv stage
Truly Shattuck, vv stage
Albert Campbell Φ 10/06 Vic 4823
Henry Burr Φ 11/06 Col 3499, 12/06 Zono 622
Eleanor Falk, vv stage

MARY'S A GRAND OLD NAME (36)
F A Mills, pub. 1905, reached #14 in April 1906
George M Cohan w & m
Featured in FORTY-FIVE MINUTES FROM BROADWAY, show (opened 01/06)
Fay Templeton, sung in show
Donald Brian, sung in show
Minnie Emmett 02/06 Col 32861 cyl

MILO (32)
J W Stern, pub. 1905, reached #9 in August 1906
Benjamin H Burt w, Alfred Solman m
Lottie Gilson, vv stage
Mamie Remington, vv stage
Bob Roberts 09/06 Col 32993 cyl, 01/07 Col 3539
The Three Troubadours, vv stage

MY GAL SAL (5)
Paul Dresser P C ΦΦΦ, pub. 1905, reached #3 in October 1906
Paul Dresser w & m
Steady seller for several years after Dresser's death, 01/06
Louise Dresser, vv stage
Lottie Gilson, vv stage
Byron G Harlan Φ 09/05 Zono 6176, 10/05 Imp 44484, 01/07 Vic 4918
The Three Troubadours, vv stage

NOBODY
Attucks, pub. 1905, reached #19 in September 1906
(Also reached #7 in September 1905)
Alex Rogers w, Bert Williams m
Bert Williams Φ vv stage, 07/06 Col 3423

NOT BECAUSE YOUR HAIR IS CURLY (19)
V Kremer, pub. 1906, reached #7 in July 1906
Bob Adams w & m
Featured in THE THREE GRACES, show (opened 04/06)
Mabel Barrison, sung in show
Trixie Fraganza, vv stage
Billy Murray Φ 09/06 Zono 546, 11/06 Vic 4861, 11/06 Col 3489
Edna Wallace Hopper, vv stage

OS-KA-LOO-SA-LOO (29)
Albright, pub. 1906, reached #11 in November 1906
Jeff T Branen w, Henry S Sawyer m
Marie Elmer, vv stage
Ruby Erwood, vv stage
Victor Orch 06/07 Vic 5114

SILVERHEELS (27)
J H Remick, pub. 1905, reached #6 in February 1906
James O'Dea w, Neil Moret m
Empire City Quartet, vv stage
Pryor's Band 01/06 Vic 4552
Harry Tally 02/06 Vic 4579
Billy Murray 02/06 Col 32876 cyl

SINCE FATHER WENT TO WORK
J W Stern, pub. 1906, reached #19 in March 1906
William Cahill w & m
William Cahill, vv stage
Arthur Collins 07/06 Imperial 44791

SINCE NELLIE WENT AWAY (25)
New York M P H, pub. 1906, reached #15 in June 1906
Herbert H Taylor w & m
Dick Jose, vv stage, 03/06 Vic 31489
J Aldrich Libbey, vv stage
Lottie Gilson, vv stage
Henry & Gallot, vv stage

SO LONG, MARY (20)
F A Mills, pub. 1905, reached #3 in May 1906
George M Cohan w & m
Featured in FORTY-FIVE MINUTES FROM BROADWAY, show (opened 01/06)
Fay Templeton, sung in show
Donald Brian, sung in show
Corinne Morgan Φ 03/06 Vic 4590, 05/06 Col 3359
Ada Jones 05/06 Ed 9288 cyl

SOMEBODY'S SWEETHEART I LONG TO BE (42)
Gus Edwards M P C, pub. 1905, reached Top 30 in Feb. 1906
Will D Cobb w, Gus Edwards m
Byron G Harlan 01/06 Ed 9171 cyl, 01/06 Zono 350, 03/06 Col 3322
Jeanette Dupree, vv stage
John W Myers 01/06 Col 3306

SOMEWHERE (18)
C K Harris, pub. 1906, reached #9 in November 1906
Charles K Harris w & m
J Aldrich Libbey, vv stage
Kelly & Violette, vv stage
Frank Coombs, vv stage
Harry Tally/Haydn Quartet 08/06 Vic 31548

STARLIGHT (16)
F B Haviland, pub. 1905, reached #5 in February 1906
Edward Madden w, Theodore F Morse m
Kathryn Miley, vv stage
Hazel Burt, vv stage
Haydn Quartet 01/06 Vic 4523
Byron G Harlan 12/05 Col 3266, 12/05 Ed 9166 cyl

SYMPATHY (46)
J H Remick, pub. 1905, reached #9 in February 1906
Jack Kendis w, Herman Paley m
Emma Carus, vv stage
Clarice Vance, vv stage
Artie Hall, vv stage
Arthur Collins 12/05 Col 32840 cyl, 01/06 Col 3298

TAKE ME BACK TO YOUR HEART AGAIN (35)
Witmark, pub. 1905, reached #10 in June 1906
Collin Davis w, Frank J Richmond m
Criterion Comedy Four, vv stage
The Musical Monarchs, vv stage
Edward Barrow 02/06 Ed 9190 cyl

TWO DIRTY LITTLE HANDS
Gus Edwards M P C, pub. 1906, reached #17 in June 1906
Will D Cobb w, Gus Edwards m
Featured in SCHOOL BOYS AND SCHOOL GIRLS, vv revue (1906)
Gus Edwards, sung in revue
Aurie Dagwell, vv stage

WAIT TILL THE SUN SHINES, NELLIE (2)
H Von Tilzer ΦΦΦ, pub. 1905, reached #1 in December 1905
Andrew Sterling w, Harry Von Tilzer m
Winona Winter, vv stage
Byron G Harlan Φ 10/05 Zono 269, 11/05 Ed 9130 cyl, 03/06 Col 3321
Harry Tally Φ 02/06 Vic 4551
Effie Brooklin, vv stage
Grace Cameron, vv stage

WAITING AT THE CHURCH (MY WIFE WON'T LET ME) (6)
Francis, D & H, pub. 1906, reached #1 in July 1906
Fred W Leigh w, Henry E Pether m
Vesta Victoria, vv stage (Later: 1907 Vic 5182)
Ada Jones ΦΦ 07/06 Vic 4714, 07/06 Zono 499, 08/06 Ed 9315 cyl, 09/06 Col 3436
Victor Orch 12/06 Vic 4870

WALTZ ME AROUND AGAIN, WILLIE (9)
F A Mills, pub. 1906, reached #1 in September 1906
Will D Cobb w, Ren Shields m
Featured in HIS HONOR, THE MAYOR, show (opened 05/06)
Blanche Ring, sung in show
Billy Murray ΦΦ 07/06 Vic 4738, 07/06 Zono 500, 09/06 Ed 9340 cyl
Emma Carus, vv stage
Della Fox, vv stage
Lottie Gilson, vv stage

WHEN THE EVENING BREEZE IS SIGHING HOME SWEET HOME (37)
J W Stern, pub. 1905, reached #14 in March 1906
J Hayden Clarendon w, Alfred Solman m
Haydn Quartet 12/05 Vic 4500
Edith Arnold, vv stage
Frank Batie, vv stage

WHEN THE MOCKING BIRDS ARE SINGING IN THE WILDWOOD (17)
J H Remick, pub. 1905, reached #6 in May 1906
Arthur Lamb w, H B Blake m
Harry Macdonough 04/06 Vic 31502, 05/06 Vic 4665
Mound City Quartet, vv stage
Frank Stanley 03/06 Col 3336

WHY DON'T YOU TRY? (30)
J H Remick, pub. 1905, reached #16 in July 1906
Harry H Williams w, Egbert Van Alstyne m
Featured in BELLE OF AVENUE A, show (opened 10/05)
Effie Fay, sung in show
Emma Carus, vv stage
Louise Dresser, vv stage
Harry Tally 02/06 Col 32880 cyl, 03/06 Vic 4593, 04/06 Col 3356

WILL YOU LOVE ME IN DECEMBER AS YOU DO IN MAY? (8)
Witmark, pub. 1905, reached #1 in April 1906
James J Walker w, Ernest Ball m
Janet Allen, vv stage
Harry Macdonough/Haydn Quartet Φ 02/06 Vic 4575
Lillian Leroy, vv stage
Albert Campbell Φ 03/06 Col 3324

WON'T YOU COME OVER TO MY HOUSE? (10)
J H Remick, pub. 1906, reached #1 in December 1906
Harry H Williams w, Egbert Van Alstyne m
Empire Comedy Four, vv stage
Orpheus Comedy Four, vv stage
Byron G Harlan 01/07 Vic 4939
Irving Gillette[1] 11/06 Ed 9394 cyl
"That" Quartet, vv stage

YOU'RE A GRAND OLD FLAG (3)
F A Mills ΦΦΦ, pub. 1906, reached #1 in June 1906
George M Cohan w & m
Featured in GEORGE WASHINGTON, JR., show (opened 02/06)
George M Cohan, sung in show
Billy Murray ΦΦ 04/06 Vic 4634[2], 04/06 Ed 9256 cyl, 04/04 Zono 425, 06/06 Col 3388
Pryor's Band 08/06 Vic 31539, 08/06 Vic 4769

[1]Irving Gillette was a pseudonym for Henry Burr.
[2]Most recordings of this song listed the title as YOU'RE A GRAND OLD RAG or THE GRAND OLD RAG.

1907

ALL IN, DOWN AND OUT (50)
Gotham-Attucks, pub. 1906, reached #13 in March 1907
Cecil Mack w, J Rosamond Johnson, Chris Smith & Elmer Bowman m
Bert Williams, vv stage, 01/07 Col 30039
Arthur Collins 03/07 Ed 9492 cyl, 04/07 Vic 5027, 04/07 Zono 687
Clarice Vance, vv stage

AND A LITTLE BIT MORE (29)
T B Harms, pub. 1907, reached #4 in June 1907
Alfred Bryan w, Fred Fisher m
Maude Lambert, vv stage
Truly Shattuck, vv stage
Ethel Levey, vv stage
Collins & Harlan 07/07 Col 3649, 07/07 Col 33150 cyl
Arthur Collins 07/07 Ed 9582 cyl, 10/07 Vic 5233

AND A LITTLE CHILD SHALL LEAD THEM (41)
C K Harris, pub. 1906, reached #13 in March 1907
Charles K Harris w & m
Byron G Harlan 12/06 Zono 615, 02/07 Ed 9472 cyl, 03/07 Vic 5003
Victor Camont, vv stage

ANY OLD TIME AT ALL
Francis, D & H, pub. 1906, reached #20 in May 1907[2]
William Jerome w, Jean Schwartz m
Featured in THE RICH MR. HOGGENHEIMER, show (opened 10/06)
Georgia Carrie & Edwin Nicander, sung in show
Arthur Collins 04/07 Col 85114 cyl

ARRAH WANNA (3)
F B Haviland, pub. 1906, reached #1 in January 1907
Jack Drislane w, Theodore F Morse m
Billy Murray/Haydn Quartet Φ 01/07 Vic 4907
Collins & Harlan 12/06 Zono 616, 01/07 Ed 9447 cyl
Effie Brooklin, vv stage
Bert Fitzgibbon, vv stage

BECAUSE I'M MARRIED NOW (13)
Shapiro, B, pub. 1907, reached #2 in July 1907
Herbert Ingraham w & m
Featured in THE WHITE HEN, show (opened 02/07)
Mabel Hite, vv stage
Maude Raymond, sung in show
Billy Murray Φ 06/07 Vic 5115, 07/07 Ed 9586 cyl, 08/07 Col 3670

BECAUSE YOU'RE YOU (23)
Witmark, pub. 1906, reached #8 in February 1907
Henry Blossom w, Victor Herbert m
Featured in THE RED MILL, show (opened 09/06)
Neal McCay & Aline Carter, sung in show
Elise Stevenson & Harry Macdonough 03/07 Vic 5020
Florence Hinkle & Harry Macdonough 02/07 Ed 9478 cyl
Elise Stevenson & Frank Stanley 04/07 Col 3590, 04/07 Col 33096 cyl, 05/07 Zono 735

THE BEST THING IN LIFE
C K Harris, pub. 1907, reached #14 in April 1907
Charles K Harris w & m
vv singers

THE BIRD ON NELLIE'S HAT (7)
J W Stern, pub. 1906, reached #1 in March 1907
Arthur Lamb w, Alfred Solman m
Eddie Foy, vv stage
Trix Sisters Φ 01/07 Vic 4904, 01/07 Ed 9450 cyl
Tom Seabrooke, vv stage

BUDWEISER'S A FRIEND OF MINE (46)
Shapiro, B, pub. 1907, reached #8 in October 1907
Vincent Bryan w, Seymour Furth m
Featured in ZIEGFELD FOLLIES OF 1907, show (opened 07/07)
Grace LaRue, sung in show
Billy Murray 01/08 Vic 5320

DON'T GET MARRIED ANY MORE, MA
Francis, D & H, pub. 1907, reached #18 in December 1907
Fred W Leigh w, Henry E Pether m
Ada Jones 01/08 Vic 5316, 01/08 Ed 9729 cyl, 03/08 Zono 984
vv singers

DREAMING (16)
J H Remick, pub. 1906, reached #2 in September 1907
L W Heiser w, J Anton Daily m
Harry Macdonough 09/07 Vic 5189
Empire City Quartet, vv stage
Albert Campbell 10/07 Col 3701

EVERY DAY IS LADIES' DAY WITH ME (35)
Witmark, pub. 1906, reached #9 in January 1907
Henry Blossom w, Victor Herbert m
Featured in THE RED MILL, show (opened 09/06)
Neal McCay, sung in show
vv singers

EVERY LITTLE BIT ADDED TO WHAT YOU'VE GOT MAKES JUST A LITTLE BIT MORE
Helf & Hager, pub. 1907, reached #15 in August 1907
William A Dillon & Lawrence M Dillon w & m
Lew Dockstader, vv stage
Collins & Harlan 08/07 Ed 9611 cyl, 09/07 Col 3678, 09/07 Zono 846

FLOATING ALONG (48)
Pillsbury, pub. 1906, reached #18 in April 1907
C C Pillsbury w, Edward Buffington m
concert bands
vv singers

GOLDEN ROD (34)
McKinley Mus Co, pub. 1907, reached #12 in June 1907
Mabel McKinley w & m
Mabel McKinley, vv stage (Later: 1909 Ed Amb 122)
Edison Concert Band 06/07 Ed 9554 cyl
Billy Murray 11/07 Vic 5247

HARRIGAN (2)
F A Mills, pub. 1907, reached #1 in October 1907
George M Cohan w & m
Featured in FIFTY MILES FROM BOSTON, show (opened 02/08)
Billy Murray ΦΦ 09/07 Vic 5197, 09/07 Zono 827
George M Cohan, vv stage
James C Marlowe, sung in show
Edward Meeker 08/07 Ed 9616 cyl

HE GOES TO CHURCH ON SUNDAY (38)
Shapiro, B, pub. 1907, reached #6 in July 1907
Vincent Bryan w, E Ray Goetz m
Featured in THE ORCHID, show (opened 04/07)
Eddie Foy, sung in show
Billy Murray Φ 06/07 Vic 5124, 07/07 Zono 786, 08/07 Col 3671, 08/07 Ed 9612 cyl

HE'S A COUSIN OF MINE (6)
Gotham-Attucks, pub. 1906, reached #2 in March 1907
Cecil Mack w, Chris Smith & Silvio Hein m
Featured in MARRYING MARY, show (opened 08/06)
Marie Cahill, sung in show
Bert Williams Φ 01/07 Col 3536
Clarice Vance, vv stage, 01/07 Vic 4931
Emma Carus, vv stage
Tascott, vv stage

HONEY BOY (5)
York Mus Co ΦΦΦ, pub. 1907, reached #2 in November 1907
Jack Norworth w, Albert Von Tilzer m
Jack Norworth, vv stage
Louise Dresser, vv stage
Columbia Quartet[1] Φ 08/07 Col 3669, 11/07 Zono 897
Billy Murray Φ 10/07 Vic 5207

HYMNS OF THE OLD CHURCH CHOIR
J W Stern, pub. 1907, reached #13 in July 1907
Arthur Lamb w, Alfred Solman m
Reidy & Currier, vv stage
Columbia Male Quartet[1] 10/07 Col 3693
Frank Stanley 07/07 Ed 9592 cyl

I JUST CAN'T MAKE MY EYES BEHAVE (15)
Gus Edwards M P C, pub. 1906, reached #4 in March 1907
Will D Cobb w, Gus Edwards m
Featured in A PARISIAN MODEL, show (opened 11/06)
Anna Held, sung in show
Ada Jones 03/07 Col 33097 cyl, 04/07 Col 3588
vv singers

I LOVE YOU TRULY (30)
C Jacobs-Bond ΦΦΦ, pub. 1906, reached Top 40 in May 1907
(Also reached #9 in October 1912)
Carrie Jacobs-Bond w & m
Steady seller for next twenty years
concert singers
wedding singers

I'M A POPULAR MAN (47)
F A Mills, pub. 1907, reached #11 in October 1907
George M Cohan w & m
Featured in THE HONEYMOONERS, show (opened 06/07)
George M Cohan, sung in show
vv singers

I'VE MADE MY PLANS FOR THE SUMMER
John Church Co, pub. 1907, reached #20 in August 1907
John Philip Sousa m
John Philip Sousa, band concerts
other concert bands

IN MONKEYLAND (22)
F B Haviland, pub. 1907, reached #5 in November 1907
Jack Drislane w, Theodore F Morse m
Collins & Harlan Φ 11/07 Vic 5270, 12/07 Ed 9700 cyl
Kitty Morris, vv stage
Devere & Hayes, vv stage

IN OLD NEW YORK (36)
Witmark, pub. 1907, reached #6 in January 1907
Henry Blossom w, Victor Herbert m
Featured in THE RED MILL, show (opened 9/06)
Dave Montgomery & Fred Stone, sung in show
Billy Murray Φ 01/07 Col 33062 cyl, 01/07 Col 3544
vv singers

IN THE EVENING BY THE MOONLIGHT, DEAR LOUISE
H Von Tilzer, pub. 1906, reached #20 in January 1907
Andrew Sterling w, Harry Von Tilzer m
Harry Macdonough 12/06 Vic 4871
Frank Stanley 01/07 Col 3521

IN THE WILDWOOD WHERE THE BLUE BELLS GREW (33)
New York Mus Co, pub. 1907, reached #6 in May 1907
Herbert H Taylor w & m
Dick Jose, vv stage
J Aldrich Libbey, vv stage
Harlan & Stanley 06/07 Ed 9567 cyl
Haydn Quartet 08/07 Vic 5168

THE ISLE OF OUR DREAMS (49)
Witmark, pub. 1906, reached #16 in December 1906
Henry Blossom w, Victor Herbert m
Featured in THE RED MILL, show (opened 09/06)
Joseph M Ratliff & Augusta Greenleaf, sung in show
stage singers

IT'S DELIGHTFUL TO BE MARRIED (28)
J W Stern, pub. 1906, reached #5 in July 1907
Anna Held w, Vincent Scotto m
Featured in THE PARISIAN MODEL, show (opened 11/06)
Anna Held, sung in show
vv singers

IT'S GREAT TO BE A SOLDIER MAN (20)
F B Haviland, pub. 1907, reached #9 in July 1907
Jack Drislane w, Theodore F Morse m
Billy Murray 05/07 Zono 739, 08/07 Vic 5161
Byron C Harlan 07/07 Ed 9600 cyl
Crawford & Stutzman, vv stage

JUST BECAUSE I LOVED YOU SO
C K Harris, pub. 1907, reached #19 in July 1907
Charles K Harris w & m
Harry Anthony 09/07 Ed 9636 cyl
vv singers

A LEMON IN THE GARDEN OF LOVE (18)
Witmark, pub. 1906, reached #4 in February 1907
M E Rourke w, Richard Carle m
Featured in THE SPRING CHICKEN, show (opened 10/06)
Richard Carle, sung in show
Billy Murray Φ 01/07 Vic 4902, 01/07 Zono 643,
02/07 Ed 9462 cyl, 03/07 Col 3579

LET IT ALONE (14)
Gotham-Attucks, pub. 1906, reached #3 in April 1907
Alex Rogers w, Bert Williams m
Featured in ABYSSINIA, show (opened 02/06)
Bert Williams Φ sung in show, 12/06 Col 3504,
12/06 Col 33025 cyl
Ada Jones 04/07 Ed 9507 cyl

MOONBEAMS (42)
Witmark, pub. 1906, reached #14 in March 1907
Henry Blossom w, Victor Herbert m
Featured in THE RED MILL, show (opened 09/06)
Augusta Greenleaf, sung in show
stage singers

MY IRISH ROSIE (19)
Francis, D & H, pub. 1906, reached #7 in February 1907
William Jerome w, Jean Schwartz m
Featured in THE LITTLE CHERUB, show (opened 08/06)
Hattie Williams, sung in show
Ada Jones 03/07 Ed 9684 cyl
Kathryn Trayer, vv stage
Kathryn Miley, vv stage

MY MARIUCCIA TAKE A STEAMBOAT (17)
Shapiro, B, pub. 1906, reached #3 in January 1907
George Ronklyn w, Al Piantadosi m
Kathryn Miley, vv stage
Billy Murray 12/06 Vic 4872
Broadway Quartet, vv stage
Arthur Collins 01/07 Col 3537, 01/07 Col 33055 cyl

NO WEDDING BELLS FOR ME (21)
M Shapiro, pub. 1906, reached #5 in September 1907
Will Heelan & Ed Moran w, Seymour Furth m
Featured in THE ORCHID, show (opened 04/07)
Trixie Fraganza, vv stage
Billy Murray Φ 05/07 Zono 742, 06/07 Vic 5123
Flavia Arcaro, sung in show
Bob Roberts 05/07 Ed 9538 cyl, 07/07 Col 3659

NOBODY'S LITTLE GIRL (27)
F B Haviland, pub. 1907, reached #6 in June 1907
Jack Drislane w, Theodore F Morse m
Byron G Harlan 05/07 Ed 9539 cyl, 06/07 Col 85123 cyl, 07/07 Vic 5147
Quaker City Four, vv stage

OLD FAITHFUL (25)
L Feist, pub. 1907, reached #7 in November 1907
Abe Holzmann m
Edison Military Band 12/07 Ed 9721 cyl
other concert bands, band concerts

POOR JOHN! (11)
Francis, D & H, pub. 1906, reached #1 in April 1907
Fred W Leigh w, Henry E Pether m
Vesta Victoria, vv stage, 09/07 Vic 5183
Ada Jones Φ 04/07 Vic 5029, 05/07 Ed 9531, 05/07 Col 3604
other vv singers

SAN ANTONIO (4)
J H Remick, pub. 1907, reached #1 in May 1907
Harry H Williams w, Egbert Van Alstyne m
Billy Murray ΦΦ 04/07 Vic 5049, 04/07 Col 33014 cyl, 05/07 Col 3608, 05/07 Ed 9547 cyl
Clarice Vance, vv stage
Avon Comedy Four, vv stage
Ethel Levey, vv stage

SCHOOL DAYS (1)
Gus Edwards M P C ΦΦΦ, pub. 1906, reached #1 in June 1907
Will D Cobb w, Gus Edwards m
Featured in SCHOOL DAYS, show (opened 09/08)
Byron G Harlan ΦΦ 05/07 Vic 5086, 06/07 Col 33128 cyl, 06/07 Ed 9562 cyl, 11/07 Zono 900
Gus Edwards, vv stage, sung in show
Julia Sanderson, vv stage
Broadway Quartet, vv stage

SHE WAS A GRAND OLD LADY (43)
J W Stern, pub. 1907, reached #20 in October 1907
William C Davies w, S R Henry m
William C Davies, vv stage
Bert Morphy, vv stage
Harvey Hindermeyer 08/07 Ed 9614 cyl

SOME DAY WHEN DREAMS COME TRUE (9)
W Jacobs, pub. 1907, reached #8 in January 1908
Philip Statts w & m
Henry Burr Φ 11/07 Zono 890, 12/07 Ed 9702 cyl, 06/08 Col 3784, 06/08 Col 33234 cyl
Trocadero Quartet, vv stage
"That" Quartet, vv stage

SOMEBODY'S WAITING FOR YOU (40)
J H Remick, pub. 1906, reached #12 in April 1907
Vincent Bryan w, Albert Gumble m
Bessie Wynn, vv stage
Trixie Fraganza, vv stage
Frank Stanley 03/07 Col 3577
Aurie Dagwell, vv stage

SPANGLES (44)
Witmark, pub. 1907, reached #16 in July 1907
John W Bratton m
Zon-o-phone Concert Band 03/07 Zono 685
Edison Symphony Orch 04/08 Ed 9801 cyl

SPRING, BEAUTIFUL SPRING
J W Stern, pub. 1903, reached #14 in November 1907
Paul Lincke m
concert orchestras

TAKE ME BACK TO NEW YORK TOWN (10)
H Von Tilzer, pub. 1907, reached #3 in November 1907
Andrew Sterling w, Harry Von Tilzer m
Harry Tally Φ 10/07 Vic 5230, 10/07 Zono 873
Billy Murray 11/07 Col 3717
Nellie Florede, vv stage
Cecilia Weston, vv stage

THE TALE THE CHURCH BELLS TOLLED (31)
J H Remick, pub. 1907, reached #4 in May 1907
Harry H Williams w, Egbert Van Alstyne m
Harry Macdonough 04/07 Ed 9522 cyl, 06/07 Vic 5121
Harry Ellis, vv stage
Frank Stanley 05/07 Col 33111 cyl, 05/07 Zono 7022

THE TEDDY BEARS' PICNIC (45)
Witmark, pub. 1907, reached #19 in August 1907
(Also reached #11 in June 1908)
John W Bratton m
Hager's Orch 05/07 Zono 731
Victor Orch[3] 09/07 Vic 5202
Collins & Jewel, vv stage

THAT'S WHAT THE ROSE SAID TO ME (12)
Gus Edwards M P C, pub. 1907, reached #5 in December 1907
B F Barnett w, Leo Edwards m
Avon Comedy Four, vv stage
Bessie Wynn, vv stage
Henry Burr 12/06 Zono 624
Frank Morrell, vv stage

UNDER THE TROPICAL MOON (37)
V Kremer, pub. 1907, reached #19 in October 1907
Christie Macdonald w, Percy Wenrich m
Phyllis Allen, vv stage
Ida Emerson, vv stage

VESTI LA GIUBBA (39)
G Schirmer, pub. 1892, reached #9 in October 1907
Ruggiero Leoncavallo w & m
Featured in PAGLIACCI, opera (opened 05/92)
Enrico Caruso ΦΦ 05/04 Vic 81032, 07/07 Vic 88061

WHEN BOB WHITE IS WHISTLING IN THE MEADOW
J W Stern, pub. 1906, reached #11 in March 1907
Monroe H Rosenfeld w & m
Emma Carus, vv stage
Haydn Quartet 04/07 Vic 5025
Byron Harlan & Frank Stanley 04/07 Ed 9515 cyl

WHEN YOU KNOW YOU'RE NOT FORGOTTEN BY THE GIRL YOU CAN'T FORGET (32)
Helf & Hager, pub. 1906, reached #5 in August 1907
Ed Gardenier w, J Fred Helf m
Emma Carus, vv stage
Albert Campbell 05/07 Col 3617, 05/07 Col 33126 cyl
Haydn Quartet 09/07 Vic 5166

WITH YOU IN ETERNITY (26)
J W Stern, pub. 1907, reached #8 in September 1907
Arthur Lamb w, Alfred Solman m
Henry Burr Φ 06/07 Ed 9555 cyl, 07/07 Col 3661, 08/07 Zono 822
vv singers

WON'T YOU BE MY HONEY? (8)
F B Haviland, pub. 1907, reached #3 in September 1907
Jack Drislane w, Theodore F Morse m
Ada Jones & Billy Murray ΦΦ 09/07 Col 3682, 09/07 Col 33164 cyl
Marion & Deane, vv stage
Devere & Hayes, vv stage

YESTERDAY
C K Harris, pub. 1907, reached #13 in November 1907
Charles K Harris w & m
Reinald Werrenrath 12/07 Ed 9694 cyl
vv singers

YOU SPLASH ME AND I'LL SPLASH YOU (24)
J W Stern, pub. 1907, reached #2 in August 1907
Arthur Lamb w, Alfred Solman m
Alice Lloyd, vv stage, 10/07 Vic 5225
Adele Richie, vv stage
Ada Jones 09/07 Col 3675, 09/07 Col 33160 cyl
Kitty Johnson, vv stage

[1]The Columbia Male Quartet (or Columbia Quartet) was the label's name for the Peerless Quartet.
[2]Reached #20 on monthly chart only.
[3]Label carried title FROLIC OF THE TEDDY BEARS.

1908

ANY OLD PORT IN A STORM (40)
F A Mills, pub. 1908, reached #9 in November 1908
Arthur Lamb w, Kerry Mills m
Featured in COHAN & HARRIS MINSTRELS, show (opened 08/08)
Frank Stanley 07/08 Ind 799 cyl, 09/08 Zono 1153, 10/08 Vic 5547
John P Rogers, sung in show
Edward Metcalfe, vv stage

ARE YOU SINCERE? (41)
J H Remick, pub. 1908, reached #10 in August 1908
Alfred Bryan w, Albert Gumble m
Elise Stevenson 07/08 Vic 5467, 09/08 Zono 1142
Byron G Harlan 11/08 Ed 9973 cyl, 01/09 Ind 929 cyl
vv singers

AS LONG AS THE WORLD ROLLS ON (3)
Witmark, pub. 1907, reached #2 in February 1908
George Graff w, Ernest Ball m
Alan Turner Φ 02/08 Vic 31693
American Quartet, vv stage
Anna Palmer, vv stage
Henry Burr 06/08 Col 3804

THE BEST I GET IS MUCH OBLIGED TO YOU (23)
J H Remick, pub. 1907, reached #1 in February 1908
Benjamin H Burt w & m
May Irwin, vv stage
Louise Dresser, vv stage
Billy Murray Φ 02/08 Vic 5335

BON BON BUDDY (9)
Gotham-Attucks, pub. 1907, reached #4 in October 1908
Alex Rogers w, Will M Cook m
Featured in BANDANA LAND, show (opened 02/08)
Bert Williams & George Walker, sung in show
Billy Murray Φ 06/08 Vic 5433, 07/08 Ind 794 cyl
vv singers

CONSOLATION (49)
F B Haviland, pub. 1908, reached #13 in July 1908
Edward Madden w, Theodore F Morse m
Bowery Comedy Four, vv stage
Robinson & Parquette, vv stage

CUDDLE UP A LITTLE CLOSER (8)
Witmark, pub. 1908, reached #2 in October 1908
Otto Harbach w, Karl Hoschna m
Featured in THE THREE TWINS, show (opened 06/08)
Ada Jones & Billy Murray ΦΦ 09/08 Vic 5532, 10/08 Ed 9950 cyl, 10/08 Ind 876 cyl
Alice Yorke, sung in show
Daisy Leon, vv stage
Van Brothers, vv stage

DON'T TAKE ME HOME (27)
H Von Tilzer, pub. 1908, reached #10 in December 1908
Vincent Bryan w, Harry Von Tilzer m
Eddie Morton 10/08 Vic 5545, 10/08 Zono 1176, 10/08 Ed 9949 cyl
Bob Roberts 11/08 Ind 889 cyl
vv singers

DOWN IN JUNGLE TOWN (6)
F B Haviland ΦΦΦ, pub. 1908, reached #1 in September 1908
Edward Madden w, Theodore F Morse m
Josie Sabel, vv stage
Collins & Harlan ΦΦ 08/08 Vic 5484, 09/08 Ed 9941 cyl, 09/08 Zono 1143
Clara Moore, vv stage
Gotham Comedy Four, vv stage

THE GLOW-WORM (2)
J W Stern ΦΦΦ, pub. 1907, reached #1 in May 1908
(Also reached #16 in April 1910)
(Also reached #2 in December 1952, with modernized lyrics)
Lilla Cayley Robinson w, Paul Lincke m
Featured in THE GIRL BEHIND THE COUNTER, show (opened 10/07)
May Naudain, sung in show
Lucy Isabel Marsh Φ 06/08 Col 3791
Victor Orch 05/08 Vic 5408
Elise Stevenson 02/09 Vic 5657
vv singers

HOO-OO (AIN'T YOU COMIN' OUT TONIGHT?) (18)
M Shapiro, pub. 1907, reached #7 in July 1908
Herbert Ingraham w & m
Bessie Wynn, vv stage
Byron G Harlan Φ 05/08 Vic 5396, 05/08 Ed 9834 cyl
May Belfort, vv stage

I LOVE A LASSIE (12)
Francis, D & H, pub. 1906, reached #13 in December 1907
Gerald Grafton w, Harry Lauder m
Steady seller 1907-1912
Harry Lauder Φ vv stage, 11/07 Vic 52002
Sandy Shaw 03/09 Col A-639

I LOVE YOU SO (MERRY WIDOW WALTZ) (11)
Chappell & Co, pub. 1907, reached #1 in February 1908
Adrian Ross w, Franz Lehar m
Featured in THE MERRY WIDOW, show (opened 10/07)
Donald Brien & Ethel Jackson, sung in show
Elise Stevenson & Harry Macdonough Φ 02/08 Vic 5340
Victor Orch Φ 10/07 Vic 5208
Prince's Orch 03/08 Col 30106

I WANT YOU
F A Mills, pub. 1907, reached #13 in April 1908
George M Cohan w & m
Henry Burr 07/08 Vic 5463
Billy Murray 07/08 Ind 806 cyl

I WISH I HAD A GIRL (4)
Thompson Mus Co, pub. 1907, reached #2 in December 1908
Gus Kahn w, Grace LeBoy m
Featured in NEARLY A HERO, show (opened 02/08)
Grace LaRue, sung in show
Billy Murray 05/09 Vic 16291
Harry Tally 04/09 Col A-642
George Austin Moore, vv stage
Manuel Romain 02/09 Ed 10068 cyl

I'M AFRAID TO COME HOME IN THE DARK (13)
J H Remick, pub. 1907, reached #1 in April 1908
Harry H Williams w, Egbert Van Alstyne m
Clarice Vance Φ vv stage, 04/08 Vic 5373
Billy Murray Φ 03/08 Vic 5355, 03/08 Ed 9780 cyl, 04/08 Zono 1030, 05/08 Col 3767
May Irwin, vv stage
Trixie Fraganza, vv stage

I'M STARVING FOR ONE SIGHT OF YOU (50)
C K Harris, pub. 1907, reached #12 in April 1908
Charles K Harris w & m
Frank Stanley & Henry Burr 07/08 Vic 5464, 08/08 Zono 1119
Manuel Romain 11/08 Ed 9977 cyl
vv singers

I'VE TAKEN QUITE A FANCY TO YOU (22)
F B Haviland, pub. 1908, reached #5 in September 1908
Edward Madden w, Theodore F Morse m
Ada Jones & Billy Murray Φ 07/08 Ind 801 cyl, 08/08 Zono 1130, 09/08 Vic 5515, 09/08 Ed 9933 cyl
Devere & Wilson, vv stage
Elise Stevenson & Frank Stanley 11/08 Col A-589

IT LOOKS LIKE A BIG NIGHT TONIGHT (17)
J H Remick, pub. 1908, reached #4 in December 1908
Gus Kahn w, Egbert Van Alstyne m
Billy Murray Φ 10/08 Vic 5550, 10/08 Ind 864 cyl
Lew Dockstader, vv stage
Clarice Vance, vv stage, 06/09 Vic 16295
Collins & Harlan 11/08 Ed 9985 cyl

JUST SOMEONE (19)
Witmark, pub. 1908, reached #3 in June 1908
Will R Anderson w & m
Featured in LONESOME TOWN, show (opened 01/08)
Maude Lambert, sung in show
Anna Palmer, vv stage
Harry Macdonough 08/08 Vic 5488
Manuel Romain 06/08 Ed 9847 cyl

THE LANKY YANKEE BOYS IN BLUE (46)
F B Haviland, pub. 1908, reached #7 in May 1908
Edward Madden w, Theodore F Morse m
Billy Murray Φ 05/08 Ind 758 cyl, 06/08 Zono 1074, 07/08 Vic 5472
McAvoy & Martin, vv stage
Ida May, vv stage

LOVE DAYS (34)
Cohan & Harris, pub. 1908, reached #19 in September 1908
William Jerome w, Jean Schwartz m
Featured in COHAN & HARRIS MINSTRELS, show (opened 08/08)
Frank Morrell, sung in show
Thomas Quigley, vv stage

LOVE'S ROUNDELAY (48)
J W Stern, pub. 1908, reached #10 in June 1908
Joseph Herbert w, Oscar Straus m
Featured in THE WALTZ DREAM, show (opened 01/08)
Edward Johnson & Edwin Wilson, sung in show
Frank Stanley & Henry Burr 05/08 Ind 760 cyl, 06/08 Col 3765
vv singers

MAKE BELIEVE (24)
F B Haviland, pub. 1907, reached #4 in March 1908
Jack Drislane w, Theodore F Morse m
Ada Jones & Billy Murray Φ 01/08 Vic 5317, 03/08 Zono 987
Devere & Wilson, vv stage
Elise Stevenson & Frank Stanley 03/08 Col 3742, 03/08 Col 33210 cyl

MORNING CY (26)
V Kremer, pub. 1908, reached #9 in February 1909
Harold Atteridge w, Bert Peters m
Victor Dance Orch 10/08 Vic 5569
Pryor's Band 04/09 Vic 35066

MUSETTE
J H Remick, pub. 1907, reached #20 in February 1908
Neil Moret m
Zon-O-Phone Band 05/08 Zono 1043
other concert bands, band concerts

MY BRUDDAH SYLVEST' (29)
F Fisher, pub. 1908, reached #7 in December 1908
Jesse Lasky w, Fred Fisher m
Mabel Hite, vv stage
Collins & Harlan 11/08 Ind 896 cyl, 12/08 Ed 10013 cyl
Sam Dody, vv stage

OH, YOU KID! (38)
M Shapiro, pub. 1908, reached #14 in October 1908
Edgar Selden w, Melville J Gideon m
Thomas J Quigley, vv stage
Violet Dale, vv stage
Ada Jones & Billy Murray 03/09 Ed 10090 cyl, 03/09 Ind 1000 cyl, 04/09 Vic 5673

OVER THE HILLS AND FAR AWAY
M Shapiro, pub. 1908, reached #20 in June 1908
William Jerome w, Jean Schwartz m
Alice Lloyd, vv stage
Harry Macdonough & John H Bieling 09/08 Vic 5506

RAINBOW (25)
J H Remick, pub. 1908, reached #9 in August 1908
Alfred Bryan w, Percy Wenrich m
Billy Murray/Haydn Quartet 12/08 Vic 5608
Henry Burr & Frank Stanley 11/08 Col A-600
Victor Orch 12/08 Vic 5608
vv singers

RED WING (7)
F A Mills, pub. 1907, reached #3 in January 1908
Thurland Chattaway w, Kerry Mills m
Frank Stanley & Henry Burr Φ 09/07 Col 3681
Sam Dudley & Harry Macdonough Φ 03/08 Vic 5368
Prince's Band 01/08 Col 3748
vv singers

ROSES BRING DREAMS OF YOU (10)
M Shapiro, pub. 1908, reached #3 in July 1908
Herbert Ingraham w & m
Bessie Wynn, vv stage
Thomas Quigley, vv stage
Harry Macdonough/Haydn Quartet Φ 07/08 Vic 5477
Columbia Quartet[1] 05/09 Col A-641
Orpheus Comedy Four, vv stage

SAFTEST O' THE FAMILY (28)
Francis, D & H, pub. 1904, reached #19 in January 1908
Bobry Beaton w, Harry Lauder m
Steady seller, 1907 to 1912
Harry Lauder, vv stage, 10/09 Vic 58014

SHE IS MA DAISY (21)
Francis, D & H, pub. 1905, reached #17 in January 1908
J D Harper w, Harry Lauder m
Steady seller, 1907 to 1912
Harry Lauder Φ vv stage, 06/09 Vic 58007, 12/09 Ed 12065 cyl, 02/10 Vic 70006
Donald Mackay 04/09 Col A-651

SMARTY (14)
York Mus Co, pub. 1908, reached #2 in June 1908
Jack Norworth w, Albert Von Tilzer m
Jack Norworth, vv stage
Ada Jones & Billy Murray Φ 06/08 Vic 5455
Trixie Fraganza, vv stage
Byron G Harlan 07/08 Zono 1108, 07/08 Ind 791 cyl

SOMEBODY LIED (33)
Will Rossiter, pub. 1907, reached #16 in October 1908
Jeff T Branen w, Evans Lloyd m
Featured in BANDANA LAND, show (opened 02/08)
Bert Williams, sung in show
Eddie Morton 10/08 Vic 5546
Josephine Gassman, vv stage
Stella Mayhew, vv stage

STOP YER TICKLIN', JOCK! (30)
Francis, D & H, pub. 1904, reached #20 in December 1907
Frank Folley w, Harry Lauder m
Harry Lauder, vv stage, 11/07 Vic 52003
Helen Trix 07/07 Zono 796

SUNBONNET SUE (1)
Gus Edwards M P C ΦΦΦ, pub. 1906, reached #1 in October 1908
Will D Cobb w, Gus Edwards m
Featured in SCHOOL BOYS AND SCHOOL GIRLS, vv revue (1908)
Harry Macdonough/Haydn Quartet ΦΦ 10/08 Vic 5568
Avon Comedy Four, vv stage
Byron G Harlan Φ 10/08 Ed 9958 cyl, 10/08 Ind 866 cyl
Gus Edwards, sung in revue
Arlington Quartet, vv stage

THE SWEETEST MAID OF ALL (42)
J W Stern, pub. 1908, reached #7 in June 1908
Joseph Herbert w, Oscar Straus m
Featured in THE WALTZ DREAM, show (opened 01/08)
Sophie Brandt & Edward Johnson, sung in show
vv singers

SWEETHEART DAYS (45)
J H Remick, pub. 1908, reached #9 in June 1908
L W Heiser w, J Anton Dailey m
May Irwin, vv stage
Marie Lloyd, vv stage
Trixie Fraganza, vv stage
Harry Macdonough 05/08 Vic 5407

TAKE ME OUT TO THE BALL GAME (15)
York Mus Co ΦΦΦ, pub. 1908, reached #1 in August 1908
(Also reached #20 in June 1909)
Jack Norworth w, Albert Von Tilzer m
Seasonal seller for many years
Norworth & Bayes, vv stage
Billy Murray/Haydn Quartet Φ 10/08 Vic 5570
Harvey Hindermeyer Φ 09/08 Col A-418

THE TEDDY BEARS' PICNIC (47)
Witmark, pub. 1907, reached #11 in June 1908
(Also reached #19 in August 1907)
John W Bratton m
Victor Orch 09/07 Vic 5202
Lasky's Pianopheinds, vv stage
Collins & Jewel, vv stage

THAT'S GRATITUDE (35)
F B Haviland, pub. 1907, reached #12 in February 1908
George A Norton w, Sheppard Camp m
Eddie Morton, vv stage, 10/07 Vic 31661
Bob Roberts 10/07 Ed 9654 cyl

THERE NEVER WAS A GIRL LIKE YOU (20)
J H Remick, pub. 1907, reached #4 in August 1908
Harry H Williams w, Egbert Van Alstyne m
Byron G Harlan 04/08 Ed 9795 cyl
Harry Macdonough 01/09 Vic 5630
Myrtle Dale, vv stage
Victoria Murray, vv stage

TIPPERARY
Helf & Hager, pub. 1908, reached #20 in May 1908
Leo Curley & James Φ Fulton w, J Fred Helf m
Blanche Ring, vv stage
Clara Morton, vv stage
Billy Murray 09/08 Vic 5507, 09/08 Zono 1147, 09/08 Ind 847 cyl

TRUE HEART (44)
Witmark, pub. 1908, reached #8 in June 1908
George Graff w, Ernest Ball m
Anna Palmer, vv stage
Albert Campbell 06/08 Vic 5450
Theis' Harmonists, vv stage

TWO BLUE EYES (16)
F B Haviland, pub. 1907, reached #1 in January 1908
Edward Madden w, Theodore F Morse m
Byron G Harlan Φ 01/08 Vic 5310
Shepherd & Ward, vv stage
Billy Murray 12/07 Col 3733
Robinson & Parquette, vv stage

TWO LITTLE BABY SHOES
F B Haviland, pub. 1907, reached #14 in April 1908
Edward Madden w, Theodore F Morse m
Byron G Harlan 02/08 Ed 9766 cyl, 03/08 Vic 5349
Genevieve Homer, vv stage
Sabel Deane, vv stage

UNDER ANY OLD FLAG AT ALL
F A Mills, pub. 1907, reached #15 in April 1908
George M Cohan w & m
Featured in THE TALK OF NEW YORK, show (opened 12/07)
Billy Murray Φ 02/08 Vic 5389, 04/08 Ed 9796 cyl, 05/08 Zono 1058, 06/08 Col 33226 cyl
Victor Moore, sung in show

VILIA (43)
Chappell & Co, pub. 1907, reached #7 in February 1908
Adrian Ross w, Franz Lehar m
Featured in THE MERRY WIDOW, show (opened 10/07)
Rosemary Glosz, sung in show
Helene Noldi 01/08 Vic 31688
Elise Stevenson 04/08 Vic 5391

WHEN A FELLOW'S ON THE LEVEL WITH A GIRL WHO'S ON THE SQUARE (39)
F A Mills, pub. 1907, reached #8 in April 1908
George M Cohan w & m
Featured in THE TALK OF NEW YORK, show (opened 12/07)
Victor Moore, sung in show
Billy Murray 01/09 Vic 5626

WHEN SWEET MARIE WAS SWEET SIXTEEN (31)
Witmark, pub. 1907, reached #4 in June 1908
Raymond Moore w, Ernest Ball m
Field's Minstrels, vv stage
Harry Macdonough & John H Bieling 08/08 Vic 5505
Marjorie Prescott, vv stage

WHEN THE MOON PLAYS PEEK-A-BOO WITH YOU (36)
F Fisher, pub. 1907, reached #20 in July 1908
Ed Gardenier w, Fred Fisher m
Featured in WINE, WOMEN AND SONG, show (opened 09/07)
Bonita Armstrong, sung in show
Stella Mayhew, vv stage
Maude Lambert, vv stage
Josephine Gassman, vv stage

WHEN WE ARE M-A-DOUBLE-R-I-E-D (32)
F A Mills, pub. 1907, reached #5 in May 1908
George M Cohan w & m
Featured in THE TALK OF NEW YORK, show (opened 12/07)
Ada Jones & Billy Murray 07/08 Ed 9875 cyl, 08/08 Zono 1135
Osborne Searle & Mildred Elaine, sung in show
vv singers

WHEN YOU WORE A PINAFORE
F B Haviland, pub. 1908, reached #20 in June 1908
Edward Madden w, Theodore F Morse m
Harry Macdonough & Frank Stanley 08/08 Vic 5508
Robinson & Parquette, vv stage

WON'T YOU WALTZ HOME SWEET HOME WITH ME? (37)
M Shapiro, pub. 1907, reached #7 in April 1908
Herbert Ingraham w & m
Anna Driver, vv stage
Byron G Harlan 12/07 Ed 9710 cyl, 05/08 Zono 1061
Pauline Hall, vv stage

THE YAMA-YAMA MAN (5)
Witmark, pub. 1908, reached #5 in August 1908
(Reached second peak at #8 in August 1909)
George Collin Davis w, Karl Hoschna m
Featured in THE THREE TWINS, show (opened 06/08)
Bessie McCoy, sung in show
Ada Jones ΦΦ 05/09 Col A-664, 07/09 Vic 16326
Pryor's Band 12/08 Vic 5596
Lyric Quartet, vv stage

[1]The Columbia Quartet was the label's name for the Peerless Quartet.

1909

AMINA (14)
J W Stern, pub. 1909, reached #6 in October 1909
Ballard MacDonald w, Paul Lincke m
Featured in MIDNIGHT SONS, show (opened 05/09)
Maude Lambert, sung in show
Pryor's Band Φ 05/09 Vic 5685
Prince's Orch 08/09 Col A-709
vv singers

ASK HER WHILE THE BAND IS PLAYING (38)
C K Harris, pub. 1908, reached #8 in February 1909
Glen MacDonough w, Victor Herbert m
Featured in ALGERIA, show[1] (opened 08/08)
Ethel Green, sung in show
Dorothy Kingsley 01/09 Zono 1191
vv singers

BEAUTIFUL EYES (30)
Ted Snyder, pub. 1909, reached #5 in June 1909
George Whiting & Carter DeHaven w, Ted Snyder m
Featured in MR. HAMLET OF BROADWAY, show (opened 12/08)
Ada Jones Φ 05/09 Ed 10123 cyl, 07/09 Ind 1100 cyl, 09/09 Vic 16339, 11/09 Col A-742
Emma Carus, vv stage
Mabel Hite, vv stage
Laura Guerite, sung in show

"BL-ND" AND "P-G" SPELLS "BLIND PIG"
York Mus Co, pub. 1908, reached #18 in March 1909
Junie McCree w, Albert Von Tilzer m
Ada Jones 06/09 Zono 5477
vv singers

BY THE LIGHT OF THE SILVERY MOON (1)
Gus Edwards M P C ΦΦΦ, pub. 1909, reached #1 in Dec. 1909
Edward Madden w, Gus Edwards m
Featured in ZIEGFELD FOLLIES OF 1909, show (opened 06/09)
Also featured in SCHOOL BOYS AND SCHOOL GIRLS, vv revue (1909)
Billy Murray/Haydn Quartet ΦΦ 03/10 Vic 16460
Lillian Lorraine, sung in show (ZF)
Columbia Quartet[2] Φ 04/10 Col A-799
Georgie Price, sung in show (SBSG)
Avon Comedy Four, vv stage

CARRIE (MARRY HARRY) (28)
York Mus Co, pub. 1909, reached #4 in December 1909
Junie McCree w, Albert Von Tilzer m
Billy Murray Φ 01/10 Vic 5758
Sophie Tucker, vv stage
Walter Van Brunt 04/10 Ind 1316 cyl

DAISIES WON'T TELL (22)
J H Remick, pub. 1908, reached #10 in November 1909
Anita Owen w & m
Anita Owen, vv stage
Arthur Clough 03/10 Col A-792
Elizabeth Wheeler & Harry Anthony 02/10 Ed 10302 cyl

DOWN AMONG THE SUGAR CANE (8)
Gotham-Attucks, pub. 1908, reached #2 in October 1909
Avery & Hart w, Cecil Mack & Chris Smith m
Avery & Hart, vv stage
Collins & Harlan Φ 03/09 Vic 5670, 03/09 Ind 1015 cyl, 04/09 Ed 10110 cyl, 07/09 Zono 5504
Clara Morton, vv stage

DOWN AT THE HUSKING BEE (29)
J W Stern, pub. 1908, reached #11 in April 1909
Monroe Rosenfeld w, S R Henry m
Collins & Harlan 07/09 Ind 1096[3] cyl, 09/09 Zono 5528, 10/09 Ed 10234 cyl, 11/09 Vic 16365
Pryor's Band 09/09 Vic 5722
The Continentals, vv stage

EVERYBODY LOVES ME BUT THE ONE I LOVE (46)
Gus Edwards M P C, pub. 1908, reached #8 in March 1909
Ed Gardenier w, Gus Edwards m
Byron G Harlan 01/09 Vic 16010
Arlington Four, vv stage

FROM THE LAND OF THE SKY-BLUE WATER (45)
White-Smith Mus Co, pub. 1909, reached Top 40 in August 1909
Nellie R Eberhart w, Charles W Cadman m
Steady seller as one of Four Indian Love Lyrics 1909-1916
Alma Gluck 08/11 Vic 64190
concert singers

GAMES OF CHILDHOOD DAYS (49)
Will Rossiter, pub. 1908, reached #14 in May 1909
Will J Harris & Harry I Robinson w & m
Bessie Taylor, vv stage
Ada Jones 01/10 Col A-766

GEE, BUT THERE'S CLASS TO A GIRL LIKE YOU (42)
Will Rossiter, pub. 1909, reached #9 in October 1909
W R Williams w & m
Maude Lambert, vv stage
Columbia Four, vv stage
Manuel Romain 10/10 Ed Amb 528 cyl

GOOD EVENING, CAROLINE (32)
York Mus Co, pub. 1908, reached #5 in January 1909
Jack Norworth w, Albert Von Tilzer m
Elise Stevenson & Frank Stanley Φ 01/09 Vic 5629, 03/09 Col A-5080
Albert Von Tilzer, vv stage
Billy Murray 01/09 Ed 10038 cyl

GOOD NIGHT, DEAR (31)
Witmark, pub. 1908, reached #10 in January 1910
Will R Anderson w & m
Featured in LOVE WATCHES, show (opened 08/08)
Billie Burke, sung in show
Harvey Hindermeyer 08/09 Col A-717
Grace Belmont, vv stage
Elizabeth Wheeler 08/09 Vic 5709

I LOVE, I LOVE, I LOVE MY WIFE, BUT OH, YOU KID (26)
H Von Tilzer, pub. 1909, reached #5 in July 1909
Jimmy Lucas w, Harry Von Tilzer m
Billy Murray 07/09 Vic 5706
Arthur Collins 08/09 Col A-707, 09/09 Zono 5523
Bob Roberts 08/09 Ind 1129 cyl
Harry Von Tilzer, vv stage

I LOVE MY WIFE, BUT OH, YOU KID! (27)
V Kremer, pub. 1909, reached #7 in July 1909
Harry Armstrong & Billy Clark w & m
Armstrong & Clark, vv stage
Doric Trio, vv stage
Edward M Favor 09/09 Ed 10201 cyl

I WISH I HAD MY OLD GIRL BACK AGAIN (12)
J W Stern, pub. 1909, reached #5 in November 1909
Ballard MacDonald w, Paul Wallace m
Manuel Romain 10/09 Ed Amb 216 cyl
Glen Ellison, vv stage
The Continentals, vv stage

I WONDER WHO'S KISSING HER NOW (3)
C K Harris ΦΦΦ, pub. 1909, reached #1 in September 1909 (Also reached #2 in October 1947)
Will Hough & Frank Adams w, Joe Howard & Harold Orlob m
Featured in THE PRINCE OF TONIGHT, show (opened 03/09 in Chicago)
Henry Burr ΦΦ 08/09 Col A-707, 01/10 Ind 1256 cyl
Joe E Howard, sung in show (later: 1936 Voc 3357)
Billy Murray 01/10 Vic 16426, 03/10 Zono 5607
vv singers

I'M AWFULLY GLAD I MET YOU (43)
F B Haviland, pub. 1909, reached #17 in July 1909
Jack Drislane w, George W Meyer m
Ada Jones & Billy Murray 09/09 Ed 10202 cyl, 10/09 Vic 16346
May Ward, vv stage

I'VE GOT A PAIN IN MY SAWDUST (37)
J W Stern, pub. 1909, reached Top 30 in July 1909
Henry Warner w, Herman Wade m
Steady seller 1909 & 1910
Kitty Cheatham, stage, 06/10 Col A-5168
other stage singers

I'VE GOT RINGS ON MY FINGERS (4)
Francis, D & H, pub. 1909, reached #1 in November 1909
R P Weston & F J Barnes w, Maurice Scott m
Featured in THE MIDNIGHT SONS, show (opened 05/09)
Also featured in THE YANKEE GIRL, show (opened 02/10)
Blanche Ring ΦΦ sung in both shows, 10/09 Vic 5737
Ada Jones Φ 09/09 Ind 1156 cyl, 11/09 Col A-741
Billy Murray 10/09 Ed Am 218 cyl, 08/10 Vic 16510
vv singers

IF I HAD A THOUSAND LIVES TO LIVE (13)
J W Stern, pub. 1908, reached #2 in April 1909
Sylvester Maguire w, Alfred Solman m
Allen Waterous 07/08 Ed 9884 cyl
Nellie Vesta, vv stage
The Continentals, vv stage
Edward Hamilton 07/09 Vic 16321

KERRY MILLS BARN DANCE (15)
F A Mills, pub. 1908, reached #13 in June 1909
Thurland Chattaway w, Kerry Mills m
Edison Symphony Orch 08/08 Ed 9909 cyl
Prince's Military Band 01/09 Col A-5082
other concert bands

LET'S GO BACK TO BABY DAYS
F B Haviland, pub. 1909, reached #13 in May 1909
Jack Drislane w, George W Meyer m
Byron G Harlan 07/09 Ind 1097 cyl
Ada Jones 09/09 Zono 5524

LONESOME (36)
F A Mills, pub. 1909, reached #13 in August 1909
Edgar Leslie w, George W Meyer m
Featured in MLLE. MISCHIEF, show (opened 09/08)
Lulu Glazer, sung in show
Harry Macdonough/Haydn Quartet 10/09 Vic 5743
Byron G Harlan 10/09 Ed 10219 cyl, 10/09 Ind 1184 cyl
Still City Quartet, vv stage

LOVE IS LIKE A CIGARETTE (35)
C K Harris, pub. 1908, reached #11 in February 1909
Glen MacDonough w, Victor Herbert m
Featured in ALGERIA, show[1] (opened 08/08)
Frank Pollock, sung in show
concert singers

MY COUSIN CARUS' (11)
Gus Edwards M P C, pub. 1909, reached #2 in August 1909
Edward Madden w, Gus Edwards m
Featured in MISS INNOCENCE, show (opened 11/08)
Also feat. in ZIEGFELD FOLLIES OF 1909, show (opened 06/09)
Billy Murray ΦΦ 06/09 Vic 16327
Anna Held, sung in show (MI)
Eddie Morton, vv stage
Arthur Deagon, sung in show (ZF)

MY OWN UNITED STATES (19)
Witmark, pub. 1902, reached #7 in January 1909
(Also reached #3 in March 1903)
Stanislaus Stange w, Julian Edwards m
Harry Wise, vv stage
other vv singers

MY PONY BOY (10)
J H Remick, pub. 1909, reached #1 in August 1909
Bobby Heath w, Charlie O'Donnell m
Featured in MISS INNOCENCE, show (opened 11/08)
Lillian Lorraine, sung in show
Columbia Quartet[2] Φ 08/09 Col A-713, 11/09 Ind 1198 cyl
Ada Jones Φ 10/09 Ed Amb 221 cyl, 11/09 Vic 16356
Empire City Quartet, vv stage

MY WIFE'S GONE TO THE COUNTRY (HURAH! HURAH!) (16)
Ted Snyder, pub. 1909, reached #3 in September 1909
George Whiting & Irving Berlin[5] w, Ted Snyder m
Orpheus Comedy Four, vv stage
Collins & Harlan Φ 09/09 Vic 5736, 09/09 Col A-724
Mabel Hite, vv stage

NEXT TO YOUR MOTHER, WHO DO YOU LOVE? (47)
Ted Snyder, pub. 1909, reached #9 in December 1909
Irving Berlin[5] w, Ted Snyder m
Kathryn Miley, vv stage
Kate Elinore, vv stage

NOBODY KNOWS, NOBODY CARES (17)
C K Harris, pub. 1909, reached #4 in May 1909
Charles K Harris w & m
Imogene Comer, vv stage
Franklyn Wallace, vv stage
Harvey Hindermeyer 07/09 Vic 16321

OH, MISS MALINDA (25)
Will Rossiter, pub. 1908, reached #4 in April 1909
Max Armstrong & Bonita Armstrong w & m
Added to WINE, WOMEN & SONG, show (opened 09/07)
Bonita Armstrong, sung in show
Maude Lambert, vv stage
Doric Trio, vv stage
Lola Lee 12/09 Ind 1234 cyl

PANSIES MEAN THOUGHTS, AND THOUGHTS MEAN YOU (44)
Witmark, pub. 1909, reached #19 in August 1909
Fleita Jan Brown w, Herbert Spencer m
Harry Macdonough 05/09 Vic 16292
Frances Gerard, vv stage
Nell Capron, vv stage

RED, RED ROSE (41)
Gotham-Attucks, pub. 1908, reached #15 in July 1909
Alex Rogers w, Will M Cook m
Featured in BANDANA LAND, show (opened 02/08)
Minnie Brown, sung in show
Arthur Clough/Haydn Quartet 12/09 Vic 35085

RED HEAD (23)
L Feist, pub. 1908, reached #9 in September 1909
Irene Franklin w, Burt Green m
Irene Franklin, vv stage
Ada Jones 11/09 Vic 16360, 1/10 Ed Amb 326 cyl, 1/10 Zono 5580
Victor Orch 10/09 Vic 16346

(YOU'RE IN) THE RIGHT CHURCH BUT THE WRONG PEW (9)
Gotham-Attucks, pub. 1908, reached #1 in February 1909
Cecil Mack w, Chris Smith m
Featured in BANDANA LAND, show (opened 02/08)
Walker & Williams, sung in show
Eddie Morton Φ 09/08 Vic 5501, 09/08 Ind 854 cyl
Collins & Harlan Φ 02/09 Col A-621
Clarice Vance, vv stage

ROSE OF THE WORLD (21)
C K Harris, pub. 1908, reached #5 in February 1909
Glen MacDonough w, Victor Herbert m
Featured in ALGERIA, show[1] (opened 08/08)
Ida Brooks Hunt, sung in show
Alice C Stevenson 01/10 Zono 5582
Victor Herbert Orch 02/10 Ed Amb 345 cyl

SADIE SALOME, GO HOME (39)
Ted Snyder, pub. 1909, reached #18 in September 1909
Irving Berlin[5] & Edgar Leslie w & m
Fanny Brice, vv stage
Bob Roberts, vv stage, 03/10 Col A-789
Edward M Favor 11/09 Ed 10243 cyl, 11/09 Ind 1211 cyl
Lillian Shaw, vv stage

SCHOOL MATES (33)
Gus Edwards M P C, pub. 1909, reached #6 in June 1909
Ed Gardenier w, Gus Edwards m
Harry Macdonough/Haydn Quartet 07/09 Vic 5704
Byron G Harlan 06/09 Zono 5488, 06/09 Ind 1053 cyl, 07/09 Ed 10159 cyl
vv singers

SENORA (48)
L Feist, pub. 1907, reached #12 in December 1909
Felix Feist w, Joseph S Nathan m
Pryor's Band 07/09 Vic 16325
Almont & Dumont, vv stage

SHINE ON, HARVEST MOON (2)
J H Remick ΦΦΦ, pub. 1908, reached #1 in March 1909
(Also reached #16 in October 1931)
Jack Norworth & Nora Bayes w & m
Featured in ZIEGFELD FOLLIES OF 1908, show (opened 06/08)
Nora Bayes & Jack Norworth, sung in show
Miss Walton & Mr. Macdonough[4] ΦΦ 04/09 Vic 16259
Ada Jones & Billy Murray Φ 05/09 Ed 10134 cyl
Frank Stanley & Henry Burr 05/09 Ind 1075 cyl, 06/09 Zono 5509
Anna Held, vv stage

TAKE ME OUT TO THE BALL GAME
York Mus Co ΦΦΦ, pub. 1908, reached #20 in June 1909
(Also reached #1 in August 1908)
Jack Norworth w, Albert Von Tilzer m
Billy Murray 07/09 Vic 5570 (ri)
vv singers

TAKE ME UP WITH YOU, DEARIE (34)
York Mus Co, pub. 1909, reached #10 in August 1909
Junie McCree w, Albert Von Tilzer m
Billy Murray/Haydn Quartet Φ 08/09 Vic 5718, 09/09 Ed 10213 cyl
Frank Stanley 09/09 Ind 1153 cyl
vv singers

THAT LOVIN' RAG (40)
F B Haviland, pub. 1907, reached Top 30 in June 1909
Victor H Smalley w, Bernie Adler m
Steady seller 1908-1910
Sophie Tucker, vv stage, 05/10 Ed 10360 cyl
Nora Bayes, vv stage, 09/10 Vic 60023
Empire City Quartet, vv stage

THAT'S A-PLENTY (18)
Will Rossiter, pub. 1909, reached #4 in November 1909
Bert Williams & Henry Creamer w & m
Featured in MR. LODE OF KOAL, show (opened 11/09)
Bert Williams, sung in show
Arthur Collins, ΦΦ 09/09 Vic 16344, 09/09 Col A-724, 09/09 Zono 5523, 09/09 Ind 1150
Al Jolson, vv stage
George Alexander, vv stage

THIS ROSE BRINGS MY HEART TO YOU (50)
Gus Edwards M P C, pub. 1909, reached #15 in May 1909
Leo Edwards w, Leo Wood m
Harry Macdonough 08/09 Vic 16337
vv singers

TO THE END OF THE WORLD WITH YOU (5)
Witmark, pub. 1908, reached #5 in September 1909
George Graff & Dave Reed w, Ernest Ball m
Henry Burr ΦΦ 04/09 Col A-648, 05/09 Vic 16292
Phyllis Allen, vv stage
Manuel Romain 1909 Ed Amb 118 cyl

UP, UP, UP IN MY AEROPLANE
Gus Edwards M P C, pub. 1909, reached #12 in November 1909
Edward Madden w, Gus Edwards m
Featured in ZIEGFELD FOLLIES OF 1909, show (opened 06/09)
Lillian Lorraine, sung in show
Haydn Quartet 09/09 Vic 16340

WHEN I DREAM IN THE GLOAMING OF YOU (6)
Shapiro, B, pub. 1908, reached #2 in July 1909
Herbert Ingraham w & m
Harry Tally Φ vv stage, 10/09 Col A-733
Byron G Harlan Φ 08/09 Zono 5500
Frank Morrell, vv stage
Anna Driver, vv stage
Thomas Quigley, vv stage

WILD CHERRIES RAG (24)
Ted Snyder, pub. 1909, reached #7 in December 1909
Irving Berlin[5] w, Ted Snyder m
Featured in ZIEGFELD FOLLIES OF 1910, show (opened 06/10)
Fanny Brice, sung in show
Maude Raymond, vv stage
Eddie Morton 10/09 Col A-737

YIP-I-ADDY-I-AY! (7)
M Shapiro, pub. 1908, reached #1 in June 1909
Will D Cobb w, John H Flynn m
Blanche Ring ΦΦ vv stage, 06/09 Vic 5692
Collins & Harlan Φ 03/09 Ed 10094 cyl, 03/09 Zono 5197
Thomas Quigley, vv stage

YOU AIN'T TALKIN' TO ME (20)
Will Rossiter, pub. 1909, reached #15 in September 1909
Shelton Brooks w & m
Lew Dockstader, vv stage
Al Jolson, vv stage
Eddie Morton, vv stage, 02/10 Col A-777
George Alexander, vv stage

[1]ALGERIA was renamed ROSE OF ALGERIA and reopened 09/09.
[2]The Columbia Quartet was the label's name for the Peerless Quartet.
[3]Arthur Collins sang solo on Ind 1096.
[4]Miss Walton is believed to be Elise Stevenson. Mr. Macdonough is Harry Macdonough.
[5]Irving Berlin's given name was Israel Baline.

1910

ALL THAT I ASK OF YOU IS LOVE (16)
M Shapiro, pub. 1910, reached #5 in November 1910
Edgar Selden w, Herbert Ingraham m
Frank Morrell, vv stage
Bessie Wynn, vv stage
Henry Burr 11/10 Ind 1419 cyl
Edgar Selden, vv stage
Collins & Harlan 01/11 Vic 5806

ANY LITTLE GIRL THAT'S A NICE LITTLE GIRL (9)
M Shapiro ΦΦΦ, pub. 1910, reached #1 in September 1910
Thomas J Gray w, Fred Fisher m
Billy Murray/American Quartet ΦΦ 10/10 Vic 16560
Della Fox, vv stage
May Ward, vv stage
Walter Van Brunt Φ 10/10 Col A-897

ARE YOU LONESOME? (46)
Thompson Mus Co, pub. 1909, reached #15 in March 1910
Gus Kahn w, Grace LeBoy m
Manuel Romain, vv stage

BIG BASS VIOL (50)
Ted Snyder Co, pub. 1910, reached Top 30 in July 1910
M T Bohannon w & m
Frank Stanley/Peerless Quartet 08/10 Vic 16507, 07/10 Zono 5634
vv singers

CALL ME UP SOME RAINY AFTERNOON (22)
Ted Snyder Co, pub. 1910, reached #5 in July 1910
Irving Berlin w & m
Ada Jones Φ 08/10 Vic 16508, 08/10 Ed Amb 485 cyl, 08/10 Ind 1386 cyl, 09/10 Col A-855
Emma Carus, vv stage
Maude Raymond, vv stage

CASEY JONES (6)
Southern Calif Mus Co, pub. 1909, reached #3 in January 1911
T Lawrence Seibert w, Eddie Newton m
Became folk and country standard
Billy Murray ΦΦ 05/10 Vic 16483, 06/10 Ed Amb 450
Seibert & Newton, vv stage
Collins & Harlan 11/10 Col A-907

THE CHANTICLEER RAG (47)
J H Remick, pub. 1910, reached #18 in August 1910
Edward Madden w, Albert Gumble m
Collins & Harlan 09/10 Col A-854, 09/10 Ind 1395 cyl, 09/10 Ed 10415 cyl
vv singers

CHINATOWN, MY CHINATOWN (45)
J H Remick ΦΦΦ, pub. 1906, reached Top 30 in October 1910
(Also reached #5 in February 1915)
William Jerome w, Jean Schwartz m
Featured in UP AND DOWN BROADWAY, show (opened 07/10)
Eddie Foy, sung in show

CIRIBIRIBIN (26)
Eclipse Mus Co, pub. 1909, reached #11 in March 1910
(Also reached #20 in January 1940)
Rudolf Thaler w, Alberto Pestalozza m
Victor Orch 11/09 Vic 16357
Prince's Orch 01/11 Col A-5235
Enrico Caruso, stage

COME AFTER BREAKFAST, BRING 'LONG YOUR LUNCH, AND LEAVE ' FORE SUPPER TIME (21)
J W Stern, pub. 1909, reached #3 in February 1910
James T Brymn, Chris Smith & Jim Burris w & m
Arthur Collins Φ 03/10 Col A-789, 06/10 Ind 1345 cyl
Chris Smith, vv stage
Weston & Young, vv stage
Stewart & Marshall, vv stage

COME ALONG, MY MANDY! (29)
T B Harms & FDH, pub. 1910, reached #7 in May 1910
Tom Mellor, Alfred J Lawrence, Harry Gifford w & m
Featured in THE JOLLY BACHELORS, show (opened 01/10)
Nora Bayes & Jack Norworth, sung in show, 06/10 Vic 70016
Ada Jones & Billy Murray 07/10 Ed Amb 468 cyl
vv singers

THE CUBANOLA GLIDE (10)
H Von Tilzer, pub. 1909, reached #2 in January 1910
Alfred Bryan w, Harry Von Tilzer m
Featured in THE GIRL FROM RECTOR'S, show (opened 05/09)
Harriet Raymond, sung in show
Sophie Tucker, vv stage
Billy Murray Φ 04/10 Vic 5769
Collins & Harlan 04/10 Ind 1305 cyl, 05/10 Ed Amb 432 cyl

DANCE OF THE GRIZZLY BEAR (48)
Ted Snyder M C, pub. 1910, reached Top 30 in September 1910
Irving Berlin w, George Botsford m
Stella Mayhew 08/10 Ed Amb 479 cyl
Billy Murray 01/11 Vic 16681
Pryor's Band 12/10 Vic 5802

DEAR OLD MOONLIGHT (43)
Gotham-Attucks, pub. 1909, reached Top 30 in April 1910
Henry Creamer w, Tom Lemonier m
vv singers

EV'RY DAY (44)
Witmark, pub. 1909, reached #20 in March 1910
Lou Weslyn w, Ted S Barron m
Barron & Weslyn, vv stage
Nanette Wallach, vv stage

EVERY LITTLE MOVEMENT (4)
Witmark, pub. 1910, reached #1 in January 1911
Otto Harbach w, Karl Hoschna m
Featured in MADAME SHERRY, show (opened 08/10)
Lucy Isabel Marsh & Harry Macdonough ΦΦ 08/10 Vic 5784[1]
Jack Reinhard & Florence Mackie, sung in show
Inez Barbour & Reinald Werrenrath Φ 08/10 Vic 5784[1]
Nat Wills, vv stage
Henry Burr & Margaret Mayhew[2] 10/10 Col A-894

THE GARDEN OF ROSES (33)
J H Remick, pub. 1909, reached #11 in January 1910
J E Dempsey w, Johann C Schmid m
Haydn Quartet 04/10 Vic 16467
vv singers

THE GLOW-WORM (39)
J W Stern, pub. 1907, reached #16 in April 1910
(Also reached #1 in May 1908)
(Also reached #2 in December 1952, with modernized lyrics)
Lilla Cayley Robinson w, Paul Lincke m
Prince's Orch 08/09 Col A-711
Vienna Quartet Φ 07/10 Vic 16503

GO ON, GOOD-A-BYE (35)
V Kremer, pub. 1910, reached #19 in June 1910
A W Brown w, M Joseph Murphy m
Brown & Cooper, vv stage
Terry & Lambert, vv stage

HAS ANYBODY HERE SEEN KELLY? (7)
T B Harms & F D H, pub. 1909, reached #1 in June 1910
C W Murphy, Will Letters & William C McKenna w & m
Featured in THE JOLLY BACHELORS, show (opened 01/10)
Nora Bayes Φ sung in show, 05/10 Vic 60013
Emma Carus, vv stage
Ada Jones 05/10 Col A-810, 08/10 Vic 16510
Billy Murray 05/10 Ed Amb 416 cyl, 09/10 Zono 5651

HEAVEN WILL PROTECT THE WORKING GIRL (30)
C K Harris, pub. 1909, reached #13 in October 1910
Edgar Smith w, A Baldwin Sloane m
Featured in TILLIE'S NIGHTMARE, show (opened 05/10)
Marie Dressler, sung in show, 09/10 Ed 10416 cyl
vv singers

I'D RATHER SAY HELLO THAN SAY GOODBYE (49)
J F Helf, pub. 1910, reached Top 30 in December 1910
Alfred Bryan w, J Fred Helf m
Excelsior Trio, vv stage
John Vogel's Minstrels, vv stage

I'LL MAKE A RING AROUND ROSIE (36)
J H Remick, pub. 1910, reached #8 in June 1910
William Jerome w, Jean Schwartz m
Blanche Ring, vv stage
Haydn Quartet 07/10 Vic 16498

I'M NOT THAT KIND OF GIRL (42)
J W Stern, pub. 1910, reached #20 in June 1910
A Seymour Brown w, Nat Ayer m
Maida Dupree, vv stage
Two Quaker Maids, vv stage

I'VE GOT THE TIME, I'VE GOT THE PLACE, BUT IT'S HARD TO FIND THE GIRL (15)
J W Stern, pub. 1910, reached #2 in August 1910
Ballard MacDonald w, S R Henry m
Hetty King, vv stage
Frank Coombs, vv stage
Walter Van Brunt Φ 09/10 Ind 3122 cyl, 10/10 Col A-897
Henry Burr 11/10 Vic 16727

IF HE COMES IN, I'M GOING OUT (23)
Gotham-Attucks, pub. 1910, reached #8 in November 1910
Cecil Mack w, Chris Smith m
Featured in A BARNYARD ROMEO, revue (1910)
Stella Mayhew, sung in revue
Leighton Brothers, vv stage
Eddie Morton 12/10 Vic 16650
Arthur Collins 08/10 Col A-845, 08/10 Ind 1381 cyl

IN THE GARDEN OF MY HEART (8)
Witmark, pub. 1908, reached #8 in April 1910
Caro Roma w, Ernest Ball m
Caro Roma, stage
Ernest Ball, stage
Reed Miller Φ 03/10 Vic 5765
Chauncey Olcott, stage
Frank Stanley & Henry Burr Φ 03/09 Col A-641, 06/09 Ind 1107 cyl

JUST FOR A GIRL (32)
Witmark, pub. 1910, reached #9 in July 1910
Ren Shields w, Ernest Ball m
Empire City Quartet, vv stage
Edward M Favor 10/10 Ed Amb 533 cyl
Frank Coombs, vv stage

MEET ME TONIGHT IN DREAMLAND (1)
Will Rossiter ΦΦΦ, pub. 1909, reached #1 in July 1910
Beth Slater Whitson w, Leo Friedman m
Maude Lambert, vv stage
Frank Morrell, vv stage
Elizabeth Wheeler & Harry Anthony Φ 01/10 Ed 10290 cyl
Henry Burr Φ 11/10 Col A-905
Primrose Four, vv stage

THE MORNING AFTER THE NIGHT BEFORE
J F Helf, pub. 1910, reached #20 in August 1910
Ed Moran w, J Fred Helf m
Lew Dockstader, vv stage
Billy Murray 09/10 Vic 16557

MY HEART HAS LEARNED TO LOVE YOU, NOW DO NOT SAY GOODBYE (11)
Witmark, pub. 1910, reached #5 in October 1910
Dave Reed w, Ernest Ball m
Harry Macdonough/Haydn Quartet Φ 08/10 Vic 16503
Victoria Four, vv stage
Longacre Quartet, vv stage

PLAY THAT BARBERSHOP CHORD (5)
J F Helf, pub. 1910, reached #1 in November 1910
William Tracey & Ballard MacDonald w, Lewis Muir m
Bert Williams ΦΦ vv stage, 12/10 Col A-929
Billy Murray/American Quartet ΦΦ 11/10 Vic 5799
Lew Dockstader, vv stage
Avery & Hart, vv stage

PUT ON YOUR OLD GRAY BONNET (3)
J H Remick ΦΦΦ, pub. 1909, reached #1 in March 1910
Stanley Murphy w, Percy Wenrich m
Haydn Quartet ΦΦ 12/09 Vic 16377
Stella Arlington, vv stage
Arthur Clough Φ 02/10 Col A-778
Byron G Harlan 04/10 Ind 1303 cyl

SHAKY EYES (18)
Witmark, pub. 1909, reached #4 in April 1910
Harry Armstrong & Billy Clark w & m
Empire City Quartet, vv stage
Arlington Four, vv stage
Arthur Collins Φ 05/10 Col A-811, 07/10 Ind 1360 cyl
Billy Murray Φ 08/10 Vic 16504

SILVER BELL (14)
J H Remick, pub. 1910, reached #5 in January 1911
Edward Madden w, Percy Wenrich m
Peerless Quartet Φ 11/10 Vic 16646
"That Girl" Quartette Φ 01/11 Vic 16695
Frank Stanley & Henry Burr Φ 12/10 Col A-917
Ada Jones & Billy Murray 12/10 Ed Amb 576 cyl, 05/11 Ed 10492 cyl

SOME OF THESE DAYS (2)
Will Rossiter ΦΦΦ, pub. 1910, reached #1 in October 1910
Shelton Brooks w & m
Sophie Tucker, vv stage, 06/11 Ed Amb 691 cyl
Belle Baker, vv stage
American Quartet Φ 03/11 Vic 16834
Primrose Four, vv stage

SOMEBODY ELSE, IT'S ALWAYS SOMEBODY ELSE (25)
F B Haviland, pub. 1910, reached #9 in October 1910
Jack Drislane w, George Meyer m
Elida Morris, vv stage
The Leightons, vv stage
American Quartet 02/11 Vic 16707

SUGAR MOON (27)
J H Remick, pub. 1910, reached #14 in December 1910
Stanley Murphy w, Percy Wenrich m
Collins & Harlan Φ 09/10 Col A-853, 09/10 Ed Amb 496 cyl, 09/10 Zono 5646, 09/10 Ind 3121 cyl, 10/10 Vic 16540
vv singers

TAKE ME BACK TO BABYLAND (31)
Witmark, pub. 1909, reached #17 in December 1910
Frank J Tannehill w, Pat Rooney m
Louise Dresser, vv stage
Grace Belmont, vv stage
Arthur Deagan, vv stage

TEMPTATION RAG (20)
Witmark, pub. 1909, reached #7 in August 1910
Lou Weslyn w, Henry Lodge m
Featured in ZIEGFELD FOLLIES OF 1910, show (opened 06/10)
Lillian Lorraine, sung in show
Arthur Collins Φ 06/10 Col A-826, 07/10 Ind 1389 cyl, 12/10 Sonora 5052
Pryor's Band Φ 08/10 Vic 16511

THAT ITALIAN RAG (28)
L Feist, pub. 1910, reached #8 in May 1910
Edgar Leslie w, Al Piantadosi m
Billy Murray 10/10 Vic 16608
Ben Walsh, vv stage
Estelle Edwards, vv stage

THAT MESMERIZING MENDELSSOHN TUNE (17)
Ted Snyder Co, pub. 1909, reached #2 in March 1910
Irving Berlin w & m
Collins & Harlan ΦΦ 04/10 Vic 16472, 04/10 Col A-801, 04/10 Ed Amb 395, 05/10 Ind 3065
Sophie Tucker, vv stage
Con Conrad, vv stage

THAT'S YIDDISHA LOVE (24)
Witmark, pub. 1910, reached #8 in November 1910
James Brockman w & m
Monroe Silver, vv stage, 05/11 Vic 16846
Arlington Four, vv stage
Edward Meeker 01/11 Ed Amb 597 cyl

TIE YOUR LITTLE BULL OUTSIDE (40)
Witmark, pub. 1909, reached #11 in April 1910
James Brockman w & m
Dolly White, vv stage
Three White Kuhns, vv stage
Kerr & Haskell, vv stage

WAY DOWN IN COTTON TOWN (41)
L Feist, pub. 1909, reached #13 in March 1910
Edgar Leslie w, Al Piantadosi m
Empire City Quartet, vv stage
Dawson & Gillette, vv stage
Walter Van Brunt & Fred Hillebrand 07/10 Ind 1370 cyl

WHAT'S THE MATTER WITH FATHER? (13)
J H Remick, pub. 1910, reached #3 in August 1910
Harry H Williams w, Egbert Van Alstyne m
Billy Murray ΦΦ 06/10 Ed 10369 cyl, 07/10 Vic 16499
Eddie Morton 11/10 U-S 328 cyl
Harry Morgan, vv stage
Fred Duprez 09/10 Ind 1400 cyl

WHERE THE RIVER SHANNON FLOWS (12)
Witmark, pub. 1905, reached #11 in November 1910
James J Russell w & m
Harry Macdonough ΦΦ 02/10 Vic 16440
John McCormack, stage
Henry Burr Φ 05/10 Col A-815
Will Oakland 03/11 Ed Amb 623 cyl
John McClosky, vv stage

WITHOUT YOU THE WORLD DON'T SEEM THE SAME (34)
Head-Westman, pub. 1910, reached #17 in November 1910
Charles Shackford w, Maurice Wolfe m
Metropolitan Four, vv stage
Peerless Quartet 01/11 Vic 16689
Durand Trio, vv stage

YIDDLE ON YOUR FIDDLE (37)
Ted Snyder Co, pub. 1909, reached #7 in February 1910
Irving Berlin w & m
Fanny Brice, vv stage
Jimmie Lucas, vv stage
Grace Leonard, vv stage

YOU ARE THE IDEAL OF MY DREAMS (19)
Shapiro, B, pub. 1910, reached #4 in June 1910
Herbert Ingraham w & m
Manuel Romain, vv stage
Frank Morrell, vv stage
Henry Burr 08/10 Ind 3103 cyl

YOU TAUGHT ME HOW TO LOVE YOU, NOW TEACH ME TO FORGET (38)
F B Haviland, pub. 1909, reached #11 in June 1910
Jack Drislane w, George Meyer m
May Ward, vv stage
Joe Maxwell 07/10 Ed Amb 456 cyl

[1] Victor used the same issue number, 5784, for two different duos performing this song on record.
[2] Margaret Mayhew was a pseudonym for Elise Stevenson.

1911

AH! SWEET MYSTERY OF LIFE (39)
Witmark ΦΦΦ, pub. 1910, reached Top 30 in May 1911
(Also reached #9 in April 1928)
(Also reached #19 in July 1935)
Rida Johnson Young w, Victor Herbert m
Featured in NAUGHTY MARIETTA, show (opened 11/10)
Steady seller, peaking in late 1920's and mid-1930's
Emma Trentini & Orville Harrold, sung in show
stage singers

ALEXANDER'S RAGTIME BAND (1)
Ted Snyder Co ΦΦΦ, pub. 1911, reached #1 in October 1911
(Also reached #3 in September 1938)
Irving Berlin w & m
All time pop standard
Emma Carus, vv stage
Collins & Harlan ΦΦ 08/11 Zono 5766, 09/11 Col A-1032, 10/11 Vic 16908
Irving Berlin, vv stage
Billy Murray Φ 11/11 Ed Amb 817 cyl, 11/11 Ed 10522 cyl

ALL ABOARD FOR BLANKET BAY (7)
H Von Tilzer, pub. 1910, reached #4 in June 1911
Andrew Sterling w, Harry Von Tilzer m
Belle Baker, vv stage
Ada Jones Φ 05/11 Col A-989
Anna Chandler, vv stage
Walter Van Brunt Φ 07/11 Vic 16868, 07/11 Ind 3227 cyl

ALL ALONE (15)
H Von Tilzer, pub. 1911, reached #2 in August 1911
Will Dillon w, Harry Von Tilzer m
Ada Jones & Billy Murray ΦΦ 07/11 Zono 5750, 07/11 Vic 5846, 08/11 Vic 16884
Elsie Tuell, vv stage
Ada Jones & Walter Van Brunt Φ 07/11 Col A-1010

ALMA (WHERE DO YOU LIVE?) (19)
J H Remick, pub. 1910, reached #17 in September 1911
George V Hobart w, Adolph Philipp m
Featured in ALMA, WHERE DO YOU LIVE? show (opened 09/10)
Kitty Gordon, sung in show
Truly Shattuck, sung in show, 02/12 Col A-1092
Inez Barbour and Harry Anthony Φ 12/10 Vic 5805, 07/11 Ind 1488 cyl

BABY ROSE (8)
Witmark, pub. 1911, reached #3 in August 1911
Lou Weslyn w, George Christie m
Maude Lambert, vv stage
Emma Carus, vv stage
American Quartet Φ 06/11 Vic 16859
The Leightons, vv stage
Collins & Harlan Φ 08/11 Col A-1023, 07/11 Zono 5748

BILLY (17)
Kendis & Paley, pub. 1911, reached #4 in December 1911
(Also reached #11 in April 1958)
Joe Goodwin, James Kendis & Herman Paley w & m
Anna Chandler, vv stage, 11/11 Ed Amb 833 cyl
Ada Jones Φ 12/11 Col A-1071
American Quartet Φ 11/11 Vic 16965

BY THE SASKATCHEWAN (45)
Chappell, pub. 1911, reached #17 in July 1911
C M S McLellan w, Ivan Caryll m
Featured in THE PINK LADY, show (opened 03/11)
John Young & Ida Adams, sung in show
Reinald Werrenrath 06/11 Vic 5839
Andrea Sarto 08/11 Col A-1024

CAN'T YOU TAKE IT BACK AND CHANGE IT FOR A BOY? (44)
F B Haviland, pub. 1911, reached #19 in August 1911
Thurland Chattaway w & m
Lottie Gilson, vv stage, 01/12 Ed Amb 890 cyl
Byron G Harlan 11/11 Col A-1056

CHICKEN RAG
J F Helf, pub. 1911, reached #18 in January 1912
James Brockman w & m
Lew Dockstader, vv stage
Spook Minstrels, vv stage
Doc Baker, vv stage

CHICKEN REEL (25)
J M Daly, pub. 1910, reached #10 in October 1911
Joseph Mittenthal w, Joseph M Daly m
Eddie Morton, vv stage
Arthur Collins 09/11 Vic 16897, 10/11 Col A-1044

CHILD LOVE
J W Stern, pub. 1911, reached #20 in October 1911
Dave Oppenheim w, Joe Cooper m
Mabel Howard, vv stage
Sydney Reynolds, vv stage
Ed Wilson, vv stage

COME, JOSEPHINE, IN MY FLYING MACHINE (9)
Shapiro, B ΦΦΦ, pub. 1910, reached #1 in March 1911
Alfred Bryan w, Fred Fisher m
Blanche Ring ΦΦ vv stage, 03/11 Vic 60032
Ada Jones/American Quartet ΦΦ 05/11 Vic 16844
Blossom Seeley, vv stage
Estelle Hart, vv stage
Harry Tally 03/11 Col A-966

DAY DREAMS (VISIONS OF BLISS) (16)
J W Stern, pub. 1910, reached #6 in May 1911
Robert B Smith w, Heinrich Reinhardt m
Featured in THE SPRING MAID, show (opened 12/10)
Christie MacDonald, sung in show, 01/12 Vic 60061
Henry Burr & Elise Stevenson Φ 04/11 Vic 5830, 04/11 Zono 5707, 05/11 Col A-990[1]

DOCTOR TINKLE TINKER (46)
Witmark, pub. 1910, reached #20 in September 1911
Otto Harbach w, Karl Hoschna m
Featured in THE GIRL OF MY DREAMS, show (opened 08/11)
John Hyams & Leila McIntyre, sung in show
Alice C Stevenson 04/11 Zono 5703

DON'T WAKE ME UP, I'M DREAMING (26)
Shapiro, B, pub. 1910, reached #9 in June 1911
Beth Slater Whitson w, Henry Ingraham m
Bessie Wynn, vv stage
Frank Morrell, vv stage
Walter Van Brunt Φ 08/11 Vic 16880, 08/11 Ind 1498 cyl
Savoy Girl Quartet 06/11 Col A-1001

DOWN BY THE OLD MILL STREAM (3)
Tell Taylor M P ΦΦΦ, pub. 1910, reached #1 in July 1911
Tell Taylor w & m
Harry Macdonough ΦΦ 12/11 Vic 17000
Frank Morrell, vv stage
Arthur Clough ΦΦ 10/11 Ed Amb 796 cyl, 11/11 Col A-1047
Frank Coombs, vv stage, 11/11 U-S 1310 cyl

GEE, BUT IT'S GREAT TO MEET A FRIEND FROM YOUR OWN HOME TOWN (14)
J F Helf, pub. 1910, reached #3 in June 1911
William Tracey w, James McGavisk m
Billy Murray Φ 03/11 Ed Amb 631 cyl, 09/11 Vic 16897
Sophie Tucker, vv stage
Will Oakland 02/11 U-S 346 cyl
Spook Minstrels, vv stage

GIRL OF MY DREAMS (50)
Harold Rossiter, pub. 1910, reached Top 30 in January 1911
Gene Emerson w & m
Richard Jose, vv stage
Simpsel & Reilly, vv stage

THE HARBOR OF LOVE (24)
J H Remick, pub. 1911, reached #5 in November 1911
Earl C Jones w, Charlotte Blake m
Frank Coombs & William H Thompson Φ 01/12 Col A-1087
Irving Gillette[4] 11/11 Ed Amb 824 cyl
Walter Van Brunt 03/12 Vic 17069
Rena Aubrey, vv stage

I LIKE THE HAT, I LIKE THE DRESS, AND I LIKE THE GIRL THAT'S IN IT (13)
J W Stern, pub. 1911, reached #6 in September 1911
Alfred Bryan w, S R Henry m
Byron G Harlan Φ 08/11 Zono 5763, 10/11 Vic 16911
Frank Ritter, vv stage
DeHaven & Sydney, vv stage

I LOVE THE NAME OF MARY (40)
Witmark, pub. 1910, reached Top 30 in April 1911
George Graff w, Ernest Ball & Chauncey Olcott m
Featured in BARRY OF BALLYMORE, show (opened 01/10)
Chauncey Olcott, sung in show
Will Oakland 03/11 Col A-969, 03/11 U-S 1133
Ernest Ball, vv stage

I WANT A GIRL (JUST LIKE THE GIRL WHO MARRIED DEAR OLD DAD) (4)
H Von Tilzer ΦΦΦ, pub. 1911, reached #2 in November 1911
Will Dillon w, Harry Von Tilzer m
American Quartet ΦΦ 11/11 Vic 16962
Columbia Quartet[3] ΦΦ 09/11 Col A-1034
Al Jolson, vv stage
Henry Burr 08/11 U-S 1282 cyl
Walter Van Brunt 11/11 Ed Amb 832 cyl, 11/11 Zono 5810

I'LL CHANGE THE THORNS TO ROSES (48)
C Laemmle, pub. 1910, reached #18 in January 1911
Arthur Lamb w, H Howard Cheney & Alfred Fredericks m
Will Oakland, vv stage, 04/11 Col A-980

I'M FALLING IN LOVE WITH SOMEONE (18)
Witmark, pub. 1910, reached #7 in April 1911
(Also reached #15 in July 1935)
Rida Johnson Young w, Victor Herbert m
Featured in NAUGHTY MARIETTA, show (opened 11/10)
John McCormack Φ 05/11 Vic 64179
Orville Harrold, sung in show
Henry Burr 04/11 Zono 5708

I'M LOOKING FOR A NICE YOUNG FELLOW (28)
J W Stern, pub. 1910, reached #3 in March 1911
Jeff T Branen w, S R Henry m
Ada Jones Φ 02/11 Ed Amb 605 cyl, 06/11 Col A-1000
Tempest & Sunshine, vv stage
Peerless Quartet Φ 02/11 Vic 5811
Muriel Window, vv stage

IN ALL MY DREAMS I DREAM OF YOU (38)
L Feist, pub. 1911, reached Top 30 in August 1911
Joseph McCarthy w, Al Piantadosi m
Will Oakland 08/11 Ed Amb 752 cyl
Frank Coombs & William H Thompson 11/11 Zono 5804, 12/11 Col A-1075
Lewis & Doty, vv stage

IN THE LAND OF HARMONY (31)
Ted Snyder Co, pub. 1911, reached #10 in August 1911
Bert Kalmar w, Ted Snyder m
Anna Chandler, vv stage, 08/11 Ed Amb 741 cyl
American Quartet Φ 09/11 Vic 16896
Arthur Collins Φ 07/11 Col A-1010
Josie Flynn, vv stage

ITALIAN STREET SONG (42)
Witmark, pub. 1910, reached #11 in March 1911
Rida Johnson Young w, Victor Herbert m
Featured in NAUGHTY MARIETTA, show (opened 11/10)
Emma Trentini, sung in show
Lucy Isabel Marsh Φ 02/11 Vic 60031

JIMMY VALENTINE (22)
J H Remick, pub. 1911, reached #14 in June 1911
Edward Madden w, Gus Edwards m
Gus Edwards, vv stage
Peerless Quartet Φ 10/11 Col A-1043[2], 04/12 Vic 17036, 07/12 Ed Amb 1042 cyl

KISS ME, MY HONEY, KISS ME (21)
Ted Snyder Co., pub. 1910, reached #4 in April 1911
Irving Berlin w, Ted Snyder m
Elida Morris Φ vv stage, 11/10 Col A-906, 12/10 Vic 16807
"Little" Amy Butler, vv stage
Ada Jones & Billy Murray 02/11 Ed Amb 617 cyl

KNOCK WOOD
H Von Tilzer, pub. 1911, reached #16 in December 1911
Andrew Sterling w, Harry Von Tilzer m
Sophie Tucker, vv stage, 12/11 Ed Amb 852 cyl
Ada Jones & Billy Murray 01/12 Vic 17008
Ada Jones & Walter Van Brunt 11/11 Col A-1058

LET ME CALL YOU SWEETHEART (2)
Harold Rossiter ΦΦΦ, pub. 1910, reached #1 in February 1911 (Also reached #9 in October 1925)
Beth Slater Whitson w, Leo Friedman m
Empire State Quartet, vv stage
Frank Morrell, vv stage
Arthur Clough Φ 03/11 Ed Amb 637 cyl
Columbia Quartet[3] Φ 11/11 Col A-1057

(HONKY TONKY) MONKEY RAG (36)
Thompson & Co, pub. 1911, reached #12 in January 1912
Chris Smith w & m
Sophie Tucker, vv stage
Rae Samuels, vv stage

MY BEAUTIFUL LADY (11)
Chappell, pub. 1911, reached #7 in December 1911
C M S McLellan w, Ivan Caryll m
Featured in THE PINK LADY, show (opened 03/11)
Lucy Isabel Marsh Φ 06/11 Vic 60040
Hazel Dawn, sung in show
Grace Kerns Φ 09/11 Col A-5307

MY HERO (12)
J H Remick, pub. 1909, reached #11 in August 1911
Stanislaus Stange w, Oscar Straus m
Featured in THE CHOCOLATE SOLDIER, show (opened 09/09)
Steady seller, 1910-1912
Lucy Isabel Marsh ΦΦ 04/10 Vic 60012
Rene Vivienne, sung in show
Inez Barbour 08/10 Col A-843

MY LOVIN' HONEY MAN (30)
L Feist, pub. 1911, reached #7 in December 1911
Joseph McCarthy w, Al Piantadosi m
Belle Baker, vv stage
Sophie Tucker, vv stage
Al Jolson, vv stage
American Quartet 01/12 Vic 16979

OCEANA ROLL (6)
J H Remick, pub. 1911, reached #2 in September 1911
Roger Lewis w, Lucien Denni m
Eddie Morton ΦΦ 10/11 Vic 16908
Six Musical Cuttys, vv stage
Arthur Collins Φ 10/11 Zono 5788, 12/11 Col A-1071

OH, YOU BEAR CAT RAG (34)
J F Helf, pub. 1910, reached Top 30 in February 1911
Fred Watson w & m
Sophie Tucker, vv stage
Blanche Ring, vv stage
Tascott, vv stage

ON MOBILE BAY (29)
J H Remick, pub. 1910, reached #10 in June 1911
Earle C Jones w, Neil Moret m
Will Oakland, vv stage, 05/11 Ed 10495
Albert Campbell & Henry Burr Φ 04/11 Col A-976
Collins & Harlan 08/11 Vic 16878

A PERFECT DAY (41)
C Jacobs-Bond ΦΦΦ, pub. 1910, reached Top 30 in May 1911 (Also reached #13 in August 1916)
Carrie Jacobs-Bond w & m
Steady seller, 1910's and 1920's
Cecil Fanning 09/11 Col A-5306
stage singers

PUT YOUR ARMS AROUND ME, HONEY (5)
York Mus Co ΦΦΦ, pub. 1910, reached #1 in May 1911 (Also reached #5 in October 1943)
Junie McCree w, Albert Von Tilzer m
Elizabeth Murray, vv stage
Collins & Harlan ΦΦ 03/11 Vic 16708, 04/11 Col A-978
Blossom Seeley, vv stage
"That Girl" Quartette Φ 03/11 Vic 5827
Ada Jones Φ 05/11 Ed Amb 669 cyl

ROAMIN' IN THE GLOAMIN' (47)
Francis D & H, pub. 1911, reached #19 in December 1911
George Grafton w, Harry Lauder m
Harry Lauder, vv stage, 08/11 Ed Amb 12320 cyl, 01/12 Vic 70061

SILVER THREADS AMONG THE GOLD (20)
H S Gordon ΦΦΦ, pub. 1873, reached Top 30 in March 1911
Eben E Rexford w, H P Danks m
Steady seller and stage favorite 1900's and 1910's
Richard Jose Φ stage, 1911 Vic 2556, 1911 Vic 31342[5]
John McCormack Φ 07/12 Vic 64260
Will Oakland, stage, 06/09 Vic 5691, 06/11 Ind 3227 cyl

STEAMBOAT BILL (10)
F A Mills, pub. 1910, reached #3 in July 1911
Ren Shields w, Bert Leighton & Frank Leighton m
Leighton Brothers Φ vv stage, 06/11 Zono 5729
Sophie Tucker, vv stage
Arthur Collins Φ 07/11 Vic 16867, 07/11 Col A-1005

THAT BEAUTIFUL RAG
Ted Snyder Co, pub. 1910, reached #20 in January 1911
Irving Berlin w, Ted Snyder m
Featured in UP AND DOWN BROADWAY, show (opened 07/10)
Ted Snyder & Irving Berlin, sung in show
Arthur Collins 09/10 Col A-853, 09/10 Zon 5653
Stella Mayhew 11/10 Ed 10438 cyl

THAT DREAMY ITALIAN WALTZ (37)
L Feist, pub. 1910, reached #17 in March 1911
Joe McCarthy w, Al Piantadosi m
Isabel D'Armond, vv stage
Ruth Thorp 10/11 U-S 405 cyl

THAT MINOR STRAIN
Gotham-Attucks, pub. 1910, reached #19 in January 1911
Cecil Mack w, Ford Dabney m
Featured in ZIEGFELD FOLLIES OF 1910, show (opened 06/10)
Bert Williams, sung in show
Eddie Morton, vv stage

THAT RAILROAD RAG (33)
Head M P C, pub. 1911, reached #18 in July 1911
Nat Vincent w, Ed Bimberg m
Lottie Gilson, vv stage
Walter Van Brunt Φ 08/11 Vic 16876
Collins & Harlan 07/11 U-S 390 cyl, 08/11 Zono 5760

THAT WAS BEFORE I MET YOU (43)
F B Haviland, pub. 1911, reached #15 in May 1911
Alfred Bryan w, George Meyer m
Ada Jones & Walter Van Brunt 06/11 Col A-998
Steele & Carr, vv stage

THERE'LL COME A TIME (32)
Harold Rossiter, pub. 1911, reached #13 in May 1911
Shelton Brooks w & m
Sophie Tucker, vv stage
Quaker City Quartet, vv stage
Arlington Four, vv stage

THEY ALWAYS PICK ON ME (35)
H Von Tilzer, pub. 1911, reached #12 in October 1911
Stanley Murphy w, Harry Von Tilzer m
Ada Jones Φ 11/11 Col A-1056, 01/12 Vic 17008, 01/12 Ed Amb 871 cyl
Mabel Howard 07/11 U-S 1247 cyl
vv singers

TWO LITTLE LOVE BEES (27)
J W Stern, pub. 1910, reached #11 in July 1911
Robert B Smith w, Heinrich Reinhardt m
Featured in THE SPRING MAID, show (opened 12/10)
Christie MacDonald, sung in show, 01/12 Vic 60060
Elizabeth Wheeler & Reinald Werrenrath Φ 05/11 Vic 5836
vv singers

UNDER THE YUM YUM TREE (23)
H Von Tilzer, pub. 1910, reached #4 in February 1911
Andrew Sterling w, Harry Von Tilzer m
Collins & Harlan Φ 01/11 Col A-943, 03/11 Vic 16836, 04/11 Ed Amb 646 cyl
Belle Baker, vv stage
Anna Chandler, vv stage

WOODMAN, WOODMAN, SPARE THAT TREE! (49)
T Snyder, pub. 1911, reached Top 30 in September 1911
Irving Berlin w & m
Featured in ZIEGFELD FOLLIES OF 1911, show (opened 06/11)
Bert Williams, sung in show (Later: 1913 Col A-1321)
Bob Roberts 10/11 Vic 16909, 11/11 Ed Amb 837 cyl
Arthur Collins 10/11 U-S 1333 cyl

[1]Columbia listed the duo as Henry Burr and Margaret Mayhew, the latter being a pseudonym for Elise Stevenson.
[2]Listed on Columbia as the Columbia Quartette.
[3]The Columbia Quartette was actually the Peerless Quartet.
[4]Irving Gillette was a pseudonym for Henry Burr.
[5]Richard Jose's recordings were reissued c. 01/11.

1912

AFTER ALL THAT I'VE BEEN TO YOU
F B Haviland, pub. 1912, reached #20 in January 1913
Jack Drislane w, Chris Smith m
Harry Ellis, vv stage
other vv singers

ALL NIGHT LONG (33)
Harold Rossiter, pub. 1912, reached #13 in December 1912
Shelton Brooks w & m
Belle Baker, vv stage
Ada Jones & Billy Murray Φ 04/13 Vic 17278
Ada Jones 05/13 Col A-1297

HER RAG
Morse Mus Co, pub. 1911, reached #12 in March 1912
Theodore F Morse w & m
Josie Sabel, vv stage
American Quartet Φ 02/12 Vic 17027
Albert Campbell & Henry Burr 03/12 Ed 455 cyl

AT THE RAGTIME BALL
Forster M P, pub. 1911, reached #18 in May 1912
Roger Lewis w, James V Monaco m
Surrey & Lynne, vv stage
other vv singers

DEAR OLD ROSE
F B Haviland, pub. 1912, reached #20 in July 1912
Jack Drislane w, George W Meyer m
Charles Harrison 08/12 U-S 1534 cyl
James Gillespie, vv stage

DREAMS OF LONG AGO (34)
L Feist, pub. 1912, reached #8 in October 1912
John Focaci & Earl Carroll w, Enrico Caruso m
Enrico Caruso ΦΦ 08/12 Vic 88376

EVERYBODY TWO-STEP (20)
J H Remick, pub. 1912, reached #5 in December 1912
Earl C Jones w, Wallie Herzer m
American Quartet Φ 11/12 Vic 17171
Victor Military Band 03/13 Vic 17271
vv singers

EVERYBODY'S DOIN' IT NOW (7)
Ted Snyder Co, pub. 1911, reached #1 in May 1912
Irving Berlin w & m
Lydia Barry, vv stage
Collins & Harlan ΦΦ 02/12 Vic 17020, 02/12 U-S 445 cyl
Columbia Quartet[1] 04/12 Col A-1123
Ruby Raymond, vv stage
Maude Tiffany, vv stage

THE GABY GLIDE (8)
Shapiro, B, pub. 1911, reached #2 in May 1912
Harry Pilcer w, Louis A Hirsch m
Featured in VERA VIOLETTA, show (opened 11/11)
Gaby Deslys, sung in show
Billy Murray ΦΦ 02/12 Zono 5847, 06/12 Vic 17077, 07/12 Ed Amb 1049 cyl
Pryor's Band 05/12 Vic 17063
Blossom Seeley, vv stage

A GARLAND OF OLD FASHIONED ROSES (35)
Forster M P, pub. 1912, reached #15 in October 1912
C H Musgrove w, E Clinton Keithley m
Victoria Four, vv stage
Elk's Minstrels, vv stage
Walter Van Brunt 03/13 Vic 17266

THE GHOST OF THE VIOLIN (37)
Waterson, B & S, pub. 1912, reached #9 in January 1913
Bert Kalmar w, Ted Snyder m
Walter Van Brunt & Maurice Burkhart 12/12 Vic 17195
Peerless Quartet 02/13 Col A-1244
Courtney Sisters, vv stage

GOODBYE, ROSE (25)
Shapiro, B, pub. 1910, reached #10 in June 1912
Addison Burkhart w, Herbert Ingraham m
Marshall & Montgomery, vv stage
Lyons & Yosco, vv stage
Walter Van Brunt 06/12 Vic 17072

HITCHY KOO (16)
F A Mills, pub. 1912, reached #4 in December 1912
L Wolfe Gilbert w, Lewis F Muir & Maurice Abrahams m
American Quartet Φ 12/12 Vic 17196
L Wolfe Gilbert, vv stage
Collins & Harlan 12/12 Ed Amb 1605 cyl, 01/13 Col A-1236

I LOVE LOVE
Witmark, pub. 1911, reached #20 in February 1912[8]
Channing Pollock & Rennald Wolf w, Charles J Gebest m
Featured in THE RED WIDOW, show (opened 11/11)
Flora Zabelle & Theodore Martin, sung in show
Caroline Vaughn & Henry Burr 02/12 Col A-1099
Lyric Quartet 02/12 Vic 5868

I LOVE YOU TRULY (39)
C. Jacobs-Bond ΦΦΦ, pub. 1906, reached #9 in October 1912
Carrie Jacobs-Bond w & m
Elsie Baker ΦΦ 08/12 Vic 17121

I'D LOVE TO LIVE IN LOVELAND WITH A GIRL LIKE YOU (26)
Will Rossiter, pub. 1910, reached #13 in March 1912
W R Williams, Leon M Block & Harry L Alford w & m
Walter Van Brunt 07/12 Vic 17089, 07/12 Ed Amb 1062 cyl
Maud Lambert, vv stage
Nonette, vv stage

I'M THE LONESOMEST GAL IN TOWN (46)
York Mus Co, pub. 1912, reached #20 in October 1912
Lew Brown w, Albert Von Tilzer m
Rena Santos, vv stage
Gypsy Countess, vv stage

IF YOU TALK IN YOUR SLEEP, DON'T MENTION MY NAME (17)
J H Remick, pub. 1911, reached #5 in February 1911
A Seymour Brown w, Nat D Ayer m
Billy Murray Φ 02/12 Vic 17025
Lucy Weston, vv stage
Dolly Connolly 03/12 Col A-1116

"IN THE GLOAMING" WAS THE SONG SHE SANG TO ME (40)
J W Stern, pub. 1911, reached #16 in June 1912
Arthur Gillespie w, George Ade-Davis m
Four Scots, vv stage
Interstate Four, vv stage

IN THE SHADOWS (5)
J W Stern, pub. 1910, reached #4 in March 1912
E Ray Goetz w, Herman Finck m
Nellie V Nichols, vv stage
Helen Clark & Walter Van Brunt Ф 01/12 Vic 17009
Prince's Orch 11/11 Col A-5322
Ed Connelly, vv stage

KENTUCKY DAYS (36)
Wenrich & Mahoney, pub. 1912, reached #11 in September 1912
Jack Mahoney w, Percy Wenrich m
Peerless Quartet Ф 12/12 Col A-1223
Billy Murray 11/12 Ed Amb 1597 cyl, 05/13 Vic 17316
vv singers

LADY ANGELINE (30)
Witmark, pub. 1912, reached #15 in June 1912
Dave Reed w, George Christie m
Collins & Harlan Ф 05/12 Vic 17061, 05/12 Col A-1137
Willie & Eugene Howard, vv stage
Maude Lambert & Ernest Ball, stage

LOVE IS MINE (44)
Schuberth, pub. 1911, reached #13 in June 1912
Edward Teschemacher w, Clarence Gartner m
Enrico Caruso ФФ 05/12 Vic 87095

MACUSHLA (50)
Boosey & Co, pub. 1910, reached Top Thirty in January 1912
Josephine V Rowe w, Dermot Macmurrough m
John McCormack, stage, 12/11 Vic 64205
Chauncey Olcott, stage

MOONLIGHT BAY (3)
J H Remick ФФФ, pub. 1912, reached #1 in July 1912
(Also reached #19 in May 1951)
Edward Madden w, Percy Wenrich m
American Quartet ФФ 03/12 Vic 17034, 04/12 Ed 10550[2], 04/12 Ed Amb 962 cyl[2]
George Primrose, vv stage
Dolly Connolly[9], vv stage, 04/12 Col A-1128
Elsie Ward, vv stage

MOTHER MACHREE (9)
Witmark ФФФ, pub. 1910, reached #9 in February 1912
(also reached #17 in October 1914)
Rida Johnson Young w, Chauncey Olcott & Ernest Ball m
Featured in BARRY OF BALLYMORE, show (opened 01/10)
Steady seller 1910-1915
Chauncey Olcott, sung in show, 08/13 Col A-1337
John McCormack ФФ 06/11 Vic 64181
Will Oakland Ф 01/11 Ed Amb 580 cyl, 11/12 Col A-1204

NATIONAL EMBLEM MARCH
W Jacobs, pub. 1906, reached #20 in August 1912
E E Bagley m
Sousa's Band, band concerts
other concert bands

OH, MR. DREAM MAN (15)
H Von Tilzer, pub. 1911, reached #6 in June 1912
James V Monaco w & m
Ada Jones Ф 06/12 Vic 17076, 06/12 Zono 5907, 07/12 Ed Amb 1047 cyl, 08/12 Ed 10567 cyl
Cy Morgan & Coombs Baker, vv stage
Dolly Connolly 01/12 Col A-1083

OH, YOU BEAUTIFUL DOLL (2)
J H Remick ФФФ, pub. 1911, reached #1 in February 1912
A Seymour Brown w, Nat D Ayer m
Billy Murray/American Quartet ФФ 01/12 Vic 16979, 02/12 Ed Amb 921 cyl[2], 03/12 Ed 10545[2]
Six Musical Cuttys, vv stage
Carmen Sisters, vv stage
Pryor's Band 05/12 Vic 17063

OH! YOU CIRCUS DAY (13)
Will Rossiter, pub. 1911, reached #2 in August 1912
Edith Maida Lessing & James V Monaco w & m
Featured in HANKY PANKY, show (opened 08/12)
Florence Moore & Bill Montgomery, sung in show
Blossom Seeley, vv stage
Collins & Harlan Ф 08/12 U-S 1545 cyl, 09/12 Col A-1187
Maude Lambert, vv stage

RAGGING THE BABY TO SLEEP (21)
F A Mills, pub. 1912, reached #5 in September 1912
L Wolfe Gilbert w, Lewis F Muir m
Al Jolson ФФ 07/12 Vic 17081
Elida Morris, vv stage
Bonita, vv stage

RAGTIME COWBOY JOE (29)
F A Mills, pub. 1912, reached #12 in October 1912
(Also reached #19 in October 1949)
(Also reached #15 in August 1959)
Grant Clarke w, Lewis F Muir & Maurice Abrahams m
Bob Roberts ФФ 07/12 Vic 17090, 11/12 U-S 509 cyl
Edward Meeker 10/12 Ed Amb 1140 cyl
vv singers

RAGTIME VIOLIN (12)
Ted Snyder Co, pub. 1911, reached #3 in June 1912
Irving Berlin w & m
American Quartet ФФ 02/12 Vic 17025, 06/12 Ed 10560[2]
Victor Military Band 04/12 Vic 17044
Gene Greene, vv stage
Arthur Collins 02/12 Ed Amb 446 cyl, 02/12 Zono 5854

ROLL DEM ROLY BOLY EYES (43)
H Von Tilzer, pub. 1912, reached #20 in June 1912
Eddie Leonard w & m
Eddie Leonard, vv stage
other vv singers

RUM TUM TIDDLE (14)
Jerome & Schwartz, pub. 1911, reached #3 in April 1912
Edward Madden w, Jean Schwartz m
Featured in VERA VIOLETTA, show (opened 11/11)
Al Jolson Φ sung in show, 02/12 Vic 17037
Emma Carus, vv stage
Bessie Clayton, vv stage

THE SONG THAT REACHES IRISH HEARTS (49)
York Mus Co, pub. 1911, reached Top 30 in May 1912
Bartley Costello w, Albert Von Tilzer m
John W Myers 03/12 U-S 1219 cyl
John E Meyer 08/12 Col A-1174
Ruby Norton, vv stage
Spiegel & Dunn, vv stage

SPIRIT OF INDEPENDENCE (45)
J H Remick, pub. 1912, reached #18 in October 1912
Abe Holzmann m
Sousa's Band, band concerts
other concert bands

TAKE A LITTLE TIP FROM FATHER (27)
Ted Snyder Co, pub. 1912, reached #6 in August 1912
Irving Berlin & Ted Snyder w & m
Maud Tiffany, vv stage
Billy Murray Φ 04/12 Zono 5866
Lillian Bradley, vv stage
William H Thompson 08/12 U-S 505 cyl

TAKE ME BACK TO THE GARDEN OF LOVE (31)
Ted Snyder Co, pub. 1911, reached #10 in May 1912
E Ray Goetz w, Nat Osborne m
Charles W Harrison Φ 05/12 Col A-1141
Walter Van Brunt Φ 06/12 Vic 17076
Bonita Armstrong & Lew Hearn, vv stage

TAKE ME IN YOUR ARMS AGAIN (48)
C K Harris, pub. 1912, reached #20 in May 1912
Charles K Harris w & m
vv singers

THAT BABOON BABY DANCE (47)
M Shapiro, pub. 1911, reached #18 in June 1912
Dave Oppenheim w, Joe Cooper m
Featured in HANKY PANKY, show (opened 08/12)
Emma Carus, vv stage
Collins & Harlan 05/12 Zono 5895, 06/12 Vic 17077,
07/12 Ed Amb 1050 cyl, 08/12 Col A-1172
Harry Cooper, sung in show

THAT DAFFYDIL RAG
J Morris, pub. 1912, reached #20 in March 1912
Bill Mueller & Frank Mueller w & m
Four Yankee Girls, vv stage
Frank & Bill Mueller, vv stage

THAT HAUNTING MELODY (23)
Jerome & Schwartz, pub. 1911, reached #6 in April 1912
George M Cohan w & m
Al Jolson Φ 03/12 Vic 17037
Five Melody Maids, vv stage
LaBelle Blanche, vv stage

THAT MELLOW MELODY (22)
G W Meyer, pub. 1912, reached #7 in November 1912
Sam Lewis w, George W Meyer m
Walter Van Brunt Φ 11/12 Vic 17170
Belle Baker, vv stage
Anna Chandler, vv stage, 12/12 Ed Amb 1588 cyl

THAT MYSTERIOUS RAG (10)
Ted Snyder Co, pub. 1911, reached #2 in March 1912
Irving Berlin & Ted Snyder w & m
Albert Campbell & Arthur Collins ΦΦ 12/11 Zono 5822,
01/12 Col A-1086, 01/12 Ed Amb 893 cyl,
01/12 U-S 436 cyl
Premier Quartet[4] 02/12 Ed 10539 cyl
Belle Travers, vv stage
Eddy Canton, vv stage

THAT'S HOW I NEED YOU (6)
L Feist ΦΦΦ, pub. 1912, reached #1 in January 1913
Joe McCarthy & Joe Goodwin w, Al Piantadosi m
Henry Burr ΦΦ 11/12 Vic 17173, 11/12 Ed Amb 1589 cyl[3]
Belle Baker, vv stage
Emma Carus, vv stage
Tilford, vv stage

THERE'S A GIRL IN HAVANA (38)
Ted Snyder Co, pub. 1911, reached #14 in February 1912
E Ray Goetz w, Irving Berlin & A Baldwin Sloane m[7]
Featured in THE NEVER HOMES, show (opened 10/11)
Lyric Quartet Φ 12/11 Vic 16985
Bessie Clifford & Joe Santly, sung in show
vv singers

THEY GOTTA QUIT KICKIN' MY DAWG AROUND (28)
Witmark, pub. 1912, reached #11 in May 1912
Webb M Oungst w, Cy Perkins m
Byron G Harlan Φ 05/12 Vic 17065, 05/12 Zono 5891,
06/12 Col A-1150, 06/12 Ed Amb 1023 cyl
Senator Champ Clark (presidential campaign song)
vv singers

TILL THE SANDS OF THE DESERT GROW COLD (4)
Witmark ⓁⓁⓁ, pub. 1911, reached #4 in September 1912
George Graff w, Ernest Ball m
Maude Lambert & Ernest Ball, stage
Alan Turner Ⓛ 12/12 Vic 35259
Donald Chalmers Ⓛ 07/12 Ed Amb 1043 cyl
Wilford Glenn, stage, 03/13 Vic 17268
Schubert Quartet, stage

WAITING FOR THE ROBERT E. LEE (1)
F A Mills, pub. 1912, reached #1 in September 1912
L Wolfe Gilbert w, Lewis F Muir m
Al Jolson, vv stage
Heidelberg Quintet ⓁⓁ 09/12 Vic 17141
Dolly Connolly Ⓛ 10/12 Col A-1197
Eddie Cantor, vv stage
Collins & Harlan 10/12 Ed Amb 1144 cyl

WAY DOWN SOUTH (32)
Tell Taylor M P, pub. 1912, reached #11 in October 1912
George Fairman w & m
Mabel Hite, vv stage
Heidelberg Quintet Ⓛ 09/12 Vic 17146
Gene Greene, vv stage

A WEE LITTLE DROP O' THE CRUISKEEN LAWN (42)
J F Helf, pub. 1911, reached #13 in March 1912
Ed Moran w, J Fred Helf m
William H Thompson 06/12 Zono 5912
vv singers

WHEN I GET YOU ALONE TONIGHT (11)
L Feist, pub. 1912, reached #2 in November 1912
Joe Goodwin & Joe McCarthy w, Fred Fisher m
Belle Baker, vv stage
Walter Van Brunt Ⓛ 11/12 Vic 17172
Tilford, vv stage
Ada Jones & Walter Van Brunt 01/13 Col A-1237

WHEN I WAS TWENTY-ONE AND YOU WERE SWEET SIXTEEN (18)
J H Remick, pub. 1911, reached #3 in May 1912
Harry Williams w, Egbert Van Alstyne m
Harry Macdonough/American Quartet Ⓛ 05/12 Vic 17057
Albert Campbell & Henry Burr Ⓛ 04/12 Col A-1138
vv singers

WHEN UNCLE JOE PLAYS A RAG ON HIS OLD BANJO (24)
Morse Mus Co, pub. 1912, reached #9 in December 1912
D A Esrom[5] w, Theodore F Morse m
Arthur Collins Ⓛ 07/12 Zono 5924, 08/12 Vic 17118, 12/12 Col A-1222
Six Musical Cuttys, vv stage
Clifford & Rose, vv stage

WHEN YOU'RE AWAY (41)
J H Remick, pub. 1911, reached #9 in November 1912
Joe Young & A Seymour Brown w, Bert Grant m
Edna Brown[6]/American Quartet 09/12 Vic 17139
Helen Clark & Harvey Hindermeyer 12/12 Ed Amb 1505 cyl
vv singers

YOU'RE MY BABY (19)
J H Remick, pub. 1912, reached #4 in November 1912
A Seymour Brown w, Nat D Ayer m
American Quartet Ⓛ 08/12 Vic 17114, 09/12 Ed Amb 1119 cyl[2]
Belle Baker, vv stage
Ada Jones & Walter Van Brunt 02/13 Col A-1252

[1]The Columbia Quartet was actually the Peerless Quartet.
[2]Listed on Edison as the Premier Quartet.
[3]Listed on Edison as Irving Gillette.
[4]The Premier Quartet (Edison) was actually the American Quartet.
[5]D A Esrom was a pseudonym for Mrs. Theodore F Morse, later known as Dorothy Terriss.
[6]Edna Brown was a pseudonym for Elsie Baker.
[7]Although this song is credited to Goetz & Sloane, it is believed that Irving Berlin alone was the writer.
[8]Reached #20 on monthly chart only.
[9]Dolly Connolly was the wife of this song's composer, Percy Wenrich.

1913

AND THE GREEN GRASS GREW ALL AROUND (39)
H Von Tilzer, pub. 1912, reached #4 in April 1913
William Jerome w, Harry Von Tilzer m
Eddie Foy, vv stage
Walter Van Brunt Ⓛ 04/13 Col A-1277
American Quartet Ⓛ 07/13 Vic 17344, 07/13 Ed Amb 1808 cyl[1]

THE ANGELUS (46)
G Schirmer, pub. 1913, reached Top 30 in August 1913
Robert B Smith w, Victor Herbert m
Featured in SWEETHEARTS, show (opened 09/13)
Christie MacDonald, sung in show
Christie MacDonald & Reinald Werrenrath 07/13 Vic 70099
Prince's Orchestra 06/13 Col A-5422

AT THE DEVIL'S BALL (40)
Waterson, B & S, pub. 1913, reached #6 in April 1913
Irving Berlin w & m
Peerless Quartet Ⓛ 05/13 Vic 17315
Maurice Burkhart/Peerless Quartet Ⓛ 04/13 Col A-1282
Jim Doherty, vv stage
Weber & Burns, vv stage

BAGDAD
Witmark, pub. 1912, reached #16 in February 1913
Anne Caldwell & James O'Dea w, Victor Herbert m
Featured in BAGDAD, show (opened 10/12)
Dave Montgomery, sung in show
Billy Murray 01/13 Vic 17220
Victor Herbert Orch 01/14 Vic 55039

BE MY LITTLE BABY BUMBLE BEE (16)
J H Remick, pub. 1912, reached #3 in January 1913
Stanley Murphy w, Henry I Marshall m
Featured in A WINSOME WIDOW, show (opened 04/12)
Ada Jones & Billy Murray ΦΦ 10/12 Vic 17152
Elizabeth Brice & Charles King, sung in show
Dolly Sisters, vv stage
Courtney Sisters, vv stage
Ada Jones & Walter Van Brunt Φ 11/12 Col A-1210

BOBBIN' UP AND DOWN (38)
Morse Mus Co, pub. 1913, reached #13 in August 1913
D A Esrom[2] w & m
Van & Schenck, vv stage
Peerless Quartet Φ 05/13 Col A-1298, 06/13 Vic 17335
Bert Fitzgibbons, vv stage

THE CURSE OF AN ACHING HEART (11)
L Feist, pub. 1913, reached #2 in August 1913
Henry Fink w, Al Piantadosi m
Will Oakland ΦΦ 08/13 Vic 17372, 11/13 Ed Amb 2022 cyl
Emma Carus, vv stage
Eva Shirley, vv stage
Manuel Romain 10/13 Col A-1380
Tilford, vv stage

DADDY HAS A SWEETHEART, AND MOTHER IS HER NAME (36)
Penn Mus Co, pub. 1912, reached #5 in May 1913
Gene Buck w, Dave Stamper m
Featured in ZIEGFELD FOLLIES OF 1912, show (opened 10/12)
Lillian Lorraine, sung in show
Edna Brown[3] 05/13 Vic 17320
Manuel Romain 06/13 Col A-1320, 09/13 Ed Amb 1845 cyl

DEAR OLD GIRL (45)
Morse Mus Co, pub. 1903, reached Top 30 in June 1913
(Also reached #2 in November 1903)
Richard H Buck w, Theodore F Morse m
Harry Macdonough 10/13 Vic 17397
Clifford & Rose, vv stage

DOWN IN DEAR OLD NEW ORLEANS
J H Remick, pub. 1912, reached #18 in April 1913
Joe Young w, Con Conrad & Jay Whidden m
Featured in ZIEGFELD FOLLIES OF 1912, show (opened 11/12)
Rae Samuels, sung in show
American Quartet 03/13 Vic 17248, 03/13 Ed Amb 1645 cyl[1]
Collins & Harlan 03/13 Col A-1260

GIANNINA MIA (43)
G Schirmer, pub. 1912, reached Top 30 in September 1913
Otto Harbach w, Rudolf Friml m
Featured in THE FIREFLY, show (opened 12/12)
Emma Trentini, sung in show
concert singers

GOOD NIGHT, NURSE (33)
J H Remick, pub. 1912, reached #4 in May 1913
Thomas J Gray w, W Raymond Walker m
Billy Murray Φ 04/13 Vic 17286
Mae West, vv stage
Walter Van Brunt 05/13 Col A-1301

GOODBYE, BOYS (10)
H Von Tilzer ΦΦΦ, pub. 1913, reached #4 in July 1913
Andrew Sterling & Will Dillon w, Harry Von Tilzer m
Featured in HONEYMOON EXPRESS, show (opened 02/13)
Al Jolson, sung in show
Eddie Foy, vv stage
Billy Murray Φ 06/13 Vic 17341, 06/13 Ed Amb 1749 cyl
Peerless Quartet Φ 05/13 Col A-1301

HERE COMES MY DADDY NOW (44)
F A Mills, pub. 1912, reached #12 in May 1913
L Wolfe Gilbert w, Lewis F Muir m
Collins & Harlan Φ 04/13 Col A-1277, 05/13 Vic 17315
George Austin Moore, vv stage

I HEAR A THRUSH AT EVE (47)
White-Smith, pub. 1913, reached Top 30 in December 1913
Nelle R Eberhardt w, Charles W Cadman m
John McCormack Φ stage, 12/13 Vic 64340
other stage singers

I HEAR YOU CALLING ME (30)
Boosey & Co, pub. 1908, reached #17 in March 1914
Harold Herford w, Charles Marshall m
Steady seller, 1910-1915
John McCormack Φ stage, 06/10 Vic 64120, 02/14 Vic 64375
Charles W Harrison Φ 08/11 Col A-5303, 06/13 Vic 17321
Helen Ruggles, stage

IN MY HAREM (12)
Waterson, B & S, pub. 1913, reached #2 in August 1913
Irving Berlin w & m
Elizabeth Murray, vv stage
Josie Flynn, vv stage
Walter Van Brunt Φ 05/13 Col A-1302
Victor Military Band Φ 06/13 Vic 17325

ISLE O'DREAMS (42)
Witmark, pub. 1912, reached Top 30 in June 1913
George Graff & Chauncey Olcott w, Ernest Ball m
Featured in THE ISLE O'DREAMS, show (opened 01/13)
Chauncey Olcott, sung in show
stage singers

IT TAKES A LITTLE RAIN WITH THE SUNSHINE TO MAKE THE WORLD GO 'ROUND (41)
Shapiro, B, pub. 1913, reached #8 in October 1913
Ballard MacDonald w, Harry Carroll m
Marshall Montgomery, vv stage
Walter Van Brunt 09/13 Vic 17361, 09/13 Ed Amb 1824 cyl
Adele Richie, vv stage
Henry Burr & Edgar Stoddard 09/13 Col A-1353

LAST NIGHT WAS THE END OF THE WORLD (9)
H Von Tilzer ΦΦΦ, pub. 1912, reached #6 in November 1913
Andrew Sterling w, Harry Von Tilzer m
Henry Burr ΦΦ 06/13 Vic 17339, 06/13 Col A-1303
Lina Cavalieri, vv stage
Clare Rochester, vv stage
Victor Military Band 08/13 Vic 17362

A LITTLE BUNCH OF SHAMROCKS (28)
H Von Tilzer, pub. 1913, reached #10 in July 1913
William Jerome & Andrew Sterling w, Harry Von Tilzer m
Bessie Wynn, vv stage
Henry Burr & Edgar Stoddard Φ 06/13 Col A-1315
William Jerome, vv stage
Arthur Clough 11/13 Vic 17434

MAMMY JINNY'S JUBILEE (22)
F A Mills, pub. 1913, reached #9 in December 1913
L Wolfe Gilbert w, Lewis F Muir m
Elizabeth Murray, vv stage
L Wolfe Gilbert, vv stage
Collins & Harlan Φ 10/13 Vic 17411, 11/13 Ed Amb 2032 cyl
Charles Falke, vv stage

MELINDA'S WEDDING DAY (24)
L Feist, pub. 1913, reached #5 in June 1913
Joe Goodwin & Joe McCarthy w, Al Piantadosi m
Emma Carus, vv stage
Collins & Harlan Φ 04/13 Vic 17295, 04/13 Col A-1285, 09/13 Ed Amb 1844 cyl
Elizabeth Murray, vv stage
Nellie V Nichols, vv stage

OH! OH! DELPHINE
Chappell, pub. 1912, reached #19 in January 1913
C M S McLellan w, Ivan Caryll m
Featured in OH! OH! DELPHINE, show (opened 09/12)
Frank McIntyre & Grace Edmond, sung in show
Victor Concert Orch 01/13 Vic 35266

OH, YOU MILLION DOLLAR DOLL (37)
M Abrahams, pub. 1913, reached #12 in December 1913
Grant Clarke, Edgar Leslie w, Maurice Abrahams m
Peerless Quartet Φ 01/14 Col A-1443
Lillian Bradley, vv stage

ON THE MISSISSIPPI (14)
Shapiro, B ΦΦΦ, pub. 1912, reached #1 in February 1913
Ballard MacDonald w, Harry Carroll & Arthur Fields m
Featured in HANKY PANKY, show (opened 08/12)
American Quartet ΦΦ 02/13 Vic 17237
Harry Cooper, sung in show
Billy Murray 03/13 Ed Amb 1637 cyl
Frank Hale, vv stage

ON THE OLD FALL RIVER LINE (27)
H Von Tilzer, pub. 1913, reached #6 in November 1913
William Jerome & Andrew Sterling w, Harry Von Tilzer m
Billy Murray Φ 11/13 Vic 17427
Melville & Higgins, vv stage
Collins & Harlan 12/13 Col A-1419
Hoyt's Minstrels, vv stage

PEG O' MY HEART (2)
L Feist ΦΦΦ, pub. 1913, reached #1 in December 1913
(Also reached #1 in July 1947)
Alfred Bryan w, Fred Fisher m
Featured in ZIEGFELD FOLLIES OF 1913, show (opened 06/13)
Charles W Harrison ΦΦ 10/13 Vic 17412
Henry Burr ΦΦ 11/13 Col A-1404
Jose Collins, sung in show
Van & Schenck, vv stage
Charlotte Ravenscroft, vv stage

THE PULLMAN PORTERS ON PARADE (31)
M Abrahams, pub. 1913, reached #12 in December 1913
Irving Berlin w, Maurice Abrahams m
Belle Baker, vv stage
Al Jolson Φ 10/13 Col A-1374
Clarice Vance, vv stage

ROW, ROW, ROW (6)
H Von Tilzer, pub. 1912, reached #1 in March 1913
William Jerome w, James V Monaco m
Featured in ZIEGFELD FOLLIES OF 1912, show (opened 10/12)
Ada Jones ΦΦ 01/13 Vic 17205
Elizabeth Brice, sung in show
Eddie Foy, vv stage
American Quartet 04/13 Vic 17295
Arthur Collins 02/13 Col A-1244

SAILING DOWN THE CHESAPEAKE BAY (13)
J H Remick, pub. 1913, reached #5 in January 1914
Jean Havez w, George Botsford m
Avon Comedy Four, vv stage
Will Oakland, vv stage
American Quartet Φ 10/13 Vic 17411, 11/13 Ed Amb 2039 cyl[1]
Albert Campbell & Henry Burr Φ 11/13 Col A-1378
Adele Ritchie, vv stage

SNOOKEY OOKUMS (20)
Waterson, B & S, pub. 1913, reached #6 in July 1913
Irving Berlin w & m
Billy Murray Φ 05/13 Vic 17313
Clark & Bergman, vv stage
Natalie Normand, vv stage
Collins & Harlan Φ 06/13 Col A-1317, 07/13 Ed Amb 1776 cyl

SOME BOY (34)
Penn Mus Co, pub. 1913, reached #7 in May 1913
Gene Buck w, Dave Stamper m
Featured in ZIEGFELD FOLLIES OF 1912, show (opened 10/12)
Lillian Lorraine, sung in show
Bessie Wynn, vv stage
Ada Jones Φ 05/13 Vic 17313

SOMEBODY'S COMING TO MY HOUSE (17)
Waterson, B & S, pub. 1913, reached #4 in November 1913
Irving Berlin w & m
Sophie Tucker, vv stage
Walter Van Brunt Φ 09/13 Vic 17381, 10/13 Ed Amb 1941 cyl
Avon Comedy Four, vv stage
Ada Jones Φ 11/13 Col A-1401

THE SPANIARD THAT BLIGHTED MY LIFE (29)
Witmark, pub. 1911, reached #7 in July 1913
Billy Merson w & m
Featured in HONEYMOON EXPRESS, show (opened 02/13)
Al Jolson ΦΦ sung in show, 05/13 Vic 17318

SUNSHINE AND ROSES (25)
J H Remick, pub. 1913, reached #15 in December 1913
Gus Kahn w, Egbert Van Alstyne m
Avon Comedy Four, vv stage
Edna Brown[3] & James F Harrison 08/13 Vic 17359
Peerless Quartet 08/13 Col A-1343

SWEETHEARTS (32)
G Schirmer, pub. 1913, reached #14 in August 1913
(Also reached #18 in February 1939 with new lyrics)
Robert B Smith w, Victor Herbert m
Featured in SWEETHEARTS, show (opened 09/13)
Christie MacDonald Φ sung in show, 07/13 Vic 60101
Grace Kerns 09/13 Col A-1359
Victor Herbert Orch 03/14 Vic 55093

SYMPATHY (23)
G Schirmer, pub. 1912, reached #18 in August 1913
Otto Harbach w, Rudolf Friml m
Featured in THE FIREFLY, show (opened 12/12)
Melville Stewart & Audrey Maple, sung in show
Walter Van Brunt & Helen Clark Φ 03/13 Vic 17270

THAT INTERNATIONAL RAG (8)
Waterson, B & S, pub. 1913, reached #3 in November 1913
Irving Berlin w & m
Sophie Tucker, vv stage
Belle Baker, vv stage
Collins & Harlan ΦΦ 11/13 Vic 17431, 11/13 Col A-1406
Clarice Vance, vv stage
Victor Military Band 01/14 Vic 17487

THAT OLD GIRL OF MINE (26)
J H Remick, pub. 1913, reached #2 in March 1913
Earl C Jones w, Egbert Van Alstyne m
American Quartet 03/13 Vic 17264
Henry Burr & Edgar Stoddard 04/13 Col A-1279
vv singers

THEN I'LL STOP LOVING YOU
L Feist, pub. 1913, reached #13 in April 1913
Joe Goodwin & Joe McCarthy w, Al Piantadosi m
Hurst, Watts & Hurst, vv stage
Henry Burr & Edgar Stoddard 05/13 Col A-1303

THERE'S A GIRL IN THE HEART OF MARYLAND (7)
Shapiro, B ΦΦΦ, pub. 1913, reached #1 in January 1914
Ballard MacDonald w, Harry Carroll m
Harry Macdonough Φ 10/13 Vic 17401
Avon Comedy Four, vv stage
Frederick V Bowers, vv stage
Henry Burr & Edgar Stoddard Φ 09/13 Col A-1360

TO HAVE, TO HOLD, TO LOVE (21)
Witmark, pub. 1913, reached #8 in August 1913
Daryl McBoyle w, Ernest Ball m
Ernest Ball & Maude Lambert, vv stage
Harry Macdonough 06/13 Vic 17338
Truly Shattuck, vv stage
Henry Burr 06/13 Col A-1319

TOO MUCH MUSTARD (48)
Schuberth, pub. 1911, reached Top 30 in June 1913
Allen Roberts w, Cecil Macklin m
Words added 1913
Victor Military Band 04/13 Vic 17292
Herron & Gaylord, vv stage
Prince's Band 06/13 Col A-1307

THE TRAIL OF THE LONESOME PINE (3)
Shapiro, B ΦΦΦ, pub. 1913, reached #1 in July 1913
Ballard MacDonald w, Harry Carroll m
Albert Campbell & Henry Burr ΦΦ 06/13 Col A-1315
James F Harrison & Edna Brown[3] Φ 06/13 Vic 17338
Merratt & Douglas, vv stage
Manuel Romain 06/13 Ed Amb 1743 cyl

WE HAVE MUCH TO BE THANKFUL FOR (50)
Waterson, B & S, pub. 1913, reached #18 in November 1913
Irving Berlin w & m
"That Girl" Quartette 10/13 Vic 17409
McMahon, Diamond & Clemence, vv stage
Manuel Romain 12/13 Ed Amb 2081 cyl

WHEN I LOST YOU (4)
Waterson, B & S ΦΦΦ, pub. 1912, reached #1 in June 1913
Irving Berlin w & m
Henry Burr ΦΦ 03/13 Vic 17275
Irving Berlin, vv stage
Six Musical Cuttys, vv stage
Lillian Washburn, vv stage
Manuel Romain Φ 05/13 Col A-1288

WHEN IRISH EYES ARE SMILING (18)
Witmark ΦΦΦ, pub. 1912, reached #15 in July 1913
Chauncey Olcott & George Graff w, Ernest Ball m
Featured in THE ISLE O'DREAMS, show (opened 01/13)
Steady seller, 1913-1919
Chauncey Olcott Φ sung in show, 06/13 Col A-1310
Harry Macdonough Φ 05/13 Vic 17317
John McCormack, stage (Later: 1917 Vic 64631)
vv singers

WHEN IT'S APPLE BLOSSOM TIME IN NORMANDY (5)
J H Remick, pub. 1912, reached #3 in September 1913
Harry Gifford, Huntley Trevor & Tom Mellor w & m
Nora Bayes, vv stage
Will Oakland, vv stage
Marguerite Dunlap & Harry Macdonough Φ 03/13 Vic 17245
Edna Brown[3] & James F Harrison Φ 10/13 Col A-1383

WHEN THE MIDNIGHT CHOO CHOO LEAVES FOR ALABAM' (15)
Waterson, B & S, pub. 1912, reached #1 in May 1913
Irving Berlin w & m
Collins & Harlan ΦΦ 02/13 Vic 17246, 02/13 Col A-1246
Victor Military Band 04/13 Vic 35277
Babette, vv stage
Madge Maitland, vv stage

YOU CAN'T STOP ME FROM LOVING YOU (49)
J H Remick, pub. 1913, reached #18 in December 1913
Alex Gerber & Stanley Murphy w, Henry I Marshall m
Henry Burr 07/13 Col A-1332
vv singers

YOU MADE ME LOVE YOU (1)
Broadway Mus Co ΦΦΦ, pub. 1913, reached #1 in September 1913
(Also reached #12 in December 1941)
Joe McCarthy w, James V Monaco m
Al Jolson ΦΦ vv stage, 10/13 Col A-1374
Belle Baker, vv stage
Will Halley Φ 09/13 Vic 17381
Santley & Norton, vv stage
Ruth Roye, vv stage

YOU'RE A GREAT BIG BLUE-EYED BABY (19)
J H Remick, pub. 1913, reached #3 in June 1913
A Seymour Brown w & m
Al Jolson, vv stage
Peerless Quartet Φ 05/13 Col A-1300
Heidelberg Quintet 07/13 Vic 17344

YOU'VE GOT YOUR MOTHER'S BIG BLUE EYES (35)
Waterson, B & S, pub. 1913, reached #10 in January 1914
Irving Berlin w & m
Elida Morris, vv stage
Al Jolson, vv stage
Lillian Davis[4] 01/14 Vic 17482

[1]Listed on Edison as the Premier Quartet.
[2]D A Esrom was a pseudonym for Mrs. Theodore F Morse, later known as Dorothy Terriss.
[3]Edna Brown was a pseudonym for Elsie Baker.
[4]Lillian Davis was a pseudonym for Marguerite Dunlap.

1914

ABA DABA HONEYMOON (20)
L Feist, pub. 1914, reached #1 in October 1914
(Also reached #3 in March 1951)
Arthur Fields & Walter Donovan w & m
Collins & Harlan ΦΦ 10/14 Vic 17620, 11/14 Col A-1600
Ruth Roye, vv stage
Elizabeth Brice & Charles King, vv stage
Eddie Foy, vv stage
Sophie Tucker, vv stage

ALL ABOARD FOR DIXIE LAND (14)
J H Remick, pub. 1913, reached #3 in July 1914
Jack Yellen w, George L Cobb m
Featured in HIGH JINKS, show (opened 12/13)
Elizabeth Murray, sung in show
Avon Comedy Four, vv stage
American Quartet Φ 03/14 Vic 17535
Ada Jones Φ 04/14 Ed Amb 2212 cyl
Nora Bayes 06/14 Vic 60117

AT A MISSISSIPPI CABARET (26)
J H Remick, pub. 1914, reached #6 in January 1915
A Seymour Brown w, Albert Gumble m
Ruth Roye, vv stage
American Quartet Φ 12/14 Vic 17650
Adele Ritchie, vv stage
Miss Patricola, vv stage

BALLIN' THE JACK (7)
J W Stern, pub. 1913, reached #1 in November 1914
Jim Burris w, Chris Smith m
Eddie Cantor, vv stage
Fanny Brice, vv stage
Lillian Lorraine, vv stage
Prince's Band Φ 11/14 Col A-5595

BY THE BEAUTIFUL SEA (2)
Shapiro, B ⴲⴲⴲ, pub. 1914, reached #1 in August 1914
Harold Atteridge w, Harry Carroll m
Bessie Wynn, vv stage
Heidelberg Quintet ⴲⴲ 08/14 Vic 17560
Bert Fitzgibbon, vv stage
Ada Jones & Billy Watkins ⴲ 09/14 Col A-1563
Prince's Band 09/14 Col A-5582

CALIFORNIA AND YOU (22)
Kalmar & Puck, pub. 1914, reached #5 in October 1914
Edgar Leslie w, Harry Puck m
Courtenay Sisters, vv stage
Irving Kaufman ⴲ 10/14 Vic 17613
Albert Campbell & Henry Burr 11/14 Col A-1601

CAMP MEETING BAND (42)
F A Mills, pub. 1913, reached #18 in June 1914
L Wolfe Gilbert w, Lewis F Muir m
Six Brown Brothers, vv stage
Elizabeth Murray, vv stage
Collins & Harlan 04/14 Vic 17537, 04/14 Col A-1496, 05/14 Ed Amb 2268 cyl

CAN'T YOU HEAR ME CALLING, CAROLINE? (8)
Witmark, pub. 1914, reached #4 in October 1914
William H Gardner w, Caro Roma m
George MacFarlane ⴲ vv stage, 10/14 Vic 60123
Caro Roma, vv stage
Frank Coombs ⴲ 07/14 Col A-1530

COHEN ON THE TELEPHONE (47)
Comic monologue, 1914, reached #11 in September 1914
Joe Hayman w
Joe Hayman ⴲⴲ 06/14 Col A-1516

DO YOU TAKE THIS WOMAN (38)
H Von Tilzer, pub. 1913, reached #4 in April 1914
Andrew Sterling w, Harry Von Tilzer m
Featured in THE PASSING SHOW OF 1913, show (opened 07/13)
American Quartet ⴲ 05/14 Vic 17554
George Whiting, sung in show
Fred Duprez, vv stage
Tascott, vv stage

DON'T BLAME IT ALL ON BROADWAY (43)
Harry Wms Mus Co, pub. 1913, reached #11 in February 1914
Joe Young & Harry Williams w, Bert Grant m
Peerless Quartet ⴲ 04/14 Vic 17539, 04/14 Col A-1497
Arthur Deagan, vv stage
Florence Tempest, vv stage

FIDO IS A HOT DOG NOW
L Feist, pub. 1914, reached #19 in October 1914
Charles McCarron & Thomas J Gray w, Raymond Walker m
Fred Duprez, vv stage
Billy Murray 10/14 Vic 17620
Lina Abarbanell, vv stage

HE'D HAVE TO GET UNDER, GET OUT AND GET UNDER, TO FIX UP HIS AUTOMOBILE (1)
M Abrahams, pub. 1913, reached #1 in February 1914
Grant Clarke & Edgar Leslie w, Maurice Abrahams m
Featured in THE PLEASURE SEEKERS, show (opened 11/13)
Billy Murray ⴲⴲ 01/14 Vic 17491, 03/14 Ed Amb 2194 cyl
Al Jolson, vv stage
Belle Baker, vv stage
Bobby North, sung in show
Six Brown Brothers, vv stage

HE'S A DEVIL IN HIS OWN HOME TOWN (16)
Waterson, B & S, pub. 1914, reached #2 in June 1914
Grant Clarke & Irving Berlin w & m
Billy Murray ⴲ 07/14 Vic 17576
Eddie Morton ⴲ 06/14 Col A-1525
Fanny Brice, vv stage
Belle Baker, vv stage
Ruth Roye, vv stage

HE'S A RAG PICKER (46)
Waterson, B & S, pub. 1914, reached #10 in January 1915
Irving Berlin w & m
Sophie Tucker, vv stage
Peerless Quartet ⴲ 01/15 Vic 17655, 01/15 Col A-1628
Helen Trix, vv stage

I LOVE THE LADIES (11)
Waterson, B & S, pub. 1914, reached #1 in July 1914
Grant Clarke w, Jean Schwartz m
Featured in OUR AMERICAN BOY, revue (1914)
Collins & Harlan ⴲ 05/14 Col A-1513
Florence Tempest, sung in revue
Will Halley ⴲ 05/14 Vic 17560
Fox & Dolly, vv stage

I MISS YOU MOST OF ALL (29)
Broadway Mus Co, pub. 1913, reached #3 in March 1914
Joe McCarthy w, James V Monaco m
Avon Comedy Four, vv stage
Manuel Romain ⴲ 02/14 Col A-1454, 05/14 Ed Amb 2258 cyl
Edna Brown[1] ⴲ 04/14 Vic 17552
Yvette, vv stage

I WANT TO GO BACK TO MICHIGAN (DOWN ON THE FARM) (10)
Waterson, B & S, pub. 1914, reached #1 in December 1914
Irving Berlin w & m
Elida Morris ⴲ 11/14 Col A-1592
Belle Baker, vv stage
Morton Harvey ⴲ 12/14 Vic 17650
Irving Berlin, vv stage
Yvette, vv stage

I'LL DO IT ALL OVER AGAIN (44)
J H Remick, pub. 1914, reached #20 in June 1914
A Seymour Brown w, Albert Gumble m
Jack Norworth, vv stage
Billy Murray 04/14 Vic 17637
Elizabeth Murray, vv stage
Adele Ritchie, vv stage

I'M ON MY WAY TO MANDALAY (6)
L Feist ΦΦΦ, pub. 1913, reached #2 in March 1914
Alfred Bryan w, Fred Fisher m
Will Oakland[2], Albert Campbell & Henry Burr ΦΦ 02/14 Vic 17503, 03/14 Col A-1484, 04/14 Ed Amb 2233 cyl
Van & Schenck, vv stage
Avon Comedy Four, vv stage
Aurie Dagwell, vv stage

IF I HAD MY WAY (39)
J Kendis, pub. 1913, reached #13 in June 1914
(Also reached #19 in July 1939)
Lou Klein w, James Kendis m
Peerless Quartet Φ 05/14 Vic 17534
Ethel Green, vv stage

IN THE CANDLELIGHT (41)
Witmark, pub. 1913, reached #17 in June 1914
Fleta Jan Brown w & m
Edna Brown[1] & James F Harrison 03/14 Vic 17529
Bessie Wynn, vv stage
Victoria Four, vv stage

IN THE TOWN WHERE I WAS BORN
F B Haviland, pub. 1914, reached #20 in September 1914[5]
Dick Howard & Billy Tracey w, Al Harriman m
Owen J McCormack, vv stage, 06/14 Ed Amb 2304 cyl
George Wilton Ballard, vv stage
Larry Ball, vv stage

ISLE D'AMOUR (12)
L Feist, pub. 1913, reached #5 in February 1914
Earl Carroll w, Leo Edwards m
Featured in ZIEGFELD FOLLIES OF 1913, show (opened 06/13)
Jose Collins, sung in show
Olive Kline Φ 02/14 Vic 17509
Daisy Leon, vv stage
Victor Military Band 02/14 Vic 35346

LITTLE GREY HOME IN THE WEST (17)
Chappell, pub. 1911, reached #10 in May 1914
D Eardly-Wilmot w, Herman Lohr m
Featured in MARRIAGE MARKET, show (opened 09/13)
Veneta Fitz-Hugh, sung in show
Alma Gluck Φ 05/14 Vic 64412
John McCormack 07/14 Vic 64425
Grace LaRue, vv stage
Charles W Harrison 03/14 Vic 17522

A LITTLE LOVE, A LITTLE KISS (19)
Chappell, pub. 1912, reached #18 in March 1914
Adrian Ross w, Lao Silesu m
Featured in ZIEGFELD FOLLIES OF 1913, show (opened 06/13)
John McCormack Φ 09/13 Vic 64343
Jose Collins, sung in show
Charles W Harrison 02/14 Vic 17509

LOVE'S OWN SWEET SONG (37)
J W Stern, pub. 1914, reached #19 in August 1914
C C S Cushing & E P Heath w, Emmerich Kalman m
Featured in SARI, show (opened 01/14)
Mitzi Hajos, sung in show
Grace Kerns & Charles W Harrison 08/14 Col A-5574

MARY, YOU'RE A LITTLE BIT OLD FASHIONED (23)
J H Remick, pub. 1914, reached #7 in August 1914
Marion Sunshine w, Henry I Marshall m
Tempest & Sunshine, vv stage
Walter Van Brunt Φ 09/14 Ed Amb 2386 cyl
Jose Collins, vv stage
Charles W Harrison 11/14 Vic 17638

THE MEMPHIS BLUES (28)
Theron C Bennett, pub. 1912, reached #17 in November 1914
William C Handy w & m
Steady seller, 1913-23, jazz & blues standard
George Evans Minstrels, vv stage
Victor Military Band 10/14 Vic 17619
Morton Harvey 01/15 Vic 17657
Collins & Harlan 07/15 Col A-1721

MOTHER MACHREE (36)
Witmark ΦΦΦ, pub. 1910, reached #17 in October 1914
(Also reached #9 in February 1912)
Rida Johnson Young w, Chauncey Olcott & Ernest Ball m
Featured in ISLE O'DREAMS, show (opened 01/13)
Steady seller 1910-1915
John McCormack, stage, 06/11 Vic 64181
Chauncey Olcott, sung in show, 08/13 Col A-1337
Ernest Ball & Maude Lambert, vv stage
George MacFarlane, vv stage

MY CROONY MELODY
Waterson, B & S, pub. 1914, reached #11 in October 1914
Joe Goodwin & E Ray Goetz w & m
Collins & Harlan 09/14 Vic 17610, 10/14 Col A-1578, 11/14 Ed Amb 2456 cyl
Victor Military Band 10/14 Vic 17617
Ashley & Canfield, vv stage

NIGHTS OF GLADNESS (13)
J W Stern, pub. 1913, reached #7 in March 1914
Ballard MacDonald w, Charles Ancliff m
Victor Military Band Φ 08/13 Vic 35304
Prince's Orch 10/13 Col A-5494
Sunday & Monday, vv stage

ON THE GOOD SHIP MARY ANN (31)
J H Remick, pub. 1914, reached #7 in April 1914
Gus Kahn w, Grace LeBoy m
Al Jolson, vv stage
Nora Bayes Ⴔ 04/14 Vic 60113
Elizabeth Murray, vv stage
Van & Schenck, vv stage

POOR PAULINE (30)
Broadway Mus Co, pub. 1914, reached #7 in December 1914
Charles McCarron w, Raymond Walker m
Fanny Brice, vv stage
Billy Murray Ⴔ 01/15 Vic 17655
Cantor & Lee, vv stage

REBECCA OF SUNNYBROOK FARM (3)
J H Remick, pub. 1914, reached #1 in April 1914
A Seymour Brown w, Albert Gumble m
Featured in ZIEGFELD FOLLIES OF 1913, show (opened 06/13)
Jose Collins, sung in show
Albert Campbell & Irving Gillette[3] ႴႴ
03/14 Col A-1483, 05/14 Ed Amb 2270 cyl
Adele Ritchie, vv stage
American Quartet Ⴔ 05/14 Vic 17534

ROLL THEM COTTON BALES (34)
J W Stern, pub. 1914, reached #8 in September 1914
James W Johnson & Bob Cole w, J Rosamond Johnson m
Trixie McCoy, vv stage
Cole & Johnson, vv stage
Heidelberg Quintet Ⴔ 10/14 Vic 17633

SARI WALTZ
J W Stern, pub. 1913, reached #17 in April 1914
C C S Cushing & E P Heath w, Emmerich Kalman m
Featured in SARI, show (opened 01/14)
Mitzi Hajos, sung in show
Victor Military Band 03/14 Vic 35364

SIT DOWN, YOU'RE ROCKING THE BOAT (33)
Harry Wms Mus Co, pub. 1913, reached #16 in March 1914
William Jerome & Grant Clarke w, Jean Schwartz m
Montgomery & Moore, vv stage
Eddie Foy, vv stage
Billy Murray Ⴔ 02/14 Vic 17516, 04/14 Ed Amb 2216 cyl

SOMEWHERE A VOICE IS CALLING (45)
T B Harms & F D H, pub. 1911, reached #20 in April 1914
Eileen Newton w, Arthur F Tate m
Steady seller, 1911-1917
John McCormack, stage (Later: 1916 Vic 64405)
Harry McClaskey[4] 01/14 Vic 17475

THEY ALL HAD A FINGER IN THE PIE (49)
H Von Tilzer, pub. 1914, reached #17 in December 1914
Vincent Bryan w, Harry Von Tilzer m
Ruth Roye, vv stage
Whiting & Burt, vv stage
American Quartet 03/15 Vic 17704

THEY'RE ON THEIR WAY TO MEXICO (50)
Waterson, B & S, pub. 1914, reached Top 30 in July 1914
Irving Berlin w & m
Belle Baker, vv stage
Heidelberg Quintet 08/14 Vic 17599
Winona Winter, vv stage

THIS IS THE LIFE (4)
Waterson, B & S, pub. 1914, reached #1 in June 1914
Irving Berlin w & m
Belle Baker, vv stage
Al Jolson, vv stage
Peerless Quartet ႴႴ 05/14 Col A-1509
Billy Murray Ⴔ 06/14 Vic 17584, 08/14 Ed Amb 2368 cyl
Mae West, vv stage

TOO-RA LOO-RA LOO-RAL (18)
Witmark, pub. 1914, reached #10 in March 1914
(Also reached #13 in December 1944)
James Royce Shannon w & m
Chauncey Olcott Ⴔ stage, 12/13 Col A-1410
George MacFarlane, stage, 11/14 Vic 60125
vv singers

WEDDING OF THE WINDS (48)
Carl Fisher, pub. 1897, reached Top 30 in March 1914
John T Hall m
Steady seller, 1900-1920
Prince's Orch 05/12 Col A-5371
Pietro Deiro 11/14 Col A-1598

WHEN IT'S NIGHT TIME DOWN IN BURGUNDY (35)
J H Remick, pub. 1914, reached #7 in October 1914
Alfred Bryan w, Herman Paley m
George MacFarlane Ⴔ vv stage, 09/14 Vic 60121
Helen Clark & Walter Van Brunt 11/14 Ed Amb 2437 cyl
Miss Chee Toy, vv stage

WHEN THE ANGELUS IS RINGING (27)
Waterson, B & S, pub. 1914, reached #8 in June 1914
Joe Young w, Bert Grant m
Jose Collins, vv stage
Lyric Quartet 07/14 Vic 17587
Peerless Quartet 07/14 Col A-1533
Kelly & Violette, vv stage

WHEN YOU PLAY IN THE GAME OF LOVE (21)
L Feist, pub. 1913, reached #2 in August 1914
Joe Goodwin w, Al Piantadosi m
Edna Brown[1] & James F Harrison Ⴔ 08/14 Vic 17594
Lyons & Yosco, vv stage
George W Ballard 08/14 Col A-1553

WHEN YOU'RE A LONG, LONG WAY FROM HOME (5)
Broadway Mus Co ႴႴႴ, pub. 1914, reached #1 in December 1914
Sam Lewis w, George Meyer m
Henry Burr ႴႴ 11/14 Vic 17632, 03/15 Col A-1681
Bessie Wynn, vv stage
Nellie V Nichols, vv stage
Van & Schenck, vv stage

WHEN YOU'RE ALL DRESSED UP AND NO PLACE TO GO (25)
T B Harms, pub. 1913, reached #5 in August 1914
Benjamin H Burt w, Silvio Hein m
Featured in THE BEAUTY SHOP, show (opened 04/14)
Raymond Hitchcock, sung in show
Billy Murray Φ 04/14 Vic 17527, 05/14 Ed Amb 2256 cyl
vv singers

WHERE DID YOU GET THAT GIRL? (9)
Kalmar & Puck, pub. 1913, reached #2 in March 1914
Bert Kalmar w, Harry Puck m
Walter Van Brunt Φ 10/13 Vic 17414, 11/13 Col A-1407
Diamond & Brennan, vv stage
Wheeler & Wilson, vv stage
Billy Murray 11/13 Ed Amb 2035 cyl

WHILE THEY WERE DANCING AROUND (40)
Broadway Mus Co, pub. 1913, reached #5 in April 1914
Joe McCarthy w, James V Monaco m
Fanny Brice, vv stage
Anna Chandler, vv stage
Eddie Morton 03/14 Col A-1484
Peerless Quartet 05/14 Vic 17571

WHO PAID THE RENT FOR MRS. RIP VAN WINKLE? (24)
L Feist, pub. 1914, reached #6 in June 1914
Alfred Bryan w, Fred Fisher m
Featured in HONEYMOON EXPRESS, show (opened 02/13)
Also featured in THE BELLE OF BOND STREET, show (opened 03/14)
Al Jolson, sung in show (HE)
Gaby Deslys & Sam Bernard, sung in show (BELLE)
Elizabeth Murray, vv stage
Marie Lloyd, vv stage
Billy Watkins Φ 07/14 Col A-1532

YOU PLANTED A ROSE IN THE GARDEN OF LOVE (32)
Witmark, pub. 1914, reached #8 in August 1914
J Will Callahan w, Ernest Ball m
Henry Burr Φ 08/14 Col A-1549
Maude Lambert & Ernest Ball, vv stage
Fields' Minstrels, vv stage
Charles W Harrison 11/14 Vic 17638

YOU'RE HERE AND I'M HERE (15)
L Feist, pub. 1914, reached #3 in September 1914
Harry B Smith w, Jerome Kern m
Featured in THE LAUGHING HUSBAND, show (opened 02/14)
Venita Fitz-Hugh & Nigel Barrie, sung in show
Olive Kline & Harry Macdonough Φ 05/14 Vic 17555
Nora Bayes, vv stage
Nellie V Nichols, vv stage
Grace LaRue, vv stage

[1]Edna Brown was a pseudonym for Elsie Baker.
[2]The trio of Oakland, Campbell & Burr sang only on the Victor record. On Columbia and Edison, only Campbell & Burr sang.
[3]Irving Gillette was a pseudonym for Henry Burr.
[4]Harry McClaskey was a pseudonym for, and real name of, Henry Burr.
[5]Reached #20 on monthly chart only.

1915

AFTER THE ROSES HAVE FADED AWAY (37)
Witmark, pub. 1914, reached #12 in March 1915
Bessie Buchanan w, Ernest Ball m
Ernest Ball & Maude Lambert, vv stage
Henry Burr Φ 12/14 Col A-1611

ALABAMA JUBILEE (26)
J H Remick, pub. 1915, reached #3 in August 1915
(Also reached #15 in July 1955)
Jack Yellen w, George L Cobb m
Collins & Harlan ΦΦ 07/15 Col A-1721, 09/15 Vic 17825, 09/15 Ed Amb 2663 cyl
Elizabeth Murray, vv stage

AUF WIEDERSEH'N (15)
G Schirmer, pub. 1915, reached #3 in January 1916
Herbert Reynolds w, Sigmund Romberg m
Featured in THE BLUE PARADISE, show (opened 08/15)
Vivian Segal & Cecil Lean, sung in show
Alice Green[1] & Harry Macdonough ΦΦ 11/15 Vic 17858
Victor Dance Orch 02/16 Vic 35514

BACK HOME IN TENNESSEE (7)
Waterson, B & S ΦΦΦ, pub. 1915, reached #1 in December 1915
William Jerome w, Walter Donaldson m
Featured in ROBINSON CRUSOE JR., show (opened 02/16)
Al Jolson, sung in show
Collins & Harlan ΦΦ 10/15 Vic 17841, 12/15 Col A-1848, 02/16 Pathe 10053
Prince's Band 12/15 Col A-5729

BACK TO THE CAROLINA YOU LOVE (29)
Waterson, B & S, pub. 1914, reached #7 in January 1915
Grant Clarke w, Jean Schwartz m
Al Jolson Φ 01/15 Col A-1621
Truly Shattuck, vv stage
Rae Samuels, vv stage
Peerless Quartet Φ 01/15 Vic 17666

BY HECK (19)
J W Stern, pub. 1914, reached #5 in May 1915
L Wolfe Gilbert w, S R Henry m
Fanny Brice, vv stage
Victor Dance Orch Φ 04/15 Vic 35435
Prince's Band 04/15 Col A-5643
Byron Harlan & Will Robbins 07/15 Col A-1722

CARRY ME BACK TO OLD VIRGINNY (30)
G Schirmer, pub. 1878, reached #11 in May 1915
James A Bland w & m
Alma Gluck ΦΦΦ 12/14 Vic 88481, 02/15 Vic 74420

CHINATOWN, MY CHINATOWN (17)
J H Remick ΦΦΦ, pub. 1906, reached #5 in February 1915
William Jerome w, Jean Schwartz m
American Quartet ΦΦ 02/15 Vic 17684
Grace Kerns & John Barnes Wells Φ 01/15 Col A-1624
Prince's Band 06/15 Col A-5674

CLOSE TO MY HEART (24)
H Von Tilzer, pub. 1915, reached #7 in December 1915
Andrew Sterling w, Harry Von Tilzer m
Albert Campbell & Henry Burr Φ 09/15 Col A-1790
vv singers

DOWN AMONG THE SHELTERING PALMS (5)
L Feist, pub. 1915, reached #4 in May 1915
James Brockman w, Abe Olman m
Lyric Quartet Φ 07/15 Vic 17778
Columbia Quartet[2] 07/15 Col A-1770
Al Jolson, vv stage

DOWN IN BOM-BOMBAY (21)
Shapiro, B, pub. 1915, reached #2 in October 1915
Ballard MacDonald w, Harry Carroll m
Emma Carus, vv stage
Collins & Harlan Φ 10/15 Vic 17841, 10/15 Col A-1807
Al Jolson, vv stage
Conway's Band 12/15 Vic 35495

EVERYBODY RAG WITH ME (35)
J H Remick, pub. 1914, reached #11 in May 1915
Gus Kahn w, Grace LeBoy m
Featured in DANCING AROUND, show (opened 10/14)
Al Jolson, sung in show
Sophie Tucker, vv stage
Courtenay Sisters, vv stage
American Quartet Φ 06/15 Vic 17769

GOODBYE, GIRLS, I'M THROUGH (13)
Chappell, pub. 1914, reached #4 in March 1915
John Golden w, Ivan Caryll m
Featured in CHIN-CHIN, show (opened 10/14)
Fred Stone, sung in show
Raymond Dixon[3] Φ 03/15 Vic 17715
Prince's Band 03/15 Col A-5634
vv singers

HELLO, FRISCO! (18)
Witmark, pub. 1915, reached #1 in October 1915
Gene Buck w, Louis A Hirsch m
Featured in ZIEGFELD FOLLIES OF 1915, show (opened 06/15)
Ina Claire, sung in show
Alice Green[1] & Ed Hamilton[4] ΦΦ 10/15 Vic 17837
Elida Morris & Sam Ash Φ 10/15 Col A-1801
Eva Tanguay, vv stage

I DIDN'T RAISE MY BOY TO BE A SOLDIER (3)
L Feist ΦΦΦ, pub. 1914, reached #1 in March 1915
Alfred Bryan w, Al Piantadosi m
Morton Harvey ΦΦ 03/15 Vic 17716
Eddie Morton, vv stage
Nellie V Nichols, vv stage
Peerless Quartet Φ 04/15 Col A-1697
Gene Greene, vv stage

I'M ON MY WAY TO DUBLIN BAY (16)
J H Remick, pub. 1915, reached #1 in July 1915
Stanley Murphy w & m
Peerless Quartet Φ 05/15 Vic 17736
Victor Military Band Φ 07/15 Vic 35458
Irene & Bobby Smith, vv stage

IF WE CAN'T BE THE SAME OLD SWEETHEARTS (38)
L Feist, pub. 1915, reached #5 in September 1915
Joe McCarthy w, Jimmy Monaco m
Irving Kaufman Φ 08/15 Vic 17813
Ed & Jack Smith, vv stage
Rose Bryant & Henry Burr Φ 07/15 Col A-1770

IT'S A LONG, LONG WAY TO TIPPERARY (2)
Chappell ΦΦΦ, pub. 1912, reached #1 in January 1915
Jack Judge & Harry H Williams w & m
John McCormack ΦΦ 02/15 Vic 64476
American Quartet ΦΦ 11/14 Vic 17639
Blanche Ring, vv stage
Ruth Roye, vv stage
Prince's Band & Chorus Φ 01/15 Col A-1620

IT'S TULIP TIME IN HOLLAND (6)
J H Remick ΦΦΦ, pub. 1915, reached #1 in November 1915
Dave Radford w, Richard A Whiting m
Fritzie Scheff, vv stage
Henry Burr Φ 12/15 Vic 17874
Prince's Band Φ 11/15 Col A-5724
Harry Macdonough Φ 12/15 Vic 17874
Ethel Costello & Andrea Sarto 10/15 Col A-1792

A LITTLE BIT OF HEAVEN (1)
Witmark ΦΦΦ, pub. 1914, reached #1 in May 1915
J Keirn Brennan w, Ernest Ball m
Featured in THE HEART OF PADDY WHACK, show (opened 11/14)
Chauncey Olcott, sung in show
George MacFarlane Φ 04/15 Vic 60132
John McCormack Φ stage, 04/16 Vic 64543
Charles W Harrison Φ 07/15 Vic 17780
Ernest Ball, vv stage

THE LITTLE GREY MOTHER (32)
Witmark, pub. 1915, reached #11 in December 1915
Bernie Grossman w, Harry DeCosta m
James Reed[5] & James F Harrison Φ 10/15 Vic 17839, 10/15 Col A-1804
Jim Doherty 01/16 Ed Amb 2762 cyl, 02/16 Ed 50310
vv singers

THE LITTLE HOUSE UPON THE HILL (22)
Shapiro, B, pub. 1915, reached #7 in May 1915
Ballard MacDonald & Joe Goodwin w, Harry Puck m
James Reed[5] & James F Harrison Ф 04/15 Vic 17732, 05/15 Col A-1700
Harry & Eva Puck, vv stage
Emma Carus, vv stage
Bessie Wynn, vv stage
Van & Schenck, vv stage

LOVE, HERE IS MY HEART (43)
L Feist, pub. 1915, reached #14 in December 1915
Adrian Ross w, Lao Silesu m
Reed Miller 12/15 Col A-1860, 02/16 Vic 17916
vv singers

THE MAGIC MELODY
T B Harms & F D H, pub. 1915, reached #19 in July 1915
Guy Bolton w, Jerome Kern m
Featured in NOBODY HOME, show (opened 04/15)
Adele Rowland, sung in show
Billy Murray 08/15 Vic 17790

MY BIRD OF PARADISE (28)
Waterson, B & S, pub. 1915, reached #3 in July 1915
Irving Berlin w & m
Peerless Quartet Ф 06/15 Vic 17770, 06/15 Col A-1760
Blossom Seeley, vv stage
Byal & Early, vv stage

MY LITTLE DREAM GIRL (8)
J W Stern, pub. 1915, reached #1 in September 1915
L Wolfe Gilbert w, Anatole Friedland m
James Reed[5] & James F Harrison ФФ 06/15 Col A-1755, 07/15 Vic 17789
Tilford, vv stage
Anatole Friedland, vv stage
Victoria Four, vv stage

MY LITTLE GIRL (33)
Broadway Mus Co, pub. 1915, reached #6 in September 1915
Sam Lewis & Will Dillon w, Albert Von Tilzer m
Albert Campbell & Henry Burr Ф 08/15 Vic 17810
Ada Jones & Bill C Robbins Ф 07/15 Col A-1724
vv singers

MY SWEET ADAIR (10)
J W Stern, pub. 1915, reached #1 in December 1915
L Wolfe Gilbert w, Anatole Friedland m
James Reed[5] & James F Harrison ФФ 11/15 Vic 17852, 11/15 Col A-1831
Anatole Friedland, vv stage
Walter Van Brunt 01/16 Ed 50301

NORWAY (42)
L Feist, pub. 1915, reached #17 in October 1915
Joe McCarthy w, Fred Fisher m
Kitty Gordon, vv stage
Albert Campbell & Henry Burr 09/15 Vic 17827, 09/15 Col A-1783

ON THE 5:15 (14)
J H Remick, pub. 1914, reached #2 in March 1915
Stanley Murphy w, Henry I Marshall m
Elizabeth Murray, vv stage
American Quartet Ф 03/15 Vic 17704
Collins & Harlan Ф 03/15 Col A-1675
Henry Marshall, vv stage

PINEY RIDGE
Shapiro, B, pub. 1915, reached #20 in January 1916
Ballard MacDonald w, Halsey K Mohr m
Albert Campbell & Henry Burr 11/15 Col A-1827
Irving Kaufman 01/16 Vic 17896
vv singers

PLAY A SIMPLE MELODY (50)
Waterson, B & S, pub. 1914, reached #17 in July 1915
(Also reached #3 in August 1950)
Irving Berlin w & m
Featured in WATCH YOUR STEP, show (opened 12/14)
Charles King & Sallie Fisher, sung in show
Mary Carson & Walter Van Brunt 06/15 Ed Amb 2607

PUT ME TO SLEEP WITH AN OLD FASHIONED MELODY (48)
Broadway Mus Co, pub. 1915, reached #19 in November 1915
Sam Lewis & Dick Howard w, Harry Jentes m
Irving Kaufman 11/15 Vic 17853
vv singers

RAGGING THE SCALE (34)
Artmusic Inc, pub. 1915, reached #7 in October 1915
Edward B Claypoole m
Prince's Band Ф 09/15 Col A-5702
Conway's Band Ф 11/15 Vic 17851

RAILROAD JIM
F B Haviland, pub. 1915, reached #18 in July 1915
Nat H Vincent w & m
Nat Vincent, vv stage

SHADOWLAND (45)
L Feist, pub. 1914, reached #10 in July 1915
Lawrence B Gilbert m
Prince's Band Ф 07/15 Col A-5680
Jaudas' Society Orch 09/15 Ed Amb 2666 cyl

SISTER SUSIE'S SEWING SHIRTS FOR SOLDIERS (25)
T B Harms & F D H, pub. 1914, reached #9 in February 1915
R P Weston w, Hermann E Darewski m
Al Jolson, stage, 03/15 Col A-1671
Billy Murray 01/15 Vic 17659, 02/15 Ed Amb 2530 cyl
Josie Heather, vv stage

THE SONG OF SONGS (41)
Chappell, pub. 1914, reached #15 in April 1915
Clarence Lucas w, Harold Vicars m
Featured in THE DANCING DUCHESS, show (opened 08/14)
Dorothy Jardon, sung in show
Josie Collins, vv stage
Grace Kerns 02/15 Col A-5625

SWEET KENTUCKY LADY (39)
Witmark, pub. 1914, reached #12 in May 1915
William Jerome w, Louis A Hirsch m
Harry Macdonough Φ 04/15 Vic 17723
George Evans' Honey Boys, vv stage
Fields' Minstrels, vv stage

SYNCOPATED WALK
Waterson, B & S, pub. 1914, reached #18 in April 1915
Irving Berlin w & m
Featured in WATCH YOUR STEP, show (opened 12/14)
Vernon & Irene Castle, sung and danced in show
Prince's Band 03/15 Col A-5632
Peerless Quartet 05/15 Vic 17748

TAKE ME TO THE MIDNIGHT CAKE WALK BALL (49)
M Abrahams, pub. 1915, reached Top 30 in December 1915
Eddie Cox, Arthur Jackson, Maurice Abrahams w & m
Featured in THE PASSING SHOW OF 1915, show (opened 05/15)
Daphne Pollard, sung in show
Prince's Band 04/16 Col A-5780
vv singers

THAT'S THE SONG OF SONGS FOR ME
Shapiro, B, pub. 1915, reached #12 in November 1915
Joe Goodwin w, Nat Osborne m
Harvey Hindermeyer 11/15 Vic 17857
Billy Burton[6] & Herbert Stuart 11/15 Col A-1831
vv singers

THERE'S A LITTLE LANE WITHOUT A TURNING ON THE WAY TO HOME SWEET HOME (27)
Broadway Mus Co, pub. 1915, reached #5 in November 1915
Sam Lewis w, George Meyer m
Henry Burr Φ 10/15 Col A-1791, 12/15 Vic 17878
vv singers

THERE'S A LITTLE SPARK OF LOVE STILL BURNING (11)
L Feist ΦΦΦ, pub. 1914, reached #2 in May 1915
Joe McCarthy w, Fred Fisher m
Featured in ALMA'S RETURN, show (1914)
Henry Burr ΦΦ 03/15 Vic 17697
Kitty Gordon, sung in show
vv singers

TIP TOP TIPPERARY MARY (31)
Shapiro, B, pub. 1914, reached #11 in February 1915
Ballard MacDonald w, Harry Carroll m
Emma Carus, vv stage
Bessie Wynn, vv stage
Truly Shattuck, vv stage
Peerless Quartet Φ 02/15 Vic 17678

UNDER THE AMERICAN FLAG
H Von Tilzer, pub. 1915, reached #19 in September 1915
Andrew Sterling w, Harry Von Tilzer m
vv singers

WHEN I LEAVE THE WORLD BEHIND (9)
Waterson, B & S, pub. 1915, reached #1 in September 1915
Irving Berlin w & m
Al Jolson, vv stage
Sam Ash Φ 08/15 Col A-1772
Fritzie Scheff, vv stage
Henry Burr Φ 12/15 Vic 17874

WHEN I WAS A DREAMER (AND YOU WERE MY DREAM) (36)
J H Remick, pub. 1914, reached #6 in August 1915
George A Little & Roger Lewis w, Egbert Van Alstyne m
Harry Macdonough Φ 07/15 Vic 17718
The Volunteers, vv stage
Sam Ash 07/15 Col A-1725

WHEN IT'S NIGHT TIME IN DIXIE LAND (47)
Waterson, B & S, pub. 1914, reached #20 in April 1915
Irving Berlin w & m
Belle Baker, vv stage
Primrose Four, vv stage

WHEN MY SHIP COMES IN (46)
H Von Tilzer, pub. 1915, reached #17 in April 1915
Vincent Bryan w, Harry Von Tilzer m
Albert Campbell & Henry Burr 04/15 Vic 17732
Claire Rochester, vv stage
Primrose Four, vv stage

WHEN OLD BILL BAILEY PLAYS THE UKULELE (40)
Broadway Mus Co, pub. 1915, reached #15 in January 1916
Charles McCarron & Nat Vincent w & m
Peerless Quartet Φ 01/16 Vic 17904, 01/16 Col A-1865
Billy Murray 02/16 Ed 2776 cyl, 03/16 Ed 50315

WHEN THE GROWN UP LADIES ACT LIKE BABIES (44)
M Abrahams, pub. 1914, reached #16 in February 1915
Joe Young & Edgar Leslie w, Maurice Abrahams m
Featured in DANCING AROUND, show (opened 10/14)
Al Jolson, sung in show, 03/15 Col A-1671
Billy Murray 02/15 Vic 17678
Willie Weston, vv stage
Sally Fields, vv stage

WHEN YOU WORE A TULIP (4)
L Feist, pub. 1914, reached #2 in January 1915
Jack Mahoney w, Percy Wenrich m
American Quartet ΦΦ 12/14 Vic 17652
Connolly & Wenrich, vv stage
Van & Schenck, vv stage
Victor Military Band 02/15 Vic 35421

WHEN YOU'RE AWAY (20)
Witmark, pub. 1914, reached #9 in June 1915
Henry Blossom w, Victor Herbert m
Featured in THE ONLY GIRL, show (opened 11/14)
Olive Kline Φ 02/15 Vic 17690
Wilda Bennett, sung in show
Grace Kerns Φ 02/15 Col A-5625

YOU KNOW AND I KNOW (AND WE BOTH UNDERSTAND)
T B Harms & F D H, pub. 1915, reached #15 in August 1915
Schuyler Greene w, Jerome Kern m
Featured in NOBODY HOME, show (opened 04/15)
Alice Dovey & George Anderson, sung in show
vv singers

YOU'LL ALWAYS BE THE SAME SWEET GIRL (12)
H Von Tilzer, pub. 1915, reached #8 in December 1915
Andrew Sterling w, Harry Von Tilzer m
James Reed[5] & James F Harrison Ф 11/15 Col A-1826, 12/15 Vic 17878
Manuel Romain, vv stage, 05/16 Ed Amb 2859
Henry Burr 05/16 Pathe 30364

YOU'RE MORE THAN THE WORLD TO ME (23)
J Morris, pub. 1914, reached #5 in January 1915
Jeff Branen w, Alfred Solman m
Manuel Romain Ф 10/14 Col A-1577, 10/14 Ed Amb 2425 cyl
George W Ballard 12/14 Vic 17654
Courtenay Sisters, vv stage
Mayo & Tally, vv stage

[1]Alice Green was a pseudonym for Olive Kline.
[2]Columbia Quartet was actually the Peerless Quartet.
[3]Raymond Dixon was a pseudonym for Lambert Murphy.
[4]Ed Hamilton was a pseudonym for Reinald Werrenrath.
[5]James Reed was a pseudonym for Reed Miller.
[6]Billy Burton was a pseudonym for Charles Harrison

1916

ALONG THE ROCKY ROAD TO DUBLIN (20)
Waterson, B & S, pub. 1915, reached #2 in February 1916
Joe Young w, Bert Grant m
American Quartet ФФ 01/16 Vic 17900, 03/16 Ed Amb 2817 cyl[1]
Blanche Ring, vv stage
Marguerite Farrell 03/16 Col A-1920

AMERICA, I LOVE YOU (13)
Kalmar & Puck, pub. 1915, reached #2 in January 1916
(Also reached #16 in March 1941)
Edgar Leslie w, Archie Gottler m
American Quartet Ф 12/15 Vic 17902
Eva Tanguay, vv stage
Sam Ash Ф 12/15 Col A-1842

ARABY (38)
Waterson, B & S, pub. 1915, reached #13 in January 1916
Irving Berlin w & m
Eddie Cantor, vv stage
Harry Macdonough Ф 12/15 Vic 17889
Prince's Orch 11/15 Col A-5715

ARE YOU FROM DIXIE? (22)
Witmark, pub. 1915, reached #6 in May 1916
Jack Yellen w, George L Cobb m
Billy Murray & Jack Kaufman Ф 03/16 Vic 17942, 09/16 Ed Amb 2942 cyl, 12/16 Ed 50357
Honey Boy Minstrels, vv stage
Peerless Quartet 03/16 Col A-1921, 04/16 Pathe 30381

ARRAH, GO ON, I'M GONNA GO BACK TO OREGON (27)
Waterson, B & S, pub. 1916, reached #5 in July 1916
Joe Young & Sam Lewis w, Bert Grant m
Peerless Quartet Ф 07/16 Vic 18046
Marguerite Farrell 06/16 Col A-1981
Maggie Cline, vv stage

AT THE END OF A BEAUTIFUL DAY (50)
F B Haviland, pub. 1916, reached #19 in September 1916
William H Perkins w & m
Jane Kenyon[2] 08/16 Vic 18065
Henry Burr 09/16 Pathe 20005
vv singers

BABES IN THE WOOD (31)
T B Harms & F D H, pub. 1915, reached #8 in July 1916
Schuyler Greene w, Jerome Kern m
Featured in VERY GOOD, EDDIE, show (opened 12/15)
Ernest Truex & Alice Dovey, sung in show
Gladys Rice & Walter Van Brunt 07/16 Ed Amb 2900 cyl, 07/16 Ed 80306
Prince's Band 07/16 Col A-5816
Harry Macdonough & Anna Howard 12/16 Vic 18172

BABY SHOES (15)
Shapiro, B ФФФ, pub. 1916, reached #1 in August 1916
Joe Goodwin & Ed Rose w, Al Piantadosi m
Henry Burr Ф 07/16 Col A-2001
Edna Brown[3] Ф 07/16 Vic 18052
vv singers

DON'T BITE THE HAND THAT'S FEEDING YOU (43)
L Feist, pub. 1915, reached #10 in March 1916
Thomas Hoier w, James Morgan m
Albert Campbell & Henry Burr 02/16 Col A-1898
Irving Kaufman 03/16 Vic 17942
Ed Morton, vv stage

DOWN WHERE THE SWANEE RIVER FLOWS
Broadway Mus Co, pub. 1916, reached #19 in October 1916
Charles S Alberte & Charles McCarron w, Albert Von Tilzer m
Featured in ROBINSON CRUSOE JR, show (opened 02/16)
Al Jolson, sung in show, 07/16 Col A-2007
Peerless Quartet 05/16 Vic 17983

GOODBYE, GOOD LUCK, AND GOD BLESS YOU (5)
Witmark ΦΦΦ, pub. 1916, reached #1 in May 1916
J Keirn Brennan w, Ernest Ball m
Henry Burr ΦΦ 05/16 Vic 17984
Ernest Ball Φ vv stage, 06/16 Col A-1978
Maude Lambert, vv stage
Chauncey Olcott, vv stage
Van & Schenck, vv stage

HELLO, HAWAII, HOW ARE YOU? (10)
Waterson, B & S, pub. 1915, reached #2 in March 1916
Bert Kalmar & Edgar Leslie w, Jean Schwartz m
Willie & Gene Howard, vv stage
Billy Murray ΦΦ 03/16 Vic 17944
Anna Chandler, vv stage, 04/16 Col A-1939
Prince's Band 04/16 Col A-5780

I CAN DANCE WITH EVERYBODY BUT MY WIFE (26)
T B Harms & F D H, pub. 1916, reached #2 in July 1916
John L Golden w, Joseph Cawthorn m
Featured in SYBIL, show (opened 01/16)
Joseph Cawthorn Φ sung in show, 05/16 Vic 55074
Billy Murray Φ 07/16 Ed Amb 2897 cyl, 09/16 Ed 50350
vv singers

I KNOW I GOT MORE THAN MY SHARE
L Feist, pub. 1916, reached #17 in January 1917
Grant Clarke & Howard Johnson w & m
Irving Kaufman 01/17 Vic 18186
Kate Elinore, vv stage
Robert Lewis[4] 12/16 Col A-2108

I LOVE A PIANO (45)
Waterson, B & S, pub. 1915, reached #15 in July 1916
Irving Berlin w & m
Featured in STOP, LOOK & LISTEN, show (opened 12/15)
Billy Murray Φ 03/16 Vic 17945
Harry Fox, sung in show
M J O'Connell 04/16 Col A-1955, 05/16 Pathe 30378, 06/16 Emer 742

I LOVE YOU, THAT'S ONE THING I KNOW (37)
J W Stern, pub. 1915, reached #11 in May 1916
L Wolfe Gilbert w, Anatole Friedland m
William Barnes 04/16 Vic 17970
Henry Burr 06/16 Emer 738, 07/16 Col A-2001
Marie Cahill, vv stage

I'VE BEEN FLOATING DOWN THE OLD GREEN RIVER (34)
Waterson, B & S, pub. 1915, reached #10 in January 1916
Bert Kalmar w, Joe Cooper m
Featured in MAID IN AMERICA, show (opened 02/15)
Billy Murray Φ 01/16 Vic 17885, 04/16 Ed Amb 2642 cyl, 04/16 Ed 50327
Florence Moore, sung in show
Sam Ash 11/15 Col A-1825
vv singers

IF I KNOCK THE "L" OUT OF KELLY (23)
Waterson, B & S, pub. 1916, reached #3 in September 1916
Joe Young & Sam Lewis w, Bert Grant m
Featured in STEP THIS WAY, show (opened 05/16)
Marguerite Farrell Φ sung in show and 09/16 Vic 18105, 09/16 Col A-2040
Ada Jones 09/16 Ed Amb 2940 cyl, 12/16 Ed 50364
Dan Quinn 09/16 Operaphone 1087
Nellie V Nichols, vv stage

IRELAND MUST BE HEAVEN FOR MY MOTHER CAME FROM THERE (9)
L Feist ΦΦΦ, pub. 1916, reached #2 in November 1916
Joe McCarthy & Howard Johnson w, Fred Fisher m
Charles W Harrison Φ 10/16 Vic 18111, 01/17 Col A-2123
John McCormack, stage
Avon Comedy Four, vv stage
Emma Carus, vv stage

KEEP THE HOME FIRES BURNING (44)
Chappell ΦΦΦ, pub. 1915, reached #14 in March 1916
(Also reached #7 in October 1917)
Lena Guilbert Ford w, Ivor Novello m
Frederick J Wheeler[5] Φ 12/15 Vic 17881, 01/16 Ed Amb 2773 cyl, 03/16 Ed 80283
Reed Miller & Frederick Wheeler[5] 01/16 Col A-1869
vv and stage singers

KISS ME AGAIN (30)
Witmark ΦΦΦ, pub. 1905, reached #17 in October 1916
Henry Blossom w, Victor Herbert m
Featured in THE CENTURY GIRL, show (opened 11/16)
Also featured in MISS 1917, show (opened 11/17)
Steady seller 1906-1920
Alice Green[6] 03/16 Vic 17954
Grace Kerns 06/16 Col A-1982
Vivienne Segal, sung in show (Miss 1917)
Arthur Cunningham & John Slavin, sung in show (CG)

THE LADDER OF ROSES
T B Harms & F D H, pub. 1915, reached #12 in April 1916
R H Burnside w, Raymond Hubbell m
Featured in HIP HIP HOORAY, show (opened 09/15)
Olive Kline Φ 02/16 Vic 17922
Howard Marsh, sung in show
Prince's Band 05/16 Col A-5794

MAMMY'S LITTLE COAL BLACK ROSE (18)
J H Remick, pub. 1916, reached #1 in January 1917
Raymond Egan w, Richard Whiting m
Al Jolson, vv stage
Blossom Seeley, vv stage
Orpheus Quartet Φ 01/17 Vic 18183
Broadway Quartet Φ 12/16 Col A-2114
Adele Rowland, vv stage

MEMORIES (4)
J H Remick ΦΦΦ, pub. 1915, reached #1 in April 1916
Gus Kahn w, Egbert Van Alstyne m
John Barnes Wells Φ 04/16 Vic 17968
Harry McClaskey[7] Φ 03/16 Col A-1923
Marx Brothers, vv stage
Carolina White, vv stage

MISSOURI WALTZ (HUSH-A-BYE MA BABY) (39)
Forster M P ΦΦΦ, pub. 1914, reached #19 in August 1916,
(Reached second peak at #19 in April 1917)
(Also reached #4 in May 1918)
James R Shannon w, Frederick K Logan & John V Eppell m
Steady seller, 1915-1919
Edna Brown[3] Φ 03/17 Vic 18214
Victor Military Band Φ 06/16 Vic 18026
Prince's Orch 09/16 Col A-5838

MOLLY DEAR, IT'S YOU I'M AFTER (32)
J H Remick, pub. 1915, reached #8 in February 1916
Frank Wood w, Henry E Pether m
Elizabeth Murray, vv stage
Orpheus Quartet Φ 01/16 Vic 17900
Sophie Tucker, vv stage
Blanche Ring, vv stage
Edith Chapman 11/15 Col A-1819

M-O-T-H-E-R (2)
L Feist ΦΦΦ, pub. 1915, reached #1 in February 1916
Howard Johnson w, Theodore F Morse m
Henry Burr ΦΦ 02/16 Vic 17913, 02/16 Col A-1899,
06/16 Emerson 720
George MacFarlane, vv stage
Sophie Tucker, vv stage
Eva Tanguay, vv stage

MY DREAMY CHINA LADY
J H Remick, pub. 1916, reached #20 in June 1916
Gus Kahn w, Egbert Van Alstyne m
Lyric Quartet 06/16 Vic 18034
Grace Nash & Henry Burr 07/16 Col A-2002
vv singers

MY MOTHER'S ROSARY (11)
Waterson, B & S, pub. 1915, reached #3 in May 1916
Sam Lewis w, George Meyer m
Charles W Harrison Φ 03/16 Vic 17948
Avon Comedy Four, vv stage, 08/16 Vic 18081
Harry McClaskey[7] 03/16 Col A-1923

MY OWN IONA (6)
J W Stern, pub. 1916, reached #2 in September 1916
L Wolfe Gilbert w, Anatole Friedland & Carey Morgan m
Charles King & Elizabeth Brice Φ 10/16 Col A-2059
May Naudain, vv stage
Henry Burr/Louise & Ferrera Φ 09/16 Pathe 35045
William Barnes Φ 07/16 Vic 18054
Rene Dietrich & Horace Wright 12/16 Vic 18171

NAT'AN, FOR WHAT ARE YOU WAITIN', NAT'AN? (49)
Kendis M P C, pub. 1916, reached #16 in June 1916
James Kendis w & m
Rhoda Bernard Φ 05/16 Pathe 30395, 06/16 Vic 18023,
06/16 Col A-1973
Sophie Tucker, vv stage
Belle Baker, vv stage
Van & Schenck, vv stage

OH! HOW SHE COULD YACKI, HACKI, WICKI, WACKI, WOO (36)
Broadway Mus Co, pub. 1916, reached #6 in November 1916
Stanley Murphy & Charles McCarron w, Albert Von Tilzer m
Eddie Cantor, vv stage
Collins & Harlan Φ 09/16 Col A-2043, 10/16 Vic 18110,
11/16 Operaphone 1928, 12/16 Ed 50372
Avon Comedy Four, vv stage

ON THE BEACH AT WAIKIKI (46)
Bergstrom Mus Co, pub. 1915, reached #19 in July 1916
G H Stover w, Henry Kailimai m
Helen Louise & Frank Ferrera Φ 04/16 Col A-1935,
06/16 Pathe 30393
vv singers

ON THE SOUTH SEA ISLE (48)
H Von Tilzer, pub. 1916, reached #13 in October 1916
Harry Von Tilzer w & m
Al Jolson, vv stage
Sterling Trio 09/16 Col A-2045, 10/16 Vic 18113
Irene Bordoni, vv stage

OUT OF THE CRADLE, INTO MY HEART
J W Stern, pub. 1916, reached #11 in January 1917
L Wolfe Gilbert w, Anatole Friedland m
Elizabeth Brice & Charles King, vv stage
Sterling Trio Φ 11/16 Pathe 20040, 12/16 Vic 18170,
01/17 Col A-2123

A PERFECT DAY (17)
C Jacobs-Bond ΦΦΦ, pub. 1910, reached #13 in August 1916
Carrie Jacobs-Bond w & m
Steady seller, 1910's and 1920's
Alma Gluck Φ 01/17 Vic 64607
Imperial Quartet 01/16 Vic 17872
Elizabeth Spencer 05/17 Vic 18250
stage singers

PRAY FOR THE LIGHTS TO GO OUT (28)
Skidmore Mus Co, pub. 1916, reached #12 in October 1916
Renton Tunnah w, Will E Skidmore m
Bert Williams, vv stage
George O'Connor 02/17 Col A-2143
Gene Rogers 11/16 Emer 787
The Cabaret Girls, vv stage

PRETTY BABY (1)
J H Remick ΦΦΦ, pub. 1916, reached #1 in September 1916
Gus Kahn w, Tony Jackson & Egbert Van Alstyne m
Featured in THE PASSING SHOW OF 1916, show (opened 06/16)
Billy Murray ΦΦ 09/16 Vic 18102
Dolly Hackett, sung in show
Orpheus Quartet, vv stage, 12/16 Vic 18162
Collins & Harlan Φ 10/16 Col A-2069
other vv singers

RACKETY COO!
G Schirmer, pub. 1915, reached #12 in May 1916
Otto Harbach w, Rudolf Friml m
Featured in KATINKA, show (opened 12/15)
Adele Rowland, sung in show
Alice Green[6] Φ 03/16 Vic 17954
Grace Nash & Sam Ash 04/16 Col A-1952

SHADES OF NIGHT (16)
J W Stern, pub. 1916, reached #5 in August 1916
L Wolfe Gilbert & Malvin Franklin w, Anatole Friedland m
Mme. Chilson Ohrman, stage
May Naudain, stage
Grace LaRue, vv stage
Sterling Trio Φ 07/16 Vic 18028, 07/16 Col A-2002
Henry Burr 06/16 Emerson 720

SHE IS THE SUNSHINE OF VIRGINIA (25)
Shapiro, B, pub. 1916, reached #3 in December 1916
Ballard MacDonald w, Harry Carroll m
Albert Campbell & Henry Burr ΦΦ 10/16 Vic 18112, 10/16 Col A-2067
vv singers

SHE'S THE DAUGHTER OF MOTHER MACHREE (33)
Witmark, pub. 1915, reached #7 in March 1916
Jeff Branen w, Ernest Ball m
Charles Harrison Φ 03/16 Vic 17948
Manuel Romain 04/16 Col A-1951, 06/16 Emerson 744
vv singers

SIAM (41)
L Feist, pub. 1915, reached #10 in May 1916
Howard Johnson w, Fred Fisher m
American Quartet 05/16 Vic 17993
Prince's Band 08/16 Col A-5827
Emma Carus, vv stage

SO LONG, LETTY (29)
Witmark, pub. 1915, reached #15 in April 1916
Earl Carroll w & m
Featured in SO LONG, LETTY, show (opened 10/16)
Charlotte Greenwood & Sydney Grant, sung in show
Alice Green[6] & Lambert Murphy 04/16 Vic 17974
Prince's Orch 05/16 Col A-5796

THE SUNSHINE OF YOUR SMILE (19)
T B Harms & F D H, pub. 1915, reached #4 in September 1916
Leonard Cooke w, Lillian Ray m
John McCormack Φ 12/16 Vic 64622
Lambert Murphy Φ 03/16 Vic 55069
vv singers

THERE'S A BROKEN HEART FOR EVERY LIGHT ON BROADWAY (40)
L Feist, pub. 1915, reached #8 in April 1916
Howard Johnson w, Fred Fisher m
Edna Brown[3] 04/16 Vic 17943
Dolly Connolly, vv stage
Manuel Romain 05/16 Col A-1964

THERE'S A LITTLE BIT OF BAD IN EVERY GOOD LITTLE GIRL (7)
L Feist, pub. 1916, reached #1 in December 1916
Grant Clarke w, Fred Fisher m
Billy Murray ΦΦ 11/16 Vic 18143
Emma Carus, vv stage
Elizabeth Brice & Charles King, vv stage
Sophie Tucker, vv stage
Avon Comedy Four, vv stage

THERE'S A LONG, LONG TRAIL (3)
Witmark ΦΦΦ, pub. 1913, reached #6 in October 1916
(Also reached #3 in March 1918)
Stoddard King w, Zo Elliott m
Steady seller, 1915-1919
James Reed[8] & James F Harrison ΦΦ 12/15 Vic 17882, 03/17 Vic 17882 (RI)
Dorothy Jardon, vv stage
Billy Burton[9] & Herbert Stuart 10/15 Col A-1791
Kathryn Dahl, vv stage

THERE'S A QUAKER DOWN IN QUAKER TOWN (24)
J H Remick, pub. 1916, reached #3 in August 1916
David Berg w, Alfred Solman m
Albert Campbell & Henry Burr Φ 06/16 Vic 18034
Peerless Quartet Φ 07/16 Col A-2005
vv singers

THEY DIDN'T BELIEVE ME (12)
J H Remick, pub. 1914, reached #2 in February 1916
Herbert Reynolds w, Jerome Kern m
Featured in THE GIRL FROM UTAH, show, (opened 08/14)
Julia Sanderson & Donald Brian, sung in show
Alice Green[6] & Harry Macdonough Φ 11/15 Vic 35491
Adele Rowland, vv stage
Gladys Rice & Walter Van Brunt 01/16 Ed Amb 2759, 04/16 Ed 80279
Grace Kerns & Reed Miller 06/16 Col A-1982

TURN BACK THE UNIVERSE AND GIVE ME YESTERDAY (21)
Witmark, pub. 1916, reached #3 in November 1916
J Keirn Brennan w, Ernest Ball m
Harry Macdonough/Orpheus Quartet Φ 10/16 Vic 18112
Maude Lambert, stage
Morton Harvey 11/16 Emerson 785

UNDERNEATH THE STARS (14)
J H Remick, pub. 1915, reached #4 in March 1916
Fleta Jan Brown w, Herbert Spencer m
Raymond Dixon[10] Φ 03/16 Vic 17946
Prince's Band 04/16 Col A-5780
vv singers

WHAT A WONDERFUL MOTHER YOU'D BE (42)
Shapiro, B, pub. 1915, reached #9 in April 1916
Joe Goodwin w, Al Piantadosi m
Henry Burr Φ 03/16 Vic 17953
Manuel Romain 03/16 Col A-1922
vv singers

WHEN THE BLACK SHEEP RETURNS TO THE FOLD
Waterson, B & S, pub. 1916, reached #19 in December 1916
Irving Berlin w & m
Avon Comedy Four, vv stage, 10/16 Vic 18126
Belle Baker, vv stage

WHERE DID ROBINSON CRUSOE GO WITH FRIDAY ON SATURDAY NIGHT? (35)
Waterson B & S, pub. 1916, reached #7 in June 1916
Joe Young & Sam Lewis w, George Meyer m
Featured in ROBINSON CRUSOE, JR, show (opened 02/16)
Al Jolson Φ sung in show, 06/16 Col A-1976
Billy Murray 08/16 Ed Amb 2931 cyl, 12/16 Ed 50356

YAAKA HULA, HICKEY DULA (8)
Waterson, B & S ΦΦΦ, pub. 1916, reached #1 in June 1916
E Ray Goetz, Joe Young & Pete Wendling w & m
Featured in ROBINSON CRUSOE, JR, show (opened 02/16)
Al Jolson ΦΦ sung in show, 04/16 Col A-1956
Collins & Harlan 06/16 Vic 18014, 07/16 Pathe 30426
Avon Comedy Four, vv stage, 08/16 Vic 18081

YOU'RE A DANGEROUS GIRL (47)
L Feist, pub. 1916, reached #10 in September 1916
Grant Clarke w, James V Monaco m
Al Jolson Φ 09/16 Col A-2041
Avon Comedy Four, vv stage, 09/16 Vic 18088

[1]Billed as the Premier Quartet on Edison.
[2]Jane Kenyon was a pseudonym for Elizabeth Wheeler.
[3]Edna Brown was a pseudonym for Elsie Baker.
[4]Robert Lewis was a pseudonym for Lewis James.
[5]Frederick J Wheeler was a pseudonym for James F Harrison.
[6]Alice Green was a pseudonym for Olive Kline.
[7]Harry McClaskey was a pseudonym for, and real name of, Henry Burr.
[8]James Reed was a pseudonym for Reed Miller.
[9]Billy Burton was a pseudonym for Charles Harrison.
[10]Raymond Dixon was a pseudonym for Lambert Murphy.

1917

ALL THE WORLD WILL BE JEALOUS OF ME (15)
Witmark, pub. 1917, reached #1 in August 1917
Al Dubin w, Ernest Ball m
Charles W Harrison Φ 07/17 Vic 18302
Henry Burr Φ 07/17 Imperial 5454, 08/17 Col A-2275, 11/17 Emerson 7249
Bison City Four, vv stage
Ernest Ball, vv stage

ALLAH'S HOLIDAY (29)
G Schirmer, pub. 1916, reached #7 in June 1917
Otto Harbach w, Rudolf Friml m
Featured in KATINKA, show (opened 12/15)
Edith Day, sung in show
Joseph C Smith's Orch Φ 05/17 Vic 18246
Prince's Band 05/17 Col A-5945

BREAK THE NEWS TO MOTHER (18)
C K Harris, pub. 1897, reached #10 in November 1917
Charles K Harris w & m
Belle Baker, vv stage
Eva Tanguay, vv stage
Shannon Four 11/17 Vic 18358
Henry Burr 02/18 Col A-2436

COME OUT OF THE KITCHEN, MARY ANN (36)
Kendis M P C, pub. 1917, reached #7 in May 1917
James Kendis & Charles Bayha w & m
Featured in HAVE A HEART, show (opened 01/17)
Louise Dresser, sung in show
M J O'Connell Φ 03/17 Vic 18221, 04/17 Col A-2189
Van & Schenck, vv stage
Elizabeth Murray, vv stage

THE DARKTOWN STRUTTERS' BALL (2)
L Feist ΦΦΦ, pub. 1917, reached #1 in February 1918
(Also reached #13 in March 1954 in comic version)
Shelton Brooks w & m
Jazz standard, 1920's to 1950's
Original Dixieland Jazz Band Φ 09/17 Col A-2297
Sophie Tucker, vv stage
Collins & Harlan Φ 04/18 Col A-2478
Six Brown Brothers Φ vv stage, 11/17 Vic 18376
Blossom Seeley, vv stage

FOR ME AND MY GAL (3)
Waterson, B & S ΦΦΦ, pub. 1917, reached #1 in May 1917
(Also reached #6 in March 1943)
Edgar Leslie & E Ray Goetz w, George Meyer m
Van & Schenck ΦΦ vv stage, 05/17 Vic 18258
Al Jolson, vv stage
Elizabeth Brice & Charles King, vv stage
George Jessel, vv stage
Billy Murray Φ 07/17 Ed Amb 3222 cyl

FOR YOU A ROSE (28)
J H Remick, pub. 1917, reached #7 in July 1917
Will D Cobb w, Gus Edwards m
Edna Brown[1] Φ 07/17 Vic 18301
Conway's Band 10/17 Vic 18345
vv singers

GOODBYE BROADWAY, HELLO FRANCE! (5)
L Feist ΦΦΦ, pub. 1917, reached #2 in September 1917
C Francis Reisner & Benny Davis w, Billy Baskette m
Featured as finale in THE PASSING SHOW OF 1917, show (opened 04/17)
American Quartet ΦΦ 09/17 Vic 18335
Peerless Quartet Φ 10/17 Col A-2333
Brown Brothers Band, vv stage
vv singers

HAWAIIAN BUTTERFLY (37)
L Feist, pub. 1917, reached #9 in July 1917
George A Little w, Billy Baskette & Joe Santly m
Elizabeth Brice & Charles King Φ 06/17 Col A-2226
Blossom Seeley, vv stage
Emma Carus, vv stage
Sterling Trio Φ 06/17 Vic 18272, 06/17 Starr 7591
Earl Fuller's Novelty Orch, dance halls

HOW'S EVERY LITTLE THING IN DIXIE? (43)
J H Remick, pub. 1916, reached #10 in February 1917
Jack Yellen w, Albert Gumble m
Arthur Fields 02/17 Col A-2153
American Quartet 03/17 Vic 18225
vv singers

HUCKLEBERRY FINN (26)
Waterson, B & S, pub. 1917, reached #9 in August 1917
Cliff Hess, Sam Lewis, Joe Young w & m
Van & Schenck Φ vv stage, 08/17 Vic 18318
Avon Comedy Four, vv stage
Sam Ash 07/17 Col A-2245

I AIN'T GOT NOBODY (14)
Craig & Co, pub. 1916, reached #3 in March 1917
(Also reached #8 in Feb 1928)
(Also reached #12 in June 1985 as part of medley)
Roger Graham & Dave Payton w, Spencer Williams m
Jazz standard 1920's and 1930's
Marion Harris Φ 11/16 Vic 18133
Sophie Tucker, vv stage
Bert Williams, vv stage
Conway's Band 09/17 Vic 35646

I DON'T KNOW WHERE I'M GOING, BUT I'M ON MY WAY (25)
H Von Tilzer, pub. 1917, reached #9 in December 1917
George Fairman w & m
Peerless Quartet Φ 10/17 Col A-2329, 10/17 Lyraphone 5110, 12/17 Vic 18383
Henry Burr 09/17 Imperial 5475, 12/17 Paroquette 116
vv singers

I DON'T WANT TO GET WELL (21)
L Feist, pub. 1917, reached #3 in January 1918
Harry Pease & Howard Johnson w, Harry Jentes m
Van & Schenck Φ vv stage, 01/18 Vic 18413
Eddie Cantor, vv stage
Arthur Fields Φ 01/18 Col A-2409, 01/18 Ed Amb 3378 cyl, 04/18 Ed 50457, 04/18 Pathe 20314

I MAY BE GONE FOR A LONG, LONG TIME (17)
Broadway Mus Co ΦΦΦ, pub. 1917, reached #2 in December 1917
Lew Brown w, Albert Von Tilzer m
Featured in HITCHY KOO, show (opened 06/17)
Grace LaRue, sung in show
Peerless Quartet Φ 09/17 Col A-2306
Shannon Four Φ 09/17 Vic 18333
vv singers

IF YOU HAD ALL THE WORLD AND ITS GOLD (35)
Piantadosi Mus Co, pub. 1916, reached #12 in March 1917
Bartley Costello & Harry Edelheit w, Al Piantadosi m
Eva Tanguay, vv stage
Belle Baker, vv stage
Stewart Jackson 06/17 Vic 18281

INDIANA (12)
Shapiro, B, pub. 1917, reached #3 in June 1917
Ballard MacDonald w, James F Hanley m
Original Dixieland Jazz Band Φ stage, 09/17 Col A-2297
Knickerbocker Quartet Φ 06/17 Col A-2221
Henry Burr 05/17 Starr 7585, 06/17 Imperial 5444
vv singers

IT TAKES A LONG, TALL, BROWN-SKIN GAL (33)
Skidmore Mus Co, pub. 1917, reached #8 in July 1917
Marshall Walker w, Will E Skidmore m
Rae Samuels, vv stage
Arthur Collins 07/17 Emerson 7188
vv singers

JOAN OF ARC, THEY ARE CALLING YOU (6)
Waterson, B & S, pub. 1917, reached #4 in November 1917
Alfred Bryan & Willie Weston w, Jack Wells m
Henry Burr Φ 08/17 Col A-2273, 10/17 Lyraphone 5112
Willie Weston 08/17 Vic 18307, 11/17 Pathe 20224
Vernon Dalhart 11/17 Ed Amb 3323 cyl

KEEP THE HOME FIRES BURNING (7)
Chappell ΦΦΦ, pub. 1915, reached #7 in October 1917
(Also reached #14 in March 1916)
Lena Guilbert Ford w, Ivor Novello m
John McCormack ΦΦ 10/17 Vic 64696
Frederick Wheeler[2] Φ 04/17 Vic 17881 (RI)
Oscar Seagle 05/18 Col A-6028
vv and stage singers

LADDIE BOY (30)
Witmark, pub. 1907, reached #11 in November 1917
Will D Cobb w, Gus Edwards m
Nora Bayes, vv stage, 10/17 Vic 45130
Albert Campbell & Henry Burr 10/17 Col A-2336
vv singers

LILY OF THE VALLEY (10)
J W Stern, pub. 1917, reached #3 in July 1917
L Wolfe Gilbert w, Anatole Friedland m
Adele Rowland, vv stage
Collins & Harlan Φ 07/17 Imperial 5456, 09/17 Col A-2296, 12/17 Vic 18398
Sophie Tucker, vv stage
Kathryn Miley, vv stage
Henry Lewis Φ 07/17 Emerson 7197

LIVERY STABLE BLUES (47)
R Graham, pub. 1917, reached #20 in October 1917
Marvin Lee w, Ray Lopez & Alcide Nunez m
Original Dixieland Jazz Band Φ 05/17 Vic 18255
W C Handy Orch 02/18 Col A-2419

LONG BOY (GOODBYE, MA! GOODBYE, PA! GOODBYE, MULE) (40)
Shapiro, B, pub. 1917, reached #16 in January 1918
William Herschell w, Barclay Walker m
Byron G Harlan/Peerless Quartet 01/18 Vic 18413, 01/18 Col A-2409
Steve Porter 01/18 Ed Amb 3365 cyl
vv singers

THE MAGIC OF YOUR EYES (31)
Witmark, pub. 1917, reached #15 in July 1917
Arthur A Penn w & m
Charles W Harrison, stage, 04/17 Vic 18244, 07/17 Col A-5963
Frances Alda, stage, 08/18 Vic 64782

M-I-S-S-I-S-S-I-P-P-I (9)
Wm Jerome Pub Co, pub. 1916, reached #3 in May 1917
Bert Hanlon & Benny Ryan w, Harry Tierney m
Featured in MIDNIGHT FROLICS OF 1916, revue 1916
Also featured in HITCHY KOO OF 1917, show (opened 06/17)
Frances White, sung in show (MF), 10/17 Vic 18537, 11/17 Vic 45137
Grace LaRue, sung in show (HK)
Ada Jones Φ 03/17 Emerson 7128, 03/17 Emerson 5169, 08/17 Pathe 20074
Anna Wheaton Φ 06/17 Col A-2224

MOTHER
G Schirmer, pub. 1916, reached #19 in April 1917
Rida Johnson Young w, Sigmund Romberg m
Featured in HER SOLDIER BOY, show (opened 12/16)
Lambert Murphy 04/17 Vic 45111
Frank Ridge, sung in show
Charles W Harrison 06/17 Col A-2227

MY HAWAIIAN SUNSHINE (32)
J W Stern, pub. 1916, reached #4 in February 1917
L Wolfe Gilbert w, Carey Morgan m
Van & Schenck, vv stage, 12/16 Emerson 798
Albert Campbell & Henry Burr Φ 02/17 Vic 18202
Gene & Willie Howard, vv stage

MY SUNSHINE JANE (50)
Witmark, pub. 1917, reached Top 30 in December 1917
J Keirn Brennan w, Ernest Ball m
Bison City Four, vv stage
Sterling Trio 12/17 Vic 18403
Frederick J Wheeler[2] & Reed Miller 01/18 Col A-2412

NAUGHTY! NAUGHTY! NAUGHTY!
Shapiro, B, pub. 1916, reached #12 in February 1917
Joe Goodwin & William Tracey w, Nat Vincent m
Featured in THE SHOW OF WONDERS, show (opened 10/16)
Grace Fisher, sung in show
Sam Ash 02/17 Col A-2149
Marguerite Farrell 03/17 Vic 18213

OH JOHNNY, OH JOHNNY, OH! (8)
Forster M P ΦΦΦ, pub. 1917, reached #2 in June 1917 (Also reached #3 in January 1940)
Ed Rose w, Abe Olman m
Featured in FOLLOW ME, show (opened 11/16)
American Quartet ΦΦ 06/17 Vic 18279
Elizabeth Brice, vv stage, 08/17 Col A-2265
Joseph C Smith's Orch 08/17 Vic 18313
Nora Bayes, vv stage
Henry Jackson, sung in show

OVER THERE (1)
L Feist ΦΦΦ, pub. 1917, reached #1 in August 1917
George M Cohan w & m
Nora Bayes ΦΦ vv stage, 10/17 Vic 45130
American Quartet ΦΦ 09/17 Vic 18333
Enrico Caruso, stage, 09/18 Vic 87294
Peerless Quartet Φ 09/17 Col A-2306
Belle Baker, vv stage

PACK UP YOUR TROUBLES IN YOUR OLD KIT BAG (11)
T B Harms & F D H, pub. 1915, reached #2 in June 1917
George Asaf w, Felix Powell m
Featured in HER SOLDIER BOY, show (opened 12/16)
Adele Rowland, sung in show
James F Harrison/Knickerbocker Quartet ΦΦ 04/17 Col A-2181
Victor Military Band Φ 03/17 Vic 18218
Edward Hamilton[3] Φ 03/17 Vic 18222
vv singers

POOR BUTTERFLY (4)
T B Harms & F D H ⊕⊕⊕, pub. 1916, reached #1 in Feb. 1917
(Also reached #19 in May 1954)
John L Golden w, Raymond Hubbell m
Featured in THE BIG SHOW, show (opened 08/16)
Edna Brown[1] ⊕⊕ 02/17 Vic 18211
Victor Military Band ⊕⊕ 02/17 Vic 35605
Sophie Bernard, sung in show
Katherine Clark[4] ⊕ 03/17 Col A-2167
Elizabeth Spencer 03/17 Ed Amb 3039 cyl, 03/17 Ed 50386

ROLLING STONES (ALL COME ROLLING HOME AGAIN) (39)
Kalmar, P & A, pub. 1916, reached #8 in April 1917
Edgar Leslie w, Archie Gottler m
American Quartet ⊕ 03/17 Vic 18215
Eva Tanguay, vv stage
Sophie Tucker, vv stage

SAILIN' AWAY ON THE HENRY CLAY (27)
J H Remick, pub. 1917, reached #6 in October 1917
Gus Kahn w, Egbert Van Alstyne m
Featured in GOOD NIGHT, PAUL, show (opened 09/17)
Elizabeth Murray, sung in show
American Quartet ⊕ 10/17 Vic 18353
Marx Brothers, vv stage
George O'Connor 11/17 Col A-2364

SEND ME AWAY WITH A SMILE (38)
Piantadosi Mus Co, pub. 1917, reached #15 in November 1917
Lou Weslyn w, Al Piantadosi m
John McCormack ⊕ 11/17 Vic 64741
Marguerite Farrell, vv stage
M J O'Connell 11/17 Col A-2355

SHE'S DIXIE ALL THE TIME
J H Remick, pub. 1916, reached #17 in April 1917
Alfred Bryan w, Harry Tierney m
Nora Bayes, vv stage
Belle Baker, vv stage
Blossom Seeley, vv stage
American Quartet 05/17 Vic 18257

SHIM-ME-SHA-WABBLE (46)
J W Stern, pub. 1917, reached #19 in August 1917
Spencer Williams w & m
Jazz standard, 1920's
National Promenade Band 02/17 Ed Amb 3071 cyl
George L Thompson 11/17 Emerson 7256

SING ME LOVE'S LULLABY (41)
L Feist, pub. 1917, reached Top 30 in October 1917
Dorothy Terriss w, Theodore F Morse m
Henry Burr 11/17 Col A-2358
Frances Alda 12/17 Vic 64716
Belle Story, vv stage

SOME SUNDAY MORNING (23)
J H Remick, pub. 1917, reached #2 in December 1917
Gus Kahn w, Richard Whiting m
M J O'Connell & Ada Jones ⊕ 10/17 Col A-2330
Elizabeth Brice & Charles King, vv stage
Ada Jones & Billy Murray 12/17 Vic 18393

SWEET EMALINA, MY GAL (45)
Broadway Mus Co, pub. 1917, reached #16 in October 1917
Henry Creamer w, Turner Layton m
Henry Burr 10/17 Col A-2314
Peerless Quartet 10/17 Lyraphone 5111, 11/17 Vic 18377

THERE'S EGYPT IN YOUR DREAMY EYES (42)
J H Remick, pub. 1917, reached #8 in April 1917
Fleta Jan Brown w, Herbert Spencer m
Raymond Dixon[5] 04/17 Vic 18238
George Wilson 03/17 Col A-2168
vv singers

THERE'S SOMEONE MORE LONESOME THAN YOU (44)
H Von Tilzer, pub. 1916, reached #13 in April 1917
Lou Klein w, Harry Von Tilzer m
James Reed[6] & James F Harrison 08/16 Vic 18064,
09/16 Col A-2044
vv singers

THEY GO WILD, SIMPLY WILD, OVER ME (19)
McCarthy & Fisher, pub. 1917, reached #3 in October 1917
Joe McCarthy w, Fred Fisher m
Marion Harris ⊕ 10/17 Vic 18343
Eddie Cantor, vv stage
vv singers

THEY'RE WEARIN' 'EM HIGHER IN HAWAII (22)
Shapiro, B, pub. 1916, reached #2 in February 1917
Joe Goodwin w, Halsey K Mohr m
Eddie Cantor, vv stage
Collins & Harlan ⊕ 02/17 Vic 18210
Al Jolson, vv stage
Morton Harvey 02/17 Col A-2143
Billy Murray, vv stage

THROW ME A ROSE (48)
T B Harms & F D H, pub. 1915, reached #9 in January 1917
Herbert Reynolds & P G Wodehouse w, Emmerich Kalman m
Featured in MISS SPRINGTIME, show (opened 09/16)
Charles Meakins & John Hazzard, sung in show
Reed Miller 01/17 Col A-2128

TILL THE CLOUDS ROLL BY (34)
T B Harms & T B H, pub. 1917, reached #9 in August 1917
Guy Bolton & P G Wodehouse w, Jerome Kern m
Featured in OH, BOY, show (opened 02/17)
Anna Wheaton & Lynn Overman, sung in show
Anna Wheaton & James Harrod ⊕ 08/17 Col A-2261
Vernon Dalhart 07/17 Emerson 7192

WE'RE GOING OVER
J Morris, pub. 1917, reached #20 in December 1917
Andrew Sterling, Bernie Grossman, Arthur Lange w & m
Peerless Quartet 12/17 Vic 18383, 01/18 Col A-2399
Harry Evans[7] 12/17 Emerson 7275
vv singers

WHAT DO YOU WANT TO MAKE THOSE EYES AT ME FOR? (13)
L Feist, pub. 1916, reached #2 in March 1917
Joe McCarthy & Howard Johnson w, James V Monaco m
Featured in FOLLOW ME, show (opened 11/16)
Ada Jones & Billy Murray ΦΦ 03/17 Vic 18224
Henry Lewis, sung in show
Emma Carus, vv stage

WHEN YANKEE DOODLE LEARNS TO PARLEZ-VOUS FRANCAIS (24)
A J Stasny, pub. 1917, reached #11 in November 1917
William Hart w, Ed Nelson m
Anna Chandler, vv stage
Elsie Janis, vv stage
Arthur Fields Φ vv stage, 02/18 Col A-2451
Empire Comedy Four, vv stage

WHERE DO WE GO FROM HERE? (16)
L Feist, pub. 1917, reached #3 in September 1917
Howard Johnson w, Percy Wenrich m
Arthur Fields Φ 09/17 Col A-2299, 09/17 Ed Amb 3260 cyl, 10/17 Ed 50433, 10/17 Lyraphone 5110
American Quartet Φ 09/17 Vic 18335
Emma Carus, vv stage
Brown Brothers Band, vv stage

WHERE THE BLACK-EYED SUSANS GROW (20)
J H Remick, pub. 1917, reached #4 in May 1917
Dave Radford w, Richard A Whiting m
Featured in ROBINSON CRUSOE, JR, show (opened 02/16)
Al Jolson, sung in show
Albert Campbell & Henry Burr Φ 04/17 Vic 18239
vv singers

WHERE THE MORNING GLORIES GROW (49)
J H Remick, pub. 1917, reached #16 in December 1917
Gus Kahn & Raymond Egan w, Richard A Whiting m
Elizabeth Spencer 12/17 Vic 18403
vv singers

YOU SAID SOMETHING
Francis D & H, pub. 1916, reached #14 in May 1917
Guy Bolton & P G Wodehouse w, Jerome Kern m
Featured in HAVE A HEART, show (opened 01/17)
Alice Green[8] & Harry Macdonough 05/17 Vic 18260
Donald McDonald & Marjorie Gateson, sung in show

[1]Edna Brown was a pseudonym for Elsie Baker.
[2]Frederick Wheeler was a pseudonym for James F Harrison.
[3]Edward Hamilton was a pseudonym for Reinald Werrenrath.
[4]Katherine Clark was a pseudonym for Grace Kerns.
[5]Raymond Dixon was a pseudonym for Lambert Murphy.
[6]James Reed was a pseudonym for Reed Miller.
[7]Harry Evans was a pseudonym for Evan Williams.
[8]Alice Green was a pseudonym for Olive Kline.

1918

AFTER YOU'VE GONE (22)
Broadway Mus Co, pub. 1918, reached #7 in November 1918
(Also reached #16 in August 1927)
Henry Creamer w, Turner Layton m
Jazz standard, 1920-1950
Sophie Tucker, vv stage
Belle Baker, vv stage
Marion Harris Φ 01/19 Vic 18509
Albert Campbell & Henry Burr Φ 09/18 Col A-2582
Al Jolson, vv stage

ARE YOU FROM HEAVEN? (23)
Gilbert & Friedland, pub. 1917, reached #2 in April 1918
L Wolfe Gilbert w, Anatole Friedland m
Henry Burr ΦΦ 04/18 Vic 18435, 04/18 Pathe 20310[1], 05/18 Col A-2513
Charles King, vv stage
Belle Baker, vv stage
Vernon Dalhart, vv stage, 03/18 Ed Amb 3433 cyl

BEALE STREET BLUES (28)
Pace & Handy, pub. 1917, reached Top 30 in January 1918
William C Handy w & m
Steady seller 1917-1919, jazz standard 1920's and 1930's
Earl Fuller's Novelty Orch 11/17 Vic 18369
Prince's Orch 10/17 Col A-2327
Al Bernard 08/19 Ed Amb 3764 cyl, 09/19 Ed 50536
Jazz bands

BLUE BIRD (BRING BACK MY HAPPINESS) (43)
Waterson, B & S, pub. 1917, reached #15 in May 1918
George Groff w, Bert Grant m
Elizabeth Spencer 05/18 Vic 18452
Sam Ash 04/18 Col A-2492

BRING BACK MY DADDY TO ME (39)
L Feist, pub. 1917, reached #5 in June 1918
William Tracey & Howard Johnson w, George Meyer m
Robert Lewis[2] 05/18 Col A-2506
Madge Evans, vv stage
Harry McClaskey[3] 07/18 Pathe 20363

(SHE'S) THE DAUGHTER OF ROSIE O'GRADY (24)
Witmark, pub. 1918, reached #4 in June 1918
Monty C Brice w, Walter Donaldson m
Pat Rooney, vv stage
Henry Burr Φ 06/18 Pathe 20350
Robert Lewis[2] Φ 07/18 Col A-2561

EVERYBODY OUGHT TO KNOW HOW TO DO THE TICKLE TOE (40)
L Feist, pub. 1917, reached #7 in June 1918
Otto Harbach w, Louis Hirsch m
Featured in GOING UP, show (opened 12/17)
Edith Day & Alice Fagan, sung in show
Victor Military Band Φ 04/18 Vic 18437
Vernon Dalhart 06/18 Ed Amb 3474 cyl, 09/18 Ed 50473

EVERYBODY'S (GONE) CRAZY 'BOUT THE DOGGONE BLUES (48)
Broadway Mus Co, pub. 1917, reached #17 in August 1918
Henry Creamer w, Turner Layton m
Featured in ZIEGFELD FOLLIES OF 1918, show (opened 06/18)
Marion Harris Φ 05/18 Vic 18443
Bert Williams, sung in show
Wilbur Sweatman's Original Jazz Band 07/18 Col A-2548

EVERYTHING IS PEACHES DOWN IN GEORGIA (12)
L Feist, pub. 1918, reached #2 in November 1918
Grant Clarke w, Milt Ager & George W Meyer m
American Quartet Φ 11/18 Vic 18497
Farber Sisters, vv stage, 11/18 Pathe 20435
Collins & Harlan 11/18 Okeh 1096, 12/18 Ed Amb 3617 cyl

FOREVER IS A LONG, LONG TIME (21)
Artmusic, pub. 1916, reached #8 in June 1918
Darl MacBoyle w, Albert Von Tilzer m
Charles Hart Φ 11/17 Vic 18283
Lillian Russell, vv stage
Mme Chilson Ohrman, vv stage
George Wilson 04/18 Col A-2492

GIVE ME THE MOONLIGHT, GIVE ME THE GIRL (50)
Broadway Mus Co, pub. 1917, reached #18 in February 1918
Lew Brown w, Albert Von Tilzer m
Sam Ash 01/18 Col A-2415
Henry Jordan 02/18 Vic 18410
vv singers

GOOD MORNING, MR. ZIP-ZIP-ZIP! (25)
L Feist, pub. 1918, reached #4 in July 1918
Robert Lloyd w & m
Arthur Fields Φ vv stage, 06/18 Para 2052, 09/18 Okeh 1074, 01/19 Vic 18510
Eugene Buckley Φ 06/18 Col A-2530

HAIL, HAIL, THE GANG'S ALL HERE (38)
L Feist, pub. 1908, reached #11 in January 1918
D A Esrom[4] w, Theodore F Morse & Arthur Sullivan m
Shannon Four 01/18 Vic 18414, 01/18 Ed Amb 3375 cyl, 04/18 Ed 50460
Irving Kaufman 02/18 Col A-2443
vv singers

HELLO, CENTRAL, GIVE ME NO-MAN'S-LAND (11)
Waterson, B & S, pub. 1918, reached #2 in August 1918
Sam Lewis & Joe Young w, Jean Schwartz m
Featured in SINBAD, show (opened 02/19)
Al Jolson ΦΦ sung in show, 07/18 Col A-2542
Edna Brown[5] 08/18 Vic 18479
Frank Carter, vv stage

HINDUSTAN (8)
Forster M P, pub. 1918, reached #3 in December 1918
Oliver G Wallace w, Harold Weeks m
Joseph C Smith's Orch Φ 11/18 Vic 18507
Albert Campbell & Henry Burr Φ 01/19 Col A-2661
Jack LaFollette, vv stage
dance bands

HOW'D YOU LIKE TO BE MY DADDY?
Waterson, B & S, pub. 1918, reached #20 in July 1918
Sam Lewis & Joe Young w, Ted Snyder m
Featured in SINBAD, show (opened 02/18)
Al Jolson, sung in show
Farber Sisters 06/18 Col A-2525

I HATE TO LOSE YOU (31)
Waterson, B & S, pub. 1918, reached #6 in June 1918
Grant Clarke w, Archie Gottler m
Peerless Quartet Φ 06/18 Vic 18460, 07/18 Pathe 20364
vv singers

I'M ALL BOUND 'ROUND WITH THE MASON-DIXON LINE (18)
Waterson, B & S, pub. 1917, reached #6 in January 1918
Sam Lewis & Joe Young w, Jean Schwartz m
Al Jolson Φ vv stage, 03/18 Col A-2478
Belle Baker, vv stage
Irving Kaufman Φ 10/17 Vic 18353, 12/17 Imperial 5509

I'M ALWAYS CHASING RAINBOWS (3)
McCarthy & Fisher ΦΦΦ, pub. 1918, reached #1 in January 1919 (Also reached #4 in February 1946)
Joe McCarthy w, Frederic Chopin m, Harry Carroll adpt
Featured in OH, LOOK! show (opened 03/18)
Charles W Harrison ΦΦ 10/18 Vic 18496
Dolly Sisters, sung in show
Harry Fox Φ 08/18 Col A-2557
Harry Carroll, vv stage
Prince's Orch Φ 10/18 Col A-6064

I'M GLAD I CAN MAKE YOU CRY (37)
J W Stern, pub. 1918, reached #16 in January 1919
Charles McCarron w, Carey Morgan m
Henry Burr 01/19 Vic 18509
Bessie Hamilton, vv stage
Harry Cooper, vv stage
"Banjo" Wallace, vv stage

I'M GOING TO FOLLOW THE BOYS
Witmark, pub. 1917, reached #10 in April 1918
George J Trinkhaus w, James V Monaco m
Elizabeth Murray, vv stage
Elizabeth Spencer & Henry Burr 03/18 Vic 18433

I'M GONNA PIN MY MEDAL ON THE GIRL I LEFT BEHIND
Waterson, B & S, pub. 1918, reached #14 in September 1918
Irving Berlin w & m
Peerless Quartet 09/18 Vic 18486
vv singers

I'M SORRY I MADE YOU CRY (4)
L Feist, pub. 1918, reached #1 in June 1918
N J Clesi w & m
Henry Burr ΦΦ 05/18 Pathe 20198[6], 06/18 Vic 18462
Emma Carus, vv stage
Belle Baker, vv stage
Anna Chandler, vv stage

IF HE CAN FIGHT LIKE HE CAN LOVE, GOOD NIGHT GERMANY! (33)
L Feist, pub. 1918, reached #9 in September 1918
Grant Clarke & Howard E Rogers w, George W Meyer m
Farber Sisters Φ 08/18 Col A-2556
Ray Samuels, vv stage
Eddie Cantor, vv stage

IF YOU LOOK IN HER EYES
Witmark, pub. 1917, reached #20 in May 1918
Otto Harbach w, Louis Hirsch m
Featured in GOING UP, show (opened 12/17)
Edith Day & Marion Sunshine, sung in show
Elizabeth Spencer & Henry Burr 05/18 Vic 18452

INDIANOLA (7)
J W Stern, pub. 1917, reached #3 in April 1918
S R Henry & Domenico Savino w & m
Billy Murray Φ vv stage, 08/18 Vic 18474
Victor Military Band Φ 04/18 Vic 18442
Prince's Band Φ 03/18 Col A-6018
Caroline Meredith, vv stage

JUST A BABY'S PRAYER AT TWILIGHT (5)
Waterson, B & S ΦΦΦ, pub. 1918, reached #1 in April 1918
Sam Lewis & Joe Young w, M K Jerome m
Henry Burr ΦΦΦ 04/18 Vic 18439, 04/18 Col A-2490, 04/18 Pathe 20307[6]
Prince's Orch 05/18 Col A-6029
vv singers

JUST LIKE WASHINGTON CROSSED THE DELAWARE (45)
L Feist, pub. 1918, reached #6 in July 1918
Howard Johnson w, George W Meyer m
Peerless Quartet Φ 07/18 Vic 18469
Arthur Fields/Peerless Quartet 07/18 Col A-2545
Elinore & Williams, vv stage

K-K-K-KATY (2)
L Feist, pub. 1918, reached #1 in July 1918
Geoffrey O'Hara w & m
Billy Murray ΦΦ 05/18 Vic 18455
Geoffrey O'Hara, vv stage
Eugene Buckley 06/18 Col A-2530
George Stewart, vv stage

KEEP YOUR HEAD DOWN, FRITZIE BOY (46)
T B Harms & F D H, pub. 1918, reached #11 in August 1918
Gitz Rice w & m
American Quartet Φ 07/18 Vic 18467
Arthur Fields, vv stage, 10/18 Col A-2600, 10/18 Pathe 20423
Lt. Gitz Rice, vv stage

LI'L LIZA JANE (30)
Sherman Clay, pub. 1916, reached #13 in March 1918
Ada DeLachau w & m
Earl Fuller's Novelty Orch 12/17 Vic 18394
Prince's Band 04/18 Col A-2483
vocal groups

LIBERTY BELL, IT'S TIME TO RING AGAIN
Shapiro, B, pub. 1917, reached #20 in March 1918
Joe Goodwin w, Halsey K Mohr m
Peerless Quartet 03/18 Vic 18434, 04/18 Pathe 20313
Arthur Fields 03/18 Col A-2473

LORRAINE (MY BEAUTIFUL ALSACE LORRAINE) (32)
McCarthy & Fisher, pub. 1917, reached #6 in May 1918
Alfred Bryan w, Fred Fisher m
Henry Burr Φ 04/18 Col A-2490
Reinald Werrenrath, stage, 04/18 Vic 45148

MAMMY'S CHOCOLATE SOLDIER (36)
Waterson, B & S, pub. 1918, reached #13 in November 1918
Sidney Mitchell w, Archie Gottler m
Marion Harris 10/18 Vic 18493
Sophie Tucker, vv stage
Nora Bayes 08/18 Col A-6051

MISSOURI WALTZ (HUSH-A-BYE MA BABY) (20)
Forster M P ΦΦΦ, pub. 1914, reached #4 in May 1918
(Also reached #19 in August 1916 and April 1917)
James R Shannon w, Frederick K Logan & John V Eppell m
Steady seller, 1915-1919
Albert Campbell & Henry Burr Φ 11/17 Col A-2358, 03/18 Pathe 20293
Joseph C Smith's Orch 02/18 Vic 35663
Helen Louise & Frank Ferrera 02/18 Col A-2450, 06/18 Pathe 20344

MY BELGIAN ROSE (19)
L Feist, pub. 1918, reached #4 in September 1918
George Benoit, Robert Levenson, Ted Garton w & m
Charles Hart & Elliott Shaw Φ 08/18 Vic 18479
Albert Campbell & Henry Burr Φ 08/18 Col A-2559
Yvette, vv stage

N'EVERYTHING
J H Remick, pub. 1917, reached #11 in July 1918
Al Jolson, Buddy DeSylva, Gus Kahn w & m
Featured in SINBAD, show (opened 02/18)
Al Jolson Φ sung in show, 06/18 Col A-2519

OH! FRENCHY (13)
Broadway Mus Co, pub. 1918, reached #9 in October 1918
Sam Ehrlich w, Con Conrad m
Arthur Fields Φ 09/18 Vic 18489, 09/18 Col A-2569, 09/18 Pathe 20411
Adelaide & Hughes, vv stage
Joseph C Smith's Orch 02/19 Vic 18511

OH! HOW I HATE TO GET UP IN THE MORNING (10)
Waterson, B & S, pub. 1918, reached #3 in November 1918
Irving Berlin w & m
Featured in ZIEGFELD FOLLIES OF 1918, show (opened 06/18)
Also featured in YIP, YIP, YAPHANK, show (opened 08/18)
Irving Berlin, sung in show (YYY)
(Later: 1927 Bruns 3492)
Arthur Fields Φ 09/18 Vic 18489, 11/18 Col A-2617, 11/18 Pathe 20431
Eddie Cantor, sung in show (ZF), vv stage
Addy Britt, vv stage

OH! HOW I WISH I COULD SLEEP UNTIL MY DADDY COMES HOME (16)
Waterson, B & S, pub. 1918, reached #3 in November 1918
Sam Lewis & Joe Young w, Pete Wendling m
Henry Burr Φ 11/18 Vic 18506, 01/19 Col A-2656, 01/19 Pathe 22004[6]
Al Jolson, vv stage
Tenny Hilson, vv stage

THE OLD GREY MARE (49)
J Morris, pub. 1915, reached #15 in February 1918
Traditional w & m, Frank Panella arr.
Collins & Harlan Φ 12/17 Vic 18387, 12/17 Imperial 5512, 01/18 Col A-2382

ON THE ROAD TO HOME SWEET HOME
J H Remick, pub. 1917, reached #18 in April 1918
Gus Kahn w, Egbert Van Alstyne m
Percy Hemus 04/18 Vic 18439
Albert Campbell & Henry Burr 05/18 Col A-2506

OUI, OUI, MARIE (15)
McCarthy & Fisher, pub. 1918, reached #10 in December 1918
Alfred Bryan & Joe McCarthy w, Fred Fisher m
Arthur Fields Φ 10/18 Pathe 20414, 11/18 Vic 18505
Adelaide & Hughes, vv stage
Irving Kaufman 12/18 Col A-2637
Rachel Grant & Billy Murray 11/18 Ed Amb 3596 cyl

ROCK-A-BYE YOUR BABY WITH A DIXIE MELODY (6)
Waterson, B & S, pub. 1918, reached #3 in September 1918
(Also reached #12 in January 1957)
Sam Lewis & Joe Young w, Jean Schwartz m
Featured in SINBAD, show (opened 02/18)
Al Jolson ΦΦ sung in show, 08/18 Col A-2560
Vernon Dalhart 11/18 Ed Amb 3586 cyl, 02/19 Vic 18512
Arthur Fields 06/18 Pathe 20360
Norma Bell, vv stage

ROSES OF PICARDY (14)
Chappell, pub. 1916, reached #19 in October 1918
(Also reached #7 in December 1923)
Frederick E Weatherly w, Haydn Wood m
Steady seller, 1917-1924
John McCormack Φ 09/19 Vic 64825
Lambert Murphy Φ 05/18 Vic 45150
Grace LaRue, stage
Charles Harrison 11/18 Col A-2618

SMILES (1)
J H Remick, pub. 1917, reached #1 in September 1918
J Will Callahan w, Lee G Roberts m
Featured in THE PASSING SHOW OF 1918, show (opened 07/18)
Joseph C Smith's Orch/Harry Macdonough ΦΦ 08/18 Vic 18473
Nell Carrington, sung in show
Albert Campbell & Henry Burr Φ 11/18 Col A-2616
Elizabeth Brice, vv stage
Adelaide & Hughes, vv stage

SOMEWHERE IN FRANCE IS THE LILY (34)
Witmark, pub. 1917, reached #11 in February 1918
Philander Johnson w, Joseph E Howard m
Henry Burr 01/18 Col A-2408
Charles Hart 01/18 Vic 18409
Dorothy Jardon, vv stage

SWEET LITTLE BUTTERCUP (41)
J H Remick, pub. 1917, reached #9 in April 1918
Alfred Bryan w, Herman Paley m
Elizabeth Spencer Φ 03/18 Vic 18427
Peerless Quartet 04/18 Pathe 20309
vv singers

THERE'S A LONG, LONG TRAIL (9)
Witmark ΦΦΦ, pub. 1913, reached #3 in March 1918
(Also reached #6 in October 1916)
Stoddard King w, Zo Elliott m
Steady seller, 1914-1919
John McCormack Φ 08/17 Vic 64694
Oscar Seagle 02/18 Col A-2451
Bessie Gilbert, vv stage
James Reed[7] & James F Harrison 03/17 Vic 17882 (RI)

THEY WERE ALL OUT OF STEP BUT JIM (27)
Waterson, B & S, pub. 1918, reached #5 in August 1918
Irving Berlin w & m
Billy Murray Φ 08/18 Vic 18465
Blanche Ring, vv stage
Connie Farber 08/18 Pathe 20388

THREE WONDERFUL LETTERS FROM HOME (47)
Shapiro, B, pub. 1918, reached #13 in June 1918
Ballard MacDonald & Joe Goodwin w, James F Hanley m
Charles Hart 05/18 Gennett 7642, 06/18 Vic 18461
Henry Burr 06/18 Col A-2529, 07/18 Pathe 20366[6]
vv singers

TIGER RAG (42)
L Feist, pub. 1917, reached #15 in October 1918
(Also reached #17 in December 1931)
(Also reached #8 in February 1952)
Nick LaRocca, et al (Original Dixieland Jazz Band) m
Jazz standard, 1918 onward
Original Dixieland Jazz Band Φ jazz concerts and 08/18 Vic 18472

TISHOMINGO BLUES (35)
J W Stern, pub. 1918, reached #14 in July 1918
Spencer Williams w & m
Arthur Mack 07/18 Pathe 20365
"Banjo" Wallace, vv stage
Yerkes American Marimba Band 12/18 Col A-2634

WAIT TILL THE COWS COME HOME (26)
Chappell, pub. 1917, reached #2 in March 1918
Anne Caldwell w, Ivan Caryll m
Featured in JACK O'LANTERN, show (opened 10/17)
Harry Macdonough & Alice Green[8] Φ 01/18 Vic 18408
Helen Falconer & Douglas Stevenson, sung in show
Henry Burr Φ 01/18 Col A-2422

WATERS OF VENICE (44)
Artmusic, pub. 1916, reached #16 in November 1918
Neville Fleeson w, Albert Von Tilzer m
Albert Campbell & Henry Burr 11/18 Col A-2616
Bessie Wynn, vv stage
Christie MacDonald, stage

WHEN YOU COME BACK (AND YOU WILL COME BACK) (17)
Witmark, pub. 1918, reached #5 in October 1918
George M Cohan w & m
Featured in COHAN REVUE OF 1918, show (opened 12/17)
George M Cohan & Nora Bayes, sung in show
John McCormack, stage, 01/19 Vic 64791
Raymond Dixon[9]/Orpheus Quartet Φ 10/18 Vic 18494

WILL YOU REMEMBER (SWEETHEART) (29)
G Schirmer, pub. 1917, reached #14 in January 1918
(Also reached #8 in May 1937)
Rida Johnson Young w, Sigmund Romberg m
Featured in MAYTIME, show (opened 08/17)
Peggy Wood & Charles Purcell, sung in show
Alice Green[8] & Raymond Dixon[9] Φ 01/18 Vic 18399
James Harrod 12/17 Col A-2393

[1]Henry Burr was listed on Pathe as Irving Gillette.
[2]Robert Lewis was a pseudonym for Lewis James.
[3]Harry McClaskey was a pseudonym for, and real name of, Henry Burr.
[4]D A Esrom was a pseudonym for Mrs. Theodore Morse (Dorothy Terriss)
[5]Edna Brown was a pseudonym for Elsie Baker.
[6]Henry Burr was listed on Pathe as Harry McClaskey.
[7]James Reed was a pseudonym for Reed Miller.
[8]Alice Green was a pseudonym for Olive Kline.
[9]Raymond Dixon was a pseudonym for Lambert Murphy.

1919

ALCOHOLIC BLUES
Broadway Mus Co, pub. 1919, reached #13 in July 1919
Edward Laska w, Albert Von Tilzer m
Billy Murray Φ 04/19 Vic 18522, 05/19 Col A-2707
Vernon Dalhart 06/19 Ed Amb 3735 cyl, 07/19 Ed 50529
vv stage

ALEXANDER'S BAND IS BACK IN DIXIE LAND (28)
J H Remick, pub. 1919, reached #10 in November 1919
Jack Yellen w, Albert Gumble m
Featured in SINBAD, show (opened 02/18)
Farber Sisters, sung in show
Harry Fox, vv stage, 11/19 Col A-2787
Miss Patricola 12/19 Pathe 22218
Anna Armstrong, vv stage

AND HE'D SAY OOH-LA-LA! WEE WEE (27)
Waterson, B & S, pub. 1919, reached #9 in November 1919
George Jessel w, Harry Ruby m
Billy Murray Φ 09/19 Pathe 22156, 10/19 Col A-2765, 11/19 Vic 18610
Eddie Cantor, vv stage
Belle Baker, vv stage
George Jessel, vv stage

BEAUTIFUL OHIO (3)
Shapiro, B ΦΦΦ, pub. 1918, reached #2 in March 1919
Ballard MacDonald w, Robert A King m
Waldorf-Astoria Dance Orch ΦΦ 03/19 Vic 18526
Henry Burr ΦΦ 05/19 Col A-2701
Olive Kline Φ 03/19 Vic 45161
Prince's Orch Φ 01/19 Col A-6081
Fritz Kreisler 09/19 Vic 64817

THE BELLS OF ST. MARYS (38)
Chappell, pub. 1917, reached #15 in September 1919
(Also reached #15 in February 1946)
Douglas Furber w, A Emmett Adams m
Steady seller, 1918-1920
Olga Peterson, stage
Mme Petrova, stage
Frances Alda 02/20 Vic 64844

BLUES (MY NAUGHTY SWEETIE GIVES TO ME) (19)
J W Stern, pub. 1919, reached #4 in September 1919
Charles McCarron w, Carey Morgan m
Ted Lewis Band Φ vv stage, 12/19 Col A-2798
Irving Kaufman Φ 08/19 Emerson 9198
Esther Walker 12/19 Vic 18619
Grace Howard, vv stage

CAROLINA SUNSHINE (31)
H Von Tilzer, pub. 1919, reached #9 in December 1919
Erwin R Schmidt w, Walter Hirsch m
Sterling Trio 10/19 Col A-2770, 10/19 Pathe 22173, 10/19 Aeolian 12187
Billee Hill, vv stage
Vernon Dalhart 12/19 Ed 50595, 02/20 Ed Amb 3915 cyl
Joseph C Smith's Orch 03/20 Vic 18646

CHINESE LULLABY (32)
G Schirmer, pub. 1919, reached #9 in October 1919
Robert H Bowers w & m
Featured in EAST IS WEST, play (opened 12/18)
Fay Bainter, sung in play
Olive Kline Φ 09/19 Vic 45167
Waldorf-Astoria Dance Orch 01/20 Col A-2817

CHONG, HE COME FROM HONG KONG (20)
L Feist, pub. 1919, reached #4 in May 1919
Harold Weeks w & m
Joseph C Smith's Orch/Billy Murray Φ 05/19 Vic 35684
Columbia Saxophone Sextet 07/19 Col A-2730
Billy Murray 05/19 Aeolian 12109
Irving Kaufman 05/19 Emer 9160, 06/19 Col A-2714
vv singers

COME ON, PAPA (36)
Waterson, B & S, pub. 1918, reached #7 in April 1919
Edgar Leslie & Harry Ruby w & m
Featured in ZIEGFELD FOLLIES OF 1918, show (opened 06/18)
Eddie Cantor, sung in show
Joseph C Smith's Orch Φ 04/19 Vic 18533
Avon Comedy Four, vv stage, 04/19 Col A-2692
Nellie Watson, vv stage

DADDY LONG LEGS (44)
Waterson, B & S, pub. 1919, reached #11 in September 1919
Sam Lewis & Joe Young w, Harry Ruby m
Henry Burr 09/19 Pathe 22148
Pauline Haver, vv stage
Sam Ash 11/19 Emerson 1058

DEAR LITTLE BOY OF MINE (9)
Witmark, pub. 1918, reached #7 in February 1919
J Keirn Brennan w, Ernest Ball m
Charles W Harrison Φ 11/18 Col A-2613
Elsie Baker Φ 03/19 Vic 45161
Will Oakland 07/19 Ed 50526, 08/19 Ed Amb 3781 cyl
Maude Lambert & Ernest Ball, vv stage
George MacFarlane, vv stage

DEAR OLD PAL OF MINE (39)
G Ricordi, pub. 1918, reached #10 in February 1919
Harold Robe w, Lt. Gitz Rice m
John McCormack Φ stage, 09/18 Vic 64785
Oscar Seagle 04/19 Col A-2684
Joseph C Smith's Orch 06/19 Vic 18543
stage singers

DON'T CRY, FRENCHY, DON'T CRY (48)
Waterson, B & S, pub. 1919, reached #19 in May 1919
Sam Lewis & Joe Young w, Walter Donaldson m
Charles Hart & Elliot Shaw 05/19 Vic 18538
Lewis James 05/19 Col A-2704
Monica Redmond, vv stage

DREAMY ALABAMA (46)
Shapiro, B, pub. 1919, reached #15 in November 1919
Ballard MacDonald w, Robert A King m
Charles Hart & Lewis James 09/19 Pathe 22162, 10/19 Vic 18596
Albert Campbell & Henry Burr 11/19 Col A-2781

EVERY DAY WILL BE SUNDAY WHEN THE TOWN GOES DRY
L Feist, pub. 1918, reached #20 in April 1919
William Jerome & Jack Mahoney w & m
Herbert Corthell, vv stage
Billy Murray 04/19 Aeolian 13003
Babette & Hilton, vv stage

EVERYBODY SHIMMIES NOW (41)
C K Harris, pub. 1918, reached #15 in March 1919
Eugene West w, Joe Gold & Edmund S Penney m
Sophie Tucker, vv stage, 04/19 Aeolian 12099
Mae West, vv stage
Trixie Fraganza, vv stage
Synco Jazz Band 07/19 Pathe 22099

EVERYBODY WANTS A KEY TO MY CELLAR
McCarthy & Fisher, pub. 1919, reached #20 in September 1919
Billy Rose w, Billy Baskette & Lew Pollack m
Featured in ZIEGFELD FOLLIES OF 1919, show (opened 06/19)
Bert Williams, sung in show, 09/19 Col A-2750
Billy Rose, vv stage
Al Bernard 08/19 Ed Amb 3790 cyl, 09/19 Ed 50545

A GOOD MAN IS HARD TO FIND (11)
Pace & Handy, pub. 1918, reached #11 in May 1919
Eddie Green w & m
Sophie Tucker, vv stage
Marion Harris Ф 05/19 Vic 18535
Mae West, vv stage
Bert Williams, vv stage

HOW YA GONNA KEEP 'EM DOWN ON THE FARM? (4)
Waterson, B & S ФФФ, reached #1 in May 1919
Sam Lewis & Joe Young w, Walter Donaldson m
Nora Bayes Ф vv stage, 04/19 Col A-2687
Eddie Cantor, vv stage
Sophie Tucker, vv stage
Byron G Harlan Ф 04/19 Okeh 1133, 04/19 Emer 9140, 05/19 Ed Amb 3726 cyl, 06/19 Pathe 22078
Arthur Fields 05/19 Vic 18537

I'LL BE HAPPY WHEN THE PREACHER MAKE YOU MINE (22)
Waterson, B & S, pub. 1919, reached #7 in December 1919
Sam Lewis & Joe Young w, Walter Donaldson m
Adele Rowland, vv stage, 12/19 Vic 18621
Irving & Jack Kaufman 11/19 Col A-2780
Kline & Barbour, vv stage
Helen Spencer, vv stage

I'LL SAY SHE DOES (25)
J H Remick, pub. 1918, reached #5 in June 1919
Buddy DeSylva, Gus Kahn, Al Jolson w & m
Featured in SINBAD, show (opened 02/18)
Al Jolson Ф sung in show, 08/19 Col A-2746
May Hamilton, vv stage
All Star Trio 04/19 Vic 18527
Sweatman's Original Jazz Band 09/19 Col A-2752

I'M FOREVER BLOWING BUBBLES (2)
J H Remick ФФФ, pub. 1919, reached #1 in June 1919 (Also reached #11 in October 1950)
James Kendis, James Brockman & Nat Vincent w, John W Kellette m
Featured in THE PASSING SHOW OF 1918, show (opened 07/18)
Albert Campbell & Henry Burr ФФ 05/19 Col A-2701
Charles Hart & Elliot Shaw Ф 06/19 Vic 18540
June Caprice, sung in show
James Brockman, vv stage

I'VE GOT MY CAPTAIN WORKING FOR ME NOW (30)
Berlin, pub. 1919, reached #6 in November 1919
Irving Berlin w & m
Billy Murray Ф 10/19 Vic 18604, 12/19 Aeolian 12208
Al Jolson Ф 12/19 Col A-2794
Eddie Cantor, vv stage, 11/19 Pathe 22201
Billee Hill, vv stage

IT'S NOBODY'S BUSINESS BUT MY OWN (45)
Skidmore Mus Co, pub. 1919, reached #8 in August 1919
Marshall Walker w, Will Skidmore m
Featured in ZIEGFELD FOLLIES OF 1919, show (opened 06/19)
Bert Williams, sung in show, 09/19 Col A-2750
Arthur Collins 06/19 Emerson 9177
vv singers

JA-DA (10)
L Feist, pub. 1918, reached #2 in March 1919
Bob Carleton w & m
Arthur Fields ФФ 02/19 Col A-2672, 04/19 Vic 18522
Violet Penney, vv stage
Wilbur Sweatman's Original Jazz Band 06/19 Col A-2707

KENTUCKY DREAM WALTZ (16)
J W Stern, pub. 1918, reached #10 in May 1919
Domenico Savino & Frank H Warren w, S R Henry m
Nicholas Orlando Orch 05/19 Vic 18539
Yerkes Jazzarimba Orch 04/19 Col A-6092
Frank & Dorothy, vv stage
Leola Lucey & Charles Hart 07/19 Ed 80458, 09/19 Ed Amb 3804 cyl

KISSES, THE SWEETEST KISSES OF ALL (37)
McCarthy & Fisher, pub. 1918, reached #10 in March 1919
Alex Sullivan w, Lynn Cowan m
Albert Campbell & Henry Burr 03/19 Col A-2676, 04/19 Pathe 22048
Sophie Tucker, vv stage
Joseph C Smith's Orch/Henry Burr 04/19 Vic 18532
Adelaide & Hughes, vv stage

MADELON (26)
J H Remick, pub. 1918, reached #5 in April 1919
Alfred Bryan w, Camille Robert m
French Army Band Ф 03/19 Col A-2675
Arthur Fields 03/19 Emer 9128, 04/19 Pathe 29234
Victor Military Band 05/19 Vic 18534
vv singers

MAMMY O' MINE (23)
J W Stern, pub. 1919, reached #2 in July 1919
William Tracey w, Maceo Pinkard m
Adele Rowland Ф 07/19 Vic 18560
Sterling Trio Ф 06/19 Col A-2718
Sam Ash 06/19 Aeolian 12120

MANDY (5)
Berlin, pub. 1919, reached #1 in October 1919
Irving Berlin w & m
Featured in ZIEGFELD FOLLIES OF 1919, show (opened 06/19)
Van & Schenck Ф sung in show, 11/19 Col A-2780
Marilyn Miller, sung in show
Eddie Cantor, vv stage
Shannon Four Ф 10/19 Vic 18605
Ben Selvin's Orch 11/19 Vic 18614

ME-OW (49)
Sam Fox, pub. 1918, reached #19 in July 1919
Harry D Kerr w, Mel B Kaufman m
Joseph C Smith's Orch Ⲫ 02/19 Vic 18511
Jockers Brothers 12/18 Col A-2639

MICKEY (13)
Waterson, B & S, pub. 1918, reached #2 in February 1919
(Also reached #11 in November 1947)
Harry H Williams w, Neil Moret m
First ever title song for a film; played live during MICKEY, silent film (rel. 08/18)
Prince's Orch Ⲫ 01/19 Col A-2662
Joseph C Smith's Orch/Henry Burr Ⲫ 04/19 Vic 18532
Sterling Trio 01/19 Col A-2662
Eddie Cantor, vv stage
Rae Samuels, vv stage

MY BABY'S ARMS (35)
L Feist, pub. 1919, reached #19 in January 1920
Joe McCarthy w, Harry Tierney m
Featured in ZIEGFELD FOLLIES OF 1919, show (opened 06/19)
John Steel Ⲫ sung in show, 11/19 Vic 18611
Delyle Alda & John Steel, sung in show
Van & Schenck, sung in show

MY BARNEY LIES OVER THE OCEAN (JUST THE WAY HE LIED TO ME) (50)
Waterson, B & S, pub. 1919, reached #18 in July 1919
Sam Lewis & Joe Young w, Bert Grant m
Nora Bayes, vv stage, 03/19 Col A-2678
Billy Murray 04/19 Vic 18530
Nellie Crawford, vv stage

NOBODY KNOWS, AND NOBODY SEEMS TO CARE (17)
Berlin, pub. 1919, reached #2 in December 1919
Irving Berlin w & m
Irving & Jack Kaufman Ⲫ 12/19 Col A-2795
Esther Walker Ⲫ 11/19 Vic 18613
Duncan Sisters, vv stage
Billee Hill, vv stage

O DEATH, WHERE IS THY STING?
Pace & Handy, pub. 1918, reached #20 in February 1919
Clarence Stout w & m
Bert Williams Ⲫ vv stage, 01/19 Col A-2652

OH! WHAT A PAL WAS MARY (8)
Waterson, B & S ⲪⲪⲪ, pub. 1919, reached #1 in December 1919
Edgar Leslie & Bert Kalmar w, Pete Wendling m
Henry Burr ⲪⲪ 10/19 Vic 18606, 10/19 Aeolian 12186, 10/19 Pathe 22173, 11/19 Col A-2786
Joseph C Smith's Orch Ⲫ 01/20 Vic 18630
Hilda LeRoy, vv stage
Edward Allen 12/19 Ed Amb 3872 cyl, 12/19 Ed 50594

A PRETTY GIRL IS LIKE A MELODY (7)
Berlin, pub. 1919, reached #1 in September 1919
Irving Berlin w & m
Featured in ZIEGFELD FOLLIES OF 1919, show (opened 06/19)
John Steel ⲪⲪ sung in show, 09/19 Vic 18588
Ben Selvin's Orch 11/19 Vic 18614
vv singers

ROSE OF NO MAN'S LAND (14)
L Feist, pub. 1918, reached #1 in January 1919
Jack Caddigan w, Joseph A Brennan m
Charles Hart & Elliot Shaw ⲪⲪ 01/19 Vic 18508
Hugh Donovan[1] Ⲫ 02/19 Col A-2670
Bob Miller, vv stage

SALVATION LASSIE OF MINE (47)
L Feist, pub. 1918, reached #18 in April 1919
Jack Caddigan w, Chick Story m
Charles Hart & Lewis James 04/19 Vic 18524
Charles Harrison 05/19 Col A-2699
vv singers

SIPPING CIDER THROUGH A STRAW (43)
J W Stern, pub. 1919, reached #8 in October 1919
Lee David & Carey Morgan w & m
Fatty Arbuckle, vv stage
Collins & Harlan 09/19 Pathe 22157, 10/19 Aeolian 12190

SMILIN' THROUGH (15)
Witmark, pub. 1918, reached #2 in September 1919
(Also reached #14 in August 1922)
Arthur A Penn w & m
Featured in SMILIN' THROUGH, play (1919)
Reinald Werrenrath Ⲫ 09/19 Vic 45166
Jane Cowl, sung in play
Alma Beck 07/19 Pathe 25028

SWEET HAWAIIAN MOONLIGHT (24)
McKinley Mus Co, pub. 1918, reached #3 in July 1919
Harold G Frost w, F Henri Klickmann m
Joseph C Smith's Orch Ⲫ 04/19 Vic 18531
Holt & Rosedale, vv stage, 09/19 Vic 18597
Emma Carus, vv stage
Grace LaRue, vv stage

TAKE ME TO THE LAND OF JAZZ (34)
Waterson, B & S, pub. 1919, reached #14 in November 1919
Edgar Leslie & Bert Kalmar w, Pete Wendling m
Marion Harris 09/19 Vic 18593
Billy Murray 10/19 Col A-2766
Grace Tremont, vv stage
Mary McPherson, vv stage

TELL ME (WHY NIGHTS ARE LONELY) (6)
J H Remick, pub. 1919, reached #2 in November 1919
J Will Callahan w, Max Kortlander m
Featured in THE PASSING SHOW OF 1919, show (opened 10/19)
Joseph C Smith's Orch/Arthur Fields ΦΦ 09/19 Vic 18594
Al Jolson Φ 01/20 Col A-2821
Lambert Murphy 12/19 Vic 45171
Brice & Moore, vv stage
Leta Corder, sung in show

THAT TUMBLEDOWN SHACK IN ATHLONE
Waterson, B & S, pub. 1918, reached #18 in May 1919
(Also reached #17 in April 1920)
Richard W Pascoe w, Monte Carlo & Alma M Sanders m
John McCormack, stage
Sterling Trio 04/19 Aeolian 13002, 05/19 Col A-2698, 06/19 Vic 18545

THAT WONDERFUL MOTHER OF MINE (18)
Witmark, pub. 1918, reached #5 in April 1919
Clyde Hager w, Walter Goodwin m
Henry Burr Φ 04/19 Vic 18524, 04/19 Aeolian 13000, 06/19 Col A-2711
Frank Morrell, vv stage
Will Oakland 07/19 Ed Amb 3758 cyl, 07/19 Ed 50526

THEY'RE ALL SWEETIES (42)
H Von Tilzer, pub. 1919, reached #19 in December 1919
Andrew Sterling w, Harry Von Tilzer m
Van & Schenck 12/19 Col A-2792
Billy Murray 12/19 Pathe 22213
Norma Bell, vv stage
Flo McFadden, vv stage

TILL WE MEET AGAIN (1)
J H Remick ΦΦΦ, pub. 1918, reached #1 in February 1919
Raymond B Egan w, Richard A Whiting m
Albert Campbell & Henry Burr ΦΦ 01/19 Emer 9109, 02/19 Col A-2668
Charles Hart & Lewis James ΦΦ 02/19 Vic 18518, 03/19 Pathe 22036
Nicholas Orlando's Orch Φ 03/19 Vic 18526
Muriel Window, vv stage
Gitz Rice & Vernon Dalhart 03/19 Ed Amb 3670 cyl

TULIP TIME (29)
T B Harms & F D H, pub. 1919, reached #6 in October 1919
Gene Buck w, Dave Stamper m
Featured in ZIEGFELD FOLLIES OF 1919, show (opened 06/19)
John Steel Φ 09/19 Vic 18588
Delyle Alda & John Steel, sung in show
Joseph C Smith's Orch 12/19 Vic 18618

THE VAMP (21)
L Feist, pub. 1919, reached #5 in October 1919
Byron Gay w & m
Added to OH, LOOK!, show (opened 03/18)
Dolly Sisters, sung in show
Joseph C Smith's Orch/w.vocal duo[2] Φ 09/19 Vic 18594
Eddie Cantor, vv stage
Waldorf-Astoria Orch/w.vocal duo 09/19 Col A-2758
Ethel Shutta, vv stage

WAIT TILL YOU GET THEM UP IN THE AIR, BOYS (33)
Broadway Mus Co, pub. 1919, reached #8 in December 1919
Lew Brown w, Albert Von Tilzer m
Billy Murray Φ 12/19 Col A-2794, 01/20 Vic 18628, 02/20 Pathe 22262
May Hamilton, vv stage
Irving Kaufman 11/19 Emerson 1080

WHEN YOU LOOK IN THE HEART OF A ROSE (12)
L Feist, pub. 1918, reached #3 in August 1919
Marian Gillespie w, Florence Methven m
Featured in THE BETTER OLE, show (opened 10/18)
John McCormack ΦΦ 07/19 Vic 64818
Charles W Harrison Φ 05/19 Col A-2699
Nonette, vv stage
Joseph C Smith's Orch Φ 06/19 Vic 18543
Lark Taylor, sung in show

WOULD YOU RATHER BE A COLONEL WITH AN EAGLE ON YOUR SHOULDER OR A PRIVATE WITH A CHICKEN ON YOUR KNEE?
L Feist, pub. 1918, reached #16 in January 1919
Sidney D Mitchell w, Archie Gottler m
Featured in ZIEGFELD FOLLIES OF 1918, show (opened 06/18)
Eddie Cantor, sung in show and vv stage
Eugene Buckley 02/19 Col A-2669
Arthur Fields, vv stage, 12/18 Okeh 1109, 02/19 Pathe 22018

YOU DIDN'T WANT ME WHEN YOU HAD ME (40)
J W Stern, pub. 1919, reached #16 in December 1919
Ben Russell & Bernie Grossman w, George J Bennett m
Irving Kaufman 12/19 Col A-2796
Henry Burr 12/19 Operaphone 21132[3], 01/20 Vic 18620
Arthur Fields 09/19 Emerson 9209
Nat Morton, vv stage

[1]Hugh Donovan was a pseudonym for Charles Harrison.
[2]Duo consisted of Harry Macdonough & Billy Murray.
[3]Henry Burr was listed on Operaphone as Irving Gillette.

1920

AFGHANISTAN
Shapiro, B, pub. 1920, reached #15 in April 1920
William Wilander w, Harry Donnelly m
Prince's Orch 05/20 Col A-2883
All Star Trio 04/20 Voc 14040
Jack Landauer, vv stage

AFTER YOU GET WHAT YOU WANT, YOU DON'T WANT IT (38)
Berlin, pub. 1920, reached #7 in October 1920
Irving Berlin w & m
Van & Schenck Φ 10/20 Col A-2966
Anna Armstrong, vv stage
Billy Jones 08/20 Pathe 22378

ALABAMA MOON (45)
Sam Fox, pub. 1920, reached #13 in July 1920
George H Green w & m
Hawaiian Trio 06/20 Vic 18669
Green's Novelty Orch[1] 06/20 Emer 10169
Olive Kline, stage, 01/21 Vic 45203

ALICE BLUE GOWN (34)
L Feist, pub. 1919, reached #10 in June 1920
(Reached second peak at #20 in January 1921)
(Also reached #12 in May 1940)
Joe McCarthy w, Harry Tierney m
Featured in IRENE, show (opened 11/19)
Edith Day Φ sung in show, 04/20 Vic 45176
Adele Rowland, vv stage
Joseph C Smith's Orch Φ 01/21 Vic 18700

ALL THE QUAKERS ARE SHOULDER SHAKERS (DOWN IN QUAKER TOWN)
Waterson, B & S, pub. 1919, reached #9 in February 1920
Bert Kalmar & Edgar Leslie w, Pete Wendling m
Kitty Warren, vv stage
Miss Patricola, vv stage, 01/20 Pathe 22241
All Star Trio 01/20 Vic 18626
Billy Murray 01/20 Aeo/Voc 12241

THE ARGENTINES, THE PORTUGUESE, AND THE GREEKS
J W Stern, pub. 1920, reached #13 in August 1920
Arthur Swanstrom & Carey Morgan w & m
Herbert Corthell, vv stage
Eddie Cantor, vv stage, 08/20 Emer 10200
Nora Bayes, vv stage, 11/20 Col A-2980

BABY, WON'T YOU PLEASE COME HOME (43)
Wms & Piron, pub. 1919, reached #17 in February 1920
Clarence Williams & Charles Warfield w & m
Clarence Williams, vv stage
Bessie Smith, vv stage (Later: 1923 Col A-3888)
Emily Zemar, vv stage

CHILI BEAN (15)
Broadway Mus Co, pub. 1920, reached #5 in December 1920
Lew Brown w, Albert Von Tilzer m
Featured in SILKS AND SATINS, show (opened 07/20)
Frank Crumit Φ 09/20 Col A-2952
Billy Murray 09/20 Aeo/Voc 14086, 09/20 Pathe 22404
Aileen Stanley, sung in show
Betty Palmer, vv stage

CUBAN MOON (49)
J Mills, pub. 1920, reached #19 in November 1920
Norman Spencer w, Joe McKiernan m
Art Hickman Orch 11/20 Col A-2982
Joseph C Smith's Orch 10/20 Vic 35698
Carl Fenton Orch 10/20 Bruns 2048

DADDY, YOU'VE BEEN A MOTHER TO ME (26)
McCarthy & Fisher, pub. 1920, reached #3 in May 1920
Fred Fisher w & m
Henry Burr Φ 04/20 Aeo/Voc 14037, 05/20 Vic 18656, 05/20 Pathe 22333
Lewis James 05/20 Col A-2894
vv singers

DARDANELLA (7)
McCarthy & Fisher ΦΦΦ, pub. 1919, reached #1 in February 1920
Fred Fisher w, Felix Bernard & Johnny S Black m
Selvin's Orch ΦΦΦ 02/20 Vic 18633
Prince's Orch 03/20 Col A-2851
Campbell & Burr 03/20 Pathe 22291
Helen Spencer, vv stage

DIXIE MADE US JAZZ BAND MAD (46)
L Feist, pub. 1920, reached #16 in December 1920
Howard Johnson, William K Wells & Irwin Dash w & m
Eddie Cantor, vv stage
Mabel Howard, vv stage
Gussie White, vv stage

FRECKLES (37)
L Feist, pub. 1919, reached #7 in February 1920
Howard Johnson w, Milt Ager & Cliff Hess m
Nora Bayes Φ 01/20 Col A-2816
Billy Murray Φ 02/20 Vic 18634
Grace Howard, vv stage

HIAWATHA'S MELODY OF LOVE (31)
J H Remick, pub. 1920, reached #3 in September 1920
Alfred Bryan & Artie Mehlinger w, George Meyer m
Featured in MIDNIGHT ROUNDERS OF 1920, show (opened 07/20)
Vivian Holt & Lillian Rosedale, sung in show
Lewis James Φ 06/20 Col A-2914
Mae Hamilton, vv stage
Charles Hart & Elliot Shaw 08/20 Aeo/Voc 14075, 09/20 Okeh 4131

HOLD ME (6)
Sherman Clay, pub. 1920, reached #1 in July 1920
Art Hickman & Ben Black w & m
Featured in ZIEGFELD FOLLIES OF 1920, show (opened 06/20)
Art Hickman Orch ФФ played in show, 06/20 Col A-2899
Florence Talbot, vv stage
Palace Trio 09/20 Vic 18682

I LOVE THE LAND OF OLD BLACK JOE (27)
Berlin, pub. 1920, reached #10 in November 1920
Grant Clarke w, Walter Donaldson m
Featured in ED WYNN'S CARNIVAL, revue (opened 04/20)
Billy Murray Ф 08/20 Vic 18677
Marion Davies, sung in revue
Van & Schenck, vv stage, 11/20 Col A-2976

I LOVE YOU SUNDAY
Forster M P, pub. 1920, reached #20 in November 1920
Charles E Byrne w, Charley Straight m
Ted Lewis Band, vv stage, 01/21 Col A-3306
Palace Trio 10/20 Emer 10240

I MIGHT BE YOUR ONCE-IN-A-WHILE (33)
T B Harms & F D H, pub. 1919, reached #9 in February 1920
Robert B Smith w, Victor Herbert m
Featured in ANGEL FACE, show (opened 12/19)
Joseph C Smith's Orch Ф 01/20 Vic 18629
Olive Kline Ф 03/20 Vic 45173
John E Young & Ada Meade, sung in show

I'LL BE WITH YOU IN APPLE BLOSSOM TIME (10)
Broadway Mus Co MMM, pub. 1920, reached #4 in November 1920
(Also reached #7 in June 1941)
Neville Fleeson w, Albert Von Tilzer m
Campbell & Burr M 10/20 Col A-2967
Nora Bayes, vv stage
Charles W Harrison M 11/20 Vic 18693
Mae Hamilton, vv stage

I'LL SEE YOU IN C-U-B-A (25)
Berlin, pub. 1919, reached #4 in May 1920
Irving Berlin w & m
Featured in GREENWICH VILLAGE FOLLIES OF 1919, show (opened 07/19)
Ted Lewis Band Ф perf. in show, 06/20 Col A-2927
Billy Murray Ф 04/20 Vic 18652, 04/20 Aeo/Voc 14035, 05/20 Pathe 22322
Grace Howard, vv stage

I'M A JAZZ VAMPIRE (44)
J W Stern, pub. 1920, reached #7 in September 1920
Arthur Swanstrom & Carey Morgan w & m
Aileen Stanley Ф vv stage, 07/20 Pathe 22389, 09/20 Pathe 22407
Marion Harris, vv stage, 02/21 Col A-3328
Babe Quinn, vv stage

IRENE (29)
L Feist, pub. 1919, reached #7 in July 1920
Joe McCarthy w, Harry Tierney m
Featured in IRENE, show (opened 11/19)
Edith Day Ф sung in show, 04/20 Vic 45176
Joseph C Smith's Orch Ф 06/20 Vic 35695
vv singers

THE JAPANESE SANDMAN (5)
J H Remick ФФФ, pub. 1920, reached #2 in November 1920
Raymond Egan w, Richard Whiting m
Nora Bayes Ф vv stage, 12/20 Col A-2997
Paul Whiteman Orch Ф 11/20 Vic 18690
Holt & Rosedale, vv stage
Sophie Tucker, vv stage
Olive Kline Ф 12/20 Vic 45201

JAZZ BABIES' BALL
Shapiro, B, pub. 1920, reached #18 in July 1920
Charles Bayha w, Maceo Pinkard m
Added to SCHUBERT GAIETIES OF 1919, show (opened 07/19)
Sophie Tucker, sung in show
Peerless Quartet 03/20 Aeo/Voc 14029
Hattie Beall, vv stage
Rose Gordon, vv stage

JUST LIKE A GYPSY (20)
J H Remick, pub. 1919, reached #7 in May 1920
Seymour B Simons & Nora Bayes w & m
Added to LADIES FIRST, show (opened 10/18)
Nora Bayes Ф sung in show, 03/20 Col A-6138
Ernest Hare, vv stage, 08/20 Bruns 2039
Irving Fisher, vv stage

LA VEEDA (17)
M Richmond, pub. 1920, reached #2 in July 1920
Nat Vincent w, John Aldan m
Green Brothers Novelty Band Ф 06/20 Vic 18667, 06/20 Pathe 22365
Yerkes' Dance Orch 05/20 Aeo/Voc 14052
Ray Miller Orch, db dates
Isham Jones Orch 09/20 Bruns 5011

LEFT ALL ALONE AGAIN BLUES (42)
T B Harms, pub. 1920, reached #8 in July 1920
Anne Caldwell w, Jerome Kern m
Featured in THE NIGHT BOAT, show (opened 02/20)
Stella Hobson, sung in show
Joseph C Smith's Orch Ф 05/20 Vic 18661
Marion Harris 08/20 Col A-2939

LET THE REST OF THE WORLD GO BY (2)
Witmark ФФФ, pub. 1919, reached #1 in January 1920
J Keirn Brennan w, Ernest Ball m
Elizabeth Spencer & Charles Hart Ф 02/20 Vic 18638
Campbell & Burr Ф 02/20 Col A-2829, 02/20 Okeh 4053
Maude Lambert & Ernest Ball, vv stage
Frank Morrell, vv stage
McFarlane Sisters, vv stage

THE LOVE NEST (4)
Victoria Pub Co, pub. 1920, reached #1 in September 1920
Otto Harbach w, Louis Hirsch m
Featured in MARY, show (opened 10/20)
John Steel ΦΦ 08/20 Vic 18676
Joseph C Smith's Orch Φ 08/20 Vic 18678
Janet Velie & Jack McGowan, sung in show
Art Hickman Orch Φ 09/20 Col A-2955
Frank Crumit 10/20 Col A-2973

THE MOON SHINES ON THE MOONSHINE
Shapiro, B, pub. 1920, reached #20 in May 1920
Francis DeWitt w, Robert Hood Bowers m
Featured in BROADWAY BREVITIES, show (opened 09/20)
Bert Williams, sung in show, 03/20 Col A-2849
Ted Lewis/<vocal 06/20 Col A-2927

MY HOME TOWN IS A ONE-HORSE TOWN (30)
Witmark, pub. 1920, reached #7 in January 1921
Alex Gerber w, Abner Silver m
Van & Schenck, vv stage
Victor Roberts[2] Φ 02/21 Vic 18712
The Harmoniers 12/20 Pathe 20471, 01/21 Aeo/Voc 14123

MY ISLE OF GOLDEN DREAMS (9)
J H Remick, pub. 1919, reached #3 in February 1920
Gus Kahn w, Walter Blaufuss m
Added to OH, LOOK! show (opened 03/18)
Dolly Sisters, sung in show
Selvin's Orch Φ 02/20 Vic 18633
Ryan & Orlob, vv stage
Columbia Orch Φ 04/20 Col A-6139

MY LITTLE BIMBO (FROM THE BAMBOO ISLE) (47)
Berlin, pub. 1920, reached #9 in November 1920
Grant Clarke w, Walter Donaldson m
Featured in SILKS AND SATINS, show (opened 07/20)
Aileen Stanley, sung in show, 11/20 Vic 18691
Frank Crumit, vv stage, 11/20 Col A-2981
Ernest Hare 10/20 Bruns 2045, 11/20 Aeo/Voc 14103

OH!
L Feist, pub. 1919, reached #12 in April 1920
(Also reached #3 in October 1953)
Arnold Johnson w, Byron Gay m
Ted Lewis/Jack Kaufman 03/20 Col A-2844
Paul Biese Orch 03/20 Vic 18647
Ethel Devereaux, vv stage

OH BY JINGO, OH BY GEE! (YOU'RE THE ONLY GIRL FOR ME) (23)
Broadway Mus Co, pub. 1919, reached #4 in June 1920
Lew Brown w, Albert Von Tilzer m
Featured in LINGER LONGER LETTY, show (opened 11/19)
Charlotte Greenwood, sung in show
Frank Crumit Φ 07/20 Col A-2935
Margaret Young Φ 06/20 Vic 18666
Babe Quinn, vv stage

OH! HOW I LAUGH WHEN I THINK HOW I CRIED OVER YOU (50)
Waterson, B & S, pub. 1919, reached #7 in May 1920
Roy Turk & George Jessel w, Willy White m
Nora Bayes Φ 04/20 Col A-2852
George Jessel, vv stage
Victor Roberts[3] 06/20 Vic 18670

OLD MAN JAZZ
J W Stern, pub. 1920, reached #19 in June 1920
Gene Quaw w & m
Saxy Holtsworth, vv stage
Babe Quinn, vv stage
Webb's Novelty Orch 06/20 Pathe 22367

ON MIAMI SHORE (19)
Chappell, pub. 1919, reached #5 in February 1920
William LeBaron w, Victor Jacobi m
Joseph C Smith's Orch Φ 02/20 Vic 18632
Victor Jacobi, vv stage
Prince's Orch 05/20 Col A-6144

PEGGY (14)
L Feist, pub. 1919, reached #3 in March 1920
Harry Williams w, Neil Moret m
Added to CENTURY MIDNIGHT WHIRL, revue (1919)
Art Hickman Orch Φ 01/20 Col A-2812
Dorothy Dickson, sung in revue
Joseph C Smith's Orch Φ 02/20 Vic 18632
Mabel Normand, vv stage

PRETTY KITTY KELLY (35)
A J Stasny, pub. 1920, reached #3 in August 1920
Harry Pease w, Ed Nelson m
Charles W Harrison Φ 08/20 Col A-2948, 09/20 Vic 18679
Miss Patricola, vv stage, 09/20 Pathe 22405
Babe Quinn, vv stage

ROSE OF WASHINGTON SQUARE (13)
Shapiro, B, pub. 1919, reached #1 in June 1920
Ballard MacDonald w, James F Hanley m
Added to ZIEGFELD MIDNIGHT FROLICS OF 1919, revue (opened 10/19)
Fanny Brice, sung in revue
Henry Burr Φ 06/20 Col A-2928
Kentucky Serenaders Φ 05/20 Col A-2908
Adrian Rollini, vv stage
All Star Trio Φ 06/20 Vic 18659

SO LONG! OO-LONG (41)
Waterson, B & S, pub. 1920, reached #4 in July 1920
Bert Kalmar & Harry Ruby w & m
Victor Roberts[2] Φ 07/20 Vic 18672
Frank Crumit Φ 07/20 Col A-2935
Kalmar & Ruby, vv stage

ST. LOUIS BLUES (22)
Pace & Handy ΦΦΦ, pub. 1914, reached #16 in September 1920
(Also reached #11 in May 1948 as a march)
William C Handy w & m
Steady seller 1915-1955 and jazz & blues standard
Marion Harris 08/20 Col A-2944
Al Bernard 07/19 Aeolian 12148, 03/20 Ed 50620, 03/20 Ed Amb 3930 cyl, 01/21 Pathe 22466
Original Dixieland Jazz Band 08/21 Vic 18772
Lt. Jim Europe's Band 09/19 Pathe 22087

SWANEE (3)
T B Harms & F D H ΦΦΦ, pub. 1919, reached #1 in May 1920
Irving Caesar w, George Gershwin m
Added to SINBAD, show (opened 02/18)
Al Jolson ΦΦ sung in show, 05/20 Col A-2884
Sousa's Band, band concerts
Nicholas Orlando Orch 02/20 Pathe 22266
Grace Howard, vv stage
All Star Trio 04/20 Vic 18651

TELL ME, LITTLE GYPSY (12)
Berlin, pub. 1920, reached #4 in October 1920
Irving Berlin w & m
Featured in ZIEGFELD FOLLIES OF 1920, show (opened 06/20)
John Steel Φ sung in show, 10/20 Vic 18687
Art Hickman Orch Φ 10/20 Col A-2972
Helen Adair, vv stage
Elliot Shaw 09/20 Pathe 22406

THAT NAUGHTY WALTZ (11)
Forster M P, pub. 1919, reached #6 in May 1920
Edwin Stanley w, Sol P Levy m
Featured in HELLO, ALEXANDER, show (opened 10/19)
Joseph C Smith's Orch Φ 04/20 Vic 18650
Vivian Holt & Lillian Rosedale, sung in show
Olive Kline Φ stage, 01/21 Vic 45203
Columbia Orch/Campbell & Burr 04/20 Col A-6139
Joseph Samuels, vv stage, 04/20 Pathe 22309

THAT OLD IRISH MOTHER OF MINE (28)
H Von Tilzer, pub. 1920, reached #12 in November 1920
William Jerome w, Harry Von Tilzer m
Charles W Harrison Φ 07/20 Col A-2937
John McCormack, stage
Sterling Trio 07/20 Pathe 22379, 12/20 Vic 18696

THAT TUMBLEDOWN SHACK IN ATHLONE
Waterson, B & S, pub. 1918, reached #17 in April 1920
(Also reached #18 in May 1919)
Richard W Pascoe w, Monte Carlo & Alma M Sanders m
John McCormack, stage, 03/20 Vic 64837
Will Oakland 12/19 Ed Amb 3876 cyl, 12/19 Ed 50586

TRIPOLI (32)
Witmark, pub. 1920, reached #7 in November 1920
Paul Cunningham & Al Dubin w, Irving Weill m
Louise Terrell & William Robyn Φ 11/20 Vic 18693
Joseph C Smith's Orch 01/21 Vic 18700
stage singers

TWELFTH STREET RAG (39)
Jenkins Mus Co, pub. 1916, reached #15 in November 1920
(Also reached #2 in October 1948)
James S Summer w, Euday L Bowman m
Jazz standard 1916-1950's
Euday L Bowman, vv stage
Max Kortlander & Victor Arden 11/20 Pathe 20467
All Star Trio, stage, 02/21 Vic 18713

VENETIAN MOON (24)
J H Remick, pub. 1919, reached #4 in August 1920
Gus Kahn w, Frank Magine & Phil Goldberg m
Featured in THE PASSING SHOW OF 1919, show (opened 10/19)
Willie & Eugene Howard, sung in show
All Star Trio Φ 04/20 Vic 18651
Kentucky Serenaders Φ 05/20 Col A-2895
Harry Jolson, vv stage

WAS THERE EVER A PAL LIKE YOU
Berlin, pub. 1920, reached #12 in March 1920
Irving Berlin w & m
Henry Burr Φ 02/20 Aeo/Voc 14004, 03/20 Vic 18645, 04/20 Col A-2861, 04/20 Pathe 22303
vv singers

WHEN MY BABY SMILES AT ME (8)
H Von Tilzer, pub. 1919, reached #1 in May 1920
Andrew Sterling & Ted Lewis w, Bill Munro m
Featured in GREENWICH VILLAGE FOLLIES OF 1919, revue (opened 07/19)
Ted Lewis/<vocal ΦΦ sung in revue, 05/20 Col A-2908
Billy Murray & Rachel Grant Φ 04/20 Aeo/Voc 14035
Helen Adair, vv stage

WHEN YOU'RE GONE I WON'T FORGET
F B Haviland, pub. 1920, reached #18 in November 1920
Ivan Reid w, Peter DeRose m
Answer song to WHEN I'M GONE YOU'LL SOON FORGET (pub. 1911)
Shannon Four 01/21 Col A-3318
Louise Terrell & George Wilton Ballard 08/20 Ed/Amb 4040 cyl
vv singers

WHISPERING (1)
Sherman Clay ΦΦΦ, pub. 1920, reached #1 in October 1920
(Also reached #18 in November 1944)
(Also reached #11 in Sept 1951 and #11 in Jan 1964)
Malvin Schonberger w, John Schonberger m
All-time pop standard
Paul Whiteman Orch ΦΦΦ 11/20 Vic 18690
John Steel 12/20 Vic 18695
Art Hickman Orch 12/20 Col A-3301
Nicholas Orlando Orch 10/20 Pathe 22426
Yerkes' Dance Orch 10/20 Voc 14100

WHOSE BABY ARE YOU? (48)
T B Harms, pub. 1920, reached #7 in June 1920
Anne Caldwell w, Jerome Kern m
Featured in THE NIGHT BOAT, show (opened 02/20)
Hal Skelly & Louise Groody, sung in show
Joseph C Smith's Orch 05/20 Vic 18661
Henry Burr & John Meyers 06/20 Pathe 22367

YELLOW DOG BLUES
Pace & Handy, pub. 1914, reached #16 in March 1920
William C Handy m
Joseph C Smith's Orch 12/19 Vic 18618
Handy's Orch, vv stage
Selvin's Orch, db dates

YOU AIN'T HEARD NOTHIN' YET (40)
J H Remick, pub. 1919, reached #14 in April 1920
Gus Kahn, Al Jolson, Bud DeSylva w & m
Al Jolson Φ vv stage and 03/20 Col A-2836
Ernest Hare 01/20 Pathe 22237
Georgie Price, vv stage

YOU CAN'T KEEP A GOOD MAN DOWN
P Bradford Inc, pub. 1920, reached #19 in August 1920
Perry Bradford w & m
Sophie Tucker, vv stage
Mamie Smith 08/20 Okeh 4113, 06/21 Okeh 4305

YOU'D BE SURPRISED (21)
Berlin, pub. 1919, reached #2 in January 1920
(Also reached #14 in February 1940)
Irving Berlin w & m
Featured in ZIEGFELD FOLLIES OF 1919, show (opened 06/19)
Also feat. in SHUBERT GAIETIES OF 1919, show (opened 07/19)
Eddie Cantor Φ sung in show (ZF), 12/19 Emer 10102
Billy Murray Φ 02/20 Vic 18634, 02/20 Okeh 4042, 04/20 Ed 50638
George Jessel, sung in show (SG)
Irving Kaufman 01/20 Col A-2815

YOU'RE A MILLION MILES FROM NOWHERE (36)
Waterson, B & S, pub. 1919, reached #5 in March 1920
Sam Lewis & Joe Young w, Walter Donaldson m
Charles W Harrison Φ 03/20 Vic 18645
Fred Hughes 04/20 Col A-2862
Walter Scanlon[4] 05/20 Emer 10145

A YOUNG MAN'S FANCY (18)
L Feist, pub. 1920, reached #3 in September 1920
Jack Yellen & John M Anderson w, Milt Ager m
Featured in WHAT'S IN A NAME, show (opened 03/20)
Rosalind Fuller, sung in show
Joseph C Smith's Orch Φ 08/20 Vic 18678
Isham Jones Orch 09/20 Bruns 5014
Helen Adair, vv stage

YOUR EYES HAVE TOLD ME SO (16)
J H Remick, pub. 1919, reached #8 in April 1920
Gus Kahn w, Egbert Van Alstyne & Walter Blaufuss m
John McCormack Φ stage, 04/20 Vic 64860
Grace LaRue, stage
Leona St Clair, vv stage
Margaret Romain 07/20 Col A-2933

[1]George H Green, the composer, fronted Green's Novelty Orchestra.
[2]Victor Roberts was a pseudonym for Billy Jones.
[3]Original 1914 title was Yellow Dog Rag.
[4]Walter Scanlon was a pseudonym for Walter Van Brunt.

1921

AIN'T WE GOT FUN? (6)
J H Remick ΦΦΦ, pub. 1921, reached #1 in July 1921
Gus Kahn & Raymond Egan w, Richard Whiting m
Benson Orch ΦΦ 07/21 Vic 18757
Van & Schenck ΦΦ vv stage, 08/21 Col A-3412
Ruth Roye, vv stage
Mabel Howard, vv stage

ALL BY MYSELF (1)
Berlin ΦΦΦ, pub. 1921, reached #1 in August 1921
Irving Berlin w & m
Ted Lewis Band ΦΦ 09/21 Col A-3434
Aileen Stanley ΦΦ 08/21 Vic 18774
Frank Crumit Φ 08/21 Col A-3415
Charles King, vv stage
Bennie Krueger Orch 10/21 Bruns 2130

ALL SHE'D SAY WAS "UMH-HUM" (45)
H Von Tilzer, pub. 1920, reached #7 in February 1921
Jack Dill, Mac Emery, Gus Van & Joe Schenck w & m
Featured in ZIEGFELD FOLLIES OF 1920, show (opened 06/20)
Van & Schenck Φ sung in show, 01/21 Col A-3319
Mabel Faleer vv stage

AVALON (11)
J H Remick, pub. 1920, reached #1 in January 1921
Al Jolson & Bud DeSylva w, Vincent Rose m
Al Jolson ΦΦ vv stage, 12/20 Col A-2995
Blossom Seeley, vv stage
Sophie Tucker, vv stage
Paul Whiteman Orch Φ 11/20 Vic 35701
Ernest Hare 12/20 Pathe 22449, 01/21 Emer 10274

BEAUTIFUL ANNABELLE LEE (44)
J H Remick, pub. 1920, reached #12 in February 1921
Alfred Bryan w, George Meyer m
Charles Hart & Elliot Shaw 02/21 Aeo/Voc 14133, 02/21 Okeh 4223, 03/21 Vic 18726
vv singers

BIMINI BAY (34)
J H Remick, pub. 1921, reached #11 in January 1922
Gus Kahn & Raymond Egan w, Richard Whiting m
Benson Orch 12/21 Vic 18824
Eddie Cantor, vv stage
Ted Lewis Band, vv stage, 12/21 Col A-3473
Aileen Stanley, vv stage

BRIGHT EYES (16)
Waterson, B & S, pub. 1920, reached #1 in April 1921
Harry B Smith w, Otto Motzan & M K Jerome m
Paul Whiteman Orch ΦΦ 04/21 Vic 18735
Leo Reisman Orch Φ 04/21 Col A-3366
Paul Specht, db dates
Casino Dance Orch 03/21 Pathe 20486

BROADWAY ROSE (20)
F Fisher, pub. 1920, reached #4 in February 1921
Eugene West w, Otis Spencer & Martin Fried m
Henry Burr/Peerless Quartet Φ 02/21 Vic 18722
Peerless Quartet Φ 02/21 Col A-3373
Yvette, vv stage
Emma Carus, vv stage

CANADIAN CAPERS (38)
J H Remick, pub. 1915, reached #10 in December 1921
(Also reached #19 in Nov. 1949)
Gus Chandler, Bert White & Harry Cohen w & m
Paul Whiteman Orch Φ 12/21 Vic 18824
Paul Biese Orch 12/21 Col A-3470
Selvin's Orch 09/21 Aeolian/Voc 14217

CHERIE (26)
L Feist, pub. 1921, reached #5 in August 1921
Leo Wood w, Irving Bibo m
Paul Whiteman Orch ΦΦ 07/21 Vic 18758
Lina Abarbanel, vv stage
Carl Fenton Orch 07/21 Bruns 2106

CRAZY BLUES (40)
P Bradford Inc, pub. 1920, reached #10 in April 1921
Perry Bradford w & m
First blues song recorded by black singer (Mamie Smith)
Mamie Smith Φ 10/20 Okeh 4169
Hattie Beall, vv stage
Original Dixieland Jazz Band 04/21 Vic 18729
Noble Sissle 03/21 Pathe 20484

CROONING (35)
Witmark, pub. 1921, reached #8 in September 1921
Al Dubin & Herbert Weise w, William F. Caesar m
Benson Orch Φ 07/21 Vic 18765
Sousa's Band, concert dates
Paul Biese Orch 10/21 Col A-3439
Dorothy Ward, vv stage

DO YOU EVER THINK OF ME? (36)
Sherman Clay, pub. 1920, reached #8 in May 1921
Harry D Kerr & John Cooper w, Earl Burtnett m
Paul Whiteman Orch Φ 04/21 Vic 18734
Happy Six 05/21 Col A-3372

DOWN BY THE O-HI-O (33)
Forster M P, pub. 1920, reached #5 in March 1921
Jack Yellen w, Abe Olman m
Featured in ZIEGFELD FOLLIES OF 1920, show (opened 06/20)
Also featured in GEORGE WHITE'S SCANDALS OF 1920, show (opened 06/20)
Billy Murray & Victor Roberts[2] Φ 03/21 Vic 18723
Al Jolson Φ 04/21 Col A-3361
Van & Schenck, sung in show (ZF)
Lou Holtz, sung in show (GWS)
Eddie Cantor, vv stage

DOWN YONDER (22)
L W Gilbert Mus Co, pub. 1921, reached #5 in August 1921
(Also reached #3 in December 1951)
L Wolfe Gilbert w & m
Added to TIP TOP, show (opened 10/20)
Also added to SINBAD, show (opened 02/18)
Ernest Hare duets[3] Φ 06/21 Emer 10377, 07/21 Bruns 2101, 08/21 Okeh 4347
Six Brown Brothers, vv stage and sung in show (TT)
Peerless Quartet Φ 08/21 Vic 18775
Happy Six 09/21 Col A-3423
Al Jolson, vv stage and sung in show (SB)

EMALINE
J H Remick, pub. 1921, reached #17 in October 1921
George A Little w, Jimmy McHugh m
Vernon Dalhart 09/21 Vic 18782
Florence Talbot, vv stage

FEATHER YOUR NEST (17)
L Feist, pub. 1920, reached #3 in January 1921
James Kendis, James Brockman, Howard Johnson w & m
Featured in TIP TOP, show (opened 10/20)
Campbell & Burr ΦΦ 12/20 Okeh 4185, 01/21 Vic 18708
Duncan Sisters, sung in show
Eddie Cantor, vv stage
Anna Chandler, vv stage

HOME AGAIN BLUES (29)
Berlin, pub. 1920, reached #12 in July 1921
Harry Akst & Irving Berlin w & m
Original Dixieland Jazz Band Φ 04/21 Vic 18729
Aileen Stanley 07/21 Vic 18760
Frank Crumit 05/21 Col A-3375
Mabel Howard, vv stage

HUMMING (47)
T B Harms, pub. 1921, reached #9 in June 1921
Louis Breau & Ray Henderson w & m
Paul Whiteman Orch 05/21 Vic 18737
Happy Six 04/21 Col A-3358
Helen Adair, vv stage

I AIN'T NOBODY'S DARLING (39)
Skidmore, pub. 1921, reached #7 in November 1921
Elmer Hughes w, Robert A King m
Frank Crumit/Paul Biese Trio 11/21 Col A-3459
All Star Trio 11/21 Vic 18802
Byron G Harlan 12/21 Okeh 4429

I FOUND A ROSE IN THE DEVIL'S GARDEN (25)
F Fisher, pub. 1921, reached #4 in May 1921
Willie Raskin w, Fred Fisher m
Sam Ash Φ 05/21 Col A-3374
Sterling Trio 06/21 Vic 18746
Paul Specht Orch, db dates

I NEVER KNEW (I COULD LOVE ANYBODY) (21)
L Feist, pub. 1920, reached #2 in April 1921
Tom Pitts, Ray Egan, Roy Marsh w & m
Paul Whiteman Orch Φ 04/21 Vic 18734
Eddie Cantor, vv stage, 05/21 Emer 10349
Rene Vivian, vv stage

I USED TO LOVE YOU, BUT IT'S ALL OVER NOW (19)
Broadway Mus Co, pub. 1920, reached #3 in May 1921
Lew Brown w, Albert Von Tilzer m
Henry Burr Φ 03/21 Vic 18725
Aileen Stanley 02/21 Aeolian/Voc 14134
Frank Crumit 06/21 Col A-3388
Rene Vivian, vv stage

I'M MISSIN' MAMMY'S KISSIN' (46)
Waterson, B & S, pub. 1921, reached #10 in May 1921
Sidney Clare w, Lew Pollack m
Arthur Fields 05/21 Emer 10349
Peerless Quartet 06/21 Vic 18751
Babe Lopez, vv stage

I'M NOBODY'S BABY (12)
L Feist ΦΦΦ, pub. 1921, reached #3 in September 1921
(Also reached #4 in September 1940)
Benny Davis, Milton Ager, Lester Santly w & m
Marion Harris Φ 09/21 Col A-3433
All Star Trio Φ 08/21 Vic 18773
Aileen Stanley 06/21 Aeo/Voc 14172, 09/21 Ed 50791
Happy Six 08/21 Col A-3410

THE JAZZ ME BLUES (42)
E B Marks, pub. 1921, reached #8 in August 1921
Tom Delaney w & m
Original Dixieland Jazz Band Φ 08/21 Vic 18772
Hattie Beall, vv stage
Vivian Lawrence, vv stage

JUST LIKE A RAINBOW (37)
Shapiro, B., pub. 1921, reached #17 in November 1921
Robert A King & Ted FioRito w & m
The Columbians 12/21 Col A-3472
Benson Orch 12/21 Vic 18825
Vivian Segal, vv stage

LEARN TO SMILE (43)
Harms, pub. 1921, reached #5 in September 1921
Otto Harbach w, Louis A Hirsch m
Featured in THE O'BRIEN GIRL, show (opened 10/21)
Paul Whiteman Orch Φ 08/21 Vic 18778
John McCormack 09/21 Vic 64982
Finita DeSoria, Elizabeth Hines & Carl Hammer, sung in show

LOOK FOR THE SILVER LINING (32)
T B Harms ΦΦΦ, pub. 1920, reached #6 in April 1921
Bud DeSylva w, Jerome Kern m
Featured in SALLY, show (opened 12/20)
Featured in GOOD MORNING DEARIE, show (opened 11/21)
Steady seller, 1920's
Marilyn Miller & Irving Fisher, sung in show (SALLY)
Marion Harris Φ 04/21 Col A-3367
Edna Brown[1] & Charles Harrison Φ 04/21 Vic 18731
Casino Dance Orch 03/21 Pathe 20486

LOVE BIRD (48)
Shapiro, B, pub. 1920, reached #11 in April 1921
Robert A King w, Ted FioRito m
Paul Whiteman Orch Φ 04/21 Vic 18735
Ernest Hare 04/21 Bruns 2074
Carlotta Stockdill, vv stage

LOVE SENDS A LITTLE GIFT OF ROSES
Francis D & H, pub. 1919, reached #12 in September 1921
(Also reached #12 in April 1923)
Leslie Cooke w, John Openshaw m
Reinald Werrenrath 07/21 Vic 64964
Sam Ash 9/21 Aeo/Voc 14214, 10/21 Okeh 4387

LOVE WILL FIND A WAY
Witmark, pub. 1921, reached #15 in October 1921
Noble Sissle & Eubie Blake w & m
Featured in SHUFFLE ALONG, show (opened 05/21)
Roger Matthews & Lottie Gee, sung in show
Leroy Smith's Dance Orch 09/21 Aeolian/Voc 14218
Selvin's Orch 12/21 Bruns 2144

MA! (HE'S MAKIN' EYES AT ME) (8)
F Fisher, pub. 1921, reached #1 in November 1921
Sidney Clare w, Con Conrad m
Added to THE MIDNIGHT ROUNDERS OF 1921, revue (opened 02/21)
Eddie Cantor, sung in revue and vv stage
Benson Orch Φ 12/21 Vic 18819
Furman & Nash[5] Φ 10/21 Col A-3445
Ted Lewis Band Φ 12/21 Col A-3473
Isham Jones Orch 12/21 Bruns 5065

MAKE BELIEVE (18)
Waterson, B & S, pub. 1921, reached #2 in June 1921
Benny Davis w, Jack Shilkret m
Paul Whiteman Orch Φ 05/21 Vic 18742
Nora Bayes Φ 06/21 Col A-3392
Anna Armstrong, vv stage

MANDY 'N' ME (30)
Shapiro, B, pub. 1921, reached #16 in December 1921
Bert Kalmar w, Con Conrad & Otto Motzan m
American Quartet 01/22 Vic 18832
Aileen Stanley 11/21 Okeh 4415
Babe Austin, vv stage

MARGIE (9)
Waterson, B & S, pub. 1920, reached #1 in February 1921
Benny Davis w, Con Conrad & J Russel Robinson m
Eddie Cantor Φ vv stage, 02/21 Emerson 10301
Original Dixieland Jazz Band Φ 02/21 Vic 18717
Ted Lewis Band Φ 03/21 Col A-3351
Frank Crumit Φ 02/21 Col A-3332

MAZIE
J Mills, pub. 1921, reached #15 in April 1921
Sidney Caine & Eli Dawson w, Lou Gold m
Green Brothers Novelty Band 04/21 Aeo/Voc 14154, 04/21 Pathe 20498, 05/21 Bruns 2086
Hattie Beall, vv stage

MOONLIGHT (41)
Waterson, B & S, pub. 1921, reached #12 in October 1921
Con Conrad w & m
Paul Whiteman Orch 07/21 Vic 18765
Frank Crumit 09/21 Col A-3431
Rose Lee, vv stage

MY MAMMY (5)
Berlin, pub. 1920, reached #1 in May 1921
(Also reached #13 in August 1967)
Sam Lewis & Joe Young w, Walter Donaldson m
Added to SINBAD, show (opened 02/18)
Featured in BOMBO, show (opened 10/21)
Al Jolson, sung in both shows and on vv stage (Later: 1928 Bruns 3912)
Paul Whiteman Orch ΦΦ 04/21 Vic 18737
Peerless Quartet Φ 04/21 Vic 18730

MY MAN (2)
L Feist, pub. 1921, reached #2 in September 1921
Channing Pollock w, Maurice Yvain m
Featured in ZIEGFELD FOLLIES OF 1921, show (opened 06/21)
Fanny Brice, sung in show, 02/22 Vic 45263
Paul Whiteman Orch ΦΦ 07/21 Vic 18758
Aileen Stanley 07/21 Okeh 4326

MY SUNNY TENNESSEE (14)
Waterson, B & S, pub. 1921, reached #5 in December 1921
Bert Kalmar, Harry Ruby, Herman Ruby, w & m
Featured in THE MIDNIGHT ROUNDERS OF 1921, revue (opened 02/21)
Eddie Cantor, sung in revue
Peerless Quartet Φ 12/21 Vic 18812
Benson Orch Φ 12/21 Vic 18819
Sophie Tucker, vv stage
Mabel Howard, vv stage

OH ME! OH MY! (OH YOU!)
T B Harms & F D H, pub. 1921, reached #13 in September 1921
Arthur Francis w, Paul Lannin & Vincent Youmans m
Featured in TWO LITTLE GIRLS IN BLUE, show (opened 05/21)
Oscar Shaw & Marion Fairbanks, sung in show
Paul Whiteman Orch 08/21 Vic 18778

OLD PAL, WHY DON'T YOU ANSWER ME? (28)
Waterson, B & S, pub. 1920, reached #3 in February 1921
Sam Lewis & Joe Young w, M K Jerome m
Henry Burr Φ 12/20 Col A-2995, 01/21 Vic 18708
Ernest Hare 02/21 Bruns 2057
Goldie Mantell, vv stage

PALE MOON
Forster M P C, pub. 1920, reached #14 in July 1921
Jesse G M Glick w, Frederick Knight Logan m
George Meader 06/21 Col A-3380
Lucy Isabel Marsh, stage, 10/21 Vic 45252
Fritzi Scheff, stage

(LENA FROM) PALESTEENA (13)
Shapiro, B, pub. 1920, reached #2 in January 1921
Con Conrad & J Russel Robinson w & m
Original Dixieland Jazz Band Φ 02/21 Vic 18717
Eddie Cantor Φ vv stage, 01/21 Emer 10292
Frank Crumit Φ 01/21 Col A-3324
Babe Lopez, vv stage

PEGGY O'NEILL (7)
L Feist, pub. 1921, reached #2 in July 1921
Harry Pease, Ed Nelson, Gilbert Dodge w & m
Victor Roberts[2] Φ 07/21 Vic 18764
Clara Norton, vv stage
Mabel Howard, vv stage
Prince's Orch 09/21 Col A-6188
Vincent Lopez Orch, db dates

SAY IT WITH MUSIC (4)
Berlin ΦΦΦ, pub. 1921, reached #1 in December 1921
Irving Berlin w & m
Featured in MUSIC BOX REVUE, show (opened 09/21)
Paul Whiteman Orch ΦΦ 11/21 Vic 18803
Paul Frawley & Wilda Bennett, sung in show
John Steel Φ 01/22 Vic 18828
Selvin's Orch 11/21 Aeo/Voc 14239

SECOND HAND ROSE (24)
Shapiro, B, pub. 1921, reached #7 in December 1921
Grant Clarke w, James F Hanley m
Featured in ZIEGFELD FOLLIES OF 1921, show (opened 06/21)
Fanny Brice, sung in show, 02/22 Vic 45263
Ted Lewis Band Φ 11/21 Col A-3453
Paul Whiteman Orch Φ 12/21 Vic 18818

SOME LITTLE BIRD
Van Alstyne & Curtis, pub. 1920, reached #19 in May 1921
Haven Gillespie, Egbert Van Alstyne, Lindsay McPhail w & m
Based on LISTEN TO THE MOCKING BIRD, pub. 1855;
Septimus Winner w & m
Paul Whiteman Orch 05/21 Vic 18742
Coon-Sanders Orch 07/21 Col A-3403
Larry Funk Orch, vv stage

SPREAD YO' STUFF
Triangle Mus Co, pub. 1921, reached #16 in June 1921
Al Bernard w, Jules Levy & Paul Crane m
Bennie Krueger Orch 05/21 Bruns 2083
Daisy Martin, vv stage, 06/21 Gen 4712

STOLEN KISSES (50)
Waterson, B & S, pub. 1921, reached Top 30 in November 1921
Francis Wheeler w, Ted Snyder m
Emil Coleman Orch 10/21 Vic 18797

STRUT, MISS LIZZIE (15)
J Mills, pub. 1921, reached #5 in July 1921
Henry Creamer w, Turner Layton m
Featured in ZIEGFELD FOLLIES OF 1921, show (opened 06/21)
Van & Schenck, sung in show
Sissle & Blake, vv stage
Blossom Seeley, vv stage
Al Bernard Φ 05/21 Bruns 2084, 05/21 Ed 50761, 06/21 Emer 10354
Ernest Hare Φ 03/21 Aeo/Voc 14144, 03/21 Pathe 22497

SWEET LADY (23)
L Feist, pub. 1921, reached #3 in November 1921
Howard E Johnson w, Dave Zoob & Frank Crumit m
Featured in TANGERINE, show (opened 08/21)
Frank Crumit & Julia Sanderson, sung in show
Paul Whiteman Orch Φ 11/21 Vic 18803
Frank Crumit Φ 12/21 Col A-3475
Billy Jones & Vaughn DeLeath 01/22 Okeh 4454
Eubie Blake 12/21 Emerson 10450

SWEET MAMA (PAPA'S GETTIN' MAD)
J Mills, pub. 1920, reached #17 in February 1921
Fred Rose, George A Little, Peter L Frost w & m
Marion Harris 12/20 Col A-3300
Original Dixieland Jazz Band 03/21 Vic 18722
Blossom Seeley, vv stage
Sissle & Blake, vv stage

TIMBUCTOO (49)
Waterson, B & S, pub. 1920, reached #12 in May 1921
Bert Kalmar w, Harry Ruby m
Frank Crumit 03/21 Col A-3352
Avon Comedy Four, vv stage
Eddie Cantor 06/21 Emerson 10352

TUCK ME TO SLEEP IN MY OLD 'TUCKY HOME (3)
Berlin ΦΦΦ, pub. 1921, reached #2 in January 1922
Sam Lewis & Joe Young w, George Meyer m
Benson Orch ΦΦ 12/21 Vic 18820
Al Jolson, vv stage
Vernon Dalhart/Criterion Trio Φ 11/21 Vic 18807
Henry Burr/Peerless Quartet Φ 12/21 Vic 18821
Billy Jones 10/21 Bruns 2127, 11/21 Okeh 4409

THE WANG WANG BLUES (10)
L Feist, pub. 1921, reached #5 in April 1921
Leo Wood w, Gus Mueller, Buster Johnson & Henry Busse m
Featured in ZIEGFELD FOLLIES OF 1921, show (opened 06/21)
Paul Whiteman Orch/Henry Busse[4] ΦΦ db dates and 12/20 Vic 18694
Van & Schenck, sung in show, 09/21 Col A-3427
Courtney Sisters, vv stage
Kitty Warren, vv stage
Bennie Krueger Orch 05/21 Bruns 2083, 07/21 Gennett 4722

WHEN FRANCES DANCES WITH ME (27)
L Feist, pub. 1921, reached #8 in December 1921
Benny Ryan w, Sol Ginsberg m
Ada Jones & Billy Murray Φ 01/22 Vic 18830
Frank Crumit 01/22 Col A-3521
Miss Patricola 12/21 Pathe 20639
Rose Gordon, vv stage
Violet Buckley, vv stage

WHIP-POOR-WILL
T B Harms, pub. 1920, reached #11 in May 1921
Bud DeSylva w, Jerome Kern m
Featured in SALLY, show (opened 12/20)
Marilyn Miller & Irving Fisher, sung in show
Isham Jones Orch 04/21 Bruns 5045
Gladys Rice 04/21 Pathe 22505

WHO'LL BE THE NEXT ONE TO CRY OVER YOU? (31)
E B Marks, Pub. 1921, reached #8 in October 1921
Johnny Black w & m
Charles W Harrison Φ 11/21 Col A-3463
Vaughn DeLeath 08/21 Okeh 4355
Van & Schenck, vv stage
Arthur Fields 12/21 Vic 18821

WYOMING
Witmark; orig. pub. 1920, reached #20 in July 1921
Gene Williams w & m
Charles Hart & Elliot Shaw 05/21 Vic 18740, 06/21 Bruns 2091
vv singers

[1]Edna Brown was a pseudonym for Elsie Baker.
[2]Victor Roberts was a pseudonym for Billy Jones.
[3]For this song, Ernest Hare sang duet with Al Bernard on Emerson and with Billy Jones on Brunswick and Okeh.
[4]Henry Busse on trumpet
[5]Edward Furman & William Nash

1922

ALL OVER NOTHING AT ALL (24)
Witmark, pub. 1922, reached #7 in August 1922
J Keirn Brennan & Paul Cunningham w, James Rule m
Nora Bayes Ф 07/22 Col A-3601
Aileen Stanley & Billy Murray 11/22 Vic 18943
Warren Sisters, vv stage
Vincent Lopez Orch, db dates

ANGEL CHILD (12)
Witmark, pub. 1922, reached #1 in May 1922
George Price, Abner Silver, Benny Davis w & m
Featured in SPICE OF 1922, revue (opened 07/22)
Al Jolson ФФ vv stage, 05/22 Col A-3568
Georgie Price, sung in revue
Campbell & Burr Ф 07/22 Vic 18903
Eddie Cantor, vv stage

APRIL SHOWERS (8)
Harms ФФФ, pub. 1921, reached #1 in February 1922
(Also reached #6 in May 1947)
Bud DeSylva w, Louis Silvers m
Featured in BOMBO, show (opened 10/21)
Al Jolson ФФ sung in show, 01/22 Col A-3500
Paul Whiteman Orch Ф 01/22 Vic 18825
Ernest Hare 04/22 Bruns 2188

BANDANA DAYS (40)
Witmark, pub. 1921, reached #12 in April 1922
Eubie Blake & Noble Sissle w & m
Featured in SHUFFLE ALONG, show (opened 05/21)
Eubie Blake Orch Ф 10/21 Vic 18791
Arthur Porter, sung in show
Mabel Faleer, vv stage
James P Johnson 03/22 Okeh 4504

BLUE (AND BROKEN-HEARTED) (36)
Stark & Cowan, pub. 1922, reached #4 in November 1922
Grant Clarke & Edgar Leslie w, Lou Handman m
The Virginians Ф 10/22 Vic 18933
Marion Harris/Isham Jones Orch 10/22 Bruns 2310
Waring's Pennsylvanians, db dates
Mary Duncan & Gertrude Murphy, vv stage

BLUE DANUBE BLUES
Harms, pub. 1921, reached #20 in April 1922
Anne Caldwell w, Jerome Kern m
Featured in GOOD MORNING DEARIE, show (opened 11/21)
Louise Groody, sung in show
Knickerbocker Orch 02/22 Col A-3516

CALIFORNIA (47)
J H Remick, pub. 1922, reached #4 in June 1922
Cliff Friend & Con Conrad w & m
Club Royal Orch Ф 06/22 Vic 18890
Blossom Seeley, vv stage
Arthur Fields 05/22 Pathe 20733
Van & Schenck 07/22 Col A-3614

CHICAGO (THAT TODDLIN' TOWN) (19)
F Fisher ФФФ, pub. 1922, reached #2 in December 1922
Fred Fisher w & m
All-time jazz & pop standard
Paul Whiteman Orch Ф 11/22 Vic 18946
Aileen Stanley, vv stage, 06/23 Okeh 4792
Blossom Seeley, vv stage
Bar Harbor Society Orch 10/22 Voc 14412
Waring's Pennsylvanians, db dates

COAL-BLACK MAMMY (49)
Francis, D & H, pub. 1921, reached #6 in November 1922
Laddie Cliff w, Ivy St. Helier m
Paul Whiteman Orch Ф 10/22 Vic 18939
Aunt Jemima, vv stage
Isham Jones Orch 10/22 Bruns 2302
Al Jolson, vv stage, 06/23 Col A-3854

DANCING FOOL (17)
Waterson, B & S, pub. 1922, reached #3 in September 1922
Harry B Smith & Francis Wheeler w, Ted Snyder m
Club Royal Orch 09/22 Vic 18923
Bar Harbor Society Orch 10/22 Voc 14394
Emily Keeler, vv stage

DAPPER DAN (15)
Broadway Mus Co, pub. 1921, reached #4 in January 1922
Lew Brown w, Albert Von Tilzer m
Added to MIDNIGHT ROUNDERS OF 1921, revue
(opened 02/21)
Eddie Cantor, sung in revue
Frank Crumit Ф 12/21 Col A-3477
Club Royal Orch Ф 01/22 Vic 18831
Rose Gordon, vv stage

DEAR OLD SOUTHLAND (14)
J Mills, pub. 1921, reached #2 in April 1922
Henry Creamer w, Turner Layton m
Paul Whiteman Orch Ф 03/22 Vic 18856
Sophie Tucker, vv stage
Ernest Hare Ф 03/22 Bruns 2179
James P Johnson 03/22 Okeh 4504

DO IT AGAIN (33)
Harms, pub. 1922, reached #5 in August 1922
Bud DeSylva w, George Gershwin m
Featured in THE FRENCH DOLL, show (opened 02/22)
Irene Bordoni, sung in show
Paul Whiteman Orch Ф 06/22 Vic 18882
Ray Miller Orch 06/22 Col A-3595

DOO DAH BLUES
Shapiro, B, pub. 1922, reached #19 in May 1922
Fred Rose w, Ted FioRito m
Mamie Smith, vv stage, 06/22 Okeh 4578
Ray Miller Orch 05/22 Col A-3563
Bennie Krueger Orch 04/22 Bruns 2194

DOWN THE OLD CHURCH AISLE
Witmark, pub. 1921, reached #20 in May 1922
Ray Perkins w & m
Featured in GREENWICH VILLAGE FOLLIES OF 1921, show (opened 06/21)
Ted Lewis Band, perf. in show, 03/22 Col A-3538

EVERYBODY STEP (42)
Berlin, pub. 1921, reached #4 in March 1922
Irving Berlin w & m
Featured in MUSIC BOX REVUE, show (opened 09/21)
Brox Sisters, sung in show
Ted Lewis Band Φ 01/22 Col A-3499
Paul Whiteman Orch Φ 01/22 Vic 18826

GEE, BUT I HATE TO GO HOME ALONE
Shapiro, B, pub. 1922, reached #11 in August 1922
Joe Goodwin & James F Hanley w & m
Featured in THE FRENCH DOLL, show (opened 02/22)
Irene Bordoni, sung in show
Billy Jones[1] Φ 06/22 Vic 18892, 09/22 Col A-3611
Dorothy Jardon 07/22 Bruns 5140

GEORGETTE (30)
Shapiro, B, pub. 1922, reached #4 in October 1922
Lew Brown w, Ray Henderson m
Featured in GREENWICH VILLAGE FOLLIES of 1922, show (opened 09/22)
Ted Lewis Φ sung in show, 10/22 Col A-3662
Club Royal Orch Φ 09/22 Vic 18919
Emil Coleman Orch 09/22 Voc 14386
Milt Britton, vv stage

GEORGIA (22)
L Feist, pub. 1922, reached #2 in June 1922
Howard Johnson w, Walter Donaldson m
Peerless Quartet Φ 05/22 Vic 18876
Paul Whiteman Orch Φ 07/22 Vic 18899
Carl Fenton Orch 06/22 Bruns 2259

GRANNY, YOU'RE MY MAMMY'S MAMMY
Berlin, pub. 1921, reached #16 in February 1922
Sam Lewis & Joe Young w, Harry Akst m
Club Royal Orch 02/22 Vic 18843
Yvette Rugel, vv stage, 03/22 Vic 18854
Charles Hart, Elliot Shaw & Everett Clark 04/22 Col A-3556

HOMESICK (34)
Berlin, pub. 1922, reached #10 in December 1922
Irving Berlin w & m
Paul Whiteman Orch Φ 12/22 Vic 18963
Nora Bayes 12/22 Col A-3711
Ted Lewis Band 12/22 Col A-3709
Ethel Levey, vv stage

HOT LIPS (18)
L Feist, pub. 1922, reached #2 in October 1922
Henry Busse, Henry Lange, Lou Davis w & m
Paul Whiteman Orch/Henry Busse[2] ΦΦ 09/22 Vic 18920
Henry Busse, stage (and 1934 Col 2937-D, 1934 Dec 198)
Cotton Pickers 09/22 Bruns 2292
Ted Lewis Band 11/22 Col A-3676

I WISH I COULD SHIMMY LIKE MY SISTER KATE (26)
Clarence Wms M P C, pub. 1922, reached #7 in December 1922
Armand J Piron w & m
Jazz standard, 1920's to 1940's
The Virginians Φ 12/22 Vic 18965
Piron's Novelty Orch, stage
Original Memphis Five, stage, 01/22 Para 20161
Cotton Pickers 01/23 Bruns 2338

I WISH I KNEW (YOU REALLY LOVED ME)
Sherman Clay, pub. 1922, reached #20 in December 1922
Robert E Spencer & Frank Anderson w, Harry Bryant m
Clyde Doerr Orch 11/22 Vic 18947
Frank Crumit 11/22 Col A-3699

I'LL BUILD A STAIRWAY TO PARADISE (43)
Harms, pub. 1922, reached #8 in November 1922
Ira Gershwin & Bud DeSylva w, George Gershwin m
Featured in GEORGE WHITE'S SCANDALS OF 1922, show (opened 08/22)
Paul Whiteman Orch Φ played in show and 11/22 Vic 18949
Winnie Lightner, sung in show

I'M JUST WILD ABOUT HARRY (13)
Witmark, pub. 1921, reached #4 in September 1922
Noble Sissle & Eubie Blake w & m
Featured in SHUFFLE ALONG, show (opened 05/21)
Lottie Gee, sung in show
Marion Harris/Isham Jones Orch Φ 10/22 Bruns 2309
Al Jolson, vv stage
Ray Miller Orch Φ 09/22 Col A-3640
Paul Whiteman Orch Φ 10/22 Vic 18938

IN THE LITTLE RED SCHOOL HOUSE (38)
E B Marks, pub. 1922, reached #5 in July 1922
Al Wilson & James Brennan w & m
American Quartet Φ 07/22 Vic 18904
Billy Jones & Ernest Hare Φ 06/22 Ed 50962, 07/22 Bruns 2270
Wilson & Brennan, vv stage
Duncan Sisters, vv stage

JUST A LITTLE LOVE SONG
Berlin, pub. 1921, reached #10 in April 1922
Sam Lewis & Joe Young w, Joe Cooper m
Paul Whiteman Orch Φ 02/22 Vic 18842
Isham Jones Orch 04/22 Bruns 5084
Ben Selvin Orch 02/22 Voc 14277

KA-LU-A (16)
T B Harms, pub. 1921, reached #2 in March 1922
Anne Caldwell w, Jerome Kern m
Featured in GOOD MORNING DEARIE, show (opened 11/21)
Paul Whiteman Orch Φ 01/22 Vic 18826
Oscar Shaw, sung in show
Edna Brown & Elliott Shaw Φ 03/22 Vic 18854
Mabel Faleer, vv stage

KITTEN ON THE KEYS (9)
J Mills, pub. 1921, reached #3 in August 1922
Zez Confrey m
Zez Confrey ΦΦ 05/21 Bruns 2082, 02/22 Emerson 10480, 04/22 Ed 50898, 07/22 Vic 18900
Vincent Lopez Orch, db dates
Carl Fenton Orch 06/22 Bruns 2261

LEAVE ME WITH A SMILE (21)
Waterson, B & S, pub. 1921, reached #9 in February 1922
Charles Koehler & Earl Burtnett w & m
Alma Gluck, stage
Happy Six 02/22 Col A-3512
All Star Trio 01/22 Vic 18834
Selvin's Orch 10/21 Voc 14233
Charles W Harrison 04/22 Vic 18862

MOON RIVER
Forster M P C, pub. 1922, reached #15 in June 1922
Lee David w & m
Bar Harbor Society Orch 03/22 Voc 14287
Rega Dance Orch 03/22 Okeh 4514

MR. GALLAGHER AND MR. SHEAN (2)
J Mills ΦΦΦ, pub. 1922, reached #1 in November 1922
Ed Gallagher & Al Shean w & m
Featured in ZIEGFELD FOLLIES OF 1922, show (opened 06/22)
Gallagher & Shean ΦΦ sung in show, 10/22 Vic 18941
Billy Jones & Ernest Hare Φ 07/22 Bruns 2270, 08/22 Okeh 4608
Furman & Nash[4] Φ 07/22 Col A-3609
Paul Whiteman/Billy Murray 03/23 Vic 19007
vv duos

MY HONEY'S LOVIN' ARMS
F Fisher, pub. 1922, reached #13 in July 1922
Herman Ruby w, Joseph Meyer m
The Virginians Φ 06/22 Vic 18881
California Ramblers 06/22 Voc 14329
Frank Crumit 11/22 Col A-3699

'NEATH THE SOUTH SEA MOON (28)
Harms, pub. 1922, reached #2 in September 1922
Gene Buck, Louis Hirsch, Dave Stamper w & m
Featured in ZIEGFELD FOLLIES OF 1922, show (opened 06/22)
Paul Whiteman Orch ΦΦ 08/22 Vic 18911
Gilda Gray, sung in show
Ray Miller Orch Φ 09/22 Col A-3649
Lambert Murphy, stage, 01/23 Vic 45332

NELLIE KELLY, I LOVE YOU (29)
Witmark, pub. 1922, reached #5 in November 1922
George M Cohan w & m
Featured in LITTLE NELLIE KELLY, show (opened 11/22)
Charles King, sung in show
American Quartet Φ 12/22 Vic 18957
Prince's Dance Orch Φ 11/22 Col A-3698

NOBODY LIED (41)
J H Remick, pub. 1922, reached #8 in September 1922
Karyl Norman & Hyatt Berry w, J Edwin Weber m
The Virginians Φ 08/22 Vic 18913
Karyl Norman, vv stage
Marion Harris 09/22 Col A-3646

NOLA (48)
Sam Fox, pub. 1916, reached #8 in July 1922
(Also reached #14 in July 1924)
(Also reached #11 in August 1950)
Felix Arndt m
Vincent Lopez Orch Φ 06/22 Okeh 4579, 06/22 Ed 50960
Felix Arndt, stage, 06/22 Vic 18056 (RI)
Carl Fenton Orch 06/22 Br 2261

O-OO, ERNEST (ARE YOU EARNEST WITH ME?) (50)
J H Remick, pub. 1922, reached #7 in June 1922
Sidney Clare & Harry Tobias w, Cliff Friend m
Eddie Cantor, vv stage
Margaret Young Φ 06/22 Bruns 2265
Emily White, vv stage

ON THE ALAMO (46)
Forster M P C, pub. 1922, reached #8 in August 1922
Gus Kahn & Joe Lyons w, Isham Jones m
Isham Jones Orch Φ 06/22 Bruns 2245
Paul Biese Orch 06/22 Col A-3586
Emil Coleman Orch 05/22 Voc 14319

ON THE GIN-GIN-GINNY SHORE (31)
Shapiro, B, pub. 1921, reached #1 in April 1922
Edgar Leslie w, Walter Donaldson m
Paul Whiteman Orch ΦΦ 03/22 Vic 18859
Ray Miller Orch 04/22 Col A-3550
Adele Rowland, vv stage
Lillian Harvey, vv stage

OOGIE OOGIE WA WA
Stark & Cowan, pub. 1922, reached #19 in June 1922
Grant Clarke & Edgar Leslie w, Archie Gottler m
Al Jolson, vv stage, 06/22 Col A-3588
Margaret Young, vv stage, 06/22 Bruns 2265

PARADE OF THE WOODEN SOLDIERS (3)
E B Marks ΦΦΦ, pub. 1922, reached #3 in March 1923
Ballard MacDonald w, Leon Jessel m
Featured by ensemble in CHAUVE SOURIS, show (opened 02/22)
Paul Whiteman Orch ΦΦ 03/23 Vic 19007
Vincent Lopez Orch Φ 08/22 Ed 50987, 09/22 Okeh 4638
Duncan Sisters, vv stage
Ray Miller Orch Φ 08/22 Col A-3628

SAY IT WHILE DANCING (27)
Witmark, pub. 1922, reached #3 in October 1922
Benny Davis w, Abner Silver m
Benson Orch Ф 10/22 Vic 18938
Isham Jones Orch Ф 11/22 Bruns 2314
Vincent Lopez Orch, vv stage

THE SHEIK (OF ARABY) (5)
Waterson, B & S, pub. 1921, reached #1 in February 1922
Harry B Smith & Francis Wheeler w, Ted Snyder m
Featured in MAKE IT SNAPPY, show (opened 04/21)
Club Royal Orch ФФ 01/22 Vic 18831
Eddie Cantor, sung in show
Ray Miller Orch 02/22 Col A-3519
Monica Redmond, vv stage
Charles Hart & Elliot Shaw 04/22 Col A-3556

SMILIN' THROUGH (45)
Witmark, pub. 1918, reached #14 in August 1922
(Also reached #2 in September 1919)
Arthur A Penn w & m
Reinald Werrenrath 05/22 Vic 45166 (RI)
George Reardon 10/22 Voc 14399
stage singers

THE SNEAK
Sherman Clay, pub. 1922, reached #18 in September 1922
Harry D Kerr w, Nacio Herb Brown m
Club Royal Orch 09/22 Vic 18921
Eddie Elkins Orch 10/22 Col A-3660

SOME SUNNY DAY (20)
Berlin, pub. 1922, reached #3 in July 1922
Irving Berlin w & m
Marion Harris Ф 06/22 Col A-3593
Paul Whiteman Orch Ф 06/22 Vic 18891
Isham Jones Orch 07/22 Bruns 2274
Brox Sisters 07/22 Bruns 2268

SONG OF LOVE (35)
L Feist, pub. 1921, reached #12 in February 1922
Based on theme from Schubert's UNFINISHED SYMPHONY
Dorothy Donnelly w, Sigmund Romberg m
Featured in BLOSSOM TIME, show (opened 09/21)
Lucy Isabel Marsh & Royal Dadmun Ф 04/22 Vic 45304
Bertram Peacock & Olga Cook, sung in show
Prince's Orch 01/22 Col A-3504
Ben Selvin 12/21 Pathe 20654

STEALING
L Feist, pub. 1921, reached #15 in April 1922
Dan J Sullivan w & m
Featured in THE PERFECT FOOL, revue (opened 11/21)
Joseph C Smith's Orch 02/22 Vic 18845
The Three Meyakos, sung in revue
Newport Society Orch 02/22 Voc 35009

STUMBLING (6)
L Feist ФФФ, pub. 1922, reached #1 in July 1922
Zez Confrey w & m
Paul Whiteman Orch ФФ db dates, 07/22 Vic 18899
Billy Murray Ф 08/22 Vic 18906
Zez Confrey, vv stage
Frank Crumit 08/22 Col A-3626
Ray Miller Orch 07/22 Col A-3611

SUEZ
Triangle Mus Co, pub. 1922, reached #17 in September 1922
Will Panacoast w, Ferde Grofe & Peter DeRose m
Rudy Wiedoeft Orch 08/22 Bruns 2283
Vincent Lopez Orch, db dates
Clyde Doerr Orch 11/22 Vic 18947

SWANEE RIVER MOON (23)
L Feist, pub. 1921, reached #4 in May 1922
H Pitman Clarke w & m
Columbia Stellar Quartet Ф 09/21 Col A-3432
Charles Hart & Elliot Shaw Ф 11/21 Voc 14238,
12/21 Bruns 2141
International Novelty Orch Ф 06/22 Vic 18882

SWEET INDIANA HOME (44)
J H Remick, pub. 1922, reached #14 in September 1922
Walter Donaldson w & m
Aileen Stanley, vv stage, 09/22 Vic 18922
Van & Schenck 07/22 Col A-3614
Karyl Norman, vv stage
George Olsen Orch, db dates

TEN LITTLE FINGERS AND TEN LITTLE TOES (7)
L Feist, pub. 1921, reached #5 in January 1922
Harry Pease & Johnny White w, Ira Schuster & Ed Nelson m
Billy Murray & Ed Smalle ФФ 01/22 Vic 18830
Billy Jones & Ernest Hare Ф 12/21 Bruns 2140,
12/21 Aeo/Voc 14247, 01/22 Okeh 4456
Belle Baker, vv stage
Betty Palmer, vv stage
Irving Kaufman 12/21 Col A-3477

THREE O'CLOCK IN THE MORNING (1)
L Feist ФФФ, pub. 1921, reached #1 in June 1922
Dorothy Terriss w, Julian Robledo m
Featured in GREENWICH VILLAGE FOLLIES, revue
(opened 08/21)
Paul Whiteman Orch ФФФ 10/22 Vic 18940
John McCormack, stage
Frank Crumit Ф 10/21 Col A-3431
Joseph C Smith's Orch Ф 04/22 Vic 18866
Richard Bold, sung in revue

WABASH BLUES (11)
L Feist, pub. 1921, reached #1 in January 1922
Dave Ringle w, Fred Meinken m
Added to TIP TOP, show (opened 10/20)
Isham Jones Orch ⵀⵀ 11/21 Bruns 5065
Benson Orch ⵀⵀ 01/22 Vic 18820
Mamie Smith, vv stage, 06/22 Okeh 4578
Hattie Beall, vv stage
Six Brown Brothers, sung in show

WHEN BUDDHA SMILES
Harms, pub. 1921, reached #7 in March 1922
Arthur Freed w, Nacio Herb Brown m
Paul Whiteman Orch ⵀ 02/22 Vic 18839
Rudy Wiedoeft Orch 01/22 Bruns 2157, 01/22 Voc 14251
Eddie Elkins Orch 03/22 Col A-3528

WHEN SHALL WE MEET AGAIN? (39)
J H Remick, pub. 1921, reached #8 in March 1922
Raymond B Egan w, Richard Whiting m
Added to TIP TOP, show (opened 10/20)
Duncan Sisters, sung in show
Edna Brown[3] & Elliot Shaw ⵀ 02/22 Vic 18841
Hackel-Berge Orch ⵀ 03/22 Vic 18858
Willie & Eugene Howard, vv stage

WHEN YOU AND I WERE YOUNG MAGGIE BLUES
J Mills, pub. 1922, reached #19 in December 1922
(Also reached #13 in May 1951)
Harold G Frost & Jimmy McHugh w & m
Includes, as counter-melody, WHEN YOU AND I WERE YOUNG, MAGGIE, pub. 1866; George W Johnson w, J A Butterfield m
Van & Schenck, vv stage, 11/22 Col A-3694
Aunt Jemima, vv stage
Duncan Sisters, vv stage
Billy Jones 08/22 Ed 50985, 09/22 Okeh 4632

WHY SHOULD I CRY OVER YOU? (32)
L Feist, pub. 1922, reached #4 in September 1922
Ned Miller w, Chester Conn m
Billy Jones[1] ⵀ 09/22 Vic 18922, 09/22 Col A-3650
The Virginians 10/22 Vic 18933
Belle Baker, vv stage
Jack Benny, vv stage

THE WORLD IS WAITING FOR THE SUNRISE (10)
Chappell, pub. 1919, reached #15 in May 1922
(Reached second peak at #14 in January 1923)
(Also reached #6 in September 1951)
Eugene Lockhart w, Ernest Seitz m
Steady seller, 1920-25
John Steel ⵀ 03/22 Vic 18844
Isham Jones Orch 11/22 Bruns 2313
Benson Orch 01/23 Vic 18980
Adele Rowland, stage
George McFarlane, stage

YANKEE DOODLE BLUES (37)
Berlin, pub. 1922, reached #7 in October 1922
Irving Caesar & Bud DeSylva w, George Gershwin m
Featured in SPICE OF 1922, show (opened 07/22)
Georgie Price, sung in show
The Virginians ⵀ 08/22 Vic 18913
Van & Schenck 10/22 Col A-3668

YOO-HOO (4)
M Richmond, pub. 1921, reached #2 in February 1922
Bud DeSylva w, Al Jolson m
Featured in BOMBO, show (opened 10/21)
Al Jolson ⵀ sung in show, 02/22 Col A-3513
Hackel-Berge Orch ⵀ 11/21 Vic 18802
Willie & Eugene Howard, vv stage
Happy Six 12/21 Col A-3482

YOU CAN HAVE EVERY LIGHT ON BROADWAY
Berlin, pub. 1922, reached #11 in May 1922
Benny Davis w, Seymour B Simons m
Billy Jones ⵀ 05/22 Col A-3574
International Novelty Orch 06/22 Vic 18889
vv singers

YOU REMIND ME OF MY MOTHER (25)
Witmark, pub. 1922, reached #4 in November 1922
George M Cohan w & m
Featured in LITTLE NELLIE KELLY, show (opened 11/22)
Charles King & Elizabeth Hines, sung in show
Henry Burr ⵀ 12/22 Vic 18957
Paul Whiteman Orch ⵀ 11/22 Vic 18949

[1]Billy Jones was billed as Victor Roberts on Victor.
[2]Henry Busse on trumpet
[3]Edna Brown was a pseudonym for Elsie Baker.
[4]Edward Furman & William Nash

1923

AFTER EVERY PARTY
Sherman Clay, pub. 1923, reached #19 in May 1923
Arthur Freed w, Earl Burtnett m
The Troubadours 04/23 Vic 19011
Bar Harbor Society Orch 05/23 Voc 14530
The Columbians 06/23 Col A-3853

AGGRAVATIN' PAPA (25)
Waterson, B & S, pub. 1922, reached #1 in April 1923
Roy Turk, J Russel Robinson, Addie Britt w & m
Sophie Tucker, vv stage, 07/23 Okeh 4817
Marion Harris ⵀ 01/23 Bruns 2345
The Virginians ⵀ 04/23 Vic 19021
Bessie Smith ⵀ 07/23 Col A-3877
Alberta Hunter ⵀ 04/23 Paramount 12013

ANNABELLE (48)
Shapiro, B, pub. 1923, reached #6 in October 1923
Lew Brown w, Ray Henderson m
Brooke Johns Φ 09/23 Vic 19108
Ted Lewis, vv stage, 10/23 Col A-3957
Anna Chandler, vv stage
Waring's Pennsylvanians, db dates

AUNT HAGAR'S CHILDREN (BLUES)
Richmond-Robbins, pub. 1923, reached #19 in May 1923
William C Handy & Tim Brymn w & m
The Virginians 04/23 Vic 19021
Handy's Orch 06/23 Okeh 4789
Ted Lewis Band 07/23 Col 3879

BAMBALINA (13)
Harms, pub. 1923, reached #1 in May 1923
Otto Harbach & Oscar Hammerstein 2nd w, Vincent Youmans & Herbert Stothart m
Featured in THE WILDFLOWER, show (opened 02/23)
Paul Whiteman Orch ΦΦ 05/23 Vic 19035
Edith Day, sung in show
Ray Miller Orch 06/23 Col A-3860

BARNEY GOOGLE (12)
J H Remick ΦΦΦ, pub. 1923, reached #2 in July 1923
Billy Rose & Con Conrad w & m
Georgie Price ΦΦ vv stage, 07/23 Vic 19066
Billy Jones & Ernest Hare[1] Φ 07/23 Col A-3876, 07/23 Bruns 2425, 07/23 Okeh 4828
Olsen & Johnson, vv stage
Great White Way Orch/Billy Murray Φ 08/23 Vic 19093

BEBE (46)
Witmark, pub. 1923, reached #11 in September 1923
Sam Coslow w, Abner Silver m
Brooke Johns 08/23 Vic 19092
Billy Jones 08/23 Col A-3913
Eddie Cantor, vv stage

BESIDE A BABBLING BROOK (26)
J H Remick, pub. 1923, reached #4 in July 1923
Gus Kahn w, Walter Donaldson m
Georgie Price Φ 07/23 Vic 19065
Great White Way Orch Φ 07/23 Vic 19058
Van & Schenck Φ 07/23 Col A-3887
Karyl Norman, vv stage

CAROLINA IN THE MORNING (4)
J H Remick ΦΦΦ, pub. 1922, reached #1 in January 1923
Gus Kahn w, Walter Donaldson m
Featured in THE PASSING SHOW OF 1922, show (opened 09/22)
Van & Schenck ΦΦ 12/22 Col A-3712
Paul Whiteman Orch ΦΦ 12/22 Vic 18962
Willie & Gene Howard, sung in show
Marion Harris 12/22 Bruns 2329
Bill Frawley, vv stage

CRINOLINE DAYS (18)
Berlin, pub. 1922, reached #4 in February 1923
Irving Berlin w & m
Featured in MUSIC BOX REVUE 1922-23, show (opened 10/22)
Paul Whiteman Orch ΦΦ 01/23 Vic 18983
Grace LaRue, sung in show
Vincent Lopez Orch, db dates, 04/23 Okeh 4762

CRYING FOR YOU
L Feist, pub. 1923, reached #15 in May 1923
Ned Miller & Chester Conn w & m
Belle Baker, vv stage
Isham Jones Orch 05/23 Bruns 2400
Paul Whiteman Orch 05/23 Vic 19034
Harry Jolson, vv stage

CUT YOURSELF A PIECE OF CAKE
L Feist, pub. 1923, reached #18 in October 1923
Billy James & Theodore F Morse w & m
Billy Murray 10/23 Vic 19114
Ted Lewis Band 10/23 Col A-3944
Billy Jones & Ernest Hare[1] 10/23 Col A-3954

DEAREST, YOU'RE THE NEAREST TO MY HEART (28)
Berlin, pub. 1922, reached #4 in June 1923
Benny Davis w, Harry Akst m
Paul Whiteman Orch Φ 05/23 Vic 19030
Nora Bayes Φ 06/23 Col A-3862
Georgie Price 06/23 Vic 19047

DIRTY HANDS! DIRTY FACE! (49)
Clarke & Leslie, pub. 1923, reached #15 in September 1923
Al Jolson, Grant Clarke & Edgar Leslie w, James V Monaco m
Added to BOMBO, show (opened 10/21)
Al Jolson, sung in show
Marion Harris 09/23 Bruns 2458
Nora Bayes, vv stage
Irving Kaufman/Selvin's Orch 08/23 Voc 14602

DOWNHEARTED BLUES
J Mills, pub. 1922, reached #18 in September 1923
Alberta Hunter w, Lovie Austin m
Bessie Smith Φ 06/23 Col A-3844
Alberta Hunter, vv stage, 10/22 Paramount 12005
Noble Sissle & Eubie Blake 08/23 Vic 19086

DREAMY MELODY (32)
J H Remick, pub. 1922, reached #4 in November 1923
Ted Koehler, Frank Magine, Clayton Naset w & m
Art Landry Orch ΦΦ 05/23 Gennett 5052, 12/23 Gennett 5255
The Troubadours 07/23 Vic 19077
Yvette Rugel, vv stage
The Misses Dennis, vv stage

FAREWELL BLUES (43)
Jack Mills, pub. 1923, reached #6 in June 1923
Elmer Schoebel, Paul Mares, Leon Rappolo w & m
The Virginians 05/23 Vic 19032
Isham Jones Orch 05/23 Bruns 2406
Friar's Society Orch 12/22 Gennett 4966

GULF COAST BLUES
Clarence Wms M P C, pub. 1923, reached #15 in August 1923
Clarence Williams w & m
Bessie Smith Ф 06/23 Col A-3844
Viola McCoy 08/23 Gennett 5151
Fletcher Henderson Orch 09/23 Voc 14636

I CRIED FOR YOU (40)
Sherman Clay, pub. 1923, reached #5 in August 1923
(Also reached #5 in March 1939)
Arthur Freed, Gus Arnheim, Abe Lyman w & m
Blossom Seeley, vv stage
Belle Baker, vv stage
The Collegians Ф 08/23 Vic 19093
Bennie Krueger Orch Ф 09/23 Bruns 2453
Cliff Edwards[2], vv stage

I GAVE YOU UP JUST BEFORE YOU THREW ME DOWN (47)
Waterson, B & S, pub. 1922, reached #14 in March 1923
Bert Kalmar, Harry Ruby, Fred Ahlert w & m
Ohman-Reser Orch/Frank Crumit Ф 03/23 Col A-3785
Paul Whiteman Orch 03/23 Vic 19003
Rachel Grant[3] & Billy Murray 04/23 Vic 19023

I LOVE YOU (2)
L Feist ФФФ, pub. 1923, reached #1 in December 1923
Harlan Thompson w, Harry Archer m
Featured in LITTLE JESSE JAMES, show (opened 08/23)
Paul Whiteman Orch ФФ 11/23 Vic 19151
Margaret Wilson & John Boles, sung in show
Lewis James Ф 01/24 Col 25-D, 01/24 Okeh 4955
Carl Fenton Orch Ф 12/23 Bruns 2487

INDIANA MOON (35)
Berlin, pub. 1923, reached #2 in October 1923
Benny Davis w, Isham Jones m
The Troubadours Ф 10/23 Vic 19115
The Columbians Ф 08/23 Col A-3908
John McCormack, stage, 07/24 Vic 1071
Ben Selvin Orch 09/23 Voc 14621

JUST A GIRL THAT MEN FORGET (21)
J Mills, pub. 1923, reached #1 in September 1923
Al Dubin, Fred Rath, Joe Garren w & m
Henry Burr ФФ 10/23 Vic 19131
Belle Baker, vv stage
Billy Jones Ф 09/23 Voc 14630
Morton Downey, vv stage

JUST FOR TONIGHT (44)
E B Marks, pub. 1923, reached #15 in November 1923
Ballard MacDonald w, Oskar Geiger m
Benson Orch Ф 09/23 Vic 19101
Grace LaRue, vv stage
Southampton Serenaders 10/23 Voc 14642

A KISS IN THE DARK (3)
Harms ФФФ, pub. 1922, reached #5 in May 1923
Bud DeSylva w, Victor Herbert m
Featured in ORANGE BLOSSOMS, show (opened 09/22)
Edith Day, sung in show
Olive Kline Ф 06/23 Vic 45348
The Serenaders Ф 01/23 Vic 18972
Amelita Galli-Curci 01/24 Vic 959

LADY OF THE EVENING (22)
Berlin, pub. 1922, reached #5 in March 1923
Irving Berlin w & m
Featured in MUSIC BOX REVUE OF 1922-23, show (opened 10/22)
John Steel Ф 02/23 Vic 18990
Paul Whiteman Orch Ф 04/23 Vic 19016
Paul Specht Orch 03/23 Col A-3778

LAST NIGHT ON THE BACK PORCH (15)
Skidmore Mus Co, pub. 1923, reached #2 in December 1923
Lew Brown & Carl Schraubstader w & m
Featured in GEORGE WHITE'S SCANDALS OF 1923, show (opened 06/23)
Paul Whiteman/American Quartet ФФ 11/23 Vic 19139
Winnie Lightner, sung in show
Billy Jones & Ernest Hare[1] Ф 01/24 Bruns 2499, 01/24 Okeh 4948
Shannon Four 11/23 Col A-3976
Aileen Stanley, vv stage

LOST (A WONDERFUL GIRL)
Shapiro, B, pub. 1922, reached #20 in February 1923
Benny Davis & James F Hanley w & m
Al Jolson 01/23 Col A-3744
Great White Way Orch 02/23 Vic 18986
Belle Baker, vv stage

LOUISVILLE LOU, THE VAMPIN' LADY (30)
Yellen & B, pub. 1923, reached #3 in September 1923
Jack Yellen w, Milt Ager m
Ted Lewis Band, vv stage, 08/23 Col A-3892
Arthur Gibbs Band 07/23 Vic 19070
Sophie Tucker, vv stage
Belle Baker, vv stage

LOVE SENDS A LITTLE GIFT OF ROSES (24)
Francis, D & H, pub. 1919, reached #12 in April 1923
(Also reached #12 in September 1921)
Leslie Cooke w, John Openshaw m
Carl Fenton Orch Ф 04/23 Bruns 2392
John McCormack, stage, 12/23 Vic 961
Bar Harbor Society Orch 03/23 Voc 14500
Sam Ash 05/23 Voc 14534

LOVE TALES
L Feist, pub. 1923, reached #11 in November 1923
Ben Ryan & Vincent Rose w & m
Great White Way Orch 10/23 Vic 19122
Eddie Elkins Orch 10/23 Col A-3940

LOVIN' SAM, THE SHEIK OF ALABAM' (11)
Ager, Y & B, pub. 1922, reached #2 in February 1923
Jack Yellen w, Milt Ager m
Added to MAKE IT SNAPPY, show (opened 04/21)
Nora Bayes Φ 02/23 Col A-3757
Miss Patricola Φ vv stage, 01/23 Vic 18976
Sophie Tucker, vv stage
Anna Chandler, vv stage
Eddie Cantor, sung in show

MARCHETA (7)
J Franklin, pub. 1913, reached #5 in October 1923
Victor Schertzinger w & m
Steady seller, 1920's
Great White Way Orch Φ 06/23 Vic 19046
Olive Kline & Elsie Baker Φ 06/22 Vic 45309
Isham Jones Orch Φ 08/23 Bruns 2439
John McCormack, stage, 07/24 Vic 1011

MIDNIGHT ROSE
Witmark, pub. 1923, reached #13 in November 1923
Lew Pollack & Sidney D Mitchell w & m
Benson Orch 11/23 Vic 19148
Charles Hart 10/23 Col A-3945
Henry Burr 01/24 Vic 19186
Courtney Sisters, vv stage

MY BUDDY (6)
J H Remick, pub. 1922, reached #1 in December 1922
Gus Kahn w, Walter Donaldson m
Henry Burr ΦΦ 11/22 Vic 18930
Al Jolson, vv stage
Ernest Hare Φ 11/22 Bruns 2320
Georgie Price, vv stage
International Novelty Orch 01/23 Vic 18995

MY SWEETIE WENT AWAY (29)
Waterson, B & S, pub. 1923, reached #3 in October 1923
Roy Turk w, Lou Handman m
Joe Raymond Φ 10/23 Vic 19110
Billy Murray & Ed Smalle Φ 11/23 Vic 19144
Anna Chandler, vv stage, 09/23 Ed 51193
Cotton Pickers 09/23 Bruns 2461

NO, NO, NORA (16)
L Feist, pub. 1923, reached #2 in November 1923
Gus Kahn w, Ted FioRito & Ernie Erdman m
Eddie Cantor Φ vv stage, 11/23 Col A-3964
Benson Orch Φ 10/23 Vic 19121
Al Jolson, vv stage
Ted FioRito Orch, db dates
Abe Lyman's Orch/Charles Kaley 11/23 Bruns 2476

OH! GEE, OH! GOSH, OH! GOLLY, I'M IN LOVE (31)
Waterson, B & S, pub. 1923, reached #2 in September 1923
Ole Olsen & Chick Johnson w, Ernest Breuer m
Featured in ZIEGFELD FOLLIES OF 1922, show (opened 06/22)
Eddie Cantor Φ vv stage, 09/23 Col A-3934
Olsen & Johnson, sung in show
Billy Jones & Ernest Hare[1] Φ 08/23 Emerson 10642, 09/23 Ed 51193, 10/23 Voc 14644

PACK UP YOUR SINS (AND GO TO THE DEVIL)
Berlin, pub. 1922, reached #14 in February 1923
Irving Berlin w & m
Featured in MUSIC BOX REVUE OF 1922-23, show (opened 10/22)
Paul Whiteman Orch Φ 01/23 Vic 18983
McCarthy Sisters, sung in show

ROSE OF THE RIO GRANDE (38)
Stark & Cowan, pub. 1922, reached #4 in April 1923
Edgar Leslie w, Ross Gorman & Harry Warren m
Marion Harris Φ 03/23 Bruns 2370
The Virginians Φ 03/23 Vic 19001
Barney Bernard, vv stage

ROSES OF PICARDY (23)
Chappell, pub. 1916, reached #7 in December 1923 (Also reached #19 in October 1918)
Frederick E Weatherly w, Haydn Wood m
The Troubadours Φ 11/23 Vic 19117
Paul Specht Orch 07/23 Col A-3870
Vincent Lopez Orch, db dates
John McCormack, stage

RUNNIN' WILD (27)
L Feist, pub. 1922, reached #2 in April 1923
Joel Gray & Leo Wood w, A Harrington Gibbs m
Ted Lewis Band Φ 03/23 Col A-3790
Miss Patricola Φ 05/23 Vic 19027
Belle Baker, vv stage
Sophie Tucker, vv stage

SAW MILL RIVER ROAD (42)
L Feist, pub. 1921, reached #10 in July 1923
Joe McCarthy w, Harry Tierney m
Isham Jones Orch Φ 05/23 Bruns 2406
Great White Way Orch 07/23 Vic 19074
The Columbians 04/23 Col A-3809

SEVEN OR ELEVEN (MY DIXIE PAIR O'DICE)
Shapiro, B, pub. 1923, reached #11 in June 1923
Lew Brown w, Walter Donaldson m
Featured in MAKE IT SNAPPY, show (opened 04/22)
Eddie Cantor, sung in show
Billy Murray & Ed Smalle 06/23 Vic 19048
Sophie Tucker, vv stage, 07/23 Okeh 4818

STELLA (50)
Waterson, B & S, pub. 1923, reached #9 in August 1923
Harry Akst, Benny Davis, Al Jolson w & m
Al Jolson Ф vv stage, 08/23 Col A-3913
Fatty Arbuckle, vv stage
Irving Kaufman 08/23 Voc 14597

SWINGIN' DOWN THE LANE (10)
L Feist, pub. 1923, reached #2 in August 1923
Gus Kahn w, Isham Jones m
Isham Jones Orch Ф db dates, 08/23 Bruns 2438
Great White Way Orch Ф 07/23 Vic 19058
Cliff Edwards[2], vv stage
Ben Bernie Orch Ф 05/23 Voc 14537

TEN THOUSAND YEARS FROM NOW (45)
Witmark, pub. 1923, reached #8 in November 1923
J Keirn Brennan w, Ernest Ball m
Henry Burr 09/23 Vic 19104
George MacFarlane, stage
Lewis James 11/23 Ed 51214

THAT OLD GANG OF MINE (1)
Berlin, pub. 1923, reached #1 in October 1923
Billy Rose & Mort Dixon w, Ray Henderson m
Featured in ZIEGFELD FOLLIES OF 1923, show (opened 10/23)
Billy Murray & Ed Smalle ФФ 09/23 Vic 19095
Van & Schenck, sung in show
Benson Orch Ф 11/23 Vic 19136
Criterion Quartet 10/23 Voc 14646
Wright & Bessinger, radio

THAT RED-HEAD GAL
F Fisher, pub. 1922, reached #17 in June 1923
Fred Fisher w, Henry Lodge m
Van & Schenck, vv stage
The Collegians 06/23 Vic 19049
Ruth Roye, vv stage

TOOT, TOOT, TOOTSIE! (GOODBYE) (14)
L Feist, pub. 1922, reached #2 in January 1923
Gus Kahn, Ernie Erdman, Dan Russo, Ted FioRito, & Robert A King w & m
Added to BOMBO, show (opened 10/21)
Al Jolson ФФ sung in show, 12/22 Col A-3705
Benson Orch Ф 12/22 Vic 18954
Ted Lewis, vv stage
Billy Jones & Ernest Hare[1] 02/23 Okeh 4726

UNDERNEATH THE MELLOW MOON
Dellwoods Mus Hs, pub. 1922, reached #14 in July 1923
Wendell Hall w & m
Paul Whiteman Orch Ф 04/23 Vic 19019
Alice Green[4] and Edna Brown[4] 07/23 Vic 19071
Ben Selvin Orch 04/23 Voc 14508

WAY DOWN YONDER IN NEW ORLEANS (19)
Shapiro, B, pub. 1922, reached #5 in February 1923
(Also reached #4 in January 1960)
Henry Creamer & Turner Layton w & m
Peerless Quartet Ф 11/22 Vic 18942
Blossom Seeley Ф vv stage, 01/23 Col A-3731
Paul Whiteman Orch Ф 05/23 Vic 19030
Miss Patricola, vv stage
Creamer & Layton, vv stage

THE WEST, A NEST, AND YOU
Sherman Clay, pub. 1923, reached #11 in December 1923
Larry Yoell & Billy Hill w & m
Waring's Pennsylvanians 12/23 Vic 19172
Lewis James 02/24 Vic 19214

WHEN HEARTS ARE YOUNG (20)
Harms, pub. 1922, reached #1 in March 1923
Cyrus Wood w, Sigmund Romberg & Al Goodman m
Featured in THE LADY IN ERMINE, show (opened 10/22)
Paul Whiteman Orch Ф 02/23 Vic 18985
Wilda Bennett, sung in show
Paul Specht Orch 02/23 Col A-3760

WHEN IT'S NIGHT TIME IN ITALY, IT'S WEDNESDAY OVER HERE
Shapiro, B, pub. 1923, reached #20 in November 1923
Lew Brown & James Kendis w & m
Jimmy Kendis, radio
Phil Baker, vv stage
Lou Holtz 02/24 Vic 19205

WHEN THE LEAVES COME TUMBLING DOWN (37)
L Feist, pub. 1922, reached #7 in January 1923
Richard Howard w & m
Clyde Doerr Orch Ф 11/22 Vic 18945
Aileen Stanley & Billy Murray 04/23 Vic 19026
McEnelly's Singing Orch, vv stage

WHEN YOU WALKED OUT, SOMEONE ELSE WALKED RIGHT IN (41)
Berlin, pub. 1923, reached #6 in August 1923
Irving Berlin w & m
Brooke Johns Ф 08/23 Vic 19092
Frank Crumit 09/23 Col A-3933
Isham Jones Orch 09/23 Bruns 2456

WHO CARES? (34)
Ager, Y & B, pub. 1922, reached #9 in February 1923
Jack Yellen w, Milt Ager m
Featured in BOMBO, show (opened 10/21)
Al Jolson, sung in show, 03/23 Col A-3779
Great White Way Orch Ф 02/23 Vic 18993
Barney Bernard, vv stage

WHO'S SORRY NOW? (8)
Waterson, B & S ΦΦΦ, pub. 1923, reached #1 in June 1923
(Also reached #5 in April 1958)
Bert Kalmar & Harry Ruby w, Ted Snyder m
Memphis Five Φ 06/23 Vic 19052
Ben Bernie Orch 06/23 Voc 14555
Irving Kaufman 05/23 Emer 10594
Isham Jones Orch 08/23 Bruns 2438
Marion Harris 08/23 Bruns 2443

WILDFLOWER (33)
Harms, pub. 1923, reached #5 in July 1923
Otto Harbach & Oscar Hammerstein 2nd w, Vincent Youmans & Herbert Stothart m
Featured in THE WILDFLOWER, show (opened 02/23)
Guy Robertson, sung in show
Great White Way Orch 07/23 Vic 19077
Ben Bernie Orch 06/23 Voc 14555

WONDERFUL ONE (9)
L Feist, pub. 1922, reached #2 in June 1923
Dorothy Terriss w, Paul Whiteman, Ferde Grofe & Marshall Neilan m
Paul Whiteman Orch ΦΦ 04/23 Vic 19019
John McCormack, stage, 12/23 Vic 961
Carl Fenton Orch 04/23 Bruns 2392

YES! WE HAVE NO BANANAS (5)
Skidmore Mus Co, pub. 1923, reached #1 in July 1923
Frank Silver & Irving Cohn w & m
Great White Way Orch/Billy Murray ΦΦ 07/23 Vic 19068
Billy Jones ΦΦ 07/23 Voc 14579, 07/23 Ed 51183, 07/23 Emerson 10623, 08/23 Bruns 2445
Eddie Cantor, vv stage
Furman & Nash[5] Φ 07/23 Col A-3873

YOU GAVE ME YOUR HEART
Waterson, B & S, pub. 1922, reached #12 in January 1923
Harry B Smith & Francis Wheeler w, Ted Snyder m
Great White Way Orch Φ 12/22 Vic 18964

YOU'VE GOT TO SEE MAMMA EV'RY NIGHT (17)
L Feist, pub. 1923, reached #1 in May 1923
Billy Rose w, Con Conrad m
Aileen Stanley & Billy Murray Φ 05/23 Vic 19027
Sophie Tucker, vv stage, 07/23 Okeh 4817
Marion Harris Φ 04/23 Bruns 2410
Dolly Kay, vv stage, 04/23 Col A-3808
Mamie Smith 05/23 Okeh 4781

YOU KNOW YOU BELONG TO SOMEBODY ELSE (39)
Berlin, pub. 1922, reached #7 in April 1923
Eugene West w, James V Monaco & Ira Schuster m
Henry Burr Φ 04/23 Vic 19026
The Virginians 05/23 Vic 19040
Irving Kaufman 04/23 Voc 14513

YOU TELL HER, I S-T-U-T-T-E-R (36)
Berlin, pub. 1922, reached #5 in April 1923
Billy Rose & Cliff Friend w & m
Billy Murray Φ 01/23 Vic 18982
Van & Schenck Φ vv stage, 03/23 Col A-3770
Billy Jones & Ernest Hare[1] Φ 01/23 Voc 14459, 01/23 Ed 51079, 02/23 Gennett 5007, 04/23 Okeh 4756

[1]Jones & Hare were also known as The Happiness Boys.
[2]Cliff Edwards was also known as Ukulele Ike.
[3]Rachel Grant was a pseudonym for Gladys Rice.
[4]Alice Green was Olive Kline; Edna Brown was Elsie Baker.
[5]Edward Furman & William Nash

1924

BAGDAD
Ager, Y & B, pub. 1924, reached #11 in November 1924
Jack Yellen w, Milt Ager m
Paul Whiteman Orch 11/24 Vic 19447
Paul Specht Orch 11/24 Col 188-D
Waring's Pennsylvanians, db dates

CALIFORNIA, HERE I COME (10)
Witmark ΦΦΦ, pub. 1924, reached #1 in April 1924
Joseph Meyer, Al Jolson, Bud DeSylva w & m
Added to BOMBO, show (opened 10/21)
All-time pop standard
Al Jolson ΦΦ sung in show, 04/24 Bruns 25692
Paul Whiteman Orch Φ 04/24 Vic 19267
Georgie Price 04/24 Vic 19261

CHANSONETTE (45)
Harms, pub. 1923, reached #13 in December 1923
Dailey Paskman, Sigmund Spaeth, Irving Caesar w, Rudolf Friml m
Paul Whiteman Orch 11/23 Vic 19145
Paul Specht Orch 12/23 Col A-3992
Lambert Murphy, stage, 05/24 Vic 45395

THE CHARLESTON
Harms, pub. 1923, reached #20 in January 1924
(Also reached #10 in December 1925)
Cecil Mack & James P Johnson w & m
Featured in RUNNIN' WILD, show (opened 10/23)
Later became the dance sensation of the mid-1920's
Arthur Gibbs Band 12/23 Vic 19165
Edith Spencer & May Barnes, sung in show

CHARLEY, MY BOY (6)
Berlin, pub. 1924, reached #1 in October 1924
(Also reached #13 in January 1950)
Gus Kahn & Ted FioRito w & m
Eddie Cantor Φ vv stage, 10/24 Col 182-D
Benny Krueger/Billy Jones Φ 10/24 Bruns 2667
Billy Murray Φ 10/24 Vic 19411
Red and Black Boys, vv stage

COLORADO (39)
E B Marks, pub. 1924, reached #8 in June 1924
Walter Hirsch w, Harold A Dellon m
State song of Colorado
Campbell & Burr Φ 05/24 Vic 19283
Jan Garber Orch, db dates
Paul Specht Orch, db dates

COVERED WAGON DAYS (50)
Waterson, B & S, pub. 1923, reached #10 in February 1924
Will Morrissey & Joe Burrowes w & m
Ted Weems Orch Φ 02/24 Vic 19212
Vincent Lopez Orch 01/24 Okeh 4946

DIZZY FINGERS
J Mills, pub. 1923, reached #16 in June 1924
Zez Confrey m
Zez Confrey, vv stage (Later: 1927 Vic 20777)
Piano rolls

DON'T MIND THE RAIN
L Feist, pub. 1924, reached #7 in June 1924
Chester Conn & Ned Miller w & m
Paul Whiteman Orch Φ 04/24 Vic 19273
Blossom Seeley, vv stage, 07/24 Col 114-D
White Sisters, vv stage

DOO WACKA DOO (48)
L Feist, pub. 1924, reached #7 in December 1924
Clarence Gaskill, Walter Donaldson, George Horther w & m
Paul Whiteman/Billy Murray Φ 12/24 Vic 19462
Isabel Patricola, vv stage, 01/25 Voc 14906
Isham Jones Orch 02/25 Bruns 2767

DOODLE DOO DOO (40)
L Feist, pub. 1924, reached #10 in September 1924
Art Kassel & Mel Stitzel w & m
Eddie Cantor, vv stage, 12/24 Col 213-D
Paul Whiteman Orch, db dates
Benson Orch Φ 06/24 Vic 19318
Margaret Young 10/24 Bruns 2673

DREAM DADDY (43)
J Morris, pub. 1923, reached #8 in April 1924
Louis Herscher w, George Keefer m
Jack Chapman/Raymond Davis Φ 02/24 Vic 19201
Carl Fenton Orch 02/24 Bruns 2525
Lewis James Orch 04/24 Col 72-D
Ted Weems Orch, db dates

FOLLOW THE SWALLOW (15)
J H Remick, pub. 1924, reached #2 in November 1924
Billy Rose & Mort Dixon w, Ray Henderson m
Al Jolson ΦΦ 10/24 Bruns 2671
George Olsen/w.vocal group Φ 11/24 Vic 19428
Wright & Bessinger, radio
Peerless Quartet Φ 12/24 Vic 19455

HARD-HEARTED HANNAH (31)
Ager, Y & B, pub. 1924, reached #8 in September 1924
Jack Yellen, Bob Bigelow, Charles Bates w & m
Featured in INNOCENT EYES, show (opened 05/24)
Belle Baker, vv stage, 11/24 Vic 19436
Cliff Edwards[3] 08/24 Pathe 32054
Frances Williams, sung in show
Paul Whiteman Orch 11/24 Vic 19447

HOW COME YOU DO MY LIKE YOU DO? (33)
Stark & Cowan, pub. 1924, reached #9 in September 1924
Roy Bergere & Gene Austin w & m
Marion Harris Φ 07/24 Bruns 2610
Gene Austin, vv stage
Frank Crumit 11/24 Vic 19437

I WANT TO BE HAPPY (28)
Harms, pub. 1924, reached #6 in December 1924
(Also reached #20 in January 1926)
Irving Caesar w, Vincent Youmans m
Featured in NO, NO, NANETTE, show (opened 05/24 in Chicago)
Charles Winninger & Louise Groody, sung in show
Jan Garber Orch Φ 10/24 Vic 19404
Vincent Lopez Orch Φ 11/24 Okeh 40175
Carl Fenton/w.vocal group 09/24 Bruns 2640

I WONDER WHAT'S BECOME OF SALLY (2)
Ager, Y & B ΦΦΦ, pub. 1924, reached #1 in November 1924
Jack Yellen w, Milt Ager m
Al Jolson Φ vv stage, 10/24 Bruns 2671
Shannon Quartet Φ 10/24 Vic 19415
Ted Lewis Band Φ vv stage, 09/24 Col 157-D
Joe Schenck Φ 09/24 Col 148-D
Cliff Edwards[3] Φ 12/24 Pathe 32079

I'M GOIN' SOUTH (21)
Witmark, pub. 1923, reached #3 in April 1924
Abner Silver & Harry Woods w & m
Featured in KID BOOTS, show (opened 12/23)
Added to BOMBO, show (opened 10/21)
Al Jolson Φ sung in show (B), 04/24 Col 61-D,
04/24 Bruns 25692
Eddie Cantor, sung in show (KB)
Paul Whiteman Orch Φ 03/24 Vic 19229
Georgie Price 04/24 Vic 19261

I'M SITTING PRETTY IN A PRETTY LITTLE CITY (34)
Witmark, pub. 1923, reached #5 in January 1924
Lou Davis, Abel Baer, Henry Santly w & m
Campbell & Burr Φ 01/24 Vic 19180
Paul Whiteman Orch Φ 02/24 Vic 19217
Jan Garber Orch, db dates
Marshall Montgomery, vv stage

IT AIN'T GONNA RAIN NO MO' (4)
Forster M P, pub. 1923, reached #1 in May 1924
Wendell Hall w & m
Wendell Hall ΦΦΦ 12/23 Vic 19171, 12/23 Gennett 5271, 01/24 Ed 51261, 02/24 Ed Amb 4824
Billy Jones & Ernest Hare[4] 05/24 Col 87-D
Carl Fenton Orch 04/24 Bruns 2568

IT HAD TO BE YOU (5)
J H Remick, pub. 1924, reached #2 in August 1924
(Also reached #5 in September 1944)
Gus Kahn w, Isham Jones m
Isham Jones Orch Φ 07/24 Bruns 2614
Marion Harris Φ 06/24 Bruns 2610
Cliff Edwards[3] Φ 06/24 Perfect 12126, 06/24 Pathe 32047
Aunt Jemima, vv stage
Aileen Stanley & Billy Murray Φ 09/24 Vic 19373

JEALOUS (8)
H Waterson, pub. 1924, reached #2 in September 1924
Tommy Malie & Dick Finch w, Jack Little m
International Novelty Orch ΦΦ 06/24 Vic 19332
Marion Harris Φ 07/24 Bruns 2622
Little Jack Little, vv stage
Ben Selvin Orch 07/24 Voc 14398
Lewis James 10/24 Col 178-D

JUNE NIGHT (9)
L Feist, pub. 1924, reached #2 in October 1924
Cliff Friend w, Abel Baer m
Waring's Pennsylvanians ΦΦ 09/24 Vic 19380
Ted Lewis Band Φ 09/24 Col 157-D
Cliff Edwards[3] 11/24 Pathe 32074
Bennie Krueger Orch 09/24 Bruns 2642
Fred Dempsey, vv stage

LA ROSITA (47)
Sam Fox, pub. 1923, reached #14 in February 1924
Allan Stuart w, Paul DuPont m
International Novelty Orch 02/24 Vic 19218
Paul Ash 01/24 Bruns 2517
Helen Moore, vv stage

LAZY (29)
Berlin, pub. 1924, reached #5 in June 1924
Irving Berlin w & m
Blossom Seeley, vv stage, 07/24 Col 114-D
Paul Whiteman Orch Φ 06/24 Vic 19299
Al Jolson Φ 06/24 Bruns 2595
Brox Sisters, vv stage, 06/24 Vic 19298

LIMEHOUSE BLUES (20)
Harms, pub. 1922, reached #2 in May 1924
Douglas Furber w, Philip Braham m
Featured in CHARLOT'S REVUE OF 1924, revue (opened 01/24)
Paul Whiteman Orch Φ 04/24 Vic 19264
Gertrude Lawrence, sung in show
The Columbians 05/24 Col 88-D

LINGER AWHILE (3)
L Feist, pub. 1923, reached #1 in February 1924
Harry Owens w, Vincent Rose m
Paul Whiteman Orch ΦΦΦ 01/24 Vic 19211
Marcia Freer & Lewis James 03/24 Vic 19259
Bennie Krueger Orch 02/24 Bruns 4526
Miss Patricola, vv stage
Balmoral Club Orch, db dates

LITTLE BUTTERFLY
Berlin, pub. 1923, reached #19 in February 1924
Irving Berlin w & m
Featured in MUSIC BOX REVUE OF 1923-24, show (opened 09/23)
John Steel, sung in show, 02/24 Vic 19219
Paul Whiteman Orch Φ 12/23 Vic 19162

LOVEY CAME BACK (36)
Berlin, pub. 1923, reached #5 in February 1924
Sam Lewis & Joe Young w, Lou Handman m
Marion Harris Φ 12/23 Bruns 2494
Lou Holtz Φ 02/24 Vic 19205
Cliff Edwards[3] 02/24 Pathe 21097

MAMMA GOES WHERE PAPA GOES (38)
Ager, Y & B, pub. 1923, reached #5 in January 1924
Jack Yellen w, Milt Ager m
Sophie Tucker, vv stage
The Georgians Φ 12/23 Col A-3996
Rae Samuels, vv stage
The Virginians/Jane Green 02/24 Vic 19215

MAMMA LOVES PAPA (PAPA LOVES MAMMA) (49)
L Feist, pub. 1923, reached #7 in February 1924
Cliff Friend & Abel Baer w & m
Van & Schenck, vv stage
Paul Whiteman Orch 01/24 Vic 19191
Isham Jones Orch 01/24 Bruns 2506

MANDALAY (14)
J H Remick, pub. 1924, reached #3 in September 1924
Earl Burtnett, Abe Lyman, Gus Arnheim w & m
Al Jolson Φ 09/24 Bruns 2650
Paul Whiteman Orch Φ 07/24 Vic 35744
Abe Lyman Orch 08/24 Bruns 2631
Art Hickman Orch 10/24 Vic 19379

MAYTIME
L Feist, pub. 1924, reached #17 in October 1924
Bud DeSylva w, Vincent Rose m
Waring's Pennsylvanians 10/24 Vic 19367
Lewis James 09/24 Col 162-D

MEMORY LANE (7)
Harms, pub. 1924, reached #4 in October 1924
Bud DeSylva w, Con Conrad & Larry Spier m
Waring's Pennsylvanians/Tom Waring ΦΦ 07/24 Vic 19303
Romancers Orch 07/24 Col 121-D
May Meredith & Lewis James 08/24 Col 138-D
Lambert Murphy 10/24 Vic 45453

MEXICALI ROSE
W A Quincke, pub. 1923, reached #15 in June 1924
(Also reached #16 in November 1938)
Helen Stone w, Jack B Tenny m
Lewis James 01/24 Okeh 4952
Bar Harbor Society Orch 05/24 Voc 14763

MINDIN' MY BUS'NESS
Berlin, pub. 1923, reached #11 in May 1924
Gus Kahn w, Walter Donaldson m
Frank Crumit ⓓ 04/24 Vic 19259
The Virginians ⓓ 04/24 Vic 19269
Ernest Hare 04/24 Okeh 40055

MY DREAM GIRL (32)
Harms, pub. 1924, reached #8 in November 1924
Rida Johnson Young w, Victor Herbert m
Featured in THE DREAM GIRL, show (opened 08/24)
Walter Woolf King, sung in show
The Troubadours ⓓ 10/24 Vic 19402
Lambert Murphy 10/24 Vic 45453

NOBODY'S SWEETHEART (11)
J Mills, pub. 1924, reached #3 in June 1924
Gus Kahn, Ernie Erdman, Billy Meyers, Elmer Schobel w & m
Added to THE PASSING SHOW OF 1923, show (opened 06/23)
Jazz standard 1920's and 1930's
Ted Lewis Band, performed in show
Isham Jones Orch ⓓ 05/24 Bruns 2578
Frank Westphal Orch ⓓ 07/24 Col 112-D
Margaret Young 06/24 Bruns 2596

NOLA
Sam Fox, pub. 1916, reached #14 in July 1924
(Also reached #8 in July 1922)
(Also reached #11 in August 1950)
Words added 1924
James F Burns w, Felix Arndt m
Vincent Lopez Orch, db dates, 01/24 Okeh 4777
Eddie Foy, vv stage
Phil Baker Orch, db dates

OLD FASHIONED LOVE
Harms, pub. 1923, reached #18 in February 1924
Cecil Mack w, James P Johnson m
Featured in RUNNIN' WILD, show (opened 10/23)
Adelaide Hall, sung in show
Frank Crumit 12/23 Col A-3997
Cliff Edwards[3] 02/24 Pathe 21097
Noble Sissle & Eubie Blake 03/24 Vic 19253

THE ONE I LOVE BELONGS TO SOMEBODY ELSE (22)
M Weil, pub. 1924, reached #2 in April 1924
Gus Kahn w, Isham Jones m
Isham Jones/Ray Miller Orch[5] ⓓ 03/24 Bruns 2555
Al Jolson/Isham Jones Orch ⓓ 04/24 Bruns 2567
Sophie Tucker, vv stage, 05/24 Okeh 40054
Paul Whiteman Orch ⓓ 03/24 Vic 19245
Ted Lewis Band 04/24 Col 52-D

AN ORANGE GROVE IN CALIFORNIA (37)
Berlin, pub. 1923, reached #6 in February 1924
Irving Berlin w & m
Featured in MUSIC BOX REVUE OF 1923-24, show (opened 09/23)
John Steel & Grace Moore, sung in show
Paul Whiteman Orch ⓓ 12/23 Vic 19169
John Steel ⓓ 02/24 Vic 19219

PUT AWAY A LITTLE RAY OF GOLDEN SUNSHINE FOR A RAINY DAY
H Waterson, pub. 1924, reached #5 in December 1924
Sam Lewis & Joe Young w, Fred Ahlert m
Aileen Stanley ⓓ 11/24 Vic 19443
Lewis James ⓓ 12/24 Col 214-D
Arden-Ohman Orch 11/24 Bruns 2670

RAGGEDY ANN (41)
T B Harms, pub. 1923, reached #5 in March 1924
Anne Caldwell w, Jerome Kern m
Featured in THE STEPPING STONES, show (opened 11/23)
Dorothy & Fred Stone, sung in show
Paul Whiteman Orch ⓓ 01/24 Vic 19187
Vincent Lopez Orch 02/24 Okeh 40009

RED HOT MAMMA
Berlin, pub. 1924, reached #11 in August 1924
Gilbert Wells, Bud Cooper, Fred Stone w & m
Sophie Tucker ⓓ vv stage, 08/24 Okeh 40129
Coon-Sanders Orch, db dates, 06/24 Vic 19316
Original Memphis Five 09/24 Col 155-D
Ben Bernie Orch, db dates

REMEMB'RING (18)
Berlin, pub. 1923, reached #2 in March 1924
Rosetta & Vivian Duncan w & m
Featured in TOPSY AND EVA, show
(opened 07/23 San Francisco, 12/23 Chicago, 12/24 New York)
Duncan Sisters ⓓ sung in show, 02/24 Vic 19206
Paul Ash Orch ⓓ 01/24 Bruns 2498
Joe Raymond Orch ⓓ 01/24 Vic 19178

RHAPSODY IN BLUE (46)
Harms, pub. 1924, reached #14 in October 1924
(Also reached #18 in November 1943)
George Gershwin m
Paul Whiteman/George Gershwin[1] 10/24 Vic 55225
George Gershwin, stage

ROCK-A-BYE MY BABY BLUES
Sherman Clay, pub. 1924, reached #15 in November 1924
Larry Yoell & Billy Hill w & m
The Troubadours 09/24 Vic 19387
The Cavaliers 12/24 Col 208-D
Carl Fenton Orch 12/24 Bruns 2690

SAN
Van Alstyne & Curtis, pub. 1920, reached #11 in Sept. 1924
Lindsay McPhail & Walter Michels w & m
Ted Lewis Band 07/24 Col 122-D
Paul Whiteman Orch 09/24 Vic 19381

SHE WOULDN'T DO (WHAT I ASKED HER TO)
Richmond-Robbins, pub. 1923, reached #10 in April 1924
Sam Gottlieb, Philip Boutelje, Al Burt, Sidney D Mitchell w & m
The Virginians/Billy Murray Φ 03/24 Vic 19241
Original Memphis Five 03/24 Col 37-D
Warner's Seven Aces, vv stage

SHINE (35)
Shapiro, B, pub. 1924, reached #5 in July 1924
(Also reached #14 in April 1948)
Cecil Mack & Lew Brown w, Ford Dabney m
The Virginians 07/24 Vic 19334
Van & Schenck, vv stage, 09/24 Col 149-D
California Ramblers 07/24 Col 127-D

SINCE MA IS PLAYING MAH JONG
Witmark, pub. 1924, reached #15 in June 1924
Billy Rose w, Con Conrad m
Featured in KID BOOTS, show (opened 12/23)
Eddie Cantor, sung in show
Original Memphis Five 05/24 Col 74-D
Jim Doherty 04/24 Ed 51299

SITTIN' IN A CORNER (12)
Berlin, pub. 1923, reached #2 in January 1924
Gus Kahn w, George Meyer m
Van & Schenck Φ vv stage, 01/24 Col 6-D
Paul Whiteman Orch Φ 12/23 Vic 19161
Brox Sisters/Isham Jones Orch 01/24 Bruns 2538

SLEEP (13)
Sherman Clay, pub. 1923, reached #2 in February 1924
(Also reached #14 in November 1960)
Earl Lebieg w & m
Waring's Pennsylvanians/w.vocal duo ΦΦ 01/24 Vic 19172
Romancers Orch 01/24 Col 29-D
Ben Selvin Orch 01/24 Voc 14695

A SMILE WILL GO A LONG, LONG WAY (17)
Waterson, B & S ΦΦΦ, pub. 1923, reached #2 in April 1924
Benny Davis & Harry Akst w & m
Ted Weems Orch Φ 04/24 Vic 19258
Henry Santrey, vv stage
Leo Reisman Orch 04/24 Col 71-D
Sam Lanin's Orch, db dates, 04/24 Okeh 40053

SOMEBODY LOVES ME (16)
Harms, pub. 1924, reached #4 in November 1924
Ballard MacDonald & Bud DeSylva w, George Gershwin m
Featured in GEORGE WHITE'S SCANDALS OF 1924, show (opened 06/24)
All-time pop standard
Paul Whiteman Orch Φ 10/24 Vic 19414
Cliff Edwards[3] Φ vv stage, 11/24 Pathe 32073
Blossom Seeley, vv stage
Winnie Lightner, sung in show
Marion Harris Φ 12/24 Bruns 2735

SOMEBODY STOLE MY GAL (26)
Denton & Haskins, pub. 1918, reached #4 in March 1924
(Also reached #17 in May 1953)
Leo Wood w & m
Ted Weems Orch ΦΦ 02/24 Vic 19212
Aileen Stanley, vv stage

SPAIN (24)
M Weil, pub. 1924, reached #4 in July 1924
Gus Kahn w, Isham Jones m
Isham Jones Orch Φ 06/24 Bruns 2600
Paul Whiteman Orch Φ 07/24 Vic 19330
Leo Reisman Orch 08/24 Col 134-D

SWEET LITTLE YOU
M Abrahams, pub. 1924, reached #20 in November 1924
Fred Phillips w, Irving Bibo m
Abe Lyman/Charles Kaley 08/24 Bruns 2631
Belle Baker, vv stage, 11/24 Vic 19436
Ted Lewis Band, vv stage, 11/24 Col 195-D

TAKE OH TAKE THOSE LIPS AWAY
L Feist, pub. 1923, reached #11 in February 1924
Joe McCarthy w, Harry Tierney m
Featured in ZIEGFELD FOLLIES OF 1923, show (opened 10/23)
Ann Pennington, sung in show
Brooke Johns Orch, db dates, 02/24 Vic 19204
Paul Specht Orch 01/24 Col 27-D

TEA FOR TWO (27)
Harms ΦΦΦ, pub. 1924, reached #3 in December 1924
(Also reached #19 in January 1926)
(Also reached #6 in October 1958)
Irving Caesar w, Vincent Youmans m
Featured in NO, NO, NANETTE, show (opened 05/24 in Chicago)
Steady seller, 1920's, and all-time pop standard
John Barker & Louise Groody, sung in show
Benson Orch Φ 11/24 Vic 19438
Marion Harris Φ 01/25 Bruns 2747

THERE'LL BE SOME CHANGES MADE
E B Marks, pub. 1921, reached #17 in Dec 1924
(Also reached #1 in April 1941)
Billy Higgins w, W Benton Overstreet m
Jazz standard 1920's to 1940's
Ethel Waters, vv stage (Earlier: 1921 Black Swan 2021)
Sophie Tucker, vv stage (Later: 1927 Okeh 40921)
Ted Lewis Orch 10/24 Col 170-D
Marion Harris, vv stage, 09/24 Bruns 2651

THERE'S YES! YES! IN YOUR EYES (19)
J H Remick, pub. 1924, reached #2 in July 1924
(Also reached #15 in September 1949)
Cliff Friend w, Joe Santly m
Paul Whiteman Orch ΦΦ 06/24 Vic 19309
Art Kahn 06/24 Col 109-D
Wendell Hall, vv stage
Nick Lucas, vv stage

THE WALTZ OF LONG AGO (42)
Berlin, pub. 1923, reached #7 in March 1924
Irving Berlin w & m
Featured in MUSIC BOX REVUE OF 1923-24, show (opened 09/23)
Grace Moore, sung in show
The Troubadours Φ 01/24 Vic 19174
Paul Specht Orch 01/24 Col 13-D

WHAT HAS BECOME OF HINKY DINKY PARLAY VOO (44)
J Mills, pub. 1924, reached #9 in August 1924
Al Dubin, Irving Mills, Jimmy McHugh, Irwin Dash w & m
Billy Jones & Ernest Hare[4] 08/24 Col 132-D, 08/24 Okeh 40128
Billy Murray & Ed Smalle 09/24 Vic 19388
Vincent Lopez Orch, db dates

WHAT'LL I DO? (1)
Berlin ΦΦΦ, pub. 1924, reached #1 in June 1924
Irving Berlin w & m
Added to MUSIC BOX REVUE OF 1923-24, show (opened 09/23)
Paul Whiteman Orch ΦΦ 06/24 Vic 19299
Grace Moore & John Steel, sung in show
Marcia Freer & Henry Burr ΦΦ 06/24 Vic 19301
Lewis James Φ 07/24 Col 115-D
Elsie Janis, vv stage

WHEN LIGHTS ARE LOW (30)
L Feist, pub. 1923, reached #7 in April 1924
Gus Kahn & Ted Koehler w, Ted FioRito m
Benson Orch Φ 01/24 Vic 19198
Ted FioRito Orch, db dates
Carl Fenton Orch 02/24 Bruns 2520
Romancers Orch 03/24 Col 41-D

WHERE THE LAZY DAISIES GROW (23)
J H Remick, pub. 1924, reached #2 in May 1924
Cliff Friend w & m
Frank Crumit Φ 05/24 Vic 19275
Cliff Edwards[3], vv stage, 04/24 Banner 1328, 04/24 Regal 9620
Van & Schenck, vv stage
Jean Goldkette Orch 06/24 Vic 19308

WHY DID I KISS THAT GIRL? (25)
Shapiro, B, pub. 1924, reached #5 in June 1924
Lew Brown w, Robert King & Ray Henderson m
Paul Whiteman/American Quartet Φ 04/24 Vic 19267
Bennie Krueger/w.vocal duo 05/24 Bruns 2576
Billy Jones/Columbia Novelty Orch 08/24 Col 131-D

[1]George Gershwin on piano
[2]Jolson's Brunswick recording was with the Isham Jones Orch.
[3]Cliff Edwards was also known as Ukulele Ike.
[4]Jones and Hare were also known as The Happiness Boys.
[5]Isham Jones leading the Ray Miller Orchestra

1925

ALABAMY BOUND (12)
Shapiro, B ΦΦΦ, pub. 1925, reached #1 in May 1925
Bud DeSylva & Bud Green w, Ray Henderson m
Blossom Seeley Φ vv stage, 04/25 Col 304-D
Al Jolson, vv stage
Paul Whiteman Orch ΦΦ 03/25 Vic 19557
Eddie Cantor, vv stage
Isham Jones Orch Φ 03/25 Bruns 2789

ALL ALONE (1)
Berlin ΦΦΦ, pub. 1924, reached #1 in January 1925
Irving Berlin w & m
Featured in MUSIC BOX REVUE OF 1924-25, show (opened 12/24)
Paul Whiteman Orch ΦΦ 12/24 Vic 19487
John McCormack Φ 02/25 Vic 1067
Al Jolson Φ 12/24 Bruns 2743
Grace Moore & Oscar Shaw, sung in show
Lewis James 01/25 Vic 19495, 01/25 Col 235-D

ANGRY (38)
Ted Browne, pub. 1925, reached #7 in November 1925
Dudley Mecum w, Henry Brunies, Merritt Brunies & Jules Cassard m
Ted Lewis Band 09/25 Col 416-D
Art Gillham 09/25 Col 411-D
Wendell Hall 01/26 Vic 19819

BROWN EYES, WHY ARE YOU BLUE? (14)
H Waterson, pub. 1925, reached #2 in December 1925
Alfred Bryan w, George W Meyer m
Nick Lucas Φ vv stage, 12/25 Bruns 2461
Franklyn Baur Φ 12/25 Vic 19806
Carl Fenton/Frank Munn Φ 11/25 Bruns 2950
Selvin's Orch 11/25 Voc 15110

BY THE LIGHT OF THE STARS
J H Remick, pub. 1925, reached #20 in August 1925
George A Little, Arthur Sizemore, Larry Shay w & m
Harry Reser Orch 07/25 Col 366-D
Jan Garber Orch 08/25 Vic 19689
Nick Lucas, vv stage, 09/25 Bruns 2906

CECILIA (22)
Berlin, pub. 1925, reached #2 in November 1925
Herman Ruby w, Dave Dreyer m
"Whispering" Jack Smith ΦΦ vv stage, 12/25 Vic 19787
Art Gillham Φ 10/25 Col 411-D
Johnny Hamp/w.vocal trio 11/25 Vic 19756

THE CHARLESTON (16)
Harms, pub. 1923, reached #10 in December 1925
(Also reached #20 in January 1924)
Cecil Mack & James P Johnson w & m
Became the dance sensation of the mid-1920's
Paul Whiteman Orch ФD 07/25 Vic 19671
Aunt Jemima, vv stage
Isham Jones Orch ФD 12/25 Bruns 2970
The Knickerbockers[1] 06/25 Col 355-D
Tennessee Tooters 10/25 Voc 15086

CHEATIN' ON ME (39)
Ager, Y & B, pub. 1925, reached #7 in June 1925
Jack Yellen w, Lew Pollack m
Warner's Seven Aces ФD 04/25 Col 305-D
Sophie Tucker, vv stage
Don Clark Orch ФD 06/25 Vic 19622
The Melody Sheiks 05/25 Okeh 40326

CLOSE YOUR EYES
Sherman Clay, pub. 1925, reached #17 in November 1925
Larry Yoell w, Charles Vincent m
Leo Reisman Orch 11/25 Col 456-D
Max Dolin Orch, db dates, 12/25 Vic 19789

COLLEGIATE (9)
Shapiro, B, pub. 1925, reached #1 in August 1925
Moe Jaffe & Nat Bonx w & m
Waring's Pennsylvanians /vocal group ФDФD 07/25 Vic 19648
Jones & Hare[2] ФD 07/25 Col 410-D, 08/25 Pathe 32129
The Knickerbockers[1] 08/25 Col 391-D
Lasky Players, vv stage

COPENHAGEN (28)
Melrose, pub. 1924, reached #2 in February 1925
Walter Melrose w, Charlie Davis m
Benson Orch ФD db dates, 12/24 Vic 19470
Arkansas Travellers 01/25 Okeh 40236
California Ramblers 02/25 Col 236-D

DEEP IN MY HEART, DEAR
Harms, pub. 1924, reached #9 in March 1925
Dorothy Donnelly w, Sigmund Romberg m
Featured in THE STUDENT PRINCE, show (opened 12/24)
Ilse Marvenga & Howard Marsh, sung in show
The Troubadours ФD 02/25 Vic 19529

DON'T BRING LULU (18)
J H Remick, pub. 1925, reached #2 in July 1925
Billy Rose & Lew Brown w, Ray Henderson m
Billy Murray ФD 06/25 Vic 19628
Bennie Krueger/Billy Jones ФD 06/25 Bruns 2859
Van & Schenck, vv stage
Avon Comedy Four, vv stage
Jones & Hare[2] 06/25 Okeh 40354

EVERYBODY LOVES MY BABY (21)
Clarence Wms M P C, pub. 1924, reached #2 in March 1925
Jack Palmer & Spencer Williams w & m
Aileen Stanley ФD vv stage, 12/24 Vic 19486
Ruth Etting, vv stage and radio
Blossom Seeley ФD 04/25 Col 304-D
Alberta Hunter 01/25 Gennett 5594
Clarence Williams/Eva Taylor 02/25 Okeh 8181

EVERYTHING IS HOTSY-TOTSY NOW
J Mills, pub. 1925, reached #16 in August 1925
Irving Mills w, Jimmy McHugh m
Gene Austin 07/25 Vic 19656
Cliff Edwards[3], stage
Hotsy-Totsy Boys, radio
Van & Schenck 07/25 Col 352-D

FASCINATING RHYTHM (33)
Harms, pub. 1924, reached #6 in March 1925
Ira Gershwin w, George Gershwin m
Featured in LADY BE GOOD!, show (opened 12/24)
Cliff Edwards[3] ФD sung in show, 02/25 Pathe 25126
Adele & Fred Astaire, sung and danced in show
Paul Whiteman Orch ФD 03/25 Vic 19551

I MISS MY SWISS (24)
L Feist, pub. 1925, reached #5 in October 1925
L Wolfe Gilbert w, Abel Baer m
Jones & Hare[2] ФD 09/25 Vic 19718, 09/25 Col 410-D
Paul Whiteman/John Sperzel ФD 11/25 Vic 19753
Ted Lewis Band 09/25 Col 406-D

I'LL SEE YOU IN MY DREAMS (3)
L Feist, pub. 1924, reached #1 in April 1925
Gus Kahn w, Isham Jones m
Isham Jones[4]/Frank Bessinger ФDФD 02/25 Bruns 2788
Paul Whiteman Orch ФD 03/25 Vic 19553
Marion Harris ФD 02/25 Bruns 2784
Ford & Glenn 04/25 Col 303-D
Yvette Rugel, vv stage

I'M GONNA CHARLESTON BACK TO CHARLESTON
J H Remick, pub. 1925, reached #20 in November 1925
Roy Turk & Lou Handman w & m
The Revelers 11/25 Vic 19778
Goofus Five 10/25 Okeh 40442
California Ramblers, db dates

IF YOU KNEW SUSIE (13)
Shapiro, B ФDФDФD, pub. 1925, reached #1 in July 1925
Bud DeSylva & Joseph Meyer w & m
Featured in BIG BOY, show (opened 01/25)
Eddie Cantor ФD vv stage, 07/25 Col 364-D
Al Jolson, sung in show
Cliff Edwards[3] ФD 07/25 Pathe 25141, 07/25 Perf 11575
Jones & Hare[2] ФD 08/25 Bruns 2888
The Melody Sheiks 06/25 Okeh 40357

IN SHADOWLAND (47)
H Waterson, pub. 1924, reached #13 in June 1925
Sam Lewis & Joe Young w, Ruth Brooks & Fred Ahlert m
The Troubadours 05/25 Vic 19612
Ben Selvin Orch 04/25 Voc 14963
Jan Garber Orch, db dates

INDIAN LOVE CALL (6)
Harms ΦΦΦ, pub. 1924, reached #7 in March 1925
(Also reached #20 in January 1937)
(Also reached #13 in September 1952)
Otto Harbach & Oscar Hammerstein 2nd w, Rudolf Friml m
Featured in ROSE MARIE, show (opened 09/24)
Dennis King & Mary Ellis, sung in show
Paul Whiteman Orch Φ 01/25 Vic 19517
Olive Kline Φ 01/25 Vic 45456
Leo Reisman Orch 02/25 Col 242-D

JUNE BROUGHT THE ROSES (30)
Harms, pub. 1924, reached #7 in April 1925
Ralph Stanley w, John Openshaw m
The Troubadours 12/24 Vic 19458
Marcia Freer 08/24 Vic 19347
John McCormack 07/25 Vic 1086

JUST A LITTLE DRINK
Villa Moret, pub. 1925, reached #19 in August 1925
Byron Gay w & m
Paul Whiteman/w.vocal quartet 07/25 Vic 19666
Ray Miller Orch 07/25 Bruns 2866

KEEP SMILING AT TROUBLE (43)
Harms, pub. 1924, reached #8 in April 1925
Al Jolson & Bud DeSylva w, Lewis Gensler m
Featured in BIG BOY, show (opened 01/25)
Al Jolson, sung in show
Shannon Quartet Φ 04/25 Vic 19588
The Columbians 05/25 Col 313-D

LET IT RAIN! LET IT POUR! (I'LL BE IN VIRGINIA IN THE MORNING) (48)
L Feist, pub. 1925, reached #17 in June 1925
Cliff Friend w, Walter Donaldson m
Added to THE GRAB BAG, show (opened 10/24)
Earl & Bell, sung in show, 05/25 Voc 14976
International Novelty Orch/Vernon Dalhart 06/25 Vic 19624
Cliff Edwards[3] 04/25 Harmograph 1015, 05/25 Perfect 11563

LET ME CALL YOU SWEETHEART (25)
Harold Rossiter ΦΦΦ, pub. 1910, reached #9 in October 1925
(Also reached #1 in February 1911)
Beth Slater Whitson w, Leo Friedman m
Steady seller, 1924-26
International Novelty Orch/Lewis James Φ 12/24 Vic 19475
Halfway House Dance Orch 12/25 Col 476-D
Shannon Quartet 04/26 Vic 19941

LET ME LINGER (LONGER) IN YOUR ARMS
L Feist, pub. 1924, reached #14 in August 1925
Cliff Friend w, Abel Baer m
Paul Whiteman/Lewis James 08/25 Vic 19692
Cliff Edwards[3] 04/25 Pathe 25132, 05/25 Perf 11566
Eva Shirley, vv stage

LISTENING
Berlin, pub. 1925, reached #20 in May 1925
Irving Berlin w & m
Featured in MUSIC BOX REVUE OF 1924-25, show (opened 12/24)
Grace Moore, sung in show, 06/25 Vic 19613
Phil Spitalny Orch 02/25 Vic 19541

MANDY, MAKE UP YOUR MIND
Berlin, pub. 1924, reached #12 in January 1925
Grant Clarke & Roy Turk w, George Meyer & Arthur Johnston m
Featured in DIXIE TO BROADWAY, show (opened 10/24)
Brox Sisters 01/25 Vic 19510
Paul Whiteman Orch 01/25 Vic 19492
Florence Mills, sung in show

MANHATTAN (26)
E B Marks, pub. 1925, reached #5 in October 1925
Lorenz Hart w, Richard Rodgers m
Featured in GARRICK GAIETIES, show (opened 05/25)
Paul Whiteman Orch Φ 11/25 Vic 19769
Sterling Holloway & June Cochrane, sung in show
The Knickerbockers[1] 10/25 Col 422-D

MIDNIGHT WALTZ (27)
L Feist, pub. 1925, reached #8 in July 1925
Gus Kahn w, Walter Donaldson m
International Novelty Orch/w.vocal duo Φ 05/25 Vic 19612
The Cavaliers[5] 05/25 Col 331-D
Lewis James 07/25 Col 375-D
Jan Garber Orch, db dates

MILENBERG JOYS (34)
Melrose, pub. 1925, reached #11 in September 1925
Walter Melrose w, Leon Rappolo, Paul Mares & Ferdinand "Jelly Roll" Morton m
Tennessee Tooters 09/25 Voc 15068
Jimmy Joy Orch 03/25 Okeh 40251
Ted Lewis Band 10/25 Col 439-D
Art Landry Orch, db dates

MONTMARTRE ROSE (45)
E B Marks, pub. 1925, reached #9 in October 1925
Tommy Lyman w & m
Tommy Lyman, radio, 09/25 Vic 19712
Jan Garber/Jack Gifford 08/25 Vic 19676
Victor Salon Orch 08/25 Vic 19695

MOONLIGHT AND ROSES (2)
Villa Moret ΦΦΦ, pub. 1925, reached #2 in October 1925
Ben Black, Neil Moret, Edwin Lemare w & m
John McCormack ΦΦ 08/25 Vic 1092
Ray Miller/w.vocal duo Φ 06/25 Bruns 2866
Henry Halstead/Marion Fonville 06/25 Vic 19579
Austin Wylie Orch 05/25 Voc 14993
Paul Ash Orch, db dates

MY BEST GIRL (23)
J H Remick, pub. 1924, reached #2 in February 1925
Walter Donaldson w & m
Georgie Price Φ 12/24 Vic 19465
Cliff Edwards[3] Φ 12/24 Pathe 32088
Isham Jones Orch Φ 01/25 Bruns 2750
Nick Lucas 02/25 Bruns 2768

MY SWEETIE TURNED ME DOWN (41)
Berlin, pub. 1925, reached #6 in October 1925
Gus Kahn w, Walter Donaldson m
Frank Crumit Φ 08/25 Vic 19701
J Russel Robinson 08/25 Col 389-D
Ponce Sisters, vv stage

NOBODY KNOWS WHAT A RED-HEADED MAMA CAN DO (50)
J Mills, pub. 1925, reached #16 in March 1925
Irving Mills & Al Dubin w, Sammy Fain m
Margaret Young 03/25 Bruns 2806
Ray Miller Orch 02/25 Bruns 2778
Original Memphis Five 04/25 Col 308-D

OH, HOW I MISS YOU TONIGHT (11)
Berlin ΦΦΦ, pub. 1925, reached #3 in July 1925
Benny Davis, Joe Burke, Mark Fisher w & m
Lewis James ΦΦ 06/25 Vic 19623, 07/25 Col 365-D
The Cavaliers[5] Φ 06/25 Col 359-D
Benson Orch Φ 08/25 Vic 19685
Irving Kaufman 07/25 Voc 15023
Joseph M White, radio

OH, KATHARINA! (7)
L Feist, pub. 1924, reached #2 in May 1925
Fritz Lohner & L Wolfe Gilbert w, Richard Fall m
Featured in CHAUVE SOURIS OF 1924-25, show (1924)
Ted Lewis Band ΦΦ vv stage, 04/25 Col 295-D
Billy Murray Φ 06/25 Vic 19628
Eddie Cantor, vv stage
Nikita Balieff, sung in show
International Novelty Orch/Vernon Dalhart Φ 04/25 Vic 19586

OH, LADY BE GOOD (46)
Harms, pub. 1924, reached #8 in March 1925
Ira Gershwin w, George Gershwin m
Featured in LADY BE GOOD, show (opened 12/24)
Walter Catlett, sung in show
Paul Whiteman Orch Φ 03/25 Vic 19551
Cliff Edwards[3] Φ 03/25 Pathe 25130

OH, MABEL (49)
Berlin, pub. 1924, reached #12 in April 1925
Gus Kahn w, Ted FioRito m
Waring's Pennsylvanians 03/25 Vic 19533
Billy Murray 04/25 Vic 19563
California Ramblers 03/25 Col 268-D, 04/25 Ed 51491

PAL OF MY CRADLE DAYS (15)
L Feist ΦΦΦ, pub. 1925, reached #4 in October 1925
Marshall Montgomery w, Al Piantadosi m
Lewis James Φ 07/25 Col 375-D
Paul Whiteman/Lewis James Φ 08/25 Vic 19690
Frank Munn 09/25 Bruns 2922
Sylvia Froos, vv stage

THE PAL THAT I LOVED STOLE THE GAL THAT LOVED (32)
L Feist, pub. 1924, reached #4 in January 1925
Harry Pease w, Ed Nelson m
Lewis James Φ 12/24 Vic 19473, 12/24 Col 225-D
Vernon Dalhart 10/24 Pathe 32072, 11/24 Okeh 40177
Charles Dornberger/Franklyn Baur 02/25 Vic 19500
Sylvia Froos, vv stage

REMEMBER (4)
Berlin ΦΦΦ, pub. 1925, reached #1 in November 1925
Irving Berlin w & m
Henry Burr ΦΦ 11/25 Vic 19780
Paul Whiteman/Elliot Shaw ΦΦ 10/25 Vic 19726
Isham Jones Orch Φ 12/25 Bruns 2963
Belle Baker, vv stage
Lewis James Φ 11/25 Col 451-D

RIVERBOAT SHUFFLE (35)
J Mills, pub. 1925, reached #11 in August 1925
Hoagy Carmichael, Dick Voynow & Irving Mills m
The Wolverines, db dates, 08/24 Gennett 5454
Isham Jones Orch 06/25 Bruns 2854
Cotton Club Orch 07/25 Col 374-D

ROSE-MARIE (19)
Harms, pub. 1924, reached #3 in February 1925
Otto Harbach & Oscar Hammerstein 2nd w, Rudolf Friml m
Featured in ROSE-MARIE, show (opened 09/24)
Paul Whiteman Orch ΦΦ 12/24 Vic 19461
Dennis King & Arthur Deagon, sung in show
John McCormack Φ 02/25 Vic 1067
Lambert Murphy 01/25 Vic 45456

SAVE YOUR SORROW (FOR TOMORROW) (40)
Shapiro, B, pub. 1925, reached #6 in November 1925
Bud DeSylva w, Al Sherman m
Shannon Four Φ 09/25 Col 404-D
George Olsen/Billy Murray Φ 10/25 Vic 19715
Gene Austin, stage, 02/26 Vic 19857
Radio Franks[6], radio

SENTIMENTAL ME (AND ROMANTIC YOU) (42)
E B Marks, pub. 1925, reached #8 in November 1925
Lorenz Hart w, Richard Rodgers m
Featured by ensemble in GARRICK GAIETIES, show (op. 05/25)
The Knickerbockers[1] ⏀ 10/25 Col 422-D
Arden-Ohman Orch 01/26 Bruns 2984
Paul Whiteman Orch, db dates

SERENADE
Harms, pub. 1924, reached #14 in March 1925
Dorothy Donnelly w, Sigmund Romberg m
Featured in THE STUDENT PRINCE, show (opened 12/24)
Howard Marsh, sung in show
Victor Male Chorus 03/25 Vic 19550

SHOW ME THE WAY
Berlin, pub. 1924, reached #13 in February 1925
Benny Davis w, Ted Lewis & Frank Ross m
Ted Lewis Band, db dates, 02/25 Col 241-D
Coon-Sanders' Night Hawks 02/25 Vic 19525

SOMETIME (31)
J H Remick, pub. 1925, reached #3 in December 1925
(Also reached #16 in September 1950)
Gus Kahn w, Ted FioRito m
Jack Shilkret's Orch ⏀ 10/25 Vic 19745
Elsie Baker ⏀ 09/25 Vic 45489
Amelita Galli-Curci 06/26 Vic 1144
Ipana Troubadours, db dates

SWANEE BUTTERFLY
J H Remick, pub. 1925, reached #16 in June 1925
Billy Rose w, Walter Donaldson m
Isham Jones Orch 06/25 Bruns 2854
Waring's Pennsylvanians 07/25 Vic 19636
Georgie Price 07/25 Vic 19654

SWEET GEORGIA BROWN (17)
J H Remick, pub. 1925, reached #2 in August 1925
(Also reached #15 in February 1949)
Maceo Pinkard, Kenneth Casey, Ben Bernie w & m
Ethel Waters ⏀ 07/25 Col 379-D
Ben Bernie Orch ⏀ db dates, 06/25 Voc 15002
Isham Jones Orch ⏀ 09/25 Bruns 2913
Helen Morgan, stage

TELL HER IN THE SPRINGTIME
Berlin, pub. 1924, reached #18 in March 1925
Irving Berlin w & m
Featured in MUSIC BOX REVUE OF 1924-25, show (opened 12/24)
Grace Moore, sung in show, 06/25 Vic 19613
Paul Whiteman Orch 01/25 Vic 19517

UKULELE LADY (10)
Berlin, pub. 1925, reached #2 in August 1925
Gus Kahn w, Richard Whiting m
Paul Whiteman/Southern Fall Colored Quartet ⏀⏀ 08/25 Vic 19690
Vaughn DeLeath ⏀ radio, 07/25 Col 361-D
Frank Crumit ⏀ 08/25 Vic 19701
Nick Lucas, vv stage
Duncan Sisters, vv stage

WEST OF THE GREAT DIVIDE (37)
Witmark, pub. 1924, reached #11 in May 1925
George Whiting w, Ernest Ball m
Charles Hart ⏀ 05/25 Col 273-D
Henry Burr 07/25 Vic 19651

WHEN MY SUGAR WALKS DOWN THE STREET (29)
J Mills, pub. 1925, reached #6 in June 1925
Irving Mills, Gene Austin, Jimmy McHugh w & m
Aileen Stanley & Gene Austin ⏀ 04/25 Vic 19585
Waring's Pennsylvanians ⏀ 05/25 Vic 19610
Gene Austin, vv stage
Warner's Seven Aces 04/25 Col 305-D

WHEN YOU AND I WERE SEVENTEEN (20)
Berlin, pub. 1924, reached #5 in April 1925
Gus Kahn w, Charles Rosoff m
Helen Clark & Lewis James ⏀ 04/25 Vic 19588
Marion Harris 04/25 Bruns 2836
Ruth Etting, vv stage and radio
Phil Spitalny Orch 02/25 Vic 19541

WHO TAKES CARE OF THE CARETAKER'S DAUGHTER (WHILE THE CARETAKER'S BUSY TAKING CARE) (36)
Shapiro, B, pub. 1924, reached #8 in June 1925
Chick Endor w & m
Featured in LADY BE GOOD, show (opened 12/24)
Cliff Edwards[3] ⏀ sung in show, 03/25 Pathe 25128
Whitey Kaufman Orch 06/25 Vic 19638
Jones & Hare[2] 07/25 Bruns 2888

WHY DO I LOVE YOU SO?
Harms, pub. 1925, reached #20 in August 1925
Ira Gershwin & Bud DeSylva w, George Gershwin m
Featured in TELL ME MORE, show (opened 04/25)
Esther Howard & Lou Holtz, sung in show
Paul Whiteman Orch 08/25 Vic 19682

YEARNING (JUST FOR YOU) (8)
Berlin, pub. 1925, reached #1 in June 1925
Benny Davis & Joe Burke w & m
Gene Austin ⏀⏀ 05/25 Vic 19625
Roger Wolfe Kahn/Elliot Shaw ⏀ 05/25 Vic 19616
Harry Reser Orch 05/25 Col 319-D
Paul Whiteman Orch, db dates

YES SIR! THAT'S MY BABY (5)
Berlin ΦΦΦ, pub. 1925, reached #1 in September 1925
Gus Kahn w, Walter Donaldson m
Gene Austin ΦΦ 07/25 Vic 19656
Eddie Cantor, vv stage
Blossom Seeley Φ vv stage, 08/25 Col 386-D
Ben Bernie Orch Φ 10/25 Voc 15080
Ace Brigode/w.vocal duo 08/25 Col 398-D

YOU'RE JUST A FLOWER FROM AN OLD BOUQUET (44)
J W Jenkins, pub. 1924, reached #7 in February 1925
Gwynne Denni w, Lucien Denni m
Vincent Lopez/Bruce Wallace Φ 01/25 Okeh 40218
Lewis James 02/25 Col 250-D
Helen Clark & Elliot Shaw 04/25 Vic 19555

[1]The Knickerbockers were actually the Ben Selvin Orch.
[2]Jones & Hare were also known as The Happiness Boys.
[3]Cliff Edwards was also known as Ukulele Ike.
[4]Isham Jones conducting the Ray Miller Orch with vocal as indicated.
[5]The Cavaliers were actually the Ben Selvin Orch.
[6]The Radio Franks were Frank Bessinger and Frank White.

1926

(WHAT CAN I SAY) AFTER I SAY I'M SORRY (10)
L Feist, pub. 1926, reached #2 in May 1926
Abe Lyman w, Walter Donaldson m
Abe Lyman/Charles Kaley Φ 04/26 Bruns 3069
Jean Goldkette/Frank Bessinger Φ 04/26 Vic 19947
Bee Palmer, stage
Ruth Etting, stage and radio

ALWAYS (1)
Berlin ΦΦΦ, pub. 1925, reached #1 in April 1926
(Also reached #6 in November 1944)
Irving Berlin w & m
Henry Burr ΦΦ 04/26 Vic 19959
George Olsen/w.vocal trio ΦΦ 04/26 Vic 19955
Vincent Lopez Orch Φ 04/26 Okeh 40567
Nick Lucas 04/26 Bruns 3088
Irving Berlin, stage

AM I WASTING MY TIME ON YOU? (48)
Stasny, pub. 1926, reached #12 in August 1926
Irving Bibo & Howard Johnson w & m
Lewis James 07/26 Col 629-D
Elliot Shaw 08/26 Vic 20070
Phil Romano, stage

AT PEACE WITH THE WORLD (43)
Berlin, pub. 1926, reached #7 in July 1926
Irving Berlin w & m
Al Jolson Φ vv stage, 07/26 Bruns 3196
Roger Wolfe Kahn/Henry Burr Φ 07/26 Vic 20045
Lewis James & Franklyn Baur Φ 07/26 Vic 20057
Isham Jones Orch 07/26 Bruns 3199

BABY FACE (9)
J H Remick ΦΦΦ, pub. 1926, reached #1 in October 1926
(Also reached #4 in May 1948)
(Also reached #14 in February 1976)
Benny Davis w, Harry Akst m
Jan Garber/Benny Davis ΦΦ 09/26 Vic 20105
Eddie Cantor, stage
"Whispering" Jack Smith Φ stage, 12/26 Vic 20229
Ruth Etting, stage and radio
Ben Selvin/<vocal Φ 09/26 Bruns 3253

BAM, BAM, BAMY SHORE (37)
J H Remick, pub. 1925, reached #9 in January 1926
Mort Dixon w, Ray Henderson m
Roger Wolfe Kahn Orch Φ 12/25 Vic 19808
Ted Lewis Band Φ 12/25 Col 478-D
The Revelers 02/26 Vic 19848

BARCELONA
L Feist, pub. 1926, reached #15 in October 1926
Gus Kahn w, Tolchard Evans m
Ben Selvin/Irving Kaufman 09/26 Bruns 3284
Nat Shilkret/Billy Murray 10/26 Vic 20113
Fred Rich/Lewis James 09/26 Col 690-D

BECAUSE I LOVE YOU (15)
Berlin, pub. 1926, reached #1 in December 1926
Irving Berlin w & m
Henry Burr ΦΦ 12/26 Vic 20258
Al Jolson, stage
John McCormack 03/27 Vic 1215
The Radiolites 12/26 Col 755-D

THE BIRTH OF THE BLUES (34)
Harms, pub. 1926, reached #6 in December 1926
Bud DeSylva & Lew Brown w, Ray Henderson m
Featured in GEORGE WHITE'S SCANDALS OF 1926, show (opened 06/26)
All-time pop standard
Harry Richman Φ sung in show, 09/26 Voc 15412
Paul Whiteman/w.vocal trio Φ 11/26 Vic 20138
The Revelers 10/26 Vic 20111

BLACK BOTTOM (14)
Harms, pub. 1926, reached #1 in December 1926
Bud DeSylva & Lew Brown w, Ray Henderson m
Featured in GEORGE WHITE'S SCANDALS OF 1926, show (opened 06/26)
Johnny Hamp Orch ΦΦ 09/26 Vic 20101
Ann Pennington, sung in show
Arden-Ohman Orch/w.vocal quartet 09/26 Bruns 3242
Howard Lanin/Frank Harris[1] 09/26 Col 689-D

THE BLUE ROOM (31)
Harms, pub. 1926, reached #8 in September 1926
Lorenz Hart w, Richard Rodgers m
Featured in THE GIRL FRIEND, show (opened 03/29)
Eva Puck & Sammy White, sung in show
The Revelers Φ 08/26 Vic 20082
Arden-Ohman Orch 07/26 Bruns 3197
The Melody Sheiks[2] 06/26 Okeh 40603

BREEZIN' ALONG WITH THE BREEZE (21)
J H Remick, pub. 1926, reached #2 in November 1926
Haven Gillespie, Seymour Simons, George Whiting w & m
Al Jolson, vv stage
Johnny Marvin Φ 10/26 Col 699-D, 10/26 Ed 51793
Helen Morgan, stage
The Revelers Φ 11/26 Vic 20140
Abe Lyman/Frank Sylvano Φ 08/26 Bruns 3240

BYE, BYE, BLACKBIRD (4)
J H Remick, pub. 1926, reached #1 in September 1926
Mort Dixon w, Ray Henderson m
Gene Austin ΦΦ 07/26 Vic 20044
Eddie Cantor, stage
George Olsen/w.vocal trio Φ 08/26 Vic 20089
Duncan Sisters, stage
Georgie Price, stage

CHERIE, I LOVE YOU (22)
Harms, pub. 1926, reached #5 in September 1926
Lillian Rosedale Goodman w & m
Ben Bernie/w.vocal duo Φ 06/26 Bruns 3170
Waring's Pennsylvanians/Tom Waring Φ 08/26 Vic 20074
Grace Moore, stage
Ross Gorman Orch Φ 07/26 Col 631-D

CLIMBING UP THE LADDER OF LOVE
Robbins-Engel, pub. 1926, reached #12 in December 1926
Raymond Klages w, Jesse Greer m
Featured in EARL CARROLL'S VANITIES, 5TH ED, show (opened 08/26)
Ted Weems/Dusty Rhodes Φ 12/26 Vic 20230
Don Voorhees/Hal Yates 12/26 Col 765-D
Thelma White & Muke de Jari, sung in show

COSSACK LOVE SONG (DON'T FORGET ME)
Harms, pub. 1925, reached #14 in May 1926
Otto Harbach & Oscar Hammerstein 2nd w, Herbert Stothart & George Gershwin m
Featured in SONG OF THE FLAME, show (opened 12/25)
Guy Robertson & Tessa Kosta, sung in show
Ipana Troubadours 04/26 Col 565-D
International Novelty Orch 04/26 Vic 19965

CROSS YOUR HEART
Harms, pub. 1926, reached #11 in December 1926
Bud DeSylva w, Lewis E Gensler m
Featured in QUEEN HIGH, show (opened 09/26)
Roger Wolfe Kahn/Henry Burr Φ 08/26 Vic 20071
Vaughn DeLeath & Ed Smalle 10/26 Col 711-D
Clarence Nordstrom & Mary Lawlor, sung in show

A CUP OF COFFEE, A SANDWICH, AND YOU (29)
Harms, pub. 1925, reached #7 in February 1926
Billy Rose & Al Dubin w, Joseph Meyer m
Featured in ANDRE CHARLOT'S REVUE OF 1926, show (opened 11/25)
Gertrude Lawrence & Jack Buchanan Φ sung in show and 02/26 Col 512-D
Leo Reisman Orch 02/26 Col 517-D
Helen Clark & Franklyn Baur 03/26 Vic 19903

DINAH (6)
H Waterson, pub. 1925, reached #1 in March 1926
(Also reached #11 in February 1932)
Sam Lewis & Joe Young w, Harry Akst m
Featured in NEW PLANTATION REVUE, revue (1925)
Added to KID BOOTS, show (opened 12/23)
Ethel Waters Φ sung in revue, 01/26 Col 487-D
The Revelers ΦΦ 01/26 Vic 19796
Eddie Cantor, sung in show
Jean Goldkette Orch Φ 04/26 Vic 19947
Cliff Edwards[3] 02/26 Pathe 25164, 02/26 Perfect 11598

DON'T WAKE ME UP (LET ME DREAM)
L Feist, pub. 1925, reached #20 in February 1926
L Wolfe Gilbert w, Mabel Wayne & Abel Baer m
Howard Lanin Orch 01/26 Vic 19797
Franklyn Baur, stage, 02/26 Col 518-D
Henry Burr 03/26 Vic 19933

DOWN BY THE WINEGAR WOIKS (47)
Shapiro, B, pub. 1925, reached #10 in March 1926
Don Bestor, Roger Lewis, Walter Donovan w & m
Aileen Stanley & Billy Murray Φ 01/26 Vic 19838
Al Bernard 01/26 Voc 15179
Don Bestor Orch, db dates

DRIFTING AND DREAMING (26)
L B Curtis, pub. 1925, reached #6 in August 1926
Haven Gillespie w, Egbert Van Alstyne, Erwin R Schmidt & Loyal Curtis m
George Olsen/w.vocal trio Φ 05/26 Vic 19569
Ted Lewis Band Φ stage, 05/26 Col 620-D
Art Gillham, stage
May Breen & Peter DeRose, radio

FIVE FOOT TWO, EYES OF BLUE (11)
L Feist, pub. 1925, reached #3 in February 1926
(Also reached #15 in June 1949)
Sam Lewis & Joe Young w, Ray Henderson m
Gene Austin ΦΦ 02/26 Vic 19899
Art Landry/Denny Curtis Φ 02/26 Vic 19850
Lanin's Redheads/Art Gillham 01/26 Col 483-D
"Whispering" Jack Smith, stage

FOR MY SWEETHEART
J H Remick, pub. 1926, reached #13 in December 1926
Gus Kahn w, Walter Donaldson m
Gene Austin 10/26 Vic 20143
Art Landry/w.vocal trio 10/26 Vic 20126
Ruth Etting, stage and radio

GIMME A LITTLE KISS, WILL YA, HUH? (23)
Berlin, pub. 1926, reached #2 in June 1926
Roy Turk, Jack Smith, Maceo Pinkard w & m
"Whispering" Jack Smith ΦΦ 06/26 Vic 19978
Jean Goldkette/w.vocal group Φ 07/26 Vic 20031
Billy Jones 05/26 Okeh 40585
Guy Lombardo Orch, db dates
Thornton Sisters, stage

THE GIRL FRIEND (40)
Harms, pub. 1926, reached #14 in September 1926
Lorenz Hart w, Richard Rodgers m
Featured in THE GIRL FRIEND, show (opened 03/26)
Eva Puck & Sammy White, sung in show
George Olsen/w.vocal trio Φ 07/26 Vic 20029
Arden-Ohman Orch 07/26 Bruns 3197

HELLO, ALOHA! HOW ARE YOU? (50)
L Feist, pub. 1926, reached #12 in September 1926
L Wolfe Gilbert w, Abel Baer m
George Olsen/Fran Frey 07/26 Vic 20060
The Radiolites/w.vocal duo 07/26 Col 646-D
The Singing Sophomores[4] 08/26 Col 652-D

HORSES (20)
L Feist, pub. 1926, reached #1 in June 1926
Byron Gay & Richard Whiting w & m
George Olsen/Fran Frey ΦΦ 05/26 Vic 19977
Ed Smalle 05/26 Bruns 3147
Paul Whiteman Orch, db dates
Roger Wolfe Kahn Orch, db dates

HOW MANY TIMES (30)
Berlin, pub. 1926, reached #9 in October 1926
Irving Berlin w & m
Bennie Krueger Orch 09/26 Bruns 3237
Nick Lucas 09/26 Bruns 3229
Brox Sisters 10/26 Vic 20123
Jones & Hare[5] 10/26 Col 700-D, 10/26 Okeh 40669

I LOVE MY BABY (28)
Shapiro, B, pub. 1925, reached #5 in March 1926
Bud Green w, Harry Warren m
Waring's Pennsylvanians/w.vocal group Φ 03/26 Vic 19905
Belle Baker, stage
Brox Sisters, stage
Aileen Stanley 04/26 Vic 19950

I NEVER KNEW (THAT ROSES GREW) (39)
Berlin, pub. 1925, reached #11 in February 1926
(Also reached #14 in August 1947)
Gus Kahn w, Ted FioRito m
Roger Wolfe Kahn Orch Φ 01/26 Vic 19845
Gene Austin Φ 02/26 Vic 19864
Sophie Tucker, stage
Radio Franks[6], radio, 01/26 Col 500-D

I WANT TO BE HAPPY
Harms, pub. 1924, reached #20 in January 1926
(Also reached #6 in December 1924)
Irving Caesar w, Vincent Youmans m
Featured in NO, NO, NANETTE, show (re-opened 09/25, NY)
Charles Winninger & Louise Groody, sung in show
Jan Garber Orch 12/25 Vic 19404

I'D CLIMB THE HIGHEST MOUNTAIN (16)
Berlin, pub. 1926, reached #2 in July 1926
Lew Brown & Sidney Clare w & m
Lillian Roth, stage
Al Jolson Φ stage, 06/26 Bruns 3183
Sophie Tucker, stage
"Whispering" Jack Smith 09/26 Vic 20038

I'M JUST WILD ABOUT ANIMAL CRACKERS
H Waterson, pub. 1926, reached #20 in September 1926
Fred Rich, Sam Coslow, Harry Link w & m
Irving Aaronson/w.vocal group 09/26 Vic 20094
Duke Ellington Orch 09/26 Gennett 3342
Lee Morse 10/26 Pathe 25190
Dell Lampe Orch, db dates

I'M SITTING ON TOP OF THE WORLD (5)
L Feist ΦΦΦ, pub. 1925, reached #2 in February 1926
(Also reached #14 in April 1953)
Sam Lewis & Joe Young w, Ray Henderson m
Al Jolson ΦΦ stage, 02/26 Bruns 3014
Roger Wolfe Kahn Orch ΦΦ 01/26 Vic 19845
Ross Gorman Orch 01/26 Col 498-D
Art Gillham 01/26 Col 505-D
Frank Crumit 03/26 Vic 19928

IN THE MIDDLE OF THE NIGHT
Berlin, pub. 1925, reached #14 in June 1926
Billy Rose w, Walter Donaldson m
Vincent Lopez Orch 04/26 Okeh 40567
Tom Waring 06/26 Vic 20004

JUST A COTTAGE SMALL (BY A WATERFALL) (27)
Harms, pub. 1925, reached #4 in May 1926
Bud DeSylva w, James F Hanley m
John McCormack Φ stage, 03/26 Vic 1133
Franklyn Baur Φ 01/26 Col 499-D
Frank Munn 04/26 Bruns 3057

JUST AROUND THE CORNER (35)
H Von Tilzer, pub. 1925, reached #10 in January 1926
Dolph Singer w, Harry Von Tilzer m
Ted Lewis/<vocal Φ 01/26 Col 504-D
Art Landry Orch 03/26 Vic 19930
Wendell Hall, stage, 04/26 Bruns 3085

KATINKA
L Feist, pub. 1926, reached #16 in August 1926
Ben Russell w, Henry Tobias m
George Olsen/w.vocal trio 09/26 Vic 20100
Ed Smalle 08/26 Col 661-D
Fred Rich/Ray Stilwell 08/26 Col 660-D

LET'S TALK ABOUT MY SWEETIE (44)
L Feist, pub. 1926, reached #7 in June 1926
Walter Donaldson w & m
Ruth Etting, radio, 05/26 Col 580-D
Wendell Hall, stage, 04/26 Bruns 3085
Charles Correll & Freeman Gosden 05/26 Vic 19986
Confidential Charlie 05/26 Harmony 132-H

LONESOME AND SORRY (17)
H Waterson, pub. 1926, reached #2 in July 1926
Benny Davis & Con Conrad w & m
Jean Goldkette/w.vocal duo ΦΦ 07/26 Vic 20031
Ruth Etting 07/26 Col 644-D
Ted Lewis Band, stage
Benny Davis, stage
Milton Berle, stage

THE LONESOMEST GIRL IN TOWN
J Mills, pub. 1925, reached #16 in January 1926
Al Dubin w, Jimmy McHugh & Irving Mills m
Franklyn Baur 01/26 Vic 19846
Cliff Edwards[3] 01/26 Perfect 11594
Morton Downey, stage, 12/25 Bruns 2975

LOOKING AT THE WORLD THROUGH ROSE-COLORED GLASSES (46)
M Weil, pub. 1926, reached #8 in October 1926
Tommy Malie & Jimmy Steiger w & m
Featured in A NIGHT IN PARIS, 2ND ED, revue (opened 08/26)
Waring's Pennsylvanians/w.vocal duo Φ 08/26 Vic 20076
Nick Lucas 09/26 Bruns 3283
Jack Osterman, sung in revue
Abe Lyman/w.vocal 09/26 Bruns 3268

LUCKY DAY (24)
Harms, pub. 1926, reached #3 in November 1926
Bud DeSylva & Lew Brown w, Ray Henderson m
Featured in GEORGE WHITE'S SCANDALS OF 1926, show (opened 06/26)
Harry Richman, sung in show, 09/26 Voc 15412
George Olsen/w.vocal trio Φ 09/26 Vic 20101
The Revelers Φ 10/26 Vic 20111
Howard Lanin/Frank Harris[1] 09/26 Col 689-D
Arden-Ohman Orch/w.vocal quartet 09/26 Bruns 3242

ME TOO (36)
Shapiro, B, pub. 1926, reached #5 in November 1926
Harry Woods, Charles Tobias, Al Sherman w & m
Gene Austin Φ 10/26 Vic 20143
Paul Whiteman/Wilbur Hall Φ 11/26 Vic 20197
California Ramblers/Irving Kaufman 10/26 Col 704-D

MOUNTAIN GREENERY
Harms, pub. 1926, reached #20 in September 1926
Lorenz Hart w, Richard Rodgers m
Featured in GARRICK GAIETIES, show (opened 05/26)
Bobbie Perkins & Sterling Holloway, sung in show
Roger Wolfe Kahn Orch 08/26 Vic 20071
Frank Crumit 10/26 Vic 20124

MY DREAM OF THE BIG PARADE
J Mills, pub. 1926, reached #14 in August 1926
Al Dubin w, Jimmy McHugh m
Billy Murray/Peerless Quartet 09/26 Vic 20098
Frank Harris[1] 08/26 Col 666-D

MY LITTLE NEST OF HEAVENLY BLUE (33)
E B Marks, pub. 1923, reached #5 in August 1926
A M Wilner, Heinz Reichert & Sigmund Spaeth w, Franz Lehar m
Fritz Kreisler Φ 07/26 Vic 1158
Jeritza, stage
Ernie Golden Orch 08/26 Bruns 3220

NEAPOLITAN NIGHTS
Sam Fox, pub. 1925, reached #17 in July 1926
(also reached #9 in November 1928)
Harry D Kerr w, J S Zamecnik m
Jack Denny Orch 05/26 Bruns 3129
Don Clark Orch 01/26 Vic 19789
Victor Salon Orch 10/26 Vic 20035

ONLY A ROSE (45)
H Waterson, pub. 1925, reached #18 in February 1926
Brian Hooker w, Rudolf Friml m
Featured in THE VAGABOND KING, show (opened 09/25)
Dennis King, sung in show
Carolyn Thomson 02/26 Vic 19897
International Novelty Orch 03/26 Vic 19901

PADDLIN' MADELIN' HOME
Shapiro, B, pub. 1925, reached #12 in January 1926
Harry Woods w & m
Featured in SUNNY, show (opened 09/25)
Cliff Edwards[3] Φ sung in show, 10/25 Pathe 25149
Ipana Troubadours/Billy Jones 02/26 Col 503-D
Wendell Hall, stage, 02/26 Bruns 3006

PLAY GYPSIES - DANCE GYPSIES
Harms, pub. 1926, reached #11 in November 1926
Julius Brummer, Alfred Grunwald & Harry B Smith w, Emmerich Kalman m
Featured in COUNTESS MARITZA, show (opened 09/26)
Walter Woolf King, sung in show
Fred Rich Orch 11/26 Col 734-D
Carl Fenton/Franklyn Baur 10/26 Bruns 3281

POOR PAPA, HE GOT NUTHIN' AT ALL (41)
Berlin, pub. 1926, reached #5 in May 1926
Billy Rose w, Harry Woods m
Jones & Hare[5] Φ 05/26 Col 596-D
"Whispering" Jack Smith 06/26 Vic 19998
Jay C Flippen, stage
Irving Aaronson/w.vocal trio 06/26 Vic 20002

THE PRISONER'S SONG (2)
Shapiro, B ΦΦΦ, pub. 1924, reached #1 in January 1926
Guy Massey[9] w & m
Vernon Dalhart ΦΦΦ 11/24 Vic 19427, 12/24 Pathe 32085, 02/25 Gennett 5588, 03/25 Col 257-D, 03/25 Ed 51459, 04/25 Emer 10850, 04/25 Ed Amb 4954, 08/25 Bruns 2900, 03/26 Okeh 40549, 04/26 Col 563-D
International Novelty Orch/Vernon Dalhart 09/25 Vic 19754
George Reneau 05/25 Voc 14991

REACHING FOR THE MOON
E B Marks, pub. 1926, reached #15 in July 1926
Benny Davis & Jesse Greer w & m
Ben Bernie/Paul Hagan 06/26 Bruns 3170
Goodrich-Silvertown Orch/Joseph White[7] 06/26 Vic 20016
Belle Brooks, stage

(I DON'T BELIEVE IT BUT) SAY IT AGAIN
Berlin, pub. 1926, reached #7 in June 1926
Harry Richman w, Abner Silver m
Nick Lucas Φ 04/26 Bruns 3088
"Whispering" Jack Smith Φ 07/26 Vic 20038
Russo-FioRito Orch 05/26 Vic 19989

SHOW ME THE WAY TO GO HOME (19)
Campbell, Connelly, pub. 1925, reached #4 in January 1926
Jimmy Campbell & Reg Connelly w & m
International Novelty Orch/Revelers Φ 12/25 Vic 19809
Wendell Hall 02/26 Bruns 3007
Vincent Lopez Orch 01/26 Okeh 40516
The Singing Sophomores[8] 01/26 Col 485-D

SLEEPY HEAD (38)
Shapiro, B, pub. 1926, reached #4 in August 1926
Benny Davis & Jesse Greer w & m
Ford & Glenn Φ 05/26 Col 583-D
Lewis James Φ 08/26 Vic 20077, 08/26 Voc 15389, 12/26 Col 753-D
Nick Lucas 09/26 Bruns 3229
Paul Ash Orch, db dates

SLEEPY TIME GAL (7)
L Feist ΦΦΦ, pub. 1925, reached #2 in February 1926
Joseph R Alden & Raymond B Egan w, Ange Lorenzo & Richard A Whiting m
Gene Austin Φ 02/26 Vic 19899
Nick Lucas Φ 02/26 Bruns 2990
Ben Bernie/Arthur Fields Φ 02/26 Bruns 2992
Lewis James Φ 01/26 Col 499-D
Art Landry/Henry Burr Φ 02/26 Vic 19843

SONG OF THE FLAME
Harms, pub. 1925, reached #13 in April 1926
Otto Harbach & Oscar Hammerstein 2nd w, George Gershwin & Herbert Stothart m
Featured in SONG OF THE FLAME, show (opened 12/25)
Tessa Kosta, sung in show, 06/26 Col 618-D
Roger Wolfe Kahn Orch 03/26 Vic 19935
Ipana Troubadours 04/26 Col 565-D

SONG OF THE VAGABONDS (32)
H Waterson, pub. 1925, reached #13 in February 1926
Brian Hooker w, Rudolf Friml m
Featured in THE VAGABOND KING, show (opened 09/25)
Dennis King, sung in show, 02/26 Vic 19897
International Novelty Orch/w.vocal group 03/26 Vic 19901
Vincent Lopez Orch 02/26 Okeh 40540

SWEET AND LOW-DOWN
Harms, pub. 1925, reached #12 in April 1926
Ira Gershwin w, George Gershwin m
Featured in TIP-TOES, show (opened 12/25)
Paul Whiteman Orch 03/26 Vic 19920
The Singing Sophomores[4] 04/26 Col 568-D
Andrew Tombes, Levey Lee & Gertrude McDonald, sung in show

TAMIAMI TRAIL
J H Remick, pub. 1926, reached #9 in May 1926
Joe Santly & Cliff Friend w & m
Ben Selvin/w.vocal Φ 04/26 Voc 15277
Whitey Kaufman Orch 06/26 Vic 19996
Gene Austin, stage, 08/26 Vic 20084

TEA FOR TWO
Harms ΦΦΦ, pub. 1924, reached #19 in January 1926
(Also reached #3 in December 1924)
(Also reached #6 in October 1958)
Irving Caesar w, Vincent Youmans m
Featured in NO, NO, NANETTE, show (re-opened 09/25, NY)
Leo Henning & Louise Groody, sung in show
Brunswick Hour Orch 02/26 Bruns 2998

THANKS FOR THE BUGGY RIDE (42)
Villa Moret, pub. 1925, reached #6 in May 1926
Jules Buffano w & m
Waring's Pennsylvanians/w.vocal group Φ 03/26 Vic 19913
Jones & Hare[5] Φ 05/26 Banner 1719
Johnny Marvin, stage, 06/26 Col 606-D
Mary Raines, radio

THAT CERTAIN FEELING
Harms, pub. 1925, reached #12 in April 1926
Ira Gershwin w, George Gershwin m
Featured in TIP-TOES, show (opened 12/25)
Allen Kearns & Queenie Smith, sung in show
Paul Whiteman Orch 03/26 Vic 19920
Arden-Ohman Orch 04/26 Bruns 3035

THAT CERTAIN PARTY (25)
Berlin, pub. 1925, reached #4 in February 1926
(Also reached #14 in November 1948)
Gus Kahn w, Walter Donaldson m
Jones & Hare[5] Φ 02/26 Vic 19865
Eddie Cantor, stage
Ponce Sisters 01/26 Col 501-D
Ted Lewis/<vocal 03/26 Col 531-D

THEN I'LL BE HAPPY (13)
Berlin ΦΦΦ, pub. 1925, reached #5 in April 1926
Sidney Clare & Lew Brown w, Cliff Friend m
"Whispering" Jack Smith Φ 02/26 Vic 19856
California Ramblers/Billy Jones Φ 02/26 Col 522-D
Ponce Sisters, stage
Russo-FioRito Orch 03/26 Vic 19917
Radio Franks[6], radio, 02/26 Col 522-D

THERE'S A NEW STAR IN HEAVEN TONIGHT (RUDOLPH VALENTINO)
J Mills, pub. 1926, reached #18 in November 1926
Irving Mills & J Keirn Brennan w, Jimmy McHugh m
Vernon Dalhart Φ 11/26 Vic 20193, 11/26 Col 718-D, 11/26 Ed 51827
Frank Munn 10/26 Bruns 3300

TING-A-LING (THE WALTZ OF THE BELLS) (49)
H Waterson, pub. 1926, reached #13 in October 1926
Addy Britt w, Jack Little m
Little Jack Little, stage
Waring's Pennsylvanians/w.vocal duo 10/26 Vic 20141
Francis Craig Orch 08/26 Col 649-D

VALENCIA (3)
Harms, pub. 1925, reached #1 in July 1926
(Also reached #18 in May 1950)
Lucienne Boyer, Jacques Charles & Clifford Grey w, Jose Padilla m
Featured in THE GREAT TEMPTATIONS, show (opened 05/26)
Paul Whiteman/Franklyn Baur ΦΦ 06/26 Vic 20007
The Revelers Φ 08/26 Vic 20082
Hazel Dawn, sung in show
Ben Selvin/Irving Kaufman Φ 06/26 Bruns 3712
Jesse Crawford Φ 08/26 Vic 20075

WHEN THE RED, RED, ROBIN COMES BOB, BOB, BOBBIN' ALONG (8)
Berlin, pub. 1926, reached #2 in October 1926
Harry Woods w & m
Al Jolson Φ stage, 08/26 Bruns 3222
"Whispering" Jack Smith Φ 08/26 Vic 20069
Paul Whiteman/w.vocal trio Φ 11/26 Vic 20177
Harry Richman, stage
Lillian Roth, stage

WHERE'D YOU GET THOSE EYES? (18)
L Feist, pub. 1926, reached #4 in September 1926
Walter Donaldson w & m
Ted Lewis/<vocal Φ 08/26 Col 667-D
George Olsen/Fran Frey Φ 10/26 Vic 20112
Vaughn DeLeath Φ radio, 09/26 Gennett 3347
Jones & Hare[5] 10/26 Okeh 40669

WHO? (12)
T B Harms, pub. 1925, reached #5 in February 1926
Otto Harbach & Oscar Hammerstein 2nd w, Jerome Kern m
Featured in SUNNY, show (opened 09/25)
George Olsen/w.vocal trio ΦΦ 01/26 Vic 19840
Marilyn Miller & Paul Frawley, sung in show
Eddie Elkins Orch 01/26 Col 493-D

[1]Frank Harris was a pseudonym for Irving Kaufman.
[2]The Melody Sheiks were led by Sam Lanin.
[3]Cliff Edwards was also known as Ukulele Ike.
[4]The Singing Sophomores were actually the Revelers.
[5]Jones and Hare were also known as The Happiness Boys.
[6]The Radio Franks were Frank Bessinger and Frank White.
[7]Joseph White was known as the Silver Masked Tenor.
[8]On Columbia, Lewis James sang as vocalist for the Cavaliers, the Cavaliers being a pseudonym for Ben Selvin's Orch.
[9]Guy Massey was a pseudonym for Vernon Dalhart, whose real name was Marion Try Slaughter.

1927

AFTER YOU'VE GONE (37)
Broadway Mus Co, pub. 1918, reached #16 in August 1927
(Also reached #7 in November 1918)
Henry Creamer w, Turner Layton m
Sophie Tucker, stage, 08/27 Okeh 40837
Charleston Chasers 04/27 Col 861-D
Bessie Smith 08/27 Col 14197

AIN'T SHE SWEET (17)
Ager, Y & B, pub. 1927, reached #2 in June 1927
(Also reached #19 in August 1949)
(Also reached #19 in August 1964)
Jack Yellen w, Milt Ager m
Ben Bernie/w.vocal duo Φ 04/27 Bruns 3444, 04/27 Voc 15525[1]
Eddie Cantor, stage
Gene Austin Φ 06/27 Vic 20568
Harry Richman Φ 04/27 Bruns 3435
Nat Shilkret/Franklyn Baur 05/27 Vic 20508

ALL ALONE MONDAY
Harms, pub. 1926, reached #8 in January 1927
Bert Kalmar w, Harry Ruby m
Featured in THE RAMBLERS, show (opened 06/26)
Nat Shilkret/Johnny Marvin Φ 12/26 Vic 20259
Marie Saxon & Jack Whiting, sung in show
Esther Walker 01/27 Bruns 3349

ARE YOU LONESOME TONIGHT? (32)
Berlin, pub. 1926, reached #6 in October 1927
(Also reached #1 in December 1960)
(Also reached #18 in May 1950 and #15 in January 1974)
Roy Turk & Lou Handman w & m
Henry Burr Φ 10/27 Vic 20873
Al Jolson, stage (Later: 1950 Dec 27043)
Vaughn DeLeath, radio, 09/27 Ed 52044
Jacques Renard/Franklyn Baur 12/27 Vic 20978

AT SUNDOWN (7)
L Feist, pub. 1927, reached #2 in July 1927
Walter Donaldson w & m
George Olsen/w.vocal trio ΦΦ 04/27 Vic 20476
Franklyn Baur 05/27 Vic 20504
Cliff Edwards, stage
Ruth Etting, radio, 09/27 Col 1052-D
Arden-Ohman Orch/w.vocal 06/27 Bruns 3481

THE BEST THINGS IN LIFE ARE FREE (33)
DeSylva, B & H, pub. 1927, reached #7 in December 1927
(Also reached #9 in March 1948)
Bud DeSylva & Lew Brown w, Ray Henderson m
Featured in GOOD NEWS, show (opened 09/27)
George Olsen/Bob Borger Φ 11/27 Vic 20872
John Price Jones & Mary Lawlor, sung in show
Frank Black/w.vocal 12/27 Bruns 3657
"Whispering" Jack Smith 01/28 Vic 21039

BLUE SKIES (5)
Berlin ΦΦΦ, pub. 1927, reached #1 in March 1927
(Also reached #12 in November 1946)
Irving Berlin w & m
Featured in BETSY, show (opened 12/26)
Featured in THE JAZZ SINGER, film (rel. 10/27)
All-time pop standard
George Olsen/w.vocal trio Φ 04/27 Vic 20455
Belle Baker, sung in show
Al Jolson, sung in film
The Knickerbockers[2]/Charles Kaley Φ 03/27 Col 860-D
Vaughn DeLeath, radio, 03/27 Okeh 40750, 05/27 Ed 51498

(HERE AM I) BROKEN HEARTED (18)
DeSylva, B & H, pub. 1927, reached #2 in October 1927
(Also reached #13 in March 1952)
Bud DeSylva & Lew Brown w, Ray Henderson m
Paul Whiteman/w.vocal trio ΦΦ 09/27 Vic 20757
Nick Lucas 10/27 Bruns 3602
Aileen Stanley, stage, 10/27 Vic 20825
Belle Baker, stage

C'EST VOUS (IT'S YOU)
Berlin, pub. 1927, reached #7 in October 1927
Abner Greenberg, Abner Silver, Harry Richman w & m
Harry Richman Φ stage, 08/27 Bruns 3538
Jacques Renard/Gene Austin Φ 08/27 Vic 20716

CHARMAINE (1)
Sherman Clay, pub. 1926, reached #1 in September 1927
(Also reached #7 in January 1952)
Erno Rapee & Lew Pollack w & m
Played during WHAT PRICE GLORY, silent film (rel. 11/26)
Lewis James ΦΦ 06/27 Vic 20590
Guy Lombardo/Weston Vaughn ΦΦ 09/27 Col 1043-D
Goodrich-Silvertown Orch/Joseph White[3] Φ 11/27 Vic 20892
Franklyn Baur 11/27 Col 1119-D
John Steel, stage

CLAP YO' HANDS
Harms, pub. 1926, reached #10 in March 1927
Ira Gershwin w, George Gershwin m
Featured in OH, KAY! show (opened 11/26)
Roger Wolfe Kahn Orch Φ 01/27 Vic 20327
"Whispering" Jack Smith Φ 02/27 Vic 20372
George Gershwin 02/27 Col 809-D
Harland Dixon, sung in show

CRAZY WORDS, CRAZY TUNE (41)
Ager, Y & B, pub. 1927, reached #9 in May 1927
Jack Yellen w, Milt Ager m
Frank Crumit Φ 04/27 Vic 20462
Irving Aaronson/w.vocal trio 04/27 Vic 20473
Six Jumping Jacks/w.vocal trio 04/27 Bruns 3434
Vaughn DeLeath, radio, 04/27 Bruns 3443

DANCING TAMBOURINE (39)
Harms, pub. 1927, reached #7 in December 1927
Phil Ponce w, W C Polla m
Paul Whiteman Orch Φ 12/27 Vic 20972
The Radiolites Φ 11/27 Col 1114-D
Waring's Pennsylvanians, db dates
Sam Lanin Orch 10/27 Okeh 40874

DO, DO, DO (47)
Harms, pub. 1926, reached #9 in February 1927
Ira Gershwin w, George Gershwin m
Featured in OH, KAY! show (opened 11/26)
Gertrude Lawrence Φ sung in show, 02/27 Vic 20331
George Olsen/w.vocal trio Φ 01/27 Voc 20327
George Gershwin 02/27 Col 809-D

THE DOLL DANCE (10)
Sherman Clay, pub. 1927, reached #5 in July 1927
Nacio Herb Brown m
Featured in HOLLYWOOD MUSIC BOX REVUE OF 1927, revue
(opened 02/27 in Hollywood)
Nat Shilkret Orch ΦΦ 06/27 Vic 20503
Vincent Lopez Orch, db dates
Earl Burtnett Orch 06/27 Col 934-D
Eddie Peabody Orch 08/27 Vic 20698

DOWN SOUTH (45)
E B Marks, pub. 1927, reached #16 in October 1927
(Instrumental version pub. 1901)
Sigmund Spaeth w, William H Myddleton m
Eveready Hour Ensemble 08/27 Vic 35823
Emil Seidel/Hoagy Carmichael 02/28 Gennett 6309

FIFTY MILLION FRENCHMEN (CAN'T BE WRONG)
Shapiro, B, pub. 1927, reached #13 in July 1927
Willie Raskin & Billy Rose w, Fred Fisher m
Sophie Tucker, stage, 07/27 Okeh 40813
Ted Lewis/<vocal 07/27 Col 988-D
Nat Shilkret/Joe Sherman 07/27 Vic 20634

FOLLOWING THE SUN AROUND
L Feist, pub. 1926, reached #15 in May 1927
Joe McCarthy w, Harry Tierney m
Featured in RIO RITA, show (opened 02/27)
J Harold Murray, sung in show
Victor Light Opera Co. 05/27 Vic 35816
Jacques Renard/w.vocal trio 06/27 Vic 20557

FORGIVE ME (35)
Ager, Y & B, pub. 1927, reached #5 in June 1927
(Also reached #10 in May 1952)
Jack Yellen w, Milt Ager m
Gene Austin Φ 06/27 Vic 20561
Lillian Roth, stage
Howard Lanin/Lewis James 04/27 Col 882-D

GIVE ME A NIGHT IN JUNE (31)
J H Remick, pub. 1927, reached #4 in November 1927
Cliff Friend w & m
Ipana Troubadours/Frank Harris[4] Φ 11/27 Col 1098-D
Johnny Marvin Φ 12/27 Vic 20984
Ernie Golden/w.vocal duo 11/27 Bruns 3829

GOOD NEWS (42)
DeSylva, B & H, pub. 1927, reached #8 in December 1927
Bud DeSylva, Lew Brown w, Ray Henderson m
Featured in GOOD NEWS, show (opened 09/27)
George Olsen/w.vocal trio Φ 11/27 Vic 20875
Zelma O'Neill, sung in show
Fred Rich/w.vocal trio 11/27 Col 1108-D

HALLELUJAH! (25)
Harms, pub. 1927, reached #8 in October 1927
Leo Robin & Clifford Grey w, Vincent Youmans m
Featured in HIT THE DECK, show (opened 04/27)
Stella Mayhew, sung in show
Nat Shilkret/Franklyn Baur Φ 07/27 Vic 20599
The Revelers Φ 07/27 Vic 20609
Harry Richman 09/27 Bruns 3569

HELLO, BLUEBIRD
J H Remick, pub. 1926, reached #10 in January 1927
Cliff Friend w & m
Art Landry/w.vocal trio Φ 01/27 Vic 20285
Vincent Lopez/Keller Sisters 02/27 Bruns 3368
Nick Lucas 02/27 Bruns 3370

HERE COMES THE SHOW BOAT
Shapiro, B, pub. 1927, reached #9 in January 1928
Billy Rose w, Maceo Pinkard m
Featured by ensemble in THE SHOW BOAT, film (rel. 05/29)
Vaughn DeLeath, radio, 12/27 Ed 52104
Six Jumping Jacks/Tom Stacks 01/28 Bruns 3699
Jean Goldkette/w.vocal trio 03/28 Vic 21166

I CAN'T BELIEVE THAT YOU'RE IN LOVE WITH ME (36)
J Mills, pub. 1926, reached #15 in September 1927
Clarence Gaskill & Jimmy McHugh w & m
Featured in GAY PAREE, show (opened 11/26)
Roger Wolfe Kahn Orch Φ 06/27 Vic 20573
Winnie Lightner, sung in show
Ben Bernie/w.vocal duo 04/27 Bruns 3442

I KNOW THAT YOU KNOW (48)
Harms, pub. 1926, reached #4 in March 1927
Anne Caldwell w, Vincent Youmans m
Featured in OH, PLEASE! show (opened 12/26)
Charles Purcell & Bea Lillie, sung in show
The Revelers Φ 02/27 Vic 20380
Ipana Troubadours/Charles Kaley 03/27 Col 829-D

I'M COMING, VIRGINIA
Robbins, pub. 1927, reached #8 in October 1927
Will Marion Cook w, Donald Heywood m
Featured in AFRICANA, show (opened 07/27)
Ethel Waters Φ sung in show, 09/27 Col 14170-D
Paul Whiteman/w.vocal trio[5] 09/27 Vic 20751
Frankie Trumbauer Orch 09/27 Okeh 40843

I'M IN LOVE AGAIN
DeSylva, B & H; orig. pub. 1925, reached #8 in July 1927
(Also reached #11 in June 1951)
Cole Porter w & m
Added to GREENWICH VILLAGE FOLLIES OF 1924, show (opened 09/24)
Ben Bernie/w.vocal duo Φ 06/27 Bruns 3496, 06/27 Voc 15541[1]
The Revelers Φ 08/27 Vic 20678
Dolly Sisters, sung in show

I'M LOOKING OVER A FOUR LEAF CLOVER (14)
Tell Taylor ΦΦΦ, pub. 1927, reached #1 in June 1927
(Also reached #1 in February 1948)
Mort Dixon w, Harry Woods m
All-time pop standard
Jean Goldkette/Billy Murray ΦΦ 04/27 Vic 20466
Ben Bernie/Scrappy Lambert ΦΦ 04/27 Bruns 3444, 04/27 Voc 15519[1]
Nick Lucas, stage, 04/27 Bruns 3439
Sam Lanin/w.vocal 04/27 Okeh 40766

I'VE GOT THE GIRL
L Feist, pub. 1926, reached #20 in February 1927
Walter Donaldson w & m
George Olsen/Fran Frey 02/27 Vic 20359
Don Clark/w.vocal duo[13] 02/27 Col 824-D
Gene Austin 03/27 Vic 20397

IF YOU SEE SALLY
L Feist, pub. 1927, reached #19 in May 1927
Gus Kahn w, Walter Donaldson m
Ted Lewis/<vocal 03/27 Col 844-D
Franklyn Baur 05/27 Col 888-D
Ruth Etting, stage and radio

IN A LITTLE SPANISH TOWN (2)
L Feist ΦΦΦ, pub. 1926, reached #1 in January 1927
Sam Lewis & Joe Young w, Mabel Wayne m
Paul Whiteman/Jack Fulton ΦΦ 12/26 Vic 20266
The Cavaliers[6]/Frank Harris[4] Φ 02/27 Col 805-D
Sam Lanin/Irving Kaufman 03/27 Okeh 40740
Jimmy Carr Orch, db dates
Nick Lucas, stage, 04/27 Bruns 3433

IT ALL DEPENDS ON YOU (12)
DeSylva, B & H, pub. 1926, reached #1 in May 1927
Bud DeSylva & Lew Brown w, Ray Henderson m
Added to BIG BOY, show (opened 01/25)
Ruth Etting ΦΦ stage, 05/27 Col 908-D
Paul Whiteman Orch ΦΦ 05/27 Vic 20513
Al Jolson, sung in show
Franklyn Baur/Jesse Crawford[7] 04/27 Vic 20463
Harry Richman, stage, 06/27 Bruns 3501

IT MADE YOU HAPPY WHEN YOU MADE ME CRY (49)
L Feist, pub. 1926, reached #5 in February 1927
Walter Donaldson w & m
Waring's Pennsylvanians/Tom Waring Φ 01/27 Vic 20315
Isham Jones/Frank Munn Φ 12/26 Bruns 3335
Gene Austin Φ 02/27 Vic 20371
Vaughn DeLeath, radio, 05/27 Ed 51966

IT WAS ONLY A SUN SHOWER
Waterson, B & S, pub. 1927, reached #9 in December 1927
Irving Kahal & Francis Wheeler w, Ted Snyder m
Ted Weems/Dusty Rhodes Φ 11/27 Vic 20910
Jim Miller & Charlie Farrell 11/27 Vic 20906
Johnny Johnson Orch, db dates

JUST A BIRD'S-EYE VIEW OF MY OLD KENTUCKY HOME
L Feist, pub. 1926, reached #15 in January 1927
Gus Kahn w, Walter Donaldson m
Jean Goldkette Orch 12/26 Vic 20268
Wendell Hall, stage, 12/26 Bruns 3331
Abe Lyman/w.vocal 12/26 Bruns 3322

JUST A MEMORY (13)
Harms, pub. 1926, reached #1 in December 1927
Bud DeSylva & Lew Brown w, Ray Henderson m
Added to MANHATTAN MARY, show (opened 09/27)
Paul Whiteman Orch ΦΦ 11/27 Vic 20881
Franklyn Baur 10/27 Bruns 3590
Vincent Lopez Orch 11/27 Bruns 3633
The Singing Sophomores[8] 01/28 Col 1178-D

JUST ANOTHER DAY WASTED AWAY (WAITING FOR YOU) (30)
Shapiro, B, pub. 1927, reached #7 in September 1927
Charles Tobias & Roy Turk w & m
Waring's Pennsylvanians/Tom Waring Φ 08/27 Vic 20724
Johnny Marvin & Ed Smalle Φ 09/27 Vic 20758
Nora Bayes, stage
Ethel Merman, stage

JUST LIKE A BUTTERFLY (THAT'S CAUGHT IN THE RAIN) (26)
J H Remick, pub. 1927, reached #4 in September 1927
Harry Woods & Mort Dixon w & m
The Troubadours/Johnny Marvin Φ 08/27 Vic 20732
Ipana Troubadours/Vaughn DeLeath Φ 08/27 Col 1018-D
Franklyn Baur Φ 09/27 Vic 20758
Blossom Seeley, stage

JUST ONCE AGAIN
L Feist, pub. 1927, reached #14 in November 1927
Walter Donaldson & Paul Ash w & m
Paul Whiteman/Austin Young 09/27 Vic 20751
Ruth Etting 10/27 Col 1075-D
Paul Ash/Franklyn Baur 11/27 Col 1090-D

THE KINKAJOU (44)
L Feist, pub. 1926, reached #12 in May 1927
Joe McCarthy w, Harry Tierney m
Featured in RIO RITA, show (opened 02/27)
Nat Shilkret/Billy Murray Φ 04/27 Vic 20474
Ada May, sung in show
The Knickerbockers[2]/Johnny Marvin 05/27 Col 893-D

LINDBERGH, THE EAGLE OF THE U.S.A.
Shapiro, B, pub. 1927, reached #10 in August 1927
Howard Johnson & Al Sherman w & m
Vernon Dalhart Φ 08/27 Vic 20674, 08/27 Col 1000-D, 08/27 Ed 52029
Jim Courtney, stage

THE LITTLE WHITE HOUSE (AT THE END OF HONEYMOON LANE) (29)
Shapiro, B, pub. 1926, reached #2 in January 1927
Eddie Dowling w, James F Hanley m
Featured in HONEYMOON LANE, show (opened 09/26)
Waring's Pennsylvanians/Tom Waring ΦΦ 01/27 Vic 20289
Eddie Dowling, sung in show
Raymond Dixon[9] Φ 12/26 Vic 20271
Howard Lanin/Frank Harris[4] 12/26 Col 762-D

LUCKY IN LOVE
DeSylva, B & H, pub. 1927, reached #7 in November 1927
Bud DeSylva & Lew Brown w, Ray Henderson m
Featured in GOOD NEWS, show (opened 09/27)
George Olsen/w.vocal trio Φ 11/27 Vic 20872
Mary Lawlor & John Price Jones, sung in show
Freddie Rich/w.vocal trio 11/27 Col 1108-D

LUCKY LINDY
L Feist, pub. 1927, reached #13 in August 1927
L Wolfe Gilbert w, Abel Baer m
Vernon Dalhart 08/27 Col 1000-D, 08/27 Ed 52029, 09/27 Bruns 3572, 09/27 Voc 5168
Nat Shilkret/w.vocal group 08/27 Vic 20681

MAGNOLIA
DeSylva, B & H, pub. 1927, reached #12 in August 1927
Bud DeSylva & Lew Brown w, Ray Henderson m
Paul Whiteman/w.vocal trio[5] Φ 08/27 Vic 20679
Johnny Marvin 08/27 Vic 20731
Harry Richman, stage, 10/27 Bruns 3583

MARY LOU (22)
H Waterson, pub. 1926, reached #4 in January 1927
Abe Lyman, George Waggner & J Russel Robinson w & m
Ipana Troubadours Φ 11/26 Col 738-D
Abe Lyman/Charles Kaley Φ 06/26 Bruns 3135
The Revelers Φ 02/27 Vic 20380
Ford & Glenn 12/26 Col 749-D
Anna Chandler, stage

ME AND MY SHADOW (3)
Berlin, pub. 1927, reached #1 in August 1927
Billy Rose w, Al Jolson & Dave Dreyer m
Featured in HARRY DELMAR'S REBELS, show (opened 11/27)
"Whispering" Jack Smith ΦΦ 07/27 Vic 20626
Ted Lewis Band, stage
Al Jolson, stage & radio
Frank Fay, sung in show
Johnny Marvin[10] ΦΦ 08/27 Vic 20675, 08/27 Col 1020-D

MISS ANNABELLE LEE (21)
Berlin, pub. 1927, reached #1 in November 1927
Sidney Clare, Lew Pollack, Harry Richman w & m
Ted Weems/w.vocal duo Φ 10/27 Vic 20846
Harry Richman, stage
The Knickerbockers[2]/Irving Kaufman Φ 10/27 Col 1088-D

MOONBEAM! KISS HER FOR ME
J H Remick, pub. 1927, reached #16 in May 1927
Mort Dixon w, Harry Woods m
Goodrich Silvertown Orch/Joseph White[3] Φ 03/27 Vic 20419
Nick Lucas 06/27 Bruns 3492
Ben Bernie Orch, db dates
Swanson Sisters, stage

MOONLIGHT ON THE GANGES (20)
Harms, pub. 1926, reached #3 in January 1927
Chester Wallace w, Sherman Myers m
Paul Whiteman/Austin Young ΦΦ 11/26 Vic 20139
The Revelers Φ 11/26 Vic 20140
Franklyn Baur 11/26 Bruns 3318

MUDDY WATER (8)
Broadway Mus Co, pub. 1926, reached #3 in June 1927
Jo Trent w, Peter DeRose & Harry Richman m
Harry Richman Φ stage, 04/27 Bruns 3435
Paul Whiteman/Bing Crosby Φ 05/27 Vic 20508
Bessie Smith Φ 04/27 Col 14197-D
Ben Bernie/Frank Munn Φ 03/27 Bruns 3414, 03/27 Voc 15509[1]
Nora Bayes, stage

ONE ALONE
Harms, pub. 1926, reached #11 in March 1927
Oscar Hammerstein 2nd w, Sigmund Romberg m
Featured in THE DESERT SONG, show (opened 11/26)
Robert Halliday, sung in show
Nat Shilkret Orch Φ 02/27 Vic 20373
Don Voorhees/Charles Kaley 03/27 Col 835-D

THE RANGER'S SONG
L Feist, pub. 1926, reached #11 in May 1927
Joe McCarthy w, Harry Tierney m
Featured in RIO RITA, show (opened 02/27)
Harry Ratcliffe & J Harold Murray, sung in show
Victor Light Opera Co/J Harold Murray 05/27 Vic 35816

RED LIPS, KISS MY BLUES AWAY
H Waterson, pub. 1927, reached #9 in July 1927
James V Monaco, Alfred Bryan, Pete Wendling w & m
Charles Dornberger/Franklyn Baur Φ 07/27 Vic 20615
Aileen Stanley & Johnny Marvin 08/27 Vic 20714
Leo Reisman/w.vocal duo 07/27 Col 973-D

RIO RITA (24)
L Feist, pub. 1926, reached #4 in May 1927
Joe McCarthy w, Harry Tierney m
Featured in RIO RITA, show (opened 02/27)
Ethelind Terry & J Harold Murray, sung in show
Nat Shilkret/Lewis James Φ 04/27 Vic 20474
Victor Light Opera Co/J Harold Murray Φ 05/27 Vic 35816
The Knickerbockers[2]/Charles Kaley Φ 05/27 Col 893-D
Sam Lanin/w.vocal 05/27 Okeh 40781

RUSSIAN LULLABY (6)
Berlin ΦΦΦ, pub. 1927, reached #1 in July 1927
Irving Berlin w & m
Roger Wolfe Kahn/Henry Garden ΦΦ 07/27 Vic 20602
The Singing Sophomores[8] Φ 07/27 Col 985-D
Franklyn Baur Φ 07/27 Vic 20611
Jesse Crawford 09/27 Vic 20791
Sascha Jacobsen 08/27 Col 133-M

SAM, THE OLD ACCORDION MAN (19)
L Feist, pub. 1927, reached #2 in April 1927
Walter Donaldson w & m
Ruth Etting Φ stage, 05/27 Col 908-D
George Olsen/w.vocal trio Φ 03/27 Vic 20425
Williams Sisters, stage, 04/27 Vic 20452
Ben Selvin/<vocal 04/27 Bruns 3425

SHAKING THE BLUES AWAY
Berlin, pub. 1927, reached #6 in November 1927
Irving Berlin w & m
Featured in ZIEGFELD FOLLIES OF 1927, show (opened 08/27)
Ruth Etting Φ sung in show, 11/27 Col 1113-D
Paul Whiteman Orch Φ 10/27 Vic 20885
Harry Reser/Franklyn Baur 11/27 Col 1109-D

SIDE BY SIDE (15)
Shapiro, B, pub. 1927, reached #3 in August 1927
(Also reached #6 in April 1953)
Harry Woods w & m
Paul Whiteman/w.vocal trio[5] ΦΦ 07/27 Φ Vic 20627
Duncan Sisters, stage
Nick Lucas 07/27 Bruns 3512
Cliff Edwards[11] 05/27 Perfect 11640
Aileen Stanley & Johnny Marvin 08/27 Vic 20714

SILVER MOON (50)
Harms, pub. 1927, reached #20 in August 1927
Dorothy Donnelly w, Sigmund Romberg m
Featured in MY MARYLAND, show (opened 09/27)
Paul Whiteman Orch Φ 05/27 Vic 20505
Nathaniel Wagner & Evelyn Herbert, sung in show
The Columbians 07/27 Col 975-D

SLOW RIVER
E B Marks, pub. 1927, reached #19 in September 1927
Henry Myers w, Charles M Schwab m
The Singing Sophomores[8] 09/27 Col 1032-D
Jean Goldkette Orch 11/27 Vic 20926
Jean Sothern, stage

SO BLUE (43)
DeSylva, B & H, pub. 1927, reached #10 in June 1927
Bud DeSylva, Lew Brown, Ray Henderson w & m
Paul Whiteman/Austin Young Φ 06/27 Vic 20570
Nick Lucas 06/27 Bruns 3492
Vincent Lopez/Frank Munn 05/27 Bruns 3473

SOMEONE TO WATCH OVER ME (46)
Harms, pub. 1926, reached #5 in March 1927
Ira Gershwin w, George Gershwin m
Featured in OH, KAY! show (opened 11/26)
Gertrude Lawrence Φ sung in show, 02/27 Vic 20331
George Olsen Orch Φ 02/27 Vic 20392
George Gershwin 02/27 Col 812-D

SOMETIMES I'M HAPPY (28)
Harms, pub. 1927, reached #8 in August 1927
Irving Caesar w, Vincent Youmans m
Featured in HIT THE DECK, show (opened 04/27)
Charles King & Louise Groody Φ sung in show and 07/27 Vic 20609
Roger Wolfe Kahn/Franklyn Baur Φ 07/27 Vic 20599
Gladys Rice & Franklyn Baur 07/27 Col 998-D
Vaughn DeLeath, radio, 10/27 Bruns 3608

SONG OF THE WANDERER (34)
Villa Moret, pub. 1926, reached #10 in April 1927
Neil Moret w & m
Earl Burtnett Orch Φ 01/27 Col 787-D
Art Landry/Al Marineau Φ 01/27 Vic 20300
Paul Whiteman Orch 06/27 Vic 20570
Aileen Stanley, stage

SUNDAY (40)
L Feist, pub. 1926, reached #7 in February 1927
Ned Miller, Chester Conn, Jule Styne, Bennie Krueger w & m
Cliff Edwards[11] Φ 01/27 Perfect 11633
Jean Goldkette/Keller Sisters Φ 01/27 Vic 20273
Gene Austin 03/27 Vic 20411

THERE'S EVERYTHING NICE ABOUT YOU
H Waterson, pub. 1927, reached #12 in June 1927
Alfred Bryan & Arthur Terker w, Pete Wendling m
Arden-Ohman Orch/w.vocal 05/27 Bruns 3457
Johnny Marvin 07/27 Vic 20612
Nat Shilkret/w.vocal duo 07/27 Vic 20603

(I'VE GROWN SO LONESOME) THINKING OF YOU
L Feist, pub. 1926, reached #6 in March 1927
Paul Ash w, Walter Donaldson m
Ruth Etting Φ 02/27 Col 827-D
Gene Austin 03/27 Vic 20411
George Olsen/w.vocal trio 03/27 Vic 20394

TONIGHT YOU BELONG TO ME (9)
H Waterson, pub. 1926, reached #2 in February 1927
(Also reached #3 in October 1956)
Billy Rose w, Lee David m
Gene Austin ΦΦ stage, 02/27 Vic 20371
Franklyn Baur Φ 12/26 Bruns 3319
Little Jack Little, stage
Ponce Sisters 01/27 Col 791-D
Anna Chandler, stage

TWO BLACK CROWS, PARTS 1 AND 2
Comic dialogue 1927, reached #15 in August 1927
George Moran & Charles Mack w
Moran & Mack ΦΦ 06/27 Col 935-D

UNDER THE MOON
J Mills, pub. 1927, reached #15 in October 1927
Francis Wheeler & Evelyn Hiller w, Ted Snyder m
Aileen Stanley & Johnny Marvin Φ 09/27 Vic 20787
Jan Garber/Leroy Montesanto 09/27 Vic 20754
Ponce Sisters 09/27 Col 1039-D

THE VARSITY DRAG (16)
DeSylva, B & H, pub. 1927, reached #4 in December 1927
Bud DeSylva, Lew Brown, Ray Henderson w & m
Featured in GOOD NEWS, show (opened 09/27)
George Olsen/Fran Frey ΦΦ 11/27 Vic 20875
Zelma O'Neill, sung in show, 06/28 Bruns 3864
The Revelers Φ 01/28 Vic 21039
Cass Hagan/w.vocal trio 11/27 Col 1114-D

WHAT DO WE DO ON A DEW-DEW-DEWY DAY? (11)
Berlin, pub. 1927, reached #2 in September 1927
Howard Johnson, Charles Tobias, Al Sherman w & m
Ruth Etting ΦΦ 07/27 Col 979-D
Nat Shilkret/Johnny Marvin Φ 10/27 Vic 20819
Vaughn DeLeath, radio, 09/27 Okeh 40844
Little Jack Little, stage
Gladys Rice, stage

WHAT DOES IT MATTER? (27)
Berlin, pub. 1927, reached #7 in June 1927
Irving Berlin w & m
Nat Shilkret/Elliot Shaw Φ 04/27 Vic 20471
Henry Burr 05/27 Vic 20490
Harry Richman Φ 06/27 Bruns 3501
Lucrezia Bori, stage

WHEN DAY IS DONE (4)
Harms, pub. 1926, reached #2 in September 1927
Bud DeSylva w, Robert Katscher m
Paul Whiteman Orch ΦΦ 09/27 Vic 35828
Nat Shilkret Orch Φ 05/27 Vic 20456
Franklyn Baur Φ 08/27 Vic 20719
Harry Archer/Franklyn Baur 02/27 Bruns 3399
Emma Carus, stage

WHERE DO YOU WORK-A JOHN? (23)
Shapiro, B, pub. 1926, reached #2 in March 1927
Mortimer Weinberg, Charley Marks, Harry Warren w & m
Waring's Pennsylvanians/w.vocal group ΦΦ 02/27 Vic 20378
Six Jumping Jacks/Tom Stacks 02/27 Bruns 3374
Jones & Hare[12] 04/27 Col 875-D

YANKEE ROSE (38)
Berlin, pub. 1926, reached #5 in April 1927
Sidney Holden w, Abe Frankel m
Roger Wolfe Kahn Orch Φ 04/27 Vic 20466
Sam Lanin/Vaughn DeLeath 04/27 Okeh 40754
Paul Specht/w.vocal group 04/27 Col 880-D

YOU DON'T LIKE IT, NOT MUCH
L Feist, pub. 1927, reached #18 in September 1927
Chester Conn, Art Kahn, Ned Miller w & m
Jones & Hare[12] 09/27 Vic 20756
Jan Garber/w.vocal duo 08/27 Vic 20676
Paul Ash/Paul Small 09/27 Col 1034-D

[1]Ben Bernie's releases on Vocalion were listed as Al Goering's Orch.
[2]The Knickerbockers were actually the Ben Selvin Orch.
[3]Joseph White was known as The Silver-Masked Tenor.
[4]Frank Harris was a pseudonym for Irving Kaufman.
[5]Whiteman's vocal group included Bing Crosby on this record.
[6]The Cavaliers were actually the Ben Selvin Orch.
[7]Jesse Crawford on organ.
[8]The Singing Sophomores were actually the Revelers.
[9]Raymond Dixon was a pseudonym for Lambert Murphy.
[10]Johnny Marvin's Victor recording included Nat Shilkret's Orch.
[11]Cliff Edwards was also known as Ukulele Ike.
[12]Jones & Hare were also known as The Happiness Boys.
[13]Clark's vocal duo was composed of Bing Crosby and Al Rinker. This was Crosby's first recording.

1928

AH! SWEET MYSTERY OF LIFE (14)
Witmark ΦΦΦ, pub. 1910, reached #9 in April 1928
Reached second peak at #11 in September 1928
(Also reached #19 in July 1935)
Rida Johnson Young w, Victor Herbert m
Waring's Concert Orch/Tom Waring Φ 08/28 Vic 35921
The Troubadours Φ 07/28 Vic 21371
Leo Reisman/w.vocal 07/28 Col 1377-D
Victor Salon Orch 02/28 Vic 9145 (album record)

AMONG MY SOUVENIRS (3)
DeSylva, B & H ΦΦΦ, pub. 1927, reached #1 in March 1928
(Also reached #6 in January 1960)
Edgar Leslie w, Horatio Nicholls m
Paul Whiteman/w.vocal trio Φ 02/28 Vic 35877
Ben Selvin/w.vocal trio Φ 01/28 Col 1188-D
Roger Wolfe Kahn/Scrappy Lambert Φ 01/28 Vic 21084
Belle Baker, stage
The Revelers Φ 02/28 Vic 21100

ANGELA MIA (MY ANGEL) (6)
DeSylva, B & H ΦΦΦ, pub. 1928, reached #1 in August 1928
Erno Rapee & Lew Pollack w & m
Played during STREET ANGEL, silent film (rel. 04/28)
Paul Whiteman/w.vocal trio ΦΦ 07/28 Vic 21388
Vincent Lopez/Lewis James Φ 07/28 Bruns 3927
James Melton Φ stage, 10/28 Col 1493-D
Franklyn Baur 10/28 Vic 21591

AWAY DOWN SOUTH IN HEAVEN (41)
Shapiro, B, pub. 1927, reached #4 in March 1928
Bud Green w, Harry Warren m
Ted Lewis/<vocal Φ stage, 02/28 Col 1242-D
Waring's Pennsylvanians, db dates
Tom Waring 03/28 Vic 21164

BACK IN YOUR OWN BACK YARD (18)
Berlin, pub. 1927, reached #2 in May 1928
Dave Dreyer, Al Jolson, Billy Rose w & m
Ruth Etting ΦΦ 04/28 Col 1288-D
Al Jolson Φ stage, 06/28 Bruns 3867
Paul Whiteman Orch Φ 04/28 Vic 21240
Gus Arnheim/Russ Columbo 06/28 Okeh 41037

BECAUSE MY BABY DON'T MEAN MAYBE NOW
Donaldson, D & G, pub. 1928, reached #20 in August 1928[1]
Walter Donaldson w & m
Ruth Etting 08/28 Col 1420-D
George Olsen/Bob Borger 08/28 Vic 21452

BELOVED (21)
Berlin, pub. 1928, reached #5 in July 1928
Gus Kahn & Joe Sanders w & m
Guy Lombardo/Carmen Lombardo Φ 06/28 Col 1345-D
The Troubadours/Lewis James Φ 06/28 Vic 21339
Ruth Etting Φ stage, 08/28 Col 1420-D
Lillian Roth, stage

CAN'T HELP LOVIN' DAT MAN (37)
T B Harms, pub. 1927, reached #11 in April 1928
Oscar Hammerstein 2nd w, Jerome Kern m
Featured in SHOW BOAT, show (opened 12/27)
Helen Morgan Φ sung in show, 04/28 Vic 21238
Nat Shilkret/Franklyn Baur Φ 04/28 Vic 21215
Ben Bernie/Vaughn DeLeath 04/28 Bruns 3808

CHERRY
United, pub. 1928, reached #16 in December 1928
(Also reached #12 in February 1944 with new lyrics)
Don Redman w & m
McKinney's Cottonpickers/Don Redman 12/28 Vic 21730

CHIQUITA (24)
L Feist, pub. 1928, reached #3 in October 1928
L Wolfe Gilbert w, Mabel Wayne m
Paul Whiteman/Jack Fulton Φ 09/28 Col 1448-D
Arden-Ohman Orch/Lewis James Φ 09/28 Vic 21513
Bernie Cummins/Walter Cummins 09/28 Bruns 3996

CHLOE (10)
Villa Moret, pub. 1927, reached #3 in April 1928
(Also reached #12 in May 1945 in comic version)
Gus Kahn w, Neil Moret m
The Singing Sophomores[2] Φ 03/28 Col 1257-D
All Star Orch Φ 02/28 Vic 21149
Shilkret's Rhyth-Melodists Φ 05/28 Vic 21298
Paul Whiteman/Austin Young 08/28 Vic 35921
Bessie Brown 04/28 Bruns 3817

C-O-N-S-T-A-N-T-I-N-O-P-L-E (40)
DeSylva, B & H, pub. 1928, reached #8 in August 1928
Harry Carleton w & m
Paul Whiteman/w.vocal group Φ 08/28 Col 1402-D
California Humming Birds 08/28 Vic 21477
Six Jumping Jacks/Tom Stacks 08/28 Bruns 3940

COQUETTE (32)
L Feist, pub. 1928, reached #5 in June 1928
Gus Kahn w, Carmen Lombardo & John Green m
Guy Lombardo/Carmen Lombardo ΦΦ stage and 06/28 Col 1345-D
Paul Whiteman Orch 05/28 Vic 21301
Dorsey Brothers Orch/Bill Dutton 05/28 Okeh 41007

CRAZY RHYTHM (28)
Harms, pub. 1928, reached #8 in August 1928
Irving Caesar w, Joseph Meyer & Roger Wolfe Kahn m
Featured in HERE'S HOWE, show (opened 05/28)
Roger Wolfe Kahn/Franklyn Baur Φ 07/28 Vic 21368
Ben Bernie/<vocal Φ 07/28 Bruns 3913
Harry Reser/Tom Stacks 09/28 Col 1378-D

DIANE (9)
Sherman Clay, pub. 1927, reached #3 in December 1927
(Also reached #10 in June 1964)
Erno Rapee & Lew Pollack w & m
Played during SEVENTH HEAVEN, silent film (rel. 05/27)
The Troubadours/w.vocal trio ΦΦ 12/27 Vic 21000
Franklyn Baur Φ 12/27 Vic 21019
James Melton Φ 02/28 Col 1206-D
Jesse Crawford Φ 02/28 Vic 21146
Sam Lanin/w.vocal 12/27 Okeh 40902

DID YOU MEAN IT? (43)
Shapiro, B, pub. 1927, reached #8 in January 1928
Phil Baker, Sid Silvers, Abe Lyman w & m
Featured in A NIGHT IN SPAIN, revue (opened 15/27)
Aileen Stanley, sung in revue
Abe Lyman/Phil Neely Φ 12/27 Bruns 3648
The Virginians/Lewis James 02/28 Vic 21105

DIGA-DIGA-DOO (27)
J Mills, pub. 1928, reached #6 in October 1928
Dorothy Fields w, Jimmy McHugh m
Featured in BLACKBIRDS OF 1928, show (opened 05/28)
Adelaide Hall, sung in show
Duke Ellington/Irving Mills Φ 10/28 Okeh 41096, 10/28 Okeh 8602, 01/29 Vic 38008
Irving Mills[3]/Elizabeth Walsh 10/28 Bruns 4014

DOIN' THE NEW LOW DOWN
J Mills, pub. 1928, reached #14 in October 1928
Dorothy Fields w, Jimmy McHugh m
Featured in BLACKBIRDS OF 1928, show (opened 05/28)
Bill Robinson, sung and danced in show, 11/29 Bruns 4535
Duke Ellington/Irving Mills 10/28 Okeh 41096, 10/28 Okeh 8602
Jack Pettis & His Pets 10/28 Vic 21599

DOIN' THE RACCOON
Remick, pub. 1928, reached #5 in December 1928
Raymond Klages w, J Fred Coots m
George Olsen/w.vocal group Φ 12/28 Vic 21701
The Knickerbockers[4]/w.vocal Φ 01/29 Col 1596-D
Rudy Vallee/<vocal 12/28 Velvetone 1759-V, 12/28 Harmony 759-H[5]

DREAM HOUSE (29)
Sherman Clay, pub. 1928, reached #9 in October 1928
Earle Foxe w, Lynn F Cowan m
Anson Weeks Orch Φ 08/28 Col 1409-D
Art Hickman[6]/Scrappy Lambert Φ 11/28 Vic 21392
Ben Selvin/w.vocal 10/28 Col 1490-D

DUSKY STEVEDORE (35)
Triangle M C, pub. 1928, reached #6 in November 1928
Andy Razaf w, J C Johnson m
Nat Shilkret/w.vocal duo Φ 09/28 Vic 21515
Thelma Terry and Her Playboys 12/28 Col 1588-D
Vaughn DeLeath, radio, 09/28 Ed 52341

GET OUT AND GET UNDER THE MOON (16)
Berlin, pub. 1928, reached #2 in August 1928
Charles Tobias & William Jerome w, Larry Shay m
Paul Whiteman/Bing Crosby Φ 08/28 Col 1402-D
Helen Kane Φ 09/28 Vic 21557
Nat Shilkret/w.vocal duo Φ 07/28 Vic 21432
Annette Hanshaw 07/28 Perfect 12444

GIRL OF MY DREAMS (5)
J Mills, pub. 1927, reached #2 in June 1928
Sunny Clapp w & m
Gene Austin ΦΦ 06/28 Vic 21334
Blue Steele/Tom Summers, db dates, 03/28 Vic 20971
Seger Ellis/<vocal 04/28 Col 1239-D
Rudy Vallee, stage

HALFWAY TO HEAVEN
Waterson, B & S, pub. 1928, reached #7 in December 1928
Al Dubin w, J Russel Robinson m
Johnny Hamp/Frank Munn Φ 10/28 Vic 21615
Cliff Edwards[7] Φ 11/28 Col 1523-D

HAPPY-GO-LUCKY LANE
J H Remick, pub. 1928, reached #7 in July 1928
Sam Lewis & Joe Young w, Joseph Meyer m
Johnny Johnson/Bob Treaster Φ 06/28 Vic 21366
Vaughn DeLeath, radio, 07/28 Ed 52288
Ponce Sisters 07/28 Col 1347-D

I AIN'T GOT NOBODY (17)
Triangle M C, pub. 1916, reached #8 in February 1928
(also reached #3 in March 1917)
(also reached #12 in June 1985 as part of medley)
Roger Graham & Dave Payton w, Spencer Williams m
Steady seller 1926-1929
Coon-Sanders Night Hawks Φ 09/27 Vic 20785
Ruth Etting Φ 05/28 Col 1312-D
Bessie Smith, stage, 02/26 Col 14095-D
Vaughn DeLeath, radio, 02/29 Ed 52408
Sophie Tucker, stage, 08/27 Okeh 40837

I CAN'T DO WITHOUT YOU (49)
Berlin, pub. 1928, reached #4 in June 1928
Irving Berlin w & m
Waring's Pennsylvanians/Tom Waring Φ 06/28 Vic 21327
Guy Lombardo/Carmen Lombardo Φ 07/28 Col 1395-D
James Melton 06/28 Col 1329-D

I CAN'T GIVE YOU ANYTHING BUT LOVE (7)
J Mills ΦΦΦ, pub. 1928, reached #2 in October 1928
Dorothy Fields[8] w, Jimmy McHugh[8] m
Briefly featured in HARRY DELMAR'S REVELS, revue
(opened 11/27)
Featured in BLACKBIRDS OF 1928, show (opened 05/28)
All-time pop standard
Cliff Edwards[7] Φ 09/28 Col 1471-D
Aida Ward & Willard McLean, sung in show
Harry Richman Φ stage, 11/28 Bruns 4035
Johnny Hamp/w.vocal trio Φ 09/28 Vic 21514
The Knickerbockers[4]/Vaughn DeLeath Φ 08/28 Col 1424-D

I JUST ROLL ALONG (HAVIN' MY UPS AND DOWNS) (46)
Berlin, pub. 1927, reached #9 in May 1928
Jo Trent w, Peter DeRose m
Vaughn DeLeath Φ radio, 04/28 Ed 52222,
05/28 Col 1323-D
Ben Bernie/w.vocal duo 05/28 Bruns 3837
Annette Hanshaw 04/28 Perfect 12419

I MUST HAVE THAT MAN
J Mills, pub. 1928, reached #14 in October 1928
Dorothy Fields w, Jimmy McHugh m
Featured in BLACKBIRDS OF 1928, show (opened 05/28)
Adelaide Hall, sung in show, 11/28 Bruns 4031
The Knickerbockers[4]/Vaughn DeLeath 08/28 Col 1424-D
Grace Hayes 09/28 Vic 21571

I SCREAM, YOU SCREAM, WE ALL SCREAM FOR ICE CREAM
Shapiro, B, pub. 1927, reached #7 in February 1928
Howard Johnson, Billy Moll, Robert King w & m
Waring's Pennsylvanians/w.vocal group Φ 02/28 Vic 21099
Jimmy Durante, stage
Van & Schenck, stage

I STILL LOVE YOU
Ager, Y & B, pub. 1928, reached #11 in June 1928
Jack Yellen w, Milt Ager m
Nick Lucas 06/28 Bruns 3850
Radiolites/Harold Lambert[9] 05/28 Col 1301-D
Sophie Tucker, stage

IDA (SWEET AS APPLE CIDER)
E B Marks, pub. 1903, reached #11 in January 1928
(Also reached #14 in July 1904)
Eddie Leonard & Eddie Munson w & m
Red Nichols & His Five Pennies ΦΦ stage and
11/27 Bruns 3626, 12/27 Voc 15622

JEANNINE, I DREAM OF LILAC TIME (8)
L Feist, pub. 1928, reached #1 in October 1928
L Wolfe Gilbert w, Nat Shilkret m
Featured in LILAC TIME, film (rel. 08/28)
Gene Austin ΦΦ 10/28 Vic 21564
Nat Shilkret/Franklyn Baur Φ 10/28 Vic 21572
Dolores Del Rio, sung in film
Ben Selvin/Frank Munn 10/28 Col 1512-D
John McCormack, stage, 02/29 Vic 1360

JUST LIKE A MELODY OUT OF THE SKY (20)
Donaldson, D & G, pub. 1928, reached #2 in September 1928
Walter Donaldson w & m
Gene Austin Φ 08/28 Vic 21454
George Olsen/Fran Frey Φ 08/28 Vic 21452
Cliff Edwards[7] Φ 08/28 Col 1427-D
Paul Whiteman/w.vocal trio 09/28 Col 1441-D

KEEP SWEEPING THE COBWEBS OFF THE MOON
J H Remick, pub. 1927, reached #7 in March 1928
Sam Lewis & Joe Young w, Oscar Levant m
Ted Lewis/Ruth Etting Φ 02/28 Col 1242-D
Waring's Pennsylvanians/Fred Waring Φ 03/28 Vic 21165
Johnny Marvin 02/28 Vic 21153
Frankie Masters Orch, db dates

KING FOR A DAY
Remick, pub. 1928, reached #14 in November 1928
Sam Lewis & Joe Young w, Ted FioRito m
George Olsen/<vocal 10/28 Vic 21566
Ted Lewis/<vocal 10/28 Col 1485-D
Harry Richman 11/28 Bruns 4035

LAST NIGHT I DREAMED YOU KISSED ME
L Feist, pub. 1928, reached #19 in September 1928
Gus Kahn w, Carmen Lombardo m
Johnny Johnson/Franklyn Baur 08/28 Vic 21498
Paul Whiteman/Jack Fulton 08/28 Col 1401-D
Dick Powell 09/28 Voc 15699

LAUGH! CLOWN, LAUGH! (12)
Remick, pub. 1928, reached #3 in June 1928
Sam Lewis & Joe Young w, Ted FioRito m
Played as theme for silent film LAUGH! CLOWN, LAUGH, (rel. 06/28)
Ted Lewis/<vocal Φ stage, 06/28 Col 1346-D
Waring's Pennsylvanians/Fred Waring Φ 06/28 Vic 21308
Harry Richman Φ 06/28 Bruns 3889
Ted FioRito Orch, stage

LET A SMILE BE YOUR UMBRELLA (19)
Waterson, B & S, pub. 1927, reached #3 in April 1928
Irving Kahal & Francis Wheeler w, Sammy Fain m
Roger Wolfe Kahn/Franklyn Baur ΦΦ 04/28 Vic 21233
Sam Lanin/Irving Kaufman 03/28 Okeh 40977
Dolly Kay, stage, 03/28 Harmony 581-H
Milton Berle, vv stage

LOUISIANA
A Piantadosi, pub. 1928, reached #16 in November 1928
Andy Razaf & Bob Schafer w, J C Johnson m
Paul Whiteman/w.vocal group[10] Φ 08/28 Vic 21438
Duke Ellington Orch 01/29 Bruns 4110
Bix Beiderbecke Orch 03/29 Okeh 41173

MAKE BELIEVE (48)
T B Harms, pub. 1927, reached #15 in April 1928
(Also reached #18 in September 1951)
Oscar Hammerstein 2nd w, Jerome Kern m
Featured in SHOW BOAT, show (opened 12/27)
Paul Whiteman/Bing Crosby Φ 03/28 Vic 21218
Norma Terriss & Howard Marsh, sung in show
Ben Bernie/Scrappy Lambert 04/28 Bruns 3808

THE MAN I LOVE (23)
Harms, pub. 1924, reached #4 in May 1928
Ira Gershwin w, George Gershwin m
Marion Harris Φ 03/28 Vic 21116
Vaughn DeLeath Φ radio, 03/28 Bruns 3748
Helen Morgan, stage
Sophie Tucker, stage

MANHATTAN SERENADE
Robbins, pub. 1928, reached #19 in June 1928
(Also reached #6 in November 1942)
Louis Alter m (words added 1942)
Paul Whiteman Orch, stage
Victor Salon Orch 05/28 Vic 35914

MARY ANN (45)
Berlin, pub. 1928, reached #5 in May 1928
Benny Davis w, Abner Silver m
Cliff Edwards[7] Φ 04/28 Col 1295-D
Jacques Renard/w.vocal duo Φ 04/28 Vic 21234
Ted Lewis/<vocal Φ 05/28 Col 1313-D

MEMORIES OF FRANCE (39)
Waterson, B & S, pub. 1928, reached #4 in October 1928
Al Dubin w, J Russel Robinson m
Gene Austin Φ 09/28 Vic 21545
The Troubadours/w.vocal trio 10/28 Vic 21590
Seger Ellis/<vocal 09/28 Col 1453-D

MISSISSIPPI MUD (44)
Shapiro, B, pub. 1927, reached #15 in June 1928
Harry Barris w & m
Paul Whiteman/w.vocal group[10] Φ 09/27 Vic 20783[11], 05/28 Vic 21274
Frankie Trumbauer/Bing Crosby 03/28 Okeh 40979
Charleston Chasers/Scrappy Lambert 06/28 Col 1335-D

MY BLUE HEAVEN (2)
L Feist ΦΦΦ, pub. 1927, reached #1 in January 1928
George Whiting w, Walter Donaldson m
Added to ZIEGFELD FOLLIES OF 1927, show (opened 08/27)
Gene Austin ΦΦΦ 12/27 Vic 20964
Paul Whiteman/w.vocal group[10] Φ 10/27 Vic 20828
Eddie Cantor, sung in show
Tommy Lyman, radio
Don Voorhees/Lewis James Φ 12/27 Col 1129-D

MY BLUE RIDGE MOUNTAIN HOME
Triangle M C, pub. 1927, reached #17 in January 1928
Carson Robison w & m
Vernon Dalhart & Carson Robison Φ 09/27 Vic 20539[13] 03/28 Okeh 45190

MY HEART STOOD STILL (34)
Harms, pub. 1927, reached #4 in February 1928
Lorenz Hart w, Richard Rodgers m
Featured in A CONNECTICUT YANKEE, show (opened 11/27)
George Olsen/w.vocal trio Φ 01/28 Vic 21034
William Gaxton & Constance Carpenter, sung in show
Broadway Nitelites[12]/Franklyn Baur Φ 01/28 Col 1187-D
James Melton, stage, 04/28 Col 1294-D

MY MELANCHOLY BABY
J Morris, pub. 1912, reached #15 in March 1928
(Also reached #10 in May 1947)
George A Norton w, Ernie Burnett m
Steady seller and jazz standard, 1928 through the 1940's
Gene Austin Φ 01/28 Vic 21015
Tommy Lyman, radio
Freddie Rose 04/28 Bruns 3768

NAGASAKI
Remick, pub. 1928, reached #13 in November 1928
Mort Dixon w, Harry Warren m
Ipana Troubadours/w.vocal 09/28 Col 1463-D
Nat Shilkret/Frank Crumit 10/28 Vic 21603
Bill "Bojangles" Robinson, stage

NEAPOLITAN NIGHTS (50)
Sam Fox, pub. 1925, reached #9 in November 1928
(also reached #17 in July 1926)
Harry D Kerr w, J S Zamecnik m
Theme music for FAZIL, film (rel. 05/28)
The Troubadours/Franklyn Baur Φ 10/28 Vic 21633
Eddie Dunstedter 02/29 Bruns 4148

OL' MAN RIVER (25)
T B Harms, pub. 1927, reached #8 in May 1928
Oscar Hammerstein 2nd w, Jerome Kern m
Featured in SHOW BOAT, show (opened 12/27)
All-time pop standard
Paul Whiteman/Bing Crosby Φ 03/28 Vic 21218
Jules Bledsoe, sung in show
Paul Whiteman/Paul Robeson Φ 05/28 Vic 35912
The Revelers 04/28 Vic 21241
Al Jolson 06/28 Bruns 3867

OLD MAN SUNSHINE (42)
Remick, pub. 1928, reached #5 in November 1928
Mort Dixon w, Harry Warren m
George Olsen/Fran Frey Φ 10/28 Vic 21566
Johnny Marvin Φ 10/28 Vic 21609
Leo Reisman/w.vocal 10/28 Col 1506-D

OUT OF THE DAWN
Donaldson, D & G, pub. 1928, reached #20 in November 1928
Walter Donaldson w & m
Featured in WARMING UP, film (rel. 07/28)
Nat Shilkret/Franklyn Baur 10/28 Vic 21572
Bernie Cummins/w.vocal trio 09/28 Bruns 3996
Richard Dix, sung in film

PERSIAN RUG
Villa Moret, pub. 1927, reached #10 in June 1928
Gus Kahn w, Neil Moret m
Dorsey Brothers Orch Φ 04/28 Okeh 40995
Louisiana Sugar Babies 06/28 Vic 21346

RAIN (30)
Robbins, pub. 1927, reached #3 in March 1928
(Also reached #15 in May 1950)
Eugene Ford w & m
Jacques Renard/w.vocal duo Φ 02/28 Vic 21107
Don Voorhees/Billy Day Φ 12/27 Col 1126-D
Johnny Marvin & Ed Smalle Φ 03/28 Vic 21172
Frankie Masters Orch, db dates

RAMONA (1)
L Feist ΦΦΦ, pub. 1928, reached #1 in May 1928
L Wolfe Gilbert w, Mabel Wayne m
Played during silent film RAMONA (rel. 05/28)
Gene Austin ΦΦΦ 06/28 Vic 21334
Paul Whiteman/Austin Young Φ 04/28 Vic 21214
Dolores Del Rio Φ 07/28 Vic 4053
Ruth Etting Φ 06/28 Col 1352-D

READY FOR THE RIVER
Villa Moret, pub. 1928, reached #10 in July 1928
Gus Kahn w, Neil Moret m
Scrappy Lambert Φ 07/28 Bruns 3926
Coon-Sanders Orch/Joe Sanders Φ 09/28 Vic 21501
Gus Arnheim Orch, db dates

REVENGE
Remick, pub. 1928, reached #8 in November 1928
Sam Lewis & Joe Young w, Harry Akst m
Franklyn Baur Φ 10/28 Vic 21591
The Troubadours/Cooper Lawley Φ 11/28 Vic 21654
Scrappy Lambert 11/28 Bruns 4043

ROSES OF YESTERDAY
Berlin, pub. 1928, reached #7 in November 1928
Irving Berlin w & m
Waring's Pennsylvanians/Tom Waring Φ 11/28 Vic 21676
Paul Whiteman/Austin Young Φ 11/28 Col 1553-D
Lewis James 12/28 Vic 21700

SALLY OF MY DREAMS
DeSylva, B & H, pub. 1928, reached #8 in December 1928
William B Kernell w & m
Featured in MOTHER KNOWS BEST, film (rel. 09/28)
Franklyn Baur Φ 12/28 Vic 21734
James Melton 01/29 Col 1614-D

THE SIDEWALKS OF NEW YORK (38)
Paull-Pioneer; orig. pub. 1894, reached #9 in Sept. 1928
(Also a top seller in 1895)
Charles B Lawlor & James W Blake w & m
Campaign song for Al Smith, candidate for U.S. President
Shannon Quartet Φ 07/28 Col 1358-D
Nat Shilkret/Lewis James Φ 08/28 Vic 21493

THE SONG IS ENDED (BUT THE MELODY LINGERS ON) (15)
Berlin, pub. 1927, reached #3 in February 1928
Irving Berlin w & m
"Whispering" Jack Smith Ф 01/28 Vic 21028
Ruth Etting Ф 01/28 Col 1196-D
Al Jolson, stage
George Olsen/w.vocal trio Ф 01/28 Vic 21040

SONNY BOY (4)
DeSylva, B & H ФФФ, pub. 1928, reached #1 in November 1928
Al Jolson, Bud DeSylva, Lew Brown, Ray Henderson w & m
Featured in THE SINGING FOOL, film (rel. 09/28)
Al Jolson ФФ sung in show, 11/28 Bruns 4033
Ruth Etting Ф 12/28 Col 1563-D
Gene Austin Ф 01/29 Vic 21779
John McCormack, stage, 02/29 Vic 1360

SUNSHINE
Berlin, pub. 1928, reached #8 in May 1928
Irving Berlin w & m
Paul Whiteman/w.vocal group[10] Ф 04/28 Vic 21240
Ipana Troubadours/Harold Lambert[9] 05/28 Col 1308-D
Vincent Lopez/Scrappy Lambert 05/28 Bruns 3835

SWEET LORRAINE
J Mills, pub. 1928, reached #15 in August 1928
(Also reached #18 in July 1944)
Mitchell Parish w, Cliff Burwell m
Rudy Vallee, stage
Johnny Johnson/Franklyn Baur 09/28 Vic 21514
The Radiolites/w.vocal 08/28 Col 1432-D

SWEET SUE (JUST YOU) (31)
Shapiro, B, pub. 1928, reached #11 in September 1928
Will J Harris w, Victor Young m
Jazz standard, 1928 through 1940's
Ben Pollack/Franklyn Baur Ф 08/28 Vic 21437
Earl Burtnett/Biltmore Trio Ф 08/28 Col 1361-D
Sue Carol, stage
Bennie Krueger Orch, db dates

THE SWEETHEART OF SIGMA CHI (22)
Melrose; orig. pub. 1912, reached #6 in January 1928
Byron D Stokes w, F Dudleigh Vernor m
Waring's Pennsylvanians/Tom Waring Ф 10/27 Vic 20820
Rudy Vallee, stage
Gene Austin Ф 12/27 Vic 20977
Eddie Thomas Collegians/Franklyn Baur Ф 08/27 Col 1019-D
college glee clubs

'S WONDERFUL
New World M C, pub. 1927, reached #20 in May 1928
Ira Gershwin w, George Gershwin m
Featured in FUNNY FACE, show (opened 11/27)
Allen Kearns & Adele Astaire, sung in show
Frank Crumit 01/28 Vic 21029
Ipana Troubadours/Scrappy Lambert 02/28 Col 1213-D
Arden-Ohman Orch/Johnny Marvin 02/28 Vic 21114

TAKE YOUR TOMORROW (AND GIVE ME TODAY)
Triangle M C, pub. 1928, reached #9 in January 1929
Andy Razaf w, J C Johnson m
Frankie Trumbauer/w.vocal duo 01/29 Okeh 41145
Rudy Vallee, stage
Vaughn DeLeath, radio
Ed McEnelly/w.vocal duo 01/29 Vic 21773

TEN LITTLE MILES FROM TOWN
Berlin, pub. 1928, reached #15 in October 1928
Gus Kahn w, Elmer Schoebel m
George Olsen/w.vocal duo 10/28 Vic 21589
Ben Bernie/Frank Luther 10/28 Bruns 4020

THAT'S MY WEAKNESS NOW (13)
Shapiro, B, pub. 1928, reached #2 in September 1928
Bud Green & Sam Stept w & m
Helen Kane Ф 09/28 Vic 21557
Nat Shilkret/Frank Munn Ф 08/28 Vic 21497
Paul Whiteman/w.vocal trio[10] Ф 09/28 Col 1444-D
Cliff Edwards[7] Ф 09/28 Col 1471-D

THERE'S A RAINBOW 'ROUND MY SHOULDER (11)
Berlin, pub. 1928, reached #2 in December 1928
Al Jolson, Billy Rose, Dave Dreyer w & m
Featured in THE SINGING FOOL, film (rel. 09/28)
Al Jolson ФФ 11/28 Bruns 4033
Johnny Marvin 01/29 Vic 21780
All Star Orch 11/28 Vic 21667

THOU SWELL (33)
Harms, pub. 1927, reached #6 in March 1928
Lorenz Hart w, Richard Rodgers m
Featured in A CONNECTICUT YANKEE, show (opened 11/27)
William Gaxton & Constance Carpenter, sung in show
Broadway Nite Lites[12]/Franklyn Baur Ф 01/28 Col 1187-D
Johnny Johnson/w.vocal trio Ф 02/28 Vic 21113
The Revelers, stage

TOGETHER (26)
DeSylva, B & H, pub. 1927, reached #1 in April 1928
(Also reached #2 in November 1944)
(Also reached #6 in August 1961)
Bud DeSylva & Lew Brown w, Ray Henderson m
Franklyn Baur Ф 03/28 Vic 21220
Cliff Edwards[7] Ф 04/28 Col 1295-D
Paul Whiteman/Jack Fulton Ф 04/28 Vic 35883
Nick Lucas 04/28 Bruns 3749

TOGETHER, WE TWO
Berlin, pub. 1927, reached #15 in February 1928
Irving Berlin w & m
Isham Jones/Keller Sisters 01/28 Bruns 3685
Vaughn DeLeath & Ed Smalle 01/28 Vic 21042
Ruth Etting 01/28 Col 1196-D

UP IN THE CLOUDS
Harms, pub. 1927, reached #12 in January 1928
Bert Kalmar w, Harry Ruby m
Featured in THE FIVE O'CLOCK GIRL, show (opened 10/27)
Oscar Shaw & Mary Eaton, sung in show
Nat Shilkret/Franklyn Baur 12/27 Vic 20996
Broadway Nite Lites[12]/Franklyn Baur 12/27 Col 1164-D

WAS IT A DREAM?
Harms, pub. 1928, reached #5 in July 1928
Larry Spier & Sam Coslow w & m
Waring's Pennsylvanians/Tom Waring Φ 05/28 Vic 21297
Jan Garber/Sonny Faircloth 07/28 Col 1372-D
Frank Munn 07/28 Bruns 3929

WHY DO I LOVE YOU?
T B Harms, pub. 1927, reached #18 in April 1928
Oscar Hammerstein 2nd w, Jerome Kern m
Featured in SHOW BOAT, show (opened 12/27)
Norma Terriss, Howard Marsh, Charles Winninger & Edna May Oliver, sung in show
Nat Shilkret/Franklyn Baur 04/28 Vic 21215
Kenn Sisson/Franklyn Baur 04/28 Bruns 3766

YOU TOOK ADVANTAGE OF ME (36)
Harms, pub. 1928, reached #8 in September 1928
Lorenz Hart w, Richard Rodgers m
Featured in PRESENT ARMS, show (opened 04/28)
Paul Whiteman/w.vocal group[10] Φ 08/28 Vic 21398
Busby Berkeley & Joyce Barbour, sung in show
Morton Downey, radio

YOU'RE A REAL SWEETHEART (47)
L Feist, pub. 1928, reached #15 in September 1928
Irving Caesar w, Cliff Friend m
Nick Lucas 08/28 Bruns 3966
George Jessel, stage
Roger Wolfe Kahn/Frank Munn 09/28 Vic 21510
Earl & Bell, stage

[1]Reached #20 on monthly chart only.
[2]The Singing Sophomores were actually the Revelers.
[3]Irving Mills and his Hotsy Totsy Gang
[4]The Knickerbockers were actually the Ben Selvin Orch.
[5]On the Harmony label, Vallee is listed as Frank Mater.
[6]Though listed as Art Hickman, the orchestra was actually that of Nat Shilkret.
[7]Cliff Edwards was also known as Ukulele Ike.
[8]Some believe this song was actually written by Andy Razaf w, Thomas "Fats" Waller m, for the 1927 revue.
[9]Harold Lambert was better known as Scrappy Lambert.
[10]Whiteman's vocal group included Bing Crosby on this record.
[11]The 1927 record was a medley of several songs. The 1928 record was the hit record.
[12]The Broadway Nite Lites were actually the Ben Selvin Orch.
[13]The Victor label bears the title MY BLUE MOUNTAIN HOME.

1929

AIN'T MISBEHAVIN'
Mills, pub. 1929, reached #11 in October 1929
Andy Razaf w, Thomas "Fats" Waller & Harry Brooks m
Featured in CONNIE'S HOT CHOCOLATES, show (opened 06/29)
Jazz standard since 1930
Thomas "Fats" Waller 11/29 Vic 22118
Louis Armstrong, sung in show, 09/29 Okeh 8714, 09/29 Okeh 41276
Leo Reisman/Lew Conrad 09/29 Vic 22047
Ruth Etting 11/29 Col 1958-D
Gene Austin 09/29 Vic 22068

ALL THAT I'M ASKING IS SYMPATHY
J Morris, pub. 1929, reached #20 in January 1930
Benny Davis w, Joe Burke m
Gene Austin 01/30 Vic 22223
Kate Smith, stage
Ted Weems Orch, db dates

AM I BLUE (7)
Witmark, pub. 1929, reached #1 in September 1929
Grant Clarke w, Harry Akst m
Featured in ON WITH THE SHOW, film (rel. 06/29)
Ethel Waters ΦΦ sung in film, 07/29 Col 1837-D
Libby Holman Φ 09/29 Bruns 4445
Nat Shilkret/Don Howard 08/29 Vic 22004
Gay Ellis[1] 10/29 Harmony 940-H
Jimmie Noone/May Alix 10/29 Voc 1296

AVALON TOWN (42)
Sherman Clay, pub. 1928, reached #8 in March 1929
Grant Clarke w, Nacio Herb Brown w
Johnny Hamp/Roy Cropper Φ 02/29 Vic 21829
Gus Arnheim/w.vocal 03/29 Okeh 41174
Cliquot Club Eskimos/Tom Stacks 01/29 Col 1592-D
Owen Fallon Orch, db dates

BIG CITY BLUES
DeSylva, B & H, pub. 1929, reached #17 in July 1929
Sidney D Mitchell & Archie Gottler w, Con Conrad m
Featured in WILLIAM FOX MOVIETONE FOLLIES OF 1929, film (rel. 05/29)
Lola Lane, sung in film
Annette Hanshaw 06/29 Col 1812-D
George Olsen/Fran Frey 07/29 Vic 21961

THE BREAKAWAY
DeSylva, B & H, pub. 1929, reached #14 in July 1929
Sidney D Mitchell & Archie Gottler w, Con Conrad m
Featured in WILLIAM FOX MOVIETONE FOLLIES OF 1929, film (rel. 05/29)
George Olsen/Fran Frey 07/29 Vic 21961
Janet Dancey & Sue Carol, sung in film
Arnold Johnson/w.vocal 07/29 Bruns 4348

BROADWAY MELODY (28)
Robbins, pub. 1929, reached #7 in May 1929
Arthur Freed w, Nacio Herb Brown m
Featured in BROADWAY MELODY, film (rel. 02/29)
Charles King Φ sung in film, 07/29 Vic 21964
Ben Selvin/w.vocal 04/29 Col 1738-D
Nat Shilkret/Four Rajahs 04/29 Vic 21886

BUTTON UP YOUR OVERCOAT (35)
DeSylva, B & H, pub. 1928, reached #4 in April 1929
Bud DeSylva & Lew Brown w, Ray Henderson m
Featured in FOLLOW THRU, show (opened 01/29)
Helen Kane Φ 04/29 Vic 21863
Zelma O'Neill & Jack Haley, sung in show
Paul Whiteman/Vaughn DeLeath Φ 04/29 Col 1736-D
Ruth Etting 05/29 Col 1762-D

CAN'T WE BE FRIENDS?
Harms, pub. 1929, reached #14 in October 1929
Paul James w, Kay Swift m
Featured in THE LITTLE SHOW, show (opened 04/29)
Libby Holman, sung in show, 11/29 Bruns 4506
Leo Reisman/Lew Conrad 10/29 Vic 22070
Bing Crosby 12/29 Col 2001-D

CAROLINA MOON (4)
J Morris, pub. 1928, reached #1 in March 1929
Benny Davis & Joe Burke w & m
Gene Austin ΦΦ 03/29 Vic 21833
Guy Lombardo Orch, stage
Morton Downey, radio
Ben Selvin/w.vocal Φ 03/29 Col 1719-D
The Troubadours[2]/Scrappy Lambert Φ 04/29 Vic 21847

COQUETTE
Berlin, pub. 1928, reached #20 in May 1929
Irving Berlin w & m
Promo song for COQUETTE, film (rel. 04/29)
Rudy Vallee/<vocal 04/29 Vic 21880
Paul Whiteman/Bing Crosby 05/29 Col 1775-D

DEEP NIGHT (43)
Ager, Y & B, pub. 1929, reached #6 in May 1929
Rudy Vallee w, Charlie Henderson m
Rudy Vallee/<vocal Φ stage, 04/29 Vic 21868
Ruth Etting 06/29 Col 1801-D
Ipana Troubadours/Smith Ballew 04/29 Col 1747-D

THE DESERT SONG
Harms, pub. 1926, reached #12 in July 1929
Otto Harbach w, Sigmund Romberg m
Featured in THE DESERT SONG, film (rel. 05/29)
John Boles & Carlotta King, sung in film
Broadway Broadcasters[3]/Scrappy Lambert 06/29 Cameo 9169

DON'T BE LIKE THAT
Shapiro, B, pub. 1928, reached #18 in February 1929
Archie Gottler, Charles Tobias, Maceo Pinkard w & m
Helen Kane 02/29 Vic 21830
Lee Morse 01/29 Col 1621-D

DON'T HOLD EVERYTHING
DeSylva, B & H, pub. 1928, reached #15 in January 1929
Bud DeSylva, Lew Brown, Ray Henderson w & m
Featured in HOLD EVERYTHING, show (opened 10/28)
Alice Boulden, sung in show
High Hatters/w.vocal trio 02/29 Vic 21791

DREAM TRAIN
M Weil, pub. 1929, reached #20 in April 1929
Billy Baskette & Charles Newman w & m
Abe Lyman/Phil Neely 02/29 Bruns 4137
Ford & Glenn 03/29 Col 1720-D

A GARDEN IN THE RAIN
Campbell, Connelly, pub. 1928, reached #13 in June 1929
(Also reached #16 in January 1952)
James Dyrenforth w, Carroll Gibbons m
Gene Austin 05/29 Vic 21915
John McCormack, stage, 08/29 Vic 1400
George Olsen/Fran Frey 06/29 Vic 21942

HAPPY DAYS AND LONELY NIGHTS
Ager, Y & B, pub. 1928, reached #19 in March 1929[11]
Billy Rose w, Fred Fisher m
Featured in SIMPLE SIMON, show (opened 02/30)
Ruth Etting, sung in show, 09/28 Col 1454-D
Johnny Marvin 01/29 Vic 21780

HONEY (14)
L Feist ΦΦΦ, pub. 1928, reached #1 in May 1929
Seymour Simons, Haven Gillespie, Richard Whiting w & m
Rudy Vallee/<vocal ΦΦ 04/29 Vic 21869
Ben Selvin/w.vocal 06/29 Col 1800-D
Wendell Hall, stage
Guy Lombardo Orch, db dates
Broadway Broadcasters[3]/Scrappy Lambert 04/29 Cameo 9130

HOW ABOUT ME?
Berlin, pub. 1928, reached #8 in February 1929
Irving Berlin w & m
Waring's Pennsylvanians/Clare Hanlon Φ 02/29 Vic 21792
Morton Downey 02/29 Vic 21806

HOW AM I TO KNOW? (41)
Robbins, pub. 1929, reached #5 in November 1929
Dorothy Parker w, Jack King m
Featured in DYNAMITE, film (rel. 08/29)
Russ Columbo, sung in film
Arden-Ohman Orch/Scrappy Lambert Φ 11/29 Vic 22111
Gene Austin 11/29 Vic 22128

I FAW DOWN AN' GO BOOM!
Donaldson, D & G, pub. 1928, reached #12 in March 1929
Leonard Stevens & James Brockman w & m
Eddie Cantor, stage, 04/29 Vic 21862
George Olsen/w.vocal group 03/29 Vic 21832
Ponce Sisters 03/29 Col 1698-D

I GET THE BLUES WHEN IT RAINS (38)
Forster, pub. 1928, reached #9 in August 1929
Marcy Klauber w & m
Guy Lombardo/Carmen Lombardo 08/29 Col 1888-D
Johnny Marvin 07/29 Vic 21959
Ford & Glenn, stage, 06/29 Col 1720-D

I KISS YOUR HAND, MADAME (31)
Harms, pub. 1929, reached #7 in June 1929
Fritz Rotter, Sam Lewis & Joe Young w, Ralph Erwin m
Rudy Vallee, stage
Leo Reisman/Ran Weeks Φ 05/29 Vic 21920
Ben Bernie/Scrappy Lambert 06/29 Bruns 4315

I MAY BE WRONG (BUT I THINK YOU'RE WONDERFUL)
Ager, Y & B, pub. 1929, reached #20 in December 1929
Harry Ruskin w, Henry Sullivan m
Featured in JOHN MURRAY ANDERSON'S ALMANAC, revue (opened 08/29)
Jimmy Savo & Trixie Fraganza, sung in revue
High Hatters/Frank Luther 11/29 Vic 22105
Libby Holman 11/29 Bruns 4506

I WANNA BE LOVED BY YOU (36)
Harms, pub. 1928, reached #4 in January 1929
Bert Kalmar w, Harry Ruby & Herbert Stothart m
Featured in GOOD BOY, show (opened 09/28)
Helen Kane ΦΦ 12/28 Vic 21684
Helen Kane & Dan Healy, sung in show
High Hatters/Sam Coslow 12/28 Vic 21682

I'LL ALWAYS BE IN LOVE WITH YOU (10)
Shapiro, B, pub. 1929, reached #4 in August 1929
Bud Green, Harry Ruby, Sam Stept w & m
Featured in STEPPING HIGH, film (rel. 12/28)
Also featured in SYNCOPATION, film (rel. 03/29)
Waring's Pennsylvanians/Clare Hanlon Φ 04/29 Vic 21870
Morton Downey Φ sung in film (SYNC), 04/29 Vic 21860

I'LL GET BY (AS LONG AS I HAVE YOU) (15)
Berlin ΦΦΦ, pub. 1928, reached #1 in March 1929 (Also reached #2 in July 1944)
Roy Turk w, Fred Ahlert m
Irving Aaronson/w.vocal group ΦΦ 01/29 Vic 21786
Ruth Etting Φ stage, 04/29 Col 1733-D
Nick Lucas 02/29 Bruns 4156

I'M BRINGING A RED, RED ROSE
Donaldson, D & G, pub. 1928, reached #14 in March 1929
Gus Kahn w, Walter Donaldson m
Featured in WHOOPEE, show (opened 12/28)
George Olsen/Bob Borger 02/29 Vic 21808
Ruth Etting 02/29 Col 1680-D
Frances Upton & Paul Gregory, sung in show

I'M JUST A VAGABOND LOVER (11)
L Feist, pub. 1929, reached #2 in July 1929
Rudy Vallee & Leon Zimmerman w & m
Featured in THE VAGABOND LOVER, film (rel. 12/29)
Also Featured in GLORIFYING THE AMERICAN GIRL, film (rel. 01/30)
Rudy Vallee ΦΦ stage, both films, 07/29 Vic 21967
Al Goodman/Frank Luther 07/29 Bruns 4362

I'M SORRY, SALLY
L Feist, pub. 1928, reached #8 in January 1929
Gus Kahn w, Ted FioRito m
Waring's Pennsylvanians/Clare Hanlon Φ 12/28 Vic 21755
Shilkret's Rhyth-Melodists 12/28 Vic 21688

I'VE GOT A FEELING I'M FALLING (44)
Santly Bros, pub. 1929, reached #12 in August 1929
Billy Rose w, Harry Link & Thomas "Fats" Waller m
Featured in APPLAUSE, film (rel. 10/29)
Ben Bernie/Scrappy Lambert Φ 06/29 Bruns 4315
Thomas "Fats" Waller 10/29 Vic 22092
Gene Austin 09/29 Vic 22033

IF I HAD A TALKING PICTURE OF YOU (8)
DeSylva, B & H, pub. 1929, reached #3 in December 1929
Bud DeSylva, Lew Brown, Ray Henderson w & m
Featured in SUNNY SIDE UP, film (rel. 10/29)
Johnny Hamp/Don Howard ΦΦ 11/29 Vic 22124
Janet Gaynor & Charles Farrell, sung in film
Paul Whiteman/Bing Crosby Φ 12/29 Col 2010-D
Belle Baker 12/29 Bruns 4550
Johnny Marvin 12/29 Vic 22148

IF I HAD YOU (23)
Robbins, pub. 1928, reached #5 in March 1929
Ted Shapiro, James Campbell, Reginald Connelly w & m
Rudy Vallee/<vocal Φ stage and 03/29 Harmony 825-H[4], 03/29 Velvetone 1825-V
Irving Aaronson/Burt Lorin[5] 04/29 Vic 21867
Ben Selvin/w.vocal 04/29 Col 1719-D

JERICHO
Harms, pub. 1929, reached #10 in May 1929
Leo Robin w, Richard Myers m
Featured in SYNCOPATION, film (rel. 03/29)
Waring's Pennsylvanians/Fred Waring Φ perf. in film , 04/29 Vic 21870
Ted Wallace/Smith Ballew 07/29 Col 1833-D

LET'S DO IT (LET'S FALL IN LOVE) (45)
Harms, pub. 1928, reached #5 in January 1929
Cole Porter w & m
Featured in PARIS, show (opened 10/28)
Irene Bordoni, sung in show
Irving Aaronson/w.vocal duo Φ 12/28 Vic 21745
Rudy Vallee/<vocal, stage, 02/29 Harmony 808-H[4], 02/29 Velvetone 1808-V

LITTLE PAL (33)
DeSylva, B & H, pub. 1929, reached #7 in September 1929
Al Jolson, Bud DeSylva, Lew Brown w, Ray Henderson m
Featured in SAY IT WITH SONGS, film (rel. 08/29)
Al Jolson, sung in film, 08/29 Bruns 4400
Gene Austin 07/29 Vic 21952
George Olsen/Fran Frey 08/29 Vic 21954
Paul Whiteman/Bing Crosby 08/29 Col 1877-D

LONELY TROUBADOUR (39)
Santly Bros, pub. 1929, reached #5 in November 1929
John Klenner w & m
Rudy Vallee/<vocal Φ radio, 11/29 Vic 22136
Ted Lewis/<vocal Φ 11/29 Col 1957-D
Nick Lucas, stage

LOUISE (19)
Remick, pub. 1929, reached #3 in June 1929
Leo Robin w, Richard Whiting m
Featured in INNOCENTS OF PARIS, film (rel. 04/29)
Maurice Chevalier Φ sung in film, 05/29 Vic 21918
Paul Whiteman/Bing Crosby Φ 05/29 Col 1771-D
Ben Pollack/Smith Ballew Φ 06/29 Vic 21941
Frankie Trumbauer/Smith Ballew 07/29 Okeh 41231

LOVE (YOUR MAGIC SPELL IS EVERYWHERE) (25)
Berlin, pub. 1929, reached #4 in December 1929
Elsie Janis w, Edmund Goulding m
Featured in THE TRESPASSER, film (rel. 09/29)
Gloria Swanson, sung in film, 10/29 Vic 22079
Arden-Ohman Orch/Frank Luther Φ 11/29 Vic 22114
Ben Selvin/Smith Ballew 11/29 Col 1994-D
Kate Smith 01/30 Harmony 1050-H, 01/30 Velvetone 2050-V

LOVE ME (27)
L Feist, pub. 1929, reached #4 in November 1929
Hale Byers w, Ernie Golden m
Paul Whiteman/Jack Fulton Φ 11/29 Col 1974-D
Nat Shilkret/Frank Munn Φ 12/29 Vic 22152
Lee Morse 11/29 Col 1972-D

LOVE ME OR LEAVE ME
Donaldson, D & G, pub. 1928, reached #15 in May 1929
(Also reached #17 in June 1955)
Gus Kahn w, Walter Donaldson m
Featured in WHOOPEE, show (opened 12/28)
Also featured in SIMPLE SIMON, show (opened 02/30)
Ruth Etting Φ sung in both shows, 03/29 Col 1680-D
Guy Lombardo/Carmen Lombardo 05/29 Col 1782-D
Leo Reisman/Ran Weeks 07/29 Vic 21966

LOVER, COME BACK TO ME (22)
Harms, pub. 1928, reached #3 in April 1929
Oscar Hammerstein 2nd w, Sigmund Romberg m
Featured in THE NEW MOON, show (opened 09/28)
Paul Whiteman/Jack Fulton Φ 04/29 Col 1731-D
Evelyn Herbert, sung in show
Rudy Vallee/<vocal Φ 04/29 Vic 21880
Arden-Ohman Orch/The Revelers Φ 03/29 Vic 21776
Jessica Dragonette 07/29 Bruns 4355

MAKIN' WHOOPIE (32)
Donaldson, D & G, pub. 1928, reached #6 in March 1929
Gus Kahn w, Walter Donaldson m
Featured in WHOOPEE, show (opened 12/28)
Eddie Cantor Φ sung in show, 02/29 Vic 21831
Paul Whiteman/w.vocal group[10] Φ 03/29 Col 1683-D
Ben Bernie/Scrappy Lambert 02/29 Bruns 4142
Harry Richman 03/29 Bruns 4197

MARIE (16)
Berlin ΦΦΦ, pub. 1928, reached #2 in February 1929
(Also reached #11 in April 1937)
(Also reached #17 in January 1954 and #15 in July 1965)
Irving Berlin w & m
Featured in THE AWAKENING, film (rel. 11/28)
The Troubadours/Lewis James ΦΦ 12/28 Vic 21746
Franklyn Baur Φ 01/29 Vic 21787
Rudy Vallee/<vocal, stage, 03/29 Harmony 834-H, 03/29 Velvetone 1834-V

ME AND THE MAN IN THE MOON
Donaldson, D & G, pub. 1928, reached #18 in March 1929[12]
Edgar Leslie w, James V Monaco m
Ted Weems/Art Jarrett 02/29 Vic 21809
Helen Kane 02/29 Vic 21830
Guy Lombardo/Carmen Lombardo 02/29 Col 1679-D

MEAN TO ME (24)
DeSylva, B & G, pub. 1929, reached #3 in May 1929
(Also reached #19 in July 1937)
Roy Turk w, Fred Ahlert m
Ruth Etting ΦΦ stage, 05/29 Col 1762-D
Helen Morgan, stage, 05/29 Vic 21930
Ted Wallace/Smith Ballew 05/29 Col 1756-D
Dorsey Brothers Orch/Smith Ballew 05/29 Okeh 41210

MISS YOU
Santly Bros, pub. 1929, reached #12 in September 1929
(Also reached #5 in April 1942)
Charles Tobias, Harry Tobias, Henry Tobias w & m
Rudy Vallee/<vocal, stage, 08/29 Vic 22029
Ben Selvin/Smith Ballew 08/29 Col 1875-D
Lee Morse 09/29 Col 1896-D

MOANIN' LOW (18)
Harms, pub. 1929, reached #5 in September 1929
Howard Dietz w, Ralph Rainger m
Featured in THE LITTLE SHOW, show (opened 04/29)
Libby Holman Φ sung in show, 09/29 Bruns 4445
Leo Reisman/Lew Conrad 09/29 Vic 22047
Sophie Tucker, stage, 09/29 Vic 22049

MY BLACKBIRDS ARE BLUEBIRDS NOW
L Feist, pub. 1928, reached #14 in January 1929
Irving Caesar w, Cliff Friend m
Featured in WHOOPIE, show (opened 12/28)
Eddie Cantor, sung in show
Ruth Etting 01/29 Col 1595-D
Bernie Cummins/<vocal 12/28 Bruns 4083

MY LUCKY STAR
DeSylva, B & H, pub. 1928, reached #19 in April 1929
Bud DeSylva, Lew Brown, Ray Henderson w & m
Featured in FOLLOW THRU, show (opened 01/29)
John Barker, sung in show
Waring's Pennsylvanians/Roy Cropper 04/29 Vic 21861
Paul Whiteman/Norman Clark 04/29 Col 1736-D

MY MOTHER'S EYES (50)
L Feist, pub. 1928, reached #10 in April 1929
L Wolfe Gilbert w, Abel Baer m
Featured in LUCKY BOY, film (rel. 01/29)
George Jessel, sung in film, 03/29 Vic 21852
Waring's Pennsylvanians/Clare Hanlon 04/29 Vic 21857
Jack Denny/Jack Parker 03/29 Bruns 4170

MY SIN (30)
DeSylva, B & H, pub. 1929, reached #4 in July 1929
Bud DeSylva & Lew Brown w, Ray Henderson m
Featured in SHOW GIRL IN HOLLYWOOD, film (rel. 04/30)
Waring's Pennsylvanians/Clare Hanlon Φ 07/29 Vic 21977
Ben Selvin/w.vocal Φ 06/29 Col 1800-D
Belle Baker Φ 07/29 Bruns 4343

MY SONG OF THE NILE (9)
Witmark, pub. 1929, reached #2 in October 1929
Alfred Bryan w, George Meyer m
Sung by unbilled tenor in DRAG, film (rel. 06/29)
The Melody Three Φ 08/29 Vic 22028
The Troubadours/Scrappy Lambert Φ 10/29 Vic 22073
Ben Selvin/Smith Ballew Φ 09/29 Col 1900-D

PAGAN LOVE SONG (3)
Robbins ΦΦΦ, pub. 1929, reached #1 in July 1929
Arthur Freed w, Nacio Herb Brown m
Featured in THE PAGAN, film (rel. 05/29)
Ramon Novarro, sung in film
The Troubadours/Frank Munn ΦΦ 05/29 Vic 21931
The Columbians/w.vocal Φ 07/29 Col 1817-D
Copley Plaza Orch[7]/Frank Munn Φ 06/29 Bruns 4321
James Melton 08/29 Col 1853-D

PAINTING THE CLOUDS WITH SUNSHINE (6)
Witmark, pub. 1929, reached #2 in November 1929
Al Dubin w, Joe Burke m
Featured in GOLD DIGGERS OF BROADWAY, film (rel. 09/29)
Nick Lucas ΦΦ sung in film, 09/29 Bruns 4418
Jean Goldkette/Frank Munn Φ 08/29 Vic 22027
Smith Ballew/<vocal 11/29 Okeh 41299
Johnny Marvin 11/29 Vic 22113

PICCOLO PETE (34)
J W Jenkins, pub. 1929, reached #6 in November 1929
Phil Baxter w & m
Ted Weems/Parker Gibbs ΦΦ 09/29 Vic 22037
Six Jumping Jacks/Tom Stacks 10/29 Bruns 4457
Freddie Rich/Irving Kaufman 09/29 Cameo 9233

A PRECIOUS LITTLE THING CALLED LOVE (20)
Remick, pub. 1928, reached #1 in April 1929
J Fred Coots & Lou Davis w & m
Featured in THE SHOPWORN ANGEL, film (rel. 01/29)
George Olsen/Ethel Shutta ΦΦ 03/29 Vic 21832
Nancy Carroll, sung in film
Johnny Marvin & Ed Smalle 04/29 Vic 21892
Ipana Troubadours/w.vocal 03/29 Col 1717-D

SATISFIED
L Feist, pub. 1929, reached #11 in December 1929
Irving Caesar w, Cliff Friend m
Henry Busse/Barry Stacey 11/29 Vic 22116
Johnny Marvin 12/29 Vic 22180

SHE'S FUNNY THAT WAY (49)
Villa Moret, pub. 1928, reached #7 in February 1929
Richard Whiting w, Neil Moret m
Gene Austin Φ stage, 01/29 Vic 21779
Ted Lewis/<vocal, stage, 02/29 Col 1656-D
Ben Bernie/Scrappy Lambert 02/29 Bruns 4132

SINGIN' IN THE RAIN (5)
Robbins, pub. 1929, reached #3 in November 1929
Arthur Freed w, Nacio Herb Brown m
Featured in HOLLYWOOD REVUE OF 1929, film (rel. 08/29)
Cliff Edwards[8] & Brox Sisters, sung in film
Cliff Edwards[8] ΦΦ 08/29 Col 1869-D
Gus Arnheim Orch Φ 08/29 Vic 22012
Nick Lucas 08/29 Bruns 4378
Earl Burtnett/Paul Gibbons 08/29 Bruns 4375

SLEEPY VALLEY (17)
Harms, pub. 1928, reached #4 in September 1929
Andrew Sterling w, James F Hanley m
Featured in THE RAINBOW MAN, film (rel. 04/29)
Gus Arnheim/Buster Dees Φ 07/29 Vic 21986
James Melton Φ 06/29 Col 1797-D
Eddie Dowling, sung in film

SOME SWEET DAY
Remick, pub. 1929, reached #20 in May 1929
Nat Shilkret & Lew Pollack w & m
Theme song for CHILDREN OF THE RITZ, film (rel. 04/29)
Nat Shilkret/Franklyn Baur 04/29 Vic 21896
Ipana Troubadours/Smith Ballew 04/29 Col 1747-D

S'POSIN'
Triangle M C, pub. 1929, reached #14 in August 1929
Andy Razaf w, Paul Denniker m
Rudy Vallee/<vocal Φ stage, 07/29 Vic 21998
Paul Whiteman/Bing Crosby 08/29 Col 1862-D

SUNNY SIDE UP (37)
DeSylva, B & H, pub. 1929, reached #9 in December 1929
Bud DeSylva, Lew Brown, Ray Henderson w & m
Featured in SUNNY SIDE UP, film (rel. 10/29)
Janet Gaynor & Charles Farrell, sung in film
Johnny Hamp/Frank Luther Φ 11/29 Vic 22124
Earl Burnett/w.vocal 11/29 Bruns 4501

(I LOVE YOU) SWEETHEART OF ALL MY DREAMS (47)
Shapiro, B, pub. 1928, reached #9 in March 1929
(Also reached #17 in May 1945)
Art Fitch, Kay Fitch, Bert Lowe w & m
Rudy Vallee[4]/<vocal Φ stage and 03/29 Harmony 811-H, 03/29 Velvetone 1811-V
Irving Aaronson/w.vocal group Φ 03/29 Vic 21834
Johnny Marvin 03/29 Vic 21851

SWEETHEARTS ON PARADE (12)
M Weil, pub. 1928, reached #1 in February 1929
Charles Newman w, Carmen Lombardo m
Guy Lombardo/Carmen Lombardo ΦΦ stage and 02/29 Col 1628-D
Jean Goldkette/Van Fleming 02/29 Vic 21800
Abe Lyman/w.vocal 02/29 Bruns 4117
Johnny Marvin 02/29 Vic 21820

THROUGH
Donaldson, D & G, pub. 1929, reached #12 in December 1929
Joe McCarthy w, James V Monaco m
Ted Lewis/<vocal Φ 11/29 Col 1957-D
Roger Wolfe Kahn/w.vocal 12/29 Bruns 4571

TIP TOE THROUGH THE TULIPS WITH ME (2)
Witmark ΦΦΦ, pub. 1929, reached #1 in October 1929
(Also reached #17 in June 1968)
Al Dubin w, Joe Burke m
Featured in GOLD DIGGERS OF BROADWAY, film (rel. 09/29)
Nick Lucas ΦΦ 09/29 Bruns 4418
Jean Goldkette/Frank Munn Φ 08/29 Vic 22027
Johnny Marvin Φ 11/29 Vic 22113
Smith Ballew/<vocal 11/29 Okeh 41299

TRUE BLUE LOU
Spier & Coslow, pub. 1929, reached #12 in October 1929
Leo Robin & Sam Coslow w, Richard Whiting m
Featured in THE DANCE OF LIFE, film (rel. 08/29)
Ethel Waters Φ 08/29 Col 1871-D
Hal Skelly, sung in film
Johnny Marvin 11/29 Vic 22125

TURN ON THE HEAT
DeSylva, B & H, pub. 1929, reached #13 in December 1929
Bud DeSylva, Lew Brown, Ray Henderson w & m
Featured in SUNNY SIDE UP, film (rel. 10/29)
Frank Richardson & Sharon Lynn, sung in film
Earl Burtnett/w.vocal 12/29 Bruns 4573
Charleston Chasers/Eva Taylor 12/29 Col 1989-D

WAITING AT THE END OF THE ROAD
Berlin, pub. 1929, reached #14 in November 1929
Irving Berlin w & m
Featured in HALLELUJAH, film (rel. 08/29)
Ethel Waters 10/29 Col 1933-D
Paul Whiteman/Bing Crosby 11/29 Col 1974-D
Dixie Jubilee Singers, sung in film

WALKING WITH SUSIE
DeSylva, B & H, pub. 1929, reached #16 in July 1929
Sidney D Mitchell & Archie Gottler w, Con Conrad m
Featured in WILLIAM FOX MOVIETONE FOLLIES OF 1929, film (rel. 05/29)
George Olsen/Fran Frey 06/29 Vic 21927
Frank Richardson, sung in film
Milt Shaw/w.vocal 06/29 Col 1811-D

WEARY RIVER (21)
Berlin, pub. 1929, reached #1 in April 1929
Grant Clarke w, Louis Silvers m
Sung by unbilled vocalist in WEARY RIVER, film (rel. 01/29)
Rudy Vallee/<vocal Φ 04/29 Vic 21868
Gene Austin Φ 04/29 Vic 21856
Jan Garber/w.vocal 04/29 Col 1724-D

WEDDING BELLS (ARE BREAKING UP THAT OLD GANG OF MINE) (40)
Waterson, B & S, pub. 1929, reached #5 in April 1929
(Also reached #17 in April 1955)
Irving Kahal & Willie Raskin w, Sammy Fain m
Sammy Fain Φ stage, 04/29 Harmony 843-H, 04/29 Velvetone 1843-V
Billy Murray & Walter Scanlon[9], radio, 04/29 Ed 52516
Gene Austin Φ 05/29 Vic 21893

THE WEDDING OF THE PAINTED DOLL (1)
Sherman Clay ΦΦΦ, pub. 1929, reached #1 in June 1929
Arthur Freed w, Nacio Herb Brown m
Featured in BROADWAY MELODY, film (rel. 02/29)
Leo Reisman/Smith Ballew Φ 06/29 Col 1780-D
Earl Burtnett/Paul Gibbons Φ 04/29 Bruns 4232
James Burrows, sung in film
Charles King Φ 07/29 Vic 21964
Horace Heidt Orch 07/29 Vic 21957

WHEN MY DREAMS COME TRUE (29)
Berlin, pub. 1929, reached #8 in October 1929
Irving Berlin w & m
Featured in THE COCOANUTS, film (rel. 06/29)
Paul Whiteman/Jack Fulton Φ 07/29 Col 1822-D
Waring's Pennsylvanians/w.vocal trio Φ 07/29 Vic 21977
Oscar Shaw & Mary Eaton, sung in film
Franklyn Baur 07/29 Vic 21989

WHEN YOU'RE SMILING (46)
H Rossiter, pub. 1928, reached Top 30 in November 1928
Mark Fisher, Joe Goodwin, Larry Shay w & m
Steady seller, 1928-1930. Jazz Standard, 1930-1950
Louis Armstrong/<vocal 11/29 Okeh 41298, 12/29 Okeh 8729
King Oliver/Frank Marvin 04/30 Vic 22298
Rudy Vallee, stage
Seger Ellis/<vocal 10/28 Col 1494-D

WHERE IS THE SONG OF SONGS FOR ME?
Berlin, pub. 1928, reached #16 in April 1929
Irving Berlin w & m
Featured in LADY OF THE PAVEMENTS, film (rel. 03/29)
Lupe Velez, sung in film, 06/29 Vic 21932
Paul Whiteman/Jack Fulton Φ 02/29 Col 1630-D
James Melton 02/29 Col 1640-D
Johnny Hamp/Joe Cassidy 03/29 Vic 21838

WHERE THE SHY LITTLE VIOLETS GROW
Remick, pub. 1928, reached #9 in March 1929
Gus Kahn w, Harry Warren m
Guy Lombardo/w.vocal trio Φ 02/29 Col 1679-D
George Olsen/Fran Frey Φ 02/29 Vic 21819
Johnny Marvin 02/29 Vic 21820

WITH A SONG IN MY HEART (48)
Harms, pub. 1929, reached #8 in July 1929
Lorenz Hart w, Richard Rodgers m
Featured in SPRING IS HERE, show (opened 03/29)
Leo Reisman/Ran Weeks Φ 06/29 Vic 21923
Lillian Taiz & John Hundley, sung in show
James Melton 08/29 Col 1853-D

YOU WERE MEANT FOR ME (26)
Robbins, pub. 1929, reached #4 in May 1929
(Also reached #11 in April 1948)
Arthur Freed w, Nacio Herb Brown m
Featured in BROADWAY MELODY, film (rel. 02/29)
Also featured in HOLLYWOOD REVUE OF 1929, film (rel. 08/29)
Also featured in THE SHOW OF SHOWS, film (rel. 11/29)
Charles King Φ sung in film (BM), 07/29 Vic 21965
Nat Shilkret/Scrappy Lambert Φ 04/29 Vic 21886
Broadway Nitelites[6]/w.vocal Φ 04/29 Col 1738-D
Helen Morgan, stage

YOU'RE THE CREAM IN MY COFFEE (13)
DeSylva, B & H, pub. 1928, reached #1 in January 1929
Bud DeSylva, Lew Brown, Ray Henderson w & m
Featured in HOLD EVERYTHING, show (opened 10/28)
Ted Weems/Parker Gibbs ΦΦ 01/29 Vic 21767
Jack Whiting, sung in show
Broadway Nitelites[6]/Jack Parker Φ 01/29 Col 1604-D
Ruth Etting 03/29 Col 1707-D

YOUR MOTHER AND MINE
Robbins, pub. 1929, reached #19 in September 1929
Joe Goodwin w, Gus Edwards m
Featured in HOLLYWOOD REVUE OF 1929, film (rel. 08/29)
Also featured in THE SHOW OF SHOWS, film (rel. 11/29)
Charles King, sung in film (HR)
Nat Shilkret/Frank Munn 08/29 Vic 22012
Nick Lucas 08/29 Bruns 4378

[1]Gay Ellis was a pseudonym for Annette Hanshaw.
[2]The name Troubadours was a pseudonym used by many orchestras. In this case, it is that of Nat Shilkret.
[3]The Broadway Broadcasters were actually Sam Lanin's Orch.
[4]Rudy Vallee was listed on the Harmony label as Frank Mater.
[5]Burt Lorin was a pseudonym for Scrappy Lambert.
[6]The Broadway Nitelites were actually the Ben Selvin Orch.
[7]Actually the Bob Haring Orch.
[8]Cliff Edwards was also known as Ukulele Ike.
[9]Walter Scanlon was a pseudonym for Walter Van Brunt.
[10]Whiteman's vocal group included Bing Crosby on this record.
[11]Reached #19 on monthly chart only.
[12]Reached #18 on monthly chart only.

1930

ABSENCE MAKES THE HEART GROW FONDER (FOR SOMEBODY ELSE)
Donaldson, D & G, pub. 1929, reached #11 in August 1930
Sam Lewis & Joe Young w, Harry Warren m
Bernie Cummins/Paul Small 07/30 Vic 22425
Gene Austin 08/30 Vic 22451

(I'M A DREAMER) AREN'T WE ALL? (5)
DeSylva, B & H, pub. 1929, reached #1 in February 1930
Bud DeSylva & Lew Brown w, Ray Henderson m
Featured in SUNNY SIDE UP, film (rel. 10/29)
Paul Whiteman/Bing Crosby Φ 01/30 Col 2010-D
Janet Gaynor & Charles Farrell, sung in film
Belle Baker 12/29 Bruns 4550
Johnny Marvin 12/29 Vic 22148

AROUND THE CORNER
L Feist, pub. 1930, reached #15 in August 1930
Gus Kahn w, Art Kassel m
Ben Selvin/Smith Ballew 07/30 Col 2221-D
Leo Reisman/Philip Steele 08/30 Vic 22459
Art Kassel Orch, db dates

BABY'S BIRTHDAY PARTY
Famous, pub. 1930, reached #18 in December 1930
Ann Ronell w & m
Guy Lombardo/w.vocal trio 12/30 Col 2319-D
Nat Shilkret Orch 01/31 Vic 22581

BESIDE AN OPEN FIREPLACE
Santly Bros, pub. 1929, reached #18 in April 1930
Will Osborne & Paul Denniker w & m
Rudy Vallee/<vocal 04/30 Vic 22284
Vaughn DeLeath, radio

BETTY CO-ED (12)
Carl Fischer, pub. 1930, reached #4 in October 1930
J Paul Fogarty & Rudy Vallee w & m
Rudy Vallee/<vocal ΦΦ radio, 09/30 Vic 22473
Bob Haring/w.vocal 09/30 Bruns 4852
Phil Spitalny/Scrappy Lambert, stage, 09/30 Hit of Wk 1097

BEYOND THE BLUE HORIZON (41)
Famous, pub. 1930, reached #6 in December 1930
Leo Robin w, Richard A Whiting & W Franke Harding m
Featured in MONTE CARLO, film, (rel. 08/30)
Jeanette MacDonald Φ sung in film, 10/30 Vic 22514
George Olsen/Bob Borger 12/30 Vic 22530
Phil Spitalny/w.vocal 11/30 Bruns 4917

BODY AND SOUL (15)
Harms, pub. 1930, reached #5 in December 1930
Edward Heyman, Robert Sour & Frank Eyton w, John Green m
Featured in THREE'S A CROWD, show (opened 10/30)
Libby Holman Φ sung in show, 11/30 Bruns 4910
Paul Whiteman/Jack Fulton Φ 11/30 Col 2297-D
Helen Morgan, stage, 11/30 Vic 22532
Ruth Etting 11/30 Col 2300-D
Louis Armstrong/<vocal 01/31 Okeh 41468

BYE BYE BLUES (43)
Berlin, pub. 1930, reached #7 in September 1930
(Also reached #14 in February 1953)
Bert Lown, Chauncey Gray, David Bennett, Fred Hamm w & m
Bert Lown/Biltmore Rhythm Boys 09/30 Col 2258-D, 09/30 Hit of Wk 1090
Leo Reisman/Don Howard 09/30 Vic 22459
Tom Clines/w.vocal 08/30 Bruns 4864

CHANT OF THE JUNGLE (16)
Robbins, pub. 1929, reached #1 in January 1930
Arthur Freed w, Nacio Herb Brown m
Featured in UNTAMED, film (rel. 11/29)
Nat Shilkret/Frank Munn Φ 01/30 Vic 22203
Joan Crawford, sung in film
Roy Ingraham/w.vocal Φ 01/30 Bruns 4586
Vaughn DeLeath, radio, 12/29 Bruns 4533
Paul Specht/w.vocal 12/29 Col 2002-D

CONGRATULATIONS
DeSylva, B & H, pub. 1929, reached #16 in January 1930
Maceo Pinkard, Coleman Goetz, Bud Green, Sam Stept w & m
Jack Denny/w.vocal 01/30 Bruns 4604
Jim Miller & Charlie Farrell 03/30 Vic 22277
Nat Shilkret/Frank Munn 04/30 Vic 22291

A COTTAGE FOR SALE (21)
DeSylva, B & H, pub. 1930, reached #3 in May 1930
(Also reached #15 in October 1945)
Willard Robison w, Larry Conley m
Guy Lombardo/Carmen Lombardo Φ 05/30 Col 2156-D
Ruth Etting 05/30 Col 2172-D
The Revelers 06/30 Vic 22382

CRYIN' FOR THE CAROLINES (20)
Remick, pub. 1929, reached #3 in March 1930
Sam Lewis & Joe Young w, Harry Warren m
Featured in SPRING IS HERE, film (rel. 07/30)
Guy Lombardo/Carmen Lombardo Φ radio, 03/30 Col 2062-D
Waring's Pennsylvanians/Will Morgan Φ 03/30 Vic 22272
Lawrence Gray, sung in film

DANCING WITH TEARS IN MY EYES (3)
Witmark, pub. 1930, reached #1 in July 1930
Al Dubin w, Joe Burke m
Nat Shilkret/Lewis James ΦΦ 07/30 Vic 22425
Ruth Etting Φ 07/30 Col 2206-D[1], 07/30 Col 2216-D
Rudy Vallee/<vocal, radio and stage
Nick Lucas 07/30 Bruns 4834

DON'T EVER LEAVE ME
T B Harms, pub. 1929, reached #20 in February 1930
Oscar Hammerstein 2nd w, Jerome Kern m
Featured in SWEET ADELINE, show (opened 09/29)
Helen Morgan & Robert Chisholm, sung in show
Helen Morgan 01/30 Vic 22199
Roger Wolfe Kahn/w.vocal 01/30 Bruns 4614

DON'T TELL HER (HIM) WHAT HAPPENED TO ME
DeSylva, B & H, pub. 1930, reached #14 in October 1930
Bud DeSylva, Lew Brown, Ray Henderson w & m
Ruth Etting 10/30 Col 2280-D
Nat Shilkret/Scrappy Lambert 11/30 Vic 22526

DOWN THE RIVER OF GOLDEN DREAMS (36)
L Feist, pub. 1930, reached #9 in August 1930
John Klenner & Nat Shilkret w & m
Johnny Marvin 07/30 Vic 22418
Hilo Hawaiian Orch/Johnny Marvin 05/30 Vic 22339

EXACTLY LIKE YOU (39)
Shapiro, B, pub. 1930, reached #8 in June 1930
(Also reached #19 in December 1936)
Dorothy Fields w, Jimmy McHugh m
Featured in LEW LESLIE'S INTERNATIONAL REVUE, show (opened 02/30)
Harry Richman, sung in show, 06/30 Bruns 4747
Bernie Cummins/<vocal 05/30 Vic 22354
Ruth Etting 07/30 Col 2199-D

FINE AND DANDY
Harms, pub. 1930, reached #13 in December 1930
Paul James w, Kay Swift m
Featured in FINE AND DANDY, show (opened 09/30)
Arden-Ohman Orch/Frank Luther 12/30 Vic 22552
Joe Cooke & Alice Boulden, sung in show

FUNNY, DEAR, WHAT LOVE CAN DO
L Feist, pub. 1929, reached #20 in February 1930[7]
Charley Straight, Joe Bennett, George A Little w & m
Marion Harris 02/30 Bruns 4663
Ben Selvin/w.vocal 03/30 Col 2096-D

GET HAPPY
Remick, pub. 1930, reached #13 in July 1930
Ted Koehler w, Harold Arlen m
Featured in 9:15 REVUE, revue (opened 02/30)
Ruth Etting, sung in revue
Nat Shilkret/w.vocal trio 07/30 Vic 22444
Frankie Trumbauer/<vocal 07/30 Okeh 41431

GO HOME AND TELL YOUR MOTHER (23)
Robbins, pub. 1930, reached #3 in October 1930
Dorothy Fields w, Jimmy McHugh m
Featured in LOVE IN THE ROUGH, film (rel. 09/30)
Gus Arnheim/Bobby Burns Φ 09/30 Vic 22505
Robert Montgomery & Dorothy Jordan, sung in film
Guy Lombardo/w.vocal trio Φ 10/30 Col 2276-D
Johnny Marvin 09/30 Vic 22502

GREAT DAY (45)
V Youmans, Inc, pub. 1929, reached #9 in January 1930
Billy Rose & Edward Eliscu w, Vincent Youmans m
Featured in GREAT DAY, show (opened 10/29)
Paul Whiteman/w.vocal group Φ 12/29 Col 2023-D
Lois Deppe & Jubilee Singers, sung in show

HAPPY DAYS ARE HERE AGAIN (8)
Ager, Y & B, pub. 1929, reached #1 in February 1930
Jack Yellen w, Milt Ager m
Featured in CHASING RAINBOWS, film (rel. 02/30)
Charles King Φ sung in film, 01/30 Bruns 4615
Leo Reisman/L Levin Φ 02/30 Vic 22221
Johnny Marvin Φ 01/30 Vic 22186
Ben Selvin/w.vocal group 03/30 Col 2116-D
Benny Meroff/Dusty Rhodes 02/30 Bruns 4709

HERE COMES THE SUN
Robbins, pub. 1930, reached #20 in October 1930
Arthur Freed w, Harry Woods m
Ted Wallace/Elmer Feldkamp 09/30 Col 2236-D
Bert Lown/Biltmore Rhythm Boys 10/30 Vic 22541
Vincent Lopez/Jack Parker, stage, 10/30 Hit of Wk 1089

I LOVE YOU SO MUCH
Harms, pub. 1930, reached #14 in August 1930
Bert Kalmar w, Harry Ruby m
Featured in THE CUCKOOS, film (rel. 04/30)
Bert Wheeler, sung in film
Arden-Ohman Orch/Frank Luther 06/30 Vic 22383
Bob Haring/w.vocal 08/30 Bruns 4852

I NEVER DREAMT
Santly Bros, pub. 1928, reached #19 in June 1930
Vivian Ellis & Donovan Parsons w & m
Rudy Vallee/<vocal 05/30 Vic 22361
Ipana Troubadours/Smith Ballew 05/30 Col 2147-D

I STILL GET A THRILL (44)
Davis, Coots & Engel, pub. 1930, reached #6 in October 1930
Benny Davis w, J Fred Coots m
Ozzie Nelson/<vocal Φ 10/30 Bruns 4897
Guy Lombardo/Carmen Lombardo Φ 11/30 Col 2286-D
Ted Weems/Art Jarrett 11/30 Vic 22515
Gladys Rice, stage

I STILL REMEMBER
J Morris, pub. 1930, reached #19 in June 1930
Charles Tobias & Sam Ward w, Peter DeRose m
Rudy Vallee/<vocal, radio, 05/30 Vic 22361

I'LL BE BLUE JUST THINKING OF YOU
L Feist, pub. 1930, reached #15 in November 1930
George A Whiting w, Pete Wendling m
Bert Lown Orch/Elmer Feldkamp 11/30 Col 2292-D
Nat Shilkret/Scrappy Lambert 11/30 Vic 22529
Ruth Etting 11/30 Col 2307-D
Harry Richman, stage

I'LL SEE YOU AGAIN
Chappell, pub. 1929, reached #20 in March 1930
Noel Coward w & m
Featured in BITTER SWEET, show (opened 11/29)
Evelyn Laye & Gerald Nodin, sung in show
Leo Reisman/L Levin 02/30 Vic 22246

I'M CONFESSIN' (THAT I LOVE YOU) (38)
Berlin, pub. 1930, reached #7 in October 1930
(Also reached #12 in February 1945)
(Also reached #14 in May 1952)
Al J Neiberg w, Doc Daugherty & Ellis Reynolds m
Rudy Vallee/<vocal 09/30 Vic 22506
Guy Lombardo/Carmen Lombardo 09/30 Col 2259-D
Louis Armstrong/<vocal 11/30 Okeh 41448

I'M FOLLOWING YOU (13)
Berlin, pub. 1929, reached #4 in February 1930
Ballard MacDonald & Dave Dreyer w & m
Featured in IT'S A GREAT LIFE, film (rel. 01/30)
Duncan Sisters, sung in film, 03/30 Vic 22269
The High Hatters/Frank Luther 02/30 Vic 22218
Paul Specht/w.vocal 02/30 Col 2056-D

I'M IN THE MARKET FOR YOU (24)
Red Star Mus Co, pub. 1930, reached #5 in June 1930
Joe McCarthy w, James F Hanley m
Featured in HIGH SOCIETY BLUES, film (rel. 04/30)
Janet Gaynor & Charles Farrell, sung in film
George Olsen/Bob Borger 06/30 Vic 22391
Columbia Photo Players[2]/Don Howard 07/30 Col 2187-D

I'M YOURS (18)
Famous, pub. 1930, reached #2 in November 1930
E Y Harbourg w, John Green m
Featured in LEAVE IT TO LESTER, film (rel. 10/30)
Added to SIMPLE SIMON, show (opened 02/30)
Bert Lown/Biltmore Rhythm Boys Φ 11/30 Vic 22541
Ruth Etting, sung in show, 12/30 Col 2318-D
Ben Bernie/w.vocal 10/30 Bruns 4898

IF I COULD BE WITH YOU (ONE HOUR TONIGHT) (6)
J H Remick, pub. 1926, reached #2 in September 1930
Henry Creamer & James P Johnson w & m
McKinney's Cotton Pickers/George Thomas ΦΦ 08/30 Vic 38118
Louis Armstrong/<vocal, stage, 10/30 Okeh 41448
Ben Pollack/Roland Lance[3] 08/30 Perfect 15325, 08/30 Banner 0747

IF I HAD A GIRL LIKE YOU (25)
L Feist, pub. 1930, reached #4 in June 1930
Louis McDermott w & m
Rudy Vallee/<vocal Φ radio, 06/30 Vic 22419
Guy Lombardo Orch, db dates
Anson Weeks/Warren Luce 06/30 Col 2211-D

IT HAPPENED IN MONTEREY (19)
L Feist, pub. 1930, reached #3 in May 1930
Billy Rose w, Mabel Wayne m
Featured in KING OF JAZZ, film (rel. 03/30)
Paul Whiteman/Jack Fulton Φ 03/30 Col 2163-D
Jeanette Loff & John Boles, sung in film
John Boles 05/30 Vic 22372
George Olsen/Bob Borger 05/30 Vic 22370

IT MUST BE TRUE (26)
Freed & Powers, pub. 1930, reached #6 in December 1930
Gus Arnheim & Gordon Clifford w, Harry Barris m
Gus Arnheim/Bing Crosby Φ 12/30 Vic 22561
Earl Burtnett/w.vocal 01/31 Bruns 4984
Ted Weems Orch, db dates

JUST A LITTLE CLOSER
Robbins, pub. 1930, reached #16 in September 1930
Howard Johnson w, Joseph Meyer m
Featured in REMOTE CONTROL, film (rel. 11/30)
Charles King, sung in film
Rudy Vallee/<vocal 09/30 Vic 22489
Ruth Etting 11/30 Col 2307-D

THE KISS WALTZ (27)
Witmark, pub. 1930, reached #3 in October 1930
Al Dubin w, Joe Burke m
Featured in DANCING SWEETIES, film (rel. 08/30)
George Olsen/Bob Borger Φ 08/30 Vic 22462
Sue Carol, sung in film
Ben Bernie/w.vocal 09/30 Bruns 4837

KITTY FROM KANSAS CITY
L Feist, pub. 1921, reached #14 in July 1930
Harry Rose, Jesse Greer, Rudy Vallee, George Bronson w & m
Rudy Vallee/<vocal 06/30 Vic 22419
Milt Coleman 09/30 Harmony 1185-H

LAZY LOU'SIANA MOON (42)
Donaldson, D & G, pub. 1930, reached #8 in April 1930
Walter Donaldson w & m
Guy Lombardo/Carmen Lombardo 04/30 Col 2135-D
Hilo Hawaiian Orch/w.vocal trio 04/30 Vic 22334

A LITTLE KISS EACH MORNING (17)
Harms, pub. 1929, reached #3 in January 1930
Harry Woods w & m
Featured in THE VAGABOND LOVER, film (rel. 11/29)
Rudy Vallee Φ sung in film, 01/30 Vic 22193
Guy Lombardo/Carmen Lombardo Φ 12/29 Col 2017-D
Lee Morse 02/30 Col 2063-D

LITTLE WHITE LIES (4)
Donaldson, D & G, pub. 1930, reached #1 in September 1930
(Also reached #3 in June 1948)
Walter Donaldson w & m
Waring's Pennsylvanians/Clare Hanlon ΦΦ 09/30 Vic 22492
Ted Wallace/Elmer Feldkamp 09/30 Col 2254-D
Rudy Vallee, stage and radio
Guy Lombardo Orch, stage and radio
Johnny Marvin 09/30 Vic 22502

LIVIN' IN THE SUNLIGHT, LOVIN' IN THE MOONLIGHT
Famous, pub. 1930, reached #10 in July 1930
Al Lewis w, Al Sherman m
Featured in THE BIG POND, film (rel. 04/30)
Maurice Chevalier Φ sung in film, 06/30 Vic 22405
Paul Whiteman/Bing Crosby 06/30 Col 2171-D

THE MAN FROM THE SOUTH (50)
Shapiro, B, pub. 1929, reached #9 in February 1930
Rube Bloom & Harry Woods w & m
Ted Weems/w.vocal group Φ db dates and 02/30 Vic 22238
Rube Bloom/w.vocal duo 02/30 Col 2103-D

THE MOON IS LOW (34)
Robbins, pub. 1930, reached #5 in May 1930
Arthur Freed w, Nacio Herb Brown m
Featured in MONTANA MOON, film (rel. 04/30)
Cliff Edwards, sung in film, 06/30 Col 2169-D
Guy Lombardo/Carmen Lombardo 04/30 Col 2135-D
Frank Luther 04/30 Vic 22330

MOONLIGHT ON THE COLORADO (11)
Shapiro, B, pub. 1930, reached #3 in December 1930
Billy Moll w, Robert A King m
Ben Selvin/w.vocal Φ 10/30 Col 2266-D
Nat Shilkret/w.vocal duo 11/30 Vic 22526

MORE THAN YOU KNOW
V Youmans, pub. 1929, reached #17 in January 1930
Billy Rose & Edward Eliscu w, Vincent Youmans m
Featured in GREAT DAY, show (opened 10/29)
Helen Morgan 12/29 Vic 22149
Libby Holman 01/30 Bruns 4613
Mayo Methot, sung in show
Jane Froman, stage and radio

MY BABY JUST CARES FOR ME (46)
Donaldson, D & G, pub. 1928, reached #10 in October 1930
Gus Kahn w, Walter Donaldson m
Featured in WHOOPEE, film (rel. 09/30)
Eddie Cantor, sung in film
Ted Weems/Art Jarrett 09/30 Vic 22499
Isham Jones/Frank Sylvano 10/30 Bruns 4907

MY FATE IS IN YOUR HANDS
Santly Bros, pub. 1929, reached #14 in January 1930
Andy Razaf w, Thomas "Fats" Waller m
Guy Lombardo/Carmen Lombardo 12/29 Col 2017-D
Gene Austin 01/30 Vic 22223
Nat Shilkret/Franklyn Baur 01/30 Vic 22222

MY FUTURE JUST PASSED (33)
Famous, pub. 1930, reached #6 in August 1930
George Marion w, Richard A Whiting m
Featured in SAFETY IN NUMBERS, film (opened 06/30)
Charles "Buddy" Rogers, sung in film, 06/30 Col 2183-D
The High Hatters/Frank Luther 08/30 Vic 22444
Columbia Photo Players[2]/Lew Conrad 06/30 Col 2187-D
Boswell Sisters 09/30 Okeh 41444

MY SWEETER THAN SWEET
Harms, pub. 1929, reached #11 in January 1930
George Marion w, Richard A Whiting m
Featured in SWEETIE, film (rel. 10/29)
Helen Kane, sung in film
Leo Reisman/L Levin 12/29 Vic 22194
Ipana Troubadours/Smith Ballew 12/29 Col 2006-D

OLD NEW ENGLAND MOON
Berlin, pub. 1930, reached #14 in August 1930
George P Howard w, Dave Vance m
Rudy Vallee/<vocal, radio, 07/30 Vic 22445
Paul Whiteman/Jack Fulton 07/30 Col 2224-D

ON THE SUNNY SIDE OF THE STREET (49)
Shapiro, B, pub. 1930, reached #12 in May 1930
Dorothy Fields w, Jimmy McHugh m
Featured in LEW LESLIE'S INTERNATIONAL REVUE, show (opened 02/30)
Harry Richman, sung in show, 05/30 Bruns 4747
Ted Lewis/<vocal 05/30 Col 2144-D
Bernie Cummins/<vocal 05/30 Vic 22354

PUTTIN' ON THE RITZ (37)
Berlin, pub. 1928, reached #6 in May 1930
(Also reached #4 in September 1983)
Irving Berlin w & m
Featured in PUTTIN' ON THE RITZ, film (rel. 02/30)
Harry Richman Φ sung in film, 03/30 Bruns 4677
Leo Reisman/Lew Conrad 04/30 Vic 22306

ROMANCE
Donaldson, D & G, pub. 1929, reached #19 in April 1930
Edgar Leslie w, Walter Donaldson m
Featured in CAMEO KIRBY, film (rel. 02/30)
Norma Terriss & J Harold Murray, sung in film
John Boles 03/30 Vic 22230

SHOULD I? (10)
Robbins, pub. 1929, reached #2 in March 1930
(Also reached #16 in August 1952)
Arthur Freed w, Nacio Herb Brown m
Featured in LORD BYRON OF BROADWAY, film (rel. 03/30)
Arden-Ohman Orch/Scrappy Lambert Φ 03/30 Vic 22255
Ethelind Terry, sung in film
Paul Whiteman/Jack Fulton 02/30 Col 2047-D

SING SOMETHING SIMPLE
Harms, pub. 1930, reached #12 in November 1930
Herman Hupfeld w & m
Featured in THE SECOND LITTLE SHOW, show (opened 09/30)
Ruth Tester, sung in show
Leo Reisman/Frank Luther 11/30 Vic 22538
Jacques Renard/w.vocal 11/30 Bruns 4918

SING, YOU SINNERS (32)
Famous, pub. 1930, reached #8 in May 1930
Sam Coslow & W Franke Harling w & m
Featured in HONEY, film (rel. 03/30)
Lillian Roth, sung in film
The High Hatters/Frank Luther 04/30 Vic 22322
Belle Baker 06/30 Bruns 4765

SINGIN' IN THE BATHTUB (30)
Witmark, pub. 1929, reached #7 in January 1930
Herb Magidson, Ned Washington, Michael H Cleary w & m
Featured in THE SHOW OF SHOWS, film (rel. 11/29)
Winnie Lightner, sung in film
Guy Lombardo/w.vocal trio Φ 01/30 Col 2045-D
The High Hatters/Frank Luther 02/30 Vic 22219

SINGING A SONG TO THE STARS (40)
Robbins, pub. 1930, reached #7 in August 1930
Howard Johnson w, Joseph Meyer m
Featured in WAY OUT WEST, film (rel. 08/30)
Cliff Edwards, sung in film
Guy Lombardo/Carmen Lombardo 07/30 Col 2205-D
Lewis James 08/30 Vic 22458

SINGING A VAGABOND SONG
Santly Bros, pub. 1929, reached #20 in April 1930[7]
Val Burton, Harry Richman, Sam Messenheimer w & m
Featured in PUTTIN' ON THE RITZ, film (rel. 02/30)
Harry Richman, sung in film, 03/30 Bruns 4678
Ted Lewis/<vocal 05/30 Col 2144-D

SO BEATS MY HEART FOR YOU (22)
DeSylva, B & H, pub. 1930, reached #4 in August 1930
Tom Waring, Charles Henderson, Pat Ballard w & m
Waring's Pennsylvanians/Stuart Churchill Φ stage and 08/30 Vic 22486
Earl Burtnett/w.vocal 07/30 Bruns 4830
Fred Rich Orch, stage

SOMETHING TO REMEMBER YOU BY
Harms, pub. 1930, reached #20 in December 1930
Howard Dietz w, Arthur Schwartz m
Featured in THREE'S A CROWD, show (opened 10/30)
Libby Holman, sung in show, 11/30 Bruns 4910
Paul Whiteman/King's Jesters 11/30 Col 2297-D
Helen Morgan 01/31 Vic 22532

SOMEWHERE IN OLD WYOMING
J Morris, pub. 1930, reached #17 in September 1930
Charles Tobias & Peter DeRose w & m
Ben Selvin/w.vocal 09/30 Col 2266-D
Carson Robison & Bud Billings[4] 12/30 Vic 22556
Guy Lombardo Orch, db dates

SOUTH SEA ROSE
DeSylva, B & H, pub. 1929, reached #17 in March 1930
L Wolfe Gilbert w, Abel Baer m
Featured in SOUTH SEA ROSE, film (rel. 12/29)
George Olsen/Ethel Shutta 02/30 Vic 22213
A & P Gypsies 02/30 Bruns 4656

ST. JAMES INFIRMARY (47)
Mills, pub. 1929, reached #8 in March 1930
(Also reached #19 in June 1931)
Irving Mills w & m
King Oliver/Frank Marvin 03/30 Vic 22298
Gene Austin 03/30 Vic 22299

STEIN SONG (2)
Carl Fischer, pub. 1910, reached #1 in April 1930
Lincoln Colcord w, E A Fenstad & A W Sprague m
Rudy Vallee/<vocal ΦΦ radio, 04/30 Vic 22321
Ted Wallace/Smith Ballew 05/30 Col 2151-D
Jesse Crawford 06/30 Vic 22394

STRIKE UP THE BAND
Harms; orig. pub. 1927, reached #13 in April 1930
Ira Gershwin w, George Gershwin m
Featured in STRIKE UP THE BAND, show (opened 01/30)
Red Nichols/w.vocal 02/30 Bruns 4695
Jim Townshend & Jerry Goff, sung in show
Arden-Ohman Orch/w.vocal group 04/30 Vic 22308

SWEET JENNIE LEE
Donaldson, D & G, pub. 1930, reached #9 in December 1930
Walter Donaldson w & m
Isham Jones/w.vocal 11/30 Bruns 4909
Ted Wallace/w.vocal 12/30 Col 2301-D
Guy Lombardo Orch, stage

SWEETHEART OF MY STUDENT DAYS (48)
L Feist, pub. 1930, reached #8 in December 1930
Gus Kahn w, Seymour Simons m
Rudy Vallee/<vocal Φ 12/30 Vic 22560
Wayne King Orch, db dates
Belle Baker 12/30 Bruns 4962

SWINGIN' IN A HAMMOCK (35)
Berlin, pub. 1930, reached #6 in September 1930
Tot Seymour & Charles O'Flynn w, Pete Wendling m
Guy Lombardo/Carmen Lombardo Φ 08/30 Col 2237-D
Leo Reisman/Lew Conrad 08/30 Vic 22453
Lee Morse 08/30 Col 2225-D
Husk O'Hare Orch, db dates

'TAIN'T NO SIN (TO DANCE AROUND IN YOUR BONES)
Donaldson, D & G, pub. 1929, reached #15 in March 1930
Edgar Leslie w, Walter Donaldson m
George Olsen/Dick Gardner 03/30 Vic 22279
Ben Selvin/w.vocal 03/30 Col 2096-D

TELLING IT TO THE DAISIES
Remick, pub. 1930, reached #18 in June 1930
Joe Young w, Harry Warren m
Ted Wallace/Smith Ballew 05/30 Col 2151-D
Gene Austin 07/30 Vic 22416

TEN CENTS A DANCE
Harms, pub. 1930, reached #9 in July 1930
Lorenz Hart w, Richard Rodgers m
Featured in SIMPLE SIMON, show (opened 02/30)
Also featured in TEN CENTS A DANCE, film (rel. 03/31)
Ruth Etting Φ sung in show, 05/30 Col 2146-D
The High Hatters/Welcome Lewis 05/30 Vic 22353

THAT WONDERFUL SOMETHING
Robbins, pub. 1929, reached #19 in February 1930
Joe Goodwin w, Louis Alter m
Featured in UNTAMED, film (rel. 12/29)
Joan Crawford, sung in film
Nat Shilkret/w.vocal group 01/30 Vic 22203

THERE'S DANGER IN YOUR EYES, CHERIE (29)
Berlin, pub. 1929, reached #4 in April 1930
Harry Richman, Jack Meskill, Pete Wendling w & m
Featured in PUTTIN' ON THE RITZ, film (rel. 02/30)
Harry Richman Φ sung in film, 03/30 Bruns 4677
Guy Lombardo/Carmen Lombardo 03/30 Col 2107-D
Waring's Pennsylvanians/Clare Hanlon 04/30 Vic 22293
James Melton 05/30 Vic 22335

THREE LITTLE WORDS (7)
Harms, pub. 1930, reached #1 in November 1930
Bert Kalmar w, Harry Ruby m
Featured in CHECK AND DOUBLE CHECK, film (rel. 10/30)
Duke Ellington/w.vocal trio[5] ΦΦ sung in film and 11/30 Vic 22528
Jacques Renard/Chester Gaylord 12/30 Bruns 4939
Ethel Waters 02/31 Col 2346-D
Rudy Vallee, stage and radio
Ipana Troubadours/w.vocal 12/30 Col 2317-D

UNDER A TEXAS MOON (28)
Remick, pub. 1929, reached #4 in May 1930
Ray Perkins w & m
Featured in UNDER A TEXAS MOON, film (rel. 03/30)
Guy Lombardo/Carmen Lombardo Φ 03/30 Col 2089-D
Frank Fay, sung in film
Ted FioRito/Pedro Espino 03/30 Vic 22252

WHAT IS THIS THING CALLED LOVE? (31)
Harms, pub. 1929, reached #4 in March 1930
Cole Porter w & m
Featured in WAKE UP AND DREAM, show (opened 12/29)
Leo Reisman/Lew Conrad Φ 03/30 Vic 22282
Frances Shelley, sung in show
Libby Holman 04/30 Bruns 4700

WHEN I'M LOOKING AT YOU
Robbins, pub. 1930, reached #17 in April 1930
Clifford Grey w, Herbert Stothart m
Featured in THE ROGUE SONG, film (rel. 01/30)
Lawrence Tibbett, sung in film, 04/30 Vic 1447
Columbia Photo Players[2] 02/30 Col 2080-D

WHEN IT'S SPRINGTIME IN THE ROCKIES (1)
Villa Moret, pub. 1929, reached #1 in June 1930
Mary Hale Woolsey & Milton Taggart w, Robert Sauer m
Hilo Hawaiian Orch/Frank Luther-Carson Robison ΦΦ 05/30 Vic 22339
Ford and Glenn Φ 08/29 Col 1828-D
Rudy Vallee, stage and radio
Ben Selvin/w.vocal duo 07/30 Col 2206-D

WHEN THE BLOOM IS ON THE SAGE
M M Preeman, pub. 1930, reached #10 in June 1930
Fred Howard & Nat Vincent w & m
The Beverly Hillbillies, stage, 05/30 Bruns 421
Happy Chappies, radio, 05/30 Col 2194-D
Bud Billings[4] & Carson Robison 09/30 Vic 40282

WHEN THE LITTLE RED ROSES GET THE BLUES
DeSylva, B & H, pub. 1930, reached #17 in May 1930
Al Dubin w, Joe Burke m
Featured in HOLD EVERYTHING, film (rel. 03/30)
Al Jolson 04/30 Bruns 4722
Winnie Lightner, sung in film

WHEN THE ORGAN PLAYED AT TWILIGHT (9)
Santly Bros, pub. 1929, reached #4 in December 1930
Raymond Wallace w, Jimmy Campbell & Reg Connelly m
Jack Hylton/Sam Browne 09/30 Vic 22434
The Cavaliers[6]/w.vocal 10/30 Col 2279-D
Jesse Crawford 10/30 Vic 22510
Ruth Etting, stage

WHY?
Davis, C & E, pub. 1929, reached #14 in March 1930
Arthur Swanstrom & Benny Davis w, J Fred Coots m
Featured in SONS O' GUNS, show (opened 11/29)
Jack Donahue & Lily Damita, sung in show
Arden-Ohman Orch/Frank Luther 01/30 Vic 22205

WHY WAS I BORN?
T B Harms, pub. 1929, reached #16 in February 1930
Oscar Hammerstein 2nd w, Jerome Kern m
Featured in SWEET ADELINE, show (opened 09/29)
Helen Morgan, sung in show, 01/30 Vic 22199
Libby Holman 01/30 Bruns 4570
Leo Reisman/L Levin 12/29 Vic 22187

WITHOUT A SONG
V Youmans, pub. 1929, reached #20 in January 1930[7]
Billy Rose & Edward Eliscu w, Vincent Youmans m
Featured in GREAT DAY, show (opened 10/29)
Paul Whiteman/Bing Crosby 12/29 Col 2023-D
Lois Deppe, sung in show

YOU BROUGHT A NEW KIND OF LOVE TO ME (14)
Famous, pub. 1930, reached #3 in August 1930
Sammy Fain, Irving Kahal, Pierre Norman w & m
Featured in THE BIG POND, film (rel. 04/30)
Maurice Chevalier, sung in film, 07/30 Vic 22405
Paul Whiteman/Bing Crosby Φ 06/30 Col 2171-D
The High Hatters/Frank Luther 07/30 Vic 22409
Belle Baker 07/30 Bruns 4765

YOU'VE GOT THAT THING
Harms, pub. 1929, reached #11 in February 1930
Cole Porter w & m
Featured in FIFTY MILLION FRENCHMEN, show (opened 11/29)
Ted Lewis/<vocal 02/30 Col 2088-D
Jack Thompson & Betty Compton, sung in show
Maurice Chevalier 04/30 Vic 22294

[1]Col 2206-D was by Ben Selvin's Orch w/Ruth Etting on vocal.
[2]The Columbia Photo Players were actually Ben Selvin's Orch.
[3]Roland Lance was a pseudonym for Jack Teagarten.
[4]Bud Billings was a pseudonym for Frank Luther
[5]Vocal trio included Bing Crosby both in film and on record.
[6]The Cavaliers were actually Ben Selvin's Orch.
[7]Reached #20 on monthly chart only.

1931

AT YOUR COMMAND (37)
Robbins, pub. 1931, reached #6 in August 1931
Harry Tobias & Bing Crosby w, Harry Barris m
Bing Crosby Φ 08/31 Bruns 6145
Gus Arnheim/Donald Novis 09/31 Vic 22758
Fred Rich/Bunny Berigan 08/31 Col 2484-D

BLUE AGAIN (30)
Robbins, pub. 1930, reached #7 in February 1931
Dorothy Fields w, Jimmy McHugh m
Featured in THE VANDERBILT REVUE, show (opened 11/30)
Duke Ellington/Sid Garry Φ 02/31 Vic 22603
Evelyn Hoey, sung in show
Red Nichols/Dick Robertson 02/31 Bruns 6014
Guy Lombardo Orch, stage and radio

BY THE RIVER STE. MARIE (28)
Robbins, pub. 1931, reached #6 in April 1931
Edgar Leslie w, Harry Warren m
Guy Lombardo/Carmen Lombardo Φ 04/31 Col 2401-D
Kate Smith, stage and radio
Henry Busse/Richard Barry 05/31 Vic 22651

CALL ME DARLING (39)
Santly Bros, pub. 1931, reached #6 in December 1931
Dorothy Dick, Bert Reisfeld, Mart Fryberg, Rolf Marbot w & m
Russ Columbo 12/31 Vic 22861
The Cavaliers[1]/w.vocal 12/31 Col 2555-D
Arthur Tracy 12/31 Bruns 6216

CHEERFUL LITTLE EARFUL
Remick, pub. 1930, reached #9 in January 1931
Ira Gershwin & Billy Rose w, Harry Warren m
Featured in SWEET AND LOW, show (opened 11/30)
The High Hatters/Johnny Marvin 01/31 Vic 22566
Hannah Williams, sung in show
Tom Gerun/w.vocal 12/30 Bruns 4971

COME TO ME
DeSylva, B & H, pub. 1931, reached #9 in August 1931
Bud DeSylva, Lew Brown, Ray Henderson w & m
Featured in INDISCREET, film (opened 05/31)
Gloria Swanson, sung in film
Jacques Renard/Paul Small 06/31 Bruns 6106
The High Hatters/Chick Bullock 08/31 Vic 22756

DANCING IN THE DARK (24)
Harms, pub. 1931, reached #5 in August 1931
Howard Dietz w, Arthur Schwartz m
Featured in THE BAND WAGON, show (opened 06/31)
Waring's Pennsylvanians/Three Waring Girls Φ 08/31 Vic 22708
Bing Crosby 09/31 Bruns 6169
John Barker, sung in show
Ben Selvin/Scrappy Lambert 08/31 Col 2473-D

DREAM A LITTLE DREAM OF ME (6)
Davis, C & E, pub. 1931, reached #3 in June 1931
(Also reached #18 in November 1950)
(Also reached #12 in August 1968)
Gus Kahn w, Wilbur Schwandt & Fabian Andre m
Wayne King/Ernie Birchill Φ 04/31 Vic 22643
Kate Smith, stage and radio
Ozzie Nelson/<vocal 04/31 Bruns 6060

EMBRACEABLE YOU
Harms, pub. 1930, reached #18 in January 1931
Ira Gershwin w, George Gershwin m
Featured in GIRL CRAZY, show (opened 10/30)
Ginger Rogers & Allen Kearns, sung in show
Arden-Ohman Orch/Frank Luther 12/30 Vic 22558
Red Nichols/Dick Robertson 12/30 Bruns 4957

AN EVENING IN CAROLINE (25)
Donaldson, D & G, pub. 1931, reached #5 in December 1931
Walter Donaldson w & m
Ted Lewis/<vocal Φ 12/31 Col 2560-D
Boswell Sisters 12/31 Bruns 6218
Ted Black/Chick Bullock 02/32 Vic 22872

A FADED SUMMER LOVE (19)
L Feist, pub. 1931, reached #2 in December 1931
Phil Baxter w & m
Paul Whiteman/Jack Fulton Φ 12/31 Vic 22827
Bing Crosby 12/31 Bruns 6200
Ruth Etting 12/31 Col 2557-D

FOR YOU
Witmark, pub. 1930, reached #15 in May 1931
(Also reached #20 in January 1949)
(Also reached #6 in February 1964)
Al Dubin w, Joe Burke m
Featured in CAPTAIN OF THE GUARD, film (rel. 03/30)
Also featured in HOLY TERROR, film (rel. 07/31)
John Boles, sung in film (CG), 05/30 Vic 22373
Joe Green/w.vocal 05/31 Col 2429-D
Leo Reisman/Frank Munn 06/31 Vic 22670

GOODNIGHT, SWEETHEART (2)
Robbins, pub. 1931, reached #1 in November 1931
Ray Noble, James Campbell, Reg Connelly, Rudy Vallee w & m
Featured in EARL CARROLL'S VANITIES, revue[2] (opened 08/31)
Guy Lombardo/w.vocal ΦΦ 12/31 Col 2547-D
Wayne King Orch ΦΦ 11/31 Vic 22825
Rudy Vallee, stage and radio
Russ Columbo Φ 12/31 Vic 22826
Bing Crosby 11/31 Bruns 6203

GOT THE BENCH, GOT THE PARK
Berlin, pub. 1931, reached #16 in April 1931
Al Lewis, Al Sherman, Fred Phillips w & m
Henry Busse/Richard Barry 05/31 Vic 22651
Noble Sissle/<vocal 04/31 Bruns 6073

GUILTY (23)
L Feist, pub. 1931, reached #2 in November 1931
(Also reached #5 in March 1947)
Gus Kahn w, Richard Whiting & Harry Akst m
Russ Columbo Φ 11/31 Vic 22801
Ruth Etting 11/31 Col 2529-D
Wayne King/Ernie Birchill 11/31 Vic 22817

HEARTACHES
Olman M C, pub. 1931, reached #13 in April 1931
(Also reached #1 in April 1947)
(Also reached #9 in November 1961)
John Klenner w, Al Hoffman m
Guy Lombardo/w.vocal trio 03/31 Col 2390-D
Bert Lown/Biltmore Trio 04/31 Vic 22612
Will Osborne/<vocal 03/31 Melotone 12078

HELLO, BEAUTIFUL
Donaldson, D & G, pub. 1931, reached #10 in April 1931
Walter Donaldson w & m
Maurice Chevalier, stage, 04/31 Vic 22634
Wayne King/w.vocal trio 04/31 Vic 22642
Nick Lucas 03/31 Bruns 6049

HIGH AND LOW
Harms, pub. 1931, reached #16 in August 1931
Howard Dietz & Desmond Carter w, Arthur Schwartz m
Featured in THE BAND WAGON, show (opened 06/31)
Waring's Pennsylvanians/Three Waring Girls 08/31 Vic 22708
Roberta Robinson & John Barker, sung in show
Jacques Renard/Frank Munn 08/31 Bruns 6136

HO-HUM (35)
Famous, pub. 1931, reached #5 in June 1931
Edward Heyman w, Dana Suesse m
Gus Arnheim/Bing Crosby 06/31 Vic 22691
Ted Lewis/<vocal 06/31 Col 2452-D
Hal Kemp/Skinnay Ennis 06/31 Bruns 6108

I APOLOGIZE (29)
DeSylva, B & H, pub. 1931, reached #6 in November 1931
(Also reached #6 in May 1951)
Al Hoffman, Ed Nelson, Al Goodman w & m
Bing Crosby Φ 11/31 Bruns 6179
Nat Shilkret/Paul Small 11/31 Vic 22781
Sam Lanin/Tom Brown 10/31 Perfect 15508

I DON'T KNOW WHY (I JUST DO) (13)
L Feist, pub. 1931, reached #2 in November 1931
(Also reached #10 in September 1946)
(Also reached #11 in December 1961)
Roy Turk w, Fred Ahlert m
Russ Columbo Φ 11/31 Vic 22801
Wayne King/w.vocal trio 11/31 Vic 22817
Bennie Krueger/Smith Ballew 11/31 Bruns 6185
Kate Smith, radio, 12/31 Col 2539-D

I FOUND A MILLION-DOLLAR BABY (17)
Remick, pub. 1931, reached #2 in August 1931
(First pub. 1926 with different melody)
Billy Rose & Mort Dixon w, Harry Warren m
Featured in BILLY ROSE'S CRAZY QUILT, show (opened 05/31)
Waring's Pennsylvanians/Clare Hanlon Φ 07/31 Vic 22707
Boswell Sisters/Victor Young Orch 07/31 Bruns 6128
Bing Crosby 08/31 Bruns 6140
Fanny Brice, sung in show

I GOT RHYTHM
Harms, pub. 1930, reached #16 in January 1931
(Also reached #3 in May 1967)
Ira Gershwin w, George Gershwin m
Featured in GIRL CRAZY, show (opened 10/30)
Ethel Merman, sung in show
Red Nichols/Dick Robertson 12/30 Bruns 4957
Arden-Ohman Orch/Frank Luther 12/30 Vic 22558
Ethel Waters 01/31 Col 2346-D

I LOVE LOUISA (44)
Harms, pub. 1931, reached #6 in September 1931
Howard Dietz w, Arthur Schwartz m
Featured in THE BAND WAGON, show (opened 06/31)
Fred Astaire, sung in show
Leo Reisman/Fred Astaire Φ 08/31 Vic 22755
Smith Ballew/<vocal 09/31 Col 2503-D

I SURRENDER, DEAR (20)
Freed & Powers, pub. 1931, reached #3 in March 1931
Gordon Clifford w, Harry Barris m
Gus Arnheim/Bing Crosby Φ 03/31 Vic 22618
Russ Columbo, stage and radio
Earl Burtnett/Don Dewey 03/31 Bruns 6034

I WANNA SING ABOUT YOU (31)
Berlin, pub. 1931, reached #3 in July 1931
Dave Dreyer & Cliff Friend w & m
Bert Lown/Biltmore Trio Φ 06/31 Vic 22689
Guy Lombardo Orch, db dates
Lloyd Keating[14]/Paul Small 06/31 Velvetone 2388-V

I'M ALONE BECAUSE I LOVE YOU (15)
Witmark, pub. 1930, reached #2 in February 1931
Joe Young & John Siras w & m
Bud Billings[3] 02/31 Vic 22588
The Cavaliers[1]/w.vocal 01/31 Col 2339-D
Leo Reisman/Ben Gordon 03/31 Vic 22606

I'M THROUGH WITH LOVE (27)
Robbins, pub. 1931, reached #4 in August 1931
Gus Kahn w, Matty Malneck & Fud Livingston m
Bing Crosby Φ 08/31 Bruns 6140
Henry Busse/Richard Barry 07/31 Vic 22677
Lee Morse 08/31 Col 2474-D

I'VE GOT FIVE DOLLARS
Harms, pub. 1931, reached #19 in April 1931
Lorenz Hart w, Richard Rodgers m
Featured in AMERICA'S SWEETHEART, show (opened 02/31)
Jack Whiting & Ann Sothern, sung in show
Arden-Ohman Orch/Frank Luther 04/31 Vic 22627
Emil Coleman/w.vocal 03/31 Bruns 6036

IT'S THE GIRL
L Feist, pub. 1931, reached #14 in September 1931
Dave Oppenheim w, Abel Baer m
Boswell Sisters/Dorsey Brothers Orch 08/31 Bruns 6151
Leo Reisman/<vocal 09/31 Vic 22757

JUST A GIGOLO (9)
DeSylva, B & H, pub. 1930, reached #1 in February 1931
(Also reached #12 in May 1985 as part of medley)
Irving Caesar & Julius Brammer w, Leonello Casucci m
Ted Lewis/<vocal Φ 02/31 Col 2378-D
Bing Crosby Φ stage, 04/31 Vic 22701
Ben Bernie/w.vocal Φ 02/31 Bruns 6023
Vincent Lopez/Jack Parker, stage, 02/31 Hit of Wk 1128
Leo Reisman/Ben Gordon 02/31 Vic 22606

JUST ONE MORE CHANCE (8)
Famous, pub. 1931, reached #1 in July 1931
(Also reached #11 in November 1951)
Sam Coslow w, Arthur Johnston m
Bing Crosby ΦΦ stage, 07/31 Bruns 6120
Russ Columbo, stage and radio
Abe Lyman/Phil Neely Φ 06/31 Bruns 6125
Gus Arnheim/Donald Novis 09/31 Vic 22758
Ruth Etting 08/31 Perfect 12219, 08/31 Banner 32231

KICKIN' THE GONG AROUND
Mills, pub. 1931, reached #15 in December 1931
Ted Koehler w, Harold Arlen m
Featured in RHYTHMANIA, revue (opened 03/31)
Cab Calloway/<vocal Φ sung in revue, 11/31 Bruns 6209
Louis Armstrong/<vocal 03/32 Okeh 41550

THE KING'S HORSES
L Feist, pub. 1930, reached #13 in March 1931
Noel Gay & Harry Graham w & m
Ben Bernie/w.vocal 03/31 Bruns 6024
Jack Hylton/Pat O'Malley 03/31 Vic 22619

LADY OF SPAIN
Sam Fox, pub. 1931, reached #9 in November 1931
(Also reached #19 in March 1949)
(Also reached #5 in December 1952)
Erell Reaves w, Tolchard Evans m
London Mayfair Orch[4]/Al Bowlly 10/31 Vic 22774
Guy Lombardo Orch, db dates
The Rondoliers 11/31 Col 2546-D

LADY, PLAY YOUR MANDOLIN
Harms, pub. 1930, reached #9 in February 1931
Irving Caesar w, Oscar Levant m
Nick Lucas 02/31 Bruns 6013
Blossom Seeley, stage
Havana Novelty Orch/Paul Small 02/31 Vic 22597

LIFE IS JUST A BOWL OF CHERRIES (47)
DeSylva, B & H, pub. 1931, reached #9 in November 1931
Lew Brown & Ray Henderson w & m
Featured in GEORGE WHITE'S SCANDALS, 11TH EDITION, show (opened 09/31)
Rudy Vallee/<vocal Φ 10/31 Vic 22783
Ethel Merman, sung in show
Bing Crosby & The Boswell Sisters, stage and radio

LITTLE GIRL
Olman M C, pub. 1931, reached #11 in August 1931
Madeline Hyde & Francis Henry w & m
Eubie Blake 08/31 Vic 22735
Red Nichols/Smith Ballew 08/31 Bruns 6138
Joe Venuti/Harold Arlen 08/31 Col 2488-D

THE LITTLE THINGS IN LIFE (26)
Berlin, pub. 1930, reached #4 in January 1931
Irving Berlin w & m
Gus Arnheim/Bing Crosby Φ 01/31 Vic 22580
Lewis James 02/31 Vic 22594
Ted Wallace/Dick Dixon[5] 01/31 Col 2334-D

LONESOME LOVER (41)
L Feist, pub. 1930, reached #6 in February 1931
Alfred Bryan w, James V Monaco m
Isham Jones/Frank Sylvano 02/31 Bruns 6015
Bert Lown/Elmer Feldkamp 03/31 Vic 22602
Guy Lombardo Orch, db dates

LOVE FOR SALE
Harms, pub. 1930, reached #20 in March 1931
Cole Porter w & m
Featured in THE NEW YORKERS, show (opened 12/30)
Libby Holman 03/31 Bruns 6044
Waring's Pennsylvanians/Three Waring Girls 02/31 Vic 22598
Kathryn Crawford, sung in show

LOVE LETTERS IN THE SAND (11)
Berlin, pub. 1931, reached #4 in October 1931
(Also reached #1 in June 1957)
Nick Kenny & Charles Kenny w, J Fred Coots m
Ted Black/Tom Brown Φ 10/31 Vic 22799
Russ Columbo, stage and radio
Lee Morse 11/31 Col 2530-D

MAMA INEZ
E B Marks, pub. 1931, reached #19 in May 1931
L Wolfe Gilbert w, Eliseo Grenet m
Enric Madriguera[6]/w.vocal group 04/31 Col 2422-D
Maurice Chevalier 08/31 Vic 22731
Xavier Cugat Orch, db dates
Vincent Lopez Orch, db dates

MANY HAPPY RETURNS OF THE DAY (16)
Witmark, pub. 1931, reached #2 in September 1931
Al Dubin w, Joe Burke m
Bing Crosby Φ 08/31 Bruns 6145
Rudy Vallee/<vocal 08/31 Vic 22752
Ipana Troubadours/Dick Robertson 09/31 Col 2486-D

ME! (43)
Berlin, pub. 1931, reached #6 in October 1931
Irving Berlin w & m
The High Hatters/Frank Luther 10/31 Vic 22780
Ben Bernie/<vocal 10/31 Bruns 6166
The Knickerbockers[7]/Dick Robertson 10/31 Col 2502-D

MINNIE THE MOOCHER
Gotham M S, pub. 1931, reached #18 in May 1931
Cab Calloway, Irving Mills, Clarence Gaskill w & m
Cab Calloway/<vocal Φ 04/31 Bruns 6074

MOOD INDIGO
Mills, pub. 1931, reached #16 in March 1931
Edward Kennedy "Duke" Ellington, Irving Mills, & Barney Bigard w & m
Duke Ellington Orch[8] Φ 12/30 Bruns 4952, 01/31 Okeh 8840, 02/31 Vic 22587
Clyde McCoy Orch 11/31 Col 2531-D
Lee Morse 11/31 Col 2530-D

MOONLIGHT SAVING TIME (7)
L Feist, pub. 1931, reached #1 in June 1931
Irving Kahal & Harry Richman w & m
Guy Lombardo/Carmen Lombardo ΦΦ 06/31 Col 2457-D
Hal Kemp/Skinnay Ennis 06/31 Bruns 6108
The High Hatters/Frank Luther 07/31 Vic 22703
Maurice Chevalier 07/31 Vic 22723
Roy Carroll[9]/Paul Small 07/31 Harmony 1322-H

MY IDEAL
Famous, pub. 1930, reached #16 in January 1931
(Also reached #5 in January 1944)
Leo Robin w, Richard Whiting & Newell Chase m
Featured in PLAYBOY OF PARIS, film (rel. 10/30)
Maurice Chevalier, sung in film, 11/30 Vic 22542
Isham Jones/Frank Sylvano 03/31 Bruns 6041

MY SONG
DeSylva, B & H, pub. 1931, reached #15 in November 1931
Lew Brown & Ray Henderson w & m
Featured in GEORGE WHITE'S SCANDALS, 11TH EDITION, show (opened 09/31)
Rudy Vallee/<vocal 10/31 Vic 22784
Ethel Merman, sung in show

NEVERTHELESS (49)
DeSylva, B & H, pub. 1931, reached #8 in July 1931
(Also reached #2 in December 1950)
Bert Kalmar w, Harry Ruby m
Jack Denny/Rob May 06/31 Bruns 6114
Rudy Vallee, stage and radio
Bing Crosby, stage and radio
Johnny Hamp/w.vocal trio 07/31 Vic 22722

NEW SUN IN THE SKY
Harms, pub. 1931, reached #19 in August 1931
Howard Dietz w, Arthur Schwartz m
Featured in THE BAND WAGON, show (opened 06/31)
Fred Astaire, sung in show
Leo Reisman/Fred Astaire 08/31 Vic 22755

99 OUT OF 100 (WANNA BE LOVED)
Robbins, pub. 1931, reached #17 in April 1931
Al Lewis & Al Sherman w & m
Rudy Vallee/<vocal, radio, 03/31 Vic 22611
Ben Bernie/Frank Sylvano 04/31 Bruns 6062

NOW THAT YOU'RE GONE (42)
Witmark, pub. 1931, reached #7 in November 1931
Gus Kahn w, Ted FioRito m
Guy Lombardo/Carmen Lombardo Φ 10/31 Col 2528-D
Ruth Etting 10/31 Col 2529-D
Ted Black/Tom Brown 11/31 Vic 22807

NOW YOU'RE IN MY ARMS (48)
Remick, pub. 1931, reached #6 in July 1931
Morton Downey & Allie Wrubel w & m
Bert Lown/Elmer Feldkamp Φ 06/31 Vic 22689
James Melton 07/31 Col 2465-D

ON THE BEACH WITH YOU
Davis, C & E, pub. 1931, reached #16 in July 1931
Tot Seymour w, Jesse Greer m
Johnny Hamp/Carl Graub 07/31 Vic 22730
Ozzie Nelson/<vocal 07/31 Bruns 6131

ONE MORE TIME
DeSylva B & H, pub. 1931, reached #12 in June 1931
Bud DeSylva, Lew Brown, Ray Henderson w & m
Gus Arnheim/Bing Crosby 04/31 Vic 22700
Ted Lewis/<vocal 06/31 Col 2452-D

(YOU CAME ALONG) OUT OF NOWHERE (21)
Famous, pub. 1931, reached #3 in May 1931
(Also reached #8 in October 1945)
Ed Heyman w, Johnny Green m
Featured in DUDE RANCH, film (rel. 04/31)
Bing Crosby Φ 05/31 Bruns 6090
Leo Reisman/Frank Munn 06/31 Vic 22668

OVERNIGHT
Robbins, pub. 1930, reached #20 in February 1931
Billy Rose & Charlotte Kent w, Louis Alter m
Featured in SWEET AND LOW, show (opened 11/30)
Fanny Brice, sung in show
The High Hatters/Johnny Marvin 01/31 Vic 22566

THE PEANUT VENDOR (5)
E B Marks, pub. 1928, reached #2 in January 1931
L Wolfe Gilbert & Marion Sunshine w, Moises Simons m
Featured in CUBAN LOVE SONG, film (rel. 12/31)
Don Azpiazu/Arturo Machin ΦΦ 11/30 Vic 22483
Lupe Velez & Lawrence Tibbett, sung in film
California Ramblers/w.vocal group 02/31 Col 2351-D
Red Nichols/Paul Small 03/31 Bruns 6035

PLEASE DON'T TALK ABOUT ME (WHEN I'M GONE) (22)
Remick, pub. 1930, reached #2 in May 1931
Sidney Clare w, Sam Stept m
Gene Austin Φ 05/31 Vic 22635
Ethel Waters, stage, 04/31 Col 2409-D
Bert Lown/Elmer Feldkamp 05/31 Vic 22652
Kate Smith, stage and radio

REACHING FOR THE MOON (38)
Berlin, pub. 1930, reached #5 in March 1931
Irving Berlin w & m
Featured in REACHING FOR THE MOON, film (rel. 12/30)
Bing Crosby, sung in film
Ruth Etting 02/31 Col 2377-D
The Troubadours[6]/Lew Conrad 03/31 Vic 22613

RIVER, STAY 'WAY FROM MY DOOR
Shapiro, B, pub. 1931, reached #13 in December 1931
Mort Dixon w, Harry Woods m
Featured in MUM'S THE WORD, revue (1931)
Boswell Sisters 12/31 Bruns 6218
Jimmie Savo, sung in revue
Kate Smith/Guy Lombardo Orch 01/32 Col 2578-D
Paul Robeson 01/32 Vic 22889

ROLL ON, MISSISSIPPI, ROLL ON
Shapiro, B, pub. 1931, reached #16 in June 1931
Eugene West, James McCaffrey, Dave Ringle w & m
Boswell Sisters, radio, 06/31 Bruns 6109
Baby Rose Marie, radio
Buddy Campbell[11]/Paul Small 06/31 Okeh 41499

SHINE ON, HARVEST MOON
J H Remick, pub. 1908, reached #16 in October 1931
(Also reached #1 in March 1909)
Jack Norworth & Nora Bayes w & m
Featured in ZIEGFELD FOLLIES OF 1931, show (opened 07/31)
Ruth Etting, sung in show, 08/31 Perfect 12737, 08/31 Banner 32229
Boswell Sisters/Dorsey Brothers Orch 10/31 Bruns 6173
Ethel Waters 10/31 Col 2511-D

SIBONEY
L Feist, pub. 1929, reached #20 in June 1931
Dolly Morse w, Ernesto Lecuona m
Alfredo Brito Orch 06/31 Vic 22685
Enric Madriguera Orch 05/31 Col 2434-D
Grace Moore, stage

ST. JAMES INFIRMARY
Mills, pub. 1929, reached #19 in June 1931
(Also reached #8 in March 1930)
Irving Mills w & m
Cab Calloway/<vocal Φ 05/31 Bruns 6105

STAR DUST
Mills ΦΦΦ, pub. 1929, reached #12 in July 1931
(Also reached #8 in February 1941)
(Also reached #16 in August 1957)
Mitchell Parish w, Hoagy Carmichael m
All-time jazz & pop standard
Isham Jones Orch Φ 12/30 Bruns 4856
Bing Crosby 10/31 Bruns 6169
Wayne King Orch 07/31 Vic 22656

SUGAR BLUES
Clarence Williams M C, pub. 1923, reached #20 in April 1931
(Also reached #16 in August 1935)
(Also reached #15 in November 1947)
Lucy Fletcher w, Clarence Williams m
Clyde McCoy Orch Φ 03/31 Col 2389-D
Blanche Calloway 06/31 Vic 22661

SWEET AND LOVELY (10)
Robbins, pub. 1931, reached #1 in October 1931
(Also reached #15 in October 1944)
Gus Arnheim, Harry Tobias, Jules Lemare w & m
Gus Arnheim/Donald Novis ΦΦ 08/31 Vic 22770
Russ Columbo 10/31 Vic 22802
Bing Crosby 11/31 Bruns 6179
Guy Lombardo/Carmen Lombardo 09/31 Col 2500-D

TEARS
Shapiro, B, pub. 1930, reached #13 in February 1931
Frank Capano & Billy Uhr w & m
Rudy Vallee/<vocal 02/31 Vic 22585
Gus Arnheim Orch, db dates
Bob Haring/w.vocal 02/31 Bruns 6009

THIS IS THE MISSUS
DeSylva, B & H, pub. 1931, reached #14 in October 1931
Lew Brown & Ray Henderson w & m
Featured in GEORGE WHITE'S SCANDALS, 11TH ED, show (opened 09/31)
Rudy Vallee/<vocal, sung in show, 10/31 Vic 22783
Ben Selvin/Paul Small 10/31 Bruns 6165

THE THRILL IS GONE
DeSylva, B & H, pub. 1931, reached #14 in October 1931
Lew Brown & Ray Henderson w & m
Featured in GEORGE WHITE'S SCANDALS, 11TH ED., show (opened 09/31)
Rudy Vallee/<vocal 10/31 Vic 22784
Everett Marshall, sung in show
Bing Crosby, radio, 12/31 Bruns 20102

TIGER RAG
L Feist, pub. 1917, reached #17 in December 1931
(Also reached #15 in October 1918)
(Also reached #8 in February 1952)
Nick La Rocca, et al (Original Dixieland Jazz Band) w & m
Mills Brothers ΦΦ 11/31 Bruns 6197
Louis Armstrong/<vocal 04/32 Col 2631-D[12]

TIME ON MY HANDS (34)
Miller Mus, pub. 1930, reached #4 in December 1931
Harold Adamson & Mack Gordon w, Vincent Youmans m
Featured in SMILES, show (opened 11/30)
Leo Reisman/Lee Wiley 12/31 Vic 22839
Marilyn Miller & Paul Gregory, sung in show
Russ Columbo 12/31 Vic 22826
Smith Ballew/<vocal 11/31 Col 2544-D

TO WHOM IT MAY CONCERN
DeSylva, B & H, pub. 1931, reached #13 in February 1931
Sidney Mitchell w, George Meyer & Archie Gottler m
Ben Bernie/w.vocal 02/31 Bruns 6008
Bert Lown/Biltmore Trio 02/31 Vic 22603

TWO HEARTS IN THREE-QUARTER TIME (33)
Harms, pub. 1930, reached #8 in May 1931
Joe Young, W Reisch & A Robinson w, Robert Stolz m
Featured in TWO HEARTS IN 3/4 TIME, film (rel. 09/30)
Johnny Hamp/Carl Graub 04/31 Vic 22638
Bob Haring/Smith Ballew 04/31 Bruns 6031
Society Night Club Orch 05/31 Perfect 15445

WABASH MOON (40)
Berlin, pub. 1931, reached #9 in May 1931
Dave Dreyer, Morton Downey, Billy McKenny w & m
Morton Downey, stage, radio, 06/31 Vic 22673
Wayne King/w.vocal group 05/31 Vic 22643
The Cavaliers[1]/w.vocal 04/31 Col 2399-D

WALKIN' MY BABY BACK HOME (18)
DeSylva, B & H, pub. 1930, reached #2 in April 1931
(Also reached #3 in August 1952)
Roy Turk & Fred Ahlert w & m
Nick Lucas 03/31 Bruns 6048
Ted Weems/Parker Gibbs 04/31 Vic 22637
Harry Richman, stage and radio
The Foursome 02/31 Bruns 4996

THE WALTZ YOU SAVED FOR ME (3)
L Feist, pub. 1930, reached #1 in May 1931
Gus Kahn w, Wayne King & Emil Flindt m
Wayne King Orch Φ 01/31 Vic 22575
Roy Smeck 03/31 Col 2391-D, 06/31 Melotone 12134
Society Night Club Orch 04/31 Perfect 15433

WERE YOU SINCERE?
Robbins, pub. 1931, reached #16 in May 1931
Jack Meskill w, Vincent Rose m
Bert Lown/Elmer Feldkamp 05/31 Vic 22653
Ruth Etting 06/31 Col 2445-D
Bing Crosby 07/31 Bruns 6120

WHEN I TAKE MY SUGAR TO TEA
Famous, pub. 1931, reached #13 in May 1931
Sammy Fain, Irving Kahal, Pierre Norman w & m
Featured in MONKEY BUSINESS, film (rel. 09/31)
Boswell Sisters/Dorsey Brothers Orch 05/31 Bruns 6083
Bert Lown/Biltmore Trio 05/31 Vic 22654
Casa Loma Orch/Kenny Sargent 05/31 Bruns 6085

WHEN IT'S SLEEPY TIME DOWN SOUTH (14)
Freed-Powers, pub. 1931, reached #2 in January 1932
Leon Rene, Otis Rene, Clarence Muse w & m
Louis Armstrong, stage, radio, 06/31 Okeh 41504
Paul Whiteman/Mildred Bailey Φ 12/31 Vic 22828
Jimmie Noone/Art Jarrett 11/31 Bruns 6174

WHEN THE MOON COMES OVER THE MOUNTAIN (1)
Robbins ΦΦΦ, pub. 1931, reached #1 in August 1931
Kate Smith, Harry Woods, Howard Johnson w & m
Kate Smith ΦΦ 09/31 Col 2516-D, 09/31 Clarion 5359
The Radiolites 08/31 Col 2485-D
Nick Lucas 09/31 Bruns 6147
Leo Reisman/Ben Gordon 08/31 Vic 22746

WHEN YOUR HAIR HAS TURNED TO SILVER (4)
J Morris, pub. 1930, reached #1 in April 1931
Charles Tobias w, Peter DeRose m
Bud and Joe Billings[13] Φ 03/31 Vic 22588
Rudy Vallee/<vocal, stage, radio, 03/31 Vic 22595
Phil Spitalny/w.vocal 03/31 Hit of Wk 1132

WHEN YOUR LOVER HAS GONE
Remick, pub. 1931, reached #14 in May 1931
Einar A Swan w & m
Featured in BLONDE CRAZY, film (rel. 11/31)
Gene Austin 04/31 Vic 22635
Ethel Waters 04/31 Col 2409-D
Bert Lown/Biltmore Trio 05/31 Vic 22652

WHEN YUBA PLAYS RUMBA ON THE TUBA (50)
Harms, pub. 1931, reached #9 in August 1931
Herman Hupfeld w & m
Featured in THE THIRD LITTLE SHOW, show (opened 06/31)
Rudy Vallee/<vocal Φ 08/31 Vic 22742
Walter O'Keefe, sung in show
The Knickerbockers[7]/w.vocal 08/31 Col 2483-D

WHISTLING IN THE DARK (36)
Olman M C, pub. 1931, reached #4 in June 1931
Allen Boretz w, Dana Suesse m
Guy Lombardo/Carmen Lombardo Φ 05/31 Col 2444-D
Rudy Vallee/<vocal 06/31 Vic 22672
Ben Bernie/w.vocal 06/31 Bruns 6097
Ted Weems Orch, db dates

WHY DANCE?
Berlin, pub. 1931, reached #20 in October 1931
Roy Turk w, Fred Ahlert m
Rudy Vallee/<vocal 10/31 Vic 22774
Abe Lyman/Phil Neely 08/31 Bruns 6154

WITHOUT THAT GAL (45)
Donaldson, D & G, pub. 1931, reached #7 in August 1931
Walter Donaldson w & m
Guy Lombardo/Carmen Lombardo Φ 08/31 Col 2475-D
Leo Reisman/<vocal 08/31 Vic 22746

WOULD YOU LIKE TO TAKE A WALK? (32)
Remick, pub. 1930, reached #5 in March 1931
Mort Dixon & Billy Rose w, Harry Warren m
Featured in SWEET AND LOW, show (opened 11/30)
Rudy Vallee/<vocal Φ 03/31 Vic 22611
Hannah Williams & Hal Thompson, sung in show
Frank Crumit & Julia Sanderson 04/31 Vic 22630
Hal Kemp/<vocal 04/31 Bruns 6055

WRAP YOUR TROUBLES IN DREAMS (46)
Shapiro, B, Pub. 1931, reached #8 in June 1931
Billy Moll & Ted Koehler w, Harry Barris m
Bing Crosby 05/31 Vic 22701
Abe Lyman/Phil Neely 06/31 Bruns 6125
Lloyd Keating[14]/w.vocal 06/31 Velvetone 2388-V

(I AM THE WORDS) YOU ARE THE MELODY
DeSylva, B & H, pub. 1930, reached #18 in January 1931
Bud DeSylva, Lew Brown, Ray Henderson w & m
Featured in JUST IMAGINE, film (rel. 10/30)
Also featured in HOLY TERROR, film (rel. 07/31)
Wayne King/Ernie Birchill 01/31 Vic 22573
Ben Selvin/w.vocal 12/30 Col 2298-D

YOU CALL IT MADNESS (BUT I CALL IT LOVE)
J Morris, pub. 1931, reached #10 in November 1931
Gregory DuBois & Paul Gregory w, Con Conrad & Russ Columbo m
Russ Columbo Φ 10/31 Vic 22802
Bert Lown/Elmer Feldkamp 10/31 Vic 22804
Kate Smith, radio, 11/31 Col 2539-D

YOU FORGOT YOUR GLOVES
Robbins, pub. 1931, reached #17 in November 1931
Edward Eliscu w, Ned Lehak m
Featured in THE THIRD LITTLE SHOW, show (opened 06/31)
Waring's Pennsylvanians/Clare Hanlon 10/31 Vic 22706
Jerry Norris & Constance Carpenter, sung in show
Victor Young/w.vocal duo 09/31 Bruns 6123

YOU TRY SOMEBODY ELSE
DeSylva, B & H, pub. 1931, reached #9 in January 1932
Bud DeSylva, Lew Brown, Ray Henderson w & m
Russ Columbo 12/31 Vic 22861
Guy Lombardo/Carmen Lombardo 01/32 Col 2567-D
Rudy Vallee/<vocal 12/31 Hit of Wk MM-4-5

YOU'RE DRIVING ME CRAZY (12)
Donaldson, D & G, pub. 1930, reached #1 in January 1931
Walter Donaldson w & m
Featured in SMILES, show (opened 11/30)
Guy Lombardo/Carmen Lombardo ΦΦ 12/30 Col 2335-D
Eddie Foy Jr. & Adele Astaire, sung in show
Rudy Vallee/<vocal Φ 01/31 Vic 22572
Nick Lucas 01/31 Bruns 4987

YOU'RE THE ONE I CARE FOR
Santly Bros, pub. 1930, reached #11 in February 1931
Harry Link w, Bert Lown & Chauncey Gray m
Bert Lown/Elmer Feldkamp 01/31 Vic 22583
Tom Gerun/w.vocal 02/31 Bruns 6002

YOURS AND MINE
Villa Moret, pub. 1930, reached #14 in January 1931
Johnny Burke w, Steve Nelson m
Ben Selvin/Smith Ballew 01/31 Col 2366-D
Red Nichols/Eddy Thomas 01/31 Bruns 4982
The Southerners/Frank Luther 02/31 Vic 22592

[1]The Cavaliers were actually Ben Selvin's Orch.
[2]Sung in revue by M H Walson and Woods Miller.
[3]Bud Billings was a pseudonym for Frank Luther.
[4]The London Mayfair Orch was led by Ray Noble.
[5]Dick Dixon is believed to be a pseudonym for Dick Robertson.
[6]The orchestra leader was actually Ben Selvin, not Madriguera.
[7]The Knickerbockers were actually the Ben Selvin Orch.
[8]Duke Ellington was listed on Brunswick as the Jungle Band, and Brunswick used the title "Dreamy Blues."
[9]Roy Carroll was a pseudonym for the Ben Selvin Orch.
[10]Although labeled as The Troubadours, this was actually the Hilo Hawaiian Orch.
[11]Buddy Campbell was a pseudonym for the Ben Selvin Orch.
[12]The Columbia record bore the title "New Tiger Rag."
[13]Bud and Joe Billings were actually Frank Luther and Carson Robison.
[14]Lloyd Keating was a pseudonym for the Ben Selvin Orch.

1932

ALL-AMERICAN GIRL (14)
L Feist, pub. 1932, reached #3 in November 1932
Al Lewis w & m
George Olsen/Fran Frey Φ stage, 10/32 Vic 24125
Ben Bernie/<vocal 11/32 Bruns 6389
Wayne King Orch, db dates

ALL OF ME (12)
Berlin, pub. 1931, reached #1 in February 1932
(Also reached #18 in August 1952)
Seymour Simons & Gerald Marks w & m
Featured in CARELESS LADY, film (rel. 04/32)
Paul Whiteman/Mildred Bailey ΦΦ 02/32 Vic 22879
Belle Baker, sung in film
Louis Armstrong/<vocal Φ 03/32 Col 2606-D, 03/32 Okeh 41552
Russ Columbo 02/32 Vic 22903
Ruth Etting 01/32 Perfect 12771

ALONE TOGETHER
Harms, pub. 1932, reached #17 in October 1932
Howard Dietz w, Arthur Schwartz m
Featured in FLYING COLORS, show (opened 09/32)
Leo Reisman/Frank Luther 10/32 Vic 24131
Jean Sargent, sung in show
Victor Young/Frank Munn 10/32 Bruns 6382

AS YOU DESIRE ME (36)
Keit-Engel, pub. 1932, reached #4 in September 1932
Allie Wrubel w & m
Russ Columbo Φ 09/32 Vic 24076
Donald Novis 09/32 Vic 24071
Arthur Tracy, radio, 09/32 Bruns 6356

AUF WIEDERSEH'N, MY DEAR (3)
Ager, Y & B, pub. 1931, reached #1 in March 1932
Al Hoffman, Ed Nelson, Al Goodhart, Milton Ager w & m
Jack Denny/w.vocal Φ 03/32 Vic 22917
Russ Columbo, stage, 05/32 Vic 22976
Morton Downey, radio, 03/32 Perfect 12788

BETWEEN THE DEVIL AND THE DEEP BLUE SEA
Mills, pub. 1931, reached #18 in March 1932
Ted Koehler w, Harold Arlen m
Featured in RHYTHMANIA, revue (opened 03/31)
Aida Ward, sung in revue
Cab Calloway/<vocal 01/32 Bruns 6209
Guy Lombardo/Carmen Lombardo 04/32 Bruns 20104
Boswell Sisters 05/32 Bruns 6291

A BOY AND A GIRL WERE DANCING
DeSylva, B & H, pub. 1932, reached #18 in January 1933
Mack Gordon w, Harry Revel m
Paul Whiteman/Jack Fulton 12/32 Vic 24188
Guy Lombardo/Carmen Lombardo 12/32 Bruns 6441
Ruth Etting, stage and radio
Lanny Ross, stage and radio

BROTHER, CAN YOU SPARE A DIME? (41)
Harms, pub. 1932 reached #8 in December 1932
E Y Harbourg w, Jay Gorney m
Featured in AMERICANA, revue (opened 10/32)
Bing Crosby Φ 12/32 Bruns 6414
Rudy Vallee/<vocal Φ 12/32 Col 2725-D
Ray Weber, sung in revue

BUGLE CALL RAG
Mills, pub. 1923, reached #17 in September 1932
(Also reached #16 in November 1934)
Jack Pettis, Billy Meyers, Elmer Schoebel m
Mills Brothers Φ 08/32 Bruns 6357

BY A RIPPLING STREAM (46)
Witmark, pub. 1932, reached #10 in June 1932
Bernice Petkere w & m
Johnny Hamp/w.vocal trio 06/32 Vic 22999
Aileen Stanley, stage and radio

BY THE FIRESIDE (22)
Robbins, pub. 1932, reached #4 in April 1932
Ray Noble, Jimmy Campbell, Reg Connelly w & m
George Olsen/w.vocal duo 04/32 Vic 22947
Eddy Duchin/Lew Sherwood 04/32 Col 2626-D

BY THE SYCAMORE TREE
Berlin, pub. 1931, reached #8 in February 1932
Haven Gillespie w, Pete Wendling m
Paul Whiteman/Jack Fulton 02/32 Vic 22879
Rudy Vallee/<vocal, radio, 03/32 Hit of Wk B-1-12
Dorsey Brothers Orch/Tony Starr 02/32 Col 2581-D

CABIN IN THE COTTON
Mills, pub. 1932, reached #12 in July 1932
Mitchell Parish w, Frank Perkins m
Cab Calloway/<vocal 05/32 Bruns 6272
Bing Crosby, radio, 08/32 Bruns 6329
Johnny Hamp/Charles Socci 06/32 Vic 22999

CAN'T WE TALK IT OVER?
Remick, pub. 1931, reached #9 in March 1932
Ned Washington w, Victor Young m
Bing Crosby & Mills Brothers 02/32 Bruns 6240
Eddy Duchin/Lew Sherwood 05/32 Col 2625-D
Ben Bernie/w.vocal 03/32 Bruns 6250

CUBAN LOVE SONG (43)
Robbins, pub. 1931, reached #7 in January 1932
Dorothy Fields, Jimmy McHugh, Herbert Stothart w & m
Featured in THE CUBAN LOVE SONG, film (rel. 12/31)
Lawrence Tibbett, sung in film, 02/32 Vic 1550
Paul Whiteman/Jack Fulton 12/31 Vic 22834
Jacques Renard/w.vocal 12/31 Bruns 6206

DANCING ON THE CEILING
Harms, pub. 1930, reached #8 in March 1932
Lorenz Hart w, Richard Rodgers m
Jack Hylton/Pat O'Malley 03/32 Vic 22912
Smith Ballew/<vocal 02/32 Banner 32368
Ben Selvin/Chester Gaylord 04/32 Col 2618-D

DELISHIOUS
Harms, pub. 1931, reached #15 in February 1932
Ira Gershwin w, George Gershwin m
Featured in DELICIOUS, film (rel. 12/31)
Janet Gaynor & Charles Farrell, sung in film
Nat Shilkret/Paul Small 02/32 Vic 22902
Bob Causer[1]/Kenny Sargent 02/32 Perfect 15556

DINAH
Mills; orig. pub. 1925, reached #11 in February 1932
(Also reached #1 in March 1926)
Sam Lewis & Joe Young w, Harry Akst m
Featured in RHYTHMANIA, revue (opened 03/31)
Bing Crosby & Mills Brothers Φ 02/32 Bruns 6240
Rudy Vallee, radio
Cab Calloway/<vocal 05/32 Perfect 15623

FIT AS A FIDDLE (18)
L Feist, pub. 1932, reached #3 in January 1933
Al Goodhart, Al Hoffman, Arthur Freed w & m
Featured in GEORGE WHITE'S MUSIC HALL VARIETIES, show (opened 11/32)
Waring's Pennsylvanians/Frank Zullo Φ 12/32 Vic 24168
Harry Richman, sung in show
Roger Wolfe Kahn/The Kahn-a-Sirs 12/32 Col 2726-D

GOOFUS (11)
L Feist, pub. 1930, reached #5 in July 1932
Gus Kahn w, Wayne King & William Harold m
Wayne King Orch Φ 08/32 Vic 22600[7]
Dan Russo/w.vocal Φ 06/32 Col 2641-D
Red Nichols/Dick Robertson 07/32 Bruns 6312

GOT A DATE WITH AN ANGEL
Harms, pub. 1931, reached #19 in June 1932[5]
Cliff Grey & Sonny Miller w, Jack Waller & Joe Tunbridge m
London Mayfair Orch[2]/Al Bowlly 05/32 Vic 22953
Debroy Somers 07/32 Col 2663-D

HELL'S BELLS
L Feist, pub. 1932, reached #13 in November 1932
Art Kassel w & m
Art Kassel/w.vocal trio Φ 08/32 Col 2682-D
Hal Kemp/w.vocal group 01/33 Bruns 6436

HERE LIES LOVE
Famous, pub. 1932, reached #12 in December 1932
Leo Robin & Ralph Rainger w & m
Featured in THE BIG BROADCAST, film (rel. 10/32)
Bing Crosby, sung in film, 12/32 Bruns 6406
Arthur Tracy, sung in film
Jimmie Grier/Ray Hendricks 12/32 Vic 24174

HOLD MY HAND (42)
Harms, pub. 1931, reached #6 in August 1932
Maurice Elwin, Harry Graham, Noel Gay w & m
London Mayfair Orch[2]/Al Bowlly 08/32 Vic 24034
Arthur Lally/The Million-aires 08/32 Bruns 6328

HOME (WHEN SHADOWS FALL) (8)
Marlo Mus, pub. 1931, reached #1 in February 1932
Peter Van Steeden, Harry Clarkson, Jeff Clarkson w & m
Peter Van Steeden/Dick Robertson Φ 01/32 Vic 22868
Rudy Vallee/<vocal, radio, 02/32 Hit of Week A-3-4
Mildred Bailey 02/32 Vic 22874
Arthur Tracy, radio, 01/32 Bruns 6227
Louis Armstrong/<vocal 03/32 Col 2606-D

HOW DEEP IS THE OCEAN? (24)
Berlin, pub. 1932, reached #3 in November 1932
(Also reached #9 in November 1945)
Irving Berlin w & m
Bing Crosby Φ radio, 12/32 Bruns 6406
Guy Lombardo/Carmen Lombardo Φ 11/32 Bruns 6399
Paul Whiteman/Jack Fulton 11/32 Vic 24141
Rudy Vallee/<vocal 12/32 Col 2724-D

HUMMIN' TO MYSELF (37)
DeSylva, B & H, pub. 1932, reached #7 in July 1932
Herb Magidson w, Sammy Fain m
Johnny Hamp/Carl Graub 06/32 Vic 24000
Ben Selvin/w.vocal 07/32 Col 2669-D

I CAN'T BELIEVE IT'S TRUE (38)
L Feist, pub. 1932, reached #7 in September 1932
Charles Newman, Ben Bernie, Isham Jones w & m
Isham Jones/Eddie Stone 09/32 Bruns 6308
Bert Lown Orch 09/32 Vic 24086
Frances Langford 09/32 Col 2696-D

I GUESS I'LL HAVE TO CHANGE MY PLAN
Harms, pub. 1929, reached #14 in October 1932
Howard Dietz w, Arthur Schwartz m
Rudy Vallee/<vocal 10/32 Col 2700-D
Paul Whiteman/Ramona Davies 10/32 Vic 24097
Guy Lombardo/Carmen Lombardo 10/32 Bruns 6363

I HEARD
Mills, pub. 1932, reached #15 in April 1932
Don Redman w & m
Don Redman/<vocal 02/32 Bruns 6233
Mills Brothers 04/32 Bruns 6269

I'LL NEVER BE THE SAME (29)
Robbins, pub. 1932, reached #5 in September 1932
Gus Kahn w, Matty Malneck & Frank Signorelli m
Paul Whiteman/Mildred Bailey Φ 10/32 Vic 24088
Ruth Etting 08/32 Perfect 12828, 08/32 Banner 32499, 08/32 Melotone 12450
Guy Lombardo/Carmen Lombardo 09/32 Bruns 6350

I'M SURE OF EVERYTHING BUT YOU (47)
Words & Music, pub. 1932, reached #9 in January 1933
Charles O'Flynn w, George W Meyer & Pete Wendling m
Guy Lombardo/w.vocal trio 12/32 Bruns 6426
Don Bestor/Neil Buckley 12/32 Vic 24176
Ruth Etting, stage and radio

IF IT AIN'T LOVE
Keit-Engel, pub. 1932, reached #18 in July 1932
Val Burton & Will Jason w & m
Isham Jones/w.vocal 05/32 Bruns 6270
Leo Reisman/Frank Luther 07/32 Vic 24011
Boswell Sisters/Dorsey Brothers Orch 07/32 Bruns 6302

IN A SHANTY IN OLD SHANTY TOWN (1)
Witmark, pub. 1932, reached #1 in July 1932
Joe Young w, Little Jack Little & John Siras m
Featured in THE CROONER, film (rel. 08/32)
Ted Lewis/<vocal ΦΦ 07/32 Col 2652-D
Teddy Joyce, sung in film
Ted Black/Chick Bullock Φ 08/32 Vic 24050
Little Jack Little, stage and radio

IN MY HIDEAWAY
Berlin, pub. 1932, reached #17 in July 1932
K L Binford w & m
Buddy Rogers/Frank Parrish 07/32 Vic 24015
Ralph Kinbery, stage

IS I IN LOVE? I IS
DeSylva, B & H, pub. 1932, reached #14 in July 1932
Mercer Cook w, J Russel Robinson m
Ben Selvin/w.vocal 07/32 Col 2661-D
Roane's Pennsylvanians/Cliff Nazarro 08/32 Vic 24036

IT DON'T MEAN A THING (IF IT AIN'T GOT THAT SWING)
Gotham, pub. 1932, reached #18 in May 1932
(Reached second peak at #20 in November 1932)
Irving Mills w, Duke Ellington m
All-time jazz standard
Duke Ellington/Ivie Anderson 03/32 Bruns 6265
Mills Brothers 10/32 Bruns 6377
Boswell Sisters 01/33 Bruns 6442

IT WAS SO BEAUTIFUL (33)
DeSylva, B & H, pub. 1932, reached #5 in September 1932
Arthur Freed w, Harry Barris m
Featured in THE BIG BROADCAST, film (rel. 10/32)
Harry Richman, stage, 09/32 Col 2701-D
Kate Smith, sung in film
Ruth Etting 08/32 Banner 32499, 08/32 Melotone 12450, 11/32 Perfect 12858
Enric Madriguera 09/32 Col 18006-D
George Olsen/Paul Small 09/32 Vic 24070

JUST A LITTLE HOME FOR THE OLD FOLKS
Donaldson, D & G, pub. 1932, reached #12 in December 1932
Edgar Leslie w, Fred Ahlert m
Don Bestor/Neil Buckley 12/32 Vic 24177
Guy Lombardo/Carmen Lombardo 01/33 Bruns 6440
Kate Smith, radio

JUST FRIENDS (25)
Robbins, pub. 1931, reached #3 in March 1932
Sam Lewis w, John Klenner m
Russ Columbo Φ 03/32 Vic 22909
Jack Denny/w.vocal 03/32 Vic 22907
Ben Selvin/w.vocal 04/32 Col 2618-D

KEEPIN' OUT OF MISCHIEF NOW
Conrad Mus, pub. 1932, reached #9 in May 1932
Andy Razaf w, Thomas "Fats" Waller m
Louis Armstrong/<vocal 05/32 Col 2646-D, 05/32 Okeh 41560
Coon-Sanders Night Hawks/Joe Sanders 05/32 Vic 22969
Fats Waller, stage

KISS ME GOODNIGHT (35)
DeSylva, B & H, pub. 1931, reached #8 in April 1932
Horatio Nicholls w, Archie Gottler m
Ruth Etting 04/32 Col 2630-D
George Olsen/Jerry Baker 04/32 Vic 22935

LAWD, YOU MADE THE NIGHT TOO LONG (40)
Shapiro, B, pub. 1932, reached #5 in June 1932
Sam Lewis w, Victor Young m
Guy Lombardo/Carmen Lombardo 05/32 Bruns 6300
Louis Armstrong/<vocal 05/32 Col 2646-D, 05/32 Okeh 41560
Paul Whiteman/Red McKenzie 06/32 Vic 22984

LAZY DAY (27)
Robbins, pub. 1932, reached #5 in July 1932
George Posford w & m
Bing Crosby Φ 06/32 Bruns 6306
Jack Denny/June Pursell 07/32 Vic 24012
Roger Wolfe Kahn/Dick Robertson 07/32 Col 2653-D

LET'S HAVE ANOTHER CUP OF COFFEE
Berlin, pub. 1932, reached #14 in April 1932
Irving Berlin w & m
Featured in FACE THE MUSIC, show (opened 02/32)
Waring's Pennsylvanians/Chick Bullock 04/32 Vic 22936
J Harold Murray & Katherine Carrington, sung in show
Phil Spitalny/Helen Rowland 05/32 Hit of Wk D-3-4

LET'S PUT OUT THE LIGHTS (AND GO TO SLEEP) (17)
Harms, pub. 1932, reached #1 in November 1932
Herman Hupfeld w & m
Featured in GEORGE WHITE'S MUSIC HALL VARIETIES, show (opened 11/32)
Paul Whiteman/Ramona Davies Φ 11/32 Vic 24140
Rudy Vallee/<vocal Φ 11/32 Col 2715-D
Harry Richman, Lili Damita & Bert Lahr, sung in show
Ben Bernie/<vocal Bruns 6385
Ozzie Nelson/Harriet Hilliard, stage

LIES
Shapiro, B, pub. 1931, reached #14 in January 1932
George Springer w, Harry Barris m
Gene Austin/Ben Pollack Orch 12/31 Perfect 15542, 12/31 Banner 32325
Ben Selvin/Dick Robertson 12/31 Harmony 1384-H, 12/31 Velvetone 2461-V
Russ Columbo, stage

A LITTLE STREET WHERE OLD FRIENDS MEET (4)
J Morris, pub. 1932, reached #1 in January 1933
Gus Kahn w, Harry Woods m
Isham Jones/Frank Hazzard Φ 12/32 Vic 24161
Gene Austin 12/32 Melotone 12529
Ozzie Nelson/<vocal 01/33 Bruns 6443
Owen Fallon/Harlan Lattimore 11/32 Perfect 15691

LOUISIANA HAYRIDE
Harms, pub. 1932, reached #15 in December 1932
Howard Dietz w, Arthur Schwartz m
Featured in FLYING COLORS, show (opened 09/32)
Clifton Webb & Tamara Geva, sung in show
Leo Reisman/Arthur Schwartz 12/32 Vic 24157

LOVABLE
Robbins, pub. 1932, reached #10 in May 1932
Gus Kahn w, Harry Woods m
Rudy Vallee/<vocal 05/32 Hit of Wk D-2-3
Leo Reisman/<vocal 05/32 Vic 22954

LOVE ME TONIGHT (30)
Famous, pub. 1932, reached #4 in October 1932
Lorenz Hart w, Richard Rodgers m
Featured in LOVE ME TONIGHT, film (rel. 08/32)
Jeanette MacDonald & Maurice Chevalier, sung in film
Bing Crosby 09/32 Bruns 6351
George Olsen/Paul Small 10/32 Vic 24124
Jeanette MacDonald 09/32 Vic 24067

LOVE, YOU FUNNY THING (49)
L Feist, pub. 1932, reached #8 in May 1932
Roy Turk w, Fred Ahlert m
Louis Armstrong/<vocal 04/32 Col 2631-D, 04/32 Okeh 41557
Bing Crosby 04/32 Bruns 6268
George Olsen/Fran Frey 05/32 Vic 22947

LULLABY OF THE LEAVES (5)
Berlin, pub. 1932, reached #1 in June 1932
Joe Young w, Bernice Petkere m
George Olsen/w.vocal group ΦΦ 06/32 Vic 22998
Ben Selvin/w.vocal 06/32 Col 2654-D
Enric Madriguera/Richard Barry 07/32 Bruns 6310

MASQUERADE (21)
L Feist, pub. 1932, reached #3 in August 1932
Paul Francis Webster w, John Jacob Loeb m
Ted Black/Dick Robertson Φ 08/32 Vic 24046
Jacques Renard/Smith Ballew 08/32 Bruns 6326

MIMI
Famous, pub. 1932, reached #17 in September 1932
Lorenz Hart w, Richard Rodgers m
Featured in LOVE ME TONIGHT, film (rel. 08/32)
Maurice Chevalier, sung in film, 09/32 Vic 24063

MY EXTRAORDINARY GAL (44)
Olman M C, pub. 1932, reached #7 in June 1932
Terry Shand w & m
Guy Lombardo/Carmen Lombardo 05/32 Bruns 6290
Gene Kardos/Dick Robertson 06/32 Vic 22986

MY MOM (26)
Donaldson, D & G, pub. 1932, reached #4 in May 1932
Walter Donaldson w & m
Kate Smith 05/32 Col 2637-D
George Olsen/Jerry Baker 05/32 Vic 22967
Morton Downey, radio, 06/32 Hit of Wk E-2-3

MY SILENT LOVE (15)
Famous, pub. 1932, reached #2 in July 1932
Edward Heyman w, Dana Suesse m
Isham Jones/Billy Scott Φ 06/32 Bruns 6308
Ruby Newman/Gordon Graham 07/32 Vic 24042
Roger Wolfe Kahn/Elmer Feldkamp 07/32 Col 2653-D

THE NIGHT WHEN LOVE WAS BORN
L Feist, pub. 1932, reached #18 in August 1932
Abel Baer, Joe Young, Dave Oppenheim w & m
Ruth Etting 08/32 Col 2681-D
Eddie Duchin/Lew Sherwood 08/32 Col 2677-D
Connie Boswell/Dorsey Brothers Orch 08/32 Bruns 6332

NOW'S THE TIME TO FALL IN LOVE
DeSylva, B & H, pub. 1931, reached #11 in February 1932
Al Sherman & Al Lewis w & m
Featured in PALMY DAYS, film (rel. 09/32)
Eddie Cantor, sung in film and on radio
Gene Kardos/Dick Robertson 01/32 Vic 22865
Ben Selvin/Dick Robertson 02/32 Col 2575-D

OF THEE I SING
New World Mus, pub. 1932, reached #20 in March 1932[6]
Ira Gershwin w, George Gershwin m
Featured in OF THEE I SING, show (opened 12/31)
Lois Morgan & William Gaxton, sung in show
Arden-Ohman Orch/Frank Luther 03/32 Vic 22911
The Knickerbockers[3]/w.vocal 03/32 Col 2598-D

ONE HOUR WITH YOU (10)
Famous, pub. 1932, reached #2 in May 1932
Leo Robin w, Richard Whiting m
Featured in ONE HOUR WITH YOU, film (rel. 03/32)
Jimmie Grier/Donald Novis Φ 05/32 Vic 22971
Maurice Chevalier, sung in film
Eddie Cantor, radio
Morton Downey, radio, 04/32 Perfect 12797

OOH! THAT KISS
Harms, pub. 1931, reached #10 in January 1932
Mort Dixon & Joe Young w, Harry Warren m
Featured in THE LAUGH PARADE, revue (opened 11/31)
Lawrence Gray & Jean Aubert, sung in revue
Arden-Ohman Orch/w.vocal duo 12/31 Vic 22818
Abe Lyman/Dick Robertson 12/31 Bruns 6208

PARADISE (2)
L Feist, pub. 1931, reached #1 in April 1932
Gordon Clifford w, Nacio Herb Brown m
Featured in A WOMAN COMMANDS, film (rel. 02/32)
Russ Columbo, sung in film, 05/32 Vic 22976
Leo Reisman/Frances Maddux ΦΦ 03/32 Vic 22904
Guy Lombardo/Carmen Lombardo Φ 06/32 Bruns 6290
Bing Crosby 05/32 Bruns 6285
Morton Downey, radio, 04/32 Perfect 12797

PINK ELEPHANTS (19)
Words & Mus, pub. 1932, reached #3 in December 1932
Mort Dixon w, Harry Woods m
George Olsen Orch Φ 11/32 Vic 24138
Guy Lombardo/w.vocal trio Φ 11/32 Bruns 6399

PLEASE (7)
Famous, pub. 1932, reached #1 in December 1932
Leo Robin w, Ralph Rainger m
Featured in THE BIG BROADCAST, film (rel. 10/32)
Bing Crosby ΦΦ sung in film, 11/32 Bruns 6394
George Olsen/Bob Borger 11/32 Vic 24139
Rudy Vallee/<vocal 12/32 Col 2724-D

PU-LEEZE, MR. HEMINGWAY!
Olman M C, pub. 1932, reached #14 in November 1932
Milt Drake, Walter Kent, Abner Silver w & m
Guy Lombardo/w.vocal trio 10/32 Bruns 6390
George Olsen/Fran Frey 10/32 Vic 24138

RAIN ON THE ROOF
Famous, pub. 1932, reached #13 in March 1932
Ann Ronell w & m
Nat Shilkret/Scrappy Lambert 03/32 Vic 22925
Casa Loma Orch[4]/Kenny Sargent 03/32 Bruns 6252
Paul Whiteman Orch, stage

ROCKIN' CHAIR
Southern, pub. 1930, reached #18 in June 1932
Hoagy Carmichael w & m
Mills Brothers 05/32 Bruns 6278
Mildred Bailey, stage, 10/32 Vic 24117
Hoagy Carmichael & Louis Armstrong 09/32 Col 2688-D

SAY IT ISN'T SO (13)
Berlin, pub. 1932, reached #1 in October 1932
Irving Berlin w & m
George Olsen/Paul Small Φ 10/32 Vic 24124
Rudy Vallee/<vocal Φ stage, radio, 10/32 Col 2714-D
Ozzie Nelson/<vocal 10/32 Bruns 6372
Connie Boswell 11/32 Bruns 6393

SHE DIDN'T SAY "YES"
T B Harms, pub. 1931, reached #19 in February 1932
Otto Harbach w, Jerome Kern m
Featured in THE CAT AND THE FIDDLE, show (opened 10/31)
Bettina Hall, sung in show
Leo Reisman/Frank Luther 02/32 Vic 22869

A SHINE ON YOUR SHOES
Harms, pub. 1932, reached #17 in December 1932
Howard Dietz w, Arthur Schwartz m
Featured in FLYING COLORS, show (opened 09/32)
Buddy Ebsen & Vilma Ebsen, sung in show
Leo Reisman/Frank Luther 11/32 Vic 24131
Roger Wolfe Kahn/w.vocal 12/32 Col 2722-D

SNUGGLED ON YOUR SHOULDER (23)
L Feist, pub. 1931, reached #6 in April 1932
Joe Young w, Carmen Lombardo m
Bing Crosby, stage, radio, 03/32 Bruns 6248
Eddy Duchin/Lew Sherwood 04/32 Col 2625-D
Kate Smith 04/32 Col 2624-D
Isham Jones/w.vocal 03/32 Bruns 6249

SO ASHAMED
Ager, Y & B, pub. 1932, reached #17 in August 1932
Milt Ager & Benny Davis w & m
Ruby Newman/Gordon Graham 09/32 Vic 24073
radio singers

SOFT LIGHTS AND SWEET MUSIC
Berlin, pub. 1932, reached #11 in May 1932
Irving Berlin w & m
Featured in FACE THE MUSIC, show (opened 02/32)
J Harold Murray & Katherine Carrington, sung in show
Waring's Pennsylvanians/Three Waring Girls
05/32 Vic 22936
Eddy Duchin/Lew Sherwood 05/32 Col 2626-D

SOMEBODY LOVES YOU (6)
J Morris, pub. 1932, reached #3 in April 1932
Charles Tobias w, Peter DeRose m
Ted Lewis/<vocal Φ 05/32 Col 2635-D
Peter Van Steeden/Chick Bullock 04/32 Vic 22948
Pickens Sisters 05/32 Vic 22965

STARLIGHT
Santly Bros, pub. 1931, reached #19 in March 1932
Joe Young w, Bernice Petkere m
Casa Loma Orch[4]/Kenny Sargent 03/32 Bruns 6252
Ted Wallace/w.vocal 03/32 Col 2601-D

STRANGE INTERLUDE (34)
Miller Mus, pub. 1932, reached #6 in September 1932
Ben Bernie & Walter Hirsch w, Phil Baker m
Rudy Vallee/<vocal Φ 09/32 Col 2702-D
Ruby Newman/Gordon Graham 09/32 Vic 24072
Morton Downey, radio, 01/33 Perfect 12874

SWEETHEARTS FOREVER (39)
Witmark, pub. 1932, reached #7 in October 1932
Irving Caesar w, Cliff Friend m
Featured in THE CROONER, film (rel. 07/32)
Wayne King/Gordon Graham 10/32 Vic 24115
David Manners, sung in film
Tom Gerun/Smith Ballew 10/32 Bruns 6365

THREE ON A MATCH (45)
DeSylva, B & H, pub. 1932, reached #9 in September 1932
Raymond B Egan w, Ted FioRito m
Featured in BLONDIE OF THE FOLLIES, film (rel. 08/32)
Paul Whiteman/Red McKenzie 09/32 Vic 24089
Freddy Martin/Elmer Feldkamp 11/32 Col 2708-D

THREE'S A CROWD (28)
Witmark, pub. 1932, reached #5 in October 1932
Al Dubin & Irving Kahal w, Harry Warren m
Featured in THE CROONER, film (rel. 07/32)
Wayne King/Gordon Graham 10/32 Vic 24115
David Manners, sung in film
Rudy Vallee/<vocal 11/32 Col 2714-D
Tom Gerun/Smith Ballew 10/32 Bruns 6365

TOO MANY TEARS (31)
Witmark, pub. 1932, reached #6 in May 1932
Al Dubin w, Harry Warren m
Guy Lombardo/Carmen Lombardo Φ 04/32 Bruns 6261
Pickens Sisters 05/32 Vic 22965
Leo Reisman/Fran Frey 05/32 Vic 22961

TRY TO FORGET
T B Harms, pub. 1931, reached #19 in January 1932
Otto Harbach w, Jerome Kern m
Featured in THE CAT AND THE FIDDLE, show (opened 10/31)
Doris Carson, Bettina Hall & Eddie Foy Jr, sung in show
Leo Reisman/Frank Luther 01/32 Vic 22870
Abe Lyman/Frank Luther 01/32 Bruns 6217

UNDERNEATH THE HARLEM MOON (50)
DeSylva, B & H, pub. 1932, reached #9 in December 1932
Mack Gordon w, Harry Revel m
Joe Rines/<vocal 01/33 Vic 24151
Don Redman/Harlan Lattimore 12/32 Bruns 6401
Chick Bullock 12/32 Perfect 15678
Fletcher Henderson/Katherine Handy 01/33 Col 2732-D

THE VOICE IN THE OLD VILLAGE CHOIR
Robbins, pub. 1932, reached #14 in July 1932
Gus Kahn w, Harry Woods m
Paul Whiteman/Jack Fulton 06/32 Vic 22998
Donald Novis 07/32 Vic 24021
Ruth Etting 07/32 Col 2660-D

WAS THAT THE HUMAN THING TO DO? (16)
Witmark, pub. 1931, reached #1 in March 1932
Joe Young w, Sammy Fain m
Bert Lown/Elmer Feldkamp Φ 02/32 Vic 22908
Guy Lombardo Orch, stage and radio
Rudy Vallee/<vocal 03/32 Hit of Wk C-1-2
Boswell Sisters 03/32 Bruns 6257

WE JUST COULDN'T SAY GOODBYE (9)
Keit-Engel, pub. 1932, reached #1 in September 1932
Harry Woods w & m
Guy Lombardo/Carmen Lombardo Φ 09/32 Bruns 6350
Paul Whiteman/Mildred Bailey Φ 09/32 Vic 24088
Freddy Martin/Terry Shand 10/32 Col 2703-D

WHEN WE'RE ALONE (PENTHOUSE SERENADE) (32)
Famous, pub. 1931, reached #4 in February 1932
Val Burton & Will Jason w & m
Arden-Ohman Orch/Frank Munn Φ 02/32 Vic 22910
Tom Gerun/Scrappy Lambert 02/32 Bruns 6236
Ruth Etting 04/32 Col 2630-D

WHERE THE BLUE OF THE NIGHT MEETS THE GOLD OF THE DAY (20)
DeSylva, B & H, pub. 1931, reached #3 in January 1932
Roy Turk, Bing Crosby, Fred Ahlert w & m
Featured in THE BIG BROADCAST, film (rel. 10/32)
Bing Crosby Φ sung in film, on radio, 01/32 Bruns 6226
Russ Columbo 01/32 Vic 22867

(I'M STILL WITHOUT A SWEETHEART) WITH SUMMER COMIN' ON
Keit-Engel, pub. 1932, reached #10 in July 1932
Roy Turk w, Fred Ahlert m
Waring's Pennsylvanians/w.vocal group 07/32 Vic 24016
Guy Lombardo/Carmen Lombardo 07/32 Bruns 6315
Bing Crosby 08/32 Bruns 6329

THE WOODEN SOLDIER AND THE CHINA DOLL
L Feist, pub. 1932, reached #10 in March 1932
Charles Newman w, Isham Jones m
Nat Shilkret/Scrappy Lambert 03/32 Vic 22925
Rudy Vallee/<vocal 04/32 Hit of Wk C-3-4
Ben Bernie/w.vocal 03/32 Bruns 6250

YOU CAN DEPEND ON ME
Southern, pub. 1932, reached #16 in March 1932
Charles Carpenter, Louis Dunlap, Earl Hines w & m
Louis Armstrong/<vocal 02/32 Col 2590-D,
02/32 Okeh 41538

(I'LL BE GLAD WHEN YOU'RE DEAD) YOU RASCAL YOU
Mills, pub. 1931, reached #19 in January 1932
Sam Theard w & m
Louis Armstrong/<vocal 12/31 Okeh 41504
Mills Brothers 01/32 Bruns 6225
Cab Calloway/<vocal 11/31 Bruns 6196

YOU'RE BLASE (48)
Harms, pub. 1932, reached #7 in August 1932
Bruce Sievier w, Ord Hamilton m
Gus Arnheim/Meri Bell 08/32 Vic 24054
Jack Hylton/Pat O'Malley 08/32 Bruns 6328
Eddy Duchin/Lew Sherwood 08/32 Col 2677-D

YOU'RE MY EVERYTHING
Harms, pub. 1931, reached #10 in February 1932
Mort Dixon & Joe Young w, Harry Warren m
Featured in THE LAUGH PARADE, show (opened 11/31)
Lawrence Gray & Jean Aubert, sung in show
Arden-Ohman Orch/Frank Luther 12/31 Vic 22818
Russ Columbo 03/32 Vic 22909

YOU'RE THE ONE (YOU BEAUTIFUL SON-OF-A-GUN)
DeSylva, B & H, pub. 1931, reached #17 in May 1932
Arthur B Fields & Gerald Marks w & m
Waring's Pennsylvanians/w.vocal group 05/32 Vic 22966
Victor Young/Scrappy Lambert 05/32 Bruns 6286

YOU'VE GOT ME IN THE PALM OF YOUR HAND
Donaldson, D & G, pub. 1932, reached #11 in September 1932
Cliff Friend & Edgar Leslie w, James V Monaco m
Gus Arnheim/w.vocal trio 08/32 Vic 24061
Bennie Krueger/Scrappy Lambert 08/32 Bruns 6334

[1]On most records where Bob Causer is listed as leader, it is not known who actually led the band.
[2]The London Mayfair Orch was led by Ray Noble.
[3]The Knickerbockers were actually the Ben Selvin Orch.
[4]The Casa Loma Orch was led by Glen Gray.
[5]Reached #19 on monthly chart only.
[6]Reached #20 on monthly chart only.
[7]King's recording was originally issued, with moderate success, in early 1931.

1933

ADORABLE (32)
Sam Fox, pub. 1933, reached #8 in June 1933
George Marion Jr w, Richard A Whiting m
Featured in ADORABLE, film (rel. 05/33)
Little Jack Little/<vocal 06/33 Blu 5065
Wayne King/<vocal 07/33 Bruns 6581
Henry Garat, sung in film

AFTER ALL, YOU'RE ALL I'M AFTER
Harms, pub. 1933, reached #18 in December 1933
Edward Heyman w, Arthur Schwartz m
Featured in SHE LOVES ME NOT, play (opened 01/34)
Eddy Duchin/Lew Sherwood 01/34 Vic 24477
John Beal, sung in play
Bing Crosby, radio

AH, BUT IS IT LOVE?
Harms, pub. 1933, reached #13 in October 1933
E Y Harbourg w, Jay Gorney m
Featured in MOONLIGHT AND PRETZELS, film (rel. 08/33)
Paul Whiteman/Jack Fulton 09/33 Vic 24365
Lillian Miles & Roger Pryor, sung in film

ANNIE DOESN'T LIVE HERE ANYMORE (21)
Berlin, pub. 1933, reached #2 in December 1933
Joe Young & Johnny Burke w, Harold Spina m
Guy Lombardo/Carmen Lombardo Φ 11/33 Bruns 6662
Ramona Davies/Roy Bargy Orch 12/33 Vic 24445

APRIL IN PARIS
Harms, pub. 1932, reached #11 in December 1933
E Y Harbourg w, Vernon Duke m
Featured in WALK A LITTLE FASTER, show (opened 12/32)
All-time pop standard
Marian Chase, stage, 10/33 LMS L-153
Freddy Martin/Elmer Feldkamp 01/34 Bruns 6717
Henry King/Joe Sudy 01/34 Vic 24478
Evelyn Hoey, sung in show

ARE YOU MAKIN' ANY MONEY?
Harms, pub. 1933, reached #16 in October 1933
Herman Hupfeld w & m
Featured in MOONLIGHT AND PRETZELS, film (rel. 08/33)
Lillian Miles, sung in film
Paul Whiteman/Ramona Davies 09/33 Vic 24365

BLESS YOUR HEART
Donaldson, D & G, pub. 1933, reached #19 in November 1933
Milton Drake, Harry Stride, Duke Easton w & m
Freddy Martin/Elmer Feldkamp 09/33 Bruns 6631
George Olsen/Joe Morrison 10/33 Col 2803-D

BLUE PRELUDE (33)
Keit-Engel, pub. 1933, reached #7 in August 1933
Gordon Jenkins & Joe Bishop w & m
Isham Jones, stage, 06/33 Vic 24298
Bing Crosby 08/33 Bruns 6601
Casa Loma Orch[1] 05/33 Bruns 6513

BY A WATERFALL (26)
Witmark, pub. 1933, reached #4 in December 1933
Irving Kahal w, Sammy Fain m
Featured in FOOTLIGHT PARADE, film (rel. 09/33)
Guy Lombardo/Carmen Lombardo Φ 11/33 Bruns 6653
Ruby Keeler & Dick Powell, sung in film
Leo Reisman/Arthur Wright 12/33 Vic 24399
Dick Powell 11/33 Bruns 6667

CLOSE YOUR EYES
Sherman Clay, pub. 1933, reached #17 in November 1933
Bernice Petkere w & m
Eddy Duchin/Lew Sherwood 10/33 Vic 24376
Freddy Martin/Elmer Feldkamp 10/33 Bruns 6620

DARKNESS ON THE DELTA
Santly Bros, pub. 1932, reached #17 in March 1933
Marty Symes & Al J Neiberg w, Jerry Livingston m
Isham Jones/Eddie Stone 02/33 Vic 24209
Ted FioRito/Muzzy Marcellino 03/33 Bruns 6478
Mildred Bailey, stage

THE DAY YOU CAME ALONG (25)
Famous, pub. 1933, reached #4 in October 1933
Arthur Johnston & Sam Coslow w & m
Featured in TOO MUCH HARMONY, film (rel. 09/33)
Bing Crosby Φ sung in film, 10/33 Bruns 6644
Victor Young/Scrappy Lambert 10/33 Bruns 6652
Leo Reisman/Frank Luther 12/33 Vic 24417

DID YOU EVER SEE A DREAM WALKING? (19)
DeSylva, B & H, pub. 1933, reached #1 in December 1933
Mack Gordon w, Harry Revel m
Featured in SITTING PRETTY, film (rel. 11/33)
Eddy Duchin/Lew Sherwood Φ 01/34 Vic 24477
Guy Lombardo/Carmen Lombardo Φ 01/34 Bruns 6713
Bing Crosby Φ 01/34 Bruns 6724
Ginger Rogers & Art Jarrett, sung in film
Meyer Davis/w.vocal 12/33 Col 2852-D

DINNER AT EIGHT (42)
Robbins, pub. 1933, reached #8 in November 1933
Dorothy Fields w, Jimmy McHugh m
Featured as theme in DINNER AT EIGHT, film (rel. 08/33)
Connie Boswell/Victor Young 10/33 Bruns 6640
Leo Reisman/Frank Luther 11/33 Vic 24419

DOIN' THE UPTOWN LOWDOWN
DeSylva, B & H, pub. 1933, reached #20 in December 1933
Mack Gordon w, Harry Revel m
Featured in BROADWAY THROUGH A KEYHOLE, film (rel. 10/33)
Isham Jones/Joe Martin 11/33 Vic 24409
Frances Williams, sung in film

DON'T BLAME ME (29)
Robbins, pub. 1933, reached #5 in September 1933
Dorothy Fields w, Jimmy McHugh m
Ethel Waters 09/33 Bruns 6617
Guy Lombardo/Carmen Lombardo 08/33 Bruns 6608
Rudy Vallee/<vocal 08/33 Blu 5115
Leo Reisman/Howard Phillips 09/33 Vic 24359

DOWN THE OLD OX ROAD
Famous, pub. 1933, reached #10 in August 1933
Sam Coslow w, Arthur Johnston m
Featured in COLLEGE HUMOR, film (rel. 06/33)
Bing Crosby, sung in film, 07/33 Bruns 6601
Paul Whiteman/w.vocal duo 09/33 Vic 24368

EADIE WAS A LADY (44)
Harms, pub. 1932, reached #7 in February 1933
Bud DeSylva w, Richard A Whiting & Nacio Herb Brown m
Featured in TAKE A CHANCE, show (opened 11/32)
Ethel Merman, sung in show, 02/33 Bruns 6456
Paul Whiteman/Ramona Davies 02/33 Vic 24202
Cab Calloway/<vocal 01/33 Perfect 15715, 01/33 Banner 32647

EVENIN'
Mills, pub. 1933, reached #16 in December 1933
Mitchell Parish w, Harry White m
Cab Calloway/<vocal, stage, 11/33 Vic 24414

FAREWELL TO ARMS (22)
Words & Mus, pub. 1933, reached #3 in April 1933
Allie Wrubel & Abner Silver w & m
Paul Whiteman/Jack Fulton Φ 03/33 Vic 24236
Arthur Tracy, radio, 04/33 Bruns 6512
Morton Downey, radio, 04/33 Melotone 12644

A FOOL IN LOVE
Berlin, pub. 1933, reached #18 in July 1933
George McQueen w, Sid Lippman m
Eddy Duchin/Lew Sherwood 07/33 Vic 24326
George McQueen[2]/Elmer Feldkamp 07/33 Perfect 15780, 07/33 Melo 12717, 07/33 Banner 32782

FORTY-SECOND STREET (17)
Witmark, pub. 1932, reached #2 in April 1933
Al Dubin w, Harry Warren m
Featured in FORTY-SECOND STREET, film (rel. 01/33)
Don Bestor/Dudley Mecum ΦΦ 04/33 Vic 24253
Ruby Keeler, sung in film
Hal Kemp/Skinnay Ennis 03/33 Bruns 6471
Boswell Sisters 05/33 Bruns 6545

THE GIRL IN THE LITTLE GREEN HAT
Bibo & Lange, pub. 1933, reached #10 in February 1933
Bradford Browne & Jack Scholl w, Max Rich m
George Olsen/Fran Frey 02/33 Vic 24220
Rudy Vallee/<vocal 03/33 Col 2744-D

GOOD MORNING, GLORY
DeSylva, B & H, pub. 1933, reached #11 in January 1934
Mack Gordon w, Harry Revel m
Featured in SITTING PRETTY, film (rel. 11/33)
Pickens Sisters, sung in film, 01/34 Vic 24468
Tom Coakley/Carl Ravazza 01/34 Vic 24480
Jay Whidden/Lee Norton 12/33 Bruns 6688

GOOD NIGHT, LITTLE GIRL OF MY DREAMS (3)
J Morris, pub. 1933, reached #1 in December 1933
Charles Tobias & Joe Burke w & m
Henry King/Joe Sudy Φ 12/33 Vic 24457
Victor Young/Red McKenzie 12/33 Bruns 6692
Elton Britt 12/33 Melotone 12873

GYPSY FIDDLES
Words & Mus, pub. 1933, reached #15 in June 1933
Allie Wrubel w & m
Arthur Tracy, radio, 06/33 Bruns 6561
Don Bestor/Neil Buckley 06/33 Vic 24317

HAVE YOU EVER BEEN LONELY? (12)
Shapiro, B, pub. 1933, reached #4 in May 1933
Billy Hill w, Peter DeRose m
Ted Lewis/<vocal Φ 04/33 Col 2753-D
Guy Lombardo Orch, radio and stage
George Hall/Glenn Cross 04/33 Blu 5021
Ozzie Nelson/<vocal 05/33 Bruns 6547

HEAT WAVE
Berlin, pub. 1933, reached #10 in December 1933
Irving Berlin w & m
Featured in AS THOUSANDS CHEER, show (opened 09/33)
Ethel Waters, sung in show, 11/33 Col 2826-D
Glen Gray[3]/Mildred Bailey 12/33 Bruns 6679
Meyer Davis/Charlotte Murray 11/33 Col 2821-D

HEY! YOUNG FELLA
Robbins, pub. 1933, reached #15 in April 1933
Dorothy Fields w, Jimmy McHugh m
Featured in CLOWNS IN CLOVER, revue (1933)
Featured in DANCING LADY, film (rel. 11/33)
Walter Woolf King, sung in revue
Glen Gray[3]/Pee Wee Hunt 03/33 Vic 24222
Rudy Vallee/<vocal 03/33 Col 2744-D

HOLD ME (16)
Robbins, pub. 1933, reached #3 in June 1933
Little Jack Little, Dave Oppenheim, Ira Schuster w & m
Eddy Duchin/Lew Sherwood Φ 05/33 Vic 24280
Hotel Commodore Orch 05/33 Col 2767-D
Ted FioRito/w.vocal 06/33 Bruns 6555

HOLD YOUR MAN (36)
Robbins, pub. 1933, reached #7 in August 1933
Arthur Freed w, Nacio Herb Brown m
Featured in DANCING LADY, film (rel. 11/33)
Don Bestor/Florence Case 07/33 Vic 24345
Winnie Lightner, sung in film
Gertrude Niesen 08/33 Col 2787-D

HONEYMOON HOTEL (40)
Witmark, pub. 1933, reached #8 in December 1933
Al Dubin w, Harry Warren m
Featured in FOOTLIGHT PARADE, film (rel. 09/33)
Ruby Keeler & Dick Powell, sung in film
Leo Reisman/Frank Luther 11/33 Vic 24399
Dick Powell 11/33 Bruns 6667
Rudy Vallee Orch/Alice Faye 11/33 Blu 5171

I COVER THE WATERFRONT (49)
Harms, pub. 1933, reached #11 in July 1933
Edward Heyman w, Johnny Green m
Eddy Duchin/Lew Sherwood 07/33 Vic 24325
Ben Bernie Orch, stage and radio
Joe Haymes/w.vocal 07/33 Col 2781-D

I GOTTA RIGHT TO SING THE BLUES
Harms, pub. 1932, reached #18 in March 1933
Ted Koehler w, Harold Arlen m
Featured in EARL CARROLL'S VANITIES 10th ED, show (opened 09/32)
Louis Armstrong/<vocal 03/33 Vic 24233
Lillian Shade, sung in show
Ethel Merman 11/32 Vic 24145
Cab Calloway/<vocal 02/33 Bruns 6460

I WAKE UP SMILING
Donaldson, D & G, pub. 1933, reached #15 in May 1933
Edgar Leslie w, Fred Ahlert m
Guy Lombardo/Carmen Lombardo 04/33 Bruns 6509
Joe Green/w.vocal 04/33 Col 2760-D
Paul Whiteman/Jack Fulton 04/33 Vic 24226

I'LL BE FAITHFUL (35)
Robbins, pub. 1933, reached #6 in December 1933
Ned Washington w, Allie Wrubel m
Jan Garber/Lew Palmer 11/33 Vic 24412
Bernie Cummins/w.vocal 11/33 Col 2827-D

I'LL TAKE AN OPTION ON YOU (45)
Harms, pub. 1933, reached #7 in April 1933
Leo Robin w, Ralph Rainger m
Featured in TATTLE TALES, show (opened 06/33)
Frank Fay & Betty Doree, sung in show
Ted FioRito/w.vocal 04/33 Bruns 6505
Paul Whiteman/Peggy Healy 06/33 Vic 24304

I'M YOUNG AND HEALTHY
Witmark, pub. 1932, reached #12 in March 1933
Al Dubin w, Harry Warren m
Featured in FORTY-SECOND STREET, film (rel. 01/33)
Dick Powell, sung in film
Bing Crosby/Guy Lombardo 03/33 Bruns 6472
Waring's Pennsylvanians/Tom Waring 02/33 Vic 24214

I'VE GOT THE WORLD ON A STRING
Mills, pub. 1932, reached #19 in March 1933
Ted Koehler w, Harold Arlen m
Featured in COTTON CLUB PARADE 21ST ED, revue (opened 10/32)
Pop and jazz standard, 1930's to 1960's
Aida Ward, sung in revue
Bing Crosby 03/33 Bruns 6491

I'VE GOT TO SING A TORCH SONG
Remick, pub. 1933, reached #18 in July 1933
Al Dubin w, Harry Warren m
Featured in GOLD DIGGERS OF 1933, film (rel. 05/33)
Dick Powell, sung in film, 07/33 Perfect 12919
Paul Whiteman/Ramona Davies 06/33 Vic 24304
Bing Crosby 08/33 Bruns 6599
Rudy Vallee/<vocal 07/33 Col 2773-D

I'VE TOLD EVERY LITTLE STAR
T B Harms, pub. 1932, reached #17 in January 1933
(Also reached #4 in May 1961)
Oscar Hammerstein 2nd w, Jerome Kern m
Featured in MUSIC IN THE AIR, show (opened 11/32)
Jack Denny/Paul Small 01/33 Vic 24183
Walter Slezak, sung in show
Eddy Duchin/Lew Sherwood 12/32 Bruns 6425

IN THE PARK IN PAREE
Famous, pub. 1933, reached #18 in June 1933
Leo Robin w, Ralph Rainger m
Featured in A BEDTIME STORY, film (rel. 04/33)
Maurice Chevalier, sung in film
Hotel Bossert Orch[4]/Elmer Feldkamp 05/33 Col 2769-D
Paul Whiteman/Jane Vance 06/33 Vic 24285

IN THE VALLEY OF THE MOON (1)
J Morris, pub. 1933, reached #1 in July 1933
Charles Tobias & Joe Burke w & m
George Hall/Glenn Cross Φ 05/33 Blu 5021
Joe Green/w.vocal 05/33 Col 2768-D
Ozzie Nelson/<vocal 06/33 Bruns 6551
Singin' Sam, radio, 06/33 Melotone 12681

ISN'T IT HEAVENLY? (37)
Harms, pub. 1933, reached #7 in July 1933
E Y Harbourg w, Joseph Meyer m
Eddy Duchin/Lew Sherwood 07/33 Vic 24325
Victor Young/Paul Small 06/33 Bruns 6589
Bert Lown/Ted Holt 06/33 Blu 5067

IT'S ONLY A PAPER MOON (50)
Harms, pub. 1933, reached #11 in November 1933
(Also reached #8 in November 1945)
Billy Rose & E Y Harbourg w, Harold Arlen m
Added to THE GREAT MAGOO, play (opened 12/32)
Featured in TAKE A CHANCE, film (rel. 11/33)
Buddy Rogers & June Knight, sung in film
Paul Whiteman/Peggy Healy 10/33 Vic 24400
Cliff Edwards 12/33 Voc 2587
Claire Carlton, sung in play

IT'S THE TALK OF THE TOWN (38)
Santly Bros, pub. 1933, reached #6 in November 1933
Marty Symes & Al J Neiberg w, Jerry Livingston m
Glen Gray[3]/Kenny Sargent 09/33 Bruns 6626
Eddy Duchin/Lew Sherwood 10/33 Vic 24377
Dick Robertson 09/33 Blu 5153

JUST AN ECHO IN THE VALLEY (4)
Robbins, pub. 1932, reached #1 in March 1933
Reg Connelly, Jimmy Campbell, Harry Woods w & m
Bing Crosby ΦΦ 02/33 Bruns 6454
Rudy Vallee/<vocal Φ 02/33 Col 2733-D
Paul Whiteman/Jack Fulton 02/33 Vic 24201

THE LAST ROUNDUP (2)
Shapiro, B, pub. 1933, reached #1 in October 1933
Billy Hill w & m
Featured in ZIEGFELD FOLLIES OF 1934, revue (opened 01/34)
George Olsen/Joe Morrison Φ stage and 08/33 Col 2791-D
Bing Crosby Φ 11/33 Bruns 6663
Guy Lombardo/Carmen Lombardo Φ 11/33 Bruns 6662
Don Bestor/Neil Buckley 10/33 Vic 24391
Gene Autry, radio, 11/33 Melotone 12832

LAZY BONES (6)
Southern M P C, pub. 1933, reached #1 in August 1933
Hoagy Carmichael & Johnny Mercer w & m
Ted Lewis/<vocal Φ 08/33 Col 2786-D
Mildred Bailey Φ 08/33 Bruns 6587
Hoagy Carmichael 11/33 Vic 24402
Glen Gray[3]/Pee Wee Hunt 08/33 Vic 24338
Don Redman/Harlan Lattimore 09/33 Bruns 6622

LEARN TO CROON (20)
Famous, pub. 1933, reached #4 in August 1933
Sam Coslow w, Arthur Johnston m
Featured in COLLEGE HUMOR, film (rel. 06/33)
Bing Crosby Φ sung in film, 07/33 Bruns 6594
Don Bestor/Maurice Cross 08/33 Vic 24344
Fran Frey/Ben Selvin Orch 08/33 Col 2788-D

LET'S CALL IT A DAY
Elar M C, pub. 1932, reached #17 in May 1933
Lew Brown w, Ray Henderson m
Featured in STRIKE ME PINK, show (opened 03/33)
Milton Watson & Carolyn Nolte, sung in show
Hotel Commodore Orch/w.vocal 05/33 Col 2767-D

LOVE IN THE MOONLIGHT (39)
Sherman Clay, pub. 1933, reached #10 in March 1933
Charley Kisco & J C Lewis w & m
Gus Arnheim/Loyce Whiteman 03/33 Vic 24235

LOVE IS A DREAM
L Feist, pub. 1933, reached #11 in March 1933
Charley Kisco & J C Lewis w & m
Gus Arnheim/Bud Struck 03/33 Vic 24234
Will Osborne[5]/<vocal 05/33 Perfect 15745,
05/33 Banner 32718, 05/33 Melotone 12647

LOVE IS THE SWEETEST THING (11)
Harms, pub. 1933, reached #3 in October 1933
Ray Noble w & m
Ray Noble's Mayfair Orch/Al Bowlly Φ 08/33 Vic 24333
Rudy Vallee/<vocal 09/33 Blu 5175
Richard Himber/Joey Nash 10/33 Voc 2526

LOVE SONGS OF THE NILE (23)
Robbins, pub. 1933, reached #4 in June 1933
Arthur Freed w, Nacio Herb Brown m
Featured in THE BARBARIAN, film (rel. 05/33)
Ramon Novarro, sung in film
Leo Reisman/Howard Phillips Φ 06/33 Vic 24312
Wayne King/w.vocal 07/33 Bruns 6580

LOVER (30)
Famous, pub. 1933, reached #4 in May 1933
(Also reached #12 in July 1952)
Lorenz Hart w, Richard Rodgers m
Featured in LOVE ME TONIGHT, film (rel. 08/32)
Jeanette MacDonald, sung in film
Paul Whiteman/Jack Fulton Φ 05/33 Vic 24283
Guy Lombardo Orch 05/33 Bruns 6535

LYING IN THE HAY (47)
Mills, pub. 1933, reached #10 in June 1933
Henry Roberts & Harry S Pepper w, Mireille Legrand m
Ray Noble/Al Bowlly 05/33 Vic 24297
Abe Lyman/Frank Sylvano 06/33 Bruns 6572

MAYBE (IT'S BECAUSE) I LOVE YOU TOO MUCH
Berlin, pub. 1933, reached #12 in June 1933
Irving Berlin w & m
Fred Astaire/Leo Reisman Orch 04/33 Vic 24262
Rudy Vallee/<vocal 04/33 Col 2756-D
Guy Lombardo/Carmen Lombardo 05/33 Bruns 6535

MINE
New World M C, pub. 1933, reached #19 in December 1933
Ira Gershwin w, George Gershwin m
Featured in LET 'EM EAT CAKE, show (opened 10/33)
Lois Moran & William Gaxton, sung in show
Leo Reisman/Phil Dewey 12/33 Vic 24429

MOON SONG (10)
Famous, pub. 1933, reached #2 in February 1933
Sam Coslow w, Arthur Johnston m
Featured in HELLO, EVERYBODY, film (rel. 01/33)
Jack Denny/Paul Small Φ 02/33 Vic 24217
Kate Smith, sung in film, 04/33 Bruns 6497
Wayne King/w.vocal trio Φ 03/33 Bruns 6474
Art Kassel/w.vocal 03/33 Col 2742-D

MY DARLING (18)
Harms, pub. 1932, reached #4 in February 1933
Edward Heyman w, Richard Myers m
Featured in EARL CARROLL'S VANITIES, 10TH ED, show (opened 09/32)
Don Bestor/Neil Buckley Φ 01/33 Vic 24142
John Hale & Josephine Houston, sung in show
Owen Fallon/Paul Small 02/33 Perfect 15719, 02/33 Melo 12581

MY MOONLIGHT MADONNA
Carl Fischer, pub. 1933, reached #10 in September 1933
Paul Francis Webster w, William Scotti m
Paul Whiteman/Jack Fulton 09/33 Vic 24364
Rudy Vallee/<vocal 08/33 Blu 5097
Victor Young Orch 09/33 Bruns 6630

NIGHT AND DAY (7)
Harms, pub. 1932, reached #1 in January 1933
Cole Porter w & m
Featured in GAY DIVORCE, show (opened 11/32)
Fred Astaire/Leo Reisman Orch ΦΦ 01/33 Vic 24193
Fred Astaire & Claire Luce, sung in show
Eddy Duchin Orch Φ 01/33 Bruns 6445
Bing Crosby, radio

AN ORCHID TO YOU
DeSylva, B & H, pub. 1933, reached #12 in July 1933
Mack Gordon & Harry Revel w & m
Eddy Duchin/Lew Sherwood 07/33 Vic 24326
Golden Bears/w.vocal 06/33 Crown 3486

PLAY, FIDDLE, PLAY (15)
E B Marks, pub. 1932, reached #4 in January 1933
Jack Lawrence w, Emery Deutsch & Arthur Altman m
Emery Deutsch, stage
Ted Lewis/<vocal 01/33 Col 2728-D
George Olsen/Dave Marshall 12/32 Vic 24165

PUDDIN' HEAD JONES
Remick, pub. 1933, reached #20 in January 1934
Alfred Bryan w, Lou Handman m
Rudy Vallee/<vocal 01/34 Vic 24475
Hal Kemp/Deane Janis 12/33 Bruns 6703

REMEMBER ME
MGM Corp, pub. 1933, reached #13 in May 1933
Gus Kahn w, Jack O'Brien m
Eddy Duchin/Lew Sherwood 05/33 Vic 24275
Victor Young/Smith Ballew 05/33 Bruns 6549

RISE 'N SHINE
Harms, pub. 1932, reached #16 in February 1933
Bud DeSylva w, Vincent Youmans m
Featured in TAKE A CHANCE, show (opened 11/32)
Featured in TAKE A CHANCE, film (rel. 11/33)
Ethel Merman, sung in show
Paul Whiteman/Ramona Davies 01/33 Vic 24197
Lillian Roth, sung in film

ROCKABYE MOON (24)
Robbins, pub. 1932, reached #6 in February 1933
Fred Steele, Morton Lang, Howard Johnson w & m
George Olsen/Ethel Shutta 12/32 Vic 24165
Victor Young/Frank Munn 12/32 Bruns 6398

SHADOW WALTZ (5)
Remick, pub. 1933, reached #1 in July 1933
Al Dubin w, Harry Warren m
Featured in GOLD DIGGERS OF 1933, film (rel. 05/33)
Bing Crosby Φ 07/33 Bruns 6599
Dick Powell & Ruby Keeler, sung in film
Dick Powell Φ 08/33 Perfect 12920
Rudy Vallee/<vocal Φ 07/33 Col 2773-D
Don Bestor/Neil Buckley 08/33 Vic 24346

SHANGHAI LIL
Witmark, pub. 1933, reached #17 in December 1933
Al Dubin w, Harry Warren m
Featured in FOOTLIGHT PARADE, film (rel. 09/33)
James Cagney & Ruby Keeler, sung in film
Rudy Vallee/<vocal 10/33 Blu 5172
Guy Lombardo/Carmen Lombardo 11/33 Bruns 6653

SHUFFLE OFF TO BUFFALO (9)
Witmark, pub. 1932, reached #1 in April 1933
Al Dubin w, Harry Warren m
Featured in FORTY-SECOND STREET, film (rel. 01/33)
Ginger Rogers & Ruby Keeler, sung in film
Hal Kemp/Skinnay Ennis Φ 03/33 Bruns 6471
Don Bestor/Maurice Cross Φ 04/33 Vic 24253
Boswell Sisters 05/33 Bruns 6545

SMOKE RINGS
Lawrence M P I, pub. 1932, reached #13 in August 1933
(Also reached #19 in July 1952)
Ned Washington w, H Eugene Clifford m
Casa Loma Orch[1], stage, radio, 07/33 Bruns 6289
Clyde McCoy Orch 08/33 Col 2794-D
Mills Brothers 06/33 Bruns 6525

THE SONG IS YOU
T B Harms, pub. 1932, reached #19 in February 1933[6]
Oscar Hammerstein 2nd w, Jerome Kern m
Featured in MUSIC IN THE AIR, show (opened 11/32)
Tullio Carminate & Natalie Hall, sung in show
Eddy Duchin/Frank Munn 01/33 Bruns 6425
Jack Denny/Paul Small 01/33 Vic 24183

SOPHISTICATED LADY (43)
Mills, pub. 1933, reached #12 in August 1933
Mitchell Parish & Irving Mills w, Duke Ellington m
Duke Ellington Orch Φ 07/33 Bruns 6600
Glen Gray & The Casa Loma Orch 08/33 Vic 24338
Don Redman Orch 07/33 Col 6560-D

SPEAK TO ME OF LOVE
Harms, pub. 1932, reached #13 in February 1933
Bruce Siever w, Jean Lenoir m
Don Bestor/Neil Buckley 01/33 Vic 24176
Eddy Duchin/Lew Sherwood 01/33 Bruns 6431

STORMY WEATHER (8)
Mills, pub. 1933, reached #1 in May 1933
Ted Koehler w, Harold Arlen m
Featured in COTTON CLUB PARADE, 22ND ED, revue
(opened 04/33)
All time pop standard
Ethel Waters Φ sung in revue, 06/33 Bruns 6564
Leo Reisman/Harold Arlen ΦΦ 04/33 Vic 24262
Guy Lombardo/Carmen Lombardo 05/33 Bruns 6550
Duke Ellington Orch 07/33 Bruns 6600
Ted Lewis/Shirley Jay 06/33 Col 2774-D

STREET OF DREAMS
L Feist, pub. 1932, reached #9 in February 1933
Sam Lewis w, Victor Young m
Guy Lombardo/Carmen Lombardo 02/33 Bruns 6455
Ben Selvin/w.vocal 02/33 Col 2734-D
Morton Downey, radio, 02/33 Perfect 12874

SWEETHEART, DARLIN' (13)
Robbins, pub. 1933, reached #3 in July 1933
Gus Kahn w, Herbert Stothart m
Featured in PEG O' MY HEART, film (rel. 05/33)
Marion Davies, sung in film
Don Bestor/Neil Buckley Φ 07/33 Vic 24317
Ben Selvin/w.vocal 07/33 Col 2778-D

TELL ME TONIGHT
Chappell, pub. 1932, reached #20 in July 1933
Frank Eyton w, Mischa Spoliansky m
Featured in BE MINE TONIGHT, film (rel. 03/33)
Bert Ambrose/Sam Browne 05/33 Vic 24279

THANKS (27)
Famous, pub. 1933, reached #3 in November 1933
Sam Coslow w, Arthur Johnston m
Featured in TOO MUCH HARMONY, film (rel. 09/33)
Bing Crosby Φ 10/33 Bruns 6643
Bing Crosby & Judith Allen, sung in film
Victor Young/Scrappy Lambert 11/33 Bruns 6652

THIS TIME IT'S LOVE (48)
L Feist, pub. 1933, reached #9 in October 1933
Sam Lewis w, J Fred Coots m
Guy Lombardo/Carmen Lombardo 12/33 Bruns 6641
Isham Jones/Joe Martin 10/33 Vic 24392

TROUBLE IN PARADISE
Ager, Y & B, pub. 1933, reached #16 in August 1933
Ned Wever w, Milt Ager & Jean Schwartz m
Eddy Duchin/Lew Sherwood 08/33 Vic 24377
Glen Gray[3]/Kenny Sargent 08/33 Bruns 6602

TRY A LITTLE TENDERNESS (28)
Robbins, pub. 1932, reached #5 in April 1933
Harry Woods, Jimmy Campbell, Reg Connelly w & m
Ted Lewis/<vocal Φ 03/33 Col 2748-D
Ruth Etting, stage, 03/33 Melotone 12625,
03/33 Perfect 12887

TWO TICKETS TO GEORGIA
Berlin, pub. 1933, reached #12 in May 1933
Joe Young, Charles Tobias, J Fred Coots w & m
Ben Pollack/Nappy Lamare 05/33 Vic 24284
Pickens Sisters, stage & radio
Victor Young/Dick Robertson 05/33 Bruns 6554

UNDER A BLANKET OF BLUE (31)
Santly Bros, pub. 1933, reached #6 in August 1933
Marty Symes & Al J Neiberg w, Jerry Livingston m
Casa Loma Orch[1]/Kenny Sargent 07/33 Bruns 6584
Don Bestor/Florence Case 08/33 Vic 24345

WE'RE IN THE MONEY (THE GOLD DIGGERS' SONG)
Remick, pub. 1933, reached #14 in July 1933
Al Dubin w, Harry Warren m
Featured in GOLD DIGGERS OF 1933, film (rel. 05/33)
Ginger Rogers, sung in film
Fred Astaire/Leo Reisman Orch 06/33 Vic 24315
Ted Lewis/<vocal 06/33 Col 2775-D

WHO'S AFRAID OF THE BIG BAD WOLF? (14)
Berlin, pub. 1933, reached #2 in October 1933
Ann Ronell w, Frank E Churchill m
Featured in THE THREE LITTLE PIGS, film (1933)
The Three Little Pigs, sung in film
Don Bestor/w.vocal group Φ 11/33 Vic 24410
Victor Young/Songsmiths 10/33 Bruns 6651
Ben Bernie/w.vocal group 11/33 Col 2824-D

WILLOW, WEEP FOR ME (34)
Berlin, pub. 1932, reached #5 in January 1933
(Also reached #16 in January 1965)
Ann Ronell w & m
Paul Whiteman/Irene Taylor Φ 01/33 Vic 24187
Ruth Etting, stage & radio
Ted FioRito/Muzzy Marcellino 12/32 Bruns 6422

YOU'RE AN OLD SMOOTHIE
Harms, pub. 1932, reached #15 in February 1933
Bud DeSylva, Richard A Whiting, Nacio Herb Brown w & m
Featured in TAKE A CHANCE, show (opened 11/32)
Ethel Merman, sung in show
Paul Whiteman/Ramona Davies 01/33 Vic 24202
Victor Young/w.vocal duo 03/33 Bruns 6484

YOU'RE GETTING TO BE A HABIT WITH ME (46)
Witmark, pub. 1932, reached #9 in April 1933
Al Dubin w, Harry Warren m
Featured in FORTY-SECOND STREET, film (rel. 01/33)
Bing Crosby/Guy Lombardo Orch Φ 03/33 Bruns 6472
Bebe Daniels, sung in film
Waring's Pennsylvanians/w.vocal 04/33 Vic 24214

YOU'RE GONNA LOSE YOUR GAL (41)
Ager, Y & B, pub. 1933, reached #7 in December 1933
Joe Young w, James V Monaco m
Jan Garber/Fritz Heilbron 12/33 Vic 24444
Glen Gray[3]/Pee Wee Hunt 01/34 Bruns 6708

YOU'VE GOT EVERYTHING
E B Marks, pub. 1933, reached #19 in November 1933[6]
Gus Kahn w, Walter Donaldson m
Anson Weeks/Bob Crosby 11/33 Bruns 6661
Jan Garber/Lee Bennett 12/33 Vic 24444

YOU'VE GOT ME CRYING AGAIN
I Jones Inc, pub. 1933, reached #14 in April 1933
Charles Newman w, Isham Jones m
Ruth Etting, stage, radio, 05/33 Perfect 12904, 05/33 Melotone 12668, 05/33 Banner 32595
Bing Crosby 04/33 Bruns 6515
Isham Jones/Joe Martin 04/33 Vic 24255

[1]The Casa Loma Orch was led by Glen Gray.
[2]George McQueen was a pseudonym for Freddy Martin
[3]Glen Gray's 1933 records were billed either as Glen Gray & The Casa Loma Orch or simply as The Casa Loma Orch.
[4]The Hotel Bossert Orch was actually the Freddy Martin Orch.
[5]Although Will Osborne's Orch is named on the label, it is believed this was the Freddy Martin Orch with Will Osborne on vocal.
[6]Reached #19 on monthly chart only.
[7]Sung in revue by Don Ross.

1934

ALL I DO IS DREAM OF YOU (5)
Robbins, pub. 1934, reached #1 in August 1934
Arthur Freed w, Nacio Herb Brown m
Featured in SADIE McKEE, film (rel. 05/34)
Jan Garber/Fritz Heilbron ΦΦ 07/34 Vic 24629
Gene Raymond, sung in film
Freddy Martin/Elmer Feldkamp 07/34 Bruns 6888
Henry Busse/w.vocal 08/34 Col 2932-D

BE STILL, MY HEART
Broadway M C, pub. 1934, reached #11 in December 1934
Allan Flynn & Jack Egan w & m
Freddy Martin/Elmer Feldkamp 12/34 Bruns 6998
Pickens Sisters 12/34 Vic 24751
Gertrude Niesen 12/34 Col 2972-D

THE BEAT OF MY HEART
Berlin, pub. 1934, reached #12 in June 1934
Johnny Burke w, Harold Spina m
Ben Pollack/Doris Robbins 04/34 Col 2905-D
Leo Reisman/George Beucler 05/34 Bruns 6869
Ramona Davies/Paul Whiteman Orch 05/34 Vic 24597

BLUE SKY AVENUE
Harms, pub. 1934, reached #20 in November 1934
Herb Magidson w, Con Conrad m
Jan Garber/Lee Bennett 11/34 Vic 24730
Gene Austin 11/34 Vic 24725
Ted Weems/Red Ingle 11/34 Col 2957-D

BOULEVARD OF BROKEN DREAMS (41)
J H Remick, pub. 1933, reached #7 in April 1934
Al Dubin w, Harry Warren m
Featured in MOULIN ROUGE, film (rel. 01/34)
Jan Garber/Lee Bennett 02/34 Vic 24498
Constance Bennett, sung in film
Ted Weems/Elmo Tanner 02/34 Blu 5288

BUGLE CALL RAG
Mills, pub. 1923, reached #16 in November 1934
(Also reached #17 in September 1932)
Jack Pettis, Billy Meyers, Elmer Schoebel m
Benny Goodman Orch Φ 10/34 Col 2958-D

CARIOCA (9)
T B Harms, pub. 1933, reached #4 in February 1934
(Also reached #15 in May 1952)
Gus Kahn & Edward Eliscu w, Vincent Youmans m
Featured in FLYING DOWN TO RIO, film (rel. 12/33)
Fred Astaire & Ginger Rogers, performed in film
Enric Madriguera Orch Φ 03/34 Col 2885-D
Harry Sosnik Orch Φ 02/34 Vic 24488
Dolores Del Rio & Etta Moten, sung in film
RKO Studio Orch, played in film, 04/34 Vic 24515

THE CHAMPAGNE WALTZ
Famous, pub. 1934, reached #10 in June 1934
Con Conrad, Ben Oakland, Milton Drake w & m
Glen Gray[2]/Kenny Sargent 05/34 Bruns 6858
Smith Ballew/<vocal 05/34 Melotone 12968, 05/34 Perfect 15907

COCKTAILS FOR TWO (7)
Famous, pub. 1934, reached #3 in July 1934
(Also reached #9 in February 1945 in comic version)
Arthur Johnston & Sam Coslow w & m
Featured in MURDER AT THE VANITIES, film (rel. 05/34)
Duke Ellington Orch ΦΦ 06/34 Vic 24617
Carl Brisson, sung in film, 07/34 Bruns 6887
Johnny Green/Howard Phillips 05/34 Bruns 6797

THE CONTINENTAL (10)
Harms, pub. 1934, reached #1 in November 1934
Herb Magidson w, Con Conrad m
Featured in THE GAY DIVORCEE, film (rel. 09/34)
Ginger Rogers, sung in film
Leo Reisman Orch Φ 10/34 Bruns 6973
Jolly Coburn/w.vocal duo Φ 11/34 Vic 24735
Lud Gluskin/Joe Host 11/34 Col 2952-D

DAMES
J H Remick, pub. 1934, reached #14 in August 1934
Al Dubin w, Harry Warren m
Featured in DAMES, film (rel. 08/34)
Dick Powell, sung in film
Eddy Duchin/Lew Sherwood 08/34 Vic 24666
Joe Haymes/Cliff Weston 08/34 Melotone 13067, 08/34 Perfect 15957, 08/34 Banner 33099

DON'T LET IT BOTHER YOU
DeSylva, B & H, pub. 1934, reached #17 in November 1934
Mack Gordon w, Harry Revel m
Featured in THE GAY DIVORCEE, film (rel. 09/34)
Fred Astaire & Ginger Rogers, performed in film
Fats Waller 11/34 Vic 24714
Leo Reisman/Sally Singer 10/34 Bruns 6963

THE DRUNKARD SONG (50)
Shapiro, B, pub. 1934, reached #8 in November 1934
Based on THERE IS A TAVERN IN THE TOWN, pub. 1883
William H Hills & Rudy Vallee w & m
Rudy Vallee/<vocal Φ 11/34 Vic 24721, 11/34 Vic 24739[3]
Fred Hillebrand 11/34 Dec 216

DUST ON THE MOON
E B Marks, pub. 1934, reached #11 in August 1934
Stanley Adams w, Ernesto Lecuona m
Eddy Duchin/Lew Sherwood 08/34 Vic 24664
Castilian Troubadours[1] 10/34 Bruns 6961, 10/34 Melotone 13110

EASTER PARADE (38)
Berlin ΦΦΦ, pub. 1933, reached #5 in January 1934
(Also reached #16 in April 1946)
Irving Berlin w & m
Featured in AS THOUSANDS CHEER, film (rel. 09/33)
All-time pop standard
Clifton Webb & Marilyn Miller, sung in film
Leo Reisman/Clifton Webb Φ 11/33 Vic 24418
Freddy Martin/w.vocal trio 01/34 Bruns 6678

EASY COME, EASY GO (45)
Harms, pub. 1934, reached #7 in June 1934
Edward Heyman w, John Green m
Featured in BACHELOR OF ARTS, film (rel. 12/34)
Eddy Duchin/DeMarco Sisters 06/34 Vic 24611
Johnny Green/Lee Wiley 05/34 Bruns 6855

EMALINE
Mills, pub. 1934, reached #20 in July 1934
Mitchell Parish w, Frank Perkins m
Benny Goodman/Mildred Bailey, stage, 04/34 Col 2907-D
Frankie Trumbauer/Jack Teagarten 04/34 Bruns 6788

EVERYTHING I HAVE IS YOURS (37)
Robbins, pub. 1933, reached #4 in February 1934
Harold Adamson w, Burton Lane m
Featured in DANCING LADY, film (rel. 11/33)
Rudy Vallee/<vocal Φ 01/34 Vic 24458
Art Jarrett & Joan Crawford, sung in film
George Olsen/w.vocal 12/33 Col 2842-D

FLYING DOWN TO RIO
T B Harms, pub. 1933, reached #14 in March 1934
Gus Kahn & Edward Eliscu w, Vincent Youmans m
Featured in FLYING DOWN TO RIO, film (rel. 12/33)
Fred Astaire, sung in film, 05/34 Col 2912-D
Rudy Vallee/<vocal 02/34 Vic 24459

FOR ALL WE KNOW (27)
L Feist, pub. 1934, reached #3 in September 1934
Sam Lewis w, J Fred Coots m
Hal Kemp/Skinnay Ennis Φ 08/34 Bruns 6947
Isham Jones/Joe Martin 09/34 Vic 24681, 10/34 Dec 170
Morton Downey, stage and radio

FRECKLE FACE, YOU'RE BEAUTIFUL
Witmark, pub. 1934, reached #19 in July 1934
Carmen Lombardo & Cliff Friend w & m
Ben Pollack/Joe Harris 07/34 Col 2931-D
Ted FioRito/Muzzy Marcellino 08/34 Bruns 6919

GOIN' TO HEAVEN ON A MULE (44)
Witmark, pub. 1934, reached #9 in March 1934
Al Dubin w, Harry Warren m
Featured in WONDER BAR, film (rel. 02/34)
Al Jolson, sung in film
Rudy Vallee/<vocal 03/34 Vic 24554

GOODNIGHT, LOVELY LITTLE LADY (30)
DeSylva, B & H, pub. 1934, reached #3 in May 1934
Mack Gordon & Harry Revel w & m
Featured in WE'RE NOT DRESSING, film (rel. 04/34)
Bing Crosby Φ sung in film, 05/34 Bruns 6854
Hal Kemp/Bob Allen 04/34 Bruns 6790

HA-CHA-CHA
Movietone, pub. 1934, reached #20 in November 1934
Gus Kahn w, Werner R Heyman m
Featured in CARAVAN, film 09/34
Rudy Vallee/<vocal 11/34 Vic 24722
Joe Reichman/Chick Bullock 11/34 Perfect 16007, 11/34 Melotone 13188, 11/34 Banner 33221

HANDS ACROSS THE TABLE (48)
Mills, pub. 1934, reached #8 in January 1935
Mitchell Parish w, Jean DeLettre m
Featured in CONTINENTAL VARIETIES, revue (opened 10/34)
Lucienne Boyer, sung in revue, 12/34 Col 2971-D
Eddy Duchin/Lew Sherwood 12/34 Vic 24805
Hal Kemp/Skinnay Ennis 12/34 Bruns 7315

I AIN'T LAZY, I'M JUST DREAMIN'
I Jones M C, pub. 1934, reached #11 in June 1934
Dave Franklin w & m
Isham Jones/Eddie Stone 05/34 Vic 24606
Benny Goodman/Jack Teagarten 06/34 Col 2923-D
Freddy Martin/Terry Shand 06/34 Bruns 6876

I NEVER HAD A CHANCE (12)
Berlin, pub. 1934, reached #2 in August 1934
Irving Berlin w & m
Eddy Duchin/Lew Sherwood Φ 07/34 Vic 24664
Glen Gray[2]/Kenny Sargent Φ 08/34 Bruns 6927

I ONLY HAVE EYES FOR YOU (19)
J H Remick, pub. 1934, reached #2 in September 1934
(Also reached #13 in July 1959)
(Also reached #18 in November 1975)
Al Dubin w, Harry Warren m
Featured in DAMES, film (rel. 08/34)
Dick Powell & Ruby Keeler, sung in film
Eddy Duchin/Lew Sherwood Φ 08/34 Vic 24665
Ben Selvin/w.vocal 08/34 Col 2936-D
Jane Froman, radio, 10/34 Dec 181

I SAW STARS (20)
Robbins, pub. 1934, reached #3 in October 1934
Maurice Sigler, Al Goodhart, Al Hoffman w & m
Guy Lombardo/Carmen Lombardo Φ 10/34 Dec 105
Freddy Martin/Elmer Feldkamp Φ 09/34 Bruns 6948
Paul Whiteman/Peggy Healy Φ 10/34 Vic 24705

I WISH I WERE TWINS
Donaldson, D & G, pub. 1934, reached #14 in July 1934
Frank Loesser & Eddie DeLange w, Joseph Meyer m
Fats Waller, stage, 07/34 Vic 24641
Henry "Red" Allen 07/34 Perf 15948
Emil Coleman/Stanley Worth 08/34 Col 2933-D

I'LL FOLLOW MY SECRET HEART
T B Harms, pub. 1934, reached #18 in December 1934
Noel Coward w & m
Featured in CONVERSATION PIECE, show (opened 10/34)
Noel Coward, sung in show
Ray Noble/Al Bowlly 12/34 Vic 24749
Leo Reisman/Sally Singer 12/34 Bruns 7304

I'LL STRING ALONG WITH YOU (3)
Witmark, pub. 1934, reached #1 in June 1934
Al Dubin w, Harry Warren m
Featured in TWENTY MILLION SWEETHEARTS, film (rel. 04/34)
Dick Powell, sung in film, 05/34 Bruns 6793
Ted FioRito/Muzzy Marcellino Φ 05/34 Bruns 6859
Tom Coakley/Carl Ravazza Φ 05/34 Vic 24600

I'VE HAD MY MOMENTS
Robbins, pub. 1934, reached #17 in July 1934
Gus Kahn w, Walter Donaldson m
Featured in HOLLYWOOD PARTY, film (rel. 05/34)
Jimmy Durante, sung in film
Eddy Duchin/Lew Sherwood 06/34 Vic 24613

ILL WIND
Mills, pub. 1934, reached #15 in May 1934
Ted Koehler w, Harold Arlen m
Featured in COTTON CLUB PARADE, 24TH ED, revue (opened 03/34)
Eddy Duchin/Harold Arlen 04/34 Vic 24579
Adelaide Hall, sung in revue
Leo Reisman/Thelma Nevins 05/34 Bruns 6789

IT'S ALL FORGOTTEN NOW
Campbell, Connelly, pub. 1934, reached #13 in October 1934
Ray Noble w & m
Ray Noble/Al Bowlly 10/34 Vic 24724
Hal Kemp/Bob Allen 10/34 Bruns 6974

KEEP YOUNG AND BEAUTIFUL
Witmark, pub. 1933, reached #13 in February 1934
Al Dubin w, Harry Warren m
Featured in ROMAN SCANDALS, film (rel. 12/33)
Eddie Cantor, sung in film
Abe Lyman/w.vocal trio 12/33 Bruns 6698
Meyer Davis/Arlene Jackson 01/34 Col 2854-D

LET'S FALL IN LOVE (35)
Berlin, pub. 1933, reached #6 in March 1934
Ted Koehler w, Harold Arlen m
Featured in LET'S FALL IN LOVE, film (rel. 01/34)
Eddy Duchin/Lew Sherwood Φ 02/34 Vic 24510
Ann Sothern, sung in film
Harold Arlen/Ray Sinatra Orch 01/34 Vic 24467
Art Jarrett, sung in film

A LITTLE DUTCH MILL (11)
Santly Bros, pub. 1934, reached #1 in May 1934
Ralph Freed w, Harry Barris m
Bing Crosby ΦΦ 04/34 Bruns 6794
Don Bestor/Neil Buckley 05/34 Vic 24587
Guy Lombardo/w.vocal trio 04/34 Bruns 6781, 04/34 Perfect 15978, 04/34 Melotone 13117
Arthur Tracy, radio, 04/34 Voc 2671

LITTLE MAN, YOU'VE HAD A BUSY DAY (16)
T B Harms, pub. 1934, reached #2 in July 1934
Maurice Sigler & Al Hoffman w, Mabel Wayne m
Isham Jones/Eddie Stone Φ 06/34 Vic 24633
Emil Coleman/w.vocal Φ 07/34 Col 2930-D
Pickens Sisters 06/34 Vic 24630

LOST IN A FOG (24)
Robbins, pub. 1934, reached #4 in November 1934
Dorothy Fields w, Jimmy McHugh m
Rudy Vallee/<vocal Φ 10/34 Vic 24721
Dorsey Brothers Orch/Bob Crosby 11/34 Dec 195
Jane Froman 11/34 Dec 180

LOVE IN BLOOM (2)
Famous, pub. 1934, reached #1 in September 1934
Leo Robin & Ralph Rainger w & m
Featured in SHE LOVES ME NOT, film (rel. 07/34)
Bing Crosby ΦΦ 08/34 Bruns 6936
Bing Crosby & Kitty Carlisle, sung in film
Paul Whiteman/Jack Fulton 08/34 Vic 24672
Hal Kemp/Skinnay Ennis 09/34 Bruns 6943
Guy Lombardo/Carmen Lombardo 10/34 Dec 102

LOVE LOCKED OUT
Harms, pub. 1933, reached #15 in February 1934
Max Kester w, Ray Noble m
Ray Noble/Al Bowlly 02/34 Vic 24485
Bert Ambrose/Sam Browne 02/34 Bruns 6755

LOVE THY NEIGHBOR (17)
DeSylva, B & H, pub. 1934, reached #1 in June 1934
Mack Gordon w, Harry Revel m
Featured in WE'RE NOT DRESSING, film (rel. 04/34)
Bing Crosby ΦΦ sung in film, 05/34 Bruns 6852
Raymond Paige/Three Rhythm Kings 06/34 Vic 24604
Richard Himber/Joey Nash 05/34 Blu 5419

THE MAN ON THE FLYING TRAPEZE (33)
Robbins, pub. 1933, reached #8 in July 1934
(Original version pub. 1868)
George Leybourne & Walter O'Keefe w & m
Walter O'Keefe Φ stage, 06/34 Vic 24172
Eddie Cantor 05/34 Melotone 13001
Bing Crosby, radio

MAY I?
DeSylva, B & H, pub. 1934, reached #10 in May 1934
Mack Gordon w, Harry Revel m
Featured in WE'RE NOT DRESSING, film (rel. 04/34)
Bing Crosby Φ sung in film, 05/34 Bruns 6853
Eddy Duchin/Lew Sherwood 04/34 Vic 24591
Richard Himber/Joey Nash 05/34 Blu 5419

MOONGLOW (18)
Mills, pub. 1934, reached #6 in August 1934
(Also reached #1 in June 1956 as part of medley)
Will Hudson, Eddie DeLange, Irving Mills w & m
Benny Goodman Orch ΦΦ 07/34 Col 2927-D
Cab Calloway Orch 09/34 Vic 24690
Glen Gray[2]/Kenny Sargent 09/34 Bruns 6937
Duke Ellington Orch 10/34 Bruns 6987

MR. AND MRS. IS THE NAME
Witmark, pub. 1934, reached #15 in December 1934
Mort Dixon w, Allie Wrubel m
Featured in FLIRTATION WALK, film (rel. 10/34)
Dick Powell & Ruby Keeler, sung in film
Dick Powell 12/34 Bruns 7328
Victor Young/Paul Small 12/34 Dec 279

MUSIC MAKES ME
T B Harms, pub. 1933, reached #17 in March 1934
Gus Kahn & Edward Eliscu w, Vincent Youmans m
Featured in FLYING DOWN TO RIO, film (rel. 12/33)
Ginger Rogers, sung in film
Emil Coleman/w.vocal 03/34 Col 2893-D
Fred Astaire 05/34 Col 2912-D

MY HAT'S ON THE SIDE OF MY HEAD
Shapiro, B, pub. 1933, reached #18 in August 1934
Harry Woods & Claude Hulbert w & m
Featured in JACK AHOY, film (rel. 02/35)
Ray Noble/Al Bowlly 07/34 Vic 24624
Vincent Lopez/Frances Hunt 07/34 Blu 5537
Jack Hulbert, sung in film

MY LITTLE GRASS SHACK IN KEALEKUA, HAWAII (4)
Sherman Clay, pub. 1933, reached #1 in April 1934
Bill Cogswell, Tommy Harrison, Johnny Noble w & m
Ted FioRito/w.vocal Φ 02/34 Bruns 6736
Ben Pollack/w.vocal trio 03/34 Col 2886-D
Paul Whiteman/Vocordians 03/34 Vic 24514
Roy Smeck 04/34 Melotone 12948

NASTY MAN
Sam Fox, pub. 1934, reached #12 in May 1934
Jack Yellen & Irving Caesar w, Ray Henderson m
Featured in GEORGE WHITE'S SCANDALS OF 1935, film (rel. 03/35)
Rudy Vallee/w.vocal trio 05/34 Vic 24581
Alice Faye, sung in film
Frances Langford 05/34 Perf 12994, 05/34 Melo 12986

A NEEDLE IN A HAYSTACK
Harms, pub. 1934, reached #13 in November 1934
Herb Magidson w, Con Conrad m
Featured in THE GAY DIVORCEE, film (rel. 09/34)
Fred Astaire, sung in film
Leo Reisman/Lew Conrad 10/34 Bruns 6973

NEIGHBORS
Keit-Engel, pub. 1934, reached #15 in April 1934
Charles O'Flynn & James Cavanaugh w, Frank Weldon m
Isham Jones/Eddie Stone 04/34 Vic 24582
Freddy Martin Orch 04/34 Bruns 6777

A NEW MOON IS OVER MY SHOULDER
Robbins, pub. 1934, reached #19 in September 1934
Arthur Freed w, Nacio Herb Brown m
Featured in STUDENT TOUR, film (rel. 10/34)
Phil Regan, sung in film, 09/34 Col 2948-D
Isham Jones/Joe Martin 09/34 Vic 24682
Johnny Green/Bernice Park 09/34 Col 2940-D

THE OBJECT OF MY AFFECTION (14)
Berlin, pub. 1934, reached #1 in January 1935
Pinky Tomlin, Coy Poe, Jimmy Grier w & m
Jimmy Grier/Pinky Tomlin ΦΦ 12/34 Bruns 7308
Boswell Sisters Φ 01/35 Bruns 7348
Glen Gray[2]/Pee Wee Hunt 01/35 Dec 298
Jan Garber/Lee Bennett 01/35 Vic 24809

THE OLD SPINNING WHEEL (1)
Shapiro, B ΦΦΦ, pub. 1933, reached #1 in January 1934
Billy Hill w & m
Ray Noble/Al Bowlly ΦΦ 11/33 Vic 24357
Victor Young/Scrappy Lambert 02/34 Bruns 6725
Emil Velasco 02/34 Col 2864-D

ONE MINUTE TO ONE
L Feist, pub. 1933, reached #16 in January 1934
Sam Lewis w, J Fred Coots m
Harry Sosnik/Bob Hannon 01/34 Vic 24481
Harry Richman, radio
Hal Kemp/Diana Janis 01/34 Bruns 6707

ONE NIGHT OF LOVE (47)
Berlin, pub. 1934, reached #7 in November 1934
Gus Kahn w, Victor Schertzinger m
Featured in ONE NIGHT OF LOVE, film (rel. 07/34)
Grace Moore Φ sung in film, 11/34 Bruns 6994
Freddy Martin/Elmer Feldkamp 10/34 Bruns 6970
Victor Young/Frank Luther 11/34 Dec 238

ORCHIDS IN THE MOONLIGHT (34)
T B Harms, pub. 1933, reached #6 in February 1934
Gus Kahn & Edward Eliscu w, Vincent Youmans m
Featured in FLYING DOWN TO RIO, film (rel. 12/33)
Rudy Vallee/<vocal Φ 01/34 Vic 24459
Fred Astaire & Dolores Del Rio, danced in film
Enric Madriguera/w.vocal 03/34 Col 2885-D
Raul Roulien, sung in film

OUT IN THE COLD AGAIN (46)
Santly Bros, pub. 1934, reached #8 in November 1934
(Also reached #20 in December 1951)
Ted Koehler w, Rube Bloom m
Glen Gray[2]/Kenny Sargent 10/34 Bruns 6964
Ruth Etting, radio, 11/34 Col 2955-D
Rudy Vallee/<vocal 10/34 Vic 24722

OVER SOMEBODY ELSE'S SHOULDER
Donaldson, D & G, pub. 1934, reached #17 in April 1934
Al Lewis & Al Sherman w & m
Isham Jones/Joe Martin 04/34 Vic 24582
Eddie Cantor, radio, 04/34 Melotone 13001
Freddy Martin/Elmer Feldkamp 03/34 Bruns 6777

PARDON MY SOUTHERN ACCENT (39)
Berlin, pub. 1934, reached #6 in October 1934
Johnny Mercer w, Matty Malneck m
Glen Gray[2]/Pee Wee Hunt 09/34 Bruns 6945
Paul Whiteman/Johnny Mercer-Peggy Healy 10/34 Vic 24704
Irving Aaronson/Ernie Mathias 10/34 Col 2946-D

PLAY TO ME, GYPSY
Berlin, pub. 1934, reached #18 in May 1934
Jimmy Kennedy & Beda Fritz Lohner w, Karel Vacek m
Arthur Tracy, radio, 04/34 Voc 2659
Smith Ballew/w.vocal group 05/34 Melotone 12968
Jack Jackson/Sam Costa 05/34 Vic 24594

POP GOES YOUR HEART
Witmark, pub. 1934, reached #12 in December 1934
Mort Dixon w, Allie Wrubel m
Featured in HAPPINESS AHEAD, film (rel. 09/34)
Dick Powell, sung in film, 11/34 Bruns 6979
Ted Lewis/<vocal 11/34 Dec 239

THE PRIZE WALTZ
Harms, pub. 1934, reached #16 in August 1934
Maurice Sigler w, Al Goodhart & Al Hoffman m
Ben Selvin/w.vocal 08/34 Col 2935-D
Don Bestor/Neil Buckley 09/34 Vic 24693

P. S. I LOVE YOU
Kornheiser, pub. 1934, reached #20 in December 1934
(Also reached #6 in August 1953)
Johnny Mercer w, Gordon Jenkins m
Rudy Vallee/<vocal 11/34 Vic 24723
Glen Gray[2]/Kenny Sargent 11/34 Dec 200

RAIN (31)
Shapiro, B, pub. 1934, reached #5 in December 1934
Billy Hill w, Peter DeRose m
Jan Garber/Lee Bennett 11/34 Vic 24730
Don Bestor/Neil Buckley 11/34 Bruns 6981
Larry Funk/Vaughn Monroe 11/34 Melotone 13186, 11/34 Banner 33219

RIDIN' AROUND IN THE RAIN
Santly Bros, pub. 1934, reached #8 in June 1934
Gene Austin & Carmen Lombardo w & m
Bing Crosby 05/34 Bruns 6852
Gene Austin, stage, 08/34 Vic 24663
Glen Gray[2]/Pee Wee Hunt 06/34 Bruns 6870

RIPTIDE (49)
Robbins, pub. 1934, reached #6 in June 1934
Gus Kahn w, Walter Donaldson m
Eddy Duchin/w.vocal duo 05/34 Vic 24613
Guy Lombardo/Carmen Lombardo 06/34 Bruns 6866, 06/34 Perfect 15978, 06/34 Melotone 13117

SANTA CLAUS IS COMIN' TO TOWN (42)
L Feist, pub. 1934, reached #3 in December 1934
(Also reached Top 20 in December 1935, 1936, 1947, 1948)
Haven Gillespie w, J Fred Coots m
All-time Christmas standard
Eddie Cantor, stage and radio
George Hall/Sonny Schuyler 12/34 Blu 5711
Harry Reser/Tom Stacks 12/34 Dec 264

SHE REMINDS ME OF YOU
DeSylva, B & H, pub. 1934, reached #11 in May 1934
Mack Gordon w, Harry Revel m
Featured in WE'RE NOT DRESSING, film (rel. 04/34)
Bing Crosby, sung in film, 05/34 Bruns 6853
Eddy Duchin/Lew Sherwood 04/34 Vic 24591
Earl Burtnett/Stanley Hickman 07/34 Col 2922-D

SLEEPY HEAD (28)
Robbins, pub. 1934, reached #6 in August 1934
Gus Kahn w, Walter Donaldson m
Featured in OPERATOR 13, film (rel. 06/34)
Mills Brothers Φ sung in film, 08/34 Bruns 6913, 10/34 Melotone 13177
Ben Pollack/Joe Harris 07/34 Col 2929-D
Vincent Lopez/Frances Hart 07/34 Blu 5524

SMOKE GETS IN YOUR EYES (6)
T B Harms, pub. 1933, reached #2 in February 1934
(Also reached #1 in January 1959)
Otto Harbach w, Jerome Kern m
Featured in ROBERTA, show (opened 11/33)
All-time pop standard
Paul Whiteman/Bob Lawrence Φ 01/34 Vic 24455
Leo Reisman/Tamara Φ 01/34 Bruns 6715
Tamara, sung in show
Emil Coleman/Jerry Cooper 01/34 Col 2846-D
Ruth Etting 03/34 Bruns 6769

SPELLBOUND
Santly Bros, pub. 1934, reached #15 in August 1934
Stanley Adams w, Jesse Greer m
Glen Gray[2]/Kenny Sargent 07/34 Bruns 6910
Vincent Lopez/Jack Campbell 07/34 Blu 5523

STARS FELL ON ALABAMA (8)
Mills, pub. 1934, reached #2 in November 1934
Mitchell Parish w, Frank Perkins m
Guy Lombardo/Carmen Lombardo ΦΦ 10/34 Dec 104
Jack Teagarten, stage, 11/34 Bruns 6993
Richard Himber/Joey Nash Φ 11/34 Vic 24745
Freddy Martin/Buddy Clark 10/34 Bruns 6976

STAY AS SWEET AS YOU ARE (15)
DeSylva, B & H, pub. 1934, reached #1 in December 1934
Mack Gordon w, Harry Revel m
Featured in COLLEGE RHYTHM, film (rel. 10/34)
Lanny Ross Φ sung in film, 12/34 Bruns 7318
Jimmie Grier/w.vocal Φ 11/34 Bruns 7307
Guy Lombardo/Carmen Lombardo Φ 12/34 Dec 274
Jolly Coburn/Roy Strom 11/34 Vic 24743
Little Jack Little/<vocal 12/34 Col 2969-D

SWEETIE PIE
L Feist, pub. 1934, reached #14 in November 1934
John J Loeb w & m
Fats Waller 11/34 Vic 24737
Anson Weeks/Kay St.Germaine 10/34 Bruns 6965

TALKIN' TO MYSELF
Harms, pub. 1934, reached #12 in October 1934
Herb Magidson w, Con Conrad m
Featured in GIFT OF GAB, film (rel. 09/34)
Raymond Paige/Rhythm Kings 09/34 Vic 24703
Ted Weems/Red Ingle 10/34 Col 2957-D
Leo Reisman/Sally Singer 10/34 Bruns 6980

TEMPTATION (32)
Robbins, pub. 1933, reached #8 in February 1934
(Also reached #7 in July 1947 in comic version)
Arthur Freed w, Nacio Herb Brown m
Featured in GOING HOLLYWOOD, film (rel. 12/33)
Bing Crosby Φ sung in film, 01/34 Bruns 6695
Ted FioRito/w.vocal 12/33 Bruns 6705
Jan Garber/Lee Bennett 02/34 Vic 24498

THANK YOU FOR A LOVELY EVENING
Robbins, pub. 1934, reached #17 in August 1934
Dorothy Fields w, Jimmy McHugh m
Featured in GIRL FROM MISSOURI, film (rel. 07/34)
Also featured in HAVE A HEART, film (rel. 10/34)
Leah Ray & Phil Harris, stage
Don Bestor/Neil Buckley 07/34 Vic 24667
Ted FioRito/w.vocal 08/34 Bruns 6924

THEN I'LL BE TIRED OF YOU
Harms, pub. 1934, reached #15 in October 1934
E Y Harbourg w, Arthur Schwartz m
Fats Waller 10/34 Vic 24708
Freddy Martin/Elmer Feldkamp 09/34 Bruns 6948
Isham Jones/Joe Martin 10/34 Dec 171

THERE GOES MY HEART
L Feist, pub. 1934, reached #19 in March 1934
Benny Davis w, Abner Silver m
Isham Jones/Joe Martin 03/34 Vic 24519
Enric Madriguera/Tony Sacco 03/34 Col 2888-D
Freddy Martin/Elmer Feldkamp 03/34 Bruns 6766

THIS LITTLE PIGGIE WENT TO MARKET (23)
DeSylva, B & H, pub. 1933, reached #2 in March 1934
Sam Coslow w, Harold Lewis m
Featured in EIGHT GIRLS IN A BOAT, film (rel. 01/34)
Eddie Duchin/Lew Sherwood Ⴔ 02/34 Vic 24512
Victor Young/Peg LaCentra 03/34 Bruns 6747
Ruth Etting 03/34 Bruns 6769

A THOUSAND GOODNIGHTS (26)
Robbins, pub. 1934, reached #2 in May 1934
Walter Donaldson w & m
Don Bestor/Neil Buckley Ⴔ 04/34 Vic 24587
Richard Himber/Joey Nash 05/34 Blu 5418
Adrian Rollini/Joey Nash 05/34 Voc 2672

THROW ANOTHER LOG ON THE FIRE (36)
L Feist, pub. 1933, reached #6 in March 1934
Jack Scholl, Charles Tobias, Murray Mencher w & m
Don Bestor/The Chanters 03/34 Vic 24523
George Olsen/w.vocal 01/34 Col 2857-D

TRUE
Santly Bros, pub. 1934, reached #11 in April 1934
Leonard Whitcup & Walter Samuels w & m
Enric Madriguera/w.vocal 03/34 Col 2896-D
Paul Whiteman/Jack Fulton 04/34 Vic 24566
Guy Lombardo/Carmen Lombardo 04/34 Bruns 6784

TUMBLING TUMBLEWEEDS
Williamson M C, pub. 1934, reached #18 in September 1934
Bob Nolan w & m
Featured in TUMBLING TUMBLEWEEDS, film (rel. 09/35)
Steady seller, 1934-35
Sons of the Pioneers, stage, 12/34 Dec 5047
Gene Autry, sung in film, 01/35 Conqueror 8465, 02/35 Melo 13315

TWO CIGARETTES IN THE DARK (13)
DeSylva, B & H, pub. 1934, reached #2 in October 1934
Paul Francis Webster w, Lew Pollack m
Featured in KILL THAT STORY, play (opened 08/34)
Gloria Grafton, sung in play, 10/34 Vic 24717
Bing Crosby Ⴔ radio, 11/34 Dec 245
Jerry Johnson/Dick Robertson Ⴔ 10/34 Vic 24710
Johnny Green/George Beucler 09/34 Col 2943-D
Frank Parker 10/34 Col 2944-D

THE VERY THOUGHT OF YOU (25)
Witmark, pub. 1934, reached #9 in October 1934
(Also reached #18 in December 1944)
Ray Noble w & m
Ray Noble/Al Bowlly Ⴔ 08/34 Vic 24657
Victor Young/George Beucler 08/34 Bruns 6931
Bing Crosby 11/34 Dec 179

WAGON WHEELS (22)
Shapiro, B, pub. 1933, reached #3 in April 1934
Billy Hill w, Peter DeRose m
Featured in THE NEW ZIEGFELD FOLLIES, show (opened 01/34)
Paul Whiteman/Bob Lawrence Ⴔ 03/34 Vic 24517
Everett Marshall, sung in show
George Olsen/w.vocal duo 03/34 Col 2881-D
Paul Robeson 07/34 Vic 24635

WE'LL MAKE HAY WHILE THE SUN SHINES (40)
Robbins, pub. 1933, reached #8 in February 1934
Arthur Freed w, Nacio Herb Brown m
Featured in GOING HOLLYWOOD, film (rel. 12/33)
Bing Crosby & Marion Davies, sung in film
Bing Crosby 01/34 Bruns 6695
Ted FioRito/w.vocal 11/33 Bruns 6706
Enric Madriguera/w.vocal 01/34 Col 2849-D

WHEN TOMORROW COMES
Witmark, pub. 1933, reached #15 in March 1934
Irving Kahal w, Sammy Fain m
Featured in MANDALAY, film (rel. 02/34)
Kay Francis, sung in film
Don Bestor/Maurice Cross 03/34 Vic 24524
Freddy Martin Orch 03/34 Bruns 6760

WHY DO I DREAM THOSE DREAMS? (43)
Witmark, pub. 1934, reached #6 in May 1934
Al Dubin w, Harry Warren m
Featured in WONDER BAR, film (rel. 02/34)
Dick Powell, sung in film, 04/34 Bruns 6792
Eddy Duchin/Lew Sherwood 04/34 Vic 24576
Freddy Martin/Terry Shand 04/34 Bruns 6770

WITH MY EYES WIDE OPEN, I'M DREAMING (21)
DeSylva, B & H, pub. 1934, reached #3 in August 1934
(Also reached #15 in February 1950)
Mack Gordon w, Harry Revel m
Featured in SHOOT THE WORKS, film (rel. 07/34)
Leo Reisman/George Beucler Φ 07/34 Bruns 6896
Isham Jones/Joe Martin Φ 07/34 Vic 24643
Jack Oakie & Dorothy Dell, sung in film
Ruth Etting 08/34 Bruns 6914

WITHOUT THAT CERTAIN THING
Harms, pub. 1933, reached #15 in March 1934
Max Nesbitt & Harry Nesbitt w & m
Bert Ambrose/Sam Browne 02/34 Bruns 6755
Emil Coleman/Jerry Cooper 03/34 Col 2882-D
Ted Black/Edith Caldwell 04/34 Blu 5370

YESTERDAYS
T B Harms, pub. 1933, reached #20 in January 1934
Otto Harbach w, Jerome Kern m
Featured in ROBERTA, show (opened 11/33)
Fay Templeton, sung in show
Leo Reisman/Frank Luther 01/34 Bruns 6701

YOU OUGHTA BE IN PICTURES (29)
Harms, pub. 1934, reached #4 in May 1934
Edward Heyman w, Dana Suesse m
Added to ZIEGFELD FOLLIES OF 1934, show (opened 01/34)
Rudy Vallee/<vocal Φ 04/34 Vic 24580
Jane Froman, sung in show
Little Jack Little/<vocal 04/34 Col 2895-D
Boswell Sisters 04/24 Bruns 6798

YOU'RE A BUILDER UPPER
Harms, pub. 1934, reached #13 in November 1934
E Y Harbourg & Ira Gershwin w, Harold Arlen m
Featured in LIFE BEGINS AT 8:40, show (opened 08/34)
Ray Bolger & Dixie Dunbar, sung in show
Leo Reisman/Harold Arlen 09/34 Bruns 6941
Glen Gray[2]/Pee Wee Hunt 11/34 Dec 193
Richard Himber/Joey Nash 09/34 Vic 24679

YOU'RE DEVASTATING
T B Harms, pub. 1933, reached #19 in January 1934
Otto Harbach w, Jerome Kern m
Featured in ROBERTA, show (opened 11/33)
Bob Hope & Tamara, sung in show
Emil Coleman/Jerry Cooper 01/34 Col 2847-D

[1] The Castilian Troubadours were actually Terig Tucci and his Latin American Orch.
[2] From 1934 on, virtually all Glen Gray records were billed as Glen Gray & The Casa Loma Orch.
[3] Vic 24739 was entitled THE LAUGHING SONG, but it was actually another take of THE DRUNKARD SONG, during which Vallee botched the lyrics and started laughing.

1935

ABOUT A QUARTER TO NINE (8)
Witmark, pub. 1935, reached #1 in June 1935
Al Dubin w, Harry Warren m
Featured in GO INTO YOUR DANCE, film (rel. 03/35)
Al Jolson, sung in film and on radio
Victor Young/Hal Burke Φ 05/35 Dec 418
Ozzie Nelson/<vocal Φ 06/35 Bruns 7425
Johnny Green/Jimmy Farrell 05/35 Col 3029-D

ACCENT ON YOUTH (34)
Famous, pub. 1935, reached #3 in September 1935
Tot Seymour w, Vee Lawnhurst m
Featured in ACCENT ON YOUTH, film (rel. 08/35)
Jan Garber/Lee Bennett Φ 09/35 Vic 25110
Duke Ellington Orch Φ 10/35 Bruns 7514
Paul Pendarvis/w.vocal 09/35 Col 3082-D
George Hall/Dolly Dawn 10/35 Blu 6099

AH! SWEET MYSTERY OF LIFE
Witmark, pub. 1910, reached #19 in July 1935
(Also reached #9 in April 1928)
Rida Johnson Young w, Victor Herbert m
Featured in NAUGHTY MARIETTA, film (rel. 02/35)
Jeanette MacDonald & Nelson Eddy, sung in film
Nelson Eddy Φ 05/35 Vic 4281

AND THEN SOME (41)
Famous, pub. 1935, reached #4 in August 1935
Tot Seymour w, Vee Lawnhurst m
Ozzie Nelson/<vocal Φ 07/35 Bruns 7464
Bob Crosby/<vocal 08/35 Dec 502
Paul Whiteman/Durelle Alexander 08/35 Vic 25088

ANIMAL CRACKERS IN MY SOUP
Movietone Mus, pub. 1935, reached #13 in September 1935
Ted Koehler & Irving Caesar w, Ray Henderson m
Featured in CURLY TOP, film (1934)
Shirley Temple, sung in film
Don Bestor/Joy Lynne 08/35 Bruns 7495

ANYTHING GOES
Harms, pub. 1934, reached #13 in February 1935
Cole Porter w & m
Featured in ANYTHING GOES, show (opened 11/34)
Ethel Merman, sung in show
Paul Whiteman/Ramona Davies 12/34 Vic 24770
Dorsey Brothers Orch/w.vocal trio 01/35 Dec 318

BELIEVE IT, BELOVED (45)
Broadway Mus Co, pub. 1934, reached #5 in February 1935
George Whiting & Nat Schwartz w, J C Johnson m
Fats Waller Φ 01/35 Vic 24808
Isham Jones/Eddie Stone 01/35 Dec 327
Freddy Martin/w.vocal trio 03/35 Bruns 7368

BLUE DANUBE WALTZ
Mills; orig. pub. 1867, reached #17 in December 1934
Johann Strauss m
Ray Noble Orch Φ 12/34 Vic 24806

BLUE MOON (12)
Robbins, pub. 1934, reached #2 in February 1935
(Also reached #1 in April 1961)
Lorenz Hart w, Richard Rodgers m
Glen Gray/Kenny Sargent Φ 01/35 Dec 312
Benny Goodman/Helen Ward Φ 02/35 Col 3003-D
Al Bowlly/Ray Noble Orch 03/35 Vic 24849
Frankie Trumbauer/w.vocal 01/35 Vic 24812
Frank Parker 02/35 Col 2996-D

CHASING SHADOWS (18)
Crawford, pub. 1935, reached #2 in July 1935
Benny Davis w, Abner Silver m
Dorsey Brothers Orch/Bob Eberle Φ 07/35 Dec 476
Enric Madriguera/Bob Bunch 07/35 Vic 25047
Jack Shilkret/Dick Robertson 08/35 Blu 5986
Louis Prima/<vocal 07/35 Bruns 7448

CHEEK TO CHEEK (6)
Berlin, pub. 1935, reached #1 in September 1935
Irving Berlin w & m
Featured in TOP HAT, film (rel. 08/35)
Fred Astaire, sung in film
Fred Astaire/Leo Reisman Orch Φ 08/35 Bruns 7486
Eddy Duchin/Lew Sherwood Φ 08/35 Vic 25093
Guy Lombardo/w.vocal trio Φ 10/35 Dec 549
Boswell Sisters 11/35 Dec 574

CLOUDS (27)
Robbins, pub. 1935, reached #6 in March 1935
Gus Kahn w, Walter Donaldson m
Ray Noble/Al Bowlly 03/35 Vic 24865
Benny Goodman/Ray Hendricks 04/35 Col 3015-D
Art Kassel/Norm Ruvell 03/35 Blu 5800
Emil Coleman/w.vocal 03/35 Dec 366

DANCING WITH MY SHADOW
J Morris, pub. 1934, reached #8 in February 1935
Harry Woods w & m
Dorsey Brothers Orch/Kay Weber 02/35 Dec 335
Richard Himber/Joey Nash 01/35 Vic 24829
Henry King/Joe Sudy 02/35 Col 2992-D

THE DIXIELAND BAND
Miller Mus, pub. 1935, reached #20 in May 1935
Johnny Mercer w, Bernie Hanighen m
Benny Goodman/Helen Ward 03/35 Col 3033-D, 05/35 Vic 25009
Bob Crosby/<vocal 07/35 Dec 479

DON'T GIVE UP THE SHIP
J H Remick pub. 1935, reached #8 in December 1935
Al Dubin w, Harry Warren m
Featured in SHIPMATES FOREVER, film (rel. 10/35)
Dick Powell, sung in film, 12/35 Dec 613
Tommy Dorsey/Cliff Weston 12/35 Vic 25183

DOWN BY THE RIVER
Famous, pub. 1935, reached #16 in April 1935
Lorenz Hart w, Richard Rodgers m
Featured in MISSISSIPPI, film (rel. 04/35)
Bing Crosby, sung in film, 04/35 Dec 392
Guy Lombardo/Carmen Lombardo 04/35 Dec 393

EAST OF THE SUN (17)
Santly Bros, pub. 1934, reached #1 in September 1935
Brooks Bowman w & m
Tom Coakley/Carl Ravazza ΦΦ 07/35 Vic 25069
Bob Crosby/Frank Tennille 08/35 Dec 502
Arthur Tracy, radio, 12/35 Dec 606

EV'RY DAY (28)
J H Remick, pub. 1934, reached #4 in March 1935
Irving Kahal w, Sammy Fain m
Featured in SWEET MUSIC, film (rel. 02/35)
Rudy Vallee/<vocal Φ sung in film, 02/35 Vic 24827
Victor Young/w.vocal 03/35 Dec 350

EVERY LITTLE MOMENT
Robbins, pub. 1935, reached #13 in August 1935
Dorothy Fields w, Jimmy McHugh m
Dorsey Brothers Orch/Kay Weber 07/35 Dec 480
Eddy Duchin/Lew Sherwood 06/35 Vic 25029
Wingy Manone/<vocal 07/35 Voc 2963

EVERY NOW AND THEN
T B Harms, pub. 1935, reached #16 in October 1935
Al Lewis & Al Sherman w, Abner Silver m
Ramona[1] 10/35 Vic 25138
George Hall/Sonny Schuyler 11/35 Blu 6099

EVERYTHING'S BEEN DONE BEFORE
Robbins, pub. 1935, reached #10 in May 1935
Harold Adamson w, Jack King & Edwin H Knopf m
Featured in RECKLESS, film (rel. 04/35)
Freddy Martin/Elmer Feldkamp 04/35 Bruns 7395
Guy Lombardo/Carmen Lombardo 04/35 Dec 424
Richard Himber/Joey Nash 04/35 Vic 24886

FARE THEE WELL, ANNABELLE (48)
J H Remick, pub. 1934, reached #4 in March 1935
Mort Dixon w, Allie Wrubel m
Featured in SWEET MUSIC, film (rel. 02/35)
Rudy Vallee/<vocal Φ sung in film, 02/35 Vic 24833
Glen Gray/Pee Wee Hunt Φ 02/35 Dec 352
Ted FioRito/Muzzy Marcellino 03/35 Bruns 7379

FLIRTATION WALK
Witmark, pub. 1934, reached #9 in January 1935
Mort Dixon w, Allie Wrubel m
Featured in FLIRTATION WALK, film (rel. 11/34)
Dick Powell, sung in film, 12/34 Bruns 7328
Victor Young/Paul Small 12/34 Dec 279
Eddy Duchin/Lew Sherwood 12/34 Vic 24786

FLOWERS FOR MADAME
T B Harms, pub. 1935, reached #12 in June 1935
Charles Tobias & Charles Newman w, Murray Mencher m
Ray Noble/Al Bowlly 04/35 Vic 24865
Bob Crosby/Frank Tennille 07/35 Dec 478
Jack Shilkret/w.vocal 05/35 Blu 5886

FOOTLOOSE AND FANCY FREE
Robbins, pub. 1935, reached #13 in July 1935
Gus Kahn w, Carmen Lombardo m
Richard Himber/Stuart Allen 06/35 Vic 25037
Henry King/Joe Sudy 08/35 Col 3048-D
Smith Ballew/<vocal 06/35 Melotone 13423

(LOOKIE LOOKIE LOOKIE) HERE COMES COOKIE
Crawford, pub. 1935, reached #8 in April 1935
Mack Gordon w, Harry Revel m
Featured in LOVE IN BLOOM, film (rel. 04/35)
Gracie Allen, sung in film
Glen Gray/Pee Wee Hunt 04/35 Dec 386
Jan Garber/Fritz Heilbron 04/35 Vic 24880

I BELIEVE IN MIRACLES (37)
L Feist, pub. 1934, reached #3 in February 1935
Sam Lewis w, George Meyer & Pete Wendling m
Dorsey Brothers Orch/Bob Crosby Φ 02/35 Dec 335
Fats Waller Φ 02/35 Vic 24853
Dick Powell 03/35 Bruns 7374

I COULDN'T BELIEVE MY EYES
Shapiro, B, pub. 1935, reached #14 in September 1935
Walter Samuels, Leonard Whitcup, Teddy Powell w & m
Freddy Martin/Elmer Feldkamp 07/35 Bruns 7462
Rudy Vallee/<vocal 08/35 Vic 25089
Dorsey Brothers Orch/Kay Weber 09/35 Dec 519

I FOUND A DREAM
Movietone Mus, pub. 1935, reached #15 in December 1935
Don Hartman w, Jay Gorney m
Featured in REDHEADS ON PARADE, film (rel. 09/35)
John Boles & Dixie Lee, sung in film
Enric Madriguera/Tony Sacco 11/35 Vic 25162
Bob Crosby/Frank Tennille 12/35 Dec 615

I GET A KICK OUT OF YOU
Harms, pub. 1934, reached #17 in January 1935
Cole Porter w & m
Featured in ANYTHING GOES, show (opened 11/34)
Ethel Merman & William Gaxton, sung in show
Paul Whiteman/Ramona Davies 12/34 Vic 24769
Ethel Merman 01/35 Bruns 7342
Leo Reisman/Sally Singer 01/35 Bruns 7332

I WAS LUCKY
Robbins, pub. 1935, reached #8 in April 1935
Jack Meskill & A Hornez w, Jack Stern m
Featured in FOLIES BERGERE, film (rel 03/35)
Maurice Chevalier & Ann Sothern, sung in film
Dorsey Brothers Orch/Bob Crosby 02/35 Dec 358
Benny Goodman/Helen Ward 04/35 Col 3018-D
Maurice Chevalier 05/35 Vic 24882

I WISH I WERE ALADDIN
Crawford, pub. 1935, reached #14 in October 1935
Mack Gordon w, Harry Revel m
Featured in TWO FOR TONIGHT, film (rel. 08/35)
Bing Crosby, sung in film, 10/35 Dec 547
Enric Madriguera/Tony Sacco 09/35 Vic 25118
Glen Gray/Kenny Sargent 10/35 Dec 553

I WISHED ON THE MOON
Famous, pub. 1935, reached #9 in October 1935
Dorothy Parker w, Ralph Rainger m
Featured in THE BIG BROADCAST OF 1936, film (rel. 09/35)
Bing Crosby Φ sung in film, 10/35 Dec 543
Ray Noble/Al Bowlly 09/35 Vic 25104
Little Jack Little/<vocal 08/35 Col 3068-D
Teddy Wilson/Billie Holiday 09/35 Bruns 7501

I WON'T DANCE (31)
T B Harms, pub. 1935, reached #7 in April 1935
Otto Harbach & Oscar Hammerstein 2nd w, Jerome Kern m
Featured in ROBERTA, film (rel. 02/35)
Fred Astaire & Ginger Rogers, sung in film
Eddy Duchin/Lew Sherwood Φ 04/35 Vic 24871
Leo Reisman/Phil Dewey 04/35 Bruns 7393
Johnny Green/w.vocal duo 04/35 Col 3022-D
George Hall/w.vocal duo 04/24 Blu 5863

I'D RATHER LISTEN TO YOUR EYES
J H Remick, pub. 1935, reached #18 in November 1935
Al Dubin w, Harry Warren m
Featured in SHIPMATES FOREVER, film (rel. 10/35)
Dick Powell, sung in film
Jacques Renard/Smith Ballew 11/35 Col 3086-D
Enric Madriguera/Tony Sacco 11/35 Vic 25153

I'LL NEVER SAY "NEVER AGAIN" AGAIN (15)
Donaldson, D & G, pub. 1935, reached #3 in August 1935
Harry Woods w & m
Ozzie Nelson/<vocal Φ 06/35 Bruns 7426
Dorsey Brothers Orch/w.vocal trio 07/35 Dec 480

I'M FALLING IN LOVE WITH SOMEONE
Witmark, pub. 1910, reached #15 in July 1935
(Also reached #7 in April 1911)
Rida Johnson Young w, Victor Herbert m
Featured in NAUGHTY MARIETTA, film (rel. 02/35)
Nelson Eddy Φ sung in film, 06/35 Vic 4280

I'M IN THE MOOD FOR LOVE (9)
Robbins, pub. 1935, reached #2 in September 1935
Dorothy Fields w, Jimmy McHugh m
Featured in EVERY NIGHT AT EIGHT, film (rel. 07/35)
All-time pop standard
Frances Langford, sung in film, 10/35 Bruns 7513
Little Jack Little/<vocal Φ 08/35 Col 3069-D
Paul Whiteman/Ramona Davies Φ 08/35 Vic 25091
Louis Armstrong/<vocal 11/35 Dec 579
Leo Reisman/Frank Luther 08/35 Bruns 7482

I'M LIVIN' IN A GREAT BIG WAY
Berlin, pub. 1935, reached #18 in July 1935
Dorothy Fields w, Jimmy McHugh m
Featured in HOORAY FOR LOVE, film (rel. 05/35)
Benny Goodman/Buddy Clark 05/35 Vic 25011
Bill Robinson & Jeni LeGon, sung in film
Louis Prima/<vocal 06/35 Bruns 7419

I'M ON A SEE SAW (24)
Chappell, pub. 1934, reached #3 in October 1935
Desmond Carter w, Vivian Ellis m
Bert Ambrose/Sam Browne Φ 09/35 Dec 467
Fats Waller Φ 09/35 Vic 25120
Joe Haymes/Cliff Weston 10/35 Perfect 351025

I'M SITTIN' HIGH ON A HILLTOP
Robbins, pub. 1935, reached #8 in December 1935
Gus Kahn w, Arthur Johnston m
Featured in THANKS A MILLION, film (rel. 10/35)
Dick Powell, sung in film, 12/35 Dec 613
Guy Lombardo/w.vocal trio 12/35 Dec 589
Paul Whiteman/John Hauser 11/35 Vic 25151

I'VE GOT A FEELIN' YOU'RE FOOLIN' (33)
Robbins, pub. 1935, reached #5 in November 1935
Arthur Freed w, Nacio Herb Brown m
Featured in BROADWAY MELODY OF 1936, film (rel. 08/35)
Dorsey Brothers Orch/Bob Eberle Φ 10/35 Dec 560
Robert Taylor & June Knight, sung in film
Eddy Duchin/Lew Sherwood 09/35 Vic 25125

I'VE GOT AN INVITATION TO A DANCE
Berlin, pub. 1934, reached #11 in January 1935
Marty Symes & Al Neiberg w, Jerry Levinson m
Hal Kemp/Skinnay Ennis 12/34 Bruns 7323
Glen Gray/Kenny Sargent 12/34 Dec 287
Paul Pendarvis/w.vocal 12/34 Col 2974-D

IF THE MOON TURNS GREEN
Berlin, pub. 1935, reached #9 in April 1935
Paul Coates w, Bernie Hanighen m
Paul Whiteman/Ramona Davies 03/35 Vic 24860
Henry Busse/Steve Bowers 04/35 Dec 398

IN A LITTLE GYPSY TEAROOM (2)
J Morris, pub. 1935, reached #1 in July 1935
Edgar Leslie w, Joe Burke m
Jan Garber/Lee Bennett Φ 06/35 Vic 25013
Bob Crosby/Frank Tennille Φ 07/35 Dec 478
Louis Prima/<vocal Φ 08/35 Bruns 7479
Arthur Tracy, stage and radio

IN THE MIDDLE OF A KISS (16)
Famous, pub. 1935, reached #3 in July 1935
Sam Coslow w & m
Featured in COLLEGE SCANDAL, film (rel. 07/35)
Hal Kemp/Skinnay Ennis Φ 06/35 Bruns 7437
Jan Garber/Lee Bennett 06/35 Vic 25025
Johnny Downs, sung in film

ISLE OF CAPRI (3)
T B Harms, pub. 1934, reached #1 in February 1935
(Also reached #12 in June 1954)
Jimmy Kennedy w, Will Grosz m
Ray Noble/Al Bowlly ΦΦ 01/35 Vic 24771
Freddy Martin/Elmer Feldkamp Φ 01/35 Bruns 7344
Lew Stone/Al Bowlly Φ 02/35 Dec 247
Wingy Manone/<vocal 04/35 Voc 2913

ISN'T THIS A LOVELY DAY (TO BE CAUGHT IN THE RAIN)? (32)
Berlin, pub. 1935, reached #4 in October 1935
Irving Berlin w & m
Featured in TOP HAT, film (rel. 08/35)
Fred Astaire, sung in film
Fred Astaire/Johnny Green Orch Φ 08/35 Bruns 7487
Eddy Duchin/Lew Sherwood 08/35 Vic 25093
Phil Ohman/w.vocal 09/35 Col 3076-D

IT'S AN OLD SOUTHERN CUSTOM
Movietone Mus, pub. 1935, reached #9 in May 1935
Jack Yellen w, Joseph Meyer m
Featured in GEORGE WHITE'S 1935 SCANDALS, film (rel. 04/35)
Alice Faye, James Dunn, Cliff Edwards, sung in film
Eddy Duchin/Lew Sherwood 04/35 Vic 24875
George Hall/Loretta Lee 04/35 Blu 5865

IT'S DARK ON OBSERVATORY HILL
Berlin, pub. 1934, reached #16 in January 1935
Johnny Burke w, Harold Spina m
Ozzie Nelson/<vocal, stage, 12/34 Bruns 6999
Dorsey Brothers Orch/Bob Crosby 01/35 Dec 314
Will Osborne/<vocal 01/35 Melotone 13255, 01/35 Perfect 16043

IT'S EASY TO REMEMBER
Famous, pub. 1935, reached #10 in April 1935
Lorenz Hart w, Richard Rodgers m
Featured in MISSISSIPPI, film (rel. 04/35)
Bing Crosby, sung in film, 04/35 Dec 391
Jan Garber/Lee Bennett 04/35 Vic 24880
Guy Lombardo/Carmen Lombardo 04/35 Dec 394

JUNE IN JANUARY (11)
Famous, pub. 1934, reached #1 in January 1935
Leo Robin w, Ralph Rainger m
Featured in HERE IS MY HEART, film (rel. 12/34)
Bing Crosby ΦΦ sung in film, 01/35 Dec 310
Guy Lombardo/Carmen Lombardo 01/35 Dec 307
Ted FioRito/Howard Phillips 01/35 Bruns 7327
Little Jack Little/<vocal 12/34 Col 2978-D
Richard Himber/Joey Nash 01/35 Vic 24811

THE LADY IN RED (22)
J H Remick, pub. 1935, reached #6 in July 1935
Mort Dixon w, Allie Wrubel m
Featured in IN CALIENTE, film (rel. 06/35)
Xavier Cugat/Don Reid Φ 06/35 Vic 25012
Judy Canova, sung in film
Louis Prima/<vocal 07/35 Bruns 7448
Joe Haymes/Cliff Weston 05/35 Blu 5918, 05/35 Melotone 13406, 05/35 Perfect 16121

LET'S SWING IT
T B Harms, pub. 1935, reached #12 in July 1935
Charles Newman, Charles Tobias, Murray Menscher w & m
Featured in EARL CARROLL'S SKETCH BOOK OF 1935, show (opened 06/35)
Ray Noble/The Freshmen 07/35 Vic 25070
Lillian Carmen, sung in show
Wingy Manone/<vocal 08/35 Voc 2990

LIFE IS A SONG (19)
Robbins, pub. 1935, reached #3 in June 1935
Joe Young w, Fred Ahlert m
Ruth Etting Φ 05/35 Col 3031-D
Joe Haymes/Skeeter Palmer 05/35 Blu 5916
Freddy Martin/Elmer Feldkamp 05/35 Bruns 7422

A LITTLE BIT INDEPENDENT (14)
Donaldson, D & G, pub. 1935, reached #1 in January 1936
Edgar Leslie w, Joe Burke m
Fats Waller ΦΦ 01/36 Vic 25196
Freddy Martin/w.vocal trio Φ 12/35 Bruns 7559
Bob Crosby/<vocal 01/36 Dec 629

A LITTLE WHITE GARDENIA
Famous, pub. 1935, reached #6 in March 1935
Sam Coslow w & m
Featured in ALL THE KING'S HORSES, film (rel. 02/35)
Carl Brisson & Mary Ellis, sung in film
Hal Kemp/Skinnay Ennis 03/35 Bruns 7370
Al Bowlly/Ray Noble 03/35 Vic 24855

LOVE AND A DIME
Santly-Joy, pub. 1935, reached #14 in June 1935
Brooks Bowman w & m
Jan Garber/Fritz Heilbron 04/35 Vic 24885
Glen Gray & The Casa Loma Orch 04/35 Dec 387
Hal Kemp/Skinnay Ennis 04/35 Bruns 7334

LOVE IS JUST AROUND THE CORNER
Famous, pub. 1934, reached #12 in February 1935
Leo Robin w, Louis Genzler m
Featured in HERE IS MY HEART, film (rel. 12/34)
Bing Crosby, sung in film, 01/35 Dec 310
Dorsey Brothers Orch/Bob Crosby 01/35 Dec 311

LOVE ME FOREVER (46)
Berlin, pub. 1935, reached #4 in August 1935
Gus Kahn w, Victor Schertzinger m
Featured in LOVE ME FOREVER, film (rel. 06/35)
Grace Moore, sung in film
Richard Himber/Stuart Allen Φ 06/35 Vic 25049
Russ Morgan/Audrey Marsh 08/35 Col 3063-D
Victor Young/Milt Watson 07/35 Dec 490

LOVELY TO LOOK AT (23)
T B Harms, pub. 1935, reached #3 in April 1935
Dorothy Fields & Jimmy McHugh w, Jerome Kern m
Featured in ROBERTA, film (rel. 02/35)
Irene Dunn, sung in film, 06/35 Bruns 7420
Eddy Duchin/Lew Sherwood Φ 04/35 Vic 24871
Leo Reisman/Phil Dewey 04/35 Bruns 7393
Guy Lombardo/w.vocal trio 05/35 Dec 406

LULLABY OF BROADWAY (7)
Witmark, pub. 1935, reached #1 in April 1935
Al Dubin w, Harry Warren m
Featured in GOLD DIGGERS OF 1935, film (rel. 03/35)
All-time pop standard
Dorsey Brothers Orch/Bob Crosby ΦΦ 03/35 Dec 370
Dick Powell & Wini Shaw, sung in film
Dick Powell 03/35 Bruns 7374
Wini Shaw/Dick Jurgens Orch 04/35 Dec 408
Little Jack Little/<vocal 03/35 Col 3009-D

LULU'S BACK IN TOWN
Witmark, pub. 1935, reached #10 in August 1935
Al Dubin w, Harry Warren m
Featured in BROADWAY GONDOLIER, film (rel. 07/35)
Fats Waller 07/35 Vic 25063
Dick Powell & The Mills Brothers, sung in film
Dick Powell 08/35 Bruns 7469
Wingy Manone/<vocal 07/35 Voc 2972

NO OTHER ONE
Famous, pub. 1935, reached #7 in December 1935
Tot Seymour w, Vee Lawnhurst m
Little Jack Little/<vocal 12/35 Col 3095-D
Benny Goodman/Helen Ward 01/36 Vic 25193
Bob Crosby/<vocal 01/36 Dec 629

NO STRINGS (I'M FANCY FREE)
Berlin, pub. 1935, reached #18 in October 1935
Irving Berlin w & m
Featured in TOP HAT, film (rel. 08/35)
Fred Astaire, sung in film
Fred Astaire/Leo Reisman Orch 08/35 Bruns 7486
Dorsey Brothers Orch/w.vocal trio 09/35 Dec 516

OLE FAITHFUL
Shapiro, B, pub. 1934, reached #11 in March 1935
Michael Carr & Joseph H Kennedy w & m
Gene Autry 02/35 Melotone 13354
Don Bestor/Neil Buckley 01/35 Bruns 7339

ON THE GOOD SHIP LOLLIPOP (13)
Movietone Mus, pub. 1934, reached #3 in February 1935
Sidney Clare w, Richard Whiting m
Featured in BRIGHT EYES, film (rel. 12/34)
Shirley Temple, sung in film
Rudy Vallee/Stewart Sisters Φ 02/25 Vic 24838
Ted FioRito/w.vocal 02/35 Bruns 7364

ON TREASURE ISLAND (5)
J Morris, pub. 1935, reached #2 in November 1935
Edgar Leslie w, Joe Burke m
Tommy Dorsey/Edythe Wright ΦΦ 11/35 Vic 25144
Bing Crosby Φ 12/35 Dec 617
Little Jack Little/<vocal 12/35 Col 3095-D
Teddy Wilson/<piano 01/36 Bruns 7572
Bob Crosby/<vocal 12/35 Dec 614

PAGE MISS GLORY
T B Harms, pub. 1935, reached #12 in September 1935
Al Dubin w, Harry Warren m
Featured in PAGE MISS GLORY, film (rel. 07/35)
Dick Powell & Marion Davies, sung in film
Hal Kemp/Skinnay Ennis 08/35 Bruns 7493

PARIS IN THE SPRING (49)
Crawford, pub. 1935, reached #6 in August 1935
Mack Gordon w, Harry Revel m
Featured in PARIS IN THE SPRING, film (rel. 05/35)
Ray Noble/Al Bowlly Φ 06/35 Vic 25040
Mary Ellis, sung in film
Freddy Martin/Elmer Feldkamp 07/35 Bruns 7459

THE PICCOLINO
Berlin, pub. 1935, reached #19 in October 1935
Irving Berlin w & m
Featured in TOP HAT, film (rel. 08/35)
Ginger Rogers, sung in film
Ray Noble/Al Bowlly 09/35 Vic 25094
Fred Astaire/Leo Reisman Orch 09/35 Bruns 7488

RED SAILS IN THE SUNSET (4)
Shapiro, B, pub. 1935, reached #1 in November 1935
Jimmy Kennedy w, Hugh Williams m
Featured in PROVINCETOWN FOLLIES, show (opened 11/35)
Bing Crosby Φ 12/35 Dec 616
Guy Lombardo/Carmen Lombardo Φ 11/35 Dec 585
Mantovani Orch/George Barclay Φ 12/35 Col 3097-D
Al Bowlly/Ray Noble Orch Φ stage, 11/35 Vic 25142
Phyllis Austin, sung in show

RHYTHM AND ROMANCE
Broadway M C, pub. 1935, reached #13 in October 1935
George Whiting & Nat Schwartz w, J C Johnson m
Fats Waller Φ 10/35 Vic 25131
Lud Gluskin/Buddy Clark 11/35 Bruns 7535

RHYTHM IS OUR BUSINESS
Select M P I, pub. 1935, reached #14 in July 1935
Sammy Cahn w, Jimmie Lunceford & Saul Chaplin m
Jimmie Lunceford/Willie Smith Φ 06/35 Dec 369
Wingy Manone/<vocal 08/35 Voc 2990
Tom Coakley/Dudley Nix 07/35 Vic 25062

ROLL ALONG, PRAIRIE MOON (30)
Robbins, pub. 1935, reached #6 in November 1935
Harry McPherson w, Ted FioRito & Albert Von Tilzer m
Featured in HERE COMES THE BAND, film (rel. 09/35)
George Hall/Sonny Schuyler 09/35 Blu 6017
Harry Stockwell, sung in film
Smith Ballew/<vocal 10/35 Melotone 351006

THE ROSE IN HER HAIR (36)
Witmark, pub. 1935, reached #6 in September 1935
Al Dubin w, Harry Warren m
Featured in BROADWAY GONDOLIER, film (rel. 07/35)
Dick Powell, sung in film, 08/35 Bruns 7469
Russ Morgan/w.vocal 08/35 Col 3063-D
Eddy Duchin/Lew Sherwood 07/35 Vic 25057

SANTA CLAUS IS COMIN' TO TOWN
L Feist, pub. 1934, reached #11 in December 1935
(Also reached Top 20 in December 1934, 1936, 1947, 1948)
Haven Gillespie w, J Fred Coots m
All-time Christmas standard
Tommy Dorsey/w.vocal duo 12/35 Vic 25145
Eddie Cantor, stage and radio
George Hall/Sonny Schuyler 12/35 Blu 5711
Joe Moss/Dick Robertson 12/35 Bruns 7544

SHE'S A LATIN FROM MANHATTAN (47)
Witmark, pub. 1935, reached #6 in June 1935
Al Dubin w, Harry Warren m
Featured in GO INTO YOUR DANCE, film (rel. 03/35)
Victor Young/w.vocal duo Φ 05/35 Dec 418
Al Jolson, sung in film
Johnny Green/Jimmy Farrell 05/35 Col 3029-D
Ozzie Nelson/<vocal 06/35 Bruns 7425

SILENT NIGHT
First pub. in English in 1871, reached #19 in December 1935
Joseph Mohr w, Franz Gruber m
All-time Christmas standard
Bing Crosby Φ 12/35 Dec 621

SOLITUDE (43)
Mills, pub. 1934, reached #8 in March 1935
Eddie DeLange & Irving Mills w, Duke Ellington m
Duke Ellington Φ 11/34 Bruns 6987, 12/34 Vic 24755
Mills Blue Rhythm Band/Chuck Richards 02/35 Col 2994-D
The Modernists[2] 11/34 Melotone 13159, 11/34 Perfect 16002, 11/34 Conqueror 8526
Dorsey Brothers Orch/Kay Weber 03/35 Dec 15013

SOON (29)
Famous, pub. 1935, reached #5 in April 1935
Lorenz Hart m, Richard Rodgers m
Featured in MISSISSIPPI, film (rel. 04/35)
Bing Crosby ΦΦ sung in film, 04/35 Dec 392
Ray Noble/Al Bowlly 03/35 Vic 24879
Guy Lombardo/Carmen Lombardo 04/35 Dec 394

STAR GAZING
L Feist, pub. 1935, reached #20 in July 1935
Al Neiberg & Marty Symes w, Jerry Levinson m
Enric Madriguera/Tony Sacco 07/35 Vic 25064
Joe Reichman/Joe Martin 07/35 Melotone 13446, 07/35 Perfect 16138

SUGAR BLUES
Clarence Williams M C, pub. 1923, reached #16 in August 1935
(Also reached #20 in April 1931)
(Also reached #15 in November 1947)
Lucy Fletcher w, Clarence Williams m
Clyde McCoy Orch Φ 04/35 Dec 381

SWEET AND SLOW
J H Remick, pub. 1935, reached #15 in August 1935
Al Dubin w, Harry Warren m
Fats Waller 07/35 Vic 25063
Wingy Manone/<vocal 07/35 Voc 2972

SWEET MUSIC
J H Remick, pub. 1934, reached #16 in March 1935
Al Dubin w, Harry Warren m
Featured in SWEET MUSIC, film (rel. 02/35)
Rudy Vallee/<vocal, sung in film, 02/35 Vic 24827
Victor Young/w.vocal 02/35 Dec 350

TAKE ME BACK TO MY BOOTS AND SADDLE (20)
Schuster & Miller, pub. 1935, reached #4 in December 1935
Teddy Powell, Walter Samuels, Leonard Whitcup w & m
Tommy Dorsey/Cliff Weston Φ 11/35 Vic 25144
Bing Crosby Φ 12/35 Dec 616
Victor Young/Frank Luther 11/35 Dec 581

TELL ME THAT YOU LOVE ME (25)
T B Harms, pub. 1935, reached #7 in June 1935
Al Stillman w, Cesare A Bixio m
Freddy Martin/Elmer Feldkamp 06/35 Bruns 7438
Victor Young/Milt Watson 06/35 Dec 485
Frank Parker, stage

THANKS A MILLION (39)
Robbins, pub. 1935, reached #6 in December 1935
Gus Kahn w, Arthur Johnston m
Featured in THANKS A MILLION, film (rel. 10/35)
Dick Powell Φ sung in film, 12/35 Dec 612
Paul Whiteman/John Hauser Φ 11/35 Vic 25151
Paul Pendarvis/w.vocal 10/35 Col 3091-D
Guy Lombardo/Carmen Lombardo 12/35 Dec 589

THRILLED
Crawford, pub. 1935, reached #12 in July 1935
Mort Greene w, Harry Barris m
Hal Kemp/Maxine Grey 06/35 Bruns 7437
Victor Young/Milt Watson 06/35 Dec 458

TINY LITTLE FINGERPRINTS
DeSylva, B & H, pub. 1934, reached #7 in March 1935
Charles Newman & Charles Tobias w, Sam Stept m
Dorsey Brothers Orch/Kay Weber 03/35 Dec 367
Don Bestor/Neil Buckley 02/35 Bruns 7366

TOP HAT, WHITE TIE, AND TAILS (35)
Berlin, pub. 1935, reached #6 in September 1935
Irving Berlin w & m
Featured in TOP HAT, film (rel. 08/35)
Fred Astaire, sung in film
Fred Astaire/Johnny Green Orch Φ 08/35 Bruns 7487
Ray Noble/Al Bowlly Φ 07/35 Vic 25094
Dorsey Brothers Orch/w.vocal trio 09/35 Dec 516

TRUCKIN' (44)
Mills, pub. 1935, reached #8 in November 1935
Ted Koehler w, Rube Bloom m
Fats Waller Φ 09/35 Vic 25116
Mills Blue Rhythm Band/Henry "Red" Allen 10/35 Col 3078-D
Duke Ellington/Ivie Anderson 10/35 Bruns 7514

TWENTY-FOUR HOURS A DAY (38)
T B Harms, pub. 1935, reached #5 in December 1935
Arthur Swanstrom w, James F Hanley m
Featured in SWEET SURRENDER, film (rel. 12/35)
Teddy Wilson/Billie Holiday Φ 12/35 Bruns 7550
Joe Venuti/Tony Pasteur 01/36 Col 3103-D
Jan Garber/Fritz Heilbron 12/35 Blu 6338

WAY BACK HOME
Donaldson, D & G, pub. 1935, reached #12 in June 1935
Al Lewis & Tom Waring w & m
Victor Young/Milt Watson 06/35 Dec 452
Fred Waring's Pennsylvanians, stage
Paul Whiteman/w.vocal duo 06/35 Vic 25022

WHAT A LITTLE MOONLIGHT CAN DO
T B Harms, pub. 1934, reached #15 in August 1935
Harry Woods w & m
Teddy Wilson/Billie Holiday, stage, 08/35 Bruns 7498
Jack Jackson/Fred Latham 07/35 Vic 25069

WHAT'S THE REASON? (10)
Berlin, pub. 1935, reached #2 in June 1935
Jimmie Grier & Coy Poe w, Pinky Tomlin & Earl Hatch m
Featured in TIMES SQUARE LADY, film (rel. 03/35)
Guy Lombardo/Carmen Lombardo Φ 04/35 Dec 393
Pinky Tomlin, sung in film
Fats Waller Φ 05/35 Vic 24889
Mills Brothers 04/35 Dec 402

WHEN I GROW TOO OLD TO DREAM (1)
Robbins, pub. 1935, reached #1 in May 1935
Oscar Hammerstein 2nd w, Sigmund Romberg m
Featured in THE NIGHT IS YOUNG, film (rel. 01/35)
Evelyn Laye & Ramon Novarro, sung in film
Glen Gray/Kenny Sargent Φ 02/35 Dec 349
Nelson Eddy Φ 02/35 Vic 4285
Paul Whiteman/The King's Men 02/35 Vic 24844

WHEN THE LEAVES BID THE TREES GOODBYE
Chappell, pub. 1935, reached #17 in November 1935
Tot Seymour w, Vee Lawnhurst m
Victor Young/Frank Luther 11/35 Dec 582
Enric Madriguera/Bob Bunch 11/35 Vic 25163

WHERE AM I?
Harms, pub. 1935, reached #13 in January 1936
Al Dubin w, Harry Warren m
Featured in STARS OVER BROADWAY, film (rel. 11/35)
James Melton, sung in film, 12/35 Vic 25185
Ray Noble/Al Bowlly 12/35 Vic 25187
Little Jack Little/<vocal 12/35 Col 3096-D
Hal Kemp/Bob Allen 12/35 Bruns 7565

WHOSE HONEY ARE YOU?
L Feist, pub. 1935, reached #18 in April 1935
J Fred Coots & Haven Gillespie w & m
Fats Waller 04/35 Vic 24892
Freddy Martin/w.vocal trio 03/35 Bruns 7382

WHY SHOULDN'T I?
Harms, pub. 1935, reached #19 in December 1935
Cole Porter w & m
Featured in JUBILEE, show (opened 10/35)
Paul Whiteman/Ramona Davies 10/35 Vic 25134
Margaret Adams, sung in show
Jimmy Dorsey/w.vocal duo 11/35 Dec 571

WINTER WONDERLAND (40)
Donaldson, D & G, pub. 1934, reached #4 in January 1935
(Also reached Top 20 in December of 1946, 1950 and 1952)
Richard B Smith w, Felix Bernard m
All-time seasonal standard
Guy Lombardo/w.vocal trio Φ 12/34 Dec 294
Richard Himber/Joey Nash 12/34 Vic 24757
Ted Weems/Parker Gibbs 12/34 Col 2976-D

WITH EVERY BREATH I TAKE
Famous, pub. 1934, reached #7 in February 1935
L Robin & Ralph Rainger w & m
Featured in HERE IS MY HEART, film (rel. 12/34)
Bing Crosby Φ sung in film, 01/35 Dec 309
Guy Lombardo/Carmen Lombardo 01/35 Dec 307
Connie Boswell 02/35 Bruns 7354

WITHOUT A WORD OF WARNING (50)
Crawford, pub. 1935, reached #7 in October 1935
Mack Gordon & Harry Revel w & m
Featured in TWO FOR TONIGHT, film (rel. 08/35)
Bing Crosby Φ sung in film, 10/35 Dec 548
Richard Himber/Stuart Allen 10/35 Vic 25119
Hal Kemp/Bob Allen 09/35 Bruns 7509

YOU ARE MY LUCKY STAR (21)
Robbins, pub. 1935, reached #2 in November 1935
Arthur Freed w, Nacio Herb Brown m
Featured in BROADWAY MELODY OF 1936, film (rel. 08/35)
Eddy Duchin/Lew Sherwood ΦΦ 09/35 Vic 25125
Dorsey Brothers Orch/Bob Eberle Φ 10/35 Dec 559
Eleanor Powell, sung in film
Eleanor Powell/Tommy Dorsey Orch 11/35 Vic 25158
Louis Armstrong/<vocal 11/35 Dec 580

YOU'RE A HEAVENLY THING
Shapiro, B, pub. 1935, reached #13 in June 1935
Joe Young & Little Jack Little w & m
Benny Goodman/Helen Ward 06/35 Vic 25021
Little Jack Little, stage
Orville Knapp/Edith Caldwell 05/35 Dec 413

YOU'RE ALL I NEED (26)
Robbins, pub. 1935, reached #3 in September 1935
Gus Kahn w, Bronislaw Kaper & Walter Jurmann m
Featured in ESCAPADE, film (rel. 07/35)
Eddy Duchin/Lew Sherwood Φ 07/35 Vic 25029
Lorraine Bridges, sung in film
Dorsey Brothers Orch/Bob Eberle 07/35 Dec 482

YOU'RE THE TOP (42)
Harms, pub. 1934, reached #6 in January 1935
Cole Porter w & m
Featured in ANYTHING GOES, show (opened 11/34)
Ethel Merman & William Gaxton, sung in show
Paul Whiteman/w.vocal duo Φ 12/34 Vic 24769
Ethel Merman 01/35 Bruns 7342
Cole Porter 02/35 Vic 24766

[1]Ramona was Ramona Davies, former Paul Whiteman vocalist.
[2]The name Modernists was a pseudonym for the Benny Goodman Orch.

1936

ALL MY LIFE (36)
Sam Fox, pub. 1936, reached #4 in June 1936
Sidney D Mitchell w, Sam Stept m
Featured in LAUGHING IRISH EYES, film (rel. 03/36)
Fats Waller ΦΦ 05/36 Vic 25296
Teddy Wilson/Ella Fitzgerald Φ 05/36 Bruns 7640
Phil Regan, sung in film
Benny Goodman/Helen Ward 06/36 Vic 25324

ALONE (9)
Robbins, pub. 1935, reached #1 in February 1936
Arthur Freed w, Nacio Herb Brown m
Featured in A NIGHT AT THE OPERA, film (rel. 10/35)
Tommy Dorsey/Cliff Weston ΦΦ 01/36 Vic 25191
Allan Jones & Kitty Carlisle, sung in film
Hal Kemp/Maxine Grey 12/35 Bruns 7552
Al Donahue/Barry McKinley 01/36 Dec 626

ALONE AT A TABLE FOR TWO
Shapiro, B, Pub. 1935, reached #10 in March 1936
Billy Hill, Daniel Richman, Ted FioRito w & m
Guy Lombardo/Carmen Lombardo Φ 02/36 Vic 25210
Ted FioRito/Stanley Hickman 02/36 Dec 679

A BEAUTIFUL LADY IN BLUE (6)
Chappell, pub. 1935, reached #3 in March 1936
Sam Lewis w, J Fred Coots m
Jan Garber/Lew Palmer ΦΦ 01/36 Dec 651
Ray Noble/Al Bowlly Φ 01/36 Vic 25209
Jan Peerce, stage, 05/36 Bruns 7635

THE BROKEN RECORD
Chappell, pub. 1935, reached #7 in January 1936
Charles Tobias & Boyd Bunch w, Cliff Friend m
Guy Lombardo/w.vocal trio Φ 01/36 Vic 25210
Freddy Martin/w.vocal group 02/36 Bruns 7591

BYE BYE BABY (40)
Berlin, pub. 1936, reached #5 in September 1936
Walter Hirsch w, Lou Handman m
Fats Waller Φ 09/36 Vic 25388
Charlie Barnet/w.vocal group 09/36 Blu 6504
Ted Weems/Parker Gibbs 10/36 Dec 895

CHRISTOPHER COLUMBUS (50)
Joe Davis, pub. 1936, reached #11 in May 1936
Andy Razaf w, Leon Berry m
Jazz standard, 1930's onward
Andy Kirk Orch Φ 04/36 Dec 729
Fletcher Henderson Orch 05/36 Voc 3211
Benny Goodman Orch 05/36 Vic 25279
Fats Waller 05/36 Vic 25295

CLING TO ME
Donaldson, D & G, pub. 1935, reached #11 in March 1936
Edgar Leslie w, Joe Burke m
Richard Himber/Stuart Allen 02/36 Vic 25235
Ozzie Nelson/w.vocal 02/36 Bruns 7597
Ted FioRito/The Debutantes 02/36 Dec 679

CLOSE TO ME
T B Harms, pub. 1936, reached #14 in November 1936
Sam Lewis w, Peter DeRose m
Tommy Dorsey/Jack Lawrence 11/36 Vic 25447
Reggie Childs/Billy Pritchard 11/36 Dec 978

CROSS PATCH
Famous, pub. 1936, reached #12 in July 1936
Tot Seymour w, Vee Lawnhurst m
Fats Waller 06/36 Vic 25315
Louis Prima/<vocal 07/36 Bruns 7680

DID I REMEMBER (4)
L Feist, pub. 1936, reached #1 in August 1936
Harold Adamson w, Walter Donaldson m
Featured in SUZY, film (rel. 07/36)
Shep Fields/Charles Chester ΦΦ 08/36 Blu 6476
Tommy Dorsey/Edythe Wright Φ 08/36 Vic 25341
Cary Grant & Jean Harlow[1], sung in film
Billie Holiday Orch/<vocal 08/36 Voc 3276
Dick Powell 09/26 Dec 889

DID YOU MEAN IT?
Berlin, pub. 1936, reached #10 in December 1936
Mort Dixon w, Jesse Greer m
Charlie Barnet/w.vocal 11/36 Blu 6605
Reggie Childs/Stephanie Dale 12/36 Dec 978

DINNER FOR ONE, PLEASE, JAMES
Chappell, pub. 1935, reached #11 in February 1936
Michael Carr w & m
Ray Noble/Al Bowlly 01/36 Vic 25187
Hal Kemp/w.vocal duo 02/36 Bruns 7587

EASY TO LOVE
Chappell, pub. 1936, reached #12 in January 1937
Cole Porter w & m
Featured in BORN TO DANCE, show (rel. 11/36)
Frances Langford, sung in film, 11/36 Dec 940
Ray Noble/Al Bowlly 11/36 Vic 25422
Shep Fields/Dick Robertson 10/36 Blu 6592
Jimmy Stewart, sung in film

EENY MEENY MINEY MO
Berlin, pub. 1935, reached #7 in January 1936
Johnny Mercer w, Matty Malneck m
Featured in TO BEAT THE BAND, film (rel. 11/35)
Benny Goodman/Helen Ward Φ 01/36 Vic 25195
Johnny Mercer, sung in film
Ginger Rogers & Johnny Mercer 01/36 Dec 638

EMPTY SADDLES
Shapiro, B, pub. 1936, reached #11 in September 1936
J Keirn Brennan & Billy Hill w & m
Featured in RHYTHM ON THE RANGE, film (rel. 07/36)
Bing Crosby Φ sung in film, 08/36 Dec 870
Sons of the Pioneers 08/36 Dec 5247
Ray Noble/Al Bowlly 08/36 Vic 25346

EVERY MINUTE OF THE HOUR
Schuster & Miller, pub. 1936, reached #11 in April 1936
Charles Kenny & Nick Kenny w & m
George Hall/Dolly Dawn 03/36 Blu 6282
Tommy Dorsey/Edythe Wright 03/36 Vic 25256

EXACTLY LIKE YOU
Shapiro, B, pub. 1930, reached #19 in December 1936
(Also reached #8 in June 1930)
Dorothy Fields w, Jimmy McHugh m
Benny Goodman/Lionel Hampton[4] 10/36 Vic 25406

A FINE ROMANCE (29)
T B Harms, pub. 1936, reached #3 in October 1936
Dorothy Fields w, Jerome Kern m
Featured in SWING TIME, film (rel. 08/36)
Fred Astaire & Ginger Rogers, sung in film
Fred Astaire/Johnny Green Orch Φ 09/36 Bruns 7716
Billie Holiday Orch/<vocal 11/36 Voc 3333
Guy Lombardo/Carmen Lombardo 10/36 Vic 25372
Bing & Dixie Lee Crosby 10/36 Dec 907

THE GLORY OF LOVE (14)
Shapiro, B, pub. 1936, reached #2 in July 1936
Billy Hill w & m
Benny Goodman/Helen Ward ΦΦ 06/36 Vic 25316
Ted FioRito/Muzzy Marcellino 06/36 Dec 793
Rudy Vallee/<vocal 06/36 Melotone 60609

GOODY-GOODY (8)
Crawford, pub. 1936, reached #1 in March 1936
Johnny Mercer w, Matty Malneck m
Benny Goodman/Helen Ward ΦΦ 03/36 Vic 25245
Freddy Martin/Terry Shand Φ 03/36 Bruns 7621
Bob Crosby/<vocal 04/36 Dec 727

HERE'S LOVE IN YOUR EYES
Famous, pub. 1936, reached #12 in December 1936
Leo Robin & Ralph Rainger w & m
Featured in THE BIG BROADCAST OF 1937, film (rel. 10/36)
Benny Goodman Orch 10/36 Vic 25391
Benny Fields, sung in film
Henry "Red" Allen/<vocal 01/37 Voc 3389

I CAN'T ESCAPE FROM YOU (45)
Famous, pub. 1936, reached #9 in September 1936
Leo Robin w, Richard Whiting m
Featured in RHYTHM ON THE RANGE, film (rel. 07/36)
Bing Crosby Φ sung in film, 09/36 Dec 871
Shep Fields/Charles Chester 08/36 Blu 6475
Eddy Duchin/Jerry Cooper 08/36 Vic 25347
Jimmie Lunceford/Dan Grissom 11/36 Dec 980

I FEEL LIKE A FEATHER IN THE BREEZE
Famous, pub. 1935, reached #6 in February 1936
Mack Gordon w, Harry Revel m
Featured by chorus in COLLEGIATE, film (rel. 02/36)
Jan Garber/Lee Bennett Φ 02/36 Dec 647
Richard Himber/Stuart Allen 01/36 Vic 25189

I'LL SING YOU A THOUSAND LOVE SONGS (13)
J H Remick, pub. 1936, reached #3 in November 1936
Al Dubin w, Harry Warren m
Featured in CAIN AND MABEL, film (rel. 10/36)
Tempo King/<vocal Φ 10/36 Blu 6535
Eddy Duchin/Jimmy Newell Φ 10/36 Vic 25393
Robert Paige, sung in film

I'M AN OLD COWHAND
L Feist, pub. 1936, reached #7 in September 1936
Johnny Mercer w & m
Featured in RHYTHM ON THE RANGE, film (rel. 07/36)
Bing Crosby Φ sung in film, 09/36 Dec 871
Sons of the Pioneers 07/36 Dec 5247
Eddy Duchin/Jerry Cooper 07/36 Vic 25347

I'M BUILDING UP TO AN AWFUL LETDOWN
Berlin, pub. 1935, reached #10 in February 1936
Johnny Mercer w, Fred Astaire m
Fred Astaire/Johnny Green Orch 03/36 Bruns 7610
Eddy Duchin/Lew Sherwood 02/36 Vic 25218
Red McKenzie/<vocal 01/36 Dec 667

I'M GONNA SIT RIGHT DOWN AND WRITE MYSELF A LETTER (43)
Crawford, pub. 1935, reached #4 in March 1936
(Also reached #4 in August 1957)
Joe Young w, Fred Ahlert m
Fats Waller Φ 07/35 Vic 25044
Boswell Sisters Φ 02/36 Dec 671
Hal Kemp/Skinnay Ennis 03/36 Bruns 7601

I'M IN A DANCING MOOD (41)
Crawford, pub. 1936, reached #5 in January 1937
Al Hoffman, Al Goodhart, Maurice Sigler w & m
Tommy Dorsey/Jack Leonard Φ 01/37 Vic 25476
Russ Morgan/<vocal Φ 12/36 Bruns 7777
Bert Ambrose/Jack Cooper 12/36 Dec 911

I'M PUTTING ALL MY EGGS IN ONE BASKET (28)
Berlin, pub. 1936, reached #2 in April 1936
Irving Berlin w & m
Featured in FOLLOW THE FLEET, film (rel. 02/36)
Fred Astaire Φ sung in film, 03/36 Bruns 7609
Guy Lombardo/Carmen Lombardo Φ 03/36 Vic 25242
Jan Garber/Fritz Heilbron Φ 03/36 Dec 699

I'M SHOOTING HIGH
Robbins, pub. 1935, reached #6 in February 1936
Ted Koehler w, Jimmy McHugh m
Featured in KING OF BURLESQUE, film (rel. 12/35)
Jan Garber/Lee Bennett Φ 02/36 Dec 647
Alice Faye, sung in film, 03/36 Melo 60308
Tommy Dorsey/Edythe Wright 02/36 Vic 25216
Little Jack Little/<vocal 02/36 Col 3108-D

I'M TALKING THROUGH MY HEART
Famous, pub. 1936, reached #15 in December 1936
Leo Robin w, Ralph Rainger m
Featured in THE BIG BROADCAST OF 1937, film (rel. 10/36)
Shirley Ross, sung in film
Shep Fields/Dick Robertson 10/36 Blu 6547
Eddy Duchin/Lew Sherwood 10/36 Vic 25390

I'VE GOT YOU UNDER MY SKIN (31)
Chappell, pub. 1936, reached #4 in December 1936
(Also reached #9 in October 1966)
Cole Porter w & m
Featured in BORN TO DANCE, film (rel. 11/36)
Ray Noble/Al Bowlly Φ 11/36 Vic 25422
Virginia Bruce, sung in film
Hal Kemp/Skinnay Ennis 11/36 Bruns 7745
Frances Langford/Jimmy Dorsey Orch 11/36 Dec 939

IF I SHOULD LOSE YOU
Famous, pub. 1935, reached #20 in January 1936
Leo Robin & Ralph Rainger w & m
Featured in ROSE OF THE RANCHO, film (rel. 01/36)
Gladys Swarthout & John Boles, sung in film
Richard Himber/Stuart Allen 12/35 Vic 25179
Isham Jones/Woody Herman 12/35 Dec 605

IN THE CHAPEL IN THE MOONLIGHT (1)
Shapiro, B, pub. 1936, reached #1 in December 1936
(Also reached #6 in August 1954)
Billy Hill w & m
Shep Fields/w.vocal ΦΦ 12/36 Blu 6640
Richard Himber/Stuart Allen 12/36 Vic 25441
Ruth Etting 01/37 Dec 1084
Mal Hallett/Jerry Perkins 12/36 Dec 1033

IS IT TRUE WHAT THEY SAY ABOUT DIXIE? (7)
Irving Caesar Inc, pub. 1936, reached #1 in June 1936
Irving Caesar & Sammy Lerner w, Gerald Marks m
Jimmy Dorsey/Bob Eberle ΦΦ 05/36 Dec 768
Al Jolson, stage and radio
Ozzie Nelson/<vocal Φ 05/36 Bruns 7651
Rudy Vallee, stage, radio, 04/36 Vic 25313
Willie Bryant/<vocal 05/36 Blu 6362

IT'S A SIN TO TELL A LIE (5)
Donaldson, D & G, pub. 1936, reached #2 in July 1936
(Also reached #9 in July 1955)
Billy Mayhew w & m
Fats Waller Φ 07/36 Vic 25342
Bobby Breen, stage, 06/36 Dec 798
Victor Young/Dick Robertson Φ 05/36 Dec 751
Kate Smith, stage and radio
Russ Morgan/Dick Robertson 05/36 Bruns 7637

IT'S BEEN SO LONG (17)
L Feist, pub. 1935, reached #4 in March 1936
Harold Adamson w, Walter Donaldson m
Benny Goodman/Helen Ward ΦΦ 03/36 Vic 25245
Freddy Martin/Terry Shand 03/36 Bruns 7631
Bunny Berigan/Chick Bullock 04/36 Voc 3179
Ruth Etting 04/36 Bruns 7646

IT'S DE-LOVELY (18)
Chappell, pub. 1936, reached #3 in December 1936
Cole Porter w & m
Featured in RED, HOT AND BLUE, show (opened 10/36)
Bob Hope & Ethel Merman, sung in show
Eddy Duchin/Jerry Cooper Φ 11/36 Vic 25432
Ethel Merman 01/37 Liberty Mus Shop 206
Leo Reisman/Sally Singer 11/36 Bruns 7753
Will Osborne/w.vocal duo 01/37 Dec 1058

KNOCK, KNOCK, WHO'S THERE?
L Feist, pub. 1936, reached #14 in September 1936
Bill Tipton, Bill Davies, Johnny Morris, Vincent Lopez w & m
Ted Weems/w.vocal group 09/36 Dec 885
Fletcher Henderson/w.vocal duo 09/36 Vic 25373
Dolly Dawn/George Hall 09/36 Blu 6507

LET YOURSELF GO (49)
Berlin, pub. 1936, reached #5 in April 1936
Irving Berlin w & m
Featured in FOLLOW THE FLEET, film (rel. 02/36)
Fred Astaire & Ginger Rogers, sung in film
Fred Astaire/Johnny Green Orch Φ 03/36 Bruns 7608
Boswell Sisters 03/36 Dec 709
Ray Noble/Al Bowlly 03/36 Vic 25241

LET'S FACE THE MUSIC AND DANCE
Berlin, pub. 1936, reached #8 in March 1936
Irving Berlin w & m
Featured in FOLLOW THE FLEET, film (rel. 02/36)
Fred Astaire, sung in film, 03/36 Bruns 7608
Ted FioRito/Stanley Hickman 03/36 Dec 697
Ray Noble/Al Bowlly 03/36 Vic 25241

LET'S SING AGAIN
L Feist, pub. 1936, reached #14 in July 1936
Gus Kahn w, Jimmy McHugh m
Featured in LET'S SING AGAIN, film (rel. 04/36)
Bobby Breen, sung in film, 07/36 Dec 798
Fats Waller 07/36 Vic 25348
Ted Weems/Elmo Tanner 07/36 Dec 820

LIGHTS OUT (10)
Shapiro, B, pub. 1935, reached #2 in March 1936
Billy Hill w & m
Eddy Duchin/Lew Sherwood Φ 02/36 Vic 25212
Victor Young/Dick Robertson Φ 03/36 Dec 703
George Hall/Johnny McKeever 02/36 Blu 6215
Ozzie Nelson, stage

A LITTLE RENDEZVOUS IN HONOLULU
J Morris, pub. 1935, reached #16 in March 1936
Edgar Leslie w, Joe Burke m
Tommy Dorsey/Jack Leonard 03/36 Vic 25246
Jan Garber/Lee Bennett 03/36 Dec 693

LOST (11)
Robbins, pub. 1936, reached #1 in May 1936
Johnny Mercer & Macy Teetor w, Phil Ohman m
Guy Lombardo/Carmen Lombardo Φ 04/36 Vic 25271
Jan Garber/Lee Bennett Φ 04/36 Dec 739
Hal Kemp/Bob Allen 04/36 Bruns 7626

LOVE IS LIKE A CIGARETTE
Shapiro, B, pub. 1935, reached #12 in May 1936
Richard Jerome w, Walter Kent m
Duke Ellington/Ivie Anderson 04/36 Bruns 7627
Eddy Duchin/Pete Woolery 04/36 Vic 25264

LOVELY LADY
Robbins, pub. 1935, reached #20 in April 1936
Ted Koehler w, Jimmy McHugh m
Featured in KING OF BURLESQUE, film (rel. 12/35)
Kenny Baker, sung in film
Tommy Dorsey/Buddy Gately 03/36 Vic 25216
Bing Crosby 05/36 Dec 756

ME AND THE MOON (27)
Santly-Joy, pub. 1936, reached #6 in October 1936
Walter Hirsch w, Lou Handman m
Bing Crosby Φ 10/36 Dec 912
Hal Kemp/Maxine Grey Φ 09/36 Bruns 7707
Shep Fields/Dick Robertson 10/36 Blu 6548

A MELODY FROM THE SKY (12)
Famous, pub. 1936, reached #1 in May 1936
Sidney D Mitchell w, Louis Alter m
Featured in THE TRAIL OF THE LONESOME PINE, film (rel. 02/36)
Jan Garber/Lee Bennett Φ 05/36 Dec 761
Fuzzy Knight, sung in film
Eddy Duchin/Pete Woolery Φ 04/36 Vic 25254
Bunny Berigan/Chick Bullock 06/36 Voc 3224
Sons of the Pioneers 05/36 Dec 5222

MIDNIGHT BLUE
Robbins, pub. 1936, reached #14 in December 1936
Edgar Leslie w, Joe Burke m
Russ Morgan/w.vocal 10/36 Bruns 7737
Shep Fields/Charles Chester 10/36 Blu 6511
Henry "Red" Allen/<vocal 12/36 Voc 3339

MOON OVER MIAMI (22)
Berlin, pub. 1935, reached #2 in February 1936
Edgar Leslie w, Joe Burke m
Eddy Duchin/Lew Sherwood Φ 02/36 Vic 25212
Jan Garber/Lee Bennett Φ 02/36 Dec 651
Lud Gluskin/Buddy Clark 02/36 Bruns 7590
Connie Boswell 02/36 Dec 657
Ted FioRito Orch, stage

THE MUSIC GOES 'ROUND AND AROUND (24)
Select M P I, pub. 1935, reached #1 in January 1936
"Red" Hodgson w, Mike Riley & Ed Farley m
Featured in SING, BABY, SING, film (rel. 08/36)
Riley-Farley Orch/<vocal duo Φ 12/35 Dec 578
Tommy Dorsey/Edythe Wright Φ 01/36 Vic 25201
Ritz Brothers, sung in film
Hal Kemp/Saxie Dowell 02/36 Bruns 7587
Wingy Manone/<vocal 01/36 Voc 3134

NO REGRETS (44)
Sherman Clay, pub. 1936, reached #7 in August 1936
Harry Tobias w, Roy Ingraham m
Tommy Dorsey/Jack Leonard 08/36 Vic 25349
Billie Holiday Orch/<vocal 08/36 Voc 3276
Glen Gray & The Casa Loma Orch, stage

ON THE BEACH AT BALI BALI (26)
J Morris, pub. 1936, reached #3 in August 1936
Al Sherman & Jack Meeskill w, Abner Silver m
Connie Boswell Φ 07/36 Dec 829
Tommy Dorsey/Edythe Wright Φ 07/36 Vic 25349
Leo Reisman/Larry Stewart 08/36 Bruns 7696
Shep Fields/Charles Chester 07/36 Blu 6417

ONE NIGHT IN MONTE CARLO
Santly-Joy, pub. 1935, reached #14 in January 1936
Al Sherman & Al Lewis w, Abner Silver m
Freddy Martin/Elmer Feldkamp 12/35 Bruns 7559
Tommy Dorsey/Edythe Wright 02/36 Vic 25220

ORGAN GRINDER'S SWING (16)
Exclusive, pub. 1936, reached #5 in November 1936
Mitchell Parish & Irving Mills w, Will Hudson m
Jimmie Lunceford Orch Φ 10/36 Dec 908
Benny Goodman Orch Φ 11/36 Vic 25442
Hudson-DeLange Orch 06/36 Bruns 7656
Tempo King/<vocal 10/36 Blu 6533

PLEASE BELIEVE ME
Sherman Clay, pub. 1935, reached #8 in March 1936
Larry Yoell w, Al Jacobs m
Al Donahue/Barry McKinley 02/36 Dec 665
Wingy Manone/<vocal 03/36 Voc 3159
Jane Froman 03/36 Dec 710

RENDEZVOUS WITH A DREAM (35)
Famous, pub. 1936, reached #5 in August 1936
Leo Robin & Ralph Rainger w & m
Featured in POPPY, film (rel. 06/36)
Rachelle Hudson, sung in film
Jan Garber/Russell Brown 08/36 Dec 867
Johnny Green/w.vocal 07/36 Bruns 7662
Shep Fields/Charles Chester 07/36 Blu 6418

RHYTHM IN MY NURSERY RHYMES
Select M P I, pub. 1935, reached #8 in February 1936
Sammy Cahn & Don Raye w, Jimmie Lunceford & Saul Chaplin m
Tommy Dorsey/Edythe Wright Φ 01/36 Vic 25201
Jimmie Lunceford/Willie Smith 11/35 Dec 572

RIDE, RED, RIDE
Milson's M P C, pub. 1935, reached #20 in March 1936
Irving Mills w, Lucky Millinder m
Mills Blue Rhythm Band/Lucky Millinder Φ 10/35 Col 3087-D

ROBINS AND ROSES (20)
Berlin, pub. 1936, reached #2 in June 1936
Edgar Leslie w, Joe Burke m
Bing Crosby Φ 05/36 Dec 791
Tommy Dorsey/Edythe Wright 05/36 Vic 25284
Orville Knapp/w.vocal 05/36 Bruns 7649
Dolly Dawn/George Hall Orch[3] 06/36 Blu 6381

SANTA CLAUS IS COMIN' TO TOWN
L Feist, pub. 1934, reached #11 in December 1936
(Also reached Top 20 in December 1934, 1935, 1947, 1948)
Haven Gillespie w, J Fred Coots m
All-time Christmas standard
Tommy Dorsey/w.vocal duo 12/36 Vic 25145
George Hall/Sonny Schuyler 12/36 Blu 5711

SHE SHALL HAVE MUSIC (39)
Chappell, pub. 1935, reached #7 in June 1936
Maurice Sigler, Al Goodhart, Al Hoffman w & m
Lud Gluskin/Buddy Clark 06/36 Bruns 7658
Jack Hylton/Sam Costa 04/36 Vic 25275
Louis Levy/Robert Ashley 05/36 Col 3130-D

SHOE SHINE BOY
Mills, pub. 1936, reached #17 in July 1936
Sammy Cahn w, Saul Chaplin m
Featured in CONNIE'S HOT CHOCOLATES, revue (revival) (1936)
Louis Armstrong, sung in revue
Wingy Manone/<vocal 05/36 Voc 3192
Duke Ellington/Ivie Anderson 09/36 Bruns 7710

SING AN OLD FASHIONED SONG
Crawford, pub. 1935, reached #14 in April 1936
Joe Young w, Fred Ahlert m
Fats Waller 03/36 Vic 25253
Jack Shilkret/Chick Bullock 03/36 Bruns 7603

SING, BABY, SING (37)
Sam Fox, pub. 1936, reached #6 in November 1936
Jack Yellen w, Lew Pollack m
Featured in SING, BABY, SING, film (rel. 08/36)
Alice Faye, sung in film
Ruby Newman/Barry McKinley Φ 10/36 Vic 25401
Charlie Barnet/<vocal 11/36 Blu 6593
Teddy Wilson/Red Harper 10/36 Bruns 7736

SING ME A SWING SONG (AND LET ME DANCE)
Southern M P C, pub. 1936, reached #15 in July 1936
Stanley Adams w, Hoagy Carmichael m
Chick Webb/Ella Fitzgerald 07/36 Dec 830
Benny Goodman/Helen Ward 07/36 Vic 25340

SING, SING, SING
Robbins, pub. 1936, reached #12 in October 1936
Louis Prima w & m
All-time jazz standard
Louis Prima/<vocal, stage, 04/36 Bruns 7628
Fletcher Henderson/Arthur Lee "Georgia Boy" Simpkins 09/36 Vic 25375

SOUTH SEA ISLAND MAGIC (25)
Select M P I, pub. 1936, reached #7 in November 1936
Lysle Tomerlyn w, Andy Iona Long m
Bing Crosby Φ 09/36 Dec 886
George Hall/Johnny McKeever 09/36 Blu 6509

SPREADIN' RHYTHM AROUND
Robbins, pub. 1935, reached #20 in March 1936
Ted Koehler w, Jimmy McHugh m
Featured in KING OF BURLESQUE, film (rel. 12/35)
Alice Faye, sung in film, 03/36 Melo 60308
Fats Waller 02/36 Vic 25211

A STAR FELL OUT OF HEAVEN (15)
Crawford, pub. 1936, reached #2 in September 1936
Mack Gordon w, Harry Revel m
Featured in POOR LITTLE RICH GIRL, film (rel. 06/36)
Tony Martin, sung in film, 10/36 Dec 884
Hal Kemp/Bob Allen Φ 09/36 Bruns 7707
Ben Bernie/Ray Hendricks 09/36 Dec 878

STOMPIN' AT THE SAVOY
Robbins, pub. 1936, reached #17 in July 1936
Andy Razaf w, Benny Goodman, Chick Webb & Edgar Sampson m
Big band classic
Benny Goodman Orch 06/36 Vic 25247, 03/37 Vic 25521[2]
Chick Webb Orch 05/36 Col 2926-D, 07/36 Voc 3246

SWINGTIME IN THE ROCKIES
Robbins, pub. 1936, reached #18 in August 1936
Jimmy Mundy & Benny Goodman m
Benny Goodman Orch Φ 08/36 Vic 25355

TAKE MY HEART (33)
Crawford, pub. 1936, reached #4 in July 1936
Joe Young w, Fred Ahlert m
Eddy Duchin/Jerry Cooper Φ 07/36 Vic 25343
Nat Brandwynne/Buddy Clark Φ 07/36 Bruns 7676
Jan Garber/Russell Brown 08/36 Dec 851

THERE IS NO GREATER LOVE
I Jones M C, pub. 1936, reached #15 in May 1936
Marty Symes w, Isham Jones m
Isham Jones/Woody Herman 04/36 Dec 704
Guy Lombardo/Carmen Lombardo 04/36 Vic 25271
Duke Ellington/Ivie Anderson 04/36 Bruns 7625

THERE'S A SMALL HOTEL (42)
Chappell, pub. 1936, reached #5 in July 1936
Lorenz Hart w, Richard Rodgers m
Featured in ON YOUR TOES, show (opened 04/36)
Ray Bolger, sung in show
Hal Kemp/Maxine Grey Φ 05/36 Bruns 7634
Paul Whiteman/Durelle Alexander 05/36 Vic 25270

THESE FOOLISH THINGS (19)
Berlin, pub. 1935, reached #1 in July 1936
Holt Marvell w, Jack Strachey & Harry Link m
Featured in SPREAD IT ABROAD, revue (opened 04/36)
Benny Goodman/Helen Ward Φ 07/36 Vic 25351
Teddy Wilson/Billie Holiday Φ 08/36 Bruns 7699
Madge Elliot & Cyril Richard, sung in revue
Nat Brandwynne/Buddy Clark 07/36 Bruns 7676

THROUGH THE COURTESY OF LOVE
Witmark, pub. 1936, reached #20 in October 1936
Jack Scholl w, M K Jerome m
Featured in HERE COMES CARTER, film (rel. 11/36)
Ross Alexander, sung in film
Bob Crosby/<vocal 10/36 Dec 903

TORMENTED (47)
Mills, pub. 1936, reached #7 in May 1936
Will Hudson w & m
Richard Himber/Stuart Allen Φ 05/36 Vic 25293
Hudson-DeLange Orch/Ruth Gaylor 03/36 Bruns 7598
Wingy Manone/<vocal 05/36 Blu 6359

THE TOUCH OF YOUR LIPS (46)
Santly Bros, pub. 1936, reached #6 in May 1936
Ray Noble w & m
Ray Noble/Al Bowlly Φ stage, 04/36 Vic 25277
Bing Crosby Φ 05/36 Dec 757
Hal Kemp/Skinnay Ennis Φ 04/36 Bruns 7626

TWILIGHT ON THE TRAIL
Famous, pub. 1936, reached #18 in July 1936
Sidney D Mitchell w, Louis Alter m
Featured in TRAIL OF THE LONESOME PINE, film (rel. 02/36)
Fuzzy Knight, sung in film
Bing Crosby 05/36 Dec 757

UNTIL THE REAL THING COMES ALONG (23)
Chappell, pub. 1936, reached #3 in September 1936
Sammy Cahn, Saul Chaplin, L E Freeman, Mann Holiner, Alberta Nichols w & m
Andy Kirk/Pha Terrell Φ 07/36 Dec 809
Fats Waller Φ 09/36 Vic 25374
Jan Garber/Russell Brown Φ 09/36 Dec 891

UNTIL TODAY
Marlo Mus, pub. 1936, reached #20 in September 1936
Benny Davis w, J Fred Coots & Oscar Levant m
Fletcher Henderson Orch 09/36 Vic 25373
Nat Brandwynne/Buddy Clark 09/36 Bruns 7712
Ted Weems/Perry Como 10/36 Dec 895

US ON A BUS
Famous, pub. 1936, reached #16 in May 1936
Tot Seymour w, Vee Lawnhurst m
Fats Waller Φ 05/36 Vic 25295
Shep Fields/Mary Jane Walsh 07/36 Blu 6418
Rudy Vallee/<vocal 06/36 Melotone 60608

WAH-HOO!
Crawford, pub. 1936, reached #6 in April 1936
Cliff Friend w & m
Paul Whiteman/Durelle Alexander Φ 03/36 Vic 25252
Top Hatters 04/36 Dec 711
Jimmy Dorsey/w.vocal trio 05/36 Dec 762

THE WAY YOU LOOK TONIGHT (3)
T B Harms, pub. 1936, reached #1 in November 1936
(Also reached #13 in October 1961)
Dorothy Fields w, Jerome Kern m
Featured in SWING TIME, film (rel. 08/36)
Fred Astaire ΦΦ sung in film, 09/36 Bruns 7717
Guy Lombardo/Carmen Lombardo Φ 09/36 Vic 25372
Teddy Wilson/Billie Holiday Φ 12/36 Bruns 7762
Bing & Dixie Lee Crosby 10/36 Dec 907
Shep Fields/Charles Chester 09/36 Blu 6505

WEST WIND
Ager, Y & B, pub. 1936, reached #13 in April 1936
Charles Newman w, Murray Mencher & Milt Ager m
Fats Waller Φ 03/36 Vic 25253
Joe Moss/w.vocal 03/36 Bruns 7617

WHAT'S THE NAME OF THAT SONG?
Pop Melodies, pub. 1936, reached #9 in April 1936
Tot Seymour w, Vee Lawnhurst m
Ozzie Nelson/<vocal 03/36 Bruns 7620
Bob Crosby/<vocal 04/36 Dec 727

WHEN A LADY MEETS A GENTLEMAN DOWN SOUTH
Pop Melodies, pub. 1936, reached #13 in October 1936
Jacques Krakeur, Dave Oppenheim, Michael Cleary w & m
Dolly Dawn/George Hall Orch[3] 09/36 Blu 6507
Ted Weems/Red Ingle 10/36 Dec 885
Russ Morgan/Linda Lee 10/36 Bruns 7728

WHEN DID YOU LEAVE HEAVEN? (2)
Robbins, pub. 1936, reached #1 in October 1936
Walter Bullock w, Richard Whiting m
Featured in SING, BABY, SING, film (rel. 03/36)
Guy Lombardo/Carmen Lombardo ΦΦ 08/36 Vic 25357
Tony Martin, sung in film, 10/36 Dec 884
Ben Bernie/Ray Hendricks 09/36 Dec 878
Hal Kemp/Skinnay Ennis 09/36 Bruns 7711
Henry "Red" Allen/<vocal 11/36 Voc 3302

WHEN I'M WITH YOU (32)
Robbins, pub. 1936, reached #2 in August 1936
Mack Gordon w, Harry Revel m
Featured in POOR LITTLE RICH GIRL, film (rel. 06/36)
Shirley Temple & Tony Martin, sung in film
Hal Kemp/Skinnay Ennis Φ 07/36 Bruns 7681
Ray Noble/Al Bowlly 07/36 Vic 25336

WHO LOVES YOU?
J Morris, pub. 1936, reached #10 in November 1936
Benny Davis w, J Fred Coots m
Teddy Wilson/Billie Holiday 11/36 Bruns 7768
George Hall/Dolly Dawn 11/36 Blu 6591
Rudy Vallee/<vocal 01/37 Melotone 70101

WITH ALL MY HEART
L Feist, pub. 1935, reached #8 in February 1936
Gus Kahn w, Jimmy McHugh m
Featured in HER MASTER'S VOICE, film (rel. 02/36)
Hal Kemp/Maxine Grey Φ 01/36 Bruns 7565
Glen Gray/Kenny Sargent 02/36 Dec 652
Peggy Conklin, sung in film

WOULD YOU? (21)
Robbins, pub. 1936, reached #6 in June 1936
Arthur Freed w, Nacio Herb Brown m
Featured in SAN FRANCISCO, film (rel. 06/36)
Jeanette MacDonald, sung in film
Bing Crosby 05/36 Dec 756
George Hall/Johnny McKeever Φ 06/36 Blu 6378
Henry King/Joe Sudy 05/36 Dec 760

YOU (30)
L Feist, pub. 1936, reached #4 in May 1936
Harold Adamson w, Walter Donaldson m
Sung by chorus in THE GREAT ZIEGFELD, film (rel. 04/36)
Tommy Dorsey/Edythe Wright Φ 05/36 Vic 25291
Jimmy Dorsey/Bob Eberle 05/36 Dec 764
Freddy Martin/Elmer Feldkamp 03/36 Bruns 7631

YOU CAN'T PULL THE WOOL OVER MY EYES (48)
Ager, Y & B, pub. 1936, reached #7 in August 1936
Charles Newman w, Murray Mencher & Milt Ager m
Benny Goodman/Helen Ward Φ 06/36 Vic 25316
Ted Weems/Perry Como 07/36 Dec 820
Dolly Dawn/George Hall Orch[3] 06/36 Blu 6382

YOU DO THE DARNDEST THINGS, BABY
Movietone Mus, pub. 1936, reached #16 in November 1936
Sidney D Mitchell w, Lew Pollack m
Featured in PIGSKIN PARADE, film (rel. 10/36)
Jack Haley, sung in film
Guy Lombardo/w.vocal trio 11/36 Vic 25421
Charlie Barnet/<vocal 11/36 Blu 6594

YOU STARTED ME DREAMING (38)
Marlo Mus, pub. 1936, reached #4 in May 1936
Benny Davis w, J F Coots m
Tommy Dorsey/Joe Dixon Φ 05/36 Vic 25284
Wingy Manone/<vocal 05/36 Blu 6359
Connie Boswell 06/36 Dec 794

YOU TURNED THE TABLES ON ME (34)
Sam Fox, pub. 1936, reached #5 in November 1936
Sidney D Mitchell w, Louis Alter m
Featured in SING, BABY, SING, film (rel. 08/36)
Benny Goodman/Helen Ward Φ 10/36 Vic 25391
Alice Faye, sung in film
Jan Garber/Russell Brown 09/36 Dec 891

YOU'RE NOT THE KIND
Mills, pub. 1936, reached #16 in August 1936
Irving Mills w, Will Hudson m
Hudson-DeLange Orch/Ruth Gaylor 06/36 Bruns 7656
Fats Waller 07/36 Vic 25353

YOURS TRULY IS TRULY YOURS
Mills, pub. 1936, reached #17 in May 1936
Benny Davis, Ted FioRito, J Fred Coots w & m
Ted FioRito/Muzzy Marcellino 03/36 Dec 746
Leo Reisman/Benny Davis 03/36 Bruns 6514

[1]Virginia Verrill's voice was dubbed for Jean Harlow.
[2]Goodman's 1937 recording was done by his quartet, not his orchestra.
[3]Billed on record as Dolly Dawn and her Dawn Patrol.
[4]Lionel Hampton on vibes and vocal

1937

AFRAID TO DREAM
Miller, pub. 1937, reached #8 in September 1937
Mack Gordon & Harry Revel w & m
Featured in YOU CAN'T HAVE EVERYTHING, film (rel. 07/37)
Tony Martin & Alice Faye, sung in film
Benny Goodman/Betty Van Φ 08/37 Vic 25627

THE BIG APPLE
Crawford, pub. 1937, reached #11 in October 1937
Buddy Bernier w, Bob Emmerich m
Tommy Dorsey & His Clambake Seven/Edythe Wright Φ 09/37 Vic 25652
Teddy Wilson/Frances Hunt 10/37 Bruns 7954
Clyde Lucas Orch 10/37 Variety 631, 12/37 Voc 3782

BLOSSOMS ON BROADWAY (32)
Famous, pub. 1937, reached #5 in November 1937
Leo Robin & Ralph Rainger w & m
Featured in BLOSSOMS ON BROADWAY, film (rel. 11/37)
Guy Lombardo/Lebert Lombardo Φ 10/37 Vic 25659
Shirley Ross, sung in film
Dick Robertson/<vocal Φ 10/37 Dec 1415
Dolly Dawn/George Hall Orch 11/37 Voc 3790

BLUE HAWAII (21)
Famous, pub. 1937, reached #7 in July 1937
Leo Robin & Ralph Rainger w & m
Featured in WAIKIKI WEDDING, film (rel. 03/37)
Bing Crosby Φ sung in film, 04/37 Dec 1175
George Hall/Dolly Dawn 04/37 Blu 6859

BOB WHITE (WHATCHA GONNA SWING TONIGHT?) (44)
Remick, pub. 1937, reached #6 in January 1938
Johnny Mercer w, Bernie Hanighen m
Bing Crosby & Connie Boswell Φ 11/37 Dec 1483
Johnny Mercer 12/37 Bruns 7988
Benny Goodman/Martha Tilton 11/37 Vic 25683
Mildred Bailey Orch/<vocal 11/37 Voc 3712

BOO-HOO (16)
Shapiro, B, pub. 1937, reached #1 in April 1937
Edward Heyman w, Carmen Lombardo & John Jacob Loeb m
Guy Lombardo/w.vocal trio ΦΦ 03/37 Vic 25522
Mal Hallett/Jerry Perkins Φ 04/37 Dec 1162
Wingy Manone/<vocal 03/37 Blu 6806

CAN I FORGET YOU?
Chappell, pub. 1937, reached #17 in October 1937
Oscar Hammerstein 2nd w, Jerome Kern m
Featured in HIGH, WIDE AND HANDSOME, film (rel. 07/37)
Irene Dunn, sung in film
Guy Lombardo/Carmen Lombardo 08/37 Vic 25615
Bing Crosby 11/37 Dec 1462

CARAVAN
Exclusive, pub. 1937, reached #11 in August 1937
(Also reached #11 in April 1953)
Irving Mills w, Juan Tizol & Duke Ellington m
Duke Ellington Orch Φ 07/37 Master 131
Barney Bigard & His Jazzopators 06/37 Variety 515, 12/37 Voc 3809

CARELESSLY (29)
Berlin, pub. 1937, reached #2 in May 1937
Charles Kenny & Nick Kenny w, Norman Ellis m
Teddy Wilson/Billie Holiday ΦΦ 05/37 Bruns 7867
Lennie Hayton/Paul Barry 06/37 Dec 1248
Kay Thompson/<vocal 05/37 Vic 25564

'CAUSE MY BABY SAYS IT'S SO
J H Remick, pub. 1937, reached #16 in July 1937
Al Dubin w, Harry Warren m
Featured in THE SINGING MARINE, film (rel. 06/37)
Dick Powell, sung in film, 07/37 Dec 1310
Bunny Berigan/<vocal 06/37 Vic 25562
Kay Kyser/w.vocal 07/37 Bruns 7891

THE DREAM IN MY HEART
T B Harms, pub. 1937, reached #17 in July 1937
Joe Thompson w, Edna Fischer m
The Musical Musketeers/Jimmy Ray 08/37 Blu 7080

EBB TIDE
Pop Melodies, pub. 1937, reached #12 in December 1937
Leo Robin w, Ralph Rainger m
Bunny Berigan/Gail Reese 10/37 Vic 25664
Claude Thornhill/Barry McKinley 10/37 Bruns 7957
Dick Robertson/<vocal 10/37 Dec 1407

FAREWELL, MY LOVE
T B Harms, pub. 1937, reached #12 in December 1937
Harry Kogen & Lou Holzer w, Henry Busse m
Russ Morgan/Mert Curtis 12/37 Bruns 8009
Guy Lombardo/Carmen Lombardo 12/37 Vic 25713
Glen Gray/Kenny Sargent 12/37 Dec 1519

THE FIRST TIME I SAW YOU (45)
Select M P I, pub. 1937, reached #6 in September 1937
Allie Wrubel w, Nat Shilkret m
Featured in THE TOAST OF NEW YORK, film (rel. 07/37)
Bunny Berigan/Ford Leary Φ 07/37 Vic 25593
Jimmie Lunceford/Dan Grissom Φ 08/37 Dec 1364
Frances Farmer, sung in film

A FOGGY DAY
Gershwin P C, pub. 1937, reached #14 in Dec 1937
Ira Gershwin w, George Gershwin m
Featured in DAMSEL IN DISTRESS, film (rel. 11/37)
Fred Astaire, sung in film, 12/37 Bruns 7982
Bob Crosby/Kay Weber 12/37 Dec 1539
Shep Fields/Bob Goday 11/37 Blu 7195

GETTING SOME FUN OUT OF LIFE
Donaldson, D & G, pub. 1937, reached #20 in November 1937
Edgar Leslie w, Joe Burke m
Billie Holiday Orch/<vocal 10/37 Voc 3701
Tommy Dorsey/Edythe Wright 11/37 Vic 25694
Dick Robertson/<vocal 11/37 Dec 1487

GONE WITH THE WIND (49)
Berlin, pub. 1937, reached #8 in August 1937
Herb Magidson w, Allie Wrubel m
Guy Lombardo/Carmen Lombardo Φ 08/37 Vic 25594
Horace Heidt/Larry Cotton Φ 08/37 Bruns 7913
Shep Fields/Bob Goday 07/37 Blu 7016

GOODNIGHT, MY LOVE (7)
Robbins, pub. 1936, reached #1 in February 1937
Mack Gordon w, Harry Revel m
Featured in STOWAWAY, film (rel. 12/36)
Benny Goodman/Ella Fitzgerald ΦΦ 12/36 Vic 25461
Shirley Temple, sung in film
Alice Faye, sung in film, 03/37 Bruns 7821
Hal Kemp/Bob Allen 01/37 Bruns 7783
Benny Goodman/Frances Hunt 02/37 Vic 25461

HARBOR LIGHTS (5)
Marlo Mus, pub. 1937, reached #5 in October 1937
(Also reached #1 in November 1950)
(Also reached #8 in April 1960)
Jimmy Kennedy w, Will Grosz m
Rudy Vallee/<vocal Φ 09/37 Blu 7067
Frances Langford Φ 10/37 Dec 1441
Claude Thornhill/Jimmy Farrell Φ 08/37 Voc 3595

HAVE YOU GOT ANY CASTLES, BABY? (36)
Harms, pub. 1937, reached #4 in October 1937
Johnny Mercer w, Richard Whiting m
Featured in VARSITY SHOW, film (rel. 08/37)
Dolly Dawn/George Hall Orch[2] Φ 09/37 Voc 3780, 09/37 Variety 621
Dick Powell, sung in film, 10/37 Dec 1430
Tommy Dorsey/Jack Leonard Φ 09/37 Vic 25635
Priscilla Lane, sung in film

HOW COULD YOU?
J H Remick, pub. 1937, reached #17 in May 1937
Al Dubin w, Harry Warren m
Anson Weeks/Margie Dee 03/37 Dec 1134
Tommy Dorsey/Edythe Wright 03/37 Vic 25513
Teddy Wilson/Billie Holiday 05/37 Bruns 7867

I KNOW NOW (26)
J H Remick, pub. 1937, reached #4 in August 1937
Al Dubin w, Harry Warren m
Featured in THE SINGING MARINE, film (rel. 07/37)
Dick Powell, sung in film, 07/37 Dec 1310
Guy Lombardo/Carmen Lombardo Φ 06/37 Vic 25566
Lennie Hayton/Paul Barry 07/37 Dec 1267
Doris Weston, sung in film

I STILL LOVE TO KISS YOU GOODNIGHT
L Feist, pub. 1937, reached #7 in December 1937
Walter Bullock w, Harold Spina m
Featured in FIFTY-SECOND STREET, film (rel. 11/37)
Bing Crosby Φ 11/37 Dec 1451
Shep Fields/Bob Goday Φ 10/37 Blu 7139
Pat Peterson, sung in film

I'VE GOT MY LOVE TO KEEP ME WARM (39)
Berlin, pub. 1937, reached #4 in April 1937
(Also reached #5 in February 1949)
Irving Berlin w & m
Featured in ON THE AVENUE, film (rel. 02/37)
Ray Noble/Howard Phillips Φ 02/37 Vic 25507
Dick Powell, sung in film, 03/37 Dec 1149
Alice Faye, sung in film, 03/37 Bruns 7821
Billie Holiday Orch/<vocal 02/37 Voc 3431
Glen Gray/Kenny Sargent 03/37 Dec 1126

IF IT'S THE LAST THING I DO
Crawford, pub. 1937, reached #6 in December 1937
Sammy Cahn w, Saul Chaplin m
Tommy Dorsey/Jack Leonard Φ 10/37 Vic 25686
Frances Langford 11/37 Dec 1464

INDIAN LOVE CALL
T B Harms, pub. 1924, reached #20 in January 1937
(Also reached #7 in March 1925)
(Also reached #13 in September 1952)
Otto Harbach & Oscar Hammerstein 2nd w, Rudolf Friml m
Featured in ROSE MARIE, film (rel. 01/36)
Jeanette MacDonald & Nelson Eddy Φ sung in film and 12/36 Vic 4323

IT LOOKS LIKE RAIN IN CHERRY BLOSSOM LANE (4)
J Morris, pub. 1937, reached #1 in July 1937
Edgar Leslie w, Joe Burke m
Guy Lombardo/Lebert Lombardo ΦΦ 06/37 Vic 25572
Shep Fields/Bob Goday Φ 06/37 Blu 6953
Lennie Hayton/Paul Barry 06/37 Dec 1248

IT'S THE NATURAL THING TO DO
Select M P I, pub. 1937, reached #12 in September 1937
Johnny Burke w, Arthur Johnston m
Featured in DOUBLE OR NOTHING, film (rel. 08/37)
Bing Crosby Φ sung in film, 08/37 Dec 1376
Mildred Bailey/<vocal 08/37 Voc 3626
Horace Heidt/King Sisters 09/37 Bruns 7927

JOSEPHINE (48)
L Feist, pub. 1937, reached #16 in April 1937
(Reached second peak at #12 in October 1937)
(Also reached #16 in July 1951)
Gus Kahn w, Wayne King & Burke Bivins m
Wayne King Orch Φ 03/37 Vic 25518
Tommy Dorsey Orch Φ 10/37 Vic 25676
Sammy Kaye Orch 10/37 Voc 3681

LET'S CALL THE WHOLE THING OFF
Gerswhin P C, pub. 1937, reached #14 in May 1937
Ira Gershwin w, George Gershwin m
Featured in SHALL WE DANCE, film (rel. 04/37)
Fred Astaire & Ginger Rogers, sung in film
Fred Astaire 04/37 Bruns 7857
Shep Fields/Bob Goday 05/37 Blu 6878
Eddy Duchin/Jerry Cooper 06/37 Vic 25569

LITTLE OLD LADY (8)
Chappell, pub. 1936, reached #2 in April 1937
Stanley Adams w, Hoagy Carmichael m
Featured in THE SHOW IS ON, revue (opened 12/36)
Ray Noble/Al Bowlly Φ 12/36 Vic 25448
Mitzi Mayfair & Charles Walters, sung in revue
Shep Fields/Bob Goday Φ 02/37 Blu 6747
Abe Lyman/Sonny Schuyler Φ 03/37 Dec 1120

LOVE AND LEARN
Chappell, pub. 1936, reached #15 in February 1937
Edward Heyman w, Arthur Schwartz m
Featured in THE GIRL FROM PARIS, film (rel. 01/37)
Eddy Duchin/Jerry Cooper 01/37 Vic 25472
Shep Fields/Bob Goday 02/37 Blu 6749
Artie Shaw/Peg LaCentra 01/37 Bruns 7787

THE LOVE BUG WILL BITE YOU (42)
Santly Bros, pub. 1937, reached #4 in May 1937
Pinky Tomlin w & m
Pinky Tomlin Φ 04/37 Bruns 7849
Guy Lombardo/w.vocal trio Φ 05/37 Vic 25548
Jimmy Dorsey/Ray McKinley 05/37 Dec 1187
Teddy Hill/w.vocal group 05/37 Blu 6897

MARIE
Berlin, pub. 1928, reached #11 in April 1937
(Also reached #2 in February 1929)
(Also reached #17 in January 1954 and #15 in July 1965)
Irving Berlin w & m
Big band classic
Tommy Dorsey/Jack Lawrence ΦΦ 03/37 Vic 25523

MAY I HAVE THE NEXT ROMANCE WITH YOU?
L Feist, pub. 1936, reached #13 in March 1937
Mack Gordon w, Harry Revel m
Featured in HEAD OVER HEELS, film (rel. 02/37)
Tommy Dorsey/Jack Leonard 01/37 Vic 25487
Jessie Matthews & Louis Borrell, sung in film
Shep Fields/Bob Goday 01/37 Blu 6689

ME, MYSELF AND I (ARE ALL IN LOVE WITH YOU)
Words & Mus, pub. 1937, reached #20 in August 1937[1]
Irving Gordon, Allan Roberts, Al Kaufman w & m
Billie Holiday Orch/<vocal 07/37 Voc 3593
Bob Howard/<vocal 06/37 Dec 1205

MEAN TO ME
Crawford; orig. pub. 1929, reached #19 in July 1937
(Also reached #3 in May 1929)
Roy Turk w, Fred Ahlert m
Teddy Wilson/Billie Holiday Φ 06/37 Bruns 7903

THE MERRY-GO-ROUND BROKE DOWN (22)
Harms, pub. 1937, reached #1 in July 1937
Cliff Friend & Dave Franklin w & m
Eddy Duchin/Lew Sherwood Φ 06/37 Vic 25585
Russ Morgan/Jimmy Lewis Φ 06/37 Bruns 7888
Shep Fields/Bob Goday Φ 07/37 Blu 7015
Jimmie Lunceford/Sy Oliver 08/37 Dec 1318

THE MOON GOT IN MY EYES (31)
Select M P I, pub. 1937, reached #3 in October 1937
Johnny Burke w, Arthur Johnston m
Featured in DOUBLE OR NOTHING, film (rel. 08/37)
Bing Crosby Φ sung in film, 09/37 Dec 1375
Mildred Bailey/<vocal 08/37 Voc 3626
Shep Fields/Bob Goday 09/37 Blu 7099
Horace Heidt/Larry Cotton 08/37 Bruns 7927

MOONLIGHT AND SHADOWS (12)
Pop Melodies, pub. 1936, reached #1 in March 1937
Leo Robin & Fred Hollander w & m
Featured in JUNGLE PRINCESS, film (rel. 11/36)
Dorothy Lamour, sung in film, 03/37 Bruns 7829
Shep Fields/Bob Goday Φ 03/37 Blu 6803
Eddy Duchin/Lew Sherwood Φ 03/37 Vic 25514
Bing Crosby 04/37 Dec 1186

MY CABIN OF DREAMS (15)
Berlin, pub. 1937, reached #3 in September 1937
Al Frazzini & Nat Madison w & m
Tommy Dorsey/Edythe Wright Φ 08/37 Vic 25620
Gus Arnheim/Jimmy Farrell 09/37 Bruns 7933
Frances Langford 11/37 Dec 1441

(THIS IS) MY LAST AFFAIR
T B Harms, pub. 1936, reached #17 in April 1937
Haven Johnson w & m
Featured in NEW FACES OF 1936, revue (opened 05/36)
Billy Haywood, sung in revue
Jimmie Lunceford/Dan Grissom 01/37 Dec 1035
Teddy Wilson/Billie Holiday 04/37 Bruns 7840
Mildred Bailey/<vocal 03/37 Voc 3449

MY LITTLE BUCKAROO
Witmark, pub. 1937, reached #19 in April 1937
Jack Scholl w, M K Jerome m
Bing Crosby 05/37 Dec 1234
Russ Morgan/Mert Curtis 03/37 Bruns 7833

NEVER IN A MILLION YEARS (28)
Robbins, pub. 1937, reached #4 in June 1937
Mack Gordon w, Harry Revel m
Featured in WAKE UP AND LIVE, film (rel. 04/37)
Bing Crosby/Jimmy Dorsey Orch Φ 04/37 Dec 1210
Alice Faye, sung in film, 05/37 Bruns 7860
Glen Gray/Kenny Sargent 05/37 Dec 1211
Guy Lombardo/Carmen Lombardo 04/37 Vic 25545

NICE WORK IF YOU CAN GET IT (23)
Gershwin P C, pub. 1937, reached #3 in December 1937
Ira Gershwin w, George Gershwin m
Featured in DAMSEL IN DISTRESS, film (rel. 11/37)
Fred Astaire Φ sung in film, 12/37 Bruns 7983
Tommy Dorsey/Edythe Wright 11/37 Vic 25695
Teddy Wilson/Billie Holiday 12/37 Bruns 8015
Shep Fields/Bob Goday 11/37 Blu 7195

THE NIGHT IS YOUNG AND YOU'RE SO BEAUTIFUL (37)
Words & Mus, pub. 1936, reached #5 in February 1937
Billy Rose & Irving Kahal w, Dana Suesse m
George Hall/Johnny McKeever Φ 01/37 Blu 6702
Wayne King Orch 02/37 Vic 25495
Jan Garber/Russ Brown 01/37 Bruns 7800

ON A LITTLE BAMBOO BRIDGE
J Morris, pub. 1936, reached #10 in March 1937
Archie Fletcher & Al Sherman w & m
Shep Fields/Bob Goday 02/37 Blu 6781
Tommy Dorsey/Edythe Wright 03/37 25513
Abe Lyman/Sonny Schuyler 03/37 Dec 1130

ON A LITTLE DREAM RANCH
Shapiro, B, pub. 1937, reached #20 in June 1937
Billy Hill w & m
Guy Lombardo/Carmen Lombardo 05/37 Vic 25560
Russ Morgan/Mert Curtis 05/37 Bruns 7866
Dick Robertson/<vocal 07/37 Dec 1283

ONCE IN AWHILE (10)
Miller Mus, pub. 1937, reached #1 in December 1937
(Also reached #16 in July 1952)
(Also reached #15 in January 1961)
Bud Green w, Michael Edwards m
Tommy Dorsey/w.vocal group ΦΦ 10/37 Vic 25686
Horace Heidt/Larry Cotton Φ 11/37 Bruns 7977
Louis Armstrong/<vocal 01/38 Dec 1560
Ozzie Nelson/Harriet Hilliard 12/37 Blu 7256
Frances Langford 01/38 Dec 1542

THE ONE ROSE (30)
Shapiro, B, pub. 1937, reached #6 in November 1937
Del Lyon & Lani McIntire w & m
Bing Crosby Φ 10/37 Dec 1201
Art Kassel/Billy Leach 11/37 Blu 7184
Larry Clinton/Bea Wain 01/38 Vic 25724

ONE, TWO, BUTTON YOUR SHOE
Select M P I, pub. 1936, reached #11 in January 1937
Johnny Burke w, Arthur Johnston m
Featured in PENNIES FROM HEAVEN, film (rel. 11/36)
Bing Crosby, sung in film, 12/36 Dec 948
Ray Noble/Al Bowlly 11/36 Vic 25428
Shep Fields/Charles Chester 11/36 Blu 6604

OUR PENTHOUSE ON THIRD AVENUE
L Feist, pub. 1937, reached #15 in August 1937
Lew Brown w, Sammy Fain m
Featured in NEW FACES OF 1937, film (rel. 06/37)
Ozzie Nelson/Harriet Hilliard 07/37 Blu 6987
Harriet Hilliard & William Brady, sung in film
Tommy Dorsey/Jack Leonard 07/37 Vic 25591

PENNIES FROM HEAVEN (2)
Select M P I, pub. 1936, reached #1 in January 1937
Johnny Burke w, Arthur Johnston m
Featured in PENNIES FROM HEAVEN, film (rel. 11/36)
Bing Crosby ΦΦ sung in film, 11/36 Dec 947
Eddy Duchin/Lew Sherwood Φ 11/36 Vic 25431
Teddy Wilson/Billie Holiday Φ 01/37 Blu 6721
Hal Kemp/Maxine Gray 11/36 Bruns 7749
Jimmy Dorsey/Bob Eberle 11/36 Dec 951

RAINBOW ON THE RIVER
L Feist, pub. 1936, reached #10 in February 1937
Paul Francis Webster w, Louis Alter m
Featured in RAINBOW ON THE RIVER, film (rel. 12/36)
Bobby Breen, sung in film, 01/37 Dec 1053
Guy Lombardo/Carmen Lombardo 12/36 Vic 25435
Ted Weems/Perry Como 12/36 Dec 969

REMEMBER ME? (24)
Witmark, pub. 1937, reached #2 in October 1937
Al Dubin w, Harry Warren m
Featured in MR. DODD TAKES TO THE AIR, film (rel. 07/37)
Hal Kemp/Skinnay Ennis ΦΦ 09/37 Vic 25633
Bing Crosby Φ 11/37 Dec 1451
Teddy Wilson/Boots Castle 09/37 Bruns 7940
Kenny Baker, sung in film

ROSES IN DECEMBER (38)
Berlin, pub. 1937, reached #5 in November 1937
Herb Magidson & George Jessel w, Ben Oakland m
Featured in LIFE OF THE PARTY, film (rel. 08/37)
Ozzie Nelson/Harriet Hilliard Φ 08/37 Blu 7034
Harriet Hilliard & Gene Raymond, sung in film
Jan Garber/Russ Brown 08/37 Bruns 7929
Bunny Berigan/Ruth Gaylor 09/37 Vic 25613

A SAILBOAT IN THE MOONLIGHT (9)
Crawford, pub. 1937, reached #1 in August 1937
Carmen Lombardo & John Jacob Loeb w & m
Guy Lombardo/Carmen Lombardo ΦΦ 07/37 Vic 25594
Billie Holiday Orch/<vocal Φ 08/37 Voc 3605
Dick Robertson/<vocal 08/37 Dec 1367
Johnny Hodges/Buddy Clark 08/37 Variety 586

SATAN TAKES A HOLIDAY
Lincoln M C, pub. 1937, reached #12 in August 1937
Larry Clinton m
Tommy Dorsey Orch Φ 07/37 Vic 25570
Edgar Hayes Orch 09/37 Dec 1382

SEPTEMBER IN THE RAIN (6)
J H Remick pub. 1937, reached #1 in May 1937
Al Dubin w, Harry Warren m
Featured in MELODY FOR TWO, film (rel. 01/37)
Guy Lombardo/Carmen Lombardo ΦΦ 04/37 Vic 25526
James Melton, sung in film, 06/37 Dec 1247
Jan Garber/Russell Brown 04/37 Bruns 7850

SERENADE IN THE NIGHT (40)
Mills Mus, pub. 1936, reached #9 in March 1937
Jimmy Kennedy w, Cesare A Bixio & Bixio Cherubini m
Shep Fields/Bob Goday Φ 02/37 Blu 6747
Mantovani/George Barclay 01/37 Col 3159-D
Connie Boswell 03/37 Dec 1160

SLUMMING ON PARK AVENUE
Berlin, pub. 1937, reached #16 in March 1937
Irving Berlin w & m
Featured in ON THE AVENUE, film (rel. 01/37)
Alice Faye, sung in film, 03/37 Bruns 7825
Ray Noble/Merry Macs 02/37 Vic 25507
Jimmie Lunceford/w.vocal trio 03/37 Dec 1128

(YOU KNOW IT ALL) SMARTY
Paramount, pub. 1937, reached #20 in August 1937
Ralph Freed w, Burton Lane m
Featured in DOUBLE OR NOTHING, film (rel. 08/37)
Fats Waller Φ 07/37 Vic 25608
Bing Crosby, sung in film, 10/37 Dec 1375
Count Basie Orch 09/37 Dec 1379

SMOKE DREAMS
Robbins, pub. 1936, reached #17 in March 1937
Arthur Freed w, Nacio Herb Brown m
Featured in AFTER THE THIN MAN, film (rel. 12/36)
Benny Goodman/Helen Ward Φ 02/37 Vic 25486
Penny Singleton, sung in film

SO MANY MEMORIES
Shapiro, B, pub. 1937, reached #11 in October 1937
Harry Woods w & m
Richard Himber/Stuart Allen 09/37 Vic 25645
Frances Langford 10/37 Dec 1440
Russ Morgan/Mert Curtis 10/37 Bruns 7959

SO RARE (17)
Robbins, pub. 1937, reached #1 in September 1937
(Also reached #2 in July 1957)
Jack Sharpe w, Jerry Herst m
Guy Lombardo/Carmen Lombardo ΦΦ 09/37 Vic 25626
Gus Arnheim/Jimmy Farrell Φ 08/37 Bruns 7919
Jimmy Dorsey, stage (Later: 1957 Frat 755)
Jimmy Ray/<vocal 09/37 Blu 7077

STARDUST ON THE MOON
E B Marks, pub. 1937, reached #14 in September 1937
Jimmy Rogan w, Emery Deutsch m
Tommy Dorsey/Edythe Wright 08/37 Vic 25630
Emery Deutsch, stage, 10/37 Bruns 7961
Woody Herman/<vocal 09/37 Dec 1385

STOP! YOU'RE BREAKING MY HEART
Famous, pub. 1937, reached #18 in August 1937
Ted Koehler w, Burton Lane m
Featured in ARTISTS AND MODELS, film (rel. 08/37)
Judy Canova & Ben Blue, sung in film
Russ Morgan/w.vocal duo 07/37 Bruns 7910
Hal Kemp/Skinnay Ennis 07/37 Vic 25598

SWEET IS THE WORD FOR YOU
Famous, pub. 1937, reached #15 in May 1937
Leo Robin w, Ralph Rainger m
Featured in WAIKIKI WEDDING, film (rel. 03/37)
Bing Crosby, sung in film, 04/37 Dec 1184
Tommy Dorsey/Jack Leonard 04/37 Vic 25532

SWEET LEILANI (3)
Select M P I, pub. 1937, reached #3 in May 1937
Harry Owens w & m
Featured in WAIKIKI WEDDING, film (rel. 03/37)
Bing Crosby/Lani McIntyre ΦΦ 04/37 Dec 1175
Bing Crosby, sung in film
Jan Garber/Russ Brown 04/37 Bruns 7839

SWING HIGH, SWING LOW
Famous, pub. 1937, reached #19 in April 1937
Ralph Freed w, Burton Lane m
Featured in SWING HIGH, SWING LOW, film (rel. 03/37)
Dorothy Lamour, sung in film, 04/37 Bruns 7838
Russ Morgan/Judy Richards 03/37 Bruns 7833
Ink Spots 05/37 Dec 1236

THAT OLD FEELING (14)
L Feist, pub. 1937, reached #1 in October 1937
Lew Brown & Sammy Fain w & m
Featured in VOGUES OF 1938, film (rel. 08/37)
Shep Fields/Bob Goday Φ 08/37 Blu 7066
Guy Lombardo/Carmen Lombardo Φ 09/37 Vic 25629
Virginia Verrill, sung in film
Jan Garber/Russ Brown 09/37 Bruns 7935

THERE'S A LULL IN MY LIFE (43)
Robbins, pub. 1937, reached #5 in June 1937
Mack Gordon w, Harry Revel m
Featured in WAKE UP AND LIVE, film (rel. 04/37)
Alice Faye, sung in film, 06/37 Bruns 7876
Teddy Wilson/Billie Holiday Φ 06/37 Bruns 7884
Duke Ellington/Ivie Anderson 05/37 Master 117
George Hall/w.vocal 05/37 Variety 536
Mildred Bailey/<vocal 05/37 Voc 3508

THERE'S FROST ON THE MOON
Berlin, pub. 1936, reached #16 in January 1937
Joe Young w, Fred Ahlert m
Tommy Dorsey/Edythe Wright 01/37 Vic 25482
Artie Shaw/Peg LaCentra 12/36 Bruns 7771

THERE'S SOMETHING IN THE AIR (41)
Robbins, pub. 1936, reached #7 in February 1937
Harold Adamson w, Jimmy McHugh m
Featured in BANJO ON MY KNEES, film (rel. 12/36)
Tony Martin, sung in film, 12/36 Bruns 7782
Shep Fields/Bob Goday Φ 01/37 Blu 6683
Ray Noble/Al Bowlly 01/37 Vic 25459

THEY ALL LAUGHED
Chappell, pub. 1937, reached #16 in May 1937
Ira Gershwin w, George Gershwin m
Featured in SHALL WE DANCE, film (rel. 04/37)
Fred Astaire & Ginger Rogers, sung in film
Fred Astaire 05/37 Bruns 7856
Tommy Dorsey/Edythe Wright 05/37 Vic 25544
Ozzie Nelson/<vocal 04/37 Blu 6873

THEY CAN'T TAKE THAT AWAY FROM ME (34)
Gershwin P C, pub. 1937, reached #6 in June 1937
Ira Gershwin w, George Gershwin m
Featured in SHALL WE DANCE, film (rel. 04/37)
Fred Astaire Φ sung in film, 05/37 Bruns 7855
Ozzie Nelson/<vocal 04/37 Blu 6873
Billie Holiday Orch/<vocal 05/37 Voc 3520
Tommy Dorsey/Jack Leonard 05/37 Vic 25549

THIS YEAR'S KISSES (35)
Berlin, pub. 1937, reached #2 in March 1937
Irving Berlin w & m
Featured in ON THE AVENUE, film (rel. 01/37)
Alice Faye, sung in film, 03/37 Bruns 7825
Benny Goodman/Margaret McCrae Φ 02/37 Vic 25505
Hal Kemp/Skinnay Ennis Φ 02/37 Bruns 7812
Shep Fields/Bob Goday Φ 02/37 Blu 6757
Teddy Wilson/Billie Holiday 03/37 Bruns 7824

TOO MARVELOUS FOR WORDS (33)
Harms, pub. 1937, reached #3 in May 1937
Johnny Mercer w, Richard Whiting m
Featured in READY, WILLING AND ABLE, film (rel. 03/37)
Bing Crosby/Jimmy Dorsey Orch Φ 04/37 Dec 1185
Ross Alexander, Winnie Shaw, Ruby Keeler & Lee Dixon, sung in film
Shep Fields/Bob Goday 03/37 Blu 6779
Eddy Duchin/Jerry Cooper 03/37 Vic 25517

TOODLE-OO
Words & Mus, pub. 1937, reached #14 in July 1937
John Jacob Loeb & Carmen Lombardo w & m
Guy Lombardo/w.vocal trio 06/37 Vic 25572
Dick Robertson/<vocal 06/37 Dec 1260

TRUST IN ME (19)
Ager, Y & B, pub. 1934, reached #5 in March 1937
Ned Wever w, Milt Ager & Jean Schwartz m
Wayne King Orch Φ 02/37 Vic 25495
Mildred Bailey Φ 03/37 Voc 3449
Connie Boswell/Ben Pollack Orch 04/37 Dec 1161

VIENI, VIENI (18)
Witmark, pub. 1937, reached #1 in November 1937
Rudy Vallee w, Vincent Scotto m
Rudy Vallee ΦΦ 10/37 Blu 7069
Emery Deutsch/Barry McKinley 11/37 Bruns 7972

WAS IT RAIN?
Santly Joy, pub. 1937, reached #11 in June 1937
Walter Hirsch w, Lou Handman m
Featured in THE HIT PARADE, film (rel. 04/37)
Frances Langford, sung in film, 05/37 Dec 1262
Johnny Hamp/Jack Campbell 05/37 Blu 6848

WHAT WILL I TELL MY HEART (27)
Crawford, pub. 1937, reached #4 in April 1937
Jack Lawrence, Peter Tinturin, Irving Gordon w & m
Andy Kirk/Pha Terrell Φ 02/37 Dec 1085
Hal Kemp/Bob Allen Φ 02/37 Bruns 7830
Bing Crosby/Jimmy Dorsey Orch Φ 04/37 Dec 1185
Guy Lombardo/Carmen Lombardo 03/37 Vic 25526
Dolly Dawn/George Hall Orch[2] 03/37 Blu 6796

WHEN MY DREAM BOAT COMES HOME (1)
Witmark, pub. 1936, reached #2 in February 1937
Cliff Friend & Dave Franklin w & m
Guy Lombardo/Lebert Lombardo ΦΦ 12/36 Vic 25435
Shep Fields/Bob Goday Φ 01/37 Blu 6661
Henry "Red" Allen/<vocal 02/37 Voc 3389

WHEN THE POPPIES BLOOM AGAIN
Shapiro, B, pub. 1936, reached #6 in April 1937
Leo Towers, Don Pelosi, Morton Morrow w & m
Bert Ambrose/Jack Cooper 03/37 Dec 1142
George Hall/Dolly Dawn 03/37 Blu 6801
Russ Morgan/Mert Curtis 04/37 Bruns 7845

WHERE ARE YOU? (47)
L Feist, pub. 1936, reached #9 in June 1937
Harold Adamson w, Jimmy McHugh m
Featured in TOP OF THE TOWN, film (rel. 03/37)
Gertrude Niesen, sung in film, 06/37 Bruns 7837
Mildred Bailey Φ 05/37 Voc 3456
Tommy Dorsey/Jack Leonard 04/37 Vic 25474

WHERE OR WHEN (25)
Chappell, pub. 1937, reached #4 in July 1937
(Also reached #5 in February 1960)
Lorenz Hart w, Richard Rodgers m
Featured in BABES IN ARMS, show (opened 04/37)
Hal Kemp/Bob Allen Φ 05/37 Bruns 7865
Mitzi Greene & Ray Heatherton, sung in show
Shep Fields/Bob Goday 05/37 Blu 6895

WHISPERS IN THE DARK (13)
Famous, pub. 1937, reached #1 in September 1937
Leo Robin w, Frederick Hollander m
Featured in ARTISTS AND MODELS, film (rel. 08/37)
Connie Boswell, sung in film, 10/37 Dec 1420
Bob Crosby/Kay Weber Φ 08/37 Dec 1346
Hal Kemp/Bob Allen Φ 07/37 Vic 25598

WHO'S AFRAID OF LOVE
Hollywood Mus, pub. 1936, reached #20 in February 1937
Sidney Mitchell w, Lew Pollack m
Featured in ONE IN A MILLION, film (rel. 12/36)
Don Ameche & Leah Ray, sung in film
Fats Waller 02/37 Vic 25499

WILL YOU REMEMBER (SWEETHEART) (46)
G Schirmer, pub. 1917, reached #8 in May 1937
(Also reached #14 in January 1918)
Rida Johnson Young w, Sigmund Romberg m
Featured in MAYTIME, film (rel. 03/37)
Jeanette MacDonald & Nelson Eddy Φ sung in film and 04/37 Vic 4329
Victor Young/Tommy Harris 05/37 Dec 1199

WITH PLENTY OF MONEY AND YOU (20)
T B Harms, pub. 1936, reached #2 in February 1937
Al Dubin w, Harry Warren m
Featured in GOLD DIGGERS OF 1937, film (rel. 12/36)
Dick Powell Φ sung in film, 01/37 Dec 1067
Henry Busse/Bob Hannon Φ 01/37 Dec 1076
Hal Kemp/Skinnay Ennis 01/37 Bruns 7769
George Hamilton 01/37 Vic 25458

YOU AND I KNOW
Robbins, pub. 1937, reached #19 in November 1937
Al Stillman & Laurence Stallings w, Arthur Schwartz m
Featured in VIRGINIA, show (opened 09/37)
Anne Booth & Ronald Graham, sung in show
Tommy Dorsey/Edythe Wright 10/37 Vic 25648
Claude Thornhill/Barry McKinley 10/37 Bruns 7951

THE YOU AND ME THAT USED TO BE (50)
Berlin, pub. 1937, reached #6 in July 1937
Walter Bullock w, Allie Wrubel m
Dolly Dawn/George Hall Orch[2] 06/37 Variety 557
Mal Hallett/Teddy Grace 06/37 Dec 1281
Eddy Duchin/Jerry Cooper 06/37 Vic 25576

YOU CAN'T STOP ME FROM DREAMING (11)
J H Remick, pub. 1937, reached #1 in November 1937
Cliff Friend & Dave Franklin w & m
Guy Lombardo/w.vocal trio Φ 10/37 Vic 25656
Ozzie Nelson/<vocal Φ 10/37 Blu 7159
Teddy Wilson Orch 10/37 Bruns 7954
Dick Robertson/<vocal 10/37 Dec 1415

YOU'RE LAUGHING AT ME
Berlin, pub. 1937, reached #14 in March 1937
Irving Berlin w & m
Featured in ON THE AVENUE, film (rel. 02/37)
Dick Powell, sung in film, 03/37 Dec 1150
Wayne King Orch 02/37 Vic 25506
Fats Waller 03/37 Vic 25530

YOURS AND MINE
Robbins, pub. 1937, reached #15 in September 1937
Arthur Freed w, Nacio Herb Brown m
Featured in BROADWAY MELODY OF 1938, film (rel. 08/37)
Teddy Wilson/Billie Holiday 07/37 Bruns 7917
Judy Garland, sung in film
Eleanor Powell, sung in film
Hudson-DeLange Orch/Nan Wynn 09/37 Master 138, 12/37 Bruns 8002

[1]Reached #20 on monthly chart only.
[2]Billed on record as Dolly Dawn and her Dawn Patrol.

1938

A-TISKET, A-TASKET (7)
Robbins, pub. 1938, reached #1 in August 1938
Ella Fitzgerald & Al Feldman w & m
Chick Webb/Ella Fitzgerald ΦΦΦ 07/38 Dec 1840
Tommy Dorsey/Edythe Wright 08/38 Vic 25899
Teddy Wilson/Nan Wynn 09/38 Bruns 8199

ALEXANDER'S RAGTIME BAND (17)
ABC Music; orig. pub. 1911, reached #3 in September 1938
(Also reached #1 in October 1911)
Irving Berlin w & m
Featured in ALEXANDER'S RAGTIME BAND, film (rel. 05/38)
Bing Crosby & Connie Boswell Φ 08/38 Dec 1887
Alice Faye, sung in film
Boswell Sisters 08/38 Voc 4239
Ray Noble Orch 09/38 Bruns 8180

ALL ASHORE (25)
Shapiro, B, pub. 1938, reached #2 in December 1938
Billy Hill w & m
Sammy Kaye/Tommy Ryan Φ 10/38 Vic 26059
Jan Garber/Lee Bennett 11/38 Bruns 8235
Paul Whiteman/Four Modernaires 11/38 Dec 2075

ALWAYS AND ALWAYS
L Feist, pub. 1937, reached #18 in May 1938
Bob Wright & Chet Forrest w, Edward Ward m
Featured in MANNEQUIN, film (rel. 12/37)
Joan Crawford, sung in film
Larry Clinton/Bea Wain 03/38 Vic 25768
George Hall/w.vocal 03/38 Voc 3943

AT A PERFUME COUNTER
Donaldson, D & G, pub. 1938, reached #14 in May 1938
Edgar Leslie w, Joe Burke m
Jimmy Dorsey/Bob Eberle 04/38 Dec 1724
Blue Barron/Russ Carlyle 04/38 Blu 7419
Larry Clinton/Bea Wain 04/38 Vic 25773

AT LONG LAST LOVE
Chappell, pub. 1938, reached #9 in November 1938
Cole Porter w & m
Featured in YOU NEVER KNOW, show (opened 09/38)
Ozzie Nelson/<vocal Φ 10/38 Blu 7825
Clifton Webb, sung in show
Larry Clinton/Bea Wain 10/38 Vic 26014

BAMBINA
L Spier, pub. 1938, reached #17 in September 1938
Larry Spier, Al Stillman, Serge Walter w & m
Jan Garber/Lee Bennett 09/38 Bruns 8206
Henry Busse/Don Huston 10/38 Dec 1976

BEGIN THE BEGUINE
Harms, pub. 1935, reached #12 in October 1938
Cole Porter w & m
Big-band classic
Artie Shaw Orch ΦΦ 09/38 Blu 7746
Tony Martin 04/39 Dec 2375

BEI MIR BIST DU SCHOEN (22)
Harms, pub. 1937, reached #1 in January 1938
Sammy Cahn & Saul Chaplin w, Sholum Secunda m
Featured in LOVE, HONOR AND BEHAVE, film (rel. 02/38)
Andrews Sisters ΦΦ 01/38 Dec 1562
Guy Lombardo/w.vocal trio Φ 01/38 Vic 25739
Priscilla Lane, sung in film
Benny Goodman/Martha Tilton 02/38 Vic 25751
Russ Morgan/<vocal 01/38 Bruns 8037

BEWILDERED
Miller Mus, pub. 1938, reached #17 in May 1938
Leonard Whitcup w, Teddy Powell m
Tommy Dorsey/Jack Leonard 04/38 Vic 25795
Mildred Bailey Orch/<vocal 05/38 Voc 4036

BOOGIE WOOGIE
Melrose; orig. pub. 1929, reached #18 in November 1938
(Also reached #12 in January 1944)
(Also reached #16 in September 1945)
Pinetop Smith m
Big-band classic and steady seller, 1938 through the 1940's
Tommy Dorsey Orch Φ 10/38 Vic 26054

CATHEDRAL IN THE PINES (15)
Berlin, pub. 1938, reached #4 in June 1938
Charles Kenny & Nick Kenny w & m
Shep Fields/Jerry Stewart Φ 05/38 Blu 7553
Horace Heidt/Larry Cotton 06/38 Bruns 8133
Dick Todd 06/38 Vic 25839

CHANGE PARTNERS (24)
Berlin, pub. 1938, reached #2 in October 1938
Irving Berlin w & m
Featured in CAREFREE, film (rel. 08/38)
Fred Astaire Φ sung in film, 09/38 Bruns 8189
Jimmy Dorsey/Bob Eberle Φ 09/38 Dec 2002
Ozzie Nelson/<vocal 09/38 Blu 7734
Larry Clinton/Dick Todd 10/38 Vic 26010
Lawrence Welk/Lois Best 10/38 Voc 4270

CRY, BABY, CRY (21)
Shapiro, B, pub. 1938, reached #1 in June 1938
Jimmy Eaton w, Terry Shand m
Larry Clinton/Bea Wain Φ 05/38 Vic 25819
Kay Kyser/Sully Mason Φ 05/38 Bruns 8114
Dick Robertson/<vocal 05/38 Dec 1726

DAY AFTER DAY
Green Bros/Knight, pub. 1938, reached #19 in December 1938
Bud Green w, Richard Himber m
Richard Himber/Stuart Allen 12/38 Vic 26106
Barry Wood 12/38 Bruns 8269

DAY DREAMING (ALL NIGHT LONG)
J H Remick, pub. 1938, reached #17 in July 1938
Johnny Mercer w, Harry Warren m
Featured in GOLD DIGGERS IN PARIS, film (rel. 05/38)
Rudy Vallee/<vocal, sung in film, 06/38 Vic 25836
Jimmie Grier/Dick Webster 06/38 Dec 1813

THE DIPSY DOODLE (14)
Lincoln Mus, pub. 1937, reached #2 in February 1938
Larry Clinton w & m
Tommy Dorsey/Edythe Wright 12/37 Vic 25693
Larry Clinton Orch, stage
Russ Morgan Orch 12/37 Bruns 8005
Chick Webb/Ella Fitzgerald 01/38 Dec 1587

DON'T BE THAT WAY (26)
Robbins, pub. 1938, reached #4 in May 1938
Mitchell Parish w, Edgar Sampson & Benny Goodman m
Benny Goodman Orch ΦΦ 04/38 Vic 25792
Mildred Bailey Orch/<vocal 05/38 Voc 4016

THE DONKEY SERENADE
G Schirmer, pub. 1937, reached #20 in May 1938
Bob Wright & Chet Forrest w, Rudolf Friml & Herbert Stothart m
Featured in THE FIREFLY, film (rel. 09/37)
Allan Jones/Nat Shilkret Orch 04/38 Vic 4380

FLAT FOOT FLUGEY (45)
Green Bros/Knight, pub. 1938, reached #7 in July 1938
Slim Gaillard, Slam Stewart, Bud Green w & m
Slim & Slam ΦΦ 04/38 Voc 4021
Benny Goodman/w.vocal group 07/38 Vic 25871
Mills Brothers & Louis Armstrong 07/38 Dec 1876
Wingy Manone/<vocal 07/38 Blu 7621

GARDEN OF THE MOON
J H Remick, pub. 1938, reached #17 in September 1938
Al Dubin & Johnny Mercer w, Harry Warren m
Featured in GARDEN OF THE MOON, film (rel. 09/38)
Red Norvo/Mildred Bailey 09/38 Bruns 8202
Jimmy Dorsey/Bob Eberle 09/38 Dec 1970
Mabel Todd, sung in film

THE GIRL IN THE BONNET OF BLUE
I Dash, pub. 1938, reached #15 in June 1938
Ross Parker w & m
Dick Todd 06/38 Vic 25839
Dick Powell 06/38 Dec 1782
Horace Heidt/Charles Goodwin 06/38 Bruns 8133

GOODNIGHT, ANGEL (23)
Berlin, pub. 1937, reached #4 in March 1938
Herb Magidson w, Allie Wrubel m
Artie Shaw/Anita Bradley Φ 02/38 Bruns 8054
Shep Fields/Bob Goday 02/38 Blu 7355
Hal Kemp/Bob Allen 02/38 Vic 25722

A GYPSY TOLD ME
Crawford, pub. 1938, reached #12 in March 1938
Jack Yellen w, Samuel Pockrass m
Featured in HAPPY LANDING, film (rel. 01/38)
Larry Clinton/Bea Wain 04/38 Vic 25800
Ted Weems/Perry Como 04/38 Dec 1695

HAVE YOU FORGOTTEN SO SOON?
Berlin, pub. 1938, reached #9 in December 1938
Edward Heyman & Sam Coslow w, Abner Silver m
Mildred Bailey Orch/<vocal 11/38 Voc 4432
Sammy Kaye/Charlie Wilson 11/38 Vic 26067
Kay Kyser/Ginny Simms 11/38 Bruns 8244

HEART AND SOUL (28)
Famous, pub. 1938, reached #2 in November 1938
(Also reached #18 in December 1952)
(Also reached #18 in July 1961)
Frank Loesser w, Hoagy Carmichael m
Featured in A SONG IS BORN, film short (1938)
All-time pop standard
Larry Clinton/Bea Wain ΦΦ 10/38 Vic 26046
Al Donahue/Paula Kelly 10/38 Voc 4398
Eddy Duchin/Stanley Worth 11/38 Bruns 8238

HEIGH-HO (20)
Berlin, pub. 1937, reached #3 in April 1938
Larry Morey w, Frank Churchill m
Featured in SNOW WHITE AND THE SEVEN DWARFS, film (rel. 12/37)
The Seven Dwarfs Φ sung in film, 02/38 Vic 25735
Horace Heidt/w.vocal duo 03/38 Bruns 8074
Fred Rich/The Clubmen 03/38 Dec 1632

HOWDJA LIKE TO LOVE ME (49)
Famous, pub. 1938, reached #10 in April 1938
Frank Loesser w, Burton Lane m
Featured in COLLEGE SWING, film (rel. 04/38)
Bob Hope & Martha Raye, sung in film
Jimmy Dorsey/Don Mattison 04/38 Dec 1671
Dolly Dawn/George Hall Orch[2] 04/38 Voc 4018

I CAN DREAM, CAN'T I?
Chappell, pub. 1937, reached #9 in March 1938
(Also reached #1 in January 1950)
Irving Kahal w, Sammy Fain m
Featured in RIGHT THIS WAY, revue (opened 01/38)
Tommy Dorsey/Jack Leonard Φ 02/38 Vic 25741
Tamara, sung in revue
Glen Gray/Kenny Sargent 02/38 Dec 1607

I DOUBLE DARE YOU (19)
Shapiro, B, pub. 1938, reached #2 in February 1938
Terry Shand & Jimmy Eaton w & m
Larry Clinton/Bea Wain Φ 02/38 Vic 25740
Russ Morgan/Bernice Parks Φ 01/38 Bruns 8037
Louis Armstrong/<vocal 03/38 Dec 1636
Woody Herman/<vocal 01/38 Dec 1523

I FALL IN LOVE WITH YOU EVERY DAY
Famous, pub. 1938, reached #11 in April 1938
Frank Loesser w, Manning Sherman & Arthur Altman m
Featured in COLLEGE SWING, film (rel. 04/38)
Jimmy Dorsey/Bob Eberle Φ 03/38 Dec 1671
Florence George & John Payne, sung in film
Larry Clinton/Bea Wain 03/38 Vic 25725

I HADN'T ANYONE TILL YOU (36)
ABC Music, pub. 1938, reached #4 in July 1938
Ray Noble w & m
Ray Noble/Tony Martin Φ 05/38 Bruns 8079
Tommy Dorsey/Jack Leonard Φ 06/38 Vic 25848
Jimmy Dorsey/Bob Eberle 06/38 Dec 1834

I LET A SONG GO OUT OF MY HEART (3)
Mills, pub. 1938, reached #2 in June 1938
Irving Mills, Henry Nemo & John Redmond w, Duke Ellington m
Duke Ellington Orch ΦΦ 04/38 Bruns 8108
Benny Goodman/Martha Tilton ΦΦ 06/38 Vic 25840
Connie Boswell 07/38 Dec 1896
Mildred Bailey Orch/<vocal 06/38 Voc 4083

I LOVE TO WHISTLE (48)
Robbins, pub. 1938, reached #7 in May 1938
Harold Adamson w, Jimmy McHugh m
Featured in MAD ABOUT MUSIC, film (rel. 02/38)
Fats Waller Φ 04/38 Vic 25806
Deanna Durbin, sung in film

I MARRIED AN ANGEL
Robbins, pub. 1938, reached #6 in July 1938
Lorenz Hart w, Richard Rodgers m
Featured in I MARRIED AN ANGEL, show (opened 05/38)
Larry Clinton/Bea Wain Φ 06/38 Vic 25837
Dennis King, sung in show
Sammy Kaye/Jimmy Brown 07/38 Voc 4140

I WON'T TELL A SOUL (44)
Crawford, pub. 1938, reached #6 in December 1938
Ross Parker & Hughie Childs w & m
Andy Kirk/Pha Terrell Φ 10/38 Dec 2127
Lawrence Welk/Walter Bloom 11/38 Voc 4435
Roy Fox/Denny Dennis 11/38 Blu 7840

I'M GONNA LOCK MY HEART (35)
Shapiro, B, pub. 1938, reached #4 in September 1938
Terry Shand & Jimmy Eaton w & m
Billie Holiday/<vocal Φ 08/38 Voc 4238
Larry Clinton/Bea Wain Φ 08/38 Vic 25885
Kay Kyser/Sully Mason 08/38 Bruns 8170

I'VE GOT A DATE WITH A DREAM
L Feist, pub. 1938, reached #7 in October 1938
Mack Gordon w, Harry Revel m
Featured in MY LUCKY STAR, film (rel. 09/38)
Benny Goodman/Martha Tilton Φ 09/38 Vic 26000
Buddy Ebsen & Joan Davis, sung in film
Horace Heidt/Larry Cotton 09/38 Bruns 8184

I'VE GOT A POCKETFUL OF DREAMS (2)
Santly-Joy, pub. 1938, reached #1 in September 1938
Johnny Burke w, James V Monaco m
Featured in SING YOU SINNERS, film (rel. 08/38)
Bing Crosby ΦΦ sung in film, 08/38 Dec 1933
Russ Morgan/<vocal Φ 08/38 Dec 1936
Shep Fields/Phyllis Kenny 08/38 Blu 7697

IN THE STILL OF THE NIGHT
Chappell, pub. 1937, reached #12 in January 1938
Cole Porter w & m
Featured in ROSALIE, film (rel. 12/37)
Nelson Eddy, sung in film
Tommy Dorsey/Jack Leonard 11/37 Vic 25663
Leo Reisman/Lee Sullivan 11/37 Bruns 7985

IT'S WONDERFUL
Robbins, pub. 1938, reached #13 in March 1938
Mitchell Parish & C S Wells w, Stuff Smith m
Benny Goodman/Martha Tilton 02/38 Vic 25727
Red Norvo/Mildred Bailey 03/38 Bruns 8069

THE LAMBETH WALK (31)
Mills, pub. 1937, reached #5 in October 1938
Douglas Furber w, Noel Gay m
Russ Morgan/Jimmy Lewis Φ 10/38 Dec 2009
Duke Ellington Orch Φ 09/38 Bruns 8204
Arthur Murray 09/38 Bruns 8218
Mills Brothers 10/38 Dec 2008
Al Donahue/Paula Kelly 10/38 Voc 4318

LET ME WHISPER (I LOVE YOU)
Chappell, pub. 1938, reached #16 in June 1938
Pat Pattison, Electo Roselle, Richard Gasparre, & Edward Heyman w & m
Bing Crosby 06/38 Dec 1819
Guy Lombardo/Carmen Lombardo 05/38 Vic 25818

LET'S SAIL TO DREAMLAND
L Spier, pub. 1938, reached #10 in April 1938
Harry Kogen, Henry Busse, Larry Spier w & m
Guy Lombardo/Carmen Lombardo 03/38 Vic 25786
Dick Robertson/<vocal 04/38 Dec 1707

LITTLE LADY MAKE BELIEVE
Olman Inc pub. 1936, reached #11 in July 1938
Charles Tobias w, Nat Simon m
Guy Lombardo/Carmen Lombardo 06/38 Vic 25823
Bing Crosby 06/38 Dec 1794
Dorothy Lamour 06/38 Bruns 8132

LOVE WALKED IN (10)
Gershwin P C, pub. 1938, reached #1 in May 1938
(Also reached #13 in November 1953)
Ira Gershwin w, George Gershwin m
Featured in THE GOLDWYN FOLLIES, film (rel. 01/38)
Sammy Kaye/Tommy Ryan Φ 05/38 Voc 4017
Kenny Baker, sung in film, 05/38 Dec 1795
Jan Garber/Russ Brown Φ 04/38 Bruns 8060
Jimmy Dorsey/Bob Eberle Φ 05/38 Dec 1724

LOVELIGHT IN THE STARLIGHT (37)
Paramount, pub. 1938, reached #5 in June 1938
Ralph Freed w, Fred Hollander m
Featured in HER JUNGLE LOVE, film (rel. 04/38)
Dorothy Lamour, sung in film, 06/38 Bruns 8132
Horace Heidt/Larry Cotton Φ 05/38 Bruns 8110
Charles "Buddy" Rogers/<vocal 06/38 Voc 4058

MAMA, THAT MOON IS HERE AGAIN
Paramount, pub. 1937, reached #15 in February 1938
Leo Robin w, Ralph Rainger m
Featured in THE BIG BROADCAST OF 1938, film (rel. 02/38)
Martha Raye, sung in film
Shep Fields/Bob Goday 01/38 Blu 7318
Benny Goodman/Martha Tilton 01/38 Vic 25720

MARTHA
(public domain); orig. pub. 1847, reached #13 in June 1938
Friedrich Von Flotow w & m
Larry Clinton/Bea Wain ΦΦ 04/38 Vic 25789
Wingy Manone/<vocal 06/38 Blu 7621

MEXICALI ROSE
M M Cole; orig. pub. 1923, reached #16 in November 1938
(Also reached #15 in June 1924)
Helen Stone w, Jack B Tenney m
Bing Crosby Φ 10/38 Dec 2001
Roy Smeck/Donald King 01/39 Dec 2235

THE MOON OF MANAKOORA
Kalmar & Ruby, pub. 1937, reached #13 in March 1938
Frank Loesser w, Alfred Newman m
Featured in THE HURRICANE, film (rel. 12/37)
Dorothy Lamour, sung in film, 02/38 Bruns 8027
Bing Crosby Φ 03/38 Dec 1649
Ray Noble/Tony Martin 03/38 Bruns 8079

MORE THAN EVER
Miller Mus, pub. 1937, reached #11 in March 1938
Bud Green w, Isham Jones m
Tommy Dorsey/Jack Leonard 03/38 Vic 25774
Bob Crosby/<vocal 03/38 Dec 1657
Red Norvo/Mildred Bailey 03/38 Bruns 8085

MUSIC, MAESTRO, PLEASE (6)
Berlin, pub. 1938, reached #1 in July 1938
(Also reached #19 in September 1950)
Herb Magidson w, Allie Wrubel m
Tommy Dorsey/Edythe Wright ΦΦ 07/38 Vic 25866
Kay Kyser/Ginny Simms 07/38 Bruns 8149
Art Kassel/Billy Leach 07/38 Blu 7619

MY MARGARITA
L Feist, pub. 1938, reached #19 in July 1938
Walter Hirsch w, Maria Grever m
Horace Heidt/w.vocal trio 06/38 Bruns 8129
Jan Savitt/Bon Bon 07/38 Blu 7593

MY OWN (43)
Robbins, pub. 1938, reached #6 in December 1938
Harold Adamson w, Jimmy McHugh m
Featured in THAT CERTAIN AGE, film (rel. 10/38)
Deanna Durbin, sung in film, 02/39 Dec 2274
Tommy Dorsey/Edythe Wright Φ 10/38 Vic 26005
George Hall/Dolly Dawn 10/38 Voc 4297

MY REVERIE (1)
Robbins, pub. 1938, reached #1 in November 1938
Larry Clinton w & adpt, Claude Debussy m
Larry Clinton/Bea Wain ΦΦ 09/38 Vic 26006
Bing Crosby Φ 11/38 Dec 2123
Mildred Bailey 11/38 Voc 4406
Eddy Duchin/Stanley Worth 11/38 Bruns 8224
Glenn Miller/Ray Eberle 11/38 Blu 7853

(DON'T WAIT TILL) THE NIGHT BEFORE CHRISTMAS
Chappell, pub. 1938, reached #10 in December 1938
Sam Lewis w, Abel Baer m
Eddy Duchin/Stanley Worth 12/38 Bruns 8264
Sammy Kaye/Three Barons 12/38 Vic 26104

NOW IT CAN BE TOLD (27)
Berlin, pub. 1938, reached #2 in September 1938
Irving Berlin w & m
Featured in ALEXANDER'S RAGTIME BAND, film (rel. 05/38)
Tommy Dorsey/Jack Leonard Φ 07/38 Vic 25856
Alice Faye, sung in film
Bing Crosby Φ 07/38 Dec 1888
Tony Martin/Ray Noble Orch 07/38 Bruns 8153

OH! MA-MA
Shapiro, B, pub. 1938, reached #8 in July 1938
Lew Brown & Rudy Vallee w, Paolo Citorello m
Rudy Vallee Orch/Red Stanley Φ 05/38 Blu 7543
Guy Lombardo/w.vocal trio 06/38 Vic 25857
Dick Robertson/<vocal 05/38 Dec 1726
Andrews Sisters 07/38 Dec 1859

OL' MAN MOSE
Santly-Joy-Select, pub. 1936, reached #12 in September 1938
Louis Armstrong & Zilmer Randolph w & m
Eddy Duchin/Patricia Norman ΦΦ 07/38 Bruns 8155
Louis Armstrong/<vocal, stage, 07/38 Dec 622

THE OLD APPLE TREE
Witmark, pub. 1938, reached #14 in April 1938
M K Jerome & Jack Scholl w & m
Featured in SWING YOUR LADY, film (rel. 01/38)
Guy Lombardo/w.vocal trio 03/38 Vic 25728
Ozzie Nelson/<vocal 03/38 Blu 7430

ON THE SENTIMENTAL SIDE (47)
Select M P I, pub. 1938, reached #5 in May 1938
Johnny Burke w, James V Monaco m
Featured in DOCTOR RHYTHM, film (rel. 04/38)
Bing Crosby Φ 03/38 Dec 1648
Billie Holiday/<vocal 03/38 Voc 3947
Guy Lombardo/Carmen Lombardo 02/38 Vic 25764

PLEASE BE KIND (4)
T B Harms, pub. 1938, reached #2 in April 1938
Sammy Cahn & Saul Chaplin w & m
Red Norvo/Mildred Bailey Φ 03/38 Bruns 8088
Benny Goodman/Martha Tilton Φ 04/38 Vic 25814
Bob Crosby/Kay Weber 04/38 Dec 1693

ROSALIE (9)
Chappell, pub. 1937, reached #1 in January 1938
Cole Porter w & m
Featured in ROSALIE, film (rel. 12/37)
Nelson Eddy, sung in film
Sammy Kaye/Tommy Ryan ΦΦ 11/37 Voc 3700
Horace Heidt/w.vocal group Φ 01/38 Bruns 8028
Jan Garber/w.vocal 12/37 Bruns 7969

SAIL ALONG, SILV'RY MOON
Select M P I, pub. 1937, reached #14 in January 1938
(Also reached #3 in February 1958)
Harry Tobias w, Percy Wenrich m
Bing Crosby Φ 12/37 Dec 1518
Gene Autry 02/38 Voc 03358

SAYS MY HEART (12)
Famous, pub. 1938, reached #1 in June 1938
Frank Loesser w, Burton Lane m
Featured in COCOANUT GROVE, film (rel. 05/38)
Red Norvo/Mildred Bailey Φ 06/38 Bruns 8135
Harriet Hilliard, sung in film
Ozzie Nelson/Harriet Hilliard Φ 05/38 Blu 7528
Tommy Dorsey/Edythe Wright Φ 05/38 Vic 25828
Andrews Sisters Φ 07/38 Dec 1875

SIXTY SECONDS GOT TOGETHER
Santly-Joy, pub. 1938, reached #14 in November 1938
Mack David w, Jerry Livingston m
Mills Brothers Φ 10/38 Dec 1964
Kay Kyser/Harry Babbitt 11/38 Bruns 8225
Dick Todd 11/38 Vic 26057

SMALL FRY (41)
Famous, pub. 1938, reached #6 in October 1938
Frank Loesser w, Hoagy Carmichael m
Featured in SING YOU SINNERS, film (rel. 08/38)
Bing Crosby & Johnny Mercer Φ 09/38 Dec 1960
Bing Crosby, Fred MacMurray & Donald O'Connor, sung in film
Mildred Bailey/<vocal 08/38 Voc 4224

SO HELP ME (IF I DON'T LOVE YOU) (33)
J H Remick, pub. 1938, reached #3 in October 1938
Eddie DeLange w, Jimmy Van Heusen m
Mildred Bailey/<vocal Φ 09/38 Voc 4253
Russ Morgan/Gloria Whitney Φ 08/38 Dec 1922
Kay Kyser/Harry Babbitt 09/38 Bruns 8197
Dick Todd 09/38 Vic 26004

SO LITTLE TIME
Shapiro, B, pub. 1938, reached #19 in June 1938
Peter DeRose & Billy Hill w & m
Guy Lombardo/Carmen Lombardo 05/38 Vic 25823
Blue Barron/Russ Carlyle 06/38 Blu 7540

SOMETHING TELLS ME
Witmark, pub. 1938, reached #19 in May 1938
Johnny Mercer w, Harry Warren m
Fats Waller 05/38 Vic 25817
Kay Kyser/Sully Mason 05/38 Bruns 8114

STOP BEATIN' 'ROUND THE MULBERRY BUSH (40)
Bregman, V & C, pub. 1938, reached #6 in September 1938
S Bickley Reichner w, Clay A Boland m
Tommy Dorsey/Edythe Wright Φ 08/38 Vic 26012
Count Basie/Jimmy Rushing Φ 10/38 Dec 2004
Kay Kyser/Sully Mason Φ 09/38 Bruns 8197
Al Donahue/Paula Kelly 09/38 Voc 4318

SUMMER SOUVENIRS
Bregman, V & C, pub. 1938, reached #9 in November 1938
Charles Newman w, J Fred Coots m
Larry Clinton/Bea Wain Φ 10/38 Vic 26042
Russ Morgan/<vocal 10/38 Dec 2053
Connie Boswell 10/38 Dec 2055

SUNDAY IN THE PARK
Mills, pub. 1938, reached #18 in April 1938
Harold Rome w & m
Sung by ensemble in PINS AND NEEDLES, show (opened 11/37)
Hudson-DeLange Orch/Mary McHugh 04/38 Bruns 8077
Ted Weems/Perry Como 04/38 Dec 1694

SWEET AS A SONG (46)
Robbins, pub. 1937, reached #4 in March 1938
Mack Gordon w, Harry Revel m
Featured in SALLY, IRENE AND MARY, film (rel. 02/38)
Tony Martin, sung in film
Horace Heidt/Larry Cotton Φ 02/38 Bruns 8043
Guy Lombardo Orch 01/38 Vic 25731
Glen Gray/Kenny Sargent 02/38 Dec 1597

SWEET SOMEONE
L Feist, pub. 1937, reached #10 in February 1938
Mack Gordon w, Harry Revel m
Featured in LOVE AND HISSES, film (rel. 12/37)
Horace Heidt/Larry Cotton 12/37 Bruns 8013
Simone Simon, sung in film
Guy Lombardo/Carmen Lombardo 12/37 Vic 25709
Ozzie Nelson/<vocal 12/37 Blu 7267

TEN PRETTY GIRLS
Crawford, pub. 1937, reached #13 in February 1938
Jimmy Kennedy w, Will Grosz m
Guy Lombardo/w.vocal trio 12/37 Vic 25702
Dick Robertson/<vocal 01/38 Dec 1585
Jan Garber/w.vocal 02/38 Bruns 8060

THANKS FOR THE MEMORY (13)
Paramount, pub. 1937, reached #1 in March 1938
Leo Robin w, Ralph Rainger m
Featured in THE BIG BROADCAST OF 1938, film (rel. 02/38)
Bob Hope & Shirley Ross, sung in film, 01/39 Dec 2219
Shep Fields/Bob Goday Φ 01/38 Blu 7318
Benny Goodman/Martha Tilton Φ 01/38 Vic 25727
Dorothy Lamour 01/38 Bruns 8017

THERE'S A FARAWAY LOOK IN YOUR EYE
Tenney Mus, pub. 1938, reached #15 in September 1938
Irving Taylor w, Vic Mizzy m
Jimmy Dorsey/Bob Eberle 08/38 Dec 1834
Dick Todd 09/38 Vic 26004

THERE'S A GOLD MINE IN THE SKY (5)
Berlin, pub. 1937, reached #4 in January 1938
Charles Kenny & Nick Kenny w & m
Featured in GOLD MINE IN THE SKY, film (rel. 07/38)
Bing Crosby Φ 01/38 Dec 1565
Gene Autry, sung in film, 02/38 Voc 03358
Horace Heidt/Larry Cotton Φ 01/38 Bruns 8021
Isham Jones/Joe Martin 02/38 Voc 3910

THERE'S HONEY ON THE MOON TONIGHT
Miller Mus, pub. 1938, reached #13 in July 1938
Mack David & Haven Gillespie w, J Fred Coots m
Vincent Lopez/Johnny Morris 07/38 Voc 4141
Fats Waller 08/38 Vic 25891

THIS TIME IT'S REAL

L Spier, pub. 1938, reached #12 in July 1938
Buddy Bernier, Walter Shivers, Bob Emmerich w & m
Horace Heidt/Larry Cotton 06/38 Bruns 8121
Ella Fitzgerald/<vocal 06/38 Dec 1806
Tommy Dorsey/Jack Leonard 06/38 Vic 25862, 07/38 Vic 25879

TI-PI-TIN (8)

L Feist, pub. 1938, reached #1 in April 1938
Raymond Leveen w, Maria Grever m
Guy Lombardo/w.vocal trio ΦΦ 03/38 Vic 25786
Horace Heidt/w.vocal trio Φ 03/38 Bruns 8078
Andrews Sisters 04/38 Dec 1703
Jerry Blaine/Phyllis Kenny 04/38 Blu 7443

TRUE CONFESSION (32)

Famous, pub. 1937, reached #3 in January 1938
Sam Coslow & Fred Hollander w & m
Featured in TRUE CONFESSION, film (rel. 11/37)
Larry Clinton/Bea Wain Φ 12/37 Vic 25706
Russ Morgan/Lewis Julian 12/37 Bruns 8009
Sammy Kaye/Charlie Wilson 01/38 Voc 3871

TULIE TULIP TIME

Chappell, pub. 1938, reached #19 in September 1938
Jack Lawrence w, Maria Grever m
Andrews Sisters 09/38 Dec 1974
Horace Heidt/w.vocal group 09/38 Bruns 8192

TWO DREAMS GOT TOGETHER

J H Remick, pub. 1938, reached #18 in February 1938
Dave Franklin & Cliff Friend w & m
Larry Clinton/Bea Wain 02/38 Vic 25740
Dolly Dawn/George Hall Orch[2] 02/38 Voc 3908

TWO SLEEPY PEOPLE (16)

Famous, pub. 1938, reached #2 in December 1938
Frank Loesser & Hoagy Carmichael w & m
Featured in THANKS FOR THE MEMORY, film (rel. 11/38)
Bob Hope & Shirley Ross Φ sung in film, 01/39 Dec 2219
Fats Waller Φ 11/38 Blu 10000
Hoagy Carmichael & Ella Logan 11/38 Bruns 8250
Lawrence Welk/Walter Bloom 12/38 Voc 4435
Kay Kyser/w.vocal duo 11/38 Bruns 8244

WHAT GOES ON HERE IN MY HEART (50)

Paramount, pub. 1938, reached #9 in September 1938
Leo Robin w, Ralph Rainger m
Featured in GIVE ME A SAILOR, film (rel. 07/38)
Benny Goodman/Martha Tilton Φ 08/38 Vic 25878
Jack Whiting & Betty Grable, sung in film

WHAT HAVE YOU GOT THAT GETS ME?

Famous, pub. 1938, reached #12 in December 1938
Leo Robin w, Ralph Rainger m
Featured by ensemble[1] in ARTISTS AND MODELS ABROAD, film (rel. 11/38)
Benny Goodman/Martha Tilton 11/38 Vic 26053
Kay Kyser/Ginny Simms 11/38 Bruns 8228

WHEN MOTHER NATURE SINGS HER LULLABY (30)

Santly-Joy-Select, pub. 1938, reached #4 in August 1938
Glenn Brown w, Larry Yoell m
Bing Crosby Φ 07/38 Dec 1874
Al Donahue/Barry McKinley 08/38 Voc 4178
Dick Robertson/<vocal 08/38 Dec 1914

WHEN THE (MIGHTY) ORGAN PLAYED "OH PROMISE ME"

J Morris, pub. 1937, reached #11 in January 1938
Jack Meskill & Al Sherman w, Abner Silver m
Guy Lombardo/Carmen Lombardo 12/37 Vic 25702
Bing Crosby 12/37 Dec 1554
Emery Deutsch/Barry McKinley 11/37 Bruns 7979

WHEN THEY PLAYED THE POLKA

Robbins, pub. 1938, reached #10 in August 1938
Lou Holzer w, Fabian Andre m
Sammy Kaye/w.vocal group 07/38 Voc 4152
Horace Heidt/King Sisters 07/38 Bruns 8148

WHERE IN THE WORLD

L Feist, pub. 1938, reached #16 in August 1938
Mack Gordon & Harry Revel w & m
Featured in JOSETTE, film (rel. 06/38)
Don Ameche, sung in film
Hal Kemp/Bob Allen 08/38 Vic 25855
Shep Fields/Hal Derwin 08/38 Blu 7604

WHILE A CIGARETTE WAS BURNING (34)

ABC Music, pub. 1938, reached #3 in November 1938
Charles Kenny & Nick Kenny w & m
Charles "Buddy" Rogers/<vocal Φ 10/38 Voc 4408
Paul Whiteman/Joan Edwards Φ stage, 10/38 Dec 2083
Sammy Kaye/Charlie Wilson 12/38 Vic 26075

WHISTLE WHILE YOU WORK (11)

Berlin, pub. 1937, reached #2 in March 1938
Larry Morey w, Frank Churchill m
Featured in SNOW WHITE AND THE SEVEN DWARFS, film (rel. 12/37)
The Seven Dwarfs Φ sung in film, 02/38 Vic 25736
Shep Fields/Bob Goday Φ 02/38 Blu 7343
Guy Lombardo/w.vocal trio 02/38 Vic 25748

WHO BLEW OUT THE FLAME?

L Feist, pub. 1938, reached #11 in December 1938
Mitchell Parish w, Sammy Fain m
Larry Clinton/Bea Wain Φ 11/38 Vic 26073
Dolly Dawn/George Hall Orch[2] 11/38 Voc 4383
Ozzie Nelson/<vocal 11/38 Blu 7814

WILL YOU REMEMBER TONIGHT TOMORROW?

Bregman, V & C, pub. 1938, reached #20 in August 1938
Dave Franklin & Cliff Friend w & m
Russ Morgan/<vocal 06/38 Bruns 8119
Larry Clinton/Jack Chesleigh 08/38 Vic 25875

YOU COULDN'T BE CUTER
T B Harms, pub. 1938, reached #6 in May 1938
Dorothy Fields w, Jerome Kern m
Featured in JOY OF LIVING, film (rel. 03/38)
Tommy Dorsey/Edythe Wright Φ 03/38 Vic 25766
Irene Dunn, sung in film
Ray Noble/Tony Martin 05/38 Bruns 8076

YOU GO TO MY HEAD (38)
J H Remick, pub. 1938, reached #4 in September 1938
Haven Gillespie w, J Fred Coots m
Larry Clinton/Bea Wain Φ 07/38 Vic 25849
Billie Holiday Orch/<vocal 07/38 Voc 4126
Glen Gray/Kenny Sargent, stage, 07/38 Dec 1783
Teddy Wilson/Nan Wynn 07/38 Bruns 8141

YOU LEAVE ME BREATHLESS (39)
Famous, pub. 1938, reached #4 in July 1938
Ralph Freed w, Fred Hollander m
Featured in COCOANUT GROVE, film (rel. 05/38)
Tommy Dorsey/Jack Leonard Φ 05/38 Vic 25828
Fred MacMurray, sung in film
Ozzie Nelson/<vocal 06/38 Blu 7528

YOU MUST HAVE BEEN A BEAUTIFUL BABY (18)
J H Remick, pub. 1938, reached #1 in January 1939
(Also reached #4 in October 1961)
Johnny Mercer w, Harry Warren m
Featured in HARD TO GET, film (rel. 11/38)
Bing Crosby Φ 12/38 Dec 2147
Dick Powell, sung in film
Tommy Dorsey/Edythe Wright Φ 11/38 Vic 26066
Russ Morgan/<vocal 11/38 Dec 2125

YOU TOOK THE WORDS RIGHT OUT OF MY HEART
Paramount M C, pub. 1937, reached #11 in February 1938
Leo Robin & Ralph Rainger [1] w & m
Featured in THE BIG BROADCAST OF 1938, film (rel. 02/38)
Dorothy Lamour, sung in film, 01/38 Bruns 8017
Benny Goodman/Martha Tilton 01/38 Vic 25720
Shep Fields/Bob Goday 01/38 Blu 7304

YOU'RE A SWEETHEART (29)
Robbins, pub. 1937, reached #3 in February 1938
Harold Adamson w, Jimmy McHugh m
Featured in YOU'RE A SWEETHEART, film (rel. 12/37)
Dolly Dawn/George Hall Orch [2] Φ 01/38 Voc 3874
Tommy Dorsey/Edythe Wright Φ 12/37 Vic 25695
Alice Faye, sung in film
Ethel Waters 02/38 Dec 1613

YOU'RE AN EDUCATION (42)
J H Remick pub. 1938, reached #6 in May 1938
Al Dubin w, Harry Warren m
Larry Clinton/Bea Wain Φ 04/38 Vic 25794
Russ Morgan/Bernice Parks 03/38 Bruns 8084
Ozzie Nelson/<vocal 03/38 Blu 7432

[1]Ensemble included Joan Bennett and Jack Benny.
[2]Billed on record as Dolly Dawn & her Dawn Patrol.

1939

ADDRESS UNKNOWN
Olman, pub. 1939, reached #13 in November 1939
Carmen Lombardo, Johnny Marks, Dedette Lee Hill w & m
The Ink Spots Φ 10/39 Dec 2707
Horace Heidt/Larry Cotton 10/39 Bruns 8441
Guy Lombardo/Carmen Lombardo 10/39 Dec 2520

AND THE ANGELS SING (23)
Bregman, V & C, pub. 1939, reached #1 in May 1939
Johnny Mercer w, Ziggy Elman adpt, music traditional
Benny Goodman/Martha Tilton ΦΦ 04/39 Vic 26170
Bing Crosby 05/39 Dec 2413
Count Basie/Helen Humes 05/39 Voc 4784

ANGELS WITH DIRTY FACES
Fischer Mus, pub. 1938, reached #15 in January 1939
Maurice Spitalny w, Fred Fisher m
Cab Calloway Φ 12/38 Voc 4498
Tommy Dorsey/Edythe Wright 01/39 Vic 26115
Blue Barron/Russ Carlyle 12/38 Blu 7856

AN APPLE FOR THE TEACHER (39)
Santly-Joy, pub. 1939, reached #4 in October 1939
Johnny Burke w, James V Monaco m
Featured in THE STAR MAKER, film (rel. 08/39)
Bing Crosby & Connie Boswell Φ 08/39 Dec 2640
Bing Crosby & Linda Ware, sung in film
Larry Clinton/Ford Leary 09/39 Vic 26332

ARE YOU HAVIN' ANY FUN?
Crawford, pub. 1939, reached #11 in November 1939
Jack Yellen w, Sammy Fain m
Featured in GEORGE WHITE'S SCANDALS OF 1939, show (opened 08/39)
Tommy Dorsey/Edythe Wright 10/39 Vic 26335
Ella Logan, sung in show
Jimmy Dorsey/Helen O'Connell 10/39 Dec 2761

BEER BARREL POLKA (1)
Shapiro, B, pub. 1939, reached #2 in June 1939
Lew Brown, Vasek Zemen & Wladimir Timm w, Jaromir Vejvoda m
Featured in YOKEL BOY, show (opened 07/39)
Will Glahe Orch ΦΦΦ 05/39 Vic V-710
Andrews Sisters Φ 05/39 Dec 2462
Minute Men of Lexington, sung in show
Lawrence Welk Orch 05/39 Voc 4788

BLUE EVENING
Miller Mus, pub. 1939, reached #18 in June 1939
Gordon Jenkins & Joe Bishop w & m
Woody Herman/<vocal 06/39 Dec 2250
Glenn Miller/Ray Eberle 07/39 Blu 10290
Frances Langford 05/39 Dec 2438

BLUE ORCHIDS (17)
Famous, pub. 1939, reached #3 in November 1939
Hoagy Carmichael w & m
Glenn Miller/Ray Eberle Φ 09/39 Blu 10372
Benny Goodman/Louise Tobin Φ 10/39 Col 35211
Bob Crosby/Teddy Grace Φ 10/39 Dec 2734
Tommy Dorsey/Jack Leonard 10/39 Vic 26339

CINDERELLA, STAY IN MY ARMS (43)
Shapiro, B, pub. 1938, reached #8 in August 1939
Jimmy Kennedy & Michael Carr w & m
Guy Lombardo/Carmen Lombardo Φ 07/39 Dec 2520
Glenn Miller/Ray Eberle 08/39 Blu 10303
Jack Teagarten/<vocal 06/39 Bruns 8378

COMES LOVE (41)
Chappell, pub. 1939, reached #7 in September 1939
Charles Tobias & Lew Brown w, Sam Stept m
Featured in YOKEL BOY, show (opened 07/39)
Artie Shaw/Helen Forrest Φ 08/39 Blu 10324
Judy Canova, sung in show
Larry Clinton/Ford Leary 07/39 Vic 26277
Eddy Duchin/Durelle Alexander 08/39 Bruns 8434
Benny Goodman/Louise Tobin 09/39 Col 35201

CONCERT IN THE PARK
Witmark, pub. 1939, reached #12 in July 1939
Dave Franklin & Cliff Friend w & m
Kay Kyser/w.vocal duo 07/39 Bruns 8385
Jan Garber/Fritz Heilbron 07/39 Voc 4889

COULD BE (31)
Santly-Joy, pub. 1938, reached #4 in March 1939
Johnny Mercer w, Walter Donaldson m
Johnny Messner/Jeanne d'Arcy Φ 02/39 Blu 10107
Sammy Kaye/Three Barons Φ 02/39 Vic 26150

DAY IN - DAY OUT (25)
Bregman, V & C, pub. 1939, reached #3 in October 1939
Johnny Mercer w, Rube Bloom m
Bob Crosby/Helen Ward Φ 09/39 Dec 2703
Artie Shaw/Helen Forrest 10/39 Blu 10406
Kay Kyser/Harry Babbitt 09/39 Col 35202
Tommy Dorsey/Jack Leonard 10/39 Vic 26339

DEEP IN A DREAM (15)
T B Harms, pub. 1938, reached #3 in February 1939
Eddie DeLange w, Jimmy Van Heusen m
Artie Shaw/Helen Forrest Φ 12/38 Blu 10046
Bob Crosby/Marion Mann 12/38 Dec 2151
Kay Kyser/Ginny Simms 12/38 Bruns 8267

DEEP PURPLE (9)
Robbins, pub. 1934, reached #1 in March 1939
(Also reached #1 in November 1963)
(Also reached #14 in March 1976)
Mitchell Parish w, Peter DeRose m
All-time pop standard
Larry Clinton/Bea Wain ΦΦ 02/39 Vic 26141
Jimmy Dorsey/Bob Eberly Φ 03/39 Dec 2295
Guy Lombardo Orch 02/39 Dec 2215
Bing Crosby 04/39 Dec 2374
Artie Shaw/Helen Forrest 04/39 Blu 10178

DON'T WORRY 'BOUT ME (40)
Mills, pub. 1939, reached #6 in June 1939
Ted Koehler w, Rube Bloom m
Featured in COTTON CLUB PARADE OF 1939, revue (opened 03/39)
Cab Calloway, sung in revue
Hal Kemp/Bob Allen Φ 04/39 Vic 26188
Count Basie/Helen Humes 05/39 Voc 4734

THE EAST SIDE OF HEAVEN
Santly-Joy, pub. 1939, reached #11 in May 1939
Johnny Burke w, Jimmy Van Heusen m
Featured in EAST SIDE OF HEAVEN, film (rel. 04/39)
Bing Crosby Φ sung in film, 04/39 Dec 2359
Kay Kyser/Harry Babbitt 04/39 Bruns 8338

(ALLA EN) EL RANCHO GRANDE (35)
E B Marks, pub. 1934, reached #7 in November 1939
J D DelMoral & Bartley Costello w, Emilio D Uranga m
Bing Crosby Φ 10/39 Dec 2494
Dick Robertson/<vocal 10/39 Dec 1979
Gene Autry, radio, 03/40 Conqueror 9388

ESPECIALLY FOR YOU
Shapiro, B, pub. 1938, reached #17 in August 1939
Orrin Tucker & Phil Grogan w & m
Jimmy Dorsey/Helen O'Connell 07/39 Dec 2554
Orrin Tucker/Bonnie Baker, stage, 07/39 Voc 4241

F.D.R. JONES
Chappell, pub. 1938, reached #10 in February 1939
Harold Rome w & m
Featured in SING OUT THE NEWS, revue (opened 09/38)
Chick Webb/Ella Fitzgerald Φ 12/38 Dec 2105
Rex Ingram, sung in revue
Cab Calloway/<vocal 12/38 Voc 4498

FERDINAND THE BULL
ABC Music, pub. 1938, reached #17 in January 1939
Larry Morey w, Albert Hay Malotte m
Featured in FERDINAND THE BULL, film cartoon (1938)
Larry Clinton/Bea Wain 07/38 Vic 25841
Merry Macs 02/39 Dec 2238

THE FUNNY OLD HILLS
Paramount, pub. 1938, reached #15 in February 1939
Leo Robin & Ralph Rainger w & m
Featured in PARIS HONEYMOON, film (rel. 01/39)
Bing Crosby ⒫ sung in film, 01/39 Dec 2201
Jan Garber/Fritz Heilbron 03/39 Voc 4644

GET OUT OF TOWN
Chappell, pub. 1938, reached #13 in February 1939
Cole Porter w & m
Featured in LEAVE IT TO ME, show (opened 01/39)
Tamara, sung in show
Eddy Duchin Orch 01/39 Bruns 8252
Frances Langford 02/39 Dec 2229

GO FLY A KITE
Famous, pub. 1939, reached #19 in September 1939[2]
Johnny Burke w, James V Monaco m
Featured in THE STAR MAKER, film (rel. 08/39)
Bing Crosby, sung in film, 08/39 Dec 2641
Artie Shaw/Tony Pastor 08/39 Blu 10347

GOD BLESS AMERICA
Berlin ⒫⒫⒫ pub. 1939, reached #11 in April 1939
(Also reached #8 in August 1940)
Irving Berlin w & m
Steady seller, 1939-1945
All-time patriotic standard
Kate Smith ⒫ stage, 04/39 Vic 26198
Bing Crosby 05/39 Dec 2400

GOOD FOR NOTHIN' BUT LOVE
Witmark, pub. 1939, reached #16 in March 1939
Eddie DeLange w, Jimmy Van Heusen m
Fats Waller 02/39 Blu 10129
Benny Goodman/Martha Tilton 02/39 Vic 26159

GOOD MORNING
Chappell, pub. 1939, reached #12 in November 1939
Arthur Freed w, Nacio Herb Brown m
Featured in BABES IN ARMS, film (rel. 09/39)
Judy Garland & Mickey Rooney, sung in film
Abe Lyman/Rose Blane 10/39 Blu 10424
Jan Savitt/Bon Bon 11/39 Dec 2805

GOODY GOODBYE
Olman M C, pub. 1939, reached #11 in December 1939
James Cavanaugh & Nat Simon w & m
Dolly Dawn/George Hall Orch[3] 11/39 Voc 5160
Ted Weems/Perry Como 12/39 Dec 2794

GOTTA GET SOME SHUTEYE
Berlin, pub. 1939, reached #10 in April 1939
Johnny Mercer w, Walter Donaldson m
Kay Kyser/Harry Babbitt ⒫ 03/39 Bruns 8312
Glen Gray/Pee Wee Hunt 04/39 Dec 2307

HEAVEN CAN WAIT (24)
J H Remick, pub. 1939, reached #2 in April 1939
Eddie DeLange w, Jimmy Van Heusen m
Kay Kyser/Harry Babbitt ⒫ 03/39 Bruns 8317
Glen Gray/Clyde Burke ⒫ 04/39 Dec 2321
Tommy Dorsey/Jack Leonard 03/39 Vic 26154

HOLD TIGHT, HOLD TIGHT (48)
Exclusive, pub. 1939, reached #8 in April 1939
Leonard Kent, Edward Robinson, Leonard Ware, Jerry Brandow, Willie Spotswood w & m
Andrews Sisters ⒫ 02/39 Dec 2214
Fats Waller ⒫ 03/39 Blu 10116
Tommy Dorsey/Skeets Herfurt 03/39 Vic 26163

HURRY HOME (49)
L Spier, pub. 1938, reached #9 in February 1939
Joseph Meyer, Buddy Bernier, Bob Emmerich w & m
Sammy Kaye/Charlie Wilson ⒫ 12/38 Vic 26084
Kay Kyser/Harry Babbitt 12/38 Bruns 8263

I CRIED FOR YOU (47)
Miller Mus; orig. pub. 1923, reached #5 in March 1939
(Also reached #5 in August 1923)
Arthur Freed, Gus Arnheim, Abe Lyman w & m
Featured in BABES IN ARMS, film (rel. 09/39)
Glen Gray/Kenny Sargent ⒫ 01/39 Dec 1864
Judy Garland, sung in film
Bing Crosby 02/39 Dec 2273
Bunny Berigan/Kathleen Lane 01/39 Vic 26116

I DIDN'T KNOW WHAT TIME IT WAS
Chappell, pub. 1939, reached #6 in December 1939
Lorenz Hart w, Richard Rodgers m
Featured in TOO MANY GIRLS, show (opened 10/39)
Benny Goodman/Louise Tobin ⒫ 11/39 Col 35230
Jimmy Dorsey/Bob Eberly 12/39 Dec 2813
Marcy Westcott & Richard Kollmar, sung in show

I GET ALONG WITHOUT YOU VERY WELL (37)
Famous, pub. 1939, reached #3 in April 1939
Mrs. James Brown Thompson w, Hoagy Carmichael m
Jimmy Dorsey/Bob Eberly ⒫ 03/39 Dec 2322
Red Norvo/Terry Allen ⒫ 03/39 Voc 4648
Larry Clinton/Bea Wain 03/39 Vic 26151

I HAVE EYES (19)
Famous, pub. 1938, reached #3 in February 1939
Leo Robin & Ralph Rainger w & m
Featured in PARIS HONEYMOON, film (rel. 01/39)
Bing Crosby ⒫ 01/39 Dec 2201
Bing Crosby & Shirley Ross, sung in film
Benny Goodman/Martha Tilton ⒫ 12/38 Vic 26071
Artie Shaw/Helen Forrest ⒫ 01/39 Blu 7889

I MUST SEE ANNIE TONIGHT
Bregman, V & C, pub. 1938, reached #9 in January 1939
Dave Franklin & Cliff Friend w & m
Guy Lombardo/w.vocal trio Φ 01/39 Dec 2195
Benny Goodman/Martha Tilton 01/39 Vic 26110

I NEVER KNEW HEAVEN COULD SPEAK
Robbins, pub. 1939, reached #13 in June 1939
Mack Gordon w, Harry Revel m
Featured in ROSE OF WASHINGTON SQUARE, film (rel. 05/39)
Alice Faye, sung in film
Bob Crosby/Marion Mann 05/39 Dec 2464
Hal Kemp/Bob Allen 04/39 Vic 26194

I POURED MY HEART INTO A SONG (38)
Berlin, pub. 1939, reached #4 in August 1939
Irving Berlin w & m
Featured in SECOND FIDDLE, film (rel. 07/39)
Artie Shaw/Helen Forrest Φ 07/39 Blu 10307
Rudy Vallee, sung in film
Jimmy Dorsey/Bob Eberly 07/39 Dec 2553

I PROMISE YOU
ABC Music, pub. 1938, reached #13 in March 1939
Sammy Lerner & Alice Faye w, Ben Oakland m
Kay Kyser/Harry Babbitt 03/39 Bruns 8317
Glen Gray/Clyde Burke 03/39 Dec 2307
Dolly Dawn/George Hall 03/39 Voc 4682

I UPS TO HER (AND SHE UPS TO ME)
Olman M C, pub. 1938, reached #19 in January 1939
Al Hoffman, Al Goodhart, Manny Kurtz w & m
Guy Lombardo/w.vocal trio Φ 01/39 Dec 2196
Eddie DeLange/<vocal 01/39 Blu 10074

I'M BUILDING A SAILBOAT OF DREAMS
Shapiro, B, pub. 1939, reached #10 in May 1939
Dave Franklin & Cliff Friend w & m
Dick Robertson/<vocal 04/39 Dec 2364
Sammy Kaye/Tommy Ryan 04/39 Vic 26183
Bing Crosby 05/39 Dec 2447

IF I DIDN'T CARE (29)
Chappell, pub. 1939, reached #6 in July 1939
Jack Lawrence w & m
The Ink Spots ΦΦ 05/39 Dec 2286
Kate Smith 06/39 Vic 26245
Count Basie/Helen Humes 05/39 Voc 4784

IF I HAD MY WAY
Paull-Pioneer; orig. pub. 1913, reached #19 in July 1939
(Also reached #13 in June 1914)
Lou Klein w, James Kendis m
Glen Gray/Kenny Sargent 05/39 Dec 2437
Kate Smith 06/39 Vic 26245
Bing Crosby 06/39 Dec 2448

IN AN EIGHTEENTH CENTURY DRAWING ROOM
Circle Mus, pub. 1939, reached #9 in October 1939
Jack Lawrence w, Raymond Scott w & adpt, W A Mozart m
Guy Lombardo Orch Φ 10/39 Dec 2701
Raymond Scott Quintet 09/39 Bruns 8404
Horace Heidt/Larry Cotton 09/39 Bruns 8450

IN THE MIDDLE OF A DREAM
L Spier, pub. 1939, reached #11 in July 1939
Al Stillman w, Einar A Swann & Tommy Dorsey m
Tommy Dorsey/Jack Leonard Φ 06/39 Vic 26226
Red Norvo/Terry Allen 07/39 Voc 4953

IT'S A HUNDRED TO ONE (I'M IN LOVE)
Miller Mus, pub. 1939, reached #13 in October 1939
Dick Jurgens & Ronnie Kemper w & m
Dick Todd 09/39 Blu 10398
Dick Jurgens/Eddy Howard 09/39 Voc 5063
Tommy Dorsey/Edythe Wright 10/39 Vic 26363

JEEPERS CREEPERS (20)
Witmark, pub. 1938, reached #1 in February 1939
Johnny Mercer w, Harry Warren m
Featured in GOING PLACES, film (rel. 12/38)
Al Donahue/Paula Kelly ΦΦ 01/39 Voc 4513
Louis Armstrong, sung in film, 02/39 Dec 2267
Gene Krupa/Irene Daye 01/39 Bruns 8280
Larry Clinton/Ford Leary 01/29 Vic 26108

THE JUMPIN' JIVE
E B Marks, pub. 1939, reached #10 in September 1939
Cab Calloway, Frankie Froeba, Jack Palmer w & m
Cab Calloway/<vocal ΦΦ stage, 08/39 Voc 5005
Lionel Hampton/<vocal 09/39 Vic 26304
Jimmy Dorsey/Helen O'Connell 09/39 Dec 2612

THE LADY'S IN LOVE WITH YOU (33)
Paramount, pub. 1939, reached #3 in July 1939
Frank Loesser w, Burton Lane m
Featured in SOME LIKE IT HOT, film (rel. 05/39)
Glenn Miller/Tex Beneke ΦΦ 05/39 Blu 10229
Bob Hope & Shirley Ross, sung in film
Bob Crosby/<vocal 06/39 Dec 2465
Benny Goodman/Martha Tilton 06/39 Vic 26211

THE LAMP IS LOW (44)
Robbins, pub. 1939, reached #6 in August 1939
Mitchell Parish w, Peter DeRose & Bert Shefter adpt,
Maurice Ravel m
Tommy Dorsey/Jack Leonard Φ 07/39 Vic 26259
Glenn Miller/Ray Eberle 07/39 Blu 10290
Dorothy Lamour 07/39 Blu 10302

(WHY COULDN'T IT LAST) LAST NIGHT
L Feist, pub. 1939, reached #8 in November 1939
Nick Kenny & Charles Kenny w, Austen Herbert Croom-Johnson m
Glenn Miller/Ray Eberle Φ 10/39 Blu 10423
Bob Crosby/<vocal 11/39 Dec 2812
Hal Kemp/Bob Allen 11/39 Vic 26397

LILACS IN THE RAIN (26)
Robbins, pub. 1939, reached #4 in December 1939
Mitchell Parish w, Peter DeRose m
Bob Crosby/<vocal Φ 10/39 Dec 2763
Charlie Barnet/Del Casino Φ 10/39 Blu 10439
Tony Martin 11/39 Dec 2791

THE LITTLE MAN WHO WASN'T THERE
Robbins, pub. 1939, reached #16 in October 1939
Harold Adamson w, Bernie Hanighen m
Glenn Miller/Tex Beneke 09/39 Blu 10358
Larry Clinton/Ford Leary 09/39 Vic 26308

LITTLE SIR ECHO (8)
Bregman, V & C; orig. pub. 1917, reached #2 in May 1939
J S Fearis w, Laura Smith & Joe Marsala m
Guy Lombardo/Carmen Lombardo Φ 03/39 Dec 2306
Bing Crosby Φ 05/39 Dec 2385
Horace Heidt/w.vocal duo Φ 03/39 Bruns 8309
Dick Todd 04/39 Blu 10169

LITTLE SKIPPER (28)
L Feist, pub. 1939, reached #5 in May 1939
Nick Kenny & Charles Kenny w & m
Tommy Dorsey/Jack Leonard Φ 04/39 Vic 26195
Ozzie Nelson/<vocal Φ 04/39 Blu 10187
Al Donahue/Paula Kelly 05/39 Voc 4736

A MAN AND HIS DREAM
Santly-Joy, pub. 1939, reached #8 in October 1939
Johnny Burke w, James V Monaco m
Featured in THE STAR MAKER, film (rel. 08/39)
Bing Crosby Φ sung in film, 08/39 Dec 2641
Kay Kyser/Harry Babbitt 08/39 Bruns 8439

THE MAN WITH THE MANDOLIN (12)
Santly, pub. 1939, reached #2 in September 1939
James Cavanaugh & John Redmond w, Frank Weldon m
Glenn Miller/Marion Hutton Φ 08/39 Blu 10358
Wayne King/w.vocal trio Φ 08/39 Vic 26314
Horace Heidt/Larry Cotton Φ 08/39 Bruns 8430

THE MASQUERADE IS OVER (34)
Crawford, pub. 1938, reached #5 in April 1939
Herb Magidson w, Allie Wrubel m
Jimmy Dorsey/Bob Eberly Φ 03/39 Dec 2293
Larry Clinton/Bea Wain 03/39 Vic 26151
Horace Heidt/Larry Cotton 03/39 Bruns 8329

THE MOON IS A SILVER DOLLAR
Robbins, pub. 1939, reached #10 in April 1939
Mitchell Parish w, Sammy Fain m
Lawrence Welk/Walter Bloom Φ 03/39 Voc 4681
Gray Gordon/Cliff Grass 03/39 Blu 10142

MOON LOVE (11)
Paramount, pub. 1939, reached #1 in September 1939
Andre Kostelanetz, Mack David & Mack Davis w & adpt,
Peter I Tschaikovsky m,
Glenn Miller/Ray Eberle ΦΦ 07/39 Blu 10303
Al Donahue/Paula Kelly Φ 07/39 Voc 4888
Paul Whiteman/Joan Edwards Φ 08/39 Dec 2578
Mildred Bailey/<vocal 08/39 Voc 4939
Sammy Kaye/Clyde Burke 08/39 Vic 26279

MOONLIGHT SERENADE (50)
Robbins, pub. 1939, reached #9 in September 1939
Mitchell Parish w, Glenn Miller m
Big band classic
Glenn Miller Orch Φ 08/39 Blu 10214

MY HEART BELONGS TO DADDY
Chappell, pub. 1938, reached #15 in March 1939
Cole Porter w & m
Featured in LEAVE IT TO ME, show (opened 11/38)
Mary Martin, sung in show
Larry Clinton/Bea Wain 01/39 Vic 26100
Mary Martin/Eddy Duchin Orch 01/39 Bruns 8282

MY LAST GOODBYE
Berlin, pub. 1939, reached #19 in July 1939
Eddy Howard w & m
Dick Jurgens/Eddy Howard, stage, 06/39 Voc 4874
Henry Busse/Dick Wharton 06/39 Dec 2454
Glenn Miller/Ray Eberle 06/39 Blu 10229

MY PRAYER (10)
Shapiro, B, pub. 1939, reached #3 in November 1939
(Also reached #1 in August 1956)
Jimmy Kennedy w, Georges Boulanger m
Glenn Miller/Ray Eberle Φ 10/39 Blu 10404
The Ink Spots Φ 10/39 Dec 2790
Sammy Kaye/Clyde Burke 11/39 Vic 26369

A NEW MOON AND AN OLD SERENADE
Berlin, pub. 1939, reached #9 in June 1939
Abner Silver, Sam Coslow, Martin Block w & m
Tommy Dorsey/Jack Leonard Φ 04/39 Vic 26181
Charlie Barnet/Judy Ellington 04/39 Blu 10153

NIGHT MUST FALL (OVER ALL)
Sam Fox, pub. 1938, reached #20 in May 1939
Barnett Shaw w, Xavier Cugat m
Xavier Cugat Orch 04/39 Vic 26074
Blue Barron/Russ Carlyle 06/39 Blu 10221

OH JOHNNY, OH JOHNNY OH! (16)
Forster ΦΦΦ pub. 1917, reached #3 in January 1940
(Also reached #2 in June 1917)
Ed Rose w, Abe Olman m
Orrin Tucker/Bonnie Baker ΦΦΦ 11/39 Col 35228
Andrews Sisters 12/39 Dec 2840
Glenn Miller/Marion Hutton 12/39 Blu 10507

OH, YOU CRAZY MOON (30)
Witmark, pub. 1939, reached #3 in September 1939
Johnny Burke w, Jimmy Van Heusen m
Tommy Dorsey/Jack Leonard Φ 08/39 Vic 26287
Glenn Miller/Ray Eberle Φ 08/39 Blu 10329
Bea Wain/Walter Gross Orch 09/39 Vic 26311

OUR LOVE (21)
Chappell, pub. 1939, reached #1 in May 1939
Buddy Bernier & Bob Emmerich w, Larry Clinton adpt, Peter I Tchaikovsky m
Tommy Dorsey/Jack Leonard ΦΦ 04/39 Vic 26202
Jimmy Dorsey/Bob Eberly Φ 04/39 Dec 2352
Larry Clinton Orch, stage

OVER THE RAINBOW (4)
L Feist, pub. 1939, reached #1 in September 1939
(Also reached #17 in September 1960)
E Y Harbourg w, Harold Arlen m
Featured in THE WIZARD OF OZ, film (rel. 08/39)
All-time pop standard
Judy Garland Φ sung in film, 09/39 Dec 2672
Glenn Miller/Ray Eberle ΦΦ 08/39 Blu 10366
Bob Crosby/Teddy Grace Φ 09/39 Dec 2657
Larry Clinton/Bea Wain 08/39 Vic 26174

PENNY SERENADE (13)
Shapiro, B, pub. 1938, reached #2 in March 1939
Hal Halifax w, Melle Weersma m
Guy Lombardo/w.vocal trio Φ stage, 03/39 Dec 2291
Sammy Kaye/Jimmy Brown Φ 03/39 Vic 26150
Horace Heidt/Larry Cotton Φ 03/39 Bruns 8313

PLEASE COME OUT OF YOUR DREAM
Words & Mus, pub. 1938, reached #20 in January 1939
Carl Sigman w & m
Seger Ellis/<vocal 12/38 Bruns 8275
Ruby Newman/<vocal 01/39 Dec 2191
Johnny Messner/<vocal 01/39 Blu 10058

SCATTERBRAIN (6)
Bregman, V & C, pub. 1939, reached #1 in December 1939
Johnny Burke, Frankie Masters, Carl Bean, Kahn Keene w & m
Featured in THAT'S RIGHT, YOU'RE WRONG, film (rel. 11/39)
Frankie Masters/<vocal ΦΦ 10/39 Voc 4915
Freddy Martin/Glenn Hughes Φ 11/39 Blu 10436
Kay Kyser Orch, played in film
Benny Goodman/Louise Tobin 11/39 Col 35241
Guy Lombardo/w.vocal trio 11/39 Dec 2767

THE SHABBY OLD CABBY
Shapiro, B, pub. 1939, reached #16 in August 1939
Al Stillman w, Nat Simon m
Horace Heidt/Larry Cotton 07/39 Bruns 8409
Sammy Kaye/Three Barons 08/39 Vic 26298
Jan Savitt/Phil Brito 08/39 Dec 2600

SOUTH AMERICAN WAY
T B Harms, pub. 1939, reached #18 in August 1939
Al Dubin w, Jimmy McHugh m
Featured in STREETS OF PARIS, revue (opened 06/39)
Carmen Miranda, sung in revue
Guy Lombardo/w.vocal trio 07/39 Dec 2566
Al Donahue/Paula Kelly 07/39 Voc 4902

SOUTH OF THE BORDER (2)
Shapiro, B, pub. 1939, reached #1 in November 1939
Jimmy Kennedy w, Michael Carr m
Shep Fields/Hal Derwin ΦΦ 10/39 Blu 10376
Gene Autry, radio, 11/39 Voc 5122
Guy Lombardo/Carmen Lombardo 11/39 Dec 2768
Bert Ambrose/Denny Dennis 11/39 Dec 2732
Tony Martin 12/39 Dec 2788

SPEAKING OF HEAVEN
Miller Mus, pub. 1939, reached #15 in January 1940
Mack Gordon w, Jimmy Van Heusen m
Glenn Miller/Ray Eberle 12/39 Blu 10455
Will Bradley/Larry Southern 12/39 Voc 5182
Eddy Duchin/Johnny McAfee 12/39 Col 35296

STAIRWAY TO THE STARS (14)
Robbins, pub. 1939, reached #1 in July 1939
Mitchell Parish w, Matty Malneck & Frank Signorelli m
Glenn Miller/Ray Eberle ΦΦ 06/39 Blu 10276
Kay Kyser/Harry Babbitt Φ 06/39 Bruns 8381
Jimmy Dorsey/Bob Eberly 07/39 Dec 2567
Al Donahue/Paula Kelly 07/39 Voc 4846

STOP! IT'S WONDERFUL (46)
L Spier, pub. 1939, reached #7 in December 1939
Bickley Reichner w, Clay Boland m
Orrin Tucker/Bonnie Baker Φ 12/39 Col 35249
Tommy Dorsey/Edythe Wright 10/39 Vic 26325
Eddie DeLange/<vocal 11/39 Blu 10441

STRANGE ENCHANTMENT
Famous, pub. 1939, reached #7 in July 1939
Frank Loesser w, Fred Hollander m
Featured in MAN ABOUT TOWN, film (rel. 06/39)
Dorothy Lamour Φ sung in film, 06/39 Blu 10265
Ozzie Nelson/Rose Ann Stevens Φ 06/39 Blu 10196
Bob Crosby/Marion Mann 05/39 Dec 2415

SUNRISE SERENADE (5)
Jewel, pub. 1938, reached #4 in June 1939
Jack Lawrence w, Frankie Carle m
Big band classic
Glen Gray Orch ΦΦ 04/39 Dec 2321
Glenn Miller Orch ΦΦ 05/39 Blu 10214
Connie Boswell 05/39 Dec 2450

SWEETHEARTS
Schirmer, pub. 1913, reached #18 in February 1939
Pub. w. new lyrics 1938
(Also reached #14 in August 1913 with original lyrics)
Bob Wright & Chet Forrest w[1], Victor Herbert m
Featured in SWEETHEARTS, film (rel. 12/38)
Jeanette Macdonald, sung in film
Bing Crosby 01/39 Dec 2315

TEARS FROM MY INKWELL
Witmark, pub. 1939, reached #18 in May 1939
Mort Dixon w, Harry Warren m
Glen Gray/Kenny Sargent 05/39 Dec 2388
Red Nichols/Bill Darnell 05/39 Blu 10200
Sammy Kaye/Tommy Ryan 04/39 Vic 26199

THANKS FOR EVERYTHING (45)
Robbins, pub. 1938, reached #7 in February 1939
Mack Gordon w, Harry Revel m
Featured in THANKS FOR EVERYTHING, film (rel. 12/38)
Artie Shaw/Helen Forrest Φ 01/39 Blu 10055
Tony Martin, sung in film
Tommy Dorsey/Edythe Wright 12/38 Vic 26119

THEY SAY (32)
Witmark, pub. 1938, reached #7 in February 1939
Edward Heyman w, Stephen Weiss & Paul Mann m
Artie Shaw/Helen Forrest Φ 01/39 Blu 10075
Sammy Kaye/Tommy Ryan 12/38 Vic 26075
Mildred Bailey Orch/<vocal 01/39 Voc 4548

THIS CAN'T BE LOVE (18)
Chappell, pub. 1938, reached #4 in January 1939
Lorenz Hart w, Richard Rodgers m
Featured in THE BOYS FROM SYRACUSE, show (opened 11/38)
Benny Goodman/Martha Tilton Φ 12/38 Vic 26099
Marcy Westcott & Eddie Albert, sung in show
Horace Heidt/Larry Cotton Φ 12/38 Bruns 8257

THIS IS IT
Chappell, pub. 1939, reached #12 in April 1939
Dorothy Fields w, Arthur Schwartz m
Featured in STARS IN YOUR EYES, show (opened 02/39)
Ethel Merman, sung in show
Tommy Dorsey/Jack Leonard 03/39 Vic 26149
Artie Shaw/Helen Forrest 03/39 Blu 10141

THIS IS NO DREAM
Bregman, V & C, pub. 1939, reached #13 in August 1939
Benny Davis w, Ted Shapiro & Tommy Dorsey m
Tommy Dorsey/Jack Leonard 07/39 Vic 26234
Horace Heidt/Larry Cotton 06/39 Bruns 8382
Charlie Barnet/Judy Ellington 07/39 Blu 10273

THIS NIGHT (WILL BE MY SOUVENIR)
Bregman, V & C, pub. 1939, reached #19 in April 1939
Gus Kahn w, Harry Warren m
Featured in HONOLULU, film (rel. 02/39)
Glen Gray/Clyde Burke 03/39 Dec 2308
Tommy Dorsey/Jack Leonard 03/39 Vic 26172

THREE LITTLE FISHIES (ITTY BITTY POO) (22)
Santly-Joy, pub. 1939, reached #1 in June 1939
Saxie Dowell w & m
Kay Kyser/w.vocal trio ΦΦ 05/39 Bruns 8358
Hal Kemp/The Smoothies Φ 05/39 Vic 26204
Paul Whiteman/Four Modernaires 05/39 Dec 2417

TO YOU
Famous, pub. 1939, reached #11 in August 1939
Benny Davis w, Ted Shapiro & Tommy Dorsey m
Tommy Dorsey/Jack Leonard 07/39 Vic 26234
Glenn Miller/Ray Eberle 07/39 Blu 10276
Al Donahue/Paula Kelly 07/39 Voc 4888

THE UMBRELLA MAN (3)
T B Harms, pub. 1938, reached #2 in February 1939
James Cavanaugh w, Vincent Rose & Larry Stock m
Kay Kyser/w.vocal duo ΦΦ 12/38 Bruns 8225
Guy Lombardo/w.vocal trio Φ 01/39 Dec 2221
Sammy Kaye/w.vocal trio 01/39 Vic 26117
Johnny Messner/Three Jacks 01/39 Blu 10048

UNDECIDED
Leeds, pub. 1939, reached #20 in April 1939
(Also reached #5 in December 1951)
Sid Robin w, Charlie Shavers m
Chick Webb/Ella Fitzgerald Φ 03/39 Dec 2323
Benny Goodman Orch 03/39 Vic 26134
John Kirby & His Onyx Club Boys 03/39 Dec 2216

WE'VE COME A LONG WAY TOGETHER
L Feist, pub. 1939, reached #18 in April 1939
Ted Koehler w, Sam Stept m
Sammy Kaye/Tommy Ryan 03/39 Vic 26178
Mitchell Ayres/Mary Ann Mercer 03/39 Voc 4665

WELL, ALL RIGHT!
Leeds, pub. 1939, reached #13 in August 1939
Frances Faye, Don Raye, Dan Howell w & m
Andrews Sisters Φ 06/39 Dec 2462
Tommy Dorsey/Edythe Wright 07/39 Vic 26281

WHAT'S NEW? (42)
Witmark, pub. 1939, reached #7 in October 1939
Johnny Burke w, Bob Haggart m
Bing Crosby Φ 10/39 Dec 2671
Benny Goodman/Louise Tobin 11/39 Col 35211
Bob Crosby Orch 09/39 Dec 2205
Hal Kemp/Nan Wynn 10/39 Vic 26336

WHITE SAILS (27)
L Feist, pub. 1939, reached #3 in July 1939
Harry Archer, Nick Kenny, Charles Kenny w & m
Sammy Kaye/Clyde Burke Φ 06/39 Vic 26267
Ozzie Nelson/<vocal Φ 07/39 Blu 10311
Al Donahue/Paula Kelly 08/39 Voc 4956

WISHING (7)
Crawford, pub. 1939, reached #1 in June 1939
Buddy DeSylva w & m
Featured in LOVE AFFAIR, film (rel. 03/39)
Glenn Miller/Ray Eberle ΦΦ 05/39 Blu 10219
Irene Dunn, sung in film
Russ Morgan/Mert Curtis Φ 06/39 Dec 2436
Horace Heidt/w.vocal duo 06/39 Bruns 8382
Orrin Tucker/<vocal 06/39 Voc 4762

WOODCHOPPERS' BALL
Leeds, pub. 1939, reached #19 in June 1939
Woody Herman & Joe Bishop m
Big band classic
Woody Herman Orch Φ 05/39 Dec 2440

YODELIN' JIVE
Leeds, pub. 1939, reached #17 in January 1940
Hughie Prince w, Don Raye m
Bing Crosby & The Andrews Sisters Φ 11/39 Dec 2800
Abe Lyman/Rose Blane 01/40 Blu 10533

YOU'RE A SWEET LITTLE HEADACHE (36)
Paramount, pub. 1938, reached #5 in March 1939
Leo Robin & Ralph Rainger w & m
Featured in PARIS HONEYMOON, film (rel 01/39)
Bing Crosby Φ sung in film, 01/39 Dec 2200
Benny Goodman/Martha Tilton Φ 01/39 Vic 26071
Artie Shaw/Helen Forrest 01/39 Blu 7889

YOU'RE THE ONLY STAR (IN MY BLUE HEAVEN)
Shapiro, B, pub. 1938, reached #17 in January 1939
Gene Autry w & m
Featured in THE OLD BARN DANCE, film (rel. 01/38)
Gene Autry, sung in film, 11/38 Conqueror 9098
Dick Todd 12/38 Blu 10034

[1]Original lyrics by Robert B Smith, 1913.
[2]Reached #19 on monthly chart only.
[3]Billed on record as Dolly Dawn & her Dawn Patrol.

1940

ALICE BLUE GOWN
L Feist, pub. 1919, reached #12 in May 1940
(Also reached #10 in June 1920)
Joe McCarthy w, Harry Tierney m
Frankie Masters/Marion Francis 04/40 Voc 5455
Glenn Miller Orch 05/40 Blu 10701
Ozzie Nelson/Rose Ann Stevens 05/40 Blu 10659

ALL THE THINGS YOU ARE (22)
Chappell, pub. 1939, reached #1 in January 1940
Oscar Hammerstein 2nd w, Jerome Kern m
Featured by vocal quartet in VERY WARM FOR MAY, show (opened 11/39)
Tommy Dorsey/Jack Leonard ΦΦ 12/39 Vic 26401
Artie Shaw/Helen Forrest Φ 01/40 Blu 10492
Frankie Masters/Harlan Rogers 01/40 Voc 5265

ALL THIS AND HEAVEN TOO
Remick, pub. 1939, reached #9 in August 1940
Eddie DeLange w, Jimmy Van Heusen m
Jimmy Dorsey/Bob Eberly 07/40 Dec 3259
Tommy Dorsey/Frank Sinatra 08/40 Vic 26653
Charlie Barnet/Larry Taylor 08/40 Blu 10751
Dick Todd 08/40 Blu 10789

AN ANGEL IN DISGUISE
Witmark, pub. 1939, reached #20 in June 1940
Kim Gannon w, Paul Mann & Stephan Weiss m
Featured in IT ALL CAME TRUE, film (rel. 04/40)
Ann Sheridan, sung in film
Dick Todd 04/40 Blu 10636
Ozzie Nelson/<vocal 05/40 Blu 10659
Horace Heidt/Larry Cotton 04/40 Col 35421

AT THE BALALAIKA (33)
L Feist, pub. 1939, reached #4 in February 1940
Eric Maschwitz, Bob Wright & Chet Forrest w, George Posford & Herbert Stothart m
Featured in BALALAIKA, film (rel. 12/39)
Orrin Tucker/Gil Mershon Φ 01/40 Col 35332
Ilona Massey, sung in film
Abe Lyman/Ed Holly 02/40 Blu 10533

BEAT ME, DADDY, EIGHT TO THE BAR (34)
Leeds, pub. 1940, reached #11 in November 1940
Hughie Prince & Eleanore Sheehy w, Don Raye m
Will Bradley/Ray McKinley Φ 08/40 Col 35530
Andrews Sisters Φ 11/40 Dec 3375
Glenn Miller/Jack Lathrop 11/40 Blu 10876

BLUEBERRY HILL (5)
Chappell, pub. 1940, reached #1 in October 1940
(Also reached #4 in January 1957)
Al Lewis, Larry Stock, Vincent Rose w & m
Glenn Miller/Ray Eberle ΦΦ 08/40 Blu 10768
Kay Kyser/Harry Babbitt 08/40 Col 35554
Russ Morgan/Carol Kay 09/40 Dec 3290

BLUEBIRDS IN THE MOONLIGHT
Famous, pub. 1939, reached #18 in January 1940
Leo Robin w, Ralph Rainger m
Featured in MAN ABOUT TOWN, film (rel. 06/39)
Glenn Miller/Marion Hutton 12/39 Blu 10465
Dick Jurgens/Eddy Howard 12/39 Voc 5181
Benny Goodman/Mildred Bailey 01/40 Col 35289

BLUE LOVEBIRD
L Feist, pub. 1940, reached #10 in July 1940
Gus Kahn w, Bronislaw Kaper m
Featured in LILLIAN RUSSELL, film (rel. 05/40)
Alice Faye, sung in film
Kay Kyser/Ginny Simms Φ 06/40 Col 35488
Mitchell Ayres/Mary Ann Mercer 07/40 Blu 10738

BOOG-IT
Regent, pub. 1940, reached #19 in June 1940
Cab Calloway, Jack Palmer, Buck Ram w & m
Glenn Miller/Marion Hutton Φ 05/40 Blu 10689
Gene Krupa/Irene Daye 05/40 Col 35415
Cab Calloway/<vocal 05/40 Voc 5444

THE BREEZE AND I (25)
E B Marks, pub. 1940, reached #3 in July 1940
(Also reached #13 in May 1955)
Al Stillman w, Ernesto Lecuona & Toots Camarata m
Based on Lecuona's ANDALUCIA: SUITE ESPAGNOLE, pub. 1928
Jimmy Dorsey/Bob Eberly ΦΦ 05/40 Dec 3150
Charlie Barnet/Mary Ann McCall 06/40 Blu 10696
Xavier Cugat/Dinah Shore 08/40 Vic 26641
Frankie Masters/Marion Francis 06/40 Voc 5528

THE CALL OF THE CANYON
Shapiro, B, pub. 1940, reached #11 in October 1940
Billy Hill w & m
Glenn Miller/Ray Eberle Φ 09/40 Blu 10845
Tommy Dorsey/Frank Sinatra 09/40 Vic 26678
Kay Kyser/Ginny Simms 09/40 Col 35627

CAN'T GET INDIANA OFF MY MIND
Santly-Joy, pub. 1940, reached #14 in September 1940
Robert DeLeon w, Hoagy Carmichael m
Bing Crosby 08/40 Dec 3321
Horace Heidt/Larry Cotton 08/40 Col 35555
Hal Kemp/Bob Allen 08/40 Vic 26655

CARELESS (13)
Berlin, pub. 1939, reached #1 in February 1940
Dick Jurgens, Eddy Howard, Lew Quadling w & m
Glenn Miller/Ray Eberle ΦΦ 12/39 Blu 10520
Dick Jurgens/Eddy Howard Φ 12/39 Voc 5235
Tommy Dorsey/Allan DeWitt 04/40 Vic 26433

CHATTERBOX
Chappell, pub. 1940, reached #13 in January 1940
Allan Roberts w, Jerome Brainin m
Featured in THAT'S RIGHT, YOU'RE WRONG, film (rel. 11/39)
Kay Kyser/Ginny Simms 12/39 Col 35307
Guy Lombardo/w.vocal trio 01/40 Dec 2910

CIRIBIRIBIN
Paramount; orig. pub. 1909, reached #20 in January 1940
(Also reached #12 in March 1910)
Rudolf Thaler w, Alberto Pestalozza m
Bing Crosby & Andrews Sisters 12/39 Dec 2800
Harry James/Frank Sinatra 01/40 Col 35316
Harry James Orch 11/39 Bruns 8327

CONFUCIUS SAY
Olman M C, pub. 1939, reached #13 in March 1940
Carmen Lombardo & Cliff Friend w & m
Guy Lombardo/w.vocal trio 02/40 Dec 2917
Kay Kyser/Sully Mason 02/30 Col 35343

CROSSTOWN
Shapiro, B, pub. 1940, reached #17 in October 1940
James Cavanaugh, John Redmond, Nat Simon w & m
Glenn Miller/Jack Lathrop 09/40 Blu 10832
Horace Heidt Orch 11/40 Col 35709

DARN THAT DREAM (39)
Bregman, V & C, pub. 1939, reached #4 in March 1940
Eddie DeLange w, Jimmy Van Heusen m
Featured by ensemble in SWINGIN' THE DREAM, show (opened 11/39)
Benny Goodman/Mildred Bailey Φ 02/40 Col 35331
Blue Barron/Russ Carlyle 02/40 Blu 10525
Tommy Dorsey/Anita Boyer 03/40 Vic 26433

DEVIL MAY CARE
Witmark, pub. 1940, reached #12 in July 1940
Johnny Burke w, Jimmy Van Heusen m
Glenn Miller/Ray Eberle Φ 06/40 Blu 10717
Bing Crosby 06/40 Dec 3064
Benny Goodman/Helen Forrest 06/40 Col 35461
Tommy Dorsey/Frank Sinatra 06/40 Vic 26593

DO I LOVE YOU?
Chappell, pub. 1939, reached #8 in March 1940
Cole Porter w & m
Featured in DuBARRY WAS A LADY, show (opened 13/39)
Ethel Merman & Ronald Graham, sung in show
Leo Reisman/Lee Sullivan Φ 01/40 Vic 26421

DOWN ARGENTINA WAY (27)
Miller Mus, pub. 1940, reached #3 in January 1941
Mack Gordon w, Harry Warren m
Featured in DOWN ARGENTINA WAY, film (rel. 10/40)
Bob Crosby/Bonnie King Φ 11/40 Dec 3404
Leo Reisman/Sara Horn 11/40 Vic 26765
Eddy Duchin/The Earbenders 12/40 Col 35774
Gene Krupa/Irene Day 12/40 Okeh 5826
Don Ameche[1], film

DREAM VALLEY (38)
L Feist, pub. 1940, reached #8 in December 1940
Nick Kenny & Charles Kenny w, Joe Burke m
Sammy Kaye/Tommy Ryan Φ 12/40 Vic 26795
Eddy Duchin/Johnny Drake 12/40 Col 35780

FAITHFUL FOREVER (37)
Famous, pub. 1939, reached #5 in February 1940
Leo Robin & Ralph Rainger w & m
Featured in GULLIVER'S TRAVELS, cartoon film (rel. 12/39)
Glenn Miller/Ray Eberle Φ 12/39 Blu 10465
Dick Jurgens/Eddy Howard 12/39 Voc 5181
Jessica Dragonette & Lanny Ross, dubbed in film

FERRY-BOAT SERENADE (6)
Robbins, pub. 1940, reached #1 in November 1940
Mario Panzeri & Harold Adamson w, Eldo di Lazzaro m
Andrews Sisters ΦΦ 10/40 Dec 3328
Kay Kyser/Harry Babbitt Φ 10/40 Col 35627
Gray Gordon/Meredith Blake Φ 09/40 Blu 10819
Frankie Masters/w.vocal duo 10/40 Okeh 5716
Leo Reisman/Anita Boyer 11/40 Vic 26718

FIVE O'CLOCK WHISTLE
Advanced, pub. 1940, reached #15 in December 1940
Josef Myrow, Kim Gannon, Gene Irwin w & m
Glenn Miller/Marion Hutton Φ 11/40 Blu 10900
Ella Fitzgerald Φ 11/40 Dec 3420
Erskine Hawkins Orch 11/40 Blu 10854

FOOLS RUSH IN (28)
Bregman, V & C, pub. 1940, reached #3 in August 1940
(Also reached #11 in November 1963)
Johnny Mercer w, Rube Bloom m
Glenn Miller/Ray Eberle Φ 06/40 Blu 10728
Tommy Dorsey/Frank Sinatra 08/40 Vic 26593
Tony Martin 08/40 Dec 3119

THE GAUCHO SERENADE (43)
Remick, pub. 1939, reached #6 in April 1940
James Cavanaugh, John Redmond, Nat Simon w & m
Featured in IT ALL CAME TRUE, film (rel. 04/40)
Dick Todd Φ 02/40 Blu 10559
Glenn Miller/Ray Eberle Φ 02/40 Blu 10570
Ann Sheridan, sung in film
Eddy Duchin/Johnny McAfee 03/40 Col 35360

GOD BLESS AMERICA (24)
Berlin ΦΦΦ, pub. 1939, reached #8 in August 1940
(Also reached #11 in April 1939)
Irving Berlin w & m
Steady seller, 1939-1945
All-time patriotic standard
Kate Smith Φ 07/40 Vic 26198
Bing Crosby 07/40 Dec 2400

HEAR MY SONG, VIOLETTA
Crawford, pub. 1938, reached #17 in August 1940
Ermengildo Carosio, Buddy Bernier & Bob Emmerich w, Rudolf Luckesch & Othmar Klose m
Glenn Miller/Ray Eberle 07/40 Blu 10684
Tommy Dorsey/Frank Sinatra 06/40 Vic 26616

HOW HIGH THE MOON
Chappell, pub. 1940, reached #10 in April 1940
(Also reached #1 in May 1951)
Nancy Hamilton w, Morgan Lewis m
Featured in TWO FOR THE SHOW, show (opened 02/40)
Benny Goodman/Helen Forrest Φ 03/40 Col 35391
Frances Comstock & Alfred Drake, sung in show
Mitchell Ayres/Mary Ann Mercer 04/40 Blu 10609

I AM AN AMERICAN
Mercer, pub. 1940, reached #13 in November 1940
Paul Cunningham, Ira Schuster, Leonard Whitcup w & m
Gray Gordon/w.vocal duo Φ 08/40 Blu 10783
Dick Robertson/<vocal 09/40 Dec 3323

I CAN'T LOVE YOU ANY MORE (THAN I DO) (47)
Olman M C, pub. 1940, reached #7 in July 1940
Herb Magidson w, Allie Wrubel m
Benny Goodman/Helen Forrest 05/40 Col 35487
Mitchell Ayres/Tommy Taylor 07/40 Blu 10653
Terry Shand/<vocal 07/40 Dec 3127

I'LL NEVER SMILE AGAIN (3)
Sun Mus Co ΦΦΦ, pub. 1939, reached #1 in August 1940
Ruth Lowe w & m
Tommy Dorsey/Frank Sinatra ΦΦΦ 07/40 Vic 26628
The Ink Spots 09/40 Dec 3346
Glenn Miller/Ray Eberle 08/40 Blu 10673

I'M NOBODY'S BABY (29)
L Feist ΦΦΦ, pub. 1921, reached #4 in September 1940
(Also reached #3 in September 1921)
Milt Ager, Lester Santly, Benny Davis w & m
Featured in ANDY HARDY MEETS DEBUTANTE, film (rel. 07/40)
Judy Garland Φ sung in film, 07/40 Dec 3174
Bea Wain/Walter Gross Orch 08/40 Vic 26603
Ozzie Nelson/Rose Ann Stevens 08/40 Blu 10722
Tommy Dorsey/Connie Haines 08/40 Vic 26609

I'M STEPPING OUT WITH A MEMORY TONIGHT
Robbins, pub. 1940, reached #11 in August 1940
Herb Magidson w, Allie Wrubel m
Glenn Miller/Ray Eberle Φ 06/40 Blu 10717
Kate Smith 07/40 Col 35398
Al Donahue/Phil Brito 07/40 Voc 5519

I'VE GOT MY EYES ON YOU
Crawford, pub. 1939, reached #8 in March 1940
Cole Porter w & m
Featured in BROADWAY MELODY OF 1940, film (rel. 02/40)
Fred Astaire, sung in film
Tommy Dorsey/Allan DeWitt Φ 02/40 Vic 26470
Bob Crosby/Marion Mann 03/40 Dec 2991

IMAGINATION (23)
ABC Music, pub. 1940, reached #1 in June 1940
Johnny Burke w, Jimmy Van Heusen m
Glenn Miller/Ray Eberle ΦΦ 05/40 Blu 10622
Tommy Dorsey/Frank Sinatra Φ 06/40 Vic 26581
Ella Fitzgerald/<vocal 05/40 Dec 3078

IN AN OLD DUTCH GARDEN (4)
T B Harms, pub. 1939, reached #2 in April 1940
Mack Gordon w, Will Grosz m
Dick Jurgens/Eddy Howard ΦΦ 01/40 Voc 5263
Glenn Miller/Ray Eberle Φ 02/40 Blu 10553
Eddy Duchin/Stanley Worth 02/40 Col 35329
Sammy Kaye/Charlie Wilson 02/40 Vic 26436

IN THE MOOD (9)
Shapiro, B, pub. 1939, reached #5 in February 1940
(Also reached #5 in December 1959)
(Also reached #11 in January 1990 as part of medley)
Andy Razaf w, Joe Garland m
Big band classic
All-time pop standard
Glenn Miller Orch ΦΦΦ 11/39 Blu 10416
Merry Macs 12/39 Dec 2842
Al Donahue/Paula Kelly 12/39 Voc 5238

INDIAN SUMMER (10)
T B Harms, pub. 1919, reached #2 in January 1940
(words added 1939)
Al Dubin w, Victor Herbert m
Tommy Dorsey/Jack Leonard ΦΦ 12/39 Vic 26390
Glenn Miller/Ray Eberle Φ 01/40 Blu 10495
Kay Kyser/Ginny Simms 01/40 Col 35337

IT'S A BLUE WORLD (31)
ABC Music, pub. 1939, reached #2 in March 1940
Bob Wright & Chet Forrest w & m
Featured in MUSIC IN MY HEART, film (rel. 01/40)
Tony Martin Φ sung in film, 02/40 Dec 2932
Glenn Miller/Ray Eberle Φ 03/40 Blu 10536
Tommy Dorsey/Anita Boyer 03/40 Vic 26465

IT'S A WONDERFUL WORLD
ABC Music, pub. 1939, reached #19 in June 1940
Harold Adamson w, Jan Savitt & Johnny Watson m
Charlie Barnet/Mary Ann McCall 05/40 Blu 10610
Jan Savitt/Bon Bon 05/40 Dec 2836

LEANIN' ON THE OLE TOP RAIL (48)
L Feist, pub. 1939, reached #10 in April 1940
Nick Kenny & Charles Kenny w & m
Featured in RIDE, TENDERFOOT, RIDE, film (rel. 08/40)
Bob Crosby/<vocal Φ 03/40 Dec 3027
Gene Autry, sung in film
Ozzie Nelson/Rose Ann Stevens 02/40 Blu 10499

LET THERE BE LOVE (49)
Shapiro, B, pub. 1940, reached #6 in May 1940
Ian Grant w, Lionel Rand m
Sammy Kaye/Tommy Ryan Φ 04/40 Vic 26564
Kay Kyser/Harry Babbitt 05/40 Col 35439
Al Donahue/Phil Brito 05/40 Voc 5454

LITTLE CURLY HAIR IN A HIGH CHAIR
L Feist, pub. 1940, reached #9 in June 1940
Charles Tobias w, Nat Simon m
Featured in FORTY LITTLE MOTHERS, film (rel. 04/40)
Eddie Cantor, sung in film
Fats Waller Φ 05/40 Blu 10698
Jimmy Dorsey/Helen O'Connell 06/40 Dec 3150

THE LITTLE RED FOX (44)
L Feist, pub. 1939, reached #9 in February 1940
James V Kern, Hy Heath & Johnny Lange w, Lew Porter m
Featured in THAT'S RIGHT, YOU'RE WRONG, film (rel. 11/39)
Kay Kyser/Harry Babbitt Φ performed in film, 12/39 Col 35295
Hal Kemp/The Smoothies 01/40 Vic 26416

A LOVER'S LULLABY
Jewel, pub. 1940, reached #13 in May 1940
Andy Razaf w, Frankie Carle & Larry Wagner m
Glen Gray & The Casa Loma Orch 04/40 Dec 3053
Frankie Masters Orch 05/40 Voc 5443
Horace Heidt/Larry Cotton 05/40 Col 35446

MAKE BELIEVE ISLAND (17)
Miller Mus, pub. 1940, reached #1 in July 1940
Nick Kenny & Charles Kenny w, Will Grosz & Sam Coslow m
Mitchell Ayres/Mary Ann Mercer ΦΦ 05/40 Blu 10687
Jan Savitt/Bon Bon 07/40 Dec 3188
Dick Todd 06/40 Blu 10729
Dick Jurgens/Harry Cool 07/40 Voc 5540
Sammy Kaye/Tommy Ryan 07/40 Vic 26594

MAYBE (20)
Robbins, pub. 1940, reached #2 in October 1940
(Also reached #8 in August 1952)
Allan Flynn & Frank Madden w & m
The Ink Spots ΦΦ 08/40 Dec 3258
Sammy Kaye/Tommy Ryan 09/40 Vic 26643
Bob Chester/Dolores O'Neill 09/40 Blu 10752
Bobby Byrne/Jimmy Palmer 09/40 Dec 3392

A MILLION DREAMS AGO
ABC Music, pub. 1940, reached #18 in November 1940
Dick Jurgens, Eddy Howard, Lew Quadling w & m
Dick Jurgens/Harry Cool 09/40 Okeh 5628
Glenn Miller/Ray Eberle 10/40 Blu 10768

THE NEARNESS OF YOU (41)
Famous, pub. 1940, reached #6 in September 1940
Ned Washington w, Hoagy Carmichael m
Glenn Miller/Ray Eberle Φ 07/40 Blu 10745
Kay Kyser/Harry Babbitt 08/40 Col 35488
Dinah Shore/Paul Wetstein Orch 08/40 Blu 10793
Eddy Howard/Lou Adrian Orch 07/40 Col 35511

A NIGHTINGALE SANG IN BERKELEY SQUARE (19)
Shapiro, B, pub. 1940, reached #2 in December 1940
Eric Maschwitz w, Manning Sherwin m
Featured in NEW FACES OF 1940, revue (1940)
Glenn Miller/Ray Eberle ΦΦ 12/40 Blu 10931
Guy Lombardo/Carmen Lombardo Φ 12/40 Dec 3453
Judy Campbell, sung in revue
Ray Noble/Larry Stewart 12/40 Col 35733
Sammy Kaye/Tommy Ryan 12/40 Vic 26795

NOW I LAY ME DOWN TO DREAM
Remick, pub. 1940, reached #9 in November 1940
Ted FioRito & Eddy Howard w & m
Guy Lombardo/Carmen Lombardo 10/40 Dec 3330
Bob Chester/Dolores O'Neill 10/40 Blu 10821
Andy Kirk/Pha Terrell 11/40 Dec 3306

ON THE ISLE OF MAY (35)
Famous, pub. 1940, reached #3 in April 1940
Mack David w, Andre Kostelanetz adpt, Peter I Tschaikovsky m
Connie Boswell Φ 02/40 Dec 3004
Dick Jurgens/Eddy Howard 03/40 Voc 5361
Kay Kyser/w.vocal duo 03/40 Col 35375
Blue Barron/Russ Carlyle 03/40 Blu 10594

ONLY FOREVER (2)
Santly-Joy, pub. 1940, reached #1 in October 1940
Johnny Burke w, James V Monaco m
Featured in RHYTHM ON THE RIVER, film (rel. 08/40)
Bing Crosby ΦΦ sung in film, 09/40 Dec 3300
Tommy Dorsey/Alton Starr Φ 09/40 Vic 26666
Eddy Duchin/June Robbins 10/40 Col 35624
Freddy Martin/Eddie Stone 09/40 Blu 10809

ORCHIDS FOR REMEMBRANCE
Miller Mus, pub. 1940, reached #17 in August 1940
Mitchell Parish w, Peter DeRose m
Eddy Howard/Lou Adrian Orch 08/40 Col 35558
Bob Chester/Dolores O'Neill 07/40 Blu 10735
Sammy Kaye/Clyde Burke 08/40 Vic 26633

OUR LOVE AFFAIR (42)
L Feist, pub. 1940, reached #6 in November 1940
Arthur Freed w, Roger Edens m
Featured in STRIKE UP THE BAND, film (rel. 09/40)
Judy Garland & Mickey Rooney, sung in film
Tommy Dorsey/Frank Sinatra Φ 10/40 Vic 26736
Glenn Miller/Ray Eberle Φ 10/40 Blu 10845
Dick Jurgens/Harry Cool 10/40 Okeh 5759

PENNSYLVANIA 6-5000
Robbins, pub. 1940, reached #14 in August 1940
Carl Sigman w, Jerry Gray m
Big band classic
Glenn Miller Orch Φ 07/40 Blu 10754
Andrews Sisters 10/40 Dec 3375

PLAYMATES (21)
Santly-Joy, pub. 1940, reached #5 in June 1940
Saxie Dowell w & m
Kay Kyser/Sully Mason ΦΦ 05/40 Col 35375
Mitchell Ayres/w.vocal duo 05/40 Blu 10585
Hal Kemp/The Smoothies 05/40 Vic 26469

POMPTON TURNPIKE
Santly-Joy, pub. 1940, reached #15 in January 1941
Will Osborne & Dick Rogers w & m
Big band classic
Charlie Barnet Orch Φ 10/40 Blu 10825
Louis Jordan/<vocal 12/40 Dec 8500

PRACTICE MAKES PERFECT (26)
BMI, pub. 1940, reached #5 in October 1940
Don Roberts & Ernest Gold w & m
Bob Chester/Al Stuart Φ 09/40 Blu 10838
Al Kavelin/Bill Darnell 10/40 Okeh 5746
Eddy Duchin/June Robbins 10/40 Col 35702

THE SAME OLD STORY
BMI, pub. 1940, reached #15 in October 1940
Michael Schwartz & Newt Oliphant w & m
Frankie Masters/w.vocal duo 10/40 Okeh 5716
Eddy Duchin/Johnny Drake 10/40 Col 35724

SAY IT (36)
Famous, pub. 1940, reached #4 in June 1940
Frank Loesser w, Jimmy McHugh m
Featured in BUCK BENNY RIDES AGAIN, film (rel. 04/40)
Glenn Miller/Ray Eberle Φ 05/40 Blu 10631
Tommy Dorsey/Frank Sinatra 05/40 Vic 26535
Ellen Drew, sung in film

SAY SI SI (PARA VIGO ME VOY)
E B Marks, pub. 1936, reached #11 in April 1940
(Also reached #19 in June 1953)
Francia Luban & Al Stillman w, Ernesto Lecuona m
Featured in CAROLINA MOON, film (rel. 07/40)
Andrews Sisters Φ 03/40 Dec 3013
Gene Autry, sung in film
Glenn Miller/Ray Eberle 04/40 Blu 10622

SCRUB ME, MAMA, WITH A BOOGIE BEAT
Leeds, pub. 1940, reached #12 in December 1940
Don Raye w & m
Will Bradley/Ray McKinley Φ 11/40 Col 35743
Andrews Sisters 01/41 Dec 3553
Charlie Barnet/Ford Leary 01/41 Blu 10975

SHAKE DOWN THE STARS
Bregman, V & C, pub. 1940, reached #11 in June 1940
Eddie DeLange w, Jimmy Van Heusen m
Glenn Miller/Ray Eberle Φ 04/40 Blu 10689
Ella Fitzgerald 06/40 Dec 3199
Benny Goodman/Helen Forrest 05/40 Col 35426

SIERRA SUE (12)
Shapiro, B, pub. 1940, reached #2 in July 1940
Joseph Buell Carey & Elliott Shapiro w & m
Bing Crosby ΦΦ 06/40 Dec 3133
Glenn Miller/Ray Eberle 07/40 Blu 10638
Gene Autry, radio, 11/40 Okeh 5780
Sammy Kaye/Tommy Ryan 06/40 Vic 26540

THE SINGING HILLS (14)
Santly-Joy, pub. 1940, reached #3 in May 1940
Mack David, Dick Sanford, Sammy Mysels w & m
Bing Crosby Φ 03/40 Dec 3064
Gene Autry, radio, 04/40 Conqueror 9388
Dick Todd 04/40 Blu 10596

SIX LESSONS FROM MADAME LA ZONGA (45)
Bregman, V & C, pub. 1940, reached #9 in September 1940
Charles Newman w, James V Monaco m
Jimmy Dorsey/Helen O'Connell Φ 07/40 Dec 3152
Charlie Barnet/Mary Ann McCall 08/40 Blu 10743
King Sisters 07/40 Blu 10733

SO FAR, SO GOOD
Miller Mus, pub. 1940, reached #17 in April 1940
Jack Lawrence w, Jimmy Mundy & Eddie White m
Bob Crosby/Marion Mann 04/40 Dec 3055
Duke Ellington/Ivie Anderson 04/40 Vic 26537
Charlie Barnet/Mary Ann McCall 04/40 Blu 10618

THE STARLIT HOUR (46)
Robbins, pub. 1939, reached #5 in April 1940
Mitchell Parish w, Peter DeRose m
Featured in EARL CARROLL'S VANITIES, show (opened 01/40)
Glenn Miller/Ray Eberle Φ 03/40 Blu 10553
Tommy Dorsey/Jack Leonard Φ 02/40 Vic 26445
Ella Fitzgerald 04/40 Dec 2988

TENNESSEE FISH FRY
Chappell, pub. 1940, reached #19 in July 1940
Oscar Hammerstein 2nd w, Arthur Schwartz m
Featured in AMERICAN JUBILEE, World's Fair, show (opened 05/40)
Kay Kyser/Sully Mason 06/40 Col 35518
Wynn Murray, sung in show
Jimmy Dorsey/Helen O'Connell 07/40 Dec 3197

THAT'S FOR ME
Famous, pub. 1940, reached #10 in October 1940
Johnny Burke w, James V Monaco m
Featured in RHYTHM ON THE RIVER, film (rel. 08/40)
Bing Crosby & Mary Martin, sung in film
Bing Crosby Φ 09/40 Dec 3309
Tommy Dorsey/Connie Haines 09/40 Vic 26736

THERE I GO (7)
BMI, pub. 1940, reached #3 in November 1940
Hy Zaret w, Irving Weiser m
Vaughn Monroe/<vocal Φ 10/40 Blu 10848
Will Bradley/Jimmy Valentine Φ 11/40 Col 35743
Tommy Tucker/Amy Arnell 11/40 Okeh 5789
Woody Herman/<vocal 11/40 Dec 3454
Kenny Baker 12/40 Vic 27207

THIS CHANGING WORLD
Robbins, pub. 1939, reached #13 in February 1940
Harold Adamson w, Dana Suesse m
Glenn Miller/Ray Eberle 01/40 Blu 10526
Will Bradley/Carlotta Dale 01/40 Voc 5262
Kay Kyser/Ginny Simms 01/40 Col 35307

TO YOU, SWEETHEART, ALOHA
Santly-Joy, pub. 1936, reached #13 in February 1940
Harry Owens w & m
Harry Owens, stage
Dick Todd 01/40 Blu 10445
Gray Gordon/Cliff Grass 01/40 Vic 26396

(I'M) TOO ROMANTIC (40)
Paramount, pub. 1940, reached #5 in May 1940
Johnny Burke w, James V Monaco m
Featured in ROAD TO SINGAPORE, film (rel. 02/40)
Bing Crosby & Dorothy Lamour, sung in film
Bing Crosby Φ 03/40 Dec 2998
Dorothy Lamour 04/40 Blu 10608
Tommy Dorsey/Frank Sinatra 04/40 Vic 26500

TRADE WINDS (8)
Harms, pub. 1940, reached #2 in October 1940
Charles Tobias w, Cliff Friend m
Bing Crosby ΦΦ 09/40 Dec 3299
Tommy Dorsey/Frank Sinatra 09/40 Vic 26666
Eddy Duchin/Tony Leonard 09/40 Col 35628

TUXEDO JUNCTION (30)
Lewis, pub. 1940, reached #7 in April 1940
Buddy Feyne w, Erskine Hawkins, William Johnson & Julian Dash m
Big band classic
Glenn Miller Orch ΦΦ 02/40 Blu 10612
Erskine Hawkins Orch Φ 12/39 Blu 10409
Jan Savitt Orch 05/40 Dec 2989

TWO DREAMS MET
Miller Mus, pub. 1940, reached #13 in November 1940
Mack Gordon & Carlos Albert w, Harry Warren m
Featured in DOWN ARGENTINA WAY, film (rel. 10/40)
Don Ameche & Betty Grable, sung in film
Mitchell Ayres/Mary Ann Mercer 11/40 Blu 10877
Tommy Dorsey/Connie Haines 11/40 Vic 26764
Eddy Duchin/Johnny Drake 11/40 Col 35774

WE THREE (18)
Mercer Mus, pub. 1940, reached #1 in December 1940
Dick Robertson, Nelson Cogane, Sammy Mysels w & m
The Ink Spots ΦΦ 10/40 Dec 3379
Tommy Dorsey/Frank Sinatra Φ 11/40 Vic 26747
Bob Chester/Dolores O'Neill 11/40 Blu 10865

WHEN THE SWALLOWS COME BACK TO CAPISTRANO (16)
Witmark, pub. 1940, reached #2 in September 1940
Leon Rene w & m
The Ink Spots Φ 07/40 Dec 3195
Glenn Miller/Ray Eberle Φ 07/40 Blu 10776
Gene Autry, radio, 11/40 Okeh 5780
Guy Lombardo/Carmen Lombardo 08/40 Dec 3213
Xavier Cugat/Dinah Shore 08/40 Vic 26641

WHEN YOU WISH UPON A STAR (11)
Berlin, pub. 1940, reached #1 in March 1940
Ned Washington w, Leigh Harline m
Featured in PINOCCHIO, film (rel. 01/40)
Cliff Edwards, sung in film
Glenn Miller/Ray Eberle ΦΦ 02/40 Blu 10570
Guy Lombardo/Carmen Lombardo 03/40 Dec 2969
Horace Heidt/Larry Cotton 03/40 Col 35351
Sammy Kaye/Tommy Ryan 03/40 Vic 26455

WHERE WAS I? (32)
Remick, pub. 1939, reached #4 in June 1940
Al Dubin w, W Franke Harling m
Featured in TILL WE MEET AGAIN, film (rel. 04/40)
Charlie Barnet/Mary Ann McCall Φ 05/40 Blu 10669
Sammy Kaye/Clyde Burke 07/40 Vic 26594
Jan Savitt/Allan DeWitt 06/40 Dec 3153

WITH THE WIND AND THE RAIN IN YOUR HAIR (15)
Paramount, pub. 1940, reached #2 in May 1940
(Also reached #19 in February 1959)
Jack Lawrence & Clara Edwards w & m
Bob Crosby/Marion Mann Φ 03/40 Dec 3018
Kay Kyser/Ginny Simms Φ 04/40 Col 35350
Bob Chester/Dolores O'Neill 04/40 Blu 10614
Sammy Kaye/Tommy Ryan 04/40 Vic 26515

THE WOODPECKER SONG (1)
Robbins, pub. 1940, reached #1 in May 1940
Harold Adamson & C Bruno-DiLazzaro w, Eldo DiLazzaro m
Featured in RIDE, TENDERFOOT, RIDE, film (rel. 08/40)
Glenn Miller/Marion Hutton ΦΦ 03/40 Blu 10598
Andrews Sisters Φ 04/40 Dec 3065
Gene Autry, sung in film
Will Glahe Orch 02/40 Vic V-743
Kate Smith 03/40 Col 35398

YOU, YOU, DARLIN'
Harms, pub. 1940, reached #17 in May 1940
Jack Scholl w, M K Jerome m
Kay Kyser/Ginny Simms 04/40 Col 35395
Duke Ellington/Herb Jeffries 05/40 Vic 26537
Bob Crosby/Marion Mann 05/40 Dec 3018

YOU'D BE SURPRISED
Berlin, pub. 1919, reached #14 in February 1940
(Also reached #2 in January 1920)
Irving Berlin w & m
Orrin Tucker/Bonnie Baker Φ 01/40 Col 35344

YOU'RE LONELY AND I'M LONELY
Berlin, pub. 1940, reached #13 in July 1940
Irving Berlin w & m
Featured in LOUISIANA PURCHASE, show (opened 05/40)
Zorina & Victor Moore, sung in show
Tommy Dorsey/Frank Sinatra 06/40 Vic 26596

YOURS IS MY HEART ALONE
Harms, pub. 1929, reached #18 in June 1940
Ludwig Herzer, Fritz Lohner & Harry B Smith w, Franz Lehar m
Glen Gray/Kenny Sargent 05/40 Dec 3053
Glenn Miller Orch 06/40 Blu 10728
Tommy Dorsey/Frank Sinatra 06/40 Vic 26616

[1]Carlos Albert's voice was dubbed for Don Ameche.

1941

ALEXANDER THE SWOOSE
A-1 Mus, pub. 1941, reached #14 in May 1941
Ben Forrest & Glenn Burrs w, Frank Furlett & Leonard Keller m
Kay Kyser/w.vocal group 04/41 Col 36040
Art Kassel/Marion Holmes 04/41 Blu 10990

ALONG THE SANTA FE TRAIL (48)
Witmark, pub. 1940, reached #9 in January 1941
Al Dubin & Edwina Coolidge w, Will Grosz m
Featured in SANTA FE TRAIL, film (rel. 12/40)
Bing Crosby Φ 01/41 Dec 3565
Glenn Miller/Ray Eberle Φ 12/40 Blu 10970
Dick Jurgens/Harry Cool Φ 01/41 Okeh 5858
Sammy Kaye/Jimmy Brown 12/40 Vic 27220

AMAPOLA (8)
E B Marks; orig. pub. 1924, reached #1 in April 1941
Albert Gamse w, Joseph M Lacalle m
Jimmy Dorsey/Bob Eberly-Helen O'Connell ΦΦΦ 03/41 Dec 3629
Xavier Cugat/Carmen Castillo 04/41 Col 36013

AMERICA, I LOVE YOU
Mills; orig. pub. 1915, reached #16 in March 1941
(Also reached #2 in January 1916)
Edgar Leslie w, Archie Gottler m
Dick Powell/Victor Young Orch 02/41 Dec 3458
Horace Heidt/w.vocal group 02/41 Col 35865

ANVIL CHORUS (43)
Mutual; orig. pub. 1853, reached #11 in March 1941
Guiseppi Verdi m, Jerry Gray arr
Glenn Miller Orch Φ 01/41 Blu 10970
Les Brown Orch 02/41 Okeh 6011

AURORA
Robbins, pub. 1941, reached #18 in July 1941
Harold Adamson w, Mario Lago & Roberto Roberti m
Featured in HOLD THAT GHOST, film (rel. 07/41)
Andrews Sisters, sung in film, 06/41 Dec 3732
Jimmy Dorsey/Helen O'Connell 07/41 Dec 3772
Xavier Cugat/Machito 07/41 Col 36139

THE BAND PLAYED ON (45)
Leeds; orig. pub. 1895, reached #11 in June 1941
(Also major hit in 1895)
John F Palmer w, Charles B Ward m
Guy Lombardo/Kenny Gardner Φ 04/41 Dec 3675
The Jesters 06/41 Dec 3676
Mitchell Ayres/Mary Ann Mercer 06/41 Blu 11101

BLUE CHAMPAGNE (28)
Encore, pub. 1941, reached #7 in August 1941
Grady Watts & Frank Ryerson w & m
Jimmy Dorsey/Bob Eberly Φ 07/41 Dec 3775
Frankie Masters/Phyllis Miles 07/41 Okeh 6279
Freddy Martin Orch 08/41 Blu 11256

BLUE FLAME
Charling, pub. 1942, reached #16 in April 1941
Leo Cordray w, Joe Bishop & James A Noble m
Woody Herman Orch Φ 03/41 Dec 3643

THE BOOGIE WOOGIE BUGLE BOY
Leeds, pub. 1941, reached #15 in March 1941
(Also reached #8 in July 1973)
Don Raye & Hughie Prince w & m
Featured in BUCK PRIVATES, film (rel. 02/41)
Andrews Sisters Φ sung in film, 03/41 Dec 3598
Woody Herman/<vocal 03/41 Dec 3617

THE BOOGLIE-WOOGLIE PIGGY
Mutual, pub. 1941, reached #15 in August 1941
Roy Jacobs w & m
Glenn Miller/Tex Beneke-Modernaires Φ 07/41 Blu 11163
Will Bradley/w.vocal duo 08/41 Col 36231
Andrews Sisters 09/41 Dec 3960

BY-U, BY-O (46)
Majestic, pub. 1941, reached #9 in January 1942
Jack Owens, Ted McMichael, Leo V Killion, Mark Fenton w & m
Woody Herman/Muriel Lane Φ 11/41 Dec 4024
Merry Macs 11/41 Dec 4023

CHATTANOOGA CHOO CHOO (4)
L Feist, pub. 1941, reached #1 in December 1941
Mack Gordon w, Harry Warren m
Featured in SUN VALLEY SERENADE, film (rel. 07/41)
Glenn Miller/Tex Beneke-Modernaires ΦΦΦ perf. in film, 09/41 Blu 11230
Andrews Sisters 12/41 Dec 4094

A CITY CALLED HEAVEN
B Warren, pub. 1941, reached #16 in November 1941
Bob Warren w & m
Shep Fields/Pat Fry 10/41 Blu 11255
Glen Gray/Kenny Sargent 12/41 Dec 4048

CONCERTO FOR TWO
Shapiro, B, pub. 1941, reached #13 in December 1941
Jack Lawrence w & adpt, Peter I Tschaikovsky m
Claude Thornhill/Danny Hurd 11/41 Col 36371
Tommy Tucker/Don Brown 11/41 Okeh 6402

DADDY (11)
Republic, pub. 1941, reached #2 in August 1941
Bob Troup w & m
Featured in TWO LATINS FROM MANHATTAN, film (rel. 09/41)
Sammy Kaye/The Kaye Choir ΦΦ 06/41 Vic 27391
Joan Davis & Jim Falkenburg, sung in film
Joan Merrill 08/41 Blu 11171
Frankie Masters/The Swingmasters 07/41 Okeh 6232
Harry James/Helen Ward 07/41 Col 36171

DO I WORRY? (24)
Melody Lane, pub. 1941, reached #3 in May 1941
Stanley Cowan & Bobby Worth w & m
Tommy Dorsey/Frank Sinatra-Pied Pipers Φ 04/41 Vic 27338
The Ink Spots Φ 05/41 Dec 3432
Bea Wain 04/41 Vic 27353

DO YOU CARE? (36)
Campbell, pub. 1941, reached #8 in October 1941
Jack Elliott w, Lew Quadling m
Sam Donahue/Irene Day 09/41 Blu 11198
Bob Crosby/<vocal 10/41 Dec 3860
Dinah Shore 09/41 Blu 11191

DOLORES (35)
Paramount, pub. 1941, reached #6 in May 1941
Frank Loesser w, Louis Alter m
Featured in LAS VEGAS NIGHTS, film (rel. 04/41)
Tommy Dorsey/Frank Sinatra-Pied Pipers Φ 04/41 Vic 27317
Bing Crosby Φ 04/41 Dec 3644
Bert Wheeler, sung in film
Frankie Masters/<vocal 05/41 Okeh 6142

ELMER'S TUNE (3)
Robbins, pub. 1941, reached #2 in December 1941
Elmer Albrecht, Sammy Gallop, Dick Jurgens w & m
Glenn Miller/Ray Eberle-Modernaires ΦΦ 10/41 Blu 11274
Dick Jurgens Orch Φ 09/41 Okeh 6209
Benny Goodman/Peggy Lee 11/41 Col 36359
Andrews Sisters 11/41 Dec 4008

EVERYTHING HAPPENS TO ME
Embassy, pub. 1941, reached #19 in June 1941
Tom Adair w, Matt Dennis m
Tommy Dorsey/Frank Sinatra 04/41 Vic 27359
Woody Herman/<vocal 05/41 Dec 3693

FRENESI (2)
Southern, pub. 1939, reached #1 in January 1941
Ray Charles & S K Russell w, Alberto Dominguez m
Artie Shaw Orch ΦΦΦ 10/40 Vic 26542
Glenn Miller Orch 02/41 Blu 10994
Woody Herman/<vocal 01/41 Dec 3427
Al Donahue Orch 01/41 Okeh 5888

FRIENDLY TAVERN POLKA
BMI, pub. 1941, reached #17 in June 1941
Jerry Bowne w, Frank DeVol m
Horace Heidt/Jerry Bowne 05/41 Col 36006
Sammy Kaye/Maury Cross 05/41 Vic 27381

G'BYE NOW (41)
BMI, pub. 1941, reached #9 in May 1941
John S Olsen, Harold Johnson, Jay Levison, Ray Evans w & m
Featured in HELLZAPOPPIN, film (rel. 12/41)
Horace Heidt/Ronnie Kemper Φ 04/41 Col 36026
Woody Herman/Muriel Lane 06/41 Dec 3745
Frankie Masters/<vocal 05/41 Okeh 6155

GEORGIA ON MY MIND
Southern, pub. 1930, reached #11 in April 1941
(Also reached #3 in November 1960)
Stuart Gorrell w, Hoagy Carmichael m
Gene Krupa/Anita O'Day 04/41 Okeh 6118
Mildred Bailey 05/41 Dec 3691
Billy Holiday 05/41 Okeh 6134

GREEN EYES (16)
Southern; orig. pub. 1931, reached #3 in September 1941
Adolfo Utrera, E Rivera & Eddie Woods w, Nilo Menendez m
Jimmy Dorsey/Bob Eberly-Helen O'Connell ΦΦ 06/41 Dec 3698
Xavier Cugat/w.vocal group 08/41 Vic 27443
Tony Pastor/Dorsey Anderson 07/41 Blu 11168

HI, NEIGHBOR!
BMI, pub. 1941, reached #17 in October 1941
Jack Owens w & m
Featured in SAN ANTONIO ROSE, film (rel. 06/41)
Orrin Tucker/The Bodyguards 10/41 Col 36362
Jane Frazee & The Merry Macs, sung in film
Al Donahue/Phil Brito 11/41 Okeh 6378

HIGH ON A WINDY HILL (22)
BMI, pub. 1940, reached #1 in March 1941
Alex Kramer & Joan Whitney w & m
Jimmy Dorsey/Bob Eberly Φ 02/41 Dec 3585
Gene Krupa/Howard Dulaney Φ 02/41 Okeh 5883
Will Bradley/Jimmy Valentine 02/41 Col 35912
Vaughn Monroe/<vocal 02/41 Blu 10976

THE HUT-SUT SONG (15)
Schumann, pub. 1941, reached #2 in June 1941
Leo V Killion, Ted McMichael, Jack Owens w & m
Freddy Martin/Eddie Stone Φ 05/41 Blu 11147
Horace Heidt/Don Juans Φ 05/41 Col 36138
King Sisters 06/41 Blu 11154
Merry Macs 06/41 Dec 3810

I DON'T WANT TO SET THE WORLD ON FIRE (12)
Cherio, pub. 1941, reached #1 in October 1941
Eddie Seiler, Sol Marcus, Bennie Benjamin, Eddie Durham w & m
Horace Heidt/Larry Cotton Φ 09/41 Col 36295
The Ink Spots Φ 10/41 Dec 3987
Tommy Tucker/Amy Arnell Φ 09/41 Okeh 6320
Mitchell Ayres/Meredith Blake 10/41 Blu 11275

I DREAMT I DWELT IN HARLEM
Fowler M C, pub. 1941, reached #12 in March 1941
Robert B Wright w, Jerry Gray, Ben Smith & Leonard Ware m
Glenn Miller Orch Φ 03/41 Blu 11063
King Sisters 07/41 Blu 11184

I GIVE YOU MY WORD (25)
BMI, pub. 1940, reached #3 in February 1941
Art Kavelin & Merril Lyn w & m
Eddy Duchin/June Robbins Φ 12/40 Col 35812
Mitchell Ayres/Tommy Taylor Φ 12/40 Blu 10895
Al Kavelin/Bill Darnell 11/40 Okeh 5734
Jack Leonard 01/41 Okeh 5886

I GUESS I'LL HAVE TO DREAM THE REST (30)
Block, pub. 1941, reached #5 in October 1941
Mickey Stoner & Martin Block w, Harold Green m
Glenn Miller/Ray Eberle-Modernaires Φ 09/41 Blu 11187
Tommy Dorsey/Frank Sinatra-Pied Pipers 09/41 Vic 27526
Tony Martin 10/41 Dec 3988

I HEAR A RHAPSODY (10)
BMI, pub. 1940, reached #1 in February 1941
(Also reached #20 in May 1952)
George Fragos, Jack Baker, Dick Gasparre w & m
Jimmy Dorsey/Bob Eberly ΦΦ 01/41 Dec 3570
Charlie Barnet/Bob Carroll Φ 01/41 Blu 10934
Dinah Shore 03/41 Blu 11003
Al Donahue/Phil Brito 02/41 Okeh 5888

I SEE A MILLION PEOPLE
Radio Tunes, pub. 1941, reached #14 in November 1941
Robert Sour w, Una Mae Carlisle m
Una Mae Carlisle, stage, 10/41 Blu 11181
Cab Calloway/<vocal 11/41 Okeh 6341
Benny Goodman/Peggy Lee 11/41 Col 36379

I WENT OUT OF MY WAY
BMI, pub. 1941, reached #13 in September 1941
Helen Bliss w & m
Teddy Powell/Ruth Gaylor 08/41 Blu 11152
Jan Savitt/Allan DeWitt 08/41 Vic 27423

I'LL BE WITH YOU IN APPLE BLOSSOM TIME (33)
Broadway Mus Co, pub. 1920, reached #7 in June 1941
(Also reached #4 in November 1920)
Neville Fleeson w, Albert Von Tilzer m
Featured in BUCK PRIVATES, film (rel. 02/41)
Andrews Sisters Φ sung in film, 04/41 Dec 3622
Wayne King Orch 04/41 Vic 27336

INTERMEZZO (A LOVE STORY) (5)
Schuberth, pub. 1940, reached #1 in June 1941
Robert Henning w, Heinz Provost m
Theme music from INTERMEZZO, film (rel. 10/39)
Wayne King Orch[1] Φ 04/41 Vic 26659
Guy Lombardo Orch Φ 05/41 Dec 3674
Freddy Martin/Clyde Rogers Φ 05/41 Blu 11123
Benny Goodman Orch 05/41 Col 36050
Charlie Spivak Orch 06/41 Okeh 6120

IT ALL COMES BACK TO ME NOW (23)
BMI, pub. 1940, reached #4 in March 1941
Alex Kramer, Joan Whitney, Hy Zaret w & m
Gene Krupa/Howard Dulaney Φ 02/41 Okeh 5883
Hal Kemp/Bob Allen Φ 02/41 Vic 27255
Eddy Duchin/June Robbins Φ 02/41 Col 35867
Ted Weems/Perry Como 03/41 Dec 3627

JIM (20)
Leeds, pub. 1941, reached #2 in October 1941
Nelson Shawn w, Edward Ross & Caesar Petrillo m
Jimmy Dorsey/Bob Eberly-Helen O'Connell Φ 09/41 Dec 3963
Dinah Shore 09/41 Blu 11204
Ella Fitzgerald 11/41 Dec 4007

JINGLE BELLS
Oliver Ditson, pub. 1857, reached #15 in December 1941
(Also reached #16 in December 1951)
J S Pierpont w & m
All-time Christmas standard
Glenn Miller/w.vocal group Φ 12/41 Blu 11353

JUST A LITTLE BIT SOUTH OF NORTH CAROLINA (38)
Porgie, D & F, pub. 1940, reached #7 in July 1941
Sunny Skylar, Bette Cannon, Arthur Shaftel w & m
Gene Krupa/Anita O'Day Φ 06/41 Okeh 6130
Mitchell Ayres/Mary Ann Mercer 07/41 Blu 11101
Raymond Scott/Clyde Burke 07/41 Col 36103

KISS THE BOYS GOODBYE (50)
Famous, pub. 1941, reached #11 in September 1941
Frank Loesser w, Victor Schertzinger m
Featured in KISS THE BOYS GOODBYE, film (rel. 06/41)
Mary Martin, sung in film
Bea Wain 07/41 Vic 27445
Tommy Dorsey/Connie Haines 08/41 Vic 27461

THE LAST TIME I SAW PARIS
Chappell, pub. 1940, reached #12 in February 1941
Oscar Hammerstein 2nd w, Jerome Kern m
Featured in LADY BE GOOD, film (rel. 07/41)
Kate Smith 01/41 Col 35802
Ann Sothern, sung in film
Vaughn Monroe/<vocal 02/41 Blu 10976

LET ME OFF UPTOWN
Reis & Taylor, pub. 1941, reached #20 in August 1941
Redd Evans & Earl Bostic w & m
Gene Krupa/Anita O'Day 07/41 Okeh 6210
Larry Clinton/Butch Stone 08/41 Blu 11240

LET'S DREAM THIS ONE OUT
BMI, pub. 1940, reached #20 in February 1941
Edward Lane w, Robert Reed m
Frankie Masters/The Swingmasters 02/41 Okeh 5998
Eddy Duchin/Tony Leonard 02/41 Col 35913

LET'S GET AWAY FROM IT ALL
Embassy, pub. 1941, reached #17 in May 1941
Tom Adair w, Matt Dennis m
Tommy Dorsey/Pied Pipers 05/41 Vic 27377
Gene Krupa/Anita O'Day 05/41 Okeh 6130

MARIA ELENA (1)
Southern, pub. 1941, reached #1 in July 1941
(Also reached #6 in November 1963)
S K Russell w, Lorenzo Barcelata m
Jimmy Dorsey/Bob Eberly ΦΦ 05/41 Dec 3698
Wayne King Orch Φ 05/41 Vic 26767
Tony Pastor/Dorsey Anderson 06/41 Blu 11127
Lawrence Welk/Jayne Walton 02/41 Okeh 5939

MAY I NEVER LOVE AGAIN
BMI, pub. 1940, reached #13 in February 1941
Sano Marco & Jack Erickson w & m
Bob Chester/Dolores O'Neill 02/41 Blu 10904
Ginny Simms 03/41 Okeh 6025
Ted Weems/Perry Como 03/41 Dec 3627

MUSIC MAKERS
Paramount, pub. 1941, reached #20 in May 1941
Harry James & Don Raye w & m
Harry James Orch 04/41 Col 35932
Andrews Sisters 05/41 Dec 3732
Count Basie Orch 05/41 Okeh 6047

MY SISTER AND I (17)
BMI, pub. 1941, reached #2 in June 1941
Alex Kramer, Joan Whitney, Hy Zaret w & m
Jimmy Dorsey/Bob Eberly ΦΦ 05/41 Dec 3710
Bea Wain 05/41 Vic 27363
Bob Chester/Bill Darnell 06/41 Blu 11088
Benny Goodman/Helen Forrest 05/41 Col 36022

NUMBER TEN LULLABY LANE
BMI, pub. 1940, reached #12 in May 1941
Bob Carleton & Bob Warren w & m
Eddy Duchin/June Robbins 04/41 Col 35917
Guy Lombardo/w.vocal trio 05/41 Dec 3699

OH, LOOK AT ME NOW (40)
Embassy, pub. 1941, reached #4 in April 1941
John DeVries w, Joe Bushkin m
Tommy Dorsey/Frank Sinatra-Connie Haines Φ 03/41 Vic 27274
Benny Goodman/Helen Forrest 04/41 Col 36012

ORANGE BLOSSOM LANE
Robbins, pub. 1941, reached #16 in December 1941
Mitchell Parish & Nick Kenny w, Peter DeRose m
Glenn Miller/Ray Eberle 12/41 Blu 11326
Claude Thornhill/Danny Hurd 12/41 Col 36391

PIANO CONCERTO (7)
Mayfair, pub. 1941, reached #2 in November 1941
Freddy Martin & Ray Austin adpt, Peter I Tschaikovsky m
Freddy Martin/Jack Fina[2] ΦΦΦ 08/41 Blu 11211
Woody Herman Orch 10/41 Dec 3973

PERFIDIA (TONIGHT) (21)
Southern, pub. 1939, reached #4 in February 1941
(Also reached #13 in May 1952)
(Also reached #16 in December 1960)
Milton Leeds w, Alberto Dominguez m
Xavier Cugat Orch Φ 01/41 Vic 26334
Glenn Miller/Dorothy Claire-Modernaires Φ 04/41 Blu 11095
Jimmy Dorsey Orch[5] Φ 03/41 Dec 3198
Benny Goodman/Helen Forrest 03/41 Col 35962
Gene Krupa/Howard Dulaney 02/41 Okeh 5715

SAN ANTONIO ROSE (31)
Berlin, pub. 1940, reached #5 in April 1941
(Also reached #7 in July 1961)
Bob Wills w & m
Featured in SAN ANTONIO ROSE, film (rel. 06/41)
Bob Wills[3]/Tommy Duncan Φ stage, 12/40 Okeh 5694
Bing Crosby[4] ΦΦ 03/41 Dec 3590

SHEPHERD SERENADE (29)
Mercer-Morris, pub. 1941, reached #3 in December 1941
Kermit Goell w, Fred Spielman m
Bing Crosby Φ 12/41 Dec 4065
Horace Heidt/w.vocal trio Φ 11/41 Col 36370
Art Jarrett 11/41 Vic 27527

A SINNER KISSED AN ANGEL
Famous, pub. 1941, reached #19 in December 1941
Mack David w, Ray Joseph m
Harry James/Dick Haymes 12/41 Col 36296
Tommy Dorsey/Frank Sinatra 12/41 Vic 27611

SO YOU'RE THE ONE (39)
BMI, pub. 1940, reached #8 in February 1941
Alex Kramer, Joan Whitney, Hy Zaret w & m
Eddy Duchin/Johnny Drake Φ 12/40 Col 35812
Hal Kemp/Janet Blair 02/41 Vic 27222
Vaughn Monroe/<vocal 02/41 Blu 10901

SONG OF THE VOLGA BOATMEN (44)
Mutual; orig. pub. 1926, reached #10 in March 1941
Russian folk song
Glenn Miller Orch ΦΦ 02/41 Blu 11029

STAR DUST (47)
Mills, pub. 1929, reached #8 in February 1941
(Also reached #12 in July 1931)
(Also reached #16 in August 1957)
Mitchell Parish w, Hoagy Carmichael m
All-time pop standard
Artie Shaw Orch ΦΦ 01/41 Vic 27230
Tommy Dorsey/Frank Sinatra-Pied Pipers Φ 01/41 Vic 27233
Glenn Miller Orch 11/40 Blu 10665

THERE'LL BE SOME CHANGES MADE (19)
E B Marks, pub. 1921, reached #1 in April 1941
(Also reached #17 in December 1924)
Billy Higgins w, W Benton Overstreet m
Benny Goodman/Louise Tobin ΦΦ 03/41 Col 35210
Ted Weems/Mary Lee 03/41 Dec 3044
Gene Krupa/Irene Day 04/41 Okeh 6021
Vaughn Monroe/Marilyn Duke 03/41 Blu 11025

THE THINGS I LOVE (18)
Campbell, pub. 1941, reached #5 in July 1941
Lew Harris & Harold Barlow w & adpt, Peter I Tschaikovsky m
Jimmy Dorsey/Bob Eberly Φ 06/41 Dec 3737
Teddy Powell/Ruth Gaylor 06/41 Blu 11113
Gene Krupa/Howard Dulaney 06/41 Okeh 6143
Barry Wood 06/41 Vic 27369

THIS LOVE OF MINE (14)
Embassy, pub. 1941, reached #4 in December 1941
Frank Sinatra w, Sol Parker & Henry Sanicola m
Tommy Dorsey/Frank Sinatra ΦΦ 09/41 Vic 27508
Tommy Tucker/Amy Arnell 10/41 Okeh 6320
Bob Chester/Betty Bradley 11/41 Blu 11316

THIS TIME THE DREAM'S ON ME
Remick, pub. 1941, reached #14 in December 1941
Johnny Mercer w, Harold Arlen m
Featured in BLUES IN THE NIGHT, film (rel. 10/41)
Priscilla Lane, sung in film
Woody Herman/<vocal 11/41 Dec 4030
Glenn Miller/Ray Eberle 11/41 Blu 11315

'TIL REVEILLE (13)
Melody Lane, pub. 1941, reached #2 in September 1941
Stanley Cowan & Bobby Worth w & m
Kay Kyser/w.vocal group ΦΦ 08/41 Col 36137
Bing Crosby Φ 08/41 Dec 3886
Freddy Martin/Clyde Rogers 06/41 Blu 11167
Wayne King/w.vocal 08/41 Vic 27511

TIME WAS (49)
Southern, pub. 1941, reached #12 in October 1941
S K Russell & Gabriel Luna w, Miguel Prado m
Jimmy Dorsey/Bob Eberly-Helen O'Connell 08/41 Dec 3859
Charlie Spivak/Gary Stevens 09/41 Okeh 6257
Tito Guizar 09/41 Vic 27513

TONIGHT WE LOVE (27)
Maestro, pub. 1941, reached #5 in November 1941
Bobby Worth w, Ray Austin & Freddy Martin adpt,
Peter I Tschaikovsky m
Tony Martin Φ 10/41 Dec 3988
Freddy Martin/Clyde Rogers 11/41 Blu 11320
Jane Froman 12/41 Col 36414

TWO HEARTS THAT PASS IN THE NIGHT
E B Marks, pub. 1941, reached #17 in July 1941
Forman Brown w, Ernesto Lecuona m
Charlie Spivak/Gary Stevens 06/41 Okeh 6110
Sammy Kaye/Arthur Wright 06/41 Vic 27391
Kate Smith 06/41 Col 36043

TWO IN LOVE
Willson, pub. 1941, reached #10 in December 1941
Meredith Willson w & m
Tommy Dorsey/Frank Sinatra Φ 11/41 Vic 27611
Vaughn Monroe/<vocal 12/41 Blu 11273
Gene Krupa/Johnny Desmond-Anita O'Day 12/41 Okeh 6447

UNTIL TOMORROW
Republic, pub. 1940, reached #14 in July 1941
Sammy Kaye w & m
Sammy Kaye/Three Kadets 05/41 Vic 27262
Woody Herman/<vocal 06/41 Dec 3745
Bob Chester/Bill Reynolds 07/41 Blu 11144

WALKING BY THE RIVER (34)
BMI, pub. 1940, reached #4 in May 1941
Robert Sour w, Una Mae Carlisle m
Una Mae Carlisle Φ 04/41 Blu 11033
Ginny Simms 04/41 Okeh 6025
Hal Kemp/Janet Blair 05/41 Vic 27222

WHY DON'T WE DO THIS MORE OFTEN?
Bregman, V & C, pub. 1941, reached #13 in November 1941
Charles Newman w, Allie Wrubel m
Freddy Martin/Eddie Stone 09/41 Blu 11211
Kay Kyser/w.vocal duo 10/41 Col 36253
Russ Morgan/<vocal 11/41 Dec 3982

A WISE OLD OWL (32)
BMI, pub. 1940, reached #2 in April 1941
Joe Ricardel w & m
Al Donahue/Dee Keating Φ 03/41 Okeh 6037
Teddy Powell/Ruth Gaylor 04/41 Blu 11089
Kay Kyser/Sully Mason 05/41 Col 36051

YES, INDEED! (42)
Embassy, pub. 1941, reached #13 in October 1941
Sy Oliver w & m
Tommy Dorsey/Joe Stafford-Sy Oliver Φ 07/41 Vic 27421
Connie Boswell & Bing Crosby/Bob Crosby 07/41 Dec 3689
Tommy Tucker/Amy Arnell 08/41 Okeh 6290

YES, MY DARLING DAUGHTER
Chappell, pub. 1940, reached #16 in February 1941
Jack Lawrence & Albert Sirmay w & m
Dinah Shore 01/41 Blu 10920
Glenn Miller/Marion Hutton 02/41 Blu 10970
Gene Krupa/Irene Day 01/41 Okeh 5909

YOU AND I (6)
Willson, pub. 1941, reached #1 in September 1941
Meredith Willson w & m
Glenn Miller/Ray Eberle ΦΦ 08/41 Blu 11215
Bing Crosby Φ 09/41 Dec 3840
Tommy Dorsey/Frank Sinatra Φ 09/41 Vic 27532
Kay Kyser/w.vocal group 08/41 Col 36244

YOU ARE MY SUNSHINE (37)
Southern, pub. 1940, reached #10 in July 1941
(Also reached #7 in December 1962)
Jimmie Davis & Charles Mitchell w & m
Featured in TAKE ME BACK TO OKLAHOMA, film (1940)
All-time pop and country standard
Bing Crosby 08/41 Dec 3952
Gene Autry, radio, 08/41 Okeh 6274
Tex Ritter, sung in film
Wayne King/<vocal 11/40 Vic 26767

YOU WALK BY (26)
BMI, pub. 1940, reached #3 in February 1941
Ben Raleigh w, Bernie Wayne m
Eddy Duchin/Johnny Drake Φ 01/41 Col 35903
Blue Barron/Russ Carlyle Φ 01/41 Blu 10894
Tommy Tucker/w.vocal duo Φ 02/41 Okeh 5973
Wayne King Orch 02/41 Vic 27206

YOU'VE GOT ME THIS WAY
Bregman, V & C, pub. 1940, reached #19 in January 1941
Johnny Mercer w, Jimmy McHugh m
Featured in YOU'LL FIND OUT, film (rel. 11/40)
Kay Kyser/Harry Babbitt, performed in film,
12/40 Col 35762
Tommy Dorsey/Pied Pipers 11/40 Vic 26770

YOURS (QUIEREME MUCHO) (9)
E B Marks, pub. 1931, reached #3 in September 1941
(Also reached #12 in November 1952)
Jack Sherr & Agustin Rodriguez w, Gonzalo Roig m
Jimmy Dorsey/Bob Eberly-Helen O'Connell ΦΦ 06/41 Dec 3657
Xavier Cugat/Dinah Shore 08/41 Vic 26384
Vaughn Monroe/Marilyn Duke 08/41 Blu 11146
Benny Goodman/Helen Forrest 08/41 Col 36067

[1]The Wayne King recording was entitled SOUVENIR DE VIENNE.
[2]Jack Fina on piano
[3]Bob Wills made several recordings of SAN ANTONIO ROSE over many years. The recording on Okeh 5694 was entitled NEW SAN ANTONIO ROSE.
[4]Crosby's record, too, bore the title NEW SAN ANTONIO ROSE.
[5]The Dorsey record bears the title TONIGHT.

1942

ALWAYS IN MY HEART (29)
Remick, pub. 1942, reached #9 in July 1942
Kim Gannon w, Ernesto Lecuona m
Featured in ALWAYS IN MY HEART, film (rel. 03/42)
Glenn Miller/Ray Eberle Φ 04/42 Blu 11438
Jimmy Dorsey/Bob Eberly 05/42 Dec 4277
Gloria Warren, sung in film
Kenny Baker 07/42 Dec 18262

AMEN (40)
Olman M C, pub. 1942, reached #12 in October 1942
Roger Segure, Bill Hardy, Vic Schoen w & m
Featured in WHAT'S COOKIN'? film (rel. 02/42)
Woody Herman/<vocal Φ sung in film and 07/42 Dec 18346
Abe Lyman/Rose Blane Φ 08/42 Blu 11542

THE ARMY AIR CORPS SONG (38)
Carl Fischer, pub. 1939, reached #11 in September 1942
Robert M Crawford w & m
Featured in ICE CAPADES REVUE, film (rel. 12/42)
Also featured in FOLLOW THE BAND, film (rel. 03/43)
Featured as theme in WINGED VICTORY, revue (opened 11/43)
Steady seller, 1942-1945
Alvino Rey/w.vocal group 08/42 Blu 11476
Dick Powell 08/42 Dec 2875
Four Clubmen 06/42 Vic 27815
The Bombardiers, sung in film (FTB)

AT LAST (47)
L Feist, pub. 1942, reached #11 in October 1942
(Also reached #14 in March 1952)
Mack Gordon w, Harry Warren m
Featured in ORCHESTRA WIVES, film (rel. 08/42)
Glenn Miller/Ray Eberle Φ sung in film and 09/42 Vic 27934
Charlie Spivak/Gary Stevens 10/42 Col 36642

BE CAREFUL, IT'S MY HEART (28)
Berlin, pub. 1942, reached #5 in September 1942
Irving Berlin w & m
Featured in HOLIDAY INN, film (rel. 06/42)
Bing Crosby ΦΦ sung in film, 08/42 Dec 18424
Tommy Dorsey/Frank Sinatra 08/42 Vic 27923
Kate Smith 08/42 Col 36618

THE BELLS OF SAN RAQUEL (39)
Peer, pub. 1941, reached #8 in January 1942
Fred Wise & Milton Leeds w, Lorenzo Barcelata m
Dick Jurgens/Harry Cool Φ 12/41 Okeh 6456
Glen Gray/Kenny Sargent 12/41 Dec 4067
Xavier Cugat/Carmen Castillo 01/42 Col 36447

BLUES IN THE NIGHT (5)
Remick, pub. 1941, reached #1 in February 1942
Johnny Mercer w, Harold Arlen m
Featured in BLUES IN THE NIGHT, film (rel. 10/41)
Woody Herman/<vocal ΦΦ 12/41 Dec 4030
Dinah Shore Φ 02/42 Blu 11436
Jimmie Lunceford/Willie Smith Φ 02/42 Dec 4125
Cab Calloway/<vocal 01/42 Okeh 6422
William Gillespie, sung in film

BREATHLESS
Campbell, L & P, pub. 1942, reached #17 in June 1942
Eddie Cherkose w, Jacques Press m
Shep Fields/Ken Carter 05/42 Blu 11497
The Merry Macs 05/42 Dec 4265
Les Brown/Betty Bonney 05/42 Okeh 6653

COW-COW BOOGIE
Leeds, pub. 1941, reached #18 in August 1942
(Also reached #18 in April 1944)
Don Raye, Gene DePaul, Benny Carter w & m
Featured in REVEILLE WITH BEVERLY, film (rel. 04/43)
Freddie Slack/Ella Mae Morse 08/42 Cap 102
Ella Mae Morse, sung in film

DAY DREAMING
T B Harms, pub. 1941, reached #17 in February 1942
Gus Kahn w, Jerome Kern m
Glenn Miller/Ray Eberle-Modernaires 02/42 Blu 11382
Bing Crosby, stage and radio

DAYBREAK
L Feist, pub. 1942, reached #12 in December 1942
Harold Adamson w, Ferde Grofe m
Featured in THOUSANDS CHEER, film (rel. 09/43)
Tommy Dorsey/Frank Sinatra Φ 10/42 Vic 27974
Kathryn Grayson, sung in film
Harry James/Johnny McAfee 12/42 Col 36644
Jimmy Dorsey/Bob Eberly 10/42 Dec 18460

DEAR MOM
Republic, pub. 1941, reached #18 in March 1942
Maury Coleman Harris w & m
Sammy Kaye/Allan Foster 02/42 Vic 27738
Charlie Spivak/Gary Stevens 02/42 Okeh 6555

DEARLY BELOVED (23)
Chappell, pub. 1942, reached #5 in November 1942
Johnny Mercer w, Jerome Kern m
Featured in YOU WERE NEVER LOVELIER, film (rel. 10/42)
Glenn Miller/Skip Nelson Φ 10/42 Vic 27953
Dinah Shore Φ 11/42 Vic 27970
Fred Astaire, sung in film
Benny Goodman/Buzz Alston 11/42 Col 36641

DEEP IN THE HEART OF TEXAS (17)
Melody Lane, pub. 1941, reached #1 in March 1942
June Hershey w, Don Swander m
Featured in HEART OF THE RIO GRANDE, film (rel. 03/42)
Alvino Rey/w.vocal duo ΦΦ 02/42 Blu 11391
Bing Crosby Φ 02/42 Dec 4162
Horace Heidt/w.vocal group Φ 03/42 Col 36525
Gene Autry, sung in film
The Merry Macs 03/42 Dec 4136

DER FUEHRER'S FACE (42)
Disney Prod, pub. 1942, reached #8 in December 1942
Oliver Wallace w & m
Featured in DONALD DUCK IN NUTZI LAND, cartoon film (1942)
Spike Jones & His City Slickers./w.vocal duo ΦΦΦ 10/42 Blu 11586

DON'T SIT UNDER THE APPLE TREE (WITH ANYONE ELSE BUT ME) (12)
Robbins, pub. 1942, reached #1 in June 1942
Lew Brown, Charles Tobias, Sam Stept w & m
Featured in PRIVATE BUCKAROO, film (rel. 06/42)
Glenn Miller/w.vocal group ΦΦ 04/42 Blu 11474
Andrews Sisters, sung in film, 05/42 Dec 18312
Kay Kyser/w.vocal group 05/42 Col 36567

EV'RYTHING I LOVE (45)
Chappell, pub. 1941, reached #10 in February 1942
Cole Porter w & m
Featured in LET'S FACE IT, show (opened 10/41)
Glenn Miller/Ray Eberle Φ 01/42 Blu 11365
Danny Kaye & Mary Jane Walsh, sung in show
Jimmy Dorsey/Bob Eberly 02/42 Dec 4123

FULL MOON
Southern, pub. 1942, reached #18 in May 1942
Bob Russell w, Gonzalo Curiel & Marcelene Odette m
Jimmy Dorsey/Bob Eberly 04/42 Dec 4312
Benny Goodman/Peggy Lee 04/42 Okeh 6652, 06/42 Col 36590

GOBS OF LOVE
Paramount, pub. 1942, reached #20 in November 1942
Redd Evans w & m
King Sisters 10/42 Blu 11576
Guy Lombardo/Rose Marie Lombardo 10/42 Dec 18435

HAPPY IN LOVE
L Feist, pub. 1941, reached #19 in April 1942
Jack Yellen w, Sammy Fain m
Featured in SONS O' FUN, show (opened 12/41)
Ella Logan, sung in show
Dick Jurgens/Buddy Moreno 03/42 Col 36586
Glenn Miller/Marion Hutton 03/42 Blu 11401

HE WEARS A PAIR OF SILVER WINGS (11)
Shapiro, B, pub. 1941, reached #1 in September 1942
Eric Maschwitz w, Michael Carr m
Kay Kyser/Harry Babbitt ΦΦ 07/42 Col 36604
Dinah Shore 08/42 Vic 27931
Gordon Jenkins/Connie Haines 08/42 Cap 106

HE'S MY GUY
Leeds, pub. 1942, reached #11 in October 1942
Don Raye w, Gene DePaul m
Featured in HI YA, CHUM, film (rel. 02/43)
Harry James/Helen Forrest Φ 09/42 Col 36614
Dinah Shore 10/42 Vic 27963
Freddie Slack/Ella Mae Morse 09/42 Cap 113

HERE YOU ARE
Robbins, pub. 1942, reached #19 in July 1942
Leo Robin w, Ralph Rainger m
Featured in MY GAL SAL, film (rel. 04/42)
Sammy Kaye/Elaine Beatty 05/42 Vic 27870
Freddy Martin/Stuart Wade 06/42 Blu 11509

HOW ABOUT YOU? (44)
L Feist, pub. 1941, reached #8 in March 1942
Ralph Freed w, Burton Lane m
Featured in BABES ON BROADWAY, film (rel. 12/41)
Judy Garland & Mickey Rooney, sung in film
Tommy Dorsey/Frank Sinatra Φ 02/42 Vic 27749
Judy Garland 01/42 Dec 4072
Dick Jurgens/Buddy Moreno 02/42 Okeh 6535

HOW DO I KNOW IT'S REAL?
Chappell, pub. 1942, reached #15 in April 1942
Lester Lee Seelen & Dan Shapiro w & m
Kay Kyser/Dorothy Dunn 04/42 Col 36526
Kate Smith 04/42 Col 36534

I CAME HERE TO TALK FOR JOE
Shapiro, B, pub. 1942, reached #11 in November 1942
Lew Brown & Charles Tobias w, Sam Stept m
Sammy Kaye/Don Cornell Φ 10/42 Vic 27994
Kay Kyser/Harry Babbitt 11/42 Col 36640

I DON'T WANT TO WALK WITHOUT YOU (18)
Paramount, pub. 1941, reached #3 in March 1942
Frank Loesser w, Jule Styne m
Featured in SWEATER GIRL, film (rel. 05/42)
Harry James/Helen Forrest ΦΦ 02/42 Col 36478
Bing Crosby Φ 03/42 Dec 4184
Dinah Shore 03/42 Blu 11423
Betty Jane Rhodes, sung in film

I GOT IT BAD (AND THAT AIN'T GOOD)
Robbins, pub. 1941, reached #20 in February 1942
Paul Francis Webster w, Duke Ellington m
Featured in JUMP FOR JOY, revue (opened 07/41)
Duke Ellington/Ivie Anderson, performed in revue and 11/41 Vic 27531
Benny Goodman/Peggy Lee 12/41 Col 36421

I LEFT MY HEART AT THE STAGE DOOR CANTEEN (22)
U.S. Army, pub. 1942, reached #4 in September 1942
Irving Berlin w & m
Featured in THIS IS THE ARMY, show (opened 07/42)
Sammy Kaye/Don Cornell Φ 08/42 Vic 27932
Charlie Spivak/Gary Stevens Φ 09/42 Col 36620
Pvt. Earl Oxford, sung in show

I MET HER ON MONDAY
ABC Music, pub. 1942, reached #17 in October 1942
Charles Newman w, Allie Wrubel m
Freddy Martin/Eddie Stone 10/42 Vic 27909
Horace Heidt/w.vocal group 10/42 Col 36636

I REMEMBER YOU (48)
Paramount, pub. 1942, reached #10 in May 1942
(Also reached #6 in October 1962)
Johnny Mercer w, Victor Schertzinger m
Featured in THE FLEET'S IN, film (rel. 01/42)
Dorothy Lamour, sung in film
Jimmy Dorsey/Bob Eberly Φ 04/42 Dec 4132
Harry James/Helen Forrest 05/42 Col 36518

I SAID NO! (43)
Paramount, pub. 1941, reached #10 in February 1942
Frank Loesser w, Jule Styne m
Featured in SWEATER GIRL, film (rel. 02/42)
Alvino Rey/Yvonne King Φ 01/42 Blu 11391
Betty Jane Rhodes, sung in film
Jimmy Dorsey/Helen O'Connell 01/42 Dec 4102

I THREW A KISS IN THE OCEAN (41)
Berlin, pub. 1942, reached #11 in June 1942
Irving Berlin w & m
Kate Smith Φ radio, 06/42 Col 36552
Jimmy Dorsey/Helen O'Connell 06/42 Dec 4304
Benny Goodman/Peggy Lee 06/42 Okeh 6652

I'LL KEEP THE LOVELIGHT BURNING
Remick, pub. 1942, reached #15 in July 1942
Harold Levey, Nick Kenny, Harry Tobias w & m
Freddy Martin/Stuart Wade 06/42 Blu 11503
Dick Jurgens/Harry Cool 06/42 Col 36600

I'LL PRAY FOR YOU
Harms, pub. 1942, reached #13 in April 1942
Kim Gannon w, Arthur Altman m
Andrews Sisters 03/42 Dec 4153
Tommy Tucker/w.vocal group 04/42 Okeh 6620

IDAHO (33)
Mills, pub. 1942, reached #3 in August 1942
Jesse Stone w & m
Featured in IDAHO, film (rel. 02/43)
Alvino Rey/Yvonne King Φ 07/42 Blu 11311
Benny Goodman/Dick Haymes 08/42 Col 36613
The Merry Macs 07/42 Dec 4313
Roy Rogers, sung in film

JERSEY BOUNCE (10)
Lewis, pub. 1941, reached #3 in June 1942
Robert B Wright w, Bobby Plater, Tiny Bradshaw & Edward Johnson m
Big-band classic
Benny Goodman Orch ΦΦ 04/42 Okeh 6590
Jimmy Dorsey Orch Φ 05/42 Dec 4288
Shep Fields Orch 06/42 Blu 11490

JINGLE, JANGLE, JINGLE (8)
Paramount, pub. 1942, reached #1 in July 1942
Frank Loesser w, Joseph J Lilley m
Featured in FOREST RANGERS, film (rel. 10/42)
Kay Kyser/w.vocal duo ΦΦΦ 07/42 Col 36604
The Merry Macs Φ 06/42 Dec 18361
Gene Autry 08/42 Okeh 6690
Freddy Martin/w.vocal duo 08/42 Vic 27909

JOHNNY DOUGHBOY FOUND A ROSE IN IRELAND (6)
Chappell, pub. 1942, reached #2 in June 1942
Al Goodhart & Kay Twomey w & m
Featured in JOHNNY DOUGHBOY, film (rel. 12/42)
Kay Kyser/w.vocal group ΦΦ 05/42 Col 36558
Guy Lombardo/Kenny Gardner 06/42 Dec 4278
Kenny Baker 06/42 Dec 18274
Freddy Martin/Clyde Rogers 06/42 Blu 11503

JUKE BOX SATURDAY NIGHT
Mutual, pub. 1942, reached #15 in January 1943
Al Stillman w, Paul McGrane m
Glenn Miller/w.vocal group Φ 11/42 Vic 20-1509

JUST AS THOUGH YOU WERE HERE (49)
Yankee, pub. 1942, reached #11 in August 1942
Eddie DeLange w, John Benson Brooks m
Tommy Dorsey/Frank Sinatra-Pied Pipers Φ 07/42 Vic 27903
Russ Morgan/<vocal 08/42 Dec 18374

(I'VE GOT A GAL IN) KALAMAZOO (16)
Bregman, V & C, pub. 1942, reached #1 in October 1942
Mack Gordon w, Harry Warren m
Featured in ORCHESTRA WIVES, film (rel. 08/42)
Glenn Miller/w.vocal group ΦΦΦ performed in film and 08/42 Vic 27934
Benny Goodman/Dick Haymes 08/42 Col 36622

MADELAINE
Santly-Joy, pub. 1941, reached #11 in January 1942
Joe Capwell & Phil Spitalny w & m
Sammy Kaye/Allan Foster Φ 01/42 Vic 27704
Bob Chester/Bob Haymes 01/42 Blu 11355
Dick Jurgens/Harry Cool 01/42 Okeh 6499

MANHATTAN SERENADE (36)
Robbins, pub. 1928, reached #6 in November 1942
(Also reached #19 in June 1928)
Harold Adamson w, Louis Alter m
(words added 1942)
Tommy Dorsey/Jo Stafford Φ 10/42 Vic 27962
Harry James/Helen Forrest Φ 11/42 Col 36644
Jimmy Dorsey/Bob Eberly 10/42 Dec 18462

THE MARINES' HYMN
E B Marks; orig. pub. 1919, reached #17 in July 1942
L Z Phillips w & m
Steady seller, 1942-45
The Four Clubmen 06/42 Vic 27814
Dick Powell 07/42 Dec 2875
Tony Pastor/Johnny McAfee 06/42 Blu 11452

ME AND MY MELINDA
Berlin, pub. 1942, reached #16 in April 1942
Irving Berlin w & m
Gene Krupa/Johnny Desmond 04/42 Okeh 6619
Vaughn Monroe/John Turnbull 04/42 Blu 11483
Kay Kyser/w.vocal group 05/42 Col 36558

MISS YOU (32)
Santly-Joy-Select, pub. 1929, reached #5 in April 1942
(Also reached #12 in September 1929)
Charles Tobias, Henry Tobias, Harry Tobias w & m
Dinah Shore Φ 03/42 Blu 11322
Bing Crosby Φ 03/42 Dec 4183
Eddy Howard/<vocal 02/42 Col 36432
Freddy Martin/Clyde Rogers 03/42 Blu 11286

MOONLIGHT COCKTAIL (4)
Jewel, pub. 1941, reached #1 in April 1942
Kim Gannon w, Lucky Roberts m
Glenn Miller/Ray Eberle ΦΦΦ 02/42 Blu 11401
Glen Gray & The Casa Loma Orch 04/42 Dec 4114
Tommy Tucker/Don Brown 02/42 Okeh 6526

MR. FIVE BY FIVE (21)
Leeds, pub. 1942, reached #3 in December 1942
Don Raye w, Gene DePaul m
Featured in BEHIND THE EIGHT BALL, film (rel. 12/42)
Harry James/Helen Forrest ΦΦ 11/42 Col 36650
Freddie Slack/Ella Mae Morse Φ 10/42 Cap 115
Andrews Sisters 10/42 Dec 18470
Sonny Dunham/Grace McDonald, performed in film

MY DEVOTION (9)
Santly-Joy, pub. 1942, reached #1 in September 1942
Roc Hillman & Johnny Napton w & m
Vaughn Monroe/<vocal ΦΦ 08/42 Vic 27925
Charlie Spivak/Gary Stevens ΦΦ 09/42 Col 36620
Jimmy Dorsey/Bob Eberly Φ 08/42 Dec 18392
King Sisters 09/42 Blu 11555

NIGHTINGALE
E B Marks, pub. 1942, reached #16 in June 1942
Fred Wise & Emilio deTorre w, Xavier Cugat & George Rosner m
Xavier Cugat/w.vocal group 05/42 Col 36559
Orrin Tucker/<vocal 05/42 Col 36597

ONE DOZEN ROSES (30)
Famous, pub. 1942, reached #5 in June 1942
Roger Lewis & Country Washburn w, Dick Jurgens
& Walter Donovan m
Dick Jurgens/Buddy Moreno Φ 04/42 Okeh 6636
Harry James/Jimmy Saunders Φ 05/42 Col 36566
Glen Gray/Pee Wee Hunt 05/42 Dec 4299
Dinah Shore 06/42 Vic 27881

PRAISE THE LORD AND PASS THE AMMUNITION (15)
Famous, pub. 1942, reached #2 in November 1942
Frank Loesser w & m
Kay Kyser/w.vocal group ΦΦΦ 10/42 Col 36640
The Merry Macs 11/42 Dec 18498

REMEMBER PEARL HARBOR (35)
Republic, pub. 1941, reached #5 in February 1942
Don Reid & Sammy Kaye w & m
Sammy Kaye/w.vocal group Φ 01/42 Vic 27738
Charlie Spivak/Gary Stevens 02/42 Okeh 6555
Eddy Howard Orch/w.vocal group 03/42 Col 36497

ROSE O'DAY (19)
Tobias-Lewis, pub. 1941, reached #3 in February 1942
Charles Tobias & Al Lewis w & m
Freddy Martin/Eddie Stone ΦΦ 01/42 Blu 11286
Kate Smith Φ 01/42 Col 36448
Guy Lombardo/Kenny Gardner 02/42 Dec 4143
Tommy Tucker/w.vocal duo 01/42 Okeh 6448
King Sisters 01/42 Blu 11349

SERENADE IN BLUE (24)
20th Century Mus, pub. 1942, reached #3 in November 1942
Mack Gordon w, Harry Warren m
Featured in ORCHESTRA WIVES, film (rel. 08/42)
Glenn Miller/Ray Eberle-Modernaires ΦΦ perf. in film,
09/42 Vic 27935
Benny Goodman/Dick Haymes 10/42 Col 36622

SHE'LL ALWAYS REMEMBER
Witmark, pub. 1942, reached #19 in April 1942
Edward Pola & Johnny Marks w & m
Dick Jurgens/Harry Cool 04/42 Okeh 6611
Glenn Miller/Ray Eberle-Modernaires 05/42 Blu 11493

THE SHRINE OF ST. CECILIA (25)
Braun, pub. 1941, reached #4 in February 1942
Carroll Loveday w, Nils Perne[1] m
Andrews Sisters Φ 01/42 Dec 4097
Sammy Kaye/Allan Foster Φ 01/42 Vic 27691
Vaughn Monroe/<vocal 01/42 Blu 11344

SING ME A SONG OF THE ISLANDS
Bregman, V & C, pub. 1942, reached #19 in June 1942
Mack Gordon w, Harry Owens m
Featured in SONG OF THE ISLANDS, film (rel. 02/42)
Betty Grable, sung in film
Alvino Rey/Bill Schallen 05/42 Blu 11448
Dick Todd 05/42 Blu 11440

SKYLARK (31)
Mayfair, pub. 1942, reached #5 in May 1942
Johnny Mercer w, Hoagy Carmichael m
Glenn Miller/Ray Eberle Φ 04/42 Blu 11462
Dinah Shore Φ 05/42 Blu 11473
Harry James/Helen Forrest 05/42 Col 36533
Bing Crosby 07/42 Dec 4193

SLEEPY LAGOON (3)
Chappell, pub. 1940, reached #1 in June 1942
Jack Lawrence w, Eric Coates m
Harry James Orch ΦΦ 04/42 Col 36549
Dinah Shore 06/42 Vic 27875
Vaughn Monroe/<vocal 06/42 Blu 11496

SOMEBODY ELSE IS TAKING MY PLACE (14)
Shapiro, B, pub. 1937, reached #1 in May 1942
Dick Howard, Bob Ellsworth, Russ Morgan w & m
Featured in STRICTLY IN THE GROOVE, film (rel. 01/43)
Benny Goodman/Peggy Lee ΦΦ 03/42 Okeh 6497
Russ Morgan/The Morganaires Φ 03/42 Dec 4098
Sammy Kaye/Allan Foster 03/42 Vic 27757
Vaughn Monroe/<vocal, radio, 04/42 Blu 11454

SOMETIMES
Berlin, pub. 1941, reached #10 in April 1942
Gus Kahn w, Carmen Lombardo m
Eddy Duchin/June Robbins 03/42 Col 36501
Sammy Kaye/Tommy Ryan 03/42 Vic 27725
Tommy Tucker/Amy Arnell 04/42 Okeh 6571

STRICTLY INSTRUMENTAL
Cherio, pub. 1942, reached #12 in September 1942
Eddie Seiler w, Sol Marcus, Benny Benjamin & Edgar Battle m
Harry James Orch Φ 08/42 Col 36579
Bob Chester Orch 08/42 Blu 11548
Jimmie Lunceford Orch 10/42 Dec 18423

A STRING OF PEARLS (27)
Mutual, pub. 1941, reached #6 in March 1942
Eddie DeLange w, Jerry Gray m
Big-band classic
Glenn Miller Orch ΦΦ 01/42 Blu 11382
Benny Goodman Orch 03/42 Okeh 6590
Connie Boswell 03/42 Dec 4163

STRIP POLKA (26)
E H Morris, pub. 1942, reached #4 in October 1942
Johnny Mercer w & m
Kay Kyser/Jack Martin ΦΦΦ 09/42 Col 36635
Johnny Mercer Φ 08/42 Cap 103
Andrews Sisters Φ 10/42 Dec 18470
Alvino Rey/King Sisters Φ 09/42 Blu 11573

SWEET ELOISE (50)
Shapiro, B, pub. 1942, reached #13 in July 1942
Mack David w, Russ Morgan m
Glenn Miller/Ray Eberle Φ 07/42 Vic 27879
Russ Morgan/Walter Link 07/42 Dec 4300
Kay Kyser/w.vocal group 06/42 Col 36589

TAKE ME (37)
Bregman, V & C, pub. 1942, reached #6 in September 1942
Mack David w, Rube Bloom m
Tommy Dorsey/Frank Sinatra Φ 08/42 Vic 27923
Jimmy Dorsey/Helen O'Connell Φ 08/42 Dec 18376
Benny Goodman/Dick Haymes 08/42 Col 36613

TANGERINE (20)
Famous, pub. 1942, reached #3 in May 1942
(Also reached #18 in April 1976)
Johnny Mercer w, Victor Scherztinger m
Featured in THE FLEET'S IN, film (rel. 01/42)
Jimmy Dorsey/Bob Eberly-Helen O'Connell ΦΦ performed in film, 04/42 Dec 4123
Vaughn Monroe/<vocal 05/42 Blu 11433
Tommy Tucker/Amy Arnell 05/42 Okeh 6583
Hal McIntyre/Carl Dennis 05/42 Vic 27803

THERE WILL NEVER BE ANOTHER YOU
Robbins, pub. 1942, reached #16 in December 1942
Mack Gordon w, Harry Warren m
Featured in ICELAND, film (rel. 08/42)
John Payne, sung in film
Sammy Kaye/Nancy Norman 12/42 Vic 27949
Woody Herman/<vocal 12/42 Dec 18469

THIS IS NO LAUGHING MATTER
Block, pub. 1941, reached #10 in January 1942
Buddy Kaye w, Al Frisch m
Charlie Spivak/Gary Stevens Φ 12/41 Okeh 6458
Glenn Miller/Ray Eberle 01/42 Blu 11369
Jimmy Dorsey/Bob Eberly 01/42 Dec 4102

THIS IS WORTH FIGHTING FOR
Harms, pub. 1942, reached #12 in August 1942
Eddie DeLange w, Sam Stept m
Featured in WHEN JOHNNY COMES MARCHING HOME, film (rel. 12/42)
Jimmy Dorsey/Bob Eberly 07/42 Dec 18376
Vaughn Monroe/<vocal 08/42 Vic 27921
Kate Smith 08/42 Col 36605

THREE LITTLE SISTERS (34)
Santly-Joy-Select, pub. 1942, reached #7 in July 1942
Irving Taylor w, Vic Mizzy m
Featured in PRIVATE BUCKAROO, film (rel. 06/42)
Andrews Sisters Φ sung in film, 05/42 Dec 18319
Vaughn Monroe/Four V's 06/42 Blu 11508
Horace Heidt/w.vocal trio 06/42 Col 36576

'TIS AUTUMN
Witmark, pub. 1941, reached #13 in February 1942
Henry Nemo w & m
Woody Herman/w.vocal group Φ 01/42 Dec 4095
Les Brown/Ralph Young 01/42 Okeh 6430
Eddy Duchin/Larry Taylor 01/42 Col 36454

WE DID IT BEFORE (AND WE CAN DO IT AGAIN)
Witmark, pub. 1941, reached #9 in February 1942
Charles Tobias w, Cliff Friend m
Featured in BANJO EYES, show (opened 12/41)
Also featured in SWEETHEART OF THE FLEET, film (rel. 08/42)
Eddie Cantor, sung in show
Dick Robertson/<vocal 02/42 Dec 4117
Eddy Howard Orch/w.vocal group 03/42 Col 36497

WE'LL MEET AGAIN
Dash-Connelly, pub. 1942, reached #15 in June 1942
Hugh Charles w, Albert R Parker m
Benny Goodman/Peggy Lee 05/42 Okeh 6644
Woody Herman/Billy Rogers 05/42 Dec 18314

WE'RE THE COUPLE IN THE CASTLE
Famous, pub. 1941, reached #15 in March 1942
Frank Loesser w, Hoagy Carmichael m
Featured in MR. BUG GOES TO TOWN, cartoon film (rel. 12/41)
Glenn Miller/Ray Eberle 02/42 Blu 11397
King Sisters 02/42 Blu 11398
Sammy Kaye/Allan Foster 02/42 Vic 27722

WHEN THE LIGHTS GO ON AGAIN (1)
Campbell, L & P, pub. 1942, reached #1 in January 1943
Eddie Seiler, Sol Marcus, Bennie Benjamin w & m
Vaughn Monroe/<vocal ΦΦ 10/42 Vic 27945
Lucky Millinder/Trevor Bacon Φ 12/42 Dec 18496
Les Brown/Jack Carroll 12/42 Okeh 6696

WHITE CHRISTMAS (7)
Berlin ΦΦΦ, pub. 1942, reached #1 in November 1942
(Also reached Top 20 every December 1943-1955, 1960 & 1961)
Irving Berlin w & m
Featured in HOLIDAY INN, film (rel. 06/42)
All-time pop standard
All-time Christmas standard
Bing Crosby ΦΦΦ sung in film, 10/42 Dec 18429
Charlie Spivak/Gary Stevens 11/42 Col 36649
Gordon Jenkins/Bob Carroll 11/42 Cap 124
Freddy Martin/Clyde Rogers 11/42 Vic 27946

THE WHITE CLIFFS OF DOVER (2)
Shapiro, B, pub. 1941, reached #1 in January 1942
Nat Burton w, Walter Kent m
Kay Kyser/Harry Babbitt ΦΦ 12/41 Col 36445
Glenn Miller/Ray Eberle Φ 01/42 Blu 11397
Kate Smith Φ radio, 01/42 Col 36448
Sammy Kaye/Arthur Wright 01/42 Vic 27704
Jimmy Dorsey/Bob Eberly 02/42 Dec 4103

WHO WOULDN'T LOVE YOU (13)
Maestro, pub. 1942, reached #4 in July 1942
Bill Carey w, Carl Fischer m
Kay Kyser/w.vocal duo ΦΦΦ 04/42 Col 36526
Freddy Martin/Stuart Wade 06/42 Vic 27891
Guy Lombardo/Kenny Gardner 06/42 Dec 4208

WONDER WHEN MY BABY'S COMING HOME
Crawford, pub. 1942, reached #14 in November 1942
Kermit Goell w, Arthur Kent m
Sammy Kaye/Nancy Norman 09/42 Vic 27922
Jimmy Dorsey/Helen O'Connell 09/42 Dec 18362
Kay Kyser/Dorothy Dunn 09/42 Col 36615

YOU MADE ME LOVE YOU (46)
Broadway M C, pub. 1913, reached #12 in December 1941
(Also reached #1 in September 1913)
Joe McCarthy w, James V Monaco m
Featured in SYNCOPATION, film (rel. 05/42)
Big-band classic
Harry James Orch ΦΦ 11/41 Col 36296
Judy Garland 12/41 Dec 1463
Jimmy Dorsey/Helen O'Connell 02/42 Dec 4142

A ZOOT SUIT
Greene-Revel, pub. 1941, reached #13 in April 1942
Ray Gilbert & Bob O'Brien w & m
Kay Kyser/w.vocal group Φ 03/42 Col 36517
Andrews Sisters 04/42 Dec 4182
Benny Goodman/Art Lund 04/42 Okeh 6606

[1]Nils Perne used the pseudonym "Jokern."

1943

ALL OR NOTHING AT ALL (19)
Leeds, pub. 1940, reached #3 in September 1943
Jack Lawrence w, Arthur Altman m
Harry James/Frank Sinatra ΦΦΦ 06/43 Col 35587
Jimmy Dorsey/Bob Eberly 08/43 Dec 2580
Count Basie/Helen Humes 08/43 Okeh 5884

AS TIME GOES BY (5)
Remick, pub. 1931, reached #1 in May 1943
(Also reached #20 in June 1952)
Herman Hupfeld w & m
Featured in CASABLANCA, film (rel. 11/42)
Rudy Vallee ΦΦ 04/43 Vic 20-1526
Dooley Wilson, sung in film (Later: 1946 Dec 40006)
Jacques Renard/Frank Munn Φ 04/43 Bruns 6205

BIG BOY
Advanced; orig. pub. 1924, reached #20 in June 1943
Jack Yellen w, Milt Ager m
Ray McKinley/Imogene Lynn 05/43 Cap 131
Bud Freeman Combo 06/43 Dec 18064

BLUE RAIN (47)
Melrose, pub. 1939, reached #15 in October 1943
Johnny Mercer w, Jimmy Van Heusen m
Glenn Miller/Ray Eberle 09/43 Vic 20-1536
Tommy Dorsey/Jack Leonard 10/43 Vic 26418
Del Courtney/Joe Martin 10/43 Voc 5279

BOOGIE WOOGIE (40)
Melrose; orig. pub. 1929, reached #12 in January 1944
(Also reached #18 in November 1938)
(Also reached #16 in September 1945)
Pinetop Smith m
Big-band classic and steady seller, 1938 through the 1940's
Tommy Dorsey Orch ΦΦ 02/43 Vic 26054
Count Basie Orch 02/43 Dec 2355
Les Brown Orch 03/43 Blu 7818

BRAZIL (14)
Southern, pub. 1942, reached #3 in March 1943
(Also reached #10 in November 1975)
S K Russell w, Ary Barroso m
Xavier Cugat/w.vocal group ΦΦ 01/43 Col 36651
Jimmy Dorsey/Bob Eberly-Helen O'Connell Φ 01/43 Dec 18460
Eddy Duchin/Tony Leonard 02/43 Col 36400

CAN'T GET OUT OF THIS MOOD (42)
Southern, pub. 1942, reached #9 in January 1943
Frank Loesser w, Jimmy McHugh m
Featured in SEVEN DAYS' LEAVE, film (rel. 10/42)
Kay Kyser/w.vocal group Φ 12/42 Col 36657
Ginny Sims, sung in film
Johnny Long/Four Teens 12/42 Dec 4369

CLOSE TO YOU
Barton M C, pub. 1943, reached #14 in October 1943
Al Hoffman & Jay Livingston w & m
Frank Sinatra Φ 08/43 Col 36678
Radio singers

COMIN' IN ON A WING AND A PRAYER (7)
Robbins, pub. 1943, reached #1 in June 1943
Harold Adamson w, Jimmy McHugh m
The Song Spinners ΦΦ 06/43 Dec 18553
Eddie Cantor, stage and radio
Willie Kelly/w.vocal Φ 06/43 Hit 7046
Four Vagabonds 07/43 Blu 30-0815

DON'T CRY, BABY
Advanced, pub. 1943, reached #19 in October 1943
Jimmy Mitchelle & Sammy Lowe w & m
Erskine Hawkins/Jimmy Mitchelle 09/43 Blu 30-0813
Lucky Millinder/Judy Carol 12/43 Dec 18569

DON'T GET AROUND MUCH ANYMORE (12)
Robbins, pub. 1942, reached #2 in May 1943
Bob Russell w, Duke Ellington m
The Ink Spots ΦΦ 02/43 Dec 18503
Duke Ellington Orch[1] Φ 05/43 Vic 26610
Glen Gray/Kenny Sargent Φ 01/43 Dec 18479

THE DREAMER (50)
Harms, pub. 1943, reached #15 in January 1944
Frank Loesser w, Arthur Schwartz m
Featured in THANK YOUR LUCKY STARS, film (rel. 08/43)
Dinah Shore, sung in film
Kay Armen Φ 11/43 Dec 18566
Peter Piper/w.vocal 10/43 Hit 7061

FAT MEAT IS GOOD MEAT
Beacon Mus, pub. 1942, reached #19 in February 1943
Irene Higginbotham w & m
Jimmy Lytell/Savannah Churchill Φ 01/43 Beacon 104

FOR ME AND MY GAL (20)
Mills; orig. pub. 1917, reached #6 in March 1943
(Also reached #1 in May 1917)
Edgar Leslie & E Ray Goetz w, George Meyer m
Featured in FOR ME AND MY GAL, film (rel. 09/42)
Judy Garland & Gene Kelly ΦΦ sung in film, 01/43 Dec 18480
Guy Lombardo/Kenny Gardner 01/43 Dec 4371
Abe Lyman/Billy Sherman 01/43 Blu 11549

FOR THE FIRST TIME (35)
Shapiro, B, pub. 1943, reached #11 in January 1944
Charles Tobias w, Dave Kapp m
Dick Haymes/Song Spinners Φ 11/43 Dec 18565
Glenn Miller/Johnny Desmond, military stage
Vaughn Monroe, military stage, V-Disc 94-A
Sid Peltyn/w.vocal 12/43 Hit 7068

THE FUDDY DUDDY WATCHMAKER
Paramount, pub. 1943, reached #18 in June 1943
Frank Loesser w, Jimmy McHugh m
Featured in HAPPY GO LUCKY, film (rel. 01/43)
Betty Hutton, sung in film
Kay Kyser/Julie Conway 05/43 Col 36673

HOW SWEET YOU ARE (39)
Remick, pub. 1943, reached #11 in December 1943
Frank Loesser w, Arthur Schwartz m
Featured in THANK YOUR LUCKY STARS, film (rel. 08/43)
Dinah Shore, sung in film
Kay Armen Φ 11/43 Dec 18566
Jo Stafford 01/44 Cap 142

I HAD THE CRAZIEST DREAM (18)
Bregman, V & C, pub. 1942, reached #3 in January 1943
Mack Gordon w, Harry Warren m
Featured in SPRINGTIME IN THE ROCKIES, film (rel. 09/42)
Harry James/Helen Forrest ΦΦΦ, performed in film and 11/42 Col 36659
Tony Martin 01/43 Dec 4394
Four Vagabonds 01/43 Blu 30-0810

I HEARD YOU CRIED LAST NIGHT (25)
Campbell, L & P, pub. 1943, reached #4 in October 1943
Jerrie Kruger w, Ted Grouya m
Featured in CINDERELLA SWINGS IT, film (rel. 01/43)
Harry James/Helen Forrest ΦΦ 08/43 Col 36677
Allen Miller/w.vocal 09/43 Hit 7053
Dick Haymes/Song Spinners 09/43 Dec 18558

I JUST KISSED YOUR PICTURE GOODNIGHT
Crawford, pub. 1942, reached #13 in April 1943
Mack David w, Walter Kent m
Allen Miller/w.vocal 03/43 Hit 7034
radio singers

I NEVER MENTION YOUR NAME (44)
Berlin, pub. 1943, reached #12 in September 1943
Mack Davis & Don George w, Walter Kent m
Jack Leonard/Ray Bloch 09/43 Okeh 6715
Dick Haymes 09/43 Dec 18558
Allen Miller/w.vocal 09/43 Hit 7048

I'LL BE HOME FOR CHRISTMAS (41)
E H Morris, pub. 1943, reached #7 in December 1943
(Also reached #17 in December 1944)
Kim Gannon, Buck Ram, Walter Kent w & m
All-time Christmas standard
Bing Crosby ΦΦ 12/43 Dec 18570
Sid Peltyn/w.vocal 12/43 Hit 7068

I'M GETTING TIRED SO I CAN SLEEP
Berlin, pub. 1942, reached #16 in February 1943
Irving Berlin w & m
Featured in THIS IS THE ARMY, show (opened 07/43)
Jimmy Dorsey/Bob Eberly 02/43 Dec 18462
Pvt. William Horne, sung in show
Hal McIntyre/Jerry Stuart 02/43 Vic 27951

I'VE HEARD THAT SONG BEFORE (8)
E H Morris, pub. 1942, reached #1 in March 1943
Sammy Cahn w, Jule Styne m
Featured in YOUTH ON PARADE, film (rel. 10/42)
Harry James/Helen Forrest ΦΦΦ 01/43 Col 36668
Frank Sinatra, sung in film
Johnny Jones/w.vocal 03/43 Hit 7038

IF YOU PLEASE (33)
Famous, pub. 1943, reached #8 in October 1943
Johnny Burke w, Jimmy Van Heusen m
Featured in DIXIE, film (rel. 06/43)
Bing Crosby Φ sung in film, 09/43 Dec 18561
Frank Sinatra 10/43 Col 36679
Peter Piper/w.vocal 10/43 Hit 7057

IN MY ARMS (21)
Pacific, pub. 1943, reached #5 in August 1943
Frank Loesser w, Ted Grouya m
Featured in SEE HERE, PRIVATE HARGROVE, film (rel. 02/44)
Dick Haymes/Song Spinners Φ 07/43 Dec 18557
Bob Crosby, sung in film
Peter Piper/w.vocal 09/43 Hit 7055

IN THE BLUE OF THE EVENING (16)
Shapiro, B, pub. 1942, reached #2 in August 1943
Tom Adair w, Alfred D'Artega m
Tommy Dorsey/Frank Sinatra ΦΦ 07/43 Vic 20-1530
Allen Miller/w.vocal 07/43 Hit 7048
D'Artega Orch, stage

IT CAN'T BE WRONG (11)
Harms, pub. 1942, reached #3 in May 1943
Kim Gannon w, Max Steiner m
Featured as theme in NOW VOYAGER, film (rel. 08/42)
Dick Haymes/Song Spinners ΦΦ 06/43 Dec 18557
Allen Miller/w.vocal Φ 05/43 Hit 7045
Four Vagabonds 06/43 Blu 30-0815

IT STARTED ALL OVER AGAIN (38)
Yankee, pub. 1942, reached #10 in April 1943
Bill Carey w, Carl Fischer m
Tommy Dorsey/Frank Sinatra-Pied Pipers Φ 02/43 Vic 20-1522
Johnny Jones/w.vocal 04/43 Hit 7041

IT'S ALWAYS YOU (29)
Famous, pub. 1941, reached #5 in July 1943
Johnny Burke w, Jimmy Van Heusen m
Featured in ROAD TO ZANZIBAR, film (rel. 04/41)
Tommy Dorsey/Frank Sinatra Φ 07/43 Vic 20-1530
Benny Goodman/Helen Forrest 07/43 Col 36680
Glenn Miller/Ray Eberle 07/43 Blu 11079
Bing Crosby, sung in film, 07/43 Dec 3636

JOHNNY ZERO (28)
Santly-Joy, pub. 1943, reached #4 in July 1943
Mack David w, Vee Lawnhurst m
The Song Spinners Φ 06/43 Dec 18553
Johnny Jones/w.vocal 06/43 Hit 7050
radio singers

LET'S GET LOST (23)
Paramount, pub. 1943, reached #3 in June 1943
Frank Loesser w, Jimmy McHugh m
Featured in HAPPY GO LUCKY, film (rel. 01/43)
Vaughn Monroe/<vocal ΦΦ 05/43 Vic 20-1524
Kay Kyser/w.vocal group Φ 05/43 Col 36673
Mary Martin, sung in film
Jimmy Dorsey/Bob Eberly 06/43 Dec 18532

MOONLIGHT BECOMES YOU (15)
Famous, pub. 1942, reached #1 in February 1943
Johnny Burke w, Jimmy Van Heusen m
Featured in ROAD TO MOROCCO, film (rel. 10/42)
Bing Crosby ΦΦ sung in film, 12/42 Dec 18513
Glenn Miller/Skip Nelson Φ 12/42 Vic 20-1520
Harry James/Johnny McAfee 01/43 Col 36668

MOONLIGHT MOOD (34)
Robbins, pub. 1942, reached #8 in February 1943
Harold Adamson w, Peter DeRose m
Glenn Miller/Skip Nelson 01/43 Vic 20-1520
Kay Kyser/w.vocal group 02/43 Col 36657
Connee Boswell 01/43 Dec 18509
Glen Gray/Kenny Sargent 01/43 Dec 18508

MOVE IT OVER
Santly-Joy, pub. 1942, reached #20 in February 1943
Sunny Skylar w & m
Ethel Merman 02/43 Vic 20-1521
Sammy Kaye/Sally Stewart, stage, 12/43 V-Disc 71-B

"MURDER" HE SAYS (45)
Paramount, pub. 1942, reached #14 in May 1943
Frank Loesser w, Jimmy McHugh m
Featured in HAPPY GO LUCKY, film (rel. 01/43)
Betty Hutton, sung in film (Later: 1951 Vic 20-4179)
Dinah Shore 04/43 Vic 20-1525
Jimmy Dorsey/Helen O'Connell 04/43 Dec 18532

NEVER A DAY GOES BY
Miller Mus, pub. 1943, reached #20 in July 1943
Peter DeRose, Mitchell Parish, Walter Donaldson w & m
Geraldo Orch/Dorothy Carless 07/43 Parlophone MPE 164
radio singers

NO LETTER TODAY
Peer, pub. 1943, reached #17 in September 1943
Frankie Brown w & m
Ted Daffan/w.vocal duo Φ 07/43 Okeh 6706
Dick Robertson/<vocal 07/43 Dec 4436

OH, WHAT A BEAUTIFUL MORNIN' (17)
Crawford, pub. 1943, reached #4 in December 1943
Oscar Hammerstein 2nd w, Richard Rodgers m
Featured in OKLAHOMA, show (opened 03/43)
Bing Crosby Φ 10/43 Dec 18564
Alfred Drake, sung in show, 12/43 Dec 23283 (in album)
Frank Sinatra 11/43 Col 36682

PAPER DOLL (1)
E B Marks, pub. 1930, reached #1 in October 1943
Johnny Black w & m,
Mills Brothers ΦΦΦ 07/43 Dec 18318
Willie Kelly/w.vocal 11/43 Hit 7067

PEOPLE WILL SAY WE'RE IN LOVE (2)
Crawford, pub. 1943, reached #3 in November 1943
Oscar Hammerstein 2nd w, Richard Rodgers m
Featured in OKLAHOMA, show (opened 03/43)
Bing Crosby ΦΦ 10/43 Dec 18564
Frank Sinatra ΦΦ 10/43 Col 36682
Alfred Drake & Joan Roberts, sung in show and 12/43 Dec 23287 (in album)
Hal Goodman/w.vocal 09/43 Hit 7059

PISTOL PACKIN' MAMA (3)
E H Morris, pub. 1943, reached #1 in November 1943
Al Dexter w & m
Al Dexter ΦΦΦ 06/43 Okeh 6708
Bing Crosby & The Andrews Sisters ΦΦΦ 11/43 Dec 23277
Freddy "Schnickelfritz" Fisher 06/43 Dec 4425

PLEASE THINK OF ME
Witmark, pub. 1942, reached #16 in March 1943
Russ Morgan, Murray Menscher, Benny Davis w & m
Russ Morgan/w.vocal group 01/43 Dec 18482
Shep Fields/Ralph Young 03/43 Blu 30-0807

PRINCE CHARMING
E H Morris, pub. 1943, reached #19 in June 1943
Al Dubin w, Leroy Holmes m
Harry James Orch 05/43 Col 36672

PUT YOUR ARMS AROUND ME, HONEY (24)
Broadway M C; orig. pub. 1910, reached #5 in October 1943
(Also reached #1 in May 1911)
Junie McCree w, Albert Von Tilzer m
Featured in CONEY ISLAND, film (rel. 05/43)
Dick Kuhn/w.vocal trio Φ 09/43 Dec 4337
Betty Grable, sung in film
Dick Haymes/Song Spinners Φ 10/43 Dec 18565
Hal Goodman/w.vocal 10/43 Hit 7056

RHAPSODY IN BLUE
Harms, pub. 1924, reached #18 in November 1943
(Also reached #14 in October 1924)
George Gershwin m
Glenn Miller Orch 10/43 Vic 20-1529

ROSE ANN OF CHARING CROSS (43)
Shapiro, B, pub. 1942, reached #11 in February 1943
Kermit Goell w, Mabel Wayne m
Kate Smith, radio
Peter Piper Orch/Black Pepper 02/43 Hit 7033
Four Vagabonds 04/43 Blu 30-0811

SAY A PRAYER FOR THE BOYS OVER THERE (32)
Southern, pub. 1943, reached #10 in October 1943
Herb Magidson w, Jimmy McHugh m
Featured in HERS TO HOLD, film (rel. 07/43)
Deanna Durbin, sung in film, 12/43 Dec 18575
radio singers

SUNDAY, MONDAY, OR ALWAYS (10)
Mayfair, pub. 1943, reached #1 in October 1943
Johnny Burke w, Jimmy Van Heusen m
Featured in DIXIE, film (rel. 06/43)
Bing Crosby ΦΦΦ sung in film, 08/43 Dec 18561
Frank Sinatra Φ 08/43 Col 36679
Peter Piper/w.vocal 08/43 Hit 7057

TAKE IT FROM THERE
Miller Mus, pub. 1943, reached #16 in July 1943
Leo Robin w, Ralph Rainger m
Featured in CONEY ISLAND, film (rel. 05/43)
Betty Grable, sung in film
Hal Goodman/w.vocal 07/43 Hit 7056

TAKING A CHANCE ON LOVE (26)
L Feist, pub. 1940, reached #6 in June 1943
Jack LaTouche & Ted Fetter w, Vernon Duke m
Featured in CABIN IN THE SKY, film (rel. 02/43)
Benny Goodman/Helen Forrest ΦΦ 04/43 Col 35869
Ethel Waters, sung in film
Sammy Kaye/Three Kaydets 04/43 Vic 20-1527

THAT OLD BLACK MAGIC (13)
Famous, pub. 1942, reached #2 in March 1943
(Also reached #20 in July 1955)
Johnny Mercer w, Harold Arlen m
Featured in STAR-SPANGLED RHYTHM, film (rel. 12/42)
Glenn Miller/Skip Nelson ΦΦ 02/43 Vic 20-1523
Johnny Johnston, sung in film
Freddie Slack/Margaret Whiting Φ 02/43 Cap 126
Horace Heidt/Charles Goodman Φ 03/43 Col 36670

THERE ARE SUCH THINGS (9)
Yankee, pub. 1942, reached #1 in January 1943
Stanley Adams w, Abel Baer & George Meyer m
Tommy Dorsey/Frank Sinatra-Pied Pipers ΦΦΦ 11/42 Vic 27974
Earl Hines/Billy Eckstine, stage
Emil Davis/w.vocal 02/43 Hit 7031

THERE'S A HARBOR OF DREAMBOATS (49)
Shapiro, B, pub. 1943, reached #12 in May 1943
Nat Burton, Al Sherman, Arthur Altman w & m
Peter Piper/w.vocal 05/43 Hit 7043
radio singers

THERE'S A STAR-SPANGLED BANNER WAVING SOMEWHERE (6)
Bob Miller Mus, pub. 1942, reached #8 in December 1942
Paul Roberts & Shelley Darnell w & m
Steady seller, 1942-44
Elton Britt ΦΦΦ 09/42 Blu 9000
Jimmy Wakely 03/43 Dec 6059

THEY'RE EITHER TOO YOUNG OR TOO OLD (30)
Witmark, pub. 1943, reached #6 in December 1943
Frank Loesser w, Arthur Schwartz m
Featured in THANK YOUR LUCKY STARS, film (rel. 08/43)
Jimmy Dorsey/Kitty Kallen ΦΦ 12/43 Dec 18571
Bette Davis, sung in film
Hildegarde, stage and radio

A TOUCH OF TEXAS
Melody Lane, pub. 1942, reached #17 in January 1943
Frank Loesser w, Jimmy McHugh m
Featured in SEVEN DAYS' LEAVE, film (rel. 10/42)
Freddy Martin/w.vocal trio, performed in film and 12/42 Vic 20-1504
Kay Kyser/w.vocal group 01/43 Col 36671

VELVET MOON (36)
Witmark, pub. 1943, reached #11 in May 1943
Eddie DeLange w, Josef Myrow m
Harry James Orch ΦΦ 04/43 Col 36672

VICT'RY POLKA (31)
Chappell, pub. 1943, reached #9 in December 1943
Sammy Cahn w, Jule Styne m
Bing Crosby & the Andrews Sisters Φ 11/43 Dec 23277

WAIT FOR ME, MARY
Remick, pub. 1942, reached #16 in October 1943
Harry Tobias w, Charles Tobias & Nat Simon m
Dick Haymes/Song Spinners 07/43 Dec 18556
Willie Kelly/w.vocal 08/43 Hit 7049

WARSAW CONCERTO
Chappell, pub. 1942, reached #17 in August 1943
Richard Addinsell m
Featured in SUICIDE SQUADRON, film (rel. 04/42)
Freddy Martin Orch 08/43 Vic 20-1535
Louis Kentner, played in film
Alec Templeton Orch 08/43 Dec 18484

WHAT'S THE GOOD WORD, MR. BLUEBIRD? (48)
Berlin, pub. 1943, reached #14 in May 1943
Al Hoffman, Allan Roberts, Jay Livingston w & m
Peter Piper/w.vocal 05/43 Hit 7043
Bob Crosby/<vocal, stage, 10/43 V-Disc 36-B
radio singers

WHITE CHRISTMAS (46)
Berlin, pub. 1942, reached #8 in December 1943
(Also reached #1 in November 1942)
(Also reached Top 20 every December 1944-1955, 1960 & 1961)
Irving Berlin w & m
Bing Crosby Φ 12/43 Dec 18429

WHY DON'T YOU DO RIGHT? (37)
Mayfair, pub. 1942, reached #11 in March 1943
Joe McCoy w & m
Featured in STAGE DOOR CANTEEN, film (rel. 05/43)
Benny Goodman/Peggy Lee ΦΦ performed in film and 01/43 Col 36652
Lil Green, stage, 03/43 Blu 8714
Nora Lee King 03/43 Dec 7866

WHY DON'T YOU FALL IN LOVE WITH ME? (27)
Harms, pub. 1942, reached #4 in February 1943
Al Lewis w, Mabel Wayne m
Dinah Shore Φ 01/43 Vic 27970
Dick Jurgens/Harry Cool Φ 01/43 Col 36643
Johnny Long/Bob Houston 01/43 Dec 4375
Connee Boswell 01/43 Dec 18483

YOU'D BE SO NICE TO COME HOME TO (22)
Chappell, pub. 1942, reached #5 in April 1943
Cole Porter w & m
Featured in SOMETHING TO SHOUT ABOUT, film (rel. 02/43)
Dinah Shore ΦΦ 02/43 Vic 20-1519
Janet Blair & Don Ameche, sung in film
Six Hits and a Miss 03/43 Cap 127
Dick Jurgens/Harry Cool 02/43 Col 36669

YOU'LL NEVER KNOW (4)
Bregman, V & C, pub. 1943, reached #1 in August 1943
Mack Gordon w, Harry Warren m
Featured in HELLO, FRISCO, HELLO, film (rel. 03/43)
Dick Haymes/Song Spinners ΦΦΦ 07/43 Dec 18556
Frank Sinatra ΦΦ 07/43 Col 36678
Alice Faye, sung in film
Willie Kelly/w.vocal 06/43 Hit 7046

[1]Originally recorded by Duke Ellington in 1940 as NEVER NO LAMENT.

1944

ALWAYS (30)
Berlin, pub. 1925, reached #6 in November 1944
(Also reached #1 in April 1926)
Irving Berlin w & m
Featured in CHRISTMAS HOLIDAY, film (rel. 06/44)
Deanna Durbin, sung in film
Sammy Kaye/Tony Alamo Φ 12/44 Vic 20-1610
Guy Lombardo/Stuart Foster Φ 01/45 Dec 18634
Gordon Jenkins/Dennis Day 12/44 Cap 125

AMOR (15)
Melody Lane, pub. 1943, reached #4 in July 1944
(Also reached #19 in September 1961)
Ricardo Lopez Mendez & Sunny Skylar w, Gabriel Ruiz m
Featured in BROADWAY RHYTHM, film (rel. 01/44)
Bing Crosby ΦΦ 07/44 Dec 18608
Andy Russell Φ 06/44 Cap 156
Xavier Cugat/Carmen Castillo 07/44 Col 36718
Ginny Simms, sung in film

AND HER TEARS FLOWED LIKE WINE (42)
Robbins, pub. 1944, reached #13 in November 1944
Joe Greene w, Stan Kenton & Charles Lawrence m
Stan Kenton/Anita O'Day Φ 09/44 Cap 166
Ella Fitzgerald/Johnny Long Orch 12/44 Dec 18633
Phil Moore Four 01/45 Vic 20-1624

AND THEN YOU KISSED ME
Miller Mus, pub. 1944, reached #19 in August 1944
Sammy Cahn w, Jule Styne m
Featured in STEP LIVELY, film (rel. 06/44)
Frank Sinatra, sung in film, 09/44 V-Disc 262-A
Bob Strong/Don Carmichael 09/44 Hit 7097

BESAME MUCHO (7)
Southern, pub. 1943, reached #1 in March 1944
Sunny Skylar w, Consuelo Velasquez m
Jimmy Dorsey/Bob Eberly-Kitty Kallen ΦΦ 01/44 Dec 18574
Andy Russell Φ 04/44 Cap 149
Abe Lyman/Rose Blane 02/44 Hit 7072
Phil Brito/Paul LaValle Orch 03/44 Musicraft 15017

BY THE RIVER OF THE ROSES (44)
Shapiro, B, pub. 1943, reached #12 in April 1944
Marty Symes w, Joe Burke m
Woody Herman/<vocal 04/44 Dec 18578
Abe Lyman/Frank Connors 03/44 Hit 7071
Phil Hanna/Harry Sosnik Orch 05/44 Dec 4435

CHERRY (46)
Melody Lane, pub. 1928, reached #12 in February 1944
(Also reached #16 in December 1928)
Ray Gilbert w, Don Redman m
Harry James Orch Φ 01/44 Col 36683
Erskine Hawkins/Jimmy Mitchelle 02/44 Blu 30-0819

COW-COW BOOGIE
Leeds, pub. 1941, reached #18 in April 1944
(Also reached #18 in August 1942)
Don Raye w, Gene DePaul m
Ella Fitzgerald & The Ink Spots Φ 03/44 Dec 18587
Freddie Slack/Ella Mae Morse 03/44 Cap 102

DANCE WITH A DOLLY (11)
Shapiro, B, pub. 1940, reached #2 in December 1944
Cool White, Terry Shand, Jimmy Eaton, Mickey Leader w & m
Russ Morgan/Al Jennings Φ 10/44 Dec 18625
Evelyn Knight Φ 09/44 Dec 18614
Tony Pastor/<vocal Φ 10/44 Blu 30-0827
Louis Prima/<vocal 11/44 Hit 7107

THE DAY AFTER FOREVER
Burke-Van Heusen, pub. 1944, reached #19 in September 1944
Joe Burke w, Jimmy Van Heusen m
Featured in GOING MY WAY, film (rel. 02/44)
Bing Crosby, sung in film, 09/44 Dec 18580
Andy Russell 09/44 Cap 156

DO NOTHIN' TILL YOU HEAR FROM ME (47)
Robbins, pub. 1943, reached #15 in March 1944
Bob Russell w, Duke Ellington m
Duke Ellington Orch[1] Φ 01/44 Vic 20-1547
Woody Herman/<vocal Φ 02/44 Dec 18578
Stan Kenton/Red Dorris Φ 02/44 Cap 145

DON'T SWEETHEART ME (28)
Advanced, pub. 1944, reached #7 in May 1944
Charles Tobias w, Cliff Friend m
Lawrence Welk/Wayne Marsh Φ 03/44 Dec 4434
Blue Barron/Tommy Ryan 05/44 Hit 7080
Ozie Waters/Colorado Hillbillies 04/44 Coast 2003

A FELLOW ON A FURLOUGH
Block, pub. 1943, reached #13 in September 1944
Bobby Worth w & m
Featured in MEET MISS BOBBY SOX, film (rel. 12/44)
Phil Hanna/Leonard Joy 08/44 Dec 4445
Bob Crosby Orch, performed in film
Louis Prima/Lily Ann Carol 09/44 Hit 7096

G. I. JIVE (20)
Capitol Mus, pub. 1943, reached #8 in July 1944
Johnny Mercer w & m
Louis Jordan ΦΦ 04/44 Dec 8659
Johnny Mercer 04/44 Cap 141

GOING MY WAY
Burke & Van H, pub. 1944, reached #15 in August 1944
Johnny Burke w, Jimmy Van Heusen m
Featured in GOING MY WAY, film (rel. 02/44)
Bing Crosby, sung in film, 08/44 Dec 18597
Vaughn Monroe/<vocal 08/44 V-Disc 244-B

GOODNIGHT, WHEREVER YOU ARE (23)
Shapiro, B, pub. 1944, reached #6 in July 1944
Dick Robertson, Al Hoffman, Frank Weldon w & m
Russ Morgan/<vocal Φ 05/44 Dec 18598
Mary Martin 06/44 Dec 23340
Blue Barron's Orch/Tommy Ryan 05/44 Hit 7081

HIS ROCKING HORSE RAN AWAY (50)
Famous, pub. 1944, reached #14 in September 1944
Johnny Burke w, Jimmy Van Heusen m
Featured in AND THE ANGELS SING, film (rel. 04/44)
Betty Hutton Φ sung in film, 07/44 Cap 155

HOLIDAY FOR STRINGS (32)
Bregman, V & C, pub. 1944, reached #10 in March 1944
Sammy Gallop w, David Rose m
David Rose Orch ΦΦΦ 01/44 Vic 27853
Jimmy Dorsey Orch 04/44 Dec 18593
Waring's Pennsylvanians 04/44 Dec 23311

AN HOUR NEVER PASSES
Shapiro, B, pub. 1944, reached #14 in October 1944
Jimmy Kennedy w & m
Jimmy Dorsey/Gladys Tell 09/44 Dec 18616
Clyde Lucas/Jean LaSalle 09/44 Hit 7099

HOW BLUE THE NIGHT
Robbins, pub. 1944, reached #18 in July 1944
Harold Adamson w, Jimmy McHugh m
Featured in FOUR JILLS AND A JEEP, film (rel. 03/44)
Dick Haymes, sung in film, 06/44 Dec 18604
Bob Chester/Betty Bradley 07/44 Hit 7088

HOW MANY HEARTS HAVE YOU BROKEN (29)
Advanced, pub. 1943, reached #4 in October 1944
Marty Symes w, Al Kaufman m
The Three Suns/Artie Dunn Φ 08/44 Hit 7092
Stan Kenton/Gene Howard 10/44 Cap 166
Tiny Hill/<vocal 10/44 Dec 4447

I COULDN'T SLEEP A WINK LAST NIGHT (25)
T B Harms, pub. 1943, reached #3 in April 1944
Harold Adamson w, Jimmy McHugh m
Featured in HIGHER AND HIGHER, film (rel. 12/43)
Frank Sinatra Φ sung in film, 02/44 Col 36687
Woody Herman/Frances Wayne 03/44 Dec 18577
Dinah Shore 04/44 Vic 20-1562

I LOVE YOU (12)
Chappell, pub. 1943, reached #1 in May 1944
Cole Porter w & m
Featured in MEXICAN HAYRIDE, show (opened 12/43)
Bing Crosby ΦΦ 04/44 Dec 18595
Jo Stafford Φ 05/44 Cap 153
Enric Madriguera/Bob Lido Φ 04/44 Hit 7077
Wilbur Evans, sung in show
Perry Como 05/44 Vic 20-1569

I WISH THAT I COULD HIDE INSIDE THIS LETTER
Shapiro, B, pub. 1943, reached #17 in April 1944
Charles Tobias w, Nat Simon m
Lawrence Welk/Jayne Walton 02/44 Dec 4428
radio singers

I'LL BE HOME FOR CHRISTMAS
E H Morris, pub. 1943, reached #17 in December 1944
(Also reached #7 in December 1943)
Walter Kent, Kim Gannon, Buck Ram w & m
Bing Crosby 12/44 Dec 18570

I'LL BE SEEING YOU (2)
Williamson, pub. 1938, reached #1 in June 1944
Irving Kahal w, Sammy Fain m
Featured as theme in I'LL BE SEEING YOU, film (rel. 12/44)
Bing Crosby ΦΦ 04/44 Dec 18595
Tommy Dorsey/Frank Sinatra Φ 05/44 Vic 20-1574
Hildegarde/Harry Sosnik Orch 05/44 Dec 23291
Louis Prima/<vocal 07/44 Hit 7082
Billie Holiday, stage, 11/44 Commodore 553

I'LL GET BY (AS LONG AS I HAVE YOU) (4)
Berlin ΦΦΦ, pub. 1928, reached #2 in July 1944
(Also reached #1 in March 1929)
Roy Turk w, Fred Ahlert m
Featured in A GUY NAMED JOE, film (rel. 12/43)
Harry James/Dick Haymes ΦΦ 04/44 Col 36698[2]
Irene Dunn, sung in film
The Ink Spots Φ 05/44 Dec 18579
King Sisters 04/44 Blu 30-0821

I'LL WALK ALONE (1)
E H Morris, pub. 1944, reached #1 in September 1944
(Also reached #6 in May 1952)
Sammy Cahn w, Jule Styne m
Featured in FOLLOW THE BOYS, film (rel. 03/44)
Dinah Shore ΦΦ sung in film, 07/44 Vic 20-1586
Martha Tilton Φ 07/44 Cap 157
Mary Martin Φ 08/44 Dec 23340
Louis Prima/Lily Ann Carol 07/44 Hit 7083

I'M MAKING BELIEVE (18)
Bregman, V & C, pub. 1944, reached #3 in December 1944
Mack Gordon w, James V Monaco m
Featured in SWEET AND LOWDOWN, film (rel. 08/44)
Ella Fitzgerald & The Ink Spots ΦΦ 11/44 Dec 23356
Hal McIntyre/Ruth Gaylor 01/45 Blu 30-0831
The Three Suns/Artie Dunn 01/45 Hit 7105

INTO EACH LIFE SOME RAIN MUST FALL (33)
Sun Mus Co, pub. 1944, reached #7 in January 1945
Allan Roberts & Doris Fisher w & m
Ella Fitzgerald & The Ink Spots Φ 11/44 Dec 23356
Charlie Barnet/Kay Starr 01/45 Dec 18638

IS YOU IS OR IS YOU AIN'T (MA' BABY) (22)
Leeds, pub. 1943, reached #3 in September 1944
Louis Jordan & Billy Austin w & m
Featured in FOLLOW THE BOYS, film (rel. 03/44)
Louis Jordan ΦΦ sung in film, 07/44 Dec 8659
Bing Crosby & The Andrews Sisters Φ 09/44 Dec 23350
Cootie Williams/Eddie Vinson 10/44 Hit 7108

IT COULD HAPPEN TO YOU (36)
Famous, pub. 1944, reached #8 in September 1944
Johnny Burke w, Jimmy Van Heusen m
Featured in AND THE ANGELS SING, film (rel. 04/44)
Dorothy Lamour & Fred MacMurray, sung in film
Jo Stafford Φ 08/44 Cap 158
Bing Crosby 09/44 Dec 18580

IT HAD TO BE YOU (21)
Remick, pub. 1924, reached #5 in September 1944
(Also reached #2 in August 1924)
Gus Kahn w, Isham Jones m
Featured in IS EVERYBODY HAPPY, film (rel. 11/43)
Also featured in SHOW BUSINESS, film (rel. 04/44)
Eddie Cantor, sung in film (SB)
Helen Forrest & Dick Haymes Φ 08/44 Dec 23349
Betty Hutton Φ 07/44 Cap 155
Nan Wynn, sung in film (IEH)
Artie Shaw Orch 09/44 Vic 20-1593

IT'S LOVE, LOVE, LOVE (17)
Santly-Joy, pub. 1943, reached #1 in April 1944
Alex Kramer, Joan Whitney, Mack David w & m
Featured in STARS ON PARADE, film (rel. 06/44)
Guy Lombardo/Skip Nelson ΦΦ 03/44 Dec 18589
King Sisters Φ 04/44 Blu 30-0822
Jan Garber/Liz Tilton 04/44 Hit 7078

LET ME LOVE YOU TONIGHT
Robbins, pub. 1940, reached #15 in December 1944
Mitchell Parish w, Rene Touzet m
Woody Herman/Billie Rogers 12/44 Dec 18619
Xavier Cugat/Carmen Castillo 11/44 Col 36718
Frances Langford 12/44 ARA 109

LITTLE DID I KNOW
Lincoln M C, pub. 1943, reached #19 in January 1944
Charles Kenny & Nick Kenny w, Abner Silver m
Phil Brito/Paul Lavalle Orch 01/44 Musicraft 15015
radio singers

LONG AGO AND FAR AWAY (9)
Crawford, pub. 1944, reached #1 in June 1944
Ira Gershwin w, Jerome Kern m
Featured in COVER GIRL, film (rel. 03/44)
Helen Forrest & Dick Haymes Φ 04/44 Dec 23317
Bing Crosby Φ 07/44 Dec 18608
Jo Stafford Φ 05/44 Cap 153
Rita Hayworth[3], film
Perry Como Φ 05/44 Vic 20-1569

A LOVELY WAY TO SPEND AN EVENING (39)
Crawford, pub. 1943, reached #9 in March 1944
Harold Adamson w, Jimmy McHugh m
Featured in HIGHER AND HIGHER, film (rel. 12/43)
Frank Sinatra Φ sung in film, 03/44 Col 36687
The Ink Spots 03/44 Dec 18583

MAIRZY DOATS (10)
Miller Mus, pub. 1943, reached #1 in April 1944
Milton Drake, Al Hoffman, Jerry Livingston w & m
The Merry Macs ΦΦ 02/44 Dec 18588
Al Trace/Red Maddox Φ 02/44 Hit 8079
Lawrence Welk/Bobby Beers 04/44 Dec 4434
The Pied Pipers 04/44 Cap 148
King Sisters 04/44 Blu 30-0822

MILKMAN, KEEP THOSE BOTTLES QUIET (34)
L Feist, pub. 1944, reached #9 in July 1944
Don Raye w, Gene DePaul m
Featured in BROADWAY RHYTHM, film (rel. 01/44)
Ella Mae Morse Φ 05/44 Cap 151
Woody Herman/<vocal 06/44 Dec 18603
Nancy Walker, sung in film
King Sisters 06/44 Blu 30-0824

MY HEART TELLS ME (5)
Bregman, V & C, pub. 1943, reached #1 in January 1944
Mack Gordon w, Harry Warren m
Featured in SWEET ROSIE O'GRADY, film (rel. 09/43)
Glen Gray/Eugenie Baird ΦΦ 12/43 Dec 18567
Betty Grable, sung in film
Jan Garber/Bob Davis 02/44 Hit 7070
Phil Brito/Paul Lavalle Orch 02/44 Musicraft 15015

MY IDEAL (31)
Paramount; orig. pub. 1930, reached #5 in January 1944
(Also reached #16 in January 1931)
Leo Robin w, Richard Whiting & Newell Chase m
Jimmy Dorsey/Bob Eberly Ф 01/44 Dec 18574
Billy Butterfield/Margaret Whiting 11/43 Cap 134
Maxine Sullivan 11/43 Dec 18555

MY SHINING HOUR (37)
E H Morris, pub. 1943, reached #8 in January 1944
Johnny Mercer w, Harold Arlen m
Featured in THE SKY'S THE LIMIT, film (rel. 07/43)
Glen Gray/Eugenie Baird Ф 12/43 Dec 18567
Fred Astaire, sung in film
Frank Sinatra, stage, 02/44 V-Disc 166-B

NO LOVE, NO NOTHIN' (26)
Triangle M C, pub. 1943, reached #4 in March 1944
Leo Robin w, Harry Warren m
Featured in THE GANG'S ALL HERE, film (rel. 11/43)
Alice Faye, sung in film
Ella Mae Morse Ф 01/44 Cap 143
Johnny Long/Patti Dugan Ф 02/44 Dec 4427
Jan Garber/Liz Tilton 04/44 Hit 7070

THE PATTY-CAKE MAN
Capitol Mus, pub. 1944, reached #18 in October 1944
Roy Jordan w & m
Ella Mae Morse 09/44 Cap 163

POINCIANA (24)
E B Marks, pub. 1936, reached #4 in April 1944
Manuel Lliso & Buddy Bernier w, Nat Simon m
Bing Crosby Ф 03/44 Dec 18586
David Rose Orch 02/44 Vic 20-1554
Benny Carter Orch 02/44 Cap 144

PRETTY KITTY BLUE EYES (40)
Santly-Joy, pub. 1944, reached #10 in September 1944
Mann Curtis w, Vic Mizzy m
The Merry Macs Ф 08/44 Dec 18610
Dennis Day, stage and radio
Art Kassel/Gloria Hart 09/44 Hit 7091

SAN FERNANDO VALLEY (16)
E H Morris, pub. 1943, reached #2 in May 1944
Gordon Jenkins w & m
Featured in SAN FERNANDO VALLEY, film (rel. 08/44)
Bing Crosby ФФ 03/44 Dec 18586
Roy Rogers, sung in film (Later: 1948 Vic 20-3075)
Johnny Mercer 04/44 Cap 150
Johnny Long/Gene Williams 05/44 Dec 4437
Four King Sisters 05/44 Blu 30-0824

SHOO-SHOO BABY (8)
Leeds, pub. 1943, reached #1 in February 1944
Phil Moore w & m
Featured in THREE CHEERS FOR THE BOYS, film (1943)
Also featured in FOLLOW THE BOYS, film (rel. 03/44)
Also featured in SOUTH OF DIXIE, film (rel. 06/44)
Andrews Sisters ФФ sung in films (3Ch & FTB) and 12/43 Dec 18572
Ella Mae Morse Ф sung in film (SOD), 12/43 Cap 143
Jan Garber/Liz Tilton 02/44 Hit 7069
Jerry Wald/Ginny Powell 02/44 Dec 4431

SMOKE ON THE WATER
Adams, V & A, pub. 1943, reached #17 in October 1944
Earl Nunn & Zeke Clements w & m
Red Foley Ф 09/44 Dec 6102
Bob Wills/Tommy Duncan 04/45 Okeh 6736
Boyd Heath 02/45 Blu 31-0522

SOMEDAY I'LL MEET YOU AGAIN (48)
Witmark, pub. 1944, reached #12 in July 1944
Ned Washington w, Max Steiner m
Featured in PASSAGE TO MARSEILLES, film (rel. 02/44)
The Ink Spots 05/44 Dec 18579
Enric Madriguera/Bob Lido 05/44 Hit 7077
Johnny Long/Gene Williams 05/44 Dec 4437

SPEAK LOW (45)
Chappell, pub. 1943, reached #11 in February 1944
Ogden Nash w, Kurt Weill m
Featured in ONE TOUCH OF VENUS, show (opened 10/43)
Guy Lombardo/Billy Leach Ф 01/44 Dec 18573
Mary Martin & Kenny Baker, sung in show, 02/44 Dec 23296
Frank Sinatra, radio, 02/44 V-Disc 154-A

SPRING WILL BE A LITTLE LATE THIS YEAR
Saunders, pub. 1944, reached #20 in May 1944
Frank Loesser w & m
Featured in CHRISTMAS HOLIDAY, film (rel. 06/44)
Deanna Durbin, sung in film, 4/45 Dec 23397
Johnnie Johnston/Paul Weston Orch 06/44 Cap 152
Morton Downey 06/44 Dec 18607

STAR EYES (35)
L Feist, pub. 1943, reached #8 in February 1944
Don Raye w, Gene DePaul m
Featured in I DOOD IT, film (rel. 07/43)
Jimmy Dorsey/Bob Eberly-Kitty Kallen ФФ perf. in film, 12/43 Dec 18571
radio singers

STRAIGHTEN UP AND FLY RIGHT (49)
Am Acad Mus, pub. 1944, reached #15 in July 1944
Irving Mills w, Nat Cole m
Featured in HERE COMES ELMER, film (rel. 10/43)
King Cole Trio, sung in film, 05/44 Cap 154
Andrews Sisters 06/44 Dec 18606

STRANGE MUSIC
Chappell, pub. 1944, reached #19 in November 1944
Robert Wright & George Forrest w & m, Edvard Grieg m
Featured in SONG OF NORWAY, show (opened 08/44)
Lawrence Brooks & Helena Bliss, sung in show
Freddy Martin/Artie Wayne 01/45 Vic 20-1615
James Melton 04/45 Vic 11-8746

SUDDENLY IT'S SPRING
Famous, pub. 1943, reached #14 in June 1944
Johnny Burke w, Jimmy Van Heusen m
Featured in LADY IN THE DARK, film (rel. 02/44)
Ginger Rogers, sung in film
Hildegarde 05/44 Dec 23297
Glen Gray/Eugenie Baird 05/44 Dec 18596

SWEET AND LOVELY
L Feist; orig. pub. 1931, reached #15 in October 1944
(Also reached #1 in October 1931)
Gus Arnheim, Harry Tobias, Jules Lemare w & m
Featured in TWO GIRLS AND A SAILOR, film (rel. 04/44)
June Allyson & Gloria DeHaven, sung in film
Bing Crosby 09/44 Dec 18429
Tommy Dorsey/Bob Allen, stage, 11/44 V-Disc 320-A

SWEET LORRAINE
Mills, pub. 1928, reached #18 in July 1944
(Also reached #15 in August 1928)
Mitchell Parish w, Cliff Burwell m
King Cole Trio, stage, 07/44 Dec 8520 (RI),
07/44 Cap 20009 (in album)

SWINGING ON A STAR (3)
Burke & Van H, pub. 1944, reached #1 in August 1944
Johnny Burke w, Jimmy Van Heusen m
Featured in GOING MY WAY, film (rel. 02/44)
Bing Crosby ΦΦΦ sung in film, 05/44 Dec 18597
Gray Rains/w.vocal duo 07/44 Hit 7086
Freddie Slack/Brian Sisters 09/44 Cap 160

TAKE IT EASY
Santly-Joy, pub. 1943, reached #20 in March 1944
Albert DeBru, Irving Taylor, Vic Mizzy w & m
Featured in TWO GIRLS AND A SAILOR, film (rel. 04/44)
Xavier Cugat/w.vocal group, performed in film
Guy Lombardo/w.vocal trio 02/44 Dec 18573
Vincent Lopez/Karole Singer 04/44 National 7003

TESS'S TORCH SONG
Harms, pub. 1943, reached #19 in June 1944
Ted Koehler w, Harold Arlen m
Featured in UP IN ARMS, film (rel. 02/44)
Dinah Shore, sung in film
Ella Mae Morse 05/44 Cap 151
Cootie Williams/Pearl Bailey 05/44 Hit 7075

THERE'LL BE A HOT TIME IN THE TOWN OF BERLIN (38)
Barton M C, pub. 1943, reached #10 in November 1944
Jack DeVries w, Joe Bushkin m
Bing Crosby & The Andrews Sisters Φ 09/44 Dec 23350
Frank Sinatra, stage, 04/44 V-Disc 103-B

TILL THEN
Sun Mus Co, pub. 1944, reached #17 in September 1944
(Also reached #11 in March 1954)
Eddie Seiler, Sol Marcus, Guy Wood w & m
Mills Brothers Φ 06/44 Dec 18599
radio singers

TIME ALONE WILL TELL
Bregman, V & C, pub. 1944, reached #17 in June 1944
Mack Gordon w, James V Monaco m
Featured in PIN-UP GIRL, film (rel. 04/44)
Charlie Spivak Orch, performed in film
Ella Fitzgerald, radio, 07/44 Dec 18605
Vaughn Monroe/<vocal, radio, 08/44 V-Disc 244-A

TIME WAITS FOR NO ONE (13)
Remick, pub. 1944, reached #3 in September 1944
Charles Tobias w, Cliff Friend m
Featured in SHINE ON HARVEST MOON, film (rel. 03/44)
Helen Forrest ΦΦ 07/44 Dec 18600
Johnny Long/Patti Dugan Φ 08/44 Dec 4439
Woody Herman/<vocal, stage, 02/45 V-Disc 357-A

TOGETHER (19)
Crawford; orig. pub. 1928, reached #2 in November 1944
(Also reached #1 in April 1928)
(Also reached #6 in August 1961)
Bud DeSylva & Lew Brown w, Ray Henderson m
Featured in SINCE YOU WENT AWAY, film (rel. 07/44)
Halen Forrest & Dick Haymes Φ 10/44 Dec 23349
Guy Lombardo/Tony Craig Φ 10/44 Φ Dec 18617
Dinah Shore 11/44 Vic 20-1594

TOO-RA LOO-RA LOO-RAL (43)
Witmark, pub. 1914, reached #13 in December 1944
(Also reached #10 in March 1914)
James Royce Shannon w & m
Featured in GOING MY WAY, film (rel. 02/44)
Bing Crosby Φ sung in film, 10/44 Dec 18621
Dennis Day, stage and radio (Later: 03/46 Vic 20-1813)
Charlie Spivak Orch 12/44 Vic 20-1603

THE TROLLEY SONG (14)
L Feist, pub. 1944, reached #1 in December 1944
Ralph Blane & Hugh Martin w & m
Featured in MEET ME IN ST. LOUIS, film (rel. 11/44)
Judy Garland Φ sung in film, 11/44 Dec 23361
The Pied Pipers ΦΦ 10/44 Cap 168
Vaughn Monroe/w.vocal duo Φ 12/44 Vic 20-1605
King Sisters 11/44 Blu 30-0829
Guy Lombardo/Stuart Foster 01/45 Dec 18634

THE VERY THOUGHT OF YOU
Witmark, pub. 1934, reached #18 in December 1944
(Also reached #9 in October 1934)
Ray Noble w & m
Featured as theme in THE VERY THOUGHT OF YOU, film (rel. 12/44)
Vaughn Monroe/<vocal 12/44 Vic 20-1605
Kitty Carlisle 12/44 Dec 23359

WHAT A DIFF'RENCE A DAY MADE
E B Marks, pub. 1934, reached #18 in November 1944
(Also reached #9 in August 1959)
(Also reached #20 in November 1975)
Stanley Adams w, Maria Grever m
Andy Russell 10/44 Cap 167
Charlie Barnet/Kay Starr 10/44 Dec 18620
Art Kassel/Jimmie Featherstone 10/44 Hit 7090

WHEN THEY ASK ABOUT YOU (27)
Berlin, pub. 1943, reached #4 in March 1944
Sam Stept w & m
Jimmy Dorsey/Kitty Kallen Φ 02/44 Dec 18582
Sonny Dunham/Don Darcy 03/44 Hit 7073
Phil Hanna/Harry Sosnik 03/44 Dec 4435

WHISPERING
Miller Mus; orig. pub. 1920, reached #18 in November 1944
(Also reached #1 in October 1920)
(Also reached #11 in Sept. 1951 and #11 in Jan. 1964)
Malvin Schonberger w, John Schonberger m
Featured in GREENWICH VILLAGE, film (rel. 08/44)
Tommy Dorsey/Frank Sinatra-Pied Pipers 09/44 Vic 20-1579
Vivian Blaine, sung in film
Horace Heidt/Fred Lowery[4] 09/44 Col 36727

WHITE CHRISTMAS (41)
Berlin, pub. 1942, reached #7 in December 1944
(Also reached #1 in November 1942)
(Also reached Top 20 every December 1943-1955, 1960 & 1961)
Irving Berlin w & m
Bing Crosby Φ 12/44 Dec 18429
Frank Sinatra Φ 12/44 Col 36756

YOU ALWAYS HURT THE ONE YOU LOVE (6)
Sun Mus Co, pub. 1944, reached #7 in September 1944
(Also reached #12 in June 1961)
Allan Roberts & Doris Fisher w & m
Mills Brothers ΦΦΦ 06/44 Dec 18599
The Three Suns/Artie Dunn 10/44 Hit 7105
Sammy Kaye/Tony Alamo 01/45 Vic 20-1606
Charlie Barnet/Kay Starr 01/45 Dec 18638

[1]Originally recorded by Duke Ellington in 1940 as CONCERTO FOR COOTIE.
[2]Reissue of recording originally on Col 36285.
[3]Nan Wynn's voice was dubbed for Rita Hayworth.
[4]Whistling by Fred Lowery.

1945

AC-CENT-TCHU-ATE THE POSITIVE (14)
E H Morris, pub. 1944, reached #1 in February 1945
Johnny Mercer w, Harold Arlen m
Featured in HERE COME THE WAVES, film (rel. 12/44)
Johnny Mercer ΦΦ 01/45 Cap 180
Bing Crosby & The Andrews Sisters ΦΦ 02/45 Dec 23379
Bing Crosby & Sonny Tufts, sung in film
Artie Shaw/Imogene Lynn Φ 01/45 Vic 20-1612
Kay Kyser/Dolly Mitchell 02/45 Col 36771

ALL OF MY LIFE (35)
Berlin, pub. 1945, reached #9 in May 1945
Irving Berlin w & m
Sammy Kaye/Billy Williams 04/45 Vic 20-1642
The Three Suns/Artie Dunn 04/45 Hit 7092
Bing Crosby 05/45 Dec 18658
Kate Smith, stage and radio

ALONG THE NAVAJO TRAIL (25)
Leeds, pub. 1942. reached #4 in October 1945
Larry Markes, Dick Charles, Eddie DeLange w & m
Featured in DON'T FENCE ME IN, film (rel. 10/45)
Bing Crosby & The Andrews Sisters ΦΦ 09/45 Dec 23437
Roy Rogers, sung in film, 12/45 Vic 20-1730
Dinah Shore Φ 09/45 Vic 20-1666
Gene Krupa/Buddy Stewart Φ 10/45 Col 36846

AND THERE YOU ARE
L Feist, pub. 1945, reached #14 in October 1945
Ted Koehler w, Sammy Fain m
Featured in WEEKEND AT THE WALDORF, film (rel. 07/45)
Xavier Cugat Orch, performed in film
Andy Russell 09/45 Cap 198
Kate Smith 10/45 Col 36821

BAIA
Peer, pub. 1944, reached #16 in June 1945
Ray Gilbert w, Ary Barroso m
Featured in THE THREE CABALLEROS, film (rel. 12/44)
Bing Crosby/Xavier Cugat Orch Φ 06/45 Dec 23413
Nestor Amoral, sung in film
Tommy Tucker/Don Brown 06/45 Col 36799

BELL-BOTTOM TROUSERS (9)
Santly-Joy, pub. 1944, reached #2 in June 1945
Moe Jaffee w & m
Tony Pastor/w.vocal duo ΦΦ 05/45 Vic 20-1661
Guy Lombardo/Jimmy Brown ΦΦ 06/45 Dec 18683
Kay Kyser/w.vocal duo Φ 06/45 Col 36801
Louis Prima/Lily Ann Carol Φ 05/45 Majestic 7134
Jerry Colonna 07/45 Cap 204

THE BLOND SAILOR
Mills, pub. 1945, reached #18 in October 1945
Mitchell Parish, Benny Bell & Joseph Lieb w, Jacob Pfeil m
Andrews Sisters Φ 10/45 Dec 18700

BOOGIE WOOGIE
Melrose; orig. pub. 1929, reached #16 in September 1945
(Also reached #18 in November 1938)
(Also reached #12 in January 1944)
Pinetop Smith m
Big band classic and steady seller, 1938 through the 1940's
Tommy Dorsey Orch Φ 09/45 Vic 20-1715

BUT I DID
Remick, pub. 1945, reached #20 in December 1945
Al Jacobs w, Joseph Meyer m
Dinah Shore 11/45 Vic 20-1732
Connee Boswell 12/45 Dec 18727

CALDONIA (36)
E H Morris, pub. 1945, reached #7 in June 1945
Fleecie Moore w & m
Woody Herman/<vocal ΦΦ 05/45 Col 36789
Louis Jordan[4] Φ 06/45 Dec 8670
Erskine Hawkins/Ace Harris 05/45 Vic 20-1659
Louis Prima/<vocal 06/45 Majestic 7134

CANDY (11)
L Feist, pub. 1944, reached #2 in April 1945
Mack David, Joan Whitney, Alex Kramer w & m
Johnny Mercer-Jo Stafford-Pied Pipers ΦΦ 02/45 Cap 183
Dinah Shore Φ 03/45 Vic 20-1632
Johnny Long/Dick Robertson 05/45 Dec 18661
King Sisters 04/45 Vic 20-1633
Jerry Wald/Kay Allen 05/45 Majestic 7129

CHICKERY CHICK (23)
Santly-Joy, pub. 1945, reached #4 in December 1945
Sylvia Dee w, Sidney Lippman m
Sammy Kaye/w.vocal duo ΦΦ 10/45 Vic 20-1726
Gene Krupa/Anita O'Day Φ 12/45 Col 36877
Evelyn Knight 12/45 Dec 18725
George Olsen/w.vocal duo 12/45 Majestic 7155

CHLOE
Villa Moret, pub. 1927, reached #12 in May 1945 (in comic version)
(Also reached #3 in April 1928 in its original version)
Gus Kahn w, Neil Moret m
Featured in BRING ON THE GIRLS, film (rel. 02/45)
Spike Jones & His City Slickers/Red Ingle Φ sung in film, 04/45 Vic 20-1654
Duke Ellington Orch 02/45 Vic 20-1547

CHOPIN'S POLONAISE (37)
Boston Mus Co; orig. pub. 1843, reached #8 in August 1945
Frederic Chopin m
Featured in A SONG TO REMEMBER, film (rel. 01/45)
Steady seller, 1945-50
Jose Iturbi Φ played in film, 09/45 Vic 11-8848
Carmen Cavallaro Orch ΦΦ 07/45 Dec 18677

COCKTAILS FOR TWO (40)
Famous, pub. 1934, reached #9 in February 1945 (in comic version)
(Also reached #3 in July 1934 in its original version)
Arthur Johnston & Sam Coslow w & m
Spike Jones & His City Slickers/Carl Grayson Φ 01/45 Vic 20-1628[1]

A COTTAGE FOR SALE
Crawford; orig. pub. 1930, reached #15 in October 1945
(Also reached #3 in May 1930)
Willard Robison w, Larry Conley m
Billy Eckstine Φ 10/45 National 9014
Phil Brito 12/45 Musicraft 15047

DON'T FENCE ME IN (10)
Harms, pub. 1944, reached #1 in January 1945
Cole Porter w & m
Featured in HOLLYWOOD CANTEEN, film (rel. 12/44)
Bing Crosby & The Andrews Sisters ΦΦΦ 11/44 Dec 23364
Roy Rogers, sung in film
Sammy Kaye/Billy Williams Φ 01/45 Vic 20-1610
Kate Smith 01/45 Col 36759
Horace Heidt/Gene Walsh 01/45 Col 36761

DON'T FORGET TONIGHT, TOMORROW
Barton M C, pub. 1945, reached #19 in November 1945
Jay Milton & Ukie Sherin w & m
Frank Sinatra/The Charioteers 11/45 Col 36854
Buzz Adlam/Don Leslie 11/45 Black & White 764-A

DREAM (2)
Capitol Songs, pub. 1944, reached #3 in June 1945
Johnny Mercer w & m
Featured in HER HIGHNESS AND THE BELLBOY, film (rel. 07/45)
The Pied Pipers ΦΦ 03/45 Cap 185
Frank Sinatra Φ 06/45 Col 36797
Freddy Martin/Artie Wayne Φ 04/45 Vic 20-1645
Jimmy Dorsey/Teddy Walters 06/45 Dec 18670

EVELINA
Crawford, pub. 1944, reached #17 in February 1945
E Y Harbourg w, Harold Arlen m
Featured in BLOOMER GIRL, show (opened 10/44)
David Brooks & Celeste Holm, sung in show and 01/45 Dec 23369 (in album)
Bing Crosby Φ 01/45 Dec 18635
Frankie Carle/Paul Allen 02/45 Col 36764

A FRIEND OF YOURS
Burke & Van H, pub. 1944, reached #12 in August 1945
Johnny Burke w, Jimmy Van Heusen m
Featured in THE GREAT JOHN L, film (rel. 06/45)
Tommy Dorsey/Stuart Foster 07/45 Vic 20-1657
Lee Sullivan, sung in film
Jo Stafford 08/45 Cap 199

FUZZY WUZZY
Drake, H & L, pub. 1944, reached #20 in August 1945
Milton Drake, Al Hoffman, Jerry Livingston w & m
Al Trace/Nate Hexler, stage, 07/45 National 7008
The Jesters/Milt Herth Trio 07/45 Dec 18688

GOOD, GOOD, GOOD
Berlin, pub. 1944, reached #14 in June 1945
Allan Roberts & Doris Fisher w & m
Xavier Cugat/Del Campo Φ 06/45 Col 36793
Sammy Kaye/w.vocal duo 08/45 Vic 20-1684
Bing Crosby & The Andrews Sisters 09/45 Dec 23437

GOTTA BE THIS OR THAT (15)
Harms, pub. 1945, reached #4 in August 1945
Sunny Skylar w & m
Benny Goodman/<vocal ΦΦ 07/45 Col 36813
Sammy Kaye/Nancy Norman Φ 08/45 Vic 20-1684
Glen Gray/Fats Daniels Φ 09/45 Dec 18691

HONG KONG BLUES
L Spier, pub. 1945, reached #15 in August 1945
Hoagy Carmichael w & m
Hoagy Carmichael Φ 08/45 ARA 123
Tommy Dorsey/Skeets Herfurt Φ 09/45 Vic 20-1722

HOW DEEP IS THE OCEAN? (46)
Berlin, pub. 1932, reached #9 in November 1945
(Also reached #3 in November 1932)
Irving Berlin w & m
Benny Goodman/Peggy Lee 10/45 Col 36754
Paul Weston/Margaret Whiting 11/45 Cap 214

I CAN'T BEGIN TO TELL YOU (6)
Bregman, V & C, pub. 1945, reached #2 in December 1945
Mack Gordon w, James V Monaco m
Featured in THE DOLLY SISTERS, film (rel. 09/45)
Bing Crosby/Carmen Cavallaro ΦΦ 11/45 Dec 23457
Harry James/Betty Grable[2] Φ performed in film and 12/45 Col 36867
Andy Russell Φ 12/45 Cap 221
Sammy Kaye/Nancy Norman Φ 12/45 Vic 20-1720

I DON'T CARE WHO KNOWS IT (50)
Robbins, pub. 1944, reached #16 in April 1945
(Reached second peak at #9 in September 1945)
Harold Adamson w, Jimmy McHugh m
Featured in NOB HILL, film (rel. 05/45)
Harry James/Kitty Kallen Φ 04/45 Col 36778
Vivian Blaine, sung in film
Glen Gray/Skip Nelson 06/45 Dec 18665

I DON'T WANT TO LOVE YOU (LIKE I DO)
Chelsea, pub. 1944, reached #11 in January 1945
Henry Pritchard w & m
Phil Brito/Paul LaValle Orch 11/44 Musicraft 15018
Dick Haymes/Victor Young Orch 02/45 Dec 18645
Sammy Kaye/Billy Williams 03/45 Vic 20-1635

I DREAM OF YOU (18)
Embassy, pub. 1944, reached #3 in January 1945
Marjorie Goetschius & Edna Osser w & m
Tommy Dorsey/Freddy Stewart Φ 01/45 Vic 20-1608
Andy Russell Φ 12/44 Cap 175
Frank Sinatra Φ 01/45 Col 36762
Perry Como 01/45 Vic 20-1629

I SHOULD CARE (38)
Dorsey Bros Mus, pub. 1945, reached #10 in June 1945
(Also reached #19 in October 1952)
Sammy Cahn, Axel Stordahl, Paul Weston w & m
Featured in THRILL OF A ROMANCE, film (rel. 05/45)
Frank Sinatra/Axel Stordahl Orch Φ 06/45 Col 36791
Martha Tilton/Eddie Miller Orch 04/45 Cap 184
Tommy Dorsey/Bonnie Lou Williams 05/45 Vic 20-1625
Robert Allen, sung in film
Jimmy Dorsey/Teddy Walters 05/45 Dec 18656

I WANNA GET MARRIED
Robbins, pub. 1944, reached #16 in March 1945
Dan Shapiro, Milton Pascal, Phil Charig w & m
Featured in FOLLOW THE GIRLS, show (opened 04/44)
Gertrude Niesen, sung in show, 03/45 Dec 23382
Louis Prima/Lily Ann Carol 03/45 Hit 7125

I WISH
Northern, pub. 1945, reached #15 in June 1945
Allan Roberts & Doris Fisher w & m
Mills Brothers 05/45 Dec 18663
radio singers

I WISH I KNEW (26)
Triangle M C, pub. 1945, reached #6 in September 1945
Mack Gordon w, Harry Warren m
Featured in BILLY ROSE'S DIAMOND HORSESHOE, film (rel. 04/45)
Dick Haymes Φ sung in film, 07/45 Dec 18662
Harry James/Kitty Kallen 08/45 Col 36794
Jan Garber/Bob Davis 08/45 ARA 122

I'LL BUY THAT DREAM (21)
Burke & Van H, pub. 1944, reached #2 in October 1945
Herb Magidson w, Allie Wrubel m
Featured in SING YOUR WAY HOME, film (rel. 11/45)
Helen Forrest & Dick Haymes ΦΦ 09/45 Dec 23434
Harry James/Kitty Kallen ΦΦ 08/45 Col 36833
Hal McIntyre/Frankie Lester 06/45 Vic 20-1679
Anne Jeffreys, sung in film

I'M BEGINNING TO SEE THE LIGHT (13)
Grande, pub. 1944, reached #2 in April 1945
Harry James, Duke Ellington, Johnny Hodges, Don George w & m
Harry James/Kitty Kallen ΦΦ 01/45 Col 36758
Duke Ellington/Joya Sherrill Φ 02/45 Vic 20-1618
Ella Fitzgerald & The Ink Spots Φ 04/45 Dec 23399

I'M CONFESSIN' (THAT I LOVE YOU) (44)
Bourne; orig. pub. 1930, reached #12 in February 1945
(Also reached #7 in October 1930)
(Also reached #14 in May 1952)
Al J Neiberg w, Doc Daugherty & Ellis Reynolds m
Perry Como Φ 02/45 Vic 20-1629
Ella Fitzgerald/Song Spinners 02/45 Dec 18633

I'M GONNA LOVE THAT GAL (GUY) (28)
Bourne, pub. 1945, reached #4 in October 1945
Frances Ash w & m
Perry Como Φ 08/45 Vic 20-1676
Benny Goodman/Dottie Reid Φ 10/45 Col 36843
Marion Hutton/Randy Brooks Orch 10/45 Dec 18703

I'M GONNA SEE MY BABY
Santly-Joy, pub. 1944, reached #19 in March 1945
Phil Moore w & m
Featured in EADIE WAS A LADY, film (rel. 02/45)
Johnny Mercer 03/45 Cap 183
Ann Miller, sung in film
Phil Moore Four/Phil Moore 02/45 Vic 20-1613

I'M WASTIN' MY TEARS ON YOU
Peer, pub. 1944, reached #16 in January 1945
Tex Ritter & Frank Harford w & m
Tex Ritter Φ 11/44 Cap 174

IF I LOVED YOU (7)
Williamson, pub. 1945, reached #2 in August 1945
Oscar Hammerstein 2nd w, Richard Rodgers m
Featured in CAROUSEL, show (opened 04/45)
Perry Como ΦΦ 07/45 Vic 20-1676
John Raitt & Jan Clayton, sung in show
Frank Sinatra Φ 09/45 Col 36825
Bing Crosby Φ 08/45 Dec 18686
Harry James/Buddy DiVito 08/45 Col 36806

IT MIGHT AS WELL BE SPRING (16)
Williamson, pub. 1945, reached #3 in December 1945
Oscar Hammerstein w, Richard Rodgers m
Featured in STATE FAIR, film (rel. 08/45)
Dick Haymes Φ 11/45 Dec 18706
Sammy Kaye/Billy Williams Φ 12/45 Vic 20-1738
Paul Weston/Margaret Whiting Φ 11/45 Cap 214
Jeanne Crain[3], film

IT'S BEEN A LONG, LONG TIME (12)
E H Morris, pub. 1945, reached #1 in November 1945
Sammy Cahn w, Jule Styne m
Harry James/Kitty Kallen ΦΦ 10/45 Col 36838
Bing Crosby/Les Paul Trio ΦΦ 10/45 Dec 18708
Charlie Spivak/Irene Daye Φ 10/45 Vic 20-1721
Stan Kenton/June Christy Φ 11/45 Cap 219

IT'S ONLY A PAPER MOON (34)
Harms, pub. 1933, reached #8 in November 1945
(Also reached #11 in November 1933)
Billy Rose & E Y Harbourg w, Harold Arlen m
Featured in TOO YOUNG TO KNOW, film (rel. 11/45)
King Cole Trio, stage, 09/45 Cap 20012 (in album)
Ella Fitzgerald/Delta Rhythm Boys Φ 09/45 Dec 23425
Benny Goodman/Dottie Reid Φ 09/45 Col 36843

JUNE IS BUSTIN' OUT ALL OVER
Williamson, pub. 1945, reached #16 in August 1945
Oscar Hammerstein 2nd w, Richard Rodgers m
Featured in CAROUSEL, show (opened 04/45)
Christine Johnson & Jan Clayton, sung in show
Hildegarde/Guy Lombardo Orch 08/45 Dec 23428

JUST A PRAYER AWAY (27)
Shapiro, B, pub. 1944, reached #5 in April 1945
Charles Tobias w, Dave Kapp m
Bing Crosby Φ 04/45 Dec 23392
Sammy Kaye/Billy Williams 04/45 Vic 20-1642
Kate Smith 04/45 Col 36783

A KISS GOODNIGHT
Miller Mus, pub. 1945, reached #19 in August 1945
Freddie Slack, Floyd Victor, Reba Nell Herman w & m
Woody Herman/<vocal 07/45 Col 36815
Freddy Slack/Liza Morrow 08/45 Cap 203

LAURA (19)
Robbins, pub. 1945, reached #2 in June 1945
Johnny Mercer w, David Raskin m
Featured as theme in LAURA, film (rel. 10/44)
Woody Herman/<vocal ΦΦ 04/45 Col 36785
Johnnie Johnston/Paul Baron Orch Φ 06/45 Cap 196
Freddy Martin Orch Φ 05/45 Vic 20-1655
Jerry Wald/Dick Merrick 04/45 Majestic 7129
Dick Haymes 05/45 Dec 18666

LET'S TAKE THE LONG WAY HOME
E H Morris, pub. 1944, reached #20 in February 1945
Johnny Mercer w, Harold Arlen m
Featured in HERE COME THE WAVES, film (rel. 12/44)
Bing Crosby & Betty Hutton, sung in film
Jo Stafford/Paul Weston Orch 02/45 Cap 181
Cab Calloway/<vocal 03/45 Col 36786

LILY BELLE
Martin Mus, pub. 1945, reached #16 in December 1945
Dave Franklin & Irving Taylor w & m
Freddy Martin/Gene Conklin Φ 10/45 Vic 20-1712
The Pied Pipers/Paul Weston Orch 10/45 Cap 207
Andrews Sisters 12/45 Dec 18700

A LITTLE ON THE LONELY SIDE (22)
Advanced, pub. 1944, reached #4 in February 1945
Dick Robertson, James Cavenaugh, Frank Weldon w & m
Frankie Carle/Paul Allen Φ 01/45 Col 36760
Guy Lombardo/Jimmy Brown Φ 02/45 Dec 18642
Phil Moore Four/Billy Daniels 05/45 Vic 20-1641

LOVE LETTERS (43)
Famous, pub. 1945, reached #12 in November 1945
(Also reached #19 in July 1966)
Edward Heyman w, Victor Young m
Dick Haymes/Victor Young Orch 10/45 Dec 18699
Victor Young Orch 01/46 Dec 23468

MEET ME IN ST. LOUIS, LOUIS
Vogel Mus Co; orig. pub. 1904, reached #19 in January 1945
(Also reached #1 in July 1904)
Andrew Sterling w, Kerry Mills m
Featured in MEET ME IN ST. LOUIS, film (rel. 11/44)
Judy Garland, sung in film, 12/44 Dec 23360
Guy Lombardo/w.vocal group 12/44 Dec 18626

MOONLIGHT IN VERMONT
Capitol Songs, pub. 1944, reached #20 in February 1945
John Blackburn w, Karl Suessedorf m
Billy Butterfield/Margaret Whiting 02/45 Cap 182
radio singers

MORE AND MORE (49)
T B Harms, pub. 1944, reached #10 in March 1945
E Y Harbourg w, Jerome Kern m
Featured in CAN'T HELP SINGING, film (rel. 12/44)
Deanna Durbin, sung in film, 03/45 Dec 23389
Tommy Dorsey/Bonnie Lou Williams Φ 03/45 Vic 20-1614
Perry Como 03/45 Vic 20-1630
Bing Crosby 04/45 Dec 18649

THE MORE I SEE YOU (31)
Bregman, V & C, pub. 1945, reached #7 in July 1945
(Also reached #16 in June 1966)
Mack Gordon w, Harry Warren m
Featured in BILLY ROSE'S DIAMOND HORSESHOE, film
(rel. 04/45)
Dick Haymes Φ 06/45 Dec 18662
Harry James/Buddy DiVito 05/45 Col 36794
Carmen Cavallaro/Gloria Foster 06/45 Dec 18671

MY DREAMS ARE GETTING BETTER ALL THE TIME (5)
Santly-Joy, pub. 1944, reached #1 in April 1945
Mann Curtis w, Vic Mizzy m
Featured in IN SOCIETY, film (rel. 08/44)
Les Brown/Doris Day ΦΦ 03/45 Col 36779
Marion Hutton, sung in film
Johnny Long/Dick Robertson Φ 04/45 Dec 18661
Phil Moore Four/Billy Daniels Φ 03/45 Vic 20-1641

(ALL OF A SUDDEN) MY HEART SINGS
Leeds, pub. 1943, reached #15 in March 1945
(Also reached #14 in February 1959)
Harold Rome & Jean M Blanvillain w, Henri Laurent Herpin m
Featured in ANCHORS AWEIGH, film (rel. 07/45)
Kathryn Grayson, sung in film
Johnnie Johnston/Paul Baron Orch 03/45 Cap 186
Martha Stewart 02/45 Blu 30-0832

NANCY (WITH THE LAUGHING FACE)
Stanwood, pub. 1944, reached #20 in December 1945
Phil Silvers w, Jimmy Van Heusen m
Frank Sinatra, radio, 12/45 Col 36868

NO CAN DO
Robbins, pub. 1945, reached #15 in November 1945
Charles Tobias w, Nat Simon m
Guy Lombardo/w.vocal duo 11/45 Dec 18712
Xavier Cugat/Leah Roy 10/45 Col 36836
King Sisters 11/45 Vic 20-1719

ON THE ATCHISON, TOPEKA, AND THE SANTA FE (3)
L Feist, pub. 1945, reached #1 in August 1945
Johnny Mercer w, Harry Warren m
Featured in THE HARVEY GIRLS, film (rel. 01/46)
Johnny Mercer ΦΦ 07/45 Cap 195
Bing Crosby ΦΦ 07/45 Dec 18690
Judy Garland, sung in film, 09/45 Dec 23436
Tommy Dorsey/The Sentimentalists Φ 08/45 Vic 20-1682
Tommy Tucker/Don Brown 08/45 Col 36829

OPUS NO. 1
Embassy, pub. 1945, reached #16 in March 1945
Sy Oliver & Sid Garris w & m
Big-band classic
Tommy Dorsey Orch Φ 02/45 Vic 20-1608

(YOU CAME ALONG) OUT OF NOWHERE (45)
Paramount; orig. pub. 1931, reached #8 in October 1945
(Also reached #3 in May 1931)
Edward Heyman w, Johnny Green m
Featured in YOU CAME ALONG, film (rel. 07/45)
Helen Forrest, sung in film, 09/45 Dec 18694
Tommy Dorsey/Stuart Foster 09/45 Vic 20-1722
Lena Horne/Teddy Wilson, stage, 09/45 Col 36737

POOR LITTLE RHODE ISLAND
Skidmore Mus, pub. 1944, reached #19 in May 1945
Sammy Cahn w, Jule Styne m
Featured in CAROLINA BLUES, film (rel. 12/44)
Guy Lombardo/Stuart Foster Φ 04/45 Dec 18651
Ann Miller, sung in film

RUM AND COCA COLA (17)
L Feist, pub. 1944, reached #2 in March 1945
Morey Amsterdam w, Lionel Belasco, Paul Baron & Jeri Sullavan m
Andrews Sisters ΦΦΦ 01/45 Dec 18636
Abe Lyman/Rose Blane Φ 03/45 Col 36775
Louis Prima/Lilyann Carol 02/45 Hit 7125

SATURDAY NIGHT (IS THE LONELIEST NIGHT OF THE WEEK) (29)
Barton M C, pub. 1945, reached #5 in March 1945
Sammy Cahn w, Jule Styne m
Frank Sinatra Φ 02/45 Col 36762
Sammy Kaye/Nancy Norman Φ 02/45 Vic 20-1635
Frankie Carle/Phyllis Lynne 03/45 Col 36777

SENTIMENTAL JOURNEY (1)
E H Morris, pub. 1944, reached #1 in June 1945
Bud Green, Les Brown, Ben Homer w & m
All-time pop standard
Les Brown/Doris Day ΦΦΦ 03/45 Col 36769
Hal McIntyre Orch Φ 04/45 Vic 20-1643
The Merry Macs Φ 06/45 Dec 18684
Louis Prima/Lilyann Carol 06/45 Majestic 7140

SLEIGH RIDE IN JULY
Burke & Van H, pub. 1944, reached #15 in February 1945
Johnny Burke w, Jimmy Van Heusen m
Featured in BELLE OF THE YUKON, film (rel. 12/44)
Dinah Shore, sung in film, 02/45 Vic 20-1617
Bing Crosby 02/45 Dec 18640
Tommy Dorsey/Bonnie Lou Williams 02/45 Vic 20-1622
Les Brown/Gordon Drake 03/45 Col 36763

STUFF LIKE THAT THERE (47)
Capitol Songs, pub. 1945, reached #13 in May 1945
Redd Evans w, Jay Livingston m
Featured in ON STAGE EVERYBODY, film (rel. 07/45)
Betty Hutton Φ 04/45 Cap 188
King Sisters, sung in film

SWEET DREAMS, SWEETHEART (33)
Remick, pub. 1944, reached #7 in February 1945
Ted Koehler w, M K Jerome m
Featured in HOLLYWOOD CANTEEN, film (rel. 12/44)
Kitty Carlisle, sung in film, 01/45 Dec 23359
Stan Kenton/Gene Howard 02/45 Cap 178
Jimmy Dorsey/Teddy Walters 02/45 Dec 18627
Ray Noble/Larry Stewart 03/45 Col 36765

(I LOVE YOU) SWEETHEART OF ALL MY DREAMS
Shapiro, B, pub. 1928, reached #17 in May 1945
(Also reached #9 in March 1929)
Art Fitch, Kay Fitch, Bert Lowe w & m
Featured in THIRTY SECONDS OVER TOKYO, film (rel. 11/44)
Charlie Spivak/Irene Daye 05/45 Vic 20-1646
Benny Goodman/Bob Hayden 05/45 Col 36790

TAMPICO (39)
Capitol Songs, pub. 1945, reached #12 in August 1945
Allan Roberts & Doris Fisher w & m
Stan Kenton/June Christy ΦΦ 07/45 Cap 202

(DID YOU EVER GET) THAT FEELING IN THE MOONLIGHT (41)
Paull-Pioneer, pub. 1944, reached #9 in December 1945
James Cavanaugh, Larry Stock, Ira Schuster w & m
Perry Como Φ 09/45 Vic 20-1709
Gene Krupa/w.vocal duo 11/45 Col 36862
Russ Morgan/w.vocal 01/45 Dec 18724

THAT'S FOR ME (20)
Williamson, pub. 1945, reached #4 in November 1945
Oscar Hammerstein 2nd w, Richard Rodgers m
Featured in STATE FAIR, film (rel. 08/45)
Dick Haymes Φ 10/45 Dec 18706
Vivian Blaine, sung in film
Jo Stafford 11/45 Cap 213
Kay Kyser/Michael Douglas 11/45 Col 36844

THERE! I'VE SAID IT AGAIN (8)
Valiant, pub. 1941, reached #3 in July 1945
(Also reached #1 in January 1964)
Redd Evans & Dave Mann w Φ m
Vaughn Monroe/<vocal ΦΦΦ 03/45 Vic 20-1637
Jimmy Dorsey/Teddy Walters 06/45 Dec 18670
Modernaires/Paula Kelly 07/45 Col 36800

THERE GOES THAT SONG AGAIN (24)
Shapiro, B, pub. 1944, reached #2 in January 1945
Sammy Cahn w, Jule Styne m
Featured in CAROLINA BLUES, film (rel. 12/44)
Kay Kyser/Georgia Carroll Φ performed in film and 01/45 Col 36757
Russ Morgan/<vocal Φ 11/44 Dec 18625
Sammy Kaye/Nancy Norman 01/45 Vic 20-1606
Billy Butterfield/Margaret Whiting 01/45 Cap 182
Kate Smith 01/45 Col 36759

THERE MUST BE A WAY (42)
Stevens Mus, pub. 1945, reached #8 in September 1945
Sammy Gallop, David Saxon, Robert Cook w & m
Charlie Spivak/Jimmy Saunders Φ 05/45 Vic 20-1663
Johnnie Johnston/Paul Baron Orch Φ 07/45 Cap 196

THERE'S NO YOU
Barton M C, pub. 1944, reached #16 in September 1945
Tom Adair w, Hal Hopper m
Jo Stafford 08/45 Cap 191
Frank Sinatra 08/45 Col 36797

THE THREE CABALLEROS
C K Harris, pub. 1944, reached #12 in March 1945
Ray Gilbert & Ernesto Cortazar w, Manuel Esperon m
Featured in THE THREE CABALLEROS, cartoon film (rel. 12/44)
Bing Crosby & The Andrews Sisters Φ 02/45 Dec 23364
Charles Wolcott/Ray Gilbert 01/45 Dec 23341

TILL THE END OF TIME (4)
Santly-Joy, pub. 1945, reached #1 in September 1945
Buddy Kaye & Ted Mossman w & adpt, Frederic Chopin m
Perry Como ΦΦΦ 08/45 Vic 20-1709
Les Brown/Doris Day Φ 08/45 Col 36828
Dick Haymes Φ 09/45 Dec 18699

TIPPIN' IN
Advanced, pub. 1945, reached #19 in May 1945
Marty Symes w, Bobby Smith m
Big-band classic
Erskine Hawkins Orch Φ 04/45 Vic 20-1639

TWILIGHT TIME
Campbell-Porgie, pub. 1944, reached #14 in February 1945
(Also reached #2 in April 1958)
Buck Ram w, Morty Nevins, Al Nevins & Artie Dunn m
The Three Suns 11/44 Hit 7092
Les Brown Orch 03/45 Col 36769
Jimmy Dorsey Orch 03/45 Dec 18656

WAITIN' FOR THE TRAIN TO COME IN (30)
M Block Mus, pub. 1945, reached #5 in December 1945
Sunny Skylar & Martin Block w & m
Peggy Lee/Dave Barbour[5] Φ 11/45 Cap 218
Harry James/Kitty Kallen Φ 11/45 Col 36867
Johnny Long/Dick Robertson Φ 11/45 Dec 18718

(I'LL BE) WALKIN' WITH MY HONEY
Republic, pub. 1945, reached #17 in December 1945
Buddy Kaye w, Sam Medoff m
Sammy Kaye/w.vocal duo 11/45 Vic 20-1713
Ray Noble/Frances Hunt 01/46 Col 36883

WHITE CHRISTMAS (48)
Berlin, pub. 1942, reached #7 in December 1945
(Also reached #1 in November 1942)
(Also reached Top 20 every December 1943-1955, 1960 & 1961)
Irving Berlin w & m
Bing Crosby Φ 12/45 Dec 18429
Frank Sinatra Φ 12/45 Col 36860
Freddy Martin/Clyde Rogers 12/45 Vic 27946

WHO THREW THE WHISKEY IN THE WELL?
Advanced, pub. 1942, reached #17 in August 1945
Lucky Millinder, Eddie DeLange, Johnny Brooks w & m
Lucky Millinder/Wynonie Harris Φ 06/45 Dec 18674
Louis Prima/<vocal 10/45 Majestic 7151

YAH-TA-TA, YAH-TA-TA (TALK, TALK, TALK)
Burke & Van H, pub. 1945, reached #12 in May 1945
Johnny Burke w, Jimmy Van Heusen m
Bing Crosby & Judy Garland Φ 05/45 Dec 23410
Harry James/Kitty Kallen 05/45 Col 36788

YOU BELONG TO MY HEART (32)
C K Harris, pub. 1943, reached #5 in July 1945
Ray Gilbert w, Augistin Lara m
Featured in THE THREE CABALLEROS, cartoon film (rel. 12/44)
Bing Crosby Φ 06/45 Dec 23413
Dora Luz, sung in film
Charlie Spivak/Jimmy Saunders Φ 05/45 Vic 20-1663
Phil Brito/Paul Lavalle Orch 06/45 Musicraft 15018

[1]Spike Jones eventually sold a million copies of COCKTAILS FOR TWO, a feat aided by his appearance in LADIES' MAN, film (rel. 01/47) in which he performed the song.
[2]Betty Grable was listed as Ruth Haag on the Columbia record.
[3]Louanne Hogan's voice was dubbed for Jeanne Crain.
[4]Louis Jordan's version was entitled CALDONIA BOOGIE.
[5]Dave Barbour on guitar

1946

ALL THROUGH THE DAY (14)
Williamson, pub. 1946, reached #4 in May 1946
Oscar Hammerstein 2nd w, Jerome Kern m
Featured in CENTENNIAL SUMMER, film (rel. 05/46)
Perry Como Φ 05/46 RCA Vic 20-1814
Frank Sinatra Φ 05/46 Col 36962
Cornel Wilde, sung in film
Margaret Whiting Φ 04/46 Cap 240

ALONG WITH ME
Witmark, pub. 1946, reached #18 in August 1946
Harold Rome w & m
Featured in CALL ME MISTER, show (opened 04/46)
Margaret Whiting 08/46 Cap 269
Danny Scholl & Paula Bane, sung in show
Artie Shaw/Mel Torme 08/46 Musicraft 365

AND THEN IT'S HEAVEN
Remick, pub. 1946, reached #10 in November 1946
Eddie Seiler, Sol Marcus, Al Kaufman w & m
Featured in SWEETHEART OF SIGMA CHI, film (rel. 11/46)
Phil Brito, sung in film, 09/46 Musicraft 15080
Harry James/Buddy DiVito 10/46 Col 37060

AREN'T YOU GLAD YOU'RE YOU? (31)
Burke & Van H, pub. 1945, reached #6 in February 1946
Johnny Burke w, Jimmy Van Heusen m
Featured in THE BELLS OF ST. MARY'S, film (rel. 11/45)
Bing Crosby Φ sung in film, 12/45 Dec 18720
Les Brown/Doris Day Φ 11/45 Col 36875
Tommy Dorsey/Stuart Foster 01/46 Vic 20-1728
Pied Pipers 12/45 Cap 225

ATLANTA, G.A. (45)
Stevens Mus, pub. 1945, reached #10 in April 1946
Sunny Skylar w, Arthur Shaftel m
Sammy Kaye/Billy Williams Φ 03/46 Vic 20-1795
Woody Herman/<vocal 04/46 Col 36949

THE BELLS OF ST. MARY'S
T B Harms, pub. 1917, reached #15 in February 1946
(Also reached #15 in September 1919)
Douglas Furber w, A Emmett Adams m
Featured in THE BELLS OF ST. MARY'S, film (rel. 11/45)
Bing Crosby, sung in film, 02/46 Dec 18721
Charlie Spivak/Jimmy Saunders 02/46 Vic 20-1791

BLUE SKIES (47)
Berlin, pub. 1927, reached #12 in November 1946
(Also reached #1 in March 1927)
Irving Berlin w & m
Featured in BLUE SKIES, film (rel. 09/46)
Bing Crosby, sung in film, 10/46 Dec 23646
Count Basie/Jimmy Rushing 09/46 Col 37070
Benny Goodman/Art Lund 08/46 Col 37053

BUMBLE BOOGIE
Martin Mus, pub. 1946, reached #20 in May 1946
(Also reached #15 in May 1961)
Jack Fina & Nikolai Rimsky-Korsakov m
Freddy Martin/Jack Fina[2] Φ 05/46 RCA Vic 20-1829
Alvino Rey Orch 08/46 Cap 262

BUZZ ME
Cherio, pub. 1945, reached #18 in February 1946
Danny Baxter & Fleecie Moore w & m
Louis Jordan Φ 01/46 Dec 18734
Ella Mae Morse 01/46 Cap 226

CEMENT MIXER (PUT-TI, PUT-TI) (44)
Am Acad Mus, pub. 1946, reached #10 in May 1946
Slim Gaillard & Lee Ricks w & m
Alvino Rey/Rocky Coluccio Φ 04/46 Cap 248
Slim Gaillard Trio 05/46 Cadet 201
Charlie Barnet/Art Robey 06/46 Dec 18862
Jimmie Lunceford/Joe Thomas 06/46 Majestic 1045

CHOO CHOO CH'BOOGIE
Rytvoc, pub. 1945, reached #14 in September 1946
Vaughn Horton, Denver Darling, Milton Gabler w & m
The top rhythm & blues song of 1946
Louis Jordan ΦΦ 08/46 Dec 23610

THE CHRISTMAS SONG
Burke & Van H, pub. 1946, reached #11 in December 1946
Mel Torme & Robert Wells w & m
All-time Christmas standard
Nat "King" Cole Φ 12/46 Cap 311
Mel Torme, stage
Les Brown/Doris Day 12/46 Col 37174

COAX ME A LITTLE BIT
Bourne, pub. 1946, reached #18 in June 1946
Charles Tobias w, Nat Simon m
Andrews Sisters 05/46 Dec 18833
Dinah Shore 05/46 Col 36944

THE COFFEE SONG
Valiant, pub. 1946, reached #12 in November 1946
Bob Hilliard & Dick Miles w & m
Featured by ensemble in COPACABANA REVUE, revue (1946)
Frank Sinatra Φ 09/46 Col 37089
King Sisters 11/46 RCA Vic 20-1943
Louis Prima/<vocal 10/46 Majestic 7191

COME RAIN OR COME SHINE (50)
Crawford, pub. 1946, reached #13 in July 1946
Johnny Mercer w, Harold Arlen m
Featured in ST. LOUIS WOMAN, show (opened 03/46)
Ruby Hill & Harold Nicholas, sung in show
Margaret Whiting 06/46 Cap 247
Helen Forrest & Dick Haymes 07/46 Dec 23548

COME TO BABY, DO!
Leeds, pub. 1945, reached #14 in February 1946
Inez James & Sidney Miller w & m
Les Brown/Doris Day 12/45 Col 36884
Duke Ellington/Joya Sherrill 02/46 Vic 20-1748
King Cole Trio 01/46 Cap 224

DAY BY DAY (28)
Barton M C, pub. 1945, reached #6 in March 1946
Sammy Cahn, Axel Stordahl, Paul Weston w & m
Frank Sinatra Φ 02/46 Col 36905
Jo Stafford Φ radio, 03/46 Cap 227
Les Brown/Doris Day 03/46 Col 36945
Bing Crosby & Mel Torme 03/46 Dec 18746

DIG YOU LATER (A HUBBA-HUBBA-HUBBA) (37)
Robbins, pub. 1945, reached #9 in January 1946
Harold Adamson w, Jimmy McHugh m
Featured in DOLL FACE, film (rel. 12/45)
Perry Como ΦΦ sung in film, 12/45 Vic 20-1750

DO YOU LOVE ME?
Bregman, V & C, pub. 1946, reached #9 in June 1946
Harry Ruby w & m
Featured in DO YOU LOVE ME?, film (rel. 04/46)
Dick Haymes, sung in film, 05/46 Dec 18792
Harry James/Ginnie Powell 06/46 Col 36965

DOCTOR, LAWYER, INDIAN CHIEF (15)
Burke & Van H, pub. 1945, reached #3 in March 1946
Paul Francis Webster w, Hoagy Carmichael m
Featured in STORK CLUB, film (rel. 10/45)
Betty Hutton ΦΦ 12/45 Cap 220
Les Brown/Butch Stone Φ 03/46 Col 16945
Hoagy Carmichael 03/46 ARA 128

DOIN' WHAT COMES NATUR'LLY (11)
Berlin, pub. 1946, reached #2 in August 1946
Irving Berlin w & m
Featured in ANNIE GET YOUR GUN, show (opened 05/46)
Freddy Martin/Glen Hughes ΦΦ 06/46 RCA Vic 20-1878
Dinah Shore ΦΦ 06/46 Col 35976
Ethel Merman, sung in show, 09/46 Dec 23584 (in album)
Jimmy Dorsey/Dee Parker 06/46 Dec 18872

EASTER PARADE
Berlin, pub. 1933, reached #16 in April 1946
(Also reached #5 in January 1934)
Irving Berlin w & m
Harry James Orch 04/46 Col 36545

FIVE MINUTES MORE (6)
Melrose, pub. 1946, reached #2 in September 1946
Sammy Cahn w, Jule Styne m
Featured in THE SWEETHEART OF SIGMA CHI, film (rel. 11/46)
Frank Sinatra ΦΦ 08/46 Col 37048
Tex Beneke/<vocal Φ 08/46 RCA Vic 20-1922
Phil Brito, sung in film
The Three Suns/Artie Dunn Φ 09/46 Majestic 7197
Skitch Henderson/Ray Kellogg 10/46 Cap 257

FULL MOON AND EMPTY ARMS (36)
Barton M C, pub. 1946, reached #8 in June 1946
Buddy Kaye & Ted Mossman w & adpt, Serge Rachmaninoff m
Frank Sinatra 04/46 Col 36947
Ray Noble/Snooky Lanson 04/46 Col 36893
Carmen Cavallaro/Bob Eberly 05/46 Dec 18813

THE GIRL THAT I MARRY (48)
Berlin, pub. 1946, reached #16 in January 1947
Irving Berlin w & m
Featured in ANNIE GET YOUR GUN, show (opened 05/46)
Steady seller, 1946-47
Frank Sinatra 06/46 Col 36975
Ray Middleton, sung in show, 09/46 Dec 23588 (in album)
Eddy Howard/<vocal 02/47 Majestic 1083
Dick Haymes 04/47 Dec 23780

THE GYPSY (1)
Leeds, pub. 1945, reached #1 in June 1946
Billy Reid w & m
The Ink Spots ΦΦΦ 04/46 Dec 18817
Dinah Shore ΦΦ 04/46 Col 36964
Sammy Kaye/Mary Marlowe Φ 05/46 RCA Vic 1844
Hildegarde/Guy Lombardo Orch Φ 05/46 Dec 23511
Hal McIntyre/Frankie Lester 06/46 Cosmo 475

HERE COMES HEAVEN AGAIN
Robbins, pub. 1945, reached #16 in March 1946
Harold Adamson w, Jimmy McHugh m
Featured in DOLL FACE, film (rel. 12/45)
Perry Como 01/46 Vic 20-1750
Kate Smith 03/46 Col 36915

HEY! BA-BA-RE-BOP
Leeds, pub. 1945, reached #13 in June 1946
Lionel Hampton & Curley Hamner w & m
Tex Beneke/<vocal Φ 05/46 RCA Vic 20-1859
Lionel Hampton/w.vocal group Φ 04/46 Dec 18754

THE HOUSE OF BLUE LIGHTS
Robbins, pub. 1946, reached #18 in July 1946
(Also reached #19 in August 1955)
Don Raye & Freddie Slack w & m
Freddie Slack/Ella Mae Morse Φ 05/46 Cap 251
Andrews Sisters 09/46 Dec 23641

I DON'T KNOW ENOUGH ABOUT YOU (21)
Campbell-Porgie, pub. 1931, reached #6 in July 1946
Peggy Lee & Dave Barbour w & m
Peggy Lee/Dave Barbour's Orch Φ 05/46 Cap 236
Mills Brothers Φ 05/46 Dec 18834
Benny Goodman/Art Lund 08/46 Col 37053

I DON'T KNOW WHY (I JUST DO) (35)
L Feist, pub. 1946, reached #10 in September 1946
(Also reached #2 in November 1931)
(Also reached #11 in December 1961)
Roy Turk w, Fred Ahlert m
Tommy Dorsey/Stuart Foster 07/46 RCA Vic 20-1901
Frank Sinatra 05/46 Col 36918
Skinnay Ennis 07/46 Signature 15033

I GOT THE SUN IN THE MORNING (30)
Berlin, pub. 1946, reached #8 in July 1946
Irving Berlin w & m
Featured in ANNIE GET YOUR GUN, show (opened 05/46)
Les Brown/Doris Day Φ 06/46 Col 36977
Ethel Merman, sung in show, 09/46 Dec 23587 (in album)
Artie Shaw/Mel Torme 07/46 Musicraft 365

I GUESS I'LL GET THE PAPERS AND GO HOME
Campbell-Porgie, pub. 1946, reached #14 in October 1946
Hughie Prince & Hal Kanner w & m
Mills Brothers 09/46 Dec 23638
Les Brown/Jack Haskel 09/46 Col 37066

I'D BE LOST WITHOUT YOU (41)
Advanced, pub. 1946, reached #9 in October 1946
Sunny Skylar w & m
Guy Lombardo/Don Rodney 08/46 Dec 18901
Frankie Carle/Marjorie Hughes 08/46 Col 36994
Buddy Morrow/Johnny McAfee 06/46 Merc 3015

I'M A BIG GIRL NOW (43)
World Mus, pub. 1946, reached #9 in May 1946
Al Hoffman, Milton Drake, Jerry Livingston w & m
Sammy Kaye/Betty Barclay 03/46 Vic 20-1812
Gertrude Niesen 04/46 Dec 23499

I'M ALWAYS CHASING RAINBOWS (23)
Miller Mus; orig. pub. 1918, reached #4 in February 1946
(Also reached #1 in January 1919)
Joe McCarthy w, Harry Carroll adpt, Frederic Chopin m
Featured in THE DOLLY SISTERS, film (rel. 09/45)
Perry Como Φ 02/46 Vic 20-1788
Helen Forrest & Dick Haymes Φ 01/46 Dec 23472
Harry James/Buddy DiVito Φ 02/46 Col 36899
John Payne, sung in film
Guy Lombardo/Erno Rapee 04/46 Dec 18789

I'M GLAD I WAITED FOR YOU
Shapiro, B, pub. 1945, reached #17 in March 1946
Sammy Cahn w, Jule Styne m
Featured in TARS AND SPARS, film (rel. 01/46)
Alfred Drake, sung in film
Peggy Lee 03/46 Cap 218
Helen Forrest 01/46 Dec 18723

IF YOU WERE THE ONLY GIRL (27)
Mutual; orig. pub. 1916, reached #6 in September 1946
Clifford Grey w, Nat Ayer m
Perry Como Φ 06/46 RCA Vic 20-1857
Dick Haymes, radio, 01/47 Dec 23752
Claude Thornhill/Buddy Hughes 10/46 Col 37092

IN LOVE IN VAIN (32)
T B Harms, pub. 1946, reached #8 in August 1946
Leo Robin w, Jerome Kern m
Featured in CENTENNIAL SUMMER, film (rel. 05/46)
Helen Forrest & Dick Haymes 08/46 Dec 23528
Margaret Whiting 05/46 Cap 240
Jeanne Crain[1], film

IN THE MIDDLE OF MAY
Crawford, pub. 1945, reached #15 in January 1946
Fred Ahlert & Al Stillman w & m
Freddy Martin/w.vocal group 12/45 Vic 20-1747
Pied Pipers/Paul Weston Orch 01/46 Cap 225

IN THE MOON MIST
Shapiro, B, pub. 1945, reached #18 in June 1946
Jack Lawrence w & adpt, Louis P Benjamin Godard m
Pied Pipers/Paul Weston Orch 04/46 Cap 243
Les Brown/Doris Day 05/46 Col 36961

IT'S ALL OVER NOW
BMI, pub. 1946, reached #17 in December 1946
Sunny Skylar & Don Marcotte w & m
Frankie Carle/Marjorie Hughes Φ 11/46 Col 37146
Peggy Lee Φ 11/46 Cap 292

JUST A LITTLE FOND AFFECTION (39)
Shapiro, B, pub. 1944, reached #9 in February 1946
Elton Box, Desmond Cox, Lewis Ilda w & m
Featured in SWING PARADE OF 1946, film (rel. 01/46)
Connee Boswell, sung in film
Gene Krupa/ Buddy Stewart 12/45 Col 36877
Charlie Barnet/Fran Warren 01/46 Dec 18722

JUST THE OTHER DAY
Shapiro, B, pub. 1946, reached #20 in September 1946
Redd Evans w, Austen Herbert Croom-Johnson m
Sam Donahue/Mynell Allen Φ 08/46 Cap 275
Vaughn Monroe/Betty Norton 09/46 RCA Vic 20-1920

LAUGHING ON THE OUTSIDE (13)
BMI, pub. 1946, reached #1 in May 1946
Ben Raleigh w, Bernie Wayne m
Dinah Shore ΦΦ 04/46 Col 36964
Sammy Kaye/Billy Williams Φ 05/46 RCA Vic 1856
Andy Russell Φ 05/46 Cap 252
Teddy Walters/Lou Bring Φ 04/46 ARA 135
Merry Macs 04/46 Dec 18811

LET IT SNOW! LET IT SNOW! LET IT SNOW! (18)
E H Morris, pub. 1945, reached #2 in February 1946
Sammy Cahn w, Jule Styne m
Seasonal standard
Vaughn Monroe/<vocal ΦΦ 12/45 Vic 20-1757
Woody Herman/<vocal Φ 02/46 Col 36909
Connee Boswell/Russ Morgan Φ 02/46 Dec 18741

LINGER IN MY ARMS A LITTLE LONGER, BABY (49)
Bourne, pub. 1946, reached #11 in October 1946
Herb Magidson w & m
Peggy Lee 09/46 Cap 263
Woody Herman/Lynn Stevens 09/46 Col 36995
Helen Forrest/The Chickadees 10/46 Dec 18908

MacNAMARA'S BAND
S O'Connor, pub. 1917, reached #16 in March 1946
John Stamford w, Shamus O'Connor m
Seasonal best-seller, 1940's to 1970's
Bing Crosby/The Jesters Φ 03/46 Dec 23495

THE MAD BOOGIE
Bregman, V & C, pub. 1946, reached #20 in June 1946
Count Basie & Buster Harding m
Count Basie Orch Φ 04/46 Col 36946

THE MOMENT I MET YOU
Embassy, pub. 1946, reached #19 in February 1946
Buck Ram & Gail Meredith w & m
Tommy Dorsey/The Sentimentalists 01/46 Vic 20-1761

MONEY IS THE ROOT OF ALL EVIL (TAKE IT AWAY)
Sun Mus Co pub. 1945, reached #18 in February 1946
Joan Whitney & Alex Kramer w & m
Andrews Sisters Φ 02/46 Dec 23474

OH! WHAT IT SEEMED TO BE (10)
Santly-Joy, pub. 1945, reached #1 in March 1946
Bennie Benjamin, George Weiss, Frankie Carle w & m
Frankie Carle/Marjorie Hughes ΦΦ 01/46 Col 36892
Frank Sinatra ΦΦ 02/46 Col 36095
Helen Forrest & Dick Haymes Φ 03/46 Dec 23481
Charlie Spivak/Jimmy Saunders Φ 03/46 RCA Vic 20-2047

THE OLD LAMP-LIGHTER (5)
Shapiro, B, pub. 1946, reached #1 in December 1946
(Also reached #6 in May 1960)
Charles Tobias w, Nat Simon m
Sammy Kaye/Billy Williams ΦΦ 11/46 RCA Vic 20-1963
Kay Kyser/Michael Douglas Φ 11/46 Col 37095
Hal Derwin/Frank DeVol's Orch Φ 11/46 Cap 288
Kenny Baker/Russ Morgan Orch 02/47 Dec 23781
Morton Downey 12/46 Majestic 1061

OLE BUTTERMILK SKY (3)
Burke & Van H, pub. 1946, reached #1 in December 1946
Hoagy Carmichael & Jack Brooks w & m
Featured in CANYON PASSAGE, film (rel. 07/46)
Kay Kyser/Michael Douglas ΦΦ 09/46 Col 37073
Hoagy Carmichael ΦΦ sung in film, 10/46 ARA 155
Paul Weston/Matt Dennis Φ 11/46 Cap 285
Helen Carroll Φ 11/46 RCA Vic 20-1982
Connee Boswell 11/46 Dec 18913

ONE MORE TOMORROW (46)
Remick, pub. 1945, reached #14 in August 1946
Ernesto Lecuona, Eddie DeLange, Josef Myrow w & m
Featured in ONE MORE TOMORROW, film (rel. 05/46)
Frankie Carle/Marjorie Hughes Φ 06/46 Col 36978
Tex Beneke/Artie Malvin 06/46 RCA Vic 20-1835
Glen Gray/Eugenie Baird 07/46 Dec 18843

ONE-ZY, TWO-ZY (I LOVE YOU-ZY) (29)
Martin Mus, pub. 1946, reached #2 in April 1946
Dave Franklin & Irving Taylor w & m
Phil Harris ΦΦ 03/46 ARA 136
Freddy Martin/w.vocal group Φ 03/46 RCA Vic 1826
Kay Kyser/The Moonbeams 04/46 Col 36960
Hildegarde/Guy Lombardo Orch 04/46 Dec 23531

PASSE
L Feist, pub. 1942, reached #20 in November 1946
Jean Sablon, Jean Geiringer, Eddie DeLange, Carl Sigman, Joseph Meyer w & m
Tex Beneke/Lillian Lane Φ 10/46 RCA Vic 20-1951
Margaret Whiting 10/46 Cap 294

PERSONALITY (19)
Burke & Van H, pub. 1945, reached #2 in March 1946
Johnny Burke w, Jimmy Van Heusen m
Featured in ROAD TO UTOPIA, film (rel. 12/45)
Johnny Mercer/Pied Pipers ΦΦ 01/46 Cap 230
Dorothy Lamour, sung in film
Bing Crosby Φ 04/46 Dec 18790
Dinah Shore Φ 03/46 Vic 20-1781
Pearl Bailey 03/46 Col 36030

PRETENDING
Criterion, pub. 1946, reached #19 in September 1946
Marty Symes w, Al Sherman m
Andy Russell Φ 08/46 Cap 271
Kate Smith 08/46 Col 36991

PRISONER OF LOVE (9)
Mayfair; orig. pub. 1931, reached #3 in June 1946
(Also reached #18 in June 1963)
Leo Robin w, Russ Columbo & Clarence Gaskill m
Perry Como ΦΦΦ 03/46 RCA Vic 20-1814
The Ink Spots Φ 06/46 Dec 18864
Billy Eckstine Φ 04/46 National 9017
Gordon MacRae 05/46 Musicraft 15065

RUMORS ARE FLYING (8)
Oxford, pub. 1946, reached #1 in November 1946
Bennie Benjamin & George Weiss w & m
Frankie Carle/Marjorie Hughes ΦΦ 09/46 Col 37069
Andrews Sisters/Les Paul Φ 10/46 Dec 23656
Betty Jane Rhodes Φ 09/46 RCA Vic 20-1944
Billy Butterfield/Pat O'Connor Φ 10/46 Cap 282
The Three Suns Φ 11/46 Majestic 7205

SEEMS LIKE OLD TIMES (38)
L Feist, pub. 1946, reached #11 in May 1946
Carmen Lombardo & John Jacob Loeb w & m
Guy Lombardo/Don Rodney Φ 03/46 Dec 18737
Vaughn Monroe/<vocal Φ 03/46 RCA Vic 1811
Kate Smith 04/46 Col 36950

SEPTEMBER SONG (20)
Crawford, pub. 1938, reached #12 in December 1946
Maxwell Anderson w, Kurt Weill m
All-time pop standard
Walter Huston, stage, 09/46 Dec 40001
Frank Sinatra 12/46 Col 37161
Jimmy Durante, stage and radio
Dardanelle Trio/Dardanelle 12/46 RCA Vic 20-1993
Bing Crosby 01/47 Dec 23754

SHOO-FLY PIE AND APPLE PAN DOWDY (25)
Capitol Songs, pub. 1945, reached #3 in May 1946
Sammy Gallop w, Guy Wood m
Stan Kenton/June Christy Φ 03/46 Cap 235
Dinah Shore Φ 03/46 Col 36943
Guy Lombardo/Don Rodney Φ 04/46 Dec 18809

SIOUX CITY SUE (17)
E H Morris, pub. 1945, reached #6 in May 1946
Ray Freedman w, Dick Thomas m
Bing Crosby/The Jesters Φ 04/46 Dec 23508
Dick Thomas, stage, 03/46 National 9007
Tony Pastor/Stubby Pastor 03/46 Cosmo 471
Zeke Manners/Curly Gribbs 03/46 Vic 20-1797

SOME SUNDAY MORNING (33)
Harms, pub. 1945, reached #8 in January 1946
Ted Koehler w, M K Jerome & Ray Heindorf m
Featured in SAN ANTONIO, film (rel. 11/45)
Helen Forrest & Dick Haymes Φ 11/45 Dec 23434
Alexis Smith, sung in film
Kate Smith 11/45 Col 36839

SOUTH AMERICA, TAKE IT AWAY (16)
Witmark, pub. 1946, reached #3 in September 1946
Harold Rome w & m
Featured in CALL ME MISTER, show (opened 04/46)
Bing Crosby & Andrews Sisters ΦΦΦ 08/46 Dec 23569
Xavier Cugat/Buddy Clark Φ 08/46 Col 37051
Betty Garrett, sung in show

STONE COLD DEAD IN DE MARKET
Northern, pub. 1946, reached #18 in July 1946
Wilmoth Houdini w & m
Ella Fitzgerald & Louis Jordan Φ 07/46 Dec 23546
King Sisters/Billy May 10/46 RCA Vic 20-1943

SURRENDER (12)
Santly-Joy, pub. 1946, reached #3 in August 1946
Bennie Benjamin & George Weiss w & m
Perry Como ΦΦ 06/46 RCA Vic 20-1877
Woody Herman/Blue Flames Φ 06/46 Col 36985
Randy Brooks/Harry Prime 09/46 Dec 18893

SYMPHONY (7)
Chappell, pub. 1945, reached #1 in January 1946
Jack Lawrence, Andre Tabet & Roger Bernstein w Alex Alstone m
Freddy Martin/Clyde Rogers ΦΦ 12/45 Vic 20-1747
Benny Goodman/Liza Morrow ΦΦ 12/45 Col 36874
Bing Crosby Φ 01/46 Dec 18735
Jo Stafford Φ 12/45 Cap 227
Guy Lombardo Orch Φ 01/46 Dec 18737

THERE'S NO ONE BUT YOU
Shapiro, B, pub. 1946, reached #17 in August 1946
Redd Evans & Austen Herbert Croom-Johnson w & m
Mills Brothers 07/46 Dec 18834
Hal McIntyre/Frankie Lester 07/46 Cosmo 479
Kay Kyser/The Moonbeams 07/46 Col 36960

THEY SAY IT'S WONDERFUL (4)
Berlin, pub. 1946, reached #2 in July 1946
Irving Berlin w & m
Featured in ANNIE GET YOUR GUN, show (opened 05/46)
Frank Sinatra ΦΦ 05/46 Col 36975
Ethel Merman & Ray Middleton, sung in show and 09/46 Dec 23586 (in album)
Perry Como Φ 06/46 RCA Vic 20-1857
Andy Russell Φ 06/46 Cap 252
Bing Crosby 06/46 Dec 18829

THE THINGS WE DID LAST SUMMER (34)
E H Morris, pub. 1946, reached #9 in November 1946
Sammy Cahn w, Jules Styne m
Jo Stafford 11/46 Cap 297
Vaughn Monroe/<vocal 11/46 RCA Vic 20-1972
Frank Sinatra 11/46 Col 37089

THIS IS ALWAYS (40)
Bregman, V & C, pub. 1946, reached #8 in November 1946
Mack Gordon w, Harry Warren m
Featured in THREE LITTLE GIRLS IN BLUE, film (rel. 09/46)
June Haver, sung in film
Harry James/Buddy DiVito 09/46 Col 37052
Jo Stafford 09/46 Cap 277
Dick Haymes 09/46 Dec 18878

TO EACH HIS OWN (2)
Paramount, pub. 1946, reached #1 in August 1946
Jay Livingston & Redd Evans w & m
Eddy Howard/<vocal ΦΦΦ 06/46 Majestic 7188
The Ink Spots ΦΦΦ 08/46 Dec 23615
Freddy Martin/Stuart Wade ΦΦ 08/46 RCA Vic 20-1921
Modernaires w/Paula Kelly Φ 08/46 Col 37063
Tony Martin/The Starlighters Φ 07/46 Merc 3022

WAIT AND SEE
L Feist, pub. 1945, reached #18 in March 1946
Johnny Mercer w, Harry Warren m
Featured in THE HARVEY GIRLS, film (rel. 01/46)
Kenny Baker, sung in film, 03/46 Dec 23459
Johnnie Johnston/Carl Kress Orch 01/46 Cap 212
Ginny Simms 04/46 ARA 130

WE'LL GATHER LILACS
Chappell, pub. 1945, reached #12 in June 1946
Ivor Novello w & m
Tommy Dorsey/Stuart Foster 05/46 RCA Vic 20-1809
Gene Krupa/Buddy Stewart 05/46 Col 36954
Bing Crosby 05/46 Dec 23510

WHITE CHRISTMAS (42)
Berlin, pub. 1942, reached #3 in December 1946
(Also reached #1 in November 1942)
(Also reached Top 20 every December 1943-1955, 1960 & 1961)
Irving Berlin w & m
Bing Crosby ΦΦ 12/46 Dec 23778
Frank Sinatra Φ 12/46 Col 37132
Jo Stafford 12/46 Cap 319
Freddy Martin/Clyde Rogers 12/46 Vic 27946

WHO DO YOU LOVE, I HOPE?
Berlin, pub. 1946, reached #19 in July 1946
Irving Berlin w & m
Featured in ANNIE GET YOUR GUN, show (opened 05/46)
Betty Nyman & Kenny Bowers, sung in show
Elliot Lawrence/Rosalind Patton 07/46 Col 37047
Andy Russell 08/46 Cap 271

WHO TOLD YOU THAT LIE?
Stevens Mus, pub. 1946, reached #14 in August 1946
Jack O Segal & Eddie Cantor w, Bee Walker m
Vaughn Monroe/<vocal 07/46 RCA Vic 20-1896
Connee Boswell/Paulette Sisters 08/46 Dec 18881

THE WHOLE WORLD IS SINGING MY SONG (24)
Robbins, pub. 1946, reached #4 in December 1946
Mann Curtis w, Vic Mizzy m
Les Brown/Doris Day Φ 10/46 Col 37066
Jimmy Dorsey/Bob Carroll 12/46 Dec 18917

WINTER WONDERLAND
Donaldson, D & G, pub. 1934, reached #14 in January 1947
(Also reached #4 in January 1935)
(Also reached Top 20 in December of 1950 and 1952)
Richard B Smith w, Felix Bernard m
All-time seasonal standard
Andrews Sisters/Guy Lombardo Orch Φ 12/46 Dec 23722
Johnny Mercer Φ 12/46 Cap 316
Perry Como/The Satisfiers 12/46 RCA Vic 20-1968

WITHOUT YOU
Peer, pub. 1945, reached #18 in September 1946
Ray Gilbert w, Osvaldo Farres m
Featured in MAKE MINE MUSIC, film (rel. 04/46)
Andy Russell, sung in film, 06/46 Cap 234
Frankie Carle/Marjorie Hughes 09/46 Col 37069

YOU KEEP COMING BACK LIKE A SONG (26)
Berlin, pub. 1943, reached #5 in November 1946
Irving Berlin w & m
Featured in BLUE SKIES, film (rel. 09/46)
Dinah Shore Φ 11/46 Col 37072
Bing Crosby Φ sung in film, 11/46 Dec 23647
Jo Stafford Φ 11/46 Cap 297
Dennis Day 11/46 RCA Vic 20-1947

YOU WON'T BE SATISFIED (UNTIL YOU BREAK MY HEART) (22)
Mutual, pub. 1945, reached #3 in April 1946
Freddy James & Larry Stock w & m
Les Brown/Doris Day Φ 01/46 Col 36884
Perry Como Φ 02/46 Vic 20-1788
Ella Fitzgerald & Louis Armstrong 04/46 Dec 23496
Louis Prima 01/46 Majestic 7144

[1]Louanne Hogan's voice was dubbed for Jeanne Crain.
[2]Jack Fina on piano

1947

ACROSS THE ALLEY FROM THE ALAMO (22)
Capitol Songs, pub. 1947, reached #5 in July 1947
Joe Green w & m
Mills Brothers ΦΦ 05/47 Dec 23863
Stan Kenton/June Christy 05/47 Cap 387
Woody Herman/<vocal 05/47 Col 37289

AIN'T NOBODY HERE BUT US CHICKENS
Sun Mus Co, pub. 1946, reached #17 in February 1947
Joan Whitney & Alex Kramer w & m
Louis Jordan Φ 01/47 Dec 23741

ALL MY LOVE
Remick, pub. 1947, reached #15 in October 1947
Al Jolson, Saul Chaplin, Harry Akst w & m
Al Jolson 09/47 Dec 23943
Dinah Shore 09/47 Col 37555

ALMOST LIKE BEING IN LOVE (50)
Sam Fox, pub. 1947, reached #14 in July 1947
Alan Jay Lerner w, Frederick Loewe m
Featured in BRIGADOON, show (opened 03/47)
Frank Sinatra 07/47 Col 37382
David Brooks & Marion Bell, sung in show
Mildred Bailey 08/47 Majestic 1140
Mary Martin 10/47 Dec 24156

--AND MIMI (34)
Shapiro, B, pub. 1947, reached #8 in December 1947
Nat Simon & Jimmy Kennedy w & m
Art Lund Φ 11/47 MGM 10082
Dick Haymes Φ 11/47 Dec 24172
Frankie Carle/Gregg Lawrence 11/47 Col 37819

ANNIVERSARY SONG (6)
Mood Mus Co, pub. 1946, reached #1 in March 1947
Al Jolson & Saul Chaplin w & adpt, Jan Ivanovici m
Featured in THE JOLSON STORY, film (rel. 09/46)
Al Jolson ΦΦΦ sung in film, 02/47 Dec 23714
Dinah Shore ΦΦ 03/47 Col 37234
Guy Lombardo/Kenny Gardner ΦΦ 02/47 Dec 23799
Tex Beneke/Gary Stevens Φ 02/47 RCA Vic 20-2126
Andy Russell 03/47 Cap 368

AN APPLE BLOSSOM WEDDING (29)
Shapiro, B, pub. 1947, reached #6 in November 1947
Jimmy Kennedy w, Nat Simon m
Sammy Kaye/Don Cornell Φ 10/47 RCA Vic 20-2330
Eddy Howard/<vocal Φ 10/47 Majestic 1156
Buddy Clark/Mitchell Ayres 11/47 Col 37488
Kenny Baker/Russ Morgan Orch 11/47 Dec 24117

APRIL SHOWERS (37)
Harms, pub. 1921, reached #6 in May 1947
(Also reached #1 in February 1922)
Buddy DeSylva w, Louis Silvers m
Featured in THE JOLSON STORY, film (rel. 09/46)
Al Jolson, sung in film, 04/47 Dec 23470
Guy Lombardo/Jimmy Brown Φ 05/47 Dec 23845

ASK ANYONE WHO KNOWS (32)
Witmark, pub. 1947, reached #7 in August 1947
Al Kaufman, Sol Marcus, Eddie Seiler w & m
Featured in WALLFLOWER, film (rel. 05/48)
Eddy Howard/<vocal Φ 07/47 Majestic 1124
The Ink Spots 08/47 Dec 23900
Margaret Whiting 08/47 Cap 410

BLESS YOU (FOR BEING AN ANGEL)
Shapiro, B, pub. 1939, reached #12 in April 1947
Edward Lane w, Don Baker m
The Ink Spots 03/47 Dec 23757
Eddy Howard/<vocal 03/47 Majestic 1089

CHI-BABA, CHI-BABA (21)
Santly-Joy, pub. 1947, reached #3 in July 1947
Mack David, Al Hoffman, Jerry Livingston w & m
Perry Como ΦΦ 05/47 RCA Vic 20-2259
Peggy Lee Φ 06/47 Cap 419
Blue Barron/w.vocal group 05/47 MGM 10027
The Charioteers 07/47 Col 37384

CHRISTMAS ISLAND
Northern, pub. 1946, reached #13 in January 1947
Lyle L Moraine w & m
Andrews Sisters/Guy Lombardo 12/46 Dec 23722

CIVILIZATION (25)
E H Morris, pub. 1947, reached #5 in December 1947
Bob Hilliard & Carl Sigman w & m
Featured in ANGEL IN THE WINGS, show (opened 12/47)
Andrew Sisters & Danny Kaye Φ 11/47 Dec 23940
Louis Prima/w.vocal group Φ 10/47 RCA Vic 20-2400
Elaine Stritch, sung in show
Ray McKinley/w.vocal Φ 11/47 Majestic 7274
Jack Smith Φ 10/47 Cap 465

DON'T YOU LOVE ME ANYMORE?
Oxford, pub. 1947, reached #12 in January 1948
Mack David, Al Hoffman, Jerry Livingston w & m
Buddy Clark 11/47 Col 37920
Freddy Martin/Clyde Rogers 11/47 RCA Vic 20-2473
Jose Melis/Jeannie Williams 11/47 Merc 5070

FEUDIN' AND FIGHTIN' (19)
Chappell, pub. 1947, reached #4 in October 1947
Al Dubin w, Burton Lane m
Dorothy Shay Φ 07/47 Col 37189
Jo Stafford Φ 08/47 Cap 443
Bing Crosby Φ 09/47 Dec 23975

(I LOVE YOU) FOR SENTIMENTAL REASONS (4)
Duchess, pub. 1945, reached #1 in February 1947
Deek Watson w, William Best m
Nat "King" Cole ΦΦ 11/46 Cap 304
Eddy Howard/<vocal ΦΦ 11/46 Majestic 7204
Dinah Shore ΦΦ 01/47 Col 37188
Charlie Spivak/Jimmy Saunders Φ 12/46 RCA Vic 20-1981
Ella Fitzgerald Φ 12/46 Dec 23670

FOR YOU, FOR ME, FOREVERMORE
Chappell, pub. 1946, reached #12 in January 1947
Ira Gershwin w, George Gershwin m
Featured in THE SHOCKING MISS PILGRIM, film (rel. 01/47)
Dick Haymes & Betty Grable, sung in film
Dick Haymes & Judy Garland 01/47 Dec 23687
Mel Torme/Artie Shaw Orch 12/46 Musicraft 412
Margaret Whiting 12/46 Cap 294

FREE EATS
Bregman, V & C, pub. 1947, reached #16 in May 1947
Count Basie, Eugene Young, Freddy Green, Ted Donnelly, & Harry E Edison w & m
Count Basie/vocal group 04/47 Vic 20-2148

A GAL IN CALICO (20)
Remick, pub. 1946, reached #3 in February 1947
Leo Robin w, Arthur Schwartz m
Featured in THE TIME, THE PLACE AND THE GIRL, film (rel. 12/46)
Johnny Mercer Φ 12/46 Cap 316
Tex Beneke/<vocal Φ 12/46 RCA Vic 20-1991
Benny Goodman/Eve Young Φ 01/47 Col 37187
Bing Crosby 01/47 Dec 23739
Jack Carson, Dennis Morgan, & Martha Vickers, sung in film

GUILTY (26)
L Feist, pub. 1931, reached #5 in March 1947
(Also reached #2 in November 1931)
Gus Kahn w, Harry Akst & Richard Whiting m
Margaret Whiting Φ 12/46 Cap 324
Ella Fitzgerald 04/47 Dec 23844
Johnny Desmond 03/47 RCA Vic 20-2109

HEARTACHES (8)
Leeds, pub. 1931, reached #1 in April 1947
(Also reached #13 in April 1931)
(Also reached #9 in November 1961)
John Klenner w, Al Hoffman m
Ted Weems/Elmo Tanner[1] ΦΦΦ 03/47 Dec 25017, 04/47 RCA Vic 20-2175
Harry James Orch Φ 04/47 Col 37305
Eddy Howard/<vocal 04/47 Majestic 1111
Jimmy Dorsey/w.vocal duo 03/47 MGM 10001

HERE COMES SANTA CLAUS
Western M P C, pub. 1947, reached #18 in December 1947
(Also reached #13 in December 1948 & #16 in December 1949)
Gene Autry & Oakley Haldeman w & m
Gene Autry Φ 12/47 Col 37942

HOW ARE THINGS IN GLOCCA MORRA? (23)
Crawford, pub. 1946, reached #4 in March 1947
E Y Harbourg w, Burton Lane m
Featured in FINIAN'S RAINBOW, show (opened 01/47)
Buddy Clark Φ 03/47 Col 37223
Ella Logan, sung in show
Martha Tilton Φ 03/47 Cap 345
Tommy Dorsey/Stuart Foster Φ 03/47 RCA Vic 20-2121
Dick Haymes Φ 03/47 Dec 23830

HOW SOON (WILL I BE SEEING YOU) (7)
Supreme, pub. 1944, reached #2 in January 1948
Carroll Lucas & Jack Owens w & m
Jack Owens ΦΦ 09/47 Tower 1258
Vaughn Monroe/<vocal Φ 11/47 RCA Vic 20-2523
Bing Crosby Φ 11/47 Dec 24101
Dinah Shore Φ 12/47 Col 37952

HUGGIN' AND CHALKIN' (27)
Hudson, pub. 1946, reached #5 in February 1947
Clancy Hayes & Kermit Goell w & m
Hoagy Carmichael ΦΦ 11/46 Dec 23675
Kay Kyser/Jack Martin-Campus Kids Φ 11/46 Col 37095
Johnny Mercer Φ 01/47 Cap 334
Herbie Fields 01/47 RCA Vic 20-2036

I AIN'T MAD (AT YOU)
Bregman, V & C, pub. 1947, reached #20 in August 1947
Count Basie, Milt Ebbins, Freddy Green w & m
Count Basie/Taps Miller Φ 08/47 RCA Vic 20-2314

I BELIEVE (44)
Sinatra Songs, pub. 1947, reached #8 in May 1947
Sammy Cahn w, Jules Styne m
Featured in IT HAPPENED IN BROOKLYN, film (rel. 03/47)
Frank Sinatra Φ 05/47 Col 37300
Frank Sinatra, Jimmy Durante & Billy Roy, sung in film
Mel Torme/Artie Shaw Orch 05/47 Musicraft 492

I HAVE BUT ONE HEART (43)
Barton M C, pub. 1945, reached #11 in October 1947
Marty Symes w, Johnny Farrow m
Vic Damone Φ 08/47 Merc 5053
Frank Sinatra 09/47 Col 37554
Pied Pipers 10/46 Cap 460

I NEVER KNEW (THAT ROSES GREW)
Bourne; orig. pub. 1925, reached #14 in August 1947
(Also reached #11 in February 1926)
Gus Kahn w, Ted FioRito m
Sam Donahue/Bill Lockwood Φ 05/47 Cap 405

I WISH I DIDN'T LOVE YOU SO (12)
Paramount, pub. 1947, reached #2 in October 1947
Frank Loesser w & m
Featured in THE PERILS OF PAULINE, film (rel. 05/47)
Betty Hutton Φ sung in film, 09/47 Cap 409
Vaughn Monroe/<vocal ΦΦ 09/47 RCA Vic 20-2294
Dinah Shore ΦΦ 10/47 Col 37506
Dick Haymes Φ 10/47 Dec 23977
Dick Farney/Paul Baron Orch 11/47 Majestic 7225

I WONDER, I WONDER, I WONDER (10)
Robbins, pub. 1947, reached #2 in July 1947
Darwin Frank Hutchins w & m
Eddy Howard/<vocal ΦΦ 05/47 Majestic 1124
Guy Lombardo/Don Rodney ΦΦ 05/47 Dec 23865
Martha Tilton Φ 07/47 Cap 395
Tony Pastor/<vocal Φ 06/47 Col 37353
Louis Armstrong 06/47 RCA Vic 20-2228

I WONDER WHO'S KISSING HER NOW (11)
E B Marks; orig. pub. 1909, reached #2 in October 1947
(Also reached #1 in September 1909)
Will Hough & Frank Adams w, Joe Howard & Harold Orlob m
Featured in I WONDER WHO'S KISSING HER NOW, film (rel. 06/47)
Perry Como/Ted Weems Orch ΦΦ 08/47 Dec 25078
Ray Noble/Snooky Lanson Φ 09/47 Col 37544
Dinning Sisters 10/47 Cap 433
Mark Stevens[2], sung in film

I'LL CLOSE MY EYES (30)
P Maurice, pub. 1945, reached #8 in April 1947
Buddy Kaye w, Billy Reid m
Andy Russell 03/47 Cap 342
Johnny Desmond 03/47 RCA Vic 20-2109
Hildegarde 02/47 Dec 23756

IF I HAD MY LIFE TO LIVE OVER (42)
General, pub. 1939, reached #12 in July 1947
Henry Tobias, Larry Vincent, Moe Jaffe w & m
Larry Vincent/Feilden Foursome 04/47 20th Century 13
Kate Smith, radio, 04/47 MGM 10003
Buddy Clark 06/47 Col 37302

IT'S A GOOD DAY (39)
Capitol Songs, pub. 1946, reached #9 in April 1947
Peggy Lee & Dave Barbour w & m
Peggy Lee Φ 01/47 Cap 322
Phil Harris/<vocal 04/47 RCA Vic 20-2163
Gene Krupa/Carolyn Grey 03/47 Col 37209

IVY
Burke & Van H, pub. 1947, reached #13 in August 1947
Hoagy Carmichael w & m
Featured as theme in IVY, film (rel. 06/47)
Jo Stafford 08/47 Cap 443
Vic Damone 07/47 Merc 5053
Dick Haymes 08/47 Dec 23877
Vaughn Monroe/<vocal 08/47 RCA Vic 20-2275

KATE (HAVE I COME TOO EARLY, TOO LATE)
Berlin, pub. 1947, reached #14 in October 1947
Irving Berlin w & m
Eddy Howard/<vocal Φ 09/47 Majestic 1160
Ray Bloch/Alan Dale 09/47 Signature 15114
Tommy Dorsey/Town Criers 10/47 RCA Vic 20-2362

KOKOMO, INDIANA
Bregman, V & C, pub. 1947, reached #16 in October 1947
Mack Gordon w, Josef Myrow m
Featured in MOTHER WORE TIGHTS, film (rel. 08/47)
Betty Grable & Dan Dailey, sung in film
Vaughn Monroe/<vocal 10/47 RCA Vic 20-2361

THE LADY FROM 29 PALMS (33)
Martin Mus, pub. 1947, reached #8 in October 1947
Allie Wrubel w & m
Freddy Martin/w.vocal group Φ 08/47 RCA Vic 20-2347
Tony Pastor/<vocal Φ 08/47 Col 37562
Andrews Sisters 10/47 Dec 23976

LINDA (5)
E H Morris, pub. 1946, reached #2 in April 1947
Jack Lawrence w & m
Ray Noble/Buddy Clark ΦΦ 02/47 Col 37215
Charlie Spivak/Tommy Mercer Φ 03/47 RCA Vic 20-2047
Paul Weston/Matt Dennis Φ 04/47 Cap 362
Larry Douglas/Ray Bloch Orch 05/47 Signature 15106

MAM'SELLE (9)
L Feist, pub. 1946, reached #1 in May 1947
Mack Gordon w, Edmund Goulding m
Featured as theme in THE RAZOR'S EDGE, film (rel. 11/46)
Art Lund ΦΦΦ 04/47 MGM 10011
Frank Sinatra ΦΦ 05/47 Col 37343
Dick Haymes Φ 05/47 Dec 23861
Pied Pipers Φ 05/47 Cap 396
Ray Dorey/Paul Baron Orch Φ 05/47 Majestic 7217

MANAGUA, NICARAGUA (13)
Encore, pub. 1946, reached #2 in March 1947
Albert Gamse w, Irving Fields m
Freddy Martin/Stuart Wade ΦΦ 01/47 RCA Vic 20-2026
Guy Lombardo/Don Rodney ΦΦ 01/47 Dec 23782
Kay Kyser/Gloria Wood Φ 02/47 Col 37214

MICKEY (38)
Harms; orig. pub. 1918, reached #11 in November 1947
(Also reached #2 in February 1919)
Harry Williams w, Neil Moret m
Ted Weems/w.vocal duo Φ 10/47 Merc 5062
Dennis Day 01/48 RCA Vic 20-2441
Blue Barron/Clyde Burke 03/48 MGM 10106

MIDNIGHT MASQUERADE (47)
Shapiro, B, pub. 1946, reached #10 in July 1947
Bernard Bierman, Arthur Bierman, Jack Manus w & m
Frankie Carle/Marjorie Hughes 05/47 Col 37337
Sammy Kaye/Don Cornell 05/47 RCA Vic 20-2122
Monica Lewis/Ray Bloch Orch 05/47 Signature 15078

MOON-FACED, STARRY-EYED
Chappell, pub. 1947, reached #20 in May 1947
Langston Hughes w, Kurt Weill m
Featured in STREET SCENE, show (opened 01/47)
Freddy Martin/Murray Arnold 05/47 RCA Vic 20-2176
Benny Goodman/Johnny Mercer 04/47 Cap 376
Danny Daniels & Sheila Bond, sung in show

MY ADOBE HACIENDA (18)
Peer, pub. 1941, reached #4 in May 1947
Louise Massey & Lee Penny w & m
Eddy Howard/<vocal ΦΦ 04/47 Majestic 1117
Dinning Sisters 05/47 Cap 389
Billy Williams Quartet 04/47 RCA Vic 20-2150
Kenny Baker/Russ Morgan 05/47 Dec 23846

MY MELANCHOLY BABY
Shapiro, B, pub. 1912, reached #10 in May 1947
(Also reached #15 in March 1928)
George A Norton w, Ernie Burnett m
Sam Donahue Orch Φ 04/47 Cap 357

NEAR YOU (2)
Supreme, pub. 1947, reached #1 in October 1947
(Also reached #8 in October 1958)
Kermit Goell w, Francis Craig m
All-time pop standard
Francis Craig/Bob Lamm ΦΦΦ 08/47 Bullet 1001
Andrews Sisters ΦΦ 09/47 Dec 24171
Larry Green/w.vocal trio Φ 10/47 RCA Vic 20-2421
Alvino Rey/Jimmy Joyce Φ 09/47 Cap 452
Elliot Lawrence/Rosalind Patton Φ 10/47 Col 37838

OH, BUT I DO! (36)
Witmark, pub. 1946, reached #7 in January 1947
Leo Robin w, Arthur Schwartz m
Featured in THE TIME, THE PLACE, AND THE GIRL, film
(rel. 12/46)
Margaret Whiting Φ 12/46 Cap 324
Tex Beneke/Artie Malvin 02/47 RCA Victor 20-1991
Harry James/Buddy DiVito 01/47 Col 37156

OLD DEVIL MOON
Crawford, pub. 1946, reached #15 in June 1947
E Y Harbourg w, Burton Lane m
Featured in FINIAN'S RAINBOW, show (opened 01/47)
Ella Logan & Donald Richards, sung in show
Margaret Whiting 06/47 Cap 410
Gene Krupa/Carolyn Grey 05/47 Col 37270

OPEN THE DOOR, RICHARD! (31)
Duchess, pub. 1947, reached #1 in March 1947
Dusty Fletcher & John Mason w, Jack McVea & Don Howell m
Count Basie/w.vocal duo ΦΦ 02/47 Vic 20-2127
The Three Flames ΦΦ 02/47 Col 37268
Jack McVea Φ 01/47 Black & White 792
Dusty Fletcher Φ 02/47 National 4012
Louis Jordan Φ 03/47 Dec 23841

PEG O' MY HEART (1)
Robbins; orig. pub. 1913, reached #1 in July 1947
(Also reached #1 in December 1913)
Alfred Bryan w, Fred Fisher m
All-time pop standard
The Harmonicats ΦΦΦ 04/47 Vitacoustic 1
Buddy Clark ΦΦ 06/47 Col 37392
The Three Suns ΦΦ 06/47 RCA Vic 20-2212
Art Lund Φ 06/47 MGM 10037
Ted Weems/Bob Edwards Φ 06/47 Merc 5052

A RAINY NIGHT IN RIO
Witmark, pub. 1946, reached #13 in April 1947
Leo Robin w, Arthur Schwartz m
Featured in THE TIME, THE PLACE, AND THE GIRL, film (rel. 12/46)
Jack Carson & Janis Paige, sung in film
Sam Donahue/w.vocal Φ 12/46 Cap 325
Dinah Shore 02/47 Col 37157

RED SILK STOCKINGS AND GREEN PERFUME
E H Morris, pub. 1947, reached #13 in June 1947
Bob Hilliard, Sammy Mysels, Dick Sanford w & m
Sammy Kaye/Don Cornell Φ 05/47 RCA Vic 10-2251
Tony Pastor/<vocal 05/47 Col 37330
Ray McKinley/w.vocal group 05/47 Majestic 7216

ROSES IN THE RAIN
Barton M C, pub. 1947, reached #14 in May 1947
Al Frisch & Fred Wise w, Frankie Carle m
Frankie Carle/Marjorie Hughes Φ 04/47 Col 37252
Matt Dennis/Paul Weston Orch 04/47 Cap 362

SANTA CLAUS IS COMIN' TO TOWN
L Feist, pub. 1934, reached #16 in December 1947
(Also reached #3 in December 1934)
(Also reached Top 20 in December 1935, 1936, 1948)
Haven Gillespie w, J Fred Coots m
Bing Crosby & The Andrews Sisters 12/47 Dec 23281
Johnny Mercer & The Pied Pipers 12/47 Cap 15004

SMOKE! SMOKE! SMOKE! (THAT CIGARETTE) (24)
American Mus. pub. 1947, reached #4 in September 1947
Merle Travis & Tex Williams w & m
Tex Williams ΦΦΦ 07/47 Cap 40001
Phil Harris Φ 08/47 RCA Vic 20-2370

SO FAR (48)
Williamson, pub. 1947, reached #12 in December 1947
Oscar Hammerstein 2nd w, Richard Rodgers m
Featured in ALLEGRO, show (opened 10/47)
Gloria Wills, sung in show, 01/48 RCA Vic 45-0044 (in album)
Frank Sinatra 11/47 Col 37883
Perry Como 10/47 RCA Vic 20-2402

SONATA (40)
Oxford, pub. 1946, reached #12 in February 1947
Ervin Drake & Jimmy Shirl w, Alex Alstone m
Perry Como Φ 12/46 RCA Vic 20-2033
Jo Stafford 01/47 Cap 337
The Three Suns/Artie Dunn 02/47 Majestic 1090

SOONER OR LATER (41)
Santly-Joy, pub. 1946, reached #11 in January 1947
Ray Gilbert w, Charles Wolcott m
Featured in SONG OF THE SOUTH, film (rel. 11/46)
Hattie McDaniel, sung in film
Sammy Kaye/Betty Barclay Φ 11/46 RCA Vic 20-1976
Les Brown/Doris Day 01/47 Col 37153

SUGAR BLUES
Pickwick; orig. pub. 1923, reached #15 in November 1947
(Also reached #20 in April 1931)
(Also reached #16 in August 1935)
Lucy Fletcher w, Clarence Williams m
Johnny Mercer Φ 09/47 Cap 448
Clyde McCoy Orch 08/47 Dec 25014

A SUNDAY KIND OF LOVE
P Maurice, pub. 1946, reached #14 in June 1947
Barbara Belle, Louis Prima, Anita Leonard, Stan Rhodes w & m
Claude Thornhill/Fran Warren 05/47 Col 37219
Jo Stafford 06/47 Cap 388
Ella Fitzgerald 06/47 Dec 23866

TALLAHASSEE (45)
Famous, pub. 1947, reached #11 in August 1947
Frank Loesser w & m
Featured in VARIETY GIRL, film (rel. 07/47)
Bing Crosby & The Andrews Sisters Φ 07/47 Dec 23885
Alan Ladd & Dorothy Lamour, sung in film
Dinah Shore & Woody Herman/Sunny Burke Orch 07/47 Col 37387

TEMPTATION (TIM-TAY-SHUN) (28)
Robbins, pub. 1933, reached #7 in July 1947 (comic version)
(Also reached #8 in February 1934 in its original version)
Arthur Freed, Nacio Herb Brown, Red Ingle w & m
Red Ingle & The Natural Seven/Cinderella G Stump[3] ΦΦΦ 06/47 Cap 412
Eddie Heywood 06/47 Dec 23811
Perry Como 06/47 RCA Vic 20-1658

THAT'S HOW MUCH I LOVE YOU
Vogue Mus, pub. 1946, reached #20 in April 1947
Eddy Arnold, Wally Fowler, J Graydon Hall w & m
Frank Sinatra Φ 03/47 Col 37231
Eddy Arnold 01/47 RCA Vic 20-1948

THAT'S MY DESIRE (3)
Mills, pub. 1931, reached #2 in August 1947
Carroll Loveday & Helmy Kresa w & m
Frankie Laine ΦΦΦ 03/47 Merc 5007
Sammy Kaye/Don Cornell ΦΦ 05/47 RCA Vic 20-2251
Martha Tilton Φ 06/47 Cap 395
Woody Herman/<vocal 06/47 Col 37329
Ella Fitzgerald 07/47 Dec 23866

THAT'S WHERE I CAME IN
Robbins, pub. 1947, reached #18 in May 1947
Charles Tobias w, Peter DeRose m
Perry Como 05/47 RCA Vic 20-2117
Mel Torme 05/47 Musicraft 15111
Jack Fina 04/47 Merc 5021

TIME AFTER TIME
Sinatra Songs, pub. 1947, reached #17 in July 1947
Sammy Cahn w, Jule Styne m
Featured in IT HAPPENED IN BROOKLYN, film (rel. 03/47)
Frank Sinatra, sung in film, 05/47 Col 37300
Tommy Dorsey/Stuart Foster 06/47 RCA Vic 20-2210

TOO FAT POLKA (17)
Shapiro, B, pub. 1947, reached #4 in December 1947
Ross MacLean & Arthur Richardson w & m
Arthur Godfrey/w.vocal trio ΦΦΦ 11/47 Col 37921
Andrews Sisters 02/48 Dec 24268
Louis Prima 02/48 RCA Vic 20-2609

WHEN YOU WERE SWEET SIXTEEN (16)
Shapiro, B; orig. pub. 1898, reached #7 in September 1947
(Also reached #2 in April 1900)
James Thornton w & m
Perry Como ΦΦ 07/47 RCA Vic 20-2259
Mills Brothers 10/47 Dec 23627
Dick Jurgens/Jimmy Castle 10/47 Col 37803

THE WHIFFENPOOF SONG (35)
Miller Mus; orig. pub. 1936, reached #6 in November 1947
George S Pomeroy & Meade Minnigerode w, Tod B Galloway m
Bing Crosby/Fred Waring Glee Club Φ 10/47 Dec 23990
Rudy Vallee/Gentlemen Songsters, stage, 12/47 Col 36461
Robert Merrill 12/47 RCA Vic 10-1313

THE WHISTLER
J L Lester, pub. 1947, reached #19 in January 1948
Hal Dickinson w, Wilbur Hatch m
Sam Donahue/Shirley Lloyd Φ 11/47 Cap 472
The Modernaires/Paula Kelly 12/47 Col 37980

WHITE CHRISTMAS (49)
Berlin, pub. 1942, reached #10 in December 1947
(Also reached #1 in November 1942)
(Also reached Top 20 every December 1943-1955, 1960 & 1961)
Irving Berlin w & m
Bing Crosby Φ 12/47 Dec 23778
Eddy Howard/<vocal 12/47 Majestic 1175
Perry Como 12/47 RCA Vic 20-1970

YOU CAN'T SEE THE SUN WHEN YOU'RE CRYIN' (46)
George Simon, pub. 1946, reached #10 in April 1947
Allan Roberts & Doris Fisher w & m
Vaughn Monroe/<vocal 02/47 RCA Vic 20-2053
The Ink Spots 04/47 Dec 23809

YOU DO (14)
Bregman, V & C, pub. 1947, reached #2 in December 1947
Mack Gordon w, Josef Myrow m
Featured in MOTHER WORE TIGHTS, film (rel. 08/47)
Dinah Shore Φ 10/47 Col 37587
Margaret Whiting Φ 11/47 Cap 438
Vaughn Monroe/<vocal Φ 11/47 RCA Vic 20-2361
Dan Dailey, sung in film
Vic Damone Φ 11/47 Merc 5056

YOU'LL ALWAYS BE THE ONE I LOVE
Sinatra Songs, pub. 1947, reached #17 in March 1947
Sunny Skylar w, Ticker Freeman m
Frank Sinatra, stage and radio
Dinah Shore 02/47 Col 37188
Hal Derwin 02/47 Cap 336

ZIP-A-DEE-DOO-DAH (15)
Santly-Joy, pub. 1945, reached #5 in January 1947
(Also reached #8 in January 1963)
Ray Gilbert w, Allie Wrubel m
Featured in SONG OF THE SOUTH, film (rel. 11/47)
Johnny Mercer/Pied Pipers Φ 12/46 Cap 323
Sammy Kaye/Three Kaydets 12/46 RCA Vic 20-1976
James Baskett, sung in film
Modernaires/Paula Kelly 01/47 Col 37147

[1]Whistling solo by Elmo Tanner.
[2]Buddy Clark's voice was dubbed for Mark Stevens.
[3]Cinderella G Stump was a pseudonym for Jo Stafford.

1948

ALL DRESSED UP WITH A BROKEN HEART
Leeds, pub. 1946, reached #20 in April 1948
Fred Patrick, Claude Reese, Jack Val w & m
Peggy Lee 02/48 Cap 15022
Buddy Clark 02/48 Col 37985
Russ Morgan/Pat Laird 03/48 Dec 24339

ALL I WANT FOR CHRISTMAS (IS MY TWO FRONT TEETH) (36)
Witmark, pub. 1946, reached #5 in December 1948
Don Gardner w & m
Seasonal standard, 1948 through 1950's
Spike Jones/George Rock ΦΦ 11/48 RCA Vic 20-3177

BABY FACE (23)
Remick, pub. 1926, reached #4 in May 1948
(Also reached #1 in October 1926)
(Also reached #14 in February 1976)
Benny Davis w, Harry Akst m
All-time pop standard
Art Mooney/w.vocal group ΦΦ 04/48 MGM 10156
Sammy Kaye/Three Kaydets 05/48 RCA Vic 20-2879
Jack Smith 05/48 Cap 15078
Henry King/Siggy Lane 05/48 Dec 25356

BALLERINA (6)
Jefferson M C, pub. 1947, reached #1 in January 1948
Bob Russell & Carl Sigman w & m
Vaughn Monroe/<vocal ΦΦΦ 11/47 RCA Vic 20-2433
Buddy Clark Φ 01/48 Col 38040
Bing Crosby Φ 01/48 Dec 24278
Jimmy Dorsey/Bob Carroll 01/48 MGM 10035

BECAUSE (41)
Chappell, pub. 1902, reached #11 in April 1948
(Also reached #20 in September 1951)
Edward Teschemacher w, Guy DeHardelot m
Perry Como ΦΦ 03/48 RCA Vic 20-2653
Jan Peerce, stage, (Later: 1949 RCA Vic 10-1454)
Deanna Durbin 03/48 Dec 24295

BEG YOUR PARDON (15)
Robbins, pub. 1947, reached #3 in March 1948
Francis Craig & Beasley Smith w & m
Francis Craig/Bob Lamm ΦΦ 01/48 Bullet 1012
Frankie Carle/Marjorie Hughes Φ 02/48 Col 38036
Larry Green/Don Grady Φ 03/48 RCA Vic 200-3647
Dinning Sisters 02/48 Cap 490

THE BEST THINGS IN LIFE ARE FREE (34)
Crawford; orig. pub. 1927, reached #9 in March 1948
(Also reached #7 in December 1927)
Buddy DeSylva & Lew Brown w, Ray Henderson m
Featured in GOOD NEWS, film (rel. 12/47)
June Allyson & Peter Lawford, sung in film
Dinah Shore 02/48 Col 37984
Jo Stafford 01/48 Cap 15017

BLUEBIRD OF HAPPINESS (29)
Harms, pub. 1934, reached #10 in October 1948
Edward Heyman & Harry Parr Davies w, Sander Harmati m
Art Mooney/Bud Brees Φ 07/48 MGM 10207
Jan Peerce, stage, 10/48 RCA Vic 11-9007,
06/49 RCA Vic 10-1454
Jo Stafford & Gordon MacRae 10/48 Cap 15207

BOUQUET OF ROSES
Hill & Range, pub. 1948, reached #17 in August 1948
Steve Nelson & Bob Hilliard w & m
Eddy Arnold Φ 06/48 RCA Vic 20-2806
Dick Haymes 01/49 Dec 24506
Jimmy Wakely 07/48 Cap 40107

BUT BEAUTIFUL (32)
Burke & Van H, pub. 1947, reached #5 in April 1948
Johnny Burke w, Jimmy Van Heusen m
Featured in ROAD TO RIO, film (rel. 11/47)
Bing Crosby, sung in film, 02/48 Dec 24283
Frank Sinatra Φ 02/48 Col 38053
Frankie Laine 02/48 Merc 5096
Margaret Whiting 02/48 Cap 15024
Art Lund 02/48 MGM 10126

BUTTONS AND BOWS (5)
Famous, pub. 1948, reached #1 in November 1948
Jerry Livingston & Redd Evans w & m
Featured in PALEFACE, film (rel. 10/48)
Dinah Shore ΦΦΦ 09/48 Col 38284
Bob Hope, sung in film
Dinning Sisters Φ 10/48 Cap 15184
Betty Garrett Φ 11/48 MGM 10244
Betty Jane Rhodes Φ 10/48 RCA Vic 20-1944

CARAMBA! IT'S THE SAMBA!
Martin Mus, pub. 1948, reached #20 in June 1948
Irving Taylor, George Wyle, Eddie Pola w & m
Peggy Lee 06/48 Cap 15090
Freddy Martin/Stuart Wade 07/48 RCA Vic 20-2867

CONFESS (43)
Oxford, pub. 1948, reached #12 in August 1948
Bennie Benjamin & George Weiss w & m
Doris Day & Buddy Clark 06/48 Col 38174
Patti Page 06/48 Merc 5129
Tony Martin 07/48 RCA Vic 20-2812

COOL WATER (33)
American Mus, pub. 1936, reached #12 in September 1948
Bob Nolan w & m
Vaughn Monroe/<vocal w. Sons of the Pioneers Φ
07/48 RCA Vic 20-2923
Sons of the Pioneers 08/48 Dec 46027
Tex Ritter/Dinning Sisters 08/48 Cap 48026

CUANTO LE GUSTA (35)
Peer, pub. 1948, reached #10 in January 1949
Ray Gilbert w, Gabriel Ruiz m
Featured in A DATE WITH JUDY, film (rel. 06/48)
Carmen Miranda, sung in film
Andrews Sisters & Carmen Miranda Φ 10/48 Dec 24479
Jack Smith/Clark Sisters 12/48 Cap 15280
Eve Young/Drugstore Cowboys 12/48 RCA Vic 20-3077
Xavier Cugat Orch 01/49 Col 38239

CUCKOO WALTZ
C Hanson, pub. 1948, reached #19 in July 1948
Buddy Kaye w, Emanuel Jonasson m
Ken Griffin 06/48 Rondo 128
Jack Smith/Clark Sisters 08/48 Cap 15156

THE DICKEY-BIRD SONG (24)
Robbins, pub. 1947, reached #7 in May 1948
Howard Dietz w, Sammy Fain m
Featured in THREE DARING DAUGHTERS, film (rel. 02/48)
Freddy Martin/Glen Hughes Φ 04/48 RCA Vic 20-2617
Jeanette MacDonald & Jane Powell, sung in film
Larry Clinton/Helen Lee 05/48 Dec 24301
Blue Barron/Charlie Fisher 04/48 MGM 10138

EV'RY DAY I LOVE YOU (JUST A LITTLE BIT MORE)
Harms, pub. 1948, reached #13 in October 1948
Sammy Cahn w, Jule Styne m
Featured in TWO GUYS FROM TEXAS, film (rel. 08/48)
Dennis Morgan, sung in film
Dick Haymes 09/48 Dec 24457
Vaughn Monroe/<vocal 10/48 RCA Victor 20-2957
Jo Stafford 09/48 Cap 15139

GOLDEN EARRINGS (18)
Paramount, pub. 1947, reached #4 in January 1948
Jay Livingston & Redd Evans w, Victor Young m
Featured in GOLDEN EARRINGS, film (rel. 08/47)
Peggy Lee ΦΦ 11/47 Cap 15009
Marlene Dietrich, sung in film
Dinah Shore 11/47 Col 37932
Bing Crosby 02/48 Dec 24278

HAIR OF GOLD, EYES OF BLUE (27)
Mellin Mus, pub. 1948, reached #7 in October 1948
Sunny Skylar w & m
Gordon MacRae/Starlighters Φ 08/48 Cap 15178
The Harmonicats/The Honeydreamers 08/48 Universal 121
Jack Emerson/Chet Howard Orch 08/48 Metronome 2018
Jack Lathrop/Drugstore Cowboys 10/48 RCA Vic 20-3109
Art Lund 09/49 MGM 10126

HAUNTED HEART
Williamson, pub. 1948, reached #15 in July 1948
Howard Dietz w, Arthur Schwartz m
Featured in INSIDE U.S.A., show (opened 04/48)
Perry Como 03/48 RCA Vic 20-2713
Jo Stafford 02/48 Cap 15023
John Tyers, sung in show

HEARTBREAKER
Leeds, pub. 1947, reached #19 in June 1948
Morty Berk, Frank Campano, Max C Freedman w & m
Andrews Sisters 05/48 Dec 24427
Ferko String Band 04/48 Palda 109

HERE COMES SANTA CLAUS
Western M P C, pub. 1947, reached #13 in December 1948
(Also reached #18 in December 1947 & #16 in December 1949)
Gene Autry & Oakley Haldeman w & m
Gene Autry Φ 12/48 Col 20337
Cliffie Stone 12/48 Cap 15205

HOW LUCKY YOU ARE
P Maurice, pub. 1946, reached #16 in February 1948
Desmond O'Connor w, Eddie Cassen m
Andrews Sisters 12/47 Dec 24171
Charlie Spivak/Tommy Mercer 12/47 RCA Vic 20-2500

I LOVE YOU, YES I DO
Lois M P C, pub. 1947, reached #19 in April 1948
Sally Nix & Henry B Glover w & m
Sammy Kaye/Don Cornell 03/48 RCA Vic 20-2674
Bull Moose Jackson 11/47 King 4181
Dinah Washington 12/47 Mercury 8065

I'LL DANCE AT YOUR WEDDING (25)
George Simon, pub. 1947, reached #5 in January 1948
Herb Magidson w, Ben Oakland m
Ray Noble/Buddy Clark Φ 12/47 Col 37967
Peggy Lee Φ 12/47 Cap 15009
Tony Martin 12/47 RCA Vic 20-2512

I'M A-COMIN' A-COURTIN', CORABELLE
Dreyer, pub. 1947, reached #18 in March 1948
Charles Newman w, Allie Wrubel m
Frankie Carle/Gregg Lawrence 01/48 Col 37972
Hoagy Carmichael/The Chickadees 02/48 Dec 24307
Korn Kobblers/Stanley Fritts 03/48 MGM 10120

I'M LOOKING OVER A FOUR LEAF CLOVER (11)
Remick; orig. pub. 1927, reached #1 in February 1948
(Also reached #1 in June 1927)
Mort Dixon w, Harry Woods m
All-time pop standard
Art Mooney/w.vocal group ΦΦΦ 01/48 MGM 10119
Russ Morgan/Ames Brothers Φ 02/48 Dec 24319
Alvino Rey/w.vocal group Φ 02/48 Cap 491
The Three Suns/Artie Dunn Φ 02/48 RCA Vic 20-2688
Uptown String Band/Joseph Giardino 01/48 Merc 5100

I'M MY OWN GRANDPAW (GRANDMAW) (40)
General, pub. 1947, reached #11 in February 1948
Dwight Latham & Moe Jaffe w & m
Guy Lombardo/Kenny Gardner 03/48 Dec 24288
Lonzo & Oscar 02/48 RCA Vic 20-2583
Jo Stafford 02/48 Cap 15023

IT ONLY HAPPENS WHEN I DANCE WITH YOU (49)
Berlin, pub. 1947, reached #10 in August 1948
Irving Berlin w & m
Featured in EASTER PARADE, film (rel. 06/48)
Fred Astaire, sung in film, 07/49 MGM 30187 (in album)
Frank Sinatra 08/48 Col 38192
Perry Como 08/48 RCA Vic 20-2888

IT'S MAGIC (10)
Witmark, pub. 1948, reached #3 in August 1948
Sammy Cahn w, Jule Styne m
Featured in ROMANCE ON THE HIGH SEAS, film (rel. 06/48)
Doris Day ΦΦΦ sung in film, 07/48 Col 38188
Dick Haymes Φ 07/48 Dec 23826
Gordon MacRae Φ 07/48 Cap 15072
Tony Martin Φ 08/48 RCA Vic 20-2862
Sarah Vaughan/Richard Maltby Orch 08/48 Musicraft 557

JUST BECAUSE (50)
Leeds; orig. pub. 1937, reached #13 in June 1948
Bob Shelton, Joe Shelton, Sydney Robin w & m
Frankie Yankovic/w.vocal duo Φ 05/48 Col 12359
Eddy Howard/<vocal 05/48 Majestic 1231

LAROO, LAROO, LILLI BOLERO
Shapiro, B, pub. 1948, reached #15 in May 1948
Sylvia Dee & Elizabeth Moore w, Sidney Lippman m
Peggy Lee 04/48 Cap 15048
Perry Como 04/48 RCA Vic 20-2734

LIFE GITS TEE-JUS, DON'T IT?
Bob Miller Mus, pub. 1948, reached #19 in November 1948
Carson Robison w & m
Carson Robison Φ 09/48 MGM 10224

LITTLE WHITE LIES (17)
Bregman, V & C; orig. pub. 1930, reached #3 in June 1948
(Also reached #1 in September 1930)
Walter Donaldson w & m
Dick Haymes/Gordon Jenkins Orch ΦΦΦ 04/48 Dec 24280
Dinah Shore Φ 06/48 Col 38114
Mel Torme 06/48 Musicraft 558

LOVE SOMEBODY (16)
Kramer-Whitney, pub. 1947, reached #6 in September 1948
Joan Whitney & Alex Kramer w & m
Doris Day & Buddy Clark ΦΦΦ 05/48 Col 38174
Barbara Frank 07/48 Variety 102

THE MAHARAJAH OF MAGADOR
Mutual, pub. 1947, reached #19 in August 1948
Lewis Harris & John Jacob Loeb w & m
Vaughn Monroe Orch/Ziggy Talent Φ
06/48 RCA Vic 20-2851

MANANA (9)
Capitol Songs, pub. 1948, reached #2 in April 1948
Peggy Lee & Dave Barbour w & m
Peggy Lee ΦΦΦ 01/48 Cap 15009
Mills Brothers 04/48 Dec 24333
Edmundo Ros/w.vocal group 05/48 London 187

MAYBE YOU'LL BE THERE (14)
Triangle M C, pub. 1947, reached #5 in November 1948
Sammy Gallop w, Rube Blume m
Gordon Jenkins/Charles Levere ΦΦΦ 06/48 Dec 24403
Eddy Howard/<vocal 07/48 Majestic 1120
Betty Jane Rhodes 07/48 RCA Vic 20-2189

MY DARLING, MY DARLING (19)
E H Morris, pub. 1948, reached #3 in December 1948
Frank Loesser w & m
Featured in WHERE'S CHARLEY? show (opened 10/48)
Jo Stafford & Gordon MacRae ΦΦ 11/48 Cap 15270
Doris Day & Buddy Clark Φ 11/48 Col 38353
Byron Palmer & Doretta Morrow, sung in show
Peter Lind Hayes 01/49 Dec 24519
Jack Lathrop & Eve Young 01/49 RCA Vic 20-3187

MY HAPPINESS (1)
Blasco Mus, pub. 1948, reached #1 in August 1948
(Also reached #3 in January 1959)
Betty Peterson w, Borney Bergantine m
Jon & Sondra Steele ΦΦΦ 05/48 Damon 11133
Pied Pipers Φ 06/48 Cap 15094
Ella Fitzgerald Φ 06/48 Dec 24446
Marlin Sisters 07/48 Col 38217
John Laurenz 08/48 Merc 5144

NATURE BOY (20)
Burke & Van Heusen, pub. 1948, reached #1 in May 1948
Eden Ahbez w & m
Nat "King" Cole ΦΦΦ 04/48 Cap 15054
Frank Sinatra Φ 05/48 Col 38210
Dick Haymes 06/48 Dec 24439
Sarah Vaughan 07/48 Musicraft 567

NOW IS THE HOUR (2)
Leeds, pub. 1946, reached #1 in March 1948
Dorothy Stewart, Maewa Kaihan, Clement Scott w & m
Bing Crosby ΦΦΦ 01/48 Dec 24279
Margaret Whiting ΦΦ 02/48 Cap 15024
Gracie Fields ΦΦ 01/48 London 110
Buddy Clark Φ 03/48 Col 38115
Eddy Howard/<vocal Φ 02/48 Majestic 1191

ON A SLOW BOAT TO CHINA (13)
Melrose, pub. 1948, reached #2 in November 1948
Frank Loesser w & m
Kay Kyser/Harry Babbitt & Gloria Wood ΦΦΦ
10/48 Col 38301
Freddy Martin/Glen Hughes Φ 11/48 RCA Vic 20-3123
Eddy Howard/<vocal Φ 11/48 Merc 5210
Benny Goodman/Al Hendrickson Φ 11/48 Cap 15208
Art Lund 11/48 MGM 10269

ONE HAS MY NAME (THE OTHER HAS MY HEART)
Peer, pub. 1948, reached #20 in November 1948
(Also reached #13 in January 1966)
Eddie Dean, Dearest Dean, Hal Blair w & m
Jimmy Wakely Φ 10/48 Cap 15162
Bob Eberly 12/48 Dec 24492

PASS THAT PEACE PIPE
Crawford, pub. 1943, reached #16 in January 1948
Roger Edens, Hugh Martin, Ralph Blane w & m
Featured in GOOD NEWS, film (rel. 12/47)
Margaret Whiting Φ 12/47 Cap 15010
Joan McCracken, sung in film
Bing Crosby 01/48 Dec 24269

PIANISSIMO
Santly-Joy, pub. 1947, reached #18 in April 1948
George Weiss & Bennie Benjamin w & m
Perry Como 01/48 RCA Vic 20-2593
Buddy Clark 02/48 Col 38031

PUT 'EM IN A BOX, TIE 'EM WITH A RIBBON (47)
Remick, pub. 1948, reached #11 in August 1948
Sammy Cahn w, Jule Styne m
Featured in ROMANCE ON THE HIGH SEAS, film (rel. 06/48)
Doris Day, sung in film, 06/48 Col 38188
Eddy Howard/<vocal 05/48 Majestic 1252
Nat "King" Cole 07/48 Cap 15060

RAMBLING ROSE (44)
Laurel M C, pub. 1948, reached #12 in October 1948
Joseph McCarthy Jr w, Joe Burke m
Perry Como 08/48 RCA Vic 20-2947
Gordon MacRae 10/48 Cap 15178

SABRE DANCE (31)
Leeds; orig. pub. 1942, reached #6 in April 1948
Allan Roberts & Lester Lee w, Aram Khachaturian m
Woody Herman Orch Φ 03/48 Col 38102
Freddy Martin[1]/Barclay Allen Φ 04/48 RCA Vic 20-2721
Victor Young Orch 04/48 Dec 24338

SANTA CLAUS IS COMIN' TO TOWN
L Feist, pub. 1934, reached #18 in December 1948
(Also reached #3 in December 1934)
(Also reached Top 20 in December 1935, 1936, 1947)
Haven Gillespie w, J Fred Coots m
Bing Crosby & The Andrews Sisters 12/48 Dec 23281
Frank Sinatra 12/48 Col 38259

SAY SOMETHING SWEET TO YOUR SWEETHEART
Mills, pub. 1948, reached #17 in November 1948
Sid Tepper & Roy Brodszky w & m
Jo Stafford & Gordon MacRae Φ 10/48 Cap 15207
Vic Damone & Patti Page 10/48 Merc 5192
The Ink Spots 11/48 Dec 24507

SERENADE OF THE BELLS (12)
Melrose, pub. 1947, reached #3 in January 1948
Kay Twomey, Al Goodhart, Al Urbano w & m
Sammy Kaye/Don Cornell ΦΦ 11/47 RCA Vic 20-2372
Jo Stafford Φ 12/47 Cap 15007
Kay Kyser/Harry Babbitt 01/48 Col 37956
Dick Haymes 03/48 Dec 24305

SHINE (45)
Shapiro, B, pub. 1924, reached #14 in April 1948
(Also reached #5 in July 1924)
Cecil Mack & Lew Brown w, Ford Dabney m
Frankie Laine Φ 01/48 Merc 5091
Ella Fitzgerald 03/48 Dec 25354
Mills Brothers 04/48 Dec 24382

SLAP 'ER DOWN AGIN, PAW (37)
Choice Mus, pub. 1947, reached #10 in March 1948
Polly Arnold, Alice Cornett, Eddie Asherman w & m
Arthur Godfrey/w.vocal trio Φ 02/48 Col 38066
Patsy Montana 03/48 RCA Vic 20-2686

ST. LOUIS BLUES (MARCH) (39)
Handy Bros; orig. pub. 1914, reached #11 in May 1948
(Also reached #16 in September 1920 in its original version)
William C Handy w & m
Tex Beneke Orch Φ 04/48 RCA Vic 20-2722
Danny Kaye/Vic Schoen Orch 05/48 Dec 24401

THE STARS WILL REMEMBER (SO WILL I) (42)
Harms, pub. 1947, reached #13 in March 1948
Leo Towers w, Don Pelosi m
Vaughn Monroe/<vocal 12/47 RCA Vic 20-2433
Frank Sinatra 01/48 Col 37809
Guy Lombardo/Don Rodney 01/48 Dec 24179

TEA LEAVES
E H Morris, pub. 1948, reached #20 in August 1948
Morty Berk, Frank Campano, Max C Freedman w & m
Jack Smith 06/48 Cap 15102
Ella Fitzgerald 06/48 Dec 24446
Emile Cole Serenaders 05/48 Col 38230

TELL ME A STORY (38)
Laurel M C, pub. 1948, reached #10 in June 1948
Maurice Sigler w, Larry Stock m
Sammy Kaye/Don Cornell Φ 05/48 RCA Vic 20-2761
Ames Brothers 05/48 Dec 24329
Vic Damone 05/48 Merc 5120

THAT CERTAIN PARTY
Bourne; orig. pub. 1925, reached #14 in November 1948
(Also reached #4 in February 1926)
Gus Kahn w, Walter Donaldson m
Benny Strong/<vocal Φ 09/48 Tower 1271
Dean Martin & Jerry Lewis 12/48 Cap 15249

TOOLIE OOLIE DOOLIE (THE YODEL POLKA) (22)
C K Harris, pub. 1948, reached #4 in May 1948
Vaughn Horton w, Arthur Beul m
Andrews Sisters ΦΦ 04/48 Dec 24380
The Sportsmen 06/48 Cap 15077
Vaughn Horton 05/48 Continental 1223
Marlin Sisters 06/48 Col 38211

A TREE IN THE MEADOW (4)
Shapiro, B, pub. 1948, reached #1 in October 1948
Billy Reid w & m
Margaret Whiting ΦΦΦ 07/48 Cap 15122
John Laurenz 08/48 Merc 5148
Monica Lewis/Ames Brothers 08/48 Dec 24411
Paul Fennelly/Reggie Goff 09/48 MGM 10211
Sam Browne/Bert Thompson Orch 07/48 London 123

TWELFTH STREET RAG (8)
Shapiro, B; orig. pub. 1916, reached #2 in October 1948
(Also reached #15 in November 1920)
Andy Razaf w, Euday L Bowman m
Pee Wee Hunt Orch ΦΦΦ 06/48 Cap 15105
Frankie Carle Orch 12/48 Col 35572
Milt Herth Trio 08/48 Dec 24450

UNDERNEATH THE ARCHES (30)
Robbins, pub. 1933, reached #6 in October 1948
Reg Connelly, Bud Flanagan, Joe McCarthy w & m
Andrews Sisters Φ 09/48 Dec 24490
Primo Scala/The Keynotes Φ 08/48 London 238
Andy Russell/Pied Pipers 09/48 Cap 15183

UNTIL (26)
Dorsey Bros Mus, pub. 1945, reached #7 in December 1948
Jack Fulton, Bob Crosby, Hunter Kahler w & m
Tommy Dorsey/Harry Prime Φ 09/48 Vic 20-3061
The Charioteers 11/48 Col 38329

WHITE CHRISTMAS (46)
Berlin, pub. 1942, reached #9 in December 1948
(Also reached #1 in November 1942)
(Also reached Top 20 every December 1943-1955, 1960 & 1961)
Irving Berlin w & m
Bing Crosby Φ 12/48 Dec 23778

WILLIAM TELL OVERTURE (IT'S A BEAUTIFUL DAY FOR THE RACES) (48)
Lindley M P C; melody pub. 1829, reached #12 in June 1948
Spike Jones w, Gioachino Rossini m
Spike Jones/Doodles Weaver Φ 06/48 RCA Vic 20-2861

WOODY WOODPECKER (21)
Leeds, pub. 1947, reached #1 in July 1948
George Tibbles & Ramey Idress w & m
Featured in WET BLANKET POLICY, cartoon film (1948)
Kay Kyser/Gloria Wood ΦΦΦ 06/48 Col 38197
Mel Blanc/The Sportsmen ΦΦ 07/48 Cap 15145
Andrews Sisters 07/48 Dec 24462

YOU CALL EVERYBODY DARLIN' (7)
Mayfair, pub. 1946, reached #1 in September 1948
Sam Martin, Ben Trace, Clem Watts w & m
Al Trace/Bob Vincent ΦΦΦ 06/48 Regent 117, 09/48 Sterling 3023
Anne Vincent Φ 07/48 Merc 5155
Andrews Sisters Φ 09/48 Dec 24490
Jack Smith 08/48 Cap 15280
Jerry Wayne 09/48 Col 38286

YOU CAME A LONG WAY FROM ST. LOUIS
Jewel, pub. 1948, reached #16 in September 1948
Bob Russell w, John Benson Brooks m
Ray McKinley/w.vocal group Φ 08/48 RCA Vic 20-2913
Lee Martin Orch 09/48 Varsity 113

YOU CAN'T BE TRUE, DEAR (3)
Biltmore, pub. 1948, reached #1 in June 1948
Gerhard Ebeler & Hal Cotton w, Hans Otten & Ken Griffin m
Ken Griffin/Jerry Wayne ΦΦΦ 04/48 Rondo 228
The Sportsmen Φ 05/48 Cap 15077
Dick Haymes Φ 06/48 Dec 24439
Vera Lynn Φ 05/48 London 202
Will Glahe/w.vocal group 06/48 RCA Vic 25-1117

YOU WERE MEANT FOR ME
Miller Mus; orig. pub. 1929, reached #11 in April 1948
(Also reached #4 in May 1929)
Arthur Freed w, Nacio Herb Brown m
Featured in YOU WERE MEANT FOR ME, film (rel. 01/48)
Dan Dailey, sung in film
Connee Boswell 03/48 Dec 25313
Gordon MacRae 03/48 Cap 15027

YOU WERE ONLY FOOLING (28)
Shapiro, B, pub. 1946, reached #4 in December 1948
William E Faber & Fred Meadows w, Larry Fotine m
Blue Barron/Clyde Burke Φ 10/48 MGM 10185
The Ink Spots Φ 11/48 Dec 24507
Kay Starr 12/48 Cap 15226

YOU'RE ALL I WANT FOR CHRISTMAS
Porgie, pub. 1948, reached #19 in December 1948
Glen Moore & Seger Ellis w & m
Frankie Laine 12/48 Merc 5177
Frank Gallagher 12/48 Dana 2026

[1]Freddy Martin's version was entitled SABRE DANCE BOOGIE.

1949

"A"-YOU'RE ADORABLE (21)
Laurel M C, pub. 1948, reached #3 in May 1949
Buddy Kaye, Fred Wise, Sidney Lippman w & m
Perry Como/Fontane Sisters ΦΦ 04/49 RCA Vic 20-3381
Jo Stafford & Gordon MacRae Φ 04/39 Cap 15393
Tony Pastor/Clooney Sisters 05/49 Col 38449
Buddy Kaye Quintet/Artie Malvin 05/49 MGM 10310

AGAIN (2)
Robbins, pub. 1948, reached #2 in June 1949
Dorcas Cochran w, Lionel Newman m
Featured in ROAD HOUSE, film (rel. 09/48)
Gordon Jenkins/Joe Graydon ΦΦ 04/49 Dec 24602
Doris Day ΦΦ 05/49 Col 38467
Mel Torme ΦΦ 04/49 Cap 15428
Vic Damone Φ 04/49 Merc 5261
Ida Lupino, sung in film

AIN'T SHE SWEET
Advanced; orig. pub. 1927, reached #19 in August 1949
(Also reached #2 in June 1927)
Jack Yellen w, Milt Ager m
Mr. Goon Bones & Mr. Ford Φ 07/49 Crystalette 1803

BABY, IT'S COLD OUTSIDE (17)
E H Morris, pub. 1948, reached #4 in July 1949
Frank Loesser w & m
Featured in NEPTUNE'S DAUGHTER, film (rel. 05/49)
Johnny Mercer & Margaret Whiting ΦΦ 05/49 Cap 567
Dinah Shore & Buddy Clark Φ 05/49 Col 38463
Ella Fitzgerald & Louis Jordan Φ 06/49 Dec 24644
Esther Williams & Ricardo Montalban, sung in film
Sammy Kaye/w.vocal duo 06/49 RCA Vic 20-3448

BALI HA'I (22)
Williamson, pub. 1949, reached #5 in July 1949
Oscar Hammerstein 2nd w, Richard Rodgers m
Featured in SOUTH PACIFIC, show (opened 04/49)
Perry Como Φ 05/49 RCA Vic 20-3402
Juanita Hall, sung in show, 05/49 Col 4562-M (in album)
Peggy Lee 05/49 Cap 543
Bing Crosby 06/49 Dec 24609
Paul Weston 06/49 Cap 629

BEAUTIFUL EYES
Leeds, pub. 1948, reached #20 in March 1949
Frankie Adams, Leonard Rosen, Neal Madaglia w & m
Art Mooney/w.vocal group 02/49 MGM 10357

BLACK COFFEE
Blossom, pub. 1948, reached #20 in June 1949
Sonny Burke & Paul Francis Webster w & m
Sarah Vaughan 06/49 Col 38462
Ella Fitzgerald 06/49 Dec 24646

BLUE CHRISTMAS
Choice Mus, pub. 1948, reached #12 in December 1949
Billy Hayes & Jay Johnson w & m
Seasonal standard, 1949 onward
Hugo Winterhalter/w.vocal group Φ 12/49 Col 38635
Russ Morgan/The Morganaires 12/49 Dec 24766
Ernest Tubb 12/49 Dec 46186

THE BLUE SKIRT WALTZ (32)
Mills, pub. 1948, reached #11 in June 1949
Mitchell Parish w, Vaclav Blaha m
Frankie Yankovic/Marlin Sisters ΦΦ 03/49 Col 12394
Guy Lombardo/w.vocal group 10/49 Dec 24714
Lawrence Duchow/Red Raven Orch 04/49 RCA Vic 20-3356

BRUSH THOSE TEARS FROM YOUR EYES
Leeds, pub. 1949, reached #15 in January 1949
Oakley Haldeman, Al Trace, Jimmy Lee w & m
Evelyn Knight Φ 11/48 Dec 24514
Barry Green 11/48 Rainbow 10090
Buddy Clark 01/49 Col 38364

CANADIAN CAPERS
Remick; orig. pub. 1915, reached #19 in November 1949
(Also reached #10 in December 1921)
Gus Chandler, Bert White, Harry Cohen orig. w & m
Ralph Blane & Harry Warren additional w & m
Featured in MY DREAM IS YOURS, film (rel. 03/49)
Doris Day, sung in film, 10/49 Col 38595
Guy Lombardo Orch 11/49 Dec 24624
Art Mooney Orch 10/49 MGM 10466

CANDY KISSES
Hill & Range, pub. 1948, reached #16 in May 1949
George Morgan w & m
Eddy Howard/<vocal 04/49 Merc 5272
George Morgan 04/49 Col 20547

CARELESS HANDS (16)
Melrose, pub. 1949, reached #4 in April 1949
Bob Hilliard & Carl Sigman w & m
Mel Torme ΦΦ 03/49 Cap 15379
Sammy Kaye/Don Cornell ΦΦ 02/49 RCA Vic 20-3321
Bing Crosby 05/49 Dec 24616
Bob & Jeanne 05/49 Dec 24563

CONGRATULATIONS
Criterion, pub. 1949, reached #20 in February 1949
Paul Weston & Sid Robin w & m
Jo Stafford/Paul Weston Orch 01/49 Cap 15319
Tex Beneke/Gary Stevens 01/49 RCA Vic 20-3237

CRUISING DOWN THE RIVER (3)
Spitzer, pub. 1945, reached #1 in March 1949
Eily Beadell & Nell Tollerton w & m
Russ Morgan/The Skylarks ΦΦΦ 02/49 Dec 24568
Blue Barron/w.vocal group ΦΦΦ 01/49 MGM 10346
Jack Smith Φ 02/49 Cap 15372
Frankie Carle/w.vocal group Φ 03/49 Col 38411
Primo Scala/The Keynotes 03/49 London 356

DANCE OF THE HOURS
Alfred; orig. pub. 1876, reached #20 in September 1949
Spike Jones w & adpt, Amilcare Ponchielli m
Spike Jones/Doodles Weaver Φ 08/49 Vic 20-3516

DON'T CRY, JOE (25)
Harms, pub. 1949, reached #5 in November 1949
Joe Marsala w & m
Gordon Jenkins/Betty Brewer ΦΦ 09/49 Dec 24720
Frank Sinatra Φ 10/49 Col 38555
Ralph Flanagan/Harry Prime 11/49 Vic/Blu 30-0007
Juanita Hall 11/49 RCA Victor 20-3557
Johnny Desmond 12/49 MGM 10518

DOWN BY THE STATION (45)
Am Acad Mus, pub. 1948, reached #15 in February 1949
Lee Ricks & Slim Gaillard w & m
Tommy Dorsey/w.vocal group Φ 01/49 RCA Vic 20-3317
Guy Lombardo/w.vocal trio Φ 02/49 Dec 24555
Slim Gaillard Trio 02/49 MGM 10309

A DREAMER'S HOLIDAY (19)
Skidmore Mus, pub. 1949, reached #4 in December 1949
Kim Gannon w, Mabel Wayne m
Perry Como/Fontane Sisters ΦΦ 10/49 RCA Vic 20-3543
Buddy Clark 11/49 Col 38599
Ray Anthony/Dick Noel 11/49 Cap 761
Gordon Jenkins/Eileen Wilson 12/49 Dec 24638

ENVY
Regent, pub. 1947, reached #20 in November 1949
Eve Sherman w, David Gussin m
Fran Warren 10/49 RCA Vic 20-3551

EVERYWHERE YOU GO
Lombardo Mus; orig. pub. 1927, reached #16 in June 1949
Larry Shay, Joe Goodwin, Mark Fisher w & m
Guy Lombardo/Don Rodney 04/49 Dec 24549
Doris Day 06/49 Col 38467
Bing Crosby & Evelyn Knight 06/49 Dec 24612

FAR AWAY PLACES (6)
Laurel M C, pub. 1948, reached #1 in February 1949
Joan Whitney & Alex Kramer w & m
Margaret Whiting ΦΦ 12/48 Cap 15278
Bing Crosby ΦΦ 01/49 Dec 24532
Perry Como Φ 01/49 RCA Vic 20-3316
Dinah Shore 01/49 Col 38356

FIDDLE DEE DEE
Harms, pub. 1949, reached #18 in October 1949
Sammy Cahn w, Jule Styne m
Sung by quartet in IT'S A GREAT FEELING, film (rel. 08/49)
Sammy Kaye/Three Kaydets 09/49 RCA Vic 20-3483
Guy Lombardo/w.vocal trio 11/49 Dec 24763
Jimmy Dorsey/Claire Hogan 09/49 Col 38523

FIVE FOOT TWO, EYES OF BLUE
L Feist, pub. 1925, reached #15 in June 1949
(Also reached #3 in February 1926)
Sam Lewis & Joe Young w, Ray Henderson m
Benny Strong/<vocal 05/49 Tower 1456
Art Mooney/w.vocal group 06/49 MGM 10398
Guy Lombardo/Kenny Gardner 06/49 Dec 24615

FOR YOU
Witmark, pub. 1930, reached #20 in January 1949
(Also reached #15 in May 1931)
(Also reached #6 in February 1964)
Al Dubin w, Joe Burke m
Artie Wayne 11/48 Cap 15140
Gordon Jenkins/w.vocal group 11/48 Dec 24478
Perry Como 12/48 RCA Vic 20-3099

FOREVER AND EVER (4)
Robbins, pub. 1948, reached #1 in May 1949
Malia Rosa w, Franz Winkler m
Russ Morgan/The Skylarks ΦΦ 03/49 Dec 24569
Perry Como ΦΦ 03/49 RCA Vic 20-3347
Margaret Whiting Φ 04/49 Cap 15386
Dinah Shore 04/49 Col 3841
Gracie Fields 04/49 London 362

THE FOUR WINDS AND THE SEVEN SEAS (36)
Lombardo Mus, pub. 1949, reached #7 in August 1949
Hal David w, Don Rodney m
Sammy Kaye/Tony Alamo, Φ 06/49 RCA Vic 20-3459
Mel Torme Φ 07/49 Cap 671
Vic Damone 07/49 Merc 5271
Herb Jeffries 07/49 Col 38511
Guy Lombardo/Don Rodney 08/49 Dec 24648

GALWAY BAY (24)
Leeds, pub. 1947, reached #4 in March 1949
Arthur Colahan w & m
Bing Crosby ΦΦ 01/49 Dec 24295
Anne Shelton 02/49 London 287
Dennis Day, radio, 04/49 RCA Vic 20-3413

GLORIA
Leon Rene, pub. 1948, reached #16 in December 1948
Leon Rene w & m
Mills Brothers 11/48 Dec 24509
Buddy Clark/Modernaires 01/49 Col 38352

GRIEVING FOR YOU
L Feist, pub. 1920, reached #19 in February 1949
Joe Gibson, Joe Ribaud, Joe Gold w & m
Tony Pastor/Rosemary Clooney 02/49 Col 38383

HERE COMES SANTA CLAUS
Western M P C, pub. 1947, reached #16 in December 1949
(Also reached #18 in December 1947 & #13 in December 1948)
Gene Autry & Oakley Haldeman w & m
Gene Autry Φ 12/49 Col 20377
Doris Day 12/49 Col 38584

HOP-SCOTCH POLKA (42)
Cromwell Mus, pub. 1949, reached #11 in October 1949
Billy Whitlock, Carl Sigman, Gene Rayburn w & m
Art Mooney/w.vocal group 09/49 MGM 10500
Guy Lombardo/Kenny Gardner 10/49 Dec 24704

THE HOT CANARY
Leeds, pub. 1948, reached #20 in March 1949
(Also reached #18 in April 1951)
Paul Nero & Paul Yakim m
Paul Weston/Paul Nero[1] 03/49 Cap 15373

THE HUCKLE BUCK (29)
United M C, pub. 1949, reached #7 in September 1949
(Also reached #18 in November 1960)
Roy Alfred w, Andy Gibson m
Tommy Dorsey/Charlie Shavers Φ 06/49 RCA Vic 20-3427
Frank Sinatra Φ 06/49 Col 38486
Paul Williams 07/49 Savoy 683
Lionel Hampton Orch 07/49 Dec 24652

I CAN DREAM, CAN'T I? (7)
Chappell, pub. 1937, reached #1 in January 1950
(Also reached #9 in March 1938)
Irving Kahal w, Sammy Fain m
Andrews Sisters ΦΦΦ 09/49 Dec 24705
Toni Arden Φ 11/49 Col 39612
Tex Beneke/Glenn Douglas Φ 11/49 RCA Vic 20-3553
Glen Gray/Kenny Sargent 11/49 Coral 60106

I DON'T SEE ME IN YOUR EYES ANYMORE (28)
Laurel M C, pub. 1949, reached #7 in July 1949
Bennie Benjamin & George Weiss w & m
Gordon Jenkins/The Stardusters Φ 04/49 Dec 24576
Perry Como Φ 04/49 RCA Vic 20-3347
Vera Lynn 06/49 London 403

I LOVE YOU SO MUCH IT HURTS (37)
Melody Lane, pub. 1948, reached #11 in February 1949
Floyd Tillman w & m
Mills Brothers Φ 02/49 Dec 24550
Jimmy Wakely 12/48 Cap 15243
Reggie Goff 02/49 London 312
Buddy Clark 03/49 Col 38406

I NEVER SEE MAGGIE ALONE (40)
Bourne; orig. pub. 1926, reached #11 in November 1949
Henry B Tilsley w, Everett Lynton & Horatio Nicholls m
Kenny Roberts Φ 09/49 Coral 64012
Art Mooney/Tex Fletcher 11/49 MGM 10548
Eddie Cantor, TV, 11/49 Vic/Blu 30-0010
Benny Strong/<vocal 11/49 Cap 750

I YUST GO NUTS AT CHRISTMAS
Beechwood M C, pub. 1949, reached #14 in December 1949
Harry Stewart w & m
Seasonal seller, 1949-1954
Yogi Yorgesson[2] Φ 12/49 Cap 781

I'LL NEVER SLIP AROUND AGAIN (44)
Peer, pub. 1949, reached #13 in November 1949
Floyd Tillman w & m
Margaret Whiting & Jimmy Wakely Φ 11/49 Cap 40246
Floyd Tillman 11/49 Col 20613

I'VE GOT A LOVELY BUNCH OF COCONUTS (33)
Cornell Mus, pub. 1949, reached #10 in November 1949
Fred Heatherton w & m
Freddy Martin/Merv Griffin Φ 10/49 RCA Vic 20-3554
Danny Kaye 01/50 Dec 24784
Primo Scala/w.vocal group 10/49 London 449

I'VE GOT MY LOVE TO KEEP ME WARM (30)
Berlin, pub. 1937, reached #5 in February 1949
(Also reached #4 in April 1937)
Irving Berlin w & m
Les Brown ΦΦΦ 12/48 Col 38324
Mills Brothers Φ 02/49 Dec 24550
Art Lund 02/49 MGM 10348
The Starlighters 02/49 Cap 15330

IT'S A BIG, WIDE, WONDERFUL WORLD
BMI, pub. 1940, reached #19 in May 1949
John Rox w & m
Buddy Clark 03/49 Col 38370
Hildegarde 05/49 Dec 24628

JEALOUS HEART (18)
Acuff-Rose, pub. 1944, reached #5 in October 1949
Jennie Lou Carson w & m
Al Morgan ΦΦ 07/49 London 500
Hugo Winterhalter/Johnny Thompson 10/49 Col 38593
Jack Owens 10/49 Dec 24711
Bill Lawrence/Henri Rene Orch 10/49 RCA Vic 20-3539
Jan Garber/Don Grabeau 11/49 Cap 759

JUST ONE WAY TO SAY I LOVE YOU
Berlin, pub. 1949, reached #15 in September 1949
Irving Berlin w & m
Featured in MISS LIBERTY, show (opened 07/49)
Eddie Albert & Allyn McLerie, sung in show
Jo Stafford 08/49 Cap 665
Perry Como 07/49 RCA Vic 20-3469

KISS ME SWEET
Advanced, pub. 1949, reached #14 in June 1949
Milton Drake w & m
Sammy Kaye/w.vocal duo 05/49 RCA Vic 20-2420
Kitty Kallen 05/49 Merc 5265

LADY OF SPAIN
Sam Fox, pub. 1931, reached #19 in March 1949
(Also reached #9 in November 1931)
(Also reached #5 in December 1952)
Erell Reaves w, Tolchard Evans m
Ray Noble/w.vocal trio 02/49 RCA Vic 20-3302

THE LAST MILE HOME
Leeds, pub. 1949, reached #20 in October 1949
Walter Kent & Walton Farmer w & m
Jo Stafford Φ 10/49 Cap 710
Gracie Fields, stage

LAVENDER BLUE (20)
Santly-Joy, pub. 1948, reached #4 in February 1949
(Also reached #4 in August 1959)
Larry Morey w, Elliot Daniel m
Featured in SO DEAR TO MY HEART, film (rel. 12/48)
Dinah Shore Φ sung in film, 12/48 Col 38299
Sammy Kaye/Three Kaydets Φ 12/48 RCA Vic 20-3100
Jack Smith 01/49 Cap 15225
Vera Lynn 12/48 London 310
Burl Ives 02/49 Dec 24547

LET'S TAKE AN OLD-FASHIONED WALK (35)
Berlin, pub. 1949, reached #8 in September 1949
Irving Berlin w & m
Featured in MISS LIBERTY, show (opened 07/49)
Perry Como 07/49 RCA Vic 20-3469
Eddie Albert & Allyn McLerie, sung in show
Frank Sinatra & Doris Day 08/49 Col 38513
Dick Haymes/Gordon Jenkins Orch 08/49 Dec 24666

A LITTLE BIRD TOLD ME (11)
Bourne, pub. 1947, reached #1 in January 1949
Harvey O Brooks w & m
Evelyn Knight ΦΦΦ 11/48 Dec 24514
Blu Lu Barker Φ 12/48 Cap 15308
Paula Watson Φ 11/48 Supreme 1507
Jerry Wayne 01/49 Col 38386

MAYBE IT'S BECAUSE (27)
Bregman, V & C, pub. 1949, reached #5 in September 1949
Harry Ruby w, Johnny Scott m
Dick Haymes Φ 07/49 Dec 24650
Eddy Howard/<vocal Φ 08/49 Merc 5314
Connie Haines 09/49 Coral 60070
Bob Crosby/Marion Morgan 10/49 Col 38504

MERRY-GO-ROUND WALTZ
Shapiro, B, pub. 1949, reached #17 in June 1949
Jimmy Kennedy & Arthur Finn w & adpt, Juventino Rosas m
Guy Lombardo/Kenny Gardner 05/49 Dec 24624
Art Mooney/w.vocal group 06/49 MGM 10405

MULE TRAIN (23)
Walt Disney M C, pub. 1949, reached #1 in December 1949
Johnny Lange, Hy Heath, Fred Glickman w & m
Featured in SINGING GUNS, film (rel. 03/50)
Frankie Laine ΦΦΦ 11/49 Merc 5345
Vaughn Monroe Φ sung in film, 11/49 RCA Vic 20-3600
Bing Crosby Φ 11/49 Dec 24798
Tennessee Ernie Φ 11/49 Cap 40258
Gordon MacRae 11/49 Cap 777

MY BOLERO
Shapiro, B, pub. 1949, reached #19 in September 1949
Jimmy Kennedy w, Nat Simon m
Featured in COME TO THE STABLE, film (rel. 06/49)
Vic Damone Φ 08/49 Merc 5313
Reggie Goff 09/49 London 491
Eddie Fisher 09/49 Vic/Blu 30-0011

MY ONE AND ONLY HIGHLAND FLING
H Warren, pub. 1948, reached #18 in July 1949
Ira Gershwin w, Harry Warren m
Featured in THE BARKLEYS OF BROADWAY, film (rel. 04/49)
Fred Astaire & Ginger Rogers, sung in film and 06/49 MGM 50016
Dinah Shore & Buddy Clark 06/49 Col 38463
Jo Stafford & Gordon MacRae 06/49 Cap 566

NEED YOU (43)
Choice Mus, pub. 1949, reached #11 in May 1949
Johnny Blackburn, Teepee Mitchell, Lew Porter w & m
Jo Stafford & Gordon MacRae Φ 04/49 Cap 15393
Guy Lombardo/Kenny Gardner 06/49 Dec 24614

NOW THAT I NEED YOU (50)
Famous, pub. 1949, reached #13 in October 1949
Frank Loesser w & m
Featured in RED, HOT AND BLUE, film (rel. 07/49)
Betty Hutton, sung in film, 08/49 Cap 620
Doris Day 08/49 Col 38507
Frankie Laine 09/49 Merc 5311

ONCE IN LOVE WITH AMY
E H Morris, pub. 1948, reached #20 in May 1949
Frank Loesser w & m
Featured in WHERE'S CHARLEY? show (opened 10/48)
Ray Bolger, sung in show, 04/49 Dec 40065
Dean Martin 02/49 Cap 15329
Freddy Martin/Merv Griffin 03/49 RCA Vic 20-3324

POWDER YOUR FACE WITH SUNSHINE (15)
Lombardo Mus, pub. 1948, reached #3 in February 1949
Carmen Lombardo & Stanley Rochinski w & m
Evelyn Knight ΦΦ 12/48 Dec 24530
Dean Martin Φ 02/49 Cap 15351
Guy Lombardo, stage and radio
Sammy Kaye/Three Kaydets 02/49 RCA Vic 20-3312
Blue Barron/w.vocal group 02/49 MGM 10346

THE PUSSY CAT SONG (47)
Leeds, pub. 1948, reached #13 in February 1949
Dick Manning w & m
Patty Andrews & Bob Crosby 01/49 Dec 24533
Perry Como/Fontane Sisters 01/49 RCA Vic 20-3288
Joy Nichols & Benny Lee 02/49 London 365
Jo Stafford & Gordon MacRae 02/49 Cap 15342

RAGTIME COWBOY JOE
Alfred Mus Co; orig. pub. 1912, reached #19 in October 1949
(Also reached #11 in October 1912)
(Also reached #15 in August 1959)
Grant Clarke w, Lewis F Muir & Maurice Abrahams m
Jo Stafford Φ 09/49 Cap 710
Eddy Howard/<vocal 09/49 Majestic 1155

RED ROSES FOR A BLUE LADY (14)
Mills, pub. 1948, reached #3 in April 1949
(Also reached #5 in March 1965)
Sid Tepper & Roy Brodszky w & m
Vaughn Monroe/<vocal w. Moon Maids ΦΦ 01/49 RCA Vic 20-3319
Guy Lombardo/Don Rodney Φ 02/49 Dec 24549
John Laurenz 04/49 Merc 5201

RIDERS IN THE SKY (8)
Mayfair, pub. 1949, reached #1 in June 1949
Stan Jones w & m
Featured in RIDERS IN THE SKY, film (rel. 12/49)
Vaughn Monroe/<vocal ΦΦΦ 04/49 RCA Vic 20-3411
Gene Autry, sung in film
Peggy Lee Φ 05/49 Cap 608
Bing Crosby 05/49 Dec 24618
Burl Ives 04/49 Col 38445

ROOM FULL OF ROSES (9)
Hill & Range, pub. 1949, reached #1 in September 1949
Tim Spencer w & m
Sammy Kaye/Don Cornell ΦΦ 06/49 RCA Vic 20-3441
Eddy Howard/<vocal ΦΦ 07/49 Merc 5296
Dick Haymes Φ 06/49 Dec 24632
Jerry Wayne Φ 08/49 Col 38525
George Morgan 10/49 Col 20594

RUDOLPH, THE RED-NOSED REINDEER (41)
St. Nicholas M P C, pub. 1949, reached #6 in December 1949
(Also reached Top 20 every December, 1950 to 1954)
Johnny Marks w & m
All-time Christmas standard
Gene Autry ΦΦ 12/49 Col 38610
Eddy Howard/w.vocal trio 12/49 Merc 5360

SLIPPING AROUND (12)
Peer, pub. 1949, reached #3 in November 1949
Floyd Tillman w & m
Margaret Whiting & Jimmy Wakely ΦΦΦ 09/49 Cap 40224
Ernest Tubb Φ 11/49 Dec 46173
Floyd Tillman 10/49 Col 20581

SO IN LOVE (39)
Harms, pub. 1948, reached #11 in April 1949
Cole Porter w & m
Featured in KISS ME KATE, show (opened 12/48)
Alfred Drake, sung in show, 04/49 RCA Vic 20-3352
Patti Page 02/49 Merc 5230
Gordon MacRae 03/49 Cap 15357
Dinah Shore 03/49 Col 28299

SO TIRED (26)
Glenmore, pub. 1943, reached #8 in March 1949
Russ Morgan & Jack Stuart w & m
Russ Morgan/<vocal Φ 12/48 Dec 24521
Kay Starr Φ 01/49 Cap 15314
Freddy Martin/Merv Griffin 03/49 RCA Vic 20-3350

SOME ENCHANTED EVENING (1)
Williamson, pub. 1949, reached #1 in July 1949
(Also reached #13 in October 1965)
Oscar Hammerstein 2nd w, Richard Rodgers m
Featured in SOUTH PACIFIC, show (opened 04/49)
Perry Como ΦΦΦ 04/49 RCA Vic 20-3402
Ezio Pinza, sung in show and 05/49 Col 4559-M (album), 09/49 Col 4559-M (single)
Bing Crosby ΦΦ 05/49 Dec 24609
Jo Stafford Φ 05/49 Cap 544
Frank Sinatra Φ 06/49 Col 38446

SOMEDAY (YOU'LL WANT ME TO WANT YOU) (13)
Duchess; orig. pub. 1940, reached #2 in October 1949
Jimmie Hodges w & m
Vaughn Monroe/<vocal ΦΦ 08/49 RCA Vic 20-3510
Mills Brothers Φ 08/49 Dec 24694
Elton Britt 08/49 RCA Vic 20-3090

SOMEONE LIKE YOU
Harms, pub. 1949, reached #13 in May 1949
Ralph Blane w, Harry Warren m
Featured in MY DREAM IS YOURS, film (rel. 03/49)
Doris Day, sung in film, 03/49 Col 38375
Peggy Lee 03/49 Cap 15349
Eddy Howard/<vocal 05/49 Merc 5254
Tommy Dorsey/Denny Dennis 04/49 RCA Vic 20-3348

SUNFLOWER (31)
Famous, pub. 1948, reached #4 in April 1949
Mack David w & m
Russ Morgan/The Skylarks Φ 02/49 Dec 24568
Jack Fulton 03/49 Tower 1454
Jack Smith 04/49 Cap 15394
Frank Sinatra 03/49 Col 38391
Ray McKinley/Jean Friley 03/49 RCA Vic 20-3334

SWEET GEORGIA BROWN (46)
Remick, pub. 1925, reached #15 in February 1949
(Also reached #2 in August 1925)
Ben Bernie, Maceo Pinkard, Kenneth Casey w & m
Brother Bones & His Shadows Φ 11/48 Tempo 652
Whistling Mr. Jones 09/49 National 9063
Benny Strong/<vocal 11/48 Tower 1255

TARA TALARA TALA
Oxford, pub. 1948, reached #19 in February 1949
Marty Symes & Johnny Farrow w & m
Frankie Laine 12/48 Merc 5177
Johnny Desmond 01/49 MGM 10287

THAT LUCKY OLD SUN (10)
Robbins, pub. 1949, reached #1 in November 1949
(Also reached #20 in January 1964)
Haven Gillespie w, Beasley Smith m
Frankie Laine ΦΦΦ 08/49 Merc 5316
Vaughn Monroe/<vocal Φ 09/49 RCA Vic 20-3531
Louis Armstrong 10/49 Dec 24752
Sarah Vaughan 09/49 Col 38559
Frank Sinatra 10/49 Col 38608

THERE'S YES! YES! IN YOUR EYES (48)
Remick, pub. 1924, reached #15 in September 1949
(Also reached #2 in July 1924)
Cliff Friend w, Joe Santly m
Eddy Howard/<vocal 08/49 Merc 5296
Carmen Cavallaro/w.vocal group 09/49 Dec 24678
Blue Barron/w.vocal group 08/49 MGM 10417
Tony Pastor/<vocal 08/49 Col 38521

THROUGH A LONG AND SLEEPLESS NIGHT
Miller Mus, pub. 1949, reached #18 in November 1949
Mack Gordon & Alfred Newman m
Featured in COME TO THE STABLE, film (rel. 06/49)
Vic Damone 09/49 Merc 5313
Dinah Shore 09/49 Col 38539

TWENTY-FOUR HOURS OF SUNSHINE
Advanced, pub. 1949, reached #11 in September 1949
Carl Sigman w, Peter DeRose m
Art Mooney/w.vocal group 07/49 MGM 10405
Carmen Cavallaro/The Cavaliers 08/49 Dec 24676

WHISPERING HOPE (38)
Oliver Ditson, orig. pub. 1868, reached #10 in October 1949
Septimus Winner[3] w & m
Jo Stafford & Gordon MacRae ΦΦ 08/49 Cap 690
Ralph Flanagan/Harry Prime 09/49 Vic/Blu 30-0008
Andrews Sisters 11/49 Dec 24717

WHITE CHRISTMAS (49)
Berlin, pub. 1942, reached #10 in December 1949
(Also reached #1 in November 1942)
(Also reached Top 20 every December 1943-1955, 1960 & 1961)
Irving Berlin w & m
Bing Crosby Φ 12/49 Dec 23778

A WONDERFUL GUY (34)
Williamson, pub. 1949, reached #9 in July 1949
Oscar Hammerstein 2nd w, Richard Rodgers m
Featured in SOUTH PACIFIC, show (opened 04/49)
Mary Martin, sung in show, 05/49 Col 4561 (in album)
Margaret Whiting Φ 05/49 Cap 542
Fran Warren 07/49 RCA Vic 20-3403
Dinah Shore 06/49 Col 38460

YINGLE BELLS (JINGLE BELLS)
Beechwood M C, pub. 1949, reached #17 in December 1949
J S Pierpont & Harry Stewart w & m
Yogi Yorgesson[2] Φ 12/49 Cap 781

YOU'RE BREAKING MY HEART (5)
Algonquin Mus, pub. 1948, reached #1 in September 1949
Peter Genaro & Sunny Skylar w & adpt, Ruggiero Leoncavallo m
Vic Damone ΦΦΦ 06/49 Merc 5271
Buddy Clark Φ 08/49 Col 38546
The Ink Spots Φ 08/49 Dec 24693
Ralph Flanagan/Harry Prime 09/49 Vic/Blu 30-0001
Jan Garber/Don Grabeau 09/49 Cap 719

YOU'RE SO UNDERSTANDING
Barron-Pemora, pub. 1949, reached #18 in August 1949
Bernie Wayne & Ben Raleigh w & m
Evelyn Knight 08/49 Dec 24636
Blue Barron/Bobby Beers 05/49 MGM 10369

[1]Paul Nero on violin.
[2]Yogi Yorgesson was a pseudonym for Harry Stewart.
[3]For this song, Septimus Winner used pen name "Alice Hawthorne."

APPENDIX

APPENDIX

ABBREVIATIONS USED IN SECTION 4

PUBLISHERS

20th Century Mus	Twentieth Century Music Corp.
A J Stasny	A. J. Stasny Music Co.
A Scull	A. Scull Music Co.
A W Tams	Arthur W. Tams
A-1 Mus	A-1 Music Publishers
ABC Music	ABC Music Corp.
Acuff-Rose	Acuff-Rose Publications
Adams, V & A	Adams, Vee & Abbott, Inc.
Advanced	Advanced Music Corp.
Ager, Y & B	Ager, Yellen & Bornstein, Inc.
Albright	Albright Music Co.
Alfred Mus Co	Alfred Music Co.
Algonquin	Algonquin Music, Inc.
Am Acad Mus	American Academy of Music, Inc.
American Advance	American Advance Music Co.
American Mus	American Music, Inc.
Artmusic	Artmusic Inc.
Attucks	The Attucks Music Publishing Co.
B Warren	Bob Warren Publishers
Barron-Pemora	Barron-Pemora Music Co.
Barton M C	Barton Music Corp.
Beacon Mus	Beacon Music Co.
Beechwood M C	Beechwood Music Corp.
Bell Mus Co	Bell Music Co.
Berge Mus Co	Berge Music Co.
Bergstrom Mus Co	Bergstrom Music Co.
Berlin	Irving Berlin, Inc.
Bibo & Lange	Bibo, Lange, Inc.
Biltmore	Biltmore Music Corp.
Blasco Mus	Blasco Music, Inc.
Blossom	Blossom Music Corp.
BMI	Broadcast Music, Inc.
Bob Miller	Bob Miller Music, Inc.
Boston Mus Co	Boston Music Co
Bourne	Bourne, Inc.
Braun	Braun Music, Inc.
Bregman, V & C	Bregman, Vocco & Conn, Inc.
Broadway Mus Co	Broadway Music Co. (orig. Will Von Tilzer)
Burke & Van H	Burke & Van Heusen, Inc.
C Hanson	Charles Hanson Music Corp.
C Jacobs-Bond	Carrie Jacobs-Bond & Son
C K Harris	Charles K. Harris
C Laemmle	Carl Laemmle Music Co.
Campbell	Campbell Music Co.
Campbell, Connelly	Campbell, Connelly & Co.
Campbell, L & P	Campbell, Loft & Porgie, Inc.
Campbell-Porgie	Campbell-Porgie, Inc.
Capitol Mus	Capitol Music, Inc.
Capitol Songs	Capitol Songs, Inc.
Carl Fischer	Carl Fischer, Inc.
Chappell	Chappell & Co.
Charling	Charling Music Corp.
Chelsea	Chelsea Music Corp.
Cherio	Cherio Music Publishers, Inc.
Choice Mus	Choice Music Inc.
Circle Mus	Circle Music Publications, Inc.
Clarence Wms M P C	Clarence Williams Music Publ. Co. Inc.
Conrad Mus	Con Conrad Music Corp.
Cooper, K & P	Cooper, Kendis & Paley
Cornell Mus	Cornell Music, Inc.
Craig & Co	Craig & Co.
Crawford	Crawford Music Corp.
Criterion	Criterion Music Corp.
Cromwell Mus	Cromwell Music, Inc.
Dash-Connelly	Dash-Connelly, Inc.
Davis, C & E	Davis, Coots & Engle
Dellwoods Mus Hs	Dellwoods Music House
Denton & Haskins	Denton & Haskins Music Co.
DeSylva, B & H	DeSylva, Brown & Henderson, Inc.
Disney Prod	Disney Productions, Inc.
Donaldson, D & G	Donaldson, Douglas & Gumble, Inc.
Dorsey Bros	Dorsey Brothers' Music, Inc.
Doty & Brill	(Charles) Doty & (Edward) Brill Publishers
Drake, H & L	Drake, Hoffman & Livington
Dreyer	Dreyer Music Corp.
Duchess	Duchess Music Corp.
E B Marks	Edw(ard) B Marks Co.
E H Morris	Edwin H. Morris & Co.
E T Paull	E(dward) T. Paull Music Co.
Eclipse Mus Co	Eclipse Music Co.
Elar M C	Elar Music Corp.
Ellis Mus Co	Ellis Music Co.
Embassy	Embassy Music Corp.
Encore	Encore Music Publishers, Inc.
Exclusive	Exclusive Publications, Inc.

F A Mills	F. A. Mills
F B Haviland	F. B. Haviland Publishing Co.
F Fisher	Fred Fisher, Inc.
Famous	Famous Music Corp.
Famous	Famous Music Corp.
Forster M P	(F. A.) Forster Music Publisher
Forster M P C	Forster Music Publishing Co.
Fowler M C	Fowler Music Corp.
Francis, D & H	Francis, Day & Hunter
Freed & Powers	Freed & Powers, Ltd.
G M Krey	George M. Krey
G Ricordi	G. Ricordi & Co.
G Schirmer	G. Schirmer, Inc.
G W Fager	George W. Fager Music Co.
G W Meyer	George W. Meyer Music Co.
General M P C	General Music Publishing Co., Inc.
George P Jennings	George P. Jennings Music Co.
George Simon	George Simon, Inc.
Gershwin P C	Gershwin Publishing Co.
Gilbert & Friedland	Gilbert & Friedland Inc.
Glenmore	Glenmore Music Inc.
Gotham M S	Gotham Music Service, Inc.
Gotham-Attucks	Gotham-Attucks Music Co.
Grande	Grande Music Corp.
Green Bros/Knight	Green Brothers & Knight
Greene-Revel	Greene-Revel Inc.
Gus Edwards M P C	Gus Edwards Music Publishing Co.
H F Odell	H. F. Odell
H S Gordon	Hamilton S. Gordon
H Von Tilzer	Harry Von Tilzer Music Publishing Co.
H Warren	(Harry) Warren Music Inc.
H Waterson	Henry Waterson, Inc.
Handy Bros	Handy Brothers Music Co.
Harms	Harms, Inc.
Harold Rossiter	Harold Rossiter Music Co.
Harry Wms Mus Co	Harry Williams Music Co.
Head M P C	Head Music Publishing Co.
Head-Westman	Head-Westman Publishing Co.
Helf & Hager	Helf & Hager Co., Inc.
Hill & Range	Hill and Range Songs, Inc.
Hill, H & B	Hill, Horwitz & Bowers
Hollywood Mus	Hollywood Music Corp.
Howley, H & D	Howley, Haviland & Dresser
Howley, Haviland	Howley, Haviland
Howley-Dresser	Howley-Dresser Co.
Hudson	Hudson Music Corp.
Hugo V Schlam	Hugo V. Schlam
Hylands, S & Y	Hylands, Spencer & Yeager
I Dash	The Irwin Dash Music Co.
I Jones Inc.	Isham Jones, Inc.
I Jones M C	Isham Jones Music Corp.
Irving Caesar Inc	Irving Caesar, Inc.
J F Helf	J. Fred Helf Co.
J Franklin	John Franklin Music Co.
J H Remick	Jerome H. Remick & Co.
J L Lester	J. L. Lester
J M Daly	(Joseph) M Daly
J Mills	Jack Mills, Inc.
J Morris	The Joe Morris Co.
J W Stern	Jos(eph) W. Stern & Co.
J W York	J. W. York & Sons
Jefferson M C	Jefferson Music Co.
Jenkins Mus Co	J. W. Jenkins Music Co.
Jenkins Sons	J. W. Jenkins Sons Music Co.
Jerome & Schwartz	(Wm.) Jerome & (Jean) Schwartz Music Co.
Jewel	Jewel Music Publishing Co.
Joe Davis	Joe Davis, Inc.
John Church Co	John Church Co.
John T Hall	John T. Hall Publishing Co.
Kalmar & Puck	Kalmar & Puck Music Co.
Kalmar & Ruby	Kalmar & Ruby Corp.
Kalmar, P & A	Kalmar, Puck & Abrahams
Keit-Engel	Keit-Engel, Inc.
Kendis & Paley	Kendis & Paley
Kendis M P C	Kendis Music Publishing Co.
Kendis Mus Co	Kendis Music Co.
Keystone Mus Co	Keystone Music Co.
Kornheiser	Phil Kornheiser, Inc.
Kramer-Whitney	Kramer-Whitney, Inc.
L B Curtis	(Loyal) B. Curtis
L Feist	Leo Feist, Inc.
L Spier	Larry Spier, Inc.
L W Gilbert M C	L. Wolfe Gilbert Music Co.
Laurel M C	Laurel Music Co.
Lawrence M P I	Lawrence Music Publishers Inc.
Leeds	Leeds Music Corp.
Leon Rene	Leon Rene Publications
Lewis	Lewis Music Publishing Co., Inc.
Lincoln M C	Lincoln Music Corp.
Lindley M P C	Lindley Music Publishing Co.
Lois P C	Lois Publishing Co.
Lombardo Mus	Lombardo Music, Inc.
Loomis P C	C. M. Loomis Publishing Co.
M Abrahams	Maurice Abrahams Music Co.
M Block Mus	Martin Block Music
M M Cole	M. M. Cole Publishing Co.
M M Preeman	M. M. Preeman
M Richmond	Maurice Richmond Co.
M Shapiro	(Maurice) Shapiro Music Publisher
M Weil	Milton Weil Music Co.

Maestro	Maestro Music Co.
Majestic	Majestic Music Co.
Marlo Mus	Marlo Music Corp.
Martin Mus	(Freddy) Martin Music
Mayfair	Mayfair Music Corp.
McCarthy & Fisher	McCarthy & Fisher, Inc.
McKinley Mus Co	McKinley Music Co.
Mellin Mus	Mellin Music, Inc.
Melody Lane	Melody Lane Publications, Inc.
Melrose	Melrose Music Corp.
Melrose Bros	Melrose Brothers Music Co.
Mercer Mus	Mercer Music Co.
Mercer-Morris	Mercer & Morris, Inc.
MGM Corp.	Metro-Goldwyn-Mayer Corp.
Miller Mus	Miller Music Co.
Mills	(Jack?) Mills Music, Inc.
Milson's M P C	Milson's Music Publishing Corp.
Mood Mus Co	Mood Music Co.
Morse Mus Co	Morse Music Co.
Movietone Mus	Movietone Music Corp.
Mutual	Mutual Music Society, Inc.
New World M C	New World Music Corp.
New York M P H	New York Music Publishing House
New York Mus Co	New York Music Co.
New York Mus Co	New York Music Co.
Northern	Northern Music Corp.
Oliver Ditson	Oliver Ditson Co.
Olman M C	Olman Music Corp.
Oxford	Oxford Music Corp.
P Bradford Inc	Perry Bradford, Inc.
P Maurice	Peter Maurice, Inc.
Pace & Handy	Pace & Handy Music Co.
Paramount	Paramount Music Corp.
Paul Dresser P C	Paul Dresser Publishing Co.
Paull-Pioneer	Paull-Pioneer Music Co.
Peer	Peer International Corporation
Penn Mus Co	Penn Music Co.
Piantadosi Mus Co	(Al) Piantadosi Music Co.
Pickwick	Pickwick Music Corp.
Pillsbury	(C. C.) Pillsbury Co.
Pop Melodies	Popular Melodies, Inc.
Porgie, D & F	Porgie, Debin & Friedman, Inc.
R Graham	(Roger) Graham
Radio Tunes	Radio Tunes, Inc.
Red Star Mus Co	Red Star Music Co.
Regent	Regent Music Corp.
Reis & Taylor	Reis & Taylor, Inc.
Remick	(J. H.) Remick Music Corp.
Republic	Republic Music Corp.
Robbins	Robbins Music Corp.
Robbins-Engel	Robbins-Engel, Inc.
Rytvoc	Rytvoc, Inc.
S O'Connor	Shamus O'Connor
Sam Fox	Sam Fox Publishing Co.
Sam Fox	Sam Fox Publishing Co.
Santly Bros	Santly Brothers
Santly-Joy	Santly-Joy, Inc.
Santly-Joy-Select	Santly-Joy-Select, Inc.?
Saunders	Saunders Publications
Schuberth	Edward Schuberth & Co.
Schumann	Schumann Music Co.
Schuster & Miller	Schuster & Miller Inc
Select M P I	Select Music Publications, Inc.
Shapiro, B	Shapiro, Bernstein & Co.
Shapiro, B & Von T	Shapiro, Bernstein & Von Tilzer
Shapiro, Remick	Shapiro, Jerome H Remick Co.
Sherman Clay	Sherman Clay & Co.
Sinatra Songs	Sinatra Songs, Inc.
Skidmore Mus	Skidmore Music Co., Inc.
Sol Bloom	Sol Bloom
Southern	Southern Music Publishing Co.
Southern Calif Mus Co	Southern California Music Co.
Spier & Coslow	Spier & Coslow, Inc.
Spitzer	(Henry) Spitzer Music Publishing Co.
St Nicholas M P C	St. Nicholas Music Publishing Co.
Stanwood	Stanwood Music Corp.
Stark & Cowan	Stark & Cowan, Inc.
Stasny	(A. J.) Stasny Music Corp.
Stevens Mus	Stevens Music Corp.
Sun Mus Co	Sun Music Co, Inc.
Supreme	Supreme Music Corp.
T B Harms	T. B. Harms & Co.
T B Harms & F D H	T. B. Harms & Francis, Day & Hunter
Ted Snyder	Ted Snyder Co.
Tell Taylor M P	Tell Taylor, Music Publisher
Tenney Mus	Tenney Music
Theron C Bennett	Theron C Bennett Co.
Thompson & Co	Thompson & Co.
Thompson Mus Co	Thompson Music Co.
Tobias-Lewis	Tobias-Lewis Music Publishers
Triangle M C	Triangle Music Co.
U S Army	This is the Army, Inc.
United M C	United Music Corp.
V Kremer	Victor Kremer Music Publisher
V Youmans Inc	Vincent Youmans, Inc.
Valiant	Valiant Music Co.
VanAlstyne & Curtis	VanAlstyne & Curtis
Vandersloot	Vandersloot Music Co.
Victoria Pub Co	Victoria Publsishing Co.
Villa Moret	Villa Moret, Inc.

Vogel Mus Co.	Vogel Music Co, Inc.
Vogue Mus	Vogue Music, Inc.
W A Quincke	W. A. Quincke Co.
W B Gray	W(illiam) B. Gray Publishing Co.
W H Anstead	W. H. Anstead Music Co.
W Jacobs	Walter Jacobs Publishing Co.
W Rolfe	W(alter) Rolfe Publishing Co.
Walt Disney M C	Walt Disney Music Co.
Waterson, B & S	Waterson, Berlin & Snyder Co.
Wenrich & Mahoney	(Percy) Wenrich & Mahoney Music Co.
Western M P C	Western Music Publishing Co.
White-Smith	White-Smith Music Co.
Whitney-Warner	Whitney-Warner Publishing Co.
Will Rossiter	Will Rossiter
Williamson	Williamson Music, Inc.
Williamson M C	Williamson Music Corp.
Willis Woodward	Willis Woodward & Co.
Willson	(Meredith) Willson
Windsor Mus Co	Windsor Music Co.
Witmark	M. Witmark & Sons
Wm Jerome Pub Co	Wm Jerome Publishing Co.
Wms & Piron	(Clarence) Williams & (Armand) Piron
Words & Mus	Words and Music, Inc.
World Mus	World Music, Inc.
Yankee	Yankee Music Publishing Corp.
Yellen & B	Yellen & Bornstein, Inc.
York Mus Co	York Music Co.

RECORD LABELS

Aeo Voc	Aeolian Vocalion
ARA	ARA
Ban	Banner
Beacon	Beacon
Bell	Bell
Ber	Berliner
Blu	Bluebird
Bruns	Brunswick
Bullet	Bullet
Cameo	Cameo
Cap	Capitol
Champion	Champion
Coast	Coast
Col	Columbia
Commodore	Commodore
Conqueror	Conqueror
Cor	Coral
Crown	Crown
Damon	Damon
Dana	Dana
Dec	Decca
Deluxe	Deluxe
Domino	Domino
Ed	Edison
Ed Amb	Edison Blue Amberol
Emer	Emerson
Gen	Gennett
Gram	Gram-O-Phone
Har	Harmony
Hit	Hit
Hit of Wk	Hit of the Week
King	King
Liberty Mus Shop	Liberty Music Shop
Lon	London
Majestic	Majestic
Melo	Melotone
Merc	Mercury
MGM	MGM
Musicraft	Musicraft
National	National
Okeh	Okeh
Operaphone	Operaphone
Palda	Palda
Para	Paramount
Pathe	Pathe Actuelle
Perf	Perfect
RCA	RCA
Rondo	Rondo
Sig	Signature
Starr	Starr
Tower	Tower
V-Disc	V-Disc*
Variety	Variety
Varsity	Varsity
Velvet Tone	Velvet Tone
Vic	Victor
Voc	Vocalion
Zono	Zonophone

*It should be noted that V-Disks were issued for the benefit of U.S. servicemen around the world during World War II but never sold over the counter in the U.S.

BIBLIOGRAPHY

BIBLIOGRAPHY

Books and Articles

A.S.C.A.P., ASCAP BIOGRAPHICAL DICTIONARY, 4th Edition, New York: R. R. Bowker, 1980

A.S.C.A.P., ASCAP HIT TUNES INDEX, New York: ASCAP, 1967

A.S.C.A.P., ASCAP INDEX OF PERFORMED COMPOSITIONS, 1952 Ed. (Volumes 1 and 2), New York: ASCAP, 1952

A.S.C.A.P., ASCAP INDEX OF PERFORMED COMPOSITIONS, 1963 Ed. (Volumes 1 to 3), New York: ASCAP, 1963

Alvarez, M. J., INDEX TO MOTION PICTURES REVIEWED BY VARIETY, 1907-1980, Metuchen, NJ: Scarecrow Press, 1982

Barr, Steven C., THE ALMOST COMPLETE 78 rpm RECORD DATING GUIDE, Toronto: Steven C. Barr, 1980

Barr, Steven C., THE ALMOST COMPLETE 78 rpm RECORD DATING GUIDE, Revised Edition, Toronto: Steven C. Barr, 1993

Benjamin, Ruth, & Arthur Rosenblatt, MOVIE SONG CATALOG, Jefferson, NC: McFarland, 1993

Billboard Magazine, FIFTY YEARS OF SONG HITS, Cincinnati: Billboard Publishers, issue of October 22, 1948

Bloom, Ken, AMERICAN SONG: THE COMPLETE MUSICAL THEATER COMPANION, 2nd Ed. 1877-1995, Vol. 1 and 2, New York: Schirmer Books/Prentice Hall International, 1996

Bordman, Gerald, AMERICAN MUSICAL THEATER - A CHRONICLE, New York: Oxford University Press, 1978

Bordman, Gerald, AMERICAN MUSICAL THEATER – A CHRONICLE, 2nd Ed., New York: Oxford University Press, 1992

Burton, Jack, THE BLUE BOOK OF BROADWAY MUSICALS, Watkins Glen, NY: Century House, 1952

Burton, Jack, THE BLUE BOOK OF HOLLYWOOD MUSICALS , Watkins Glen, NY: Century House, 1953

Burton, Jack, THE BUE BOOK OF TIN PAN ALLEY, Watkins Glen, NY: Century House, 1951

Chipman, John H., INDEX TO TOP-HIT TUNES, Boston: Bruce Humphries, 1962

Cohen-Stratyner, Barbara, POPULAR MUSIC 1900-1919, Detroit: Gale Research Inc., 1988

Connor, D. Russell & Warren W. Hicks, B. G. ON THE RECORD: A BIO-DISCOGRAPHY OF BENNY GOODMAN, New Rochelle, NY: Arlington House, 1969

Downey, Pat, George Albert & Frank Hoffman, THE CASH BOX POP SINGLES CHARTS, 1950-1993, Englewood CO, Libraries Unlimited, 1994

Ewen, David, AMERICAN POPULAR SONGS FROM THE REVOLUTIONARY WAR TO THE PRESENT, New York: Random House, 1966

Flower, John, MOONLIGHT SERENADE, A BIO-DISCOGRAPHY OF THE GLENN MILLER CIVILIAN BAND, New Rochelle, NY: Arlington House, 1972

Fuld, James J., AMERICAN POPULAR MUSIC, 1875-1950, Philadelphia: Musical Americana, 1955

Fuld, James J, BOOK OF WORLD FAMOUS MUSIC, New York: Crown Publishers, 1971

Jackson, Arthur, & John Russell Taylor, THE HOLLYWOOD MUSICAL, New York: McGraw Hill Book Co, 1971

Jacobs, Dick, WHO WROTE THAT SONG? 2nd Ed., Cincinnati: Writer's Digest Books, 1994

Jasen, David, TIN PAN ALLEY, New York: Donald I. Fine Inc., 1988

Kinkle, Roger D., THE COMPLETE ENCYCLOPEDIA OF POPULAR MUSIC AND JAZZ,

New Rochelle, NY: Arlington House, 1974
Kobbe, Gustav, KOBBE'S COMPLETE OPERA BOOK, 10th Ed., London: Bodley Head, 1987
Lax, Roger & Frederick Smith, THE GREAT SONG THESAURUS, 2nd Ed., New York: Oxford University Press, 1989
Lissauer, Robert, LISSAUER'S ENCYCLOPEDIA OF POPULAR MUSIC IN AMERICA, 1888 TO PRESENT, New York: Paragon House, 1991
Marco, Guy A., ENCYCLOPEDIA OF RECORDED SOUND IN THE U.S., New York: Garland Publishers, 1993
Marks, Edward, THEY ALL SANG, New York: Viking Press, 1934
Mattfeld, Julius, VARIETY MUSIC CAVALCADE, Englewood Cliffs, NJ: Prentice-Hall, 1962
MCA Records, Complete listings of SONGS OF OUR TIMES, 1917-1934, as featured on Decca Record albums issued 1940-1950
Murrels, Joseph, THE BOOK OF GOLDEN DISCS 3rd. Ed., London: Barrie & Jenkins, 1978
Rust, Brian, THE AMERICAN RECORD LABEL BOOK, New Rochelle, NY: Arlington House, 1978
Shapiro, Nat, POPULAR MUSIC (1920-1969), New York: Adrian Press, 1973
Shapiro, Nat & Bruce Pollack, POPULAR MUSIC, 1920-1979 - A REVISED CUMULATION, Detroit: Gale Research Inc., 1985
Spaeth, Sigmund, A HISTORY OF POPULAR MUSIC IN AMERICA, New York: Random House, 1948
Sutton, Allan, A GUIDE TO PSEUDONYMS ON AMERICAN RECORDS, 1892-1942, Westport, CT: Greenwood Press, 1993
Weaver, John T., FORTY YEARS OF SCREEN CREDITS, 1929-1969, Metuchen, NJ: Scarecrow Press, 1970
Whitburn, Joel, POP MEMORIES, 1890-1954, Menomonee Falls, WI: Record Research Inc., 1986
Whitburn, Joel, TOP POP SINGLES, 1955-1990, Menomonee Falls, WI: Record Research Inc., 1991
Whiteman, Paul, RECORDS FOR THE MILLIONS, New York: Hermitage Press, 1948
Wier, Albert E., MACMILLAN ENCYCLOPEDIA OF MUSIC AND MUSICIANS, New York: The Macmillan & Co., 1938
Williams, John R., THIS WAS YOUR HIT PARADE, Camden, Maine: John R. Williams, 1973
FILM DAILY YEARBOOK, 52nd Ed., New York: Wids Film and Film Folk Inc., 1970
NEW YORK TIMES FILM REVIEWS 1913-1988, New York: New York Times, 1971
VARIETY FILM REVIEWS, New York: Garland Publishers, 1983

Discographies

Fagan, Ted, & William R. Moran, ENCYCLOPEDIC DISCOGRAPHY OF VICTOR RECORDINGS, 1900-1903, New York: Greenwood Press, 1983
Fagan, Ted, & William R. Moran, ENCYCLOPEDIC DISCOGRAPHY OF VICTOR RECORDINGS, Matrix 1-4999, 1903-1907, New York: Greenwood Press, 1986
Koenigsberg, Allen, EDISON CYLINDER RECORDS, 1889-1912, New York: Stellar Publications, 1969
Lorenz, Kenneth M., PIONEER DISCOGRAPHY SERIES, VOL. II, TWO-MINUTE BROWN WAX AND XP CYLINDER RECORDS OF COLUMBIA RECORDS, Wilmington, DE: Kastlemusick Inc., 1981
Rust, Brian, THE AMERICAN DANCE BAND DISCOGRAPHY, 1917-1942, New Rochelle, NY: Arlington House, 1975
Rust, Brian, THE COMPLETE ENTERTAINMENT DISCOGRAPHY, 2nd Edition, New York: Da Capo Press, 1989
Rust, Brian, JAZZ RECORDS, 1897-1942, New Rochelle, NY: Arlington House, 1978
Rust, Brian, THE VICTOR MASTER BOOK, Vol. 2, 1925-1936, Stanhope, NJ: W. C. Allen, 1970
Rust, Brian & Sandy Forbes, BRITISH DANCE BANDS ON RECORD, 1911-1945, Harrow: Middlesex, Great Britain: General Gramophone Publications, Ltd., 1987

THE RIGLER AND DEUTSCH RECORD INDEX, Washington, DC: Association for Recorded Sound Collections, 1983

Periodicals

BILLBOARD, Cincinnati, 1908-1961; New York, 1961-1999
CATALOG OF U.S. COPYRIGHT ENTRIES, Washington, DC: U.S. Copyright Office, Library of Congress, 1899-1977
METRONOME, New York, Vol. 15-54, 1899-1938
MUSIC TRADE REVIEW, New York, 1900-1934, published by Edward Lyman Bill
THE MUSIC TRADES, New York, 1899-1929, published by John C. Freund
NEW YORK CLIPPER, New York, 1899-1924
PHONOSCOPE, New York, 1899
RECORD RESEARCH, Brooklyn, NY: Nos. 144-246, 1977-1991
TALKING MACHINE WORLD, New York, 1905-1930, publ. by Edward Lyman Bill
VARIETY, New York, 1907-1999
VAUDEVILLE NEWS AND NEW YORK STAR, New York, 1918-1927

Record Catalogs and Sheet Music

SHEET MUSIC COLLECTION OF THE FREE LIBRARY OF PHILADELPHIA
SHEET MUSIC COLLECTION OF THE LIBRARY OF CONGRESS, MUSIC DIVISION
SHEET MUSIC COLLECTION OF THE NEW YORK PUBLIC LIBRARY, MUSIC DIVISION
BERLINER GRAMOPHONE RECORD CATALOGS, 1899-1900
COLUMBIA RECORDS CATALOGS, 1900-1934
VICTOR RECORDS CATALOGS, 1901-1934

Libraries

The Annenberg Communications Library of the University of Pennsylvania, Philadelphia, PA
Boston Public Library, Boston, MA
  Music Department
Broadcasting Pioneers Library, Washington DC
The Free Library of Philadelphia, Philadelphia, PA
  Music Department
  Theater Collection
  Business, Science & Industry
  Government Publications
  Newspaper/Microfilm Center
The Library of Congress
  Music Division
  Recorded Sound Center
The New York Public Library, Performing Arts Library, Lincoln Center Plaza, New York
  Music Division
  Rodgers & Hammerstein Archives of Recorded Sound
  Billy Rose Theater Collection
The Van Pelt Library of the University of Pennsylvania, Philadelphia, PA
  Music Department